PAGE 38

ON THE ROAD

TOP EXPERIENCES MAP NEXT PAGE

THIS EDITION WRITTEN AND RESEARCHED BY

Ryan Ver Berkmoes

Alexis Averbuck, Kerry Christiani, Mark Elliott, David Else, Duncan Garwood, Anthony Ham, Virginia Maxwell, Craig McLachlan, Miles Roddis, Caroline Sieg, Regis St Louis, Nicola Williams, Neil Wilson

›Western Europe

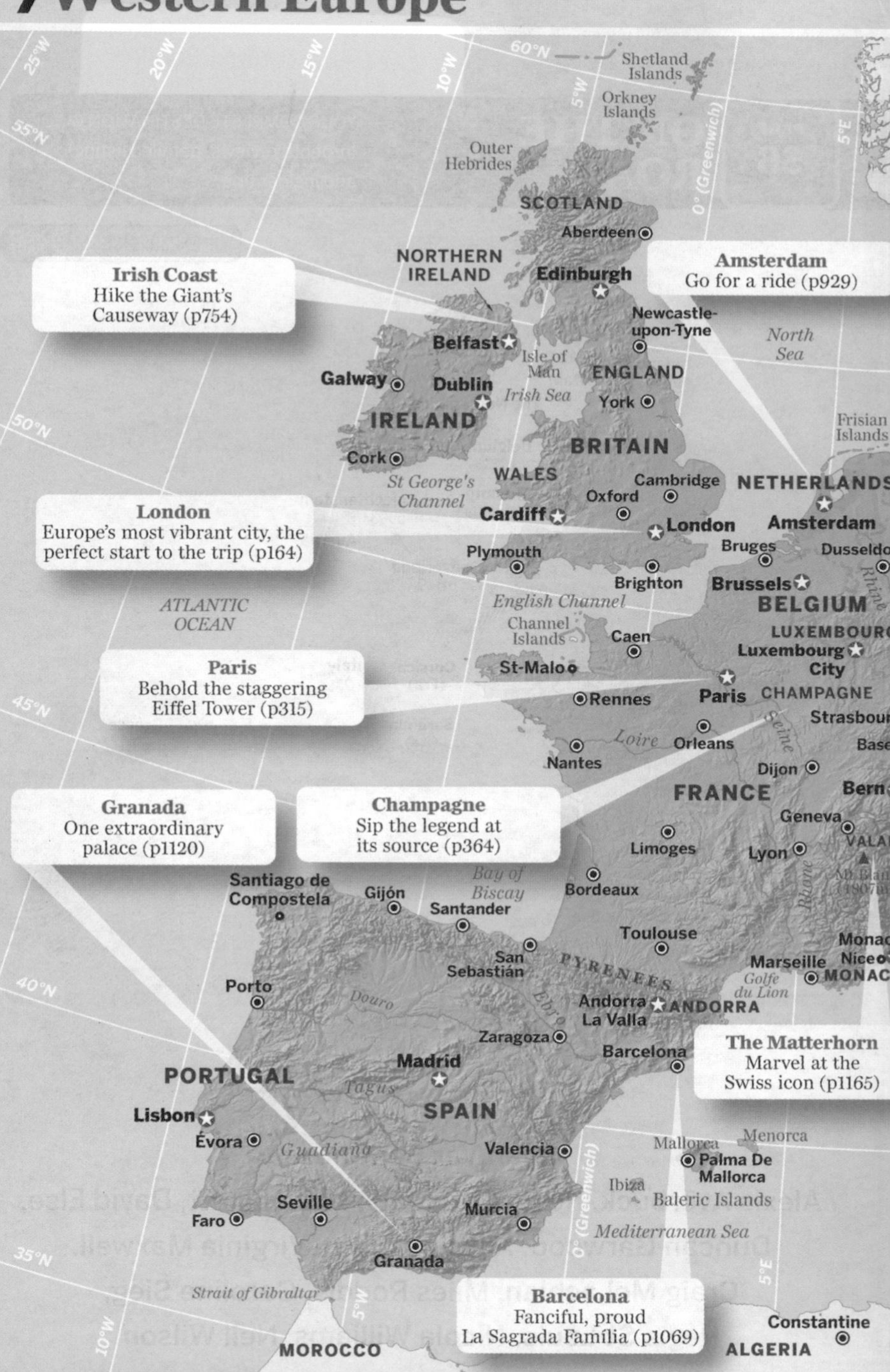

Top Experiences ›

26 TOP EXPERIENCES

Eiffel Tower, Paris

1 Seven million people visit the Eiffel Tower (p315) annually, but few disagree that each visit is unique. From an evening ascent amid twinkling lights to lunch in the company of a staggering city panorama, there are 101 ways to 'do' it. Pedal beneath it, skip the lift and hike up, buy a crêpe from a stand or a key ring from the street, snap yourself in front of it, visit at night or even – our favourite – experience the lucky chance to see all 324m of it glow in a different colour for a light show on a special occasion.

CHRISTER FREDRIKSSON / LONELY PLANET IMAGES ©

London

2 Can you hear that, music lovers? That's London (p164) calling – from the numerous theatres, concert halls, nightclubs, pubs and even tube stations, where on any given night hundreds, if not thousands, of performers are taking to the stage. Search for your own iconic London experience, whether it's the Proms at the Royal Albert Hall, an East End singalong around a clunky pub piano, a performance of *Oliver!* in the West End, a superstar DJ set at Fabric or a floppy-fringed guitar band at a Hoxton boozer. BBC Proms concert, Royal Albert Hall

Ancient Rome

3 Rome's famous seven hills (there are really nine) offer superb vantage points. The Palatino (p778) is a gorgeous green expanse of evocative ruins, towering pines and unforgettable views over the Roman Forum. This is where Romulus supposedly founded the city; where ancient Roman emperors lived in unimaginable luxury. As you walk the gravel paths you can almost sense the ghosts in the air. The Roman Forum from the Palatino

Venice

4 There's something magical about Venice (p818) on a sunny winter's day. With far fewer tourists around and the light sharp and clear, it's the perfect time to lap up the city's unique and magical atmosphere. Ditch your map and wander Dorsoduro's shadowy backlines while imagining secret assignations and whispered conspiracies at every turn. Then visit two of Venice's top galleries, the Galleria dell'Accademia and the Collezione Peggy Guggenheim (both p822), the latter of which houses works by many of the giants of 20th-century art.

Imperial Vienna

5 Imagine what you could do with unlimited riches and Austria's top architects at your hands and you have the Vienna of the Habsburgs. The monumentally graceful Hofburg (p55) whisks you back to the age of empires as you marvel at the treasury's imperial crowns, the equine ballet of the Spanish Riding School and the chandelier-lit apartments fit for an empress. The palace is rivalled in grandeur only by the 1441-room Schloss Schönbrunn (p58), a Unesco World Heritage site, and the baroque Schloss Belvedere (p59), both set in exquisite landscaped gardens. The Hofburg

Remembering the Wall, Berlin

6 Even after 20 years, the sheer magnitude and disbelief that the Berlin Wall really cut through this city doesn't sink in. But the best way to examine its role in Berlin is to make your way – on foot or by bike – along the Berlin Wall Trail (p481). Passing the Brandenburg Gate, analysing graffiti at the East Side Gallery or learning about its history at the Documentation Centre: the path brings it all into context. It's heartbreaking and hopeful and sombre, but integral to trying to understand Germany's capital.

Berlin Wall monument at Gedenkstatte Berliner Mauer

DAVID TOMLINSON / LONELY PLANET IMAGES ©

Gaping at the Matterhorn

7 Sure, it graces Toblerone packages and evokes stereotypical 'Heidi' scenes, but nothing prepares you for the allure of the Matterhorn (p1165). As soon as you step into the timber-chalet-filled village of Zermatt, this loner looms above you, mesmerising you with its chiselled, majestic peak. Gaze at it from a tranquil sidewalk cafe, hike in its shadow along the tangle of alpine paths above town with cowbells clinking in the distance, or pause on a ski slope and admire its magnetic stance.

Alhambra, Granada

8 The Alhambra (p1121), the world's most refined example of Islamic art, is the most enduring symbol of 800 years of the Moorish rule of Al-Andalus. The Alhambra's red fortress towers dominate the Granada skyline against the Sierra Nevada's snow-capped peaks, while its perfectly proportioned Generalife gardens complement the exquisite detail of the Palacio Nazariés. Put simply, this is Spain's most beautiful monument.

Barcelona's La Sagrada Família

9 One of Spain's top sights, the Modernista brainchild of Antoni Gaudí remains a work in progress more than 80 years after its creator's death. Fanciful and profound, inspired by nature and barely restrained by a Gothic style, Barcelona's quirky temple (p1069) soars skyward with an almost playful majesty. The improbable angles and departures from architectural convention will have you shaking your head in disbelief, but the detail of the decorative flourishes on the Passion and Nativity Facades are worth studying for hours.

Beer-drinking in Munich

10 It's not so much the idea that you can drink beer in Munich (p520) – everybody knows you can – it's the variety of places where you can drink that astounds and makes this a must-stop for everyone. There's Oktoberfest, of course, and then there are the famous beer halls, from the huge and infamous (Hofbräuhaus) to the huge and merely wonderful (Augustiner Bräustuben). And why stay inside for your frothy, refreshing litre of lager? You can drink it in a park (Chinesischer Turm) or in the city centre (Viktualienmarkt) – or really just about anywhere. Oktoberfest beer hall

DAVID TOMLINSON / LONELY PLANET IMAGES ©

Tuscany

11 Don't dismiss a travel cliché out of hand without investigating fully; for example, the gently rolling hills of Tuscany (p838), bathed in golden light and dotted with ancient vineyards. Battalions of books, postcards and lifestyle TV shows try to do this magical region justice, but nothing really succeeds except a visit. Here, picture-perfect towns full of Renaissance treasures vie with magnificent scenery and Italy's best food and wine. Once you've had a taste of Tuscany, every cliché will ring absolutely true.

Coastal Exploring

12 Hiking the Causeway Coast (p754) between Ballycastle and Bushmills will take you through some of Northern Ireland's most inspiring and impressive coastal scenery. Its grand geological centrepiece is the Giant's Causeway, a strange and beautiful natural wonder that has been pulling in international visitors for a couple of centuries. But there's also the nerve-testing challenge of the spectacular Carrick-a-Rede rope bridge – and, waiting at journey's end, a well-deserved dram at Bushmills' whiskey distillery. Giant's Causeway

Santorini

13 On first view, startling Santorini (p654) grabs your attention and doesn't let it go. The submerged caldera, surrounded by lava-layered cliffs topped by villages that look like a sprinkling of icing sugar, is one of nature's great wonders, best experienced by a walk along the clifftops from the main town of Fira to the northern village of Oia. The precariousness and impermanence of the place is breathtaking. Recover from your efforts with an ice-cold Mythos beer in Oia as you wait for its famed picture-perfect sunset.

Champagne

14 Name-brand Champagne (p364) houses such as Mumm, Mercier and Moët & Chandon, in the main towns of Reims and Épernay, are known the world over. Our secret tip? Much of Champagne's best liquid gold is made by almost 5000 small-scale vignerons (wine makers) in 320-odd villages. Dozens welcome visitors for a taste, tipple and shop at producer's prices, rendering the region's scenic driving routes the best way to taste fine bubbly amid rolling vineyards and drop-dead-gorgeous villages. Vineyard near Épernay

WILL SALTER / LONELY PLANET IMAGES ©

Navigating Amsterdam's Canals

15 To say Amsterdammers love the water is an understatement. Sure, the city (p929) made its first fortune in maritime trade, but that's ancient history. You can stroll next to the canals and check out some of the city's 3300 houseboats. Or, better, go for a ride. From boat level you'll get to see a whole new set of architectural details, like the ornamentations bedecking the bridges. And when you pass the canalside cafe terraces, you can just look up and wave.

Luxembourg's Capital Castles

16 Beyond the banks that help make Luxembourg Europe's wealthiest country, the little Grand Duchy is an unexpectedly attractive rural patchwork of undulating fields, wooded hills and deep-cut river valleys. The extraordinary fortifications of Luxembourg City (p912), the fascinating Unesco-listed capital, still astound. And many of the nation's neat little country villages retain highly impressive castle ruins. None are more dramatic than those at Bourscheid or Vianden. Bridge over Alzette River, Luxembourg City

GLENN VAN DER KNIJFF / LONELY PLANET IMAGES ©

IZZET KERIBAR / LONELY PLANET IMAGES ©

Holland by Bike

18 The Netherlands equals nirvana for bike riders. The nation where everyone rides bikes to commute, to visit friends, to shop or just to have fun is perfectly designed for cyclists. Consider: it's flat (mostly); you can glide alongside canals spotting windmills; there are over 20,000km of dedicated bike paths; and except for motorways there's virtually nowhere bicycles can't go. Whether you spend an entire trip cycling Holland or even just the occasional jaunt, it'll be a highlight of your trip.

FRANS LEMMENS / LONELY PLANET IMAGES ©

Alfama, Lisbon

17 The Alfama (p978), with its labyrinthine alleyways, hidden courtyards and curving, shadow-filled lanes, is a magical place to lose all sense of direction and delve into the soul of the city. On the journey, you'll pass breadbox-sized grocers, brilliantly tiled buildings and cosy taverns filled with easy-going chatter, with the scent of chargrilled sardines and the mournful rhythms of fado drifting in the breeze. Then you round a bend and catch sight of steeply pitched rooftops leading down to the glittering Tejo and you know you're hooked...

Edinburgh

19 Edinburgh (p269) is a city of many moods, famous for its amazing range of festivals and especially lively in the summer. The Scottish capital is also well worth visiting out of season, for sights like the castle silhouetted against the blue spring sky with a yellow haze of daffodils misting the slopes below; or for the fog snagging the spires of the Old Town, with rain on the cobblestones and a warm glow beckoning from the window of a pub on a chill December morning.

LEANNE LOGAN / LONELY PLANET IMAGES ©

Beer & Chocolate

20 Belgium has a brew for all seasons. And then some. From tangy lambics to full-flavoured Trappists, the range of beer styles is quite exceptional and each is served in its own special glass. Best of all, you can sip a selection in timeless cafes, hidden away in the atmospheric cores of Belgium's great 'art' cities – Ghent, Bruges, Antwerp and Brussels – with their appealing mixtures of medieval and art nouveau architecture. For non-drinkers, there's an unparalleled range of chocolate shops selling melt-in-the-mouth pralines incorporating ever-more-intriguing flavour combinations.

Bath

21 Britain can boast many great cities, but Bath (p208) stands out as the belle of the ball. The Romans built a health resort to take advantage of the hot water bubbling to the surface here; the springs were rediscovered in the 18th century and Bath became the place to see and be seen by British high society. Today, the stunning Georgian architecture of grand townhouses, sweeping crescents and Palladian mansions (not to mention Roman remains, a beautiful cathedral and a 21st-century spa) means Bath demands your undivided attention. Exterior, Roman Baths

SIMON GREENWOOD / LONELY PLANET IMAGES ©

OLIVER STREWE / LONELY PLANET IMAGES ©

Dublin

22 Ireland's capital city (p703) can boast all the attractions and distractions of a major international metropolis, but manages to retain the friendliness, intimacy and atmosphere of a small town. Whether wandering the leafy Georgian terraces of St Stephen's Green or getting up close and personal with the past at Kilmainham Gaol, you're never far from a friendly pub where the beer is grand and the craic is flowing. And, of course, there's the chance to sink a pint of the black stuff at that fountainhead of froth, the original Guinness brewery. Stag's Head Pub

Baroque Salzburg

23 A fortress on a hill; 17th-century cobbled streets; Mozart; the ultimate singalong: if Salzburg (p80) didn't exist, someone would have to invent it just to keep all the acolytes who visit each year happy. It's hard to say what's more popular, but you just have to see all the DVDs for sale to know that this is Sound of Music country, and faster than you can say 'Do-re-mi' you can be whisked into the gorgeous steep hills that are alive with tour groups year-round.

RICHARD NEBESKY / LONELY PLANET IMAGES ©

Skiing in Chamonix

24 Sure, 007 did it, but so can you: the Vallée Blanche (p395) is a once in a lifetime experience. You won't regret the €70-odd it costs to do the 20km off-piste descent from the spike of the Aiguille du Midi to mountaineering mecca Chamonix – every minute of the five hours it takes to get down will pump more adrenalin in your body than anything else you've ever done. Craving more? Hurl yourself down Europe's longest black run (16km) at Alpe d'Huez.

Ancient Landmarks

25 From Athens' renowned Acropolis to the monastery-crowned rock spires of Meteora, Greece offers some of Europe's most impressive historical sights, such as the oracular Temple of Delphi, perched above the Gulf of Corinth; Olympia, home to the first Olympic Games; Epidavros' acoustically perfect theatre; and the mystical Sanctuary of Asclepius, an ancient healing centre. Olive and orange groves surround the vast ruins of Mystras, the one-time capital of the Byzantine Empire. Start with the Acropolis and follow the path of history over Greece's landscape. The Acropolis

LEE FOSTER / LONELY PLANET IMAGES ©

Slow-boating the Rhine

26 It sounds hokey: sitting on a boat bobbing along looking at the sights. Well, we dare anyone to take a cruise on the Rhine (p563) and not be utterly sold, captivated and ready to do it again. Sitting up on deck, you'll see the busy river is framed by vineyard-clad hills on either side. Here and there pops up the ruins of a castle. (Who doesn't like a castle?) And in between are cute little towns with half-timbered buildings; don't be fooled by fakes elsewhere – these are the real thing.

welcome to Western Europe

Charm, fascination, pleasure, wonderment – just a few of the emotions you'll feel in Europe, the continent with the most of everything travellers want.

Perfect First Big Trip

You haven't been anywhere until you've been to Europe – and this means the countries at its core: Western Europe. There is no other place on Earth with so many different nations so close together, with so much history connecting them all – touring this patchwork quilt of tiny dots has enthralled travellers for generations.

Europe is easy; it's as simple as that. It's the perfect reason to get your passport, book your flight and go. Paris, Rome and London are just the start. You could wash up on a rocky Mediterranean beach with little more than a credit card and some cash and enjoy yourself quite nicely. Yes, it can be expensive, but probably not much more than you're used to paying at home. And home was never like this.

Perfect First Dream

Think back to your first thoughts of Europe. Was it building the Leaning Tower of Pisa out of Lego blocks? Or wondering why the best toast was called French? Or quaffing a Heineken behind the neighbour's shed? But try to remember all the impressions and thoughts you had about Europe before you ever set foot on the continent… Good luck!

For a place that's not very big, the range and breadth of Europe's impact is extraordinary. The Western European countries covered in this book occupy less than one-third the space of the US or Australia and yet have still managed to produce Plato, da Vinci and Churchill.

Nowhere else has Europe's variety of cultures, places and experiences all crammed together in such a tight space. Fast trains mean you can wake up on the Mediterranean coast, have lunch in Paris and see a show that night in London. Have a dab of this and a dab of that as it suits your mood.

Perfect Every Time

Whether this is your fifth trip to Western Europe or a first-time dream come true – or even if you live there – surprises await. Feel the chill on your spine when you see that iconic work of art. Find yourself standing right on the spot where *that* happened. Or catch yourself on a beach or on a glacier, at a cafe or in a club thinking, 'These people really know how to live'.

Sure, the continent is experiencing challenges to the monumental effort of coexistence called the EU. But compared to the events of the 20th century, the Western Europe of today couldn't be more peaceful and prosperous, with old-world manners that visitors are always charmed to discover – and which will charm you long after your trip.

So grab that passport. Go. Enjoy. Love every minute.

need to know

Buses

» There are some long-distance buses; most useful for day trips to small places outside cities.

Trains

» Trains go almost everywhere; often fast and usually frequent.

When to Go

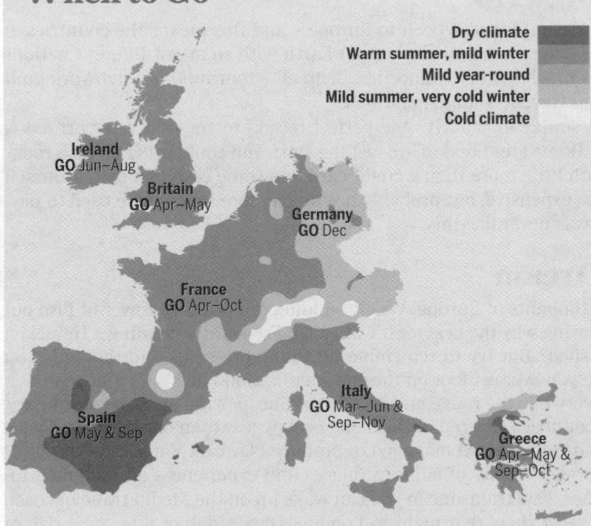

High Season (Jun–Aug)

» Everybody comes to Europe and all of Europe hits the road.

» With everybody needing a bed, prices peak.

» Beautiful weather means that everybody is outside in cafes.

Shoulder (Apr–May & Sep–Oct)

» Moderate weather means days can be bright and clear.

» Europe is popular but not overrun and prices are moderate: Europeans are sleeping at home.

» Almost everything is open.

Low Season (Nov–Mar)

» Outside of ski resorts and Christmas markets, most regions are quiet; much is closed.

» Prices reflect hope more than greed.

» Secret time to enjoy major cities where the pleasures indoors don't close.

Your Daily Budget

Budget less than €60

» Dorm beds: €15–20

» Excellent markets and local quick eats hold costs down

» Look for museum free days, walk and absorb city culture

Midrange €60–€200

» Double room in a nice midrange hotel: €60–€150

» Stay at small hotels for a special experience

» Lunch at top restaurants can be great value

Top End over €200

» Stays at iconic hotels: €150 and up

» Look for tastings menus at hot restaurants

» Enjoy the duty-free refund from an afternoon's stylish shopping

Driving
» Car hire readily available throughout Europe.

Ferries
» Relax at sea between Ireland and Britain, Britain and the Continent, Italy and Greece.

Bicycles
» From the two-wheel heaven of The Netherlands to the mountainous thrills of Italy, Western Europe is pure cycling joy.

Planes
» Cheap airfares take you from one end of the continent to the other.

Websites
» **Lonely Planet** (www.lonelyplanet.com/europe) Destination information, hotel bookings, traveller forums and more.

» **Train Information** (www.seat61.com) All about getting around Europe by train.

» **Michelin** (www.viamichelin.com) Calculates the best route from A to B by car.

» **BBC News** (www.bbc.co.uk/news) Find out what's happening before you arrive.

» **Tourist Office Directory** (www.towd.com) Links to tourist offices everywhere.

Money
Credit cards are widely accepted, with a few exceptions. See the chapters on individual countries for more information on money and the current exchange rates.

» **Euro (€)** Andorra, Austria, Belgium, France, Germany, Greece, Ireland, Italy, Liechtenstein, Luxembourg, The Netherlands, Portugal, Spain

» **Pound (£)** Britain

» **Swiss franc (Sfr)** Switzerland

Visas
Generally not required for stays of up to 90 days for citizens of most Western countries (Australia, Canada, New Zealand, USA etc). The Schengen Agreement (no passport controls at borders between member countries) applies to some areas; see p1217.

Arriving in Europe
» **Schiphol Airport, Amsterdam**
Trains to the centre (20min).

» **Heathrow Airport, London**
Trains (15min) and Tube (1hr) to the centre.

» **Aéroport Roissy Charles de Gaulle**
Many buses (1hr) and trains (30min) to the centre.

» **Frankfurt Airport**
Trains (15min) to the centre.

» **Leonardo da Vinci Airport, Rome**
Buses (1hr) and trains (30min) to the centre.

What to Take
» **Sandals or thongs (flip-flops)** for that rocky yet alluring Mediterranean beach

» **Raincoat, waterproof jacket or umbrella** for the weather that keeps Europe green

» **A good pair of earplugs** for sleeping in the heart of boisterous culture

» **Menu phrasebook** so you don't just order boring stuff or get an offal surprise

» **Map** so you can show new friends where you come from

» **Extra duffel bag** for the booty from your Paris shopping spree

» **Sunglasses** to protect your eyes and to look so, so cool while checking out the action from a sidewalk cafe

» **Bottle-opener** for when the perfect bottle of wine calls your name

» **Condoms** because you never know when the moment will be just right

» **Smart set of clothes** for blowing the budget

if you like...

Castles & Palaces

First there were castles, the A-bombs of their day, designed to frustrate enemies and make their owners impervious. Later there were armies, and royalty could define flamboyance through vast palaces and grounds that continue to astound.

Versailles The palace against which all others are measured, from the Hall of Mirrors to Marie Antoinette's refuge (p349)

Neuschwanstein So what if it's not even 200 years old? In the heart of the Bavarian Alps, this is everybody's (including Disney's) castle fantasy (p540)

Conwy Castle What a serious castle should look like, right down to the eight defensive towers. No frippery here, just grim walls, awhiff of boiling oil and the echo of a catapault (p265)

Vienna's palaces At imperial spectacles like the Hofburg, you can see the royal excess that impoverished a continent and fuelled revolutions (p55)

Beer & Wine

Europe packs a large variety of beer and wine into a small space: every region seems to have at one least liquid creation it's known for.

Belgian beer As varied and diverse as it gets, with over 400 breweries and zillions of beers; some brewed by monks, others flavoured by fruit, all worth trying (p155)

Bordeaux The centre of Burgundy might as well be the centre of the wine universe – at least the red one (p411)

English Ales Not warm, just not ice cold, which means that the flavours – from fruity to bitter – come through. Best enjoyed in a country pub (p302)

Tuscany's best chianti You can almost taste the warm burnt-umber colours of the iconic Italian region of Tuscany in every glass. Don't skimp: go for the Classico (p838)

Historic Places

When you were 13 you learned more about Western European history than you hoped to know, but now that you're on the ultimate field trip, you'll want to see more history than you'll have time to find.

Pompeii Rome's elite literally frozen in time. Wander the streets and alleys of this great ancient city, buried by a volcanic eruption two millennia ago (p865)

Athens Acropolis, Ancient Agora, Roman Agora, Temple of Olympian Zeus, Hadrian's Arch et al. You'll yearn for a toga (p614)

Bruges Beautiful Renaissance town in Belgium with gables, canals, bell towers and an overall harmony that's still beguiling (p143)

Dachau The first WWII concentration camp is close to Munich, and a harrowing introduction to one of the 20th century's worst horrors (p531)

» The ruins of Pompeii, Italy (p865)

GREG ELMS / LONELY PLANET IMAGES ©

Cultural Cuisine

Europeans love their food and you'll love it too, in all its tasty variations. Saving room for dessert is mandatory, despite all the temptations day in and day out.

Spanish tapas Little plates of treats of every description; savoury Iberian ham or a perfect stuffed olive or a little deep-fried… (p1042)

Fish & chips Cod battered, fried and served with a scoop of fresh chips may seem humdrum but in the right hands – and with the right vinegar – the results are sublime (p249)

German wursts The long and the short of it is simple: sausages are delicious and Germany has hundreds of varieties – often the source of great local pride (p603)

Belgian chocolate The only thing that might melt quicker is your heart when you ponder a box of these extravagant confections: a dose of perfection in your mouth (p156)

Cafes & Bars

Whether it's a coffee savoured for an hour or a drink with a roomful of new friends, you'll find plenty of places for liquid joy.

Vienna's coffee houses Unchanged in decades and redolent with the air of refinement; pause for a cup served just so (p68).

Irish pubs Guinness would have you believe otherwise but their iconic stout tastes best at home when served in the most gregarious places on the planet (p712)

Parisian cafes What's more clichéd? The practised curtness of the waiter or the studied boredom of the customer? Probably both, and we wouldn't miss the show for anything (p336)

Dutch brown cafes So called for the stains on the walls from legions of smokers, they should just be called cozy, for the warm and friendly atmosphere (p969)

Beaches

They rim the Mediterranean: lovely strands of blindingly white sand moistened by lapping waves of azure. You can find solitude or join an entire community, and seldom will you need much fabric or coin for what you wear.

St-Tropez The name means beach, and at the Plage de Pampelonne the beautiful people are really the extra-beautiful people (p442)

Lefkada Cliffs drop to broad swaths of white sand and turquoise waters on the west coast of this untrammelled Greek island (p682)

Karpathos Apella and Ammoöpi beaches on this snug island avoid cliché and deliver the goods in a package that includes white sand backed by tidy ancient villages (p669)

Menorca Beaches so beautiful you'll think they may merely be dreams are tucked away in little coves like pearls in oysters. In fact, dig a little and you may find an archaeological treasure (p1110)

If you like... roller coasters
Austria's serpentine Grossglockner Road is one of Europe's greatest drives. Snow-capped mountains, plunging waterfalls and lakes scattered like gemstones are just the start (p101)

If you like... Roman ruins
The Forum in Rome is the ultimate seven hills of fantasy (p775)

If you like... gardens
The magnificent Alhambra will spoil you for any other garden you'll ever see (p1121)

Outdoor Fun

Don't just stare at the beautiful scenery, dive right into it. Legendary places across the continent come alive when you get active and take that hill or surmount that wave. There's something to do no matter the season.

An English stroll The entire countryside seems to have been made for beautiful, memorable walking (p305)

Biking the Loire Valley There's a gorgeous chateau around every bend in the river in this beautiful valley (p376)

Ski year-round Experience Olympic-sized skiing in Innsbruck, the Austrian alpine city ringed by famous pistes. Head to the glaciers in August for downhill action (p95)

Big blow The wind is always howling in Tarifa, which windsurfers have proclaimed to be the best spot on the Mediterranean (p1130)

Great Dining

Europe is where the sly concept of 'slow food' was invented: we love to eat well, so why rush it? And eat well you can!

Paris dining The city and culture that taught the rest of the world about refined food (p336)

Pizza in Naples The peasant dish that ate the world – or vice versa – is most vibrant in the city of its birth (p863)

San Sebastián Spain's Basque powerhouse boasts more Michelin stars per capita than anywhere else in the world (p1087)

Provence glory It has been known to cause people to swoon: the market at Carpentras bursts with hundreds of stalls laden with the produce of Provence, the province of food (p432)

Nightlife

The best clubs in the world, the stars on stage and moody haunts of night owls are all part of the scene after dark.

Berlin More cutting edge clubs than seems possible, where DJs experiment with the sounds of tomorrow (p492)

London The stages of London have been graced by some famous types through the years; remember that Shakespeare guy? On any given night – or afternoon – there are dozens of theatre productions, from crowd-pleasing musicals to edgy drama (p193)

Rotterdam Holland's second city doesn't play second fiddle (or synthesizer) after midnight, when its massive clubs draw the best tune talent of Europe (p951)

Paris The City of Light is just that after dark, when romantic strolls amidst the lit-up splendor can end in jazz clubs, idiosyncratic cafes, cabarets and much more (p343)

» The foyer of the Staatsoper opera house, Vienna, Austria (p68)

GREG ELMS / LONELY PLANET IMAGES ©

Art

From Greek statues to works that defy description or even understanding, Europe's art is ever-evolving. Great art museums – and artfully great cities – are reason enough for a trip.

The Louvre It's not really France's museum, it's the world's; treasures from everywhere in exhaustive quantity (p327)

Tate Modern London's modern art museum barely fits into a huge old power station on the banks of the Thames; its works always stir imaginations and controversy (p172)

Florence It starts with the Duomo, continues through the Uffizi Gallery and crosses the Ponte Vecchio – the entire Renaissance embodied in one city (p838)

Van Gogh Musuem He left his mark everywhere, but remnants of Van Gogh's troubled life and glorious creations are best found at his namesake Amsterdam museum (p931)

Music

Classical music of royalty, soulful songs of the masses, pop culture that changed the world: just some of the ways the European love of music will get into your beat.

Vienna's state opera The Staatsoper is the premier venue in a city synonymous with opera and classical music. Wait! Is that Mozart I hear? (p68)

The Beatles They sprang – and sang – from Liverpool and now the city does them proud at the Beatles Story, which recounts the lives and work of the Fab Four(p257)

Irish music The Irish love their music and it takes little – sometimes just the pull of a pint – to get them singing. The west coast hums with music pubs, especially in Galway (p738)

Fado Portuguese love the melancholy, nostalgic songs of fado. Hear it in Lisbon's Alfama district (p991)

Scenic Journeys

There are beautiful journeys aplenty in Europe, from the Highlands of Scotland to the high lands of the Swiss Alps.

Cinque Terre Five picture-perfect seaside villages are linked by a trail along beaches, hillside vineyards and olive groves (p808)

Rugged Scotland The route between Inverness and remote Kyle is one of Britain's great scenic train journeys (p290)

Rhine by rail The slow train between Mainz and Koblenz has stunning views and lets you hopscotch through every quaint little half-timbered village (p563)

Glacier Express Two of Switzerland's most fabled alpine resorts, Zermatt and St Moritz, are linked by its most fabled train; hold your breath as you cross the soaring Landwasser Viaduct (p1195)

month by month

Top Events

1. **Christmas Markets,** December
2. **Oktoberfest,** September
3. **Carnevale,** February
4. **Edinburgh International Festival,** August
5. **Notting Hill Carnival,** August

January

The first month of the year is the coldest and most quiet. People are literally working off the holidays and even the Greek beaches are chilled to the teens (centigrade). What to do? Ski!

A Hot Cold New Year

An enormous, raucous Edinburgh street party (Hogmanay) sees in the New Year in Scotland. It's replicated Europe-wide as main squares resonate with champagne corks and fireworks.

February

Carnival in all its manic glory sweeps through the Catholic regions of Continental Europe. Cold temperatures – even in Venice – are forgotten amid masquerades, street festivals and general bacchanalia. Expect to be kissed by a stranger.

Carnaval

Pre-Lent is celebrated with greater vigour in Maastricht than anywhere else in Northern Europe. While the rest of the Netherlands hopes the canals will freeze for ice-skating, this Dutch corner cuts loose with a celebration that would have done its former Roman residents proud.

Carnevale

In the period before Ash Wednesday, Venice goes mad for masks. Costume balls, many with traditions centuries old, enliven the social calendar in this storied old city like no other event. Even those without a coveted invite are swept up in the pageantry.

Karneval/ Fasching

Germany doesn't leave the pre-Lent season solely to its neighbours. Karneval is celebrated with abandon in the traditional Catholic regions of the country including Bavaria, along the Rhine and deep in the Black Forest. It's the wild bookend to Oktoberfest in Munich.

March

Let's hear it for the crocus, the tiny bulb whose purple flower breaks through the ice-crusted soil to let Europe know that there's a thaw in the air and spring will soon come.

St Patrick's Day

Parades and celebrations are held on March 17 in Irish towns big and small to honour their beloved St Patrick. While elsewhere the day is a commercialised romp of green beer, in his home country it's time to celebrate with friends and family.

April

Spring arrives with a burst of colour, from the glorious bulb fields of Holland to the blooming orchards of Spain. On the most southern beaches it's time to shake the sand out of the umbrellas.

Semana Santa

Procession of penitents and holy icons in Spain, notably in Seville, during Easter week. Throughout the week thousands of members of religious brotherhoods parade in traditional garb. Look for the pointed *capirotes* (hoods).

Settimana Santa

Italy celebrates Holy Week with processions and passion plays. By Holy Thursday, Rome is thronged with the faithful and even non-believers are swept up in the emotion and piety of hundreds of thousands of faithful flocking to the Vatican and St Peter's Basilica.

Greek Easter

The most important festival in the Greek Orthodox calendar. The emphasis is on the Resurrection so it's a celebratory event – the most significant part is midnight on Easter Saturday when candles are lit and a fireworks and candlelit procession hits the streets.

Feria de Abril

Hoods off! A week-long party held in Seville, Spain, in late April to counterbalance the religious peak of Easter. The many beautiful old squares of this gorgeous city come alive during the long, warm nights the nation is known for.

Koninginnedag (Queen's Day)

Nationwide celebration in the Netherlands on 30 April, but especially in Amsterdam, which becomes awash in orange costumes and fake afros, beer, balloon animals, beer, dope, Red Bull, beer, leather boys, skater grrrls, temporary roller coasters, clogs, beer, fashion victims, grannies…

May

Expect nice weather anywhere but especially in the south where the Mediterranean summer is already full steam ahead. Yachts prowl the harbours while beautiful people ply the sands.

Cannes Film Festival

The famous, not-so-famous and the merely topless converge for a year's worth of movies in little more than one week in Cannes. Join the sun-drenched crowds strolling the strand and soaking up the glitz.

Brussels Jazz Marathon

Around-the-clock jazz performances hit Brussels, during the second-last weekend in May (www.brusselsjazzmarathon.be). The saxophone becomes the instrument of choice for this international-flavoured city's most joyous celebration. Look for gigs on huge open-stages and in divey little clubs.

Queima das Fitas

Coimbra's annual highlight is this boozy week of fado music and revelry that begins on the first Thursday in May when students celebrate the end of the academic year. These are clearly honour students as they do it in this Portuguese town better than anywhere.

June

The huge summer travel season hasn't started yet but the sun has busted through the clouds and the weather is gorgeous, from the hot shores in the south to the cool climes of the north.

Festa de Santo António

In Portugal there's feasting, drinking and dancing in Lisbon's Alfama in honour of St Anthony (12 to 13 June). This caps off the even grander three-week-long Festas de Lisboa, which features processions and dozens of street parties.

Festa de São João

Elaborate processions, live music on Porto's plazas and merry-making all across Portugal's second city. Squeaky plastic hammers (available for sale everywhere) come out for the unusual custom of whacking one another. Everyone is fair game – expect no mercy.

Luxembourg National Day

Held on 23 June, this is the Grand Duchy's biggest event – a celebration of the birth of the Grand Duke (though it doesn't actually fall on a Grand Ducal birthday). Fireworks in Luxembourg City kick it off on the evening of 22 June.

Glastonbury Festival

The town's youthful summer vibe peaks at this long weekend of music, theatre and New Age shenanigans (www.glastonburyfestivals.co.uk), one of England's favourite outdoor events. More than 100,000 turn up to writhe in Pilton Farm's grassy fields (or deep mud).

July

Visitors have arrived from around the world and outdoor cafes, beer

gardens and beach clubs are hopping. Expect beautiful – even steamy – weather anywhere you go.

Il Palio

Siena's great annual event is the Palio (2 July & 16 August), a pageant culminating in a bareback horse race round Il Campo. The city is divided into 17 *contrade* (districts), of which 10 compete for the *palio* (silk banner) and emotions explode.

Montreux Jazz Festival

It's not all that jazz as big-name rock acts also hit town for this famous festival held during the first two weeks of July (www.montreuxjazz.com). Glitterai from across the globe gather for a top-end celebration of top-flight music on the shores of Lake Geneva.

Sanfermines (aka 'Running of the Bulls')

Huge male bovines and people who want to be close to them invade Pamplona, Spain for the famous Sanfermines festival 6 to 14 July, when the city is overrun with thrill-seekers, curious onlookers and, oh yeah, bulls. Its most famous event, the Encierro (Running of the Bulls), begins at 8am daily.

B-Parade

A huge techno street parade in Berlin, usually held the second weekend of July (www.b-parade.de). Enormous trucks filled with speakers literally make the earth move for the hundreds of thousands of partiers who line the route, dancing the entire time.

Bastille Day

Fireworks, balls, processions and more for France's national day, 14 July. Celebrated in every French town and city: go to the heart of town and get caught up in this patriotic festival that, of course, has wonderful food and wine.

De Gentse Feesten

Belgium's Ghent is transformed into a 10-day party of music and theatre, a highlight is a vast techno celebration called 10 Days Off (www.gentsfeesten.be). This under-appreciated gem of the low country is high on fine bars serving countless kinds of beer.

August

Everybody's going someplace as half of Europe shuts down to go enjoy the traditional month of holiday with the other half. If it's near the beach, from Germany's Baltic to Spain's Balearic, it's mobbed.

Salzburg Festival

Austria's most renowned classical music festival, the Salzburg Festival (www.salzburgfestival.at) attracts international stars from late July to the end of August. That urbane person who looks like a famous cellist sitting by you having a glass of wine probably is.

Street Parade

In Switzerland, it's Zürich's turn to let its hair down with an enormous techno parade (www.street-parade.ch). All thoughts of numbered accounts are forgotten as bankers and everybody else in this otherwise staid burg parties to orgasmic deep-base thump, thump, thump.

Notting Hill Carnival

Held over two days in August, this is Europe's largest and London's most vibrant outdoor carnival, where the local Caribbean community shows the city how to party. Food, frolic and fun are just a part of a vast multicultural celebration.

Edinburgh International Festival

Three weeks of innovative drama, comedy, dance, music and more from around the globe, held in Edinburgh (www.eif.co.uk). Two weeks overlap with the celebrated Fringe Festival (www.edfringe.com) which draws innovative acts from around the globe. Expect cutting-edge comedy, drama and productions that defy description.

September

It's cooling off in every sense, from the northern countries to the romance started on a dance floor in Ibiza. It's maybe the best time to visit: the weather's still good and the crowds have thinned.

Venice International Film Festival

The Mostra del Cinema di Venezia is Italy's top film festival and one of the world's top indie film fests (www.labiennale.org). The judging here is seen as an early indication of what to look for at the next year's Oscars.

Oktoberfest

Germany's legendary beer-swilling party (www.oktoberfest.de) starts mid-September in Munich (don't ever tell anyone you turned up for it in October, even if you did). Millions descend for litres of beer and carousing that has no equal. If you don't plan ahead, you'll sleep in Austria.

Festes de la Mercè

Barcelona knows how to party until dawn and it outdoes itself for the Festes de la Mercè (around 24 September), the city's biggest celebration, with four days of concerts, dancing, *castellers* (human-castle builders), fireworks and *correfocs* – a parade of firework-spitting dragons and devils.

October

Although your beach fantasies may go unfulfilled, this is another good month to visit. Almost everything is still open and prices and visitor numbers are way down. Look for sales on rain coats, you'll need them.

Festival at Queen's

Belfast hosts the second-largest arts festival (www.belfastfestival.com) in the UK for three weeks in late October/early November in and around Queen's University. It's a time for the city to shed its gritty legacy and celebrate the intellectual and the creative without excessive hype.

November

Leaves have fallen and snow is about to in much of Europe. Even in the temperate zones around the Mediterranean it can get chilly, rainy and blustery. Most seasonal attractions have closed for the year.

Guy Fawkes Night

Bonfires and fireworks erupt across Britain on 5 November recalling a failed antigovernment plot from the 1600s. Go to high ground in London to see glowing explosions erupt everywhere.

December

Christmas is a good excuse for warm cheer despite the cold weather in virtually every city and town. Decorations transform even the drabbest shopping street and every region has its own traditions.

Christmas Markets

Christkindlmarkts are held across Germany and Austria. The most famous are in Nuremberg and Vienna but every town has one. Warm your hands through your mittens holding a hot mug of mulled wine and find that special (or kitsch) present.

Natale

Italian churches set up intricate cribs or *presepi* (nativity scenes) in the lead-up to celebrating Christmas. Some are quite famous, most are works of art and many date back hundreds of years and are venerated for their spiritual ties.

itineraries

Whether you've got six days or 60, these itineraries provide a starting point for the trip of a lifetime. Want more inspiration? Head online to lonelyplanet.com/thorntree to chat with other travellers.

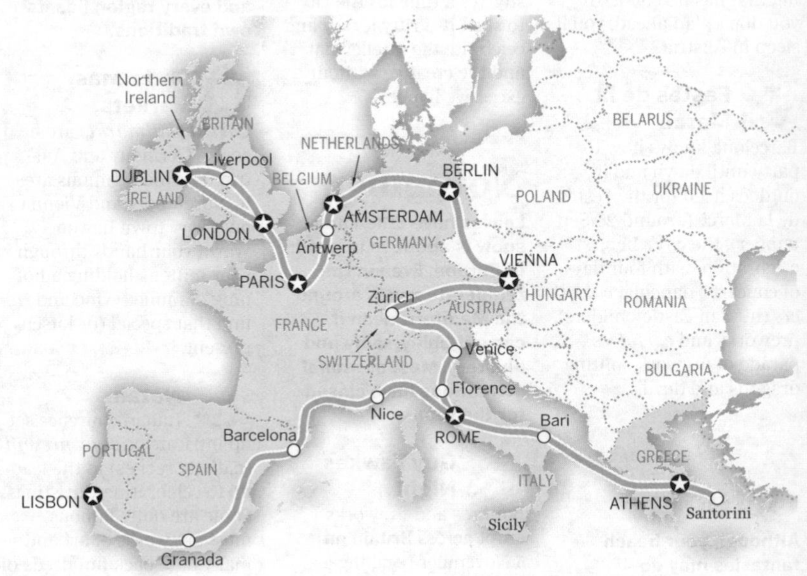

One to Two Months

Ultimate Europe

Have limited time but want to see a bit of everything? Start in **Dublin**, sampling the vibrant pubs and traditional Irish craic. From Ireland, take a ferry to **Liverpool** or fly to **London** for some great theatre. From London, take the Eurostar train to **Paris**.

Head north from Paris to **Antwerp** for amazing beer, and then further north to **Amsterdam**, not forgetting to ride a canal boat. Go east, stopping for a cruise on the Rhine, and spend a few days exploring (and surviving) the nightlife in **Berlin**. Next, **Vienna** beckons with classical-music riches. Step west to **Zürich** and the Alps for awe-inspiring ski slopes and vistas.

Head to the canals of **Venice** and through **Florence** to historic **Rome**. Train it to **Bari** and take a ferry to **Athens**, then explore island beaches, starting with the stunning **Santorini**. Off to the south of France then, and to Mediterranean towns such as **Nice**. Continue to **Barcelona** before heading to the Moorish towns of southern Spain, perhaps **Granada**. End your trip in laid-back **Lisbon**, enjoying a glass of local port wine to celebrate completing your grand journey!

One to Two Months
Mediterranean Europe

Beautiful weather and scenery are the draw of this comprehensive tour that follows famous towns and cities from antiquity to the present.

Start in southern Spain with some British flavour in **Gibraltar**, where you can view the only wild primates in Europe. Go north to the city that defines lovely: **Seville**. Make your way up the eastern coast past the Moorish town of **Málaga** and on to the ever-beautiful **Granada** and **Córdoba**. Then it's back to the coast at **Valencia**, for a ferry hop to the parties and beaches of the **Balearic Islands**.

Back on the mainland, **Barcelona** is filled with the architecture of Gaudí. From here, head into France's Provence region, where in **Marseille** you can see the fortress that was inspiration for the novel *The Count of Monte Cristo*. Leave the sea for the hills and lavender-scented towns like **Orange**. On to the **Côte d'Azur** and its playground for the rich and famous, **St-Tropez**. A quick stop in the capital of the French Riviera, **Nice**, makes a good jumping-off point for other nearby hot spots such as **Cannes**.

Take a ferry to **Corsica** and experience the traditional lifestyle of quiet fishing villages. Hit the snowy peaks at **Calvi** and the groves of **Les Calanques** before hopping down to **Sardinia**. From here, take a long ferry ride or a quick flight to **Sicily** to visit colossal Greek temples and its famous volcano, Mt Etna.

Catch a ferry to **Naples**, on the Italian mainland, and take a trip to **Pompeii**. Move east to **Brindisi** for a ferry to Greece that passes rocky coasts seen by mariners for millennia, landing in **Patra**. Head to **Athens** to wonder at ancient treasures before getting a plane or ferry to islands such as **Crete** and **Mykonos**. Retrace your steps to Italy. Head north to **Rome**, taking time to wander amid its ruins and piazzas. Continue through Tuscany, stopping at **Pisa** to see its famous 'leaning tower'. Finish up along the Ligurian coast in the port city of **Genoa** via the coastal towns of the Cinque Terre, where you can stroll along the Via dell'Amore.

Three Weeks

Backroads of Europe

You've already done the major capitals and ticked every must-see box. Now start seeing the rest of Europe. The far north of Ireland is rugged and uncrowded; start yourself in **Donegal**, then head to the very welcoming Northern Ireland – **Belfast** in particular. Head southeast to the gritty yet charming town of **Newcastle-upon-Tyne** in England, then catch the ferry to the Netherlands, where **Rotterdam** combines edgy modern architecture with rocking charm.

Go east to the former East German cities of **Leipzig** and **Dresden**, each of which are creating a new future from their historic pasts. Turn south via the amazing **Regensburg** to the temperate Swiss town of **Lugano**. Traverse Italy and the hidden gem of **Mantua**, followed by beautiful Umbria and towns such as **Perugia**. In the far south, take time to wander frenetic **Naples** and the ruin-filled **Amalfi Coast** before pressing on to **Sicily** and its ancient and colourful culture.

Hop a ferry to Greece and enjoy some of the less-visited islands, such as **Naxos** or **Lesvos**. From here you can fly home or enjoy the ultimate carefree holiday, exploring other Greek islands as the ferries and your whims take you.

Two Weeks

A Sample of Europe

Watching Europe from the window of a train, gazing at the sea rolling past the handrail of a ferry – that's the way generations of travellers have explored the continent, and you can, too. To stick to tradition you might even grab a kiss on a misty station platform or share a hug on deck as the land slips away behind you. Start in the Scottish castle-town of **Edinburgh**, then take the train to **London** and on to **Harwich** for a ferry crossing to **Hoek van Holland**. From here, trains connect to fabled, gabled **Amsterdam**.

Take a fast train to **Cologne** and then mellow out on a river cruise down the alluring Rhine River. Alight at **Mainz** and connect by train through **Basel** to **Interlaken** for the slow-moving trains and trams that wend through glaciers of the Alps. Next take a train past rugged scenery to connect with stylish **Milan**, where a fast Italian Eurostar train zips to **Florence**, the heart of the Slow Food Movement. Reserve a sleeping compartment and snuggle up tight on the night train to **Paris**, feeling the romance in the rhythm of the rails.

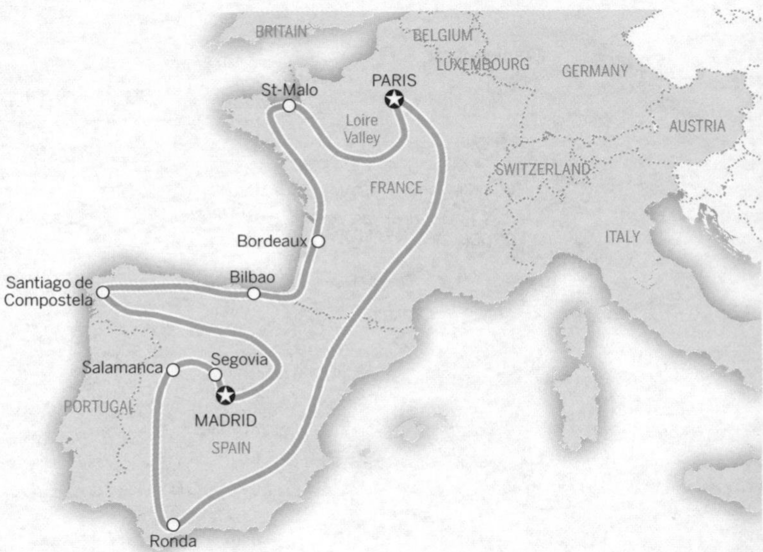

Two Weeks

France & Iberia

Get a feel for two of Europe's most distinct countries on this relatively compact jaunt. Start in **Paris**, of course. Sample the chateaux of the **Loire Valley**, then take the fast TGV train to Brittany, where the battlements of **St-Malo** always astound. Although the apple ciders of the region delight, you'll want to continue south to Burgundy, where red wine reaches its pinnacle in the region around **Bordeaux**. Head across the border to the Basque city of **Bilbao** before continuing to the pilgrimage shrine of **Santiago de Compostela**.

If you think you eat late at home, you've got nothing on **Madrid**, where an evening of tapas and drinks in tiny bars can postpone dinner until midnight. Find your favourite square and become a regular. Spend a day inside the walls of the beautiful hill town of **Segovia**. And don't let the sandstone splendour of **Salamanca** pass without a stop. Go south and plan on using a car to explore the many hill towns of Andalucía. Little winding roads traverse stark landscapes and olive orchards before reaching places like **Ronda**, with its whitewashed buildings gleaming in the distance. End at the coast or return to Paris.

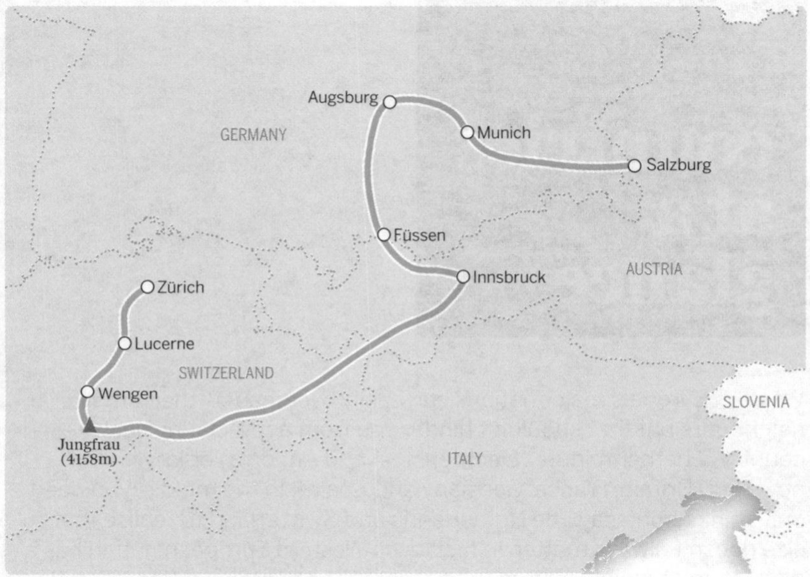

One to Two Weeks

Europe's Mountains

Fly into **Zürich**, the tidy banking town, where (besides the smell of money) you'll get a whiff of the Alps. Move onwards to the ever-cute lakeside city of **Lucerne**, where iconic half-timbered bridges cross glacier-cold waters. Start your ascent by setting up in one of the cosy chalets of **Wengen**, where an imposing wall of Alps looms before you. Go by train to the top of **Jungfrau** and walk everywhere on wildflower-framed trails (in spring). Let the cowbells serenade you.

Leave Switzerland for its immediate eastern neighbour, Austria. In **Innsbruck**, which has hosted the Winter Olympics twice, you can ski year-round and dine in cute mountain huts. Cross the spine of the Alps into Germany and behold the cutest castle on a hilltop you'll ever find: the wildly popular Neuschwanstein, in **Füssen**. If you have time, you could take a side drive on the Romantic Road starting at **Augsburg**. The beer halls of **Munich** are a short hop away; this is a good stop to spend a couple of days – when it's clear, you can see the Alps. A short final jaunt brings you to the perfect combination of hills and music: **Salzburg**.

countries at a glance

Western Europe's major nations can easily overshadow their smaller neighbours but that shouldn't hinder you from appreciating each country, whether minute (Liechtenstein and Andorra) or large and powerful (Britain, France, Germany and Spain). In the middle, you need only think about, say, the Netherlands and Switzerland to realise that size doesn't always matter. In fact, each Western European nation has a distinct and tangible culture (often more than one) and differs from its neighbours in myriad ways. And that's the real joy of a vacation to the continent: so much in such a small space.

Andorra

Shopping ✓
Dramatic Scenery ✓✓
Skiing ✓

A tiny country hidden like a pea in a mattress between France and Spain in the Pyrenees, Andorra is popular with bargain-shoppers, land-speculators and skiers – not necessarily in that order. Stop only if nearby.
p40

Austria

Music ✓✓✓
Skiing ✓✓
History ✓✓

Regal and elegant, Vienna is a grand capital for a grand empire that no longer exists. Enjoy its faded elegance along with the baroque wonders of Salzburg and the skiing of Innsbruck and the Alps.
p50

Belgium

Beer ✓✓✓
Chocolate ✓✓
History ✓

Belgians can't agree on a language but they do agree that they have the best beer variety in the world and that their chocolate rivals anyone. Plus there's Brussels cafes, Ghent, Antwerp and Bruges.
p113

Britain

History ✓✓✓
Culture ✓✓✓
Nature ✓

British history reads like the history of the world, from Roman times on. Concurrently it has given English-speakers their language and much of their literature and music. Corners of the island are as beautiful as anywhere.

p160

France

Food ✓✓✓
Cities ✓✓✓
Wine ✓✓✓

There's Paris and then there's Paris and that's enough reason to visit France. But consider all the other extraordinary towns and regions (such as Lyon and Provence). In all of them you can enjoy fabulous French food and wine.

p313

Germany

History ✓✓✓
Beer ✓✓
Festivals ✓

Germany has been at the heart of critical moments in history for more than 100years, an inescapable fact for visitors. Today it is a forward-looking nation that enjoys its pleasures like beer and festivals.

p471

Greece

Monuments ✓✓✓
Islands ✓✓✓
Food ✓

The Acropolis is the iconic symbol of an ancient civilization that's a basis for so much of Western culture. But civilization is of little concern at the scores of beguiling islands with their beaches, tavernas and ultra-fresh seafood.

p611

Ireland

People ✓✓✓
Culture ✓✓✓
Nature ✓

The Irish are linked to their culture on the Emerald Isle (it *is* green and has a brutal beauty on the west coast) like few places. Their gift of language spins yarns and creates memorable literature.

p700

Italy

History ✓✓✓
Culture ✓✓✓
Food ✓✓✓

History (Roman Empire), tick. Culture (Renaissance et al), tick. Food (Italian cuisine), tick, tick, tick! Really, there's so much to love about the Boot that who knows where to begin, so just take the plunge.

p771

Liechtenstein

Smallness ✓✓✓
Nature ✓
Castle ✓

Thanks to a monarchy that refuses entreaties from neighbours, this pea-sized principality remains staunchly independent. It's got pretty hikes, a royal castle (not open) and a booming business in two industries: false teeth and passport stamps.
p903

Luxembourg

Forests ✓✓
Fortresses ✓
Towns ✓

Interesting initially for its size, Luxembourg surprises by having more than you'd think. The deep Ardennes forests hide old fortified towns like Echternach while the namesake capital was once the toughest fortress in Europe.
p909

Netherlands

Biking ✓✓✓
History ✓✓
Towns ✓✓

Pedalling along bikeways between Holland's quaint towns (Delft, Leiden etc) you pass windmills and tulip fields. Should a lovely day be this easy? Reflect in Amsterdam where fun, frolic and culture are all easy to find.
p926

Portugal

Towns ✓✓
Culture ✓✓
Beaches ✓

Coimbra has it all: a lively university town where the medieval backstreets yield odd little clubs for fado music. It's an intoxicating mix – if you can escape the pull of Lisbon or the beaches.
p975

Spain

Cities ✓✓✓
Food ✓✓
Beaches ✓

Ever sunny, Spain works its spell from Basque tapas bars to the never-ending nights of vibrant Barcelona to the impossibly photogenic hill towns and famous beaches of Andalucía. Plus you really can smell the orange blossoms in Seville.
p1025

Switzerland

Mountains ✓✓✓
Beauty ✓✓✓
Skiing ✓✓

Even if Switzerland was flat, it would still have chocolate. But add in the Alps and you might forget your sweet tooth. Traversing, climbing, hiking, skiing or just contemplating are regular highlights, with Lake Geneva, Lucerne, the chocolate being added bonuses.
p1149

Look out for these icons:

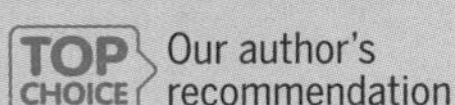

Our author's recommendation

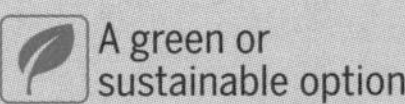
A green or sustainable option

FREE No payment required

See the Index for a full list of destinations covered in this book.

On the Road

Andorra

Includes »

Best Places to Eat

» Borda Pairal 1630 (p43)
» Ca la Conxita (p43)
» Borda del Rector (p46)

Best Places to Stay

» Hotel Pyrénées (p43)
» Hotel Bonavida (p46)
» Hostal Pobladó (p47)

Why Go?

Some say Andorra's nothing but skiing and shopping. They may add that Andorra la Vella, its capital and only town, is a fuming traffic jam bordered by palaces of consumerism. (Fact: Andorra has over 2000 shops – that's more than one for every 40 inhabitants.)

They're right to a point, but also way off course. Shake yourself free of Andorra la Vella's tawdry embrace, take one of the principality's three secondary roads and you're very soon amid dramatic mountain scenery.

This minicountry wedged between France and Spain offers by far the best ski slopes and resort facilities in all the Pyrenees. Once the snows melt, there's an abundance of great walking, ranging from easy strolls to demanding day hikes in the principality's higher, more remote reaches. Strike out above the tight valleys and you can walk for hours, almost alone.

When to Go

Andorra La Vella

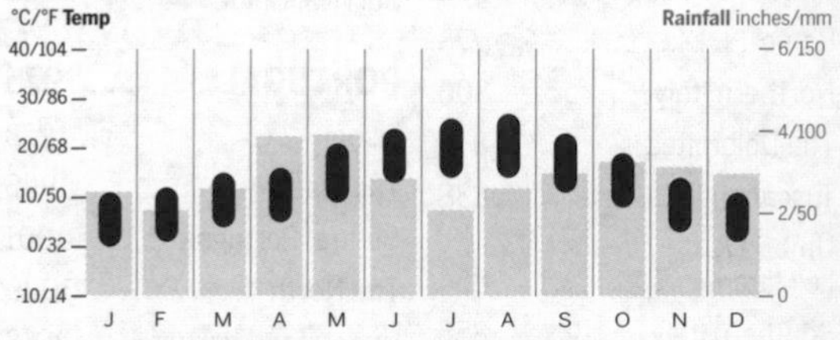

Mid-Jan to mid-Feb Ski slopes are at their quietest after New Year and before French school holidays.

Mid-Jun to mid-Jul & Sep Camp and hike either side of the summer peak, before new snow falls.

8 Sep Every hamlet and village celebrates Fiesta de Meritxell, also marking Andorra's national day.

ANDORRA LA VELLA

POP 20,400 / ELEV 1030M

Andorra la Vella (pronounced 'vey-yah'; literally 'old') is both capital and sole town of this tiny principality. Its main preoccupation is retailing electronic and luxury goods.

Sights & Activities

The small **Barri Antic** (Historic Quarter) was all there was of Andorra la Vella until well after WWII. The rooftop **Plaça del Poble** (accessible by a public lift), a popular gathering place, gives good views of the valley.

FREE **Casa de la Vall** PARLIAMENT
(☎tour reservations 829 129; Carrer de la Vall; ⊙10am-2pm & 3-6pm Tue-Sat, 10am-2pm Sun) Built as a private home, the House of the Valley has served as Andorra's parliament building since 1702. **El Tribunal de Corts** is the country's only courtroom. The **Sala del Consell**, upstairs, must be one of the world's cosiest parliament chambers. Free guided tours (optionally in English).

La Caldea SPA
(☎800 999; www.caldea.ad; Parc de la Mola 10; adult/child €34/25; ⊙variable, consult website) What a sensual delight after a tough day

Andorra Highlights

1. Ski the snowfields of **Grandvalira** (p48)
2. Tramp a sample of the walking trails that thread through the principality, especially above **Ordino** (p46) and **Soldeu** (p45)
3. Steep yourself in the warm mineral waters of space-age **La Caldea** (p41)
4. At **Casa Rull** (p46) see how Andorrans lived before skiing and shopping.

Andorra la Vella

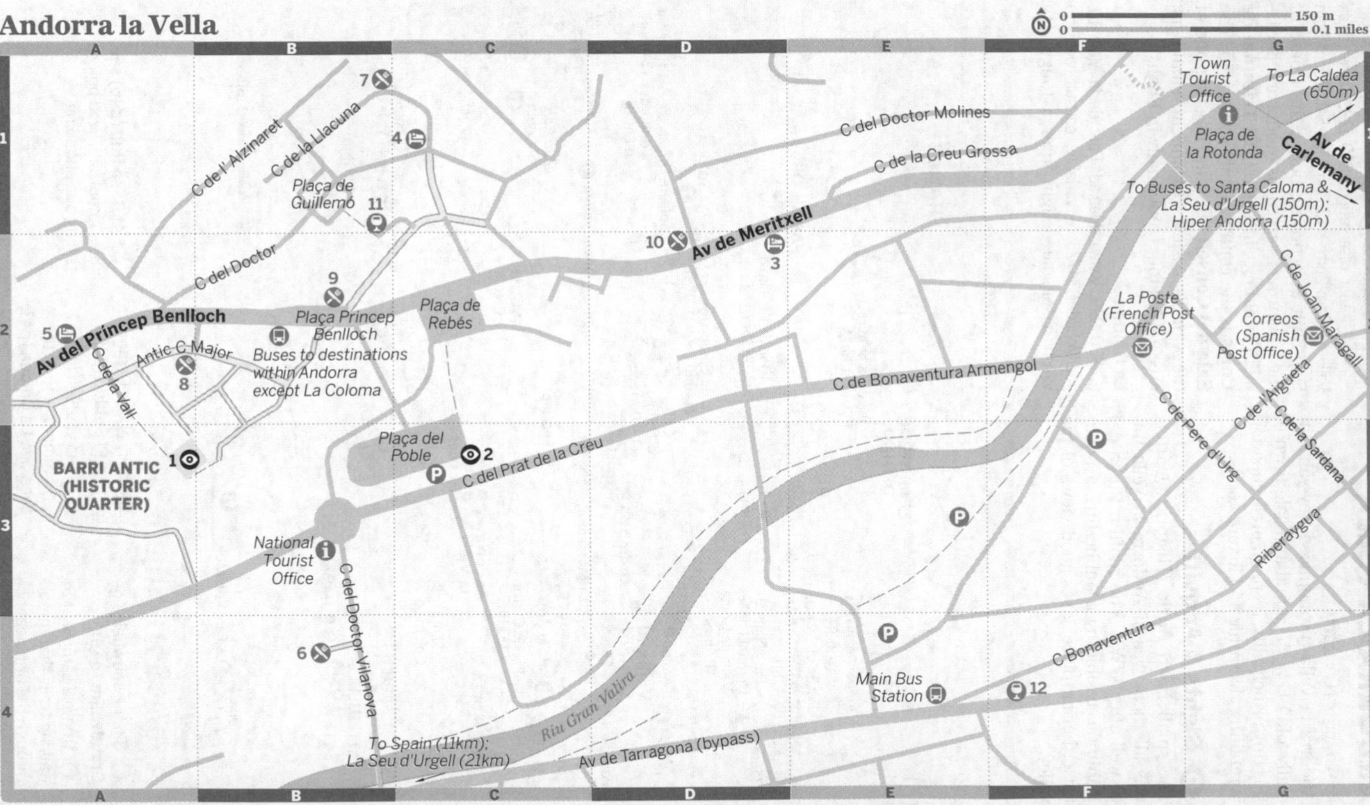

on the ski slopes or walking trails! All glass and gleaming like some futuristic cathedral, Europe's largest spa complex offers lagoons, giant jacuzzis, vapour baths and saunas, fed by warm thermal springs. It's in Escaldes, just a 10-minute walk upstream from Plaça de la Rotonda.

Sleeping

TOP CHOICE Hotel Pyrénées HOTEL €€

(☎879 879; www.hotelpyrenees.com; Avinguda del Príncep Benlloch 20; incl breakfast s €39.50-61, d €53.50-103; P@≋☜) Constructed in 1940, Hotel Pyrénées ranks among Andorra's very few venerable buildings. Snuggle down in its cosy bar which, like the 70 attractively furnished rooms and quality restaurant, has plenty of appealing dark woodwork.

Hôtel de L'Isard HOTEL €€

(☎876 800; www.hotelisard.com in French & Spanish; Avinguda de Meritxell 36; incl breakfast s €60-97, d €70-143; P@☜) At this comfortable, family-run hotel, ask for a room at the rear, overlooking the valley and mountain beyond. There are also six split-level rooms, ideal for families. It runs a good **restaurant** (set menu €16.10, mains €7.50-9.75).

Hotel Florida HOTEL €€

(☎820 105; www.hotelflorida.ad; Carrer de la Llacuna 15; s/d incl breakfast from €53/58; ⊙closed Jun & Nov; @☜) This welcoming modern hotel sits on a quiet side street. Its 27 rooms vary in size; ask for one of the larger ones, which cost no more. After a day's activity, relax in the hotel's sauna – free for guests.

Andorra la Vella

Sights

1	Casa de la Vall	A3
	El Tribunal de Corts	(see 1)
2	Plaça del Poble Public Lift	C3
	Sala del Consell	(see 1)

Sleeping

3	Hôtel de L'Isard	D2
4	Hotel Florida	C1
5	Hotel Pyrénées	A2

Eating

6	Borda Pairal 1630	B4
7	Ca la Conxita	B1
8	Can Benet	A2
	Hotel Pyrénées Restaurant	(see 5)
9	Papanico	B2
10	Pyrénées Department Store	D2

Drinking

11	Cervesería L'Abadia	B1
12	La Borsa	F4

HAVE YOUR SAY

Found a fantastic restaurant that you're longing to share with the world? Disagree with our recommendations? Or just want to talk about your most recent trip?

Whatever your reason, head to lonelyplanet.com, where you can post a review, ask or answer a question on the Thorntree forum, comment on a blog, or share your photos and tips on Groups. Or you can simply spend time chatting with like-minded travellers. So go on, have your say.

Eating

TOP CHOICE Ca la Conxita MEDITERRANEAN €€

(☎829 948; Carrer de la Llacuna 12; three-course meal €25-30; ⊙Mon-Sat) The pink neon sign hints at the kitsch interior with its winsome dolls and cases of classic brandies and spirits. Disregard them. There's no menu, only the freshest produce of the day. Conxita, your exuberant host, will explain. Should her minimal English fail, she'll drag you into her open kitchen and simply show you.

TOP CHOICE Borda Pairal 1630 MOUNTAIN CUISINE €€

(☎869 999; www.labordapairal1630.com; Carrer Doctor Vilanova 7; set menu €16, mains €14-21.50, tapas €3.20-7.25; ⊙Tue-Sun) Overlooked by bleak high-rises, this converted stone farm house survives as a gourmet restaurant with a strong wine list and plenty of hearty meat dishes such as suckling pig and roast goat.

Hotel Pyrénées' restaurant INTERNATIONAL €

(☎879 879; www.hotelpyrenees.com; Avinguda del Príncep Benlloch 20; set menus €9.60 & 13; ⊙closed Jun) Haunting black-and-white photos of a long-lost Andorra flank the walls of this restaurant, which serves quality French and Spanish cuisine beneath sparkling chandeliers. Its €13 *menu*, with plenty of choice and imaginative dishes, is excellent value. For more modest fare, it offers tasty *platos combinados* (€4.70–8.70).

Can Benet MEDITERRANEAN €€

(☎828 922; Antic Carrer Major 9; set menu/mains €35/14-31; ⊙Tue-Sun) At this long-established restaurant, you can eat in the intimate ground-floor bar or the attractively stone-clad upstairs dining room.

Pyrénées Department Store SELF-SERVICE €
(Avinguda de Meritxell 21) Top-floor cafeteria **El Grill** (salads/mains from €3.85/4.90) offers great fare at reasonable prices. Beside it is gourmet **La Bohéme** (set menu €17, mains €14.50-18.50), while one floor down there's a well-stocked **supermarket** for self-caterers.

Papanico TAPAS €€
(☎867 333; www.papanico.es; Avinguda del Príncep Benlloch 4; mains €12.50-20.50) It's quick service at Papanico, where you can snack on tapas and sandwiches (around €5) or enjoy a full meal. Retreat to the rear restaurant with its vast collection of beer bottles arranged around the walls.

Drinking

La Borsa BAR
(Avinguda de Tarragona 36; ⊙11pm-3am Tue-Sun) Like a drink and the chance to dance? Enjoy a little flutter? At the Stock Exchange you can indulge in all three. The price of each drink varies according to the night's consumption, so keep a close eye on that electronic screen.

Cervesería L'Abadia PUB
(Cap del Carrer 2; ⊙6pm-2am Mon-Sat) Here's a place for serious beer drinkers, with over eight classics on draught and many more in the bottle.

Shopping

With prices about 25% lower here than those in Spain and France, you can find big savings on items such as sporting gear, luggage, photographic equipment, shoes, clothing and electronic goods.

Information

Post Office

Correos (Carrer de Joan Maragall 10) The Spanish post office.

La Poste (Carrer de Pere d'Urg 1) The French post office.

Tourist Information

National tourist office (☎820 214; Edificio Davi, Local C, Carrer Doctor Vilanova 13; ⊙10am-1.30pm & 3-7pm Mon-Sat)

Town tourist office (☎873 103; Plaça de la Rotonda; ⊙9am-9pm mid-Jun–mid-Sep; 9am-1pm & 3-7pm Mon-Sat, 9am-1pm Sun rest of year) Besides local knowledge, this office also carries pan-Andorra information.

Getting There & Around

All long-distance buses come and go from the **main bus station** (Avinguda de Tarragona). Buses for destinations around Andorra (with the exception of Santa Coloma) all stop just west of Plaça Princep Benlloch.

La Hispano Andorrana (☎807 000; www.hispanoandorrana.com, in Spanish) runs hourly buses to La Seu d'Urgell (€2.75, 45 minutes) in Spain, stopping outside Hiper Andorra on Avinguda de Meritxell.

Andorra la Vella is a traffic nightmare. Leave your vehicle in the huge open-air car park just north of the main bus station.

Call ☎863 000 for a taxi. For car hire, ring **Avis** (☎871 855).

NUTS & BOLTS

- **Capital** Andorra la Vella
- **Currency** euro (€)
- **Area** 468 sq km
- **Telephone** country code ☎376; international access code ☎00
- **Emergency telephone number** ☎112
- **Official language** Catalan (Spanish is widely used, French less so)
- **Visas** Schengen rules do not apply; see p49 for information.
- **Exchange rates** A$1 = €0.74; C$1 = €0.74; ¥100 = €0.87; NZ$1 = €0.56; UK£1 = €1.16; US$1 = €0.67
- **Budget hotel room (double)** €40–60
- **Two-course dinner** €15–30
- **Connections** The nearest airports are in Barcelona (Spain) and Toulouse (France). Daily buses connect Andorra with each city's airport and train station.

AROUND ANDORRA LA VELLA

Naturlandia

At 2050m, **Naturlandia** (☎741 444; www.naturlandia.ad, in Catalan), north of Andorra la Vella, is a great little winter cross-country skiing centre with over 15km of marked forest trails, snow shoe circuits and Tobotronc, a 5.3km toboggan run through the woods that's the world's longest. Summer fun includes skating on its synthetic ice rink, horse riding, dog sledding and mountain biking.

Sant Julià de Lòria

Sant Julià de Lòria lies 6km south of Andorra la Vella.

Museu del Tabac MUSEUM
(☎741 545; www.museudeltabac.com; Carrer Doctor Palau 17; adult/child €5/3.50; ⏲10am-8pm Tue-Sat, 10am-2.30pm Sun) Occupying a one-time tobacco factory, this museum recalls the (to some) pleasurable sins of tobacco and smuggling, both mainstays of the Andorran economy until the mid 20th century. Rooms are furnished with the trappings of tobacco cultivation, cigarette and cigar making. There's an optional English audio accompaniment and a 15-minute film. Allow at least an hour.

Encamp

Encamp has a couple of places that merit a visit.

Casa Cristo MUSEUM
(Carrer dels Cavallers 2; adult/child €3/1.50; ⏲10am-2pm & 3-6pm Tue-Sat, 10am-2pm Sun) A 30-minute guided tour takes you through this four-storey farmer's house, furnished and equipped as though the last occupants had just walked out.

Museu Nacional de l'Automòbil MUSEUM
(National Automobile Museum; adult/child €3/1.50; ⏲10am-2pm & 3-6pm Tue-Sat, 10am-2pm Sun) One of Europe's finest collections of classic cars includes gleaming Bentleys, a Cadillac, Bugattis, Buicks – and a tinny Citroen 2CV once used as a hearse. Upstairs is an unlabelled jumble of equally antique bikes and motorcycles. In summer its evening hours are extended to 8pm.

ANDORRA ITINERARY

After a day spent pounding the winter ski slopes, drop down to Andorra la Vella for dinner and some intensive shopping. In summer, you can explore each of Andorra's three valleys on separate day walks. Year-round, steep your weary limbs in the warm and soothing waters of La Caldea spa.

Canillo & Soldeu

Canillo (elevation 1500m), 11km northeast of Andorra la Vella, shares a helpful **tourist office** (☎751 090; www.vdc.ad; ⏲9am-1pm & 3-7pm Mon-Sat, 8am-4pm Sun) with Soldeu, a further 7km up the valley along the CG2.

Sights

Museu de les Dues Rodes (☎853 444; www.m2r.ad; Canillo; adult/child €3/free; ⏲3-7pm Tue-Sat, 10am-1pm Sun) With its vintage Ducatis, BSAs, Triumphs and Harley-Davidsons, this is an homage to the motorbike and power-assisted cycles, all restored to pristine, gleaming condition.

Activities

Skiing

Soldeu–El Tarter and Canillo, together with Grau Roig and Pas de la Casa, to the east, constitute the combined snowfields of **Grandvalira** (☎808 900; www.grandvalira.com). With 193km of runs and a combined lift system that can shift over 100,000 skiers per hour, it's the largest ski area in the Pyrenees.

Summer Activities

The tourist office's comprehensive *Mountain, Nature and Sports Guide* (€2) has a wealth of practical information and route descriptions for walkers, climbers and canyon clamberers.

From mid-July to mid-September, the Canillo and Soldeu **cabin lifts** (€3) whisk you up to the higher reaches, from where you can walk or hire a mountain bike to whizz back down.

Canillo's **Palau de Gel** (Ice Palace) has an ice rink, Olympic-sized swimming pool, Italian restaurant and bar with wi-fi.

Up at 2250m, only the magnificent panorama will distract you from your swing at the new nine-hole course **Grandvalira Golf Soldeu** (€30), Europe's highest.

Sleeping & Eating

TOP CHOICE Hotel Bonavida HOTEL €€
(☎751 300; www.hotelbonavida.com; Plaça Major; per person incl breakfast €32-55; ⏱Nov–mid-Apr & mid-May–Sep; P@≋) Most of the cosy rooms, right beside Canillo's cabin lift, have balconies overlooking the river and mountain beyond. The welcome's warm, the cuisine excellent and the copious buffet breakfast includes real espresso coffee.

Hotel Roc de Sant Miquel HOTEL €
(☎851 079; www.hotel-roc.com; per person incl breakfast €32-53, half-board €44-65 Dec-Apr, s/d without breakfast €19/30 Jun-Oct; ⏱closed May & Nov) This friendly, relaxed Soldeu hotel, run by a young Anglo-Andorran couple, makes for a great skiing base. In summer, they hire out mountain bikes to guests and can arrange nature walks and hikes. Half-board is compulsory during most winter months; in summer breakfast (€6) is not included.

Camping Santa Creu CAMPING GROUND €
(☎851 462; camping_santa creu@yahoo.com; per person/tent/car €4/4/4; ⏱Jun-Sep) The greenest, smallest and quietest of Canillo's five camping grounds.

TOP CHOICE Borda del Rector GRILLS €€
(☎852 606; www.bordarector.com; mains €13.50-15.50; ⏱Wed-Mon mid-Nov–Apr & Jun–mid-Oct) At Soldeu's northwestern limit, this low-beamed barn has been imaginatively converted. Meats sizzle on the open fire and the French chef uses only fresh produce.

Fat Albert's BAR, RESTAURANT €€
(☎851 765; meals around €25; ⏱4-11pm mid-Nov–mid-Apr) Also in Soldeu and in another cosy, converted hay barn, Fat Albert's is a favourite with locals and visitors alike. Pizzas cost around €10.

Cal Lulu CATALAN, FRENCH €€
(☎851 427; set menu €15, mains €13-18, pizzas €8.50-13.50; ⏱closed Mon & Tue except Dec–mid-Apr & Jul-Aug) Intimate (it's divided into small booths), Cal Lulu in Canillo is strong on meat dishes, such as grilled rabbit and *pierrade* – three kinds of meat sizzled on a heated stone.

HIGH ON LIFE

Andorra is a proven rejuvenator. All that fresh mountain air? Regular doses of retail therapy? What's uncontested is that average life expectancy in Andorra, at 83.5 years, is the world's highest.

Getting There & Around

Buses L3 and L4 link Canillo with Andorra la Vella and Soldeu every 20 minutes.

Sispony

Tiny Sispony is about 5km north of Andora la Vella and 1km off the CG3.

Casa Rull MUSEUM
(Carrer Major; adult/child incl audioguide €3/1.50; ⏱10am-2pm & 3-6pm Tue-Sat, 10am-2pm Sun) This restored home of a rich farming family captures life in Andorra when all was agriculture and livestock rearing. Allow a full hour to roam the house and view the two audiovisual presentations.

Ordino & Around

Ordino, 8km north of Andorra la Vella on highway CG3, is Andorra's most attractive village. At an elevation of 1300m, it's a good starting point for summer activity holidays. The **tourist office** (☎878 173; www.ordino.ad; ⏱8am-6pm Mon-Sat Jul & Aug, 8.30am-1pm & 3-6.30pm Mon-Sat Sep-Jun, 9am-1pm Sun yearround) is within the Centre Esportiu d'Ordino sports complex beside the CG3.

Sights

Museu d'Areny i Plandolit MUSEUM
(☎836 908; adult/child €3/1.50; ⏱10am-2pm & 3-6pm Tue-Sat, 10am-2pm Sun) For a sense of the life of the very few rich Andorrans of past times, take a half-hour guided visit (in Spanish) around the richly furnished interior of this originally 17th-, mainly 19th-century manor house.

In its grounds, the **Museo Postal de Andorra** (same times & tariffs) is fun, even for non-philatelists. The museum has a 15-minute audiovisual presentation (available in English) and displays set upon set of stamps issued by France and Spain specifically for Andorra.

Activities

There are plenty of excellent walking trails around Ordino. Pick up *Thirty-six Interesting Itineraries on the Paths of the Vall d'Ordino & the Parish of La Massana* from the tourist office. Walk descriptions are altogether tauter than the title.

Mina de Llorts IRON MINE
(adult/child €3/2; ⏱9.30am-1.30pm & 3.30-6.30pm Tue-Sat, 9.30am-1.30pm Sun, mid-Jun–mid-Oct)

North of Ordino, this mine recalls the valley's long-abandoned iron-mining and charcoal-burning heritage. From the mine, you can follow, independently and year round, the **Camino de los Hombres de Hierro** (Iron Miners' Route) – a 3km walk with interpretive panels, well worth supplementing with the tourist office's guide (€2).

El Bosc de Segudet ADVENTURE CIRCUIT
(€35; ⏲9am-1pm & 3-6pm Jun–mid-Sep) Here in the woods, you can play Tarzan on wobbling bridges, swaying rope links and rocky climbs. Book at Ordino's tourist office.

Sleeping & Eating

Hotel Santa Bàrbara de la Vall d'Ordino HOTEL €€
(☎738 100; www.hotelstabarbara.com; Plaça d'Ordino; s/d incl breakfast from €50/70; P) Above the main square and facing the church, this 19-room hotel with its small, attractive bar is excellent value. Its two large split-level rooms are ideal for a family.

Camping Borda d'Ansalonga CAMPING GROUND €
(☎850 374; www.campingansalonga.com; per person/tent/car €6.75/4.75/4.75; ⏲mid-Jun–Apr; 🏊) This large, grassy option enjoys an attractive valley site 1.25km from the village.

Casa León BAR, RESTAURANT €
(☎835 977; http://resto-andorra.com, in French; set menus €9-20; ⏲Tue-Sun) French-owned, this friendly bar-restaurant offers varied tapas, homemade desserts and plentiful à la carte grilled meat dishes.

Getting There & Away

Bus L6 runs to and from Andorra la Vella every half hour.

Arinsal & Pal

Arinsal, 10km northwest of Andorra la Vella, has good skiing and snowboarding and a lively après-ski scene. It's linked with the smaller ski station of Pal, in turn part of the **Vallnord complex** (☎878 000; www.vallnord.com). Their combined slopes have 63km of pistes with a vertical drop of 1010m.

In summer the **Vallnord Bike Park** (☎878 000; www.vallnordbikepark.com; adult/child per day €21/14.50) has a pulse-racing choice of downhill and cross-country mountain-bike tracks.

Arinsal's a good departure point for mountain walks within the scenic **Parc Natural Comunal de les Valls de Comapedrosa**. One particularly popular trail leads to

BUS TURÍSTIC

This tourist bus follows four routes that between them cover the major sights of the principality (including several of its lovely Romanesque churches that are normally closed). Days vary according to the season and tours last around four hours. For information and reservations, call ☎805 151 or visit any tourist office.

Estany de les Truites (2260m) – a natural lake and a staffed mountain hut with beds, refreshments and meals.

Sleeping & Eating

TOP CHOICE **Hostal Pobladó** HOSTEL, RESTAURANT €
(☎835 122; www.hotpoblado.com; per person incl breakfast €20-25; ⏲closed Nov; @) Located next to the cabin lift on Arinsal's main street, this is a great place to meet other skiers or walkers. It has a small, sunny terrace, a restaurant serving Tex-Mex and à la carte dishes and a lively bar with free internet for guests.

Camping Xixerella CAMPING GROUND €
(☎738 613; www.campingxixerella.com, in Spanish; per person/tent/car €6.30/6.30/6.30; ⏲closed Oct; 🏊) Between Pal and Arinsal, this large, well-equipped camping ground has plenty of shade and greenness.

All of the following are on the main street in Arinsal.

Pampa ARGENTINIAN €€
(☎839 630; mains €10-14, pizzas & pastas around €9; ⏲daily) This newcomer offers your standard pastas and pizzas. Its juicy, grilled meats, more enticing and scarcely more expensive, are prepared to perfection by the cheery Argentinian team.

Vertical Limit Café CAFE, RESTAURANT €
(☎835 057; ⏲Mon-Sat) Snack on salads and crêpes (around €10), cold cuts and cheeses, plus tender grilled meat.

Café Everest FONDUES €€
(☎839 599; mains & fondues €13-19; ⏲from 8pm daily) This chalet restaurant is run by Everest adventurer Ian Woodall; in honour of its namesake it's bedecked with Himalayan posters and magazine covers. Also known by its previous name of Refugi de la Fondue, it has meat, cheese and even chocolate fondues on offer, and it also serves up tasty bistro fare.

Getting There & Away

Bus L5 runs between Andorra la Vella and Arinsal via La Massana every half hour. There are also at least 12 local buses daily between La Massana and Arinsal.

UNDERSTAND ANDORRA

History

From the Middle Ages until 1993, Andorra's sovereignty was vested in two 'princes': the bishop of the Spanish border town of La Seu d'Urgell and the French president (who inherited the job from France's pre-Revolutionary kings). Nowadays, democratic Andorra is styled as a 'parliamentary co-princedom', in which the bishop and president remain joint but nominal heads of state.

People

A mere 36% of Andorra's inhabitants are Andorran nationals, a percentage almost equalled by the number of Spanish residents. The official language is Catalan, closely related to both Spanish and French. Many Andorrans speak a couple of these languages and most younger people can manage more than a smattering of English too.

Environment

Andorra is essentially three valleys hugged by steep mountains.

Size 25km north-south, 29km east-west.

Main river Riu Gran Valira, formed near Andorra la Vella by the confluence of the Valira d'Orient and the Valira del Nord.

Highest point Coma Pedrosa (2942m).

Food & Drink

Most restaurants serve dishes that you'll also find in neighbouring France and Spain.

WANT MORE?

Head to Lonely Planet (www.lonelyplanet.com/andorra/andorra-la-vella) for planning advice, author recommendations, traveller reviews and insider tips.

If you're lucky, your menu will feature a dish or two of hearty, meat-based mountain fare.

Escudella A thick soup of *albondigas* (meat balls), perhaps with chicken and a lump or two of sausage, chick peas, carrots, and potatoes. Almost the national dish.

Cabrito con picadillo de frutos secos Goat roasted with almonds and pine nuts.

Pato con pera de invierno Roast duck with pears.

SURVIVAL GUIDE

Directory A–Z

Accommodation

Tourist offices stock a free booklet – *Guia d'Allotjaments Turístics* (Guide to Tourist Accommodation).

Outside Andorra la Vella, there are very few budget options for independent travellers. To compensate, there are plenty of camping grounds, often beautifully situated. During the ski season, many resort hotels won't take independent travellers and may insist upon half-board (breakfast and either lunch or dinner included).

For hikers, Andorra has 27 off-the-beaten-track *refugis* (mountain refuges); all except one are unstaffed and free.

PRICE RANGES

We classify rates in Andorra for a double room with private bathroom like this:

€€€ more than €100

€€ €60 to €100

€ less than €60

Activities

Above the main valleys, you'll find attractive lake-dotted mountain country, great for skiing in winter and walking in summer.

SKIING

Andorra has three ski areas (rental for downhill ski gear is €10–18 per day; for snowboards it's €16–22):

Grandvalira (p48) The largest and best.

Vallnord (p47) Cheaper but generally colder and windier.

Naturlandia (p45) Great for cross-country.

DIVING IN ANDORRA

Seriously, scuba? At 2000m above sea level and 200km from the sea? And in winter? Yes, all of these. **Diving Andorra** (☎868 053; www.divingandorra.com) offers diving beneath the pure ice of high mountain tarns.

WALKING & CYCLING

Lonely Planet's *Hiking in Spain* features more information on a week's worth of hikes within Andorra.

The most reliable map for walkers is *Andorra,* published by Editorial Alpina at 1:40,000.

In summer, most resorts rent mountain bikes (around €15 per day).

Business Hours

Banks 9am-1pm & 3-5pm Mon-Fri, 9am-noon Sat

Restaurants 1-3.30pm & 8-10.30pm

Shops 10am-1pm & 4-8pm Mon-Sat, 9.30am-1pm Sun, major stores 9.30am-8pm

Food

We indicate prices for a main course in Andorra in the following way:

€€€ more than €20

€€ €10 to €20

€ less than €10

Legal Matters

There are no smoking bans in Andorra.

Money

Andorra's official currency is the euro (€).

Post

France and Spain each have their own post boxes and issue their own Andorran stamps (available at tourist offices). You can't use regular French or Spanish stamps.

Telephone

Domestic numbers have no area codes. To call internationally, buy a *teletarja* (phonecard; from €3) at tourist offices and kiosks.

Visas

Visas are not necessary to visit Andorra, but you'll need a passport (EU citizens can opt for their national ID cards instead).

Getting There & Away

Unless you hike over the mountains, the only way to reach Andorra is by road from Spain or France. If driving, fill up in Andorra; fuel is substantially cheaper there.

All bus services arrive at and leave from Andorra la Vella.

To/From Spain

Alsa (www.alsa.es) Eight buses daily to/from Barcelona's Estació del Nord (€28.50; three hours).

Autocars Novatel (☎803 789; www.andorrabybus.com) Five minibuses daily to/from Barcelona's airport El Prat de Llobregat (€32; 3½ hours) .

Direct Bus (☎805 151; www.andorradirectbus.es, in Spanish) Up to eight buses daily to/from Barcelona's airport (€31) via the city's Estació Sants train station.

Viatges Montmantell (☎807 444; www.montmantell.com, in Spanish) Five buses daily to/from Lleida bus and train stations (€19, 2¾ hours), connecting with the Madrid-bound high-speed AVE train. Services stop outside La Caldea.

To/From France

Autocars Novatel ☎803 789; www.andorrabybus.com) Up to four minibuses daily to/from the Toulouse-Blagnac Airport and Gare Matabiau train station (€35, 3½ hours).

Getting Around

Bus routes Six radiate from Andorra la Vella along the principality's three main roads.

Timetables Tourist offices carry *Andorra en Bus,* a free leaflet giving routes, tariffs and timetables. Online, consult www.transportpublic.ad.

Speed limit 40km/h in villages, 90km/h elsewhere.

ONLINE RESOURCES

» **Andorra Mania** (www.andorramania.com)

» **Ministry of Tourism & Environment** (www.andorra.ad)

» **Ski Andorra** (www.skiandorra.ad)

Austria

Includes »

Best Places to Eat

» Figlmüller (p65)
» Deuring-Schlössle (p102)
» Chez Nico (p97)
» Aiola Upstairs (p78)
» Alter Fuchs (p86)

Best Places to Stay

» Hotel Kaertnerhof (p64)
» Villa Trapp (p85)
» Nepomuks (p96)
» Hotel Schloss Dürnstein (p73)
» Seehotel Grüner Baum (p91)

Why Go?

For such a small country, Austria has made it big. This is, after all, the land where Mozart was born, Strauss taught the world to waltz and Julie Andrews grabbed the spotlight with her twirling entrance in the *Sound of Music*. This is where the Habsburgs built their 600-year empire, and where past glories still shine in the resplendent baroque palaces and chandelier-lit coffee houses of Vienna, Innsbruck and Salzburg. This is a perfectionist of a country and whatever it does – mountains, classical music, new media, castles, cake, you name it – it does exceedingly well.

Beyond its grandiose cities, Austria's allure lies outdoors. And whether you're schussing down the legendary slopes of Kitzbühel, climbing high in the Alps of Tirol or pedalling along the banks of the sprightly Danube, you'll find the kind of inspiring landscapes that no well-orchestrated symphony, camera lens or singing nun could ever quite do justice.

When to Go

Vienna

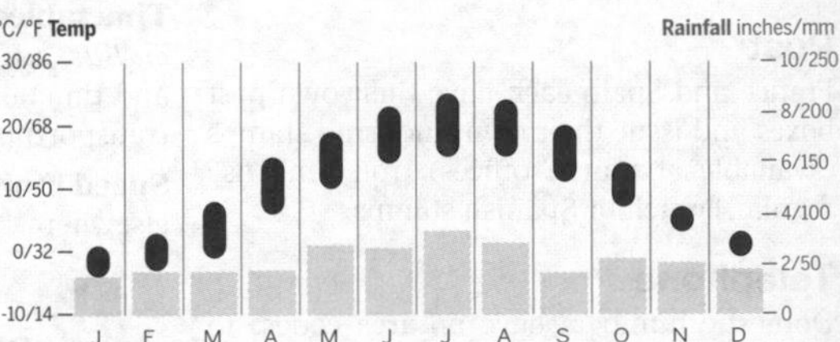

Jul–Aug Alpine hiking in Tirol, lake swimming in Salzkammergut and lots of summer festivals.

Sep–Oct New wine in vineyards near Vienna, golden forest strolls and few crowds.

Dec–Jan Christmas markets, skiing in the Alps and Vienna waltzing into the New Year.

Connections

Bang in the heart of Europe, Austria has speedy connections to its eight neighbouring countries. Trains (p112) from Vienna run to many Eastern European destinations, including Bratislava, Budapest, Prague and Warsaw; there are also connections south to Italy via Klagenfurt and north to Berlin. Salzburg is within sight of the Bavarian border, and there are many trains Munich-bound and beyond from the baroque city. Innsbruck is on the main rail line from Vienna to Switzerland, and two routes also lead to Munich. Look out for the fast, comfortable RailJet services to Germany and Switzerland.

ITINERARIES

Two Days

Spend this entire time in Vienna, making sure to visit the Habsburg palaces and Stephansdom before cosying up in a *Kaffeehäus* (coffee house). At night, check out the pumping bar scene.

One Week

Spend two days in Vienna, plus another day exploring the Wachau wine region, a day each in Salzburg and Innsbruck, one day exploring the Salzkammergut lakes, and finally one day in St Anton am Arlberg or Kitzbühel hiking or skiing (depending on the season).

Essential Food & Drink

» **Make it meaty** Go for a classic Wiener schnitzel, *Tafelspitz* (boiled beef with horseradish sauce) or *Schweinebraten* (pork roast). The humble wurst (sausage) comes in various guises.

» **On the side** Lashings of potatoes, either fried (*Pommes*), roasted (*Bratkartoffeln*), in a salad (*Erdapfelsalat*) or boiled in their skins *(Quellmänner)*; *Knödel* (dumplings) and *Nudeln* (flat egg noodles).

» **Kaffee und Kuchen** Coffee and cake is Austria's sweetest tradition. Must-trys: flaky apple strudel, rich, chocolaty *Sacher Torte* and *Kaiserschmarrn* (sweet pancakes with raisins).

» **Wine at the source** Jovial locals gather in rustic *Heurigen* (wine taverns) in the wine-producing east, identified by an evergreen branch above the door. Sip crisp Grüner Veltiner whites and spicy Blaufränkisch wines.

» **Cheese fest** Dig into gooey *Käsnudeln* (cheese noodles) in Carinthia, *Kaspressknodel* (fried cheese dumplings) in Tirol and *Käsekrainer* (cheesy sausages) in Vienna. The hilly Bregenzerwald is studded with dairies.

AT A GLANCE

» **Currency** euro (€)

» **Language** German

» **Money** ATMs widely available; banks open Mon-Fri

» **Visas** Schengen rules apply

Fast Facts

» **Area** 83,855 sq km

» **Population** 8,217,280

» **Capital** Vienna

» **Telephone** country code ☎43; international access code ☎00

» **Emergency** ☎112

Exchange Rates

Australia	A$1	€0.74
Canada	C$1	€0.74
Japan	¥100	€0.87
New Zealand	NZ$1	€0.56
UK	UK£1	€1.16
USA	US$1	€0.67

Set Your Budget

» **Budget hotel room** €50

» **Two-course dinner** €15

» **Museum entrance** €7

» **Beer** €3

» **City transport ticket** €2

Resources

» **ÖAV** (www.alpenverein.at, in German) Austrian Alpine Club

» **ÖBB** (www.oebb.at) Austrian Federal Railways

» **Österreich Werbung** (www.austria.info) National tourism authority

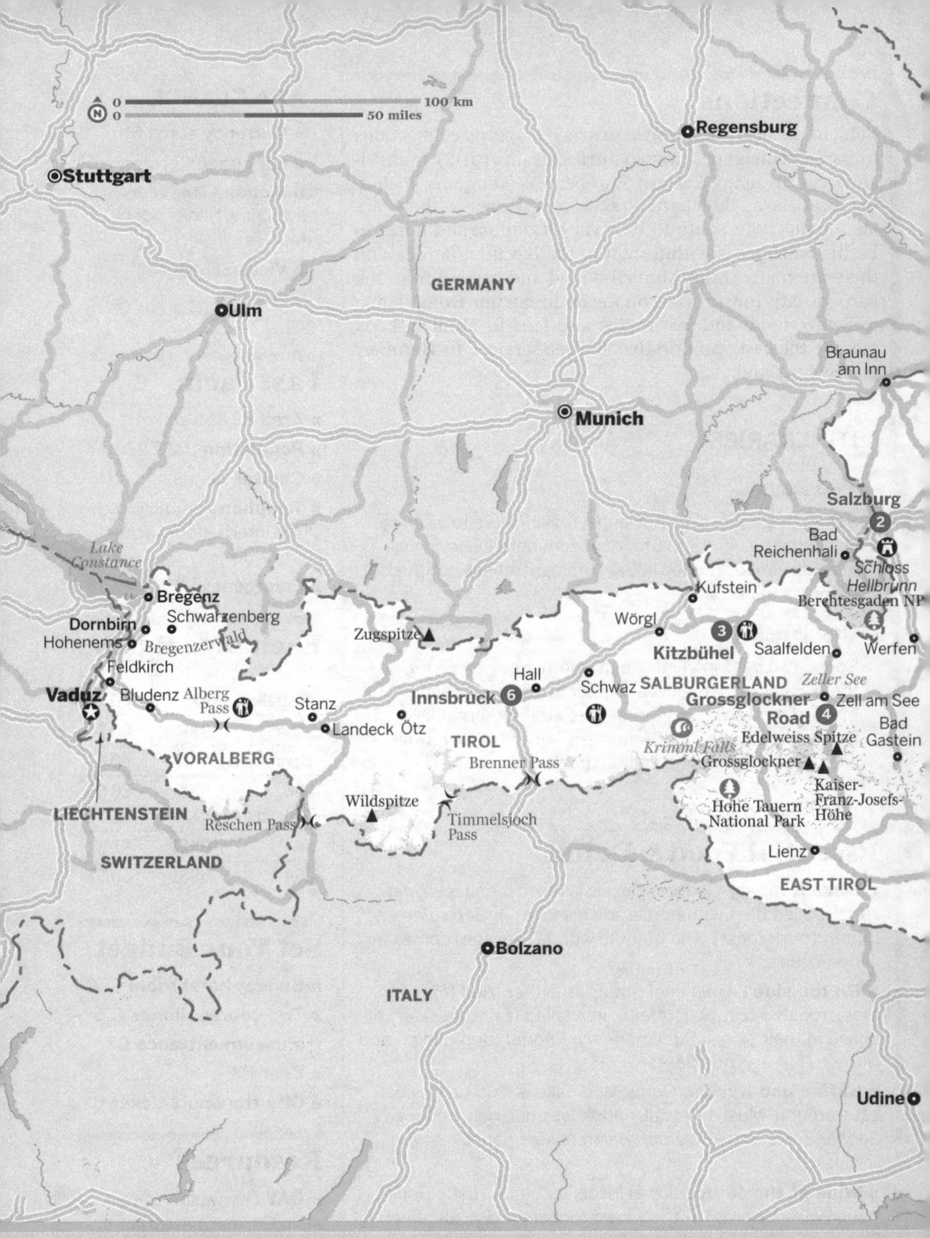

Austria Highlights

❶ Discover the opulent Habsburg palaces, coffee houses and cutting-edge galleries of **Vienna** (p54)

❷ Survey the baroque cityscape of **Salzburg** (p80) from the giddy height of 900-year-old Festung Hohensalzburg

❸ Send your spirits soaring from peak to peak hiking and skiing in **Kitzbühel** (p99)

❹ Buckle up for a rollercoaster ride of Alps and glaciers on the **Grossglockner Road** (p101), one of Austria's greatest drives

5 Dive into the crystal clear lakes of **Salzkammergut** (p88), Austria's summer playground

6 Whiz up to the Tyrolean Alps in Zaha Hadid's space-age funicular from picture-perfect **Innsbruck** (p93)

7 Explore the romantic Wachau and technology trailblazer Linz in the **Danube Valley** (p72)

VIENNA

☎01 / POP 1.68 MILLION

Few cities in the world glide so effortlessly between the present and the past like Vienna. Its splendid historical face is easily recognised: grand imperial palaces and bombastic baroque interiors, museums flanking magnificent squares.

But Vienna is also one of Europe's most dynamic urban spaces. A stone's throw from Hofburg (the Imperial Palace), the MuseumsQuartier houses some of the world's most provocative contemporary art behind a striking basalt facade. Outside, a courtyard buzzes on summer evenings with throngs of Viennese drinking and chatting.

The city of Mozart is also the Vienna of Falco, who immortalised its urban textures in song. It's a city where sushi and Austro-Asian fusion restaurants stand alongside the traditional *Beisl* (small taverns). In this Vienna, it's OK to mention poetry slam and Stephansdom in one breath.

Throw in the mass of green space within the confines of the city limits (almost half the city expanse is given over to parkland) and the 'blue' Danube cutting a path east of the historical centre, and this a capital that is distinctly Austrian.

History

Vienna was probably an important trading post for the Celts when the Romans arrived around 15 BC. They set up camp and named it Vindobona, after the Celtic tribe Vinid, and by the 3rd century it had developed into a town and vineyards were introduced to the area. It was first officially recorded as 'Wenia' in 881 and became a Babenberg stronghold in the 11th century. The Babenberg's ruled for 200 years, until the Habsburgs took control of the city's reins and held them firm until the end of WWI.

Over the centuries Vienna suffered Ottoman sieges in 1529 and 1683, and occupation in 1805 and 1809 by Napoleon and his armies. In the years in between, it received a major baroque makeover, the remnants of which can be seen in many buildings throughout the city. The mid-19th century saw Vienna blossom again, and the royal coffers were emptied to build the celebrated Ringstrasse and accompanying buildings.

Between the two world wars Vienna's political pendulum swung from one extreme to the other – the 1920s saw the influx of socialism and the 1930s the rise of fascism. Vienna suffered heavily under Allied bombing, and on 11 April 1945 advancing Russian troops liberated the city. The Allies joined them until Austria became independent in 1955, and since then it has gone from the razor's edge of Cold War to the focal point between new and old EU member nations.

Sights

Vienna's stately buildings and beautifully tended parks are made for the aimless ambler. Humming with street entertainers, pedestrian-only shopping lanes in the Innere Stadt (inner city) like Kärntner Strasse and Graben are great for a shop 'n' stroll.

Some former homes of the great composers, including those of Mozart and Beethoven, are open to the public; ask at the tourist office.

Many of the following sights and attractions open slightly later in July and August, and close earlier from November to March.

FREE **Stephansdom** CHURCH
(Map p60; www.stephanskirche.at; 01, Stephansplatz; ⌚6am-10pm Mon-Sat, 7am-10pm

ADDRESSES & ORIENTATION

Many of the historic sights such as Stephansdom (St Stephen's Cathedral) are in Vienna's walkable heart, the Innere Stadt (inner city; 1st District), south of the river on a diversion of the Danube, the Danube Canal (Donaukanal). It's encircled on three sides by the Ringstrasse, a series of broad boulevards sporting an extravaganza of architectural delights.

In terms of addresses, Vienna is divided into 23 *Bezirke* (districts), fanning out in approximate numerical order clockwise around the Innere Stadt. Note that when reading addresses, the number of a building within a street *follows* the street name. Any number *before* the street name denotes the district. The middle two digits of postcodes correspond to the district. Thus a postcode of 1010 means the place is in district one, and 1230 refers to district 23.

VIENNA IN...

One Day

Jump on tram 1 or 2 and circle the **Ringstrasse** (Ring road) for a brief but rewarding tour of the boulevard's buildings. Get out at Kärntner Strasse and wander towards the Gothic **Stephansdom** before heading to the **Hofburg** and the breathtaking art collection of the **Kunsthistorisches Museum**. Dine at an **Innere Stadt restaurant** before a night at the **Staatsoper**.

Two Days

On day two, visit imperial palace **Schönbrunn** before a feast of Austrian art at the **Leopold Museum**. Eat at Vienna's celebrated **Naschmarkt**, then cross the city for a twilight ride on the **Riesenrad**. Finish the day with local wine and food at a **Heuriger**.

Sun) Rising high and mighty above Vienna with its dazzling mosaic tiled roof is Stephansdom, or Steffl (little Stephen) as the Viennese call it. The cathedral was built on the site of a 12th-century church but its most distinctive features are Gothic.

Taking centre stage inside is the magnificent Gothic **stone pulpit**, fashioned in 1515 by Anton Pilgram. The baroque **high altar** in the main chancel depicts the stoning of St Stephen; the left chancel contains a winged altarpiece from Wiener Neustadt, dating from 1447; the right chancel houses the Renaissance-style red marble tomb of Friedrich III.

Dominating the cathedral is the skeletal, 136.7m-high **Südturm** (adult/child €3.50/1; ⏲9am-5.30pm). Negotiating 343 steps brings you to a cramped viewing platform for a stunning panorama of Vienna. You can also explore the cathedral's **Katakomben** (catacombs; tours adult/child €4/1.50; ⏲10-11.30am & 1.30-4.30pm Mon-Sat, 1.30-4.30pm Sun), housing the remains of plague victims in a bone house and urns containing some of the organs of Habsburg rulers – gripping stuff.

TOP CHOICE **Hofburg** PALACE

(Imperial Palace; www.hofburg-wien.at) Nothing symbolises the culture and heritage of Austria more than its Hofburg, home base of the Habsburgs for six centuries, from the first emperor (Rudolf I in 1273) to the last (Karl I in 1918). The Hofburg owes its size and architectural diversity to plain old one-upmanship; the oldest section is the 13th-century **Schweizerhof** (Swiss Courtyard; Map p60).

The **Kaiserappartements** (Imperial Apartments; Map p60; adult/child €9.90/5.90; ⏲9.30am-5.30pm), once occupied by Franz Josef I and Empress Elisabeth, are extraordinary for their chandelier-lit opulence. Included in the entry price, the **Sisi Museum** (Map p60) is devoted to the life of Austria's beauty-obsessed Empress Elisabeth, nicknamed 'Sisi'. Highlights include a reconstruction of her luxurious coach and the dress she wore on the eve of her wedding. A ticket to the Kaiserappartements also includes entry to the **Silberkammer** (Silver Chamber; Map p60), showcasing fine silverware and porcelain.

Among several other points of interest within the Hofburg you'll find the **Burgkapelle** (Royal Chapel; Map p60), where the Vienna Boys' Choir performs; the **Spanische Hofreitschule** (Spanish Riding School; Map p60; see p69); and the **Schatzkammer** (Imperial Treasury; Map p60; 01, Schweizerhof; adult/child €12/free; ⏲10am-6pm Wed-Mon), which holds all manner of wonders including the 10th-century Imperial Crown, a 2860-carat Columbian emerald and even a thorn from Christ's crown.

MORE FOR YOUR MONEY

If you're planning on doing a lot of sightseeing, consider purchasing the **Wien-Karte** (Vienna Card; €18.50) for 72 hours of unlimited travel plus discounts at selected museums, attractions, cafes and shops. It's available from hotels and ticket offices.

The City of Vienna runs some 20 **municipal museums** (www.museum.vienna.at), which are included in a free booklet available at the Rathaus. Permanent exhibitions in all are free on Sundays.

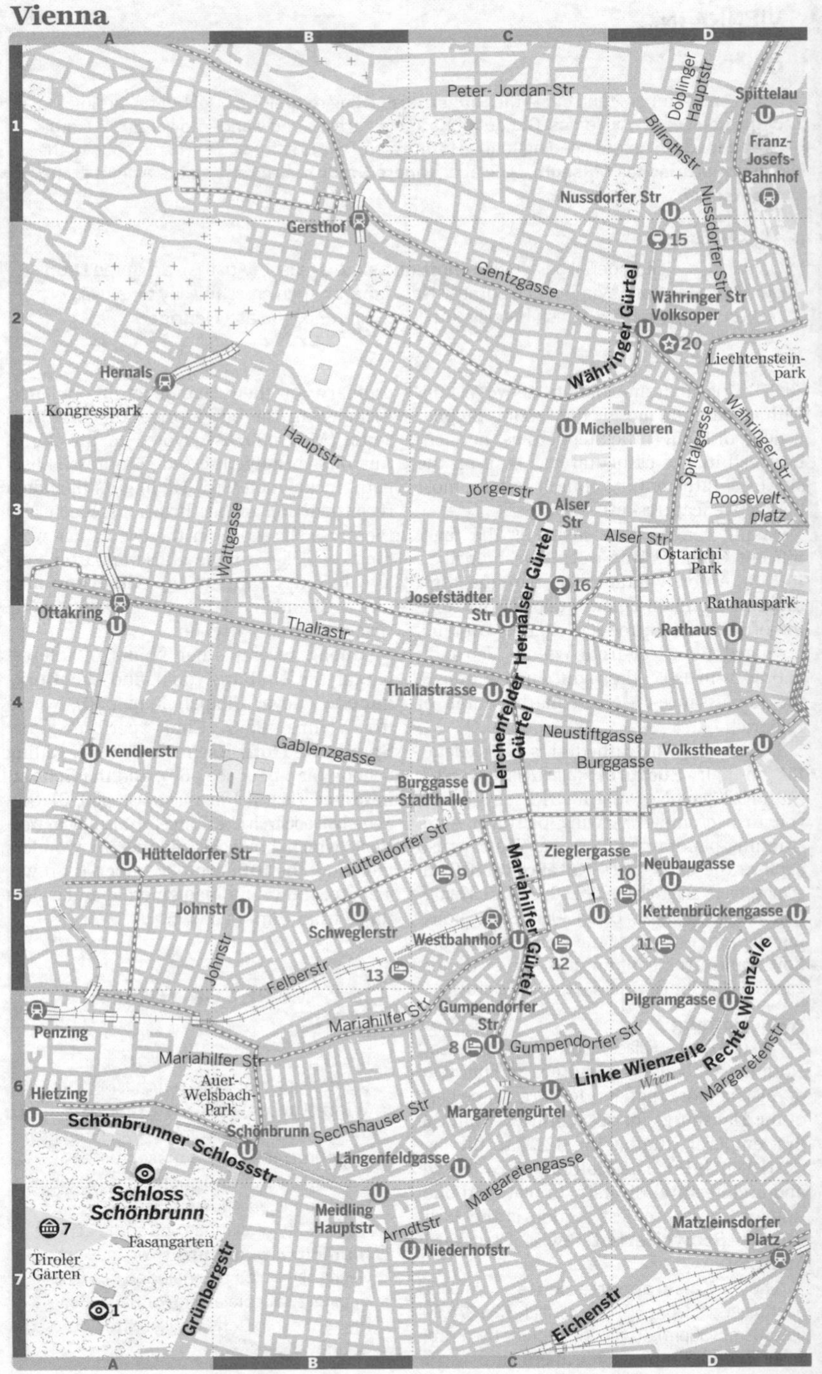
A
B
C
D
1
2
3
4
5
6
7
Peter-Jordan-Str
Döblinger Hauptstr
Spittelau
Billrothstr
Franz-Josefs-Bahnhof
Nussdorfer Str
Gersthof
15
Nussdorfer Str
Gentzgasse
Währinger Gürtel
Währinger Str Volksoper
20
Liechtenstein-park
Hernals
Kongresspark
Michelbueren
Währinger Str
Hauptstr
Spitalgasse
Jörgerstr
Alser Str
Roosevelt-platz
Wattgasse
Alser Str
Ostarichi Park
16
Josefstädter Str
Rathauspark
Ottakring
Thaliastr
Rathaus
Hernalser Gürtel
Thaliastrasse
Lerchenfelder Gürtel
Neustiftgasse
Volkstheater
Kendlerstr
Gablenzgasse
Burggasse
Burggasse Stadthalle
Hütteldorfer Str
Zieglergasse
Hütteldorfer Str
Mariahilfer Gürtel
Neubaugasse
9
10
Johnstr
Kettenbrückengasse
Schweglerstr
Westbahnhof
12
11
Johnstr
Felberstr
13
Pilgramgasse
Rechte Wienzeile
Mariahilfer Str
Gumpendorfer Str
Penzing
Mariahilfer Str
8
Gumpendorfer Str
Linke Wienzeile
Auer-Welsbach-Park
Wien
Margaretenstr
Hietzing
Margaretengürtel
Schönbrunner Schlossstr
Schönbrunn
Sechshauser Str
Längenfeldgasse
Margaretengasse
Schloss Schönbrunn
Meidling Hauptstr
Arndtstr
Matzleinsdorfer Platz
7
Fasangarten
Niederhofstr
Tiroler Garten
Grünbergstr
1
Eichenstr

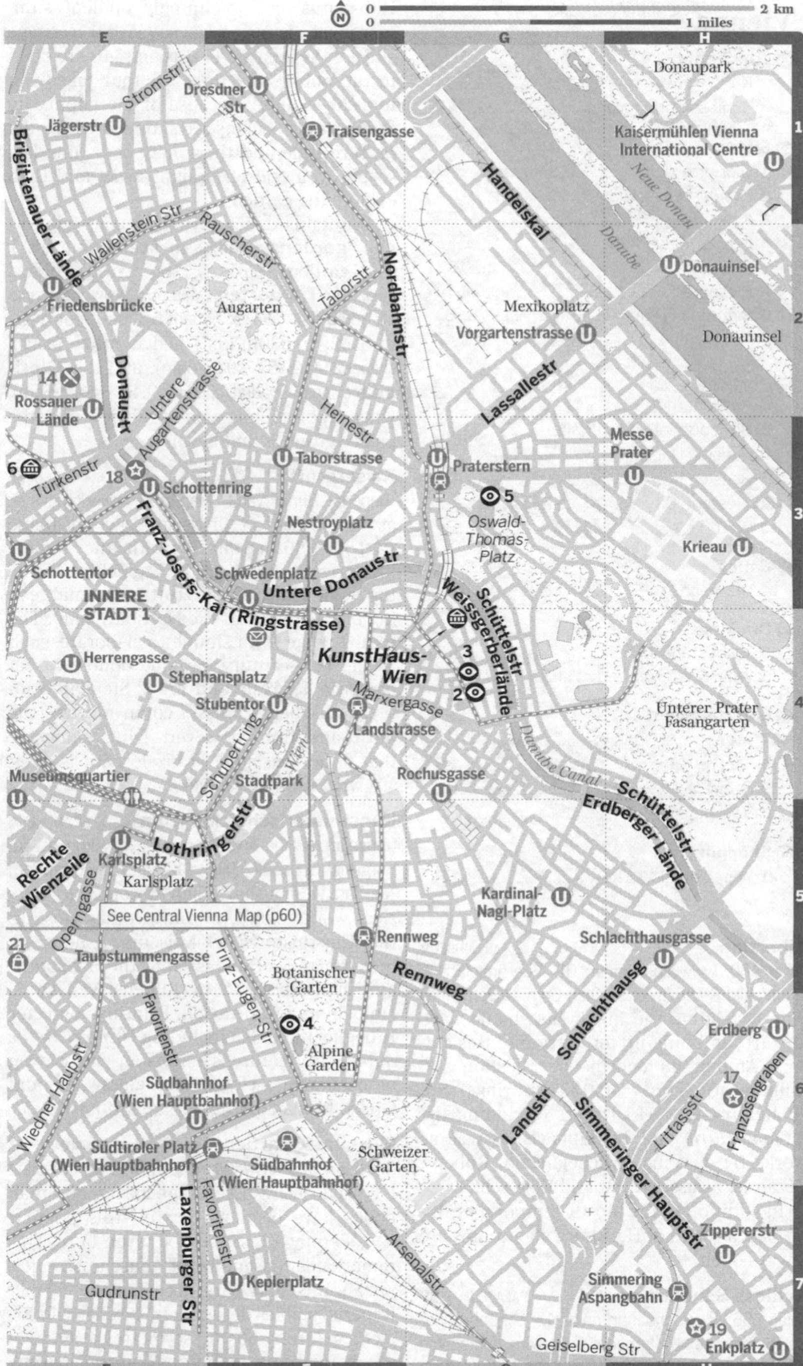
0 2 km
0 1 miles
E
F
G
H
1
2
3
4
5
6
7
Donaupark
Stromstr
Dresdner Str
Jägerstr
Traisengasse
Kaisermühlen Vienna International Centre
Brigittenauer Lände
Neue Donau
Handelskai
Danube
Wallenstein Str
Rauscherstr
Nordbahnstr
Donauinsel
Friedensbrücke
Augarten
Taborstr
Mexikoplatz
Vorgartenstrasse
Donauinsel
Donaustr
Untere Augartenstrasse
14
Rossauer Lände
Lassallestr
Heinestr
Messe Prater
6
Türkenstr
18
Taborstrasse
Praterstern
Schottenring
5
Franz-Josefs-Kai (Ringstrasse)
Nestroyplatz
Oswald-Thomas-Platz
Krieau
Schottentor
Schwedenplatz
Untere Donaustr
INNERE STADT 1
Weissgerberlände
Schüttelstr
KunstHaus-Wien
3
Herrengasse
Stephansplatz
2
Stubentor
Marxergasse
Unterer Prater Fasangarten
Landstrasse
Schubertring
Wien
Danube Canal
Museumsquartier
Stadtpark
Rochusgasse
Schüttelstr
Erdberger Lände
Lothringerstr
Rechte Wienzeile
Karlsplatz
Karlsplatz
Kardinal-Nagl-Platz
Operngasse
See Central Vienna Map (p60)
21
Prinz-Eugen-Str
Rennweg
Schlachthausgasse
Taubstummengasse
Botanischer Garten
Rennweg
Schlachthausg
Favoritenstr
4
Alpine Garden
Erdberg
Wiedner Hauptstr
Südbahnhof (Wien Hauptbahnhof)
17
Franzosengraben
Landstr
Littasstr
Simmeringer Hauptstr
Südtiroler Platz (Wien Hauptbahnhof)
Südbahnhof (Wien Hauptbahnhof)
Schweizer Garten
Laxenburger Str
Favoritenstr
Arsenalstr
Zippererstr
Gudrunstr
Keplerplatz
Simmering Aspangbahn
19
Geiselberg Str
Enkplatz

Vienna

Top Sights

KunstHausWien ... G4
Schloss Schönbrunn ... A6

Sights

1 Gloriette ... A7
2 Hundertwasserhaus ... G4
3 Kalke Village ... G4
4 Oberes Belvedere ... F6
5 Prater ... G3
Riesenrad ... (see 5)
6 Sigmund Freud Museum ... E3
7 Tiergarten ... A7

Sleeping

8 Altwienerhof ... C6
9 Boutiquehotel Stadthalle ... C5
10 Pension Hargita ... D5
11 Pension Kraml ... D5
12 Westend City Hostel ... C5
13 Wombat's ... B5

Eating

14 Stomach ... E2

Drinking

15 Halbestadt Bar ... D2
16 Wein & Wasser ... C3

Entertainment

17 Arena ... H6
18 Flex ... E3
19 Szene Wien ... H7
20 Volksoper ... D2

Shopping

21 Wie Wien ... E5

Albertina ART MUSEUM

(Map p60; www.albertina.at; 01, Albertinaplatz 3; adult/child €9.50/free; 10am-6pm, to 9pm Wed) Simply reading the highlights should have any art fan lining up for entry into this gallery. Among its enormous collection (1.5 million prints and 50,000 drawings) are 70 Rembrandts, 145 Dürers (including the famous *Hare*) and 43 Raphaels, as well as works by da Vinci, Michelangelo, Rubens, Cézanne, Picasso, Klimt and Kokoschka.

In addition to the mostly temporary exhibitions, a series of Habsburg staterooms are always open.

Schloss Schönbrunn PALACE, MUSEUM

(Map p56; www.schoenbrunn.at; 13, Schönbrunner Schlossstrasse 47; Imperial Tour with audioguide adult/child €9.50/6.50; 8.30am-5pm) The Habsburgs' overwhelmingly opulent summer palace is now a Unesco World Heritage site. Of the palace's 1441 rooms, 40 are open to the public; the Imperial Tour takes you into 26 of these. Because of the popularity of the palace, tickets are stamped with a departure time and there may be a time lag, so buy your ticket straight away and then explore the gardens.

Fountains dance in the French-style formal **gardens** (admission free; 6am-dusk). The gardens harbour the world's oldest zoo, the **Tiergarten** (Map p56; www.zoovienna.at; adult/child €14/6; 9am-6.30pm), founded in 1752; a 630m-long hedge **maze** (adult/child €2.90/1.70; 9am-6pm); and the **Gloriette** (Map p56; adult/child €2/1.40; 9am-6pm), whose roof offers a wonderful view over the palace grounds and beyond.

Kaisergruft CHURCH

(Imperial Burial Vault; Map p60; www.kapuziner.at/wien, in German; 01 Neuer Markt; adult/child €4/1.50; 10am-6pm) Beneath the Kapuzinerkirche (Church of the Capuchin Friars), the high-peaked Kaisergruft is the final resting place of most of the Habsburg elite. The tombs range from simple to elaborate, such as the 18th-century baroque double casket of Maria Theresia and Franz Stephan. Empress Elisabeth's ('Sissi') coffin receives the most attention, however: lying alongside that of her husband, Franz Josef, it is often strewn with fresh flowers.

Kunsthistorisches Museum ART MUSEUM

(Museum of Fine Arts; Map p60; www.khm.at; 01, Burgring 5; adult/child €12/free; 10am-6pm Tue-Sun, to 9pm Thu) When it comes to classical works of art, nothing comes close to the Kunsthistorisches Museum. It houses a huge range of art amassed by the Habsburgs and includes works by Rubens, Van Dyck, Holbein and Caravaggio. Paintings by Peter Brueghel the Elder, including *Hunters in the Snow,* also feature. There is an entire wing of ornaments, clocks and glassware, and Greek, Roman and Egyptian antiquities.

MuseumsQuartier MUSEUM COMPLEX

(Museum Quarter; www.mqw.at; 07, Museumsplatz 1, information & ticket centre 10am-7pm) Small books have been written on this popular site, so only a taste can be given here. This remarkable ensemble of museums, cafes, restaurants and bars occupies the former imperial stables designed by Fischer von Erlach. Spanning 60,000 sq metres, it's one of the world's most ambitious cultural spaces.

The highpoint is undoubtedly the **Leopold Museum** (Map p60; www.leopoldmuseum.org; adult/child €10/free; ⏲10am-6pm, to 9pm Thu), which showcases the world's largest collection of Egon Schiele paintings, alongside some fine works by Austrian artists like Klimt, Kokoschka and Albin Egger-Lienz.

The dark basalt **MUMOK** (Map p60; www.mumok.at; 07, Museumsplatz 1; adult/child €9/free; ⏲10am-6pm, to 9pm Thu) is alive with Vienna's premier collection of 20th-century art, centred on fluxus, nouveau realism, pop art and photo-realism.

Schloss Belvedere PALACE, ART MUSEUM

(Map p60; www.belvedere.at; combined ticket adult/child €13.50/free) Belvedere is a masterpiece of total art and one of the world's finest baroque palaces, designed by Johann Lukas von Hildebrandt (1668–1745).

The first of the palace's two main buildings is the **Oberes Belvedere** (Upper Belvedere; Map p56; 03, Prinz-Eugen-Strasse 27; adult/child €9.50/free; ⏲10am-6pm). Pride and joy of the gallery is Gustav Klimt's rich gold *The Kiss* (1908), which perfectly embodies Viennese art nouveau, accompanied by other late-19th- to early-20th-century Austrian works. The second is the grandiose **Unteres Belvedere** (Lower Belvedere; Map p60; 03, Rennweg 6; adult/child €9.50/free; ⏲10am-6pm Thu-Tue, to 9pm Wed), which contains a baroque museum. The buildings sit at opposite ends of a manicured garden.

KunstHausWien MUSEUM

(Map p56; www.kunsthauswien.com; 03, Untere Weissgerberstrasse 13; adult/child €9/4.50) Like something out of a toy shop, this gallery was designed by eccentric Viennese artist and architect Friedensreich Hundertwasser (1928–2000), whose love of uneven floors, colourful mosaic ceramics, irregular corners and rooftop greenery shines through. The permanent collection is a tribute to Hundertwasser, showcasing his paintings, graphics and philosophy on ecology and architecture.

Down the road there's a block of residential flats by Hundertwasser, the **Hundertwassershaus** (Map p56; cnr Löwengasse &Kegelgasse). It's not possible to see inside, but you can visit the **Kalke Village** (Map p56; www.kalke-village.at; ⏲9am-7pm), also the handiwork of Hundertwasser, created from an old Michelin factory. It contains overpriced cafes, souvenir shops and art shops, all in typical Hundertwasser fashion with a distinct absence of straight lines.

FREE **Prater** AMUSEMENT PARK

(Map p56; www.wien-prater.at; 02) This large park encompasses grassy meadows, woodlands, an amusement park known as the **Würstelprater** and one of the city's icons, the **Riesenrad** (www.wienerriesenrad.com; 02, Prater 90; adult/child €8.50/3.50; ⏲9am-11.45pm). Built in 1897, this 65m-high Ferris wheel takes about 20 minutes to rotate its 430-tonne weight, offering far-reaching views of Vienna. It achieved celluloid fame in *The Third Man*.

Palais Liechtenstein ART MUSEUM

(www.liechtensteinmuseum.at; 09, Fürstengasse 1; adult/child €10/free; ⏲10am-5pm Fri-Tue) The collection of Duke Hans-Adam II of Liechtenstein is on show at Vienna's gorgeous baroque Liechtenstein Palace. It's one of the largest private collections in the world, and presents a feast of classical paintings including Raphael's *Portrait of a Man* (1503) and Rubens' *Decius Mus* cycle (1618).

Secession Building LANDMARK

(Map p60; www.secession.at; 01, Friedrichstrasse 12; exhibition & frieze adult/child €8.50/5; ⏲10am-6pm Tue-Sun) This popular art nouveau 'temple of art' building was built in 1898 and bears an intricately woven gilt dome that the Viennese nickname the 'golden cabbage'. The highlight inside is the 34m-long *Beethoven Frieze* by Klimt.

Haus der Musik MUSEUM

(Map p60; www.hdm.at; 01, Seilerstätte 30; adult/child €10/5.50; ⏲10am-10pm) Delving into the physics of sounds and paying tribute to Austria's great composers, this interactive museum is a fascinating journey through music. Most fun of all is the room where you can virtually conduct the Vienna Philharmonic.

Pestsäule MEMORIAL

(Map p60; Plague Column; 01, Graben) Graben is dominated by the knobbly outline of

WANT MORE?

For in-depth information, reviews and recommendations at your fingertips, head to the Apple App Store to purchase Lonely Planet's *Vienna City Guide* iPhone app.

Alternatively, head to **Lonely Planet** (www.lonelyplanet.com/austria/vienna) for planning advice, author recommendations, traveller reviews and insider tips.

Central Vienna

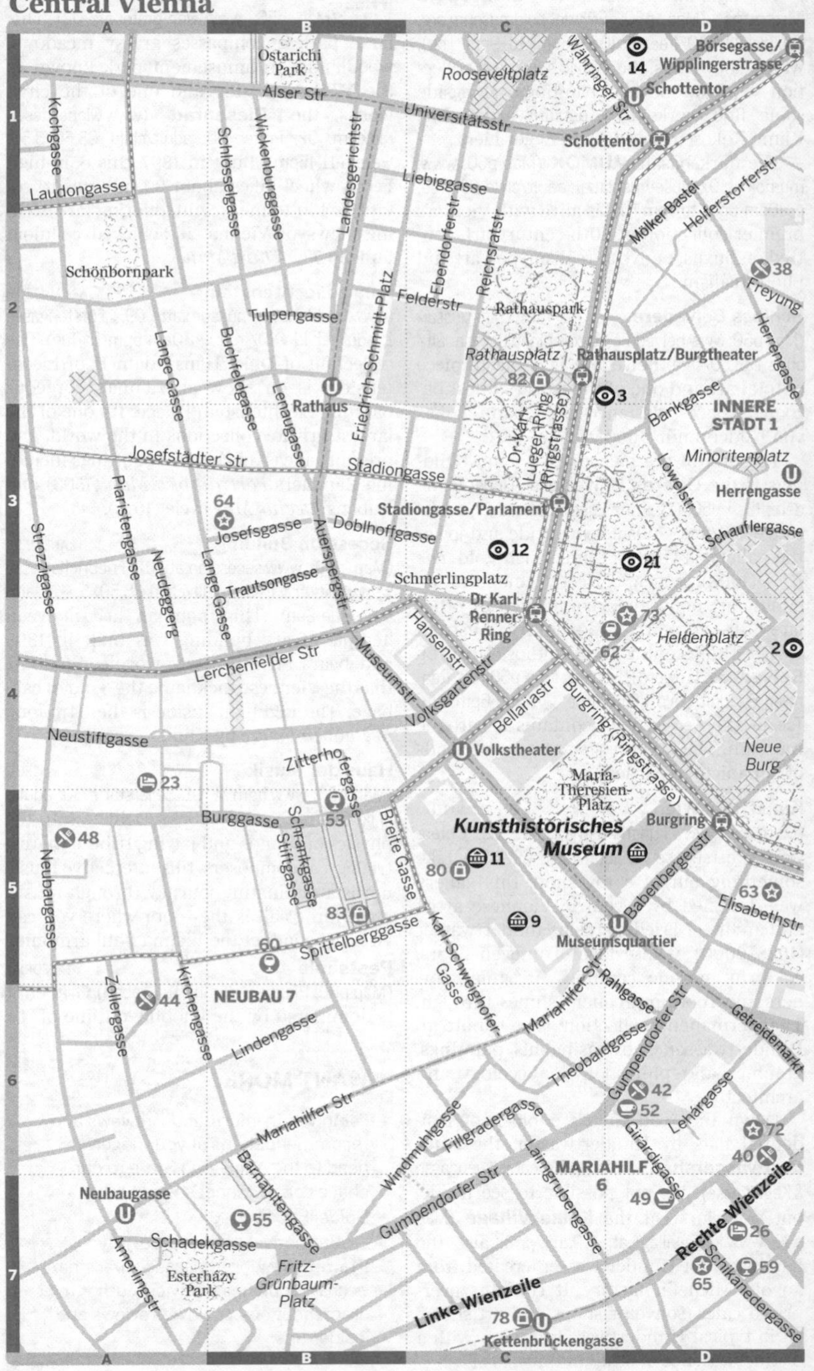

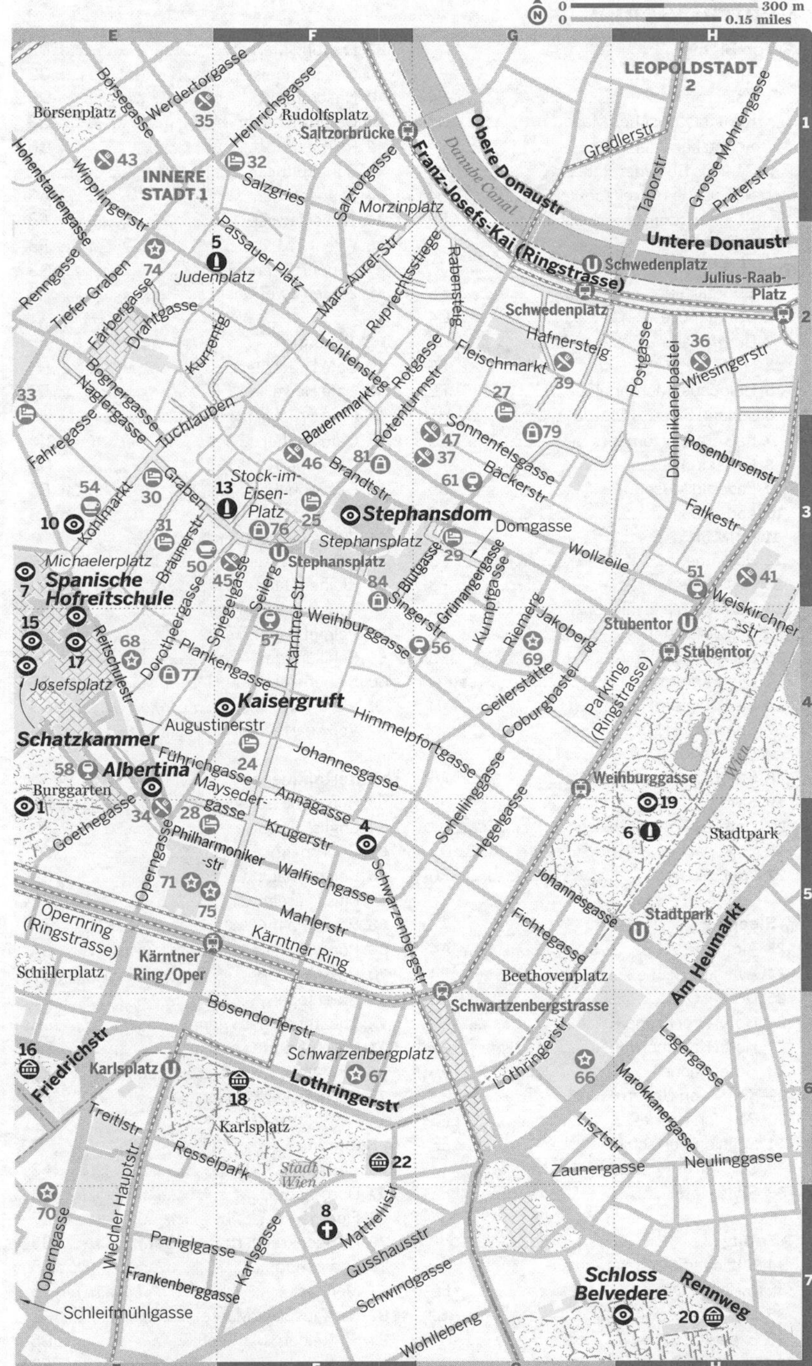

0 300 m
0 0.15 miles
LEOPOLDSTADT 2
INNERE STADT 1
Börsenplatz
Rudolfsplatz
Saltzorbrücke
Obere Donaustr
Danube Canal
Franz-Josefs-Kai (Ringstrasse)
Untere Donaustr
Schwedenplatz
Julius-Raab-Platz
Morzinplatz
Judenplatz
Stephansdom
Stephansplatz
Stock-im-Eisen-Platz
Domgasse
Michaelerplatz
Spanische Hofreitschule
Josefsplatz
Schatzkammer
Kaisergruft
Albertina
Burggarten
Stubentor
Weihburggasse
Stadtpark
Opernring (Ringstrasse)
Kärntner Ring/Oper
Kärntner Ring
Schillerplatz
Schwartzenbergstrasse
Beethovenplatz
Schwarzenbergplatz
Karlsplatz
Lothringerstr
Resselpark
Stadt Wien
Friedrichstr
Am Heumarkt
Schloss Belvedere
Rennweg
VIENNA CENTRAL VIENNA

Central Vienna

Top Sights

Albertina ... E4
Kaisergruft ... F4
Kunsthistorisches Museum ... D5
Schatzkammer ... E4
Schloss Belvedere ... H7
Spanische Hofreitschule ... E4
Stephansdom ... F3

Sights

1 Burggarten ... E5
2 Burgkapelle ... D4
3 Burgtheater ... D2
4 Haus der Musik ... F5
5 Holocaust Memorial ... F2
6 Johann Strauss Statue ... H5
7 Kaiserappartements ... E3
8 Karlskirche ... F7
9 Leopold Museum ... C5
10 Loos Haus ... E3
11 MUMOK ... C5
12 Parliament ... C3
13 Pestsäule ... F3
14 Rathaus ... D1
15 Schweizerhof ... E4
16 Secession Building ... E6
Silberkammer ... (see 7)
Sisi Museum ... (see 7)
17 Spanische Hofreitschule Entrance ... E4
18 Stadtbahn Pavillons ... F6
19 Stadtpark ... H5
20 Unteres Belvedere ... H7
21 Volksgarten ... D3
22 Wien Museum ... F6

Sleeping

23 Altstadt ... A4
24 Aviano ... F4
25 DO & CO ... F3
26 Hotel Drei Kronen ... D7
27 Hotel Kaertnerhof ... G2
28 Hotel Sacher ... E5
29 König von Ungarn ... G3
30 Pension Nossek ... E3
31 Pension Pertschy ... E3
32 Schweizer Pension ... F1
33 Style Hotel ... E2

Eating

34 Bitzinger Würstelstand am Albertinaplatz ... E5
35 En ... E1
36 Expedit ... H2
37 Figlmüller ... G3
38 Freyung Market ... D2
39 Griechenbeisl ... G2
40 Naschmarkt ... D6
41 Österreicher im MAK ... H3
42 Ra'mien ... D6
43 Soupkultur ... E1
44 St Josef ... A6
45 Trzesniewski ... F3
46 Wrenkh ... F3
47 Zanoni & Zanoni ... G3
48 Zu den Zwei Liesln ... A5

Drinking

49 Café Drechsler ... D7
50 Café Hawelka ... E3
51 Café Prückel ... H3
Café Sacher ... (see 28)
52 Café Sperl ... D6
53 Das Möbel ... B5
54 Demel ... E3
55 Futuregarden Bar & Art Club ... B7
56 Kleines Café ... G4
57 Loos American Bar ... F4
58 Palmenhaus ... E4
59 Schikaneder ... D7
60 Siebensternbräu ... B5
61 Vis-à-vis ... G3
62 Volksgarten Pavillon ... D4

Entertainment

63 Burg Kino ... D5
64 English Theatre ... B3
65 Goodmann ... D7
66 Konzerthaus ... G6
67 Musikverein ... F6
68 Palais Palffy ... E4
69 Porgy & Bess ... G4
70 Roxy ... E7
71 Staatsoper ... E5
72 Theater an der Wien ... D6
73 Volksgarten ... D4
74 Why Not? ... E2
75 Wien-Ticket Pavillon ... E5

Shopping

76 Altmann & Kühne ... F3
77 Dorotheum ... E4
78 Flohmarkt ... C7
79 Heiligenkreuzerhof Market ... G3
80 Lomoshop ... C5
81 Manner ... F3
82 Rathausplatz Market ... C2
83 Spittelberg Market ... B5
84 Woka ... F3

this memorial, designed by Fischer von Erlach in 1693 to commemorate the 75,000 victims of the Black Death.

Holocaust Memorial MEMORIAL
(Map p60; 01, Judenplatz) This is Austria's first Holocaust memorial, the 'Nameless Library'. This squat, boxlike structure pays homage to the 65,000 Austrian Jews who were killed during the Holocaust.

Sigmund Freud Museum MUSEUM
(Map p56; www.freud-museum.at; 09, Berggasse 19; adult/child €7/2.50; 9am-5pm) Former house of the famous psychologist, now housing a small museum featuring some of his personal belongings.

Wien Museum MUSEUM
(Map p60; www.museum.vienna.at, in German; 04, Karlsplatz 5; adult/child €6/free; 10am-6pm Tue-Sun) Provides a snapshot of the city's history, and contains a handsome art collection with paintings by Klimt and Schiele.

Loos Haus LANDMARK
(Map p60; 01, Michaelerplatz) A perfect example of the clean lines of Loos' work. Franz Josef hated it and described the windows, which lack lintels, as 'windows without eyebrows'.

Stadtbahn Pavilions LANDMARK
(Map p60; 04, Karlsplatz; adult/child €2/1; 10am-6pm Tue-Sun Apr-Oct) Jugendstil pavilions designed by Otto Wagner for Vienna's first public transport system.

Activities

Dividing the Danube from the Neue Donau is the svelte Donauinsel (Danube Island), which stretches some 21.5km from opposite Klosterneuburg in the north to the Nationalpark Donau-Auen in the south. The island features long sections of **swimming** areas, concrete paths for **walking** and **cycling**, and restaurants and snack bars. The Alte Donau is a landlocked arm of the Danube, a favourite of **sailing** and boating enthusiasts, swimmers, walkers, fisherfolk and, in winter (when it's cold enough), for **ice skating**.

Tours

The tourist office publishes a monthly list of guided walks, *Wiener Spaziergänge*, and can advise on bus tours and river cruises.

Vienna Tour Guides WALKING TOURS
(www.wienguide.at; adult/child €14/7) Conducts 60 different guided walking tours, some of which are in English, from art nouveau architecture to Jewish traditions and the ever-popular *Third Man* Tour.

Festivals & Events

Pick up a copy of the monthly booklet of events from the tourist office. Tickets for many events are available at **Wien-Ticket Pavillon** (Map p60) in the hut by the Staatsoper.

Opernball (01, Staatsoper) Of the 300 or so balls held in January and February, the Opernball (Opera Ball) is the ultimate. It's a supremely lavish affair, with the men in tails and women in shining white gowns.

Wiener Festwochen (www.festwochen.or.at) Wide-ranging program of arts from around the world, from May to mid-June.

Donauinselfest Free three-day festival of rock, pop, hardcore, folk and country music on the Donauinsel in June.

Musikfilm Festival (01, Rathausplatz) Screenings of operas, operettas and concerts outside the Rathaus in July and August.

Viennale (www.viennale.at) The country's biggest and best film festival, featuring fringe and independent films from around the world in October.

Christkindlmärkte Vienna's much-loved Christmas market season runs from mid-November to Christmas Day.

Sleeping

Cosy guesthouses, minimalist-chic hotels, funky hostels – it's all in the mix in Vienna.

WORTH A TRIP

LATE GREATS

The **Zentralfriedhof** (11, Simmeringer Hauptstrasse 232-244; admission free; 7am-7pm May-Aug, to 6pm Mar, Apr, Sep & Oct, 8am-5pm Nov-Feb; 6 or 71 to Zentralfriedhof), about 4km southeast of the city centre, is one of Europe's largest cemeteries. With two and a half million graves, it has more 'residents' than Vienna. Beethoven, Schubert and Brahms have memorial tombs here, and in addition to the clump of famous composers, those pushing up daisies include architect Adolf Loos and the man of Austrian Pop, Falco.

DON'T MISS

SPIN OF THE RING

The Ringstrasse, often just called the Ring, is a wide, tree-lined boulevard encircling much of the Innere Stadt. The best way to see its monumental buildings is by jumping on tram 1 or 2 for a brief but rewarding self-guided tour. For the price of a single ticket you'll take in the neo-Gothic **Rathaus** (city hall; Map p60), the Greek Revival-style **Parliament** (Map p60), the 19th-century **Burgtheater** (Map p60) and the baroque **Karlskirche** (St Charles' Church; Map p60), among others.

Or hop off to relax in one of the Ring's three parks: flower-strewn **Burggarten** (Map p60), **Volksgarten** (Map p60) and **Stadtpark** (Map p60) with its **gold statue of Johann Strauss**.

Central Vienna is first to fill up, especially in summer, so book well ahead if you're keen to be close to the major sights.

TOP CHOICE **Hotel Kaertnerhof** HOTEL €€
(Map p60; ☎512 19 23; www.karntnerhof.com; 01, Grashofgasse 4; s/d from €95/140; @) Tucked away from the bustle, this treasure oozes old Vienna charm, from the period paintings to the wood- and frosted-glass-panelled lift to the roof terrace. Rooms mix a few plain pieces with antiques, chandeliers and elegant curtains. With Stephansplatz less than five minutes away, this place is a steal.

Pension Hargita PENSION €
(Map p56; ☎526 19 28; www.hargita.at; 07, Andreasgasse 1; s/d from €57/68;) Ignore the bland exterior – stepping into the wood-panelled lobby is like entering a mountain chalet. This Hungarian–Austrian family-operated space is tasteful simplicity. Fresh colours and flowers decorate the homey rooms, and the breakfast room has a country feel.

Schweizer Pension PENSION €
(Map p60; ☎533 81 56; www.schweizerpension.com; 01, Heinrichsgasse 2; s/d from €48/65;) This small, family-run pension is a superb deal, with homely touches and eco credentials. Book in advance, though, as it has only 11 rooms and is popular among those on squeezed budgets. Wi-fi is only available in the common areas.

Boutiquehotel Stadthalle HOTEL €€
(Map p56; ☎982 42 72; www.hotelstadthalle.at; 15, Hackengasse 20; s/d from €68/98) Welcome to Vienna's most sustainable hotel, which makes the most of solar power, rainwater collection and LED lighting. Rooms are a blend of modern with polished antiques. You'll get a 10% discount if you arrive by bike or train.

Hotel Sacher HOTEL €€€
(Map p60; ☎514 56-0; www.sacher.com; 01, Philharmonikerstrasse 4; d from €375; @) Walking into the Sacher is like turning back the clock a hundred years. The reception, with its dark-wood panelling, deep red shades and heavy gold chandelier, recalls an expensive *fin-de-siècle* bordello. All rooms boast baroque furnishings and 19th-century oil paintings, and the top-floor spa pampers with chocolate treatments.

Altstadt PENSION €€
(Map p60; ☎522 66 66; www.altstadt.at; 07, Kirchengasse 41; s/d from €149/249; @) One of Vienna's finest pensions, Altstadt has charming, individually decorated rooms, with high ceilings, plenty of space and a cosy lounge with free afternoon tea and cakes. Staff are genuinely affable and artworks are from the owner's personal collection.

Wombat's HOSTEL €
(Map p56; ☎897 36 23; www.wombats.at; 05, Mariahilfer Strasse 137; dm/r €20/56; @) For a relaxed Aussie hostel vibe in central Vienna, it has to be Wombat's. Interiors are rainbow bright, dorms modern with en suite, and common areas include a bar and pool tables. Bike rental is also available.

Pension Nossek PENSION €€
(Map p60; ☎533 70 41-0; www.pension-nossek.at, in German; 01, Graben 17; s/d from €65/120;) Overlooking the Graben and just steps from Stephansdom, Nossek has an enviable location and polite service. Rooms are spacious, spotless and enhanced with baroque-style furnishings. Credit cards are not accepted.

Altwienerhof HOTEL €€
(Map p56; ☎892 60 00; www.altwienerhof.at; 15, Herklotzgasse 6; s/d €79/99) This pseudo-plush family-run hotel, just outside the Gürtel ring, offers ridiculously romantic abodes –

think miniature chandeliers, antique pieces, floral bedding and lace tablecloths. Breakfast is taken in the conservatory or large inner courtyard.

Aviano PENSION €€
(Map p60; ☎512 83 30; www.secrethomes.at; 01, Marco-d'Aviano-Gasse 1; s/d €104/148;) Aviano is a supremely central, good-value choice. The small high-ceilinged rooms feature whitewashed antique furnishings and decorative moulding. In summer, the sunny breakfast room opens onto a small balcony.

Pension Pertschy PENSION €€
(Map p60; ☎534 49-0; www.pertschy.com; 01, Habsburgergasse 5; s/d €79/119;) This quiet pension, just off the Graben, is hard to beat. The spacious rooms sport bright colours and period pieces, the staff are friendly, and children are welcomed with gusto (toys and highchairs are available).

Westend City Hostel HOSTEL €
(Map p56; ☎597 67 29; www.westendhostel.at; 06, Fügergasse 3; dm/s/d €20.50/52/62; @) This independent hostel received a bright and funky head-to-toe revamp in 2009. All of the spacious dorms are en suite and the ivy-clad inner courtyard is superb.

Hotel Drei Kronen PENSION €€
(Map p60; ☎587 32 89; www.hotel3kronen.at; 04, Schleifmühlegasse 25; s/d €79/100; @) A sweet family-run abode near the Naschmarkt, with rooms decked out in Jugendstil furnishings. There's even free *Sekt* (sparkling wine) at breakfast.

Pension Kraml PENSION €
(Map p56; ☎587 85 88; www.pensionkraml.at; 06, Brauergasse 5; s/d from €35/76, apt from €99;) A quiet and cosy family-run pension, where old-school politeness and comfort are paramount. Rooms are large (if a little dated).

König von Ungarn HOTEL €€
(Map p60; ☎515 84-0; www.kvu.at; 01, Schulerstrasse 10; s/d €150/219;) Vienna's oldest hotel (1746) balances class and informality. Rooms are individually furnished with antiques (the best face Domgasse) and the inner courtyard is wonderful.

Eating

Vienna has thousands of restaurants covering all budgets and styles of cuisine, but dining doesn't stop there. *Kaffeehäuser* (coffee houses), *Beisl* (small taverns) and *Heurigen* (wine taverns) are just as fine for a good meal. *Würstel Stande* (sausage stands) are conveniently located on street corners and squares.

TOP CHOICE **Figlmüller** BEISL €€
(Map p60; ☎512 61 77; 01, Wollzeile 5; mains €7-15; lunch & dinner, closed Aug) This famous *Beisl* serves some of the biggest (and best) schnitzels in town. Sure, the rural decor is contrived and beer isn't served (only wine from the owner's own vineyard), but it doesn't get more Viennese than this.

Stomach AUSTRIAN €€
(Map p56; ☎310 20 99; 09, Seegasse 26; mains €10-18; dinner Wed-Sat, lunch & dinner Sun) Once a butcher's shop, Stomach serves seriously good Austrian food, from Styrian roast beef to pumpkin soup. The interior is rural Austrian, and the overgrown garden creates a picturesque backdrop. Reservations are recommended.

Griechenbeisl BEISL €€
(Map p60; ☎533 19 77; 01, Fleischmarkt 11; mains €11-24; 11am-1am) This is Vienna's oldest *Beisl* (dating from 1447), once frequented by the likes of Beethoven, Schubert and Brahms. The vaulted, wood-panelled rooms are a cosy setting for classic Viennese dishes. Bag a spot in the front garden in summer.

Wrenkh VEGETARIAN €€
(Map p60; ☎533 15 26; 01, Bauernmarkt 10; lunch menus €9.50-10.50, mains €8.50-19.50; lunch & dinner Mon-Fri, dinner Sat;) Glass-walled Wrenkh serves beautifully presented vegetarian food prepared with organic produce. The sleek-looking customers come for the lip-smacking fare that ranges from risotto to tofu.

DESIGNER SPLURGE

Vienna is making architectural waves with its ultra-sleek design hotels, including these two favourites:

DO & CO HOTEL €€€
(Map p60; ☎241 88; www.doco.com; 01, Stephansplatz 12; r from €310) Swanky & sexy with views of Stephansdom.

Style Hotel HOTEL €€€
(Map p60; ☎22 780 0; www.stylehotel.at; 01, Herrengasse 12; r from €250) Top contender for the title of Vienna's most fashionable hotel, with art nouveau and art deco overtones.

Zu den Zwei Liesln BEISL €
(Map p60; ☎523 32 82; 07, Burggasse 63; lunch menus €4.90-5.30, mains €6-11.90) Six varieties of schnitzel crowd the menu at this classic budget *Beisl* of legendary status. The quaint and cosy wood-panelled interior is complemented by a tree-shaded inner courtyard.

En JAPANESE €€
(Map p60; ☎532 44 90; 01, Werdertorgasse 8; lunch menus €8.20-9.70, mains €9-23; ⏲closed Sun) En offers some of the best sushi in Vienna, and its lunch menus are a bargain considering the quality. Outdoor seating is available in summer; in winter sit at the bar and watch the skilled sushi-makers prepare your meal.

St Josef VEGETARIAN €
(Map p60; ☎526 68 18; 07, Mondscheingasse 10; small/large plates €6.80/8.20; ⏲breakfast & lunch Mon-Sat; ⊜☑) This canteen-like vegetarian place that cooks to a theme each day (Indian, for instance) has a sparse, industrial character and super-friendly staff.

Expedit ITALIAN €€
(Map p60; ☎512 33 13 23; 01, Wiesingerstrasse 6; mains €8-25; ⏲10am-1am Mon-Sat, to 10pm Sun) Expedit has moulded itself on a Ligurian *osteria*. Its warehouse decor creates a busy yet informal atmosphere and a clean, smart look. Every day brings new, seasonal dishes to the menu. Reservations are recommended.

Österreicher im MAK AUSTRIAN €€
(Map p60; ☎7140 121; 01, Stubenring 5; lunch €6.40, mains €14.50-20.80; ⏲8.30am-1am) This is the brainchild of Helmut Österreicher, one of Austria's leading chefs. He jazzes up back-to-the-roots Austrian dishes such as *Tafelspitz* with exotic or nonregional ingredients. Sleek architectural lines create a modern flourish.

Ra'mien ASIAN €€
(Map p60; ☎585 47 98; 06, Gumpendorfer Strasse 9; mains €7-16; ⏲Tue-Sun, closed Aug) Bright young things gravitate towards this minimalist-chic noodle bar, with a choice of Thai, Japanese, Chinese and Vietnamese noodle soups and rice dishes. The lounge bar downstairs has regular DJs and stays open until at least 2am.

Bitzinger Würstelstand am Albertinaplatz SAUSAGE STAND €
(Map p60; 01, Albertinaplatz; sausages €2.80-3.50; ⏲24hr) Located behind the Staatsoper, this is one of Vienna's best sausage stands. Watch ladies and gents dressed to the nines while enjoying your wurst and a beer.

Trzesniewski SANDWICHES €
(Map p60; Dorotheergasse 1; sandwiches from €2.80; ⏲8.30am-7.30pm Mon-Fri, 9am-5pm Sat) Possibly Austria's finest sandwich shop, with 21 delectably thick spreads, from tuna with egg to Swedish herring. Plan on sampling a few; two bites and they're gone.

Soupkultur SOUP & SALAD €
(Map p60; Wipplingerstrasse 32; soups €3.90-4.50, salads €5.80-7.20; ⏲lunch Mon-Fri) Organic produce and aromatic spices are used to create eight different soups and eight varieties of salads each week.

Zanoni & Zanoni ICE CREAM €
(Map p60; Lugeck 7; ice cream from €2; ⏲7am-midnight) An Italian gelataria and *pasticceria* open 365 days a year. Great for creamy gelati and late-night desserts.

Quick Eats & Self-Catering

Self-caterers can stock up at the Hofer, Billa and Spar **supermarkets** in the centre. Some have well-stocked delis that make sandwiches to order – the perfect cheap lunch on the run. The city is also dotted with markets.

Freyung Market MARKET
(Map p60; 01, Freyung; ⏲9am-6pm Fri & Sat 1st & 3rd weekend of month) Sells fresh organic produce.

Drinking

Vienna is riddled with late-night drinking dens, with concentrations of pulsating bars north and south of the Naschmarkt, around Spittelberg (many double as restaurants) and along the Gürtel (mainly around the U6 stops of Josefstädter Strasse and Nussdorfer Strasse). The Bermuda Dreieck (Bermuda Triangle), near the Danube Canal in the Innere Stadt, also has many bars, but they are more touristy.

Vienna's age-old *Heurigen* are identified by a *Busch'n* (a green wreath or branch) hanging over the door; many have outside tables in large gardens or courtyards, while inside the atmosphere is rustic. Some serve a hot or cold buffet. *Heurigen* cluster in the wine-growing suburbs to the north, southwest, west and northwest of the city. Opening times are approximately from 4pm to 11pm, and wine costs around €2.50 per *Viertel* (250mL).

TOP CHOICE **Palmenhaus** BAR, CAFE
(Map p60; 01, Burggarten; ⌚10am-2am, closed Mon & Tue Jan-Feb) Housed in a beautifully restored Victorian palm house, the Palmenhaus has a relaxed vibe. In summer, tables spill out onto the pavement overlooking the green of the Burggarten, and there are occasional club nights.

Das Möbel BAR, CAFE
(Map p60; 07, Burggasse 10; ⌚10am-1am;) The interior is never dull at this bar near the MuseumsQuartier. It's remarkable for its funky decor and furniture – cube stools, assorted moulded lamps – and everything is up for sale.

Vis-à-vis WINE BAR
(Map p60; 01, Wollzeile 5; ⌚4.30-10.30am Tue-Sat) Hidden down a narrow, atmospheric passage is this wee wine bar – it may only seat close to 10 but it makes up for it with over 350 wines on offer (strong emphasis on Austrian faves) and great antipasti.

Loos American Bar COCKTAIL BAR
(Map p60; 01, Kärntner Durchgang 10; ⌚noon-4am Sun-Wed, to 5am Thu-Sat) Designed by Adolf Loos in 1908, this tiny box decked head-to-toe in onyx is *the* spot for a classic cocktail in the Innere Stadt, expertly whipped up by talented mixologists.

10er Marie HEURIGER
(16, Ottakringerstrasse 222-224; ⌚3pm-midnight Mon-Sat) Vienna's oldest *Heuriger* has been going strong since 1740 – Schubert, Strauss and Crown Prince Rudolf all kicked back a glass or three here. The usual buffet is available.

Wein & Wasser WINE BAR
(Map p56; 08, Laudongasse 57; ⌚6pm-1am Mon-Sat) At 'Wine & Water', the staff warmly guide you through the lengthy list, including over 20 Austrian wines served by the glass. The brick arches, lit by flickering candles, create a cosy space for imbibing.

Halbestadt Bar COCKTAIL BAR
(Map p56; 09, Stadtbogen 155; ⌚6pm-2am Mon-Thu, 7pm-2am Fri, to 4am Sat & Sun) Impeccable hospitality, with no trace of snobbery, is what this sleek little bar under the subway arches is about. Mixologists hold court creating tongue-enticing works of art with glasses to match.

Futuregarden Bar & Art Club BAR, CLUB
(Map p60; 06, Schadekgasse 6; ⌚6pm-2am Mon-Sat, from 8pm Sun) A white, spartan space with a cool atmosphere and up-to-the-minute electronic tracks.

DON'T MISS

NASCHMARKT NIBBLES

The sprawling **Naschmarkt** (Map p60; 06, Linke & Rechte Wienzeile; ⌚6am-6.30pm Mon-Fri, to 5pm Sat) is *the* place to *nasch* (snack) in Vienna. Big and bold, the market is a foodie's dream. The food stalls selling meats, fruits, vegetables, cheeses and spices are perfect for assembling your own picnic. There are also plenty of people-watching cafes, restaurants dishing up good-value lunches, delis and takeaway stands where you can grab a falafel or baguette.

Siebensternbräu PUB
(Map p60; www.7stern.at; 07, Siebensterngasse 19; ⌚10am-midnight) Large brewery with all the main varieties, plus hemp beer, chilli beer and smoky beer. The hidden back garden is sublime in summer.

Schikaneder BAR
(Map p60; 04, Margareten Strasse 22-24; ⌚6pm-4am) A grungy bar with a buzzing vibe that attracts students and an arty crowd. Also hosts movie nights.

Volksgarten Pavillon BAR
(Map p60; 01, Burgring 1; ⌚11am-2am Apr–mid-Sep) A lovely 1950s-style pavilion with views of Heldenplatz and an ever-popular garden.

☆ Entertainment

Vienna is, and probably will be till the end of time, the European capital of opera and classical music. The program of music events is never-ending and even the city's buskers are often classically trained musicians. The tourist office produces a handy monthly listing of concerts and other events.

Flex CLUB
(Map p56; www.flex.at; 01, Donaukanal, Augartenbrücke; ⌚6pm-4am) Vienna's most celebrated low-life club, Flex has one of the best sound systems in Europe, puts on great shows and features the top DJs from Vienna and abroad. Messed Up (techno) on Monday and London Calling (alternative and indie) on Wednesday and Friday are always popular.

DON'T MISS

COFFEE HOUSE CULTURE

Vienna's legendary *Kaffeehäuser* (coffee houses) are wonderful places for people-watching, daydreaming and catching up on gossip or world news. Most serve light meals alongside a mouth-watering array of cakes and tortes. Expect to pay around €7 for a coffee with a slice of cake. These are just some of our favourites.

Café Sperl CAFE

(Map p60; 06, Gumpendorfer Strasse 11; ⏲7am-11pm Mon-Sat, 11am-8pm Sun, closed Sun in summer;) With its gorgeous Jugendstil fittings, grand dimensions, cosy booths and unhurried air, Sperl is one of Vienna's finest coffee houses. The must-try is *Sperl Torte* – an almond and chocolate cream dream.

Café Hawelka CAFE

(Map p60; 01, Dorotheergasse 6; ⏲8am-2am Mon & Wed-Sat, from 10am Sun) A traditional haunt for artists and writers, this shabby-chic coffee house attracts the gamut of Viennese society. There's a convivial vibe between friends and complete strangers.

Café Sacher CAFE

(Map p60; 01, Philharmonikerstrasse 4; ⏲8am-11:30pm) This opulent coffee house is celebrated for its *Sacher Torte* (€4), a rich chocolate cake with apricot jam once favoured by Emperor Franz Josef.

Café Prückel CAFE

(Map p60; 01, Stubenring 24; ⏲8.30am-10pm) Intimate booths, strong coffee and diet-destroying cakes are all attractions at this 1950s gem. There's live piano music from 7pm to 10pm Monday, Wednesday and Friday.

Demel CAFE

(Map p60; 01, Kohlmarkt 14; ⏲10am-7pm) An elegant, regal cafe near the Hofburg. Demel's speciality is the *Anna Torte*, a chocolate and nougat calorie-bomb.

Café Drechsler CAFE

(Map p60; 06, Linke Wienzeile 22; ⏲8am-2am Mon, 3am-2am Tue-Sat, 3am-midnight Sun) Sir Terence Conran revamped this stylish yet distinctly Viennese cafe. Its goulash is legendary, as are the DJ tunes that keep the vibe hip and upbeat.

Kleines Café CAFE

(Map p60; 01, Franziskanerplatz 3; ⏲10am-2am) Tiny bohemian cafe with wonderful summer seating on Franziskanerplatz.

Staatsoper CONCERT VENUE

(Map p60; ☎514 44 7880; www.wiener-staatsoper.at; 01, Opernring 2; ⏲box office closed Sun) Performances at Vienna's premier opera and classical music venue are lavish, formal affairs, where people dress up. Standing-room tickets (€3 to €4) are sold 80 minutes before performances begin.

Musikverein CONCERT VENUE

(Map p60; ☎505 81 90; www.musikverein.at; 01, Bösendorferstrasse 12; ⏲box office closed Sun) The opulent Musikverein, home to the Vienna Philharmonic Orchestra, is celebrated for its acoustics. Standing-room tickets in the main hall cost €4 to €6.

Porgy & Bess JAZZ CLUB

(Map p60; www.porgy.at; 01, Riemergasse 11; ⏲7pm-late) Quality is the cornerstone of Porgy & Bess' popularity. The sophisticated club presents a top-drawer line-up of modern jazz acts and DJs fill spots on weekends.

Volksoper CONCERT VENUE

(People's Opera; Map p56; ☎514 44 3670; www.volksoper.at; 09, Währinger Strasse 78; ⏲box office closed Sun) Vienna's second opera house features operettas, dance and musicals. Standing tickets go for as little as €2 to €6.

Szene Wien LIVE MUSIC VENUE

(Map p56; www.szenewien.at; 11, Hauffgasse 26; ⏲7.30pm-late) Good things happen in small places – this small venue hauls out a mixed bag that includes rock, reggae, funk, jazz and world music.

Roxy CLUB

(Map p60; www.sunshine.at; 04, Operngasse 24; ⏲11pm-4am Thu-Sat) Roxy's tiny dance floor reaches bursting point when DJs from the electronic scene guest here, though everything from Brazilian to jazzy grooves can be heard.

Konzerthaus CONCERT VENUE
(Map p60; ☎242 002; www.konzerthaus.at; 03, Lothringerstrasse 20; ⊙box office closed Sun) This is a major venue in classical music circles, but throughout the year ethnic music, rock, pop or jazz can also be heard in its hallowed halls.

Volksgarten CLUB
(Map p60; 01, Burgring 1; ⊙Tue-Sat) This club attracts a well-dressed crowd, keen to strut their stuff and scan for talent from the long bar. The quality sound system pumps out an array of music styles.

Theater an der Wien THEATRE
(Map p60; www.musicalvienna.at; 06, Linke Wienzeile 6). Once the host of monumental premiers such as Mozart's *Die Zauberflöte,* this theatre now showcases opera, dance and concerts. Tickets start from €7 for standing room.

Palais Palffy CLUB
(Map p60; www.palais-palffy.at; 01, Josefsplatz 6; ⊙from 9pm Thu-Sat) DJs spin electro, pop, house and oldies at this club housed in an illustrious old building. The 1st-floor lounge bar glitters under an enormous Swarovski crystal chandelier.

Burg Kino CINEMA
(Map p60; www.burgkino.at; 01, Opernring 19) English films; has regular screenings of *The Third Man*.

Goodmann CLUB
(Map p60; www.goodmann.at, in German; 04, Rechte Wienzeile 23; ⊙3am-10am Mon-Sat) This is where clubbers go for a snack when the clubs close (food is served till 8am).

English Theatre THEATRE
(Map p60; www.englishtheatre.at; 08, Josefsgasse 12; ⊙box office closed Sun) Stages performances in English.

Why Not? CLUB
(Map p60; www.why-not.at; 01, Tiefer Graben 22; ⊙10pm-4am Fri & Sat) This small, central club fills quickly mainly with young gay guys on weekends.

Arena LIVE MUSIC
(Map p56; www.arena.co.at, in German; 03, Baumgasse 80; ⊙2pm-late) Hard rock and metal in a former slaughterhouse. Arena also shows films outdoors in summer.

Shopping

The Innere Stadt sells designer labels, sweets and jewellery; head to Mariahilfer Strasse for high-street brands. Idiosyncratic local stores cluster in Neubau, and Neubaugasse is good for secondhand hunters. Josefstädter Strasse has a quaint, old-fashioned shopping experience.

Wie Wien GIFTS
(Map p56; www.wiewien.at; 05, Kettenbrückegasse 5; ⊙2-7pm Mon-Fri, 11am-6pm Sat) A Vienna concept store like no other – each piece in the shop represents the city in some way, from delicate ceramics with a picture of the Riesenrad to T-shirts depicting the Naschmarkt.

DON'T MISS

IMPERIAL ENTERTAINMENT

Founded over five centuries ago by Maximilian I as the imperial choir, the world-famous **Vienna Boys' Choir** (Wiener Sängerknaben; www.wsk.at) is the original boy band. These cherubic angels in sailor suits still hold a fond place in Austrian hearts. **Tickets** (☎533 99 27; www.bmbwk.gv.at, in German) for their Sunday performances at 9.15am (October to June) in the Burgkapelle (Royal Chapel) in the Hofburg should be booked around six weeks in advance. The group also performs regularly in the Musikverein.

Another throwback to the Habsburg glory days is the **Spanische Hofreitschule** (Spanish Riding School; Map p60; ☎533 90 31; www.srs.at; 01, Michaelerplatz 1; ⊙performances 11am Sat & Sun mid-Feb–Jun & late Aug-Dec). White Lipizzaner stallions gracefully perform equine ballet to classical music, while chandeliers shimmer from above and the audience cranes to see from pillared balconies. Tickets, costing between €23 and €143, are ordered through the website, but be warned that performances usually sell out months in advance. Unclaimed tickets are sold about two hours before performances). **Morning Training** (adult/child/family €12/6/24; ⊙10am-noon Tue-Sat Feb-Jun & mid-Aug–Dec) same-day tickets are available at the **visitor centre** (⊙9am-4pm Tue-Fri) on Michaelerplatz.

DON'T MISS

TO MARKET

Vienna's atmospheric **Flohmarkt** (flea market; Map p60; 05, Kettenbrückengasse; ⊙dawn-4pm Sat) shouldn't be missed, with goods piled up in apparent chaos on the walkway. Books, clothes, records, ancient electrical goods, old postcards, ornaments, carpets…you name it, it's all here. Come prepared to haggle.

From mid-November, *Christkindlmärkte* (Christmas markets) bring festive sparkle to Vienna, their stalls laden with gifts, *glühwein* (mulled wine) and *Maroni* (roasted chestnuts). Some of the best include the pretty but touristy **Rathausplatz market** (Map p60), the traditional **Spittelberg market** (Map p60) in Spittelberg's cobbled streets, where you can pick up quality crafts, and the authentic, oft-forgotten **Heiligenkreuzerhof market** (Map p60).

Dorotheum AUCTION HOUSE
(Map p60; www.dorotheum.com; 01, Dorotheergasse 17; ⊙10am-6pm Mon-Fri, 9am-5pm Sat) One of Europe's largest auction houses, where surprisingly not every item is priced out of this world. Stop by and simply browse – it's as entertaining as visiting many of Vienna's museums.

Lomoshop PHOTOGRAPHY
(Map p60; 07, Museumsplatz 1; ⊙11am-7pm Mon-Sun) Cult Lomo cameras, gadgets and accessories in the MuseumsQuartier.

Manner CONFECTIONERY
(Map p60; www.manner.com; 01, Stephansplatz 7; ⊙10am-6.30pm Sun-Fri, 9.30am-8.30pm Sat) One bite and you'll be hooked on the *Manner Schnitten* (wafers filled with hazelnut cream) sold at this old-world confectionery store since 1898.

Woka PORCELAIN
(Map p60; www.woka.at; 01, Singerstrasse 16) Accurate re-creations of Wiener Werkstätte lamps are the hallmark of Woka.

Altmann & Kühne PORCELAIN
(Map p60; Graben 30) Altmann & Kühne have been producing handmade bonbons for over 100 years using a well-kept secret recipe. The packaging is designed by Wiener Werkstätte.

Information

Many cafes and bars offer free wi-fi for their customers.

Airport Information Office (⊙6am-11pm) Located in the arrival hall.

Allgemeines Krankenhaus (☎404 00; 09, Währinger Gürtel 18-20) Hospital with a 24-hour casualty ward.

Jugendinfo (Vienna Youth Information; ☎1799; www.jugendinfowien.at; 01, Babenbergerstrasse 1; ⊙noon-7pm Mon-Sat) Offers various reduced-price tickets for 14- to 26-year-olds.

Main post office (01, Fleischmarkt 19; ⊙6am-10pm)

Police station (☎313 10; 01, Deutschmeisterplatz 3)

Tourist Info Wien (☎211 14-555; www.wien.info; 01, Albertinaplatz; ⊙9am-7pm) Vienna's main tourist office, with a ticket agency, hotel booking service, free maps and every brochure you could ever wish for.

Getting There & Away

Air

Vienna is the main centre for Austrian international flights. Although there are frequent flights to Graz, Klagenfurt, Salzburg, Linz and Innsbruck with **Austrian Airlines** (www.austrian.com) from Vienna, flying domestic routes offers few benefits over trains. Book early for the cheapest fares. For further details, see p109.

Boat

Fast hydrofoils travel eastwards to Bratislava (one way €19 to €31, return €38 to €62, 1¼ hours) daily from April to October and on Saturdays and Sundays in March. They also travel daily to Budapest (one way/return €89/109, 5½ hours). Bookings can be made through **DDSG Blue Danube** (☎58 880-0; www.ddsg-blue-danube.at; 02, Handelskai 265).

Heading west, a series of boats ply the Danube between Krems and Melk, with a handful of services originating in Vienna. Two respectable operators include DDSG Blue Danube and **Brandner** (☎07433-25 90; www.brandner.at), the latter located in Wallsee. Both run trips from April through October that start at around €11 one way. For trips into Germany, contact **Donauschiffahrt Wurm + Köck** (☎0732 783607; www.donauschiffahrt.de; Untere Donaulände 1, Linz).

Bus

Vienna currently has no central bus station. National Bundesbuses arrive and depart from several different locations, depending on the destination. Bus lines serving Vienna include **Eurolines** (www.eurolines.com).

Car & Motorcycle

The Gürtel is an outer ring road that joins up with the A22 on the north bank of the Danube and the A23 southeast of town. All the main road routes intersect with this system, including the A1 from Linz and Salzburg, and the A2 from Graz.

Train

Vienna is one of central Europe's main rail hubs. **Österreiche Bundesbahn** (ÖBB; Austrian Federal Railway; www.oebb.at) is the main operator. There are direct services and connections to many European cities. Sample destinations include Berlin (nine to 10 hours), Budapest (2¾ to four hours), Munich (four to five hours), Paris (12 to 13 hours), Prague (4½ to 5½ hours) and Venice (eight to nine hours).

Vienna has multiple train stations. At press time, a massive construction project was in progress at Vienna's former Südbahnhof: essentially the station was shut but an eastern section had been set up as a temporary station to serve some regional trains to/from the east, including Bratislava. The complex is due to reopen as Hauptbahnhof Wien (Vienna Central Station) in late 2012/early 2013, and as the main station it will receive international trains. As a result, all long-distance trains are being rerouted among the rest of Vienna's train stations. Additionally, Westbahnhof is undergoing major renovation; at press time, a provisional station had been created so that the station could remain in operation – it is slated to reopen in late 2011. Further train stations include Franz-Josefs-Bahnhof (which handles trains to/from the Danube Valley), Wien Mitte, Wien Nord and Meidling.

ℹ Getting Around

To/From the Airport

It is 19km from the city centre to **Vienna International Airport** (VIE; www.viennaairport.com) in Schwechat. The **City Airport Train** (CAT; www.cityairporttrain.com; return adult/child €18/free; ⏲5.38am-11.08pm) runs every 30 minutes and takes 16 minutes between the airport and Wien Mitte; book online for a €2 discount. The **S-Bahn (S7)** does the same journey (single €3.60) but in 26 minutes.

Buses run every 20 or 30 minutes, between 5am and 11pm, from the airport (one way/return €6/11). Services run to Meidling, Westbahnhof and Schwedenplatz.

Taxis cost about €35. **C&K Airport Service** (☎44 444) charges €33 one way for shared vans.

Bicycle

Cycling is an excellent way to get around and explore the city – over 800km of cycle tracks criss-cross the capital. Popular cycling areas include the 7km path around the Ringstrasse, the Donauinsel, the Prater and along the Donaukanal (Danube Canal).

Vienna's city bike scheme is called **Vienna City Bike** (www.citybikewien.at, in German; 1st/2nd/3rd hour free/€1/2, per hour thereafter €4), with more than 60 bicycle stands across the city. A credit card is required to rent bikes – just swipe your card in the machine and follow the instructions (in a number of languages).

Car & Motorcycle

Due to a system of one-way streets and expensive parking, you're better off using the excellent public transport system. If you do plan to drive in the city, take special care of the trams; they always have priority and vehicles must wait behind trams when they stop to pick up or set down passengers.

Fiakers

More of a tourist novelty than anything else, a *Fiaker* is a traditional-style horse-drawn carriage. Bowler-hatted drivers generally speak English and point out places of interest en route. Expect to pay a cool €65/95 for a 40-/60-minute ride from Stephansplatz, Albertinaplatz or Heldenplatz.

Public Transport

Vienna has a unified public transport network that encompasses trains, trams, buses, and underground (U-Bahn) and suburban (S-Bahn) trains. Free maps and information pamphlets are available from **Wiener Linien** (www.wienerlinien.at, in German).

Before use, all tickets must be validated at the entrance to U-Bahn stations and on buses and trams (except for weekly and monthly tickets). Tickets are cheaper to buy from ticket machines

MEDIA

Tune into Vienna's cultural scene on the following websites:

» **About Vienna** (www.aboutvienna.org) General website with cultural and sightseeing information.

» **City of Vienna** (www.wien.gv.at) Comprehensive government-run website.

» **Falter** (www.falter.at, in German) Online version of the ever-popular Falter magazine.

» **Vienna Online** (www.vienna.at, in German) Site with info on parties, festivals and news.

in U-Bahn stations and in *Tabak* (tobacconist) shops, where singles cost €1.80. On board, they cost €2.20. Singles are valid for an hour, and you may change lines on the same trip.

A 24-hour ticket costs €5.70, a 48-hour ticket €10, a 72-hour ticket €13.60 and an eight-day ticket €28.80 (validate the ticket once per day as and when you need it). Weekly tickets (valid Monday to Sunday) cost €14; the Vienna Card (€18.50) includes travel on public transport for up to three days. The Strip Ticket (*Streifenkarte*) costs €7.20 and gives you four single tickets.

Ticket inspection is infrequent, but fare dodgers pay an on-the-spot fine of €62.

Taxi

Taxis are metered for city journeys and cost €2.60 flag fall during the day and €2.70 at night, plus a small per km fee. It's safe to hail taxis from the street, and there's generally an abundance of choice.

THE DANUBE VALLEY

The stretch of Danube between Krems and Melk, known locally as the Wachau, is arguably the loveliest along the entire length of the mighty river. Both banks are dotted with ruined castles and medieval towns, and lined with terraced vineyards. Further upstream is the industrial city of Linz, Austria's avant-garde art and new technology trailblazer.

Krems an der Donau

☎02732 / POP 23,800

Sitting on the northern bank of the Danube against a backdrop of terraced vineyards, Krems marks the beginning of the Wachau. It has an attractive cobbled centre, a small university, some good restaurants and the gallery-dotted Kunstmeile (Art Mile).

Sights & Activities

It's a pleasure to wander the cobblestone streets of Krems and Stein, especially at night – don't miss the baroque treasures of Schürerplatz and Rathausplatz squares in Stein.

Kunsthalle ART MUSEUM

(www.kunsthalle.at; Franz-Zeller-Platz 3; adult/child €9/3.50; ⏲10am-6pm) The flagship of Krems' **Kunstmeile** (www.kunstmeile-krems.at), an eclectic collection of galleries and museums, the Kunsthalle has a program of small but excellent changing exhibitions.

Sleeping & Eating

Arte Hotel Krems HOTEL €€

(☎711 23; www.arte-hotel.at, in German; Dr-Karl-Dorrek-Strasse 23; s €89-105, d €128-162; P⊖☎) This comfortable new art hotel close to the university has large, well-styled rooms in bright colours and with open-plan bathrooms.

Jugendherberge HOSTEL €

(☎834 52; oejhv.noe.krems@aon.at; Ringstrasse 77; dm €18; ⏲closed Nov-Mar; P⊖) This popular HI (Hostelling International) hostel close to the tourist office is well geared for cyclists; it features a climbing wall, a garage for bicycles and packed lunches.

Mörwald Kloster Und AUSTRIAN €€

(☎704 930; www.moerwald.at; Undstrasse 6; mains €20-33, 5-course menu €85, 3-course lunch €25; ⏲closed Sun & Mon; ⊖) Run by celebrity chef and winemaker Toni Mörwald, this is one of the Wachau's best restaurants. Delicacies from roast pigeon breast to fish dishes with French touches are married with top wines. There's a lovely garden.

Information

Krems Tourismus (☎826 76; www.krems.info; Utzstrasse 1; ⏲9am-6pm Mon-Fri, 11am-5pm Sat, 11am-4pm Sun, closed Sat & Sun Nov-Apr) Has excellent city walk and vineyard maps, and stocks a *Heurigen* calendar.

Getting There & Away

Frequent daily trains connect Krems with Vienna's Franz-Josefs-Bahnhof (€13.90, one hour). The quickest way to Melk is by train to Spitz, continuing by bus (€7.30, one hour, five times

WORTH A TRIP

THROUGH THE GRAPEVINE

The 830km **Weinstrasse Niederösterreich** (Lower Austria Wine Rd; www.weinstrassen.at) wends through eight wine-producing regions in Lower Austria, including the Kremstal, Kamptal and Weinviertel, passing beautiful terraced vineyards, bucolic villages, castles and abbeys. Visit the website for the low-down on local wineries (some with accommodation), wine shops and rustic *Heurigen* (wine taverns) where you can taste the region's pinot blanc (Weissburgunder), grüner veltliner, Riesling and red wines. Autumn is the time for semifermented *Sturm* (new wine).

daily). The boat station is near Donaustrasse, about 2km west of the train station.

Dürnstein

☎02711 / POP 900

The pretty town of Dürnstein, on a supple curve in the Danube, is not only known for its beautiful buildings but also for the castle above the town where Richard I (the Lionheart) of England was imprisoned in 1192. His unscheduled stopover on the way home from the Crusades came courtesy of Austrian archduke Leopold V, whom he had insulted.

There's not much left of **Kuenringerburg castle** today. It's basically just a pile of rubble. Still, it's worth snapping a picture and the views from the top are breathtaking.

Sleeping & Eating

The tourist office has a list of private rooms and *Gasthöfe* (guesthouses) in Dürnstein.

TOP CHOICE **Hotel Schloss Dürnstein** HOTEL €€€
(☎212; www.schloss.at; Dürnstein 2; s €166, d €198-276, apt €355-380; P) This castle is the last word in luxury in town, with antique-furnished rooms, a sauna and a high-end restaurant (mains €16 to €30) with staggering views over the river.

Hotel Sänger Blondel HOTEL €€
(☎253; www.saengerblondel.at; Klosterplatz/Dürnstein 64; s €68, d €86-112; P@) This hotel's good-sized rooms have views to the Danube, castle or garden.

Pension Böhmer GUESTHOUSE €
(☎239; Hauptstrasse 22; s/d €42/62; P) A small, reasonably priced guesthouse in the heart of town and just a quick hop from the castle.

Restaurant Loibnerhof AUSTRIAN €€
(☎828 90; Unterloiben 7; mains €15-26, 3- & 4-course menu €26-52; closed Mon & Tue) Situated 1.5km east of Dürnstein in Unterloiben, this family-run restaurant inside a 400-year-old building has a leafy garden for enjoying local specialities such as *Kalbsbeuschel* (veal lights).

Information

For more about Dürnstein, contact the **tourist office** (☎200; www.duernstein.at; 9am-5pm) in the train station.

Getting There & Away

Dürnstein can be reached from Krems by train (€2, 11 minutes, hourly).

ON YOUR BIKE

Many towns in the Danube Valley are part of a bike hire network called **Leihradl**. After registering using a credit card (either by calling the hotline on ☎02742-229 901 or on the website www.leihradl.at, in German), a refunded €1 is deducted and you can begin renting bicycles for €1/5 per hour/24 hours.

Melk

☎02752 / POP 5200

With its sparkling and majestic abbey-fortress, Melk is a highlight of any visit to the Danube Valley. Many visitors cycle here for the day – wearily pushing their bikes through the cobblestone streets.

Sights

Stift Melk ABBEY
(Benedictine Abbey of Melk; ☎5550; www.stiftmelk.at; Abt Berthold Dietmayr Strasse 1; adult/child/family €7.70/4.50/15.40, with guided tour €9.50/6.30/19; 9am-5.30pm) Rising like a vision on a hill overlooking the town, Stift Melk is Austria's most famous abbey. It has been home to Benedictine monks since the 11th century, though it owes its current good looks to 18th-century mastermind Jakob Prandtauer.

The interior of the twin-spired monastery church is baroque gone barmy, with endless prancing angels and gold twirls. Other highlights include the **Bibliothek** (Library) and the **Marmorsaal** (Marble Hall); the trompe l'oeil on the ceiling (by Paul Troger) gives the illusion of greater height. Eleven of the imperial rooms, where dignitaries (including Napoleon) stayed, now house a **museum**.

From around November to March, the monastery can only be visited by guided tour (11am and 2pm daily). Always phone ahead to ensure you get an English-language tour.

Sleeping & Eating

Restaurants and cafes with alfresco seating line the Rathausplatz.

Hotel Restaurant zur Post HOTEL €€
(☎523 45; www.post-melk.at, in German; Linzer Strasse 1; s €61-71, d €98-112, apt €155-210; P@) This bright hotel in the heart of

town has large, comfortable rooms. There's a sauna, free bike use for guests and a decent restaurant serving Austrian classics.

Hotel Wachau HOTEL €€
(☎525 31; www.hotel-wachau.at; Am Wachberg 3; s €65, d €95-125; P@) For comfortable, modern rooms, try this hotel 2km southeast of the train station. The restaurant (mains €12 to €20, gourmet menu €45) is open for dinner Monday to Saturday and specialises in well-prepared regional cuisine.

Information

The **tourist office** (☎523 07-410; www.niederoesterreich.at/melk; Babenbergerstrasse 1; ⏲9am-noon & 2-6pm Mon-Fri, 10am-noon Sat & Sun), east of Rathausplatz, has maps and plenty of useful information.

Getting There & Away

Boats leave from the canal by Pionierstrasse, 400m north of the abbey. There are hourly trains to Vienna (€15.70, 1¼ hours).

Linz

☎0732 / POP 189,000

In Linz beginnt's (It begins in Linz) goes the Austrian saying, and it's spot on. Linz is blessed with a leading-edge cyber centre and world-class contemporary-art gallery, both signs that Upper Austria kick-started the country's technological industry. Beyond the industrial outskirts you'll find plenty of culture, so much so that it gained the title of European Capital of Culture 2009.

Sights & Activities

Linz' baroque Hauptplatz and sculpture-strewn Danube Park are made for aimless ambling. The **Linz Card**, giving entry to major sights and unlimited use of public transport, costs €15/25 for one/three days.

Ars Electronica Center MUSEUM
(www.aec.at; Ars Electronica Strasse 1; adult/child €7/4; ⏲9am-5pm Wed-Fri, to 9pm Thu, 10am-6pm Sat & Sun) Ars Electronica Center zooms in on tomorrow's technology, science and digital media. In themed labs you can interact with robots, animate digital objects and (virtually) travel the world. The shipshape centre kaleidoscopically changes colour after dark.

Lentos ART MUSEUM
(www.lentos.at; Ernst-Koref-Promenade 1; adult/child €6.50/4.50; ⏲10am-6pm Wed-Mon, to 9pm Thu) Ars Electronica's rival icon across the Danube is the rectangular glass-and-steel Lentos, also strikingly illuminated by night. The gallery guards one of Austria's finest modern art collections, including works by Warhol, Schiele and Klimt, which sometimes feature in the large-scale exhibitions.

Neuer Dom CHURCH
(New Cathedral; Herrenstrasse 26; ⏲8am-7pm) This neo-Gothic giant of a cathedral was designed in the mid-19th century by Vinzenz Statz of Cologne Dom fame. The tower's height was restricted to 134m, so as not to outshine Stephansdom in Vienna.

Landesgalerie ART MUSEUM
(State Museum; www.landesgalerie.at; Museumstrasse 14; adult/child €6.50/4.50; ⏲9am-6pm Tue-Fri, to 9pm Thu, 10am-5pm Sat & Sun) Cutting-edge art exhibitions in neoclassical surrounds and a sculpture garden.

Schlossmuseum MUSEUM
(Castle Museum; www.schlossmuseum.at; Schlossberg 1; adult/child €6.50/4.50; ⏲9am-6pm Tue-Fri, to 9pm Thu, 10am-5pm Sat & Sun) Linz' hilltop castle is a treasure trove of art and history. The Gothic ecclesiastical paintings are a highlight.

Festivals & Events

The **Ars Electronica Festival** (www.aec.at) in early September showcases cyberart, computer music, and other marriages of technology and art. This leads into the **Brucknerfest** (www.brucknerhaus.at), which pays homage to native son Anton Bruckner with a month of classical music between

DON'T MISS

RECORD-BREAKING RAILWAY

From Linz' Hauptplatz, the narrow-gauge **Pöstlingbergbahn** (adult/child €5.60/2.80; ⏲6am-10pm Mon-Sat, 7.30am-10pm Sun) hauls you up to Pöstlingberg (537m), departing every 30 minutes. This gondola features in the Guinness Book of Records as the world's steepest mountain railway – quite some feat for such a low-lying city! Far-reaching city and Danube views await at the summit, and kids love to take a spin on the century-old fairytale train.

mid-September and early October. Be sure to book early.

Sleeping & Eating

The tourist office offers a free accommodation-booking service, but only face-to-face and not over the phone.

Pavement cafes, bistros and lively bars line up on and around Hauptplatz, on the main shopping thoroughfare Landstrasse and the cobbled Altstadt.

Spitz Hotel HOTEL €€
(☎73 37 33; www.spitzhotel.at; Fiedlerstrasse 6; r €130-250; P@) Much-lauded Austrian architect Isa Stein has left her avant-garde imprint on the Spitz. Each of the hotel's rooms has unique artworks. Minimalism rules here, with clean lines, open-plan bathrooms and hardwood floors.

Hotel am Domplatz HOTEL €€
(☎77 30 00; www.hotelamdomplatz.at; Stifterstrasse 4; s €120-140, d €150-180; P@) Sidling up to the Neuer Dom, this glass-and-concrete design hotel reveals light, streamlined interiors. Wind down with a view at the rooftop spa.

Wolfinger HISTORIC HOTEL €€
(☎77 32 91; www.hotelwolfinger.at; Hauptplatz 19; s/d €85/126; P@) This 500-year-old hotel, located on the main square, has an air of old-world grandeur. Archways, stuccowork and period furniture give the rooms some character.

Sommerhaus Hotel HOTEL €
(☎24 57 376; www.sommerhaus-hotel.at; Julius-Raab-Strasse 10; s/d €49/74; P@) Sitting between the city and open fields, this revamped uni hotel has simple, comfy rooms and a big indoor pool. Take tram 1 or 2 to Schumpeterstrasse and walk five minutes.

k.u.k. Hofbäckerei CAFE €
(Pfarrgasse 17; coffee & cake €3-6; 6.30am-6pm Mon-Fri, 7am-12.30pm Sat) The empire lives on at this gloriously stuck-in-time cafe. Here Fritz Rath bakes *the* best *Linzer Torte* in town – rich, spicy and with lattice pastry that crumbles just so.

Cubus FUSION €€
(Ars-Electronica-Strasse 1; mains €8.50-14.50; 9am-1am Mon-Sat, to 6pm Sun;) On the 3rd floor of the Ars Electronica Center, this glass cube has stellar Danube views. The menu is strictly fusion and the two-course lunch a snip at €7.

Alte Welt AUSTRIAN €€
(☎77 00 53; www.altewelt.at, in German; Hauptplatz 4; mains €9-16; lunch Mon-Sat, dinner daily) Set around an arcaded inner courtyard, Alte Welt serves hearty fare like roast pork and beef ragout, and a good-value two-course lunch for €6.50. It sometimes hosts live jazz and jam sessions.

Information

Atlas Media (Graben 17; internet per hour €2.50; 9.30am-11pm Mon-Sat, 1-11pm Sun) Internet and discount international calls.

Hotspot Linz (www.hotspotlinz.at, in German) Free wi-fi at 120 hotspots in the city, including Ars Electronica Center and Lentos.

Post office (Domgasse 1; 8am-6pm Mon-Fri, 9am-noon Sat) Handy to the centre.

Tourist Information Linz (☎7070 2009; www.linz.at; Hauptplatz 1; 9am-7pm Mon-Sat, 10am-7pm Sun, shorter hours winter) Free city maps and room reservation service.

Getting There & Around

AIR Austrian Airlines, Lufthansa, Ryanair and Air Berlin fly to the **Blue Danube Airport** (www.linz-airport.at), 13km southwest of Linz. An hourly shuttle bus (€2.60, 20 minutes) links the airport to the main station from Monday to Saturday.

WORTH A TRIP

ST FLORIAN

One of Austria's finest Augustinian abbeys is St Florian's **Augustiner Chorherrenstift** (www.stift-st-florian.at; Stiftstrasse 1; tours adult/child €8/5; tours 11am, 1pm, 3pm May-Sep), 18km southeast of Linz. The abbey dates back to at least 819 but is now overwhelmingly baroque in style. A guided tour leads you through the opulent library, Marble Hall and the Altdorfer Gallery, displaying 14 paintings by Albrecht Altdorfer (1480–1538) of the Danube School. A vision of pink marble and gilding, the resplendent abbey church harbours the huge 18th-century organ upon which famous Romantic composer Anton Bruckner played during his stint as organist (1850 to 1855).

Buses run frequently between St Florian and Linz Hauptbahnhof (€2.60, 22 minutes); there is a reduced service on Sunday.

PUBLIC TRANSPORT Bus and tram tickets are bought before you board from pavement dispensers or *Tabak* (tobacconist) shops. Single tickets cost €1.80 and day passes €3.60. Some of the bus services stop early in the evening.

TRAIN Linz is halfway between Salzburg and Vienna on the main road and rail routes. Trains to Salzburg (€22, 1¼ hours) and Vienna (€31.20, 1½ hours) leave approximately twice hourly.

THE SOUTH

Austria's two main southern states, Styria (Steiermark) and Carinthia (Kärnten), often feel worlds apart from the rest of the country, both in climate and attitude. Styria is a blissful amalgamation of genteel architecture, rolling green hills, vine-covered slopes and soaring mountains. Its capital, Graz, is one of Austria's most attractive cities.

A jet-setting, fashion-conscious crowd heads to sun-drenched Carinthia for summer holidays. The region (which is right on the border with Italy) exudes an atmosphere that's as close to Mediterranean as this staunch country gets.

Graz

0316 / POP 257,350

Austria's second-largest city is probably its most relaxed and, after Vienna, its liveliest for after-hours pursuits. It's an attractive place with bristling green parkland, red rooftops and a small, fast-flowing river gushing through its centre. Architecturally, it has Renaissance courtyards and provincial baroque palaces complemented by innovative modern designs.

The surrounding countryside, a mixture of vineyards, mountains, forested hills and thermal springs, is within easy striking distance, and Graz has a beautiful bluff connected to the centre by steps, a funicular and a glass lift. Last but not least, a large student population (some 50,000) propels

Central Graz

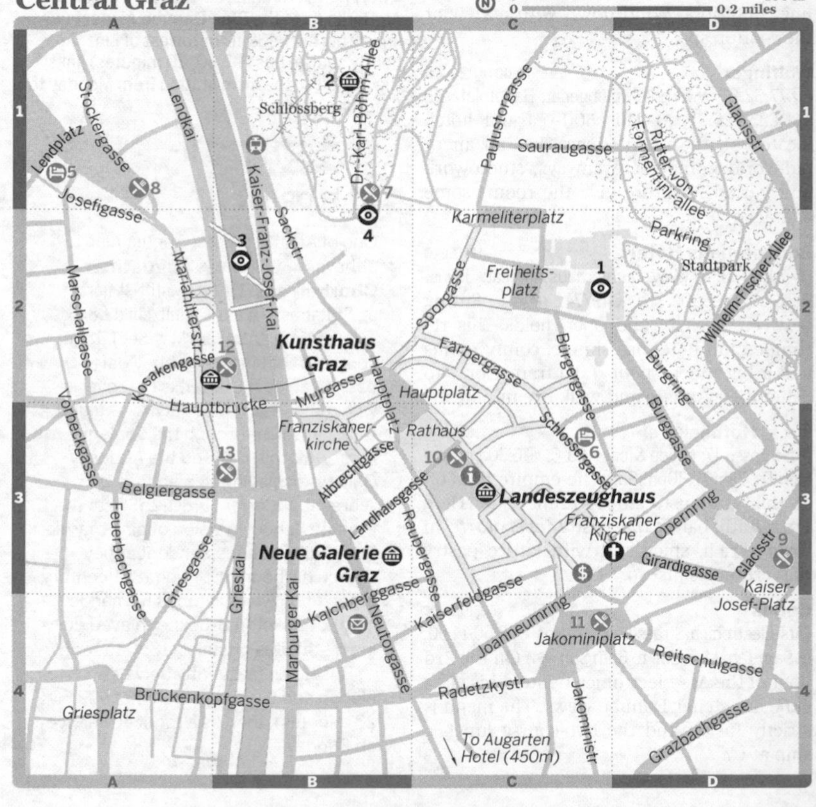

the nightlife and vibrant arts scene, creating a loveable and liveable city.

Sights & Activities

Graz is a city easily enjoyed by simply wandering aimlessly. Admission to all of the major museums with a 24-hour ticket costs €11/14 for adults/children.

Universalmuseum Joanneum MUSEUM
(www.museum-joanneum.at; Raubergasse 10) With its 19 locations, this ensemble of museums is the gardener of Graz' rich cultural landscape. Until work is completed, some museums will be closed until late 2011, including **Neue Galerie Graz** (adult/child €8/3; 10am-6pm, closed Mon), Styria's most important historical and contemporary art collection.

Kunsthaus Graz ART MUSEUM
(www.kunsthausgraz.at; Lendkai 1; adult/child €7/3; 10am-6pm, closed Mon) Designed by British architects Peter Cook and Colin Fournier, this world-class contemporary art space looks something like a space-age sea slug. Exhibitions change every three to four months.

Schloss Eggenberg PALACE
(Eggenberger Allee 90; adult/child €7/3; 10am-5pm, closed Mon & Nov-Palm Sunday) A blend of gothic, Renaissance and baroque styles, this beautiful palace can be reached by tram 1 from Hauptplatz. Admission includes a guided tour (from 10am to 4pm on the hour except at 1pm), taking in 24 *Prunkräume* (staterooms), which are based around astronomy, the zodiac and classical or religious mythology.

FREE **Murinsel** BRIDGE
This artificial island-cum-bridge in the River Mur is an open seashell of glass, concrete and steel, by New York artist Vito Acconci. It houses a trendy cafe-bar in aqua blue and a small stage. In summer, further downstream a beach bar is set up.

Schlossberg VIEWPOINT
The wooded slopes of Schlossberg (473m) can be reached on foot, with the funicular **Schlossbergbahn** (Castle Hill Railway; 1hr ticket €1.90) from Kaiser-Franz-Josef-Kai, or by **Glass Lift** (1hr ticket €1.90) from Schlossbergplatz. Napoleon was hard-pressed to raze this fortress, but raze it he did. Today the medieval **Uhrturm** (Clock Tower) and a small **Garrison Museum** (Schlossberg 5a; adult/child €1/free; 10am-4pm, closed Mon-Wed & Nov–mid-May) are the legacy.

Landeszeughaus ARMOURY
(www.zeughaus.at; Herrengasse 16; adult/child €7/3; 10am-6pm) A must-see for fans of armour and weapons, housing an astounding array of 30,000 gleaming exhibits.

FREE **Burg** CASTLE, PARK
(Hofgasse) At the far end of Graz' 15th-century castle is an ingenious **double staircase** (1499). Adjoining it is the **Stadtpark**, the city's largest green space.

Sleeping

Hotel Daniel HOTEL €€
(711 080; www.hoteldaniel.com; Europaplatz 1; r €59-79, breakfast €9 per person; P@) Perched at the top of Annenstrasse, the Daniel is an exclusive design hotel. All rooms are tastefully furnished in minimalist designs; you can rent a Vespa (€15 per day) and there's a 24-hour espresso bar.

Hotel Strasser HOTEL €
(71 39 77; www.hotel-strasser.at; Eggenberger Gürtel 11; s/d/tr/apt €45/65/93/180; P@) Strasser has some fascinating pseudo-neoclassical and Mediterranean touches, with Tuscan gold blending with mirrors and cast-iron balustrades. It's handy to the train station.

Central Graz

Top Sights

	Kunsthaus Graz	A2
	Landeszeughaus	C3
	Neue Galerie Graz	B3

Sights

1	Burg	C2
2	Garrison Museum	B1
3	Murinsel	B2
4	Uhrturm	B2

Sleeping

5	Gasthof-Pension zur Steirer-Stub'n	A1
6	Hotel zum Dom	C3

Eating

7	Aiola Upstairs	B1
8	Farmers Market	A1
9	Farmers Market	D3
10	Fast-Food Stands	C3
11	Fast-Food Stands	C4
12	iku	B2
13	Mangolds	B3

Drinking

	Insel Café	(see 3)

WORTH A TRIP

HUNDERTWASSER SPA

East Styria is famed for its thermal springs. Fans of Friedensreich Hundertwasser's playful architectural style won't want to miss the surreal **Rogner-Bad Blumau** (☎03383-51 00-0; www.blumau.com; adult/child €39/21; ⏰9am-11pm), 50km east of Graz. The spa has all the characteristics of his art, including uneven floors, grass on the roof, colourful ceramics and golden spires. Overnight accommodation includes entry to the spa. Call ahead to book treatments from sound meditation to invigorating Styrian elderberry wraps.

Hotel zum Dom HOTEL €€
(☎82 48 00; www.domhotel.co.at; Bürgergasse 14; s €83-93, d €170-220, ste €227-332; P📶) Hotel zum Dom's individually furnished rooms come with power showers or whirlpools, and one suite even has a terrace whirlpool.

Augarten Hotel HOTEL €€
(☎20 800; www.augartenhotel.at; Schönaugasse 53; s/d €115-165, d €140-190; P❄📶🏊) The arty Augarten is decorated with the owner's private collection. All rooms are bright and modern, and the pool and sauna round off an excellent option.

Gasthof-Pension zur Steirer-Stub'n GUESTHOUSE €
(☎71 68 55; www.pension-graz.at; Lendplatz 8; s/d €43/78, apt €110-160; 📶) A bright and breezy guesthouse where many of the good-sized rooms have patios overlooking Lendplatz.

Jugend und Familiengästehaus Graz HOSTEL €
(☎70 83 210; graz@jufa.at, Idlhofgasse 74; dm €22, s €39-46.50, d €64-77; P@📶) Take bus 31, 32 or 33 from Jakominiplatz for this HI hostel about 800m south of the main train station.

Eating

With leafy salads dressed in delicious pumpkin-seed oil, fish specialities and *Pfand'l* (pan-grilled) dishes, Styrian cuisine is Austrian cooking at its light and healthy best.

Aside from the following listings, there are plenty of cheap eats near Universität Graz, particularly on Halbärthgasse, Zinzendorfgasse and Harrachgasse.

Stock up for a picnic at the **farmers markets** (⏰4.30am-1pm, closed Sun) on Kaiser-Josef-Platz and Lendplatz. For **fast-food stands**, head for Hauptplatz and Jakominiplatz.

TOP CHOICE **Aiola Upstairs** INTERNATIONAL €€
(www.aiola.at, in German; Schlossberg 2; pasta €9.50-15, mains €17.50-25; ⏰9am-midnight, closed Sun) This wonderful restaurant on Schlossberg has great views, delicious international flavours, a superb wine list, spot-on cocktails and very chilled music.

Der Steirer BEISL €€
(www.dersteirer.at, in German; Belgiergasse 1; mains €9-18.50, tapas €2, lunch menu €6.90; ⏰11am-midnight) This Styrian neo-*Beisl* and wine bar has a small but excellent selection of local dishes and a large choice of wines. The goulash with fried polenta is easily one of the best in the country.

Mangolds VEGETARIAN €
(www.mangolds.at, in German; Griesgasse 11; meals €5-10; ⏰11am-7pm Mon-Fri, to 4pm Sat; 🖉) Tasty patties, rice dishes and over 40 different salads are served at this pay-by-weight vegetarian cafeteria.

iku INTERNATIONAL €
(☎8017 9292; www.iku-graz.at, in German; Lendkai 1; lunch menu €7; ⏰9am-1am) This sleek restaurant inside the surrealistic Kunsthaus does great breakfasts, salads and lunch specials (11.30am to 3pm). Reserve ahead for the Sunday brunch with music.

Drinking & Entertainment

The bar scene in Graz is split between three main areas: around the university; adjacent to the Kunsthaus; and on Mehlplatz and Prokopigasse (dubbed the 'Bermuda Triangle').

Insel Café CAFE
(Murinsel; ⏰9.30am-midnight) This cafe offers a unique experience – you can sip on your drink as the Mur River splashes below your feet.

Orange BAR/CLUB
(www.cafe-bar-orange.at, in German; Elisabethstrasse 30; ⏰8pm-3am) A student crowd flocks to this modern bar and club, with a patio for summer evenings. DJs spin regularly here.

Kulturhauskeller BAR, BEISL
(Elisabethstrasse 30; ⏰9pm-5am, closed Sun & Mon) Next to Orange, the Kulturhauskeller is a cavernous cellar bar that heaves with

raunchy students on weekends. After 11pm admission is €3.

Information

Graz Tourismus (☎80 75-0; www.graztourismus.at; Herrengasse 16; ⏰10am-6pm) Graz' main tourist office, with loads of free information on the city. Inside the train station is an information stand and terminal, and free hotline to the tourist office.

High Speed Internet-Selfstore (Herrengasse 3; per 30min €1; ⏰7am-10pm) A coin-operated internet space inside the passage.

Main post office (Neutorgasse 46; ⏰8am-7pm Mon-Fri, 9am-noon Sat)

Getting There & Away

AIR **Ryanair** (www.ryanair.com) has regular flights from London Stansted to **Graz airport** (☎290 20; www.flughafen-graz.at), 10km south of the centre, while **Air Berlin** (www.airberlin.com) connects the city with Berlin.

BICYCLE Bicycle rental is available from **Bicycle** (☎68 86 45; Körösistrasse 5; per 24hr €10; ⏰7am-1pm & 2-6pm, closed Sat & Sun).

PUBLIC TRANSPORT Single tickets (€1.90) for buses, trams and the Schlossbergbahn are valid for one hour, but you're usually better off buying a 24-hour pass (€4.10).

TRAIN Trains to Vienna depart hourly (€34, 2½ hours), and six daily go to Salzburg (€48, four hours). International train connections from Graz include Ljubljana (€34, 3½ hours) and Budapest (€46, 5½ hours).

Klagenfurt

☎0463 / POP 94,000

With its salacious location on Wörthersee and more Renaissance than baroque beauty, Carinthia's capital Klagenfurt has a distinct Mediterranean feel. While there isn't a huge amount here to see, it makes a handy base for exploring Wörthersee's lakeside villages and elegant medieval towns to the north.

Sights & Activities

Boating and swimming are usually possible from May to September.

Wörthersee LAKE

Owing to its thermal springs, the Wörthersee is one of the region's warmer lakes (an average 21°C in summer) and is great for swimming, lakeshore frolicking and water sports. The 50km **cycle path** around the lake is one of the 'Top 10' in Austria. In summer the tourist office cooperates with a hire company for bicycles (per 24 hours €10 to €19), which can also be picked up and dropped off at various points around the lake.

Europapark PARK

The green expanse and its *Strandbad* (beach) on the shores of the Wörthersee are centres for splashy fun, and especially good for kids. The park's biggest draw is **Minimundus** (www.minimundus.at; Villacher Strasse 241; adult/child €12/7; ⏰9am-6pm), a 'miniature world' with 140 replicas of the world's architectural icons, downsized to a scale of 1:25. To get there, take bus 10, 11, 12 or 22 from Heiligengeistplatz.

Sleeping & Eating

When you check into accommodation in Klagenfurt, ask for a *Gästekarte* (guest card), entitling you to discounts.

Arcotel Moser Verdino HOTEL €€

(☎578 78; www.arcotel.at/moserverdino; Domgasse 2; s €80-144, d €104-256, ste €128-180, apt €148-1920; ⊖@) This excellent pick has high-quality modern rooms with flair, very helpful staff and often discounted rates.

Hotel Liebetegger HOTEL €€

(☎569 35; www.liebetegger.com, in German; Völkermarkter Strasse 8; s €60, d €85-95, apt €110-200; P⊖@) Original artwork spruces up this hotel. The apartments can sleep up to four guests and it offers free use of bikes.

Jugendgästehaus Klagenfurt HOSTEL €

(☎23 00 20; www.oejhv.or.at; Neckheimgasse 6; dm/s/d €20.50/28.50/49; P⊖@) This modern HI hostel near Europapark is reached by bus 10, 12, 13 or 22.

Restaurant Maria Loretto AUSTRIAN €€

(☎244 65; Lorettoweg 54; mains €15-25; ⏰lunch & dinner Mar-Dec; P⊖) A wonderful restaurant situated on a headland above Wörthersee near the *Strandbad*. Reserve for evenings or an outside table.

Zauberhutt'n ITALIAN/AUSTRIAN €€

(Osterwitzgasse 6; mains €10-17; ⏰Mon-Sat, closed lunch Sat; ⊖) Pasta, pizza, delicious

FREE GUIDED WALKS

Tailor your own Klagenfurt walking tour by picking up the brochure in English from the tourist office. It has a map and descriptions of monuments, historic buildings and hidden courtyards. Free guided tours depart from the tourist office at 10am during July and August.

grilled squid and classic meat dishes all feature at this inexpensive, family-run restaurant.

Information

Café-bar G@tes (Waagplatz 7; per 10min €1; 9am-1am Mon-Fri, 7pm-1am Sat & Sun;) Wi-fi is free if you buy a drink.

Tourist office (53 722 23; www.info.klagenfurt.at; Rathaus, Neuer Platz 1; 8am-6pm Mon-Fri, 10am-5pm Sat, 10am-3pm Sun) Sells Kärnten cards and books accommodation.

Getting There & Around

AIR Klagenfurt's **airport** (www.klagenfurt-airport.com; Flughafenstrasse 60-66) is served by Ryanair from London Stansted and Frankfurt-am-Main, and **TUIfly** (www.tuifly.com) from major German cities.

BUS Bus drivers sell single tickets (€1.80) and 24-hour passes (€4.20). To get to the airport, take bus 40 from the main train station to Annabichl (€1.80, 25 minutes, four times hourly), then change to bus 45 (10 minutes).

TRAIN Two hourly direct trains run from Klagenfurt to Vienna (€48, 3¾ hours) and Salzburg (€35.50, three hours). Trains to Graz depart every two to three hours (€35.50, 2¾ hours). Trains to western Austria, Italy, Slovenia and Germany go via Villach (€7.20, 30 to 40 minutes, two to four per hour).

SALZBURG

0662 / POP 147,600

The joke 'If it's baroque, don't fix it' is a perfect maxim for Salzburg; the tranquil Old Town burrowed below steep hills looks much as it did when Mozart lived here 250 years ago. Second only to Vienna in numbers of visitors, this compact city is centred on a tight grouping of narrow, cobbled streets overshadowed by ornate 17th-century buildings, which are in turn dominated by the medieval Hohensalzburg fortress from high above. Across the fast-flowing Salzach River rests the baroque Schloss Mirabell, surrounded by gorgeous manicured gardens.

If this doesn't whet your appetite, then bypass the grandeur and head straight for kitsch-country by joining a tour of *The Sound of Music* film locations.

Sights

Old Town HISTORIC AREA

A Unesco World Heritage site, Salzburg's Old Town centre is equally entrancing whether viewed from ground level or the hills above.

The grand **Residenzplatz**, with its horse-drawn carriages and mythical fountain, is a good starting point for a wander. The overwhelmingly baroque **Dom** (cathedral; Domplatz; admission free; 8am-7pm Mon-Sat, 1-7pm Sun), slightly south, is entered via bronze doors symbolising faith, hope and charity. The adjacent **Dommuseum** (adult/child €6/2; 10am-5pm Mon-Sat, 11am-6pm Sun) is a treasure-trove of ecclesiastical art.

From here, head west along Franziskanergasse and turn left into a courtyard for **Stiftskirche St Peter** (St Peter Bezirk 1/2; admission free; 8.30am-noon & 2.30-6.30pm), an abbey church founded around 700. Among the lovingly tended graves in the grounds you'll find the **Katakomben** (catacombs; adult/student €1/0.60; 10.30am-5pm Tue-Sun).

The western end of Franziskanergasse opens out into Max Reinhardt Platz, where you'll see the back of Fisher von Erlach's **Kollegienkirche** (Universitätsplatz; admission free; 8am-6pm), another outstanding example of baroque architecture. The **Stift Nonnberg** (Nonnberg Convent; admission free; 7am-dusk), where Maria first appears in *The Sound of Music*, is back in the other direction, a short climb up the hill to the east of the Festung Hohensalzburg.

Festung Hohensalzburg FORTRESS

(www.salzburg-burgen.at; Mönchsberg 34; adult with/without funicular €10.50/7.40, child €6/4.20; 9am-8pm) Salzburg's most visible icon is this mighty clifftop fortress, one of the best preserved in Europe. Built in 1077, it was home to many prince-archbishops who ruled Salzburg from 798. Inside are the impressively ornate staterooms, torture chambers and two museums.

It takes 15 minutes to walk up the hill to the fortress, or you can catch the **Festungsbahn funicular** (Festungsgasse 4; adult/child one way €3.60/1.80, return €6/3.20; 9am-8pm).

SALZBURG CARD

The money-saving **Salzburg Card** (1-/2-/3-day card €25/33/38) gets you entry to all of the major sights and attractions, a free river cruise, unlimited use of public transport (including cable cars) plus numerous discounts on tours and events. The card is half-price for children and €3 cheaper in the low season.

Salzburg Museum MUSEUM
(www.smca.at; Mozartplatz 1; adult/child €7/3; ⏲9am-5pm Tue-Sun, to 8pm Thu) Housed in the baroque Neue Residenz palace, Salzburg's flagship museum hosts contemporary art exhibitions and celebrates the city's famous citizens, like 16th-century physician Paracelsus, in an interactive way. Salzburg's famous 35-bell **glockenspiel**, which chimes daily at 7am, 11am and 6pm, is on the palace's western flank.

Schloss Mirabell PALACE
(⏲dawn-dusk) Prince-Archbishop Wolf Dietrich built this splendid palace in 1606 for his beloved mistress Salome Alt. The only way to see the sublime baroque interior is by attending an evening concert in the **Marmorsaal** (Marble Hall).

It's free to visit the manicured, fountain-dotted **gardens**, which are less overrun first thing in the morning and early evening. The *Tänzerin* (dancer) sculpture is a great spot from which to take photographs. *Sound of Music* fans will of course recognise the Pegasus statue, the gnomes and the steps where the mini von Trapps practised 'Do-Re-Mi'.

Mozarts Geburtshaus MUSEUM
(Mozart's Birthplace; www.mozarteum.at; Getreidegasse 9; adult/child €7/2.50; ⏲9am-5.30pm) Mozart was born in this bright-yellow townhouse in 1756 and spent the first 17 years of his life here. The museum today harbours a collection of memorabilia, including the miniature violin the child prodigy played, plus a lock of his hair and buttons from his jacket.

Mozart-Wohnhaus MUSEUM
(Mozart's Residence; www.mozarteum.at; Makartplatz 8; adult/child €7/2.50; ⏲9am-5.30pm) The Mozart family moved to this more spacious abode in 1773, where a prolific Mozart composed works such as the *Shepherd King* and *Idomeneo*. Alongside family portraits and documents, you'll find Mozart's original fortepiano.

The museum also houses the free **Mozart Ton-und Filmmuseum** (⏲9am-1pm Mon, Tue & Fri, 1-5pm Wed & Thu), a film and music archive for the ultra-enthusiast.

Residenz PALACE, ART MUSEUM
(www.residenzgalerie.at; Residenzplatz 1; adult/child €8.50/2.70; ⏲10am-5pm Tue-Sun) This resplendent baroque palace is where the prince-archbishops held court until the 19th century. You can visit their opulently frescoed staterooms, while the gallery spotlights Dutch and Flemish masters of the Rubens and Rembrandt ilk.

WANT MORE?

Head to **Lonely Planet** (www.lonelyplanet.com/austria/salzburg) for planning advice, author recommendations, traveller reviews and insider tips.

Museum der Moderne ART MUSEUM
(www.museumdermoderne.at; Mönchsberg 32; adult/child €8/6; ⏲10am-6pm, to 8pm Wed) Straddling Mönchsberg's cliffs, this ultramodern gallery shows first-rate modern art exhibitions. The works of Gerhard Richter, Max Ernst and Hiroshi Sugimoto have previously featured.

The **Mönchsberg Lift** (Gstättengasse 13; with/without gallery ticket return €1.70/2.90; ⏲8am-7pm, to 9pm Wed) whizzes up to the gallery year-round.

FREE **Friedhof St Sebastian** CEMETERY
(Nonnberggasse 2; ⏲7am-dusk) Tucked away behind the baroque St Sebastian's Church, this peaceful cemetery is the final resting place of Mozart family members and 16th-century physician Paracelsus. Outpomping them all, though, is Prince-Archbishop Wolf Dietrich von Raitenau's mosaic-tiled **mausoleum**, an elaborate memorial to himself.

Tours

The horse-drawn carriages (*Fiaker*) in front of Residenz do guided Altstadt (Old Town) tours; prices depend on your itinerary.

One-hour guided tours of the historic centre depart daily at 12.15pm and 2pm on Mozartplatz and cost €9. You can borrow a two-hour iGuide from the tourist office (€7.50) to take in the sights at your own speed.

How much fun you have on a *Sound of Music* tour depends on whether your group gets into the yodel-eh-hee-hee spirit of things. If you can, try to get together your own little posse.

Fräulein Maria's Bicycle Tours BICYCLE TOURS
(www.mariasbicycletours.com; adult/child incl bike hire €24/15; ⏲9.30am May-Sep) Wannabe Marias on bicycles. No booking is required; just turn up at the Mirabellplatz meeting point.

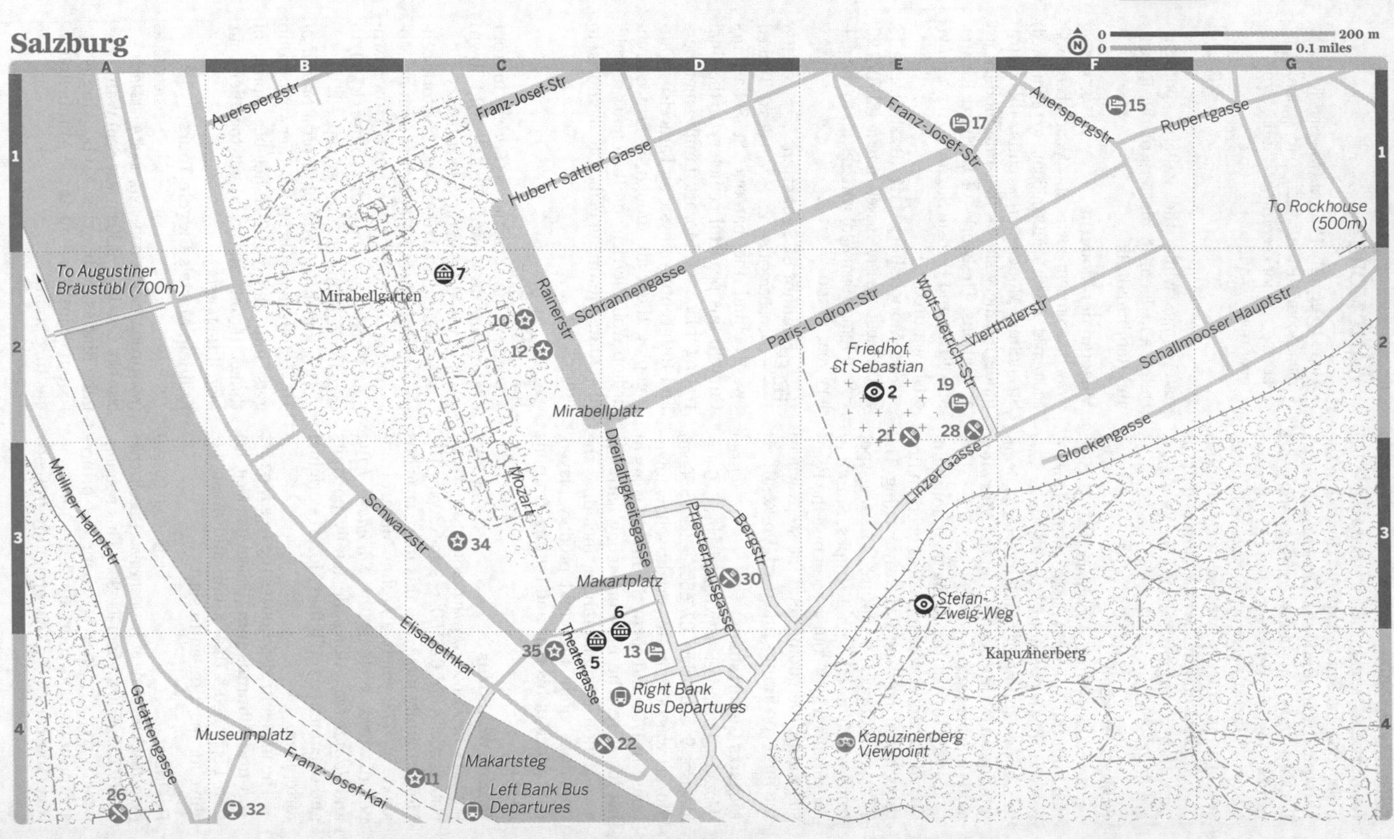
Salzburg
0 200 m
0 0.1 miles
A
B
C
D
E
F
G
1
2
3
4
Auerspergstr
Franz-Josef-Str
Hubert Sattier Gasse
Franz-Josef-Str
Auerspergstr
Rupertgasse
To Rockhouse (500m)
To Augustiner Bräustübl (700m)
Mirabellgarten
7
Rainerstr
Schrannengasse
Paris-Lodron-Str
Wolf-Dietrich-Str
Vierthalerstr
Schallmooser Hauptstr
10
12
Friedhof St Sebastian
2
19
21
28
Mirabellplatz
Glockengasse
Linzer Gasse
Mozart
Dreifaltigkeitsgasse
Priesterhausgasse
Bergstr
Schwarzstr
34
30
Müllner Hauptstr
Makartplatz
6
5
13
35
Theatergasse
Elisabethkai
Stefan-Zweig-Weg
Kapuzinerberg
Right Bank Bus Departures
Gstättengasse
Museumplatz
Franz-Josef-Kai
22
Kapuzinerberg Viewpoint
11
Makartsteg
Left Bank Bus Departures
26
32

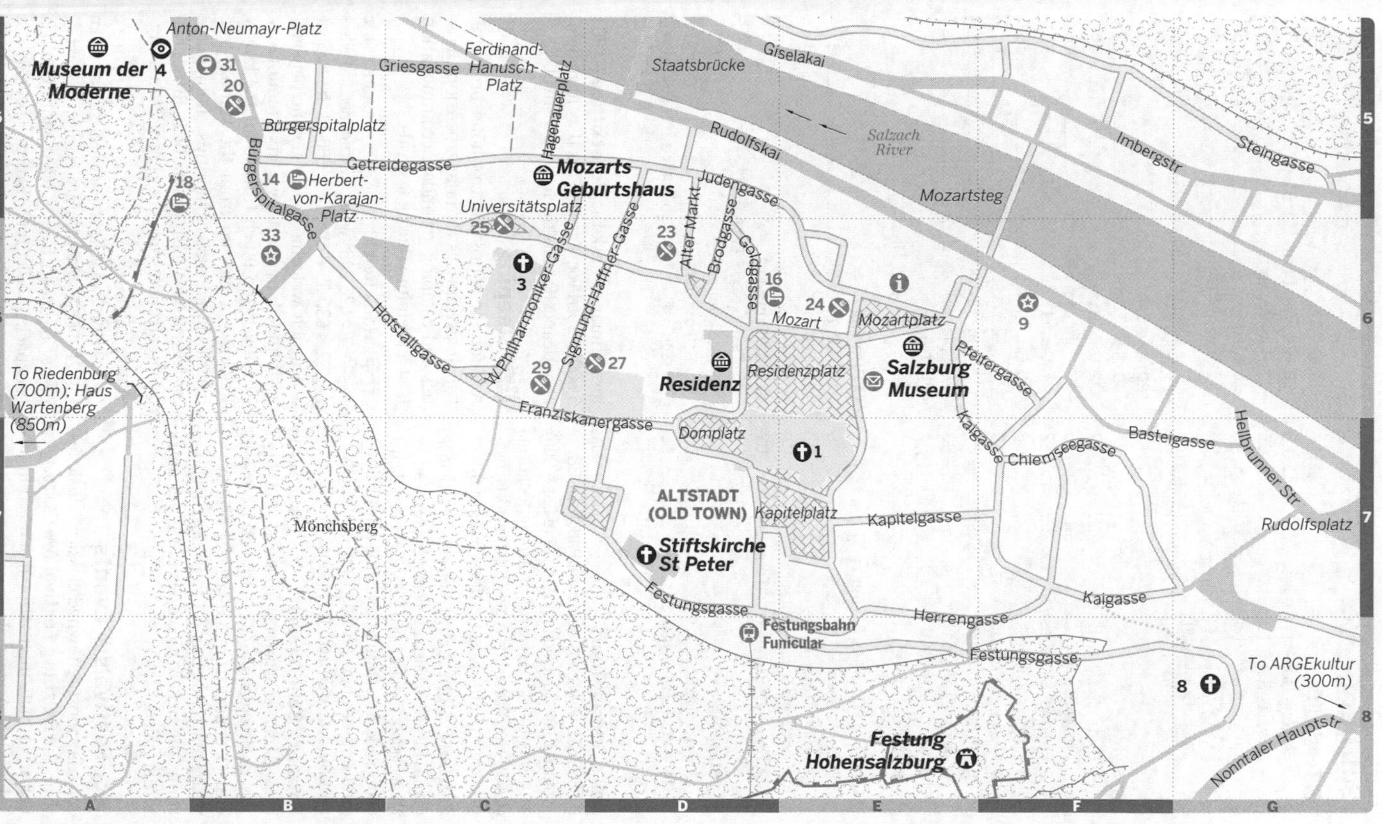
Museum der Moderne
4
Anton-Neumayr-Platz
31
20
Griesgasse
Ferdinand-Hanusch-Platz
Staatsbrücke
Giselakai
Salzach River
Imbergstr
Steingasse
Mozartsteg
Rudolfskai
Bürgerspitalplatz
Bürgerspitalgasse
Getreidegasse
Hagenauerplatz
Mozarts Geburtshaus
Judengasse
14
Herbert-von-Karajan-Platz
18
Universitätsplatz
25
33
3
23
Alter Markt
Brodgasse
Goldgasse
16
24
Mozart
Mozartplatz
9
W Philharmoniker-Gasse
Sigmund-Haffner-Gasse
Hofstallgasse
29
27
Residenz
Residenzplatz
Salzburg Museum
Pfeifergasse
Kaigasse
Chiemseegasse
Basteigasse
Hellbrunner Str
Rudolfsplatz
To Riedenburg (700m); Haus Wartenberg (850m)
Franziskanergasse
Domplatz
1
ALTSTADT (OLD TOWN)
Kapitelplatz
Kapitelgasse
Mönchsberg
Stiftskirche St Peter
Festungsgasse
Festungsbahn Funicular
Herrengasse
Kaigasse
To ARGEkultur (300m)
8
Festung Hohensalzburg
Nonntaler Hauptstr
A
B
C
D
E
F
G
5
6
7
8

Salzburg

Top Sights
Festung Hohensalzburg E8
Mozarts Geburtshaus C5
Museum der Moderne A5
Residenz D6
Salzburg Museum E6
Stiftskirche St Peter D7

Sights
1 Dom E7
Dommuseum (see 1)
2 Friedhof St Sebastian E2
3 Kollegienkirche C6
4 Mönchsberg Lift A5
5 Mozart-Wohnhaus C4
6 Mozart Ton-und Filmmuseum D3
7 Schloss Mirabell C2
8 Stift Nonnberg G8

Activities, Courses & Tours
9 Bob's Special Tours F6
10 Fräulein Maria's Bicycle Tours C2
11 Salzburg Schiffsfahrt C4
12 Salzburg Sightseeing Tours C2

Sleeping
13 Arte Vida D4
14 Arthotel Blaue Gans B5
15 Hotel & Villa Auersperg F1
16 Hotel am Dom D6
17 Hotel Mozart E1
18 Stadtalm A5
19 Wolf Dietrich E2

Eating
20 Afro Café B5
21 Alter Fuchs E2
22 Café Bazar D4
23 Café Tomaselli D6
24 Demel E6
25 Grüner Markt C6
26 M32 A4
27 Mensa Toskana D6
28 Spicy Spices E2
29 Triangel C6
30 zum Fidelen Affen D3

Drinking
31 Humboldt Stub'n B5
32 Republic B4

Entertainment
33 Festspiele Ticket Office B6
34 Mozarteum C3
Schlosskonzerte (see 7)
35 Schlosskonzerte Box Office C4

Bob's Special Tours COACH TOURS
(☎849 511; www.bobstours.com; Rudolfskai 38; ⊙office 10am-3pm Mon-Fri, noon-2pm Sat & Sun) Minibus tours to *Sound of Music* locations (€40), the Bavarian Alps (€40) and Grossglockner (€80). Reservations essential.

Salzburg Sightseeing Tours COACH TOURS
(☎881 616; www.salzburg-sightseeingtours.at; Mirabellplatz 2; adult/child €20/7; ⊙office 8am-6pm) Sells a 24-hour ticket for a multilingual hop-on, hop-off bus tour of the city and *Sound of Music* locations.

Salzburg Schiffsfahrt RIVER CRUISES
(www.salzburgschifffahrt.at; adult/child €13/7, to Schloss Hellbrunn €16/10; ⊙Apr-Oct) Hour-long cruises depart from Makartsteg bridge, with some chugging on to Schloss Hellbrunn (the ticket price does not cover entry to the palace).

Festivals & Events

Austria's most renowned classical music festival, the **Salzburg Festival** (www.salzburgfestival.at) attracts international stars from late July to late August. Book on its website before January, or ask the **ticket office** (☎804 5-500; Herbert-von- Karajan-Platz 11; ⊙10am-6pm) about cancellations during the festival.

Sleeping

Ask for the tourist office's hotel brochure, which gives prices for hotels, pensions, hostels and camping grounds. Accommodation is at a premium during festivals.

TOP CHOICE **Haus Reichl** GUESTHOUSE €
(☎826 248; www.privatzimmer.at; Reiterweg 52; s €30-35, d €48-52, tr €66-72; P) Expect a heartfelt welcome at this terrific pension, surrounded by meadows and mountains. Nothing is too much trouble for the kindly Reichls – a pick-up from the station, free bicycle hire, sightseeing tips, homemade pastries at breakfast, you name it. Bus 21 frequently trundles into the centre, 2km away.

YOHO Salzburg HOSTEL €
(☎879 649; www.yoho.at; Paracelsusstrasse 9; dm €19-21, d €50; @ wi-fi) Comfy bunks, free wi-fi, plenty of cheap beer – what more could a backpacker ask for? Except, perhaps, a merry sing-along with the *Sound of Music*

screened at 10.30am daily (yes, *every* day). The friendly crew can arrange tours, adventure sports and bike hire.

Arte Vida GUESTHOUSE €€
(☎873 185; www.artevida.at; Dreifaltigkeitsgasse 9; s €50-110, d €70-120; 📶) Arte Vida has the boho-chic feel of a Marrakesh riad, with its lantern-lit salon, communal kitchen and individually designed rooms done out in rich colours and fabrics. Markus arranges yoga sessions in the quiet garden, and outdoor activities.

Haus Wartenberg GUESTHOUSE €€
(☎848 400; www.hauswartenberg.com; Riedenburgerstrasse 2; s/d €65/95; P@) Set in vine-strewn gardens, this 17th-century chalet guesthouse is a 10-minute stroll from the Altstadt. Country-style rooms done out in chunky pinewood and florals are in keeping with the character of the place.

Hotel & Villa Auersperg HOTEL €€
(☎889 440; www.auersperg.at; Auerspergstrasse 61; s €109-139, d €145-188, ste €205; P@📶) This charismatic villa-hotel hybrid fuses late-19th-century flair with contemporary design. Relax by the lily pond in the garden or in the rooftop wellness area with mountain views. Free bike hire is a bonus.

Hotel am Dom HOTEL €€
(☎842 765; www.hotelamdom.at; Goldgasse 17; s €90-180, d €140-260; ❄@📶) Antique meets boutique at this Altstadt hotel, where the original vaults and beams of the 800-year-old building contrast with razor-sharp design features. Artworks inspired by the Salzburg Festival grace the strikingly lit rooms.

Hotel Schloss Mönchstein HISTORIC HOTEL €€€
(☎848 555-0; www.monchstein.at; Mönchsberg Park 26; d €335-445, ste €595-1450; P❄📶) On a fairytale perch atop Mönchsberg, this 16th-century castle is honeymoon (and second mortgage) material. Rooms are lavishly decorated with Persian rugs and oil paintings. A massage in the spa, a candlelit tower dinner for two, a helicopter ride – just say the word.

Arthotel Blaue Gans HISTORIC HOTEL €€
(☎842 491-50; www.hotel-blaue-gans-salzburg.at; Getreidegasse 43; s €120-140, d €140-200; ❄📶) Contemporary design blends harmoniously with the original vaulting and beams of this 650-year-old hotel, with sleek yet comfortable rooms.

Wolf Dietrich HISTORIC HOTEL €€
(☎871 275; www.salzburg-hotel.at; Wolf-Dietrich-Strasse 7; s/d €130/190; P@🏊) Old-world elegance in the rooms, plus an ultramodern spa and pool. Organic produce is served at breakfast.

Hotel Mozart HISTORIC HOTEL €€
(☎872 274; www.hotel-mozart.at; Franz-Josef-Strasse 27; s/d/tr/q €95/140/160/180; P📶) An antique-filled lobby gives way to spotless rooms with comfy beds and sizeable bathrooms. Breakfast is worth the extra €10.

Stadtalm HOSTEL €
(☎841 729; www.diestadtalm.com; dm €19) A recently revamped hostel atop Mönchsberg, where the big draw is the incredible view over Salzburg.

Camping Schloss Aigen CAMPING GROUND €
(☎622 079; www.campingparadies.at; Weberbartlweg 20; campsites per adult/child/tent €5/3/4.60; ⏲May-Sep) A leafy camping ground overlooking Gaisberg mountain, with a playground, minimarket and restaurant. Bus 10 runs into town from the stop 700m away.

Eating

Old-fashioned taverns, world flavours, kitschy Mozart dinners – you'll find the lot in the Altstadt. Sidestep Getreidegasse's crowds and head for right-bank Linzer Gasse and its tributaries, and quieter right-bank backstreets such as those east of Residenzplatz.

If you're on a budget, go for the lunchtime *Tagesmenü* (fixed menu) served at most places. The Altstadt's mazy streets are scattered with delis, supermarkets and sausage stands. Self-caterers can find picnic fixings at the **Grüner Markt** (Universitätsplatz; ⏲Mon-Sat).

DON'T MISS

NO TOURIST TRAPP

Did you know that there were 10 (not seven) von Trapp children? Or that Rupert was the eldest (so long Liesl) and the captain a gentle-natured man? For the truth behind the Hollywood legend, stay at **Villa Trapp** (☎63 08 60; www.villa-trapp.com; Traunstrasse 34; d €109-500) in Aigen district, 3km from the Altstadt. Marianne and Christopher have transformed the von Trapp's elegant 19th-century villa into a beautiful guesthouse, brimming with family heirlooms and snapshots. The villa sits in Salzburg's biggest private park.

DON'T MISS

COFFEE BREAK

Get *gemütlich* (comfy) over coffee, cake and people-watching in Salzburg's grandest cafes:

Demel CAFE
(www.demel.at; Mozartplatz 2; ⏲9am-8pm; 📶) Demel's 1st-floor balcony has a prime view of Mozartplatz. The must-try here is the *Anna Torte:* a moist chocolate sponge with a splash of orange liqueur, topped with a chocolate-nougat swirl.

Café Bazar CAFE
(www.cafe-bazar.at; Schwarzstrasse 3; ⏲7.30am-11pm Mon-Sat, 9am-6pm Sat) All chandeliers, polished wood and intelligent conversation. Enjoy breakfast or a cream-filled torte on the terrace overlooking the Salzach River.

Café Tomaselli CAFE
(www.tomaselli.at, in German; Alter Markt 9; ⏲7am-9pm) Going strong since 1705, this marble and wood-panelled cafe is a former Mozart haunt. It's famous for having Salzburg's flakiest strudels, best *Einspänner* (coffee with whipped cream) and grumpiest waiters.

Alter Fuchs AUSTRIAN €
(☎882 022; Linzer Gasse 47-49; mains €9-16; ⏲Mon-Sat) This old fox prides itself on serving up old-fashioned Austrian fare, such as schnitzels fried to golden perfection. Foxes clad in bandanas guard the bar in the vaulted interior and there's a courtyard for good-weather dining.

Afro Café AFRICAN €€
(☎844 888; Bürgerspitalplatz 5; lunch €6.90, mains €10-14; ⏲10am-midnight Mon-Sat) Hot-pink walls, beach-junk art and *big* hair… this afro-chic cafe keeps the good vibes and food coming. Fruity cocktails wash down favourites like grilled chicken with honey-lime glaze.

Riedenburg GOURMET €€€
(☎830 815; www.riedenburg.at, in German; Neutorstrasse 31; lunch €18, mains €26-35; ⏲Tue-Sat) At this romantic Michelin-starred pick, Richard Brunnauer's creative Austrian signatures, such as venison and guinea fowl crêpes with wild herbs, are expertly matched with top wines.

zum Fidelen Affen AUSTRIAN €€
(☎877 361; Priesterhausgasse 8; mains €10.50-16.50; ⏲dinner Mon-Sat) At the jovial monkey you'll dine heartily on Austrian classics like goulash and sweet curd dumplings in the vaulted interior or on the pavement terrace. Reservations are recommended.

M32 FUSION €€
(☎841 000; www.m32.at, in German; Mönchsberg 32; mains €14-26; ⏲9am-1am Tue-Sun) Bold colours and a forest of stag antlers reveal architect Matteo Thun's imprint at Museum der Moderne's glass-walled restaurant. The seasonal food and views are fantastic.

Triangel AUSTRIAN €€
(☎842 229; www.triangel-salzburg.at; Wiener-Philharmoniker-Gasse 7; mains €9-20) Arty bistro near the Festspielhaus, with a market-fresh menu.

Mensa Toskana INTERNATIONAL €
(Sigmund-Haffner-Gasse 11; lunch €4.20-5.10; ⏲lunch Mon-Fri) Atmospheric university cafe in the Altstadt, with a sunny terrace and decent lunches.

Spicy Spices INDIAN €
(Wolf-Dietrich-Strasse 1; mains €6.50; 🖉) 'Healthy heart, lovely soul' is the mantra of this all-organic, all-vegetarian haunt.

Drinking

Nobody's pretending Salzburg is rave city, but the days of lights out by 11pm are long gone. You'll find the biggest concentration of bars along both banks of the Salzach and the hippest around Gstättengasse and Anton-Neumayr-Platz.

TOP CHOICE **Augustiner Bräustübl** BREW PUB
(Augustinergasse 4-6; ⏲3-11pm Mon-Fri, 2.30-11pm Sat & Sun) Who says monks can't enjoy themselves? This hillside complex of beer halls and gardens is not to be missed. The local monks' brew keeps the huge crowd of up to 2800 humming.

Republic BAR
(Anton-Neumayr-Platz 2; ⏲8am-1am Sun-Thu, 8am-4am Fri & Sat) One of Salzburg's most happening haunts, with regular DJs and free events from tango on Sundays to salsa on Tuesdays.

Humboldt Stub'n BAR
(Gstättengasse 4-6; ⏲10am-4am) A nail-studded Mozart punk guards this upbeat bar

opposite Republic. Try a sickly Mozart cocktail (liqueur, cherry juice, cream and chocolate). Beers are €2.50 at Wednesday's student night.

Entertainment

Some of the high-brow venues include the **Schlosskonzerte** (848 586; www.salzburger-schlosskonzerte.at), in Schloss Mirabell's sublime baroque Marble Hall, and the **Mozarteum** (www.mozarteum.at; Schwarzstrasse 26). Marionettes bring the *Sound of Music* and Mozart's operas magically to life at **Salzburger Marionettentheater** (87 24 06; www.marionetten.at; Schwarzstrasse 24; May-Sep, Christmas, Easter).

Most bands with a modern bent will invariably play at either the **Rockhouse** (www.rockhouse.at, in German; Schallmooser Hauptstrasse 46) or **ARGEkultur** (www.argekultur.at, in German; Josef-Preis-Allee 16); both double as popular bars.

Information

Many hotels and bars offer free wi-fi, and there are several cheap internet cafes near the train station. Bankomaten (ATMs) are all over the place; there are also exchange booths at the airport and downtown, but beware of high commission rates.

Hospital (44 82; Müllner Hauptstrasse 48) Just north of Mönchsberg.

International Telephone Discount (Kaiserschützenstrasse 8; internet per hour €2; 9am-8pm Mon-Sat, 1-8pm Sun) Near the station. Also offers discount calls.

Police headquarters (63 83; Alpenstrasse 90)

Post office Main branch (Residenzplatz 9); station (Südtiroler Platz 1)

STA Travel (www.statravel.at; Rainerstrasse 2) Student and budget travel agency.

Tourist office (889 87-330; www.salzburg.info; Mozartplatz 5; 9am-7pm) Has plenty of information about the city and its immediate surrounds; there's a ticket booking agency in the same building. For information on the rest of the province, visit the **Salzburgerland Tourismus** (www.salzburgerland.com) website.

Western Union (8am-8.30pm Mon-Fri, to 2pm Sat, 1-6pm Sun) Changes money at its branch in the station post office.

Getting There & Away

Air

Salzburg airport (www.salzburg-airport.com), a 20-minute bus ride from the centre, has regular scheduled flights to destinations all over Austria and Europe. Low-cost flights from the UK are provided by **Ryanair** (www.ryanair.com) and **easyJet** (www.easyjet.com). Other airlines include **British Airways** (www.britishairways.com) and **KLM** (www.klm.com).

Bus

Buses depart from just outside the Hauptbahnhof on Südtiroler Platz, where timetables are displayed. Bus information and tickets are available from the information points on the main concourse.

Hourly buses leave for the Salzkammergut including Bad Ischl (€9.10, 1½ hours), Mondsee (€5.70, 50 minutes), St Wolfgang (€8.40, 1¾ hours) and St Gilgen (€5.70, 50 minutes). For more information on buses in Salzburgerland and the Salzkammergut and an online timetable, see www.svv.at.

Car & Motorcycle

Three motorways converge on Salzburg to form a loop around the city: the A1/E60 from Linz, Vienna and the east; the A8/E52 from Munich and the west; and the A10/E55 from Villach and the south. The quickest way to Tirol is to take the road to Bad Reichenhall in Germany and continue to Lofer (B178) and St Johann in Tirol.

Train

Salzburg's Hauptbahnhof was undergoing extensive renovation at the time of research.

Fast trains leave hourly for Vienna (€47.50, three hours) via Linz (€22, 1¼ hours). The express service to Klagenfurt (€35.50, three hours) goes via Villach. The quickest way to Innsbruck (€37.80, two hours) is by the 'corridor' train through Germany via Kufstein; trains depart at least every two hours. There are trains every hour or so to Munich (€34).

Getting Around

TO/FROM THE AIRPORT **Salzburg airport** (www.salzburg-airport.com) is located 4km west of the city centre. Bus 2 goes there from the Hauptbahnhof (€2.10, 19 minutes). A taxi costs about €15.

BICYCLE **Top Bike** (www.topbike.at; 2hr/4hr/day €6/10/15, 20% discount with all train tickets) rents bikes from just outside the train station.

BUS Bus drivers sell singles for €2.10. Other tickets, including day (€5) and week (€12.80) passes, must be bought from the automatic machines at stops or *Tabak* shops.

CAR & MOTORCYCLE The majority of the Old Town is pedestrianised. The nearest central parking area is the Altstadt Garage under the Mönchsberg. Attended car parks cost €1.40 to €2.40 per hour. On streets with automatic ticket machines (blue zones), a three-hour maximum applies (€0.50 for 30 minutes) between 9am and 7pm Monday to Friday and 9am and 4pm Saturday.

AROUND SALZBURG

Schloss Hellbrunn

A prince-archbishop with a wicked sense of humour, Markus Sittikus built Italianate **Schloss Hellbrunn** (www.hellbrunn.at; Fürstenweg 37; adult/child €9.50/4.50; ⌚9am-5.30pm, to 9pm Jul & Aug) as a 17th-century summer palace and an escape from his Residenz functions.

The ingenious trick fountains and water-powered figures are the big draw. When the tour guides set them off, expect to get wet! Admission includes entry to the baroque palace. The rest of the sculpture-dotted gardens are free to visit. Look out for the *Sound of Music* pavilion of 'Sixteen Going on Seventeen' fame.

Bus 25 runs to Hellbrunn, 4.5km south of Salzburg, every 20 minutes from Rudolfskai in the Altstadt.

Werfen

☎06468 / POP 3020

The world's largest accessible ice caves, the soaring limestone turrets of the Tennengebirge mountains and a formidable medieval fortress are but the tip of the superlative iceberg in Werfen. Such salacious natural beauty hasn't escaped Hollywood producers – Werfen stars in WWII action film *Where Eagles Dare* (1968) and makes a cameo appearance in the picnic scene of *The Sound of Music*.

Both the ice caves and fortress can be visited as a day trip from Salzburg if you start early (tour the caves first and be at the fortress by 3pm for the falconry show), otherwise consult the **tourist office** (☎53 88; www.werfen.at; Markt 24; ⌚9am-noon & 2-5pm Mon-Fri) for accommodation options.

Sights & Activities

Eisriesenwelt ICE CAVES

(www.eisriesenwelt.at; adult/child €8.50/4.50, with cable car €19/9.50; ⌚9am-3.30pm May-Oct) Billed as the world's largest accessible ice caves, more than 1000m above Werfen in the Tennengebirge mountains, this glittering ice empire is a once seen, never forgotten experience. The 1¼-hour tour takes you through twinkling passageways and chambers, the carbide lamps picking out otherworldly ice sculptures. Dress for subzero temperatures.

Burg Hohenwerfen FORTRESS

(adult/child €14/7.50; ⌚9am-5pm Apr-Oct) High on a wooded cliff top, Burg Hohenwerfen has kept watch over the Salzach Valley since 1077, although its current appearance dates from the 16th century. Highlights include far-reaching views over Werfen from the belfry, dungeons containing some pretty nasty torture instruments, and a dramatic falconry show (11am and 3pm). The walk up from the village takes 20 minutes.

Getting There & Around

Werfen can be reached from Salzburg on the A10/E55 motorway or by train (€9.20, 40 minutes). In summer, minibuses (single/return €2.90/5.80) run every 25 minutes between Eisriesenstrasse in Werfen and the car park, a 20-minute walk from the cable car to Eisriesenwelt.

SALZKAMMERGUT

A picture-perfect wonderland of glassy blue lakes and tall craggy peaks, Austria's Lake District is a long-time favourite holiday destination, attracting visitors in droves from Salzburg and beyond.

Whether you're looking for a way to entertain the kids or hoping to commune with nature, the area is big on variety. The peaceful lakes offer limitless opportunities for boating, fishing, swimming or just lazing on the shore. Favourite waterside beauty spots include the picturesque villages of Hallstatt and St Wolfgang, and the Riviera-style port of Gmunden. You can also tour the salt mines that made the region wealthy or plunge into the depths of the fantastic Dachstein caves, where glittering towers of ice are masterfully illuminated in the depths of a mountain.

Getting There & Around

BOAT Passenger boats ply the waters of the Attersee, Traunsee, Mondsee, Hallstätter See and Wolfgangsee.

BUS Regular buses connect the region's towns and villages, though less frequently on weekends. Timetables are displayed at stops, and tickets can be bought from the driver.

CAR & MOTORCYCLE To reach Salzkammergut from Salzburg by car or motorcycle, take the A1 or Hwy 158.

Salzkammergut

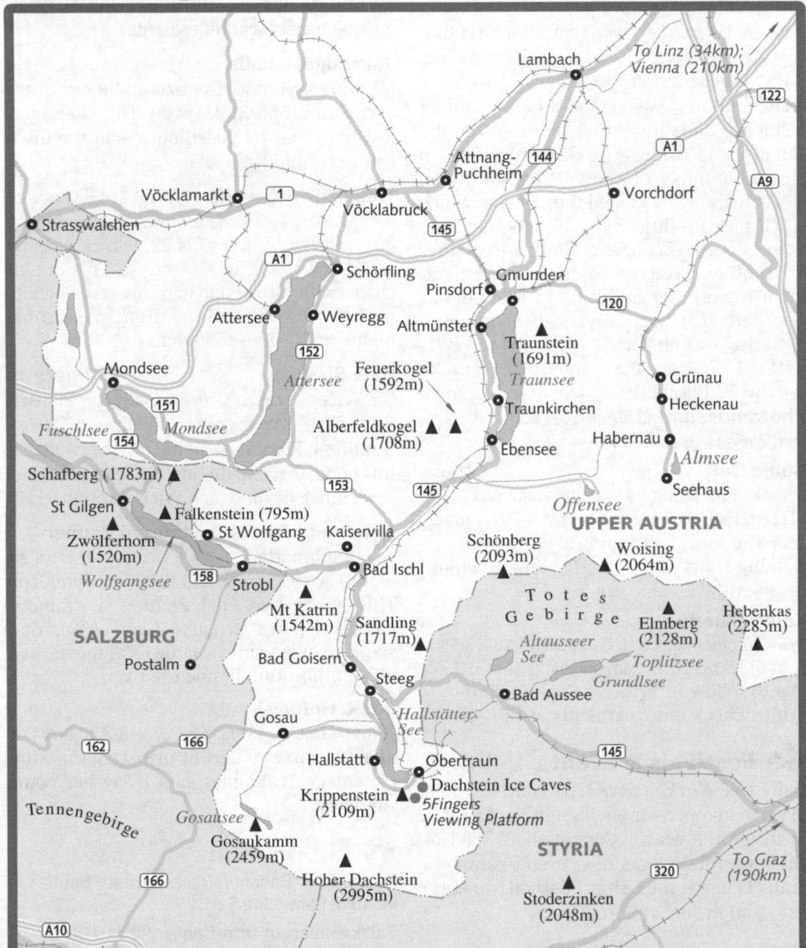

TRAIN The country's major rail routes bypass the heart of Salzkammergut, but regional trains cross through the area from north to south. This route begins at Attnang-Puchheim on the Salzburg–Linz line. The track from here connects to Bad Ischl, Hallstatt and Obertraun in one direction and to Gmunden in another. At the smaller, unattended stations *(unbesetzter Bahnhof)* you'll have to buy tickets from a machine on the platform or else purchase them from staff on the train (no surcharge applies).

After leaving Obertraun, the railway continues eastwards via Bad Aussee before connecting with the main Bischofshofen–Graz line at Stainach-Irdning.

Bad Ischl

☎06132 / POP 14,050

During the last century of the Habsburg reign, Bad Ischl became the favourite summertime retreat for the imperial family and their entourage. Today the town and many of its dignified buildings still have a stately aura, and a perhaps surprisingly high proportion of the local women still go about their daily business in *Dirndl* (Austria's traditional full pleated skirt). It makes a good base for exploring the entire Salzkammergut region.

Sights & Activities

Kaiservilla PALACE

(Jainzen 38; www.kaiservilla.com; adult/child €12/7.50, grounds only €4.50/3.50; 9.30am-4.45pm, closed Thu-Tue Jan-Mar, closed Nov) This Italianate building was Franz Josef's summer residence and shows that he loved huntin', shootin' and fishin' – it's decorated with an obscene number of animal trophies. It can be visited only by guided tour, during which you'll pick up little gems, like the fact that Franz Josef was conceived in Bad Ischl after his mother, Princess Sophie, took a treatment to cure her infertility in 1828. It was also here that the Kaiser signed the letter declaring war on Serbia, which led to WWI.

What was once the teahouse of Franz Josef's wife, Elisabeth, now contains a small **Photomuseum** (adult/child €2/1.50; 9.30am-5pm, closed Nov-Mar).

Cable Car CABLE CAR

(www.katrinseilbahn.com; return adult/child €17.50/11.50, closed Apr–mid-May & Nov–mid-Dec) The local mountain (1542m) with walking trails and limited skiing in winter is served by a cable car.

Kaiser Therme SPA

(www.eurothermen.co.at; Bahnhofstrasse 1; adult/child €13.50/9.50; 9am-midnight) If you'd like to follow in Princess Sophie's footprints, check out treatments at this spa.

Festivals & Events

Daily free *Kurkonzerte* (spa concerts) take place in an open-air pavilion in the Kurpark or inside the nearby Congresshaus. Bad Ischl stages the works of operetta composer Franz Lehár at the **Lehár Festival** (www.leharfestival.at) in July and August.

Sleeping & Eating

Staff at both the tourist offices can help find rooms.

Hotel Garni Sonnhof HOTEL €€

(230 78; www.sonnhof.at; Bahnhofstrasse 4; s €65-95, d €90-150; P) Nestled in a leafy glade of maple trees next to the station, this hotel has cosy, traditional decor, a beautiful garden, chickens that deliver breakfast eggs, and a sunny conservatory. There's a sauna and a steam bath on-site.

Goldenes Schiff HOTEL €€

(242 41; www.goldenes-schiff.at; Adalbert Stifterkai 3; s €98-109, d €144-176, apt €192; P@) The best rooms at this comfortable pick have large windows overlooking the river. There's also a wellness centre and an excellent restaurant (mains €14 to €18) serving Austrian cuisine using local ingredients.

Jugendgästehaus HOSTEL €

(265 77; jgh.badischl@oejhv.or.at; Am Rechensteg 5; dm/s/d €16.50/31/47; @) The characterless but clean HI guesthouse is in the town centre behind Kreuzplatz.

Weinhaus Attwenger AUSTRIAN €€

(233 27; www.weinhaus-attwenger.com, in German; Lehárkai 12; mains €14-22; lunch & dinner, closed Mon, closed Tue Nov-Apr;) This quaint chalet with a riverside garden serves prime-quality Austrian cuisine from a seasonal menu, with wines to match.

Café Sissy AUSTRIAN €€

(www.cafe-sissy.at, in German; Pfarrgasse 2; mains €11-18.50; 8am-midnight) Pictures of Sissy (Empress Elisabeth) hang on the walls of this popular riverside cafe. You can breakfast here, lunch or dine on a Wiener schnitzel.

Grand Café & Restaurant Zauner Esplanade AUSTRIAN €€

(Hasner Allee 2; mains €10-18.50; 10am-10pm) This offshoot of Café Zauner, the famous pastry shop at Pfarrgasse 7, serves Austrian staples, some using organic local meats, in a pleasant location beside the river.

K.u.K. Hofbeisl BEISL €

(Wirerstrasse 4; mains €8-20; 8-3.30am) For quality grub at a decent price, try this simple eatery. It doubles as a lively bar come sundown.

Information

Post office (Bahnhofstrasse; 8am-6pm Mon-Fri, 9am-noon Sat)

Salzkammergut Info-Center (240 00-0; www.salzkammergut.co.at; Götzstrasse 12; 9am-8pm, closed Sun Oct-Mar) Has bike rental (per 24 hours €13) and internet (per 10 minutes €1.10).

Tourist office (277 57-0; www.badischl.at; Auböckplatz 5; 8am-6pm Mon-Fri, 9am-6pm Sat, 10am-1pm Sun) Has a telephone service (8am to 10pm) for rooms and information.

Getting There & Around

BUS Buses depart from outside the train station, with hourly buses to Salzburg (€9.10, 1½ hours) via St Gilgen (€4.80, 40 minutes). Buses to St Wolfgang (€3.60, 30 minutes) go via Strobl.

CAR & MOTORCYCLE Most major roads in the Salzkammergut go to or near Bad Ischl; Hwy 158 from Salzburg and the north–south Hwy 145 intersect just north of the town centre.

TRAIN Hourly trains to Hallstatt (€3.60, 25 minutes) go via Steeg/Hallstätter See, at the northern end of the lake, and continue on the eastern side via Hallstatt station to Obertraun (€4.30, 30 minutes). A boat from Hallstatt station (€2.20) takes you to the township. There are also frequent trains to Gmunden (€7.20, 40 minutes) and Salzburg (€21, two hours) via Attnang-Puchheim.

Hallstatt

06134 / POP 840

With pastel-hued homes, swans and towering mountains on either side of a glassy green lake, Hallstatt looks like some kind of greeting card for tranquillity. Boats chug lazily across the water from the train station to the village itself, which clings precariously to a tiny bit of land between mountain and shore. So small is the patch of land occupied by the village that its annual Corpus Christi procession takes place largely in small boats on the lake.

Sights & Activities

Hallstatt has been classified a Unesco World Heritage site for its natural beauty and for evidence of human settlement dating back 4500 years. Over 2000 graves have been discovered in and around the village, most dating from 1000 to 500 BC.

Salzbergwerk SALT MINE

(funicular return plus tour adult/child €24/12, tour only €12/6; 9.30am-4.30pm, closed mid-Oct–Apr) The region's major cultural attraction is situated high above Hallstatt on Salzberg (Salt Mountain). In 1734 the fully preserved body of a prehistoric miner was found and today he is known as the 'Man in Salt'. The standard tour revolves around his fate, with visitors travelling down an underground railway and miner's slides (a photo is taken of you while sliding) to an illuminated subterranean salt lake.

The mine can be reached on foot or with the **funicular railway** (one way adult/child €7/3.50).

Beinhaus CHURCH

(Bone House; Kirchenweg 40; admission €1; 10am-6pm, closed Nov-Apr) Don't miss the macabre yet beautiful Beinhaus behind Hallstatt's parish church. It contains rows of stacked skulls painted with flowery designs and the names of the deceased. The old Celtic pagan custom of mass burial has been practised here since 1600 (mainly due to the lack of graveyard space), and the last skull in the collection was added in 1995.

WORTH A TRIP

OBERTRAUN

At nearby Obertraun you'll find the intriguing **Dachstein Rieseneishöhle** (www.dachsteinwelterbe.at; cable car return plus one cave adult/child €27/15, one cave only adult/child €10.80/6). The caves are millions of years old and extend into the mountain for almost 80km in places. The ice itself is around 500 years old, but is increasing in thickness each year – the 'ice mountain' is 8m high, twice as high now as it was when the caves were first explored in 1910.

From Obertraun it's also possible to catch a cable car to **Krippenstein** (return adult/child €23/14; closed mid-Oct–Nov & Easter–mid-May), where you'll find the freaky **5Fingers viewing platform**, which protrudes over a sheer cliff face. Not for sufferers of vertigo.

Hallstätter See LAKE

You can hire boats and kayaks (per hour from €11) on the lake, or scuba dive with the **Tauchclub Dachstein** (0676/644 99 89; www.zauner-online.at; 2-3-hr course from €35).

Sleeping & Eating

Rooms fill quickly in summer, so book ahead, arrive early, or go straight for the tourist office and they'll help you find something, either in Hallstatt or Lahn (the southern part of the village).

Seehotel Grüner Baum HOTEL €€

(8263; Marktplatz 104; s €80, d without view €140, d or ste with lake view €170-210; P@) This hotel has its own pontoon and tastefully furnished rooms (most with balconies). Breakfast delivered to your bedside and sparkling lake views make this ideal for romantic sojourns.

Bräugasthof am Hallstätter See GUESTHOUSE €€

(8221; www.brauhaus-lobisser.com; Seestrasse 120; s €49-55, d €98, tr €130-135) A central, friendly guesthouse with a lakeside restaurant (mains €14 to €19) serving trout and other local specialities.

Gasthaus Mühle HOSTEL €
(☎8318; www.hallstatturlaub.at, in German; Kirchenweg 36; dm €23; ⊙closed Tue & Nov) This hostel with decent (if basic) dorms is handily situated on the way up to the church.

Balthazar im Rudolfsturm CAFE €
(Rudolfsturm; mains €10-13.50; ⊙9am-6pm, closed Nov–Apr;) With the most spectacular terrace in the region, Balthazar is situated 855m above Hallstatt. Both the views over the lake and the food are excellent.

Information

Tourist office (☎8208; www.dachstein-salzkammergut.at; Seestrasse 169; ⊙9am-6pm Mon-Fri, to 4pm Sat, to noon Sun, closed Sat & Sun Sep-Jun) Turn left from the ferry to reach the office. It stocks the free leisure map of lakeside towns, and hiking and cycling trails.

Getting There & Away

BOAT The last ferry connection leaves Hallstatt train station at 6.55pm (€2.20, 10 minutes). Ferry excursions do the circuit Hallstatt Lahn via Hallstatt Markt, Obersee, Untersee and Steeg return (€9.50, 90 minutes) three times daily from mid-July to August.

BUS Eight to 10 buses connect Hallstatt (Lahn) town with Obertraun (€1.90, eight minutes) daily.

CAR Access into the village is restricted by electronic gates from early May to late October. Staying overnight in town gives free parking and a pass to open the gates.

TRAIN Hallstatt train station is across the lake. The boat service from there to the village coincides with train arrivals. About a dozen trains daily connect Hallstatt and Bad Ischl (€3.60, 22 minutes) and Hallstatt with Bad Aussee (€3.60, 15 minutes).

Wolfgangsee

Wolfgangsee is a hugely popular place to spend the summer swimming, boating, walking or simply lazing by its soothing waters. Its two main resorts are St Wolfgang and St Gilgen, the first of which takes first prize in the beauty stakes.

Coming from Salzburg, the first town you come across is **St Gilgen**. It's a fine point from which to explore the surrounding region, and its **tourist office** (☎2348; www.wolfgangsee.at; Mondsee Bundesstrasse 1a; ⊙9am-8pm Mon-Fri, to 6pm Sat, 10am-5pm Sun) can help with accommodation and activities.

St Wolfgang, towards the southern end of Wolfgangsee, is squeezed between the northern shoreline of the lake and the towering peak of Schafberg (1783m). Its **tourist office** (☎8003; www.wolfgangsee.at; Au 140; ⊙9am-8pm Mon-Fri, to 6pm Sat, 10am-5pm Sun) has plenty of information for travellers.

In the heart of the village you'll find the 14th-century **Pilgrimage Church** (donation €1; ⊙9am-6pm), a highly ornate example that still attracts pilgrims. Reaching the top of **Scharfberg** is an easy exercise – from May to October, a cogwheel railway climbs to its summit in 40 minutes (one way/return €19.60/28.60). Otherwise it's a three- to four-hour walk.

Both St Wolfgang and St Gilgen have numerous pensions, starting from about €25 per person; the local tourist offices have details.

On the lakefront, 1km east of St Wolfgang, **Camping Appesbach** (☎2206; www.appesbach.at; Au 99; campsite per adult/child/tent €7/4/7; ⊙closed Oct-Easter; P) is a favourite with Austrian holidaymakers. A plusher option with lake views, a wellness area and two pools is **Im Weissen Rössl** (☎2306-0; www.weissesroessl.at; Im Stöckl 74; s €130-160, d €190-280; P@), the setting for Ralph Benatzky's operetta *The White Horse*.

A ferry operates May to October between Strobl and St Gilgen (one way €8.80, 75 minutes), stopping at points en route. Services are most frequent from June to early September. Boats run from St Wolfgang to St Gilgen almost hourly during the day (one way €6.50, 50 minutes); the free *Eintauchen & Aufsteigen* timetable from local tourist offices gives exact times.

A Postbus service from St Wolfgang via Strobl to St Gilgen (€3.90, 50 minutes) is frequent out of season, but tails off somewhat in summer when the ships run. For Salzburg (€6.40, 1¾ hours) you need to connect in St Gilgen or Strobl (€2.10, 12 minutes).

Northern Salzkammergut

Mondsee is popular for two reasons – its close proximity to Salzburg (only 30km) and its warm water. The main village on the lake, also called Mondsee, is home to an attractive 15th-century church that was used in the wedding scene of *The Sound of Music* and a small and helpful **tourist office** (☎2270; www.mondsee.at; Dr Franz Müller Strasse 3; ⊙8am-6pm Mon-Fri, 9am-6pm Sat & Sun, closed Sat & Sun Oct-May).

Lying to the east of Mondsee is **Attersee**, Salzkammergut's largest lake and a favourite with sailors. East again from Attersee you'll find **Traunsee** and its three main resorts: Gmunden, Traunkirchen and Ebensee. **Gmunden** is famous for its twin castles, linked by a causeway on the lake, and its green and white ceramics. Contact the local **tourist office** (☎643 05; www.traunsee.at; Toscanapark 1; ⊙8am-8pm Mon-Fri, 10am-7pm Sat & Sun) for information on accommodation and activities on and around the lake.

Buses run every hour to Mondsee from Salzburg (€5.70, 55 minutes). Gmunden is connected to Salzburg by train (€15.70, 1¼ hours), via Attnang-Puchheim.

TIROL

With converging mountain ranges behind lofty pastures and tranquil meadows, Tirol (also Tyrol) captures a quintessential Alpine panoramic view. Occupying a central position is Innsbruck, the region's jewel, while in the northeast and southwest are superb ski resorts. In the southeast, separated somewhat from the main state since part of South Tirol was ceded to Italy at the end of WWI, lies the protected natural landscape of the Hohe Tauern National Park, an Alpine wonderland of 3000m peaks, including the country's highest, the Grossglockner (3798m).

Innsbruck

☎0512 / POP 118,000

Tirol's capital is a sight to behold. The mountains are so close that within 25 minutes it's possible to travel from the heart of the city to over 2000m above sea level. Summer and winter outdoor activities abound, and it's understandable why some visitors only take a peek at Innsbruck proper before heading for the hills. But to do so is a shame, for Innsbruck has its own share of gems, including an authentic medieval Altstadt (Old Town), inventive architecture and vibrant student-driven nightlife.

Sights

Innsbruck's atmospheric, medieval Altstadt is ideal for a lazy stroll. Many of the sights listed below close an hour or two earlier in winter.

TOP CHOICE **Goldenes Dachl & Museum** MUSEUM
(Golden Roof; Herzog-Friedrich-Strasse 15; adult/child €4/2; ⊙10am-5pm, closed Mon Oct-Apr) Innsbruck's golden wonder is this Gothic oriel, built for Emperor Maximilian I and glittering with 2657 fire-gilt copper tiles. An audioguide whizzes you through the history in the museum; look for the grotesque tournament helmets designed to resemble the slit-eyed Turks of the rival Ottoman Empire.

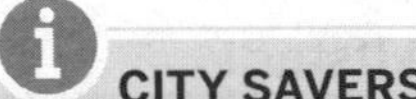

CITY SAVERS

The **Innsbruck Card** gives one visit to Innsbruck's main sights and attractions, a return journey on all cable cars and unlimited use of public transport including the Sightseer bus, which makes getting to some of the more remote sights easier. It's available at the tourist office and costs €29/34/39 for 24/48/72 hours (half-price for children).

Stay overnight in Innsbruck and you'll receive a **Club Innsbruck Card**, giving discounts on transport and activities, and allows you to join the tourist office's free guided hikes in summer.

Hofkirche CHURCH
(www.tiroler-landesmuseum.at; Universitätstrasse; combined Volkskunstmuseum ticket adult/child €8/4; ⊙10am-6pm Mon-Sat, 12.30am-6pm Sun) The 16th-century Hofkirche is one of Europe's finest royal court churches. Top billing goes to the empty **sarcophagus** of Emperor Maximilian I (1459–1519), a masterpiece of German Renaissance sculpture, guarded by 28 giant bronze figures including Dürer's legendary King Arthur. You're now forbidden to touch the statues, but numerous inquisitive hands have already polished parts of the dull bronze, including Kaiser Rudolf's codpiece!

Volkskunstmuseum MUSEUM
(Folk Art Museum; www.tiroler-landesmuseum.at; Universitätstrasse; combined Hofkirche ticket adult/child €8/4; ⊙10am-6pm Mon-Sat, 12.30am-6pm Sun) Next door to the Hofkirche, the Volkskunstmuseum houses Tyrolean folk art from handcarved sleighs and Christmas cribs to carnival masks and cow bells.

Hofburg PALACE
(Imperial Palace; www.hofburg-innsbruck.at; Rennweg 1; adult/child €8/free; ⊙9am-5pm) Empress Maria Theresia gave this Habsburg palace a total baroque makeover in the 16th century. The highlight of the state apartments is the Riesensaal (Giant's Hall), lavishly adorned with frescos and paintings of

Innsbruck Altstadt

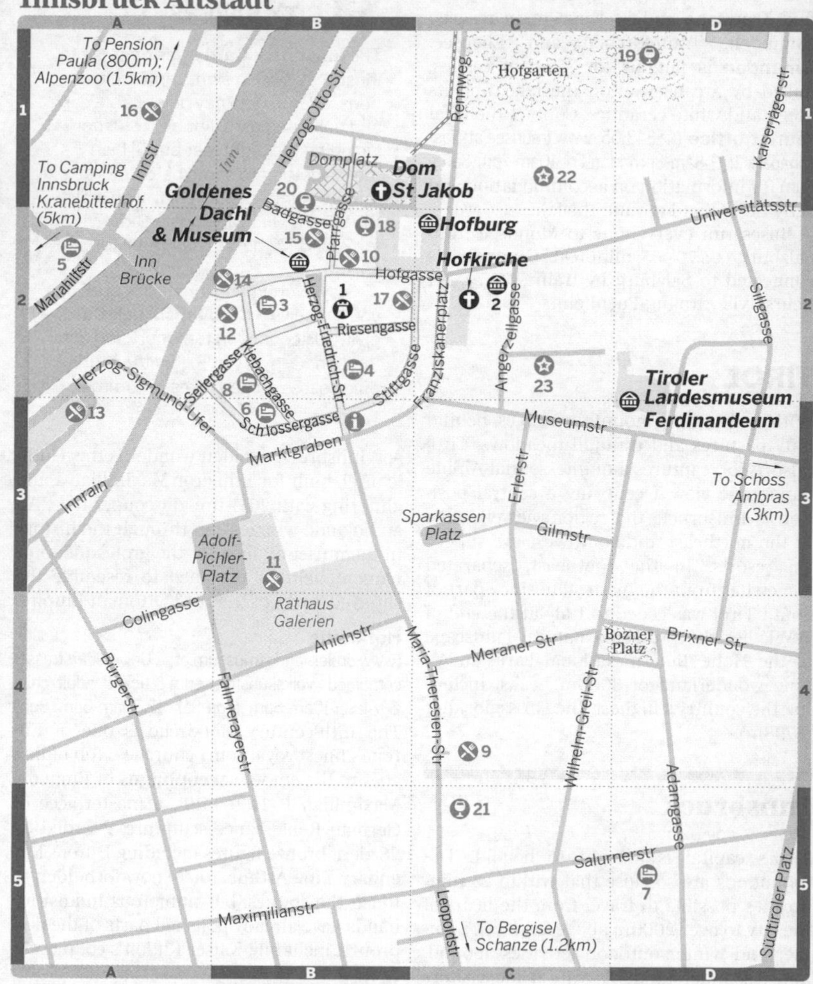

Maria Theresia and her 16 children, including Marie Antoinette.

Tucked behind the palace is the **Hofgarten** (admission free; ⌚daylight hr), an attractive garden for a botanical stroll.

Bergisel SKI JUMP

(www.bergisel.info; adult/child €8.50/4; ⌚10am-6pm) Rising above Innsbruck like a celestial staircase, this glass-and-steel ski jump was designed by much-lauded Iraqi architect Zaha Hadid. From May to July, fans pile in to see athletes train, while preparations step up a gear in January for the World Cup Four Hills Tournament.

It's 455 steps or a two-minute funicular ride to the 50m-high **viewing platform**. Here, the panorama of the Nordkette range, Inn Valley and Innsbruck is breathtaking, though the cemetery at the bottom has undoubtedly made a few ski jumping pros quiver in their boots.

Bus 4143 and line TS run from the Hauptbahnhof to Bergisel.

Tiroler Landesmuseum Ferdinandeum ART MUSEUM

(www.tiroler-landesmuseum.at; Museumstrasse 15; adult/child €8/4; ⌚10am-6pm Tue-Sun) This treasure-trove of Tyrolean history and art

Innsbruck Altstadt

Top Sights
- Dom St Jakob B1
- Goldenes Dachl & Museum B2
- Hofburg C2
- Hofkirche C2
- Tiroler Landesmuseum Ferdinandeum D3

Sights
1. Stadtturm B2
2. Volkskunstmuseum C2

Sleeping
3. Goldener Adler B2
4. Hotel Weisses Kreuz B2
5. Mondschein A2
6. Nepomuks B3
7. Pension Stoi D5
8. Weisses Rössl B2

Eating
- Cafe Munding .... (see 6)
9. Chez Nico C4
10. Gasthaus Goldenes Dachl B2
11. Lichtblick B3
12. Mamma Mia B2
13. Markthalle A3
14. Ottoburg B2
15. s'Culinarium B2
16. Shere Punjab A1
17. s'Speckladele B2

Drinking
- 360° .... (see 11)
18. Elferhaus B2
19. Hofgarten Café D1
20. Moustache B1
21. Thereisenbräu C5

Entertainment
22. Tiroler Landestheater C1
23. Treibhaus C2

contains the original reliefs used to design the Goldenes Dachl. In the gallery you'll find old master paintings, Gothic altarpieces, a handful of Kokoschka and Klimt originals, and Viennese actionism works with shock factor.

Schloss Ambras CASTLE
(www.khm.at/ambras; Schlossstrasse 20; adult/child €10/free; 10am-5pm) Archduke Ferdinand II transformed Schloss Ambras from a fortress into a Renaissance palace in 1564. A visit takes in the ever-so-grand banquet hall, shining armour (look out for the 2.60m suit created for giant Bartlmä Bon) and room upon room of Habsburg portraits, with Titian, Velázquez and van Dyck originals. It's free to stroll or picnic in the expansive **gardens** (6am-8pm).

Schloss Ambras is 4.5km southeast of the centre. Take bus 4134 from the Hauptbahnhof to the castle for discounted entry and a free return journey.

FREE **Dom St Jakob** CHURCH
(St James' Cathedral; Domplatz; 7.30am-9.30pm Mon-Sat, 8am-7.30pm Sun) Innsbruck's 18th-century cathedral is a feast of over-the-top baroque. The Madonna above the high altar is by the German Renaissance painter Lukas Cranach the Elder.

Alpenzoo ZOO
(Weiherburggasse 37; adult/child €8/4; 9am-6pm) Home to Alpine wildlife like golden eagles, chamois and ibex. To get there, walk up the hill from Rennweg or take bus W from Marktplatz.

Stadtturm TOWER
(city tower; Herzog-Friedrich-Strasse 21; adult/child €3/1.50; 10am-8pm) Climb this tower's 148 steps for 360-degree views of the city's rooftops, spires and surrounding mountains.

Activities

Anyone who loves playing in the great outdoors will be itching to head up into the Alps in Innsbruck.

Nordketten Bahnen FUNICULAR
(www.nordkette.com; 8.30am-5.30pm) Zaha Hadid's space-age funicular runs every 15 minutes, whizzing you from the Congress Centre to the slopes in just 25 minutes. Tickets cost €14.10/23.40 one way/return to Seegrube and €15.60/26 to Hafelekar. Both afford superb views of Innsbruck and the Alps, and appeal to walkers and mountain bikers.

Guided Hikes WALKING
(Innsbruck Information; ☎535 60; www.innsbruck.info; Burggraben 3; 9am-6pm) From late May

WORTH A TRIP

AROUND INNSBRUCK

Just 9km east of Innsbruck is the town of Hall in Tirol. The labyrinth of pretty cobbled streets at its medieval heart pays testament to the massive wealth it accumulated from silver mines over the centuries. You can learn more about this legacy at **Burg Hasegg** (Burg Hasegg 6; adult/child €8/6; ⏲10am-5pm Tue-Sun), a 14th-century castle that had a 300-year career as a mint for silver *Thalers* (coins, the root of the modern word 'dollar').

Another 9km east along the valley in Wattens is **Swarovski Kristallwelten** (Swarovski Crystal Worlds; http://kristallwelten.swarovski.com; Kristallweltenstrasse 1; adult/child €9.50/free; ⏲9am-6.30pm), one of Austria's most-visited attractions. A crystal winterscape by Alexander McQueen, a kaleidoscopic crystal dome and a striking Terence Conran–designed shop are part of the fabulously glittering experience.

From Innsbruck, trains run frequently to Hall in Tirol (€2, eight minutes) and Fritzens-Wattens (€3.60, 16 minutes), 3km north of Swarovski Kristallwelten.

to October, Innsbruck Information arranges daily guided hikes from sunrise walks to lantern-lit strolls, free to those with a Club Innsbruck Card (see the boxed text, p93). Pop into the tourist office to register and browse the program.

Inntour ADVENTURE SPORTS
(www.inntour.com; Leopoldstrasse 4; ⏲9am-6.30pm Mon-Fri, to 5pm Sat) A one-stop adrenalin shop, taking you canyoning (€75), tandem paragliding (€95), white-water rafting (€45) and bungee jumping from the 192m Europabrücke (Europe Bridge).

Olympia SkiWorld Innsbruck SKIING
(www.ski-innsbruck.at) Innsbruck is the gateway to this massive ski arena, covering nine surrounding resorts and 282km of slopes to test all abilities. The most central place to pound powder is the **Nordpark**, accessed by **cable car** (⏲8am-7pm) running every 15 minutes. A three-/seven-day Innsbruck Glacier Ski Pass covering all areas costs €105/200; ski buses are free to anyone with an Innsbruck Card.

Sleeping

The tourist office has lists of private rooms costing between €20 and €40 per person.

TOP CHOICE **Nepomuks** HOSTEL €
(☎584 118; www.nepomuks.at; Kiebachgasse 16; dm/d €22/54; 📶) Could this be backpacker heaven? Nepomuks sure comes close, with its Altstadt location, well-stocked kitchen and high-ceilinged dorms with homely touches like CD players. The delicious breakfast in attached Café Munding, with homemade pastries, jam and fresh-roasted coffee, gets your day off to a grand start.

Hotel Weisses Kreuz HISTORIC HOTEL €€
(☎594 79; www.weisseskreuz.at; Herzog-Friedrich-Strasse 31; s €36-72, d €100-132; P@📶) Beneath the Altstadt's arcades, this atmospheric 500-year-old hotel has played host to famous guests including a 13-year-old Mozart. It remains comfortable to this day.

Pension Paula GUESTHOUSE €
(☎292 262; www.pensionpaula.at; Weiherburggasse 15; s/d €39/62; P) Nestled in the hills above Innsbruck and with great city views, this family-run pension has super-clean, homely rooms (most with balcony). It's 1km north of the Altstadt, near the Alpenzoo.

Romantik Hotel Schwarzer Adler HOTEL €€€
(☎587 109; www.deradler.com; Kaiserjägerstrasse 2; s €110-159, d €150-211, ste €295-480; P@🏊) This boutique hotel's fabulously over-the-top suites glitter with Swarovski crystals; one features the solid marble bed Gianni Versace once slept in. Asian-inspired treatments pamper in the spa. It's about a five-minute walk west of the Hofburg along Universitätsstrasse.

Goldener Adler HISTORIC HOTEL €€
(☎571 111; www.goldeneradler.com; Herzog-Friedrich-Strasse 6; s/d €92/135; P❄📶) Since opening in 1390, the grand Goldener Adler has welcomed kings, queens and Salzburg's two biggest exports: Mozart and Mrs von Trapp. Rooms are elegant with gold drapes and squeaky-clean marble bathrooms.

Weisses Rössl GUESTHOUSE €€
(☎583 057; www.roessl.at; Kiebachgasse 8; s/d/tr/q €80/120/135/160; P⊖@📶) An antique rocking horse greets you at this 600-year-old guesthouse, with vaulted interiors and bright, spacious rooms. Host Mr Plank is a keen

hunter and the restaurant (mains €7 to €18) has a meaty menu.

Pension Stoi GUESTHOUSE €
(☎585 434; www.pensionstoi.at, in German; Salurnerstrasse 7; s/d/tr/q €44/69/85/98; P wi-fi) This central, family-run guesthouse occupies a rambling art nouveau villa. You'll need to schlep your bags (there's no lift) and buy your own breakfast.

Mondschein HOTEL €€
(☎227 84; www.mondschein.at; Mariahilfstrasse 6; s €87-105, d €105-180; P air-con wi-fi) Like its name, the moon lights the way to this riverside hotel, set in a 15th-century fisherman's house. The cheery rooms sport Swarovski crystal-studded bathrooms.

Camping Innsbruck Kranebitterhof CAMPING GROUND €
(Herzog-Friedrich-Strasse 21; adult/child €3/1.50; ⏲10am-8pm) Modern camping ground west of town, with Alpine views, a pizzeria and playground. Bus line O stops nearby or you can cycle along the River Inn.

Eating

Bistros, cafes and traditional taverns line Altstadt lanes like Herzog-Friedrich-Strasse, Hofgasse and Kiebachgasse; most have alfresco seating in summer. Maria-Theresien-Strasse, the Rathaus Galerien mall and Universitätsstrasse are other good picks; the latter attracts students. Self-caterers will find **supermarkets** like Hofer and Billa on Museumstrasse.

TOP CHOICE **Chez Nico** VEGETARIAN €€
(☎586 398; www.chez-nico.at; Maria-Theresien-Strasse 49; lunch €12.50, 7-course menu €45; ⏲lunch & dinner Tue-Fri, dinner Sat; ✎) Take a creative Parisian chef with an artistic eye and a passion for herbs, *et voilà,* you get Chez Nico. Nicolas Curtil (Nico) cooks seasonal vegetarian delights like chanterelle-apricot goulash and porcini-sage ravioli at this intimate bistro.

Lichtblick FUSION €€€
(☎566 550; Rathaus Galerien; www.restaurant-lichtblick.at; lunch €8-13, set menus €35-46; ⏲10am-1am Mon-Sat) On the 7th floor of the Rathaus Galerien, this glass-walled restaurant is a glamorous setting for fusion cuisine and sweeping Innsbruck views.

Gasthaus Goldenes Dachl TYROLEAN €€
(☎589 370; www.gasthaus-goldenesdachl.at; Hofgasse 1; mains €10-18) Portions are generous and the menu typically Tyrolean at this tavern, a cosy spot to try *Gröstl* (potatoes and bacon topped with a fried egg).

Ottoburg AUSTRIAN €€
(☎584 338; www.ottoburg.at; Herzog-Friedrich-Strasse 1; lunch €6-9, mains €17-26; ⏲Tue-Sun; no-smoking) This 12th-century castle hides a warren of wood-panelled *Stuben* (parlours). Dig into tournedos of venison, *Topfenknödel* (cottage cheese dumplings) and other hearty fare.

Cafe Munding CAFE €
(☎584 118; Kiebachgasse 16; cake €2-4; ⏲8am-8pm) Divine cakes, pastries and home-roasted coffee.

Mamma Mia PIZZERIA €
(☎562 902; Kiebachgasse 2; mains €5-8) No-frills Italian bistro with a great buzz, huge pizzas and a shady terrace.

Shere Punjab INDIAN €€
(☎282 755; www.sherepunjab.eu; Innstrasse 19; mains €9-12) Authentic Indian. Word has it even Bollywood stars come here for flavoursome biryanis and kormas.

> DON'T MISS
>
> ### PICNIC GOODIES
>
> **s'Speckladele** MEAT €
> (Stiftgasse 4; ⏲9am-1pm & 2-6pm Tue-Fri, 9am-3pm Sat) This hole-in-the-wall shop has been doing a brisk trade in regional sausages, hams and speck made from 'happy pigs' for the past 60 years. Mini *Teufel* sausages with a chilli kick are the must-try.
>
> **s'Culinarium** WINE €
> (Pfarrgasse 1; ⏲10am-6pm Mon-Fri, 3-6pm Sat) Herby Signor will help you pick an excellent bottle of Austrian wine at his shop-cum-bar.
>
> **Markthalle** MARKET €
> (www.markthalle-innsbruck.at; Innrain; ⏲7am-6.30pm Mon-Fri, to 1pm Sat) Freshly baked bread, Tyrolean cheese, organic fruit, smoked ham and salami – it's all under one roof at this riverside covered market.

Drinking

Besides a glut of bars in the Altstadt, a string of bars huddle under the railway arches on Ingenieur-Etzel-Strasse, otherwise known as the Viaduktbögen.

Moustache BAR
(www.cafe-moustache.at, in German; Herzog-Otto-Strasse 8; ⏲11am-2am Tue-Sun) You too can try your hand at playing Spot-the-Moustache (Einstein, Charlie Chaplin and others), the preferred pastime at this retro newcomer. It has a terrace overlooking pretty Domplatz, as well as Club Aftershave in the basement.

Hofgarten Café BAR
(Rennweg 6a; ⏲11am-2am Tue-Thu, to 4am Fri-Sun) DJs spin at this tree-shaded beer garden and star-studded pavilion. The happening events line-up skips from summer festivals to weekend house parties.

360° BAR
(Rathaus Galerien; ⏲10am-1am Mon-Sat) There's no better place to see Innsbruck start to twinkle. Grab a cushion and drink in 360-degree views of the city and Alps from the balcony skirting the circular bar.

Theresienbräu PUB
(Maria-Theresien-Strasse 53; ⏲10am-1am Mon-Wed, to 2am Thu-Sat, to midnight Sun) A lively microbrewery with a big beer garden for quaffing a cold one.

Elferhaus PUB
(Herzog-Friedrich-Strasse 11; ⏲10am-2am) Nurse a beer beside gothic gargoyles at the bar or take a church-like pew to hear live rock bands play.

☆ Entertainment

For more entertainment options, pick up a copy of *Innsider,* found in cafes across town, or visit www.innsider.at (in German).

Tiroler Landestheater THEATRE
(Maria-Theresien-Strasse 53; ⏲10am-1am Mon-Wed, to 2am Thu-Sat, to midnight Sun) This neoclassical theatre is the city's main stage for opera, dance and drama.

Weekender Club CLUB
(www.weekenderclub.net, in German; Tschamlerstrasse 3; ⏲9pm-4am Mon, Fri & Sat) Happening warehouse club, with top DJs and concerts. It's a 10-minute walk south of Maria-Theresien-Strasse along Leopoldstrasse.

Treibhaus CULTURAL CENTRE
(www.treibhaus.at, in German; Angerzellgasse 8; ⏲10am-1am) Young Innsbruckers flock to this cultural complex to enjoy the big garden terrace, the chilled atmosphere and regular DJs. There's free live music on Friday evenings.

ℹ Information

Innsbruck Information (☎535 60; www.innsbruck.info; Burggraben 3; ⏲9am-6pm) Main tourist office with truckloads of info on the city and surrounds, including skiing and walking. Sells ski passes, public-transport tickets and city maps (€1); will book accommodation (€3 commission) and has an attached ticketing service.

International Telephone Discount (Südtirolerplatz 1; internet access per hour €2.50; ⏲9am-9pm Mon-Sat, 10am-9pm Sun) Cheap phone calls as well.

Landeskrankenhaus (☎50 40; Anichstrasse 35) The *Universitätklinik* (University Clinic) at the city's main hospital has emergency services.

Main post office (Maximilianstrasse 2)

ℹ Getting There & Away

AIR Innsbruck Airport (www.innsbruck-airport.com), 4km to the west of the city centre, caters to national and international flights, handled mostly by Austrian Airlines, BA, easyJet and Welcome Air.

CAR & MOTORCYCLE The A12 and the parallel Hwy 171 are the main roads heading west and east. The B177, to the west of Innsbruck, continues north to Munich (Germany). The A13 is a toll road (€8) running south through the Brenner Pass to Italy and crossing the 192m Europabrücke, spanning the Sill River. Toll-free Hwy 182 follows the same route, passing under the bridge.

TRAIN Fast trains depart every two hours for Bregenz (€31.30, 2¾ hours), Salzburg (€37.80, two hours), Kitzbühel (€17.60, 1¾ hours) and Munich (€37, two hours). Six daily trains head for Lienz (€31.20, three to five hours); some pass through Italy while others take the long way round via Salzburgerland.

ℹ Getting Around

TO/FROM THE AIRPORT The airport is 4km west of the centre and served by bus F. Buses depart every 15 or 20 minutes from Maria-Theresien-Strasse (€1.80); taxis charge about €8 to €10 for the same trip.

CAR & BICYCLE Street parking is very limited in the city centre. Parking garages (eg under the Altstadt) cost around €17 per day. **Inntour** (Leopoldstrasse 4; ⏲9am-6.30pm Mon-Fri, 9am-5pm Sat) rents city, mountain, freeride and children's bikes for €19/24/35/12 per day respectively.

PUBLIC TRANSPORT Single tickets on buses and trams cost €1.80 (from the driver; valid upon issue). A 24-hour ticket is €4.10.

Mayrhofen

☎05285 / POP 3850

Tirol is ribbed by beautiful valleys, but the Zillertal is among the best, its soaring peaks begging outdoor escapades. A central place to base yourself is Mayrhofen, a mecca to skiers and après-skiers in winter, and mountain bikers, hikers and *Lederhosen*-clad *Volksmusik* (folk music) fans in summer.

Snow-sure Mayrhofen has varied skiing on 166km of slopes, one of Europe's best terrain parks for snowboarders and the infamous Harakiri, Austria's steepest piste with a 78% gradient. A ski pass, valid for all cable cars and lifts, costs €41.50 for one day.

The ultramodern **tourist office** (☎676 00; www.mayrhofen.at; Europahaus; ⏲8am-6pm Mon-Fri, 9am-6pm Sat, 9am-noon Sun) should be your first port of call for free *Info von A-Z* booklets in English.

To work your taste buds instead of your legs, pay a visit to **Sennerei Zillertal** (www.sennerei-zillertal.at; Hollenzen 116; admission with/without tasting €11.20/5.80; ⏲10am-3pm, closed Nov–mid-Dec), a grass-roots dairy. See how local cheeses are made on the production facility tour and then enjoy the chance to taste them.

DON'T MISS

SUMMER IN THE ZILLERTAL

The Zillertal is one of Austria's greatest outdoor playgrounds. Come summer the valley buzzes with cyclists, with 800km of well-marked trails reaching from easygoing valley jaunts to gruelling mountain passes. Bicycles are available for hire at train stations throughout the Zillertal for €8/12 per half-/full day; www.zillertal.at has maps, route descriptions and GPS downloads.

Hikers head for the pristine Alpine landscapes of **Naturpark Zillertaler Alpen** (www.naturpark-zillertal.at, in German). From May to October, the nature reserve runs guided walks, most costing around €5, from llama trekking to sunrise photo excursions. For adrenalin-fuelled pursuits like rock climbing, rafting and paragliding, try **Action Club Zillertal** (☎629 77; www.actionclub-zillertal.com; Hauptstrasse 458; ⏲9am-noon & 3-6pm) in Mayrhofen.

Pick up a handy accommodation booklet at the tourist office. Right in the centre, 500-year-old **Hotel Kramerwirt** (☎67 00; www.kramerwirt.at; Am Marienbrunnen 346; s/d €89/154, mains €8-21; P ☒) has spacious rooms, a whirlpool for relaxing moments and a traditional restaurant.

To gorge on *Schlutzkropf'n* (fresh pasta filled with cheese) and the like in the cosiest of surrounds, head to woodsy chalet **Wirtshaus zum Griena** (☎67 67; Dorfhaus 768; mains €7-15). Or assemble your own meaty snack at **Metzgerei Kröll** (Scheulingstrasse 382; snacks €3-8; ⏲7.30am-12.30pm & 2.30-6pm Mon-Fri, 7am-noon Sat), famous for its aromatic *Schlegeis-Speck* ham cured at 1800m. Pizza and pasta dominate the menu at **Mamma Mia** (☎67 68; Einfahrt Mitte 432; mains €7-9; ⏲11am-midnight).

Trains run regularly to Jenbach (55 minutes, €6.30), where they connect with services to Innsbruck (20 minutes; €7.20).

Kitzbühel

☎05356 / POP 8450

Kitzbühel began life in the 16th century as a silver- and copper-mining town, and today preserves a charming medieval centre despite its other persona – as a fashionable and prosperous winter resort. It's renowned for the white-knuckled Hahnenkamm downhill ski race in January and the excellence of its slopes.

Activities

There's an Alpine **flower garden** (free) on Kitzbüheler Horn (note there's a toll road for drivers). The forest-fringed Schwarzsee, 3km to the northwest, is a fine location for summer **swimming**.

Skiing SKIING

In winter there's first-rate intermediate skiing and freeriding on Kitzbüheler Horn to the north and Hahnenkamm to the south of town. A one-day ski pass costs €41.50, though some pensions and hotels offer reductions before mid-December or after mid-March.

Hiking HIKING

Dozens of summer hiking trails thread through the Kitzbühel Alps; the tourist office gives walking maps and runs free guided hikes for guests staying in town. The Flex-Ticket covering all cable cars costs €33.50 (€42.50 with bus) for three out of seven days.

Sleeping & Eating

The tourist office can help with accommodation, but it's best to book well ahead. Rates leap up to 50% in the high winter season.

For self-caterers, there's a **Spar supermarket** (Bichlstrasse 22) and **Metzgerei Huber** (Bichlstrasse 14; snacks €3.50-7; Mon-Fri, 8am-12.30pm Sat) for carnivorous snacks.

Villa Licht HOTEL €€
(☎622 93; www.villa-licht.at; Franz-Reich-Strasse 8; s/d €85/150; P 🛜 ≋) Pretty gardens, warm-hued rooms with pine trappings, mountain views – this charming Tyrolean chalet has the lot. Kids love the tree house and outdoor pool.

Snowbunny's Hostel HOSTEL €
(☎067-6794 0233; www.snowbunnys.co.uk; Bichlstrasse 30; dm/d €25/60; @ 🛜) Friendly, laid-back hostel, a bunny-hop from the slopes. Dorms are fine, if a tad dark; breakfast is DIY-style in the kitchen. There's a TV lounge, ski storage room and a shop for backpacker staples (Vegemite, Jägermeister etc).

Pension Kometer PENSION €€
(☎622 89; Gerbergasse 7; www.pension-kometer.com; s/d €57/94; P) Make yourself at home in the bright, sparklingly clean rooms at this family-run guesthouse. There's a relaxed lounge with games and DVDs. Breakfast is a treat with fresh breads, fruit and eggs.

Hosteria ITALIAN €€
(☎753 02; Alf Petzoldweg 2; mains €8-16) Authentic antipasti and wood-fired pizzas are matched with fine wines and genuine smiles at this stylish little Italian.

Lois Stern ASIAN €€
(☎748 82; www.loisstern.com, in German; Josef-Pirchl-Strasse 3; mains €17-25; ⊙Tue-Sat) Lois works his wok in the show kitchen of this intimate bistro. On the menu: Asian fusion cuisine from fiery tom-yam soup to stir-fried gambas.

Information

The **tourist office** (☎666 60; www.kitzbuehel.com; Hinterstadt 18; ⊙8.30am-6pm Mon-Wed, to 7.30pm Thu-Fri, 9am-6pm Sat, 10am-noon & 4-6pm Sun, closed Sun btwn seasons) has loads of info in English and a 24-hour accommodation board.

Getting There & Away

BUS It's quicker and cheaper to get from Kitzbühel to Lienz by bus (€13.80, two hours, twice daily) than by train.

CAR & MOTORCYCLE Kitzbühel is on the B170, 30km east of Wörgl and the A12/E45 motorway. Heading south to Lienz, you pass through some marvellous scenery. Hwy 108 (Felber Tauern Tunnel) and Hwy 107 (Grossglockner Rd; closed in winter) both have toll sections.

TRAIN The main train station is 1km north of central Vorderstadt. Trains run frequently from Kitzbühel to Innsbruck (€17.60, 1½ hours) and Salzburg (€25.60, 2½ hours). For Kufstein (€9.20, one hour), change at Wörgl.

Lienz

☎04852 / POP 11,950

The Dolomites rise like an amphitheatre around Lienz, straddling the Isel and Drau Rivers, and just 40km north of Italy. Those same arresting river and mountain views welcomed the Romans, who settled here some 2000 years ago. Lienz is also a stopover for skiers and hikers passing through or on the way to the Hohe Tauern National Park.

Sights & Activities

Schloss Bruck FORTRESS
(Schlossberg 1; adult/child €7.50/2.50; ⊙10am-6pm mid-May–late Oct) Lienz' biggest crowd-puller is its medieval fortress. The museum displays everything from Tyrolean costumes to emotive paintings by famous local son Albin Egger-Lienz.

Stadtpfarrkirche St Andrä CHURCH
(Pfarrgasse 4; ⊙daylight hr) More of Albin Egger-Lienz' sombre works can be seen at the Gothic St Andrew's Church.

Aguntum ANCIENT SITE
(www.aguntum.info; Stribach 97; adult/child €5/3; ⊙9.30am-6pm, closed Nov–mid-Apr) For an insight into Lienz' Roman past, visit the Aguntum archaeological site.

Skiing SKIING
A €36 day pass covers skiing on the nearby **Zettersfeld** and **Hochstein** peaks. However, the area is more renowned for its 100km of cross-country trails; the town fills up for the annual **Dolomitenlauf** cross-country skiing race in mid-January.

Dolomiten Lamatrekking LLAMA TREKKING
(☎680 87; www.dolomitenlama.at, in German) The Dolomites make for highly scenic hiking, with cable cars rising to Hochstein (return €13) and Zettersfeld (€10). From this outfitter you can enlist a gentle-natured llama to accompany you.

Sleeping & Eating

The tourist office can point you in the direction of good-value guesthouses and camping grounds.

Hotel Haidenhof HOTEL €€
(☎624 40; www.haidenhof.at, in German; Grafendorferstrasse 12; s/d €86/142; P) High above Lienz, this country retreat has a dress-circle view of the Dolomites. The spacious rooms and roof terrace maximise those views. Home-grown produce features in the restaurant (mains €7 to €20).

Romantik Hotel Traube HOTEL €€
(☎644 44; www.hoteltraube.at; Hauptplatz 14; s €68, d €128-152; P @) Right on the main square, Traube races you back to the Biedermeier era with its high ceilings and antique-meets-boutique rooms. The 6th-floor pool affords views over Lienz to the Dolomites.

Kirchenwirt AUSTRIAN €€
(☎625 00; Pfarrgasse 7; mains €8.50-16; ⏲9am-1am) Up on a hill opposite Stadtpfarrkirche St Andrä, this is Lienz' most atmospheric restaurant. Dine under the vaults or on the streamside terrace on local dishes like East Tyrolean milk-fed lamb.

Information

The **tourist office** (☎050-212 400; www.stadt-lienz.at; Europaplatz 1; ⏲8am-6pm Mon-Fri, 9am-noon & 5-7pm Sat) will find rooms free of charge, or you can use the hotel board (free telephone) outside. Free internet access is available at the local **library** (Muchargasse 4; ⏲9am-noon & 3-6pm Tue-Fri, 9am-noon Sat).

Getting There & Away

Except for the 'corridor' route through Italy to Innsbruck (€31.20, four hours), trains to the rest of Austria connect via Spittal Millstättersee to the east, including hourly trains to Salzburg (€33.70, 3½ hours). To head south by car, you must first divert west or east along Hwy 100.

Hohe Tauern National Park

If you thought Mother Nature pulled out all the stops in the Austrian Alps, Hohe Tauern National Park was her magnum opus. Straddling Tirol, Salzburg and Carinthia, this national park is the largest in the Alps; a 1786-sq-km wilderness of 3000m peaks, Alpine meadows and waterfalls. At its heart lies **Grossglockner** (3798m), Austria's highest mountain, which towers over the 8km-long **Pasterze Glacier**, best seen from the outlook at **Kaiser-Franz-Josefs-Höhe** (2369m).

The 48km **Grossglockner Road** (Hwy 107; www.grossglockner.at, in German) from Bruck in Salzburgerland to Heiligenblut in Carinthia is one of Europe's greatest Alpine drives. A feat of 1930s engineering, the road swings giddily around 36 switchbacks, passing jewel-coloured lakes, forested slopes and wondrous glaciers.

If you have wheels, you'll have more flexibility, although the road is open only between May and October, and you must pay tolls (per car/motorcycle €28/18).

The major village on the Grossglockner Road is **Heiligenblut**, dominated by mountain peaks and the needle-thin spire of its 15th-century pilgrimage church. Here you'll find a **tourist office** (☎20 01; www.heiligenblut.at, in German; Hof 4; ⏲9am-6pm Mon-Fri, 9am-noon & 4-6pm Sat), which can advise on guided ranger hikes, mountain hiking and skiing. The village also has a campsite, a scattering of restaurants and a spick-and-span **Jugendherberge** (☎22 59; www.oejhv.or.at; Hof 36; dm/s/d €20/28/48; P).

Bus 5002 runs frequently between Lienz and Heiligenblut on weekdays (€7.40, one hour); less frequently at weekends. From late June to late September, four buses run from Monday to Friday, three at weekends

WORTH A TRIP

KRIMML FALLS

The thunderous, three-tier **Krimml Falls** (www.wasserfaelle-krimml.at; adult/child €2/0.50, free Dec-Apr; ⏲ticket office 8am-6pm mid-Apr–late Oct) is Europe's highest waterfall at 380m, and one of Austria's most unforgettable sights. The pretty Alpine village of Krimml has a handful of places to sleep and eat; contact the **tourist office** (☎72 39; www.krimml.at; Oberkrimml 37; ⏲8am-noon, 2.30-6pm Mon-Fri, 8.30-10.30am & 4.30-6pm Sat) for more information.

Krimml is on Hwy 168 (which becomes Hwy 165). Buses run year-round from Krimml to Zell am See (€8.40, 1¼ hours, hourly).

between Heiligenblut and Kaiser-Franz-Josefs-Höhe (€4.10, 30 minutes). Timetables change regularly here though, so it's best to check with the tourist office in Lienz before setting off.

VORARLBERG

Vorarlberg has always been a little different. Cut off from the rest of Austria by the snow-capped Arlberg massif, this westerly region has often associated itself more with Switzerland than Vienna far to the east, and its citizens have developed a strong dialect Tyroleans even find hard to decipher.

Alluringly beautiful, this region is an aesthetic mix of mountains, hills and valleys. Trickling down from the Alps to the shores of Bodensee (Lake Constance), Vorarlberg is a destination in its own right, attracting everyone from classical-music buffs to skiers. It's also a gateway, by rail or water, to Germany, Liechtenstein and Switzerland.

Bregenz

05574 / POP 27,000

Bregenz has been a ritzy address for generations, which is not surprising considering its pretty location on the shores of Bodensee. Boating, cycling, and lounging on the lake's shores are the general activities here, and many visitors time a stay in Vorarlberg's capital to catch the annual Bregenzer Festspiele in summer.

Sights

Kunsthaus ART MUSEUM

(www.kunsthaus-bregenz.at; Karl-Tizian-Platz; adult/child €8/free; 10am-6pm Tue-Sun, to 9pm Thu) The architecturally eye-catching Kunsthaus, by award-winning Swiss architect Peter Zumthor, hosts first-rate contemporary art exhibitions.

Oberstadt HISTORIC AREA

Set high above the modern centre is the Oberstadt, the storybook old town; look for the enormous onion dome of the **Martinsturm** (St Martin's Tower; www.martinsturm.at; Martinsgasse; adult/child €1/0.50; 10am-5pm Tue-Sun Apr-Oct), reputedly the largest in central Europe.

Pfänder Cable Car CABLE CAR

(Steinbruchgasse 4; one-way adult/child €6.30/3.10, return €10.80/5.40; 8am-7pm) For spectacular views of the lake, town and not-so-distant Alps, catch the cable car which rises to 1064m.

Activities

Bregenz' shimmering centrepiece is the **Bodensee**, Europe's third-largest lake, straddling Austria, Switzerland and Germany. Lakeside activities include **sailing** and **diving** at Lochau, 5km north of town, and **swimming**. The most central place for a quick dip or a barbecue is the **Pipeline**, a stretch of pebbly beach north of Bregenz, so-named for the large pipeline running parallel to the lake.

Bodensee Radweg CYCLING

(www.bodensee-radweg.com) In summer, the well-marked Bodensee Radweg that circumnavigates the Bodensee becomes an autobahn for lycra-clad *Radfahrer* (cyclists). Hire your own set of wheels at **Fahrradverleih Bregenz** (Bregenz Harbour; 9am-7pm May-Sep) for €16.50 per day.

Festivals & Events

The **Bregenzer Festspiele** (Bregenz Festival; 407-6; www.bregenzerfestspiele.com), running from late July to late August, is the city's premier cultural festival. World-class operas and orchestral works are staged on the Seebühne, a floating stage on the lake, in the Festspielhaus and at the Vorarlberger Landestheater. Information and tickets are up for grabs about nine months before the festival.

Sleeping & Eating

Stop by the tourist office for a list of private rooms (around €30 per person). Prices soar and beds are at a premium during the Bregenzer Festspiele – book ahead.

Restaurants and cafes huddle along the lakefront and the streets of the Unterstadt. In summer, little beats a picnic on the banks of the Bodensee.

TOP CHOICE **Deuring-Schlössle** HISTORIC HOTEL €€€

(478 00; www.deuring-schloessle.at; Ehre-Guta-Platz 4; s/d/ste €111/222/386; P@) Bregenz' best rooms are found in this fabulously renovated old castle. Each one is decorated differently, but all have loads of medieval charm and grace. Its restaurant (mains around €30) is also Bregenz' best, with a sophisticated look and a market-fresh menu.

JUFA Gästehaus Bregenz HOSTEL €

(05708-35 40; www.jufa.at/bregenz; Mehrerau-erstrasse 5; dm €27; P@) Housed in a former needle factory near the lake, this HI hostel now reels backpackers in with its super-clean dorms and excellent facilities including a common room and restaurant.

Hotel Weisses Kreuz HOTEL €€

(☎498 80; www.hotelweisseskreuz.at; Römerstrasse 5; s/d €119/146, mains €14-29; P❄@🛜) Service is attentive at this central pick, with a restaurant rolling out seasonal Austrian fare. The smart rooms sport cherry wood furnishings, flat-screen TVs and organic bedding.

Cafesito CAFE €

(Maurachgasse 6; bagels €3-4; ⌚7.45am-6.30pm Mon-Fri, 9am-4.30pm Sat) Tiny Cafesito does the best create-your-own bagels and smoothies in town. Lilac-yellow walls and modern art create a funky backdrop for a light lunch or cup of fair-trade coffee.

Wirtshaus am See AUSTRIAN €€

(☎422 10; www.wirtshausamsee.at; Seepromenade 2; mains €11-18) Snag a table on the lakefront terrace at this mock half-timbered villa, dishing up local specialities like buttery Bodensee whitefish and venison ragout. It's also a relaxed spot for quaffing a cold one.

Information

Bregenz' **tourist office** (☎49 59-0; www.bregenz.ws; Rathausstrasse 35a; ⌚9am-6pm Mon-Fri, to noon Sat) has information on the city and the surrounding area, and can help with accommodation.

Getting There & Away

BOAT From April to mid-October, there's a frequent boat service between Bregenz and a number of towns and cities on the Bodensee, including Konstanz (one way €15, 4¼ hours) and Friedrichshafen (€12.40, two hours) in Germany. For information, consult www.bodenseeschifffahrt.at (in German).

TRAIN Four daily trains go to Munich (€43.50, three hours) via Lindau, and Zürich (€33, 2¼ hours) via St Gallen (€12, 50 minutes). Nine trains daily depart for Innsbruck (€31, 2½ hours). Trains to Konstanz (€11.40, 1¾ hours) may be frequent, but require between one and four changes.

St Anton am Arlberg

☎05446 / POP 2270

At the heart of the wild and austerely beautiful Arlberg region lies St Anton am Arlberg. In 1901 the first ski club in the Alps was founded here, downhill skiing was born and the village never looked back. Today the resort has legendary slopes and is Austria's unrivalled king of après ski.

Activities

Skiing SKIING

St Anton attracts both intermediate and advanced skiers and boarders, with 280km of slopes, fantastic backcountry opportunities and a freestyle park on Rendl. A ski pass covering the whole Arlberg region and valid for all 84 ski lifts costs €44.50/239 for one/seven days in high season.

Hiking HIKING

Naturally, hiking is the number-one summer pastime: the Wanderpass (€28/33 for three/seven days) gives you a head start with access to all lifts.

H20 Adventures ADVENTURE SPORTS

(☎05446-39 37; Arlrock, Bahnhofstrasse 1; ⌚May–mid-Oct) H20 Adventures gets adrenalin pumping, with activities from rafting to canyoning and mountain biking.

Sleeping & Eating

Rates can be almost double those quoted below in high winter season, when you'll need to book well ahead. Hit Dorfstrasse for

WORTH A TRIP

BREGENZERWALD

Only a few kilometres southeast of Bregenz, the forest-cloaked slopes, velvet-green pastures and limestone peaks of the Bregenzerwald unfold. In summer it's a glorious place to spend a few days hiking the hills and filling up on all manner of home-made cheeses in Alpine dairies. Winter brings plenty of snow, and the area is noted for its downhill and cross-country skiing.

The **Bregenzerwald tourist office** (☎05512-23 65; www.bregenzerwald.at; Impulszentrum 1135, Egg; ⌚9am-5pm Mon-Fri, 8am-1pm Sat & Sun) has information on the region, and cheese-lovers can consult www.kaesestrasse.at (in German) for the low-down on the **Cheese Road**. From Bregenz, buses travel to Bezau (€4.40, one hour), one of the region's main villages, at least every two hours; however, this offbeat region is easier to explore by car.

snack bars and restaurants serving everything from tapas to Tex-Mex with a side order of après-ski. Most restaurants and bars close in summer.

TOP CHOICE **Altes Thönihaus** GUESTHOUSE €
(☎28 10; www.altes-thoenihaus.at; Im Gries 1; s/d/q €28/52/80; 📶) Dating to 1465, this listed wooden chalet oozes Alpine charm from every last beam. Fleecy rugs and pine keep the mood cosy in rooms with mountain-facing balconies. Downstairs there's a superb little spa and restored *Stube* (parlour).

Himmlhof GUESTHOUSE €€
(☎232 20; www.himmlhof.com; Im Gries 9; d €94-126; P) This *himmlisch* (heavenly) Tyrolean chalet has wood-clad rooms brimming with original features (tiled ovens, four-poster beds and the like). An open fire and spa beckon after a day's skiing.

Museum Restaurant AUSTRIAN €€
(☎24 75; Rudi-Matt-Weg 10; mains €10-16; ⊙dinner) Arlberger hay soup, succulent Tyrolean beef and fresh-from-the-pond trout land on your plate at this wood-panelled restaurant, picturesquely housed in the village museum.

Information

The **tourist office** (☎226 90; www.stantonamarlberg.com; Arlberg Haus; ⊙8.30am-7pm Mon-Fri, 9am-6pm Sat, 9am-noon & 3-5pm Sun) has information on accommodation, activities, maps and an accommodation board with free telephone outside.

Getting There & Away

St Anton is on the main railway route between Bregenz (€16.90, 1½ hours) and Innsbruck (€20, 1¼ hours). The town is close to the eastern entrance of the Arlberg Tunnel, the toll road connecting Vorarlberg and Tirol. The tunnel toll is €8.50 one way. You can avoid the toll by taking the B197, but no vehicles with trailers are allowed on this winding road.

UNDERSTAND AUSTRIA

History

Austria has been a galvanic force in shaping Europe's history. This landlocked little country was once the epicentre of the mighty Habsburg empire and, in the 20th century, a pivotal player in the outbreak of WWI.

Civilisation & Empire

Like so many European countries, Austria has experienced invasions and struggles since time immemorial. There are traces of human occupation since the ice age, but it was the Celts who made the first substantial mark on Austria around 450 BC. The Romans followed 400 years later, and in turn were followed by Bavarians and, in 1278, the House of Habsburg, who took control of the country by defeating the head of the Bavarian royalty.

The Habsburg Monarchy

For six centuries the Habsburgs used strategic marriages to maintain their hold over a territory that encompassed much of central and Eastern Europe and, for a period, even Germany. But defeat in WWI brought that to an end, when the Republic of Austria was formed in 1918.

The 16th and 17th centuries saw the Ottoman threat reach the gates of Vienna, and in 1805 Napoleon defeated Austria at Austerlitz. Austrian Chancellor Metternich cleverly reconsolidated Austria's power in 1815 after Waterloo, but the loss of the 1866 Austro-Prussian War, and creation of the Austro-Hungarian empire in 1867, diminished the Habsburg's influence in Europe.

However, these setbacks pale beside Archduke Franz Ferdinand's assassination by Slavic separatists in Sarajevo on 28 June 1914. When his uncle, the Austro-Hungarian emperor Franz Josef, declared war on Serbia in response, the ensuing 'Great War' (WWI) would prove the Habsburgs' downfall.

WWII & Postwar Austria

During the 1930s the Nazis began to influence Austrian politics, and by 1938 the recession-hit country was ripe for picking. Invading German troops met little resistance and Hitler was greeted on Heldenplatz as a hero by 200,000 Viennese.

Austria was heavily bombed during WWII, but the country recovered well, largely through the Marshall Plan and sound political and economic decisions (excluding its foray with the far-right Freedom Party and its controversial leader, Jörg Haider, in the 1990s). Austria has maintained a neutral stance since 1955, been home to a number of international organisations, including the UN, since 1979, and joined the EU in 1995.

Austria today enjoys the kind of economic, social and political stability that many other nations would dream of. Cities forging ahead include Linz, which seized the reins as European Capital of Culture in 2009, and Innsbruck, which is gearing up to host the first Winter Youth Olympics in 2012. Vienna, too, has plenty to look pleased about, topping the Mercer Quality of Living List in 2010 and with a shiny new Hauptbahnhof in the making. Meanwhile, up in the mountains, sustainability is the watchword, with an increasing number of resorts polishing their eco-credentials and using clean energy.

Arts & Architecture

Classical Music

What other country can match the musical heritage of Austria? Great composers were drawn to Vienna by the Habsburgs' generous patronage during the 18th and 19th centuries. The era most strongly associated with Austrian music is *Wiener Klassik* (Vienna Classic), which dates back to the mid- and late 18th century and has defined the way we perceive classical music today. It began life as a step down from the celestial baroque music of the royal court and church, and shifted the focus of performance onto the salons and theatres of upper middle-class society.

Joseph Haydn (1732–1809) is considered to be the first of the great composers of the *Wiener Klassik* era, followed by Salzburg wunderkind Wolfgang Amadeus Mozart (1756–91). Beethoven's musical genius reached its zenith in Vienna. *Lieder* (song) master Franz Schubert (1797–1828) was the last of the heavyweight *Wiener Klassik* composers.

Vienna Secession & Expressionism

In 1897, 19 progressive artists broke away from the conservative artistic establishment and formed the Vienna Secession (*Sezession*) movement, synonymous with art nouveau. Vienna turned out such talents as the painter Gustav Klimt (1862–1918); Schloss Belvedere showcases one of his finest works, *The Kiss*. Vienna-born architect Otto Wagner (1841–1918) ushered in a new, functional direction around the turn of the 20th century and gave the capital a metro system replete with attractive art nouveau stations.

Gustav Klimt strongly influenced the work of well-known Austrian expressionists like Egon Schiele (1890–1918), who was obsessed with capturing the erotic on canvas, and Oskar Kokoschka (1886–1980). The paintings of these three Austrian greats hang out in the Leopold Museum in Vienna's MuseumsQuartier.

Baroque Heyday

Thanks to the Habsburg monarchy and its obsession with pomp and splendour, Austria is packed with high-calibre architecture, which reached giddy heights of opulence during the baroque era of the late 17th and early 18th century. It took the graceful column and symmetry of the Renaissance and added elements of the grotesque, burlesque and the saccharin.

Johann Bernhard Fischer von Erlach (1656–1723), the mastermind behind Schloss Schönbrunn, was the country's greatest baroque architect. Like Fischer von Erlach, Austria's second architect of the era, Johann Lukas von Hildebrandt (1668–1745), was famous for his interior decorative work of palaces for the aristocracy such as Schloss Belvedere. Paul Troger (1698–1762) is Austria's master of the baroque fresco and his work is best appreciated at Stift Melk. Other baroque highlights include Karlskirche in Vienna, Salzburg's Dom and the Hofburg in Innsbruck.

Food & Drink

Staples & Specialities

Austria is famous for its Wiener schnitzel, for its tender goulash and for desserts like *Sacher Torte* (Sacher cake) and *Kaiserschmarrn* (sweet pancake with raisins). Certainly, these legendary classics are not to be missed, but the Austrian table offers a host of other regional and seasonal delights. Throw in excellent red wines from Burgenland and quality whites and reds from Lower Austria, Styria and elsewhere, and you have the makings of an exciting and unexpected culinary experience.

In Lower Austria try Waldviertel game, beef and poppy dishes, tangy cider from the Mostviertel, and pike and carp from Burgenland. The Wachau goes mad for *Marillen* (apricots) around mid-July. Styria is renowned for its *Almochsen* (meadow beef) and healthy, nutty pumpkin oil. Upper Austria is *Knödel* (dumpling) country, while the must-eat in neighbouring Salzburgerland is *Salzburger Nockerln,* a sweet soufflé. Freshwater fish in Carinthia, *Heumilchkäse* (hay

PRACTICALITIES

» **Opening Hours** Most sights and tourist offices operate on reduced hours from November to March. Opening hours we provide are for the high season, so outside those months it can be useful to check ahead.

» **Seasonal Closures** In the Alps, many hotels, restaurants and sometimes tourist offices close between seasons, from around May to mid-June and mid-September to early December.

» **Concessions** Museums and sights have concessions for families, children (generally under-16-year-olds), students and senior citizens; you may need to show proof of age. Children under 12 years usually receive a substantial discount on rooms they share with parents.

» **Smoking** Unless a separate room has been set aside, smoking is not allowed in restaurants. It's legal to smoke anywhere on outdoor terraces. Whenever a hotel has designated nonsmoking rooms, we've included an icon to show this.

milk cheese) from Vorarlberg and Tirol's hearty *Gröstl* (a fry-up from leftover potatoes, pork and onions) are other regional specialities.

Where to Eat & Drink

Beyond the traditional restaurant, *Gasthaus* or *Gasthof*, you'll find coffee houses serving a handful of light or classic dishes like goulash, ethnic eat-in and take-away joints, and often corner Italian pizzerias. Solid Austrian fare is on the menu in Vienna's homely, good-value inns called *Beisl* (small taverns; from the Yiddish word for 'little houses'). In the winegrowing regions, rustic *Heurigen* (wine taverns) sell their wine directly from their own premises and food is available buffet-style. They open on a roster so pick up the local *Heurigenkalendar* (*Heurigen* calendar) from the tourist offices.

For cheap food, try *Mensen* (university canteens). Another money-saving trick is to make lunch the main meal of the day, as many Austrians do; many restaurants provide a good-value *Tagesteller* or *Tagesmenü* (set meal) at this time. You can assemble your own picnic at local farmers' markets, where the freshest produce is sold.

SURVIVAL GUIDE

Directory A–Z

Accommodation

From simple mountain huts to five-star hotels fit for kings – you'll find the lot in Austria. Tourist offices invariably keep lists and details, and some arrange bookings for free or for a nominal fee. Some useful points:

» It's wise to book ahead at all times, particularly during the high seasons: July and August and December to April (in ski resorts).

» Some places require email confirmation but many are bookable online. Be aware that confirmed reservations in writing are considered binding, and cancellations within several days of arrival often involve a fee or full payment.

» Most hotel rooms in Austria have their own shower, although hostels and some rock-bottom digs have an *Etagendusche* (corridor shower).

» Very often a hotel won't have lifts; if this is important, always check ahead.

» In mountain resorts, high-season prices can be up to double the prices charged in the low season (May to June and October to November). In other towns, the difference may be 10% or less.

» In some resorts (not often in cities), a *Gästekarte* (guest card) is issued if you stay overnight, which offers discounts on things such as cable cars and admission.

» Locally, always check the city or region website, as many (such as in Vienna, Salzburg and Graz) have an excellent booking function.

Some useful websites:

Austrian Hotelreservation (www.austrian-hotelreservation.at)

Austrian National Tourist Office (www.austria.info)

Booking.com (www.booking.com)

Hostelling International (www.hihostels.com)

Hostelworld (www.hostelworld.com)

PRICE RANGES

Our reviews refer to double rooms with a private bathroom, except in hostels or where otherwise specified. Listings are arranged in order of preference, and quoted rates are for high season, which is April to October.

€€€ more than €200

€€ €80 to €200

€ less than €80

Activities

Austria is a wonderland for outdoorsy types, with much of the west given over to towering Alpine peaks. Opportunities for hiking and mountaineering are boundless in Tirol, Salzburgerland and the Hohe Tauern National Park, all of which have extensive Alpine hut networks (see www.alpenverein.at). Names like St Anton, Kitzbühel and Mayrhofen fire the imagination of serious skiers, but you may find cheaper accommodation and lift passes in little-known resorts; visit www.austria.info for the lowdown.

Business Hours

Banks 9am-3pm Mon-Fri, to 5.30pm Thu

Clubs 10pm to late

Cafes 7.30am-8pm; hours vary widely

Pubs till midnight or later

Restaurants noon-3pm, 7-11pm

Shops 9am-6.30pm Mon-Fri, 9am-5pm Sat

Supermarkets 9am to 7pm or 8pm Mon-Sat

Discount Cards

Regional Various discount cards are available, many of them covering a whole region or province. Some are free with an overnight stay. See destinations for details.

Student & Youth Cards International Student Identity Cards (ISIC) and European Youth Card (Euro<26; check www.euro26.org for discounts) will get you discounts at most museums, galleries and theatres. Admission is generally a little higher than the price for children.

Discount Rail Cards See p112.

WHERE TO STAY

Hotels & Pensions Hotels and pensions (B&Bs) are rated by the same criteria from one to five stars. Hotels offer more services, including bars, restaurants and parking, whereas pensions tend to be smaller and less standardised.

Hostels In Austria over 100 hostels (*Jugendherberge*) are affiliated with Hostelling International (HI). Facilities are often excellent. Four- to six-bed dorms with shower/toilet are the norm, though some places also have doubles and family rooms. See www.oejhv.or.at or www.oejhw.at for details.

Private Rooms *Privatzimmer* (private rooms) are cheap (often about €40 per double). On top of this, you will find *Bauernhof* (farmhouses) in rural areas, and some *Öko-Bauernhöfe* (organic farms).

Alpine Huts There are over 530 of these huts in the Austrian Alps; most are maintained by the Österreichischer Alpenverein (ÖAV; Austrian Alpine Club; www.alpenverein.at, in German). Meals are often available. Bed prices for nonmembers are around €26 to €44 in a dorm; ÖAV members pay half-price. Contact the ÖAV for lists of huts and to make bookings.

Rental Accommodation *Ferienwohnungen* (self-catering apartments) are ubiquitous in Austrian mountain resorts; advance booking is recommended. Contact a local tourist office for lists and prices.

Camping Austria has over 490 camping grounds, many well equipped and scenically located. Prices can be as low as €4 per person or small tent and as high as €10. Many close in winter, so phone ahead to check. Search for camping grounds by region at www.camping-club.at (in German).

Eco-Hotels To search *Bio-* or *Öko-* ('eco') hotels by region, see www.biohotels.info.

Embassies & Consulates

All of the embassies and consulates listed below are located in Vienna (telephone prefix ☎01). For a complete listing of other embassies and consulates, look in the Austrian telephone book under *Botschaften* (embassies) or *Konsulate* (consulates).

Australia (☎506 74-0; www.australian-embassy.at; Mattiellistrasse 2-4)

Canada (☎531 38-3000; www.kanada.at; Laurenzerberg 2)

New Zealand (consulate-general; ☎318 85 05; www.nzc.at; Salesianergasse 15/3)

UK (☎716 13-0; www.britishembassy.at; Jaurèsgasse 12)

USA (☎313 39-0; http://austria.usembassy.gov; Boltzmanngasse 16)

Food

Price ranges for restaurants listed in this book are indicated by the following:

€€€ more than €30

€€ €15 to €30

€ below €15

Gay & Lesbian Travellers

Austria is close to the Western European par on attitudes towards homosexuality. Vienna is more tolerant towards gays and lesbians than the rest of the country.

The *Spartacus International Gay Guide,* published by Bruno Gmünder (Berlin), is a good directory of gay entertainment venues worldwide (mainly for men). Online resources:

Gay.de (www.gay.at)

Gayboy (www.gayboy.at)

Gaynet (www.gayguide.at)

Rainbow (www.rainbow.or.at)

Language Courses

Many places, including some of Austria's universities, offer German courses, usually with the option of accommodation. Well-known course providers:

Berlitz (www.berlitz.at) Offers private, intensive day and evening courses in Vienna, Wiener Neustadt, Klagenfurt, Linz and Graz.

Inlingua Sprachschule (www.inlingua.at) Courses run for a minimum of two weeks and can either be taken in the morning or some evenings. Classes are limited to seven students and individual tuition is also available. Offices in Linz, Graz, Salzburg, Innsbruck, Klagenfurt and Vorarlberg.

Money

ATMs Some *Bankomaten* (ATMs) are 24 hours. Most accept at the very least Maestro debit cards and Visa and MasterCard credit cards.

Credit Cards Visa and MasterCard (Eurocard) are accepted a little more widely than American Express (Amex) and Diners Club.

Currency Austria's currency is the euro. Major train stations have currency offices, and there are also plenty of banks and *bureaux de changes*.

Taxes *Mehrwertsteuer* (MWST; value-added tax) is set at 20% for most goods. Prices are always displayed inclusive of all taxes. Shops with a 'Global Refund Tax Free Shopping' sticker have the paperwork to reclaim about 13% of this tax on single purchases over €75 by non-EU citizens or residents. See www.globalrefund.com for more information. Vienna and Salzburg airports have refund desks. It's easiest to claim this before leaving the country, rather than at home.

Tipping It's customary to tip about 10% in restaurants, bars and cafes, and in taxis; hand over the bill and the tip together. It also doesn't hurt to tip hairdressers, hotel porters, cloak-room attendants, cleaning staff and tour guides €1 or €2.

Transfers For emergency transfers, **Western Union** (www.westernunion.com) money offices are available in larger towns.

Public Holidays

New Year's Day (Neujahr) 1 January

Epiphany (Heilige Drei Könige) 6 January

Easter Monday (Ostermontag) March/April

Labour Day (Tag der Arbeit) 1 May

Whit Monday (Pfingstmontag) Sixth Monday after Easter

Ascension Day (Christi Himmelfahrt) Sixth Thursday after Easter

Corpus Christi (Fronleichnam) Second Thursday after Whitsunday

Assumption (Maria Himmelfahrt) 15 August

National Day (Nationalfeiertag) 26 October

All Saints' Day (Allerheiligen) 1 November

Immaculate Conception (Mariä Empfängnis) 8 December

Christmas Day (Christfest) 25 December

St Stephen's Day (Stephanitag) 26 December

Telephone

Area Codes Area codes begin with '0' (eg '01' for Vienna). Drop this when calling from outside Austria; use it for all landline calls inside Austria except for local calls or to special toll and toll-free numbers.

Directory Enquiries Call ☎0900 11 88 77 for international directory assistance.

Free & Toll Numbers 0800 numbers are free, 0810 and 0820 cost 0.10c and 0.20c respectively per minute, and 0900 numbers are exorbitant and best avoided.

Mobile Numbers Austrian mobile (*Handy*) telephone numbers begin with 0650 or higher up to 0683.

Public Telephones These take phonecards or coins; €0.20 is the minimum for a local call. Call centres are also widespread, and many internet cafes are geared for Skype calls.

Roaming The network works on GSM 1800 and is compatible with GSM 900 phones; it is not compatible with systems from the USA unless the mobile phone is at least a tri-band model. Roaming can get very expensive if your provider is outside the EU.

SIM Cards Phone shops sell prepaid SIM cards for about €10 (calls for about 0.10c per minute) that can be refilled at kiosks anywhere.

Tourist Information

Tourist offices, which are dispersed far and wide in Austria, tend to adjust their hours from one year to the next, so the hours listed in this chapter are a guide only and may have changed slightly by the time you arrive.

The **Austrian National Tourist Office** (ANTO; www.austria.info) has a number of overseas offices. There is a comprehensive listing on the ANTO website.

Visas

Visas for stays of up to three months are not required for citizens of the EU, much of Eastern Europe, Israel, USA, Canada, the majority of Central and South American nations, Japan, Korea, Malaysia, Singapore, Australia or New Zealand. All other nationalities require a visa; the Ministry of Foreign Affairs website at www.bmaa.gv.at has a list of Austrian embassies where you can apply for one.

Getting There & Away

Entering the Country

Paperwork A valid passport is required. The only exception to this rule is when entering from another Schengen country (all EU states minus Britain and Ireland); in this case, only a national identity card is required.

Border Procedures Formal border controls have been abolished if entering from another EU country and Switzerland, but spot checks may be carried out at the border or inside Austria itself.

Air

Vienna is the main transport hub for Austria, but Graz, Linz, Klagenfurt, Salzburg and Innsbruck all receive international flights. Flights to these cities are often a cheaper option than those to the capital, as are flights to Airport Letisko (Bratislava Airport), 60km east of Vienna in Slovakia.

Among the low-cost airlines, Ryanair and Air Berlin fly to Graz, Innsbruck, Klagenfurt, Linz, Salzburg and Vienna (Ryanair to Bratislava for Vienna).

Following are the key international airports in Austria:

Airport Letisko Bratislava (BTS; ☎421 2 3303 33 53; www.airportbratislava.sk) Serves Bratislava and has good transport connections to Vienna. Used by Ryanair.

Graz (GRZ; ☎0316-29 02-0; www.flughafen-graz.at)

Innsbruck (INN; ☎0512-225 25-0; www.innsbruck-airport.com)

Klagenfurt (KLU; ☎0463-41 5 00-0; www.klagenfurt-airport.com)

Linz (LNZ; ☎07221-600-0; www.flughafen-linz.at)

Salzburg (SZG; ☎0662-85800; www.salzburg-airport.com)

Vienna (VIE; ☎01-7007 22233; www.viennaairport.com)

Land

BUS

Buses depart from Austria for as far afield as England, the Baltic countries, the Netherlands, Germany and Switzerland. But most significantly, they provide access to Eastern European cities small and large – from the likes of Sofia and Warsaw, to Banja Luka, Mostar and Sarajevo.

Services operated by **Eurolines** (www.eurolines.at) leave from Vienna and from several regional cities.

CAR & MOTORCYCLE

There are numerous entry points into Austria by road from Germany, the Czech Republic, Slovakia, Hungary, Slovenia, Italy and Switzerland. All border-crossing points are open 24 hours.

Insurance Third-party insurance is a minimum requirement in Europe and you'll need to carry proof of this in the form of a Green Card. The car must also display a sticker indicating the country of origin.

Paperwork Proof of ownership of a private vehicle and a driver's licence should always be carried while driving. EU licences are accepted in Austria while all other nationalities require a German translation or an International Driving Permit (IDP).

Safety Requirements Carrying a warning triangle and first-aid kit in your vehicle is compulsory.

TRAIN

Austria has excellent rail connections. The main services in and out of the country from the west normally pass through Bregenz, Innsbruck or Salzburg en route to Vienna. Trains to Eastern Europe invariably leave from Südbahnhof in Vienna (closed for reconstruction 2011–12; see p112). Express services to Italy go via Innsbruck or Villach; trains to Slovenia are routed through Graz.

Express & High-Speed Trains Express trains are identified by the symbols EC (EuroCity; serving international routes) or IC (InterCity; serving national routes). The French TGV and the German InterCityExpress (ICE) trains are high-speed trains. Surcharges are levied for these.

London The fastest connection between London and Vienna by rail is on **Eurostar** (www.eurostar.com) via Brussels and Frankfurt am Main. It takes a total of 14 hours.

Online Timetables **ÖBB** (www.oebb.at) Austrian National Railways, with national and international connections. Only national connections have prices online.

Reservations Extra charges can apply on fast trains and international trains, and it is a good idea (sometimes obligatory) to make seat reservations for peak times.

> **MOVING ON?**
>
> For tips, recommendations and reviews, head to shop.lonelyplanet.com to purchase downloadable PDFs of the Czech Republic, Hungary and Slovenia chapters from Lonely Planet's *Eastern Europe* guide.

River & Lake

Hydrofoils run to Bratislava and Budapest from Vienna; slower boats cruise the Danube between the capital and Passau. The **Danube Tourist Commission** (www.danube-river.org) has a country-by-country list of operators and agents who can book tours. Germany and Switzerland can be reached from Bregenz.

Getting Around

Transport systems in Austria are highly developed and efficient. Individual bus and train *Fahrplan* (timetables) are readily available, as are helpful annual timetables.

Air

Flying within a country the size of Austria is not usually necessary. A couple of airlines serving longer routes:

Austrian Airlines (www.austrian.com) The national carrier and its subsidiaries Tyrolean Airways and Austrian Arrows offer several flights daily between Vienna and Graz, Innsbruck, Klagenfurt, Linz and Salzburg.

Welcome Air (www.welcomeair.at) Flights from Innsbruck to Graz.

Bicycle

Austria is an efficiently run paradise for cyclists, criss-crossed by plenty of designated cycling paths.

Bike Hire All cities have at least one bike shop that doubles as a rental centre; expect to pay around €10 to €15 per day.

Bike Touring Most tourist boards have brochures on cycling facilities and routes within their region. Separate bike tracks are common in cities, and long-distance tracks and routes also run along major rivers such as the Danube and lakes such as Wörthersee in Carinthia.

Bike Transport You can take bicycles on any train with a bicycle symbol at the top of its timetable. A day ticket costs €5 for regional, €10 for national (InterCity) and €12 for international trains. You can't take bicycles on buses.

Boat

The Danube serves as a thoroughfare between Vienna and Lower and Upper Austria. Services are generally slow, scenic excursions rather than functional means of transport.

Bus

Rail routes are often complemented by Postbus services, which usually depart from outside train stations. In remote regions, there are fewer services on Saturday and often none on Sunday. Generally, you can only buy tickets from the drivers. For information inside Austria, call ☎0810 222 333 (6am to 8pm); from outside Austria, call ☎+43 1 71101; or visit the website, www.postbus.at.

Car & Motorcycle

Autobahns ('A') and *Bundesstrassen* ('B') are major roads, while *Landstrassen* ('L') let you enjoy the ride and are usually good for cyclists. A daily motorail service links Vienna to Innsbruck, Salzburg and Villach.

AUTOMOBILE ASSOCIATIONS

Annual membership for Austria's two automobile associations costs €66 and includes a free 24-hour breakdown service. Nonmembers incur a fee for call-outs which varies, depending on the time of day. The two associations:

ARBÖ (☎24hr emergency assistance 123, office 050/123 123; www.arboe.at)

ÖAMTC (☎24hr emergency assistance 120, office 01-711 99-0; www.oeamtc.at)

HIRE

Multinational car-hire firms **Avis** (www.avis.at), **Budget** (www.budget.at), **Europcar** (www.europcar.co.at) and **Hertz** (www.hertz.at) all have offices in major cities; ask at tourist offices for details. The minimum age for hiring small cars is 19 years, or 25 years for larger, 'prestige' cars. Customers must have held a driving licence for at least a year. Many contracts forbid customers to take cars outside Austria, particularly into Eastern Europe.

MOTORWAY & TUNNEL TOLLS

A *vignette* (motorway tax) is imposed on all autobahn; charges for cars/motorbikes are €7.90/4.50 for 10 days and €22.90/11.50 for two months. *Vignette* can be purchased at border crossings, petrol stations and *Tabak* shops. There are additional tolls (usually €2.50 to €10) for some mountain tunnels.

ROAD RULES

Children Under the age of 14 who are shorter than 1.5m must have a special seat or restraint.

Crash Helmet Compulsory for motorcyclists and their passengers, not for cyclists.

Drinking & Driving The penalty for drink-driving – over 0.05% – is a hefty on-the-spot fine and confiscation of your driving licence.

Driving Licence A licence should always be carried. If it's not in German, you need to carry a translation or International Driving Permit (IDP) as well.

Fines Can be paid on the spot, but ask for a receipt.

Give Way Rules Give way to the right at all times except when a priority road sign indicates otherwise. Trams always have priority.

Hitchhiking It's illegal to hitchhike on Austrian motorways.

Minimum Driving Age 18.

Parking Most town centres have *Kurzparkzone* (short-term parking zones) during office hours. *Parkschein* (parking vouchers) for such zones can be purchased from *Tabak* shops or pavement dispensers. Parking is unrestricted on unmarked streets.

Seat Belts Compulsory.

Snow Chains Carrying snow chains in winter is recommended (compulsory in some areas).

Speed Limits The speed limit is 50km/h in built-up areas, 130km/h on motorways and 100km/h on other roads. Except for the A1 (Vienna–Salzburg) and the A2 (Vienna–Villach), the speed limit is 110km/h on the autobahn from 10pm to 5am.

Which Side of the Road Drive on the right-hand side.

Train

Austria has a clean, efficient rail system, and if you use a discount card it's very inexpensive.

Disabled Passengers Use the ☎05-1717 number from 7am to 10pm for special travel assistance; do this at least 24 hours ahead of travel (72 hours ahead for international services). Staff at stations will help with boarding and alighting.

Fares The fares quoted in this chapter are for 2nd-class tickets.

Information **ÖBB** (☎05 17 17; www.oebb.at) is the main operator, supplemented with a handful of private lines. Tickets and timetables are available online.

RailJet It's worth seeking out RailJet train services connecting Vienna, Graz, Villach, Salzburg and Innsbruck, as they travel up to 200km/h.

Reservations In 2nd class within Austria this costs €3.50 for most express services; recommended for travel on weekends.

RAIL PASSES

Depending on the amount of travelling you intend to do in Austria, and your residency status, rail passes can be a good deal.

Eurail Austria Pass This handy pass is available to non-EU residents; prices start at €112 for three days' unlimited 1st-class travel within one month, and youths under 26 receive substantial discounts. See the website at www.eurail.com for all options (eg Austria–Germany Pass).

Interrail Passes are for European citizens and include One Country Pass Austria (three/four/six/eight days €172/191/252/290). Youths under 26 receive substantial discounts. See www.interrailnet.com for all options.

Vorteilscard Reduces fares by at least 45% and is valid for a year, but not on buses. Bring a photo and your passport or ID. It costs adult/under 26 years/senior €100/20/27).

Belgium

Includes »

Best Places to Eat

» Den Gouden Harynck (p146)

» House of Eliott (p141)

» L'Ogenblik (p126)

Best Places to Stay

» Guesthouse Nuit Blanche (p145)

» Chambres d'Hôtes Verhaegen (p140)

» Relais Bourgondisch Cruyce (p146)

» Hotel Julien (p134)

Why Go?

Stereotypes of comic books, remarkable beers and sublime chocolates are just the start in this eccentric little country, whose self-deprecating people have quietly spent centuries producing some of Europe's finest art and architecture. Bilingual Brussels is the dynamic yet personable EU capital, but also sports what's arguably the world's most beautiful city square. Flat, Dutch-speaking Flanders has many other alluring medieval city cores, all easily linked by regular train hops. In hilly, French-speaking Wallonia, the attractions are contrastingly rural – castle villages, outdoor activities and extensive cave systems that prove a major draw for Dutch caravanners but are hard to fully appreciate by public transport. War buffs will find Belgium full of moving battlefield sites from all eras. And anyone with a love of the good life will quickly come to appreciate a country where cafe-culture is king and fine food is almost a birthright.

When to Go

Brussels

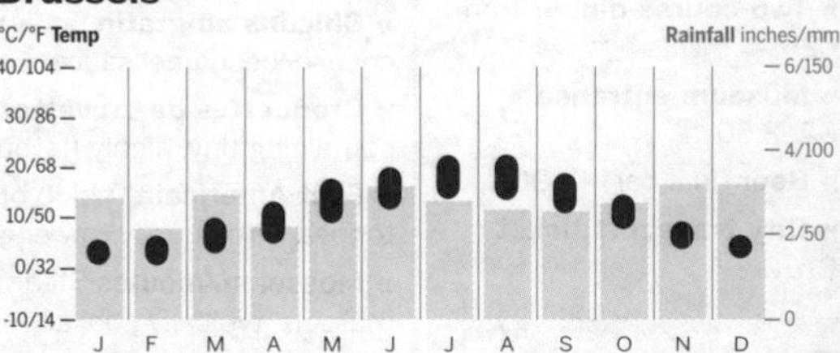

Pre-Easter weekends Belgium hosts many of Europe's weirdest carnivals, not just at Mardi Gras.

Mid-June Scenes from the battle are recreated. at Waterloo by uniformed armies of volunteers.

Mid-Aug, even years Brussels' Grand Place hosts an ornate, multicoloured 'carpet' of flower petals.

AT A GLANCE

» **Currency** euro (€)

» **Languages** Dutch, French, German

» **Money** ATMs common; credit cards widely accepted

» **Visas** Schengen rules apply

Fast Facts

» **Area** 30,278 sq km

» **Population** 10.4 million

» **Capital** Brussels

» **Telephone** country code ☎32; international access code ☎00

» **Emergency** ☎112

Exchange Rates

Australia	A$1	€0.74
Canada	C$1	€0.74
Japan	¥100	€0.87
New Zealand	NZ$1	€0.56
UK	UK£1	€1.16
USA	US$1	€0.67

Set Your Budget

» **Budget hotel double** under €60

» **Two-course dinner** from €25

» **Museum entrance** €2–8.50

» **Beer** (in a bar) €1.90

» **City transport ticket** €1.70

Resources

» **Belgium** (www.belgiumtheplaceto.be)

» **Brussels** (www.visitbrussels.be)

Connections

Amsterdam, Paris, Cologne and London are all under 2½ hours from Brussels by high-speed train. Liège and Antwerp are also on high-speed international routes. Go via Tournai or Ghent to reach France by train if you want to avoid such lines and their compulsory reservations (or if you have a railcard that requires it). Budget airlines offer cheap deals to numerous European destinations particularly from Charleroi.

ITINERARIES

Four Days

Just long enough to get a first taste of Belgium's four finest 'art cities': Bruges, Ghent, Brussels and Antwerp, all easy jump-offs or short excursions while you're train-hopping between Paris and Amsterdam. Bruges is the fairy-tale 'Venice of the north', Ghent has similar canal-side charms without the tourist hordes, and Brussels' incomparable Grand Place is worth jumping off any train for, even if you have only a few hours to spare. Cosmopolitan Antwerp goes one further, adding in fashion and diamonds. If you're overnighting make sure to hit Brussels on a weekend and Bruges on a weekday to get the best deals on accommodation.

Ten Days

Add an extra night in each of the above and consider stops in the moving WWI sites of historic Ypres, hopping to Antwerp via Leuven, Mechelen and Lier, and possibly driving around rural Wallonia to visit a selection of fascinating caves and castles.

Essential Food & Drink

Classic, home-style Belgian dishes include the following:

» **Ballekes/bouletten** Meatballs.

» **Chicons au gratin** Endive rolled in ham and cooked in cheese/béchamel sauce.

» **Croquettes de crevettes grises** Like fish cakes, but containing tiny, highly flavoured North Sea shrimps.

» **Filet Américain** A blob of raw minced beef, typically topped with equally raw egg yolk.

» **Mosselen/moules** Steaming cauldrons of in-the-shell mussels, typically cooked in white wine and served with a mountain of *frites* (chips).

» **Paling in 't groen** Eel in a sorrel or spinach sauce.

» **Stoemp** Mashed veg-and-potato dish.

» **Vlaamse stoverij/carbonade flamande** Semi-sweet beer-based beef casserole.

» **Waterzooi** A cream-based chicken or fish stew.

BRUSSELS

POP 1.03 MILLION

Like the country it represents, Brussels (Bruxelles, Brussel) is a surreal, multilayered place pulling several disparate identities into one enigmatic core. It subtly seduces with great art, tempting chocolate shops and classic cafes. Meanwhile a confusing architectural smorgasbord pits awesome art-nouveau and 17th-century masterpieces against shabby suburbanism and the disappointingly soulless glass-faced anonymity of the EU area. Note that Brussels is officially bilingual, so all names – from streets to train stations – have both Dutch and French versions, but for simplicity we use only the French versions in this chapter.

Sights

CENTRAL BRUSSELS

Although Brussels is very spread out, most key sights and numerous unmissable cafes are within leisurely walking distance of the fabulous Grand Place.

Grand Place NEIGHBOURHOOD

Brussels' incomparable central square tops any itinerary. Its splendidly spired Gothic **Hôtel de Ville** was the only building to escape bombardment by the French in 1695, quite ironic considering that it was their main target. Today the pedestrianised square's splendour is due largely to its intact collection of **guildhalls**, rebuilt by merchant guilds after 1695 and fancifully adorned with gilded statues. Several now host tempting **cafes**, though similarly historic drinking spots are somewhat less expensive around the nearby **Bourse** (Map p122). That's Brussels' 1873 stock exchange whose neoclassical stone facade features sculptures by the young Rodin. A block northeast of Grand Place, the 1847 **Galeries St-Hubert** (Map p122; www.galeries-saint-hubert.com) was Europe's first shopping arcade and remains a must-visit. Enchantingly colourful lanes of close-packed fish restaurants lead south from here down the **Rue des Bouchers**, but beware that (with some exceptions) many are notorious tourist traps (see p126).

Manneken Pis MONUMENT

Making a suitably surreal national symbol, the **Manneken Pis** (Map p122) is a diminutive fountain in the form of a little boy cheerfully taking a leak into a fountain pool. Sexual equality is ensured by his lesser-known squatting sister, the **Jeanneke Pis** (Map p122; www.jeannekepisofficial.be; Impasse de la Fidélité).

Musées Royaux des Beaux-Arts ART MUSEUM

(Map p122; www.fine-arts-museum.be; Rue de la Régence 3; adult/student/BrusselsCard €8/2/free; ⏲10am-5pm Tue-Sun) Belgium's premier collection of both ancient and modern art is remarkably well endowed with works by Flemish Primitives, the Breugel (Breughel) family and Rubens. However, many rooms are currently closed for long-term renovation. Headphones (for English explanations) cost an extra €2.50; special exhibitions also cost extra. A €13 combination ticket includes the Magritte Museum next door.

Magritte Museum ART MUSEUM

(Map p122; www.musee-magritte-museum.be; Place Royale; adult/under 26yr/BrusselsCard €8/2/free; ⏲10am-5pm Tue-Sun) This state-of-the-art 2009 museum celebrates the life and work of Belgian surrealist artist René Magritte, taking visitors well beyond his stereotypically witty canvases of pipes and bowler hats. Consider pre-purchasing tickets online to save queuing.

MIM MUSEUM

(Map p122; Musical Instrument Museum; www.mim.be; Rue Montagne de la Cour 2; adult/BrusselsCard €5/free; ⏲10am-5pm Tue-Sun) MIM makes one

BRUSSELSCARD

The **BrusselsCard** (www.bitc.be; 24/48/72hr €24/34/40) allows free visits to 32 Brussels-area museums (including those indicated in reviews) and gives a few bar and restaurant discounts, plus unlimited free use of city public transport. Only seriously hyperactive museum fans will save much money, but if you do buy a BrusselsCard, the following (not reviewed) are central and worth adding to your busy schedule:

» **Brewery Museum** (Map p122) On the Grand Place; visit if only for the free beer.

» **Lace Museum** (Map p122)

» **Maison du Roi** (Map p122) Includes the Manneken Pis' costumes.

» **Money Museum** (Map p122)

» **Porte de Hal** (Map p118) Ancient city gate-fort.

Belgium Highlights

1 Come on weekdays off-season to appreciate the picture-perfect canal scenes of medieval **Bruges** (p143), without the tourist overload

2 Be wooed by underappreciated **Ghent** (p137), one of Europe's greatest all-round discoveries

3 Savour the 'world's most beautiful square', then seek out the remarkable cafes and chocolate shops of the capital, **Brussels** (p115)

4 Follow fashion to hip yet historic **Antwerp** (p130)

5 Drive Flanders' back lanes to St-Sixtus Abbey in **Westvleteren** (p150) to find the holy grail of beer lovers

6 Climb a lion to survey the classic battlefield at **Waterloo** (p130)

7 Ponder the heartbreaking futility of WWI in Flanders' fields around meticulously rebuilt **Ypres** (p148)

8 Explore the caves and castles of rural Wallonia around **Rochefort** (p152)

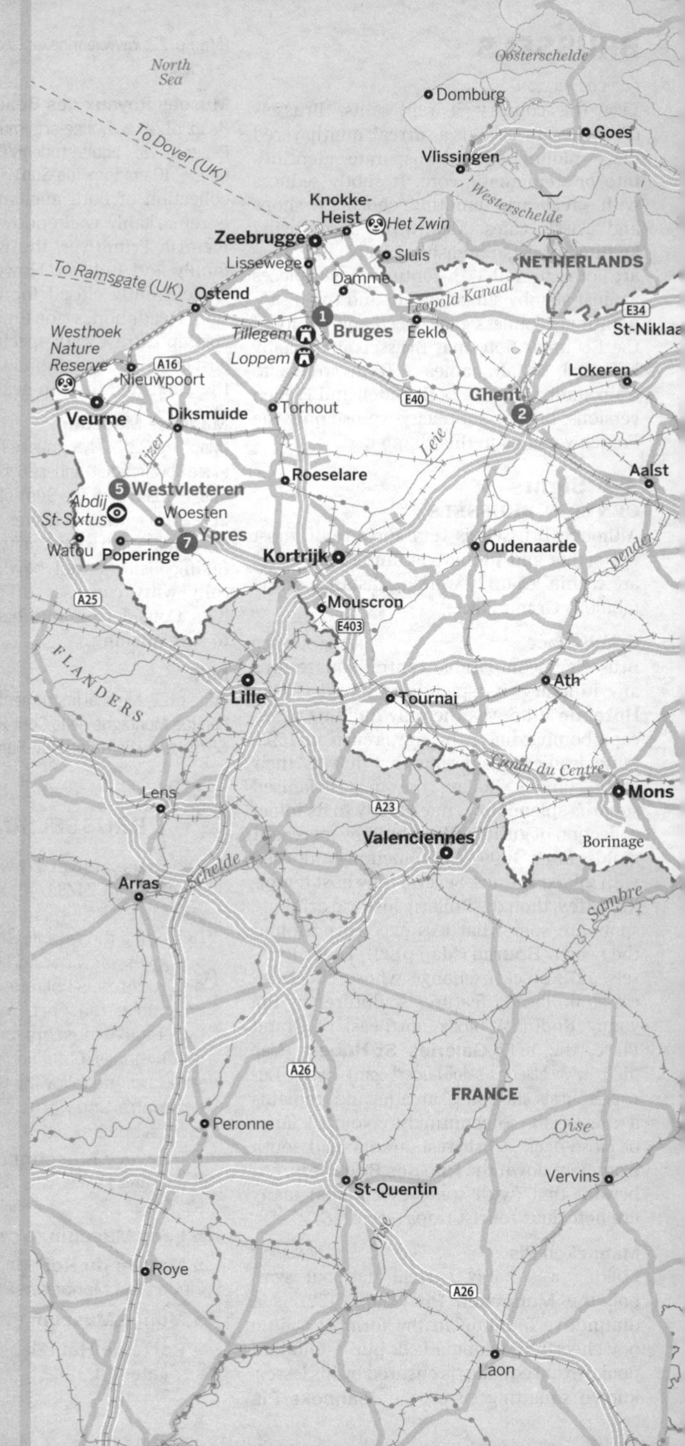

0 30 km
0 20 miles
Tilburg
NETHERLANDS
Roosendaal
Eindhoven
Venlo
A1
N1
Kanaal Antwerpen - Turnhout
Turnhout
A12
A21
Antwerp
4
Antwerp Airport
Herentals
Mol
Neerpelt
Roermond
Maas
Albert Kanaal
Lier
Nete
Fort van Breendonk
E313
Mechelen
National Park Hoge Kempen
GERMANY
Diest
A2
Genk
Hasselt
Bokrijk Openluchtmuseum
Brussels Airport
E19
Leuven
Maastricht
3
Brussels
E313
A2
Aachen
E19
Waterloo
Louvain-la-Neuve
A3
Braine l'Alleud
6
Ottignies
Waterloo Battlefield
Liège Airport
Liège
Verviers
Hautes Fagnes-Eifel Nature Park
Nivelles
Jehay
E411
Vesdre
Hautes Fagnes
Huy
Meuse
Remouchamps
Charleroi Airport
E42
Namur
Modave
Hautes Fagnes Nature Reserve
Coo
Stavelot
Charleroi
Amblève
Durbuy
Barvaux
Godinne
E25
Hotton
N5
Ourthe
Dinant
E421
Marloie
Rochefort
Houyet
La Roche-en-Ardenne
8
Jemelle
Botte de Hainaut
Lavaux-Ste-Anne
Han-sur-Lesse
Champlon
Clervaux
Lesse
Chimay
Couvin
E46
Bastogne
E411
Vianden
Libramont
ARDENNES
Semois
E46
Ettelbrück
Rochehaut
Gutland
Bouillon
LUXEMBOURG
Charleville-Mezières
Findel Airport
Arlon
Orval
Meuse
Luxembourg City
Virton
Rodange
Aisne

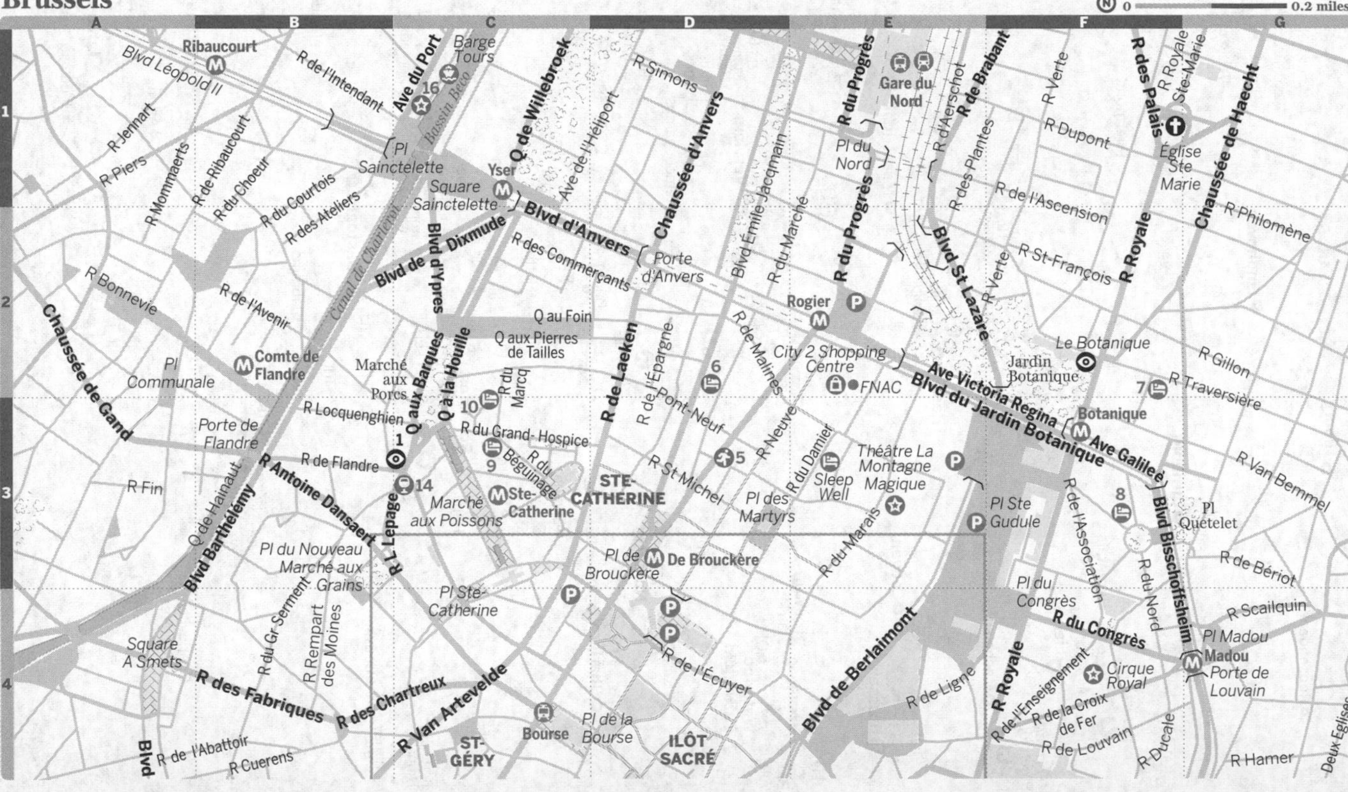
Brussels
400 m
0.2 miles
Ribaucourt
Blvd Léopold II
R de l'Intendant
Ave du Port
Barge Tours
16
Bassin Béco
Q de Willebroek
R Simons
Chaussée d'Anvers
R du Progrès
Gare du Nord
R d'Aerschot
R de Brabant
R Verte
R des Palais
R Royale
Ste-Marie
Chaussée de Haecht
R Jennart
R Piers
R Mommaerts
R de Ribaucourt
R du Choeur
R du Courtois
R des Ateliers
Pl Sainctelette
Yser
Square Sainctelette
Ave de l'Héliport
Blvd Émile Jacqmain
R du Marché
Pl du Nord
R du Progrès
R des Plantes
R Dupont
Église Ste Marie
R de l'Ascension
R Philomène
Canal de Charleroi
Blvd de Dixmude
Blvd d'Ypres
Blvd d'Anvers
R des Commerçants
Porte d'Anvers
Blvd St Lazare
R Verte
R St-François
R Royale
R Bonnevie
Chaussée de Gand
R de l'Avenir
Rogier
Q au Foin
Q aux Pierres de Tailles
R de Laeken
R de Malines
City 2 Shopping Centre
FNAC
Ave Victoria Regina
Blvd du Jardin Botanique
Jardin Botanique
Le Botanique
R Gillon
Pl Communale
Comte de Flandre
Marché aux Porcs
Q aux Barques
Q à la Houille
R du Marcq
10
6
7
R Traversière
R Locquenghien
Porte de Flandre
R de l'Épargne
R Pont-Neuf
R Neuve
Botanique
Ave Galilée
R du Grand-Hospice
1
R de Flandre
R Antoine Dansaert
9
R du Béguinage
R St Michel
5
R du Damier
Théâtre La Montagne Magique
Sleep Well
R Van Bemmel
R Fin
Q de Hainaut
Blvd Barthélémy
R L Lepage
14
Marché aux Poissons
Ste-Catherine
STE-CATHERINE
Pl des Martyrs
R du Marais
Pl Ste Gudule
R de l'Association
8
Blvd Bisschoffsheim
Pl Quetelet
Pl du Nouveau Marché aux Grains
Pl de Brouckère
De Brouckère
R du Nord
R de Bériot
Pl Ste-Catherine
Pl du Congrès
R du Congrès
R Scailquin
Pl Madou
Madou
Porte de Louvain
R du Gr Serment
R Rempart des Moines
Square A Smets
R des Fabriques
R des Chartreux
R Van Artevelde
R de l'Écuyer
Blvd de Berlaimont
R de Ligne
R Royale
R de l'Enseignement
R de la Croix de Fer
Cirque Royal
R de Louvain
R Ducale
R Hamer
Deux Églises
Blvd
R de l'Abattoir
R Cuerens
ST-GÉRY
Bourse
Pl de la Bourse
ÎLOT SACRÉ

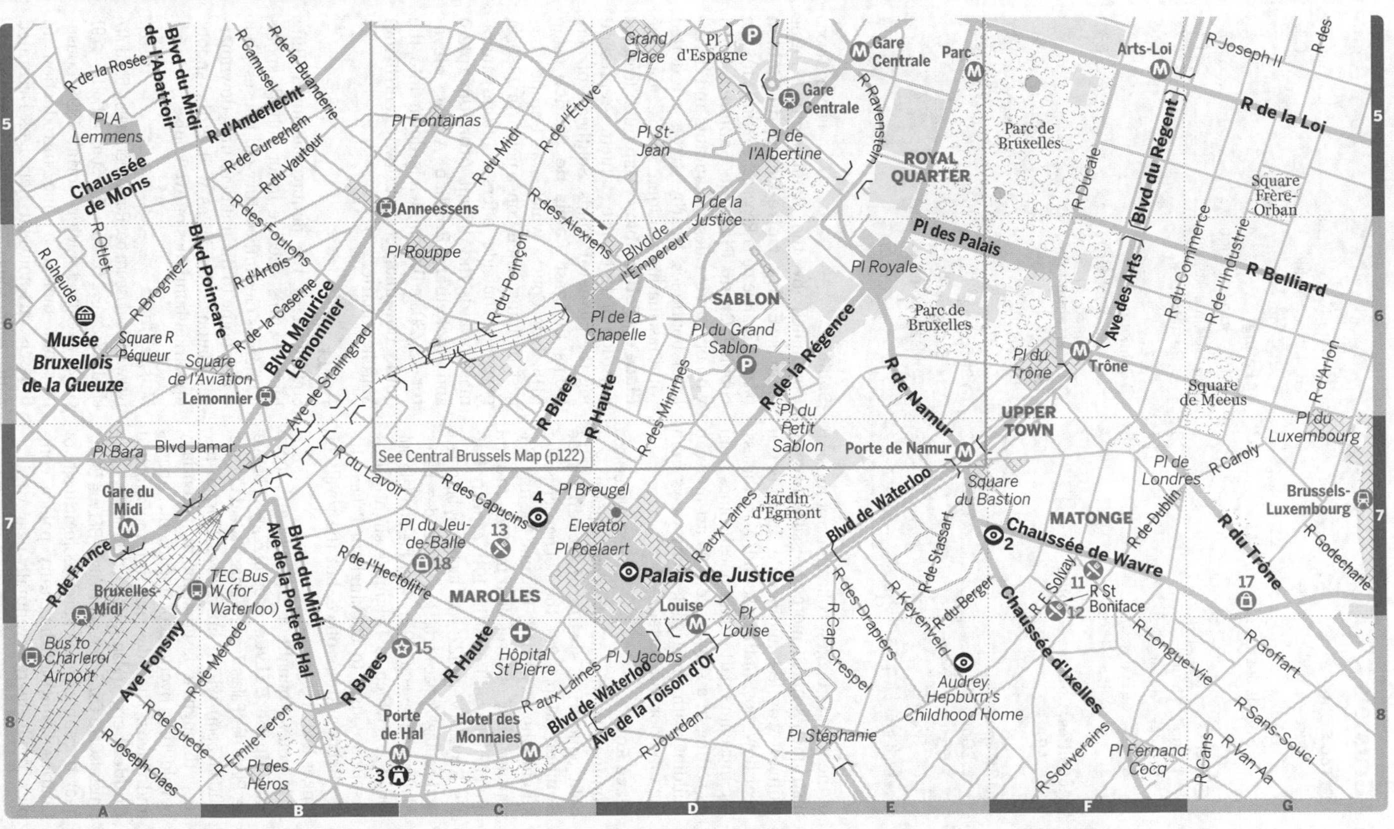
Grand Place
Pl d'Espagne
Gare Centrale
Parc
Arts-Loi
R Joseph II
R des
R de la Rosée
Blvd du Midi de l'Abattoir
R Camusel
R de la Buanderie
R d'Anderlecht
R de Cureghem
R du Vautour
Pl A Lemmens
Chaussée de Mons
Pl Fontainas
R du Midi
R de l'Etuve
Pl St-Jean
Pl de l'Albertine
R Ravenstein
ROYAL QUARTER
Parc de Bruxelles
R de la Loi
Blvd du Régent
Square Frère-Orban
R Otlet
R Gheude
Blvd Poincare
R des Foulons
R d'Artois
R Brogniez
Anneessens
Pl Rouppe
R des Alexiens
Blvd de l'Empereur
Pl de la Justice
Pl des Palais
R Ducale
Ave des Arts
R du Commerce
R de l'Industrie
R Belliard
Pl Royale
SABLON
Pl du Grand Sablon
Parc de Bruxelles
Musée Bruxellois de la Gueuze
Square R Péqueur
Square de l'Aviation
Lemonnier
R de la Caserne
Blvd Maurice Lemonnier
Ave de Stalingrad
R du Poinçon
Pl de la Chapelle
R de la Régence
R de Namur
Pl du Trône
Trône
Square de Meeus
R d'Arlon
Pl du Luxembourg
R Blaes
R Haute
R des Minimes
Pl du Petit Sablon
UPPER TOWN
Porte de Namur
Pl Bara
Blvd Jamar
See Central Brussels Map (p122)
R du Lavoir
R des Capucins
4
Pl Breugel
Jardin d'Egmont
Blvd de Waterloo
Square du Bastion
Pl de Londres
R Caroly
Brussels-Luxembourg
Gare du Midi
Pl du Jeu-de-Balle
13
Elevator
Pl Poelaert
R aux Laines
MATONGE
R de Dublin
R du Trône
R Godecharle
R de France
18
R de l'Hectolitre
Palais de Justice
2
Chaussée de Wavre
R de Stassart
Bruxelles-Midi
TEC Bus W (for Waterloo)
MAROLLES
Louise
Pl Louise
R des Drapiers
R Keyenveld
R du Berger
R E Solvay
11
R St Boniface
12
17
Bus to Charleroi Airport
Ave Fonsny
R de Mérode
Ave de la Porte de Hal
Blvd du Midi
Hôpital St Pierre
Pl J Jacobs
R Cap Crespel
Chaussée d'Ixelles
R Longue-Vie
R Goffart
15
R Blaes
R Haute
R aux Laines
Blvd de Waterloo
Ave de la Toison d'Or
Audrey Hepburn's Childhood Home
R de Suede
R Emile Feron
Porte de Hal
Hotel des Monnaies
R Jourdan
Pl Stéphanie
R Sans-Souci
R Joseph Claes
Pl des Héros
3
R Souverains
Pl Fernand Cocq
R Cans
R Van Aa
A
B
C
D
E
F
G
5
6
7
8

Brussels

Top Sights
Musée Bruxellois de la Gueuze ... A6
Palais de Justice ... D7

Sights
1 Cubitus Mural ... C3
2 Galerie d'Ixelles ... F7
3 Porte de Hal ... B8
4 Quick & Flupke Mural ... C7

Activities, Courses & Tours
5 ARAU ... D3

Sleeping
6 2Go4 ... D2
7 Centre Vincent van Gogh ... F2
8 Hostel Jacques Brel ... F3
9 Hôtel Noga ... C3
10 Maison Noble ... C3

Eating
11 Le Soleil d'Áfrique ... F7
12 L'Ultime Atome ... F7
13 Restobières ... C7

Drinking
14 Au Laboureur ... C3

Entertainment
15 Fuse ... C8
16 K-Nal ... C1

Shopping
17 Beermania ... G7
18 Flea Market ... C7

of the world's biggest collections of musical instruments much more accessible by providing a wordless audioguide that lets you hear how most of them sound. Nonetheless, the museum's particular appeal comes from its setting in a showpiece 1899 art-nouveau building with unparalleled city views from the top-floor cafe terrace.

Place Royale NEIGHBOURHOOD
Dominating this neoclassical square is a bold equestrian **statue of Godefroid de Bouillon** (Map p122), the Belgian crusader knight who very briefly became the first European 'king' of Jerusalem in 1099. Around the corner you'll find the 19th-century **Palais Royal** (Map p122; www.monarchy.be/palace-and-heritage/palace-brussels; Place des Palais; admission free; 10.30am-4pm Tue-Sun late Jul-early Sep), which is Belgium's slightly less-inspired cousin to Buckingham Palace. It's the Belgian king's office, but the royals no longer live here.

If you've bought a BrusselsCard, peep into **Musée BELvue** (Map p122; www.belvue.be; Place des Palais 7; adult/BrusselsCard €5/free; 10am-5pm), which introduces Belgian history through a fascinating, if potentially bewildering, overload of documents, images and videos. Then descend into the attached **Coudenberg** (Map p122; adult/under 26yr/BrusselsCard €5/3/free, with Musée BELvue €8/4/free), the subterranean archaeological site of Charles Quint's 16th-century palace complex. You'll emerge eventually near MIM.

Sablon NEIGHBOURHOOD
Dominated by the flamboyantly Gothic church, **Église Notre-Dame du Sablon** (Map p122; Rue de la Régence; 9am-7pm), the cobbled **Grand Place du Sablon** is lined with upmarket cafes, restaurants and chocolatier boutiques. Nearby streets are dotted with fascinating antique shops, and the **Place du Petit Sablon** (Map p122) features a garden of 48 bronze statuettes representing the medieval guilds. Southeast of here looms the vast **Palais de Justice** (Map p118; Law Court), which was Europe's biggest building when constructed in 1883. A pavement outside offers rooftop panoramas towards the distant **Atomium** (p125) and **Koekelberg Basilica**. A glass **elevator** (7.30am-11.45pm) leads down into the quirky, downmarket (but slowly gentrifying) Marolles quarter.

IXELLES

Southwest of the pentagonal Inner Ring highway, this sizeable inner suburb sports numerous elegant, century-old houses – but is also home to the multicultural, downmarket Matonge district as well as the snooty, upmarket boutiques of Ave Louise.

Musée Horta MUSEUM
(www.hortamuseum.be; Rue Américaine 25; adult/child €7/3; 2-5.30pm Tue-Sun; M Horta, 91 or 92) Architect Victor Horta's 1898 house-museum makes a fine introduction to Brussels' art-nouveau heritage. Decorated with numerous century-old ornaments,

the building's sinuous wrought iron and shaped wood are augmented by a partially stained-glass roof. The ticket stub includes a small map, helping you to seek out other art-nouveau monuments scattered around the surrounding area. For more, see www.brusselsartnouveau.be or buy the €3 Brussels art-nouveau guide from tourist offices.

Matonge NEIGHBOURHOOD
Nicknamed for a square in Kinshasa, Congo, Matonge is home to Brussels' African community. The architecture includes its fair share of tired old 1960s concrete, but **Chaussée de Wavre** and the dreary **Galerie d'Ixelles** (Map p118) come to life with African hairstylists, exotic groceries, outlets for Congolese CDs and DVDs, and many inexpensive places to sample African foods.

CINQUANTENAIRE

Hop off metro line 1 or 5 at Mérode to see Leopold II's triumphal arch and associated grand museums.

Arcade du Cinquantenaire MONUMENT
Designed to celebrate Belgium's 50th anniversary, this arch's construction went over-schedule…by 25 years! You can climb it from stairs within the **Military Museum** (www.klm-mra.be; Parc du Cinquantenaire 3; admission/audioguide free/€3; ⌚9am-11.45 & 1-4.30pm Tue-Sun), which boasts a vast collection.

Musée du Cinquantenaire MUSEUM
(www.kmkg-mrah.be; Parc du Cinquantenaire 10; adult/concession/BrusselsCard €5/4/free; ⌚10am-5pm Tue-Sun) Belgium's most underestimated museum has an astonishingly rich, global collection ranging from ancient Egyptian sarcophagi to Meso-American masks, to icons to wooden bicycles. You'd need days to appreciate it all. The English-language audioguide (€3 extra) is worth considering.

Autoworld MUSEUM
(www.autoworld.be; adult/concession/BrusselsCard €6/4.70/free; ⌚10am-6pm Apr-Sep, 10am-5pm Oct-Mar) One of Europe's biggest collections of vintage and 20th-century cars.

COMIC-STRIP CULTURE

In Belgium, comic strips *(bande dessinée)* are revered as the 'ninth art' and each September Brussels hosts a major **Comic-Strip Festival** (www.fetedelabd.be) at the splendid St-Gilles town hall. Internationally, the country's best-known comic-book hero is quiff-headed boy-detective Tintin, whose creator is celebrated at the superb **Hergé Museum** (www.museeherge.com; adult/concession €9.50/7; ⌚10.30am-5.30pm Tue-Sun), an hour south of Brussels by train in the otherwise uninteresting student town of Louvain-la-Neuve. Changing trains at Ottignies can save time.

Serious comic fans might also enjoy Brussels' comprehensive **Centre Belge de la Bande Dessinée** (Map p122; www.comicscenter.net; Rue des Sables 20; adult/concession/BrusselsCard €7.50/6/free; ⌚10am-6pm Tue-Sun) in a distinctive Horta-designed art-nouveau building, though relatively little is in English.

Comic Murals

Over 40 comic-strip murals enliven Brussels buildings. Their locations are mapped on www.visitbrussels.be (look for the 'Walks' section) and on free brochures available from Brussels International tourist office. Our favourites include the following:

» **Cubitus** (Map p118; Rue de Flandre)

» **Néron** (Map p122; Place St-Géry)

» **Quick & Flupke** (Map p118; Rue Haute)

» **Tibet & Duchâteau** (Map p122; Rue du Bon Secours 9)

Comic Shops

» **Brüsel** (Map p122; www.brusel.com; Blvd Anspach 100; ⌚10.30am-6.30pm Mon-Sat, noon-6.30pm Sun)

» **La Maison de la BD** (Map p122; www.jije.org; Blvd de l'Impératrice 1; museum admission €2; ⌚10am-6pm Tue-Sun)

» **Multi-BD** (Map p122; www.multibd.com; Blvd Anspach 122-124; ⌚10.30am-7pm Mon-Sat, 12.30-6.30pm Sun)

» **Nine City** (www.ninecity.be, www.moof-museum.be)

Central Brussels

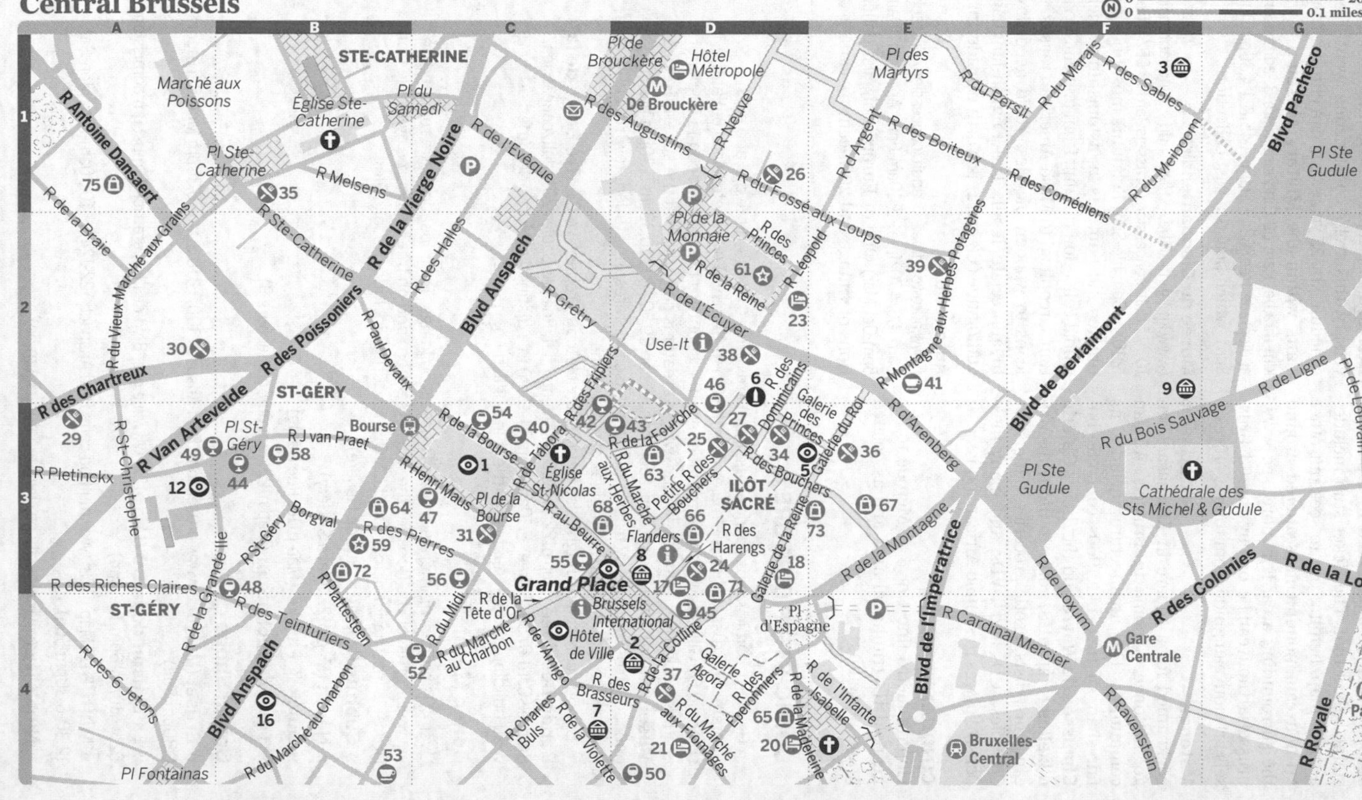

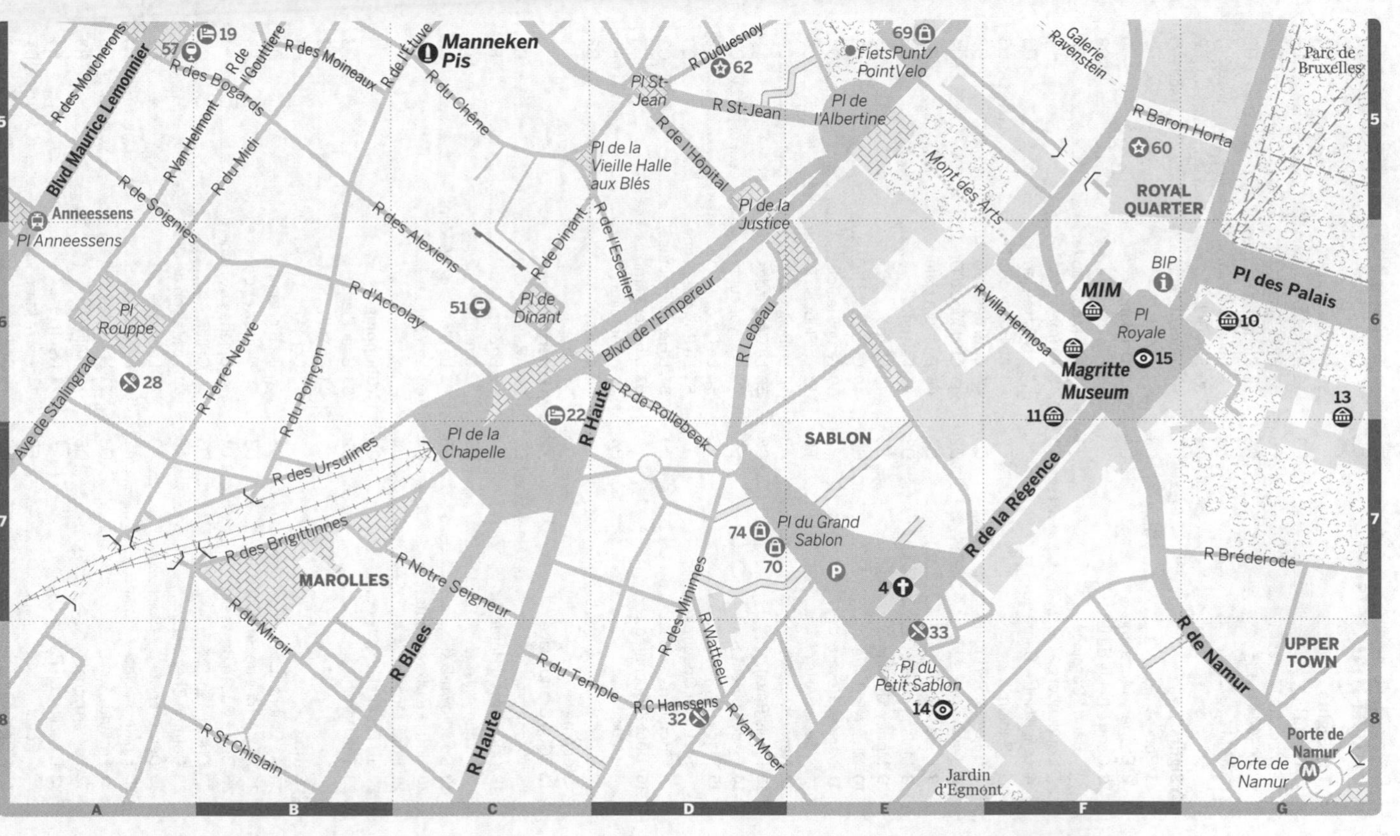

BRUSSELS BRUSSELS

Central Brussels

Top Sights

Grand Place C3
Magritte Museum F6
Manneken Pis C5
MIM F6

Sights

1 Bourse C3
2 Brewery Museum D4
3 Centre Belge de la Bande Dessinée F1
Coudenberg .... (see 10)
4 Église Notre-Dame du Sablon E7
5 Galeries St-Hubert D3
6 Jeanneke Pis D2
7 Lace Museum C4
8 Maison du Roi D3
9 Money Museum F2
10 Musée BELvue G6
11 Musées Royaux des Beaux-Arts F6
12 Néron Mural A3
13 Palais Royal G6
14 Place du Petit Sablon E8
15 Place Royale F6
Statue of Godefroid de Bouillon .... (see 15)
16 Tibet & Duchâteau Mural B4

Sleeping

17 2Go4 Grand Place Rooms D3
18 Chambres d'Hotes du Vaudevillle D3
19 Downtown-BXL B5
20 Hôtel Le Dixseptième D4
21 Hotel Mozart D4
22 JH Bruegel C6
23 The Dominican D2

Eating

24 A l'Ombra D3
25 Aux Armes de Bruxelles D3
26 Belga Queen Brussels D1
27 Chez Léon D3
28 Comme Chez Soi A6
29 Den Teepot A3
30 Fin de Siècle A2
31 Fritland C3
32 Le Perroquet D8
33 L'Ecailler du Palais Royal E8
34 L'Ogenblik D3
35 Mer du Nord B1
36 Mokafé E3
37 Pitta Street D4
38 Ricotta & Parmesan D2
Scheltema .... (see 34)
39 Sea Grill E2
Vincent .... (see 27)

Drinking

40 À la Bécasse C3
41 À la Mort Subite E2
42 A l'Image de Nostre-Dame C3
43 Au Bon Vieux Temps D3
44 Café des Halles B3
45 Chaloupe d'Or D4
46 Délirium Café D2
47 Falstaff C3
48 Floreo B3
49 Gecko A3
50 Goupil le Fol D4
51 La Fleur en Papier Doré C6
52 Le Belgica C4
53 Le Cercle des Voyageurs B4
54 Le Cirio C3
55 Le Roy d'Espagne C3
56 L'Homo Erectus C3
57 Moeder Lambic Fontainas A5
58 Zebra B3

Entertainment

59 AB B3
60 BoZar F5
Cinematek .... (see 60)
61 La Monnaie/De Munt D2
62 Le You D5

Shopping

63 Beer Planet D3
64 Brüsel B3
65 Corné Port Royal D4
66 De Biertempel D3
67 Délices et Caprices E3
Galeries St-Hubert .... (see 5)
68 Galler C3
69 La Maison de la BD E5
70 Leonidas D7
Leonidas .... (see 71)
71 Leonidas D3
72 Multi-BD B3
73 Neuhaus E3
74 Pierre Marcolini D7
75 Stijl A1

TERVUREN

Africa Museum MUSEUM
(www.africamuseum.be; Leuvensesteenweg 13; adult/concession/BrusselsCard €5/4/free, audioguide €2; ⏲10am-5pm Tue-Sun) In a vast formal park of lakes and manicured lawns, this veritable palace of a building was purpose-built by King Léopold II to show off Europe's most impressive array of African artefacts. Of course, much of the collection was plundered from Léopold's then-private 'garden' (Congo) where his rule saw a staggering percentage of the Congolese population die. From Montgomery metro station, take tram 44 to its eastern terminus.

ANDERLECHT

Internationally best known for its **football team** (www.rsca.be, www.anderlecht-online.be; Van den Stock Stadium, Avenue Théo Verbeeck 2; Ⓜ St-Guidon), this sprawling western suburb now has a grimy, run-down reputation. However, back in 1521 it was still a country village when the world-famous humanist Erasmus came to 'play at farming'.

Musée Bruxellois de la Gueuze BREWERY
(Map p118; www.cantillon.be; Rue Gheude 56; admission €5; ⏲9am-5pm Mon-Fri, 10am-5pm Sat; Ⓜ Bruxelles-Midi) In this fascinating working brewery, cobwebs and 19th-century equipment contribute to a curious spontaneous fermentation process that produces ultra-tart lambic beers, a Brussels speciality. Two tasters are included in the price of a self-guided tour. From Bruxelles-Midi station walk 800m north via Place Bara and Rue Limnander.

HEYSEL

A 15-minute metro ride to Brussels' northern edge brings you to an area of trade fairs, the national stadium and curious **Mini Europe** (www.minieurope.com; adult/child €13.40/10, with Atomium €19.90/13.90; ⏲10am-5pm Apr-Jun & Sep-Dec, 9.30am-8pm Jul-Aug), featuring walk-through recreations of the continent's top tourist sights at 1:25 scale.

Atomium MONUMENT, MUSEUM
(www.atomium.be; Sq de l'Atomium; adult/concession/BrusselsCard €11/8/9; ⏲10am-7pm May-Sep, 10am-6pm Oct-Apr; Ⓜ Heyzel, 🚍51) This Brussels icon is a space-age leftover from the 1958 World Fair consisting of nine gigantic gleaming balls impressively representing an iron crystal lattice enlarged 165 billion times. However, the interior exhibitions are less compelling and you might be happy just glimpsing the Atomium distantly from outside the vast Palais de Justice (p120) in central Brussels.

> **WANT MORE?**
>
> Head to **Lonely Planet** (www.lonelyplanet.com/belgium/brussels) for planning advice, author recommendations, traveller reviews and insider tips.

Tours

On the last Saturday of most months, **ARAU** (Map p118; ☎02 219 33 45; www.arau.org; Blvd Adolphe Max 55) tours visit some of Brussels' otherwise private art-nouveau showpieces.

Sleeping

Brussels' countless business hotels drop prices dramatically at weekends, during the July and August summer holidays and whenever the 'Eurocrats' are away. At such times, internet deals can get you a top-end room for little more than a mediocre midrange option, and €69 walk-in deals become possible at several options around the southern entrance of the Galeries St-Hubert. There are various cheap, basic choices around Bruxelles-Midi but, although slowly improving, that area can be somewhat intimidating. Around Rogier and Bruxelles-Nord, several upper-range hotels lie uncomfortably close to a seedy red-light district.

Bed & Brussels (www.bnb-brussels.be) allows you to filter 75 B&Bs by theme and location.

Hôtel Le Dixseptième BOUTIQUE HOTEL €€€
(Map p122; ☎02 502 57 44; www.ledixseptieme.be; Rue de la Madeleine 25; d weekday/weekend from €200/100; ❄) This alluring boutique hotel occupies part of a 17th-century ambassadorial mansion. Its understated opulence reigns in all but the very cheapest rooms.

Dominican BUSINESS HOTEL €€€
(Map p122; ☎02 203 08 08; www.thedominican.be; Rue Léopold 9; r weekday/weekend from €180/115; ❄@📶) The Dominican combines classic elegance with understated modern chic on the site of a former abbey. The location is brilliantly central, albeit on a side street favoured by beggars.

Downtown-BXL B&B €€
(Map p122; ☎0475 290721; www.downtownbxl.com, www.lacasabxl.com; Rue du Marché au

Charbon 118-120; r €77-109;) The excellent-value rooms here feature zebra-striped cushions and Warhol/Marilyn prints in 'Downtown', or Moroccan-Oriental–style decor in the adjacent 'Casa-BXL'. Gay-friendly.

Chambres d'Hôtes du Vaudeville B&B €€
(Map p122; 0471 473837; www.chambresdhotesduvaudeville.be; Galerie de la Reine 11; d from €115;) This luxury B&B has arty decor and a thrilling location, but, in the bigger front rooms, light sleepers might suffer from noise that reverberates all night around the gorgeous *galeries*. Get the keys from Theatre du Vaudeville next door. Breakfast is delivered at 8am; make your own Nespresso.

Maison Noble B&B €€
(Map p118; 02 219 23 39; www.maison-noble.eu; Rue du Marcq 10; r €139-159;) This splendidly refined four-room guest house, in a quiet street near Place St-Catherine, features a steam room and a piano lounge.

Hôtel Noga FAMILY HOTEL €€
(Map p118; 02 218 67 63; www.nogahotel.com; Rue du Béguinage 38; r weekday/weekend from €95/70;) Model yachts, sepia photos of Belgian royalty and assorted random kitsch lead up to rooms that are neat and clean without any particular luxuries. Prices include breakfast and one hour's wi-fi.

Hotel Mozart KITSCH HOTEL €€
(Map p122; 02 502 66 61; www.hotel-mozart.be; Rue du Marché aux Fromages 23; s/d/q €80/100/150;) Mashing Turkish mosaic work, gilt rococo-styled chairs and endless imitation antiques into a kitschy sensory overload, this place is inexpensive, super-central and unforgettable, but expect spongy mattresses, unsophisticated bathrooms and constant street noise if your room faces the 'pitta strip'. Walk-in discounts of around 20% are possible.

Hostel Jacques Brel HOSTEL €
(Map p118; 02 218 01 87; www.laj.be; Rue de la Sablonnière 30; HI members dm €16.40-20.50, s/d €34/49.60;) This neat, presentable and reasonably spacious hostel lies in a quiet, pleasant area less than 15-minutes' walk from Grand Place. The sociable bar has occasional live music and there's a 2nd-floor terrace. No lockout.

JH Bruegel HOSTEL €
(Map p122; 02 511 04 36; www.jeugdherbergen.be; Rue du St-Esprit 2; HI members dm/s/d €21.30/35.50/51.40;) Brussels' most central hostel has a cellar bar, several sitting areas and decent, gender-segregated dorms with showers (toilets shared). However, the 10am to 2pm lockout is infuriating; read the regulations carefully and ask for a night key (deposit €20) if staying out beyond 1am.

Centre Vincent van Gogh HOSTEL €
(Map p118; 02 217 01 58; www.chab.be; Rue Traversière 8; dm €18.50-21.50, s/d/q €33.50/53/86;) The lobby bar and pool-table veranda here are unusually hip for a hostel, but the rooms are less glamorous, and from some reaching the toilets means crossing the garden courtyard. No membership needed, and no lockout.

2GO4 HOSTEL €
(02 219 30 19; www.2GO4.be) Hostel (Map p118; Blvd Émile Jacqmain 99; dm €22-29, s/d/q €55/69/116; reception 7am-1pm & 4-11pm); Grand Place Rooms (Map p122; Rue des Harengs 6; d €59-70) The well-equipped hostel, featuring zany ground-floor furnishings, is toward the slightly sleazier end of town. Check in here even if you're staying in the wonderfully central, if haphazardly decorated, 'Grand Place Rooms'. Rates include coffee but not breakfast or towels (€1). No lockout, no curfew.

Eating

CENTRAL BRUSSELS

Several interesting options are dotted along Rue de Flandre, with reliable seafood restaurants around nearby Place Ste-Catherine and Marché aux Poissons. Inexpensive, if rarely authentic, Asian restaurants line Rue J van Praet between the Bourse and Place St-Géry. Restaurants reviewed here focus on value for money, but with formal attire, advance bookings and a plutonium credit card, central gourmet options include **Comme Chez Soi** (Map p122; www.commechezsoi.be), **Sea Grill** (Map p122; www.seagrill.be) and **L'Ecailler du Palais Royal** (www.lecaillerdupalaisroyal.be).

L'Ogenblik SEAFOOD €€€
(Map p122; 02 511 61 51; www.ogenblik.be; Galerie des Princes 1; lunch €11, mains €23-28; noon-2.30pm & 7pm-midnight) This archetypal historic bistro-restaurant has sawdust floors, close-packed tables and feels more convivially casual than most upmarket Brussels fish restaurants. Nonetheless the seafood quality challenges the best, while steaks and duck dishes are also available. Book ahead. Nearby, similarly priced recommendations include **Scheltema**, **Vincent**, **Chez Léon** and **Aux Armes de Bruxelles**. However,

beware of many other outwardly cheaper options that give a brilliant buzz to the Rue des Bouchers and Petite Rue des Bouchers – several have been known to operate sneaky tourist-catching scams.

Fin de Siècle BELGIAN €€
(Map p122; Rue des Chartreux 9; mains €11-19; bar 4.30pm-1am, kitchen 6pm-12.30am) A low-lit cult place with rough tables, youthful cafe-ambience and great-value Belgian favourites, along with meze and tandoori chicken. There's no sign and, with no reservations accepted, you might need to queue.

Belga Queen Brussels BELGIAN €€
(Map p122; 02 217 21 87; www.belgaqueen.be; Rue du Fossé aux Loups 32; mains €16-25, weekday lunch €16; noon-2.30pm & 7pm-midnight) Belgian cuisine is given a chic, modern twist within a magnificent, if reverberant, 19th-century bank building with classical stained-glass ceilings. There's a good wine and beer list.

A l'Ombra ITALIAN €€
(Map p122; Rue des Harengs 2; pastas €8.50-13, mains €14-18; noon-3pm Mon-Fri & 6.30pm-11.30pm Mon-Sat) Take a tiny, tile-walled 1920s shop-house, keep the original decor, insert a narrow communal table and see if the customers finally communicate over their delicious fresh pasta. Perhaps…at least with the farewell grappa.

Ricotta & Parmesan ITALIAN €
(Map p122; www.ricottaparmesan.com; Rue de l'Écuyer 31; mains €9-15; noon-2.30pm & 6.30pm-11pm Mon-Sat) Reliable, sensibly priced Italian cuisine in a pair of antique buildings decorated with olive-oil bottles and old cooking implements, some fancifully framed.

Mer du Nord SEAFOOD €
(Map p122; Rue Ste-Catherine 1; 8am-6pm Tue-Sun; M Ste-Catherine) Stand and nibble seafood snacks outside this popular fishmongers if the numerous nearby fish restaurants seem too pricey.

Den Teepot VEGAN €
(Map p122; Rue des Chartreux 66; noon-2pm Mon-Sat;) Above an organic food grocery, this macrobiotic eatery serves a one-choice vegetarian lunch of the day (€8.80).

Pitta Street KEBABS €
(Map p122; Rue du Marché aux Fromages; 11am-3am) Snacks from €3 in a bustling pedestrian street just behind the Grand Place.

Mokafé WAFFLES €
(Map p122; Galerie du Roi; 7.30am-11.30pm) This timeless cafe in the awesome Galeries St-Hubert is ideal for coffee and cakes or €2.60 Brussels waffles.

Fritland CHIPS €
(Map p122; Rue Henri Maus 49; 11am-1am Sun-Thu, 10am-3am Fri & Sat) Sit-down or takeaway *frites* (chips).

MARROLES & SABLON

The Sablon has many interesting, relatively upmarket eateries. Dotted along Rue Haute are several more idiosyncratic choices.

Restobières BELGIAN €€
(Map p118; 02 502 72 51; www.restobieres.eu; Rue des Renards 32; mains €12-22, menus €18-38; noon-3pm Tue-Sat, 6.30pm-11pm Thu-Sat, 4pm-11pm Sun) Beer-based Belgian meals served in a Marolles backstreet amid bottles, grinders and countless antique souvenir biscuit tins featuring Belgian royalty.

Le Perroquet CAFE €
(Map p122; Rue Watteeu 31; light meals €6.50-11; noon-1am) This glorious yet relaxed art-nouveau cafe serves drinks, good-value salads and an imaginative range of stuffed pittas, some vegetarian.

IXELLES

Many ever-buzzing options line Rue St-Boniface while numerous inexpensive world cuisines can be found in the neighbouring streets of Matonge. There are many fashion-conscious restaurants further south around Flagey and Place du Châtelain.

Le Soleil d'Afrique AFRICAN €
(Map p118; Rue Longue-Vie 10; meals €5-8; noon-midnight) Low, low prices for big, big portions of various African favourites – *moambe, yassa, mafé* – best enjoyed on a summer day at the street-side bench tables, which are colourfully graffitied with hippie colours and motifs.

L'Ultime Atome BELGIAN €€
(Map p118; 02 513 13 67; www.ultime-atome.com; Rue St-Boniface 14; mains €11-17; 8.30am-1am Mon-Fri, 10am-1am Sat & Sun; M Porte de Namur) This cavernous brasserie attracts a youthful crowd and the non-stop kitchen turns out great value meals, including mussels, Moroccan *tajines* and cheesy endives.

Drinking

Cafe culture is one of Brussels' greatest attractions. On the Grand Place itself, 300-year-old gems, like **Le Roy d'Espagne**

(Map p122; Grand Place 1) and **Chaloupe d'Or** (Map p122; Grand Place 24) are magnificent but predictably pricey. Somewhat cheaper classics lie around the Bourse, several down easily missed, shoulder-wide alleys. Livelier pubs are ranged around Place St-Géry. The fashion-conscious head further south to Flagey.

Around the Bourse AREA
Many of Brussels's most iconic cafes are within stumbling distance of the Bourse. Don't miss century-old masterpieces **Falstaff** (Map p122; Rue Henri Maus 17; ⌚10am-1am; 🚭), with its festival of stained glass ceilings, and **Le Cirio** (Map p122; Rue de la Bourse 18; ⌚10am-midnight; 🚭), a sumptuous yet affordable 1866 marvel full of polished brasswork and serving great-value pub meals. Three more classics are hidden up shoulder-wide alleys: the medieval yet unpretentious **A l'Image de Nostre-Dame** (Map p122; off Rue du Marché aux Herbes 5; ⌚noon-midnight Mon-Fri, 3pm-1am Sat, 4-10.30pm Sun); the 1695 Rubenseque **Au Bon Vieux Temps** (Map p122; Impasse Saint Michel; ⌚11am-midnight), which sometimes stocks ultra-rare Westvletteren beers (albeit charging €10!); and the 1877 lambic specialist **À la Bécasse** (Map p122; Rue de Tabora 11; ⌚11am-midnight; 🚭), with its vaguely Puritanical rows of wooden tables.

Délirium Café PUB
(Map p122; www.deliriumcafe.be; Impasse de la Fidélité 4A; ⌚10am-4am Mon-Sat, 10am-2am Sun) The smoky main cellar pub has barrel tables, beer-tray ceilings and over 2000 beers. Upstairs, the smoke-free **Tap House** (www.deliriumtaphouse.be) features copper stills, metal panelling and 25 beers on draft. Neighbouring buildings house associated bars (from 8pm) serving hundreds of *jenevers* (Dutch-style gins), vodkas, rums and absinthes. No wonder the little alley's so vibrant. Live music at 10.15pm.

Place St-Géry AREA
Sip a quiet coffee by day or be buffeted by music at night in youthful yet characterful bars – like **Zebra** (Map p122), **Gecko** (Map p122) and **Floreo** (Map p122) – that ring **Café des Halles** (Map p122; www.cafedeshalles.be), an 1881 market hall that's now part cafe, part exhibition hall and hosts a free weekend nightclub in its cellars.

Moeder Lambic Fontainas PUB
(Map p122; Place Fontainas 8; ⌚10am-4am Mon-Sat, 10am-2am Sun; 🚭) A pub with designer decor, dangling trumpet lamps, backlit wall panels and an incredible 40 brews on draft including Cantillon lambics and gueuze.

À la Mort Subite CAFE
(Map p122; Rue Montagne aux Herbes Potagères 7; ⌚11am-midnight; 🚭) Unchanged since 1928, with lined-up wooden tables, arched mirror panels and entertainingly brusque service.

Le Cercle des Voyageurs BAR
(Map p122; www.lecercledesvoyageurs.be; Rue des Grands Carmes 18; ⌚8am-11pm Wed-Mon; 🚭) This high-ceilinged lounge-bar feels like a gentlemen's club and has a library of travel books for browsing.

Goupil le Fol BAR
(Map p122; Rue de la Violette 22; ⌚9pm-5am) A sensory overload of rambling acid-trip passageways, ragged old sofas and inexplicable beverages mostly based on madly fruit-flavoured wines. Soft French chanson music rules.

La Fleur en Papier Doré CAFE
(Map p122; www.goudblommekeinpapier.be; Rue des Alexiens 53; ⌚11am-midnight Tue-Sat, 11am-7pm Sun) Once Magritte's local cafe.

☆ Entertainment

AB LIVE MUSIC
(Map p122; Ancienne Belgique; www.abconcerts.be; Blvd Anspach 110) Great venue for international and home-grown bands.

La Monnaie/De Munt OPERA
(Map p122; www.demunt.be; Place de la Monnaie) Opera, theatre and dance.

BoZar LIVE MUSIC
(Map p122; www.bozar.be; Palais des Beaux-Arts, Rue Ravenstein 23) Music, dance, exhibitions, theatre and more.

Cinematek CINEMA
(Map p122; www.cinematek.be; Rue Baron Horta 9; admission €3; ⌚from 5pm) Classic talkies, plus silent movies with live piano accompaniment.

Nightclubs

Fuse CLUB
(Map p118; www.fuse.be; Rue Blaes 208; admission €5-12; ⌚11pm-7am Fri & Sat; Ⓜ Porte de Hal) The Marolles club that 'invented' European techno still crams in the punters. Half-price entry before midnight.

K-Nal CLUB
(Map p118; www.libertinesupersport.be; Avenue du Port 1; ⌚11pm-6am Sat) On Saturday nights

GAY & LESBIAN BRUSSELS

Brussels' compact, thriving Rainbow Quarter is clustered around Rue du Marché au Charbon, where you'll find two LGBT information centres. A dozen gay-oriented bars here include **L'Homo Erectus** (Map p122; www.lhomoerectus.com; Rue des Pierres 57; ⌚4pm-dawn) and classic 'brown cafe' **Le Belgica** (Map p122; www.lebelgica.be; Rue du Marché au Charbon 32; ⌚10pm-3am Thu-Sun). **Belgian Gay & Lesbian Pride** (www.blgp.be; ⌚1st Sat in May) culminates in this area with a vast-scale all-night party. Sunday, it's gay party night at **Le You** (Map p122; www.leyougayteadance.com; entry €9, free before 10pm). Once a month, **La Démence** (www.lademence.com) at Fuse (p128) is one of Europe's major raves for gay men. Try www.noctis.com/pages/events/gay.php for more information on events and venues.

from 11pm, K-Nal's Libertine Supersport spins house, disco and lounge music and invites the biggest names in electro. Expect queues.

Le You CLUB
(Map p122; www.leyou.be; Rue Duquesnoy 18; admission €10; ⌚from 11pm Thu-Sat, from 9pm Sun) A central labyrinth of dance floors and chill-out rooms, where Thursday is for under 25s and Sunday is gay night.

Shopping

Tourist-oriented shops selling chocolate, beer, lace and Atomium baubles stretch between the Grand Place and Manneken Pis. For better **chocolate shops** (see the boxed text, p156) in calmer, grander settings, peruse the resplendent **Galeries St-Hubert** or the upmarket Sablon area. In the Marolles, Rue Haute and Rue Blaes are full of quirky **interior design shops** while Place du Jeu-de-Balle has a daily **flea market** (Map p118; ⌚6am-2pm). Rue Antoine Dansaert has most of Brussels' **high-fashion boutiques**, with **Stijl** (Map p122; Rue Antoine Dansaert 74) hosting many cutting-edge collections.

Supermarkets sell a range of **Belgian beers** relatively cheaply. For wider selections and the relevant glasses, try the following:

Délices et Caprices (Map p122; www.the-belgian-beer-tasting-shop.be; Rue des Bouchers 68; ⌚2-8pm Thu-Mon) Small, friendly and personal.

Beermania (Map p118; www.beermania.be; Chaussée de Wavre 174; ⌚11am-9pm Mon-Sat)

De Biertempel (Map p122; www.biertempel.be; Rue du Marché aux Herbes 56b; ⌚9.30am-7pm)

Beer Planet (Map p122; www.beerplanet.eu; Rue de la Fourche 45; ⌚1-9pm Tue-Sun)

Information

Internet Access

Free at Use-It (see the boxed text, p130) and upstairs within **Bibliothèque des Riches Claires** (Rue des Riches Claires 24; ⌚12.30pm-3.30pm Tue, 12.30-5.30pm Wed, 10am-3pm Thu, 10am-5pm Fri, 9.30-11.30am Sat).

Money

ATMs are widespread. Exchange agency rates are usually best around the Bourse.

Tourist Information

There are info counters at Brussels Airport and Bruxelles-Midi station.

Brussels International (☎02 513 89 40; www.visitbrussels.be; Grand Place; ⌚9am-6pm Mon-Sat, plus Sun in summer) Cramped and often packed city info office within the town hall.

Flanders Info (☎02 504 03 90; www.visitflanders.com; Rue du Marché aux Herbes 61; ⌚9am-6pm Mon-Sat, 10am-5pm Sun; 📶)

Getting There & Away

AIR See p157.

BUS Eurolines (☎02 274 13 50; www.eurolines.be; Rue du Progrès 80; ⌚5.45am-8.45pm; 🚉Gare du Nord) International buses depart from Bruxelles-Nord train station; see p158.

TRAIN Eurostar, TGV and Thalys high-speed trains stop only at **Bruxelles-Midi** (Brussel-Zuid). Jump on any local service for the four-minute hop to conveniently central **Bruxelles-Central**. All domestic trains (p159), plus some Amsterdam services, stop there anyway. Consult www.b-rail.be for timetable information.

Getting Around

To/From the Airport

For Brussels-South Charleroi airport, see p157.

TRAIN Four trains depart each hour from 5.30am to 11.50pm. It costs €5.10 and takes 16 minutes from Bruxelles-Central, 20 minutes from Bruxelles-Midi.

TAXI Fares cost around €35. Bad idea in rush hour traffic.

USE-IT!

Use-It (Map p122; www.use-it.be; Rue de la Fourche 50; ⏲10am-1pm & 2-6pm Mon-Sat) creates brilliant info maps, full of irreverent, spot-on tips from locals. They're available as downloads or free from hostels and tourist info places (ask!). Cities covered so far are Brussels, Bruges, Antwerp, Ghent, Leuven, Charleroi and Mechelen.

Bicycle

SHORT-TERM HIRE With **Villo!** (www.villo.be; ⏲24hrs), you can ride a bike from A to B, drop it off, then take a new one for the next hop. The first 30 minutes is free, but costs, charged automatically to your credit card, rise rapidly if you keep it longer (one/two/three hours €0.50/3.50/7.50). Keep the bike 24hr and you've automatically 'bought' it (€150). Some of the 180 automated rental pick-up/drop-off stations are credit-card equipped for paying the initial membership subscription (per day/week/year €1.50/7/30). High-toll helpline ☎078 05 11 10 works only during office hours.

LONGER HIRE **FietsPunt/PointVelo** (www.recyclo.org; per 1/3 days €7.50/15; ⏲7am-7pm Mon-Fri) is located outside Bruxelles-Central's Madeleine exit. You'll need ID, plus a credit card or a €150 cash deposit.

TOURS **Brussels Bike Tours** (www.brusselsbiketours.com; tour incl bicycle rental adult/student €30/25; ⏲10am & 3pm Apr-Sep, 11am Oct), with a maximum group size of 12, start from the Grand Place tourist office and take around 3½ hours, including stops for beer and *frites*.

Public Transport

INFORMATION Fare/route information at www.stib.be.

COSTS Tickets, once validated, can be used on any combination of the metro, trams and city buses, with the exception of reaching the airport. A one-hour 'jump' ticket costs €1.70/2 when pre-purchased/bought aboard. Booklets of five/10 tickets cost €7.30/11.20. A one-/three-day unlimited pass costs €4.50/9.50.

OPERATING HOURS From 6am to midnight daily. Limited 'Noctis' buses (€3) run from midnight to 3am Friday and Saturday.

Taxi

Taxis cost €2.40 flag fall plus €1.35 per kilometre in Brussels, €2.70 per beyond city limits (eg airport, Tervuren). Taxis ranks are located at Bruxelles-Midi and Madeleine, or pre-book on ☎02 268 00 00 or ☎02 349 49 49.

AROUND BRUSSELS

Leuven

POP 92,000

Home to Leffe and Stella Artois, Leuven (Louvain in French; www.leuven.be) is Flanders' premier university town and is a lively, self-confident ancient city. Although the town was heavily damaged in 20th-century wars, Leuven's flamboyant 15th-century **Stadhuis** (Grote Markt 9; admission €2) survived. Covered in statuary, it's one of Europe's most architecturally ornate city halls.

Leuven adds only a minor detour to the train ride between Brussels (€4.80, 30 minutes, five hourly) and Antwerp (€6.60, 45 minutes, hourly). In between also consider stops in historic **Mechelen** or very pretty **Lier**.

Waterloo

POP 31,000

European history changed course in June 1815 when Napoleon was definitively defeated at the Battle of Waterloo, 20km south of Brussels. The battlefield, a vast patchwork of rolling fields, has a hamlet of visitor attractions. Most striking is a grassy hill topped with a great bronze **lion**, which you can climb (€6) to survey the scene. Enter through the large **visitor centre** (www.waterloo1815.be; ⏲10am-5pm); the 'Lion Pass' (adult/concession €8.50/6.50) adds in a 20-minute film. Guided truck tours to some outer battle sites cost €5.50 or combine all the above for €12. Check out the hamlet's 19th-century cafes too.

Despite the name, the battlefield-hamlet is some 5km south of Waterloo town (www.waterloo-tourisme.be). Instead of arriving at Waterloo's inconvenient train station, get within 800m of the battlefield by TEC bus W from either Avenue Fonsny (outside Bruxelles-Midi in Brussels) or from the much closer Braine l'Alleud train station on the Brussels–Charleroi line.

FLANDERS

Antwerp

POP 457,000

Cosmopolitan, confident and full of contrasts, Antwerp (Antwerpen in Dutch, Anvers in French) was one of northern Europe's foremost cities in the 17th century when it also was home to Pieter Paul Rubens, diplomat, philosopher and northern Europe's greatest baroque artist. Today it once again revels in fame and fortune attracting art lovers and mode moguls, club queens and diamond dealers.

Sights

CITY CENTRE

Grote Markt SQUARE
Antwerp's photogenic epicentre, this pedestrianised square is graced by a Renaissance-style **Stadhuis** and the baroque **Brabo Fountain**, featuring a bronze hero throwing the severed hand of a dastardly giant. This illustrates the legend that romantics still use to explain Antwerp's disputed etymology, 'Hand Werpen' (hand throwing) becoming Antwerpen.

Onze-Lieve-Vrouwekathedraal CATHEDRAL
(www.dekathedraal.be; Handschoenmarkt; adult/concession €5/3; ⏲10am-5pm Mon-Fri, 10am-3pm Sat, 10am-4pm Sun) Belgium's largest Gothic cathedral, built between 1352 and 1521, still dominates the city skyline thanks to a steeple that is arguably the most magnificent in Europe. Priceless artworks inside include two world-famous Rubens tableaux.

Museum Plantin-Moretus HISTORIC BUILDING
(www.museumplantinmoretus.be; Vrijdag Markt 22; adult/under 26yr €6/4; ⏲10am-5pm Tue-Sun) Antwerp has saved numerous historic homes as art-filled museums, but none can compare with this enchanting medieval building that once housed the world's first industrial printing works, which published books including those by Rubens' brother. Highlights include the formal courtyard garden, 1640 library and historic print shop.

ANTWERP MONEYSAVERS

Sold at tourist offices, the two-day **Museumkaart (€20)** provides free city transport and entrance to 15 museums and five significant churches, including all sights reviewed below. Most city-run museums are free anyway if you're under 19 or over 65. Many, including Museum Plantin-Moretus and Rubenshuis, are free for everyone on the last Wednesday of each month.

Rubenshuis HISTORIC BUILDING
(www.museum.antwerpen.be; Wapper 9-11; adult/concession €6/4; ⏲10am-5pm Tue-Sun) Rubens' Antwerp home and studio has been meticulously restored and rebuilt along original lines and filled with 17th-century artworks, albeit relatively few by the master himself. The full 90-minute audioguide visit may prove overly detailed for many visitors.

Scheldt Riverbank NEIGHBOURHOOD
The Scheldt River (Schelde in Dutch), Antwerp's economic lifeline, offers a riverside stroll along **Zuiderterras**, a raised promenade that runs south from **Het Steen** castle. At the tree-lined square **St-Jansvliet**, a lift descends to the **St-Annatunnel** (free), allowing pedestrians and cyclists to cross 570m beneath the river to the **Linkeroever** (Left Bank) for a city panorama.

Meir NEIGHBOURHOOD
If walking from the main train station to Groenplaats, revel in the grand, statue-draped architecture of pedestrianised Meir and Leystraat. The gilt-overloaded **Stadsfeestzaal** (Meir 76) is one of the world's most indulgently decorated shopping malls. Watch top-quality chocolates being made at **Chocolate Line** (www.thechocolateline.be; ⏲10.30am-6.30pm) in the 1745 **Paleis op de Meir** (www.paleisopdemeir.be; Meir 50).

STATION AREA

Antwerpen-Centraal train station is an attraction in itself and the famous **Antwerp zoo** is just outside.

The Diamond Quarter NEIGHBOURHOOD
(www.awdc.be) An astounding 80% of all the world's uncut diamonds are traded in Antwerp's architecturally miserable diamond district, immediately southwest of Antwerpen-Centraal station. For the cost of a smile you can see gem polishers at work at **Diamondland** (www.diamondland.be; Appelmansstraat 33a; admission free; ⏲9.30am-5pm Mon-Sat), which is essentially a zero-pressure lure to get visitors into a diamond salesroom. The well explained **Diamond Museum** (Koningin Astridplein 19-23; adult/concession €8/4; ⏲10am-5.30pm Tue-Thu) has changing jewellery 'treasure shows' and similar live gem-polishing demonstrations.

'T ZUID

Around 1km south of the fashion quarter, 't Zuid is a conspicuously prosperous area dotted with century-old architecture, hip bars, fine restaurants and interesting museums.

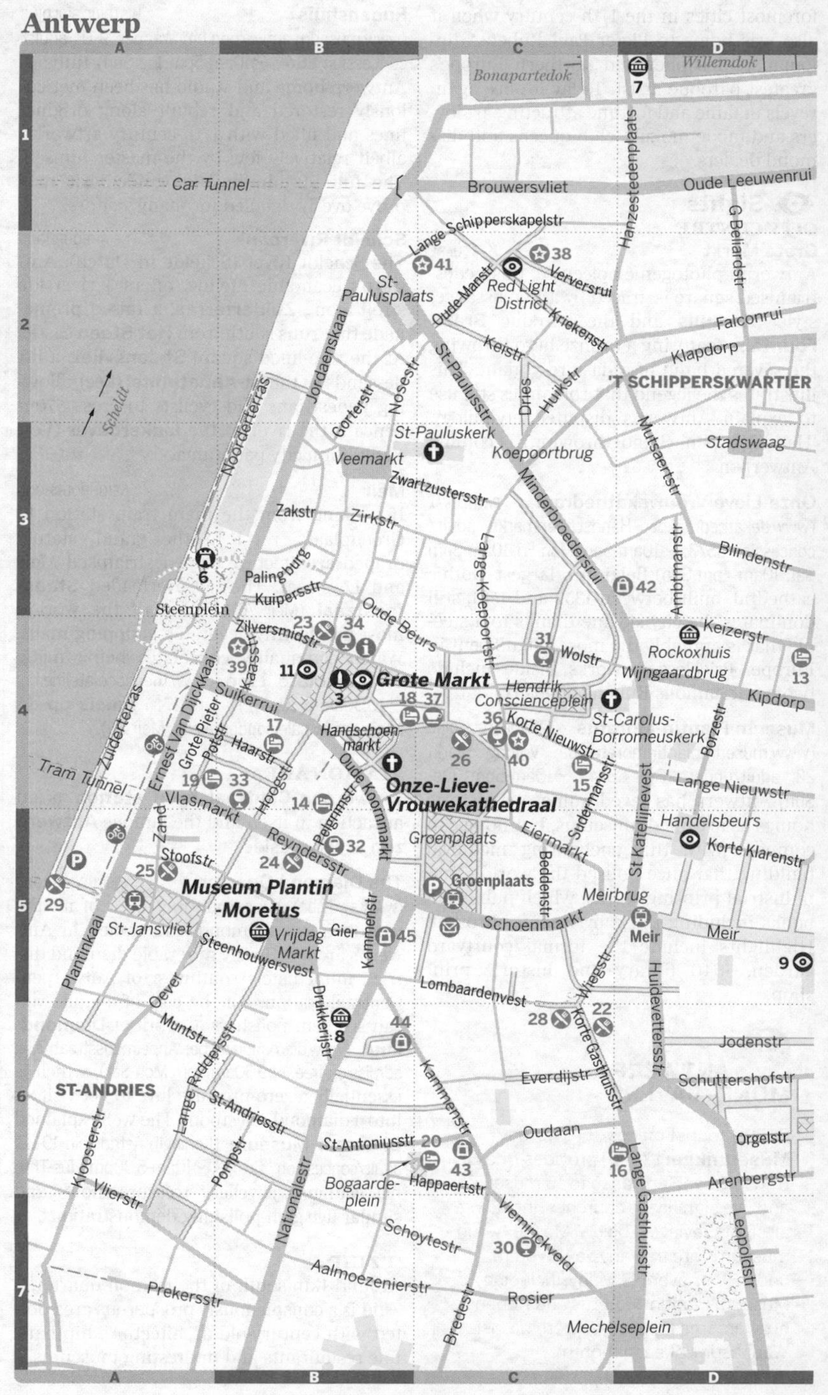
A
B
C
D
1
2
3
4
5
6
7
Bonapartedok
Willemdok
7
Car Tunnel
Brouwersvliet
Oude Leeuwenrui
Hanzestedenplaats
G Beliardstr
Lange Schipperskapelstr
38
41
Red Light District
Verversrui
St-Paulusplaats
Oude Manstr
Kriekenstr
Falconrui
Keistr
Klapdorp
St-Paulusstr
Dries
Huikstr
'T SCHIPPERSKWARTIER
Jordaenskaai
Nosestr
Gorterstr
Noorderterras
Scheldt
St-Pauluskerk
Koepoortbrug
Mutsaertstr
Stadswaag
Veemarkt
Zwartzustersstr
Minderbroedersrui
Zakstr
Zirkstr
Lange Koepoortstr
Blindenstr
6
Palingburg
42
Ambtmanstr
Kuipersstr
Steenplein
Oude Beurs
23
34
Keizerstr
Zilversmidstr
Rockoxhuis
31
13
39
Wolstr
Wijngaardbrug
11
Grote Markt
3
Hendrik Conscienceplein
Kaasstr
Suikerrui
18
37
Kipdorp
17
Handschoenmarkt
36
St-Carolus-Borromeuskerk
Borzestr
Zuiderterras
Korte Nieuwstr
Haarstr
26
40
Tram Tunnel
Ernest Van Dijckkaai
Grote Pieter Potstr
Oude Koornmarkt
15
19
33
Hoogstr
Onze-Lieve-Vrouwekathedraal
Lange Nieuwstr
Vlasmarkt
14
Pelgrimstr
Sudermanstr
Handelsbeurs
Zand
Reyndersstr
Groenplaats
Eiermarkt
Korte Klarenstr
32
Stoofstr
24
Beddenstr
25
St Katelijnevest
Museum Plantin -Moretus
Groenplaats
Meirbrug
29
Schoenmarkt
St-Jansvliet
Vrijdag Markt
Gier
45
Meir
Meir
Steenhouwersvest
Kammenstr
9
Plantinkaai
Oever
Lombaardenvest
Wiegstr
Huidevettersstr
Drukkerijstr
22
Muntstr
8
44
28
Korte Gasthuisstr
Jodenstr
Everdijstr
Schuttershofstr
ST-ANDRIES
Lange Ridderstr
Kammenstr
St-Andriesstr
Oudaan
Orgelstr
St-Antoniusstr
20
Kloosterstr
43
16
Lange Gasthuisstr
Arenbergstr
Pompstr
Bogaardeplein
Happaertstr
Vlierstr
Nationalestr
Schoytestr
Vleminckveld
Leopoldstr
30
Aalmoezenierstr
Prekersstr
Rosier
Bredestr
Mechelseplein

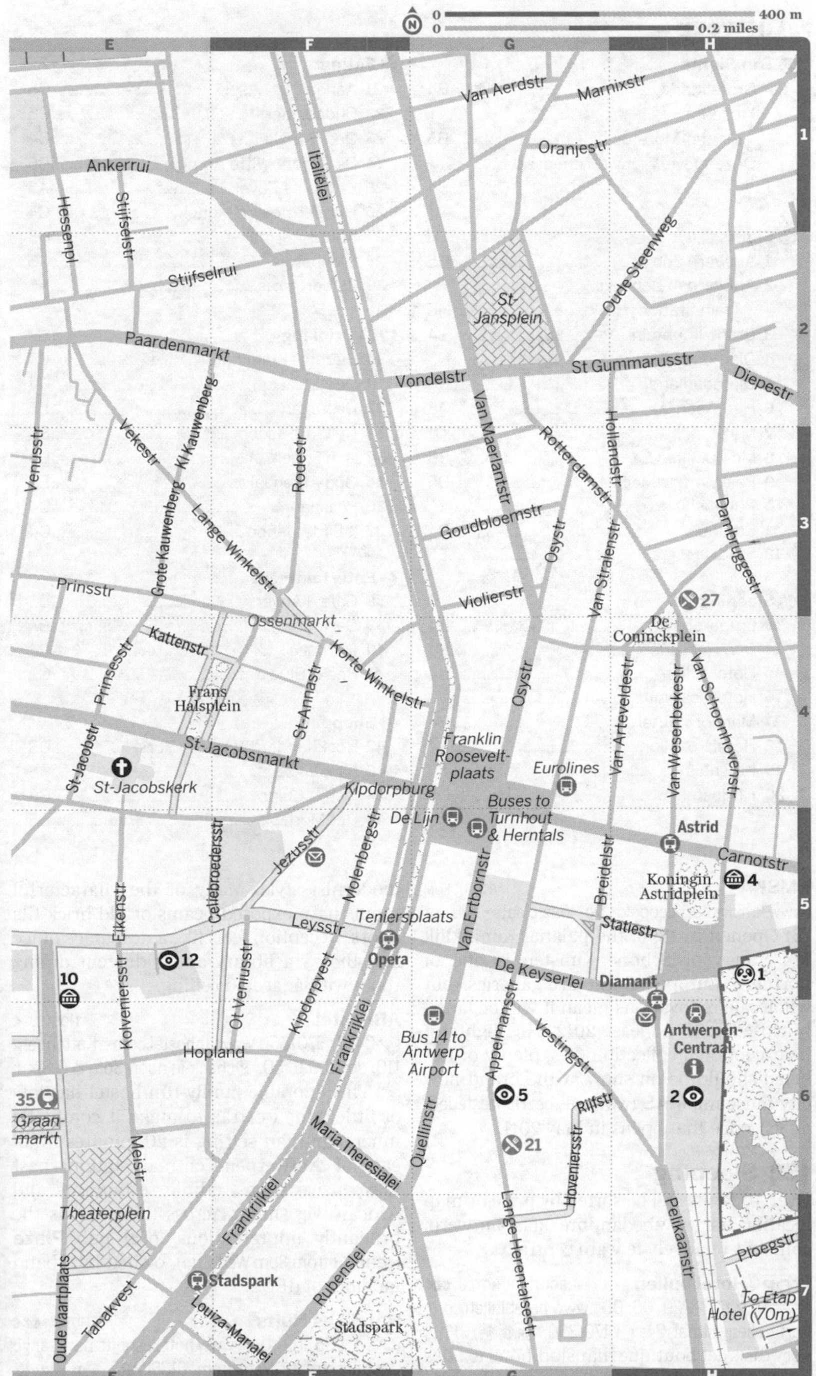
0 400 m
0 0.2 miles
E
F
G
H
1
2
3
4
5
6
7
Van Aerdstr
Marnixstr
Oranjestr
Ankerrui
Italiëlei
Hessenpl
Stijfselstr
Stijfselrui
Oude Steenweg
St-Jansplein
Paardenmarkt
Vondelstr
St Gummarusstr
Diepestr
Venusstr
Vekestr
Kl Kauwenberg
Rodestr
Van Maerlantstr
Rotterdamstr
Hollandstr
Damburggestr
Grote Kauwenberg
Lange Winkelstr
Goudbloemstr
Osystr
Van Stralenstr
Prinsstr
Violierstr
27
Ossenmarkt
Kattenstr
De Coninckplein
Korte Winkelstr
Prinsesstr
Frans Halsplein
St-Annastr
Osystr
Van Arteveldestr
Van Wesenbekestr
Van Schoonhovenstr
St-Jacobsmarkt
Franklin Rooseveltplaats
Eurolines
St-Jacobstr
St-Jacobskerk
Kipdorpburg
Buses to Turnhout & Herntals
De Lijn
Astrid
Carnotstr
Jezusstr
Molenbergstr
Van Ertbornstr
Breidelstr
Koningin Astridplein
4
Cellebroedersstr
Eikenstr
Leysstr
Teniersplaats
Opera
Statiestr
12
De Keyserlei
Diamant
1
10
Ot Veniusstr
Kipdorpvest
Appelmansstr
Vestingstr
Kolveniersstr
Frankrijklei
Bus 14 to Antwerp Airport
Antwerpen-Centraal
Hopland
35
Graanmarkt
5
Rijfstr
2
Meistr
Maria Theresialei
Quellinstr
21
Hoveniersstr
Theaterplein
Frankrijklei
Lange Herentalsestr
Pelikaanstr
Ploegstr
Rubenslei
Oude Vaartplaats
Tabakvest
Stadspark
Louiza-Marialei
Stadspark
To Etap Hotel (70m)

Antwerp

Top Sights
Grote Markt B4
Museum Plantin-Moretus B5
Onze-Lieve-Vrouwekathedraal B4

Sights
1 Antwerp Zoo H5
2 Antwerpen Centraal Train Station H6
3 Brabo Fountain B4
4 Diamond Museum H5
5 Diamondland G6
6 Het Steen A3
7 MAS D1
8 MoMu B6
9 Paleis op de Meir D5
10 Rubenshuis E5
11 Stadhuis B4
12 Stadsfeestzaal E5

Sleeping
13 Emperor's 48 .... D4
14 Den Heksenketel B4
15 Hotel Julien C4
16 Hotel Les Nuits D6
17 Matelote Hotel B4
18 Hotel Postiljon B4
19 Katshuis A4
20 HI Hostel C6

Eating
21 Aahaar G6
22 Chocolatiers C6
23 De 7 Schaken B4
24 De Groote Witte Arend B5
25 De Kleine Zavel A5
26 Het Vermoeide Model C4
27 Kubus Permeke H3
28 Lombardia C6
29 Zuiderterras A5

Drinking
30 Bierhuis Kulminator C7
31 De Kat C4
32 De Vagant B5
33 De Ware Jacob B4
34 Den Engel B4
35 Oud Arsenaal E6
36 Pelikaan C4
37 't Elfde Gebod C4

Entertainment
38 Café d'Anvers C2
39 Cartoons B4
40 De Muze C4
41 Red & Blue C2

Shopping
42 Boekhandel 't Verschil Burie D3
43 Fans C6
44 Fish & Chips B6
45 Het Modepaleis B5

KMSKA ART MUSEUM
(www.kmska.be; Leopold De Waelplaats; 1 or 23) Opened in 1890, the palatial Koninklijk Museum voor Schone Kunsten is one of northern Europe's finest art galleries, but wholesale renovations mean it will be largely closed until at least 2012. Highlights of its exceptional collection (yes, plenty of Rubens) should be on show at the brand new city museum, **MAS** (www.mas.be; Hanzestedenplaats), once that opens in May 2011.

Sleeping

Over 40 B&Bs can be sorted by price or map location on www.bedandbreakfast-antwerp.com, but relatively few are central.

TOP CHOICE **Hotel Julien** BOUTIQUE HOTEL €€€
(03 229 06 00; www.hotel-julien.com; Korte Nieuwstraat 24; r €170-290;) This very discreet boutique mansion-hotel exudes a tastefully understated elegance and subtle modernist style. Many of the characterful rooms have exposed beams or old brick-tile floors. Reception feels like a designer's office and there's a library and indulgent dining room with a faceted ceiling.

ABhostel HOSTEL €
(0473 570166; www.abhostel.com; Kattenberg 110; dm/d €21/50; check-in noon-3pm & 6-8pm;) This adorable family-run hostel has lots of little added extras to make it comfy. Its inner-suburban setting is 20-minutes' walk east of Antwerpen-Centraal station, past inexpensive shops, ethnic restaurants and African wig shops. Across the street is the brilliantly unpretentious local pub **Plaza Real** (from 8pm Wed-Sun), owned by a band member of dEUS.

Hotel Les Nuits HOTEL €€€
(03 225 02 04; www.hotellesnuits.be; Lange Gasthuisstraat; d/ste from €135/215;) Black-

on-black corridors that are fashionable fantasies more than Halloween howlers lead to 24 designer-modernist rooms, each with its own special touches, super-comfy bed and rainforest shower. Sauna and *hamam* (Turkish baths) are free. Breakfast (€12.50) is taken in the casually suave restaurant where you check in; there's no reception.

Hotel Postiljon FAMILY HOTEL **€€**
(☎03 231 75 75; www.hotelpostiljon.be; Blauwmoezelstraat 6; s/d €65/75, with shared toilet from €45/60; 📶) You can't be closer to the cathedral than this! The 21 older rooms are simple and staid, albeit with partly stained-glass windows. However, the 10 'business rooms' at the back (from s/d €90/120) are new and contrastingly modernist. Free wi-fi; breakfast €10.

Katshuis GUEST HOUSE **€**
(☎0476 206947; www.katshuis.be; Grote Pieter Potstraat 18 & 19; s/d/tr €35/50/80) Stairs are steep and rooms vary here. While none are overly polished, some have a microwave, chandeliers and wooden beams and all are remarkably good value. Phone ahead to arrange a check-in time (after 4pm). Check-out is a luxuriously late 2pm. Coffee but not breakfast is included.

HI Hostel HOSTEL **€**
(Jeugdherberg; ☎03 238 02 73; www.vjh.be/antwerpen.htm) The old Op Sinjoorke hostel is tatty and very inconveniently located, but, from Easter 2011, a brand new custom-built hostel should (if not delayed again) replace it on helpfully central Bogaardeplein. Most locals haven't a clue where that is, so use our map!

Den Heksenketel HOSTEL **€**
(☎0489 395780; www.denheksenketel.com; Pelgrimstraat 22; dm €20; 📶) Rough-edged but super-central two-dorm backpacker hostel above a decent bar on a buzzing, pedestrianised street that has an unbeatable cathedral view. Only two toilets. New management plans improvements in 2011.

Matelote Hotel BOUTIQUE HOTEL **€€**
(☎03 201 88 00; www.hotel-matelote.be; Haarstraat 11; r €90-190; @📶) Discreet new design hotel on a pedestrianised backstreet in the heart of the city, with 10 contemporary rooms, tastefully arranged in a 16th-century building. Breakfast costs €12.

Emperor's 48 B&B **€€**
(☎03 288 73 37; www.emperors48.com; Keizerstraat 48; s/d €60/80, apt €150; @) If you like his distinctive photographic art (www.bartmichielsen.net), you'll love Bart Michielsen's stylishly low-lit, gay-friendly B&B in a well-located 1878 town house.

Eating

For cheap, central snacks, stroll Hoogstraat, near the cathedral. For cosy, pricier options look in parallel Pelgrimstraat (with it's 'secret' medieval alley, Vlaaikeusgang) or the picturesque lanes leading to Rubens' wonderful but fire-damaged St-Carolus-Borromeuskerk. For confectioners and **chocolatiers**, try the lanes around Lombardia. In 't Zuid (off our map, to the south) you'll find a great mix of options, both hip and historic, north and west of KMSKA.

De Groote Witte Arend BELGIAN **€€**
(☎03 233 50 33; www.degroottewittearend.be; Braderijstraat 24; snacks €4-9, mains €12-20; ⏰10.30am-midnight) Well-cooked Belgian classics, including *stoemp*, eel, shrimp croquettes and rabbit in Westmalle, are served around the open cloister of a partly 16th-century former convent with its own preserved chapel. The bar stocks more than 80 Belgian beers.

FASHION FRENZY

Now snapping at the heels of Milan and New York, Antwerp has emerged as an avant-garde fashion capital thanks to talented alumni of the Flanders Fashion Institute, which now hosts a style museum, **MoMu** (www.momu.be; Nationalestraat 28; adult/concession €7/5; ⏰10am-6pm Tue-Sun), featuring regularly changing exhibitions. This is the epicentre of Antwerp's 'fashion district'. Designer boutiques huddle here, around the striking **Toneelhuis** theatre and line Schuttershofstraat, Huidevettersstraat and Nationalestraat, where **Het Modepaleis** (www.driesvannoten.be; Nationalestraat 16) is the elegant flat-iron shaped flagship outlet of Dries Van Noten. Kammenstraat focuses more on street wear (**Fans**, **Fish'n'Chips**). There's also plenty of choice scattered around 't Zuid, including **Ann Demeulemeester** (www.anndemeulemeester.be; Verlatstraat 38) and the cutting-edge multi-designer outlet **Hospital** (www.hospital-antwerp.com; De Burburestraat 4a; ⏰1-6.30pm Tue-Sun).

Het Vermoeide Model BELGIAN €€
(☎03 233 52 61; Lijnwaadmarkt 2; mains €16.50-25, set menu €26; ⏲4-10pm Tue-Sun) This atmospheric medieval house-restaurant is full of exposed brickwork and chandeliers, with a creaky stairway leading up to a secret little roof terrace (advance bookings advised in summer). The menu includes steaks, ribs, *waterzooi* (€17.50) and seasonal mussels in Calvados.

Lombardia ORGANIC, VEGAN €€
(www.lombardia.be; Lombaardenvest 78; sandwiches €7.20-12, vegan/non-veg lunch €13.50/15.50; ⏲7.45am-6pm Mon-Sat; ☑) Experience frothy Ginger Love (www.gingerlove.be; €4) at this legendary health-food shop-cum-cafe, whose owner has cooked for Sting and Moby. The mostly vegie food is 100% organic and the colourful decor has a simple if whacky comic-book feel.

De Kleine Zavel MEDITERRANEAN €€€
(☎03 231 96 91; www.kleinezavel.be; Stoofstraat 2; mains €23-30; ⏲noon-2.30pm & 6-11pm Wed-Sun) The informal bistro-style decor belies this restaurant's high gastronomic standing for fusion cuisine with an accent on fish and Mediterranean flavours.

Zuiderterras EUROPEAN €€
(☎03 234 12 75; www.zuiderterras.be; Ernest van Dijckkaai 37; mains €16-25; ⏲9am-midnight) This bustling contemporary cafe-restaurant is an Antwerp landmark, with summer terrace and year-round river views, if somewhat patchy service. Reservations advised.

De 7 Schaken BISTRO €€
(www.de7schaken.be; Braderijstraat 24; snacks €7-10, mains €12-22; ⏲11am-11pm) Entered through a wood-panelled pub just off Grote Markt, this traditionally styled bistro serves sensibly priced Belgian classics and stays open all day. Multilingual menus.

Aahaar INDIAN, VEGAN €
(www.aahaar.com; Lange Herentalsestraat 23; mains/buffet €6.80/9; ⏲noon-3pm & 6-9.30pm; ☑) You don't need to be one of the neighbourhood's diamond dealers to afford Aahaar's highly recommended five-dish buffets that are 100% vegetarian.

Kubus Permeke BUDGET €
(www.casvzw.eu; De Coninckplein 25; sandwiches/mains/set menu from €2.40/8.70/10.50; ⏲10am-8.30pm Mon-Thu, 10am-2.30pm Fri-Sun) This architecturally interesting glass cube serves bargain meals, primarily to low income families, but they're available to all...And far better than you might anticipate.

Drinking

To sound like a local, stride into a pub and ask for a *bolleke*. Don't worry, that means a 'little bowl' (ie glass) of De Koninck, the city's favourite ale. Cheap places to try it include classic, smoky 'brown cafes' **Oud Arsenaal** (Pijpelincxstraat 4; ⏲9am-7.30pm Fri-Wed), **De Kat** (Wolstraat 22), **De Ware Jacob** (Vlasmarkt 19) and the livelier **Pelikaan** (Melkmarkt 14).

Den Engel BAR
(Grote Markt 5; ⏲9am-2am) Historic watering hole whose terrace provides perfect views across the main square.

De Vagant GIN CAFE
(www.devagant.be; Reyndersstraat 25; ⏲11am-2am) More than 200 types of *jenever* (Dutch gin; €2.20 to €7.50) served in a bare-boards local cafe or sold by the bottle from their bottle shop, which resembles an old-style pharmacy.

't Elfde Gebod BAR
(www.kathedraalcafe.be; Torfbrug 10; ⏲noon-11pm Mon-Sat, noon-10pm Sun; ⊖) This ivy-clad medieval masterpiece has an utterly astounding interior decked with angels, saints, pulpits and several deliciously sacrilegious visual jokes.

Bierhuis Kulminator BEER PUB
(Vleminckveld 32; ⏲8pm-midnight Mon, 11am-midnight Tue-Fri, 5pm-late Sat) Classic pub boasting 700 mostly Belgian brews, including rare vintage bottles.

Bar Tabac BAR
(www.bartabac.be; Waalsekaai 43; ⏲9pm-7am Wed-Sat) Unpretentious, low-lit one-room bar in 't Zuid that tries hard not to try hard. If you prefer smoother lounge-style bars, there's half a dozen close by. Westmalle on tap goes for just €2.40.

GAY ANTWERP

Antwerp's vibrant LGBT scene is widely diffused around town, with relevant places usually flying rainbow flags. Tourism Antwerp produces a useful multilingual map-guide *Gay Antwerpen*, with more information available from gay-and-lesbian bookshop-cafe **Boekhandel 't Verschil** (www.verschil.be; Minderbroedersrui 33; ⏲11am-6pm).

TRAINS FROM ANTWERPEN-CENTRAAL

DESTINATION	FARE (€)	DURATION (MIN)	FREQUENCY (PER HR)
Amsterdam	26.90	190	1
Bruges	14.20	70	1
Brussels	6.30	35-50	5
Ghent	9.90	50	2
Leuven	6.60	45	2
Liège	14.80	125	1
Lier	2.50	15	2
Mechelen	2.90	15	2

☆ Entertainment

For listings consult www.weekup.be/antwerpen/week; www.zva.be in summer; and www.gratisinantwerpen.be for free events.

Café Local CLUB

(www.cafelocal.be; Waalsekaai 25; members/non-members €9/10; ⌚10pm-late Thu-Sat; 🚋8) This large, unintimidating nightclub in 't Zuid takes a salsa-merengue turn on the first Sunday of each month. Several nearby lounges and music-bars on Waalsekaai and Luikstraat also crank up the music till the wee hours.

De Muze LIVE MUSIC

(☎03 226 01 26; Melkmarkt 15; ⌚noon-4am) This two-level cafe is a bastion of live jazz Monday to Saturday from 10pm. There's also a heavy-rock joint across the street and various live-music alternatives a block north.

Cartoons CINEMA

(www.cartoons-cinema.be; Kaasstraat 4-6) Art-house and quality foreign movies.

Café d'Anvers CLUB

(www.cafe-d-anvers.com; Verversrui 15; ⌚11pm-7.30am Fri & Sat; 🚋7) A club not a cafe, this legendary place pumps out funk, house, disco and soul in the city's red-light district. Many of Belgium's top DJs started here.

Red & Blue CLUB

(www.redandblue.be; Lange Schipperskapelstraat 11; ⌚11pm-7am Fri & Sat; 🚋7) On Saturday nights it's one of Europe's best-loved gay discos for men. It goes mixed on Fridays.

ℹ Information

TOURIST INFORMATION Tourism Antwerp (☎03 232 01 03; www.visitantwerpen.be; Grote Markt 13; ⌚9am-5.45pm Mon-Sat, 9am-4.45pm Sun) is a central tourist office with a branch on level zero of Antwerpen-Centraal train station.

ℹ Getting There & Away

BUS Regional **De Lijn** (www.delijn.be) and international **Eurolines** (☎03 233 86 62; www.eurolines.com; Van Stralenstraat 8; ⌚9am-5.45pm Mon-Fri, 9am-3.15pm Sat) buses both depart from points near Franklin Rooseveltplaats. **Ecolines** (www.ecolines.net) buses for Eastern Europe depart from near Antwerpen-Berchem train station, 2km southeast of Antwerpen-Centraal.

TRAIN Antwerpen-Centraal Station (🚋Diamant), 1.5km east of the historic centre, is a veritable cathedral of a building, considered by many to be among the world's most handsome stations. Seven daily high-speed trains run to Paris (from €48, 125 minutes).

ℹ Getting Around

Franklin Rooseveltplaats and Koningin Astridplein are hubs for the integrated network of **De Lijn** (www.delijn.be) buses and trams.

Ghent

POP 235,000

Known as Gent in Dutch and Gand in French, Ghent is Flanders' unsung historic city. Like a grittier Bruges without the crush of tourists, it sports photogenic canals, medieval towers, great cafes and some of Belgium's most inspired museums. Always a lively student city, things go crazy in mid-July during the 10-day **Gentse Feesten** (www.gentsefeesten.be), a citywide party of music and theatre incorporating **10 Days Off** (www.10daysoff.be), one of Europe's biggest techno parties.

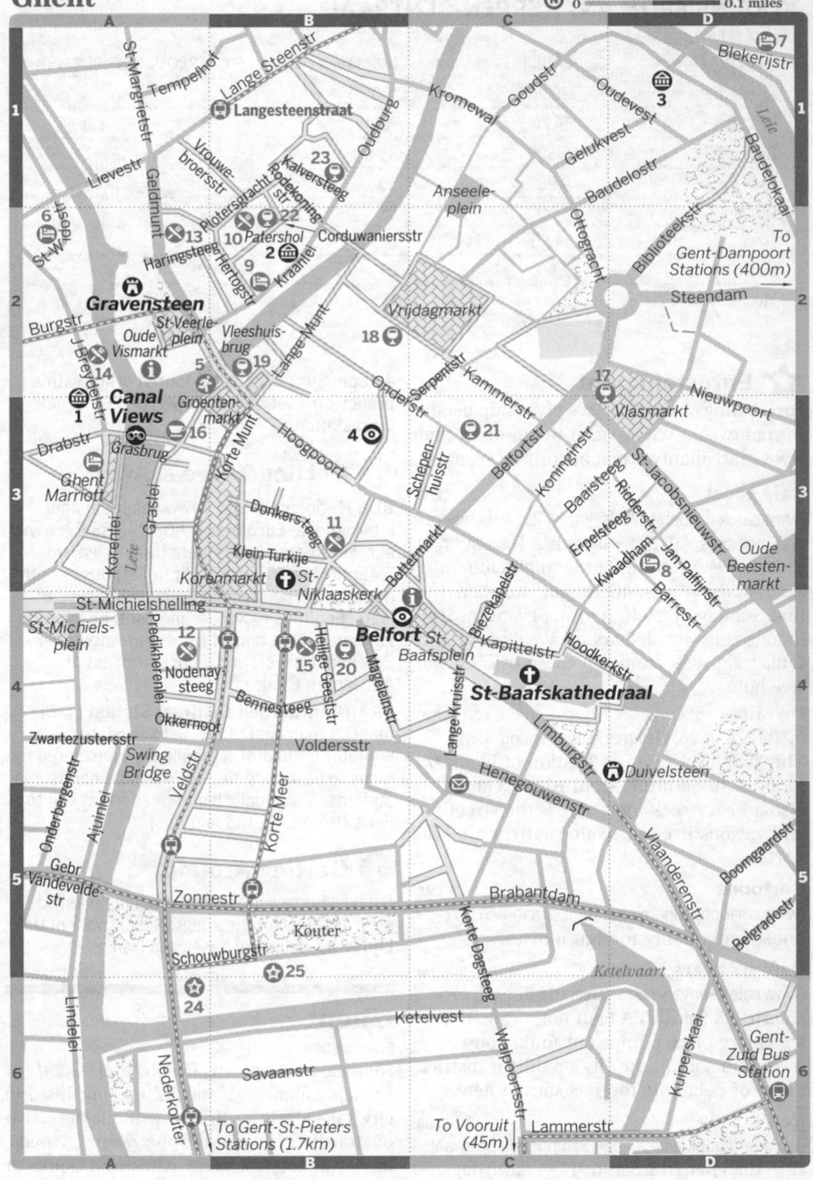

BELGIUM FLANDERS

Sights

CITY CENTRE

The main sights are strolling distance from Korenmarkt, the westernmost of three interlinked squares that form the heart of Ghent's historic core.

TOP CHOICE Graslei & Patershol NEIGHBOURHOOD
For one of Belgium's most picturesque views, cross **Grasbrug** bridge and look towards **Graslei**, the city's favoured waterfront promenade, lined with archetypal step-gabled warehouses and town houses.

Ghent

Top Sights
Belfort............B4
Canal Views............A3
Gravensteen............A2
St-Baafskathedraal............C4

Sights
1 Design Museum............A3
2 Huis van Alijn............B2
3 MIAT............D1
4 Werregarensteeg............B3

Activities, Courses & Tours
5 Canal Tours............A2

Sleeping
6 De Draecke............A2
7 Hostel 47............D1
8 Hotel Flandria............D3
9 Hotel Harmony............B2

Eating
10 Amadeus............B2
11 Amadeus............B3
12 Brasserie Pakhuis............A4
13 Eethuis Avalon............A2
14 House of Eliott............A2
15 Soup'r............B4

Drinking
16 Callisto Tearoom............A3
17 Charlatan............C2
18 Herberg de Dulle Griet............B2
19 Het Waterhuis aan de Bierkant............B2
Hot Club de Gand............(see 19)
20 Limonada............B4
21 Pink Flamingo's............C3
22 Rococo............B2
't Caffetse............(see 2)
't Dreupelkot............(see 19)
23 't Velootje............B1

Entertainment
24 De Vlaamse Opera............A6
25 Handelsbeurs............B5

Touristy **canal tours** (adult/child €6/3.50; ⌚10am-6pm Mar–mid-Oct, weekends only mid-Oct–Feb) depart regularly from near here or you can stroll aimlessly around the picturesque alleys of the medieval **Patershol district**. If you have a Museumpass, don't miss the delightful **Huis van Alijn** (www.huisvanalijn.be; Kraanlei 65; adult/under 26yr €5/1; ⌚11am-5pm Tue-Sat, 10am-5pm Sun) in a restored 1363 children's hospice. The museum's theme is life in the 20th century and, although little is in English, the engrossing exhibits are self explanatory and family home videos prove unexpectedly moving.

St-Baafskathedraal CHURCH
(St-Baafsplein; ⌚8.30am-6pm) Massive without magnificence, this vast cathedral is an essential stop for fans of Flemish Primitive art who flock in to see Jan van Eyck's world-famous 1432 masterpiece the **Adoration of the Mystic Lamb** (adult/child €3/1.50; ⌚9.30am-4.30pm Mon-Sat, 1-4.30pm Sun). To see what the fuss is about without queuing or paying, see the photo replica in side-chapel 30.

Belfort HISTORIC BUILDING
(Botermarkt; adult/concession €3/2.50; ⌚10am-5.30pm mid-Mar–mid-Nov) Ghent's 14th-century belfry affords spectacular views of the city, while an audioguide provides historical commentary. A lift takes you most of the way up, but there are still some narrow stairs to negotiate.

Gravensteen CASTLE
(St-Veerleplein; adult/concession €8/6; ⌚9am-5pm) Lovingly restored, the Gravensteen once more looks like a quintessential 12th-century castle, even though it spent the 19th century recycled as a factory. An imaginative video story-tour compensates for a relative lack of period furnishings.

MIAT MUSEUM
(www.miat.gent.be; Minnemeers 9; adult/under 26yr €5/1; ⌚10am-6pm Tue-Sun) In a five-floor 19th-century mill-factory building, this innovative museum celebrates Ghent's history of textile production with thought-provoking exhibits about industrialisation's effects on society (mostly in Dutch). Prepare for sensory overload on Tuesday or Thursday mornings when the working machinery is unleashed.

Design Museum MUSEUM
(www.designmuseumgent.be; J Breydelstraat 5; adult/child €5/free; ⌚10am-6pm Tue-Sun) One of Ghent's lesser-known gems, the Design Museum displays furnishings from the Renaissance through to contemporary styles.

Werregarensteeg OFFBEAT SIGHTS
Graffiti-filled alley.

GHENT MONEYSAVERS

The good value **Museumpass** (www.visitgent.be; €20) provides three days' free entrance to all the sights reviewed below (except for boat tours), six more attractions and all city transport. It's sold at museums, De Lijn booths and the tourist office.

OUT OF THE CENTRE

Museum Dr Guislain MUSEUM
(www.museumdrguislain.be; Jozef Guislainstraat 43; adult/under 26yr €5/1; ⏲9am-5pm Tue-Fri, 1-5pm Sat & Sun; 🚊1) Hidden away in a spooky 1857 neo-Gothic lunatic asylum, this enthralling museum takes visitors on a trilingual, multicultural journey through the history of psychiatry from gruesome neolithic trepanning to contemporary brain scans via cage beds and phrenology. Tram 1 stops outside.

STAM MUSEUM
(www.stamgent.be; Bijloke Complex; adult/concession €6/4.50; ⏲10am-6pm Tue-Sun; 🚊4) Brand-new interactive museum explaining the city's evolution through history.

SMAK ART MUSEUM
(www.smak.be; Citadelpark; adult/under 26yr €6/1, 10am-1pm Sun free; ⏲10am-6pm Tue-Sun; 🚌5) Regularly changing exhibitions of cutting-edge installation art.

Museum voor Schone Kunsten ART MUSEUM
(www.mskgent.be; Citadelpark; adult/under 26yr €5/1; ⏲10am-6pm Tue-Sun; 🚌5) This stately maze of light, airy rooms houses a good selection of Belgian art from the 14th to 20th centuries.

Sleeping

Complete B&B listings and a booking service are organised by **Bed & Breakfast Ghent** (www.bedandbreakfast-gent.be).

TOP CHOICE Chambres d'Hôtes Verhaegen B&B €€€
(☎09 265 07 60; www.hotelverhaegen.be; Oude Houtlei 110; d €195-265; ⏲reception 2-6pm) This 1770s rococo mansion is a sumptuous blend of historical restoration and certain well-placed modernist and retro touches. There's a dazzling salon, 18th-century dining room and neatly manicured parterre garden. Superb 'Paola's Room' has hosted Belgian royalty. Breakfast costs €15 extra.

Hotel Harmony BOUTIQUE HOTEL €€€
(☎09 324 26 80; www.hotel-harmony.be; Kraanlei 37; s/d/ste from €135/150/225; @≋) This old-meets-new boutique hotel offers luxuriously heaped pillows, fine white linens, Miró-inspired art and chocolate-and-raspberry colour schemes beneath antique beams. River views from 'exceptional' rooms (s/d €160/185) are possibly the best in Ghent. The rear deck has an 8m-by-4m outdoor pool. Breakfast is included; wi-fi costs €2/10 per hour/day.

Atlas B&B B&B €€
(☎09 233 49 91; www.atlasbenb.be; Rabotstraat 40; s/d from €57/73; P@📶) This fine 1865 town house has some gorgeous belle-époque, art-deco and art-nouveau touches and features plentiful maps and globes. Smaller rooms – 'Africa' and retro-colourful 'America' – have mini shower booths. Stylishly exotic 'Asia' is much bigger, while Tuscan 'Europe' (s/d €72/93) comes with four-poster bed and a new jacuzzi bathroom on an intermediate stairway. Free covered parking.

Hostel 47 HOSTEL €
(☎0478 712827; www.hostel47.com; Blekerijstraat 47-51; dm €26.50-29.50, d/tr €71/97.50) With white-on-white fashion decor in a refitted, high-ceilinged classical house, this is one of Europe's calmest and most stylish hostels. Phone ahead as reception is often not staffed.

Limited.Co GUEST HOUSE €€
(☎09 225 14 95; www.limited-co.be; Hoogstraat 58; s/d/q €55/80/125; 📶) Above a cafe-restaurant of modern pared-back simplicity are five great-value, gently fashionable rooms with lime-green walls, black floors and smart white bathrooms. Call to make arrangements if arriving outside restaurant hours.

Hotel Flandria BUDGET HOTEL €€
(☎09 223 06 26; www.hotelflandria-gent.be; Barrestraat 3; s/d/tr/q €58/68/100/125; @📶) Friendly owners are gradually ironing out the dowdier features of this basic but traveller-friendly hotel with comfy beds and a central location on a dark, narrow lane. The six cheapest rooms (s/d €43/53) share two bathrooms. Reception usually closes at 10pm, although sometimes earlier.

Accipio B&B
(☎0486 559498; www.accipio.be; St-Elisabethplein 26; s/d/q €80/95/160; @) Two super-stylish family-sized suites in an historic house with 19th-century beams and lots

of personality. Each includes a kitchenette with Senseo coffee-maker.

De Draecke HOSTEL €

(☎09 233 70 50; www.vjh.be; St-Widostraat 11; HI members dm/tw €21.80/52) Behind a traditional pseudo-medieval facade, this modern, HI-affiliated hostel is slightly institutional but ideally central and faces a peaceful willow-lined canal. Breakfast is included; towels, lockers and internet cost extra. No lockout.

Eating

As well as our recommendations, there's an endlessly tempting selection of eateries in the alleys of Patershol, along Graslei's photogenic canal and up Oudburg, where prices fall the further north you walk. Ghent is vegetarian-friendly, encouraging the population to eat meat-free on Thursdays and producing a useful free map, downloadable at www.visitgent.be/documenten/visit_gent/veggie/veggieplan_en.pdf.

House of Eliott LOBSTER €€

(☎09 225 21 28; www.thehouseofeliott.be; J Breydelstraat 36; mains €15-24; ⏲noon-2pm & 6-11pm Thu-Mon, closed Sep) Flapper mannequins and sepia photos exude pseudo-1920s charm in this canal-side gem with an exceptional waterside terrace. The speciality is lobster in multifarious preparations.

Brasserie Pakhuis EUROPEAN, OYSTERS

(☎09 223 55 55; www.pakhuis.be; Schuurkenstraat 4; mains €13.50-29, set lunch €12.90, set dinners €25-42; ⏲lunch & dinner Mon-Sat, bar from lunch to 1am) This hip (if mildly ostentatious) brasserie and bar is set in an elegantly restored former textile warehouse, whose century-old wrought ironwork is well worth admiring, even if you only stop for a drink.

Amadeus RIBS €€

(www.amadeusspareribrestaurant.be; mains €12.50-17; ⏲6.30pm-11pm) Patershol (☎09 225 13 85; Plotersgracht 8/10); Botermarkt (☎09 223 37 75; Goudenleeuwplein 7) Great value all-you-can-eat spare ribs (€13.95) served at two equally enticing addresses, both dressed up like Parisian brasseries, full of mirrors, stained glass, and the bustle of cheerful conversation.

Eethuis Avalon VEGETARIAN €

(☎09 224 37 24; www.restaurantavalon.be; Geldmunt 32; meals €9-13; ⏲lunch Mon-Sat; ✎) Reliably delicious, organic vegetarian food served in a warren of little rooms or outside on a small, tree-shaded terrace.

Soup'r SOUP €

(St-Niklaasstraat 9; small/large soup €3/4.50, sandwiches €2.70-4; ⏲11.30am-5pm Mon-Sat) Attractive modern soup kitchen.

Drinking

For character, variety and eccentricity, Ghent's cafes are world-beaters.

't Velootje BAR

(Kalversteeg 2; beer €4; ⏲usually from 9pm) Crammed from floor to ceiling with all manner of junk and riches, from antique bicycles to dusty virgins, this bewildering cafe has dodgy toilets, a temperamental owner and only two types of unreliably chilled beer. But you won't forget it.

Hotsy Totsy CAFE

(www.hotsytotsy.be; Hoogstraat 1; ⏲6pm-1am Mon-Fri, 8pm-2am Sat & Sun; 🚊1) This 'artists cafe' sports a classic zinc bar, silver-floral wallpaper and black-and-white film photos. There are chess sets, poetry nights and free live jazz most Thursday evenings, October to April.

Het Waterhuis aan de Bierkant BEER PUB

(www.waterhuisaandebierkant.be; Groentenmarkt 12; ⏲11am-1am) Draped in dried hop fronds and serving exclusive house beers, the building is a photogenic sight in its own right. It shares an enticing waterfront terrace with **'t Dreupelkot** (⏲4pm-late) a *jenever* (Dutch gin) specialist.

Rococo CAFE

(Corduwaniersstraat 5; ⏲from 10pm) Brilliantly lavish late-night cafe-bar with carved wooden ceilings and lighting provided entirely by candles.

Pink Flamingo's PUB, CAFE

(www.pinkflamingos.be; Onderstraat 55; ⏲noon-midnight Sun-Thu, 2pm-3am Fri & Sat) Kitsch-overloaded cafe with Barbie-lamps, 1970s wallpaper and oodles of plastic fruit.

Hot Club de Gand LIVE MUSIC

(www.hotclubdegand.be; Schuddevisstraatje; ⏲3pm-late) Around 9pm most nights while uni's in session, you'll hear live acoustic music (jazz, gypsy, blues, flamenco...) at this hidden cafe down a tiny alley behind 't Dreupelkot.

Herberg de Dulle Griet BEER PUB

(Vrijdagmarkt 50; ⏲4.30pm-1am Tue-Sat, noon-7.30pm Mon) Heavy beams, heraldic ceilings, barrel tables, lacy lampshades and the odd boar's head all add character to one of Ghent's best-known beer pubs.

't Caffetse CAFE
(Kraanlei 65; ⌚11am-5pm Tue-Sat) This remarkably inexpensive cafe is set within the cloister of the 14th-century Huis van Alijn (p139). There's lawn seating in summer.

Limonada LOUNGE
(www.limonada.be; Heilige Geeststraat 7; ⌚10pm-3am Mon-Sat) Unthreatening yet hip 70s-retro chill-out lounge with beanbag seats around low luminous tables.

Callisto Tearoom CAFE
(Hooiaard; ⌚varies seasonally) Tourist-oriented perch, with unbeatable waterway views, balloon lanterns, funky colours and traditional glass chandeliers.

Charlatan PUB
(www.charlatan.be; Vlasmarkt 9; ⌚7pm-late Tue-Sun) Lively, late-night music bar with live gigs in virtually any genre starting around 10pm. Several similarly raucous alternatives lie nearby.

☆ Entertainment

For listings of what's on, see *Week-Up* (www.weekup.be/gent/week); *Zone 09* magazine (free), which can be found in distribution boxes around town; or www.democrazy.be. All are in Dutch.

Vooruit THEATRE
(www.vooruit.be; St-Pietersnieuwstraat 23; 🚍5) This prominent venue for dance, rock concerts, film and visiting theatre companies occupies a striking 1912 building, whose architecture was a visionary premonition of art deco.

Culture Club CLUB
(www.cultureclub.be; Afrikalaan 174; ⌚Thu-Sat Oct-May) Once rated the 'world's hippest club', themes and cover charges vary (check the website). It's roughly 1.5km north of Gent-Dampoort station via Koopvaardijlaan.

De Bijloke LIVE MUSIC
(www.debijloke.be; Jozef Kluyskensstraat 2) Medieval abbey-hospital recycled into a classical music venue.

De Vlaamse Opera OPERA
(www.vlaamseopera.be; Schouwburgstraat 3) An 1840 beauty with horseshoe-shaped tiered balconies and elegant salons.

Handelsbeurs LIVE MUSIC
(www.handelsbeurs.be; Kouter 29) Anything from classics to Latin to blues.

ℹ Information

TOURIST INFORMATION The **tourist office** (☎09 266 52 32; www.visitgent.be; Botermarkt 17; ⌚9.30am-6.30pm) should move to the old fish-market building on St-Veerleplein during late 2011.

ℹ Getting There & Away

Bus

INTERNATIONAL There's a **Eurolines Office** (☎09 220 90 24; www.eurolines.be; Koningin Elisabethlaan 73; ⌚8.30am-noon & 1.30-5.30pm Mon-Fri, 8.30am-noon Sat) near Gent-St-Pieters, but their international buses (eg to London at 11.35pm) currently depart from **Gent-Dampoort**, bus-platform 15.

REGIONAL Many **De Lijn** (www.delijn.be) services currently depart from **Gent-Zuid bus station** (Woodrow Wilsonplein), but a new bus station is under construction beside Gent-St-Pieters.

Train

Gent-Dampoort, 1km west of the old city, is the handiest station, with useful trains to Antwerp (€8.60, fast/slow 42/64 minutes, three per hour), Bruges (€5.90, 35 minutes, hourly) and Lille, France (€15.20, 68 minutes, hourly), via Kortrijk.

Ghent's main station, **Gent-St-Pieters** (2.5km south of centre) has more choice of destinations, including Brussels (€8.10, 36 minutes, twice hourly) and Bruges (fast/slow 24/42 minutes, five per hour).

ℹ Getting Around

Driving a car in Ghent is purgatory. Park it and walk or ride.

Bicycle

HIRE Hire bicycles from Gent-St-Pieters **station luggage room** (bagagekantoor; per day €9.50, deposit €12.50) or **Biker** (Steendam 16; per half/full day €6.50/9; ⌚9am-12.30pm & 1.30-6pm Tue-Sat). ID required.

WARNING Police confiscate illegally parked bikes (look for the bicycle parking areas to be safe).

Bus & Tram

TICKETS One-hour/all-day tickets cost €1.20/5 if purchased ahead of time from ticket machines or **De Lijn offices** Gent-St-Pieters Kiosk (⌚7am-7pm Mon-Fri); Botermarkt (⌚7am-7pm Mon-Fri, 10.30am-5.30pm Sat).

TRAM 1 Picks up within the tunnel to the left as you exit Gent-St-Pieters station then runs to Korenmarkt, Gravensteen and beyond.

BUS 5 From Vlasmarkt passing Vooruit, the university quarter and Heuvelpoort (a handy bus stop for accessing the Citadelpark galleries).

Bruges

POP 117,000

Cobblestone lanes, dreamy canals, soaring spires and whitewashed old almshouses combine to make central Bruges (Brugge in Dutch) one of Europe's most picture-perfect historic cities. The only problem is that everyone knows.

Sights

Beyond the sights listed, the real joy of Bruges is simply wandering alongside the canals, soaking up the atmosphere. To avoid the worst crowds, explore east of pretty Jan van Eyckplein. Or maybe seek out the windmills beside the city's eastern 'moat', heading north of the fortified Kruispoort gate-tower at Langestraat's eastern end.

TOP CHOICE **Groeningemuseum** ART MUSEUM
(Dijver 12; adult/concession €8/6; 9.30am-5pm Tue-Sun) This small but extraordinarily valuable collection covers Flemish art from the 14th to 20th centuries, including some priceless Renaissance and Flemish Primitive works. Some gruesome scenes include a flaying in Gerard David's *Judgement of Cambyses* (1498, room 1) and the multiple tortures of *St George* (room 3) – the saint manages to keep his bright white underpants remarkably unsoiled nonetheless. In room 2 are much more meditative works, including Jan Van Eyck's radiant (if rather odd) masterpiece *Madonna with Canon George Van der Paele* (1436) and Hans Memling's *Moreel Triptych*. Later artistic genres include a typically androgynous figure by superstar symbolist Fernand Khnopff, plus a surrealist canvas each from Magritte and Delvaux.

Markt SQUARE
The heart of ancient Bruges, the old market square is lined with pavement cafes beneath step-gabled facades. The buildings aren't always quite as medieval as they look, but together they create a fabulous scene and even the neo-Gothic **post office** is architecturally magnificent. The scene is dominated by the **Belfort**, Belgium's most famous belfry whose iconic octagonal tower is arguably better appreciated from afar than by climbing 366 claustrophobic **steps to the top** (adult/concession €8/6; 9.30am-5pm, last tickets 4.15pm).

Burg SQUARE
Bruges' 1420 **Stadhuis** (City Hall; Burg 12) is smothered in statuettes and contains a breathtaking **Gotishe Zaal** (Gothic Hall; adult/concession €2/1; 9.30am-4.30pm), featuring dazzling polychromatic ceilings, hanging vaults and historicist murals. Tickets include entry to part of the early baroque **Brugse Vrije** (Burg 11a; 9.30am-noon & 1.30-4.30) next door. With its gilt highlights and golden statuettes, this palace was once the administrative centre for a large autonomous territory ruled from Bruges between 1121 and 1794.

The easily missed **Basilica of the Holy Blood** (Burg 5; 9.30-11.50am & 2-5.50pm) is named for its highly revered relic, a few coagulated drops of Christ's blood, venerated daily (usually 2pm). Pay €1.50 to see the one-room treasury housing a reliquary used to display the phial of blood during the elaborate Heilig-Bloedprocessie (Holy Blood Procession) every Ascension Day (17 May 2012, 9 May 2013).

Onze-Lieve-Vrouwekerk CHURCH
(Mariastraat; 9.30am-4.50pm Mon-Sat, 1.30-4.50pm Sun) This large, sober 13th-century church is best known for Michelangelo's serenely contemplative 1504 *Madonna and Child* statue. The church's **treasury section** (adult/concession €2/1) houses royal graves plus 15th- and 16th-century artworks

St-Janshospitaal MUSEUM
(Mariastraat 38; adult/concession €8/6; 9.30am-5pm Tue-Sun) The chapel of a 12th-century hospital displays historical medical implements, medically themed paintings and six masterpieces by 15th-century artist Hans

BRUGES MONEYSAVERS

A three-day **Musea Brugge Pass** (adult/child €15/5) allows free entry to 16 city-owned attractions. Even if you only visit the Belfort and Groeningemuseum, you'll already save money.

Private attractions like Choco-Story and De Halve Maan (plus an interesting **diamond museum** and a less-successful **chip museum**) aren't included, but you can save a little on each of those using a **Bruges Card** (www.brugescard.be) or **Welkom@ Brugge Card** (www.welkom-brugge.be), given free to guests by most hostels and hotels.

Bruges

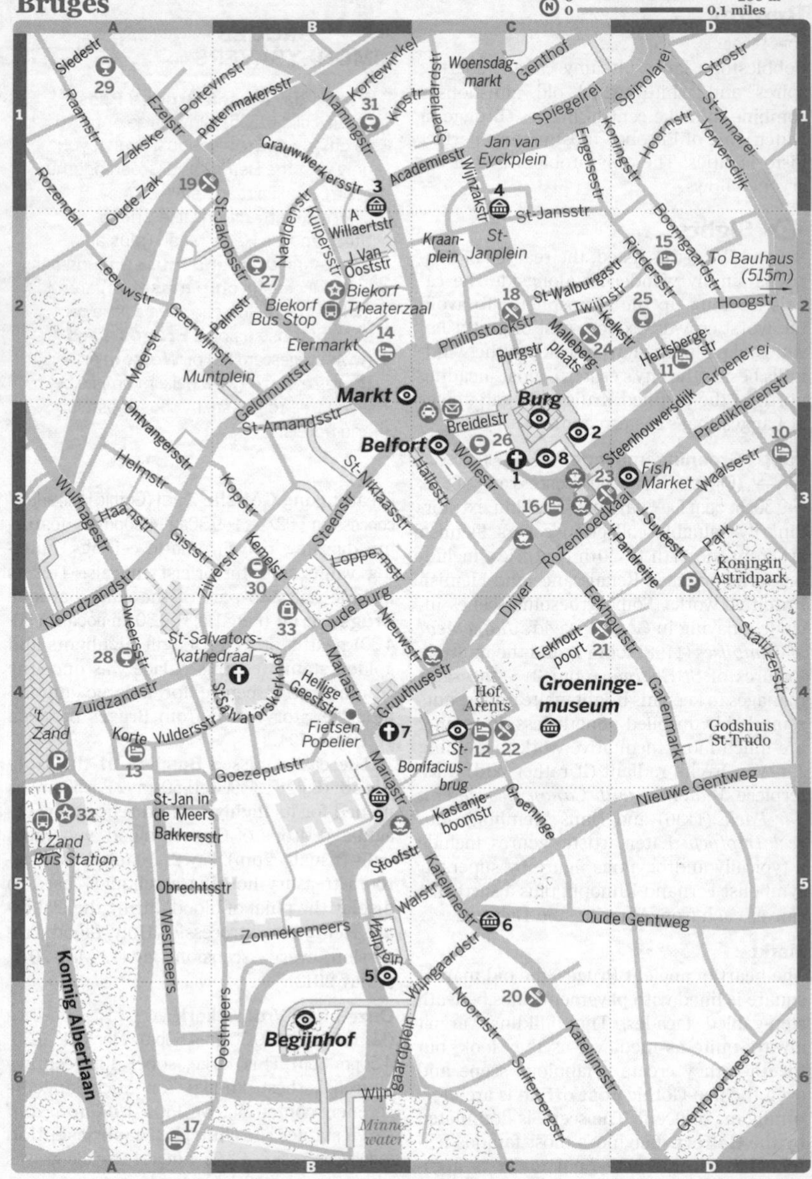

Memling. Tickets allows visits to a restored 17th-century pharmacy, poorly signposted off a small courtyard beside.

Begijnhof GARDEN

(admission free; ⏲6.30am-6.30pm) This is undoubtedly one of Bruges' quaintest spots. The walled *begijnhof* (a courtyard surrounded by historic dwellings that was originally built to house lay sisters) is an area of hushed calm found just 10 minutes' walk south of the Markt, and close to the romantic **Minnewater** (Lake of Love).

Bruges

Choco-Story MUSEUM
(www.choco-story.be; Wijnzakstraat 2; adult/child €6/4; ⏲10am-5pm) Trace the cocoa bean's crooked path from Aztec currency to a dieter's dilemma in this absorbing museum that culminates in tasting a praline that's made as you watch. The last demonstration is at 4.45pm.

De Halve Maan BREWERY
(www.halvemaan.be; Walplein 26) Find where the 'Bruges Fool' *(Brugse Zot)* originated on crowded 45-minute **guided tours** (tour incl 1 drink €5.50; ⏲hourly 11am-4pm) of this 1856 brewery. Or just sip a 'Strong Henry' (*Straffe Hendrik*; 9%) in the appealing cafe.

Museum voor Volkskunde MUSEUM
(Balstraat 43; adult/concession €2/1; ⏲9.30am-5pm Tue-Sun) In an attractive former almshouse, 18 themed tableaux illustrate Flemish life in times past. Although less engrossing than the Ghent equivalent, the surroundings are relatively free of tourists and the entry fee is quickly offset if you drink enough beer at the museum's time-warp cafe, **De Zwarte Kat** (⏲closed 11.45am-2pm): only €1.25 a pop.

Sleeping

Brilliantly comprehensive, **Hotel Bruges** (http://hotels.brugge.be/en) helps you filter around 250 hotels and B&Bs. Nonetheless, all accommodation can prove oppressively overbooked from Easter to September, over Christmas and, especially, at weekends, when two-night minimum stays are commonly required. Cheaper B&Bs often offer discounts of around €10 per room per night for stays longer than one night. In the lowest seasons (early November, late January), midrange options sometimes give big last-minute discounts. An all-night touch-screen computer outside the main tourist office displays hotel availability and contact information.

TOP CHOICE **Guesthouse Nuit Blanche** B&B €€€
(☎0494 400447; www.bruges-bb.com; Groeninge 2; d €175-195) Step into a Van Eyck painting where original gothic fireplaces and period furniture cunningly hide many of the modern fittings. The historic house once hosted Churchill, as well as Belgian royalty, and room rates cover the bottle of bubbly in your minibar. Drink it in the picture-postcard

canal-side garden or on 'lovers bridge', to which Guesthouse Nuit Blanche has a much-prized private entrance.

Relais Bourgondisch Cruyce BOUTIQUE HOTEL €€€
(050 33 79 26; www.relaisbourgondischcruyce.be; Wollestraat 41-47; d €185-375; Mar-Dec) Luxury and history intertwine in this part-timbered medieval house full of designer fittings, genuine antiques, trunks, Persian rugs and even an original Matisse. Watch the tourists drool enviously as they pass in their cruise barges. Room sizes vary significantly.

Hostel Lybeer HOSTEL €
(050 33 43 55; www.hostellybeer.com; Korte Vuldersstraat 31; dm from €15, s/d without bathroom €27.50/55;) 'Clean enough to be healthy, dirty enough to be happy', Lybeer has plenty of tatty edges, but few hostels have such a homely feeling or such congenially good-humoured staff. There's a large common room, small kitchen, free internet and laundry available (€3.50).

Bauhaus HOSTEL €
(050 34 10 93; www.bauhaus.be; Langestraat 135; dm €15-22, s €30-34, tw €38-50;) This well-run backpacker 'village' incorporates a bustling hostel, apartments, a night club, bike hire, internet cafe and a little chill-out room and garden, well hidden behind the reception and laundrette (at Langestraat 145). The atmospheric bar-restaurant is excellent... except when you're trying to sleep above it. Take bus 6 or 16 from the train station.

Hotel Patritius FAMILY HOTEL €€
(050 33 84 54; www.hotelpatritius.be; Riddersstraat 11; d €80-122, tr €129-147;) This proud 1830s town house has high ceilings, a snug bar-lounge, a historic spiral staircase and a pleasant garden. The 16 guest rooms vary radically in size and style: some new, some with exposed beams, some mildly chintzy. A decent breakfast is included.

B&B Huyze Hertsberge B&B €€
(050 33 35 42; www.huyzehertsberge.be; Hertsbergestraat 8; r €125-165) Oozing with good taste, this late-17th-century house has a tranquil little canal-side garden and gorgeous period salon decked with antiques and sepia photos. Rooms are comfortably grand.

B&B Dieltiens B&B €€
(050 33 42 94; www.bedandbreakfastbruges.be; Waalsestraat 40; s/d/tr €70/80/100) Art old and new fills this classical house, which remains an appealingly real home run by charming musician hosts. Central yet quiet.

't Keizershof FAMILY HOTEL €
(050 33 87 28; www.hotelkeizershof.be; Oostermeers 126; s €25-44, d/tr/q €44/66/80;) Seven simple rooms with shared bathrooms are remarkably tasteful and well kept for this price. Downstairs, a typical former brasserie-cafe is now used as the breakfast room. Free parking.

Etap Hotel CHAIN HOTEL €
(050 40 51 20; www.etaphotel.com; Bruges Station; tr €49-59) This brand-new, 184-room hotel has retro fittings that are unexpectedly hip for a budget chain. Reception is manned 24 hours. Parking costs €2.50; wi-fi €4.50/9.90 per hour/day.

Hotel Central HOTEL €€
(050 33 18 05; www.hotelcentral.be; Markt 30; d €80-100, without bathroom €60-80) Walls are thin, there's no lift and 'reception' means finding a waiter at the typical tourist restaurant downstairs. But, hey, you're right on Markt (though only room 9 has a view towards the belfry).

Eating

Touristy terraces crowd the Markt and line pedestrianised St-Amandsstraat where there are many cheaper eateries. Along eclectic Langestraat (the eastward extension of Hoogstraat), you'll find everything from kebabs to Michelin stars. About town, numerous taverns and bakeries serve snacks and several hostels offer great meal deals.

TOP CHOICE **Den Gouden Harynck** FINE DINING €€€
(050 33 76 37; www.dengoudenharynck.be; Groeninge 25; mains €38-45, set lunch menu €35, 3-/4-course menus €74/89; lunch & dinner Tue-Sat) Jackets or pearls are appropriate garb in this uncluttered Michelin-starred restaurant, where even the set lunch is a faultless exercise in artistic nouveau cuisine.

De Bottelier MEDITERRANEAN €€
(050 33 18 60; www.debottelier.com; St-Jakobsstraat 63; pasta/veg dishes from €8.80/13.50, other mains from €16; lunch & dinner Tue-Fri, dinner Sat) Decorated with hats and old clocks, this adorable little restaurant overlooks a handkerchief of canal-side garden. It's consistently popular with local diners, so book ahead.

Est Wijnbar TAPAS €
(050 33 38 39; www.wijnbarest.be; Braambergstraat 7; mains €9.50-12.50, tapas €3.50-9.50;

⏲4pm-midnight Wed-Sun; ✍) Partly stripped paintwork on heavy 17th-century beams creates an ancient-yet-modern feel in this tiny two-tiered wine bar, whose tempting light meals include seven vegetarian options. Live music Sundays.

Cambrinus BRASSERIE €€
(www.cambrinus.eu; Philipstockstraat 19; snacks €7, mains €17-23; ⏲noon-11pm) Cambrinus keeps its kitchen open all day for mussels and other Belgian favourites, including many beer-based meals, and offers hundreds of brews to wash it all down with. It's family friendly, but the decor and service are in stereotypical British pub style.

De Bron VEGETARIAN €
(☎050 33 45 26; Katelijnestraat 82; ⏲lunch Mon-Fri; ✍) This bright, functional vegetarian restaurant essentially serves just soup (€2) or their daily changing lunch-of-the-day (small/medium/large €8.50/9/10.50). Add soy sauce and sesame seeds to taste.

't Gulden Vlies BELGIAN €€
(☎050 33 47 09; www.tguldenvlies.be; Mallebergplaats 17; mains €14-22, 2-/3-course menu €16/27; ⏲7pm-3am Wed-Sun) Intimate late-night restaurant with old-fashioned decor and good-value Belgian cuisine.

De Twijfelaar BISTRO €€
(Eekhoutstraat 24; lunch €10, dinner mains €16-23; ⏲noon-2.30pm & 6-11pm Tue-Sat) Combining a 1717 town house and an art-nouveau shop-building this 'art bistro' serves fair-value meals, including simple, inexpensive lunches.

Drinking & Entertainment

Hostels Bauhaus (p146), **Passage** (www.passagebruges.com), **Charlie Rockets** (www.charlierockets.com) and **Snuffel Hostel** (www.snuffel.be) all have congenial backpacker-oriented pubs, most serving decent yet inexpensive food. Bauhaus also has Bruges' one nightclub. Eiermarkt, just north of Markt, has many plain but lively bars, with DJs and seemingly endless happy hours.

De Garre PUB
(Garre 1; ⏲noon-midnight) Hidden down a minuscule alley between candy shops, this antique pub serves dozens of Belgian ales. Served nowhere else, Garre Tripel (€3) is a magnificent 11% mind-blower.

De Republiek PUB
(www.derepubliek.be; St-Jakobsstraat 36; ⏲from 11am) Spacious local favourite with candlelit tables, backlit bottles and a youthful buzz, it has a garden terrace and cheap food till late.

't Brugs Beertje PUB
(Kemelstraat 5; ⏲4pm-1am Thu-Tue) Classic brew pub decorated with time-yellowed beer mats and enamel brewery signs.

't Poatersgat PUB
(Vlaamingstraat 82; ⏲5pm-late) With mood-lit vaulted cellars decorated with old pianos and hop fronds, it's popular with 20-something locals. Beers cost from €2.

Concertgebouw CONCERT HALL
(☎050 47 69 99; www.concertgebouw.be; 't Zand 34) The 21st-century architecture is discordantly brash and contemporary, but the acoustics and top-floor views are hard to beat.

Information

TOURIST INFORMATION The **Tourist Office** (☎050 44 46 46; www.brugge.be) Concertgebouw ('t Zand 34; ⏲10am-6pm); Train Station (⏲10am-5pm Mon-Fri, 10am-2pm Sat & Sun) has standard city maps for €0.50, but the arguably better *Use-It* maps (www.use-it.be) are free if you ask for one.

WEBSITES **Bruggecentraal** (www.bruggecentraal.be) has events listings.

Getting There & Away

Bruges' train station is about 1.5km south of the Markt, a lovely walk via the Begijnhof. Every hour, trains run twice to Brussels (€12.90, one hour), five times to Ghent (€5.60, fast/slow 23/39 minutes), and once to Antwerp (€12.90, 70 minutes). For Ypres (Ieper in Dutch), take a train to Roeselare (€4.50, fast/slow 22/33 minutes), then bus 94 or 95: both buses pass key WWI sites en route.

Getting Around

BUS To get from the train station to Markt, take any bus marked 'Centrum'. For the way back, buses stop at Biekorf, just northwest of Markt on Kuiperstraat.

BICYCLE **Bauhaus hostel** (per half/full day €6/9), **Fietsen Popelier** (Mariastraat 26; per hr/half-day/full-day €3.50/7/10; ⏲10am-7pm), and **Rent-a-Bike** (Bruges Station; per day/week €12/72; ⏲7.30am-7pm Mon-Fri, 9am-9pm Sat & Sun) all offer bicycle hire.

Quasimundo (☎050 33 07 75; www.quasimundo.eu; adult/student €24/22; ⏲mid-Mar–mid-Oct) offers half-day bicycle tours around Bruges and its surroundings, with rental included. Book ahead.

BOAT Canal Tours (adult/child €6.90/3.20; ⌚10am-6pm Easter-early Nov) depart every 20 minutes from several jetties, notably on Dijver. Tours last 30 minutes.

HORSE-DRAWN CARRIAGE Up to five people per carriage (€36) on a well-trodden, 35-minute route from the Markt. Includes a five-minute nosebag stop near the Begijnhof.

Around Bruges

Historic, quaint but often tourist-jammed, the inland port-village of **Damme** (www.toerismedamme.be) makes a popular summer excursion by canal **paddle steamer** (⌚10am-5pm Easter–mid-Oct; one-way/return €6/7.50), departing every two hours from Bruges' Noorweegse Kaai (bus 4 from Markt). Consider cycling instead: it's only 5km and, by continuing 2km further along the idyllic canal, you'll escape from the worst of the visitor overload. If you're fit, consider then heading 10km northwest via Dudzele and **Hof Ter Doest** (www.terdoest.be) to sweet little **Lissewege** (www.lissewege.be), an artists village, which runs hourly trains to Bruges.

Quasimodo (☎050 37 04 70, 0800 97525; www.quasimodo.be) visits most of these on **Triple Treat tours** (under/over 26yr €45/55; ⌚9am Mon, Wed & Fri Feb–mid-Dec), adding castles at **Loppem** and **Tillegem** and fascinating **WWII coastal defences** near Ostend. The same company's **Flanders Fields tours** (under/over 26yr €45/55; ⌚9am Tue-Sun Apr-Oct) visit Ypres Salient.

Ypres

POP 35,500

Especially when viewed from the southeast, Ypres' Grote Markt is one of the most breathtaking market squares in Flanders. It's all the more astonishing once you discover that virtually all of its convincingly 'medieval' buildings are in fact 20th-century copies. The originals had been brutally bombarded into oblivion between 1914 and 1918 when the historic city failed to capitulate to German WWI advances. WWI battles in the surrounding poppy fields, known as the Ypres Salient, killed hundreds of thousands of soldiers. A century later, countless lovingly tended cemeteries remain, along with numerous widely spread WWI-based museums and trench remnants. Together they present a thoroughly moving introduction to the horrors and futility of war.

Sights

CENTRAL YPRES

Grote Markt SQUARE

The brilliantly rebuilt **Lakenhallen**, a vast Gothic edifice originally serving as the 13th-century cloth market, dominates this very photogenic central square. It sports a 70m-high belfry, reminiscent of London's Big Ben, and hosts the gripping museum **In Flanders Fields** (www.inflandersfields.be; Grote Markt 34; adult/child €8/4; ⌚10am-6pm), a multimedia WWI experience honouring ordinary people's experiences of wartime horrors. It's very highly recommended, but will be closed from mid-September 2011 till April 2012 for refitting. The ticket allows free entry to three other minor city museums.

Menin Gate & City Ramparts NEIGHBOURHOOD

A block east of Grote Markt, the famous **Menin Gate** is a large stone gateway straddling the main road at the city moat. It's inscribed with the names of 54,896 'lost' British and other Commonwealth WWI troops whose bodies were never found. Every evening at 8pm, traffic is halted while buglers sound the **Last Post** (www.lastpost.be) in moving remembrance.

A pleasant 20-minute parkland stroll takes you south atop the hefty city **rampart remnants**, emerging at **Rijselpoort** where there's a pretty moat-side **war cemetery**. Beneath is the intriguing little **Ramparts War Museum** (Rijselsestraat 208; admission €3; ⌚11am-8pm), which displays WWI mementos through a series of subterranean mannequin scenes. Enter through the inexpensive **'t Klein Rijsel** pub, which serves its own caramel-rich beer (€2) in specially made tankards.

YPRES SALIENT

Many Salient sites are awkward to reach without a car or tour bus. However, the following are accessible by the Ypres–Roeselare bus routes 94 and 95, so could be visited en route to or from Bruges.

Memorial Museum Passchendaele 1917 MUSEUM

(www.passchendaele.be; Ieperstraat 5, Zonnebeke; admission €5; ⌚10am-6pm Feb-Nov) The highlight of this slick, very informative WWI museum is walking through recreated dugouts and trench emplacements in the basement. It's in the 1922 'castle' of Zonnebeke village, 6km east of Ypres. Bus 94 stops 200m away.

Tyne Cot CEMETERY
(admission free; ⌚24hrs) The world's largest Commonwealth war cemetery, 11,956 soldiers are buried here in maudlin straight rows. A further 35,000 names of the missing are engraved on the rear wall. The name Tyne Cot was coined by Northumberland Fusiliers who fancied that German bunkers on the hillside here looked like Tyneside cottages (two remain sitting amid the graves). Enter via a sparse but well designed **visitor centre** (⌚9am-6pm Feb-Nov). It's 3km beyond Zonnebeke, 500m from the nearest 94 bus stop.

Deutscher Soldatenfriedhof CEMETERY
The Salient's small, intensely moving German cemetery has up to 10 bodies per grave and is eerily watched over by the silhouettes of four shadowy statues. Enter through a black concrete 'tunnel' that clanks and hisses spookily with distant war sounds while four short video montages commemorate the tragedy of war. Bus 95 stops outside at 'Duits Kerkhof'. That's 1km north of Langemark, 17 minutes from Ypres.

Tours

There are dozens more WWI sites to seek out. If you have wheels, the tourist office has useful pamphlets. The following two bookshops between Grote Markt and Menin Gate sell a range of specialist books and offer twice-daily, half-day guided mini-bus tours of selected war sites. Advance booking is wise.

Over the Top (☎057 42 43 20; www.overthetoptours.be; Meensestraat 41; ⌚9am-12.30pm, 1.30-5.30pm & 7.30-8.30pm)

British Grenadier (☎057 21 46 57; www.salienttours.com; Meensestraat 5; ⌚9.30am-1pm, 2-6pm & 7.30-8.30pm)

Sleeping & Eating

The nearest youth hostel is located in Kortrijk.

Yoaké B&B B&B €€
(☎057 20 35 14; www.yoake-ieper.be/bedhome.htm; Tempelstraat 35; d €85; ❄📶) Two smart rooms, one almost an apartment, are attached to a hip wellness centre. At weekends it's only for guests taking the full €147 wellness package.

Ariane Hotel HOTEL €€
(☎057 21 82 18; www.ariane.be; Slachthuisstraat 58; s/d from €94/120; P📶) Peaceful, professionally managed larger hotel with contemporary designer rooms, wartime memorabilia in common rooms and a swish restaurant that's a popular Ypres institution.

WWI GRAVESITE SEARCHES

If your relative died in the region's WWI battles, find out which cemetery or memorial they're commemorated at using www.cwgc.org (for UK and other Commonwealth soldiers), www.ambc.gov (for Americans) or www.volksbund.de (for Germans).

B&B Ter Thuyne B&B €€
(☎057 36 00 42; www.terthuyne.be; Gustave de Stuersstraat 19; s/d €60/75; @) The three comfortable rooms are luminously bright, scrupulously clean and modern without fashion consciousness.

Hotel Regina HOTEL €€
(☎057 21 88 88; www.hotelregina.be; Grote Markt 45; s/d from €70/85) Right on the Markt, the location is ideal. Attempts at 'artistic' decor generally backfire, but the Ensor room is a worthy exception, with an old-world timber interior and unbeatable views.

B&B Zonneweelde B&B €
(☎057 20 27 23; Adjudant Masscheleinlaan 18; s/d €28/50) Cheap, basic rooms with a hotchpotch of furniture and scrappy shared bathroom facilities in an old-fashioned suburban home. It faces the canal, three blocks north of Grote Markt.

In 't Klein Stadhuis CAFE, RESTAURANT €€
(www.kleinstadhuis.be; Grote Markt 32; mains €12-21; ⌚closed Sun Oct-May) Tucked away in an eccentrically decorated historic guildhall beside the Stadhuis, this split-level cafe serves gigantic, good-value meals and offers limited options even when the main kitchen is closed.

Information

INTERNET ACCESS Temple.com (Tempelstraat 18; per hr €2; ⌚11am-7pm Fri-Wed) has computers with internet in a grocery shop run by a Cameroonian princess.

TOURIST INFORMATION The well-equipped tourist office **Toerisme Ieper** (☎057 23 92 20; www.ieper.be; Grote Markt 34; ⌚9am-6pm) is located inside the Lakenhallen.

WORTH A TRIP

BEER COUNTRY

Dotted with windmills, the almost pan-flat hop fields north and west of Ypres produce many of Belgium's most sought-after beers. **De Dolle** (www.dedollebrouwers.be; ⏲brewery visits 2pm Sun) creates **Oerbier** at Esen near attractive Diksmuide which, like Ypres, had its historic core totally rebuilt after WWI. Watou is known for the full-flavoured **St-Bernardus** (www.sintbernardus.be). Like liquid alcoholic chocolate, extraordinary **Pannepot** (www.struise.noordhoek.com/eng) is brewed at the dreary-looking **Deca Brewery** in Woesten on the windmill-dotted road between Ypres and the gorgeous medieval town of Veurne. But the 'holy grail' of pubs is **In de Vrede** (www.indevrede.be; Donkerstraat 13, Westvleteren; ⏲10am-8pm Sat-Wed), opposite **Abdij St-Sixtus** (St Sixtus Abbey; www.sintsixtus.be; ⏲closed to visitors). While the pub's decor is far from memorable, it's the only place anywhere on earth where there's a reasonably assured chance of drinking (not taking away) the rarest of Trappist beers, **Westvleteren 12°** (€4.50). It's often cited as the world's best brew. Once you've tasted its fruity complexity, you might well agree.

Getting There & Around

BUS Services pick up passengers in Grote Markt's northeast corner (check the direction of the bus carefully!) including Roeselare-bound routes 94 (roughly twice hourly on weekdays, five daily on weekends) and 95 (hourly on weekdays, five daily on weekends).

TRAIN Services run hourly to Ghent (€9.90, one hour) and Brussels (€15.20, 1½ hours) via Kortrijk (€4.50, 30 minutes), where you could change for Bruges or Antwerp.

BICYCLE Hire bicycles from **Hotel Ambrosia** (☎057 36 63 66; www.ambrosiahotel.be; D'Hondtstraat 54; per day €10; ⏲9am-7pm); a credit card is required as a guarantee.

WALLONIA

Tournai

POP 68,000

Pleasant Tournai (Doornik in Dutch) is Wallonia's oldest city. It was battered by WWII bombs, but the photogenic **Grand Place** has since been convincingly rebuilt. The city might not merit a long detour, but if you want to reach Lille (France) from Brussels by train without paying high-speed supplements, coming this way can save you money.

Sights include the five iconic towers of the striking, if sober and scaffolding-filled, **Cathédrale Notre Dame** (admission free; ⏲9.15am-noon & 2-6pm) and the 72m-high **belfry**, which is Belgium's oldest. Both are Unesco World Heritage Sites. Facing the belfry, the **Tourist Office** (☎069 22 20 45; www.tournai.be; Vieux Marché aux Poteries 14) can point you towards a cache of enjoyable museums, all free on the first Sunday of each month.

The **Auberge de Jeunesse** (☎069 21 61 36; www.laj.be; Rue St-Martin 64; dm/s/d €17.50/31/44) is one of Belgium's friendliest hostels (take bus 7 or 88). Central though hidden, the likeable **Hôtel d'Alcantara** (☎069 21 26 48; www.hotelalcantara.be; Rue des Bouchers St-Jacques 2; s/d from €84/94; P@) experiments semi-successfully with '70s-retro design within a regal old town house.

The train station, 1km northeast of the centre, has connections twice hourly to Brussels (€11.70, fast/slow 61/73 minutes) and hourly to Lille-Flandres (€6, 25 minutes).

Liège

POP 189,000

Beneath its brutally disfigured, post-industrial surface, sprawling Liège (Luik in Dutch) is a living architectural onion concealing layer upon layer of history. Fine churches abound, as befits a city that spent 800 years as the capital of an independent principality run by bishops. Proudly free-spirited citizens are disarmingly friendly and no Belgian city bubbles with more joie de vivre. Love it or loathe it, Liège is quirky and oddly compulsive.

Sights

The historic zone and main **museums** (free the first Sunday of each month) are a short walk west of Liège-Palais train station: walk east past the vast, dour former Bishops' Palace (Place St-Lambert) through attractive Place du Marché. For a **panoramic view** of the city, climb to the top of the **Montagne de Bueren stairway**.

Musée de la Vie Wallonne MUSEUM
(www.viewallonne.be; Cour des Mineurs; adult/child €5/3; ⏲10am-5pm Tue-Sat, 10am-4pm Sun) In an adapted convent-cloister building, this quirkily imaginative multimedia experience examines Wallonia's economic rise and fall, from 12th-century Mosan metalwork to 1960s room decor to the late-20th-century post-industrial demise.

Grand Curtius MUSEUM
(www.grandcurtiusliege.be; Féronstrée 136; adult/concession €5/3; ⏲10am-6pm Wed-Mon) This engrossing, ambitious museum has interwoven tales of Liège artists and industries with a wide-ranging history of the visual arts. Allow several hours to do it justice.

Musée de l'Art Wallon ART MUSEUM
(Féronstrée 86; adult/child €5/3; ⏲1-6pm Tue-Sat, 11am-6pm Sun) Behind a brutally ugly exterior, discover this truly excellent collection of art by Francophone Belgian artists.

Sleeping

Hôtel Hors Château GUEST HOUSE €€
(☎04 250 60 68; www.hors-chateau.be; Rue Hors Château 62; s/d/ste €78/95/125, breakfast €12; 📶) Nine stylish new rooms tucked into an old half-timbered building ideally situated in the historic quarter. Call ahead to arrange arrival times.

Auberge de Jeunesse HOSTEL €
(☎04 344 56 89; www.laj.be; Rue Georges Simenon 2; HI members dm/s/d €18.80/33/46; @) Great hostel across the river in the Outremeuse 'republic'.

Hôtel Les Acteurs FAMILY HOTEL €€
(☎04 223 00 80; www.lesacteurs.be; Rue des Urbanistes 10; s/d/tr €46/66/83) Simple but cheap, well-maintained old rooms above a very inexpensive cafe.

Eating & Drinking

There are terrace restaurants on Place du Marché, many good-value sandwich shops along Rue Hors Château and an interesting range of little eateries on Rue Roture, hidden away near the hostel in Outremeuse. Tread carefully on Rue du Pot d'Or, which has dozens of (overly) lively late-night bars.

La Maison du Peket/Amon Nanesse PUB, RESTAURANT €€
(www.maisondupeket.be; Rue de l'Epée 4; meals €10.50-18.50; ⏲10am-2am, kitchen noon-2.30pm & 6-10.30pm) Just behind Place du Marché, this rambling antique house with bare brick walls and heavy beams combines a lively bar specialising in Walloon *genièvre* (*jenever;* Dutch gin) with a restaurant serving satisfying pub meals, including *boulets à la liègeoise* (meatballs in raisin-sweetened gravy).

Le Pot au Lait PUB
(www.potaulait.be; Rue Sœurs de Hasque; ⏲10am-2am Mon-Sat, 2pm-2am Sun; 📶) Watch aliens landing in Liège's wackiest pub-cafe, hidden in an alley 100m east of the cathedral. La Chouffe draft costs only €2.30. No food.

Information

TOURIST INFORMATION The **Maison de Tourisme** (☎04 237 92 92; www.liege.be, www.ftpl.be; Place St-Lambert 32; ⏲9am-5.30pm) and **Office du Tourisme** (☎04 221 92 21; Féronstrée 92; ⏲9am-5pm Mon-Fri, 10am-4.30pm Sat, 10am-2.30pm Sun) can suggest dozens of additional city attractions.

Getting There & Away

Trains from Liège-Palais

Brussels (€13.60, 125 minutes, hourly) via **Huy** (€4.40, 29 minutes)

Coo (€7.70, one hour)

Luxembourg City (€38.20, 2½ hours, 18 daily) via **Clervaux** (€20.60, 1½ hours, every two hours)

Trains from Liège-Guillemins

Aachen (€11.70, 54 minutes, every two hours)

Brussels (€13.60, one hour, hourly) via **Leuven** (€9.90, 35 minutes)

Maastricht (€4.30, 30 minutes, hourly)

High-speed Services

Reservations are compulsory for the following:

Cologne (standard/pre-booked €33/19, one hour, six daily) via **Aachen** (€23/14, 23 minutes)

Frankfurt (€94.60/39, 2½ hours, three daily)

Paris (€89/45, 2¼ hours, seven daily)

Bastogne

POP 14,200

In late 1944 allied forces were sweeping east across Europe. But WWII wasn't yet over. Hitler's last gasp was a midwinter counter-attack that devastated the Ardennes and nearby Luxembourg, creating a 'bulge' in the allied frontline. During this pivotal 'Battle of the Bulge', plucky Bastogne was surrounded but refused to capitulate. Today the town isn't lovely, but it's a must-see for

ON THE ROAD IN WALLONIA

Without a car you'll spend longer reaching most of the Wallonia's rural sites than actually enjoying them. But by car, combining a handful of destinations can make for a very enjoyable day out. There's a very wide choice of accommodation, but much is packed full in summer and closed in winter. For in-depth coverage, see Lonely Planet's *Belgium & Luxembourg*.

Kayaking & Outdoor Activities

Durbuy (www.durbuyinfo.be, www.durbuyadventure.be) The 'world's smallest town' is quaint if touristy and is well set up for all manner of sporting fun. Plenty of hotels.

La Roche-en-Ardenne (www.ardenne-aventures.be, www.brandsport.be, www.la-roche-tourisme.com) Water sports and mountain biking from a charmingly compact town nestled around a medieval castle ruin.

Coo (www.coo-adventure.com) The hamlet's famous 15m 'waterfall' is underwhelming but outdoor options are numerous and there's a family amusement park (see www.plopsa.be). Accommodation is limited in Coo but is more plentiful in nearby Stavelot.

Caves

Belgium's publicly accessible cave systems each have their own character. Visits take over an hour with set departure times that vary seasonally (check websites). There's no 'escape' once you've started so don't forget appropriate footwear, warm clothes and a pre-emptive bathroom stop.

Han-sur-Lesse (www.grotte-de-han.be) Belgium's foremost stalactite-rich caves are accessed by a little train ride, but it's often over-stuffed with tourists. Nearby hotels are lacklustre; a hostel is available (see www.gitesdetape.be).

Rochefort (www.valdelesse.be) This attractive town is famous for its Trappist beers. Walking distance from the town centre, the Grotte de Lorette is remarkable for its depth, not its stalagmites. Good choice of accommodation.

WWII buffs. The main square – a car park adorned with a tank – has been renamed Place McAuliffe after the American general whose famous reply to the German call to surrender was one word, 'Nuts!' Here you'll find the **Maison du Tourisme** (☎061 21 27 11; www.paysdebastogne.be; Place McAuliffe 60; ⏲9am-6pm).

Of numerous WWII museums, Bastogne's best is 800m northeast of here: **J'avais 20 ans en '45** (☎061 50 20 02; www.bastogne.be/20ansen45; adult/child €6.50/5; ⏲10am-6pm, closed Fri Oct-Apr, last entry 5pm) is an imaginative exhibition giving movingly balanced insights into the conflict through dozens of eyewitness video accounts. Keep the entry ticket to get a €1 discount at **Bastogne Historical Centre** (www.bastognehistoricalcenter.be; Colline du Mardasson; entry incl audioguide adult/child €8.50/6; ⏲9.30am-5.30pm Mar-Dec), a much more standard war museum full of uniforms, weapons, a couple of dioramas and a movie. It's located on a gentle hilltop 1.5km further northeast and is beside a big star-shaped **American War Memorial**, beneath which is a chapel-cave with mosaics by Fernand Léger.

Right on Bastogne's main square, the warm and friendly **Hôtel Collin** (☎061 21 48 88; www.hotel-collin.com; Place McAuliffe 8; s/d/tr €67/85/105) is a pleasant family hotel with a pseudo-art-nouveau cafe and a Mediterranean-styled restaurant.

Bus 163b (€3.80, 45 minutes) runs every two hours to Libramont on the Brussels–Luxembourg train line. Buses also run hourly (except Sundays) to Ettelbrück (one hour) in Luxembourg.

UNDERSTAND BELGIUM

History

Bruges, Ghent and Ypres boomed in the 13th and 14th centuries as northern Europe's foremost cloth-trading cities. Crafts-

Hotton (www.grottesdehotton.com, www.si-hotton.be) Great grottoes and a jaw-dropping vertical subterranean chasm, yet relatively uncommercial.

Remouchamps (www.grottes.be; www.ourthe-ambleve.be) Lacks the drama of the three 'greats' above, but you get to ride down an underground river in a boat.

Castles

Wallonia's capital **Namur** (www.namurtourisme.be, www.mtpn.be) is dominated by a massive, sober fortified **citadel** (www.citadelle.namur.be; admission free), but the region has many more romantic castles including the following:

Château de Jehay (www.chateaujehay.be; adult/student €5/2.50, audioguide €1; ⌚2-6pm Tue-Fri, 11am-6pm Sat & Sun Apr-Sep) A 1550 gingerbread fantasy of alternating brick and stone layers rising from a tree-ringed moat between Liège and patchily historic Huy (bus 85).

Château de Modave (www.modave-castle.be; adult/student €7.50/4; ⌚10am-5pm Tue-Sun Apr–mid-Nov) Palatial chateau with 20 majestically furnished rooms and 17th-century stucco ceilings.

Château de Lavaux-Sainte-Anne (www.chateau-lavaux.com; adult/child €6.50/4; ⌚9am-5.30pm) Partly furnished 1450 moated fortress visible west of the E411 motorway as you pass junction 22a just 10km from Han-sur-Lesse.

Semois Valley

Eccentric loops of river valley flanked by vividly green waterside meadow extend either side of **Bouillon**, whose looming central castle ruin once belonged to the crusader conqueror of Jerusalem. The Ardennes' finest panoramic viewpoints overlook the Semois at **Rochehaut** and at harder-to-reach **Tombeau du Géant**. A relatively short drive southeast is **Orval**, with its highly photogenic, part-ruined abbey, which is most famous for its Trappist beer. A unique if understrength variant of the beer is available at the monastery pub, **Auberge de l'Ange Gardien** (⌚11am-8pm).

people established powerful guilds that built elaborate guildhouses around fine market squares, typically adorned with a belfry as a symbol of civic pride.

When Protestantism swept across Europe in the 16th century, the Low Countries (present-day Belgium, the Netherlands and Luxembourg) embraced it, much to the chagrin of their ruler, the fanatically Catholic Philip II of Spain. The result, from 1568, was a war that lasted 80 years and in the end roughly laid the region's present-day borders. Holland and its allied provinces victoriously expelled the Spaniards, while Belgium and Luxembourg stayed under their strict Catholic rule.

For the next 200 years Belgium remained a battlefield for successive foreign powers. After the Spaniards came the Austrians, and, in turn, the French. After Napoleon was trounced in 1815 at Waterloo near Brussels, the Dutch took over for 15 years until, in 1830, the Catholic Belgians split from protestant Holland and finally formed their own kingdom.

From the late 19th century, Belgium rapidly grew wealthy, both through industrialisation and through King Léopold II's disgraceful profiting from the Congo, which was brutal even by the colonial standards of that era.

When WWI kicked off in 1914 Belgium was officially neutral, but the Germans invaded anyway. Western Flanders became a blood-soaked killing field and whole towns, including historic Ypres, were bombarded into the mud. Incredibly Ypres' ancient heart has since been meticulously rebuilt and tours of the Ypres Salient offer poignant WWI reminders.

During WWII, the country was taken over within three weeks of a surprise German attack in May 1940 and, even after an initial 1944 liberation, suffered a second devastation during Hitler's last-gasp counter-attack in the Ardennes. A Belgian government in exile was formed in London, but King

Léopold III remained in Nazi-occupied Belgium. Questions over this perceived collaboration led to his abdication in 1950 in favour of his son, King Baudouin. Baudouin's popular reign ended with his abrupt death in 1993. Childless, Baudouin was succeeded by his brother, the present King Albert II.

Despite the wars, for much of the 20th century Wallonia's mining, glassware, steel and other heavy industries made it the powerhouse of one of Europe's strongest economies. However, since the 1970s, the old economic balance has reversed with a serious post-industrial decline affecting much of Wallonia, while formerly agricultural Flanders has boomed with new higher-tech industries. A parallel series of political changes have increasingly emphasised the north–south linguistic divide. With ever less communication between the regions, forming a national consensus has proved ever more difficult in recent years. In 2007 the country was without a government for nearly a year. And the 2010 federal elections saw months more deadlock. The immediate sticking point has been the arcane case of BHV, an anomalous boundary question affecting a voting district in Flemish Brabant. But, at a more fundamental level, Flemish politicians want greater autonomy for their wealthy region, while French speakers fear that further separation of powers will reduce subsidies to the struggling south. Politicians' increasing inability to compromise threatens to break the nation irrevocably in two. However, the risk of Flanders rapidly declaring unilateral independence is probably overstated since nobody quite knows what would then become of Brussels. And it would all be very expensive. For many citizens the issues are seen as mere political point scoring and, as a result, public confidence in politics in general has sunk to an all-time low.

People

Belgium's population is split north–south by language. In Flanders (Vlaanderen) the language is the Flemish dialect of Dutch. South of the divide in Wallonia (La Wallonie), people speak French with some Belgian peculiarities, though a tiny enclave of the eastern Ardennes is German speaking. Brussels is officially bilingual, though in day-to-day reality spoken French (and English) predominates there. Politically, the two main language communities have long been at loggerheads. But they share a low-key form of tolerant Roman Catholicism. Religious-based traditions remain strong but, to a great extent, being Catholic is more a badge of social status than a spiritual dogma. Many Belgian cities have large immigrant communities, notably from Italy and France, but more conspicuously from Morocco, Turkey and the former Belgian colony of Congo. Belgium's small Jewish community is most visible in Antwerp's diamond district.

Arts

Literature

One of Belgium's foremost novelists was Hugo Claus, whose masterpiece, *The Sorrow of Belgium*, weaves a beautifully nuanced examination of Nazi collaboration during WWII. Georges Simenon, the 'shagaholic' creator of Inspector Maigret, was born in Liège.

Music & Dance

Belgium owes its independence to an 1830 revolution that started with an opera at La Monnaie/De Munt, still Brussels' foremost classical venue. Jazz owes much to Belgium's Adolphe Sax who invented the saxophone. Brussels' three-day **Jazz Marathon** (www.brusselsjazzmarathon.be; ⏲late May) remains one of the capital's most joyous events.

In the 1950s Flemish-born chanson star Jacques Brel took the French-speaking world by storm and remains widely revered. Among more contemporary names, keep an ear out for Puggy, Arid, Ghinzu and dEUS (alternative rock), Soulwax/2manyDJs (electro/mash-up), Axelle Red (pop-chanson) and Hooverphonic (trip hop).

Foremost in Belgian dance are the **Royal Flanders Ballet** (www.kbvv.be) and dynamic contemporary groups **Rosas** (www.rosas.be) and **Danses/Plan K** (www.charleroi-danses.be).

Architecture

Dozens of Belgium's earliest buildings feature on Unesco's World Heritage list, including many a great belfry (belfort, beffroi) and *begijnhof* (courtyard surrounded by historic dwellings built to house lay sisters). Belgium was at the forefront of sinuously beautiful art nouveau, the design wave that swept across Europe at the end of the 19th century. Although later 20th-century neglect put much of this heritage under the demolition ball, there are still some fine examples in Brussels (Musée Horta, MIM) and Antwerp ('t Zuid and Zurenborg areas).

Apart from the mind-boggling 1958 Atomium, later 20th-century architecture proved far less inspired. Brussels' glass-tower EU quarter tragically wasted a great opportunity for city re-invention, but the last decade has seen a few contemporary masterpieces, such as Santiago Calatrava's Guillemins train station in Liège.

Visual Arts

In the late Middle Ages, sophisticated artists known quite misleadingly as the Flemish Primitives were at the forefront of a secularisation of painting. Key players included Jan van Eyck and Hans Memling, whose works are prominent in Belgian art galleries. Brussels' Breugel (Breughel) family created some of the 16th century's most memorable art, from peasant scenes to terrifying Bosch-like allegories of hell and damnation. However, styles changed radically with the 17th-century Counter-Reformation. To remind upstart citizens of the Catholic God's mystical power, baroque altarpieces and giant paintings burst forth with chubby cherubs and angelic awe. That era's foremost artist was Antwerp-based Pieter Paul Rubens, whose works are still an essential feature of numerous Antwerp museums and churches.

In the 19th and early 20th centuries, Belgian art greats included sculptor and social realist painter Constantin Meunier, expressionist pioneer James Ensor, fauvist Rik Wouters and multitalented Jean Brusselmans. Symbolist Fernand Khnopff produced beguiling work echoing the contemporary pre-Raphaelites and giving a foretaste of surrealism, whose foremost Belgian star was René Magritte, now celebrated in an excellent new Brussels museum.

Amongst Belgium's best-known contemporary artists are Panamarenko, Luc Tuymans and Jan Fabre, notable for covering a ceiling in Brussels' Palais Royal with 1.4 million iridescent beetle wing cases.

Sport

In an unexpected double comeback, Belgium's 'retired' tennis greats, Justine Henin and Kim Clijsters, have returned to the global top twenty, closely followed by up-and-coming star Yanina Wickmayer. However, Belgium's beloved sport, cycling, is in the doldrums, while the nation's hopes of co-hosting the 2018 soccer World Cup came to nothing.

Food & Drink

Dining is a treat in Belgium, where meals are often described as being French in quality, German in quantity. Though Belgian home-cooking is making a resurgence (see p114 for typical local dishes), many upper-range restaurants still prefer French-influenced cuisine. Here starters regularly include pâtés, garlic snails and possibly scallops. Main courses typically offer relatively unfussy fresh-fish dishes (monkfish, sole or perhaps cod) and quality meats. Steaks are generally served bloodier than English-speaking visitors anticipate: *à point* translates in phrase books as 'medium' but tends to approach what many Anglophones consider as rare. 'Blue' steaks have barely bounced off the grill. Locals show no qualms at tucking into frog's legs, veal, rabbit, foie gras, tripe or horse meat *(paardenfilet/steack de cheval)*.

Although restaurants can be pricey, you can save money by taking a weekday lunchtime *dagschotel/plat du jour* (dish of the day) or *dagmenu/menu du jour* (multi-course meal of the day). Or by eating in cafes or Asian places (where rice is generally included in menu prices). A *belegd broodje/sandwich garni* (half a baguette with filling) makes a great, inexpensive quick lunch.

Belgian cafes always serve alcohol, as well as coffee, and are convivial places to sample the nation's amazing range of beers. Belgium's famous lagers (eg Stella Artois) and white beers (Hoegaarden) are now global brands. But what has connoisseurs really drooling are the robust, rich 'abbey' beers (which were originally brewed in monasteries), and the 'Trappist beers' (that still are). Chimay, Rochefort, Westmalle and Orval are the best known, but, for beer maniacs, the one that really counts is Westvleteren 12° (see p150), which, like Chimay Blue and Rochefort 8, should ideally be aged a year or two. A Belgian beer oddity is spontaneously fermented lambic, a startlingly acidic brew made more palatable by aging then blending into gueuze or macerating with cherries to produce *kriek*.

Although tap water is always drinkable, in restaurants it's never served. Buy the bottled stuff – or beer, which is often cheaper.

Note that smoking is banned in restaurants and in cafes that serve meals.

BUYING BELGIAN CHOCOLATES

Mouth-watering Belgian chocolate is some of the world's best as it always uses 100% pure cocoa butter and involves lengthy 'conching' (stirring) to create a silky smooth texture. Within any specialist chocolatier shop, archetypal pralines (filled, bite-size chocolates) cost the same whether you select piece-by-piece or take a pre-mixed ballotin selection pack. However, prices vary radically between brands. So which to pick?

Leonidas (Map p122; www.leonidas.com; per kg €20.20) Ubiquitous. Although maligned by Belgian choco snobs, its price-quality ratio is hard to beat.

Corné Port Royal (Map p122; www.corneportroyal.be; per kg €40) Great *manons* (short-shelf-life pralines filled with flavoured crème-fraiche).

Galler (Map p122; www.galler.com; per kg €48) Innovative Kaori chocolate sticks that you dip in provided flavour pots.

Chocolate Line (Map p144; www.thechocolateline.be; per kg €50) Dominique Persoone's wild experiments have included using chilli, oregano and wasabi: the chocolate shooters were originally created for the Rolling Stones. Antwerp and Bruges only.

Neuhaus (Map p122; www.neuhaus.be; per kg €52) Established in 1857 in Brussels' gorgeous Galerie de la Reine, Neuhaus created Belgium's original pralines.

Pierre Marcolini (off Map p122; www.marcolini.be; per kg €70) Chic chocolatier famed for using exclusive chocolate beans, experimental flavours (eg tea) and fashion-conscious black-box packaging.

SURVIVAL GUIDE

Directory A–Z

Accommodation

In **hotel** rooms under €60 for a double expect shared bathroom facilities. Midrange hotels (under €150) can be fairly functional, but many top-end establishments in Brussels cut prices radically at weekends and in summer.

Rooms rented in local homes *(gastenkamers/chambres d'hôtes)* can be cheap and cheerful (from €35/45 per single/double), but many **B&Bs** offer standards equivalent to a boutique hotel (up to €160 double).

Holiday houses *(gîtes)* are easily rented in Wallonia, but minimum stays apply and there's a hefty 'cleaning fee' on top of quoted rates; see **Belsud** (www.belsud.be).

Dorm beds in **hostels** cost from €15 to 29. Hostels (*jeugdherbergen* in Dutch, *auberges de jeunesse* in French) affiliated with **Hostelling International** (HI; www.jeugdherbergen.be, www.laj.be) charge €3 extra for non-members, and around €2 less for under-26-year-olds (prices include sheets and a basic breakfast). Always read the conditions.

Camping opportunities are plentiful, especially in the Ardennes. For extensive listings see www.campingbelgique.be (Wallonia) and www.camping.be (Flanders).

PRICE RANGES

Our sleeping reviews refer to double rooms with a private bathroom, except in hostels or where otherwise specified. The rates quoted are for **high season**, which is May to September in Bruges, Ypres and the Ardennes, and September to June in business cities.

€€€ more than €150

€€ €60 to €150

€ less than €60

Activities

In **Flanders** (www.fietsroute.org), **bicycles** are a popular means of everyday travel and many roads have dedicated cycle lanes. In **Wallonia** (www.ravel.wallonie.be), the hilly terrain favours mountain bikes (*VTT/vélo tout-terrain* in French). Brussels offers a forward-thinking bike-rental scheme, but its drivers are notorious for disregarding bicycles – beware!

Canoeing and **kayaking** are best in the Ardennes, but don't expect rapids of any magnitude.

Local tourist offices have copious information about footpaths and sell regional **hiking** maps. Hilly Wallonia is more inspiring than flat Flanders.

Many **museums** in Flanders offer €1 tickets for 'youths' under 26 years.

Business Hours

Opening hours given in the text are for high season. Many tourism-based businesses reduce their hours off season.

Banks 9am-3.30pm Mon-Fri

Brasseries 11am-1am

Clubs 11pm-6am Fri-Sun

Pubs & cafes till 1am or later

Restaurants 11.30am-2.30pm & 6.30-10.30pm

Shops 10am-6pm Mon-Sat, limited opening Sun; some close for lunch

Supermarkets 9am-8pm Mon-Sat, some open Sundays

Embassies

All are in Brussels.

Australia (☎02 286 05 00; www.eu.mission.gov.au; Rue Guimard 6/8)

Canada (☎02 741 06 11; www.ambassade-canada.be; Ave de Tervuren 2)

Japan (☎02 513 23 40; www.be.emb-japan.go.jp; Sq de Meeûs 5–6)

New Zealand (☎02 512 10 40; www.nzembassy.com; Ave des Nerviens 9–31)

UK (☎02 287 62 11; www.ukinbelgium.fco.gov.uk; Ave Auderghem 10)

US (☎02 811 40 00; http://belgium.usembassy.gov; Blvd du Régent 27)

Food

Price ranges for average main courses are as follows:

€€€	more than €25
€€	€14 to €25
€	less than €14

Money

Banks usually offer better exchange rates than **exchange bureaux** (*wisselkantoren* in Dutch, *bureaux de change* in French), though sometimes only for their banking clients.

ATMs are widespread, but often hidden within bank buildings.

Tipping is not expected in restaurants (service and VAT is always included).

Public Holidays

School holidays are July and August; one week in November; two weeks at Christmas; one week around Carnival; two weeks at Easter; one week in May.

ENTERTAINMENT RESOURCES

Nightlife listings www.theclubbing.com, www.noctis.com

Cinema listings www.cinenews.be

Concerts & tickets www.fnacagenda.be

Public holidays are as follows:

New Year's Day 1 January

Easter Monday March/April

Labour Day 1 May

Ascension Day Fortieth day after Easter

Whit Monday Seventh Monday after Easter

Flemish Community Festival 11 July (Flanders only)

National Day 21 July

Assumption 15 August

Francophone Community Festival 27 September (Wallonia only)

All Saints' Day 1 November

Armistice Day 11 November

German-Speaking Community Festival 15 November (eastern cantons only)

Christmas Day 25 December

Telephone

Dial full numbers: there's no optional area code.

International operator ☎1324

Directory assistance ☎1405; costs a hefty €3

Reverse-charge ☎1224

Toll-free ☎0800

High toll ☎0900, ☎070

Visas

Schengen visa rules apply. See p1217 for more information. Embassies are listed at www.diplomatie.belgium.be/en.

Getting There & Away

Air

Antwerp airport (ANR; www.antwerpairport.be) is tiny with just a few flights to the UK on **CityJet** (www.cityjet.com).

EUROLINES SERVICES

LINE	STANDARD PRICE (€)	SUPER-PROMO PRICE (€)	DURATION (HR)	FREQUENCY
Brussels–Amsterdam	17	10	3¾-4½	8 daily
Brussels–Frankfurt	44	38	6	1 or 2 daily
Brussels–London	41	22	6-8½	5 daily
Bruges–London	41	22	4¼	2 weekly, daily in summer
Brussels–Paris	29	9	4	12 daily

Brussels airport (BRU; www.brusselsairport.be) is Belgium's main long-haul gateway. Domestic airline **Brussels Airlines** (www.brusselsairlines.com) flies from here to numerous European and African destinations. Brussels is also a European hub for Chinese airline **Hainan Airlines** (www.global.hnair.com), Gulf-based **Etihad** (www.etihadairways.com), and Indian airline **Jet Airways** (www.jetairways.com), with useful connections to North America and throughout Asia.

Budget airlines **Ryanair** (www.ryanair.com), **JetAirFly** (www.jetairfly.com) and **WizzAir** (www.wizzair.com) use the misleadingly named **Brussels-South Charleroi Airport** (CRL; www.charleroi-airport.com), which is actually 55km south of Brussels, 6km north of the ragged, post-industrial city of Charleroi. **L'Elan** (www.voyages-lelan.be) runs direct buses to/from a stop near Bruxelles-Midi station roughly every half hour (single/return €13/22, one hour); the last northbound services departs at 11.30pm, the first southbound at 4.30am. Alternatively **buses** (www.infotec.be; €2.70, 18 minutes) run to Charleroi-Sud train station twice hourly on weekdays, hourly at weekends. A combined bus-and-rail ticket purchased before leaving the airport is never more than €11 to anywhere in Belgium. If planning to sleep at the airport, bring a good mat and something warm or use one of eight mostly generic hotels around 2km away, such as the bare-bones Formule 1.

Liège airport (LGG; www.liegeairport.com) has mostly charter flights

Land

BUS

Ecolines (☎02 279 20 57; www.ecolines.net) and **Eurobus** (☎02 527 50 12; www.eurobus.pl) operate from Brussels and Antwerp to various destinations in Eastern Europe.

Eurolines (☎02 274 13 50; www.eurolines.be ⏱telephone booking line 9am-7.30pm Mon-Fri, 9am-5pm Sat) is part of the Europe-wide network. Pre-bookings are compulsory but, although nine Belgian cities are served, only Brussels, Antwerp, Ghent and Liège have ticket offices. Special tickets adding a connecting bus to major cities in England/Scotland (from €15/22 total) are available through ticket offices but not available online. See the boxed text for some examples of standard/'super-promo' (off peak, advance purchase) fares.

CAR & MOTORCYCLE

Border crossings are not usually controlled. Petrol is cheaper in Luxembourg, so fill up there if passing by. **Car-share EuroStop** (www.taxistop.be; €3 per 100km) matches paying hitchhikers with drivers for long-distance international rides. A **driving licence** from your home country will usually suffice for foreign drivers. As in France, there is **priorité à droite** (give way to the right); see the boxed text, p468.

TRAIN

For comprehensive timetables and international bookings, see www.b-rail.be.

High-speed Trains

International high-speed trains have compulsory pre-booking requirements and charge radically different prices according to availability, so advance booking can save a packet. Operating companies:

Thalys (www.thalys.com) Paris–Brussels–Antwerp–Rotterdam–Schipol–Amsterdam runs eight times daily; the Brussels–Amsterdam section takes 113 minutes. Brussels–Paris takes 80 minutes with summer-only connections to Avignon and Marseille (5¾ hours). Brussels–Liège–

Aachen–Cologne (108 minutes) runs four times daily.

Eurostar (www.eurostar.com) Brussels–Lille–London St Pancras (two hours) runs up to nine times daily.

ICE (www.db.de) Brussels–Liège–Aachen–Cologne–Frankfurt (3¼ hours) runs six times daily via Frankfurt airport (three hours).

TGV (www.sncf.com) Has numerous Belgium–France routes, including Brussels–CDG airport (100 minutes, seven daily), but no service to central Paris.

FYRA (www.fyra.com) The Brussels–Amsterdam high-speed service (1¾ hours) is due to start in 2013.

Other International Trains

NMBS/SNCB trains have fixed fares, accept rail passes without a surcharge and don't require advanced booking. Useful international connections include Brussels–Luxembourg (€34.60, 3¼ hours) every two hours; and Brussels–Antwerp–Amsterdam (€37.80, three hours), currently hourly at least until FYRA services start. There's no NMBS/SNCB Brussels–Paris train but NMBS/SNCB trains run regularly to Lille from Tournai (€6, 30 minutes), Ypres (via Kortrijk) and Antwerp (via Ghent).

Sea

Most UK-bound motorists drive a couple of hours west to Dunkirk (Dunkerque) or Calais in France. However there are two direct options from Belgium:

Zeebrugge–Hull P&O (www.poferries.com) runs the 14-hour overnight service, which costs from €159 one-way. Pedestrians can reach Zeebrugge port on a bus leaving Bruges train station at 7.30pm (€3.50).

Ostend–Ramsgate TransEuropa Ferries (www.transeuropaferries.com) runs this service (€55-62 one-way, four hours, four daily). No pedestrians carried.

Getting Around

Bicycle

Cycling is a great way to get around in flat Flanders, less so in chaotic Brussels or undulating Wallonia. The Belgian countryside is riddled with cycling routes (see www.veloroutes.be) and most tourist offices sell helpful regional cycling maps.

Bikes on the train cost €5 one-way (or €8 all day) on top of the rail fare. A few busy city-centre train stations don't allow bicycle transportation.

Bike hire is available from private operators and many major train stations from around €6.50/9.50 per half/full day. A deposit and/or ID is usually required.

Bus & Tram

Regional buses are well coordinated with Belgium's rail network, but in rural regions you can still find that relatively short distances can involve long waits. In Brussels and Antwerp, trams that run underground are marked *'premetro'*. Bus companies:

De Lijn (www.delijn.be, in Dutch) In Flanders.

STIB (www.stib.be) In Brussels.

TEC (www.infotec.be) In Wallonia.

Car & Motorcycle

Motorways are toll free. **Speed limits** are 50km/h in most towns (30km/h near schools), 70km/h to 90km/h on inter-town roads, and 120km/h on motorways. The maximum legal **blood alcohol limit** is 0.05%. **Car hire** is available at airports and major train stations, but is usually cheaper from city centre offices.

Taxi

Taxis must usually be pre-booked but there are ranks near main stations. Tips and taxes are always included in metered fares.

Train

NMBS/SNCB (Belgian Railways; ☎02 528 28 28; www.b-rail.be) trains are completely non-smoking. Special fare categories:

Children After 9am, kids under 12 travel for free if accompanied by an adult.

Seniors People over 65 pay only €5 for a return 2nd-class trip anywhere in Belgium (some exclusions apply).

B-Excursions Good-value one-day excursion fares including return rail ticket plus selected entry fees.

Go Pass/Rail Pass Ten one-way 2nd-class trips to anywhere in Belgium (except frontier points) cost €46/74 for people under/over 26 years.

Weekend Return Tickets Valid from 7pm Friday to Sunday night, for just 20% more than a single.

Britain

Includes »

Best Places to Eat

- Smiths of Smithfield (p189)
- Terre à Terre (p203)
- Marlborough Tavern (p211)
- Llys Meddyg (p264)
- Fishers Bistro (p274)

Best Places to Stay

- Hoxton (p187)
- St Anne's House (p207)
- Ambleside YHA (p260)
- NosDa Budget Hotel (p263)
- Trafford Bank (p289)

Why Go?

The Tower of London, Edinburgh Castle, Buckingham Palace, Manchester United, The Beatles...Britain does icons like nowhere else on earth, and the astounding variety is a major reason to travel here. City streets tempt with shops and restaurants, and some of the finest museums in the world. Next day, you're deep in the countryside, high in the hills or enjoying a classic seaside resort.

Along with variety, a journey through Britain is a journey through history. You can lay your hands on the ancient megaliths of a 5000-year-old stone circle or walk through Roman ruins, then fast forward to the future and admire 21st-century architecture or explore the space-age domes of Cornwall's Eden Project.

And it's all so easy. In this compact country you're never far from the next welcoming pub, the next scenic national park or the next impressive castle on your hit list of highlights.

When to Go

London

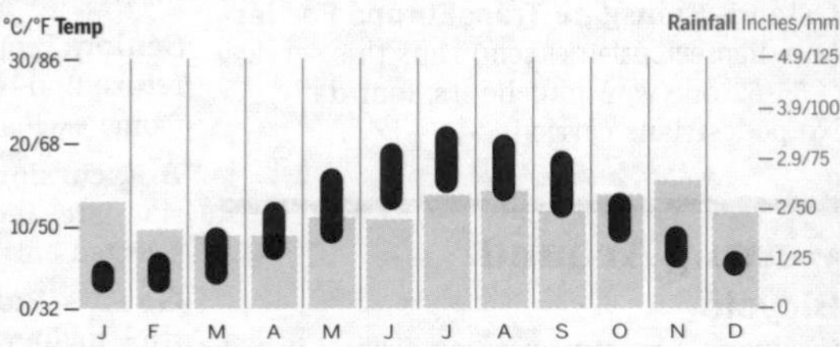

Easter–May Fewer crowds, especially in popular spots like Bath, York and Edinburgh

June–Aug The weather is at its best but the coast and national parks are busy

Mid-Sep–Oct Prices drop and the weather is often surprisingly good

Connections

As an island on the edge of Western Europe, Britain's overland transport options to neighbouring countries were limited to ferries before the opening of the Channel Tunnel in 1994 introduced direct Eurostar rail services from Paris and Brussels. Ferries still sail from southern England across to France in a couple of hours, from eastern England to the Netherlands, Germany or northern Spain, from northern England to Scandinavia, from southwest Scotland to Northern Ireland and from Wales to the Republic of Ireland. For details on Eurostar and ferry routes, see p308 and p309.

ITINERARIES

One Week

With just seven days, you're pretty much limited to sights in England. Start in London, then branch out to Canterbury and Brighton, or Salisbury and Stonehenge (or all four). Sample the delights of historic Bath, tootle up to Oxford and Stratford-upon-Avon, then head east to Cambridge before returning to London.

Two Weeks

Start in London, then do a southeast–southwest loop via the grand cathedral cities of Canterbury, Winchester and Salisbury. Marvel at the iconic menhirs of Stonehenge and nearby Avebury, then enjoy more history in beautiful Bath. Head over to Cardiff for a taste of Wales, then cruise across the classic English countryside of the Cotswolds to reach Oxford. Not far away is Stratford-upon-Avon, for everything Shakespeare. Strike out north to Scotland's capital Edinburgh, before recrossing the border down to Durham and York, then Cambridge and back to London.

Essential Food & Drink

» **Roast beef with Yorkshire pudding** Iconic English dish: beef with baked-batter pudding.

» **Bangers and mash** Another icon: sausages and mashed potato.

» **Fish and chips** Once the nation's most popular takeaway food, though nowadays a curry is the favourite.

» **Haggis** Scottish speciality of sheep-offal pudding served with 'tatties and neeps' (potatoes and turnips).

» **Cawl and bara lafwr** Welsh treats: a broth made with lamb and leeks; savoury scones made with oatmeal and seaweed.

AT A GLANCE

» **Currency** pound sterling (£)

» **Languages** English, Welsh, Scottish Gaelic

» **Money** Change bureaus and ATMs widely available.

» **Visas** Schengen rules do not apply; see p308.

Fast Facts

» **Area** 88,500 sq miles

» **Population** 58 million

» **Telephone** country code ☎44; international access code ☎00

» **Emergency** ☎999

Exchange Rates

Australia	A$1	UK£0.65
Canada	C$1	UK£0.63
Euro Zone	€1	UK£0.87
Japan	¥100	UK£0.77
New Zealand	NZ$1	UK£0.45
USA	US$1	UK£0.60

Set Your Budget

» **Hostel dorm bed** £10–25

» **Midrange B&B** £50–100

» **Two-course pub dinner** £8–13

» **Pint of beer** £3

» **Long-distance coach** £10–30 (200-mile trip)

» **Long-distance train** £15–50 (200-mile trip)

Resources

» **Visit Britain** (www.visitbritain.com)

» **National Traveline** (www.traveline.org.uk)

Britain Highlights

1 Walk the streets of **London** (p164), one of the world's greatest capital cities

2 Take in **Bath** (p208), Britain's belle of the ball

3 Wander Britain's most dramatic Roman ruin, **Hadrian's Wall** (p251)

4 Enjoy mountains, valleys and – of course – lakes in the **Lake District** (p259)

5 Find hiking heritage, medieval city walls and the spectacular cathedral at **York** (p242)

6 See classic chocolate-box countryside at its best in the **Cotswolds** (p228)

7 Marvel at the iconic prehistoric site of **Stonehenge** (p208)

8 Get acquainted with **Edinburgh** (p269), the city of many moods, famous for festivals

9 Experience jaw-dropping moments at every turn in Scotland's **Northwest Highlands** (p289)

10 Discover the best of wild and wonderful West Wales in **Pembrokeshire** (p263)

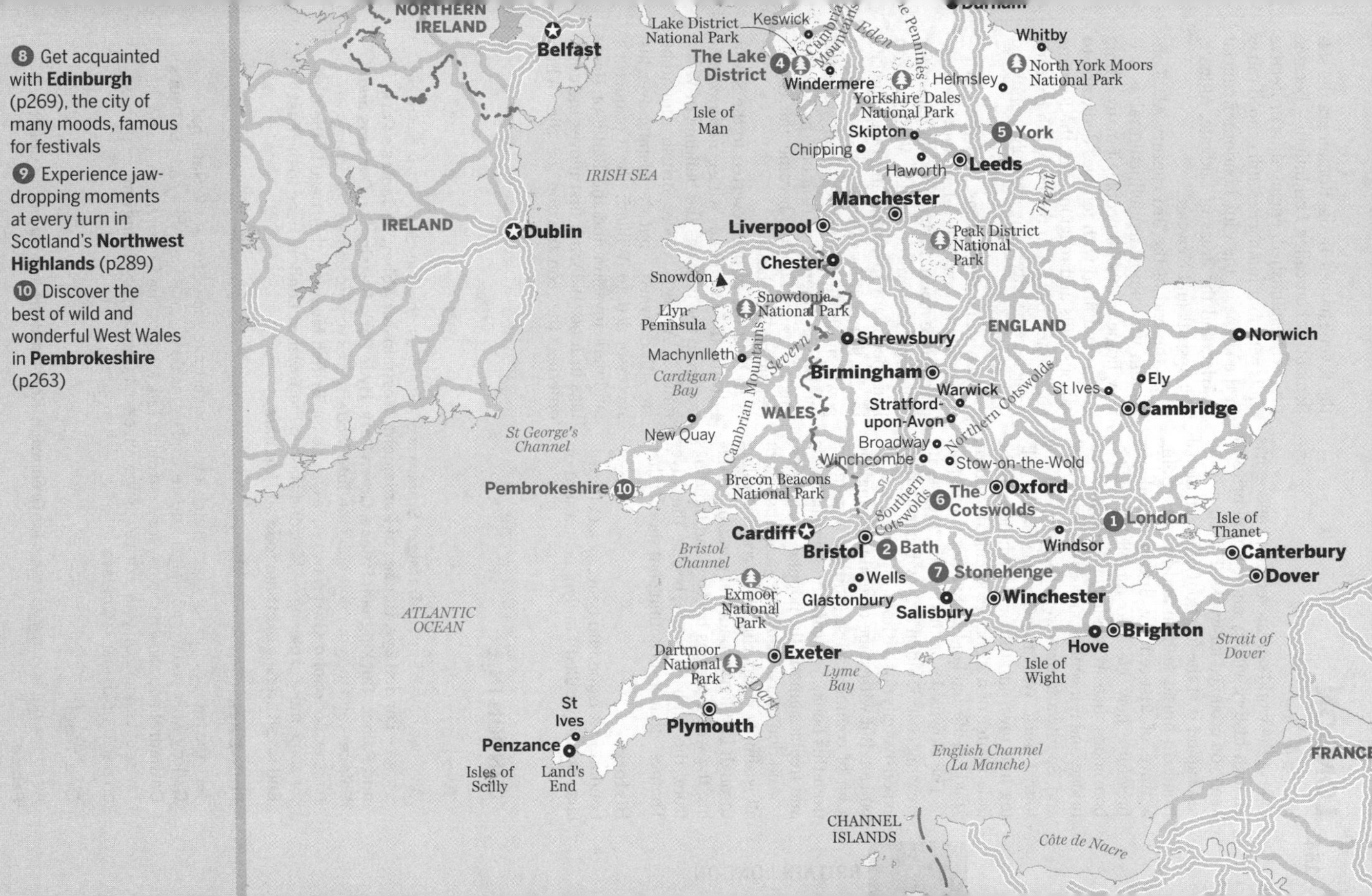

LONDON

POP 7.51 MILLION

One of the world's greatest cities, London has enough history, vitality and cultural drive to keep you occupied for weeks. This cosmopolitan capital is at the forefront of international trends in music, fashion and the arts, riding a wave of 21st-century British confidence, breathing new life into established neighbourhoods like Westminster and Knightsbridge, and reinventing areas like Clerkenwell and Southwark that were formerly off the tourist track. With the Olympic Games rolling into town in 2012, and even despite the little matter of a global economic downturn, London's life and landscape never stands still.

The downside of this renaissance is increasing cost: London is now Europe's most expensive city for visitors – whatever their budget. But with some careful planning and a bit of common sense (and a few pointers from this book), you can find great bargains and freebies among the popular attractions.

And don't forget that the greatest show of all is simply wandering the streets, strolling through London's wonderful parks or admiring the world-famous bridges and buildings from the embankments beside the River Thames – that costs nothing but shoe leather.

History

London first came into being as a Celtic village, possibly called Lundyn, near a ford on the River Thames. In the Roman era the settlement – then called Londinium – became properly established, enclosed in protective walls with four main gates still echoed today in the shape of the City, London's financial district, and the areas of Ludgate, Aldgate, Bishopsgate and Newgate.

By the end of the 3rd century AD, Londinium was almost as multicultural as it is now, home to 30,000 people of many ethnic groups and filled with temples dedicated to various cults and religions. But the Romans abandoned Britain in the early 5th century, reducing the city to a sparsely populated backwater.

Then came the Saxons, and the town – which was by now called Lundenwic – prospered once again. Perhaps too much so, for it caught the eye of Danish Vikings, who launched many invasions and razed the city in the 9th century. The Saxons held on to power until 1016, when they finally accepted the Danish ruler Knut (Canute) as King of England, and London became the capital (replacing Winchester).

In 1042 the throne reverted to the Saxon Edward the Confessor, whose main contribution to the city was the building of Westminster Abbey – where British monarchs are still crowned – but the dispute over his successor led to William the Conqueror's landmark invasion and the Battle of Hastings in 1066. William's first moves included ordering the construction of the White

LONDON IN...

Two Days

Only two days? Start in **Trafalgar Square** and see at least the outside of all the big-ticket sights – **London Eye, Houses of Parliament, Westminster Abbey, St James's Park and Palace, Buckingham Palace, Green Park, Hyde Park, Kensington Gardens and Palace** – and then motor around the **Tate Modern** until you get booted out. In the evening, explore **Soho**. On day two, race around the **British Museum**, then head to **the City** for some more exploring on foot, and finish in the **Tower of London**. Head to the **East End** for an evening of **ethnic food** and **hip bars**.

Four Days

Take the two-day itinerary but stretch it to a comfortable pace. Stop at the **National Gallery** while you're in Trafalgar Square, explore inside Westminster Abbey and **St Paul's Cathedral** and allow half a day for each of the Tate Modern, the British Museum and the Tower of London. On your extra evenings, check out **Camden** and **Islington** or splurge on a slap-up dinner in **Chelsea**.

One Week

As above, but add in a day each for **Greenwich**, **Kew Gardens** and **Hampton Court Palace**.

London

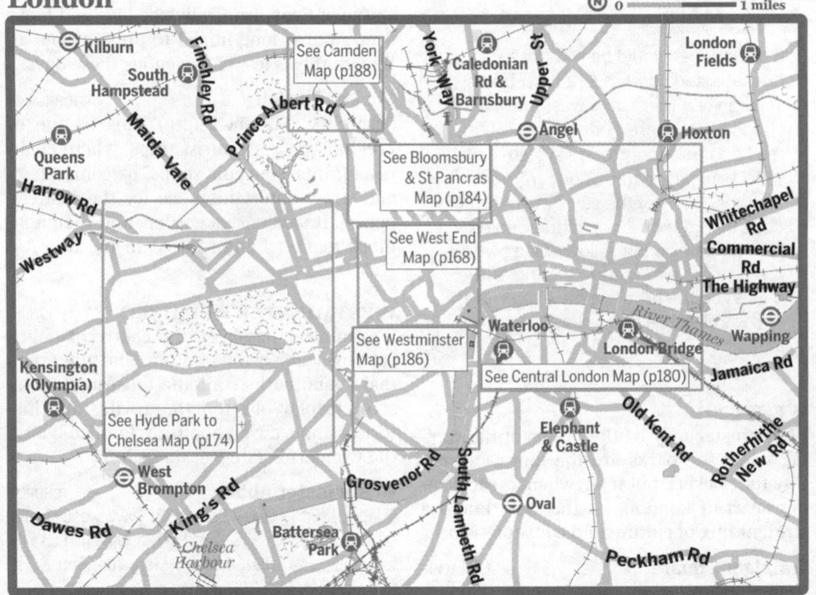

Tower (the core of today's Tower of London), negotiating taxes with the merchants, and affirming the city's independence and right to self-government.

With this foundation, London grew prosperous and increased in global importance throughout the medieval period, surviving devastating challenges like the 1665 Plague and 1666 Great Fire. Instead, the city simply shrugged and reinvented itself – many of its landmarks such as St Paul's Cathedral were built at this time by visionary architect Christopher Wren.

By 1720 London had 750,000 inhabitants and was the centre of a growing world empire. Fuelled by mercantile wealth, the Victorian era was the city's golden age. In contrast, WWII was London's darkest hour, with the city on the edge of destruction after the relentless bombings known as the Blitz. Several museums recall this period, still fresh in the memory of many elderly locals.

The ugly postwar rebuilding phase of the 1950s gave way to the cultural renaissance of the 1960s, when London became the planet's undisputed swinging capital. Things dipped again during the 1970s, while the 1980s heralded a time of great plenty for some Londoners and hardship for others. The pendulum swung again in the 1990s, and London was the focus of the Cool Britannia phenomenon of new politics, arts and music.

In 2000 the modern metropolis of London got its first elected Mayor (as opposed to the Lord Mayor of the City of London – a largely ceremonial role), and through the early years of the 21st century the city rediscovered a self-confidence that fuelled its selection as 2012 Olympic Games host.

But for every period of success, tragedy has never been far away. The day after winning its Olympic bid in 2005, four terrorist bombs killed dozens of people on buses and underground trains around the city. While deep anxiety initially gripped many Londoners, most soon returned to their daily routines – a stoic response mirrored throughout the capital's turbulent history.

Sights

London is teeming with magnificent buildings, world-leading museums (many of which offer free admission) and cutting-edge attractions. With so much to see and do, it can be hard to know where to start. Weather will be a determining factor: if it's raining, it's a day for museums and galleries; if the sun shines, make like a Londoner and include the parks on your itinerary.

MAPS

No Londoner would be without a pocket-sized *London A–Z* map-book – you can buy them at newsstands and shops everywhere. For getting around the London Underground system ('the tube'), maps are free at underground stations. Many of the city's main attractions lie within the loop of the Circle Line (colour-coded yellow). Don't worry if you take a wrong turn: getting a little bit lost on the tube is a rite of passage, and it's always easy to retrace your steps.

WEST END

Westminster may be the brains of the capital, while the parks are the lungs and the City the pockets, but if anywhere is the beating heart of London, it's the West End – a strident mix of culture and consumerism.

Trafalgar Square LANDMARK

(Map p168; ⊖Charing Cross) Trafalgar Square is a great place to start any visit to London. Frequently the venue for rallies and marches (and feverish New Year's festivities), Londoners congregate here to celebrate anything from football victories to the ousting of political leaders. Dominating the square is the 43m-high **Nelson's Column**, erected in 1843 to commemorate British hero Admiral Nelson's 1805 victory over Napoleon. Around the square are four plinths; three have permanent statues, the **fourth plinth** has temporary installations.

FREE **National Gallery** ART MUSEUM

(Map p168; www.nationalgallery.org.uk; Trafalgar Sq WC2; ⏲10am-6pm Sat-Thu, to 9pm Fri; ⊖Charing Cross) Gazing grandly over Trafalgar Square, this is Britain's most important art repository. Seminal paintings from every epoch are here, including works by Giotto, Leonardo da Vinci, Michelangelo and Van Gogh. It can be daunting, so arrive early and take your time, or target your visit.

FREE **National Portrait Gallery** ART MUSEUM

(Map p168; www.npg.org.uk; St Martin's Pl WC2; ⏲10am-6pm Sat-Wed, to 9pm Thu & Fri; ⊖Charing Cross) A visit here is like stepping into a picture book of British history.

Piccadilly Circus LANDMARK

(Map p168; ⊖Piccadilly Circus) Neon-lit, turbo-charged Piccadilly Circus is home to a popular but unremarkable London landmark, the statue of **Eros**. Ironically, the love god looks over an area long linked to prostitution, although this is less conspicuous these days.

Covent Garden HISTORIC AREA

(Map p168; ⊖Covent Garden) This is one of London's biggest tourist traps, where chain restaurants, souvenir shops, balconied bars and street entertainers vie for the punters' pound. It *was* once a garden, and then a famous market immortalised in the film *My Fair Lady*.

WESTMINSTER & PIMLICO

Westminster has been the centre of political power for a millennium, and the area's many landmarks combine to form an awesome display of strength, gravitas and historical import. Neighbouring Pimlico boasts the wonderful Tate Britain gallery.

Westminster Abbey CHURCH

(Map p186; ☎020-7222 5152; www.westminster-abbey.org; 20 Dean's Yard SW1; adult/child £15/6, tours £3; ⏲9.30am-4.30pm Mon, Tue, Thu & Fri, to 7pm Wed, to 2.30pm Sat; ⊖Westminster) Not merely a beautiful place of worship, Westminster Abbey serves up history cold on slabs of stone. This is where most monarchs have been crowned since 1066 (look out for the incongruously ordinary-looking **Coronation Chair**), and for centuries the great and the good have been interred here; in **Poet's Corner** you'll find the resting places of Chaucer, Dickens, Hardy, Tennyson, Dr Johnson and Kipling as well as memorials to Shakespeare, Jane Austen, Emily Brontë and more.

Westminster Cathedral CHURCH

(Map p186; www.westminstercathedral.org.uk; Victoria St SW1; ⏲7am-7pm; ⊖Victoria) Not to be confused with the eponymous abbey, the neo-Byzantine Westminster Cathedral dates from 1895, and is the headquarters of Britain's Roman Catholic Church. It's still a work in progress, the vast interior part dazzling marble and mosaic, and part bare brick; new sections are completed as funds allow. The distinctive 83m red-brick and white-stone **tower** (adult/child £5/2.50) offers splendid views of London, and unlike St Paul's, you can take the lift.

Houses of Parliament HISTORIC BUILDING

(Map p186; www.parliament.uk; Parliament Sq SW1; ⊖Westminster) Coming face to face with one of the world's most recognisable landmarks is always a surreal moment, but in the case of the Houses of Parliament it's a revelation. Officially called the Palace of Westminster, the oldest part of the interior is **Westminster Hall** (dating from 1097), but much of the visible building today dates from 1840. The palace's most famous feature is its clock tower, known (erroneously) as **Big Ben** – actually the name of the 13-tonne bell inside the tower. When parliament is in recess (three months over the summer, and a couple of weeks over Easter and Christmas) there are guided **tours** (☎0844 847 1672; www.ticketmaster.co.uk/housesofparliament; 75min tours adult/child £14/6) of the **House of Commons**, the **House of Lords** and other historic areas.

FREE **Tate Britain** ART MUSEUM
(Map p186; www.tate.org.uk; Millbank SW1; 10am-5.40pm; Pimlico) Reaching through time from 1500 to the present, this gallery is crammed with local heavyweights such as Blake, Hogarth, Gainsborough, Whistler, Spencer and, especially, Turner, whose 'interrupted visions' – unfinished canvases of moody skies – wouldn't look out of place in the contemporary section, alongside works by David Hockney, Francis Bacon, Tracey Emin and Damien Hirst. There are free hour-long guided tours taking in different sections of the gallery daily at midday and 3pm, plus additional tours at 11am and 2pm on weekdays.

Churchill Museum & Cabinet War Rooms MUSEUM
(Map p186; www.iwm.org.uk/cabinet; Clive Steps, King Charles St SW1; adult/child £15/free; 9.30am-6pm; Westminster) The Cabinet War Rooms were Prime Minister Winston Churchill's underground military headquarters during WWII. Now a wonderfully evocative and atmospheric museum, the restored and preserved rooms (including Churchill's bedroom) capture the drama of the time.

ST JAMES'S & MAYFAIR

Put on your best rah-rah voice to wander this aristocratic enclave of palaces, gentlemen's clubs, famous hotels, historic shops and elegant buildings.

Buckingham Palace PALACE
(Map p186; ☎020-7766 7300; www.royalcollection.org.uk; Buckingham Palace Rd SW1; adult/child £17/9.75; late Jul-Sep; Victoria) With so many imposing buildings in the capital, the Queen's relatively plain city pad can be an anticlimax. When she's not visiting far-flung parts of the world, Elizabeth II splits her time between here, Windsor and Balmoral. A handy way of telling whether she's home is to check whether the 'royal standard' flag is flying on the roof. The somewhat gaudily furnished **State Rooms** are open in summer for the hordes of Royal-loving tourists, but it's more fun outside watching the **changing of the guard** (11.30am May-Jul, alternate days rest of yr).

St James's Park & Green Park PARKS
(Map p186) With its manicured flowerbeds and ornamental lake, **St James's Park** is a wonderful place to stroll and take in the views of Westminster, Buckingham Palace and St James's Palace. The expanse of **Green Park** links St James's Park to Hyde Park and Kensington Gardens, creating a green corridor from Westminster all the way to Kensington. Although it doesn't have lakes, fountains or formal gardens, it's blanketed with daffodils in spring and seminaked bodies whenever the sun shines.

THE CITY

For centuries, the City (note the capital C) *was* London. Its boundaries have changed little from the Roman walls built in this area two millennia ago, and today it's London's central business district (also known as the 'square mile'). Only about 10,000 people actually live in the City, although some 300,000 more come to work here each weekday, generating almost three-quarters of Britain's entire GDP before squeezing back onto the tube to head home. On Sundays the City becomes a virtual ghost town, which is a good time to walk around and explore its ancient churches, intriguing architecture, hidden gardens and atmospheric laneways (although you'll miss the smell of fear as the planet's leading bankers cope with the fallout from the global credit crunch).

WANT MORE?

For in-depth information, reviews and recommendations at your fingertips, head to the Apple App Store to purchase Lonely Planet's *London City Guide* iPhone app.

Alternatively, head to **Lonely Planet** (www.lonelyplanet.com/england/london) for planning advice, author recommendations, traveller reviews and insider tips.

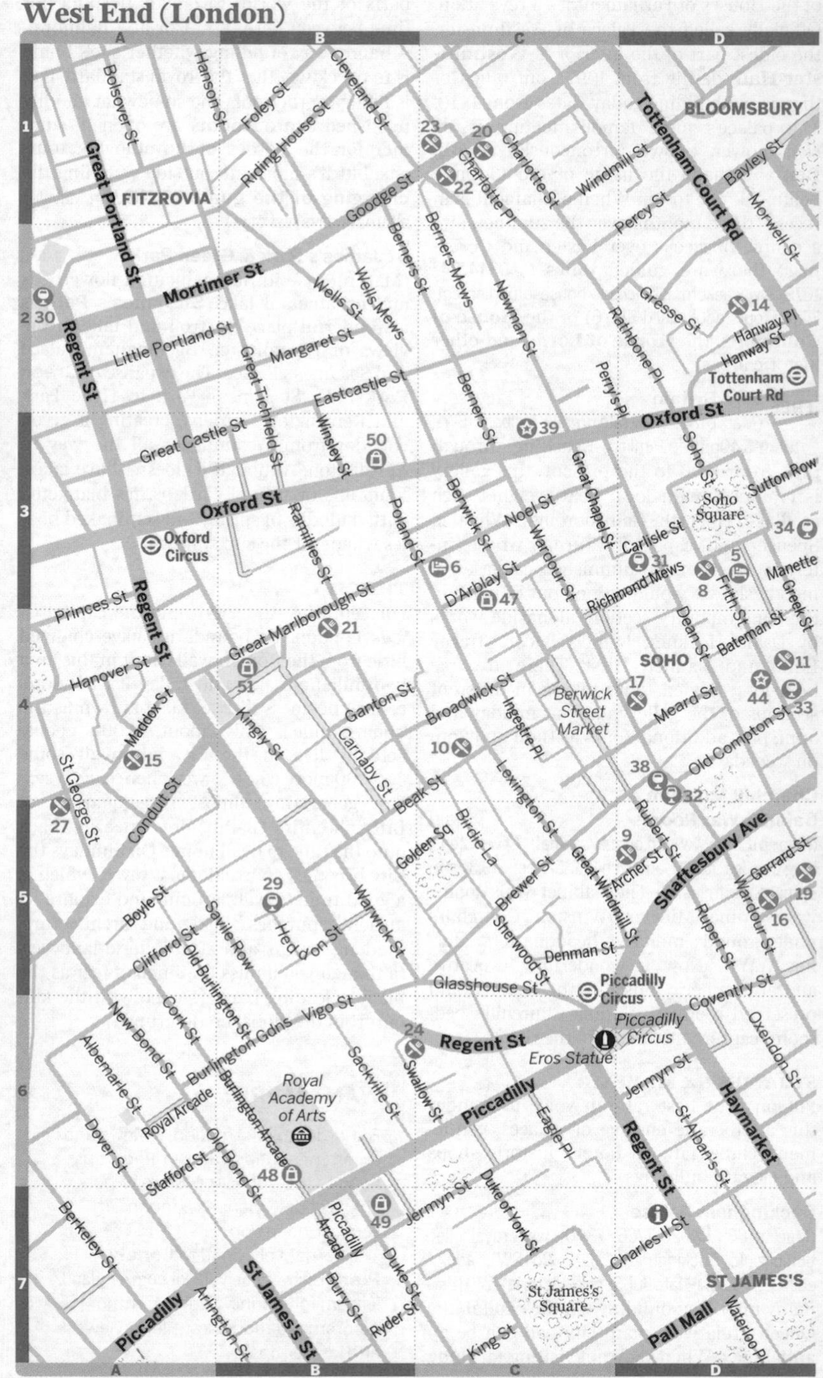

BLOOMSBURY
FITZROVIA
SOHO
ST JAMES'S
Great Portland St
Tottenham Court Rd
Oxford St
Regent St
Mortimer St
Goodge St
Charlotte St
Oxford Circus
Tottenham Court Rd
Piccadilly Circus
Soho Square
Berwick Street Market
Royal Academy of Arts
Eros Statue
St James's Square
Shaftesbury Ave
Piccadilly
Haymarket
Pall Mall

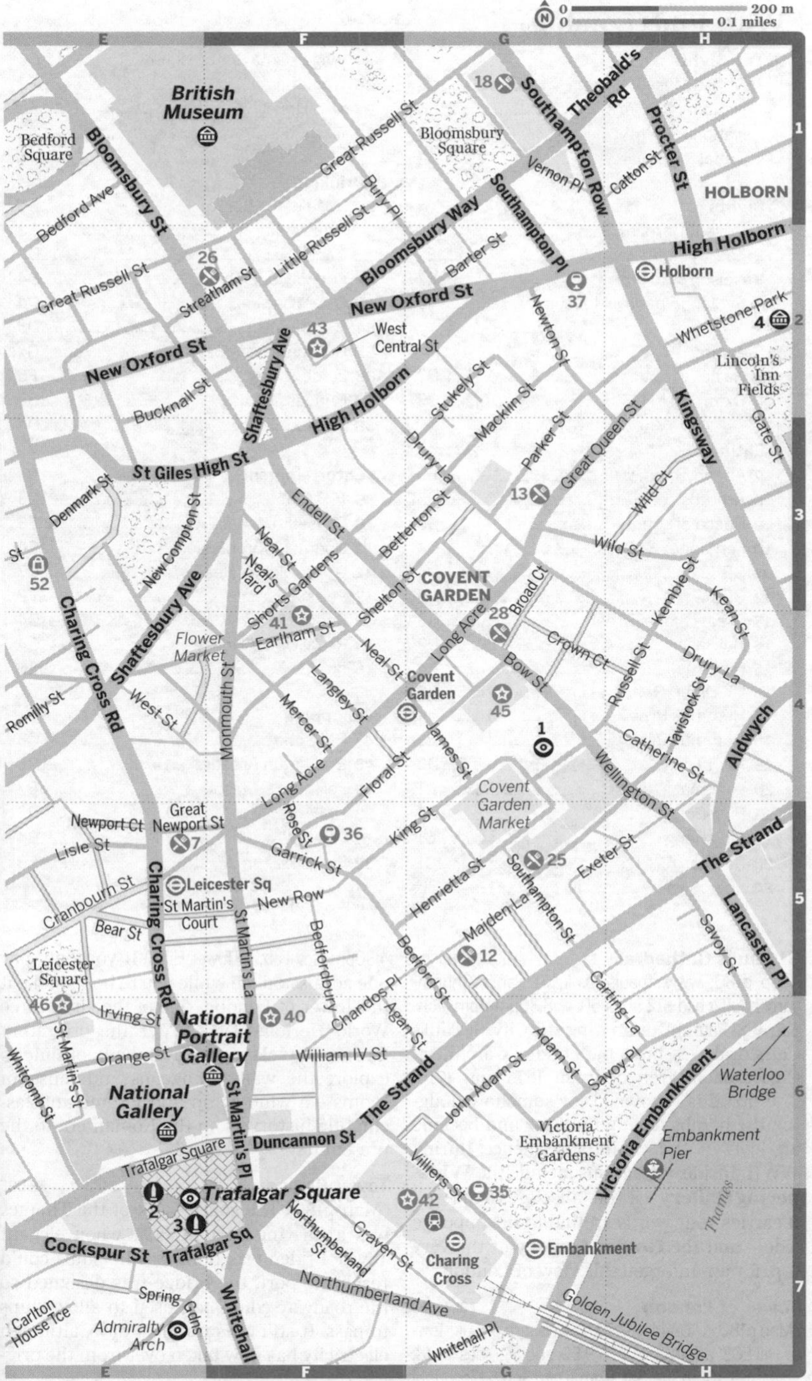
British Museum
Bedford Square
Bloomsbury Square
HOLBORN
High Holborn
Holborn
New Oxford St
West Central St
Lincoln's Inn Fields
Kingsway
COVENT GARDEN
Covent Garden
Covent Garden Market
Flower Market
Charing Cross Rd
Shaftesbury Ave
Leicester Sq
Leicester Square
National Portrait Gallery
National Gallery
Trafalgar Square
The Strand
Aldwych
Lancaster Pl
Victoria Embankment
Victoria Embankment Gardens
Embankment Pier
Waterloo Bridge
Embankment
Charing Cross
Northumberland Ave
Golden Jubilee Bridge
Whitehall
Admiralty Arch
Cockspur St
Thames

West End (London)

Top Sights

British Museum F1
National Gallery E6
National Portrait Gallery F6
Trafalgar Square E7

Sights

1 Covent Garden G4
2 Fourth Plinth E7
3 Nelson's Column E7
4 Sir John Soane's Museum H2

Sleeping

5 Hazlitt's D3
6 Oxford St YHA C3

Eating

7 Abeno Too E5
8 Arbutus D3
9 Bocca di Lupo D5
10 Fernandez & Wells C4
11 GBK D4
12 GBK G5
13 Great Queen Street G3
14 Hakkasan D2
15 Hibiscus A4
16 HK Diner D5
17 Hummus Bros D4
18 Hummus Bros G1
19 Kam Tong D5
20 Lantana C1
21 Ping Pong B4
22 Ping Pong C1
23 Salt Yard C1
24 Veeraswamy B6
25 Wagamama G5
26 Wagamama F2
27 Wild Honey A5
28 Zizzi G4

Drinking

29 Absolut Ice Bar B5
30 Artesian A2
31 Candy Bar D3
32 Friendly Society D4
33 G-A-Y Bar D4
34 G-A-Y Late D3
35 Gordon's Wine Bar G7
36 Lamb & Flag F5
37 Princess Louise G2
38 Village D4

Entertainment

39 100 Club C3
40 Coliseum F6
41 Donmar Warehouse F4
42 G-A-Y Club @ Heaven G7
43 Popstarz F2
44 Ronnie Scott's D4
45 Royal Opera House G4
46 tkts E6

Shopping

47 BM Soho C3
48 Burlington Arcade B6
49 Fortnum & Mason B7
50 HMV B3
51 Liberty B4
52 Ray's Jazz E3

St Paul's Cathedral CHURCH

(Map p180; www.stpauls.co.uk; St Paul's Churchyard; adult/child £12.50/4.50; ⏲8.30am-4pm Mon-Sat; ⊖St Paul's) Dominating the City, St Paul's Cathedral was built by 'London's architect' Christopher Wren between 1675 and 1710. The dome is renowned for somehow dodging the bombs during the Blitz and became an icon of the capital's resilience during WWII. Inside, attractions include the **Whispering Gallery** – if you talk close to the wall it carries your words around to the opposite side – and the **Golden Gallery** at the very top, for an unforgettable view of London.

Tower of London FORTRESS

(Map p180; ☎0844 482 7777; www.hrp.org.uk; Tower Hill EC3; adult/child £17/9.50, audio guides £4/3; ⏲9am-5.30pm Tue-Sat, from 10am Sun & Mon, until 4.30pm Nov-Feb; ⊖Tower Hill).) If you only pay one admission fee while you're here, make it the Tower of London, one of the city's three World Heritage sites. After the obligatory **Crown Jewels** visit, leave plenty of time to explore the walls, dungeons and museum rooms – a window on a gruesome and fascinating history, from the Roman era to the present day.

Tower Bridge BRIDGE

(Map p180) The south bank of the Thames was a thriving port in 1894 when elegant Tower Bridge was built. So the ships could reach the port, the bridge was designed so the roadway could be raised to allow ships to pass. It still goes up most days, although electricity has now taken over from the original steam engines. Walking across is free. For more insights, the **Tower Bridge Exhibition** (www.towerbridge.org.uk; adult/child £7/3; ⌚10am-5.30pm Apr-Sep, 9.30am-5pm Oct-Mar; ⊖Tower Hill) recounts the story with videos and animatronics.

Monument MONUMENT

(Map p180; www.themonument.info; Monument St EC4; adult/child £3/1; ⌚9.30am-5.30pm; ⊖Monument) Designed by Wren to commemorate the Great Fire, the Monument is 60.6m high, the exact distance from its base to the bakery on Pudding Lane where the blaze began. Climb the 311 tight spiral steps for an eye-watering view from beneath the symbolic vase of gold-leaf flames.

FREE **Museum of London** MUSEUM

(Map p180; www.museumoflondon.org.uk; 150 London Wall EC2; ⌚10am-6pm; ⊖Barbican) A visit to the fascinating Museum of London early in your stay helps to make sense of the layers of history that make up this great city.

CLERKENWELL & HOLBORN

In these now fashionable streets it's hard to find an echo of the notorious 'rookeries' of the 19th century, where families lived in probably the worst conditions in the city's long history, as documented so vividly in the novels of Charles Dickens.

Sir John Soane's Museum MUSEUM

(Map p168; www.soane.org; 13 Lincoln's Inn Fields WC2; tours £5; ⌚10am-5pm Tue-Sat, 6-9pm 1st Tue of month; ⊖Holborn) Not all of this area's inhabitants were poor, aptly demonstrated by the remarkable home of a celebrated architect, now the Sir John Soane's Museum. Stuffed with his eclectic collections, the house is largely as it was when Sir John was taken out in a box. Tours are run at 11am on Saturdays.

Charles Dickens Museum MUSEUM

(Map p184; www.dickensmuseum.com; 48 Doughty St WC1; adult/child £6/3; ⌚10am-5pm Mon-Sat, 11am-5pm Sun; ⊖Russell Sq) Dickens' sole surviving London residence is where his work really flourished – *The Pickwick Papers, Nicholas Nickleby* and *Oliver Twist* were all written here. Visitors can stroll through rooms choc-a-bloc with fascinating memorabilia.

SOUTHWARK

Outside the walls (and rules) of the city, Londoners once crossed to the areas south of the river for a wide range of diversions. This was the perfect spot to drink yourself silly, hook up with a prostitute, watch a bear being tortured for your amusement, then head to the theatre. The area is much more seemly now, but the theatre and entertainment tradition remains. A stroll along the **South Bank** beside the Thames is a great way to pass a couple of hours.

Shakespeare's Globe HISTORIC THEATRE

(Map p180; ☎020-7401 9919; www.shakespeares-globe.org; 21 New Globe Walk SE1; adult/child £11/7; ⌚10am-5pm; ⊖London Bridge) An authentic 1997 rebuild of the original London theatre where many Shakespeare plays were performed, the Globe has become a pilgrimage destination for fans of the Bard. Admission includes a guided tour of the open roofed theatre, faithfully reconstructed from oak beams, handmade bricks, lime plaster and thatch. There's also an extensive exhibition about Shakespeare and his times. Plays are still performed here (seats £15 to £35). As in Elizabethan times, 'groundlings' can watch for a modest price (£5) but there's no protection from the elements and you'll have to stand.

London Eye VIEWS

(Map p186; ☎0871 781 3000; www.londoneye.com; adult/child £18/9.50; ⌚10am-8pm; ⊖Waterloo) Originally designed as a temporary structure to celebrate the millennium, the Eye is a 135m-tall, slow-moving wheel with passengers riding in pods. The wheel takes 30 minutes to rotate completely and offers 25-mile views on a clear day. Book your ticket online to speed up your wait (you also get a 20% discount), or you can pay an additional £10 to jump the queue.

Southwark Cathedral CHURCH

(Map p180; ☎020-7367 6700; Montague Close SE1; suggested donation £4-6.50; ⌚8am-6pm Mon-Fri, 9am-6pm Sat & Sun; ⊖London Bridge) Although the central tower dates from 1520 and the choir from the 13th century, Southwark Cathedral is largely Victorian. Inside are monuments galore, including a Shakespeare Memorial. It's also worth visiting to hear **Evensong** (⌚5.30pm Tue, Thu & Fri, 4pm Sat, 3pm Sun).

City Hall LANDMARK

(Map p180; www.london.gov.uk; Queen's Walk SE1; ⌚8.30am-6pm Mon-Fri; ⊖London Bridge) The wonky-egg-shaped City Hall is an architectural feast, as well as home to the mayor's office and the London Assembly.

Design Museum MUSEUM

(Map p180; www.designmuseum.org; 28 Shad Thames SE1; adult/child £8.50/5; ⏲10am-5.45pm; ⊖Tower Hill) A must for anyone interested in beautiful, practical things; the permanent collection has displays of modern British design and there are regular temporary exhibitions including the annual *Designs of the Year* competition.

HMS *Belfast* SHIP

(Map p180; http://hmsbelfast.iwm.org.uk; Queen's Walk SE1; adult/child £13/free; ⏲10am-5pm; ⊖London Bridge) Launched in 1938, this battleship took part in the D-day landings and saw action in Korea. Explore the engine room, gun decks, galley, chapel and cells.

London Dungeon OFFBEAT SIGHT

(Map p180; ☎020-7403 7221; www.thedungeons.com; 28-34 Tooley St SE1; adult/child £20/15; ⏲10.30am-5pm, extended hr during holidays; ⊖London Bridge) Older kids tend to love the London Dungeon, as the terrifying queues during school holidays and weekends testify. It's all spooky music, ghostly boat rides, macabre hangman's-drop rides, fake blood and actors dressed up as gory criminals.

Sea Life AQUARIUM

(Map p186; ☎0871 663 1678; www.sealife.co.uk/london; County Hall SE1; adult/child £18/13; ⏲10am-6pm; ⊖Waterloo) One of the largest aquariums in Europe, with all sorts of aquatic creatures organised into different zones (coral cave, rainforest, River Thames), culminating with the shark walkway.

Hayward Gallery ART MUSEUM

(Map p180; www.southbankcentre.co.uk; Belvedere Rd SE1; ⏲10am-6pm Sat-Thu, to 10pm Fri; ⊖Waterloo) Part of the 1960s 'brutalist' Southbank Centre, the Hayward hosts a changing roster of modern art – video, installations, photography, collage, painting etc. Admission charges vary.

TATE-A-TATE

To get between London's Tate galleries in style, the **Tate Boat** (www.thames-clippers.com) will whisk you from one to the other, stopping en route at the **London Eye**. Services run from 10.10am to 5.28pm daily at 40-minute intervals. A River Roamer hop-on hop-off ticket (purchased on board) costs £12, single tickets £5.

FREE **Tate Modern** ART MUSEUM

(Map p180; www.tate.org.uk; Queen's Walk SE1; ⏲10am-6pm Sun-Thu, to 10pm Fri & Sat; ⊖Southwark) This surprisingly elegant former power station is now a tremendous museum. Focusing on modern art in all its wacky and wonderful permutations, it has been extraordinarily successful in bringing challenging work to the masses, becoming one of London's most popular attractions.

CHELSEA, KENSINGTON & KNIGHTSBRIDGE

It's called the Royal Borough of Kensington and Chelsea, and residents are certainly paid royally, earning the highest incomes in the UK (shops and restaurants will presume you do too). Knightsbridge has some of London's best-known department stores, while Kensington High St has a lively mix of chains and boutiques. Away from mammon, South Kensington boasts some of London's most beautiful and interesting museums.

FREE **Victoria & Albert Museum** MUSEUM

(V&A; Map p174; www.vam.ac.uk; Cromwell Rd SW7; ⏲10am-5.45pm Sat-Thu, to 10pm Fri; ⊖South Kensington) A vast and wonderful museum of decorative art and design, the V&A is like the nation's attic, comprising four million objects collected from Britain and around the globe. In its 150 galleries you'll see ancient Chinese ceramics, Japanese swords, Asian and Islamic art, Rodin sculptures, Elizabethan gowns, an all-wooden Frank Lloyd Wright study and a pair of Doc Martens. Yes, you'll need to plan.

FREE **Natural History Museum** MUSEUM

(Map p174; www.nhm.ac.uk; Cromwell Rd SW7; ⏲10am-5.50pm; ⊖South Kensington) A sure-fire hit with kids of all ages, the Natural History Museum is crammed full of interesting stuff, starting with the giant dinosaur skeleton that greets you in the main hall. The **Earth Galleries** are equally impressive. The **Darwin Centre** houses a team of biologists and a staggering 20-million species of animal and plant specimens. Take a lift to the top of the **Cocoon**, a seven-storey egg-shaped structure encased within a glass pavilion, and make your way down through the floors of interactive displays. Glass windows let you to watch the scientists at work.

FREE **Science Museum** MUSEUM

(Map p174; www.sciencemuseum.org.uk; Exhibition Rd SW7; ⏲10am-6pm; ⊖South Kensington) With seven floors of educational exhibits, the Science Museum covers everything from the Industrial Revolution to the exploration of space. There is something for all ages, from vintage cars to a flight simulator. Kids particularly love the interactive sections.

Hyde Park PARK

(Map p174; 5.30am- midnight; Marble Arch, Hyde Park Corner or Queensway) At 145 hectares, this is central London's largest open space. Henry VIII expropriated it from the Church in 1536, when it became a hunting ground and later a venue for duels, executions and horse racing. The 1851 Great Exhibition was held here and during WWII the park became an enormous potato field. These days, it serves as an occasional concert venue and a full-time green space. There's boating on the **Serpentine** and **Speaker's Corner** for oratorical acrobats. Nearby **Marble Arch** was designed as the entrance to Buckingham Palace, and moved here in 1851. A soothing structure, the **Diana, Princess of Wales Memorial Fountain** is a circular stream that cascades gently and reassembles in a pool at the bottom; paddling is encouraged. It was unveiled in mid-2004, instigating an inevitable debate over matters of taste and gravitas.

Kensington Palace PALACE

(Map p174; www.hrp.org.uk/kensingtonpalace; Kensington Gardens W8; adult/child £13/6.25; 10am-6pm; High St Kensington) Once the monarch's main residence, until George III moved across the park to Buckingham Palace, various members of the extended royal family still live here. In popular imagination it's most associated with three princesses: Victoria (born here in 1819), Margaret (sister of the current queen, who lived here until her 2002 death) and Diana (more than a million bouquets were left outside the gates following her death in 1997).

The palace building is undergoing major restoration work until January 2012, but rather than closing completely, various open sections have been transformed into a giant art installation. Leading artists and fashion designers have been given free rein to create their own enchanted spaces within the ornately painted and gilded rooms. There are no information panels, display cases, audio guides or tours. If you're hungry for historical information, ask the warders, who have been rebranded as 'explainers' for this very purpose.

Kensington Gardens PARK

(Map p174; dawn-dusk; High St Kensington) Blending in with Hyde Park, these royal gardens are part of Kensington Palace. Diana devotees can visit the **Diana, Princess of Wales Memorial Playground** in its northwest corner. The **Albert Memorial** is a lavish marble, mosaic and gold affair opposite the Royal Albert Hall, built to honour Queen Victoria's husband, Albert (1819–61).

The gardens also house the **Serpentine Gallery** (www.serpentinegallery.org; admission free; 10am-6pm), one of London's edgiest contemporary art spaces. The **Sunken Garden**, near the palace, is at its prettiest in summer, while tea in the **Orangery** is a treat any time of the year.

MARYLEBONE

With one of London's best high streets and plenty of green space, increasingly hip Marylebone is a great area to wander.

Regent's Park PARK

(Map p188; Regent's Park) This is London's finest open space – at once lively and serene, cosmopolitan and local – with football pitches, tennis courts and a boating lake. **Queen Mary's Gardens** are particularly pretty, with spectacular roses in summer, and the **Open Air Theatre** (020-7935 5756; www.openairtheatre.org) hosts performances of Shakespeare, comedy and concerts on summer evenings.

London Zoo ZOO

(Map p188; www.londonzoo.co.uk; Outer Circle, Regent's Park NW1; adult/child £18/14; 10am-5.30pm Mar-Oct, to 4pm Nov-Feb; Camden Town) A huge amount of money has been spent to bring London Zoo, established in 1828, into the modern world. It now has a swanky £5.3 million gorilla enclosure and is involved in gorilla conservation in Gabon. Feeding times, reptile handling and the petting zoo are guaranteed winners with the kids.

Madame Tussauds WAXWORKS

(Map p174; 0870 400 3000; www.madame-tussauds.co.uk; Marylebone Rd NW1; adult/child £26/22; 9.30am-5.30pm; Baker St) With so much fabulous free stuff to do in London, it's a wonder that people still join lengthy queues to visit Madame Tussauds, but in a celebrity-obsessed world the opportunity to pose beside Prince Charles and Camilla, or that other regal couple, Posh and Becks, is not short on appeal. The wax figures are life-size and lifelike, and as close to the real thing as most of us will get.

Hyde Park to Chelsea (London)

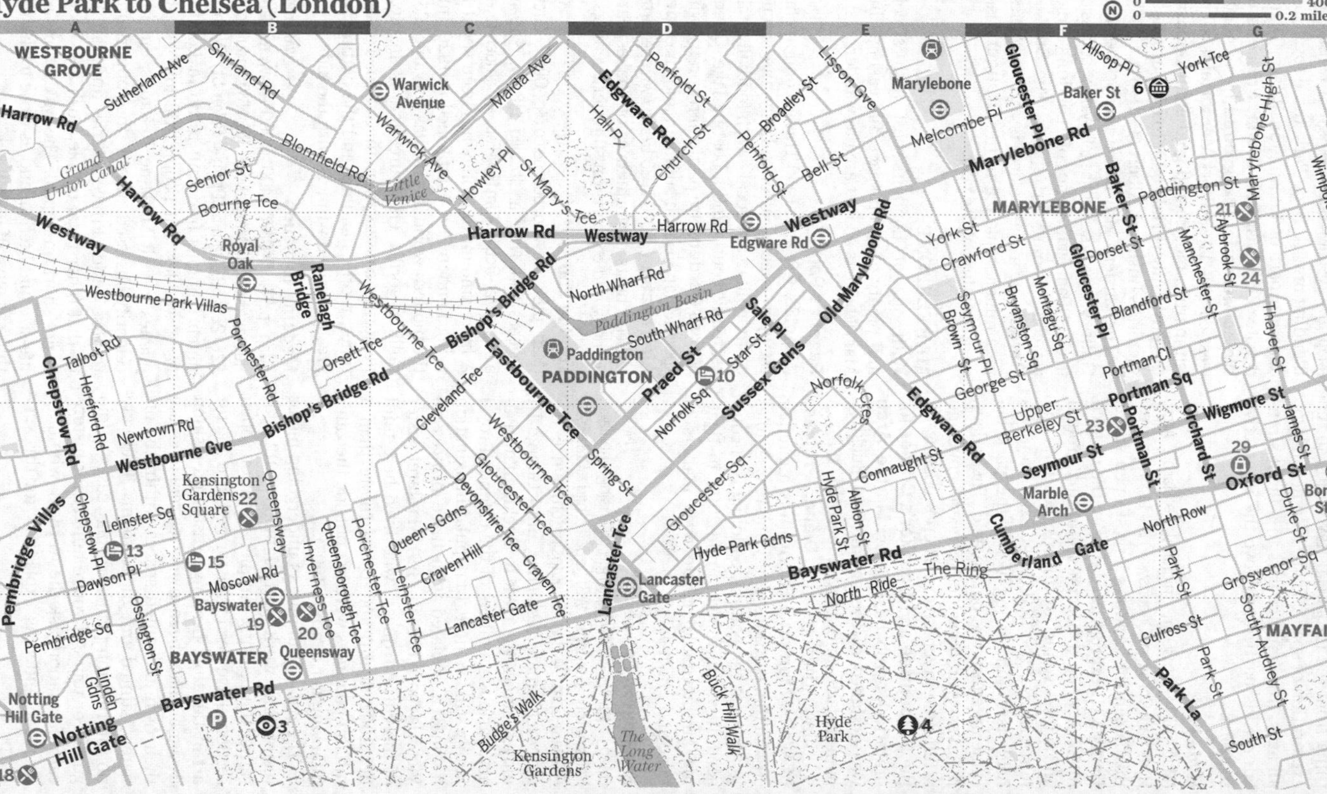

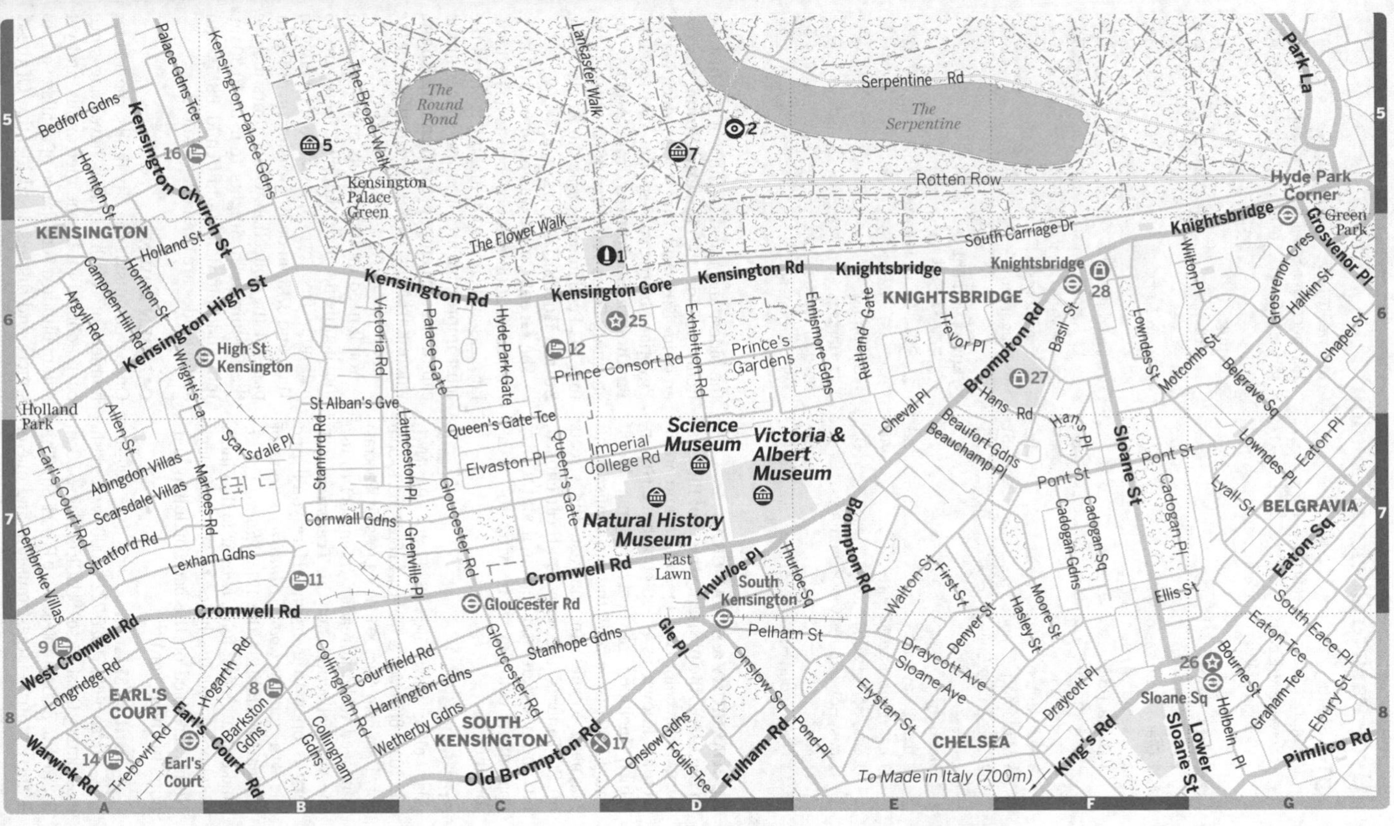
Bedford Gdns
Kensington Church St
Palace Gdns Tce
Kensington Palace Gdns
The Broad Walk
The Round Pond
Lancaster Walk
Serpentine Rd
The Serpentine
Park La
16
Hornton St
5
Kensington Palace Green
7
2
Rotten Row
Hyde Park Corner
Green Park
Grosvenor Pl
KENSINGTON
Holland St
The Flower Walk
1
South Carriage Dr
Knightsbridge
Campden Hill Rd
Hornton St
Argyll Rd
Kensington High St
Kensington Rd
Kensington Gore
Kensington Rd
Knightsbridge
Knightsbridge
28
Wilton Pl
Grosvenor Cres
Halkin St
Chapel St
KNIGHTSBRIDGE
Victoria Rd
Palace Gate
Hyde Park Gate
25
12
Exhibition Rd
Ennismore Gdns
Rutland Gate
Trevor Pl
Brompton Rd
Basil St
Lowndes St
Motcomb St
Belgrave Sq
High St Kensington
Wright's La
Prince Consort Rd
Prince's Gardens
27
Hans Rd
Cheval Pl
Holland Park
Allen St
St Alban's Gve
Launceston Pl
Queen's Gate Tce
Queen's Gate
Imperial College Rd
Science Museum
Victoria & Albert Museum
Beaufort Gdns
Beauchamp Pl
Hans Pl
Sloane St
Pont St
Pont St
Lowndes Pl
Eaton Pl
Lyall St
BELGRAVIA
Scarsdale Pl
Abingdon Villas
Scarsdale Villas
Marloes Rd
Stanford Rd
Elvaston Pl
Gloucester Rd
Earl's Court Rd
Cornwall Gdns
Grenville Pl
Natural History Museum
Brompton Rd
Cadogan Gdns
Cadogan Sq
Cadogan Pl
Eaton Sq
Pembroke Villas
Stratford Rd
Lexham Gdns
11
Cromwell Rd
East Lawn
Thurloe Pl
Thurloe Sq
South Kensington
Walton St
First St
Denyer St
Hasley St
Moore St
Ellis St
South Eace Pl
Cromwell Rd
Gloucester Rd
Pelham St
9
West Cromwell Rd
Longridge Rd
Hogarth Rd
8
Collingham Rd
Courtfield Rd
Harrington Gdns
Gloucester Rd
Stanhope Gdns
Gle Pl
Onslow Sq
Draycott Ave
Sloane Ave
Eaton Tce
26
Bourne St
Graham Tce
Ebury St
EARL'S COURT
Earl's Court Rd
Barkston Gdns
Wetherby Gdns
SOUTH KENSINGTON
Elystan St
Draycott Pl
Sloane Sq
Holbein Pl
14
Warwick Rd
Trebovir Rd
Earl's Court
Collingham Gdns
Old Brompton Rd
17
Onslow Gdns
Foulis Tce
Fulham Rd
Pond Pl
CHELSEA
To Made in Italy (700m)
King's Rd
Lower Sloane St
Pimlico Rd
A
B
C
D
E
F
G
5
6
7
8

Hyde Park to Chelsea (London)

Top Sights
- Natural History Museum ... D7
- Science Museum ... D7
- Victoria & Albert Museum ... D7

Sights
- 1 Albert Memorial ... D6
- 2 Diana, Princess of Wales Memorial Fountain ... D5
- 3 Diana, Princess of Wales Memorial Playground ... B4
- 4 Hyde Park ... E4
- 5 Kensington Palace ... B5
- 6 Madame Tussauds ... F1
- 7 Serpentine Gallery ... D5

Sleeping
- 8 base2stay ... B8
- 9 easyHotel Earl's Court ... A8
- 10 easyHotel Paddington ... D2
- 11 easyHotel South Kensington ... B7
- 12 Gore ... C6
- 13 New Linden Hotel ... A3
- 14 Twenty Nevern Square ... A8
- 15 Vancouver Studios ... B3
- 16 Vicarage Private Hotel ... A5

Eating
- 17 GBK ... D8
- 18 Geales ... A4
- 19 Kam Tong ... B4
- 20 Kiasu ... B4
- 21 La Fromagerie ... G1
- 22 Le Café Anglais ... B3
- 23 Locanda Locatelli ... F3
- 24 Providores & Tapa Room ... G2
- Wagamama ... (see 28)

Entertainment
- 25 Royal Albert Hall ... D6
- 26 Royal Court Theatre ... G8

Shopping
- 27 Harrods ... F6
- 28 Harvey Nichols ... F6
- 29 Selfridges ... G3

BLOOMSBURY & ST PANCRAS

In the 1930s, the pleasant streets of Bloomsbury were colonised by artists and intellectuals known as the Bloomsbury Group, which included novelists Virginia Woolf and EM Forster and the economist John Maynard Keynes. In contrast, the streets of St Pancras are grey and car-choked, but the new Eurostar terminal and a ritzy apartment complex is reviving the area's fortunes.

British Library LIBRARY

(Map p184; www.bl.uk; 96 Euston Rd NW1; 9.30am-6pm Mon & Wed-Fri, to 8pm Tue, to 5pm Sat, 11am-5pm Sun; King's Cross St Pancras) You need to be a 'reader' (member) to use the vast collection, but the **Treasures gallery** is open to everyone. Here you'll find the 4th-century *Codex Sinaiticus* (one of the earliest Bibles), the 1215 *Magna Carta*, Shakespeare's first folio, Leonardo da Vinci's notebooks and the lyrics to 'A Hard Day's Night' scribbled on the back of Julian Lennon's birthday card.

FREE **British Museum** MUSEUM

(Map p168; 020-7323 8000; www.britishmuseum.org; Great Russell St WC1; 10am-5.30pm Sat-Wed, to 8.30pm Thu & Fri; Russell Sq) This is the country's largest museum and one of the oldest and finest in the world. Must-see items include the **Rosetta Stone**, discovered in 1799 and the key to deciphering Egyptian hieroglyphics; the controversial **Parthenon Sculptures** from Athens; the stunning **Oxus Treasure** of 7th- to 4th-century BC Persian gold; and the Anglo-Saxon **Sutton Hoo** burial relics.

The **Great Court** was restored and augmented in 2000 and now boasts a spectacular glass-and-steel roof, making it one of the most impressive architectural spaces in the capital. In the centre is the **Reading Room**, where Karl Marx wrote the *Manifesto of the Communist Party*.

You'll need multiple visits to savour even the highlights here; happily there are 15 half-hour free 'eye opener' tours between 11am and 3.45pm daily, focusing on different parts of the collection. Other tours include the 90-minute highlights tour at 10.30am, 1pm and 3pm daily (adult/child £8/5), and audio guides are available (£4.50).

CAMDEN TOWN

Once well outside the city limits, the former hamlets of North London have long since been gobbled up by the metropolis, and yet still maintain a semblance of a village atmosphere and distinct local identity. Of these, the enclave of Camden Town is a lively neighbourhood of pubs, live-music venues, boutiques, technicolour hairstyles, facial furniture, intricate tattoos, ambitious platform shoes and, most famously, **Camden Market** (p196). There are often a few cartoon punks hanging around earning a few bucks for being photographed by tourists, as well as none-too-discreet dope dealers.

HOXTON, SHOREDITCH & SPITALFIELDS

The East End suburbs of Hoxton, Shoreditch and Spitalfields are traditionally working class but increasingly trendy these days. They're a great place for diverse ethnic cuisine, thanks to the waves of immigrants that have arrived here over the centuries.

FREE **Geffrye Museum** MUSEUM
(off Map p180; www.geffrye-museum.org.uk; 136 Kingsland Rd E2; 10am-5pm Tue-Sat, noon-5pm Sun; Old St) Devoted to domestic interiors, this former almshouse has been converted into a series of living rooms dating from 1630 to the current Ikea generation.

FREE **White Cube** ART MUSEUM
(Map p180; www.whitecube.com; 48 Hoxton Sq N1; 10am-6pm Tue-Sat; Old St) In an industrial building with an impressive glazed-roof extension, White Cube offers contemporary art exhibitions from sculptures to video, installations and painting.

DOCKLANDS

East of the centre, London's port was once the global trade hub of the enormous British Empire. In the 40 years following WWII, the port and surrounding Docklands area went downhill, but massive redevelopment spearheaded by the towers of Canary Wharf means crusty seadogs have been replaced with battalions of dark-suited office workers.

FREE **Museum of London Docklands** MUSEUM
(www.museumoflondon.org.uk/docklands; Hertsmere Rd, West India Quay E17; 10am-6pm; DLR West India Quay) In a heritage-listed warehouse, this museum uses a combination of artefacts and multimedia to chart the history of the city through its river and docks. There's a lot to see here, including a section on the slave trade.

GREENWICH

More than any of the former villages swamped by the metropolis, Greenwich (*gren*-itch) has retained its own sense of identity based on splendid architecture and strong connections with the sea and science. An extraordinary cluster of buildings have earned 'Maritime Greenwich' its place on Unesco's World Heritage list. It's also famous for straddling the hemispheres; this is degree zero, the home of Greenwich Mean Time.

Greenwich is easily reached on the DLR train. Or go by boat: **Thames River Services** (www.thamesriverservices.co.uk; single/return £9.50/12.50) depart half-hourly from Westminster Pier (one hour, every 40 minutes). **Thames Clippers** (www.thamesclippers.com; adult/child £5.30/2.65) are cheaper.

FREE **Old Royal Naval College** HISTORIC BUILDINGS
(www.oldroyalnavalcollege.org; 2 Cutty Sark Gardens SE10; 10am-5pm; DLR Cutty Sark) This magnificent example of monumental classical architecture is now partly used by the University of Greenwich and Trinity College of Music, but you can visit the **chapel** and the extraordinary **Painted Hall**, which took artist Sir James Thornhill 19 years to complete.

The college complex was built on the site of the 15th-century Palace of Placentia, the

BRITAIN & GREECE SQUABBLE OVER MARBLES

Wonderful though it is, the British Museum can sometimes feel like one vast repository for stolen booty. Much of what's on display wasn't just 'picked up' by Victorian explorers, but taken or purchased under dubious circumstances. Foreign governments occasionally demand the return of their property. The British Museum says 'no' and the problem goes away until the next time. Not the Greeks, however. They consistently demand the return of the so-called Elgin Marbles (brought to Britain by Lord Elgin), the ancient marble sculptures that once adorned the Parthenon. The British Museum, and successive British governments, steadfastly refuses to hand over the priceless works that were removed and shipped to England by the British ambassador to the Ottoman Empire, the Lord Elgin, between 1801 and 1805. When Elgin blew all his dough, he sold the marbles to the government. The diplomatic spat continues.

birthplace of both Henry VIII and Elizabeth I. This Tudor connection is explored in **Discover Greenwich**, along with Greenwich's industrial and maritime history. Tours of the complex leave at 2pm daily, taking in areas not otherwise open to the public (£5, 90 minutes).

FREE **National Maritime Museum** MUSEUM
(020-8858 4422; www.nmm.ac.uk; Romney Rd SE10; 10am-5pm; DLR Cutty Sark) Directly behind the old college, the National Maritime Museum completes Greenwich's trump hand of historic buildings. Exhibits range from interactive displays to humdingers like Cook's journals and Nelson's uniform, complete with a hole from the bullet that killed him. The mood changes abruptly between galleries (one is devoted to toy ships while another examines the slave trade).

At the centre of the site, the elegant Palladian **Queen's House** has been restored to something like Inigo Jones' intention when he designed it in 1616 for the wife of Charles I. It's a refined setting for a gallery focusing on illustrious seafarers and historic Greenwich.

Behind Queen's House, idyllic **Greenwich Park**, affords great views of London, and is capped by the **Royal Observatory** (10am-5pm), which Charles II had built in 1675 to help solve the riddle of longitude. Success was confirmed in 1884 when Greenwich was designated as the prime meridian of the world, and Greenwich Mean Time (GMT) became the universal measurement of standard time. Here you can stand with your feet straddling the western and eastern hemispheres.

O2 VENUE
(www.theo2.co.uk; Peninsula Sq SE10; North Greenwich) The world's largest dome (365m in diameter) opened on 1 January 2000 as the Millennium Dome, but closed on 31 December. Renamed The O2, it's now a 20,000-seater sports and entertainment arena surrounded by shops and restaurants. There are ferry services from central London on concert nights.

WEST LONDON

Kew Gardens BOTANIC GARDENS
(www.kew.org.uk; Kew Rd; adult/child £14/free; 9.30am-6.30pm Apr-Aug, earlier closing other months; Kew Gardens) In 1759 botanists began collecting specimens to plant in the 3-hectare plot known as the Royal Botanic Gardens. They never stopped collecting, and the gardens have bloomed to 120 hectares, the most comprehensive botanical collection on earth. You can easily spend a whole day wandering around, but if you're pressed for time, the **Kew Explorer** (adult/child £4/1) is a hop-on hop-off road train that leaves from Victoria Gate and takes in the gardens' main sights. Highlights include the enormous **Palm House**, a hothouse of metal and curved sheets of glass; the impressive **Princess of Wales Conservatory**; the celebrated **Great Pagoda**; and the **Temperate House**, which is the world's largest ornamental glasshouse and home to its biggest indoor plant, the 18m Chilean Wine Palmand.

Hampton Court Palace PALACE
(www.hrp.org.uk/HamptonCourtPalace; adult/child £14/7; 10am-6pm Apr-Oct, to 4.30pm Nov-Mar; Hampton Court) Built by Cardinal Thomas Wolsey in 1514 but coaxed out of him by Henry VIII, this is England's largest and grandest Tudor structure. It was already one of the most sophisticated palaces in Europe when, in the 17th century, Wren was commissioned to build an extension. The result is a beautiful blend of Tudor and 'restrained baroque' architecture.

Take a themed tour led by costumed historians or, if you're in a rush, visit the highlights: **Henry VIII's State Apartments**, including the **Great Hall** with its spectacular hammer-beamed roof; the **Tudor Kitchens**; and the **Wolsey Rooms**. You could easily spend a day exploring the palace and its hectares of riverside gardens, especially if you get lost in the 300-year-old **maze**.

Hampton Court is 13 miles southwest of central London and is easily reached by train from Waterloo. Alternatively, the riverboats that head from Westminster to Kew continue here (return adult/child £23/12, three hours).

Tours

One of the best ways to orientate yourself when you first arrive in London is with a 24-hour hop-on/hop-off pass for the double-decker bus tours. The buses loop around interconnecting routes throughout the day, providing a commentary as they go, and the price includes a river cruise and three walking tours. You'll save a couple of pounds by booking online.

Original London Sightseeing Tour BUS
(020-8877 1722; www.theoriginaltour.com; adult/child £25/12)

Big Bus Company BUS
(☎020-7233 9533; www.bigbustours.com; adult/child £26/10)

London Walks WALKING
(☎020-7624 3978; www.walks.com)

London Mystery Walks WALKING
(☎07957 388280; www.tourguides.org.uk)

Festivals & Events

University Boat Race BOAT RACE
(www.theboatrace.org) Held annually since 1829 between Oxford and Cambridge universities. In late March.

London Marathon RUNNING RACE
(www.london-marathon.co.uk) Half a million spectators gather to watch whippet-thin champions and bizarrely clad amateurs run this race in late April.

Trooping the Colour ROYAL PARADE
Pomp and pageantry overload to celebrating the Queen's official birthday in June.

Meltdown Festival MUSIC FESTIVAL
(www.southbankcentre.co.uk) The Southbank Centre hands over curatorial reins to a legend of contemporary music (such as David Bowie, Morrissey or Patti Smith) to create a full program of concerts, talks and films in late June.

Wimbledon Lawn Tennis Championships TENNIS TOURNAMENT
(www.wimbledon.org; tickets by public ballot) The world's most splendid tennis event takes place in late June.

GAY & LESBIAN LONDON

London's had a thriving gay scene since at least the 18th century, when the West End's 'Mollie houses' were the forerunners of today's gay bars. The West End, particularly Soho, remains the visible centre of gay and lesbian London, with numerous venues clustered around Old Compton St. However, Soho doesn't hold a monopoly; there are local gay bars in many neighbourhoods. Vauxhall (south of the Thames) has taken off as a hub for the hirsute, hefty and generally harder-edged sections of the community. Earl's Court (West London), Islington (North London) and Limehouse (East End) have their own mini scenes.

Generally, London's a safe place for lesbians and gays. It's rare to encounter any problem with sharing rooms or holding hands in the inner city, although it would pay to keep your wits about you at night and be conscious of your surroundings.

The easiest way to find out what's going on is to pick up the free press from a venue *(Pink Paper, Boyz, QX)*, but be warned: the ads can be somewhat...confronting. The gay section of *Time Out* is useful, as are www.gaydarnation.com (for men) and www.ginger-beer.co.uk (for women). The hardcore circuit club nights run on a semi-regular basis at a variety of venues: check out **DTPM**, **Fiction** (both at www.dtpmevents.co.uk), **Matinee**, **SuperMartXé** (both at www.loganpresents.com) and **Megawoof!** (www.megawoof.com).

Here are some venues to get you started:

Candy Bar (Map p168; www.candybarsoho.co.uk; 4 Carlisle St W1; ⊖Tottenham Court Rd) Long-running lesbian hang-out.

Friendly Society (Map p168; 79 Wardour St W1; ⊖Piccadilly Circus) Soho's quirkiest gay bar.

G-A-Y (Map p168; www.g-a-y.co.uk) G-A-Y Bar (30 Old Compton St W1; ⊖Leicester Sq); G-A-Y Late (5 Goslett Yard WC2; ⏲11pm-3am; ⊖Tottenham Court Rd); G-A-Y Club @ Heaven (The Arches, Villiers St WC2; ⏲11pm-4am Thu-Sat; ⊖Charing Cross) Too camp to be restricted to one venue, G-A-Y now operates bars and club nights at one of gaydom's most internationally famous venues, Heaven.

Gay's the Word (Map p184; 66 Marchmont St WC1; ⊖Russell Sq) Books and mags of all descriptions.

Popstarz (Map p168; www.popstarz.org; The Den, 18 West Central St WC1; ⏲10pm-4am Fri; ⊖Tottenham Court Rd) London's legendary indie pop club night. The online flyer gets you in free.

Village (Map p168; www.village-soho.co.uk; 81 Wardour St W1; ⊖Piccadilly Circus) Glitzy gay bar.

Central London

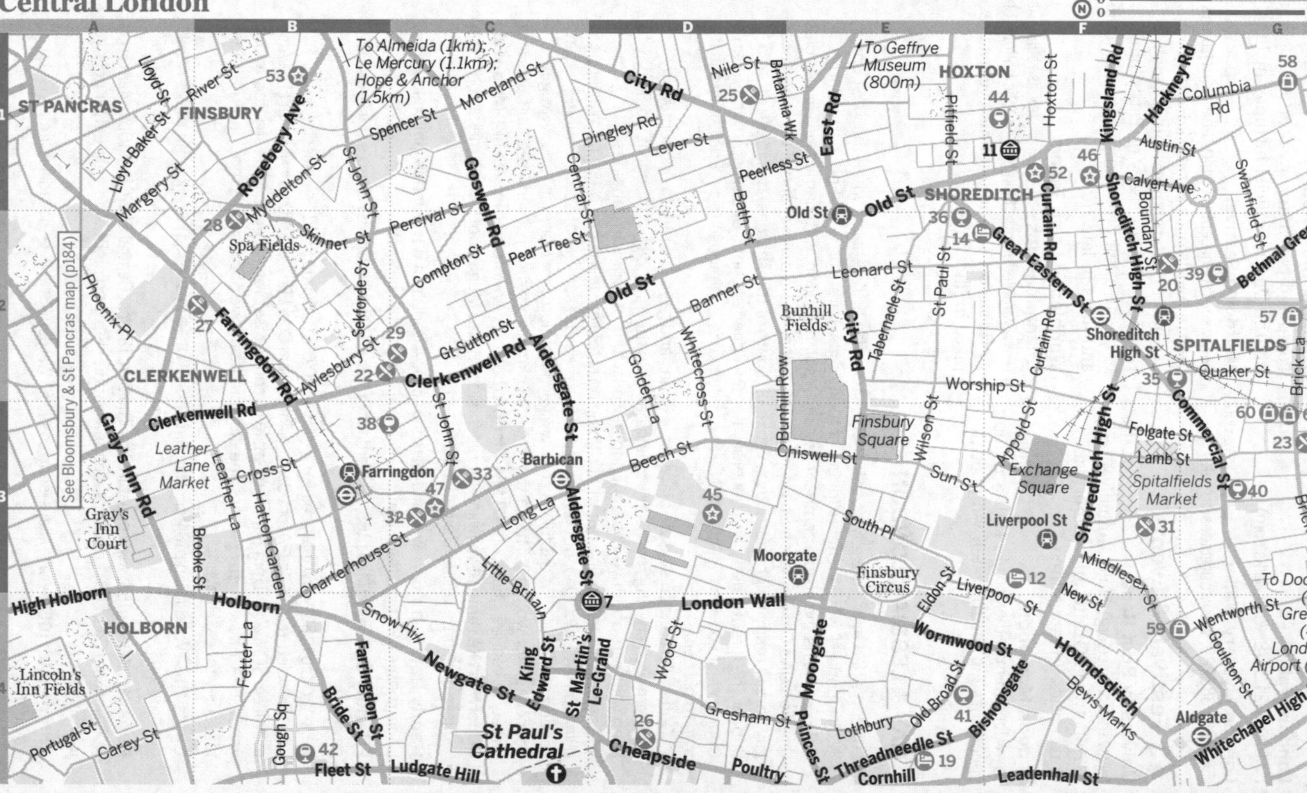

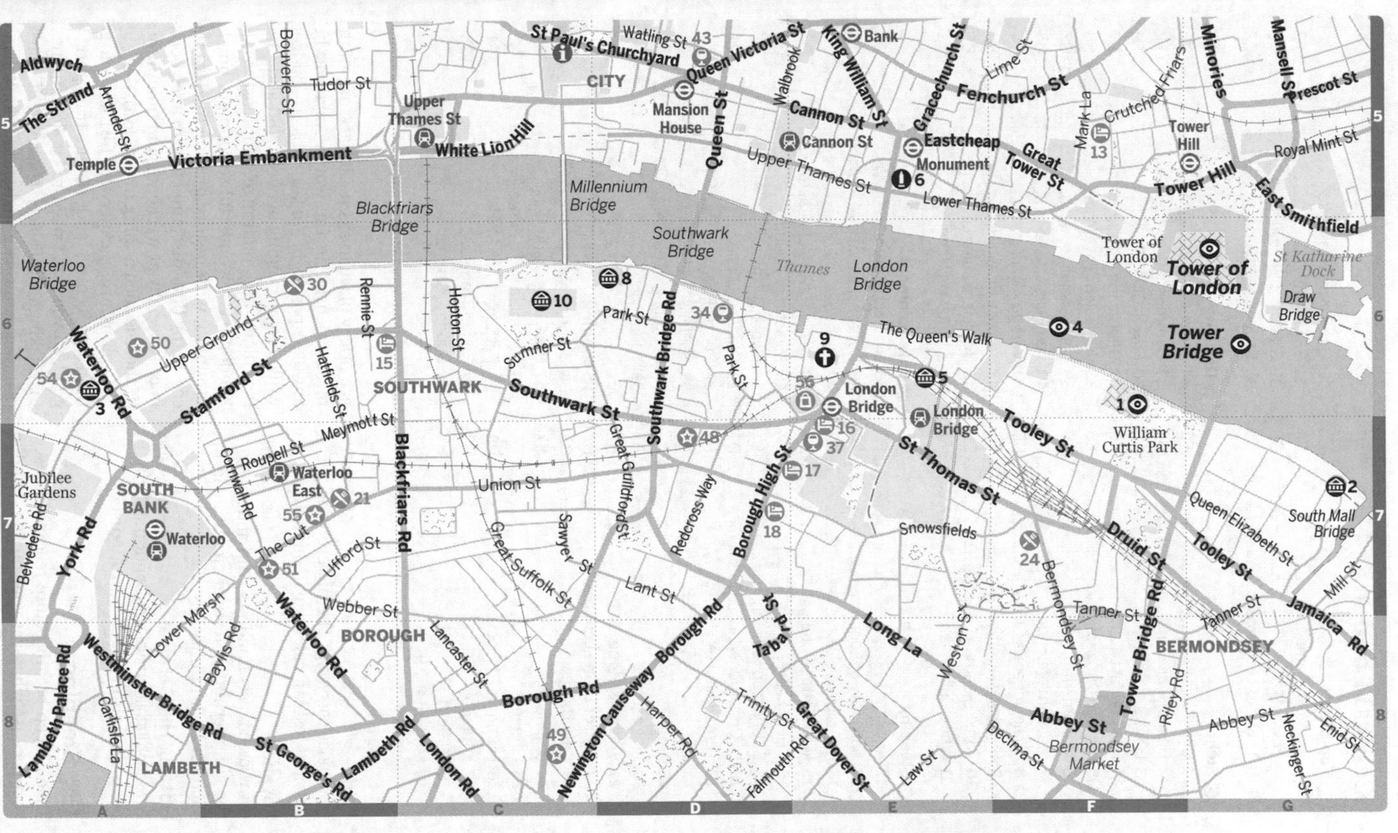
Aldwych
The Strand
Arundel St
Bouverie St
Tudor St
Upper Thames St
White Lion Hill
Temple
Victoria Embankment
St Paul's Churchyard
CITY
Watling St
43
Queen Victoria St
Mansion House
Queen St
Walbrook
Cannon St
Cannon St
King William St
Bank
Gracechurch St
Eastcheap
Monument
6
Upper Thames St
Lower Thames St
Fenchurch St
Lime St
Mark La
13
Crutched Friars
Great Tower St
Minories
Tower Hill
Tower Hill
Mansell St
Prescot St
Royal Mint St
East Smithfield
Blackfriars Bridge
Millennium Bridge
Southwark Bridge
Thames
London Bridge
Tower of London
Tower of London
St Katharine Dock
Draw Bridge
Waterloo Bridge
30
Rennie St
Hopton St
10
8
Park St
Southwark Bridge Rd
34
Park St
9
The Queen's Walk
4
Tower Bridge
50
Upper Ground
54
3
Waterloo Rd
Stamford St
Hatfields St
15
SOUTHWARK
Sumner St
Southwark St
56
London Bridge
5
London Bridge
Tooley St
1
William Curtis Park
Meymott St
Roupell St
Waterloo East
Cornwall Rd
21
Blackfriars Rd
Union St
Great Guildford St
48
16
37
17
Borough High St
St Thomas St
2
Queen Elizabeth St
South Mall Bridge
Jubilee Gardens
SOUTH BANK
Waterloo
55
The Cut
51
Ufford St
Great Suffolk St
Sawyer St
Redcross Way
18
Snowsfields
24
Druid St
Tooley St
Mill St
Belvedere Rd
York Rd
Lower Marsh
Baylis Rd
Waterloo Rd
Webber St
BOROUGH
Lancaster St
Lant St
Borough Rd
Tabard St
Long La
Weston St
Bermondsey St
Tanner St
Tower Bridge Rd
Tanner St
Jamaica Rd
BERMONDSEY
Lambeth Palace Rd
Westminster Bridge Rd
Carlisle La
LAMBETH
St George's Rd
Lambeth Rd
London Rd
Borough Rd
49
Newington Causeway
Harper Rd
Trinity St
Falmouth Rd
Great Dover St
Law St
Decima St
Abbey St
Bermondsey Market
Riley Rd
Abbey St
Neckinger St
Enid St
A
B
C
D
E
F
G
5
6
7
8

Central London

Top Sights

	St Paul's Cathedral	C4
	Tower Bridge	G6
	Tower of London	G6

Sights

1	City Hall	F6
2	Design Museum	G7
3	Hayward Gallery	A6
4	HMS Belfast	F6
5	London Dungeon	E6
6	Monument	E5
7	Museum of London	D4
8	Shakespeare's Globe	D6
9	Southwark Cathedral	E6
10	Tate Modern	C6
11	White Cube	F1

Sleeping

12	Andaz	F3
13	Apex City of London	F5
14	Hoxton	E2
15	Mad Hatter Hotel	B6
16	Orient Express	E7
17	St Christopher's Inn	E7
18	St Christopher's Village	D7
19	Threadneedles	E4

Eating

20	Albion	F2
21	Anchor & Hope	B7
22	Bistrot Bruno Loubet	B2
23	Cafe Bangla	G3
24	Delfina	F7
25	Fifteen	D1
26	Hummus Bros	D4
27	Little Bay	B2
28	Medcalf	B2
29	Modern Pantry	C2
30	Oxo Tower Brasserie	B6
31	S&M Café	F3
32	Smiths of Smithfield	C3
33	St John	C3

Drinking

34	Anchor	D6
35	Commercial Tavern	F2
36	Favela Chic	E2
37	George Inn	E7
38	Jerusalem Tavern	B3
39	Loungelover	G2
40	Ten Bells	G3
41	Vertigo 42	E4
42	Ye Olde Cheshire Cheese	B4
43	Ye Olde Watling	D5
44	Zigfrid Von Underbelly	F1

Entertainment

45	Barbican Centre	D3
46	Cargo	F1
47	Fabric	C3
48	Menier Chocolate Factory	D7
49	Ministry of Sound	C8
50	National Theatre	A6
51	Old Vic	B7
52	Plastic People	F1
53	Sadler's Wells	B1
54	Southbank Centre	A6
55	Young Vic	B7

Shopping

56	Borough Market	E6
57	Brick Lane Market	G2
58	Columbia Road Flower Market	G1
59	Petticoat Lane Market	F4
60	Rough Trade	G3
61	Sunday (Up)market	G3

Pride GAY & LESBIAN
(www.pridelondon.org) The big event on the gay and lesbian calendar in June/July.

Lovebox MUSIC FESTIVAL
(www.lovebox.net) London's contribution to the summer music festival circuit, held in Victoria Park in mid-July.

Notting Hill Carnival STREET PARADES
(www.nottinghillcarnival.biz) London's Caribbean community parties in August.

Sleeping

Take a deep breath before reading this section because whatever your budget, London is a pricey place to sleep – in fact, one of the most expensive in the world. Anything below £80 per night for a double is 'budget', while rooms ranging between £80 and £180 per night are 'midrange'. But cost aside, London has a wonderful selection of hotels, brimming with history or zany modern decor. Many offer discounts for advance bookings, especially at weekends and quiet times (if there is such a thing in London).

Options are cheaper the further you go from the centre, and public transport is good, so you don't need to be sleeping next to Buckingham Palace. However, if you're planning some late nights and don't fancy night buses (a consummate London experience, but one you'll want only once), it'll make sense not to bed down too far from the action.

It's now becoming the norm for budget and midrange places to offer free wireless internet. The expensive places will offer it too, but often charge. If your hotel or hostel charges for breakfast, check the prices; anything over £8 just isn't worth it when there are so many eateries to explore.

WEST END

This is the heart of the action, so accommodation comes at a price, and a hefty one at that. A couple of hostels cater for would-be Soho hipsters of more modest means.

Hazlitt's HOTEL £££
(Map p168; ☎020-7434 1771; www.hazlittshotel.com; 6 Frith St W1; s £206, d/ste from £259/646; @📶; ⊖Tottenham Court Rd) Staying in this charming house is a trip back into a time when four-poster beds and claw-footed baths were the norm for gentlefolk.

Oxford St YHA HOSTEL £
(Map p168; ☎0845 371 9133; www.yha.org.uk; 14 Noel St W1; dm/tw from £18/44; @📶; ⊖Oxford Circus) In most respects, this is a bog-standard YHA hostel with tidy rooms and all the usual facilities, but it's got a terrific (albeit noisy) location and decent views from some of the rooms.

WESTMINSTER & PIMLICO

Handy for the major sights, these areas have some good-value options.

Luna Simone Hotel B&B ££
(Map p186; ☎020-7834 5897; www.lunasimonehotel.com; 47-49 Belgrave Rd SW1; s £70-75, d £95-120; @📶; ⊖Pimlico) The blue-and-yellow rooms aren't huge but they're clean and calming; the ones at the back are quieter.

Windermere Hotel B&B ££
(Map p186; ☎020-7834 5163; www.windermere-hotel.co.uk; 142-144 Warwick Way SW1; s £105-155, d £129-165; @📶; ⊖Victoria) Chintzy but comfortable early-Victorian townhouse; the cheapest rooms share bathrooms.

THE CITY

Bristling with bankers during the week; you can often pick up a considerable bargain at weekends.

Apex City of London HOTEL ££
(Map p180; ☎020-7702 2020; www.apexhotels.co.uk; 1 Seething Lane EC3; r from £100; 📶; ⊖Tower Hill) Business-focused but close enough to the Tower to hear the heads roll.

Threadneedles HOTEL £££
(Map p180; ☎020-7657 8080; www.theetoncollection.com; 5 Threadneedle St EC2; r weekend/weekday from £175/345; @📶; ⊖Bank) Popular with suits, but the atmosphere is chic rather than stuffy.

SOUTHWARK

Immediately south of the river is good if you want to immerse yourself in workaday London and still be central.

Mad Hatter Hotel HOTEL ££
(Map p180; ☎020-7401 9222; www.fullershotels.com; 3-7 Stamford St SE1; r £155; ⊖Southwark) There's nothing particularly mad (or even unusual) here, but this is a good hotel with decent-sized rooms and unassuming decor.

St Christopher's Village HOSTEL £
(Map p180; ☎020-7939 9710; www.st-christophers.co.uk; 163 Borough High St SE1; dm/r from £14/62; @📶; ⊖London Bridge) The Village is a huge, up-for-it party hostel, with a club that opens until 4am on the weekends and a roof terrace bar. It's either heaven or hell, depending on what you're looking for.

Nearby are two satellites that are smaller, quieter and, frankly, more pleasant: **St Christopher's Inn** (121 Borough High St) is above a very nice pub; **The Oasis** (59 Borough High St) is a female-only hostel.

CHELSEA, KENSINGTON & KNIGHTSBRIDGE

These classy zones offer easy access to the museums and big-name fashion stores. It's all a bit sweetie-darling, along with the prices.

Gore HOTEL ££
(Map p174; ☎020-7584 6601; www.gorehotel.com; 190 Queen's Gate SW7; r from £135; @📶; ⊖Gloucester Rd) A short stroll from the Royal Albert Hall, the Gore serves up British grandiosity (antiques, carved four-posters, a secret bathroom in the Tudor room) with a large slice of camp.

Vicarage Private Hotel B&B ££
(Map p174; ☎020-7229 4030; www.londonvicaragehotel.com; 10 Vicarage Gate W8; s/d £95/125, without bathroom £56/95; @📶; ⊖High St Kensington) You can see Kensington Palace from the doorstep of this grand Victorian town house. The cheaper rooms are on floors three and four, so you may get a view as well as a workout.

Bloomsbury & St Pancras (London)

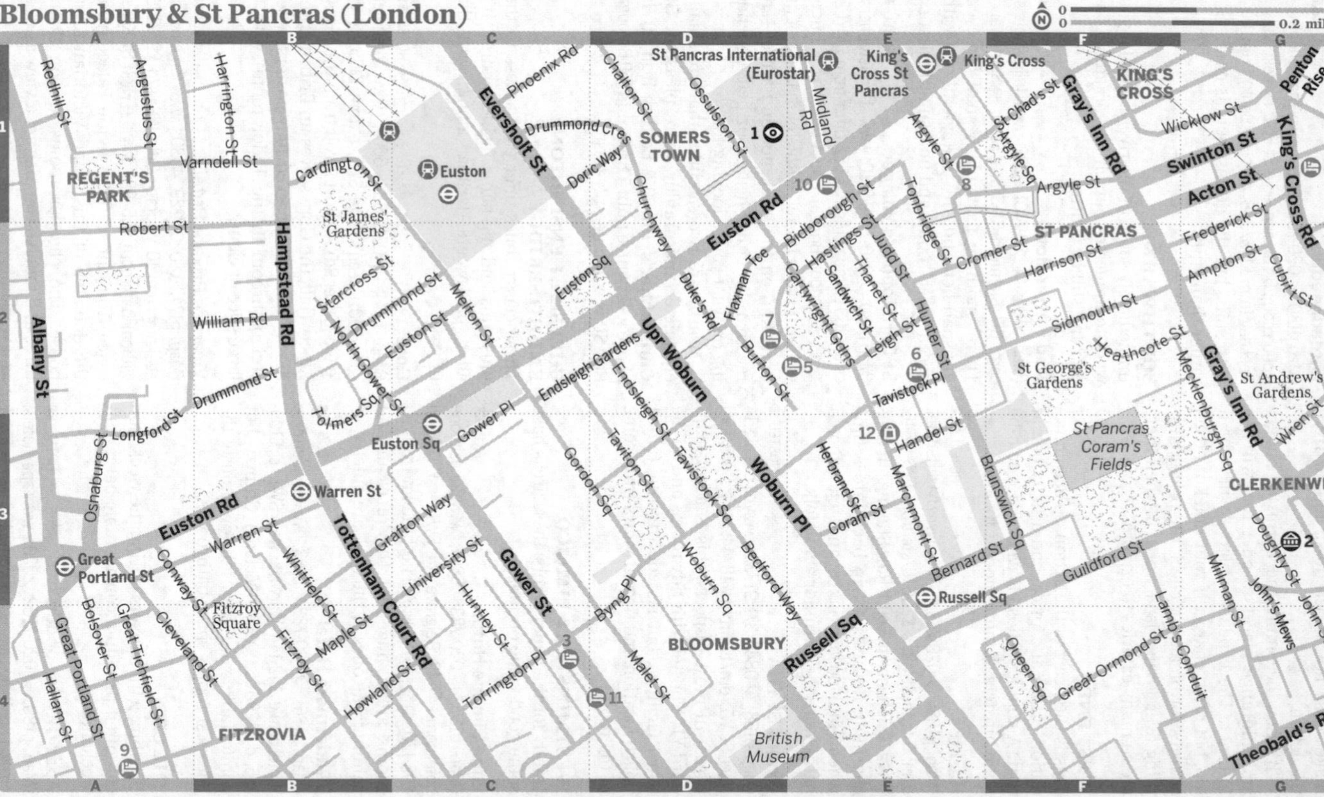

Bloomsbury & St Pancras (London)

Sights

Sleeping

Shopping

BLOOMSBURY & ST PANCRAS

Only one step removed from the West End, the neighbourhoods of Bloomsbury and adjoining Fitzrovia offer good value. You'll find a stretch of lower-priced hotels along Gower St and on pretty Cartwright Gardens. The nearby area of St Pancras is hardly salubrious but handy to absolutely everything, with some excellent budget options.

London Central YHA HOSTEL £

(Map p184; ☎0845 371 9154; www.yha.org.uk; 104-108 Bolsover St W1; dm £21-32, q from £70; @📶; ⊖Great Portland St) One of London's new breed of YHA hostels, most of the four- to six-bed rooms have en suites. There's a cafe-bar attached to reception and a wheelchair-accessible kitchen downstairs.

Arran House Hotel B&B ££

(Map p184; ☎020-7636 2186; www.arranhotel-london.com; 77-79 Gower St WC1; s/d/tr/q £70/110/128/132, without bathroom £60/80/105/111; @📶; ⊖Goodge St) Period features, a pretty back garden and a comfy lounge lift this hotel from average to attractive. Squashed en suites or shared bathrooms are the trade-off for reasonable rates.

Arosfa Hotel B&B ££

(Map p184; ☎020-7636 2115; www.arosfalondon.com; 83 Gower St WC1; s £60-65, d/tr/q £90/102/110; @📶; ⊖Goodge St) Immaculate if unremarkable rooms, blinged-up lounge and en suites to all 15 bedrooms – but they're tiny.

Jesmond Dene Hotel B&B ££

(Map p184; ☎020-7837 4654; www.jesmonddenehotel.co.uk; 27 Argyle St WC1; s/d incl breakfast from £60/65; P@📶; ⊖Kings Cross) A surprisingly pleasant option close to busy King's Cross station, with clean but small rooms, some of which share bathrooms.

London St Pancras YHA HOSTEL £

(Map p184; ☎020-7388 9998; www.yha.org.uk; 79 Euston Rd NW1; dm/r from £20/61; @📶; ⊖Kings Cross) A renovation in 2009 has made this 185-bed hostel one of the best in central London. Rooms range from private doubles to six-bed dorms; most have bathrooms. There's a good bar and cafe but no kitchen.

Ridgemount Hotel B&B ££

(Map p184; ☎020-7636 1141; www.ridgemounthotel.co.uk; 65-67 Gower St WC1; s/d/tr/q £55/78/96/108, without bathroom £43/60/81/96; @📶; ⊖Goodge St) There's a comfortable, welcoming feel at this old-fashioned, slightly chintzy place that's been in the same family for 40 years.

Jenkins Hotel B&B ££

(Map p184; ☎020-7387 2067; www.jenkinshotel.demon.co.uk; 45 Cartwright Gardens WC1; s/d from £52/95; ⊖Russell Sq) This modest hotel has featured in the TV series of Agatha Christie's *Poirot*. Rooms are small but the hotel has charm.

Crescent Hotel B&B ££

(Map p184; ☎020-7387 1515; www.crescenthotelofllondon.com; 49-50 Cartwright Gardens WC1; s/d from £52/105; @📶; ⊖Russell Sq) One of the cheaper options on Cartwright Gardens, there's a homely feel to this humble hotel, despite the odd saggy beds.

Clink78 HOSTEL £

(Map p184; ☎020-7183 9400; www.clinkhostel.com; 78 Kings Cross Rd WC1; dm/r from £12/60; @📶; ⊖Kings Cross) If anyone can think of a more right-on London place to stay than the courthouse where The Clash went on trial, please let us know. You can watch TV from the witness box or sleep in the cells, but the majority of the rooms are custom-built and quite comfortable.

Generator HOSTEL £

(Map p184; ☎020-7388 7666; www.generatorhostels.com/London; 37 Tavistock Pl WC1; dm/r from £18/55; @📶; ⊖Russell Sq) Lashings of primary colours and shiny metal are the

Westminster (London)

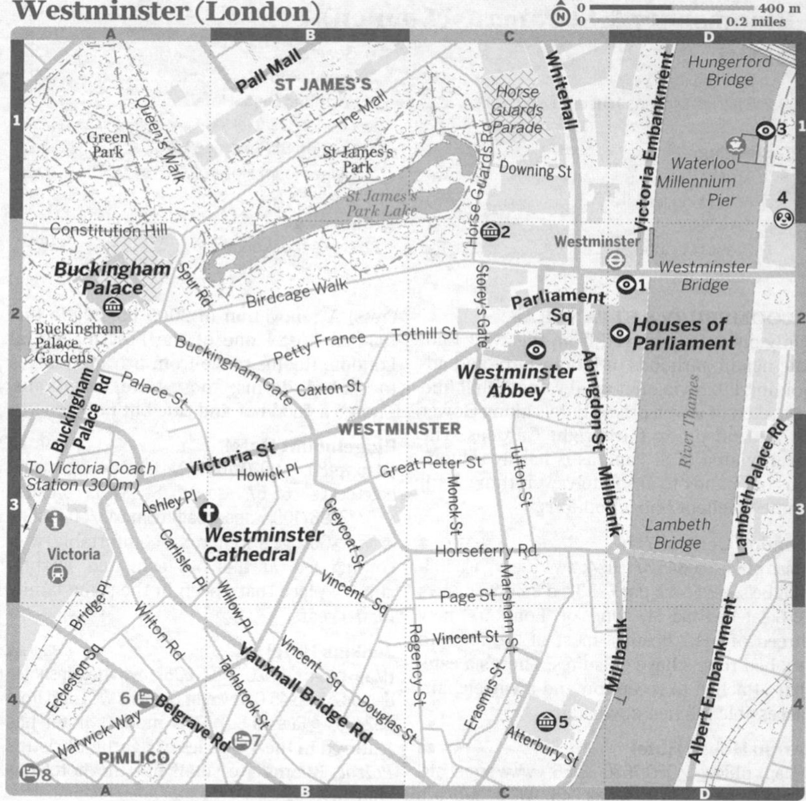

hallmarks of this futuristic 820-bed hostel. The bar stays open until 2am and hosts quizzes, karaoke and DJs. Come to party.

EARL'S COURT & FULHAM

Earl's Court is lively, cosmopolitan and so popular with travelling antipodeans that it's been nicknamed Kangaroo Valley. There are no real sights as such, but it does have inexpensive digs and an infectious holiday atmosphere.

Barclay House B&B ££
(☎020-7384 3390; www.barclayhouselondon.com; 21 Barclay Rd SW6; s/d £69/89, @📶; ⊖Fulham Broadway) A proper homestay B&B, with just two comfy bedrooms and an exceptionally welcoming host.

Twenty Nevern Square HOTEL ££
(Map p174; ☎020-7565 9555; www.20nevernsquare.com; 20 Nevern Sq SW5; r from £95; @📶; ⊖Earl's Court) An Ottoman theme runs through this townhouse hotel, with wooden furniture and luxurious fabrics, while natural light helps maximise space.

base2stay APARTMENT HOTEL ££
(Map p174; ☎020-7244 2255; www.base2stay.com; 25 Courtfield Gardens SW5; s/d from £93/99; @📶; ⊖Earl's Court) With smart decor, power showers, flat-screen TVs with internet access and artfully concealed kitchenettes, this boutique establishment feels like a four-star hotel without the hefty price tag.

easyHotel BUDGET HOTEL £
(www.easyhotel.com; r from £25; @📶) Earl's Court (Map p174; 44 West Cromwell Rd SW5; ⊖Earl's Court); Paddington (Map p174; 10 Norfolk Pl W2; ⊖Paddington); South Kensington (Map p174; 14 Lexham Gardens W8; ⊖Gloucester Rd); Victoria (Map p186; 36 Belgrave Rd SW1; ⊖Victoria) Run along the same principles as its sibling business easyJet, this no-frills chain has tiny rooms with even tinier bathrooms.

Westminster (London)

Top Sights

Sights

Sleeping

NOTTING HILL, BAYSWATER & PADDINGTON

Don't be fooled by the movie. Notting Hill and the areas immediately north of Hyde Park are as shabby as they are chic, while scruffy Paddington has lots of cheap hotels, with a major strip along Sussex Gardens, worth checking if you're short on options.

New Linden Hotel HOTEL ££
(Map p174; 020-7221 4321; www.newlinden.co.uk; 58-60 Leinster Sq W2; s/d from £79/105; @; Bayswater) Cramming in a fair amount of style for the price, with modern art in the rooms and carved wooden fixtures in the guest lounge. The quiet location, helpful staff and monsoon shower heads in the deluxe rooms make this an excellent proposition.

Vancouver Studios APARTMENT HOTEL ££
(Map p174; 020-7243 1270; www.vancouverstudios.co.uk; 30 Prince's Sq W2; apt £89-170; @; Bayswater) Reasonably priced studios (sleeping one to three people) with kitchenettes and a self-service laundry.

HOXTON, SHOREDITCH & SPITALFIELDS

It's always had a rough-edged reputation, but London's East End is being speedily gentrified, with some good options close to the nightlife.

TOP CHOICE **Hoxton** HOTEL £
(Map p180; 020-7550 1000; www.hoxtonhotels.com; 81 Great Eastern St EC2; d & tw £59-199; @; Old St) All rooms are identical, but the pricing structure means the first ones each day cost £59: an absolute steal for a hotel of this calibre.

Andaz HOTEL ££
(Map p180; 020-7961 1234; www.london.liverpoolstreet.andaz.com; 40 Liverpool St EC2; r from £145; @; Liverpool St) The former Great Eastern Hotel is now the London flagship for Hyatt's youth-focused Andaz chain, where black-clad staff check you in on laptops. Rooms are a little generic but have free juice, snacks and wi-fi.

AIRPORTS

Yotel BUDGET HOTEL £
(020-7100 1100; www.yotel.com; s/d £69/85, or per 4hr £29/45 then per additional hr £8; @) Gatwick (South Terminal); Heathrow (Terminal 4) The best news for early-morning flyers since coffee-vending machines, Yotel's smart 'cabins' offer pint-sized luxury: comfy beds, soft lights, internet-connected TVs, monsoon showers and fluffy towels. Swinging cats isn't recommended, but when is it ever?

Eating

Dining out in London has become so fashionable that you can hardly open a menu without banging into a celebrity chef, while the range and quality of eating options has increased massively over the last few decades.

BOOKING SERVICES

» **At Home in London** (020-8748 1943; www.athomeinlondon.co.uk) B&Bs.
» **British Hotel Reservation Centre** (020-7592 3055; www.bhrconline.com)
» **GKLets** (020-7613 2805; www.gklets.co.uk) Apartments.
» **London Homestead Services** (020-7286 5115; www.lhslondon.com) B&Bs.
» **LondonTown** (020-7437 4370; www.londontown.com) Hotels and B&Bs.
» **Uptown Reservations** (020-7937 2001; www.uptownres.co.uk) Upmarket B&Bs.
» **Visit London** (0871 222 3118 per min 10p; www.visitlondonoffers.com) Hotels.

Camden (London)

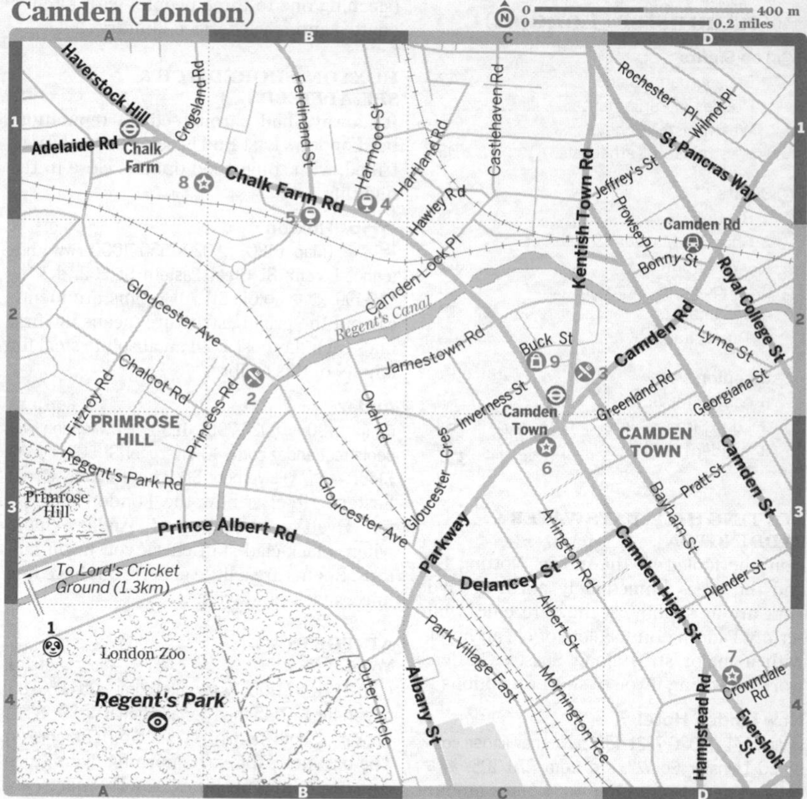

In this section, we steer you towards restaurants and cafes distinguished by their location, value for money, unique features, original settings and, of course, good food.

WEST END

Between them, Mayfair, Soho and Covent Garden are the gastronomic heart of London, with stacks of restaurants and cuisines at a wide range of budgets.

TOP CHOICE **Hibiscus** FRENCH £££
(Map p168; ☎020-7629 2999; www.hibiscusrestaurant.co.uk; 29 Maddox St W1; 3-course lunch/dinner £30/70; ⊖Oxford Circus) Claude and Claire Bosi have generated an avalanche of praise and two Michelin stars for their restaurant. Expect adventurous, intricate dishes and perfect service.

Great Queen Street BRITISH ££
(Map p168; ☎020-7242 0622; 32 Great Queen St WC2; mains £9-19; ⏲lunch daily, dinner Mon-Sat; ⊖Holborn) There's no tiara on this Great Queen, but the food's still the best of British.

Veeraswamy INDIAN ££
(Map p168; ☎020-7734 1401; www.veeraswamy.com; 99 Regent St W1, enter Swallow St; mains £15-30, pre- & post-theatre 2-/3-course £18/21; ⊖Piccadilly Circus) This is Britain's longest-running Indian restaurant. The excellent food, engaging service and exotic but elegant decor make for a memorable eating experience.

Wild Honey MODERN EUROPEAN ££
(Map p168; ☎020-7758 9160; www.wildhoneyrestaurant.co.uk; 12 St George St W1; mains £15-24; ⊖Oxford Circus) For a good-value meal with the oak-panelled ambience of a top Mayfair restaurant, try the excellent pre-theatre set menu (£22 for three courses).

Abeno Too JAPANESE £
(Map p168; www.abeno.co.uk; 17-18 Great Newport St WC2; mains £8-13; ⊖Leicester Sq) Specialists

Camden (London)

Top Sights

Regent's Park ... A4

Sights

1 London Zoo (Entrance) ... A4

Eating

2 Engineer ... B2
3 Mango Room ... C2

Drinking

4 Lock Tavern ... B1
5 Proud ... B1

Entertainment

6 Jazz Cafe ... C3
7 Koko ... D4
8 Roundhouse ... A1

Shopping

9 Camden Market ... C2

in *okonomi-yaki* (Japanese-style pancakes) and soba (noodles), which are cooked in front of you on a hotplate. Sit at the bar or by the window and feast.

Arbutus MODERN EUROPEAN ££
(Map p168; 020-7734 4545; www.arbutusrestaurant.co.uk; 63-64 Frith St W1; mains £14-20; Tottenham Court Rd) Focusing on seasonal produce, inventive dishes and value for money, Anthony Demetre's Michelin-starred restaurant just keeps getting better.

Fernandez & Wells DELICATESSEN, CAFE £
(Map p168; www.fernandezandwells.com; 73 Beak St W1; mains £4-5; Piccadilly Circus) There's no shortage of delicious charcuterie and cheese to fill the fresh baguettes on the counter of this teensy cafe.

HK Diner CHINESE £
(Map p168; 22 Wardour St W1; mains £6-13; lunch & dinner; Piccadilly Circus) For soft-shell crab or barbecue pork in the wee hours of the morning (it's open till 4am), this Hong Kong–style cafe (delicious food, no-nonsense decor) is the place to come.

Bocca di Lupo ITALIAN ££
(Map p168; 020-7734 2223; www.boccadilupo.com; 12 Archer St W1; mains £11-25; Piccadilly Circus) Although this restaurant can be found hiding down a dark Soho backstreet, it radiates an elegant sophistication.

Hummus Bros CAFE £
(www.hbros.co.uk; mains £4-8;); Soho (Map p168; 88 Wardour St W1; Piccadilly Circus); Holborn (Map p168; 37-63 Southampton Row W1; Holborn); Cheapside (Map p180; 128 Cheapside EC2; St Pauls) This informal place is hummus heaven. It comes in small or regular bowls with a choice of meat or vegie toppings and a side of pita bread.

CLERKENWELL & FARRINGDON

Clerkenwell's hidden gems are well worth digging for; Exmouth Market is a good place to start.

TOP CHOICE **Bistrot Bruno Loubet** FRENCH ££
(Map p180; 020-7324 4455; www.bistrotbrunoloubet.com; 86-88 Clerkenwell Rd EC1; mains £12-17; breakfast, lunch & dinner; Farringdon) An informal but stylish bistro below the Zetter Hotel. There are London restaurants charging double for food half as good.

St John BRITISH ££
(Map p180; 020-7251 0848; www.stjohnrestaurant.com; 26 St John St EC1; mains £14-22; Farringdon) Whitewashed walls and simple wooden furniture keep diners free to concentrate on world-famous 'nose-to-tail' treats. Expect offal, ox tongue and bone marrow.

Smiths of Smithfield BRITISH ££
(Map p180; 020-7251 7950; www.smithsofsmithfield.co.uk; 67-77 Charterhouse St EC1; mains 1st fl £13-15, top fl £19-30; Farringdon) This converted meat-packing warehouse is all things to all people. Hit the ground-floor bar for a beer, go upstairs to a relaxed dining space, or continue up for two more floors of feasting, each slightly smarter and pricier than the last.

Little Bay EUROPEAN £
(Map p180; 020-7278 1234; www.little-bay.co.uk; 171 Farringdon Rd EC1; mains before/after 7pm £6.45/8.45; Farringdon) The crushed-velvet ceiling, handmade twisted lamps and elaborately painted tables are bonkers but fun; the hearty food is very good value.

Modern Pantry FUSION ££
(Map p180; 020-7553 9210; www.themodernpantry.co.uk; 47-48 St John's Sq EC1; mains £15-22; breakfast, lunch & dinner; Farringdon)

One of London's most talked-about eateries, with an innovative menu.

Medcalf BRITISH ££
(Map p180; ☎020-7833 3533; www.medcalfbar.co.uk; 40 Exmouth Market EC1; mains £10-16; ⊙closed dinner Sun; ⊖Farringdon) In a beautifully converted 1912 butcher's shop, serving excellent-value and well-realised fare.

SOUTHWARK

You'll find plenty of touristy eateries on the riverside, making the most of the constant foot traffic and iconic London views. For a feed with a local feel, head to **Borough Market** (boxed text, p196) or **Bermondsey St**.

Oxo Tower Brasserie FUSION £££
(Map p180; ☎020-7803 3888; www.harveynichols.com/restaurants/oxo-tower-london; Barge House St SE1; mains £18-26; ⊖Waterloo) The spectacular views are the big drawcard here. Choose from the restaurant, the less extravagantly priced brasserie or if you're not hungry, the bar. Set price menus are offered at lunchtime, before 6.15pm and after 10pm (three-courses £27).

Delfina MODERN EUROPEAN ££
(Map p180; ☎020-7357 0244; www.thedelfina.co.uk; 50 Bermondsey St SE1; mains £10-15; ⊙lunch Sun-Fri, dinner Fri; ⊖London Bridge) This white-walled restaurant in a converted chocolate factory serves delicious food to a backdrop of contemporary canvases. Sunday roasts are popular.

Anchor & Hope GASTROPUB ££
(Map p180; 36 The Cut SE1; mains £12-17; ⊙lunch Tue-Sun, dinner Mon-Sat; ⊖Southwark) The hope is that you'll get a table because you can't book at this quintessential gastropub serving unashamedly meaty British food.

CHELSEA, KENSINGTON & KNIGHTSBRIDGE

These highbrow neighbourhoods have some of London's very best (and priciest) restaurants.

Made in Italy ITALIAN £
(off Map p174; ☎020-7352 1880; www.madeinitalygroup.co.uk; 249 King's Rd SW3; pizzas £5-11, mains £8-17; ⊙dinner Mon-Fri, lunch & dinner Sat & Sun; ⊖Sloane Sq) Pizza is served by the tasty quarter-metre at this traditional trattoria. Sit on the roof terrace and dream of Napoli.

Gordon Ramsay FRENCH £££
(☎020-7352 4441; www.gordonramsay.com; 68 Royal Hospital Rd SW3; 3-course lunch/dinner £45/90; ⊖Sloane Sq) Whether you like or loathe the ubiquitous celeb-chef, his eponymous restaurant is one of Britain's finest – one of only four in the country with three Michelin stars. Book ahead and dress up: jeans and T-shirts are forbidden – if you've seen the chef on the telly, you won't argue.

NOTTING HILL, BAYSWATER & PADDINGTON

Notting Hill teems with good places to eat, from cheap takeaways to atmospheric pubs and restaurants worthy of the fine-dining tag. Queensway has the best strip of Asian restaurants this side of Soho.

Kiasu SOUTHEAST ASIAN £
(Map p174; www.kiasu.co.uk; 48 Queensway W2; mains £6-9; ⊖Bayswater) Local Malaysians and Singaporeans rate this place highly, as do those who know a tasty good-value bite when they see it.

Geales SEAFOOD ££
(Map p174; ☎020-7727 7528; www.geales.com; 2 Farmer St W8; 2-course lunch £10, mains £10-18; ⊙closed lunch Mon; ⊖Notting Hill Gate) Fresh fish in a variety of guises – either battered and British or with an Italian sensibility.

Kam Tong CHINESE £
(www.kam-tong.co.uk; yum cha £3-4, mains £8-17) Bayswater (Map p174; 59-63 Queensway W2; ⊖Bayswater); Chinatown (Map p168; 14 Lisle St WC2; ⊖Leicester Sq) When most of the clientele are Chinese, you know you're on to a good thing.

Le Café Anglais MODERN EUROPEAN ££
(☎020-7221 1415; www.lecafeanglais.co.uk; 8 Porchester Gardens W2; mains £13-25, 3-course menu £30; ⊖Bayswater) This bustling restaurant has a very eclectic menu (from gigantic roasts to Thai curries) which aims to please everybody – and usually does.

MARYLEBONE

Marylebone's charming High St has a huge range of eateries. You won't go too far wrong planting yourself on a table anywhere.

Providores & Tapa Room FUSION £££
(Map p174; ☎020-7935 6175; www.theprovidores.co.uk; 109 Marylebone High St W1; 2/3/4/5 courses £30/43/53/60; ⊖Baker St) New Zealand's greatest culinary export since kiwifruit, chef Peter Gordon works magic here, matching his creations with NZ wines.

La Fromagerie CAFE £
(Map p174; www.lafromagerie.co.uk; 2-6 Moxon St W1; mains £6-13; ⊖Baker St) This providore-

cafe has bowls of delectable salads, antipasto and beans scattered about the long communal table. Huge slabs of bread invite you to tuck in, while the heavenly waft from the cheese room beckons.

Locanda Locatelli ITALIAN ££
(Map p174; 020-7935 9088; www.locandalocatelli.com; 8 Seymour St W1; mains £11-30; Marble Arch) Known for its sublime pasta dishes, this dark but quietly glamorous restaurant in an otherwise unremarkable hotel is one of London's hottest tables.

FITZROVIA

Tucked away behind busy Tottenham Court Rd, Fitzrovia's Charlotte and Goodge Sts form one of central London's most vibrant eating precincts.

Hakkasan CHINESE ££
(Map p168; 020-7927 7000; www.hakkasan.com; 8 Hanway Pl W1; mains £11-58; Tottenham Court Rd) The first Chinese restaurant to get a Michelin star is hidden down a lane – like all fashionable haunts need to be.

Salt Yard SPANISH, ITALIAN ££
(Map p168; 020-7637 0657; www.saltyard.co.uk; 54 Goodge St W1; tapas £4-8; Goodge St) Named after the place where cold meats are cured, this softly lit joint serves delicious Spanish and Italian tapas.

Lantana CAFE £
(Map p168; www.lantanacafe.co.uk; 13 Charlotte Pl W1; mains £4-10; breakfast & lunch Mon-Sat; Goodge St) Excellent coffee and substantial, inventive brunches induce queues on Saturday mornings outside this Australian-style cafe.

CAMDEN TOWN

Camden's great for cheap eats, while neighbouring Chalk Farm and Primrose Hill are salted with gastropubs and upmarket restaurants.

Engineer GASTROPUB ££
(Map p188; 020-7722 0950; 65 Gloucester Ave NW1; mains £13-21; Chalk Farm) One of London's original gastropubs, serving consistently good international cuisine to hip North Londoners. The courtyard garden is a real treat on balmy summer nights.

Mango Room CARIBBEAN ££
(Map p188; 020-7482 5065; www.mangoroom.co.uk; 10-12 Kentish Town Rd NW1; mains £11-14; Camden Town) An upmarket Caribbean experience serving modern and traditional dishes. The rum-based happy hour cocktails (£4; 6pm to 8pm) will get you in the tropical mood.

ISLINGTON

Allow at least an evening to explore Islington's Upper St and the lanes leading off it.

TOP CHOICE **Le Mercury** FRENCH £
(off Map p180; 020-7354 4088; www.lemercury.co.uk; 140a Upper St N1; mains £7-10; Highbury & Islington) A cosy Gallic haunt that appears much more expensive than it is. Sunday lunch by the open fire upstairs is a treat.

Regent PIZZA £
(201 Liverpool Rd N1; mains £7-11; Angel) Loved by the young crowd, the ambience is more pub than pizzeria, and the jukebox is loaded with indie pop gems.

Duke of Cambridge GASTROPUB ££
(020-7359 3066; www.dukeorganic.co.uk; 30 St Peter's St N1; mains £14-18; Angel;) This tucked-away gastropub serves only organic food and drink, fish from sustainable sources and locally sourced vegetables and meat.

HOXTON, SHOREDITCH & SPITALFIELDS

From the hit-and-miss Bangladeshi restaurants of Brick Lane to the Vietnamese strip on Kingsland Rd, via the Jewish, Spanish, French, Italian and Greek eateries in between, the East End's cuisine is as multicultural as its residents.

Fifteen ITALIAN ££
(Map p180; 0871 330 1515; www.fifteen.net; 15 Westland Pl N1; breakfast £2-8.50, trattoria £6-11, restaurant £11-25; breakfast, lunch & dinner; Old St) TV-chef Jamie Oliver's culinary philanthropy started here. The food is beyond excellent and even those on limited budgets can afford a visit.

Albion BRITISH ££
(Map p180; www.albioncaff.co.uk; 2-4 Boundary St E2; mains £9-13; Old St) Self-consciously retro, serving up top-quality British classics: bangers and mash, steak and kidney pies, devilled kidneys and, of course, fish and chips.

Cafe Bangla BANGLADESHI £
(Map p180; 128 Brick Lane E1; mains £5-15; Liverpoool St) Amongst the hordes of practically interchangeable Brick Lane restaurants, this one stands out for its murals of scantily clad women riding dragons, alongside a tribute to Princess Di.

CHAIN GANG

It's an unnerving, but not uncommon, experience to discover an idiosyncratic cafe or pub, then find it again (and again) on completely different streets. But chain eateries shouldn't automatically be sneered at; some offer jolly good food at fair prices. Some of the best:

GBK GOURMET BURGERS
(www.gbk.co.uk; ⏲lunch & dinner) Covent Garden (Map p168; 13-14 Maiden Lane WC2); Soho (Map p168; 15 Frith St W1); South Kensington (Map p174; 107 Old Brompton Rd SW7)

Ping Pong CHINESE
(www.pingpongdimsum.com; ⏲lunch & dinner) Goodge St (Map p168; 48 Newman St W1); Soho (Map p168; 45 Great Marlborough St W1)

S&M Café BRITISH
(www.sandmcafe.co.uk; ⏲breakfast, lunch & dinner) Islington (4-6 Essex Rd N1); Spitalfields (Map p180; 48 Brushfield St E1)

Wagamama JAPANESE
(www.wagamama.com; ⏲lunch & dinner) Bloomsbury (Map p168; 4 Streatham St WC1); Covent Garden (Map p168; 1 Tavistock St WC2); Knightsbridge (Map p174; Harvey Nichols, 109-125 Brompton Rd SW1)

Zizzi ITALIAN
(Map p168; www.zizzi.co.uk; 20 Bow St WC2; ⏲lunch & dinner)

Drinking

As long as there's been a city, Londoners have loved to drink – and, as history shows, often immoderately. Soho is undoubtedly the heart of London's bar culture, with enough variety to cater to all tastes. Camden's great for grungy boozers, losing ground on the cool front to venues around Hoxton and Shoreditch. Other places with pub-crawl potential include Clerkenwell, Islington, Southwark, Notting Hill, Earl's Court… Hell, it's just not that difficult. The reviews below are simply to make sure you don't miss out on some of the most historic, unusual, best-positioned or excellent examples of the genre.

WEST END

Gordon's Wine Bar BAR
(Map p168; www.gordonswinebar.com; 47 Villiers St WC2; ⊖Embankment) What's not to love about this cavernous wine cellar lit by candles and practically unchanged over the last 120 years?

Princess Louise PUB
(Map p168; 208 High Holborn WC1; ⊖Holborn) Arguably London's most beautiful pub, decorated with fine tiles, etched mirrors and a gorgeous central horseshoe bar, often packed with the after-work crowd.

Lamb & Flag PUB
(Map p168; 33 Rose St WC2; ⊖Covent Garden) Everyone's favourite Covent Garden 'find', this historic pub is often jammed.

Absolut Ice Bar BAR
(Map p168; ☎020-7478 8910; www.belowzerolondon.com; 31-33 Heddon St W1; admission Thu-Sat £16, Sun-Wed £13; ⊖Piccadilly Circus) At -6°C, this bar made entirely of ice is literally the coolest in London. It's a gimmick, sure, but a good one.

THE CITY

Vertigo 42 CHAMPAGNE BAR
(Map p180; ☎020-7877 7842; www.vertigo42.co.uk; Tower 42, Old Broad St EC2; ⊖Liverpool St) Book a two-hour slot in this 42nd-floor bar with top views across London.

Ye Olde Cheshire Cheese PUB
(Map p180; Wine Office Ct, 145 Fleet St EC4; ⊖Holborn) *Re*-built in 1667, this place is a bit touristy but always atmospheric and enjoyable.

Ye Olde Watling PUB
(Map p180; 29 Watling St EC4; ⊖Mansion House) Another atmospheric olde pub from the 1660s.

CLERKENWELL & FARRINGDON

Jerusalem Tavern PUB
(Map p180; www.stpetersbrewery.co.uk; 55 Britton St EC1; ⊖Farringdon) Pick a wood-panelled cubbyhole at this 1720 coffee shop-turned-inn, and choose from a selection of St Peter's beers and ales.

SOUTHWARK

George Inn PUB
(Map p180; www.nationaltrust.org.uk/main/w-georgeinn; 77 Borough High St SE1; ⊖London Bridge) London's last surviving galleried coaching inn, dating in its current form from 1677. Dickens and Shakespeare used to prop up the bar here (not together, obviously).

Anchor PUB
(Map p180; 34 Park St SE1; ⊖London Bridge) An 18th-century boozer replacing the 1615

version where Samuel Pepys witnessed the Great Fire; it still has a terrace offering superb views across the Thames.

MARYLEBONE

Artesian BAR
(Map p168; www.artesian-bar.co.uk; Langham Hotel, 1C Portland Pl W1; ⊖Oxford Circus) For a dose of colonial glamour with a touch of the orient, try this sumptuous bar at the Langham.

CAMDEN TOWN

Lock Tavern PUB, MUSIC
(Map p188; www.lock-tavern.co.uk; 35 Chalk Farm Rd NW1; ⊖Camden Town) The archetypal Camden pub, with a rooftop terrace and a beer garden, with an interesting crowd, ready conviviality and regular live music.

Proud BAR, MUSIC
(Map p188; www.proudcamden.com; Stables Market NW1; admission free-£10; ⊖Camden Town) This place has booths, rock photography on the walls and deckchairs printed with images of Pete Doherty and Blondie. Enjoy the gallery by day or bands by night. No, despite the name it's not a gay bar.

HOXTON, SHOREDITCH & SPITALFIELDS

TOP CHOICE **Loungelover** COCKTAIL BAR
(Map p180; ☎020-7012 1234; www.lestriosgarcons.com; 1 Whitby St E1; ⏲6pm-midnight Sun-Thu, to 1am Fri & Sat; ⊖Liverpool St) Book a table, sip your cocktail and admire the Louis XIV chairs, the huge hippo head, the cage-turned-living room, the jewel-encrusted stag's head and the loopy chandeliers. Utterly fabulous.

Ten Bells PUB
(Map p180; cnr Commercial & Fournier Sts E1; ⊖Liverpool St) The most famous Jack the Ripper pub; admire the wonderful 18th-century tiles and ponder the past over a pint.

TOP CHOICE **Commercial Tavern** PUB
(Map p180; 142 Commercial St E1; ⊖Liverpool St) The zany decor's a thing of wonder in this reformed East End boozer.

Favela Chic BAR
(Map p180; www.favelachic.com; 91-93 Great Eastern St EC2; entry £5-10 after 8pm; ⊖Old St) Hip young things; crazy theme nights; fun and funky music.

Zigfrid Von Underbelly BAR
(Map p180; www.zigfrid.com; 11 Hoxton Sq N1; ⊖Old St) Furnished like an oversized lounge room, the kookiest of the Hoxton Sq venues.

> **LOO STOP**
>
> While facilities are available at most museums and sights, many foreign visitors are surprised at London's lack of public toilets (also coyly called 'public conveniences' on signs) out on the street. If you're caught short, here are some tips: very few tube stations have facilities but bigger rail stations usually do (although they're often coin-operated, so yes it's 20p to pee). The smarter department stores are a good bet, if you can face five floors on an escalator, as are fast-food outlets. In a busy pub, you might be able to sneak in to use the loo, but it's polite to order a drink afterwards – which kinda defeats the purpose.

☆ Entertainment

From West End luvvies to East End geezers, Londoners have always loved a spectacle. With bear baiting and public executions no longer an option, they've learnt to make do with having the world's best theatres, nightclubs and live music. For comprehensive listings see *Time Out* or the free papers at tube stations.

Theatre

London is a world capital for theatre and there's a lot more than mammoth musicals to tempt you into the West End. On performance days, you can buy half-price tickets for West End productions (cash only) from the official agency **tkts** (Map p168; www.tkts.co.uk; Leicester Sq WC2; ⏲10am-7pm Mon-Sat, noon-4pm Sun; ⊖Leicester Sq). The booth is the one with the clock tower; beware of touts selling dodgy tickets. For more, see www.officiallondontheatre.co.uk or www.theatremonkey.com.

The term 'West End' – as with 'Broadway' – generally refers to big-money productions like musicals, but also includes some heavyweights:

Royal Court Theatre THEATRE
(Map p174; ☎020-7565 5000; www.royalcourttheatre.com; Sloane Sq SW1; ⊖Sloane Sq) Patron of new British writing.

National Theatre THEATRE
(Map p180; ☎020-7452 3000; www.nationaltheatre.org.uk; South Bank SE1; ⊖Waterloo)

Cheaper tickets for classics and new plays from some of the world's best companies.

Royal Shakespeare Company THEATRE
(RSC; ☎0844 800 1110; www.rsc.org.uk) The Bard's classics and other quality stuff.

Old Vic THEATRE
(Map p180; ☎0844 871 7628; www.oldvictheatre.com; The Cut SE1; ⊖Waterloo) Kevin Spacey continues his run as artistic director (and occasional performer).

Donmar Warehouse THEATRE
(Map p168; ☎0844 871 7624; www.donmarwarehouse.com; 41 Earlham St WC2; ⊖Covent Garden) A not-for-profit company with a West End reputation.

You'll generally find the most original works off the West End, at several venues:

Almeida THEATRE
(off Map p180; ☎020-7359 4404; www.almeida.co.uk; Almeida St N1; ⊖Highbury & Islington)

Young Vic THEATRE
(Map p180; ☎020-7922 2922; www.youngvic.org; 66 The Cut SE1; ⊖Waterloo)

Menier Chocolate Factory THEATRE
(Map p180; ☎020-7907 7060; www.menierchocolatefactory.com; 55 Southwark St SE1; ⊖London Bridge)

Nightclubs

London's had a lot of practice perfecting the art of clubbing – Samuel Pepys used the term in 1660 – and the variety of venues today is staggering. Some run their own regular weekly schedule, while others host promoters on an ad hoc basis. The big nights are Friday and Saturday, although you'll find some of the most cutting-edge sessions midweek. Admission prices vary widely; it's often cheaper to arrive early or prebook tickets.

Fabric CLUB
(Map p180; www.fabriclondon.com; 77a Charterhouse St EC1; admission £8-18; ⏲10pm-6am Fri, 11pm-8am Sat, 11pm-6am Sun; ⊖Farringdon) Consistently rated as one of the world's greatest clubs, Friday's FabricLive offers drum'n'bass, breakbeat and hip hop; Saturdays see house, techno and electronica; while hedonistic Sundays are delivered by the Wetyourself crew.

Plastic People CLUB
(Map p180; www.plasticpeople.co.uk; 147-149 Curtain Rd EC2; admission £5-10; ⏲10pm-3.30am Fri & Sat, to 2am Sun; ⊖Old St) Taking the directive 'underground club' literally – a low-ceilinged subterranean den of dubsteppy, wonky, funky, no-frills, fun times.

Ministry of Sound CLUB
(Map p180; www.ministryofsound.com; 103 Gaunt St SE1; admission £13-22; ⏲11pm-6.30am Fri & Sat; ⊖Elephant & Castle) Where the global brand started, it's London's most famous club and still packs in a diverse crew with big local and international names.

Cargo CLUB
(Map p180; www.cargo-london.com; 83 Rivington St EC2; admission free-£16; ⊖Old St) A popular club with a courtyard where you can simultaneously enjoy big sounds and the great outdoors. It also hosts live bands and gay bingo.

Rock, Pop & Jazz

While London may have stopped swinging in the 1960s, every subsequent generation has given birth to a new set of bands in the city's thriving live venues: punk in the 1970s, New Romantics in the 1980s, Brit Pop in the 1990s and the current crop of skinny-jeaned rockers and electro acts thrilling scenesters today. Big-name gigs sell out quickly, so check www.seetickets.com before you travel. See also the pubs with music listed under Drinking reviews.

Koko CLUB
(Map p188; www.koko.uk.com; 1a Camden High St NW1; ⊖Mornington Cres) Occupying the Camden Palace, with live bands most nights and the regular Club NME (£5) on Friday.

O2 Academy Brixton LIVE MUSIC
(☎0844 477 2000; www.o2academybrixton.co.uk; 211 Stockwell Rd SW9; ⊖Brixton) Always winning awards for 'best live venue', hosting big-name acts in a relatively intimate setting (5000 capacity).

Jazz Cafe CLUB
(Map p188; www.jazzcafe.co.uk; 5 Parkway NW1; ⊖Camden Town) Intimate club that stages a full roster of jazz, rock, pop, hip hop and dance, including famous names.

Ronnie Scott's CLUB
(Map p168; ☎020-7439 0747; www.ronniescotts.co.uk; 47 Frith St W1; ⊖Leicester Sq) London's legendary jazz club, pulling in the hep cats since 1959.

100 Club CLUB
(Map p168; ☎020-7636 0933; www.the100club.co.uk; 100 Oxford St W1; ⊖Oxford Circus) This legendary London venue once showcased the Stones and was at the centre of the punk

revolution; it now features jazz, rock and even a little swing.

Hope & Anchor PUB
(off Map p180; ☎020-7700 0550; 207 Upper St N1; admission free-£6; ⊖Angel) Live music's still the focus of the pub that hosted the first London gigs of Joy Division and U2.

Roundhouse LIVE MUSIC, THEATRE
(Map p188; ☎0844 482 8008; www.roundhoues.org.uk; Chalk Farm Rd NW1; ⊖Chalk Farm) An iconic concert venue since the 1960s, hosting the likes of the Rolling Stones, Led Zeppelin and The Clash. It's also used for theatre and comedy.

Classical Music, Opera & Dance

With four world-class symphony orchestras, two opera companies, various smaller ensembles, brilliant venues, reasonable prices and high standards of performance, London is a classical capital. Keep an eye out for the free (or cheap) lunchtime concerts held in many of the city's churches.

Royal Albert Hall CONCERT HALL
(Map p174; ☎020-7589 8212; www.royalalberthall.com; Kensington Gore SW7; ⊖South Kensington) Beautiful Victorian venue that hosts classical concerts and contemporary artists.

Barbican Centre ARTS CENTRE
(Map p180; ☎0845 121 6823; www.barbican.org.uk; Silk St EC2; ⊖Barbican) This hulking complex has a full program of film, music, theatre, art and dance, including loads of concerts from the **London Symphony Orchestra** (www.lso.co.uk), which is based here.

Southbank Centre CONCERT HALLS
(Map p180; ☎0844 875 0073; www.southbankcentre.co.uk; Belvedere Rd SE1; ⊖Waterloo) Home to the **London Philharmonic Orchestra** (www.lpo.co.uk), **Sinfonietta** (www.londonsinfonietta.org.uk) and the **Philharmonia Orchestra** (www.philharmonia.co.uk), amongst others, this centre hosts classical, opera, jazz and choral music in three premier venues: the **Royal Festival Hall**, the smaller **Queen Elizabeth Hall** and the **Purcell Room**. Look out too for free recitals in the foyer.

Royal Opera House OPERA, BALLET
(Map p168; ☎020-7304 4000; www.roh.org.uk; Bow St WC2; tickets £5-195; ⊖Covent Garden) Covent Garden is synonymous with opera thanks to this world-famous venue, also the home of the **Royal Ballet**. Backstage tours on weekdays (£10, book ahead).

Sadler's Wells DANCE
(Map p180; ☎0844 412 4300; www.sadlers-wells.com; Rosebery Ave EC1; tickets £10-49; ⊖Angel) A glittering modern venue, Sadler's Wells has been given much credit for bringing modern dance to the mainstream.

Coliseum OPERA
(Map p168; ☎0871 911 0200; www.eno.org; St Martin's Lane WC2; tickets £10-87; ⊖Leicester Sq) Home of the progressive **English National Opera**; all performances are in English.

Shopping

Napoleon famously described Britain as a nation of shopkeepers, which doesn't sound at all bad to us! From world-famous department stores to quirky backstreet retail revelations, London is a mecca for shoppers with an eye for style and a card to exercise. If you're looking for something distinctly British, eschew the Union Jack–emblazoned kitsch of the tourist thoroughfares and fill your bags with London fashion, music, books and antiques.

In the West End, Oxford St is the place for High St fashion, while Regent St cranks it up a notch. Carnaby St is no longer the hip hub that it was in the 1960s, but the lanes around it still have good boutiques. Bond St has designers galore, Savile Row is famous for bespoke tailoring and Jermyn St is the place for Sir to buy his smart clobber (particularly shirts).

Department Stores

London's famous department stores are an attraction in themselves, even if you're not interested in buying.

Selfridges DEPARTMENT STORE
(Map p174; www.selfridges.com; 400 Oxford St W1; ⊖Bond St) The funkiest and most vital of London's one-stop shops, where fashion runs the gamut from street to formal.

Fortnum & Mason DEPARTMENT STORE
(Map p168; www.fortnumandmason.com; 181 Piccadilly W1; ⊖Piccadilly Circus) The byword for quality and service from a bygone era, steeped in 300 years of tradition.

Liberty DEPARTMENT STORE
(Map p168; www.liberty.co.uk; Great Marlborough St W1; ⊖Oxford Circus) An irresistible blend of contemporary styles and indulgent pampering in a mock-Tudor fantasyland of carved dark wood.

Harrods DEPARTMENT STORE
(Map p174; www.harrods.com; 87 Brompton Rd SW1; ⊖Knightsbridge) A pricy but fascinating

ROLL OUT THE BARROW

London has more than 350 markets selling everything from antiques and curios to flowers and fish. Some, such as Camden and Portobello Rd, are full of tourists, while others exist just for the locals. Here's a sample:

Columbia Road Flower Market FLOWERS, PLANTS
(Map p180; Columbia Rd E2; 8am-2pm Sun; Old St) The best place for East End barrow boy banter ('We got flowers cheap enough for ya muvver-in-law's grave'). Unmissable.

Borough Market FOOD
(Map p180; www.boroughmarket.org.uk; 8 Southwark St SE1; 11am-5pm Thu, noon-6pm Fri, 8am-5pm Sat; London Bridge) A farmers' market sometimes called London's Larder; everything from organic falafel to boars' heads.

Camden Market MARKET
(Map p188; 10am-5.30pm; www.camdenmarkets.org; Camden Town) Actually a series of markets spread along Camden High St; the Lock and Stables markets are still the place for punk fashion, cheap food, hippy-dippy stuff and a whole lotta craziness.

Portobello Road Market CLOTHES, ANTIQUES
(www.portobellomarket.org; Portobello Rd W10; 8am-6.30pm Mon-Sat, to 1pm Thu; Notting Hill Gate or Ladbroke Grove) One of London's most famous (and crowded) street markets; new and vintage clothes, antiques and food.

Broadway Market FOOD
(www.broadwaymarket.co.uk; 9am-5pm Sat; Bethnal Green) Graze from the organic food stalls or choose a cooked meal.

Brixton Market MARKET
(www.brixtonmarket.net; Electric Ave & Granville Arcade; 8am-6pm Mon-Sat, to 3pm Wed; Brixton) Immortalised in the Eddie Grant song, Electric Ave is a cosmopolitan treat that mixes everything from reggae music to exotic spices.

Sunday (Up)market CLOTHES, ACCESSORIES
(Map p180; www.sundayupmarket.co.uk; The Old Truman Brewery, Brick Lane E1; 10am-5pm Sun; Liverpool St) Handmade handbags, jewellery, new and vintage clothes and shoes.

Brick Lane Market MARKET
(Map p180; www.visitbricklane.org; Brick Lane E1; 8am-2pm Sun; Liverpool St) A sprawling East End bazaar featuring everything from fruit to paintings and bric-a-brac.

Petticoat Lane Market MARKET
(Map p180; Wentworth St & Middlesex St E1; 9am-2pm Sun-Fri; Aldgate) A cherished East End institution overflowing with cheap consumer durables and jumble sale ware.

theme park for fans of Britannia, Harrods is always crowded with slow tourists.

Harvey Nichols DEPARTMENT STORE
(Map p174; www.harveynichols.com; 109-125 Knightsbridge SW1; Knightsbridge) London's temple of high fashion, jewellery and perfume.

Music

As befitting a global music capital, London has a wide range of music stores.

HMV MUSIC
(Map p168; www.hmv.com; 150 Oxford St W1; Oxford Circus) Giant store selling music, DVDs and magazines.

Ray's Jazz JAZZ, BLUES
(Map p168; www.foyles.co.uk; Foyles, 113-119 Charing Cross Rd WC2; Tottenham Court Rd) Where aficionados find those elusive back catalogues.

BM Soho DANCE
(Map p168; www.bm-soho.com; 25 D'Arblay St W1; Oxford Circus) If they haven't got what you're after, they'll know who does.

Rough Trade ALTERNATIVE, PUNK, INDIE
(www.roughtrade.com); East (Map p180; Dray Walk, 91 Brick Lane E1; Liverpool St); West (130 Talbot Rd W11; Ladbroke Grove) The best place to come for anything of an indie or alternative bent.

Information

Britain & London Visitor Centre (www.visitbritain.com; 1 Regent St SW1; 9am-6.30pm Mon-Fri, 10am-4pm Sat & Sun; Piccadilly Circus) Accommodation and theatre bookings, transport tickets, *bureau de change*, international telephones and internet terminals. Longer hours in summer.

City of London Information Centre (020-7332 1456; www.visitthecity.co.uk; 9.30am-5.30pm Mon-Sat, 10am-4pm Sun; St Paul's Churchyard EC4; St Paul's) Tourist information, fast-track tickets to City attractions and guided walks (adult/child £6/4).

Getting There & Away

London is the country's major gateway; for more details on transport connections, see p308.

Bus & Coach

The London terminus for long-distance buses (called 'coaches' in Britain) is **Victoria Coach Station** (020-7824 0000; 164 Buckingham Palace Rd SW1; Victoria).

Train

Most of London's main-line rail terminals are linked by the Circle line on the tube.

Charing Cross Canterbury

Euston Manchester, Liverpool, Carlisle, Glasgow

King's Cross Cambridge, Hull, York, Newcastle, Scotland

Liverpool Street Stansted airport (Express), Cambridge

London Bridge Gatwick airport, Brighton

Marylebone Birmingham

Paddington Heathrow airport (Express), Oxford, Bath, Bristol, Exeter, Plymouth, Cardiff

St Pancras Gatwick and Luton airports, Brighton, Nottingham, Sheffield, Leicester, Leeds, Paris Eurostar

Victoria Gatwick airport (Express), Brighton, Canterbury

Waterloo Windsor, Winchester, Exeter, Plymouth

Getting Around

To/From the Airports

GATWICK Mainline trains run every 15 minutes between Gatwick's South Terminal and Victoria (from £12, 37 minutes), hourly at night, or to/from St Pancras (from £12, 66 minutes) via London Bridge, City Thameslink, Blackfriars and Farringdon. **Gatwick Express** (0845 850 1530; www.gatwickexpress.com) trains run to/from Victoria every 15 minutes from 5am to 11.45pm (one way/return £16/26, 30 minutes, first/last train 3.30am/12.32am). The **EasyBus** (www.easybus.co.uk) minibus service between Gatwick and Earl's Court (every 30 minutes from 4.25am to 1am, about 1¼ hours) costs from £2 to £10, depending on when you book. You're charged extra if you have more than one carry-on and one check-in bag.

HEATHROW The cheapest option to central London is the Piccadilly line on the tube, accessible from every terminal (£4.50, one hour, departing every five minutes from around 5am to 11.30pm). If it's your first time in London, it's a good chance to practise using the tube as it's at the beginning of the line and therefore not too crowded when you get on. If there are vast queues at the ticket office, use the automatic machines instead; some accept credit cards as well as cash.

Quicker is the dedicated **Heathrow Express** (0845 600 1515; www.heathrowexpress.co.uk), an ultramodern train to/from Paddington (one way/return £16.50/32, 15 minutes, every 15 minutes 5.12am to 11.42pm). You can purchase tickets on board (£5 extra), from self-service machines (cash and credit cards accepted) at both stations or online.

LONDON CITY The Docklands Light Railway (DLR) connects London City Airport to the tube network, taking 22 minutes to reach Bank station (£4).

LUTON Mainline trains run between St Pancras (£9.50, 29 to 39 minutes) and Luton Airport Parkway station, where a shuttle bus (£1) will get you to the airport within 10 minutes. The **EasyBus** (www.easybus.co.uk) minibus service between Victoria and Luton Airport (via Baker St) costs from £2 to £10 (about 1½ hours, every 30 minutes).

STANSTED The **Stansted Express** (0845 850 0150; www.stanstedexpress.com) connects with Liverpool St station (one way/return £18/27, 46 minutes, every 15 minutes 6am to 12.30am). The **EasyBus** (www.easybus.co.uk) minibus between Stansted and Baker St costs £2 to £10 (1¼ hours, every 20 minutes). The **Airbus A6** (0870 580 8080; www.nationalexpress.com) links with Victoria Coach Station (£11, allow 1¾ hours, at least every 30 minutes).

Bus

Travelling round London by double-decker bus is an enjoyable way to get a feel for the city, but usually slower than the tube. Buses run regularly during the day, while less-frequent night buses (prefixed with the letter 'N') wheel into action when the tube stops. Single-journey bus tickets (valid for two hours) cost £2 (£1.20 on Oyster, capped at £3.90 per day); a weekly pass is £17. Children ride for free. At stops with yellow signs, you have to buy your ticket from the automatic machine *before* boarding (unless you have an Oyster or Travelcard). Buses stop on request, so clearly signal the driver with an outstretched arm.

The classic London bus, the red double-decker 'Routemaster', has been pensioned off and replaced with more modern varieties on most routes. For a taste of history, **Routemasters** still operate on route 9 (between Aldwych and Royal Albert Hall) and route 15 (Trafalgar Sq and Tower Hill); these are the only buses without wheelchair access.

Bicycle

Central London is mostly flat, relatively compact and the traffic moves slowly – all of which make it surprisingly good for cyclists. It can get terribly congested though, so you'll need to keep your wits about you – and lock your bike (including both wheels) securely. Bikes can be hired from numerous self-service docking stations through the **Cycle Hire** (www.tfl.gov.uk; free 1st 30min, then 1/2/3/6/24hr £1/6/15/35/50) scheme.

Car

Don't even think about it. London was recently rated Western Europe's second most congested city (congratulations Brussels). In addition, you'll pay £8 per day simply to drive into central London from 7am to 6pm on a weekday. If you're hiring a car to continue your trip around Britain after sightseeing in London, take the tube or train to a major airport and pick it up from there.

Taxi

London's famous black cabs are available for hire when the yellow light above the windscreen is lit. To get a licence, cabbies must do 'The Knowledge', which tests them on 25,000 streets and points of interest. Fares are metered, with flag fall of £2.20 and additional rate dependent on time of day, distance travelled and taxi speed. A one-mile trip will cost between £4.60 and £8.60.

Minicabs quote trip fares in advance and are a cheaper alternative to black cabs. They're licensed (recognisable by the 't' symbol displayed in the window) but drivers don't do 'The Knowledge' so they may not know every street. Minicabs operate via booking agencies (most busy areas have a walk-in office with drivers waiting). See p307 for safety advice.

Train

As well as the tube, London is served by regular urban train services, particularly south of the Thames. To use the train, buy a one-off ticket at a station – from the ticket desk or a machine (or on the train if there's no desk or machine) – or use a Travelcard or Oyster card. Most urban train stations are fitted with Oyster readers, but not all have turnstiles: it's important to remember to tap in and tap out at the Oyster reader, otherwise your card will register an unfinished journey and you'll be charged extra.

Underground & DLR

London's underground train network (universally known as the tube) extends its subterranean tentacles across the city and into the surrounding counties, with services running every few minutes from roughly 5.30am to 12.30am (from 7am to 11.30pm Sunday). It's easy to use. Tickets or Travelcards (or Oyster card top-ups) can be purchased from counters or machines at each station using either cash or credit card. They're then inserted into the slot on the turnstiles (or you touch your Oyster card on the yellow reader) and the barrier opens. Once you're

LONDON'S YOUR OYSTER

Although locals love to complain, London's public transport is excellent, with tubes, trains, buses and boats all covering the capital. **Transport for London** (TFL; www.tfl.gov.uk) binds it all together; the website also has information on taxis and rental bikes – plus journey planners.

London is divided into concentric transport zones, with almost all places in this book in Zones 1 and 2. You can save money and avoid queues at ticket machines by getting a Travelcard (£7.20 per day for Zones 1 and 2; £5.60 if you avoid peak hours: 6.30am to 9.30am and 4pm to 7pm), available from ticket machines or counters at stations. It's valid on bus, tube and most urban trains – and much cheaper than buying two tube tickets or three bus tickets.

If you're in London for a few days, get an Oyster card, a reusable smartcard preloaded with credit to give unlimited transport on tube, bus and some rail services. Touch your card to the yellow sensors at the station turnstiles or bus entrance, and the fare is deducted from your card, at a much lower rate than a one-off paper ticket. For four days or fewer, opt for the daily rate (as per Travelcard above). If you're here for a week, load up your Oyster card as a weekly season ticket (£26). The card itself is £3, fully refundable when you leave.

through you can jump on and off different lines as often as you need to get to your destination.

Also included within the tube network are some urban train lines (branded as 'Overground' and shown on tube maps) and the Docklands Light Railway (DLR), linking the City to Docklands, Greenwich and London City Airport. It's worth taking just for the view, especially when it hurtles between the skyscrapers of Canary Wharf; try to get the front row seat in the driverless front carriage.

Waterbus

The myriad boats that ply the Thames are a great way to travel, avoiding traffic jams and giving great views. Passengers with Travelcards (including an Oyster) get a third off all fares. **Thames Clippers** (www.thamesclippers.com) runs regular commuter services between Embankment, Waterloo, Blackfriars, Bankside, London Bridge, Tower, Canary Wharf, Greenwich, North Greenwich and Woolwich piers (adult/child £5.30/2.65) from 7am to midnight (from 9.30am weekends).

MAPPING THE TUBE

The London tube map is an acclaimed graphic design work, using coloured lines to show 14 different routes. However, it's not remotely to scale. On the map, distances between stations are more or less the same. In reality, central stations can be just 250m apart while in the outer suburbs it may be miles between one station and the next.

AROUND LONDON

'When you're tired of London, you're tired of life' opined 18th-century Londoner Samuel Johnson. But he wasn't living in an age when too many days on the tube can leave you exhausted and grouchy. Luckily, the capital is surprisingly close to some excellent day escapes. Well-known day-trip haunts like Brighton and Oxford are covered in the Southeast England and Southwest England sections. Two other gems an easy train ride from the capital are covered here.

Windsor & Eton

POP 31,000

Dominated by the massive bulk and heavy influence of Windsor Castle, these twin towns have a rather surreal atmosphere, with the morning pomp and ceremony of the changing of the guards in Windsor and the sight of school boys dressed in formal tail coats wandering the streets of Eton.

Windsor Castle CASTLE

(www.royalcollection.org.uk; adult/child £16/9.50; ⏲9.45am-5.15pm) The largest and oldest occupied fortress in the world, Windsor Castle is a majestic vision of battlements and towers used for state occasions and as the Queen's weekend retreat. But that doesn't mean visitors have to be content with peering through the gates outside. Instead, you can enter large sections of the castle complex, now fully restored after the devastating 1992 fire. Highlights include **Queen Mary's giant dolls' house**, designed by Sir Edward Lutyens, and **St George's Chapel**, containing the tombs of several monarchs, including Henry VIII.

Eton College HISTORIC SCHOOL

(www.etoncollege.com; adult/child £6.20/5.20; ⏲guided tours 2pm & 3.15pm daily during school holidays, Wed, Fri, Sat & Sun during term time) A short walk through Windsor and across the River Thames brings you to this famous public school – which in Britain means a *private* school – where 18 prime ministers and endless royals were educated. Several buildings date from the mid-15th century when Henry VI founded the school. As you wander round you may recognise some of the buildings; *Chariots of Fire, The Madness of King George, Mrs Brown* and *Shakespeare in Love* are just some of the classics filmed here.

ℹ Information

Royal Windsor Information Centre (☎01753-743900; www.windsor.gov.uk; Old Booking Hall, Windsor Royal Shopping Arcade; ⏲9.30am-5pm Mon-Sat, 10am-4pm Sun)

ℹ Getting There & Away

Trains from Windsor Central station on Thames St go to London Paddington (27 to 43 minutes). Trains from Windsor Riverside station go to London Waterloo (56 minutes). Services run half-hourly from both stations and tickets cost £7.90.

SOUTHEAST ENGLAND

Traditionally a day-trip playground for Londoners escaping overcrowded streets, England's southeast offers fascinating historic towns, sweeping greenbelt vistas and some vibrant seaside resorts – many just an hour or so by train from the capital. This section covers the counties of Kent, Sussex and Hampshire, with places listed roughly east to west. For visitor information, see www.visitsoutheastengland.com.

Canterbury

POP 43,432

With its jaw-dropping cathedral surrounded by medieval cobbled streets, this World Heritage city has been a Christian pilgrimage site for several centuries, and a tourist attraction for almost as long. Today's visitors come to immerse themselves in religious and secular history, including Thomas Becket's murder and the bawdy works of Geoffrey Chaucer, but this is no mothballed outdoor museum: Canterbury is surprisingly vibrant, and a good base for exploring the wider region.

Sights

Canterbury Cathedral CHURCH

(www.canterbury-cathedral.org; adult/concession £8/7; ⏲9am-5pm Mon-Sat, 12.30pm-2.30pm Sun) The Anglican faith could not have a more imposing mother church than this extraordinary early-Gothic cathedral. It's an overwhelming edifice filled with enthralling stories, striking architecture and an enduring sense of spirituality. This ancient structure is packed with monuments commemorating the nation's battles. The spot in the northwest transept where Archbishop Thomas Becket met his grisly end has been drawing pilgrims for more than 800 years and is marked by a flickering candle and striking modern altar. The wealth of detail in the cathedral is immense and unrelenting, so it's well worth joining a one-hour **tour** (adult/child £5/3; ⏲10.30am, noon & 2.30pm Mon-Fri, 10.30am, noon & 1.30pm Sat Easter-Oct), or you can take a 40-minute self-guided **audio tour** (adult/concessions £3.50/2.50).

Museum of Canterbury MUSEUM

(www.canterbury-museums.co.uk; Stour St; adult/child £3.60/2.30; ⏲11am-4pm Mon-Sat, also 1.30-4pm Sun Jun-Sep) A fine 14th-century building now houses the city's absorbing museum which has a jumble of exhibits from pre-Roman times to the assassination of Becket, via Joseph Conrad to locally born celebs.

Canterbury Tales CHAUCER ATTRACTION

(www.canterburytales.org.uk; St Margaret's St; adult/child £7.75/5.75; ⏲10am-5pm Mar-Oct) This three-dimensional interpretation of Chaucer's classic tales through jerky animatronics and audio guides is a lively and fun introduction for the young or uninitiated.

THE CANTERBURY TALES

If English literature has a father figure, it is Geoffrey Chaucer (1342/3–1400), the first English writer to introduce characters – rather than 'types' – into fiction. Written in the now hard-to-decipher Middle English of the day, Chaucer's *Tales* is a series of 24 vivid stories as told by a party of pilgrims on their journey from London to Canterbury. It remains one of the pillars of the literary canon, as well as a collection of rollicking good yarns about adultery, debauchery, crime and edgy romance, all filled with Chaucer's witty observances of human nature.

Sleeping

House of Agnes HOTEL ££

(☎01227-472185; www.houseofagnes.co.uk; 71 St Dunstan's St; r from £83; @📶) This 13th-century beamed inn has eight themed rooms such as 'Venice' (carnival masks), 'Boston' (light and airy) and 'Canterbury' (antiques and heavy fabrics).

White House B&B ££

(☎01227-761836; www.whitehousecanterbury.co.uk; 6 St Peter's Lane; s/d from £60/80; 📶) An elegant Regency town house with a friendly welcome, period rooms with modern touches and a grand guest lounge.

Kipp's Independent Hostel HOSTEL £

(☎01227-786121; www.kipps-hostel.com; 40 Nunnery Fields; dm/s/d £16/22/36; @) Popular for its laid-back, homely atmosphere, with lots of communal areas, clean though cramped dorms, bike hire and garden.

Canterbury Cathedral Lodge HOTEL ££

(☎01227-865350; www.canterburycathedrallodge.org; Canterbury Cathedral precincts; r from £65; @📶) Modern rooms have excellent facilities but best of all are the views and the unlimited access to the cathedral for guests.

Eating & Drinking

TOP CHOICE **Deeson's** BRITISH ££

(☎01227-767854; 25-27 Sun St; mains £4.50-16; ⏲lunch & dinner) Local fruit and veg,

CANTERBURY ATTRACTIONS PASSPORT

The **Canterbury Attractions Passport** (adult/child £19/15.25) gives entry to the cathedral and The Canterbury Tales, plus St Augustine's Abbey and one of the city's museums. It's available from the tourist office.

local wines and beers, local fish and the odd ingredient from the proprietor's allotment, all served in a contemporary setting a Kentish apple's throw from the Cathedral gates. What more do you want?

Veg Box Cafe VEGETARIAN £
(1 Jewry Lane; soups/specials £4.95/6.95; breakfast & lunch Mon-Sat;) This welcoming, laid-back spot uses only the freshest, locally sourced organic ingredients in its dishes, served at stocky timber tables under red paper lanterns.

Thomas Beckett PUB
(21 Best Lane) A classic English pub with a garden of hops hanging from its timber frame, quality ales, comfy seating, decent grub and a cosy fireplace for winter nights.

Parrot PUB
(1-9 Church Lane) Canterbury's oldest boozer is a snug pub downstairs and a much-lauded dining room upstairs.

Information

Tourist office (01227-378100; www.canterbury.co.uk; 12 Sun St; 9.30am-5pm Mon-Sat, to 4.30pm Sun) Situated opposite the cathedral gate.

Getting There & Away

The bus station is on St George's Lane. There are two train stations: Canterbury East for London Victoria, and Canterbury West for London Charing Cross and London St Pancras.

Bus & Coach

Dover National Express, £5, 40 minutes, hourly

London Victoria National Express, £13.40, two hours, hourly

Train

Dover Priory £6.50, 25 minutes, every 30 minutes

London St Pancras £27.80, one hour, hourly

London Victoria £23.40, one hour 40 minutes, two to three hourly

Dover

POP 39,078

Dover's shabby town centre is a sad introduction to Britain for travellers arriving by boat, but the town has a couple of stellar attractions to redeem it.

Sights

Dover Castle CASTLE
(English Heritage; www.english-heritage.org.uk; adult/child £13.90/7; 10am-6pm Apr-Sep; P) The almost impenetrable Dover Castle, one of the most impressive in England, was built to bolster defences at the shortest sea crossing to mainland Europe. The site has been in use for 2000 years and sprawls across the hilltop, commanding a tremendous view of the English Channel as far as the French coastline. Highlights include the remains of a **Roman lighthouse**, a restored **Saxon church**, the robust 12th-century **Great Tower**, with walls up to 7m thick, and the warren of claustrophobic **secret wartime tunnels** under the castle.

White Cliffs of Dover LANDMARK
Immortalised in song, film and literature, these iconic cliffs are embedded in the national consciousness, a big 'Welcome Home' sign to generations of travellers and soldiers. The cliffs rise to 100m high and extend on either side of Dover, but the best bit is the 6-mile stretch that starts about 2 miles east of town, properly known as the Langdon Cliffs. The area is managed by the National Trust and there's a small information office, from where you can take the stony path east along the cliff tops for a bracing 2-mile walk to the **South Foreland Lighthouse** (National Trust; www.nationaltrust.org.uk; adult/child £4/2; guided tours 11am-5.30pm Fri-Mon mid-Mar–Oct).

Sleeping

B&Bs cluster along Castle St, Maison Dieu Rd and Folkestone Rd.

Hubert House B&B ££
(01304-202253; www.huberthouse.co.uk; 9 Castle Hill Rd; s/d from £40/55; P@) The comfortable bedrooms may be overly flowery but the welcome is warm. It has its own little bistro downstairs which opens out onto a front terrace.

Number One Guest House B&B ££
(01304-202007; www.number1guesthouse.co.uk; 1 Castle St; d from £50; P) At the foot of Dover Castle, with rooms decorated in traditional

WORTH A TRIP

LEEDS CASTLE

Leeds Castle (www.leeds-castle.com; adult/child £17.50/10; ⏲10am-6pm Apr-Sep) is one of the most visited attractions in Britain. This impressive structure balancing on two islands amid a large lake has been transformed from fortress to lavish palace over the centuries, and the vast estate is ideal for peaceful walks.

Leeds Castle is just east of Maidstone in Kent. Trains run from London Victoria to Bearsted (£17.10, one hour), from where you catch a special shuttle coach to the castle (£5 return).

Victorian style, this place also has a garden with lovely views.

East Lee Guest House B&B ££
(☎01304-210176; www.eastlee.co.uk; 108 Maison Dieu Rd; d £60; P📶) Energetic hosts, renovated rooms and excellent breakfasts.

Eating & Drinking

TOP CHOICE **Allotment** BRITISH ££
(9 High St; www.theallotmentdover.com; mains £7.50-16; ⏲breakfast, lunch & dinner Tue-Sat) Dover's best dining spot plates up local fish and meat in a relaxed, understated setting. Swab the decks with a Kentish wine as you admire the view.

La Salle Verte CAFE £
(14-15 Cannon St; snacks £2-5.50; ⏲breakfast & lunch Mon-Sat) The funkiest little coffee shop in Dover serves great coffee and snacks.

Information

Tourist office (☎01304-205108; www.whitecliffscountry.org.uk; Biggin St; ⏲9am-5.30pm Jun-Aug, 9am-5.30pm Mon-Fri & 10am-4pm Sat & Sun Apr, May & Sep, closed Sun Oct-Mar)

Getting There & Away

Bus & Coach

Canterbury Bus 15, 45 minutes, twice hourly

London Victoria Coach 007, £13.50, 2¾ hours, 19 daily

Train

London Charing Cross £18.50, two hours, twice hourly

London St Pancras £31.70, one hour, hourly

Getting Around

The ferry companies run regular shuttle buses between the docks and the train station (five minutes) as they're a long walk apart.

Taxis offering 24-hour services include **Heritage** (☎01304-204420) and **Star Taxis** (☎01304-228822).

Brighton & Hove

POP 247, 817

While some British seaside resorts are paint-peeled reminders of an earlier era, Brighton and Hove – two towns combined to form a new city in 2000 – has successfully moved on. It's now a cosmopolitan centre with a bohemian spirit, exuberant gay community, dynamic student population and a healthy number of ageing and new-age hippies, as well as traditional candy-floss fun – although the beach has never been the main attraction, mainly because it's stones not sand. But Brighton rocks all year-round, and really comes to life in summer.

Sights

Royal Pavilion HISTORIC BUILDING
(www.royalpavilion.org.uk; adult/child £9.50/5.40; ⏲9.30am-5.45pm Apr-Sep, 10am-5.15pm Oct-Mar) The city's must-see attraction is the glittering palace and party-pad of the Prince Regent (later King George IV), still an apt symbol of Brighton's reputation for hedonism. The domes and minarets outside are only a prelude to the palace's lavish oriental-themed interior.

Brighton Pier PIER
(www.brightonpier.co.uk) This grand old centenarian pier is the place to come to experience the tackier side of Brighton. There are plenty of stomach-churning fairground rides and dingy amusement arcades, plus candy floss and Brighton rock to chomp.

The Lanes SHOPPING
Brighton's original fishing-village heart is the Lanes, a cobblestone web of 17th-century cottages housing a gentrified cornucopia of independent shops, pubs and one-of-a-kind eateries. The adjacent **North Laine** has a funkier vibe with streets of multicoloured shops, secondhand record stores and vegetarian cafes for local hipsters.

Festivals

There's always something fun going on in Brighton, but the main events include **Gay**

Pride (www.brightonpride.org) in early August and the **Brighton Festival** (☎01273-709 709; www.brightonfestival.org) in May, the biggest in Britain after Edinburgh, drawing theatre, dance, music and comedy performers from around the globe.

Sleeping

Traditional B&Bs line the streets radiating from Brighton Pier, but there are also some new boutique properties and a good selection of backpacker joints – several cater to raucous stag/hen nights, while others are more traditional, so choose wisely!

TOP CHOICE **Neo Hotel** BOUTIQUE HOTEL ££
(☎01273-711104; www.neohotel.com; 19 Oriental Pl; d from £100; wi-fi) With nine rooms straight out of the pages of a design magazine, other temptations include satin kimono robes and wonderful breakfasts with fruit pancakes.

Baggies Backpackers HOSTEL £
(☎01273-733740; www.baggiesbackpackers.com; 33 Oriental Pl; dm/d £13/35; wi-fi) A warm atmosphere, on-site owners and clean dorms have made this long-established hostel something of an institution.

Snooze HOTEL ££
(☎01273-605797; www.snoozebrighton.com; 25 St George's Tce; s/d from £60/85; @wi-fi) This eccentric Kemp Town pad is very fond of retro styling. It's more than just a gimmick though – rooms are comfortable and spotless, and there are great vegie breakfasts.

Seadragon Backpackers HOSTEL £
(☎01273-711854; www.seadragonbackpackers.co.uk; 36 Waterloo St; dm/tw £20/50; wi-fi) Perched on the edge of Hove, this simple and well-equipped hostel lacks vibe but is ideal for budget nomads who like to party elsewhere then snooze in peace.

Eating & Drinking

Brighton easily has the best choice on the south coast, with cafes, restaurants, pubs and bars to fulfil every whim. Drunken stag parties and tacky nightclubs rule on West St, but there are many other options, including the unique mix of seafront clubs and bars. For pointers, visit www.drinkinbrighton.co.uk.

TOP CHOICE **Terre à Terre** VEGETARIAN ££
(71 East St; mains £10-15; ⊙lunch & dinner Tue-Sun; vegetarian) Even staunch meat eaters will come out raving about this legendary vegetarian restaurant, famous for its modern space and inventive dishes full of robust flavours.

JB's American Diner DINER £
(31 King's Rd; burgers £7, mains £6.50-12; ⊙lunch & dinner) Shiny red leather booths, stars and stripes, and a '50s soundtrack provide the background for colossal portions of burgers, fries and milkshakes.

English's Oyster Bar SEAFOOD ££
(www.englishs.co.uk; 29-31 East St; mains £11-25; ⊙lunch & dinner) A 60-year institution, this Brightonian seafood paradise dishes up everything from oysters and lobster to Dover sole.

GAY & LESBIAN BRIGHTON

For more than 100 years Brighton has been a gay haven, and with over 35,000 gay men and lesbians living here, it is the most vibrant queer community in the country outside London. Kemp Town (aka Camptown), on and off St James' St, is where it's all at. For information, see www.gay.brighton.co.uk and www.realbrighton.com or the free monthly magazine **Gscene** (www.gscene.com).

Hub (129 St James' St; ⊙8am-6pm Mon-Fri, 10am-6pm Sat & Sun) Cool coffee-shop hang-out.

Amsterdam (www.amsterdam.uk.com; 11-12 Marine Pde; ⊙noon-2am) Hotel, sauna, restaurant and extremely hip bar.

Candy Bar (www.thecandybar.co.uk; 129 St James' St; ⊙9pm-2am) Slick cafe-bar-club for the girls.

Queen's Arms (www.queensarmsbrighton.com; 7 George St; ⊙3pm-late) Plenty of camp cabaret and karaoke.

Revenge (www.revenge.co.uk; 32-34 Old Steine; ⊙10.30pm-3am) Nightly disco with occasional cabaret.

Basement Club (31-34 Marine Pde; ⊙9am-2am) Located beneath gay Legends Hotel, winner of the Golden Handbag award 2009.

Brighton

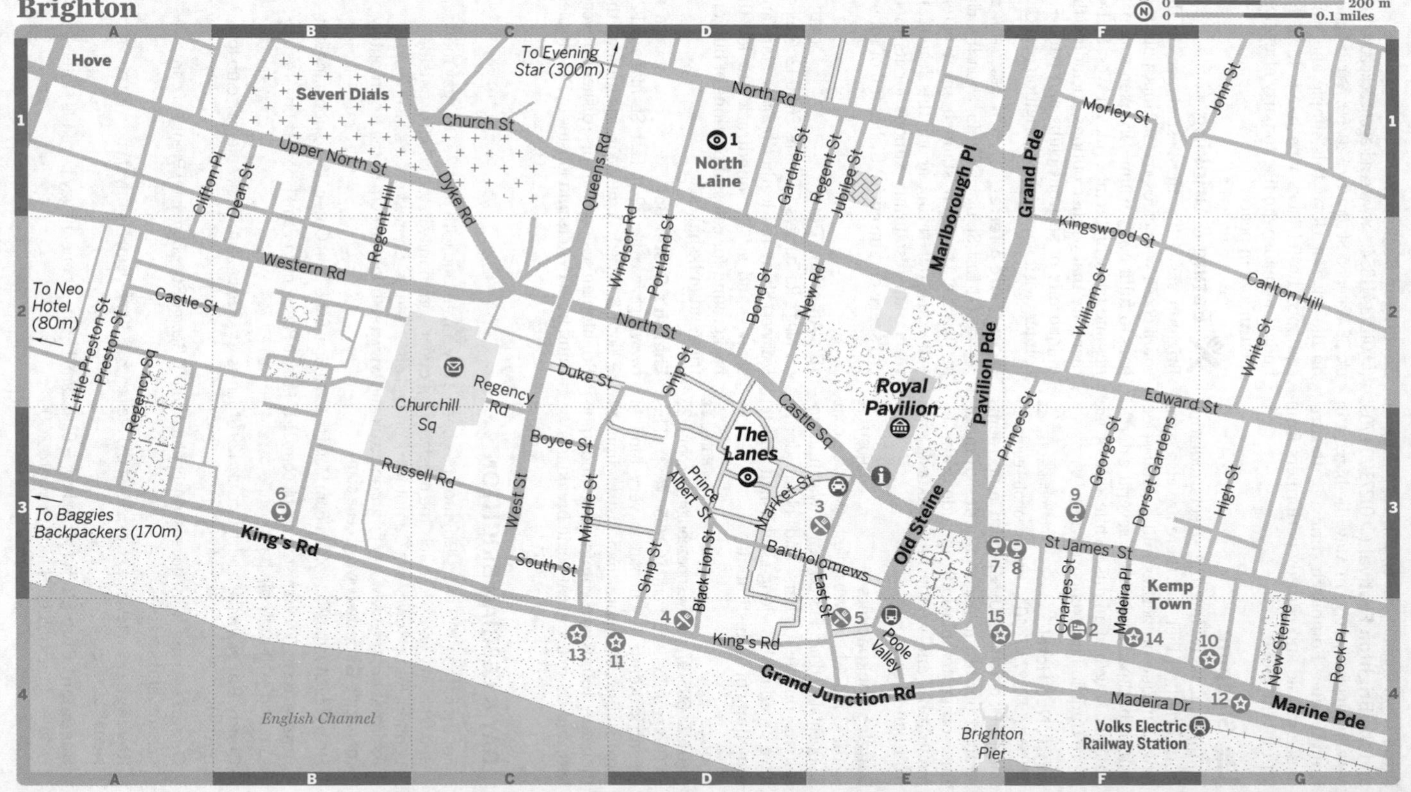
Hove
Seven Dials
North Laine
The Lanes
Royal Pavilion
Kemp Town
Poole Valley
English Channel
Brighton Pier
Volks Electric Railway Station
To Evening Star (300m)
To Neo Hotel (80m)
To Baggies Backpackers (170m)
King's Rd
Grand Junction Rd
Marine Pde
Madeira Dr
Old Steine
Pavilion Pde
Grand Pde
Marlborough Pl
North Rd
North St
Queens Rd
Dyke Rd
Church St
Upper North St
Western Rd
Regent Hill
Dean St
Clifton Pl
Castle St
Regency Sq
Preston St
Little Preston St
Churchill Sq
Russell Rd
Regency Rd
West St
South St
Boyce St
Duke St
Middle St
Ship St
Black Lion St
Prince Albert St
Bartholomews
Market St
East St
Castle Sq
Windsor Rd
Portland St
Bond St
Gardner St
Regent St
Jubilee St
New Rd
Kingswood St
William St
Edward St
Carlton Hill
White St
John St
Morley St
Princes St
George St
Dorset Gardens
High St
St James' St
Charles St
Madeira Pl
New Steine
Rock Pl
200 m
0.1 miles

Brighton

Top Sights

Evening Star PUB
(www.eveningstarbrighton.co.uk; 55/56 Surrey St) This cosy pub is a beer-drinker's nirvana, with a wonderful selection of award-winning real ales.

106 Bar & Brasserie BAR
(www.106brasseries.com; Kings Rd; ⏲3pm-11pm Fri, noon-11pm Sat, 11am-5pm Sun) Huge sea-view windows deluge this weekend venue in light as you sip a preclub cocktail and watch the sun go down.

Entertainment

Brighton offers the best entertainment line-up on the south coast. When Britain's top DJs aren't plying their trade in London, Ibiza or Aya Napia, chances are you'll spy them here.

Coalition BAR, CLUB
(171-181 Kings Rd Arches) All sorts happen here, from comedy to live music to club nights.

Funky Buddha NIGHTCLUB
(Kings Rd Arches) Subterranean tunnels playing funky house, '70s, R & B and disco to a stylish and attitude-free crowd.

Funky Fish Club NIGHTCLUB
(www.funkyfishclub.co.uk; 19-23 Marine Pde) Friendly and unpretentious little club playing soul, funk, jazz, Motown and old-skool.

Concorde 2 NIGHTCLUB
(www.concorde2.co.uk; Madeira Dr, Kemp Town) Brighton's best-known and best-loved club is a disarmingly unpretentious den, where DJ Fatboy Slim pioneered the Big Beat Boutique and still occasionally graces the decks.

Information

Tourist office (☎0300-300 0088; www.visitbrighton.com; Royal Pavilion Shop, Royal Pavilion; ⏲10am-5.30pm) The guys to turn to for anything Brighton-related, from tide times to train times.

Getting There & Away

Bus & Coach

London Victoria National Express, £11.80, two hours, hourly

Train

All London-bound services pass through Gatwick airport.

London St Pancras £16.90, 1¼ hours, half-hourly

London Victoria £13.90, 50 to 70 minutes, half-hourly

Portsmouth £13.90, 1½ hours, hourly

Winchester

POP 41,420

Calm, collegiate Winchester is a mellow must-see for all visitors. The past still echoes around the flint-flecked walls of this ancient cathedral city. It was the capital of Saxon kings, and its statues and sights evoke two of England's mightiest myth-makers: Alfred the Great and King Arthur (yes, he of the round table).

Sights

Winchester Cathedral CHURCH
(www.winchester-cathedral.org.uk; adult/child £6/free, combined admission & tower tour £9; ⏲9am-5pm Sat, 12.30-3pm Sun) Almost 1000 years of history are crammed into Winchester's cathedral. The exterior isn't at first glance appealing but the interior is awe inspiring, with one of the longest medieval naves (164m) in Europe and a fascinating collection of features from all eras. Jane Austen, one of England's best-loved authors, is buried near the entrance in the northern aisle.

FREE **Great Hall & Round Table** HISTORIC BUILDING
(Castle Ave; suggested donation adult/child £1/50p; ⏲10am-5pm) The cavernous Great Hall is the only part of 11th-century Winchester Castle that Oliver Cromwell spared from destruction. Crowning the wall is what centuries of mythology have dubbed King Arthur's Round Table. It's actually a 700-year-old copy, but is fascinating nonetheless.

Hospital of St Cross HISTORIC BUILDING
(www.stcrosshospital.co.uk; St Cross Rd; adult/child £3/1; ⏲9.30am-5pm Mon-Sat, 1-5pm Sun Apr-Oct, 10.30am-3.30pm Mon-Sat Nov-Mar) Established in 1132 to house pilgrims and crusaders en route to the Holy Land, this hospital is the oldest charitable institution in the country. It's about a mile outside the centre (a pretty walk through water meadows) and all visitors can claim the centuries-old 'Wayfarer's Dole' – a crust of bread and swig of beer from the Porter's Gate.

Sleeping

Wykeham Arms HISTORIC HOTEL ££
(☎01962-853834; www.fullershotels.com; 75 Kingsgate St; s/d/ste £70/119/150; P 📶) This place is bursting with history – it used to be a brothel and also put up Nelson for a night (some say the two events coincided). Creaking, winding stairs lead to the cosy, traditionally styled bedrooms above the pub, while sleeker rooms opposite look out onto a pocked-sized courtyard garden.

Dolphin House B&B ££
(☎01962-853284; www.dolphinhousestudios.co.uk; 3 Compton Rd; s/d £55/70; P 📶) At this place your continental breakfast is delivered to a compact kitchen – perfect for lazy lie-ins – while the terrace overlooks a gently sloping lawn.

No 21 B&B ££
(☎01962-852989; St Johns St; s/d £45/90) Gorgeous cathedral views, a flower-filled cottage garden and rustic-chic rooms (think painted wicker and woven bedspreads) make this art-packed house a tranquil city bolthole.

Eating & Drinking

TOP CHOICE **Chesil Rectory** MODERN BRITISH ££
(☎01962-851555; www.chesilrectory.co.uk; 1 Chesil St; mains £16; ⏲lunch & dinner Mon-Sat, lunch Sun) Duck through the hobbit-sized door, settle down amid the 15th-century beams and savour perfectly prepared modern British cuisine.

Black Rat BRITISH ££
(☎01962-844465; www.theblackrat.co.uk; 88 Chesil St; mains £17-20; ⏲dinner daily, lunch & dinner Sat & Sun) Worn wooden floorboards and warm red-brick walls give this relaxed restaurant a cosy feel.

Black Boy PUB
(www.theblackboypub.com; 1 Wharf Hill; ⏲noon-11pm, to midnight Fri & Sat) This adorable old pub is filled with obsessive and sometimes freaky collections, from pocket watches to bear traps.

Information

Tourist office (☎01962-840500; www.visitwinchester.co.uk; High St; ⏲10am-5pm Mon-Sat, also 11am-4pm Sun May-Sep)

Getting There & Away

BUS Regular, direct National Express buses shuttle to London Victoria (£14.40, 1¾ hours).

TRAIN Trains leave every 30 minutes for London Waterloo (£26, 1¼ hours). There are also fast links to the Midlands.

SOUTHWEST ENGLAND

Southwest England offers the pick of Britain's cities, coast and countryside – all on one verdant, sea-fringed platter. Here you'll find the golden sands and surging waves of Cornwall, your very own fossil on Dorset's Jurassic Coast, Wiltshire's prehistoric sites, Bath's exquisite Georgian cityscape, Bristol's buzzing nightlife, Somerset's hippy-chic ambience and Devon's beguiling blend of moors and shores.

The places in this section are listed roughly east to west. For information, see www.visitsouthwest.com.

Salisbury

POP 43,335

Centred on a majestic cathedral topped by the tallest spire in England, the gracious city of Salisbury has been an important provincial city for more than 1000 years. Its streets form an architectural timeline ranging from medieval walls and half-timbered Tudor townhouses to Georgian mansions and Victorian villas. It's also a lively modern town with plenty of bars, restaurants and terraced cafes, as well as a concentrated cluster of excellent museums.

WORTH A TRIP

JANE AUSTEN'S HOUSE

There's more than a touch of period drama at the former home of Jane Austen (1775–1817), where she wrote *Mansfield Park, Emma* and *Persuasion*, and revised *Sense and Sensibility, Pride and Prejudice* and *Northanger Abbey*. This appealing red-brick house, where the celebrated English novelist lived from 1809 to 1817, is now a **museum** (www.jane-austens-house -museum.org.uk; Chawton; adult/child £7/2; ⌚10.30am-4.30pm mid-Feb–Dec). Highlights include elegant furniture and copper pans in the kitchen, the occasional table Austen used as a desk, first editions of her novels and the delicate handkerchief she embroidered for her sister.

The museum is 18 miles east of Winchester; take bus 64 from Winchester to Chawton roundabout (50 minutes, hourly Monday to Saturday, six on Sunday) then walk the 500m to Chawton village.

Sights

Salisbury Cathedral CHURCH

(www.salisburycathedral.org.uk; requested donation adult/child £5/3; ⌚7.15am-6.15pm) England is endowed with countless stunning churches, but few can hold a candle to the grandeur and sheer spectacle of Salisbury Cathedral. Tours run throughout the day and best illuminate the intricate interior of flying buttresses and vaulted ceilings. Work out the crick in your neck in the octagonal **chapter house** – where one of only four original versions of the Magna Carta is displayed – before heading out into **Cathedral Close**, an impressive medieval perimeter of small museums and restored period houses. The **Evensong** (⌚5.30pm Mon-Sat, 3pm Sun) held here (during term time only) is intensely atmospheric.

Old Sarum HISTORIC SITE

(EH; adult/child £3.50/1.80; ⌚10am-5pm Apr-Sep, 11am-3pm Oct-Mar) A 2-mile walk or 10-minute bus ride from the centre, Old Sarum was a hill fort during the Iron Age, later occupied by Romans and Saxons. By the mid-11th century it was one of the most important towns in England, with the first cathedral built in 1092. But within 30 years the cathedral was moved, founding the new city of Salisbury, and by 1331 Old Sarum was abandoned. Today its grassy knoll is perfect for a summer stroll or picnic.

Festivals

Salisbury Festival ARTS FESTIVAL

(www.salisburyfestival.co.uk) A prestigious, eclectic event encompassing classical, world and pop music, plus theatre, literature and art, held late May to early June.

Sleeping

TOP CHOICE **St Anne's House** BOUTIQUE B&B ££

(☎01722-335657; www.stannshouse.co.uk; 32 St Ann St; s/d £60/110) For some perfectly priced indulgence, head to this sumptuous town house which overflows with antiques, fine silk and linen direct from Istanbul.

Rokeby Guesthouse B&B ££

(☎01722-329800; www.rokebyguesthouse.co.uk; 3 Wain-a-long Rd; s/d from £50/60; P@) Fancy furnishings, free-standing baths and lovely bay windows make this a stand-out from the crowd. The decking overlooking the lawn helps too.

Salisbury YHA HOSTEL £

(☎0845 371 9537; www.yha.org.uk; Milford Hill; dm £18; P@) A real gem, with neat rooms in a rambling Victorian building. Choose from doubles or dorms. A cafe-bar, laundry and dappled gardens add to the appeal.

Eating & Drinking

There's a wide choice of eateries around the main square, and near the cathedral.

Lemon Tree BRITISH ££

(☎01722-333471; www.thelemontree.co.uk; 92 Crane St; mains £10; ⌚lunch & dinner Mon-Sat) The menu at this tiny eatery is packed with character, and the patio garden makes warm weather dining a delight.

One BRITISH ££

(☎01722-411313; www.haunchofvenison.uk.com; 1 Minster St; mains £9-13; ⌚lunch & dinner) Sloping floors, slanting beams and fake pony-hide chairs surround you in this chic eatery, located above the Haunch of Venison pub. The menu is equally eclectic.

Haunch of Venison PUB
(www.haunchofvenison.uk.com; 1 Minster St) Featuring wood-panelled snugs, spiral staircases and wonky ceilings, this 14th-century drinking den is packed with atmosphere – and ghosts.

Information

Tourist office (☎01722-334956; www.visitwiltshire.co.uk/salisbury; Fish Row, Market Sq; ⊙9.30am-6pm Mon-Sat, to 5pm Mon-Sat Oct-Apr, 10am-4pm Sun Jun-Sep)

Getting There & Away

BUS National Express operates coaches to/from London via Heathrow (£16, three hours, three daily), and Bath (£10, 1¼ hours, one daily) and Bristol (£10, 2¼ hours, one daily). Regular buses serve Shaftesbury, Devizes and Avebury.

TRAIN Trains run half-hourly to/from London Waterloo (£32, 1½ hours) and hourly to Exeter (£27, two hours) and further west. Another line provides hourly connections to Bath (£8, one hour) and Bristol (£9, 1¼ hours).

Stonehenge

Britain's most iconic archaeological site, this compelling ring of monolithic stones has attracted a steady stream of pilgrims, poets and philosophers for the last 5000 years. Despite the constant flow of traffic from the main road beside the monument, and the huge numbers of visitors who traipse around the perimeter on a daily basis, **Stonehenge** (EH; www.english-heritage.org.uk; adult/child £6.90/3.50; ⊙9am-7pm Jun-Aug, 9.30am-6pm Mar-May & Sep-Oct, 9.30am-4pm Oct-Feb) still manages to be a mystical, ethereal place – a haunting echo from Britain's forgotten past, and a reminder of the people who once walked the many ceremonial avenues across Salisbury Plain. Even more intriguingly, it's still one of Britain's great archaeological mysteries: despite countless theories about what the site was used for, ranging from a sacrificial centre to a celestial timepiece, in truth, no one really knows what drove prehistoric Britons to expend so much time and effort on its construction.

STONE CIRCLE ACCESS VISITS

Visitors normally have to stay outside the stone circle itself. But on **Stone Circle Access Visits** (☎01722-343830; www.english-heritage.org.uk; adult/child £14.50/7.50) you get to wander round the core of the site, getting up-close views of the iconic bluestones and trilithons. The walks take place in the evening or early morning, so the quieter atmosphere and the slanting sunlight add to the effect. Each visit only takes 26 people; to secure a place book at least two months in advance.

Getting There & Around

BUS No regular buses go to the site. The **Stonehenge Tour** (☎01722-336855; www.thestonehengetour.info; return adult/child £11/5) leaves Salisbury's railway and bus stations half-hourly in June and August, and hourly between September and May. Tickets last all day, so you can hop off at Old Sarum on the way back.

TAXI Taxis charge £35 to go to the site from Salisbury, wait for an hour and come back.

Bath

POP 90,144

A cultural trendsetter and fashionable haunt for the last 300 years, the honey-stoned city of Bath is especially renowned for its architecture. Along its stately streets you'll find a celebrated set of Roman bathhouses, a grand medieval abbey and some fine Georgian terraces. In fact, Bath has so many listed buildings the entire place has been named a World Heritage Site. Throw in some fabulous restaurants, gorgeous hotels and top-class shopping, and you have a city that demands your undivided attention – just don't expect to dodge the crowds.

History

Bath's existence is based upon geological luck. Hot springs bubble to the surface here, and legend has it King Bladud, father of King Lear, founded the city some 2800 years ago when his pigs were cured of leprosy by a dip in the warm swampy water. In AD 44, along came the Romans; they established the town of Aquae Sulis and built an extensive baths complex and a temple to the goddess Sulis-Minerva. Through the Middle Ages, Bath was a wool-trading town, but it wasn't until the early 18th century that Ralph Allen and the celebrated dandy Richard 'Beau' Nash made Bath the centre of fashionable society. More recently, the city's futuristic (and controversial) Thermae Bath Spa has been joined by a huge new shopping centre

WORTH A TRIP

AVEBURY

While the tour buses usually head straight to Stonehenge, prehistoric purists make for Avebury Stone Circle. Though it lacks the dramatic trilithons ('gateways') of its sister site across the plain, Avebury is the largest stone circle in the world and a more rewarding place to visit simply because you can get closer to the giant boulders. A large section of Avebury village is actually inside the circle, meaning you can sleep, or at least have lunch and a pint, inside the mystic ring. To get here, bus 5/6/96 runs from Salisbury (1¾ hours, hourly Monday to Saturday, five on Sunday).

at SouthGate, seamlessly blending in with the rest of Bath's amber-coloured buildings.

Sights

Roman Baths MUSEUM
(www.romanbaths.co.uk; Abbey Churchyard; adult/child £12/7.80; 9am-8pm Jul & Aug, to 6pm Mar-Jun, Sep & Oct, 9.30am-5.30pm Jan, Feb, Nov & Dec) In typically ostentatious style, the Romans constructed a glorious complex of bathhouses above the thermal waters, and 2000 years later this is one of the best-preserved ancient Roman spas in the world. The site gets very busy in summer; you can usually dodge the worst crowds by visiting early on a midweek morning.

Bath Abbey CHURCH
(www.bathabbey.org; requested donation £2.50; 9am-6pm Mon-Sat Easter-Oct, to 4.30pm Nov-Easter, 1-2.30pm & 4.30-5.30pm Sun year-round) Constructed between 1499 and 1616, this is the last great medieval church built in England. Inside, the nave's wonderful **fan vaulting** was erected in the 19th century. Outside, the most striking feature is the west facade, where angels climb up and down stone ladders, commemorating a dream of the founder, Bishop Oliver King.

Royal Crescent & The Circus ARCHITECTURE
Bath's crowning glory is the Royal Crescent, a semicircular terrace of majestic houses originally built for wealthy socialites overlooking the green sweep of Royal Victoria Park. For a glimpse into the splendour of Georgian life, head for **No 1 Royal Crescent** (www.bath-preservation-trust.org.uk; adult/child £6/2.50; 10.30am-5pm Tue-Sun mid-Feb–mid-Oct, to 4pm mid-Oct–Dec), restored using only 18th-century materials. Nearby is **The Circus**, a ring of 30 houses divided into three terraces; plaques commemorate famous residents such as Thomas Gainsborough, Clive of India and David Livingstone.

FREE **Assembly Rooms** ARCHITECTURE
(Bennett St; 10.30am-5pm Mar-Oct, to 4pm Nov-Feb) Opened in 1771, this was where fashionable Bath socialites gathered to waltz, play cards and listen to the latest chamber music. Today you're free to wander around the rooms, if they haven't been reserved for a special function. Highlights include the card room, tearoom and ballroom, all lit by their original 18th-century chandeliers.

Fashion Museum MUSEUM
(www.fashionmuseum.co.uk; adult/child £7/5, joint ticket with Roman Baths £15/9; 10.30am-5pm Mar-Oct, to 4pm Nov-Feb) In the basement of the Assembly Rooms, this museum displays costumes worn from the 16th to late-20th centuries, including some alarming crinolines that forced women to approach doorways side on.

Jane Austen Centre MUSEUM
(www.janeausten.co.uk; 40 Gay St; adult/child £6.50/3.50; 9.45am-5.30pm Apr-Sep, 11am-4.30pm Oct-Mar) Bath is a location in Jane Austen's novels including *Persuasion* and *Northanger Abbey,* and the author's connections with the city are celebrated here. Other displays include period costumes.

DON'T MISS

THE THERMAE BATH SPA

Larking about in the Roman Baths might be off the agenda, but you can still sample the city's curative waters at **Thermae Bath Spa** (0844 888 0844; www.thermaebathspa.com; Hot Bath St; New Royal Bath spa session per 2hr/4hr/day £24/34/54, spa packages from £65; New Royal Bath 9am-10pm), where the old Cross Bath is now incorporated into an ultramodern shell of local stone and plate glass. The New Royal Bath ticket includes steam rooms, waterfall shower and a choice of bathing venues – including the open-air rooftop pool, where you can swim in the thermal waters with a backdrop of Bath's stunning cityscape.

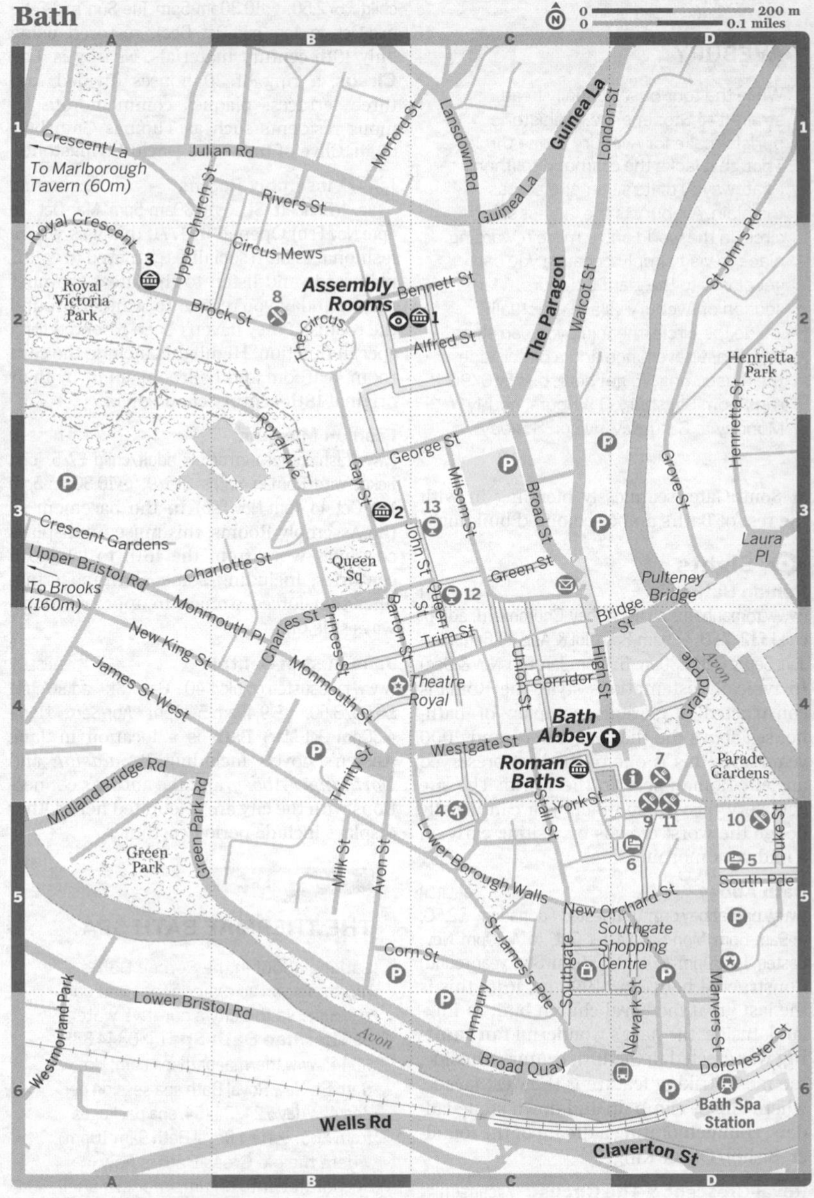

Festivals

Bath International Music Festival MUSIC
(www.bathmusicfest.org.uk) Mainly classical and opera, plus smaller gigs of jazz, folk and world. Mid-May to early June.

Sleeping

TOP CHOICE Halcyon HOTEL ££
(☎01225-444100; 2/3 South Pde; www.thehalcyon.com; d £99-125; 🛜) A shabby terrace has been knocked through, polished up and totally reinvented, making this hotel far and

Bath

Top Sights

	Assembly Rooms	B2
	Bath Abbey	C4
	Roman Baths	C4

Sights

1	Fashion Museum	C2
2	Jane Austen Centre	B3
3	No 1 Royal Crescent	A2

Activities, Courses & Tours

4	Thermae Bath Spa	C5

Sleeping

5	Halcyon	D5
6	Three Abbey Green	D5

Eating

7	Café Retro	D4
8	Circus	B2
9	Demuth's	D5
10	Onefishtwofish	D5
11	Sally Lunn's	D5

Drinking

12	Raven	C3
13	Salamander	C3

away the best in the city centre. It's style on a budget; studio rooms even have kitchens. We like it a lot.

Brooks HOTEL ££
(☎01225-425543; www.brooksguesthouse.com; 1 & 1a Crescent Gardens; d £69-175; 📶) On the west side of Bath, this is a plush option, attractively blending heritage fixtures with snazzy finishes.

Three Abbey Green B&B ££
(☎01225-428558; www.threeabbeygreen.com; 3 Abbey Green; d £85-135; 📶) Considering the location, this place is a steal – tumble out of the front door practically onto the abbey's doorstep.

Appletree Guest House B&B ££
(☎01225-337642; www.appletreeguesthouse.co.uk; 7 Pulteney Gardens; s £55-66, d £85-110, f £120-132; 📶) It's absolutely tiny, but recommended for the sunny disposition of its owners.

Bath YHA HOSTEL £
(bath@yha.org.uk; dm £14, d from £35; P @) Hostels don't come much grander than this Italianate mansion, a steep climb (or a short hop on bus 18) heading west from the city centre.

Eating & Drinking

Bath is full of eating and drinking options. The narrow lanes off Milsom St, the quieter streets around the Theatre Royal and the area around Walcot St are good places to start exploring.

TOP CHOICE **Circus** BRITISH ££
(☎01225-318918; www.thecircuscafeandrestaurant.co.uk; 34 Brock St; lunch £5.50-9.70; dinner mains £11-13.90; ⌚lunch & dinner) In a city that's often known for its snootiness, The Circus manages to be posh but not in the slightest pretentious. Quite simply, our favourite place to eat in Bath.

TOP CHOICE **Marlborough Tavern** GASTROPUB ££
(☎01225-423731; www.marlborough-tavern.com; 35 Marlborough Bldg; mains £10.95-15.95; ⌚lunch & dinner) This is Bath's best gastropub, especially if you like your food flavours rich and rustic.

Demuth's VEGETARIAN ££
(☎01225-446059; 2 North Pde Passage; mains £9.75-14.25; ⌚lunch & dinner; 🌿) For the last two decades this brilliant meat-free bistro has been turning out some of Bath's most creative and imaginative food.

Onefishtwofish SEAFOOD ££
(☎01225-330236; 10a North Pde; mains £13-18; ⌚dinner Tue-Sun) Pescetarians can plump for this super seafooderie, with cute little tables crammed in under a barrel-brick roof dotted with twinkly lights.

Café Retro CAFE £
(18 York St; mains £5-11; ⌚breakfast, lunch & dinner Tue-Sat, breakfast & lunch Mon) The paint job's scruffy, the crockery's ancient, but that's all part of the charm, and there's nowhere better for a stonking burger, a crumbly cake or a good mug of tea.

Sally Lunn's TEA HOUSE £
(4 North Pde Passage; lunch mains £5-6, dinner mains from £8; ⌚lunch & dinner) Classic chintzy tearoom serving the trademark Sally Lunn's bun.

Raven PUB
(Queen St) Highly respected by real ale aficionados, this fine city drinking den commands a devoted following for its well-kept beer and trad atmosphere.

Salamander PUB
(3 John St) The city's bespoke brewery, Bath Ales, owns this place, and you can sample all of its produce here.

Information

Tourist office (☎0906-711 2000, accommodation 0844-847-5256; www.visitbath.co.uk; Abbey Churchyard; ⌚9.30am-6pm Mon-Sat Jun-Sep, to 5pm Oct-May, 10am-4pm Sun year-round) Phone enquiries to the main office are charged at premium rate (50p per minute).

Getting There & Away

BUS Bath's new **bus and coach station** (enquiries office ⌚9am-5pm Mon-Sat) is on Dorchester St near the train station. **National Express** (www.nationalexpress.com) coaches run to/from London (£21.25, 3½ hours, 10 daily) via Heathrow (£17.50, 2¾ hours), and to Bristol (45 minutes, every 30 minutes).

TRAIN Direct trains go to/from London Paddington (£22 to £39, 1½ hours, at least hourly) and Bristol (£5.80, 11 minutes, four per hour), which has connections to most major British cities.

Bristol

POP 393,300

Bristol's buzzing. After decades of neglect, there's change happening everywhere you look in the southwest's biggest city: the historic docks have been redeveloped, the harbourside is crammed with galleries and urban pieds-à-terre, and the tired old city centre is now almost unrecognisable thanks to the addition of one of Britain's largest new shopping centres at Cabot's Circus. Long known for its industrial connections, more recently Bristol has garnered a reputation as one of the southwest's most creative corners, thanks to its thriving media industry and its lively music, theatre and art scenes.

Sights

SS Great Britain (TOP CHOICE) MUSEUM

(www.ssgreatbritain.org; Great Western Dock, Gas Ferry Rd; adult/child £11.95/9.50; ⌚10am-5.30pm Apr-Oct, to 4.30pm Nov-Mar) In 1843 Bristol's favourite engineer, Isambard Kingdom Brunel, designed the mighty SS *Great Britain*, the first transatlantic steamship to be driven by a screw propeller. By 1937 she was no longer watertight and was abandoned in the Falkland Islands, before finally being towed back to Bristol in 1970. Since then a massive 30-year restoration program has brought the SS *Great Britain* back to stunning life. The ship's rooms have been refurbished in impeccable detail, including the galley, surgeon's quarters, mess hall and the great engine room. The highlight is the amazing 'glass sea' on which the ship sits, enclosing an airtight dry dock that preserves the delicate hull and allows visitors to see the ground-breaking screw propeller up close. Moored nearby is a replica of John Cabot's ship *Matthew*, which sailed from Bristol to Newfoundland in 1497.

> **DANGERS**
>
> As in any big city, it pays to keep your wits about you after dark, especially around the suburb of St Paul's, just northeast of the centre.

Clifton HISTORIC AREA

During the 18th and 19th centuries, wealthy Bristol merchants transformed Clifton into an elegant hilltop suburb packed with porticoed mansions – especially around **Cornwallis Cres** and **Royal York Cres**. These days, Clifton is still the poshest postcode in Bristol, with a wealth of streetside cafes and designer shops, and a villagey atmosphere far removed from the rest of the city.

Clifton Suspension Bridge BRIDGE

(www.clifton-suspension-bridge.org.uk) Clifton's most famous (and photographed) landmark is another Brunel masterpiece, spanning the Avon Gorge on the edge of the city centre. Built in 1864, it was designed to carry light horse-drawn traffic and foot passengers, but these days around 12,000 cars cross every day – testament to the quality of the construction. It's free to walk or cycle across the bridge; car drivers pay a 50p toll. There's a **visitor information point** (visitinfo@clifton-suspension-bridge.org; ⌚10am-5pm) near the tower on the Leigh Woods side.

At-Bristol SCIENCE MUSEUM

(www.at-bristol.org.uk; Anchor Rd; adult/child £10.80/7; ⌚10am-5pm Mon-Fri, to 6pm Sat & Sun) Bristol's interactive science museum has several zones spanning space, technology and the human brain. It's fun, highly interactive and keeps kids enthralled for hours.

Arnolfini Arts Centre (FREE) ART MUSEUM

(www.arnolfini.org.uk; 16 Narrow Quay; ⌚10am-6pm Tue-Sun) The city's avant-garde gallery remains the top venue in town for modern art, as well as occasional exhibitions of dance, film and photography.

Sleeping

Bristol YHA HOSTEL £

(bristol@yha.org.uk; 14 Narrow Quay; dm £20, s £25-35, d £40-45; @) This warehouse hostel

BANKSY

Bristol brings you closer to the guerrilla graffiti artist Banksy. Acknowledged as a local boy, his true identity is a secret, though his work is well known. Headline-grabbing works include issuing spoof British £10 notes (with Princess Diana's head instead of the Queen's); replacing 500 copies of Paris Hilton's debut album in record shops with remixes (featuring tracks titled 'Why Am I Famous?' and 'What Have I Done?'); painting an image of a ladder going up and over the Israeli West Bank Barrier; and covertly inserting his own version of a primitive cave painting (with a human hunter-gatherer pushing a shopping trolley) into the British Museum in London.

Around Bristol, a few of his early works survive. Look out for his notorious *Love Triangle* (featuring an angry husband, a two-timing wife, and a naked man dangling from a window) at the bottom of Park St, and the large mural called *Mild Mild West* featuring a Molotov cocktail–wielding teddy bear on Cheltenham Rd, opposite the junction with Jamaica St. For more, see www.banksy.co.uk.

overlooking the harbour has one of the best locations in town. The facilities here are superb, including the modern four-bed dorms and doubles and an excellent coffee lounge. There's a kitchen for self-caterers.

Premier Inn, King St HOTEL ££
(☎0117-910 0619; www.premiertravelinn.com; The Haymarket; r £59-79; ❄📶) Swallow those preconceptions. In the absence of any decent B&Bs near the city centre, this budget chain is a real find. It's literally steps from the harbour – although the pub next door can get rowdy on weekends.

Future Inn Cabot Circus HOTEL ££
(☎0845 094 5588; www.futureinns.co.uk; Bond St South; d £59-89; P📶) Modern, functional and businessy, the concrete skin is charmless but the rooms are clean, and the rates are fantastic this close to the centre.

Eating & Drinking

Eating and drinking in Bristol is a real highlight – the city is jammed with restaurants, bars and pubs of every description. The areas around Park St and the waterfront are good options if you want to stroll and see what takes your fancy.

TOP CHOICE **Bordeaux Quay** BRITISH ££
(☎0117-943 1200; www.bordeaux-quay.co.uk; Canons Way; brasserie mains £10, restaurant mains £17-21; ⏲lunch & dinner) Top-class dining with sustainable credentials in a fabulous converted warehouse overlooking the harbour; there's a restaurant, brasserie, bar, deli, bakery and even a cookery school.

TOP CHOICE **Riverstation** MODERN BRITISH ££
(☎0117-914 4434; www.riverstation.co.uk; 2-/3-course lunch £12/14.75; dinner mains £13-19; ⏲lunch & dinner) The city's original, riverside restaurant, renowned for super-sophisticated modern British cooking. The downstairs cafe's good for light lunches too.

Primrose Café BISTRO ££
(☎0117-946 6577; www.primrosecafe.co.uk; 1-2 Boyce's Ave; dinner mains £12.50-16.50, 2-/3-course menu £15.95/18.95; ⏲breakfast & lunch) The classic Clifton cafe, popular for coffee with the Sunday papers or for a late-night treat of British food with a French accent.

Apple PUB
(Welsh Back) Bristol's legendary cider-boat stocks an impressive 40 varieties of the golden elixir.

Albion PUB
(Boyce's Ave) Lovely old-fashioned pub packed with evening drinkers from Clifton's well-heeled streets.

Zerodegrees PUB
(www.zerodegrees.co.uk; 53 Colston St) Plentiful glass, chrome and steel in Bristol's boutique brewery.

Entertainment

Bristol's nightclub scene moves fast, so check the latest listings at **Venue** (www.venue.co.uk).

Thekla CLUB
(www.thekla.co.uk; The Grove) Bristol's venerable club-boat has something to suit all moods: electro-punk, indie, disco and new wave, plus regular live gigs.

Colston Hall VENUE
(www.colstonhall.org; Colston St) Bristol's biggest concert hall hosts everything from big-name comedy to touring bands.

BRISTOL FERRY

A fun way to get around is on the boat run by **Bristol Ferry Boat Co** (☎0117-927 3416; www.bristolferry.com; adult/child return £3.30/2.70, day pass £7/5). Two routes go from the city centre dock, near the tourist office. The blue route goes east to Temple Meads via Millennium Sq, Welsh Back and Castle Park (for Broadmead and Cabot Circus); the red route goes west to Hotwells via Millennium Sq and the SS *Great Britain*.

Information

Bristol Visitor Information Centre (☎0333 321 0101; www.visitbristol.co.uk; E-Shed, 1 Canons Rd; ⏰10am-6pm) In a new purpose-built location on the harbour.

Getting There & Away

BUS The main bus station on Marlborough St has an **enquiry office** (⏰7.30am-6pm Mon-Fri, 10am-6pm Sat). National Express coaches serve Birmingham (£17, two hours, nine daily), London (£18, 2½ hours, at least hourly), Cardiff (£7, 1¼ hours, nine daily) and Exeter (£12.40, two hours, four daily).

TRAIN Bristol is an important rail hub. Services include London (£34, 1¾ hours, hourly), Birmingham (£40,1½ hours, hourly) and Edinburgh (£82, 6½ hours, four daily).

Wells

POP 10,406

With Wells, small is beautiful. This tiny, picturesque metropolis is England's smallest city, and only qualifies for the 'city' title thanks to a magnificent medieval cathedral. Wells has been the main seat of ecclesiastical power in this part of Britain since the 12th century, and is still the official residence of the Bishop of Bath and Wells. Medieval buildings and cobbled streets radiate out from the cathedral green to a marketplace that has been the bustling heart of Wells for some nine centuries (Wednesday and Saturday are market days).

Sights

Wells Cathedral CHURCH
(www.wellscathedral.org.uk; Chain Gate, Cathedral Green; requested donation adult/child £5.50/2.50; ⏰7am-7pm Apr-Sep, to dusk Oct-Mar) Set in a marvellous medieval close, the Cathedral Church of St Andrew was built in stages between 1180 and 1508. The building incorporates several Gothic styles, but its most famous asset is the wonderful **west front**, an immense sculpture gallery decorated with more than 300 figures, restored to its original splendour in 1986. Inside, the most striking feature is the pair of **scissor arches** that separate the nave from the choir. High up in the north transept you'll come across a wonderful **mechanical clock** dating from 1392 – the second-oldest surviving in England. Guided tours (Monday to Saturday) are free, and usually take place every hour. Regular concerts and choir recitals are held here throughout the year.

Bishop's Palace HISTORIC BUILDINGS
(www.bishopspalacewells.co.uk; adult/child £5/2; ⏰10.30am-6pm summer, to 4pm winter) Beyond the cathedral, the 13th-century Bishop's Palace is a real delight. Purportedly the oldest inhabited building in England, it's ringed by water and surrounded by a huge fortified wall. The natural wells that gave the city its name bubble up in the palace's grounds, feeding the moat, while the swans have been trained to ring a bell outside one of the windows when they want to be fed.

Sleeping & Eating

Beryl B&B ££
(☎01749-678738; www.beryl-wells.co.uk; Hawkers Lane; d £75-130; P) A mile from the city centre, this gabled Victorian mansion has a great eccentric atmosphere, with grandfather clocks and stately four-posters aplenty. Outside there's a private garden and a heated pool to enjoy.

Stoberry House B&B ££
(☎01749-672906; www.stoberry-park.co.uk; Stoberry Park; d £70-95, supplement for 1-night stays £10-15; P 📶) Supremely posh B&B, with four rooms richly furnished in silky fabrics. The truly gorgeous art-filled garden is the icing on the cake.

TOP CHOICE **Old Spot** BRITISH ££
(☎01749-689099; 12 Sadler St; 2/3-course lunch £15/17.50, dinner £21.50/26.50; ⏰lunch Wed-Sun, dinner Tue-Sat) A favourite with the foodie guides, this place specialises in old country favourites with a modern twist.

Goodfellows BISTRO, CAFE ££
(☎01749-673866; 5 Sadler St; cafe mains £7-10, restaurant mains £11.50-25, 3-course dinner £35; ⏰cafe breakfast & lunch Mon-Sat, dinner Wed-Sat, restaurant lunch Tue-Sat, dinner Wed-Sat) Down-

stairs is a super cafe-bakery, while upstairs is a more formal seafood bistro – a favourite with the local ladies-who-lunch.

Information

Tourist office (☎01749-672552; www.wellstourism.com; Market Pl; ⏰9.30am-5.30pm Apr-Oct, 10am-4pm Nov-Mar)

Getting There & Away

The bus station is south of Cuthbert St, on Princes Rd.

173 To/from Bath (one hour, hourly)

376/377 Between Bristol (one hour, hourly) and Glastonbury (15 minutes) via Wells

Glastonbury

POP 8429

If you suddenly feel the need to get your third eye cleansed or your chakras realigned, there's really only one place in England which fits the bill: good old Glastonbury, a long-time bohemian haven and still a favourite hang-out for mystics and countercultural types of all descriptions. The main street is lined with crystal sellers, vegie cafes, mystical bookshops and bong emporiums, but Glastonbury has been a spiritual centre since long before the hippies arrived. It's supposedly the birthplace of Christianity in England, and several of Britain's most important ley lines are said to converge on nearby Glastonbury Tor.

Sights

Glastonbury Abbey RUINS

(www.glastonburyabbey.com; Magdalene St; adult/child £5.50/3.50; ⏰9.30am-6pm or dusk Sep-May, from 9am Jun-Aug) Legend has it that Joseph of Arimathea, great-uncle of Jesus, returned here with the Holy Grail after the death of Christ, founding England's first church, now occupied by the ruined abbey dating from 1184. It's still possible to make out some of the nave walls and the remains of the crossing arches. The grounds also contain a small **museum**, as well as the **Holy Thorn tree**, which supposedly sprung from Joseph's staff and mysteriously blooms twice a year, at Christmas and Easter.

FREE **Glastonbury Tor** LANDMARK

The iconic 160m-high grassy hump of Glastonbury Tor looms up from flat fields to the northwest of town, providing glorious views over the surrounding countryside. It's a focal point for a bewildering array of myths, being variously the home of a faerie king, the stronghold of Gwyn ap Nudd (ruler of the Underworld) and the mythic Isle of Avalon where King Arthur was taken after being mortally wounded in battle, and where the 'once and future king' sleeps until his country calls again.

Festivals

The town is famous for June's **Glastonbury Festival** (www.glastonburyfestivals.co.uk), a massive, often mud-soaked extravaganza of music, dance, spirituality, good times and general all-round weirdness.

Sleeping

Shambhala Healing Retreat B&B ££

(☎01458-831797; www.shambhala.co.uk; Coursing Batch; s £44, d £76-112) If you're not in touch with your inner goddess, this spiritual sanctuary probably isn't for you. It's New Age through and through, from the 'clear energy' bedrooms to the meditation tent on the top floor.

Parsnips B&B ££

(☎01458-835599; www.parsnips-glastonbury.co.uk; 99 Bere Lane; s/d £50/65; P @) This solid, modern B&B is a decent bet if you're looking for an escape from tie-dye and crystals.

Glastonbury Backpackers HOSTEL £

(☎01458-833353; www.glastonburybackpackers.com; 4 Market Pl; dm £14-16, tw £35-45, d £45-50; P @) Pretty basic, but very friendly, with a TV lounge, kitchen and cafe-bar downstairs.

Eating & Drinking

Rainbow's End CAFE £

(17a High St; mains £4-7; ⏰lunch; 🌱) A Glasto classic, this wholefood cafe serves up hearty soups and generous portions of vegie chilli in a cheery dining room dotted with potted plants.

Hundred Monkeys Cafe BISTRO ££

(52 High St; mains £8-15; ⏰lunch Mon-Wed & Sun, lunch & dinner Thu-Sat) Surprisingly sleek bistro, decked out with leather sofas, pine tables and a big blackboard listing fresh pastas, salads and mains.

Who'd a Thought It Inn PUB ££

(17 Northload St; mains £8.25-16.95; ⏰lunch & dinner) In keeping with Glastonbury's spirit, this pub is brimming with wacky character, from the bike on the ceiling to the reclaimed red telephone box tucked in one corner.

Information

Glastonbury Tourist Office (☎01458-832954; www.glastonburytic.co.uk; The Tribunal, 9 High St; ⊙10am-5pm Apr-Sep, to 4pm Oct-Mar)

Getting There & Away

There is no train station in Glastonbury, so buses are the only public transport option.

Bus 29 To Taunton (50 minutes, nine daily Monday to Saturday, six on Sunday)

Bus 376/377 Northwest to Wells (30 minutes, hourly Monday to Saturday, seven on Sundays) and Bristol (1¼ hours), and south to Street (15 minutes)

Exmoor National Park

Barely 21 miles wide and 12 miles north to south, Exmoor may be tiny but the scenery more than makes up for it. Part wilderness expanse, part rolling fields, dotted with meadows, valleys and crumbling cliffs, Exmoor seems to sum up everything that's green and pleasant about the English landscape. Below, we list some of our favourite sleeping options. For information, see www.visit-exmoor.info.

DULVERTON

Dulverton is the southern gateway to Exmoor National Park.

Sleeping

Town Mills B&B ££

(☎01398-323124; www.townmillsdulverton.co.uk; High St; s/d £60/85; P 📶) This converted mill is livened up by bits of art and crisp fabrics, and you can hear the rush of the river from your window.

LYNTON & LYNMOUTH

Lynmouth is a busy harbour town lined with pubs, souvenir sellers and fudge shops. At the top of the cliffs is the more genteel resort of Lynton, reached via an amazing water-operated railway, or a stiff walk.

Sleeping

Chough's Nest B&B £

(☎01598-753315; www.choughsnesthotel.co.uk; North Walk, Lynton; d £94-110; P) For cliff-top position and sea views, this place is unbeatable.

St Vincent House B&B ££

(☎01598-752244; www.st-vincent-hotel.co.uk; Castle Hill, Lynton; d £75-80; P) No sea view, but this classy lodge was built by a sea captain who sailed with Nelson – hence the heritage decor.

PORLOCK

The small village of Porlock is one of the prettiest on the Exmoor coast; the huddle of thatched cottages on its main street is framed on one side by the sea, and on the other by steeply sloping hills.

Sleeping & Eating

Ship Inn PUB £

(www.shipinnporlock.co.uk; High St; s £40, d £60, mains £7.75-11.95) A venerable pub with 10 surprisingly light rooms, also serving substantial food – mainly steaks, roasts and stews – in the wood-filled bar.

Exeter

POP 116,393

Well heeled and comfortable, Exeter exudes evidence of its centuries-old role as the spiritual and administrative heart of Devon. The city's gloriously Gothic cathedral presides over stretches of cobbled streets, fragments of the terracotta Roman city wall, and a tumbling of medieval and Georgian buildings. A snazzy new shopping centre brings bursts of the modern, while thousands of university students ensure a buzzing nightlife.

Sights

Exeter Cathedral CHURCH

(www.exeter-cathedral.org.uk; The Close; adult/child £5/free; ⊙9.30am-4.45pm Mon-Sat) Magnificent in warm, honey-coloured stone, Exeter's Cathedral Church of St Peter is framed by lawns and wonky half-timbered buildings – a quintessentially English scene. There's been a religious site here since at least the 5th century but the Normans started the current building in 1114. Like many English cathedrals, there's evidence of Victorian renovation but the best ancient quirks remain, including carvings of a man standing on his head and an angel playing bagpipes.

The Quay LANDMARK

A highlight of any visit to Exeter, this cobbled, quaintly gentrified former port area situated on a curve of the River Exe is now home to galleries, cafes and pubs. Even on sunny days, it's not hard to find an outdoor seating spot.

Sleeping

Raffles B&B ££

(☎01392-270200; www.raffles-exeter.co.uk; 11 Blackall Rd; s/d £42/72; P) Creaking with antiques, this late-Victorian townhouse is an appealing blend of old and new, while the walled garden and much-coveted parking make it a great-value choice.

Woodbine B&B ££
(☎01392-203302; www.woodbineguesthouse.co.uk; 1 Woodbine Tce; s/d £38/66; 📶) A bit of a surprise sits behind this archetypal flower-framed terrace: modern rooms featuring low beds and underfloor heating in the showers.

White Hart HOTEL ££
(☎01392-279897; www.english-inns.co.uk; 66 South St; s £60, d £60-70; P) They've been putting people up here since the 14th century. Rooms are either traditional (dark woods and rich drapes) or contemporary (laminate floors and light fabrics).

Globe Backpackers HOSTEL £
(☎01392-215521; www.exeterbackpackers.co.uk; 71 Holloway St; dm/d £16.50/42; @📶) A spotlessly clean, relaxed, rambling house near the Quay.

Eating & Drinking

Herbies VEGETARIAN £
(15 North St; mains £5-9; ⏰lunch Mon-Sat, dinner Tue-Sat; 🥕) Cosy and gently groovy, this is *the* place in town to tuck into delicious butterbean and vegetable pie or cashew nutloaf. The menu's strong on vegan dishes too.

Harry's BISTRO ££
(www.harrys-exeter.co.uk; 86 Longbrook St; mains £8-12; ⏰lunch & dinner Mon-Sat) The decor is all wooden chairs, blackboards and gilt mirrors, making Harry's the kind of welcoming neighbourhood bistro you wish was on your own doorstep, but rarely is.

On the Waterfront BAR
(www.waterfrontexeter.co.uk; The Quay) In 1835 this was a warehouse, now its red-brick ceilings stretch back from a thoroughly modern bar, and the tables outside are a popular spot for a riverside pint.

Double Locks PUB
(www.doublelocks.com; Canal Banks) About 2 miles south of town beside the Exeter Ship Canal, this excellent pub has scarred floorboards, excellent ale, good bar food (mains £9), real fires and a relaxed atmosphere.

Information

Tourist office (☎01392-665700; www.exeterandessentialdevon.com; Paris St; ⏰9am-5pm Mon-Sat, 10am-4pm Sun Jul & Aug)

Getting There & Away

BUS Express bus X38 goes to/from Plymouth (£6, 1¼ hours, hourly Monday to Saturday, three on Sunday). On Sundays between June and mid-September Bus 82, the Transmoor Link, makes five trips between Exeter and Plymouth via Moretonhampstead, Postbridge, Princetown and Yelverton.

TRAIN Trains run between Exeter St Davids station and London Paddington (£45, 2½ hours, hourly), via Bristol (£18, 1¼ hours, half-hourly).

Plymouth

POP 256,633

If parts of Devon are costume dramas or nature programs, Plymouth is a healthy dose of reality TV. It's gritty, and certainly not always pretty, but this is a city huge in spirit and it comes with some great assets: handy access to the wild expanse of Dartmoor; a rich maritime history; and a decidedly lively nightlife.

Sights

Plymouth Hoe LANDMARK
Francis Drake supposedly spied the Spanish fleet from this grassy strip overlooking Plymouth Sound; the fabled bowling green where he finished his game was probably where his **statue** now stands. Dominating the scene is the red-and-white-striped former lighthouse, **Smeaton's Tower** (The Hoe; adult/child £2/1; ⏰10am-noon & 1-4pm Tue-Sat Apr-Oct, to 3pm Nov-Mar). Climbing its 93 steps provides an illuminating insight into lighthouse keepers' lives and stunning views.

Barbican HISTORIC AREA
(www.plymouthbarbican.com) With cobbled streets and Tudor and Jacobean buildings, many now converted into galleries and restaurants, this is the historic heart of Plymouth. The **Mayflower Steps** mark where the Pilgrim Fathers set sail for America on 16 September 1620. Scores of other famous voyages are marked by plaques, including one led by a certain Captain James Cook.

Sleeping

Bowling Green HOTEL ££
(☎01752-209090; www.bowlinggreenhotel.co.uk; 10 Osborne Pl; s/d/f £47/68/78; P📶) Some of the airy cream-and-white rooms in this family-run hotel look out onto the modern incarnation of Drake's famous bowling green.

Jewell's B&B £
(☎01752-254760; www.jewellsguesthouse.com; 220 Citadel Rd; s/d/f £28/50/65) Traces of the Victorian era linger in the high ceilings of this friendly townhouse. Rooms are bright and modern, and top-quality bathrooms add another layer of class.

Berkeleys of St James B&B ££
(☎01752-221654; www.onthehoe.co.uk; 4 St James Pl East; s/d/f £40/60/75) A cosy terrace, dishing up breakfasts full of local goodies.

Eating & Drinking

TOP CHOICE **Barbican Kitchen** BRITISH ££
(☎01752-604448; 60 Southside St; mains £11; ⊙lunch & dinner Mon-Sat, lunch Sun) The interior of this bistro-style restaurant fizzes with bursts of shocking pink and lime. The food is attention-grabbing too.

Cap'n Jaspers CAFE £
(www.capn-jaspers.co.uk; Whitehouse Pier, Quay Rd; snacks £3-5; ⊙breakfast, lunch & dinner) Unique, quirky and slightly insane, this cabin has been delighting bikers, tourists, locals and fishermen for decades with its motorised gadgets and teaspoons attached by chains. The menu is of the burger and bacon butty school.

Platters SEAFOOD ££
(12 The Barbican; mains £16; ⊙lunch & dinner) A down-to-earth eatery with fish so fresh it's just stopped flapping.

Dolpin PUB
(14 The Barbican) Wonderfully unreconstructed boozer with scuffed tables, bench seats and no-nonsense atmosphere.

Information

Tourist office (☎01752-306330; www.visitplymouth.co.uk; Plymouth Mayflower, 3 The Barbican; ⊙9am-5pm Mon-Sat, 10am-4pm Sun Apr-Oct, 9am-5pm Mon-Fri, 10am-4pm Sat Nov-Mar)

Getting There & Away

Bus

National Express services run to/from Bristol (£29, three hours, five daily), London (£33, five to six hours, eight daily) and Penzance (£8, t, six daily). Bus X38 goes to/from Exeter (£6, 1¼ hours, one to three daily). On Sundays between June and mid-September Bus 82, the Transmoor Link, makes five trips between Plymouth and Exeter, via Yelverton, Princetown, Postbridge and Moretonhampstead.

Train

Services include London (£40, 3¼ hours, half-hourly), Bristol (£32, two hours, two or three per hour), Exeter (£7.40, one hour, two or three per hour) and Penzance (£8, two hours, half-hourly).

Dartmoor National Park

Dartmoor is a compelling landscape, very different from the rest of Devon. Exposed granite hills (called 'tors') crest the horizon, linked by swathes of moorland. On the fringes, streams tumble over boulders in woods of twisted trees. The centre of this 368-sq-mile wilderness is the higher moor; vast, treeless, moody and utterly empty. Naturally, Dartmoor's charms include superb walking and cycling, rustic pubs and country-house hotels – perfect boltholes when the mist rolls in. We've listed a few favourites below. For information, see www.dartmoor.co.uk.

POSTBRIDGE

A good base for exploring the park, this quaint village has a couple of shops and pubs and is best known for its 13th-century **clapper bridge**.

Sleeping

Two Bridges HOTEL £££
(☎01822-890581; www.twobridges.co.uk; Two Bridges; s £95-125, d £140-190; P) A classic moorland hotel, 3 miles southwest of Postbridge, with gently elegant rooms, huge inglenook fireplaces and squishy leather sofas; former guests Wallace Simpson, Winston Churchill and Vivien Leigh probably liked it too.

Bellever YHA HOSTEL £
(☎0845 371 9622; www.yha.org.uk; dm £14; ⊙Mar-Oct; P) A characterful former farm, a mile south of Postbridge, with a huge kitchen, lots of rustic stone walls and cosy dorms.

WIDECOMBE-IN-THE-MOOR

This is archetypal Dartmoor, down to the ponies grazing on the village green. Widecombe's honey-grey, 15th-century buildings circle a church whose 40m tower has seen it dubbed the Cathedral of the Moor.

Sleeping & Eating

Higher Venton Farm B&B ££
(☎01364-621235; www.ventonfarm.com; Widecombe; d £50-60; P) This 16th-century farmhouse defines the 'picture-postcard thatch' architectural style.

WORTH A TRIP

EDEN PROJECT

If any one thing is emblematic of Cornwall's regeneration, it's the **Eden Project** (☎01726-811911; www.edenproject.com; Bodelva; adult/child £15/5; ⏰10am-6pm Apr-Oct, to 4.30pm Nov-Mar). Ten years ago the site was an exhausted clay pit; a symbol of the county's industrial decline. Now it's home to the largest plant-filled greenhouses on the planet – a monumental education project about the natural world. Tropical, temperate and desert environments have been recreated inside the massive biomes, so a single visit carries you from the steaming rainforests of South America to the dry deserts of northern Africa.

Rugglestone Inn PUB £
(www.rugglestoneinn.co.uk; mains £4-9; ⏰lunch & dinner) You'll find plenty of locals in front of this intimate old pub's wood-burning stove.

Newquay

POP 19,423

Bright, breezy and unashamedly brash, Newquay is the undisputed capital of British surfing. All summer, a nonstop parade of beach-lovers and boozed-up clubbers create a drink-till-dawn party atmosphere that's more Costa del Sol than Cornwall. If you've come to catch the waves, the best-known beach is **Fistral** – the venue for the annual Boardmasters surfing festival. Below town are **Great Western** and **Towan**; a little further up the coast you'll find **Tolcarne**, **Lusty Glaze**, **Porth** and **Watergate Bay**. All these beaches are good for swimming and supervised by lifeguards in summer.

Sleeping

The Hotel, Watergate Bay HOTEL ££
(☎01637-860543; www.watergatebay.co.uk; Watergate Bay; d £95-295, ste £205-400; P) Fresh from a multimillion-pound refit, the old Watergate has been reinvented as a beachside beauty. The dazzling rooms boast mini sea-view balconies.

Goofys HOSTEL £
(☎01637-872684; www.goofys.co.uk; 5 Headland Rd; r per person £32.50-40; P@) The town's top surf lodge bills itself as a 'boutique hostel'. All the dorms are nicely furnished, and there are doubles too.

Carlton Hotel B&B ££
(☎01637-872658; www.carltonhotelnewquay.co.uk; 6 Dane Rd; s £45, d £68-94; P) Swanky rooms, frilly edged beds, DVD players and country-cream furnishings run throughout this upmarket B&B.

Eating & Drinking

Beach Hut BISTRO ££
(☎01637-860877; Watergate Bay; mains £9.75-19.95; ⏰breakfast, lunch & dinner) Beachy in feel, with classic surf 'n' turf menu: burgers and a different fresh fish dish every day.

Café Irie CAFE £
(☎01637-859200; www.cafeirie.co.uk; 38 Fore St; lunch £3-8; ⏰breakfast & lunch Mon-Sat) Run by surfers for surfers, with vintage vinyl on the walls, multicoloured plates, and chalkboards scrawled with specials.

Chy BAR
(www.thekoola.com/the-chy-bar; 12 Beach Rd) Chrome, wood and leather dominate this stylish cafe-bar overlooking Towan Beach. The patio is perfect for a gourmet breakfast or lunchtime salad. Later, DJs take to the decks and the beers start to flow.

Information

Tourist office (☎01637-854020; www.newquay.co.uk; Marcus Hill; ⏰9.30am-5.30pm Mon-Sat, to 12.30pm Sun)

Getting There & Away

AIR Newquay Airport (☎01637-860600; www.newquaycornwallairport.com) has regular flights to UK airports, including London, Birmingham, Cardiff and Edinburgh.

BUS The 585/586 is the fastest service to Truro (50 minutes, twice hourly Monday to Saturday), where you can connect with other services.

TRAIN There are trains every couple of hours between Newquay and Par (£3.80, 45 minutes) on the main London–Penzance line.

St Ives

POP 9870

Sitting on the fringes of a glittering arc-shaped bay, St Ives was once a pilchard-fishing harbour but it's better known today as a centre of the arts. Cobbled alleyways lead through a jumble of galleries, cafes and brasseries that cater for thousands of summer visitors. It's an intriguing mix of boutique chic and traditional seaside, and while the high-season traffic can be heavy, St Ives is still an essential stop on any Cornish tour. Nearby, receding tides reveal 3 miles of golden beach at **Gwithian** and **Godrevy Towans**, both popular spots for kiteboarders and surfers.

Sights

Tate St Ives ART MUSEUM
(☎01736-796226; www.tate.org.uk/stives; Porthmeor Beach; adult/child £5.75/3.25, joint ticket with Barbara Hepworth Museum £8.75/4.50; ⊙10am-5pm Mar-Oct, to 4pm Tue-Sun Nov-Feb) This landmark gallery contains work by celebrated local artists, including Terry Frost, Patrick Heron and Barbara Hepworth, and hosts regular special exhibitions.

Barbara Hepworth Museum & Sculpture Garden ART MUSEUM
(☎01736-796226; www.tate.org.uk/stives/hepworth; Barnoon Hill; adult/child £5.75/3.25, joint ticket with Tate £8.75/4.50; ⊙10am-5pm Mar-Oct, to 4pm Tue-Sun Nov-Feb) Barbara Hepworth (1903–75) was a leading abstract sculptor and a key figure in the St Ives art scene. Fittingly, her former studio has been transformed into a moving archive and museum.

Sleeping

Primrose Valley HOTEL £££
(☎01736-794939; www.primroseonline.co.uk; Porthminster Beach; d £105-155, ste £175-225; P) A swash of sexy style on the St Ives seafront, this classy location is full of spoils –therapy room, metro-modern bar, and locally sourced breakfasts.

Treliska B&B ££
(☎01736-797678; www.treliska.com; 3 Bedford Rd; d £60-80;) The smooth decor is attractive – chrome taps, wooden furniture, cool sinks – but what really sells it is the fantastic position, literally steps from St Ives' centre.

Eating & Drinking

Alba SEAFOOD ££
(☎01736-797222; Old Lifeboat House; mains £11-18; ⊙lunch & dinner) Split-level sophistication serving excellent seafood. Tables five, six and seven have the best harbour views.

Blas Burgerworks CAFE £
(The Warren; burgers £5-10; ⊙dinner Tue-Sun) This pocket-sized joint has a big reputation: sustainable sourcing, eco-friendly packaging and lots of wacky burger variations have earned it a loyal following.

Hub CAFE-BAR
(www.hub-stives.co.uk; The Wharf) This is the heart of St Ives' (admittedly limited) nightlife, with lattes by day, cocktails and boutique beers after-dark, plus sliding doors that open onto the harbour when the sun shines.

Sloop Inn PUB
(The Wharf) A classic fishermen's boozer, complete with low ceilings, tankards behind the bar and a comprehensive selection of Cornish ales.

Information

Tourist office (☎01736-796297; ivtic@penwith.gov.uk; Street-an-Pol; ⊙9am-5.30pm Mon-Fri, 9am-5pm Sat, 10am-4pm Sun) Inside the Guildhall.

Getting There & Away

BUS Quickest bus to Penzance is the 17 (30 minutes, twice hourly Monday to Saturday, hourly on Sunday). In summer the open-top 300 takes the scenic route via Zennor, Land's End and St Just.

TRAIN The gorgeous branch line from St Ives is worth taking just for the coastal views: trains terminate at St Erth (£3, 14 minutes, half-hourly), where you can catch connections along the Penzance–Paddington main line.

Penzance

POP 21,168

The historic harbour town of Penzance is a hotchpotch of winding streets, old shopping arcades and a grand seafront promenade. It's much more, er, authentic than prettified St Ives, and makes an excellent base for exploring the rest of west Cornwall.

Sights

St Michael's Mount LANDMARK
(NT; ☎01736-710507; castle & gardens adult/child £8.75/4.25; ⊙house 10.30am-5.30pm Sun-Fri late Mar-Oct) Looming up from the waters of Mount's Bay is the unmistakeable silhouette of St Michael's Mount, a craggy island topped by an ancient monastery – one of Cornwall's most iconic landmarks. Highlights include the original **armoury**, the 14th-century **priory church** and the abbey's subtropical **gardens** teetering dramatically above the sea. The island is reached from

the little town of **Marazion**, 3 miles from Penzance; you can walk across the causeway at low tide, or catch a ferry at high tide in the summer.

Sleeping

Summer House B&B ££
(01736-363744; www.summerhouse-cornwall.com; Cornwall Tce; d £120-150; closed Nov-Mar; P) For a touch of Chelsea-on-Sea, check into this elegant Regency house. Cheery colours characterise the bedrooms, and downstairs there's a Mediterranean restaurant with an alfresco terrace.

Camilla House B&B ££
(01736-363771; www.camillahouse.co.uk; 12 Regent Tce; s £37.50, d £75-95; P) One of several quality B&Bs on Regent's Tce, this place stands out for its classy rooms, period features and eco-conscious stance. Fluffy bathrobes, pillow treats and views over the prom will tempt you too.

Penzance YHA HOSTEL £
(penzance@yha.org.uk; Castle Horneck, Alverton; dm £14; P@) An 18th-century manor house on the outskirts of town, this hostel has an on-site cafe, laundry and four- to 10-bed dorms.

Eating &Drinking

Bakehouse BISTRO ££
(01736-331331; www.bakehouserestaurant.co.uk; Chapel St; mains £8.95-19.50; lunch Wed-Sat, dinner daily) This funky double-floored diner caters for seafood-lovers and vegies, but the carnivores do best.

Archie Brown's CAFE £
(01736-362828; Bread St; mains £3-10; breakfast & lunch Mon-Sat) A cosier wholefood cafe you couldn't hope to find. Archie has been serving Penzance's earth mothers and artsy crowd for years and shows no signs of flagging.

Turk's Head PUB
(Chapel St) The oldest pub in town, covered in maritime memorabilia.

Zero Lounge BAR
(Chapel St) More urban chic than olde-worlde, plus the town's best beer patio.

Information

Tourist office (01736-362207; penzancetic@cornwall.gov.uk; Station Approach; 9am-5pm Mon-Sat, 10am-1pm Sun) Next to the bus station.

Getting There & Away

BUS The 17/17A/17B runs to St Ives (30 minutes, twice hourly Monday to Saturday, hourly on Sunday).

TRAIN

Bristol £37, four hours

Exeter £11.50, three hours

London Paddington £57.50, 5½ hours, hourly

St Ives £3.30, 30 minutes

Land's End

Just 9 miles from Penzance, Land's End is the most westerly point of mainland England, where cliffs plunge dramatically

WORTH A TRIP

ST JUST MINES & ENGINE HOUSES

It's hard to imagine today, but this area was once a booming tin and copper mining industry. Since 2006 this legacy has been recognised by the formation of the UK's newest Unesco World Heritage Site, the **Cornwall and West Devon Mining Landscape** (www.cornish-mining.org.uk). Highlights include the **Geevor Tin Mine** (01736-788662; www.geevor.com; adult/child £9.50/4.50; 9am-5pm Sun-Fri Mar-Oct, to 4pm Nov-Feb) at Pendeen, just north of St Just, where hourly tours of the underground shafts provide amazing insights into the harsh conditions once faced by Cornwall's miners. More mining heritage comes to life at the **Levant Mine & Beam Engine** (www.nationaltrust.org.uk/main/w-levantmineandbeamengine; adult/child £5.80/2.90; 11am-5pm Tue-Fri & Sun Jul-Sep, Wed-Fri & Sun Jun, Wed & Fri Apr, May & Oct), while clinging to the cliffs nearby is **Botallack Mine** (not open to the public), one of Cornwall's most dramatic engine houses, where abandoned mine shafts extend beneath the raging Atlantic waves.

St Just is 6 miles north of Land's End. Buses 17/17A/17B travel from St Ives (1¼ hours, half-hourly Monday to Saturday, five on Sunday) via Penzance.

into the pounding Atlantic surf. Unfortunately, the **Legendary Land's End** (☎0870 458 0099; www.landsend-landmark.co.uk; adult/child £11/7; ⏲10am-5pm summer, to 3pm winter) theme park hasn't done much to enhance the view. Take our advice: skip the tacky multimedia shows and opt for an exhilarating cliff-top stroll instead.

Bus 1/1A travels from Penzance (one hour, eight daily, five on Saturday) to Land's End; half the buses go via Sennen, the other half via Treen and Porthcurno.

CENTRAL ENGLAND

The geographic heartland of England is a mix of wildly differing scenes, with historic towns like Oxford and Stratford-upon-Avon, flower-decked villages in the Cotswolds, and rejuvenated former industrial cities like Birmingham. In this section we also cover the lush dales and peaty moors of the Peak District. Places are listed roughly south to north. For information, see www.visitheartofengland.com (covering Birmingham and around, Warwickshire and Shropshire), www.oxfordshirecotswolds.org and www.visitpeakdistrict.com.

Oxford

POP 134,300

Renowned as one of the world's most famous university towns, Oxford lives up to its advance billing as a colourful, history-flavoured place. It's also a hot spot in summer – so bypass jostling tour groups by coming early or late in the season if you can.

For visitors short on time, 'Oxford or Cambridge?' is a common conundrum. If we're blunt we'd say Oxford is not quite as quaint or pretty as Cambridge, but it more than makes up for this by being far more vibrant, with a wider array of attractions.

History

Oxford is the oldest university in Britain, with the first of its 39 separate colleges dating from the 13th century. This august institution's history includes a 14th-century riot over the quality of a local innkeeper's wine, which suggests that students have changed little over the centuries. Its plethora of notable graduates includes William Morris, Oscar Wilde, Lewis Carroll and, as the evidence suggests, Sherlock Holmes. All men, you note. Women were not admitted to Oxford's closeted halls until 1878 and even then were not allowed to receive degrees until the 1920s.

Sights

Much of the centre of Oxford is taken up by graceful university buildings, each one individual in its appearance and academic specialities. Not all are open to the public. For those that are, visiting hours change with the term and exam schedule. Check www.ox.ac.uk/colleges for full details.

Christ Church College COLLEGE
(www.chch.ox.ac.uk; St Aldate's; adult/child £6/4.50; ⏲9am-5pm Mon-Sat, 2-5pm Sun) The largest and grandest of all of Oxford's colleges, and most popular thanks to the magnificent buildings and latter-day fame as a location for the *Harry Potter* films.

Magdalen College COLLEGE
(www.magd.ox.ac.uk; High St; adult/child £4.50/3.50; ⏲1-6pm) Set amid 40 hectares of lawns and river walks, Magdalen (*mawd*-len) is one of the wealthiest and most beautiful of Oxford's colleges.

Merton College COLLEGE
(www.merton.ox.ac.uk; Merton St; admission £2; ⏲2-5pm Mon-Fri, 10am-5pm Sat & Sun) From the High St, follow the wonderfully named Logic Lane to Merton College, one of Oxford's original three colleges, founded in 1264.

Bodleian Library LIBRARY
(www.bodley.ox.ac.uk; Broad St; ⏲9am-5pm Mon-Fri, to 4.30pm Sat, 11am-5pm Sun) One of the oldest public libraries in the world, this historic building holds more than seven million items on 118 miles of shelving.

Radcliffe Camera LIBRARY
(Radcliffe Sq) Another library and quintessential Oxford landmark – and one of its most photographed buildings (no public access).

FREE **Ashmolean Museum** MUSEUM
(www.ashmolean.org; Beaumont St; ⏲10am-6pm Tue-Sun) Britain's oldest public museum, the Ashmolean reopened in late 2009 after a massive £61 million redevelopment that makes the once intimidating building and stuffy collection a real joy to browse.

Oxford Covered Market INDOOR MARKET
(www.oxford-covered-market.co.uk; ⏲9am-5.30pm) A haven of traditional butchers, fishmongers, cobblers and barbers, this is the place to go for Sicilian sausage, handmade chocolates,

DON'T MISS

PUNTING

A quintessential Oxford experience is punting. A punt is a flat-bottomed boat, propelled (if that's the word) with a pole instead of oars. Punts are available to rent (£13/15 per hour weekdays/weekends, £65 deposit, mid-March to mid-October, 10am to dusk), and hold five people including the punter. The most central location is **Magdalen Bridge Boathouse** (www.oxfordpunting.co.uk; High St). From here, you can punt downstream around the Botanic Gardens and Christ Church Meadow or upstream around Magdalen Deer Park. Be prepared to spend much of your time struggling to get out of a tangle of low branches or avoiding the path of an oncoming boat.

traditional pies, funky T-shirts and expensive brogues.

Sleeping

There are strings of B&Bs along the Iffley, Abingdon, Banbury and Headington roads. The following places stand out for their value for money.

Oxford Rooms COLLEGE ROOMS £
(www.oxfordrooms.co.uk; r from £40) Didn't quite make the cut for a place at uni here? At least you can experience life inside the hallowed college grounds and breakfast in a grand college hall by staying overnight in one of the student rooms.

TOP CHOICE **Malmaison** HOTEL £££
(01865-268400; www.malmaison-oxford.com; Oxford Castle; d/ste from £160/245; P @ wi-fi) Lock yourself up for the night in one of Oxford's most spectacular settings, a former Victorian prison that has been converted into a sleek and slinky hotel.

Ethos Hotel HOTEL ££
(01865-245800; www.ethoshotels.co.uk; 59 Western Rd; d from £80; @ wi-fi) This funky new hotel has spacious rooms, marble bathrooms, mini kitchen, breakfast basket and free wi-fi – all just 10 minutes' walk from the city centre. Incredible value.

Buttery Hotel HOTEL ££
(01865-811950; www.thebutteryhotel.co.uk; 11-12 Broad St; s/d from £55/95; @) It's a modest enough place but a great deal, with spacious modern rooms, decent bathrooms and the pick of the city's attractions on your doorstep.

Oxford YHA HOSTEL £
(01865-727275; www.yha.org.uk; 2a Botley Rd; dm/d from £18/46; @) Bright, well kept, clean and tidy, this is Oxford's best budget option with simple but comfortable dorm accommodation, private rooms and loads of facilities.

Central Backpackers HOSTEL £
(01865-242288; www.centralbackpackers.co.uk; 13 Park End St; dm £17-20; @) A good budget option right in the centre of town, with bright and simple rooms that sleep four to 12 people, plus a decent lounge, a rooftop terrace and free internet.

Eating

Oxford has plenty of choice, but ubiquitous chain restaurants dominate the scene, especially along George St and around the pedestrianised square at the castle. Head to Walton St in Jericho, to St Clements, Summertown or up the Cowley Rd for a more quirky selection of restaurants.

The Trout MODERN BRITISH ££
(01865-510930; www.thetroutoxford.co.uk; 195 Godstow Rd, Wolvercote; mains £8-16) Possibly the prettiest location in Oxford, this charming old-world pub has been a favourite haunt of town and gown for many years. Book ahead.

Door 74 MODERN BRITISH ££
(01865-203374; www.door74.co.uk; 74 Cowley Rd; mains £8-13; closed Mon & Sun dinner) This cosy little place woos its fans with a rich mix of British and Mediterranean flavours, and friendly service.

Café Coco MEDITERRANEAN £
(www.cafe-coco.co.uk; 23 Cowley Rd; mains £6-10.50) Chilled but always buzzing, this place has classic posters on the walls and a bald clown in an ice bath. The food can be a bit hit and miss but most people come for the atmosphere.

Georgina's CAFE £
(Ave 3, Oxford Covered Market; mains £3-6; 8.30am-5pm Mon-Sat, 10am-4pm Sun) Hidden up a scruffy staircase in the covered market, this funky little cafe serves a bumper crop of salads, soups and such goodies as goat's cheese quesadillas.

Oxford

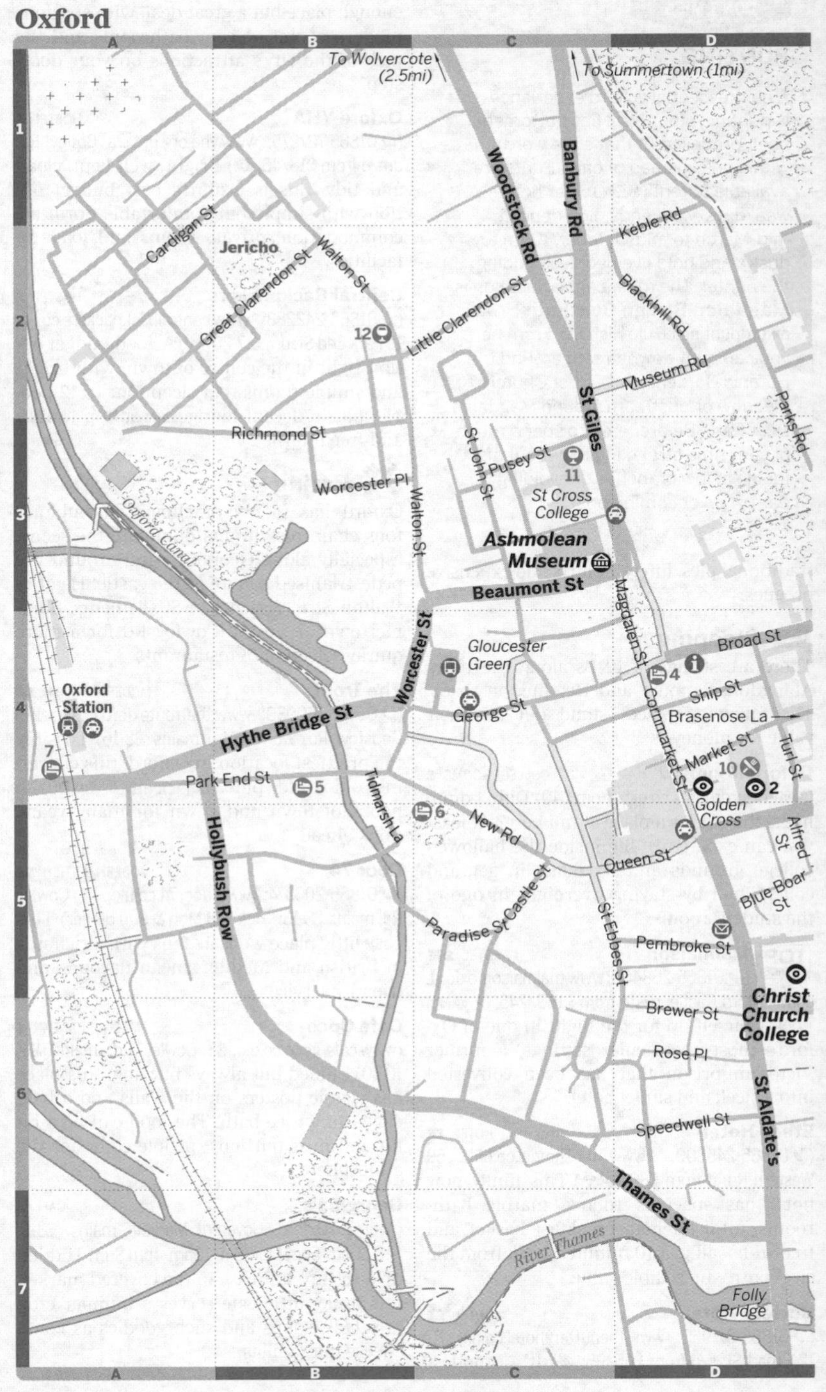
A
B
C
D
1
2
3
4
5
6
7
To Wolvercote (2.5mi)
To Summertown (1mi)
Jericho
Cardigan St
Great Clarendon St
Walton St
12
Little Clarendon St
Woodstock Rd
Banbury Rd
Keble Rd
Blackhall Rd
Museum Rd
Parks Rd
St Giles
Richmond St
Worcester Pl
St John St
Pusey St
11
St Cross College
Oxford Canal
Ashmolean Museum
Beaumont St
Magdalen St
Broad St
Gloucester Green
4
Ship St
Brasenose La
George St
Cornmarket St
Market St
Turl St
10
2
Golden Cross
Oxford Station
7
Hythe Bridge St
Worcester St
Park End St
5
6
Tidmarsh La
New Rd
Hollybush Row
Alfred St
Queen St
Castle St
Blue Boar St
Paradise St
St Ebbes St
Pembroke St
Christ Church College
Brewer St
Rose Pl
St Aldate's
Speedwell St
Thames St
River Thames
Folly Bridge

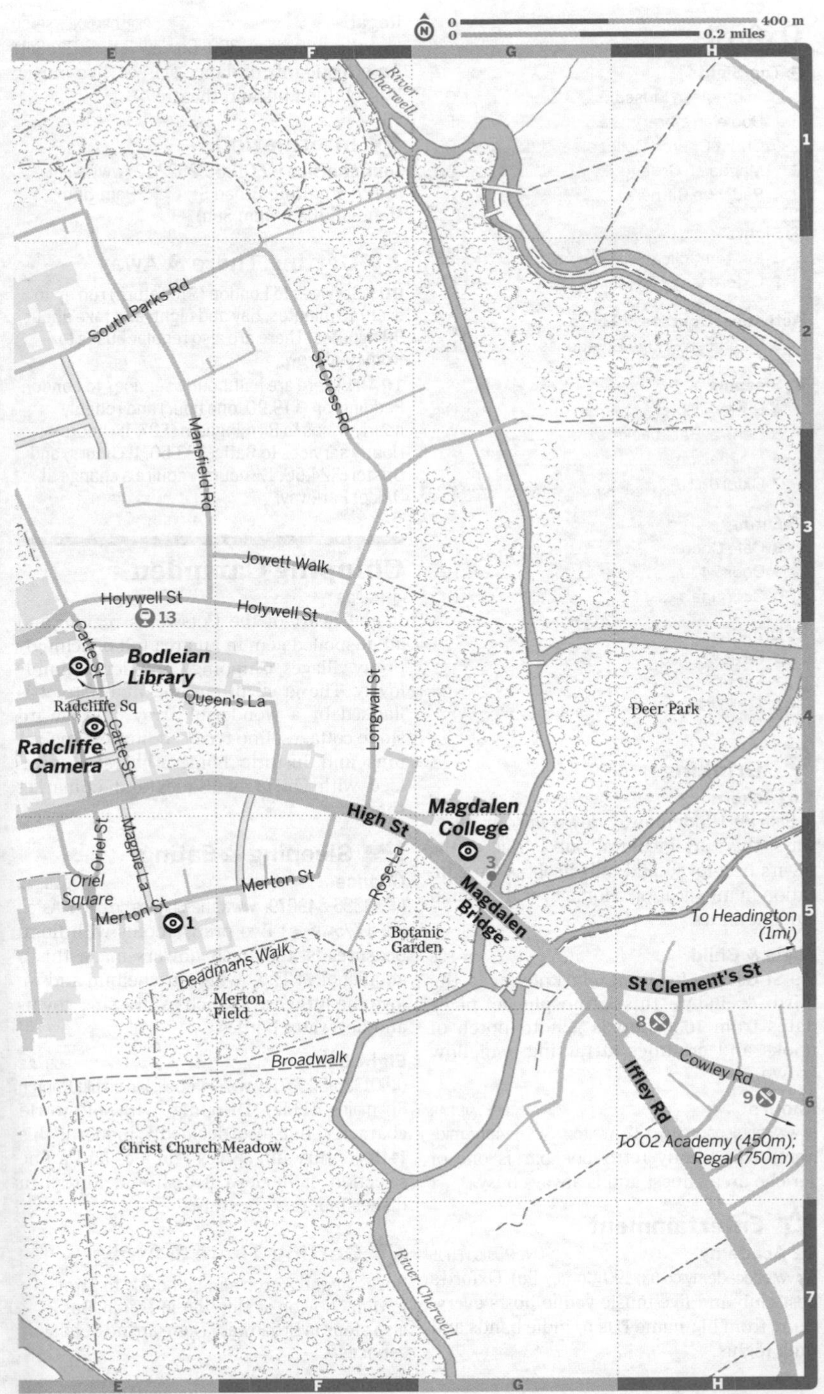
0 400 m
0 0.2 miles
E
F
G
H
River Cherwell
South Parks Rd
St Cross Rd
Mansfield Rd
Jowett Walk
Holywell St
Holywell St
13
Catte St
Bodleian Library
Radcliffe Sq
Queen's La
Catte St
Radcliffe Camera
Longwall St
High St
Magdalen College
3
Deer Park
Oriel St
Magpie La
Oriel Square
Merton St
Merton St
1
Rose La
Magdalen Bridge
Botanic Garden
To Headington (1mi)
Deadmans Walk
St Clement's St
Merton Field
8
Broadwalk
Cowley Rd
Iffley Rd
9
Christ Church Meadow
To O2 Academy (450m); Regal (750m)
River Cherwell
1
2
3
4
5
6
7

Oxford

Top Sights

	Ashmolean Museum	C3
	Bodleian Library	E4
	Christ Church College	D5
	Magdalen College	G5
	Radcliffe Camera	E4

Sights

1	Merton College	E5
2	Oxford Covered Market	D4

Activities, Courses & Tours

3	Magdalen Bridge Boathouse	G5

Sleeping

4	Buttery Hotel	D4
5	Central Backpackers	B4
6	Malmaison	C5
7	Oxford YHA	A4

Eating

8	Café Coco	H6
9	Door 74	H6
10	Georgina's	D4

Drinking

11	Eagle & Child	C3
12	Raoul's	B2
13	Turf Tavern	E3

Drinking

Turf Tavern PUB

(4 Bath Pl) Hidden away down narrow alleyways, this tiny medieval pub is one of the town's best-loved and bills itself as 'an education in intoxication'. Home to real ales and student antics.

Eagle & Child PUB

(49 St Giles) Affectionately known as the 'Bird & Baby', this atmospheric place dates from 1650 and is a hotchpotch of nooks and crannies attracting a mellow crowd.

Raoul's COCKTAIL BAR

(www.raoulsbar.co.uk; 32 Walton St; 4pm-midnight) This trendy retro-look bar is one of Jericho area's finest and is always busy.

Entertainment

O2 Academy LIVE MUSIC VENUE

(www.o2academy.co.uk; 190 Cowley Rd) Oxford's best club and live-music venue hosts everything from big-name DJs to indie bands and funk nights.

Regal PERFORMANCE SPACE

(www.the-regal.com; 300 Cowley Rd; Thu-Sat) An eclectic mix of dance classes, live music, DJs, club nights and theatre.

Information

Tourist office (01865-252200; www.visitoxford.org; 15-16 Broad St; 9.30am-5pm Mon-Sat, 10am-4pm Sun)

Getting There & Away

BUS Services to London (£16 return) run up to every 15 minutes, day and night, and take about 90 minutes. There are also regular buses to/from Heathrow.

TRAIN There are half-hourly services to London Paddington (£19.90, one hour) and roughly hourly trains to Birmingham (£27, 1¼ hours). Hourly services to Bath (£22.50, 1¼ hours) and Bristol (£24.50, 1½ hours) require a change at Didcot Parkway.

Chipping Campden

POP 2206

In the heart of the Cotswolds region, and an unspoiled gem in an area full of achingly pretty villages, Chipping Campden is simply lovely. The graceful curving main street is flanked by a wonderful array of wayward stone cottages, fine terraced houses, ancient inns and historic homes, liberally sprinkled with chichi boutiques and upmarket shops.

Sleeping & Eating

Chance B&B ££

(01386-849079; www.the-chance.co.uk; 1 Aston Rd; d £75; P) Two pretty rooms with floral bedspreads and fresh flowers make this a good choice. The owners are helpful and we love the little extras such as dressing gowns and hot water bottles.

Eight Bells PUB ££

(01386-840371; www.eightbellsinn.co.uk; Church St; mains £13-17) Dripping with old-world character, but also decidedly modern, this 14th-century inn serves real ales and a fine selection of modern British and European dishes in a rustic setting.

Getting There & Away

Buses 21 and 22 run almost hourly to Stratford-upon-Avon or Moreton-in-Marsh. Bus 21 also stops in Broadway. There are no Sunday services.

DON'T MISS

BLENHEIM PALACE

One of the country's greatest stately homes, **Blenheim Palace** (www.blenheimpalace.com; adult/child £18/10, park & garden only £10.30/5; ⏲10.30am-5.30pm daily mid-Feb–Oct, Wed-Sun Nov–mid-Dec) is a monumental baroque fantasy designed by Sir John Vanbrugh and Nicholas Hawksmoor between 1705 and 1722. Now a Unesco World Heritage Site, it's home to the 11th Duke of Marlborough. Inside, Blenheim (*blen*-um) is stuffed with statues, tapestries, ostentatious furniture and giant oil paintings in elaborate gilt frames. Highlights include the **Great Hall**, a vast space topped by 20m-high ceilings adorned with images of the 1st duke in battle; the opulent **Saloon**, the most important public room; the three **state rooms** with their plush decor and priceless china cabinets; and the magnificent 55m **Long Library**. You can also visit the **Churchill Exhibition**, dedicated to the life, work and writings of Sir Winston, who was born at Blenheim in 1874. Outside, you can stroll through the lavish **gardens** and vast **parklands**, parts of which were landscaped by Lancelot 'Capability' Brown.

Blenheim Place is near the town of Woodstock, a few miles northwest of Oxford. To get there, Stagecoach bus S3 runs every half-hour (hourly on Sunday) from George St in Oxford.

Broadway

POP 2496

Yet another pretty Cotswold village, set at the foot of a steep escarpment. Its main street is lined with antiques shops, tearooms and art galleries, and is justifiably popular in the summer months. Take the time to wander, and you'll be rewarded with quiet back roads lined with stunning cottages, flower-filled gardens and picturesque churches.

Broadway is littered with chintzy B&Bs, but for something more modern, try **Windrush** (☎01386 853577; www.broadway-windrush.co.uk; Station Rd; d from £90; P 📶), a stunning little B&B with newly refurbished rooms decked out in great style.

Stow-on-the-Wold

POP 2794

A popular stop on a tour of the Cotswolds, Stow is anchored by a large market square surrounded by handsome buildings and a good number of antique shops, boutiques, tearooms and delis. It can be a little too busy if you're looking for true Cotswold charm, but on a quiet day it's a wonderful place.

Sleeping

Mole End B&B ££
(☎01451-870348; www.moleendstow.co.uk; Moreton Rd; s/d from £55/80; P @) This charming B&B on the outskirts of town is a real gem, with three stunning rooms, a large garden with bucolic views, great breakfasts and amiable hosts.

Number 9 B&B ££
(☎01451-870333; www.number-nine.info; 9 Park St; s/d from £45/65; 📶) Centrally located and wonderfully atmospheric, this place has sloping floors, exposed beams, cosy but spacious rooms and brand-new bathrooms.

Stow-on-the-Wold YHA HOSTEL £
(☎0845 371 9540; www.yha.org.uk; The Square; dm £14.40; P @ 👪) Slap bang on the market square, this hostel is in a wonderful 16th-century townhouse with small dorms and a warm welcome for families.

Getting There & Away

Bus 855 links Stow with Moreton and Cirencester (eight daily Monday to Saturday). Bus 801 runs to Cheltenham and Moreton (four daily Monday to Friday, nine on Saturday).

Winchcombe

POP 4379

Winchcombe is a sleepy Cotswolds town, with butchers, bakers and small independent shops giving it a very authentic feel. It was capital of the Saxon kingdom of Mercia and important until the Middle Ages, and today the remnants of its illustrious past can still be seen. Among the sleeping and eating options, the **White Hart Inn** (☎01242-602359; www.wineandsausage.co.uk; r £40-115) is excellent.

THE COTSWOLDS – QUINTESSENTIAL ENGLAND

A soft rural landscape, filled with glorious honey-coloured villages, old mansions, thatched cottages and atmospheric churches – welcome to the Cotswolds. If you've ever dreamed of falling asleep under English-rose wallpaper or lusted after a cream tea in the mid-afternoon, there's no finer place to fulfil your fantasies.

This is prime tourist territory, however, and the most popular villages can be besieged by traffic in summer. So visit the main centres early morning or late evening, focus your attention on the southern parts of the region, or take to the hills on foot or by bike.

A handy gateway town is **Moreton-in-Marsh**: a bus service runs to/from Cheltenham (seven times daily, one hour, Monday to Saturday) via Stow-on-the-Wold (15 minutes), with two Sunday services from May to September; there are trains roughly every two hours to/from London Paddington (£26.90, one hour 40 minutes) via Oxford (£7.90, 40 minutes).

Shrewsbury

POP 67,126

On the western side of England, close to the border with Wales, Shrewsbury (*shrooz-bree*) is a delightful jumble of winding medieval streets and timbered Tudor houses leaning at precarious angles. It's also an excellent gateway to exploration in this quiet and scenic region, known as The Marches.

Sights

Shrewsbury Abbey CHURCH
(01743-232723; www.shrewsburyabbey.com; Abbey Foregate; donation adult/child £2/1; 10.30am-3pm Mon-Sat, 11.30am-2.30pm Sun) Famous as the setting for Ellis Peters' *Chronicles of Brother Cadfael*, the red-sandstone Shrewsbury Abbey is all that remains of a vast Benedictine monastery founded in 1083. You can still see some impressive Norman, Early English and Victorian features, including an exceptional 14th-century west window.

Shrewsbury Castle CASTLE
(01743-358516; adult/child £2.50/1.50; 10am-5pm Mon-Sat, to 4pm Sun May-Sep, 10am-4pm Tue-Sat Feb-Apr) Another landmark hewn from sunset-red Shropshire sandstone, the castle contains a stiff-upper-lipped **museum** dedicated to the Shropshire Regiment, plus fine views from its battlements.

Sleeping & Eating

As well as the following choices, pretty Abbey Foregate is lined with B&Bs.

Lion Hotel HOTEL ££
(01753-353107; www.thelionhotelshrewsbury.co.uk; Wyle Cop; s/d from £80/98; P) A famous coaching inn, decked with portraits of lords and ladies in powdered wigs. The lounge has a grand stone fireplace and the rooms are note-perfect, down to the period-pattern fabrics and ceramic water jugs.

Tudor House B&B ££
(01743-351735; www.tudorhouseshrewsbury.com; 2 Fish St; s/d from £69/79; @) A bowing frontage festooned with hanging baskets and window boxes sets the scene at this delightful Tudor cottage on – yes – a delightful Tudor lane.

Mad Jack's MODERN EUROPEAN ££
(01743-358870; www.madjacksuk.com; 15 St Mary's St; mains £11-16) A classy place straddling the boundary between cafe, restaurant and bar, with an elegant dining room and swish contemporary bedrooms (singles/doubles from £70/80) upstairs.

Three Fishes PUB
(4 Fish St) Quintessential creaky Tudor alehouse, with a jolly publican, some mellow regulars, and hops hanging from the 15th-century beamed ceiling.

Information

Tourist office (01743-281200; www.visitshrewsbury.com; Shrewsbury Museum & Art Gallery, Barker St; 9.30am-5.30pm Mon-Sat, 10am-4pm Sun May-Sep, 10am-5pm Mon-Sat Oct-Apr)

Getting There & Away

BUS National Express buses run to London (£21, 4½ hours, two daily) and Birmingham (£7, 1½ hours, two daily).

TRAIN Trains run direct to London Marylebone (£52, 2¾ hours, four daily Monday to Saturday, two on Sunday). If you're bound for Wales, the country line to Swansea (£33, 3¾ hours, hourly) is a treat.

Stratford-upon-Avon

POP 22,187

The author of some of the most quoted lines in the English language, William Shakespeare was born in Stratford in 1564 and died here in 1616. The five houses linked to his life form the centrepiece of a tourist attraction that verges on a cult of personality. Experiences range from the tacky (bard-themed tearooms) to the humbling (Shakespeare's modest grave in Holy Trinity Church) and the sublime (a play by the world-famous Royal Shakespeare Company). If you can leave without buying at least a Shakespeare novelty pencil, you'll have resisted one of the most keenly honed marketing machines in the nation.

Sights & Activities

Shakespeare Houses MUSEUMS

(☎01789-204016; www.shakespeare.org.uk; all 5 properties adult/child £19/12, 3 in-town houses £12.50/8; ⏰9am-5pm Apr-Oct, winter hr vary) Five important buildings associated with Shakespeare contain museums that form the core of the visitor experience, run by the Shakespeare Birthplace Trust. You can buy individual tickets, but it's more cost effective to buy a combination ticket.

Start your Shakespeare tour at **Shakespeare's Birthplace** (Henley St), the house where the world's most famous playwright supposedly spent his childhood days. When Shakespeare retired, he swapped the bright lights of London for a comfortable town house on **New Place**. It was demolished in 1759, but the adjacent **Nash's House** (☎01789-292325; cnr Chapel St & Chapel Lane), where Shakespeare's granddaughter Elizabeth lived, describes the town's history.

Shakespeare's daughter Susanna married doctor John Hall, and **Hall's Croft** (☎01789-292107, Old Town) is their fine Elizabethan residence. Deviating from the Shakespeare theme, the exhibition here offers fascinating insights into 16th-century medicine.

Before marrying Shakespeare, Anne Hathaway lived in Shottery, a mile west of the centre, in the pretty thatched farmhouse known as **Anne Hathaway's Cottage** (☎01789-292100, Cottage La, Shottery). As well as period furniture, there's an orchard and arboretum, with examples of all the trees mentioned in Shakespeare's plays.

Mary Arden's Farm (☎01789-293455; Station Rd, Wilmcote), the childhood home of Shakespeare's mum, is at Wilmcote, 3 miles west of Stratford. Aimed firmly at families, the farm has exhibits tracing country life over the centuries, with nature trails, falconry displays and a collection of rare-breed farm animals.

Holy Trinity Church CHURCH

(☎01789-266316; www.stratford-upon-avon.org; Old Town; admission to church free, Shakespeare's grave adult/child £1.50/50p; ⏰8.30am-6pm Mon-Sat, 12.30-5pm Sun Apr-Sep, shorter winter hr) The final resting place of the Bard is said to be the most visited parish church in England. Inside are handsome 16th- and 17th-century tombs, some fabulous carvings on the choir stalls (look for the man yanking a dwarf's beard) and of course the grave of the man himself with its ominous epitaph: 'cvrst be he yt moves my bones'.

Sleeping

B&Bs are plentiful along Grove Rd and Evesham Pl.

Stratford-upon-Avon YHA HOSTEL £

(☎0845 371 9661; www.yha.org.uk; Hemmingford House, Alveston; dm from £16; P @) Set in a large, 200-year-old mansion 1.5 miles east of the town centre, this superior hostel attracts travellers of all ages.

Shakespeare Hotel HOTEL ££

(☎01789-294997; www.mercure.com; Chapel St; s/d £135/150; P @) For the full Tudor inn experience, head to this atmospheric Mercure property in a timbered medieval charmer on the main street.

White Sails GUESTHOUSE ££

☎01789-264326; www.white-sails.co.uk; 85 Evesham Rd; r from £95; P @ wifi) Plush fabrics, framed prints, brass bedsteads and shabby-chic tables set the scene at this gorgeous guesthouse.

Ambleside Guest House B&B ££

(☎01789-297239; www.amblesideguesthouse.co.uk; 41 Grove Rd; s/d from £25/50; P @) Lovely, nonfrilly B&B, with spotless rooms, amiable, well-informed hosts and big organic breakfasts.

Ashgrove Guest House B&B ££

(☎01789-297278; www.ashgrovehousestratford.co.uk; 37 Grove Rd; s/d from £25/50; P) Tidy, airy rooms decked out in varying degrees of burgundy. Look for the wooden bear sculpture outside.

Broadlands Guest House B&B ££

(☎01789-299181; www.broadlandsguesthouse.co.uk; 23 Evesham Pl; s/d from £48/80; P) Prim and blue, with classic rooms and filling breakfasts.

 Eating & Drinking

Sheep St is clustered with eating options, mostly aimed at theatregoers (look out for good-value pretheatre menus).

Edward Moon's MODERN BRITISH ££
(☎01789-267069; www.edwardmoon.com/moonsrestaurant; 9 Chapel St; mains £10-15; ⊙lunch & dinner) This snug eatery serves hearty English dishes, many livened up with herbs and spices from the East.

Vintner Wine Bar MODERN BRITISH ££
(☎01789-297259; www.the-vintner.co.uk; 5 Sheep St; mains £10-20; ⊙breakfast, lunch & dinner) Set in a townhouse from 1600, this quirky place is full of exposed brickwork and low ceilings to bang your head on.

Oscar's CAFE, BAR £
(13/14 Meer St; sandwiches & lunches £4-7; ⊙lunch) A casual cafe serving appetising breakfasts, lunches and afternoon tea; it turns into a bar after hours.

Dirty Duck PUB
(Waterside) Officially called the 'Black Swan', this enchanting riverside alehouse is a favourite thespian watering hole, and has a roll-call of former regulars (Olivier, Attenborough etc) that reads like an actors' *Who's Who*.

Windmill Inn PUB
(Church St) Ale was flowing at this old pub at the same time as rhyming couplets flowed from Shakespeare's quill.

Information

Tourist office (☎01789 264293; www.shakespeare-country.co.uk; 62 Henley St; ⊙10am-5pm, to 4pm winter) By the entrance to the Bards Walk mall, the tourist office has racks of brochures and local info.

Getting There & Away

BUS National Express coaches and other bus companies run from Stratford's Riverside bus station.

Birmingham National Express £7.70, one hour, twice daily

London Victoria National Express, £17.10, three to four hours, five daily

Moreton-in-Marsh Bus 21/22, one hour, hourly

Oxford National Express £9.90, one hour, twice daily

Warwick Bus 16, 40 minutes, hourly

TRAIN Trains run to/from Birmingham (£6.30, one hour, hourly) and London Marylebone (£49.50, 2¼ hours, four daily). The **Shakespeare Express steam train** (0121-708 4960; www.shakespeareexpress.com) runs twice every Sunday in July and August between Stratford and Birmingham Snow Hill (one way adult/child £10/5).

Getting Around

A bicycle offers a handy means of transport for visiting the outlying Shakespeare properties, and **Stratford Bike Hire** (☎07711-776340; www.stratfordbikehire.com; 7 Seven Meadows Rd; per half/full day from £7/13) will deliver to your accommodation.

Warwick

POP 25,434

Regularly name-checked by Shakespeare, Warwick is a treasure-house of medieval architecture, dominated by the soaring turrets of Warwick Castle, now transformed into a major tourist attraction by the team behind Madame Tussauds. It's undeniably popular, but the summer queues can resemble a medieval siege.

Sights

Warwick Castle CASTLE
(☎0870 442 2000; www.warwick-castle.co.uk; castle adult/child £19.95/11.95, castle & dungeon adult/child £27.45/19.45; ⊙10am-6pm Apr-Sep, to 5pm Oct-Mar; P) Founded in 1068 by William the Conqueror, the stunningly preserved Warwick Castle is the biggest show in town. With waxwork-populated private apartments, sumptuous interiors, landscaped gardens, towering ramparts, displays of arms and armour, medieval jousting and a theme-park dungeon (complete with torture chamber and ham actors in grisly make-up), there's plenty to keep the family busy for a whole day. Tickets are discounted if you buy online.

Sleeping & Eating

Reasonably priced B&Bs line Emscote Rd.

Charter House B&B ££
(☎01926-496965; sheila@penon.gotadsl.co.uk; 87-91 West St; s/d incl breakfast from £65/85; P@) A cute little timbered cottage with three rooms convincingly decorated in medieval period styles, and a long list of options for breakfast.

DON'T MISS

ROYAL SHAKESPEARE COMPANY

You just can't come to Stratford without seeing one of the Bard's plays performed by the **Royal Shakespeare Company** (RSC; ☎0844 800 1110; www.rsc.org.uk; tickets £8-38). There are often special deals for under 25-year-olds, students and seniors, and a few tickets are held back for sale on the day of performance.

Rose & Crown PUB ££
(☎01926-411117; www.roseandcrownwarwick.co.uk; 30 Market Pl; mains from £8; P@) This convivial gastropub has good beer and superior food, as well as five appealing rooms (including breakfast from £70) with tasteful modern trim, some with views of the town square.

Information

Tourist office (☎01926-492212; www.warwick-uk.co.uk; Court House, Jury St; ⏲9.30am-4.30pm Mon-Fri, from 10am Sat, 10am-3.30pm Sun)

Getting There & Away

Stagecoach bus 16 goes to Stratford-upon-Avon (40 minutes, hourly). Trains run to Birmingham (£7.40, 45 minutes, every half-hour), Stratford-upon-Avon (£5.20, 30 minutes, hourly) and London (£30, 1¾ hours, every 20 minutes).

Birmingham

POP 977,087

Once a byword for bad town planning, England's second-largest city – known to locals as 'Brum' – is shaking off the legacy of industrial decline, and spending serious money replacing drab 1960s concrete architecture with gleaming glass and steel. The town centre looks better than it has in decades, helped in no small part by the revitalised Bullring centre and the iconic Selfridges building, which looks out over the city like the compound eye of a giant robot insect.

Birmingham might not leap out as a tourist attraction, but there's a lot to see, including some fine museums and galleries, and the nightlife and food are the best in the Midlands.

Sights

Victoria Square NOTABLE BUILDINGS
Birmingham's grandest civic buildings are clustered around pedestrianised Victoria Square, dominated by the stately facade of **Council House**, erected between 1874 and 1879. The square was given a facelift in 1993, with modernist sphinxes and a fountain topped by a naked female figure nicknamed 'the floozy in the Jacuzzi' overlooked by a disapproving **statue** of Queen Victoria.

Housed in the annexe at the back of Council House, the delightful **Birmingham Museum & Art Gallery** (☎0121-303 2834; www.bmag.org.uk; Chamberlain Sq; admission free; ⏲10am-5pm Mon-Thu & Sat, 10.30am-5pm Fri, 12.30-5pm Sun) houses ancient treasures and Victorian art, including an important collection of major Pre-Raphaelite works by Rossetti, Edward Burne-Jones and others, plus a treasure trove of 7th-century Anglo-Saxon gold unearthed in a field near Lichfield in 2009.

The west side of the square is marked out by the neoclassical **town hall** (☎0121-780 3333; www.thsh.co.uk), constructed in 1834 and styled after the Temple of Castor and Pollux in Rome, now used as a venue for classical concerts and stage performances.

Cathedral Church of St Philip CHURCH
(☎0121-262 1840; Colmore Row; donations requested; ⏲7.30am-6.30pm Mon-Fri, 8.30am-5pm Sat & Sun) North of the New St shopping precinct, the small but perfectly formed Cathedral Church of St Philip was constructed in a neoclassical style between 1709 and 1715.

Gas Street Basin HISTORIC AREA
During the industrial age, Birmingham was a major hub on the English canal network (the city technically has more miles of canals than Venice). Visiting narrowboats still float into Gas St Basin in the heart of the city, passing a string of swanky wharfside developments.

Sleeping

Birmingham Central Backpackers HOSTEL £
(☎0121-643 0033; www.birminghamcentralbackpackers.com; 58 Coventry St; dm from £13; @) Despite the setting in down-at-heel Digbeth, this hostel is handy for the bus station, and guests have a choice of standard dorms or funky Japanese-style pods.

Nitenite HOTEL ££
(☎0121-631 5550; www.nitenite.com; 18 Holliday St; r from £56; P@) The compact rooms

feel a little like yacht cabins, with panelled walls, floating double beds and giant plasma TV screens with webcam images of the city streets.

Westbourne Lodge B&B ££
(☎0121-429 1003; www.westbournelodge.co.uk; Fountain Rd; s/d from £49.50/69; P@🛜) Removed from the city centre, about 2 miles out in the suburb of Edgbaston, this place has spacious rooms and a pleasant terrace to enjoy in summer.

Information

Tourist office (☎0121-202 5115; www.visitbirmingham.com; The Rotunda, 150 New St; ⏲9.30am-5.30pm Mon & Wed-Sat, 10am-5.30pm Tue, 10.30am-4.30pm Sun)

Getting There & Away

Bus

Most intercity coaches run to/from the Birmingham Coach Station on Digbeth High St.

London £15.70, 2¾ hours, every 30 minutes
Manchester £12.60, 2½ hours, 12 daily
Oxford £11.60, 1½ to two hours, five daily

Bus X20 to Stratford-upon-Avon (1¼ hours, hourly, every two hours at weekends) leaves from a stop on Moor St, just north of the Pavilions mall.

Train

Most long-distance trains leave from New St Station, beneath the Pallasades shopping centre. Chiltern Railways runs to London Marylebone (£31.90; 2½ hours, two hourly) from Birmingham Snow Hill, and London Midland runs to Stratford-upon-Avon (£6.30, one hour, hourly) from Snow Hill and Moor St station.

Peak District National Park

Squeezed between the industrial Midlands to the south and the cities of Manchester and Sheffield to the west and east, the surprisingly rural Peak District is one of the finest areas in England for walking, cycling and other outdoor activities. Don't be misled by the name; there are few peaks, but plenty of wild moors, rolling farmland and deep valleys – plus hardy villages, prehistoric sites and limestone caves.

The Peak District is principally in Derbyshire but spills into five adjoining counties (including Yorkshire, Staffordshire and Cheshire). It's also one of England's best-loved national parks, but escaping the crowds is no problem if you avoid summer weekends. The region is divided into the wilder scenery of the Dark Peak in the north, and the gentler meadows and dales of the White Peak in the south. The towns of Buxton to the west or Matlock to the east are good gateways, or you can stay right in the centre at Edale, Bakewell or Castleton.

Sights

Chatsworth House PALACE
(☎01246-582204; www.chatsworth.org; adult/child £11.25/6; ⏲11am-5.30pm Mar-Dec) Known as the 'Palace of the Peak', this vast edifice has been occupied by the dukes of Devonshire for centuries. Among the prime attractions

EATING IN BIRMINGHAM – IT'S GOT TO BE BALTI

If curry is the unofficial national dish of England, then the balti is its finest interpretation – and was reputedly invented here in Birmingham. The best place to sample this Brummie delicacy is the so-called Balti Triangle, formed by Ladypool Rd, Stoney Lane and Stratford Rd. Reflecting the religious sensibilities of local residents, restaurants serve soft drinks, fruit juices and lassis (yoghurt shakes) instead of alcohol, but diners are welcome to bring their own beer and wine. Expect to pay £7 to £9 for a balti and rice or naan bread. To get here, take bus 2, 5, 5A or 6 from Corporation St and ask the driver for Ladypool Rd.

Our pick of the Birmingham baltis:

Grameen Khana (☎0121-449 9994; www.grameenkhana.com; 310-12 Ladypool Rd) Multicoloured lights and Bollywood movies provide a backdrop to Birmingham's best balti – according to a city-wide poll in 2009.

Saleem's Restaurant & Sweet House (☎0121-449 1861; 256-8 Ladypool Rd) Long established and understandably popular for its tasty milk-based Indian sweets and generous portions of balti.

Al Faisal's (☎0121-449 5695; www.alfaisal.co.uk; 136-140 Stoney Lane) Come here for delicious dishes from the mountains of Kashmir as well as classic Birmingham baltis.

BIRMINGHAM BY NIGHT

As in most large cities, it's wise to avoid walking alone late at night in unlit areas. The area around Digbeth bus station can be quite rough after dark – stick to the High St if you are walking to central Birmingham.

in the house itself are the magnificent artworks, decorated ceilings and the treasure troves of splendid furniture.

The house sits in over 42 hectares of **gardens** (adult/child £7.50/4.50), with grottoes, fountains, a maze and changing collections of modern sculptures. Beyond that is another 400 hectares of **park** (admission free), open for walking and picnicking.

Chatsworth is 3 miles northeast of Bakewell. Buses 170 and 218 run several times a day (15 minutes), plus bus 215 on Sunday. Another option is to walk from Bakewell (about 2 miles each way), following a quiet lane then footpaths through Chatsworth park down to the house.

Sleeping

The Peak District has a great selection of B&Bs, hotels and pubs. We've listed just a few favourites. For more, try local Tourist Information Centres (TICs), or see www.visitpeakdistrict.com.

BUXTON

Buxton is a picturesque sprawl of Georgian terraces, Victorian amusements and pretty parks, set in the very heart of the Peak District.

Roseleigh Hotel B&B ££
(01298-24904; www.roseleighhotel.co.uk; 19 Broad Walk; s/d incl breakfast from £38/72; P @ wi-fi) This gorgeous B&B has excellent rooms and a great location. The owners are seasoned travellers, with plenty of tales to tell.

EDALE

Surrounded by majestic countryside, this tiny cluster of cottages is an enchanting spot. Despite the remote location, the Manchester–Sheffield train line passes nearby, meaning easy access – and legions of outdoor types on summer weekends.

Stonecroft B&B ££
(01433-670262; www.stonecroftguesthouse.co.uk; Grindsbrook; r from £75; P) This handsome house has two comfortable bedrooms. Vegetarians and vegans are well catered for – the organic breakfast is excellent.

CASTLETON

Castleton is blessed with more than its fair share of visitor attractions: the streets are lined with old stone houses, a wonderfully atmospheric castle overlooks the village, walking trails criss-cross the surrounding hills, while below ground is riddled with caverns – many open to the public as 'show caves'.

Causeway House B&B ££
(01433-623921; www.causewayhouse.co.uk; Back St; s/d £33/65) The floors of this ancient, character-soaked stone cottage have been worn and warped with age, but you'll find the quaint bedrooms inside bright and welcoming.

BAKEWELL

The second-largest town in the Peak District, pretty Bakewell is a great base for exploring the White Peak. The town is probably best known for its eponymous pudding (and woe betide anyone asking for a Bakewell *tart*).

Melbourne House B&B ££
(01629-815357; Buxton Rd; r from £55; P) In a picturesque building dating back more than three centuries, this is an inviting B&B on the main road leading to Buxton.

Information

There are many TICs in and around the park.

Bakewell (01629-813227; Bridge St; 9.30am-5pm Apr-Oct, from 10am Nov-Mar)

PEAK HOSTELS

Hikers, outdoors types and shoestring travellers can take advantage of some useful YHA hostels, including the phenomenally popular **Castleton YHA Hostel** (0870 770 5758; www.yha.org.uk; Castle St; dm £14; @) and **Edale YHA Hostel** (0870 770 5808; www.yha.org.uk; dm from £11.95; @), the latter also an Activity Centre to try your hand at caving, kayaking, climbing and abseiling. There's also a series of rudimentary 'bunk barns' (beds per person from £6) in remote locations. For details, see www.yha.org.uk.

Buxton (☎01298-25106; Pavilion Gardens; ⌚9.30am-5pm Oct-Mar, 10am-4pm Apr-Sep)

Castleton (☎01433-620679; Buxton Rd; ⌚9.30am-5.30pm Mar-Oct, 10am-5pm Nov-Feb)

Peak District National Park Authority (☎01629-816200; www.peakdistrict.org)

Getting There & Around

National Express coaches run from London Victoria to Manchester and Buxton, from where you can switch to a local bus. Derby, south of the park, is another good gateway, easily reached by coach and train, and from there trains run to Matlock. Trains also run between Sheffield and Manchester via Edale and several other Peak villages.

By far the handiest local bus is the hourly **Transpeak** (www.transpeak.co.uk) service that cuts across the Peak District from Nottingham and Derby to Manchester, via Matlock, Bakewell and Buxton.

EASTERN ENGLAND

The vast flatland of Eastern England (or East Anglia, as it's usually called) is a mix of lush farms, melancholy fens, big skies and the bucolic scenery that once inspired Constable and Gainsborough. Meanwhile, the meandering coast is lined with pretty fishing villages and bucket-and-spade resorts, while inland sit the watery charms of the Norfolk Broads.

Cambridge

POP 108,863

Drowning in exquisite architecture, steeped in history and tradition, and renowned for its quirky rituals, Cambridge is a university town extraordinaire. The tightly packed core of ancient colleges, the picturesque riversides and the leafy green meadows that seem to surround the city give it a far more tranquil appeal than rival Oxford.

Sights

Cambridge University comprises 31 colleges, though not all are open to the public. Most close to visitors for the Easter term and all are closed for exams from mid-May to mid-June. Opening hours vary from day to day, and the hours given below are only a rough guide, so contact the colleges or the tourist office for information.

Trinity College COLLEGE
(www.trin.cam.ac.uk; Trinity St; adult/child £1/50p; ⌚9am-4pm) The largest of Cambridge's colleges, Trinity is entered by an impressive gateway. As you walk through, have a look at the statue of the founder, Henry VIII. His left hand holds a golden orb, while his right grips not the original sceptre but a table leg, put there by student pranksters and never replaced.

King's College Chapel CHAPEL
(www.kings.cam.ac.uk/chapel; King's Pde; adult/child/under 12yr £5/3.50/free; ⌚9.30am-4.30pm Mon-Sat, 10am-5pm Sun) In a city crammed with glorious architecture, this is the showstealer; one of the most extraordinary examples of Gothic architecture in England – most famous for its **fan-vaulted ceiling**, with intricate tracery soaring upwards before exploding into a series of stone fireworks. The lofty **stained-glass windows** still retain their original glass, rare survivors of the excesses of the Civil War; it's thought they were spared on the orders of Cromwell himself, who knew of their beauty from his own studies in Cambridge.

The Backs PARK
Behind the grandiose facades, stately courts and manicured lawns of the city's central colleges lie a series of riverside gardens and parklands collectively known as the Backs. These tranquil green spaces and shimmering waters offer unparalleled views of the colleges and are often the most enduring image of Cambridge for visitors.

FREE **Fitzwilliam Museum** MUSEUM
(www.fitzmuseum.cam.ac.uk; Trumpington St; ⌚10am-5pm Tue-Sat, noon-5pm Sun) This museum is filled with priceless treasures from ancient Egyptian sarcophagi to Greek and Roman art, Chinese ceramics to English glass, and some dazzling illuminated manuscripts. The upper galleries showcase works by Leonardo da Vinci, Titian, Rubens, Gainsborough and Constable, right through to Rembrandt and Picasso. You can join a one-hour **guided tour** (£3.50) on Saturdays at 2.30pm.

FREE **Corpus Christi College** COLLEGE
(www.corpus.cam.ac.uk; Trumpington St) Entry to this illustrious college is via the so-called New Court that dates back a mere 200 years. To your right is the **Parker Library,** which holds the finest collection of Anglo-Saxon manuscripts in the world.

PUNTING

Gliding a punt along the Backs is a blissful experience once you've got the knack, though it can also be a challenge. Renting costs £14 to £16 per hour, while safer and more relaxing chauffeured trips cost £10 to £12 (a return trip to Grantchester is £20 to £30).

Sleeping

Some of Cambridge's most central B&Bs use their convenient location as an excuse not to upgrade. Some of the better places are a bit of a hike from town but well worth the effort.

Cambridge Rooms COLLEGE ROOMS ££
(www.cambridgerooms.co.uk; r £35-120) For a taste of life inside the hallowed college grounds, you can stay in a student room. Accommodation varies from traditional singles (with shared bathroom) overlooking college quads to modern en suite rooms in nearby annexes.

Hotel Felix HOTEL £££
(01223-277977; www.hotelfelix.co.uk; Whitehouse Lane, Huntingdon Rd; d £180-305; P@) This luxurious boutique hotel occupies a lovely villa in landscaped grounds a mile from the city centre. Its 52 rooms embody designer chic with minimalist style but lots of comfort.

Tenison Towers B&B ££
(01223-363924; www.cambridgecitytenisontowers.com; 148 Tenison Rd; s/d from £40/60) This exceptionally friendly and homely place is really handy if you're arriving by train. The rooms are bright and simple with pale colours and fresh flowers.

Benson House B&B ££
(01223-311594; www.bensonhouse.co.uk; 24 Huntingdon Rd; d £85-110; P) Just a 15-minute walk from the city centre, this lovely B&B has some beautifully renovated rooms offering hotel-standard accommodation.

Cambridge YHA HOSTEL £
(0845 371 9728; www.yha.org.uk; 97 Tenison Rd; dm/tw £16/40; @) Within walking distance of the city centre, the dorms at this cheap and cheerful hostel are small and basic, and with lots of groups it can be noisy.

Eating

Cambridge is packed with chain restaurants, particularly around the city centre. You'll find upmarket chains such as Browns and Loch Fyne on Trumpington St, and plenty of Asian eateries on Regent St.

Origin8 CAFE £
(www.origin8delicafes.com; 62 St Andrew's St; mains £4-6.50; breakfast & lunch Mon-Sat, lunch Sun) Bright and airy, this cafe-deli prides itself on its local organic ingredients.

Oak Bistro MODERN BRITISH ££
(01223-323361; www.theoakbistro.co.uk; 6 Lensfield Rd; mains £11-17, set 2-/3-course lunch £12/15; closed Sun) This little place serves up classic dishes with modern flair. The atmosphere is relaxed, the decor minimalist and the food perfectly cooked.

CB2 CAFE ££
(www.cb2bistro.com; 5-7 Norfolk St; mains £6-13; @) Internet cafe, bistro, music venue and cinema all rolled into one, this lively place dishes up a great range of rustic cuisine in a relaxed and friendly atmosphere.

Rainbow Vegetarian Bistro VEGETARIAN ££
(www.rainbowcafe.co.uk; 9a King's Pde; mains £8-10; lunch & dinner Tue-Sat, lunch Mon & Sun;) First-rate vegetarian and organic dishes with a hint of the exotic are served in this snug subterranean gem.

Drinking

Cambridge is awash with historic pubs that echo with intellectual banter and rowdy merrymaking – just as they have for centuries past.

Eagle PUB
(Bene't St) Cambridge's most famous pub has loosened the tongues and pickled the grey cells of many illustrious academics; among them Nobel Prize–winning scientists Crick and Watson, who discussed their research into DNA here.

Kingston Arms PUB
(33 Kingston St;) Down to earth and full of character, this bright blue pub has real ales, decent pub grub (mains £8.50 to £13.50), a walled garden, free wi-fi and a friendly attitude.

Granta PUB
(01223-505016; Newnham Rd) If the exterior of this picturesque waterside pub looks strangely familiar, don't be surprised. It's a TV directors' favourite.

Cambridge

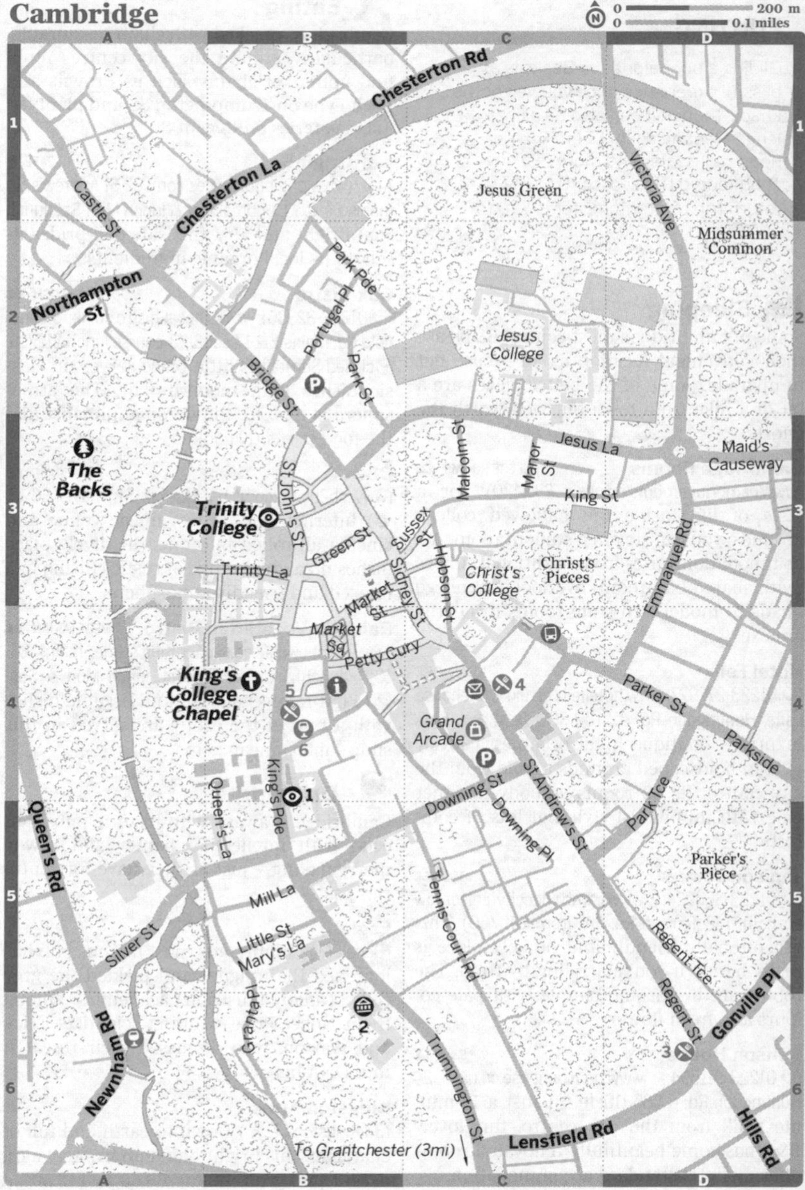

Information

Tourist office (☎0871 266 8006; www.visitcambridge.org; Old Library, Wheeler St; ⏲10am-5.30pm Mon-Fri, to 5pm Sat, 11am-3pm Sun)

Getting There & Away

BUS There are regular buses to/from Stansted (£12.40, 50 minutes), Heathrow (£29.90, 2½ to three hours) and Gatwick (£31, four hours) airports. Buses to Oxford (£10.90, 3½ hours) are regular but take a very convoluted route.

Cambridge

TRAIN Trains run at least every 30 minutes to/from London's King's Cross and Liverpool St stations (£19.10, 45 minutes to 1¼ hours).

Ely

POP 15,102

A small but charming city steeped in history and dominated by a jaw-dropping cathedral, Ely (*ee*-lee) makes an excellent day trip from Cambridge. Beyond the dizzying heights of the cathedral towers lie medieval streets, pretty Georgian houses and riverside walks reaching out into the eerie fens that surround the town.

Sights

Ely Cathedral CHURCH
(www.elycathedral.org; adult/child £6/free; ⌚9am-5pm) Dominating the town and visible across the flat farmland for vast distances, Ely Cathedral is locally dubbed the 'Ship of the Fens'. It's renowned for the uncluttered lines and lofty sense of space in its early-12th-century Romanesque **nave**, and the masterly 14th-century octagon and lantern **towers** which soar upwards in shimmering colours. For more insight into the fascinating history of the cathedral join a free guided tour. It's also worth timing a visit to attend the spine-tingling **Evensong** (⌚5.30pm Mon-Sat, 4pm Sun) or Sunday **choral service** (⌚10.30am).

Oliver Cromwell's House MUSEUM
(☎01353-662062; adult/child £4.50/4; ⌚10am-5pm Apr-Oct, 11am-4pm Nov-Mar) A short hop from the cathedral is the attractive half-timbered house where England's warty warmonger lived with his family from 1636 to 1646, now a Civil War exhibition.

Information

Tourist office (☎01353-662062; www.visitely.org.uk; 29 St Mary's St; ⌚10am-5pm)

Getting There & Away

The easiest way to get to Ely from Cambridge is by train (15 minutes, every 20 minutes); don't even consider the bus, as it takes a round-about route and is five times as long. There are also trains to/from Norwich (£12.90, one hour, every 20 minutes). If you like to stride out, the **Fen Rivers Way** is a lovely 17-mile walk between Cambridge and Ely (map available from tourist offices).

Norwich

POP 121,550

The largest city in Eastern England, affluent and easy-going Norwich (norritch) is a rich tapestry of meandering laneways liberally sprinkled with architectural gems, spoils of the city's heyday at the height of the medieval wool boom. A magnificent cathedral lords over it all from one end of the city centre and a sturdy Norman castle from the other, while grand squares, quiet lanes, thriving markets, modern shopping centres, contemporary-art galleries and a young student population give the city a genial attitude. Add easy access to the Broads and coast, and you have an excellent base for touring the area.

Sights

Norwich is a fantastic city to see on foot, with winding laneways and narrow passageways criss-crossing the centre of town. Most radiate from the candy-stripe canopied **Market Square** (⌚8am-4.30pm), one of the biggest and oldest markets in England, running since 1025. As you walk it's impossible to miss the huge number of **medieval churches** (www.norwich-churches.org) in the city. There are 36 to be precise, a testament to the city's wealth during the Middle Ages.

Norwich Cathedral CHURCH
(www.cathedral.org.uk; admission by donation; ⌚7.30am-6pm) Begun in 1096, Norwich cathedral is one of the finest in the country. The sheer size of its nave is impressive but its most renowned feature is the superb **Gothic rib-vaulting** added in 1463. Among

the spidery stonework are 1200 sculpted roof bosses depicting bible stories. Together they represent one of the finest achievements of English medieval masonry. For a deeper insight join one of the fascinating **guided tours** (donation expected), held daily at 10.45am, 12.30pm and 2.15pm.

Norwich Castle CASTLE
(www.museums.norfolk.gov.uk; castle & exhibitions adult/child £6.20/4.40, exhibitions £3.30/2.40; ⏲10am-5pm Mon-Sat, 1-5pm Sun) Perched on a hilltop, this massive Norman castle keep is a sturdy example of 12th-century aristocratic living. It's one of the best-preserved examples of Anglo-Norman military architecture in the country, despite a 19th-century facelift and a gigantic shopping centre grafted to one side. It's now also home to an excellent **art gallery** and **interactive museum**.

Sleeping

Most B&Bs are around the train station or outside the ring road. A new youth hostel is planned by the river; ask at the tourist office for details.

38 St Giles B&B ££
(☎01603-662944; www.38stgiles.co.uk; 38 St Giles St; s/d from £90/130; P) Ideally located, beautifully styled and reassuringly friendly, this boutique B&B in the centre of town is a real gem.

St Giles House HOTEL £££
(☎01603-275180; www.stgileshousehotel.com; 41-45 St Giles St; d incl breakfast £120-210;) Right in the heart of the city in a stunning 19th-century building, rooms range from fashionably art deco style to less personal modern decor.

By Appointment HOTEL ££
(☎01603-630730; www.byappointmentnorwich.co.uk; 25-29 St George's St; s/d incl breakfast from £90/120; @) This fabulously theatrical and delightfully eccentric B&B occupies three heavy-beamed 15th-century merchant's houses.

Beaufort Lodge B&B ££
(☎01603-667402; www.beaufortlodge.com; 60-62 Earlham Rd; s/d £55/70; P@) With light and airy rooms, this place is a great deal. It's about a mile west of Market Sq.

Information

Tourist office (☎01603-213999; www.visitnorwich.co.uk; The Forum; ⏲9.30am-6pm Mon-Sat, to 2.30pm Sun)

Getting There & Away

BUS National Express (www.nationalexpress.com) coaches go to/from London (£16.60, three hours, seven daily).

TRAIN Twice-hourly trains go to London Liverpool Street (£40.40, two hours), Cambridge (£13.40, 1¼ hours) and Ely (£12.90, one hour).

NORTHEAST ENGLAND

By turns wild and pretty, rural and urban, modern and historic, northeast England contains the large and varied counties of Yorkshire and Northumberland, and three of Britain's great cities: historic York, Durham, and resurgent Newcastle. This region also offers national parks with excellent walking and other outdoor activities, great expanses of empty beach, plus a hoard of world-class relics and ruins dating back two turbulent millennia – from the epic Roman construction project Hadrian's Wall to the haunting monastery island of Lindisfarne.

Places in this section are described roughly south to north. For general information, see www.yorkshirevisitor.com and www.visitnortheastengland.com.

Leeds

POP 750,200

One of the fastest-growing cities in the UK, Leeds is the glitzy, glamorous embodiment of newly rediscovered northern self-confidence. More than a decade of redevelopment has seen a transformation from near-derelict mill town into a vision of 21st-century urban chic, with skyscraping office blocks, waterfront apartments and renovated Victorian shopping arcades earning the city its much-hyped moniker: 'Knightsbridge of the North'. For visitors, it's also an excellent gateway to several major attractions.

Sleeping

There are no budget options in the city centre, and the better midrange choices are chain hotels. If you want somewhere more personal and good value, there are plenty of decent B&Bs and small hotels out in the suburbs, especially near Headingley cricket ground.

TOP CHOICE **Quebecs** BOUTIQUE HOTEL £££
(☎0113-244 8989; www.theetoncollection.com; 9 Quebec St; s/d/ste from £170/190/325; @) Victorian grace at its opulent best is

> **WORTH A TRIP**
>
> **NORFOLK BROADS**
>
> A watery mesh of navigable slow-moving rivers, freshwater lakes, wild meadows, fens, bogs and saltwater marshes make up the Norfolk and Suffolk Broads – the region's most beautiful natural attraction. Home to some of the UK's rarest plants and animals and protected as a national park, with flourishing nature reserves and bird sanctuaries, it's also very popular with boaters. Walkers and cyclists will also find a web of lanes and riverside paths, as well as the Broads' highest point, How Hill, all of a dizzying 12m above sea level.

the theme of our favourite hotel in town. The elaborate wood panelling and heraldic stained-glass windows in the public areas are complemented by the contemporary design of the bedrooms. Prebooking online can reveal excellent bargains.

Jury's Inn HOTEL ££
(☎0113-283 8800; www.jurysinns.com; Kendell St, Brewery Pl; r £69-115; P@) This chain hotel has large, functional rooms, and plenty of personal charm in the heart of the fashionable Brewery Wharf district, just a short walk from the centre.

Bewleys Hotel HOTEL ££
(☎0113-234 2340; www.bewleyshotels.com/leeds; City Walk, Sweet St; r from £69; P@) Just 10 minutes' walk from the city centre, with stylish and well-appointed rooms.

Moorlea B&B £
(☎0113-243 2653; www.moorleahotel.co.uk; 146 Woodsley Rd; s/d from £40/50;) Gay-friendly hotel northwest of the centre, near the University of Leeds.

Boundary Hotel Express HOTEL £
(☎0113-275 7700; www.boundaryhotel.co.uk; 42 Cardigan Rd; s/d £42/54; @) Basic but welcoming; 1.5 miles northwest of the centre in Headingley.

Headingley Lodge HOTEL £
(☎0113-278 5323; www.headingleylodge.co.uk; Headingley Stadium, St Michael's Lane; d/f £50/60; P@) Part of the Headingley stadium complex; rooms are smart, with cricket-ground views.

Information

Gateway Yorkshire & Leeds Visitor Centre (☎0113-242 5242; www.visitleeds.co.uk; The Arcade, Leeds City Train Station; 9am-5.30pm Mon-Sat, 10am-4pm Sun)

Getting There & Away

BUS National Express (www.nationalexpress.com) has hourly services to/from London (£22, 4½ hours) and half-hourly services to/from Manchester (£9.20, 1¼ hours). **Yorkshire Coastliner** (www.coastliner.co.uk) has useful services between Leeds and York.

TRAIN Hourly services to/from London King's Cross (£85, 2½ hours), Manchester (£16, one hour) and York (£11, 30 minutes).

Around Leeds

HAREWOOD HOUSE

The great park, sumptuous gardens and mighty stately home of **Harewood House** (www.harewood.org; adult/child £14.30/7.25; grounds 10am-6pm, house noon-4.30pm Apr-Oct) could easily fill an entire day trip from Leeds, and also makes a good port of call on the way to Harrogate.

The house and grounds were built between 1759 and 1772 by the era's superstar designers: John Carr designed the exterior, Lancelot 'Capability' Brown laid out the park, Thomas Chippendale supplied the furniture, Robert Adams designed the interior, and Italy was raided to create an appropriate art collection.

Harewood is about 7 miles north of Leeds. Take bus 36 (half-hourly Monday to Saturday, hourly on Sunday), which continues to Harrogate. Visitors coming by bus get half-price admission, so hang on to your ticket.

NATIONAL COAL MINING MUSEUM FOR ENGLAND

For three centuries, West and South Yorkshire were synonymous with coal production, until the industry came to a shuddering halt in the 1980s. This era is now remembered by the **National Coal Mining Museum for England** (www.ncm.org.uk; Overton, near Wakefield; admission free; 10am-5pm, last tour 3.15pm). The highlight of a visit is the underground tour (departing every 10 minutes) – equipped with helmet and head-torch – of the coal seam where massive drilling machines now stand idle. Former miners work as guides, and explain details – sometimes with a suitably authentic and almost impenetrable mix of local dialect and technical terminology.

The museum is about 10 miles south of Leeds, near Junction 40 on the M1. By public transport, take a train from Leeds to Wakefield (15 minutes, at least hourly), and then bus 232 towards Huddersfield (25 minutes, hourly).

YORKSHIRE SCULPTURE PARK

One of England's most impressive collections of sculpture is scattered across the formidable 18th-century estate of **Bretton Park**, 200-odd hectares of lawns, fields and trees, a bit like the art world's equivalent of a safari park. The **Yorkshire Sculpture Park** (www.ysp.co.uk; Bretton, near Wakefield; admission free, parking £4; ⏲10am-6pm Apr-Sep, to 5pm Oct-Mar) showcases the work of dozens of sculptors both national and international, but the main focus is the work of Barbara Hepworth and Henry Moore. Other highlights include pieces by Andy Goldsworthy and Eduardo Paolozzi. There's also a program of temporary exhibitions, plus a **bookshop** and **cafe**.

The park is 12 miles south of Leeds, just off Junction 38 on the M1. By public transport, take a train from Leeds to Wakefield (15 minutes, at least hourly), then bus 444 which runs between Wakefield and Barnsley via Bretton Park (30 minutes, hourly Monday to Saturday).

Haworth

POP 6100

In the canon of English literature, it seems that only Shakespeare himself is held in higher esteem than the beloved Brontë sisters, judging by the eight million visitors a year who come to this hardy northern town where the classics *Jane Eyre* and *Wuthering Heights* were born.

WORTH A TRIP

WUTHERING HEIGHTS?

Above Haworth stretch the bleak moors of the **South Pennines** – immediately familiar to Brontë fans – and the tourist office has leaflets on local walks to various Brontë-related spots. A 6.5-mile favourite leads to **Top Withins**, a ruined farm thought to have inspired *Wuthering Heights*, even though a plaque clearly states that the farmhouse bore no resemblance to the one Emily wrote about. But it's in a great position, and well worth the walk for the views alone.

Sights

Brontë Parsonage Museum MUSEUM
(www.bronte.info; Church St; adult/child £6.50/3.50; ⏲10am-5.30pm Apr-Sep, 11am-5pm Oct-Mar) Set in a pretty garden overlooking the church and graveyard, the house where the Brontë family lived from 1820 till 1861 is now a museum. The rooms are meticulously furnished and decorated exactly as they were in the Brontë era, with many personal possessions on display.

Sleeping & Eating

Virtually every second house on Main St offers B&B; we've highlighted some of our favourites. Most eating options are on (or just off) Main St too, and many of the B&Bs have small cafes that are good for a spot of lunch.

Old Registry B&B ££
(☎01535-646503; www.theoldregistryhaworth.co.uk; 2-4 Main St; r £75-120; 📶) This elegantly rustic guesthouse has carefully themed rooms with four-poster bed, whirlpool bath or valley view.

Ye Sleeping House B&B ££
(☎01535-546992; www.yesleepinghouse.co.uk; 8 Main St; s/d from £29/58) There's a cosy cottage atmosphere at this welcoming B&B, with just three small rooms and two friendly resident cats.

Aitches B&B ££
(☎01535-642501; www.aitches.co.uk; 11 West Lane; s/d from £40/58) A very classy Victorian house with four en suite rooms, and a pleasant olde-worlde atmosphere.

Apothecary Guest House B&B ££
(☎01535-643642; www.theapothecaryguesthouse.co.uk; 86 Main St; s/d £35/55; 📶) Oak beams and narrow, slanted passageways lead to smallish rooms with cheerful decor.

Old White Lion Hotel HOTEL, RESTAURANT ££
(☎01535-642313; www.oldwhitelionhotel.com; West Lane; s/d from £63/88; 📶) Pub-style accommodation – comfortable if not spectacular – above an oak-panelled bar and highly rated restaurant (mains £8 to £13).

Haworth YHA HOSTEL £
(☎0845 371 9520; www.yha.org.uk; Longlands Dr; dm £16; P@) A big old house with a games room, lounge, cycle store and laundry. It's

STEAM ENGINES & RAILWAY CHILDREN

Haworth is on the **Keighley & Worth Valley Railway** (www.kwvr.co.uk; adult/child return £9.40/4.70, adult/child Day Rover £14/7), where steam and classic diesel engines chug between Keighley and Oxenhope. It was here, in 1969, that the classic movie *The Railway Children* was shot; Mr Perks was stationmaster at Oakworth, where the Edwardian look has been meticulously maintained. Trains operate about hourly at weekends all year; daily in holiday periods.

on the northeastern edge of town, off Lees Lane.

Weaver's Restaurant with Rooms BRITISH, HOTEL ££
(☎01535-643822; www.weaversmallhotel.co.uk; 15 West Lane; mains £13-19; ⊙lunch Wed-Fri, dinner Tue-Sat) A stylish and atmospheric restaurant, with a menu featuring local produce, and three comfy bedrooms (singles/doubles £65/110) upstairs.

Information

Tourist office (☎01535-642329; www.haworth-village.org.uk; 2-4 West Lane; ⊙9am-5.30pm Apr-Sep, to 5pm Oct-Mar)

Getting There & Away

From Leeds, the easiest approach is via Keighley, which is on the Metro rail network. Bus 500 runs from Keighley bus station to Haworth (15 minutes, hourly). However, the most interesting way to get from Keighley to Haworth is via the Keighley & Worth Valley Railway.

Skipton

POP 14,300

This busy town has long been dubbed the gateway to the Yorkshire Dales. There's been a market here for centuries; Monday, Wednesday, Friday and Saturday are market days, bringing crowds to the High St and giving the town something of a festive atmosphere.

A pleasant stroll from the tourist office along the canal path leads to **Skipton Castle** (www.skiptoncastle.co.uk; High St; adult/child £6.20/3.70; ⊙10am-6pm Mon-Sat, noon-6pm Sun Mar-Sep, to 4pm Oct-Feb), one of the best-preserved medieval castles in England – a fascinating contrast to the ruins you'll see elsewhere.

The town has a good selection of B&Bs, cafes and pubs, and is easy to reach from Leeds (£7.50, 40 minutes, half-hourly, hourly on Sunday) on the local Metro rail network. If you're heading into the Dales, see the boxed text on p242.

Yorkshire Dales National Park

From well-known names such as Wensleydale and Ribblesdale, to obscure Langstrothdale and Arkengarthdale, the Yorkshire Dales is one of the most beautiful parts of northern England. It's been protected as a national park since the 1950s, assuring its status as a walker's and cyclist's paradise. For more details, see www.yorkshiredales.org.uk.

MALHAM

The pretty village of Malham is the jumping-off point for two of the national park's most spectacular features: **Malham Cove**, a huge rock amphitheatre lined with 80m-high vertical cliffs, and **Gordale Scar**, a deep limestone canyon with scenic cascades and the remains of an Iron Age settlement.

Sleeping

Beck Hall HOTEL ££
(☎01729-830332; www.beckhallmalham.com; s/d from £36/54; P ᯤ) This rambling 17th-century country house on the edge of the village has 15 individually decorated rooms.

Malham YHA HOSTEL £
(☎0845 371 9529; www.yha.org.uk; dm £18; P ♿) In the village centre is this purpose-built hostel with top-notch facilities.

HORTON-IN-RIBBLESDALE

At the heart of the park, the little village of Horton is a firm favourite with outdoor enthusiasts. Despite its remote location, access is easy thanks to the Settle–Carlisle train line. Everything centres on the excellent **Pen-y-ghent Cafe** (mains £2-6; ⊙breakfast & lunch), which acts as the village tourist office as well as filling walkers' fuel tanks with hearty grub and pint mugs of tea. It

THE SETTLE–CARLISLE LINE

The 72-mile Settle–Carlisle Line, built between 1869 and 1875, was one of the greatest engineering projects of the Victorian era and today offers one of England's most scenic railway journeys. Trains run between Leeds and Carlisle via Settle about eight times per day.

The first section of the journey from Leeds is via **Keighley**, where the Keighley & Worth Valley Railway branches off to **Haworth**. The train stops at **Skipton**, gateway to the Yorkshire Dales, and then **Settle** – where the drama really begins and the line forces its way through the landscape, clinging to valley sides or overcoming hills via tunnels, embankments and spectacular viaducts. Other stops include **Horton-in-Ribblesdale** and the remote outpost of **Ribblehead** – especially useful for walkers. The last halts are **Appleby** and **Langwathby**, just northwest of Penrith (a jumping-off point for the Lake District), before the train finally pulls into **Carlisle**.

The entire journey from Leeds to Carlisle takes just under three hours and costs £23/28 for a single/return. Various hop-on-hop-off passes for one or three days are also available. For more information, see www.settle-carlisle.co.uk.

also sells maps, guidebooks and walking gear. As well as the handful of B&Bs in the village, a good option is the **Golden Lion** (☎01729-860206; www.goldenlionhotel.co.uk; s/d from £40/60, bunkhouse per person £12), a lively pub with comfortable B&B bedrooms, a 40-bed bunkhouse, and a good menu of food and drink.

York

POP 181,100

Nowhere in northern England says 'medieval' quite like York, a city of extraordinary historical wealth that has lost little of its pre-industrial lustre. Its spider's web of narrow streets is enclosed by a magnificent circuit of 13th-century walls and the city's rich heritage is woven into virtually every brick and beam. Modern, tourist-oriented York – with its myriad museums, restaurants, cafes and traditional pubs – is a carefully maintained heir to that heritage.

Sights

York Minster CHURCH

(www.yorkminster.org; adult/child £8/free; ⏲minster 9am-5.30pm Mon-Sat Apr-Oct, 9.30am-5.30pm Mon-Sat Nov-Mar, noon-3.45pm Sun year-round) Not content with being Yorkshire's most important historic building, the awe-inspiring York Minster is also the largest medieval cathedral in all of northern Europe. If this is the only cathedral you visit in England, you'll still walk away satisfied. The first church on this spot was a wooden chapel built for the baptism of King Edwin of Northumbria on Easter Day 627; its location is marked in the crypt. It was replaced with a stone church, built on the site of a Roman basilica, parts of which can be seen in the **foundations**. The first Norman minster was built in the 11th century; again, you can see surviving fragments in the foundations and **crypt**. The present minster, built mainly between 1220 and 1480, manages to encompass all the major stages of Gothic architectural development. Highlights include the **west front**, octagonal **chapter house**, the **towers**, and the fabulous **stained-glass windows**.

Jorvik MUSEUM

(www.vikingjorvik.com; Coppergate; adult/child £8.95/6; ⏲10am-5pm Apr-Oct, to 4pm Nov-Mar) Interactive multimedia exhibits aimed at 'bringing history to life' often achieve just the opposite, but the much-hyped Jorvik – the most visited attraction in town after the minster – manages to pull it off with admirable aplomb. It's a smells-and-all reconstruction of the Viking settlement that was unearthed here during excavations in the late 1970s. The highlight for some is the **Lloyds Bank Turd** – a massive fossilised human stool that must be the only jobby in the world to have its own Wikipedia entry. You can cut queuing time by booking your tickets online and choosing the time you want to visit – it only costs £1 extra.

FREE **City Walls** CITY WALLS

(⏲8am-dusk) If the weather's good, don't miss the chance to walk the ramparts of the City Walls, to get a whole new perspective on the city. The full circuit is 4.5 miles (allow 1½ to two hours); if you're pushed for time, the short stretch from Bootham Bar to Monk Bar is worth doing for the views of the minster.

FREE **National Railway Museum** MUSEUM
(www.nrm.org.uk; Leeman Rd; ⏲10am-6pm) Many railway museums are the sole preserve of lone men in anoraks getting high on the smell of coal and nostalgia. But this place is different. York's National Railway Museum – the biggest in the world, with more than 100 locomotives – is so well presented and full of fascinating stuff that it's interesting even to folk whose eyes don't mist over at the thought of a 4-6-2 A1 Pacific class chuffing into a tunnel.

Yorkshire Museum MUSEUM
(www.yorkshiremuseum.org.uk; Museum St; adult/child £7/free; ⏲10am-5pm) Most of York's Roman archaeology is hidden beneath the medieval city, so the displays in the Yorkshire Museum are invaluable. There are excellent exhibits on Viking and medieval York too, including priceless artefacts such as the 8th-century Coppergate helmet, a 9th-century Anglian sword decorated with silver, and the 15th-century gold and sapphire Middleham Jewel pendant.

Shambles MEDIEVAL STREET
(www.yorkshambles.com) The cobbled lane known as the Shambles, lined with 15th-century Tudor buildings that overhang so much they seem to meet above your head, is the most visited street in Europe. It's quaint and picturesque certainly, and hints at what a medieval street may have looked like, but it's undeniably busy in summer.

York Castle Museum MUSEUM
(www.yorkcastlemuseum.org.uk; Tower St; adult/child £8/free; ⏲9.30am-5pm) This excellent museum contains displays of everyday life through the centuries, with reconstructed domestic interiors, a Victorian street and a less-than-homely prison cell where you can try out the condemned man's bed – in this case the highwayman Dick Turpin.

Clifford's Tower CASTLE
(EH; Tower St; adult/child £3.50/1.80; ⏲10am-6pm Apr-Sep, to 5pm Oct, to 4pm Nov-Mar) There's precious little left of York Castle except for this evocative stone tower. There's not much to see inside but the views over the city are excellent.

Tours

There's a bewildering range of tours on offer, including a host of ever more competitive night-time ghost tours – York is reputed to be England's most haunted city. For starters, check the tourist office suggestions for walking itineraries at www.visityork.org/explore.

Ghost Hunt of York WALKING
(www.ghosthunt.co.uk; adult/child £5/3; ⏲tours 7.30pm) Award-winning and highly entertaining 75-minute tour laced with authentic ghost stories; ideal for kids. Begins at the Shambles; no need to book.

Yorkwalk WALKING
(www.yorkwalk.co.uk; adult/child £5.50/3.50; ⏲tours 10.30am & 2.15pm) A series of two-hour themed walks on an ever-growing list of themes, such as Roman York, women in York, and the inevitable coffin and plague tour. Begins at Museum Gardens Gate; no need to book.

LOCAL KNOWLEDGE

ANDY DEXTROUS: GHOST TOUR GUIDE, YORK

Things I love about York include its outstanding architecture, the maze of 'snickleways' (narrow alleys), the array of small independent shops, the street entertainment and festivals, and central, green spaces like **Museum Gardens**, next to the Yorkshire Museum. All year-round the streets are full of appreciative visitors from all over the world enjoying the city, relaxing and adding to the atmosphere.

York's Spookiest Spots

Haunted pubs like the **Old White Swan**. Plus the **Antiques Centre** on Stonegate. In the streets around the Minster, you're always within a breath of a ghost tale.

Best of York

For beer and atmosphere, the **Blue Bell**. For vegie and vegan food and a place that welcomes children, **El Piano**. And for sheer ambience, **Gray's Court**.

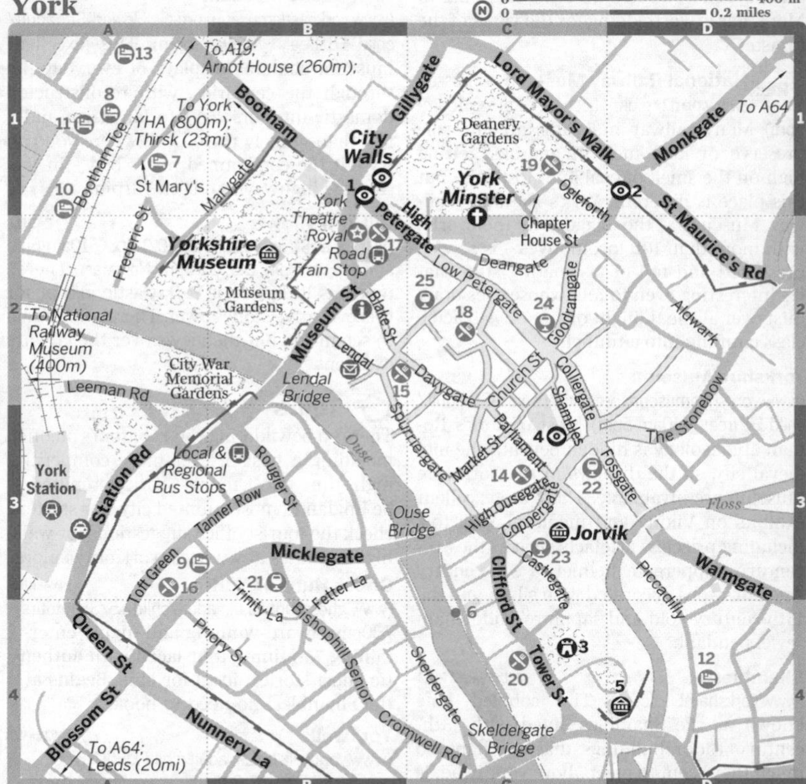

YorkBoat BOAT

(www.yorkboat.co.uk; King's Staith; adult/child £7.50/3.50) One-hour river cruises depart from King's Staith at 10.30am, noon, 1.30pm and 3pm (and Lendal Bridge 10 minutes later), February to November.

Original Ghost Walk of York WALKING

(www.theoriginalghostwalkofyork.co.uk; adult/child £4.50/3; ⏲tours 8pm) Ghoulish history from a well-established group. Departs from the King's Arms pub by Ouse Bridge.

York Citysightseeing BUS

(www.city-sightseeing.com; day tickets adult/child £10/4; ⏲9am-5pm) Hop-on hop-off route with 16 stops, calling at all the main sights; buses leave every 10 minutes from Exhibition Sq near York Minster.

FREE **Association of Voluntary Guides** WALKING

(www.visityork.org; ⏲tours 10.15am, also 2.15pm Apr-Sep & 6.45pm Jun-Aug) Free two-hour walking tours of the city starting from Exhibition Sq in front of York City Art Gallery.

Sleeping

There are plenty of decent B&Bs on the streets north and south of Bootham. South-west of the town centre, there are B&Bs clustered around Scarcroft Rd, Southlands Rd and Bishopthorpe Rd. It's also worth looking at serviced apartments if you're planning to stay two or three nights. **City Lets** (☎01904-652729; www.cityletsyork.co.uk) offers a good selection of places from around £90 a night for a two-person apartment – we particularly like the modern flats in the peaceful courtyard at Talbot Court on Low Petergate.

Abbeyfields B&B ££

(☎01904-636471; www.abbeyfields.co.uk; 19 Bootham Tce; s/d from £49/78; 📶) We rate this place for its warm welcome, thoughtfully arranged bedrooms and excellent breakfasts.

York

Top Sights

	City Walls	B1
	Jorvik	C3
	York Minster	C1
	Yorkshire Museum	B2

Sights

1	City Wall Access Steps	B1
2	City Wall Access Steps	D1
3	Clifford's Tower	C4
4	Shambles	C3
5	York Castle Museum	D4

Activities, Courses & Tours

6	YorkBoat	C4

Sleeping

7	23 St Mary's	A1
8	Abbeyfields	A1
9	Ace Hotel	A3
10	Briar Lea Guest House	A1
11	Elliotts B&B	A1
12	Hotel 53	D4
13	St Raphael	A1

Eating

14	Ate O'Clock	C3
15	Betty's	B2
16	Blake Head Vegetarian Cafe	A3
17	Café Concerto	B2
18	El Piano	C2
19	Gray's Court	C1
20	Olive Tree	C4

Drinking

21	Ackhorne	B3
22	Blue Bell	C3
23	Little John	C3
24	Old White Swan	C2
25	Ye Olde Starre	C2

Elliotts B&B B&B ££
(01904-623333; www.elliottshotel.co.uk; 2 Sycamore Pl; s/d from £55/80; P@) A beautifully converted 'gentleman's residence' towards the boutique end of the market with elegant rooms and hi-tech touches. Excellent location, both quiet and central.

Arnot House B&B ££
(01904-641966; www.arnothouseyork.co.uk; 17 Grosvenor Tce; r £70-85; P) With three beautifully decorated rooms (provided you're a fan of Victorian floral patterns) and an authentically old-fashioned look, this place appeals to a more mature clientele; children are not allowed.

23 St Mary's B&B ££
(01904-622738; www.23stmarys.co.uk; 23 St Mary's; s/d £55/90; P@) A smart and stately townhouse with nine rooms, some with hand-painted furniture, others decorated with antiques and polished mahogany.

York YHA HOSTEL £
(0845 371 9051; www.yha.org.uk; 42 Water End, Clifton; dm £18-20; P@) Originally the Rowntree (Quaker confectioners) mansion, now a spacious hostel, with mostly four-bed dorms, about a mile northwest of the city centre.

Ace Hotel HOSTEL £
(01904-627720; www.acehotelyork.co.uk; 88-90 Micklegate; dm/tw from £20/60; @) Once home to the High Sheriff of Yorkshire, this is a large and well-equipped hostel, popular with school groups and stag parties – don't come here for peace and quiet!

Briar Lea Guest House B&B ££
(01904-635061; www.briarlea.co.uk; 8 Longfield Tce; s/d from £37/62;) Clean, simple rooms and a friendly welcome in a central location.

St Raphael B&B ££
(01904-645028; www.straphaelguesthouse.co.uk; 44 Queen Annes Rd; s/d from £65/76;) Historic house with that half-timbered look, great central location and home-baked bread at breakfast.

Hotel 53 HOTEL ££
(01904-559000; www.hotel53.com; 53 Piccadilly; r from £86; P) Modern and minimalist, but very central with secure parking just across the street.

YORKSHIRE PASS

If you plan on visiting a lot of sights, you can save yourself some money by using a **Yorkshire Pass** (www.yorkshirepass.com; 1/2/3/6 days adult £28/38/44/68, child £18/22/26/44). It grants you free access to more than 70 pay-to-visit sights in Yorkshire, including all the major attractions in York. Available at York tourist office, or you can buy online.

Eating

York has a very wide range of eating options to suit all budgets.

Gray's Court CAFE ££
(grayscourtyork.com; Chapter House St; mains £6-7; lunch) An unexpected find in the very heart of York, this 16th-century house has a country atmosphere, gourmet coffee and cake, a sunny garden and an oak-panelled Jacobean gallery (extra points if you grab the alcove table above the main door).

Ate O'Clock BISTRO ££
(01904-644080; www.ateoclock.co.uk; 13a High Ousegate; mains £14-17; lunch & dinner Tue-Sat) A tempting menu has made this place hugely popular with locals. Three-course dinner for £16.75 from 6pm to 7.55pm Tuesday to Thursday.

Blake Head Vegetarian Cafe VEGETARIAN £
(104 Micklegate; mains £5-7; lunch;) A bright and airy space at the back of a bookshop, this cafe is filled with modern oak furniture and funky art.

Olive Tree MEDITERRANEAN ££
(01904-624433; www.theolivetreeyork.co.uk; 10 Tower St; mains £9-18; lunch & dinner) Local produce gets a Mediterranean makeover at this bright and breezy bistro. The lunchtime and early-evening menu offers two courses for £13.

Café Concerto CAFE, BISTRO ££
(01904-610478; www.cafeconcerto.biz; 21 High Petergate; snacks £3-8, mains £10-17; breakfast, lunch & dinner) Walls papered with sheet music and chilled jazz on the stereo set the bohemian tone in this comforting coffee shop by day, sophisticated bistro in the evening.

Betty's TEA HOUSE ££
(www.bettys.co.uk; St Helen's Sq; mains £6-11, afternoon tea £16; breakfast, lunch & dinner) Afternoon tea, old-school style, with white-aproned waitresses, linen tablecloths and a teapot collection ranged along the walls.

El Piano VEGAN £
(www.elpiano.com; 15 Grape Lane; mains £4-7; lunch & dinner Mon-Sat, lunch Sun;) With a 100% vegan, nut-free and gluten-free menu, this Hispanic-style spot has a lovely cafe downstairs and three themed rooms upstairs.

Drinking

With only a couple of exceptions, the best drinking holes in town are the older, traditional pubs.

TOP CHOICE **Blue Bell** PUB
(53 Fossgate) This is what a real English pub looks like – a tiny, wood-panelled room with a smouldering fireplace, decor (and beer and smoke stains) dating from c 1798, a pile of ancient board games in the corner, friendly and efficient bar staff, and top-notch ale.

Ye Olde Starre PUB
(40 Stonegate) Licensed since 1644, this is York's oldest pub – a warren of small rooms and a small beer garden, with half a dozen real ales on tap. It was used as a morgue by the Roundheads during the Civil War, but the atmosphere's improved a lot since then.

Ackhorne PUB
(9 St Martin's Lane) Tucked away off beery Micklegate, this locals' inn is as comfortable as slippers; some of the old guys here look like they've merged with the furniture. There's a pleasant beer garden at the back.

Little John PUB, CLUB
(5 Castlegate) This historic pub – the third oldest in York – is the city's top gay venue, with regular club nights and other events. It's also haunted by Dick Turpin. We're not sure what's scarier though – the ghost story, or the Thursday night karaoke session.

Old White Swan PUB
(80 Goodramgate) Popular and atmospheric old pub with small beer garden and a good range of guest real ales. And it's haunted...

Information

York Visitor Centre (01904-550099; www.visityork.org; 1 Museum St; 9am-6pm Mon-Sat, 10am-5pm Sun Apr-Sep, shorter hours Oct-Mar)

Getting There & Away

BUS There are National Express coaches to/from London (£26, 5½ hours, four daily), Birmingham (£26, 3¼ hours, one daily) and Newcastle (£15, 2¾ hours, four daily).

TRAIN York is a major railway hub with frequent direct services to/from Birmingham (£45, 2¼ hours), Newcastle (£15, one hour), Leeds (£11, 30 minutes), London's King's Cross (£80, two hours), and Manchester (£15, 1½ hours).

Around York

CASTLE HOWARD

Stately homes may be two a penny in England, but you'll have to try hard to find one as breathtakingly stately as **Castle Howard** (www.castlehoward.co.uk; adult/child house & grounds £12.50/7.50, grounds only £8.50/6; ⏲house 11am-4.30pm, grounds 10am-6.30pm Mar-Oct & 1st 3 weeks Dec), a work of theatrical grandeur and audacity, and one of the world's most beautiful buildings. It's instantly recognisable from its starring role in the 1980s TV series *Brideshead Revisited* and more recently in the 2008 film of the same name (both based on Evelyn Waugh's 1945 novel of nostalgia for the English aristocracy).

If you can, try to visit on a weekday, when it's easier to find the space to appreciate this hedonistic combination of art, architecture, landscaping and natural beauty. Inside, the great house is full of treasures – the breathtaking **Great Hall** with its soaring Corinthian pilasters, Pre-Raphaelite **stained glass** in the chapel, and corridors lined with classical antiquities. Outside, as you wander the grounds (populated by peacocks, naturally), views reveal Vanbrugh's playful **Temple of the Four Winds** and Hawksmoor's stately **mausoleum**, or wider vistas over the surrounding hills.

Castle Howard is 15 miles northeast of York. There are several organised tours from York – check with the tourist office. By public transport, Yorkshire Coastliner bus 840 (40 minutes from York, one daily) links Leeds, York, Castle Howard and Whitby.

Helmsley

POP 1620

Helmsley is a classic North Yorkshire market town, a handsome place full of old houses, historic coaching inns and – inevitably – a cobbled market square (market day Friday), all basking under the watchful gaze of a sturdy Norman castle.

Sights & Activities

The impressive ruin of 12th-century **Helmsley Castle** (EH; adult/child £4.70/2.40; ⏲10am-6pm Apr-Sep, to 5pm Mar & Oct, to 4pm Thu-Mon Nov-Feb) is defended by a striking series of deep ditches and banks to which later rulers added the thick stone walls and defensive towers – only one tooth-shaped tower survives today.

Nextdoor is **Helmsley Walled Garden** (www.helmsleywalledgarden.org.uk; adult/child £4/free; ⏲10.30am-5pm Apr-Oct, closed Sat & Sun Nov-Mar). If you're into horticulture with a historical twist, this is Eden.

South of town stretches the superb landscape of Duncombe Park, with the stately home of **Duncombe Park House** (www.duncombepark.com; adult/child house & gardens £8.25/3.75, gardens only £5/3; ⏲11am-5.30pm Sun-Thu Easter-Oct) at its heart. The house is 1.5 miles south of town, an easy walk through the park. You could easily spend a day here, especially if you take in one of the many **walks** set out in the parkland. Cream of the crop is the 3.5-mile route to **Rievaulx Abbey** – the tourist office can provide route leaflets and advice on buses if you don't want to walk both ways.

Sleeping & Eating

A clutch of old coaching inns on Market Pl offer B&B, decent grub and a pint of real ale. The **Feathers Hotel** (☎01439-770275; www.feathershotelhelmsley.co.uk; Market Pl; s/d from £50/90) has four-poster beds in some rooms and historical trimmings throughout. In contrast, **Helmsley YHA** (☎0845 371 9638; www.yha.org.uk; Carlton Lane; dm £18; P 👪) looks like an ordinary suburban home, but it does the job for budget travellers. For eating, as well as the pubs, Helmsley boasts a couple of quality eateries and delis on the main square.

Information

Tourist office (☎01439-770173; ⏲9.30am-5.30pm Mar-Oct, 10am-4pm Fri-Sun Nov-Feb)

Getting There & Away

Bus 31X runs between York and Helmsley (1¼ hours, two daily Monday to Saturday).

Around Helmsley

RIEVAULX

In the secluded valley, amid fields and woods loud with birdsong, stand the magnificent ruins of **Rievaulx Abbey** (EH; adult/child £5.30/2.70; ⏲10am-6pm Apr-Sep, to 5pm Thu-Mon Oct, to 4pm Thu-Mon Nov-Mar). This idyllic spot was chosen by Cistercian monks in 1132 as a base for missionary activity in northern Britain. St Aelred, the third abbot, famously described the abbey's setting as 'everywhere peace, everywhere serenity, and a marvellous freedom from the tumult of the world'. But the monks of Rievaulx (ree-voe) were far from unworldly, and soon created a network of commercial interests ranging from sheep farms to lead mines. And with the money, they built this amazing structure.

Near the abbey is an attraction from a different era: **Rievaulx Terrace & Temples** (NT; adult/child £5.25/2.90; ⌚11am-5pm Mar-Oct). Landscape-gardening fashion favoured a Gothic look in the 1750s, and many aristocrats had mock ruins built in their parks. The Duncombe family went one better, as their lands contained a real medieval ruin – Rievaulx Abbey. So the terrace was built so that lords and ladies could stroll effortlessly in the 'wilderness' and admire the abbey in the valley below. Today we can do the same, with views over Ryedale and the Hambleton Hills forming a perfect backdrop.

Rievaulx is about 3 miles west of Helmsley. Note that there's no direct access between the abbey and the terrace – their entrance gates are about a mile apart, though easily reached along a lane – steeply uphill if you're going from the abbey to the terrace.

Whitby

POP 13,600

Sitting comfortably between the sea and the hills of the North York Moors is the coastal town of Whitby. Split down the middle by the River Esk, this place is part commercial fishing port with a bustling quayside fishmarket, and part traditional seaside resort complete with sandy beach, amusement arcades and promenading holidaymakers slurping ice-cream cones in the sun. Whitby has a compelling history too; a highlight is the forbidding cliff-top abbey ruin. It was here that a young fellow called James Cook was apprenticed to a Whitby shipowner. Years later, HMS *Endeavour* was built in the harbour before setting sail to discover Australia.

WHITBY'S DARK SIDE

The famous story of *Dracula*, inspiration for a thousand lurid movies, was written by Bram Stoker while staying at a B&B in Whitby in 1897. Although most Hollywood versions of the tale concentrate on darkest Transylvania, much of the original book was set in Whitby and many sites can still be seen today. The tourist office sells an excellent *Dracula Trail* leaflet. In recent years these morbid associations have seen the rise of a series of hugely popular goth festivals.

Sights

Whitby Abbey RUINS
(EH; adult/child £5.80/2.90; ⌚10am-6pm Apr-Sep, to 4pm Thu-Mon Oct-Mar) There are ruined abbeys and there are picturesque ruined abbeys, and then there's Whitby Abbey, dominating the skyline above the East Cliff like a great Gothic tombstone silhouetted against the sky. Get here via the 199 steps of **Church Stairs**.

Captain Cook Memorial Museum MUSEUM
(www.cookmuseumwhitby.co.uk; Grape Lane; adult/child £4.50/3; ⌚9.45am-5pm Apr-Oct, 11am-3pm Mar) The former house of a shipowner, highlights include the attic where Cook lodged as a young apprentice, Cook's own maps and letters, etchings from the South Seas and a wonderful model of the *Endeavour* with all the crew and stores laid out for inspection.

Whitby Sands BEACH
Stretching west from the harbour mouth, this is the spot for donkey rides, ice cream and bucket-and-spade escapades. Atop the cliff, the **Captain Cook Monument** shows the great man looking out to sea, often with a seagull perched on his head. Nearby is the **Whalebone Arch**, recalling Whitby's days as a whaling port.

Sleeping

B&Bs are concentrated in West Cliff in the streets to the south and east of Royal Crescent; if a house here ain't offering B&B, chances are it's derelict.

TOP CHOICE **Marine Hotel** HOTEL £££
(☎01947-605022; www.the-marine-hotel.co.uk; 13 Marine Pde; r £150) Feeling more like mini suites than ordinary hotel accommodation, the four bedrooms at the Marine are quirky, stylish and comfortable – the sort of place that makes you want to stay in rather than go out. Ask for one of the two rooms that have a balcony – they have great views across the harbour.

Langley Hotel B&B ££
(☎01947-604250; www.langleyhotel.com; 16 Royal Cres; s/d from £70/100; P 📶) With a cream and crimson colour scheme, and a gilt four-poster bed in one room, this grand old guesthouse exudes a whiff of Victorian splendour. Go for room 1 or 2 to make the most of the panoramic views from West Cliff.

Whitby YHA HOSTEL £
(☎0845 371 9049; www.yha.org.uk; Church Lane; dm £18-22; P @ 📶) Having an unbeatable

position next to the abbey ruins, this hostel doesn't have to try too hard. And it doesn't.

Harbour Grange HOSTEL £
(☎01947-600817; www.whitbybackpackers.co.uk; Spital Bridge; dm £17) Overlooking the harbour and less than 10 minutes' walk from the train station, this tidy hostel is conveniently located but has an 11.30pm curfew.

Rosslyn House B&B ££
(☎01947-604086; www.guesthousewhitby.co.uk; 11 Abbey Tce; s/d £35/55) Bright and cheerful with a friendly welcome.

Bramblewick B&B ££
(☎01947-604504; www.bramblewickwhitby.com; 3 Havelock Pl; s/d £32/66; P 📶) Friendly owners, hearty breakfasts, and abbey views from the top-floor room.

Eating & Drinking

Green's SEAFOOD ££
(☎01947-600284; www.greensofwhitby.com; 13 Bridge St; bistro mains £10-19, restaurant 2-/3-course dinner £34/41; ⊙lunch & dinner) The classiest eatery in town is ideally situated to take its pick of the fish freshly landed at the harbour.

Moon & Sixpence BRASSERIE ££
(☎01947-604416; 5 Marine Pde; mains £10-18; ⊙lunch & dinner) This brand-new brasserie and cocktail bar has a prime position, with views across the harbour to the abbey ruins.

Magpie Cafe SEAFOOD ££
(www.magpiecafe.co.uk; 14 Pier Rd; mains £9-18; ⊙lunch & dinner) Flaunts its reputation for serving the 'world's best fish and chips'; damn fine they are too, but the world and his dog knows about it, and summertime queues can stretch along the street.

Java Cafe-Bar CAFE £
(2 Flowergate; mains £4-6; ⊙breakfast & lunch; 📶) A cool little diner with stainless-steel counters, retro decor, music videos on the flat screen and a healthy menu.

Humble Pie'n'Mash PIES £
(www.humblepienmash.com; 163 Church St; mains £5; ⊙lunch & dinner Mon-Sat, lunch Sun) Superb homemade pies with fillings ranging from lamb, leek and rosemary to roast veg and goat's cheese, served in a cosy cottage.

Trenchers FISH AND CHIPS ££
(www.trenchersrestaurant.co.uk; New Quay Rd; mains £10-15; ⊙lunch & dinner) Top-notch fish and chips minus the 'world's best' tagline – your best bet if you want to avoid the queues at the Magpie.

Station Inn PUB
(New Quay Rd) Best place in town for atmosphere and real ale with an impressive range of cask-conditioned beers.

WORTH A TRIP

ROBIN HOOD'S BAY

For a cracking day out, take a bus to the nearby fishing village of Robin Hood's Bay, explore the winding streets, have lunch in an old pub or delightful deli-cafe, then hike the 6-mile cliff-top footpath back to Whitby (allow three hours).

Information

Tourist office (☎01947-602674; www.visitwhitby.com; Langborne Rd; ⊙10am-6pm May-Sep, to 4.30pm Oct-Apr)

Getting There & Away

BUS The **Yorkshire Coastliner** (www.coastliner.co.uk) service runs between Leeds to Whitby.

TRAIN Coming from the north, you can get to Whitby by train along the **Esk Valley Railway** from Middlesbrough (£4.70, 1½ hours, four per day), with connections from Durham and Newcastle. From the south, it's easier to get a train from York to Scarborough, then a bus from Scarborough to Whitby.

Durham

POP 42,940

The grand city of Durham is crowned by a magnificent castle and Britain's finest Norman cathedral, together a Unesco World Heritage site. Surrounding them both is a maze of cobbled streets usually full of upper-crust students attending Durham's prestigious university. It's a place rich in history, and (thanks to those students) also packed with busy pubs and bars. We recommend that you either visit as a day trip from Newcastle or as an overnight stop on your way between north and south.

Durham Cathedral CHURCH
(www.durhamcathedral.co.uk; donation requested; ⊙7.30am-6pm, to 5.30pm Sun) Durham's most famous building has earned superlative

praise for centuries. This is, quite simply, the definitive structure of the Anglo-Norman Romanesque style, and one of the world's greatest places of worship. There are **guided tours** (adult/child £4/free; ⌚10.30am, 11am & 2pm Mon & Sat) and **Evensong** (⌚5.15pm Mon-Sat, 3.30pm Sun).

Durham Castle CASTLE
(www.dur.ac.uk; adult/concession £5/3.50; ⌚tours 2pm, 3pm & 4pm term time, 10am, 11am & noon during university vacations) Built in 1072, Durham Castle is now part of the university. Highlights of the 45-minute tour include the groaning 17th-century **Black Staircase**, the 16th-century **chapel** and the beautifully preserved **Norman chapel**.

Information

Tourist office (☎0191-384 3720; www.thisisdurham.com; 2 Millennium Pl; ⌚9.30am-5.30pm Mon-Sat, 10am-4pm Sun)

Getting There & Away

Bus

London National Express; £29.80, 6½ hours, four daily

Newcastle buses 21, 44, X41, X2, one hour to 1¾ hours, several per hour

Train

Edinburgh £50.30, two hours, hourly

London £103.60, three hours, hourly

Newcastle £5.20, 15 minutes, five hourly

York £21.90, one hour, four hourly

Newcastle-upon-Tyne

POP 189,863

Once synonymous with postindustrial decline, today's Newcastle is reborn and brimming with confidence. All of a sudden, this unfailingly friendly city, with its Geordie accent thicker than molasses, has kick-started a brand-new arts and entertainment scene, while riotous nightlife remains an established tradition.

Sights

Quayside NEIGHBOURHOOD
The Quayside, on the northern bank of the River Tyne, is ideal for a pleasant walk through the very heart of the city. You'll see the famous Tyne bridges – and the area really comes to life at night, with bars, clubs and restaurants full to bursting.

BRIDGING THE TYNE

The classic view of Newcastle is along the River Tyne to the city's iconic cluster of bridges. Most famous is the **Tyne Bridge**; its resemblance to Australia's Sydney Harbour Bridge is no coincidence as both were built by the same company, at around the same time. The quaint little **Swing Bridge** pivots in the middle to let ships through. The **High Level Bridge**, designed by Robert Stephenson, was the world's first combined road and railway bridge (1849). The most recent addition is the multiple-award-winning **Millennium Bridge** (2002), which lifts like an eyelid to let ships pass.

FREE **BALTIC – Centre for Contemporary Art** ART MUSEUM
(www.balticmill.com; Gateshead Quays; ⌚10am-6pm Wed-Mon, from 10.30am Tue) South of the Tyne is the entirely separate city of Gateshead (the local authorities bill the pair as 'NewcastleGateshead'), home to BALTIC, once a huge grain store, now a huge art gallery to rival London's Tate Modern.

Sleeping

The majority of city-centre options cater to the party people and business folk that make up the majority of Newcastle's overnight guests. Most other accommodation is in the handsome northern suburb of Jesmond, where the forces of gentrification and student power fight it out for territory. The main drag, Osborne Rd, is lined with all kinds of sleeping choices as well as bars and restaurants – making it a strong rival with the city centre for the late-night party scene.

City Centre

Backpackers Newcastle HOSTEL £
(☎0191 340 7334; www.backpackersnewcastle.com; 262 Westgate Rd; dm from £17.95; wi-fi) This well-run budget hostel has just 26 beds and a backpacker vibe. Bike storage, a kitchen and large games room make this a great kip on the Tyne.

Greystreethotel HOTEL ££
(☎0191 230 6777; www.greystreethotel.com; 2-12 Grey St; d from £109; P) The Grey Street is a bit of designer class along the classiest street in town. The rooms are gorgeous but a tad

cluttered with flat-screen TVs, big beds and modern furnishings.

Jesmond

Avenue B&B ££
(☎0191 281 1396; 2 Manor House Rd; s/d £39.50/60) Buried in a sleepy residential area but just a couple of blocks from the action on Osborne Rd, this well-run B&B is big on floral flounce and faux country style.

Newcastle YHA HOSTEL £
(☎0845 371 9335; www.yha.org.uk; 107 Jesmond Rd; dm from £18) This rambling place has small dorms but it's a good budget option.

Drinking

It's no secret that Geordies like a good night out, epitomised by the cheap and colourful cocktails of the Bigg Market. The Ouseburn area attracts a mellower crowd; the western end of Neville St has a decent mix of great bars and is home to the best of the gay scene.

Crown Posada PUB
(31 The Side) An unspoilt pub in the city centre and a favourite with more seasoned drinkers, be they the after-work or instead-of-work crowd.

Cumberland Arms PUB
(off Byker Bank, Ouseburn) Sitting above the Ouseburn, this 19th-century pub has a sensational selection of ales as well as a range of Northumberland meads. There's a terrace outside, and a bring-one/borrow-one library.

Information

Tourist offices (www.visitnewcastlegateshead.com) Main branch (☎0191-277 8000; Central Arcade, Market St; ⊙9.30am-5.30pm Mon-Sat); Guildhall (☎0191-277 8000; Newcastle Quayside; ⊙10am-5pm Mon-Fri, 9am-5pm Sat, 9am-4pm Sun); Sage Gateshead (☎0191-478 4222; Gateshead Quays; ⊙10am-5pm)

Getting There & Away

Bus

Local and regional buses leave from Haymarket or Eldon Sq bus stations. National Express services:

Edinburgh £17.50, three hours, three daily

London £10 to £27, seven hours, nine daily

Manchester £19.50, five hours, five daily

Train

Newcastle is on the main rail line between London and Edinburgh, and is the starting point of the scenic Tyne Valley Line west to Carlisle.

Carlisle £14.50, 1½ hours, hourly

Edinburgh £32, 1½ hours, half-hourly

London King's Cross £103.60, three hours, half-hourly

York £23.50, one hour, every 20 minutes

Hadrian's Wall

Built in AD 122 to mark the edge of the Roman Empire, this 73-mile coast-to-coast barrier across England remains a major feature on the landscape nearly 2000 years later. Although some parts of the wall have virtually disappeared, other stretches are remarkably well preserved and utterly spectacular. Not surprisingly, the whole wall – and several associated forts and other Roman remains – are part of a Unesco World Heritage site.

The best area to visit is just north of the modern towns of **Hexham** and **Brampton**. Good gateways include the tiny twin settlements of **Once Brewed** and **Twice Brewed**, and the small towns of **Haltwhistle** and **Greenhead**, all with accommodation (ranging from YHA hostels to B&Bs) and TICs with maps and leaflets about the wall and surrounding area. The best site for information is www.hadrians-wall.org.

Sights

As well as the wall itself you can also marvel at the Roman forts and castles along its length.

Chesters ROMAN FORT
(EH; ☎01434-681379; Chollerford; adult/child £4.80/2.40; ⊙10am-6pm Apr-Sep) Situated near

WORTH A TRIP

ANGEL OF THE NORTH

This extraordinary, gigantic, apocalyptic statue of a human frame with wings looms over the main A1 highway about 5 miles south of Newcastle. At 20m high, 200 tonnes and with a wingspan wider than a Boeing 767, it's Antony Gormley's best-known sculpture and – thanks to all those passing cars – the most viewed piece of public art in the country (though Mark Wallinger's *White Horse* in Kent may pinch the title over the next decade). You can walk right up to the base of the statue, and feel absolutely dwarfed. Buses 21 and 22 from Eldon Sq will take you there.

HADRIAN'S HISTORY

Named in honour of the emperor who ordered it built, Hadrian's Wall is one of the Roman Empire's greatest engineering projects, a spectacular testament to ambition and the practical Roman mind. Even today, almost 2000 years after the first stone was laid, the sections that are still standing remain an awe-inspiring sight, proof that when the Romans wanted something done, they just knuckled down and did it.

When completed, the mammoth structure ran from the Solway Firth (west of Carlisle) to the mouth of the Tyne (east of Newcastle). Every Roman mile (about 1500m, slightly shorter than a modern mile) there was a gateway guarded by a small fort (milecastle) and between each milecastle were two observation turrets. Milecastles are numbered right across the country, starting with Milecastle 0 in the appropriately named Newcastle suburb of Wallsend, and ending with Milecastle 80 at Bowness-on-Solway.

A series of forts was developed as bases some distance south (and may predate the wall), and 16 lie astride it. The prime remaining forts on the wall are Cilurnum (Chesters), Vercovicium (Housesteads) and Banna (Birdoswald). The best forts behind the wall are Corstopitum at Corbridge, and Vindolanda north of Bardon Mill.

Chollerford, this well-preserved fortification includes an impressive **bathhouse**, while its **museum** displays a fascinating array of Roman sculptures and drawings unearthed in the area.

Vindolanda Roman Fort & Museum ROMAN FORT
(www.vindolanda.com; adult/child £5.90/3.50, with Roman Army Museum £9/5; ⏲10am-6pm Apr-Sep, to 5pm Feb, Mar & Oct) About 1.5 miles north of Bardon Mill, and 1 mile from Once Brewed, this extensive site offers a fascinating glimpse into the daily life of a Roman garrison town.

Housesteads Roman Fort & Museum ROMAN FORT
(EH; adult/child £4.80/2.40; ⏲10am-6pm Apr-Sep) This is the best-preserved Roman fort in the whole country, and the area's most dramatic and popular ruin. The carefully preserved foundations include a public latrine, and a gateway overlooking the wild Northumbrian countryside, little changed since the legionaries pulled out in AD 410. It's 2.5 miles north of Bardon Mill, or a spectacular walk (3 miles) along the wall itself from Once Brewed.

Activities

Walkers and cyclists can follow the entire length of the wall – or just bits of it – on the **Hadrian's Wall Path** (www.nationaltrail.co.uk/hadrianswall) or **Hadrian's Wall Cycleway** (www.cycle-routes.org/hadrianscycleway).

Getting There & Away

Reaching Hadrian's Wall is straightforward. The Newcastle–Carlisle train line runs parallel to the wall a mile or two to the south, with stations at Hexham, Haydon Bridge, Bardon Mill, Haltwhistle and Brampton. There are hourly buses between Carlisle and Newcastle, via most of the same towns. From June to September the hail-and-ride Hadrian's Wall Bus (number AD 122 – geddit?) shuttles between all the major sites, towns and villages along the way.

NORTHWEST ENGLAND

A place of two halves, Northwest England offers two very contrasting experiences: culture, music and big nights out in the world-famous cities of Manchester and Liverpool; peace, quiet, fresh air and high peaks in the mountainous Lake District. So pack your dancing shoes and your hiking boots, and come on over.

Manchester

POP 394,270

'Manchester has everything but a beach.' Former Stone Roses' frontman Ian Brown's description of his native city has become the city's unofficial motto – and even accounting for a bit of northern bluster, Brown isn't far wrong. This is the uncrowned capital of the north – as well as the birthplace of capitalism and the crucible of the Industrial Revolution.

Manchester was raised on lofty ambition, and its world-class museums and heavyweight art galleries are a fitting legacy, but what makes this city truly special are its distractions of pure pleasure: this is the best place to dine, drink and dance outside London – and at a much more reasonable price.

Sights

CITY CENTRE

FREE **Museum of Science & Industry** MUSEUM
(MOSI; ☎0161-832 1830; www.msim.org.uk; Liverpool Rd; charges vary for special exhibitions; ⏲10am-5pm) If there's anything you want to know about the Industrial (and post-Industrial) Revolution, and Manchester's key role in it, you'll find the answers here.

FREE **People's History Museum** MUSEUM
(☎0161-839 6061; www.phm.org.uk; Left Bank, Bridge St) One of the city's best museums, devoted to British social history and the labour movement. It's compelling stuff, and a marvellous example of a museum's relevance to our everyday lives.

National Football Museum MUSEUM
(☎0161-907 9099; www.nationalfootballmuseum.com; Urbis, Cathedral Gardens, Corporation St) It's the world's most popular game and Manchester is home to the world's most popular team, so when this football museum needed a new home, it came to the stunning glass triangle that is Urbis. It's a major stop on any football fan's itinerary.

FREE **Manchester Art Gallery** ART MUSEUM
(☎0161-235 8888; www.manchestergalleries.org; Mosley St; ⏲10am-5pm Tue-Sun) There's a superb collection of British art and a hefty number of European masters on display here, including 37 Turner watercolours and the country's best Pre-Raphaelite collection, as well as works by Lucien Freud, Francis Bacon, Stanley Spencer and David Hockney.

SALFORD QUAYS

It's a cinch to get here from the city centre via Metrolink (£2). For the Imperial War Museum North and the Lowry, look for the Harbour City stop; get off at Old Trafford for the eponymous stadium.

WANT MORE?

For in-depth information, reviews and recommendations at your fingertips, head to the Apple App Store to purchase Lonely Planet's *Manchester City Guide* iPhone app.

GAY & LESBIAN MANCHESTER

The city's gay scene is unrivalled outside London, and caters to every taste. Its healthy heart beats loudest in the Gay Village, centred on **Canal St**. Here you'll find bars, clubs, restaurants and – crucially – karaoke joints that cater almost exclusively to the pink pound. The country's biggest gay and lesbian arts festival, **Queer Up North** (☎0161-833 2288; www.queerupnorth.com), takes place in spring every two years. **Manchester Pride** (☎0161-236 7474; www.manchesterpride.com) is a 10-day festival in the middle of August each year and attracts over 500,000 people.

FREE **Imperial War Museum North** MUSEUM
(☎0161-836 4000; www.iwm.org.uk/north; Trafford Wharf Rd; ⏲10am-6pm Mar-Oct, to 5pm Nov-Feb) War museums generally appeal to those with a fascination for military hardware but this place takes a radically different approach: war is hell, it tells us, but it's a hell we revisit with tragic regularity.

FREE **Lowry** ARTS CENTRE
(☎0161-876 2020; www.thelowry.com; Pier 8, Salford Quays; ⏲11am-8pm Tue-Fri, 10am-8pm Sat, 11am-6pm Sun & Mon) Looking more like a steel ship than an arts centre, the Lowry attracts more than a million visitors a year, for everything from exhibitions and performances to bars, restaurants and shops. The complex is home to more than 300 paintings and drawings by northern England's favourite artist, LS Lowry (1887–1976), who was born in nearby Stretford.

Old Trafford STADIUM
(☎0870 442 1994; www.manutd.com; Sir Matt Busby Way; ⏲9.30am-5pm) Home of the world's most famous club, the Old Trafford stadium is both a theatre and a temple for its millions of fans worldwide, many of whom come on a pilgrimage to pay tribute to the minor deities that others may know only as highly paid footballers. The **tour** (adult/child £12.50/8.50; ⏲every 10min 9.40am-4.30pm except match days) includes a seat in the stands, a peek at the players' lounge and a walk down the tunnel to the pitchside dugout. The **museum** (adult/child £9/7; ⏲9.30am-5pm) has a comprehensive history of the club.

Sleeping

CITY CENTRE

TOP CHOICE **Velvet Hotel** BOUTIQUE HOTEL ££
(0161-236 9003; www.velvetmanchester.com; 2 Canal St; r from £99;) Beautiful bespoke rooms make this a real contender for best in the city. Despite the location and tantalising decor, it's as popular with straight visitors as it is with the same-sex crowd.

Hatters HOSTEL £
(0161-236 9500; www.hattersgroup.com; 50 Newton St; dm/s/d/tr from £14.50/27.50/50/67.50;) The old-style lift and porcelain sinks are the only leftovers of this former milliner's factory, now one of the best hostels in town, with a location to match.

Radisson Edwardian HOTEL ££
(0161-835 9929; www.radissonedwardian.com/manchester; Peter St; r from £90;) The Free Trade Hall saw it all, from Emmeline Pankhurst's suffragette campaign to the Sex Pistols' legendary 1976 gig. Today, those rabble-rousing noisemakers wouldn't be allowed to set foot in the door of what is now a sumptuous five-star hotel.

Manchester YHA HOSTEL £
(0845 371 9647; www.yha.org.uk; Potato Wharf; dm incl breakfast from £16;) This purpose-built canalside hostel in the Castlefield area is one of the best in the country, with four- and six-bed dorms and a host of good facilities.

Palace Hotel BOUTIQUE HOTEL ££
(0161-288 1111; www.principal-hotels.com; Oxford St; s/d from £85/105;) An elegant refurbishment of one of Manchester's most magnificent Victorian palaces resulted in a special boutique hotel.

Park Inn Hotel HOTEL ££
(0161-832 6565; www.sasparkinn.com; 4 Cheetham Hill Rd; r from £99;) Spacious, modern rooms (with floor-to-ceiling windows) in a huge hotel overlooking the MEN Arena; perfect if you're going to a gig.

Midland HOTEL ££
(0161-236 3333; www.themidland.co.uk; Peter St; r from £104;) Mr Rolls and Mr Royce sealed the deal in the elegant lobby of this fancy business hotel.

Eating

Manchester has something for every palate and every budget. There are good restaurants throughout the city, including a superb selection in Chinatown and the organic havens of the Northern Quarter. To dine like an in-the-know Mancunian, go to suburbs like Didsbury, about 5 miles south of the city centre (take Bus 43 or 143 from Oxford St).

CITY CENTRE

Yang Sing CHINESE ££
(0161-236 2200; 34 Princess St; mains £9-17; lunch & dinner) A serious contender for best Chinese restaurant in England, Yang Sing attracts diners from all over with its exceptional Cantonese cuisine.

Earth Cafe VEGETARIAN £
(0161-834 1996; www.earthcafe.co.uk; 16-20 Turner St; chef's special £3.20; lunch Tue-Sat;) Below the Manchester Buddhist Centre, this gourmet vegetarian cafe's motto is 'right food, right place, right time'. The result is wonderful.

Love Saves the Day CAFE £
(0161-832 0777; Tib St; lunch £6-8; breakfast & lunch Mon-Wed, Sat & Sun, breakfast, lunch & dinner Thu & Fri) The Northern Quarter's most popular cafe is a New York–style deli, small supermarket and sit-down eatery in one large, airy room.

Trof CAFE £
(0161-832 1870; 5-8 Thomas St; sandwiches £4, mains around £8; lunch & dinner) Great music, top staff and a fab menu, plus a broad selection of beers and tunes (Tuesday night is acoustic night), make this hang-out a firm favourite with students.

DIDSBURY & SOUTHERN SUBURBS

Cachumba Cafe INTERNATIONAL £
0161-445 2479; www.cachumba.co.uk; 220 Burton Rd; mains £4-9; dinner Tue-Sat) Cachumba does for food what the 'global beats' section in a record shop does for music. Friendly, relaxed, informal and exactly the kind of cafe we like to linger in.

Fat Loaf BRITISH ££
(0161-438 0319; www.thefatloaf.co.uk; 846 Wilmslow Rd; mains £10.95-15.95; lunch & dinner Mon-Sat, lunch Sun) This increasingly popular restaurant serves locally sourced food, done to perfection.

Drinking

There's every kind of drinking hole in Manchester, from really grungy ones that smell but have plenty of character to the ones that were designed by a team of architects but have the atmosphere of a freezer. Here's a few to get you going.

Britons Protection PUB
(0161-236 5895; 50 Great Bridgewater St) Whisky – 200 different kinds of it – is the beverage of choice at this old-fashioned boozer with open fires in the back rooms and a cosy atmosphere.

Bluu BAR
(0161-839 7740; www.bluu.co.uk; Unit 1, Smithfield Market, Thomas St; noon-midnight Sun-Mon, to 1am Tue-Thu, to 2am Fri & Sat) Our favourite of the Northern Quarter's collection of great bars; cool, comfortable and with a fab terrace.

Lass O'Gowrie PUB
(0161-273 6932; 36 Charles S) A Victorian classic off Princess St, and a favourite with students, old-timers and BBC employees.

Odd BAR
(0161-833 0070; www.oddbar.co.uk; 30-32 Thomas St; 11am-11pm Mon-Sat, to 10.30pm Sun) This eclectic little bar – with its oddball furnishings, wacky tunes and antiestablishment crew of customers – is a slice of Mancuniana to be treasured.

Bar Centro BAR
(0161-835 2863; 72-74 Tib St; mains £6-9; noon-midnight Mon-Wed, to 1am Thu, to 2am Fri & Sat, 2pm-midnight Sun) A Northern Quarter stalwart, very popular with the bohemian crowd precisely because it doesn't try to be. Great beer, nice staff and a better-than-average bar menu make this one of the choice spots in the area.

Old Wellington Inn PUB
(0161-830 1440; 4 Cathedral Gates)
One of the oldest buildings in the city and a lovely spot for a pint of genuine ale.

Peveril of the Peak PUB
(0161-236 6364; 127 Great Bridgewater St)
An unpretentious pub with wonderful Victorian glazed tilework outside.

☆ Entertainment

With a terrific club scene, Manchester remains at the vanguard of dance-floor culture. Before going out, here's a handy tip: drop all mention of 'Madchester' and keep talk of being 'up for it' to strict irony.

TOP CHOICE **Sankey's** CLUB
(0161-950 4201; www.sankeys.info; Radium St, Ancoats; admission free-£12; 10pm-3am Thu & Fri, to 4am Sat) Pioneer of dance music (Chemical Brothers, Daft Punk and others got their start here), and still with an unwavering commitment to top-class DJs. Choon!

FAC 251: The Factory CLUB
(0161-272 7251; www.factorymanchester.com; 112-118 Princess St; admission £3-6; 9.30pm-3am Mon-Sat) Tony Wilson's legendary Factory Records label HQ has been converted into a brand-new club and live music venue.

South CLUB
(0161-831 7756; 4a South King St; admission £5-8; 10pm-3am Fri & Sat) An excellent basement club to kick off the weekend.

Band on the Wall BAR, LIVE MUSIC
(0161-834 1786; www.bandonthewall.org; 25 Swan St) A top-notch venue that hosts everything from rock to world music.

Ruby Lounge BAR, LIVE MUSIC
(0161-834 1392; 26-28 High St) Terrific live music venue in the Northern Quarter that features mostly rock bands.

Information

Tourist office (0871 222 8223; www.visitmanchester.com; Piccadilly Plaza, Portland St; 10am-5.15pm Mon-Sat, to 4.30pm Sun)

Getting There & Away

Air

Manchester Airport (0161-489 3000; www.manchesterairport.co.uk), south of the city, is the largest airport outside London and is served by 13 locations throughout Britain as well as over 50 international destinations.

Bus

National Express (08717 81 81 81; www.nationalexpress.com) serves most major cities almost hourly from Chorlton St coach station in the city centre. Destinations include Liverpool (£6.30, 1¼ hours, hourly), Leeds (£8.40, one hour, hourly) and London (£24.40, 3¾ hours, hourly).

Train

Manchester Piccadilly is the main station for trains to and from the rest of the country. Trains head to Liverpool Lime St (£9, 45 minutes, half-hourly), Newcastle (£35, three hours, six daily) and London (£60, three hours, seven daily).

Chester

POP 80,130

The small city of Chester is one of English history's greatest gifts to the contemporary visitor. Its red-sandstone walls gift-wrap a tidy collection of Roman remains, and Tudor and Victorian buildings.

Sights & Activities

FREE City Walls LANDMARK
A good way to get a sense of Chester's unique character is to walk the 2-mile circuit along the city walls that surround the historic centre. Originally built by the Romans around AD 70, the walls were altered substantially over the following centuries but have retained their current position since around 1200.

FREE Roman Amphitheatre RUINS
Just outside the city walls, this ruined arena once seated 7000 spectators (making it the country's largest). Now it's little more than steps buried in grass, but a great place to rest your feet after walking the walls.

The Rows ARCHITECTURE
A series of two-level galleried arcades line Chester's four main streets. The architecture is a handsome mix of Victorian and Tudor (original and mock), housing a fantastic collection of individually owned shops.

Sleeping

Except for a handful of options, most of the accommodation is outside the city walls but within easy walking distance of the centre.

Stone Villa B&B ££
(01244-345014; www.stonevillachester.co.uk; 3 Stone Pl, Hoole Rd; s/d from £45/75) Twice winner of Chester's B&B of the Year in the last 10 years, this beautiful villa has everything you need for a memorable stay.

Chester Backpackers HOSTEL £
(01244-400185; www.chesterbackpackers.co.uk; 67 Boughton; dm from £13.50;) Comfortable dorm rooms with nice pine beds in a typically Tudor white-and-black building.

Bawn Lodge B&B ££
(01244-324971; www.bawnlodge.co.uk; 10 Hoole Rd; r from £75; P) Spotless rooms with plenty of colour make this charming guesthouse a very pleasant option.

Chester Townhouse B&B ££
(01244-350021; www.chestertownhouse.co.uk; 23 King St; s/d £45/75; P) Five beautifully decorated rooms in a handsome 17th-century house within the city walls.

Grove Villa B&B ££
(01244-349713; www.grovevillachester.com; 18 The Groves; r from £65; P) A wonderfully positioned Victorian home overlooking the Dee.

Eating & Drinking

Several eateries line the Rows.

Old Harker's Arms PUB ££
(01244-344525; www.harkersarms-chester.co.uk; 1 Russell St; mains £9-14; lunch & dinner) An old-style boozer with a gourmet kitchen, this is the perfect place to tuck into Cumberland sausages or a Creole rice salad with sweet potatoes, and then rinse your palate with a pint of Waddies (as Wadworth Ale is known round here).

Albion PUB ££
(01244-340345; 4 Albion St; mains £8-11) No children, no music, and no big screens, this 'family-hostile' pub is a throwback to a time when ale-drinking still had its own *rituals* – aka ingrained prejudices. Still, this is one of the finest pubs in northwest England.

Information

Tourist office (01244-402111; www.chester.gov.uk; Town Hall, Northgate St; 9am-5.30pm Mon-Sat, 10am-4pm Sun May-Oct, 10am-5pm Mon-Sat Nov-Apr)

Getting There & Away

Bus

National Express (08717 81 81 81; www.nationalexpress.com) coaches stop on Vicar's Lane, just opposite the tourist office by the Roman amphitheatre. Destinations include Birmingham (£12.40, 2¼ hours, four daily), Liverpool (£7.20, one hour, four daily), London (£24.60, 5½ hours, three daily) and Manchester (£6.80, 1¼ hours, three daily).

Train

Trains travel to/from Liverpool (£4.35, 45 minutes, hourly), London Euston (£65.20, 2½ hours, hourly) and Manchester (£12.60, one hour, hourly).

Liverpool

POP 469,020

Beleaguered by a history of hard times and chronic misfortune, Liverpool's luck has changed dramatically in recent years. The centre is being transformed, while the city's magnificent cultural heritage is celebrated on the waterfront around Albert Dock.

Sights

CITY CENTRE

FREE World Museum MUSEUM
(0151-478 4399; www.liverpoolmuseums.org.uk/wml; William Brown St; 10am-5pm)

Natural history, science and technology are the themes of this sprawling museum. It also includes the country's only free **planetarium**.

FREE **Walker Art Gallery** ART MUSEUM
(☎0151-478 4199; www.liverpoolmuseums.org.uk/walker; William Brown St; ⊙10am-5pm) Touted as the 'National Gallery of the North', the Walker houses an outstanding collection of art from the 14th to the 21st centuries.

FREE **St George's Hall** CULTURAL CENTRE
(☎0151-707 2391; www.stgeorgesliverpool.co.uk; William Brown St; ⊙10am-5pm Tue-Sat, 1-5pm Sun) Arguably Liverpool's most impressive building – a magnificent example of neoclassical architecture. Curiously, it was built as law courts *and* a concert hall – trial by string quartet, perhaps?

Liverpool Cathedral CHURCH
(☎0151-709 6271; www.liverpoolcathedral.org.uk; Hope St; ⊙8am-6pm) This is a building of superlatives: Britain's largest church; the world's largest Anglican cathedral; the world's third-largest bell (with the world's heaviest peal); even the world's largest organ.

Metropolitan Cathedral of Christ the King CHURCH
(☎0151-709 9222; www.liverpoolmetrocathedral.org.uk; Mt Pleasant; ⊙8am-6pm Mon-Sat, to 5pm Sun Oct-Mar) Liverpool's Catholic cathedral is a mightily impressive modern building, completed in 1967. The central tower frames the world's largest stained-glass window.

ALBERT DOCK

Liverpool's biggest tourist attraction is **Albert Dock** (☎0151-708 8854; www.albertdock.com; admission free). This former port and its surrounding buildings is now a Unesco World Heritage Site.

TOP CHOICE **International Slavery Museum** MUSEUM
(☎0151-478 4499; www.liverpoolmuseums.org.uk/ism; Albert Dock; admission free; ⊙10am-5pm) This magnificent museum reveals slavery's unimaginable horrors – including Liverpool's own role in the slave trade – and it doesn't baulk at confronting racism, through a remarkable series of multimedia and other displays.

Beatles Story MUSEUM
(☎0151-709 1963; www.beatlesstory.com; Albert Dock; adult/student/child £12.95/8.50/6.50; ⊙9am-7pm, last admission 5pm) Liverpool's most popular museum tells the story of the world's most famous foursome, with plenty of genuine memorabilia – and hardly a mention of internal discord.

FREE **Merseyside Maritime Museum** MUSEUM
(☎0151-478 4499; www.liverpoolmuseums.org.uk/maritime; Albert Dock; ⊙10am-5pm) A graphic celebration of one of the world's great ports, including a fascinating emigration exhibit about the nine million migrants who came through on their way to North America and Australia.

FREE **Tate Liverpool** ART MUSEUM
(☎0151-702 7400; www.tate.org.uk/liverpool; Albert Dock; special exhibitions adult/child from £5/4; ⊙10am-5.50pm Jun-Aug, 10am-5.50pm Tue-Sun Sep-May) A substantial checklist of 20th-century artists.

NORTH OF ALBERT DOCK

The area to the north of Albert Dock is known as **Pier Head**, still the departure point for ferries across the River Mersey. The story of the millions of migrants who sailed from Liverpool will be told in the eye-catching **Museum of Liverpool** (⊙0151-207 0001; Mann Island), due to open in 2011. Until then, this area will continue to be dominated by a trio of buildings known as the 'Three Graces': the domed **Port of Liverpool Building**; the **Cunard Building**, in the style of an Italian palazzo; and the **Royal Liver Building** (*lie*-ver) crowned by the city's symbol, the famous copper Liver Bird.

Festivals

Merseyside International Street Festival CULTURE
(www.brouhaha.uk.com) A three-week extravaganza of world culture beginning in mid-July and featuring indoor and outdoor performances by artists and musicians from pretty much everywhere.

Mathew St Festival MUSIC
(☎0151-239 9091; www.mathewstreetfestival.org) The world's biggest tribute to the Beatles features six days of music, a convention and a memorabilia auction during the last week of August.

Sleeping

CITY CENTRE

Racquet Club BOUTIQUE HOTEL ££
(☎0151-236 6676; www.racquetclub.org.uk; Hargreaves Bldg, 5 Chapel St; r £110; 📶) Eight individually styled rooms make this one of the most elegant choices in town.

DOING THE BEATLES TO DEATH

It doesn't matter that half of the band are gone or that the much-visited Cavern Club is an unfaithful reconstruction of the original, nor that, if he were alive, John Lennon might have devoted much of his cynical energy to mocking the 'Cavern Quarter' that has grown up around Mathew St. No, it doesn't matter at all, because the Beatles phenomenon lives on, and a huge chunk of the city's visitors come to visit, see and touch anything – and we mean anything – even vaguely associated with the Fab Four. Which isn't to say that a wander around Mathew St isn't fun: from shucking oysters in the Rubber Soul Oyster Bar to buying a Ringo pillowcase in the From Me to You shop, virtually all of your Beatles needs can be taken care of.

True fans will also undoubtedly want to visit the National Trust–owned **Mendips**, the home where John lived with his Aunt Mimi from 1945 to 1963, and **20 Forthlin Rd**, where Paul grew up. You can only do so by prebooked **tour** (0151-427 7231; adult/child £16.80/3.15; 10.30am & 11.20am Wed-Sun Easter-Oct), from outside the National Conservation Centre.

International Inn HOSTEL £
(0151-709 8135; www.internationalinn.co.uk; 4 South Hunter St; dm/d from £15/36;) A superb converted warehouse in the middle of uni-land: heated rooms accommodate from two to 10 people with tidy wooden beds and bunks.

62 Castle St BOUTIQUE HOTEL ££
(0151-702 7898; www.62castlest.com; 62 Castle St; r from £79;) This elegant property successfully blends the traditional Victorian features of the building with a sleek, contemporary style.

Hard Days Night Hotel HOTEL £££
(0151-236 1964; www.harddaysnighthotel.com; Central Bldgs, North John St; r £110-160, ste £750;) You don't have to be a Beatles fan to stay here, but it helps: the 110 ultramodern rooms are decorated with specially commissioned drawings of the band.

AROUND ALBERT DOCK

Liverpool YHA HOSTEL £
(0845 371 9527; www.yha.org.uk; 25 Tabley St; dm from £16;) It may look like an East European apartment complex, but this award-winning hostel is very comfortable. The dorms have attached bathrooms and even heated towel rails.

Campanile Hotel HOTEL ££
(0151-709 8104; www.campanile-liverpool-queens-dock.co.uk; Chaloner St, Queen's Dock; r from £50;) Functional, motel-style rooms in a great location.

Premier Inn HOTEL ££
(0870 990 6432; www.premierinn.co.uk; Albert Dock; r from £49;) Decent chain hotel two steps away from the Beatles Story museum.

Eating & Drinking

Liverpool has plenty of choices to satisfy every taste. The best areas include Ropewalks, along Hardman St and Hope St or along Nelson St in the heart of Chinatown.

Everyman Bistro CAFE £
(0151-708 9545; www.everyman.co.uk; 13 Hope St; mains £5-8; lunch & dinner Mon-Sat, dinner Sun) Out-of-work actors and other creative types make this great cafe-restaurant (located beneath the Everyman Theatre) their second home – with good reason. Great tucker and a terrific atmosphere.

Alma de Cuba CUBAN ££
(0151-709 7097; www.alma-de-cuba.com; St Peter's Church, Seel St; mains £16-24; lunch & dinner) This extraordinary venture has seen the transformation of a Polish church into a Miami-style Cuban extravaganza. *¡Salud!*

Meet Argentinean STEAKHOUSE ££
(0151-258 1816; www.meetrestaurant.co.uk; 2 Brunswick St; mains £11-26; lunch & dinner) An elegant tribute to massive slabs of grilled beef – just as any self-respecting gaucho would demand.

Quarter WINE BAR, BISTRO ££
(0151-707 1965; 7-11 Falkner St; mains £9-13; lunch & dinner) A gorgeous little wine bar and bistro with outdoor seating for that elusive summer's day.

Magnet BAR
(0151-709 6969; 39 Hardman St) Red leather booths, plenty of velvet and a suitably seedy

New York-dive atmosphere where Tom Waits would feel right at home.

Philharmonic PUB
(☎0151-707 2837; 36 Hope St; ⊙to 11.30pm) This extraordinary pub, designed by the shipwrights who built the *Lusitania,* is one of the most beautiful in all of England.

Hannah's BAR
(☎0151-708 5959; 2 Leece St) One of the top student bars in town, with an easygoing crowd and some pretty decent music.

☆ Entertainment

Most of the city's clubs and late-night bars are concentrated in the area of Ropewalks.

Masque CLUB
(☎0151-707 6171; www.chibuku.com; 90 Seel St; admission £4-11; ⊙Mon-Sat) This converted theatre is home to our favourite club in town. The fortnightly Saturday Chibuku is one of the best club nights in all of England.

Nation CLUB
(☎0151-709 1693; 40 Slater St, Wolstenholme Sq; admission £4-13) It looks like an air-raid shelter, but it's the big-name DJs dropping the bombs at the city's premier dance club, formerly the home of Cream.

Le Bateau CLUB
(☎0151-709 6508; 62 Duke St; admission £3-8; ⊙Thu-Sat) In this superb indie club 500 punters cram the dance-floor and hear everything from techno to hard rock.

Academy LIVE MUSIC
(☎0151-794 6868; Liverpool University, 11-13 Hotham St) Good spot to see mid-size bands on tour.

Cavern Club LIVE MUSIC
(☎0151-236 1965; 8-10 Mathew St) Reconstruction of 'world's most famous club'; good selection of local bands.

Information

08 Place tourist office (☎0151-233 2008; Whitechapel; ⊙9am-8pm Mon-Sat Apr-Sep, to 6pm Mon-Sat Oct-Mar, 11am-4pm Sun year-round) The main branch of the tourist office.

Albert Dock tourist offices (☎0151-478 4599; ⊙10am-6pm) At the Anchor Courtyard and Merseyside Maritime Museum.

Getting There & Away

Bus

There are National Express services to/from most major towns, including Manchester (£6.30, 1¼ hours, hourly), London (£25.60, five to six hours, six daily), Birmingham (£12.40, 2¾ hours, five daily) and Newcastle (£21.60, 6½ hours, three daily).

Train

Liverpool's main station is Lime St. It has hourly services to almost everywhere, including Chester (£5, 45 minutes), London (£65, 3¼ hours) and Manchester (£9, 45 minutes).

Lake District National Park

A dramatic landscape of high peaks, dizzying ridges and huge lakes gouged by the march of ice age glaciers, the Lake District in Cumbria is a beautiful corner of Britain. It may not be the wildest place on earth, and there are much bigger mountains in Wales and Scotland, but for England it's as extreme as it gets. Not surprisingly, the awe-inspiring geography here shaped the literary persona of one of Britain's best-known poets, William Wordsworth.

Often called simply the Lakes (but never – note, Australians – the '*Lakes* District'), the national park and surrounding area attract around 15 million visitors annually. But if you avoid summer weekends, and especially if you do a bit of hiking, it's easy enough to miss the crush.

The key valleys of the Lake District radiate from a central high point like spokes of a wheel, with most of the larger towns at the outer edge. Principal gateways include the twin towns of Windermere and Bowness in the south, Ambleside slightly nearer the centre, and Keswick in the north. All have hostels, B&Bs, places to eat and shops selling maps and outdoor equipment.

There's a host of B&Bs and country-house hotels in the Lakes, plus over 20 YHA hostels, many of which can be linked by foot. The following is just the tip of the mountain.

BE PREPARED

The Lake District is home to England's highest peak (Scafell; 978m), the wettest inhabited place (Seathwaite; over 3m of rain a year) and notoriously changeable weather conditions – which prove fatal to a few unready souls each year – so make sure you're prepared if you're heading for the hills.

WINDERMERE & BOWNESS

POP 8432

Windermere – the lake and the town of the same name – has been a centre for Lakeland tourism since the first steam trains arrived in 1847. The station is still there, making this an excellent gateway. The town of Windermere is 1.5 miles uphill from the lake, and bustling Bowness (officially Bowness-on-Windermere) is on the lakeshore, where a bevy of boat trips, ice-cream booths and frilly teashops jostle for space.

Sleeping

TOP CHOICE **Wheatlands Lodge** B&B ££
(015394-43789; www.wheatlandslodge-windermere.co.uk; Old College Lane; d £70-150; P) Set back from the main street of Windermere town, this elegant residence looks venerably Victorian, but inside reveals some contemporary surprises.

Lake District Backpackers Lodge HOSTEL £
(015394-46374; www.lakedistrictbackpackers.co.uk; High St; dm £15-17; @) A little underwhelming, with cramped dorms, but it's cheap, near Windermere train station and the managers organise local biking/hiking trips.

Number 80 Bed Then Breakfast B&B ££
(015394-43584; www.number80bed.co.uk; 80 Craig Walk; d £80-90;) A lovely little bolthole in Bowness.

AMBLESIDE

POP 3382

Windermere and Bowness are tourist towns, but Ambleside is 100% for walkers and other outdoor types – with plenty of gear shops and the start point of several classic hikes on the surrounding high fells.

Sleeping

Lakes Lodge B&B ££
(015394-33240; www.lakeslodge.co.uk; Lake Rd; r £89-129;) A trendy cross between a mini hotel and a modern guesthouse: the rooms are all clean lines and zero clutter.

Gables
(015394-33272; www.thegables-ambleside.co.uk; Church Walk; s £40-50, d £60-80; P) Gabled by name, gabled by nature, this double-fronted house is in a quiet spot overlooking the recreation ground.

TOP CHOICE **Ambleside YHA** HOSTEL £
(0845 371 9620; ambleside@yha.org.uk; Windermere Rd; dm from £14; P) Thanks to a recent refit, this place has excellent rooms and facilities, plus top lake views and a host of organised activities.

Ambleside Backpackers HOSTEL £
(015394-32340; www.englishlakesbackpackers.co.uk; Old Lake Rd; dm £16; P@) Cottage hostel a short walk south from town.

KESWICK

POP 5257

The main town of the north Lakes, Keswick sits beside lovely Derwent Water, a silvery curve studded by wooded islands and criss-crossed by puttering cruise boats. It's crammed with B&Bs, especially around Stanger St and Helvellyn Rd.

Sleeping

TOP CHOICE **Howe Keld** B&B ££
(017687-72417; www.howekeld.co.uk; 5-7 The Heads; s £50, d £90-100;) A very stylish B&B with slate-floored bathrooms, handmade furniture and sleek decor.

Oakthwaite House B&B ££
(017687-72398; www.oakthwaite-keswick.co.uk; 35 Helvellyn St; d £60-76) Just four rooms, with power showers and cool shades throughout. Some rooms have fell views too.

Ellergill B&B ££
(017687-73347; www.ellergill.co.uk; 22 Stanger St; d £64-72) Velour bedspreads and plumped-up

WORTH A TRIP

GRASMERE

Grasmere is a gorgeous little Lakeland village, all the more famous because of its links with Britain's leading Romantic poet, William Wordsworth. Literary pilgrims come to **Dove Cottage** (015394-35544; www.wordsworth.org.uk; adult/child £7.50/4.50; 9.30am-5.30pm), his former home, where highlights include some fine portraits of the man himself, a cabinet containing his spectacles, and a set of scales used by his pal de Quincey to weigh out opium. At **St Oswald's Church** you'll see a memorial to the poet, and in the churchyard you'll find his grave. To cure any sombre thoughts, head for **Sarah Nelson's Gingerbread Shop** and stock up on Grasmere's famous confectionery.

cushions give this Victorian house an opulent edge.

Keswick YHA HOSTEL £
(☎0845 371 9746; www.yha.org.uk; Station Rd; dm £23; @) In a converted mill beside the river, this efficient hostel offers roomy dorms, doubles and triples, some with balconies.

Information

The Lake District's tourist offices are crammed with information on local hikes, activities and accommodation, and stocked with guidebooks, maps and hiking supplies.

Ambleside (☎015394-32582; tic@thehubofambleside.com; Central Buildings, Market Cross; ⏲9am-5pm)

Bowness (☎015394-42895; bownesstic@lake-district.gov.uk; Glebe Rd; ⏲9.30am-5.30pm Easter-Oct, 10am-4pm Fri-Sun Nov-Mar)

Keswick (☎017687-72645; keswicktic@lake-district.gov.uk; Moot Hall, Market Pl; ⏲9.30am-5.30pm Apr-Oct, to 4.30pm Nov-Mar)

Windermere (☎015394-46499; windermeretic@southlakeland.gov.uk; Victoria St; ⏲9am-5.30pm Mon-Sat, 9.30am-5.30pm Sun Apr-Oct)

Getting There & Away

Train

To reach the Lakes by rail, take any stopping train on the main line between London, Manchester and Glasgow, then change at Oxenholme, from where regular trains run to Windermere.

Bus

National Express coaches run direct from London and Glasgow (and various other towns around the country) to Windermere.

Getting Around

The most useful bus routes for getting around the Lakes:

505 (Coniston Rambler) Serves Kendal, Windermere, Ambleside and Coniston

555 (Lakeslink) Runs from Lancaster to Carlisle, across the heart of the Lakes via all the main towns

SOUTH & WEST WALES

Lying to the west of England, the nation of Wales is a separate country within the state of Great Britain. It's a nation with Celtic roots, its own language and a rich historic legacy. While some areas in the south are undeniably scarred by coal mining and heavy industry, overall Wales boasts a landscape of wild mountains, rolling hills, rich farmland and some of the most beautiful beaches in all of Britain. If you're on a long tour, South Wales is most easily reached from southern or central England, and is well worth the diversion.

Cardiff

POP 324,800

The capital of Wales since only 1955, Cardiff has embraced its role with vigour, emerging as one of Britain's leading urban centres. Caught between its ancient castle and its ultramodern waterfront, this compact city has entered the 21st century with confidence, flexing its new architectural muscles as if it's still astonished to have them. Day or night, a definite buzz reverberates through the streets.

Sights

CENTRAL CARDIFF

Cardiff Castle CASTLE
(www.cardiffcastle.com; Castle St; adult/child £8.95/6.35, incl guided tour £11.95/8.50; ⏲9am-6pm Mar-Oct, to 5pm Nov-Feb) The grafting of Victorian mock-Gothic extravagance onto genuine Norman relics makes Cardiff Castle the city's leading attraction. It's far from a traditional Welsh castle but it neatly encompasses the city's history.

Millennium Stadium STADIUM
(☎029-2082 2228; www.millenniumstadium.com; Westgate St; tours adult/child £6.50/4; ⏲10am-5pm Mon-Sat, to 4pm Sun) This spectacular stadium squats like a stranded spaceship in the heart of the city – and in this rugby-mad nation somehow gets away with it.

CARDIFF BAY

The redeveloped waterfront of Cardiff Bay is about 2 miles from the city centre, lined with bars, restaurants and shops – and a collection of stunning buildings

FREE **Wales Millennium Centre** ARTS CENTRE
(☎029-2063 6464; www.wmc.org.uk; Bute Pl) The premier arts complex of Wales, this architectural masterpiece of slate and bronze is a key feature of the bay (you might recognise it from the TV show *Torchwood*, too). If you can't take in a show, you can wander through the public areas at will or take an official **guided tour** (adult/child £5.50/4.50; ⏲9am-5pm).

Central Cardiff

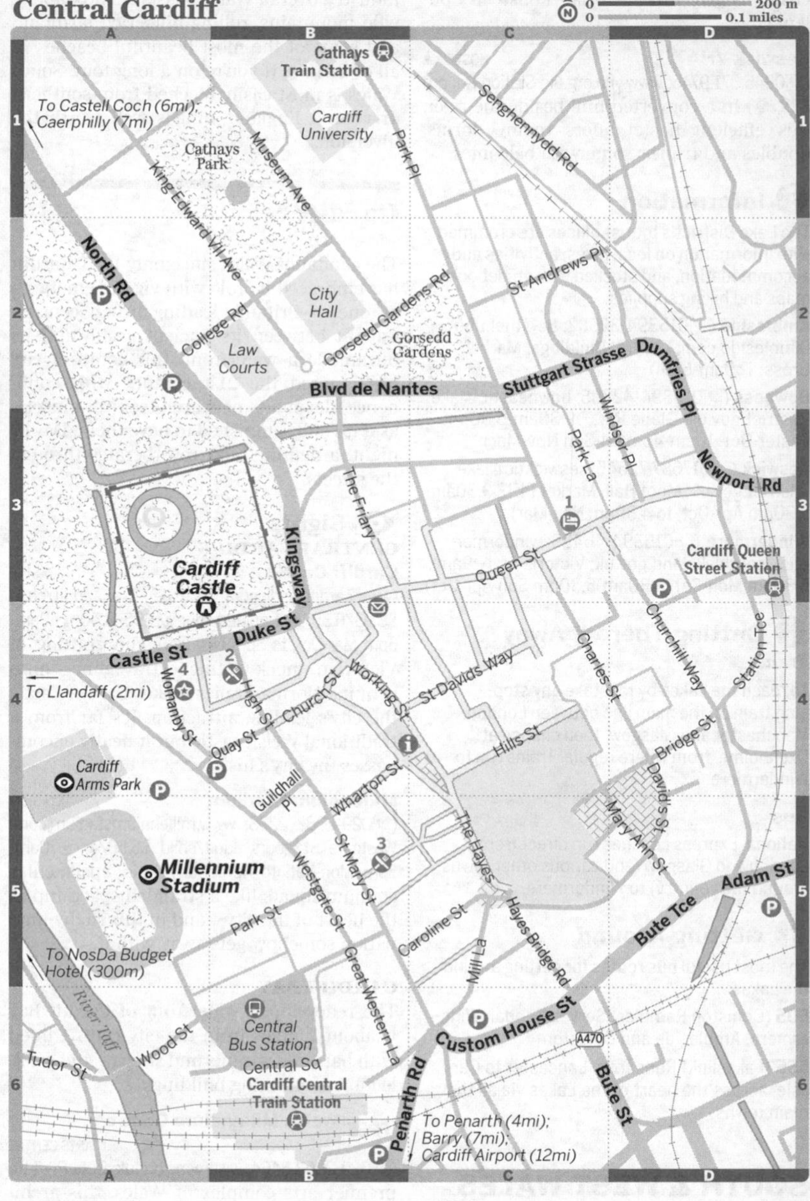

FREE **Senedd (National Assembly Building)** NOTABLE BUILDING
(☎0845 010 5500; www.assemblywales.org/sen-home; ⏲10.30am-4.30pm, extended during plenary sessions) This striking structure is home to the Welsh National Assembly. The lobby and surrounding area are littered with public artworks.

FREE **Pierhead** MUSEUM
(☎029-0845 010 5500; www.pierhead.org; ⏲10.30am-4.30pm) One of the area's few Victorian remnants, this red-brick building

Central Cardiff

Top Sights

Cardiff Castle A4
Millennium Stadium A5

Sleeping

1 Parc Hotel C3

Eating

2 Goat Major B4
3 Plan B5

Entertainment

4 Clwb Ifor Bach A4

with its famous clock tower is a long-time Cardiff icon.

Sleeping

CENTRAL CARDIFF

TOP CHOICE NosDa Budget Hotel HOSTEL £
(☎029-2037 8866; www.nosda.co.uk; 53-59 Despenser St; dm/tw from £19/43; @ 📶 P) You won't find a better budget bed any closer to the city centre than this stylishly refurbished hostel right across the river from the Millennium Stadium.

Parc Hotel HOTEL ££
(☎0871 376 9011; www.thistle.com/theparchotel; Park Pl; r from £99; @ 📶) A smart contemporary hotel located right at the heart of the main shopping area, with tasteful rooms, good facilities and helpful staff.

CARDIFF BAY

St David's Hotel & Spa HOTEL ££
(☎029-2045 4045; www.thestdavidshotel.com; Havannah St; r from £99; @ 📶 🏊) A glittering, glassy tower topped with a sail-like flourish, St David's epitomises Cardiff Bay's transformation from wasteland to stylish place-to-be. Every room has a private balcony with a harbour view.

Eating & Drinking

You'll find a diverse array of restaurants scattered around the city, with a particularly ritzy batch lining Cardiff Bay. In the city centre are bars, clubs and burger joints that cater especially to the throngs of young drinkers.

CENTRAL CARDIFF

Plan CAFE £
(28 Morgan Arcade; mains £5-8; ⏰breakfast & lunch; ✍) Serving quite possibly Wales' best coffee, and specialises in healthy, organic, locally sourced food.

Goat Major PUB £
(33 High St; mains £7-8; ⏰lunch) A solidly traditional pub with local ale and a fine selection of homemade pies.

TOP CHOICE Clwb Ifor Bach CLUB
(☎029-2023 2199; www.clwb.net; 11 Womanby St) Truly an independent music great, *Y Clwb* is Cardiff's most eclectic and important venue.

CARDIFF BAY

TOP CHOICE Woods Bar & Brasserie MODERN EUROPEAN ££
(☎029-2049 2400; Stuart St; mains £11-18; ⏰closed Sun dinner) The historic Pilotage Building has been renovated with exposed stone walls and a glass extension to accommodate Cardiff Bay's best restaurant.

Salt BAR
(Mermaid Quay, Cardiff Bay) A large, modern, nautical-themed bar with plenty of sofas and armchairs for lounging around, and a 1st-floor open-air terrace with a view of the yachts out in the bay.

Information

Tourist office (☎029-2087 3573; www.visitcardiff.com; Old Library, The Hayes; ⏰9.30am-5.30pm Mon-Sat, 10am-4pm Sun; @)

Cardiff Bay Visitor Centre (☎029-2087 7927; Harbour Dr; ⏰10am-6pm)

Getting There & Away

BUS National Express coach destinations include Fishguard (£10, three hours), Brecon (£4.10, 1¼ hours) and London (£22, 3¼ hours).

TRAIN Direct services from Cardiff include London Paddington (£43, 2¾ hours) and Fishguard Harbour (£20, 2¼ hours).

Pembrokeshire Coast National Park

At the far southwest tip of Wales sits the beautiful Pembrokeshire Coast National Park (Parc Cenedlaethol Arfordir Sir Benfro), covering the cliffs and beaches of the coast and its offshore islands, as well as the Preseli Hills and Daugleddau waterway inland. The towns of Tenby, St Davids and Newport all have sleeping and eating options. For wider travels, ferries leave the port of Goodwick near Fishguard bound for Ireland.

TENBY

POP 4900

Perched on a headland with sandy beaches and painted houses, Tenby is a postcard-maker's dream.

Sleeping

Bay House B&B ££
(☎01834-849015; www.bayhousetenby.co.uk; 5 Picton Rd; r from £70) A stylish, modern take on the seaside B&B, Bay House offers a relaxed, friendly atmosphere, airy rooms with flat-screen TVs and DVDs, and an emphasis on local, organic produce.

Lindholme House B&B ££
(☎01834-843368; www.lindholmehouse.co.uk; 27 Victoria St; s/d from £30/60) A traditional B&B with friendly owners and fry-up breakfasts, salmon-hued Lindholme is a little chintzy but clean, comfy and central.

ST DAVIDS

POP 1800

The little town of St Davids is Britain's smallest city, its status ensured by the magnificent 12-century cathedral named for the nation's patron saint – a place of pilgrimage for centuries. Today St Davids is known for its laid-back vibe and excellent hiking, surfing and wildlife-watching in the surrounding area.

Sleeping & Eating

TOP CHOICE **Ramsey House** B&B ££
(☎01437-720321; www.ramseyhouse.co.uk; Lower Moor; r £100; ᯤP) Friendly and fresh B&B on the outskirts of town.

St Davids YHA HOSTEL £
(☎0845 371 9141; www.yha.org.uk; Llaethdy, Whitesands Bay; dm £15, tw £36, q £63) Former farmhouse tucked beneath Carn Llidi, 2 miles northwest of town, with snug dorms in the cow sheds.

Bench CAFE, BISTRO £
(www.bench-bar.co.uk: 11 High St; mains £5-17; ⏲breakfast, lunch & dinner; @ᯤ) Serving snacks, ice cream and coffee during the day, and by night a bustling bar-bistro with a strong Mediterranean motif.

Farmer's Arms PUB
(14 Goat St) Authentic country pub, with a garden out back to watch the sun go down on a summer's evening.

NEWPORT (TREFDRAETH)

POP 1200

In stark contrast to the industrial city of Newport near Cardiff, the little Pembrokeshire village of Newport is a pretty cluster of flower-bedecked cottages huddled beneath a castle at the foot of the mystical Preseli Hills.

Sleeping & Eating

TOP CHOICE **Llys Meddyg** HOTEL ££
(☎01239-820008; www.llysmeddyg.om; East St; r £100-150; ᯤ@) Contemporary city cool by the seaside. Bedrooms are large and bright, and the restaurant is superb (mains £17 to £34).

Golden Lion Hotel PUB ££
(☎01239-820321; www.goldenlionpembrokeshire.co.uk; East St; mains £10-20; ᯤP) An appealing country inn (singles/doubles £60/85), with a snug traditional bar and good restaurant.

Information

Tourist offices in Pembrokeshire:

Fishguard (☎01437-776636; Town Hall, Market Sq; ⏲10am-4pm Mon-Sat; @)

Goodwick (☎01348-874737; Ocean Lab, Goodwick; ⏲10am-4pm; @)

Newport (☎01239-820912; Long St; ⏲10am-6pm Mon-Sat Easter-Oct, 10.30am-3pm Mon & Fri, 10.30am-1pm Tue-Thu & Sat Nov-Easter)

Tenby (☎01834-842402; Upper Park Rd; ⏲10am-4pm Easter-Oct, Mon-Sat Nov-Easter)

Brecon Beacons National Park

Marking the boundary between South and Mid-Wales, the Brecon Beacons National Park (Parc Cenedlaethol Bannau Brycheiniog) features a range of high mountain plateaus of grass and heather, rising above waterfall-splashed valleys and a rural landscape of tranquil farmland. A good gateway is the town of Brecon, which is easily reached from Cardiff.

BRECON (ABERHONDDU)

POP 7900

The handsome stone market town of Brecon is the main hub of the national park and a natural base for exploring the surrounding countryside. The conical hill of **Pen-y-Crug**, capped by an Iron Age hill fort, rises to the northwest of the town and makes a good objective for a short hike (2.5 miles round trip). In the second weekend in August, the town hosts the **Brecon Jazz Festival** (www.breconjazz.co.uk; concerts free-£32), one of Europe's leading jazz events.

Sleeping & Eating

TOP CHOICE Cantre Selyf B&B ££

(☎01874-622904; www.cantreselyf.co.uk; 5 Lion St; s/d from £56/72; P 📶) This elegant 17th-century townhouse, right in the middle of Brecon, has atmospheric period decor and furnishings.

Bridge Cafe B&B ££

(☎01874-622024; www.bridgecafe.co.uk; 7 Bridge St; s/d from £30/50) This friendly place offers up hearty home-cooked meals (mains £8); upstairs are some plain but comfortable bedrooms.

Brecon YHA HOSTEL £

(☎0845 371 9506; www.yha.org.uk; Groesffordd; dm from £14) Victorian farmhouse hostel, 2 miles east of Brecon.

Information

Brecon Tourist Office (☎01874-622485; Market car park; ⌚9.30am-5.30pm Mon-Sat, 10am-4pm Sun)

National Park Visitor Centre (☎01874-623366; www.breconbeacons.org; Libanus; ⌚9.30am-5pm) The park's main visitor centre is off the A470 road, 5 miles southwest of Brecon, with full details of walks, hiking and biking trails, outdoor activities, wildlife and geology.

Getting There & Away

National Express coaches run between Brecon and Birmingham (£27, 4¼ hours) and Cardiff (£4.10, 1¼ hours).

MID- & NORTH WALES

Mid-Wales is a rural region, way off the beaten track, with epic wild scenery and sturdy little market towns – it's also a crucible for the movements championing green issues and top-notch local food. In contrast, the landscape of North Wales is more mountainous, and surrounded by a beautiful coastline. Other gems are the Unesco-listed castles at Harlech, Baumaris and Conwy, while the island of Anglesey is always a good bet for fine weather when thick cloud covers the peaks inland. In many ways, North Wales distils the very essence of Welshness – you'll hear the language on the street, see the Celtic legacy in the landscape and soak up the cultural pride in local galleries (just don't mention that to the folks in Cardiff).

Snowdonia National Park

The jagged peaks of Snowdonia National Park (Parc Cenedlaethol Eryri) offer the most spectacular mountain scenery in Wales. The most popular area is in the north around Snowdon (at 1085m, the highest peak in Britain south of the Scottish Highlands), although the park extends all the way south to Machynlleth. For outdoor types, walking on the mountains is the main activity. For mountain bikers there are excellent trails in the surrounding forests. For more information, see www.visitsnowdonia.info.

Good bases and gateways include the busy village of Betws-y-Coed on the eastern side of the park, while pretty Beddgelert is handy for the south. Most convenient for Snowdon itself is the town of Llanberis – less attractive, but with all the facilities you need.

BEDDGELERT

POP 500

Charming little Beddgelert is a conservation village of rough grey stone buildings, overlooking the trickling River Glaslyn with its ivy-covered bridge.

DON'T MISS

CONWY

On the north coast of Wales, the historic town of Conwy is utterly dominated by the Unesco-designated cultural treasure of **Conwy Castle** (Cadw; adult/child £4.60/4.10; ⌚9am-5pm, 9.30am-4pm Mon-Sat, 11am-4pm Sun low season), the most stunning of all Edward I's Welsh fortresses. Built between 1277 and 1307 on a rocky outcrop, it has commanding views across the estuary and Snowdonia National Park. Exploring the castle's nooks and crannies makes for a superb, living-history visit, but best of all, head to the **battlements** for panoramic views and an overview of Conwy's majestic complexity. The 1200m-long **town wall** was built with the castle to guard Conwy's residents at night. Today you can walk part way round the wall for more excellent views; the best are to be had from Upper Gate.

Sleeping & Eating

Plas Tan Y Graig B&B ££

(☎01766-890310; www.plastanygraig.co.uk; s/d £49/78;) This bright, friendly place is the best B&B in the heart of the village.

Lyn's Cafe CAFE £

(meals £3-12; breakfast & lunch winter, plus dinner summer) A family-friendly all-rounder.

PEN-Y-PASS

Pen-y-pass is no more than a car park, information centre and YHA hostel at the highest point on the road between Llanberis and Beddgelert, but it's a popular starting point for walkers heading up Snowdon.

Sleeping & Eating

Pen-y-Gwyrd HOTEL £

(☎01286-870211; www.pyg.co.uk; Nant Gwynant; r £48, without bathroom £40; Jan-Oct) Just down the road from Pen-y-Pass, this hotel was used as a training base by the 1953 Everest team, and memorabilia includes their signatures on the ceiling. At the time of research the hotel was closed for renovations.

Pen-y-Pass YHA HOSTEL £

(☎0845 371 9534; www.yha.org.uk; dm from £16) Superbly situated on the slopes of Snowdon, 5.5 miles up the A4086 from Llanberis.

LLANBERIS

POP 1900

Llanberis is a major hub for walkers and climbers, and also the terminus for the Snowdon Mountain Railway. Yes, you can get to the top of the country's highest summit by train.

Sleeping & Eating

Dolafon B&B ££

(☎01286-870993; www.dolafon.com; High St; s/d from £30/60; P) Set back from the road, this imposing 19th-century house has good traditional rooms and tearooms.

Llanberis YHA HOSTEL £

(☎0845 371 9645; dm from £18) Former quarry manager's house on the slopes above the town.

Pete's Eats CAFE £

(☎01286-870117; www.petes-eats.co.uk; 40 High St; meals £4-6; @) A classic cafe and bunkhouse where hikers swap tips over monster portions in a hostel-like environment.

BETWS-Y-COED

POP 950

This busy tourist town has a bit of an Alpine feel, and plenty of accommodation options.

> **TONGUE-TWISTING**
>
> At first sight, Welsh looks impossibly difficult to get your tongue around. But once you know that 'dd' is pronounced 'th', and 'w' can also be a vowel pronounced 'oo', and 'f' is 'v', while 'ff' is 'f', and 'll' is roughly 'cl', you might just about be able to ask the way to Llanfairpwllgwyngyllgogerychwyrndrobwllllantysiliogogogoch – a village in Anglesey with Britain's longest place name.

Sleeping & Eating

TOP CHOICE **Tŷ Gwyn Hotel** HOTEL ££

(☎01690-710383; www.tygwynhotel.co.uk; r £52-120; P) This ex-coaching inn has been welcoming guests since 1636, its venerable age borne out by misshapen rooms and exposed beams. The menu focuses on hearty mains (£13 to £18) but lighter bar-style meals are also available.

Maes-y-Garth B&B ££

(☎01690-710441; www.maes-y-garth.co.uk; Lon Muriau; r £66-70; P) Just outside town off the A470, this new place has earned itself many fans, thanks to its warm welcome and three quietly stylish rooms.

Betws-y-Coed YHA HOSTEL £

(☎01690-710796; www.yha.org.uk; Swallow Falls; dm from £16) A functional hostel and bustling traveller hub.

Information

Beddgelert (☎01766-890615; Canolfan Hebog; 9.30am-5.30pm Easter-Oct, 9.30am-4.30pm Fri-Sun Nov-Mar; @)

Betws-y-Coed (☎01690-710426; www.betws-y-coed.co.uk; Royal Oak Stables; 9.30am-4.30pm)

LLanberis (☎01286-870765; 41 High St; 9.30am-4.30pm Apr-Oct, 9.30am-3pm Fri-Mon Nov-Mar)

Getting There & Around

The handiest train line runs along the North Wales coast between Chester and Holyhead, via Llandudno Junction and Bangor (from where you can get buses into the park itself).

An excellent local bus network called the **Snowdon Sherpa** (☎0870 608 2608) serves the park, with connections to Llandudno, Betws-y-Coed, Bangor and Llanberis.

SOUTHERN SCOTLAND

North of the border with England, and below the Central Belt region of Edinburgh and Glasgow, sits the broad region of southern Scotland. The western side of this region offers some fine scenery – high hills, moors, forests and a craggy coastline – without the attendant tour buses and crowds you might find in the Highlands. Ayrshire is immediately southwest of Glasgow, with Dumfries & Galloway beyond. Warmed by Gulf Stream currents, it also enjoys the region's mildest climate (we're speaking relatively here). This was also the home of Robbie Burns, Scotland's national poet. The eastern side of this region is called the Scottish Borders – an area of historic towns, ancient abbeys and lush glens with a unique beauty and romance that's often missed by travellers rushing through on their way to Edinburgh.

The places in this section are described roughly west to east.

Alloway

The pretty town of Alloway is best known as the birthplace of Robert Burns. The brand-new **Robert Burns Birthplace Museum** (NTS; www.nts.org.uk; adult/child £8; ⏲10am-5pm Oct-Mar, to 5.30pm Apr-Sep) displays a solid collection of Burnsiana, including manuscripts and possessions of the poet – such as the pistols he packed in order to carry out his daily work as a taxman. A Burns jukebox allows you to select readings of your favourite verses, and there are other entertaining audio and visual performances.

To get here, aim for the town of Ayr (easily reached from Glasgow), then take bus 57 (Monday to Saturday, hourly, 10 minutes).

Isle of Arran

POP 4800

Enchanting Arran lies moored in the Firth of Clyde southwest of Glasgow, strangely undiscovered by foreign tourists. The island is a visual feast, and boasts culinary delights, cosy pubs and stacks of accommodation. The variations in Scotland's dramatic landscape can all be experienced on this one small island, it's best explored by pulling on the hiking boots or jumping on a bicycle.

BRODICK

The gateway to the island, Brodick is the port for most ferries to/from Ardrossan on

THE SCOTTISH BARD

Best remembered for penning the words of 'Auld Lang Syne', Robert Burns (1759–96) is Scotland's most famous poet and a popular hero whose birthday (25 January) is celebrated as Burns Night by Scots around the world.

Burns was born in 1759 in Alloway to a poor family, who scraped a living gardening and farming. At school he soon showed an aptitude for literature and a fondness for the folk song. He later began to write his own songs and satires. When the problems of his arduous farming life were compounded by the threat of prosecution from the father of Jean Armour, with whom he'd had an affair, he decided to emigrate to Jamaica. He gave up his share of the family farm and published his poems to raise money for the journey.

The poems were so well reviewed in Edinburgh that Burns decided to remain in Scotland and devote himself to writing. He went to Edinburgh in 1787 to publish a second edition, but the financial rewards were not enough to live on and he had to take a job as an excise man in Dumfriesshire. Though he worked well, he wasn't a taxman by nature, and described his job as 'the execrable office of whip-person to the blood-hounds of justice'. He contributed many songs to collections published by Johnson and Thomson in Edinburgh, and a 3rd edition of his poems was published in 1793. In all, Burns composed more than 28,000 lines of verse over 22 years. He died of rheumatic fever in Dumfries in 1796, aged 37.

Burns wrote in Lallans, the Scottish Lowland dialect of English; perhaps this is part of his appeal. He was also very much a man of the people, satirising the upper classes and the church for their hypocrisy.

The Burns connection in southern Scotland is milked for all it's worth. Tourist offices have a *Burns Heritage Trail* leaflet leading you to every place that can claim some link. Burns fans should have a look at www.robertburns.org.

the mainland. Highlights include **Brodick Castle & Park** (NTS; www.nts.org.uk; adult/child castle & park £10.50/7.50, park only £5.50/4.50; castle 11am-4pm Sat-Wed Apr-Oct, open daily late Jun-early Sep, park 9.30am-sunset) about 2 miles from town.

Sleeping & Eating

Glenartney B&B ££
(01770-302220; www.glenartney-arran.co.uk; Mayish Rd; s/d £56/78; late Mar-Sep; P) Uplifting views and helpful hosts make this a great option. Cyclists and hikers are welcome.

Eilean Mòr CAFE £
(www.eileanmorarran.com; Shore Rd; mains £8-10; breakfast, lunch & dinner;) Upbeat and modern, this likeable little cafe is not afraid to give its pasta a Scottish twist; try the haggis ravioli.

LOCHRANZA

The village of Lochranza is in a stunning location in a small bay in the island's north. On a promontory stand the ruins of the 13th-century **Lochranza Castle** (Historic Scotland; www.historic-scotland.gov.uk; admission free), said to be the inspiration for the castle in *The Black Island*, Hergé's Tintin adventure.

Sleeping

Lochranza SYHA HOSTEL £
(01770-830631; www.syha.org.uk; Lochranza; dm/f £17.50/72; mid Feb–Oct; P@) A recent refurbishment has made a really excellent hostel of what was always a charming place. Lovely views, great facilities and welcoming management make this a top option.

Catacol Bay Hotel PUB ££
(01770-830231; www.catacol.co.uk; Catacol; r per person £30; P@) Genially run, and with a memorable position overlooking the water, this no-frills pub 2 miles south of Lochranza offers comfortable-enough rooms with shared bathroom and views to lift the heaviest heart.

LAMLASH

Lamlash boasts a dazzling setting, strung along the beachfront. Just off the coast is **Holy Island**, owned by the Samye Ling Tibetan Centre and used as a retreat, but day visits are allowed. Depending on tides, the **ferry** (01770-600998) makes around seven trips a day (adult/child return £10/5, 15 minutes).

Sleeping

Lilybank Guest House B&B ££
(01770-600230; www.lilybank-arran.co.uk; Shore Rd, Lamlash; s/d £50/70; P) Built in the 17th century, but refurbished for 21st-century needs, with comfortable rooms. The front ones have great views over Holy Island.

Information

Brodick Tourist office (01770-303774; www.ayrshire-arran.com; 9am-5pm Mon-Sat, also Sun Jul-Aug)

Getting There & Away

CalMac runs a car ferry between Ardrossan and Brodick (passenger/car return £9.70/59, 55 minutes, four to eight daily), and from April to late October runs services between Claonaig and Lochranza (passenger/car return £8.75/39.10, 30 minutes, seven to nine daily).

Getting Around

BICYCLE Several places hire out bicycles in Brodick, including **Arran Adventure Company** (01770-302244; www.arranadventure.com; Shore Rd; day/week £15/55) and the **Boathouse** (01770-302868; Brodick Beach; day/week £12.50/45).

PUBLIC TRANSPORT Four to seven buses go daily from Brodick pier to Lochranza (45 minutes); many also go from Brodick to Lamlash and Whiting Bay (30 minutes), then on to Kildonan and Blackwaterfoot.

Melrose

POP 1656

On the eastern side of southern Scotland, and epitomising the ambience of the Borders, the charming town of Melrose sits at the feet of the three heather-covered Eildon Hills, featuring a classic market square and one of the finest ruined abbeys in the region.

Sights

Melrose Abbey CHURCH
(HS; www.historic-scotland.gov.uk; adult/child £5.20/3.10; 9.30am-5.30pm Apr-Sep, to 4.30pm Oct-Mar) Perhaps the best of the great Border abbeys, the red sandstone walls and remaining broken shell of Melrose is pure Gothic – and famous for its decorative stonework (see if you can glimpse the pig gargoyle playing the bagpipes on the roof). You can also climb to the top for tremendous views.

Sleeping

Old Bank House B&B ££

(☎01896-823712; www.oldbankhousemelrose.co.uk; 27 Buccleuch St; s/d £40/60) Right in the middle of town, this noble building offers B&B that stands out for its friendly welcome and helpful attitude. Spacious rooms and inviting beds make this a top Borders base.

Melrose SYHA HOSTEL £

(☎01896-822521; www.syha.org.uk; Priorwood; dm/tw £17/36; ⊙late Mar-late Oct; P@) A short walk from the abbey, this stately Georgian house is in a quiet location with a big grassy garden to relax in. The dorms vary substantially in the number of beds and have no lockers, but it's all spotless and the common areas are good.

Information

Tourist office (☎01896-822283; melrose@visitscotland.com, Abbey St; ⊙10am-4.30pm Mon-Sat, noon-4pm Sun Apr-Oct, 10am-4pm Fri & Sat Nov-Mar) By the abbey.

Getting There & Away

First (www.firstgroup.com) buses run to/from Edinburgh (£6, 2¼ hours, hourly) via Peebles. Change in Galashiels (20 minutes, frequent) for more frequent Edinburgh services and for other Borders destinations.

EDINBURGH

POP 440,000

The Scottish capital, Edinburgh (*ed*-in-bruh), and neighbouring Glasgow, with several nearby towns, together make up the 'Central Belt' – by far the most urban area of Scotland. For many years, visitors tended to favour Edinburgh and overlook Glasgow, but recently Scotland's second city has enjoyed a cultural and architectural renaissance. Rather than weighing up which of the two cities to see, it's well worth making the effort to fit them both on your itinerary.

Scotland's proud and historic capital city is a visual delight, built on a grand scale around two hills – one topped by its impressive castle, the other by a big chunk of undeveloped mountain seemingly helicoptered in for effect. Among Edinburgh's well-proportioned buildings and tangle of walkways you'll find a rich haul of excellent museums, galleries, pubs and entertainment options to suit every taste and budget. History jumps out at you from every turn, and every house seems to have its own ghost story. And with the UK's most popular and comprehensive summer festival scene to enjoy, visitors who plan a brief stopover often end up staying longer.

Sights

Edinburgh's city centre is divided into two parts – Old Town and New Town – split by Princess Street Gardens. Most of the sights are here. A major exception is the Royal Yacht *Britannia,* in the redeveloped docklands district of Leith, 2 miles northeast of the centre.

OLD TOWN

Edinburgh's Old Town stretches along a ridge to the east of the castle, a jumbled maze of closes (alleys) and wynds (narrow lanes), stairs and vaults, and cleft along its spine by the cobbled ravine of the Royal Mile, the name of the line of streets between the castle and the Palace of Holyroodhouse.

Edinburgh Castle CASTLE

(www.edinburghcastle.gov.uk; Castle Hill; adult/child incl audio guide £14/7.50; ⊙9.30am-6pm Apr-Sep, to 5pm Oct-Mar, last admission 45min before closing) The brooding black crags of Castle Rock rising above the western end of Princes St are the very reason for Edinburgh's existence. This hill-top fortress defended the invasion route between England and central Scotland, a route followed by countless armies from the Roman legions of the 1st and 2nd centuries AD to the Jacobite troops of Bonnie Prince Charlie in 1745. Edinburgh Castle has played a pivotal role in Scottish history, both as a royal residence – King Malcolm Canmore (r 1058–93) and Queen Margaret first made their home here in the 11th century – and as a military stronghold. The castle last saw military action in 1745; from then until the 1920s it served as the British army's main

DON'T MISS

CASTLE HIT LIST

If you're pushed for time, here's a hit list of the top things to see at Edinburgh Castle:

» Views from Argyle Battery

» One O'Clock Gun

» Great Hall

» Honours of Scotland

» Prisons of War

Central Edinburgh

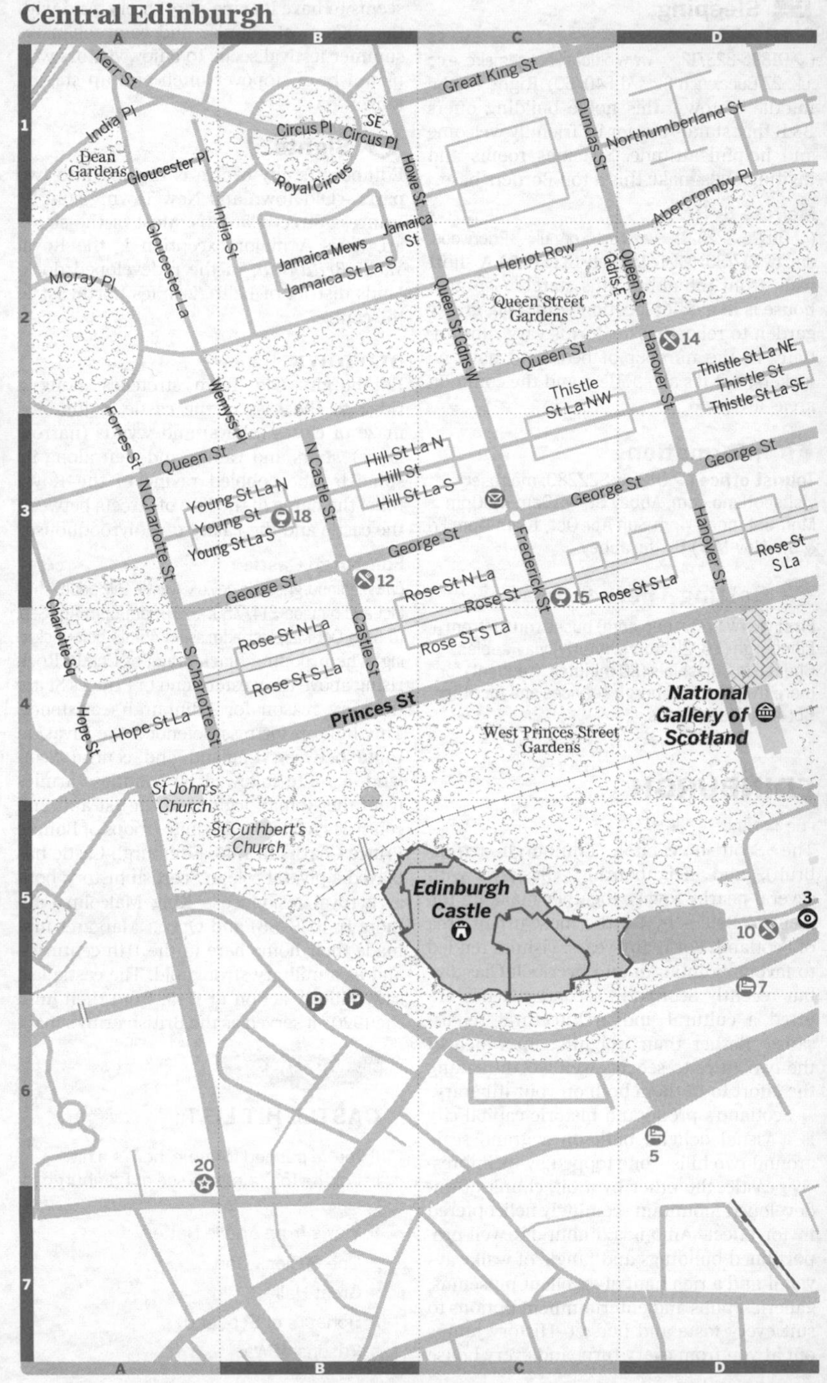

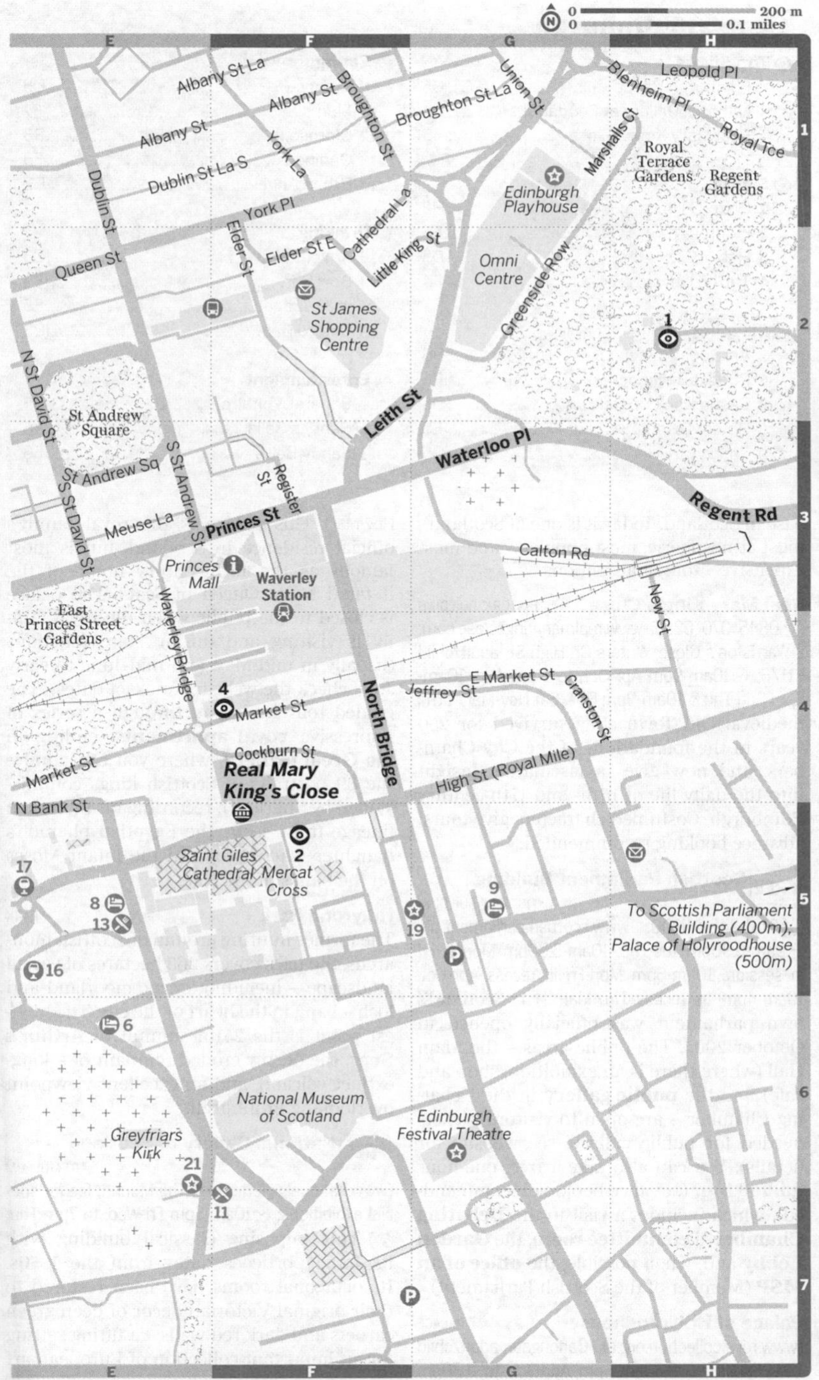
0 200 m
0 0.1 miles
E
F
G
H
Albany St La
Albany St
Broughton St
Broughton St La
Union St
Blenheim Pl
Leopold Pl
Royal Tce
Albany St
York La
Dublin St La S
Marshalls Ct
Royal Terrace Gardens
Regent Gardens
Dublin St
York Pl
Edinburgh Playhouse
Cathedral La
Elder St
Elder St E
Little King St
Queen St
Omni Centre
Greenside Row
St James Shopping Centre
1
N St David St
St Andrew Square
Leith St
Waterloo Pl
S St Andrew St
St Andrew Sq
Register St
S St David St
Regent Rd
Meuse La
Princes St
Calton Rd
Princes Mall
Waverley Station
New St
East Princes Street Gardens
Waverley Bridge
E Market St
Jeffrey St
North Bridge
Cranston St
4
Market St
Cockburn St
Market St
Real Mary King's Close
High St (Royal Mile)
N Bank St
2
Saint Giles Cathedral
Mercat Cross
17
9
8
13
19
To Scottish Parliament Building (400m); Palace of Holyroodhouse (500m)
16
6
National Museum of Scotland
Edinburgh Festival Theatre
Greyfriars Kirk
21
11
1
2
3
4
5
6
7

Central Edinburgh

Top Sights

Edinburgh Castle	C5
National Gallery of Scotland	D4
Real Mary King's Close	F5

Sights

1 Calton Hill	H2
2 Edinburgh Festival Office	F5
3 Hub	D5
4 Tattoo Office	F4

Sleeping

5 Art Roch Hostel	D6
6 Budget Backpackers	E6
7 Castle Rock Hostel	D5
8 Hotel Missoni	E5
9 Smart City Hostel	G5

Eating

10 Amber	D5
11 Mums	F7
12 Oloroso	B3
13 Ondine	E5
14 Urban Angel	D2

Drinking

15 Amicus Apple	C3
16 Bow Bar	E5
17 Jolly Judge	E5
18 Oxford Bar	B3

Entertainment

19 Cabaret Voltaire	G5
20 Henry's Cellar	A6
21 Sandy Bell's	E6

base in Scotland. Today it is one of Scotland's most atmospheric, most popular – and most expensive – tourist attractions.

Real Mary King's Close HISTORIC BUILDING
(☎0845 070 6255; www.realmarykingsclose.com; 2 Warriston's Close, Writers Ct, High St; adult/child £11/6; ⏰10am-9pm Apr-Oct, to 11pm Aug, 10am-5pm Sun-Thu & 10am-9pm Fri & Sat Nov-Mar) This medieval Old Town alley survived for 250 years in the foundations of the City Chambers, and now gives a fascinating insight into the daily life of 16th- and 17th-century Edinburgh. Costumed characters give tours; advance booking recommended.

FREE **Scottish Parliament Building** NOTABLE BUILDING
(☎0131-348 5200; www.scottish.parliament.uk; ⏰9am-6.30pm Tue-Thu, 10am-5.30pm Mon & Fri in session, 10am-6pm Mon-Fri in recess Apr-Oct, 10am-4pm in recess Nov-Mar; wi-fi) Scotland's own parliament was officially opened in October 2005. The public areas – the Main Hall (where there is an exhibition, shop and cafe) and the **public gallery** in the Debating Chamber – are open to visitors (tickets needed for public gallery; see website for details). You can also take a free, one-hour **guided tour** (advance booking recommended), which includes a visit to the **Debating Chamber**, a **committee room**, the **Garden Lobby** and, when possible, the **office of an MSP** (Member of the Scottish Parliament).

Palace of Holyroodhouse PALACE
(www.royalcollection.org.uk; Canongate; adult/child £10.25/6.20; ⏰9.30am-6pm Apr-Oct, to 4.30pm Nov-Mar) This palace is the royal family's official residence in Scotland, but is most famous as the 16th-century home of the ill-fated Mary, Queen of Scots. The palace is closed to the public when the royal family is visiting and during state functions (usually in mid-May, and mid-June to early July; check the website for exact dates). The guided tour leads you through a series of impressive **royal apartments**, ending in the **Great Gallery**, where you can admire the 89 portraits of Scottish kings commissioned by Charles II, recording his unbroken lineage from Scota, the Egyptian pharaoh's daughter who discovered the infant Moses on the banks of the Nile.

Holyrood Park PARK
The former hunting ground of Scottish monarchs, the park covers 263 hectares of varied landscape – including crags, moorland and loch – bang in the heart of the city. The highest point is the 251m summit of **Arthur's Seat**, the deeply eroded remnant of a long-extinct volcano, and an excellent viewpoint overlooking Edinburgh.

FREE **National Gallery of Scotland** ART MUSEUM
(www.nationalgalleries.org; The Mound; fee for special exhibitions; ⏰10am-5pm Fri-Wed, to 7pm Thu; wi-fi) This imposing classical building with its Ionic porticoes dates from the 1850s. Its octagonal rooms have been restored to their original Victorian decor of deep green carpets and dark red walls – a fitting setting for an important collection of European art

from the Renaissance to postimpressionism, with works by Verrocchio (Leonardo da Vinci's teacher), Tintoretto, Titian, Holbein, Rubens, Van Dyck, Vermeer, El Greco, Poussin, Rembrandt, Gainsborough, Turner, Constable, Monet, Pissaro, Gauguin and Cézanne.

Royal Yacht Britannia SHIP
(www.royalyachtbritannia.co.uk; Ocean Terminal, Leith; adult/child £10.50/6.75; 9.30am-6pm Jul-Sep, 10am-5.30pm Apr-Jun & Oct, 10am-5pm Nov-Mar, last admission 1½hr before closing;) Two miles northeast of the city centre, Leith has been Edinburgh's seaport since the 14th century. Like many of Britain's dockland areas, it fell into decay but since the late 1980s has been undergoing a revival. Here you'll find one of Scotland's biggest tourist attractions: the former Royal Yacht *Britannia*, the British royal family's floating home during their foreign travels from the time of her launch in 1953 until her decommissioning in 1997. Take a tour at your own pace with an audio guide (20 languages) for an intriguing insight into the Queen's private tastes – *Britannia* was one of the few places where the royal family could enjoy true privacy.

Tours

Bus Tours

Open-topped bus tours leave from Waverley Bridge and offer hop-on, hop-off tours of the main sights. They're a good way to get your bearings, although with a bus map and a Day Saver bus ticket (£3) you could do much the same thing but without the commentary.

City Sightseeing BUS TOUR
(www.edinburghtour.com; adult/child £12/5) Bright red buses depart every 20 minutes from Waverley Bridge.

Majestic Tour BUS TOUR
(www.edinburghtour.com; adult/child £12/5) Runs every 30 minutes (every 20 minutes in July and August) from Waverley Bridge to the Royal Yacht *Britannia* at Ocean Terminal via the New Town, returning via Holyrood and the Royal Mile.

Walking Tours

Black Hart Storytellers WALKING TOUR
(www.blackhart.uk.com; adult/concession £9.50/7.50) The 'City of the Dead' tour of Greyfriars Kirkyard is probably the scariest of Edinburgh's 'ghost' tours.

Edinburgh Literary Pub Tour WALKING TOUR
(www.edinburghliterarypubtour.co.uk; adult/student £10/8) An enlightening two-hour trawl through Edinburgh's literary history in the entertaining company of Messrs Clart and McBrain.

Rebus Tours WALKING TOUR
(www.rebustours.com; adult/student £10/9) Tours of the 'hidden Edinburgh' frequented by novelist Ian Rankin's fictional detective, John Rebus.

PARLIAMENTARY DEBATE

It's fitting that the design of the Scottish parliament has long been a topic of discussion. Enric Miralles (1955–2000), the architect, believed that a building could be a work of art. However, the weird concrete confection he created has left the good people of Edinburgh scratching their heads in confusion. What does it all mean? The strange forms of the exterior are all symbolic in some way, from the oddly shaped windows on the west wall (inspired by the silhouette of the Reverend Robert Walker Skating on Duddingston Loch, one of Scotland's most famous paintings), to the ground plan of the whole complex which apparently represents a 'flower of democracy rooted in Scottish soil'. If you look down on the complex from Salisbury Crags, you just might agree.

Sleeping

OLD TOWN

TOP CHOICE **Hotel Missoni** BOUTIQUE HOTEL £££
(0131-220 6666; www.hotelmissoni.com; 1 George IV Bridge; r £180;) The Italian fashion house has established a style icon in the heart of the medieval Old Town with this bold statement of a hotel – modernistic architecture, impeccably mannered staff and, most importantly, very comfortable bedrooms.

Smart City Hostel HOSTEL £
(0870 892 3000; www.smartcityhostels.com; 50 Blackfriars St; dm £9-22, tw £80; @) A big (620 beds), bright, modern hostel that feels more like a hotel, with a convivial cafe, excellent facilities and a central location just off the Royal Mile.

Art Roch Hostel HOSTEL £
(0131-228 9981; www.artrochhostel.com; 2 West Port, Grassmarket; dm from £10; @) This new place tries to be all things to all people, and pretty much succeeds, with mixed and

WANT MORE?

For in-depth information, reviews and recommendations at your fingertips, head to the Apple App Store to purchase Lonely Planet's *Edinburgh City Guide* iPhone app.

Alternatively, head to **Lonely Planet** (www.lonelyplanet.com/scotland/edinburgh) for planning advice, author recommendations, traveller reviews and insider tips.

female-only dorms, an executive floor, 24-hour reception and a great location close to the castle.

Castle Rock Hostel HOSTEL £
(☎0131-225 9666; www.scotlands-top-hostels.com; 15 Johnston Tce; dm from £13.50, d £40-55; @) Bright, spacious, single-sex dorms, superb views and a great location – the only way to get closer to the castle would be to pitch a tent on the esplanade.

Budget Backpackers HOSTEL £
(☎0131-226 6351; www.budgetbackpackers.com; 39 Cowgate, The Grassmarket; dm from £12.50-16, tw £48; @) This fun spot piles on the extras, with bike storage, pool tables, laundry and colourful chill-out lounge.

NEW TOWN & AROUND

TOP CHOICE **Six Mary's Place** B&B ££
(☎0131-332 8965; www.sixmarysplace.co.uk; 6 Mary's Pl, Raeburn Pl; s/d/f from £50/94/150; @📶🚭) This attractive Georgian townhouse mixes period features, contemporary furniture and modern colours, plus great (vegetarian-only) breakfasts and a comfy lounge with free coffee.

Dene Guest House B&B ££
(☎0131-556 2700; www.deneguesthouse.com; 7 Eyre Pl; per person £25-50; 👪) A friendly and informal place, with a welcoming owner and spacious bedrooms.

Eating

The last decade has been a boon for foodies – Edinburgh now has more restaurants per head of population than London. For good-value eats, head for the student-populated areas south of the city centre: Brunstfield, Marchmont and Newington. Fine dining is concentrated in the New Town, Stockbridge and Leith.

OLD TOWN

TOP CHOICE **Ondine** SEAFOOD £££
(☎0131-226 1888; www.ondinerestaurant.co.uk; 2 George IV Bridge; mains £14-24; ⊙lunch & dinner) New on the scene in 2009, Ondine has rapidly become one of Edinburgh's finest seafood restaurants, with a menu based on sustainably sourced fish. The two-course pre-theatre (5pm to 6.30pm) dinner costs £15.

Mums CAFE £
(www.monstermashcafe.co.uk; 4a Forrest Rd; mains £6-8; ⊙breakfast, lunch & dinner) The original founder of Monster Mash has reopened with a new name, serving up classic British comfort food – bangers and mash, shepherd's pie, fish and chips.

Amber SCOTTISH ££
(☎0131-477 8477; www.amber-restaurant.co.uk; 354 Castlehill; mains £12-18; ⊙lunch daily, dinner Tue-Sat) You've got to love a place where the waiter greets you with the words, 'My name is Craig, and I'll be your whisky adviser for this evening.' Located in the Scotch Whisky Experience, this restaurant manages to avoid the tourist clichés, and creates genuinely interesting and flavoursome dishes.

NEW TOWN

Urban Angel CAFE £
(☎0131-225 6215; www.urban-angel.co.uk; 121 Hanover St; mains £8-12; ⊙breakfast, lunch & dinner Mon-Sat, lunch Sun) A wholesome deli-cafe-bistro that puts the emphasis on Fairtrade, organic and locally sourced produce, serving all-day brunch, tapas, and a wide range of snacky meals.

TOP CHOICE **Oloroso** SCOTTISH £££
(☎0131-226 7614; www.oloroso.co.uk; 33 Castle St; mains £16-25; ⊙lunch & dinner) One of Edinburgh's most stylish restaurants, perched on a glass-encased rooftop with views across to the Firth of Forth, serving top-notch Scottish produce with Asian and Mediterranean touches. Two-course lunch £18.50.

LEITH

TOP CHOICE **Fishers Bistro** SEAFOOD ££
(☎0131-554 5666; www.fishersbistros.co.uk; 1 The Shore; mains £10-35; ⊙lunch & dinner) This cosy little restaurant, tucked beneath a 17th-century signal tower, is one of the city's best seafood places.

Drinking

Edinburgh has more than 700 drinking establishments, as varied as the population –

from fancy palaces to rough dives, from beardy real-ale pubs to trendy cocktail bars.

OLD TOWN

Bow Bar PUB
(80 West Bow) One of the city's best traditional-style pubs (it's not as old as it looks), serving a range of excellent real ales and a vast selection of malt whiskies in the evenings.

Jolly Judge PUB
(www.jollyjudge.co.uk; 7a James Ct;) A snug little pub tucked away down a close, exuding a cosy 17th-century atmosphere. No music or gaming machines, just the buzz of conversation.

NEW TOWN

Oxford Bar PUB
(www.oxfordbar.com; 8 Young St) The Oxford is that rarest of things these days: a real pub for real people, with no 'theme', no music, no frills and no pretensions. 'The Ox' has been immortalised by Ian Rankin, author of the Inspector Rebus novels, who is a regular here, as is his fictional detective.

Amicus Apple COCKTAIL BAR
(www.amicusapple.com; 15 Frederick St) This laid-back cocktail lounge is New Town's hippest hang-out. The drinks menu ranges from retro classics such as a Bloody Mary or mojito to original and unusual concoctions such as the Cuillin Martini (Tanqueray No 10 gin, Talisker malt whisky and smoked rosemary).

LEITH

Teuchter's Landing PUB
(1 Dock Pl) A cosy warren of timber-lined nooks and crannies housed in a single-storey red-brick building (once a waiting room for ferries across the Firth of Forth), this real ale and malt whisky bar also has outdoor tables on a floating terrace in the dock.

☆ Entertainment

The comprehensive source for what's on is *The List* (www.list.co.uk), an excellent magazine covering entertainment options in both Edinburgh and Glasgow.

Henry's Cellar LIVE MUSIC
(www.theraft.org.uk; 8a Morrison St) One of Edinburgh's most eclectic live-music venues, Henry's has something going on every night of the week.

Sandy Bell's LIVE MUSIC
(25 Forrest Rd) This unassuming bar has been a stalwart of the traditional-music scene for decades. There's music almost every evening at 9pm, and also from 3pm Saturday and Sunday.

Cabaret Voltaire CLUB, LIVE MUSIC
(www.thecabaretvoltaire.com; 36 Blair St) Edinburgh's most 'alternative' club, which eschews huge dance floors in favour of a 'creative crucible' hosting an eclectic mix of DJs, live acts, comedy, theatre, visual arts and the spoken word. Evol (Friday from 10.30pm)

FESTIVAL CITY

Edinburgh boasts a frenzy of festivals, especially in August, with half a dozen world-class events running at the same time. For the basics, see below; for more, see www.edinburghfestivals.co.uk.

Edinburgh Festival Fringe (0131-226 0026; www.edfringe.com; Edinburgh Festival Fringe Office, 180 High St) The biggest festival of the performing arts anywhere in the world, held over 3½ weeks in August, the last two weeks overlapping with the first two weeks of the Edinburgh International Festival.

Edinburgh International Festival (0131-473 2099; www.eif.co.uk) Festooned with superlatives – the oldest, the biggest, the most famous, the best in the world – with three weeks in August of diverse and inspirational music, opera, theatre and dance. Tickets can be purchased at the **Hub** (www.hubtickets.co.uk).

Edinburgh Military Tattoo (0131-225 1188; www.edintattoo.co.uk; Tattoo Office, 32 Market St) A spectacular display of military marching bands, massed pipes and drums, acrobats, cheerleaders and motorcycle display teams, all played out in front of the magnificent backdrop of the floodlit castle during the first three weeks of August.

Edinburgh International Book Festival (0845 373 5888; www.edbookfest.co.uk) A fun fortnight of talks, readings, debates, lectures, book signings and meet-the-author events, for two weeks in August (usually the first two weeks of the Edinburgh International Festival).

BUSES FROM EDINBURGH

DESTINATION	FARE (£)	DURATION (HR)	FREQUENCY
Aberdeen	26	3¼	3 daily
Dundee	14	2	hourly
Fort William	30	4-5	8 daily
Glasgow	6	1¼	every 15min
Inverness	26	4	hourly
Portree	46	7	1 daily
Stirling	7	1	hourly

is an Edinburgh institution catering to the indie-kid crowd, and is regularly voted Scotland's top club night out.

Studio 24 CLUB
(24 Calton Rd) The dark heart of Edinburgh's underground music scene, with a program that covers all bases, from house to nu metal via punk, ska, reggae, tribal, techno and dance.

Information

Edinburgh & Scotland Information Centre (ESIC; ☎0845 225 5121; www.edinburgh.org; Princes Mall, 3 Princes St; ⊙9am-9pm Mon-Sat, 10am-8pm Sun Jul & Aug, 9am-7pm Mon-Sat, 10am-7pm Sun May, Jun & Sep, 9am-5pm Mon-Wed, 9am-6pm Thu-Sun Oct-Apr)

Getting There & Away

Air

Edinburgh Airport (☎0131-333 1000; www.edinburghairport.com), 8 miles west of the city, has numerous flights to other parts of Scotland and the UK, Ireland and mainland Europe.

Bus

Scottish Citylink (☎0871 266 3333; www.citylink.co.uk) coaches connect Edinburgh with Scotland's cities and major towns.

It's also worth checking with **Megabus** (☎0900 160 0900; www.megabus.com) for cheap intercity bus fares (from as little as £3) from Edinburgh to Aberdeen, Dundee, Glasgow, Inverness and Perth.

Train

The main terminus in Edinburgh is Waverley train station, located in the heart of the city. Trains arriving from, and departing for, the west also stop at Haymarket station, which is more convenient for the West End.

First ScotRail (☎08457 55 00 33; www.scotrail.co.uk) operates a regular shuttle service between Edinburgh and Glasgow (£11, 50 minutes, every 15 minutes), and frequent daily services to all Scottish cities including Aberdeen (£40, 2½ hours), Dundee (£20, 1¼ hours) and Inverness (£55, 3¼ hours).

GLASGOW

POP: 634,680

Unpretentious and gregarious, Glasgow defines urban renewal. Once synonymous with poverty and desperation, the city is now a byword for style and chic. Gone are the rusting relics of a moribund shipbuilding industry, replaced by absorbing attractions that celebrate that very heritage. Add to this Scotland's premier eating scene, northern Britain's best range of live music, cutting-edge nightclubs, a vibrant gay culture, and an amazing collection of pubs and bars, and a night or two in Glasgow is likely to be a highlight of your visit.

Sights

CITY CENTRE

Glasgow's main square in the city centre is grand **George Sq**, built in the Victorian era to show off the city's wealth, and dignified by statues of notable Scots, including Robert Burns, James Watt, John Moore and Sir Walter Scott. The prosperity of Glasgow's 18th-century 'tobacco lords', who made vast profits importing tobacco, rum and sugar via lucrative transatlantic trade routes, is reflected in the grand buildings they erected in the area east and southeast of George Sq, now known as the **Merchant City**; many have been renewed as stylish apartments, bars and restaurants.

Glasgow School of Art MACKINTOSH BUILDING
(☎0141-353 4526; www.gsa.ac.uk/tours; 167 Renfrew St; adult/child/family £8.75/7/24; ⏲9.30am-6.30pm Apr-Sep, 10am-5pm Oct-Mar) The architect and designer Charles Rennie Mackintosh is a Glasgow icon, and this is one of his greatest buildings, still fulfilling its original function. The visitor entrance is on Dalhousie St. Excellent hour-long **guided tours** (roughly hourly in summer) are run by architecture students; this is the only way you can visit the building's interior – apart from enrolling.

FREE **Willow Tearooms** MACKINTOSH BUILDING
(www.willowtearooms.co.uk; 217 Sauchiehall St; ⏲9am-5pm Mon-Sat, 11am-5pm Sun) Admirers of the great Mackintosh will love the Willow Tearooms, an authentic reconstruction of tearooms Mackintosh designed and furnished in the early 20th century for restaurateur Kate Cranston. Relive the original splendour of this unique tearoom and admire the architect's stroke in just about everything: he had free rein and gave even the teaspoons his distinctive touch.

EAST END

The oldest part of the city, given a facelift in the 1990s, is concentrated around Glasgow Cathedral, to the east of the modern centre. It takes 20 minutes to walk from George Sq.

Glasgow Cathedral CHURCH
(HS; www.historic-scotland.gov.uk; Cathedral Sq; ⏲9.30am-5.30pm Mon-Sat, 1-5pm Sun Apr-Sep, 9.30am-4.30pm Mon-Sat, 1-4.30pm Sun Oct-Mar) A shining example of Gothic architecture, this is the only mainland Scottish cathedral to have survived the Reformation. The imposing interior conjures up medieval might and sends a shiver down your spine.

THE CLYDE

Once a thriving shipbuilding area, the River Clyde sank into dereliction in the 1980s, but is now being rejuvenated. A major campaign to redevelop Glasgow Harbour, involving the conversion of former docklands into shops and public areas, is under way.

Glasgow Science Centre MUSEUM
(www.glasgowsciencecentre.org; 50 Pacific Quay; Science Mall adult/child £9.95/7.95, IMAX, tower or planetarium £2.50; ⏲10am-5pm) Scotland's flagship millennium project brings science and technology alive through hundreds of interactive family-friendly exhibits. The main components include the **IMAX** theatre, an interactive **Science Mall,** a rotating **observation tower**, and a **planetarium**.

FREE **Riverside Museum** MUSEUM
(www.glasgowmuseums.com; 100 Pointhouse Pl; ⏲10am-5pm Mon-Thu & Sat, 11am-5pm Fri & Sun) Due to open just before this book hit the shelves, this new museum, being built along the Clyde where it meets the River Kelvin, will house a varied collection, including a display of maritime heritage and much of what was formerly in the Museum of Transport. The magnificent barque *Glenlee* (also known as the **Tall Ship**), a beautiful three-master launched in 1896, will be moored here.

WEST END

With its expectant buzz, trendy bars and nonchalant swagger, the West End is as close as Glasgow gets to bohemian. To get here from the centre, buses 9, 16 and 23 run towards Kelvingrove, 8, 11, and 16 to the university.

FREE **Kelvingrove Art Gallery & Museum**
MUSEUM, ART MUSEUM
(www.glasgowmuseums.com; Argyle St; ⏲10am-5pm Mon-Thu & Sat, 11am-5pm Fri & Sun) In a magnificent stone building, this grand Victorian cathedral of culture has been revamped into an unusual museum, with an amazing variety of exhibits. Here you'll find Micronesian shark-tooth swords beside a Spitfire plane, but it's not random mix 'n' match: rooms are thoughtfully themed, and the collection is a manageable size.

FREE **Hunterian Art Gallery** ART MUSEUM
(www.hunterian.gla.ac.uk; 82 Hillhead St; ⏲9.30am-5pm Mon-Sat) A great place to see the art of Scotland: the bold tones of the Scottish Colourists, Samuel Peploe, Francis Cadell, JD Fergusson; works by several of the Glasgow Boys; Sir William MacTaggart's impressionistic landscape; and a special collection of James McNeill Whistler's prints and paintings.

TOP CHOICE **Mackintosh House** MACKINTOSH BUILDING
(www.hunterian.gla.ac.uk; 82 Hillhead St; admission £3, after 2pm Wed free; ⏲9.30am-5pm

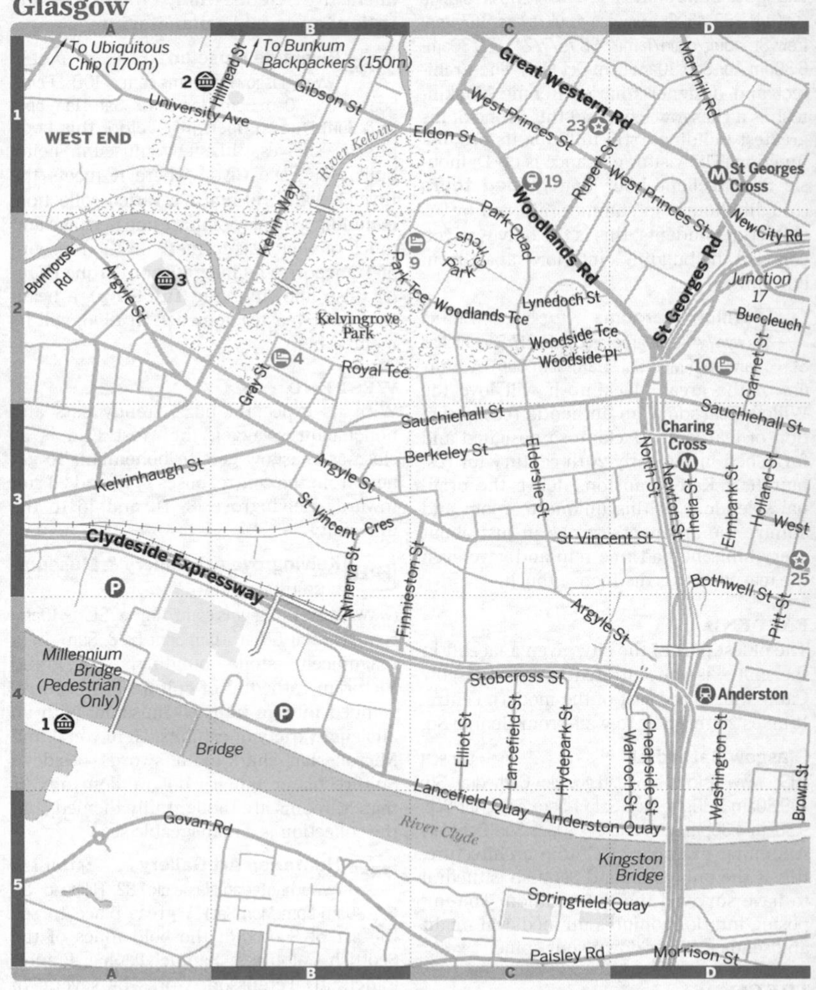

Mon-Sat) Attached to the Hunterian Art Gallery is this faithful reconstruction of Charles Rennie Mackintosh's first home. There's something otherworldly about the style of the beaten silver panels, the long-backed chairs and the surface decorations that echoes medieval Celtic manuscript illuminations. You certainly wouldn't have wanted to be a guest who spilled a glass of red wine on this pristine carpet.

Festivals & Events

Not to be outdone by Edinburgh, Glasgow has some kicking festivals of its own.

Celtic Connections MUSIC FESTIVAL
(0141-353 8000; www.celticconnections.com) Two-week music festival held in January.

West End Festival MUSIC FESTIVAL
(0141-341 0844; www.westendfestival.co.uk) Glasgow's biggest music and arts festival, running for two weeks in June.

Sleeping

CITY CENTRE

TOP CHOICE **Brunswick Hotel** HOTEL ££
(0141-552 0001; www.brunswickhotel.co.uk; 106 Brunswick St; d £50-95;) The 'com-

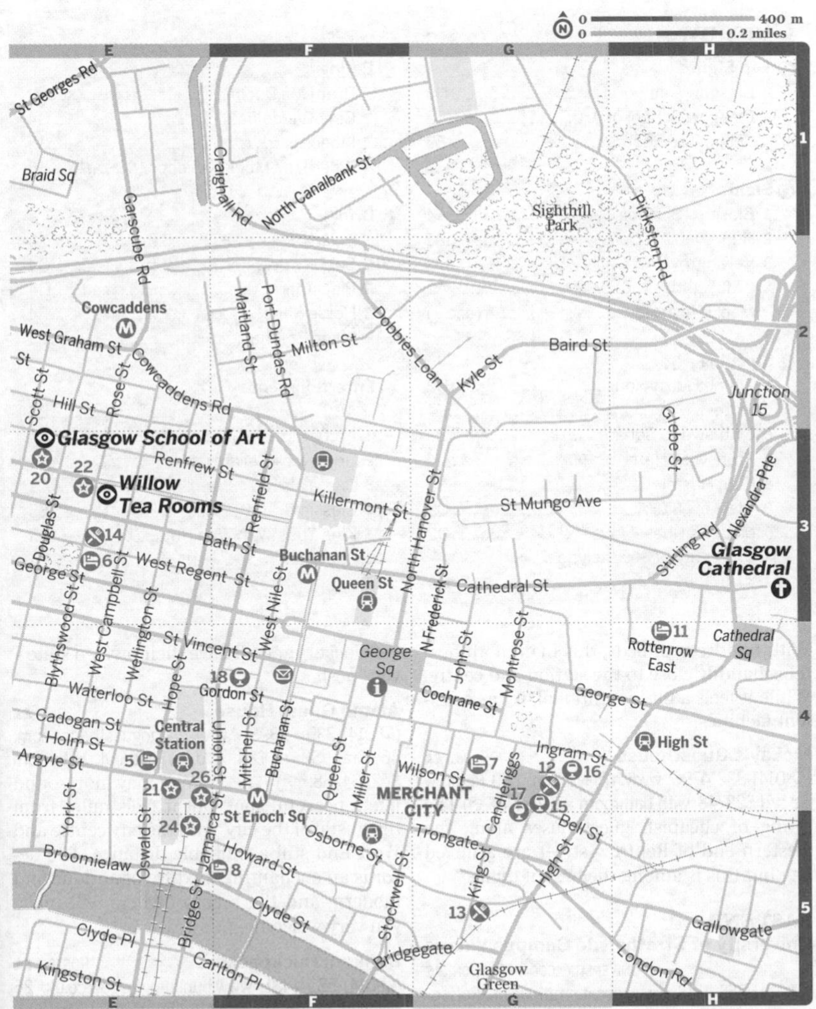

pact' and 'standard' doubles are stylish, and will do if you're here for a night out, but the king-size rooms are well worth the £10 upgrade. Every now and then the whole place converts into a party venue, with DJs in the lifts and art installations in the rooms. You couldn't ask for a more relaxed and friendly Merchant City base.

Blythswood Square HOTEL **£££**

(☎0141-248 8888; www.blythswoodsquare.com; 11 Blythswood Sq; r £195-285; @📶🏊) Recently opened in a gorgeous Georgian terrace, this elegant five-star offers plenty of inner-city luxury. There's an excellent bar and superb restaurant, and a very handsome colonnaded salon space on the 1st floor that functions as an evening spot for cocktails.

Artto HOTEL **££**

(☎0141-248 2480; www.arttohotel.com; 37 Hope St; s/d £70/90; 📶) Right by the train station, this modish, affordable hotel offers compact but attractive rooms. Large windows make staying at the front appealing but light sleepers will be happier at the rear.

Euro Hostel HOSTEL **£**

(☎0141-222 2828; www.euro-hostels.co.uk; 318 Clyde St; dm £15-25, s £35-50, d £40-70; @📶)

Glasgow

Top Sights

	Glasgow Cathedral	H3
	Glasgow School of Art	E3
	Willow Tea Rooms	E3

Sights

1	Glasgow Science Centre	A4
2	Hunterian Art Gallery	A1
3	Kelvingrove Art Gallery & Museum	A2
	Mackintosh House	(see 2)

Sleeping

4	Alamo Guest House	B2
5	Artto	E4
6	Blythswood Square	E3
7	Brunswick Hotel	G4
8	Euro Hostel	F5
9	Glasgow SYHA	C2
10	McLay's Guest House	D2
11	University of Strathclyde Campus Village	H4

Eating

	Brutti Ma Buoni	(see 7)
12	Café Gandolfi	G4
13	Mono	G5
14	Where the Monkey Sleeps	E3

Drinking

15	Artà	G4
16	Babbity Bowster	G4
17	Blackfriars	G4
18	Horse Shoe	F4
19	Uisge Beatha	C1

Entertainment

20	ABC	E3
21	Arches	E4
22	Brunswick Cellars	E3
23	Captain's Rest	C1
24	Classic Grand	E5
25	King Tut's Wah Wah Hut	D3
26	Sub Club	E4

With hundreds of beds, this mammoth hostel is handily close to the station and centre. While it feels a bit institutional, it has excellent facilities.

McLay's Guesthouse B&B ££

(☎0141-332 4796; www.mclays.com; 260 Renfrew St; s/d £28/48, with bathroom £36/56; @ wi-fi) The string of cheapish guesthouses along the western end of Renfrew street are a mixed bag but this is among the best of them.

EAST END

University of Strathclyde Campus Village UNIVERSITY ACCOMMODATION ££

(☎0141-553 4148; www.rescat.strath.ac.uk; Rottenrow East; s £36, without bathroom £30; ⊙mid-Jun–mid-Sep; wi-fi) The uni opens its halls of residence to tourists over summer. The Campus Village, opposite Glasgow Cathedral, offers B&B accommodation in single rooms at good prices. Cheaper, self-catering prices may also be available.

WEST END

Glasgow SYHA HOSTEL £

(☎0141-332 3004; www.syha.org.uk; 8 Park Tce; dm/tw £23/62; @ wi-fi) Perched on a hill overlooking Kelvingrove Park in a charming townhouse, this place is simply fabulous and one of Scotland's best official hostels. Dorms are mostly four to six beds with padlock lockers and all have their own en suite – very posh.

Alamo Guest House B&B ££

(☎0141-339 2395; www.alamoguesthouse.com; 46 Gray St; d £84, s/d/tw without bathroom £42/64/68; wi-fi) The Alamo may not sound like a peaceful spot, but it feels miles from the hustle of the city, with the city centre and West End still a walkable distance. The decor is an enchanting mixture of antique and modern, and the breezy owners will make you very welcome.

Bunkum Backpackers HOSTEL ££

(☎0141-581 4481; www.bunkumglasgow.co.uk; 26 Hillhead St; dm/tw £14/36; P wi-fi) A tempting budget headquarters for assaults on the eateries and pubs of the West End. There's no curfew, but it's not a party hostel.

Eating

Glasgow is the best place to eat in Scotland, with an excellent range of eateries. The West End is the culinary centre of the city; Merchant City also boasts an incredible concentration of quality restaurants and cafes.

CITY CENTRE

Café Gandolfi CAFE, BISTRO ££

(☎0141-552 6813; 64 Albion St; mains £8-14; ⊙breakfast, lunch & dinner Mon-Sat, lunch & dinner

Sun) In the fashionable Merchant City, this cafe-bistro has been pulling in the punters for years.

Brutti Ma Buoni BISTRO ££
(☎0141-552 0001; www.brunswickhotel.co.uk; 106 Brunswick St; mains £8-13; ⏰lunch & dinner; 👪) If you like dining in a place that has a sense of fun, Brutti's menu, with Italian and Spanish influences, draws a smile for its quirkiness and its prices.

Where the Monkey Sleeps CAFE £
(www.monkeysleeps.com; 182 West Regent St; dishes £5-7; ⏰breakfast & lunch Mon-Sat) This funky little number in the middle of the business district is just what you need to get away from the ubiquitous coffee chains.

Mono VEGETARIAN £
(www.myspace.com/monoglasgow; 12 Kings Ct, King St; mains £3-8; ⏰lunch & dinner; ✎) Combining food with music, Mono is one of Glasgow's best vegetarian-vegan eateries.

WEST END

There are numerous excellent restaurants in the West End. They cluster along Byres Rd and, just off it, on Ashton Lane and Ruthven Lane. Gibson St and Great Western Rd also have plenty to offer.

Ubiquitous Chip SCOTTISH £££
(☎0141-334 5007; www.ubiquitouschip.co.uk; 12 Ashton Lane; 2-/3-course dinner £35/40; ⏰lunch & dinner) The original champion of Scottish produce, this restaurant has won lots of awards for its unparalleled Scottish cuisine, and for its lengthy wine list.

Drinking

Some of Scotland's best nightlife is found in the din and sometimes roar of Glasgow's pubs and bars. There are as many different styles of bar as there are punters to guzzle in them; a month of solid drinking wouldn't get you past the halfway mark.

CITY CENTRE

TOP CHOICE **Artà** BAR
(www.arta.co.uk; 13-19 Walls St; ⏰until 3am) This extraordinary place is so baroque that when you hear a Mozart concerto on the stereo, you might expect to see the man himself at the other end of the bar. There's floor-to-ceiling velvet, a chilled vibe and a mixed crowd. The big cocktails are great.

Horse Shoe PUB
(www.horseshoebar.co.uk; 17 Drury St) This legendary city pub and popular meeting place dates from the late 19th century and is largely unchanged. It's a picturesque spot, but its main attraction is what's served – real ale and good food.

Blackfriars PUB
(www.blackfriarsglasgow.com; 36 Bell St) Merchant City's most relaxed and atmospheric pub; the seating area with large windows is great for people-watching.

Babbity Bowster PUB
(16-18 Blackfriars St) In a quiet corner of Merchant City, this handsome spot is perfect for a tranquil daytime drink, particularly in the adjoining beer garden.

THE GENIUS OF CHARLES RENNIE MACKINTOSH

Charles Rennie Mackintosh is to Glasgow what Gaudí is to Barcelona. His quirky, linear and geometric designs are seen everywhere, and you'll see his tall, thin, art nouveau typeface repeatedly reproduced.

Born in Glasgow in 1868, Mackintosh studied at the Glasgow School of Art. In 1896, when he was only 27 years old, he won a competition for his design of the school's new building. The first section, which was opened in 1899, is considered to be the earliest example of art nouveau in Britain, as well as Mackintosh's supreme architectural achievement.

Although Mackintosh's genius was quickly recognised on the Continent, he did not receive the same encouragement in Scotland. His architectural career in Scotland lasted only until 1914, when he moved to England to concentrate on furniture design. He died in 1928, and it is only since the last decades of the 20th century that his genius has been widely recognised.

Many of the buildings Mackintosh designed in Glasgow are open to the public. If you're a fan, the **Mackintosh Trail** ticket (£16), available at the tourist office or any Mackintosh building, gives you a day's free admission to all his creations plus unlimited bus and subway travel.

GAY & LESBIAN GLASGOW

Glasgow has a vibrant gay scene, with the gay quarter found in and around the Merchant City (particularly Virginia, Wilson and Glassford Sts). For more, check out the free **Scots Gay** (www.scotsgay.co.uk) magazine and the Glasgow section of the **GayScotland** (www.gayscotland.com) website.

FHQ (10 John St) In-fashion women-only location in the heart of the Pink Triangle.

Polo Lounge (84 Wilson St) Staff claim 'the city's best talent' is found here; a quick glance at the clientele – male and female – proves their claim.

Waterloo Bar (306 Argyle St) This traditional pub is Scotland's oldest gay bar, with punters of all ages.

WEST END

Uisge Beatha PUB
(www.uisgebeathabar.co.uk; 232 Woodlands Rd). With 100 whiskies and four quirky rooms to choose from, this unique pub is one of Glasgow's best – an antidote to style bars.

☆ Entertainment

Glasgow is Scotland's entertainment city, from fine theatres to cracking nightclubs, and venues showcasing Scottish bands at the cutting edge of modern music. Two bars where you can see the best, and worst, of Glasgow's newest bands are **Brunswick Cellars** (239 Sauchiehall St) and **Classic Grand** (18 Jamaica St).

Sub Club NIGHTCLUB
(www.subclub.co.uk; 22 Jamaica St) Saturdays at the Sub Club are one of Glasgow's legendary nights. The claustrophobic vibe is not for those faint of heart.

Arches NIGHTCLUB
(www.thearches.co.uk; 253 Argyle St) The godfather of Glaswegian clubs is a must for funk and hip-hop freaks.

King Tut's Wah Wah Hut LIVE MUSIC
(www.kingtuts.co.uk; 272a St Vincent St) One of the city's premier live-music pub venues hosts bands every night of the week.

ABC LIVE MUSIC
(O2 ABC; www.abcglasgow.com; 300 Sauchiehall St) Former cinema; medium- to large-size acts.

Captain's Rest LIVE MUSIC
(www.captainsrest.co.uk; 185 Great Western Rd) Variety of indie bands.

Information

Tourist office (0141-204 4400; www.seeglasgow.com; 11 George Sq; 9am-5pm Mon-Sat) Closes later and opens Sundays in summer.

Getting There & Away

Air

Ten miles west of the city, **Glasgow International Airport** (www.glasgowairport.com) handles domestic traffic and international flights. **Glasgow Prestwick Airport** (www.gpia.co.uk), 30 miles southwest of Glasgow, is used by budget airlines, with many connections to Britain and Europe.

Bus

All long-distance buses arrive and depart from **Buchanan bus station** (0141-333 3708; www.spt.co.uk/bus/bbs; Killermont St). For coaches to/from London, **Megabus** (www.megabus.com) has one-way fares for around £11, while **National Express** (08717 81 81 81; www.nationalexpress.com) charges £10 to £35 (eight hours). Most of these services are overnight.

Scottish Citylink (0870 550 5050; www.citylink.co.uk) has buses to most major towns in Scotland.

Aberdeen £26.50, 2¾ to four hours, hourly

Edinburgh £6.30, 1¼ hours, every 15 minutes

Fort William £20.50, three hours, seven daily

Inverness £25.50, 3½ hours, eight daily

Oban £16.40, three hours, four direct daily

Train

Glasgow has two train stations. Generally, Glasgow Central station serves southern Scotland, England and Wales; Queen St station serves the north and east. There are buses every 10 minutes between them. Trains run to/from London's King's Cross and Euston stations (advance purchase single £60, full fare £144, 4½ hours, hourly).

First ScotRail (08457 55 00 33; www.scotrail.co.uk) runs Scottish trains:

Aberdeen £40.30, 2½ hours, hourly

Dundee £22.60, 1½ hours, hourly

Edinburgh £11.50, 50 minutes, every 15 minutes

Fort William £23.40, 3¾ hours, four to five daily

Inverness £70.40, 3½ hours, 10 daily, four on Sunday

Oban £19.30, three hours, three to four daily

CENTRAL SCOTLAND

Central Scotland is less a geographical region and more a catch-all term for everything between the Glasgow–Edinburgh conurbation and the mountains of the northwestern Highlands. Anything you ever dreamed about Scotland you can find here: lochs, hills, castles, whisky distilleries and some truly beautiful islands.

Loch Lomond

The 'bonnie banks' and 'bonnie braes' of Loch Lomond have long been Glasgow's rural retreat, and today the loch's popularity shows no sign of decreasing. The main tourist focus is on the loch's western shore, along the A82. The southern end, around Balloch, is occasionally a nightmare of jet skis and motorboats. The eastern shore, followed by the West Highland Way long-distance footpath, is a little quieter. The region's importance was recognised when it became the heart of **Loch Lomond & the Trossachs National Park** (www.lochlomond-trossachs.org) – Scotland's first national park, created in 2002.

Sleeping & Eating

Loch Lomond Youth Hostel HOSTEL £
(SYHA; ☎01389-850226; Arden; dm £18; ⏲Mar-Oct; P@wifi) Forget about roughing it, this is one of the most impressive hostels in the country – an imposing 19th-century country house set in beautiful grounds overlooking the loch. It's 2 miles north of Balloch and very popular, so book in advance in summer. And yes, it *is* haunted.

TOP CHOICE **Drover's Inn** PUB £
(☎01301-704234; www.thedroversinn.co.uk; Inverarnan; bar meals £8-10, steaks £15-17; ⏲lunch & dinner; P) This low-ceilinged place has smoke-blackened stone, barmen in kilts and walls festooned with moth-eaten stag's heads. We love it as a quirky place to eat and drink. Accommodation (singles/doubles from £40/78) varies from eccentric and rather rundown rooms in the old building (including a ghost in room 6), to more comfortable rooms (with en suite bathrooms) in the modern annexe across the road.

Information

Balloch tourist office (☎0870 720 0607; Balloch Rd; ⏲9.30am-6pm Jun-Aug, 10am-6pm Apr & Sep)

National Park Gateway Centre (☎01389-751035; www.lochlomondshores.com; Loch Lomond Shores, Balloch; ⏲10am-6pm Apr-Sep, to 5pm Nov-Mar; @wifi)

Getting There & Away

BUS First Glasgow buses 204 and 215 run from Argyle St in central Glasgow to Balloch and Loch Lomond Shores (1½ hours, at least two per hour). Scottish Citylink coaches from Glasgow to Oban and Fort William stop at Luss (£8, 55 minutes, six daily).

TRAIN There are frequent trains from Glasgow to Balloch (£4.15, 45 minutes, every 30 minutes).

Stirling

POP 32,673

With an utterly impregnable position atop a mighty crag, Stirling's beautifully preserved old town is a treasure of noble buildings and cobbled streets winding up to the ramparts of its dominant castle. Also here is the brooding Wallace Monument, honouring the giant freedom fighter of *Braveheart* fame, while nearby is Bannockburn, scene of Robert the Bruce's major triumph over the English.

The castle makes a fascinating visit, but make sure you spend time exploring the old town and the picturesque path that circles it. Near the castle are a couple of very snug pubs to toast Scotland's hoary heroes. Below the old town, retail-minded modern Stirling doesn't offer the same appeal; stick to the high ground as much as possible and you'll love the place.

Sights

Stirling Castle CASTLE
(HS; www.historic-scotland.gov.uk; ⏲9.30am-6pm Apr-Sep, to 5pm Oct-Mar) Hold Stirling and you control Scotland. This maxim has ensured that a fortress of some kind has existed here since prehistoric times. You cannot help drawing parallels with Edinburgh castle, and it commands similarly superb views, but many find Stirling's fortress more atmospheric. The location, architecture and historical significance combine to make it a grand and memorable visit. This means it

draws plenty of visitors, so it's advisable to visit in the afternoon; many tourists come on day trips from Edinburgh or Glasgow, so you may have the castle to yourself by about 4pm.

National Wallace Monument MONUMENT
(www.nationalwallacemonument.com; adult/child £7.50/4.50; ⏲10am-5pm Apr-Jun, Sep & Oct, to 6pm Jul & Aug, 10.30am-4pm Nov-Mar) This nationalist memorial, commemorating the bid for Scottish independence, is so Victorian Gothic it deserves circling bats and ravens.

Bannockburn BATTLEFIELD
Though Wallace's heroics were significant, it was Robert the Bruce's defeat of the English on 24 June 1314 at Bannockburn, just outside Stirling, that eventually established lasting Scottish nationhood, sending King Edward II 'homeward, tae think again', as *Flower of Scotland* commemorates. At the **Bannockburn Heritage Centre** (NTS; www.nts.org.uk; adult/child £5.50/4.50; ⏲10am-5pm Oct-Mar, to 5.30pm Apr-Sep), the history pre- and postbattle is lucidly explained, although the battlefield itself (which never closes) is harder to appreciate; apart from a statue of the victor astride his horse and a misbegotten flag memorial, there's nothing to see.

Bannockburn is 2 miles south of Stirling; you can reach it on bus 51 from Murray Pl in the centre.

Sleeping

Castlecroft Guest House B&B ££
(☎01786-474933; www.castlecroft-uk.com; Ballengeich Rd; s/d £45/60; P@📶) Nestling into the hillside under the back of the castle, this great hideaway feels like a rural retreat but is a short, spectacular walk from the heart of historic Stirling.

Willy Wallace Backpackers Hostel HOSTEL £
(☎01786-446773; www.willywallacehostel.com; 77 Murray Pl; dm/tw £17/36; @📶) This highly convenient hostel is friendly, spacious and sociable. There are colourful dormitories, free tea and coffee, a good kitchen and a laissez-faire atmosphere. Other amenities include a laundry service and free internet and wi-fi.

Sruighlea B&B ££
(☎01786-471082; www.sruighlea.com; 27 King St; s/d £40/60; 📶) It feels like a secret hideaway – there's no sign – but is conveniently located smack bang in the centre of town, with eating and drinking places practically on the doorstep.

Stirling SYHA HOSTEL £
(☎01786-473442; www.syha.org.uk; St John St; dm/tw £17.25/45; P@📶) Right in the old town, this hostel has an unbeatable location and great facilities.

Information

Tourist office (☎01786-475019; stirling@visitscotland.com; 41 Dumbarton Rd; ⏲10am-5pm Mon-Sat, plus Sun Jun–mid-Sep; @)

Getting There & Away

BUS Citylink services:

Dundee £12.50, hourly, 1½ hours
Edinburgh £6.70, one hour, hourly
Glasgow £6.60, 45 minutes, hourly
Perth £7.70, 50 minutes, at least hourly

Some buses continue to Aberdeen, Inverness and Fort William.

TRAIN First ScotRail services:

Aberdeen £38.60, 2¼ hours, regular services
Dundee £15.80, one hour, regular services
Edinburgh £6.90, 55 minutes, twice hourly Monday to Saturday, hourly Sunday
Glasgow £7.10, 40 minutes, twice hourly Monday to Saturday, hourly Sunday
Perth £10.40, 35 minutes, regular services

Oban

POP 8120

Oban is a peaceful waterfront town on a delightful bay. There's not a huge amount to see, but it's an appealingly busy – sometimes crowded – place with some excellent restaurants and lively pubs, and it's the main gateway to the islands of Mull, Iona, Colonsay, Barra, Coll and Tiree.

Sights

FREE **McCaig's Tower** HISTORIC BUILDING
(⏲24hr) Crowning the hill above the town centre, this Victorian folly can be reached on foot, up a flight of steps called Jacob's Ladder from Argyll St. Follow the signs. The views over the bay are worth the effort.

Sleeping

As befitting a ferry town, Oban has lots of B&B accommodation.

Barriemore Hotel B&B ££
(☎01631-566356; www.barriemore-hotel.co.uk; Corran Esplanade; s/d from £65/92; P) With a

grand location overlooking Oban Bay and spacious rooms (ask for a sea view).

Heatherfield House B&B ££
(☎01631-562681; www.heatherfieldhouse.co.uk; Albert Rd; s/d from £35/70; P@) Converted 1870s rectory set in extensive grounds. Room 1 has a fireplace, sofa and great view.

Manor House HOTEL £££
(☎01631-562087; www.manorhouseoban.com; Gallanach Rd; r £154-199; P) One of Oban's finest hotels, with small but elegant rooms in Georgian style, a posh bar frequented by local and visiting yachties, and a fine restaurant serving Scottish and French cuisine.

Oban Backpackers Lodge HOSTEL £
(☎01631-562107; www.obanbackpackers.com; Breadalbane St; dm £12.50-13.50; @) A friendly place with a nice atmosphere, good facilities and a large lounge with lots of sofas.

Eating

TOP CHOICE **Waterfront Restaurant** SEAFOOD ££
(☎01631-563110; www.waterfrontoban.co.uk; Waterfront Centre, Railway Pier; mains £10-18; lunch & dinner) The stylish, unfussy decor does little to distract from the superb seafood freshly landed at the quay just a few metres away.

Shellfish Bar SEAFOOD £
(Railway Pier; mains £2-7; lunch) If you want to savour superb Scottish seafood without the expense of an upmarket restaurant, head for Oban's famous seafood stall – it's the green shack on the quayside near the ferry terminal.

Kitchen Garden CAFE £
(www.kitchengardenoban.co.uk; 14 George St; mains £3-8; lunch daily, dinner Thu-Sat) Great little cafe above a deli – good coffee, cakes, homemade soups and sandwiches.

Information

Tourist office (☎01631-563122; www.oban.org.uk; Argyll Sq; 9am-7pm Jul & Aug, 9am-5.30pm Mon-Sat, 10am-5pm Sun May, Jun & Sep, 9am-5.30pm Mon-Sat Oct-Apr)

Getting There & Away

The bus, train and ferry terminals are all grouped conveniently together next to the harbour on the southern edge of the bay.

BOAT CalMac (www.calmac.co.uk) ferries link Oban with the islands of Mull, Coll, Tiree, Lismore, Colonsay, Barra and Lochboisdale. Ferries to the Isle of Kerrera depart from a separate jetty, about 2 miles southwest of Oban town centre.

BUS Scottish Citylink buses run to/from Glasgow (£17, three hours, four daily).

TRAIN Oban is at the terminus of a scenic route that branches off the West Highland line at Crianlarich. There are up to three trains daily to/from Glasgow (£19, three hours). If you're heading north, the train to Fort William takes a very roundabout route. You're better off by bus.

THAR SHE BLOWS!

The North Atlantic Drift – a swirling tendril of the Gulf Stream – carries warm water into the cold, nutrient-rich seas off the Scottish coast, resulting in huge blooms of plankton. Small fish feed on the plankton, and bigger fish feed on the smaller fish. And this huge seafood smorgasbord attracts large numbers of marine mammals: porpoises, dolphins, minke whales and even – though sightings are rare – humpback and sperm whales. Scotland has embraced the cetaceans, and dozens of operators around the coast offer whale-spotting boat trips lasting from a couple of hours to all day. While seals, porpoises and dolphins can be seen year-round, minke whales are migratory. The best time to see them is from June to August, with August being the peak month for sightings. The website of the **Hebridean Whale & Dolphin Trust** (www.whaledolphintrust.co.uk) has lots of information on the species you are likely to see, and how to identify them.

Isle of Mull

POP 2600

From the rugged ridges of Ben More and the black basalt crags of Burg to the blinding white sand, rose-pink granite and emerald waters that fringe the Ross, lovely Mull can lay claim to some of the finest and most varied scenery in the Inner Hebrides. Add in two impressive castles and easy access from Oban, and you can see why it's sometimes impossible to find a spare bed on the island.

TOBERMORY

POP 750

Tobermory, the island's main town, is a picturesque little fishing port and yachting centre with brightly painted houses arranged around a sheltered harbour, with a grid-patterned 'upper town'. The village was the setting for the children's TV program *Balamory,* and while the series stopped filming in 2005, regular repeats mean that the town still swarms in summer with toddlers towing parents around looking for their favourite TV characters.

Sleeping

Cuidhe Leathain B&B ££
(☎01688-302504; www.cuidhe-leathain.co.uk; Salen Rd; r per person £35;) A handsome 19th-century house in the upper town, with a cosily cluttered atmosphere. The owners are a fount of knowledge about Mull and its wildlife.

2 Victoria St B&B £
(☎01688-302263; 2 Victoria St; s/d £25/40; ⏲Easter-Oct) Traditional, old-school B&B with simple, homely bedrooms (with shared bathroom) and a friendly and hospitable host.

Tobermory Youth Hostel HOSTEL £
(SYHA; ☎01688-302481; Main St; dm £15; ⏲Mar-Oct; @) Great location in a Victorian house right on the waterfront. Bookings recommended.

Information

Craignure tourist office (☎01680-812377; ⏲8.30am-5pm Mon-Sat, 10.30am-5pm Sun)

Tobermory tourist office (☎01688-302182; The Pier, Tobermory; ⏲9am-6pm Mon-Sat, 10am-5pm Sun Jul & Aug, 9am-5pm Mon-Sat, 11am-5pm Sun May & Jun, shorter hours rest of yearr)

Getting There & Around

There are frequent **CalMac** (www.calmac.co.uk) car ferries from Oban to Craignure (passenger/car £4.65/41.50, 40 minutes, every two hours), and another car-ferry link from Lochaline to Fishnish, on the east coast of Mull (£2.80/12.55, 15 minutes, at least hourly).

BICYCLE You can hire bikes for around £10 to £15 a day.

Brown's Hardware Shop (☎01688-302020; www.brownstobermory.co.uk; Main St, Tobermory)

On Yer Bike (☎01680-300501; Inverinate, Salen) Easter to October only. Also has an outlet by the ferry terminal at Craignure.

BUS **Bowman's Tours** (☎01680-812313; www.bowmanstours.co.uk) is the main operator, connecting the ferry ports and the island's main villages. Bus 495 goes from Craignure to Tobermory (£7 return, one hour, six daily Monday to Friday, four or five Saturday and Sunday), and bus 496 links Craignure to Fionnphort (£11 return, 1¼ hours, three or four daily Monday to Saturday, one Sunday).

St Andrews

POP 14,209

For a small place, St Andrews made a big name for itself, firstly as religious centre, then as Scotland's oldest university town. But its status as the home of golf has propelled it to even greater fame, and today's pilgrims arrive with a set of clubs. It's a lovely place to visit even if you've no interest in the game, with impressive medieval ruins, stately university buildings, idyllic white sands, and excellent accommodation and eating options.

Sights

British Golf Museum MUSEUM
(www.britishgolfmuseum.co.uk; Bruce Embankment; adult/child £6/3; ⏲9.30am-5pm Mon-Sat, 10am-5pm Sun Apr-Oct, 10am-4pm Nov-Mar) The museum provides an extraordinarily comprehensive overview of the history and development of the game of golf and the role of St Andrews, plus it has a large collection of memorabilia.

Opposite the museum is the **Royal & Ancient Golf Club**, which stands proudly at the head of the **Old Course**, which you can stroll on once play is finished for the day, and all day on Sundays. Beside it stretches magnificent **West Sands** beach, made famous by the film *Chariots of Fire*.

St Andrews Cathedral RUINS
(HS; www.historic-scotland.gov.uk; The Pends; adult/child £4.20/2.50, incl castle £7.20/4.30; ⏲9.30am-5.30pm Apr-Sep, to 4.30pm Oct-Mar) The ruins of this cathedral are all that's left of one of Britain's most magnificent medieval buildings, but you can still appreciate the scale and majesty of the edifice founded in 1160. The entrance fee applies only to the tower and museum; you can wander freely around the atmospheric ruins.

St Andrews Castle CASTLE
(HS; www.historic-scotland.gov.uk; The Scores; adult/child £5.20/3.10, with cathedral £7.20/4.30; ⏲9.30am-5.30pm Apr-Sep, to 4.30pm Oct-Mar) Not far from the cathedral and with dramatic coastline views, this ruined castle is very evocative.

Sleeping

TOP CHOICE **Abbey Cottage** B&B ££
(☎01334-473727; www.abbeycottage.co.uk; Abbey Walk; s £40, d £59-64; P) You know you've strayed from B&B mainstream when your charming host's hobby is photographing tigers in the wild – don't leave without browsing her albums. This engaging spot sits below the town, surrounded by stone walls which enclose a rambling garden; it feels like you are staying in the country.

Hazelbank Hotel HOTEL £££
(☎01334-472466; www.hazelbank.com; 28 The Scores; s/d £90/151; @) Offering a genuine welcome, this family-run place has front rooms with marvellous views along the beach and out to sea (rooms at the back are cheaper and more spacious).

Five Pilmour Place B&B ££
(☎01334-478665; www.5pilmourplace.com; 5 Pilmour Pl; s £75, d £105-130; @) Just around the corner from the Old Course, this luxurious and intimate spot offers stylish, compact rooms with an eclectic range of styles as well as modern conveniences such as flat-screen TV and DVD player. The king-size beds are especially comfortable, and the lounge area is a stylish treat.

St Andrews Tourist Hostel HOSTEL £
(☎01334-479911; www.standrewshostel.com; St Marys Pl; dm £13-14;) Laid-back and central, this hostel in a stately old building has high corniced ceilings and a laissez-faire approach. The dorms could use new mattresses, but are clean and bright.

University of St Andrews COLLEGE ROOMS ££
(www.discoverstandrews.com; ⊙mid-Jun–mid-Sep; P@) When the university is out of session, three student residences are opened up as visitor accommodation. There's a hotel, **New Hall** (☎01334-467000; s/d £56/83); self-catering rooms, **David Russell Hall** (☎01334-467100; apt for 3/7 days £290/560); and budget single rooms in the central **McIntosh Hall** (☎01334-467035; s/d £34/60). These prices are all good value for the standard of accommodation on offer.

Eating

Vine Leaf SCOTTISH ££
(☎01334-477497; www.vineleafstandrews.co.uk; 131 South St; 2-course dinner £23.50; ⊙dinner Tue-Sat;) Classy, comfortable, and well established, this friendly place offers a changing menu of sumptuous Scottish seafood, game and vegetarian dishes.

Grill House BISTRO £
(www.grillhouserestaurant.co.uk; St Mary's Pl; mains £6-15; ⊙lunch & dinner) This sometimes boisterous restaurant offers something for every taste and budget. The upbeat atmosphere and service are great, as is the £5 lunchtime deal.

Tailend BISTRO £
(130 Market St; mains £6-10; ⊙breakfast, lunch & dinner) Delicious fresh fish sourced from Arbroath just up the coast puts this new St Andrews arrival a class above most chippies.

Information

Tourist office (☎01334-472021; www.visit-standrews.co.uk; 70 Market St; ⊙9.15am-6.30pm Mon-Sat, 11am-4pm Sun Apr-Jun, 9.15am-6.30pm Mon-Sat, 9.30am-5pm Sun Jul-Sep, 9.15am-5pm Mon-Sat Oct-Mar; @)

Getting There & Away

BUS Frequent services:

Edinburgh via Kirkcaldy £9.40, two hours, hourly

Dundee 30 minutes, half-hourly

Glasgow £9.40, 2 ½ hours, hourly

Stirling £7.30, two hours, six to seven Monday to Saturday

TRAIN There is no train station in St Andrews itself, but you can take a train from Edinburgh to Leuchars, 5 miles to the northwest (£11.20, one hour, hourly); grab a seat on the right-hand side of the carriage for great Firth views. From here, buses leave very regularly for St Andrews.

Aberdeen

POP 197,300

Aberdeen is the powerhouse of the northeast, fuelled by the North Sea petroleum industry. Oil money has made the city as expensive as London and Edinburgh, and there are hotels, restaurants and clubs with prices to match the depth of oil-wealthy pockets. Fortunately, most of the cultural attractions, such as the excellent Maritime Museum and the Aberdeen Art Gallery, are free.

Aberdeen is known throughout Scotland as 'the granite city'. On a sunny day the granite lends an attractive glitter, but when grey rain clouds scud in off the North Sea, it can be hard to tell where the buildings stop and the sky begins.

Sights

FREE Marischal College & Museum MUSEUM
(www.abdn.ac.uk/marischal_museum; Marischal College, Broad St; ⏲10am-5pm Mon-Fri, 2-5pm Sun) Marischal College was founded in 1593 and merged with King's College in 1860 to create the modern University of Aberdeen. The impressive facade in Perpendicular Gothic style dates from 1906 and is the world's second-largest granite structure (after L'Escorial near Madrid). At the time of research, the building was being converted into Aberdeen City Council's new headquarters.

Founded in 1786, the museum houses a fascinating collection. In one room, the history of northeastern Scotland is depicted through its myths, customs, famous people, architecture and trade. The other gallery gives an anthropological overview of the world, incorporating objects from vastly different cultures, arranged thematically (Polynesian wooden masks alongside gas masks and so on). The museum was closed to the public during building work, but will reopen sometime in 2011.

FREE Aberdeen Art Gallery ART MUSEUM
(www.aagm.co.uk; Schoolhill; ⏲10am-5pm Tue-Sat, 2-5pm Sun; 📶) Behind the grand facade of Aberdeen Art Gallery is a cool, marble-lined space exhibiting the work of contemporary Scottish and English painters such as Gwen Hardie, Stephen Conroy, Trevor Sutton and Tim Ollivier.

FREE Aberdeen Maritime Museum MUSEUM
(www.aagm.co.uk; Shiprow; ⏲10am-5pm Mon-Sat, noon-3pm Sun) Overlooking the nautical bustle of the harbour is the Maritime Museum, centred on a three-storey replica of a North Sea oil production platform, with exhibits explaining all you ever wanted to know about the petroleum industry.

Sleeping

There are clusters of B&Bs on Bon Accord St and Springbank Tce (both 400m southwest of the train station), and along Great Western Rd (the A93, a 25-minute walk southwest of the city centre).

TOP CHOICE Globe Inn B&B ££
(☎01224-624258; www.the-globe-inn.co.uk; 13-15 North Silver St; s/d £65/70) This popular pub has comfortable guestrooms upstairs. There's live music on weekends so it's not a place for early-to-bed types, but the price versus location factor can't be beat.

Butler's Islander Guest House B&B ££
(☎01224-212411; www.butlersguesthouse.com; 122 Crown St; s £40-65, d £60-80; @📶) A cosy place with a big breakfast menu.

Aberdeen Youth Hostel HOSTEL £
(SYHA; ☎01224-646988; 8 Queen's Rd; dm £18-20; @📶) This budget option is a mile west of the train station.

Eating & Drinking

TOP CHOICE Café 52 BISTRO ££
(☎01224-590094; www.cafe52.net; 52 The Green; mains £12-16; ⏲breakfast, lunch & dinner Mon-Sat, breakfast & lunch Sun; 📶) A haven of laid-back industrial chic serving some of the area's finest and most inventive cuisine.

Foyer FUSION ££
(☎01224-582277; www.foyerrestaurant.com; 82a Crown St; mains £10-19; ⏲lunch & dinner Tue-Sat; 🖉) Foyer is a light and airy art gallery and restaurant, run by a charity for homeless youth. The seasonal menu fuses Scottish, Mediterranean and Asian influences, with lots of good vegetarian options.

Sand Dollar Café CAFE/BISTRO £
(www.sanddollarcafe.com; 2 Beach Esplanade; mains £4-7) This place is a cut above your usual seaside cafe – on sunny days you can sit at the wooden tables outside and share a bottle of chilled white wine, while the evening bistro menu (mains £11 to £20) offers steak and seafood dishes.

Prince of Wales PUB
(7 St Nicholas Lane) Tucked down an alley off Union St, Aberdeen's best-known pub boasts the longest bar in the city, and a great range of real ales and good-value pub grub.

Information

Tourist office (☎01224-288828; www.aberdeen-grampian.com; 23 Union St; ⏲9am-6.30pm Mon-Sat, 10am-4pm Sun Jul & Aug, 9.30am-5pm Mon-Sat Sep-Jun)

Getting There & Away

AIR **Aberdeen Airport** (www.aberdeenairport.com) is at Dyce, 6 miles northwest of the city centre. There are regular flights to numerous Scottish and UK destinations, including Orkney and Shetland, and international flights to the Netherlands, Norway, Denmark and France.

BOAT Car ferries from Aberdeen to Orkney (passenger single £17 to £26, car single £69 to £94, six hours, three or four weekly) and Shetland (passenger single £23 to £35, car single £92 to £124, 12 to 14 hours, daily) are run by **Northlink Ferries** (www.northlinkferries.co.uk). The ferry terminal is a short walk east of the train and bus stations.

BUS National Express runs direct buses to/from London (£45, 12 hours) twice daily, one of them overnight. Scottish Citylink runs services to Edinburgh (£26, 3¼ hours) and Glasgow (£26, 4¼ hours).

TRAIN Several trains run daily to/from London's King's Cross (£122, off-peak fares are cheaper, 7½ hours); some are direct, but most involve a change at Edinburgh. Other destinations include Edinburgh (£40, 2½ hours), Glasgow (£40, 2¾ hours) and Inverness (£25, 2¼ hours).

NORTHERN & WESTERN SCOTLAND

This area is a long way north, and takes effort to reach, but it is by far the best bit of Scotland, and one of the best bits of the whole of Britain too. Some folks (well, those who love mountains and wild places) would even say that it's one of the finest parts of the whole of Europe.

The western part of this area includes deep lochs, misty glens and towering snow-covered mountains. Famous name-checks include Ben Nevis, Britain's highest peak. The northern area, often called the Northwest Highlands, is the land beyond the Great Glen – the geological fault running across Scotland from Fort William to Inverness, separating this remote and ruggedly region from the rest of the country.

It's easy to underestimate the scale of this part of Scotland, so give yourself extra time to explore. See www.visithighlands.com for transport and accommodation advice.

Inverness

POP 55,000

Inverness is the capital of the Highlands, and one of the fastest-growing towns in Britain. It's a transport hub and jumping-off point for the central, western and northern Highlands, the Moray Firth coast and the Great Glen. In summer it overflows with visitors intent on monster hunting at nearby Loch Ness, but it's worth a visit in its own right for a stroll along the picturesque River Ness and a cruise on the Moray Firth in search of its famous bottlenose dolphins.

Sleeping

There are lots of B&Bs along Old Edinburgh Rd and Ardconnel St on the east side of the river, and on Kenneth St and Fairfield Rd on the west side, plus a good range of backpacker accommodation.

TOP CHOICE **Trafford Bank** B&B ££
(01463-241414; www.traffordbankguesthouse.co.uk; 96 Fairfield Rd; s/d from £85/110; P wi-fi) This place is only 10 minutes' walk from the city centre, and highly recommended for its comfortable rooms and luxurious touches.

TOP CHOICE **Rocpool Reserve** BOUTIQUE HOTEL £££
(01463-240089; www.rocpool.com; Culduthel Rd; s/d from £160/195; P wi-fi) Boutique chic meets the Highlands in this slick and sophisticated little hotel, where an elegant Georgian exterior conceals an oasis of contemporary cool.

Ardconnel House B&B ££
(01463-240455; www.ardconnel-inverness.co.uk; 21 Ardconnel St; per person from £35; wi-fi) A terraced Victorian house with six comfortable en suite rooms, a dining room with crisp white table linen, and a breakfast menu that includes Vegemite for homesick antipodeans.

Bazpackers Backpackers Hotel HOSTEL £
(01463-717663; 4 Culduthel Rd; dm/tw £14/38; @) Inverness's smallest hostel (30 beds) is hugely popular – a friendly, quiet place with a convivial lounge centred on a wood-burning stove, a small garden and great views.

Inverness Millburn SYHA Hostel HOSTEL £
(SYHA; 01463-231771; Victoria Dr; dm £18.50; Apr-Dec; P @ wi-fi) This modern 166-bed hostel is 10 minutes' walk northeast of the city centre. With its comfy beds and flashy stainless-steel kitchen, some reckon it's the best hostel in the country.

Eating & Drinking

TOP CHOICE **Café 1** BISTRO ££
(01463-226200; www.cafe1.net; 75 Castle St; mains £10-20; lunch & dinner Mon-Sat) This friendly and appealing little bistro has candle-lit tables and an international menu based on quality Scottish produce.

Mustard Seed MODERN SCOTTISH ££
(01463-220220; www.mustardseedrestaurant.co.uk; 16 Fraser St; mains £12-16; lunch &

dinner) Bright and bustling, Mustard Seed brings a dash of big-city style to Inverness. The menu changes weekly, focusing on Scottish and French cuisine with a modern twist. Grab a table on the upstairs balcony – with a great view across the river. The two-course lunch for £6 is hard to beat.

TOP CHOICE **Clachnaharry Inn** PUB £
(www.clachnaharryinn.co.uk; 17-19 High St; Clachnaharry) Just over a mile northwest of the city centre, on the bank of the Caledonian Canal, this is a delightful old coaching inn (with beer garden out back) serving an excellent range of real ales and good pub grub.

Leakey's CAFE £
(Greyfriars Hall, Church St; ⌚lunch Mon-Sat) Cafe in secondhand bookshop.

Information

Tourist office (☎01436-234353; www.visithighlands.com; Castle Wynd; ⌚9am-6pm Mon-Sat, 9.30am-5pm Sun Jul & Aug, 9am-5pm Mon-Sat, 10am-4pm Sun Jun, Sep & Oct, 9am-5pm Mon-Sat Apr & May, limited hours Nov-Mar)

Getting There & Away

AIR **Inverness airport** (www.hial.co.uk/inverness-airport) is at Dalcross, 10 miles east of the city. There are scheduled flights to London, Belfast, Stornoway, Benbecula, Orkney, Shetland and several other British airports.

BUS **National Express** (www.nationalexpress.com) operates a direct overnight bus to/from London (£45, 13 hours, one daily), with more frequent services requiring a change at Glasgow.

Citylink (www.citylink.co.uk) has connections to Glasgow (£26, 3½ to 4½ hours, hourly), Edinburgh (£26, 3½ to 4½ hours, hourly), Fort William (£11, two hours, five daily), Ullapool (£9, 1½ hours, two daily except Sunday) and Portree on the Isle of Skye (£17, 3½ hours, five daily).

TRAIN There is one direct train daily to/from London (£99, eight hours); others require a change at Edinburgh. There are several direct trains a day from Glasgow (£55, 3½ hours), Edinburgh (£55, 3¼ hours) and Aberdeen (£25, 2¼ hours). The line from Inverness to Kyle of Lochalsh (£18, 2½ hours, four daily Monday to Saturday, two Sunday) provides one of Britain's great scenic train journeys.

Loch Ness

Deep, dark and narrow, Loch Ness stretches for 23 miles between Inverness and Fort Augustus. Its bitterly cold waters have been extensively explored in search of the elusive Loch Ness monster, but most visitors see her only in cardboard cut-out form at the monster exhibitions. The village of **Drumnadrochit** is a hotbed of beastie fever, with two monster exhibitions battling it out for the tourist dollar. The **Loch Ness Exhibition Centre** (www.loch-ness-scotland.com; adult/child £6.50/4.50; ⌚9am-6.30pm Jul & Aug, to 6pm Jun & Sep, 9.30am-5pm Feb-May & Oct, 10am-3.30pm Nov-Jan; 📶) is the better of the two Nessie-themed attractions, with a scientific approach that allows you to weigh the evidence for yourself.

Getting There & Away

Scottish Citylink and Stagecoach buses from Inverness towards Fort William run along the shores of Loch Ness (six to eight daily, five on Sunday). The bus stops at Drumnadrochit (£6.20, 30 minutes) and Loch Ness Youth Hostel (£10, 45 minutes).

Glen Coe

Scotland's most famous glen is also one of the grandest and, in bad weather, the grimmest. The southern side is dominated by three massive, brooding spurs, known as the **Three Sisters**, while the northern side is enclosed by the continuous steep wall of the knife-edged **Aonach Eagach** ridge. The main road threads its lonely way through the middle of all this mountain grandeur.

Glencoe was written into the history books in 1692 when the resident MacDonalds were murdered by Campbell soldiers in what became known as the Glencoe Massacre.

The little village of Glencoe stands on the south shore of Loch Leven at the western end of the glen.

Sleeping & Eating

TOP CHOICE **Clachaig Inn** HOTEL ££
(☎01855-811252; www.clachaig.com; Clachaig, Glencoe; s/d £70/88; P📶) A favourite haunt of hill walkers and climbers (bar meals £8 to £12).

Glencoe Independent Hostel HOSTEL £
(☎01855-811906; www.glencoehostel.co.uk; Glencoe; dm £12-15, bunkhouse £11-12; P) This handily located hostel is just 10 minutes' walk from the Clachaig Inn.

Getting There & Away

Scottish Citylink buses run to Glencoe from Fort William (£7, 30 minutes, eight daily) and Glasgow (£19, 2½ hours, eight daily).

Fort William

POP 9910

Basking on the shores of Loch Linnhe amid magnificent mountain scenery, Fort William has one of the most enviable settings in the whole of Scotland. If it wasn't for the busy dual carriageway crammed between the town centre and the loch, and one of the highest rainfall records in the country, it would be almost idyllic. Even so, 'Fort Bill' has carved out a reputation as 'Outdoor Capital of the UK' (www.outdoorcapital.co.uk), and its easy access by rail and bus makes it a good launch-pad for Highland exploration.

Sleeping &Eating

TOP CHOICE Lime Tree HOTEL ££
(☎01397-701806; www.limetreefortwilliam.co.uk; Achintore Rd; s/d from £70/100; P) This former Victorian manse overlooking Loch Linnhe is an 'art gallery with rooms', decorated throughout with atmospheric Highland landscapes. Foodies rave about the restaurant, and the gallery space – a triumph of sensitive design – stages everything from serious exhibitions to folk concerts.

Grange B&B ££
(☎01397-705516; www.grangefortwilliam.com; Grange Rd; r per person £56-59; P) An exceptional 19th-century villa set in its own landscaped grounds, fitted with log fires, chaise longues and Victorian roll-top baths.

Fort William Backpackers HOSTEL £
(☎01397-700711; www.scotlands-top-hostels.com; Alma Rd; dm/tw from £14/38; @) A 10-minute walk from the bus and train stations, this lively and welcoming hostel is perched on a hillside with great views over Loch Linnhe.

Bank Street Lodge HOSTEL £
(☎01397-700070; www.bankstreetlodge.co.uk; Bank St; dm/tw £14.50/48) Part of a modern hotel and restaurant complex, Bank Street Lodge is the most central budget option, only 250m from the train station.

Grog & Gruel PUB ££
(www.grogandgruel.co.uk; 66 High St; mains £9-12) A traditional-style, wood-panelled pub with an excellent range of cask ales from regional Scottish and English microbreweries. Bar meals are served and upstairs the lively Tex-Mex restaurant is open for dinner.

Information

Tourist office (☎01397-703781; www.visithighlands.com; 15 High St; ⌚9am-6pm Mon-Sat, 10am-5pm Sun Apr-Sep, limited hours Oct-Mar)

Getting There & Away

BUS Scottish Citylink buses link Fort William with Glasgow (£21, three hours, eight daily) and Edinburgh (£30, 4½ hours, one daily direct, seven with a change at Glasgow) via Glencoe and Crianlarich, as well as Oban (£9, 1½ hours, three daily), Inverness (£11, two hours, five daily) and Portree on the Isle of Skye (£28, three hours, four daily).

CLIMBING BEN NEVIS

Looming over Fort William is Ben Nevis (1344m). As the highest peak in the British Isles, it attracts thousands of people who would not normally go anywhere near the summit of a Scottish mountain. Many get to the top with no trouble, but every year a surprisingly large number people have to be rescued. Even if you're climbing 'the Ben' on a fine summer's day, an ascent should not be undertaken lightly. You will need proper walking boots (the path is rough and stony, and there may be wet snowfields on the summit), warm clothing, waterproofs, a map and compass, and plenty of food and water. And don't forget to check the weather forecast (see www.bennevisweather.co.uk). In thick cloud, visibility at the summit can be 10m or less; in such conditions, the only safe way off the mountain requires careful use of a map and compass to avoid walking over 700m cliffs.

There are three possible starting points for the tourist track ascent (the easiest route to the top) – Achintee Farm; the footbridge at Glen Nevis Youth Hostel; and the car park at Glen Nevis visitor centre. The path climbs gradually to the shoulder at Lochan Meall an t-Suidhe (known as the Halfway Lochan), then zigzags steeply up beside the Red Burn to the summit plateau. The total distance to the summit and back is 8 miles; allow at least four or five hours to reach the top, and another 2½ to three hours for the descent. Afterwards, as you celebrate in the pub with a pint, consider the fact that the record time for the annual Ben Nevis Hill Race is just under 1½ hours – up *and* down. Then have another pint.

TRAIN The spectacular West Highland line runs from Glasgow to Mallaig via Fort William. There are three trains daily (two on Sunday) from Glasgow to Fort William (£24, 3¾ hours), and four daily (three on Sunday) between Fort William and Mallaig (£10, 1½ hours). If you're travelling from Edinburgh (£40, five hours), you'll have to change at Glasgow's Queen St station.

The overnight Caledonian Sleeper service connects Fort William and London Euston (£103 sharing a twin-berth cabin, 13 hours).

Isle of Skye

POP 9900

The Isle of Skye is the biggest of Scotland's islands, a 50-mile-long smorgasbord of velvet moors, jagged mountains, sparkling lochs and towering sea cliffs. It takes its name from the old Norse *sky-a,* meaning 'cloud island', a Viking reference to the often mist-enshrouded Cuillin Hills. The stunning scenery is the main attraction, but there are plenty of cosy pubs to retire to when the mist closes in.

Sleeping

Portree, the island's capital, has the largest selection of accommodation, eating places and other services. A small selection of favourites is listed here, but there are many more hostels and B&Bs dotted around the island.

TOP CHOICE **Ben Tianavaig B&B** B&B ££
(01478-612152; www.ben-tianavaig.co.uk; 5 Bosville Tce; r £65-75; P wi-fi) You'll get a warm welcome at this appealing B&B bang in the centre of town. All four bedrooms have a view across the harbour to the hill that gives the house its name.

Peinmore House B&B ££
(01478-612574; www.peinmorehouse.co.uk; r per person £55; P) Located around 2 miles south of Portree, this former manse has recently been cleverly converted into a stylish and comfortable guesthouse with enormous bedrooms, excellent breakfasts and panoramic views.

Bayfield Backpackers HOSTEL £
(01478-612231; www.skyehostel.co.uk; Bayfield; dm from £13; @ wi-fi) Clean, central and modern, this hostel provides the best backpacker accommodation in town. The owner really makes you feel welcome, and is a fount of advice on what to do and where to go in Skye.

Bayview House B&B £
(01478-613340; www.bayviewhouse.co.uk; Bayfield; r per person from £23; P wi-fi) This is a modern house with spartan but sparklingly clean rooms, and bathrooms with power showers. At this price and location, it's a bargain.

Eating & Drinking

TOP CHOICE **Café Arriba** CAFE £
(www.cafearriba.co.uk; Quay Brae; light meals £5-8, dinner mains £10-13; breakfast, lunch & dinner May-Sep, breakfast & lunch Oct-Apr;) This funky little cafe, brightly decked out in primary colours, has the best choice of vegetarian grub on the island, as well as carnivorous treats and excellent coffee.

Sea Breezes SEAFOOD ££
(01478-612016; 2 Marine Buildings, Quay St; mains £10-20; lunch & dinner Tue-Sun, closed Nov, Jan & Feb) An informal, no-frills restaurant specialising in local fish and shellfish – fresh from the boat.

Granary Bakery CAFE £
(Somerled Sq; light mains £5-8; breakfast & lunch Mon-Sat) Most of Portree seems to congregate at this cosy coffee shop to snack on tasty sandwiches, filled rolls, pies, cakes and pastries.

Information

Portree tourist office (01478-612137; Bayfield Rd, Portree; 9am-6pm Mon-Sat, 10am-4pm Sun Jun-Aug, 9am-5pm Mon-Fri, 10am-4pm Sat Apr, May & Sep, limited hours Oct-Mar)

Getting There & Away

Boat

The Isle of Skye became permanently tethered to the Scottish mainland when the Skye Bridge opened in 1995. Despite the bridge, there are still a couple of ferry links between Skye and the mainland:

CalMac (www.calmac.co.uk) operates the Mallaig to Armadale ferry (driver or passenger £3.85, car £20.30, 30 minutes, eight daily Monday to Saturday, five to seven on Sunday). It's very popular in July and August, so book ahead if you're travelling by car.

Skye Ferry (www.skyeferry.co.uk) runs a tiny vessel (six cars only) on the short Glenelg to Kylerhea crossing (car and up to four passengers £12, five minutes, every 20 minutes). The ferry operates from 10am to 6pm daily from Easter to October only, till 7pm June to August.

Bus

Scottish Citylink runs buses from Glasgow to Portree (£38, seven hours, four daily) via Crianlarich, Fort William and Kyle of Lochalsh. Buses also run from Inverness to Portree (£17, 3½ hours, five daily).

John O'Groats

POP 500

The most northeasterly extreme spot on mainland Britain, John O'Groats is nothing more than a car park surrounded by tourist shops, and offers little to the visitor beyond a means to get across to Orkney. Even the famous pub has been shut for a while now (although there are a couple of cafes). John O'Groats is best known as the endpoint of the 874-mile trek from Land's End in Cornwall, a popular if arduous challenge for cyclists and walkers, many of whom raise money for charitable causes. If you see someone stagger in, give them a round of applause.

Orkney Islands

POP 19,300

Just 6 miles off the northern coast of Scotland, this archipelago is renowned for its dramatic coastal scenery – from soaring cliffs to sandy beaches – abundant bird life, Viking heritage and a plethora of prehistoric sites. There are about 70 islands in all (16 inhabited); the largest goes by the imaginative name of Mainland, with Kirkwall the capital and Stromness the major port.

For information, contact Kirkwall's **TIC** (872856; www.visitorkney.com; West Castle St; 9am-5pm Mon-Fri, 10am-4pm Sat Oct-Apr, 9am-6pm May & Sep, 8.30am-8pm Jun-Aug).

Stenness, a short bus ride from Kirkwall or Stromness, is the most accessible spot for exploring prehistoric Orkney, including **Skara Brae**, a 5000-year-old village, the **Standing Stones of Stenness** and **Barnhouse Neolithic Village**. Particularly recommended is **Maes Howe** (HS; 01856-761606; www.historic-scotland.gov.uk; adult/child £5.20/3.10; tours hourly 10am-3pm Oct-Mar, also 4pm Apr-Sep), an ancient – and atmospheric – Stone Age tomb. Creeping down the long stone passageway to the central chamber, you feel the indescribable gulf of years that separate us from the architects of this mysterious place. The long journey to Orkney is worth it for this alone.

There's a good selection of low-priced B&Bs and hostels across the Orkneys – especially on Mainland – and plenty of cafes, restaurants and pubs.

Tours

Wildabout Orkney BUS TOURS
(01856-851011; www.wildaboutorkney.com) This outfit operates tours covering Orkney's history, ecology, folklore and wildlife. Day trips operate year-round and cost £49, with pick-ups in Stromness and Kirkwall.

John O'Groats Ferries BUS TOURS
(01955-611353; www.jogferry.co.uk; John O'Groats) If you're in a hurry, these guys run a one-day tour of the main Orkney sites for £46, including the ferry from John O'Groats. You can do the whole thing as a long day trip from Inverness.

Information

Tourist office (01856-872856; www.visitorkney.com; 6 Broad St; 9am-6pm summer, 9am-5pm Mon-Fri, 10am-4pm Sat winter)

Getting There & Away

AIR **Flybe/Loganair** (0871 700 0535; www.flybe.com) flies daily from Kirkwall to Aberdeen, Edinburgh, Glasgow, Inverness and Sumburgh (Shetland).

BOAT **NorthLink Ferries** (0845 600 0449; www.northlinkferries.co.uk) run to/from Aberdeen, while **John O'Groats Ferries** (01955-611353; www.jogferry.co.uk) operates a passenger shuttle to/from John O'Groats. **Pentland Ferries** (01856-831226; www.pentlandferries.co.uk) offers a cheap car-ferry crossing (passenger/car £13/30, one hour) from Gills Bay, about 3 miles west of John O'Groats, landing at St Margaret's Hope in Orkney.

Getting Around

BICYCLE Various locations on Mainland hire bikes, including **Cycle Orkney** (01856-875777; www.cycleorkney.com; Tankerness Lane, Kirkwall; per day £15; Mon-Sat;) and **Orkney Cycle Hire** (01856-850255; www.orkneycyclehire.co.uk; 54 Dundas St, Stromness; per day £7.50-10).

BOAT **Orkney Ferries** (01856-872044; www.orkneyferries.co.uk; Shore St, Kirkwall) operates car ferries from Mainland to the islands.

BUS Buses run on Mainland. Dayrider (£7.25) and 7-Day Megarider (£16.25) tickets allow unlimited travel.

History

It may be a small island on the edge of Western Europe, but Britain was never on the sidelines of history. For thousands of years, invaders and incomers have arrived, settled and made their mark. The result is Britain's fascinating mix of landscape, culture and language – a dynamic pattern that shaped the nation and continues to evolve today.

Celts & Romans

Populated by bands of hunter-gatherers for centuries, the island now called Britain changed significantly around 4000 BC when a group of migrants wielding new-fangled stone tools crossed the land bridge from the European mainland (sea levels were lower then – and it was long before the Channel Tunnel).

These early settlers built massive burial mounds and passage graves, such as Maes Howe on the Scottish island of Orkney (p293), but perhaps the most enduring legacy left by these nascent Britons are the great stone circles of Avebury (p209) and Stonehenge (p208) in southern England, still clearly visible today.

The next important gene pool influx came from the Celts of central Europe, whose bronze- and iron-smelting skills launched a mini cultural revolution. London's British Museum, along with many town and city museums across the country, display artefacts from this period.

Even more numerous are the excavated discoveries from Britain's colourful Roman era. Although there had been some earlier expeditionary campaigns, the main Roman invasion of the region they called Britannia was in AD 43, quickly overcoming local resistance to establish dominion over much of the land for the next 350 years. The Romans were a major influence, building villas, forts and bath houses that can still be seen in cities like Bath (p208) and at Hadrian's Wall (p251), once the northernmost border of the entire empire.

The Dark Ages

With its empire crumbling across Europe, the Romans abandoned Britain in AD 410, and the province entered a period known by some historians as the Dark Ages. Towns were abandoned and rural areas became no-go zones as local warlords fought over fiefdoms. The vacuum didn't go unnoticed and once again invaders crossed from the European mainland – this time Germanic tribes called Angles and Saxons.

By the late 6th century much of southern and central Britain was predominantly Anglo-Saxon, divided into separate kingdoms dominated by Wessex (in today's southern England), Mercia (today's central England) and Northumbria (today's northern England and southern Scotland), with the Celtic culture pushed to the western and northern edges (today's Wales and northern Scotland).

Anglo-Saxon expansion forced the disparate tribes of Wales to band together and sow the seeds of nationhood. They called themselves *cymry* (fellow countrymen), and today *Cymru* is the Welsh word for Wales. In the north of Britain, a people called the Picts, and their kingdom of Alba, were invaded from the south by the Anglo-Saxons, and from the west by the Scotti tribe from Ireland – the latter group eventually became dominant, giving their name to the region we call Scotland.

Not surprisingly, while the tribal kingdoms of Britain ebbed and flowed, yet again the island was invaded by a bunch of pesky Continentals – this time the Nordic people known as Vikings. By the end of the first millennium, Vikings from modern-day Denmark and Norway occupied large swaths of land across much of Scotland – including the islands – and northern and eastern England, where they made the city of York (p242) their capital.

Meanwhile, Wales was also dealing with the Nordic intruders. Building on the initial cooperation forced upon them by Anglo-Saxon oppression, in the 9th and 10th centuries the small kingdoms of Wales began cooperating to repel the Vikings.

And while the Welsh were forming their own nation, similar events were being played out in the north. In the 9th century, the king of the Scotti declared himself ruler of both the Scotti *and* the Picts, and therefore king of all Alba. In the 11th century, Scottish nation-building was further consolidated by King Malcolm III (whose most famous act was the 1057 murder of Macbeth – as immortalised by William Shakespeare), who founded the Canmore dynasty that would rule Scotland for the next two centuries.

1066 & All That

While Wales and Scotland laid the foundations of nationhood, back in England things remained unsettled until the Battle of Hastings of 1066 – the most memorable of dates for anyone who studied British history, or for anyone who hasn't. King William of Normandy, with an army of Norman soldiers, landed near the town of Hastings, on England's southern coast. The Saxons were defeated and their king, Harold, was killed – according to tradition by an arrow in the eye. William became king of England, earning himself the prestigious epithet Conqueror.

The Normans had a great influence on England, importing French aristocrats to take charge, and building an imposing network of hulking castles and astonishing cathedrals. Many architectural landmarks you'll see on your travels in Britain date from this period, such as Windsor Castle (p199) near London and Durham Cathedral (p249) in northeast England – although of course they've undergone changes over the centuries.

In Scotland, King Malcolm III was more accommodating to Norman ways – or, at least, he liked the way they ran a country. By 1212 a courtier called Walter of Coventry remarked that the Scottish court was 'French in race and manner of life, in speech and in culture'. But while the French–Norman effect changed England and lowland Scotland over the following centuries, further north the Highland clans remained isolated in their glens – a law unto themselves for another 600 years.

Medieval Britain

The centuries after the Norman invasion saw England racked with intrigue and conspiracy as aristocratic families squared off against each other to influence the royal succession. The era also introduced an equally enduring tendency of bickering between royalty and the church – epitomised in 1170 when King Henry II had 'turbulent priest' Thomas Becket murdered in Canterbury Cathedral (p200) – still an important shrine and tourist attraction today.

The following century saw King Edward I come to the throne of England. An ambitious general, he led a bloody invasion of Wales that lasted much of the 1270s, ending with the defeat of Welsh Prince Llewellyn and Wales becoming a dependent principality, owing allegiance to England. There were no more Welsh kings, and just to make it clear who was boss, Edward made his own son Prince of Wales. (Ever since, the British sovereign's eldest son has been automatically given the title. Most recently, Prince Charles was formally proclaimed Prince of Wales at Caernarfon Castle in 1969, much to the displeasure of Welsh nationalists.)

Edward had less luck in Scotland. In 1297, at the Battle of Stirling Bridge, the English were defeated by a Scots army under the leadership of William Wallace. More than 700 years later, Wallace is still remembered as the epitome of Scottish patriots.

Great Dynasties

In 1399 Henry IV – the first monarch of the House of Lancaster – came to the throne, but his rule was disrupted by a final cry of resistance from the downtrodden Welsh, led by Owain Glyndŵr (Owen Glendower to the English). The rebellion was crushed, vast areas of farmland were destroyed, Glyndŵr died an outlaw and the Welsh elite were barred from public life for many years.

By 1485 King Henry VII had been crowned, the first of the Tudor dynasty – a period characterised by the timber-framed buildings of English towns like Chester (p255) and Stratford-upon-Avon (p229). Henry diligently mended fences with his northern neighbours by marrying off his daughter to James IV of Scotland. He also withdrew many of the anti-Welsh restrictions imposed after the Glyndŵr uprising.

Matrimony may have been more useful than warfare for Henry VII, but the multiple marriages of his successor, Henry VIII, were a very different story. Fathering a male heir was his problem – hence the famous six wives – but the pope's disapproval of divorce led to a split with the Roman Catholic Church, and parliament made Henry the head of the Protestant Church of England. It was the beginning of a pivotal division between Catholics and Protestants that still exists in some areas of Britain.

In 1536 Henry's next step was the 'dissolution' of many abbeys and monasteries, and the romantic ruins of some of these – including Whitby Abbey (p248) and Glastonbury Abbey (p215) – can still be visited. At the same time, Henry signed the Acts of Union (1536–43), formally uniting England and Wales for the first time.

The Elizabethan Age

When Henry VIII died, he was succeeded by his son Edward VI, then by daughter Mary

I, but their reigns were short. So, unexpectedly, the third child, Elizabeth, came to the throne. As Elizabeth I, she inherited a nasty mess of religious strife and divided loyalties, but after an uncertain start she gained confidence and turned the country round. Refusing marriage, she borrowed biblical imagery and became known as the Virgin Queen – perhaps the first English monarch to create a cult image.

Highlights of Elizabeth's 45-year reign included the naval defeat of the Spanish Armada, the far-flung explorations of English seafarers Walter Raleigh and Francis Drake, the expansion of England's increasingly global trading network, including the newly established colonies on the east coast of America, not to mention a cultural flourishing thanks to writers such as William Shakespeare and Christopher Marlowe.

Mary Queen of Scots

Meanwhile, Elizabeth's cousin Mary (daughter of Scottish King James V, and a Catholic) had become queen of Scotland. She'd spent her childhood in France and had married the French *dauphin* (crown prince), thereby becoming queen of France as well. Why stop at two? After her husband's death, Mary returned to Scotland, and from there ambitiously claimed the English throne as well – on the grounds that Elizabeth was illegitimate.

Mary's plans failed; she was imprisoned and forced to abdicate, but then escaped to England and appealed to Elizabeth for help. This could have been a rookie error, or she might have been advised by courtiers with their own agenda. Either way, it was a bad move. Mary was – not surprisingly – seen as a security risk and imprisoned once again. In an uncharacteristic display of indecision, Elizabeth held Mary under arrest for 19 years before finally ordering her execution, moving her frequently from house to house, so that today England has many stately homes (and even a few pubs) proclaiming 'Mary Queen of Scots slept here'.

Britain United

When Elizabeth died in 1603, despite a bountiful reign, one thing the Virgin Queen failed to provide was an heir. She was succeeded by her closest relative, the Scottish (and safely Protestant) King James, son of the murdered Mary. He became James I of England and VI of Scotland, the first English monarch of the House of Stuart (Mary's time in France had Gallicised the Stewart name). Most importantly, James united England, Wales and Scotland into one kingdom – another step towards British unity, at least on paper – although the terms 'Britain' and 'British' were still not yet widely used in this context.

A century later, in 1707, the Act of Union was passed, bringing an end to the independent Scottish parliament, and finally linking the countries of England, Wales and Scotland under one parliament (based in London) for the first time in history. The nation of Britain was now established as a single state, with a bigger and more powerful parliament, and a constitutional monarchy with clear limits on the power of the king or queen.

Scotland's cultural and intellectual life flourished throughout the 18th century, and Edinburgh in particular became an important centre of Enlightenment thinking. Philosophers Adam Smith and David Hume along with poet Robert Burns influenced generations of thinkers, and the city became one of Europe's most beautiful examples of the new rational approach to architecture. Much of this heritage is still intact, making modern-day Edinburgh (p269) one of the world's most picturesque cities.

The Empire Strikes Out

Unity in Britain was mirrored by expansion abroad. Vast swaths of territory in America, Canada and India became part of the British Empire, and the first claims were made to Australia after Captain James Cook's epic voyage in 1768.

The empire's first major setback came when the American colonies won the War of Independence (1776–83). This forced Britain to withdraw from the world stage for a while, a gap not missed by French ruler Napoleon. He threatened to invade Britain and hinder the power of the British overseas, before his ambitions were curtailed by navy hero Viscount Horatio Nelson and military hero the Duke of Wellington at the famous battles of Trafalgar (1805) and Waterloo (1815), and everything – from Britain's point of view – was wonderfully back on track again.

The Industrial Age

While the empire expanded abroad, at home Britain had become the crucible of the Industrial Revolution. Steam power (patented by James Watt in 1781) and steam trains (launched by George Stephenson in 1830) transformed methods of production and transport, and the towns of the English Midlands became the first industrial cities.

This population shift in England was mirrored in Scotland. From about 1750 onwards, much of the Highlands region had been emptied of people, as landowners casually expelled entire farms and villages to make way for more profitable sheep farming, a seminal event in Scotland's history known as the Clearances. Industrialisation just about finished off the job. Although many of the dispossessed left for the New World, others came from the glens to the burgeoning factories of the Lowlands. The tobacco trade with America boomed, and then gave way to textile and engineering industries, as the cotton mills of Lanarkshire and the Clyde shipyards around Glasgow expanded rapidly.

The same happened in Wales. By the early 19th-century copper, iron and slate were being extracted in the Merthyr Tydfil and Monmouth areas. The 1860s saw the Rhondda valleys opened up for coal mining, and Wales soon became a major exporter of coal, as well as the world's leading producer of tin plate.

Across Britain, industrialisation meant people were on the move as never before. People left the land and villages their families had occupied for generations. Often they went to the nearest factory, but not always. People from rural Dorset migrated to the English Midlands, for example, while farmers from Scotland and England settled in South Wales and became miners. The rapid change from rural to urban society caused great dislocation, and although knowledge of science and medicine also improved alongside industrial advances, it meant a rapid rise in population. For many people, the side effects of Britain's economic blossoming were poverty and deprivation.

Nevertheless, by the time Queen Victoria took the throne in 1837, Britain's factories dominated world trade and Britain's fleets dominated the oceans. The rest of the 19th century was seen as Britain's golden age (for some people, it still is) – a period of confidence not seen since the days of the last great queen, Elizabeth I.

The lasting cultural impact of the Victorian era is still evident throughout the country in the great red-brick factories, enormous glass-roofed train stations and magnificent public buildings in cities such as London, Newcastle, Manchester, Edinburgh and Glasgow.

The Modern Era

Most of Britain's 20th century was a period of conflict and decline. Two world wars brought the nation almost to its knees, although many still recall the 1940 Battle of Britain, when the country resisted a three-month air attack from Germany, as its finest hour.

In the 1950s and '60s, the once-great manufacturing industries started to falter, and the 1970s and '80s saw them pretty much die completely.

By the 1990s, though, Britain had bounced back and entered the new millennium with one of the world's strongest economies and a cultural scene dubbed (briefly) 'Cool Britannia'. In the general election of 1997, after nearly 18 years of Conservative rule, 'New' Labour swept to power under a fresh-faced leader called Tony Blair.

New Millennium

In the early part of the 21st century, Britain's role on the world stage was exemplified by its relationship with the USA and participation in military campaigns in Afghanistan and Iraq – not that everyone agreed with such moves; millions of people took to the streets of London and other major British cities to protest their nation's involvement.

Meanwhile, on the home front, history turned full circle as the state of Britain began to divide into its three constituent nations, with the Labour government announcing a referendum on Scottish devolution. The Scots voted overwhelmingly in favour, and representatives to the new Scottish parliament – which has limited but increasing law-making powers – were elected in 1999. Today the new parliament building in Edinburgh (p272) is one of the city's main sights. Concurrently, in a step towards greater political autonomy, the people of Wales voted to be governed by a Welsh Assembly, which now meets in a landmark new building in Cardiff (p262).

Britain Today

June 2007 saw the resignation of Tony Blair, allowing Gordon Brown, the Chancellor of the Exchequer (the British term for Minister of Finance) and for so long the prime-minister-in-waiting, to finally get the top job. His first year in office was initially a disappointment, but his handling of the global economic crisis towards the end of 2008 earned many plaudits and restored public support.

But it wasn't enough. In 2010, a record 14 years of Labour rule came to an end, and a new coalition between the Conservative and Liberal-Democrat parties became the new government, with David Cameron as the prime minister. Despite coming from opposite sides of the centre ground, the 'Con-Lib' coalition impressed most observers with laudable displays of collaboration. Crunch time came in October 2010, when the new chancellor, George Osborne, set out his money-saving plans for Britain. In headlines terms, Health was safe and Education and Defence scraped through, while departments such as the Foreign Office and areas such as the police and welfare, plus local councils, were hit big-time. Over the next year or so the detail will trickle through. For the people of Britain, it remains to be seen exactly what gets cut and what gets spared.

People

Britain's population is 58 million (England around 50 million, Wales around three million and Scotland around five million), making it one of the world's most densely populated countries.

Several big towns and cities in Britain – particularly London, Glasgow, Birmingham and Manchester – have large South Asian and Afro-Caribbean communities, many established for three or more generations. In recent years, large numbers of people from Eastern Europe have also come to Britain for work.

Historically, the three nations that make up Britain have long been dominated by England – which is why many visitors confuse 'Britain' with 'England', and 'British' with 'English', but of course you should take care you use the right term – especially in Wales and Scotland. Calling a Scot 'English' is like calling a New Zealander 'Australian' or a Canadian 'American'.

Religion

In the 2001 national census, around 35 million people in Britain stated their religion as Christian. Although many write 'C of E' (Church of England) when filling in forms, only a million or so of these attend Sunday services. Other Christian faiths include Roman Catholic (about 10% of the population), plus sizeable groups of Methodists, Baptists and other nonconformists – most notably in Wales and Scotland.

The census also recorded around 1.5 million Muslims in Britain (about 3% of the population). Other faiths include Hindus (1%), Sikhs (0.7%), Jews (0.5%) and Buddhists (0.3%). Nowadays more non-Christians regularly visit their places of worship than do all the Anglicans, Catholics, Methodists and Baptists combined – especially if you include the druids at Stonehenge, and all those wags who amusingly wrote 'Jedi Knight' on the census form.

Arts

Britain has a colourful artistic history – most notable for its theatre and literature – that stretches back centuries, while its modern popular culture – especially pop and rock music – resonates throughout the world.

Literature

Travelling in the footsteps of English, Scottish or Welsh writers can be the highlight of any trip to Britain. Ambling through the cobbled streets of Canterbury recalls Chaucer's ribald comedy, a trip to Bath evokes Jane Austen, while strolling in the Scottish glens might summon up the spirit of Robbie Burns. Spirits of a different variety should be sampled in the pubs of Wales, some of which inspired the poetry of Dylan Thomas.

For most lit lovers, a visit to Stratford-upon-Avon is a must. As well as being the birthplace of William Shakespeare, one of the world's greatest playwrights, it's also the world centre of Shakespeare performance and the home of the renowned Royal Shakespeare Company.

Britain's best-known contemporary writer is probably JK Rowling, author of the *Harry Potter* stories, closely followed in a similar genre by Philip Pullman's *His Dark Materials* trilogy. But away from parallel worlds, some British novels set in Britain to sample while you're travelling here might include Muriel Spark's *The Prime of Miss Jean Brodie,* Irvine Welsh's *Trainspotting* or Zadie Smith's *White Teeth* and *On Beauty*. Other star novelists covering (loosely defined) 'multicultural Britain' themes include Monica Ali, whose *Brick Lane* was shortlisted for the 2003 Man Booker Prize, and Andrea Levy, winner of the Orange Prize for her novel *Small Island,* about a Jamaican couple settled in 1950s London.

At the more popular end of the shelf is the best-selling author Nick Hornby, chronicling the fragilities and insecurities of the British middle-class male in novels like *Fever Pitch* and *High Fidelity,* while Sebastian Faulks (best known for his wartime novel *Birdsong*) wrote the first new James Bond novel in over 50 years; the resulting *Devil May Care* became one of the fastest-selling hardbacks ever published.

But even James Bond can't hold a candle to the literary phenomenon that is celebrity autobiographies – penned by everyone from footballers to talent show also-rans – a reminder of the increasing importance of hype over merit in the modern book market. But whatever you make of the literary qualities of these memoirs, it's hard to argue with the figures – the British public buys them by the bucketload.

Cinema & TV

Britain's home-grown film industry ebbs and flows, with most of its contemporary worldwide hits – including *Shakespeare in Love* and *Bend It Like Beckham* – occupying the heart-warming side of film narrative. For a whiff of originality try *The Full Monty, Secrets and Lies, Vera Drake, Billy Elliot, East is East* or *Atonement*. For a great laugh, try *Shaun of the Dead* or *Hot Fuzz.*

The BBC is Britain's leading broadcaster and a venerable institution, with several channels of the world's best programming dominating national radio and free-to-air TV. Foreigners are frequently amazed that public service broadcasting can produce such a range of professional, innovative, up-to-date and stimulating programs. All this – and without adverts too! In TV comedy alone, its legendary gems range from *Monty Python's Flying Circus* to *The Office* and *Gavin & Stacey.*

Music

There's a great depth of classical music performance in Britain, with several cities hosting their own renowned symphony orchestras, but the music this country is best known for is pop and rock, with venerable juggernauts like Elton John and the Rolling Stones routinely topping lists of high-grossing concert tours around the world.

In recent decades, the '90s was notable for the rise of British 'indie' bands, with the likes of Blur, Elastica, Suede, Supergrass, Ocean Colour Scene, Manic Street Preachers, the Verve, Pulp, Travis, Feeder, Super Furry Animals, Stereophonics, Catatonia, Radiohead and, above all, Oasis, reviving the guitar-based format. Heralded as the 'Britpop' revolution, part of the even bigger Cool Britannia phenomenon that combined new music, new art, new fashion and New Labour politics, it was over almost as soon as it started, but a host of bands such as Coldplay, Badly Drawn Boy, Snow Patrol and Razorlight played on, and spawned a wave of imitators.

Today British pop music is as fast-moving and varied as ever, divided into a host of genres mixing a wide range of influences including glam, punk, electronica and folk (while British folk itself, thanks largely to the rise of world music, enjoys its biggest revival since the 1960s). Big names like Muse, Dizzee Rascal and Franz Ferdinand continue to headline summer festivals, backed up by current favourites like Mumford & Sons, Bombay Bicycle Club, Foals and The XX. Beyond the festivals, Britain's live music scene continues to thrive, a vital opportunity for bands to make money in a business squeezed by free file-sharing. Meanwhile, commercial pop acts like Leona Lewis and Diana Vickers are produced by endless – and obsessively followed – reality TV talent shows.

By the time you read this book, half of the 'great new bands' of last year will have sunk without a trace, and a fresh batch of unknowns will have risen to dominate the airwaves and download sites. One thing's for sure, the British music scene has never stood still, and it doesn't look like settling down any time soon.

Sport

If you want to take a shortcut into the heart of British culture, watch the British at play. They're fierce and passionate about their sport, whether participating or spectating. The mood of the nation is more closely aligned to the success of its international teams in major competition than to budget announcements from the chancellor of the exchequer, or even the weather. This is no more clearly evidenced than by the massive support for Team GB, especially the phenomenal cyclists and swimmers, in the 2008 Beijing Olympics. Sometimes it's the success of the *nations* that matters; the separate rugby teams of England, Wales and Scotland,

and the English and Scottish national football sides, have supporters with passion that borders on the insane.

But although the British invented – or at least laid down the modern rules for – many of the world's most popular spectator sports, including cricket, tennis, golf, rugby and football, the national teams aren't always so good at playing them (as the newspapers continually like to remind us), although recent years have seen some notable success stories. But a mixed result doesn't dull the fans' enthusiasm. Every weekend thousands of people turn out to cheer their favourite club or side, and sporting highlights such as tennis at Wimbledon or the Grand National horse race keep the entire nation enthralled. And Team GB will have a chance to shine again, this time on home soil, when the next Olympics come to London in 2012.

Environment

The island of Britain sits on the eastern edge of the North Atlantic and consists of three nations: England in the south and centre, Scotland to the north and Wales to the west – together making up the state of Great Britain.

The Land

When it comes to topology, Britain is not a place of extremes – there are no Himalayas or Lake Baikals – but even a short journey can take you through a surprising mix of landscapes.

Southern England's countryside is gently undulating, with hilly areas such as the Cotswolds and a mix of cities, towns and farmland. East Anglia is mainly low and flat, while the southwest peninsula has wild moors and rich pastures – hence Devon's world-famous cream – plus a rugged coast with sheltered beaches, making it a favourite holiday destination.

In the north of England, farmland remains interspersed with towns and cities, but the landscape is noticeably more bumpy. A line of large hills called the Pennines (fondly tagged 'the backbone of England'), runs from Derbyshire to the Scottish border, and includes the peaty plateaus of the Peak District, the wild moors around Haworth (immortalised in Brontë novels) and the delightful valleys of the Yorkshire Dales.

Perhaps England's best-known landscape is the Lake District, a small but spectacular cluster of mountains in the northwest, where Scafell Pike (a towering 978m) is England's highest peak.

The landscape of Wales is also defined by hills and mountains: notably the Brecon Beacons in the south, and the spiky peaks of Snowdonia in the north, with Snowdon (1085m) the highest peak in Wales. In between lie the wild Cambrian Mountains of Mid-Wales, rolling towards a west coast of spectacular cliffs and shimmering river estuaries.

For real mountains, though, you've got to go to Scotland, especially the wild, remote and thinly populated northwest Highlands. Ben Nevis (1344m) is Scotland's – and Britain's – highest mountain, but there are many more to choose from. The Highlands are further enhanced by the vast cluster of beautiful islands that lie off the loch-indented west coast.

UK OK?

The nation of Great Britain consists of England, Wales and Scotland. So far, so good. So what's the UK? The United Kingdom (UK) consists of the three countries of Great Britain plus Northern Ireland. And just for the record, the island of Ireland consists of Northern Ireland and the Republic of Ireland (also called Eire), while the British Isles is a *geographical* term for the whole group of islands that make up the UK and the Republic of Ireland, plus some autonomous and semiautonomous islands such as the Isle of Man and Channel Islands.

Wildlife

For a small country, Britain has a diverse range of plants and animals. Some native species are hidden away, but easy-to-see gems include woods carpeted in shimmering bluebells or a stately herd of deer in the mountains. This wildlife is part of the fabric of Britain, and having a closer look will enhance your trip enormously.

In farmland areas, rabbits are everywhere, but if you're hiking through the countryside look out for brown hares, an increasingly rare species, related to rabbits but much larger. Males battle for territory by boxing on their hind legs in early spring and are, of course, as 'mad as a March hare'.

Between the fields, hedges provide cover for flocks of finches, but these seed-eaters must watch out for sparrowhawks – birds of prey that come from nowhere at tremendous speed. Other predators include barn owls, a wonderful sight as they fly silently along hedgerows listening for the faint rustle of a vole or shrew. In rural Wales or Scotland you may see a buzzard, Britain's most common large raptor.

A classic British mammal is the red fox. Traditionally a rural animal, these wily beasts adapt well to any situation, so you're just as likely to see them scavenging in towns and city suburbs. A controversial law banning the hunting of foxes with dogs was introduced in 2005, but as this activity (a traditional country pursuit or savage blood sport, depending on who you talk to) killed only a small proportion of the total fox population, opinion is still divided if the ban has had any impact on numbers.

In woodland areas, mammals include the small white-spotted fallow deer and the even smaller roe deer. If you hear rustling among the fallen leaves it might be a hedgehog – a cute-looking, spiny-backed insect-eater – but it's an increasingly rare sound these days; conservationists say that hedgehogs will be extinct in Britain by 2025, possibly due to increased building in rural areas, the use of insecticides in farming, and the changing nature of both the countryside and the city parks and gardens that once made up the hedgehog's traditional habitat.

You're much more likely to see grey squirrels; this species was introduced from North America and has proved so adaptable that native British red squirrels are severely endangered.

The most visible moorland mammal is the red deer. Herds survive on Exmoor and Dartmoor, in the Lake District, and in larger numbers in Scotland. The males are most spectacular after June, when their antlers have grown ready for the rutting season. The stags keep their antlers through the winter and then shed them again in February.

National Parks & Conservation Areas

Way back in 1810, poet and outdoors-lover William Wordsworth suggested that the Lake District should be 'a sort of national property, in which every man has a right'. More than a century later, the Lake District became a national park (although quite different from Wordsworth's vision), along with the Brecon Beacons, Cairngorms, Dartmoor, Exmoor, Loch Lomond & The Trossachs, New Forest, Norfolk & Suffolk Broads, Northumberland, North York Moors, Peak District, Pembrokeshire Coast, South Downs Snowdonia and Yorkshire Dales.

Combined, Britain's national parks now cover over 10% of the country. It's an impressive total, but the term 'national park' can cause confusion. First, these areas are not state owned: nearly all land is private, belonging to farmers, companies, estates and conservation organisations. Second, they are not total wilderness areas, as in many other countries. In Britain's national parks you'll see roads, railways, villages and even towns. Development is strictly controlled, but about 250,000 people live and work inside national-park boundaries. Some of them work in industries such as quarrying, which ironically does great damage to these supposedly protected landscapes. On the flip side, these industries provide vital jobs (although sometimes for people outside the park), and several wildlife reserves have been established on former quarry sites.

Despite these apparent anomalies, national parks still contain vast tracts of wild mountains and moorland, rolling downs and river valleys, and other areas of quiet countryside, all ideal for long walks, cycle rides, easy rambles, sightseeing or just lounging around. To help you get the best from the parks, they all have information centres and facilities (walking trails, car parks, campsites etc) for visitors. For more details, see www.nationalparks.gov.uk.

Environmental Issues

With Britain's long history of human occupation, it's not surprising that the land's appearance is almost totally the result of people's interactions with the environment. Ever since Neolithic farmers learnt how to make axes, trees have been cleared so that crops could be planted – a trend that has continued into our own time.

The most dramatic environmental changes hit rural areas after WWII in the late 1940s, continuing into the '50s and '60s, especially in England, when a drive to be self-reliant in food meant new – intensive and large-scale – farming methods. This changed the landscape from a patchwork of small fields to a scene of vast prairies as walls were demolished, trees felled, ponds filled, wetlands drained and, most notably, hedgerows ripped up.

Hedgerows have come to symbolise many other environmental issues in rural areas, and in recent years the destruction has abated, partly because farmers recognise their anti-erosion qualities, partly because they don't need to remove any more, and partly because they're encouraged to 'set aside' such areas as wildlife havens – although in 2008 set-aside land was under threat as farmers sought to take advantage of soaring grain prices. Nonetheless, subsidies from government or European agencies encourage farmers to replant hedgerows. Ironic, when only 20 years ago there were subsidies to pull them out.

Of course, environmental issues are not exclusive to rural areas. In Britain's towns and cities, topics such as air pollution, light pollution, levels of car use, road building, airport construction, public-transport provision and household-waste recycling are never far from the political agenda, although some might say they're not near enough to the top of the list.

Food & Drink

The words 'British' and 'cuisine' never used to be uttered in the same sentence without a nervous laugh or gagging reflex. Those days are long gone and there's now a rich variety of well-prepared regional dishes alongside an impressive array of cosmopolitan options, reflecting the nation's burgeoning ethnic diversity.

Staples & Specialities

Britain's traditional meals include roast beef, fish and chips, bangers and mash, and steak and kidney pie – many of these revered dishes have been reinvented for foodies at some of the nation's finest restaurants, as well as in more straightforward restaurants and cafes.

Another British speciality – especially if you're staying at B&Bs – is the big fry-up breakfast, containing bacon, sausage, egg, beans, mushrooms, toast and more, often called the 'full English' (in England). In Scotland you may get offered haggis or black pudding, and oatcakes instead of toast.

Alongside the home-grown favourites, most Brits have also embraced a huge variety of ethnic cuisines, with Chinese and Indian restaurants now more common than traditional chippies, and cities like Glasgow, Birmingham and Manchester vying to be the nation's curry capital.

Where to Eat & Drink

You'll find a good variety of eateries in most British towns and cities – whether you're vegetarian, vegan or carnivore.

As well as restaurants and cafes, in country areas you'll find teashops (essentially a smart cafe), and across Britain pubs are often a good option for good-value no-nonsense food. Look out for the ploughman's lunch, a faux traditional plate of bread, cheese and pickles, which goes down well with a pint or two of 'real ale' (traditional beer).

For many foreigners, traditional British beer can be a bit of a shock – a warm, flat and expensive shock – but that's because taste is the key; the beer doesn't need to be cold or pressurised to make it palatable. Once you've got used to that idea you can start experimenting with the many different regional tastes and textures.

Across Britain, smoking is banned in all enclosed public places, and that includes all bars, pubs, cafes and restaurants – which is why you'll often see small groups of smokers huddled on the pavement outside.

SURVIVAL GUIDE

Directory A–Z

Accommodation

Accommodation in Britain is as varied as the sights you visit. From hip hotels to basic barns, the wide choice is all part of the attraction. There's a wide range of prices too; like-for-like, London tends to be the most expensive part of the country. Some other points:

» Across Britain, whatever the budget-level, rates tend to drop in low season (generally October to April).

» Breakfast is usually included in midrange and top-end options, but it'll be an extra at hostels and other bargain options.

» Prices for B&Bs and hotels are generally for rooms with private bathroom – either en suite or across the landing from the room.

» Smoking is banned in all enclosed places in Britain, including hotels, B&Bs and other accommodation.

» In summer, popular spots (York, Canterbury, Bath etc) get very crowded, so booking ahead is often essential.
» Accommodation can be impossible to get (or very costly) when towns and cities hold festivals or major sporting events, such as the Edinburgh Fringe, Brecon Jazz, Chester Races, Cardiff rugby internationals, etc.

PRICE RANGES

Our reviews refer to double rooms with a private bathroom, except in hostels or where otherwise specified. Quoted rates are for **high season**, which is May to September.

£££	more than £130
££	£50 to £130
£	less than £50

CAMPING

Free camping is rare in Britain, but there are many camping grounds on the edge of towns and in the countryside. Rates range from £5 to £10 per person, depending on location, season and facilities. We don't list specific camping grounds; hostels are often preferred since they charge only slightly more and offer more facilities (not to mention shelter from the sometimes inclement British weather).

HOSTELS

Britain has two national hostelling organisations: **Youth Hostels Association** (YHA; www.yha.org.uk), covering England and Wales, and **Scottish Youth Hostels Association** (SYHA; www.syha.org.uk). Dorm beds range from £9 to £20 per night, and many hostels also have double and four-bed rooms. You don't *have* to be a member of YHA or SHYA (or another Hostelling International – HI – organisation) to stay at YHA/SYHA hostels, but nonmembers pay extra: £3 extra per person per night in England and Wales; £1 per person per night in Scotland. Annual YHA membership costs £16; SYHA costs £10. Under 16s, under 26s, seniors and families get discounts.

Most hostel prices vary according to demand and season. Book early for an off-peak Tuesday night in May and you'll get a cheap rate. Book late for a weekend in August and you'll pay top whack – if there's space at all. Throughout this chapter, we've generally quoted the cheaper rates (in line with those on YHA's and SYHA's websites); you may pay more. Some hostels also have varying opening times and days, especially in remote locations or out of the tourist season, so check before turning up.

BOOKING THROUGH TICS

Local Tourist Information Centres (TICs) will find and book accommodation for you ahead of your arrival if you tell them what you're after. This service is sometimes free but there's usually a fee (around £4). It's often worth the money as it saves you hiking or phoning loads of places, and sometimes the fee is deducted from your accommodation cost, meaning no extra charge to you.

There's a growing array of independent hostels and backpackers across Britain, varying widely in quality, facilities and price (typically from £10 to £25 per night). Some are quiet and cosy, while others are for serious party travellers. The print and online **Independent Hostel Guide** (www.independenthostelguide.co.uk) is the best listing. North of the English border, an excellent site is www.hostel-scotland.co.uk.

HOTELS

A hotel in Britain might be a small and simple place, perhaps a former farmhouse now stylishly converted, where peace and quiet – along with luxury – are guaranteed. Or it might be a huge country house with fancy facilities, grand staircases, acres of grounds and the requisite row of stag heads on the wall. Charges vary as much as quality and atmosphere. At the bargain end, you can find singles/doubles costing £30/40 per night. Move up the scale and you'll pay £100/150 per night or beyond.

If all you want is a place to put your head down, budget chain hotels can be a good option. Most are totally lacking in style or ambience, but who cares? You'll only be there for eight hours, and six of them you'll be asleep. Most offer rooms at variable prices based on demand; on a quiet night in November twin-bed rooms with private bathroom start at around £20, and at the height of the tourist season you'll pay £45 or more.

Etap Hotels (www.etaphotel.com)

Hotel Formule 1 (www.hotelformule1.com)

Premier Inn (www.premierinn.com)

Travelodge (www.travelodge.co.uk)

ROOM RATES

In Britain there's often no such thing as a 'standard' hotel rate. Many hotels, especially larger places or chains, vary prices according to demand – or have different rates for online, phone or walk-in bookings – just like airlines and train operators. So if you book early for a night when the hotel is likely to be quiet, rates are cheap. If you book late, or aim for a public holiday weekend, you'll pay a lot. However, if you're prepared to be flexible and leave booking to the very last minute, you can sometimes get a bargain as rates drop again. The end result: you can pay anything from £19 to £190 for the very same hotel room. With that in mind, the hotel rates we quote are often guide prices only (B&B prices tend to be much more consistent).

B&BS & GUESTHOUSES

The B&B ('bed and breakfast') is a great British institution. Smaller places may have just one guest room, and you'll feel like part of the family. Larger B&Bs may have around 10 rooms and more facilities. 'Guesthouse' is sometimes just another name for a B&B, or something in between B&B and hotel. Room rates are nearly always quoted per person, but based on two people sharing. Single rooms cost more. Bottom-end you'll pay around £20 per person per night; in the midrange you're looking at around £35 or £40. Most B&Bs serve enormous breakfasts, included in the rate; some also offer packed lunches (around £5) and evening meals (around £10 to £15).

PUBS & INNS

As well as selling drinks, many pubs and inns offer lodging, particularly in country areas. Staying in a pub can be good fun – you're automatically at the centre of the community – although accommodation varies enormously.

» Expect to pay around £20 per person per night at the cheap end, and around £30 to £35 for something better.

» An advantage for solo tourists: pubs are more likely to have single rooms.

» If a pub does B&B, it normally does evening meals, served in the bar or an adjoining restaurant.

UNIVERSITY ACCOMMODATION

Many universities offer student accommodation to visitors during vacations. You usually get a functional single bedroom with private bathroom, and self-catering flats are also available. Prices range from £15 to £30 per person. A handy portal is www.universityrooms.co.uk.

Activities

Britain is a great destination for outdoor enthusiasts. Walking and cycling are the most popular activities – you can do them on a whim, and they're the perfect way to open up some beautiful corners of the country. Britain supplies the goods for thrill-seekers, too: the coast has excellent spots for surfing and the whacky sport of coasteering, while inland you might try mountain boarding. A good site for inspiration is www.visitbritain.com – follow links to Holiday Ideas and Outdoor Activities.

COASTEERING

It's like mountaineering, but instead of going up a mountain, you go along the coast – a steep rocky coast, often with waves breaking around your feet. And if the rock gets too steep, you jump in and start swimming. It's not the thing to do on your own, but joining an organised group is easy enough. Outdoor centres – notably in Cornwall and Pembrokeshire – provide wetsuits, helmets and buoyancy aids. You provide an old pair of training shoes and a sense of adventure. For more information see www.coasteering.org.

CYCLING

Compact Britain is an excellent destination to explore by bike, whether you're pottering around a cycle-friendly city such as Oxford or Bristol, or heading into the countryside. Popular regions to tour include southwest England, the Yorkshire Dales, Derbyshire's Peak District, Mid-Wales and the Scottish Borders. There are cycle-hire outlets in most tourist centres; rates range from £6 per half-day to £60 per week. The 10,000-mile **National Cycle Network** (www.nationalcyclenetwork.org.uk) is a web of quiet roads and traffic-free tracks that pass through busy cities and remote rural areas. The **Cyclists' Touring Club** (☎0870 873 0060; www.ctc.org.uk) is the leading national organisation, and its website includes a cycle-hire directory and mail-order service for maps and books.

MOUNTAIN BOARDING & KITE BOARDING

Imagine hurtling down a grassy hillside on a gigantic skateboard, and you've pretty much got mountain boarding. Add a wing-shaped parachute, and it's a kite board – so you can get the wind to pull you around whenever gravity gives up. There are mountain-boarding centres in Yorkshire, Derbyshire, Shropshire, Cornwall and the Brecon Beacons (among other places). See www.atbauk.org for more info.

SURFING & KITESURFING

If you've come from the other side of the world, you'll be delighted to learn that summer water temperatures in Britain are equivalent to winter temperatures in southern Australia (about 13°C). But as long as you've got a wetsuit, there are many excellent surfing opportunities where the west coast is exposed to the Atlantic, including southwest Wales, Cornwall and Devon. For info, see www.britsurf.co.uk.

Britain is great for kitesurfing too, thanks to brisk winds, decent waves and great beaches. Once again, Cornwall and Pembrokeshire are favourite spots, but it's possible on other beaches along the British coastline. See www.kitesurfing.org.

WALKING & HIKING

Britain's picturesque terrain is great for walking – whether you want an easy stroll or an energetic hike. Every country town is surrounded by a network of footpaths, with even more choice in the national parks and mountain areas such as the Lake District, North Wales and the Highlands of Scotland.

Some long routes are designated National Trails; for more info see www.nationaltrails.co.uk. But you don't have to do the whole route; many people follow sections of the classics for a day or two, or a just few hours. It still makes for a great day out.

The **Ramblers Association** (020-7339 8500; www.ramblers.org.uk) is the country's leading organisation for walkers, and its website is a mine of background information.

For keen walkers and hikers, Britain boasts many multiday routes:

Coast to Coast Popular hike across three northern England national parks.

Cotswold Way Delightful ramble through southern hills and countryside.

Dales Way Through Yorkshire's charming countryside to the Lake District.

Pembrokeshire Coast Path Rollercoaster romp around the west Wales peninsula.

West Highland Way Classic route through southern Scotland.

> **FIRST STEPS**
>
> So, you've arrived in a new area and want to know more about local options for walking, hiking, cycling or other outdoor activities. Step 1: find the local tourist office. Step 2: pick up leaflets, maps and guidebooks, find out about bike hire or guided walks, and get information on other activities in the region, such as surf schools. Step 3: head out, and enjoy!

Business Hours

Reviews in this chapter won't list business hours unless they differ from the following standards:

Banks 9.30am to 4pm or 5pm Monday to Friday, 9.30am to 1pm Saturday

Museums Smaller museums may close Monday and/or Tuesday, and close on weekdays in the low season

Nightclubs to 2am or beyond

Post offices 9am to 5pm Monday to Friday, 9am to 12.30pm Saturday (main branches to 5pm)

Pubs 11am to 11pm Sunday to Thursday, sometimes to midnight or 1am Friday and Saturday; some pubs close between 3pm and 6pm; bars open to midnight or later

Restaurants Lunch noon to 3pm, dinner 6pm to 11pm or later; some restaurants close on Sunday evenings or all day Monday; cafes open 7am to 6pm; teashops open for lunch until 5pm or later in summer; country cafes may close between October and April

Shops 9am to 5pm Monday to Saturday (to 5.30pm or 6pm in cities), 10am to 4pm Sunday; in smaller towns or country areas, shops may close for lunch from 1pm to 2pm and on Wednesday or Thursday afternoon

Embassies & Consulates

This is a selection of embassies, consulates and high commissions in London. For a complete list of embassies in Britain, see the website of the **Foreign & Commonwealth Office** (www.fco.gov.uk), which also lists Britain's diplomatic missions overseas.

Australia (☎020-7379 4334; www.australia.org.uk; Australia House, The Strand, WC2B 4LA)

Canada (☎020-7258 6600; www.canada.org.uk; 1 Grosvenor Sq, W1X 0AB)

Japan (☎020-7465 6500; www.uk.emb-japan.go.jp; 101 Piccadilly, W1J 7JT)

New Zealand (☎020-7930 8422; www.nzembassy.com/uk; 80 Haymarket, SW1Y 4TQ)

USA (☎020-7499 9000; www.usembassy.org.uk; 24 Grosvenor Sq, W1A 1AE)

Food

Prices for eateries in this chapter are for a main meal unless otherwise indicated. The symbols used in each review indicate the following prices:

£££ more than £18

££ £9 to £18

£ less than £9

Gay & Lesbian Travellers

Most major cities – especially London, Brighton, Manchester and Glasgow – have gay and lesbian scenes, but there can still be some intolerance in smaller towns (and tabloid newspapers). Resources:

Diva (www.divamag.co.uk)

Gay Times (www.gaytimes.co.uk)

London Lesbian & Gay Switchboard (☎020-7837 7324; www.llgs.org.uk or www.queery.org.uk)

Pink Paper (www.pinkpaper.com)

Heritage Organisations

A highlight of a journey through Britain is visiting the numerous castles and historic sites that pepper the country. Membership of a heritage organisation gets you free admission (usually a good saving) as well as information handbooks and so on. If you join an English heritage organisation, it covers you for Wales and Scotland, and vice versa.

We have included the relevant acronym (NT, NTS, EH etc) in the information for properties listed in this chapter. You can join at the first NT/NTS/EH/HS/Cadw site you visit.

English Heritage (EH; www.english-heritage.org.uk) Annual membership costs £44. An Overseas Visitors Pass allows free entry to most sites for seven/14 days for £20/25. In Wales and Scotland the equivalent organisations are **Cadw** (www.cadw.wales.gov.uk) and **Historic Scotland** (HS; www.historic-scotland.gov.uk).

National Trust (NT; www.nationaltrust.org.uk) Annual membership costs £49 (with discounts for under-26s). A Touring Pass allows free entry to NT properties for one/two weeks (£21/26 per person). The **National Trust for Scotland** (NTS; www.nts.org.uk) is similar.

Language

The dominant language of Britain is English. In Wales about 600,000 people (20% of the population) speak Welsh as a first language, and many more as a strong second tongue, especially in the north – although everyone speaks English as well. Welsh is a Celtic language, entirely different from English. It almost died out in the 1960s, but today Welsh-language TV, radio and literature are increasingly popular, and all signs on roads and in public places are in both languages. In Scotland, Gaelic – another Celtic language – is spoken by about 80,000 people, mainly in the Highlands and Islands, while Lallans (or Lowland Scots) is much closer to English.

Money

ATMs ATMs (often called 'cash machines') are easy to find in cities and even small towns. Watch out for ATMs that might have been tampered with; a common ruse is to attach a card-reader to the slot.

Changing Money Cities and larger towns have banks and bureaus for changing your money (cash or travellers cheques) into pounds. Check rates first; some bureaus may claim 'no commission' but they change at poor rates. You can change money at some post offices for fair rates – very handy in country areas.

Credit & Debit Cards Smaller businesses, such as pubs or B&Bs, prefer debit cards (or charge a fee for credit cards), and some take cash or cheque only. Nearly all credit and debit cards use a 'Chip and PIN' system (instead of signing). If your card isn't Chip and PIN enabled, you should be able to sign in the usual way, but some places may not accept your card.

Currency The currency of Britain is the pound sterling (£). Paper money ('notes')

SCOTTISH POUNDS

Scotland issues its own currency (including a £1 note), interchangeable with the money used in the rest of the UK. However, you'll find shops more readily accept Scottish money in the north of England than in the south. Banks will always change Scottish pounds.

comes in £5, £10, £20 and £50 denominations, although some shops don't accept £50 notes because fakes circulate.

Tipping In Britain, you're not obliged to tip if service or food was unsatisfactory (even if it's been added to your bill as a 'service charge').

» Restaurants – around 10%; also teashops and smarter cafes with full table service; at smarter restaurants, waiters can get a bit sniffy if the tip isn't nearer 12% or even 15%

» Taxis – 10%, or rounded up to the nearest pound), especially in London; it's less usual to tip minicab drivers

» Toilet attendants – around 50p

» Pubs – around 10% if you order food at the table and your meal is brought to you; if you order and pay at the bar (food or drinks), tips are not expected

Travellers Cheques Travellers cheques are rarely used in Britain, as credit/debit cards and ATMs have become preferred.

Public Holidays

New Year's Day 1 January

Easter March/April (Good Friday to Easter Monday inclusive)

May Day First Monday in May

Spring Bank Holiday Last Monday in May

Summer Bank Holiday Last Monday in August

Christmas Day 25 December

Boxing Day 26 December

» If a public holiday falls on a weekend, the nearest Monday is usually taken instead.

» In England and Wales, most businesses and banks close on official public holidays (hence the quaint term 'bank holiday').

» In Scotland, bank holidays are just for the banks, and many businesses stay open.

» Many Scottish towns have a spring and autumn holiday, but the dates vary.

» On public holidays (and Sundays), some small museums and sights close, but larger attractions have their busiest times.

» Virtually everything – attractions, shops, banks, offices – closes on Christmas Day, although pubs are open at lunchtime.

» There's usually no public transport on Christmas Day, and a very minimal service on Boxing Day.

Safe Travel

Britain is a remarkably safe country, but crime does occur in London and other cities. When travelling by tube, tram or urban train service at night, choose a carriage containing other people.

Unlicensed minicabs – a bloke with a car earning money on the side – operate in large cities, and are worth avoiding unless you know what you're doing. Scams include driving round in circles, then charging an enormous fare. Dangers include driving to a remote location then subjecting you to robbery or rape. To avoid this, use a metered taxi or phone a reputable minicab company and get an up-front quote for the ride.

Telephone

In this chapter, area codes and individual numbers are listed together, separated by a hyphen.

Area codes in Britain do not have a standard format or length; eg ☎020 for London, ☎0161 for Manchester, ☎01225 for Bath, ☎015394 for Ambleside, followed as usual by the individual number.

Other codes:

» ☎0500 or ☎0800 – free calls

» ☎0845 – calls at the local rate, wherever you're dialling from within the UK

» ☎087 – calls at the national rate

» ☎089 or ☎09 – premium rate

» ☎07 – mobile phones, more expensive than calling a landline

To call outside the UK, dial ☎00, then the country code (☎1 for USA, ☎61 for Australia etc), the area code (you usually drop the initial zero) and the number.

» operator ☎100

» international operator ☎155 – also for reverse-charge (collect) calls

For directory enquiries, a host of agencies compete for your business and charge from 10p to 40p; numbers include ☎118 192, ☎118 118, ☎118 500 and ☎118 811.

VISIT BRITAIN

Before leaving home, check the informative, comprehensive and wide-ranging website of Britain's official tourist board, VisitBritain (www.visitbritain.com).

Tourist Information

All British cities and towns, and some villages, have a tourist information centre (TIC) with helpful staff, books and maps, free leaflets and loads of advice on things to see or do. They can also assist with booking accommodation. Most tourist offices keep regular business hours; in quiet areas they close from October to March, while in popular areas they open daily year-round. For a list see www.visitmap.info/tic.

Visas

If you're a European Economic Area (EEA) national, you don't need a visa to visit (or work in) Britain. Citizens of Australia, Canada, New Zealand, South Africa and the USA are given leave to enter the UK at their point of arrival for up to six months (three months for some nationalities), but are prohibited from working. For more info see www.ukvisas.gov.uk or www.ukba.homeoffice.gov.uk.

Getting There & Away

Entering the Country

AIR

You can easily fly to Britain from just about anywhere in the world. London is a global hub, but major regional airports such as Manchester and Glasgow also handle international flights. In recent years other regional airports around Britain have massively increased their choice – especially on budget ('no-frills') airlines to/from mainland Europe – very handy for travels around the continent.

London Airports

London is served by five airports; Heathrow and Gatwick are the busiest.

London City (LCY; www.londoncityairport.com)

London Gatwick (LGW; www.gatwickairport.com)

London Heathrow (LHR; www.heathrowairport.com)

Luton (LTN; www.london-luton.co.uk)

Stansted (STN; www.stanstedairport.com)

Regional Airports

Regional airports with international flights:

Birmingham (BHM; www.bhx.co.uk)

Bristol (BRS; www.bristolairport.co.uk)

Cardiff (CWL; www.cwlfly.com)

Edinburgh (EDI; www.edinburghairport.com)

Glasgow (GGW; www.glasgowairport.com)

Liverpool (LPL; www.liverpooljohnlennonairport.com)

Manchester (MAN; www.manchesterairport.co.uk)

Newcastle (NCL; www.newcastleairport.com)

Southampton (SOU; www.southamptonairport.com)

LAND

Bus & Coach

You can easily travel between Britain and other European countries via long-distance bus or coach. The international network **Eurolines** (www.eurolines.com) connects a huge number of destinations; buy tickets online via one of the national operators.

Services to/from Britain are operated by **National Express** (www.nationalexpress.com). Some sample journey times to/from London:

Amsterdam 12 hours

Barcelona 24 hours

Dublin 12 hours

Paris eight hours

If you're flexible with timings (ie travel when few other people want to) and book early, you can get some very good deals; eg London to Paris or Amsterdam one way starts at just £18, although paying nearer £25 is more usual.

Train

The Channel Tunnel makes direct train travel between Britain and mainland Europe a fast and enjoyable option.

Eurostar (www.eurostar.com) High-speed passenger services hurtle at least 10 times daily between London and Paris (2½ hours) or Brussels (two hours). You can buy tickets from travel agencies, major train stations or direct from the Eurostar website. The normal single fare between London and Paris/Brussels is around £150, but if you buy in advance and travel at a less busy period, deals drop to around £90 return or even less.

'Through fare' tickets are also available for purchase for many cities in Britain; eg York to Paris, or Manchester to Brussels. You can also get very good train and hotel combination deals – bizarrely sometimes cheaper than train fare only.

Eurotunnel (www.eurotunnel.com) Drivers use the Eurotunnel at Folkestone in England or Calais in France: you drive onto a train, get carried through the tunnel and drive off at the other end. The trains run four times an hour from 6am to 10pm, then hourly. Loading and unloading takes an hour; the journey takes 35 minutes. You can book in advance online or pay on the spot. The one-way cost for a car and passengers is around £90 to £150 depending on the time of day (less busy times are cheaper); promotional fares bring it nearer to £50.

Many 'normal' trains also run between Britain and mainland Europe. You buy one ticket, but get off the train at the port, walk onto a ferry, then get another train on the other side. Routes include Amsterdam–London (via Hook of Holland and Harwich).

Travelling between Ireland and Britain, the main train–ferry–train route is Dublin to London, via Dun Laoghaire and Holyhead. Ferries also run between Rosslare and Fishguard or Pembroke (Wales), with train connections on either side.

SEA

The main ferry routes between Britain and mainland Europe include Dover to Calais or Boulogne (France), Harwich to Hook of Holland (Netherlands), Hull to Zeebrugge (Belgium) or Rotterdam (Netherlands), Rosyth to Zeebrugge, Portsmouth to Santander or Bilbao (Spain), Newcastle to Bergen (Norway) or Gothenberg (Sweden). Routes to/from Ireland include Holyhead to Dun Laoghaire.

Competition from the Eurotunnel and budget airlines means ferry operators discount heavily and offer flexible fares, with great bargains at quiet times of the day or year. For example, the short cross-channel routes such as Dover to Calais or Boulogne can be as low as £20 for a car plus up to five passengers, although around £50 is more likely. If you're a foot passenger, or cycling, there's often less need to book ahead, and cheap fares on the short crossings start from about £10 each way.

HOLIDAY SEASONS

Roads get busy and hotel prices go up during school holidays. Exact dates vary from year to year and region to region, but are roughly:

» **Easter Holiday** Week before and week after Easter

» **Summer Holiday** Third week of July to first week of September

» **Christmas Holiday** Mid-December to first week of January.

There are also three week-long 'half-term' school holidays – usually late February (or early March), late May and late October. These vary between Scotland, England and Wales.

Main operators:

Brittany Ferries (www.brittany-ferries.com)

DFDS Seaways (www.dfds.co.uk)

Irish Ferries (www.irishferries.com)

Norfolkline (www.irishferries.com)

P&O Ferries (www.poferries.com)

Speedferries (www.speedferries.com)

Stena Line (www.stenaline.com)

Transmanche (www.transmancheferries.com)

Broker sites covering all routes and options include www.ferrybooker.com and www.directferries.co.uk.

Getting Around

For getting around Britain, your first main choice is going by car or public transport. Having your own car makes the best use of time and helps reach remote places, but rental and fuel costs can be expensive for budget travellers – while the hassles of parking and traffic jams in major cities hit everyone – so public transport is often the better way to go.

Your main public transport options are train and long-distance bus (called coach in Britain). Services between major towns and cities are generally good, although at 'peak' (busy) times you must book in advance to be sure of getting a ticket. Conversely, if you book ahead early or travel at 'off-peak' periods, train and coach tickets can be very cheap.

As long as you have time, by using a mix of train, coach, local bus, the odd taxi, walking and occasionally hiring a bike, you can get almost anywhere in Britain without having to drive. You'll certainly see more of the countryside than you might slogging along grey motorways.

Air

If you're pushed for time, flights on longer routes across Britain (eg Exeter or Southampton to Edinburgh or Inverness) are handy. With advance booking, fares start as low as £20 one way, but up to £100 is more likely. On shorter or direct routes (eg London to Newcastle), train durations compare favourably with planes – once airport downtime is factored in.

AIRLINES IN BRITAIN

Airlines operating domestic flights within Britain:

Air Southwest (WOW; www.airsouthwest.com) Serving Bristol, Cardiff, Leeds-Bradford, Gatwick, Manchester, Newquay, Plymouth.

bmibaby (WW; www.bmibaby.com) Birmingham, East Midlands, Cardiff, Edinburgh, Glasgow, Manchester, Newquay.

British Airways (BA; www.britishairways.com) Birmingham, Edinburgh, Glasgow, Manchester and more.

Eastern Airways (EZE; www.easternairways.com) Aberdeen, Newcastle, Norwich, Cardiff, Southampton and more.

easyJet (EZY; www.easyjet.com) Aberdeen, Bristol, Edinburgh, Glasgow, Inverness, Liverpool, Luton, Stansted, Newcastle.

Flybe (BE; www.flybe.com) Airports served include Aberdeen, Bristol, Edinburgh, Exeter, Glasgow, Liverpool, Manchester, Newcastle, Newquay, Southampton and many Scottish islands.

TRAVELINE

Traveline (0871 200 2233; www.traveline.org.uk) is a very useful information service covering bus, coach, taxi and train services nationwide. By phone, you get transferred automatically to an advisor in the region you're phoning *from;* for details on another part of the country, you need to key in a code number (81 for London, 874 for Cumbria etc). For a full list of codes, go to the Traveline website.

Ryanair (FR; www.ryanair.com) Aberdeen, Birmingham, Bournemouth, Edinburgh, Glasgow, Inverness, Liverpool, Stansted and Newquay.

Bus

If you're on a tight budget, long-distance buses (coaches) nearly always offer the cheapest, though also the slowest, way to get around. Many towns have separate bus and coach stations; make sure you're in the right place!

National Express (08717 818181; www.nationalexpress.com) is the main coach operator, with a wide network and frequent services between main centres. North of the border, **Scottish Citylink** (08705 505050; www.citylink.co.uk) is the leading coach company. Fares vary: they're cheaper if you book in advance and travel at quieter times (special off-peak fares cost as low as £1). As a guide, a 200-mile trip (eg London to York) will cost around £15 to £20 if you book a few days in advance, and a lot more if booking's left to the last minute.

Also offering fares from £1 is **Megabus** (www.megabus.com), a budget coach service serving about 30 destinations in Britain.

BUS PASSES

National Express offers discount passes to full-time students and under-26s, called **Young Persons Coachcards**. They cost £10 and get you 30% off standard adult fares. Also available are coachcards for people over 60, families and disabled travellers.

For touring the country, National Express offers **Brit Xplorer passes**, allowing unlimited travel for seven days (£79), 14 days (£139) and 28 days (£219). You don't need to book journeys in advance; if the coach has a spare seat, you can take it.

Car & Motorcycle

Most overseas driving licences are valid in Britain for up to 12 months from the date of entry.

RENTAL

Compared to many countries (especially the USA), car rental is expensive in Britain; you'll pay around £250 per week for a small car (including insurance and unlimited mileage) but rates rise at busy times and drop at quiet times. All of the major players are available, such as Avis and Budget.

Many international websites have separate web pages for customers in different countries, and the prices for a car in Britain on the UK web pages can differ from the same car's prices on the USA or Australia pages. You have to surf a lot of sites to find the best deals.

Another option is to look online for small local car-hire companies in Britain who can undercut the international franchises. Generally, those in cities are cheaper than in rural areas. Rental-broker sites include **UK Car Hire** (www.ukcarhire.net).

You can also hire a motorhome or campervan. It's more expensive than hiring a car, but saves on accommodation costs and gives almost unlimited freedom. Sites to check:

Cool Campervans (www.coolcampervans.com)

Just Go (www.justgo.uk.com)

Wild Horizon (www.wildhorizon.co.uk)

HOW MUCH TO...?

When travelling long-distance by train or bus/coach in Britain, it's important to realise that there's no such thing as a standard fare. Prices vary according to demand and when you buy your ticket. Book long in advance and travel on Tuesday mid-morning, and it's cheap. Buy your ticket on the spot late Friday afternoon, and it'll be a lot more expensive. Ferries use similar systems. Throughout this book, we have generally quoted sample fares somewhere in between the very cheapest and most expensive options. The price you pay will almost certainly be different.

ROAD RULES

The *Highway Code*, available in bookshops (or at www.direct.gov.uk/en/TravelAndTransport/Highwaycode), contains everything you need to know about Britain's road rules. The main ones:

» Drive on the left

» Wear fitted seat belts in cars

» Wear crash helmets on motorcycles

» Give way to your right at junctions and roundabouts

» Always use the left-hand lane on motorways and dual-carriageways, unless overtaking (passing)

» Don't use a mobile phone while driving unless it's fully hands-free

» Distances are in miles (not kilometres)

Speed limits are 30mph in built-up areas, 60mph on main roads, and 70mph on motorways and most (but not all) dual carriageways. Drinking and driving is taken very seriously; the maximum blood-alcohol level allowed is 80mg/100mL.

Train

For long-distance travel around Britain, trains are faster and more comfortable than coaches but can be more expensive – although with discount tickets they're competitive – and often take you through beautiful countryside. The British like to moan about their trains, but around 85% run on time. The other 15% that get delayed or cancelled mostly impact commuters rather than long-distance services

Around 20 companies operate train services in Britain, including **First Great Western** (www.firstgreatwestern.co.uk), which runs from London to Bristol; **National Express East Coast** (www.eastcoast.co.uk), which runs from London to Edinburgh; and **Virgin Trains** (www.virgintrains.co.uk), which runs the 'west coast' route from London to Birmingham and Glasgow. **Network Rail** (www.networkrail.co.uk) operates tracks and stations.

This system can seem confusing, but information and ticket-buying are mostly centralised. If you have to change trains, or use two train operators, you usually still buy one ticket valid for the whole journey. The main railcards are also accepted by all operators.

PLANNING

Your first stop should be **National Rail Enquiries** (☎08457 48 49 50; www.nationalrail.co.uk), Britain's timetable and fare-information service. Enter your start and end destinations to see a range of routes, times and fares, plus links to the relevant train operator or centralised ticketing services (www.thetrainline.com, www.qjump.co.uk and www.raileasy.co.uk). Train-travel websites can be confusing at first (you always have to state an approximate preferred time and day of travel, even if you don't mind *when* you go), but with a little delving they offer some real bargains.

Handy maps of the UK rail network are available for download from the National Rail Enquiries website.

CLASSES

Rail travel has two classes: 1st and standard. Travelling 1st class costs around 50% more than standard and, except on crowded

BREAK FOR THE BORDER

When travelling around Britain, getting between the three constituent nations of England, Scotland and Wales is easy. The bus and train systems are fully integrated and in most cases you won't even know you've crossed the border. Passports are not required.

trains, isn't worth it. At weekends some train operators offer 'upgrades' for an extra £10 to £15 on top of your standard-class fare.

COSTS & RESERVATIONS

For short journeys (under about 50 miles), it's usually best to buy tickets on the spot at rail stations. For longer journeys, on-the-spot fares are always available, but tickets are much cheaper to buy in advance: the earlier you book, the cheaper it is. You can also save if you travel 'off-peak' (ie days and times that aren't busy). Advance purchase usually gets a reserved seat too. The cheapest fares are nonrefundable, so if you miss your train you'll have to buy a new ticket.

If you buy online, you can have the ticket posted (UK addresses only), or collect it from station machines on the day of travel.

Regardless of operator, these are the three main fare types:

Anytime Buy anytime, travel anytime – usually the most expensive option

Off-peak Buy anytime, travel off-peak

Advance Buy in advance, travel only on specific trains (usually the cheapest option)

An Anytime single ticket from London to York will cost around £100 or more and an Off-peak around £80, while an Advance is around £20 (even less if you book early enough or don't mind arriving at midnight).

TRAIN PASSES

If you're staying in Britain for a while, passes known as 'railcards' are available. For full details see www.railcard.co.uk.

16–25 Railcard For those aged 16 to 25, or full-time UK students

Family & Friends Railcard Covers up to four adults and four children

Senior Railcard For anyone aged over 60 years

Disabled Person's Railcard £18 (application forms from stations or from the railcard website)

Most railcards cost around £26 (valid for one year, available from major stations or online) and get you a 33% discount on most train fares, except those already heavily discounted. With the Family card, adults get 33% and children get 60% discounts, so the fee is easily repaid in a couple of journeys.

Regional Passes

For those touring mainly southeast England (eg London to Dover, Weymouth, Cambridge or Oxford), a **Network Railcard** covers up to four adults and up to four children travelling together outside peak times.

National Passes

For country-wide travel, **BritRail** (www.britrail.com) passes are available for visitors from overseas. They must be bought in your country of origin (not in Britain) from a specialist travel agency. They're available in three different versions (England only; all Britain; UK and Ireland) and for periods from four to 30 days. Of the other international passes, **Eurail** cards are not accepted in Britain, and **InterRail** cards are only valid if bought in another mainland European country.

PLUSBUS

If train doesn't get you all the way to your destination, a **PlusBus** (www.plusbus.info) supplement (usually around £2) validates your train ticket for onwards travel by bus – more convenient, and usually cheaper, than buying a separate bus ticket.

France

Includes »

Best Places to Eat

» Chez Janou (p337)

» Pink Flamingo (boxed text, p341)

» La Table de Ventabren (boxed text, p428)

» Auberge de la Truffe (boxed text, p406)

» Les Vieilles Luges (p396)

Best Places to Stay

» Hôtel Amour (p336)

» L'Apostrophe (p334)

» Hôtel de l'Illwald (boxed text, p371)

» L'Épicerie (p427)

» Hôtel 7e Art (p441)

Why Go?

Few countries provoke such passion as La Belle France. Love it or loathe it, everyone has their own opinion about this Gallic goliath. Snooty, sexy, superior, chic, infuriating, arrogant, officious and inspired in equal measures, the French have long lived according to their own idiosyncratic rules, and if the rest of the world doesn't always see eye-to-eye with them, well, *tant pis* (too bad) – that's the price you pay for being a culinary trendsetter, artistic pioneer and cultural icon.

If ever there was a country of contradictions, this is it. France is a deeply traditional place: castles, chateaux and ancient churches litter the landscape, while centuries-old principles of rich food, fine wine and joie de vivre underpin everyday life. Yet it is also a country that has one of Western Europe's most multicultural make-ups, not to mention a well-deserved reputation for artistic experimentation and architectural invention. Enjoy!

When to Go

Paris

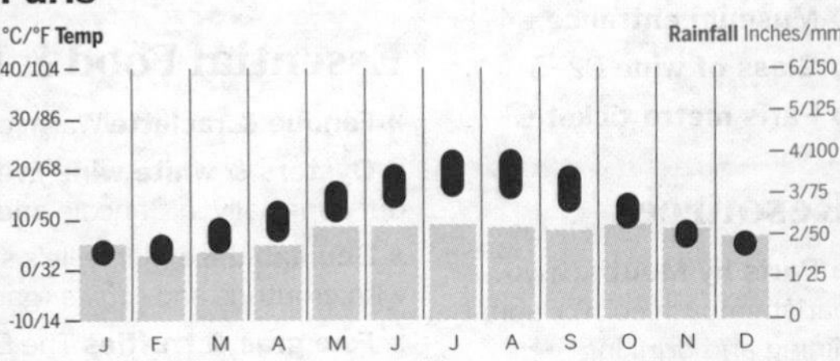

Dec–Mar Hit the French Alps, Jura or Pyrenees for some serious ski action. Or eat truffles.

Apr–Jun France at springtime best, *sans* crowds; June's Fête de la Musique gets you jigging.

Sep Cooling temperatures, abundant produce and the grape harvest; perfect for cycling through Provence.

AT A GLANCE

» **Currency** euro (€)

» **Language** French

» **Money** ATMs can be found everywhere.

» **Visas** Schengen rules apply

Fast Facts

» **Area** 551,000 sq km

» **Population** 64.4 million

» **Capital** Paris

» **Telephone** country code ☎33; international access code ☎00

» **Emergency** ☎112

Exchange Rates

Australia	A$1	€0.74
Canada	C$1	€0.74
Japan	¥100	€0.87
New Zealand	NZ$1	€0.56
UK	UK£1	€1.16
USA	US$1	€0.67

Set Your Budget

» **Budget hotel room** from €70

» **Two-course dinner** €15–50

» **Museum entrance** €4–8

» **Glass of wine** €2–5

» **Paris metro ticket** €1.70

Resources

» **Paris by Mouth** (www.parisbymouth.com) Capital dining and drinking

» **France 24** (www.france24.com/en/france) French news in English

» **France.fr** (www.france.fr) Official country website

Connections

High-speed trains link Paris' Gare du Nord with London St Pancras (via the Channel Tunnel/Eurostar rail service) in just over two hours; Gare du Nord is also the point of departure for speedy trains to Brussels, Amsterdam and Cologne. Many more trains make travelling between the French capital and pretty much any city in every neighbouring country a real pleasure. Ferry links from Cherbourg, St-Malo, Calais and other north-coast ports travel to England and Ireland; and ferries from Marseille and Nice provide regular links with seaside towns in Corsica, Italy and North Africa.

Regular bus and rail links cross the French–Spanish border via the Pyrenees, and the French–Italian border via the Alps and the southern Mediterranean coast. For more see p463.

ITINERARIES

One Week

Start with a few days exploring Paris, taking in the Louvre, Eiffel Tower, Musée d'Orsay, Notre Dame, Montmartre and a boat trip along the Seine. Then head out to Normandy, Monet's garden at Giverny, and Versailles; or throw yourself into the Renaissance high life at chateaux in the Loire Valley.

Two Weeks

With Paris and surrounds having taken up much of the first week, concentrate on exploring one or two regions rather than trying to do too much in a whistlestop dash. High-speed TGV *(train à grande vitesse)* trains zip from Paris to practically every province: for prehistoric interest, head to the Dordogne; for architectural splendour, you can't top the Loire Valley; for typical French atmosphere, try the hilltop villages of Provence; and for sunshine and seafood, the French Riviera on the sparkling Med is the only place to be.

Essential Food & Drink

» **Fondue & raclette** Warm cheese dishes in the French Alps.

» **Oysters & white wine** Everywhere on the Atlantic coast, but especially in Cancale and Bordeaux.

» **Bouillabaisse** Marseille's signature hearty fish stew, eaten with croutons and *rouille* (garlic-and-chilli mayonnaise).

» **Foie gras & truffles** The Dordogne features goose and 'black diamonds' from December to March. Provence is also good for indulging in the aphrodisiacal fungi.

» **Piggy-part cuisine** Lyon is famous for its juicy *andouillette* (pig-intestine sausage) and Côtes du Rhône red.

» **Champagne** Tasting in century-old cellars is an essential part of Champagne's bubbly experience.

PARIS

POP 2.21 MILLION

What can be said about the sexy, sophisticated City of Lights that hasn't already been said a thousand times before? Quite simply, this is one of the world's great metropolises – a trendsetter, market leader and cultural capital for over a thousand years and still going strong. This is the place that gave the world the cancan and the cinematograph, a city that reinvented itself during the Renaissance, bopped to the beat of the jazz age and positively glittered during the belle époque (literally, 'beautiful era').

As you might expect, Paris is strewn with historic architecture, glorious galleries and cultural treasures galore. But the modern-day city is much more than just a museum piece: it's a heady hotchpotch of cultures and ideas – a place to stroll the boulevards, shop till you drop, flop riverside, or simply do as Parisians do and watch the world buzz by from a streetside cafe. Savour every moment.

History

The Parisii, a tribe of Celtic Gauls, settled the Île de la Cité in the 3rd century BC. Paris prospered during the Middle Ages and flourished during the Renaissance, when many of the city's most famous buildings were erected.

The excesses of Louis XVI and his queen, Marie-Antoinette, led to an uprising of Parisians on 14 July 1789, and the storming of the Bastille prison – kick-starting the French Revolution.

In 1851 Emperor Napoleon III oversaw the construction of a more modern Paris, complete with wide boulevards, sculptured parks and a sewer system. Following the disastrous Franco-Prussian War and the establishment of the Third Republic, Paris entered its most resplendent period, the belle époque, famed for its art nouveau architecture and artistic and scientific advances. By the beginning of the 1930s, Paris had become a centre for the artistic avant-garde, and it remained so until the Nazi occupation of 1940–44.

After WWII, Paris regained its position as a creative centre and nurtured a revitalised liberalism that climaxed in student-led uprisings in 1968.

During the 1980s President François Mitterrand initiated several *grands projets*, building projects that garnered widespread approval even when the results were popular failures. In 2001 Bertrand Delanoë, a socialist with support from the Green Party, became Paris' – and a European capital's – first openly gay mayor. He returned to power for another term in the 2008 elections.

Sights

LEFT BANK

Eiffel Tower LANDMARK

(Map p318; www.tour-eiffel.fr; lifts to 2nd fl adult/child €8.10/4, to 3rd fl €13.10/9, stairs to 2nd

PARIS IN…

Two Days

Join a **morning tour** then focus on those Parisian icons: **Notre Dame**, the **Eiffel Tower** and the **Arc de Triomphe**. Late afternoon have a coffee or pastis on **av des Champs-Élysées**, then mooch to **Montmartre** for dinner. Next day enjoy the **Musée d'Orsay**, **Ste-Chapelle** and the **Musée Rodin**. Brunch on **place des Vosges** and enjoy a night of mirth and gaiety in the nightlife-buzzy **Marais**.

Four Days

With another two days, consider a **cruise** along the Seine or **Canal St-Martin** and meander further afield to **Cimetière du Père Lachaise** or **Parc de la Villette**. By night take in a concert or opera at the **Palais Garnier** or **Opéra Bastille**, and go on a bar-and-club crawl along Ménilmontant's **rue Oberkampf**. The **Bastille** area also translates as another great night out.

A Week

Seven days allows you to see a good many of the major sights listed in this chapter and also visit places around Paris, such as **Chartres** with its beautiful cathedral, and the queen of French chateaux, **Versailles**.

France Highlights

1. Gorge on the iconic sights and sophistication of Europe's most hopelessly romantic city, **Paris** (p315)
2. Relive the French Renaissance with extraordinary chateaux built by kings and queens in the **Loire Valley** (p375)
3. Do a Bond swooshing down slopes in the shadow of Mont Blanc in **Chamonix** (p394)
4. Dodge tides, stroll moonlit sand and immerse yourself in legend at island abbey **Mont St-Michel** (p359)
5. Savour ancient ruins, modern art, markets, lavender and hilltop villages in slow-paced **Provence** (p420)
6. Taste bubbly in ancient *caves* (cellars) in **Reims** (p364) and **Épernay** (p366), the heart of Champagne
7. Tuck into France's halest, piggy-driven cuisine in traditional **Lyonnais bouchons** (p392)
8. Soak up the mystery of the world's best megaliths from the back of a Breton bicycle around **Carnac** (boxed text, p361)

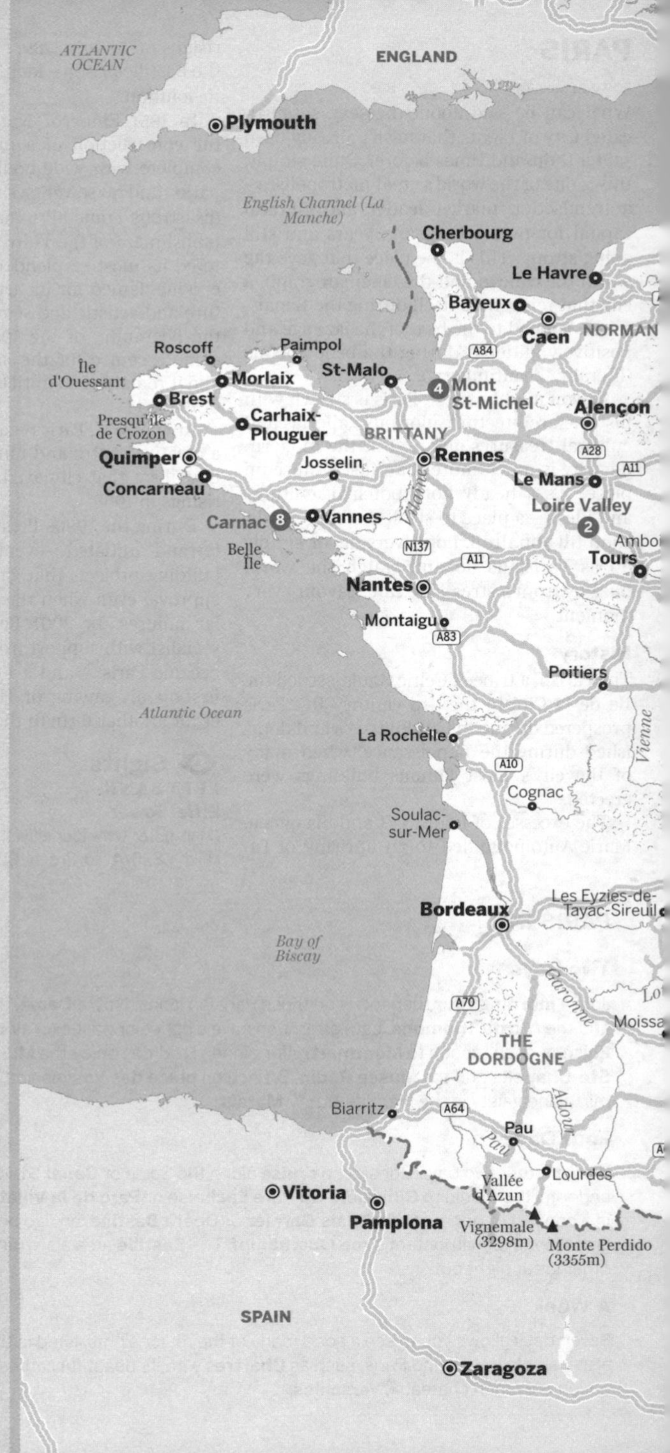

0 200 km
0 100 miles
Dunkirk
Calais
Brussels
NETHERLANDS
BELGIUM
Lille
GERMANY
Meuse
Mainz
LUXEMBOURG
Luxembourg
SOMME
Paris
Versailles
Vernon
Dreux
Reims
Épernay
CHAMPAGNE
Troyes
Metz
ALSACE
Nancy
Strasbourg
Stuttgart
LORRAINE
Sélestat
Schnellenbuhl
Katzenthal
BURGUNDY
Orléans
Beaugency
Chambord
Auxerre
LA SOLOGNE
Dijon
CÔTE D'OR
Beaune
Besançon
Arc-et-Senans
Arbois
Métabief Mont d'Or
Les Rousses
Basel
AUSTRIA
SWITZERLAND
Le Creusot
JURA
Lausanne
Lake Geneva
Les Portes du Soleil
Chamonix
Mont Blanc (4810m)
Gueret
Clermont-Ferrand
Lyon
Annecy
Chambéry
FRENCH ALPS
St-Étienne
Grenoble
ITALY
Puy Mary (1787m)
Valence
Sestriere
Vaison la Romaine
Mt Lozère (1699m)
Mt Ventoux (1912m)
THE LOT
Pont du Gard
Nîmes
Avignon
Les Baux de Provence
Arles
Provence
Cannes
Nice
Monaco
Ligurian Sea
Toulouse
Montpellier
LANGUEDOC
Aix-en-Provence
Marseille
St-Tropez
ROUSILLON
Perpignan
Golfe de Beauduc
ANDORRA
Puig Neulós
SPAIN
Barcelona
Mediterranean Sea
Île Rousse
Bastia
Calvi
Monte Cinto (2706m)
CORSICA
Ajaccio
Bonifacio
ITALY

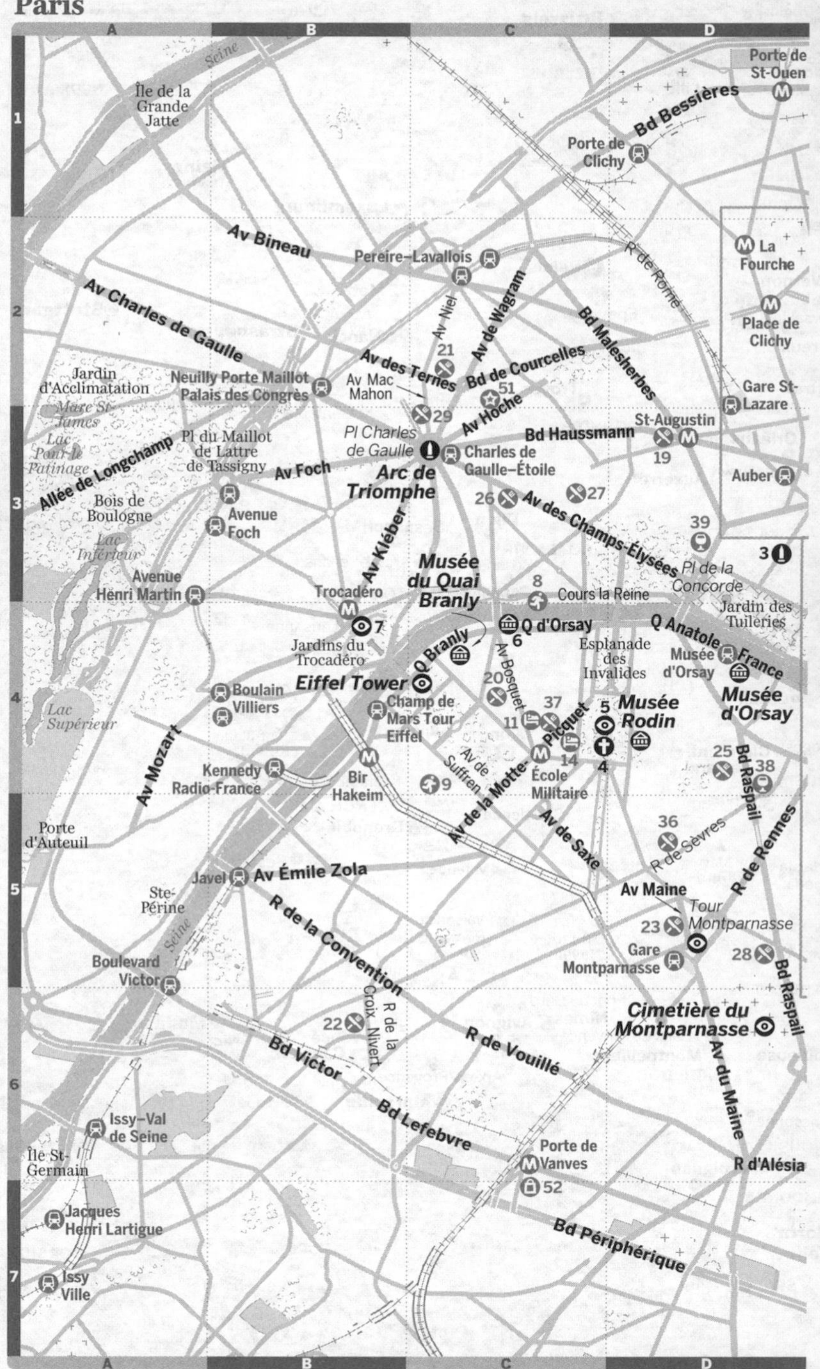

FRANCE PARIS

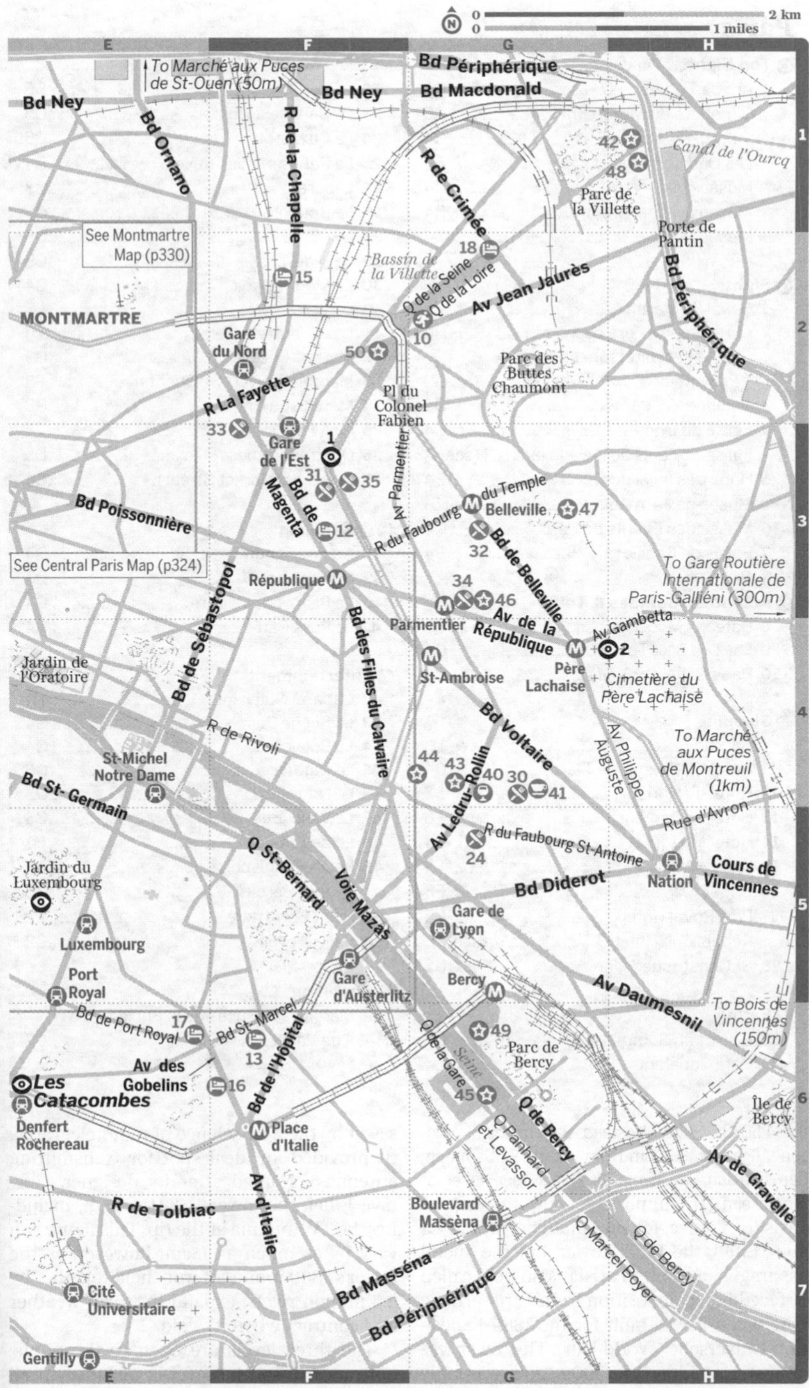

0 2 km
0 1 miles
To Marché aux Puces de St-Ouen (50m)
Bd Périphérique
Bd Ney
Bd Macdonald
Bd Ornano
R de la Chapelle
R de Crimée
Canal de l'Ourcq
Parc de la Villette
Porte de Pantin
See Montmartre Map (p330)
Bassin de la Villette
Q de la Seine
Q de la Loire
Av Jean Jaurès
Bd Périphérique
MONTMARTRE
Gare du Nord
Parc des Buttes Chaumont
R La Fayette
Pl du Colonel Fabien
Gare de l'Est
Av Parmentier
Bd de Magenta
Bd Poissonnière
R du Faubourg du Temple
Belleville
Bd de Belleville
See Central Paris Map (p324)
République
To Gare Routière Internationale de Paris-Galliéni (300m)
Bd de Sébastopol
Bd des Filles du Calvaire
Parmentier
Av de la République
Av Gambetta
Père Lachaise
Cimetière du Père Lachaise
Jardin de l'Oratoire
St-Ambroise
Bd Voltaire
R de Rivoli
To Marché aux Puces de Montreuil (1km)
St-Michel Notre Dame
Av Ledru-Rollin
Av Philippe Auguste
Bd St-Germain
Rue d'Avron
R du Faubourg St-Antoine
Q St-Bernard
Voie Mazas
Jardin du Luxembourg
Bd Diderot
Nation
Cours de Vincennes
Luxembourg
Gare de Lyon
Port Royal
Gare d'Austerlitz
Bercy
Av Daumesnil
To Bois de Vincennes (150m)
Bd de Port Royal
Bd St-Marcel
Bd de l'Hôpital
Q de la Gare
Seine
Parc de Bercy
Av des Gobelins
Les Catacombes
Q de Bercy
Île de Bercy
Denfert Rochereau
Place d'Italie
Q Panhard et Levassor
Av de Gravelle
R de Tolbiac
Av d'Italie
Boulevard Massèna
Q Marcel Boyer
Q de Bercy
Bd Masséna
Bd Périphérique
Cité Universitaire
Gentilly
PARIS PARIS

Paris

Top Sights
Arc de Triomphe C3
Cimetière du Montparnasse D6
Eiffel Tower C4
Les Catacombes E6
Musée d'Orsay D4
Musée du Quai Branly C4
Musée Rodin D4

Sights
1 Canal St-Martin F3
2 Cimetière du Père Lachaise H4
Cité de l'Architecture et du Patrimoine .... (see 7)
3 Colonne Vendôme D3
4 Église du Dôme C4
Église St-Louis des Invalides .... (see 4)
5 Hôtel des Invalides C4
Musée de l'Armée .... (see 5)
6 Musée des Égouts de Paris C4
7 Palais de Chaillot B4

Activities, Courses & Tours
8 Bateaux Mouches C3
9 Fat Tire Bike Tours Office C4
10 Paris Canal Croisières G2

Sleeping
Cadran Hôtel .... (see 11)
11 Hôtel du Champ-de-Mars C4
12 Hôtel du Nord F3
13 Hôtel La Demeure F6
14 Hôtel Muguet C4
15 Kube Hôtel F2
16 Oops F6
17 Port Royal Hôtel E6
République Hôtel .... (see 12)
18 St Christopher's Inn G2

Eating
19 Bistrot du Sommelier D3
20 Café Constant C4
21 Fromagerie Alléosse C2
22 Jadis B6
23 La Cabane à Huîtres D5
24 La Gazzetta G5
25 La Pâtisserie des Rêves D4
26 Ladurée C3
27 Le Boudoir C3
28 Le Dôme D5
29 Le Hide C3
30 Le Mouton Noir G4
31 Le Verre Volé F3
Les Cocottes .... (see 20)
32 Marché Belleville G3
33 Marché Couvert St-Quentin F3
34 Marche ou Crêpe G3
35 Pink Flamingo F3
36 Quatrehommes D5
37 Rue Cler (Market Street) C4

Drinking
38 Au Sauvignon D4
39 Buddha Bar D3
40 Le Bistrot du Peintre G4
41 Le Pure Café G4

Entertainment
42 Cabaret Sauvage H1
43 La Scène Bastille G4
44 Le Balajo G4
45 Le Batofar G6
46 Le Nouveau Casino G3
47 Le Vieux Belleville G3
48 Le Zénith H1
49 Palais Omnisports de Paris-Bercy G6
50 Point Éphémère F2
51 Salle Pleyel C2

Shopping
52 Marché aux Puces de la Porte de Vanves C7

fl €4.50/3; lifts & stairs 9am-midnight mid-Jun–Aug, lifts 9.30am-11pm, stairs 9.30am-6pm Sep–mid-Jun; MChamp de Mars–Tour Eiffel or Bir Hakeim) It's impossible now to imagine Paris (or France, for that matter) without La Tour Eiffel, the Eiffel Tower, but the 'metal asparagus', as some Parisians snidely called it, faced fierce opposition from Paris' artistic elite when it was built for the 1889 Exposition Universelle (World Fair). The tower was almost torn down in 1909, and was only saved by the new science of radiotelegraphy (it provided an ideal spot for transmitting antennas). Named after its designer, Gustave Eiffel, the tower is 324m high, including the TV antenna at the tip. This figure can vary by as much as 15cm, however, as the tower's 7300 tonnes of iron, held together by 2.5 million rivets, expand in warm weather and contract when it's cold.

The three levels are open to the public (entrance to the 1st level is included in all admission tickets), though the top level closes in heavy wind. You can either take the lifts (east, west and north pillars), or, if you're feeling fit – don't blame us if you run out of steam halfway up – the stairs in the south pillar up to the 2nd platform. Buy tickets in advance online to avoid monumental queues at the ticket office.

Spreading out around the Eiffel Tower are the **Jardins du Trocadéro** (MTrocadéro), whose fountains and statue garden are grandly illuminated at night.

Musée du Quai Branly MUSEUM
(Map p318; www.quaibranly.fr; 37 quai Branly, 7e; adult/child €8.50/free; 11am-7pm Tue, Wed & Sun, to 9pm Thu-Sat; MPont de l'Alma or Alma-Marceau) The architecturally impressive but unimaginatively named Quai Branly Museum introduces the art and cultures of Africa, Oceania, Asia and the Americas through innovative displays, film and musical recordings. With *'Là où dialoguent les cultures'* ('Where cultures communicate') as its motto, the museum is one of the most dynamic and forward-thinking in the world. The anthropological explanations are kept to a minimum; what is displayed here is meant to be viewed as art. Don't miss the views from the 5th-floor restaurant, **Les Ombres**.

Musée d'Orsay ART MUSEUM
(Map p318; www.musee-orsay.fr; 62 rue de Lille, 7e; adult/child €8/free; 9.30am-6pm Tue, Wed & Fri-Sun, 9.30am-9.45pm Thu; MMusée d'Orsay or Solférino) The Musée d'Orsay, housed in a turn-of-the-century train station overlooking the Seine, displays France's national collection of paintings, sculptures and other art produced between the 1840s and 1914. The museum is especially renowned for its Impressionist and art nouveau collections: the upper level contains a celebrated collection of Impressionist paintings by Monet, Pissarro, Renoir, Sisley, Degas and Manet, plus post-Impressionist works by Cézanne, Van Gogh, Seurat and Matisse. Art nouveau aficionados will want to linger on the middle level, while on the ground floor, look out for early works by Manet, Monet, Renoir and Pissarro.

Tickets are valid all day, so you can come and go as you please. A reduced entrance fee of €5.50 applies to everyone after 4.15pm (6pm on Thursday). A combined ticket including the Musée Rodin costs €12.

TOP CHOICE **Jardin du Luxembourg** PARK
(Map p324; 7.30 or 8.15am–5 or 10pm according to the season; MLuxembourg) When the weather is fine, Parisians of all ages come flocking to the formal terraces and chestnut groves of this 23-hectare city park to read, relax, stroll through urban **orchards** and visit the honey-producing **Rucher du Luxembourg** (Luxembourg Apiary).

The **Palais du Luxembourg** (Map p324; rue de Vaugirard, 6e), at the northern end of the garden, was built for Marie de Médicis, Henri IV's consort; it has housed the **Sénat** (Senate), the upper house of the French parliament, since 1958.

Top spot for sun-soaking – always loads of chairs here – is the southern side of the palace's 19th-century, 57m-long **Orangery** (1834), where lemon and orange trees, palms, grenadiers and oleanders shelter from the cold.

TOP CHOICE **Musée Rodin** GARDEN, ART MUSEUM
(Map p318; www.musee-rodin.fr; 79 rue de Varenne, 7e; adult/child incl garden €7-10/free, garden only €1; 10am-5.45pm Tue-Sun; MVarenne) One of our favourite cultural attractions, the Rodin Museum is both a sublime museum and one of the most relaxing spots in the city, with a lovely sculpture garden in which to lounge. The 18th-century house displays some of Rodin's most famous works, including *The Burghers of Calais (Les Bourgeois de Calais), Cathedral, The Thinker (Le Penseur)* and *The Kiss (Le Baiser)*.

Les Catacombes OSSUARY
(Map p318; www.catacombes.paris.fr, in French; 1 av Colonel Henri Roi-Tanguy, 14e; adult/child €8/4; 10am-5pm Tue-Sun; MDenfert Rochereau)

PLANNING TIP

Most Paris museums are closed on Mondays, but a dozen-odd, including the Louvre and Centre Pompidou, are closed on Tuesdays instead.

PARIS MUSEUM PASS

Valid for some 38 sights including the Louvre, Centre Pompidou, Musée d'Orsay, St-Denis basilica, parts of Versailles and Fontainebleau, the **Paris Museum Pass** (www.parismuseumpass.fr; 2/4/6 days €32/48/64) can be purchased online, from the Paris Convention & Visitors Bureau (p346), Fnac outlets, major metro stations and all participating venues.

WANT MORE?

For in-depth information, reviews and recommendations at your fingertips, head to the Apple App Store to purchase Lonely Planet's *Paris City Guide* iPhone app.

Alternatively, head to **Lonely Planet** (www.lonelyplanet.com/france/paris) for planning advice, author recommendations, traveller reviews and insider tips.

There are few spookier sights in Paris than the Catacombes, one of three underground cemeteries created in the late 18th century to solve the problems posed by Paris' overflowing cemeteries. Twenty metres below street level, the catacombs consist of 1.7km of winding tunnels stacked from floor to ceiling with the bones and skulls of millions of Parisians – guaranteed to send a shiver down your spine.

If your ghoulish appetite yearns for more, check out lots more famous graves at **Cimetière du Montparnasse** (Map p318; cnr blvd Edgar Quinet & rue Froidevaux, 14e; ⌚8am-5.30 or 6pm Mon-Fri, 8.30am-6pm Sat, 9am-6pm Sun; Ⓜ Edgar Quinet or Raspail), including French crooner Serge Gainsbourg, poet Charles Baudelaire, writer Guy de Maupassant, playwright Samuel Beckett, photographer Man Ray and philosopher Jean-Paul Sartre.

Musée des Égouts de Paris MUSEUM
(Map p318; place de la Résistance, 7e; adult/child €4.20/3.40; ⌚11am-5pm Sat-Wed May-Sep, 11am-4pm Sat-Wed Oct-Dec & Feb-Apr; Ⓜ Pont de l'Alma) A working museum whose entrance – a rectangular maintenance hole topped with a kiosk – is across the street from 93 quai d'Orsay, 7e. Raw sewage flows beneath your feet as you walk through 480m of odoriferous tunnels, passing artefacts illustrating the development of Paris' waste-water disposal system. A visit here quite takes your breath away.

Panthéon MONUMENT
(Map p324; place du Panthéon, 5e; adult/child €8/free; ⌚10am-6.30pm Apr-Sep, to 6pm Oct-Mar; Ⓜ Luxembourg) This domed landmark was commissioned around 1750 as an abbey church, but because of financial and structural problems it wasn't completed until 1789 (not a good year for opening churches in France). The crypt houses the tombs of Voltaire, Jean-Jacques Rousseau, Victor Hugo, Émile Zola, Jean Moulin and Nobel Prize–winner Marie Curie, among many others. Inside the gloomy Panthéon itself, a working model of Foucault's Pendulum demonstrates the rotation of the earth; it wowed the scientific establishment when it was presented here in 1851.

Hôtel des Invalides MONUMENT, MUSEUM
(Map p318; Ⓜ Varenne or La Tour Maubourg) Hôtel des Invalides was built in the 1670s as housing for 4000 *invalides* (disabled war veterans). On 14 July 1789, a mob forced its way into the building and seized 28,000 rifles before heading to the prison at Bastille, starting the French Revolution.

North of the main courtyard is the **Musée de l'Armée** (Map p318; Army Museum; www.invalides.org; 129 rue de Grenelle, 7e; adult/child €9/free; ⌚10am-6pm Mon & Wed-Sat, to 9pm Tue), home to the nation's largest collection on the history of the French military.

South are **Église St-Louis des Invalides**, once used by soldiers, and **Église du Dôme**, which contains the extraordinarily extravagant **Tombeau de Napoléon 1er** (Napoleon I's Tomb; ⌚10am-6pm Apr-Sep, 10am-5pm Oct-Mar): six coffins fit into one another rather like a Russian stacking doll.

Palais de Chaillot PALACE, MUSEUM
(Map p318; 17 place du Trocadéro et du 11 Novembre, 16e; Ⓜ Trocadéro) The two curved, colonnaded wings of this palace and the terrace in between them afford an exceptional panorama of the **Jardins du Trocadéro**, the Seine and the Eiffel Tower. The palace's eastern wing houses the standout **Cité de l'Architecture et du Patrimoine** (Map p318; www.citechaillot.fr, in French; 1 place du Trocadéro et du 11 Novembre, 16e; adult/child €8/free; ⌚11am-7pm Mon, Wed & Fri-Sun, to 9pm Thu), devoted to French architecture and heritage.

Jardin des Plantes GARDEN
(Map p324; 57 rue Cuvier & 3 quai St-Bernard, 5e; ⌚7.30am-7pm; Ⓜ Gare d'Austerlitz, Censier Daubenton or Jussieu) Paris' 24-hectare Jardin des Plantes was founded in 1626 as a medicinal herb garden for Louis XIII. On its southern fringe is the city's main natural-history museum, the **Musée National d'Histoire Naturelle** (Map p324; www.mnhn.fr, in French; ⌚10am-5pm Wed-Mon; Ⓜ Censier Daubenton or Gare d'Austerlitz), with several galleries covering evolution, geology, palaeontology and the history of human evolution.

Église St-Germain des Prés CHURCH
(Map p324; 3 place St-Germain des Prés, 6e; ⌚8am-7pm Mon-Sat, 9am-8pm Sun; Ⓜ St-Germain des Prés) Paris' oldest church, the Romanesque Église St-Germain des Prés, was built in the 11th century on the site of a 6th-century abbey and was the dominant church in Paris until the arrival of Notre Dame.

Église St-Sulpice CHURCH
(Map p324; place St-Sulpice, 6e; ⌚7.30am-7.30pm; Ⓜ St-Sulpice) Lined with 21 side chapels, this beautiful Italianate church was built between 1646 and 1780. The facade, designed by a Florentine architect, has two rows of superimposed columns and is topped by two towers. The neoclassical decor of the vast interior is influenced by the Counter-Reformation.

THE ISLANDS

Paris' twin set of islands could not be more different. **Île de la Cité** is bigger, full of sights and very touristed (few people live here).

Smaller **Île St-Louis** is residential and quieter, with just enough boutiques and restaurants – and a legendary ice-cream maker – to attract visitors. The area around **Pont St-Louis**, the bridge across to the Île de la Cité, and **Pont Louis Philippe**, the bridge to the Marais, is one of the most romantic spots in Paris.

ÎLE DE LA CITÉ

The site of the first settlement in Paris, around the 3rd century BC, and later the Roman town of Lutèce (Lutetia), Île de la Cité remained the centre of royal and ecclesiastical power throughout the Middle Ages. The seven decorated arches of Paris' oldest bridge, **Pont Neuf** (Map p324; Ⓜ Pont Neuf), have linked Île de la Cité with both banks of the River Seine since 1607.

Cathédrale de Notre Dame de Paris CHURCH
(Map p324; www.cathedraledeparis.com; 6 place du Parvis Notre Dame, 4e; audioguide €5; ⌚8am-6.45pm Mon-Fri, 8am-7.15pm Sat & Sun; Ⓜ Cité) Notre Dame is the true heart of Paris: distances from Paris to all parts of metropolitan France are measured from **place du Parvis Notre Dame**, the square in front of this masterpiece of French Gothic architecture.

Notre Dame – the most visited site in Paris, with 10 million people crossing its threshold each year – is famed for its stunning stained-glass rose windows, leering gargoyles and elegant flying buttresses, as well as a monumental 7800-pipe organ. Constructed on a site occupied by earlier churches (and, a millennium before that, a Gallo-Roman temple), it was begun in 1163 but not completed until the mid-14th century. Architect Viollet-le-Duc carried out extensive renovations in the mid-19th century. Free 1½-hour tours in English run at noon on Wednesday, 2pm Thursday and 2.30pm Saturday.

The entrance to its famous towers, the **Tours de Notre Dame** (Map p324; rue du Cloître Notre Dame; adult/child €7.50/free; ⌚10am-6.30pm daily Apr-Jun & Sep, 9am-7.30pm Mon-Fri, 9am-11pm Sat & Sun Jul & Aug, 10am-5.30pm daily Oct-Mar) is from the North Tower, to the right and around the corner as you walk out of the cathedral's main doorway. A narrow spiral staircase – 422 steps – takes you to the top of the west facade for face-to-face views of countless gargoyles, the massive 13-tonne 'Emmanuel' bell in the South Tower and an unforgettable bird's-eye view of Paris. No hunchbacks, though, despite what you may have heard from Victor Hugo.

TOP CHOICE **Ste-Chapelle** CHURCH
(Map p324; 4 blvd du Palais, 1er; adult/child €8/free; ⌚9.30am-6pm Mar-Oct, 9am-5pm Nov-Feb; Ⓜ Cité) Paris' most exquisite Gothic monument is tucked within the Palais de Justice (Law Courts). The 'walls' of the **upper chapel** are sheer curtains of richly coloured and finely detailed **stained glass**, which bathe the chapel in extraordinary coloured light on a sunny day. Conceived by Louis IX to house his sacred relics, the chapel was consecrated in 1248.

IT'S FREE

Paris' national museums are something of a bargain: admission is reduced for those aged over 60 years and 18 to 25; and completely free for **EU residents under 26** years of age, anyone **under 18** years, and **everyone on the first Sunday of each month**. These include: the Louvre, Musée National d'Art Moderne in the Pompidou, Musée du Quai Branly, Musée d'Orsay, Musée Rodin and Cité de l'Architecture et du Patrimoine.

Ditto for the following except they are only free the first Sunday of the month from November to March: Arc de Triomphe, Conciergerie, Panthéon, Ste-Chapelle and the Tours de Notre Dame.

Central Paris

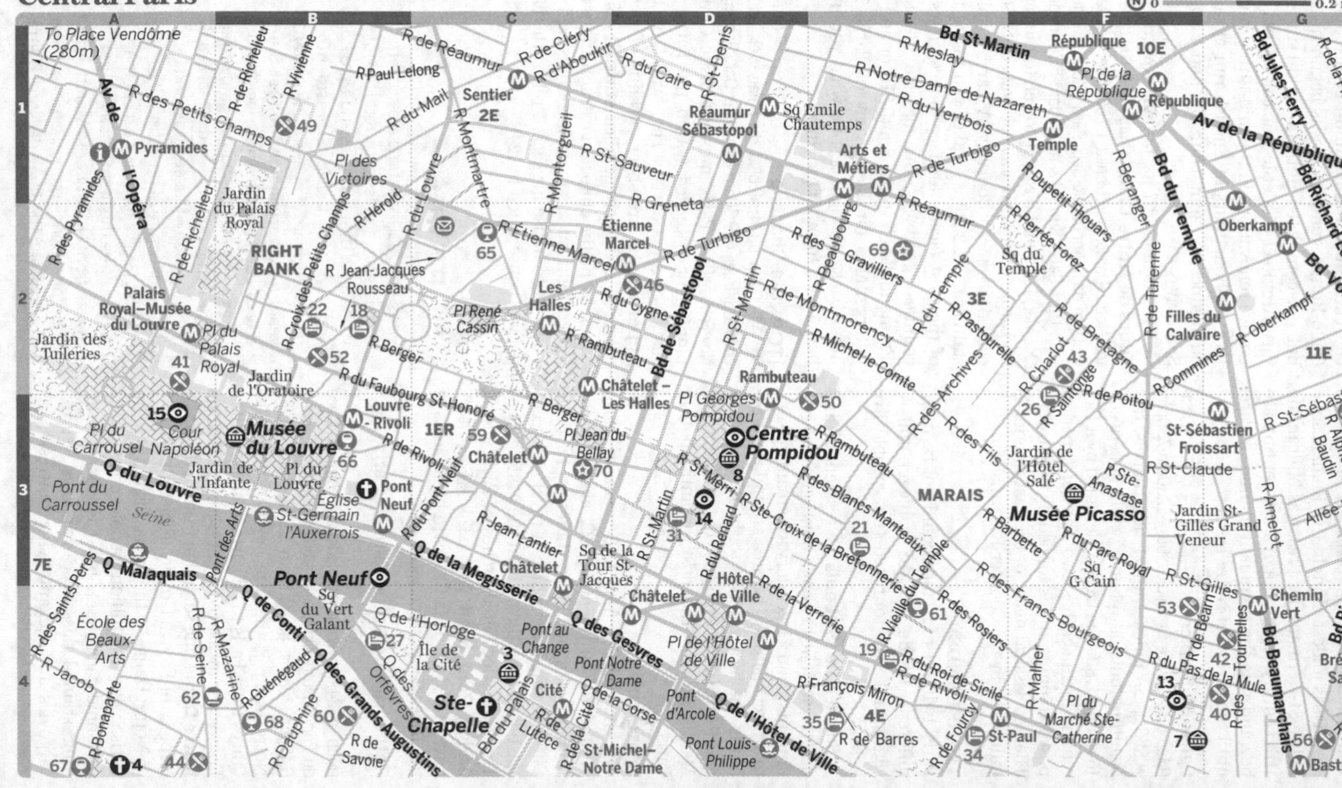

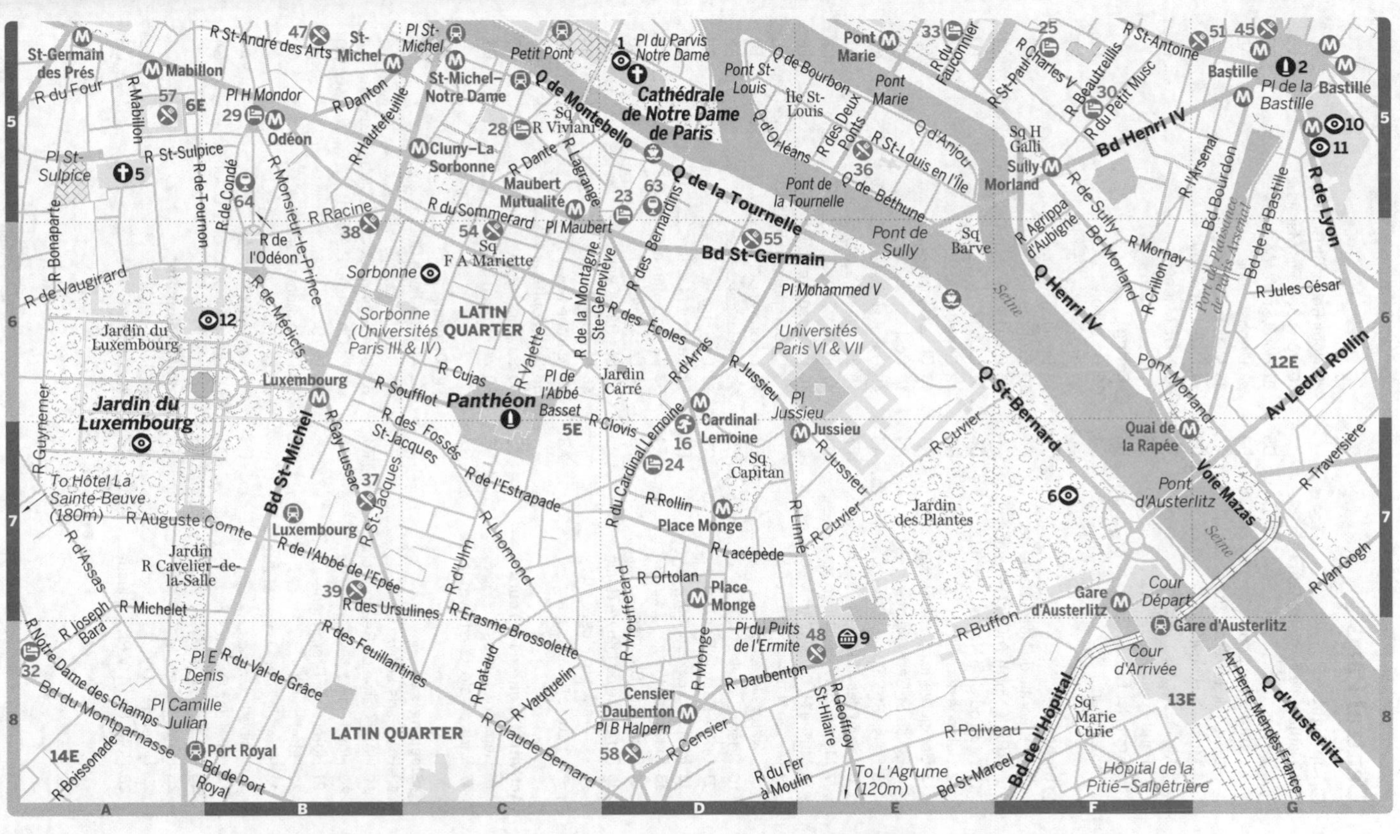
St-Germain des Prés
R du Four
Mabillon
R Mabillon
57
6E
Pl St-Sulpice
5
R St-Sulpice
R Bonaparte
R de Tournon
R de Condé
64
R St-André des Arts
47
St-Michel
Pl H Mondor
29
Odéon
R Danton
R Hautefeuille
Pl St-Michel
St-Michel–Notre Dame
Cluny–La Sorbonne
Petit Pont
28
R Viviani
Sq
Q de Montebello
R Dante
R Lagrange
Maubert Mutualité
1
Pl du Parvis Notre Dame
Cathédrale de Notre Dame de Paris
23
63
Pl Maubert
R du Sommerard
54
Sq F A Mariette
R Racine
38
R de l'Odéon
R Monsieur-le-Prince
Sorbonne
R de Vaugirard
12
Jardin du Luxembourg
R de Médicis
Sorbonne (Universités Paris III & IV)
LATIN QUARTER
R de la Montagne Ste-Geneviève
R des Bernardins
Q de la Tournelle
Pont de la Tournelle
55
Bd St-Germain
Pont St-Louis
Île St-Louis
Q d'Orléans
Q de Bourbon
R des Deux Ponts
36
Pont Marie
Q de Béthune
R St-Louis en l'Île
Q d'Anjou
Pont de Sully
Sq Barye
33
R du Fauconnier
R St-Paul
25
R Charles V
30
R Beautreillis
R du Petit Musc
R St-Antoine
51
45
Bastille
2
Pl de la Bastille
10
11
R de Lyon
Bd Henri IV
Sq H Galli
Sully Morland
R de Sully
R Agrippa d'Aubigné
Bd Morland
R Mornay
R Crillon
R l'Arsenal
Bd Bourdon
Port de Plaisance de Paris-Arsenal
Bd de la Bastille
R Jules César
Q Henri IV
Seine
Pl Mohammed V
Universités Paris VI & VII
R des Écoles
R d'Arras
R Jussieu
Pl Jussieu
Jussieu
Q St-Bernard
12E
Pont Morland
Av Ledru Rollin
Quai de la Rapée
R Traversière
Voie Mazas
Pont d'Austerlitz
R Van Gogh
Jardin du Luxembourg
Luxembourg
R Cujas
R Soufflot
Panthéon
R Valette
Pl de l'Abbé Basset
5E
Jardin Carré
R Clovis
R du Cardinal Lemoine
Cardinal Lemoine
16
24
Sq Capitan
R Cuvier
6
Jardin des Plantes
R Guynemer
To Hôtel La Sainte-Beuve (180m)
Bd St-Michel
R Gay Lussac
37
R St-Jacques
R des Fossés St-Jacques
R de l'Estrapade
R Lhomond
R Rollin
Place Monge
R Linné
R Lacépède
R Auguste Comte
Luxembourg
Jardin R Cavelier-de-la-Salle
R d'Assas
R de l'Abbé de l'Épée
39
R des Ursulines
R d'Ulm
R Erasme Brossolette
R Mouffetard
R Ortolan
Place Monge
Gare d'Austerlitz
Cour Départ
Gare d'Austerlitz
R Buffon
R Michelet
R Joseph Bara
32
R Notre Dame des Champs
Bd du Montparnasse
Pl E Denis
R du Val de Grâce
R des Feuillantines
R Rataud
R Vauquelin
R Monge
Pl du Puits de l'Ermite
48
9
R Daubenton
Cour d'Arrivée
Av Pierre Mendès France
Q d'Austerlitz
13E
Pl Camille Julian
Port Royal
Bd de Port Royal
14E
R Boissonade
LATIN QUARTER
R Claude Bernard
Censier Daubenton
Pl B Halpern
58
R Censier
R Geoffroy St-Hilaire
R du Fer à Moulin
To L'Agrume (120m)
Bd St-Marcel
R Poliveau
Bd de l'Hôpital
Sq Marie Curie
Hôpital de la Pitié–Salpêtrière
A
B
C
D
E
F
G
5
6
7
8

Central Paris

Top Sights

Cathédrale de Notre Dame de Paris D5
Centre Pompidou D3
Jardin du Luxembourg A7
Musée du Louvre B3
Musée Picasso F3
Panthéon C6
Pont Neuf B3
Ste-Chapelle C4

Sights

1 Cathédrale de Notre Dame de Paris North Tower (Entrance to Tours de Notre Dame) D5
2 Colonne de Juillet G5
3 Conciergerie C4
4 Église St-Germain des Prés A4
5 Église St-Sulpice A5
6 Jardin des Plantes F7
7 Maison de Victor Hugo F4
8 Musée National d'Art Moderne D3
9 Musée National d'Histoire Naturelle E8
10 Opéra Bastille G5
11 Opéra Bastille Box Office G5
12 Palais du Luxembourg B6
13 Place des Vosges F4
14 Place Igor Stravinsky D3
15 Pyramide du Louvre (Main Entrance to Musée du Louvre) A3

Activities, Courses & Tours

16 Gepetto et Vélos D7
17 Paris à Vélo, C'est Sympa! G3

Sleeping

18 BVJ Paris-Louvre B2
19 Hôtel Caron de Beaumarchais E4
20 Hôtel Daval G4
21 Hôtel de la Bretonnerie E3
22 Hôtel de Lille B2
23 Hôtel de Notre Dame Maître Albert D5
24 Hôtel des Grandes Écoles D7
25 Hôtel du 7e Art F5
26 Hôtel du Petit Moulin F3
27 Hôtel Henri IV B4
28 Hôtel Henri IV Rive Gauche C5
29 Hôtel Relais St-Germain B5
30 Hôtel St-Louis Marais F5
31 Hôtel St-Merry D3
32 L'Apostrophe A8
33 MIJE Le Fauconnier E5
34 MIJE Le Fourcy E4
35 MIJE Maubuisson E4

Eating

36 Berthillon E5
37 Bistroy Les Papilles B7
38 Bouillon Racine B6
39 Bruno Solques B7
40 Café Hugo G4
41 Café Marly A2
42 Chez Janou G4
43 Chez Nénesse F2
44 Cosi A4
45 Dalloyau G5
46 Joe Allen D2
47 KGB B5
48 La Mosquée de Paris E8
Le Comptoir du Relais .... (see 29)
49 Le Grand Colbert B1
50 Le Hangar E3
51 Le Nôtre G5
52 Le Petit Mâchon B2
53 Le Petit Marché F4
54 Le Pré Verre C6
55 Les Pâtes Vivantes D6
56 Marché Bastille G4
57 Marché St-Germain A5
58 Rue Mouffetard (Market Street) D8
59 Saveurs Végét' Halles C3
60 Ze Kitchen Galerie B4

Drinking

61 Au Petit Fer à Cheval E4
62 Café La Palette A4
63 Curio Parlor Cocktail Club D5
La Chaise au Plafond .... (see 61)
64 Le 10 .... B5
65 Le Cochon à l'Oreille C2
66 Le Fumoir B3
67 Les Deux Magots A4
68 Prescription Cocktail Club B4

Entertainment

69 L'Attirail E2
70 Le Baiser Salé C3

Conciergerie MONUMENT
(Map p324; 2 blvd du Palais, 1er; adult/child €7/free; ⏲9.30am-5 or 6pm; ⓂCité) Built as a royal palace in the 14th century for the concierge of the Palais de la Cité, this was the main prison during the Reign of Terror (1793–94), used to incarcerate alleged enemies of the Revolution before they were brought before the Revolutionary Tribunal in the Palais de Justice next door. Among the 2700 prisoners held here before being sent to the guillotine was Queen Marie-Antoinette – see a reproduction of her cell.

The Rayonnant Gothic, 14th-century **Salle des Gens d'Armes** (Cavalrymen's Hall) is the largest surviving medieval hall in Europe.

A joint ticket with Ste-Chapelle costs €11.

RIGHT BANK

Musée du Louvre ART MUSEUM
(Map p324; www.louvre.fr; permanent collections/permanent collections & temporary exhibits €9.50/14, after 6pm Wed & Fri €6/12; ⏲9am-6pm Mon, Thu, Sat & Sun, 9am-10pm Wed & Fri; ⓂPalais Royal-Musée du Louvre) The vast Palais du Louvre, overlooking the fashionable **Jardin des Tuileries** gardens, was constructed as a fortress by Philippe-Auguste in the 13th century and rebuilt in the mid-16th century for use as a royal residence. In 1793 the Revolutionary Convention transformed it into the nation's first national museum.

The Louvre's staggering 35,000 exhibits are spread across three wings: Sully, Denon and Richelieu. It's reckoned you'd need about nine months to see everything, so trying to pack it all into a single afternoon isn't a particularly clever idea: you'll get much more out if it by concentrating on a single section or period that interests you.

The collection is mind-bogglingly diverse, ranging from Islamic art works and Egyptian artefacts through to a fabulous collection of Greek and Roman antiquities (including the *Venus de Milo* and the *Winged Victory of Samothrace*). But it's the celebrated paintings that draw most visitors; highlights include signature works by Raphael, Botticelli, Delacroix, Titian, Géricault and of course Leonardo da Vinci's slyly smiling *Mona Lisa* (Denon Wing, 1st floor, room 6). If you have time, peek at the section devoted to objets d'art, which houses a series of fabulously extravagant salons, including the apartments of Napoleon III's Minister of State, a collection of priceless Sèvres porcelain and Louis XV's dazzling crown jewels.

The gallery's main entrance and ticket windows in the Cour Napoléon are covered by the iconic 21m-high **Pyramide du Louvre**, a glass pyramid designed by the Chinese-American architect IM Pei. Skip the pyramid-entrance queue by entering via the Porte des Lions entrance or the Carrousel du Louvre shopping centre.

Arc de Triomphe LANDMARK
(Map p318; viewing platform adult/child €9/free; ⏲10am-10.30 or 11pm; ⓂCharles de Gaulle-Étoile) The Arc de Triomphe stands in the middle of the world's largest traffic roundabout, **place de l'Étoile**, officially known as place Charles de Gaulle. The 'triumphal arch' was commissioned in 1806 by Napoleon to commemorate his victories, but remained unfinished when he started losing battles, and wasn't completed until 1836. Since 1920, the body of an **unknown soldier** from WWI has lain beneath the arch; a memorial flame is rekindled each evening around 6.30pm.

The **viewing platform** (50m up via 284 steps and well worth the climb) affords wonderful views of the dozen avenues that radiate out from the arch, many of which are named after Napoleonic generals. **Av Foch** is Paris' widest boulevard, while **av des Champs Élysées** leads south to **place**

THE LOUVRE: TICKETS & TOURS

Buy tickets in advance from ticket machines in the Carrousel du Louvre shopping centre (99 rue de Rivoli) or, for an extra €1 to €1.60, from Fnac or Virgin Megastores *billetteries* (ticket offices), and walk straight in without queuing. Tickets are valid for the whole day, meaning you can come and go as you please. By 2012 you should be able to buy tickets direct on www.louvre.fr.

Before hitting the collections, pick up a free English-language *plan* (map) of the labyrinthine Louvre from the information desk in the centre of the Hall Napoléon. At the entrance to each wing rent a self-paced audioguide (€6).

English-language **guided tours** (☎01 40 20 52 63) depart at 11am, 2pm and (sometimes) 3.45pm Monday and Wednesday to Saturday. Tickets cost €5 in addition to the cost of admission. Sign up at least 30 minutes before departure time.

DON'T MISS

BOHEMIAN SOULS IN MONTMARTRE

No address better captures the quartier's rebellious, bohemian and artsy past than **Musée de Montmartre** (Map p330; www.museedemontmartre.fr; 12 rue Cortot, 18e; adult/child €7/free; ⏲11am-6pm Tue-Sun; Ⓜ Lamarck Caulaincourt), one-time home to painters Renoir, Utrillo and Raoul Dufy. The 17th-century manor house–museum displays paintings, lithographs and documents; hosts art exhibitions by contemporary artists currently living in Montmartre; and in its excellent bookshop sells bottles of the wine produced from grapes grown in the quartier's very own vineyard, **Clos Montmartre**.

Later, pay your respects to bohemian souls – writers Émile Zola, Alexandre Dumas and Stendhal, composer Jacques Offenbach, artist Edgar Degas, film director François Truffaut and dancer Vaslav Nijinsky among others – laid to rest in the **Cimetière de Montmartre** (Map p330; ⏲8am-5.30 or 6pm Mon-Fri, from 8.30am Sat, from 9am Sun; Ⓜ Place de Clichy). Around since 1798, the cemetery is Paris' most famous cemetery after Père Lachaise (p329).

de la Concorde and its famous 3300-year-old pink granite obelisk, which once stood in the Temple of Ramses at Thebes (present-day Luxor).

Centre Pompidou ART MUSEUM
(Map p324; www.centrepompidou.fr; place Georges Pompidou, 4e; Ⓜ Rambuteau) Opened in 1977, this is one of central Paris' most iconic modern buildings; it was one of the first structures to have its 'insides' turned out. Its main attraction, the **Musée National d'Art Moderne** (Map p324; adult/child €10-12/free; ⏲11am-9pm Wed-Mon), showcases France's national collection of post-1905 art, with surrealists, cubists, fauvists and pop artists all brilliantly represented.

Outside, street performers congregate around lively **place Georges Pompidou**. Nearby **place Igor Stravinsky** delights with its fanciful mechanical fountains of skeletons, a treble clef and a pair of ruby-red lips.

Basilique du Sacré Cœur LANDMARK
(Map p330; www.sacre-coeur-montmartre.com; place du Parvis du Sacré Cœur, 18e; ⏲6am-10.30pm; Ⓜ Anvers) The gleaming white **dome** (admission €5; ⏲9am-7pm daily Apr-Sep, 9am-6pm Oct-Mar) of this iconic basilica has one of Paris' most spectacular city panoramas. It sits plump in the heart of hillside Montmartre, a neighbourhood that lured bohemian writers and artists in the late 19th and early 20th centuries. Between 1908 and 1912 Picasso lived at the studio called **Bateau Lavoir** (Map p330; 11bis place Émile Goudeau; Ⓜ Abbesses).

After WWI the artsy activity shifted to Montparnasse, but Montmartre nonetheless retains an upbeat ambience that all the tourists in the world couldn't spoil. Cafes, restaurants, endless tourists and a concentrated cluster of caricaturists and painters fill its main square, **place du Tertre** (Map p330; Ⓜ Abbesses) – if you're seeking your portrait painted in Paris, this is the spot.

Just a few blocks southwest of the tranquil residential streets of Montmartre is lively, neon-lit **Pigalle** (9e and 18e), one of Paris' two main sex districts. A funicular connects it to the top of Butte de Montmartre (Montmartre Hill).

Opéra & Grands Boulevards
HISTORIC BUILDING, NOTABLE STREETS
Place de l'Opéra is the site of Paris' world-famous (and original) opera house, **Palais Garnier** (Map p330; ☎guided tours 08 25 05 44 05; www.operadeparis.fr; place de l'Opéra, 9e; Ⓜ Opéra). Around it fan out eight contiguous 'Great Boulevards' – Madeleine, Capucines, Italiens, Montmartre, Poissonnière, Bonne Nouvelle, St-Denis and St-Martin – laid out in the 17th century, and later the cultural hub of the city during the belle époque. Blvd Haussmann is the heart of the city's commercial district and boasts many famous department stores.

Place Vendôme SQUARE
(Ⓜ Tuileries or Opéra) The octagonal place Vendôme has long been one of the city's smartest addresses, famous for its 18th-century architecture, exclusive boutiques and the superposh Hôtel Ritz-Paris. The 43.5m-tall **Colonne Vendôme** (Map p318) was fashioned from cannons captured by Napoleon at the Battle of Austerlitz in 1805; the general stands on top of the column dressed in suitably imperial garb.

Musée Picasso ART MUSEUM
(Map p324; www.musee-picasso.fr, in French; 5 rue de Thorigny, 3e; ⌚9.30am-6pm Wed-Mon; Ⓜ St-Paul or Chemin Vert) One of Paris' best-loved art museums, the Picasso Museum contains more than 3500 of the *grand maître*'s engravings, paintings, ceramics and sculptures, as well as works from his own art collection by Braque, Cézanne, Matisse, Modigliani, Degas and Rousseau. At the time of printing, it was scheduled to reopen after extensive renovations in 2012.

Place des Vosges SQUARE
(Map p324; Ⓜ St-Paul or Bastille) The Marais, the area of the Right Bank north of Île St-Louis in the 3e and 4e, was originally a marsh before it was transformed into one of the city's most fashionable districts by Henri IV, who constructed elegant *hôtels particuliers* (private mansions) around place Royale – today known as place des Vosges.

Novelist Victor Hugo lived here from 1832 to 1848, and his home is now the **Maison de Victor Hugo** (Map p324; www.musee-hugo.paris.fr, in French; adult/child €7/free; ⌚10am-6pm Tue-Sun), with drawings, paintings and memorabilia relating to the author.

Place de la Bastille SQUARE
(Map p324; Ⓜ Bastille) The Bastille is the most famous monument in Paris that no longer exists; the notorious prison was demolished by a Revolutionary mob on 14 July 1789, and the place de la Bastille where the prison once stood is now a busy traffic roundabout. The 52m-high **Colonne de Juillet** (July Column) was erected in memory of Parisians killed during the July Revolution of 1830.

Opéra Bastille OPERA HOUSE
(Map p324; www.opera-de-paris.fr, in French; 2-6 place de la Bastille, 12e; Ⓜ Bastille) Paris' giant 'second' opera house, the Opéra Bastille, designed by the Canadian architect Carlos Ott, was inaugurated on 14 July 1989, the 200th anniversary of the storming of the Bastille. Check online for departure times of 1¼-hour **guided tours** (☎01 40 01 19 70; adult/child €11/6). Tickets go on sale 10 minutes before departure at the **box office** (Map p324; 130 rue de Lyon, 12e; ⌚10.30am-6.30pm Mon-Sat).

TOP CHOICE **Cimetière du Père Lachaise** CEMETERY
(Map p318; www.pere-lachaise.com; ⌚8am-6pm Mon-Fri, from 8.30am Sat, from 9am Sun; Ⓜ Philippe Auguste, Gambetta or Père Lachaise) The world's most-visited graveyard, Cimetière du Père Lachaise opened its one-way doors in 1804. Among the 800,000 people buried here are Chopin, Molière, Balzac, Proust, Gertrude Stein, Colette, Pissarro, Seurat, Modigliani, Sarah Bernhardt, Yves Montand, Delacroix, Édith Piaf and even the 12th-century lovers Abélard and Héloïse, whose remains were disinterred and reburied here together in 1817 beneath a neo-Gothic tombstone. The graves of **Oscar Wilde** (Division 89) and **Jim Morrison** (Division 6) are perennially popular.

Activities

Cycling

Paris now counts some 370km of cycling lanes in the city, plus many sections of road are shut to motorised traffic on Sundays and holidays. Pick up wheels with **Vélib'** (p347), join an organised bike tour (see p330) or rent your own wheels and DIY with:

DON'T MISS

CANAL ST-MARTIN

The shaded towpaths of the tranquil, 4.5km-long **Canal St-Martin** (Map p318; Ⓜ République, Jaurès or Jacques Bonsergent) are a wonderful place for a romantic stroll or a bike ride past nine locks, metal bridges and ordinary Parisian neighbourhoods. The canal's banks have undergone a real urban renaissance, and the southern stretch in particular is an ideal spot for cafe lounging, quayside summer picnics and late-night drinks. Hip new bistros have moved into the area (most are closed Sunday and often Monday) and if you're in Paris to tempt your taste buds, you'll wind up in these eastern suburbs sooner rather than later.

Linking the 10e arrondissement with **Parc de la Villette** in the 19e via the **Bassin de la Villette** and **Canal de l'Ourcq**, the canal makes its famous dogleg turn in the 10e arrondissement. Parts of the waterway – which was built between 1806 and 1825 in order to link the Seine with the 108km-long Canal de l'Ourcq – are actually higher than the surrounding land. If you want to savour the real flavour of the canal, take a tour on a **canal boat** (see p331).

Montmartre

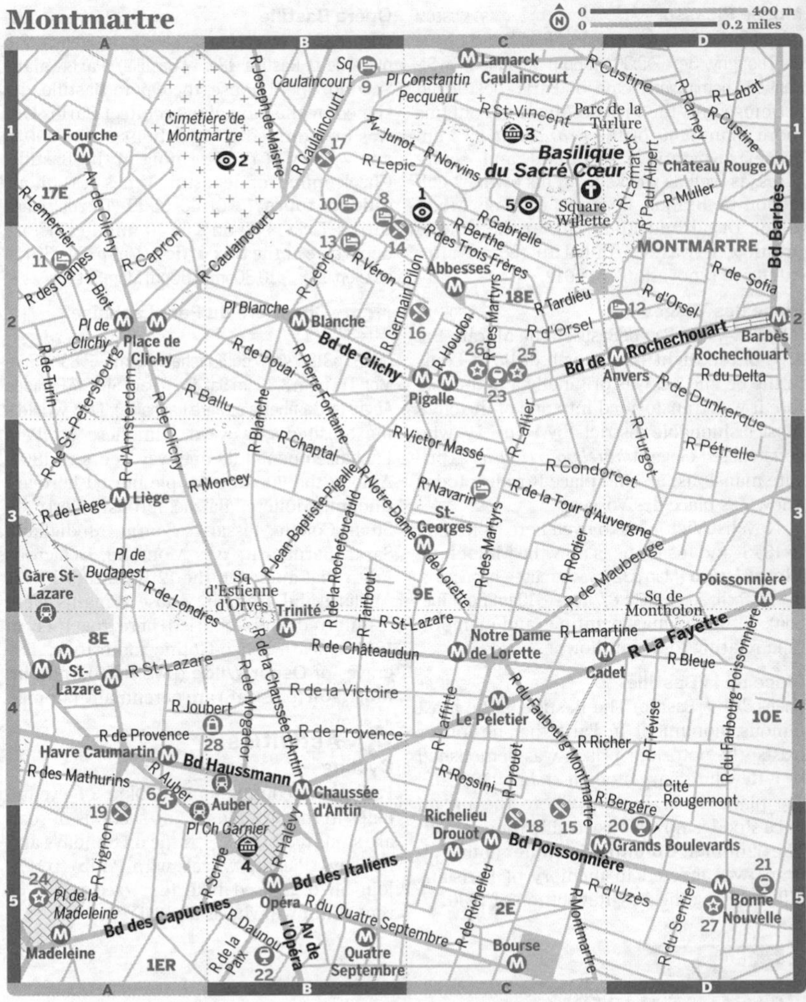

Gepetto et Vélos CYCLING
(Map p324; www.gepetto-et-velos.com, in French; 59 rue du Cardinal Lemoine, 5e; per day/weekend €15/25; ⌚9am-1pm & 2-7.30pm Tue-Sat; Ⓜ Cardinal Lemoine)

Paris à Vélo, C'est Sympa! CYCLING
(Map p324; www.parisvelosympa.com; 22 rue Alphonse Baudin, 11e; per day/weekend €15/25; ⌚9.30am-1pm & 2-6pm Mon-Fri, 9am-1pm & 2-7pm Sat & Sun, shorter hours in winter; Ⓜ St-Sébastien Froissart)

☞ Tours

Fat Tire Bike Tours BICYCLE
(Map p318; ☎01 56 58 10 54; www.fattirebiketours.com; 24 rue Edgar Faure, 15e; Ⓜ La Motte-Picquet Grenelle) Bike tours by day (€28; four hours) and night; to Versailles, Monet's garden (Giverny) and the Normandy beaches. Participants generally meet opposite the Eiffel Tower at the start of the Champ de Mars. Costs include the bicycle and rain gear. Reserve in advance.

Bateaux Mouches BOAT
(Map p318; ☎01 42 25 9610; www.bateauxmouches.com; Port de la Conférence, 8e; adult/child €10/5; ⌚Mar-Nov; Ⓜ Alma Marceau) Based on the Right Bank, Paris' most famous riverboat company runs 1000-seat tour boats. Cruises (70 minutes) run regularly from 10.15am to 11pm April to September and

Montmartre

Top Sights

Basilique du Sacré Cœur C1

Sights

1 Bateau Lavoir C1
2 Cimetière de Montmartre B1
3 Musée de Montmartre C1
4 Palais Garnier B5
5 Place du Tertre C1

Activities, Courses & Tours

6 L'Open Tour A4

Sleeping

7 Hôtel Amour C3
8 Hôtel Bonséjour Montmartre B1
9 Hôtel Caulaincourt Square B1
10 Hôtel des Arts B1
11 Hôtel Eldorado A2
12 Le Village Hostel D2
13 Plug-inn Hostel B2

Eating

14 Café Burq B2
15 Chartier C5
16 Chez Toinette C2
17 Le Café qui Parle B1
18 Le J'Go C5
19 Le Roi du Pot au Feu A5

Drinking

20 Au Limonaire D5
21 DeLaVille Café D5
22 Harry's New York Bar B5
23 La Fourmi C2

Entertainment

24 Kiosque Théâtre Madeleine A5
25 La Cigale C2
26 Le Divan du Monde C2
27 Le Rex Club D5

Shopping

28 Galeries Lafayette B4
Le Printemps .... (see 28)

13 times a day between 11am and 9pm the rest of the year.

Paris Canal Croisières BOAT
(Map p318; ☎01 42 40 96 97; www.pariscanal.com; Bassin de la Villette, 19-21 quai de la Loire, 19e; adult/child €17/10; ⏲Mar-Nov; Ⓜ Jaurès or Musée d'Orsay) This company runs daily 2½-hour cruises departing from near the Musée d'Orsay (quai Anatole France, 7e) for Bassin de la Villette, 19e, via the charming Canal St-Martin and Canal de l'Ourcq.

L'Open Tour BUS
(Map p330; ☎01 42 66 56 56; www.pariscityrama.com; 13 rue Auber, 9e; 1 day adult/child €29/15; Ⓜ Havre Caumartin or Opéra) This company runs open-deck buses along four circuits and you can jump on/off at more than 50 stops. Buy tickets from the driver.

Eye Prefer Paris WALKING
(www.eyepreferparistours.com; €195 for 3 people) New Yorker turned Parisian leads offbeat tours of the city; cooking classes too.

Paris Walks WALKING
(www.paris-walks.com; adult/child €12/8) Thematic tours (fashion, chocolate, the French Revolution) in English.

Festivals & Events

Grande Parade de Paris NEW YEAR
(www.parisparade.com) The Great Paris Parade, with marching and carnival bands, dance acts and so on, takes place on the afternoon of New Year's Day.

Fashion Week FASHION
(www.pretparis.com) Prêt-à-Porter, the ready-to-wear fashion salon that is held twice a year in late January and again in September, is a must for fashion buffs. It's held at the Parc des Expositions at Porte de Versailles, 15e (Ⓜ Porte de Versailles).

Paris Jazz Festival JAZZ
(www.parcfloraldeparis.com; www.paris.fr) Free jazz concerts every Saturday and Sunday afternoon in June and July in Parc Floral de Paris.

Paris Plages BEACH
(www.paris.fr) 'Paris Beaches' sees three waterfront areas transformed into sand-and-pebble 'beaches', complete with sunbeds, beach umbrellas, atomisers, lounge chairs and palm trees. Four weeks from mid-July to mid-August.

Nuit Blanche EVENT
(www.paris.fr) 'White Night' is when Paris becomes 'the city that doesn't sleep', with museums across town joining bars and

WORTH A TRIP

BOIS DE BOULOGNE & VINCENNES

Flee the smoke for a gad around Paris' twinset of green woods – **Bois de Vincennes** and the **Bois de Boulogne** – where Parisians picnic, sunbathe and escape the city hustle.

On Paris' western fringe, 845-hectare **Bois de Boulogne** (Map p318; blvd Maillot, 16e; MPorte Maillot) was inspired by Hyde Park in London. Attractions include formal gardens, a lake with rowing boats, **kids' amusement park** (www.jardindacclimatation.fr) and 18th-century chateau, **Château de Bagatelle** (route de Sèvres à Neuilly, 16e; adult/child €6/free; tours 3pm Sat & Sun Apr-Sep, 9am-5pm Oct-Mar), with spectacular flower gardens. The **Fondation Louis Vuitton pour la Création** (www.fondationlouisvuitton.fr), a fine-arts centre designed by Frank Gehry, will open here by the end of 2012. Steer clear after dark, when Bois de Boulogne morphs into a playground for female and transvestite prostitutes.

To the southeast of the centre is the 995-hectare **Bois de Vincennes** (off Map p318; blvd Poniatowski, 12e; MPorte de Charenton or Porte Dorée), which encompasses its own fortified castle, **Château de Vincennes** (www.chateau-vincennes.fr; av de Paris, 12e; 10am-5 or 6pm May-Aug, 10am-5pm Sep-Apr; MChâteau de Vincennes); it's free to explore the grounds, but the keep and royal chapel can only be visited by guided **tour** (adult/child €8/free). Nearby there's also a huge **floral park** (www.parcfloraldeparis.com, in French) with a butterfly garden, a **zoo** (www.mnhn.fr) and an **aquarium** (www.acquarium-portedoree.fr).

clubs and staying open till the very wee hours on the first Saturday and Sunday of October.

Fete des Vendanges de Montmartre HARVEST
(www.fetedesvendangesdemontmartre.com, in French) This five-day festival during the second weekend in October celebrates Montmartre's grape harvest with costumes, speeches and a parade.

Sleeping

The Paris Convention & Visitors Bureau (p346) can find you a place to stay (no booking fee, but you need a credit card), though queues can be long in high season.

For B&B accommodation try **Alcôve & Agapes** (www.bed-and-breakfast-in-paris.com), **Good Morning Paris** (www.goodmorningparis.fr) or **B&B Paris** (www.2binparis.com).

LOUVRE & LES HALLES

This area is central but don't expect tranquillity or many bargains. Although it's most disposed to welcoming top-end travellers, there are some decent midrange places too.

TOP CHOICE **Hôtel St-Merry** HISTORIC HOTEL €€
(Map p324; 01 42 78 14 15; www.hotelmarais.com; 78 rue de la Verrerie, 4e; r €135-230, tr €205-275; ; MChâtelet) The interior of this 12-room hostelry, with beamed ceilings, church pews and wrought-iron candelabra, is a neo-goth's wet dream; you have to see the architectural elements of room 9 (flying buttress over the bed) and the furnishings of 12 (choir-stall bed board) to believe them. Only some of the rooms come with air-conditioning.

BVJ Paris-Louvre HOSTEL €
(Map p324; 01 53 00 90 90; www.bvjhotel.com; 20 rue Jean-Jacques Rousseau, 1er; dm/d €29/70; @; MLouvre-Rivoli) This modern, 200-bed hostel has doubles and bunks in a single-sex room for four to 10 people, with showers down the corridor. Guests must be aged 18 to 35 years. Rooms are accessible from 2.30pm on the day you arrive and all day after that. No kitchen.

Hôtel de Lille BUDGET HOTEL €
(Map p324; 01 42 33 33 42; 8 rue du Pélican, 1er; s €39-43, d €50-55, tr €85; MPalais Royal-Musée du Louvre;) This old-fashioned but spotlessly clean 13-room hotel is down a quiet side street from the Louvre in a 17th-century building.

MARAIS & BASTILLE

Budget accommodation is a forte of the Marais. East of Bastille, the untouristed 11e provides a glimpse up close of working-class Paris.

TOP CHOICE **Hôtel du Petit Moulin** BOUTIQUE HOTEL €€€
(Map p324; ☎01 42 74 10 10; www.hoteldupetitmoulin.com; 29-31 rue de Poitou, 3e; r €190-290; ❄@📶; Ⓜ Filles du Calvaire) This scrumptious boutique hotel (OK, we're impressed that it was a bakery at the time of Henri IV) was designed by Christian Lacroix. Choose from medieval and rococo Marais sporting exposed beams and dressed in toile de Jouy wallpaper, to more-modern surrounds with contemporary murals and heart-shaped mirrors just this side of kitsch.

Hôtel Daval HOTEL €€
(Map p324; ☎01 47 00 51 23; www.hoteldaval.com; 21 rue Daval, 11e; s €81, d €89-98, tr/q €109/127; ❄📶; Ⓜ Bastille) Always a favourite, this 23-room property is a very central option if you're looking for almost-budget accommodation just off place de la Bastille. What's more, a refit has brought it well into the 21st century. Rooms and bathrooms are on the small side and if you're looking for some peace and quiet, choose a back room (eg room 13).

Hôtel de la Bretonnerie HOTEL €€
(Map p324; ☎01 48 87 77 63; www.bretonnerie.com; 22 rue Ste-Croix de la Bretonnerie, 4e; r €135-165, tr & q €190; 📶; Ⓜ Hôtel de Ville) This very charming midrange hotel in the heart of the Marais nightlife area dates from the 17th century. The decor of its 29 rooms and suites is unique; some have four-poster and canopy beds.

Hôtel Caron de Beaumarchais BOUTIQUE HOTEL €€
(Map p324; ☎01 42 72 34 12; www.carondebeaumarchais.com; 12 rue Vieille du Temple, 4e; r €125-162; ❄📶; Ⓜ St-Paul) Decorated like an 18th-century private house, this themed hotel must be seen to be believed. In the palatial lobby an 18th-century pianoforte, gaming tables, gilded mirrors and candelabras set the tone for a stay that will be unique.

Maison Internationale de la Jeunesse et des Étudiants HOSTEL €
(MIJE; ☎01 42 74 23 45; www.mije.com; dm/s/d/tr per person €30/49/36/32; @) The MIJE runs three hostels in attractively renovated 17th- and 18th-century *hôtels particuliers* in the heart of the Marais, and it's difficult to think of a better budget deal in Paris. **MIJE Maubuisson** (Map p324; 12 rue des Barres, 4e; Ⓜ Hôtel de Ville or Pont Marie) – the pick of the three – is half a block south of the *mairie* (town hall) of the 4e and has 99 beds. With 200 beds, **MIJE Le Fourcy** (Map p324; 6 rue de Fourcy, 4e; Ⓜ St-Paul) is the largest of the three and has a cheap eatery serving a three-course fixed-price *menu* including a drink for €10.50. **MIJE Le Fauconnier** (Map p324; 11 rue du Fauconnier, 4e; Ⓜ St-Paul or Pont Marie), two blocks south, sleeps 125.

Rooms are closed from noon to 3pm, and the curfew is 1am to 7am. Annual membership costs €2.50.

Hôtel du 7e Art THEMED HOTEL €€
(Map p324; ☎01 44 54 85 00; www.paris-hotel-7art.com; 20 rue St-Paul, 4e; s €75-150, d €95-155; 📶; Ⓜ St-Paul) Film buffs, this fun place with a black-and-white-movie theme running throughout its 23 rooms is for you.

Hôtel St-Louis Marais HISTORIC HOTEL €€
(Map p324; ☎01 48 87 87 04; www.saintlouismarais.com; 1 rue Charles V, 4e; s €99, d & tw €115-140, tr €150; 📶; Ⓜ Sully Morland) This especially charming hotel in a converted 17th-century convent sports lots of wooden beams, terracotta tiles and heavy brocade drapes. Four floors but no lift; wi-fi €5.

THE ISLANDS

Île St-Louis is the more romantic of the Seine's two islands and is strung with excellent top-end hotels. Or try:

RENTING AN APARTMENT

Be it a night, a week or longer, this is increasingly the modish way to stay in Paris. Consult agencies listed on www.parisinfo.com or try:

» **Haven in Paris** (www.haveninparis.com) Luxury apartments from €575 per week

» **Paris Accommodation Service** (www.paris-accommodation-service.com) Over 500 properties; studios from €520 per week

» **Paris Apartments Services** (www.paris-apts.com) Studios from €100 per day

» **Paris Attitude** (www.parisattitude.com) 3000 properties; studios from €325 per week

» **Paris Stay** (www.paristay.com) Over 200 vacation flats (ie convenient location), with studios from €300 per week

Hôtel Henri IV BUDGET HOTEL €
(Map p324; ☎01 43 54 44 53; www.henri4hotel.fr; 25 place Dauphine, 1er; r €42-69, tr €77-81; 📶; Ⓜ Pont Neuf or Cité) This place, known for its 15 worn and very cheap rooms, has always been popular for its romantic location on the tip of Île de la Cité. What we long expected has happened: under new management the hotel is cleaning up its act and refitting its rooms. Views over the square are wonderful. Book well in advance.

LATIN QUARTER

Midrange hotels in this good-value Left Bank neighbourhood are particularly popular with visiting academics, making rooms hardest to find during conferences (March to June and October).

Port Royal Hôtel BUDGET HOTEL €
(Map p318; ☎01 43 31 70 06; www.hotelportroyal.fr; 8 blvd de Port Royal, 5e; s €41-89, d €52.50-89; Ⓜ Les Gobelins) This 46-room hotel has been run by the same family since 1931. Its six floors are served by a lift, but the cheapest (washbasin-clad) rooms share a toilet and shower (buy a €2.50 token at reception). Rooms are spotless and quiet, especially those peeping down on a glassed-in courtyard. Predictably, this value-for-money place is no secret, so book ahead. No credit cards.

Hôtel La Demeure BOUTIQUE HOTEL €€
(Map p318; ☎01 43 37 81 25; www.hotel-paris-lademeure.com; 51 blvd St-Marcel, 13e; s/d €165/202; ❄@📶; Ⓜ Gobelins) This elegant little number is the domain of a charming father/son team who speak perfect English and are always at hand. Warm red and orange tones lend a 'clubby' feel to public areas; wraparound balconies add extra appeal to corner rooms; and then there's those extra touches – an iPod dock in every room, wineglasses for guests who like to BYO ('bring your own'), art to buy on the walls…

Oops DESIGN HOSTEL €
(Map p318; ☎01 47 07 47 00; www.oops-paris.com; 50 av des Gobelins, 13e; dm €28-35; @📶; Ⓜ Gobelins) It might be discreetly wedged between cafe terraces and shop fronts but inside there is nothing discreet about this address. A lurid candyfloss-pink lift scales its six floors. Doubles (which can be booked in advance) are well sized and stylish dorms max out at four to six beds. Breakfast is a generous affair and in keeping with that true hostel spirit guests must evacuate their room between 11am and 5pm. Reserve online.

Hôtel de Notre Dame Maître Albert HOTEL €€
(Map p324; ☎01 43 26 79 00; www.hotel-paris-notredame.com; 19 rue Maître Albert, 5e; d €170-280; ❄@📶; Ⓜ Maubert Mutualité) A lovely little number hidden down a quiet street paces from the Seine, this quaint hotel is something of a labyrinth with its long corridors bedecked in striking cobblestone-patterned carpet and rooms with low beamed ceilings; occasionally sloping.

Hôtel Henri IV Rive Gauche HOTEL €€€
(Map p324; ☎01 46 33 20 20; www.henri-paris-hotel.com; 9-11 rue St-Jacques, 5e; s/d/tr €159/185/210; ❄@📶; Ⓜ St-Michel Notre Dame or Cluny La Sorbonne) This 'country chic' hotel with 23 rooms awash with antiques, old prints and fresh flowers is steps from Notre Dame and the Seine – think manor house in Normandy. Front rooms have stunning views of Église St-Séverin and its buttresses. Rates are cheapest online.

Hôtel des Grandes Écoles GARDEN HOTEL €€
(Map p324; ☎01 43 26 79 23; www.hotel-grandes-ecoles.com; 75 rue du Cardinal Lemoine, 5e; d €115-140; @📶; Ⓜ Cardinal Lemoine or Place Monge) This wonderful 51-room hotel with its own garden is tucked in a courtyard off a medieval street. Choose a room in one of three buildings: our favourites are rooms 29 to 33 with direct garden access.

ST-GERMAIN, ODÉON & LUXEMBOURG

Staying in chic St-Germain des Prés (6e) is a delight. But beware – budget places just don't exist in this part of the Left Bank.

TOP CHOICE **L'Apostrophe** DESIGN HOTEL €€
(Map p324; ☎01 56 54 31 31; www.apostrophe-hotel.com; 3 rue de Chevreuse, 6e; d €150-350; ❄@📶; Ⓜ Vavin) This art hotel has style. Its 16 rooms pay homage to the written word: graffiti tags one wall of room U (for 'urbain'), which has a ceiling shaped like a skateboard ramp; and room P (for 'Paris parody') sits in the clouds overlooking Paris' rooftops. Clever design features such as double sets of imprinted curtains (one for day, one for night) or the 'bar table' on wheels that slots over the bed, top off this design-driven ensemble.

TOP CHOICE **Hôtel Relais St-Germain** HOTEL €€€
(Map p324; ☎01 43 29 12 05; www.hotel-paris-relais-saint-germain.com; 9 Carrefour de l'Odéon, 7e; s/d €220/285; ❄@📶; Ⓜ Odéon) What rave reports this 17th-century town

house with flower boxes and baby-pink awning gets. Ceilings are beamed, furniture is antique and fabrics are floral. Mix this with a chic contemporary air, ample art works to admire and one of Paris' most talked-about bistros, **Le Comptoir du Relais** (p339), as next-door neighbour. Delicious, darling!

Hôtel La Sainte-Beuve HOTEL €€
(off Map p324; ☎01 45 48 20 07; www.parishotelcharme.com; 9 rue Ste-Beuve, 6e; d €159-365; ❄@📶; ⓂRue Notre Dame des Champs) 'Home away from home' is the motto of this 22-room *hôtel-maison* southwest of Jardin du Luxembourg. Rooms are a riot of colour: pick from fuchsia-pink stylishly mixed with lime-green and taupe, or racing green wed with oyster-grey and burgundy.

FAUBOURG ST-GERMAIN & INVALIDES

The 7e is a lovely arrondissement to call home, although it's slightly removed from the action.

Cadran Hôtel BOUTIQUE HOTEL €€
(Map p318; ☎01 40 62 67 00; www.paris-hotel-cadran.com; 10 rue du Champ de Mars, 7e; d €144-225; ❄📶; ⓂÉcole Militaire) An address for gourmets, this concept hotel seduces guests with a clock theme and an open-plan reception spilling into a *bar à chocolat* (chocolate bar) that sells – yes – chocolate and seasonally flavoured *macarons*. Rooms are futuristic, with all the mod cons.

Hôtel Muguet FAMILY HOTEL €€
(Map p318; ☎01 47 05 05 93; www.hotelmuguet.com; 11 rue Chevert, 7e; s/d/tr €110/145/195; ❄📶; ⓂLa Tour Maubourg) Functional decor and generous-sized triples, with armchair-bed converting a separate lounge area into kid's bedroom, make this a great family choice. From the 4th floor, the Eiffel Tower starts to sneak into view. Back down on ground level, a trio of rooms opens onto a delightful courtyard garden.

Hôtel du Champ-de-Mars BUDGET HOTEL €
(Map p318; ☎01 45 51 52 30; www.hotelduchampdemars.com; 7 rue du Champ de Mars, 7e; s/d/tr €91/98/128; @📶; ⓂÉcole Militaire) This charming 25-room hotel, which lies in the shadow of the Eiffel Tower, is on everyone's wish list – you'll need to book a month or two ahead.

CLICHY & GARE ST-LAZARE

These areas have some excellent midrange choices. The best deals are away from Gare St-Lazare, but there are several places beside the station along rue d'Amsterdam worth checking out.

TOP CHOICE **Hôtel Eldorado** QUIRKY HOTEL €
(Map p330; ☎01 45 22 35 21; www.eldoradohotel.fr; 18 rue des Dames, 17e; s €35-60, d €70-80, tr €80-90; 📶; ⓂPlace de Clichy) This bohemian place is one of Paris' greatest finds: a welcoming, well-run place with 23 colourfully decorated and (often) ethnically themed rooms. We love rooms 1 and 2 in the garden annexe. Cheaper-category singles have washbasin only. The hotel's excellent **Bistro des Dames** is a bonus.

GARE DU NORD, GARE DE L'EST & RÉPUBLIQUE

The areas around the Gare du Nord and Gare de l'Est are far from the prettiest parts of Paris, but decent-value hotels are a dime a dozen.

TOP CHOICE **St Christopher's Inn** HOSTEL €
(Map p318; ☎01 40 34 34 40; www.st-christophers.co.uk; 68-74 quai de la Seine, 19e; dm incl breakfast €15-38, d from €35; @📶; ⓂRiquet or Jaurès) This is certainly one of Paris' best, biggest (300 beds) and most up-to-date hostels. It features a modern design, three types of dorms (10-bed, eight-bed, six-bed) as well as doubles with or without bathroom. Other perks include a canalside cafe, free (temperamental) wi-fi, breakfast, internet cafe, a female-only floor and bar. Seasonal prices vary wildly; check the website for an accurate quote. No kitchen.

Kube Hôtel BOUTIQUE HOTEL €€€
(Map p318; ☎01 42 05 20 00; www.muranoresort.com; 1-5 passage Ruelle, 18e; s €250, d €300-400; ❄@📶; ⓂLa Chapelle) The easternmost edge of the 18e, virtually on the lap of Gare du Nord, is the last place you'd expect to find an ubertrendy boutique hotel. The theme is, of course, three-dimensional square – from the glassed-in reception box in the entrance courtyard to the cube-shaped furnishings in the 41 guestrooms and the ice in the cocktails at its celebrated **Ice Kube** bar.

Hôtel du Nord HOTEL €
(Map p318; ☎01 42 01 66 00; www.hoteldunord-leparivelo.com; 47 rue Albert Thomas, 10e; r/q €69/105; 📶; ⓂRépublique) A cosy place with 23 personalised rooms all decorated with flea-market antiques, Hôtel du Nord's other winning attribute is its prized location near place République. Borrow a bike from reception.

République Hôtel THEMED HOTEL €€
(Map p318; ☎01 42 39 19 03; www.republiquehotel.com; 31 rue Albert Thomas, 10e; s/d/tr/q €75/88/108/159; ; MRépublique) This hip spot is heavy on the pop art and UK paraphernalia – the Union Jack and the Beatles turn up an awful lot – but you cannot fault the inexpensive rates and fantastic location off place République.

MONTMARTRE & PIGALLE

What a charmer Montmartre is with its varied accommodation scene embracing everything from boutique to bohemian, hostel to *hôtel particulier*. The area east of Sacré Cœur can be rough – avoid Château Rouge metro station at night.

Hôtel Amour BOUTIQUE HOTEL €€
(Map p330; ☎01 48 78 31 80; www.hotelamourparis.fr; 8 rue Navarin, 9e; s/d €100/150-280; ; MSt-Georges or Pigalle) Planning a romantic escapade to Paris? Say no more. One of the 'in' hotels of the moment, the inimitable black-clad Amour is very much worthy of the hype – you won't find a more original place to lay your head in Paris at these prices. Of course, you'll have to forgo TV (none), but who needs a box when you're in love?

Hôtel des Arts HOTEL €€
(Map p330; ☎01 46 06 30 52; www.arts-hotel-paris.com; 5 rue Tholozé, 18e; s/d €95/140; @; MAbbesses or Blanche) Hôtel des Arts has comfortable midrange rooms done up in a traditional style (lots of floral motifs). Just up the street is the old-style windmill Moulin de la Galette – how's that for location?

Hôtel Bonséjour Montmartre BUDGET HOTEL €
(Map p330; ☎01 42 54 22 53; www.hotel-bonsejour-montmartre.fr; 11 rue Burq, 18e; s €33-69, d €56-69; @; MAbbesses) At the top of a quiet street, the 'Good Stay' is a perennial favourite. It's simple but welcoming, comfortable and very clean. Some rooms have balconies and No 55 glimpses Sacré Cœur. Hall showers €2.

Le Village Hostel HOSTEL €
(Map p330; ☎01 42 64 22 02; www.villagehostel.fr; 20 rue d'Orsel, 18e; per person dm €28-38, d €70-90, tr €96-115, q €112-140; @; MAnvers) A fine, 25-room address with beamed ceilings, lovely terrace and Sacré Cœur views. Kitchen facilities are available, and there's a popular bar too. Rooms are closed between 11am and 4pm; no curfew.

Plug-inn Hostel HOSTEL €
(Map p330; ☎01 42 58 42 58; www.plug-inn.fr; 7 rue Aristide Bruant, 18e; dm €20-30, d €60-80, tr €90; @; MAbbesses or Blanche) This 2010 hostel has several things going for it, central Montmartre location for starters. Lockout by day; no curfew by night.

Hotel Caulaincourt Square BUDGET HOTEL €
(Map p330; ☎01 46 06 46 06; www.caulaincourt.com; 2 square Caulaincourt, 18e; dm €25, s €50-60, d & tw €63-76, tr €89; @; MLamarck Caulaincourt) This hotel with dorm rooms is perched on the backside of Montmartre, beyond the tourist hoopla in a real Parisian neighbourhood.

PARISIAN EAT STREETS

» **Av de Choisy, av d'Ivry** & **rue Baudricourt** Chinatown: cheap Chinese and Southeast Asian (especially Vietnamese) eateries

» **Blvd de Belleville** Middle Eastern (Algerian, Tunisian) food, especially couscous

» **Rue de Belleville** Asian, especially Thai and Vietnamese

» **Rue du Faubourg St-Denis** Indian, Pakistani and Bangladeshi

» **Passage Brady** Magnet for Indian, Pakistani and Bangladeshi dishes

» **Rue Cadet, rue Richer** & **rue Geoffroy Marie** Triangle of streets; Jewish (mostly Sephardic) and kosher food

» **Rue Montorgueil** Pedestrian market street packed with tip-top quality, quick eats

» **Rue Ste-Anne** The heart of Paris' Japantown

» **Rue Rosiers** Hunting ground for Ashkenazic Jewish kosher food, especially falafel

Eating

As the culinary centre of the most aggressively gastronomic country in the world, the city has more 'generic French', regional, and ethnic restaurants than any other place in France. In pricier restaurants, ordering a *menu* (set two- or three-course meal at a fixed price) at lunchtime is invariably extraordinary good value.

LOUVRE & LES HALLES

This area is filled with trendy restaurants, though few are outstanding – most cater to

TOP FIVE PÂTISSERIES

» **Ladurée** (Map p318; www.laduree.fr, in French; 75 av des Champs-Élysées, 8e; Ⓜ George V) The most famous and decadent of Parisian patisseries; inventor of the *macaron* to boot.

» **Le Nôtre** (Map p324; www.lenotre.fr, in French; 10 rue St- Antoine, 4e; Ⓜ Bastille) Delectable pastries and chocolate; 10 more outlets around town.

» **La Pâtisserie des Rêves** (Map p318; www.lapatisseriedesreves.com; 93 rue du Bac, 7e; Ⓜ Rue du Bac) Extraordinary cakes and tarts showcased beneath glass at the chic 'art' gallery of big-name *pâtissier* Philippe Conticini.

» **Bruno Solques** (Map p324; 248 rue St-Jacques, 5e; Ⓜ Luxembourg) Paris' most inventive *pâtissier*, Bruno Solques excels at oddly shaped flat tarts and fruit-filled brioches.

» **Dalloyau** (Map p324; www.dalloyau.fr; 5 blvd Beaumarchais, 4e; Ⓜ Bastille) Specialities include *pain aux raisins* (raisin bread), *millefeuille* (pastry layered with cream), *tarte au citron* (lemon tart) and *opéra* (coffee-flavoured almond cake and chocolate).

tourists. Streets lined with places to eat include rue des Lombards, the narrow streets north and east of Forum des Halles, and foodie streets rue Montorgueil and rue Ste-Anne. Find supermarkets around Forum des Halles.

Le Grand Colbert FRENCH €€€
(Map p324; ☎01 42 86 87 88; www.legrandcolbert.fr; 2-4 rue Vivienne, 2e; lunch menus €22.50 & €29.50; ⏰noon-1am; Ⓜ Pyramides) This former workers' *cafétéria* transformed into a fin-de-siècle showcase is a convenient spot for lunch if visiting the *passages couverts* (covered passages) or cruising the streets late at night (last orders: 1am).

Café Marly FRENCH, CAFÉ €€€
(Map p324; ☎01 46 26 06 60; cour Napoléon du Louvre, 93 rue de Rivoli, 1er; mains €20-30; ⏰8am-2am; Ⓜ Palais Royal-Musée du Louvre) This classic venue facing the Louvre's inner courtyard serves contemporary French fare throughout the day under the palace colonnades. Views of the glass pyramid (and French starlets) are priceless.

Saveurs Végét' Halles VEGETARIAN €
(Map p324; ☎01 40 41 93 95; www.saveursveget halles.fr; 41 rue des Bourdonnais, 1er; menus €9.90-18.90; ⏰Mon-Sat; Ⓜ Châtelet; 🌿) This strictly vegan eatery is egg-free and serves a fair few mock-meat dishes like *poulet végétal aux champignons* ('chicken' with mushrooms) and *escalope de seitan* (wheat gluten 'escalope'). No alcohol.

Le Petit Mâchon LYONNAIS €€
(Map p324; ☎01 42 60 08 06; 158 rue St-Honoré, 1er; mains €14-22; ⏰Tue-Sun; Ⓜ Palais Royal-Musée du Louvre) Close to the Louvre, this upbeat bistro serves some of the best Lyonnais specialities in town.

Joe Allen AMERICAN €€
(Map p324; ☎01 42 36 70 13; 30 rue Pierre Lescot, 1er; lunch menus €14, dinner menus €18.10 & €22.50; ⏰noon-1am; Ⓜ Étienne Marcel) An institution since 1972, Joe Allen is a little bit of New York in Paris. The ribs are particularly recommended.

MARAIS & BASTILLE

The Marais is one of Paris' premier dining neighbourhoods; book ahead for weekend dining. Towards République is decent ethnic cuisine: Chinese noodle shops and restaurants on rue Au Maire, 3e (Ⓜ Arts et Métiers); and Jewish restaurants cooking up specialities from Central Europe, North Africa and Israel along rue des Rosiers, 4e (Ⓜ St-Paul). Takeaway falafel and shawarma are available at several places along the same street.

Bastille is equally chock-a-block with restaurants; then there is its fabulous open-air market (see boxed text, p338).

TOP CHOICE **Chez Janou** PROVENÇAL €€
(Map p324; ☎01 42 72 28 41; www.chezjanou.com; 2 rue Roger Verlomme, 3e; mains €14.50-19; Ⓜ Chemin Vert) This lovely little spot just east of place des Vosges attracts celebs (last seen: John Malkovich) with its inspired cooking from the south of France, 80 types of pastis and excellent service.

TOP CHOICE **Le Hangar** FRENCH, BISTRO €€
(Map p324; ☎01 42 74 55 44; 12 impasse Berthaud, 3e; mains €16-20; ⏰Tue-Sat; Ⓜ Les Halles) Unusual for big mouths like us, we almost baulk at revealing details of this

TOP FIVE FOOD MARKETS

» **Marché Bastille** (Map p324; blvd Richard Lenoir, 11e; ⏰7am-2.30pm Thu & Sun; Ⓜ Bastille or Richard Lenoir) Paris' best outdoor food market.

» **Marché Belleville** (Map p318; blvd de Belleville btwn rue Jean-Pierre Timbaud & rue du Faubourg du Temple, 11e & 20e; ⏰7am-2.30pm Tue & Fri; Ⓜ Belleville or Couronnes) Fascinating entry into the large, vibrant communities of the eastern neighbourhoods, home to artists, students and immigrants from Africa, Asia and the Middle East.

» **Marché Couvert St-Quentin** (Map p318; 85 blvd de Magenta, 10e; ⏰8am-1pm & 3.30-7.30pm Tue-Sat, 8.30am-1pm Sun; Ⓜ Gare de l'Est) Iron-and-glass covered market built in 1866, lined with gourmet food stalls.

» **Rue Cler** (Map p318; rue Cler, 7e; ⏰8am-7pm Tue-Sat, 8am-noon Sun; Ⓜ École Militaire) Commercial street market with an almost party-like atmosphere at weekends.

» **Rue Mouffetard** (Map p324; rue Mouffetard; ⏰8am-7.30pm Tue-Sat, 8am-noon Sun; Ⓜ Censier Daubenton) The city's most photogenic market street.

perfect little restaurant. It serves all the bistro favourites – rillettes, foie gras, steak tartare – in relaxing surrounds. The terrace is a delight in fine weather.

La Gazzetta FRENCH €€€
(Map p318; ☎01 43 47 47 05; www.lagazzetta.fr; 29 rue de Cotte, 12e; lunch menus €16, dinner menus €38 & €50; ⏰lunch Tue-Sat, dinner Mon-Sat; Ⓜ Ledru Rollin) This neo-brasserie has gained a substantial following under the tutelage of Swedish chef Peter Nilsson, who is as comfortable producing dishes such as scallops with cress and milk-fed lamb confit and iced Bleu d'Auvergne cheese as he is mini anchovy pizzas. Excellent-value, lunchtime *menu*.

Le Petit Marché FRENCH, BISTRO €€
(Map p324; ☎01 42 72 06 67; 9 rue de Béarn, 3e; mains €16-24, lunch menus €12.50; Ⓜ Chemin Vert) This great little bistro just up from place des Vosges fills up at lunch and dinner with a mixed crowd who come to enjoy its hearty cooking and friendly service.

TOP CHOICE **Café Hugo** FRENCH, CAFE €€
(Map p324; ☎01 42 72 64 04; 22 place des Vosges, 4e; mains €10.70-13.30; ⏰8am-2am; Ⓜ Chemin Vert) Go for brunch (€16.20) or the *plat du jour* (dish of the day) with a glass of wine (€12.50) at our favourite affordable eatery on Paris' most beautiful square – and you'll love Paris forever.

Chez Nénesse FRENCH, BISTRO €
(Map p324; ☎01 42 78 46 49; 17 rue Saintonge, 3e; mains €18; ⏰Mon-Fri; Ⓜ Filles du Calvaire) The atmosphere here is charmingly 'old Parisian' and unpretentious. Dishes are prepared with fresh, high-quality ingredients and pose good value for money.

Marche ou Crêpe FRENCH, BRETON €
(Map p318; ☎01 43 57 04 78; www.marcheoucrepe.com; 88 rue Oberkampf, 11e; crêpes & galettes €2.20-7.80; ⏰6pm-midnight Tue-Thu, 6pm-2am Fri & Sat, 5pm-midnight Sun; Ⓜ Parmentier) This little outlet near nightlife-busy rue Jean-Pierre Timbaud serves delicious savoury galettes, sweet crêpes, homemade soups, and salads – until late, very late.

LATIN QUARTER & JARDIN DES PLANTES

From cheap-eat student haunts to chandelier-lit palaces loaded with history, the 5e has something to suit every budget and culinary taste. Rue Mouffetard is famed for its food market and food shops; while its side streets, especially pedestrianised rue du Pot au Fer, cook up fine budget dining.

TOP CHOICE **Bistroy Les Papilles** FRENCH, BISTRO €€
(Map p324; ☎01 43 25 20 79; www.lespapillesparis.fr, in French; 30 rue Gay Lussac, 5e; menus €22-31; ⏰Tue-Sat; Ⓜ Luxembourg) This hybrid bistro, wine cellar and *épicerie* (specialist grocer) is one of those fabulous dining experiences that packs out the place (reserve a few days in advance to guarantee a table). Dining is at simply dressed tables wedged beneath bottle-lined walls, and fare is market-driven. But what really sets it apart is its exceptional wine list.

TOP CHOICE **L'Agrume** FRENCH, BISTRO €€
(off Map p324; ☎01 43 31 86 48; 15 rue des Fossés St-Marcel, 5e; mains €30, lunch menus €14 & €16, dinner menu €35; ⏰Tue-Sat; Ⓜ Censier Daubenton) Lunching at this pocket-sized contemporary bistro is magnificent value and a real gourmet experience. Watch chefs work

with seasonal products in the open kitchen while you dine; reserve several days ahead.

Le Pré Verre FRENCH, BISTRO €€
(Map p324; ☎01 43 54 59 47; 25 rue Thénard, 5e; 2-/3-course menus €13.50/28; ⌚Tue-Sat; Ⓜ Maubert Mutualité) Noisy, busy and buzzing, this jovial bistro plunges diners into the heart of a Parisian's Paris. At lunchtime join the flock and go for the fabulous-value *formule déjeuner* (€13). The wine list features France's small independent vignerons.

La Mosquée de Paris NORTH AFRICAN €€
(Map p324; ☎01 43 31 38 20; 39 rue Geoffroy St-Hilaire, 5e; mains €15-20; Ⓜ Censier Daubenton or Place Monge) Dig into a couscous, *tajine* or meaty grill within the walls of the city's **central mosque**. Or spoil yourself with a peppermint tea and oriental pastry in its **tearoom** (⌚9am-11.30pm), or lunch, body scrub and massage in its *hammam* (Turkish bath).

ST-GERMAIN, ODÉON & LUXEMBOURG

There's far more to this fabled pocket of Paris than the literary cafes of Sartre or the picnicking turf of Jardin de Luxembourg. Rue St-André des Arts (Ⓜ St-Michel or Odéon) is lined with places to dine lightly or lavishly, as is the stretch between Église St-Sulpice and Église St-Germain des Prés (especially rue des Canettes, rue Princesse and rue Guisarde).

TOP CHOICE **Le Comptoir du Relais** FRENCH, BISTRO €€€
(Map p324; ☎01 44 27 07 97; 9 Carrefour de l'Odéon, 6e; dinner menus €50; Ⓜ Odéon) The culinary handiwork of top chef Yves Camdeborde, this gourmet bistro serves seasonal dishes with a creative twist. Bagging a table without an advance reservation at lunchtime is doable providing you arrive sharp at 12.30pm, but forget more gastronomic evening dining without a reservation (weeks in advance for weekends).

TOP CHOICE **Quatrehommes** CHEESE SHOP €
(Map p318; 62 rue de Sèvres, 6e; Ⓜ Vanneau) Buy the best of every French cheese, many with an original take (eg Mont d'Or flavoured with black truffles), at this king of *fromageries* (cheese shops). The smell alone upon entering is heavenly.

KGB FUSION €€
(Map p324; ☎01 46 33 00 85; http://zekitchen-galerie.fr, in French; 25 rue des Grands Augustins, 6e; lunch menus €27 & €34; ⌚Tue-Sat; Ⓜ St-Michel) KGB (as in 'Kitchen Galerie Bis') is the latest creation of William Ledeuil of **Ze Kitchen Galerie** (Map p324; 4 rue des Grands Augustins, 6e; lunch/dinner menus €26.50/65; ⌚Mon-Fri, dinner Sat; Ⓜ St-Michel) fame. Overtly art-gallery in feel, this small dining space plays to a hip crowd with its casual platters of Asian-influenced *zors d'œuvres,* creative pastas and meats cooked in a *marmite* (earthenware pot).

Bouillon Racine CLASSICAL FRENCH €€
(Map p324; ☎01 44 32 15 60; 3 rue Racine, 6e; lunch/dinner menus €14.90/29.50; Ⓜ Cluny-La Sorbonne) This 'soup kitchen' built in 1906 to feed city workers is an art nouveau palace. Age-old recipes such as roast snails, *caille confite* (preserved quail) and lamb shank with liquorice inspire the menu. End your foray into gastronomic history with an old-fashioned sherbet.

DON'T MISS

THE GOURMET GLACIER

Berthillon (Map p324; 31 rue St-Louis en l'Île, 4e; ice creams €2.10-5.40; ⌚10am-8pm Wed-Sun; Ⓜ Pont Marie) on Île St-Louis is the place to head to for Paris' finest ice cream. There are 70 flavours to choose from, ranging from fruity cassis to chocolate, coffee, *marrons glacés* (candied chestnuts), *Agenaise* (Armagnac and prunes), *noisette* (hazelnut) and *nougat au miel* (honey nougat). One just won't be enough...

DON'T MISS

HIPPY GROOVE CUISINE

Tiny but almost perfect, **Le Mouton Noir** (Map p318; ☎01 48 07 05 45; www.lemoutonnoir.fr; 65 rue de Charonne, 11e; menus €29; ⌚dinner Tue-Sat, lunch Sat & Sun; Ⓜ Charonne) is no *mouton noir* (black sheep). Fabulously unique, this dining address with a mere two dozen seats west of Bastille is a neighbourhood secret that we've just gone and blown. The idea is to use unusual products in traditional French cooking – 'cuisine hippy groove', the chef calls it. Try crab bisque with red curry and lentils, sea bass with cheese, or eggplant with thyme. Brunch (€19) is a fine weekend tradition.

Cosi SANDWICH BAR €
(Map p324; 54 rue de Seine, 6e; sandwich menus €10-15; noon-11pm; M Odéon) With sandwich names such as Stonker, Tom Dooley and Naked Willi, Cosi could easily run for Paris' most imaginative sandwich maker.

Marché St-Germain MARKET €
(Map p324; 4-8 rue Lobineau, 6e; 8.30am-1pm & 4-7.30pm Tue-Sat, 8.30am-1pm Sun; M Mabillon) Covered food market.

EIFFEL TOWER AREA & 16E

The museum- and monument-rich 16e arrondissement has some fine dines too. Around Mademoiselle Eiffel grab picnic supplies on foodie street rue Cler or pick from several restaurants on rue de Montessuy.

TOP CHOICE **Café Constant** FRENCH, CONTEMPORARY €€
(Map p318; www.cafeconstant.com, in French; 139 rue Ste-Dominique, 7e; mains €16; Tue-Sun; M École Militaire or Port de l'Alma) Take a former Michelin-starred chef, a dead-simple corner cafe and what do you get? A Christian Constant hit with original mosaic floor, worn wooden tables and a massive queue out the door every mealtime. The cafe doesn't take reservations, but you can enjoy a drink at the bar while you wait. Cuisine is creative bistro.

Les Cocottes FRENCH, CONCEPT €€
(Map p318; www.leviolondingres.com; 135 rue Ste-Dominique, 7e; starters/cocottes & mains/desserts €11/16/7; Mon-Sat; M École Militaire or Port de l'Alma) *Cocottes* are casseroles, and that is what this chic space – jam-packed day and night – is all about. Get here sharp at noon or 7.15pm (or before) to get a table; no reservations.

MONTPARNASSE

Since the 1920s, Montparnasse has been one of Paris' premier avenues for enjoying cafe life, though younger Parisians deem the quarter démodé (out of fashion) these days.

TOP CHOICE **Jadis** FRENCH, BISTRO €€€
(Map p318; 01 45 57 73 20; www.bistrot-jadis.com, in French; 202 rue de la Croix Nivert, 15e; lunch menus €25 & €32, dinner menus €45 & €65; Mon-Fri; M Boucicaut) This neo-bistro is one of Paris' most raved about. Traditional French dishes pack a modern punch thanks to rising-star chef Guillaume Delage, who dares to do things like braise pork cheeks in beer and use black rice instead of white. The lunch *menu* is extraordinary good value and the chocolate soufflé sheer heaven.

TOP CHOICE **La Cabane à Huîtres** FRENCH, OYSTERS €
(Map p318; 01 45 49 47 27; 4 rue Antoine Bourdelle, 14e; menus €18; Wed-Sat; M Montparnasse-Bienvenüe) One of Paris' best oyster addresses, this earthy wooden-styled *cabane* (cabin) with just nine tables is the pride and joy of fifth-generation oyster farmer Françis Dubourg, who splits his week between the capital and his oyster farm in Arcachon on the Atlantic coast.

Le Dôme HISTORIC BRASSERIE €€€
(Map p318; 01 43 35 25 81; 108 blvd du Montparnasse, 14e; starters/mains €20/40; M Vavin) A 1930s art deco extravaganza, the Dome is a monumental place for a meal of the formal white-tablecloth and bow-tied waiter variety. Stick with the basics at this historical venue and end on a high with *millefeuille* – a decadent extravaganza not to be missed.

ÉTOILE & CHAMPS-ÉLYSÉES

The 8e arrondissement around the Champs-Élysées is known for its big-name chefs (Alain Ducasse, Pierre Gagnaire, Guy Savoy) and culinary icons (Taillevent), but there are all sorts of under-the-radar restaurants scattered in the backstreets where Parisians who live and work in the area dine.

Bistrot du Sommelier FRENCH €€€
(Map p318; 01 42 65 24 85; www.bistrotdusommelier.com; 97 blvd Haussmann, 8e; lunch menus €33, incl wine €43, dinner menus €65-110; Mon-Fri; M St-Augustin) The whole point of this attractive eatery is to match wine with food, aided by one of the world's foremost sommeliers, Philippe Faure-Brac. Sample his wine/food pairings on Friday, when a three-course tasting lunch with wine is €50 and a five-course dinner with wine is €75.

Le Boudoir FRENCH €€€
(Map p318; 01 43 59 25 29; 25 rue du Colisée, 8e; lunch/dinner menus €19/50; lunch Mon-Fri, dinner Tue-Sat; St-Philippe du Roule or Franklin D Roosevelt) Spread across two floors, the quirky salons here – Marie Antoinette, Palme d'Or and the Red Room – are individual works of art with a style befitting the name. In a move towards yesteryear decadence, a private smoking room is hidden on the premises. The *prix fixe* (fixed-price) lunch is an excellent deal.

Le Hide FRENCH €€
(Map p318; 01 45 74 15 81; www.lehide.fr; 10 Rue du Général Lanrezac, 17e; menus €22 & €29; lunch Mon-Fri, dinner Mon-Sat; M Charles de Gaulle-Étoile) A reader favourite, Le Hide

DON'T MISS

CANAL ST-MARTIN: A PARISIAN-PERFECT PICNIC

Pink Flamingo (Map p318; ☎01 42 02 31 70; www.pinkflamingopizza.com; 67 rue Bichat, 10e; pizzas €10.50-16; ⊙until 11pm Tue-Sat, 1pm-11pm Sun; Ⓜ Jacques Bonsergent) is not just another pizza place. *Mais non, chérie!* Once the weather warms up, the Flamingo unveils its secret weapon – pink helium balloons that the delivery guy uses to locate you and your perfect canalside picnic spot. Nip into the canalside pizzeria to order Paris' most inventive pizza (duck, apple and chèvre perhaps, or what about gorgonzola, figs and cured ham?), grab a balloon, and stroll off along the canal to your perfect picnic spot.

To make your picnic Parisian perfect, buy a bottle of wine from nearby **Le Verre Volé** (Map p318; ☎01 48 03 17 34; 67 rue de Lancry, 10e; mains €12; Ⓜ Jacques Bonsergent), a wine shop with a few tables, excellent wines (€5 to €60 per bottle, €4.50 per glass) and expert advice.

is a tiny neighbourhood bistro serving scrumptious traditional French fare: snails, baked shoulder of lamb, monkfish in lemon butter.

Fromagerie Alléosse CHEESE SHOP €
(Map p318; 13 rue Poncelet, 17e; Ⓜ Ternes) This is the best cheese shop in Paris; well worth a trip across town.

OPÉRA & GRANDS BOULEVARDS

The neon-lit area around blvd Montmartre forms one of the Right Bank's most animated cafe and dining districts.

TOP CHOICE **Les Pâtes Vivantes** CHINESE €
(46 du Faubourg Montmartre, 9e; noodles €9.50-12; ⊙Mon-Sat; Ⓜ Le Peletier) This is one of the few spots in Paris for sampling hand-pulled noodles *(là miàn)* made to order in the age-old northern Chinese tradition. There's also a **Latin Quarter branch** (Map p324; ☎01 40 46 84 33; 22 blvd St-Germain, 5e; Ⓜ Cardinal Lemoine).

Le Roi du Pot au Feu FRENCH, BISTRO €€
(Map p330; 34 rue Vignon, 9e; menus €24-29; ⊙noon-10.30pm Mon-Sat; Ⓜ Havre Caumartin) The typical Parisian bistro atmosphere adds to the charm of the 'King of Hotpots', but what you really come here for is its *pot-au-feu* (beef, root vegetable and herb stew), the stock as starter and the meat and veg as main. No bookings.

Chartier FRENCH, BISTRO €
(Map p330; ☎01 47 70 86 29; www.restaurant-chartier.com; 7 rue du Faubourg Montmartre, 9e; menus with wine €19.40; Ⓜ Grands Boulevards) Chartier started life as a *bouillon* (soup kitchen) in 1896 and is a real belle époque gem. For a taste of old-fashioned Paris, it's unbeatable. No reservations.

Le J'Go SOUTHWEST FRENCH €€
(Map p330; ☎01 40 22 09 09; www.lejgo.com; 4 rue Drouot, 9e; menus €15-20; ⊙lunch Mon-Fri, dinner Mon-Sat; Ⓜ Richelieu Druot) This contemporary, Toulouse-style bistro magics diners away to southwestern France. Flavourful regional cooking revolves around a *rôtissoire* (meat on a spit) – minimum 20 minutes' roasting.

MONTMARTRE & PIGALLE

You'll still find some decent eateries in Montmartre, but beware the tourist traps. Towards place Pigalle there are plenty of grocery stores, many open until late; try side streets off blvd de Clichy such as rue Lepic.

Chez Toinette FRENCH €€
(Map p330; ☎01 42 54 44 36; 20 rue Germain Pilon, 18e; mains €17-22; ⊙dinner Mon-Sat; Ⓜ Abbesses) Chez Toinette keeps alive the tradition of old Montmartre with its simplicity and culinary expertise. Partridge, doe and duck are house specialities.

Café Burq FRENCH, BISTRO €€
(Map p330; ☎01 42 52 81 27; 6 rue Burq, 18e; menus €26 & €30; ⊙7pm-2am Tue-Sat; Ⓜ Abbesses) This convivial, retro bistro is always buzzing; book ahead. But don't come for the decor or space – both are nonexistent.

Le Café qui Parle FRENCH €€
(Map p330; ☎01 46 06 06 88; 24 rue Caulaincourt, 18e; menus €12.50 & €17; ⊙Mon-Sat, lunch Sun; 📶; Ⓜ Lamarck Caulaincourt or Blanche) We love the Talking Cafe's wall art and ancient safes below (the building was once a bank), but not as much as we love its weekend brunch (€17).

Drinking

The line between bars, cafes and bistros is blurred at best. Sitting at a table costs more than standing at the counter, more on a fancy square than a backstreet, more in the 8e than in the 18e. After 10pm many cafes charge a pricier *tarif de nuit* (night rate).

LOUVRE & LES HALLES

Le Fumoir COCKTAIL BAR
(Map p324; 6 rue de l'Amiral Coligny, 1er; ⊙11am-2am; MLouvre-Rivoli) The 'Smoking Room' is a huge, stylish colonial-style bar-cafe opposite the Louvre – a fine place to sip top-notch gin while nibbling on olives.

Le Cochon à l'Oreille BAR, CAFE
(Map p324; 15 rue Montmartre, 1er; ⊙10am-11pm Tue-Sat; MLes Halles or Étienne Marcel) A Parisian jewel, this heritage-listed hole-in-the wall retains its belle époque tiles with market scenes of Les Halles, and just eight tiny tables.

MARAIS & BASTILLE

Le Pure Café CAFE
(Map p318; 14 rue Jean Macé, 11e; ⊙7am-2am; MCharonne) This old cafe moonlights as a restaurant, but we like it as it was intended to be, especially over a *grand crème* (large white coffee) and the papers on Sunday morning.

Le Bistrot du Peintre WINE BAR
(Map p318; 116 av Ledru-Rollin, 11e; ⊙8am-2am; MBastille) Lovely belle époque bistro and wine bar, with 1902 art nouveau bar, elegant terrace and spot-on service.

Au Petit Fer à Cheval BAR
(Map p324; 30 rue Vieille du Temple, 4e; ⊙8am-2am; MHôtel de Ville or St-Paul) The original horseshoe-shaped zinc counter (1903) leaves little room for much else at this genial bar, but nobody seems to mind.

La Chaise Au Plafond BAR
(Map p324; 10 Rue du Trésor, 4e; ⊙10am-2am; ⊙Hôtel de Ville or St-Paul) The Chair on the Ceiling is a peaceful, warm place with terrace – a real oasis from the frenzy of the Marais and worth knowing about in summer.

LATIN QUARTER & JARDIN DES PLANTES

Curio Parlor Cocktail Club COCKTAIL BAR
(Map p324; 16 rue des Bernardins, 5e; ⊙7pm-2am Tue-Thu, 7pm-4am Fri & Sat; MMaubert Mutualité) This hybrid bar-club looks to the interwar *années folles* (crazy years) of 1920s Paris, London and New York for inspiration. Go to its Facebook page to track the next party.

ST-GERMAIN, ODÉON & LUXEMBOURG

TOP CHOICE **Au Sauvignon** WINE BAR
(Map p318; 80 rue des Sts-Pères, 7e; ⊙8am-midnight; MSèvres-Babylone) To savour the full flavour of this 1950s wine bar, order a plate of *casse-croûtes au pain Poilâne* – sandwiches made with the city's most famous bread.

Prescription Cocktail Club COCKTAIL CLUB
(Map p324; 23 rue Mazarine, 6e; ⊙7pm-2am Mon-Thu, 7pm-4am Fri & Sat; MOdéon) With bowler and flat-top hats as lampshades and a 1930s speakeasy New York air to the place, this cocktail club is Parisian-cool. Watch Facebook for events.

Le 10 CELLAR PUB
(Map p324; 10 rue de l'Odéon, 6e; ⊙5.30pm-2am; MOdéon) Plot the next revolution or conquer a lonely heart at this local institution that groans with students, smoky ambience and cheap sangria.

Café La Palette HISTORIC CAFE
(Map p324; 43 rue de Seine, 6e; ⊙8am-2am Mon-Sat; MMabillon) In the heart of gal-

BAR-HOPPING STREETS

Prime Parisian drinking spots, perfect for evening meandering to soak up the scene:

» **Rue Vieille du Temple** & **surrounding streets, 4e** Marais cocktail of gay bars and chic cafes.

» **Rue Oberkampf** & **rue Jean-Pierre Timbaud, 11e** Hip bars, bohemian hang-outs and atmospheric cafes.

» **Rue de la Roquette, rue Keller** & **rue de Lappe, 11e** Whatever you fancy, Bastille has the lot.

» **Rue Montmartre, 2e** Modern, slick bars and pubs.

» **Canal St-Martin, 10e** Heady summer nights in casual canalside cafes.

» **Rue Princesse** & **rue des Canettes, 6e** Pedestrian duo of student, sports 'n' tapas bars and pubs on the Left Bank.

lery land, this cafe where Cézanne and Braque drank attracts fashionable people and art dealers. Its summer terrace is as beautiful.

Les Deux Magots HISTORIC CAFE
(Map p324; www.lesdeuxmagots.fr; 170 blvd St-Germain, 6e; 7am-1am; M St-Germain des Prés) St-Germain's most famous cafe, where Sartre, Hemingway and Picasso hung out.

ÉTOILE & CHAMPS-ELYSÉES

Buddha Bar COCKTAIL BAR
(Map p318; 8-12 rue Boissy d'Anglas, 8e; noon-2am Sun-Thu, 4pm-3am Fri & Sat; M Concorde) The decor is spectacular, with a two-storey golden Buddha and millions of candles, at this A-list cocktail bar known for its Zen lounge music.

OPÉRA & GRANDS BOULEVARDS

DeLaVille Café BAR, CAFE
(Map p330; 34 blvd de Bonne Nouvelle, 10e; 11am-2.30am; ; M Bonne Nouvelle) This erstwhile brothel fuses history (original mosaic tiles, distressed walls) with industrial chic. Its terrace is among the best along the grands boulevards and DJs play Thursday to Saturday, making it a hot 'before' venue for the nearby **Rex Club** (p345).

TOP CHOICE **Harry's New York Bar** AMERICAN BAR
(Map p330; 5 rue Daunou, 2e; 10.30am-4am; M Opéra) Lean upon the bar where F Scott Fitzgerald and Ernest Hemingway drank and gossiped, while white-smocked waiters mix killer martinis and Bloody Marys.

TOP CHOICE **Au Limonaire** WINE BAR
(Map p330; 01 45 23 33 33; http://limonaire.free.fr; 18 cité Bergère, 9e; 7pm-midnight Mon, 6pm-midnight Tue-Sun; M Grands Boulevards) This little wine bar is one of the best places to listen to traditional French *chansons* (songs) and local singer/songwriters. Reservations recommended.

MONTMARTRE & PIGALLE

La Fourmi BAR
(Map p330; 74 rue des Martyrs, 18e; 8am-2am Mon-Thu, to 4am Fri & Sat, 10am-2am Sun; M Pigalle) A Pigalle stayer, 'The Ant' always hits the mark: hip but not snobby, with a laid-back crowd and a rock-oriented playlist.

☆ Entertainment

From jazz cellars to comic theatre, garage beats to go-go dancers, world-class art galleries to avant-garde artist squats, Paris is *the* capital of savoir-vivre, with spectacular entertainment to suit every budget, every taste. To find out what's on, surf **Figaroscope** (www.figaroscope.fr) or buy *Pariscope* (€0.40) or *Officiel des Spectacles* (€0.35; www.offi.fr, in French) at Parisian news kiosks. *Billeteries* (ticket offices) in **Fnac** (www.fnacspectacles.com, in French) and **Virgin Megastores** (www.virginmega.fr, in French) sell tickets.

HALF-PRICE TICKETS

If you go on the day of a performance, you can snag a half-price ticket (plus €3 commission) for ballet, theatre, opera and other performances at the discount-ticket outlet **Kiosque Théâtre Madeleine** (Map p330; www.kiosquetheatre.com; opp 15 place de la Madeleine, 8e; 12.30-8pm Tue-Sat, to 4pm Sun; M Madeleine).

French-language websites www.billetreduc.com, www.ticketac.com and www.webguichet.com all sell discounted tickets.

Live Music

Palais Omnisports de Paris-Bercy (Map p318; www.bercy.fr, in French); **Le Zénith** (Map p318; www.le-zenith.com, in French) and **Stade de France** (www.stadefrance.com) are Paris' big-name venues. But it's the smaller concert halls loaded with history and charm that most fans favour.

Le Vieux Belleville FRENCH CHANSONS
(Map p318; 01 44 62 92 66; www.le-vieux-belleville.com; 12 rue des Envierges, 20e; admission free; performances 8pm Thu-Sat; M Pyrénées) This old-fashioned bistro at the top of Parc de Belleville is an atmospheric venue for performances of *chansons,* featuring accordions and an organ grinder, three times a week. It's a lively favourite with locals; book ahead.

Cabaret Sauvage WORLD, LATINO
(Map p318; 01 42 09 03 09; www.cabaretsauvage.com; Parc de la Villette, 221 av Jean Jaurès, 19e; tickets €8-34; 7pm-2am Tue-Sun; Porte de la Villette) This super-cool space (it looks like a gigantic yurt) hosts African, reggae and raï concerts as well as DJ nights that last till dawn; occasional hip-hop and indie acts pass through.

DON'T MISS

FREE SHOWS

Paris' eclectic gaggle of clowns, mime artists, living statues, acrobats, rollerbladers, buskers and other street entertainers can be bags of fun and costs substantially less than a theatre ticket (a few coins in the hat is a sweet gesture). Some excellent musicians perform in the long echo-filled corridors of the metro, a privilege that artists have to audition for. Outside, you can be sure of a good show at:

» **Place Georges Pompidou, 4e** In front of the Centre Pompidou.

» **Pont St-Louis, 4e** Bridge linking Paris' two islands (best enjoyed with Berthillon ice cream in hand).

» **Pont au Double, 4e** Pedestrian bridge linking Notre Dame with the Left Bank (ditto; see boxed text, p339).

» **Place Jean du Bellay, 1er** Musicians and fire-eaters near the Fontaine des Innocents.

» **Parc de la Villette, 19e** African drummers at the weekend.

» **Place du Tertre, Montmartre, 18e** Montmartre's original main square wins hands down as Paris' busiest street-artist stage.

L'Attirail WORLD, LATINO

(Map p324; ☎01 42 72 44 42; www.lattirail.com; 9 rue au Maire, 3e; admission free; ⏲10.30am-1.30am Mon-Sat, 3pm-1.30am Sun; Ⓜ Arts et Métiers) There are free concerts of *chansons françaises* and world music almost every evening at this cosmopolitan enclave. Manic but friendly customers crowd the Formica bar with its cheap *pots* (460mL bottle) of wine.

Le Baiser Salé JAZZ

(Map p324; www.lebaisersale.com, in French; 58 rue des Lombards, 1er; admission free-€20; ⏲5pm-6am; ⏲Châtelet) One of several jazz clubs located on this street, the Salty Kiss hosts concerts of jazz, Afro and Latin jazz and jazz fusion, and is known for discovering new talents. Sets start at 7.30pm and 10pm. Monday's jam session is free.

Salle Pleyel CLASSICAL

(Map p318; ☎01 42 56 13 13; www.sallepleyel.fr; 252 rue du Faubourg St-Honoré, 8e; concert tickets €10-85; ⏲box office noon-7pm Mon-Sat, to 8pm on day of performance; Ⓜ Ternes) Dating from the 1920s, this highly regarded hall hosts many of Paris' finest classical-music events, including concerts by the Orchestre de Paris (www.orchestredeparis.com, in French).

Point Éphemère ROCK, INDIE

(Map p318; ☎01 40 34 02 48; www.pointephemere.org; 200 quai de Valmy, 10e; admission free-€21; ⏲bar noon-2am Mon-Sat, 1-9pm Sun; Ⓜ Louis Blanc) This 'centre for dynamic artists' has a great location by Canal St-Martin, with indie concerts and the odd electro dance night. Bar, restaurant and exhibit area too.

La Cigale ROCK, JAZZ

(Map p330; ☎01 49 25 81 75; www.lacigale.fr; 120 blvd de Rochechouart, 18e; admission €25-60; Ⓜ Anvers or Pigalle) Now classed as a historical monument, this music hall dates from 1887 but was redecorated 100 years later by Philippe Starck.

Nightclubs

Unfortunately, Paris is *not* up to the likes of London, Berlin or New York when it comes to clubbing. Lacking a mainstream scene, the scene tends to be underground and mobile, making the web the smartest way of keeping on top of it.

TOP CHOICE **La Scène Bastille** CLUB

(Map p318; www.scenebastille.com; 2bis rue des Taillandiers, 11e; admission €12-15; ⏲Mon-Sat; Ⓜ Bastille or Ledru Rollin) The unpretentious Bastille Scene is the kind of place where local DJs go to relax and listen to music.

TOP CHOICE **Le Batofar** TUGBOAT

(Map p318; www.batofar.org, in French; opp 11 quai François Mauriac, 13e; admission free-€15; ⏲9pm-midnight Mon & Tue, to 4am or later Wed-Sun; Ⓜ Quai de la Gare or Bibliothèque) This much-loved tugboat has a rooftop bar that's great in summer, while the club underneath provides memorable underwater acoustics between its metal walls and portholes.

Le Divan du Monde CULTURAL CENTRE

(Map p330; www.divandumonde.com; 75 rue des Martyrs, 18e; admission €10-15; ⏲11pm-5am Fri & Sat; Ⓜ Pigalle) Cinematographic events, Romani music gatherings, *nouvelles chansons françaises* (new French songs), air-guitar face-offs, rock parties... Inventive and open-minded is what this excellent cross-cultural venue in Pigalle is.

Le Balajo DANCE CLUB

(Map p318; www.balajo.fr; 9 rue de Lappe, 11e; admission from €12; ⏲10pm-2am Tue & Thu, 11pm-5am Fri & Sat, 3-7.30pm Sun; Ⓜ Bastille) This historic ballroom is devoted to salsa classes and Latino music on weekdays and DJ-spun rock, disco, funk, R&B and house at weekends.

Le Nouveau Casino CLUB

(Map p318; www.nouveaucasino.net, in French; 109 rue Oberkampf, 11e; admission €5-10; ⏲7.30pm or midnight to 2 or 5am Tue-Sun; Ⓜ Parmentier) This club is known for its live-music concerts and lively weekend club nights. The program is eclectic, underground and up-to-the-minute.

Le Rex Club CLUB

(Map p330; www.rexclub.com; 5 blvd Poissonnière, 2e; admission free-€12; ⏲11.30pm-6am Wed-Sat; Ⓜ Bonne Nouvelle) The Rex reigns majestic in the house and techno scene – always has and always will.

Shopping

As in most capital cities, shops are spread across different neighbourhoods, inspiring very different styles of shopping. Annual, month-long *soldes* (sales) see prices slashed by as much as 50%; they start up in mid-January and again in mid-June.

Key areas to mooch with no particular purchase in mind are the maze of backstreet lanes in the Marais (3e and 4e), around St-Germain des Prés (6e), and parts of Montmartre and Pigalle (9e and 18e). Or perhaps you have something specific to buy?

Designer haute couture The world's most famous designers stylishly jostle for window space on Av Montaigne, av Georges V and rue du Faubourg St-Honoré, 8e.

Chain-store fashion Find Gap, H&M, Zara and other major, super-sized chain stores on Rue de Rivoli in the 1er, Les Halles in the 2e, and av des Champs-Élysées, 8e.

Department stores On and around Blvd Haussmann, 9e, including Paris' famous

DIGITAL CLUBBING

Track tomorrow's hot 'n' happening soirée with these Parisian nightlife links:

» www.gogoparis.com (in English)

» www.lemonsound.com

» www.novaplanet.com

» www.parisbouge.com

» www.parissi.com

» www.tribudenuit.com

Galeries Lafayette (Map p330) at No 40 and **Printemps** (Map p330) at No 64.

Factory outlets Price-cut fashion for men, women and kids the length of Rue d'Alésia, 14e.

Hip fashion & art Young designers crowd Rue Charlot, 3e, and beyond in the northern Marais.

Fine art & antiques Right Bank place des Vosges, 4e, and Left Bank Carré Rive Gauche, 6e.

Design Eames, eat your heart out! Boutique galleries specialising in modern furniture, art and design (1950s to present) stud rue Mazarine and rue de Seine, 6e.

Information

Dangers & Annoyances

Paris is generally safe. Metro stations best avoided late at night include: Châtelet-Les Halles and its corridors; Château Rouge in Montmartre; Gare du Nord; Strasbourg St-Denis; Réaumur Sébastopol; and Montparnasse Bienvenüe.

Pickpocketing and thefts from handbags and packs is a problem wherever there are crowds (especially of tourists). Be careful around Montmartre's Sacré Cœur; Pigalle; the areas around Forum des Halles and Centre Pompidou; the Latin Quarter; below the Eiffel Tower; and on the metro during rush hour.

Internet Resources

Mairie de Paris (www.paris.fr)

Paris by Mouth (www.parisbymouth.com)

Paris Convention & Visitors Bureau (www.parisinfo.com)

My Little Paris (www.mylittleparis.com)

Medical Services

American Hospital of Paris (☎01 46 41 25 25; www.american-hospital.org; 63 blvd Victor Hugo, 92200 Neuilly-sur-Seine; Ⓜ Pont de Levallois Bécon)

DON'T MISS

FLEA MARKETS

» **Marché aux Puces de Montreuil** (off Map p318; av du Professeur André Lemière, 20e; ⏲8am-7.30pm Sat-Mon; Ⓜ Porte de Montreuil) Particularly known for its second-hand clothing, designer seconds, engravings, jewellery, linen, crockery and old furniture.

» **Marché aux Puces de St-Ouen** (off Map p318; rue des Rosiers, av Michelet, rue Voltaire, rue Paul Bert & rue Jean-Henri Fabre, 18e; ⏲9am-6pm Sat, 10am-6pm Sun, 11am-5pm Mon; Ⓜ Porte de Clignancourt) Around since the late 19th century, and said to be Europe's largest.

» **Marché aux Puces de la Porte de Vanves** (Map p318; av Georges Lafenestre & av Marc Sangnier, 14e; ⏲7am-6pm or later Sat & Sun; Ⓜ Porte de Vanves) The smallest and, some say, friendliest of the trio.

Hôpital Hôtel Dieu (☎01 42 34 82 34; www.aphp.fr; 1 place du Parvis Notre Dame, 4e; Ⓜ Cité) One of the city's main government-run public hospitals; after 8pm use the emergency entrance on rue de la Cité, 4e.

Pharmacie Les Champs (☎01 45 62 02 41; Galerie des Champs, 84 av des Champs-Élysées, 8e; ⏲24hr; Ⓜ George V)

Tourist Information

Paris Convention & Visitors Bureau (Map p324; www.parisinfo.com; 25-27 rue des Pyramides, 1er; Ⓜ Pyramides; ⏲9am-7pm Jun-Oct, 10am-7pm Mon-Sat & 11am-7pm Sun Nov-May) Main tourist office, with a clutch of smaller centres elsewhere in the city.

Getting There & Away

Air

Aéroport d'Orly (ORY; ☎01 70 36 39 50; www.aeroportsdeparis.fr) Older and smaller of Paris' two major airports, 18km south of the city.

Aéroport Roissy Charles de Gaulle (CDG; ☎01 70 36 39 50; www.aeroportsdeparis.fr) Three terminal complexes – Aérogare 1, 2 and 3 – are located 30km northeast of Paris in the suburb of Roissy.

Aéroport Beauvais (BVA; ☎08 92 68 20 66; www.aeroportbeauvais.com) Located 80km north of Paris; used by charter companies and budget airlines

Bus

Eurolines (☎01 43 54 11 99; www.eurolines.fr; 55 rue St-Jacques, 5e; Ⓜ Cluny-La Sorbonne) Reservations and tickets for international buses to Western and Central Europe, Scandinavia and Morocco.

Gare Routière Internationale de Paris-Galliéni (off Map p318; ☎08 92 89 90 91; 28 av du Général de Gaulle; Ⓜ Galliéni) Paris' international bus terminal in the eastern suburb of Bagnolet.

Train

Paris has six major train stations. For mainline train information around the clock, contact **SNCF** (☎08 91 36 20 20, timetables ☎08 91 67 68 69; www.sncf.fr).

Gare d'Austerlitz (Map p324; blvd de l'Hôpital, 13e; Ⓜ Gare d'Austerlitz) Trains to/from Spain and Portugal; Loire Valley and non-TGV trains to southwestern France (eg Bordeaux and Basque Country).

Gare de l'Est (Map p318; blvd de Strasbourg, 10e; Ⓜ Gare de l'Est) Trains to/from Luxembourg, parts of Switzerland (Basel, Lucerne, Zurich), southern Germany (Frankfurt, Munich) and points further east; regular and TGV Est trains to areas of France east of Paris (Champagne, Alsace and Lorraine).

Gare de Lyon (Map p318; blvd Diderot, 12e; Ⓜ Gare de Lyon) Trains to/from parts of Switzerland (eg Bern, Geneva, Lausanne), Italy and points beyond; regular and TGV Sud-Est and TGV Midi-Méditerranée trains to areas southeast of Paris, including Dijon, Lyon, Provence, the Côte d'Azur and the Alps.

Gare Montparnasse (Map p318; av du Maine & blvd de Vaugirard, 15e; Ⓜ Montparnasse Bienvenüe) Trains to/from Brittany and places en route from Paris (eg Chartres, Angers, Nantes); TGV Atlantique Ouest and TGV Atlantique Sud-Ouest trains to Tours, Nantes, Bordeaux and other destinations in southwestern France.

Gare du Nord (Map p318; rue de Dunkerque, 10e; Ⓜ Gare du Nord) Trains to/from the UK, Belgium, northern Germany, Scandinavia, Moscow etc (terminus of the high-speed Thalys trains to/from Amsterdam, Brussels, Cologne and Geneva and Eurostar to London); trains to the northern suburbs of Paris and northern France, including TGV Nord trains to Lille and Calais.

Gare St-Lazare (Map p318; rue St-Lazare & rue d'Amsterdam, 8e; Ⓜ St-Lazare) Normandy (eg Dieppe, Le Havre, Cherbourg).

Getting Around

To/From the Airports

Getting into town is straightforward and inexpensive thanks to a fleet of public-transport options. Bus drivers sell tickets. Children aged four to nine years pay half-price on most services.

AÉROPORT D'ORLY

Air France bus 1 (☎08 92 35 08 20; http://videocdn.airfrance.com/cars-airfrance; single/return €11.50/18.50; ⊙6.15am-11.15pm from Orly, 6am-11.30pm from Invalides) This *navette* (shuttle bus) runs every 30 minutes to/from Gare Montparnasse (rue du Commandant René Mouchotte, 15e; Ⓜ Montparnasse Bienvenüe) and Aérogare des Invalides (Ⓜ Invalides) in the 7e.

Noctilien bus 31 (☎32 46; www.noctilien.fr; adult €6.80 or 4 metro tickets; ⊙12.30am-5.30pm) Part of the RATP night service, Noctilien hourly bus 31 links Orly-Sud with Gare de Lyon, Place d'Italie and Gare d'Austerlitz (45 mins).

Orlybus (☎32 46; www.ratp.fr; adult €6.60; ⊙6am-11.20pm from Orly, 5.35am-11.05pm from Paris) RATP bus every 15 to 20 minutes to/from metro Denfert Rochereau (20 to 30 minutes) in the 14e.

Orlyval (☎32 46; www.ratp.fr; adult €10.25; ⊙6am-11pm) This RATP service links Orly with the city centre via a shuttle train and the RER (p348). Automatic rail (€7.90) to the RER B station Antony, then RER B4 north (€2.35; 35 to 40 minutes to Châtelet, every four to 12 minutes). Orlyval tickets are valid for the subsequent RER and metro journey.

RATP bus 183 (☎32 46; www.ratp.fr; adult €1.70 or 1 metro/bus ticket; ⊙5.35am-8.35pm) Cheapest way of getting to/from Orly Sud: very slow public bus linking only Orly-Sud (one hour) with metro Porte de Choisy every 30 minutes.

RATP bus 285 (☎32 46; www.ratp.fr; adult €6.80 or 4 metro tickets; ⊙5.05am-midnight from Orly, 5am-12.40am from Paris) Every 10 to 30 minutes to/from metro Villejuif Louis Aragon (55 minutes).

RER C & shuttle (☎32 46; www.ratp.fr; adult €6.20; ⊙5.30am-11.30pm) Shuttle bus every 15 to 30 minutes to RER line C station, Pont de Rungis-Aéroport d'Orly RER station, then RER C2 train to Paris' Gare d'Austerlitz (50 minutes).

AÉROPORT ROISSY CHARLES DE GAULLE

Air France bus 2 (☎08 92 35 08 20; http://videocdn.airfrance.com/cars-airfrance; single/return €15/24; ⊙5.45am-11pm) Links airport every 30 minutes with the Arc de Triomphe outside 1 av Carnot, 17e (45 minutes), and Porte Maillot metro station, 17e (35 to 50 minutes).

Air France bus 4 (☎08 92 35 08 20; http://videocdn.airfrance.com/cars-airfrance; adult single/return €16.50/27; ⊙7am-9pm from Roissy Charles de Gaulle, 6.30am-9.30pm from Paris) Links airport every 30 minutes with **Gare de Lyon** (20bis blvd Diderot, 12e; Ⓜ Gare de Lyon) and **Gare Montparnasse** (rue du Commandant René Mouchotte, 15e; Ⓜ Montparnasse Bienvenüe); journey times 50 to 55 minutes.

Noctilien buses 140 & 143 (☎32 46; www.noctilien.fr; adult €5.10 or 3 metro tickets; ⊙12.30am-5.30pm) Hourly night buses to/from Gare de l'Est (140 & 143) and Gare de Nord (143).

RATP bus 350 (☎32 46; www.ratp.fr; adult €5.10 or 3 metro tickets ⊙5.30am-11pm) Every 30 minutes to/from Gare de l'Est and Gare du Nord (both one hour).

RER B (☎32 46; www.ratp.fr; adult €8.70; ⊙5.20am-midnight) Under extensive renovation at the time of research, with replacement buses on duty; RER line B3 usually links CDG1 and CDG2 with the city every 10 to 15 minutes (30 minutes).

Roissybus (☎32 46; www.ratp.fr; adult €9.40; ⊙5.30am-11pm) Direct bus every 30 minutes to/from **Opéra** (cnr rue Scribe & rue Auber, 9e; Ⓜ Opéra).

BETWEEN ORLY & CHARLES DE GAULLE

Air France shuttle bus 3 (www.cars-airfrance.com, in French; adult €19; ⊙6am-10.30pm) Every 30 minutes; free for connecting Air France passengers; journey time one hour.

Orlyval (☎32 46; www.ratp.fr; adult €17.60; ⊙6am-11pm) RER line B3 from Charles de Gaulle to the Antony station, then Orlyval automatic metro to Orly.

AÉROPORT PARIS-BEAUVAIS

Navette Officielle (Official Shuttle Bus; ☎08 92 68 20 64, airport 08 92 68 20 66; adult €14) Leaves Parking Pershing, west of the Palais des Congrès de Paris, 3¼ hours before flight departures (board 15 minutes before) and leaves the airport 20 minutes after arrivals, dropping passengers south of the Palais des Congrès on place de la Porte Maillot. Journey time 1¼ hours; buy tickets at sales point just outside the terminal and from a kiosk in the car park.

Bicycle

Vélib' (www.velib.paris.fr; day/week subscription €1/5, bike hire per 1st/2nd/additional 30min free/€2/4) With this self-service bike scheme you can pick up a pearly-grey bike for peanuts from one roadside Vélib' station and drop it off at another. Its almost 1500 bike *stations* are accessible around the clock. iPhone users can download the Vélib' application. To get a bike, open a Vélib' account: one- and seven-day subscriptions can be done at any station with any credit card that has a microchip. If the station you want to return your bike to is full, swipe your card across the multilingual terminal to get 15 minutes for free to find another station. Bikes are geared to cyclists aged 14 and over, and are fitted with gears, antitheft lock with key, reflective strips and front/rear lights. Helmets are not compulsory; bring your own if you want to wear one.

Boat

Batobus (☎08 25 05 01 01; www.batobus.com; adult 1-/2-/3-day pass €13/17/20; ⏲10am-9.30pm May-Aug, shorter hr rest of year) A fleet of glassed-in trimarans dock at eight small piers along the Seine every 15 to 30 minutes; buy tickets at each stop or tourist offices, and jump on and off as you like.

Car & Motorcycle

If driving a car in Paris doesn't destroy your holiday sense of spontaneity, parking will. If you must drive, the fastest way to get across the city is usually via the blvd Périphérique, the ring road encircling the city.

Major car-rental companies have offices at airports and train stations. Another option is the self-service, pay-as-you-go scheme provided by **Connect by Hertz** (☎08 00 45 04 00; www.connectbyhertz.com): for a €120 annual membership fee you can use their website to book a car in your neighbourhood; rates start at €4/32 per hour/day plus €0.35 per kilometre and include insurance and petrol. The Mairie de Paris also hopes to have a fleet of 3000-odd electric rental cars parked around the city by 2012, to be called Autolib' (ie the car equivalent of Vélib').

Street parking in central Paris is limited to two hours (€1.50 to €3 per hour); to pay, buy a Paris Carte worth €10 or €30 at *tabacs* (tobacconists). Municipal car parks cost €2 to €3.50 per hour or around €25 per 24 hours.

Got the urge to look like you've just stepped into (or out of) a 1950s French film? Grab a pastel-coloured Vespa XLV 50cc scooter from **Left Bank Scooters** (www.leftbankscooters.com); they'll deliver/pick up from your hotel and arrange tours (from €130) as far as Versailles.

Public Transport

Paris' public transit system is operated by the **RATP** (www.ratp.fr). The same RATP tickets are valid on the metro, RER, buses, trams and Montmartre funicular. A single ticket/*carnet* of 10 costs €1.70/12.

One ticket covers travel between any two metro stations (no return journeys) for 1½ hours; you can transfer between buses and between buses and trams, but not from metro to bus or vice versa.

ON YOUR WAY

The official **Paris Île de France** (www.nouveau-paris-ile-de-france.fr) website is a treasure trove of information on the area.

Keep your ticket until you exit the station; ticket inspectors can fine you if you can't produce a valid ticket.

BUS Paris' bus system runs from 5.30am to 8.30pm Monday to Saturday, after which certain *service en soirée* (evening service) lines continue until midnight or 12.30am, when **Noctilien** (www.noctilien.fr) night buses, departing every hour between 12.30am and 5.30am, kick in. Two circular lines (the N01 and N02) link the four main train stations – St-Lazare, Gare de l'Est, Gare de Lyon and Montparnasse – plus popular nightspots such as Bastille, the Champs-Élysées, Pigalle and St-Germain. Look for blue *N* or 'Noctilien' signs.

Short bus rides (ie rides in one or two bus zones) cost one metro/bus ticket (€1.70 or €1.80 direct from the driver); longer rides require two. Remember to cancel *(oblitérer)* single-journey tickets in the *composteur* (cancelling machine) next to the driver.

METRO & RER Paris' underground network consists of the 14-line metro and the RER, a network of suburban train lines. Each metro train is known by the name of its terminus. The last metro train on each line begins sometime between 12.35am and 1.04am, before starting up again around 5.30am.

TOURIST PASSES The Mobilis card allows unlimited travel for one day in two to six zones (€6.10 to €17.30) on the metro, the RER, buses, trams and the Montmartre funicular; while the Paris Visite pass allows unlimited travel (including to/from airports) plus discounted entry to museums and activities and costs €8.80/14.40/19.60/28.30 for one to three zones for one/two/three/five days.

TRAVEL PASSES **Navigo** (www.navigo.fr, in French), like London's Oyster or Hong Kong's Octopus cards, consists of a weekly, monthly or yearly unlimited pass that can be recharged at Navigo machines in most metro stations; swipe the card across the electronic panel to go through turnstiles. Standard Navigo passes, available to anyone with an address in Île de France, are free but take up to three weeks to be issued. Otherwise pay €5 for a Nagivo Découverte (Navigo Discovery) card, issued on the spot. Both require a passport photo and can be recharged for periods of one week or more.

Otherwise, weekly tickets *(coupon hebdomadaire)* cost €17.20 for zones 1 and 2, valid Monday to Sunday; monthly tickets (*coupon mensuel*; €56.60 for zones 1 and 2) run from the first day of the month.

Taxi

The flag fall is €2.10, plus €0.89 per kilometre within the city limits from 10am and 5pm Monday to Saturday (Tarif A; white light on meter), and €1.14 per kilometre from 5pm to 10am, all day Sunday, and public holidays (Tarif B; orange light on meter).

Central taxi switchboard (☎01 45 30 30 30)

Alpha Taxis (☎01 45 85 85 85; www.alphataxis.com)

Taxis Bleus (☎01 49 36 29 48, 08 91 70 10 10; www.taxis-bleus.com)

Taxis G7 (☎01 47 39 47 39; www.taxisg7.fr, in French).

AROUND PARIS

Bordered by five rivers – the Epte, Aisne, Eure, Yonne and Marne – the area around Paris looks rather like a giant island, and indeed is known as Île de France. Centuries ago this was where French kings retreated to extravagant chateaux in Versailles and Fontainebleau. These days such royal castles have been joined by a kingdom of an altogether different kind.

Disneyland Paris

In 1992, Mickey Mouse, Snow White and chums set up shop on reclaimed sugar-beet fields 32km east of Paris at a cost of €4.6 billion. Though not quite as over-the-top as its American cousin, France's Disneyland packs in the crowds nonetheless.

The main **Disneyland Park** (⏲9am-11pm summer, 10am-8pm Mon-Fri, 9am-8pm Sat & Sun winter) comprises five *pays* (lands), including an idealised version of an American **Main St**, a recreation of the American Wild West in **Frontierland** with the legendary Big Thunder Mountain ride, futuristic **Discoveryland**, and the exotic-themed **Adventureland**, where you'll find the Pirates of the Caribbean and the spiralling 360-degrees roller coaster, Indiana Jones and the Temple of Peril. Pinocchio, Snow White and other fairy-tale characters come to life in candy-coated heart of the park, **Fantasyland**.

Adjacent **Walt Disney Studios Park** (⏲9am-6pm summer, 10am-6pm Mon-Fri, 9am-6pm Sat & Sun winter) has a sound stage, backlot and animation studios illustrating how films, TV programs and cartoons are produced.

Standard admission fees at **Disneyland Resort Paris** (www.disneylandparis.com; adult/child €52/44) only cover one park – to visit both buy a one-day pass costing €65/57 per adult/child. Multiday equivalents are also available, as are a multitude of special offers and accommodation/transport packages.

Marne-la-Vallée/Chessy, Disneyland's RER station, is served by line A4; trains run every 15 minutes or so from central Paris (€6.55, 35 to 40 minutes) with the last train back to Paris just after midnight. By car follow route A4 from Porte de Bercy (direction Metz-Nancy) and take exit 14.

Versailles

POP 88,930

The prosperous and leafy suburb of Versailles, 28km southwest of Paris, is the site of France's grandest and most famous chateau. It served as the kingdom's political capital and the seat of the royal court for more than a century – from 1682 until 1789 when Revolutionary mobs massacred the palace guard and dragged Louis XVI and Marie Antoinette back to Paris, where they eventually had their heads separated from their shoulders.

Dodge the worst of the crowds by visiting early morning or late afternoon, and buy your ticket in advance online (www.chateauversailles.fr) or from Fnac. Queues are longest on Tuesday (when many of Paris' museums are closed) and on Sunday.

SUMMER MAGIC

The palace gardens' largest fountains are the 17th-century **Bassin de Neptune** (Neptune's Fountain), a dazzling mirage of 99 spouting gushers 300m north of the palace. Watch them 'dance' in all their glory during summer's **Grandes Eaux Musicales** (adult/child €8/6; ⏲11am-noon & 3.30-5pm Tue, Sat & Sun Apr-Sep) or after-dark **Grandes Eaux Nocturnes** (adult/child €21/17; ⏲9-11.30pm Sat & Sun mid-Jun–Aug). Both 'dancing water' displays set to baroque and other classical music of the era are nothing sort of magical.

Sights

Château de Versailles PALACE

(www.chateauversailles.fr; adult/child & EU resident under 26yr €15/free; ⌚9am-6.30pm Tue-Sun summer, 9am-5.30pm Tue-Sun winter) Built in the mid-17th century by Louis XIV to project the absolute power of the French monarchy, Versailles palace was jointly designed by the architect Louis Le Vau, the painter and interior designer Charles Le Brun, and the landscape artist André Le Nôtre. It's a fabulous monument to the wealth and ambition of the French aristocracy.

The 580m-long palace is split into several wings, each with an astonishing array of grand halls, wood-panelled corridors and sumptuous bedchambers, including the **Grand Appartement du Roi** (King's Suite) and **Galerie des Glaces** (Hall of Mirrors), a 75m-long ballroom with 17 huge mirrors on one side. Outside are vast **landscaped gardens**, filled with canals, pools and neatly trimmed box hedges, and two outbuildings, the **Grand Trianon** and the **Petit Trianon**.

Standard admission includes an English-language audioguide and entry to the state apartments, the chapel, **Appartements du Dauphin et de la Dauphine** and various galleries. A **Passeport** (adult/child & EU resident under 26yr €18-25/free) includes the same, plus the two Trianons and, in high season, the Hameau de la Reine and the Grandes Eaux Musicales fountain displays.

The current €400-million restoration project is Versailles' most ambitious yet and until 2020 at least a part of the palace is likely to be clad in scaffolding.

Getting There & Away

RER line C5 (€2.95, every 15 minutes) goes from Paris' Left Bank RER stations to Versailles-Rive Gauche, 700m southeast of the chateau.

SNCF operates up to 70 trains daily from Paris' Gare St-Lazare (€3.70) to Versailles-Rive Droite, 1.2km from the chateau. Versailles-Chantiers is served by half-hourly SNCF trains daily from Gare Montparnasse (€2.95); trains continue to Chartres (€11.50, 30 to 60 minutes).

Chartres

POP 45,600

The magnificent 13th-century cathedral of Chartres, crowned by two very different spires – one Gothic, the other Romanesque – rises from rich farmland 88km southwest of Paris and dominates the medieval town. With its astonishing blue stained glass and other treasures, France's best-preserved medieval basilica is a must-see.

ZOOM IN

To study the extraordinary detail of Chartres' cathedral close up, rent binoculars (€2) from Chartres **tourist office** (☎02 37 18 26 26; www.chartres-tourisme.com; place de la Cathédrale; ⌚9am-7pm Mon-Sat, 9.30am-5.30pm Sun summer, 10am-6pm Mon-Sat, 10am-1pm & 2.30-4.30pm Sun winter), across the square from the cathedral's main entrance.

Sights

Cathédrale Notre Dame de Chartres CHURCH

(www.diocese-chartres.com, in French; place de la Cathédrale; ⌚8.30am-7.30pm daily, to 10pm Tue, Fri & Sun summer) The 130m-long Chartres cathedral takes your breath away. The original Romanesque cathedral was devastated in a fire in 1194, but remnants of it remain in the **Portail Royal** (Royal Portal) and the 103m-high **Clocher Vieux** (Old Bell Tower, also known as the South Tower). The rest of the cathedral predominantly dates from the 13th century, including many of the 172 glorious **stained-glass windows**, which are renowned for the depth and intensity of their 'Chartres blue' tones.

A visit up the lacy Flamboyant Gothic, 112m-tall **Clocher Neuf** (New Bell Tower; adult/child €7/free, free to all 1st Sun of certain months; ⌚9.30am-12.30pm & 2-6pm Mon-Sat, 2-6pm Sun summer, to 5pm winter) rewards with superb views of the three-tiered flying buttresses and the 19th-century copper roof, turned green by verdigris.

Getting There & Away

Some three dozen SNCF trains a day link Paris' Gare Montparnasse (€13.60, 55 to 70 minutes) with Chartres via Versailles-Chantiers (€11.50, 45 minutes to one hour).

LILLE, FLANDERS & THE SOMME

When it comes to culture, cuisine, beer, shopping and dramatic views of land and sea, the friendly Ch'tis (residents of France's northern tip) and their region compete with the best France has to offer: Flemish-style Lille, the cross-Channel shopping centre of Calais, and the moving battlefields and cemeteries of WWI.

Lille

POP 232,000

Lille (Rijsel in Flemish) may be the country's most underrated major city. In recent decades this once-grimy industrial metropolis has transformed itself – with generous government help – into a glittering and self-confident cultural and commercial hub. Highlights of the city include an attractive Old Town with a strong Flemish accent, three renowned art museums, stylish shopping and a cutting-edge, student-driven nightlife.

Sights

Vieux Lille OLD TOWN

Lille's Old Town, which begins just north of place du Général de Gaulle, is justly proud of its restored 17th- and 18th-century houses. Those along **rue de la Monnaie** house the city's chicest boutiques and the **Hospice Comtesse Museum** (32 rue de la Monnaie; adult €3.50; 10am-12.30pm & 2-6pm, closed Mon morning & Tue), featuring mainly religious art.

Nearby, the 1652 **Vieille Bourse** (Old Stock Exchange; place du Général de Gaulle; M Rihour) consists of 24 houses decorated with caryatids and cornucopia.

Palais des Beaux Arts ART MUSEUM

(Fine Arts Museum; www.pba-lille.fr; place de la République; adult/child €5.50/free; 2-6pm Mon, 10am-6pm Wed-Sun; M République Beaux Arts) Lille's world-renowned fine-arts museum has a first-rate collection of 15th- to 20th-century paintings, including works by Rubens, Van Dyck and Manet.

La Piscine Musée d'Art et d'Industrie ART MUSEUM

(www.roubaix-lapiscine.com; 23 rue de l'Espérance, Roubaix; adult/child €4.50/free; 11am-6pm Tue-Thu, 11am-8pm Fri, 1-6pm Sat & Sun; M Gare Jean Lebas) Housed in an art deco swimming pool (built 1927–32), this gallery 12km northeast of Gare Lille-Europe, showcases fine arts, applied arts and sculpture in a delightfully watery environment.

Sleeping

TOP CHOICE **L'Hermitage Gantois** DESIGN HOTEL €€€

(03 20 85 30 30; www.hotelhermitagegantois.com; 224 rue de Paris; d €215-325; @; M Mairie de Lille) We love the highly civilised atrium and 67 huge, luxurious rooms at this mix of Flemish-Gothic facade and refined ultra-modernist interiors. Starck accessories mingle with Louis XV–style chairs, and bathrooms sparkle with Carrara marble. The still-consecrated chapel was built in 1637.

Hôtel Brueghel HOTEL €€

(03 20 06 06 69; www.hotel-brueghel.com; 5 parvis St-Maurice; d €89; ; M Gare Lille-Flandres) The 65 rooms here mix vaguely antique furnishings with modern styling, though they don't have as much Flemish charm as the lobby. Some south-facing rooms have sunny views of the adjacent church.

Hôtel du Moulin d'Or HOTEL €€

(03 20 06 12 67; www.hotelmoulindor.com, in French; 15 rue du Molinel; d/tr €87/98; ; M Gare Lille-Flandres) Rich yellow and blue tones welcome you warmly to this family-run establishment with 14 rooms, some flowery, others striped. The cute little breakfast room feels like a B&B. No lift.

Auberge de Jeunesse HOSTEL €

(03 20 57 08 94; www.hihostels.com; 12 rue Malpart; dm incl breakfast €18, d €37; Feb–mid-Dec; @; M Mairie de Lille) This central former maternity hospital has 163 beds in rooms for two to eight, kitchen facilities and free parking. A few doubles have en-suite showers. Lockout 11am to 3pm (4pm Friday to Sunday).

Eating

Keep an eye out for *estaminets* (traditional eateries) serving Flemish specialities such as *carbonnade* (beef braised with Flemish beer, spice bread and brown sugar).

OLD TOWN EAT STREETS

» **Rue de Gand** Small, moderately priced French and Flemish restaurants.

» **Rue de la Monnaie** Quirky restaurants here and on neighbouring side streets.

» **Rue Royale** Ethnic cuisine (couscous, Japanese etc).

» **Rue Solférino** & **rue Masséna** Lively, student-dominated cheap eats near the Palais des Beaux-Arts.

Chez la Vieille TRADITIONAL €
(☎03 28 36 40 06; 60 rue de Gand; mains €9.50-12; ⊙Tue-Sat) One of the best places in Lille to tuck into Flemish specialities. Old-time prints, antiques and fresh hops hanging from the rafters create the ambience of a Flemish village c 1900. The vibe is informal but it's a good idea to call ahead.

À l'Huîtrière SEAFOOD €€€
(☎03 20 55 43 41; www.huitriere.fr, in French; 3 rue des Chats Bossus; lunch menus €45; ⊙Mon-Sat, lunch Sun Sep-Jul) On the 'Street of the Hunchback Cats', this sophisticated restaurant is as well known for its stunning art deco trappings – think sea-themed mosaics and stained glass – as for its fabulous seafood and wine cellar.

Meert TEAROOM €
(www.meert.fr; 27 rue Esquermoise; ⊙9.30am-7.30pm Tue-Fri, 9am-7.30pm Sat, 9am-1pm & 3-7pm Sun; MRihr) Vanilla-flavoured *gaufres* (waffles; €2.30 each) are the speciality of this luxury tearoom-cum-pastry-and-sweets-shop, in the biz since 1761. Its adjacent **chocolate shop** (per kg €89) transports you to 1839.

TOP CHOICE **Marché de Wazemmes** FOOD MARKET €
(place de la Nouvelle Aventure; ⊙8am-2pm Tue-Thu, 8am-8pm Fri & Sat, 8am-3pm Sun & holidays; MGambetta) Beloved foodie space, 1.7km southwest of the tourist office in Lille's working-class quarter of Wazemmes.

Drinking

Think two key nightlife zones: Vieux Lille's small, chic bars, and the student-oriented bars around rue Masséna and rue Solférino. In summer, pavement cafe terraces render place de la Théâtre in front of the opera prime beer-sipping terrain.

L'Illustration Café BAR, CAFE
(www.bar-lillustration.com, in French; 18 rue Royale; ⊙12.30pm-3am Mon-Sat, 2pm-3am Sun) Adorned with art nouveau woodwork and changing exhibits by local painters, this laid-back bar attracts artists, musicians, budding intellectuals and teachers in the mood to read, exchange weighty ideas – or just shoot the breeze. The mellow soundtrack mixes Western classical with jazz, French *chansons* and African beats.

DON'T MISS

NORTHERN BREWS

French Flanders brews some truly excellent *bière blonde* (lager) and *bière ambrée* (amber beer) with an alcohol content of up to 8.5%. Brands that give the Belgian brewers a run for their money include 3 Monts, Amadeus, Ambre des Flandres, Brasserie des 2 Caps, Ch'ti, Enfants de Gayant, Grain d'Orge, Hellemus, Jenlain, L'Angellus, La Wambrechies, Moulins d'Ascq, Raoul, Septante 5, St-Landelin, Triple Secret des Moines and Vieux Lille.

Information

Tourist office (☎from abroad 03 59 57 94 00, in France 08 91 56 20 04; www.lilletourism.com; place Rihour; ⊙9.30am-6.30pm Mon-Sat, 10am-noon & 2-5pm Sun; MRihr) Sells the Lille City Pass (one-/two-/three-day €20/30/45) covering Lille's museums and public transport.

Getting There & Away

Eurolines (☎08 92 89 90 91; www.eurolines.com; 23 parvis St-Maurice; MGare Lille-Flandres) Serves cities such as Brussels (€17, 1½ hours), Amsterdam (€42, five hours) and London (€35, 5½ hours; by day via the Channel Tunnel, at night by ferry). Buses depart from blvd de Leeds near Gare Lille-Europe.

Lille has two train stations: Gare Lille-Flandres for regional services and Paris' Gare du Nord (€40 to €55, one hour, 14 to 18 daily), and ultramodern Gare Lille-Europe for all other trains, including Eurostars to London and TGVs/Eurostars to Brussels-Nord (€18 to €26, 35 minutes, 12 daily).

Getting Around

Lille's two metro lines, tramways and bus lines are run by **Transpole** (www.transpole.fr). Tickets (€1.30) are sold on buses but must be purchased (and validated in the orange posts) *before* boarding a metro or tram. A Pass Journée (all-day pass) costs €3.60.

Calais

POP 76,200

As Churchill might have put it, 'Never in the field of human tourism have so many travellers passed through a place and so few stopped to visit'. Over 15 million people pass through Calais en route to the cross-Channel ferries, but few explore the town itself – it's worth it, if only to see Rodin's famous sculpture, *The Burghers of Calais*.

Sights

Burghers of Calais SCULPTURE

By the time you read this, it should be possible to ride a lift up to the top of the Unesco World Heritage–listed **belfry** crowning Calais' Flemish Renaissance-style **town hall** (1911–25). Inside is the town's main sight: Rodin's *Les Bourgeois de Calais* (The Burghers of Calais; 1895), honouring six local citizens who, in 1347, held off the besieging English forces for more than eight months. Edward III was so impressed he ultimately spared the Calaisiens and their six leaders.

TOP CHOICE **Musée de la Dentelle et de la Mode** LACE MUSEUM

(www.cite-dentelle.fr; 135 quai du Commerce; €5; ⏲10am-5 or 6pm Wed-Mon) Watch a century-old mechanical loom with 3500 vertical threads and 11,000 horizontal ones bang, clatter and clunk according to instructions given by perforated Jacquard cards at Calais' cutting-edge Lace and Fashion Museum.

Sleeping

TOP CHOICE **Hôtel Meurice** HOTEL €€

(☎03 21 34 57 03; www.hotel-meurice.fr; 5-7 rue Edmond Roche; d €85-150; @🛜) Meurice is a veteran hotel with 39 rooms and plenty of atmosphere thanks to its grand lobby staircase, antique furnishings, Hemingwayesque bar and breakfast room with garden views.

Auberge de Jeunesse HOSTEL €

(☎03 21 34 70 20; www.auberge-jeunesse-calais.com; av Maréchal de Lattre de Tassigny; s/d incl breakfast €26/38; 🛜) Modern, well equipped and just 200m from the beach. Take bus 3, 5 or 9.

Eating

Restaurants ring place d'Armes and are plentiful just south of there along rue Royale.

Histoire Ancienne BISTRO €

(☎03 21 34 11 20; www.histoire-ancienne.com; 20 rue Royale; lunch/dinner menus from €13/19; ⏲Tue-Sat, lunch Mon) Specialising in French and regional dishes, some grilled over an open wood fire, this 1930s Paris-style bistro has treats such as *escargots à l'ail* (garlic snails).

Information

Tourist office (☎03 21 96 62 40; www.calais-cotedopale.com; 12 blvd Georges Clemenceau; ⏲9 or 10am–6 or 7pm, closed Sun mid-Sep–Mar)

Getting There & Around

Boat

Daily some 40-odd car ferries from Dover dock at Calais' bustling car-ferry terminal, 1.5km northeast of place d'Armes.

P&O Ferries Calais town centre (www.poferries.com; 41 place d'Armes); car-ferry terminal (⏲6am-10pm); car-ferry car park (⏲24hr) The only ferry company that still takes foot passengers across the Strait of Dover.

SeaFrance Calais town centre (www.seafrance.com; 2 place d'Armes); car-ferry car park (⏲24hr)

Shuttle buses (€2, hourly 11am to 6 or 7pm) link Gare Calais-Ville (train station) and place d'Armes (stopping in front of Café de la Tour) with the car-ferry terminal. Departure times are posted at stops.

Bus

Ligne BCD (☎08 00 62 00 59; www.ligne-bcd.com, in French) links Calais' train station (hours posted) with Dunkirk (€8, 50 minutes, 11 daily Monday to Friday, three on Saturday).

Car & Motorcycle

To reach the Channel Tunnel's vehicle-loading area at Coquelles, 6km southwest of the town centre, follow the road signs on the A16 to 'Tunnel Sous La Manche' (exit 42).

Train

Calais has two train stations: **Gare Calais-Ville**, 650m south of main square place d'Armes; and TGV station **Gare Calais-Fréthun**, 10km southwest near the Channel Tunnel entrance. Trains and shuttle buses (€2, free with train ticket) link the two.

Gare Calais-Ville serves Amiens (€24, 2½ to 3½ hours, six to eight daily), Boulogne (€7.50, 30 minutes, up to 19 daily), Dunkirk (€8, 50 minutes, two to five Monday to Saturday) and Lille-Flandres (€16, 1¼ hours, eight to 19 daily).

Gare Calais-Fréthun is served by TGVs to Paris' Gare du Nord (€41 to €62, 1½ hours, three to six daily) and Eurostars to London St-Pancras (€149, one hour, three daily).

Dunkirk

POP 69,500

Made famous and flattened almost simultaneously in 1940, Dunkirk (Dunkerque) was unfortunately rebuilt during one of the most uninspired periods in Western architecture. Admire a spectacular view of it from the 15th-century, 58m-high **belfry** (adult €2.90) housing the **tourist office** (☎03 28 66 79 21; www.lesdunesdeflandre.fr; rue de l'Amiral Ronarc'h);

WORTH A TRIP

CÔTE D'OPALE

For a dramatic and beautiful intro to France, head to the 40km of majestic cliffs, sand dunes and beaches between Calais and Boulogne. Known as the Côte d'Opale (Opal Coast) because of the ever-changing interplay of greys and blues in the sky and sea, it is a kaleidoscope of wind-buffeted coastal peaks, wide beaches and rolling farmland. The remains of Nazi Germany's Atlantic Wall, a chain of fortifications and gun emplacements built to prevent the Allied invasion that in the end took place in Normandy, stud the shore, much loved by British beach-goers since Victorian times.

Protected by the **Parc Naturel Régional des Caps et Marais d'Opale** (www.parc-opale.fr), the area is criss-crossed by hiking paths, including the **GR120 Littoral trail** (red-and-white trail markings) that snakes along the coast – except where the cliffs are in danger of collapse. Some trails are open to mountain bikers and those on horseback. Each village along the Côte d'Opale has at least one camping ground, and most have places to eat.

By car, the D940 offers some truly spectacular vistas – or hop aboard Inglard's bus 44, which links the string of villages between Calais and Boulogne.

its melodious, 50-bell carillon inside sounds every quarter-hour.

Ship-model lovers will enjoy this port city's **Musée Portuaire** (Harbour Museum; www.museeportuaire.com; 9 quai de la Citadelle; adult/family €5/13; ⏲10am-12.45pm & 1.30-6pm Wed-Mon), housed in a one-time tobacco warehouse. **Guided tours** (adult/family incl museum €10/15) take visitors aboard a lighthouse ship, a *peniche* (barge) and a three-masted training ship built for the German merchant marine in 1901.

Malo-les-Bains, 2km northeast of Dunkirk city centre, is a turn-of-the-20th-century seaside resort whose broad, sandy beach, **Plage des Alliés**, honours Allied troops evacuated to England during Operation Dynamo. Stretching east to the Belgian border, the **Dunes Flamandes** (Flemish Dunes) represent a unique ecosystem harbouring hundreds of plant species, including rare orchids. Tides permitting, walk or cycle along the wet sand or path from Malo-les-Bains to Leffrinckoucke, Zuydcoote and Bray-Dunes.

Most trains from Dunkirk's train station, 1km southwest of the tourist office, stop at Gare Lille-Flandres (€13, 30 to 80 minutes, up to 20 daily).

NORMANDY

Famous for cows, cider and Camembert, this largely rural region (www.normandie-tourisme.fr) is one of France's most traditional – and most visited thanks to world-renowned sights such as the Bayeux Tapestry, historic D-Day beaches, Monet's garden at Giverny and spectacular Mont St Michel.

Rouen

POP 120,000

With its elegant spires, beautifully restored medieval quarter and soaring Gothic cathedral, the ancient city of Rouen is a Normandy highlight. Devastated several times during the Middle Ages by fire and plague, the city was later badly damaged by WWII bombing raids, but has been meticulously rebuilt over the last six decades. The city makes an ideal base for exploring the northern Normandy coast.

Sights

Église Jeanne d'Arc CHURCH

(place du Vieux Marché) The old city's main thoroughfare, rue du Gros Horloge, runs from the cathedral west to **place du Vieux Marché**. Dedicated in 1979, the thrillingly bizarre Église Jeanne d'Arc, with its fish-scale exterior, marks the spot where 19-year-old Joan of Arc was burned at the stake in 1431.

Cathédrale Notre Dame CATHEDRAL

(place de la Cathédrale; ⏲2-7pm Mon, 7.30am-7pm Tue-Sat, 8am-6pm Sun) Rouen's stunning Gothic cathedral, with its polished, brilliant-white facade, is the famous subject of a series of paintings by Monet. Its 75m-tall **Tour de Beurre** (Butter Tower) was financed by locals who donated to the cathedral in return for being allowed to eat butter during Lent – or so the story goes.

Musée des Beaux-Arts ART MUSEUM
(esplanade Marcel Duchamp; adult/child €5/free; ⏲10am-6pm Wed-Mon) Housed in a grand structure erected in 1870, Rouen's fine-arts museum features canvases by Caravaggio, Rubens, Modigliani, Pissarro, Renoir, Sisley (lots) and (of course) several works by Monet.

Musée Le Secq des Tournelles MUSEUM
(☎02 35 88 42 92; 2 rue Jacques Villon; adult/child €3/free; ⏲10am-1pm & 2-6pm Wed-Mon) Inside a desanctified 16th-century church, this riveting museum examines the blacksmith's craft.

DON'T MISS

THE CIDER ROAD

Normandy's signposted 40km **Route du Cidre**, about 20km east of Caen, wends its way through the Pays d'Auge, a rural area of orchards, pastures, hedgerows, half-timbered farmhouses and stud farms, through picturesque villages such as Cambremer and Beuvron-en-Auge. Along the way, signs reading 'Cru de Cambremer' indicate the way to about 20 small-scale, traditional producers who are happy to show you their facilities and sell you their home-grown cider (€3 a bottle) and Calvados.

Sleeping

Hôtel des Carmes HOTEL €
(☎02 35 71 92 31; www.hoteldescarmes.com, in French; 33 place des Carmes; d €49-65, tr €67-77; @ 📶) This sweet little number has a dozen rooms with bright, quirky decor; some have cerulean-blue cloudscapes painted on the ceilings. Burn off some Camembert calories by taking one of the cheaper, 4th-floor rooms.

TOP CHOICE **Hôtel de Bourgtheroulde** HOTEL €€€
(☎02 35 14 50 50; www.hotelsparouen.com; 15 place de la Pucelle; r €215-380; ❄ 📶 ≋) This stunning conversion of an old private mansion brings a dash of glamour and luxury to Rouen's hotel scene. Rooms are large, gorgeously designed and feature beautiful bathrooms.

Hôtel de la Cathédrale HOTEL €
(☎02 35 71 57 95; www.hotel-de-la-cathedrale.fr; 12 rue St-Romain; s €56-79, d €66-96, q €119; 📶) Hiding behind a 17th-century half-timbered facade, this atmospheric hotel has 27 stylishly refitted rooms, mostly overlooking a quiet plant-filled courtyard.

Hôtel Dandy HOTEL €€
(☎02 35 07 32 00; www.hotels-rouen.net; 93 rue Cauchoise; d €80-105; 📶) Decorated in a grand Louis XV style, this charming place has individually designed rooms brimming

WORTH A TRIP

KILLING FIELDS

The **Battle of the Somme**, a WWI Allied offensive waged northeast of Amiens, was planned with the goal of relieving the pressure on the beleaguered French troops at Verdun. On 1 July 1916, two-dozen divisions of British, Commonwealth and French troops went 'over the top' in a massive assault along a 34km front. But German positions proved virtually unbreachable, and on the first day alone 21,392 Allied troops were killed and another 35,492 were wounded.

By the time the offensive was called off in mid-November, some 1.2 million lives had been lost: the British had advanced just 12km, the French 8km. The Battle of the Somme has since become a symbol of the meaningless slaughter of war and its killing fields and cemeteries have since become a site of pilgrimage (see www.somme-battlefields.co.uk). The tourist offices in **Amiens** (☎03 22 71 60 50; www.amiens.com/tourisme) and **Arras** (☎03 21 51 26 95; www.ot-arras.fr) supply maps, guides and minibus tours.

Cheap, spartan but oozing soul are the dorm facilities in Arras at **Maison St-Vaast** (☎03 21 21 40 38; http://arras.catholique.fr/page-15065.html, in French; 103 rue d'Amiens; dm per person €21; 📶). A convent in the 1600s and rebuilt after WWI, the atmospheric building has a lovely cloister and a 1920s chapel with stained glass and a frequently played pipe organ.

Rouen

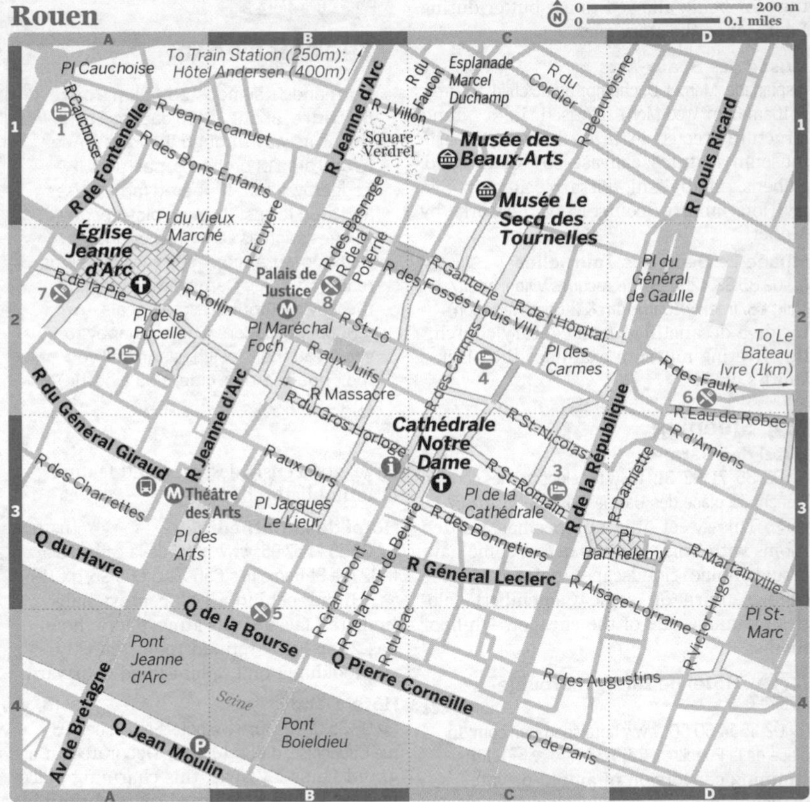

with character and is passionately run by a friendly family.

Hôtel Andersen HOTEL €
(☎02 35 71 88 51; www.hotelandersen.com; 4 rue Pouchet; s €45-56, d €56-63;) Ensconced in an early-19th-century mansion, this quietly stylish hotel with old-world atmosphere, classical music and 15 spare but imaginative rooms is one of a half-dozen hotels around the train station.

Eating

Little eateries crowd the north side of rue Martainville. For ethnic cuisine head two blocks south to rue des Augustins. More restaurants can be found along rue de Fontenelle (a block west of Église Jeanne d'Arc), and a few blocks east along rue Ecuyère.

TOP CHOICE **Les Nymphéas** NORMAN €€
(☎02 35 89 26 69; www.lesnympheas-rouen.com, in French; 7-9 rue de la Pie; menus €30-70; Tue-Sat) Its formal table settings arrayed under 16th-century beams, this fine restaurant serves cuisine based on fresh local ingredients, giving a rich Norman twist to dishes such as farm-raised wild duck, scallops and lobster.

Gill GASTRONOMIC €€
(☎02 35 71 16 14; www.gill.fr; 8-9 quai de la Bourse; menus €35-92; Tue-Sat) *The* place to go in Rouen for French cuisine of the highest order, served in an ultrachic, modern space. Specialities include Breton lobster, scallops with truffles, Rouen-style pigeon and, for dessert, *millefeuille à la vanille*.

Le P'tit Bec BISTRO €
(☎02 35 07 63 33; www.leptitbec.com, in French; 182 rue Eau de Robec; menus €13-15.50; lunch Mon-Sat, dinner Fri & Sat, also open dinner Tue-Thu Jun-Aug;) The down-to-earth menu here is stuffed with pasta, salads, *œufs cocottes* (eggs with grated cheese baked in cream),

Rouen

Top Sights

Cathédrale Notre Dame....................C3
Église Jeanne d'Arc....................A2
Musée des Beaux-Arts....................C1
Musée Le Secq des Tournelles....................C1

Sleeping

1 Hôtel Dandy....................A1
2 Hôtel de Bourgtheroulde....................A2
3 Hôtel de la Cathédrale....................C3
4 Hôtel des Carmes....................C2

Eating

5 Gill....................B4
6 Le P'tit Bec....................D2
7 Les Nymphéas....................A2
8 Pascaline....................B2

several vegetarian options and homemade desserts. Its summer terrace sits on one of Rouen's most picturesque side streets.

Pascaline BISTRO €
(☎02 35 89 67 44; 5 rue de la Poterne; mains €10-20) A top spot for a great-value lunch, this bustling bistro serves up traditional French cuisine in typically Parisian surroundings. Live piano nightly and jazz on Thursdays.

Information

Tourist office (☎02 32 08 32 40; www.rouentourisme.com; 25 place de la Cathédrale; ⏲9am-7pm Mon-Sat, 9.30am-12.30pm & 2-6pm Sun) Hotel reservations cost €3; audioguides (€5).

Getting There & Away

TRAIN Some direct train services from **Gare Rouen-Rive Droite** (rue Jeanne d'Arc):

Amiens €18.20, 1¼ hours, four or five daily.
Caen €23.30, 1½ hours, eight to 10 daily.
Dieppe €10.40, 45 minutes, up to 16 daily.
Le Havre €13.60, 50 minutes, 10 to 18 daily.
Paris St-Lazare €20.50, 1¼ hours, up to 25 daily.

Bayeux

POP 14,350

Bayeux has become famous throughout the English-speaking world thanks to a 68m-long piece of painstakingly embroidered cloth: the 11th-century Bayeux Tapestry, whose 58 scenes vividly tell the story of the Norman invasion of England in 1066. The town is also one of the few in Normandy to have survived WWII practically unscathed, with a centre crammed with 13th- to 18th-century buildings, wooden-framed Norman-style houses, and a spectacular Norman Gothic cathedral.

Sights

TOP CHOICE **Bayeux Tapestry** TAPESTRY
(www.tapisserie-bayeux.fr; rue de Nesmond; admission incl audioguide €7.80; ⏲9am-6.30pm mid-Mar–mid-Nov, to 7pm May-Aug, 9.30am-12.30pm & 2-6pm mid-Nov–mid-Mar) The world's most celebrated embroidery recounts the conquest of England from an unashamedly Norman perspective. Fifty-eight scenes fill the central canvas, and religious allegories and illustrations of everyday 11th-century life fill the borders. The final showdown at the Battle of Hastings is depicted in graphic fashion, complete with severed limbs and decapitated heads (along the bottom of scene 52); Halley's Comet, which blazed across the sky in 1066, appears in

DON'T MISS

MAISON DE CLAUDE MONET

Monet's home for the last 43 years of his life is now the delightful **Maison et Jardins de Claude Monet** (☎02 32 51 28 21; www.fondation-monet.com; adult/child €6/3.50; ⏲9.30am-6pm Apr-Oct), where you can view the Impressionist's pastel-pink house and famous gardens with lily pond, Japanese bridge draped in purple wisteria, and so on. Early to late spring, daffodils, tulips, rhododendrons, wisteria and irises bloom in the flowery gardens, followed by poppies and lilies. By June, nasturtiums, roses and sweet peas are in flower, while September is the month to see dahlias, sunflowers and hollyhocks.

The gardens are in Giverny, 66km southeast of Rouen. Several trains (€10.10, 40 minutes) leave Rouen before noon; with hourly return trains between 5pm and 10pm (9pm Sat). From Paris' Gare St-Lazare two early-morning trains run to Vernon (€12.50, 50 minutes), 7km to the west of Giverny, from where **shuttle buses** (☎08 25 07 60 27; www.mobiregion.net; €4 return) shunt passengers to Giverny.

scene 32. Scholars believe the 68.3m-long tapestry was commissioned by Bishop Odo of Bayeux, William the Conquerer's half-brother, for the opening of Bayeux' cathedral in 1077. For an animated version of the Bayeux Tapestry, check out David Newton's creative short film on YouTube.

Musée Mémorial de la Bataille de Normandie WAR MUSEUM
(Battle of Normandy Memorial Museum; blvd Fabien Ware; adult/student €6.50/3.80; ⌚9.30am-6.30pm May-Sep, 10am-12.30pm & 2-6pm Oct-Apr) Using well-chosen photos, personal accounts, dioramas and wartime objects, this first-rate museum offers an excellent introduction to WWII in Normandy. Don't miss the 25-minute film on the Battle of Normandy, screened in English up to five times daily. Nearby, the **Bayeux War Cemetery** (blvd Fabien Ware) contains the graves of 4848 soldiers from the UK and 10 other countries (including Germany).

Sleeping

Family Home HOSTEL €
(☎02 31 92 15 22; 39 rue Général de Dais; dm/s €19/30) One of France's most charming hostels, this place sports a 17th-century dining room, a delightful 16th-century courtyard, and 80 beds in rooms for one to four people. Check in any time of day – if reception isn't staffed, phone and someone will pop by.

Château de Bellefontaine CHATEAU HOTEL €€
(☎02 31 22 00 10; www.hotel-bellefontaine.com; 49 rue de Bellefontaine; d €125-150; 📶) Swans and a bubbling brook welcome you to this majestic 18th-century chateau, surrounded by a 2-hectare private park 1.5km southeast of town. Decor mixes tradition with modernity, and the rural location couldn't be more pastoral.

Hôtel Reine Mathilde HOTEL €
(☎02 31 92 08 13; www.hotel-bayeux-reinemathilde.fr; 23 rue Larcher; d €60-63, tr/q €73/85; 📶) Located above a bustling cafe, this charming little hotel is an excellent bet, right in the centre of town. Rooms, smallish but comfortable, are named after Norman folk of yore.

Eating

Rue St-Jean and rue St-Martin are home to cheap eateries and food shops. Appropriately, rue des Cuisiniers (north of the cathedral) is another handy, restaurant-busy street. Be sure to sample local speciality *cochon de Bayeux* (Bayeux-style pork).

DON'T MISS

CAEN MÉMORIAL

Caen's hi-tech, hugely impressive **Mémorial – Un Musée pour la Paix** (Memorial – A Museum for Peace; www.memorial-caen.fr; Esplanade Général Eisenhower; adult/child €17.50/free; ⌚9am-7pm Mar-Oct, 9.30am-6pm Tue-Sun Nov-Feb) uses sound, lighting, film, animation and lots of exhibits to graphically explore and evoke the events of WWII, D-Day landings and the ensuing Cold War. Tickets remain valid for 24 hours. The museum also runs D-Day beach tours.

La Reine Mathilde CAKE SHOP €
(47 rue St-Martin; cakes from €2.50; ⌚8.30am-7.30pm Tue-Sun) A sumptuous, c 1900-style patisserie and *salon de thé* (tearoom) that's ideal if you've got a hankering for something sweet. There's seating here, making it prime breakfast and afternoon-tea terrain.

La Rapière NORMAN €€
(☎02 31 21 05 45; 53 rue St-Jean; menus €15-33.50; ⌚Fri-Tue) Housed in a late-1400s mansion held together by its original oak beams, this restaurant specialises in hearty home cooking – the *timbale de pêcheur* (fisherman's stew) is served up piping hot in a cast-iron pan. For dessert, an excellent option is *trou normand* (apple sorbet with a dash of Calvados).

Information

Tourist office (☎02 31 51 28 28; www.bayeux-bessin-tourism.com; pont St-Jean; ⌚9.30am-12.30pm & 2-6pm)

Getting There & Away

Trains link Bayeux with Caen (€5.80, 20 minutes, up to 13 daily), from where there are connections to Paris' Gare St-Lazare (€31.20, two hours) and Rouen (€22.70, 1½ hours).

D-Day Beaches

The D-Day landings, code-named 'Operation Overlord', were the largest military operation in history. Early on 6 June 1944, Allied troops stormed ashore along 80km of beaches north of Bayeux, code-named (from west to east) Utah, Omaha, Gold, Juno and Sword. The landings on D-Day – called Jour J in French – were followed by the Battle of Normandy, which ultimately led to the liberation of Europe from Nazi occupation. Memorial museums in Caen (see the boxed text, p358) and Bayeux (p358) provide a comprehensive overview, and there are many small D-Day museums dotted along the coast. For context, see www.normandiememoire.com and www.6juin1944.com.

The most brutal fighting on D-Day took place 15km northwest of Bayeux along the stretch of coastline now known as **Omaha Beach**, today a glorious stretch of fine golden sand partly lined with sand dunes and summer homes. **Circuit de la Plage d'Omaha**, trail-marked with a yellow stripe, is a self-guided tour along the beach, surveyed from a bluff above by the huge **Normandy American Cemetery & Memorial** (www.abmc.gov; Colleville-sur-Mer; ⌚9am-5pm). Featured in the opening scenes of Steven Spielberg's *Saving Private Ryan*, this is the largest American cemetery in Europe.

Tours

Mémorial MINIBUS

(www.memorial-caen.fr; tours €69) Excellent year-round minibus tours (four to five hours). Rates include entry to Mémorial. Book online.

Normandy Sightseeing Tours WALKING, MINIBUS

(☎02 31 51 70 52; www.normandywebguide.com) Half-/full-day tours (€40/75) of various beaches and cemeteries.

Getting There & Away

Bus Verts (www.busverts.fr, in French) bus 70 (two or three daily Monday to Saturday, more in summer) goes northwest from Bayeux to Colleville-sur-Mer and Omaha Beach (€2.15, 35 minutes).

Mont St-Michel

On a rocky island opposite the coastal town of Pontorson, connected to the mainland by a narrow causeway, the sky-scraping turrets of the abbey of **Mont St-Michel** (☎02 33 89 80 00; www.monuments-nationaux.fr; adult/child incl guided tour €8.50/free; ⌚9am-7pm May-Aug, 9.30am-6pm Sep-Apr, last entry 1hr before closing) provide one of France's iconic sights. The surrounding bay is notorious for its fast-rising tides: at low tide the Mont is surrounded by bare sand for miles around; at high tide, just six hours later, the bay, causeway and nearby car parks can be submerged.

From the **tourist office** (☎02 33 60 14 30; www.ot-montsaintmichel.com; ⌚9am-7pm Jul & Aug, 9am-12.30pm & 2-6.30pm Mon-Sat, 9am-noon & 2-6pm Sun Apr-Jun & Sep, shorter hours winter), at the base of the mount, a cobbled street winds up to the **Église Abbatiale** (Abbey Church), incorporating elements of both Norman and Gothic architecture. Other notable sights include the arched **cloître** (cloister), the barrel-roofed **réfectoire** (dining hall), and the Gothic **Salle des Hôtes** (Guest Hall), dating from 1213. A one-hour tour is included with admission; English tours run hourly in summer, twice daily (11am and 3pm) in winter. In July and August, Monday to Saturday, there are illuminated *nocturnes* (night-time visits) with music from 7pm to 10pm.

Bus 6 (☎08 00 15 00 50; www.mobi50.com, in French) links Mont St-Michel with Pontorson (€2, 13 minutes), from where there are two to three daily trains to/from Bayeux (€20.80, 1¾hr) and Cherbourg (€25.90, three hours).

BRITTANY

Brittany is for explorers. Its wild, dramatic coastline, medieval towns, thick forests and eeriest stone circles this side of Stonehenge make a trip here well worth the detour from the beaten track. This is a land of prehistoric mysticism, proud tradition and culinary wealth, where locals still remain fiercely independent, where Breton culture (and cider) is celebrated and where Paris feels a very long way away indeed.

KNOW THE TIDE

Check the *horaire des marées* (tide table) at the tourist office. When the tide is out, you can walk all the way around Mont St-Michel, a distance of about 1km. Stray too far from the Mont and you risk getting stuck in wet sand – from which Norman soldiers are depicted being rescued in one scene of the Bayeux Tapestry – or being overtaken by the incoming tide, providing your next of kin with a great cocktail-party story.

Quimper

POP 67,250

Small enough to feel like a village – with its slanted half-timbered houses and narrow cobbled streets – and large enough to buzz as the troubadour of Breton culture, Quimper (pronounced *kam-pair*) is the thriving capital of Finistère (meaning 'land's end'; in Breton *Penn ar Bed*, meaning 'head of the world').

Sights

Most of Quimper's historic architecture is concentrated in a tight triangle formed by place Médard, rue Kéréon, rue des Gentilhommes and its continuation, rue du Sallé, to place au Beurre.

Cathédrale St-Corentin CHURCH
(9.30am-noon & 1.30-6.30pm) At the centre of the city is the cathedral with its distinctive

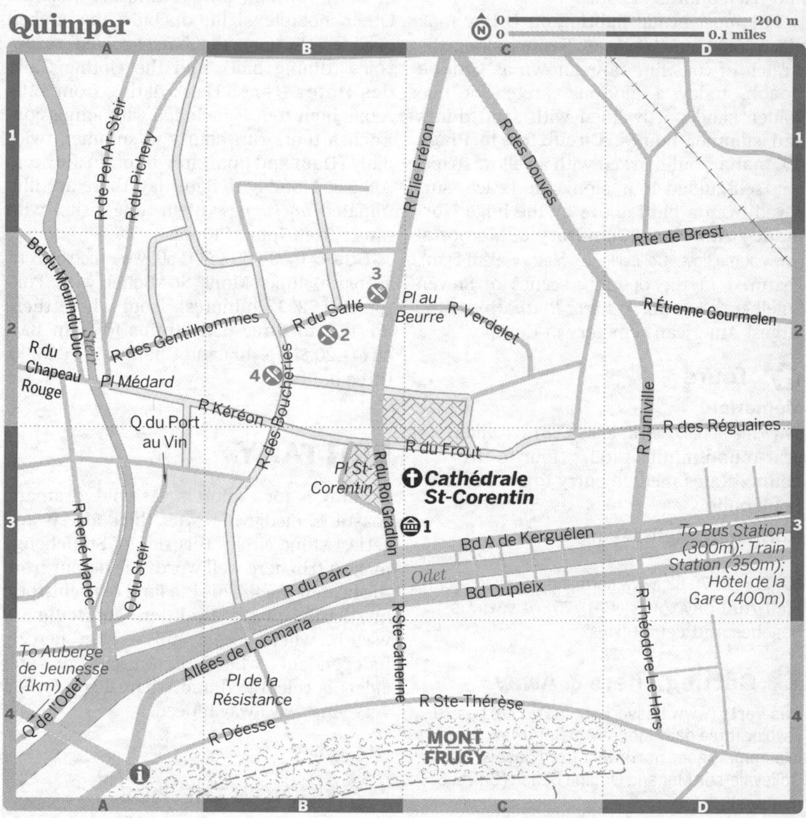

kink, said to symbolise Christ's inclined head as he was dying on the cross. Construction began in 1239 but the cathedral's dramatic twin spires weren't added until the 19th century. High on the west facade, look out for an equestrian statue of King Gradlon, the city's mythical 5th-century founder.

Musée Départemental Breton MUSEUM
(1 rue du Roi Gradlon; adult/child €4/free; 9am-6pm daily) Beside the cathedral, recessed

WORTH A TRIP

THE MORBIHAN MEGALITHS

Pre-dating Stonehenge by about a hundred years, **Carnac** comprises the world's greatest concentration of megalithic sites. There are more than 3000 of these upright stones scattered across the countryside between **Carnac-Ville** and **Locmariaquer** village, most of which were erected between 5000 BC and 3500 BC. No one's quite sure what purpose these sites served, although theories abound. A sacred site? Phallic fertility cult? Or maybe a celestial calendar? Even more mysterious is the question of their construction – no one really has the foggiest idea how the builders hacked and hauled these vast granite blocks several millennia before the wheel arrived in Brittany, let alone mechanical diggers.

Because of severe erosion, the sites are usually fenced off to allow vegetation to regrow. **Guided tours** (€4) run in French year-round and in English at 3pm Wednesday, Thursday and Friday early July to late August. Sign up at the **Maison des Mégalithes** (02 97 52 89 99; rte des Alignements; 9am-8pm Jul & Aug, to 5.15pm Sep-Apr, to 7pm May & Jun). Opposite, the largest menhir field – with no fewer than 1099 stones – is the **Alignements du Ménec**, 1km north of Carnac-Ville. From here, the D196 heads northeast for about 1.5km to the **Alignements de Kermario**. Climb the stone observation tower midway along the site to see the alignment from above. Another 500m further on are the **Alignements de Kerlescan**, while the **Tumulus St-Michel**, 400m northeast of the Carnac-Ville tourist office, dates back to at least 5000 BC.

For background, Carnac's **Musée de Préhistoire** (10 place de la Chapelle, Carnac-Ville; adult/child €5/2.50; 10am-6pm) chronicles life in and around Carnac from the Palaeolithic and neolithic eras to the Middle Ages.

behind a magnificent stone courtyard, this museum showcases Breton history, furniture, costumes, crafts and archaeology in a former bishop's palace.

Sleeping

TOP CHOICE **Hôtel Manoir des Indes** MANOR HOUSE €€
(02 98 55 48 40; www.manoir-hoteldesindes.com; 1 allée de Prad ar C'hras; s €105-150, d €150-170;) This stunning hotel conversion, located in an old manor house just a short drive from the centre of Quimper, has been restored with the original world-traveller owner in mind. Decor is minimalist and modern with Asian objets d'art and lots of exposed wood.

Hôtel de la Gare HOTEL €
(02 98 90 00 81; www.hoteldelagarequimper.com; 17 av de la Gare; s/d €49/54;) This cheap, friendly place opposite the train station is the best deal in town. There's a pleasant cafe feel to the lobby, free parking and a small courtyard garden.

Auberge de Jeunesse HOSTEL €
(02 98 64 97 97; www.fuaj.org/quimper; 6 av des Oiseaux; camping €6, dm incl breakfast from €12.70, sheets €3; Apr-Sep) Seasonal hostel with self-catering facilities.

Eating

TOP CHOICE **Le Cosy Restaurant** REGIONAL CUISINE €
(02 98 95 23 65; 2 rue du Sallé; mains €10-14.50; lunch Tue-Sat, dinner Wed, Fri & Sat) Make your way through the *épicerie* crammed with locally canned sardines, ciders and other Breton specialities to this eclectic dining room where you can tuck into top-quality gratins and *tartines*.

Crêperie La Krampouzerie CRÊPERIE €
(9 rue du Sallé; galettes €2-7; Tue-Sat, dinner Sun) Crêpes and galettes made from organic flours and regional ingredients like *algues d'Ouessant* (seaweed), Roscoff onions and homemade ginger caramel are king here. Tables on the square out front create a real street-party atmosphere.

Le Petit Gaveau BISTRO €
(02 98 64 29 86; 16 rue des Boucheries; mains €8-15 lunch Mon-Sat, dinner Wed-Sat) This sleek conversion of an old stone house plays host to simple yet excellent food. Live jazz Thursday to Saturday (€3 supplement).

Information

Tourist office (02 98 53 04 05; www.quimper-tourisme.com, in French; place de la Résistance; 9.30am-12.30pm & 1.30-6.30pm)

Getting There & Away

CAT/Viaoo (www.viaoo29.fr) bus destinations include Brest (€6.50, 1¼ hours); **Le Coeur** (☎02 98 54 40 15) runs to Concarneau (€2, 45 minutes, seven to 10 daily).

Frequent trains serve Brest (€15.40, 1¼ hours), Rennes (€38, 2½ hours) and Paris' Gare Montparnasse (€74.80, 4¾ hours).

St-Malo

POP 50,200

The mast-filled port of fortified St-Malo is inextricably tied up with the deep briny blue: the town became a key harbour during the 17th and 18th centuries, functioning as a base for merchant ships and government-sanctioned privateers, and these days it's a busy cross-Channel ferry port and summertime getaway.

Sights

Walking on top of the city's sturdy 17th-century ramparts (1.8km) affords fine views of the old walled city known as Intra-Muros ('within the walls') or Ville Close – access the ramparts from any of the city gates.

Cathédrale St-Vincent CATHEDRAL
(place Jean de Châtillon; ⌚9.30am-6pm) The city's centrepiece was constructed between the 12th and 18th centuries. The battle to liberate St-Malo destroyed around 80% of the old city during August 1944, and damage to the cathedral was particularly severe. A mosaic plaque on the floor of the nave marks the spot where Jacques Cartier received the blessing of the bishop of St-Malo before his 'voyage of discovery' to Canada in 1535.

Fort National RUINS
(www.fortnational.com; adult/child €5/3; ⌚Easter & Jun-Sep) From the city ramparts, spot the remains of St-Malo's former prison and the rocky islet of **Île du Grand Bé**, where the great St-Malo-born 18th-century writer Chateaubriand is buried. (You can walk across at low tide, but check the tide times with the tourist office.)

Musée du Château HISTORY MUSEUM
(adult/child €5/2.80; ⌚10am-noon & 2-6pm Apr-Sep, Tue-Sun Oct-Mar) Within **Château de St-Malo**, built by the dukes of Brittany in the 15th and 16th centuries, this museum looks at local cod fishing and photos of St-Malo after WWII.

Aquarium AQUARIUM
(www.aquarium-st-malo.com; av Général Patton; adult/child €15.50/9.50; ⌚10am-6pm Feb-Oct & Dec, to 8pm Jul & Aug) Allow around two hours to spend at St-Malo's excellent aquarium, 4km south of the city centre. It's a great wet-weather alternative for kids, with a minisubmarine descent and a *bassin tactile* (touch pool), where you can actually fondle sea creatures such as rays and turbot – and even a baby shark. Bus C1 from the train station passes by every half-hour.

Sleeping

Hôtel San Pedro HOTEL €
(☎02 99 40 88 57; www.sanpedro-hotel.com; 1 rue Ste-Anne; s €52-54, d €63-73; 📶) Tucked at the back of the old city, the San Pedro has cool, crisp, neutral-toned decor with subtle splashes of colour, friendly service and superb sea views.

Camping Aleth CAMPING GROUND €
(☎06 78 96 10 62; www.camping-aleth.com; allée Gaston Buy, St-Servan; €13.40 per 2-person tent; ⌚May-Sep) Perched on a peninsula, Camping Aleth has panoramic 360-degree views and is close to beaches and some lively bars.

Auberge de Jeunesse Éthic Étapes HOSTEL €
(☎02 99 40 29 80; www.centrevarangot.com; 37 av du Père Umbricht; dm incl breakfast €17.50-19.80; @) This efficient place has a self-catering kitchen and free sports facilities. Take bus C1 from the train station.

Eating

Restaurants abound between Porte St-Vincent, the cathedral and the Grande Porte.

St-Malo

Top Sights
Cathédrale St-Vincent B3

Sights
1 Château de St-Malo C2
2 Fort National B1
3 Musée du Château C2

Sleeping
4 Camping Aleth A7
5 Hôtel San Pedro A3

Eating
6 La Bouche en Folie B3
7 Le Chalut B2
8 Restaurant Delaunay B3

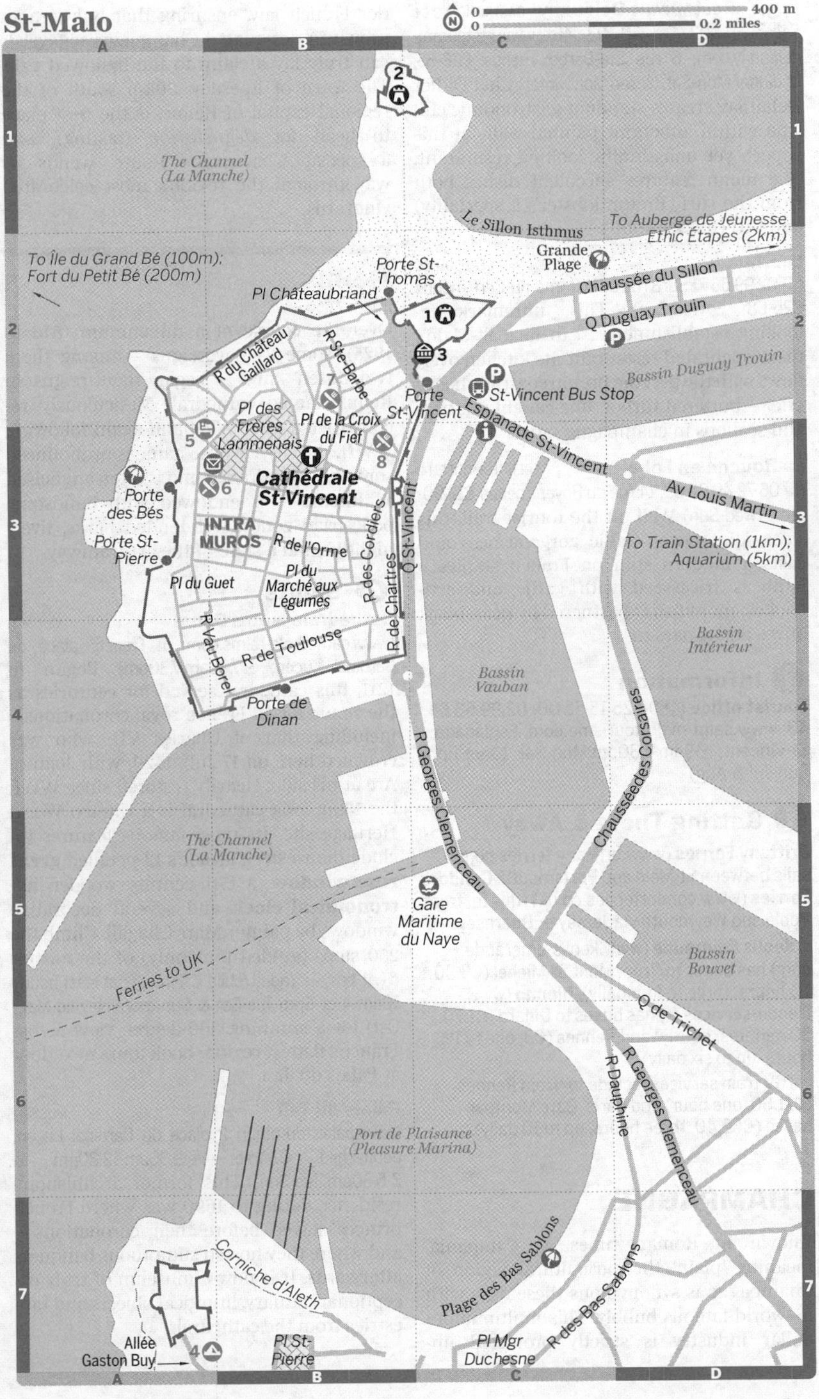

0 400 m
0 0.2 miles

A B C D

1 2 3 4 5 6 7

The Channel (La Manche)

Le Sillon Isthmus

To Auberge de Jeunesse Ethic Étapes (2km)

To Île du Grand Bé (100m); Fort du Petit Bé (200m)

Grande Plage

Porte St-Thomas

Pl Châteaubriand

Chaussée du Sillon

Q Duguay Trouin

Bassin Duguay Trouin

R du Château Gaillard

R Ste-Barbe

St-Vincent Bus Stop

Porte St-Vincent

Esplanade St-Vincent

Pl des Frères Lammenais

Pl de la Croix du Fief

Cathédrale St-Vincent

Av Louis Martin

Porte des Bés

INTRA MUROS

Porte St-Pierre

R de l'Orme

R des Cordiers

Q St-Vincent

To Train Station (1km); Aquarium (5km)

Pl du Guet

Pl du Marché aux Légumes

R de Chartres

R Vau Borel

R de Toulouse

Bassin Intérieur

Bassin Vauban

Porte de Dinan

Chaussée des Corsaires

R Georges Clemenceau

The Channel (La Manche)

Gare Maritime du Naye

Bassin Bouvet

Ferries to UK

Q de Trichet

R Dauphine

R Georges Clemenceau

Port de Plaisance (Pleasure Marina)

Corniche d'Aleth

Plage des Bas Sablons

R des Bas Sablons

Allée Gaston Buy

Pl St-Pierre

Pl Mgr Duchesne

FRANCE ST-MALO

TOP CHOICE **Restaurant Delaunay** GASTRONOMIC €€ (☎02 99 40 92 46; www.restaurant-delaunay.com; 6 rue Ste-Barbe; menus €28-65; ☎dinner Mon-Sat, closed Mon winter) Chef Didier Delaunay creates standout gastronomic cuisine within aubergine-painted walls at this superb yet unassuming-looking restaurant. The menu features succulent dishes both from the surf (Breton lobster's a speciality) and turf (tender lamb).

Le Chalut SEAFOOD €€
(☎02 99 56 71 58; 8 rue de la Corne-du-Cerf; menus €25-68; ⏲Wed-Sun) This unremarkable-looking establishment is, in fact, St-Malo's most celebrated restaurant. Its kitchen overflows with the best the Breton coastline has to offer – buttered turbot, line-caught sea bass and scallops in champagne sauce.

La Bouche en Folie FRENCH, MODERN €
(☎06 72 49 08 89; 14 rue du Boyer; menus €12.90-29; ⏲Wed-Sun) Well off the tourist trail, this sleek joint oozes Gallic gorgeousness and casts a modern spin on French staples – lamb is fricasséed with garlic and artichokes; monkfish is partnered by peas, black olives and asparagus.

Information

Tourist office (☎08 25 13 52 00, 02 99 56 64 43; www.saint-malo-tourisme.com; Esplanade St-Vincent; ⏲9am-7.30pm Mon-Sat, 10am-6pm Sun Jul & Aug)

Getting There & Away

Brittany Ferries (www.brittany-ferries.com) sails between St-Malo and Portsmouth; **Condor Ferries** (www.condorferries.co.uk) runs to/from Poole and Weymouth via Jersey or Guernsey.

Keolis Emeraude (www.keolis-emeraude.com) has buses to/from Mont St-Michel (€3.30, 1½ hours, three to four daily). **Illenno** (www.illenoo-services.fr) has buses to Dinard (€1.70, 30 minutes, hourly) and Rennes (€3, one to 1½ hours, up to six daily).

TGV train services include to/from Rennes (€11.60, one hour) and Paris' Gare Montparnasse (€62.40, three hours, up to 10 daily).

CHAMPAGNE

Known in Roman times as Campania, meaning 'plain', the agricultural region of Champagne is synonymous these days with its world-famous bubbly. This multimillion-dollar industry is strictly protected under French law, ensuring that only grapes grown in designated Champagne vineyards can truly lay a claim to the hallowed title. The town of Épernay, 30km south of the regional capital of Reims, is the best place to head for *dégustation* (tasting), and a special 'Champagne Route' wends its way through the region's most celebrated vineyards.

Reims

POP 187,650

Over the course of a millennium (816 to 1825), some 34 sovereigns – among them two dozen kings – began their reigns in Reims' famed cathedral. Meticulously reconstructed after WWI and again following WWII, the city – whose name is pronounced something like 'rance' and is often anglicised as Rheims – is endowed with handsome pedestrian zones, well-tended parks, lively nightlife and a state-of-the-art tramway.

Sights

Cathédrale Notre Dame CHURCH
(www.cathedrale-reims.com, in French; place du Cardinal Luçon; ⏲7.30am-7.30pm) Begun in 1211, this cathedral served for centuries as the venue for all French royal coronations – including that of Charles VII, who was crowned here on 17 July 1429, with Joan of Arc at his side. Heavily restored since WWI, the 139m-long cathedral is a Unesco World Heritage site. Its most famous features include the western facade's 12-petalled **great rose window**, a 15th-century wooden **astronomical clock** and several decorative windows by painter Marc Chagall. Climb the 250 steps (guided tour only) of the **cathedral tower** (adult/child €7/free; ⏲at least hourly 10am-4 or 5pm Tue-Sat & Sun morning mid-Mar–Oct) for a stunning 360-degree view across France's flattest region; book tours next door at Palais du Tau.

Palais du Tau MUSEUM
(www.palais-du-tau.fr; 2 place du Cardinal Luçon; adult/child €7/free; ⏲9.30am-12.30pm & 2-5.30pm Tue-Sun) This former archbishop's residence dating to 1690 was where French princes stayed before their coronations – and where they hosted sumptuous banquets afterwards. It is now a museum of truly exceptional statuary, liturgical objects and tapestries from the cathedral.

CENT SAVER

The **Reims City Card** (€15), sold at the tourist office, gets you a tour of a Champagne house, a DIY audioguide tour of the cathedral and admission into Reims' municipal museums.

TOP CHOICE **Basilique St-Rémi** CHURCH
(place du Chanoine Ladame) This Benedictine abbey church, a Unesco World Heritage site, mixes Romanesque elements with early Gothic. It honours Bishop Remigius, who baptised Clovis and 3000 Frankish warriors in 498. The 12th-century-style chandelier has 96 candles, one for each year of the life of St Rémi, whose tomb lies in the choir. It's situated about 1.5km south-southeast of the tourist office; take the Citadine 1 or 2 or bus A or F to the St-Rémi stop.

Activities

The bottle-filled cellars (10°C to 12°C – bring a sweater!) of eight Reims-area Champagne houses can be visited by guided tour which ends, *naturellement*, with a tasting session.

Mumm CHAMPAGNE HOUSE
(www.mumm.com; 34 rue du Champ de Mars; tours €10; 9am-11am & 2-5pm Mar-Oct, Sat Nov-Feb) Mumm (pronounced 'moom'), founded in 1827, is the world's third-largest Champagne producer. Engaging and edifying one-hour tours take you through cellars filled with 25 million bottles of bubbly. Tours with tutored tastings of special vintages cost €15 to €20.

Taittinger CHAMPAGNE HOUSE
(www.taittinger.com; 9 place St-Niçaise; tours €10; 9.30-11.50am & 2pm-4.20pm, closed Sat & Sun mid-Nov–mid-Mar) Parts of these cellars, 1.5km southeast of the cathedral, occupy 4th-century Roman stone quarries; other bits were excavated by 13th-century Benedictine monks.

Sleeping

Hôtel de la Paix HOTEL €€
(03 26 40 04 08; www.bestwestern-lapaix-reims.com; 9 rue Buirette; d €155-205;) An island of serenity just steps from hopping place Drouet d'Erlon, this modern, Best Western–affiliated hostelry has 169 classy, comfortable rooms. Mellow out in the pool, Jacuzzi, *hammam* or Japanese courtyard garden.

Hôtel de la Cathédrale HOTEL €
(03 26 47 28 46; www.hotel-cathedrale-reims.fr; 20 rue Libergier; s/d/q from €56/59/79;) Graciousness and a resident Yorkshire terrier greet guests at this hostelry, run by a music-loving couple. Rooms, spread over four floors (no lift) are smallish but pleasingly chintz; room 43 peeps at Basilique St-Rémi and the hills.

Latino Hôtel HOTEL €
(03 26 47 48 89; www.latinocafe.fr, in French; 33 place Drouet d'Erlon; d €58-79, ste €130;) Above a buzzy cafe filled with a Latin beat, this almost-boutique hotel features some fun furnishings, a warm welcome from the staff and pithy quotes from the great and the good (Gandhi, Oscar Wilde) sgraffitoed on the hall walls.

WORTH A TRIP

CULINARY CANCALE

No day trip from St-Malo is tastier than one to **Cancale** (www.cancale-tourisme.fr), an idyllic Breton fishing port 14km to the east that's famed for its offshore *parcs à huîtres* (oyster beds).

Learn all about oyster farming at the **Ferme Marine** (www.ferme-marine.com; corniche de l'Aurore; adult/child €6.80/3.60; mid-Feb–Oct, English guided tours 2pm Jul–mid-Sep) and shop for oysters fresh from their beds at the **Marché aux Huîtres** (12 oysters from €3.50, lunch platters €20; 9am-6pm), the local oyster market atmospherically clustered around the Pointe des Crolles lighthouse.

Le Coquillage (02 99 89 64 76; www.maisons-de-bricourt.com; 1 rue Duguesclin; menus €26-90; Mar-Dec), the fabulous, Michelin three-star kitchen of superchef Olivier Roellinger, is housed in the equally fabulous Château Richeux, 4km south of Cancale. Crown the culinary experience with lunch or dinner here.

Keolis (www.keolis-emeraude.com) runs buses from St-Malo (€2, 30 minutes) that stop in Cancale at Port de la Houle, next to the pungent fish market.

Eating

Place Drouet d'Erlon is lined with inexpensive restaurants and pub-cafes. More-discerning diners head to rue de Mars, adjacent to rue du Temple and place du Forum.

TOP CHOICE Le Foch FISH €€
(☎03 26 47 48 22; www.lefoch.com; 37 blvd Foch; menus €31-80; ⊙Tue-Fri, dinner Sat, lunch Sun) Considered by many to be one of France's best fish restaurants, elegant Le Foch – holder of one Michelin star – serves up classic cuisine that's as beautiful as it is delicious.

Brasserie Le Boulingrin BRASSERIE €€
(☎03 26 40 96 22; www.boulingrin.fr; 48 rue de Mars; menus €18-28; ⊙Mon-Sat) An old-time brasserie – the decor and zinc bar date to 1925 – whose ambience and cuisine make it an enduring favourite. September to June, the culinary focus is *fruits de mer* (seafood).

Côté Cuisine TRADITIONAL, FRENCH €
(☎03 26 83 93 68; 43 blvd Foch; mains €11.80-22.50; ⊙Mon-Sat) A spacious, modern place with well-regarded traditional French cuisine – especially good value for lunch. Try to snag a table overlooking Sq Colbert.

Information

Tourist office (www.reims-tourisme.com; 2 rue Guillaume de Machault; ⊙9am-7pm Mon-Sat, 10am-6pm Sun)

Getting There & Away

Direct trains link Reims with Épernay (€6, 20 to 36 minutes, at least 14 daily), Laon (€9, 35 to 55 minutes, up to eight daily) and Paris' Gare de l'Est (€24, 1¾ hours, 10 to 15 daily), half of which are speedy TGVs (€32 to €41, 45 minutes).

Épernay

POP 25,225

Prosperous Épernay, 25km south of Reims, is the self-proclaimed *capitale du champagne* and home to many of the world's most celebrated Champagne houses. Beneath the town's streets, some 200 million of bottles of Champagne are slowly being aged, just waiting around to be popped open for some fizz-fuelled celebration.

Sights & Activities

Many of Épernay's *maisons de champagne* (Champagne houses) are based along the handsome and eminently strollable av de Champagne. Cellar tours end with tasting and a visit to the factory-outlet bubbly shop.

Moët & Chandon CHAMPAGNE HOUSE
(☎03 26 51 20 20; www.moet.com; adult/child €14.50/9; 20 av de Champagne; ⊙9.30-noon & 2-4.30pm, closed Sat & Sun mid-Nov–mid-Mar, closed Jan) This prestigious *maison* offers some of the region's best cellar tours. Feeling flush? Buy a jeroboam (3L bottle) of 1998 superpremium Dom Pérignon, *millésime* (vintage Champagne) for €2100.

Mercier CHAMPAGNE HOUSE
(☎03 26 51 22 22; www.champagnemercier.com; 68-70 av de Champagne; adult/child €9/5; ⊙9.30-11.30am & 2-4.30pm, closed mid-Dec–mid-Feb) Everything here is flashy, including the 160,000L barrel that took two decades to build, the lift that transports visitors 30m underground, and the laser-guided touring train.

De Castellane CHAMPAGNE HOUSE
(☎03 26 51 19 11; www.castellane.com, in French; 64 av de Champagne; adult/child €8.50/free; ⊙10-11am & 2-5pm mid-Mar–Dec, closed Jan–mid-Mar) Tours take in an informative bubbly museum, and the reward for climbing the 237 steps up the 66m-high tower (1905) is a fine panorama.

Sleeping

Le Clos Raymi HISTORIC HOTEL €€
(☎03 26 51 00 58; www.closraymi-hotel.com; 3 rue Joseph de Venoge; d from €100; @) Staying at this delightful three-star place is like being a personal guest of Monsieur Chandon himself, who occupied this luxurious home over a century ago. Seven romantic rooms have giant beds, 3.7m-high ceilings, ornate mouldings and parquet floors.

La Villa St-Pierre HOTEL €
(☎03 26 54 40 80; www.villasaintpierre.fr; 14 av Paul Chandon; d €45-50; 📶) In an early-20th-century mansion, this homely hotel with 11 simple rooms retains much of the charm of yesteryear.

Eating

Épernay's main dining area is Rue Gambetta and adjacent place de la République.

TOP CHOICE La Cave à Champagne FRENCH, REGIONAL €€
(☎03 26 55 50 70; www.la-cave-a-champagne.com, in French; 16 rue Gambetta; menus €17-32; ⊙Thu-Mon, lunch Tue) 'The Champagne Cellar' is well regarded by locals for its *champenoise* cuisine, served in a warm, traditional, bour-

WORTH A TRIP

TROYES

What a fine and dandy spot to get a sense of what Europe looked like back when Molière was penning his finest plays and the Three Musketeers were swashbuckling! One of Champagne's historic capitals, lively little **Troyes** (www.tourisme-troyes.com) is graced with some of France's finest medieval and Renaissance half-timbered buildings. Explore lanes such as **rue Paillot de Montabert**, **rue Champeaux**, **rue de Vauluisant**, **rue de la Pierre** and **rue Général Saussier** to throw yourself in the heart of it.

Tiny **ruelle des Chats** (Alley of the Cats) feels like stepping back into the Middle Ages, while pharmacy **Apothicaire de l'Hôtel-Dieu-le-Comte** (quai des Comtes de Champagne; adult/child €2/free; ⌚10 or 11am-1pm & 2-7pm Thu-Sun & Wed afternoon May-Sep, 10am-noon & 2-5pm Fri-Sun Oct-Apr) is a fabulous blast from the past with its original wood panelling dating to 1721, and old-fashioned remedies. Traditional crafts made obsolete by the Industrial Revolution fill the **Maison de l'Outil et de la Pensée Ouvrière** (Museum of Tools & Crafts; www.maison-de-l-outil.com; 7 rue de la Trinité; adult/child €6.50/free; ⌚10am-6pm), housed in the magnificent Renaissance-style Hôtel de Mauroy, built in 1556. Then there is the **Cathédrale St-Pierre et St-Paul** (place St-Pierre) with its hotchpotch of Champenois Gothic architecture, medieval **stained glass**, fantastical baroque **organ** and tiny **treasury**.

The people of Troyes are enormously proud of their local speciality, *andouillette de Troyes* (pork or veal tripe sausage), something of an acquired taste best sampled over lunch at **Au Jardin Gourmand** (☎03 25 73 36 13; 31 rue Paillot de Montabert; mains €19-23; ⌚Tue-Sat, dinner Mon). It's elegant and intimate with a lovely summer terrace, and there are no fewer than 11 varieties of *andouillette* on the menu.

geois atmosphere. You can sample three different Champagnes for €21. To avoid disappointment, book your table a couple of weeks in advance.

Bistrot Le 7 FRENCH €€
(☎03 26 55 28 84; 13 rue des Berceaux; menus €17-23; ⌚daily) One of the restaurants at Hôtel Les Berceaux has earned a Michelin star, the other (this one) serves excellent French cuisine amid semiformal, Mediterranean-chic decor. The escargots in a basil, butter and cream sauce are superior, and the chocolate desserts are to die for.

Restaurant Le Théâtre TRADITIONAL, FRENCH €€
(☎03 26 58 88 19; www.epernay-rest-letheatre.com, in French; menus €17-46; ⌚dinner Mon & Thu-Sat, lunch Tue & Sun) Traditional cuisine is served in a corner dining room built a century ago with 4.2m ceilings and floor-to-ceiling windows. The market-driven menu changes every three weeks.

ℹ Information

Tourist office (☎03 26 53 33 00; www.ot-epernay.fr; 7 av de Champagne; ⌚9.30am-12.30pm & 1.30-7pm Mon-Sat, 11am-4pm Sun, closed Sun mid-Oct–mid-Apr) Details on cellar visits, car touring and walking/cycling options. Rents GPS units (€7 per day) with DIY vineyard-driving tours in English.

ℹ Getting There & Away

Direct trains link Reims (€6.20, 20 to 36 minutes, 11 to 18 daily) and Paris' Gare de l'Est (€21, 1¼ hours, five to 10 daily).

ALSACE & LORRAINE

Alsace is a one-off cultural hybrid. With its Germanic dialect and French sense of fashion, love of foie gras and *choucroute* (sauerkraut), fine wine *and* beer, this distinctive region often leaves you wondering quite where you are. Where are you? In the land of living fairy tales, where vineyards fade into watercolour distance, and hilltop castles mingle with the region's emblematic storks and half-timbered villages.

Lorraine has high culture and effortless grace thanks to its historic roll-call of dukes and art nouveau pioneers, who had an eye for grand designs and good living. Its blessedly underrated cities, cathedrals and art collections leave first-timers spellbound, while its WWI battlefields render visitors speechless.

DON'T MISS

FOODIE TRAILS

No matter whether you're planning to get behind the wheel for a morning or pedal leisurely through the vineyards for a week, the picture-book **Route des Vins d'Alsace** (Alsace Wine Route) is a must. Swinging 170km from Marlenheim to Thann, the road is like a 'greatest hits' of Alsace, with its pastoral views, welcoming *caves* (cellars) and half-timbered villages. Go to www.alsace-route-des-vins.com to start planning.

Fancy cheese with your wine? Hit **Munster** to taste the pungent, creamy fromage first made by Benedictine monks. The tourist office (www.la-vallee-de-munster.com) arranges farmstays and dairy tours.

Having polished off the cheese and wine, it would be rude not to pass the chocolates, or gingerbread, or macaroons, on the **Route du Chocolat et des Douceurs d'Alsace**, 200km of sweet-toothed travels. Pick up a map at Strasbourg tourist office (p371), from where the trail wends 80km north to Bad Bergzabern and 125km south to Heimsbrunn near Mulhouse. Before departure, stock up on *pain d'épices* (gingerbread) from heavenly shop **Mireille Oster** (www.mireille-oster.com; 14 rue des Dentelles), *beerawecka* (Alsatian fruit cake) from **Coco LM** (www.coco-lm.com; 16 rue du Dôme) and sumptuous truffles, pralines, macaroons and edible Strasbourg landmarks from renowned chocolatier **Christian** (www.christian.fr; 12 rue de l'Outre).

Strasbourg

POP 276,000

Prosperous, cosmopolitan Strasbourg ('City of the Roads') is the intellectual and cultural capital of Alsace, as well as the unofficial seat of European power – the European Parliament, the Council of Europe and the European Court of Human Rights are all based here. The city's most famous landmark is its pink sandstone cathedral, towering above the restaurants, *winstubs* (traditional Alsatian eateries) and pubs of the lively old city.

Mulled wine, spicy *bredele* (biscuits) and a Santa-loaded children's village make a trip to Strasbourg's sparkly Marché de Noël a must.

Sights

TOP CHOICE **Grande Île** OLD TOWN
With its bustling squares and upmarket shopping streets, the Grande Île – Unesco-listed since 1988 – is a paradise for the aimless ambler. Its narrow streets are especially enchanting at night, while the half-timbered buildings and flowery canals around **Petite France** on the Grande Île's southwestern corner are fairy-tale pretty. Drink in views of the River Ill and the mighty 17th-century **Barrage Vauban** (Vauban Dam), undergoing renovation at the time of writing, from the much-photographed **Ponts Couverts** (Covered Bridges) and their trio of 13th-century towers.

Cathédrale Notre-Dame CHURCH
(place de la Cathédrale; ⏲7am-7pm) Strasbourg's lacy, candy-coloured Gothic cathedral is one of the marvels of European architecture. Its west facade was completed in 1284, but the 142m spire wasn't finished till 1439. Inside the south entrance, the 30m-high, 16th-century **astronomical clock** (adult/child €2/free; ⏲tickets sold from 11.50am) strikes solar noon at 12.30pm, with a parade of carved wooden figures portraying the different stages of life and Jesus with his apostles.

A spiral staircase twists up to the 66m-high **platform** (adult/child €4.70/2.30; ⏲9am-7.15pm), which provides a stork's-eye view of Strasbourg.

Musée d'Art Moderne et Contemporain ART MUSEUM
(place Hans Jean Arp; adult/child €6/free; ⏲noon-7pm Tue, Wed & Fri, noon-9pm Thu, 10am-6pm Sat & Sun) This striking glass-and-steel cube showcases an outstanding collection of fine art, graphic art and photography. Kandinsky, Picasso, Magritte and Monet canvases hang out alongside curvaceous works by Strasbourg-born abstract artist Hans Jean Arp.

Palais Rohan HISTORIC RESIDENCE
(2 place du Château; adult/child €5/free; ⏲noon-6pm Mon & Wed-Fri, 10am-6pm Sat & Sun) Hailed as a mini Versailles, this opulent 18th-century residence was built for the city's princely bishops. Its basement archaeology museum spans the Palaeolithic period to AD 800; and rooms adorned with Hannong

ceramics and silverware evoke the lavish lifestyle of 18th-century nobility in the ground-floor decorative arts museum.

Tours

Cave des Hospices de Strasbourg WINE
(www.vins-des-hospices-de-strasbourg.fr, in French; 1 place de l'Hôpital; 8.30am-noon & 1.30-5.30pm Mon-Fri, 9am-12.30pm Sat) A hospice back in the days when wine was considered a cure for all ills, this brick-vaulted wine cellar produces first-rate Alsatian wines deep in the bowels of Strasbourg's hospital.

Batorama BOAT
(www.batorama.fr, in French; adult/child €8.50/4.50; half-hourly 9.30am-9pm) Scenic boat trips along the storybook canals of Petite France, taking in the Vauban Dam and the glinting EU institutions. Tours depart from in front of Palais Rohan.

Brasseries Heineken BEER
(03 88 19 57 55; 4 rue St-Charles; hourly 9am-4pm Mon-Fri) Free two-hour tours of the Heineken brewery (some in English; reserve ahead), 2.5km north of Grande Île; take bus 4 to the Schiltigheim Mairie stop.

Festivals & Events

Vin chaud (mulled wine), spicy *bredele* and a Santa-loaded children's village feature in Strasbourg's sparkly **Marché de Noël** (Christmas Market; www.noel.strasbourg.eu), from the last Saturday in November to 24 December.

Raise a glass to Alsatian beer at October's **Mondial de la Bière** (www.mondialbierestrasbourg.com) or to wine at March's **Riesling du Monde** (www.riesling-du-monde.com).

Sleeping

Camping de la Montagne Verte CAMPING GROUND €
(03 88 30 25 46; www.camping-montagne-verte-strasbourg.com; 2 rue Robert Forrer; campsites €14-18.50) Pitch up at this quiet camping ground, a 10-minute stroll from Montagne Verte tram stop, 3km west of Petite France. It's right next to the cycling lane leading into town.

Hôtel du Dragon SMALL HOTEL €€
(03 88 35 79 80; www.dragon.fr; 12 rue du Dragon; s €79-112, d €89-124;) Step through a tree-shaded courtyard into the blissful calm of this bijou hotel. Crisp interiors, attentive service and prime location near Petite France.

Hôtel Gutenberg HISTORIC HOTEL €€
(03 88 32 17 15; www.hotel-gutenberg.com; 31 rue des Serruriers; r €75-135;) Right in the flower-filled heart of Petite France, this hotel blends 250 years of history with contemporary design – think clean lines, zesty colours and the occasional antique.

Romantik Hôtel Beaucour HISTORIC HOTEL €€
(03 88 76 72 00; www.hotel-beaucour.com; 5 rue des Bouchers; s €75-110, d €135-165;) With its antique flourishes and a cosy salon centred on a fireplace, this place oozes half-timbered romance. Jacuzzi bathtubs!

Eating

Appetising restaurants abound on Grande Île: try canalside Petite France for Alsatian fare and half-timbered romance; Grand' Rue for curbside kebabs and *tarte flambée;* and rue des Veaux or rue des Pucelles for hole-in-the-wall eateries serving the world on a plate.

TOP CHOICE **La Choucrouterie** ALSATIAN €€
(03 88 36 52 87; www.choucrouterie.com, in French; 20 rue St Louis; choucroute €12-16; lunch Mon-Fri, dinner daily) Naked ladies straddling giant sausages (on the menu, we hasten to add) and eccentric chefs juggling plates of steaming *choucroute garnie* are

DON'T MISS

WHEN HELL WAS HELL

Hollywood gore seems tame compared with the tortures back when Hell really was hell. Sure to scare you into a life of chastity is *Les Amants Trépassés* (The Deceased Lovers), painted in 1470, showing a grotesque couple being punished for their illicit lust: both of their entrails are being devoured by dragon-headed snakes.

Track it down in room 23 of Strasbourg's fabulous **Musée de l'Œuvre Notre Dame** (3 place du Château; adult/child €4/free; noon-6pm Tue-Fri, 10am-6pm Sat & Sun). Occupying a cluster of sublime 14th- and 16th-century buildings, the world-renowned ecclesiastical museum boasts one of Europe's premier collections of Romanesque, Gothic and Renaissance sculptures, 15th-century paintings and stained glass.

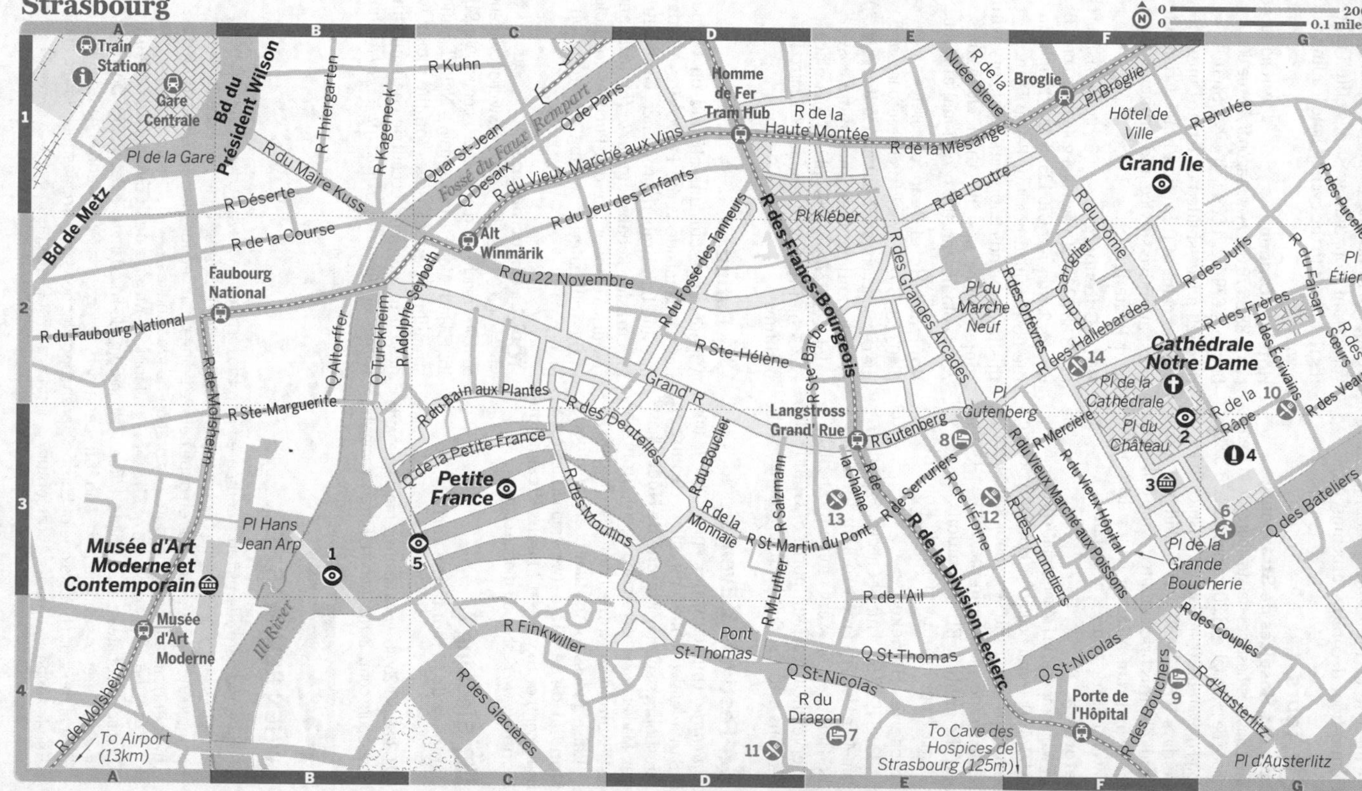
Strasbourg
0 200 m
0 0.1 miles
Train Station
Gare Centrale
Bd du Président Wilson
Bd de Metz
Pl de la Gare
R du Maire Kuss
R Thiergarten
R Kageneck
R Kuhn
Quai St-Jean
Q Desaix
Fossé du Faux Rempart
Q de Paris
R du Vieux Marché aux Vins
R du Jeu des Enfants
Alt Winmärik
R Déserte
R de la Course
Faubourg National
R du Faubourg National
R de Molsheim
R du 22 Novembre
R Adolphe Seyboth
Q Turckheim
Q Altorffer
R Ste-Marguerite
R du Bain aux Plantes
Q de la Petite France
Petite France
R des Dentelles
R des Moulins
Grand' R
R du Fossé des Tanneurs
R Ste-Hélène
Homme de Fer Tram Hub
R de la Haute Montée
R des Francs-Bourgeois
Pl Kléber
R Ste-Barbe
Langstross Grand' Rue
R Gutenberg
R du Boucliér
R de la Monnaie
R St-Martin du Pont
R Salzmann
R M Luther
R de la Chaîne
R de la Division Leclerc
R des Serruriers
R de l'Épine
R de l'Ail
Pl Hans Jean Arp
Musée d'Art Moderne et Contemporain
Musée d'Art Moderne
Ill River
R Finkwiller
Pont St-Thomas
Q St-Thomas
Q St-Nicolas
R du Dragon
R des Glacières
To Airport (13km)
To Cave des Hospices de Strasbourg (125m)
R de la Nuée Bleue
Broglie
Pl Broglie
Hôtel de Ville
R Brulée
R de la Mésange
R de l'Outre
Grand Île
R du Dôme
R des Grandes Arcades
Pl du Marché Neuf
R des Orfèvres
R du Sanglier
R des Hallebardes
R des Juifs
R des Pucelles
R du Faisan
Pl St-Étienne
R des Frères
R des Écrivains
R des Sœurs
R des Veaux
Cathédrale Notre Dame
Pl de la Cathédrale
Pl du Château
R de la Râpe
Pl Gutenberg
R Mercière
R du Vieux Marché aux Poissons
R du Vieux Hôpital
R des Tonneliers
Pl de la Grande Boucherie
Q des Bateliers
R des Couples
R des Bouchers
R d'Austerlitz
Pl d'Austerlitz
Porte de l'Hôpital
1
2
3
4
5
6
7
8
9
10
11
12
13
14

Strasbourg

just the tip of the theatrical iceberg at this inimitable bistro and playhouse double act.

La Cloche á Fromage CHEESE SHOP €€
(☎03 88 23 13 19; www.cheese-gourmet.com; 27 rue des Tonneliers; fondues €21-25; ⊙Tue-Sun) *Au revoir* diet... Loosen your belt for Strasbourg's gooiest fondues and raclette at this temple to cheese, saving an inch for the 200-variety cheeseboard of Guinness Book of World Records fame.

Maison Kammerzell ALSATIAN €€
(☎03 88 32 42 14; www.maison-kammerzell.com; 16 place de la Cathédrale; menus €27-46) Medieval icon Maison Kammerzell serves well-executed Alsatian cuisine such as *baeckeoffe* and *choucroute*. A staircase spirals up to frescoed alcoves and the 1st floor where the views – oh the views! – of the floodlit cathedral are sensational.

L'Assiette du Vin BISTRO €€
(☎03 88 32 00 92; www.assietteduvin.fr, in French; 5 rue de la Chaîne; lunch menus €19, dinner menus €32-55; ⊙Tue-Fri, dinner Sat-Mon) Market-fresh cuisine with a twist, discreet service and an award-winning wine list lure discerning foodies to this rustic-chic bistro in the Old Town. The plat du jour is a snip at €8.50.

Bistrot et Chocolat CAFE €
(www.bistrotetchocolat.net, in French; 8 rue de la Râpe; snacks €4-8, brunches €10-19; ⊙10.30am-7pm Tue-Sun) Chocolate fondue, organic hot chocolate with ginger, chocolate soup sprinkled with gingerbread croutons... This boho-chic bistro is an ode to the cocoa bean. Weekend brunches are a treat.

Information

Tourist office (☎03 88 52 28 28; www.otstrasbourg.fr; 17 place de la Cathédrale; ⊙9am-7pm) Runs an annexe in the southern wing of Strasbourg train station, 400m west of Grande Île.

Getting There & Away

Air

Strasbourg's international **airport** (www.strasbourg.aeroport.fr) is 17km southwest of the city centre (towards Molsheim), near the village of Entzheim.

Ryanair links London Stansted with **Karlsruhe/Baden Baden airport** (www.badenairpark.de), 58km northeast of Strasbourg, across the Rhine in Germany.

Train

DOMESTIC Destinations include Paris' Gare de l'Est (€67, 2¼ hours, 17 daily), Lille (€94, four hours, 13 daily), Lyon (€52, six hours, five

WORTH A TRIP

FOREST FANTASY

Get back to nature at the **Hôtel de l'Illwald** (☎03 90 56 11 40; www.illwald.fr; Schnellenbuhl; d €72-85; 📶), a dreamy hotel bordering the lushly forested Ill'Wald nature reserve, which has France's largest population of wild deer. This half-timbered, red-sandstone hotel keeps the mood intimate in gorgeous rooms: some sleek with hardwood floors and four-poster beds, others rustic with warm pine, antique furnishings and downy bedding. After a day walking or cycling, have drinks by an open fire and dinner in the frescoed restaurant. The hotel is 60km south of Strasbourg, off the D424 in Schnellenbuhl.

WORTH A TRIP

KATZENTHAL

Tiptoe off the tourist trail to Alsatian village **Katzenthal** (population 550), 9km west of Colmar and 80km south of Strasbourg. *Grand cru* vines ensnare the hillside, topped by the medieval ruins of Château du Wineck, from where walking trails into forest and vineyard begin.

Then there is the fabulous, family-run **Vignoble Klur** (☎03 89 80 94 29; www.klur.net; 105 rue des Trois Epis; d €80-110), an organic winery and guest house that hosts wine tastings, Alsatian cookery classes, herb walks in the vineyards, creative workshops and tandems to pedal through the vines *á deux*. Make yourself at home in a sunny apartment with kitchenette, read a book by an open fire in the salon, or unwind in the organic sauna. Oh, and don't miss Jean-Louis Frick's hilarious mural of hedonistic wine lovers above the entrance – it has raised a few local eyebrows, apparently.

daily), Marseille (€87, eight hours, five daily), Metz (€23, two hours, 20 daily) and Nancy (€22, 1½ hours, 25 daily).

INTERNATIONAL Cities with direct services include Basel SNCF (Bâle; €21, 1¼ hours, 25 daily), Brussels-Nord (€70, 5¼ hours, three daily), Karlsruhe (€22, 40 minutes, 16 daily) and Stuttgart (€43, 1¼ hours, four TGVs daily). If you take the Eurostar via Paris or Lille, London is just five hours and 15 minutes away, city centre to city centre.

ROUTE DES VINS From Strasbourg, there are trains to Route des Vins destinations including Colmar (€10.50, 30 minutes, 30 daily), Dambach-la-Ville (€8, one hour, 12 daily), Obernai (€5.50, 30 minutes, 20 daily) and Sélestat (€7.50, 30 minutes, 46 daily).

Nancy

POP 107,250

Delightful Nancy has a refined air found nowhere else in Lorraine. With its resplendent central square, fine museums, medieval Old Town, formal gardens and shop windows sparkling with crystal, the former capital of the dukes of Lorraine catapults visitors back to the opulence of the 18th century (when much of the city centre was built).

Sights

Place Stanislas SQUARE

This neoclassical square, laid out in the 1750s, is one of Europe's most dazzling public spaces. The rococo fountains, gilded gateways and opulent buildings form one of France's finest ensembles of 18th-century architecture.

Musée de l'École de Nancy MUSEUM

(School of Nancy Museum; www.ecole-de-nancy.com; 36-38 rue du Sergent Blandan; adult/child €6/4; ⏲10am-6pm Wed-Sun) A highlight of a visit to Nancy, the School of Nancy Museum brings together an exquisite collection of art nouveau interiors, curvaceous glass and landscaped gardens. Find it in a 19th-century villa, 2km southwest of the centre.

Musée des Beaux-Arts ART MUSEUM

(3 place Stanislas; adult/child €6/free; ⏲10am-6pm Wed-Mon) Star attractions at this fine-arts museum include a superb collection of art nouveau glass and paintings from the 14th to 18th centuries.

Sleeping

TOP CHOICE **Hôtel des Prélats** HISTORIC HOTEL €€

(☎03 83 30 20 20; www.hoteldesprelats.com; 56 place Monseigneur Ruch; s/d €69/109; ❄📶) Sleep in a 17th-century bishop's palace next to the cathedral. Prélats plays up the romance with stained-glass windows, four-poster beds and shimmery drapes.

Hôtel de Guise BOUTIQUE HOTEL €€

(☎03 83 32 24 68; www.hoteldeguise.com; 18 rue de Guise; s €63, d €75-100; 📶) Boutique chic meets 17th-century elegance at this hotel on an old-town backstreet. There's a walled garden for quiet moments.

La Résidence TRADITIONAL HOTEL €€

(☎03 83 35 42 34; www.hotel-laresidence-nancy.fr, in French; 30 blvd Jean-Jaurès; r €70-85; 📶) This convivial hotel is one of Nancy's best deals, with an inviting salon and a leafy courtyard for an alfresco breakfast.

Eating

Eats street rue des Maréchaux dishes up everything from French to Italian, tapas, seafood, Indian and Japanese. Then there's Grande Rue, peppered with sweet bistros.

FRANCE ALSACE & LORRAINE

Chez Tony DELI €
(place Henri Mengin; mains €6-11; ⏲Tue-Sat) Generously heaped plates of antipasti, freshly made pasta, colourful garden chairs, big smiles all round – it's a Tuscan garden party every lunchtime at Chez Tony in Nancy's covered market. Toast your find with a glass of olive liqueur or Chianti.

Brasserie Excelsior BRASSERIE €€
(☎03 83 35 24 57; 50 rue Henri Poincaré; menus €23-38; ⏲8am-12.30am Mon-Sat, 8am-11pm Sun) As opulent as a Fabergé egg with its stucco and stained glass, Excelsior whisks you back to the decadent era of art nouveau. Brusquely efficient waiters serve brasserie classics: oysters, steaks and seafood platters.

Aux Délices du Palais BISTRO €
(☎03 83 30 44 19; 69 Grande Rue; mains €9; ⏲Mon-Fri, dinner Sat) Purple walls and glitter balls, this shabby-chic bistro serves whatever the jovial chef fancies cooking – from flavoursome tagines to fajitas. Great value, hence the enthusiastic local following.

Information

Tourist office (☎03 83 35 22 41; www.ot-nancy.fr; place Stanislas; ⏲9am-7pm Mon-Sat, 10am-5pm Sun) Free brochures detailing walking tours of Nancy's art nouveau architecture.

Getting There & Away

The **train station** (place Thiers), 800m southwest of place Stanislas, is on the line linking Paris' Gare de l'Est (€54, 1½ hours, 11 daily) with Strasbourg (€22, 1½ hours, 12 daily). Other destinations include Baccarat (€9.50, 45 minutes, 15 daily) and Metz (€9.50, 40 minutes, 48 daily).

Metz

POP 125,720

Straddling the confluence of the Moselle and Seille Rivers, Metz is Lorraine's graceful capital. Its Gothic marvel of a cathedral, Michelin star-studded dining scene, beautiful yellow-stone Old Town and regal Quartier Impérial (up for Unesco World Heritage status) have long managed to sidestep the world spotlight. But all that has changed with the show-stopping arrival of Centre Pompidou-Metz.

DON'T MISS

CENTRE POMPIDOU-METZ

This architecturally innovative **museum** (www.centrepompidou-metz.fr; 1 parvis des Droits de l'Homme; adult/child €7/free; ⏲11am-6pm Mon, Wed & Sun, 11am-8pm Thu, Fri & Sat), dazzling white and sinuous, is the satellite branch of Paris' Centre Pompidou. Its gallery draws on Europe's largest collection of modern art to stage ambitious temporary exhibitions. The dynamic space also hosts top-drawer cultural events.

Sights

Cathédrale St-Étienne CHURCH
(place St-Étienne; ⏲8am-6pm) As delicate as Chantilly lace, the golden spires of this Gothic cathedral crown the town's skyline. Exquisitely lit by kaleidoscopic curtains of 13th- to 20th-century stained glass, the cathedral is nicknamed 'God's lantern'. Flamboyant **Chagall** windows in reds, yellows and blues in the ambulatory harbour the **treasury** (adult/child €2/1; ⏲10am-12.30pm & 2-5pm), and a sculpture of a dragon said to have terrified pre-Christian Metz lurks in the 15th-century **crypt** (adult/child €2/1; ⏲10am-12.30pm & 2-5pm).

Quartier Impérial HISTORIC QUARTER
The stately boulevards and bourgeois villas of the German Imperial Quarter, including rue Gambetta and av Foch, are the brainchild

MASSIF DES VOSGES

The sublime **Parc Naturel Régional des Ballons des Vosges** covers 3000 sq km in the southern Vosges range. In the warm months, the gentle, rounded mountains, deep forests, glacial lakes and rolling pastureland are a walker's paradise, with an astounding 10,000km of marked trails and cycle routes, and in winter you'll discover three dozen inexpensive skiing areas.

For information on the park, contact the **Maison du Parc Naturel Régional des Ballons des Vosges** (www.parc-ballons-vosges.fr, in French; 1 cour de l'Abbaye; ⏲10am-noon & 2-6pm Tue-Sun) in Munster, a small streamside town famous for its notoriously smelly and eponymous cheese, Munster (meaning 'monastery').

of Kaiser Wilhelm II. Built to trumpet the triumph of Metz' post-1871 status as part of the Second Reich, the architecture is a whimsical mix of art deco, neo-Romanesque and neo-Renaissance influences. The area's unique ensemble of Wilhelmian architecture has made it a candidate for Unesco World Heritage status. Philippe Starck lamp posts juxtapose Teutonic sculptures, whose common theme is German imperial might, at the monumental Rhenish neo-Romanesque train station (1908).

Sleeping

TOP CHOICE **Péniche Alclair** HOUSEBOAT €
(06 37 67 16 18; www.chambrespenichemetz.com; allée St Symphorien; r incl breakfast €65;) Cécile and Xavier Bonfils have transformed an old barge into this stylish blue houseboat with snazzy bathrooms and watery views. Find it moored a pleasant 15-minute riverside stroll south of the centre.

Hôtel de la Cathédrale HISTORIC HOTEL €€
(03 87 75 00 02; www.hotelcathedrale-metz.fr; 25 place de Chambre; d €75-110;) This classy little hotel occupies a 17th-century town house opposite the cathedral. Climb the wrought-iron staircase to your classically elegant room, with high ceilings, hardwood floors and antique trappings.

La Citadelle DESIGN HOTEL €€€
(03 87 17 17 17; www.citadelle-metz.com; 5 av Ney; d €205-265; @) A 16th-century citadel given a boutique makeover, luxurious La Citadelle blends history with Zen-style sleekness. The hotel's pride and joy is its Michelin-starred restaurant, **Le Magasin aux Vivres**.

Eating

Metz has scores of appetising restaurants, many along and near the river. Place St-Jacques becomes one giant open-air cafe when the sun's out. Cobbled rue Taison and the arcades of place St-Louis shelter moderately priced bistros, pizzerias and cafes.

Restaurant Thierry FUSION €€
(03 87 74 01 23; www.restaurant-thierry.fr; 5 rue des Piques; menus €24-34; Mon, Tue & Thu-Sat) Walking into this spice-scented, lantern-lit restaurant is like stepping into the glammest of Marrakchi riads. An open fire crackles in the salon, where an aperitif works up an appetite for Asian- and Moroccan-inflected dishes, such as delicate prawn *nems* (spring rolls), seafood tagines and beautifully cooked sole with tempura.

La Voile Blanche MODERN FRENCH €€
(03 87 20 66 66; 1 parvis des Droits de l'Homme; menus €25-35; Wed-Mon, lunch Sun) Art on a plate is the aim at Centre Pompidou-Metz' kaleidoscope-inspired restaurant, designed by architects Patrick Jouin and Sanjit Manku.

Maire TRADITIONAL FRENCH €€
(03 87 32 43 12; www.restaurant-maire.com, in French; 1 rue des Ponts des Morts; menus €37-45; Wed-Mon, dinner Wed) This smart riverside restaurant serves up cathedral views, market-fresh dishes and 500 bottles in its wine cellar.

Information

Tourist office (03 87 55 53 76; http://tourisme.mairie-metz.fr; 2 place d'Armes; 9am-7pm Mon-Sat, 10am-5pm Sun)

Getting There & Away

Train it from Metz' ornate early-20th-century **train station** (pl du Général de Gaulle) to Paris' Gare de l'Est (€53, 80 minutes, 13 daily), Nancy (€9.50, 40 minutes, 48 daily) and Strasbourg (€23, 1¾ hours, 14 daily).

DON'T MISS

GO TO MARKET

If only every market were like Metz' grand **Marché Couvert** (Covered Market; place de la Cathédrale; 8am-6.30pm Tue-Sat). Once a bishop's palace, now a temple to fresh local produce, this is the kind of place where you pop in for a baguette and struggle out an hour later with bags overflowing with charcuterie, ripe fruit and five different sorts of fromage.

Make a morning of it, stopping for an early, inexpensive lunch and a chat with the market's larger-than-life characters. At **Chez Mauricette** (sandwiches €2-4.50, antipasti plate €5-7), Mauricette tempts with Lorraine goodies from herby saucisson to local charcuterie and mirabelle pâté. Her neighbour is **Soupes á Soups** (soups €2.80-5.50), where Patrick ladles out homemade soups, from mussel to creamy mushroom varieties.

CHATEAUX TOURS

Many of the big-name Loire Valley chateaux are covered by the **Pass'-Châteaux**, which offers savings of between €1.20 and €5.30 depending on which chateaux you visit; contact the tourist offices in Blois, Cheverny and Chambord.

Hard-core indie travellers might baulk at the idea, but if you don't have your own wheels a minibus tour can be the most time-efficient way of taking in the Loire Valley biggies.

Blois tourist office and **TLC** (02 54 58 55 44; www.tlcinfo.net, in French; 3 morning departures Apr-Aug) run a shuttle (€6) from Blois to Chambord and Cheverny.

Several companies offer a choice of itineraries, packaging Azay-le-Rideau, Villandry, Cheverny, Chambord and Chenonceau (plus wine-tasting tours) in various combinations. Half-day trips cost €18 to €33; full-day trips €43 to €50. Admission to the chateaux isn't included, but you get discount on tickets. Reserve at Tours tourist office, from where most tours depart:

» **Acco-Dispo** (www.accodispo-tours.com)

» **Alienor** (www.alienor.com)

» **Quart de Tours** (www.quartdetours.com)

» **St-Eloi Excursions** (www.saint-eloi.com)

» **Touraine Evasion** (www.tourevasion.com)

» **Loire Valley Tours** (www.loire-valley-tours.com)

THE LOIRE VALLEY

One step removed from the French capital, the Loire was historically the place where princes, dukes and notable nobles established their country getaways, and the countryside is littered with some of the most extravagant architecture outside Versailles. From sky-topping turrets and glittering banquet halls to slate-crowned cupolas and crenellated towers, the hundreds of chateaux dotted along this valley, a Unesco World Heritage site, comprise 1000 years of astonishingly rich architectural and artistic treasures.

Blois

POP 40,057

Blois' historic chateau was the feudal seat of the powerful counts of Blois, and its grand halls, spiral staircases and sweeping courtyards provide a whistlestop tour through the key periods of French architecture. Sadly for chocoholics, the town's historic chocolate factory, Poulain, is off-limits to visitors.

Sights

Blois' old city, heavily damaged by German attacks in 1940, retains its steep, twisting medieval streets.

Château Royal de Blois CASTLE
(www.chateaudeblois.fr; place du Château; adult/child €8/4; 9am-7pm Jul & Aug, 9am-6.30pm Apr-Jun & Sep, 9am-12.30pm & 1.30-5.30pm Oct-Mar) Blois' Royal Chateau makes an excellent introduction to the chateaux of the Loire Valley, with elements of Gothic (13th century); Flamboyant Gothic (1498–1503), early Renaissance (1515–24) and classical (1630s) architecture in its four grand wings.

Maison de la Magie MUSEUM
(www.maisondelamagie.fr, in French; 1 place du Château; adult/child €9/5; 10am-12.30pm & 2-6.30pm, closed mornings Mon-Fri Sep) Opposite the chateau is the former home of watchmaker, inventor and conjurer Jean Eugène Robert-Houdin (1805–71), after whom the great Houdini named himself. It now offers daily magic shows and optical trickery.

Musée de l'Objet ART MUSEUM
(www.museedelobjet.org, in French; 6 rue Franciade; adult/child €4/2; 1.30-6.30pm Wed-Sun late Jun-Aug, Fri-Sun Mar-late Jun & Sep-Oct, closed Dec-Feb) This eye-catching museum has modern art made from everyday materials, with works by Dalí and Man Ray.

Sleeping

Côté Loire HOTEL €
(02 54 78 07 86; www.coteloire.com; 2 place de la Grève; d €55-76;) If it's charm and

THE LOIRE BY BIKE

The Loire Valley is mostly flat – it's excellent cycling country. **Loire à Vélo** (www.loireavelo.fr) maintains 800km of signposted routes. Pick up a guide from tourist offices, or download route maps, audioguides and bike-hire details online.

Détours de Loire (☎02 47 61 22 23; www.locationdevelos.com) has bike-rental shops in Tours and Blois (☎02 54 56 07 73; train station); can deliver bikes; and allows you to collect/return bikes along the route for a small surcharge. Classic bikes cost €14/59 per day/week; tandems €45 per day.

Les Châteaux à Vélo (☎02 54 78 62 52; www.chateauxavelo.com) has a bike-rental circuit between Blois, Chambord and Cheverny, 300km of marked trails and can shuttle you by minibus. Free route maps online (also 40 downloadable MP3 guides) and at tourist offices.

colours you want, head for the Loire Coast. Its rooms come in cheery checks, bright pastels and the odd bit of exposed brick; and breakfast is served on a wooden-decking patio.

Hôtel Anne de Bretagne HOTEL **€**
(☎02 54 78 05 38; http://annedebretagne.free.fr; 31 av du Dr Jean Laigret; s €45-51, d €54-56, tr €60-72; 📶) This creeper-covered hotel has friendly staff and a bar full of polished wood and vintage pictures. Modern rooms are finished in flowery wallpaper and stripy bedspreads.

Le Monarque HOTEL **€**
(☎02 54 78 02 35; 61 rue Porte Chartraine; s €38, d €58-59; ❄📶) Modern, bright and no-nonsense, this hotel sits at the edge of the old city, and offers comfort, cleanliness and a restaurant.

Eating & Drinking

L'Orangerie GASTRONOMIC **€€€**
(☎02 54 78 05 36; www.orangerie-du-chateau.fr; 1 av du Dr Jean Laigret; menus €33-77) The Orangery is cloud nine for connoisseurs of haute cuisine. Plates are artfully stacked (duck liver, langoustine, foie gras) and the sparkling *salon* would make Louis XIV envious. On summer nights, dine in the courtyard.

Les Banquettes Rouges TRADITIONAL, FRENCH **€€**
(☎02 54 78 74 92; 16 rue des Trois Marchands; menus €14.50-32; ⏰Tue-Sat) Handwritten slate menus and wholesome food distinguish the Red Benches: rabbit with marmalade, duck with lentils and salmon with apple vinaigrette, all done with a spicy twist.

Le Castelet TRADITIONAL, FRENCH **€€**
(☎02 54 74 66 09; 40 rue St-Lubin; menus €15-32; ⏰Tue-Sat & Mon; 🅥) Rusticana and rural frescos cover the walls of this country restaurant that emphasises seasonal ingredients, organics and vegetarian options.

Information

Tourist office (☎02 54 90 41 41; www.bloispaysdechambord.com; 23 place du Château; ⏰9am-7pm)

Getting There & Away

Bus

TLC (☎02 54 58 55 44; www.tlcinfo.net) runs a chateau shuttle (see boxed text, p375) and buses from Blois' train station (tickets €2 on board). Some destinations:

BEAUGENCY Line 16, 55 minutes, four Monday to Saturday, one Sunday

CHAMBORD Line 3, 40 minutes, four Monday to Saturday, one Sunday

CHEVERNY Line 4, 45 minutes, six to eight Monday to Friday, two Saturday, one Sunday

Train

AMBOISE €11, 20 minutes, 10 daily

ORLÉANS €13 to €20, 45 minutes, hourly

TOURS €13 to €19, 40 minutes, 13 daily

PARIS' GARES D'AUSTERLITZ & MONTPARNASSE €34 to €57, two hours, 26 daily

Around Blois

CHÂTEAU DE CHAMBORD

For full-blown chateau splendour, you can't top **Chambord** (☎02 54 50 50 20; www.chambord.org; adult/child €9.50/free; ⏰9am-7.30pm mid-Jul–mid-Aug, 9am-6.15pm mid-Mar–mid-Jul & mid-Aug–Sep, 9am-5.15pm Jan–mid-Mar & Oct-Dec), constructed from 1519 by François I as a lavish base for hunting game in the Sologne forests, but eventually used for just 42 days during the king's 32-year reign (1515–47). Pick up the multilingual audioguide (adult/child €4/2), if only to avoid getting lost in Chambord's endless rooms and corridors.

The chateau's most famous feature is its **double-helix staircase**, attributed by some

WORTH A TRIP

LUNCH BREAK

Need a moment to yourself between chateaux? Head to Bracieux, 7km south of Chambord, for lunch at **Au Fil de Temps** (02 54 46 03 84; 11 place de la Halle; €18-22; Fri-Wed). Its simple specialities such as tender white asparagus with beurre blanc or savoury salmon filets beat the tourist traps into the dust.

to Leonardo da Vinci, who lived in Amboise (34km southwest) from 1516 until his death three years later. The Italianate **rooftop terrace**, surrounded by cupolas, domes, chimneys and slate roofs, was where the royal court assembled to watch military exercises and hunting parties returning at the end of the day.

Several times daily there are 1½-hour **guided tours** (€4) in English, and during school holidays **costumed tours** entertain kids. The *son et lumière* show **Chambord, Rêve de Lumières** (adult/child €12/10, Jul–mid-Sep), projected on the chateau's facade nightly, is a real summer highlight, as is the daily **equestrian show** (02 54 20 31 01; www.ecuries-chambord.com, in French; adult/child €9.50/7; May-Sep).

Chambord is 16km east of Blois, 45km southwest of Orléans and 17km northeast of Cheverny. For public transport options see p376 and the boxed text, p375.

CHÂTEAU DE CHEVERNY

Thought by many to be the most perfectly proportioned chateau of all, **Cheverny** (02 54 79 96 29; www.chateau-cheverny.fr; adult/child €7.50/3.60; 9.15am-6.45pm Jul & Aug, 9.15am-6.15pm Apr-Jun & Sep, 9.45am-5.30pm Oct, 9.45am-5pm Nov-Mar) represents the zenith of French classical architecture, the perfect blend of symmetry, geometry and aesthetic order. It has hardly been altered since its construction between 1625 and 1634. Inside is a formal dining room, bridal chamber and children's playroom (complete with Napoleon III–era toys), as well as a guards' room full of pikestaffs, claymores and suits of armour.

Near the chateau's gateway, the kennels house pedigreed French pointer/English foxhound hunting dogs still used by the owners of Cheverny; feeding time is the **Soupe des Chiens** (5pm Apr-Sep, 3pm Oct-Mar).

Behind the chateau is the 18th-century **Orangerie**, where many priceless art works (including the *Mona Lisa*) were stashed during WWII. Hergé used the castle as a model for Moulinsart (Marlinspike) Hall, the ancestral home of Tintin's sidekick, Captain Haddock. **Les Secrets de Moulinsart** (combined ticket with chateau adult/child €12/7) explores the Tintin connections.

Cheverny is 16km southeast of Blois and 17km southwest of Chambord. For buses to/from Blois see its Getting There & Away section.

CHÂTEAU DE CHAUMONT

It's a brisk climb up to resolutely medieval **Château de Chaumont-sur-Loire** (www.domaine-chaumont.fr, in French; adult/child €9/3.50; 10am-6.30pm Apr-Sep, to 5 or 6pm Oct-Mar), set on a bluff overlooking the Loire. The entrance, across a wooden drawbridge between two wide towers, opens onto an inner courtyard from where there are stunning

DON'T MISS

A CHAMBORD GAD-ABOUT

Chambord is not just about its chateau: **Domaine National de Chambord**, the vast hunting reserve ensnaring it, is a must-explore. While most of its 54 sq km is reserved strictly for high-ranking French government officials (hard to imagine Sarkozy astride a galloping stallion), 10 sq km of its **walking**, **cycling** and **equestrian trails** are open to anyone.

A real highlight is **wildlife-spotting**, especially in September and October during the rutting season, when you can watch stags, boars and red deer woo and mate. Observation towers dot the park; set out at dawn or dusk to spot.

Or pedal around: hire bikes at the **rental kiosk** (02 54 33 37 54; per hr/half-/full day €6/10/13; Apr-Oct) near the jetty on the Cosson River (where you can also rent boats). **Guided bike tours** (adult/child €10/6 plus bike hire) depart mid-August to September. Alternatively, join a **Land Rover Safari** (02 54 50 50 06; adult/child €18/10; Apr-Sep).

STAYING OVER

Tucked at the foot of Cheverny's driveway amid grassland, renovated 19th-century farmhouse **La Levraudière** (☎02 54 79 81 99; http://lalevraudiere.free.fr; 1 chemin de la Levraudière; incl breakfast s €59, d €62-65, tr €80-85) is a perfect blend of tradition and modernity. Breakfast is around a slab-like wooden table laden with fabulous homemade jams, while rooms are all about crisp linens and meticulous presentation.

views. Opposite the main entrance are the luxurious stables, built in 1877.

Chaumont-sur-Loire is 17km southwest of Blois and 20km northeast of Amboise. Onzain, a 2.5km walk from Chaumont across the Loire, has trains to Blois (€11, 10 minutes, 13 daily) and Tours (€11 to €15, 35 minutes, 10 daily).

Tours

POP 140,000

Hovering somewhere between the style of Paris and the conservative sturdiness of central France, Tours is a key staging post for exploring chateaux country. It's a smart, vivacious kind of town, filled with wide 18th-century boulevards, parks and imposing public buildings, as well as a busy university of some 25,000 students.

Sights

Musée des Beaux-Arts ART MUSEUM

(18 place François Sicard; adult/child €4/2; ⌚9am-12.45pm & 2-6pm Wed-Mon) Arranged around the courtyard of the archbishop's gorgeous palace, this fine-arts museum flouts grand rooms decorated to reflect the period of the art works on display. Look for works by Delacroix, Degas and Monet, as well as a rare Rembrandt miniature and a Rubens Madonna and Child.

Cathédrale St-Gatien CHURCH

(place de la Cathédrale; ⌚9am-7pm) With its twin towers, flying buttresses and gargoyles, this cathedral's a show-stopper. It's known for its stained glass; the interior dates from the 13th to 16th centuries, and the domed tops of the two 70m-high towers are Renaissance.

TOP CHOICE **Musée du Compagnonnage** MUSEUM

(8 rue Nationale, in Cloître St-Julien; adult/child €5/3.30; ⌚9am-noon & 2-6pm, closed Tue mid-Sep–mid-Jun) France's skilled labourers, including pastry chefs, coopers and locksmiths, are celebrated here. Displays range from handmade clogs to booby-trapped locks, vintage barrels and cakes.

Sleeping

L'Adresse BOUTIQUE HOTEL €€

(☎02 47 20 85 76; www.hotel-ladresse.com; 12 rue de la Rôtisserie; s €50, d €70-100; ❄📶) Looking for Parisian style in provincial Tours? Then you're in luck – 'The Address' is a boutique bonanza, with rooms finished in sleek slates and ochres, topped off with wi-fi, flat-screen TVs and designer sinks.

Hôtel de l'Univers HOTEL €€€

(☎02 47 05 37 12; www.hotel-univers.fr; 5 blvd Heurteloup; d €198-270; ❄@📶) Everyone from Ernest Hemingway to Édith Piaf has bunked at the Universe over its 150-year history. Previous guests gaze down from the frescoed balcony above the lobby, and rooms are appropriately glitzy: huge beds, gleaming bathrooms.

Hôtel Mondial HOTEL €€

(☎02 47 05 62 68; www.hotelmondialtours.com; 3 place de la Résistance; s €52-72, d €64-87; 📶) Overlooking place de la Résistance, this hotel boasts a fantastic city-centre position. The modernised, metropolitan attic rooms in funky greys, browns and scarlets are the nicest, but even the older-style ones are decent. Reception is on the 2nd floor and there's no lift.

Hôtel Ronsard BOUTIQUE HOTEL €

(☎02 47 05 25 36; www.hotel-ronsard.com; 2 rue Pimbert; s €53-67, d €59-72; ❄@📶) This hotel translates as centrally located and comfortable value. Think sleek modern rooms dressed in slate-grey and sparkling white linen.

Eating

In the old city, place Plumereau, rue du Grand Marché and rue de la Rôtisserie are crammed with cheap eats (quality variable).

TOP CHOICE **Cap Sud** GASTRO BISTRO €€

(☎02 47 05 24 81; 88 rue Colbert; menus €14.50-36; ⌚Tue-Sat) A hot-mod red interior combines nicely with genial service here, and the food! The food! Sensitive, refined creations are made from the freshest ingredients presented in style. Reserve in advance.

Tartines & Co GOURMET SANDWICHES €
(6 rue des Fusillés; mains €9-12; ⊙lunch Tue-Sat, dinner Wed-Fri) This snazzy little bistro reinvents the traditional *croque* (toasted sandwich) amidst jazz and friendly chatter. Choose your topping and it's served up quick-as-a-flash on toasted artisanal bread.

L'Atelier Gourmand GASTRO BISTRO €€
(☎02 47 38 59 87; 37 rue Étienne Marcel; menus €23; ⊙lunch Tue-Fri, dinner Mon-Sat) Another foodie address, but bring dark glasses: the puce-and-silver colour scheme is straight out of a Brett Easton Ellis novel. There's no quibbling with the food: hunks of roast lamb, green-pepper duck and authentic bouillabaisse, delivered with a modern spin.

Le Zinc TRADITIONAL FRENCH €€
(☎02 47 20 29 00; 27 place du Grand Marché; menus €19-25.50; ⊙Mon, Tue & Thu-Sat, dinner Sun) More concerned with market-fresh classic staples than Michelin stars and haute cuisine cachet, this bistro is attractive, authentic and tasty.

Drinking

Place Plumereau and the surrounding streets are plastered with grungy bars and drinking dens, all of which get stuffed to bursting on hot summer nights.

Bistro 64 JAZZ BAR
(64 rue du Grand Marché; ⊙11am-2am Mon-Sat) One step removed from the place Plum hustle. Scuffed-up decor, jazz combos and plenty of house beers entertain a local crowd.

La Canteen WINE BAR
(10 rue de la Grosse Tour; ⊙noon-2.30pm & 7.30-11pm Mon-Sat) For something smoother and sexier, swing by this designer wine bar with rough stone walls, leather sofas, razor-sharp tables and neon-lit bar.

Information

Tourist office (☎02 47 70 37 37; www.ligeris.com; 78-82 rue Bernard Palissy; ⊙8.30am-7pm Mon-Sat, 10am-12.30pm & 2.30-5pm Sun)

Getting There & Away

Air

Tours-Val de Loire Airport (www.tours.aeroport.fr), 5km northeast, is linked to London's Stansted, Dublin, Marseille and Porto by Ryanair.

Bus

The **information desk** (⊙8am-6.30pm Mon-Fri, 8.30am-12.30pm & 1.30-6.30pm Sat) for **Touraine Fil Vert** (☎02 47 31 14 00; www.touraine-filvert.com, in French) is at the bus

WORTH A TRIP

TOP CHATEAUX TRIPS

From Tours a clutch of fabulous castles beg to be discovered:

» **Chenonceau** (www.chenonceau.com; adult/child €10.50/8; ⊙9am-8pm Jul & Aug, 9am-7.30pm Jun & Sep, 9am-7pm Apr & May, 9.30am-5 or 6pm Oct-Mar) This 16th-century castle is one of the Loire's most architecturally attractive – and busiest. Framed by a glassy moat and sweeping gardens, and topped by turrets and towers, it's straight out of a fairy tale. Don't miss the yew-tree labyrinth and the 60m-long Grande Gallerie spanning the Cher River.

» **Azay-le-Rideau** (☎02 47 45 42 04; adult/child €7.50/free; ⊙9.30am-6pm, to 7pm Jul & Aug, 10am-12.30pm & 2-5.30pm Oct-Mar) Built in the 1500s on an island in the Indre River, this romantic, moat-ringed wonder flouts geometric windows, ordered turrets and decorative stonework. Don't miss: its famous loggia staircase and summertime *son et lumière*.

» **Langeais** (☎02 47 96 72 60; adult/child €8.50/5; ⊙9.30am-6.30pm, to 5.30pm Feb & Mar, 9am-7pm Jul & Aug) For medieval atmosphere, head for this 15th-century fortress complete with working drawbridge, crenellated battlements and ruined 10th-century donjon. Don't miss the ruined keep (France's oldest) built by 10th-century warlord, Count Foulques Nerra.

» **Villandry** (www.chateauvillandry.com; adult/child €9/5, gardens only €6/3.50; ⊙chateau 9am-6pm, to 5.30pm Mar, to 5pm Feb & early Nov, gardens 9am-5pm to 7.30pm year-round) One of the last major Renaissance chateaux to be built in the Loire, this one is more famous for what's outside than in. Its gardens are nothing short of glorious. Don't miss the Ornamental Garden or the *potager* (kitchen garden).

Tours

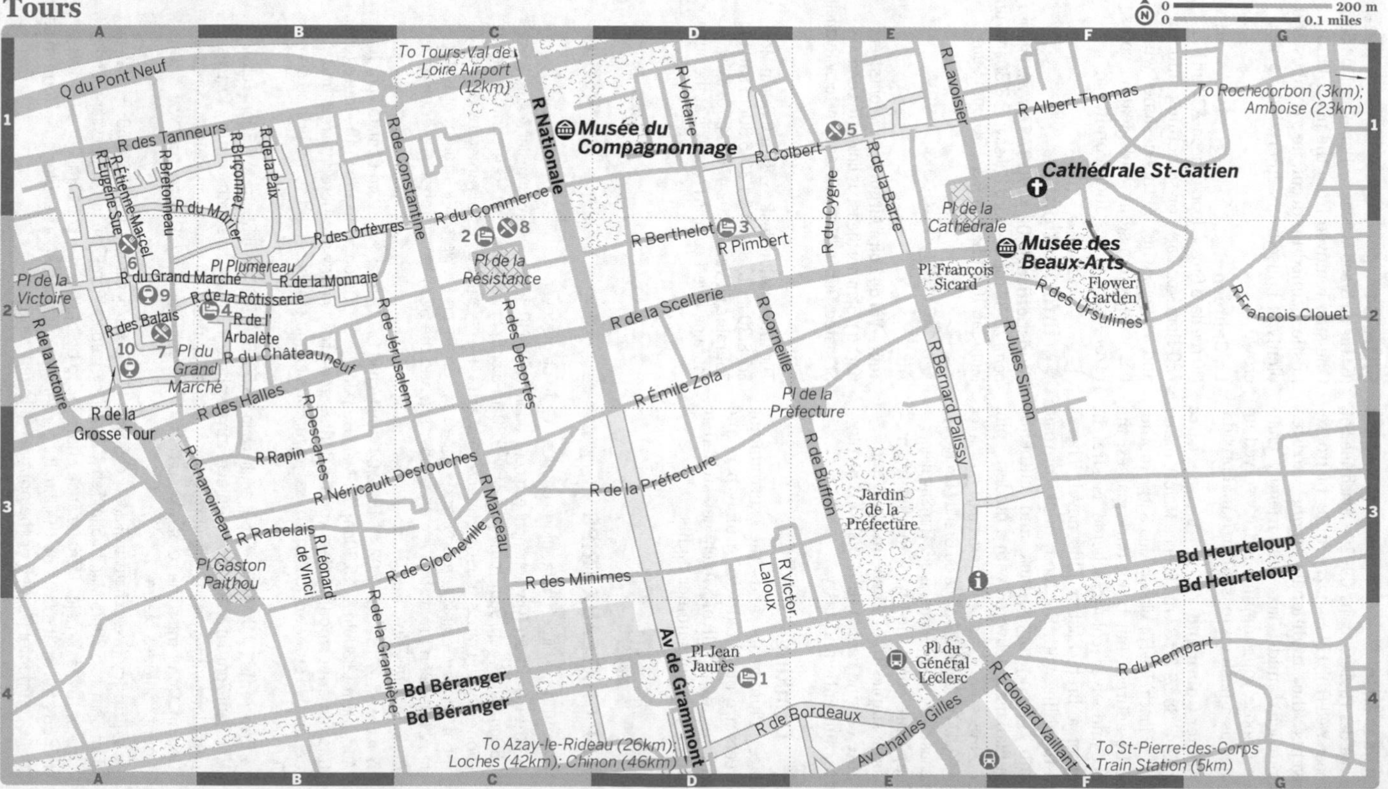
200 m
0.1 miles
To Tours-Val de Loire Airport (12km)
To Rochecorbon (3km); Amboise (23km)
To Azay-le-Rideau (26km); Loches (42km); Chinon (46km)
To St-Pierre-des-Corps Train Station (5km)
Musée du Compagnonnage
Cathédrale St-Gatien
Musée des Beaux-Arts
Flower Garden
Jardin de la Préfecture
Pl de la Cathédrale
Pl François Sicard
Pl de la Résistance
Pl de la Préfecture
Pl Plumereau
Pl de la Victoire
Pl du Grand Marché
Pl Gaston Paithou
Pl Jean Jaurès
Pl du Général Leclerc
Q du Pont Neuf
R Nationale
R Voltaire
R Lavoisier
R Albert Thomas
R Colbert
R des Tanneurs
R Bretonneau
R Briçonnet
R de la Paix
R Étienne Marcel
R Eugène Sue
R du Mûrier
R de Constantine
R du Commerce
R des Orfèvres
R Berthelot
R Pimbert
R du Cygne
R de la Barre
R du Grand Marché
R de la Monnaie
R de la Rôtisserie
R des Balais
R de l'Arbalète
R du Châteauneuf
R de la Victoire
R de la Grosse Tour
R des Halles
R de Jérusalem
R des Déportés
R de la Scellerie
R Corneille
R Bernard Palissy
R Jules Simon
R des Ursulines
R François Clouet
R Émile Zola
R Descartes
R Rapin
R Chanoineau
R Néricault Destouches
R Marceau
R de la Préfecture
R de Buffon
R Rabelais
R Léonard de Vinci
R de Clocheville
R des Minimes
R Victor Laloux
R de la Grandière
Bd Heurteloup
Bd Béranger
Av de Grammont
R du Rempart
R de Bordeaux
Av Charles Gilles
R Édouard Vaillant
A
B
C
D
E
F
G
1
2
3
4
5
6
7
8
9
10

Tours

Top Sights

Cathédrale St-Gatien F1
Musée des Beaux-Arts F2
Musée du Compagnonnage C1

Sleeping

1 Hôtel de l'Univers D4
2 Hôtel Mondial C2
3 Hôtel Ronsard D2
4 L'Adresse B2

Eating

5 Cap Sud E1
6 L'Atelier Gourmand A2
7 Le Zinc A2
8 Tartines & Co C2

Drinking

9 Bistro 64 .... A2
10 La Canteen A2

station, next to the train station. Line C links Tours with Amboise (€1.60, 35 minutes, 12 daily Monday to Saturday) and Chenonceaux (€1.60, 1¼ hours, two daily).

Train

Tours is the Loire's main rail hub. The train station is linked to St-Pierre-des-Corps, Tours' TGV train station, by frequent shuttle trains.

AMBOISE €11, 20 minutes, 12 daily
ANGERS €23 to €34, one hour, 26 daily
BLOIS €9.10, 40 minutes, 12 daily
BORDEAUX €40 to €62, 2¾ hours
CHENONCEAUX €11, 30 minutes, eight daily
LOCHES €11, 50 minutes, one or two daily
NANTES €28 to €55, 1½ hours
ORLÉANS €24 to €35, one to 1½ hours, hourly
PARIS' GARE D'AUSTERLITZ €41 to €62, two to 2¾ hours, five daily, slow trains
PARIS' GARE MONTPARNASSE €44 to €83, 1¼ hours, 30 daily, high-speed TGVs
SAUMUR €14 to €21, 35 minutes, hourly

Amboise

POP 12,900

The childhood home of Charles VIII and final resting place of Leonardo da Vinci, elegant Amboise, 23km northeast of Tours, is pleasantly perched along the southern bank of the Loire and overlooked by its fortified chateau. With some seriously posh hotels and a wonderful weekend market, Amboise is a very popular base for exploring nearby chateaux; coach tours arrive en masse to visit da Vinci's Clos Lucé.

Sights

Château Royal d'Amboise CASTLE

(place Michel Debré; adult/child €9.70/6.30; 9am-6pm Apr–mid-Nov, 9am-5.30pm Mar, 9am-12.30pm & 2-4.45pm Jan-Feb & mid-Nov–Dec) Sprawling across a rocky escarpment above town, this easily defendable castle presented a formidable prospect to would-be attackers – but saw little military action. It was more often used as a weekend getaway from the official royal seat at nearby Blois. Charles VIII (r 1483–98), born and bred here, was responsible for the chateau's Italianate remodelling in 1492. Today, just a few of the original 15th- and 16th-century structures survive, notably the **Flamboyant Gothic wing** and **Chapelle St-Hubert**, believed to be the final resting place of da Vinci. Exit the chateau through the circular **Tour Hurtault** with its ingenious sloping spiral ramp for easy carriage access.

TOP CHOICE **Le Clos Lucé** HISTORIC MANOR

(www.vinci-closluce.com; 2 rue du Clos Lucé; adult/child €12.50/7.50; 9am-7pm Feb-Oct, to 6pm Nov-Dec, 10am-6pm Jan) Leonardo da Vinci took up residence in the grand manor house at Le Clos Lucé in 1516 on the invitation of François I, and its interior and gardens are chock-a-block with scale models of the artist's many wacky inventions.

Pagode de Chanteloup PAGODA

(www.pagode-chanteloup.com, in French; adult/child €8.50/6.50; 10am-7pm) Two kilometres south of Amboise, this curiosity was built between 1775 and 1778 when the odd blend of classical French architecture and Chinese motifs were all the rage. Clamber to the top for glorious views. In summer, picnic hampers (€12 to €26) are sold, you can rent rowing boats, and play free outdoor games.

Sleeping

La Pavillon des Lys BOUTIQUE HOTEL €€

(02 47 30 01 01; www.pavillondeslys.com; 9 rue d'Orange; d €98-160;) Consider this: take

EASE THE PAIN

Buy tickets in advance at the tourist office and visit early in the day to avoid crowds.

a cappuccino-coloured, 18th-century town house and fill it with designer lamps, roll-top baths, hi-fi steroes and deep sofas – chuck in a locally renowned restaurant and an elegant patio garden and wow, you've got yourself one beautiful hotel!

Le Clos d'Amboise HISTORIC HOTEL €€
(☎02 47 30 10 20; www.leclosamboise.com; 27 rue Rabelais; r €97-149;) Another posh pad finished with oodles of style and lashings of luxurious fabrics. Features range from wood-panelling to antique beds; some rooms have separate sitting areas, others original fireplaces. Sauna and gym in the old stables.

Villa Mary B&B €€
(☎02 47 23 03 31; www.villa-mary.fr; 14 rue de la Concorde; d incl breakfast €90-120) Four tip-top rooms in an impeccably furnished 18th-century town house, crammed with beeswaxed antiques, glittering chandeliers and antique rugs.

Centre Charles Péguy-Auberge de Jeunesse HOSTEL €
(☎02 47 30 60 90; www.mjcamboise.fr; Île d'Or; dm €12; reception 2-8pm Mon-Fri, 5-8pm Sat & Sun; @) Efficient boarding-school-style hostel on Île d'Or, with 72 beds mostly in three- or four-bed dorms. Table tennis and bike hire available.

Hôtel Le Blason HOTEL €
(☎02 47 23 22 41; www.leblason.fr; 11 place Richelieu; s/d/tr €45/55/70; @) Quirky, creaky budget hotel on a quiet square with 25 higgledy-piggledy rooms, wedged in around corridors: most are titchy, flowery and timber-beamed.

Eating

Chez Bruno REGIONAL CUISINE €
(☎02 47 57 73 49; place Michel Debré; menus from €12; lunch Tue-Sun, dinner Tue-Sat) Uncork a host of local vintages in a coolly contemporary setting, accompanied by honest regional cooking.

L'Épicerie TRADITIONAL FRENCH €€
(☎02 47 57 08 94; 46 place Michel Debré; menus €22-34; Wed-Sun) A more time-honoured atmosphere with rich wood, neo-Renaissance decor and filling fare such as *cuisse de lapin* (rabbit leg) and *tournedos de canard* (duck fillet).

Bigot TEAROOM €
(2 rue Nationale; 9am-7.30pm Tue-Fri, 8.30am-7.30pm Sat & Sun) Since 1913 this award-winning chocolatier and patisserie has been whipping up some of the Loire's creamiest cakes and gooiest treats: multicoloured *macarons,* buttery biscuits, handmade chocolates and petits fours.

Information

Tourist office (☎02 47 57 09 28; www.amboise-valdeloire.com; 9am-7pm Mon-Sat, 10am-1pm & 2-6pm Sun) In a riverside building opposite 7 quai du Général de Gaulle.

Getting There & Around

Bicycle

Cycles Richard (☎02 47 57 01 79; 2 rue de Nazelles; €15/day; 9am-noon & 2.30-7pm Tue-Sat)

Bus

Touraine Fil Vert's Line C (see Tours' Getting There & Away section) links Amboise's post

WORTH A TRIP

A TRIP BETWEEN VINES

Burgundy's most renowned vintages come from the **Côte d'Or** (Golden Hillside), a range of hills made of limestone, flint and clay that runs south from Dijon for about 60km. The northern section, the **Côte de Nuits**, stretches from Marsannay-la-Côte south to Corgoloin and produces reds known for their robust, full-bodied character. The southern section, the **Côte de Beaune**, lies between Ladoix-Serrigny and Santenay and produces great reds and whites.

Tourist offices can provide local brochures: *The Burgundy Wine Road*, an excellent free booklet published by the Burgundy Tourist Board (www.bourgogne-tourisme.com); and a useful map, *Roadmap to the Wines of Burgundy* (€0.50). There's also the **Route des Grands Crus** (www.road-of-the-fine-burgundy-wines.com), a signposted road route of some of the most celebrated Côte de Nuits vineyards.

Wine & Voyages (www.wineandvoyages.com; €48-58) and **Alter & Go** (www.alterandgo.fr; €60-80), with an emphasis on history and winemaking methods, run minibus tours in English; reserve online or at the Dijon tourist office.

office with Tours' bus terminal (€1.60, 45 minutes, 12 daily Monday to Saturday). Two go to Chenonceaux (15 minutes, Monday to Saturday).

Train

BLOIS €11, 20 minutes, 14 daily

TOURS €11, 20 minutes, 10 daily

PARIS' GARE D'AUSTERLITZ €38 to €56, 2¼ hours, 14 daily

PARIS' GARE MONTPARNASSE €107, 1¼ hours, 10 daily, TGV

BURGUNDY & THE RHÔNE VALLEY

If there's one place in France where you're really going to find out what makes the nation tick, it's Burgundy. Two of the country's enduring passions – food and wine – come together in this gorgeously rural region, and if you're a sucker for hearty food and the fruits of the vine, you'll be in seventh heaven.

Dijon

POP 250,000

Dijon is one of France's most appealing cities. Filled with elegant medieval and Renaissance buildings, dashing Dijon is Burgundy's capital, and spiritual home of French mustard. Its lively Old Town is wonderful for strolling, especially if you like to leaven your cultural enrichment with excellent food, fine wine and shopping.

Dijon has plenty of green spaces including **Jardin de l'Arquebuse**, whose stream, pond and formal gardens are across the tracks from the train station.

Sights & Activities

Palais des Ducs et des États de Bourgogne PALACE

(Palace of the Dukes & States of Burgundy) Once home to Burgundy's powerful dukes, this monumental palace with neoclassical facade overlooks **place de la Libération**, Old Dijon's magnificent central square dating from 1686. The palace's eastern wing houses the outstanding **Musée des Beaux-Arts**, whose entrance is next to the **Tour de Bar**, a squat 14th-century tower that once served as a prison.

Just off the **Cour d'Honneur**, the 46m-high, mid-15th-century **Tour Philippe le Bon** (adult/child €2.30/free; guided tours every 45min 9am-noon & 1.45-5.30pm, closed Mon-Tue & morning Wed, also Thu-Fri late Nov–Easter) affords fantastic views over the city. Spot Mont Blanc on a clear day.

DON'T MISS

THE LUCKY OWL

Dijon's **Rue de la Chouette** is named after the small stone *chouette* (owl) carved into the exterior corner of the chapel, diagonally across from No 24. It's said to grant happiness and wisdom to those who stroke it, so generations of fortune-seekers have worked it quite smooth! All sorts of superstitions surround the owl: some insist that walking by the dragon in the lower left corner of the grille of the adjacent window annuls your wish; others insist that approaching the dragon helps your wish come true.

Église Notre Dame CHURCH

A block north of the Palais des Ducs, this church was built between 1220 and 1240. Its extraordinary facade's three tiers are lined with leering gargoyles separated by two rows of pencil-thin columns. Atop the church, the 14th-century **Horloge à Jacquemart**, transported from Flanders in 1383 by Philip the Bold who claimed it as a trophy of war, chimes every quarter-hour.

Cathédrale St-Bénigne CHURCH

(place St-Philibert) Built over the tomb of St Benignus (believed to have brought Christianity to Burgundy in the 2nd century), Dijon's Burgundian Gothic-style cathedral was built around 1300 as an abbey church. Some of Burgundy's great figures are buried in its crypt.

Musée de la Vie Bourguignonne MUSEUM

(17 rue Ste-Anne; 9am-noon & 2-6pm Wed-Mon) Housed in a 17th-century Cistercian convent, this museum explores village and town life in Burgundy in centuries past with evocative tableaux illustrating dress and traditional crafts.

Sleeping

Hôtel Le Jacquemart HOTEL €

(03 80 60 09 60; www.hotel-lejacquemart.fr; 32 rue Verrerie; d €49-65; @) In the heart of old Dijon, this two-star hotel has tidy, comfortable rooms; the pricier ones come with marble fireplaces.

Dijon

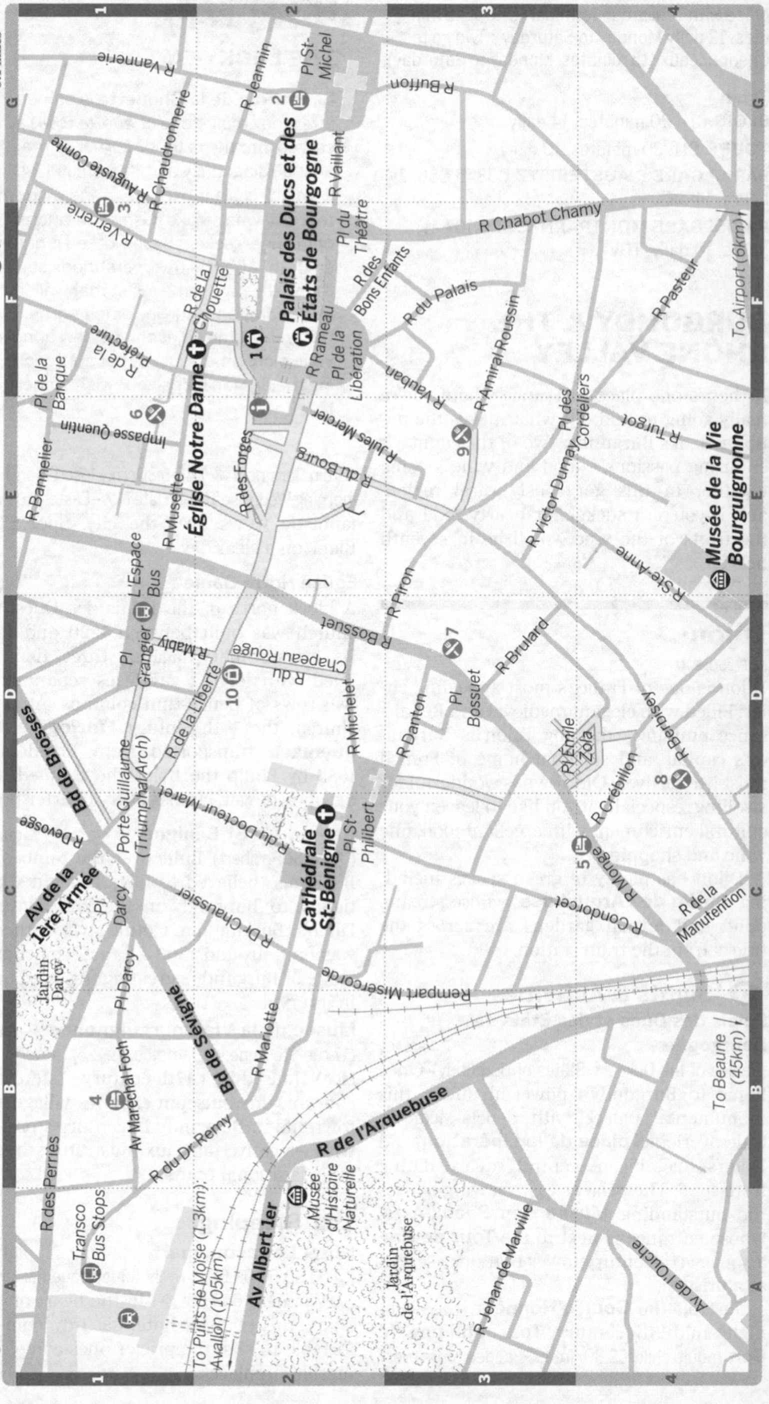

0 200 m
0 0.1 miles

A B C D E F G
1 2 3 4

R des Perriès
Transco Bus Stops
4
Av Marechal Foch
Pl Darcy
Jardin Darcy
Av de la 1ère Armée
Pl Darcy
R Devosge
Bd de Brosses
Porte Guillaume (Triumphal Arch)
Pl Grangier
L'Espace Bus
R Bannelier
Pl de la Banque
Impasse Quentin
6
R de la Préfecture
R Verrerie
3
R Auguste Comte
R Vannerie
R Chaudronnerie
R Musette
Église Notre Dame
R de la Chouette
R Jeannin
R du Dr Remy
To Puits de Moïse (1.3km); Avallon (105km)
Bd de Sévigné
R de la Liberté
R Mably
10
R des Forges
1
2
Av Albert 1er
R Mariotte
R Dr Chaussier
R du Docteur Maret
R du Chapeau Rouge
Palais des Ducs et des États de Bourgogne
Pl St-Michel
Musée d'Histoire Naturelle
R de l'Arquebuse
Cathédrale St-Bénigne
Pl St-Philibert
R Michelet
R Bossuet
R du Bourg
R Jules Mercier
R Rameau
Pl de la Libération
Pl du Théâtre
R Vaillant
R des Bons Enfants
Jardin de l'Arquebuse
Rempart Miséricorde
R Danton
R Piron
R Vauban
R du Palais
R Buffon
Pl Bossuet
7
9
R Amiral Roussin
R Chabot Charny
R Jehan de Marville
R Brulard
R Victor Dumay
Pl des Cordeliers
Pl Émile Zola
5
R Condorcet
R Monge
R Crébillon
R Ste-Anne
R Turgot
R Pasteur
8
R Berbisey
Av de l'Ouche
To Beaune (45km)
R de la Manutention
Musée de la Vie Bourguignonne
To Airport (6km)

Dijon

Top Sights

Cathédrale St-Bénigne........C2
Église Notre Dame........F2
Musée de la Vie Bourguignonne........E4
Palais des Ducs et des États de Bourgogne........F2

Sights

1 Tour Philippe le Bon........F2

Sleeping

2 Hôtel Chambellan........G2
3 Hôtel Le Jacquemart........F1
4 Hôtel Le Jura........B1
5 Hôtel Le Sauvage........C4

Eating

6 Café Chez Nous........E1
7 La Dame d'Aquitaine........D3
8 La Mère Folle........D4
9 Le Petit Roi de la Lune........E3

Shopping

10 Moutarde Maille........D2

Hôtel Chambellan HOTEL €
(03 80 67 12 67; www.hotel-chambellan.com; 92 rue Vannerie; s/d from €45/50) Built in 1730, this Old Town address has a vaguely medieval feel. Rooms come in cheerful tones of red, orange, pink and white; some have courtyard views.

Hôtel Le Sauvage HOTEL €
(03 80 41 31 21; www.hotellesauvage.com, in French; 64 rue Monge; s €46-55, d €51-61, tr €80;) Set in a 15th-century *relais de poste* (post-relay house) that ranges around a cobbled, vine-shaded courtyard, this little hotel just off the lively rue Monge is definitely good value.

Hôtel Le Jura HOTEL €€
(03 80 41 61 12; www.oceaniahotels.com; 14 av Maréchal Foch; d €70-92, q €179;) Near the train station, this no-nonsense hotel has friendly staff and some rooms overlooking a central courtyard. 'Superior' rooms are really that. Room prices fluctuate; check online.

Eating

Eat streets loaded with restaurants include buzzy rue Berbisey, place Émile Zola, rue Amiral Roussin and around the perimeter of the covered market. Outdoor cafes fill place de la Libération.

Café Chez Nous CAFE €
(impasse Quentin; lunch menus €8; lunch noon-2pm, bar 10am-2am, 11am-2pm Sun, closed Mon) This quintessentially French *bar du coin* (neighbourhood bar), often crowded, hides down an alleyway near the covered market. Lunches are generally organic and wine by the glass is a bargain (€1.20 to €2.40). Check the chalkboard for dinners and live music.

Le Petit Roi de la Lune BISTRO €€
(03 80 49 89 93; 28 rue Amiral Roussin; lunch menus €10, mains €15-18; lunch Tue-Sat, dinner Mon-Sat) A hip, younger crowd comes for French cuisine that, explains the chef, has been *revisitée, rearrangée et decalée* (revisited, rearranged and shifted). The hugely popular breaded-and-fried Camembert served with blackberry jelly tops the list.

La Mère Folle BURGUNDIAN €€
(03 80 50 19 76; 102 rue Berbisey; menus €10-23; Tue-Sat) Look past the OTT medieval decor to find Burgundian specialities such as *magret de canard au miel, thym et mirabelles* (fillet of duck with honey, thyme and cherry plums). Weekday lunches are a steal and include terrine straight from the crock.

La Dame d'Aquitaine REGIONAL CUISINE €€
(03 80 30 45 65; 23 place Bossuet; menus €21-43; lunch Tue-Sat, dinner Mon-Sat, closed lunch mid-Jul–mid-Aug) Excellent local cuisine is served under the sumptuously lit bays of a 13th-century *cave*. Classical music filters through and the wine list is extensive.

Information

Tourist office (08 92 70 05 58; www.visitdijon.com; 9am-6.30pm Mon-Sat, 10am-6pm Sun) Main office (11 rue des Forges); Annexe (train station)

DON'T MISS

DIJON MUSTARD

If there is one pilgrimage to be made on Dijon's main shopping area, rue de la Liberté, it is to **Moutarde Maille** (32 rue de la Liberté; 10am-7pm Mon-Sat), the factory boutique of the company that makes Dijon's most famous mustard. The tangy odours of the sharp sauce assault your nostrils instantly upon entering and there are 36 different kinds to buy, including cassis-, truffle- or celery-flavoured. Three on tap (from €2.40 per 200ml) can be sampled.

Getting There & Away

Bus

Transco (☎08 00 10 20 04; www.mobigo-bourgogne.com) Buses stop in front of the train station. Bus 60 (€1.50) links Dijon with the northern Côte de Nuits wine villages of Marsannay-la-Côte, Couchey, Fixin and Gevrey-Chambertin (30 minutes).

Eurolines (☎03 80 68 20 44; 53 rue Guillaume Tell) International travel.

Train

LYON-PART DIEU €36 to 90, two hours, 25 daily

PARIS' GARE DE LYON €52 to €136, 1¾ hours by TGV, three hours regular train, 20 daily

NICE €106 to €213, 6¼ hours by TGV, two direct daily

STRASBOURG €55 to €126, 3½ hours, nine daily

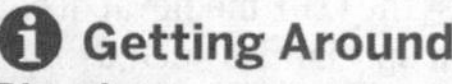

Getting Around

Bicycle

Main tourist office (€18/day) Rentals with free helmets.

Velodi (www.velodi.net, in French) 400 bikes at 33 stations around town.

Beaune

POP 22,720

Beaune (pronounced 'bone'), 44km south of Dijon, is the unofficial capital of the Côte d'Or. This thriving town's raison d'être and the source of its joie de vivre is wine: making it, tasting it, selling it, but most of all, drinking it. Consequently Beaune is one of the best places in all of France for wine tasting.

The jewel of Beaune's old city is the magnificent Hôtel-Dieu, France's most splendiferous medieval charity hospital.

Sights & Activities

Beaune's amoeba-shaped old city is enclosed by **stone ramparts** sheltering wine cellars. Lined with overgrown gardens and ringed by a pathway, they make for a lovely stroll.

TOP CHOICE **Hôtel-Dieu des Hospices de Beaune** GOTHIC HOSPITAL

(rue de l'Hôtel-Dieu; adult/child €6.50/2.80; ⏰9am-6.30pm) Built in 1443, this magnificent Gothic hospital (until 1971) is famously topped by stunning turrets and pitched rooftops covered in multicoloured tiles. Interior highlights include the barrel-vaulted **Grande Salle** (look for the dragons and peasant heads up on the roof beams); the mural-covered **St-Hughes Room**; an 18th-century **pharmacy** lined with flasks once filled with elixirs and powders such as *beurre d'antimoine* (antimony butter) and *poudre de cloportes* (woodlouse powder); and the multipanelled masterpiece **Polyptych of the Last Judgement** by 15th-century Flemish painter Rogier van der Weyden, depicting Judgment Day in glorious technicolour.

Cellar Visits WINE TASTING

Millions of bottles of wine age to perfection in cool dark cellars beneath Beaune's buildings, streets and ramparts. Tasting opportunities abound and dozens of cellars can be visited by guided tour. Our favourites include the candlelit cellars of the former Église des Cordeliers, **Marché aux Vins** (www.marcheauxvins.com, in French; 2 rue Nicolas Rolin; admission €10; ⏰9.30-11.45am & 2-5.45pm, no midday closure mid-Jun–Aug), where 15 wines can be sampled; and **Cellier de la Vieille Grange** (www.bourgogne-cellier.com, in French; 27 blvd Georges Clemenceau; ⏰9am-noon & 2-7pm Wed-Sat, by appointment Sun-Tue), where locals flock to buy Burgundy wines *en vrac* (in bulk) for as little as €1.25 per litre (from €3.40 per litre for AOC). Tasting is done direct from barrels using a pipette. Bring your own jerrycan or buy a vinibag. **Patriarche Père et Fils** (www.patriarche.com; 5 rue du Collège; audioguide tour €10; ⏰9.30-11.30am & 2-5.30pm), lined with about five million bottles of wine, has Burgundy's largest cellars.

Sleeping

Hôtel des Remparts HISTORIC HOTEL €€

(☎03 80 24 94 94; www.hotel-remparts-beaune.com; 48 rue Thiers; d €75-112; ❄@📶) Set around two delightful courtyards, rooms in this 17th-century town house have red-tiled floors, simple antique furniture and luxurious bathrooms. Friendly staff can also hire out bikes.

Hôtel Rousseau HOTEL €

(☎03 80 22 13 59; 11 place Madeleine; d incl breakfast €58, s/d with washbasin only from €40, hall shower €3) An endearingly old-fashioned, 12-room hotel where the lady who has run the place since 1959 occasionally shuts reception without warning so she can go shopping.

Abbaye de Maizières HISTORIC HOTEL €€

(☎03 80 24 74 64; www.beaune-abbaye-maizieres.com; 19 rue Maizières; d €112; @)

A ROOM WITH A VINE VIEW

It is not in town, but in beautiful stone-laced vintner villages around Dijon and Beaune that some of Burgundy's most sought-after sleeping addresses are hidden:

» **Villa Louise Hôtel** (☎03 80 26 46 70; www.hotel-villa-louise.fr, in French; Aloxe-Corton; d €100-195; @ 📶 🏊) Who needs city life when you can stow away in vineyard-side luxury? This tranquil mansion on the Côte de Beaune houses dreamy rooms, expansive garden, sauna, pool and wine cellar.

» **Domaine Corgette** (☎03 80 21 68 08; www.domainecorgette.com; rue de la Perrière, St-Romain; d incl breakfast €80-90; 📶) The sun-drenched terrace at this village winery faces dramatic cliffs. Rooms are light and airy with crisp linens, fireplaces and wooden floors.

» **Maison des Abeilles** (☎03 80 62 95 42; http://perso.wanadoo.fr/maison-des-abeilles, in French; Magny-les-Villars; d incl breakfast €58-64, q €90; @) Sweet and jolly Jocelyne maintains this impeccably clean *chambre d'hôte* (B&B) in a small village in the Haute Côte. Rooms are colourful and breakfast is a homemade feast.

Think an idiosyncratic hotel inside a 12th-century abbey with 13 rooms featuring brickwork and wooden beams.

Eating

Beaune harbours a host of excellent restaurants; you'll find many around place Carnot, place Félix Ziem and place Madeleine.

Caves Madeleine BURGUNDIAN €€
(☎03 80 22 93 30; 8 rue du Faubourg Madeleine; menus €14-24; ⏲Mon-Wed & Sat, dinner Fri) This is a convivial Burgundian restaurant where locals tuck into regional classics like *boeuf bourguignon* and *cassolette d'escargots* at long shared tables surrounded by wine racks.

Le Bistrot Bourguignon BURGUNDIAN €€
(☎03 80 22 23 24; 8 rue Monge; mains €16-19; ⏲Tue-Sat) This lively bistro and wine bar serves hearty regional cuisine and 17 Burgundy wines by the glass (€3 to €9). Hosts live jazz at least once a month.

Le P'tit Paradis MODERN BURGUNDIAN €€
(☎03 80 24 91 00; 25 rue Paradis; menus €19-36; ⏲Tue-Sat) Find this intimate restaurant, known for *cuisine elaborée* (creative cuisine) made with local products, on a medieval street. Summer terrace.

Information

Tourist office (☎03 80 26 21 30; www.beaune-burgundy.com; 6 blvd Perpreuil; ⏲9am-7pm Mon-Sat, 9am-6pm Sun)

Getting There & Away

Bus

Bus 44 links Beaune with Dijon (€1.50, 1½ hours, up to seven daily), stopping at Côte d'Or villages like Vougeot, Nuits-St-Georges and Aloxe-Corton.

Train

DIJON €11, 25 minutes, 40 daily

LYON-PART DIEU €31 to €46, 1¾ hours, 16 daily

MÂCON €12.90, 50 minutes, 16 daily

NUITS-ST-GEORGES €11, 10 minutes, 40 daily

PARIS' GARE DE LYON €64 to €118, 2¼ hours by TGV, 20 daily, two direct TGVs daily

Lyon

POP 480,660

Gourmets, eat your heart out: Lyon is *the* gastronomic capital of France, with a lavish table of piggy-driven dishes and delicacies to savour. The city has been a commercial, industrial and banking powerhouse for the past 500 years, and is still France's second-largest conurbation, with outstanding art museums, a dynamic nightlife, green parks and a Unesco-listed Old Town.

Sights

VIEUX LYON

Old Lyon, with its cobblestone streets and medieval and Renaissance houses below Fourvière hill, is divided into three quarters: St-Paul at the northern end, St-Jean in the middle and St-Georges in the south. Lovely old buildings languish on **rue du Bœuf**, **rue St-Jean** and **rue des Trois Maries**.

The partly Romanesque **Cathédrale St-Jean** (place St-Jean, 5e; ⏲8am-noon & 2-7.30pm Mon-Fri, 8am-noon & 2-7pm Sat & Sun; Ⓜ Vieux Lyon), seat of Lyon's 133rd bishop, was built from the late 11th to the early 16th centuries.

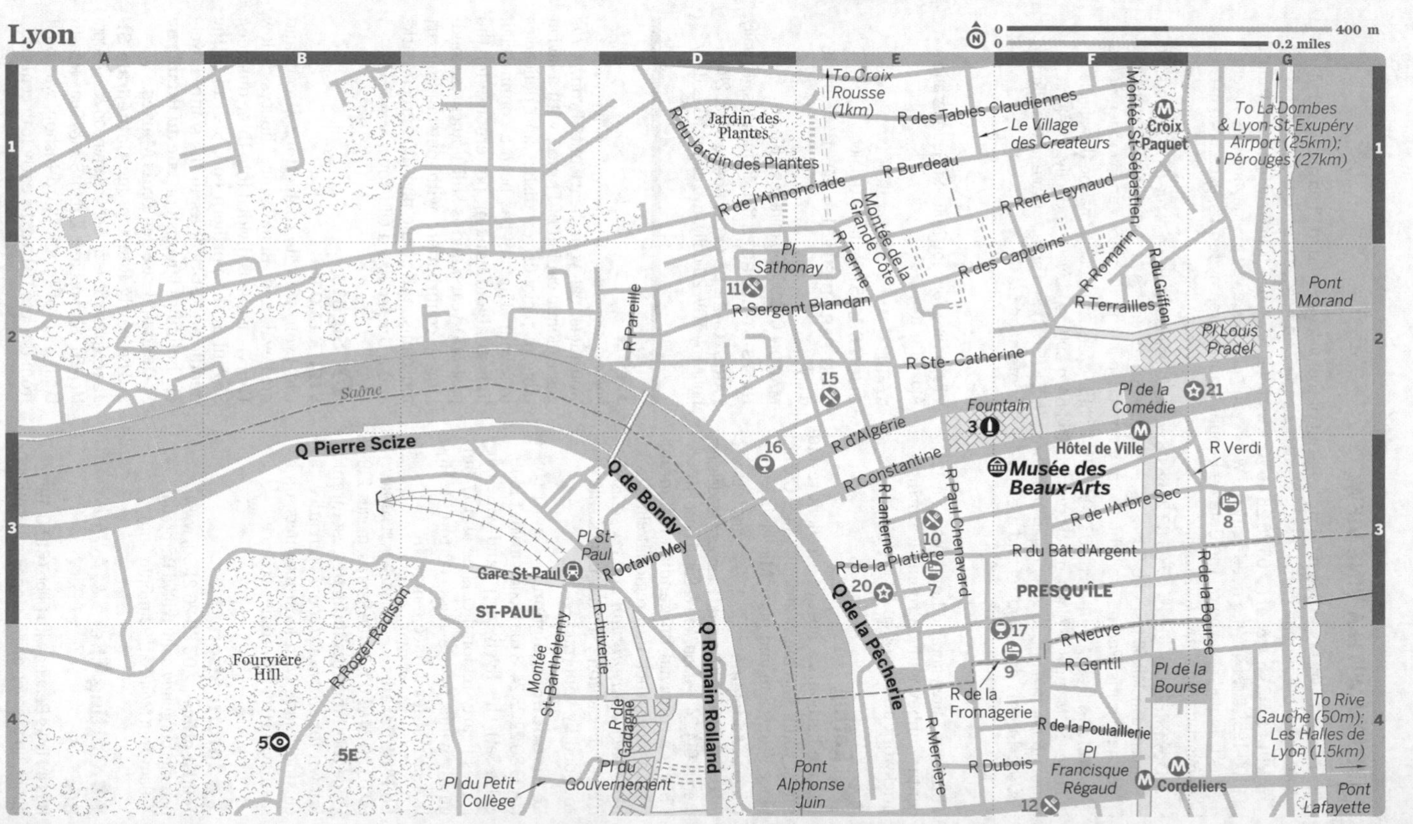
Lyon
0 400 m
0 0.2 miles
A
B
C
D
E
F
G
1
2
3
4
To Croix Rousse (1km)
To La Dombes & Lyon-St-Exupéry Airport (25km); Pérouges (27km)
Jardin des Plantes
R du Jardin des Plantes
R des Tables Claudiennes
Le Village des Createurs
Montée St-Sébastien
Croix Paquet
R de l'Annonciade
R Burdeau
R René Leynaud
Montée de la Grande Côte
R Terme
Pl Sathonay
11
R Sergent Blandan
R des Capucins
R Romarin
R du Griffon
R Terrailles
Pont Morand
Pl Louis Pradel
R Pareille
R Ste-Catherine
15
Saône
Pl de la Comédie
21
Fountain
3
Hôtel de Ville
R Verdi
Q Pierre Scize
16
R d'Algérie
R Constantine
Musée des Beaux-Arts
R de l'Arbre Sec
8
Q de Bondy
R Lanterne
R Paul Chenavard
10
R du Bât d'Argent
Pl St-Paul
R Octavio Mey
Gare St-Paul
R de la Platière
20
7
PRESQU'ÎLE
R de la Bourse
ST-PAUL
R Juiverie
Q Romain Rolland
Q de la Pêcherie
17
R Neuve
9
R Gentil
Pl de la Bourse
Fourvière Hill
R Roger Radison
Montée St-Barthélemy
R de Gadagne
R de la Fromagerie
R de la Poulaillerie
To Rive Gauche (50m); Les Halles de Lyon (1.5km)
5
5E
Pl du Gouvernement
Pl du Petit Collège
Pont Alphonse Juin
R Mercière
R Dubois
Pl Francisque Régaud
Cordeliers
Pont Lafayette
12

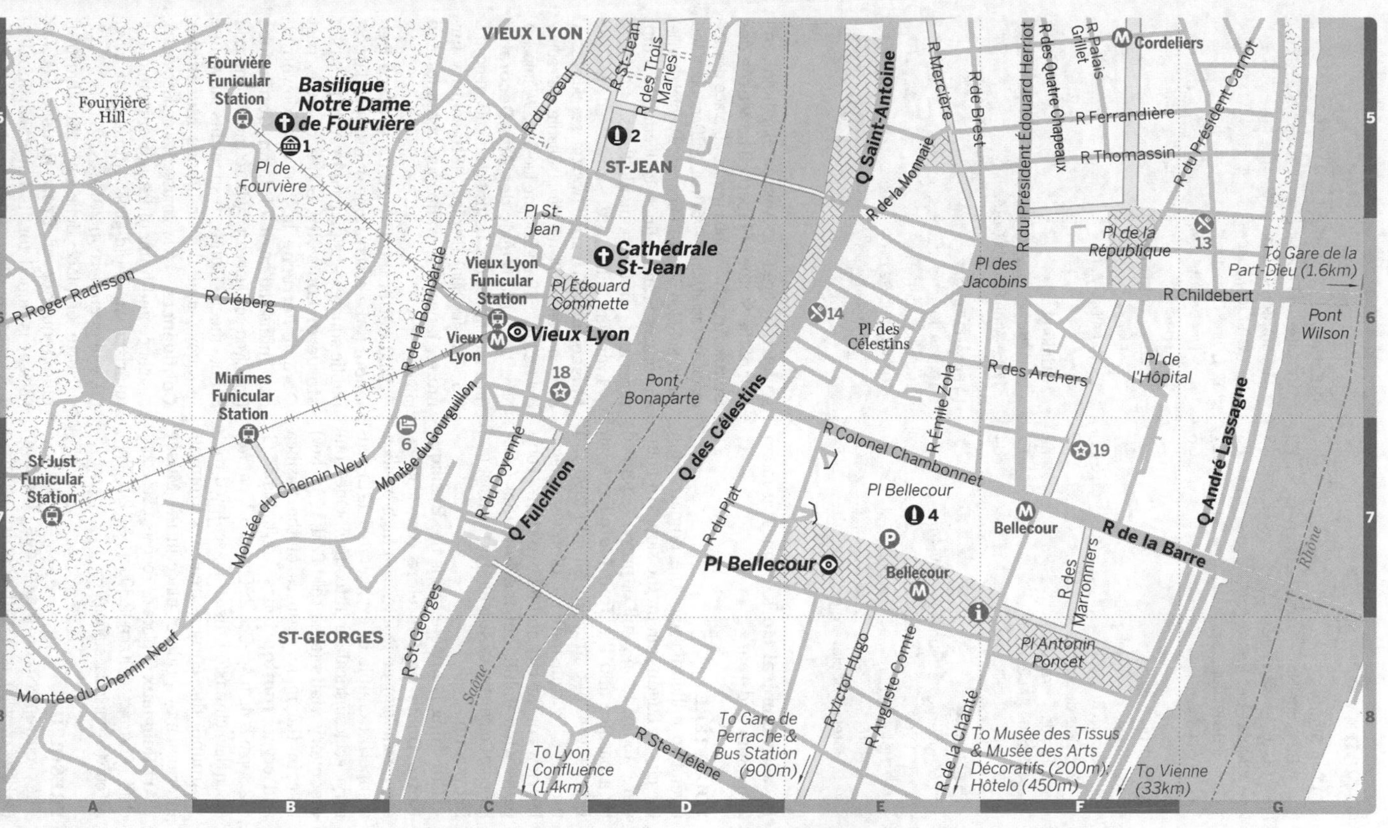
VIEUX LYON
Fourvière Hill
Fourvière Funicular Station
Basilique Notre Dame de Fourvière
1
Pl de Fourvière
R du Bœuf
R St-Jean
R des Trois Maries
2
ST-JEAN
Pl St-Jean
Cathédrale St-Jean
Vieux Lyon Funicular Station
Pl Édouard Commette
Vieux Lyon
Vieux Lyon
R Roger Radisson
R Cléberg
R de la Bombarde
Minimes Funicular Station
6
Montée du Gourguillon
18
Pont Bonaparte
St-Just Funicular Station
Montée du Chemin Neuf
R du Doyenne
Q Fulchiron
Q des Célestins
ST-GEORGES
R St-Georges
Saône
Montée du Chemin Neuf
To Lyon Confluence (1.4km)
R Ste-Hélène
To Gare de Perrache & Bus Station (900m)
R du Plat
Pl Bellecour
Q Saint-Antoine
R de la Monnaie
14
Pl des Célestins
R Mercière
R de Brest
R du Président Édouard Herriot
R des Quatre Chapeaux
R Palais Grillet
Cordeliers
R Ferrandière
R Thomassin
R du Président Carnot
Pl de la République
13
Pl des Jacobins
To Gare de la Part-Dieu (1.6km)
R Childebert
Pont Wilson
R des Archers
Pl de l'Hôpital
R Émile Zola
R Colonel Chambonnet
19
Pl Bellecour
4
Bellecour
Bellecour
Q André Lassagne
R de la Barre
Rhône
R des Marronniers
Pl Antonin Poncet
R Victor Hugo
R Auguste Comte
R de la Charité
To Musée des Tissus & Musée des Arts Décoratifs (200m); Hôtelo (450m)
To Vienne (33km)

Lyon

Top Sights

Basilique Notre Dame de Fourvière B5
Cathédrale St-Jean D6
Musée des Beaux-Arts F3
Pl Bellecour E7
Vieux Lyon C6

Sights

1 Musée d'Art Religieux B5
Opéra de Lyon ..... (see 21)
2 Palais de Justice D5
3 Pl des Terreaux E2
4 Statue of Louis XIV E7
5 Tour Métallique B4

Sleeping

6 Auberge de Jeunesse du Vieux Lyon C7
7 Hôtel de Paris E3
8 Hôtel Iris G3
9 Hôtel Le Boulevardier F4

Eating

10 Café des Fédérations E3
11 Comptoir-Restaurant des Deux Places D2
12 Grand Café des Négociants F4
13 Le Bec G6
14 Le Comptoir des Filles E6
15 Magali et Martin E2

Drinking

16 Le Voxx D3
17 Le Wine Bar d'à Côté F4

Entertainment

18 (L'A)Kroche C6
19 Fnac Billetterie F7
20 Hot Club de Lyon E3
21 Opéra de Lyon G2

Its **astronomical clock** chimes at noon, 2pm, 3pm and 4pm.

FOURVIÈRE

Over two millennia ago, the Romans built the city of Lugdunum on the slopes of Fourvière. Today, Lyon's 'hill of prayer' – topped by a basilica and the **Tour Métallique**, an Eiffel Tower–like structure built in 1893 and used as a TV transmitter – affords spectacular views of the city and its two rivers. Footpaths wind uphill, but the **funicular** (place Édouard Commette; €2.40 return) is the least taxing way up.

Crowning Fourvière hill is the **Basilique Notre Dame de Fourvière** (www.fourviere.org; 8am-7pm), an iconic, 27m-high basilica, a superb example of exaggerated 19th-century ecclesiastical architecture. One-hour **discovery visits** (adult/child €2/1; Apr-Nov) take in the main features of the basilica and crypt; **rooftop tours** (adult/child €5/3; 2.30pm & 4pm Apr-Oct, 2.30pm & 3.30pm Wed & Sun Nov) climax on the stone-sculpted roof.

Around the corner, treasures from its interior enjoy pride of place in the **Musée d'Art Religieux** (8 place de Fourvière, 5e; adult/child €5/free; 10am-12.30pm & 2-5.30pm; M Fourvière funicular station).

PRESQU'ÎLE

The centrepiece of **place des Terreaux** (M Hôtel de Ville) is a 19th-century fountain sculpted by Frédéric-Auguste Bartholdi, creator of the Statue of Liberty. The **Musée des Beaux-Arts** (www.mba-lyon.fr; 20 place des Terreaux, 1er; adult/child €76/free; 10am-6pm Wed, Thu & Sat-Mon, 10.30am-6pm Fri; M Hôtel de Ville) showcases France's finest collection of sculptures and paintings outside Paris.

Lyonnais silks are showcased at the **Musée des Tissus** (www.musee-des-tissus.com, in French; 34 rue de la Charité, 2e; adult/child €7/4; 10am-5.30pm Tue-Sun; M Ampère). Next door, the **Musée des Arts Décoratifs** (free with Musée des Tissus ticket; 10am-noon & 2-5.30pm Tue-Sun) displays 18th-century furniture, tapestries, wallpaper, ceramics and silver.

Laid out in the 17th century, **place Bellecour** (M Bellecour) – one of Europe's largest public squares – is pierced by an equestrian **statue of Louis XIV**. South of here, past **Gare de Perrache**, lies the once-downtrodden industrial area of **Lyon Confluence** (www.lyon-confluence.fr), where the Rhône and Saône meet. Trendy restaurants now line its quays, and the ambitious **Musée des Confluences** (www.museedesconfluences.fr), a science-and-humanities museum inside a futuristic steel-and-glass transparent crystal, will open here in 2014.

North of place Bellecour, the charmful hilltop quarter of **Croix Rousse** (M Croix Rousse) is famed for its bohemian inhabitants, lush outdoor food market and silk-weaving tradition, illustrated by the **Maison des Canuts** (www.maisondescanuts.com; 10-12 rue d'Ivry, 4e; adult/child €6/3; ⏲10am-6pm Tue-Sat, guided tours 11am & 3.30pm; Ⓜ Croix Rousse).

RIVE GAUCHE

Parc de la Tête d'Or PARK
(blvd des Belges, 6e; Ⓜ Masséna) Spanning 117 hectares, France's largest urban park was landscaped in the 1860s. It's graced by a lake (rent a rowing boat), botanic garden with greenhouses, rose garden, zoo and **puppet theatre** (☎04 78 93 71 75; www.theatre-guignol.com). Its northern realms are ensnared by the post-1960 art of the **Musée d'Art Contemporain** (www.moca-lyon.org; 81 quai Charles de Gaulle, 6e; adult/child €8/free; ⏲noon-7pm Wed-Fri, 10am-7pm Sat & Sun).

Buses 41 and 47 link the park with metro Part-Dieu.

Musée Lumière FILM MUSEUM
(www.institut-lumiere.org; 25 rue du Premier Film, 8e; adult/child €6/5; ⏲11am-6.30pm Tue-Sun; Ⓜ Monplaisir-Lumière) Cinema's glorious beginnings are showcased at the art nouveau home of Antoine Lumière, who moved to Lyon with sons Auguste and Louis in 1870. The brothers shot the first reels of the world's first motion picture, *La Sortie des Usines Lumières* (Exit of the Lumières Factories) here in one of their father's photographic factories in the grounds on 19 March 1895. The former factory is the Hangar du Premier Film cinema today.

Centre d'Histoire de la Résistance et de la Déportation MILITARY MUSEUM
(www.chrd.lyon.fr; 14 av Berthelot, 7e; adult/child €4/free; ⏲9am-5.30pm Wed-Sun; Ⓜ Perrache or Jean Macé) The WWII headquarters of Gestapo commander Klaus Barbie evokes Lyon's role as the 'Capital of the Resistance' through moving multimedia exhibits.

WANT MORE?

For in-depth information, reviews and recommendations at your fingertips, head to the Apple App Store to purchase Lonely Planet's *Lyon City Guide* iPhone app.

Alternatively, head to **Lonely Planet** (www.lonelyplanet.com/france/burgundy-and-the-rhone/lyon) for planning advice, author recommendations, traveller reviews and insider tips.

LYON CITY CARD

The **Lyon City Card** (www.lyon-france.com; 1/2/3 days adult €20/30/40, child €11/15/20) covers admission to every Lyon museum and the roof of Basilique Notre Dame de Fourvière, as well as a guided city tour, a river excursion (April to October) and discounts on other selected attractions, exhibitions and shops.

The card also includes unlimited travel on city buses, trams, the funicular and metro (cheaper cards not incorporating transport are available). Pre-book online or buy from the tourist office.

Festivals & Events

Les Nuits de Fourvière MUSIC
(Fourvière Nights; www.nuitsdefourviere.fr, in French) Open-air concerts atmospherically set in Fourvière's Roman amphitheatre;early June to late July.

Fête des Lumières LIGHT
(Festival of Lights; www.lumieres.lyon.fr) Over several days around the Feast of the Immaculate Conception (8 December), sound-and-light shows are projected onto key buildings.

Sleeping

Péniche Barnum B&B €€
(☎06 63 64 37 39; www.peniche-barnum.com; 3 quai du Général Sarrail, 6e; d €120-150; ❄ 📶; Ⓜ Foch) Moored on the Rhône between Pont Morand and the Passerelle du Collège footbridge, Lyon's most unique B&B is a navy-and-timber barge with two smart en suite guestrooms, a book-filled lounge, and shaded terrace on deck. Organic breakfast €10.

Hôtel Le Boulevardier HOTEL €
(☎04 78 28 48 22; www.leboulevardier.fr; 5 rue de la Fromagerie, 1er; s €45-51, d €47-53; 📶; Ⓜ Hôtel de Ville) Sporting quirky touches such as old skis and tennis racquets adorning the hallways, Le Boulevardier is a bargain 11-room hotel with snug, spotless rooms. It's up a steep spiral staircase above a cool little bistro and jazz club of the same name, which doubles as reception.

Hotelo HOTEL €€
(☎04 78 37 39 03; www.hotelo-lyon.com; 37 cours de Verdun, 2e; d from €70; Ⓜ Perrache) Our hot

choice around Gare de Perrache, this one stands out for its crisp contemporary design. Studios have a kitchenette and one room is perfectly fitted out for travellers with disabilities.

Hôtel de Paris HOTEL €€
(04 78 28 00 95; www.hoteldeparis-lyon.com; 16 rue de la Platière, 1er; s €49-59, d €65-90; ; MHôtel de Ville) At this fantastic-value hotel in a 19th-century bourgeois building, the funkiest rooms' retro '70s decor incorporates a palette of chocolate-and-turquoise or candyfloss-pink.

Auberge de Jeunesse du Vieux Lyon HOSTEL €
(04 78 15 05 50; lyon@fuaj.org; 41-45 montée du Chemin Neuf, 5e; dm incl breakfast €18; reception 7am-1pm, 2-8pm & 9pm-1am; ; MVieux Lyon) Stunning city views unfold from the terrace of Lyon's only hostel, and from many of the (mostly six-share) dorms.

Hôtel Iris HOTEL €
(04 78 39 93 80; www.hoteliris.fr; 36 rue de l'Arbre Sec, 1er; s €43-55, d €56-80; MHôtel de Ville) This basic but colourful dame in a centuries-old convent couldn't be better placed: its street brims with hip places to eat and drink.

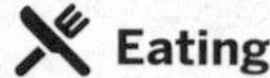

Eating

A flurry of big-name chefs presides over a sparkling restaurant line-up that embraces all genres: French, fusion, fast and international, as well as traditional Lyonnais *bouchons* (literally meaning 'bottle stopper' or 'traffic jam', but in Lyon a small, friendly bistro serving the city's local cuisine). See www.lyonresto.com (in French) for reviews, videos and ratings.

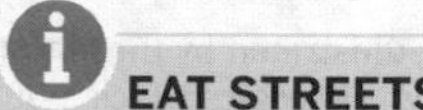

EAT STREETS

» **Rue St-Jean** A surfeit of restaurants jam Vieux Lyon's pedestrian main street.

» **Cobbled rue Mercière, rue des Marronniers** & **place Antonin Poncet, 2e** Ride the metro to Bellecour and these buzzing streets, chock-a-block with eating options (of widely varying quality) and pavement terraces overflowing in summer.

» **Rue du Garet** & **Rue Verdi, 1er** This twinset of parallel streets sits snug by Lyon's opera house on the Presqu'île.

TOP CHOICE **Le Bec** FRENCH, FUSION €€€
(04 78 42 15 00; www.nicolaslebec.com, 2e; 14 rue Grolée; lunch menus €40, dinner menus €90-135; Tue-Sat) With two Michelin stars, this is the flagship restaurant of Lyon's hottest chef Nicolas Le Bec, famed for his seasonal, world-influenced cuisine. Sunday brunch (€45) at his other address, innovative concept space **Rue Le Bec** (04 78 92 87 87; 43 quai Rambaud, 2e; mains €9-30; Tue-Sun; 1, Montrochet stop), on the Confluence, is equally hot.

TOP CHOICE **Magali et Martin** LYONNAIS €€
(04 72 00 88 01; 11 rue Augustins, 1er; lunch/dinner menus €19.60/35; Mon-Fri; MHôtel de Ville) Watch chefs turn out traditional but lighter, more varied *bouchon*-influenced cuisine, at this sharp dining address.

Café des Fédérations BOUCHON €€
(04 78 28 26 00; www.lesfedeslyon.com, in French; 8 rue Major Martin, 1er; menus €19-42; Mon-Sat; MHôtel de Ville) Black-and-white

A MARKET LUNCH

Shopping and munching some lunch at the market is an unmissable part of the Lyon experience.

Pick up a round of impossibly runny St Marcellin from legendary cheesemonger Mère Richard, or a knobbly Jésus de Lyon from pork butcher Collette Sibilia at Lyon's famed indoor market **Les Halles de Lyon** (http://halledelyon.free.fr, in French; 102 cours Lafayette, 3e; 8am-7pm Tue-Sat, 8am-noon Sun; MPart-Dieu). Or simply sit down and enjoy a lunch of local produce, lip-smacking *coquillages* (shellfish) included, at one of its stalls.

Alternatively, meander up to the hilltop quarter of Croix Rousse and, December to April, indulge in oysters and a glass of white Cotes de Rhône on a cafe pavement terrace – before or after shopping at its fabulous **outdoor food market** (blvd de la Croix Rousse, 4e; Tue-Sun morning; MCroix Rousse).

photos of old Lyon hang on wood-panelled walls at this Lyonnais bistro, unchanged for decades.

Le Comptoir des Filles LYONNAIS €€
(☎04 78 38 03 30; 8 quai des Celestins, 2e; mains €15-23; Tue-Sat; Ⓜ Bellecour) *Quenelles* (Lyonnais dumplings) are the speciality of this elegant, Saône-side spot. Six varieties are available each day along with other market-prepared dishes.

Comptoir-Restaurant des Deux Places BOUCHON €€
(☎04 78 28 95 10; 5 place Fernand Rey, 1er; lunch/dinner menus €13/28; Tue-Sat; Ⓜ Hôtel de Ville) Checked curtains, antique-crammed interior and ink-scribed menu contribute to the overwhelmingly traditional feel of this neighbourhood bistro with an idyllic terrace beneath trees.

Grand Café des Négociants BRASSERIE €€
(www.cafe-des-negociants.com, in French; 2 place Francisque Regaud, 2e; mains €17.50-34; 7am-3am; Ⓜ Cordeliers) This cafe-style brasserie with mirror-lined walls and tree-shaded terrace has been a favourite meeting point with Lyonnais since 1864. Don't miss its thick hot chocolate (cheaper before noon).

Drinking & Entertainment

Cafe terraces on place des Terreaux buzz with all-hours drinkers, as do the British, Irish and other-styled pubs on nearby rue Ste-Catherine, 1er, and rue Lainerie and rue St-Jean, 5e, in Vieux Lyon.

Weekly what's on guides include **Lyon Poche** (www.lyonpoche.com, in French; at newsagents €1) and **Le Petit Bulletin** (www.petit-bulletin.fr, in French; free on street corners). Track nightclub offerings at www.lyonclubbing.com, www.lyon2night.com and www.night4lyon.com (all in French).

You can buy theatre and concert tickets at **Fnac Billetterie** (www.fnac.com/spectacles; 85 rue de la République, 2e; 10am-7pm Mon-Sat; Ⓜ Bellecour).

Ninkasi Gerland LIVE MUSIC
(www.ninkasi.fr, in French; 267 rue Marcel Mérieux, 7e; Ⓜ Stade de Gerland) Spilling over with a fun, frenetic crowd, this microbrewery near Lyon's football stadium is one of several Ninkasi addresses around town. Entertainment ranges from DJs and bands to film projections amid a backdrop of fish-and-chips, build-your-own burgers and other un-French food.

DRINKS AFLOAT

Floating bars with DJs and live bands rock until around 3am aboard the string of *péniches* (river barges) moored along the Rhône's left bank. Scout out the section of quai Victor Augagneur between Pont Lafayette (metro Cordeliers or Guichard) and Pont de la Guillotière (metro Guillotière).

Our favourites: laid-back **Passagère** (21 quai Victor Augagneur, 7e; daily); classy **La Pie** (http://lapieresto.com, in French; 2 quai Victor Augagneur, 3e; Wed-Sat); party-hard **Le Sirius** (www.lesirius.com, in French; 4 quai Victor Augagneur, 3e; daily; wi-fi); and electro-oriented **La Marquise** (www.marquise.net, in French; 20 quai Victor Augagneur, 3e; Tue-Sun).

Le Wine Bar d'à Côté WINE BAR
(www.cave-vin-lyon.com, in French; 7 rue Pleney, 1er; Tue-Sat; Ⓜ Cordeliers) Hidden in a tiny alleyway, this cultured wine bar feels like a rustic English gentlemen's club with leather sofa seating and library.

Le Voxx BAR
(1 rue d'Algérie, 1er; Ⓜ Hôtel de Ville) Minimalist riverside bar packed with a real mix of people, from students to city slickers.

Opéra de Lyon OPERA HOUSE
(www.opera-lyon.com, in French; place de la Comédie, 1er; Ⓜ Hôtel de Ville) Premier venue for opera, ballet and classical music.

(L'A)Kroche LIVE MUSIC
(8 rue Monseigneur Lavarenne, 5e; Tue-Sun; Ⓜ Vieux Lyon) Hip concert cafe-bar with DJs spinning electro, soul, funk and disco; bands too.

Hot Club de Lyon LIVE MUSIC
(www.hotclubjazz.com, in French; 26 rue Lanterne, 1er; admission €5-18; Tue-Sat; Ⓜ Hôtel de Ville) Lyon's leading jazz club, around since 1948.

Le Transbordeur LIVE MUSIC
(www.transbordeur.fr, in French; 3 blvd de Stalingrad, Villeurbanne) In an old industrial building, Lyon's prime concert venue draws international acts on the European concert-tour circuit.

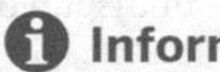

Information

Tourist office (☎04 72 77 69 69; www.lyon-france.com; place Bellecour, 2e; 9am-6pm; Ⓜ Bellecour)

Getting There & Away

Air

Lyon-St-Exupéry Airport (www.lyon.aeroport.fr), 25km east of the city, serves 120 direct destinations across Europe and beyond, including many budget carriers.

Bus

Eurolines (☎04 72 56 95 30; www.eurolines.fr; Gare de Perrache)

Linebús (☎04 72 41 72 27; www.linebus.com, in Spanish; Gare de Perrache)

Train

Lyon has two main-line train stations: **Gare de la Part-Dieu** (Ⓜ Part-Dieu) and **Gare de Perrache** (Ⓜ Perrache). Some destinations by direct TGV:

BEAUNE €23.10, 2¼ hours, up to nine daily

DIJON €30.20, two hours, at least 12 daily

LILLE-EUROPE €92, 3¼ hours, nine daily

MARSEILLE €58.60, 1¾ hours, every 30 to 60 minutes

PARIS GARE DE LYON €64.30, two hours, every 30 to 60 minutes

STRASBOURG €55.90, 4¾ hours, five daily

Getting Around

Tramway **Rhonexpress** (www.rhonexpress.net, in French) links the airport with Part-Dieu train station in under 30 minutes. Trams depart approximately every 15 minutes between 6am and 9pm, and every 30 minutes from 5am to 6am and 9pm to midnight. A single/return ticket costs €13/23.

Buses, trams, a four-line metro and two funiculars linking Vieux Lyon to Fourvière are run by **TCL** (www.tcl.fr). Public transport runs from around 5am to midnight. Tickets cost €1.60/13.70 for one/*carnet* of 10; bring coins as machines don't accept notes (or some international credit cards). Time-stamp tickets on all forms of public transport or risk a fine.

Bikes are available from 200-odd bike stations thanks to **vélo'v** (www.velov.grandlyon.com; first 30min free, first/subsequent hr €1/2).

THE FRENCH ALPS & JURA

Whether it's paragliding among the peaks, hiking the trails or hurtling down a mountainside strapped to a pair of glorified toothpicks, the French Alps is the undisputed centre of adventure sports in France. Under Mont Blanc's 4810m of raw wilderness lies the country's most spectacular outdoor playground, and if the seasonal crowds get too much, you can always take refuge in the little-visited Jura, a region of dark wooded hills and granite plateaux stretching for 360km along the French–Swiss border.

Chamonix

POP 9400 / ELEV 1037M

With the pearly white peaks of the Mont Blanc massif as sensational backdrop, being an icon comes naturally to Chamonix. First 'discovered' by Brits William Windham and Richard Pococke in 1741, this is the mecca of mountaineering. Its knife-edge peaks, plunging slopes and massive glaciers have enthralled generations of adventurers and thrill-seekers ever since. Its après-ski scene is equally pumping.

Sights

Aiguille du Midi MOUNTAIN PEAK, CABLE CAR

A jagged pinnacle of rock 8km from the domed summit of Mont Blanc, the **Aiguille du Midi** (3842m) is one of Chamonix' iconic landmarks. If you can handle the height, the 360-degree panorama from the top of the French, Swiss and Italian Alps is unforgettable.

The vertiginous **Téléphérique du l'Aiguille du Midi** (☎04 50 53 30 80, advance reservations 24hr 04 50 53 22 75; 100 place de l'Aiguille du Midi; adult/child return Aiguille du Midi €41/33, Plan de l'Aiguille €24/19.20; ⊙8.30am-4.30pm) links Chamonix with the Aiguille du Midi. Mid-station Plan de l'Aiguille (2317m) is a terrific place to start hikes or paraglide. In summer you will need to obtain a boarding card (marked with the number of your departing *and* returning cable car) in addition to a ticket. Advance phone reservations incur a €2 booking fee. Bring warm clothes, as even in summer the temperature rarely rises above -10°C at the top.

Mid-May to mid-September the unrepentant can continue for a further 30 minutes of mind-blowing scenery – think suspended glaciers and spurs, seracs and shimmering ice fields – in the smaller bubbles of the

TICKET TO RIDE

Public transport is free in the Chamonix valley if you have a **carte d'hôte** – free from your hotel or camping ground when you check in! The card includes reductions on some activities too.

LOCAL KNOWLEDGE

ERIC FAVRET: MOUNTAIN GUIDE

Ever since Mont Blanc, the highest peak in the Alps, was first climbed in 1786, Chamonix has attracted travellers worldwide. And there is something really special about it: not only does it sit amid extremely condensed mountaineering opportunities, it's also a perfectly balanced combination of pure landscape alignment and dramatic mountain views.

Aiguille du Midi

The Aiguille du Midi, with one of the highest cable cars in the world, cannot be missed. Beyond the summit ridge is a world of snow and ice offering some of the greatest intermediate off-piste terrain in the Alps.

Off-Piste Thrills

The Vallée Blanche has to be seen. But the Aiguille du Midi also has amazing off-piste runs, such as Envers du Plan, a slightly steeper and more advanced version of Vallée Blanche, offering dramatic views in the heart of the Mont Blanc range. There is also the less frequented run of the 'Virgin' or 'Black Needle'; a striking glacial run, offering different views and a close-up look at the Giant's seracs.

Best-Ever Mont Blanc View

No hesitation: the Traverse from Col des Montets to Lac Blanc. It's as popular as the Eiffel Tower for hikers in summer. I love swimming in mountain lakes, so I like to stop at Lac des Chéserys, just below, where it is quieter: what's better than a swim in pure mountain water, looking at Mont Blanc, the Grandes Jorasses and Aiguille Verte? This is what I call mountain landscape perfection!

Télécabine Panoramic Mont Blanc (adult/child return from Chamonix €65/52; ⏲8.30am-3.45pm) to **Pointe Helbronner** (3466m) on the French–Italian border. From here another cable car descends to the Italian ski resort of Courmayeur.

Le Brévent MOUNTAIN PEAK

The highest peak on the western side of the valley, **Le Brévent** (2525m) offers fabulous views of the Mont Blanc massif. It can be reached via the **Télécabine du Brévent** (29 rte Henriette d'Angeville; adult/child €24/19.50; ⏲8.50am-4.45pm Jun-Aug, 8.45am-4.45pm mid-Dec–Apr), which is found at the end of rue de la Mollard.

Mer de Glace GLACIER

The glistening **Mer de Glace** (Sea of Ice) is the second-largest glacier in the Alps, 14km long, 1800m wide and up to 400m deep. A quaint red mountain train links **Gare du Montenvers** (35 place de la Mer de Glace; adult/child €24/19; ⏲10am-4.30pm) in Chamonix with Montenvers (1913m), from where a cable car transports tourists in summer down to the glacier and the **Grotte de la Mer de Glace** (⏲Dec-May & mid-Jun–Sep), an ice cave where frozen tunnels and ice sculptures – carved anew every year since 1946 – change colour like mood rings. A quaint red mountain train trundles up from **Gare du Montenvers** (35 place de la Mer de Glace; adult/child €24/19; ⏲10am-4.30pm) in Chamonix to Montenvers (1913m), from where a cable car takes you down to the glacier and cave. Tickets cover the 20-minute journey, entry to the caves and the cable car.

The Mer de Glace can be reached on foot via the Grand Balcon Nord trail from Plan de l'Aiguille. The two-hour uphill trail from Chamonix starts near the summer luge track. Traversing the crevassed glacier requires proper equipment and an experienced guide.

Activities

The **Maison de la Montagne** (190 place de l'Église; ⏲8.30am-noon & 3-7pm), across the square from the tourist office, supplies comprehensive details on hiking, skiing and every other imaginable pastime in the Mont Blanc area.

Sleeping

TOP CHOICE **Auberge du Manoir** CHALET €€

(☎04 50 53 10 77; www.aubergedumanoir.com, in French; 8 rte du Bouchet; s €94-108, d €104-150, q €165; 📶) This beautifully converted farmhouse, ablaze with geraniums in summer, ticks all the perfect-Alpine-chalet boxes: pristine mountain views, pine-panelled rooms and an inviting bar where an open fire keeps things cosy.

Hotel Slalom BOUTIQUE HOTEL €€
(04 50 54 40 60; www.hotelslalom.net; 44 rue de Bellevue, Les Houches; r €158;) The rooms are the epitome of boutique chic – sleek, snowy white and draped with Egyptian cotton linens – at this gorgeous chalet-style hotel, situated nicely at the foot of the slopes in Les Houches.

Le Vert Hôtel PARTY HOTEL €€
(04 50 53 13 58; www.verthotel.com; 964 rte des Gaillands; s/d/tr/q €75/96/120/140, minimum 3-night stay) Self-proclaimed 'Chamonix' house of sports and creativity', this party house 1km south of town has no-frills rooms, some with microscopic bathrooms. But what people really come for is the hotel's all-happening, ultrahip bar, a regular venue for top DJs and live music.

Hôtel El Paso PARTY HOTEL €
(04 50 53 64 20; www.cantina.fr; 37 impasse des Rhododendrons; s/d/tr/q €49/64/75/90) What you'll get is a threadbare mattress and four scuffed walls reminiscent of good times – small sacrifices given that El Paso is cheap, central and *the* place to party, dude. Tex-Mex feasts and DJs downstairs keep the place rocking, so invest in earplugs if sleeping is a priority.

Hotel L'Oustalet FAMILY HOTEL €€
(04 50 55 54 99; www.hotel-oustalet.com; 330 rue du Lyret; d/q €140/180;) You'll pray for snow at this Alpine chalet near Aiguille du Midi cable car, just so you can curl up by the fire with a *chocolat chaud* (hot chocolate) and unwind in the sauna and whirlpool. Rooms are snugly decorated in solid pine and open onto balconies with Mont Blanc views. There's a pool in the garden for summertime chilling.

SAVVY SLEEPS

Book ahead in winter, when hotel beds are at a premium. Many places close from mid-April to May and from November to mid-December. Room rates nosedive in the low season and summer; expect discounts of up to 50% on high-season prices.

Hôtel Faucigny SMALL HOTEL €€
(04 50 53 01 17; www.hotelfaucigny-chamonix.com; 118 place de l'Église; s/d/tr/q €55/86/98/124;) This bijou hotel is one of the sweetest deals in town. Relax by an open fire in winter and out on the flower-clad terrace with Mont Blanc views in summer.

Les Deux Glaciers CAMPING GROUND €
(04 50 53 15 84; www.les2glaciers.com; 80 rte des Tissières; campsites €14.50; mid-Dec–mid-Nov;) Oh, what a beautiful morning! Draw back your tent flap and be dazzled by Mont Blanc and glaciated peaks at this almost year-round camping ground in Les Bossons, 3km south of Chamonix. Take the train to Les Bossons, or the Chamonix bus to Tremplin-le-Mont.

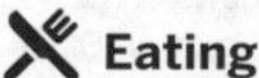

Eating

TOP CHOICE Les Vieilles Luges TRADITIONAL FRENCH €€
(www.lesvieillesluges.com; Les Houches; menus €20-35) Like a scene from a snow globe, this childhood dream of a 250-year-old farmhouse can only be reached by slipping on skis or taking a scenic 20-minute hike from Maison Neuve chairlift.

Le Bistrot GASTRONOMIC €€€
(04 50 53 57 64; www.lebistrotchamonix.com, in French; 151 av de l'Aiguille du Midi; menus €17-65) Sleek and monochromatic, this is a real foodie's place. Michelin-starred chef Mickey experiments with textures and seasonal flavours to create taste sensations like pan-seared Arctic char with chestnuts, and divine warm chocolate macaroon with raspberry and red pepper coulis.

Le GouThé TEAROOM €
(95 rue des Moulins; menus €9; 9am-6.30pm Fri-Mon) Philippe's hot chocolates with pistachio and gingerbread infusions, bright macaroons and crumbly homemade tarts are just the sugar fix for the slopes. He's a dab hand with *galettes* (buckwheat crêpes), too.

Le Chaudron REGIONAL CUISINE €€
(04 50 53 57 64; 79 rue des Moulins; menus €20-23; dinner) Funky cowskin-clad benches are the backdrop for a feast of Savoyard fondues and lamb slow-cooked in red wine to melting perfection at this chic chalet.

Munchie FUSION €€
(04 50 53 45 41; www.munchie.eu; 87 rue des Moulins; mains €18-24; dinner) Think pan-Asian fusion at this trendy Swedish-run hang-out where sittings go faster than

DON'T MISS

A LOFTY LUNCH

Feast on fine cuisine and even finer mountain views at these high-altitude favourites:

» **La Crémerie du Glacier** (www.lacremerieduglacier.fr, in French; 766 chemin de la Glacière; mains €10-19; ⏲Tue-Mon) World-famous *croûtes au fromage* (toast topped with melted cheese). Ski here with the red Pierre à Ric piste in Les Grands Montets.

» **Le 3842** (☎04 50 55 82 23; Aiguille du Midi; mains €12-21; ⏲restaurant mid-Jun–mid-Sep, snack bar all year) Dining and drinking with knockout views at what claims to be Europe's highest cafe atop the Aiguille du Midi.

» **Le Panoramic** (☎04 50 53 44 11; Le Brévent; menus from €15; ⏲mid-Dec–Apr & late Jun–Sep) Cheeses, cured meats, BBQ fare and knockout MB views.

musical chairs (making it worth a try even without a reservation).

Drinking & Entertainment

Nightlife rocks. In the centre, riverside rue des Moulins boasts a line-up of drinking holes. Get the low-down on the slopeside scene on www.lepetitcanardchx.com.

Most après-ski joints serve food as well as booze.

Chambre Neuf BAR
(272 av Michel Croz; 📶) Cover bands, raucous après-ski drinking and Swedish blondes dancing on the tables make Room Nine one of Chamonix' liveliest party haunts. Conversations about epic off-pistes and monster jumps that are, like, totally mental, man, dominate at every table.

Monkey Bar MUSIC BAR
(81 place Edmond Desailloud; ⏲1pm-2am; 📶) Slightly grungy, very cool, this party hot spot has live gigs and DJs several times a week. There's a mad rush to the bar at 4.45pm, when pints are €1.50 for 15 minutes!

MBC MICROBREWERY
(www.mbchx.com; 350 rte du Bouchet; ⏲4pm-2am) Be it with burgers, cheesecake, live music or amazing locally brewed beers, this trendy microbrewery delivers.

Information

Tourist office (☎04 50 53 00 24; www.chamonix.com; 85 place du Triangle de l'Amitié; ⏲8.30am-7pm)

Getting There & Away

Bus

From **Chamonix bus station** (www.sat-montblanc.com; place de la Gare), next to the train station, two to three buses run daily to/from Geneva airport (one way/return €33/55, 1½ to two hours) and Courmayeur (one way/return €13/20, 45 minutes). Advanced booking only.

Train

From Chamonix-Mont Blanc **train station** (place de la Gare) the Mont Blanc Express narrow-gauge train trundles to/from St-Gervais-Le Fayet (€9.50, 40 minutes, nine to 12 daily), from where there are trains to most major French cities.

Annecy

POP 53,000 / ELEV 447M

Lac d'Annecy is one of the world's purest lakes, receiving only rainwater, spring water and mountain streams. Swimming in its sapphire depths, surrounded by snowy mountains, is a real Alpine highlight. Strolling the geranium-strewn streets of the historic Vieille Ville (Old Town) is not half bad either.

Sights & Activities

Vieille Ville & Lakefront OLD TOWN, LAKE
Wandering around the Vieille Ville and the lakefront is the essence of Annecy. Behind the town hall are the **Jardins de l'Europe**, linked to the park of **Champ de Mars** by the **Pont des Amours** (Lovers' Bridge).

With labyrinthine narrow streets and colonnaded passageways, the Old Town retains much of its 17th-century appearance. On the central island, imposing **Palais de l'Isle** (3 passage de l'Île; adult/child €4.90/2.30; ⏲10.30am-6pm) was a prison, but now hosts local-history displays.

In the 13th- to 16th-century castle above town, the museum inside **Château d'Annecy** (adult/child €4.90/2.30; ⏲10.30am-6pm) explores traditional Savoyard art, crafts and Alpine natural history.

Annecy

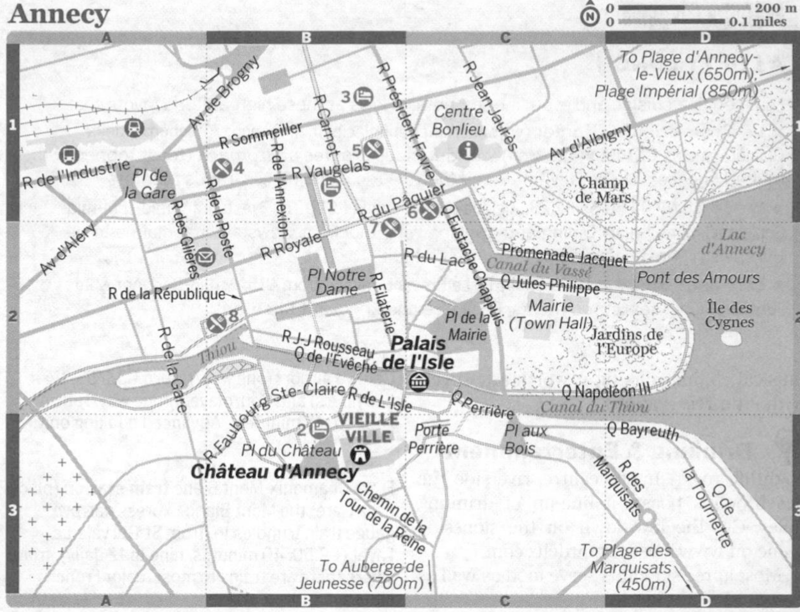

Parks line the lakefront. Public beach **Plage d'Annecy-le-Vieux** is 1km east of Champ de Mars. Closer to town, the private **Plage Impérial** (€3.50; ⏲Jul & Aug) sits beneath the pre-WWI **Impérial Palace**. **Plage des Marquisats** (⏲Jul & Aug) is 1km south of the Vieille Ville along rue des Marquisats.

Sleeping

Hôtel Alexandra FAMILY HOTEL €
(☎04 50 52 84 33; www.hotelannecy-alexandra.fr; 19 rue Vaugelas; s/d/tr/q €48/59/70/89; wifi) Nice surprise: Annecy's most charming hotel is also among its most affordable. The welcome is five-star and rooms are spotless – a few extra euros gets you a balcony and canal view.

Le Pré Carré BOUTIQUE HOTEL €€€
(☎04 50 52 14 14; www.hotel-annecy.net; 27 rue Sommeiller; s/d €172/202; ❄@wifi) Chic Le Pré Carré keeps things contemporary with Zen colours in rooms, a jacuzzi and business corner. The staff know Annecy inside out, so you're in very good hands.

Hôtel du Château HOTEL €
(☎04 50 45 27 66; www.annecy-hotel.com; 16 rampe du Château; s/d/tr/q €49/68/75/85; wifi) Nestled at the foot of the castle, this hotel's trump card is its sun-drenched, panoramic breakfast terrace. Pine-furnished rooms are small but sweet.

Camping Les Rives du Lac CAMPING GROUND €
(☎04 50 52 40 14; www.lesrivesdulac-annecy.com; 331 chemin des Communaux; campsites €21; ⏲mid-Apr–mid-Oct) Pitch your tent near the lakefront at this shady camping ground, 5km south of town in Sévrier. A cycling track runs into central Annecy from here.

Auberge de Jeunesse HOSTEL €
(☎04 50 45 33 19; www.fuaj.org, in French; 4 rte du Semnoz; dm incl breakfast & sheets €19.50;

mid-Jan–Nov;) Annecy's smart wood-clad hostel has great facilities and chipper staff. Dorms have en suite showers. It's a 10-minute walk south of the centre.

Eating

The quays along Canal du Thiou in the Vieille Ville are jam-packed with touristy cafes and pizzerias. Crêpes, kebabs, classic French cuisine – you'll find it all along pedestrianised rue Carnot, rue de L'Isle and rue Faubourg Ste-Claire.

La Cuisine des Amis BISTRO €€
(04 50 10 10 80; 9 rue du Pâquier; mains €16.50-25) Walking into this bistro is somewhat like gatecrashing a private party – everyone is treated like one big jolly *famille*. Pull up a chair, *prendre un verre* (have a drink), scoff regional fare, pat the dog and see if your snapshot ends up on the wall of merry *amis*.

Nature & Saveur ORGANIC €€
(04 50 45 82 29; place des Cordeliers; lunch menus with/without wine €42/32; lunch Tue-Sat) Laurence Salomon's 100% organic restaurant attracts a real boho-chic clientele. Inspired by the seasons, the menu uses wholesome ingredients from local farms, ranging from obscure legumes to locally reared meat.

La Ciboulette MODERN FRENCH €€
(04 50 45 74 57; www.laciboulette-annecy.com; cour du Pré Carré, 10 rue Vaugelas; menus €31-46; Tue-Sat) Such class! Crisp white linen and gold-kissed walls set the scene at this surprisingly affordable Michelin-starred place, where chef Georges Paccard cooks fresh seasonal specialities, such as slow-roasted Anjou pigeon with Midi asparagus. Reservations are essential.

Contresens FUSION €€
(04 50 51 22 10; 10 rue de la Poste; mains €15; Tue-Sat) The menu reads like a mathematic formula but it soon becomes clear: starters are A, mains B, sides C and desserts D. The food is as experimental as the menu – think sun-dried tomato, Beaufort cheese and rocket salad burger, mussel ravioli, 'deconstructed' Snickers – and totally divine. Kid nirvana.

L'Étage TRADITIONAL FRENCH €€
(04 50 51 03 28; 13 rue du Pâquier; mains €14-22, 3-course menus €18) Cheese, glorious cheese... *Fromage* is given pride of place in the spot-on fondues and raclette at L'Étage, where a backdrop of mellow music and cheerful staff keep the ambience relaxed.

FREE WHEELER

Pick up a set of wheels to gad along the silky-smooth cycling path ensnaring Lake Annecy from **Vélonecy** (place de la Gare; €15 per day) at the train station; train ticket holders pay €5 per day. Or, in summer, simply head for the water and hire a bike lakeside from one of the many open-air stalls.

Information

Tourist office (04 50 45 00 33; www.lac-annecy.com; Centre Bonlieu, 1 rue Jean Jaurès; 9am-6.30pm Mon-Sat, 10am-1pm Sun)

Getting There & Away

Bus

From the **bus station** (rue de l'Industrie), adjoining the train station, **Billetterie Crolard** (www.voyages-crolard.com) sells tickets for roughly hourly buses to villages around the lake, local ski resorts and Lyon St-Exupéry airport (one-way/return €33/50, 2¼ hours). **Autocars Frossard** (www.frossard.eu) sells tickets for Geneva (€10.50, 1¾ hours, 16 daily).

Train

From Annecy's **train station** (place de la Gare), there are frequent trains to many destinations, including Lyon (€23, 2¼ hours) and Paris' Gare de Lyon (€75, four hours).

Grenoble

POP 159,400

Wherever you turn in big-city Grenoble, you'll be treated to intoxicating Alpine views. But Grenoble isn't just a mountain base: since the 1960s the city has been a leading technology hub and cultural centre, with outstanding museums, a lively arts scene and some 60,000 students to lap it all up.

Sights

Fort de la Bastille FORTRESS
(www.bastille-grenoble.com) Looming above the old city on the northern side of the Isère River, this grand 16th-century fort is Grenoble's best-known landmark. Views are spectacular, with vast mountains on every side and the grey waters of the Isère River below. On China-blue ski days you can ogle Mont Blanc's snowy hump. To get to the fort, ride the riverside **Téléphérique Grenoble Bastille** (quai Stéphane Jay; adult/child single €4.50/2.90, return €6.50/4.05; Feb-Dec).

Grenoble

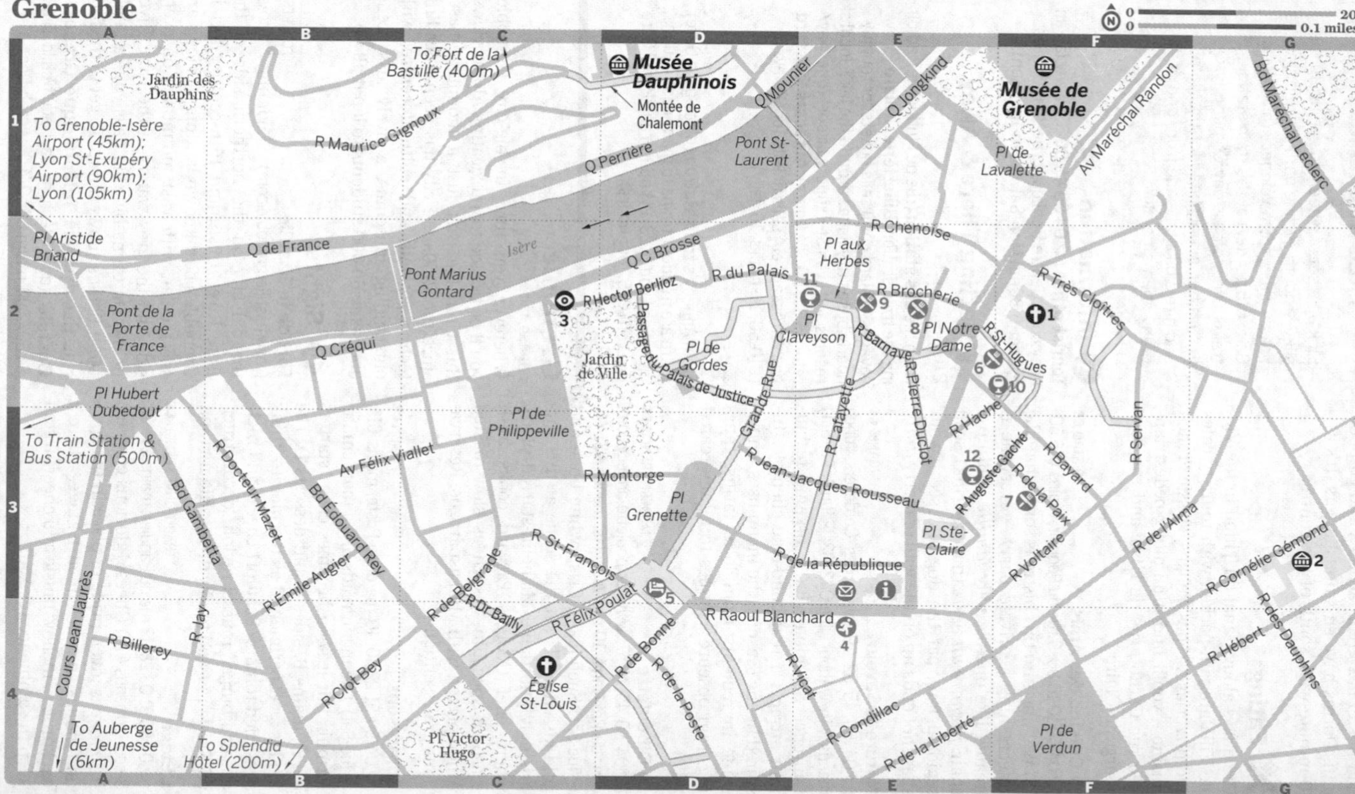
Musée Dauphinois
Montée de Chalemont
To Fort de la Bastille (400m)
Jardin des Dauphins
To Grenoble-Isère Airport (45km); Lyon St-Exupéry Airport (90km); Lyon (105km)
R Maurice Gignoux
Q Perrière
Pont St-Laurent
Q Mounier
Q Jongkind
Musée de Grenoble
Pl de Lavalette
Av Maréchal Randon
Bd Maréchal Leclerc
Pl Aristide Briand
Q de France
Isère
Pont Marius Gontard
Q C Brosse
R Chenoise
Pl aux Herbes
R du Palais
R Hector Berlioz
R Brocherie
R Très Cloîtres
Pont de la Porte de France
Q Créqui
Passage du Palais de Justice
Pl de Gordes
Pl Claveyson
R Barnave
Pl Notre Dame
R St-Hugues
Jardin de Ville
Grande Rue
R Lafayette
R Pierre Duclot
R Hache
R Servan
Pl Hubert Dubedout
To Train Station & Bus Station (500m)
Pl de Philippeville
Av Félix Viallet
R Docteur Mazet
Bd Gambetta
Bd Édouard Rey
R Montorge
Pl Grenette
R Jean-Jacques Rousseau
R Auguste Gaché
R de la Paix
R Bayard
Pl Ste-Claire
R de la République
R Voltaire
R de l'Alma
R Cornélie Gémond
R St-François
R de Belgrade
R Dr Bailly
R Émile Augier
R Félix Poulat
R Raoul Blanchard
R Jay
R Billerey
Cours Jean Jaurès
R Clot Bey
Église St-Louis
R de Bonne
R de la Poste
R Vicat
R Condillac
R de la Liberté
Pl de Verdun
R Hébert
R des Dauphins
Pl Victor Hugo
To Auberge de Jeunesse (6km)
To Splendid Hôtel (200m)
200 m
0.1 miles

Grenoble

Top Sights

Musée Dauphinois D1
Musée de Grenoble F1

Sights

Bishop's Palace .... (see 1)
1 Cathédrale Notre Dame F2
2 Musée de la Résistance et de la Déportation de l'Isère G3
Musée de l'Ancien Évêché .... (see 1)
3 Téléphérique Grenoble Bastille C2

Activities, Courses & Tours

4 Maison de la Montagne E4

Sleeping

5 Hôtel de l'Europe D3

Eating

6 Chez Mémé Paulette E2
7 Ciao a Te F3
8 La Fondue E2
9 L'Épicurien E2

Drinking

10 Le 365 .... F2
11 Le Couche Tard E2
12 Le Tord Boyaux E3

Musée de Grenoble MUSEUM
(www.museedegrenoble.fr, in French; 5 place de Lavalette; adult/child €5/free; 10am-6.30pm Wed-Mon) The sleek glass-and-steel exterior of Grenoble's boldest museum is renowned for its distinguished modern collection, including star pieces by Chagall, Matisse, Canaletto, Monet and Picasso.

Magasin Centre National d'Art Contemporain ART MUSEUM
(www.magasin-cnac.org; 155 cours Berriat; adult/child €3.50/2; 2-7pm Tue-Sun) Ensconced in a cavernous glass-and-steel warehouse built by Gustave Eiffel, this is among Europe's leading centres of contemporary art. Many of its cutting-edge exhibitions are designed specifically for the space. Ride tram A to the Berriat-Le Magasin stop.

Musée de l'Ancien Évêché MUSEUM
(www.ancien-eveche-isere.com, in French; 2 rue Très Cloîtres; 9am-6pm Wed-Sat & Mon, 10am-7pm Sun, 1.30-6pm Tue) On place Notre Dame, Grenoble's Italianate **Cathédrale Notre Dame** and adjoining 13th-century **Bishops' Palace** – originally home to Grenoble's bishops – form this history museum. Its rich collection takes visitors beneath the cathedral square to a crypt safeguarding old Roman walls and a 4th- to 10th-century baptistery.

Musée Dauphinois MUSEUM
(www.musee-dauphinois.fr, in French; 30 rue Maurice Gignoux; 10am-7pm Wed-Mon) Set in a 17th-century convent, this museum documents the cultures, crafts and traditions of Alpine life, including a fantastic exhibition devoted to the region's skiing history.

Musée de la Résistance et de la Déportation de l'Isère MUSEUM
(www.resistance-en-isere.com, in French; 14 rue Hébert; 9am-6pm Mon & Wed-Fri, 1.30-6pm Tue, 10am-6pm Sat & Sun) This emotive museum examines the deportation of Jews and other 'undesirables' from Grenoble to Nazi camps during WWII in a cool-headed way.

Sleeping

Auberge de Jeunesse HOSTEL €
(04 76 09 33 52; www.fuaj.org, in French; 10 av du Grésivaudan; dm incl breakfast €19; @) Clean and ultramodern, Grenoble's ecoconscious hostel sits in parkland, 5km from town. Top-notch facilities include bar, kitchen and sun deck. Take bus 1 to La Quinzaine stop or tram A to La Rampe stop and walk for 15 minutes.

Splendid Hôtel HOTEL €€
(04 76 46 33 12; www.splendid-hotel.com; 22 rue Thiers; s/d €59/75-95;) Colourful, fresh and jazzed up with funky paintings, this is a welcome break from Grenoble's otherwise dreary two-star scene. Take a seat in the leafy courtyard for a copious breakfast with fresh pastries and fruit.

Hôtel de l'Europe HISTORIC HOTEL €
(04 76 46 16 94; www.hoteleurope.fr; 22 place Grenette; s €31-45, d €41-70) Set on Grenoble's

ACTION!

Get the scoop on mountain activities around Grenoble – skiing, snowboarding, ice climbing, walking, mountain biking, rock climbing and more – from knowledgeable staff at Grenoble's **Maison de la Montagne** (www.grenoble-montagne.com; 3 rue Raoul Blanchard).

If you're heading out for the day to one of the town's nearby ski resorts, jump lift-pass queues by buying your pass in advance from Grenoble's tourist office.

liveliest square, this 17th-century haunt retains some charm. The snazzy hot-pink breakfast room and grand spiral staircase promise good things, making the rooms something of an anticlimax with their '70s-style wallpaper and postage-stamp bathrooms.

Eating

Grenoble's most atmospheric bistros huddle on backstreets in the *quartier des Antiquaires* (Antiques Quarter). Don't miss local dish *gratin dauphinois* (finely sliced potatoes oven-baked in cream and a pinch of nutmeg).

TOP CHOICE Chez Mémé Paulette CAFE €
(2 rue St-Hugues; mains €8; noon-midnight Tue-Sat) This is an old curiosity shop of a cafe, crammed with antique books, milk jugs, cuckoo clocks and other eye-catching collectables. It draws a young, arty crowd with its boho vibe and wallet-friendly soul food, from chunky soups to *tartines* and homemade tarts.

L'Épicurien MODERN FRENCH €€
(04 76 51 96 06; 1 place aux Herbes; menus €25-41) Chandeliers cast flattering light on the leather banquettes, exposed stone and twisting wrought-iron staircase of this chic split-level restaurant. An aperitif at the bar whets your appetite for flavours such as creamy *gratin dauphinois* and herb-crusted lamb.

Ciao a Te ITALIAN €€
(04 76 42 54 41; 2 rue de la Paix; mains €15; Tue-Sat Jul-Jun) Stylish and relaxed, this Grenoblois favourite dishes up handmade pasta, crispy *panzerotti* (filled pastries), tender veal and the freshest seafood in town.

La Fondue FRENCH €€
(04 76 15 20 72; 5 rue Brocherie; fondues €17-20; Tue-Sat, dinner Mon) Gorge on so-smooth fondues laced with kirsch, Génépi and chartreuse or chocolate.

Drinking

Like every good student city, Grenoble does a mean party. See www.grenews.com and www.petit-bulletin.fr for what's happening.

Le 365 WINE BAR
(3 rue Bayard; Tue-Sat) If Dionysus (god of wine) had a house, this is surely what it would look like: an irresistible clutter of bottles, oil paintings and candles that create an ultrarelaxed setting for quaffing wine.

Le Couche Tard BAR
(1 rue du Palais) If you're too cool for school, check out Go to Bed Late, a grungy pub that actively encourages you to graffiti its walls. The merrier you become during happy hour (until 10pm daily), the more imaginative those doodles are…

Le Tord Boyaux WINE BAR
(4 rue Auguste Gaché; 6pm-2am) More than 30 flavoured wines, some quite extrava-

WORTH A TRIP

GREAT ESCAPES

Southwest of Grenoble, the gently rolling pastures and chiselled limestone peaks of the 1750-sq-km **Parc Natural Régional du Vercors** are the stuff of soft adventure. Quieter and cheaper than neighbouring Alpine resorts, the wildlife-rich park is a magnet for enthusiasts of fresh air, cross-country skiing, snowshoeing, caving and hiking. Its accommodation, moreover, is the stuff of Alpine dreams:

» **Les Allières** (www.aubergedesallieres.com, in French; Lans-en-Vercors; half-board per person €45) This 1476m-high forest chalet offers no-frills digs (bunk beds, shared toilets) and wondrous mountain food (mains €16 to €25). The wood-fire raclette and *tarte aux myrtilles* (blueberry tart) are divine.

» **À la Crécia** (www.gite-en-vercors.com, in French; 436 chemin des Cléments, Lans-en-Vercors; s/d/tr/q €52/57/72/87) Goats, pigs and poultry rule the roost at this 16th-century, solar-powered farm. Rooms are stylishly rustic with beams, earthy hues and mosaic bathrooms. Dinner (€17) is a farm-fresh feast.

» **Gîte La Verne** (http://gite.laverne.free.fr, in French; La Verne, Méaudre; apt for 4/8 people per week €500/750) Fitted with fully equipped kitchens, this *gîte*'s beautiful apartments blend Alpine cosiness with mod cons. Whether you opt for self-catering or half-board, you'll luurv the *hammam* and outdoor Norwegian bath.

gant (violet, chestnut, Génépi, fig), and a blind test every Tuesday night to see how many your taste buds can recognise.

Information

Tourist office (☎04 76 42 41 41; www.grenoble-tourisme.com; 14 rue de la République; ⌚9am-6.30pm Mon-Sat, 10am-1pm & 2-5pm Sun)

Getting There & Away

Air

Several budget airlines, including Ryanair and easyJet, fly to/from **Grenoble Isère airport** (www.grenoble-airport.com), 45km northwest and linked by **shuttle bus** (www.grenoble-altitude.com; single/return €12.50/22, 45 minutes, twice daily Tue-Sat).

Bus

From the **bus station** (rue Émile Gueymard), next to the train station, **VFD** (www.vfd.fr, in French) and **Transisère** (www.transisere.fr, in French) run buses to/from various destinations including Geneva (€43, 2½ hours) and Lyon St-Exupéry (€22, one hour) airports.

Train

From the **train station** (rue Émile Gueymard), frequent trains run to/from Paris' Gare de Lyon (from €76, 3½ hours) and Lyon (€19, 1½ hours, five daily).

POP 121,850

Despite a swoon-worthy Old Town, first-rate restaurants and happening bars pepped up by students, this cultured capital of the Franche-Comté region – astraddle several hills and the banks of the Doubs River – is refreshingly modest and untouristy. In Gallo-Roman times, it was a key stop on trade routes between Italy, the Alps and the Rhine. Time-travel to 2012, when Besançon TGV train station opens 10km north in the village of Auxon.

Sights

Citadelle de Besançon — CITADEL

(www.citadelle.com; rue des Fusillés de la Résistance; adult/child €8/4.60; ⌚9am-6pm) Besançon's crowning glory, dramatically lit by night, is its Unesco-listed **citadel**, a formidable feat of 17th-century engineering by the prolific Vauban. Inside are three museums covering local traditions, natural history and the rather more harrowing rise of Nazism, fascism and the French Resistance movement.

VISI'PASS

Visit Besançon's top sights and museums, including the citadel and Musée des Beaux-Arts, with a **Visi'Pass** (adult/child €8/4.10). Buy it at sights, online or at the tourist office.

Musée des Beaux-Arts — MUSEUM

(www.musee-arts-besancon.org, in French; 1 place de la Révolution; adult/child €5/free; ⌚9.30am-noon & 2-6pm Wed-Mon) This is France's oldest museum, founded in 1694 when the Louvre was but a twinkle in Paris' eye. The collection spans archaeology with its Egyptian mummies, Neolithic tools and Gallo-Roman mosaics; a cavernous drawing cabinet whose 5500 works include Dürer, Delacroix and Rodin masterpieces; and 14th- to 20th-century painting with standouts by Titian, Rubens, Goya and Matisse.

Sleeping

Hôtel de Paris — DESIGN HOTEL €€

(☎03 81 81 36 56; www.besanconhoteldeparis.com; 33 rue des Granges; s €60, d €75-105; @📶) Hidden in the Old Town, this former 18th-century coaching inn reveals a razor-sharp eye for design. Corridors lit by leaded windows lead to slinky, silver-kissed rooms, a small fitness room and shady inner courtyard.

Charles Quint Hôtel — HISTORIC HOTEL €€

(☎03 81 82 05 49; www.hotel-charlesquint.com; 3 rue du Chapitre; d €89-145; @🏊) This 18th-century town house turned nine-room boutique hotel is sublime. Find it slumbering in the shade of the citadel, behind the cathedral.

Maison de Verre — B&B €€

(☎03 81 81 82 27; www.lamaisondeverre.com, in French; 26 rue Bersot; s/d 75/85; 📶) Katherine Bermond has cleverly converted a car factory into this nouveau-chic *chambre d'hôte* with industrial twist.

Eating

TOP CHOICE Le Saint-Pierre — MODERN FRENCH €€

(☎03 81 81 20 99; www.restaurant-saintpierre.com, in French; 104 rue Battant; menus €35-60; ⌚lunch Mon-Fri, dinner Mon-Sat) This arty restaurant is among Besançon's most coveted. Crisp white linen, exposed stone and subtle lighting are the backdrop for intense flavours, expertly paired with regional wines. The three-course *menu marché* is a steal at €35.

WORTH A TRIP

A WINE LOVER'S TRIP

No road trip is tastier than the **Route des Vins de Jura** (Jura Wine Rd; www.laroutedesvinsdujura.com), a driving itinerary that corkscrews through 80km of well-tended vines and pretty stone villages. Route planners and winery guide are online.

Linger in **Arbois**, Jura wine capital, over a glass of *vin jaune*. The history of this nutty 'yellow wine' is told in the **Musée de la Vigne et du Vin** (adult/child €3.50/2.70; 10am-12pm & 2-6pm Wed-Mon), in the whimsical, turreted Château Pécauld. Don't miss the 2.5km-long **Chemin des Vignes** walking trail and 8km-long **Circuit des Vignes** mountain-bike routes through vines.

TOP CHOICE **La Balance Mets et Vins** (03 84 37 45 00; 47 rue de Courcelles; menus €23-55; Thu-Mon, lunch Tue) at Arbois offers the perfect coda to this wine lover's trip; lunch here, on local, organic produce. Its signature *coq au vin jaune et aux morilles*, casserole and crème brûlée doused in *vin jaune* are musts, as is the wine menu with five glasses of either Jurassienne wine (€15) or *vin jaune* (€25, including a vintage one). Kids can sniff, swirl and sip, too, with three kinds of organic grape juice (€7.50).

High above Arbois is tiny **Pupillin**, a cuter-than-cute, yellow-stone village famous for its wine production. Several *caves* (wine cellars) can be visited.

Arbois **tourist office** (03 84 66 55 50; www.arbois.com; 17 rue de l'Hôtel de Ville; 9am-noon & 2-6pm Mon-Sat) has walking and cycling information and a list of *caves* for tastings.

Trains link Arbois and Besançon (€8.50, 45 minutes, 10 daily).

La Table des Halles MODERN FRENCH **€€**
(03 81 50 62 74; 22 rue Gustave Courbet; menus €15-29; Tue-Sat) The urban loft decor at this fashionable restaurant wouldn't look out of place in New York's meat-packing district. But what lands on your plate is resolutely French and regional.

Mirabelle CAFE **€€**
(5 rue Mégevand; mains €11-14; lunch Mon-Fri, dinner Mon-Sat) Bird boxes dangle from the ceiling and the cheese menu is chalked on a mouse-shaped blackboard at this kinda kitsch, kinda cool cafe. A boho crowd flock here for gratins, *croûtes* and scrummy tarts made with seasonal, mostly organic ingredients.

Information

Tourist office (03 81 80 92 55; www.besancon-tourisme.com; place du 8 Septembre; 10am-6pm Mon-Sat, 10am-1pm Sun)

Getting There & Away

From the **train station** (av du Général de Gaulle), trains serve Paris (€41, 2¾ hours, 26 daily), Dijon (€14, 70 minutes, 20 daily) and Lyon (€28, 3½ hours, 25 daily).

Around Besançon

SALINE ROYALE

Envisaged by its designer, Claude-Nicolas Ledoux, as the 'ideal city', the 18th-century **Saline Royale** (Royal Saltworks; www.salineroyale.com, in French; adult/child €7.50/3.50; 9am-noon & 2-6pm) in Arc-et-Senans, 35km southwest of Besançon, is a showpiece of early Industrial Age town planning. The semicircular saltworks is a Unesco World Heritage site.

Trains link Besançon and Arc-et-Senans (€6.50, 30 minutes, 10 daily).

MÉTABIEF

Métabief (population 890, elevation 1000m), 75km south of Besançon, is the Jura's leading cross-country ski resort. From atop Mont d'Or (1463m), a fantastic panorama stretches over the foggy Swiss plain to Lake Geneva, the Matterhorn and Mont Blanc.

Then there is *vacherin Mont d'Or*, the only French cheese to be wrapped in spruce bark and eaten with a spoon – hot from a box. Arrive with the milk lorry around 9am at the **Fromagerie du Mont d'Or** (www.fromageriedumontdor.com, in French; 2 rue Moulin; 9am-12.15pm & 3-7pm Mon-Sat, 9am-noon Sun) to watch it being made.

Online see www.tourisme-metabief.com.

Parc Naturel Régional du Haut-Jura

Experience the Jura at its rawest in the Haut-Jura Regional Park, an area of 757 sq km stretching from Chapelle-des-Bois almost to the western tip of Lake Geneva. Each year in February its lakes, mountains and low-lying valleys host the Transjurassienne, the world's second-longest cross-country skiing race.

Highlights include **Les Rousses** (population 2850, elevation 1100m), the park's main sports hub in winter (skiing) and summer (walking and mountain biking); and the incredible views from the **Telesiège Val Mijoux** (chairlift return €6; ⊙10.30am-1pm & 2.15-5.30pm Sat & Sun mid-Jul–mid-Aug) linking Mijoux with Mont Rond (1533m). Even more stunning is the far-reaching vista over Lake Geneva from the **Col de la Faucille**, 20km south of Les Rousses.

Château de Voltaire (allée du Château; adult/child €5/free; ⊙tours in French hourly 10.30am-4.30pm Tue-Sun mid-May–mid-Sep), where the great writer lived from 1759 until his return to Paris and death in 1778, is also worth visiting. Guided tours take in the chateau, chapel and 7-hectare park.

Public transport in the park is almost nonexistent, so you'll need wheels. A great place to start is in Lajoux at the **Maison du Parc** (www.parc-haut-jura.fr; adult/child €5/3; ⊙10am-12.30pm & 2-6.30pm Tue-Fri, 2-6.30pm Sat & Sun), an interactive sensorial museum that explores the region through sound, touch and smell.

DON'T MISS

CROSS-BORDER

TOP CHOICE **Hôtel Franco-Suisse** (☎03 84 60 02 20; www.arbezie-hotel.com; La Cure; s/d/tr/q incl half-board €88/127/166/254), a unique bistro inn right on the French-Swiss border, lets you sleep sweet with your head in Switzerland and your feet in France. At home here since 1920, the Arbez family take huge pride in their cosy rooms and regional cuisine. Find them wedged between France's Col de la Faucille and Switzerland's Col de la Givrine in the hamlet of La Cure, 2.5km from Les Rousses.

THE DORDOGNE & THE LOT

If it's French heart and soul you're after, look no further. Tucked in the country's southwestern corner, the neighbouring regions of the Dordogne and Lot combine history, culture and culinary sophistication in one unforgettably scenic package. The Dordogne is best known for its sturdy *bastides* (fortified towns), clifftop chateaux and spectacular prehistoric cave paintings, while the Mediterranean-tinged region of the Lot is home to endless vintage vineyards and the historic city of Cahors.

Sarlat-La-Canéda

POP 9950

A gorgeous tangle of honey-coloured buildings, alleyways and secret squares make up this unmissable Dordogne village – a natural if touristy launch pad into the Vézère Valley.

Part of the fun of Sarlat is getting lost in its twisting alleyways and backstreets. **Rue Jean-Jacques Rousseau** or the area around **Le Présidial** are good starting points, but for the grandest buildings and *hôtels particuliers* you'll want to explore **rue des Consuls**. Whichever street you take, sooner or later you'll hit the **Cathédrale St-Sacerdos** (place du Peyrou), a real mix

DON'T MISS

GOOSE FEST

Three gold-hued, bronze-sculpted geese on **place du Marché aux Oies** ('geese market' square) attest to the enduring economic and gastronomic role of these birds in the Dordogne. Both the covered market and Sarlat's chaotic **Saturday-morning market** (place de la Liberté & rue de la République) – a full-blown French market experience 'must' – sell a smorgasbord of goose-based goodies.

In local restaurants, feast on foie gras and other goose-based specialities such as *grillons* (coarse-textured goose pâté), *magret* (goose breast), *aiguillettes* (fine slivers of *magret*) and *civet* (stew).

Gaggles of live geese fill Sarlat during its **Fest'Oie** (goose festival) on the third Sunday in February, accompanied by stalls, music and goose-fuelled banquet.

WORTH A TRIP

TRUFFLE CAPITAL

For culinary connoisseurs there is just one reason to visit the Dordogne: black truffles *(truffes)*. A subterranean fungi that thrives on the roots of oak trees, this mysterious little mushroom is notoriously capricious. The art of truffle-hunting is a closely guarded secret and vintage crops fetch as much as €1000 per kg. Truffles are sought after by top chefs for an infinite array of gourmet dishes, but black truffles are often best eaten quite simply in a plain egg omelette, shaved over buttered pasta or sliced on fresh crusty bread.

Truffles are hunted by dogs (and occasionally pigs) from December to March and sold at special truffle markets in the Dordogne, including in Périgueux, Sarlat and most notably, the 'world's truffle capital', **Sorges** (population 1234). This tiny village, 23km northeast of Périgueux on the N21, is the place to get up on truffle culture, at the **Ecomusée de la Truffe** (www.ecomusee-truffe-sorges.com; Le Bourg, Sorges; adult/child €4/2; ⏲10am-noon & 2-5pm, closed Mon Oct-Jan) and hook yourself up with a truffle hunt. **La Truffe Noire de Sorges** (☎06 08 45 09 48; www.truffe-sorges.com; 1½hr tours €10; ⏲by reservation Dec-Feb & Jun-Sep) runs tours of *truffiéres* (the areas where truffles are cultivated), followed by tasting.

Then there is **Auberge de la Truffe** (☎05 53 05 02 05; www.auberge-de-la-truffe.com, in French; Sorges; s €52-105, d €56-120; ❄≋) in the village centre, with its stylish and renowned **restaurant** (menus €23-57) serving sensational seasonal cuisine. For culinary connoisseurs there is just one fixed menu to order, the *menu truffe* (€100).

of architectural styles and periods: the belfry and western facade are the oldest parts.

Nearby, the former **Église Ste-Marie** (place de la Liberté) houses Sarlat's mouth-watering **Marché Couvert** (covered market) and a state-of-the-art **panoramic lift** (elevator) in its bell tower. It was designed by top French architect Jean Nouvel (whose parents live in Sarlat).

The **tourist office** (☎05 53 31 45 45; www.sarlat-tourisme.com; rue Tourny; ⏲9am-6pm Mon-Sat, 10am-1pm & 2-5pm Sun) neighbours the cathedral.

Sleeping

Hôtel La Couleuvrine HOTEL €€
(☎05 53 59 27 80; www.la-couleuvrine.com; 1 place de la Bouquerie; d €56-88; @) Gables, chimneys and red-tile rooftops adorn this rambling hotel, originally part of Sarlat's city wall. It's old, odd and endearingly musty; a couple of rooms are in the hotel's turret.

Hôtel Les Récollets HOTEL €
(☎05 53 31 36 00; www.hotel-recollets-sarlat.com; 4 rue Jean-Jacques Rousseau; d €45-69; ❄📶) Lost in the Old Town medieval maze, the Récollets is a budget beauty. Nineteen topsy-turvy rooms and a charming vaulted breakfast room are rammed in around the medieval *maison*.

Clos La Boëtie BOUTIQUE HOTEL €€€
(☎05 53 29 44 18; www.closlaboetie-sarlat.com; 95-97 av de la Selves; d €210-280; ❄@📶≋) Each of the 11 rooms at this 19th-century mansion, a five-minute walk north of the Cité Médiévale, is a jewel. Some have terraces and all come with soothing, hydromassage showers and balneotherapy ('water healing') baths.

Eating

Bistro de l'Octroi REGIONAL CUISINE €€
(☎05 53 30 83 40; www.lebistrodeloctroi.fr, in French; 111 av de Selves; menus €18-26) This local's tip is a little way out of town, but don't let that dissuade you. Sarladais pack into this cosy town house for the artistically presented, accomplished cooking that doesn't sacrifice substance for style.

Le Grand Bleu GASTRONOMIC €€€
(☎05 53 29 82 14; www.legrandbleu.eu, in French; 43 av de la Gare; menus €33-90; ⏲lunch Thu-Sun, dinner Tue-Sat) Every menu at this Michelin-starred temple includes a choice of meat (such as veal sweetbreads with truffles) or seafood (such as lobster risotto with roast eggplant and truffle mousse). Cooking courses, too.

Le Présidial REGIONAL CUISINE €€
(☎05 53 28 92 47; 6 rue Landry; menus from €29; ⏲lunch Tue-Sat, dinner Mon-Sat Apr-Nov) What was a 17th-century courthouse now flaunts the city's most romantic dining terrace. Goose, duck and foie gras dominate the menu, and the wine list is packed with Sarlat and Cahors vintages.

Le Bistrot REGIONAL CUISINE €€
(☎05 53 28 28 40; place du Peyrou; menus €18.50-24.50; ⏲Mon-Sat) Red-checked tablecloths and twinkling fairy lights create an intimate atmosphere at this diminutive bistro. Don't miss the *pommes sarlardaises* (potatoes cooked in duck fat).

Getting There & Away

The **train station** (ave de la Gare), 1.3km south of the old city, serves Périgueux (change at Le Buisson; €13.90, 1¾ hours, three daily) and Les Eyzies (change at Le Buisson; €8.60, 50 minutes to 2½ hours, three daily).

Les Eyzies-de-Tayac-Sireuil

POP 860

A hot base for touring the Vezère Valley's extraordinary cave collection, this village is essentially a clutch of touristy shops strung along a central street. Its **Musée National de Préhistoire** (www.musee-prehistoire-eyzies.fr, in French; 1 rue du Musée adult/child €5/free, 1st Sun of month free; ⏲9.30am-6pm Wed-Mon), rife with amazing prehistoric finds, makes a great introduction to the area.

About 250m north of the museum is the Cro-Magnon shelter of **Abri Pataud** (www.mnhn.fr, in French; 20 rue du Moyen Âge; adult/child €5/3; ⏲10am-noon & 2-6pm Sun-Thu), with an ibex carving dating from about 19,000 BC. Admission includes a guided tour (some in English).

Train services link Les Eyzies with Sarlat-la-Canéda.

Cahors

POP 21,128

Sheltered in a U-shape curve in the Lot River, bustling Cahors has the feel of a sun-baked Mediterranean town. Pastel-coloured buildings line shaded squares in the old medieval quarter, criss-crossed by a labyrinth of alleyways, dead ends and riverside quays. The town's most famous landmark is the **Pont Valentré**, one of France's finest medieval bridges, built from six arches and three towers.

Sleeping

TOP CHOICE **Hôtel Jean XXII** HOTEL €
(☎05 65 35 07 66; www.hotel-jeanxxii.com, in French; 2 rue Edmond-Albé; s €48, d €58-65; 📶) This excellent little hotel mixes original stone, greenery and well-worn wood with a dash of metropolitan minimalism. Smart rooms have muted colours, and there's a

WORTH A TRIP

PREHISTORIC PAINTINGS

Fantastic prehistoric **caves** with some of the world's finest **cave art** is what makes the Vézère Valley so very special. Most of the caves are closed in winter, and get very busy in summer. Visitor numbers are strictly limited, so you'll need to reserve well ahead.

Of the valley's 175 known sites, the most famous include **Grotte de Font de Gaume** (www.eyzies.monuments-nationaux.fr; adult/child €7/free; ⏲9.30am-12.30pm & 2-5.30pm Sun-Fri), 1km northeast of Les Eyzies. About 14,000 years ago, prehistoric artists created the gallery of over 230 figures, including bison, reindeer, horses, mammoths, bears and wolves, of which 25 are on permanent display.

About 7km east of Les Eyzies, **Abri du Cap Blanc** (www.eyzies.monuments-nationaux.fr; adult/child €7/free; ⏲9.30am-12.30 & 2-5.30pm Sun-Fri) showcases an unusual sculpture gallery of horses, bison and deer.

Then there is **Grotte de Rouffignac** (www.grottederouffignac.fr; adult/child €6.30/4; tours in French ⏲10-11.30am & 2-5pm), sometimes known as the 'Cave of 100 Mammoths' because of its painted mammoths. Access to the caves, hidden in woodland 15km north of Les Eyzies, is aboard a trundling electric train.

Star of the show goes hands down to **Grotte de Lascaux** (Lascaux II: ☎05 53 51 95 03; www.semitour.com; adult/child €8.80/6; ⏲9.30am-6pm), 2km southeast of Montignac, featuring an astonishing menagerie including oxen, deer, horses, reindeer and mammoth, as well as an amazing 5.5m bull, the largest cave drawing ever found. The original cave was closed to the public in 1963 to prevent damage to the paintings, but the most famous sections have been meticulously recreated in a second cave nearby – a massive undertaking that required some 20 artists and took 11 years.

reading area on the 1st floor where you can unwind in leather armchairs.

Auberge de Jeunesse HOSTEL €
(☎05 65 35 64 71; fjt46@wanadoo.fr; 222 rue Joachim Murat; dm €13.20; ⏱9am-12.30pm & 2-7pm; 📶) In an old convent, Cahors' hostel is basic but friendly and functional. Dorms sleep four to ten, and there's a rambling garden.

Eating

L'O à la Bouche FRENCH €€
(☎05 65 35 65 69; 134 rue St-Urcisse; menus €19.50-26.50; ⏱Tue-Sat) *'Cuisine creative'* are the watchwords at this refined address where classic ingredients get a fresh spin: cod in a peanut crust and *'tout coco'* chocolate pudding anyone?

Le Marché FUSION €€
(☎05 65 35 27 27; www.restaurantlemarche.com; 27 place Jean-Jacques Chapon; menus €19-50; ⏱Tue-Sat) Puce-and-cream armchairs, razor-edge wood and slate walls set the designer tone at the Market, where the menu's just as swish.

Marie Colline VEGETARIAN €
(☎05 65 35 59 96; 173 rue Georges Clemenceau; mains €8.50; ⏱lunch Tue-Fri Sep-Jul; 🌿) This little bistro has such a traditional feel it's a surprise to discover that its menu is meat- and fish-free. Solo diners are seated at a sociable shared table.

Information

Tourist office (☎05 65 53 20 65; www.tourisme-cahors.com, in French; place François Mitterrand; ⏱9.30am-6.30pm Mon-Sat)

Getting There & Away

Cahors' **train station** (place Jouinot Gambetta) is on the main line (eight to 10 daily) to Paris' Gare d'Austerlitz (€67.70, five hours) via Brive-la-Gaillarde (€18.20, one hour), Limoges (€30.50, two hours) and Souillac (€13.10, 40 minutes), from where SNCF coaches continue to Sarlat (€2, 40 minutes, two daily).

THE ATLANTIC COAST

Though the French Riviera is France's most popular beach spot, the many seaside resorts along the Atlantic coast are fast catching up. If you're a surf nut or a beach bum, then the sandy bays around Biarritz will be right up your alley, while oenophiles can sample the fruits of the vine in the high temple of French winemaking, Bordeaux. Towards the Pyrenees you'll find the Basque Country, which in many ways is closer to the culture of northern Spain than to the rest of France.

Nantes

POP 291,000

You can take Nantes out of Brittany (as happened when regional boundaries were redrawn during WWII), but you can't take Brittany out of its long-time capital, Nantes ('Naoned' in Breton). Spirited and innovative, this city has a long history of reinventing itself. Founded by Celts, the city later became France's foremost port, industrial centre and shipbuilding hub, and has recently reinvented itself again as a cultural centre and youthful metropolis – one in two Nantais is under 40!

Sights

TOP CHOICE Les Machines de l'Île de Nantes GALLERY
(www.lesmachines-nantes.fr; adult/child €7/5.50, elephant ride adult/child €7/5.50; ⏱10am-8pm Jul-Aug, hours vary rest of year) Nantes' quirkiest sight! Prance around like a Maharajah on a 45-tonne elephant with a secret lounge in its belly or sail a boat through dangerous oceans rife with oversized squid at this surreal gallery that would have Jules Verne smiling in his grave! Admission covers the workshop where the larger-than-life, fantastical contraptions are built.

Musée Jules Verne MUSEUM
(www.julesverne.nantes.fr, in French; 3 rue de l'Hermitage; adult/child €3/1.50; ⏱10am-noon & 2-6pm Mon & Wed-Sat, 2-6pm Sun) Overlooking the river 2km southwest of the tourist office, this magical museum displays 1st-edition books, hand-edited manuscripts and cardboard cut-outs inspired by the work of Jules Verne of *Around the World in 80 Days* fame, born in Nantes in 1828.

Château des Ducs de Bretagne CASTLE, MUSEUM
(www.chateau-nantes.fr; adult/child €5/3; ⏱9.30am-8pm Jul-Aug, shorter hr rest of year) Forget fusty furnishings – the stripped, light-filled interior of the restored Château des Ducs de Bretagne houses multimedia-rich new exhibits detailing the city's history.

NANTES CITY PASS

Sold at the tourist office for €18/28/36 per 24/48/72 hours, this pass gets you unlimited travel on buses and trams, entry into museums and monuments, a guided tour, shopping discounts and various other handy extras.

Musée des Beaux-Arts MUSEUM
(10 rue Georges Clemenceau; adult €3.50; 10am-6pm Wed & Fri-Mon, to 8pm Thu) One of the finest collections of French paintings outside Paris hangs here, with works by Chagall, Monet, Picasso and Kandinsky among others.

Sleeping

TOP CHOICE **Hôtel Pommeraye** BOUTIQUE HOTEL €€
(02 40 48 78 79; www.hotel-pommeraye.com; 2 rue Boileau; s €54-99, d €59-129;) Sleek and chic, this is more art gallery than hotel. The rooms have shimmering short-pile carpets and textured walls, while eye-catching art seriously distracts in reception and other common areas.

Hôtel Graslin BOUTIQUE HOTEL €€
(02 40 69 72 91; www.hotel-graslin.com; 1 rue Piron; r €75-105;) An unlikely (but very Nantes) marriage of art deco and 1970s is what this refurbished hotel is all about. Love the edgy colour combos and shag carpets in the attic rooms.

La Manu HOSTEL €
(02 40 29 29 20; nanteslamanu@fuaj.org; 2 place de la Manu; dm incl breakfast €18.20; reception closed noon-4pm; @) Housed in a converted factory, this well-equipped, 123-bed hostel is a 15-minute walk from the centre. Alas, there's a lock-out from noon to 4pm. Take tram 1 to the Manufacture stop.

Hôtel des Colonies BOUTIQUE HOTEL €
(02 40 48 79 76; www.hoteldescolonies.fr; 5 rue du Chapeau Rouge; s €58-78, d €65-78;) Local art exhibitions, cherry-red public areas and rooms in purple, green and orange make this an attractive option.

Hôtel La Pérouse DESIGN HOTEL €€
(02 40 89 75 00; www.hotel-laperouse.fr; 3 allée Duquesne; r €118;) Styled to reflect the city's shipbuilding traditions, this hotel has a wooden gangway entrance, stone-and-wood lobby and 46 rooms with zigzag chairs and canvas sail curtains.

Eating

Nantes' most cosmopolitan dining is in the medieval Bouffay quarter around rue de la Juiverie, rue des Petites Écuries and rue de la Bâclerie. Rue Jean Jacques Rousseau and rue Santeuil are other busy eat streets.

In March and November, buy sardines at street stalls all over town.

TOP CHOICE **Le Bistrot de l'Écrivain** MODERN FRENCH €€
(02 51 84 15 15; 15 rue Jean Jacques Rousseau; menus €14.50-18.50; Mon-Sat) Splashed in shades of red, the Writer's Bistro is an easygoing place with bottle-lined walls and creative Nantaise cuisine.

Un Coin en Ville MODERN FRENCH €€
(02 40 20 05 97; 2 place de la Bourse; menus from €12.90; lunch Tue-Fri, dinner Tue-Sat) Flickering candles, soulful jazz and blues, and cooking that fuses local produce with exotic styles is what gives this place sex appeal.

Le 1 GASTRONOMIC €€
(02 40 08 28 00; 1 rue Olympe de Gouges; menus €14.90-23) The wine cellar – a see-through affair with 2000-odd bottles stacked on stainless-steel racks – is a big drawcard of this contemporary dining space overlooking the Loire.

Drinking

Let the party begin! Nantes has no shortage of edgy spots and there is no better place to start than the **Hangar à Bananes** (www.hangarabananes.com, in French; 21 quai des Antilles; daily till late), a rejuvenated banana-ripening warehouse on Île de Nantes with more than a dozen restaurants, bars and clubs (and combinations thereof), each hipper than the next. The front terraces of most face Daniel Buren's art installation **Anneaux de Buren** (quai des Antilles), illuminated at night.

Or try industrial-chic **Le Lieu Unique** (www.lelieuunique.com, in French; 2 rue de la Biscuiterie), the one-time LU biscuit factory-turned-performance arts space where you can catch dance, theatre and contemporary art. Its restaurant and polished concrete bar buzzes.

If you get French, **leBoost** (www.leboost.com, in French) has local listings.

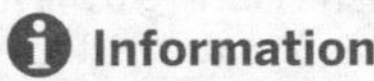

Information

Tourist office (www.nantes-tourisme.com; 2 place St-Pierre & cours Olivier de Clisson; 10am-6pm Mon-Sat, from 10.30am Thu)

Getting There & Away

Air

Aéroport International Nantes-Atlantique (www.nantes.aeroport.fr) is 12km southeast of town. Shuttle buses (€7, 20 minutes) link it with the Gare Centrale bus-tram hub and the train station's southern entrance from about 6.45am to 11pm.

Train

The **train station** (27 blvd de Stalingrad) is well connected to most of the country. Destinations include Paris' Gare Montparnasse (€57.90, two hours, 15 to 20 daily), Bordeaux (€44.60, four hours, three or four daily) and La Rochelle (€24.10, 1¾ hours, three or four daily).

Poitiers

POP 91,900

Inland from the coast, history-steeped Poitiers rose to prominence as the former capital of Poitou, the region governed by the Counts of Poitiers in the Middle Ages. Poitiers has one of the oldest universities in the country, first established in 1432 and today a lynchpin of this lively city.

Sights

Église Notre Dame la Grande CHURCH

(place Charles de Gaulle) Every evening from 21 June until the third weekend in September, spectacular colours are cinematically projected onto the western facade of this beautiful Romanesque church next to Poitier's covered market. The oldest parts date from the 11th century and the only original frescos are the faint 12th- or 13th-century works that adorn the U-shaped dome above the choir.

Baptistère St-Jean CHURCH

(rue Jean Jaurès; adult/child €2/1; ⏲10.30am-12.30pm & 3-6pm Wed-Mon Apr-Oct) Constructed in the 4th and 6th centuries on Roman foundations, this baptistery, 100m south of Poitier's Gothic-style cathedral **Cathédrale St-Pierre** (rue de la Cathédrale), was redecorated in the 10th century and used as a parish church. The octagonal hole beneath the frescos was used for total-immersion baptisms until the 7th century.

Futuroscope THEME PARK

(www.futuroscope.com; adult/child €35/26; ⏲10am-11.15pm Jul-Aug, shorter hr Sep-Dec & Feb-Jun) This cinematic theme park, 10km north of Poitiers in Jaunay-Clan, takes you whizzing through space, diving into the deep blue ocean depths and on a close encounter with futuristic creatures. To keep things cutting edge, one-third of the attractions change annually. Many are motion-seat setups requiring a minimum height of 120cm. From Poitiers' train station take bus 9 or E (€1.30, 30 minutes).

Sleeping & Eating

Hôtel de l'Europe HISTORIC HOTEL €

(☎05 49 88 12 00; www.hotel-europe-poitiers.com; 39 rue Carnot; s/d €55/61; wi-fi) The main building of this elegant hotel, with sweeping staircase, oversized rooms and refined furnishings, dates from 1710.

WORTH A TRIP

GREEN VENICE

Floating along emerald waterways – tinted green in spring and summer by duckweed – in a kayak or rowing boat is a real Zen highlight. Dubbed *Venise Verte* (Green Venice), the **Parc Naturel Interrégional du Marais Poitevin** is a tranquil, bird-filled wetland covering some 800 sq km of wet and drained marshland, threaded with canals, cycling paths and the odd waterside village.

Boating and **cycling** are the only ways to explore and there is no shortage of bikes (€6/13 per hour/half-day) and flat-bottomed boats (from €15/38) or kayaks (from €12/30) to rent from the Marais Poitevin's two main bases: tiny, honey-coloured **Coulon** and (our favourite, being a sucker for romance), the pretty village of **Arçais**. Try **Arçais Venise Verte** (www.veniseverteloisirs.fr, in French), **Au Martin Pecheur** (www.aumartinpecheur.com, in French) or **Bardet-Huttiers** (www.marais-arcais.com, in French).

To ensure complete and utter head-over-the-heels love, stay overnight at the environmentally friendly **Maison Flore** (☎05 49 76 27 11; www.maisonflore.com; rue du Grand Port, Arçais; s/d €57/72; wi-fi). Romantically set on Arçais' waterfront, the 10-room boutique hotel is painted the colours of local marsh plants such as pale-green Angelica and bright-purple Iris. Books and board games in the lounge add a cosy touch and you can rent boats.

Getting to Green Venice is painful in anything other than your own car.

ON THE WINE TRAIL

Thirsty? The 1000-sq-km wine-growing area around the city of Bordeaux is, along with Burgundy, France's most important producer of top-quality wines. Whet your palate with Bordeaux tourist office's introduction wine-and-cheese courses (€24).

Serious students of the grape can enrol in a two-hour (€25) or two- to three-day course (€335 to €600) at the *école du vin* (wine school) inside the **Maison du Vin de Bordeaux** (3 cours du 30 Juillet). Courses include chateaux visits.

Bordeaux has over 5000 estates where grapes are grown, picked and turned into wine. Smaller chateaux often accept walk-in visitors, but at many places, especially better-known ones, you have to reserve in advance. If you have your own wheels, one of the easiest to visit is **Château Lanessan** (☎05 56 58 94 80; www.lanessan.com; Cussac-Fort-Medoc; adult/child €8/2; ⊙advance reservation).

Favourite vine-framed villages brimming with charm and tasting/buying opportunities include medieval **St-Émilion** (www.saint-emilion-tourisme.com), port town **Pauillac** (www.pauillac-medoc.com) and **Listrac-Médoc**. In **Arsac-en-Médoc**, Philippe Raoux's vast glass-and-steel wine centre, **La Winery** (☎05 56 39 04 90; www.lawinery.fr, in French; Rond-point des Vendangeurs, D1), stuns with concerts and contemporary art exhibitions alongside tastings to determine your *signe œnologique* ('wine sign'; booking required).

Many chateaux close during October's *vendange* (grape harvest).

Hôtel Central HOTEL €
(☎05 49 01 79 79; www.centralhotel86.com, in French; 35 place du Maréchal Leclerc; d €38-65) At the southern edge of Poitier's charming pedestrian district of half-timbered houses, this two-star place is a terrific little bargain. Rooms are snug but sunlit.

La Serrurerie TRADITIONAL €
(☎05 49 41 05 14; 28 rue des Grandes Écoles; mains €10-17.50; ⊙8am-2am) Showcasing local art, sculpture and retro toys, this mosaic-and-steel bistro-bar is Poitiers' communal lounge-dining room. A chalked blackboard menu lists specialities such as *tournedos* (thick slices) of salmon, sensational pastas and a divine crème brûlée.

Information

Tourist office (☎05 49 41 21 24; www.ot-poitiers.fr; 45 place Charles de Gaulle; ⊙10am-11pm Mon-Sat, 10am-6pm & 7-11pm Sun 21 Jun-Aug, shorter hr rest of year)

Getting There & Away

The **train station** (blvd du Grand Cerf) has direct links to Bordeaux (€35, 1¾ hours), Nantes (€27.50, 3¼ hours) and Paris' Gare Montparnasse (€50, 1½ hours, 12 daily).

Bordeaux

POP 238,900

The new millennium was a turning point for the city long nicknamed La Belle au Bois Dormant (Sleeping Beauty), when the mayor, ex-Prime Minister Alain Juppé, roused Bordeaux, pedestrianising its boulevards, restoring its neoclassical architecture, and implementing a hi-tech public-transport system. Today the city is a Unesco World Heritage site and, with its merry student population and 2.5 million-odd annual tourists, scarcely sleeps at all.

Sights

Cathédrale St-André CHURCH
This Unesco-listed cathedral is almost overshadowed by the gargoyled, 50m-high Gothic belfry, **Tour Pey-Berland** (adult/child €5/free; ⊙10am-1.15pm & 2-6pm Jun-Sep, shorter hr rest of year). Erected between 1440 and 1466, its spire was later topped off with the statue of Notre Dame de l'Aquitaine. Scaling the tower's 232 narrow steps rewards you with a spectacular panorama of the city.

Museums MUSEUMS
Bordeaux's museums have free entry for permanent collections. Gallo-Roman statues and relics dating back 25,000 years are among the highlights at the impressive **Musée d'Aquitaine** (20 cours Pasteur; temporary exhibitions €3; ⊙11am-6pm Tue-Sun), while more than 700 post-1960s works by 140 European and American artists are on display at the **CAPC Musée d'Art Contemporain** (Entrepôt 7, rue Ferrére; ⊙11am-6pm Tue, Thu-Sun, to 8pm Wed, closed Mon).

The evolution of Occidental art from the Renaissance to the mid-20th century is on view at Bordeaux's **Musée des Beaux-Arts**

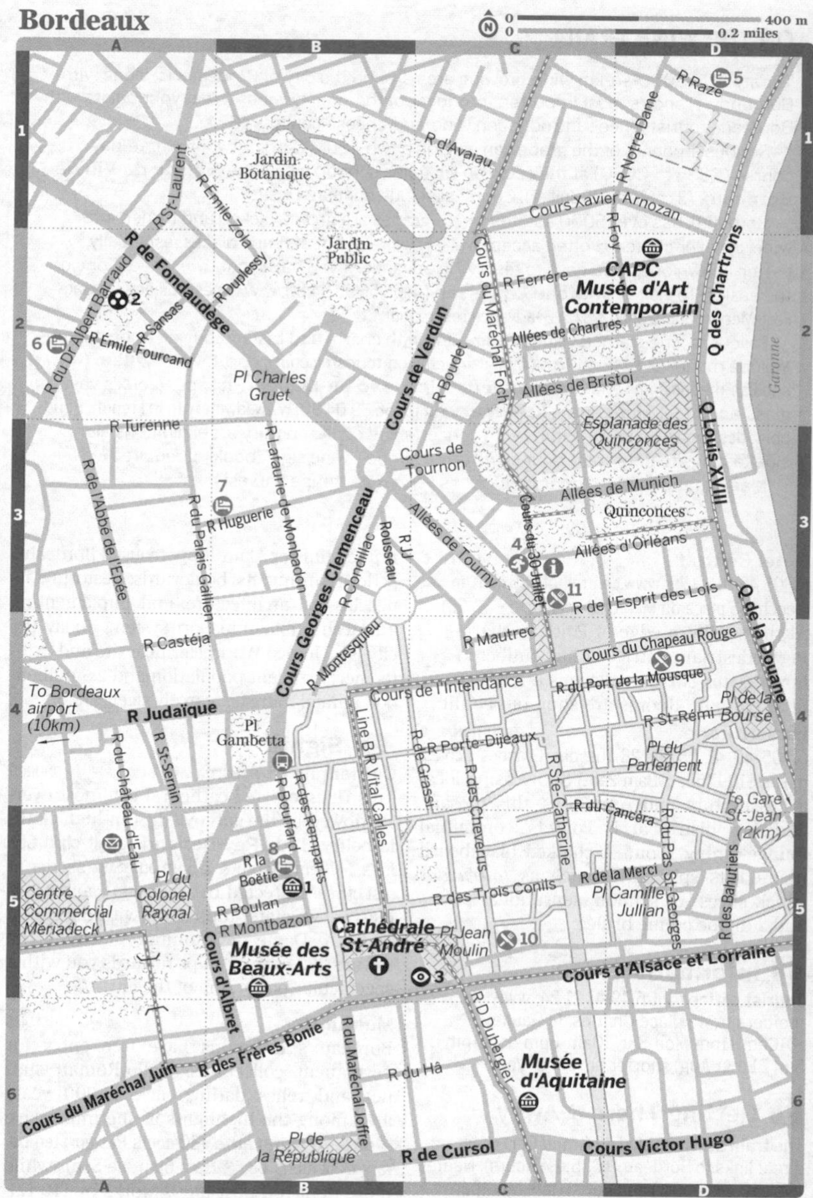

(20 cours d'Albret; ⏲11am-6pm Wed-Mon), while *faïence* pottery, porcelain, gold, iron, glass-work and furniture are displayed at the **Musée des Arts Décoratifs** (39 rue Bouffard; ⏲museum 2-6pm Wed-Mon, temporary exhibits from 11am Mon-Fri).

Palais Gallien RUINS

(rue du Docteur Albert Barraud; adult/child €3/2.50; ⏲2-7pm Jun-Sep) The only remains of the Roman city of Burdigala are these crumbling ruins of what was once its 3rd-century amphitheatre.

Bordeaux

Jardin Public GARDEN
(cours de Verdun) Home to a lovely botanical garden since 1855, the Jardin Public was laid out in 1755 and reworked in the English style a century later.

Sleeping

TOP CHOICE **Ecolodge des Chartrons** B&B €€
(☎05 56 81 49 13; www.ecolodgedeschartrons.com; 23 rue Raze; s/d incl breakfast €98/110) Hidden on a side street off the quays in Bordeaux's Chartrons wine merchants district, this *chambre d'hôte* spearheads ecofriendly sleeping in the city: think solar-heated water, hemp-based soundproofing and recycled antique furniture.

La Maison Bord'eaux BOUTIQUE HOTEL €€
(☎05 56 44 00 45; www.lamaisonbord-eaux.com; 113 rue du Docteur Albert Barraud; s/d from €130/150;) You'd expect to find a sumptuous 18th-century chateau with conifer-flanked courtyard and stable house in the countryside, but this one is smack-bang in the city. Dine after dusk on request (from €30).

La Maison du Lierre BOUTIQUE HOTEL €€
(☎05 56 51 92 71; www.maisondulierre.com; 57 rue Huguerie; d €68-128;) A beautiful Bordelaise stone staircase (no lift) leads to sunlit rooms with polished floorboards, rose-printed fabrics and sparkling bathrooms at the delightful House of Ivy. The vine-draped garden is dreamy.

Auberge de Jeunesse HOSTEL €
(☎05 56 33 00 70; www.auberge-jeunesse-bordeaux.com; 22 cours Barbey; dm incl sheets & breakfast €22; reception 7.30am-1.30pm & 3.30-9.30pm;) Bordeaux's hostel is in an ultramodern building. From the train station, follow cours de la Marne for 300m and turn left opposite the park; the hostel is about 250m further.

Une Chambre en Ville BOUTIQUE HOTEL €€
(☎05 56 81 34 53; www.bandb-bx.com; 35 rue Bouffard; s/d €103/115) A Room in Town blends in well with the antique and art shops on the same street. Each of the five rooms is a work of art.

Eating

Place du Parlement, rue du Pas St-Georges, rue des Faussets and place de la Victoire are loaded with dining addresses, as is the old waterfront warehouse district around quai des Marques – great for a sunset meal or drink.

TOP CHOICE **Le Cheverus Café** BISTRO €
(☎05 56 48 29 73; 81-83 rue du Loup; menus from €10.50; Mon-Sat) Friendly, cosy and chaotically busy (be prepared to wait for a table at lunchtime) best describes this neighbourhood bistro, smack in the city centre. Lunch in particular is an all-out bargain.

TOP CHOICE **La Tupina** REGIONAL CUISINE €€
(☎05 56 91 56 37; 6 rue Porte de la Monnaie; mains €18-40) Filled with the smell of soup simmering in an old *tupina* ('kettle' in Basque) over an open fire, this white-tableclothed place is feted far and wide for its seasonal regional specialities: minicasserole of foie gras and eggs, milk-fed lamb or goose wings with potatoes and parsley. Lunch here weekdays for €16.

L'Entrecôte BRASSERIE €€
(☎05 56 81 76 10; 4 cours du 30 Juillet; menus €16.50) Opened in 1966, this unpretentious place doesn't take reservations, and it has just one menu option: succulent thin-sliced meat, heated by tealights, cooked in a special shallot sauce and accompanied by homemade *frites* (French fries).

La Boîte à Huîtres OYSTERS €
(☎05 56 81 64 97; 36 cours du Chapeau Rouge; mains €8) This rickety wood-panelled little place is the best spot in Bordeaux to slurp fresh Arcachon oysters, traditionally served with sausage.

DON'T MISS

OYSTERS ON SATURDAY

A classic Saturday-morning Bordeaux experience is slurping oysters and white wine from one of the seafood stands at the market, **Marché des Capucins** (six oysters & glass of wine €6; 7am-noon).

L'Estaquade GASTRONOMIC €€€
(05 57 54 02 50; quai de Queyries; mains €22-26) Set on stilts jutting out from the riverbank, this restaurant is known for its seafood and magical views of Bordeaux's lovely neoclassical architecture.

Information

Tourist office (05 56 00 66 00; www.bordeaux-tourisme.com; 12 cours du 30 Juillet; 9am-7.30pm Mon-Sat, 9.30am-6.30pm Sun Jul & Aug, shorter hr rest of yr) Runs a smaller but helpful branch by the train station.

Getting There & Away

Air

Bordeaux airport (www.bordeaux.aeroport.fr) is in Mérignac, 10km west of the city centre, with domestic and some international services. **Jet'Bus** (05 56 34 50 50) shuttle buses (€7, 45 minutes, every 45 minutes) links it with the train station, place Gambetta and main tourist office in town.

Bus

Citram Aquitaine (www.citram.fr, in French) Regional buses.

Eurolines (05 56 92 50 42; 32 rue Charles Domercq) International lines.

Train

From Bordeaux's Gare St-Jean, 3km from the centre:

PARIS' GARE MONTPARNASSE €69.80, three hours, at least 16 daily

NANTES €44.60, four hours

POITIERS €35.20, 1¾ hours

TOULOUSE €33, 2¼ hours

Biarritz

POP 27,500

Edge your way south along the coast towards Spain and you arrive in stylish Biarritz, just as ritzy as its name suggests. The resort took off in the mid-19th century (Napoleon III had a rather soft spot for the place) and it still shimmers with architectural treasures from the belle époque and art deco eras. Big waves – some of Europe's best – and a beachy lifestyle are a magnet for Europe's hip surfing set.

Sights & Activities

Beaches BEACHES
Biarritz' fashionable beaches, particularly **Grande Plage** and **Plage Miramar**, are end-to-end bodies on hot summer days. Rent a stripey 1920s style beach tent for €9.50 a day. North of Pointe St-Martin, the adrenaline-pumping surfing beaches of **Anglet** continue northwards for over 4km. Ride eastbound bus 9 from av Verdun (just near av Édouard VII).

Beyond long, exposed **Plage de la Côte des Basques**, some 500m south of Port Vieux, are **Plage de Marbella** and **Plage de la Milady**. Take westbound bus 9 from rue Gambetta where it crosses rue Broquedis.

Musée de la Mer MUSEUM
(www.museedelamer.com; Esplanade du Rocher de la Vierge; adult/child €8/5.50; 9.30am-midnight Jul-Aug, shorter hr rest of year) Biarritz' history as a fishing and whaling port is explored at the Musée de la Mer, alongside underwater life collected from the Bay of Biscay (Golfe de Gascogne).

Sleeping

Hôtel Mirano BOUTIQUE HOTEL €€
(05 59 23 11 63; www.hotelmirano.fr, in French; 11 av Pasteur; d €100-110) Squiggly purple, orange and black wallpaper and oversize orange-perspex light fittings are just a few of the groovy rad '70s touches at this boutique retro hotel, found a 10-minute stroll from the town centre.

Villa Le Goëland HISTORIC HOTEL €€€
(05 59 24 25 76; www.villagoeland.com; 12 plateau de l'Atalaye; r from €170;) This stunning family home with chateau-like spires is perched high on a plateau above Pointe Atalaye. Rooms have panoramic views of town, the sea and across to Spain.

Hôtel Edouard VII HISTORIC HOTEL €€
(05 59 22 39 80; www.hotel-edouardvii.com; 21 av Carnot; d from €118;) From the ornate dining room full of tick-tocking clocks to the pots of lavender designed to match the wallpaper, this beautiful and intimate hotel screams 1920s Biarritz chic.

Hôtel Les Alizès BOUTIQUE HOTEL €
(☎05 59 24 11 74; www.alizes-biarritz.com; 13 rue du Port Vieux; s/d €62/90; 📶) With its brash and blushing shades clashing brilliantly with old-fashioned desks and wardrobes, this funky family-run hotel is one of the town's most memorable cheapies. Its beach-facing location is spot on.

Auberge de Jeunesse de Biarritz HOSTEL €
(☎05 59 41 76 00; www.hibiarritz.org; 8 rue Chiquito de Cambo; dm incl sheets & breakfast €19.50; ⏰reception 8.30-11.30am & 6-9pm, to noon & 10pm May-Sep, closed mid-Dec–early Jan; @📶) This popular place offers outdoor activities including surfing. Rooms for two to four hostellers have an en suite bathroom. To get here from the train station, follow the railway westwards for 800m.

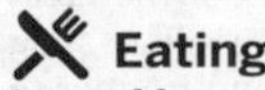

Eating

See-and-be-seen cafes and restaurants line Biarritz' beachfront. Anglet is also becoming increasingly trendy, with cafes strung along the waterfront.

TOP CHOICE **Casa Juan Pedro** SEAFOOD €
(☎05 59 24 00 86; Port des Pêcheurs; mains €5-15) Situated down by the old port – something of a hidden village of wooden fishing cottages – this cute shack restaurant cooks up tuna, sardines and squid with bags of friendly banter. There are several similar neighbouring places.

Le Crabe-Tambour SEAFOOD €€
(☎05 59 23 24 53; 49 rue d'Espagne; menus €13-18) Named after the famous 1977 film (the owner was the cook for the film set), this local address serves great seafood at a price that is hard to fault.

Bistrot des Halles BASQUE €€
(☎05 59 24 21 22; 1 rue du Centre; mains €14.50-17) One of several decent restaurants set along the rue du Centre that get their fruit and veg fresh from the nearby covered produce market, this bustling place serves up excellent fish as well as other fresh fare, in an interior adorned with old metallic advertising posters.

WORTH A TRIP

LOURDES

In the heart of the Pyrenees, **Lourdes** (www.lourdes-infotourisme.com), population 15,700, has been one of the world's most important pilgrimage sites since 1858, when 14-year-old Bernadette Soubirous (1844–79) saw the Virgin Mary in a series of 18 visions that came to her in a grotto. The town now feels dangerously close to a religious theme park, with a roll-call of over six million miracle-seeking visitors and endless souvenir shops selling statues and Virgin Mary–shaped plastic bottles (just add holy water at the shrine). But the commercialism doesn't extend to the *sanctuaires* (sanctuaries) themselves, mercifully souvenir-free.

Grotte de Massabielle (Massabielle Cave) is the most revered site in the area. The Esplanade des Processions, which is lined with enormous flickering candles left by previous pilgrims, leads along a river to the grotto's entrance, where people queue up to enter the cave or to dip in one of the 19 holy **baths** (⏰generally 9-11am & 2.30-4pm Mon-Sat, 2-4pm Sun & holy days). It's not for wallflowers: once you're behind the curtain, you're expected to strip off before being swaddled in a sheet and plunged backwards into the icy water.

The main 19th-century section of the sanctuaries is divided between the neo-Byzantine **Basilique du Rosaire**, the **crypt** and spire-topped **Basilique Supérieure** (Upper Basilica). From Palm Sunday to mid-October, nightly torchlight processions start from the Massabielle Grotto at 9pm, while at 5pm there's the **Procession Eucharistique** (Blessed Sacrament Procession) along Esplanade des Processions.

When the crowds of pilgrims get too much for you, seek refuge on the rocky 94m-high pinnacle of **Pic du Jer** – the panorama of Lourdes and the Pyrenees is inspiring. Walk three hours along a marked trail or ride six minutes in the century-old **funicular** (www.picdujer.info; blvd d'Espagne; adult/child €9.50/8; ⏰9.30am-6 or 7pm Mar-Nov). The summit is a superb picnic spot.

Lourdes is well connected by train; destinations include Bayonne (€21, 1¾ hours, up to four daily), Toulouse (€25.10, 1¾ hours, six daily) and Paris' Gare Montparnasse (€89.30, 6½ hours, four daily).

EAT STREETS

The area around covered market **Les Halles** (rue des Halles, rue du Centre, rue du Vieux Port) is the Biarritz hot spot for character-infused tapas joints, bar loaded with tasty treats.

Le Clos Basque BASQUE €€
(☎05 59 24 24 96; 12 rue Louis Barthou; menus €24; ⊙lunch Tue-Sun, dinner Tue-Sat) With its exposed stonework strung with abstract art, this tiny place could have strayed from Spain. Cuisine is traditional Basque with a contemporary twist. Reserve to snag a table on the terrace.

Drinking

Great bars stud rue du Port Vieux, place Clemenceau and the central food-market area.

Ventilo Caffé BAR €
(rue du Port Vieux; ⊙closed Tue out of season) Dressed up like a tart's boudoir, this fun and funky place continues its domination of the Biarritz bar scene.

Arena Café Bar BAR €
(Plage du Port Vieux; ⊙9am-2am Apr-Sep, 10am-2am Wed-Sun Oct-Mar) Tucked in a tiny cove, this beachfront hangout combines style-conscious restaurant (mains €15 to €22) with fuchsia- and violet-tinged bar and DJs.

Milk Bar BAR €
(17 blvd du Géneral de Gaulle; ⊙Tue-Sun) If you're on the hunt for a surfer, or are a surfer at heart, then this place just back from the beach is the place to get your wax out.

Information

Tourist office (☎05 59 22 37 00; www.biarritz.fr; Square d'Ixelles; ⊙9am-7pm Jul & Aug, 9am-6pm Mon-Sat, 10am-5pm Sun Sep-Jun)

Getting There & Away

Air

Biarritz-Anglet-Bayonne Airport (www.biarritz.aeroport.fr), 3km southeast of Biarritz, is served by easyJet, Ryanair and other low-cost carriers. STAB bus No 6 (line C on Sunday) links it once or twice hourly with Biarritz.

Bus

ATCRB buses (www.transdev-atcrb.com) runs services down the coast to the Spanish border.

Train

Biarritz-La Négresse train station, 3km south of town, is linked to the centre by buses 2 and 9 (B and C on Sundays).

LANGUEDOC-ROUSSILLON

Languedoc-Roussillon comes in three distinct flavours: Bas-Languedoc (Lower Languedoc), land of bullfighting, rugby and robust red wines, where the region's major sights are found; sunbaked Nîmes with its fine Roman amphitheatre; and fairy-tale Carcassonne, crowned with a ring of witch-hat turrets.

Inland, Haut Languedoc (Upper Languedoc) is a mountainous, sparsely populated terrain made for lovers of the great outdoors; while south sits Roussillon, snug against the rugged Pyrenees and frontier to Spanish Catalonia. Meanwhile Languedoc's traditional centre, Toulouse, was shaved off when regional boundaries were redrawn almost half a century ago, but we've chosen to include it in this section.

Carcassonne

POP 49,100

With its witch's-hat turrets and walled city, from afar Carcassonne looks like a fairy-tale fortress – but the medieval magic's more than a little tarnished by an annual influx of over four million visitors. It can be a tourist hell in high summer, so arrive out of season to see the town at its best (and quietest).

Pick up an audioguide (€3 for two hours) to **La Cité** (Old City) at the **tourist office** (☎04 68 10 24 30; www.carcassonne-tourisme.com; 28 rue de Verdun; ⊙9am-6 or 7pm Mon-Sat, 9am-noon or 1pm Sun) or its **annexe** (La Cité Porte Narbonnaise).

The old city is dramatically illuminated at night and enclosed by two **rampart walls** punctuated by 52 stone towers, Europe's largest city fortifications. Successive generations of Gauls, Romans, Visigoths, Moors, Franks and Cathars reinforced the walls, but only the lower sections are original; the rest, including the turrets, were stuck on by the 19th-century architect Viollet-le-Duc.

A drawbridge leads to the old gate of **Porte Narbonnaise** and rue Cros Mayrevieille en route to place Château and the 12th-century **Château Comtal** (adult/child €8.50/free; ⊙10am-6.30pm Apr-Sep). Admission includes a castle meander, a short film and an optional 30- to 40-minute guided tour of the ramparts (tours in English July and August). South is **Basilique St-Nazaire** (⏲9-11.45am & 1.45-5 or 5.30pm), illuminated by delicate medieval rose windows.

Carcassonne is on the main rail line to/from Toulouse (€14, 50 minutes).

Nîmes

POP 146,500

This buzzy city boasts some of France's best-preserved classical buildings, including a famous Roman amphitheatre, although the city is most famous for its sartorial export, *serge de Nîmes* – better known to cowboys, clubbers and couturiers as denim.

Sights

Les Arènes ROMAN AMPHITHEATRE
(adult/child €7.80/4.50; ⏲9am-6.30pm) Nîmes' magnificent Roman amphitheatre, the best preserved in the Roman Empire, was built around AD 100 to seat 24,000 spectators. It hosted animal fights to the death, stag hunts, man against lion or bear confrontations and, of course, gladiatorial combats. In the contemporary arena, it's only the bulls that get killed. There's a mock-up of the gladiators' quarters and, if you time it right, you'll see a couple of actors in full combat gear slugging it out in the arena.

Maison Carrée ROMAN TEMPLE
(place de la Maison Carrée; adult/child €4.50/3.70; ⏲10am-6.30pm) The Square House is a remarkably preserved rectangular Roman temple, constructed around AD 5 to honour Emperor Augustus' two adopted sons. Inside, a 22-minute 3D film staring heroes from the city's history is screened every half-hour.

Carré d'Art MUSEUM
(www.carreeartmusee.com, in French; place de la Maison Carrée; permanent collection free, temporary exhibitions adult/child €5/3.70; ⏲10am-6pm Tue-Sun) The striking glass-and-steel building facing the Maison Carrée was designed by British architect Sir Norman Foster. Inside is the **municipal library** and **Musée d'Art Contemporain**, with both permanent and temporary modern and contemporary art exhibitions from the 1960s on. End your visit with lunch (€16 to €28) on the Art Square's wonderful rooftop restaurant terrace, **Le Ciel de Nîmes**.

BILLET NÎMES ROMAINE

Buy a **combination ticket** (adult/child €9.90/7.60), valid for three days, covering all three of Nîmes major sights. Buy one at the first sight you visit.

Sleeping

Royal Hôtel HOTEL €€
(☎04 66 58 28 27; www.royalhotel-nimes.com, in French; 3 blvd Alphonse Daudet; r €60-80; ❄📶) You can't squeeze this 21-room hotel, popular with visiting artists and raffishly bohemian, into a standard mould. Rooms are furnished with flair and mainly overlook place d'Assas, a work of art in its own right.

Hôtel Amphithéâtre HOTEL €
(☎04 66 67 28 51; http://perso.wanadoo.fr/hotel-amphitheatre; 4 rue des Arènes; s €41-45, d €53-70) A pair of 18th-century mansions, the Amphitheatre Hotel just down the road from its namesake has 15 rooms, each named after a writer or painter. Montesquieu and Arrabal each have a balcony.

Auberge de Jeunesse HOSTEL €
(☎04 66 68 03 20; www.hinimes.com; 257 chemin de l'Auberge de Jeunesse, La Cigale; dm/d €13.50/34; ⏲Feb-Dec) This sterling, well-equipped hostel with self-catering facilities has houses for two to six in its extensive grounds, as well as regular dorms. Find it 3.5km northwest of the train station; take bus I, direction Alès or Villeverte, to the Stade stop.

DON'T MISS

FESTIVE NÎMES

Nîmes becomes more Spanish than French during its two *férias* (bullfighting festivals): the five-day **Féria de Pentecôte** (Whitsuntide Festival) in June, and the three-day **Féria des Vendanges** celebrating the grape harvest on the third weekend in September. Each is marked by daily *corridas* (bullfights). Buy tickets in situ or online at the **Billeterie des Arènes** (www.arenesdenimes.com; 2 rue de la Violette).

WORTH A TRIP

PONT DU GARD

A Unesco World Heritage site, this three-tiered Roman aqueduct is exceptionally well preserved. It's part of a 50km-long system of canals built about 19 BC by the Romans to bring water from near Uzès to Nîmes. The scale is huge: the 35 arches of the 275m-long upper tier, running 50m above the Gard River, contain a watercourse designed to carry 20,000 cubic metres of water per day and the largest construction blocks weigh over five tonnes.

Pick up an audioguide (€6) from the **visitors centre** (www.pontdugard.fr; ⏲9.30am-7pm May-Sep, to 5 or 6pm Oct-Apr) on the left, northern bank and allow around 1½hr to take in the vast, hugely informative and innovative museum **Musée de la Romanité** inside. Afterwards, walk the **Mémoires de Garrigue**, a 1.4km trail with explanatory panels through typical Mediterranean bush and scrubland.

A day ticket covering the above plus parking in one of the car parks on either side of the Gard River is €15 for up to five passengers (€10 November to March). In July and August pay an extra €2 to teeter along the aqueduct's top tier with a guide (every half-hour from 10am to 11.30am and 2pm to 5.30pm). Admission to the site is free once the museum has closed.

The best view of the Pont du Gard is from upstream, beside the river, where you can swim on hot days.

Eating

Nîmes' gastronomy owes as much to Provence as to Languedoc. Look out for *cassoulet* (pork, sausage and white bean stew, sometimes served with duck), aïoli and *rouille* (a spicy chilli mayonnaise).

Le Marché sur la Table FRENCH €€
(☎04 66 67 22 50; 10 rue Littré; mains €17-19; ⏲Wed-Sun) You *could* just pop in for a glass of wine at this first-class bistro, but you'd be missing out on Éric Vidal's market-fuelled food. Dining in the quiet rear courtyard is delightful.

Le 9 FRENCH €€
(☎04 66 21 80 77; 9 rue de l'Étoile; mains €15-18; ⏲Mon-Sat & lunch Sun May-Sep) Have a meal or drop in for a drink at this mildly eccentric place, tucked behind high green doors. Eat in vast, arched former stables or in the leafy, vine-clad courtyard.

Carré d'Art CLASSIC FRENCH €€
(☎04 66 67 52 40; www.restaurant-lecarredart.com, in French; 2 rue Gaston Boissier; menus €19-29; ⏲Mon-Sat) Enjoy exceptional cuisine in sublimely tasteful surroundings – gilded mirrors, moulded ceilings, fresh flowers, feather-light chandeliers and contemporary art work.

Au Plaisir des Halles FRENCH €€
(☎04 66 36 01 02; 4 rue Littré; mains €24-30; ⏲Tue-Sat) Near the covered market, ingredients here are locally sourced and the lunchtime three-course *menu* (€20) is excellent value. Local winegrowers feature both on the walls and in the wine racks.

Information

Tourist office (☎04 66 58 38 00; www.ot-nimes.fr; 6 rue Auguste; ⏲8.30am-6.30pm Mon-Fri, 9am-6.30pm Sat, 10am-5pm Sun)

Getting There & Away

Air

Ryanair is the only airline to use Nîmes' **airport** (☎04 66 70 49 49), 10km southeast of the city on the A54.

Bus

Bus station (☎04 66 38 59 43; rue Ste-Félicité)

PONT DU GARD €1.50, 30 minutes, two to seven daily

UZÈS €1.50, 45 minutes, four to 10 daily

Train

ALÈS €8.50, 40 minutes

ARLES €7.50, 30 minutes

AVIGNON €8.50, 30 minutes

MARSEILLE €19, 1¼ hours

PARIS' GARE DE LYON €52 to €99.70, three hours

Toulouse

POP 446,200

Elegantly set at the confluence of the Canal du Midi and the River Garonne, this vibrant southern city – nicknamed *la ville rose* (the pink city) after the distinctive hot-pink stone used in many buildings – is one of France's liveliest metropolises. Busy, buzzy and bustling with students, this riverside dame has a history stretching back over 2000 years and has been a hub for the aerospace industry since the 1930s. With a thriving cafe and cultural scene, a wealth of impressive *hotels particuliers* and an enormously atmospheric old quarter, France's fourth-largest city is one place you'll definitely want to linger.

Sights

Place du Capitole SQUARE

(place du Capitole) On the ceiling of the arcades on this bustling square's western side are 29 vivid **illustrations** of Toulouse history by contemporary artist Raymond Moretti. On the square's eastern side is the 128m-long facade of the **Capitole**, Toulouse's city hall built in the 1750s.

Basilique St-Sernin CHURCH

(place St-Sernin; ⊙8.30am-noon & 2-6pm Mon-Sat, 8.30am-12.30pm & 2-7.30pm Sun) The magnificent octagonal tower and spire of Toulouse's famous red-brick basilica pop up above the rooftops all over the city. This is France's largest and best-preserved example of Romanesque architecture: inside, the soaring nave and delicate pillars lead towards the ornate tomb of St-Sernin himself, sheltered beneath a sumptuous canopy.

Cité de l'Espace MUSEUM

(www.cite-espace.com/en; av Jean Gonord; adult/child €22/15.50; ⊙9.30am-7pm mid-Jul–Aug, 9.30am-5 or 6pm Sep-Dec & Feb-Jun, closed Jan) On the city's eastern outskirts, this museum explores the city's interstellar credentials with a wealth of hands-on exhibits, from space shuttle simulators and 3D-theatres to a full-scale replica of the Mir Space Station and a 53m-high Ariane 5 space rocket.

Musée des Augustins ART MUSEUM

(www.augustins.org; 21 rue de Metz; adult/child €3/free, temporary exhibitions €6/free; ⊙10am-6pm Thu-Tue, 10am-9pm Wed) Toulouse's fabulous fine-arts museum in an old Augustinian monastery with cloister gardens spans the centuries from the Romans to the early 20th century. View works by Delacroix, Ingres and Courbet, Toulouse-Lautrec and Monet.

Les Abattoirs ART MUSEUM

(www.lesabattoirs.org; 76 allées Charles de Fitte; admission €3-10; ⊙11am-7pm weekends, 10-6pm Wed-Fri) This red-brick structure was the city's main abattoir, since reinvented as cutting-edge art gallery and venue for concerts and exhibitions.

Sleeping

TOP CHOICE **Hôtel St-Sernin** BOUTIQUE HOTEL €€

(☎05 61 21 73 08; www.hotelstsernin.com; 2 rue St-Bernard; d €111-131;) A swish little number in the shade of Basilique St-Sernin, this hotel is beautifully finished with slate-grey walls, crisp white sheets and splashes of zesty colour. Book well ahead to snag a basilica view.

Le Clos des Potiers HOTEL €€

(☎05 61 47 15 15; www.le-clos-des-potiers.com; 12 rue des Potiers; d €100-125;) This little-known hideaway in a *hôtel particulier* near the cathedral is one of Toulouse's best-kept secrets. Rooms blend the bespoke feel of an upmarket B&B (antique rugs, characterful furniture, original mantelpieces) with the comfort and efficiency of a smart hotel (private garden, lovely lounge, treat tray).

Hôtel La Chartreuse HOTEL €

(☎05 61 62 93 39; www.chartreusehotel.com; 4bis blvd de Bonrepos; s/d/tr €41/47/57) This super, family-run establishment by the station is a really welcome surprise: clean, friendly and surprisingly quiet, with a lovely little breakfast room and back garden patio. Sure, rooms are a tad fusty, but for this price, what do you expect?

Eating

Blvd de Strasbourg, place St-Georges and place du Capitole are perfect spots for summer dining alfresco. Rue Pargaminières

DON'T MISS

ALL AFLOAT

Toulouse is a river city, and you couldn't possibly leave without venturing out onto the water. March to November, several operators run scenic hour-long boat trips (adult/child €8/5) along the Garonne from quai de la Daurade; in summer trips also pass through the St-Pierre lock onto the Canal du Midi and Canal de Brienne.

Buy tickets on the boat, up to 10 minutes before departure, from **Les Bateaux Toulousains** (www.bateaux-toulousains.com), **Toulouses Croisières** (www.toulouse-croisieres.com) or **L'Occitania** (www.loccitania.fr).

is the street for kebabs, burgers and other late-night student grub.

TOP CHOICE **Chez Navarre** REGIONAL CUISINE €€
(05 62 26 43 06; 49 Grande Rue Nazareth; menus €13-20; Mon-Fri) Wanna dine with locals? Then come to this wonderful *table d'hôtes* where honest Gascon cuisine is dished up beneath a hefty beamed ceiling. Dining is around communal, candlelit tables and there's usually just one main meal choice plus soup and terrine.

Au Jardins des Thés CAFE €€
(16 pl St-Georges; menus €12.50-15.50) A perennially packed terrace on one of the city's smartest squares testifies to just how good the salads, *tartes salées* (savoury tarts) and other little lunchy treats are at these Tea Gardens.

Les Halles Victor Hugo BISTRO €
(place Victor Hugo; menus €10-20; lunch Tue-Sun) For a quintessentially French experience, join the punters at the string of tiny restaurants on the 1st floor of the Victor Hugo food market. Food is simple, unfussy and full of character.

Faim des Haricots VEGETARIAN €
(www.lafaimdesharicots.fr; 3 rue du Puits Vert; Mon-Sat;) Everything's served *á volonte* (all you can eat) at this 100% veggie/wholefood restaurant, where €15.50 buys you a savoury tart, salad, hot dishes, dessert and a *pichet* (pitcher) of wine.

Drinking & Entertainment

Almost every square in the Vieux Quartier has at least one cafe, busy day and night. Other hot after-dark streets include rue Castellane, rue Gabriel Péri and near the river around place St-Pierre.

Toulouse has a cracking live music and clubbing scene. Check what's on at www.toulouse.sortir.eu.

Au Père Louis HISTORIC BAR
(45 rue des Tourneurs; 8.30am-3pm & 5-10.30pm Mon-Sat) Top of our list for irresistible old-fashioned charm, 'Father Louis' is Toulouse's oldest bar (franked 1889).

Bodega Bodega TAPAS BAR
(1 rue Gabriel Péri; tapas €4.50-10; 7pm-2am Mon-Fri, 7pm-6am Sat, 8pm-2am Sun) Revel in all the fun of the *féria* in a historic building where the tax authority once was. Weekends means live music and the tapas is tip-top.

La Maison BAR
(9 rue Gabriel Péri; 5pm-2am Sun-Fri, 5pm-5am Sat) The House is a hip, shabby-chic hangout for students and trendies, with plenty of vintage fireplace, scruffy sofas and secondhand chairs dotted around the living room.

Opus Café CLUB
(24 rue Bachelier; admission free; midnight-5am Mon-Wed, 11pm-6am Thu-Sat) Dance until dawn at this much-loved venue for seasoned clubbers.

Le Bikini MUSIC CLUB
(www.lebikini.com; rue Hermès, Ramonville St-Agne) The stuff of Toulousien legend for 25 years or so; at the end of metro line B (Ramonville metro stop).

Le Cri de la Mouette CLUB, BAR
(www.lecridelamouette.com; 78 allée de Barcelone) The Cry of the Seagull is a cool clubbar and gig venue aboard a canalboat.

Information

Tourist office (05 61 11 02 22; www.toulouse-tourisme.com; square Charles de Gaulle; 9am-7pm Mon-Sat, 10.30am-5.15pm Sun Jun-Sep, shorter hr rest of year)

Getting There & Away

Air

Toulouse-Blagnac Airport (www.toulouse.aeroport.fr/en), 8km northwest of the centre, has frequent flights to Paris and other large French and European cities. easyJet, bmibaby, Ryanair, KLM, Flybe and germanwings fly here. A **shuttle bus** (www.tisseo.fr) (€5, 20 minutes, every 20 minutes) links it with town.

Train

Gare Matabiau (blvd Pierre Sémard), 1km northeast of the centre, is served by frequent fast TGVs west to Bordeaux (€36.90, two hours), with connections to Bayonne, Paris and the southwest), and east to Carcassonne (€12, one hour) and beyond.

PROVENCE

Provence conjures up images of rolling lavender fields, blue skies, gorgeous villages, wonderful food and superb wine. It certainly delivers on all those fronts, but it's not just worth visiting for its good looks – dig a little deeper and you'll also discover the multicultural metropolis of Marseille, the artistic haven of Aix-en-Provence and the old Roman city of Arles.

Marseille

POP 860,350

There was a time when Marseille was the butt of French jokes. No more. The *cité phocéenne* has made an unprecedented comeback, undergoing a vast makeover. Marseillais will tell you that the city's rough-and-tumble edginess is part of its charm and that, for all its flaws, it is a very endearing place. They're right: Marseille grows on you with its unique history, souklike markets, millennia-old port and spectacular *corniches* (coastal roads) – all good reasons indeed why Marseille was chosen as European Capital of Culture in 2013.

Sights

Vieux Port OLD PORT

Ships have docked for more than 26 centuries at Marseille's colourful Vieux Port. Although the main commercial docks were transferred to the Joliette area on the coast north of here in the 1840s, it still overflows with fishing craft, yachts and local ferries.

Guarding the harbour are **Fort St-Nicolas** on the southern side and, across the water, **Fort St-Jean**, founded in the 13th century by the Knights Hospitaller of St John of Jerusalem. Wedged between restaurants on the cafe-lined quays is **La Maison du Pastis** (108 quai du Port), a distillery where you can sample 90 varieties of the local aniseed-flavoured firewater, pastis.

Standing guard between the old and the 'new' port, is the striking Byzantine-style **Cathédrale de la Major**, at the heart of the current dynamic dockland redevelopment around **La Joliette**. The cathedral's distinct striped facade is built from local white Cassis stone and green marble from Florence in Italy.

Basilique Notre Dame de la Garde CHURCH

(montée de la Bonne Mère; 7am-7pm, longer hr summer) Be blown away by the celestial views and knockout 19th-century architecture at the hilltop Basilique Notre Dame de la Garde, the resplendent Romano-Byzantine basilica 1km south of the Vieux Port that dominates Marseille's skyline. The domed basilica was built between 1853 and 1864 and is ornamented with coloured marble, murals and mosaics restored in 2006. Take bus 60 from the Vieux Port or walk up (30 minutes).

Château d'If ISLAND CASTLE

(www.if.monuments-nationaux.fr; adult/child €5/free; 9.30am-6.30pm, shorter hr & closed Mon winter) Immortalised in Alexandre Dumas' 1840s novel *Le Comte de Monte Cristo* (The Count of Monte Cristo), the 16th-century island prison of Château d'If sits 3.5km west of the Vieux Port. Political prisoners of all persuasions were incarcerated here, along with Protestants, the Revolutionary hero Mirabeau and the Communards of 1871.

Frioul If Express (www.frioul-if-express.com; 1 quai des Belges, 1er) boats (€10, 20 minutes) sail from the corner of quai de la Fraternité and quai de Rive Neuve at the Vieux Port.

TOP CHOICE **Le Panier** HISTORIC QUARTER

North of the Vieux Port, Marseille's old Le Panier quarter translates as 'the basket', and was the site of the Greek *agora* (marketplace). Today, its winding, narrow streets are a jumble of old stone houses, candy-coloured wooden shutters and artisans' shops: **72% Pétanque** (10 rue du Petit Puits), known for its brilliantly scented soaps, chocolate or tomato-leaf included, is a real favourite. Be prepared to get lost and don't miss the stunning **Centre de la Vieille Charité** (2 rue de la Charité, 2e; M Joliette), built as a charity shelter for the town's poor and now home to a twinset of museums covering Mediterranean archaeology and African, Oceanic and American Indian Art. Later, hang out at a cafe on people-watching square **place de Lenche**.

Sleeping

TOP CHOICE **Casa Honoré** BOUTIQUE B&B €€€

(04 96 11 01 62; www.casahonore.com; 123 rue Sainte, 7e; d incl breakfast €150-200; M Vieux Port) Los Angeles meets Marseille at this four-room *maison d'hôte,* built around a central courtyard with lap pool shaded by banana trees. The style reflects the owner's love for contemporary interior design.

CENT SAVER

The **Marseille City Pass** (1-/2-day pass €22/29) gets you admission to Marseille's museums, a guided tour of town, unlimited public transport travel, a boat trip, entrance to Château d'If and a load of discounts. Buy it at the tourist office.

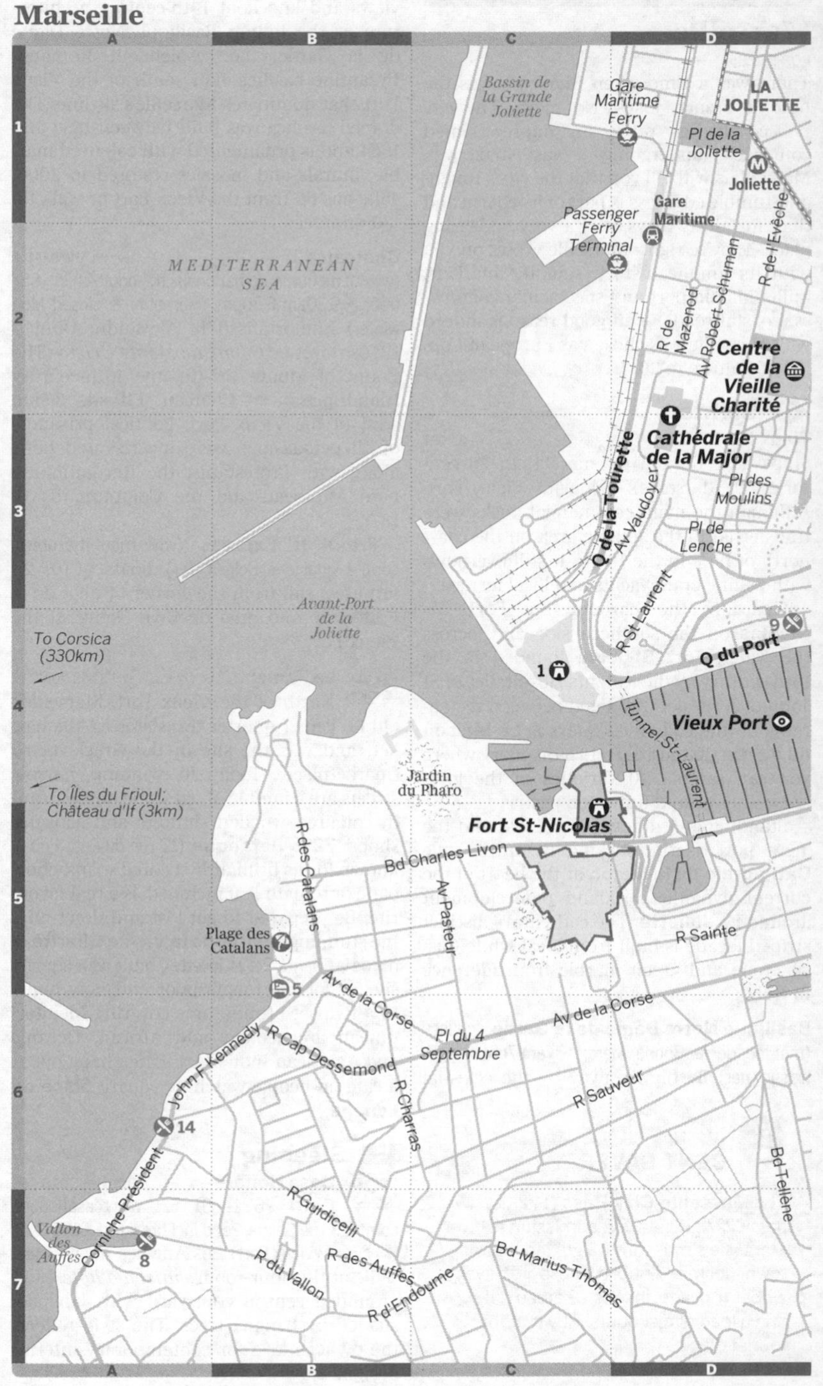
A
B
C
D
1
2
3
4
5
6
7
Bassin de la Grande Joliette
Gare Maritime Ferry
LA JOLIETTE
Pl de la Joliette
Joliette
Gare Maritime
Passenger Ferry Terminal
R de l'Evêche
Av Robert Schuman
R de Mazenod
MEDITERRANEAN SEA
Centre de la Vieille Charité
Cathédrale de la Major
Pl des Moulins
Q de la Tourette
Av Vaudoyer
Pl de Lenche
R St Laurent
Avant-Port de la Joliette
To Corsica (330km)
9
Q du Port
1
Tunnel St-Laurent
Vieux Port
Jardin du Pharo
To Îles du Frioul; Château d'If (3km)
Fort St-Nicolas
R des Catalans
Bd Charles Livon
Av Pasteur
R Sainte
Plage des Catalans
5
Av de la Corse
Av de la Corse
Pl du 4 Septembre
R Cap Dessemond
John F Kennedy
R Charras
R Sauveur
14
Corniche Président
Bd Tellène
R Guidicelli
Vallon des Auffes
8
R des Auffes
R du Vallon
R d'Endoume
Bd Marius Thomas

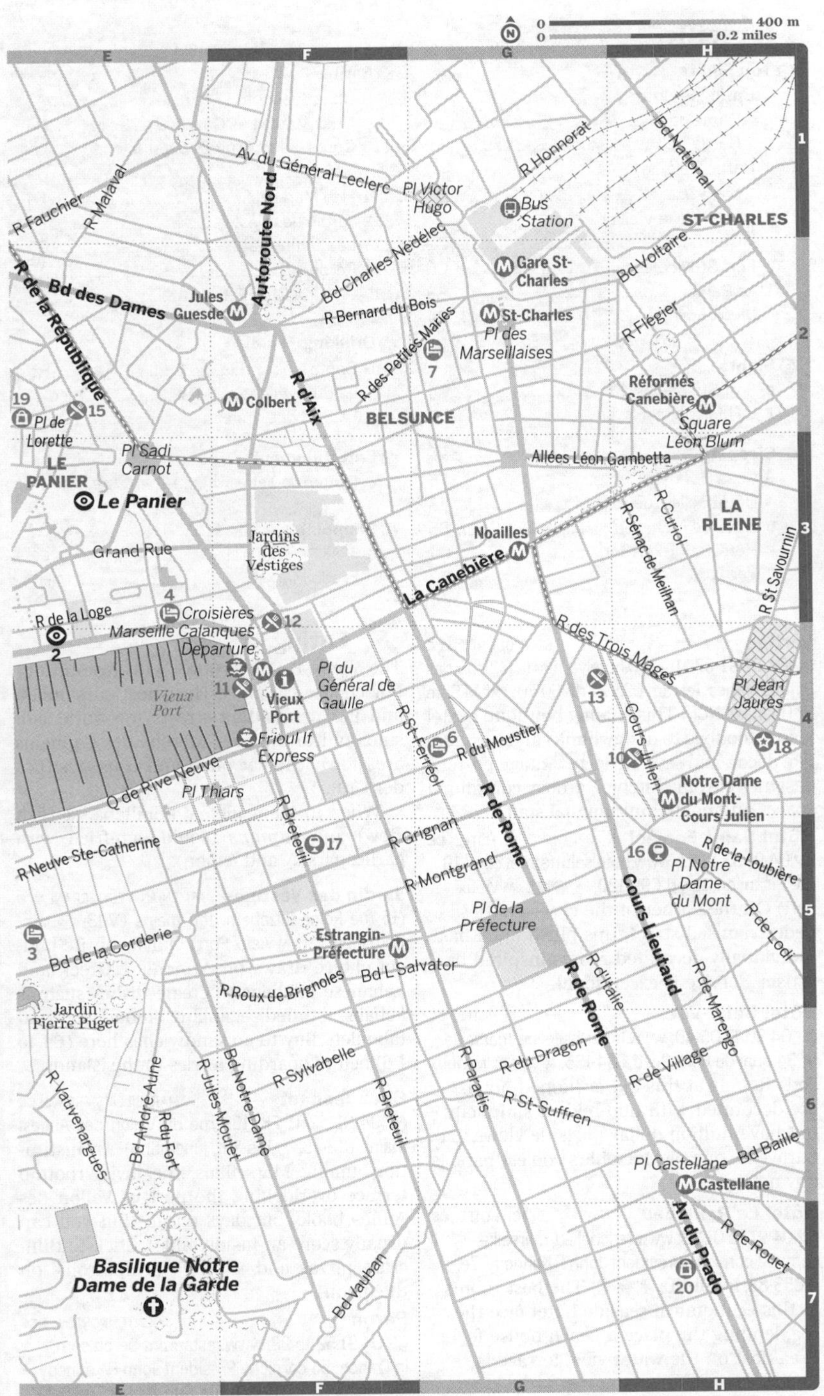
0 400 m
0 0.2 miles
ST-CHARLES
BELSUNCE
LE PANIER
LA PLEINE
Le Panier
Basilique Notre Dame de la Garde
Bus Station
Gare St-Charles
St-Charles
Jules Guesde
Colbert
Noailles
Réformés Canebière
Vieux Port
Estrangin-Préfecture
Notre Dame du Mont-Cours Julien
Castellane
Croisières Marseille Calanques Departure
Frioul If Express
Jardins des Vestiges
Jardin Pierre Puget
Av du Général Leclerc
Autoroute Nord
Bd des Dames
R de la République
R d'Aix
La Canebière
R de Rome
Cours Lieutaud
Av du Prado
Allées Léon Gambetta
Bd National
Bd Voltaire
Bd Charles Nédélec
R Bernard du Bois
R des Petites Maries
R Honnorat
R Flégier
R Curiol
R Sénac de Meilhan
R St Savournin
R des Trois Mages
Cours Julien
R de la Loubière
R de Lodi
R de Marengo
R de Village
Bd Baille
R de Rouet
R St-Ferréol
R du Moustier
R Grignan
R Montgrand
R Breteuil
R Paradis
R d'Italie
R du Dragon
R St-Suffren
R Sylvabelle
Bd Notre Dame
R Jules Moulet
R du Fort
Bd André Aune
R Vauvenargues
Bd Vauban
R Roux de Brignoles
Bd L Salvator
Bd de la Corderie
R Neuve Ste-Catherine
Q de Rive Neuve
Pl Thiars
Pl du Général de Gaulle
Pl de la Préfecture
Pl Notre Dame du Mont
Pl Jean Jaurès
Pl Castellane
Square Léon Blum
Pl des Marseillaises
Pl Victor Hugo
Pl Sadi Carnot
Pl de Lorette
Grand Rue
R de la Loge
R Fauchier
R Malaval
Vieux Port
FRANCE MARSEILLE

Marseille

Top Sights

	Basilique Notre Dame de la Garde	E7
	Cathédrale de la Major	D3
	Centre de la Vieille Charité	D2
	Fort St-Nicolas	C5
	Le Panier	E3
	Vieux Port	D4
	Sights	
1	Fort St-Jean	C4
2	La Maison du Pastis	E4
	Sleeping	
3	Casa Honoré	E5
4	Hôtel Belle-Vue	E3
5	Hôtel Le Richelieu	B5
6	Hôtel Saint-Ferréol	G4
7	Vertigo	G2
	Eating	
8	Chez Jeannot	A7
9	Chez Madie Les Galinettes	D4
10	Cours Julien Fruit & Vegetable Market	H4
11	Fish Market	F4
12	Jardin des Vestiges	F3
13	La Cantinetta	G4
14	Péron	A6
15	Pizzaria Chez Étienne	E2
	Drinking	
16	Dame Noir	H5
	La Caravelle	(see 4)
17	La Part des Anges	F5
	Entertainment	
18	L'Intermédiaire	H4
	Shopping	
19	72% Pétanque	E2
20	Prado Market	H7

Vertigo BOUTIQUE HOSTEL €
(☎04 91 91 07 11; www.hotelvertigo.fr; 42 rue des Petites Maries, 1er; dm €25-27, d €60-70; @; MGare St-Charles SNCF) This snappy boutique hostel kisses goodbye to dodgy bunks and hospital-like decor, and says 'hello' to vintage posters, designer chrome kitchen, groovy communal spaces and polite multilingual staff.

Hôtel Saint-Ferréol HOTEL €€
(☎04 91 33 12 21; www.hotelsaintferreol.com; 19 rue Pisançon, 1er; d €99-120; ❄@📶; MVieux Port) On the corner of the city's prettiest pedestrianised street, this plush hotel has individually decorated rooms inspired by artists. Service is exceptional.

Hôtel Belle-Vue HOTEL €€
(☎04 96 17 05 40; www.hotel-bellevue-marseille.fr; 34 quai du Port, 2e; d €84-135; ❄@📶; MVieux Port) Rooms at this old-fashioned hotel are decorated with mid-budget simplicity, but have million-dollar portside views. La Caravelle, one of Marseille's coolest bars, is downstairs.

Hôtel Le Richelieu BEACH HOTEL €€
(☎04 91 31 01 92; www.lerichelieu-marseille.com; 52 corniche Président John F Kennedy, 7e; d €53-88, tr €91-110; ❄@📶) The best rooms at this economical seaside hotel face the sea, lending the place a beach-house feel. Breakfast on the water-view terrace is idyllic.

Eating

The Vieux Port overflows with restaurants, but choose carefully. Head to Cours Julien and its surrounding streets for world cuisine; and to the near Marché des Capucins area for cheap-eat pizza and couscous (under €10).

When in Marseille eat bouillabaisse (fish stew) and *supions* (squid pan-fried with garlic, parsley and lemon).

Jardin des Vestiges ARMENIAN-MEDITERRANEAN €
(15 rue Reine Elizabeth, 1er; mains €7-13; ⏲9am-6pm Mon-Sat; MVieux Port) Our favourite budget choice draws on Armenian, Greek and Lebanese kitchens to create dishes such as kebabs, stuffed eggplant, moussaka and tabouleh. Buy to-go sandwiches here (€4 to €6) before boarding ferries to the islands.

Chez Jeannot MARSEILLAIS, FRENCH €€
(☎04 91 52 11 28; 129 rue du Vallon des Auffes; mains €12-25; ⏲Tue-Sat, lunch Sun) An institution among Marseillais, the jovial rooftop terrace overlooking the port of Vallon des Auffes books out days ahead (but you can usually score an inside table). Stick to thin-crust pizzas and *supions* ('chippirons' on the menu).

Péron CONTEMPORARY €€€
(☎04 91 52 15 22; www.restaurant-peron.com, in French; 56 corniche Président John F Kennedy, 7e; mains €35; ⏲lunch Tue-Sun, dinner Tue-Sat)

Perched on the sea's edge with magnificent views of Château d'If, Péron is one of Marseille's top seafood tables. Arrive before dark to watch the sunset.

La Cantinetta ITALIAN €€
(☎04 91 48 10 48; 24 cours Julien; mains €9-19; ⏲Tue-Sat; Ⓜ Notre Dame du Mont-Cours Julien) Our top choice on cours Julien serves perfectly al dente housemade pasta and other Italian goodies. Tables inside are cheek-by-jowl; we prefer the sun-dappled, tiled patio garden.

Chez Madie Les Galinettes PROVENÇAL €€
(☎04 91 90 40 87; 138 quai du Port, 2e; menus €25-35; ⏲Mon-Sat, closed Sat lunch summer; Ⓜ Vieux Port) This portside terrace is always packed, as is its arty interior when the weather isn't cooperating. Bouillabaisse needs to be ordered 48 hours ahead.

Pizzaria Chez Étienne MARSEILLAIS, ITALIAN €€
(43 rue de Lorette, 2e; mains €12-15; ⏲Mon-Sat; Ⓜ Colbert) This family-style neighbourhood haunt serves Marseille's best wood-fired pizza, beef steak and *supions* (pan-fried squid). Pop in beforehand to reserve in person (no phone). No credit cards.

Drinking & Entertainment

Options for a coffee or something stronger abound on both quays at the Vieux Port.

Cafes crowd cours Honoré d'Estienne d'Orves (1e), a large open square two blocks south of quai de Rive Neuve. Another cluster overlooks place de la Préfecture, at the southern end of rue St-Ferréol (1er).

DON'T MISS

MARSEILLE MARKETS

The small but enthralling **fish market** (quai des Belges; ⏲8am-1pm; Ⓜ Vieux Port) is a daily fixture at the Vieux Port. **Cours Julien** hosts a Wednesday-morning organic fruit and vegetable market and **Prado Market** (av du Prado; ⏲8am-1pm; Ⓜ Castellane or Périer) is the place to go for anything and everything other than food.

La Caravelle BAR
(34 quai du Port, 2e; ⏲7am-2am; Ⓜ Vieux Port) Look up or miss this upstairs hideaway with miniature portside terrace. Live jazz Friday from 9pm.

TOP CHOICE **La Part des Anges** WINE BAR
(33 rue Sainte; mains €15, ⏲lunch Mon-Sat, dinner daily) The wine list at this happening wine bar and restaurant is an oenologist's dream.

Dame Noir BAR
(30 place Notre Dame de Mont, 6e; ⏲5pm-2am Tue-Sat; Ⓜ Notre Dame du Mont-Cours Julien) Hip cats spill onto the sidewalk from this neighbourhood bar. DJs spin Thursday to Saturday. No sign; look for the red lights by the door.

L'Intermédiaire DIVE CLUB
(63 place Jean Jaurès, 6e; ⏲7pm-2am; Ⓜ Notre Dame du Mont-Cours Julien) Grungy venue

WORTH A TRIP

LES CALANQUES

Marseille abuts the wild and spectacular Les Calanques, a protected 20km stretch of high, rocky promontories rising from the bright turquoise sea. Sheer cliffs are occasionally interrupted by idyllic beach-fringed coves, many only possible to reach with kayak. They've been protected since 1975 and are slated to become a national park by 2011.

Calanque de Sormiou is the largest rocky inlet, with two seasonal restaurants cooking up fabulous views: **Le Château** (☎04 91 25 08 69; mains €18-24; ⏲Apr–mid-Oct) – the better food – and **Le Lunch** (☎04 91 25 05 39, 04 91 25 05 37; http://wp.resto.fr/lelunch; mains €16-28; ⏲Apr–mid-Oct) – nearer the water; both require advance reservation. By bus, take No 23 from the Rond Point du Prado metro stop to La Cayolle, from where it's a 3km walk (note diners with a table reservation can drive through; otherwise, the road is open to cars weekdays only September to June).

Marseille's tourist office leads guided hikes in Les Calanques and has information on walking trails (shut July and August due to forest-fire risk). For great views from out at sea hop aboard a boat trip to the wine-producing port of **Cassis** (www.ot-cassis.com), 30km east along the coast, with **Croisières Marseille Calanques** (www.croisieres-marseille-calanques.com, in French; 74 quai du Port, 2e).

WANT MORE?

Head to **Lonely Planet** (www.lonelyplanet.com/france/provence/marseille) for planning advice, author recommendations, traveller reviews and insider tips.

with graffitied walls is one of the best for live bands or DJs (usually techno or alterna).

Information

Dangers & Annoyances

Marseille isn't a hotbed of violent crime, but petty crimes and muggings are common. Avoid the Belsunce area (southwest of the train station, bounded by La Canebière, cours Belsunce and rue d'Aix, rue Bernard du Bois and blvd d'Athènes) at night. Walking La Canebiére is annoying, but generally not dangerous; expect to encounter kids peddling hash.

Tourist information

Tourist office (☎04 91 13 89 00; www.marseille-tourisme.com; 4 La Canebière, 1er; ⌚9am-7pm Mon-Sat, 10am-5pm Sun; Ⓜ Vieux Port)

Getting There & Away

Air

Aéroport Marseille-Provence (www.marseille.aeroport.fr), 25km northwest in Marignane, has numerous budget flights to various European destinations. **Shuttle buses** (Marseille ☎04 91 50 59 34; airport ☎04 42 14 31 27; www.lepilote.com) link it with Marseille train station (€8.50; 25 minutes, every 20 minutes from 5am to 11.30pm).

Boat

Gare Maritime (passenger ferry terminal; www.marseille-port.fr; Ⓜ Joliette)

SNCM (www.sncm.fr; 61 blvd des Dames, 2e; Ⓜ Joliette) Ferries to/from Corsica, Sardinia, Algeria and Tunisia.

Algérie Ferries (☎04 91 90 89 28; 58 blvd des Dames, 2e; Ⓜ Colbert) Ferries to/from Algeria.

Bus

The **bus station** (3 rue Honnorat, 3e; Ⓜ Gare St-Charles) is behind the train station.

AIX-EN-PROVENCE €4.90, 35 to 60 minutes, every five to 10 minutes

AVIGNON €18.50, two hours, one daily

CANNES €25, two hours, up to three daily

NICE €26.50, three hours, up to three daily

Train

From Marseille's **Gare St-Charles**, trains including TGVs go all over France and Europe.

AVIGNON €22.80, 35 minutes, 27 daily

LYON €47.30, 1¾ hours, 16 daily

NICE €29.70, 2½ hours, 21 daily

PARIS' GARE DE LYON €84.20, three hours, 21 daily

Getting Around

Pick up a bike from 100-plus stations across the city with **Le Vélo** (www.levelo-mpm.fr). A one-week 'subscription' costs €1; the first 30 minutes of each ride are free, then pay €1 per hour.

Marseille has two metro lines, two tram lines and an extensive bus network, all run by **RTM** (6 rue des Fabres, 1er; ⌚8.30am-6pm Mon-Fri, 9am-12.30pm & 2-5.30pm Sat; Ⓜ Vieux Port), where you can obtain information and transport tickets (€1.50). The metro runs from 5am to 10.30pm Monday to Thursday, and until 12.30am Friday to Sunday; the tram runs between 5am and 1am daily.

Aix-en-Provence

POP 146,700

Aix-en-Provence is to Provence what the Left Bank is to Paris: a pocket of bohemian chic crawling with students. It's hard to believe that 'Aix' (pronounced ex) is just 25km from chaotic, exotic Marseille. The city has been a cultural centre since the Middle Ages (two of the town's most famous sons are painter Paul Cézanne and novelist Émile Zola) but for all its polish, it's still a laid-back Provençal town at heart.

Sights

Circuit de Cézanne ARTIST TRAIL

Art, culture and architecture abound in Aix, especially thanks to local lad Paul Cézanne (1839–1906). To see where he ate, drank, studied and painted, you can follow the Circuit de Cézanne, marked by footpath-embedded bronze plaques inscribed with the letter C. A free English-language guide to the plaques, *Cézanne's Footsteps,* is available from the tourist office.

The trail takes in Cézanne's last studio, **Atelier Paul Cézanne** (www.atelier-cezanne.com; 9 av Paul Cézanne; adult/child €5.50/2; ⌚10am-noon & 2-6pm, closed Sun winter), 1.5km north of the tourist office. It's painstakingly preserved as it was at the time of his death, strewn with tools and still-life models; his admirers claim this is where Cézanne is most present.

The other two main Cézanne sights in Aix are the **Bastide du Jas de Bouffan**, the family home where Cézanne started painting, and the **Bibémus quarries**, where he did most of his Montagne Ste-Victoire paintings. Head to the tourist office for bookings (required) and information.

Cathédrale St-Sauveur CHURCH
(rue Laroque; 8am-noon & 2-6pm) A potpourri of styles, Aix cathedral was begun in the 12th century and successively enlarged over the next few hundred years: it's worth a visit for the memorable Gregorian chants, usually sung at 4.30pm Sunday.

Musée Granet MUSEUM
(www.museegranet-aixenprovence.fr, in French; place St-Jean de Malte; adult/child €4/free; 11am-7pm Tue-Sun) Housed in a 17th-century priory, this museum's pride and joy are its nine Cézanne paintings and works by Picasso, Léger, Matisse, Tal Coat and Giacometti.

Festivals & Events

Life seems to be one long festival in festive Aix; the tourist office has a festival list.

Festival International d'Art Lyrique d'Aix-en- Provence PERFORMING ARTS
(International Festival of Lyrical Art; www.festival-aix.com) The highlight of Aix's sumptuous cultural calendar. In July, this month-long festival brings classical music, opera and buskers.

Festival de le Roque d'Anthéron PIANO MUSIC
(www.festival-piano.com) Mid-July to mid-August, from Aix to the Luberon.

Sleeping

Book accommodation through the **Centrale de Réservation** (04 42 16 11 84; www.aixenprovencetourism.com).

TOP CHOICE **L'Épicerie** B&B €€
(06 08 85 38 68; www.unechambreenville.eu; 12 rue du Cancel; s incl breakfast €80-120, d €100-130;) This retro B&B is the fabulous creation of born-and-bred Aixois lad, Luc. His breakfast room recreates a 1950s grocery store, and the flowery garden out back is a dream for evening dining (book ahead). Breakfast is a veritable feast gargantuan enough to last all day.

Hôtel Cézanne BOUTIQUE HOTEL €€€
(04 42 91 11 11; http://cezanne.hotelaix.com; 40 av Victor Hugo; d €179-249;) Aix's hippest hotel is a study in clean lines, with sharp-edged built-in desks and loveseats that feel a touch Ikea. Best is breakfast (€19), which includes smoked salmon and Champagne.

Auberge de Jeunesse du Jas de Bouffan HOSTEL €
(04 42 20 15 99; www.auberge-jeunesse-aix.fr; 3 av Marcel Pagnol; dm incl breakfast & sheets €19-22; reception 7am-2.30pm & 4.30pm-midnight, closed mid-Dec–Jan) Shiny-new with a bar, tennis courts, bike shed and massive summer BBQs, this HI hostel is 2km west of the centre; shame about the motorway. Take bus 4 from La Rotonde to the Vasarely stop.

Hôtel les Quatre Dauphins SMALL HOTEL €€
(04 42 38 16 39; www.lesquatredauphins.fr; 54 rue Roux Alphéran; s €55-60, d €70-85;) Close to cours Mirabeau, this sweet 13-room hotel, a former private mansion, was redone in 2010 and looks fresh and clean, with new bathrooms and rainfall showerheads. The tall terracotta-tiled staircase (no elevator) leads to four attic rooms, with sloped beamed ceilings.

Hôtel Cardinal HOTEL €
(04 42 38 32 30; www.hotel-cardinal-aix.com; 24 rue Cardinale; s/d €60/70) Beneath stratospheric ceilings, Hôtel Cardinal's 29 romantic rooms are beautifully furnished with antiques, tasselled curtains, and newly tiled bathrooms.

Eating

Aix' sweetest treat is the marzipan-like local speciality, *calisson d'Aix,* a small, diamond-shaped, chewy delicacy made with ground almonds and fruit syrup. The daily **produce market** (place Richelme) sells olives, goat's cheese, garlic, lavender, honey, peaches, melons and other sun-kissed products.

Le Petit Verdot FRENCH €€
(04 42 27 30 12; www.lepetitverdot.fr; 7 rue Entrecasteaux; mains €15-25; dinner Mon-Sat, lunch Sat) Wine is the primary focus at this earthy restaurant, where tabletops are made of cast-off wine crates. The meat-heavy menu is designed to marry with the wines, not the other way round.

La Chimère Café SUPPER CLUB €€
(04 42 38 30 00; www.lachimerecafe.com; 15 rue Brueys; menus €28-32) Aix's party crowd laps up the cabaret feel of this former nightclub: starry-night vaulted ceiling in the underground room and grand chandeliers with crimson velvet on the main floor. Food is classic French.

WORTH A TRIP

A CULINARY DETOUR

Hilltop village **Ventabren** (population 5000), 16km west of Aix, provides the perfect lazy-day detour. Meander sun-dappled cobbled lanes; peep inside a 17th-century church; and get drunk on dizzying views of Provence from old chateau ruins before a superb lunch or dinner at **La Table de Ventabren** (☎04 42 28 79 33; www.latabledeventabren.com; 1 rue Cézanne; menus €41-50; ⊙lunch Wed-Sun, dinner Tue-Sun). Chef Dan Bessoudo, honoured with a coveted Michelin star, creates inventive wholly modern French dishes and knockout desserts – served in summer on a romantic terrace facing distant mountains and starry skies. Get here before the prices double; reservations essential.

Le Poivre d'Ane CONTEMPORARY €€
(☎04 42 21 32 66; www.restaurantlepoivredane.com; 40 place des Cardeurs; menus €28-45; ⊙dinner Thu-Tue) Fancy a haddock milkshake, duck sushi or thyme-and-cinnamon apple tart with Baileys whipped cream? Summer tables are smack dab on one of Aix's loveliest pedestrian squares; reservations essential.

Amphitryon PROVENÇAL €€
(☎04 42 26 54 10; www.restaurant-amphitryon.fr; 2-4 rue Paul Doumer; menus €25-40; ⊙Tue-Sat) Amphitryon enjoys a solid reputation, particularly in summer for its market-driven cooking and alfresco dining in the cloister-garden. Attached **Comptoir de l'Amphi** (mains €12-17) is less expensive.

Information

Tourist office (www.aixenprovencetourism.com; 2 place du Général de Gaulle; ⊙8.30am-7pm Mon-Sat, 10am-1pm & 2-6pm Sun, longer hr summer)

Getting There & Away

Bus

From Aix' **bus station** (av de l'Europe), a 10-minute walk southwest from La Rotonde, routes include Marseille (€4.90, 35 minutes via the autoroute or one hour via the D8), Arles (€9, 1½ hours) and Avignon (€14.70, 1¼ hours).

Half-hourly shuttle buses go to/from Aix TGV station and Aéroport Marseille-Provence.

Train

The only useful train from Aix' **city centre train station** (av Victor Hugo) is to/from Marseille (€7, 50 minutes). Other services use **Aix TGV station**, 15km away.

AVIGNON €6.60, 20 minutes

MARSEILLE €13, 55 minutes

NÎMES €7.50, 30 minutes

Avignon

POP 93,560

Hooped by 4.3km of superbly preserved stone ramparts, this graceful city is the belle of Provence's ball. Famed for its annual performing arts festival and fabled bridge, Avignon is an ideal spot from which to step out into the surrounding region. Wrapping around the city, Avignon's defensive ramparts were built between 1359 and 1370, and are punctuated by a series of sturdy *portes* (gates).

Sights

Palais des Papes PAPAL PALACE
(www.palais-des-papes.com; place du Palais; adult/child €6/3; ⊙9am-8pm Jul & early-mid-Sep, to 9pm Aug, to 7pm mid-Mar–Jun & mid-Sep–Oct, to 6.30pm early–mid-Mar, to 5.45pm Nov-Feb) This Unesco World Heritage site, the world's largest Gothic palace, was built when Pope Clement V abandoned Rome in 1309 and settled in Avignon. The immense scale of the palace, with its cavernous stone halls and vast courtyards, testifies to the wealth of the popes; the 3m-thick walls, portcullises and watchtowers emphasise their need for defence.

Pont St-Bénezet BRIDGE
(adult/child €4.50/3.50; ⊙9am-8pm, 9.30am-5.45pm Nov-Mar) This fabled bridge, immortalised in the French nursery rhyme *Sur le Pont d'Avignon,* was completed in 1185. The 900m-long wooden bridge was repaired and rebuilt several times before all but four of its 22 spans were washed away in the mid-1600s. If you don't feel like paying, you can see it for free from the Rocher des Doms park, Pont Édouard Daladier or from across the river on the Île de la Barthelasse's chemin des Berges.

Musée du Petit Palais MUSEUM
(www.petit-palais.org; place du Palais; adult/child €6/free; ⏲10am-1pm & 2-6pm Wed-Mon) The bishops' and archbishops' palace during the 14th and 15th centuries now houses an outstanding collection of lavish 13th- to 16th-century Italian religious paintings by artists including Botticelli, Carpaccio and Giovanni di Paolo.

Musée Angladon ART MUSEUM
(www.angladon.com; 5 rue Laboureur; adult/child €6/4; ⏲1-6pm Tue-Sun Apr-Nov, 1-6pm Wed-Sun Jan-Mar, closed Dec) This charming museum harbours Impressionist treasures, including the only Van Gogh painting in Provence *(Railway Wagons)*, and works by Cézanne, Manet, Degas and Picasso.

Festivals & Events

Hundreds of artists take to the stage and streets during the world-famous **Festival d'Avignon** (www.festival-avignon.com), held every year from early July to early August. Don't miss the more experimental (cheaper) fringe **Festival Off** (www.avignonleoff.com, in French) that runs alongside the main fest.

Sleeping

TOP CHOICE **Le Limas** B&B €€
(☎04 90 14 67 19; www.le-limas-avignon.com; 51 rue du Limas; d/tr incl breakfast from €120/200; ❄@) Behind its discreet lavender door, this chic address in an 18th-century town house is like something out of *Vogue Living*. It's everything interior designers strive for when mixing old and new. Breakfast by the fireplace or on a sun-drenched terrace!

Hôtel de l'Horloge HOTEL €€
(☎04 90 16 42 00; www.hotels-ocre-azur.com; place de l'Horloge; r €95-180; ❄🛜) Most rooms at this supercentral hotel are straightforward (comfortable, all mod cons), but the five terrace rooms have the edge with sophisticated furnishings and views: ask for 505 with its incredible view of the Palais des Papes.

YMCA-UCJG HOSTEL €€
(☎04 90 25 46 20; www.ymca-avignon.com; 7bis chemin de la Justice; dm €36, without bathroom €25; ⏲reception 8.30am-6pm, closed Dec–early Jan; 🛜🏊) This spotless hostel across the river, just outside Villeneuve-lès-Avignon, has some private rooms and a swimming pool and terrace with panoramic views of the city. Take bus 10 to the Monteau stop.

Hôtel Boquier HOTEL €
(☎04 90 82 34 43; www.hotel-boquier.com, in French; 6 rue du Portail Boquier; d €50-70; ❄🛜) The infectious enthusiasm of owners Sylvie and Pascal Sendra sweeps through this central little place, bright, airy and spacious.

Lumani B&B €€
(☎04 90 82 94 11; www.avignon-lumani.com; 37 rue du Rempart St-Lazare; d incl breakfast €100-170; ❄🛜) This fabulous *maison d'hôte* run by Elisabeth, whose art is hung throughout the stunning house, is a fount of inspiration for artists. Love the fountained garden.

Eating

Place de l'Horloge's touristy cafes have so-so food. Restaurants open seven days during summer-festival season, when reservations

WORTH A TRIP

VAN GOGH'S ARLES

If the winding streets and colourful houses of Arles seem familiar, it's hardly surprising – Vincent van Gogh lived here for much of his life in a yellow house on place Lamartine, and the town regularly featured in his canvases. His original house was destroyed during WWII, but you can still follow in Vincent's footsteps on the **Van Gogh Trail**, marked out by footpath plaques and a brochure handed out by the **tourist office** (main office ☎04 90 18 41 20; www.tourisme.ville-arles.fr; esplanade Charles de Gaulle; ⏲9am-6.45pm Apr-Sep, 9am-4.45pm Mon-Sat, 10am-12.45pm Sun Oct-Mar; train station ☎04 90 43 33 57; ⏲9am-1.30pm & 2.30-4.45pm Mon-Fri Apr-Sep).

Two millennia ago, Arles was a major Roman settlement. The town's 20,000-seat amphitheatre and 12,000-seat theatre, known as the **Arénes** and the **Théâtre Antique**, are nowadays used for cultural events and bullfights.

Telleschi (☎04 42 28 40 22) buses go to/from Aix-en-Provence (€9, 1½ hours) and there are regular trains to/from Nîmes (€7.50, 30 minutes), Marseille (€13.55, 55 minutes) and Avignon (€6.60, 20 minutes).

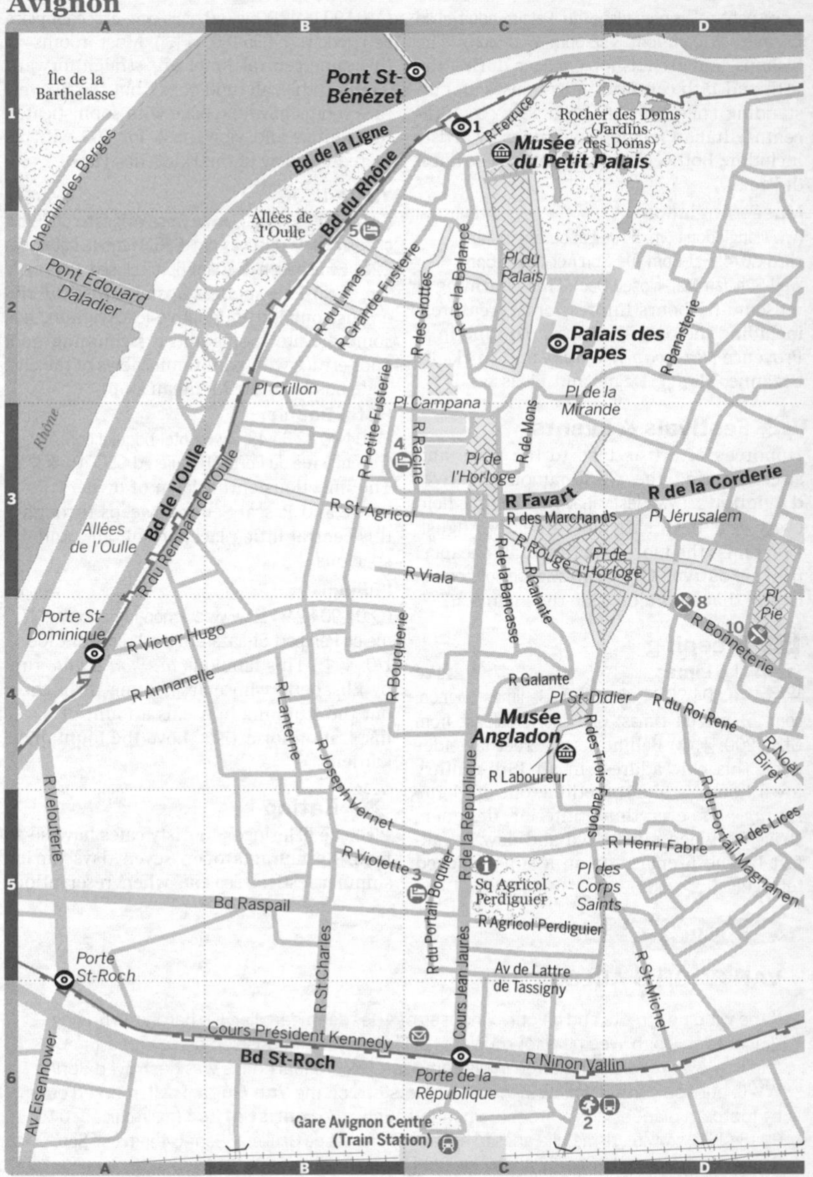

FRANCE PROVENCE

become essential. *Papaline d'Avignon* is a pink, chocolate ball filled with potent Mont Ventoux herbal liqueur.

Cuisine du Dimanche PROVENÇAL €€
(04 90 82 99 10; www.lacuisinedudimanche.com, in French; 31 rue Bonneterie; mains €15-25; closed Sun & Mon Oct-May) Spitfire chef Marie shops every morning at Les Halles to find the freshest ingredients for her earthy flavour-packed cooking. The market-driven menu changes daily, but specialities include scallops and a simple roast chicken with pan gravy.

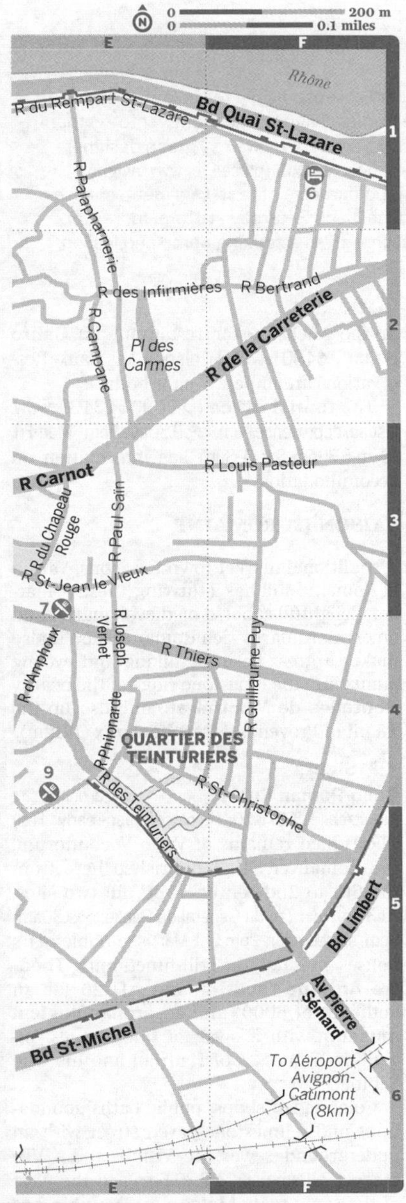

Avignon

Top Sights

Musée Angladon	C4
Musée du Petit Palais	C1
Palais des Papes	C2
Pont St-Bénézet	C1

Sights

1 Pont St-Bénézet Entrance	C1

Activities, Courses & Tours

2 Autocars Lieutaud	C6

Sleeping

3 Hôtel Boquier	C5
4 Hôtel de l'Horloge	B3
5 Le Limas	B2
6 Lumani	F1

Eating

7 Au Tout Petit	E3
8 Cuisine du Dimanche	D4
9 L'Epice and Love	E4
10 Les Halles	D4

Au Tout Petit CONTEMPORARY FRENCH €€
(☎04 90 82 38 86; 4 rue d'Amphoux; menus €11-24; ⊙Tue-Sat) This teensy place with just eight tables packs big flavours into every imaginative dish: simple, smart cooking, maximising the use of spice.

L'Epice and Love FRENCH €
(☎04 90 82 45 96, 30 rue des Lices; mains €11-12; ⊙dinner Mon-Sat) Stews, roasts and other homestyle French dishes is what makes this tiny bohemian restaurant, decorated with antique kitchen ware and mismatched chairs, so appealing. No credit cards.

Information

Tourist office (www.avignon-tourisme.com; 41 cours Jean Jaurès; ⊙9am-5pm Mon-Sat, 9.45am-5pm Sun)

Getting There & Away

Air

Aéroport Avignon-Caumont (www.avignon.aeroport.fr), 8km southeast, has seasonal flights to/from Britain and Ireland.

Bus

From the **bus station** (blvd St-Roch), down the ramp to the right as you exit the train station:

AIX-EN-PROVENCE €14, 1¼ hour
ARLES €7.70, 1½ hours
MARSEILLE €20, two hours
NÎMES €8.10, 1¼ hours

Train

Avignon has two stations: **Gare Avignon TGV**, 4km southwest in Courtine; and central **Gare**

DON'T MISS

LES HALLES

There is no better spot to shop for that perfect Provence picnic to scoff atop bluff-top park **Rocher des Doms** (tasty views of the Rhône, Avignon and Mont Ventoux) than at the market. Bursting with local life and a fabulous vegetal wall by green designer Patrick Blanc (of Musée du Quai Branly fame), **Les Halles** (place Pie; www.avignon-leshalles.com; ⏲7am-1pm Tue-Sun) is a gourmand paradise of fruit, veg, meat, cheese, herbs, olive oil and other local seasonal produce. Each Saturday at 11am, moreover, during **La Petite Cuisine des Halles**, a local chef gives a cooking demo and lesson; details online.

Avignon Centre (42 blvd St-Roch) with trains to/from:

ARLES €6.70, 20 minutes

NÎMES €8.70, 30 minutes

Some TGVs to/from Paris stop at Gare Avignon Centre, but TGVs for Marseille (€22.80, 35 minutes) and Nice (€54.40, three hours) only use Gare Avignon TGV.

In July and August there's a direct **Eurostar** (www.eurostar.com) service on Saturdays from London (from €135 return, six hours) to Gare Avignon Centre. See p464 for more details.

Around Avignon

LES BAUX DE PROVENCE

At the heart of the Alpilles, spectacularly perched above picture-perfect rolling hills of vineyards, olive groves and orchards, is the hilltop village of Les Baux de Provence. Van Gogh painted it and if you stroll around the deep dungeons, up crumbling towers and around the maze-like ruins of **Château des Baux** (www.chateau-baux-provence.com; adult/child €7.60/5.70; ⏲9am-6pm, to 8pm Jul & Aug) you'll see why.

For a real splurge lunch at legendary **L'Ousta de Baumanière** (☎04 90 54 33 07; www.oustaudebaumaniere.com; menus €95-150) or the Michelin-star restaurant **La Cabro d'Or** (☎04 90 54 33 21), also in Les Baux. Reservations are imperative for both.

The **tourist office** (☎04 90 54 34 39; www.lesbauxdeprovence.com; ⏲9.30am-5pm Mon-Fri, 10am-5.30pm Sat & Sun) has information on accommodation.

DON'T MISS

CARPENTRAS MARKET

Don't miss **Carpentras**, 25km northeast of Avignon, on a Friday morning when its streets and squares spill over with hundreds of market stalls laden with breads, honeys, cheeses, olives, fruit and a rainbow of *berlingots* (the local striped, pillow-shaped hard-boiled sweet). Late November to March, pungent black-truffle stalls murmur with hushed-tones transactions.

VAISON-LA-ROMAINE

POP 6392

A traditional market town for aeons, Vaison la Romaine still has a thriving Tuesday market, delightful cobbled medieval quarter and an extraordinarily rich Roman legacy. It also makes a great base for hiking and cycling jaunts into the limestone ridge of the nearby **Dentelles de Montmirail** and also up the 'Giant of Provence', **Mont Ventoux** (1912m).

Sights

Gallo-Roman Ruins ARCHAEOLOGICAL SITE
(adult/child €8/3.50; ⏲closed Jan–early Feb) The ruined remains of Vasio Vocontiorum, the Roman city that flourished here from the 6th to 2nd centuries BC, fill two sites. At **Puymin** (av du Général de Gaulle; ⏲9.30am-6pm, closed noon-2pm Oct-Mar) see noblemen's houses, mosaics, the still-functioning **Théâtre Antique** (built around AD 20 for an audience of 6000) and an **archaeological museum** with a swag of fine statues, including likenesses of Hadrian and his wife Sabina.

Colonnaded shops, public baths' foundations and a limestone-paved street with an underground sewer are visible at **La Villasse** (⏲10am-noon & 2.30-6pm), to the west of the same road. **Maison au Dauphin** has splendid marble-lined fish ponds.

Your ticket also includes entry to the peaceful 12th-century Romanesque cloister at **Cathédrale Notre-Dame de Nazareth** (cloister €1.50; ⏲10am-12.30pm & 2-6pm, closed Jan & Feb), found a five-minute walk west of La Villasse.

WORTH A TRIP

CHÂTEAUNEUF-DU-PAPE

Carpets of vineyards unfurl around this tiny medieval village, the summer residence of Avignon's popes who had a summer residence – all but one ruined wall today – built atop the hill here.

Most Châteauneuf-du-Pape wine is red, and strict regulations govern production. Reds come from 13 different grape varieties – grenache is the biggie – and are aged at least five years. Sample them over a free tasting *(dégustation gratuite)* at more than two dozen shops and cellars in the village, or at the **Musée du Vin** (www.brotte.com; rte d'Avignon; admission free; ⏲9am-1pm & 2-7pm). The **tourist office** (www.paysprovence.fr, in French; place du Portail; ⏲9.30am-6pm Mon-Sat Jun-Sep, closed Wed & Sun Oct-May) has a list of wine-producing estates that do cellar visits, tastings, tours and so on.

Perched beneath the ruined chateau, **Le Verger des Papes** (☎04 90 83 50 40; 4 rue du Château; menus €20-30; ⏲hours vary) has a leafy terrace with knockout vistas and the best traditional French cooking in town, with bread made in a wood-fired oven.

Cité Médiévale MEDIEVAL CITY

Across the pretty **Pont Romain** (Roman Bridge), cobblestone alleyways known as *calades* carve through the stone walls up to an imposing 12th-century **chateau** (guided tours in French, €2; ⏲check with tourist office) built by the counts of Toulouse, from where there are eagle-eye views.

Sleeping & Eating

Hôtel Le Burrhus DESIGN HOTEL €

(☎04 90 36 00 11; www.burrhus.com; 1 place de Montfort; d €55-87; 📶) Smack bang on Vaison's vibrant central square, this looks like a quaint old place from the outside, but is cutting-edge designer inside.

La Lyriste PROVENÇAL €€

(☎04 90 36 04 67; 45 cours Taulignan; menus €18-36; ⏲Wed-Sun) In summer book a table on the terrace at this tasty contemporary bistro, known for its seasonal dishes and local classics such as *bourride* (fish stew).

Getting There & Away

From the **bus station,** 400m east of the town centre on ave des Choralies, **Autocars Lieutaud/Trans Vaucluse** (www.cars-lieutaud.fr) runs buses to/from Avignon (€6, 1½ hours).

THE FRENCH RIVIERA & MONACO

With its glistening seas, idyllic beaches and lush hills, the French Riviera (Côte d'Azur in French) screams exclusivity, extravagance and excess. It has been a favourite getaway for the European jet set since Victorian times and there is nowhere more chichi or glam in France than St-Tropez, Cannes and super-rich, sovereign Monaco.

But it's not just a high-roller's playground. Every year millions of visitors descend on the southern French coast to bronze their bodies, smell the lavender and soak up that hip Mediterranean vibe.

Nice

POP 352,400

Riviera queen Nice is what good living is all about – shimmering shores, the very best of Mediterranean food, a unique historical heritage, free museums, a charming Old Town, exceptional art and Alpine wilderness within an hour's drive. No wonder so many young French people aspire to live here while the tourists just keep flooding in.

To get stuck-in straight away, make a beeline upon arrival for Promenade des Anglais, Nice's curvaceous palm-lined seafront that follows its busy pebble beach for 6km from the city centre to the airport.

Sights

Vieux Nice OLD TOWN

Ditch the map and lose yourself in the Old Town's tangle of 18th-century pedestrian passages and alleyways, historic churches and hole-in-the-wall joints selling Niçois tapas. Cours Saleya, running parallel to the seafront, hosts one of France's most vibrant, vividly hued **food markets** (⏲6am-1.30pm Tue-Sun), trestle tables groaning with shiny fruit and veg, pastries, *fruits confits* (glazed or candied fruits such as figs, ginger, pears etc). Baroque **Cathédrale Ste-Réparate** (place Rossetti) with its glazed terracotta

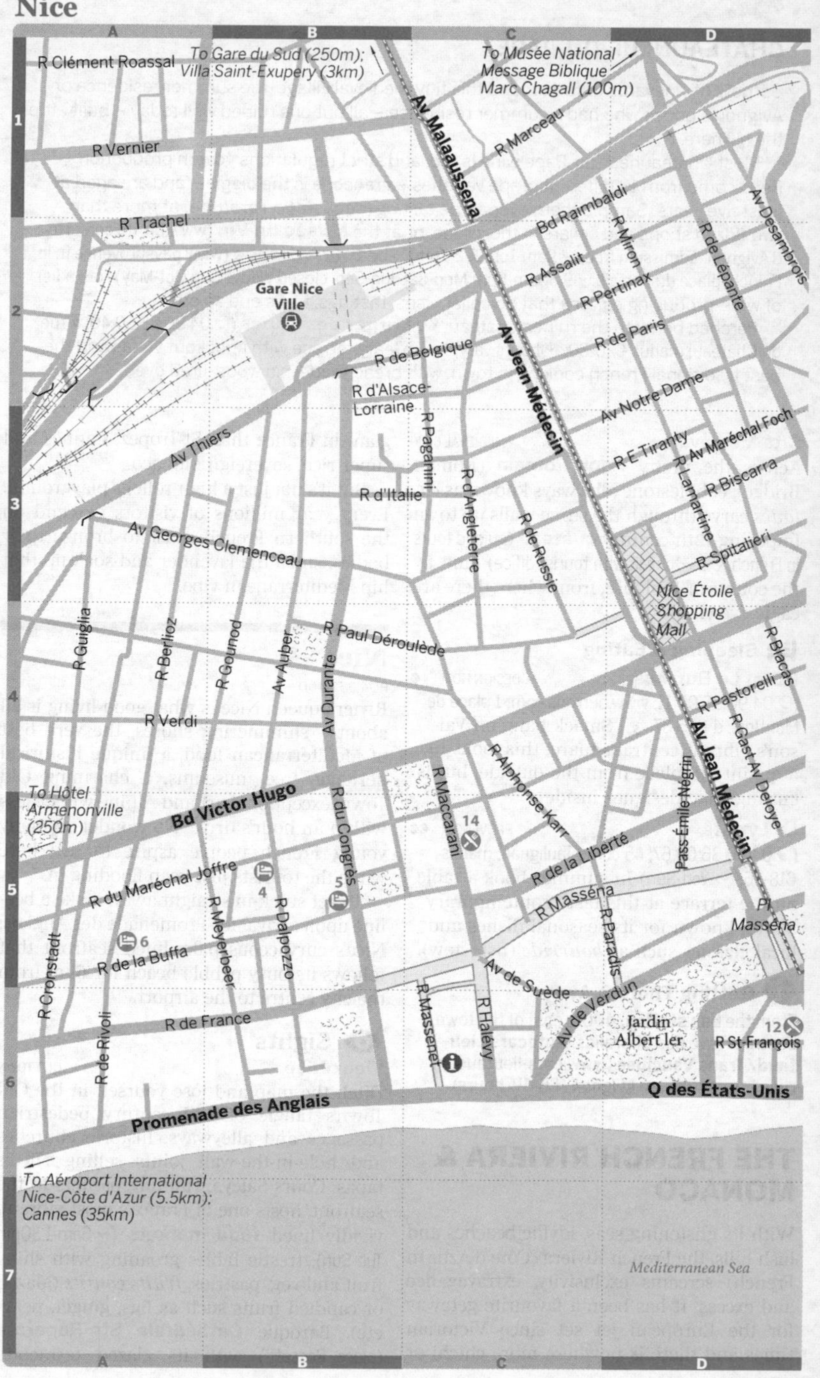

To Gare du Sud (250m); Villa Saint-Exupery (3km)
To Musée National Message Biblique Marc Chagall (100m)
R Clément Roassal
R Vernier
R Trachel
Av Malaussena
R Marceau
Bd Raimbaldi
R Miron
R de Lépante
Av Desambrois
R Assalit
R Pertinax
Gare Nice Ville
R de Paris
R de Belgique
Av Jean Médecin
R d'Alsace-Lorraine
Av Notre Dame
R Pagani
Av Maréchal Foch
R E Tiranty
Av Thiers
R Lamartine
R Biscarra
R d'Italie
R d'Angleterre
R de Russie
R Spitalieri
Av Georges Clemenceau
Nice Étoile Shopping Mall
R Paul Déroulède
R Guiglia
R Berlioz
R Gounod
Av Auber
Av Durante
R Blacas
R Pastorelli
R Verdi
R Gast Av Deloye
R Alphonse Karr
To Hôtel Armenonville (250m)
Bd Victor Hugo
R du Congrès
R Maccarani
Pass Émile Negrin
14
R de la Liberté
R du Maréchal Joffre
4
5
R Masséna
Pl Masséna
R Meyerbeer
R Dalpozzo
6
R de la Buffa
R Paradis
R Cronstadt
Av de Suède
R Massenet
R Halévy
Av de Verdun
R de France
Jardin Albert Ier
12
R St-François
R de Rivoli
Promenade des Anglais
Q des États-Unis
To Aéroport International Nice-Côte d'Azur (5.5km); Cannes (35km)
Mediterranean Sea

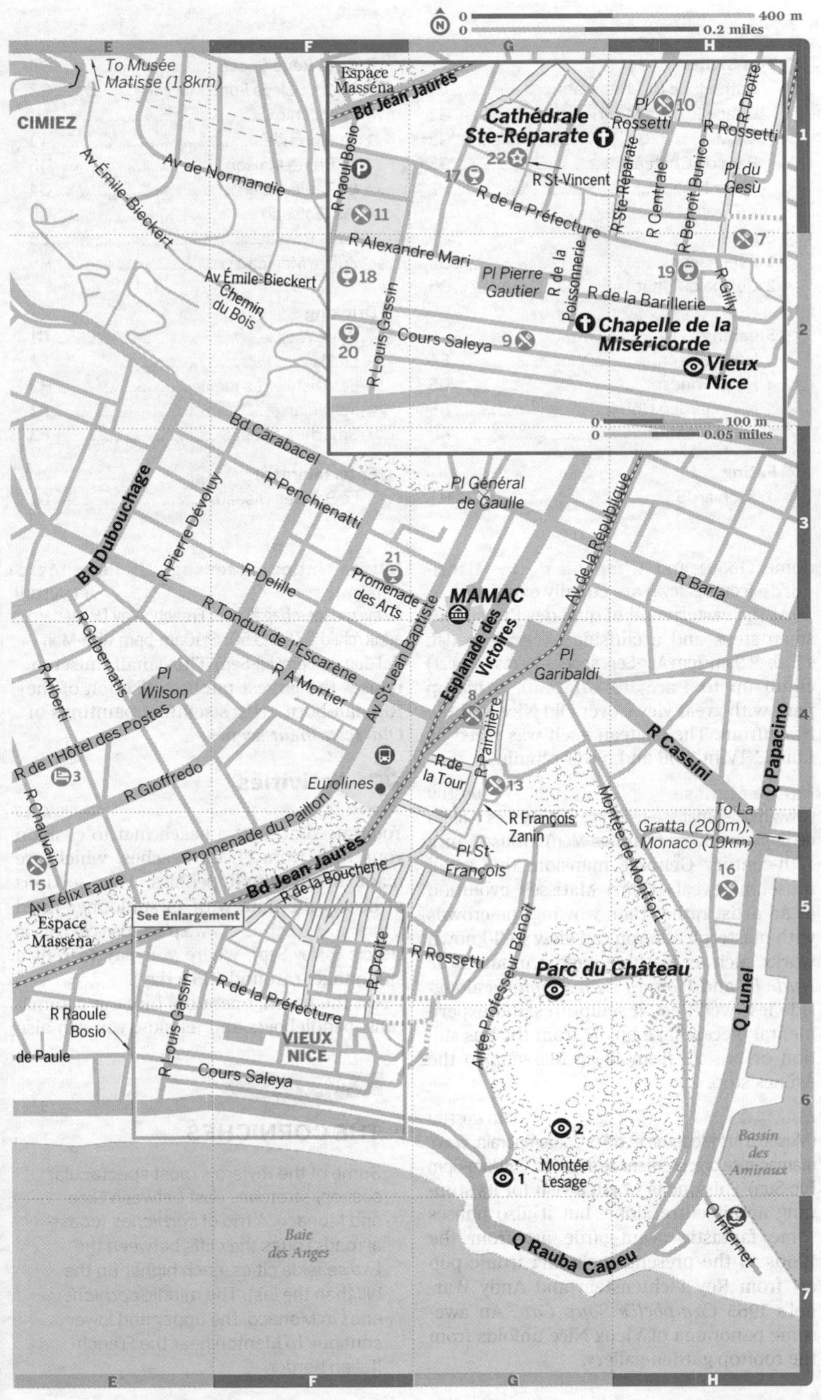
0 400 m
0 0.2 miles
E
F
G
H
To Musée Matisse (1.8km)
CIMIEZ
Av Émile-Bieckert
Av de Normandie
Av Émile-Bieckert
Chemin du Bois
Bd Carabacel
R Penchienatti
Bd Dubouchage
R Pierre Dévoluy
R Delille
R Tonduti de l'Escarène
R A Mortier
R Gubernatis
Pl Wilson
R Alberti
R de l'Hôtel des Postes
3
R Gioffredo
R Chauvain
15
Av Félix Faure
Espace Masséna
Promenade du Paillon
Bd Jean Jaurès
R de la Boucherie
See Enlargement
R Raoule Bosio
de Paule
R Louis Gassin
R de la Préfecture
VIEUX NICE
Cours Saleya
R Droite
R Rossetti
Baie des Anges
Pl Général de Gaulle
21
Promenade des Arts
MAMAC
Av St-Jean Baptiste
Esplanade des Victoires
Av de la République
Pl Garibaldi
R Barla
8
R Pairolière
R de la Tour
Eurolines
13
R François Zanin
Pl St-François
R Cassini
Q Papacino
To La Gratta (200m); Monaco (19km)
16
Montée de Montfort
Allée Professeur Benoît
Parc du Château
Q Lunel
2
1
Montée Lesage
Q Rauba Capeu
Q Infernet
Bassin des Amiraux
Espace Masséna
Bd Jean Jaurès
Cathédrale Ste-Réparate
Pl Rossetti
10
R Droite
R Rossetti
R Raoul Bosio
22
R St-Vincent
17
R Ste-Réparate
R Centrale
R Benoît Bunico
Pl du Gesù
11
R de la Préfecture
R Alexandre Mari
7
18
Pl Pierre Gautier
R de la Poissonnerie
19
R Gilly
R de la Barillerie
Chapelle de la Miséricorde
R Louis Gassin
20
Cours Saleya
9
Vieux Nice
0 100 m
0 0.05 miles
1
2
3
4
5
6
7

Nice

Top Sights

	Cathédrale Ste-Réparate	G1
	Chapelle de la Miséricorde	G2
	MAMAC	G3
	Parc du Château	G5
	Vieux Nice	H2

Sights

1	Ascenseur	G6
2	Colline du Château	G6

Sleeping

3	Hôtel Wilson	E4
4	Hôtel Windsor	B5
5	Nice Garden Hôtel	B5
6	Villa Rivoli	A5

Eating

7	Acchiardo	H2
8	Chez René Socca	G4
9	Cours Saleya Food Market	G2
10	Fenocchio	H1
11	La Merenda	F1
12	La Petite Maison	D6
13	La Table Alziari	G4
14	Luc Salsedo	C5
15	Luna Rossa	E5
16	Zucca Magica	H5

Drinking

17	Chez Wayne's	G1
18	Le Six	F2
19	Les Distilleries Idéales	H2
20	Ma Nolan's	F2
21	Smarties	F3

Entertainment

22	Le Bar des Oiseaux	G1

dome (1650) and **Chapelle de la Miséricorde** (cours Saleya) are equally exuberant.

At the eastern end of quai des États-Unis, steep steps and a cliffside **ascenseur** (lift; €1.10; 9am-7pm Apr-Sep, shorter hr rest of year) climb up to **Parc du Château**, a hilltop park with great views over Old Nice and the beachfront. The chateau itself was razed by Louis XIV in 1706 and never rebuilt.

Musée Matisse MUSEUM

(www.musee-matisse-nice.org; 164 av des Arènes de Cimiez; 10am-6pm Wed-Mon) Housed in a 17th-century Genoese mansion, this small museum reveals Henri Matisse's evolution as an artist rather than wowing the crowds with masterpieces. You can view well-known works such as his blue paper cutouts *Blue Nude IV* and *Woman with Amphora* alongside less-well-known sculptures and experimental pieces. Take bus 17 from the bus station or bus 22 from Place Masséna to the Arènes stop.

MAMAC ART MUSEUM

(Musée d'Art Moderne et d'Art Contemporain; www.mamac-nice.org; promenade des Arts; 10am-6pm Tue-Sun) This one is worth a visit for its stunning architecture alone, but it also houses some fantastic avant-garde art from the 1960s to the present, including iconic pop art from Roy Lichtenstein and Andy Warhol's 1965 *Campbell's Soup Can*. An awesome panorama of Vieux Nice unfolds from the rooftop garden-gallery.

Musée National Message Biblique Marc Chagall ART MUSEUM

(www.musee-chagall.fr, in French; 4 av Dr Ménard; adult/child €7.50/5.50; 10am-5pm Wed-Mon Oct-Jun, to 6pm Jul-Sep) This small museum houses the largest public collection of the Russian-born artist's seminal paintings of *Old Testament* scenes.

Activities

Beaches BEACHES

You'll need at least a beach mat to cushion your tush from Nice's beaches, which are made up of round pebbles. Free sections of beach alternate with 15 sunlounge-lined **private beaches** (www.plagesdenice.com, in French; May-Sep), where you pay to rent a sunlounger (around €15 a day).

On the beach, operators hire out catamarans, paddleboats and jet skis; you can also

DON'T MISS

THE CORNICHES

Some of the Riviera's most spectacular scenery stretches east between Nice and Monaco. A trio of *corniches* (coastal roads) hugs the cliffs between the two seaside cities, each higher up the hill than the last. The middle *corniche* ends in Monaco; the upper and lower continue to Menton near the French-Italian border.

parascend, waterski or paraglide. There are showers and toilets on every beach.

Festivals & Events

Carnaval de Nice CARNIVAL

(www.nicecarnaval.com) This two-week carnival, held in February, is particularly famous for its 'battles of the flowers', where thousands of blooms are tossed into the crowds from passing floats, as well as its fantastic fireworks display.

Nice Jazz Festival MUSIC

(www.nicejazzfestival.fr) In July, Nice swings to the week-long jazz festival at the Arènes de Cimiez, amid the Roman ruins.

Sleeping

Nice has a suite of places to sleep, from stellar independent backpacker hostels to international art-filled icons. Prices rocket upwards in the summer season.

TOP CHOICE **Villa Rivoli** BOUTIQUE HOTEL €€

(☎04 93 88 80 25; www.villa-rivoli.com; 10 rue de Rivoli; s/d/q from 85/99/210;) Built in 1890, this stately villa feels like your own pied-à-terre in the heart of Nice. Rooms are character-rich, some with fabric walls, gilt-edged mirrors, and marble fireplaces. Breakfast in the garden or belle-époque salon.

Hôtel Windsor BOUTIQUE HOTEL €€

(☎04 93 88 59 35; www.hotelwindsornice.com; 11 rue Dalpozzo; d €120-175; @) Graffiti casts aggressive splashes of colour on the edgy, oversize rooms of the Windsor – a real nod to contemporary art. Rooms overlooking the backyard tropical garden have a particularly lush view.

Nice Garden Hôtel BOUTIQUE HOTEL €€

(☎04 93 87 35 63; www.nicegardenhotel.com; 11 rue du Congrès; s/d €75/100;) Nine beautifully appointed rooms blend old and new and overlook a delightful garden with a glorious orange tree – pure, unadulterated charm and peacefulness just two blocks from the promenade.

Villa Saint-Exupéry HOSTEL €

(☎04 93 84 42 83; www.villahostels.com; 22 av Gravier; dm €25-30, s/d €45/90; @) Why can't all hostels be like this? Set in a lovely converted monastery in the north of the city, this backpacker palace features a 24-hour common room in a converted chapel, state-of-the-art-kitchens, barbecue terraces and lovely dorms; they'll even pick you up from the nearby Comte de Falicon tram stop or St Maurice stop for bus 23 (from the airport).

Hôtel Wilson BOUTIQUE HOTEL €

(☎04 93 85 47 79; www.hotel-wilson-nice.com; 39 rue de l'Hôtel des Postes; s/d €50/55;) Many years of travelling, an experimental nature and exquisite taste have turned Jean-Marie's rambling flat into a compelling place to stay. Mind the two resident tortoises as you sit down for a breakfast.

Hôtel Armenonville HOTEL €€

(☎04 93 96 86 00; www.hotel-armenonville.com; 20 av des Fleurs; d €86-105; @) Shielded by its large garden, this grand early-20th-century mansion has sober rooms, three (12, 13 and 14) with a huge terrace overlooking *le jardin*.

Eating

Niçois nibbles include *socca* (a thin layer of chickpea flour and olive oil batter), *salade niçoise* and *farcis* (stuffed vegetables). Restaurants in Vieux Nice are a mixed bag, so choose carefully.

La Merenda NIÇOIS €€

(4 rue Raoul Bosio; mains €12-15; ⊙Mon-Fri) This pocket-sized bistro serves some of the most unusual fare in town: stockfish (dried cod soaked in running water for a few days and then simmered with onions, tomatoes, garlic, olives and potatoes) and tripe. It also serves Bellet wines, a rare local vintage. No credit cards.

WORTH A TRIP

THE PINE CONE TRAIN

Chugging between mountains and the sea, narrow-gauge railway **Train des Pignes** (Pine Cone Train; www.trainprovence.com) is one of France's most picturesque train rides. Rising to 1000m, with breathtaking views, the 151km-long track between Nice and Digne-les-Bains passes through the scarcely populated back country of little-known Haute Provence.

Day-trip suggestion: a picnic and meander around the historical centre and citadel of the beautiful medieval village of **Entrevaux** (€18 return, 1½ hours).

DON'T MISS

NICE FAST FOOD

When locals crave a quick bite, they grab a *pan bagnat* (loosely translated as sopped bread), the local version of a tuna sandwich made with crusty round bread, chunks of cold tuna, lettuce, tomatoes, onions, radish and egg, all drizzled with loads of olive oil. The best come from portside snack-bar **La Gratta** (2 blvd Franck Pilatte; sandwiches €4.50; ⏲lunch). Find a spot by the water to dangle your feet over the quay and watch masts bob in the harbour while you drip olive oil down your chin.

Chez René Socca NIÇOIS €
(2 rue Miralhéti; dishes from €2; ⏲9am-9pm Tue-Sun, to 10.30pm Jul & Aug, closed Nov) This address is about taste, not presentation or manners. Grab some *socca* or *petits farçis* and head across the street to the bar for a *grand pointu* (glass) of red, white or rosé.

Zucca Magica VEGETARIAN €€
(☎04 93 56 25 27; www.lazuccamagica.com; 4bis quai Papacino; menus €30; ⏲Tue-Sat; 🖉) The 'Magic Pumpkin' is a rarity in France – a vegetarian restaurant that non-vegetarians like! Bring an appetite: fixed-price meals comprise four set dishes (five for dinner) plus dessert, all sourced at the market.

La Table Alziari NIÇOIS €
(☎04 93 80 34 03, 4 rue François Zanin; mains €9-15, ⏲Tue-Sat) Run by the grandson of the famous Alziari olive-oil family, this citrus-coloured restaurant chalks up local specialities such as *morue à la niçoise* (cod served with potatoes, olives and a tomato sauce) and *daube* (stew) on its blackboard.

Acchiardo BISTRO €
(38 rue Droite; mains €14-20; ⏲Mon-Fri) Going strong since 1927; locals flock here to Acchiardo for the plat du jour (daily special), a glass of wine and a load of gossip served straight up on the counter.

TOP CHOICE **Fenocchio** ICE CREAM €
(2 place Rossetti; from €2; ⏲9am-midnight Feb-Oct) Beat the summer heat with Nice's most fabulous *glacier* (ice-cream maker). Eschew predictable favourites and indulge in new tastes: black olive, tomato-basil, rhubarb, avocado, rosemary, *calisson* (almond biscuit frosted with icing sugar), lavender, ginger or liquorice. There are 50 flavours in all to choose from.

TOP CHOICE **Luc Salsedo** MODERN FRENCH €€€
(☎04 93 82 24 12; www.restaurant-salsedo.com, in French; 14 rue Maccarani; mains €26; ⏲lunch Fri & Sun-Tue, dinner Thu-Tue Jun-Sep, dinner only Jul-Aug) The cuisine of young chef Salsedo is local and seasonal, served without pomp on plates, rustic boards or cast-iron pots. The wine list is another French hit.

Luna Rossa ITALIAN €€
(☎04 93 85 55 66; www.lelunarossa.com; 3 rue Chauvain; mains €15-25; ⏲Tue-Fri, dinner Sat) The Red Moon translates as fresh pasta, perfectly cooked seafood, sun-kissed veg (artichoke hearts, sun-dried tomatoes, asparagus tips etc) and succulent meats.

La Petite Maison FRENCH, NIÇOIS €€€
(☎04 93 92 59 59; www.lapetitemaison-nice.com; 11 rue St-François de Paule; mains €20-40; ⏲Mon-Sat) Nice's hottest tables draw celebs and politicians for its happening scene and elegantly executed Nićois specialities – tops for a splashy night out.

Drinking & Entertainment

Vieux Nice's streets are stuffed with bars and cafes, serving anything from morning espresso to lunchtime pastis (the aperitif tipple in these parts).

Smarties LOUNGE BAR
(http://nicesmarties.free.fr; 10 rue Defly; ⏲6pm-2am Tue-Sat) We love Smarties' sexy-'70s swirly orange style, which draws a hot-looking straight/gay crowd. On weekends, the tiny dance floor fills when DJs spin deep house, electro, techno and occasionally disco; weekdays are mellower. Free buffet with happy hour (6pm to 9pm).

Les Distilleries Idéales CAFE
(24 rue de la Préfecture; ⏲9am-12.30am) Whether you're after a coffee on your way to cours Saleya or a sundowner, the atmosphere in this brilliant bistro is infectious: you're bound to leave with a skip in your step.

Le Bar des Oiseaux CABARET
(www.bardesoiseaux.com, in French; 5 rue St-Vincent; ⏲lunch Mon-Sat, dinner Tue-Sat) Artists dig this bohemian bar (and adjoining theatre) for live jazz, *chansons françaises* (French songs) and cabaret nights. Cover costs around €5 when there's entertainment; you can also dine here (*menus* around €20).

Ma Nolan's PUB
(www.ma-nolans.com; 2 rue St François de Paule; ⌚noon-2am Mon-Fri, 11pm-2am Sat & Sun) This Irish pub is a backpacker favourite, with a Monday-night pub quiz, televised sport, nightly live music and full English brekkie.

Le Six GAY BAR
(www.le6.fr; 6 rue Raoul Bosio; ⌚Tue-Sun 10pm-4:30am) Primped and pretty A-gays crowd shoulder to shoulder at Nice's compact, perennially popular 'mo bar. Climb the ladder to the mezzanine.

Chez Wayne's BAR
(www.waynes.fr; 15 rue de la Préfecture; ⌚2.30pm-12.30am) This raucous watering hole has live bands every night.

Information

Main tourist office (www.nicetourisme.com; 5 promenade des Anglais; ⌚8am-8pm Mon-Sat, 9am-7pm Sun Jun-Sep, 9am-6pm Mon-Sat Oct-May) By the beach.

Train station tourist office (av Thiers; ⌚8am-8pm Mon-Sat, 9am-7pm Sun Jun-Sep, 8am-7pm Mon-Sat, 10am-5pm Sun Oct-May)

Getting There & Away

Air

Aéroport International Nice-Côte d'Azur (www.nice.aeroport.fr), 6km west of the centre, is served by numerous carriers, including several low-cost ones.

Ligne d'Azur runs two airport buses (€4). Route 99 shuttles approximately every half-hour direct between Gare Nice Ville and both airport terminals daily from around 8am to 9pm. Route 98 takes the slow route and departs from the bus station every 20 minutes (30 minutes Sunday) from around 6am to around 9pm.

A second tram line is planned to connect Nice's centre with the airport.

Boat

The fastest, cheapest ferries to Corsica (p448) depart from Nice.

SNCM (www.sncm.fr; ferry terminal, quai du Commerce)

Corsica Ferries (www.corsicaferries.com; quai Lunel)

> **WANT MORE?**
>
> For in-depth information, reviews and recommendations at your fingertips, head to the Apple App Store to purchase Lonely Planet's *Nice City Guide* iPhone app.

> **CARTE ISABELLE**
>
> Between July and September, the SNCF's **Carte Isabelle** (€14) covers unlimited train trips in a single day (except TGV trains) from Fréjus to Ventimiglia in Italy, and from Nice inland to Tende.

Bus

From the **bus station** (5 blvd Jean Jaurès) a single €1 fare takes you anywhere in the Alpes-Maritimes *département* (with a few exceptions, such as the airport) and includes one connection, within 74 minutes. Buses run daily to Antibes (one hour), Cannes (1½ hours), Monaco (45 minutes), Vence (one hour) and St-Paul de Vence (55 minutes).

Eurolines (www.eurolines.com) Operates from the bus station.

Train

From **Gare Nice Ville** (av Thiers), 1.2km north of the beach, there are frequent services to Antibes (€4, 30 minutes), Cannes (€6.10, 40 minutes), Menton (€4.60, 35 minutes) and Monaco (€3.40, 20 minutes). Direct TGV trains link Nice with Paris' Gare de Lyon (€115, 5½ hours).

Cannes

POP 71,800

Everyone's heard of Cannes and its celebrity film festival. The latter only lasts for two weeks in May, but the buzz and glitz linger all year thanks to regular visits from celebrities who come here to indulge in designer shopping, beaches and the palace hotels of the Riviera's glammest seafront, blvd de la Croisette.

Offshore lie the idyllic islands, Îles de Lérins, the unexpected key to 2000-plus years of history – from Ligurian fishing communities (200 BC) to one of Europe's oldest religious communities (5th century AD) and the enigmatic Man in the Iron Mask.

Sights & Activities

Beaches BEACHES
The central, sandy beaches along blvd de la Croisette are sectioned off for hotel patrons. Many accept day guests, who pay from €20 per day for a mattress and yellow-and-white parasol on **Plage du Gray d'Albion** (⌚10am-5pm Mar-Oct), to €50-odd for a pearl-white lounge on the pier of super-stylish **Z Plage** (⌚9.30am-6pm May-Sep), the beach of Hôtel Martinez.

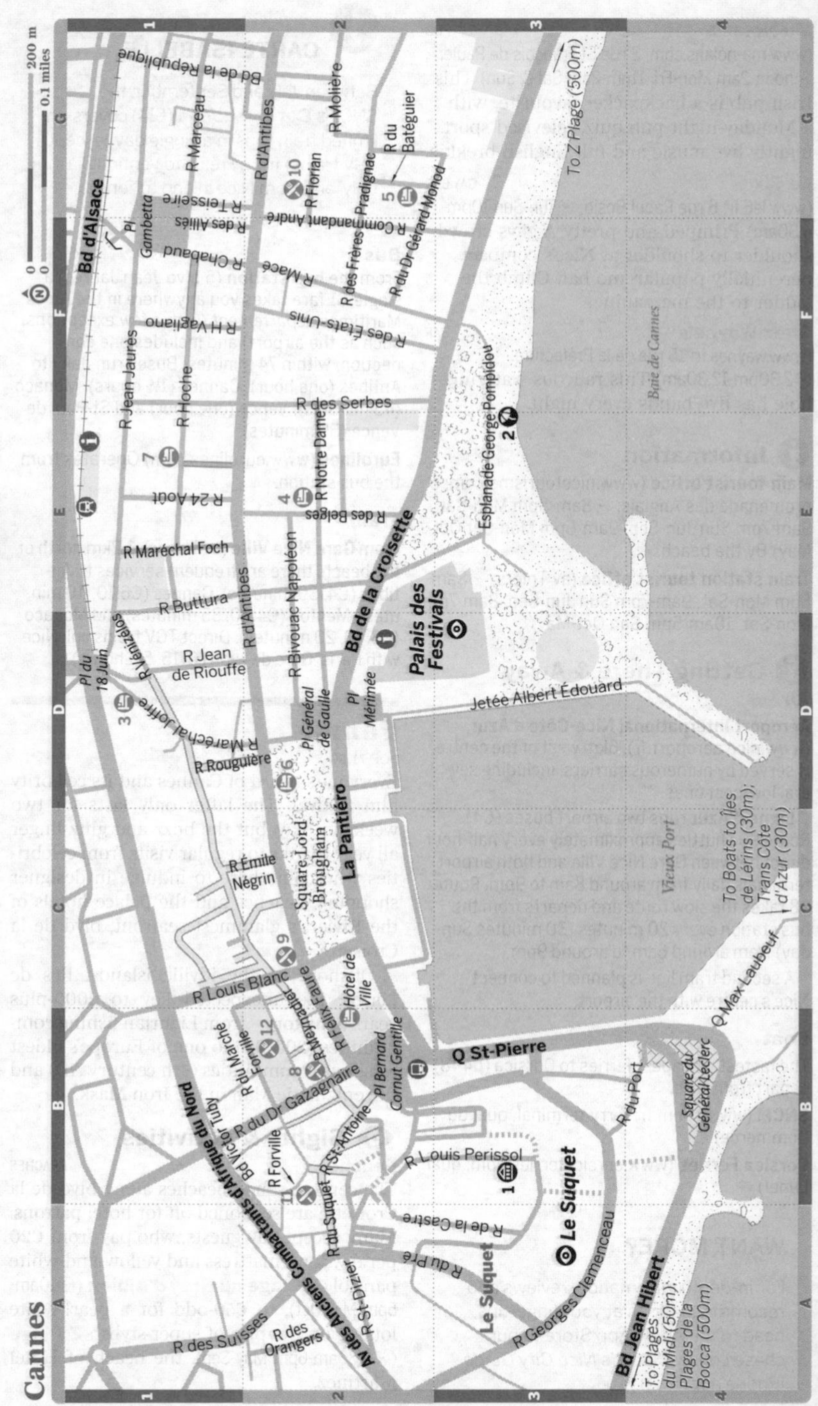
Cannes
0 200 m
0 0.1 miles
Bd d'Alsace
Bd de la République
R Marceau
R d'Antibes
R Molière
R Florian
R du Batéguier
Pl Gambetta
R Teisseire
R des Alliés
R Commandant André
R Pradignac
R Chabaud
R Macé
R des Frères
R du Dr Gérard Monod
R H Vagliano
R des États-Unis
R Jean Jaurès
R Hoche
R des Serbes
R Notre Dame
R 24 Août
R des Belges
R Maréchal Foch
R Buttura
R Bivouac Napoléon
Bd de la Croisette
Palais des Festivals
Esplanade George Pompidou
Baie de Cannes
To Z Plage (500m)
Pl du 18 Juin
R Vénizélos
R Jean de Riouffe
R Maréchal Joffre
R Rouguière
Pl Général de Gaulle
Pl Mérimée
Jetée Albert Édouard
Vieux Port
To Boats to Îles de Lérins (30m); Trans Côte d'Azur (30m)
Square Lord Brougham
La Pantiéro
R Émile Négrin
R Louis Blanc
R Meynadier
R Félix Faure
Hôtel de Ville
Q Max Laubeuf
Q St-Pierre
Pl Bernard Cornut Gentille
Marché Forville
R du Marché Forville
R du Dr Gazagnaire
Bd Victor Tuby
R St-Antoine
R Forville
R du Port
Square du Général Leclerc
Av des Anciens Combattants d'Afrique du Nord
R Louis Perissol
R du Suquet
R St-Dizier
R de la Castre
R du Pré
Le Suquet
R Georges Clemenceau
Bd Jean Hibert
To Plages du Midi (50m); Plages de la Bocca (500m)
R des Suisses
R des Orangers
1 2 3 4 5 6 7 8 9 10 11 12
A B C D E F G

Cannes

A microscopic strip of sand near the Palais des Festivals is free, but you'll find better free sand on **Plages du Midi** and **Plages de la Bocca**, west from the Vieux Port along blvd Jean Hibert and blvd du Midi.

Palais des Festivals LANDMARK

(Festival Palace; blvd de la Croisette) At the western end of La Croisette, this concrete bunker is the unlikely host of the world's most glamorous film festival. The tourist office runs **guided tours** (adult/child €3/free; 1½ hrs; 2.30pm Jun-Apr) several times a month; book ahead.

Le Suquet OLD TOWN

Cannes' historic quarter, pre-dating the glitz and glam of the town's festival days, retains a quaint village feel with its steep, meandering alleyways. There are wonderful views of the Baie de Cannes from the top of the hill, and the fascinating **Musée de la Castre** (place de la Castre; adult/child €3.20/free; 10am-7pm Jul & Aug, 10am-1pm & 2-5pm Tue-Sun Sep-Jun), an ethnographic museum.

Îles de Lérins ISLANDS

Although just 20 minutes away by boat, these tranquil islands feel far from the madding crowd. **Île Ste-Marguerite**, where the mysterious Man in the Iron Mask was incarcerated during the late 17th century, is known for its bone-white beaches, eucalyptus groves and small marine museum. Tiny **Île St-Honorat** has been a monastery since the 5th century: visit small chapels, stroll through vineyard and forest and lunch or take afternoon tea at monk-run restaurant **La Tonnelle** (04 92 99 18 07; mains €25; lunch).

Boats leave Cannes from quai des Îles on the western side of the harbour. **Riviera Lines** (www.riviera-lines.com; adult/child €11.50/6 return) runs ferries to Île Ste-Marguerite and **Compagnie Planaria** (www.cannes-ilesdelerins.com; adult/child €12/6) covers Île St-Honorat.

Sleeping

Hotel prices in Cannes fluctuate wildly according to the season, and soar during the film festival, when you'll need to book months in advance.

TOP CHOICE **Hôtel 7e Art** BOUTIQUE HOTEL €

(04 93 68 66 66; www.7arthotel.com; 23 rue Maréchal Joffre; s €68, d €60-98;) Cannes' newest star puts boutique style within reach of budgeteers. The owners schooled in Switzerland and their snappy design of putty-coloured walls, padded headboards and pop art far exceeds what you'd expect at this price.

Hôtel Le Mistral BOUTIQUE HOTEL €€

(04 93 39 91 46; www.mistral-hotel.com; 13 rue des Belges; d from €89;) This small hotel, a mere 50m from La Croisette, wins the *palme d'or* for best value in town: rooms are in red and plum tones and bathrooms feature designer fittings.

Hotel Le Romanesque BOUTIQUE HOTEL €€

(04 93 68 04 20; www.hotelleromanesque.com; 10 rue Batéguier; r €90-150;) Every room is individually decorated at this eight-room boutique charmer in the heart of Cannes' nightlife district. Favourites include Charlotte, with its sun-drenched bath; and Elizabeth, the former maid's quarters, with low, sloping, beamed ceilings.

Villa Tosca HOTEL €€

(04 93 38 34 40; www.villa-tosca.com; 11 rue Hoche; s/d €80/100;) This elegant, bourgeois town house sits on a semi-pedestrianised street in Cannes' shopping area. Rooms with balcony are perfect for people-watching.

Hôtel Splendid BOUTIQUE HOTEL €€€

(04 97 06 22 22; www.splendid-hotel-cannes.com; 4-6 rue Félix Faure; s/d from €160/190;) The hotel in this elaborate 1871 building has

WORTH A TRIP

THE SCENT OF THE CÔTE D'AZUR

Mosey some 20km northwest of Cannes to inhale the sweet smell of lavender, jasmine, mimosa and orange-blossom fields. In **Grasse**, one of France's leading perfume producers, dozens of perfumeries create essences to sell to factories (for aromatically enhanced foodstuffs and soaps) as well as to prestigious couture houses – the highly trained noses of local perfume-makers can identify 3000 scents in a single whiff.

Fragonard (www.fragonard.com; 20 blvd Fragonard; ⌚9am-6pm Feb-Oct, 9am-12.30pm & 2-6pm Nov-Jan) is the easiest perfumery to reach by foot. The tourist office has information on other perfumeries and field trips to local flower farms, including the flower-strewn **Domaine de Manon** (☎04 93 60 12 76; www.domaine-manon.com; admission €6). Roses are picked mid-May to mid-June, jasmine July to late October.

everything it takes to rival Cannes' posher palaces: beautifully decorated rooms, fabulous location, stunning views and more, in the form of self-catering kitchenettes.

Eating

You'll find the least-expensive restaurants around rue du Marché Forville. Hipper, pricier establishments are in Le Suquet and the 'Carré d'Or' (the 'golden square' streets between La Croisette and rue d'Antibes). Square Lord Brougham, next to the Vieux Port, is the place to picnic.

TOP CHOICE **Mantel** MODERN EUROPEAN €€
(☎04 93 39 13 10; www.restaurantmantel.com; 22 rue St-Antoine; menus €25-38; ⌚Fri-Mon, dinner Tue & Thu) The Italian maître d' here will make you feel like a million dollars and you'll melt for Noël Mantel's divine cuisine and great-value prices. Best of all, you get not one but two desserts with your menu (oh, the pannacotta…).

Le Riad MOROCCAN €€
(☎04 93 38 60 95; www.restaurant-le-riad.fr; 6 impasse Florian; mains €13-26; ⌚noon-midnight Tue-Sat) Le Riad imports Moroccan hospitality and authentic cooking, with *tagine* classics and a real *pastilla* (pigeon pie) – rare even in Morocco. On weekend nights a belly-dancer sets a party mood. Excellent service.

Coquillages Brun SEAFOOD €€
(☎04 93 39 21 87; www.astouxbrun.com; 27 rue Félix Faure; menus from €28; ⌚12pm-1am) Cannes' most famous brasserie is *the* place to indulge in oysters, mussels, prawns, crayfish and other delightfully fresh shells with a glass of crisp white wine.

Aux Bons Enfants TRADITIONAL FRENCH €€
(80 rue Meynadier; menus €23; ⌚Tue-Sat) This familial little place buzzes. The lucky ones who get a table (arrive early or late) can feast on top-notch regional dishes.

Information

Tourist office (☎04 92 99 84 22; www.cannes.travel; blvd de la Croisette; ⌚9am-8pm Jul & Aug, 9am-7pm Mon-Sat Sep-Jun) On the ground floor of Palais des Festivals; runs an annexe next to the train station.

Getting There & Away

Bus

From the **bus station** (place Bernard Cornut Gentille) buses serve Nice (bus 200, €1, 1½ hours) and Nice airport (bus 210, €15, 50 minutes, half-hourly)

Train

GRASSE €3.80, 30 minutes
MARSEILLE €22, two hours
NICE €6.10, 40 minutes

St-Tropez

POP 5700

In the soft autumn or winter light, it's hard to believe the pretty terracotta fishing village of St-Tropez is a stop on the Riviera celebrity circuit. It seems far removed from its glitzy siblings further up the coast, but come spring or summer, it's a different world: the population increases tenfold, prices triple and fun-seekers pile in to party till dawn, strut around the luxury-yacht-packed Vieux Port and enjoy the creature comforts of exclusive A-listers' beaches in the Baie de Pampelonne.

If you can at all avoid visiting in July and August, do. But if not, take heart: it's always fun to play 'I spy...' (a celebrity).

Sights & Activities

Musée de l'Annonciade ART MUSEUM
(place Grammont, Vieux Port; adult/child €6/4; 10am-noon & 2-6pm Wed-Mon Oct & Dec-May, 10am-noon & 3-7pm Wed-Mon Jun-Sep) Displayed in a disused chapel at the Vieux Port (Old Port), this small water-facing museum displays works by Matisse, Bonnard, Dufy and pointillist Signac, who set up his home and studio in St-Tropez.

Plage de Pampelonne BEACH
The golden sands of **Plage de Tahiti**, 4km southeast of town, morph into the 5km-long, celebrity-studded **Plage de Pampelonne**, which sports a line-up of exclusive beach restaurants and clubs in summer. The bus to Ramatuelle stops at various points along a road, 1km inland from the beach. Beach mats can be rented for around €15 per day.

Citadelle CITADEL
(admission €2.50; 10am-6.30pm Apr-Sep, 10am-12.30pm & 1.30-5.30pm Oct-Mar) The panoramas of St-Tropez's iconic church tower and glistening bay from this lofty 17th-century fortress are definitely worth the climb.

Sleeping

St-Tropez is no shoestring destination, but multistar camping grounds abound on the road to Plage de Pampelonne.

Hôtel Le Colombier HOTEL €€
(04 94 97 05 31; impasse des Conquettes; r €84-158, without bath €76;) An immaculate converted house five minutes' walk from place des Lices, the Colombier's fresh summery decor is feminine and uncluttered. Not all rooms have air-con. Rooms without baths share a toilet, but have bidet, sink and shower.

Hôtel Ermitage BOUTIQUE HOTEL €€€
(04 94 27 52 33; www.ermitagehotel.fr; av Paul Signac; r €180-300;) Kate Moss and Lenny Kravitz favour this rocker crash pad inspired by St-Tropez in the 1950s to 1970s – disco meets mid-century modern. Its out-of-town, hillside location only ups the exclusivity factor and proffers knockout views over town.

TOP CHOICE **Lou Cagnard** HOTEL €€
(04 94 97 04 24; www.hotel-lou-cagnard.com; 18 av Paul-Roussel; d/tr €69-140/160;) Book well ahead for this great-value courtyard charmer, shaded by lemon and fig trees. Rooms are spotlessly kept and five have garden terraces.

Pastis ART HOTEL €€€
(04 98 12 56 50; www.pastis-st-tropez.com; 61 av du Général Leclerc; d from €200-350;) This stunning hotel with pop-art-inspired interior is the brainchild of an English couple passionate about modern art. Swim in the emerald-green pool and snooze under centenary palm trees.

Les Palmiers BOUTIQUE HOTEL €€
(04 94 97 01 61; www.hotel-les-palmiers.com; 26 blvd Vasserot; d €89-189;) In an old villa with courtyard garden overlooking place des Lices, Les Palmiers has friendly service and simple rooms. Skip the annexe for the main building.

Eating

Quai Jean Jaurès at the Vieux Port is littered with restaurants and cafes.

DON'T MISS

TOP FIVE BEACH EATS

Book lunch (well ahead) at the following, open May to September and around €15 to €40 for a main.

» **Club 55** (www.leclub55.fr; 43 blvd Path) St-Tropez's oldest-running beach club, this 1950s address was the crew canteen for the filming of *And God Created Woman* with Brigitte Bardot. The rich and famous flock here to be seen, although the food – rather remarkably – is nothing special.

» **Nikki Beach** (www.nikkibeach.com/sttropez; rte de l'Epi) Favoured by dance-on-the-bar celebs such as Paris Hilton and Pamela Anderson, the deafening scene ends at midnight.

» **Moorea Plage** (www.moorea-plage-st-tropez.com; rte des Plages) Ideal for conversation and backgammon (supplied); tops for steak.

» **Liberty Plage** (www.plageleliberty.com; chemin des Tamaris; year-round) Clothing optional – eat naked.

WORTH A TRIP

MASSIF DE L'ESTÉREL

Punctuated by pine, oak and eucalyptus trees, the rugged red mountain range Massif de l'Estérel contrasts dramatically with the brilliant blue sea.

Extending east from St-Raphaël to Mandelieu-La Napoule (near Cannes), a curling coastal road, the famous corniche de l'Estérel (also known as the corniche d'Or and N98), passes through summer villages and dreamy inlets perfect for a quick dip. Try **Le Dramont**, where the 36th US Division landed on 15 August 1944, or **Agay**, a sheltered bay with excellent beach. More than 100 hiking trails criss-cross the Massif de l'Estérel's interior and views from the top of **Pic de l'Ours** (496m) and **Pic du Cap Roux** (452m), both accessible via marked trails, are breathtaking.

End your foray in style with dinner or a drink in neighbouring **St-Raphaël** (population 35,000) at **Les Charavins** (04 94 95 03 76; 36 rue Charabois; mains €18-26; dinner Thu-Tue, lunch Thu, Fri, Mon & Tue). Run by Philippe Furnémont, a former Michelin-starred chef and wine connoisseur, this jolly wine bar is fabulously French. The cuisine is resolutely traditional, and don't even *think* about turning down whatever wine suggestion Philippe offers you.

Brasserie des Arts MODERN FRENCH €€
(04 94 40 27 37; www.brasseriedesarts.com; 5 place des Lices; mains €20) Wedged in a line-up of eating/drinking terraces jockeying for attention on St-Tropez's people-watching square, BA, as it is known, is where the locals go. Its fixed three-course menu is gourmet and excellent value.

Auberge des Maures PROVENÇAL €€
(04 94 97 01 50; 4 rue du Docteur Boutin; mains €31-39; dinner) St-Trop's oldest restaurant remains the locals' choice for consistently good, copious portions of earthy Provençal cooking. Book a table (essential) in the leafy courtyard.

Le Sporting BRASSERIE €€
(04 94 97 00 65; place des Lices; mains €14-24; 8am-1am) There's a bit of everything on the menu at always-packed Le Sporting, but the speciality is hamburger topped with foie gras and creamy morel sauce. Reservations essential.

DON'T MISS

THE MARKET

One of southern France's busiest and best, St-Tropez's **place des Lices market** (mornings Tue & Sat) is a highlight of local life, with colourful stalls groaning under the weight of plump fruit and veg, mounds of olives, local cheeses, chestnut purée and fragrant herbs. Afterwards meander to the port and duck beneath the stone arch to the bijou **fish market** (mornings Tue-Sun, daily summer), hidden between stone walls on place aux Herbes.

Information

Tourist office (04 94 97 45 21; www.ot-saint-tropez.com; quai Jean Jaurès; 9.30am-8pm Jul & Aug, 9.30am-12.30pm & 2-7pm Apr-Jun & Sep–mid-Oct, 9.30am-12.30pm & 2-6pm mid-Oct–Mar)

Getting There & Away

Boat

Trans Côte d'Azur (www.trans-cote-azur.com) Day trips from Nice and Cannes, Easter to September.

Bus

From the **bus station** (av Général de Gaulle), buses run by **VarLib** (www.varlib.fr, in French) serve Ramatuelle (€2, 35 minutes) and St-Raphaël train station (€2, 1¼ hours) via Grimaud, Port Grimaud and Fréjus. There are four daily buses to Toulon-Hyères airport (€15; 1½ hours).

Monaco

377 / POP 32,000

Your first glimpse of this pocket-sized principality will probably make your heart sink: after all the gorgeous medieval hilltop villages, glittering beaches and secluded peninsulas of the surrounding area, Monaco's concrete high-rises and astronomic prices come as a shock.

But Monaco is beguiling. The world's second-smallest state (a smidgen bigger

RIDING A BIKE AROUND YOUR LIVING ROOM

That's what Brazilian triple-world champion Nelson Piquet famously likened driving Monaco's **Formula One Grand Prix** to! Monaco's cachet nonetheless means it's the most coveted trophy, and the narrow lanes, tortuous road layout and hairpin bends along Monaco's streets means spectators can get closer to the action than at most circuits. Buy trackside tickets (from €70/270 standing/seated) for the event, held each year in May, from the **Automobile Club de Monaco** (www.formula1monaco.com), but get in early as demand is steeper than the near-vertical streets. If you're dead keen, you can walk the 3.2km circuit; the tourist office has maps.

than the Vatican), it is as famous for its tax-haven status as for its glittering casino, sports scene (Formula One, world-famous circus festival and tennis open) and a royal family on a par with British royals for best gossip fodder. For visitors, it just means an exciting trip: from an evening at the stunning casino to a visit of the excellent Musée Océanographique to a spot of celebrity/royalty spotting, Monaco is a fun day out on the Riviera.

In terms of practicalities, Monaco is a sovereign state but has no border control. It has its own flag (red and white), national holiday (19 November) and telephone country code (377), but the official language is French and the country uses the euro even though it is not part of the European Union.

Sights & Activities

Casino de Monte Carlo CASINO

(www.casinomontecarlo.com; place du Casino; ⊙European Rooms from noon Sat & Sun, from 2pm Mon-Fri) Living out your James Bond fantasies just doesn't get any better than at Monte Carlo's monumental, richly decorated showpiece, the 1910-built casino. Admission is €10 for the European Rooms, with poker/slot machines, French roulette and *trente et quarante* (a card game), and €20 for the Private Rooms, which offer baccarat, blackjack, craps and American roulette. Jacket-and-tie dress code kicks in after 10pm. Minimum entry age for both types of rooms is 18; bring photo ID.

TOP CHOICE **Musée Océanographique de Monaco** AQUARIUM

(www.oceano.org; av St-Martin; adult/child €13/6.50; ⊙9.30am-7pm) Propped on a sheer cliff-face, this classic-looking museum was built in 1910 and houses a fantastic aquarium. The spectacular views from the rooftop terrace are especially not to be missed. Exhibit signs are translated into English, Italian and German.

Palais du Prince ROYAL PALACE

(www.palais.mc; adult/child €8/3.50; ⊙10am-6pm Apr-Sep) For a glimpse into royal life, tour the state apartments with an audioguide. The palace is what you would expect of any aristocratic abode: lavish furnishings and expensive 18th- and 19th-century art. Guards are changed outside the palace at 11.55am every day.

Cathédrale de Monaco CHURCH

(4 rue Colonel) An adoring crowd continually shuffles past Prince Rainier's and Princess Grace's graves inside the choir of Monaco's Romanesque-Byzantine cathedral. Its famous boys' choir sings Sunday Mass at 10am from September to June.

Sleeping

If your shoestring budget's fraying, stay in Nice and train it the 20 minutes to Monaco.

Ni Hôtel BOUTIQUE HOTEL €€

(☎97 97 51 51; www.nihotel.com; 1bis rue Grimaldi; s/d from €120/150; ❄📶) This uberhip design hotel makes bold use of flashy primary colours (shower walls, chairs and stairs are made of transparent coloured plastic) mixed with sobering black and white. The roof terrace is in a prime spot for evening drinks.

TRAFFIC-JAM DODGER

To skip the worst of July and August's high-season traffic, motorists get off the A8 at Le Muy (exit 35), take the D558 road through the Massif des Maures and via La Garde Freinet to Port Grimaud, park and hop aboard a **Bateaux Verts** (www.bateauxverts.com) shuttle boat (adult/child €6.50/3.50, 15 minutes) to St-Tropez.

Monaco

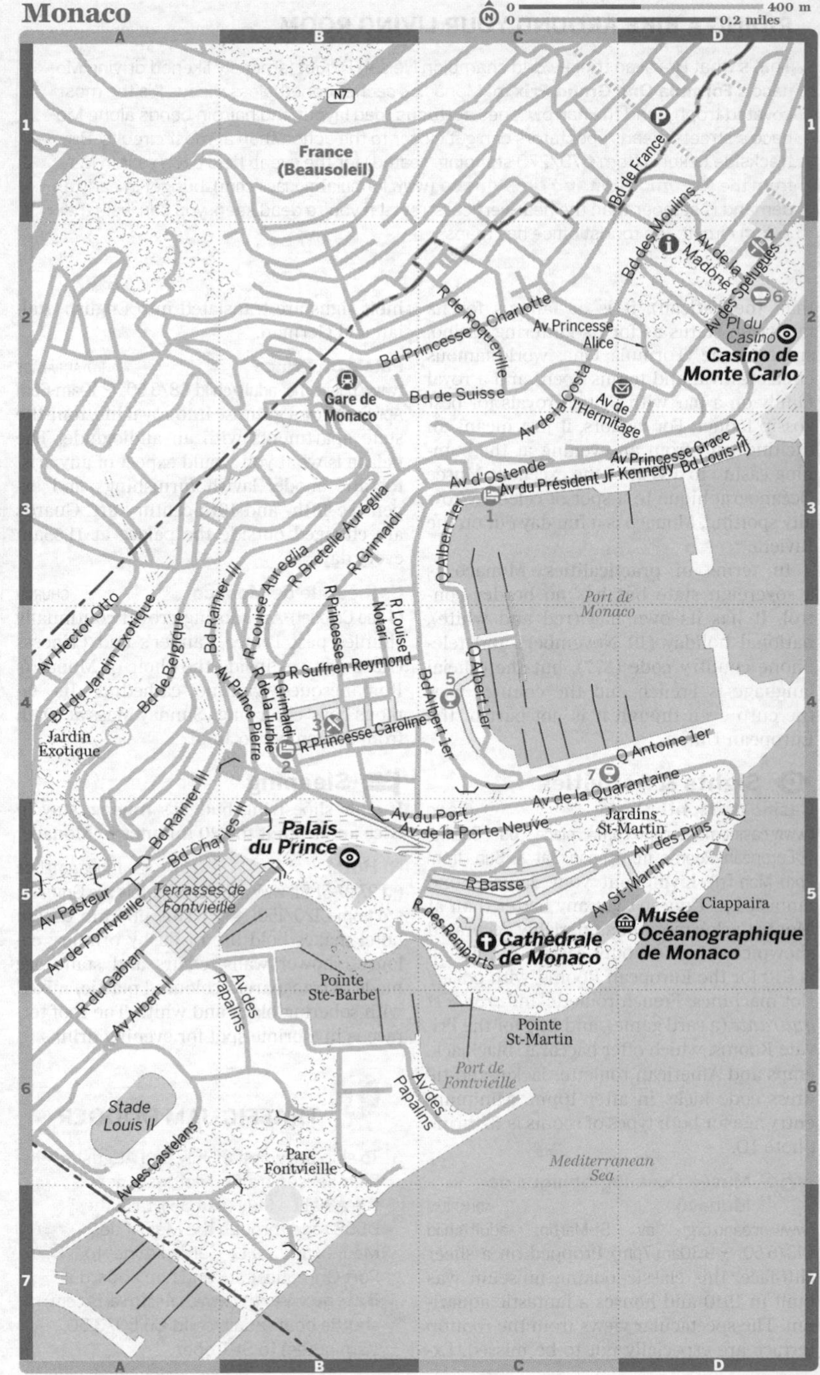
0 400 m
0 0.2 miles
France (Beausoleil)
N7
Bd de France
Bd des Moulins
Av de la Madone
Av des Spélugues
Pl du Casino
Casino de Monte Carlo
Av Princesse Alice
R de Roqueville
Bd Princesse Charlotte
Bd de Suisse
Gare de Monaco
Av de la Costa
Av de l'Hermitage
Av Princesse Grace
Bd Louis-II
Av du Président JF Kennedy
Av d'Ostende
Q Albert 1er
Port de Monaco
R Bretelle Aureglia
R Grimaldi
R Louise Aureglia
R Princesse
R Louise Notari
R Suffren Reymond
Bd Albert 1er
R Princesse Caroline
R de la Turbie
Av Prince Pierre
Bd Rainier III
Bd de Belgique
Bd du Jardin Exotique
Av Hector Otto
Jardin Exotique
Q Antoine 1er
Av de la Quarantaine
Jardins St-Martin
Av des Pins
Av du Port
Av de la Porte Neuve
Palais du Prince
Bd Charles III
Av Pasteur
Terrasses de Fontvieille
Av de Fontvieille
R Basse
R des Remparts
Av St-Martin
Ciappaira
Musée Océanographique de Monaco
Cathédrale de Monaco
R du Gabian
Av Albert II
Av des Papalins
Pointe Ste-Barbe
Pointe St-Martin
Port de Fontvieille
Stade Louis II
Av des Castelans
Parc Fontvieille
Mediterranean Sea

Monaco

Top Sights

Hôtel Miramar HOTEL €€
(☎93 30 86 48; www.miramar.monaco-hotel.com; 1 av du Président JF Kennedy; d €145; ❄📶) This 1950s-vintage seaside hotel, replete with rooftop terrace bar for lazy breakfasts, lunches and evening drinks, is a fabulous option located right by the port. Seven of the 11 rooms have fabulous balconies overlooking the yachts.

Eating & Drinking

TOP CHOICE **Le Nautique** CAFE €
(3 av Président Kennedy; mains €9-13; ⊙Mon-Sat lunch) The clubhouse of Monaco's rowing club has million-dollar views and €10 lunches, served in a sunny linoleum-floored dining room. Look for the gym equipment at street level and the inconspicuous sign marked 'Société Nautique Fédération Monégasque Sport Avion Snack Bar'.

Tip Top PIZZERIA €
(11 rue Spélugues; mains 12-24; ⊙24hr) Tip Top is where local Monégasques gather all night long for pizza, pasta and gossip.

Huit & Demi ITALIAN €€
(☎93 50 97 02; www.huit-et-demi.com; rue Princesse Caroline; mains €13-27; ⊙noon-3pm & 7-11pm Mon-Fri, 7-11pm Sat) Chic and popular, this is the hot spot to savour Italian fare amid crimson-coloured walls lined with celebrity B&W portraits. We prefer the street terrace.

Brasserie de Monaco MICROBREWERY
(www.brasseriedemonaco.com; 36 rte de la Piscine; ⊙11am-1pm Sun-Thu, 11am-3am Fri & Sat) Tourists and locals rub shoulders at Monaco's only microbrewery, which crafts rich organic ales and lager alongside tasty (pricy) antipasti plates.

Stars 'n' Bars AMERICAN
(www.starsnbars.com; 6 quai Antoine 1er; ⊙noon-2.30am, closed Mon Oct-May) Any star worth his/her reputation has partied at this American western saloon. Monstrous burgers and other food too.

Café de Paris CAFE
(www.montecarloresort.com; place du Casino; mains €17-53; ⊙7am-2am) Sip grossly overpriced coffee and limo-spot on this sprawling 300-seat terrace next to the casino.

Information

Telephone

Calls between Monaco and France are international calls. Dial 00 followed by Monaco's country code (377) when calling Monaco from France or elsewhere abroad. To phone France from Monaco, dial 00 and France's country code (33).

Tourist information

Tourist office (www.visitmonaco.com; 2a blvd des Moulins; ⊙9am-7pm Mon-Sat, 11am-1pm

THE MONACO MONARCHY

Originally from Genoa in neighbouring Italy, the Grimaldi family has ruled Monaco since 1297, except for its occupation during the French Revolution. Its independence was again recognised by France in 1860, and it's been an independent state ever since.

Since the marriage of Prince Rainier III of Monaco (r 1949–2005) to Hollywood actress Grace Kelly in 1956, Monaco's ruling family has been a non-stop feature in gossip magazines. Even Albert II, who has been prince since his father's death in 2005, hasn't escaped media scrutiny: he has two illegitimate children and no legitimate heirs, but his achievements as an athlete (he played for Monaco football team and is a judo black belt), his charity work and promotion of the arts have earned him favourable press. In mid-2010 he announced his engagement and impending marriage in 2011 to South African Olympic swimmer and former model Charlene Wittstock.

DON'T MISS

BACKPACKER PARADISE

If you're not up for the Nice–Monaco train trip, check into **Relais International de la Jeunesse Thalassa** (04 93 81 27 63; www.clajsud.fr; 2 av Gramaglia, Cap d'Ail; dm incl sheets & breakfast €18; Apr-Oct), Monaco's closest hostel, smack on the seashore in a beautiful spot on Cap d'Ail.

Sun) From mid-June to late September additional tourist-info kiosks mushroom around the harbour and train station.

Getting There & Away

Monaco's **train station** (av Prince Pierre) has frequent trains to Nice (€3.40, 20 minutes), and east to Menton (€1.90, 10 minutes) and beyond into Italy.

CORSICA

The rugged island of Corsica (Corse in French) is officially a part of France, but remains fiercely proud of its own culture, history and language. It's one of the Mediterranean's most dramatic islands, with a bevy of beautiful beaches, glitzy ports and a mountainous, maquis-covered interior to explore, as well as a wild, independent spirit all of its own.

The island has long had a love-hate relationship with the mother mainland – you'll see plenty of anti-French slogans and 'Corsicanised' road signs – but that doesn't seem to deter the millions of French tourists who descend on the island every summer. Prices skyrocket and accommodation is at a premium during the peak season between July and August, so you're much better off saving your visit for spring and autumn.

Bastia

POP 44,000

Filled with heart, soul and character, the ramshackle old port of Bastia is a good surprise. Sure, it might not measure up to Ajaccio's sexy style or the architectural appeal of Bonifacio, but this lived-in, well-loved city is what modern-day Corsica is all about. Allow yourself at least a day to climb narrow alleyways from the seething old harbour to the dramatic 16th-century citadel, currently undergoing one of the largest (and costliest) renovation projects in the island's history.

Sights & Activities

Even by Corsican standards, Bastia is a pocket-sized city. The 19th-century central square of **place St-Nicholas** sprawls along the seafront between the ferry port and harbour. Named after the patron saint of sailors – a nod to Corsica's seagoing heritage – the square is lined with plane trees, busy cafes and a **statue of Napoleon Bonaparte**, Corsica's famous son.

A network of narrow lanes leads south towards the old port and the neighbourhood of **Terra Vecchia**, a muddle of crumbling apartments and balconied blocks. Further south is the Vieux Port (Old Port), ringed by pastel-coloured tenements and buzzy brasseries, as well as the twin-towered **Église St-Jean Baptiste**. The best views of the harbour are from the **Jetée du Dragon** (Dragon Jetty) or from the hillside park of **Jardin Romieu** (Romieu Garden), reached via a twisting staircase from the waterfront. Behind the garden looms Bastia's sunbaked **citadel**, built from the 15th to 17th centuries as a stronghold for the city's Genoese masters. One of the citadel's landmarks, the **Palais des Gouverneurs** (Governors' Palace; place du Donjon) now houses Bastia's top-notch local history museum, **Musée d'Histoire de Bastia** (€5; 10am-6pm Tue-Sun).

Sleeping

Hôtel Central HOTEL €€
(04 95 31 71 12; www.centralhotel.fr; 3 rue Miot; d €85-100;) This family-run number in a stately 19th-century building has 21 rooms wrapped with a retro feel.

Hôtel Les Voyageurs HOTEL €€
(04 95 34 90 80; www.hotel-lesvoyageurs.com; 9 av Maréchal Sébastiani; s €75-95, d €90-115;) What sets The Travellers apart is the buttermilk walls, modern-art prints and blindingly white bathrooms that contrast sharply with the more austere facade.

Eating

You'll find endless restaurants around the Vieux Port and quai des Martyrs.

Chez Vincent TRADITIONAL CORSICAN €€
(04 95 31 62 50; 12 rue St-Michel; mains €9-22; Mon-Fri, dinner Sat) Corsican staples and wood-fired pizzas are what beckon here. The

assiette du bandit Corse (€18.50) features a smorgasbord of local nosh, including stewed veal chestnuts, cured meats, ewe's-milk cheese, wild boar pâté and roast *figatellu* (liver sausage).

A Casarella MODERN CORSICAN €€
(☎04 95 32 02 32; 6 rue Ste-Croix; mains €15-28; ⏲Tue-Sun) Tuck into innovative dishes built from organic produce on Bastia's loveliest terrace, poised above the port in the citadel, twinkling harbour lights below.

Information

Tourist office (www.bastia-tourisme.com; place St-Nicolas; ⏲8.30am-8pm Apr-Sep, shorter hr rest of year)

Getting There & Away

Air

Aéroport Bastia-Poretta (www.bastia.aeroport.fr) is 24km south of the city. Buses (€8.50, 30 minutes, 10 daily) depart from outside the Préfecture building; timetables are posted at the stop.

Boat

Bastia's two **ferry terminals** are connected by a free **shuttle bus**. All the ferry companies have information offices in the southern terminal, which usually open for same-day ticket sales a couple of hours before each sailing.

Ferries sail to/from Marseille, Toulon and Nice on mainland France, and several ports in Italy.

Corsica Ferries (www.corsicaferries.com; 15bis rue Chanoine Leschi)

La Méridionale (www.lameridionale.fr)

Moby Lines (www.moby.it; 4 rue du Commandant Luce de Casabianca)

SNCM (www.sncm.fr; inside Southern Terminal)

Bus

Beaux Voyages (☎04 95 65 11 35) Buses to Île Rousse (€13, 90 minutes) and Calvi (€16, 2½ hours) daily except Sunday. Buses leave from the train station.

Eurocorse (☎04 95 31 73 76) Buses to Ajaccio (€21, three hours) via Corte (€11.50, two hours) twice daily except on Sundays from Bastia's 'bus station', a car park north of place St-Nicholas.

Autocars Cortenais (☎04 95 46 02 12) Travels to Corte (€11, two hours) once daily on Monday, Wednesday and Friday. Buses leave from the train station.

Les Rapides Bleus (☎04 95 31 03 79; 1 av Maréchal Sébastiani) Buses leave from in front of the post office to Porto-Vecchio (€22, three hours) twice daily except Sundays and holidays.

Train

From the **train station** (av Maréchal Sébastiani) main destinations include Ajaccio (€25, 3¾ hours, four daily) via Corte (1¾ hours), and Calvi (three hours, three or four daily) via Île Rousse.

MONEY MATTERS

Many restaurants and hotels in Corsica don't accept credit cards, and *chambres d'hôtes* (B&Bs) hardly ever: those that do quite frequently refuse card payments for amounts typically less than €15.

Calvi

POP 5600

Basking between the fiery orange bastions of its 15th-century citadel and the glittering waters of a moon-shaped bay, Calvi feels closer to the chichi sophistication of a Côte d'Azur resort than a historic Corsican port – and has sky-high prices to match. Palatial yachts dock along its harbourside, while above the quay the watchtowers of the town's Genoese stronghold stand guard, proffering sweeping views inland to Monte Cinto (2706m). Visit in the shoulder seasons, when you can stroll the citadel's cobbled alleys in relative peace and quiet.

The **tourist office** (☎04 95 65 16 67; www.balagne-corsica.com; Port de Plaisance; ⏲9am-noon & 3-6.30pm Jul & Aug, 9am-noon & 2-6pm Mon-Sat May, Jun, Sep & Oct, 9am-noon & 2-6pm Mon-Fri Nov-Apr) is opposite the marina.

Calvi's 15th-century **citadel** – also known as the Haute Ville (Upper City) – sits on a rocky promontory above the Basse Ville (Lower Town). The **Palais des Gouverneurs** (place d'Armes), once the seat of power for the Genoese administration, now serves as a base for the French Foreign Legion. Uphill from Caserne Sampiero is the 13th-century **Église St-Jean Baptiste**, rebuilt in 1570.

Calvi's stellar 4km **beach** begins at the marina and runs east around the Golfe de Calvi. Rent out kayaks and windsurfing gear from **Calvi Nautique Club** (www.calvinc.org; Base Nautique, Port de Plaisance; ⏲May-Oct).

Sleeping

Most hotels shut in winter.

DON'T MISS

TRAMWAY DE LA BALAGNE

The best way to dip into the glittering beaches and rocky coves lacing the Balagne coast between Calvi and Île Rousse is aboard the clattering **Tramway de la Balagne** – an unforgettable train journey (€5.50, 45 minutes, up to eight daily Easter to September). Nicknamed the *trinighellu* (the trembler), the dinky little train stops at 15 stations (all by request only) en route between the two towns; for sand, leave the train at Algajola or Plage de Bodri, the last stop before Île Rousse.

Hôtel Belvedere HOTEL €€
(☎04 95 65 01 25; www.resa-hotels-calvi.com; place Christophe Colomb; d €70-120; ❄📶) With a top-town position striking distance from the citadel and 24 comfortable yet smallish rooms, the Viewpoint won't disappoint. Rooms on the 3rd floor gloat at top-notch views of the Golfe de Calvi.

Hôtel du Centre HOTEL €
(☎04 95 65 02 01; 14 rue d'Alsace Lorraine; d without bathroom €32-47; ⊙Jun-Sep) Not the most charming choice – furnishings are seriously dated – but at this price and in such a brilliant location it would be churlish to quibble.

Camping La Pinède CAMPING GROUND €
(☎04 95 65 17 80; www.camping-calvi.com; rte de la Pinède; campsites €9; ⊙Apr-Oct; 🏊) Handy for Calvi town and the beach.

Eating

Calvi's quayside is chock-a-block with restaurants, quality variable.

TOP CHOICE **Emile's** GASTRONOMIC €€€
(☎04 95 65 09 60; quai Landry; mains €38-46; ⊙Apr-Oct) This top-end darling of central Calvi overlooks the quayside. If you've never tried grilled lobster, this is *the* place to do it, washed down with an ice-cold bottle of white.

Le Tire-Bouchon BISTRO €€
(☎04 95 65 24 41; rue Clémenceau; mains €12-20; ⊙Jun-Sep, closed Wed Apr, May & Oct) This buzzy option is a gourmand's playpen. Perch yourself on the balcony overlooking the crowds milling below and order from the chalkboard: veal stew perhaps, or tagliatelle with broccius, a cheese platter and a luscious local tipple.

Getting There & Away

Air

Aéroport Calvi Ste-Catherine (www.calvi.aeroport.fr), 7km southeast, has no airport bus: allow €20-odd for a **taxi** (☎04 95 65 03 10).

Boat

SNCM and Corsica Ferries run boats to/from Nice from Calvi's **ferry terminal** (quai Landry).

Bus

Les Beaux Voyages (☎04 95 65 15 02; place de la Porteuse d'Eau) runs daily buses to Bastia (€16, 2½ hours) via Île Rousse (€4, 15 minutes).

Train

Calvi's **train station** connects with Ajaccio (five hours, two daily) via Corte (€15.10, four hours two daily) and Bastia (three hours), both with change of train in Ponte Leccia.

Ajaccio

POP 52,880

With its sweeping bay and buzzing centre replete with mellow-toned buildings, cafes and yacht-packed marina, Ajaccio, Corsica's main metropolis, is all class and seduction. Looming over this elegant port city is the spectre of Corsica's great general: Napoleon Bonaparte was born here in 1769 and the city is dotted with statues and museums relating to the diminutive dictator (starting with the main street in Ajaccio, cours Napoléon).

Sights & Activities

Musée National de la Maison Bonaparte MUSEUM
(rue St-Charles; adult/child €5/3.50; ⊙2-5.50pm Mon, 9-11.30am & 2-5.30pm Tue-Sun Apr-Sep, 2-4.15pm Mon, 10-11.30am & 2-4.15pm Tue-Sun Oct-Mar) The Napoleonic saga begins here, the grand house where Napoléon spent the first nine years of his life. View memorabilia of the emperor and his siblings, including a glass medallion containing a lock of his hair.

Palais Fesch – Musée des Beaux-Arts ART MUSEUM
(www.musee-fesch.com; adult/child €8/5; 50-52 rue du Cardinal Fesch; ⊙10.30-5pm Mon, Wed & Sat, noon-5pm Thu, Fri & Sun) Established by

Ajaccio

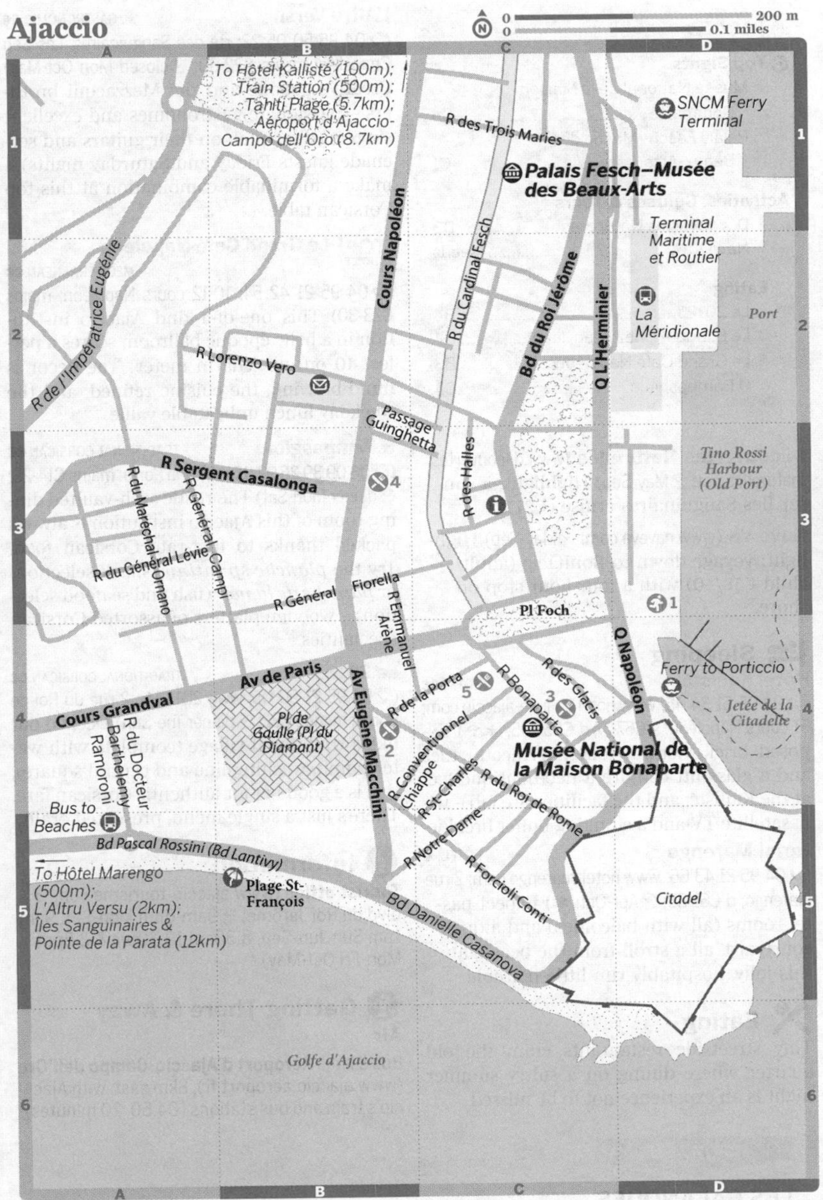

Napoléon's uncle, this Corsica must-see has France's largest collection of Italian paintings outside the Louvre. Don't miss Botticelli's *La Vierge à l'Enfant Soutenu par un Ange* (Mother & Child Supported by an Angel).

Boat Trips TOURS

Boat trips around the Golfe d'Ajaccio and Îles Sanguinaires (€27), and excursions to the Scandola Nature Reserve (adult/child €50/35), depart daily from the quay opposite place Foch.

Ajaccio

Top Sights

Activities, Courses & Tours

Eating

Découvertes Naturelles (www.decouvertes-naturelles.net; May-Sep) Highlight: a sunset Îles Sanguinaires cruise (€27).

Nave Va (www.naveva.com; May-Sep) Highlight: voyage down to Bonifacio (adult/child €58/40) with a four-hour stop on shore.

Sleeping

Hôtel Kallisté HOTEL €€
(04 95 51 34 45; www.hotel-kalliste-ajaccio.com; 51 cours Napoléon; s €67-77, d €85-105;) Exposed brick, neutral tones, terracotta tiles and a glass lift conjure a neo-boutique feel at the Kallisté, and the facilities are fab – wi-fi, satellite TV and a stonking buffet brekkie.

Hôtel Marengo HOTEL €
(04 95 21 43 66; www.hotel-marengo.com; 2 rue Marengo; d €61-83; Apr-Oct;) Expect pastel rooms (all with balconies) and a quiet courtyard, all a stroll from the beach, at this jolly, hospitably run little bolthole.

Eating

Tiny streetside restaurants cram the old quarter where dining on a sultry summer night is an experience not to be missed.

L'Altru Versu GASTRONOMIC €€
(04 95 50 05 22; rte des Sanguinaires, Les Sep Chapelles; mains €22-30; closed Mon Oct-May) Creative cuisine and the Mezzacqui brothers – passionate gastronomes and excellent singers (they hitch on their guitars and serenade guests Friday and Saturday nights) – make a formidable combination at this top Corsican table.

TOP CHOICE **Le Grand Café Napoléon** MEDITERRANEAN €€
(04 95 21 42 54; 10-12 cours Napoléon; mains €23-30) This one-of-a-kind Ajaccio institution in a belle époque ballroom scores a perfect 10 on our 'charm meter'. The decor is mind-blowing, the cuisine refined, and the weekday lunch unbeatable value.

U Pampasgiolu TRADITIONAL CORSICAN €€
(06 09 39 26 92; 15 rue de la Porta; mains €14-28; dinner Mon-Sat) The rustic arch-vaulted dining room of this Ajaccio institution is always packed thanks to first-rate Corsican food. Try the *planche spuntinu* (snack selection) or *planche de la mer* (fish and seafood selection) – wooden platters of assorted Corsican specialities.

Le 20123 TRADITIONAL CORSICAN €€
(04 95 21 50 05; www.20123.fr; 2 rue du Roi de Rome; menus €32; dinner Tue-Sun) Decked out like a traditional village (complete with water pump, washing line and central square), this is a good bet for authentic Corsican fare. There's just a single menu, presented orally.

Information

Tourist office (www.ajaccio-tourisme.com; 3 blvd du Roi Jérôme; 9am-6pm Mon-Sat, 9am-1pm Sun Jun-Sep, 8.30am-12.30pm & 2-5pm Mon-Fri Oct-May)

Getting There & Away

Air

Bus 8 links **Aéroport d'Ajaccio-Campo dell'Oro** (www.ajaccio.aeroport.fr), 8km east, with Ajaccio's train and bus stations (€4.50, 20 minutes).

WORTH A TRIP

LES CALANQUES

One of Corsica's most iconic natural sights, **Les Calanques de Piana**, 85km south of Calvi, are a spectacular landscape of flaming-red granite cliffs and spiky outcrops, carved into bizarre shapes by the sea and wind. Vivid green pine and chestnut forests on less-rocky areas contrast dramatically with the technicoloured granite.

Several walking trails wend through these dramatic rock formations, many starting near the Pont de Mezzanu road bridge, 3km from **Piana** (www.otpiana.com) along the D81.

WORTH A TRIP

RÉSERVE NATURELLE DE SCANDOLA

There's no vehicle access or footpath into the magnificent **Réserve Naturelle de Scandola** – Corsica's only Unesco-protected marine reserve, midway between Ajaccio and the coastal town of **Porto** – so the only way to get up close is by sea. From April to October several companies based on the quayside at Porto's marina sail through its shimmering sapphire waters to the base of its cliffs. Expect to pay around €40 for the privilege.

Predictably, this is paradise for **diving** and **snorkelling**, and several companies organise introductory dives for beginners (from €45) and snorkelling trips (€15) to the fringe of Scandola. At Porto's quay, try diving outfits **Centre de Plongée du Golfe de Porto** (www.plongeeporto.com), **Génération Bleue** (www.generation-bleue.com) or **Méditerranée Porto Sub** (www.plongeecose.fr).

Boat

Boats to/from Toulon, Nice and Marseille depart from/arrive at **Terminal Maritime et Routier** (quai l'Herminier):

Corsica Ferries (www.corsicaferries.com)

La Méridionale (www.lameridionale.fr)

SNCM (www.sncm.fr)

Bus

Local bus companies have kiosks inside the ferry terminal building.

Autocars Ceccaldi (☎04 95 22 41 99) Travels to Porto (2½ hours, two daily, no Sunday buses Sep-Jun) via Piana (1½ hours).

Eurocorse (☎04 95 21 06 30) Travels to Bastia (three hours, two daily) via Corte (two hours), and Bonifacio (four hours, one or two daily).

Train

From the **train station** (place de la Gare):

BASTIA (four hours, three to four daily)

CALVI (five hours, two daily; change at Ponte Leccia).

CORTE (two hours, three to four daily)

Bonifacio

POP 2700

With its glittering harbour, creamy-white cliffs and stout citadel, this dazzling port is an essential stop. Just a short hop from Sardinia, Bonifacio has a distinctly Italianate feel: sun-bleached town houses, washing lines and murky chapels cram the old citadel, while down below on the harbourside, brasseries and boat-kiosks tout their wares to the droves of day trippers.

A steep staircase links the harbour with the citadel's old gateway, the **Porte de Gênes**, complete with its original 16th-century drawbridge. Inside the gateway is the 13th-century **Bastion l'Étendard**, which houses a small historical museum exploring Bonifacio's past. Along the ramparts, fabulous panoramic views unfold from **place du Marché** and **place Manichella**. From the citadel, the **Escalier du Roi d'Aragon** (King of Aragon's stairway; admission €2.50; ⌚9am-7pm Apr-Oct) staggers down the cliff.

Boat trips to the remote beaches and gin-clear waters of the offshore **Îles Lavezzi** (Lavezzi Islands) run from the quayside. Bonifacio is surrounded by beaches, including **Piantarella** (popular with windsurfers) and shingly **Calalonga**. The horseshoe bay of **Rondinara** is about 18km northeast, and tree-fringed **Palombaggia** is about 30km northeast near Porto-Vecchio.

Sleeping

Hôtel des Étrangers HOTEL €

(☎04 95 73 01 09; www.hoteldesetrangers.fr; av Sylvère Bohn; d €46-65; ⌚Apr–mid-Oct; ❄📶) Bonifacio's only budget option is the 'Foreigners' Hotel'. Spick-and-span rooms, all with tiled floors, clean bathrooms and simple colour schemes almost make up for the road racket.

Hôtel Le Colomba HOTEL €€

(☎04 95 73 73 44; www.hotel-bonifacio-corse.fr; rue Simon Varsi; d €100-160; ⌚Mar-Nov; ❄📶) A not-quite-boutique hotel in a picturesque side street, in the heart of the citadel. Wrought-iron bedsteads and country fabrics in some rooms, carved bedheads and chequerboard tiles in others.

Eating

Swish terrace restaurants pack the quayside, but the food isn't always as fancy as the ambience suggests.

DON'T MISS

THE PERFECT SNAPSHOT

If you're after that perfect picture, don't miss the fantastic, three-hour return walk along cliffs from Bonifacio to **Phare de Pertusato** (Pertusato Lighthouse), from where the seamless views of the cliffs, Îles Lavezzi, Bonifacio and Sardinia will sweep you off your feet. The starting point (signposted) is just to the left of the sharp bend on the hill up to Bonifacio's citadel. Complete the experience with lunch at Domaine de Licetto.

Cantina Doria CORSICAN €
(☎04 95 73 50 49; 27 rue Doria; mains €10-14; ⊙Apr-Oct) This is *the* place in Bonifacio for Corsican country food, which is served at wooden benches amid copper pots, rustic tools and dented signs. Try typical *lasagnes au fromage Corse* (lasagne with Corsican cheese) or *aubergines à la Bonifacienne* (aubergines stuffed with breadcrumbs and cheese), and you'll leave patting your tummy contentedly.

Domaine de Licetto TRADITIONAL CORSICAN €€
(☎04 95 73 03 59; rte du Phare; menus €36; ⊙dinner Mon-Sat Apr-Jul & Sep–mid-Oct, daily Aug) For the authentic Corsican experience this restaurant is hard to beat. The five-course menu is a culinary feast of local ingredients (suckling lamb, cheese-stuffed eggplant...) produced by small-scale farmers. Find it in the maquis on the way to Phare de Pertusato.

Kissing Pigs MODERN CORSICAN €€
(☎04 95 73 56 09; quai Banda del Ferro; mains €8-15) Diners pack into this cosy wine bar by the harbour, famed for its platters of Corsican meats and cheeses. The wine list and swinging sausages are also hits.

Information

Tourist office (www.bonifacio.fr; 2 rue Fred Scamaroni; ⊙9am-8pm May–mid-Oct, 9am-noon & 2-6pm Mon-Fri mid-Oct–Apr)

Getting There & Away

Air

A taxi into town from **Aéroport de Figari** (www.figari.aeroport.fr), 21km north, costs about €40 (no public transport).

Boat

Saremar (www.saremar.it, in Italian) and **Moby Lines** (www.moby.it) sail between Bonifacio and Santa Teresa di Gallura (on the neighbouring island of Sardinia) in summer.

Bus

Eurocorse (☎04 95 70 13 83) runs buses to Porto-Vecchio (30 minutes), with onward connections to Ajaccio (four hours).

UNDERSTAND FRANCE

France Today

Presidential elections in 2007 ushered in big change for France in the shape of Nicolas Sarkozy (b 1955) of Chirac's centre-right party UMP *(Union pour un Mouvement Populaire)*. Dynamic, ambitious and far from media-shy, Sarko (as he was quickly dubbed by the popular press) wooed punters with big talk of job creation, lower taxes, crime crackdown and help for France's substantial immigrant population. Yet controversy dogged Sarko's first period in office, infamously marked by him splitting with his second wife and swiftly wedding sexy Italian chanteuse and multimillionaire supermodel Carla Bruni.

Beyond Sarkozy's high-profile private life, there have been major political developments too, including the banning of smoking in public places (2007) and the ratification of a new EU treaty (2008). More controversially, the wearing of crucifixes, the Islamic headscarf and other overtly religious symbols has been banned in state schools since 2004 and the wearing of face-covering veils in public since 2010 – much to the consternation of France's notable Muslim community (around 10% of the population).

For a few fleeting months in 2009 France joined much of the rest of Europe in recession and by mid-2010 the unemployment rate was hovering at a disconcerting 10%. Hard-line attempts were made the same year to raise the retirement age from 60 to 62 and full state pension age from 65 to 67, thereby reforming a pension system unchanged since 1982, which simply sparked widespread horror and a series of national strikes and protests.

Sarko's honeymoon was clearly over.

History

Prehistory

Neanderthals were the first to live in France (about 90,000 to 40,000 BC). Cro-Magnons followed 35,000 years ago and left behind cave paintings and engravings, especially around the Vézère Valley in the Dordogne. Neolithic people (about 7500 to 4000 years ago) created France's incredible menhirs (standing stones) and dolmens (megalithic tombs), especially in Brittany.

The Celtic Gauls arrived between 1500 and 500 BC, and were superseded by the Romans for around five centuries after Julius Caesar took control around 52 BC, until the Franks and Alemanii overran the country.

The Frankish Merovingian and Carolingian dynasties ruled from the 5th to the 10th century AD. In 732 Charles Martel defeated the Moors, preventing France from falling under Muslim rule. Martel's grandson, Charlemagne (742–814), extended the power and boundaries of the kingdom and was crowned Holy Roman Emperor in 800.

The Early French Kings

The tale of William the Conqueror's invasion of England in 1066 is recorded in the Bayeux Tapestry, sowing the seeds for a fierce rivalry between France and England that peaked with the Hundred Years War (1337–1453).

Following the occupation of Paris by the English-allied dukes of Burgundy, John Plantagenet was made regent of France on behalf of England's King Henry VI in 1422. Less than a decade later he was crowned king at Paris' Notre Dame cathedral. Luckily for the French, a 17-year-old warrior called Jeanne d'Arc (Joan of Arc) came along in 1429. She persuaded Charles VII that she had a divine mission from God to expel the English from France. Following her capture by the Burgundians and subsequent sale to the English in 1430, Joan was convicted of witchcraft and heresy and burned at the stake in Rouen, on the site now marked by the city's cathedral.

The arrival of Italian Renaissance culture during the reign of François I (r 1515–47) ushered in some of France's finest chateaux, especially in the Loire Valley.

The period from 1562 to 1598 was one of the bloodiest periods in French history. Ideological disagreement between the Huguenots (French Protestants) and the Catholic monarchy escalated into the French Wars of Religion.

The Sun King

Louis XIV, Le Roi Soleil (the Sun King), ascended the throne in 1643, and spent the next 60 years in a series of bloody wars. He also constructed the fabulous palace at Versailles.

Louis XV ascended to the throne in 1715 and shifted the royal court back to Paris. As the 18th century progressed, the ancien régime became increasingly out of step with the needs of the country. Antiestablishment and anticlerical ideas expressed by Voltaire, Rousseau and Montesquieu further threatened the royal regime.

Revolution to Republic

Social and economic crisis marked the 18th century. Discontent among the French populace turned violent when a Parisian mob stormed the prison at Bastille. France was declared a constitutional monarchy and Louis XVI was publicly guillotined in January 1793 on Paris' place de la Concorde.

The Reign of Terror between September 1793 and July 1794 saw religious freedoms revoked, churches closed, cathedrals turned into 'Temples of Reason' and thousands beheaded. In the chaos a dashing young Corsican general named Napoleon Bonaparte (1769–1821) stepped from the shadows.

In 1799 Napoleon assumed power and in 1804 he was crowned emperor of France at Notre Dame. Napoleon waged several wars in which France gained control over most of Europe. Two years later, Allied armies entered Paris, exiled Napoleon to Elba and restored the French throne at the Congress of Vienna (1814–15).

In 1815 Napoleon escaped, entering Paris on 20 May. His glorious 'Hundred Days' back in power ended with the Battle of Waterloo and his exile to the island of St Helena, where he died in 1821.

Second Republic to Second Empire

The subsequent years were marked by civil strife and political unrest, with monarchists and revolutionaries vying for power. Louis-Philippe (r 1830–48), a constitutional monarch, was chosen by parliament but ousted by the 1848 Revolution. The Second Republic was established and Napoleon's nephew, Louis Napoleon Bonaparte, was elected president. But in 1851 Louis Napoleon led a coup d'état and proclaimed himself Emperor Napoleon III of the Second Empire (1852–70).

France enjoyed significant economic growth. Paris was transformed under urban planner Baron Haussmann (1809–91), who created the 12 huge boulevards radiating from the Arc de Triomphe. But Napoleon III embroiled France in various catastrophic conflicts, including the Crimean War (1853–56) and the Franco-Prussian War (1870–71), which ended with Prussia taking the emperor prisoner. Upon hearing the news, defiant Parisian masses took to the streets demanding a republic be declared – enter the Third Republic.

The World Wars

The 20th century was marked by two of the bloodiest conflicts in the nation's history, beginning with the Great War (WWI). The northeastern part of France bore the brunt of the devastating trench warfare between Allied and German forces: 1.3 million French soldiers were killed and almost one million injured, and the battlefields of the Somme have become powerful symbols of the unimaginable costs and ultimate futility of modern warfare.

After the war, the Treaty of Versailles imposed heavy reparations on the defeated nations, including the return of Alsace-Lorraine, which the French had lost to Germany in 1871. These punitive terms sowed the seeds for future unrest, when the fanatic leader Adolf Hitler rose to power and promised to restore the German nation's pride, power and territory. Despite constructing a lavish series of defences (the so-called Maginot Line) along its German border, France was rapidly overrun and surrendered in June 1940. The occupying Germans divided France into an Occupied Zone (in the north and west) and a puppet state in the south, centring on the spa town of Vichy.

The British Army was driven from France during the Battle of Dunkirk in 1940. Four years later, on 6 June 1944, Allied forces stormed the coastline of Normandy in the D-Day landings. The bloody Battle of Normandy followed and Paris was liberated on 25 August.

The Fourth Republic

In the first postwar election in 1945, the wartime leader of the Free French, Général Charles de Gaulle, was appointed head of the government, but quickly sensed that the tide was turning against him and in 1946 he resigned.

Progress rebuilding France's shattered economy and infrastructure was slow. By 1947 France was forced to turn to the USA for loans as part of the Marshall Plan to rebuild Europe. The economy gathered steam in the 1950s but the decade marked the end of French colonialism in Vietnam and in Algeria. The Algerian war of independence (1954–62) was particularly brutal, characterised by torture and massacre meted out to nationalist Algerians.

The Modern Era

De Gaulle assumed the presidency again in 1958, followed by his prime minister Georges Pompidou (in power 1969–74), Valéry Giscard d'Estaing (in power 1974–81), François Mitterrand (in power 1981–95), and the centre-right president Jacques Chirac, who (among other things) oversaw the country's adoption of the euro in 1999.

Arts

Literature

France has made huge contributions to European literature. The philosophical work of Voltaire (1694–1778) and Jean-Jacques Rousseau dominated the 18th century. A century later the poems and novels of Victor Hugo – *Les Misérables* and *Notre Dame de Paris* (The Hunchback of Notre Dame) among them – became landmarks of French Romanticism.

In 1857 two literary landmarks were published: *Madame Bovary* by Gustave Flaubert (1821–80) and Charles Baudelaire's collection of poems, *Les Fleurs du Mal* (The Flowers of Evil). Émile Zola (1840–1902) meanwhile strove to convert novel-writing from an art to a science in his series *Les Rougon-Macquart*.

Symbolists Paul Verlaine (1844–96) and Stéphane Mallarmé (1842–98) aimed to express mental states through their poetry. Verlaine's poems, with those of Arthur Rimbaud (1854–91), are seen as French literature's first modern poems.

After WWII, the existentialist movement developed around the lively debates of Jean-Paul Sartre (1905–80), Simone de Beauvoir (1908–86) and Albert Camus (1913–60) over coffee and cigarettes in Paris' Left Bank cafes.

Contemporary authors include Françoise Sagan, Pascal Quignard, Anna Gavalda, Emmanuel Carrère, Stéphane Bourguignon and Martin Page, whose novel *Comment Je Suis Devenu Stupide* (How I Became Stupid) explores a 25-year-old Sorbonne student's methodical attempt to become stupid. No French writer better delves into the mind, mood and politics of the country's ethnic population than Faïza Guène (b 1985; www.faiza-guene-lesgensdubalto.fr), the latest literary sensation born and bred on a ghetto housing estate outside Paris.

Cinema

Cinematographic pioneers the Lumière brothers shot the world's first-ever motion picture in March 1895 and French film flourished in the following decades. The post-WWII *nouvelle vague* (new wave) filmmakers, such as Claude Chabrol, Jean-Luc Godard and François Truffaut, pioneered the advent of modern cinema, using fractured narratives, documentary camerawork and highly personal subjects.

Big-name stars, slick production values and nostalgia were the dominant motifs in the 1980s, as filmmakers switched to costume dramas, comedies and 'heritage movies'. Claude Berri's depiction of prewar Provence in *Jean de Florette* (1986), Jean-Paul Rappeneau's *Cyrano de Bergerac* (1990) and *Bon Voyage* (2003), set in 1940s Paris – all starring France's best-known (and biggest-nosed) actor, Gérard Depardieu – found huge audiences in France and abroad.

La Haine (1995), directed by Mathieu Kassovitz, documents the bleak reality of life in the Parisian suburbs. At the other end of the spectrum, massive international hit *Le Fabuleux Destin de Amélie Poulain* (*Amélie;* 2001) is a feel-good story about a Parisian do-gooder. Or watch *Bienvenue chez les Ch'tis* (2008), another big box-office hit of recent years, which debunks grim stereotypes about the industrialised regions of the north of France with high jinks and hilarity.

Music

French musical luminaries Charles Gounod (1818–93), César Franck (1822–90) and *Carmen* creator Georges Bizet (1838–75) among them were a dime a dozen in the 19th century. Claude Debussy (1862–1918) revolutionised classical music with *Prélude à l'Après-Midi d'un Faune* (Prelude to the Afternoon of a Faun); while Maurice Ravel (1875–1937) peppered his work, including *Boléro,* with sensuousness and tonal colour.

Jazz was the hot sound of 1920s Paris with the likes of Sidney Bechet, Kenny Clarke, Bud Powell and Dexter Gordon filling clubs in the capital.

The *chanson française,* a folkish tradition dating from medieval troubadours, was revived in the 1930s by Edith Piaf and Charles Trenet. In the 1950s Paris' Left Bank cabarets nurtured *chansonniers* (cabaret singers) like Léo Ferré, Georges Brassens, Claude Nougaro, Jacques Brel and the much-loved crooner Serge Gainsbourg.

Electronic music (think Daft Punk and Air) has a global following, while French rap never stops breaking new ground, pioneered in the 1990s by MC Solaar and continued by young French rappers such as Disiz La Peste, Monsieur R, Rohff (www.roh2f.com), the trio Malekal Morte, Marseille's home-grown IAM (www.iam.tm.fr) and five-piece band KDD from Toulouse. Cyprus-born Diam's (short for *'diamant'* meaning 'diamond'; www.diams-lesite.com), who arrived in Paris aged seven, is one of France's few female rappers, while Brittany's Manau (www.manau.com) trio engagingly fuses hip hop with traditional Celtic sounds.

French pop music has evolved massively since the 1960s *yéyé* (imitative rock) days of Johnny Hallyday. Particularly strong is world music, from Algerian raï and other North African music (artists include Natacha Atlas) to Senegalese *mbalax* (Youssou N'Dour) and West Indian zouk (Kassav, Zouk Machine). Musicians who combine many of these elements include Paris-born Manu Chao (www.manuchao.net) and Franco-Algerian Rachid Taha (www.rachidtaha.fr).

No artist has cemented France's reputation in world music more than Paris-born, Franco-Congolese rapper, slam poet and three-time Victoire de la Musique-award winner, Abd al Malik (www.abdalmalik.fr). Hot on the heels of his first two albums, *Gibraltar* (2006) and *Dante* (2008) – both classics – is his fabulous *Château Rouge* (2010).

Architecture

Southern France is the place to find France's Gallo-Roman legacy, especially at the Pont du Gard, and the amphitheatres in Nîmes and Arles.

THE MENU

In France a menu is not the card given to you in restaurants listing what's cooking (that's called *la carte* in French). Rather, *un menu* is a pre-set, three-course meal at a fixed price – by far the best-value dining around and something that is available in 99% of restaurants.

Lunch *menus* often include a glass of wine and/or coffee, and are a great way of dining at otherwise unaffordable gastronomic addresses.

All but top-end places often have *une formule* on offer too, a cheaper lunchtime option usually comprising the plat du jour (dish of the day) plus starter or dessert.

Several centuries later, architects adopted Gallo-Roman motifs in masterpieces such as Poitier's Église Notre Dame la Grande.

Impressive 12th-century Gothic structures include Avignon's pontifical palace, Chartres' cathedral, and of course, Notre Dame in Paris.

Art nouveau (1850–1910) combined iron, brick, glass and ceramics in new ways. See it for yourself at Paris' metro entrances and in the Musée d'Orsay.

Contemporary buildings to look out for include the once-reviled (now much-revered) Centre Pompidou and IM Pei's glass pyramid at the Louvre. In the provinces, notable buildings include Strasbourg's European Parliament, a 1920s art deco swimming pool-turned-art museum in Lille, and the stunning new Centre Pompidou in Metz.

Painting

An extraordinary flowering of artistic talent occurred in 19th- and 20th-century France. The Impressionists, who endeavoured to capture the ever-changing aspects of reflected light, included Edouard Manet, Claude Monet, Edgar Degas, Camille Pisarro, and Pierre-Auguste Renoir. They were followed by the likes of Paul Cézanne (who lived in Aix-en-Provence) and Paul Gauguin, as well as the fauvist Henry Matisse (a resident of Nice on the French Riviera) and cubists including Spanish-born Pablo Picasso and Georges Braque (1882–1963).

Environment

The Land

Hexagon-shaped France is the largest country in Europe after Russia and Ukraine. The country's 3200km-long coastline ranges from chalk cliffs (Normandy) to fine sand (Atlantic coast) and pebbly beaches (Mediterranean coast).

Europe's highest peak, Mont Blanc (4810m), crowns the French Alps along France's eastern border, while the rugged Pyrenees define France's 450km-long border with Spain, peaking at 3404m. The country's major river systems include the Garonne, Rhône, Seine, and France's longest river, the Loire.

Wildlife

France has more mammals (around 110) than any other country in Europe. Couple this with 363 bird species, 30 types of amphibian, 36 varieties of reptile and 72 kinds of fish, and wildlife-watchers are in paradise. Several distinctive animals can still be found in the Alps and Pyrenees, including the marmot, *chamois* (mountain antelope), *bouquetin* (Alpine ibex) and *mouflon* (wild mountain sheep), introduced in the 1950s. The *loup* (wolf) disappeared from France in the 1930s, but was reintroduced to the Parc National du Mercantour in 1992. The *aigle royal* (golden eagle) is a rare but hugely rewarding sight in the French mountain parks.

National Parks

The proportion of protected land is low relative to the country's size: six national parks (www.parcsnationaux-fr.com) fully protect just 0.8% of the country. Another 13% is protected by 45 regional parks (www.parcs-naturels-regionaux.tm.fr) and a further few per cent by 320 smaller nature reserves (www.reserves-naturelles.org).

Environmental Issues

Summer forest fires are an annual hazard. Wetlands, essential for the survival of a great number of species, are shrinking. More than two million hectares – 3% of French territory – are considered important wetlands, but only 4% of this land is protected.

France generates around 80% of its electricity from nuclear power stations – the highest ratio in the world – with the rest coming from carbon-fuelled power stations and renewable resources (mainly wind farms and hydroelectric dams). Latest projects include Europe's largest solar-powered electricity-generating station in a village in Provence (2011), and new nuclear reactor on Normandy's west coast (2012) under the world's most ambitious nuclear-power program.

Food & Drink

France means food. Every region has its distinctive cuisine, from the rich classic dishes of Burgundy, the Dordogne, Lyon and Normandy, to the sun-filled Mediterranean flavours of Provence, Languedoc and Corsica. Broadly speaking, the hot south tends to favour olive oil, garlic and tomatoes, while the cooler pastoral north favours cream and butter. Coastal areas brim with mussels, oysters and saltwater fish.

The number-one essential is *pain* (bread), typically eaten with every meal. Order in a restaurant and within minutes a basket should be on your table. Except in a handful of top-end gastronomic restaurants, butter (unsalted) is never an accompaniment. The long, thin baguette (and fatter *flûte*) is the classic 'loaf', but there are countless others.

France *is* cheese land and the local *fromagerie* (cheese shop) is always the pongiest place in town. There are nearly 500 varieties of *fromage* (cheese), ranging from world-known classics such as Brie, Camembert and Époisses de Bourgogne (France's smelliest cheese?) to local unknowns available only in the regions where they're made. At mealtimes cheese is always served after the main course and before dessert.

Charcuterie – hams, *saucissons* (salamis), sausages, black pudding and the fabulous *andouillette* (pig intestine sausage) – is the backbone of any self-respecting French picnic. Traditionally it is made only from pork, though other meats (beef, veal, chicken or goose) go into sausages, salamis, blood puddings and other cured and salted meats. Vegetarians and vegans note: specialist vegetarian restaurants are few and far between in France; most menus are meat-heavy.

There are dozens of wine-producing regions throughout France, but the principal regions are Alsace, Bordeaux, Burgundy, Champagne, Languedoc-Roussillon, the Loire region and the Rhône. Areas such as Burgundy comprise many well-known districts, including Chablis, Beaujolais and Mâcon, while Bordeaux encompasses Médoc,

WHERE TO EAT & DRINK

» **Auberge** Country inn serving traditional country fare, often attached to a rural B&B or small hotel.

» **Ferme auberge** Working farm that cooks up meals built squarely from local farm products; usually served *table d'hôte* (literally 'host's table'), meaning in set courses with little or no choice.

» **Bistro** (also spelled *bistrot*) Anything from a pub or bar with snacks and light meals to a small, fully fledged restaurant.

» **Brasserie** Very much like a cafe except it serves full meals, drinks and coffee from morning till 11pm or even later. Classic fare includes *choucroute* (sauerkraut) and *moules-frites* (mussels and fries).

» **Cafe** Serves basic food as well as drinks, most commonly a chunk of baguette filled with Camembert or pâté and *cornichons* (mini gherkins), a *croque-monsieur* (grilled ham and toasted-cheese sandwich) or *croque-madame* (a toasted-cheese sandwich topped with a fried egg).

» **Crêperie** (also *galetteries*) Casual address specialising in sweet crêpes and savoury galettes.

» **Restaurant** Born in Paris in 1765 when Monsieur Boulanger opened a small business on rue Bailleuil, 1er, selling soups, broths and other *restaurants* ('restoratives'). Restaurants today serve lunch and dinner five or six days; for standard opening hours see p461.

» **Salon de Thé** Trendy tearoom often serving light lunches (quiche, salads, cakes, tarts, pies and pastries) as well as black and herbal teas.

St-Émilion and Sauternes among many others. Northern France and Alsace meanwhile produce some excellent local beers; *bière à la pression* (draught beer) is served by the *demi* (about 33cL).

Coffee and mineral water are drunk by the gallon in France. In restaurants save cents by asking for a jug of tap water *(une carafe d'eau)* rather than pricier bottled water. The most common coffee, simply called *un café* in French, is espresso – ordering anything other than this at the end of a meal is a real faux pas.

SURVIVAL GUIDE

Directory A–Z

Accommodation

France has accommodation to suit every taste and pocket. In this guide we've listed reviews by author preference.

As a rule of thumb, budget covers everything from bare-bones hostels to simple family-run places; midrange means a few extra creature comforts such as satellite TV, air-conditioning and free wi-fi; while top-end places stretch from luxury five-star chains with the mod cons and swimming pools to boutique-chic chalets in the Alps.

Accommodation costs vary wildly between regions: what will buy you a night in a romantic *chambre d'hôte* (B&B) in the countryside may only get you a dorm bed in major cities and ski resorts; see individual sections to gauge costs.

Many tourist offices make room reservations, often for a fee of €5, but many only do so if you stop by in person. In the French Alps, ski resort tourist offices operate a central reservation service.

PRICE RANGES

Our reviews refer to the cost of a double room with a private bathroom, except in hostels or where otherwise specified. Quoted rates are for high season, which is July and August in southern France (Provence and the French Riviera, Languedoc-Roussilon, Corsica) and December to March in the French Alps. Prices exclude breakfast unless otherwise noted.

€€€ more than €175 (€180 in Paris)

€€ €70 to €175 (€80 to €180 in Paris)

€ below €70 (€80 in Paris)

B&BS

For charm, a heartfelt *bienvenue* (welcome) and home cooking, it's hard to beat a *chambre d'hôtes* (B&B). Pick up lists at local tourist offices or online:

Bienvenue à la Ferme (www.bienvenue-a-la-ferme.com) Sleep on a farm.

Chambres d'Hôtes France (www.chambresdhotesfrance.com)

Fleurs de Soleil (www.fleursdesoleil.fr, in French)

Gîtes de France (www.gites-de-france.fr) Umbrella organisation for B&Bs and self-catering properties *(gîtes);* check their catalogue *Gîtes de Charme* (www.gites-de-france-charme.com).

Samedi Midi Éditions (www.samedimidi.com)

CAMPING

Camping has never been more *en vogue.* Gîtes de France and Bienvenue à la Ferme coordinate camping on farms.

» Most camping grounds open March or April to October.

» Euro-economisers should look for good-value but no-frills *campings municipaux* (municipal camping grounds).

» Camping in nondesignated spots (*camping sauvage*) is illegal in France.

Easy-to-navigate websites with campsites searchable by location and facilities:

Camping en France (www.camping.fr)

Camping France (www.campingfrance.com)

Guide du Camping (www.guideducamping.com)

HPA Guide (http://camping.hpaguide.com)

Les Cabanes de France (www.cabanes-de-france.com, in French) Tree houses.

HOSTELS

Hostels range from funky to threadbare.

» A dorm bed in an *auberge de jeunesse* (youth hostel) costs about €25 in Paris, and anything from €10 to €28 in the provinces; sheets are always included and often breakfast too.

» To prevent outbreaks of bed bugs, sleeping bags are no longer permitted.

» All hostels are nonsmoking.

HOTELS

French hotels vary greatly in quality, ranging from low-budget no-star places to full-blown pleasure palaces.

» French hotels almost never include breakfast in their advertised nightly rates.
» Hotels in France are rated with one to five stars; ratings are based on objective criteria (eg size of entry hall), not service, decor or cleanliness.
» A double room has one double bed (or two singles pushed together); a room with twin beds is more expensive, as is a room with bathtub instead of shower.

Activities

From glaciers, rivers and canyons in the Alps to porcelain-smooth cycling trails in the Dordogne and Loire Valley – not to mention 3200km of coastline stretching from Italy to Spain and from the Basque country to the Straits of Dover – France's landscapes beg exhilarating outdoor escapes.
» The French countryside is criss-crossed by a staggering 120,000km of *sentiers balisés* (marked walking paths), which pass through every imaginable terrain in every region of the country. No permit is needed to hike.
» Probably the best-known trails are the *sentiers de grande randonnée* (GR), long-distance paths marked by red-and-white-striped track indicators.
» For details on regional activities, courses, equipment rental, clubs and companies, see this book's destination listings and contact local tourist offices.

ORGANISATIONS

Whether you are a peak bagger, surfer dude or thrill-seeking mountain biker, the following organisations can help you plan your petit adventure:

Club Alpin Français (French Alpine Club; www.ffcam.fr, in French) Groups 280 mountain-sports clubs and arranges professional guides for escapades in *alpinisme* (mountaineering), *escalade* (rock climbing), *escalade de glace* (ice climbing) and other highland activities. Runs *refuges* (mountain huts) in the French Alps too.

École du Ski Français (ESF; www.esf.net) French ski school.

Fédération Française de Cyclisme (www.ffc.fr, in French) Founded in 1881, the French Cycling Federation is *the* authority on competitive cycling in France and mountain biking (VTT; *vélo tout terrain*).

Fédération Française de Vol Libre (www.federation.ffvl.fr, in French) Groups regional clubs specialising in *deltaplane* (hang-gliding), *parapente* (paragliding) and *le kite-surf* (kitesurfing).

Véloroutes et Voies Vertes (www.af3v.org) A database of 250 signposted *véloroutes* (bike paths) and *voies vertes* (greenways) for cycling and in-line skating.

Business Hours

French business hours are regulated by a maze of government regulations, including the 35-hour working week.
» The midday break is uncommon in Paris but, in general, gets longer the further south you go.
» French law requires most businesses to close Sunday; exceptions include grocery stores, *boulangeries*, florists and businesses catering to the tourist trade.
» In many places shops close on Monday.
» Many service stations open 24 hours a day and stock basic groceries.
» Restaurants generally close one or two days of the week.
» Most (but not all) national museums are closed on Tuesday, while most local museums are closed on Monday, though in summer some open daily. Some museums close for lunch.
» In this book we've only listed business hours where they differ from the following standards:

Banks 9 or 9.30am-1pm & 2-5pm Mon-Fri or Tue-Sat

Bars 7pm to 1am Mon-Sat

Cafes 7 or 8am-10 or 11pm Mon-Sat

Nightclubs 10pm-3, 4 or 5am Thu-Sat

Post offices 8.30 or 9am to 5 or 6pm Mon-Fri, 8am-noon Sat

Restaurants lunch noon-2.30 or 3pm, dinner 7-10 or 11pm

Shops 9 or 10am-noon & 2-6 or 7pm Mon-Sat

Supermarkets 9am to 7 or 8pm Mon-Sat

Embassies & Consulates

All foreign embassies are in Paris. Many countries have consulates in other major cities such as Bordeaux, Lyon, Nice, Marseille and Strasbourg. To find a consulate or embassy visit look up *'ambassade'* in France's

Pages Jaunes (Yellow Pages; www.pagesjaunes.fr, in French).

Australia (☎01 40 59 33 00; www.france.embassy.gov.au; 4 rue Jean Rey; Ⓜ Bir Hakeim)

Canada (☎01 44 43 29 00; www.amb-canada.fr; 35 av Montaigne; Ⓜ Franklin D Roosevelt)

Japan (☎01 48 88 62 00; www.amb-japon.fr in French & Japanese; 7 av Hoche; Ⓜ Courcelles)

New Zealand (☎01 45 01 43 43; www.nzembassy.com; 7ter rue Léonard de Vinci; Ⓜ Victor Hugo)

UK (☎01 44 51 31 00; www.ukinfrance.fco.gov.uk; 35 rue du Faubourg St- Honoré; Ⓜ Concorde)

USA (☎01 43 12 22 22; http://france.usembassy.gov; 4 av Gabriel; Ⓜ Concorde)

Food

Eating reviews throughout this chapter are ordered by preference. Price ranges for a two-course evening meal are:

€€€ more than €50

€€ €15 to €50

€ below €15

Gay & Lesbian Travellers

Gay mayors (including Paris' very own Bertrand Delanoë), artists and film directors, camper-than-camp fashion designers...the rainbow flag flies high in France, one of Europe's most liberal countries when it comes to homosexuality.

» Most major gay and lesbian organisations are based in Paris.

» Bordeaux, Lille, Lyon, Toulouse and many other towns have active communities.

» Attitudes towards homosexuality tend to be more conservative in the countryside and villages.

» Gay Pride marches are held in major French cities from mid-May to early July.

» Online try:

French Government Tourist Office (www.us.franceguide.com/special-interests/gay-friendly) Information about 'the gay-friendly destination par excellence'.

France Queer Resources Directory (www.france.qrd.org, in French) Gay and lesbian directory.

Gay Travel France (www.gaytravelfrance.com) Gay and lesbian accommodation.

Paris Gay (www.paris-gay.com) Everything about gay Paree.

Language Courses

The government site www.diplomatie.gouv.fr (under 'Francophony') and www.europa-pages.com/france list language schools in France.

All manner of French language courses are available in Paris and provincial towns and cities; many arrange accommodation. Some schools you might consider:

Alliance Française (www.alliancefr.org; 101 blvd Raspail, 6e, Paris; Ⓜ St-Placide) Venerable institution for the worldwide promotion of French language and civilisation, with intensive and extensive classes, including literature and business French.

Centre Méditerranéen d'Études Françaises (www.monte-carlo.mc/centremed; chemin des Oliviers, Cap d'Ail) French Riviera school dating to 1952, with an open-air amphitheatre designed by Jean Cocteau overlooking the sparkling blue Med.

Eurocentre d'Amboise (www.eurocentres.com; 9 mail St-Thomas, Amboise) Small, well-organised school in the charming Loire Valley; branches in La Rochelle and Paris.

Université de Provence (http://sites.univ-provence.fr/wscefee; 29 av Robert Schumann, Aix-en-Provence) A hot choice in lovely Aix.

Legal Matters

French police have wide powers of stop-and-search and can demand proof of identity at any time. Foreigners must be able to prove their legal status in France (eg passport, visa, residency permit).

Money

» Credit and debit cards, accepted almost everywhere in France, are convenient, relatively secure and usually offer a better exchange rate than travellers cheques or cash exchanges.

» Some places (eg 24hr petrol stations, some autoroute toll machines) only take French-style credit cards with chips and PINs.

» Commercial banks charge €3 to €5 fee per foreign-currency transaction – if they even bother to offer exchange services any more.

» In Paris and major cities, *bureaux de change* (exchange bureaux) are faster and easier, open longer hours and give better rates.

For lost cards, call:

Amex (☎01 47 77 72 00)

Diners Club (☎08 10 31 41 59)

MasterCard (☎08 00 90 13 87)

Visa (Carte Bleue; ☎08 00 90 11 79)

Public Holidays

New Year's Day (Jour de l'An) 1 January

Easter Sunday & Monday (Pâques & lundi de Pâques)

May Day (Fête du Travail) 1 May – traditional parades.

Victoire 1945 8 May – commemorates the Allied victory in Europe that ended WWII.

Ascension Thursday (Ascension) May – celebrated on the 40th day after Easter.

Pentecost/Whit Sunday & Whit Monday (Pentecôte & lundi de Pentecôte) Mid-May to mid-June – celebrated on the seventh Sunday after Easter.

Bastille Day/National Day (Fête Nationale) 14 July – *the* national holiday.

Assumption Day (Assomption) 15 August

All Saints' Day (Toussaint) 1 November

Remembrance Day (L'onze novembre) 11 November – marks the WWI armistice.

Christmas (Noël) 25 December

Telephone

MOBILE PHONES

» French mobile phones numbers begin with ☎06 or ☎07.

» France uses GSM 900/1800, compatible with the rest of Europe and Australia but not with the North American GSM 1900 or the totally different system in Japan (though some North Americans have tri-band phones that work here).

» It may be cheaper to buy your own French SIM card (€20 to €30) sold at ubiquitous outlets run by France's three mobile phone companies, **Bouygues** (www.bouyguestelecom.fr), France Telecom's **Orange** (www.orange.com) and **SFR** (www.sfr.com, in French).

» Recharge cards are sold at most *tabacs* and newsagents; domestic prepaid calls cost about €0.50 per minute.

PHONE CODES

Calling France from abroad Dial your country's international access code, ☎33 (France's country code), and the 10-digit local number *without* the initial 0.

Calling internationally from France Dial ☎00 (the international access code), the country code, area code (without the initial zero if there is one) and local number.

Directory inquiries For France Telecom's *service des renseignements* (directory inquiries) dial ☎11 87 12. For help in English with all France Telecom's services, see www.francetelecom.com or call ☎09 69 36 39 00.

International directory inquiries For numbers outside France, dial ☎11 87 00.

Emergency number ☎112, can be dialled from public phones without a phonecard.

Toilets

» Public toilets, signposted WC or *toilettes,* are not always plentiful in France.

» Love them (sci-fi geek) or loathe them (claustrophobe), France has its fair share of 24hr self-cleaning toilets, €0.50 in Paris and free elsewhere.

» Some older cafes and restaurants still have the hole-in-the-floor squat toilets.

» The French are blasé about unisex toilets, so save your blushes when tiptoeing past the urinals to reach the ladies' loo.

Visas

For up-to-date details on visa requirements, visit the **French Foreign Affairs Ministry** (www.diplomatie.gouv.fr).

» EU nationals and citizens of Iceland, Norway and Switzerland need only a passport or national identity card to enter France and stay in the country, even for stays of over 90 days. Citizens of new EU member states may be subject to various limitations on living and working in France.

» Citizens of Australia, the USA, Canada Israel, Hong Kong, Japan, Malaysia, New Zealand, Singapore, South, Korea and many Latin American countries do not need visas to visit France as tourists for up to 90 days. For long stays of over 90 days, contact your nearest French embassy or consulate.

» Other people wishing to come to France as tourists have to apply for a **Schengen Visa** (p1217).

» Tourist visas cannot be changed into student visas after arrival. However, short-term visas are available for students sitting university-entrance exams in France.

Getting There & Away

Entering the Country

Entering France from other parts of the EU is a breeze – no border checkpoints or customs thanks to Schengen Agreements signed by all of France's neighbours except the UK, the Channel Islands and Andorra. For these three entities, old-fashioned document and customs checks remain the norm, at least when exiting France (when entering France in the case of Andorra).

Air

For a list of airports in France, see the boxed text below.

Land

BUS

Eurolines (☎08 92 89 90 91; www.eurolines.eu), a group of 32 long-haul coach operators (including the UK's National Express), links France with cities across Europe and in Morocco and Russia. Discounts are available to people under 26 and over 60. Make advance reservations, especially in July and August.

The standard Paris–London fare is €46 (€57 including high-season supplements) but the trip – including a Channel crossing either by ferry or the Chunnel – can cost as little €15 if you book 45 days ahead.

CAR & MOTORCYCLE

A right-hand-drive vehicle brought to France from the UK or Ireland must have deflectors affixed to the headlights to avoid dazzling oncoming traffic.

Departing from the UK, **Eurotunnel shuttle trains** (☎in UK 08443-35 35 35, in France 08 10 63 03 04; www.eurotunnel.com) whisk bicycles, motorcycles, cars and coaches from Folkestone through the Channel Tunnel to Coquelles, 5km southwest of Calais, in just 35 minutes. The shuttle services run 24 hours a day. The earlier you book, the cheaper the fare. Standard fares for a car, including up to nine passengers, start at UK£53.

TRAIN

Rail services link France with virtually every country in Europe. Tickets and information are handled by **Rail Europe** (www.raileurope.com) or in France, by **SNCF** (☎in France 36 35, from abroad +33 8 92 35 35 35; www.sncf.com).

Certain services between France and its continental neighbours are marketed under separate brand names:

» **Alleo** Rail travel to Germany.
» **Artésia** (www.artesia.eu) Italian cities such as Milan and, overnight, Venice, Florence and Rome.
» **Elipsos** (www.elipsos.com) Luxurious 'train-hotel' services to Spain.
» **TGV Lyria** (www.tgv-lyria.fr) Switzerland
» **Thalys** (www.thalys.com) Links Paris' Gare du Nord with Brussels (82 minutes), Amsterdam CS (3⅓hr), Cologne Hauptbahnhof (3¼ hours) and other destinations.
» **Eurostar** (☎in UK 08432 186 186, in France 08 92 35 35 39; www.eurostar.com) Runs from London St-Pancras station to Paris Gare du Nord in 2¼ hours, with easy onward connections available to destinations all over France. Ski trains connecting England with the French Alps run weekends mid-December to mid-April.

SEA

Regular ferries travel to France from Italy, the UK, Channel Islands and Ireland. Several ferry companies ply the waters between Corsica and Italy. For details, see the boxed text, p466.

INTERNATIONAL AIRPORTS

AIRPORT	PHONE	WEBSITE
Paris	France 39 50; abroad +33 1 70 36 39 50	www.aeroportsdeparis.fr
Bordeaux	05 56 34 50 50	www.bordeaux.aeroport.fr
Lille	08 91 67 32 10	www.lille.aeroport.fr
Lyon	08 26 80 08 26	www.lyon.aeroport.fr
Marseille	04 42 14 14 14	www.mrsairport.com
Nantes	02 40 84 80 00	www.nantes.aeroport.fr
Nice	08 20 42 33 33	www.nice.aeroport.fr
Strasbourg	03 88 64 67 67	www.strasbourg.aeroport.fr
Toulouse	08 25 38 00 00	www.toulouse.aeroport.fr

SAMPLE TRAIN FARES

ROUTE	FULL FARE (€)	DURATION (HR)
Amsterdam–Paris	79	3¼
Barcelona–Montpellier	57	4½
Berlin–Paris	238	8
Brussels–Paris	44–64	1½
Frankfurt–Paris	106	4
Geneva–Lyon	25	2
Geneva–Marseille	65	3½
Vienna–Strasbourg	149	9

Getting Around

Air

France's vaunted high-speed train network has made rail travel between some cities (eg from Paris to Lyon and Marseille) faster and easier than flying.

Air France (☎36 54; www.airfrance.com) and its subsidiaries **Brit Air** (☎36 54; www.britair.fr) and **Régional** (☎36 54; www.regional.com) control the lion's share of France's long-protected domestic airline industry. Good deals can be had if you buy your ticket well in advance (at least 42 days ahead for the very best deals), stay over a Saturday night and don't mind tickets that can't be changed or reimbursed.

Budget carriers offering flights within France include **easyJet** (www.easyjet.com), **Airlinair** (www.airlinair.com), **Twin Jet** (www.twinjet.net) and **CCM** (www.aircorsica.com).

Bus

You're nearly always better off travelling by train in France if possible, as the SNCF domestic railway system is heavily subsidised by the government and is much more reliable than local bus companies. Nevertheless, buses are widely used for short-distance travel within *départements,* especially in rural areas with relatively few train lines (eg Brittany and Normandy).

Bicycle

France is a great place to cycle. Not only is much of the countryside drop-dead gorgeous, but the country has a growing number of urban and rural *pistes cyclables* (bike paths and lanes; www.voiesvertes.com, in French) and an extensive network of secondary and tertiary roads with relatively light traffic. French train company SNCF does its best to make travelling with a bicycle easy and has a special website for cyclists (www.velo.sncf.com, in French).

Most French cities and towns have at least one bike shop that rents out mountain bikes (VTT; €10 to €20 a day), road bikes (VTCs) and cheaper city bikes. You have to leave ID and/or a deposit (often a credit-card slip) that you forfeit if the bike is damaged or stolen. A growing number of cities have automatic bike rental systems.

Car & Motorcycle

A car gives you exceptional freedom and allows you to visit more-remote parts of France. But it can be expensive and, in cities, parking and traffic are frequently a major headache. Motorcyclists will find France great for touring, with winding roads of good quality and lots of stunning scenery.

BRINGING YOUR OWN VEHICLE

All foreign motor vehicles entering France must display a sticker or licence plate identifying its country of registration. If you're bringing a right-hand-drive vehicle remember to fix deflectors on your headlights to avoid dazzling oncoming traffic.

Driving Licence & Documents

All drivers must carry a national ID card or passport; a valid driving licence (*permis de conduire;* most foreign licences can be used in France for up to a year); car-ownership papers, known as a *carte grise* (grey card); and proof of third party (liability) insurance.

FUEL & TOLLS

Essence (petrol), also known as *carburant* (fuel), costs around €1.40/L for 95 unleaded

INTERNATIONAL FERRY COMPANIES

CONNECTION	FERRY COMPANY	PHONE NUMBER(S)
England–Normandy, England–Brittany, Ireland–Brittany	Brittany Ferries	in UK 0871-244 0744; in Ireland 021 4277 801; in France 08 25 82 88 28
Ireland–Normandy	Celtic Link Ferries	in Ireland 053-916 2688
Morocco–France	Comanav & Comarit	in Sète (SNCM) 04 67 46 68 00
England–Normandy, England–Brittany, Channel Islands–Brittany	Condor Ferries	in UK 0845-609 1024; in France 08 25 13 51 35
Tunisia–France	CTN	Marseille 04 91 91 55 71
Ireland–Normandy, Ireland–Brittany	Irish Ferries	in Ireland 0818 300 400; in France 08 10 00 13 57; in Cherbourg 02 33 23 44 44; in Roscoff 02 98 61 17 17
England–Channel Ports, England–Normandy	LD Lines	in UK 0844-576 8836; in France 08 25 30 43 04
Channel Islands–Normandy	Manche Îles Express	on Jersey 01534-880 756; on Guernsey 01481-832 059; in France 08 25 13 10 50
England–Channel Ports	Norfolk Line	in UK 0844-847 5042; outside UK +44-208-127 8303 in France 03 28 59 01 01
England–Channel Ports	P&O Ferries	in UK 08716 645 645; in France 08 25 12 01 56
England–Channel Ports	SeaFrance	in UK 0871-423 7119; in France 08 25 82 50 00
Algeria–France, Sardinia–France, Tunisia–France	SNCM	in France 32 60; outside France +33 825 88 80 88;
England–Normandy	Transmanche Ferries	in UK 0844-576 8836; in France 08 25 30 43 04

(Sans Plomb 95 or SP95, usually available from a green pump), and €1.30 for diesel (*diesel, gazole* or *gasoil,* usually available from a yellow pump). Filling up *(faire le plein)* is most expensive along autoroutes and cheapest at supermarkets on town outskirts.

Many French motorways (autoroutes) are fitted with toll *(péage)* stations that charge a fee based on the distance you've travelled; factor in these costs when driving.

HIRE

To hire a car you'll usually need to be over 21 and in possession of a valid driving licence and a credit card. Auto transmissions are *very* rare in France; you'll need to order one well in advance.

See p1221 for a list of major car rental companies with offices across France and Europe.

INSURANCE

Unlimited third-party liability insurance is mandatory in France. Third-party liability insurance is provided by car-rental companies, but collision-damage waivers (CDW) vary between companies. When comparing rates check the *franchise* (excess). Your credit card may cover CDW if you use it to pay for the car rental.

ROAD RULES

Cars drive on the right in France. Speed limits on French roads are as follows:

» 50km/h in built-up areas

WEBSITE	PORTS OUTSIDE FRANCE	PORTS IN FRANCE
www.brittany-ferries.co.uk; www.brittanyferries.ie	Cork, Plymouth, Poole, Portsmouth	Caen (Ouistreham), Cherbourg, Roscoff, St-Malo
www.celticlinkferries.com	Rosslare	Cherbourg
www.aferry.to/comanav.htm; www.aferry.to/comarit.htm	Nador, Tanger	Sète
www.condorferries.com	Poole, Portsmouth, Weymouth, Guernsey, Jersey	Cherbourg, St-Malo
www.ctn.com.tn	Tunis	Marseille
www.irishferries.ie; www.shamrock-irlande.com, in French	Rosslare	Cherbourg, Roscoff
www.ldlines.co.uk	Dover, Portsmouth	Boulogne-sur-Mer, Le Havre
www.manche-iles-express.com	Alderney, Guernsey, Jersey	Barneville-Carteret, Diélette, Granville
www.norfolkline.com	Dover	Dunkirk (Loon Plage)
www.poferries.com	Dover	Calais
www.seafrance.com	Dover	Calais
www.sncm.fr	Alger, Annaba, Bejaia, Oran, Porto Torres, Skikda, Tunis	Marseille
www.transmancheferries.com	Newhaven	Dieppe

» 90km/h (80km/h if it's raining) on N and D highways
» 110km/h (100km/h if it's raining) on dual carriageways
» 130km/h (110km/h if it's raining) on autoroutes.

Other key rules of the road:
» All passengers must wear seatbelts.
» Children who weigh less than 18kg must travel in backward-facing child seats.
» It is illegal to drive with a blood-alcohol concentration over 0.05% – the equivalent of two glasses of wine for a 75kg adult.
» Mobile phones may only be used when accompanied by a hands-free kit or speakerphone.
» All vehicles must carry a reflective safety jacket (stored inside the car, not boot) and a reflective triangle.
» Riders of any type of two-wheeled vehicle with a motor (except motor-assisted bicycles) must wear a helmet.
» North American drivers, remember: turning right on a red light is illegal.

Train

France's superb rail network is operated by the state-owned **SNCF** (www.sncf.com); many rural towns not on the SNCF train network are served by SNCF buses.

The flagship trains on French railways are the superfast TGVs, which reach speeds in excess of 200mph and can whisk you from Paris to the Côte d'Azur in as little as three hours.

SNCF TRAIN FARES & DISCOUNTS

The Basics

» Full-fare return travel costs twice as much as a one-way fare.

» 1st-class travel, where still available, costs 20% to 30% extra.

» Ticket prices for many trains are pricier during peak periods.

» The further in advance you reserve, the lower the fare.

» Children aged 4 to 11 pay half price, under 4s travel for free.

Discount Tickets

» **Prem's** The SNCF's most heavily discounted, use-or-lose tickets, sold online, by phone and at ticket windows/machines a maximum of 90 days and minimum 14 days before you travel.

» **Bons Plans** A grab-bag of cheap options for different routes/dates, advertised online under the tab 'Dernière Minute' (Last Minute).

» **iDTGV** Cheap tickets aimed at the iPod generation on advance-purchase TGV travel between about 30 cities; only sold at www.idtgv.com.

Discount Cards

Reductions of 25% to 60% are available with several discount cards (valid for one year):

» **Carte 12-25** (www.12-25-sncf.com in, French; €49) For travellers aged 12 to 25 years.

» **Carte Enfant Plus** (www.enfantplus-sncf.com, in French; €70) For one to four adults travelling with a child aged four to 11 years.

» **Carte Escapades** (www.escapades-sncf.com, in French; €85) Discounts on return journeys of at least 200km that include a Saturday night away or only involve travel on a Saturday or Sunday; for 26- to 59-year-olds.

» **Carte Sénior** (www.senior-sncf.com, in French; €56) Over 60 years.

Many non-high-speed lines are also served by TGV trains; otherwise you'll find yourself aboard a non-TGV train, referred to as a *corail* or TER *(train express régional)*.

TGV lines and key stations:

TGV Nord, **Thalys** & **Eurostar** These link Paris' Gare du Nord with Arras, Lille, Calais, Brussels (Bruxelles-Midi), Amsterdam, Cologne and, via the Channel Tunnel, Ashford, Ebbsfleet and London St Pancras.

TGV Est Européen Connects Paris' Gare de l'Est with Reims, Nancy, Metz, Strasbourg, Zurich and Germany, including Frankfurt and Stuttgart. At present super-high-speed track stretches only as far east as Lorraine, but it's supposed to reach Strasbourg in 2016.

TGV Sud-Est & TGV Midi-Méditerranée These lines link Paris' Gare de Lyon with the southeast, including Dijon, Lyon, Geneva, the Alps, Avignon, Marseille, Nice and Montpellier.

TGV Atlantique Sud-Ouest & **TGV Atlantique Ouest** These link Paris' Gare Montparnasse with western and southwestern France, including Brittany (Rennes, Brest, Quimper), Tours, Nantes, Poitiers, La Rochelle, Bordeaux, Biarritz and Toulouse.

TICKETS

Buying online at the various SNCF websites can reward with you some great reductions

PRIORITY TO THE RIGHT

Under the *priorité à droite* (priority to the right) rule, any car entering an intersection from a road on your right has the right of way, unless the intersection is marked *'vous n'avez pas la priorité'* (you do not have right of way) or *'cédez le passage'* (give way).

VALIDATE YOURSELF

Before boarding any train, you must validate *(composter)* your ticket by time-stamping it in a *composteur*, one of those yellow posts located on the way to the platform. If you forget (or don't have a ticket for some other reason), find a conductor on the train before they find you – or risk an unwelcome fine.

on fares, but be warned – these are generally intended for domestic travellers, and if you're buying abroad be aware of the pitfalls. Many tickets can't be posted outside France, and if you buy with a non-French credit card, you might not be able to use it in the automated ticket collection machines at many French stations. Buying from a ticket office may not secure you the cheapest fare, but at least you'll be sure of being able to pick up your ticket...

RAIL PASSES

The **InterRail One Country Pass** (www.interrailnet.com; 3/4/6/8 days €194/209/269/299, 12–25 yr €126/136/175/194), valid in France, entitles residents of Europe who do not live in France to unlimited travel on SNCF trains for three to eight days over a month.

Germany

Includes »

Why Go?

Beer or wine? That sums up the German conundrum. One is at the heart of a pilsner-swilling culture, is the very reason for one of the world's great parties (Oktoberfest) and is consumed with pleasure across the land. The other is responsible for gorgeous vine-covered valleys, comes in myriad forms and is enjoyed everywhere, often from cute little green-stemmed glasses.

And the questions about Germany continue. Berlin or Munich? Castle or club? Ski or hike? East or west? BMW or Mercedes? In fact, the answers are simple: both. Why decide? The beauty of Germany is that rather than choosing, you can revel in the contrasts.

Berlin, edgy and vibrant, is a grand capital in a constant state of reinvention. Munich rules Bavaria, the centre of national traditions. Half-timbered villages bring smiles as you wander their cobblestoned and castle-shadowed lanes. Exploring this country and all its facets keeps visitors happy for weeks.

Best Places to Eat

» Cafe Jacques (p490)
» Wolfshöhle (p557)
» Bratwursthäusle (p537)
» Feynsinn (p574)
» Wurstküche (p539)

Best Places to Stay

» Michelberger Hotel (p488)
» Hotel Blauer Bock (p526)
» Kogge (p591)
» Hotel Sankt Nepomuk (p533)
» Hotel Elch (p537)

When to Go

Berlin

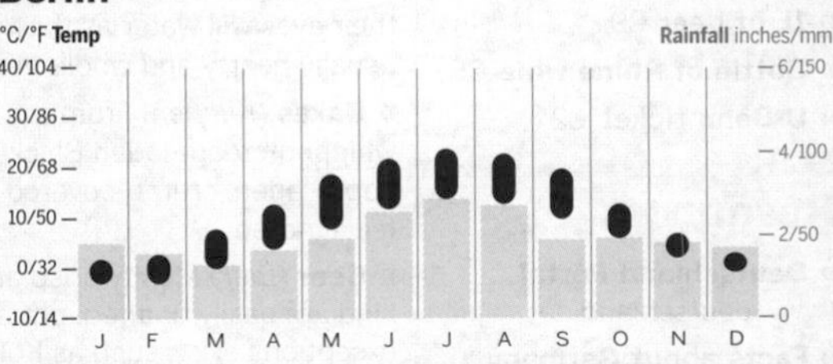

Jun–Aug Warm summers cause Germans to shed their clothes; night never seems to come.

Sep The real month of Oktoberfest; autumn celebrations are found throughout Bavaria.

Dec It's icy, it's cold and you can drink hot wine at Christmas markets countrywide.

AT A GLANCE

» **Currency** euro (€)

» **Language** German

» **Money** ATMs common, cash preferred for small purchases

» **Visas** Schengen rules apply

Fast Facts

» **Area** 356,866 sq km

» **Population** 85 million

» **Capital** Berlin

» **Telephone** country code ☎49; international access code ☎00

» **Emergency** ☎112

Exchange Rates

Australia	A$1	€0.74
Canada	C$1	€0.74
Japan	¥100	€0.87
New Zealand	NZ$1	€0.56
UK	UK£1	€1.16
USA	US$1	€0.67

Set Your Budget

» **Midrange hotel double room** €80–150

» **Two-course dinner** €12

» **1L of beer** €9

» **Bottle of Rhine wine** €6

» **U-Bahn ticket** €2

Resources

» **Deutschland Portal** (www.deutschland.de)

» **Facts about Germany** (www.tatsachen-ueber-deutschland.de)

» **German National Tourist Board** (www.germany-tourism.de)

Connections

At the heart of Europe, Germany has a superb railway that's well linked to surrounding countries. Freiburg and Stuttgart have services south to Switzerland and Italy, Munich is close to the Czech Republic and Austria (including Salzburg and Innsbruck), Berlin is close to Poland, Hamburg has frequent services to Denmark, Cologne is good for fast trains to the Netherlands and Belgium (including Brussels for Eurostar to London), and Frankfurt is the base for high-speed trains to Paris, Strasbourg and other parts of France.

ITINERARIES

One week

Starting in Berlin, spend three days in and around the city, then head south through the wonderful little Thuringian town of Weimar and the tiny Bavarian town of Bamberg before ending up in Munich.

Two weeks

Start in Munich for some Bavarian joy, then head up to the goofy castles in Füssen. Take in some of the Bavarian Alps and the fun of Freiburg. Explore the Black Forest, soak up Baden-Baden and settle in for a boat voyage down the Rhine in Mainz. Pop up to Hamburg then south to the old East and Dresden. Finish it all in Berlin.

Essential Food & Drink

» **Sausage** *(Wurst)* More than 1500 types are made countrywide. From sweet, smoky and tiny Nurnbergers to imposing Thüringers to that fast-food remedy for the munchies, the sliced and drowned currywurst.

» **Mustard** *(Senf)* The perfect accompaniment to sausages, schnitzels and more, German mustards can be hot, laced with horseradish or rich with seeds. Or all three.

» **Bread** *(Brot)* Get Germans talking about bread and often their eyes will water as they describe their favourite type – usually hearty and whole-grained in infinite variations.

» **Cakes** *(Kuchen)* From the confectionery fantasy of the whipped-cream-laden Black Forest cake to all manner of apple-laden, crumb-covered delights, sweet tooths never feel ignored.

» **Beer** *(Bier)* Mostly crisp and clear, the many lagers of the land are easily quaffed, preferably from huge steins. But exceptions exist, such as Kölsch in Cologne and Rauchbier in Bamberg.

» **Wine** *(Wein)* It's not all sweet and it's not all white; the best is superb and comes from 13 distinct regions.

BERLIN

030 / POP 3.41 MILLION

You live history in Berlin. You might be distracted by the trendy, edgy, gentrified streets, by the bars bleeding a laid-back cool factor, by the galleries sprouting talent and pushing the envelope, but make no mistake – reminders of its once-divided past assault you while modernity sits around the corner. Norman Foster's Reichstag dome, Peter Eisenman's Holocaust Memorial and the iconic Brandenburg Gate are all contained within a few neighbouring blocks. Potsdamer Platz and its shiny Sony Center hosts Berlin's star-studded film festival each year, a stone's throw from where only 20 years ago you could climb up a viewing platform in the West and peer over the wall to glimpse the alternate reality of the East. Casually strolling along Bernauerstrasse near trendy Prenzlauer Berg, you suddenly place your foot on a brick-marked line in the pavement marking where the wall once stood.

Renowned for its diversity and its tolerance, its alternative culture and its night-owl stamina, the best thing about the German capital is the way it reinvents itself and isn't shackled by its mind-numbing history. And the world knows this – expatriates and a steady increase of out-of-towners are flocking to see what all the fuss is about.

Meanwhile, creative types flock here to write that book, paint their hearts out or simply live the ultimate bohemian life (though the low price tag that often inspires these romantic lifestyle choices is steadily climbing). Still, in Berlin nobody questions artistic intentions, experimental philosophies or lofty ideas, and it's perfectly fine to try, fail and try again. Some arrive seeking (and finding) Hemingway's Paris or Warhol's New York, but everyone unearths something extraordinary that often makes home seem, well, banal and conservative.

In the midst of it all, students rub shoulders with Russian émigrés, fashion boutiques inhabit monumental German Democratic Republic (GDR) buildings, Turkish residents live next door to famous DJs and the nightlife has long left the American sector as edgy clubbers watch the sun rise over the neon-lit Universal Music headquarters in the city's east.

In short, all human life is here, and don't expect to get much sleep.

History

United, divided, united again, Berlin has a roller-coaster past. The merging of two medieval trading posts, it enjoyed its first stint as a capital in 1701, when it became the leading city of the state of Brandenburg-Prussia. Under Prussian King Friedrich I and his son, Friedrich II, Berlin flourished culturally and politically.

The Industrial Revolution, when commercial giants such as Siemens emerged, also boosted the city. As workers flooded to Berlin's factories, its population doubled between 1850 and 1870. 'Deutschland' was a latecomer to the table of nationhood, but in 1871 Berlin was again proclaimed a capital, this time of the newly unified Germany.

By 1900 the city was home to almost two million people, but after WWI it fell into decline and, like the rest of Germany, suffered an economic crisis and hyperinflation. There was a brief, early communist uprising in the capital in 1918, led by Karl Liebknecht and Rosa Luxemburg (whose names now adorn Berlin streets). However, that was quickly squashed, and during the following Weimar Republic (1919–33) Berlin

BERLIN IN TWO DAYS

Investigate the **Brandenburg Gate** area, including the **Reichstag** and the **Holocaust Memorial**. Walk east along Unter den Linden, stopping at the **Bebelplatz book-burning memorial**. Veer through the **Museumsinsel** for window-shopping and cafe-hopping through **Hackescher Markt**. In the evening, explore the bars of Prenzlauer Berg, along Kastanieanallee and Pappelallee, stopping for a drink in **Fleischmöbel**.

Start the next day at the **East Side Gallery** remnant of the Berlin Wall, before heading to **Checkpoint Charlie** and the nearby **Jewish Museum**. Take the U-Bahn to **Kurfürstendamm** and catch scenic bus 100 back to the **Fernsehturm**. Later, explore Kreuzberg nightlife around Kottbusser Tor and go clubbing – **Berghain/Panoramabar** is best if you are short on time. Alternatively, head for the **Berliner Ensemble**.

Germany Highlights

1 Party day and night in **Berlin** (p473); save sleep for somewhere else as there's no time here with the clubs, museums, bars and ever-changing zeitgeist

2 Time your journey for **Oktoberfest** (p526). Munich's orgy of suds, or just hang out in a beer garden

3 Go slow in Germany's alluring small towns like **Bamberg** (p533), with winding lanes, smoked beer (!) and a lack of cliché

4 Compare the soaring peaks of the Dom in **Cologne** (p571) with the towering glasses of the city's famous beer

5 Go cuckoo in the **Black Forest** (p552), discovering its chilly crags, misty peaks and endless trails

6 Get into the swing of **Dresden** (p496), with a creative culture beyond the restorations

7 Cycle around one of the world's great harbours in **Hamburg** (p586), then follow the trail of the Beatles

8 Discover **Regensburg** (p538), Germany's Unesco-recognised ancient gem, with traces of Rome and Tuscany (and great sausages!) around every corner

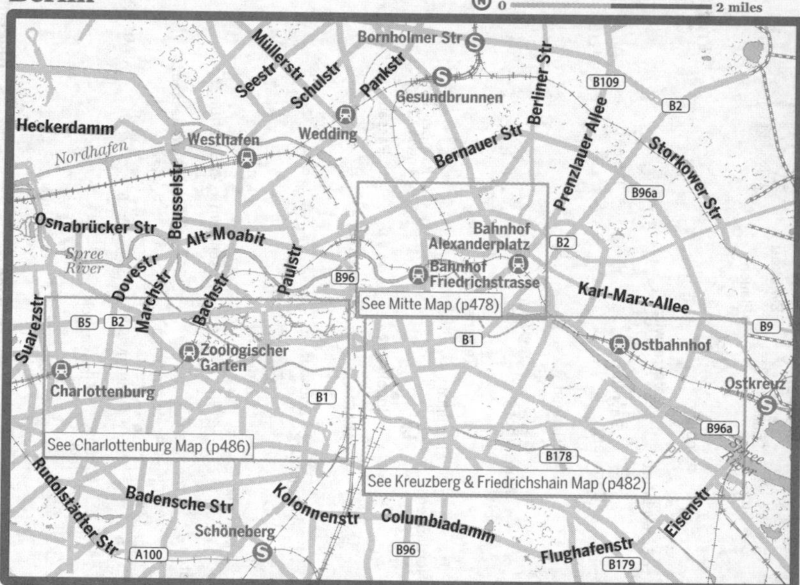

gained a reputation for decadence. Cabaret, the savage political theatre of Bertolt Brecht, expressionist art and jazz all flourished as Berliners partied to forget their troubles.

In the mid-1930s Berlin became a centrepiece of Nazi power and suffered heavily during WWII. During the Battle of Berlin from August 1943 to March 1944, British bombers targeted the city nightly. The Soviets also shelled Berlin and invaded from the east.

The Potsdam Conference took place in August 1945 and split the capital into zones occupied by the four victorious powers – the USA, Britain, France and the Soviet Union. In June 1948 the three Western Allies introduced a separate currency and administration in their sectors. In response, the Soviets blockaded West Berlin. Only a huge airlift by the Allies managed to keep the city stocked with food and supplies. In October 1949 East Berlin became the capital of the GDR, the German Democratic Republic.

The Berlin Wall, built in August 1961, was originally intended to prevent the drain of skilled labour from the East, but soon became a Cold War symbol. For decades East Berlin and West Berlin developed separately, until Hungary breached the Iron Curtain in May 1989; the Berlin Wall followed on 9 November. By 1 July 1990 the wall was being hacked to pieces. The Unification Treaty signed on 3 October that year designated Berlin the official capital of Germany, and in June 1991 the parliament voted to move the seat of government from Bonn back to Berlin. In 1999 that was finally achieved.

Times, however, have been tough. Without the huge national subsidies provided during the decades of division, the newly unified Berlin has struggled economically. In 2001 the centre-right mayor resigned amid corruption allegations, leaving the city effectively bankrupt. Current centre-left mayor Klaus Wowereit, Berlin's first openly gay mayor, first came into power in 2001 and was re-elected in 2006 – he is popular and passionately dedicated to his city, but has made few inroads into the crisis. But Wowereit remains undaunted and tries to look on the bright side, constantly reminding us of his now-famous proclamation, 'Berlin is poor, but sexy'.

Orientation

Standing at Berlin's Brandenburg Gate, on the former East-West divide, you can see many major sights. Looking east, your eye follows Unter den Linden past the Museumsinsel (Museum Island) in the Spree River, to the needle-shaped Fernsehturm (TV tower) at Alexanderplatz.

If you turn west, you face the golden Siegessäule (Victory Column) along the equally huge thoroughfare of Strasse des 17 Juni, which cuts through the middle of Berlin's central park, the Tiergarten. To your right, just near the Brandenburg Gate, is the glass-domed Reichstag and beyond that the new government district and the snazzy Hauptbahnhof (main train station). The cluster of skyscrapers diagonally off to the left, with the unusual circus-tent roof, is Potsdamer Platz.

On the other, far west side of the Tiergarten, out of sight near Zoo station, sits the one-time centre of West Berlin, including the shopping street of the Kurfürstendamm (or 'Ku'damm').

Although wealthier, more mature Berliners still happily frequent the west, the eastern districts are the most happening. Even Mitte, or the centre, now lies east of the former wall. As Mitte heads northeast, it merges into the trendy district of Prenzlauer Berg. Friedrichshain, another popular neighbourhood, is found several kilometres east of the centre, around Ostbahnhof.

Kreuzberg, south of Mitte, has two sides: western Kreuzberg was the alternative hub of West Berlin and is still hanging in there, with some interesting restaurants and bars; eastern Kreuzberg is grungier, hopping and definitely where the 'kool kids' – and adults – hang out. Further east and south is the rapidly gentrifying Kreuzkölln, which is loosely defined as the area where Kreuzberg and neighbouring Neukölln overlap. The upscale southwestern districts of Charlottenburg, Schöneberg and Wilmersdorf offer nice restaurants and a calm atmosphere, though some may find them a tad sterile in comparison with places further east.

Sights

Brandenburg Gate LANDMARK

(Brandenburger Tor; Map p478; Pariser Platz; MS-Bahn Unter den Linden) Finished in 1791 as one of 18 city gates, the neoclassical Brandenburg Gate became an East-West crossing point after the Berlin Wall was built in 1961. A symbol of Berlin's division, it was a place US presidents loved to grandstand. John F Kennedy passed by in 1963. Ronald Reagan appeared in 1987 to appeal to the Russian leader, 'Mr Gorbachev, tear down this wall!'. In 1989 more than 100,000 Germans poured through it as the wall fell. Five years later, Bill Clinton somewhat belatedly noted: 'Berlin is free'. The crowning Quadriga statue, a winged goddess in a horse-drawn chariot (once kidnapped by Napoleon and briefly taken to Paris), was cleaned in 2000 along with the rest of the structure.

Reichstag HISTORIC BUILDING

(Parliament; Map p478; 2273 2152; www.bundestag.de; Platz der Republik 1; admission free; 8am-midnight, last admission 10pm; MS-Bahn Unter den Linden) Just northwest of the Brandenburg Gate stands the glass-domed landmark with four national flags fluttering. A fire here in 1933 allowed Hitler to blame the communists and grab power, while the Soviets raised their flag here in 1945 to signal Nazi Germany's defeat. Today the building is once again the German seat of power, but it's the glass cupola added during the 1999 refurbishment that 10,000-plus people a day flock to see. Walking along the internal spiral walkway by British star architect Lord Norman Foster feels like being in a post-modern beehive. To beat the queues, book a table at the upmarket rooftop restaurant **Käfer** (2262 9935; www.feinkost-kaefer.de), which uses a separate entrance. With young children in tow, you're allowed to bypass the queue, too.

Holocaust Memorial MEMORIAL

(Denkmal für die ermordeten Juden Europas; Map p478; 2639 4336; www.stiftung-denkmal.de; Cora-Berliner-Strasse 1; admission free; field 24hr, information centre 10am-8pm Tue-Sun, last entry 7.15pm Apr-Sep, 10am-7pm Tue-Sun, last entry 6.15pm Oct-Mar; MS-Bahn Unter den Linden) Just south of the Reichstag, this grid of 2711 'stelae', or differently shaped concrete columns, is set over 19,000 sq metres of gently undulating ground. The slate-grey expanse of walkways and pillars can be

WANT MORE?

For in-depth information, reviews and recommendations at your fingertips, head to the Apple App Store to purchase Lonely Planet's *Berlin City Guide* iPhone app.

Alternatively, head to **Lonely Planet** (www.lonelyplanet.com/germany/berlin) for planning advice, author recommendations, traveller reviews and insider tips.

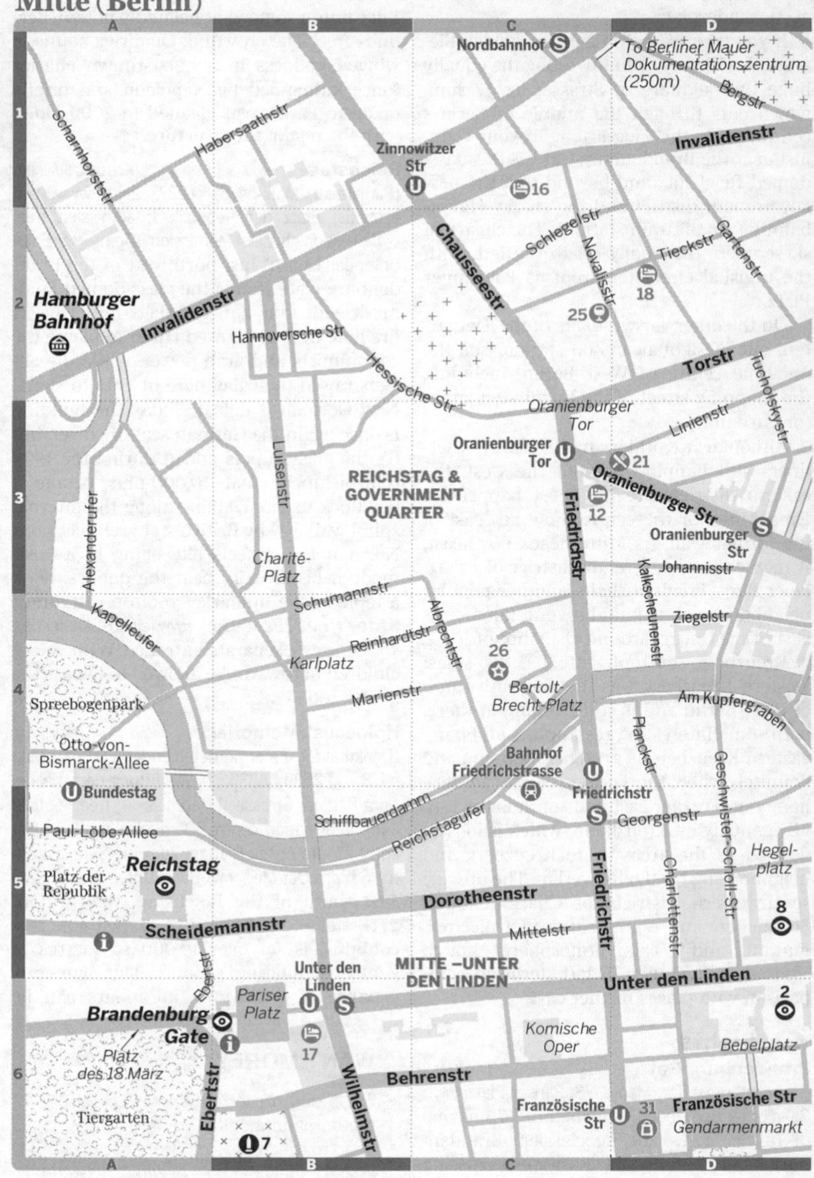

entered from any side, but presents varied sombre perspectives as you move through it. For historical background, designer Peter Eisenman has created an underground information centre in the southeast corner of the site.

Unter den Linden HISTORIC AVENUE

Celebrated in literature and lined with lime (or linden) trees, the renowned street Unter den Linden (Map p478) was the fashionable avenue of old Berlin. Today, after decades of communist neglect, it's been rebuilt and has

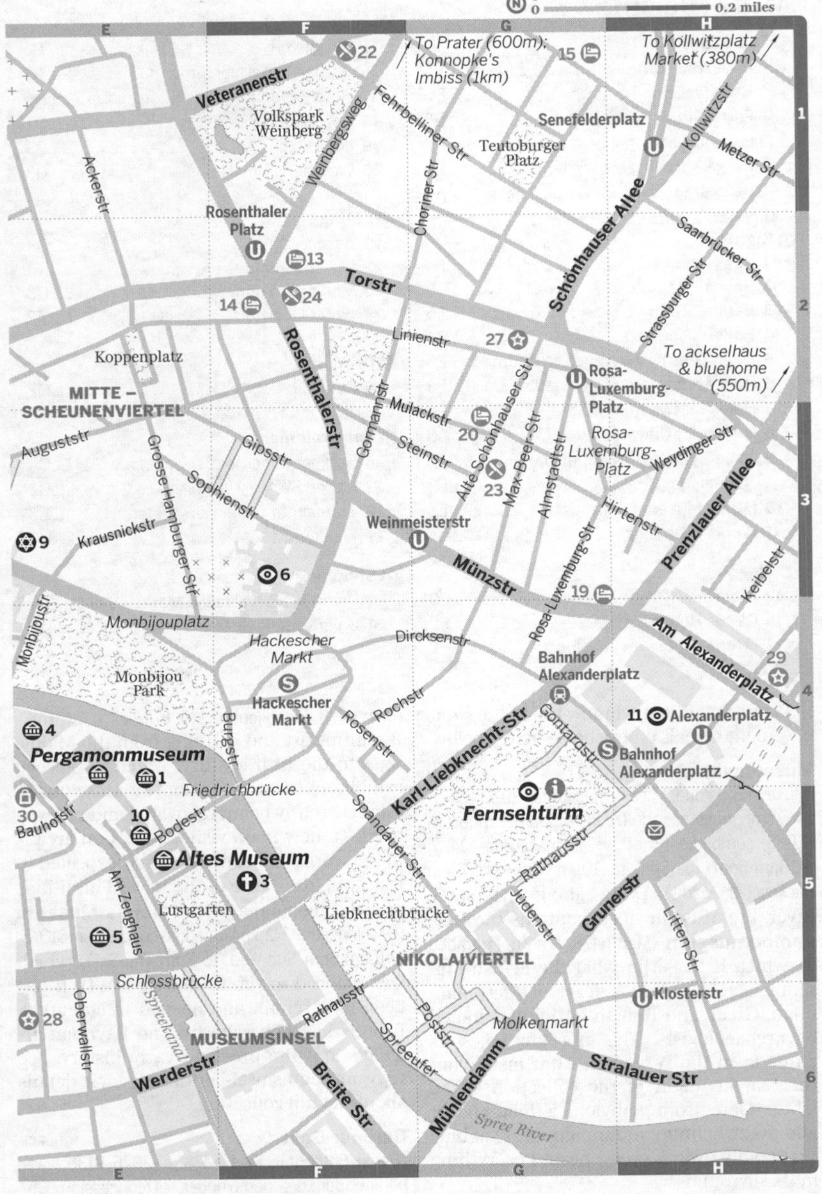

finally regained its former status. The thoroughfare stretches east from the Brandenburg Gate down to the Museumsinsel area, passing by shops, embassies, opera houses, museums and Berlin's revered **Humboldt University**.

Bebelplatz MEMORIAL

(Bebl Square; Map p478; Ⓜ Französische Strasse) Set on the Unter den Linden opposite the Humboldt University, this **book-burning memorial** is a reminder of the first major Nazi book-burning, which occurred in May

Mitte (Berlin)

Top Sights

- Altes Museum E5
- Brandenburg Gate B6
- Fernsehturm G5
- Hamburger Bahnhof A2
- Pergamonmuseum E4
- Reichstag A5

Sights

1 Alte Nationalgalerie E4
2 Bebelplatz D6
3 Berliner Dom F5
4 Bodemuseum E4
5 Deutsches Historisches Museum E5
6 Hackesche Höfe F3
7 Holocaust Memorial B6
8 Humboldt University D5
9 Neue Synagogue & Centrum Judaicum E3
10 Neues Museum E5
11 World Time Clock H4

Sleeping

12 Arcotel Velvet C3
13 Circus Hostel F2
14 Circus Hotel F2
15 Eastseven G1
16 Garden Hotel Honigmond C1
17 Hotel Adlon Kempinski B6
18 Hotel Honigmond D2
19 Lux 11 .... G3
20 Wombat's City Hostel G3

Eating

21 Assel D3
22 La Foccaceria F1
23 Monsieur Vuong G3
24 Sankt Oberholz F2

Drinking

25 Reingold C2

Entertainment

26 Berliner Ensemble C4
27 Kaffee Burger G2
28 Staatsoper Unter den Linden E6
29 Weekend H4

Shopping

30 Berlin Art & Nostalgia Market E5
31 Galeries Lafayette D6

1933. A transparent window tile in the stone pavement reveals empty bookshelves below.

Museumsinsel MUSEUM

(Museums Island; ☎all museums 2090 5577; www.smb.museum; adult/concession per museum €10/5, combined ticket for all museums €14/7; ⏰10am-6pm Tue-Sun, to 10pm Thu; Ⓜ S-Bahn Hackescher Markt) Lying along the Spree River, the Museumsinsel contains the **Pergamonmuseum** (Map p478; Am Kupfergraben 5), which is to Berlin what the British Museum is to London: a feast of Mesopotamian, Greek and Roman antiquities looted by archaeologists. The museum takes its name from the Pergamon Altar inside, but the real highlight of the collection is the Ishtar Gate from Babylon, a magnificent and overwhelming monument of royal blue that boldly dwarfs everyone and everything in its surrounds.

The **Alte Nationalgalerie** (Old National Gallery; Map p478; Bodestrasse 1-3) houses 19th-century European sculpture and painting; the **Altes Museum** (Map p478; Am Lustgarten) features classical antiquities but is scheduled for restoration and may be closed in the coming years; and the **Bodemuseum** (Map p478; Monbijoubrücke) houses sculpture, Byzantine art and painting from the Middle Ages to the 19th century. Watch for special exhibitions at each. The entire Museumsinsel is currently being renovated and redeveloped – a new main visitor reception area is in the works and construction is expected to last until 2015. One of the newest additions was the reopening of the **Neues Museum** (New Museum; Map p478; adult/concession €10/5; ⏰10am-6pm Sun-Wed, to 8pm Thu-Sat), which was reduced to rubble during WWII. It has been fully rebuilt and opened in late 2009. It houses Queen Nefertiti and Egyptian artefacts and the pre- and early history. See www.museumsinsel-berlin.de for details about the full collection.

Berliner Dom CHURCH

(Berlin Cathedral; Map p478; ☎2026 9136 www.berliner-dom.de; adult/under 14/concession €5/free/3; ⏰9am-8pm Mon-Sat, from noon Sun Apr-Sep, to 7pm Oct-Mar; Ⓜ S-Bahn Hackescher Markt) Overlooking the 'island' is this stately former royal court church – come here mainly for the exceptional view of the city from its top gallery, glass mosaics of the dome and to glimpse the Sauer organ (over 7000 pipes).

Deutsches Historisches Museum MUSEUM
(German History Museum; Map p478; ☎203 040; www.dhm.de; Unter den Linden 2; admission €6, ⏲10am-6pm; Ⓜ S-Bahn Hackescher Markt) Some come for the permanent exhibition on German history, but the museum is still arguably most notable for the glass-walled spiral staircase by modernist architect IM Pei (creator of the Louvre's glass pyramid).

Hackescher Markt HISTORIC AREA
(Ⓜ S-Bahn Hackescher Markt) A complex of shops and apartments around eight courtyards, the **Hackesche Höfe** (Map p478) is commercial and touristy, but it's definitely good fun to wander around the big-name brand shops and smaller boutiques or simply people watch in the cafes and restaurants – the atmosphere is always lively.

Neue Synagogue & Centrum Judaicum SYNAGOGUE
(Map p478; ☎8802 8300; www.cjudaicum.de; Oranienburger Strasse 28-30; adult/concession €3/2; ⏲10am-8pm Sun & Mon, to 6pm Tue-Thu, to 5pm Fri, reduced hr Nov-Apr; Ⓜ S-Bahn Hackescher Markt) The original New Synagogue, finished in 1866 in what was then predominantly Jewish part of the city, was Germany's largest synagogue at that time. It was destroyed in World War II and rebuilt after the Berlin Wall fell. Now this space doubles as a museum and cultural centre illustrating its history of local Jewish life.

Hamburger Bahnhof MUSEUM
(Map p478; ☎3978 3439; www.hamburgerbahnhof.de; Invalidenstrasse 50; adult/concession €12/6; ⏲10am-6pm Tue-Fri, 11am-8pm Sat, 11am-6pm Sun; Ⓜ Hauptbahnhof/Lehrter Stadtbahnhof) This contemporary-art museum is housed in a former neoclassical train station and showcases works by Warhol, Lichtenstein, Cy Twombly and Keith Haring.

Fernsehturm LANDMARK
(Map p478; ☎242 3333; www.berlinerfernsehturm.de; adult/concession €10/6.50; ⏲9am-midnight Mar-Oct, from 10am Nov-Feb; Ⓜ Alexanderplatz) Call it Freudian or call it *Ostalgie* (nostalgia

IF WALLS COULD TALK

Remnants of the 155km Berlin Wall are scattered across the city, but you can follow all or sections of its former path along the 160km-long **Berliner Mauerweg** (Berlin Wall Trail; www.berlin.de/mauer), a signposted walking and cycling path that follows the former border fortifications, either along customs-patrol roads in West Berlin or border-control roads used by GDR guards. Along the route, 40 multilingual information stations provide historical context, highlight dramatic events and relate stories about daily life in the divided city.

The longest surviving stretch of the wall is the **East Side Gallery** (Map p482; www.eastsidegallery.com; Mühlenstrasse; Ⓜ S-Bahn Warschauer Strasse) in Friedrichshain. Panels along this 1.3km section of graffiti and art include the famous portrait of Soviet leader Brezhnev kissing GDR leader Erich Hönecker and a Trabant car seemingly bursting through the (now crumbling) concrete.

The sombre **Berliner Mauer Dokumentationszentrum** (Berlin Wall Documentation Centre; off Map p478; ☎464 1030; www.berliner-mauer-dokumentationszentrum.de; Bernauer Strasse 111; admission free; ⏲10am-6pm Tue-Sun Apr-Oct, to 5pm Nov-Mar; Ⓜ U-Bahn Bernauersrasse) is a memorial containing a section of the original wall, photos of the surrounding area (before and during the lifespan of the wall), newspaper clippings and listening stations featuring old West and East Berlin radio programs as well as eyewitness testimonies. Be sure to climb the tower for a view of an artistic re-creation of no-man's land as well as the **Kapelle der Versöhnung** (Chapel of Reconciliation), a modern round structure of pressed earth and slim wooden planks built on the site of an 1894 red-brick church blown up in 1985 in order to widen the border strip. A 15-minute remembrance service for those killed while attempting to flee from east to west is held at noon Tuesday to Friday.

In Kreuzberg, the famous sign at **Checkpoint Charlie** (Map p482) still boasts 'You are now leaving the American sector'. But it and the reconstructed US guardhouse are just tourist attractions now. For a less light-hearted view of the past, visit **Haus am Checkpoint Charlie** (Map p482; ☎253 7250; www.mauer-museum.com; Friedrichstrasse 43-45; adult/concession €12.50/9.50; ⏲9am-10pm; Ⓜ Kochstrasse/Stadtmitte). Tales of spectacular escape attempts include through tunnels, in hot-air balloons and even using a one-man submarine.

Kreuzberg & Friedrichshain (Berlin)

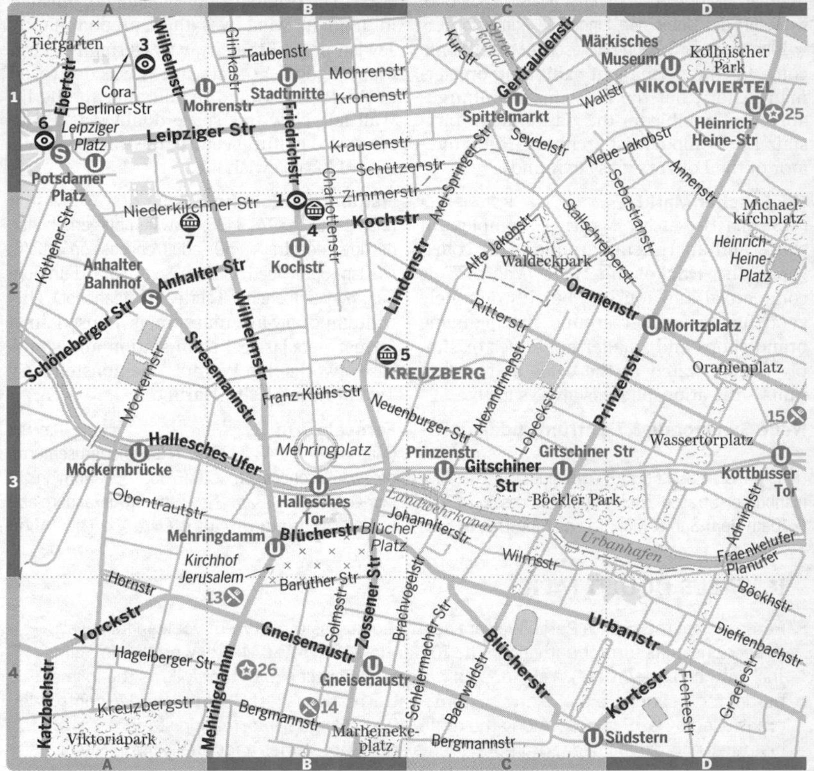

for the communist East or *Ost*), but Berlin's once-mocked socialist Fernsehturm TV tower is fast becoming its most-loved symbol. Originally erected in 1969 and the city's tallest structure, its central bauble was decorated as a giant football for the 2006 FIFA World Cup, while its 368m outline still pops up in numerous souvenirs. That said, ascending 207m to the revolving (but musty) Telecafe is a less singular experience than visiting the Reichstag dome.

The Turm dominates **Alexanderplatz**, a former livestock and wool market that became the low-life district chronicled by Alfred Döblin's 1929 novel *Berlin Alexanderplatz* and then developed as a 1960s communist showpiece. Even in a city so often described as one big building site, today's Alexanderplatz is an unusual hive of construction activity as it is transformed into the next Potsdamer Platz–style development. However, its communist past still echoes through the retro **World Time Clock** (Map p478) and along the portentous **Karl-Marx-Allee**, which leads several kilometres east from the square to Friedrichshain.

Bauhaus Archiv MUSEUM

(Map p486; ☎254 0020; www.bauhaus.de; Klingelhöferstrasse 14; adult/concession Sat-Mon €7/4, Wed-Fri €6/3; ⊙10am-5pm Wed-Mon; Ⓜ Nollendorfplatz) This avant-garde museum includes drawings, chairs and other Modernist objects from the famous Bauhaus school of design – as well as a very tempting shop. The school itself survives in Dessau (see p513).

Neue Nationalgalerie MUSEUM

(Map p486; ☎266 2951; www.neue-nationalgalerie.de; Potsdamer Strasse 50; adult/concession €10/5; ⊙10am-6pm Tue, Wed & Fri, to 10pm Thu, 11am-6pm Sat & Sun; Ⓜ S-Bahn Potzdamer Platz) Berlin's best collection of 20th-century works by Picasso, Klee, Munch, Dalí, Kandinsky and many German expressionists are housed in

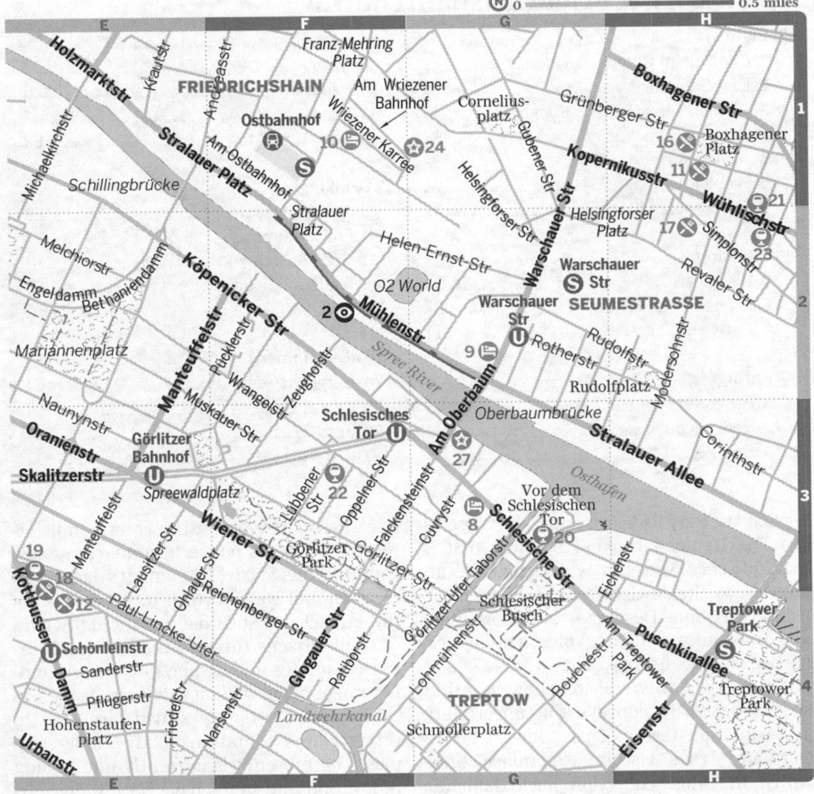

an exquisite 'temple of light and glass' built by Bauhaus-director Ludwig Mies van der Rohe.

Potsdamer Platz HISTORIC AREA

(Map p482; S-Bahn Potsdamer Platz) The lid was symbolically sealed on capitalism's victory over socialism in Berlin when this postmodern temple to Mammon was erected in 2000 over the former death strip. Under the big-top, glass-tent roof of the **Sony Center** and along the malls of the Legolike **Daimler City**, people swarm in and around shops, restaurants, offices, loft apartments, clubs, a cinema, a luxury hotel and a casino – all revitalising what was the busiest square in prewar Europe.

During the International Film Festival Berlin (see p485), Potsdamer Platz welcomes Hollywood A-listers. In between you can rub shoulders with German cinematic heroes – particularly Marlene Dietrich – at the **Filmmuseum** (300 9030; www.filmmuseum-berlin.de; Potsdamer Strasse 2; adult/concession €6/4.50; 10am-6pm Tue, Wed & Fri-Sun, to 8pm Thu). There's also 'Europe's fastest lift' to the 100m-high **Panorama Observation Deck** (www.panoramapunkt.de; adult/concession €4.50/3; 11am-8pm, last entry 7.30pm).

But, as ever in Berlin, the past refuses to go quietly. Just north of Potsdamer Platz lies the **former site of Hitler's Bunker**.

Topographie des Terrors MEMORIAL

(Map p482; 2548 6703; www.topographie.de; Niederkirchner Strasse 8; admission free; 10am-8pm May-Sep, to dusk Oct-Apr; S-Bahn Potsdamer Platz) This is an eye-opening and graphic collection of text and images surrounding WWII, mounted on the ruins of the Gestapo and SS headquarters. Note: this memorial may not be suitable for children.

TOP CHOICE **Jewish Museum** MUSEUM

(Map p482; 2599 3300; www.juedisches-museum-berlin.de; Lindenstrasse 9-14; adult/concession €5/2.50; 10am-10pm Mon, to 8pm

Kreuzberg & Friedrichshain (Berlin)

Sights
1 Checkpoint Charlie B2
2 East Side Gallery F2
3 Former Site of Hitler's Bunker A1
4 Haus am Checkpoint Charlie B2
5 Jewish Museum B2
6 Potsdamer Platz A1
7 Topographie des Terrors A2

Sleeping
8 Die Fabrik G3
9 Michelberger Hotel G2
10 Ostel F1

Eating
11 Bürgeramt Früstücksklub H1
12 Cafe Jacques E4
13 Curry 36 .... B4
14 Foodorama B4
15 Hasir D3
16 Papaya H1
17 Schneeweiss H2
18 Türkenmarkt E3

Drinking
19 Ankerklause E3
20 Freischwimmer G3
21 Hops & Barley H1
22 Madame Claude F3
23 Süss War Gestern H2

Entertainment
24 Berghain/Panoramabar G1
25 Kit Kat Club D1
26 SchwuZ B4
27 Watergate G3

Tue-Sun, last entry 1hr before closing; MHallesches Tor) The Daniel Libeskind building that is the Jüdisches Museum is as much the attraction as the Jewish-German history collection within. Designed to disorientate and unbalance with its 'voids', cul-de-sacs, barbed metal fittings, slit windows and uneven floors, this still-somehow-beautiful structure swiftly conveys the uncertainty and sometime-terror of past Jewish life in Germany. It's a visceral experience, after which the huge collection itself demands your concentration. The building's footprint is a ripped-apart Star of David.

Kaiser-Wilhelm-Gedächtniskirche & Kurfürstendamm CHURCH
(Map p486; 218 5023; www.gedaechtniskirche-berlin.de; Breitscheidplatz; memorial hall 10am-4pm Mon-Sat, hall of worship 9am-7pm; MHallesches Tor) West Berlin's legendary shopping thoroughfare and avenue, the Ku'damm (the nickname for its full name Kurfürstendamm), has lost some of its cachet since the wall fell, but is worth visiting for its landmark church, which remains in ruins – just as British bombers left it on 22 November 1943 – as an antiwar memorial. Only the broken west tower still stands. In 1961 the modern hall of worship was built adjacent to the church.

Stasi Museum MUSEUM
(553 6854; www.stasimuseum.de; House 22, Ruschestrasse 103; adult/concession €5/4; 11am-6pm Tue-Fri, 2-6pm Sat & Sun; MMagdalenenstrasse) This imposing compound, formerly the secret police headquarters, now contains the Stasi Museum. It's largely in German, but well worth it to get a sense of the impact the Stasi had on the daily lives of GDR citizens through the museum's extensive photos and displays of the astounding range of surveillance devices, as well as exhibits of the tightly sealed jars used to retain cloths containing body-odour samples. The museum is currently undergoing renovation and items have been temporarily relocated in another building (still part of the Stasi complex) – the temporary site is equally engaging – though former Stasi head Mielke's office can only be seen in photos. At the time of writing it was schedule to be reopened in its original space towards late 2011.

Tours

Guided tours in Berlin are phenomenally popular; you can choose Third Reich, Wall, bunker, communist, boat or bicycle tours, as well as guided pub crawls. Expect to pay around €15 and up.

New Berlin WALKING TOURS
(017-9973 0397; www.newberlintours.com) Free (yup, free) 3½-hour introductory walking tours. These leave at 10.30am and 12.30pm from Dunkin' Donuts opposite the Zoologisher Garten train station, and 11am and 1pm outside Starbucks at Pariser Platz near the Brandenburg Gate. Guides are enthusiastic, knowledgeable...and accept tips.

Trabi Safari CAR TOURS

(☎275 2273; www.trabi-safari.de; €30-80) Tool around Berlin in a Trabant car; operates from the Berlin Hi-Flyer near Checkpoint Charlie.

Fat Tire Bike Tours BIKE TOURS

(http://fattirebiketours.com/berlin) Offers a huge range of tours, from standard city tours to themed tours along the former course of the Berlin Wall and/or a Cold War tour, historical tours and more.

Festivals & Events

International Film Festival Berlin FILM FESTIVAL

(☎259 200; www.berlinale.de) The Berlinale, held in February, is Germany's answer to the Cannes and Venice film festivals.

Christopher Street Day GAY EVENT

(☎2362 8632; www.csd-berlin.de) Held on the last weekend in June, Germany's largest gay event has been running for more than 30 years.

Fuckparade DANCE EVENT

(www.fuckparade.org) Each August this anti-establishment, antigentrification demonstration dances to its own noncommercial techno beat.

NIGHT AT THE MUSEUMS

All museums listed on www.smb.museum are free on Thursday for four hours before closing time – this includes the **Pergamonmuseum** and the **Altes Museum** (see p480). Alternatively, museumophiles will love the **Schau-Lust Museen Berlin Pass** (☎250 025). A mere €19 gives you admission to more than 70 museums (not including Checkpoint Charlie) over three days.

Sleeping

Berlin's independent hostels are far superior to the standard DJH (www.jugendherberge.de) locations in town.

MITTE & PRENZLAUER BERG

Lette'm Sleep HOSTEL €

(☎4473 3623; www.backpackers.de; Lettestrasse 7; dm from €11, tw without bathroom from €49, apt from €69; ; MEberswalder Strasse) Located within stumbling distance of the Prenzlauer Berg nightlife action, this colourful and convenient party hostel is simply groovy, baby, groovy.

Roof APARTMENT €€

(☎6951 8833; www.roof-berlin.com; studio/1-bed apt €85/115, reduced rates after 3 nights;) Proprietor Ariane has two studios and a one-bedroom apartment – all tastefully decorated in soothing colours with comfy, contemporary touches – peppered around central Prenslauer Berg. She'll even stock the fridge for you with breakfast or snacks like wine and cheese (€25 for either) on request.

DON'T MISS

BERLIN'S TIERGARTEN, A SWATH OF GREEN

Lolling about in the grass on a sunny afternoon is the quintessential Berlin pastime. Germans adore the outdoors and flock to urban green spaces whenever the weather is fine. They also dislike tan lines, so don't be surprised if you stumble upon locals sunbathing in the nude.

The Tiergarten is criss-crossed by a series of major roads and anchored by the Brandenburg Gate and the Reichstag on its northwestern edge. It's a tangle of curved walking and cycling paths, tiny ponds, open fields and thick woods. You'll probably get lost, but there are dozens of maps scattered about to help you find your way.

From the Reichstag, the Tiergarten's **carillon** (John-Foster-Dulles-Allee; 100 or 200) and the **Haus der Kulturen der Welt** (House of World Cultures; John-Foster-Dulles-Allee) are clearly visible. The latter was the US contribution to the 1957 International Building Exposition and it's easy to see why locals call it the 'pregnant oyster'.

Further west, the wings of the **Siegessäule** (Victory Column; 100 or 200) were the *Wings of Desire* in that famous Wim Wenders film. This golden angel was built to commemorate Prussian military victories in the 19th century. Today, as the end point of the annual Christopher Street Parade, she's also a gay icon. However, there are better views than those at the column's peak.

Charlottenburg (Berlin)

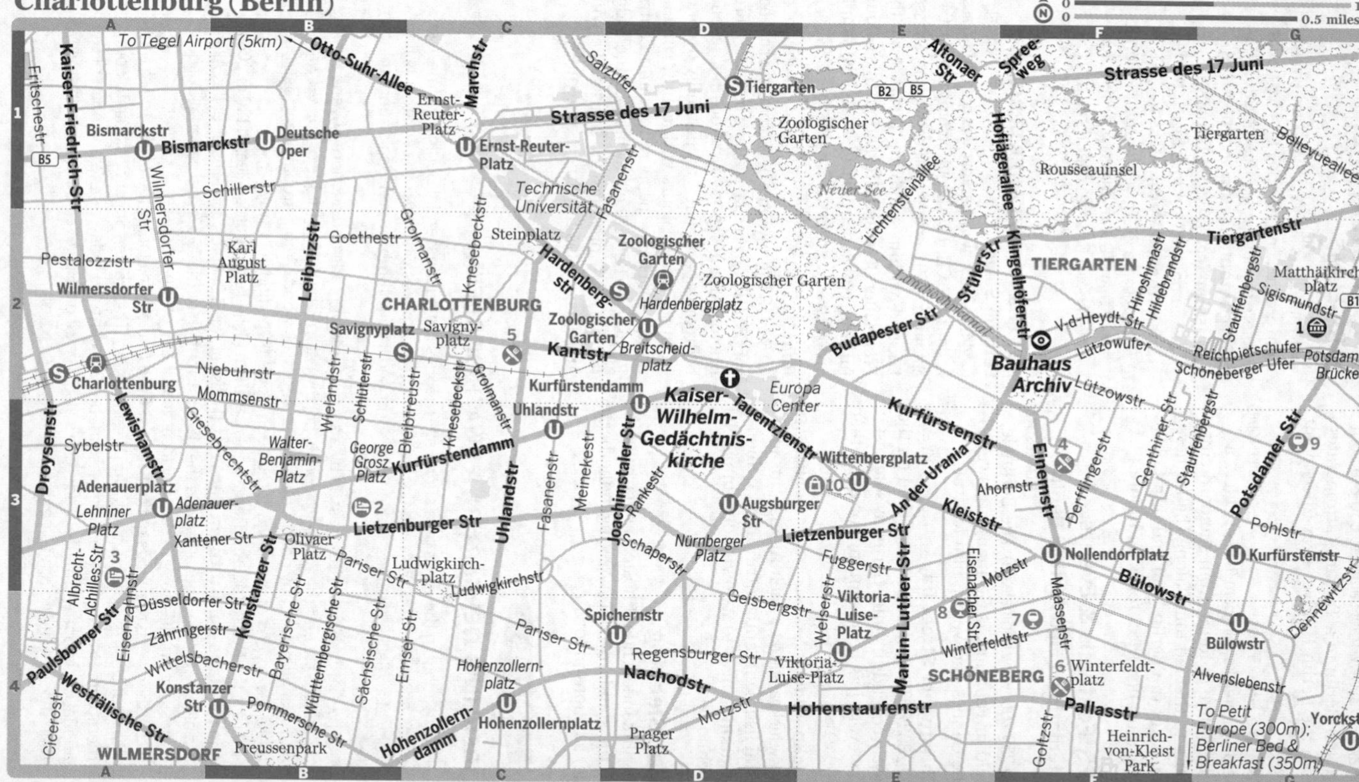

Charlottenburg (Berlin)

ackselhaus & bluehome HOTEL €€
(off Map p478; ☎4433 7633; www.ackselhaus.de; Belforter Strasse 21; ste from €105, apt from €150; @; M Senefelder Platz) This Zen oasis, spread across two buildings, offers exquisitely designed suites or apartments (most with kitchenettes). Each has a different theme, from Italian to Hollywood; all exude an element of exquisite class, calm and humour – the African suite, for example, has stuffed animal heads mounted on the wall.

Hotel Honigmond HOTEL €€
(Map p478; ☎284 4550; www.honigmond-berlin.de; Tieckstrasse 12; s/d from €105/115; @; M Oranienburger Tor) A perfect choice for a romantic weekend (or simply those seeing a touch of elegance and class). This tasteful hotel is all creaky wooden floors and four-poster beds. Sister property **Garden Hotel Honigmond** (Map p478; ☎2844 5577; www.honigmond-berlin.de; Invalidenstrasse 122; s/d from €103/113; @; M Zinnowitzer Strasse) offers similar rooms but includes a tranquil back garden.

EastSeven HOSTEL €
(Map p478; ☎9362 2240; www.eastseven.de; Schwedter Strasse 7; dm from €18, s/d from €38/52; @; M Senefelder Platz) Retro and homey, with spotless rooms and sturdy pine furniture, there is a youthful elegance here rarely present in hostels. The lovely garden is perfect for summer barbecues.

Hotel Greifswald HOTEL €
(☎4442 7888; www.hotel-greifswald.de; Greifswalderstrasse 211; s/d/tr/apt from €57.50/69/90/75; @; M Senefelder Platz) You'd never guess this informal, quiet hotel set back from the street around a sweet courtyard is regularly home to bands and even rock stars – until you see their photos in the lobby. We love the sumptuous breakfast buffet (€7.50) served until noon.

Circus Hotel HOTEL €€
(Map p478; ☎2000 3939; www.circus-berlin.de; Rosenthalerstrasse 1; s €70, d from €80, ste €100, apt €115-170; @; M U-Bahn Rosenthaler Platz) The fancier younger sister to the Circus Hostel across the intersection, this hotel has given careful attention to every detail – the result is a retro twist on minimalism, airy rooms, bold-coloured walls and super-shiny wood flooring.

Malzcafe HOTEL €€
(☎702 21357; www.malzcafe.de; Veteranenstrasse 10; s/d/q €80/110/150, apt from €109; @; M Rosenthaler Platz) A small hotel above an adjoining cafe, you'll be made to feel right at home in minimalist rooms with soft, soothing tones, high ceilings and plenty of space. A pleasant terrace is divine in warm weather, and you're a short hop to both the heart of Mitte and Prenzlauer Berg.

Arcotel Velvet HOTEL €€
(Map p478; ☎278 7530; www.arcotelhotels.com; Oranienburger Strasse 52; d/ste from €140/150; M Oranienburger Tor) Floor-to-ceiling windows give front rooms a bird's-eye view of the bustling street and, combined with bathrooms separated only by gauze curtains, create a feeling of loft living. If you plan to retire before 2am, request a room facing the back – the main road gets quite loud and rowdy at weekends.

Lux 11 HOTEL €€€
(Map p478; ☎936 2800; www.lux-eleven.com; Rosa-Luxemburg-Strasse 9-13; r/ste from €165/205; @; M Weinmeisterstrasse/Alexanderplatz) A liberal use of white makes this slick, streamlined hotel a haven of unpretentious minimalism. All rooms feature a tiny kitchenette (kettle, coffee makers, two-pot stove and a handful of cookware).

FREE PICKS

Welcome news for budget travellers: in comparison to other European capitals, Berlin is generally quite inexpensive, and several key sights and experiences are completely free:

» **Brandenburg Gate** (p477) The symbol of Berlin and of reunified Germany is a must-see on any Berlin itinerary.

» **Kaiser-Wilhelm-Gedächtniskirche** (p484) This left-as-it-was-bombed church on the Ku'damm is a vivid reminder of WWII.

» **Tiergarten** (p485) Let yourself get lost in this oasis of green.

» **New Berlin walking tours** (p484) They're free, and guides are chock-full of information about their beloved city.

» **Holocaust Memorial** (p477) An experiential monument to the victims of the Holocaust.

» **East Side Gallery** (p481) The longest remaining section of the wall is a memorial to freedom.

Hotel Adlon Kempinski HOTEL €€€
(Map p478; ☎226 10; www.kempinski.com, Am Pariser Platz, Unter den Linden 77; r from €450; ; Ⓜ S-Bahn Unter den Linden) Still remembered mostly for being the hotel where Michael Jackson had his baby-dangling episode, this luxurious hotel is situated just on the doorstep of the Brandenburg Gate. It's also known for its Schochu cocktail bar, a swanky spot featuring elegant, gold Asian touches.

Wombat's City Hostel HOSTEL €
(Map p478; ☎8471 0820; www.wombats-hostels.com; Alte Schönhauser Strasse 2; dm/d €24/65, apt with kitchen €80; @; Ⓜ Rosa-Luxemburg-Platz) A popular member of the Mitte hostel scene, rooms and dorms (all en suite) are decorated with modern touches, and doubles offer long balconies. A hopping lounge and all-you-can-eat breakfast buffet (€3.70) round out the package. Discounts are available from November to February.

Circus Hostel HOSTEL €
(Map p478; ☎2839 1433; www.circus-hostel.de; Weinbergsweg 1a; dm from €21, s/d without bathroom €42/58, with bathroom €52/72, 2-/4-person apt €95/150; @; Ⓜ U-Bahn Rosenthaler Platz) This stalwart is one of the most popular hostels in town, with a great central location and friendly staff. Rooms feature splashes of vibrant colour and modern, Ikea-like furnishings. There's a two-night minimum stay for apartments. It's quite the party hostel with free beer on Mondays and Thursdays and a kickin' on-site bar that holds regular karaoke nights.

KREUZBERG & FRIEDRICHSHAIN

Die Fabrik HOTEL €
(Map p482; ☎611 7716; www.diefabrik.com; Schlesische Strasse 18; dm €20, s/d/tr/q from €40/54/70/85; @; Ⓜ Schlesisches Tor) A cross between a hostel and a hotel (it feels more like the latter), these tidy and simple rooms are a steal. Plenty of spotless shower and toilet facilities are located on each floor; the larger doubles come with washbasins and tiny sitting areas. Solar power heats 100% of your hot water in the sunny months (and a smaller percentage in other seasons). Wi-fi is available in the lobby only.

Michelberger Hotel HOSTEL €
(Map p482; ☎2977 8590; www.michelbergerhotel.com; Warschauer Strasse 39; s/d/tr from €60/70/150; ; Ⓜ Prinzenstrasse, Hallesches Tor) This trendy design hotel is funky and fun and offers downmarket rates in stylish digs – think loft beds and sleek furniture. Minimalism dominates but the clean lines mean small spaces still feel roomy.

Ostel HOSTEL €
(Map p476; ☎2576 8660; www.ostel.eu; Wriezener Karree 5; dm/d/apt €15/56/120; @; Ⓜ Ostbahnhof) *Ostalgie* – nostalgia for the communist East – is taken to a whole new level at this hostel/hotel with original socialist GDR furnishings and portraits of Honecker and other former socialist leaders. You can even stay in a 'bugged' Stasi Suite. You might think you've entered a surreal time machine – until you access the free wi-fi that is. At the time of writing the hotel was due to open a DDR restaurant, mimicking the old-school

Interhotels, the socialist hotel chain that dominated before the wall fell.

Eastern Comfort Hostelboot HOSTEL €
(☎6676 3806; www.eastern-comfort.com; Mühlenstrasse 73-77; dm €18, s/d from €55/78, bedding €5; @; S-Bahn Warschauer Strasse) This moored boat-turned-hostel is close to the East Side Gallery, is convenient for both Kreuzberg and Friedrichshain and features cosy rooms and dorms (all en suite). If it's full ask about the 18 units in the Western Comfort boat across the river (check in at Eastern Comfort).

CHARLOTTENBURG & SCHÖNEBERG

Hotel Bogota HOTEL €€
(Map p486; ☎881 5001; www.bogota.de; Schülterstrasse 45; d without bathroom from €65, with bathroom €90-150; ; Uhlandstrasse) With oodles of charm and character at affordable prices, this is a must for vintage-furniture lovers. Ask about the landmark building's fascinating fashion history (which will explain the snazzy photos adorning the walls).

Berliner Bed & Breakfast HOTEL €
(off Map p486; ☎2437 3962; www.berliner-bed-and-breakfast.de; Langenscheidtstrasse 5; s/d/tr/q without bathroom €35/55/68/78; Kleistpark) Lofty ceilings and gorgeous wood floors dominate in this small, unique space with themed rooms (Asia, retro, fashionable). Excellent breakfast provisions are left for guests each day, which you prepare yourself in the communal kitchen.

Propeller Island City Lodge HOTEL €€€
(Map p486; ☎891 9016; www.propeller-island.de; Albrecht-Achilles-Strasse 58; r per person from €75; @; Adenauerplatz) Keen to sleep in a bed suspended by ropes, or in a coffin, or on a pile of chopped logs? If you've dreamed it you can probably find it in one of the themed rooms (oh, and slightly more standard spaces are available too).

Eating

Berliners love to eat out – it's relaxed and affordable and patrons often linger long after finishing their meals. Many of the best finds are in the budget category. Restaurants usually open from 11am to midnight, with varying *Ruhetage* or rest days. Cafes often close around 8pm, though just as many stay open until 2am or later.

Berlin is a snacker's paradise, with Turkish (your best bet), wurst (sausage), Greek, Italian and Chinese *Imbiss* stalls throughout the city. Meat eaters should not leave the city without trying Berlin's famous currywurst.

For self-caterers, there's the excellent organic **Kollwitzplatz market** (off Map p478; 9am-4pm Sat & Sun; Senefelderplatz), the relaxed **Winterfeldtplatz farmers market** (Map p486; Wed & Sat) and the bustling, ultracheap **Türkenmarkt** (Turkish market; Map p482; noon-6:30pm Tue & Fri).

MITTE & PRENZLAUER BERG

Oderquelle GERMAN €€
(☎4400 8080; Oderberger Strasse 27; mains €8-16; dinner; Eberswalder Strasse) Modern German food in such mellow, convivial digs is rare, almost as rare as snagging a table here after 7pm, so be sure to reserve. This is one of the best places in Berlin for consistently excellent service, exceptional wine and typical German dishes – think elegant, modern comfort food.

La Focacceria PIZZA €
(Map p478; Fehrbelliner Strasse 24; slices €1.75; 11am-11pm; Rosenthaler Platz) A character-filled focaccia and pizza joint with an intense local following – perfect for an afternoon snack after a hard day's shopping or sightseeing.

Konnopke's Imbiss WURST STAND €
(off Map p478; Schönhauser Allee 44a; snack €2; 6am-8pm Mon-Fri, noon-7pm Sat; Eberswalder Strasse) The quintessential wurst stand under the elevated U-Bahn tracks. We think Konnopke's serves the best currywurst in town.

Assel GERMAN €€
(Map p478; ☎281 2056; Oranienburger Strasse 21; mains €5-16; Oranienburger Strasse or Hackescher Markt) One of the few exceptional picks on a particularly touristy and busy stretch of Mitte. Come for coffee, a bite or a full meal and stretch out in the wooden booths made from old S-Bahn seats. Plus, the toilets are entertaining (you'll see).

Sankt Oberholz INTERNATIONAL €
(Map p478; Rosenthaler Strasse 72a; dishes €5-8; ; Rosenthaler Platz) Berlin's '*Urbanen Pennern*' (officeless, self-employed creative types) have been flocking here for years with their laptops for the free wi-fi access, but we like it for the people watching – especially from the lofty lifeguard chairs out front. Soups, sandwiches and salads are always satisfying.

Monsieur Vuong ASIAN €€
(Map p478; Alte Schönhauser Strasse 46; mains €7 Ⓜ Weinmeisterstrasse, Rosa-Luxemburg-Platz or Alexanderplatz) Berlin's original designer Asian soup den is trendy, packed and consistently serves amazing Vietnamese fare. Arrive early to avoid queuing.

KREUZBERG & FRIEDRICHSHAIN

Hasir TURKISH €
(Map p482; Adalbertstrasse 10; mains €5-10; 24hr; Ⓜ Kottbusser Tor) Local lore says this is the birthplace of Berlin's doner kebab – we haven't seen proof but we do know it tastes fantastic and we can indulge on proper chairs. It's also a fab spot to try simple Turkish fare.

Bürgeramt Früstücksklub BURGERS €
(Map p482; Krossenerstrasse 22; burgers €2-4; from 11am Mon-Fri, from 10am Sat & Sun; Ⓜ Samariterstrasse;) A mere 13 types of burgers, including chicken and veggie versions, are cooked up with love and a smile in this wee space – if you can't snag a seat, head to the tree-filled square opposite. Hearty breakfast fare is also available.

TOP CHOICE **Cafe Jacques** INTERNATIONAL €€
(Map p482; 694 1048; Maybachufer 8; mains €12-20; Ⓜ Schönleinstrasse) Dishes hover around French and North African mainstays but Italian fare features too – frankly, it's all so lovingly and exceptionally prepared, you can't go wrong with anything you order. No surprise then that the devoted clientele flock here and linger over top-quality wine, flickering candlelight and the relaxed vibe. Reserve or be disappointed – one peek inside and you'll want to hop in and get a piece of this unfussy space and inviting atmosphere.

Nansen INTERNATIONAL €€
(301 1438; Maybachufer 39; mains €10-19; dinner; Ⓜ Schönleinstrasse) At this local favourite in this gentrified part of town, you can dine on seasonal modern German cuisine in a romantic, candlelit space – most menu items are sourced locally.

Papaya THAI €
(Map p482; Krossener Strasse 11; mains €5-11; Ⓜ Frankfurter Tor) Don't come here for the decor (it's bland) but do come for homemade Thai specialities. It's a prime spot to fill up on quick, satisfying, budget fare before hitting the plethora of bars and clubs on its doorstep.

Foodorama INTERNATIONAL €€
(Map p482; Bergmannstrasse 94; mains €7-14; Ⓜ Mehringdamm) Germany's first climate-neutral restaurant has cafeteria-style digs but features the unlikely (organic currywurst and Wiener schnitzel) plus Asian stir-fries and German cucumber salad.

Curry 36 SAUSAGES €
(Map p482; Mehringdamm 36; snacks €2-6; 9am-4pm Mon-Sat, to 3pm Sun; Ⓜ Mehringdamm) This is Kreuzberg's most popular sausage stand, as evidenced by the daily queues (yes, it really is worth the wait).

Schneeweiss GERMAN €
(Map p482; 2904 9704; Simplonstrasse 16; day menu €7-10, Ⓜ S-Bahn Warschauer Strasse) Subtly embossed vanilla wallpaper, a long, central table and parquet flooring keep neutral 'Snow White' feeling more après-ski than icy. The vaguely German 'Alpine' food is excellent.

CHARLOTTENBURG & SCHÖNEBERG

Café Einstein Stammhaus AUSTRIAN €€
(Map p486; 261 5096; www.cafeeinstein.com, in German; Kurfürstenstrasse 58; mains €15-23; 9am-1am; Ⓜ Nollendorfplatz) You'll think you've hopped to another capital at this Viennese coffee house. Choose from schnitzel, strudel and other Austrian fare in the polished, palatial digs.

Schwarzes Café INTERNATIONAL €
(Map p486; Kantstrasse 148; dishes €5-10; Ⓜ S-Bahn Zoo or Savignyplatz) Founded in 1978, this 24-hour food 'n' booze institution must have seen half of Berlin pass through it (or pass out in it) at some point. Don't leave without checking out the toilets.

Engelbecken BAVARIAN €€
(615 2810; Witzleben Strasse 31; mains €8-20; dinner daily, lunch Sun; Ⓜ Sophie Charlotte Platz) Come here for what many rate as Berlin's best Bavarian food, with *Schweinbraten* (pork sausages), schnitzels, dumplings and sauerkraut. All meats are organic.

Petite Europe ITALIAN €€
(off Map p486; 781 2964; Langenscheidtstrasse 1; mains €5-12; dinner; Ⓜ Kleistpark) Pizzas, pastas and other straightforward Italian dishes are still going strong at this 40-year-old institution.

Drinking

Gemütlichkeit, which roughly translates as 'cosy, warm and friendly, with a decided lack of anything hectic', dominates the upscale bars of the west as well as the hipper, more underground venues in the east. Prenzlauer Berg, the first GDR sector to develop a happening nightlife, still attracts visitors, creative types and gay customers, but as its residents have aged (and produced many, many babies) its nightlife has become more subdued. Clubs and bars in Mitte around Hackescher Markt cater to a cool, slightly older and wealthier crowd. Friedrichshain boasts a young, hipster feel and Kreuzberg remains the alternative hub, becoming grungier as you move east. Charlottenburg and Winterfeldtplatz are fairly upmarket and mature, but liberal.

Bars without food open between 5pm and 8pm and may close as late as 5am (if at all).

Madame Claude BAR

(Map p482; Lübbener Strasse 19; Ⓜ Schlesiches Tor) Kick back with a beer and pretend you've stepped into the pages of Alice in Wonderland. Run by a threesome (of course), tables and chairs live on the ceiling, coat hooks are upside down and the shoes dangling above made us grin like the Cheshire cat. True to Berlin it's shabby and slightly gritty, with secondhand furniture and a DJ doling out tracks from a hip Mac.

Hops & Barley PUB

(Map p482; ☎2936 7534; Wühlisch Strasse 40; Ⓜ S-Bahn Warschauer Strasse) Excellent ciders and beers – brewed on site at this convivial microbrewery – pack them in every night. It's set inside a former butcher shop littered with aged-but-refurbished wood tables and school desks.

Kumpelnest 3000 BAR

(Map p486; Lützowstrasse 23; Ⓜ Kurfürstenstrasse) Once a brothel, always an experience: the Kumpelnest has been famed since the '80s for its wild, inhibition-free nights. Much of the original whorehouse decor remains intact.

Fleischmöbel BAR

(Oderberger Strasse 2; ⏲from noon; Ⓜ Eberswalder Strasse) Despite its odd name, which means Meat Furniture, the furniture is merely secondhand at this loungey cafe. It morphs into a convivial drinking den after dark, with serious locals engaging in intense conversations.

Ankerklause BAR

(Map p482; ☎693 5649; Kottbusser Damm 104; Ⓜ Kottbusser Tor) Slightly kitsch but always a winner, this nautical-themed bar in an old harbour master's house is worthy of a brew or two. Thursdays it turns into a casual dance floor with music suiting most tastes.

Reingold COCKTAIL BAR

(Map p478; Novalisstrasse 11; Ⓜ Oranienburger Tor) Gold walls and sleek furnishings manage to be both glam and retro in this recently revamped Mitte bar. Pricey (but exceptional) cocktails contain freshly squeezed juices and house-made fruit syrups.

Süss War Gestern BAR

(Map p482; Wülischstrasse 43; Ⓜ S-Bahn Ostkreuz). Street art–covered walls, 1970s decorations and comfortable sofas make this outpost worth the trek. Most nights feature a DJ spinning anything from funk to soul to electric music.

Rote Lotte COCKTAIL BAR

(☎017 7345 3693; Oderbergerstrasse 38; Ⓜ Eberswalder Strasse) Plush sofas and booths have an old-world feel in this stylish crowd pleaser – perfect for a quiet, civilised drink.

Prater BEER GARDEN

(off Map p478; Kastanienallee 7-9; Ⓜ Eberswalder Strasse) A summer institution, Berlin's oldest beer garden (since 1837) invites you in for a tall chilled draft under the canopy of chestnut trees.

Green Door COCKTAIL BAR

(Map p486; Winterfeldtstrasse 50; Ⓜ Nollendorfplatz) Ring the doorbell to get them to open the namesake green door and let you into this tiny neighbourhood bar. Cocktails are on offer.

Wohnzimmer BAR

(☎445 5458; Lettestrasse 6; ⏲10am-4am; Ⓜ Eberswalder Strasse) The vintage furnishings often match up well with the style of its patrons in this laid-back Prenlauer Berg stalwart.

Freischwimmer BAR

(Map p482; Vor dem Schlesischen Tor 2a; ⏲from 2pm Mon-Fri, from 11am Sat & Sun, reduced hr in winter; Ⓜ Schlesisches Tor). It was a boathouse, now it's a bar that entices with its chill vibe and a view of the tranquil canal.

☆ Entertainment

Berlin's legendary nightlife needs little introduction. Whether alternative, underground, cutting edge, saucy, flamboyant or even highbrow, it all crops up here.

Berlin also has a thriving scene of no-holds-barred sex clubs. The notorious **Kit Kat Club** (Map p482; ☎7889 9704; Bessemerstrasse 14; Ⓜ Alt-Tempelhof) is the original and best.

GAY & LESBIAN BERLIN

Berlin boasts a liberal – no, wild is more like it – gay scene where anything goes. Still going strong since the 1920s, Schöneberg is the original gay area, but these days Prenzlauer Berg is the trendiest. Friedrichshain also has a small student-y gay scene. Skim through **Berlin Gay Web** (http://berlin.gay-web.de, in German) for all things gay in Berlin, or **Girl Ports** (www.girlports.com/lesbiantravel/destinations/berlin), a lesbian travel magazine.

SchwuZ (Map p482; ☎693 7025; www.schwuz.de; Mehringdamm 61; ⏲from 11pm Fri & Sat; Ⓜ Mehringdamm) is one of the longest-running mixed nightclubs; there's a cafe here all week too.

Hafen (Map p486; ☎211 4118; Motzstrasse 19; Ⓜ Nollendorfplatz) is a Schöneberg staple with a consistent party scene. There's also an eclectic quiz night on Mondays (in English first Monday of the month).

Nightclubs

Few clubs open before 11pm (and if you arrive before midnight you may be dancing solo) but they stay open well into the early hours – usually sunrise at least. As the scene changes so rapidly, it's always wise to double-check listings magazines or ask locals. Admission charges, when they apply, range from €5 to €20.

Berghain/Panoramabar CLUB
(Map p482; www.berghain.de; Wrienzer Bahnhof; ⏲from midnight Thu-Sat; Ⓜ Ostbahnhof) If you only make it to one club in Berlin, this is where you need to go. The upper floor (Panoramabar, aka 'Pannebar') is all about house; the big factory hall below (Berghain) goes hard-core techno. Expect cutting-edge sounds in industrial surrounds.

Kaffee Burger CLUB
(Map p478; ☎2804 6495; www.kaffeeburger.de; Torstrasse 60; Ⓜ Rosa-Luxemburg-Platz) The original GDR '60s wallpaper is part of the decor at this arty bar, club and music venue in Mitte. Burger hosts popular monthly readings by local (mainly expat) writers in English, but many come here for indie, rock, punk and cult author Wladimir Kaminer's twice-monthly *Russendisko* (Russian disco; www.russendisko.de).

Watergate CLUB
(Map p482; ☎6128 0394; www.water-gate.de; Falckensteinstrasse 49a; ⏲from 11pm Fri & Sat; Ⓜ Schlesisches Tor) Watch the sun rise over the Spree River through the floor-to-ceiling windows of this fantastic lounge. The music is mainly electro, drum'n'bass and hip hop.

Weekend CLUB
(Map p478; www.week-end-berlin.de; Am Alexanderplatz 5; ⏲from 11pm Thu-Sat; Ⓜ Alexanderplatz) Tear your eyes from the beautiful people and gaze through the 12th-floor windows, across the *Blade Runner* landscape of dug-up Alexanderplatz and over Berlin. (Alexanderplatz 5 is the one with the Sanyo logo.) Thursdays are best, while Saturdays see an invasion of suburban weekend warriors. Its rooftop deck is sublime on a summer night.

Music & Theatre

Staatsoper Unter den Linden OPERA HOUSE
(Map p478; ☎information 203 540, tickets 2035 4555; www.staatsoper-berlin.de; Unter den Linden 5-7; Ⓜ S-Bahn Unter den Linden) This is the handiest and most prestigious of Berlin's three opera houses, where unsold seats go on sale cheap an hour before curtains-up.

Berliner Ensemble THEATRE
(Map p478; ☎information 284 080, tickets 2840 8155; www.berliner-ensemble.de; Bertolt-Brecht-Platz 1; Ⓜ Friedrichstrasse) 'Mack the Knife' had its first public airing here, during the *Threepenny Opera's* premiere in 1928. Bertolt Brecht's former theatrical home continues to present his plays.

Shopping

While Hackescher Markt (p481) is increasingly commercial, plenty of cutting-edge boutiques are found in Prenzlauer Berg (especially along Kastanienallee and Stargarder Strasse) and in the side streets of Kreuzberg.

Flea market–hopping is a popular local pastime on the weekend, particularly Sundays. The **Berlin Art & Nostalgia Market** (Map p478; Georgenstrasse, Mitte; ⏲8am-5pm Sat & Sun; Ⓜ S-Bahn Friedrichstrasse) is heavy on collectables, books, ethnic crafts and GDR memorabilia; the **Flohmarkt am Mauerpark** (Bernauer Strasse 63, Mauerpark; ⏲10am-5pm Sun;

Ⓜ Eberwalder Strasse) is known for its vintage wear and young-designer retro fashions; and the **Flohmarkt am Arkonaplatz** (Arkonaplatz; ⏲10am-5pm Sun; Ⓜ Bernauerstrasse) is the best spot to hit if you're looking for retro 1960s and 1970s furniture and accessories.

KaDeWe DEPARTMENT STORE
(Map p486; www.kadewe.de; Tauentzienstrasse 21-24; ⏲10am-8pm Mon-Thu, to 9pm Fri, 9.30am-8pm Sat; Ⓜ U-Bahn Wittenbergplatz) Germany's most renowned retail emporium, equivalent to Harrods. The 6th-floor gourmet food halls are extraordinary, and the store is near the principal western shopping thoroughfare of Kurfürstendamm.

Galeries Lafayette DEPARTMENT STORE
(Map p478; www.galeries-lafayette.de; Friedrichstrasse 76-78; ⏲10am-8pm Mon-Sat; Ⓜ U-Bahn Französiche Strasse) The famous Parisian department store also has a branch in Mitte, including a floor of fancy French food and swanky spots to grab a tipple after a hard day's shop.

 Information

Internet access is a breeze to find in Berlin – and the entire Sony Center at Potsdamer Platz is a free public hot spot.

Berlin Tourismus (☎250 025; http://visitberlin.de/de) Alexanderplatz (Map p478; Alexa Shopping Centre; ⏲10am-6pm); Brandenburg Gate (Map p478; ⏲10am-6pm); Hauptbahnhof (Ground floor, Europa Platz entrance; ⏲8am-10pm); Reichstag (Map p478; ⏲10am-6pm); Zoologisher Garten station (Kurfürstendamm 21; ⏲10am-8pm Mon-Sat, to 6pm Sun)

Berlin Welcome Card (www.berlin-welcomecard.de; 48/72hr €16.90/22.90, incl Potsdam & up to 3 children €18.90/25.90) Free public transport, plus museum and entertainment discounts.

Kassenärztliche Bereitschaftsdienst (Public Physicians' Emergency Service; ☎310 031; www.kvberlin.de, in German) Medical phone referral service.

Post office (Map p478; Rathausstrasse 5; ⏲8am-7pm Mon-Fri, to 4pm Sat; Ⓜ Alexanderplatz)

 Getting There & Away

Air

Berlin has two international airports, reflecting the legacy of the divided city. The larger one is in the northwestern suburb of **Tegel** (TXL), about 8km from the city centre; the other is in **Schönefeld** (SXF), about 22km southeast of town. Tegel is due to be decommissioned, with Schönefeld being expanded into **Berlin Brandenburg International** (BBI). It has an estimated completion date of mid-2012. For information about either, go to www.berlin-airport.de or call ☎0180-500 0186.

Bus

Berlin is well connected to the rest of Europe by a network of long-distance buses. Most buses arrive at and depart from the **Zentraler Omnibusbahnhof** (ZOB; ☎302 5361; Masurenallee 4-6; Ⓜ Kaiserdamm/Witzleben), opposite the Funkturm radio tower. Tickets are available from travel agencies or at the bus station.

Car

Lifts can be organised by ride-share agency **ADM Mitfahrzentrale** (www.mf24.de, in German) Hardenbergplatz (☎194 420; Hardenbergplatz 14; ⏲9am-8pm Mon-Fri, 10am-2pm Sat, 10am-4pm Sun); Bahnhof Zoo (☎194 240; ⏲9am-8pm Mon-Fri, 10am-6pm Sat & Sun).

Train

Regular long-distance services arrive at the architecturally spectacular **Hauptbahnhof** (www.berlin-hauptbahnhof.de), with many continuing east to Ostbahnhof. ICE and IC trains leave hourly to every major city in Germany and there are also connections to central Europe. Sample fares include Leipzig (€36, 1¼ hours), Hamburg (€68, 1½ to two hours), Stralsund (€38 to €46, 2¾ to 3¼ hours) and Prague (€62, 4½ to five hours).

Unfortunately the few lockers available are hidden in the parking garage.

Getting Around

Berlin's public transport system is excellent – leave your car at home. The comprehensive network of U-Bahn and S-Bahn trains, buses, trams and ferries covers most corners.

To/From the Airport

SCHÖNEFELD The S9 train travels through all the major downtown stations, taking 40 minutes to Alexanderplatz.

The faster 'Airport Express' trains travel the same route half-hourly to Bahnhof Zoo (30 minutes), Friedrichstrasse (23 minutes), Alexanderplatz (20 minutes) and Ostbahnhof (15 minutes). Note that these are regular regional RE or RB trains designated as Airport Express in the timetable. Trains stop about 400m from the terminals, which are served by a free shuttle bus every 10 minutes. Walking takes five to 10 minutes.

Buses 171 and X7 link the terminals directly with the U-Bahn station Rudow (U7), with onward connections to central Berlin.

PUBLIC TRANSPORT TICKETS

Three tariff zones exist – A, B and C. Unless venturing to Potsdam, the outer suburbs or Schönefeld Airport, you'll only need an AB ticket.

TICKET	AB (€)	BC (€)	ABC (€)
Single	2.10	2.50	2.80
Day pass	6.10	6.30	6.50
Group day pass (up to 5 people)	15.40	15.90	16.10
7-day pass	26.20	27.00	32.30

The fare for any of these trips is €2.80. A taxi to central Berlin costs about €35.

TEGEL Tegel (TXL) is connected to Mitte by the JetExpressBus TXL (30 minutes) and to Bahnhof Zoo (Zoo Station) in Charlottenburg by express bus X9 (20 minutes). Bus 109 serves the western city – it's slower but useful if you're headed somewhere along Kurfürstendamm (30 minutes). Tegel is not directly served by the U-Bahn, but both bus 109 and X9 stop at Jakob-Kaiser-Platz (U7), the station closest to the airport.

Any of these trips costs €2.10. Taxi rides cost about €20 to Bahnhof Zoo and €23 to Alexanderplatz.

Bicycle

Flat and bike-friendly, with special bike lanes, abundant green spaces and peaceful waterways, Berlin is best explored by tooling around on two wheels. For details on following the course of the former Berlin Wall by bike along the marked Berliner Mauerweg, see p481. Bicycles *(Fahrräder)* may be taken aboard designated U-Bahn and S-Bahn cars (though not on buses) for the price of a reduced single ticket.

Many hostels and hotels rent bicycles to their guests, or can refer you to an agency. Expect to pay from €10 per day and €50 per week. A minimum cash deposit and/or ID is required. One reliable outfit with English-speaking staff and six branches throughout central Berlin is **Fahrradstation** (☎0180-510 8000; www.fahrradstation.de).

Car & Motorcycle

Garage parking is expensive (about €2 per hour) and vehicles entering the environmental zone (within the S-Bahn rail ring) must display a special sticker (*Umweltplakette;* €5 to €15). Order it online at www.berlin.de/sen/umwelt/luftqualitaet/de/luftreinhalteplan/doku_umweltzone.shtml. The fine for getting caught without the sticker is €40.

Public Transport

One type of ticket is valid on all public transport, including the U-Bahn, buses, trams and ferries run by **Berliner Verkehrsbetriebe** (☎194 49; www.bvg.de), as well as the S-Bahn and regional RE, SE and RB trains operated by **Deutsche Bahn** (www.bahn.de).

For ticket prices and zones see the boxed text this page.

Most tickets are available from vending machines located in the stations, but must be validated before use. If you're caught without a validated ticket, there's a €40 on-the-spot fine.

Services operate from 4am until just after midnight on weekdays, with many *Nachtbus* (night bus) services in between. At weekends, they run all night long (except the U4).

Taxi

Taxi stands are located at all main train stations and throughout the city. Order a taxi on ☎0800-222 2255.

BRANDENBURG

Although it surrounds bustling Berlin, the Brandenburg state of mind is quiet, rural and gentle, with vast expanses of unspoilt scenery, much of it in protected nature reserves. Its landscape is quilted in myriad shades, from emerald beech forest to golden fields of rapeseed and sunflowers, but it's also rather flat, windswept and perhaps even a bit melancholic.

Potsdam

☎0331 / POP 150,000

Featuring ornate palaces and manicured gardens dotted around a huge riverside park, the Prussian royal seat of Potsdam is the most popular day trip from Berlin. Elector Friedrich Wilhelm of Brandenburg laid the ground for the town's success when he made it his second residence in the 17th century. But Friedrich II (Frederick the Great) commissioned most of the palaces in the mid-18th century.

In August 1945 the victorious WWII Allies chose nearby Schloss Cecilienhof for the Potsdam Conference, which set the stage for the division of Berlin and Germany into occupation zones.

Sights

Park Sanssouci HISTORIC SITE

(admission free; dawn to dusk) At the heart of Park Sanssouci lies a celebrated rococo palace, **Schloss Sanssouci** (969 4190; adult/concession Apr-Oct €12/8, Nov-Mar €8/5; 10am-6pm Tue-Sun Apr-Oct, to 5pm Nov-Mar). Built in 1747, it has some glorious interiors. Only 2000 visitors are allowed entry each day (a Unesco rule), so tickets are usually sold by 2.30pm, even in quiet seasons. Tours run by the tourist office guarantee entry.

The late-baroque **Neues Palais** (New Palace; 969 4255; adult/concession €6/5; 10am-6pm Wed-Mon Apr-Oct, to 5pm Nov-Mar) was built in 1769 as the royal family's summer residence. It's one of the most imposing buildings in the park and the one to see if your time is limited.

The **Bildergalerie** (Picture Gallery; 969 4181; adult/concession €2/1.50; 10am-6pm Tue-Sun mid-May–Oct) contains a rich collection of 17th-century paintings by Rubens, Caravaggio and other big names.

Many consider the **Chinesisches Haus** (Chinese House; 969 4222; admission €2; 10am-6pm Tue-Sun mid-May–Oct) to be the pearl of the park. It's a circular pavilion of gilded columns, palm trees and figures of Chinese musicians and animals, built in 1757.

Schloss Cecilienhof PALACE

(969 4244; tours adult/concession €6/5; 9am-6pm Tue-Sun Apr-Oct, to 5pm Nov-Mar) When outgoing British Prime Minister Winston Churchill and his accompanying successor Clement Attlee arrived at this palace in 1945 for the Potsdam Conference they must have immediately felt at home. Located in the separate New Garden, northeast of the centre on the bank of the Heiliger See, this is an incongruously English-style country manor in rococo-heavy Potsdam.

WORTH A TRIP

SACHSENHAUSEN CONCENTRATION CAMP

In 1936 the Nazis opened a *Konzentrationslager* (concentration camp) for men in a disused brewery in Sachsenhausen, 35km north of Berlin. By 1945 about 220,000 prisoners had passed through the gates – labelled, as at Auschwitz in Poland, *Arbeit Macht Frei* (Work Sets You Free). About 100,000 were murdered here.

After the war the Soviets and the communist leaders of the new GDR set up Speziallager No 7 (Special Camp No 7) for political prisoners, ex-Nazis, monarchists and others, jailing 60,000 and killing up to 12,000.

The **Sachsenhausen Memorial and Museum** (03301-200 200; www.stiftung-bg.de; admission free; 8.30am-6pm mid-Mar–mid-Oct, to 4pm mid-Oct–mid-Mar) consists of several parts. The **Neues Museum** (New Museum) includes a history of anti-Semitism and audiovisual material. East of it are **Barracks 38 and 39**, reconstructions of two typical huts housing most of the 6000 Jewish prisoners brought to Sachsenhausen after Kristallnacht (9–10 November 1938). Number 38 was rebuilt after being torched by neo-Nazis in September 1992. North of here is the prison and prison yard, where you'll find a **memorial** to the homosexuals who died here. The recently revamped **Lagermuseum** (Camp Museum), situated in what was once the camp kitchen, houses exhibits illustrating the everyday life in the camp during its various phases, including some artwork produced by the inmates. Left of the tall **monument** (1961), erected by the GDR in memory of political prisoners interned here, is the **crematorium** and **Station Z extermination site**, a pit for shooting prisoners in the neck with a wooden 'catch' where bullets could be retrieved and recycled.

The easiest way to get to Sachsenhausen from Berlin is to take the frequent S1 train to Oranienburg (€2.80, 50 minutes). The walled camp is a signposted 20-minute walk from Oranienburg station.

Filmpark Babelsberg MUSEUM
(☎721 2755; www.filmpark.de; Grossbeerenstrasse; adult/child/concession €19/13/16; ⏰10am-6pm Apr-Oct) Germany's **UFA Film Studios** was where Fritz Lang's *Metropolis* was shot and FW Murnau filmed the first Dracula movie, *Nosferatu*. Since a relaunch in 1999, it's helped Berlin regain its film-making crown, with Roman Polanski's *The Pianist* and Quentin Tarantino's *Inglorious Bastards* both made here. The visitor experience includes theme-park rides and a studio tour – the daily stunt show (2pm) is worth catching. The studios are east of the city centre.

Altstadt HISTORIC AREA
The **Brandenburger Tor** (Brandenburg Gate) at the western end of the Old Town on Luisenplatz isn't a patch on the one in Berlin but it is older, dating from 1770. From here, pedestrian Brandenburger Strasse runs due east, providing the town's main eating strip.

Standing out from its surrounds is the pretty **Holländisches Viertel** (Dutch Quarter). Towards the northern end of Friedrich-Ebert-Strasse, it has 134 gabled red-brick houses, built for Dutch workers who came to Potsdam in the 1730s at the invitation of Friedrich Wilhelm I. The homes have been well restored and now house all kinds of interesting galleries, cafes and restaurants.

Tours

Weisse Flotte BOAT
(☎275 9210; www.schiffahrt-in-potsdam.de; Lange Brücke 6; ⏰9.45am-7pm Apr-Oct) Boats cruise the Havel and the lakes around Potsdam, departing from the dock near Lange Brücke, with frequent trips to Wannsee (one way/return €9/12) and around the castles (€10).

Information

Potsdam tourist office (☎275 580; www.potsdamtourismus.de; Brandenburger Strasse 3; ⏰9.30am-6pm Mon-Fri, 9.30am-4pm Sat & Sun Apr-Oct, 10am-6pm Mon-Fri, 9.30am-2pm Sat & Sun Nov-Mar) Near the Hauptbahnhof.

Park Sanssouci Besucherzentrum (Park Sanssouci Visitor Centre; ☎969 4202; www.spsg.de; An der Orangerie 1; ⏰8.30am-5pm Mar-Oct, 9am-4pm Nov-Feb) Near the windmill and Schloss Sanssouci.

Getting There & Away

S-Bahn line S7 links central Berlin with Potsdam Hauptbahnhof about every 10 minutes. Some regional (RB/RE) trains from Berlin stop at all three stations in Potsdam. Your ticket must cover Berlin Zones A, B and C (€2.80) to travel here.

Potsdam Hauptbahnhof is just southeast of the city centre, across the Havel River. As this is still quite a way – 2km – from Park Sansoucci, you might like to change here for a train going one or two stops to Charlottenhof (for Schloss Sanssouci) or Sanssouci (for Neues Palais).

SAXONY

With its restored 'old German' roots, Saxony has emerged as one of the biggest draws for visitors to Germany. Restored and revitalised Dresden combines classicism with creativity. Just up the fabled Elbe River, Meissen is a gem of a medieval town with a palace and cathedral high on a hill.

Its history dating back to the Germanic tribes of over 1000 years ago, Saxony embodies many of the classic qualities associated with Germany. Dresden and Leipzig have a long tradition in the arts and are today centres of culture. And even though the local dialect can be impenetrable to those with mere schoolbook German, that same classic German traces its roots right back to here.

The state is fairly compact and high-speed rail links make the region easily accessible from all corners of Germany.

Dresden

☎0351 / POP 484,000

Proof that there is life after death, Dresden has become one of Germany's most popular attractions, and for good reason. Restorations have returned the city to the glory days when it was famous throughout Europe as 'Florence on the Elbe', owing to the efforts of Italian artists, musicians, actors and master craftsmen who flocked to the court of Augustus the Strong, bestowing countless masterpieces upon the city. Death came suddenly when, shortly before the end of WWII, Allied bombers blasted and incinerated much of the baroque centre, a beautiful jewel-like area dating from the 18th century. More than 25,000 people died, and in bookstores throughout town you can peruse texts showing the destruction (or read about it in Kurt Vonnegut's classic *Slaughterhouse Five*).

Rebuilding began under the communist regime in the 1950s and accelerated greatly after reunification. The city celebrated its 800th anniversary in 2006 and, while much focus is on the restored centre, you should cross the River Elbe to the Neustadt, where edgy new clubs and cafes open every week, joining the scores already there.

Sights

Dresden is best explored on foot, where one monument after another reveals itself and you're free to amble down alleys to make your own discoveries.

Frauenkirche CATHEDRAL
(Church of Our Lady; www.frauenkirche-dresden.org; Neumarkt; 10am-6pm) One of Dresden's most beloved icons, the Frauenkirche was rebuilt in time for the city's 800th anniversary celebrations in 2006. Initially constructed between 1726 and 1743 under the direction of baroque architect George Bähr, it was Germany's greatest Protestant church until February 1945, when bombing raids flattened it. The communists decided to leave the rubble as a war memorial; after reunification, calls for reconstruction prevailed, although the paucity of charcoal-tinged original stones shows just how much is new.

Look for the very few blackened stones on the exterior, these were salvaged from the rubble of the original. Otherwise – not surprisingly – the church feels brand new, especially inside. Most moving is the melted cross from the original. You can also climb to the top for good views. The surrounding Neumarkt is part of a massive redevelopment designed to evoke prewar Dresden, although at this point it feels all too bland and reconstituted.

Semperoper HISTORIC BUILDING
(www.semperoper-erleben.de; Theaterplatz; tour adult/child €8/4; varies) Designed by Gustav Semper, this neo-Renaissance opera house *is* Dresden. The original building opened in 1841 but burned down less than three decades later. Rebuilt in 1878, it was pummelled in WWII and reopened in 1985 after the communists invested a fortune restoring it. The best way to appreciate it is through one of the many performances (see p501).

Residenzschloss PALACE
(www.skd.museum; Schlossplatz) The Residenzschloss, a massive neo-Renaissance palace, has ongoing restoration projects. Its many features include the **Hausmannsturm** (Servants' Tower; adult/child €3/2; 10am-6pm Wed-Mon), which has sobering pictures of the complete WWII destruction.

TOP CHOICE *Grünes Gewölbe*
(Green Vault; adult/child €10/5; 10am-7pm Wed-Mon) This is one of the world's finest collections of precious objects. Treasures include the world's biggest green diamond, tiny pearl sculptures and a stunning group of 137 gem-studded figures by Johann Melchior Dinglinger, court jeweller of Augustus the Strong. Even cynics will marvel at the wafer-thin creations in amber. Buy timed tickets in advance from the office or online.

Hofkirche
(9am-5pm) This baroque Catholic church contains the heart of Augustus the Strong. Free **concerts** (11.30am Wed &Sat) are extraordinary.

Fürstenzug
(Procession of Princes; Augustusstrasse) Outside, you'd need a really wide-angle lens to get a shot of Wulhelm Walther's amazing 102m-long tiled mural on the wall of the former Stendehaus (Royal Stables). The scene, a long row of royalty on horses, was painted in 1876 and then transferred to some 24,000 Meissen porcelain tiles in 1906.

Verkehrsmuseum
(Transport Museum; Augustusstrasse 1; adult/child €4.50/2.50; 10am-5pm Tue-Sun) This transport museum is fittingly located in the Johanneum, the old stables. Motoring back towards the 20th century, this is a fascinating

NAVIGATING DRESDEN

The Elbe River splits Dresden in a rough V-shape, with the **Neustadt** (new city) to the north and the **Altstadt** (old city) to the south.

There are two main train stations: the restored **Hauptbahnhof** on the southern side of town, and **Dresden-Neustadt** north of the river. Most trains stop at both.

From the Hauptbahnhof, pedestrian-only **Prager Strasse** leads north into the Altstadt. Here there's a mix of communist-era triumphalism and modern-day commercialism. The lovely **Brühlsche Terrasse** runs along the Elbe between the Albertinum and the Zwinger, with boat docks below.

In the Neustadt, home to much of the city's nightlife, the main attractions for visitors are the **Albertplatz** and **Louisenstrasse** quarters. Here you'll find all manner of shops, galleries, funky boutiques and dozens of cafes, bars and clubs.

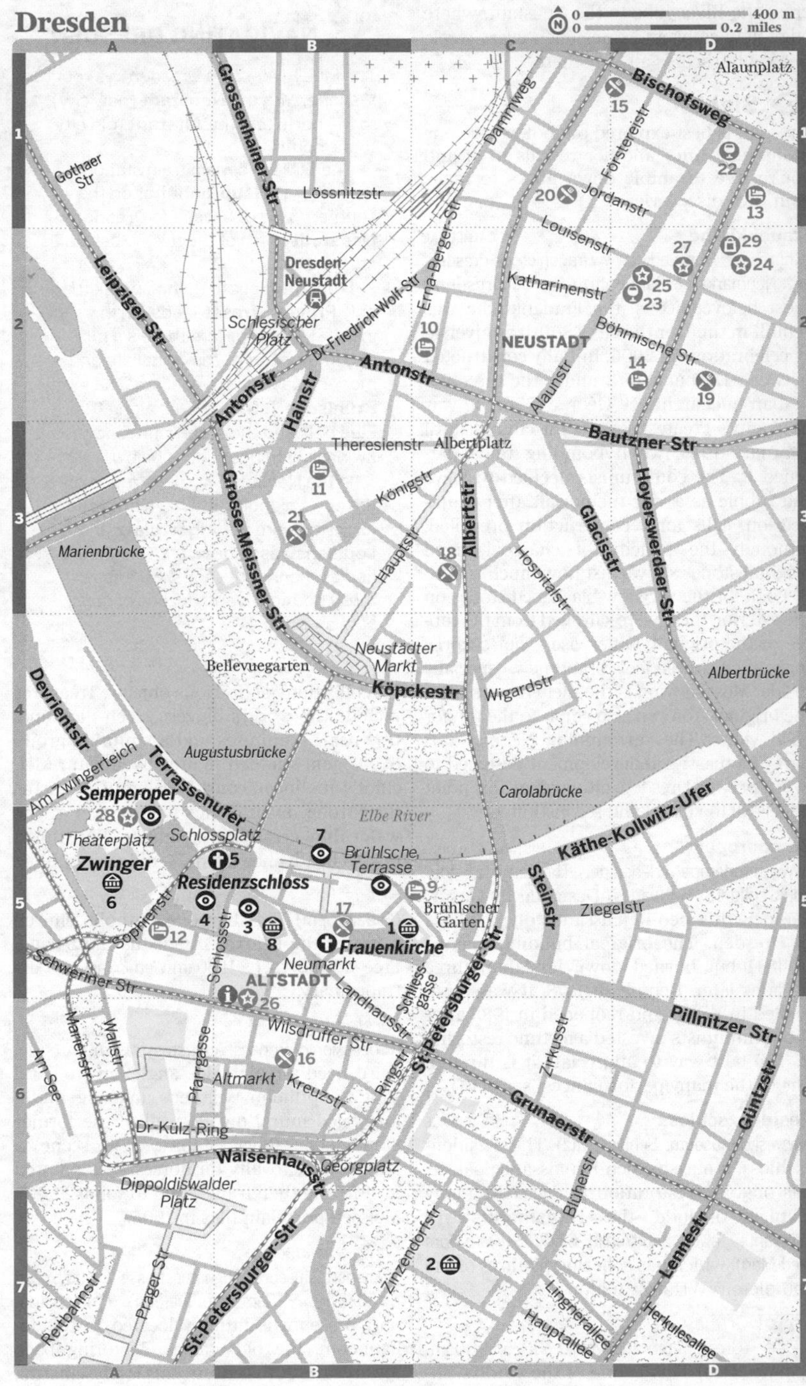

0 400 m
0 0.2 miles
A
B
C
D
1
2
3
4
5
6
7
Alaunplatz
Bischofsweg
Dammweg
Grossenhainer Str
Gothaer Str
Lössnitzstr
Förstereistr
Jordanstr
Louisenstr
Katharinenstr
Böhmische Str
Erna-Berger-Str
Dresden-Neustadt
Schlesischer Platz
Dr-Friedrich-Wolf-Str
Leipziger Str
NEUSTADT
Antonstr
Alaunstr
Hainstr
Bautzner Str
Theresienstr
Albertplatz
Königstr
Hoyerswerdaer Str
Glacisstr
Grosse Meissner Str
Albertstr
Hospitalstr
Hauptstr
Marienbrücke
Neustädter Markt
Bellevuegarten
Köpckestr
Wigardstr
Albertbrücke
Devrientstr
Augustusbrücke
Am Zwingerteich
Terrassenufer
Semperoper
Carolabrücke
Elbe River
Käthe-Kollwitz-Ufer
Theaterplatz
Schlossplatz
Brühlsche Terrasse
Zwinger
Residenzschloss
Steinstr
Brühlscher Garten
Ziegelstr
Sophienstr
Schlossstr
Frauenkirche
Neumarkt
ALTSTADT
Landhausstr
Schliessgasse
St-Petersburger-Str
Schweriner Str
Pillnitzer Str
Wilsdruffer Str
Marienstr
Wallstr
Pfarrgasse
Ringstr
Zirkusstr
Am See
Altmarkt
Kreuzstr
Grunaerstr
Güntzstr
Dr-Külz-Ring
Waisenhausstr
Georgplatz
Blüherstr
Dippoldiswalder Platz
Zinzendorfstr
Lennéstr
Reitbahnstr
Prager Str
Lingnerallee
Hauptallee
Herkulesallee
1
2
3
4
5
6
7
8
9
10
11
12
13
14
15
16
17
18
19
20
21
22
23
24
25
26
27
28
29

Dresden

Top Sights
- Frauenkirche ... B5
- Residenzschloss ... A5
- Semperoper ... A5
- Zwinger ... A5

Sights
1. Albertinum ... B5
2. Deutsches Hygiene-Museum ... C7
3. Fürstenzug ... B5
   Galerie Alte Meister ... (see 6)
4. Grünes Gewölbe ... A5
5. Hofkirche ... B5
6. Porzelansammlung ... A5
   Rüstkammer ... (see 6)
7. Sächsische Dampfschiffahrt Landing Dock ... B5
8. Verkehrsmuseum ... B5

Sleeping
9. EV-Ref Gemeinde zu Dresden ... C5
10. Hostel & Backpacker Kangaroo-Stop ... C2
11. Hotel Martha Hospiz ... B3
12. Kempinski Hotel Taschenbergpalais ... A5
13. Lollis Homestay ... D1
14. Rothenburger Hof ... D2

Eating
15. Café Europa ... D1
16. Gänsedieb ... B6
17. Grand Café ... B5
18. Neustädter Markthalle ... C3
19. Raskolnikoff ... D2
20. Villandry ... C1
21. Wenzel Prager Bierstuben ... B3

Drinking
22. Café 100 ... D1
23. Scheunecafé ... D2

Entertainment
24. Blue Note ... D2
25. Katy's Garage ... D2
26. Kulturpalast ... B6
27. Queens ... D2
28. Semperoper ... A5

Shopping
29. Thalia ... D2

collection, including penny farthings, trams, dirigibles and carriages. Visitors can watch a melancholy 40-minute film with original black-and-white footage of 1930s Dresden.

Zwinger MUSEUMS
(www.skd.museum; Theaterplatz 1; ⏲10am-6pm Tue-Sun) Dresden's elaborate 1728 fortress, an attraction in its own right with a popular ornamental courtyard, also houses six major museums. The most important is the **Galerie Alte Meister** (adult/child €10/7.50), which features masterpieces including Raphael's *Sistine Madonna*. The **Rüstkammer** (Armoury; adult/child €3/2) has a superb collection of ceremonial weapons. The dazzling **Porzelansammlung** (Porcelain Collection; adult/child €6/3.50) is filled with flamboyant breakables.

Albertinum MUSEUM
(www.skd.museum; Brühlsche Terrasse; adult/child €8/6; ⏲10am-6pm) Massive renovations ended in 2010 and the results are stunning. A light-filled enclosed courtyard welcomes you into this treasure trove of art. Highlights include the **Münzkabinett** collection of antique coins and medals, and the **Skulpturensammlung**, which includes classical and Egyptian works. The **Galerie Neue Meister** has renowned 19th- and 20th-century paintings from leading French and German Impressionists.

Deutsches Hygiene-Museum MUSEUM
(www.dhmd.de; Lingnerplatz 1; adult/child €7/3; ⏲10am-6pm Tue-Sun) Awash in displays relating to the ravages of venereal disease, the theory of eugenics and reasons to bathe.

Tours

Sächsische Dampfschiffahrt RIVER TOUR
(www.saechsische-dampfschiffahrt.de; adult/child from €16/8) Ninety-minute Elbe tours leave from the Terrassenufer dock several times daily in summer aboard the world's oldest fleet of paddle-wheel steamers. There's also service to villages along the river such as Meissen.

Stadtrundfahrt Dresden BUS TOUR
(www.stadtrundfahrt.com; adult/child €20/10) This narrated hop-on, hop-off tour has 22 stops in the centre and the elegant outer villa districts along the Elbe. It includes short tours of the Zwinger, Fürstenzug, Frauenkirche and Pfunds Molkerei.

Sleeping

Accommodation in Dresden can be very expensive in the high season. Luckily, several good-value budget places can be found in the lively Neustadt. Although rising property prices in the area are taking a toll, some quirky places soldier on.

Lollis Homestay HOSTEL €
(☎810 8458; www.lollishome.de; Görlitzer Strasse 34; dm €13-19, s €30-38, d €40-42, linen €2, breakfast €3; @ 📶) Dresden's quirkiest hostel has two contenders for Germany's most outlandish dorms: one containing a real Trabant you can bed down in for the night; the other a Giant's Room with oversize furniture that makes guests feel like Tom Thumb. In addition there's free bike rental.

Kempinski Hotel Taschenbergpalais HOTEL €€€
(☎491 20; www.kempinski-dresden.de; Taschenberg 3; r €200-400; ❄ @ 📶 🏊) This restored 18th-century mansion is Dresden's heavyweight, with views over the Zwinger, incredibly quiet corridors, and doors that seem impervious to anything outside, protecting the 214 rooms and suites. In winter the courtyard turns into an ice rink.

Hotel Martha Hospiz HOTEL €€
(☎817 60; www.hotel-martha-hospiz.de; Nieritzstrasse 11; r €80-140; 📶) Fifty rooms decked out in Biedermeier style, an attractive winter garden and a sound on-site restaurant with Saxon cooking and local wine make this a very pleasant place to lay your hat. It's all very slick.

Rothenburger Hof HOTEL €€
(☎812 60; www.rothenburger-hof.de; Rothenburger Strasse 15-17; r €75-160, apt €140-180; ❄ 📶 🏊) This quiet launch pad for Neustadt explorations counts among its assets apartments with kitchenette and balcony, a Moorish-style steam room and a great pool. The included breakfast is lavish.

Hotel Kipping HOTEL €€
(☎478 500; www.hotel-kipping.de; Winckelmannstrasse 6; s/d from €70/80; @ 📶) Just south of the Hauptbahnhof, this is a family-run, family-friendly hotel that comes with 20 comfortable rooms in a house right out of the *Addams Family*. The bar and cafe are especially appealing.

EV-Ref Gemeinde zu Dresden PENSION €
(☎438 230; www.ev-ref-gem-dresden.de; Brühlscher Garten 4; s/d from €60/75) The name is not a marketer's dream, but this pension is amazing value in a great location – on the river and overlooking the Albertinum. This historic retirement home makes rooms available for travellers whenever a resident has permanently 'checked out'. Rooms have showers and TV and often great views; breakfast is included.

Hostel & Backpacker Kangaroo-Stop HOSTEL €
(☎314 3455; www.kangaroo-stop.de; Erna-Berger-Strasse 8-10; dm/s/d from €13/29/40; @ 📶) Welcoming and low-key, with rooms spread over two buildings: one for backpackers and the other for families. So which will see more immature behaviour? The big breakfast buffet costs €5. Dresden-Neustadt station is nearby.

Ibis Dresden Lilienstein HOTEL €€
(☎4856 6663; www.ibishotel.com; Prager Strasse 13; r €60-120; ❄ 📶) Together with the adjoining Ibis Dresden Bastei and the Ibis Dresden Königstein, this enormous complex dating from the communist era has more than 900 rooms, meaning vacancies in summer. The decor is 'cheap and cheerful'. It's a three-minute walk from the Hauptbahnhof.

Campingplatz Mockritz CAMPING GROUND €
(☎471 5250; www.camping-dresden.de; Boderitzerstrasse 30; per adult/tent/car €6/3/6) Friendly little campsite 3km south of the Hauptbahnhof. Take bus 76 from the Hauptbahnhof and get off at the stop 'Campingplatz Mockritz'.

Eating

The Neustadt has oodles of cafes and restaurants, many found along Königstrasse and the streets north of Albertplatz. This is the most interesting part of town at night. South of the river, look near the Altmarkt, and Münzgasse/Terrassengasse, between Brühlsche Terrasse and the Frauenkirche.

Off Albertstrasse, the **Neustädter Markthalle** is a gorgeously restored old market hall (enter on Metzer Strasse) with food stalls good for picnics and amazingly cheap wurst lunches.

TOP CHOICE **Wenzel Prager Bierstuben** CZECH €€
(Königstrasse 1; mains €7-20; ⏲11am-midnight) This busy beer hall serves up oceans of Czech lager under arched brick ceilings. Always crowded, the menu leans towards traditional meaty mains. The garlic soup is sublime, and the cured pork with horseradish a delight.

Villandry MEDITERRANEAN €€
(Jordanstrasse 8; mains €8-20; ⏲6.30-11.30pm Mon-Sat) The folks in the kitchen here sure know how to coax maximum flavour out of even the simplest, often organic, ingredients, and to turn them into super-tasty Mediterranean treats for eyes and palate. Meals are best enjoyed in the lovely courtyard.

Raskolnikoff CAFE €
(www.raskolnikoff.de; Böhmische Strasse 34; mains €5-14) This bohemian cafe in a former artists' squat was one of the Neustadt's first post-Wende pubs. The menu is sorted by compass direction (borscht to quiche Lorraine to smoked fish) and there's a sweet little ivy-lined beer garden out back, plus a gallery and pension (rooms €40 to €55) upstairs.

Gänsedieb GERMAN €€
(Weisse Gasse 1; mains €8-18) One of nearly a dozen choices on Weisse Gasse, the 'Goose Thief' serves hearty schnitzels, goulash and steaks alongside a full range of Bavarian Paulaner beers. The name was inspired by the iconic 1880 fountain outside.

Café Europa CAFE €€
(Königsbrücker Strasse 68; mains €6-15; ⏲24hr;) Smart open-all-hours cafe with newspapers and free internet. Come here to regroup during the early hours.

Grand Café CAFE €€
(An der Frauenkirche 12; mains €10-20; ⏲10am-1am) Yummy cakes and more ambitious mains in the gold-trimmed Coselpalais, plus tables on a large patio and good views of Frauenkirche.

Drinking & Entertainment

Dresden's nightlife is ever changing and the Neustadt still has plenty of that proletariat/GDR vibe: grunge beats swank every time. Many of the places listed under Eating are also good just for a drink.

Dresden is synonymous with opera, and performances at the spectacular **Semperoper** (www.semperoper.de; Theaterplatz) are brilliant. Tickets cost from €10, but they're usually booked out well in advance. Check for returns. Some performances by the renowned philharmonic are also held here, but most are in the GDR-era **Kulturpalast** (www.kulturpalast-dresden.de; Schlossstrasse 2), which hosts a wide range of events.

TOP CHOICE **Café 100** WINE BAR
(Alaunstrasse 100) Off a courtyard, you'll pass hundreds of empty bottles on the way in, a foreshadowing of the lengthy wine list and delights that follow. Candles give the underground space a romantic yet edgy glow. The place to take that someone you met on the train.

Scheunecafé CAFE
(Alaunstrasse 36-40) Set back from the street, this place combines Indian food (mains €7 to €12), a vast beer garden, live music and DJs into a fun and funky stew.

Blue Note JAZZ
(www.jazzdepartment.com; Görlitzer Strasse 2b; ⏲until 5am) Small, smoky and smooth, this converted smithy has live jazz almost nightly until 11pm, then turns into a night-owl magnet until the wee hours. The talent is mostly regional.

Strasse E CLUB
(www.strasse-e.de; Werner-Hartmann-Strasse 2) Dresden's most high-octane party zone is in an industrial area between Neustadt and the airport. Half a dozen venues here cover the entire spectrum of danceable sound, from disco to dark wave, electro to pop. Take tram 7 to Industriegelände.

Katy's Garage LIVE MUSIC
(Alaunstrasse 48) This rockin' shanty town, a key venue for live gigs and club nights throughout the week, is centred around a former tyre shop.

Queens GAY BAR
(Görlitzer Strasse 3) The kitsch decor is the perfect backdrop for this pulsating hot spot, famous for its *Schlager* (schmaltzy German pop songs) parties.

Shopping

Altmarkt-Gallerie anchors a vast shopping area that extends along Prager Strasse and Pfarrgasse, but the most interesting oddball shops are found in the Neustadt. With one exception: **Fem2Glam** (www.fem2glam.com; Prager Strasse 8/8a) has made waves with its popular line of dildos made from polished (fear not: they're sealed!) Elbe River sandstone.

If a good book is more your style, **Thalia** (Dr-Külz-Ring 12) has loads of Dresden-related texts.

Information

Dresden City-Card (per 48hr €21) Provides admission to museums, discounted city tours and boat tours and free public transport. Buy it at the tourist office.

Dresden Regio-Card (per 72hr €32) Everything offered by the City-Card plus free transport on the entire regional transport network. Valid as far as the Czech border and Meissen.

Tourist office (www.dresden-tourist.de; Kulturpalast, Schlossstrasse; ⏲10am-7pm Mon-Fri, 10am-6pm Sat, 10am-3pm Sun) Also houses the central ticket office.

Getting There & Around

Dresden's **airport** (DRS; www.dresden-airport.de), served by Lufthansa and Air Berlin among others, is 9km north of the city centre, on S-Bahn line 2 (€1.90, 20 minutes).

Dresden is well linked with regular train services through the day to Leipzig (€29, 70 minutes), Berlin-Hauptbahnhof by IC/EC train (€36, 2¼ hours) and Frankfurt-am-Main by ICE (€89, 4½ hours).

Dresden's **public transport network** (www.dvbag.de) charges €1.90 for a single-trip ticket; day tickets cost €5 and can be bought on trams. Trams 3, 7, 8 and 9 provide good links between the Hauptbahnhof, Altstadt and Neustadt.

Around Dresden

MEISSEN

☎03521 / POP 29,000

Straddling the Elbe around 25km upstream from Dresden, Meissen is a compact, perfectly preserved Saxon town, popular with day trippers. Crowning a rocky ridge above it is the Albrechtsburg palace, which in 1710 became the cradle of European porcelain manufacture. The world-famous Meissen china, easily recognised by its trademark insignia, is still the main draw for coach parties. Fortunately, the cobbled lanes, dreamy nooks and idyllic courtyards of the Altstadt (old town) make escaping from the shuffling crowds a snap.

Sights

The **Markt** is framed by the **Rathaus** (town hall; 1472) and the Gothic **Frauenkirche**, which – fittingly – has a porcelain carillon.

Meissen's medieval fortress, the 15th-century **Albrechtsburg** (www.albrechtsburg-meissen.de; Domplatz 1; adult/child €8/4; ⏲10am-6pm Mar-Oct, to 5pm Nov-Feb), crowns a ridge high above the Elbe River and is reached by steep lanes. It contains the former **ducal palace** and **Meissen Cathedral**, a magnificent Gothic structure. It is widely seen as the birthplace of Schloss architecture, with its ingenious system of internal arches. Augustus the Strong of Saxony created Europe's first porcelain factory here in 1710.

Next door, the towering 13th-century **Albrechtsburg Cathedral** (☎452 490; Domplatz 7; adult/child €4/2; ⏲10am-6pm Mar-Oct, to 4pm Nov-Feb) contains an altarpiece by Lucas Cranach the Elder.

Meissen has long been renowned for its chinaware, with its trademark insignia of blue crossed swords. Meissen's porcelain factory is now 1km southwest of the Altstadt in an appropriately beautiful building, the **Porzellan-Museum** (www.meissen.com; Talstrasse 9; adult/child €9/4.50; ⏲9am-6pm May-Oct, to 5pm Nov-Apr), which dates to 1916. There are often long queues for the workshop demonstrations, but you can view the porcelain collection upstairs at your leisure.

Information

Tourist office (www.touristinfo-meissen.de; Markt 3; ⏲10am-6pm Mon-Fri, to 4pm Sat & Sun Apr-Oct, 10am-5pm Mon-Fri, to 3pm Sat Nov-Mar)

Getting There & Away

Half-hourly S-Bahn trains run from Dresden's Hauptbahnhof and Neustadt train stations (€5.50, 40 minutes). To visit the porcelain factory, get off at Meissen-Triebischtal (one stop after Meissen).

A more pleasant way to get here is by steamer (between May and September). Boats leave from the **Sächsische Dampfschiffahrt** (☎866 090; www.saechsische-dampfschiffahrt.de) dock in Dresden once daily (€17 return, two hours).

SAXON SWITZERLAND

Sächsische Schweiz (Saxon Switzerland; www.saechsische-schweiz.de) is a 275-sq-km national park 50km south of Dresden, near the Czech border. Its wonderfully wild, craggy country is dotted with castles and tiny towns along the mighty Elbe River. The landscape varies unexpectedly and radically: its forests can look deceptively tropical, while the worn cliffs and plateaux recall the parched expanses of New Mexico or central Spain (generally without the searing heat).

The highlight of the park is the **Bastei lookout**, on the Elbe River some 28km southeast of Dresden. One of the most breathtaking spots in the whole of Germany, it features fluted pinnacles 305m high and unparalleled views of the surrounding forests, cliffs and mountains, as well as a sweeping view along the river itself.

There are myriad routes for hiking (and cycling). Get here on the S1 train to Königstein, which makes a good base.

Leipzig

0341 / POP 515,000

In Goethe's *Faust,* a character named Frosch calls Leipzig 'a little Paris'. He was wrong – Leipzig is more fun and infinitely less self-important than the Gallic capital. It's an important business and transport centre, a trade-fair mecca and arguably the most dynamic city in eastern Germany.

Leipzig also has some of the finest classical music and opera in the country, and its fine art and literary scenes are flourishing. Once home to Bach, Wagner and Mendelssohn, and to Goethe, it more recently earned the sobriquet *Stadt der Helden* (City of Heroes) for its leading role in the 1989 democratic revolution.

You can easily fill a day or more wandering the centre of town.

Sights

Leipzig's compact centre lies within a ring road that outlines the town's medieval fortifications. To reach the city centre from the Hauptbahnhof, cross Willy-Brandt-Platz and continue south along Nikolaistrasse for five minutes. The **Markt** is the city focus and has been revamped with the installation of a new underground S-Bahn station for a cross-city line set to open in 2013.

Don't rush from sight to sight – wandering around Leipzig is a pleasure in itself, with many of the blocks around the central Markt criss-crossed by old internal shopping passages. Four good ones: **Steibs Hof** (100-year-old blue tiles and classic cafes), **Specks Hof** (soaring atrium, bookshops, cafes), **Jägerhofpassage** (galleries, theatre, antiques) and the classic **Mädlerpassage** (grand design, the famous Auerbachs Keller).

TOP CHOICE **Stasi Museum** MUSEUM
(www.runde-ecke-leipzig.de; Dittrichring 24; admission free; 10am-6pm) Former headquarters of the East German secret police, the Stasi Museum has exhibits on propaganda, amazingly hokey disguises, surveillance photos and other forms of 'intelligence', all part of the chilling machinations of the GDR's all-out zeal for controlling, manipulating and repressing its own people.

Museum der Bildenden Künste MUSEUM
(Museum of Fine Arts; www.mdbk.de; Katharinenstrasse 10; adult/child €5/free; 10am-6pm Tue & Thu-Sun, noon-8pm Wed) Leipzig's liveliest museum, the Museum der Bildenden Künste, is housed in a stunning glass cube of a building that provides both a dramatic – and echoey – backdrop to its collection, which spans old masters and the latest efforts of local artists.

Zeitgeschichtliches Forum MUSEUM
(Forum of Contemporary History; 222 20; Grimmaische Strasse 6; admission free; 9am-6pm Tue-Fri, 10am-6pm Sat & Sun) Haunting and uplifting by turns, the Zeitgeschichtliches Forum tells the story of the GDR from division and dictatorship to resistance and reform. It does a good job of chronicling the 1989 revolution, which started here, and it captures the tragic drama of the original Iron Curtain division.

Bach Museum MUSEUM
(www.bach-leipzig.de; Thomaskirchhof 16; adult/child €6/free; 10am-6pm Tue-Sun) Johann Sebastian Bach worked here from 1723 until his death in 1750. The newly revamped collection focuses on the composer's busy life in Leipzig. Multimedia displays allow you to get inside his head as he was composing music. Just across is **Thomaskirche** (Thomaskirchhof 18), where he lead the choir (and was only hired after three others turned the job down).

Other Music Sites HISTORIC BUILDINGS
Other stars of the real, real, real oldies beat in Leipzig include Felix Mendelssohn-Bartholdy, who lived (and died) in the **Mendelssohn-Haus** (www.mendelssohn-stiftung.de; Goldschmidtstrasse 12; admission €4.50; 10am-6pm); and Robert Schumann, who spent the first four years of his marriage to Leipzig pianist Clara Wieck in the **Schumann-Haus** (www.schumann-verein.de; Inselstrasse 18; admission €3; 2-5pm Wed-Fri, 10am-5pm Sat & Sun).

Neues Rathaus HISTORIC BUILDING
(New Town Hall; 1230; Martin-Luther-Ring; 7am-4.30pm Mon-Fri) Off the southern ring road is the 108m-high tower of the baroque Neues Rathaus. Though the origins date to the 16th century, its current manifestation was completed in 1905. The interior makes it one of the finest municipal buildings in Germany; the lobby houses rotating exhibitions, mostly on historical themes.

Völkerschlachtdenkmal MONUMENT
(Battle of Nations Monument; Prager Strasse; adult/child €5/3; 10am-6pm Apr-Oct, to 4pm Nov-Mar) Some 100,000 soldiers died in the epic 1813 battle that led to the decisive victory of

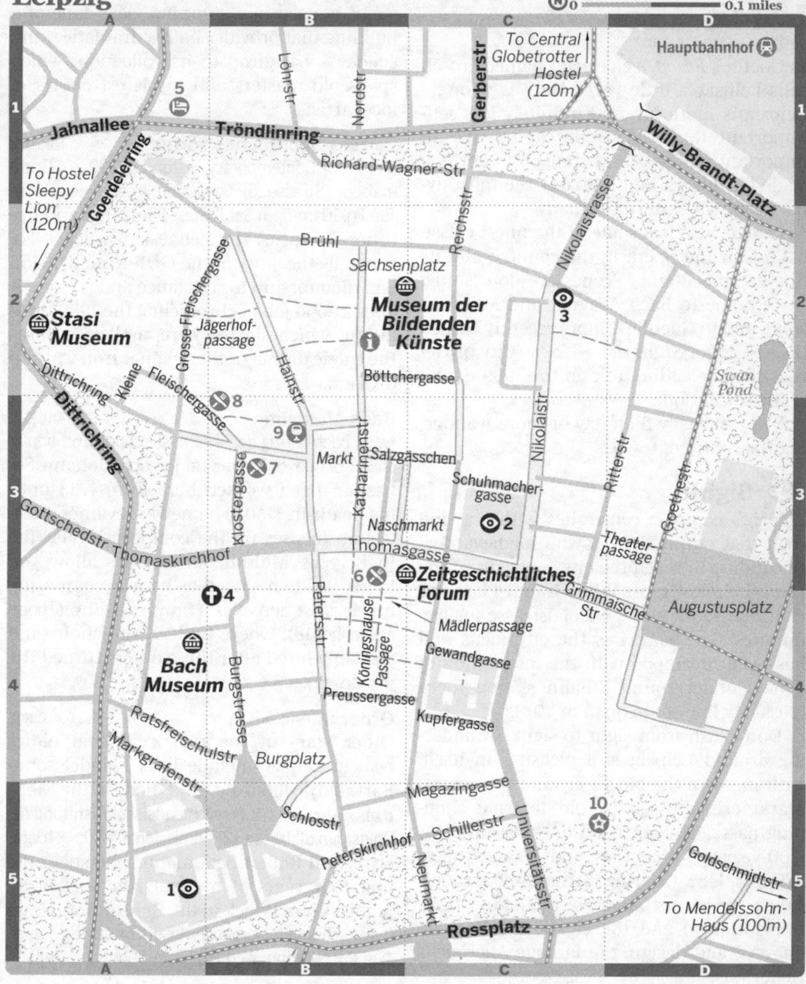

Prussian, Austrian and Russian forces over Napoleon's army. Built a century later, the Völkerschlachtdenkmal is a sombre and imposing 91m colossus that towers above southeastern Leipzig, not far from the actual killing fields. Climb the 500 steps for a view of the region. Take tram 15 from the station (direction: Meusdorf).

Alte Spinnerei ARTIST STUDIOS

(www.spinnerei.de; Spinnereistrasse 7; ⏲11am-6pm Tue-Sat) 'Cotton to culture' is the motto of this 19th-century cotton-spinning factory–turned–artist colony. Around 80 New Leipzig School artists, including Neo Rauch, have their studios in this huge pile of red-brick buildings, alongside designers, architects, goldsmiths and other creative types. Their work is displayed in about 10 galleries, including **Galerie Eigen+Art** (☎960 7886; www.eigen-art.com), internationally renowned for championing young artists. Take the S-1 to Plagwitz.

Sleeping

Midrange accommodation in the centre is fairly unexciting and usually the preserve of the big chains (particularly the many Accor brands).

Leipzig

Top Sights
Bach Museum ... A4
Museum der Bildenden Künste ... B2
Stasi Museum ... A2
Zeitgeschichtliches Forum ... B3

Sights
1 Neues Rathaus ... A5
2 Specks Hof ... C3
3 Steibs Hof ... C2
4 Thomaskirche ... B4

Sleeping
5 Hotel Fürstenhof ... A1

Eating
6 Auerbachs Keller ... B3
7 Zill's Tunnel ... B3
8 Zum Arabischen Coffe Baum ... B3

Drinking
9 Spizz ... B3

Entertainment
10 Moritz-Bastei ... C5

Hotel Fürstenhof HOTEL €€€
(☎1400; www.starwood.de; Tröndlinring 8; r from €200; ❄@✆≋) This intimate but grand hotel, with a 200-year pedigree, is part of the luxury branch of the Starwood chain. It has updated old-world flair, impeccable service, a gourmet restaurant and an oh-so-soothing grotto-style pool and spa.

Central Globetrotter Hostel HOSTEL €
(☎149 8960; www.globetrotter-leipzig.de; Kurt-Schumacher-Strasse 41; dm €14-18, s/d €28/40; @✆) In a busy location just north of the train station, this 80-room hostel offers bare-bones accommodation. Some rooms boast murals, albeit ones that won't win any scholarships to the Art Academy of Leipzig. Breakfast is €4 extra.

Hotel Markgraf HOTEL €€
(☎303 030; www.markgraf-leipzig.de; Körnerstrasse 36; r €85-100; ✆) This smartly run hotel puts you within staggering distance of the Karl-Liebknecht-Strasse nightlife. Many rooms overlook a pretty little park and there's a sauna for relaxing. Take tram 10 or 11 south to Südplatz.

Hotel Kosmos HOTEL €€
(☎233 4422; www.hotel-kosmos.de; Gottschedstrasse 1; s/d from €50/80) Right on a street with burgeoning nightlife, this low-key place in a grand building combines GDR-era furniture with murals in themed rooms. The murals next to the bed in the Marilyn Monroe room may fool the foolhardy.

Hotel Vier Jahreszeiten HOTEL €€
(☎985 10; www.guennewig.de; Kurt-Schumacher-Strasse 23-29; s €73-114, d €92-150; @✆) Close to the train station, this anonymous but well-run place has 67 comfortable rooms and serves up a good buffet breakfast in the atrium.

Hostel Sleepy Lion HOSTEL €
(☎993 9480; www.hostel-leipzig.de; Käthe-Kollwitz-Strasse 3; dm from €15, s/d €30/45; @✆) Budget-minded nomads will feel welcome at this low-key hostel, with 60 clean and comfy beds in cheerfully painted rooms with private facilities. The major sights – and bars – are just steps away.

Camping Am Auensee CAMPING GROUND €
(☎465 1600; www.motel-auensee.de; Gustav-Esche-Strasse 5; campsites per person from €6, cabins €40-60) This camping ground is in a pleasant wooded spot on the city's northwestern outskirts (take tram 10 or 11 to Anna Berger Strasse). The cabins are A-frame bungalows.

Eating

TOP CHOICE **Auerbachs Keller** GERMAN €€
(☎216 100; www.auerbachs-keller-leipzig.de; Mädlerpassage; mains €14-22) Founded in 1525, Auerbachs Keller is one of Germany's classic restaurants, serving typically hearty fare. Goethe's *Faust – Part I* includes a scene here, in which Mephistopheles and Faust carouse with some students before they ride off on a barrel. The historic section of the restaurant includes the Goethe room and the *Fasskeller;* note the carved tree trunk in the latter, depicting the whole barrel-riding adventure. There's excellent traditional chow, too.

Gosenschenke 'Ohne Bedenken' BEER GARDEN €€
(Menckestrasse 5; mains €6-16) This historic Leipzig institution, backed by the city's prettiest beer garden, is *the* place to sample Gose, a local top-fermented beer often

served with a shot of liqueur. The menu has a distinctly carnivorous bent. Take tram 12 to Fritz-Seger-Strasse.

Zill's Tunnel GERMAN **€€**
(Barfussgässchen 9; mains €9-15) Empty tables are a rare sight at this outstanding restaurant offering a classic menu of robust Saxon dishes. Sit on the outside terrace, in the rustic cellar, or in the covered 'tunnel' courtyard.

Zum Arabischen Coffe Baum CAFE **€€**
(Kleine Fleischergasse 4; mains €8-15) Leipzig's oldest coffee bar has a staid old restaurant and cafe offering excellent meals over three floors, plus a free coffee museum at the top. Composer Robert Schumann met friends here, and if you ask nicely you can sit at his regular table.

Drinking & Entertainment

Barfussgässchen and Kleine Flieschergasse, west of the Markt, form one of Leipzig's two 'pub miles', packed with outdoor tables that fill up the second the weather turns warm. The other is on Gottschedstrasse, a wider nightlife strip just west of the Altstadt.

Leipzig has a famously raw music scene. In late May, the world's largest **Goth Festival** (www.wave-gotik-treffen.de) attracts over 20,000 leather-clad, dark-side partiers.

To hear the more sedate works of native-born Bach, the Thomaskirche has frequent free recitals and performances by the boy's choir he once led. Mendelssohn-Haus has concerts on Sundays (adult/child €12/8).

TOP CHOICE **Conne Island** LIVE MUSIC
(www.conne-island.de; Koburger Strasse 3) This former squatter's haunt has morphed into the city's top venue for punk, indie, ska, rock and hip-hop concerts. It's in the southern suburb of Connewitz; take tram 9 to Koburger Brücke.

Werk II VENUE
(www.werk-2.de; Kochstrasse 132) This large cultural centre in an old factory is great for catching up-and-coming bands, alternative film and theatre, or even circus acts. It's in Connewitz; take tram 9 to Connewitzer Kreuz.

Moritz-Bastei CLUB
(www.moritzbastei.de; Universitätsstrasse 9) One of the best student clubs in Germany, in a spacious cellar below the old city walls. It has live music or DJs most nights and runs films outside in summer.

Spizz BAR
(Markt 9) Classic brass instruments dangle above the stage at this city slicker, where you might catch some cool jazz. It has three levels, a good range of wines and beers, and a fine sidewalk cafe that's good day or night.

Information

The Hauptbahnhof contains a modern mall with over 140 shops and (radically for Germany) it is open from 6am to 10pm daily. You'll find good bookshops, a post office, banks and much more.

Leipzig Card (1/3 days €9/19) Free or discounted admission to attractions, plus free travel on public transport. Available from the tourist office and most hotels.

Tourist office (www.leipzig.de; Katharinenstrasse 8; ⌚9.30am-6pm Mon-Fri, to 4pm Sat, to 3pm Sun)

Getting There & Away

Leipzig-Halle airport (LEJ; www.leipzig-halle-airport.de) has regional flights. Ryanair serves tiny **Altenburg airport** (ADC; www.flughafen-altenburg.de), some 53km from Leipzig. There's a shuttle bus (€12, 1¾ hours) timed to coincide with flights.

Leipzig is an important rail hub and fittingly has a monumental Hauptbahnhof. Regular services include Dresden (€29, 70 minutes), Munich (€87, five hours), Berlin-Hauptbahnhof by ICE (€42, 70 minutes) and Frankfurt (€70, 3½ hours).

Getting Around

Trams (www.lvb.de) are the main public-transport option, with most lines running via the Hauptbahnhof. The S-Bahn circles the city's outer suburbs. A single ticket costs €2 and a day card €5. The vast project of building an S-Bahn line under the city centre is due for completion late in 2013.

THURINGIA

Thuringia likes to trade on its reputation as the 'green heart' of Germany, an honour helped by the former GDR's dodgy economy, which limited development. These days its main towns of Erfurt and Weimar are popular for their historic centres and long histories. In fact the latter is a microcosm of German history – high and low – over the last 500 years.

While the communist era may have been relatively benign, the previous decades were not. The Nazis had numerous concentration camps here, including the notorious Buchenwald and the nightmare of Mittelbau Dora. But yet again, in contrast, Weimar was the place where Germany tried a liberal democracy in the 1920s and in previous centuries it was home to notables such as Bach, Schiller, Goethe and Thomas Mann.

Erfurt

☎0361 / POP 201,000

Thuringia's capital is a scene-stealing combo of sweeping squares, time-worn alleyways, perky church towers, idyllic river scenery, and vintage inns and taverns. On the little Gera River, Erfurt was founded by the indefatigable missionary St Boniface as a bishopric in 742. Rich merchants founded the university in 1392, allowing students to study common law, rather than religious law. Its most famous graduate was Martin Luther, who studied philosophy here before becoming a monk at the local Augustinian monastery in 1505.

This is a city to stroll. It's a five-minute walk north along Bahnhofstrasse to Anger, the main shopping and business artery. The Gera River bisects the Altstadt, spilling off into numerous creeks.

Sights

Krämerbrücke

(Merchants' Bridge) Unique in this part of Europe, this medieval bridge is an 18m-wide, 120m-long curiosity spanning the Gera River. Quaint houses and shops line both sides of the narrow road. It has a powerful magnetism for tourists.

Dom St Marien CATHEDRAL

(Domplatz; ⏲9am-5pm Mon-Fri, to 4.30pm Sat, 2-4pm Sun, shorter hr in winter) It's hard to miss Erfurt's cathedral casting its massive shadow over Domplatz from an artificial hill built specially for it. Ironically, it was originally only planned as a simple chapel in 752; by the time it was completed it was the rather strange, huge amalgam you see today. In July the stone steps leading up to the cathedral are the site of the opera festival **Domstufenfestspiele**.

Severikirche CHURCH HALL

(⏲9am-6pm Mon-Fri, shorter hr in winter) Next to the cathedral, this impressive 1280 five-aisled church hall boasts a stone Madonna (1345), a 15m-high baptismal font (1467) and the sarcophagus of St Severus, whose remains were brought to Erfurt in 836.

Augustinerkloster HISTORIC BUILDING

(www.augustinerkloster.de; Augustinerstrasse; tours adult/child €5/3; ⏲tours 10am-5pm Mon-Sat, 11am-3pm Sun) Augustinerkloster, now a nunnery, has a strong pedigree: Martin Luther was a monk here from 1505 to 1511 and, after being ordained in the chapel, read his first Mass here. You can view Luther's cell and an exhibit on the Reformation. The grounds and church are free.

Zitadelle Petersberg HISTORIC BUILDING

North of the Dom complex and west of Andreasstrasse, many of the city's lesser churches were demolished to erect this impressively tough-looking fortress – hence the reason why Erfurt has so many steeples without churches attached. There is a fascinating series of subterranean tunnels within the thick walls, which can only be seen on a guided tour from the tourist office (enquire there for times and prices).

Alte Synagoge HISTORIC BUILDING

(Old Synagogue; www.alte-synagoge.erfurt.de; Waagegasse 8; adult/child €5/1.50; ⏲10am-6pm Tue-Sun) One of the oldest Jewish houses of worship in Europe, with roots in the 12th century. After the pogrom of 1349, it was converted into a storehouse and, after later standing empty for decades, has now been restored as a museum.

Sleeping

Hotel Zumnorde HOTEL €€

(☎568 00; www.hotel-zumnorde.de; Anger 50/51; r €100-170; ❄📶) The 50 rooms and suites are modern, quite large and avoid decoration-overload in this fine hotel in the centre. There's a pretty garden hiding behind the noble facade. Enter from Weitergasse. The included breakfast buffet is vast.

Opera Hostel HOSTEL €

(☎6013 1366; www.opera-hostel.de; Walkmühlstrasse 13; dm €14-18, r €40-80; @📶) Run with smiles and aplomb, this upmarket hostel in a historic building scores big with wallet-watching global nomads. You'll sleep like a log in bright, spacious rooms, many with an extra sofa for chilling, and make friends in the communal kitchen and on-site lounge-bar.

Hotel am Kaisersaal HOTEL €€

(☎658 560; www.hotel-am-kaisersaal.de; Futterstrasse 8; r €80-100) The 36 rooms are tip-top and appointed with all expected mod cons in this highly rated hotel. Request a room facing the yard, though, if street noise disturbs. It's close to the Krämerbrücke.

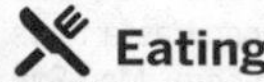

Eating

You'll find interesting and trendy restaurants and cafes along Michaelisstrasse and Marbacher Gasse. Look for *Puffbohnenpfanne* (fried broad beans with roast bacon), an Erfurt speciality. For a quick treat, have a classic Thuringer bratwurst hot off the grill from a **food stand** (Schlösserstrasse; meal €1.80) near a small waterfall.

Zum Güldenen Rade GERMAN **€€**
(Marktstrasse 50; mains €10-16) For the best potato dumplings in town, report to this gorgeous patrician town house, which centuries ago housed a tobacco factory. Aside from the classic version with gravy, you can also order them with more esoteric stuffings, such as spinach and salmon, or with black pudding and liver pâté.

Zum Goldenen Schwann GERMAN **€**
(Michaelisstrasse 9; mains €5-14) It's not so much the unpretentious traditional food that makes this place popular locally, rather the highly rated unfiltered boutique beer. Good for Thuringian cuisine.

Steinhaus GASTROPUB **€**
(Allerheiligenstrasse 20-21; mains €5-10) The ceiling beams may be ancient, but the crowd is intergenerational at this rambling gastro pub/beer garden in the historic Engelsburg. Dips, baguettes, pasta and gratins should keep your tummy filled and your brain balanced.

Information

Tourist office (www.erfurt-tourismus.de) Benediktsplatz (Benediktsplatz 1; ⏲10am-7pm Mon-Fri, 10am-6pm Sat, 10am-4pm Sun Apr-Dec, 10am-6pm Mon-Sat, 10am-4pm Sun Jan-Mar) Petersberg (⏲11am-6.30pm Apr-Oct, 11am-4pm Nov & Dec)

Getting There & Around

Erfurt's flashy Hauptbahnhof is on a line with frequent services linking Leipzig (€27, one hour) and Weimar (€8, 15 minutes). Hourly ICE/IC services go to Frankfurt (€51, 2¼ hours) and Berlin-Hauptbahnhof (€56, 2½ hours).

Eisenach

Eisenach is home to the Wartburg, the only German castle to be named a Unesco World Heritage site. Composer Johann Sebastian Bach was born here but he plays second fiddle to the awe-inspiring edifice in stone and half-timber high on the hill.

The **tourist office** (www.eisenach.info; Markt 24; ⏲10am-6pm Mon-Fri, 10am-5pm Sat & Sun) can help you find accommodation if your day trip gets extended.

The **Wartburg** (www.wartburg-eisenach.de; tour adult/child €8/5; ⏲tours 8.30am-5pm Mar-Oct, 9am-3.30pm Nov-Feb), parts of which date from the 11th century, is perched high above the town on a wooded hill. It is said to go back to Count Ludwig der Springer (the Jumper); you'll hear the story of how the castle got its name many times, but listen out for how Ludwig got his peculiar moniker as well.

The castle owes its huge popularity to **Martin Luther**, who went into hiding here from 1521 to 1522 after being excommunicated; during this time he translated the entire New Testament from Greek into German, contributing enormously to the development of the written German language. His modest, wood-panelled **study** is part of the guided tour (available in English), which is the only way to view the interior. The **museum** houses the famous Cranach paintings of Luther, and important Christian artefacts from all over Germany. Most of the rooms you'll see are extravagant 19th-century impressions of medieval life rather than original fittings; the re-imagined Great Hall inspired Richard Wagner's opera *Tannhäuser*. Between Easter and October crowds can be horrendous; arrive before 11am.

Frequent trains run to Erfurt (€12 to €15, 30 to 45 minutes) and most continue the short distance to Weimar.

Weimar

☎03643 / POP 65,000

Neither a monumental town nor a medieval one, Weimar appeals to those whose tastes run to cultural and intellectual pleasures. After all, this is the epicentre of the German Enlightenment, a symbol for all that is good and great in German culture. An entire pantheon of intellectual and creative giants lived and worked here: Goethe, Schiller, Bach, Cranach, Liszt, Nietzsche, Gropius, Herder, Feininger, Kandinsky, Klee...the list goes on.

You'll see reminders of them wherever you go – here, a statue; there, a commemorative plaque decorating a house facade –

plus scores of museums and historic sites. In summer, Weimar's many parks and gardens lend themselves to taking a break from the intellectual onslaught.

Internationally, of course, Weimar is better known as the place where the constitution of the Weimar Republic was drafted after WWI, though there are few reminders of this historical moment. The ghostly ruins of the Buchenwald concentration camp, on the other hand, provide haunting evidence of the terrors of the Nazi regime. The Bauhaus and classical Weimar locations are protected as Unesco World Heritage sites.

Sights

A good place to begin a tour is in front of the neo-Gothic 1841 **Rathaus** on the Markt. Directly east is the **Cranachhaus**, where painter Lucas Cranach the Elder lived for two years before his death in 1553. Just south is the other extreme of local history, the Nazi-era Hotel Elephant.

TOP CHOICE **Goethe Sites** HISTORIC SITES

The **Goethe Nationalmuseum** (Frauenplan 1; adult/child €8.50/2.50; ⌚9am-6pm Tue-Sun) focuses not so much on the man but his movement, offering a broad overview of German classicism, from its proponents to its patrons. Admission is included to the adjoining **Goethe Haus**, where such works as *Faust* were written, and which focuses much more on the man himself. He lived here from 1775 until his death in 1832. Goethe's original 1st-floor living quarters are reached via an expansive Italian Renaissance staircase decorated with sculpture and paintings brought back from his travels to Italy. You'll see his dining room, study and the bedroom with his deathbed. Because demand often exceeds capacity, you'll be given a time slot to enter. Once inside, you can stay as long as you want.

Goethes Gartenhaus (adult/child €4.50/2; ⌚10am-6pm Apr-Oct, to 4pm Nov-Mar) was his beloved retreat and stands in the alluring **Park an der Ilm**.

Bauhaus Museum MUSEUM

(Theaterplatz; adult/child €5/1; ⌚10am-6pm) The Bauhaus School and movement were founded here in 1919 by Walter Gropius, who managed to draw artists such as Kandinsky, Klee, Feininger and Schlemmer as teachers. The exhibition at the museum chronicles the evolution of the group and explains its design innovations, which continue to shape our lives. In 1925 the Bauhaus moved to Dessau and in 1932 to Berlin, where it was dissolved by the Nazis the following year. Once the form is in line with its function, a much grander museum is planned for 2013.

Schlossmuseum MUSEUM

(Burgplatz 4; adult/child €6/2.50; ⌚10am-6pm Tue-Sun Apr-Oct, 10am-4pm Nov-Mar) Housed in the **Stadtschloss**, the former residence of the ducal family of Saxe-Weimar, the museum boasts the **Cranach Gallery**, several portraits by **Albrecht Dürer** and collections of Dutch masters and German romanticists. A €90-million project for a full restoration is now in the works. Note that the courtyard was used by both the Nazis and the communists for interrogating political prisoners.

Other Historic Sites HISTORIC SITES

Goethe's fellow dramatist Friedrich von Schiller lived in Weimar from 1799 until his early death in 1805; his house is now the **Schiller Museum** (Schillerstrasse 12; adult/child €5/2; ⌚9am-6pm Wed-Mon). The study at the end of the 2nd floor contains the desk where he penned *Wilhelm Tell* and other works.

Liszt Haus (Marienstrasse 17; adult/child €4/1; ⌚10am-6pm Tue-Sun Apr-Oct) is on the western edge of Park an der Ilm. Composer and pianist Franz Liszt lived here in 1848 and again from 1869 to 1886, when he wrote *Hungarian Rhapsody* and *Faust Symphony*. It reopened in 2011 (the official year of Liszt!) after a major rehab.

Sleeping

The tourist office can help find accommodation, especially at busy times. There are many pensions scattered about the centre, which is where you should stay.

Hotel Anna Amalia HOTEL €

(☎495 60; www.hotel-anna-amalia.de; Geleitstrasse 8-12; r €60-90, apt €130-180; ᯤ) The Mediterranean look, with its nice, fresh colour scheme, exudes feel-good cheer in this family-run hotel near Goetheplatz. For more panache and elbow room, book one of the apartments, which sleep up to four. Good breakfast buffet.

Hotel Elephant HOTEL €€€

(☎8020; www.starwood.de; Markt 19; r from €120-250; @ᯤ) A true classic, the 1937 marble Bauhaus-Deco splendour of the 99-room, five-star Elephant has seen most of Weimar's great and good come and go. Just to make the point, a golden Thomas Mann looks out over the Markt from a balcony in front.

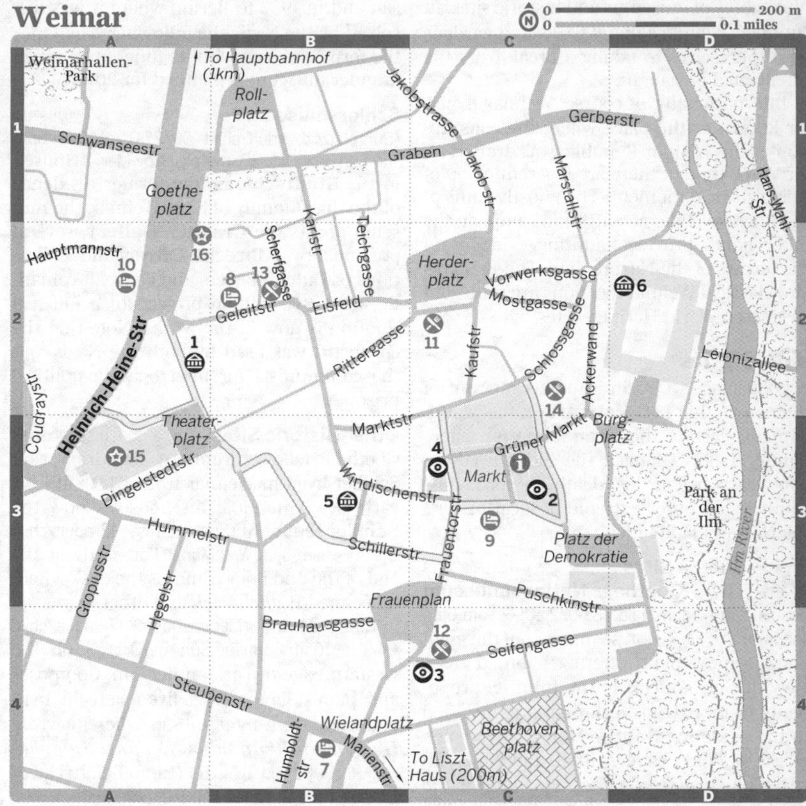

Labyrinth Hostel HOSTEL €
(☎811 822; www.weimar-hostel.com; Goetheplatz 6; dm €13-21, r €30-50; @📶) Loads of imagination has gone into this professionally run hostel with artist-designed rooms. In one double, for example, the bed perches on stacks of books, while another comes with a wooden high-platform bed. Bathrooms are shared and so are the kitchen and the lovely rooftop terrace. Dorm 8 has a balcony.

Hotel Amalienhof HOTEL €€
(☎5490; www.amalienhof-weimar.de; Amalienstrasse 2; r €90-110) This charming 35-room church-affiliated hotel has classy antique furnishings, richly styled rooms that subtly point to history, and a late breakfast buffet for those who take their holidays seriously.

Eating

Jo Hanns BISTRO €€
(Scherfgasse 1; mains €10-20) The food is satisfying but it's the 130 wines from the Saale-Unstrut region – many served by the glass – that draw people inside the cosy maroon walls or outside on the terrace. Food is inventive, with many specials.

Gasthaus zum Weissen Schwan GERMAN €€
(Frauentorstrasse 23; mains €11-20; ⊙noon-midnight Wed-Sun) At this venerable inn, you can fill your tummy with Goethe's favourite dish (boiled beef with herb sauce, red beet salad and potatoes), which actually hails from his home town of Frankfurt. The rest of the menu, though, is upmarket Thuringian.

Estragon CAFE €
(Herderplatz 3; meals €4-8; ⊙lunch) There are days when a bowl of steamy soup feels as warm and embracing as a hug from a good friend. This little soup kitchen turns mostly organic ingredients into delicious flavour combos served in three sizes. It shares digs with a small organic supermarket.

Weimar

Sights

1 Bauhaus Museum A2
2 Cranachhaus C3
3 Goethe Haus C4
Goethe Nationalmuseum .... (see 3)
4 Rathaus C3
5 Schiller Museum B3
Schlossmuseum .... (see 6)
6 Stadtschloss D2

Sleeping

7 Hotel Amalienhof B4
8 Hotel Anna Amalia B2
9 Hotel Elephant C3
10 Labyrinth Hostel A2

Eating

11 Estragon C2
12 Gasthaus zum Weissen Schwan C4
13 Jo Hanns B2
14 Residenz-Café C2

Entertainment

15 Deutsches Nationaltheater A3
16 Studentenclub Kasseturm A2

Residenz-Café CAFE €€
(Grüner Markt 4; mains €6-16;) The 'Resi', an enduring Weimar favourites, has something for everyone's taste. The Lovers' Breakfast is €20 for two; the inspired meat and vegetarian dishes may well have you swooning, too.

Entertainment

Studentenclub Kasseturm VENUE
(www.kasseturm.de; Goetheplatz 10; 6pm-late) A classic student club, the Kasseturm is a historic round tower with three floors of live music, DJs, cabaret and €2 beers.

Deutsches Nationaltheater THEATRE
(German National Theatre; www.nationaltheater-weimar.de; Theaterplatz; closed Jul & Aug) This historic venue shows classic and contemporary plays, plus ballet, opera and classical music.

Information

Stiftung Weimarer Klassik (www.klassik-stiftung.de) The organisation responsible for Weimar's Unesco monuments and museums has an info-filled website.

Tourist information (www.weimar.de; Markt 10; 9.30am-7pm Mon-Fri, to 4pm Sat & Sun) Discount cards start at €10.

Getting There & Away

Weimar's Hauptbahnhof is a 20-minute walk from the centre. It's on a line with frequent services linking Leipzig (€24, one hour) and Erfurt (€8, 15 minutes). Two-hourly ICE/IC services go to Berlin-Hauptbahnhof (€53, 2¼ hours).

Most buses serve Goetheplatz, on the northwestern edge of the Altstadt. Don't have time for the 20-minute walk before the next train departs? A cab costs €6.

Buchenwald

This **concentration-camp museum** (www.buchenwald.de; 9am-6pm Apr-Oct, 9am-4pm Nov-Mar) and memorial are located just 10km north of Weimar. The contrast between the brutality of the former and the liberal humanism of the latter is hard to comprehend.

Between 1937 and 1945, more than one-fifth of the 250,000 people incarcerated here died. The location on the side of a hill only added to the torture of the inmates, as there are sweeping views of the region – an area where people were free while those here died. Various parts of the camp have been restored and there is an essential museum with excellent exhibits. There's also a heart-breaking display of art created by the prisoners. Murals of flowers speak volumes about what was lost. A visit can occupy several hours.

After the war, the Soviets turned the tables but continued the brutality by establishing Special Camp No 2, in which 7000 so-called anticommunists and ex-Nazis were literally worked to death. Their bodies were found after the reunification in mass graves north of the camp, near the Hauptbahnhof.

In Weimar, **Buchenwald Information** (Markt 10; 9.30am-6pm Mon-Fri, to 3pm Sat & Sun) is an excellent resource.

To reach the camp, take bus 6 (€1.80, 15 minutes, hourly) from Weimar.

SAXONY-ANHALT

Once the smog-filled heart of GDR industry, Saxony-Anhalt (Sachsen-Anhalt) isn't on everyone's must-visit list. In fact, while the landscape is looking much greener these days, the flow of human traffic is mainly in an outbound direction, as many young people head west in search of jobs.

Still, the state has some strong drawcards: this is the home of the Bauhaus legacy and the wonderful bordering landscape of the Harz region.

Magdeburg

☎0391 / POP 230,000

Something old, something new: Magdeburg is constantly characterised by the juxtaposition of those two. Home to Germany's most ancient cathedral, the city also boasts the last of Austrian architect Friedensreich Hundertwasser's bonkers buildings and is a model of GDR-style wide boulevards and enormous *Plattenbauten* (concrete tower blocks) apartments. A small enclave of early-20th-century terraces and cobbled streets around Hasselbachplatz also stands out so remarkably that entering and leaving this historic district is like being transported in a time machine.

Sights

Magdeburg is most famous for its 13th-century **Dom** (☎543 2414; Domplatz; admission free; ⏲10am-4pm Mon-Sat, 11.30am-4pm Sun), which is apparently the oldest on German soil. However, the town also has a 21st-century attraction in Friedensreich Hundertwasser's **Green Citadel** (Grüne Zitadelle; ☎400 9650; www.gruene-zitadelle.de; Breiter Weg 8-10; German tours €6; ⏲information office 10am-6pm, tours 11am, 3pm & 5pm Mon-Fri, hourly 10am-5pm Sat & Sun). The last design by the famous Austrian architect, this apartment and shopping complex was completed in 2005, five years after his death. It evinces all his signature features – irregular windows, free-form walls and golden domes. The building is pink, but derives its name from its natural architecture and grass-covered roof.

The historic area surrounding **Hasselbachplatz** is an attraction in its own right and full of bars, clubs and restaurants.

Sleeping & Eating

Green Citadel HOTEL €€

(☎620 780; www.hotel-zitadelle.de; Breiter Weg 9; s €105-135, d €125-145, breakfast €11; @📶) Fans of Hundertwasser can ponder the architect's penchant for uneven, organic forms in these elegant rooms. The attached cafe (dishes €4 to €5, open 7am to 7pm) is open to the public, serving breakfast and light meals.

DJH Magdeburg HOSTEL €

(☎532 101; www.jugendherberge.de; Leiterstrasse 10; dm/s/tw €20/30/45, over 27yr extra €3; @) The smart, modern premises, generous space, good facilities and quiet but central location make this a winner.

Liebig INTERNATIONAL €

(☎555 6754; Liebigstrasse 1-3; ⏲10am-late) Private alcoves and pleated curtains lining the walls create a feeling of warmth and privacy amid this trendy bar-cafe-restaurant. Mediterranean fare, curries and steaks are all served.

Amsterdam ITALIAN €

(☎662 8680; Olvenstedter Strasse 9; mains €5-13; ⏲10am-1am Sun-Thu, 10am-2am Fri, 3pm-2am Sat; ✎) There's nothing Dutch about this welcoming bistro, with food ranging from bruschetta and panini to tuna steaks, a dedicated vegetarian selection and sumptuous breakfasts served until 5pm on weekdays and 6pm on Sundays.

Information

Tourist Information Magdeburg (☎194 33; www.magdeburg-tourist.de; Ernst-Reuter-Allee 12; ⏲10am-6.30pm Mon-Fri, to 4pm Sat Apr-Oct, 10am-6pm Mon-Fri, to 3pm Sat Nov-Mar)

Getting There & Away

There are trains to/from Berlin (€24.70, one hour and 40 minutes, hourly), while regular IC and RE trains run to Leipzig (€20.30, 1¼ hours, around every two hours).

Dessau-Rosslau

☎0340 / POP 89,000

'Less is more' and 'form follows function' – both these dictums were taught in Dessau, home of the influential Bauhaus School. Between 1925 and 1932, some of the century's greatest artists and architects breathed life into the ground-breaking principles of modernism here, among them Walter Gropius, Paul Klee, Wassily Kandinsky and Ludwig Mies Van der Rohe. Their legacy still stands proud, in the immaculate Bauhaus School building, the lecturers' purpose-built homes and other pioneering constructions.

The Bauhaus was born in Weimar in 1919, and it sought brief respite in Berlin (see p482) before being disbanded by the Nazis in 1933. But as the site of the movement's heyday and the 'built manifesto of Bauhaus ideas', Dessau is the true keeper of the flame.

Sights

Bauhaus founder Walter Gropius considered architecture the ultimate creative expression. So his first realised project, the **Bauhaus Gebäude** (Bauhaus Building; ☎650 8251; www.bauhaus-dessau.de; Gropiusallee 38; exhibition hall adult/concession €5/4, with Meisterhäuser €12/8, tours €4/3; ⊙10am-6pm, German tours 11am & 2pm, extra tours Sat & Sun), is extremely significant. Once home to the Hochschule für Gestaltung (Institute for Design), where the architect and his colleagues taught, today it houses a postgraduate college. You can visit the changing exhibitions and

DON'T MISS

BEWITCHING HARZ

The **Harz Mountains** constitute a mini-Alpine region straddling Saxony-Anhalt and Lower Saxony. Here, medieval castles overlook fairy-tale historic towns, while there are caves, mines and numerous hiking trails to explore.

The region's highest – and most famous – mountain is the Brocken, where one-time visitor Johann Wolfgang von Goethe set the 'Walpurgisnacht' chapter of his play *Faust*. His inspiration in turn came from folk tales depicting *Walpurgisnacht*, or *Hexennacht* (witches' night), as an annual witches' coven. Every 30 April to 1 May it's celebrated enthusiastically across the Harz region.

Goslar

Goslar is a truly stunning 1000-year-old city with beautifully preserved half-timbered buildings and an impressive **Markt**. The town's **Kaiserpfalz** is a reconstructed Romanesque 11th-century palace. Just below there's the restored **Domvorhalle**, which displays the 11th-century 'Kaiserstuhl' throne, used by German emperors.

Brocken's summit is an easy day trip from Goslar. Take a bus (810) or train (faster) from Goslar to Bad Harzburg and then a bus (820) to Torfhaus, where the 8km Goetheweg trail begins.

If climbing a mountain is not your thing, a mere wander around town and a stroll along the circumference of town, a green space dotted with bucolic lakes and bits of the old city wall, makes for a fine day.

The **tourist office** (☎05321-780 60; www.goslar.de; Markt 7; ⊙9.15am-6pm Mon-Fri, 9.30am-4pm Sat, to 2pm Sun Apr-Oct, 9.15am-5pm Mon-Fri, 9.30am-2pm Sat Nov-Mar) can help with accommodation, which includes a **DJH Hostel** (☎05321-222 40; www.jugendherberge.de; Rammelsbergerstrasse 25; dm €20.50-23.50) and hotels **Die Tanne** (☎05321-343 90; www.die-tanne.de; Bäringerstrasse 10; s €40-65, d €65-100) and the fancier **Kaiserworth** (☎05321-7090; www.kaiserworth.de; Markt 3; s €80-101, d €122-207, apt €182-252; @). For a special experience, don't miss **Fortezza** (☎05321-4803; Thomasstrasse 2; mains €8-17), a Spanish restaurant ensconced in a 16th-century tower attached to the old city wall.

As well as being serviced by **buses** (www.rbb-bus.de), Goslar is connected by train to Hanover (€15.20, one hour and 10 minutes).

Quedlinburg

The Unesco World Heritage town of Quedlinburg is best known for its spectacular castle district, perched on a 25m-high plateau above its historic half-timbered buildings. Originally established during the reign of Heinrich I (919–36), the present-day Renaissance **Schloss** (palace) dates from the 16th century. Its centrepiece is the restored baroque **Blauer Saal** (Blue Hall).

Contact **Quedlinburg-Tourismus** (☎03946-905 625; www.quedlinburg.de; Markt 2; ⊙9.30am-6.30pm Mon-Fri, to 3pm Sat, to 2pm Sun Apr–mid-Oct, 9.30am-5pm Mon-Fri, to 1pm Sat mid-Oct–Mar) for more information. Lodgings include a **DJH hostel** (☎03946-811 703; www.jugendherberge.de; Neuendorf 28; dm €16.50-19.50, bedding €3) and the hotels **Pension Zum Altstadtwinkel** (☎03946-91 9975; Hohe Strasse 15; s/d/apt €35/66/120; wi-fi) and **Romantik Hotel Theophano** (☎03946-963 00; www.hoteltheophano.de; Markt 13-14; s/d from €69/79).

There are hourly trains to Magdeburg (from €13.80, one hour and 10 minutes).

wander through a small section. However, taking a tour is best; it gets you into otherwise closed rooms, even if you don't understand German.

Since a key Bauhaus aim was to 'design for living', the three white, concrete **Meisterhäuser** (Master Craftsmen's Houses; www.meisterhaeuser.de; Ebertallee 63-71; admission to all 3 houses adult/concession €5/4, combination ticket with Bauhaus Gebäude €12/8; ⌚10am-6pm Tue-Sun mid-Feb–Oct, to 5pm Nov–mid-Feb) are a fascinating insight into this philosophy and style of living.

Sleeping & Eating

In Dessau-Rosslau, you really can eat, drink and sleep Bauhaus. For a different diet, investigate the main thoroughfare of Zerbster Strasse.

Bauhaus dorms HOSTEL €
(☎650 8318; kaatz@bauhaus-dessau.de; Gropiusallee 38; s/d €25/40) Since the Bauhaus school was renovated in 2006, you can really live the modernist dream by hiring the former students' dorms inside.

Hotel-Pension An den 7 Säulen HOTEL €
(☎619 620; Ebertallee 66; s €47-52, d €65-72) This relaxed pension (with an Ayurverdic spa) has a glass-fronted breakfast room overlooking the Meisterhäuser across the leafy street.

Kornhaus INTERNATIONAL €€
(☎640 4141; Kornhausstrasse 146; mains €8-15) This is Bauhaus gone a touch upscale on the edge of the Elbe River, where you can lounge on the wide balcony and contemplate the curve of the river and the building all at once.

Bauhaus Klub BAR
(Gropiusallee 38' mains €3-7) Starting to see a pattern here? The occasional cool dude in black polo-neck jumper and horn-rimmed glasses can be seen among the broad mix of people in this basement bar of the Bauhaus school. In the same building as the Klub, student favourite **Bauhaus Mensa** (☎650 8421; Gropiusallee 38; mains €3-10; ⌚8am-2pm Mon-Fri) offers cheap cafeteria-style meals.

Information

Bauhaus Foundation (☎650 8251; www.bauhaus-dessau.de; Gropiusallee 38; ⌚10am-6pm) Offers educational info on, and tours of, Bauhaus buildings, sometimes in English.

Tourist office (☎204 1442, accommodation reservations 220 3003; www.dessau-tourismus.de; Zerbster Strasse 2c; ⌚9am-6pm Mon-Fri, 9am-1pm Sat Apr-Oct, 9am-5pm Mon-Fri, 10am-1pm Sat Nov-Mar)

Getting There & Away

RE trains run to Berlin every one to two hours (€21, 1¾ hours). Dessau is equidistant from Leipzig and Magdeburg (both €10.50, 45 minutes to one hour), with frequent services to each.

MECKLENBURG-WESTERN POMERANIA

Mecklenburg-Vorpommern combines historic Hanseatic-era towns like Schwerin, Wismar and Stralsund with holiday areas such as Warnemünde and Rügen Island. It is off the path for many travellers, but in summer it seems like half the country is here, lolling on the sands in some state of undress. Outside of these somewhat mild times (this is a region where the beaches are dotted with large, wicker beach baskets to provide shelter) the intrepid visitor is rewarded with journeys far from the maddening crowds.

Schwerin

☎0385 / POP 95,860

State capital Schwerin has a modest dignity befitting its status. The oldest city in Mecklenburg-Western Pomerania, it has numerous lakes, including one that is the town's centrepiece. Buildings are an interesting mix of 16th- to 19th-century architecture. It's small enough to explore on foot and, if you're on the move, you can see it as part of a half-day break on a train journey. But Schwerin's beauty and charm are invariably infectious, and few people regret spending extra time here.

Sights

Southeast of the Alter Garten, over the causeway on the Burginsel (Burg Island), the striking neo-Gothic **Schloss Schwerin** (☎525 2920; www.schloss-schwerin.de; adult/child €4/2.50; ⌚10am-6pm mid-Apr–mid-Oct, 10am-5pm Tue-Sun mid-Oct–mid-Apr) was built in the mid-1800s around the chapel of a 16th-century ducal castle and is quite rightly the first attraction visitors head to upon arrival. The causeway is overlooked by a statue of **Niklot**, an early Slavic prince, who was defeated by Heinrich der Löwe (Henry the Lion) in 1160. The huge, graphic picture of his death is a highlight of the castle's interior.

You don't get better examples of north German red-brick architecture than the 14th-century Gothic **Dom** (☎565 014; Am Dom 4; ⏰11am-2pm Mon-Fri, 11am-4pm Sat, noon-3pm Sun), towering above the Markt. You can climb up to the platform in the 19th-century tower (adult/child €1.50/0.50).

The enormous neoclassical building in the Alter Garten, the **Staatliches Museum** (☎595 80; www.museum-schwerin.de; Alter Garten 3; adult/concession €6/4; ⏰10am-6pm Tue-Sun Apr-Oct, 10am-5pm Tue-Sun Nov-Mar), permanently displays old Dutch masters including Rembrandt, Rubens and Brueghel, as well as oils by Lucas Cranach the Elder and collections of more modern works by Marcel Duchamp and Ernst Barlach.

Sleeping & Eating

Hotel Nordlicht HOTEL €€
(☎558 150; www.hotel-nordlicht.de; Apothekerstrasse 2; s/d/apt from €54/82/86; @ 📶) Simple furnishings, helpful staff, spotless rooms (some with balconies) and walls covered with interesting old photos of Schwerin round out this excellent budget choice in a quiet part of town.

Hotel Niederländischer Hof HOTEL €€
(☎591 100; www.niederlaendischer-hof.de; Karl-Marx-Strasse 12-13; s €87-124, d €125-170 incl breakfast; 📶) You can't beat the Pfaffenteich location or the elegant rooms and marble bathrooms at this exceedingly classy hotel. There's even a library with an open fire for those contemplative German winters.

DJH Hostel HOSTEL €
(☎326 0006; www.jugendherberge.de; Waldschulweg 3; dm under/over 26yr incl breakfast €17.50/20.50) This basic hostel is about 4km south of the city centre, just opposite the zoo. Take tram 1 to Marienplatz, then bus 14 to the last stop, Jugendherberge.

Friedrich's FRENCH €
(☎555 473; Friedrichstrasse 2; mains €8-15; 🖉) Overlooking the Pfaffenteich, this Parisian-style cafe has a casual atmosphere, a classy, friendly bar area and an uncomplicated selection of salads, fish, grills and vegetarian dishes. The waterfront terrace is divine in warm weather.

Historisches Weinhaus Wöhler GERMAN €€
(☎555 830; www.weinhaus-woehler.com; Puschkinstrasse 26; mains €9-21) Stained-glass windows tell you that this place is indeed historic. Open since 1895, the building dates to the 18th century. The restaurant offers classic Mecklenburg specialities and there's even a fun tapas bar for a quick non-Germanic bite. The beer garden is alluring and you can sleep it off in the comfortable rooms (€85 to €160) upstairs.

Information

Schwerin-Information (☎592 5212; www.schwerin.de; Markt 14; ⏰9am-7pm Mon-Fri, 10am-6pm Sat & Sun Apr-Oct, 9am-6pm Mon-Fri, 10am-4pm Sat & Sun Nov-Mar)

Getting There & Away

Schwerin is on the line linking Hamburg (€21.70 to €25, 50 minutes to 1¼ hours) with Stralsund (€31.70, two hours). Services to Rostock (€14.90 to €18.80, one hour) are frequent, as are those to Wismar (€6.90, 30 minutes). There are RE trains to Berlin-Hauptbahnhof (€31.70, 2¼ hours).

Wismar

☎03841 / POP 45,200

Wismar, a Hanseatic gem that's fast being discovered, joined the powerful trading league in the 13th century – the first town east of Lübeck to do so. For centuries it was in and out of Swedish control – hence the 'Swedish heads' dotted across town. Quieter than Rostock or Stralsund, Wismar can fill up with visitors quickly in high season; it's definitely worth an overnight stay, and is also the gateway to **Poel Island**, a lovely little piece of green to the north.

Sights & Activities

The old harbour, **Alter Hafen**, with old boats swaying in the breeze, evokes trading days from centuries ago. Featured in the 1922 film *Nosferatu*, it is still a focal point of activity in Wismar. **Clermont Reederei** (☎224 646; www.reederei-clermont.de; adult/child €8/4) operates hour-long harbour cruises five times daily from May to September, four times daily in April and four times on Saturday and Sunday in March, leaving from Alter Hafen. Daily boats also go to Poel Island (adult return €14, May to September). Various other companies run tours on historic ships during summer; contact the **harbour** (☎389 082; www.alterhafenwismar.de, in German) for details.

Running through town, the **Grube** (channel) is the last artificial medieval waterway in the north and should be a part of any stroll through the historic quarter. The **Wasserkunst** is a 12-sided well from

1602 that anchors a corner of the attractive **Markt**.

The town's historical museum, **Schabbellhaus** (☎282 350; www.schabbellhaus.de; Schweinsbrücke 8; adult/child €2/1, free Fri; ⌚10am-8pm Tue-Sun May-Oct, to 5pm Nov-Apr), has taken over a former Renaissance brewery (1571), just south of the St-Nikolai-Kirche across the canal. The museum's pride and joy is the large 16th-century tapestry *Die Königin von Saba vor König Salomon* (The Queen of Sheba before King Solomon).

Wismar was a target for British and American bombers just weeks before the end of WWII. Of the three great red-brick churches that once rose above the rooftops, only **St-Nikolai-Kirche** (St-Nikolai-Kirchhof; admission €1; ⌚8am-8pm May-Sep, 10am-6pm Apr & Oct, 11am-4pm Nov-Mar), built from 1381 to 1487, remains intact. Massive **St-Georgen-Kirche** (admission by donation; ⌚10am-8pm Jul & Aug, 10am-6pm Mar-Jun & Sep-Dec, 10am-6pm Mon-Sat, 10am-4pm Sun Jan & Feb) has been extensively renovated for combined use as a church, concert hall and exhibition space. In 1945 a freezing populace was driven to burn what was left of the church's beautiful wooden statue of St George and the dragon. The great brick **steeple** (⌚10am-8pm Apr-Oct), built in 1339, of the 13th-century **St-Marien-Kirche**, towers above the city.

Sleeping & Eating

Along the Alter Hafen, seafood (including delicious fish sandwiches from as little as €2) is sold directly from a handful of bobbing boats. Most are open 9am to 6pm daily, and from 6am on Saturday during Wismar's weekly fish market.

Bio Hotel Reingard HOTEL €€
(☎284 972; www.reingard.de; Weberstrasse 18; s €58-62, d €86-88 incl breakfast) Wismar's most charming place to stay is this boutique hotel with its handful of artistic rooms, leafy little garden and gourmet *bio* (organic) restaurant (menus from €30 for two people; by arrangement). There's even a small adjoining **museum** containing the owner's 300,000-strong collection of buttons and vintage belt buckles.

Pension Chez Fasan HOTEL €
(☎213 425; www.unterkunft-pension-wismar.de; Bademutterstrasse 20a; s without bathroom €21, s/d with bathroom €24/45, breakfast €5) This is the best budget deal in town. Rooms in the three-building complex come with satellite TV and a great central location.

DJH Hostel Wismar HOSTEL €
(☎32 680; www.jugendherberge.de; Juri Gagarin Ring 30a; dm incl breakfast & linen under/over 26yr €20.50/25.10) Popular with large groups, this hostel is simple and clean. It's a 15-minute walk from the train station; alternatively take bus D to Philip Müller Strasse.

Zur Reblaus Wein- und Kaffeestube CAFE €
(www.zur-reblaus.de; Neustadt 9; snacks €4-9; ⌚2-10pm May-Sep, closed Sun Oct-Apr) A snug wine bar and cafe where locals come for a drink or a *Kaffeeklatsch* (chat over coffee); try the house speciality pie, the *Trummertorte*. Rooms are also available upstairs in the attached pension (single/double from €38/55).

Brauhaus am Lohberg SEAFOOD €€
(Kleine Hohe Strasse 15; mains €7-15) Spread over a series of warehouses dating back to the 16th century, this popular spot is honouring Wismar's long tradition of brewing by once again making its own beer. There's a good seafood menu.

Information

In the Altstadt you'll find **tourist information** (☎251 3025; www.wismar.de; Am Markt 11; ⌚9am-6pm Mar-Dec, 9am-6pm Mon-Sat, 10am-4pm Sun Jan & Feb).

Getting There & Away

Trains travel the coastal branch lines to Rostock (€10, 70 minutes, hourly) and Schwerin (€6.80, 30 minutes, hourly).

Rostock & Warnemünde

☎0381 / POP 200,400

Rostock, the largest city in sparsely populated northeastern Germany, is a major Baltic port and shipbuilding centre. Its chief suburb – and chief attraction – is Warnemünde, 12km north of the centre. Counted among eastern Germany's most popular beach resorts, it's hard to see it as a small fishing village these days, but the boats still bring in their catches, and some charming streets and buildings persist amid the tourist clutter.

First mentioned in 1161 as a Danish settlement, Rostock began taking shape as a German fishing village around 1200. In the 14th and 15th centuries, it was an important Hanseatic trading city; parts of the city centre, especially along Kröpeliner Strasse, retain the flavour of this period.

Sights

Lined with 15th- and 16th-century burghers' houses, Kröpeliner Strasse is a lively, cobbled pedestrian street that runs west from Neuer Markt to the **Kröpeliner Tor** (☎454 177; adult/child €2/1; ⏲10am-6pm), a 55m-high tower you can climb.

The **Kloster Zum Heiligen Kreuz** (Holy Cross Convent; Klosterhof 18) was established in 1270 by Queen Margrethe I of Denmark; today it houses the **Cultural History Museum** (☎203 590; admission free; ⏲10am-6pm Tue-Sun), with an excellent and varied collection, including large numbers of everyday items used by locals over the centuries.

Rostock's pride and joy, the **Marienkirche** (☎453 325; Am Ziegenmarkt; admission by donation; ⏲10am-6pm Mon-Sat, 11.15am-5pm Sun May-Sep, 10am-noon & 2-4pm Mon-Sat, 11.15am-noon Sun Oct-Apr), built in 1290, was the only one of Rostock's four main churches to survive WWII unscathed. The long north–south transept was added after the ceiling collapsed in 1398. Notable features include the 12m-high astrological clock (1470–72) and the Gothic bronze baptismal font (1290).

Warnemünde, the lively seafront to the north lined with hotels and restaurants, is where the tourists congregate. Its broad, sandy beach stretches west from the **lighthouse** (1898) and the **Teepott** exhibition centre, and is chock-a-block with bathers on hot summer days.

Sleeping

Jellyfish Hostel HOSTEL €
(☎444 3858; www.jellyfish-hostel.com; Beginenberg 25, Rostock; dm/s/d per person from €15/31/25; @📶) Set in a landmark building, this palatial place features rooms with moulded ceilings and lots of space. The buffet breakfast is €4.

Pension Zum Steuermann HOTEL €
(☎511 68; www.pension-zum-steuermann.de; Alexandrinenstrasse 57, Warnemünde; apt €45-120) These cheerful blue-and-white former fishermen's houses are tucked away down a side street. They have a relaxed, beachy feel and are popular with families.

Hotel Kleine Sonne HOTEL €€
(☎497 3153; www.die-kleine-sonne.de; Steinstrasse 7; s €52-82, d €104-164, breakfast €11; @) This lovely place lives up to its name with sunny yellow and red detailing, and semaphore prints by Berlin artist Nils Ausländer. If you're cycling, you can get two nights' accommodation, a packed lunch, three-course dinner, cycling itineraries and bike storage for €159/238 per single/double. All guests have free use of the wellness centre at the Steigenberger Hotel Sonne.

DJH hostel Warnemünde HOSTEL €
(☎548 170; www.jugendherbergen-mv.de; Parkstrasse 47; dm under/over 26yr €25.20/30.80; @📶) This fantastic hostel is in a converted weather station just minutes from the western end of the Warnemünde beach, near Diedrichshagen. The tower rooms are particularly popular with families, who tend to dominate in the July and August holiday period.

Hotel Verdi HOTEL €
(☎252 240; www.hotel-verdi.de; Wollenweberstrasse 28; s/d/studio/apt incl breakfast from €59/79/84/119; 📶) Opening to an umbrella-shaded, timber-decked terrace is this sparkling little hotel just near the Petrikirche and Alter Markt, with a handful of attractively decorated rooms, larger studios with kitchenettes, and a ground-floor holiday apartment sleeping up to four people. All are great value.

Steigenberger Hotel Sonne HOTEL €€€
(☎497 30; www.hotel-sonne-rostock.de; Neuer Markt 2; s/d from €79/158, breakfast €17; @📶) It's hard for the interior to compete with the ornate facade at this hotel – a confection of stepped gables and iron lacework topped with a golden 'sun'. However, the rooms do their best in tones of brown, red and yellow, and there's a clutch of classy restaurants.

Eating

Excellent fish and wurst stalls set up shop on Rostock's Neuer Markt and Warnemünde's harbour most mornings.

Weineckeck Krahnstöver PUB FARE €€
(Grosse Wasser Strasse 30; mains €10-18; ⏲closed Sun) One side is a wine bar with a pub feel, the other side a proper restaurant: both sides have a loyal local following and offer a lengthy list of wines that you sip in the warm, old-fashioned atmosphere between dark wood walls.

Café Kloster INTERNATIONAL €€
(☎375 7950; Klosterhof 6; mains €9-15; ⏲closed Sun; 🖉) This sweet bistro offers soups, salads and plenty of veggie fare, with seating available in its art-filled interior or under a massive pear tree in its hidden garden.

Krahnstöver Likörfabrik WINE BAR €
(Grosse Wasserstrasse 30/Grubenstrasse 1; mains €6-12) This late-15th-century former liquor factory is an excellent example of late Gothic architecture. The wine bar has an inventive menu; around the corner, the Kneipe seems as old as the building and dishes up hearty fare.

Zur Kogge GERMAN €
(☎493 4493; Wokrenterstrasse 27; mains €9-17) Touristy but still unmissable, this is Rostock's oldest restaurant. Cosy wooden booths are lined with stained-glass decorations of Hanseatic coats of arms and monster fish threatening sailing ships, while life preservers hang from the walls. The menu is dominated by fish, but you can enjoy coffee and cake between meal times if you want to avoid the crowds.

Information

Tourist information (☎381 2222; www.rostock.de; Neuer Markt 3; ⊙10am-7pm Mon-Fri, 10am-4pm Sat & Sun Jun-Aug, 10am-6pm Mon-Fri, 10am-4pm Sat & Sun May & Sep, 10am-6pm Mon-Fri, 10am-3pm Sat Oct-Apr)

Warnemünde-Information (☎548 000; www.warnemuende.de; Am Strom 59; ⊙9am-6pm Mon-Fri, 10am-4pm Sat & Sun Mar-Oct, 10am-5pm Mon-Fri, 10am-3pm Sat Nov-Feb)

Getting There & Around

Rostock is on the busy **train** line that links Hamburg (€29.90 to €38, 1¾ to 2½ hours) to Stralsund (€12.80, one hour). Services to/from Schwerin (€14.70 to €18.50, one hour) are frequent, as is the branch line to Wismar (€10, 70 minutes, hourly). There are RE trains to Berlin-Hauptbahnhof (€34.80, 2½ to 2¾ hours, every two hours).

Ferries sail to/from Denmark, Sweden, Latvia and Finland. Boats depart from the **Überseehafen** (overseas seaport; www.rostock-port.de), which is on the east side of the Warnow. Take tram 1, 2, 3 or 4 to Dierkower Kreuz (tram 3 or 4 from the Hauptbahnhof), then change for bus 49 to Seehafen. There is an S-Bahn to Seehafen, but it's a 20-minute walk from the station to the piers (not fun if you're dragging heavy bags).

There are frequent **S-Bahn** services linking Rostock to Warnemünde (€1.70, 20 minutes). In Rostock, tram lines 3, 4 and 6 link the train station with the centre. The area lends itself to bike touring. **Radstation** (☎240 1153; www.radstation-rostock.de; Hauptbahnhof; per day from €7; ⊙10am-6pm Mon-Fri, to 1pm Sat) is convenient for rentals.

Stralsund

☎03831 / POP 57,600

You instantly know you're next to the sea here. Possessing an unmistakable medieval profile, Stralsund was the second-most powerful member of the medieval Hanseatic League, after Lübeck. In 1648 Stralsund, Rügen Island and Pomerania came under the control of the Swedes – who had helped in their defence. The city remained Swedish until 1815, when it was incorporated into Prussia.

An attractive town of imposing churches and elegant town houses, Stralsund boasts more examples of classic red-brick Gothic gabled architecture than almost anywhere else in northern Germany. It has some excellent sights, including the fantastic new aquarium Ozeaneum. Stralsund is a great place to visit if you want to get a feel for Baltic culture.

Sights

Alter Markt HISTORIC AREA
One of the two structures dominating the Alter Markt is the gorgeous 14th-century **Rathaus**, with its late-Gothic decorative facade. The upper portion has slender copper turrets and gables that have openings to prevent strong winds from knocking over the facade. This ornate design was Stralsund's answer to its rival city, Lübeck, which has a similar town hall. The sky-lit gallery overhanging the vaulted walkway is held aloft by shiny black pillars on carved and painted bases.

Exit through the eastern walkway to the main portal of the other dominant presence in the Alter Markt, the 1270 **Nikolaikirche** (☎299 799; ⊙10am-4pm Mon-Sat, 2-4pm Sun). Modelled after the Marienkirche in Lübeck (p595) and bearing a fleeting resemblance to Notre Dame, it's filled with art treasures. Also worth a closer look are the **high altar** (1470), 6.7m wide and 4.2m tall, showing Jesus' entire life, and the mostly inaccurate **astronomical clock** (1394), allegedly the oldest in the world.

Neuer Markt HISTORIC AREA
The Neuer Markt is dominated by the massive 14th-century **Marienkirche** (☎298 965; ⊙10am-5pm), another superb example of north German red-brick construction. Check out the huge **F Stellwagen organ** (1659), festooned with music-making cherubs. You can climb the steep wooden steps up the

Stralsund

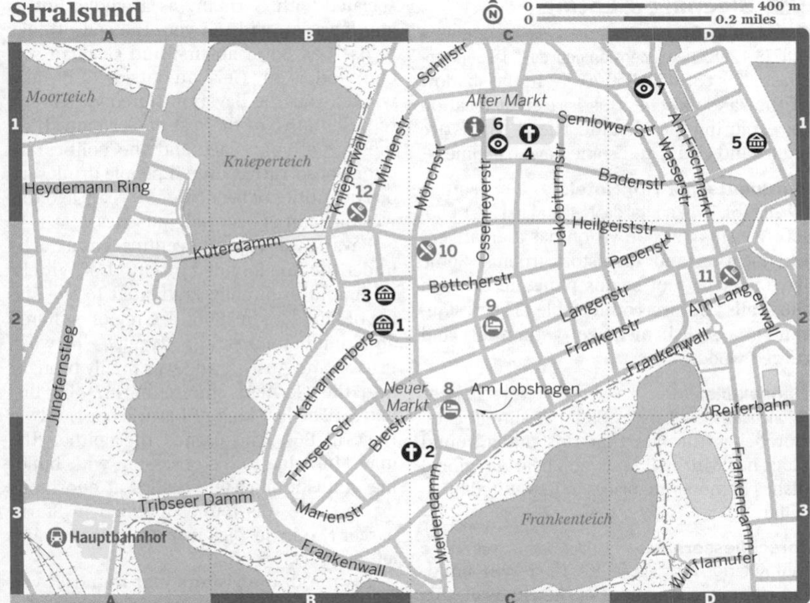

tower (adult/concession €4/2) for a sweeping view of the town and Rügen Island.

Meeresmuseum MUSEUM
(Oceanographic Museum; ☎265 010; www.meeresmuseum.de; Katharinenberg 14-20; adult/child €7.50/5, combination ticket incl Ozeaneum adult/child €18/11; ⊙10am-6pm Jun-Sep, 10am-5pm Oct-May) North of Neuer Markt, a 13th-century convent church is now a museum that showcases displays on local sea life and the people who catch it.

Ozeaneum AQUARIUM
(☎265 0610; www.ozeaneum.de; Hafeninsel Stralsund; adult/child €14/8, combination ticket incl Meeresmuseum adult/child €18/11; ⊙9.30am-9pm Jun-Sep, 9.30am-7pm Oct-May) The massive white structure on the harbour is an aquarium that takes you on a spectacular journey through the ecosystems of the Baltic, the North Sea and the North Atlantic.

Kulturhistorisches Museum MUSEUM
(☎287 90; Mönchstrasse 25-27; adult/child €4/2; ⊙10am-5pm Tue-Sun) Stralsund's cultural history museum has a large historical collection, paintings by Caspar David Friedrich and Philipp Otto Runge, faience (tin-glazed earthenware), playing cards and Gothic altars, as well as various outlying exhibitions in restored houses.

Stralsund

Sights

1 Kulturhistorisches Museum B2
2 Marienkirche C3
3 Meeresmuseum B2
4 Nikolaikirche C1
5 Ozeaneum D1
6 Rathaus C1
7 Weisse Flotte D1

Sleeping

8 Norddeutscher Hof Hotel C2
9 Pension Cobi C2

Eating

10 Hanseקeller C2
11 Tiffany D2
12 Torschliesserhaus B1

Tours

Weisse Flotte (☎0180-321 2120; www.weisse-flotte.com; Fährstrasse 16; one way adult/child €2.50/1.30; ⊙May-Oct) runs seven ferries daily to the scenic fishing village of Altefähr, on Rügen Island. One-hour **harbour cruises** (adult/child €7/4) also depart four times daily during summer months.

Sleeping & Eating

Pension Cobi PENSION €
(☎278 288; www.pension-cobi.de; Jakobiturmstrasse 15; s €35-45, d €50-70;) In the shadow of the Jakobikirche, this is a great location for exploring the Altstadt. The 14 rooms are smart and clean, and some have balconies.

Norddeutscher Hof Hotel HOTEL €
(☎293 161; www.nd-hof.de; Neuer Markt 22; r €50-100;) This maroon vision has a great central location and 13 historic rooms. Some have ancient roof beams plunging through the walls. All are comfortable. The restaurant is a stylish melange of tin walls and carved wood.

Hansekeller GERMAN €€
(Mönchstrasse 48; mains €8-14) A simple exterior belies the fact that this underground place lies within. It serves up hearty regional dishes at moderate prices in its vaulted brick cellar.

Torschliesserhaus PUB FARE €
(Am Kütertor 1; mains €8-16) In a 1281 building right by a fragment of the city wall, this restaurant-pub has a good beer garden and tasty local fare heavy on seafood.

Tiffany INTERNATIONAL €
(Am Langenwall; buffet €7; 9am-6pm Tue-Sun) This loosely themed breakfast bar is simply fantastic, darling.

Finally, there's a great stand (sausages €1.80) with grilled sausages at the **morning farmers market** (8am to 1pm Monday to Saturday) on Neuer Markt, and boats in the harbour sell just-out-of-the-ocean seafood sandwiches (€3 to €5).

Information

Tourismuszentrale (☎246 90; www.stralsundtourismus.de; Alter Markt 9; 10am-6pm Mon-Fri, to 4pm Sat & Sun May-Oct, 10am-5pm Mon-Fri, to 4pm Sat Nov-Apr)

Getting There & Away

Stralsund is on the line to Hamburg (€48, three hours) via Rostock (€12.80, one hour) and Schwerin (€32, two hours). Direct trains go to Berlin (from €36, 2¾ to 3¼ hours).

BAVARIA

Bavaria (Bayern) can seem like every German stereotype rolled into one. Lederhosen, beer halls, oompah bands and romantic castles are just some Bavarian clichés associated with Germany as a whole. But as any Bavarian will tell you, the state thinks of itself as Bavarian first and German second. And as any German outside of Bavaria will tell you, the Bavarian stereotypes aren't representative of the rest of Germany. It's a mostly Catholic place and the politics are often conservative, even if people drink serious quantities of beer (over 90 years ago this was the land of beer-hall putsches).

Bavaria was ruled for centuries as a duchy under the line founded by Otto I of Wittelsbach, and eventually graduated to the status of kingdom in 1806. The region suffered amid numerous power struggles between Prussia and Austria, and was finally brought into the German empire in 1871 by Bismarck. The last king of Bavaria was Ludwig II (1845–86), who earned the epithet 'the mad king' due to his obsession with building fantastic fairy-tale castles at enormous expense. He was found drowned in Starnberger See in suspicious circumstances and left no heirs.

Bavaria draws visitors year-round. If you only have time for one part of Germany after Berlin, this is it. Munich, the capital, is the heart and soul. The Bavarian Alps, Nuremberg and the medieval towns on the Romantic Road are other important attractions.

Munich

☎089 / POP 1.35 MILLION

Pulsing with prosperity and *Gemütlichkeit* (cosiness), Munich (München) revels in its own contradictions. Folklore and age-old traditions exist side by side with sleek BMWs, designer boutiques and high-powered industry. Its museums include world-class collections of artistic masterpieces, and its music and cultural scenes rival Berlin.

Despite all its sophistication, Munich retains a touch of provincialism that visitors find charming. The people's attitude is one of live-and-let-live, and Müncheners will be the first to admit that their 'metropolis' is little more than a *Weltdorf,* a world village. During Oktoberfest visitors descend on the Bavarian capital in their zillions to raise a glass to this fascinating city.

History

Originally settled by monks from the Benedictine monastery at Tegernsee in the 7th and 8th century, the city itself wasn't founded until 1158 by Heinrich der Löwe. In 1255 Munich became the home for the Wittelsbach dukes,

WORTH A TRIP

RÜGEN ISLAND

Germany's largest island, Rügen is at times hectic, relaxed, windblown and naked – fitting, perhaps, since the resort tradition here reflects all aspects of Germany's recent past. In the 19th century, luminaries such as Einstein, Bismarck and Thomas Mann came to unwind in the fashionable coastal resorts. Later both Nazi and GDR regimes made Rügen the holiday choice for dedicated comrades.

The island's highest point is the 117m **Königsstuhl** (king's throne), the chalk cliffs of which tower above the sea. Much of Rügen and its surrounding waters are either national park or protected nature reserves, and the **Bodden** inlet area is a bird refuge popular with birdwatchers.

Other popular tourist destinations are **Jagdschloss Granitz** (1834), a castle surrounded by lush forest, and **Prora**, the location of a 2km-long workers' retreat built by Hitler before the war. It is a surreal sight and is home to several museums, including the **Dokumentationszentrum Prora** (☎03839-313 991; www.proradok.de; Objektstrasse 1; adult/concession €5/4; ⏲9.30am-7.30pm Jun-Aug, 10am-6pm Mar-May, Sep & Oct, 11am-4pm Nov-Feb), which looks at the huge construction's history.

Tourismus Rügen (☎03838-807 70; www.ruegen.de; Am Markt 4, Bergen; ⏲8am-6pm Mon-Fri) and **Tourismusgesellschaft Binz** (☎03838-134 60; www.binz.de; Zeppelinstrasse 7, Binz; ⏲10am-6pm Mon-Fri) are your best bets for information.

The main resort town is Binz in eastern Rügen. Trains from Stralsund arrive here (€12, 45 minutes, every two hours), but to get around the island and really appreciate it, a car is vital.

princes and kings who ruled for the next 700 years. The city suffered through the Black Plague, first in 1348 and again in 1623, when two-thirds of the population died.

Munich has been the capital of Bavaria since 1503, but didn't really achieve prominence until the 19th century under the guiding hand of Ludwig I. Ludwig became more conservative and repressive, and carried on an affair with the actress and dancer Lola Montez. He was forced to abdicate in favour of his son, Maximilian II, who started a building renaissance, promoting science, industry and education.

At the turn of the last century there were 500,000 residents, but in the aftermath of WWI Munich became a hotbed of right-wing political ferment. Hitler staged a failed coup attempt in Munich in 1923, but the National Socialists seized power only a decade later. WWII brought bombing and more than 6000 civilian deaths until American forces entered the city in 1945. Then, in 1972, the Munich Olympics turned disastrous when 11 Israeli athletes were murdered.

Today it is the centre of major German industries such as Siemens and BMW.

Sights

Munich is a sprawling metropolis. Wandering the centre is rewarding but you'll need public transport to get out to some of the key sights like the palaces.

Palaces

Residenz PALACE

(Max-Joseph-Platz 3) Bavarian rulers lived in this vast pile from 1385 to 1918. Apart from the palace itself, the **Residenzmuseum** (www.residenz-muenchen.de; adult/child €6/free; ⏲9am-6pm Apr–mid-Oct, 10am-5pm mid-Oct–Mar) has an extraordinary array of 100 rooms containing no end of treasures and artworks. The entrance is on Max-Joseph-Platz. In the same building, the **Schatzkammer** (Treasure Chamber; adult/child €6/free) exhibits jewels, crowns and ornate gold.

Schloss Nymphenburg PALACE

(www.schloesser.bayern.de; adult/child €5/4; ⏲9am-6pm Apr–mid-Oct, 10am-4pm mid-Oct–Mar) This was the royal family's very impressive summer home. Parts date from 17th century. The surrounding park deserves a long, regal stroll. All this splendour is northwest of the city centre, via tram 17 from the Hauptbahnhof.

Art Museums

Alte Pinakothek ART MUSEUM

(www.pinakothek.de; Barer Strasse 27; adult/child €7/5, Sun €1; ⏲10am-8pm Tue, to 6pm Wed-Sun) A stroll northeast of the centre, this treasure

Central Munich

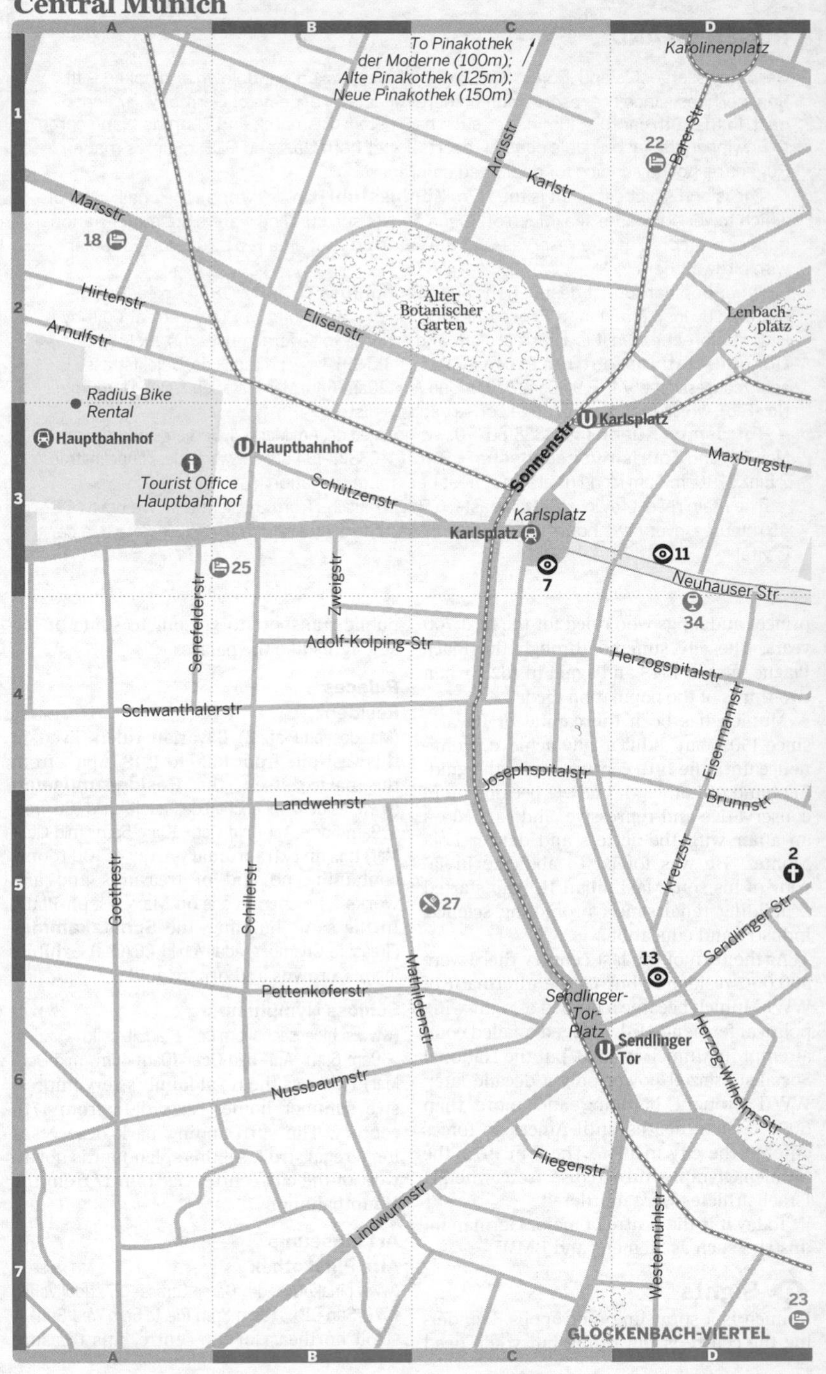

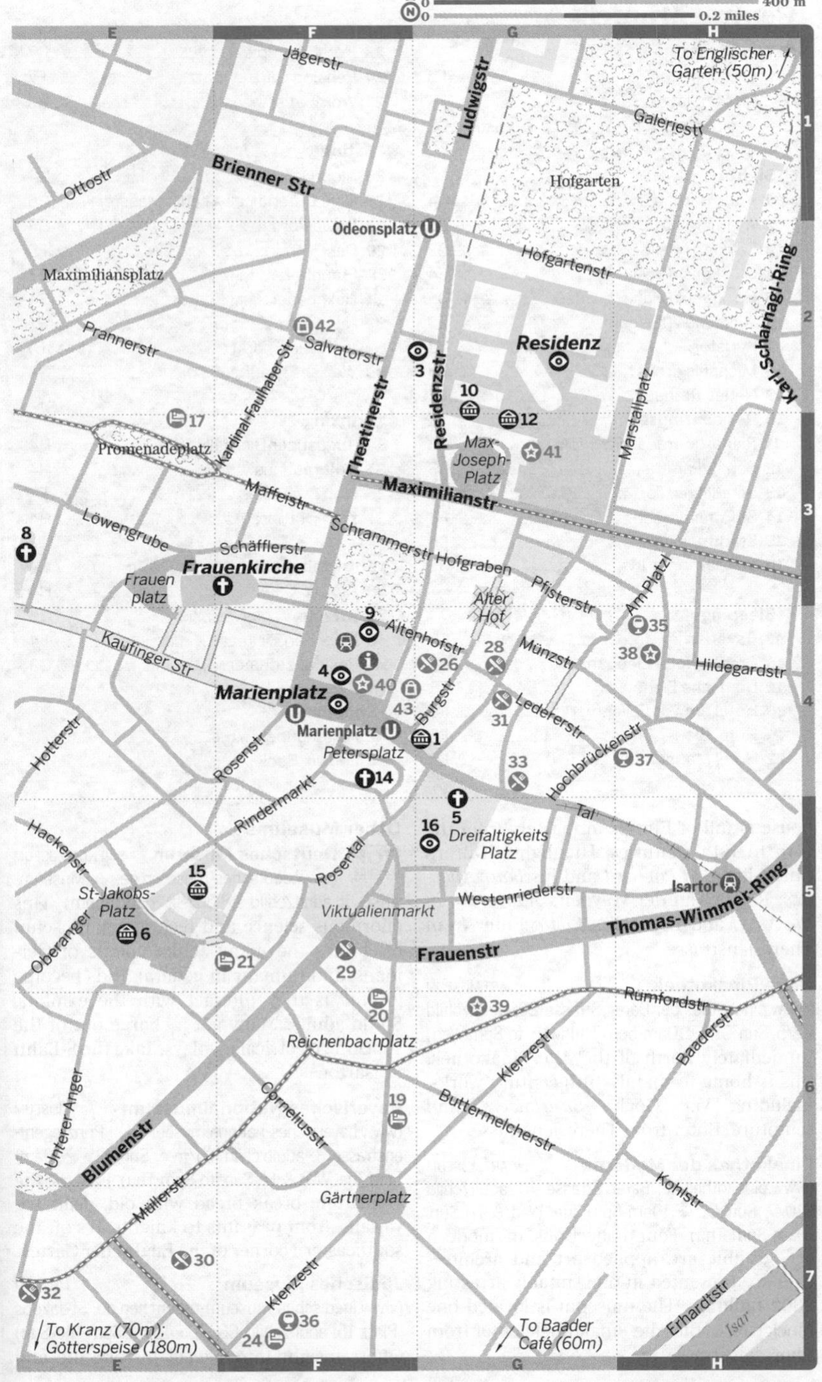

0 400 m
0 0.2 miles
To Englischer Garten (50m)
Jägerstr
Ludwigstr
Galeriestr
Hofgarten
Brienner Str
Ottostr
Odeonsplatz
Hofgartenstr
Maximiliansplatz
Karl-Scharnagl-Ring
Prannerstr
42
Salvatorstr
Residenz
3
Kardinal-Faulhaber-Str
Theatinerstr
Residenzstr
10
12
17
Promenadeplatz
Max-Joseph-Platz
41
Marstallplatz
Maffeistr
Maximilianstr
Löwengrube
Schrammerstr
Hofgraben
8
Schäfflerstr
Frauenkirche
Frauen platz
Pfisterstr
Am Platzl
Alter Hof
9
Altenhofstr
35
Kaufinger Str
28
Münzstr
38
Hildegardstr
26
4
40
Marienplatz
43
Burgstr
31
Ledererstr
Marienplatz
1
Hotterstr
Rosenstr
Petersplatz
Hochbrückenstr
37
14
33
Rindermarkt
Tal
5
16
Dreifaltigkeits Platz
Hackenstr
15
Rosental
St-Jakobs-Platz
Westenriederstr
Isartor
Viktualienmarkt
Thomas-Wimmer-Ring
Oberanger
6
Frauenstr
21
29
Rumfordstr
20
39
Reichenbachplatz
Baaderstr
Klenzestr
Unterer Anger
19
Corneliusstr
Buttermelcherstr
Blumenstr
Gärtnerplatz
Kohlstr
Müllerstr
30
32
Klenzestr
36
Erhardtstr
Isar
24
To Kranz (70m); Götterspeise (180m)
To Baader Café (60m)
GERMANY MUNICH

Central Munich

Top Sights

- Frauenkirche F3
- Marienplatz F4
- Residenz G2

Sights

1 Altes Rathaus G4
2 Asamkirche D5
3 Feldherrnhalle G2
4 Glockenspiel F4
5 Heiliggeistkirche G5
6 Jüdisches Museum E5
7 Karlstor C3
8 Michaelskirche E3
9 Neues Rathaus F4
10 Residenzmuseum G2
11 Richard Strauss Fountain D3
12 Schatzkammer G3
13 Sendlinger Tor D5
14 St Peterskirche F4
15 Stadtmuseum E5
16 Viktualienmarkt G5

Sleeping

17 Bayerischer Hof E3
18 Creatif Hotel Elephant A2
19 Deutsche Eiche F6
20 Hotel am Viktualienmarkt F6
21 Hotel Blauer Bock F5
22 Hotel Marienbad D1
23 Hotel Olympic D7
24 Pension Gärtnerplatz F7
25 Wombat's B3

Eating

26 Alois Dallmayr G4
27 Café Osteria La Vecchia Masseria C5
28 Daylesford G4
29 Der Pschorr F5
30 Fraunhofer E7
31 Haxnbauer G4
32 Nil E7
Viktualienmarkt (see 16)
33 Weisses Brauhaus G4

Drinking

34 Augustiner Bierhalle D4
35 Hofbräuhaus H4
36 Morizz F7
37 Zum Dürnbrau H4

Entertainment

38 Atomic Café H4
39 Jazzbar Vogler G6
40 München Ticket F4
41 Residenztheater G3

Shopping

42 Hugendubel F2
43 Ludwig Beck F4

house is full of European masters from the 14th to 18th centuries. Highlights: Dürer's Christ-like *Self Portrait* and his *Four Apostles,* Rogier van der Weyden's *Adoration of the Magi* and Botticelli's *Pietà*. Enter from Theresienstrasse.

Neue Pinakothek ART MUSEUM
(www.pinakothek.de; Barer Strasse 29; adult/child €7/5, Sun €1; ⏲10am-5pm Thu-Mon, to 8pm Wed) Immediately north of the Alte Pinakothek, this is home to mainly 19th-century works, including Van Gogh's *Sunflowers,* and sculpture. Enter from Theresienstrasse.

Pinakothek der Moderne ART MUSEUM
(www.pinakothek.de; Barer Strasse 40; adult/child €10/7, Sun €1; ⏲10am-6pm Tue, Wed & Fri-Sun, 10am-8pm Thu) Four collections of modern art, graphic art, applied art and architecture are presented in one suitably arresting 2002 building. The museum is located one block east of the Alte Pinakothek; enter from Theresienstrasse.

Other Museums

TOP CHOICE **Deutsches Museum** SCIENCE MUSEUM
(www.deutsches-museum.de; Museumsinsel 1; adult/child €8.50/3; ⏲9am-5pm) This enormous science and technology museum celebrates the many achievements of Germans, and humans in general. Kids become gleeful as they interact with the exhibits. So do adults. Many get a charge out of the shocking electrical displays. Take the S-Bahn to Isartor.

Bayerisches Nationalmuseum MUSEUM
(www.bayerisches-nationalmuseum.de; Prinzregentenstrasse 3; adult/child €5/free, Sun €1; ⏲10am-5pm Tue, Wed & Fri-Sun, to 8pm Thu) East of the Hofgarten, break bread with old, dead Bavarians, from peasants to knights. It's off the southeastern corner of the Englischer Garten.

Jüdisches Museum MUSEUM
(www.juedisches-museum-muenchen.de; St-Jakobs-Platz 16; adult/child €6/3; ⏲10am-6pm Tue-Sun) Offers insight into Jewish history, life and

culture in Munich. The Nazi era is dealt with, but the accent of this modern museum is clearly on contemporary Jewish culture.

Stadtmuseum MUSEUM
(www.stadtmuseum-online.de; St-Jakobs-Platz 1; adult/child €4/2, Sun free; ⏲10am-6pm Tue-Sun) You went in for an hour and spent two; this superbly redone city museum puts the foam on the stein of Munich history – good and bad. Multimedia displays bring Munich's many characters to life.

BMW Museum CAR MUSEUM
(www.bmw-welt.de; adult/child €12/6; ⏲10am-6pm Tue-Sun) North of the city, auto-fetishists get stoked at this bowl-shaped temple adjacent to BMW's headquarters and factory. Exhibits are extensive and on weekdays you can tour the factory. Take the U3 to Olympiazentrum.

Parks & Gardens

TOP CHOICE **Englischer Garten** PARK
One of the largest city parks in Europe, this grand park is a great place for strolling, especially along the Schwabinger Bach. In summer nude sunbathing is the rule rather than the exception. It's not unusual for hundreds of naked people to be in the park during a normal business day, with their clothing stacked primly on the grass. If they're not doing this, they're probably drinking merrily at one of the park's three beer gardens (see the boxed text, p529).

Botanical Gardens GARDEN
(www.botmuc.de; Menzinger Strasse 65; adult/child €4/free; ⏲varies with season, generally 9am-6pm) The gorgeous municipal gardens are two stops past Schloss Nymphenburg on tram 17.

Olympia Park Complex PARK
The glorious grounds of the 1972 Olympics continue to thrill today. If you like heights, take a ride up the lift of the 290m **Olympiaturm** (Olympic Tower; adult/child €4.50/3; ⏲9am-midnight). And if you fancy a swim, the **Olympic Pool Complex** (admission €4; ⏲7am-11pm) will have you feeling like Mark Spitz while you imagine seven gold medals around your neck – or just work on your breaststroke. Take the U3 to Olympia Zentrum.

A MUNICH STROLL

The pivotal **Marienplatz** is a good starting point for a tour of Munich's heart. Dominating the square is the towering neo-Gothic **Neues Rathaus** (new town hall), with its ever-dancing **Glockenspiel** (carillon), which performs at 11am and noon (also at 5pm from March to October), bringing the square to an expectant standstill (note the fate of the Austrian knight…). Two important churches are on this square: the baroque star **St Peterskirche** (Rindermarkt 1; church free, tower adult/child €1.50/1; ⏲9am-7pm Apr-Oct, to 6pm Nov-Mar) and, behind the **Altes Rathaus**, the often-forgotten **Heiliggeistkirche** (Tal 77; ⏲7am-6pm).

Walk north along the genteel Theatinerstrasse, a staid street today with a notorious past. On November 9, 1923, Hitler and his followers marched up the street during their 'beer hall putsch' to seize control of Bavaria. A hail of gunfire at the **Feldherrnhalle** in front of Odeonsplatz ended the revolution – but not for long.

Return south on Theatinerstrasse, and cut west to the landmark of Munich, the late-Gothic **Frauenkirche** (Church of Our Lady; Frauenplatz 1; ⏲7am-7pm Sat-Wed, 7am-8.30pm Thu, 7am-6pm Fri) with its then-trendy 16th-century twin onion domes. Go inside and join the hordes gazing at the grandeur of the place, or scale the 98m **tower** (adult/child €3/1.50; ⏲10am-5pm Mon-Sat Apr-Oct) for some Alps spotting. Continue west to the large, grey 16th-century **Michaelskirche** (Neuhauserstrasse 52; ⏲8am-7pm), Germany's earliest and grandest Renaissance church.

Further west is the **Richard Strauss Fountain** and the medieval **Karlstor**, an old city gate. Double back towards Marienplatz and turn right onto Eisenmannstrasse, which becomes Kreuzstrasse and converges with Herzog-Wilhelm-Strasse at the medieval gate of **Sendlinger Tor**. Go down the shopping street Sendlinger Strasse to the **Asamkirche** (Sendlinger Strasse 34), a flamboyant 17th-century church designed by brothers Cosmas Damian and Egid Quirin Asam. The ornate marble facade won't prepare you for the opulence inside, where scarcely an inch is left unembellished.

Walk east through St-Jakobs-Platz to buy some well-earned refreshments at the **Viktualienmarkt**.

DON'T MISS

OKTOBERFEST

Hordes come to Munich for **Oktoberfest** (www.oktoberfest.de; ⌚10am-11.30pm, from 9am Sat & Sun), running the 15 days before the first Sunday in October. Reserve accommodation well ahead and go early in the day so you can grab a seat in one of the hangar-sized beer 'tents'. The action takes place at the Theresienwiese grounds, about a 10-minute walk southwest of the Hauptbahnhof. While there is no entrance fee, those €9 1L steins of beer (called *Mass*) add up fast. Although its origins are in the marriage celebrations of Crown Prince Ludwig in 1810, there's nothing regal about this beery bacchanalia now: expect mobs, expect to meet new and drunken friends, expect decorum to vanish as night sets in and you'll have a blast.

A few tips:

» Locals call it *Weisn* (meadow)

» The Hofbräu Festhalle tent is big with tourists

» The Augustiner tent draws traditionalists

» Traditional Oktoberfest beer should be a rich copper colour; order it instead of the tourist-satisfying pale lager

Tours

Mike's Bike Tours BIKE TOURS
(www.mikesbiketours.com; tours from €24) Enjoyable (and leisurely) city cycling tours in English. Tours depart from the archway at the Altes Rathaus on Marienplatz.

Munich Walk Tours WALKING TOURS
(www.munichwalktours.de; tours from €12) Walking tours of the city on topics from Nazis to beer. Meet under the Glockenspiel on Marienplatz.

City Bus 100 BUS
Ordinary city bus that runs from the Hauptbahnhof to the Ostbahnhof via 21 of the city's museums and galleries. This includes all three Pinakothek, the Residenz and the Bayerisches Nationalmuseum.

Sleeping

Munich has no shortage of places to stay – except during Oktoberfest or some busy summer periods, when the wise (meaning those with a room) will have booked. Many budget and midrange places can be found in the cheerless streets around the train station. If you can, avoid it as you'll find hotels with more charm and atmosphere elsewhere.

Munich's youth hostels that are DJH- and HI-affiliated do not accept guests over age 26, except group leaders or parents accompanying a child.

TOP CHOICE **Hotel Blauer Bock** HOTEL €€
(☎231 780; www.hotelblauerbock.de; Sebastiansplatz 9; r €60-150;) A whiff of roasted almonds away from the Viktualienmarkt, this tidy hotel once provided shelter for Benedictine monks and has an ideal location that's the envy of more prestigious abodes. It's comfy, familiar and spacious. Cheaper rooms share bathrooms. The included breakfast buffet offers creative options beyond the norm.

Bayerischer Hof HOTEL €€€
(☎212 00; www.bayerischerhof.de; Promenadeplatz 2-6; r €180-400;) Room doors fold away into the stucco mouldings at the Hof, one of the grande dames of the Munich hotel trade. It boasts a super-central location, a pool and a jazz club. Marble, antiques and oil paintings abound, and you can dine till you drop at any one of the three fabulous restaurants. Rates include a champagne breakfast.

Pension Gärtnerplatz HOTEL €€
(☎202 5170; www.pension-gaertnerplatztheater.de; Klenzestrasse 45; r €80-130;) Escape the tourist rabble, or reality altogether, in this eccentric establishment where rooms are a stylish interpretation of Alpine pomp. The room named 'Sisi' will have you sleeping in a canopy bed guarded by a giant porcelain mastiff. The hotel is well located near trendy cafes and shops.

Deutsche Eiche HOTEL €€
(☎231 1660; www.deutsche-eiche.com; Reichenbachstrasse 13; r incl breakfast €80-160, apt from €200;) Traditionally it's been a gay outpost, but style junkies of all sexual persuasions should enjoy the plushly designed

rooms. Cheaper rooms are more utilitarian; near the trendy Gärtnerplatz. Also on the premises is a bathhouse.

Hotel am Viktualienmarkt HOTEL €€
(231 1090; www.hotel-am-viktualienmarkt.de; Utzschneiderstrasse 14; r €50-120;) Owner Elke and her daughter Stephanie run this perfectly located property with panache and a sunny attitude. A steep staircase (no lift) leads to rooms, the nicest of which have wooden floors and framed poster art. Book far ahead.

Hotel Olympic HOTEL €€
(231 890; www.hotel-olympic.de; Hans-Sachs-Strasse 4; r €95-200;) If you're into designer decor, Frette linens and chocolates on your pillow, go elsewhere. But if you like a hip location (the buzzing Glockenbach-Viertel), public areas doubling as an art gallery, and 38 spacious rooms, give this one a try. Rooms facing the inner courtyard are quieter.

Meininger City Hostel & Hotel HOSTEL, HOTEL €
(420 956 053; www.meininger-hostels.de; Landsbergerstrasse 20; dm/r from €18/45;) This hotel-hostel combo scores big points for three reasons: rooftop bar, amenities and service. About 600m west of the Hauptbahnhof, it has 380 beds in 95 cheerful rooms ranging in size from singles to 12-bed dorms. The Augustiner brewery is within stumbling distance.

Wombat's HOSTEL, HOTEL €
(5998 9180; www.wombats-hostels.com; Senefelderstrasse 1; dm €12-24, r from €70;) Style, comfort and location are hallmarks of this hotel-cum-hostel. You'll sleep well in pine beds with real mattresses (free linen), reading lamps in doubles, and dorms with en suite bathrooms. Breakfast is an extra €4.

Leonardo Boutique Hotel Savoy HOTEL €€
(287 870; www.leonardo-hotels.com; Amalienstrasse 25; r €80-180;) In a Maxvorstadt area thick with modest hotels and cafes, the Savoy stands out after a stylish refit that has given it trappings of luxury. Big windows look across to other inns so you can compare rooms. The frolic of Schwabing is just north.

Hotel Uhland HOTEL €€
(543 350; www.hotel-uhland.de; Uhlandstrasse 1; r €70-200;) The Uhland is an enduring favourite with regulars who expect their hotel to feel like a home away from home. Three generations of family members organise amenities like bike rentals or mix-your-own breakfast muesli. Make a splash in the waterbed suite after a day at the nearby Oktoberfest grounds.

Hotel Marienbad HOTEL €€
(595 585; www.hotelmarienbad.de; Barer Strasse 11, Maxvorstadt; r €50-150;) Back in the 19th century, Wagner, Puccini and Rilke shacked up in what once ranked among Munich's finest hotels. Still friendly and well maintained, it now flaunts an endearing alchemy of styles, from playful art nouveau to campy 1960s utilitarian.

Creatif Hotel Elephant HOTEL €€
(555 785; www.creatif-hotel-elephant.com; Lämmerstrasse 6; r €60-150;) The Creatif is a polychromatic and friendly place bursting with flowers. Its 44 rooms are stylish and comfortable, in an Ikea sort of way.

Campingplatz Thalkirchen CAMPING GROUND €
(7243 0808; www.camping-muenchen.de; Zentralländstrasse 49; campsites per person/tent €5/4; mid-Mar–end Oct) To get to this camping ground, southwest of the city centre, take the U3 to Thalkirchen and catch bus 135 (about 15 minutes).

Tent CAMPING GROUND €
(141 4300; www.the-tent.com; In den Kirschen 30; campsites €5.50 plus per person €5.50, bed in main tent €11; Jun-Sep) Pads and blankets provided for the bagless; bring your own lock for the lockers. Take tram 17 to the Botanic Gardens then follow the signs to a legendary international party.

Eating

Clusters of restaurants can be found anywhere there's pedestrian life. The streets in and around Gärtnerplatz and Glockenback-Viertel are the flavour of the moment. You can always do well in and around Marienplatz and the wonderful Viktualienmarkt.

WANT MORE?

For in-depth information, reviews and recommendations at your fingertips, head to the Apple App Store to purchase Lonely Planet's *Munich City Guide* iPhone app.

Alternatively, head to **Lonely Planet** (www.lonelyplanet.com/germany/munich) for planning advice, author recommendations, traveller reviews and insider tips.

Restaurants

TOP CHOICE Der Pschorr GERMAN €€
(Viktualienmarkt 15; mains €10-18) Shining like a jewel box across a square, this modern high-ceilinged restaurant, operated by one of the main local brewers, is the 21st-century version of a beer hall. Creative dishes, including new takes on old German classics, stream out from the open kitchen. There's even a bit of Med-flair to the long list of daily specials.

Daylesford ORGANIC €€
(Ledererstrasse 3; mains from €9-17; 9am-8pm Mon-Sat;) Right in the middle of pure-pork land, you can eat your veggies again and again with glee (and sneak an organic cheeseburger while you're at it). Food couldn't be fresher: luscious bakery items share space with deli salads and more.

Weisses Brauhaus BAVARIAN €€
(Tal 7; mains €9-20) The place for classic Bavarian fare in an ancient beer-hall setting. Everything from *Weissewurst* (beloved local white sausage) to hearty traditional fare such as boiled ox cheeks is on offer. The menu has changed little in decades.

Café Osteria La Vecchia Masseria ITALIAN €€
(Mathildenstrasse 3; mains €7-15) This is one of the best Italian places in Munich, loud but unquestionably romantic. Earthy wood tables, antique tin buckets, baskets and clothing irons conjure up the ambience of an Italian farmhouse. The chef comes out to greet customers in his trademark straw hat.

Haxnbauer GERMAN €€
(Sparkassenstrasse; mains €10-22) Meats of all kinds roast in the windows of this modern take on a trad restaurant. The wood is dark, as are the crispy bits on the much-favoured roast goose. Always popular; excellent quality.

Fraunhofer GERMAN €€
(Fraunhoferstrasse 9; mains €6-16; 4.30pm-1am) This classic brewpub contrasts 'ye olde worlde' atmosphere (mounted animal heads and a portrait of Ludwig II) with a menu that offers progressive takes on classical fare. Big with hipsters *and* their parents.

Cafes

Götterspeise CAFE €
(Jahnstrasse 30; snacks from €3) If the Aztecs thought of chocolate as the elixir of the gods, then this shop-cum-cafe must be heaven. Cocoa addicts satisfy their cravings with rave-worthy French chocolate cake, thick, hot drinking chocolate and chocolate-flavoured 'body paint' for those wishing to double their sins.

Uni Lounge CAFE €
(Geschwister-Scholl-Platz 1; meals €4-8) Enjoy a cheap breakfast, lazy lunch or cocktails to a soundtrack of high-minded conversation beneath the whitewashed vaulting of this student hang-out. The outdoor seating is ringed by grand university buildings.

Nil CAFE €€
(Hans-Sachs-Strasse 2; meals €8-14; 8am-4am) Right in trendy Glockenbach-Viertel, this hip place draws a straight and gay crowd in the know. Tables outside are packed when the sun shines; inside it's packed all night long.

Kranz CAFE €€
(Hans-Sachs-Strasse 12; mains €8-16) A luxe cafe in the heart of the edgy and trendy streets of the Glockenbach-Viertel. Posh desserts beg you go easy on the organic burgers. Excellent sidewalk tables.

Baader Café CAFE €
(Baaderstrasse 47; meals €6-14) This literary think-and-drink place gets everyone from short skirts to tweed jackets to mingle beneath the conversation-fuelling map of the world. Lines form early for Sunday brunch.

Markets

TOP CHOICE Viktualienmarkt OUTDOOR MARKET
(Mon-Fri & Sat morning) Just south of Marienplatz is a large open-air market, where you can put together a picnic feast to take to the Englischer Garten. The fresh produce, cheese and baked goods are hard to resist. Or relax here under the trees, at tables provided by one of the many beer and sausage vendors. This is the place to see the German's love of all things organic.

Alois Dallmayr FOOD HALL
(Dienerstrasse 14) You'll find one of the world's great delicatessens behind the mustard-yellow awnings, its sparkling cases filled with fine foods. This is the place to come if you want a pet crayfish (see their fountain home).

Drinking

Apart from the beer halls and gardens, Munich has no shortage of lively pubs. Schwabing and Glockenback-Viertel are good places to follow your ears. Many places

BEER HALLS & BEER GARDENS

Beer drinking is not just an integral part of Munich's entertainment scene, it's a reason to visit. Germans drink an average of 130L of the amber liquid each per year, while Munich residents manage much more. Locals will be happy to help ensure that you don't bring down the average.

Beer halls can be vast boozy affairs seating thousands, or much more modest neighbourhood hang-outs. The same goes for beer gardens. Both come in all shapes and sizes. What's common is a certain camaraderie among strangers, huge 1L glasses of beer (try putting one of those in your carry-on) and lots of cheap food – the saltier the better. Note that in beer gardens, tradition allows you to bring your own food, a boon if you want an alternative to pretzels, sausages and the huge white radishes served with, you guessed it, salt.

On a warm day there's nothing better than sitting and sipping among the greenery at one of the Englischer Garten's classic beer gardens. **Chinesischer Turm** is justifiably popular while the nearby **Hirschau** on the banks of Kleinhesseloher See is less crowded.

Other top choices:

Augustiner Bräustuben (Landsberger Strasse 19) Depending on the wind, an aroma of hops envelops you as you approach this ultra-authentic beer hall inside the actual Augustiner brewery. The Bavarian grub here is superb, especially the *Schweinshaxe* (pork knuckles). Giant black draught horses are stabled behind glass on your way to the loo. It's about 700m west of the Hauptbahnhof.

Hofbräuhaus (Am Platzl 9) The ultimate cliché of Munich beer halls. Tourists arrive by the busload but no one seems to mind that this could be Disneyland (although the theme park wasn't once home to Hitler's early speeches, like this place was). Wander upstairs for echoes of the past, a small museum and possibly a seat.

Zum Dürnbrau (Tal 21) Tucked into a corner off Tal, this is a great and authentic little alternative to the Hofbräuhaus. There's a small beer garden, and drinkers of dark draughts enjoy pewter-topped mugs.

Augustiner Bierhalle (Neuhauser Strasse 27) What you probably imagine an old-style Munich beer hall looks like, filled with laughter, smoke and clinking glasses.

serve food; most are open until 1am or later on weekends.

Alter Simpl PUB
(Türkenstrasse 57, Maxvorstadt; meals from €8) Thomas Mann and Hermann Hesse used to knock 'em back at this legendary thirst parlour. Alter Simpl is also a good place to satisfy midnight munchies as bar bites are available until one hour before closing time.

Morizz BAR
(Klenzestrasse 43) This mod art deco–style lounge with red leather armchairs and mirrors for posing and preening goes for a more moneyed clientele and even gets the occasional local celebrity drop-in. Packed on weekends.

Trachtenvogl LOUNGE
(Reichenbachstrasse 47, Gärtnerplatzviertel; ⏲10am-1am) At night you'll have to shoehorn your way into this buzzy lair favoured by a chatty, boozy crowd of scenesters, artists and students. Daytimes are mellower at this former folkloric garment shop.

☆ Entertainment

Munich is one of the cultural capitals of Germany; the publications and websites listed on p530 can guide you to the best events. For tickets, try **München Ticket** (www.muenchenticket.de; Neues Rathaus, Marienplatz).

Nightclubs & Live Music

Kultfabrik CLUBS
(www.kultfabrik.de; Grafingerstrasse 6; ⏲8pm-6am) There are more than 25 clubs for you to sample in this old potato factory before you end up either mashed or fried (or both). Electro and house beats charge up the crowd at the loungey **apartment 11**, the Asian-themed **Koi** and **Drei Türme** (www.dreituerme.de), a chic living-room club disguised as a Hollywood castle and lit by a forest of glass-fibre tubes. It's close to the Ostbahnhof station.

GAY & LESBIAN MUNICH

Much of Munich's gay and lesbian nightlife is around **Gärtnerplatz** and the **Glockenback-Viertel**. Any of the nightspots in this area listed earlier (such as Nil and Morizz) will have a mixed crowd.

Our Munich and *Sergej* are monthly guides easily found in this neighbourhood. Another good resource is **Max&Milian** (Ickstattstrasse 2), Munich's best gay bookstore.

Deutsche Eiche (p526) caters to gay and lesbian guests.

Jazzbar Vogler JAZZ
(Rumfordstrasse 17, Gärtnerplatzviertel) This intimate watering hole brings some of Munich's baddest cats to the stage. You never know who might show up for Monday's blues-jazz-Latin jam session.

Atomic Café CLUB
(www.atomic.de; Neuturmstrasse 5; ⏲10pm-4am, 9pm on concert nights Tue-Sun) This bastion of indie sounds with funky '60s decor is known for bookers with a knack for catching upwardly hopeful bands before their big break.

Theatre

Residenztheater (Max-Joseph-Platz 2) is the home of the **Bavarian State Opera** (www.staatsoper.de) and also the site of many cultural events (particularly during the opera festival in July).

Shopping

All shoppers converge on the Marienplatz to buy designer shoes or kitschy souvenirs. The stylish department store **Ludwig Beck** (☎236 910; Marienplatz 11) has something for everyone. Bypass Calvin et al for more unusual European choices. Nearby Maximilianstrasse is a fashionable street that is ideal for simply strolling and window shopping. Close by, **Hugendubel** (Salvatorplatz 2) is crammed with English-language titles.

To truly 'unchain' yourself, though, you should hit the Gärtnerplatzviertel and Glockenbach-Viertel, bastions of well-edited indie stores and local-designer boutiques. Hans-Sachs-Strasse and Reichenbachstrasse are especially promising. Maxvorstadt, especially Türkenstrasse, also has an interesting line-up of stores with stuff you won't find on the high street back home.

Munich has eight **Christmas markets** from late November, including a big one on Marienplatz. For more on these popular events, see p538.

Information

For late-night shopping and services such as pharmacies and currency exchange, the Hauptbahnhof's multilevel shopping arcades cannot be beaten.

Discount Cards

City Tour Card (www.citytourcard.com; 1/3 days €9.80/18.80) Includes transport and discounts of between 10% and 50% for about 30 attractions. Available at some hotels, MVV (Munich public transport authority) offices and U-Bahn and S-Bahn vending machines.

Medical Services

Ärztlicher Bereitschaftsdienst (☎01805-191 212; ⏲24hr) Emergency medical service.

Bahnhof-Apotheke (☎598 119; Bahnhofplatz 2, Ludwigsvorstadt) Pharmacy.

Tourist Information

EurAide (☎593 889; www.euraide.de; Hauptbahnhof; ⏲9am-noon & 1-5pm, longer hr in summer) Dispenses savvy travel advice in English, sells and validates rail passes, explains train-ticket savings and discounts many tours; staff work in the DB Travel Centre at counter 1.

Tourist office (www.muenchen.de) Hauptbahnhof (Bahnhofplatz 2; ⏲9.30am-6.30pm Mon-Sat, 10am-6pm Sun, longer hr in summer & during holidays); Marienplatz (Neues Rathaus, Marienplatz 8; ⏲10am-8pm Mon-Fri, to 4pm Sat) Be sure to ask for the excellent and free guides *Young and About in Munich, National Socialism in Munich* and various neighbourhood guides.

Websites

www.muenchen-tourist.de Munich's official website.

www.munichfound.com Munich's expat magazine.

www.toytowngermany.com English-language community website with specialised Munich pages; partnered with Berlin's excellent The Local.

Getting There & Away

Air

Munich's sparkling white **airport** (MUC; www.munich-airport.de) is second in importance only to Frankfurt for international and national connections. Flights will take you to all major destinations worldwide.

Bus

Munich has a new **bus station** (ZOB; www.zob-muenchen.de; Arnulfstrasse) that already looks typical of the daggy genre. Ticket windows and small waiting areas are on the top floor. It's 500m west of the Hauptbahnhof, at the S-Bahn stop Hackerbrücke. Among the operators here are **Touring** (www.touring.de), which also runs **Europabus** services.

Munich is a stop for the **Romantic Road bus** (www.romanticroadcoach.de); see p606.

Car & Motorcycle

The main hire companies have counters together on the second level of the Hauptbahnhof. For arranged rides, the **Mitfahrzentrale** (☎194 40; www.mitfahrzentrale.de; Lämmerstrasse 6; ⊙8am-8pm) is near the Hauptbahnhof. The cost is split with the driver and you can reach most parts of Germany for well under €40.

Train

Train services to/from Munich are excellent. There are rapid connections at least every two hours to all major cities in Germany, as well as daily trains to other European cities, including the following:

DESTINATION	PRICE	DURATION (HR)
Paris	€140	6
Vienna	€75	4
Zürich	€65	4¼

Hourly ICE services include the following:

DESTINATION	PRICE	DURATION (HR)
Berlin	€113	5¾
Frankfurt	€89	3
Hamburg	€115	5½

Getting Around

To/From the Airport

Munich's international airport is connected by the S8 and the S1 to Marienplatz and the Hauptbahnhof (€9.60). Service takes about 40 minutes; there's a train every 10 minutes from 4am until 12.30am or so. The S8 route is slightly faster. A ticket that's good all day costs €10.40.

Taxis make the long haul for at least €60.

Bicycle

Pedal power is popular in relatively flat Munich. **Radius Bike Rental** (www.radiustours.com; Hauptbahnhof, near track 32; ⊙10am-6pm May-Sep) rents out two-wheelers from €15 per day. Other tour companies have similar rates.

Car & Motorcycle

It's not worth driving in the city centre – many streets are pedestrian-only. The tourist office has a map that shows city parking places (€2 or more per hour).

Public Transport

Munich's excellent **public transport network** (MVV; www.mvv-muenchen.de) is zone-based, and most places of interest to tourists (except Dachau and the airport) are within the 'blue' inner zone (*Innenraum;* €2.40). MVV tickets are valid for the S-Bahn, U-Bahn, trams and buses, but they must be validated before use. The U-Bahn ceases operating around 12.30am Monday to Friday and 1.30am on Saturday and Sunday, but there are some later buses and S-Bahns. Rail passes are valid exclusively on the S-Bahn.

Kurzstrecke (short rides) cost €1.20 and are good for no more than four stops on buses and trams, and two stops on the U- and S-Bahns. *Tageskarte* (day passes) for the inner zone cost €5.20, while three-day tickets cost €12.80.

Taxi

Taxis (☎216 10) are expensive and not much more convenient than public transport.

Dachau

The first Nazi concentration camp was **Dachau** (www.kz-gedenkstaette-dachau.de; Alte-Roemerstrasse 75; admission free; ⊙9am-5pm Tue-Sun), built in March 1933. Jews, political prisoners, homosexuals and others deemed 'undesirable' by the Third Reich were imprisoned in the camp. More than 200,000 people were sent here; more than 30,000 died at Dachau, and countless others died after being transferred to other death camps. An English-language documentary is shown at 11.30am and 3.30pm. A visit includes camp relics, memorials and a very sobering museum.

Take the S2 (direction: Petershausen) to Dachau and then bus 726 to the camp. A Munich XXL day ticket (€7) will cover the trip.

Romantic Road

The popular and schmaltzily named Romantic Road (Romantische Strasse) links a series of picturesque Bavarian towns and cities. It's not actually one road per se, but rather a 353km route chosen to highlight as many quaint towns and cities as possible in western Bavaria.

From north to south it includes the following major stops:

» **Würzburg** The starting point, featuring 18th-century artistic splendour among the vineyards.

» **Rothenburg ob der Tauber** The medieval walled hub of cutesy, picturesque Bavarian touring.

» **Dinkelsbühl** Another medieval walled town replete with moat and watchtowers; a smaller Rothenburg. The town is best reached by bus or car.

» **Augsburg** A medieval and Renaissance city with many good places for a beer.

» **Wieskirche** Stunning Unesco-recognised church.

» **Füssen** The southern end of the route, and the cute and over-run home of mad King Ludwig's castles.

In addition to these principal stops, more than a dozen little towns clamour for attention – and your money. A good first stop is the info-packed website www.romanticroad.de. Also look for the excellent and free large map and route description at tourist offices.

Getting There & Around

The principal cities and towns listed above are all easily reached by train – see the individual listings for details. But to really explore the route, you are best off with your own transport. The entire length is copiously marked with brown signs in German, English and Japanese. With a car, you can blow through places of little interest and linger at those that appeal.

Bus

A popular way to tour the Romantic Road is the **Romantic Road bus** (☎069 719126-268; www.romanticroadcoach.de; ⊙phone line 9am-6pm Mon-Fri).

Starting in Frankfurt in the north and Füssen in the south, a bus runs in each direction each day covering the entire route. However, seeing the entire whack in one day is only for those with unusual fortitude and a love of buses. Stops are brief (17 minutes for Wieskirche, *Schnell!* 35 minutes for Rothenburg, *Schnell!* etc) so you'll want to choose places where you can break the trip for a day (stopovers are allowed). But of course this leads you to decide between a 30-minute visit and a 24-hour one.

The buses depart mid-April to mid-October, south from Frankfurt Hauptbahnhof at 8am and north from Füssen at 8am, and take about 12 hours. The total fare (tickets are bought on board) is a pricey €105. Rail-pass holders get a paltry 20% discount. You can also just ride individual segments (eg Rothenburg to Augsburg costs €26), which may be the best use.

Würzburg

☎0931 / POP 135,000

Nestled among river valleys lined with vineyards, Würzburg beguiles even before you reach the city centre. Three of the four largest wine-growing estates in all of Germany are here and most of the delicate whites produced locally never leave the region – the locals will always reach for a wine glass first. Over 1300 years old, Würzburg was rebuilt after being bombed late in WWII (it took only 17 minutes to almost completely destroy the city). The grand buildings are amazing, even if the town itself is a tad drab.

Sights

The magnificent, sprawling Unesco-listed **Residenz** (www.residenz-wuerzburg.de; Balthasar-Neumann-Promenade; adult/child €7/6; ⊙9am-6pm Apr-Oct, 10am-4pm Nov-Mar), a baroque masterpiece by Neumann, took a generation to build and boasts the world's largest ceiling fresco (graphic artists take note: he didn't need Photoshop); the **Hofgarten** at the back is a beautiful spot.

The interior of the **Dom St Kilian** (museum €5; ⊙10am-7pm Tue-Sun Apr-Oct, to 5pm Tue-Sun Nov-Mar) and the adjacent **Neumünster**, an 11th-century church in the old town housing the bones of St Kilian, the patron saint of Würzburg, continue the baroque themes of the Residenz.

Neumann's fortified **Alter Kranen** (old crane), which serviced a dock on the riverbank south of Friedensbrücke, is now the **Haus des Frankenweins** (Kranenkai 1), where you can taste Franconian wines (for around €3 per glass).

The medieval fortress **Marienberg**, across the river on the hill, is reached by crossing the 15th-century stone **Alte Mainbrücke** (old bridge) from the city and walking up Tellstiege, a small alley. It encloses the **Fürstenbau Museum** (adult/child €4/3; ⊙9am-6pm Tue-Sun Apr-Oct), featuring the Episcopal apartments, and the regional **Mainfränkisches Museum** (Festung Marienberg; adult/child €4/3; ⊙10am-5pm Tue-Sun Apr-Oct, to 4pm Tue-Sun Nov-Mar). For a simple thrill, wander the walls enjoying the panoramic views.

Sleeping & Eating

Würzburg's many *Weinstuben* (cosy places to enjoy wine in a traditional setting) are excellent places for sampling the local vintages. Look for crests of gilded grapes over entrances. Sanderstrasse has a good strip of lively bars.

Babelfish Hostel HOSTEL €
(☎304 0430; www.babelfish-hostel.de; Haugerring 2; dm €17-23, r €45-70; @📶) This green-powered, independent hostel has moved to new digs in a bank building across from the Hauptbahnhof. Facilities include spotless dorms, rooftop terrace and bike rental (€5 per day).

Hotel Rebstock HOTEL €€
(☎309 30; www.rebstock.com; Neubaustrasse 7; r €85-170; ❄📶) Class, hospitality and a touch of nostalgia are the characteristics of this elegant hotel, one of Würzburg's best. Meticulously restored, this rococo mansion has 70 superbly furnished rooms.

Hotel Till Eulenspiegel HOTEL €€
(☎355 840; www.hotel-till-eulenspiegel.de; Sanderstrasse 1a; r €70-120; 📶) Run by the gregarious Johannes, the 18 rooms are comfortable and some have sunny balconies. There's also a small but good *Weinstube* (wine bar) and a pub serving unusual Bavarian microbrews.

Zum Stachel GERMAN €€
(☎527 70; www.weinhaus-stachel.de; Gressengasse 1; mains €12-22; ⏲closed Sun) There's a restaurant at this 15th-century watering hole, but better yet is to just enjoy a drink on one of its stone balconies overlooking the *Romeo and Juliet*–like Renaissance courtyard.

Weinstuben Juliusspital WEINSTUBE €€
(☎540 80; Juliuspromenade 19; mains €8-20) This rambling place serves up a long list of wines (especially local whites). You can have a meal or just a drink at one of the many old wooden tables.

Information

The **tourist office** (www.wuerzburg.de; Marktplatz; ⏲10am-6pm Mon-Fri, 10am-2pm Sat & Sun May-Oct, reduced hr & closed Sun other times), in the rococo masterpiece Falkenhaus, runs 90-minute English-language **city walks** (€6; ⏲1pm Fri & Sat May-Oct).

Getting There & Away

Würzburg is served by frequent ICE trains from Frankfurt (€33, 70 minutes) and Nuremberg (€33, 69 minutes). It's a major stop for the ICE trains on the Hamburg–Munich line. It is also on the Romantic Road bus route (€19, 1½ hours to/from Rothenburg). The stop is in front of the train station.

Bamberg

☎0951 / POP 71,000

Off the major tourist routes, Bamberg is revered by those in the know. It boasts a beautifully preserved collection of 17th- and 18th-century merchants' houses, palaces and churches. It is bisected by a large canal and fast-flowing river that are spanned by cute little bridges, and it even has its own local style of beer. No wonder it has been recognised by Unesco as a World Heritage site. Could it be the best small town in Germany?

Sights

Bamberg's main appeal is its fine buildings – the sheer number, their jumble of styles and the ambience this creates. Most attractions are spread on either side of the Regnitz River, but the **Altes Rathaus** (Obere Brücke) is actually solidly perched on its own islet. Its lavish murals are among many around town.

The princely and ecclesiastical district is centred on **Domplatz**, where the Romanesque and Gothic **cathedral** (⏲8am-6pm Apr-Sep, to 5pm Oct-Mar), housing the statue of the chivalric king-knight, the *Bamberger Reiter*, is the biggest attraction. Look for the enigmatic statue, the *Lächelnde Engel* (Smiling Angel).

Across the square, the imposing 17th-century **Neue Residenz** (www.schloesser.bayern.de; Domplatz 8; adult/child €4/3; ⏲9am-6pm Apr-Sep, 10am-4pm Oct-Mar) has 40 rooms filled with treasures and opulent decor.

Above Domplatz is the former Benedictine **monastery of St Michael**, at the top of Michaelsberg. The **Kirche St Michael** (Franziskanergasse 2; ⏲9am-6pm) is a must-see for its baroque art and the herbal compendium painted on its ceiling. The garden terraces afford another marvellous overview of the city's splendour.

Sleeping

Some of the breweries also rent rooms – a major convenience.

TOP CHOICE **Hotel Sankt Nepomuk** HOTEL €€
(☎984 20; www.hotel-nepomuk.de; Obere Mühlbrücke 9; r €95-145; 📶) Named aptly after the patron saint of bridges, this is a classy

establishment in a half-timbered former mill right on the Regnitz. It has a superb restaurant (mains €15 to €30) with a terrace, 24 comfy rustic rooms and bikes for rent.

Backpackers Bamberg HOSTEL €
(☎2221 718; www.backpackersbamberg.de; Heiliggrabstrasse 4; dm €15-18, r €40-60; 📶) Newly relocated to a large and accommodating half-timbered building, this hostel is a fine budget choice. It's a five-minute walk from the train station towards the old town. Furnishings are new and the decor has a freeform flair.

Hotel Europa HOTEL €€
(☎309 3020; www.hotel-europa-bamberg.de; Untere Königstrasse 6-8; r €75-120) Smell the spaghetti from one of the 46 rooms above Bamberg's best Italian restaurant. Ask for a room at the front with views of the Dom and the red-tiled roofs of the Altstadt. Breakfast is in the restaurant or out in the sunny courtyard.

Eating & Drinking

Bamberg's unique style of beer is called *Rauchbier,* which literally means smoked beer. With a bacon flavour at first, it is a smooth brew that goes down easily.

TOP CHOICE **Schlenkerla** GERMAN €€
(Dominikanerstrasse 6; mains €8-15; ⏲Wed-Mon) Featuring a warren of rooms decked out with lamps fashioned from antlers, this 16th-century restaurant is famous for tasty Franconian specialities and *Rauchbier,* served directly from oak barrels. This should be your one stop if you only have time for one (stop, not beers...).

Klosterbräu GERMAN €
(Obere Mühlbrücke 1-3; mains €6-12) This beautiful half-timbered brewery is Bamberg's oldest. It draws *Stammgäste* (regular local drinkers) and tourists alike, who wash down filling slabs of meat and dumplings with its excellent range of ales.

Brauereigasthof Fässla GERMAN €
(☎265 16; www.faessla.de; Obere Königstrasse 19-21; mains €7-10) Chairs at the on-site restaurant are embossed with Fässla's cute coat of arms – a gnome rolling a giant beer barrel. Enjoy the light pilsner here, then head upstairs for a snooze (rooms €40 to €70).

Information

The **tourist office** (www.bamberg.info; Geyerswörthstrasse 3; ⏲9.30am-6pm Mon-Fri, 9.30am-2.30pm Sat & Sun) is in the old town.

Getting There & Away

Two trains per hour go to/from both Würzburg (€17, one hour) and Nuremberg (€20, one hour). Bamberg is also served by ICE trains running between Munich (€58, two hours) and Berlin (€74, 3¾ hours) every two hours.

Rothenburg ob der Tauber

☎09861 / POP 12,000

In the Middle Ages, Rothenburg's town fathers built strong walls to protect the town from siege; today they are the reason the town is under siege from tourists. The most stereotypical of all German walled towns, Rothenburg can't help being so cute.

Granted 'free imperial city' status in 1274, it's a confection of twisting cobbled lanes and pretty architecture enclosed by towered stone walls. Swarmed during the day, the underlying charm oozes out after the last bus leaves.

Note that the gaggle of Christmas shops and 'museums' are quite wily – once in, you have to walk the entire labyrinth in order to escape.

Sights

The **Rathaus on Markt** was commenced in Gothic style in the 14th century but completed in Renaissance style. The **tower** (admission €2) gives a majestic view over the town and the Tauber Valley.

According to legend, the town was saved during the Thirty Years War when the mayor won a challenge by the Imperial General Tilly and downed more than 3L of wine at a gulp. This **Meistertrunk** scene is re-enacted by the clock figures on the tourist office building (eight times daily in summer). Actors re-enact other famous scenes from the past (but not the mythical assault on the tour bus by fudge vendors) at 6.30pm Friday, May to September.

Totally uncommercial, **Jakobskirche** (Klingengasse 1; adult/child €2/1; ⏲9am-5pm) is sober and Gothic. Marvel at the carved *Heilige Blut Altar* (Holy Blood Altar).

The **Reichsstadt Museum** (www.reichsstadtmuseum.rothenburg.de; Klosterhof 5; adult/under 18yr €3/2; ⏲10am-5pm Apr-Oct, 1-4pm Nov-Mar), in the grandiose former convent, features the superb 1494 *Rothenburger Passion* in 12 panels.

Sleeping & Eating

Resist the temptation to try a *Schneeball,* a crumbly ball of bland dough with the taste and consistency of chalk – surely one of Europe's worst 'local specialities'.

Altfränkische Weinstube HOTEL €
(☎6404; www.altfraenkische-weinstube-rothenburg.de; Am Klosterhof 7; r €60-80;) Hiding in a quiet side street near the Reichsstadtmuseum, this enchantingly characterful inn has six atmosphere-laden rooms, all with bathtubs and most with four-poster or canopied beds. The restaurant (open for dinner only) serves up sound regional fare with a dollop of medieval cheer.

Pension Raidel HOTEL €
(☎3115; www.romanticroad.com/raidel; Wenggasse 3; r €25-60) This half-timbered inn has 500-year-old exposed beams studded with wooden nails, and musical instruments for guests to play. Some rooms share bathrooms.

Zur Höll GERMAN €€
(Burggasse 8; dishes €6-18) This medieval wine tavern, with an appreciation for slow food and a name that means hell, is in the town's oldest original building, dating back to the year 900. The menu of regional specialities is limited but refined, though it's the wine that people really come for.

Getting There & Away

There are hourly trains to/from Steinach, a transfer point for service to Würzburg (total journey €13, 70 minutes). Rothenburg is a crossroads for tourist buses. Romantic Road buses pause here for 35 minutes.

Nuremberg

☎0911 / POP 498,000

Nuremberg (Nürnberg) woos visitors with its wonderfully restored medieval Altstadt, its grand castle and its magical *Christkindlmarkt* (Christmas market). Thriving traditions also include sizzling *Nürnberger Bratwürste* (finger-sized sausages) and *Lebkuchen* – large, soft gingerbread cookies, traditionally eaten at Christmas time but available here year-round. Both within and beyond the high stone wall encircling the Altstadt is a wealth of major museums that shed light on Nuremberg's significant history.

Nuremberg played a major role during the Nazi years, as documented in Leni Riefenstahl's film *Triumph of the Will*, and during the war-crimes trials afterwards. It has done an admirable job of confronting this ugly past with museums and exhibits. And it has recaptured much of the charm lost when bombing raids flattened the centre; it is still the heart of the German toy industry.

Sights

The scenic **Altstadt** is easily covered on foot. On Lorenzer Platz there's the **St Lorenzkirche**, noted for the 15th-century tabernacle that climbs like a vine up a pillar to the vaulted ceiling.

To the north is the bustling **Hauptmarkt**, where the most famous **Christkindlmarkt** in Germany is held from the Friday before Advent to Christmas Eve. The church here is the ornate **Pfarrkirche Unsere Liebe Frau**; the clock's figures go strolling at noon. Near the Rathaus is **St Sebalduskirche** (⌚9.30am-6pm), Nuremberg's oldest church (dating from the 13th century), with the shrine of St Sebaldus.

Kaiserburg CASTLE
(www.schloesser.bayern.de; adult/child incl museum €6/5; ⌚9am-6pm Apr-Sep, 10am-4pm Oct-Mar) Climb up Burgstrasse to this enormous 15th-century fortress for good views of the city. The walls spread west to the tunnel-gate of **Tiergärtnertor**, where you can stroll behind the castle to the gardens.

Germanisches Nationalmuseum MUSEUM
(www.gnm.de; Kartäusergasse 1; adult/child €8/5; ⌚10am-6pm Tue & Thu-Sun, to 9pm Wed) The most important general museum of German culture in the country, this stunner displays works by German painters and sculptors, an archaeological collection, arms and armour, musical and scientific instruments and, of course, toys.

TOP CHOICE **Nuremberg Trials Memorial** HISTORICAL SITE
(www.memorium-nuremberg.de; Bärenschanzstrasse 72; adult/child €5/3; ⌚10am-6pm Wed-Mon) From 1945 to 1949 suspected Nazis were tried for war crimes in Nuremberg, which was chosen because it had been the spiritual home of the Third Reich. The top leaders, such as von Ribbentrop and Streicher, received death sentences; others, such as Göring, committed suicide ahead of the noose. The transcripts are still studied today and show that the rule of law can contend with evil. The courthouse where the trials were held is still in use and is now home to a compelling and comprehensive **exhibit** about the world's first efforts to prosecute genocide. **Courtroom 600**, where

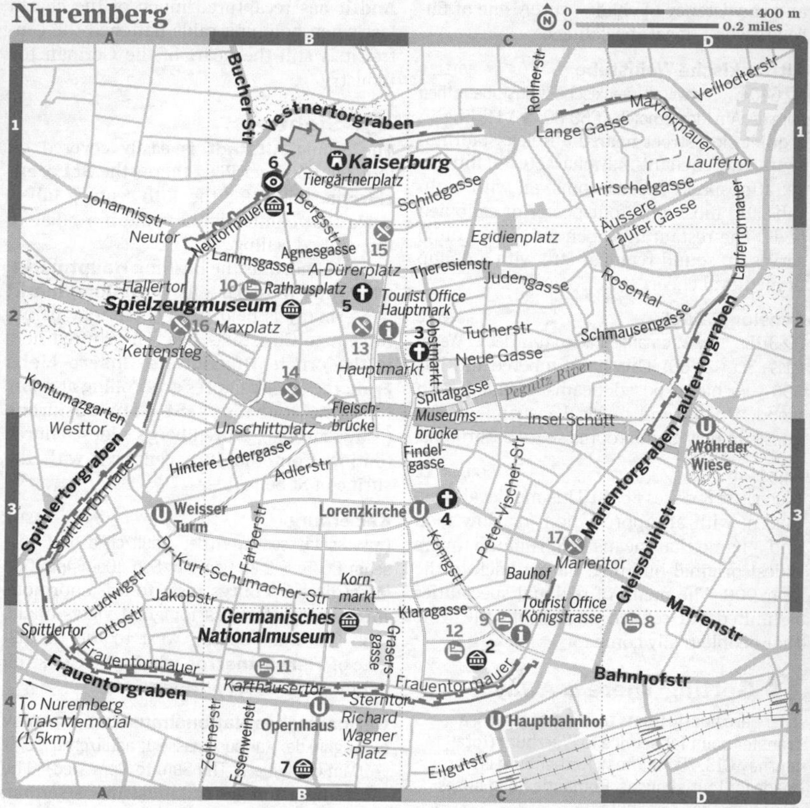

the trials were held, can be toured when it is not in use.

Other Museums MUSEUMS

Nuremberg has a lot of toy companies and the **Spielzeugmuseum** (Toy Museum; Karlstrasse 13-15; adult/child €5/3; 10am-5pm Tue-Fri, to 6pm Sat & Sun) presents their products in their infinite variety.

The **Verkehrsmuseum** (Transportation Museum; www.dbmuseum.de; Lessingstrasse 6; adult/child €4/2; 9am-5pm Tue-Sun) has a trainload of exhibits on the German railways.

Albrecht-Dürer-Haus (Albrecht-Dürer-Strasse 39; adult/child €5/2.50; 10am-5pm Fri-Wed, to 8pm Thu) is where Dürer, Germany's renowned Renaissance draughtsman, lived from 1509 to 1528. A digital version of wife Agnes leads tours.

The sleekly curving **Neues Museum** (www.nmn.de; Luitpoldstrasse 5; adult/child €4/3; 10am-8pm Tue-Fri, to 6pm Sat & Sun) contains a superb collection of contemporary art and design.

Luitpoldhain HISTORICAL SITE

Nuremberg's role during the Third Reich is well known. The Nazis chose this city as their propaganda centre and for mass rallies, which were held at Luitpoldhain, a (never completed) sports complex of megalomaniac proportions.

Don't miss the **Dokumentationzentrum** (www.museen.nuernberg.de; Bayernstrasse 110; adult/child €5/3; 9am-6pm Mon-Fri, 10am-6pm Sat & Sun) in the north wing of the massive unfinished Congress Hall, which would have held 50,000 people for Hitler's spectacles. The museum's absorbing exhibits trace the rise of Hitler and the Nazis, and the important role Nuremberg played in the mythology. Take tram 9 or 6 to Doku-Zentrum.

Sleeping

Nuremberg hosts many a trade show through the year (including a huge toy fair in February). During these times – and

Nuremberg

Top Sights

Sights

Sleeping

Eating

Christmas market weekends – rates soar like a model rocket.

TOP CHOICE **Hotel Elch** HOTEL €€
(☎249 2980; www.hotel-elch.com; Irrerstrasse 9; r €65-110; wifi) This dramatically historic hotel, with a logo of the namesake elk, occupies a 14th-century half-timbered house that wears every one of its years on its skew facade. The spotless and petite rooms are up a narrow medieval staircase. Breakfast is served in the quaint woody restaurant, the Schnitzelria, which does a good line in Franconian beers and, yes, schnitzel.

Lette 'm Sleep HOSTEL €
(☎992 8128; www.backpackers.de; Frauentormauer 42; dm €16-20, r from €50; @wifi) A backpacker favourite, this independent hostel is just five minutes' walk from the Hauptbahnhof. Private rooms share bathrooms, however you can read to your heart's content in the private facilities of several apartments (from €65), which also have kitchens.

Art & Business Hotel HOTEL €€
(☎232 10; www.art-business-hotel.com; Gleissbühlstrasse 15; r €60-150; wifi) You don't have to be an artist or a business person to stay at this stylish, up-to-the-minute place, a retro sport shoe's throw from the Hauptbahnhof. Rooms are a study in diligently composed minimalism, while technicolour art and design brings cheer to the communal spaces.

Hotel Drei Raben HOTEL €€
(☎274 380; www.hotel3raben.de; Königstrasse 63; r €100-185; wifi) This designer theme hotel builds upon the legend of three ravens perched on the building's chimney stack, who tell each other stories from Nuremberg lore. Each of the 21 rooms uses its style and humour to tell a particular tale – from the life of Dürer to the history of the locomotive.

Probst-Garni Hotel HOTEL, PENSION €€
(☎203 433; www.hotel-garni-probst.de; Luitpoldstrasse 9; r €60-100) Nuremberg's most reasonably priced pension is squeezed on the 3rd floor of a vintage building. Recent renovations have given the rooms furnishings that are prim and proper. The letters from happy guests are sweet.

Eating

Don't leave Nuremberg without trying its famous *Nürnberger Bratwürste.* Order 'em by the dozen with *meerrettich* (horseradish) on the side. Restaurants line the hilly lanes above the Burgstrasse.

TOP CHOICE **Bratwursthäusle** GERMAN €€
(http://die-nuernberger-bratwurst.de; Rathausplatz 2; meals €6-14; closed Sun) A local legend and *the* place for flame-grilled and scrumptious local sausages. Get them with *Kartoffelsalat* (potato salad). There are also nice tree-shaded tables outside.

Marientorzwinger GERMAN €€
(Lorenzer-strasse 33; mains €8-17) This is the last remaining *Zwinger* eatery (taverns built between the inner and outer walls when they relinquished their military use) in Nuremberg. Chomp on sturdy Franconian staples or a veggie dish in the simple wood-panelled dining room or the leafy beer garden, and swab the decks with a yard of Fürth-brewed Tucher.

Hütt'n GERMAN €€
(Burgstrasse 19; mains €8-15; dinner Wed-Mon) Be prepared to queue for a table at this local haunt. The special here is the *Ofenfrische*

DON'T MISS

CHRISTMAS MARKETS

Beginning in late November every year, central squares across Germany – especially those in Bavaria – are transformed into Christmas markets or *Christkindlmarkts* (also known as *Weihnachtsmärkte*). Folks stamp about between the wooden stalls, perusing seasonal trinkets (from treasures to schlock) while warming themselves with tasty *glühwein* (mulled, spiced red wine) and treats such as sausages and potato pancakes. The markets are popular with tourists but locals love 'em too, and bundle themselves up and carouse for hours. Nuremberg's **market** (www.christkindlesmarkt.de) fills much of the centre and attracts two million people.

Krustenbraten: roast pork with crackling, dumplings and sauerkraut salad. There's also a near-endless variety of schnapps and beers.

Café am Trödelmarkt CAFE €
(Trödelmarkt 42; dishes €3-5; ⏲9am-6pm) A gorgeous place on a sunny day, this multilevel waterfront cafe overlooks the covered Henkersteg bridge. It's popular for its fresh and tasty continental breakfasts.

Kettensteg BEER GARDEN €
(Maxplatz 35; mains €6-14) Right by the river and with its own suspension bridge to the other side, this beer garden and restaurant is fine on a summer day and cosy in winter. The basic fare is tasty and absorbs lots of beer.

Information

Nürnberg + Fürth Card (€21) Good for two days of unlimited public transport and admissions.

Tourist office (www.tourismus.nuernberg.de) Künstlerhaus (Königstrasse 93; ⏲9am-7pm Mon-Sat, 10am-4pm Sun); Hauptmarkt (Hauptmarkt 18; ⏲9am-6pm Mon-Sat, 10am-4pm Sun)

Getting There & Around

Nuremberg's **airport** (NUE; www.airport-nuernberg.de) is a hub for budget carrier Air Berlin, which has services throughout Germany, as well as flights to London. There's frequent service to the airport on the S-2 line (€2, 12 minutes).

The city is also a hub for train services. Sample fares:

DESTINATION	PRICE	DURATION (HR)
Berlin-Hauptbahnhof	€89	4½
Frankfurt	€48	2
Munich	€49	1
Stuttgart	€38	2¼

Tickets on the bus, tram and U-Bahn system cost €2 each. Day passes are €4.

Regensburg

☎0941 / POP 129,000

On the wide Danube River, Regensburg has relics of all periods as far back as the Romans, yet doesn't have the tourist mobs you'll find in other equally attractive German cities. Oh well, their loss. At least Unesco noticed. It recognised that Regensburg has the only intact medieval centre in Germany. Amid the half-timbers, Renaissance towers that could be in Tuscany mix with Roman ruins. Meanwhile, some 25,000 students keep things lively.

From the main train station, walk up Maximilianstrasse for 10 minutes to reach the centre.

Sights

A veritable miracle of engineering in its time, the **Steinerne Brücke** (Stone Bridge) was cobbled together between 1135 and 1146. For centuries it remained the only solid crossing along the entire Danube.

Lording over Regensburg, **Dom St Peter** (Domplatz; ⏲6.30am-6pm Apr-Oct, to 5pm Nov-Mar) ranks among Bavaria's grandest Gothic cathedrals. Construction of this green-hued twin-spired landmark began in the late 13th century, mostly to flaunt the city's prosperity. The cavernous interior's prized possessions include kaleidoscopic stained-glass windows.

The **Altes Rathaus** (adult/child incl museum €6/3; ⏲tours in English 3pm Apr-Oct, 2pm Nov, Dec & Mar) was progressively extended from medieval to baroque times and was the seat of the Reichstag for almost 150 years.

The **Roman wall**, with its **Porta Praetoria** arch, follows Unter den Schwibbögen onto Dr-Martin-Luther-Strasse.

Lavish **Schloss Thurn und Taxis** (www.thurnundtaxis.de; Emmeramsplatz 5; tours adult/child €11.50/9; ⏲11am-5pm Mon-Fri, 10am-5pm Sat & Sun) includes the castle proper (*Schloss*) and the royal stables *(Marstall)*. The adjoining **Basilika St Emmeram** is a riot of rococo and has a perfect cloister. You need to join a **tour** (⏲in German hourly, in English 1.30pm Jun-mid-Sep) to see the sights.

Sleeping & Eating

Atmospheric hotels with modern style can be found scattered through the medieval centre. Hidden around corners you'll find cafes with good wine and boisterous beer gardens.

TOP CHOICE Altstadthotel am Pach HOTEL €€
(⏲298 610; www.regensburghotel.de; Untere Bachgasse 9; r €80-150; 📶) Those who have shaped Regensburg history, from Marcus Aurelius to Emperor Karl V, are commemorated in the 21 rooms of this high-concept hotel. Rooms vary in size but all are warmly furnished with thick carpets, comfy mattresses and a minifridge.

Hotel Goldenes Kreuz HOTEL €€
(☎558 12; www.hotel-goldeneskreuz.de; Haidplatz 7; r €80-140; 📶) Surely the best deal in town, the nine fairy-tale rooms here each bear the name of a crowned head and are fit for a kaiser. Huge mirrors, dark antique and Bauhaus furnishings, four-poster beds, chubby exposed beams and parquet flooring produce a stylish opus in leather, wood, crystal and fabric.

Brook Lane Hostel HOSTEL €
(⏲690 0966; www.hostel-regensburg.de; Obere Bachgasse 21; dm €15-20, s/d/apt from €35/45/140; 📶) Regensburg's only backpacker hostel has spanking-new dorms and bathrooms, and its very own food store.

TOP CHOICE Wurstküche SAUSAGES €
(☎466 210; Thundorferstrasse 3; meals €7-10; ⏲8am-7pm) The Danube rushes past this little house that's been cooking up the addictive local version of Nuremberg sausages since 1135. Which is better? These or the northern version? (Better try both.)

Dicker Mann GERMAN €€
(Krebsgasse 6; mains €6-15) One of the oldest restaurants in town, this stylish, very traditional restaurant has dependable Bavarian food, swift service and a lively flair thanks to its young and upbeat staff. On a balmy evening, grab a table in the lovely beer garden out back.

Spitalgarten BEER GARDEN €
(St Katharinenplatz 1; meals €5-10) A veritable thicket of folding chairs and slatted tables by the Danube, this is one of the best places in town for some al fresco quaffing. It claims to have brewed beer (today's Spital) here since 1350, so it probably knows what it's doing by now.

Information

There's internet access at coin-operated terminals (€1 per 15 minutes) on the top level of the train station.

Tourist office (www.regensburg.de; Altes Rathaus; ⏲9am-6pm Mon-Fri, to 4pm Sat & Sun)

Getting There & Away

Regensburg is on the busy train line between Nuremberg (€24, one hour) and Vienna, Austria (€75, four hours). There are hourly trains to Munich (€25, 1½ hours).

Augsburg

☎0821 / POP 270,000

Originally established by the Romans in 15 BC, Augsburg later became a centre of Luther's Reformation. Today it's a lively provincial city, criss-crossed by little streams, that has an appealing ambience and vitality. It makes a good day trip from Munich or as part of a Romantic Road foray.

Sights

Look for the very impressive onion-shaped towers on the 17th-century **Rathaus** (Rathausplatz; admission to Golden Hall €2; ⏲10am-6pm) and the adjacent **Perlachturm**, a former guard tower. North of here is the 10th-century **Dom Maria Heimsuchung** (Hoher Weg; ⏲10am-6pm Mon-Sat), which has more 'modern' additions, such as the 14th-century doors showing scenes from the Old Testament.

The Fuggers – a 16th-century banking family and *not* a Renaissance version of the Fockers – left their mark everywhere. They have lavish tombs inside **St Anna Kirche** (Im Annahof 2, off Annastrasse; ⏲10am-noon Tue-Sat, 3-5pm Tue-Sun), a place also known for being a Martin Luther bolt-hole (massive renovations are ongoing so it may be closed periodically). The amazingly named 16th-century **Fuggerei** (adult/child €4/2; ⏲9am-8pm Apr-Oct,

9am-6pm Nov-Mar) was built with banking riches to house the poor, which, remarkably, it still does. The excellent **museum** (Mittlere Gasse 14; free with Fuggerei admission) shows how they've lived.

Sleeping & Eating

Hotel am Rathaus HOTEL €€
(☎346 490; www.hotel-am-rathaus-augsburg.de; Am Hinteren Perlachberg 1; r €70-125;) As central as it gets, and moments away from Rathausplatz, this boutique hotel has fresh neutral decor and a sunny little breakfast room. The trendy Italian restaurant is surprisingly good.

Ratskeller GERMAN €€
(Rathausplatz 2; mains €8-15) Avoid cliché with ambiently lit corners and anterooms and mezzanines strewn with comfy lounges. There's a wide terrace out back for serious quaffing. Ratskeller's kitchen is renowned for its *Schweinebraten* – roast pork with dumplings and red-cabbage sauerkraut.

Bauerntanz GERMAN €€
(Bauerntanzgässchen 1; mains €8-16) Framed by lace curtains, this dark-timber place with copper lamps serves big portions of creative Swabian and Bavarian food. There's outdoor seating.

Information

Tourist office (☎502 0724; www.augsburg-tourismus.de; Maximilian Strasse 57; ⏲9am-6pm Mon-Fri, 10am-5pm Sat, 10am-2pm Sun Apr-Oct, 9am-5pm Mon-Fri, 10am-2pm Sat Nov-Mar)

Getting There & Away

Trains between Munich and Augsburg are frequent (€12 to €20, 40 minutes); it's on the main line to Frankfurt. The Romantic Road bus stops at the train station and the Rathaus.

Füssen

☎08362 / POP 18,000

Never have so many come to a place with so few inhabitants by comparison. Close to the Austrian border and the foothills of the Alps, Füssen is often overlooked by the mobs swarming the two castles associated with King Ludwig II in nearby Schwangau, which fulfil everyone's fantasy image of a castle.

If Füssen anchors a fairy-tale vision of Germany through King Ludwig's castles, the town itself is not quite the ugly stepsister but rather the practical-accountant stepsister. It has some baroque architecture and you can actually sense a certain Alpine serenity after dark while locals count the change from the day's day-tripper invasion.

Sights

Neuschwanstein and **Hohenschwangau** castles provide a fascinating glimpse into the romantic king's state of mind (or lack thereof) and well-developed ego. Hohenschwangau is where Ludwig lived as a child. It's not as cute, even though both castles are 19th-century constructions, but it draws less crowds and visits are more relaxed. The adjacent Neuschwanstein is Ludwig's own creation (albeit with the help of a theatrical designer). Although it was unfinished when he died in 1886, there is plenty of evidence of Ludwig's twin obsessions: swans and Wagnerian operas. The sugary pastiche of architectural styles, alternatively overwhelmingly beautiful and just a little too much, reputedly inspired Disney's Fantasyland castle.

Tickets may only be bought from the **ticket centre** (www.ticket-center-hohenschwangau.de; Alpenseestrasse 12, Hohenschwangau; adult/child €9/free, incl Schloss Hohenschwangau €17/free; ⏲tickets 8am-5.30pm Apr-Sep, 9am-3.30pm Oct-Mar). In summer it's worth the €1.80 surcharge each to reserve ahead. To walk to Hohenschwangau from there takes about 20 minutes, while Neuschwanstein is a 45-minute steep hike. Horse-drawn carriages (€6) and shuttle buses (€2) shorten but don't eliminate the hike. The walk between the castles is a piney 45-minute stroll.

Take the bus from Füssen train station (€2, 15 minutes, hourly) or share a **taxi** (☎7700; up to 4 people €10). Go early to avoid the worst of the rush.

And remember, as soon as you leave the main trails, you're in beautiful and untrammelled Alpine wilderness.

Sleeping & Eating

A pavilion near the tourist office has a computerised list of vacant rooms in town; most of the cheapest rooms, at around €20 per person, are in private homes just a few minutes from the Altstadt.

Altstadt Hotel zum Hechten HOTEL €
(☎916 00; www.hotel-hechten.com; Ritterstrasse 6; r €50-100;) Set around a quiet inner courtyard, this child-friendly place is one of Füssen's oldest Altstadt hotels, with rustic public areas and bright, modern guest rooms in a sizes small to XL. The restaurant

is a rollicking place for a drink; skip the schnitzel.

Drinking

Giovanni's Weinladen WINE

(Lechhalde 2) Bottles line the walls of this wine store, which also sells by the glass. A few tables out front on a terrace take in some tree-clad hills and you can move on from the genteel charms of the grape to something with more of a kick like grappa.

Information

Tourist office (☎938 50; www.fuessen.de; Kaiser-Maximillian-Platz 1; ⏰9am-5pm Mon-Fri, 10am-2pm Sat, 10am-noon Sun)

Getting There & Away

Train connections to Munich and Augsburg (€23, two hours) run every hour. Füssen is the start of the Romantic Road and the **Romantic Road bus** (www.romanticroadcoach.de; ⏰8am daily mid-Apr–mid-Oct) service. Day trips from Munich are widely promoted.

RVO bus 9606 (www.rvo-bus.de) connects Füssen, via Wieskirche and Oberammergau, with Garmisch-Partenkirchen (€3, 2¼ hours, five to six daily).

BAVARIAN ALPS

While not quite as high as their sister summits further south in Austria and Switzerland, the Bavarian Alps (Bayerische Alpen) still are standouts, owing to their abrupt rise from the rolling Bavarian foothills. Stretching westward from Germany's southeastern corner to the Allgäu region near Lake Constance, the Alps take in most of the mountainous country fringing the southern border with Austria.

Berchtesgaden

☎08652 / POP 7900

Steeped in myth and legend, the Berchtesgadener Land enjoys a natural beauty so abundant that it's almost preternatural. Framed by six formidable mountain ranges and home to Germany's second-highest mountain, the Watzmann (2713m), the dreamy, fir-lined valleys are filled with gurgling streams and peaceful Alpine villages.

Much of the terrain is protected by law as the Nationalpark Berchtesgaden, which embraces the pristine Königssee, one of Germany's most photogenic lakes. Yet, Berchtesgaden's history is also indelibly entwined with the Nazi period, as chronicled at the disturbing Dokumentation Obersalzberg. The Eagle's Nest, a mountaintop lodge built for Hitler, is now a major tourist attraction.

WORTH A TRIP

WIESKIRCHE

This Unesco World Heritage–listed **church** (www.wieskirche.de; ⏰8am-7pm May-Oct, to 5pm Nov-Apr) is a jaw-dropping spectacle of 18th-century rococo excess. Its white pillars tower over a tiny village 25km northeast of Füssen. The church can be reached by the **Romantic Road bus** (www.romanticroadcoach.de) or **RVO bus 9606** (www.rvo-bus.de), which runs between Füssen and Garmisch-Partenkirchen via Wieskirche and Oberammergau (five to six daily).

Sights & Activities

Dokumentation Obersalzberg MUSEUM

(www.obersalzberg.de; Salzbergstrasse 41, Obersalzberg; adult/child & student €3/free; ⏰9am-5pm daily Apr-Oct, 10am-3pm Tue-Sun Nov-Mar) In 1933 quiet Obersalzberg (some 3km from Berchtesgaden) became the southern headquarters of Hitler's government, a dark period that's given the full historical treatment at this at-times heartbreaking and compelling museum. You can visit tunnels that were dug for a fortunately unfulfilled Nazi last stand, but the exhibits – including the erudite English audio guide (€2) – are the real draw. It shows how Hitler gained the support of the masses through his demonization of 'elites' while cigarette companies increased sales by including a picture of the dictator in every pack.

To get there take bus 838 from the 1938-vintage Hauptbahnhof in Berchtesgaden. It's hourly weekdays but infrequent at weekends. A cab costs about €20.

Eagle's Nest HISTORIC SITE

Berchtesgaden's creepiest – yet impressive – draw is the Eagle's Nest atop Mt Kehlstein, a sheer-sided peak at Obersalzberg. Perched at 1834m, the innocent-looking lodge (called Kehlsteinhaus in German) has sweeping views across the mountains and down into the valley where the Königssee shimmers. Ironically, though it was built for him, Hitler is said to have suffered from vertigo and rarely visited.

ALP-HOPPING

While the public transport network is good, the mountain geography means there are few direct routes between the top Alpine draws; sometimes a shortcut via Austria is quicker (such as by road between Füssen and Garmisch-Partenkirchen). Bus rather than rail routes are often more practical. For those driving, the **German Alpine Road** (Deutsche Alpenstrasse) is a scenic way to go.

Drive or take bus 849 from Dokumentation Obersalzberg to Kehlstein, where you board a special **bus** (www.kehlsteinhaus.de; adult/child €16/9) that drives you up the mountain. It runs between 9am and 4pm, and takes 35 minutes.

Eagle's Nest Tours (☎649 71; www.eagles-nest-tours.com; Königsseer Strasse 2; adult/6-12yr €48/30; ⏲1.30pm mid-May–Oct) has four-hour tours in English that cover the war years; they leave from near the train station.

Salzbergwerk SALT MINE
(www.salzzeitreise.de; adult/child €15/10; ⏲9am-5pm May-Oct, 11am-3pm Nov-Apr) The 1½-hour tours of this salt mine combine history with a carnival.

Alpine Beauty NATURAL ATTRACTIONS
Crossing the beautiful, emerald-green **Königssee**, an alpine lake situated 5km south of Berchtesgaden (and linked by hourly buses in summer) is sublime. There are frequent boat tours (€13) across the lake to the pixel-perfect chapel at **St Bartholomä**.

The wilds of **Berchtesgaden National Park** offer some of the best **hiking** in Germany. A good introduction to the area is a 2km path up from St Bartholomä beside the Königssee to the Watzmann-Ostwand, a massive 2000m-high rock face where scores of overly ambitious mountaineers have died.

Sleeping & Eating

Berchtesgaden town proper is just up the hill from the train station and is rather staid. You might want to make your visit a day trip from Salzburg. There's no need to linger here when there's so much nearby.

Hotel Bavaria HOTEL €€
(☎660 11; www.hotelbavaria.net; Sunklergässchen 11; r €50-130) A short hop from the station, this guest house, run by the same family for a century, has romantically beamed rooms with four-poster beds and modern bathrooms. Looking at the views from some of the pricier quarters with balconies, you'd think the hotel had been lined up specially to catch the vistas.

Information

The **tourist office** (www.berchtesgaden.de; Königsseer Strasse 2; ⏲8.30am-6pm Mon-Fri, to 5pm Sat, 9am-3pm Sun Apr–mid-Oct, reduced hr other times) is just across the river from the train station.

Getting There & Away

There is hourly train service to Berchtesgaden from Munich (€30, 2½ hours), which usually requires a change in Frilassing. There are hourly connections to nearby Salzburg in Austria (€10, one hour); bus 840 from the station takes 45 minutes.

Garmisch-Partenkirchen

☎08821 / POP 27,000

The Alpine towns of Garmisch and Partenkirchen were merged for the 1936 Winter Olympics (it's making another bid for the 2020 Games). Munich residents' favourite getaway spot, this year-round resort is also a big draw for skiers, snowboarders, hikers and mountaineers. On sunny days, an ascent of Zugspitze will astound.

Sights & Activities

The huge **ski stadium** outside town hosted the Olympics. From the pedestrian Am Kurpark, walk up Klammstrasse, cross the tracks and veer left on the first path to reach the stadium and enjoy the spectacular views.

An excellent short hike from Garmisch is to the **Partnachklamm gorge**, via a winding path above a stream and underneath the waterfalls. You take the Graseck cable car and follow the signs.

An excursion to the **Zugspitze** (www.zugspitze.de) summit, Germany's highest peak (2962m), is a spectacular outing from Garmisch. There are various ways up, including the **Bayerische Zugspitzbahn rack-railway**, just west of the main train station, summit cable car or Eibsee cable car. You can use any combination of these modes for adult/child €47/9 round trip. Or you can scale it in two days. The summit is a winter playground year-round, with glaciers, snow and on clear days (the only times you should do this), extraordinary views of the Alps.

Garmisch is bounded by three separate ski areas – **Zugspitze plateau** (the highest), **Alpspitze/Hausberg** (the largest) and **Eckbauer** (the cheapest). Day ski passes range from €19 for Eckbauer to €37 for Zugspitze. The optimistically named Happy Ski Card is a pass for the entire region (from €69 for two days). A web of cross-country ski trails runs along the main valleys.

For ski hire and courses try the following:

Skischule (☎4931; www.skischule-gap.de; Am Hausberg 8)

Sport Total (☎1425; www.agentursporttotal.de; Marienplatz 18) Also organises paragliding, mountain biking, rafting and ballooning.

Sleeping & Eating

The tourist office has a 24-hour, outdoor room-reservation board. Choices are many.

Hotel Garmischer Hof HOTEL €€
(☎9110; www.garmischer-hof.de; Chamonixstrasse 10; s €59-94, d €94-136;) Generations of athletes, artists and outdoor enthusiasts have stayed at this refined chateau, property of the Seiwald family since 1928. Tasteful and cosy are the rooms, many with incredible Alpine views. Breakfast is served in the vaulted cafe-restaurant with a garden terrace.

Hostel 2962 HOSTEL €
(☎957 50; www.hostel2962.com; Partnachauenstrasse 3; dm/d from €20/60;) An old converted hotel, this is still essentially a typical Garmisch lodge. Rooms have some rather arch detailing that has some fun with Alpine clichés.

Bräustüberl GERMAN €€
(☎2312; Fürstenstrasse 23, Garmisch; mains €6-17) Conversation flows as freely as the beer at this quintessential Bavarian brew-pub, complete with enormous enamel coal-burning stove and dirndl-clad waitresses. Opt for the beer hall in winter and the beer garden in summer.

Information

Tourist office (☎180 700; www.gapa.de; Richard-Strauss-Platz 1, Garmisch; ⊗8am-6pm Mon-Sat, 10am-noon Sun) Near the station.

Zugspitzcard (www.zugspitzcard.com; adult/child from €44/25) Includes cable-car and railway rides and discounts, admission to museums and activities.

Getting There & Away

From Garmish there is train service to Munich (€19, 80 minutes, hourly) and to Innsbruck, Austria (€15, 80 minutes, every two hours)via Mittenwald. **RVO bus 9606** (www.rvo-bus.de), from in front of the train station, runs to Füssen (€3, 2¼ hours, five to six daily), via Oberammergau and Wieskirche.

Oberammergau

☎08822 / POP 5500

A blend of genuine piety, religious kitsch and monumental commercial greed, Oberammergau sometimes seems to sink under the weight of day trippers. Sadly, the crowds may distract from the town's triple charms: its gorgeous valley setting below the jagged Kofel peak, a 500-year-old woodcarving tradition and a wealth of houses painted with *Lüftlmalerei* (idealised external murals).

Oberammergau, about 20km north of Garmisch-Partenkirchen, is known worldwide for hosting the famous **Passion Play** (www.passionplay-oberammergau.com), acted out by much of the townfolk roughly every 10 years since 1634 to give thanks for being spared from the plague. The next one is in 2020.

Hourly trains connect Munich with Oberammergau (€18, 1¾ hours) with a change at Murnau. **RVO bus 9606** (www.rvo-bus.de) links Oberammergau with Füssen and the Wieskirche as well as Garmisch-Partenkirchen five to six times daily.

BADEN-WÜRTTEMBERG

With the exception of cuckoo clocks in the Black Forest, Baden-Württemberg runs a distant second in the cliché race to Bavaria. But that's really all the better, as it leaves more for you to discover on your own.

It's a pretty land of misty hills, shadowy conifers and cute villages that rewards exploration. If you want a big and quaint German village with lots of history, there's Heidelberg. Baden-Baden is the sybaritic playground for spa-goers, and Freiburg has youthful vibrancy in an intriguing package. Finally, Lake Constance is a misty redoubt bordering Switzerland and has all the pleasures a large body of water can offer.

The prosperous modern state of Baden-Württemberg was created in 1951 out of three smaller regions: Baden, Württemberg and Hohenzollern (thank goodness the names stopped at two).

Stuttgart

0711 / POP 592,000

Hemmed in by vine-covered hills, comfortable Stuttgart enjoys a quality of life funded by its fabled car companies: Porsche and Mercedes. It's also Baden-Württemberg's state capital and the hub of its industries. At the forefront of Germany's economic recovery from the ravages of WWII, Stuttgart started life less auspiciously in 950 as a horse stud farm. About 80% of the city centre was destroyed in WWII, but there are a few historical buildings left and – no surprise – car museums.

Sights

Stretching southwest from the Neckar River to the city centre is the **Schlossgarten**, an extensive strip of parkland divided into three sections (Unterer, Mittlerer and Ober-er), complete with ponds, swans, street entertainers and modern sculptures. At the gardens' southern end they encompass the sprawling baroque **Neues Schloss** (Schlossplatz).

Next to the turreted, Renaissance-esque **Altes Schloss** is the city's oldest square, Schillerplatz, with its **Friedrich Schiller statue** in honour of the poet, and the 12th-

Stuttgart

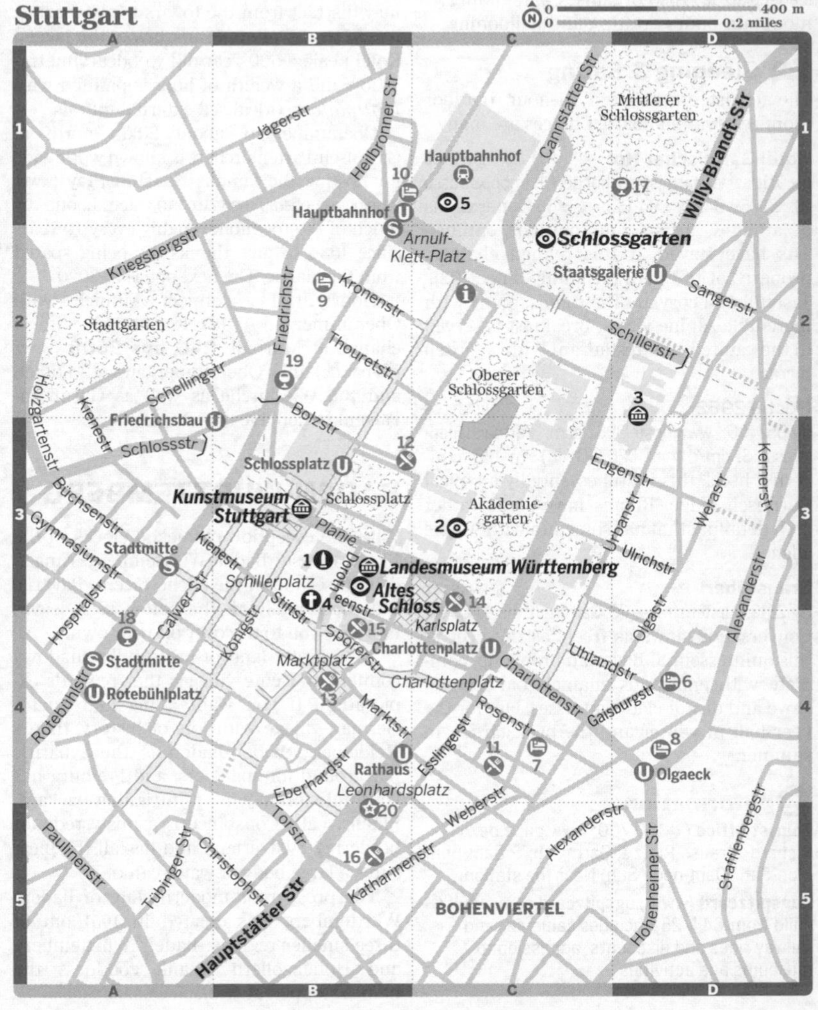

century **Stiftskirche** (Stiftstrasse 12) with its twin 61m-high late-Gothic towers.

The **tower** at the daggy main train station sports a revolving three-pointed star of the Mercedes-Benz. Get up close and personal and enjoy great views as part of the **TurmForum** (Hauptbahnhof; admission free; ⊙10am-9pm Apr-Sep, to 6pm Oct-Mar), an exhibition promoting the now notorious **Stuttgart 21 scheme** (www.bahnprojekt-stuttgart-ulm.de) to radically transform the station and surrounding tracks. When construction began in 2010, huge street protests shut down the city and the political ramifications are ongoing.

Museums & Galleries MUSEUMS

The Altes Schloss houses the **Landesmuseum Württemberg** (www.landesmuseum-stuttgart.de; Schillerplatz 6; adult/child €4.50/free; ⊙10am-5pm Tue-Sun), where exhibits include Roman-era discoveries.

Possibly more beautiful than the works within, the **Kunstmuseum Stuttgart** (www.kunstmuseum-stuttgart.de; Kleiner Schlossplatz 1; adult/child €5/3.50; ⊙10am-6pm Tue, Thu, Sat & Sun, to 9pm Wed & Fri) glows like a radioactive sugar cube at night. Highlights include works by Otto Dix, Dieter Roth and Willi Baumeister.

Adjoining the Schlossgarten you'll find the thriving **Staatsgalerie** (www.staatsgalerie.de; Konrad-Adenauer-Strasse 30; adult/child €5.50/4; ⊙10am-6pm Wed & Fri-Sun, to 8pm Tue & Thu), which houses an excellent collection from the Middle Ages to the present. It's especially rich in old German masters from the surrounding Swabia region.

TOP CHOICE **Car Museums** MUSEUMS

An arms race has broken out between the local auto giants, with both building vast and costly monuments to themselves.

The motor car was first developed by Gottlieb Daimler and Carl Benz at the end of the 19th century. The impressive **Mercedes-Benz Museum** (www.museum-mercedes-benz.com; Mercedesstrasse 100; adult/child €8/4; ⊙9am-6pm Tue-Sun) is in the suburb of Bad-Cannstatt; take S-Bahn 1 to Neckarpark. Don't mention Chrysler.

For even faster cars, cruise over to the striking **Porsche Museum** (www.porsche.com; Porscheplatz 1; adult/child €8/4; ⊙9am-6pm Tue-Sun); take S-Bahn 6 to Neuwirtshaus, north of the city. No word yet on whether they'll be adding a VW wing.

Pick up the excellent free booklet *Automotive Heritage* from the tourist office.

Sleeping

Der Zauberlehrling HOTEL €€€

(☎237 7770; www.zauberlehrling.de; Rosenstrasse 38; r €120-280; ❄📶) This consciously chic 'design hotel' in the Bohnenviertel has 17 named rooms, each unique and each a design sensation. Make a splash – or go down – in the Titanic-themed room with its waterbed. Amenities abound, including a breakfast garden.

City Hotel HOTEL €€

(☎210 810; www.cityhotel-stuttgart.de; Uhlandstrasse 18; r €80-120; 📶) Eschew the anonymity of Stuttgart's cookie-cutter chains for this intimate hotel just off Charlottenplatz.

Stuttgart

Top Sights

	Altes Schloss	B3
	Kunstmuseum Stuttgart	B3
	Landesmuseum Württemberg	B3
	Schlossgarten	C2

Sights

1	Friedrich Schiller Statue	B3
2	Neues Schloss	C3
3	Staatsgalerie	D2
4	Stiftskirche	B3
5	TurmForum	C1

Sleeping

6	City Hotel	D4
7	Der Zauberlehrling	C4
8	Hostel Alex 30	D4
9	Hotel Unger	B2
10	InterCity Hotel	B1

Eating

11	Basta	C4
12	Café Künstlerbund	B3
13	Food Market	B4
14	Grand Café Planie	C3
15	Markthalle	B4
16	Weinstube Fröhlich	B5

Drinking

17	Beer Garden	D1
18	Muttermilch	A4
19	Palast der Republik	B2

Entertainment

20	Kiste	B5

The 31 rooms are light, clean and modern, if slightly lacklustre. Breakfast on the terrace in summer is a bonus.

Hotel Unger HOTEL €€
(☎209 90; www.hotel-unger.de; Kronenstrasse 17; r €90-200; 📶) Right near the Hauptbahnhof, this hotel's corporate feel is offset by its snappy attention to detail and comfort. Guests rave about the generous breakfast with smoked fish, fresh fruit and pastries. Floors six and seven have good views.

InterCity Hotel HOTEL €€
(☎222 8233; www.intercityhotel.com; Hauptbahnhof; r €60-180; 📶) Right in the train station, the large rooms are utilitarian but a mere crawl from trains and a few steps from the centre. This is the perfect location if you plan a quick getaway or late arrival, plus you can watch any Stuttgart 21 protests.

Hostel Alex 30 HOSTEL €
(☎838 8950; www.alex30-hostel.de; Alexanderstrasse 30; dm €22, r €35-100; @📶) Tidy and orderly, near the Bohnenviertel. Take U-Bahn lines 5, 6 or 7 to Olgaeck.

Eating

Stuttgart is a great place to sample Swabian specialities such as *Spätzle* (home-made noodles) and *Maultaschen* (a hearty ravioli in broth). Local wines edge out beer in popularity.

The **food market** (Marktplatz; ⏰7.30am-1pm Tue, Thu & Sat) and the **Markthalle** (market hall; Dorotheenstrasse 4; ⏰7am-6.30pm Mon-Fri, 7am-4pm Sat), with their bounty of local produce and gourmet items, are the best features of the otherwise humdrum Marktplatz.

TOP CHOICE **Weinstube Fröhlich** SWABIAN €€
(Leonhardstrasse 5; mains €8-15) Hard in the midst of Stuttgart's paltry red-light district, this restaurant is traditional but not a period piece. Creative takes on local standards include superb *Maultaschen* and plate-covering schnitzel. The hardwood floors allow the food to shine. As the name implies, the local wine list is long.

Basta SWABIAN €€
(Wagnerstrasse 39; mains €10-18) The hum of chatter and herby smells fill this snug Bohnenviertel bistro, which has an intensely loyal following. Each flavour shines through in dishes like wild-garlic *Maultaschen*. Wine lovers have plenty of choice, and the bar is a classy place for a drink even if not dining.

DON'T MISS

BOHEMIAN BEANS

Stuttgart's most interesting neighbourhood is a short stroll from the centre. The **Bohnenviertel** (Bean District) takes its name from the diet of the poor tanners, dyers and craftsmen who lived here. Today the district's cobbled lanes and gabled houses harbour idiosyncratic galleries, workshops, bookstores, wine taverns, cafes and a red-light district.

Grand Café Planie CAFE €€
(Charlottenplatz 17; mains €5-15) Fully luxe, like a loaded E-class sedan, this fin de siècle cafe features a print of the *Grossstadt* triptych by the realist Otto Dix. You may wish the realism didn't extend to the lavish array of tortes in a long case, but have one anyway.

Café Künstlerbund CAFE €
(Schlossplatz 2; mains €7-10) Shelter under the arches facing the park or out in the sunshine at this funky cafe that's part of a large gallery. The drinks menu is huge, as are the choices for breakfast. When the weather gets nasty, duck into the groovy upstairs room.

Drinking & Entertainment

Hans-im-Glück Platz, centred on a namesake fountain depicting the caged Grimm's fairy-tale character Lucky Hans, is a hub of bars. Club- and lounge-lined Theodor-Heuss-Strasse is thronged with sashaying hipsters. A **beer garden** (Cannstatter Strasse 18) in the Mittlerer Schlossgarten, northeast of the main train station, has beautiful views over the city.

Palast der Republik BAR
(Friedrichstrasse 27) A legendary and tiny pillbox of a bar that pulls a huge crowd of laid-back, genial drinkers. Statuary and stickers abound.

Kiste JAZZ CLUB
(Hauptstätter Strasse 35; ⏰4pm-2am Mon-Thu, to 3am Fri & Sat) This hole-in-the-wall bar, often jam-packed, is the city's leading jazz venue, with concerts nightly except Sunday, starting at 9.30pm or 10pm.

Muttermilch LOUNGE
(www.muttermilch-stuttgart.de; Theodor-Heuss-Strasse 23) Good-looking Stuttgarters dance to soul and funk in nouveau Alpine chic before hopping off to other nearby clubs.

Information

Königstrasse is the spine of central Stuttgart, with most of the major stores and malls.

Stuttcard (from €18) Free museum entry and transport, plus discounts on events, activities and guided tours. Sold at the tourist office and some hotels.

Tourist office (www.stuttgart-tourist.de; Königstrasse 1a; ⌚9am-8pm Mon-Fri, 9am-6pm Sat, 11am-6pm Sun)

Getting There & Around

Stuttgart's **airport** (SGT; www.stuttgart-airport.com) is south of the city and includes service from Air Berlin, Germanwings and Lufthansa. It's served by S2 and S3 trains (€3.30, 30 minutes from the Hauptbahnhof).

There are frequent train departures for all major German cities, and many international ones, such as Zürich and Paris.

DESTINATION	PRICE	DURATION (HR)
Frankfurt	€57	1¼
Munich	€53	2¼
Nuremberg	€38	2¼

One-way fares on Stuttgart's **public transport network** (www.vvs.de) are €2 in the central zone; a central-zone day pass is €6.

Tübingen

☎07071 / POP 84,000

Forty kilometres south of Stuttgart, Tübingen mixes all the charms of a late-medieval city – a hilltop fortress, cobbled alleys and half-timbered houses – with the erudition and mischief of a university town. Wander the winding alleys of old stone walls, then take a boat ride down the Neckar River.

On **Marktplatz**, the centre of town, is the 1435 **Rathaus**, with its baroque facade and astronomical clock. The nearby late-Gothic **Stiftkirche** (Am Holz-markt; ⌚9am-5pm) houses the tombs of the Württemberg dukes and has excellent medieval stained-glass windows. The Renaissance **Schloss Hohentübingen** (Burgsteig 11), now part of the university, has fine views over the steep, red-tiled rooftops of the old town, and a museum.

Sleeping & Eating

Hotel am Schloss HOTEL €€

(☎929 40; www.hotelamschloss.de; Burgsteige 18; r €65-135; 📶) Some come for the restaurant's legendary *Maultaschen* (mains €9 to €15), some for peerless castle views, and others for the dapper rooms ensconced in a 16th-century building.

Wurstküche GERMAN €€

(Am Lustnauer Tor 8; mains €10-16) Stroll up a hill for fine local foods sourced from organic farmers.

Weinhaus Beck WINE TAVERN

(Am Markt 1) Rarely an empty table at this convivial wine tavern beside the Rathaus.

Getting There & Away

The definition of a day trip: trains between Tübingen and Stuttgart run every 30 minutes (€12, one hour).

Heidelberg

☎06221 / POP 146,000

Heidelberg's baroque old town built from rose-hued sandstone, lively university atmosphere, excellent pubs and evocative half-ruined castle make it hugely popular with visitors, 3.5 million of whom flock here each year. They are following in the footsteps of the 19th-century romantics, most notably the poet Goethe. Britain's William Turner also loved the city, which inspired him to paint some of his greatest landscapes.

Less starry-eyed was Mark Twain (www.mark-twain-in-heidelberg.de), who in 1878 began his European travels with a three-month stay in Heidelberg, recounting his bemused observations in *A Tramp Abroad.*

Sights

TOP CHOICE **Schloss** CASTLE

(www.schloss-heidelberg.de; adult/child €5/3, tours €4; ⌚8am-5.30pm) Heidelberg's imposing icon is one of Germany's finest

HEIDELBERG FAST TRACK

Heidelberg's captivating **old town** starts to reveal itself only after a charm-free 15-minute walk east from the main train station. Cut to the chase and go direct to the heart of town with bus 32 to Universitätsplatz or bus 33 to Bergbahn, whichever leaves first. Later, stroll west the length of Hauptstrasse (the town's shopping spine) to Bismarckplatz and catch a tram to the station.

Heidelberg

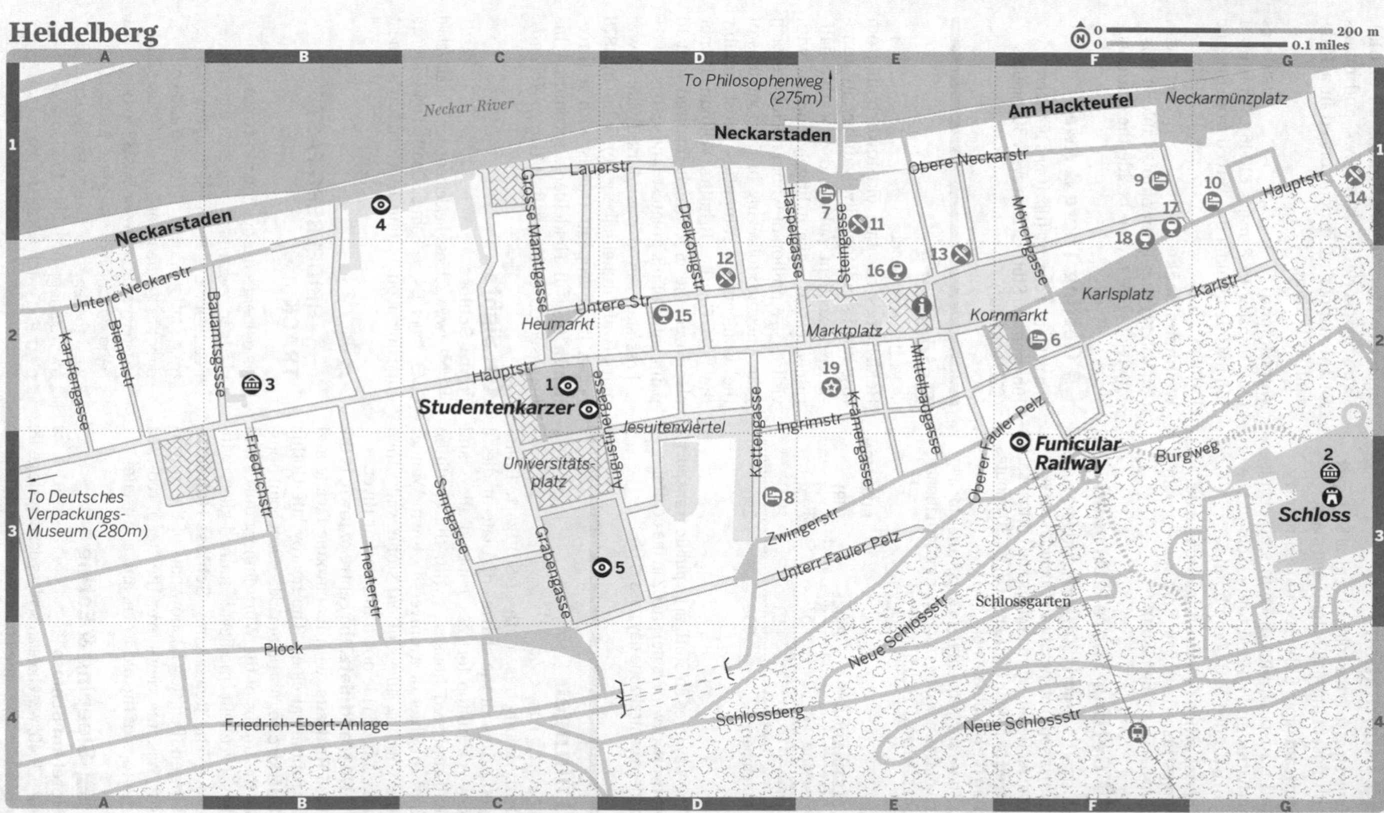
0 200 m
0 0.1 miles
To Philosophenweg (275m)
Neckar River
Am Hackteufel
Neckarmünzplatz
Neckarstaden
Neckarstaden
Lauerstr
Obere Neckarstr
Grosse Mamtlgasse
Dreikönigstr
Haspelgasse
Steingasse
Mönchgasse
Hauptstr
Untere Neckarstr
Untere Str
Heumarkt
Marktplatz
Kornmarkt
Karlsplatz
Karlstr
Karpfengasse
Bienenstr
Bauamtsgssse
Hauptstr
Studentenkarzer
Jesuitenviertel
Ingrimstr
Kettengasse
Krämergasse
Mittelbadgasse
Augustinergasse
Universitäts-platz
Friedrichstr
Sandgasse
Theaterstr
Grabengasse
Zwingerstr
Unterr Fauler Pelz
Oberer Fauler Pelz
Funicular Railway
Burgweg
Schloss
Schlossgarten
Neue Schlossstr
Neue Schlossstr
Schlossberg
Plöck
Friedrich-Ebert-Anlage
To Deutsches Verpackungs-Museum (280m)

Heidelberg

examples of grand Gothic-Renaissance architecture. The building's half-ruined state only enhances its romantic appeal (Twain called it 'the Lear of inanimate nature'). Seen from anywhere in the Altstadt, this striking red-sandstone castle dominates the hillside. The entry fee covers the castle, the **Grosses Fass** (Great Vat), an enormous 18th-century keg capable of holding 221,726L; and the **Deutsches Apothekenmuseum** (German Pharmaceutical Museum; Schlosshof 1).

Ride the **Funicular Railway** (one way €4; 9am-8pm summer, to 5pm other times) to the castle from lower Kornmarkt station, or enjoy an invigorating 15-minute walk up steep, stone-laid lanes. Either way be sure to walk down, especially through the less-crowded paths to the east. The funicular continues up to the **Königstuhl**, where there are good views (additional fare €9).

Old Town HISTORIC QUARTER

Dominating Universitätsplatz are the 18th-century **Alte Universität** and the **Neue Universität**. On the back side, find the **Studentenkarzer** (student jail; Augustinergasse 2; adult/child €3/2.50; 10am-6pm Tue-Sun Apr-Sep, 10am-4pm Tue-Sat Oct-Mar). From 1778 to 1914 this jail was used for misbehaved students (crimes included drinking, singing and womanising). The **Marstall** is the former arsenal, now a student Mensa (cafeteria).

The **Kurpfälzisches Museum** (Palatinate Museum; 583 402; Hauptstrasse 97; adult/child €3/2; 10am-6pm Tue-Sun) contains paintings, sculptures and the jawbone of the 600,000-year-old Heidelberg Man.

The Heidelberg region has been a major global supplier of printing equipment, much of it used to create packaging for products. The **Deutsches Verpackungs-Museum** (German Museum of Packaging; Hauptstrasse 22; adult/child €3.50/2.50; 1-6pm Wed-Sun) celebrates classic packages such as the Nivea jar as well as less successful items such as Titanic-brand cigarettes.

A stroll along the **Philosophenweg**, north of the Neckar River, gives a welcome respite from Heidelberg's tourist hordes.

The tourist office runs English-language **guided tours** (adult/student €7/5; tours 10.30am Fri & Sat Apr-Oct) that depart from the Löwenbrunnen (Lions Fountain) at Universtätsplatz.

Sleeping

Finding any accommodation during Heidelberg's high season can be difficult. Arrive early in the day or book ahead.

Hotel Goldener Hecht HOTEL €€

(536 80; www.hotel-goldener-hecht.de; Steingasse 2; r €65-110;) Goethe almost slept here: the hotel would have kept the famous author had the clerk on duty not been so uppity. Ever since, guests at this family-run place have received a warm welcome. Some of the 13 sparkling rooms, each unique, have views of the Neckar River.

Kulturbrauerei Hotel HOTEL €€

(502 980; www.heidelberger-kulturbrauerei.de; Leyergasse 6; r €110-180;) Great beer comes second at this swank microbrewery hotel.

The stylish rooms are decked out in soft creams with shiny parquet floors and large windows. Some rooms on the top floor have soaring A-frame ceilings.

Hotel Zum Pfalzgrafen HOTEL €€
(☎204 89; www.hotel-zum-pfalzgrafen.de; Kettengasse 21; r €70-110) Polished pine floors are a nice touch at this family-run place, which has 24 clean-lined rooms that belie the hotel's classic 18th-century facade. The breakfast buffet is included.

Hotel Am Kornmarkt HOTEL €€
(☎905 830; www.hotelamkornmarkt.de; Kornmarkt 7; r €40-110) Discreet and understated, this Altstadt favourite has 20 pleasant, well-kept rooms. The pricier rooms have great views of the Kornmarkt, while cheaper ones share spotless hall showers.

Steffi's Hostel HOSTEL €
(☎0176-2016 2200; www.hostelheidelberg.de; Alte Eppelheimer Strasse 50; dm €20-24, r €45-60; @📶) Backpackers sing the praises of this hostel, housed in a one-time brick factory near the Hauptbahnhof. Steffi greets guests warmly with bounteous perks.

Sudpfanne HOSTEL €
(☎163 636; www.heidelberger-sudpfanne.de; Hauptstrasse 223; dm €16; 📶) Right in the centre of things, the mood is set by the wine-barrel entrance (it's also a cafe).

Eating

Try heading down the small streets leading away from Marktplatz to increase your ratio of locals.

Zur Herrenmühle GERMAN €€
(Hauptstrasse 239; mains €9-24; ⊙dinner Mon-Sat) Serves traditional, classic south-German food that veers so far south that Italian flavours drift in. Dine under the ancient wood beams of a 17th-century mill or outside in a serene garden. Rustically elegant, with geraniums hanging over the windows.

Schiller's Café CAFE €
(Heiliggeiststrasse 5; snacks €2-4) Whisper quietly about this half-timbered cafe, housed in one of Heidelberg's oldest buildings, where the movie *Schille* was filmed. Hot chocolates with cinnamon, home-made cakes, quiches, and wines are mostly organic.

Brauhaus Vetter GERMAN €€
(Steingasse 9; mains €7-14) A popular brewery that serves up lots of hearty fare to absorb the suds. The copper kettles gleam. Groups of six or more can order the Brewer's feast, a sausage, pretzel, radish, meat and cheese smorgasbord.

Café Burkardt CAFE €
(Untere Strasse 27; cake & snacks €3-8) Full of doily-draped nooks and dark-wood crannies, this nostalgic cafe tempts with Heidelberg's tastiest tarts and cheesecakes. Opt for a table in the courtyard, where Weimar Republic president Friedrich Ebert was born.

Drinking & Entertainment

'German university life is a very free life; it seems to have no restraints.' So observed Mark Twain, and two centuries later little has changed; you won't have to go far to find a happening backstreet bar. Lots of the action centres on Untere Strasse.

Two ancient pubs, **Zum Roten Ochsen** (☎209 77; Hauptstrasse 213) and **Zum Sepp'l** (☎230 85; Hauptstrasse 217), are now filled with tourists reliving the uni days they never had.

Cave54 LIVE MUSIC
(www.cave54.de; Krämergasse 2; ⊙Thu-Sun) For live jazz and blues, head to this stone cellar that oozes character. Some nights there's a DJ.

MaxBar CAFE
(Marktplatz 5) A French-style cafe with classic views of the Marktplatz. Perfect for a beer or a pastis, it's especially popular on weekend nights. Wave to the Napoleon bust above the bar.

Destille BAR
(Untere Strasse 16) Known for the tree trunk behind the bar, this mellow and hugely popular pub pours stiff drinks that inspire the chess players here to make rather unorthodox moves.

Information

Heidelberg Card (from €13) Discounts and free admission to many sights.

Tourist office (☎194 33; www.heidelberg-marketing.de) Hauptbahnhof (Willy-Brandt-Platz 1; ⊙9am-7pm Mon-Sat year-round, 10am-6pm Sun Apr-Nov); Marktplatz (⊙8am-5pm Mon-Fri, 10am-5pm Sat)

Getting There & Around

There are hourly IC trains to/from Frankfurt (€19, one hour) and Stuttgart (€24, 40 minutes). The frequent service to Mannheim (€5, 15 minutes) has connections to cities throughout Germany.

Bismarckplatz is the main public-transport hub. One-way tickets for the excellent bus and tram system (www.vrn.de) are €2.20.

Baden-Baden

☎07221 / POP 55,000

Who would want to bathe naked with a bunch of strangers? That's the question at the heart of the matter in Baden-Baden, the storied and ritzy spa town. The answer, of course, should be, anyone who wants to enjoy a truly self-indulgent experience.

And let's see, shall we call them, well, prudes can still get a bit of the pleasure while staying suited and segregated. The natural hot springs have attracted visitors since Roman times, but this small city only really became fashionable in the 19th century, when it became a destination of royalty. It is stately, closely cropped and salubrious. Take the 69°C plunge.

Sights & Activities

Baths BATHS

The 19th-century **Friedrichsbad** (www.roemisch-irisches-bad.de; Römerplatz 1; bathing program €21-31; 9am-10pm) is the reason for your journey. It's decadently Roman in style and provides a muscle-melting 16-step bathing program. No clothing is allowed inside; several sections are mixed on most days.

The more modern **Caracalla-Therme** (www.caracalla.de; Römerplatz 1; entrance from €14; 8am-10pm) is a vast, modern complex of outdoor and indoor pools, and hot- and cold-water grottoes. You must wear a bathing suit and bring your own towel.

Historic Town HISTORIC BUILDINGS

The 2000-year-old **Römische Badruinen** (Roman Bath Ruins; Römerplatz 1; adult/child €2.50/1; 11am-noon & 3-6pm mid-Mar–mid-Nov) are worth a quick look, but for a real taste of Baden-Baden head to the **Kurhaus**, built in the 1820s, which houses the ornate **casino** (www.casino-baden-baden.de; Kaiserallee 1; admission €3, guided tours adult/child €4/2; tours 9.30am-noon, gambling after 2pm), which improves greatly after the entryway that looks like a meeting hall. Wear what you want for tours; for gambling men must wear a coat and tie (rentals €11).

Enjoy a taste of the warm and salty water that made Baden-Baden famous at the stolid, porticoed **Trinkhalle** (Pump Room; Kaiserallee 3). The water's free but a flimsy plastic cup (an eco nightmare!) will cost you €0.20.

Sleeping & Eating

Most restaurants huddle in the pedestrianised stretch around Leopoldsplatz. Nightlife is suited for people who've had the life boiled out of them.

Steigenberger Europäischer Hof HOTEL €€€

(☎93 30; www.badischer-hof.steigenberger.com; Kaiserallee 2; r €160-300; @) Suitably grand to go with the climes locally, this 120-bed dowager stays dolled up morning to night. Rooms span the gamut, from 'economy' with views of the courtyard to rather grand luxe options with balconies and views of the park and passing swells.

Hotel am Markt HOTEL €

(☎270 40; www.hotel-am-markt-baden.de; Marktplatz 18; r €43-80; @) This peach-fronted hotel next to the Stiftskirche is a real find. Its 23 rooms are homey, bathrooms squeaky-clean and the silence is broken only by church bells.

Rizzi ITALIAN €€€

(Augustaplatz 1; mains €16-24) A summertime Italian favourite, this stout pink villa's tree-shaded patio faces Lichtentaler Allee. Fresh seafood, saffron-infused risotto and enticing pastas pair nicely with local rieslings.

Jensens CAFE €

(Sophienstrasse 45; meals €5-9;) Opposite Caracalla-Therme, this bistro with a patio has a hip feel with its pepper-red walls, wood floors and jazzy tunes. Honour nearby Strasbourg with a *Flammkuchen* on the patio.

Information

The **tourist office** (www.baden-baden.com; Kaiserallee 3; 10am-5pm Mon-Sat, 2-5pm Sun) is in the Trinkhalle.

Getting There & Around

Baden-Airpark (FKB; www.badenairpark.de) has daily Ryanair service but, like many tiny airports served by the budget carrier, getting to/from the airport can be a challenge. Consult the airport website for details on the sketchy service.

Baden-Baden is on the busy Mannheim-Basel train line. Frequent local trains serve Karlsruhe (€8, 15 minutes) and Offenburg (€9, 20 minutes), from where you can make connections to much of Germany.

Buses 201, 216 and 245 traverse the 7km to Leopoldsplatz (€2).

BLACK FOREST

The Black Forest (Schwarzwald) gets its name from its dark canopy of evergreens, which evoke mystery and allure in many. Although some parts heave with visitors, a 20-minute walk from even the most crowded spots will put you in quiet countryside interspersed with enormous traditional farmhouses and patrolled by amiable dairy cows. It's not nature wild and remote, but bucolic and picturesque.

The Black Forest is east of the Rhine between Karlsruhe and Basel. It's shaped like

Black Forest (Schwarzwald)

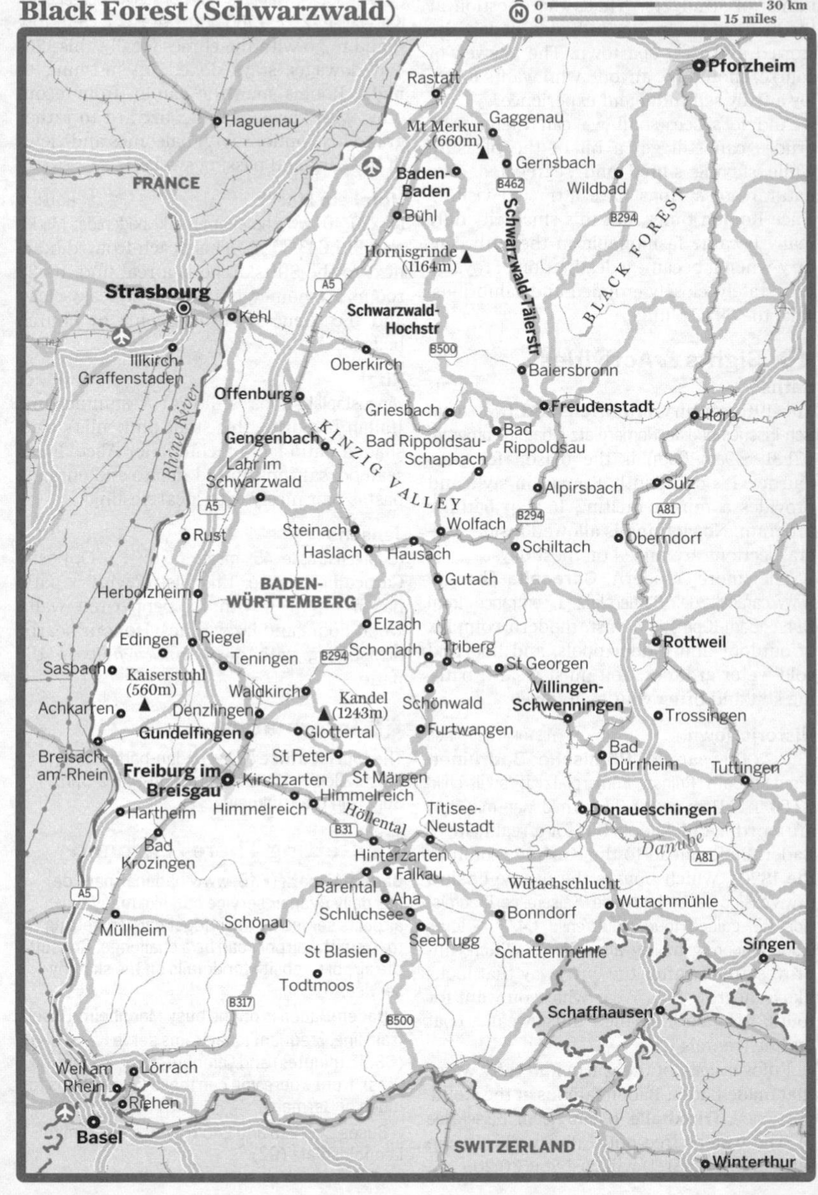

a bean, about 160km long and 50km wide. From north to south there are four good bases for your visit: Freudenstadt, Schiltach, Triberg and Titisee. Each has good train links.

With a car you'll find a visit especially rewarding, as you can wander the rolling hills and deep valleys at will. One of the main tourist roads is the Schwarzwald-Hochstrasse (B500), which runs from Baden-Baden to Freudenstadt and from Triberg to Waldshut. Other thematic roads with maps provided by tourist offices include Schwarzwald Bäderstrasse (spa town route), Schwarzwald Panoramastrasse (panoramic view route) and Badische Weinstrasse (wine route). Make certain you have an excellent commercial regional road map with you, too.

And, yes, there are many, many places to buy cuckoo clocks (you pay at least €150 for a good one).

FOREST FOODIE FAVES

Regional specialities include *Schwarz wälder Schinken* (ham), which is smoked and served in a variety of ways. Rivalling those ubiquitous clocks in fame (but not price), *Schwarzwälder Kirschtorte* (Black Forest cake) is a chocolate and cherry concoction. Most hotels and guest houses have restaurants serving traditional hearty (but expensive) German fare. Wash it all down with Rothaus, the crisp local pilsener.

Freudenstadt

07441 / POP 24,000

Freudenstadt is a good base for exploring the northern Black Forest and hikes into the surrounding countryside. It's most notable feature is a vast cafe- and shop-lined **market square** that is the largest in the country. The **tourist office** (www.freudenstadt.de; Marktplatz 64; 9am-6pm Mon-Fri, 10am-2pm Sat & Sun May-Oct, shorter hr other times) is good for local hiking ideas.

The Gaiser family extend a warm welcome at **Hotel Adler** (915 20; www.adler-fds.de; Forststrasse 15-17; r €45-95, mains €8-18;), a guesthouse with comfy, fusty rooms and a terrace. The bistro serves Swabian faves like *Spätzle* (egg noodles).

Don't judge **Hotel Schwanen** (915 50; www.schwanen-freudenstadt.de; Forststrasse 6; r €40-110, mains €9-16;) by its 1970s-style reception, as the rooms have a mod patina (dig the stripes behind the bed). The restaurant is famous for its *Riesenpfannkuchen* (giant pancakes).

From Freudenstadt, hourly trains run south to Schiltach (€7, 30 minutes) and north to the important transfer point of Karlsruhe (€16, 1½ hours). Stuttgart has hourly trains (€16, 1½ hours).

Alpirsbach

A small town, Alpirsbach, 10km north of Schiltach, is worth a trip for its 12th-century Benedictine abbey, **Kloster Alpirsbach** (admission €4; 10am-5.30pm Mon-Sat, 11am-4.30pm Sun, shorter hr in winter). It's often uncrowded and if you find yourself alone in the large Romanesque complex it can be quite eerie. The cloisters are impressive, as is the small museum that documents the lives of those who lived here.

Just across the old complex you'll find what's kept the monks busy all these years: the **Alpirsbacher Klosterbräu** (Marktplatz 1; tours €6.50; tours 2.30pm) brewery. Tours include a couple of glasses of the brew. To sample them all, head to nearby **Löwen-Post** (07444-955 95; www.loewen-post.de; Markplatz 12; r €40-70, mains €6-12), where you can get a sampling flight of six of the monks' finest. The food is top-notch Swabian and the rooms in the old inn have an unfussy, modern vibe.

Alpirsbach is a stop for the hourly trains linking Schiltach and Freudenstadt.

Schiltach

07836 / POP 4000

A contender for the prettiest town in the Black Forest is Schiltach, where there is the always-underlying roar of the intersecting Kinzig and Schiltach Rivers. Half-timbered buildings lean at varying angles along the criss-crossing hillside lanes.

The **tourist office** (www.schiltach.de; Hauptstrasse 5; 10am-5pm Mon-Fri, to 2pm Sat Apr-Oct) can help with accommodation and has a lot of English-language information. Be sure not to miss the **Schüttesäge-museum** (Hauptstrasse 1; 11am-5pm Tue-Sun Apr-Oct), which is part of an old mill built on the river. It shows what water power could do. The **Markt** has several tiny museums that cover local history and culture. Most are open in the afternoons during the tourist season.

There are numerous hotels and restaurants in the compact centre. Choosing a room is an adventure at **Gasthof Sonne** (☎957 570; www.sonneschiltach.de; Marktplatz 3; r €43-80; 📶). Shall it be a romantic rose-tinged nest or an armour-filled knight's chamber? The restaurant is excellent.

Nineteen generations of the same family have run the 16th-century inn **Weysses Rössle** (☎387; www.weysses-roessle.de; Schenkenzeller Strasse 42; r €50-70; 📶), where countrified rooms feature snazzy bathrooms. The woodsy tavern uses locally sourced, organic fare.

Schiltach is on the train line linking Offenburg (€8, 45 minutes) via Hausach to Freudenstadt (€5, 30 minutes), with hourly services. Change at Hausach for Triberg (€7, 50 minutes).

Triberg

☎07722 / POP 5400

Heir to the Black Forest cake recipe, nesting ground of the world's biggest cuckoos and spring of Germany's highest waterfall – Triberg is a torrent of Schwarzwald superlatives and attracts gushers of guests.

Start with a troll, er, we mean stroll (but trolls of the garden kind are sold in all the many gift shops). There's a one-hour walk to the stair-stepped **waterfalls**; it starts near the **tourist office** (www.triberg.de; Wallfahrtstrasse 4; ⏰10am-5pm), which also has a small museum. The duelling oversized cuckoos are at opposite ends of town (we prefer the one in Schonach).

Above the shop of master woodcarver Gerald Burger is **Kukucksnest** (☎869 487; Wallfahrtstrasse 15; r €50-60), a beautiful nest he has carved for guests.

The kirsch-scented Black Forest cake at **Café Schäfer** (www.cafe-schaefer-triberg.de; Hauptstrasse 33; ⏰9am-6pm, from 11am Sun, closed Wed) is the real deal; it has the original recipe to prove it.

Triberg is midway on the spectacular Karlsruhe (€22, 1½ hours) to Konstanz (€22, 1½ hours) train line. There are hourly services and good connections. Change at Hausach for Schiltach and Freudenstadt. The station is 1.7km from the centre; take any bus to the Markt.

BLACK FOREST SAVINGS

Most Black Forest hotels will give you a **Schwarzwald-Gästekarte** (Black Forest Guest Card) for discounts or freebies on museums, ski lifts, events and attractions. Some versions entitle you to free use of public transport.

Tourist offices in the Black Forest sell the three-day **SchwarzwaldCard** (www.blackforest-tourism.com; adult/child €32/21) for admission to around 150 attractions and activities.

Furtwangen

In Furtwangen, 17km south of Triberg, visit the **Deutsches Uhrenmuseum** (German Clock Museum; www.deutsches-uhrenmuseum.de; Gerwigstrasse 11; adult/child €4/3; ⏰9am-6pm Apr-Oct, 10am-5pm Nov-Mar) for a look at the traditional Black Forest skill of clock-making. A fun demo shows what puts the 'cuc' and the 'koo' in the namesake clock. Buses from Triberg stop here.

Titisee-Neustadt

☎07651 / POP 12,000

The iconic glacial **lake** here draws no shortage of visitors to the busy village of Titisee-Neustadt. Walking around Titisee or paddle-boating across it are major activities. If you have wheels, ride or drive into the surrounding rolling meadows to see some of the truly enormous traditional house-barn combos.

The **tourist office** (www.titisee-neustadt.de; Strandbadstrasse 4; ⏰9am-6pm Mon-Fri, 10am-1pm Sat & Sun) can help you arrange a farm stay. The short streets radiating off the lakefront are lined with clock and schlock shops. But fanciers will be in hog heaven for all the **Black Forest ham outlets**. It's time to picnic!

Titisee is linked to Freiburg by frequent train services (€10, 40 minutes). To reach Triberg to the north, there are scenic hourly connections via Neustadt and Donaueschingen (€16, two hours).

Feldberg

The Black Forest **ski season** runs from late December to March. While there is good downhill skiing, the area is more suited to cross-country skiing. The centre for winter

WORTH A TRIP

HELL TO HEAVEN

Just south of Furtwangen, look for a tiny road off to the west evocatively called the **Hexenloch** (Witch's Hole). This narrow road penetrates deep into a narrow valley of rushing white water and tall trees. It alone is worth the cost of a car hire – which is the only way to enjoy the hole. Even on warm days it's cold as a witch's you-know-what down here (one family in the valley actually installed a mirror on a mountain to shine a beam of reflected sunshine). The road follows the bends in the river and you'll see shaded banks of snow months after it has melted elsewhere. Look for small roadhouses with little spinning water wheels.

West of the south end of the Hexenloch road, **St Peter** is a tiny town that offers a start at redemption with a twin-towered, onion-domed namesake abbey. It's an 18th-century vision in gold, glitter and gilt that would do any Las Vegas designer proud.

Finish your quest with a baptism. Going northwest of Furtwangen on the Katzensteigstrasse, follow signs for the 7km drive to **Donauquelle**, a spring that is a source of the Danube. High on a knoll, a short path leads down to the water burbling forth from the ground, beginning an adventure that ends 2900km later in the Black Sea. Hikes here fan out in all directions. You can bed down amid the beauty and tranquillity at **Kolmenhof** (☎07723-931 025; www.kolmenhof.de; r from €85), a mountain chalet with a cafe with organic food and slow-food principles. Heaven indeed.

sports is around Titisee (the ski jumps are a prominent landmark), with uncrowded downhill ski runs at **Feldberg** (www.liftverbund-feldberg.de; day pass adult/child €27/15) and numerous graded cross-country trails.

In summer you can use the lifts to reach the summit of the sallow-sloped Feldberg (1493m) for a wondrous panorama that stretches to the Alps.

Feldberg is 15km south of Titisee. It can be reached by bus 7300 from Titisee (€4, 12 minutes, hourly) or in season by free ski shuttles.

Freiburg im Breisgau

☎0761 / POP 214,000

Nestled between hills and vineyards, Freiburg im Breisgau has a medieval Altstadt made timeless by a thriving university community. There's a sense of fun here exemplified by the *bächle* (tiny medieval canals) running down the middle of streets. Perhaps being Germany's sunniest city contributes to the mood.

Founded in 1120 and ruled for centuries by the Austrian Habsburgs, Freiburg has retained many traditional features, although major reconstruction was necessary following WWII. The monumental 13th-century cathedral is the city's key landmark but the real attractions are the vibrant cafes, bars and street life, plus the local wines. The best times for tasting are July, for the four days of *Weinfest* (Wine Festival), or August, for the nine days of *Weinkost* (wine tasting).

Sights

Medieval Freiburg HISTORIC QUARTER

The major sight in Freiburg is the 700-year-old **Münster** (Cathedral; Münsterplatz; tower adult/child €1.50/1; ⊙9.30am-5pm Mon-Sat, 1-5pm Sun), a classic example of both high- and late-Gothic architecture that looms over Münsterplatz, Freiburg's market square. Ascend the **west tower** to the stunning pierced spire for great views of Freiburg and, on a clear day, the Kaiserstuhl wine region and the Vosages Mountains to the west. Spend time in contemplation of the art-filled **chapels** and **choirs**, then search out the **gargoyle** outside that once spouted water from his butt.

South of the Münster stands the solid red **Kaufhaus**, the 16th-century merchants' hall. You can sense the Middle Ages – but not the smell – along **Fischerau** and **Gerberau**.

The bustling **university quarter** is northwest of the **Martinstor** (one of the old city gates). On the walk in from the station, note the field of **grape vines** from around the world.

Augustinermuseum MUSEUM

(☎201 2531; Salzstrasse 32; adult/child €6/4; ⊙10am-5pm Tue-Sun) A fine collection of

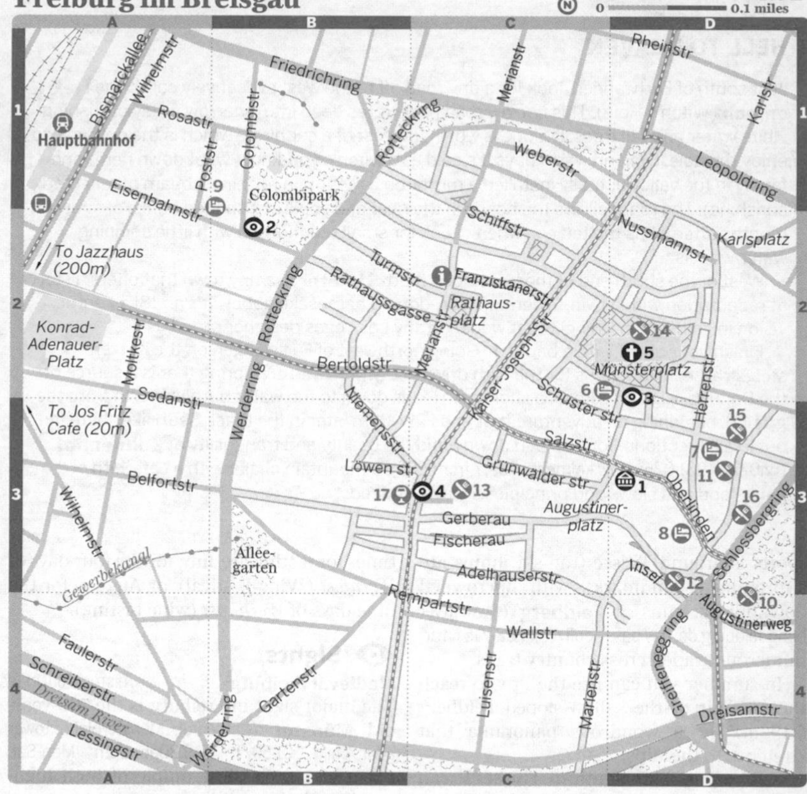

medieval art, including works by Matthias Grünewald and Cranach plus lavish stained-glass windows, is the highlight of this museum, which has reopened after a massive refit.

Schauinslandbahn CABLE CAR
(www.bergwelt-schauinsland.de; one way/return adult €8/12, child €5/7; ⏲9am-5pm Jan-Jun, to 6pm Jul-Sep, 9.30am-5pm Oct-Dec) Ride high to the **Schauinsland peak** (1284m). From these Black Forest highlands numerous easy and well-marked trails make the Schauinsland area ideal for day walks. From Freiburg take tram 4 south to Günterstal and then bus 21 to Talstation.

Sleeping

Hotel zum Roten Bären HOTEL €€
(☎387 870; www.roter-baeren.de; Oberlinden 12; r €100-180; 📶) Billed as Germany's oldest guest house, this blush-wine-pink hotel near Schwabentor dates to 1120. Though the vaulted cellar is medieval, rooms are modern, creak-free and have sleek wood furnishings.

Hotel Schwarzwälder Hof HOTEL €€
(☎380 30; www.schwarzwaelder-hof.eu; Herrenstrasse 43; r €65-110; 📶) This bijou hotel has an unrivalled style-for-euro ratio. Some of the 42 rooms have postcard views of the Altstadt. A wrought-iron staircase has such a dramatic sweep that you may be tempted to make your entrance twice. Bargain singles share bathrooms.

Hotel Oberkirch HOTEL €€
(☎202 6868; www.hotel-oberkirch.de; Münsterplatz 22; r €95-175; 📶) Our readers sing the praises of this green-shuttered, 250-year-old hotel, with the Münster views of a million postcards. The 26 countrified rooms reveal a Laura Ashley love of florals. Enjoy a floral bouquet from the excellent wine selection on offer in the garden.

Freiburg im Breisgau

Sights
1 Augustinermuseum ... D3
2 Grape Vines ... B2
3 Kaufhaus ... D2
4 Martinstor ... C3
5 Münster ... D2

Sleeping
6 Hotel Oberkirch ... C2
7 Hotel Schwarzwälder Hof ... D3
8 Hotel zum Roten Bären ... D3
9 Park Hotel Post ... B1

Eating
10 Biergarten Greiffenegg-Schlössle ... D4
11 Englers Weinkrügle ... D3
12 Hausbrauerei Feierling ... D3
13 Markthalle ... C3
14 Produce Market ... D2
15 Wolfshöhle ... D3
16 Zylinder Feinkost ... D3

Drinking
17 Schlappen ... B3

Black Forest Hostel HOSTEL €
(☎881 7870; www.blackforest-hostel.de; Kartäuserstrasse 33; dm €14-23, s/d €30/50; @) Freiburg's funkiest budget digs are five minutes' stroll from the centre. Overlooking vineyards, this former factory has been lovingly revamped as an industrial-themed hostel. Bike hire costs €5 per day.

Park Hotel Post HOTEL €€€
(☎385 480; www.park-hotel-post.de; Am Colombipark 63; r €110-200;) Slip back to the more graceful age of art nouveau at this refined pile overlooking Colombipark, with 45 summery rooms decorated in pastel blues and yellows. Attentive service and generous breakfasts sweeten the deal.

Eating & Drinking

The fragrant smoke around the Münster at lunch isn't incense, it's the smoke from dozens of grills loaded with sausages. Get one on a bun and pile it with grilled onions (€2). On Saturday you can have veggies (and fruit and cheese and...) with your wurst when the weekly **produce market** operates. It's one of Germany's best.

Otherwise, your choices are myriad. Freiburg likes a good meal out – and a drink. Or two.

TOP CHOICE **Wolfshöhle** FUSION €€€
(☎790 98; www.wolfshoehle-freiburg.de; Konvikstrasse 8; mains €18-30; lunch & dinner Thu-Tue) Fresh fare from the region – that simple philosophy guides the ever-changing menu here at one of Freiburg's best. The classic old exterior hides a thoroughly modern dining room, with sleek wood surfaces and black leather seating. Swabian favourites and dishes from neighbouring regions transcend the everyday. Book.

Markthalle MARKET HALL €
(Grünwälderstrasse 2; meals €3-8; 7am-8pm) Just when you think you've seen all the stalls here that sell food from around the world, you round a corner and there's more. Each has a speciality, whether it's South Asian, Italian or simply a bevy of the heartiest soups you could hope to warm by. Find a communal table, get a glass of local wine or beer and enjoy.

Hausbrauerei Feierling BREWERY €€
(Gerberau 46; mains €6-12;) Starring one of Freiburg's best beer gardens, this brewpub serves great vegetarian options and humungous schnitzels with *Brägele* (chipped potatoes). If you drink one too many, take care not to fall in the stream or you may become dinner for the open-jawed *Krokodil*. Huge, fun beer gardens.

Schlappen PUB €
(☎334 94; Löwenstrasse 2; 11am-1am Mon-Thu, to 3am Fri & Sat, 3pm-1am Sun) With its jazz-themed back room and poster-plastered walls, this student watering hole is a perennial fave. Try a *Flammkuche* (tasty, crispy Alsatian pizza), then forget about it with absinthe.

Englers Weinkrügle GERMAN €€
(Konviktstrasse 12; mains €8-15; Tue-Sun) A warm, woody *Weinstube* with wisteria growing out front and regional flavours on the menu. The trout in various guises is delicious. If you were wondering what's the deal with local wine, answers abound.

Zylinder Feinkost ITALIAN DELI €
(Konviktstrasse 51; snacks €5-8; lunch) Opera plays in this little Italian deli, where Matteo's passion for the minutiae of Chianti and antipasti is contagious. Pull up a stack of crates

for a glass of *prosecco* and home-made focaccia with wafer-thin prosciutto.

Biergarten Greiffenegg-Schlössle BEER GARDEN €

(Schlossbergring 3; mains €5) Perched above Freiburg, this terrace beer garden is great for watching the sun set over the city's red rooftops. Save your strength for drinking and ride the elevator up and stumble down. The restaurant inside the villa is upmarket.

Entertainment

Jazzhaus JAZZ

(www.jazzhaus.de; Schnewlinstrasse 1) Under the brick arches of a wine cellar, this venue hosts first-rate jazz, rock and hip-hop concerts (€10 to €30) at 8pm at least three nights a week. It morphs into a club on weekends.

Jos Fritz Cafe LOUNGE

(www.josfritzcafe.de; Wilhelmstrasse 15) Down a little alley past the recycling bins, this cafe hosts concerts of alternative bands and events such as political discussions (stir things up with 'Is Merkel too liberal?').

Information

The **tourist office** (www.freiburg.de; Rathausplatz 2-4; ⏲8am-8pm Mon-Fri, 9.30am-5pm Sat, 10am-noon Sun Jun-Sep, 8am-6pm Mon-Fri, 9.30am-2.30pm Sat, 10am-noon Sun Oct-May) is well stocked with hiking and cycling maps to the region.

Getting There & Around

Freiburg shares **EuroAirport** (www.euroairport.com) with Basel (Switzerland) and Mulhouse (France). It buzzes with low-cost carriers. The **Airport Bus** (www.freiburger-reisedienst.de) runs almost every hour (adult/child €20/10, 55 minutes) .

Fast trains connect Freiburg to Basel (€23, 45 minutes, hourly) and north to Frankfurt (€61, two hours, hourly) and beyond.

Cut across the Rhine to France's cute Colmar. Bus 1076 makes the run two to three times daily (€8, 1¼ hours).

Single rides on the efficient local bus and tram system cost €2.20. A 24-hour pass is €5. Trams depart from the bridge over the train tracks.

LAKE CONSTANCE

Lake Constance (Bodensee) is an oasis in landlocked southern Germany. Even if you never make contact with the water, this giant bulge in the sinewy course of the Rhine offers a splash of refreshment. Historic towns line its vineyard-dappled periphery, which can be explored by boat or bicycle or on foot. While sun is nice, the lake is best on one of the many misty days, when it is shrouded in mystery.

Constance's southern side belongs to Switzerland and Austria, where the snow-capped Alps provide backdrops across the lake so ideal that you may decide to unwisely chuck it all and start a postcard business. The German side of Lake Constance features three often-crowded tourist centres in Constance, Meersburg and the island of Lindau. It's essentially a summer area, when it abounds with aquatic joy.

Getting There & Around

Trains link Lindau and Constance, and buses fill in the gaps to places like Meersburg. By car, the B31 hugs the northern shore of Lake Constance, but it can get rather busy. The Constance–Meersburg car ferry run by BSB ferries (p559) provides a vital link for those who don't want to circumnavigate the entire lake and a chance for some watery vistas.

The most enjoyable, albeit slowest, way to get around is on the **Bodensee-Schiffsbetriebe** (BSB; www.bsb-online.com) boats, which, from Easter to late October, call several times a day at the larger towns along the lake; there are discounts for rail-pass holders.

Numerous schemes exist for discounted travel and admissions spanning the three countries surrounding the lake; ask at tourist offices.

Constance

☎07531 / POP 81,000

Constance (Konstanz) nudges the Swiss border. It's a lake town where the allure of the waters sometimes drowns the rather remarkable old town. The main attraction is fittingly named Mainau Island.

It achieved historical significance in 1414, when the Council of Constance convened to try to heal huge rifts in the Catholic Church. The consequent burning at the stake of the religious reformer Jan Hus as a heretic, and the scattering of his ashes over the lake, did nothing to block the Reformation.

Sights & Activities

TOP CHOICE **Old Town** HISTORIC QUARTER

The city's most visible feature is the Gothic spire of the **Münster** (⏲9am-6pm Mon-Sat, 10am-6pm Sun), added in 1856 to a church that was started in 1052. You'll feel like a treasure hunter as you make one find after another within. Get the brilliant walking tour brochure from the tourist office and explore the **Altstadt** (Old Town), which seems to have a medieval surprise around every corner.

Lakefront NATURAL FEATURE

Head across to **Mainau Island** (www.mainau.de; adult/child €16/free; ⏲sunrise to sunset), with its baroque castle set in vast and gorgeous gardens with seasonal displays. Take bus 4 (€2, 20 minutes) or a BSB ferry from the harbour behind the station (€6, one hour, hourly).

Five rocky shore areas optimistically called **beaches** are open from May to September, including the **Strandbad Horn** (the best and most crowded), with bush-shrouded nude bathing. Take bus 5 or walk for 20 minutes north around the shore.

Directly in front of town, the **Stadtgarten** is ideal for an idyll; paths lead past yachts, monuments, gardens and cafes.

Sleeping & Eating

The following are in the Altstadt.

Hotel Barbarossa HOTEL €€

(☎128 990; www.barbarossa-hotel.com; Obermarkt 8-12; r €50-130;) Charming old place, carefully restored (although the floors still creak). White walls set off beautiful wooden antiques. The art deco restaurant (mains €8 to €20) has fine local specialities.

Hotel Augustiner Tor HOTEL €€

(☎282 450; www.hotel-augustiner-tor.de; Bodanstrasse 18; r €80-150;) This cleverly restored turn-of-the-century hotel offers unrivalled value for money. Streamlined rooms exude Scandinavian simplicity with clean lines, creamy beige leather and wood floors.

Hafenmeisterei CAFE €€

(Hafenstrasse 8; mains €11-20) Hafenmeisterei blends beach-shack breeziness with a cool lounge vibe. Reggae grooves play as chefs sizzle up wok and fish dishes in the open kitchen. One of many bodacious outdoor terraces on the harbour.

Brauhaus Johann Albrecht BEER HALL €€

(Konradigasse 2; mains €8-16) A rambling beer hall with a rustic menu featuring daily specials. The food here offers good value and the beer, brewed on the premises in copper vats, goes down fine, especially on the terrace in summer.

DJH Hostel HOSTEL €

(☎322 60; www.jugendherberge-konstanz.de; Zur Allmannshöhe 18; dm €22) Occupying a water tower, with neat dorms, a bistro and gardens. It's 4km northeast of the Altstadt, served by buses 1 and 4.

Information

The **tourist office** (www.konstanz.de/tourismus; Bahnhofplatz 43; ⏲9am-6.30pm Mon-Fri, to 4pm Sat, 10am-1pm Sun Apr-Oct, 9.30am-12.30pm & 2-6pm Mon-Fri Nov-Mar) is in the train station.

Getting There & Away

Constance has trains to Offenburg (€29, 2¼ hours, hourly) via Triberg in the Black Forest, and Stuttgart (€38, 2¼ hours, every two hours). There are good connections into Switzerland (which is 200m south!), including Zürich (€18, 1¼ hours, hourly). All services depart from the restored landmark Gothic station. Bike-hire shops are nearby.

BSB Ferries (www.bsb-online.com) on various schedules serve numerous destinations including Meersburg (€5, 30 minutes) and Lindau (€15, three to four hours).

Meersburg

☎07532 / POP 5300

Constance is the big city compared to Meersburg across the lake. The winding, hilly, cobblestone streets, vine-patterned hills and a sunny lakeside promenade make it a good stop if travelling by ferry or car.

The **tourist office** (www.meersburg.de; Kirchstrasse 4; ⏲9am-6pm Mon-Fri, 10am-2pm Sat, reduced hr in winter) is in the Altstadt and can help find accommodation if you decide to stay.

Steigstrasse is lined with delightful half-timbered houses, each boasting a gift shop. The modest 11th-century **Altes Schloss** (adult/child €8.50/4.50; ⏲9am-6.30pm Mar-Oct) is the oldest structurally intact castle in Germany.

The Constance to Meersburg **car ferry** (www.bsb-online.com) runs from the northeastern Constance suburb of Staadand. BSB ferries stop on their shore-hopping voyages between Constance (€5, 30 minutes) and Lindau (€14, 2½ to three hours).

Lindau

☎08382 / POP 26,500

A forgotten corner of Bavaria. Most people assume this medieval little island-city is part of Baden-Württemberg but it's not. Here you'll see the blue-and-white Bavarian state colours, and sudsy brews trump the wines found elsewhere along the lake.

Connected to the nearby lakeshore by bridges, this is a charming, nearly car-free town. Key sights (often adorned with murals) include the **Altes Rathaus** (Reichsplatz), the **city theatre** (Barfüsser-platz) and the little harbour's **Seepromenade**, with its Bavarian Lion monument and **lighthouse**. When the haze clears, the Alps provide a stunning backdrop for watersports that include windsurfing and rowing.

Alte Post (☎934 60; www.alte-post-lindau.de; Fischergasse 3; r €60-140; ⊙closed late Dec–late Mar; 🛜) is a 300-year-old coaching inn that was once a stop on the Frankfurt–Milan mail run. Sitting pretty on cobbled Fischergasse, it's well-kept, light and spacious, and the rooms have chunky pine furnishings and wicker chairs.

The 18th-century **Hotel Garni Brugger** (☎934 10; www.hotel-garni-brugger.de; Bei der Heidenmauer 11; r €55-100; ⊙closed Dec; 🛜), with 23 bright rooms decked out in floral fabrics and pine, is run by a family that bends over to please. Guests can thaw out in the sauna in winter.

Carving through the centre of the island, Lindau's cobbled main street, **Maximilianstrasse**, is lined with elegant cafes, restaurants and ice-cream shops.

Information

The **tourist office** (☎260 030; www.lindau.de; Ludwigstrasse 68; ⊙9am-6pm Mon-Fri, 2-6pm Sat & Sun May-Sep, 9am-5pm Mon-Fri Oct-Apr) is opposite the train station.

Getting There & Away

Lindau has trains to Ulm (€22, 1¾ hours, hourly) on the Munich–Stuttgart line, Munich (€38, 2¼ hours, every two hours) and direct to Zürich (€25, four times daily). Trains to nearby Bregenz (€5, nine minutes, two hourly) let you connect to the rest of Austria and Switzerland.

BSB Ferries (www.bsb-online.com) on various schedules serve destinations including Meersburg (€14, 2½ to three hours) and Constance (€15, three to four hours).

RHINELAND-PALATINATE

Rhineland-Palatinate (Rheinland-Pfalz) is deeply riven by rivers, and the names of two – Rhine and Moselle – are synonymous with the wines made from the grapes growing on their hillsides. Created after WWII from parts of the former Rhineland and Rhenish Palatinate regions, its turbulent history goes all the way back to the Romans, as seen in Trier. In recent centuries it was hotly contested by the French and a variety of German states, which produced many of its now-crumbling fortresses.

This land of wine and great natural beauty reaches its apex in the verdant Moselle Valley towns, such as Cochem, and along the heavily touristed Rhine, where rich hillside vineyards provide a backdrop for noble castles and looming medieval fortresses. For this part of Germany, focus your attention on the water, the land it courses through and the fruit of the vines on its hillsides.

Moselle Valley

Exploring the vineyards and wineries of the Moselle (Mosel) Valley is an ideal way to get a taste of German culture and people – and, of course, the crisp, light wines. Take the time to slow down and savour a glass or two.

Like a vine right before harvest, the Moselle hangs heavy with visitor fruit. Castles and half-timbered towns are built along the sinuous river below steep, rocky cliffs planted with vineyards (they say locals are born with one leg shorter than the other so that they can easily work the vines). It's one of the country's most scenic regions, with a constant succession of views rewarding the intrepid hikers who brave the hilly trails.

Many winemakers have their own small pensions but accommodation is hard to find in May when people enjoy a spring awakening, on summer weekends and during the local wine harvest (mid-September to mid-October). Note also that much of the region – like the vines themselves – goes into a deep slumber from November to March, albeit after an autumn explosion of colour.

Getting There & Around

The most scenic part of the Moselle Valley runs 195km from Trier to Koblenz; it's most practical to begin your Moselle Valley trip from either of these two.

It is not possible to travel the entire length of the banks of the Moselle River via rail. Local and fast trains run every hour between Trier and Koblenz, but the only riverside stretch of this line is between Cochem and Koblenz (however, it's a scenic dandy). Apart from this run – and the scenic Moselweinbahn line taking tourists between Bullay and Traben-Trarbach – travellers use buses, ferries, bicycles or cars to travel between most of the upper Moselle towns.

Moselbahn (www.moselbahn.de) runs eight buses on weekdays (fewer at weekends) between Trier and Bullay (three hours each way), a pretty route following the river's winding course and passing through numerous quaint villages. Buses leave from outside the train stations in Trier and Bullay.

The relaxed way to explore the Moselle in the high season is by boat. From May to early October, **Köln-Düsseldorfer (KD) Line** (www.k-d.com) ferries sail daily between Koblenz and Cochem (€25 one way, 5¼ hours upstream, 4¼ hours downstream). Other smaller ferry companies also operate on the Moselle from various towns. Eurail and German Rail passes are valid for all normal KD Line services, and travel on your birthday is free.

The Moselle is a popular area among cyclists, and for much of the river's course there's a separate 'Moselroute' bike track. Most towns have a rental shop or two; ask at the tourist offices. Many of the Moselbahn buses also carry bikes.

KOBLENZ

☎0261 / POP 110,000

Koblenz is an important ferry and train junction at the confluence of the Rhine and Moselle Rivers. The **tourist office** (www.touristik-koblenz.de; Bahnhofsplatz 7; ⌚9am-6pm Mon-Sat year-round, plus 10am-6pm Sun Apr-Oct) is in a modern building in front of the Hauptbahnhof.

The **Deutsches Eck** is a park at the dramatic meeting point of the rivers. It's dedicated to German unity and is a good reason for a riverside stroll.

South of Koblenz, at the head of the beautiful Eltz Valley, **Burg Eltz** (www.burg-eltz.de; adult/child €8/5.50; ⌚9.30am-5.30pm Apr-Oct) is not to be missed. Towering over the surrounding hills, this superb medieval castle has frescoes, paintings, furniture and ornately decorated rooms. Burg Eltz is best reached by train to Moselkern on the Trier line, from where it's a 50-minute walk up through the forest. Alternatively, a shuttle bus runs in peak season.

In town, many of Koblenz' restaurants and pubs are in the Altstadt, around Münzplatz and Burgstrasse, and along the Rhine. The small towns in either river valley offer more atmospheric accommodation than those in town.

The busy KD Line ferry dock is a 10-minute walk from the train station. Trains fan out in all directions: up the Moselle to Trier (€20, 1½ hours, hourly) via Cochem and Bullay; north along the Rhine to Cologne (€20, one hour, two hourly) and south on the Rhine to Mainz (€20, one hour, two hourly).

COCHEM

☎02671 / POP 5400

This often-crowded German town has narrow alleyways and one of the most beautiful castles in the region. It's also a good base for hikes into the hills. The **tourist office** (www.cochem.de; Endertplatz; ⌚9am-5pm Mon-Sat, 10am-noon Sun, reduced hr in winter) is next to the Moselbrücke bridge.

For a great view, head up to the **Pinnerkreuz** with the chairlift on Endertstrasse (€5). The perfect crown on the 100m-high hill, **Reichsburg Castle** (www.reichsburg-cochem.de; adult/6-17yr €5/3; ⌚9am-5pm) is a 15-minute walk from town. Its idealised form can be credited to its 1877 construction (it was never needed to actually *function* as a castle).

Many local vineyards offer tours that include a chance to wander the vines, enjoy the views, have a picnic, sample some cheese, visit the gift shop and, oh, try the wine.

Hotel-Pension Garni Villa Tummelchen (☎910 520; www.villa-tummelchen.com; Schlossstrasse 22; r from €55-80; 📶) is a bit up the hill from town and thus has sweeping Moselle vistas. It's worth an extra couple of euros to get a room with a balcony and a view.

Tucked away uphill from the Markt and its fountain, **Zom Stüffje** (www.zom-stueffje.de; Oberbachstrasse 14; mains €8-18; ⌚Wed-Mon) is richly decorated with dark timber and murals, and serves classic German fare and some of the better local vintages.

This is the terminus for KD Line boats from Koblenz. Trains on the Trier–Koblenz line run twice hourly to Bullay (€5, 10 minutes), where you can pick up the Moselbahn bus.

COCHEM TO TRIER

To explore the little villages along the Moselle upstream from often-oversubscribed Cochem, take the train from there to **Bullay**, from where you can catch the Moselbahn bus and town-hop the rest of the way to Trier.

TRABEN-TRARBACH

Full of fanciful art-nouveau villas, the double town of Traben-Trarbach is a welcome relief from the 'romantic half-timbered town' circuit. Pick up a map of the town at the **tourist office** (www.traben-trarbach.de; Bahnstrasse 22). The ruined medieval **Grevenburg**, which, unlike its Cochem cousin, survived the 19th century without being 'restored', sits high in the craggy hills above Trarbach and is reached from the Markt via a steep footpath.

Weingut Caspari (www.weingut-caspari.de; Weiherstrasse 18, Trarbach; mains €5-15) is a rustic, old-time *Strausswirtschaft* (winery-cum-eatery) that serves hearty local specialities, such as *Feiner Grillschinken Moselart* (boiled ham with potato puree and sauerkraut). It's six short blocks inland from the bridge.

BERNKASTEL-KUES

The twin town of Bernkastel-Kues is at the heart of the middle Moselle region. On the right bank, Bernkastel has a charming **Markt**, a romantic ensemble of half-timbered houses with beautifully decorated gables.

On Karlstrasse, the alley to the right as you face the Rathaus, the tiny **Spitzhäuschen** resembles a giant bird's house, its narrow base topped by a much larger, precariously leaning, upper floor.

Get your heart pumping by hoofing it from the Spitzhäuschen up to **Burg Landshut**, a ruined 13th-century castle – framed by vineyards and forests – on a bluff above town; allow 30 to 60 minutes. You'll be rewarded with glorious valley views and a cold drink at the **beer garden** (⌚10am-6pm mid-Feb–Nov).

Trier

☎0651 / POP 101,000

Trier is touted as Germany's oldest town and you'll find more Roman ruins here than anywhere else north of the Alps. Although settlement of the site dates back to 400 BC, Trier itself was founded around 16 BC as Augusta Treverorum, the capital of Gaul, and was second in importance only to Rome in the Western Roman Empire. Its proximity to France can be tasted in its cuisine, while its large student population injects life among the ruins.

Sights

Like a high-school history class in a day, only now with wine at the end, Trier's sights span at least 23 centuries. A **Combi-Ticket** (adult/child €6/5) is good for most of the historical sites.

BIKE DOWN THE VALLEY

You can rent a bike in Trier and spend two to four days cycling through the villages and vineyards of the Moselle Valley to Koblenz. It's generally downhill, which helps make the trip literally a breeze. Once in Koblenz you could return with the bike on the train or, better, simply turn in your bike and continue your travels. **RadStatiuon am Hauptbahnhof Trier** (☎148 856; www.bues-trier.de; Hauptbahnhof; touring bike rental day/week €10/42) will retrieve the bike from Koblenz (or any other stop in between) for a fee of €20.

Roman Ruins HISTORICAL BUILDINGS

The town's chief landmark is the **Porta Nigra** (adult/child €3/1.50; ⌚9am-6pm Apr-Sep, to 5pm Mar & Oct, to 4pm Nov-Feb), the imposing city gate on the northern edge of the town centre. Its construction dates back to the 2nd century AD.

Additional Roman sites include the **Amphitheatre** (Olewigerstrasse; adult/child €3/1.50; ⌚9am-6pm Apr-Sep, to 5pm Mar & Oct, to 4pm Nov-Feb) and the gloomy underground caverns of the **Kaiserthermen** (Im Palastgarten).

Middle Ages Buildings HISTORICAL BUILDINGS

Trier's massive (and massively restored) Romanesque **Dom** (www.dominformation.de; Liebfrausenstrasse 12; ⌚6.30am-6pm Apr-Oct, to 5.30pm Nov-Mar) shares a 1600-year history with the nearby and equally impressive **Konstantin Basilika** (☎724 68; Konstantinplatz; ⌚10am-6pm Mon-Fri, noon-6pm Sun Apr-Oct).

The early-Gothic **Dreikönigenhaus** (Simeonstrasse 19) was built around 1230 as a protective tower. The original entrance was on the second level, accessible only by way of a retractable rope ladder.

Museums MUSEUMS

The **Karl Marx Haus** (www.fes.de/marx; Brückenstrasse 10; adult/child €3/2; ⌚10am-6pm daily Apr-Oct, 2-5pm Tue-Sun Nov-Mar) is the suitably modest birthplace of the man. It is a major pilgrimage stop for the growing numbers of mainland Chinese tourists to Europe. The walls are lined with manifestos.

Near Porta Nigra, **Städtisches Museum** (www.museum-trier.de; Simeonstrasse 60; adult/child €5/free; ⌚9.30am-6pm Tue-Sun) fills a renovated 11th-century Trier monastery with two millennia of Trier history.

Sleeping

Hotel Römischer Kaiser HOTEL €€
(☎977 00; www.friedrich-hotels.de; Am Porta-Nigra-Platz 6; r €75-150; wifi) The Kaiser is in an elegant, old corner building. The 43 rooms are comfortable, decorated in soft colours and have parquet floors; some have balconies. Ceilings are regally high. Unwind after a long day tracking Romans on the sunny terrace.

Hille's Hostel HOSTEL €
(☎710 2785; www.hilles-hostel-trier.de; Gartenfeldstrasse 7; dm €15-19, s/d €41/52; @) The rooms here are furnished with Ikea bunk beds and are set back from the road amid some hardy palms. There's a big kitchen and the chance to ponder the mugs of previous guests that line the walls.

Hotel Paulin HOTEL €€
(☎147 4010; www.hotel-paulin-trier.de; Paulinstrasse 13; r €60-120; wifi) In a low-key, modern building right across from the old centre, this tidy 24-room hotel offers something even a weary Roman can appreciate: a comfy night's sleep at a good price. As for the bacchanalia, that's up to you…

Hotel Pieper HOTEL €€
(☎230 08; www.hotel-pieper-trier.de; Thebäerstrasse 39; r €50-120; wifi) An excellent family-run hotel on a residential street with a few neighbourhood cafes, just five minutes from the station. Rooms are comfy and have free wi-fi. Best of all is the bounteous breakfast buffet that includes treats like fresh pineapple.

Eating

The narrow and historic Judengasse, near the Markt, has several small bars and clubs. There's a cluster of stylish places on Viehmarktplatz and another bunch in front of the Dom. In summer getting a seat at a cafe can feel like battling a lion.

Walderdorff's CAFE €€
(www.walderdorffs.de; Domfreihof 1a; mains €8-16) A high-concept wine bar and cafe across from the Dom. Score one of the dozens of tables out front or inside in the stylish surrounds. The food is fresh and light; look for salads, sandwiches and many seasonal specials.

Zum Domstein BISTRO €€
(www.domstein.de; Am Hauptmarkt 5; mains €10-20, Roman dinner €15-33) A touristy but fun German-style bistro where you can either feast like the ancient Romans (fried zucchini? Not bad.) or dine on more conventional German and international fare. Avoid indecision and have a wine flight (sampler).

Kartoffel Kiste SPUD CAFE €€
(www.kiste-trier.de; Fahrstrasse 13-14; mains €8-16) A local favourite, this place specialises in baked, breaded, soupified and sauce-engulfed potatoes, as well as steaks. There is an extraordinary bronze fountain fronting its many outdoor tables.

Information

Tourist office (www.trier.de; An der Porta Nigra; ⌚9am-6pm Mon-Sat, 10am-5pm Sun May-Oct, reduced hr in winter). Offers good two-hour guided city walking tours (adult/child €7/3.50, 1.30pm Saturday May to October) in English; located at the Porta Nigra, a 10-minute walk from the train station along the Theodor-Heuss-Allee.

Trier-Card (from €9) Discounts and free public transport.

Getting There & Away

Trier has a train service to Koblenz (€20, 1½ hours, hourly) via Bullay and Cochem, as well as to Luxembourg (€16, 50 minutes, hourly).

Rhine Valley – Koblenz to Mainz

A trip along the mighty Rhine is a highlight for most travellers, as it should be. The section between Koblenz and Mainz provides vistas of steep vineyard-covered mountains punctuated by brooding castles. It really is rather magical. Spring and autumn are the best times to visit the Rhine Valley; in summer it's overrun and in winter most towns go into hibernation.

Though the trails here may be a bit more crowded with day trippers than those along the Moselle, hiking along the Rhine is excellent. The slopes and trails around Bacharach are justly famous.

Every town along the route offers cute little places to stay or camp and atmospheric places to eat and drink.

Getting There & Around

Although Koblenz and Mainz are the best starting points, the Rhine Valley is also easily accessible from Frankfurt on a very long day trip, but it could drive you to drink, as it were.

Each mode of transport on the Rhine has its own advantages and all are equally enjoyable.

Try combining several. The **Köln-Düsseldorfer (KD) Line** (www.k-d.com) runs slow and fast boats daily between Koblenz and Mainz (as well as the less-interesting stretch between Cologne and Koblenz). The journey takes about four hours downstream and about 5½ hours upstream (€47, free with rail pass). Boats stop at riverside towns along the way.

Frequent train services through the area operate on both sides of the Rhine River, but are more convenient on the left bank. You can travel non-stop on IC/EC trains or by slower regional RB or RE services. The ride is amazing; sit on the right heading north and on the left heading south. Note that most stations don't have lockers.

ST GOAR & ST GOARSHAUSEN

☎06741 / POP 3100

These two towns are on opposite sides of the Rhine; St Goar is on the left bank. One of the most impressive castles on the river is **Burg Rheinfels** (www.st-goar.de; adult/child €5/2.50; ⏰9am-6pm Apr-Oct, 11am-5pm Sat & Sun in good weather Nov-Mar) in St Goar. An absolute must-see, the labyrinthine ruins reflect the greed and ambition of Count Dieter V of Katzenelnbogen, who built the castle in 1245 to help levy tolls on passing ships ('African or European?'). Across the river, just south of St Goarshausen, is the Rhine's most famous sight, the **Loreley Cliff**. Legend has it that a maiden sang sailors to their deaths against its base. It's worth the trek to the top of the Loreley for the view.

St Goar's **Jugendherberge** (☎388; www.djh.de; Bismarckweg 17; dm/s/d €18/30/50) is right below the castle. **Hotel Hauser** (☎333; www.hotelhauser.de; Heerstrasse 77; r €50-80) is relaxed like an old easy chair. Large restaurant windows and all 13 rooms overlook the Rhine. Have a drink on the patio.

> **RHINE TOWNS**
>
> Besides those listed in this section, here's the low-down on some other towns along the Rhine route. All have train and boat service.
>
> » **Boppard** Roman walls and ruins (left bank).
>
> » **Oberwesel** Numerous towers and walkable walls of a ruined castle (left bank).
>
> » **Assmannshausen** Small, relatively untouristed village with nice hotels, sweeping views and good hikes (right bank).
>
> » **Rüdesheim** Overrated and overvisited town of trinkets and hype (right bank).

BACHARACH

☎06743 / POP 2400

Walk beneath one of the thick-arched gateways in Bacharach's medieval walls and you'll find yourself in a beautifully preserved medieval village. The **tourist office** (☎919 303; www.bacharach.de; Oberstrasse 45; ⏰9am-5pm Mon-Fri, 10am-4pm Sat Apr-Oct) will mind day trippers' bags.

Bacharach's **Jugendherberge** (☎1266; www.djh.de; dm from €20) is a legendary facility housed in the Burg Stahleck castle. The **Hotel Kranenturm** (☎1308; www.kranenturm.com; Langstrasse 30; r €50-100; @) is a turreted fantasy of stone, and also offers filling meals.

Part of the old ramparts, the **Rhein Hotel** (☎1243; www.rhein-hotel-bacharach.de; Langstrasse 50; r €60-130, mains €9-18; ❄📶) has 14 well-lit, soundproofed rooms with compact bathrooms and original artwork. The restaurant serves regional dishes.

MAINZ

☎06131 / POP 185,000

A short train ride from Frankfurt, Mainz has an attractive old town that's a good day trip. It can't compare to the compact beauty of the nearby towns along the Rhine, but impresses with its massive **Dom** (Domstrasse 3; ⏰9am-6pm Tue-Fri, to 4pm Sat, 1-3pm Sun), which has a blend of Romanesque, Gothic and baroque architecture. **St Stephanskirche** (Weisspetrolse 12; ⏰10am-noon & 2-5pm) has stained-glass windows by Marc Chagall.

Mainz's museums include the standout **Gutenberg Museum** (www.gutenberg-museum.de; Liebfrauenplatz 5; adult/child €5/3; ⏰9am-5pm Tue-Sat, 11am-3pm Sun), which contains two namesake copies of the first printed Bible. For more information on attractions in Mainz, visit the **tourist office** (www.touristik-mainz.de; Brückenturm am Rathaus; ⏰9am-6pm Mon-Fri, 10am-4pm Sat, 11am-3pm Sun).

Trains along the Rhine to Koblenz (€20, one hour) run twice hourly. Heidelberg (€20, one hour, hourly) is an easy trip, as is Frankfurt via the Frankfurt airport (€10, 40 minutes, several per hour).

HESSE

The Hessians, a Frankish tribe, were among the first to convert to Lutheranism in the early 16th century. Apart from a brief period of unity in that same century under Philip the Magnanimous, Hesse (Hessen) remained a motley collection of principalities and, later, of Prussian administrative districts until proclaimed a state in 1945. Its main cities are Frankfurt-am-Main, Kassel and the capital, Wiesbaden.

Besides being a transport hub, Frankfurt-am-Main offers its own diversions, although you'll find that the rest of Germany will soon beckon.

Frankfurt-am-Main

069 / POP 645,000

Variously called 'Mainhattan' and 'Bankfurt', Frankfurt is indeed on the Main (pronounced 'mine') River and, after London, is Europe's centre of finance. Both sobriquets also refer to the city's soaring skyline of bank-owned skyscrapers.

But while all seems cosmopolitan, it is often just a small town at heart. Streets get quiet in the evenings, the long list of museums has no really outstanding stars, and it has cute old pubs you would only ever think to find in country towns. But when a major convention is in town, such as the Frankfurt Book Fair, it feels as bustling and jammed as any metropolis.

Frankfurt-am-Main is Germany's most important transport hub for air, train and road connections, so you will probably end up here at some point, though truthfully it will probably be best enjoyed as a gateway to someplace else rather than a focus of your trip. Note that Frankfurt is often officially referred to as Frankfurt-am-Main, or Frankfurt/Main, since there is another, smaller town named Frankfurt (Frankfurt-an-der-Oder) located near the Polish border.

Sights

Frankfurt has the most skyscraper-filled skyline in Europe. Banks and related firms have erected a phalanx of egotistical edifices along Mainzer Landstrasse and the Taunusanlange. Tallest (not just locally but within all the EU) at 259m is the pudgy yet pinnacled **Commerzbank Building** on Kaiserplatz. It was designed by Sir Norman Foster.

Get your head in the clouds atop the **Main Tower** (www.maintower-restaurant.de; Neue Mainzer Strasse 52-58; adult/child €5/3.50; 10am-9pm Apr-Oct, 10am-7pm Nov-Mar, weather permitting), with its open-air viewing platform 200m up. There is also a **cocktail bar** (5.30pm-1am, to 2am Fri & Sat) and restaurant.

Altstadt HISTORIC QUARTER

Frankfurt has room for all its high-rises because about 80% of the old city was wiped off the map by two Allied bombing raids in March 1944. Although postwar reconstruction was subject to the hurried demands of the new age, rebuilding efforts were more thoughtful in the **Römerberg**, the old central area of Frankfurt west of the cathedral, where ersatz 14th- and 15th-century buildings provide a glimpse of the beautiful city that once was. The old town hall, or **Römer**, is in the northwestern corner of Römerberg and consists of three 15th-century houses topped with Frankfurt's trademark stepped gables.

East of Römerberg, behind the Historischer Garten (which has the remains of

NAVIGATING FRANKFURT

The **airport** is 11 minutes by train southwest of the city centre. The **Hauptbahnhof** is on the western side of the city, but it's still within walking distance of the centre.

The best route to the centre through the sleazy train-station area is along **Kaiserstrasse**. This leads to **Kaiserplatz** and on to a large square called **An der Hauptwache**. This is the retail hub, with stores stretching along in all directions, principally along the **Zeil**.

The area between the former prison/police station (Hauptwache) and the **Römerberg**, in the tiny vestige of Frankfurt's original old city, is the centre of Frankfurt. The **Main River** flows just south of the Altstadt, with several bridges leading to one of the city's most charming areas, **Sachsenhausen**. Its northeastern corner, known as **Alt-Sachsenhausen**, has quaint old houses and narrow alleyways.

Just northeast of the centre, Frankfurt's village roots are most strongly felt in **Bornheim**. The neighbourhood's spine, **Berger Strasse**, is lined with funky small shops, cafes and pubs.

Frankfurt-am-Main

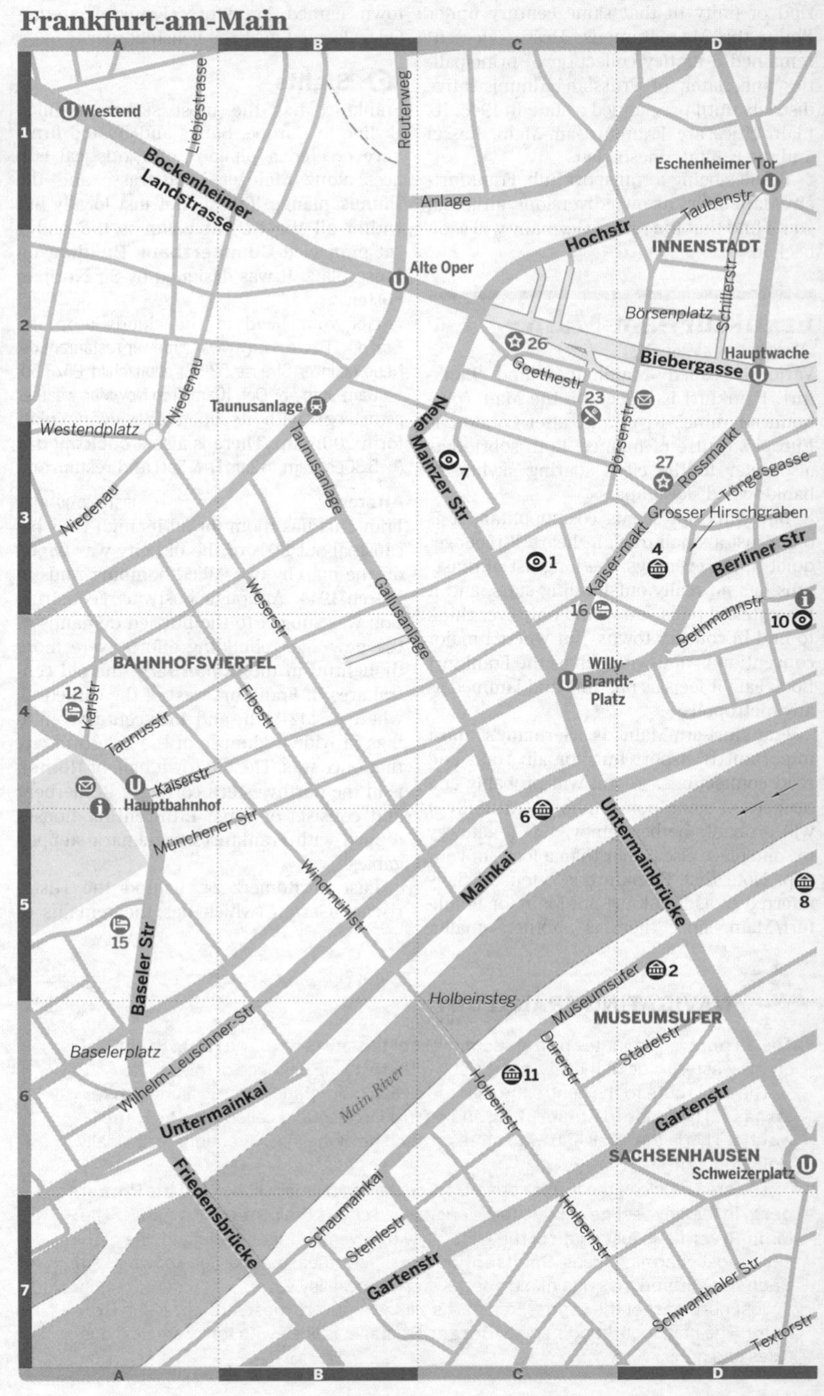

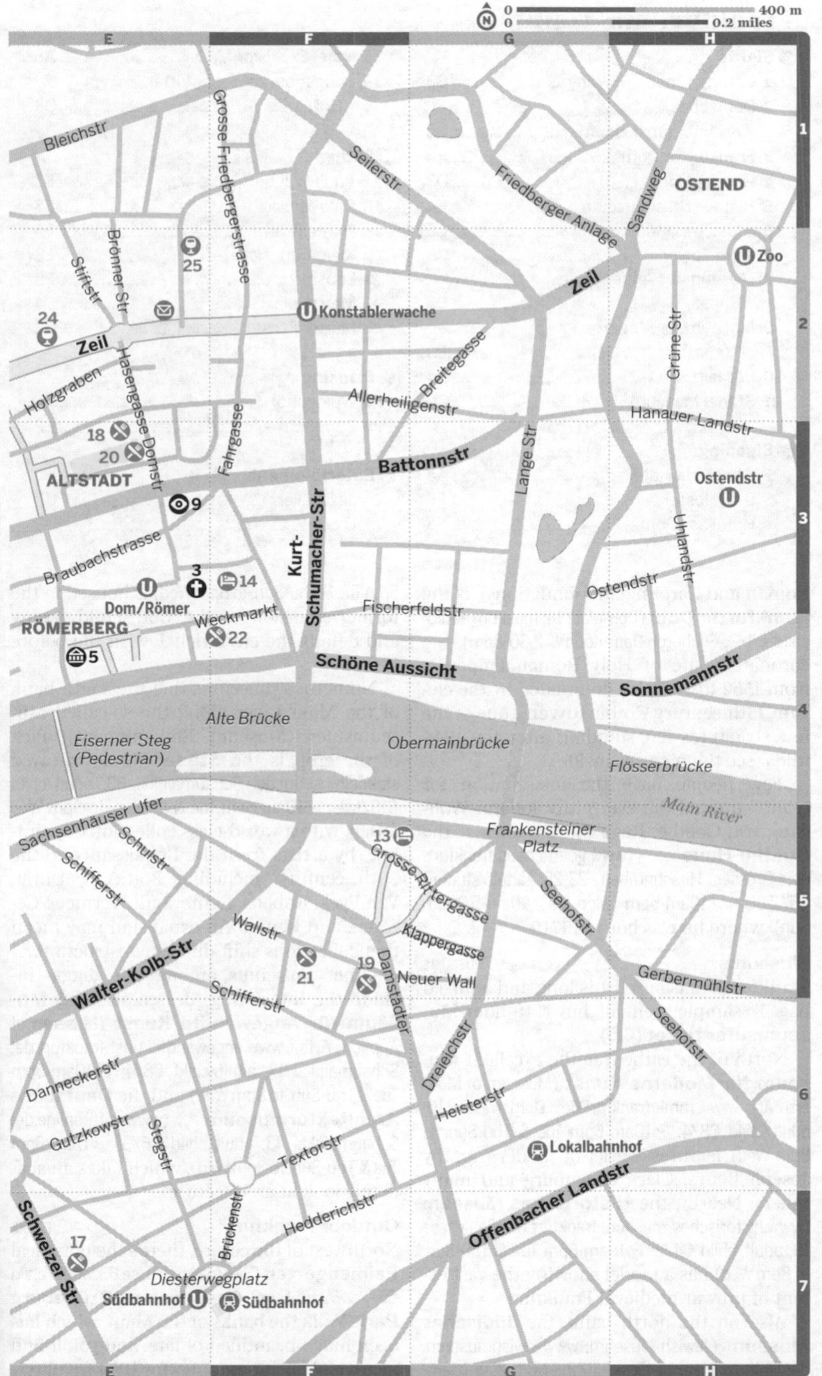

0 400 m
0 0.2 miles
E
F
G
H
1
2
3
4
5
6
7
Bleichstr
Grosse Friedbergerstrasse
Seilerstr
Friedberger Anlage
Sandweg
OSTEND
Zoo
Stiftstr
Brönner Str
25
24
Zeil
Konstablerwache
Zeil
Grüne Str
Holzgraben
Hasengasse
Breitegasse
Allerheiligenstr
Hanauer Landstr
18
20
Domstr
Fahrgasse
Battonnstr
Lange Str
Ostendstr
ALTSTADT
9
Kurt-Schumacher-Str
Uhlandstr
Braubachstrasse
3
14
Ostendstr
Dom/Römer
Weckmarkt
Fischerfeldstr
RÖMERBERG
22
5
Schöne Aussicht
Sonnemannstr
Alte Brücke
Eiserner Steg (Pedestrian)
Obermainbrücke
Flösserbrücke
Main River
Sachsenhäuser Ufer
13
Frankensteiner Platz
Schulstr
Grosse Rittergasse
Schifferstr
Seehofstr
Wallstr
Klappergasse
Walter-Kolb-Str
21
19
Darmstädter
Neuer Wall
Gerbermühlstr
Schifferstr
Seehofstr
Dreieichstr
Danneckerstr
Heisterstr
Gutzkowstr
Stegstr
Textorstr
Lokalbahnhof
Offenbacher Landstr
Schweizer Str
Hedderichstr
Brückenstr
17
Diesterwegplatz
Südbahnhof
Südbahnhof

Frankfurt-am-Main

Sights

1 Commerzbank Building C3
2 Deutsches Architekturmuseum D5
3 Frankfurter Dom E3
4 Goethe-Haus D3
5 Historisches Museum E4
6 Jüdisches Museum C5
7 Main Tower C3
8 Museum für Angewandte Kunst D5
9 Museum für Moderne Kunst E3
10 Römer D4
11 Städel Museum C6

Sleeping

12 Concorde Hotel A4
13 DJH Hostel F5
14 Hotel am Dom F3
15 Hotel Excelsior A5
16 Steigenberger Frankfurter Hof C3

Eating

17 Adolf Wagner E7
18 Cafe Mozart E3
19 Fichte Kränzi F5
20 Kleinmarkthalle E3
21 Lobster F5
22 Metropol F4
23 Mutter Ernst C2

Drinking

24 Weidenhof E2
25 Zum Schwejk E2

Entertainment

26 Jazzkeller C2
27 U 60311 .... D3

Roman and Carolingian foundations), is the **Frankfurter Dom** (Domplatz 14; museum adult/child €3/2; ⊙church 9am-noon & 2.30-8pm), the coronation site of Holy Roman emperors from 1562 to 1792. It's dominated by the elegant 15th-century Gothic **tower** – one of the few structures left standing after the 1944 raids (see the pictures inside).

'Few people have the imagination for reality' uttered the ever-pithy Johann Wolfgang von Goethe. Read more quotes at the **Goethe-Haus** (www.goethehaus-frankfurt.de; Grosser Hirschgraben 23-25; adult/student €5/2.50; ⊙10am-6pm Mon-Sat, 10am-5.30pm Sun), where he was born in 1749.

Museums MUSEUMS

Frankfurt's museum list is long and a mixed bag. To sample them all, buy a 48-hour **Museumsufer ticket** (€15).

North of the cathedral, the excellent **Museum für Moderne Kunst** (Museum of Modern Art; www.mmk-frankfurt.de; Domstrasse 10; adult/child €8/4; ⊙10am-6pm Tue & Thu-Sun, to 8pm Wed) features works of modern art by Joseph Beuys, Claes Oldenburg and many others. Nearby, the **Historisches Museum** (www.historisches-museum.frankfurt.de; Saalgasse 19; adult/child €4/2; ⊙10am-6pm Tue & Thu-Sun, to 8pm Wed) has a model showing the vast extent of prewar medieval Frankfurt.

Also on the north bank, the **Jüdisches Museum** (Jewish Museum; www.jewishmuseum.de; Untermainkai 14-15; adult/child €4/2; ⊙10am-5pm Tue & Thu-Sun, to 8pm Wed) is housed in the former mansion of the Rothschild family and details the city's rich Jewish life before WWII.

Numerous museums line the south bank of the Main River along the so-called Museumsufer (Museum Embankment). Pick of the crop is the **Städel Museum** (www.staedelmuseum.de; Schaumainkai 63; adult/child €10/free; ⊙10am-5pm Tue & Fri-Sun, to 9pm Wed & Thu), with a world-class collection of paintings by artists from the Renaissance to the 20th century, including Botticelli, Dürer, Van Eyck, Rubens, Rembrandt, Vermeer, Cézanne and Renoir. An expansion may mean that collections shift during construction.

Other museums among the gaggle include the interesting, design-oriented **Museum für Angewandte Kunst** (Museum of Applied Arts; www.angewandtekunst-frankfurt.de; Schaumainkai 17; adult/child €8/4; ⊙10am-5pm Tue & Thu-Sun, to 8pm Wed) and the **Deutsches Architekturmuseum** (www.dam-online.de; Schaumainkai 43; adult/child €6/3; ⊙11am-6pm Tue & Thu-Sun, to 8pm Wed), which takes an academic look at architecture.

Outdoor Frankfurt PARKS

Northwest of the centre, there's the botanical **Palmengarten** (Siesmayerstrasse 63; adult/child €5/2; ⊙9am-6pm), next door to **Grüneburg Park**. Walk the banks of the Main, which has been much-beautified of late, and you'll find plenty of benches popular for BYO frivolity.

Sleeping

Frankfurt's good public transport means nothing is very distant no matter where you stay.

Predictably, much of Frankfurt's budget accommodation is in the grotty Bahnhofsviertel, which surrounds the station; be sure to check out the room first. The streets north to the Messe (convention centre) are a bit better and convenient for early departures. During large trade fairs the town is booked out months in advance and rates soar.

TOP CHOICE Villa Orange HOTEL €€
(☎405 840; www.villa-orange.de; Hebelstrasse 1, Nordend; r €80-180;) Offering tranquillity, modern German design and small-hotel comforts (eg a quiet corner library), this century-old villa has 38 spacious rooms. The lavish breakfast buffet is organic. On weekends, rates fall.

Hotel am Dom HOTEL €€
(☎138 1030; www.hotelamdom.de; Kannengiessergasse 3; r €90-130;) This unprepossessing, 30-room hotel has immaculate rooms, apartments with kitchenettes and four-person suites just a few paces from the cathedral. A large breakfast buffet is included.

Steigenberger Frankfurter Hof HOTEL €€€
(☎215 02; www.steigenberger.de; Am Kaiserplatz; r from €160;) Schopenhauer used to lunch here but his pessimism is unlikely to dampen your enthusiasm for this cosmopolitan and elegant 19th-century neo-Renaissance institution, Frankfurt's most gracious and traditionally luxurious grand hotel.

Hotel Am Berg HOTEL €€
(☎660 5370; www.hotel-am-berg-ffm.de; Grethenweg 23; r €50-110) Located in a sandstone building in the quiet backstreets of Sachsenhausen, this hotel close to the Südbahnhof has large rooms (some sharing bathrooms) that could have been sets for a '70s porn movie. Seek refuge out back.

Hotel Excelsior HOTEL €
(☎256 080; www.hotelexcelsior-frankfurt.de; Mannheimer Strasse 7-9, Bahnhofsviertel; r €60-100;) Behind a newish, light-green facade, this 197-room place offers excellent value, with a free business centre; free coffee, tea, veggies and cakes in the lobby; and free landline phone calls throughout Germany.

Concorde Hotel HOTEL €€
(☎242 4220; www.hotelconcorde.de; Karlstrasse 9; r €60-120;) Understated yet well-run, this establishment in a restored art deco building near the Hauptbahnhof is a good choice any time, but especially on weekends. Multicoloured mood lights are a feature of the rooms – the red-light setting goes with the neighbourhood.

DJH Hostel HOSTEL
(☎610 0150; www.jugendherberge-frankfurt.de; Deutschherrnufer 12, Sachsenhausen; dm €17-25, r €35-75;) Advance bookings are advisable; within easy walking distance of the city centre and nightspots.

Eating

Known to the locals as Fressgasse (Munch-Alley), the Kalbächer Petrolse and Grosse Bockenheimer Strasse area, between Opernplatz and Börsenstrasse, has some medium-priced restaurants and fast-food places with outdoor tables in summer.

Wallstrasse and the surrounding streets in Alt-Sachsenhausen also have lots of lively midpriced restaurants. Bornheim, along strollable Berger Strasse, is another excellent choice.

Look for a bounty of outdoor stands serving food and drinks to gregarious crowds from April to October in the streets south of the Zeil.

Restaurants

Eckhaus GERMAN €€
(Bornheimer Landstrasse 45; mains €8-15) The smoke-stained walls, the iron fan above the door and those ancient floorboards all suggest an inelegant, long-toothed past. The hallmark rösti have been served in this restaurant-bar for over 100 years. Take the U-4 to Merianplatz.

Lobster CONTINENTAL €€
(Wallstrasse 21; mains €15-20; 6pm-1am Mon-Sat, hot dishes until 10.30pm) This cosy, friendly *Weinbistrot* (wine bistro) serves up mouth-watering meat and fish dishes that are 'a little bit French'. Offerings are listed on chalkboards. On a quiet Sachsenhausen street.

Mutter Ernst GERMAN €€
(Alte Rothofstrasse 12; mains €9-18; closed Sun) The ancient amber-coloured glass windows look into a timeless dining room. Grab a wooden table among the panelled walls for some excellent trad German fare.

Metropol BISTRO €€
(Weckmarkt 13-15; mains €8-16) Serves dishes from a changing menu that fluctuates between inspired and bistro staples. Has a

lovely courtyard out the back where children can chill out. A good place to pause and refresh while touring.

Cafes

Café Mozart CAKES €

(Töngesgasse 23; cakes from €2) Sample Frankfurt's traditional torte scene by joining the grannies and other trad-lovers who beat a path to this popular cafe to linger over coffee for hours on end.

Café Kante CAFE €

(Kantstrasse 13; breakfast €3-7; ⏲7am-7pm) Walk into this classic Bornheim cafe and you'll be overwhelmed by the delicious aroma of fantastic coffee, breads, cakes and croissants. It's half a block east of Merianplatz U-bahn station.

Apple-Wine Taverns

Apple-wine taverns are Frankfurt's great local tradition. They serve *Ebbelwoi* (Frankfurt dialect for *Apfelwein*), an alcoholic apple cider, along with local specialities like *Handkäse mit Musik* (literally, 'handcheese with music'). This is a round cheese soaked in oil and vinegar and topped with onions; your bowel supplies the music. Anything with the sensational local sauce made from herbs, *Grünesauce,* is a winner. Some good *Ebbelwoi* taverns are situated in Alt-Sachsenhausen.

TOP CHOICE **Fichte Kränzi** APPLE WINE €€

(Wallstrasse 5; mains €7-15) Just superb. A smallish place down an alley with a large, shady tree outside. The schnitzels are tops, as is the patter from the waiters.

Adolf Wagner APPLE WINE €€

(Schweizer Strasse 71; meals €8-15) This old place has one of the most atmospheric interiors in Sachsenhausen. The garden is appealing as well.

Apfelwein Solzer APPLE WINE €€

(www.solzer-frankfurt.de; Berger Strasse 260, Bornheim; mains €7-15) With wood-panelled walls and a covered courtyard.

Markets

Off Hasenpetrolse, **Kleinmarkthalle** (Hasengasse 5-7; ⏲7.30am-6pm Mon-Fri, to 3pm Sat) is a great produce market with loads of fruit, vegetables, meats and hot food.

Drinking

Many of the places listed under Eating are good for a drink, especially the apple-wine joints. Wander down the streets of Alt-Sachsenhausen to hear the echoes of the millions of American military personnel who drank at the gaudy bars here during the Cold War.

Weidenhof BAR

(Zeil 104) Drinking games here can revolve around 'spot the shopping bag' – and you'll need plenty of fortitude for this as bags abound at this high-concept bar and terrace right in the middle of Frankfurt's thronged main shopping street.

Wein-Dünker WINE BAR

(Berger Strasse 265) This musty little wine cellar, down to the right as you enter the courtyard, is not retro, it's real. Descend, rub your eyes and try some of Germany's finest. A good place to meet real Frankfurters.

Zum Schwejk GAY BAR

(Schafergasse 20) This is a popular gay bar and one of several on this street. Nice tables out front.

☆ Entertainment

Ballet, opera and theatre are strong features of Frankfurt's entertainment scene. Free *Frizz* has good listings (in German) of what's on in town.

Forsythe Company DANCE

(www.theforsythecompany.de; Bockenheimer Depot, Carlo-Schmid-Platz 1) Easily the world's most-talked-about dance company; the work of William Forsythe is often on tour.

U60311 CLUB

(Rossmarkt 6) A top club for techno, U60311 draws the best talent from around Europe. It's underground, literally, and often still going at noon from the night before.

Jazzkeller JAZZ

(www.jazzkeller.com; Kleine Bockenheimer Strasse 18a, Innenstadt) Look hard to find this place – a great jazz venue with mood – hidden in a cellar under an alley that obliquely intersects Goethestrasse. Live jazz except on Friday, when there's dancing to Latin and funk.

ℹ Information

Frankfurt Card (1/2 days €9/13) Gives 50% off admission to important attractions and unlimited travel on public transport.

Tourist office (www.frankfurt-tourismus.de) Hauptbahnhof (⏲8am-9pm Mon-Fri, 9am-6pm Sat & Sun) Römer (Römerberg 27; ⏲9.30am-5.30pm Mon-Fri, 10am-4pm Sat & Sun) The latter is at the northwest corner of the Römerberg square.

Post office airport (departure lounge B; ⏲7am-9pm); Hauptbahnhof (⏲7am-7.30pm Mon-Fri, 8am-4pm Sat); Innenstadt (Zeil 90, ground fl, Karstadt department store; ⏲9.30am-8pm)

Reisebank airport (Terminal 1, arrival hall B; ⏲6am-11pm); Hauptbahnhof (⏲7am-9pm) The train-station branch is at the head of platform 1.

Getting There & Away

Air

Germany's largest airport is **Frankfurt airport** (FRA; www.frankfurt-airport.com), a vast labyrinth with connections throughout the world. It's served by most major airlines, although not many budget ones.

Only cynics like Ryanair would say that Frankfurt has another airport. **Frankfurt-Hahn airport** (HHN; www.hahn-airport.de) is 70km west of Frankfurt. Buses from Frankfurt's Hauptbahnhof take about two hours – longer than the flight from London. Given the journey time it's fitting the bus company is called **Bohr** (☎06543-501 90; www.bohr-omnibusse.de; adult/child €12/6; ⏲hourly).

Bus

Long-distance buses leave from the south side of the Hauptbahnhof, where you'll find **Eurolines** (www.eurolines.eu; Mannheimer Strasse 15), with services to most European destinations.

The **Romantic Road bus** (www.romanticroadcoach.de) leaves from the south side of the Hauptbahnhof.

Car

Frankfurt-am-Main features the famed Frankfurter Kreuz, the biggest autobahn intersection in the country. All the main car-hire companies have offices in the main hall of the Hauptbahnhof and at the airport.

Train

The Hauptbahnhof handles more departures and arrivals than any station in Germany. Among the myriad services:

DESTINATION	PRICE	DURATION (HR)
Berlin	€111	4
Hamburg	€106	3½
Munich	€89	3¼

For Cologne take the fast (€63, 1¼ hours) ICE line or the slower and more scenic line along the Rhine (€41, 2½ hours, hourly).

Many long-distance trains also serve the airport. This station, Fernbahnhof, is 300m beyond the S-Bahn station, which is under Terminal 1.

Getting Around

To/From the Airport

S-Bahn lines S8 and S9 run every 15 minutes between the airport and Frankfurt Hauptbahnhof (€3.80, 11 minutes, 4.15am to 1am), usually continuing via Hauptwache and Konstablerwache. Taxis (about €40) take 30 minutes without traffic jams.

The airport train station has two sections: platforms 1 to 3 (below Terminal 1, hall B) handle S-Bahn connections, while IC and ICE connections are in the long-distance train station (Fernbahnhof), 300m distant.

Public Transport

Both single and day tickets for Frankfurt's excellent **transport network** (RMV; www.traffiq.de) can be purchased from automatic machines at almost any train station or stop. Single tickets cost €2.40 and a *Tageskarte* (24-hour ticket) costs €6 (€9.35 with the airport).

Taxi

Taxis are slow compared to public transport and expensive at €2.75 flag fall plus a minimum of €1.65 per km (more at night). There are numerous taxi ranks throughout the city, or you can book a cab (☎230 001).

NORTH RHINE-WESTPHALIA

From vibrant Cologne to elegant Düsseldorf to stately Bonn, the heavily populated Rhine-Ruhr region goes far beyond its coal and steels industries and offers historic towns and cities, each with a distinct life and atmosphere.

Cologne

☎0221 / POP 1 MILLION

Cologne (Köln) seems almost ridiculously proud to be the home of Germany's largest cathedral. The twin-tower shape of its weather-beaten Gothic hulk adorns the strangest souvenirs – from trifles like egg cosies and slippers to fancier fare like glassware and expensive jewellery. However, this bustling Rhine-side metropolis has much more to offer than its most recognisable and ubiquitous symbol. As early as the 1st century AD, Colonia Agrippinensis was an important Roman trading settlement. Today it's one of Germany's most multicultural spots, with a vibrant nightlife only partly fuelled by the local *Kölsch* beer.

Sights

Dom CATHEDRAL
(www.koelner-dom.de; admission free; ⏲6am-7.30pm, no visitors during services) As easy as it is to get church fatigue in Germany, the huge Kölner Dom is one you shouldn't miss. Blackened with age, this gargoyle-festooned Gothic cathedral has a footprint of 12,470 sq metres, with twin spires soaring to 157m. Although its ground stone was laid in 1248, stop-start construction meant it wasn't finished until 1880, as a symbol of Prussia's drive for unification. Just over 60 years later it escaped WWII's heavy night bombing largely intact.

Sunshine filtering softly through stained-glass windows and the weak glow of candles are the only illumination in the moody, high-ceilinged interior.

Behind the altar lies the cathedral's most precious reliquary, the **Shrine of the Three Magi** (c 1150–1210), which reputedly contains the bones of the Three Wise Men. Brought to Cologne from Milan in the 12th century, it can just be glimpsed through the gates to the inner choir.

To see the shrine properly, you need to take a **guided tour** (adult/concession €6/4; ⏲in English 10.30am & 2.30pm Mon-Sat, 2.30pm Sun). Alternatively, you can embark on the

Cologne

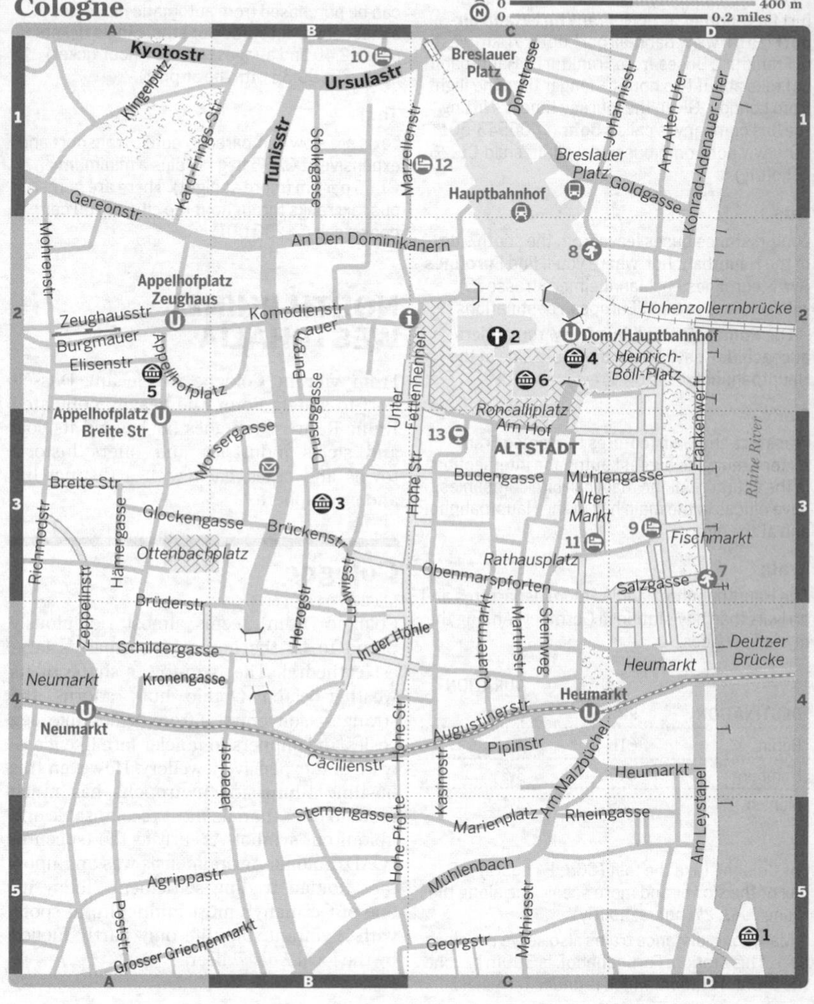

seriously strenuous endeavour of climbing the 509 steps of the Dom's **south tower** (adult/concession €2.50/1.50; ⏲9am-6pm May-Sep, to 5pm Mar, Apr & Oct, to 4pm Nov-Feb). You pass the 24-tonne **Peter Bell**, the world's largest working clanger, before emerging at 98.25m to magnificent views.

Two prominent museums sit right next to the cathedral. The **Römisch-Germanisches Museum** (Roman Germanic Museum; ☎2212 2304; www.museenkoeln.de; Roncalliplatz 4; adult/concession €8/4; ⏲10am-5pm Tue-Sun) displays artefacts from the Roman settlement in the Rhine Valley. The **Museum Ludwig** (☎2212 6165; www.museenkoeln.de; Bischofsgartenstrasse 1; adult/concession €9/6, 50% off first Thu evening of each month; ⏲10am-6pm Tue-Sun, to 10pm first Thu of each month) has an astoundingly good collection of 1960s pop art, German expressionism and Russian avant-garde painting, as well as photography.

Kolumba MUSEUM
(☎933 1930; www.kolumba.de; Kolumbastrasse 4; adult/under 18yr/concession €5/free/3; ⏲noon-5pm Wed-Mon) Encased in the ruins of the late-Gothic church St Kolumba, with layers of foundations going back to Roman times, this is a magnificent design by Swiss architect Peter Zumthor, 2009 winner of the Pritzker Prize, the 'architectural Oscar'. Exhibits span the arc of religious artistry from the early days of Christianity to the present. Coptic textiles, Gothic reliquary and medieval painting are juxtaposed with works by Bauhaus legend Andor Weininger and edgy room installations.

Cologne

Sights

Activities, Courses & Tours

Sleeping

Drinking

NS Dokumentationszentrum MUSEUM
(☎2212 6332; www.museenkoeln.de/nsdok; Appellhofplatz 23-25; adult/concession €3.60/1.50; ⏲10am-4pm Tue, Wed & Fri, 10am-6pm Thu, 11am-4pm Sat & Sun) Cologne's Third Reich history is poignantly documented here. The basement of the building was the local Gestapo prison, where scores of people were interrogated, tortured and killed. Inscriptions on the basement cell walls offer a gut-wrenching record of the emotional and physical pain endured by inmates.

Chocolate Museum MUSEUM
(☎931 8880; www.schokoladenmuseum.de; Am Schokoladenmuseum 1a; adult/concession €7.50/7; ⏲10am-6pm Tue-Fri, 11am-7pm Sat & Sun, last entry 1hr before closing) South along the riverbank is this glass-walled museum where you nibble on samples while learning the history and process of chocolate-making. Don't miss the 'Cult chocolate' floor.

Tours

Day cruises and Rhine journeys can be organised through **KD River Cruises** (☎208 8318; www.k-d.com; Frankenwerft 35). Day trips (10.30am, noon, 2pm and 6pm) cost €7.20. Sample one-way fare to Bonn is €12.50.

Festivals & Events

Held just before Lent in late February or early March, Cologne's **Carnival** (Karneval) rivals Munich's Oktoberfest for exuberance, as people dress in creative costumes and party in the streets. Things kick off the Thursday before the seventh Sunday before Easter and last until Monday *(Rosenmontag)*, when there are formal and informal parades.

Sleeping

Accommodation prices in Cologne increase by at least 20% when fairs are on. For more options, see the tourist office, which offers a room-finding service (€3).

Hotel Hopper et cetera HOTEL €€
(☎924 400; www.hopper.de; Brüsseler Strasse 26; s €80-270, d €120-295; @) Parquet flooring, white linen and red chairs lend an elegant simplicity to this former monastery's rooms. The package is rounded off with a bar and sauna in separate parts of the vaulted cellar.

Pension Jansen HOTEL €
(☎251 85; www.pensionjansen.de; 2nd fl, Richard Wagner Strasse 18; s €31-45, d €62-65) This cute, well-cared-for pension has six individually decorated rooms with cheerful colours

and motifs. Details like handmade wreaths hanging on aqua walls – or a big red rose screen-printed on the bed linen – convey a homey atmosphere. Book early.

Hotel Cristall HOTEL €€
(☎163 00; www.hotelcristall.de; Ursulaplatz 9-11; s €72-184, d €90-235; @📶) Angular red, orange and purple sofas greet you in the lobby of this recently expanded boutique hotel. Rooms in the newest wing feature luxuriously minimalist spaces with slate showers and black carpeting; the main building has simpler rooms with a stylish but less-modern look.

Das Kleine Stapelhäuschen HOTEL €
(☎272 7777; www.koeln-altstadt.de/stapelhaeuschen; Fischmarkt 1-3; s/d from €45/68; @📶) A small, friendly hotel housed in a 12th-century building in the centre of the old town, just off the riverbank. Exposed beams, antique furnishings and simple but cosy touches give rooms a homey feel.

Lint Hotel HOTEL €€
(☎920 550; www.lint-hotel.de; Lintgasse 7; s/d €85/129; 📶) Modern, clean rooms with parquet flooring and light, white bedspreads fill this ecofriendly hotel in the heart of the old town. The staff will be happy to tell you all about the solar panels and how they keep waste to a minimum.

Station Hostel for Backpackers HOSTEL €
(☎912 5301; www.hostel-cologne.de; Marzellenstrasse 44-56; dm €17-20, s/d/tr €39/55/75; @📶) You can't get more convenient than this friendly six-floor hostel around the corner from the train station. The rooms could use some sprucing up but they're perfectly simple and clean. Breakfast costs €3, or you can use the guest kitchen.

Meininger City Hostel & Hotel HOSTEL €
(☎355 332 014; www.meininger-hostels.com; Engelbertstrasse 33-35; dm €17-24, s/d/tr from €43/68/84, breakfast €3.50; @📶) Located in a former hotel, this charming hostel in the cool Zülpicher Viertel district is loaded with retro appeal coupled with modern rooms featuring lockers, reading lamps, a small TV and bathrooms.

Eating

While Cologne's beer halls serve excellent meals, the city overflows with restaurants – for the largest variety and the most happening atmosphere, head to the Zülpicher and Belgisches Viertel neighbourhoods.

Alcazar PUB FARE €
(Bismarckstrasse 39; snacks €4-9, mains €10-16; 🖉) The food and atmosphere are both hearty and warming at this old-school, slightly hippie pub. The changing menu always has one veggie option.

Metzgerei & Salon Schmitz INTERNATIONAL €
(Aachener Strasse 28; snacks €4-8) Whether you prefer sidling up to the long bar or grabbing an ultracomfy sofa in the retro lounge, Schmitz is a perfect pit stop for relaxed chats over coffee or cocktails. If hunger strikes, pop next door to **Metzgerei Schmitz**, a deli in a former butcher's shop.

MoschMosch ASIAN €
(Pfeilstrasse 25-27; dishes €7-11; ⏲11am-11pm) This sleek Japanese noodle bar offers flavourful ramen noodle soups and teppanyaki dishes in a candlelit space in the heart of the trendy Belgisches Viertel.

TOP CHOICE **Feynsinn** INTERNATIONAL €€
(☎240 9210; Rathenauplatz 7; mains €7-18) The glint of artfully arranged glasses behind the mirrored bar will catch your eye from the street, as will the broken-glass chandeliers. Inside, under murals, students, creative types and tourists tuck into seasonal cuisine (menu changes weekly) as well as traditional Cologne fare such as *Himmel and Aad* (literally Heaven and Earth, which is mashed potatoes and apple sauce). The owners have even started to raise their own pigs and cattle.

Weinstube Bacchus INTERNATIONAL €€
(☎217 986; Rathenauplatz 17; mains €9-20; ⏲dinner) Dark-wood tables, yellow walls that are lined with paintings by local artists (all pieces are for sale), a seasonal international menu and an almost exclusively German wine list make this casual wine bar–restaurant popular among the locals.

Drinking & Entertainment

As in Munich, beer in Cologne reigns supreme. More than 20 local breweries turn out a variety called *Kölsch*, which is relatively light and slightly bitter. The breweries run their own beer halls and serve their wares in skinny 200mL glasses. For more options, take a tram to Zülpicherplatz and explore.

Früh am Dom BEER HALL
(☎258 0394; Am Hof 12-14) This three-storey beer hall and restaurant (including cellar bar) is the most central, with black-and-white flooring, copper pans and tiled ovens keeping

it real, despite the souvenir shop. It's open for breakfast.

Fiffi Bar COCKTAIL BAR

(Rolandstrasse 99) Look for the pink lei-wearing bull-terrier statue mounted above the entrance of this hilarious retro, red-vinyl, dog-themed joint. We personally recommend ordering the Frozen Setter (Cuervo, pineapple and lemon) but perhaps you'd prefer the Sweet Lassie (rum, banana and cream)?

Katt-Winkel COCKTAIL BAR

(Greesbergstrasse 2) Housed in a cool, triangular space, this gay cafe-bar welcomes everyone. It's a relaxing spot to unwind to mellow music with an expertly mixed cocktail.

Päffgen BEER HALL

(Friesenstrasse 64-66) Another favourite, this thrumming wood-lined room has its own beer garden. It's not far from the bars of the Belgisches Viertel.

Hotelux VODKA BAR

(Rathenauplatz 22) Red walls, red booths and red lights; Hotelux serves cocktails and over 30 types of 'Soviet water' (ie vodka) to students and intellectual types.

Gebäude 9 CLUB

(814 637; Deutz-Mülheimer Strasse 127-129) Once a factory, this is now a Cologne nightlife stalwart spinning drum'n'bass, indie pop, gypsy music and '60s trash to film noir and puppets.

Underground LIVE MUSIC

(542 326; Vogelsanger Strasse 200; Mon & Wed-Sat) This complex combines a pub and two concert halls where indie and alt-rock bands play several times a week. Otherwise it's party time with different music nightly (no cover). There's a beer garden in summer.

Information

Köln Welcome Card (24/48/72hr €9/14/19) Discount card that includes free public transport (including Bonn) and discounted museum admission. Available from the tourist office.

Main post office (01802-3333; WDR Centre, Breite Strasse 6-26; 9am-7pm Mon-Fri, to 2pm Sat)

Tourist office (2213 0400; www.koelntourismus.de; Unter Fettenhennen 19; 9am-8pm Mon-Sat, 10am-5pm Sun)

Getting There & Away

Air

Cologne-Bonn airport (CGN; www.airport-cgn.de) is growing in importance. There are now direct flights to New York, while budget airlines German Wings and easyJet, among others, fly here.

Car

The city is on a main north–south autobahn route and is easily accessible for drivers. The popular German ride-share agency **ADM-Mitfahrzentrale** (194 40; www.citynetz-mitfahrzentrale.de; Maximinen Strasse 2) is near the train station.

Train

There are frequent RE services operating to Düsseldorf (€11 to €16, 25 to 30 minutes) and Aachen (€13.90, 50 minutes to one hour). Frequent EC, IC, or ICE trains go to Hanover (from €55, 2¾ to three hours), Frankfurt (from €39, one to 2¼ hours, three hourly) and Berlin (€104, 4¼ hours, hourly). Frequent Thalys high-speed services connect Cologne to Paris (from €95, four hours) via Brussels, and ICE trains go to Amsterdam (from €59, 2½ hours).

Getting Around

Cologne's mix of buses, trams and U-Bahn and S-Bahn trains is operated by **VRS** (01803-504 030; www.vrsinfo.de) in cooperation with Bonn's system.

Short trips (up to four stops) cost €1.60, longer ones €2.40. Day passes are €6.90 for one person and €10.10 for up to five people travelling together. Buy your tickets from the orange ticket machines at stations and aboard trams; be sure to validate them.

Cologne is flat and cycle-friendly. Bicycle hire is available next to the main train station at **Radstation** (139 7190; www.radstationkoeln.de; Am Hauptbahnhof/Breslauerplatz; per 3hr/1/3/7 days €5/10/20/40; 5.30am-10.30pm Mon-Fri, 6.30am-8pm Sat, 8am-8pm Sun).

Bonn

0228 / POP 312,000

South of Cologne on the Rhine's banks, Beethoven's birthplace became West Germany's temporary capital in 1949. But exactly 50 years later it was demoted when most (but not all) government departments returned to Berlin. These days several large company headquarters reside here, including telecommunications giant Deutsche Telekom, Deutsche Post World Net (German postal service plus international express mail service DHL) and renowned German TV broadcaster Deutsche Welle.

An excellent collection of museums and a quiet, compact old town filled with

18th-century baroque architecture make Bonn a worthwhile day trip.

The **tourist office** (☎775 000; www.bonn-regio.de; Windeckstrasse 1; ⏱9am-6.30pm Mon-Fri, 9am-4pm Sat, 10am-2pm Sun) is a three-minute walk along Poststrasse from the Hauptbahnhof, and can fill you in with any extra details.

Ludwig van Beethoven fans will head straight to the **Beethoven-Haus** (☎981 7525; www.beethoven-haus-bonn.de; Bonngasse 24-26; adult/concession €4/3; ⏱10am-6pm Mon-Sat, 11am-6pm Sun Apr-Oct, to 5pm Nov-Mar), where the composer was born in 1770. The house contains memorabilia concerning his life and music, including his last piano, with an amplified sounding board to accommodate his deafness. The annual Beethoven Festival takes place August to September.

The **Haus der Geschichte der Bundesrepublik Deutschland** (FRG History Museum; ☎916 50; www.hdg.de; Willy-Brandt-Allee 14; admission free; ⏱9am-7pm Tue-Sun) presents Germany's postwar history. It is part of the Museumsmeile, four museums that also include the **Kunstmuseum Bonn** (☎776 260; www.kunstmuseum-bonn.de; Friedrich-Ebert-Allee 2; adult/concession €5/2.50; ⏱10am-6pm Tue & Thu-Sun, to 9pm Wed) and the **Kunst-und Ausstellungshalle der Bundesrepublik Deutschland** (☎917 1200; www.bundeskunsthalle.de; Friedrich-Ebert-Allee 2; adult/concession €8/5; ⏱10am-9pm Tue & Wed, to 7pm Thu-Sun).

The unfiltered ale is a must at **Brauhaus Bönnsch** (☎650 610; Sterntorbrücke 4; mains €7-15; ⏱11am-1am), a congenial brew-pub adorned with photographs of famous politicians: Willy Brandt to, yes, Arnold Schwarzenegger. Schnitzel, spare ribs and sausage dominate the menu, but the *Flammkuchen* (Alsatian pizza) is still a perennial bestseller.

From Cologne, it's quicker to take an RE train to Bonn (€6.50, 30 minutes) than a tram (€8.50 day pass, 55 minutes). For river trips, see p573.

Düsseldorf

☎0211 / POP 585,000

'D-Town' or 'the City D', as local magazine editors like to call Düsseldorf, is Germany's fashion capital. But that means Jil Sander and Wolfgang Joop rather than cutting-edge street wear, as you'll soon discover observing fur-clad *Mesdames* with tiny dogs along the ritzy shopping boulevard of the Königsallee.

Indeed, this elegant and wealthy town could feel stiflingly bourgeois if it weren't for its lively old-town pubs, its position on the Rhine, its excellent art galleries and the postmodern architecture of its Mediahafen.

Sights

Düsseldorf has a lively **Altstadt**, which is filled with enough restaurants, beer halls and pubs to have earned it the slightly exaggerated title of the 'longest bar in the world'. In the central Marktplatz you'll find a **statue** of the former ruler, or elector, Jan Wellem.

What really sets the city apart, however, is the contemporary architecture of its **Mediahafen**. Here, in the city's south, docks have been transformed into an interesting commercial park, most notably including the **Neuer Zollhof**, three typically curved and twisting buildings by Bilbao Guggenheim architect Frank Gehry. You'll find a map of the park on a billboard located behind (ie on the street side of) the red-brick Gehry building.

For a bird's-eye view of the Mediahafen, and indeed all of Düsseldorf, catch the express elevator to the 168m viewing platform of the neighbouring **Rheinturm** (adult/child €3.50/1.90; ⏱10am-11.30pm). There's also a revolving restaurant and cocktail bar a level above, at 172.5m.

It's a pleasant stroll between the Mediahafen and the Altstadt along the riverside **Rheinuferpromenade**. Alternatively, you can join the city's elite window-shopping along the **Königsallee**, or 'Kö' – Düsseldorf's answer to Rodeo Drive.

Three excellent galleries, two sharing the same collection, form the backbone of Düsseldorf's reputation as a city of art.

Reopened in 2010, the **K20** (☎838 10; www.kunstsammlung.de; Grabbeplatz 5; adult/concession €10/5, combination ticket K20 & K21 €17/8.50; ⏱10am-6pm Tue-Fri, 11am-6pm Sat & Sun) museum features a brand-new wing and early-20th-century masters, including an extensive Paul Klee collection.

K21 (☎838 1600; www.kunstsammlung.de; Ständehausstrasse 1; adult/concession €10/5, combination ticket K20 & K21 €17/8.50; ⏱10am-6pm Tue-Fri, 11am-6pm Sat & Sun) concentrates on art from 1990 onwards. Highlights include Nam June Paik's *TV Garden*, local artist Katarina Fritsch's giant black mouse sitting on a sleeping man, the psychedelically decorated bar and the glassed-in roof.

KIT – Kunst im Tunnel (☎892 0769; www.kunst-im-tunnel.de; Mannesmannufer 1b; adult/

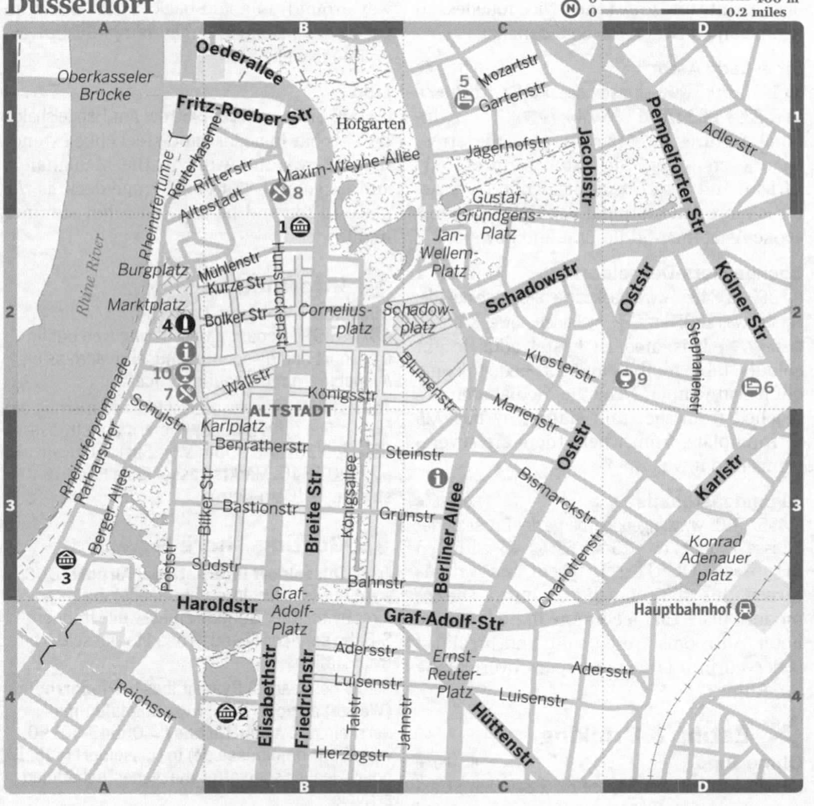

Düsseldorf

Sights

1 K20 ... B2
2 K21 ... B4
3 KIT–Kunst im Tunnel ... A3
4 Statue of Jan Wellem ... A2

Sleeping

5 Hotel Berial ... C1
6 Sir & Lady Astor ... D2

Eating

7 Libanon Express ... A2
8 Ohme Jupp ... B1

Drinking

9 Galapagoz ... D2
10 Zum Uerige ... A2

concession €4/3) literally translates as 'Art in the Tunnel', which is exactly what you get in the former road tunnel. Revolving exhibits – often by local students from the Düsseldorfer Art Academy – line the concrete curved walls of this surreal, subterranean space. The riverside cafe upstairs is a popular drinking spot during clement weather.

Sleeping

Hotel Berial HOTEL €

(☎490 0490; www.hotelberial.de; Gartenstrasse 30; s/d from €40/60; @) An inviting ambience reigns here, thanks to the friendly staff and the contemporary furnishings. Decor features lots of blue, blond wood, glass bathroom doors and some bright prints. The breakfast buffet is truly gargantuan.

Stage 47 BOUTIQUE HOTEL €€€

(☎388 030; www.stage47.de; Graf-Adolf-Strasse 47; s/d from €160/180; @) Behind the drab exterior, movie glamour meets design chic at this urban boutique hotel. Rooms are named for famous people, some of whom have actually stayed in the environs dominated by black, white and grey tones. Nice touches: an iHome and a Nespresso coffee maker.

Sir & Lady Astor HOTEL €€
(☎173 370; www.sir-astor.de; Kurfürstenstrasse 18 & 23; s €83-170, d €95-240; @ 📶) The twin-hotel features two parts across the street from each other: Sir Astor features only African and Scottish motifs, while Lady Astor is more international and themed rooms evoke Asia, the Middle East and beyond.

Backpackers-Düsseldorf HOSTEL €
(☎302 0848; www.backpackers-duesseldorf.de; Fürstenwall 180; dm €22, incl linen, towel & breakfast; @ 📶) This modern hostel adds bright colours, table football and soft beds to come out a real winner. Near the Mediahafen, it's reached from the train station by bus 725 to Kirchplatz, from where there are several trams into town.

Jugendgästehaus HOSTEL €
(☎557 310; www.jugendherberge.de; Düsseldorfer Strasse 1; dm/s/tw €25/42/62; @ 📶) Situated in upscale Oberkassel, recent renovations turned this 368-room hostel into a snazzy, modern place that feels more like a boutique hotel. All rooms are en suite and breakfast is served in a large, airy space overlooking the Rhine.

Eating & Drinking

Ohme Jupp BISTRO €
(☎326 406; Ratinger Strasse 19; ⊙8am-1am) Casual, artsy cafe serving breakfast and seasonal blackboard specials; also a popular afterwork drinking den.

Libanon Express MIDDLE EASTERN €
(Berger Strasse 19-21; cafe €3-14, restaurant €10-19) Crammed with mirrors and tiles – and with recommendations stickered on the window – this cafe serves great kebabs, falafel and other Middle Eastern specialities.

Zum Uerige BREWPUB
(☎866 990; Berger Strasse 1) In this noisy, cavernous place, the trademark Uerige Alt beer (a dark and semisweet brew typical of Düsseldorf) flows so quickly that the waiters just carry around trays and give you a glass whenever they spy one empty. It also serves hearty German fare, so it doubles as an excellent place for a bite.

Galapagoz BAR
(☎355 8983; www.galapagoz.de; Klosterstrasse 68a) Tuck into this tiny cafe-bar for fantastic cocktails, wines and snacks (the menu is written on the slate tiles that wrap their way around) in a laid-back South American space. It's primarily a gay hangout, but everyone is welcome.

Lido BAR
(☎1576 8730; www.lido1960.de; Am Handelshafen 15) This bar in a glass-and-steel cube extending out over the water in the Mediahafen, and its smooth outdoor lounge-deck, is *the* place to see and be seen on a hot summer night.

Information

Düsseldorf Welcome Card (24/48/72hr €9/14/19) Discount card offering free public transport and discounted museum admission. Available from the tourist office.

Tourist office (www.duesseldorf-tourismus.de) main office (☎172 0222; Immermannstrasse 65b; ⊙9.30am-6.30pm Mon-Sat); old town (☎1720 2840; Marktstrasse/Ecke Rheinstrasse; ⊙10am-6pm)

Getting There & Away

From **Düsseldorf International Airport** (DUS: www.duesseldorf-international.de), trains go directly to other German cities, while frequent S-Bahn services (1 and 7) head to Düsseldorf train station.

Low-cost carrier Ryanair flies to **Niederrhein (Weeze) airport** (NRN; www.flughafen-niederrhein.de). A **shuttle bus** (☎06543-501 90; www.bohr-omnibusse.de) to Düsseldorf (€15, 1¼ hours) leaves soon after the planes' scheduled arrivals.

The many **train** services from Düsseldorf include to Cologne (€10.50 to €16, 25 to 30 minutes), Frankfurt-am-Main (€70, 1½ to 1¾ hours), Hanover (€53, 2½ hours) and Berlin (€97, 4¼ hours).

Getting Around

The metro, trams and buses are useful to cover Düsseldorf's distances. Most trips within the city cost €2.30; longer trips to the suburbs are €4.50. Day passes are €5.30.

Aachen

☎0241 / POP 247,000

A spa town with a hopping student population and tremendous amounts of character, Aachen has narrow cobbled streets, quirky fountains, shops full of delectable *Printen* (local biscuit, a bit like gingerbread), and a pretty cathedral, which make for an excellent day trip from Cologne or Düsseldorf or a worthy overnight stop.

Sights

Next to the tourist office is the **Elisenbrunnen** (Elisa Fountain); despite its sulphuric, rotten-egg smell, you *can* drink the water – it's supposedly good for the digestion.

In the far left-hand corner of the park, behind the Elisenbrunnen, you'll find the **Geldbrunnen** (Gold Fountain), which represents the circulation of money. The comical figures around the pool clutch their coins or purses while the water is sucked down the central plughole (jokingly known as 'the taxman').

Head east along the top of the park here, towards Forum M, and turn left into Buchkremerstrasse. Soon you'll reach a fountain with a scary-looking creature. This is the mythological **Bahkauv**, which was rumoured to jump on the backs of those returning late from the pub and demand a lift all the way home.

Buchkremerstrasse becomes Buchel. Turn left just past Leo van den Daele, then right again, and you'll come to Hühnermarkt, with its **Hühnerdiebbrunnen** (Chicken-thief fountain). The hasty thief hasn't noticed one of his stolen chickens is a rooster that's about to unmask him by crowing.

From here, Aachen's main **Markt** is visible just to the northeast. The 14th-century **Rathaus** (adult/concession €2/1; ⌚10am-5pm Mon-Fri, 10am-1pm & 2-5pm Sat & Sun) overlooks the Markt, while a fountain statue of **Charlemagne** is in the middle.

Head back down the hill along Krämerstrasse until you come to the **Puppenbrunnen** (Puppet fountain), where you're allowed to play with the movable bronze figures.

Continuing in the same direction for 50m, you'll arrive at Aachen's famous Dom.

Dom CATHEDRAL

(Kaiserdom or Münster; www.aachendom.de; ⌚7am-7pm Apr-Oct, 7am-6pm Nov-Mar) While Cologne's cathedral wows you with its size and atmosphere, Aachen's similarly Unesco-listed Dom impresses with its shiny neatness. The small, Byzantine-inspired **octagon** at the building's heart dates from 805 but its ceiling mosaics still glitter and its marble columns still gleam.

The building's historical significance is twofold: not only did Charlemagne order it built, but 30 Holy Roman emperors were crowned here from 936 to 1531.

The brass **chandelier** hanging in the centre was donated by Emperor Friedrich Barbarossa in 1165. Standing at the main altar and looking back towards the door, it's just possible to glimpse Charlemagne's simple marble throne. The man himself lies in the golden **shrine** behind the altar. The cathedral became a site of pilgrimage after his death.

Carolus Thermal Baths BATHS

(☎182 740; www.carolus-thermen.de; Stadtgarten/Passstrasse 79; admission with/without sauna from €22/11; ⌚9am-11pm) The 8th-century Franks were first lured to Aachen for its thermal springs. And just over 1200 years later, the state-of-the-art Carolus Thermen are still reeling them in.

That's hardly surprising, for the complex is part therapeutic spa – good for rheumatism etc – and part swimming centre. Quirky currents whiz you around one pool, water jets bubble up in another and taps pour out cold water in yet another. Only diehard fans should pay for the sauna, as there's – bizarrely – a steam room accessible to all.

The baths are in the city garden, northeast of the centre.

Sleeping

Hotel Drei Könige HOTEL €€

(☎483 93; www.h3k-aachen.de, in German; Büchel 5; s €90-130, d €120-160, apt €130-240; wi-fi) The radiant Mediterranean decor is an instant mood enhancer at this family-run favourite with its doesn't-get-more-central location. Some rooms are a tad small but the two-room apartment sleeps up to four. Breakfast on the 4th floor comes with heavenly views over the rooftops and the cathedral.

Hotel Benelux HOTEL €€

(☎400 030; www.hotel-benelux.de; Franzstrasse 21-23; s €94-109, d €120-154; wi-fi) This well-run hotel is clean and uncluttered, with tasteful art in all its rooms. The rooftop garden with the enclosed gazebo is a bonus.

Jugendgästehaus HOSTEL €

(☎711 010; www.jugendherberge.de; Maria-Theresia-Allee 260; dm/s/tw €23/37/57; @) This modern DJH outpost sits on a hill overlooking the city, and gets lots of school groups. Take bus 2 to Ronheide.

Eating & Drinking

Aachen's students have their own 'Latin Quarter' along Pontstrasse, with dozens of bars and cheap eats. The street heads northeast off the Markt and runs for nearly 1km.

Leo van den Daele INTERNATIONAL €

(Büchel 18) A warren of 17th-century rooms all linked by crooked stairs across four merchants' homes, this nationally renowned cafe specialises in gingerbread, or *Printen*. You can also enjoy light meals – soups, sandwiches, quiches and *pastetchen* (vol-au-vents) – among its tiled stoves and antique knick-knacks.

Kaiser Wetter ITALIAN €€
(☎9437 9950; www.kaiserwetter-ac.de; Hof 5) Stop by for a drink, a snack or a light meal of salads and pizzas at this restaurant-lounge in the centre of town. Relax at the outdoor tables under the shadow of giant Roman pillars or step inside the modern interior.

Anna's Tafel FRENCH €€
(☎5593 5537; Pontstrasse 62; mains €10-14) This tiny, quiet wine bar–restaurant with unfinished wood tables and romantic candelabras serves seasonal French specialities, cheese and charcuterie plates and decadent desserts. A great escape from the student crowds just up the road.

Apollo Kino & Bar BAR/CLUB
(☎900 8484; Pontstrasse 141-149) This cavernous basement joint does double duty as an art-house cinema and a sweaty dance club for the student brigade. Alt sounds rule on Mondays and salsa on Tuesdays, but on other nights it could be anything from dancehall to disco, house to power pop.

Information

Tourist office (☎180 2960/1; www.aachen.de; Atrium Elisenbrunnen, Kapuzinergraben; ⌚9am-6pm Mon-Fri, 9am-2pm Sat, also 10am-2pm Sun Easter-Dec)

Getting There & Around

There are frequent trains to Cologne (€13.90 to €19.50, 30 minutes to one hour) and twice-hourly service to Düsseldorf (from €17.20, 70 minutes to 1½ hours). The high-speed Thalys train passes through regularly on its way to Brussels and Paris (from €87, three hours).

Buses cost €1.50 (trip of a few stops only), €2.20 (regular single) or €6.10 (day pass).

LOWER SAXONY

Lower Saxony (Niedersachsen) likes to make much of its half-timbered towns. Hamelin is certainly a true fairy-tale beauty, and leaning Lüneberg is quite unlike any other town you'll see. The state is also home to the global headquarters of Volkswagen and the business-minded capital, Hanover, as well as the pretty Harz mountains (see the boxed text, p513).

Hanover

☎0511 / POP 518,000

German comedians – yes, they do exist – like to dismiss Hanover as 'the autobahn exit between Göttingen and Walsrode'. However, the capital of Lower Saxony is far livelier than its reputation assumes, and its residents are remarkably friendly and proud of their small city. While it's famous for hosting trade fairs, particularly the huge CEBIT computer show in March, it also boasts acres of greenery in the Versailles-like gardens, Herrenhäuser Gärten.

Parts of the central Altstadt look medieval, but few of them are. They're mostly clever fakes built after intense WWII bombing.

Sights & Activities

The enormous **Grosser Garten** (Large Garden; admission €3, free in winter) is the highlight of the **Herrenhäuser Gärten** (☎1684 7576; www.herrenhaeuser-gaerten.de; ⌚9am-sunset). It has a small maze and Europe's tallest fountain. Check the website in summer for **Wasserspiele**, when all fountains are synchronised, and the night-time **Illuminations**. The **Niki de Saint Phalle Grotto** is a magical showcase of the artist's work. She was French – her colourful figures adorn the famous Stravinsky fountain outside the Centre Pompidou in Paris – but developed a special relationship with Hanover. There's a popular beer garden in the Grosser Garten. Alternatively, the flora of the **Berggarten** (Mountain Garden; admission €2, combined entry with Grosser Garten €4) is interesting. Adjacent lies the **Sea Life Hannover** (☎56 669 0101; adult/child €14.95/10.95, incl Grosser Garten & Berggarten adult/child €15.50/11.95; ⌚10am-5pm), a 3500-sq-metre educational aquarium with friendly staff and clever displays.

The **Neues Rathaus** (new town hall) was built between 1901 and 1913. Town models in the foyer reveal the extent of WWII devastation. Further east lies the Leine River and, since 1974, **Die Nanas** – three fluorescent-coloured, earth-mama sculptures by de Saint Phalle – have lived here. They're best seen on Saturday, when there's a flea market at their feet.

In summer, the **Machsee** (lake) has ferries (crossing €3, tour €6) and numerous boats for hire. There's a free public **swimming beach** on the southeast shore.

Sleeping

The tourist office only finds private rooms during trade fairs but can arrange hotel bookings year-round for €7.

City Hotel Flamme HOTEL €€
(☎388 8004; www.cityhotelflamme.de; Lammstrasse 3; s/d €69/99; @☎) This art hotel features endearing touches such as goodnight stories on bedside tables. Rooms are arranged around a tropical-feeling atrium that has an inviting bar. Accommodation is spotless and the staff are friendly.

City Hotel am Thielenplatz HOTEL €€
(☎327 691; www.smartcityhotel.de; Thielenplatz 2; s €58.50-68.50, d €77-87; @☎) Crisp, white, retro furnishings and high ceilings dominate in the airy space here. Some bathrooms are miniscule but overall this place is excellent value and only a short walk from the train station. The reception desk is located in the popular downstairs bar.

Jugendherberge HOSTEL €
(☎131 7674; www.jugendherberge.de; Ferdinand-Wilhelm-Fricke-Weg 1; dm under/over 27yr from €23.90/26.90; @) This large, space lab–like structure houses a modern hostel with breakfast room and terrace bar overlooking the river in an area that feels more country than city. Take U3 or U7 to Fischerhof, cross the mini red suspension bridge and turn right.

GästeResidenz PelikanViertel HOTEL €€
(☎399 90; Pelikanstrasse 11; s €46-69, d €66-89, tr €92-109; @) Upmarket student residence meets budget hotel, this huge complex (located in the former Pelikan fountain-pen factory) has a wide range of Ikea-style rooms, all with kitchenettes. Prices skyrocket during trade-fair periods. Take U3, U7 or U9 to Pelikanstrasse.

Eating & Drinking

Markthalle INTERNATIONAL €
(Karmarschstrasse 49; dishes €4-10; ⊙7am-8pm Mon-Wed, to 10pm Thu & Fri, to 4pm Sat) This huge covered market of food stalls (sausages, sushi, tapas and more), gourmet delis and standing-only 'bars' is a no-nonsense, atmospheric place for a quick bite. It's also heaving each Friday evening with people proclaiming *Prost!* (Cheers!) to the start of the weekend.

Spandau INTERNATIONAL €€
(Engelbosteler Damm 30; mains €6-14; ⊙10am-1am Sun-Wed, 10am-2am Thu-Sat) Retro-'70s Spandau in Hanover's Nordstadt is more like Berlin's Kreuzberg – a place where students from the nearby university and the local Turkish community rub shoulders.

Café-Bar Celona CAFE, BAR €€
(☎353 8576; Knochenhauerstrasse 42; mains €7-16) Latin-themed and plant-filled, this cafe-bar is fine any time of day (or night) for a bite, a drink, or both. Book ahead for its massive (and massively popular) all-you-can-eat Sunday brunch (€8.95).

Mr Phung Kabuki JAPANESE €€
(Friedrichswall 10) Boats bob by on the water-based sushi chain, and you can order all manner of pan-Asian and wok dishes in this airy, trendy restaurant with an enormous range of spirits.

Information

Hannover Tourismus (☎information 1234 5111, room reservations 1234 555; www.hannover.de; Ernst- August-Platz 8; ⊙9am-6pm Mon-Fri, 9am-2pm Sat, also 9am-2pm Sun Apr-Sep)

Getting There & Around

Hanover's **airport** (HAJ; www.hannover-airport.de) has many connections, including on low-cost carrier Air Berlin.

There are frequent IC/ICE train services running to/from Hamburg (€34 to €39, 1¼ to 1½ hours), Berlin (€53 to €58, 1½ to two hours), Cologne (€54 to €61, 2¾ to 3¼ hours) and Munich (€112, 4¼ to 4¾ hours), among other destinations.

U-Bahn lines from the Hauptbahnhof are boarded in the station's north (follow the signs towards Raschplatz), except the U10 and U17, which are overground trams leaving from near the tourist office.

Most visitors only travel in the central 'Hannover' zone. Single tickets are €2.10 and day passes €4.10.

The S-Bahn (S5) takes 17 minutes to the airport (€2.80).

Around Hanover

CELLE

☎05141 / POP 70,800

With row upon row of ornate half-timbered houses, all decorated with scrolls and allegorical figures, Celle is a pleasant place for a leisurely day trip. Even the tourist office,

Tourismus Region Celle (☎1212; www.region-celle.com; Markt 14; ⊙9am-6pm Mon-Fri, 10am-4pm Sat, 11am-2pm Sun May-Sep, 9am-5pm Mon-Fri, 10am-1pm Sat Oct-Apr), is located in a striking building, the **Altes Rathaus** (1561–79), which boasts a wonderful Weser Renaissance stepped gable, topped with the ducal coat of arms and a golden weather vane.

Lying just west of the Rathaus is the 13th-century **Stadtkirche** (☎7735; An der Stadkirche 8; tower adult/concession €1/0.50; ⊙10am-6pm Tue-Sat Apr-Dec, to 5pm Jan-Mar, tower 10-11.45am & 2-4.45pm Tue-Sat). You can climb up the 235 steps to the top of the church steeple for a view of the city, or just watch as the city trumpeter climbs the 220 steps to the white tower below the steeple for a trumpet fanfare in all four directions. The spectacle is most entertaining and takes place daily at 9.30am and 5.30pm (sometimes more frequently during the summer months – enquire at the tourist office).

Further west lies the magnificently proportioned wedding-cake **Schloss** (Ducal Palace; ☎123 73; Schlossplatz; tours adult/concession €5/3; ⊙tours hourly 11am-3pm Tue-Sun Apr-Oct, 11am & 3pm Tue-Sun, plus 1pm Sat & Sun Nov-Mar). Built in 1292 by Otto Der Strenge (Otto the Strict) as a town fortification, the building was expanded and turned into a residence in 1378. The last duke to live here was Georg Wilhelm (1624–1705), and the last royal was Queen Caroline-Mathilde of Denmark, who died here in 1775.

The Schloss can only be visited on guided tours (in German), but there are explanatory brochures in English for sale. Highlights include the magnificent baroque theatre, the private apartment of Caroline-Mathilde and, above all, the chapel. Its original Gothic form is evident in the high windows and vaulted ceiling, but the rest of the intricate interior is pure Renaissance. The duke's pew was above; the shutters were added later so His Highness could snooze during the three-hour services.

Across from the palace stands Celle's **Kunstmuseum** (Art Museum; ☎123 55; www.

WORTH A TRIP

VOLKSWAGEN CITY

Volkswagen *is* the Lower Saxon town of **Wolfsburg** – and the huge VW emblem adorning the company's global headquarters (and a factory the size of a small country) won't let you forget it. 'Golfsburg', as it's nicknamed after one of VW's most successful models, does a nice sideline in modern architecture. But really, the top reason people come here is to experience the theme park called Autostadt, which tells you everything you ever wanted to know about VW.

Spread across 25 hectares, **Autostadt** (Car City; ☎0800-2886 782 38; www.autostadt.de; Stadtbrücke; adult/child/concession/family €15/6/12/38, entry after 4pm €7; ⊙9am-6pm) is a celebration of all things Volkswagen. Exhibitions run the gamut of automotive design and engineering, the history of the Beetle and the marketing of individual marques, including VW itself, Audi, Bentley, Lamborghini, Seat and Skoda.

Included in the admission price is the **CarTower Discovery**, a fun glass lift that whisks you up to the 20th floor as if you were an actual car (vehicles are stored inside the towers). At the top you have a sweeping view of the city and complex. Most exciting for wannabe race-car drivers, there are obstacle courses and safety training (€25 to €28) where you can take an adrenalin-fuelled spin.

The space-age building beside the train station is **Phaeno** (☎0180-106 0600; www.phaeno.de; Willy Brandt-Platz 1; adult/child/concession/family €12/7.50/9/26.50; ⊙9am-5pm Mon-Fri, 10am-6pm Sat & Sun), a science centre designed by British-based Iraqi architect Zaha Hadid. Some 250 hands-on exhibits and experiments – wind up your own rocket, watch thermal images of your body – provide hours of fun. It's very physical, but also requires concentration. Instructions and explanations come in German and English.

Wolfsburg's centre lies just southeast of the Hauptbahnhof. Autostadt is north across the train tracks. Head through the 'tunnel' under the Phaeno science centre and you'll see the footbridge. **Wolfsburg tourist office** (☎05361 899 930; www.wolfsburg.de; Willy Brandt-Platz 3; ⊙9am-6pm Mon-Fri, 10am-3pm Sat & Sun) is in the train station.

Frequent RE/IC/ICE train services arrive from Hanover (from €12.90, 30 minutes to one hour) and Berlin (from €34.40, one to 1¼ hours).

kunst.celle.de; Schlossplatz 7; adult/concession incl Bomann Museum €5/3, free Fri; ⌚10am-5pm Tue-Fri, to 6pm Sat & Sun), which bills itself as 'the world's first 24-hour museum'. It's claiming this after a €4-million refurbishment created a transparent glass facade that showcases electric-light installations right through the evening – the exterior colour changes from red, orange, purple, gold and blue during the last few hours of darkness. During the day, you can visit the contemporary German paintings, sculptures and objects of collector Robert Simon.

In the older building adjacent, you'll still find the regional-history **Bomann Museum** (☎125 44; www.bomann-museum.de; Schlossplatz 7; adult/concession incl Kunstmuseum €5/3; ⌚10am-5pm Tue-Sun, last entry 4.15pm). Here, among other things, you can wander through rooms furnished in 19th-century style.

Various train services run to Celle from Hanover (€8.40 to €10.50, 20 to 35 minutes) and Hamburg (€23.80 to €28, one to 1½ hours). The Altstadt is about a 15-minute walk east of the Hauptbahnhof.

HAMELIN

☎05151 / POP 58,700

If you were to believe the 'Pied Piper of Hamelin' fairy tale, this quaint, ornate town on the Weser River ought to be devoid of both rats and children. According to legend, the Pied Piper *(Der Rattenfänger)* was employed by Hamelin's townsfolk to lure their pesky rodents into the river in the 13th century. When they refused to pay him, however, he picked up his flute again and led their kids away.

However, it is a bedtime story, after all. International tourism means the reality is very different. Everywhere you look along Hamelin's cobbled streets are – you guessed it – fake rats and happy young children.

The train station is about 800m east of the centre. To get to **Hameln Tourist Information** (☎957 823; www.hameln.com; Diesterallee 1; ⌚9am-6.30pm Mon-Fri, 9.30am-4pm Sat, 9.30am-1pm Sun May-Sep, 9am-6pm Mon-Fri, 9.30am-1pm Sat & Sun Oct & Apr) take bus 2, 3, 4, 21, or 33.

The best way to explore is to follow the **Pied Piper trail** – the line of white rats drawn on the pavements. There are information posts at various points. They're in German, but at least you know when to stop to admire the various restored 16th- to 18th-century half-timbered houses.

The detailed Weser Renaissance style dominates the Altstadt – the **Rattenfängerhaus** (Rat Catcher's House; Osterstrasse 28), from 1602, is perhaps the finest example, with its steep and richly decorated gable. Also not to be missed is the **Hochzeitshaus** (Wedding House; 1610–17) at the Markt end of Osterstrasse. The **Rattenfänger Glockenspiel** at the far end chimes daily at 9.35am and 11.35am, while a **carousel of Pied Piper figures** twirls at 1.05pm, 3.35pm and 5.35pm.

Between May and September you can watch the **Pied Piper open-air play** at noon on Sunday and the comic musical *Rats* on Wednesday at 4.30pm; both are free and are performed at the Hochzeitshausplatz in the centre of town – contact the tourist office for details.

Frequent S-Bahn trains (S5) head from Hanover to Hamelin (€10.30, 45 minutes). By car, take the B217 to/from Hanover.

BREMEN

☎0421 / POP 550,000

It's a shame the donkey, dog, cat and rooster in Grimm's *Die Bremerstadmusikanten* (Town Musicians of Bremen) never actually made it here – they would have fallen in love with the place. This little city is big on charm, from the statues of the famous fairy-tale characters to the jaw-dropping art-nouveau laneway to the impressive Markt. On top of that, the waterfront promenade along the Weser River is a relaxing refuge filled with outdoor cafes, and the student district along Ostertorsteinweg knows it's got a good thing going and leaves little to be desired.

Sights & Activities

Bremen's **Markt** is striking, particularly its ornate, gabled **Rathaus**. In front stands a 13m-tall medieval statue of the knight **Roland**, Bremen's protector. On the building's western side, you'll find a sculpture of the **Town Musicians of Bremen** (1951). Local artist Gerhard Marcks has cast them in their most famous pose, scaring the robbers who invaded their house, with the rooster atop the cat, perched on the dog, on the shoulders of the donkey.

Also on the Markt is the twin-towered **Dom St Petri**, the most interesting – and slightly macabre – feature of which is its **Bleikeller** (Lead Cellar; ☎365 0441; adult/concession €1.40/1; ⌚10am-5pm Mon-Fri, 10am-2pm Sat, noon-5pm Sun Easter-Oct) Here, open coffins

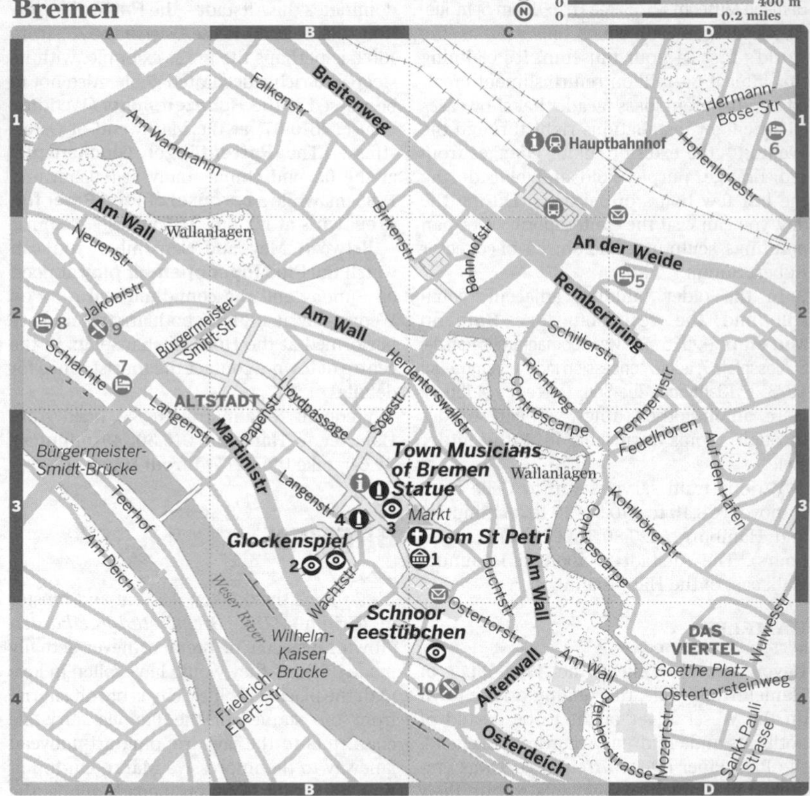

reveal eight corpses that have mummified in the dry underground air. The Bleikeller has its own entrance, south of the main cathedral door.

If the Markt is memorable, then nearby **Böttcherstrasse** is unique. It's an opulent art deco street commissioned by Ludwig Roselius, the inventor of decaffeinated coffee and founder of the company Hag. He later managed to save it from the Nazis, who thought it 'degenerate'. Under the golden relief you enter a world of tall brick houses, shops, galleries, restaurants, a **Glockenspiel** and several museums (which can easily be skipped). If you can, peek in the back door of 'Haus Atlantis' (aka the Hilton hotel), for its phantasmagorical, multicoloured, glass-walled **spiral staircase**.

The maze of narrow, winding alleys known as the **Schnoorviertel** was once the fishermen's quarter and then the red-light district. Now its doll's house–sized cottages are souvenir shops and restaurants. The cute **Schnoor Teestübchen** (Wüste Stätte 1) serves Frisian tea and cakes.

With more time, make a visit to **Beck's Brewery** (☎5094 5555; Am Deich 18-19; tours in German & English €9.50; ⏲2pm & 3.30pm Thu & Fri, 12.30pm, 2pm, 3.30pm & 5pm Sat Jan-Apr, additionally 11am & 12.30pm Thu & Fri, 9.30am & 11am Sat May-Dec) or the oyster-shaped **Universum Science Center** (☎334 60; www.usc-bremen.de; Wiener Strasse 2; adult/concession & child €18.50/12.50; ⏲9am-6pm Mon-Fri, 10am-7pm Sat & Sun, last entry 90min before closing).

Sleeping

Bremer Backpacker Hostel HOSTEL €
(☎223 8057; www.bremer-backpacker-hostel.de; Emil-Waldmannstrasse 5-6; dm/s/d €17/28/46, bedding €3; @📶) A friendly place five minutes from the train station, here you'll find simply furnished but spotless rooms spread out over several levels (each floor is named after

Bremen

Top Sights

Sights

Sleeping

Eating

a continent), a full kitchen, a living room and a cheerful courtyard.

Hotel Bölts am Park HOTEL €€
(☎346 110; www.hotel-boelts.de; Slevogtstrasse 23; s/d €70/90; @📶) This family-run hotel in a leafy neighbourhood has real character, from the old-fashioned breakfast hall to its well-proportioned rooms. A few singles with hall showers and toilets cost €48.

Hotel Überfluss HOTEL €€€
(☎322 860; www.hotel-ueberfluss.com; Langenstrasse 72/Schlachte; s €139-154, d €184-199, ste €359; ❄@📶🏊) Dragging quaint Bremen into the 21st century is this jaw-dropping design hotel. It's all green-tinted windows overlooking the Weser River, and shiny black bathrooms. The friendly staff and the lobby, which displays bits of the old city wall found when constructing the hotel, make this place feel unique and more than worth the splurge.

DJH Hostel Bremen HOSTEL €
(☎163 820; www.jugendherberge.de; Kalkstrasse 6; dm under/over 27yr €23.50/26.50, s/d €36.50/63; @📶) Looking like a work of art from outside, with a yellow-and-orange Plexiglas facade and slit rectangular windows, this refurbished building more resembles a museum than a hostel. Comfortable dorms are all en suite, there's a bar-breakfast room with huge glass windows overlooking the Weser River, and a rooftop terrace. Take tram 3 or 5 to Am Brill.

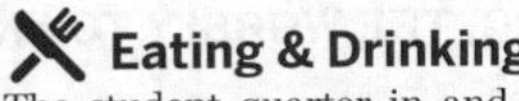

Eating & Drinking

The student quarter in and around Ostertorsteinweg, Das Viertel, is full of restaurants and cafes and has a vaguely bohemian atmosphere. The waterfront promenade, Schlachte, is more expensive and mainstream. The Marktplatz is home to oodles of cheap snack stands.

Piano CAFE/BAR
(Fehrfeld 64; mains €6-13) One of the most enduringly popular cafes in the student quarter, excellent for an evening tipple or a snack from its pizza, pasta, steaks and veggie casserole menu. Breakfast is served until 4pm.

Apadana PERSIAN €
(cnr Heinkenstrasse & Faulenstrasse; mains €6-13) This family-run, hospitable Persian restaurant serves lovingly prepared, traditional fare in a simple, quiet space. It's excellent for solo diners, with a large stack of magazines on hand to read.

Restaurant Flett GERMAN €€
(☎320 995; Böttcherstrasse 3-5) Despite all the tourists, this is the best place in Bremen to try local specialities such as *Labskaus* (a hash of beef or pork with potatoes, onion and herring) or *Knipp* (fried hash and oats).

Katzen Café INTERNATIONAL €€
(☎326 621; Schnoor 38) This Moulin Rouge–style restaurant opens out into a rear sunken terrace bedecked with flowers. The menu runs the gamut from Alsatian to Norwegian, with seafood a strong theme.

Wohnzimmer BAR
(☎163 2064; Ostertorsteinweg 99) This bar and lounge mostly gets a relaxed 20s and 30s crowd, who hang out on the sofas – which explains the name 'Living Room' – or lounge around on the mezzanine levels in non-smoker and smoker areas.

Information

Tourist office (☎01805-101030; www.bremen-tourism.de) Hauptbahnhof (⏰9am-7pm Mon-Fri, 9.30am-6pm Sat & Sun); branch office (Obernstrasse/Liebfrauenkirchhof; ⏰10am-6.30pm Mon-Fri, 10am-4pm Sat & Sun)

Getting There & Around

Flights from **Bremen airport** (BRE: www.airport-bremen.de) include low-cost carriers Air Berlin and Ryanair.

WORTH A TRIP

LÜNEBURG, THE WOBBLY TOWN

With an off-kilter church steeple, buildings leaning on each other and houses with swollen 'beer-belly' facades, it's as if charming Lüneburg has drunk too much of the Pilsener lager it used to brew.

Of course, the city's wobbly angles and uneven pavements have a more prosaic cause. For centuries until 1980, Lüneburg was a salt-mining town, and as this 'white gold' was extracted from the earth, ground shifts and subsidence knocked many buildings sideways. Inadequate drying of the plaster in the now-swollen facades merely added to this asymmetry.

But knowing the scientific explanation never detracts from the pleasure of being on Lüneburg's comic-book crooked streets.

Between Hanover (€26, one hour by train) and Hamburg (€13.20, 30 minutes), the city's an undemanding day trip from either. From the train station, head west into town towards the highly visible, 14th-century **St Johanniskirche**, the 106m-high spire of which leans 2.2m off true. Local legend has it that the architect tried to kill himself by jumping off it. (He fell into a hay cart and was saved, but celebrating his escape later in the pub he drank himself into a stupor, fell over, hit his head and died after all.)

The church stands at the eastern end of the city's oldest square, **Am Sande**, full of typically Hanseatic stepped gables. At the western end stands the beautiful black-and-white **Industrie und Handelskammer** (Trade and Industry Chamber).

Continue one block past the Handelskammer and turn right into restaurant-lined Schröderstrasse, which leads to the Markt, where the ornate **Rathaus** (town hall) contains the **tourist office** (☎04131 207 6620; www.lueneburg.de; ⌚9am-6pm Mon-Fri, to 4pm Sat, 10am-4pm Sun May-Sep, 9am-5pm Mon-Fri, to 2pm Sat Oct-Apr).

Admire the square before continuing west along Waagestrasse and down our favourite Lüneburg street, **Auf dem Meere**, en route to the **St Michaeliskirche**. Here the wonky facades and wavy pavements are like something from a Tim Burton film.

It's too late now to regain your equilibrium, so head back along Am Flock for the pubs on **Am Stintmarkt** on the bank of the Ilmenau River.

Frequent trains go to Hamburg (€20.80 to €28, one hour to 1¼ hours), Hanover (€21 to €30, one hour to 80 minutes) and Cologne (€60, three hours).

Tram 6 leaves the airport frequently, heading to the centre (€2.20, 16 minutes). Other trams cover most of the city. Single bus and tram tickets cost €2.20; a day pass (€5.90 for one adult and two children) is excellent value.

HAMBURG

☎040 / POP 1.77 MILLION

It comes as no surprise that Hamburg is stylishly expanding itself by 40% without batting an eye – this is a city where ambition flows through the ubiquitous waterways and designer-clad residents cycle to their media jobs with a self-assurance unmatched by any other German city. The site of Europe's largest urban-renewal project is a never-ending forest of cranes that are efficiently transforming old city docks into an extension of the city – it all makes you wonder: what *can't* this city achieve? Decent weather; that's one thing it can't buy, build or create. But residents are passionately dedicated to their beloved city and will rarely fret about drizzly skies – they just open up their designer umbrellas and get on with it.

Germany's leading port city has always been forward-thinking and liberal. Its dynamism, multiculturalism and hedonistic red-light district, the Reeperbahn, all arise from its maritime history. Joining the Hanseatic League trading bloc in the Middle Ages, Hamburg has been enthusiastically doing business with the rest of the world ever since. In the 1960s it nurtured the musical talent of the Beatles. Nowadays it's also a media capital and the wealthiest city in Germany.

Sights & Activities

Old Town HISTORIC AREA

Hamburg's medieval **Rathaus** (☎4283 120 10; tours adult/child €3/0.50, ⌚English-language tours hourly 10.15am-3.15pm Mon-Thu, to 1.15pm Fri, to 5.15pm Sat, to 4.15pm Sun; Ⓜ Rathausmarkt or Jungfernstieg) is one of Europe's most opulent. North of here, you can wander through the **Alsterarkaden**, the Renaissance-style arcades sheltering shops and cafes alongside a canal or 'fleet'.

For many visitors, however, the city's most memorable building is south in the Merchants' District. The 1920s, brown-brick **Chile Haus** (cnr Burchardstrasse & Johanniswall; Ⓜ Mönckebergstrasse/Messberg) is shaped like an ocean liner, with remarkable curved walls meeting in the shape of a ship's bow and staggered balconies that look like decks.

Alster Lakes LAKES

A cruise on the Binnenalster and Aussenalster is one of the best ways to appreciate the elegant side of the city. **ATG Alster-Touristik** (☎3574 2419; www.alstertouristik.de; 2hr trip adult/child €9.50/4.25; ⏲Apr-Oct; Ⓜ Jungfernstieg) is a good bet. The company also offers 'fleet' tours and winter tours through the icy waters.

Better yet, hire your own rowboat or canoe. Opposite the Atlantic Hotel you'll find **Segelschule Pieper** (☎247 578; www.segelschule-pieper.de; An der Alster; per hr from €15; ⏲Apr-Oct; Ⓜ Hauptbahnhof).

Speicherstadt & Harbour HISTORIC AREA

The beautiful red-brick, neo-Gothic warehouses lining the Elbe archipelago south of the Altstadt once stored exotic goods from around the world. Now the so-called **Speicherstadt** (Ⓜ Messberg/Baumwall) is a popular sightseeing attraction. It's best appreciated by simply wandering through its streets or taking a Barkassen boat up its canals. **Kapitän Prüsse** (☎313 130; www.kapitaen-pruesse.de; Landungsbrücke No 3; adult/child from €12.50/5.50) offers regular Speicherstadt tours, leaving from the port. Other Barkassen operators simply tout for business opposite the archipelago.

Another way to see the Speicherstadt is from the **High-Flyer Hot Air Balloon** (☎3008 6968; www.highflyer-hamburg.de; per 15min €15; ⏲10am-midnight, to 10pm winter, weather permitting) tethered nearby.

The Speicherstadt merges into the **HafenCity**, an area where the old docks are being transformed into a 155-hectare extension of the city – what looks like a never-ending construction zone is actually Europe's largest inner-city development project. When finished, the area will house a university, approximately 6000 apartments and more. It's estimated that in the next 20 years, it will extend the centre city of Hamburg by about 40%. Some 40,000 people will work here, and 12,000 will live here. The squat brown-brick former warehouse at the far west of the zone is being transformed into the new **Elbphilharmonie** (Elbe Philharmonic Hall; http://elbphilharmonie-bau.de), due for completion by 2012. Pritzker Prize–winning Swiss architects Herzog & de Meuron are responsible for the design, which, like their Tate Modern building in London, boasts a glass top. This time, however, they're being far more ambitious, as the glass facade should be taller than its brick base and the roof line will rise in wavelike peaks to reflect the waterfront location. Get details and ponder models detailing the magnitude of the project at the **HafenCity InfoCenter** (☎3690 1799; Am Sandtorkai 30; ⏲10am-6pm Tue, Wed & Fri-Sun, to 8pm Thu May-Sep). HafenCity will be connected to the Hauptbahnhof and several other central transport hubs when the new U-Bahn line (U4) opens in late 2011.

Port and Elbe River cruises start in summer at the St Pauli Landungsbrücken. **Hadag** (☎311 7070; www.hadag.de; Brücke 2; 1hr harbour trip adult/child from €10/5.50) offers some of the best deals and cruises.

Reeperbahn RED LIGHT DISTRICT

(Ⓜ Reeperbahn) No discussion of Hamburg is complete without mentioning St Pauli, home of the Reeperbahn, Europe's biggest red-light district. Sex shops, peep shows, dim bars and strip clubs line the streets, which generally start getting crowded with the masses after 8pm or 9pm. This is also where the notorious **Herbertstrasse** (a block-long street lined with brothels that's off-limits to men under 18 and to female visitors of all ages) is located as well as the **Erotic Art Museum** (☎317 4757; www.eroticartmuseum.de; Bernhard-Nocht-Strasse 69; adult €5; ⏲noon-10pm, to midnight Fri & Sat) and the **Condomerie** (☎319 3100; www.condomerie.de; Spielbudenplatz 18; ⏲noon-midnight), with its extensive collection of prophylactics and sex toys.

WANT MORE?

Head to **Lonely Planet** (www.lonelyplanet.com/germany/hamburg) for planning advice, author recommendations, traveller reviews and insider tips.

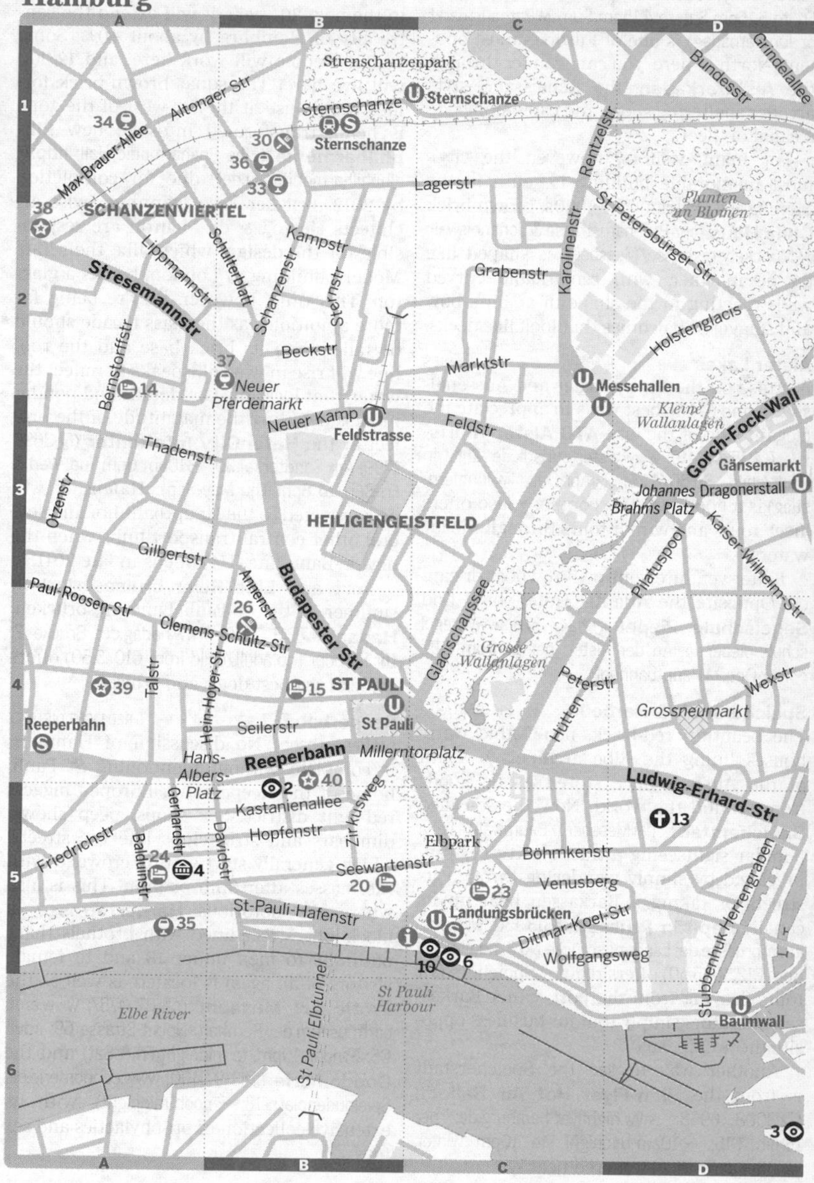

Fischmarkt MARKET

Here's the perfect excuse to stay up all Saturday night. Every Sunday between 5am and 10am, curious tourists join locals of every age and walk of life at the famous Fischmarkt in St Pauli. The market has been running since 1703, and its undisputed stars are the boisterous *Marktschreier* (market criers) who hawk their wares at full volume. Live bands also entertainingly crank out cover versions of ancient German pop songs in the adjoining *Fischauktion-*

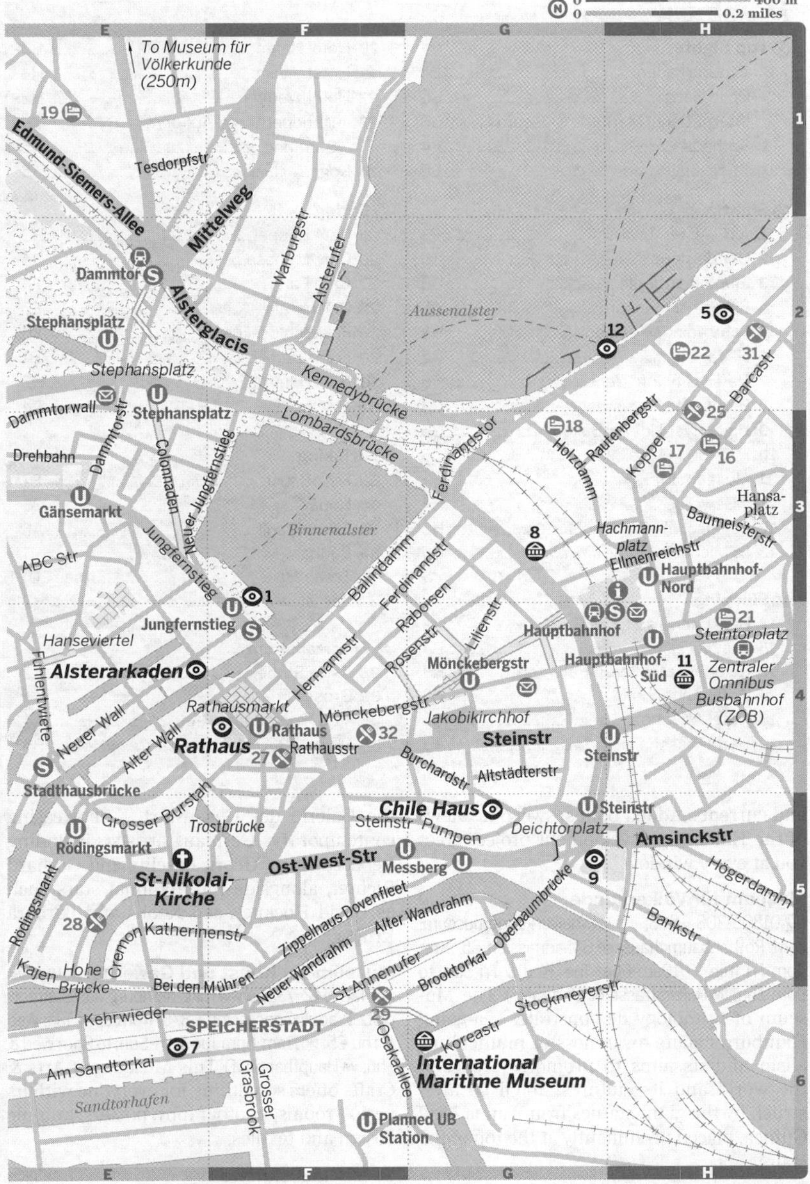

shalle (Fish Auction Hall). Take bus 112 to Hafentreppe.

International Maritime Museum MUSEUM
(☎300 93 300; www.internationales-maritimes-museum.de; Koreastrasse 1; adult/concession €10/7; ⏰10am-6pm Tue, Wed & Fri-Sun, 10am-8pm Thu; Ⓜ Messberg) Ensconced within HafenCity (p587), this nine-floor, enormous space examines 3000 years of maritime history through displays of model ships, naval paintings, navigation tools and educational exhibits explaining the seas and its tides

Hamburg

Top Sights
- Alsterarkaden ... E4
- Chile Haus ... G5
- International Maritime Museum ... G6
- Rathaus ... F4
- St-Nikolai-Kirche ... E5

Sights
1. ATG Alster-Touristik ... F3
2. Condomerie ... B5
3. Elbphilharmonie ... D6
4. Erotic Art Museum ... A5
5. Fahrradladen St Georg ... H2
6. Hadag ... C5
7. Hafen City Info Center ... E6
8. Hamburger Kunsthalle ... G3
9. High-Flyer Hot Air Balloon ... G5
10. Kapitän Prüsse ... C5
11. Museum für Kunst und Gewerbe ... H4
12. Segelschule Pieper ... H2
13. St Michaeliskirche ... D5

Sleeping
14. Backpackers St Pauli ... A2
15. East ... B4
16. Galerie-Hotel Sarah Petersen ... H3
17. Hotel Annenhof ... H3
18. Hotel Atlantic ... G3
19. Hotel Fresena ... E1
20. Hotel Hafen ... B5
21. Hotel Village ... H4
22. Hotel Wedina ... H2
23. Jugendherberge-Auf dem Stintfang ... C5
24. Kogge ... A5

Eating
25. Café Koppel ... H3
26. Café Mimosa ... B4
27. Café Paris ... F4
28. Deichgraf ... E5
29. Fleetschlösschen ... F6
30. Frank und Frei ... B1
31. Geel Haus ... H2
32. Mr Cherng ... F4

Drinking
33. Fritz Bauch ... B1
34. Nouar ... A1
35. StrandPauli ... A5
36. Südhang ... B1
- Tower Bar ... (see 20)

37. Zoë 2 ... B2

Entertainment
38. Astra Stube ... A2
39. Grosse Freiheit 36/Kaiserkeller ... A4
40. Meanie Bar/Molotow Club ... B4

and currents. Added bonus: sweeping views of the HafenCity development project greet you at every window.

Museum für Völkerkunde MUSEUM
(☎01805-308 888; www.voelkerkundemuseum.com; Rothenbaumchaussee 64; admission €5, after 4pm Fri free; ⏲10am-6pm Tue, Wed & Fri-Sun, to 9pm Thu; Ⓜ Hallerstrasse or Dammtor) The Museum of Ethnology demonstrates sea-going Hamburg's acute awareness of multiculturalism and its aims to promote respect of the world and its cultures. You'll be awestruck by the giant statues from Papua New Guinea, placed prominently at the top of the stairs.

Hamburger Kunsthalle MUSEUM
(☎428 131 200; www.hamburger-kunsthalle.de; Glockengiesserwall; adult/concession €8.50/5; ⏲10am-6pm Tue, Wed & Fri-Sun, to 9pm Thu); Ⓜ Hauptbahnhof) Consists of two buildings, the old one housing old masters and 19th-century art, and a white concrete cube – the Galerie der Gegenwart – showcasing contemporary German artists, including Rebecca Horn, Georg Baselitz and Gerhard Richter, alongside international stars such as David Hockney, Jeff Koons and Barbara Kruger.

Museum für Kunst und Gewerbe MUSEUM
(☎428 542 732; www.mkg-hamburg.de; Steintorplatz 1; adult/concession €8/5, from 5pm Tue, Wed & Thu €5; ⏲11am-6pm Tue & Fri-Sun, to 9pm Wed & Thu; Ⓜ Hauptbahnhof) This Museum of Arts & Crafts offers something for everyone with its period rooms, photography, posters, graphic design and textiles.

St Michaeliskirche CHURCH
(tower adult/concession €3/2; ⏲10am-6pm Apr-Oct, to 5pm Nov-Mar; Ⓜ Stadthausbrücke) This is one of Hamburg's most recognisable landmarks and northern Germany's largest Protestant baroque church. From the tower of 'Der Michel', as it's commonly called, you have panoramic views.

St-Nikolai-Kirche CHURCH

(Ost-West-Strasse; adult/child €3.70/3; 10.30am-5.30pm; Rödingsmarkt) This WWII-damaged church is now an antiwar memorial, with some chilling photos of the then-bombed-out city.

Sleeping

Fritz Hotel BOUTIQUE HOTEL €€

(8222 2830; www.fritzhotel.com; Schanzenstrasse 101-103; s/d €60/90; ; Sternshanze) Run by fun, friendly staff, this stylish town-house hotel is as cool as a cucumber in shades of white and grey and splashes of red. It's great for urbanistas who'll be happy finding their own breakfast at neighbourhood cafes (though the hotel offers fresh fruit and coffee) and who aren't perturbed by a bit of street noise (some rooms have balconies overlooking the action; ask for one of the quieter rooms out the back).

Backpackers St Pauli HOSTEL €

(2351 7043; www.backpackers-stpauli.de; Bernstorffstrasse 98; dm €19.50-24, d/tr from €60/75, linen €2, breakfast & snacks €2-4.30; @; Feldstrasse) Entered via a bright cafe, this is a great new addition to Hamburg's hostel scene, with a cool, subterranean, maritime-themed lounge containing a small kitchenette, a sunny outdoor terrace, table football and light-filled rooms (some with bathrooms) with good-sized lockers.

Superbude Hotel, Hostel & Lounge HOSTEL €

(380 8780; www.superbude.de; Spaldingstrasse 152; dm €16-22, d €59-89; @; Berliner Tor) This hostel-hotelnear St Georg is just about the snazziest hotel-hostel we've ever seen. Housed in a former printing factory, the modern, spacious dorms and rooms feel like trendy loft spaces. Quirky touches include plungers used as wall 'hooks', a metallic polka-dot entrance, slate stone flooring, cow-hide rugs and two entertainment rooms (one with Nintendo, Wii and table football; the other is a mini cinema). Breakfast is €7, laundry facilities are free and bike rental costs €4 per day.

Jugendherberge-Auf dem Stintfang HOSTEL €

(313 488; www.jugendherberge.de; Alfred-Wegener-Weg 5; dm from €22.90; @; Landungsbrücken) Modern, clean and convenient (head out of the U-Bahn station, up the steps to the massive modern complex at the top of the hill), this DJH hostel overlooks the Elbe River and the harbour. With lots of large, noisy school groups, however, it's very keen on rules, and you're locked out part of the day.

Kogge HOTEL €

(312 872; www.kogge-hamburg.de; Bernhard-Nocht-Strasse 59; s €29.50-33, d €48.40-55; @; Landungsbrücken or Reeperbahn) We wanna rock 'n' roll all night at this friendly, fun rock 'n' roll bar and hotel sitting on a quite street around the corner from the noisy Reeperbahn territory. Themed rooms include those named 'Bollywood', 'Punk Royal', 'Disco Dream' and all share shower and toilet facilities. Popular with musicians and perfect for travellers planning to party all night and sleep until late (standard check out is 2pm).

Hotel Annenhof HOTEL €

(243 426; www.hotelannenhof.de; Lange Reihe 23; s €40-50, d €70-80; Hauptbahnhof) The Annenhof's attractive, cheerful rooms have polished wooden floorboards and clean, simple furnishings. There's no breakfast but plenty of cafes nearby.

Hotel Village HOTEL €€

(480 6490; www.hotel-village.de; Steindamm 4; s/d from €72/95, without bathroom from €52/68; @; Hauptbahnhof) A former bordello going straight, it has boudoirs that feature various mixes of red velvet, gold flock wallpaper and leopard prints, and sometimes even blue neon–lit bathrooms or mirrors above the bed – don't be surprised if you stumble upon a photo shoot during your stay. It's a fun, functional space a stone's throw from the main train station. Breakfast is included.

Hotel Fresena HOTEL €€

(410 4892; www.hotelfresena.de; Moorweidenstrasse 34; s €75-99, d €88-130; @; Dammtor) Palatial, clean, modern rooms; high ceilings; African statues; and cool theatre photographs give this place character without clutter. If it's full the building houses four other pensions and the friendly staff will help you find a room elsewhere. Breakfast is €9.

Hotel Wedina HOTEL €€

(280 8900; www.wedina.de; Gurlittstrasse 23; s/d main bldg incl breakfast from €98/118, other bldg incl breakfast from €108/138; ; Hauptbahnhof) You might find a novel instead of a chocolate on your pillow at Wedina, a hotel that's a must for bookworms and literary groupies. Jonathan Franzen, Vladimir Nabokov and JK Rowling are just some of the authors who've stayed and left behind signed books.

The hotel is spread over four buildings, offering a choice of traditional decor in the main red building or modern, urban living in its green, blue and yellow houses. The hotel also offers bike hire (€8 per day).

Hotel Hafen HOTEL €€
(☎311 1370; www.hotel-hafen-hamburg.de; Seewartenstrasse 9; r from €120, breakfast €16; @; Landungsbrücken) Location, location, location. This privately owned behemoth of a hotel (353 rooms) looms over the heart of Hamburg's harbour from a small hill. If you're lucky enough to score a harbour-facing room (no guarantees, but it's worth asking), the views are extraordinary. In addition to the refurbished, historic main building – a former seamen's home – there are newer modern wings.

Galerie-Hotel Sarah Petersen PENSION €€
(☎249 826, 0173 200 0746; www.galerie-hotel-sarah-petersen.de; Lange Reihe 50; s €88-155, d €98-165; @; Hauptbahnhof) This delightful *pensione* (guest house) inside a historic 1790 town house is an extension of its welcoming artist-owner's personality, whose paintings decorate the walls of his 'gallery of dreams'. Furnishings include a mix of contemporary, antique and art-deco styles. Our pick of its five rooms is the top-floor terrace studio, with a romantic rooftop terrace, kitchenette and separate living area. Breakfast costs €9.50.

Schlaflounge B&B €€
(☎3868 5387; www.schlaflounge.de, in German; Vereinsstrasse 54b; s/d €65/89, breakfast €10; Christuskirche) Live like a local in this stylish, streamlined B&B in an appealing residential quarter with relaxed neighbourhood bars and excellent restaurants nearby. Attractive rooms incorporate blond wood and either brown and ochre or dark-red and aqua colour schemes. Breakfast includes organic fruit and home-made jam.

East HOTEL €€€
(☎309 933; www.east-hamburg.de; Simon-von-Utrecht-Strasse 31; d/apt/ste from €165/175/275; St Pauli) Pillars, walls and lamps emulate organic forms in the public areas of this warm, richly decorated design hotel. Floors are themed by plants and spices.

Hotel Atlantic HOTEL €€€
(☎288 80; www.kempinski.atlantic.de; An der Alster 72-79; s €270-370, d €300-500, ste from €500, breakfast €33; Hauptbahnhof Nord) Imagine yourself aboard a luxury ocean liner in this grand 252-room hotel, which opens onto Holzdamm. Built for cruise passengers, it has ornate stairwells, wide hallways and subtle maritime touches. Suites – including BMW and James Bond suites – are a big leap up from the standard accommodation. Significantly cheaper rates are often available online.

Eating

The **Schanzenviertel** (Feldstrasse/Schanzenstern) swarms with cheap eateries; try Schulterblatt for Portuguese outlets or Susanenstrasse for Asian and Turkish. Many fish restaurants around the Landungsbrücken are overrated and touristy. St Georg's **Lange Reihe** (Hauptbahnhof) offers many characterful eating spots to suit every budget, and there is a seemingly endless selection of simple but quality, high-value sushi joints all over town.

Fleetschlösschen INTERNATIONAL €€
(Brooktorkai 17; snacks €7-10; 8am-8pm Mon-Fri, 11am-6pm Sat & Sun; Messberg) This former customs post overlooks a Speicherstadt canal and the HafenCity development and has a narrow, steel spiral staircase to the toilets. There's barely room for 20 inside, but its several outdoor seating areas are brilliant in sunny weather. The owner's collection of *Kleinods* (small treasures) includes centuries-old Dutch pottery unearthed during the construction of HafenCity.

Café Paris FRENCH €€
(Rathausstrasse 4; mains €10-19; from 9am Mon-Fri, from 10am Sat & Sun; Rathaus) At this stalwart in the city centre, be sure to admire the spectacular maritime- and industry-themed ceiling murals and tiles. On weekends breakfast is served until 4pm in this bustling French brasserie.

Geel Haus GERMAN €€
(Koppel 76; dishes €5-10; from 6pm; Hauptbahnhof) A casual, homey neighbourhood favourite tucked away on a quiet street in St Georg with an emphasis on Austrian and German fare, plus plenty of veggie options.

frank und frei PUB FAR €
(Schanzenstrasse 93; mains €5-16; Sternschanze) Big, bustling and laid-back restaurant-pub, with brick walls, wooden booths, shiny pillars and a stylish curved wooden bar, offering simple German fare, salads and pastas. It's a great place to unwind with a beer, a bite or a full meal.

DON'T MISS

SOUPY EEL

Tired of wurst and dumplings? Well, you're in a port city now so specialities generally involve seafood, veering away from stereotypical German fare. *Labskaus* is a dish of boiled, marinated beef put through the grinder with mashed potatoes and herring and served with a fried egg, red beets and pickles. Or perhaps you'd prefer *Aalsuppe* (eel soup) spiced with dried fruit, ham, vegetables and herbs? **Deichgraf** (☎364 208; www.deichgraf-hamburg.de; Deichstrasse 23; mains €18-29; ⏲lunch Mon-Sat, dinner Sat; Ⓜ Rödingsmarkt) is one leading local restaurant that can acquaint you with these and other local dishes.

Café Koppel INTERNATIONAL €
(Lange Reihe 66; dishes €4.50-9; ✎; Ⓜ Hauptbahnhof) Set back from busy Lange Reihe, with a garden in summer, this largely veggie cafe is a refined oasis in an airy space housing galleries and artists' workshops. The menu includes great breakfasts, lots of salads, stews, jacket potatoes, curries and pasta.

Café Mimosa INTERNATIONAL €
(Clemens-Schultz-Strasse 87; dishes €5-12; Ⓜ St Pauli) A welcome change from the greasy fast-food joints in the nearby Reeperbahn, this gem of a neighbourhood cafe serves delicious pastas, healthy salads, proper coffee and home-made cakes in a theatrical space of stripped floors, bare wooden tables with brass candlesticks and red-and-cream-painted walls. There's a smattering of pavement tables.

Mr Cherng ASIAN €€
(Speersort 1; mains €6-11; Ⓜ Rathaus) A favourite with city office workers, high-quality Chinese, Thai and Japanese cuisine is served at impressively low prices, especially at the all-you-can-eat sushi buffet.

Drinking & Entertainment

Südhang WINE BAR
(☎4309 9099; www.suedhang-hamburg.de; Susannenstrasse 29; ⏲from noon Mon-Sat, from 4pm Sun; Ⓜ Sternschanze) Walk through the shoe store, head up the stairs and enter this friendly wine bar, with polished mahogany tables and low lighting, perched right above the hustle of the neighbourhood.

Zoë 2 BAR
(Neuer Pferdemarkt 17; ⏲from noon; Ⓜ Feldstrasse) The sister living room to the original Zoë in Berlin (which, sadly, closed years ago) is alive and kicking with battered sofas, rough-hewn walls and old lampshades.

Tower Bar COCKTAIL BAR
(www.hotel-hafen-hamburg.de; Seewartenstrasse 9; ⏲6pm-1am Mon-Thu, 6pm-2.30am Fri-Sun; Ⓜ Landungsbrücken) For an elegant, mature evening, repair to this 14th-floor eyrie at the Hotel Hafen for unbeatable harbour views.

Nouar BAR
(Max-Brauer-Allee 275; ⏲from 7pm; Ⓜ Sternschanze) A popular late-night bar with students and other denizens of the nearby Schanzenviertel, this place has that relaxed secondhand look going on and a fondness for football during the week.

Fritz Bauch BAR
(☎430 0194; Bartelstrasse 6; ⏲from 5pm; Ⓜ Sternschanze) A down-to-earth neighbourhood bar in the middle of the Schanzenviertel with yellow and pale-pink walls; wooden arched ceilings; basic, no-nonsense drinks and hopping music.

Meanie Bar/Molotow Club CLUB
(☎310 845; www.molotowclub.com; Spielbudenplatz 5; ⏲from 6pm; Ⓜ Reeperbahn) One of the few venues along the Reeperbahn with real local cred, retro Meanie Bar sits above the Molotow Club, where an independent-music scene thrives.

Grosse Freiheit 36/Kaiserkeller LIVE MUSIC
(☎3177 7811; Grosse Freiheit 36; ⏲from 10pm Tue-Sat; Ⓜ Reeperbahn) Wedged between live-sex theatres and peep shows, this is popular for live rock and pop, particularly as the Beatles played in the basement Kaiserkeller.

Astra Stube CLUB
(www.astra-stube.de; Max-Brauer-Allee 200; ⏲from 9.30pm Mon-Sat Ⓜ St Pauli) This graffiti-covered red building underneath the railway tracks looks totally unpromising, but it's actually a pioneer of Hamburg's underground scene, with DJs playing experimental electro, techno and drum 'n' bass.

Information

Dangers & Annoyances

Although safe, Hamburg contains several red-light districts around the train station and Reeperbahn. The Hansaplatz in St Georg can feel a bit dicey after dark. Fortunately, there's a strong police presence in these areas.

LIFE'S A BEACH BAR

Following the trend in Paris, Zürich and Berlin, river-beach bars in Hamburg are *the* place to be in the summer. The city beach season kicks off around April and lasts until at least September, as patrons come to drink, listen to music, dance and generally hang out on the waterfront. Leading venues, open daily, include **Lago Bay** (www.lago.cc, in German; Grosse Elbstrasse 150; Ⓜ Königstrasse), a stylish retreat where you can actually swim, while free exercise classes will help you keep fit, er, between cocktails. **StrandPauli** (www.strandpauli.de, in German; St-Pauli-Hafenstrasse 84; 🚌112) is a more laid-back stretch of sand with a youthful feel, and **Strandperle** (www.strandperle-hamburg.de, in German; Övelgönne 1; 🚌112) is the original Hamburg beach bar. It's little more than a kiosk but the people-watching is tops, as patrons linger over the newspaper with a drink or a coffee – think of it as a sandy, al fresco cafe-lounge.

Emergency

Police station Hauptbahnhof (Kirchenallee exit); St Pauli (Davidwache, Spielbudenplatz 31; Ⓜ Reeperbahn)

Post

Main post office (☎01802-3333; Dammtorstrasse 14; ⊙8.30am-6pm Mon-Fri, 9am-noon Sat; Ⓜ Jungfernstieg)
Post office (☎01802-3333; Mönckebergstrasse 7; ⊙9am-7pm Mon-Fri, to 3pm Sat; Ⓜ Hauptbahnhof)

Tourist Information

Hamburg Tourismus (☎information 3005 1200, hotel bookings 3005 1300; www.hamburg-tourismus.de) Hauptbahnhof (Kirchenallee exit; ⊙8am-9pm Mon-Sat, 10am-6pm Sun); Landungsbrücken (btwn piers 4 & 5; ⊙8am-6pm Apr-Oct, 10am-6pm Nov-Mar; Ⓜ Landungsbrücken); airport (☎5075 1010; ⊙6am-11pm) Sells the Hamburg Card (one/three/five days €8.50/19.90/34.90), which offers free public transport and museum discounts.

 Getting There & Away

Air

Hamburg's **airport** (HAM: www.flughafen-hamburg.de) has frequent flights to domestic and European cities, including on low-cost carrier Air Berlin.

For flights to/from Ryanair's so-called 'Hamburg-Lübeck' (actually an hour away) see p596.

Bus

The **Zentral Omnibus Busbahnhof** (ZOB, central bus station; ☎247 5765; www.zob-hamburg.de; Adenauer Allee 78) is most popular for services to Central and Eastern Europe. **Eurolines** (☎4024 7106; www.eurolines.com) has buses to Prague (€65) and Vilnius (€85).

Car & Motorcycle

The A1 (Bremen–Lübeck) and A7 (Hanover–Kiel) cross south of the Elbe River.

Train

When reading train timetables, remember that there are two main train stations: Hamburg Hauptbahnhof and Hamburg-Altona. There are frequent RE/RB trains to Lübeck (€11.50, 45 minutes), as well as various services to Hanover (from €35, 1¼ to 1½ hours) and Bremen (from €20.90, one to 1¼ hours). In addition there are EC/ICE trains to Berlin (from €65, 1½ to two hours), Cologne (from €78, four hours) and Munich (from €125, 5½ to six hours) as well as EC trains to Copenhagen (from €81, 4¾ hours).

Getting Around

To/From the Airport

The S1 S-Bahn connects the airport directly with the city centre, including the Hauptbahnhof. The journey takes 24 minutes and costs €2.70.

Bicycle

Hamburg is a fantastic place to explore by bike, with extensive cycle lanes (many along the water). For bike hire, try **Fahrradladen St Georg** (☎243 908; Schmilinskystrasse 6; per day €10).

Public Transport

There is an integrated system of buses and U-Bahn and S-Bahn trains. A single journey costs €2.70; day tickets, bought from machines before boarding, cost €6.30, or €5.30 after 9am. From midnight to dawn the night-bus network takes over from the trains, converging on the main metropolitan bus station at Rathausmarkt.

SCHLESWIG-HOLSTEIN

Sandwiched between the North and Baltic Seas, Schleswig-Holstein is Germany's answer to the Côte d'Azur. Of course, the weather here often makes it a pretty funny sort of answer, as dark clouds and strong winds whip in across the flat peninsula. Still, people flock to the beaches on the coasts, and the countryside in between has a stark beauty.

Lübeck

0451 / POP 220,900

Two pointed cylindrical towers of Lübeck's Holstentor (gate) greet you upon arrival – if you think they're a tad crooked, you're not seeing things: they lean towards each other across the stepped gable that joins them. Right behind them, the streets are lined with medieval merchants' homes and spired churches forming the city's so-called 'crown'. It's hardly surprising that this 12th-century gem is on Unesco's World Heritage list.

Sights

The impossibly cute city gate or **Holstentor** (122 4129; adult/concession €5/2.50; 10am-6pm Apr-Dec, 11am-5pm Tue-Sun Jan-Mar) serves as Lübeck's museum as well as its symbol. The six gabled brick buildings east of the Holstentor are the **Salzspeicher**, once used to store the salt from Lüneburg that was pivotal to Lübeck's Hanseatic trade.

Behind these warehouses, the Trave River forms a moat around the old town, and if you do one thing in Lübeck in summer, it should be a boat tour. From April to September, **Maak-Linie** (706 3859; www.maak-linie.de) and **Quandt-Linie** (777 99; www.quandt-linie.de) depart regularly from either side of the Holstentorbrücke. Prices are €9/4/6.50 per adult/child/student.

Each of Lübeck's churches offers something different. The shattered bells of the **Marienkirche** (Schüsselbuden 13; admission €1; 10am-6pm Apr-Sep, to 5pm Oct, to 4pm Tue-Sun Nov-Mar) still lie on the floor where they fell after a bombing raid. There's also a little devil sculpture outside, with an amusing fairy tale (in English). The tower lift in the **Petrikirche** (397 730; www.st-petri-luebeck.de, in German; Schüsselbuden 13; adult/concession €3/2; 9am-9pm Apr-Sep, 10am-7pm Oct-Mar) affords superb views.

The **Rathaus** (122 1005; Breite Strasse 64; adult/concession €3/1.50; tours 11am, noon & 3pm Mon-Fri) is ornate, but all the tours are in German. If you have a sweet tooth, head across the street to **JG Niederegger shop and cafe** (Breite Strasse 89) and pick up a chocolate-coated marzipan treat, a gift, or both.

In the Middle Ages, Lübeck was home to numerous craftspeople and artisans. Their presence caused demand for housing to outgrow the available space, so tiny single-storey homes were built in courtyards behind existing rows of houses. These were then made accessible via little walkways from the street.

Almost 90 such *Gänge* (walkways) and *Höfe* (courtyards) still exist, among them charitable housing estates built for the poor, the *Stiftsgänge* and *Stiftshöfe*. The most famous of the latter are the beautiful **Füchtingshof** (Glockengiesserstrasse 25; 9am-noon & 3-6pm) and the **Glandorps Gang** (Glockengiesserstrasse 41-51), which you can peer into.

If you head south along An der Obertrave southwest of the Altstadt, you'll pass one of Lübeck's loveliest corners, the **Malerwinkel** (Painters' Quarter), where you can take a break on garden benches among blooming flowers, gazing out at the houses and white picket fences across the water.

A few steps further, fans of *The Tin Drum* shouldn't miss the **Günter Grass-Haus** (122 4192; www.guenter-grass-haus.de; Glockengiesserstrasse 21; adult/concession €5/2.50, 'Kombi' card with Buddenbrookhaus €7/4; 10am-5pm Apr-Dec, 11am-5pm Jan-Mar), which includes a fine collection of manuscripts and sculptures. Fellow Nobel Prize–winning author Thomas Mann *(Death in Venice)* was born in Lübeck and he's commemorated in the award-winning **Buddenbrookhaus** (122 4190; www.buddenbrookhaus.de; Mengstrasse 4; adult/concession €5/2.50; 'Kombi' card with Günter Grass-Haus €7/4; 11am-6pm Apr-Dec, 11am-5pm Jan-Mar).

For children, there's a fantastic **Theater Figuren Museum** (786 26; www.tfm-luebeck.com; Am Kolk 14; adult/child/concession €5/2.50/3; 10am-6pm Apr-Oct, 11am-5pm Tue-Sun Nov-Mar). It's a private collection of some 1200 puppets, props, posters and more, from Europe, Asia and Africa. The adjoining cafe is also a good place to refuel.

Alternatively, ask the tourist office about the nearby seaside resort of **Travemünde**.

Sleeping

Hotel zur Alten Stadtmauer HOTEL €
(737 02; www.hotelstadtmauer.de; An der Mauer 57; s/d from €55/65, without bathroom from €37/55;) With pine furniture and splashes of red or yellow, this simple, 25-room hotel

is bright and cheerful. The wooden flooring means sound carries, but customers here tend not to be quieter types. Back rooms overlook the river.

Hotel Lindenhof HOTEL €€
(☎872 100; www.lindenhof-luebeck.de; Lindenstrasse 1a; s €65-95, d €85-135 incl breakfast; @) Its rooms are businesslike and small, but a healthy breakfast buffet, friendly service and little extras (free biscuits, newspapers and a 6am-to-midnight snack service) propel the Lindenhof into a superior league.

Hotel Jensen HOTEL €€
(☎702 490; www.hotel-jensen.de; An der Obertrave 4-5; s €75-85, d €93-115 incl breakfast; @) Classic and romantic, this old *Patrizierhaus* (mansion house) is conveniently located facing the Salzspeicher across the Trave River. Its seafood restaurant, Yachtzimmer, is also excellent.

Klassik Altstadt Hotel BOUTIQUE HOTEL €€
(☎702 980; www.klassik-altstadt-hotel.de; Fischergrube 52; s/d €76/138, ste from €135; wi-fi) Each room at this elegantly furnished boutique hotel is dedicated to a different German writer or artist, such as Thomas Mann and Johann Sebastian Bach, as well as international luminaries like Denmark's Hans Christian Andersen. It's close to many of the city's best dining options, but it also has a solid in-house restaurant (mains €11.50 to €14.50).

Rucksackhotel HOSTEL €
(☎706 892; www.rucksackhotel-luebeck.de; Kanalstrasse 70; dm €13-15, s €28, d €34-40, linen €3, breakfast €3-5; @ wi-fi) None of the rooms at this 30-bed hostel are en suite, but it has a relaxed atmosphere and good facilities, including a well-equipped kitchen, as well as round-the-clock access.

DJH Hostel Altstadt HOSTEL €
(☎702 0399; www.jugendherberge.de; Mengstrasse 33; dm from €19) Standard hostel in the old town – it isn't particularly new, but it's cosy and central.

Two very cheap and basic places are **Sleep-Inn** (☎719 20; www.cvjm-luebeck.de; Grosse Petersgrube 11; dm from €14) and the **Hotel Am Dom** (☎399 9430; www.cvjm-luebeck.de; Dankwartsgrube 43; s & d from €37).

Eating

Markgraf INTERNATIONAL €€€
(☎706 0343; www.markgraf-luebeck.de, in German; Fischergrube 18; mains €13-21; ⊙dinner Tue-Sun) This historic restaurant is the epitome of elegance, with white tablecloths and silverware laid out under the chandeliers and black ceiling beams of a 14th-century house. The cuisine displays Mediterranean and Asian influences.

Schiffergesellschaft FRISIAN €€
(☎767 76; www.schiffergesellschaft.de; Breite Strasse 2; mains €11-25) The fact it's a tourist magnet can't detract from the thrilling atmosphere of this 500-year-old guildhall. Seafood-heavy Frisian specialities and local beer are the way to go.

Nui ASIAN €€
(Beckergrube 72; mains €6-13; ⊙lunch & dinner Mon-Fri, 3-10pm Sat) Tempting aromas waft from artfully arranged plates in this trendy but relaxed Thai/Japanese restaurant.

Suppentopf INTERNATIONAL €
(Fleischerstrasse 36; soups €3.50; ⊙11am-4pm Mon-Fri) It's always bustling here, so join Lübeck's office workers for a stand-up lunch of delicious, often spicy, soup.

Information

Staff at the **Lübeck Travemünde Tourismus** (☎01805 882 233; www.lubeck-tourism.de; Holstentorplatz 1; ⊙9.30am-7pm Mon-Fri, 10am-3pm Sat, 10am-2pm Sun Jun-Sep, 9.30am-6pm Mon-Fri, 10am-3pm Sat Oct-May) can organise city tours and sell discount cards.

Getting There & Away

Lübeck's **airport** (LBC; www.flughafen-luebeck.de) is linked to several cities in Germany and to London by budget carriers Ryanair and easyJet.

Synchronised shuttle buses take passengers straight to Hamburg (one way €9, 55 minutes), while scheduled bus 6 (€2.50) serves Lübeck's Hauptbahnhof and central bus station. Frequent trains run from the airport train station (300m from the terminal) north to Lübeck's Hauptbahnhof, and south as far as Büchen, from where there are connections to Hamburg.

NORTH FRISIAN ISLANDS

Part playground of the rich and famous, part nature-lovers' utopia, the grass-covered dunes, ochre cliffs, traditional reed-thatched cottages and just-off-the-boat seafood of Germany's North Frisian Islands provide a restorative escape from the everyday. Pondering the sunset on a beach, the wind gusts blow away every inch of whatever may plague you on the mainland. Sylt, the largest island of the Frisian archipelago, is the northernmost point in the country and sees the most action. Quieter and more remote, Amrum and Föhr lie just to the south and east.

Sylt

☎04651 / POP 21,100

Sylt can't be labelled without scratching your head. Downtown **Westerland**, the largest town, is largely filled with high-rises that obscure views of the beach, although some pretty thatched houses and simple brick homes dot the outskirts. Some of the world's best **windsurfing** can also be found off this shore.

Further north, pretty **Kampen** is largely where the wealth is most obvious, with ritzy restaurants and celebrity guests. But it's also home to the 52.5m-tall, ochre-coloured **Uwe Dune**. Climb the wooden steps to the top for a stunning 360-degree view.

Towards **List**, on the island's northern tip, is the popular **Wanderdünengebiet**, where people hike between grass-covered dunes. Or try List's beach-side **sauna**.

Inside the Westerland train station, there's an **information pavilion** (☎846 1029; 9am-4pm, reduced hr in winter) or try **Westerland Tourism** (☎9980, 0180 550 9980; www.westerland.de; Strandstrasse 35; 9am-6pm Mon-Fri May-Oct, 9am-5pm Mon-Fri Nov-Apr).

MUDDY WATERS

It's a tad messy but a tonne of fun. The best *Wattwandern* – walking on tidal flats from one point to another (the same as Dutch *wadlopen*) – is between the islands of Amrum and Föhr. Full-day excursions (from €26) can be combined with various boat trips. Contact Westerland Tourism.

Sleeping

Accommodation is at a premium in summer, but ask the tourist office about cheaper private rooms. Significant discounts can be found outside the summer months. Beware that credit cards are not always accepted – even in some midrange hotels. A small *Kurtaxe*, or resort tax, will be added to your bill.

Romantik Hotel Jörg Müller BOUTIQUE HOTEL €€€
(☎277 88; www.hotel-joerg-mueller.de, in German; Südermarkt Strasse 8, Westerland; r incl breakfast €160-260) Gourmands are in for a treat at this boutique establishment run by one of Germany's best-known foodie families. Its pastel-hued rooms are romantic hideaways, but the real lure is the gourmet breakfast and three restaurants, including Jörg Müller's signature gastronomic restaurant (menus from €32 up to €118 for a six-course blowout). If you're inspired, Müller also offers cooking classes (six-hour class €240, including five-course meal and paired wines).

Long Island House Sylt B&B €€
(☎04651-995 9550; www.sylthotel.de; Eidumweg 13, Westerland; s €88-116, d €126-196 incl breakfast; @ wifi) Mirrors like portholes, unpolished wood and painted cane chairs exude simple but elegant, beachy comfort. There's a spacious garden and breakfast includes local specialities and traditional Frisian tea.

DJH Hostel HOSTEL €
(☎835 7825; www.jugendherberge.de; Fischerweg 36-40, Westerland; dm under/over 26yr incl breakfast €20.10/23.10; closed mid-late Dec) Westerland's new hostel is set amid the dunes, a 45-minute walk from the Bahnhof. Alternatively, take bus 2 in the direction of Rantum/Hörnum to the Dikjen Deel stop. If you're after something even further away from it all, there are also DJH hostels at **List-Mövenberg** (www.jugendherberge.de/jh/list) and **Hörnum** (www.jugendherberge.de/jh/hoernum).

Eating

Alte Friesenstube RESTAURANT €€€
(☎1228; Gaadt 4, Westerland; mains €19-25; from 6pm Tue-Sun) You won't find sojourning celebs at this charmingly old-fashioned, family-run restaurant. Set inside Sylt's oldest reed-thatched cottage (1648), lined with decorative wall tiles and tiled ovens, what you will find are homely regional specials listed on a largely incomprehensible handwritten menu in *Plattdütsch* dialect (helpfully translated by staff).

Kupferkanne CAFE €€
(☎410 10; Stapelhooger Wai, Kampen; meals €6-15) Giant mugs of coffee or Frisian tea and enormous, home-made slices of cake are de rigueur at this WWII bunker-turned-cafe. Dine outdoors on wooden tables surrounded by a maze of low bramble hedges overlooking the Wadden Sea, or inside where it's easy (and fun) to get lost in its cavernous nooks and crannies.

WORTH A TRIP

AMRUM & FÖHR

Tiny Amrum is renowned for its fine white *Kniepsand* (sand bank). There's a 10km stroll from the tall **lighthouse** at Wittdün to the village of Norddorf, and an 8km return hike along the beach. The **tourist office** (☎04682-94 030; www.amrum.de; ferry landing, Wittdün; ⌚hours vary) can provide accommodation.

The 'green isle' of Föhr is interesting for its Frisian culture. Its main village, **Wyk**, boasts plenty of windmills, there are 16 northern hamlets tucked behind dikes up to 7m tall, and there's the large 12th-century church of **St Johannis** in Nieblum. The **Föhr information service** (☎04681-300; www.foehr.de) can help with more details. There is no camping here.

WDR (☎800; www.wdr-wyk.de) has ferries to Föhr (€7, 45 minutes) and Amrum (€9, two hours) from Dagebüll Hafen.

Gosch SEAFOOD **€€**
(Friedrichstrasse 15b; fish sandwiches €4-7, meals €8-13) This fast-fish chain has colonised mainland Germany, but it originated in Sylt and remains here in force.

Sansibar INTERNATIONAL **€€€**
(☎964 646; Hörnumer Strasse 80; Rantum; mains €14-35) Reservations are a must at this airy grass-roof pavilion on the beach north of Hörnum, ideal for a sunset drink or dinner.

ℹ Getting There & Around

Sylt is connected to the mainland by a narrow causeway exclusively for trains. Regular services travel from Hamburg (Altona and Hauptbahnhof) to Westerland (from €32.50 return, three to 3¼ hours).

If driving, you must load your vehicle onto a **car train** (☎995 0565; www.syltshuttle.de; return €80) in Niebüll near the Danish border. There are constant crossings (usually at least once an hour) in both directions, and no reservations can be made.

There's also a **car ferry** (☎0180-310 3030; www.sylt-faehre.de; return from €61) from Havneby, Denmark to List at the north of the island.

Air Berlin has several services a week from Berlin, Düsseldorf and others to **Sylt/Westerland airport** (GWT; www.flughafen-sylt.de); Lufthansa arrives from Frankfurt, Hamburg and Munich.

Sylt's two north–south bus lines run every 20 to 30 minutes, and three other frequent lines cover the rest of the island.

UNDERSTAND GERMANY

History

Events in Germany have often dominated the European stage, but the country itself is a relatively recent invention: for most of its history Germany has been a patchwork of semi-independent principalities and city-states, occupied first by the Roman Empire, then the Holy Roman Empire and finally the Austrian Habsburgs. Perhaps because of this, many Germans retain a strong regional identity, despite the momentous events that have occurred since.

The most significant medieval events in Germany were pan-European in nature – Martin Luther brought on the Protestant Reformation with his criticism of the Catholic Church in Wittenberg in 1517, a movement that sparked the Thirty Years War. Germany became the battlefield of Europe, only regaining stability after the Napoleonic Wars with increasing industrialisation and the rise of the Kingdom of Prussia. In 1866 legendary Prussian 'Iron Chancellor' Otto von Bismarck brought the German states together, largely by force, and a united Germany emerged for the first time in 1871, under Kaiser Wilhelm I.

WWI & the Rise of Hitler

With the advent of the 20th century, Germany's rapid growth soon overtaxed the political talents of Kaiser Wilhelm II and led to mounting tensions with England, Russia and France. When war broke out in 1914, Germany's only ally was a weakened Austria-Hungary. Gruelling trench warfare on two fronts sapped the nation's resources, and by late 1918 Germany sued for peace. The kaiser abdicated and escaped to the Netherlands. Amid widespread public anger and unrest, a new republic, which became known as the Weimar Republic, was proclaimed.

The Treaty of Versailles in 1919 chopped huge areas off Germany and imposed heavy reparation payments. These were impossible to meet, and when France and Belgium occupied the Rhineland to ensure continued payments, the subsequent hyperinflation and miserable economic conditions provided fertile ground for political extremists. One of these was Adolf Hitler, an Austrian drifter, would-be artist and German army veteran.

Led by Hitler, the National Socialist German Workers' Party (or Nazi Party) staged an abortive coup in Munich in 1923. This landed Hitler in prison for nine months, during which time he wrote *Mein Kampf*.

In 1929 the worldwide economic Depression hit Germany hard, which led to unemployment, strikes and demonstrations. The Communist Party, headed by Ernst Thälmann, gained strength, but wealthy industrialists began to support the Nazi Party and police turned a blind eye to Nazi street thugs.

The Nazis increased their strength in general elections, and in 1933 replaced the Social Democrats as the largest party in the Reichstag (parliament), with about one-third of the seats. Hitler was appointed chancellor and one year later assumed absolute control as führer (leader).

WWII & the Division of Germany

From 1935 Germany began to re-arm and build its way out of the economic depression with strategic public works such as the autobahns (freeways). Hitler reoccupied the Rhineland in 1936, and in 1938 annexed Austria and, following a compromise agreement with Britain and France, parts of Czechoslovakia.

All of this took place against a backdrop of growing racism at home. The Nuremberg Laws of 1935 deprived non-Aryans – mostly Jews and Roma (sometimes called Gypsies) – of their German citizenship and many other rights. On 9 November 1938 the horror escalated into *Kristallnacht* (night of broken glass), in which synagogues and Jewish cemeteries, property and businesses across Germany were desecrated, burned or demolished.

In September 1939, after signing a pact that allowed both Stalin and himself a free hand in the east of Europe, Hitler attacked Poland, which led to war with Britain and France. Germany quickly occupied large parts of Europe, but after 1942 began to suffer increasingly heavy losses. Massive bombing reduced Germany's cities to rubble, and the country lost 10% of its population. Germany surrendered unconditionally in May 1945, soon after Hitler's suicide.

At the end of the war, the full scale of Nazi racism was exposed. 'Concentration camps', intended to rid Europe of people considered undesirable according to Nazi doctrine, had exterminated some six million Jews and one million more Roma, communists, homosexuals and others in what has come to be known as the Holocaust, history's first 'assembly line' genocide.

At conferences in Yalta and Potsdam, the Allies (the Soviet Union, the USA, the UK and France) redrew the borders of Germany, making it around 25% smaller than it had become after the Treaty of Versailles 26 years earlier. Germany was divided into four occupation zones.

In the Soviet zone of the country, the communist Socialist Unity Party (SED) won the 1946 elections and began a rapid nationalisation of industry. In September 1949 the Federal Republic of Germany (FRG) was created out of the three western zones; in response the German Democratic Republic (GDR) was founded in the Soviet zone the following month, with (East) Berlin as its capital.

From Division to Unity

As the West's bulwark against communism, the FRG received massive injections of US capital, and experienced rapid economic development (the *Wirschaftswunder* or 'economic miracle') under the leadership of Konrad Adenauer. The GDR, on the other hand, had to pay US$10 billion in war reparations to the Soviet Union and rebuild itself from scratch.

A better life in the west increasingly attracted skilled workers away from the miserable economic conditions in the East. As these were people the GDR could ill afford to lose, it built a wall around West Berlin in 1961 and sealed its border with the FRG.

In 1971 a change to the more flexible leadership of Erich Honecker in the East, combined with the *Ostpolitik* (East Politics) of FRG chancellor Willy Brandt, allowed an easier political relationship between the two Germanys. In the same year the four occupying powers formally accepted the division of Berlin.

Honecker's policies produced higher living standards in the GDR, yet East Germany barely managed to achieve a level of prosperity half that of the FRG. After Mikhail

Gorbachev came to power in the Soviet Union in March 1985, the East German communists gradually lost Soviet backing.

Events in 1989 rapidly overtook the GDR government, which resisted pressure to introduce reforms. When Hungary relaxed its border controls in May 1989, East Germans began crossing to the West. Tighter travel controls resulted in would-be defectors taking refuge in the FRG's embassy in Prague. Meanwhile, mass demonstrations in Leipzig spread to other cities and Honecker was replaced by his security chief, Egon Krenz, who introduced cosmetic reforms. Then suddenly on 9 November 1989, a decision to allow direct travel to the West was mistakenly interpreted as the immediate opening of all GDR borders with West Germany. That same night thousands of people streamed into the West past stunned border guards. Millions more followed in the next few days, and the dismantling of the Berlin Wall began soon thereafter.

The trend at first was to reform the GDR but, in East German elections held in early 1990, citizens voted clearly in favour of the pro-reunification Christian Democratic Union (CDU). A Unification Treaty was drawn up to integrate East Germany into the Federal Republic of Germany, enacted on 3 October 1990. All-German elections were held on 2 December that year and, in the midst of national euphoria, the CDU-led coalition, which strongly favoured reunification, soundly defeated the Social Democrat opposition. The CDU's leader, Helmut Kohl, earned the enviable position of 'unification chancellor'.

Two Decades Somewhat Whole

In 1998 a coalition of Social Democrats (SPD), led by Gerhard Schröder, and Bündnis 90/die Grünen (the Greens party) took political office from Kohl and the CDU amid allegations of widespread financial corruption in the unification-era government.

Schröder and the SDP-Greens only narrowly managed to retain office in the 2002 general election. In 2004 things looked even worse. The slashing of university funding brought students out in protest for several weeks, and a botched reform of the public health-insurance system was one of the most unpopular pieces of legislation ever, resulting in massive gains for the supposedly discredited CDU at subsequent local elections.

These advances paid off in 2005 as Schröder went down in national elections, although just barely. The winner by a very narrow margin was Angela Merkel and the CDU. Not only is Merkel the first woman chancellor in German history but she is also the first one who grew up in the old GDR.

During her first term in office, Merkel proved to be a cautious leader, forming a coalition with the SPD. Her style, devoid of even a trace of drama-queen, struck a chord with many Germans and her popularity remained at over 50% even as the CDU's popularity fell somewhat on increasingly harsh economic times. She was reelected in 2009 but her popularity has waned since as Germany's export-based economy has been battered by global recession. The national mood is glum, especially as German funds are a major part of EU bailouts for Greece and others.

Over two decades after reunification, the overall stereotypes of the West and the old East – that the *Wessis* are arrogant while the *Ossis* simply bitch – had become ingrained in German culture. But now both agree on one thing: times used to be better.

Arts

Germany's meticulously creative population has made major contributions to international culture, particularly during the 18th century when the Saxon courts at Weimar and Dresden attracted some of the greatest minds of Europe. With such rich traditions to fall back on, inspiration has seldom been in short supply for the new generations of German artists, despite the upheavals of the country's recent history.

Literature

The undisputed colossus of the German arts was Johann Wolfgang von Goethe: poet, dramatist, painter, politician, scientist, philosopher, landscape gardener and perhaps the last European to achieve the Renaissance ideal of excellence in many fields. His greatest work, the drama *Faust,* is the definitive version of the legend, showing the archetypal human search for meaning and knowledge.

Goethe's close friend Friedrich Schiller was a poet, dramatist and novelist. His most famous work is the dramatic cycle *Wallenstein,* based on the life of a treacherous general of the Thirty Years War who plotted to make himself arbiter of the empire. Schiller's other great play, *Wilhelm Tell,* dealt with the right of the oppressed to rise against tyranny.

On the scientific side, Alexander von Humboldt contributed much to environmentalism through his studies of the relationship of plants and animals to their physical surroundings. His contemporary, the philosopher Georg Wilhelm Friedrich Hegel, created an all-embracing classical philosophy that is still influential today.

Postwar literature was influenced by the politically focused Gruppe 47. It included writers such as Günter Grass, winner of the 1999 Nobel Prize for Literature, whose modern classic *Die Blechtrommel* (The Tin Drum) humorously follows German history through the eyes of a young boy who refuses to grow up. Christa Wolf, an East German novelist and Gruppe 47 writer, won high esteem throughout Germany. Her 1963 story *Der geteilte Himmel* (Divided Heaven) tells of a young woman whose fiancé abandons her for life in the West.

A wave of recent novelists has addressed modern history in a lighter fashion. *Helden wie wir* (Heroes Like Us) by Thomas Brussig, an eastern German, tells the story of a man whose penis brings about the collapse of the Berlin Wall, while the GDR's demise is almost incidental to the eponymous barfly in Sven Regener's *Herr Lehmann* (Mr Lehmann). Also from Berlin is Russian-born Wladimir Kaminer (a possible mayoral candidate in 2011), whose books document stranger-than-fiction lives in the capital. His *Russian Disco* has been translated into English.

Bitterness in the East over the reunification is given a full airing in the darkly satirical *New Lives* by Ingo Schulze. The same subject matter is given a more entertaining take in Christoph Hein's *Settlement*, which follows the rise of Germany's richest man.

Music

CLASSICAL

Forget brass bands and oompah music – few countries can claim the impressive musical heritage of Germany. Even a partial list of household names would have to include Johann Sebastian Bach, Georg Friedrich Handel, Ludwig van Beethoven, Richard Strauss, Robert Schumann, Johannes Brahms, Felix Mendelssohn-Bartholdy, Richard Wagner and Gustav Mahler, all of whom are celebrated in museums, exhibitions and festivals around the country.

These musical traditions continue to thrive: the Berlin Philharmonic, Dresden Opera and Leipzig Orchestra are known around the world, and musical performances are hosted almost daily in every major theatre in the country.

POP

Germany has also made significant contributions to the contemporary-music scene. Internationally renowned artists include punk icon Nina Hagen, '80s balloon girl Nena and rock bands from the Scorpions to Die Toten Hosen and current darlings Wir sind Helden. Gothic and hard rock have a disproportionately large following in Germany, largely thanks to the success of death-obsessed growlers Rammstein.

For real innovation, though, the German dance-music scene is second to none, particularly in Frankfurt and Berlin. Kraftwerk pioneered the original electronic sounds, which were then popularised in raves and clubs such as Berlin's Tresor in the early '90s. Paul van Dyk was among the first proponents of euphoric trance, which pushed club music firmly into the commercial mainstream. DJs such as Ian Pooley, Westbam and Ellen Allien now play all over the world. Germany has the largest electronic-music scene in the world and it is on full display (in every way) at Berlin's B-Parade (www.b-parade.de).

The German pop scene is led by the goth/punk/boy-band fusion Tokio Hotel. Their chart-topping songs are led by the big-haired and androgynous Bill Kaulitz. Their appeal crosses borders: they won MTV's music award for Best Group in 2009.

Architecture

The scope of German architecture is such that it could easily be the focus of an entire visit. The first great wave of buildings came with the Romanesque period (800–1200), examples of which can be found at Trier cathedral, the churches of Cologne and the chapel of Charlemagne's palace in Aachen.

The Gothic style (1200–1500) is best viewed at Freiburg's Münster cathedral, Cologne's cathedral and the Marienkirche in Lübeck. Red-brick Gothic structures are common in the north of Germany, with buildings such as Schwerin's Dom and Stralsund's Nikoliakirche.

For classic baroque, Balthasar Neumann's superb Residenz in Würzburg, the magnificent cathedral in Passau and the many classics of Dresden's old centre are must-sees. The neoclassical period of the 19th century was led by Karl Friedrich Schinkel, whose name crops up all over Germany.

In 1919 Walter Gropius founded the Bauhaus movement in an attempt to meld theoretical concerns of architecture with the practical problems faced by artists and craftspeople. The Bauhaus flourished in Dessau, but with the arrival of the Nazis, Gropius left for Harvard University.

Albert Speer was Hitler's favourite architect, known for his pompous neoclassical buildings and grand plans to change the face of Berlin. Most of his epic works ended up unbuilt or flattened by WWII.

Frankfurt shows Germany's take on the modern high-rise. For a glimpse of the future of German architecture, head to Potsdamer Platz, Leipziger Platz and the new government area north of the Reichstag in Berlin, which are glitzy swathes of glass, concrete and chrome.

Visual Arts

The Renaissance came late to Germany but flourished once it took hold, replacing the predominant Gothic style. The draughtsman Albrecht Dürer of Nuremberg was one of the world's finest portraitists, as was the prolific Lucas Cranach the Elder, who worked in Wittenberg for more than 45 years. The baroque period brought great sculpture, including works by Andreas Schlüter in Berlin, while romanticism produced some of Germany's most famous paintings, best exemplified by Caspar David Friedrich and Otto Runge.

At the turn of the 20th century, expressionism established itself with great names like Swiss-born Paul Klee and the Russian-born painter Wassily Kandinsky, who were also associated with the Bauhaus design school. By the 1920s, art had become more radical and political, with artists like George Grosz, Otto Dix and Max Ernst exploring the new concepts of Dada and surrealism. Käthe Kollwitz is one of the era's few major female artists, known for her social-realist drawings.

The only works encouraged by the Nazis were of the epic style of propaganda artists like Mjölnir; nonconforming artists such as sculptor Ernst Barlach and painter Emil Nolde were declared 'degenerate' and their pieces destroyed or appropriated for secret private collections.

Since 1945 abstract art has been a mainstay of the German scene, with key figures like Joseph Beuys, Monica Bonviciniand and Anselm Kiefer achieving worldwide reputations. Leipzig is a hot spot for art; figurative painters like Neo Rauch are generating much acclaim.

Sport

Football (soccer) is the number-one spectator sport in Germany, as in most other European countries. Germany hosted the cup in 2006 in new or rebuilt stadiums all over the country. Although Germany finished third (Italy beat France in the final in Berlin), it was widely praised for hosting a fantastic series of matches, and many Germans took great pride in their time on the world stage.

Germany did one better at Euro 2008, although it lost to Spain in the final in Vienna. Spain again proved troublesome in the 2010 World Cup, beating Germany in the semifinals.

The Bundesliga is the top national league, with seasons running from September to June. Notable top-flight teams include Bayern München, Borussia Dortmund and VfB Stuttgart. The Deutscher Fussball-Bund (DFB; www.dfb.de) is the national body responsible for all levels of the game.

International sports are also very well attended, especially when the relevant national teams are in form. Major tennis, athletics, Grand Prix, swimming, cycling and water-polo events are all features of the German sporting calendar.

Environment

Germans are wholly on board with various green schemes. Households and businesses participate enthusiastically in waste-recycling programs. A refund system applies to a wide range of glass bottles and jars, while containers for waste paper and glass can be found in each neighbourhood. The government is a signatory of the major international treaties on climate change and runs its own campaigns to save energy and reduce CO_2 emissions domestically. Despite a somewhat hostile climate for such schemes, requirements for solar power in residential and commercial buildings are proliferating.

Food & Drink

German Specialities

Wurst (sausage), in its hundreds of forms, is by far the most universal main dish. Regional favourites include bratwurst (spiced sausage), *Weisswurst* (veal sausage) and *Blutwurst* (blood sausage). Other popular main dishes include *Rippenspeer* (spare ribs), *Rotwurst* (black pudding), *Rostbrätl* (grilled meat), *Putenbrust* (turkey breast) and many forms of schnitzel (breaded pork or veal cutlet).

Potatoes feature prominently in German meals, as *Bratkartoffeln* (fried), *Kartoffelpüree* (mashed), Swiss-style rösti (grated then fried) or *Pommes Frites* (French fries). A Thuringian speciality is *Klösse,* a ball of mashed and raw potato that is then cooked into a dumpling. A similar Bavarian version is the *Knödel. Spätzle,* a noodle variety from Baden-Württemberg, is a common alternative.

Germans are keen on rich desserts. Popular choices are the *Schwarzwälder Kirschtorte* (Black Forest cherry cake) – one worthwhile tourist trap – as well as endless varieties of *Apfeltasche* (apple pastry). In the north you're likely to find berry *Mus,* a sort of compote. Desserts and pastries are often enjoyed during another German tradition, the 4pm coffee break.

Drinks

Beer is the national beverage and it's both excellent and relatively cheap. Each region and brewery has its own distinctive taste and body.

Some types:

Pils The crisp pilsener Germany is famous for, often refreshingly and slightly bitter.

Alt Dark and full-bodied.

Weizenbier Made with wheat instead of barley malt, served in a tall, 500mL glass. Light in colour, it's lovely on a hot day.

Export Tastes like bland lagers anywhere.

Bockbier Often dark and the best is seasonal.

Helles Bier Light beer.

Dunkles Bier Dark (the best is richly flavoured).

Kölsch The light, sweet beer of Cologne, served in tiny glasses.

Berliner Weisse A low-alcohol wheat beer mixed with woodruff or raspberry syrup.

Rauchbier A Bamberg speciality; smoked to a dark-red colour, it tastes like bacon. (Really.)

German wines are exported around the world, and for good reason. They are inexpensive and typically white, light and intensely fruity. A *Weinschorle* or *Spritzer* is white wine mixed with mineral water. The Rhine and Moselle Valleys are the classic wine-growing regions.

The most popular nonalcoholic choices are mineral water and soft drinks, coffee and fruit or black tea. Bottled water almost always comes bubbly *(mit Kohlensäure)* – order *ohne Kohlensäure* if you're bothered by bubbles.

Where to Eat & Drink

Besides German food in restaurants, pubs beer halls and more, you'll enjoy huge variety. Italian, Turkish, Greek and Chinese are all popular. Stand-up food stalls *(Schnellimbiss* or *Imbiss)* offer doner kebabs to traditional German sausages to the ubiquitous and wildly popular currywurst (sausage served sliced, swimming in ketchup and sprinkled with curry powder) with beer.

Eating venues are supposed to be nonsmoking, though this is not always followed in small, family-run places.

Vegetarians

Most German restaurants will have at least a couple of vegetarian dishes on the menu, although it is advisable to check anything that doesn't specifically say it's meat-free, as bacon and chicken stock are undeclared ingredients in German cuisine. Asian and Indian restaurants will generally be quite happy to make vegetarian dishes on demand. Vegans may find themselves having to explain exactly what they do and don't eat to get something suitable.

Habits & Customs

Restaurants always display their menus outside with prices, but watch for daily or lunch specials chalked onto blackboards. Lunch is the main meal of the day; getting a main meal in the evening is never a problem, but you may find that the dish or menu of the day only applies to lunch.

Rather than leaving money on the table, tip when you pay by stating a rounded-up figure or saying '*es stimmt so*' (that's the right amount). A tip of 10% is generally about right.

SURVIVAL GUIDE

Directory A–Z

Accommodation

Germany has all types of places to unpack your suitcase, from hostels, camping grounds and family hotels to chains, business hotels and luxury resorts. Reservations are a good idea, especially if you're travelling in the busy summer season (June to September). Local tourist offices will often go out of their way to find something in your price range.

Germany has more than 2000 organised camping grounds, several hundred of which stay open throughout the year. Prices are around €3 to €5 for an adult, plus €3 to €7 for a car and/or tent. Look out for ecologically responsible camping grounds sporting the Green Leaf award from the ADAC motoring association.

Deutsches Jugendherbergswerk (DJH; www.jugendherberge.de) coordinates the official Hostelling International (HI) hostels in Germany. Rates in gender-segregated dorms, or in family rooms, range from €13 to €25 per person, including linen and breakfast. People over 27 are charged an extra €3 or €4.

Indie hostels are more relaxed and can be found in most large cities.

PRICE RANGES

Prices we list include private bathroom unless otherwise stated and are quoted at high-season rates. Breakfast is not included unless specified. Most rooms are non-smoking.

€€€	more than €150
€€	€80 to €150
€	less than €80

Business Hours

Banks & government offices 9.30am to 4pm Monday to Friday

Bars & cafes 11am to 1am

Clubs Mostly 10pm to 4am

Post offices 9am to 6pm Monday to Friday

Restaurants 10am or 11am to 10pm, with a 3pm to 6pm break

Shops 9am to 6pm Monday to Saturday (also Sunday in large cities); many more are staying open to 8pm or later on days other than Thursday

Discount Cards

Many cities offer discount cards. These cards will usually combine up to three days' free use of public transport with free or reduced admission to major local museums and attractions. They're generally a good deal if you want to fit a lot in; see the Information section under the relevant destination and ask at tourist offices for full details.

Embassies & Consulates

The following embassies are all in Berlin. Many countries also have consulates in cities such as Frankfurt and Munich.

Australia (☎030-880 0880; www.australian-embassy.de; Wallstrasse 76-79)

SMOKE & MIRRORS

Germany was one of the last countries in Europe to legislate smoking, which it did in 2007–08, and, by all accounts, it hasn't done a very effective job. Each of the 16 states was allowed to introduce its own antismoking laws, creating a rather confusing patchwork. In most states, smoking is a no-no in schools, hospitals, airports, train stations and other public facilities. But when it comes to bars, pubs, cafes and restaurants, every state does it just a little differently. Bavaria has the toughest laws, which ban smoking practically everywhere, although an exception was made for Oktoberfest tents; so-called 'smoking clubs' are also permitted.

In most states, lighting up is allowed in designated smoking rooms. However, in July 2008 Germany's highest court ruled this scheme unconstitutional because it discriminates against one-room establishments. These may now allow smoking, provided they serve no food and only admit patrons over 18. So far enforcement has been sporadic, to say the least, despite the threat of fines.

Canada (☎030-203 120; www.kanada-info.de; Leipziger Platz 17)

New Zealand (☎030-206 210; www.nzembassy.com; Friedrichstrasse 60)

UK (☎030-204 570; http://ukingermany.fco.gov.uk; Wilhelmstrasse 70)

USA (☎030-830 50; http://germany.usembassy.gov/; Pariser Platz 2)

Food

The following price categories for the cost of a main course are used in the listings in this chapter.

€€€	more than €20
€€	€10 to €20
€	less than €10

Gay & Lesbian Travellers

Overall, Germans are tolerant of gays *(Schwule)* and lesbians *(Lesben)* although, as elsewhere in the world, cities (Berlin!) are more liberal than rural areas, and younger people tend to be more open-minded than older generations. Discrimination is more likely in eastern Germany and in the conservative south, where gays and lesbians tend to keep a lower profile.

Legal Matters

By law you must carry some form of photographic identification, such as your passport, national identity card or driving licence. Reporting theft to the police is usually a simple, if occasionally time-consuming, matter. Remember that the first thing to do is show some form of identification.

If driving in Germany, you should carry your driving licence and obey road rules carefully (see p608). The permissible blood-alcohol limit is 0.05%; drivers caught exceeding this amount are subject to stiff fines, a confiscated licence and even jail time. Drinking in public is not illegal, but be discreet about it.

Illegal drugs are widely available, especially in clubs. Cannabis possession is a criminal offence and punishment may range from a warning to a court appearance. Dealers face far stiffer penalties, as do people caught with any other 'recreational' drugs.

Money

ATMS

Automatic teller machines can be found outside banks and at train stations.

TIPPING

Restaurant bills always include a service charge *(Bedienung)* but most people add 5% or 10% unless the service was truly abhorrent.

» **Bellhops** €1 per bag

» **Maids** €1 per night

» **Bartenders** 5%

» **Taxi drivers** around 10%

CREDIT CARDS

All major international cards are recognised, and you will find that most hotels, restaurants and major stores accept them (although *not* all railway ticket offices). Always check first to avoid disappointment. Shops may levy a 5% surcharge (or more) on credit cards to offset the commissions charged by card providers.

EXCHANGE

The easiest places to change cash in Germany are the banks or foreign-exchange counters at airports and train stations, particularly those of the Reisebank. The main banks in larger cities generally have money-changing machines for after-hours use, although they don't often offer reasonable rates.

Public Holidays

Germany observes eight religious and three secular holidays nationwide. Shops, banks, government offices and post offices are closed on these days. States with predominantly Catholic populations, such as Bavaria and Baden-Württemberg, also celebrate Epiphany (6 January), Corpus Christi (10 days after Pentecost), Assumption Day (15 August) and All Saints' Day (1 November). Reformation Day (31 October) is only observed in eastern Germany.

The following are *gesetzliche Feiertage* (public holidays):

Neujahrstag (New Year's Day) 1 January

Ostern (Easter) Good Friday, Easter Sunday and Easter Monday

Christi Himmelfahrt (Ascension Day) Forty days after Easter

Maifeiertag/Tag der Arbeit (Labour Day) 1 May

Pfingsten (Whit/Pentecost Sunday & Monday) Fifty days after Easter.

Tag der Deutschen Einheit (Day of German Unity) 3 October

Weihnachtstag (Christmas Day) 25 December

Zweite Weihnachtstag (Boxing Day) 26 December

Safe Travel

Although the usual cautions should be taken, theft and other crimes against travellers are relatively rare in Germany. Africans, Asians and southern Europeans may encounter racial prejudice, especially in eastern Germany, where they can be singled out as convenient scapegoats for economic hardship. However, the animosity is usually directed against immigrants, not tourists.

Telephone

German phone numbers consist of an area code followed by the local number, which can be between three and nine digits long.

Country code ☎49

International access code ☎00

International directory inquiries ☎118 34 for an English-speaking operator

National directory inquiries ☎118 37 for an English-speaking operator, or www.dastelefonbuch.de

Operator assistance ☎0180-200 1033

Travellers With Disabilities

Germany is fair at best (but better than much of Europe) for the needs of travellers with disabilities, with access ramps for wheelchairs and/or lifts in some public buildings. Resources include the following:

Deutsche Bahn Mobility Service Centre (☎01805-996 633, ext 9 for English operator; www.bahn.de; ⌚8am-8pm Mon-Fri, 8am-4pm Sat) Train access and route-planning information. Useful English site content.

German National Tourism Office (www.deutschland-tourismus.de) Has an entire section (under Travel Tips) about barrier-free travel in Germany.

Natko (www.natko.de) Central clearing house for inquiries about 'tourism without barriers' in Germany.

Getting There & Away

Air

Budget carriers, Lufthansa and international airlines serve numerous German airports from across Europe and the rest of the world. Frankfurt and Munich are the hubs.

Berlin Schönefeld (SXF; www.berlin-airport.de)

Berlin Tegel (TXL; www.berlin-airport.de)

Cologne/Bonn (CGN; www.airport-cgn.de)

Düsseldorf (DUS; www.duesseldorf-international.de)

Frankfurt (FRA; www.frankfurt-airport.de)

Frankfurt-Hahn (HHN; www.hahn-airport.de)

Hamburg (HAM; www.flughafen-hamburg.de)

Munich (MUC; www.munich-airport.de)

Stuttgart (STR; www.flughafen-stuttgart.de)

For information about individual German airports, see listings within the chapter.

Land

BUS

Travelling by bus between Germany and the rest of Europe is cheaper than by train or plane, but journeys will take a lot longer.

Eurolines (www.eurolines.com) is a consortium of national bus companies operating routes throughout the continent. The German affiliate is **Touring** (www.touring.de). Sample one-way fares and travel times:

ROUTE	PRICE	DURATION (HR)
Budapest–Frankfurt	€98	13–18
Florence–Munich	€76	9
London–Cologne	€60	13
Paris–Munich	€61	13
Warsaw–Berlin	€58	11

Eurolines has a discounted youth fare for those under 26 that saves you around 10%. Tickets can be purchased throughout Germany at most train stations.

CAR & MOTORCYCLE

Germany is served by an excellent highway system. If coming from the UK, the quickest option is the Channel Tunnel. Ferries take longer but are cheaper. You can be in Germany three hours after the ferry docks.

Autobahns and highways become jammed on weekends in summer and before and after holidays.

TRAIN

A favourite way to get to Germany from elsewhere in Europe is by train. See p1223 for details on trains in Western Europe.

Conventional long-distance trains between major German cities and other countries are often called EuroCity (EC) trains. High-speed trains now also link Germany to some other parts of Europe. Often, longer international routes are served by at least one day train and sometimes a night train as well. The main German hubs with the best connections for major European cities include the following:

Cologne High-speed Thalys trains to France and Belgium (with Eurostar connections from Brussels to London), InterCity Express (ICE) trains to the Netherlands.

Frankfurt ICE trains to Paris.

Hamburg Scandinavia.

Munich High-speed trains to Paris and Vienna; regular trains to southern and southeastern Europe.

Stuttgart High-speed trains to Italy and Switzerland.

Sea

Germany's main ferry ports are Kiel, Lübeck and Travemünde in Schleswig-Holstein, and Rostock and Sassnitz (on Rügen Island) in Mecklenburg-Western Pomerania. All have services to Scandinavia and the Baltic states.

Getting Around

Air

There are lots of domestic flights, many with budget carriers such as **Air Berlin** (www.airberlin.com) and **Germanwings** (www.germanwings.com), as well as **Lufthansa** (www.lufthansa.com). But with check-in and transit times, flying is less efficient than a fast train.

Bicycle

Radwandern (bicycle touring) is very popular in Germany. Pavements are often divided into separate sections for pedestrians and cyclists – be warned that these divisions are taken very seriously. Favoured routes include the Rhine, Moselle, Elbe and Danube Rivers and the Lake Constance area.

Simple three-gear bicycles can be hired from around €15/40 per day/week, and more robust mountain bikes from €20/50.

Cycling is allowed on all roads and highways but not on the autobahns. Cyclists must follow the same rules of the road as vehicles. Helmets are not compulsory, even for children, but wearing one is still a good idea.

MOVING ON?

For tips, recommendations and reviews, head to shop.lonelyplanet.com to purchase a downloadable PDF of the Denmark chapter from Lonely Planet's Scandinavia guide, or the Poland and Czech Republic chapters from *Eastern Europe*.

Bicycles may be taken on most trains but you must buy a separate *Fahrradkarte* (bicycle ticket). These cost €9 on long-distance trains and €4.50 on regional trains (RB, RE and S-Bahn, valid all day). Bicycles are not allowed on high-speed ICE trains. There is no charge at all on some trains; for specifics enquire at a local station or call Deutsche Bahn on the **DB Radfahrer-Hotline** (bicycle hotline; ☎01805-151 415). Free lines are also listed in DB's complimentary *Bahn & Bike* brochure, as are the almost 250 stations throughout the country where you can hire bikes for between €3 and €13.

Germany's main cycling organisation is the **Allgemeiner Deutscher Fahrrad Club** (ADFC; www.adfc.de).

Boat

Boats are most likely to be used for basic transport when travelling to or between the Frisian Islands, though tours along the Rhine, Elbe and Moselle Rivers are also popular. During summer there are frequent services on Lake Constance but, with the exception of the Constance–Meersburg and the Friedrichshafen–Romanshorn car ferries, these boats are really more tourist crafts than transport options. From April to October, excursion boats ply lakes and rivers in Germany and can be a lovely way to see the country.

Bus

The bus network in Germany functions primarily in support of the train network. Bus stations or stops are usually located near the train station in any town. Consider using buses when you want to cut across two train lines and avoid long train rides to and from a transfer point. A good example of where to do this is in the Alps, where the best way to follow the peaks is by bus.

However a few buslines are vying to lure train passengers with cheap fares – even if comfort and travel times are inferior. These include the following:

Berlin Linien Bus (www.berlinlinienbus.de) Connects major cities (primarily Berlin, but also Munich, Düsseldorf and Frankfurt) with each other as well as holiday regions such as the Harz and the Bavarian Alps. Express service between Berlin and Hamburg is popular (€9 to €22, 3¼ hours, 12 daily).

Touring (www.touring.de) The German affiliate of **Eurolines** (www.eurolines.com) has services that include the popular Romantic Road bus in Bavaria and overnight buses between major cities.

Car & Motorcycle

Cars are impractical in urban areas. Vending machines on many streets sell parking vouchers that must be displayed clearly behind the windscreen. Leaving your car in a central *Parkhaus* (car park) can cost a fortune, as much as €20 per day or more.

AUTOMOBILE ASSOCIATIONS

ADAC (Allgemeiner Deutscher Automobil-Club; ☎roadside assistance 0180-222 2222, if calling from mobile phone 222 222; www.adac.de) offers roadside assistance to members of its affiliates, including British AA, American AAA and Canadian CAA.

DRIVING LICENCES

Visitors do not need an international driving licence to drive in Germany; bring your licence from home.

HIRE

You usually must be at least 21 years of age to hire a car in Germany. You'll need to show your licence and passport, and make sure you keep the insurance certificate for the vehicle with you at all times.

Rental companies are not always convenient to train stations, so check if you plan to pick up a car when you hop off. Agencies include the following:

Avis (☎0180-555 77; www.avis.de)

Europcar (☎0180-580 00; www.europcar.de)

Hertz (☎0180-533 3535; www.hertz.de)

Sixt (☎0180-526 0250; www.sixt.de)

INSURANCE

You must have third-party insurance to enter Germany with a vehicle.

ROAD CONDITIONS

The autobahn system of motorways runs throughout Germany. Road signs (and most motoring maps) indicate national autobahn routes in blue with an 'A' number, while international routes have green signs with an 'E'. Though efficient, the autobahns are often busy, and visitors frequently have trouble coping with the high speeds. Secondary roads (usually designated with a 'B' number) are easier on the nerves and much more scenic, but can be slow going.

ROAD RULES

Road rules are easy to understand, and standard international signs are in use. You drive on the right, and cars are right-hand drive. Right of way is usually signed, with major roads given priority, but at unmarked intersections traffic coming from the right always has right of way.

The blood-alcohol limit for drivers is 0.05%. Obey the road rules carefully: the German police are very efficient and issue heavy on-the-spot fines. Germany also has one of the highest concentrations of speed cameras in Europe.

Speed limits:

Towns & cities 50km/h

Open road/country 100km/h

Autobahn Unlimited but many exceptions as posted

Public Transport

Public transport is excellent within big cities and small towns, and is generally based on buses, *Strassenbahn* (trams) and the S-Bahn and/or U-Bahn (underground trains). Tickets cover all forms of transit, and fares are determined by zones or time travelled, sometimes both. Multiticket strips and day passes are generally available, offering better value than single-ride tickets.

Make certain that you have a ticket when boarding – only buses and some trams let you buy tickets from the driver. In some cases you will have to validate the ticket on the platform or once aboard. Ticket inspections are frequent (especially at night and on holidays) and the fine is a non-negotiable €50 or more.

Train

Operated almost entirely by **Deutsche Bahn** (DB; www.bahn.de), the German train system is the finest in Europe and is generally the best way to get around the country. There are independent operators, such as ALX, which runs between Munich and Regensburg.

Trains run on an interval system, so wherever you're heading, you can count on a service at least every two hours. Schedules are integrated throughout the country so that connections between trains are time-saving and tight, often only five minutes. Of course this means that when a train is late, connections are missed and you can find yourself stuck waiting for the next train.

CLASSES

It's rarely worth buying a 1st-class ticket on German trains; 2nd class is usually quite comfortable. There's more difference between the train classifications – basically the faster a train travels, the plusher (and more expensive) it is.

Train types include the following:

CNL, EN, D These are night trains, although an occasional D may be an extra daytime train.

ICE Sleek InterCityExpress services run at speeds up to 300km/h. The trains are very comfortable and feature cafe cars.

IC/EC Called InterCity or EuroCity, these are the premier conventional trains of DB. When trains are crowded, the open-seating coaches are much more comfortable than the older carriages with compartments.

RE RegionalExpress trains are local trains that make limited stops. They are fairly fast and run at one- or two-hourly intervals.

RB RegionalBahn are the slowest DB trains, not missing a single cow or town.

S-Bahn These suburban trains run frequent services in larger urban areas and rail passes are usually valid. Not to be confused with U-Bahns, which are run by local authorities that don't honour rail passes.

COSTS

Standard DB ticket prices are distance-based. You will usually be sold a ticket for the shortest distance to your destination.

Sample fares for one-way, 2nd-class ICE travel include Frankfurt–Berlin (€113), Frankfurt–Hamburg (€109) and Frankfurt–Munich (€91).

Regular full-fare tickets are good for four days from the day you tell the agent your journey will begin, and you can make unlimited stopovers along your route during that time. In this chapter train fares given between towns are all undiscounted 2nd class.

Discounts

DB sells Savings Fares that discount the high cost of regular tickets and are sold like airline tickets (ie trains with light loads may have tickets available at a discount, others none). Ask at the ticket counters, use the vending machines or book through www.bahn.de. For web purchases, the tickets arrive as email, which you then print out. It's easy.

The following are among the most popular discounts offered by DB (2nd class):

BahnCard 25/50/100 Only worthwhile for extended visits to Germany, these discount cards entitle holders to 25/50/100% off regular fares and cost €57/230/3800.

Dauer-Spezial 'Saver fare' tickets sold at a huge discount on the web.

Savings Fare 25 Round-trip tickets bought three or more days in advance and restricted to specific trains save 25%.

Savings Fare 50 Same conditions as the fare above but also including a Saturday-night stay.

Schönes Wochenende 'Happy Weekend' tickets allow unlimited use of RE, RB and S-Bahn trains on a Saturday or Sunday between midnight and 3am the next day, for up to five people travelling together, or one or both parents and all their children/grandchildren for €37. They are best suited to weekend day trips from urban areas.

RESERVATIONS

During peak periods, a seat reservation (€3.50) on a long-distance train can mean the difference between squatting near the toilet or relaxing in your own seat. Reservations can be made using vending machines or the web.

SCHEDULE INFORMATION

The DB website is excellent. There is extensive info in English and you can use it to sort out all the discount offers and schemes. In addition it has an excellent schedule feature that works not just for Germany but the rest of Europe.

Telephone information is also available: reservations ☎118 61; toll-free automated timetable ☎0800-150 7090.

TICKETS

Many train stations have a *Reisezentrum* (travel centre), where staff sell tickets and can help you plan an itinerary (ask for an English-speaking agent). Smaller stations may only have a few ticket windows and the smallest ones aren't staffed at all. In this case, you must buy tickets from multilingual vending machines. These are also plentiful at staffed stations and convenient if you don't want to queue at a ticket counter. Both agents and machines accept major credit cards.

Buying your ticket on the train carries a surcharge (€3 to €8). Not having a ticket carries a stiff penalty.

TRAIN PASSES

Agencies outside Germany sell German Rail Passes for unlimited travel on all DB trains for a number of days in a 30-day period. Sample 2nd-class prices for adults/under 26 are €188/150 for four days. With web discounts available, passes may not be good value. Try the DB website to compare.

Most Eurail and Inter-Rail passes are valid in Germany.

Greece Ελλάδα

Includes »

Best Places to Eat

- » Marco Polo Café (p667)
- » Tassia (p684)
- » Tzitzikas & Mermingas (p622)
- » Spondi (p624)
- » Taverna Lava (p656)

Best Places to Stay

- » 1700 (p643)
- » Amfitriti Pension (p632)
- » Hotel Grande Bretagne (p621)
- » Pension Sofi (p651)
- » Hotel Afendoulis (p672)

Why Go?

Don't let headline-grabbing financial woes put you off going to Greece. The elements that have made Greece one of the most popular destinations on the planet are still all there, and now is as good a time as ever to turn up for some fun in the sun. That alluring combination of history and hedonism continues to beckon. Within easy reach of magnificent archaeological sites are breathtaking beaches and relaxed tavernas serving everything from ouzo to octopus. Wanderers can island-hop to their heart's content, while party types can enjoy pulsating nightlife in Greece's vibrant modern cities and on islands such as Mykonos, Ios and Santorini. Throw in welcoming locals with an enticing culture and it's easy to see why most visitors head home vowing to come back. Travellers to Greece inevitably end up with a favourite site they long to return to – get out there and find yours.

When to Go

Athens

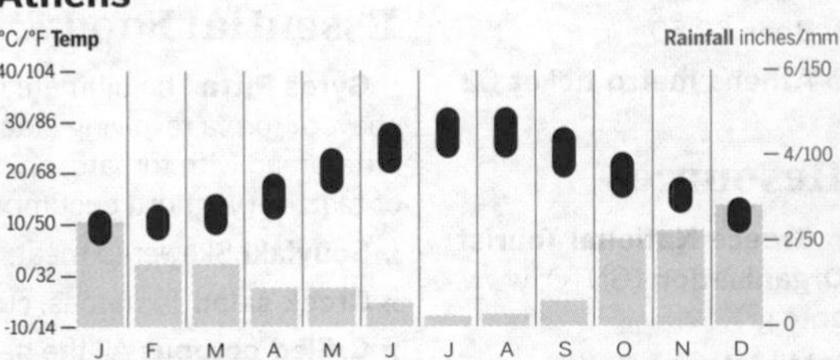

May & Jun Greece opens the shutters in time for Orthodox Easter; the best months to visit.

Jul & Aug Be prepared to battle summer crowds, high prices and soaring temperatures.

Sep & Oct The season winds down; a relaxing and pleasant time to head to Greece.

AT A GLANCE

» **Currency** euro (€)

» **Language** Greek

» **Money** ATMs all over; banks open Mon-Fri

» **Visas** Schengen rules apply

Fast Facts

» **Area** 131,944 sq km

» **Population** 11.2 million

» **Capital** Athens

» **Telephone** country code ☎30; international access code ☎00

» **Emergency** ☎112

Exchange Rates

Australia	A$1	€0.74
Canada	C$1	€0.74
Japan	¥100	€0.87
New Zealand	NZ$1	€0.56
UK	UK£1	€1.16
USA	US$1	€0.67

Set Your Budget

» **Budget hotel room** €50

» **Two-course dinner** €20

» **Museum entrance** €5

» **Beer** €2.50

» **Athens metro ticket** €2

Resources

» **Greece National Tourist Organisation** (GNTO; www.gnto.gr)

» **Ministry of Culture** (www.culture.gr)

» **Ancient Greece** (www.ancientgreece.com)

» **Greek Ferries** (www.greekferries.gr)

Connections

For those visiting Greece as part of a trip around Europe, there are various exciting options for reaching onward destinations overland or by sea.

There are regular ferry connections between Greece and the Italian ports of Ancona, Bari, Brindisi and Venice. Similarly, there are ferries operating between the Greek islands of Rhodes, Symi, Kos, Samos, Chios and Lesvos and the Aegean coast of Turkey. Island-hopping doesn't have to take you back to Athens.

Overland, it's possible to reach Albania, Bulgaria, Macedonia and Turkey from Greece. If you've got your own wheels, you can drive through border crossings with these four countries. There are bus connections with Albania, Bulgaria and Turkey, and train connections with Bulgaria, Macedonia and Turkey. In summer there are direct train services to Moscow.

ITINERARIES

One Week

Explore Athens' museums and ancient sites on day one before spending a couple of days in the Peloponnese visiting Nafplio, Mycenae and Olympia; ferry to the Cyclades and enjoy Mykonos and spectacular Santorini.

One Month

Give yourself some more time in Athens and the Peloponnese, then visit the Ionian Islands for a few days. Explore the Zagoria Villages before travelling back to Athens via Meteora and Delphi. Take a ferry from Piraeus south to Mykonos, then island-hop via Santorini to Crete. After exploring Crete, take the ferry east to Rhodes, then north to Symi, Kos and Samos. Carry on north to Chios, then head on to Lesvos. Take the ferry back to Piraeus when you're out of time or money.

Essential Food & Drink

» **Gyros Pitta** The ultimate in cheap eats. Pork or chicken shaved from a revolving stack of sizzling meat is wrapped in pitta bread with tomato, onion, fried potatoes and lashings of tzatziki (yoghurt, cucumber and garlic). Costs €2 to €3.

» **Souvlaki** Skewered meat, usually pork.

» **Greek salad** Tomatoes, cucumber, onion, feta and olives.

» **Grilled octopus** All the better with a glass of ouzo.

» **Ouzo** Sipped slowly, this legendary Greek aniseed-flavoured tipple turns a cloudy white when ice and water is added.

» **Raki** Cretan firewater produced from grape skins.

» **Greek coffee** A legacy of Ottoman rule, Greek coffee should be tried at least once by all visitors.

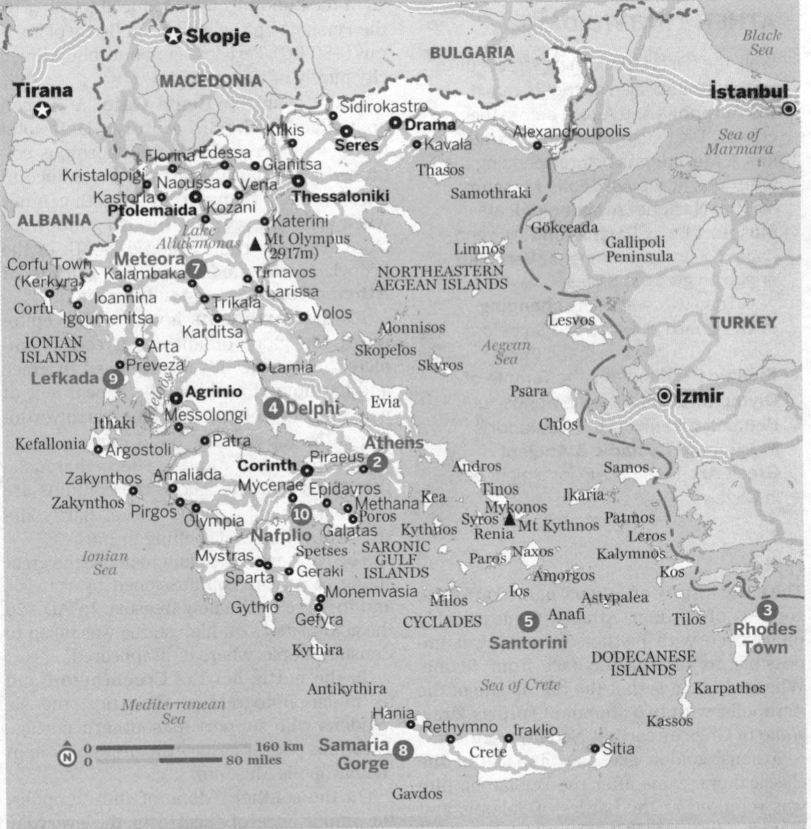

Greece Highlights

1. **Island-hop** (p698) at your own pace under the Aegean sun
2. In **Athens** (p613), trace the ancient to the modern from the Acropolis to booming nightclubs
3. Lose yourself within the medieval walls of **Rhodes Old Town** (p667)
4. Search for the oracle amidst **Delphi's** (p637) dazzling ruins
5. Stare dumbfounded at the dramatic volcanic caldera of incomparable **Santorini** (p654)
6. Sup on **ouzo** (p690) while munching on grilled octopus
7. Climb russet rock pinnacles to the exquisite monasteries of **Meteora** (p638)
8. Hike through Crete's stupendous **Samaria Gorge** (p663)
9. Let your cares float away from the pristine west-coast beaches of **Lefkada** (p682)
10. Use quaint **Nafplio** (p632) as a base for exploring the back roads and ruins of the Pelopponese

ATHENS ΑΘΗΝΑ

POP 3.8 MILLION

Stroll around Athens and you'll quickly stumble across breathtaking archaeological treasures, reminders of the city's enormous historical influence on Western civilisation. With the makeover that accompanied the 2004 Olympics, Athens presented its cosmopolitan-modern side to the world, and with Greece's financial difficulties in 2010 it has revealed its more restive aspect. Though the city still suffers from traffic congestion, pollution and urban sprawl, take the time to look beneath her skin and you will discover a complex metropolis full of vibrant subcultures.

ATHENS IN TWO DAYS

Walk the deserted morning streets of the charming Plaka district to reach the **Acropolis** and **Agora** before the crowds. Dig in to *mezedhes* at **Tzitzikas & Mermingas** before spending the afternoon at the **Acropolis Museum** and the **National Archaeological Museum**. Enjoy **Parthenon** views and haute cuisine over dinner at **Varoulko** or sup on gyros at **Savas**.

On day two, watch the **changing of the guard** at Syntagma Sq before crossing the gardens to the **Panathenaic Stadium** and the **Temple of Olympian Zeus**. Visit the wonderful **Benaki Museum** or the **Goulandris Museum of Cycladic & Ancient Greek Art**, then rest up for a night out in **Gazi**.

History

The early history of Athens, named after the goddess of wisdom, Athena, is inextricably interwoven with mythology, making it impossible to disentangle fact from fiction. What is known is that the hilltop site of the Acropolis, with two abundant springs, drew some of Greece's earliest Neolithic settlers.

Athens' golden age, the pinnacle of the classical era, came after the Persian empire was repulsed at the battles of Salamis and Plataea (480–479 BC). The city has passed through many hands and cast off myriad invaders from Sparta to Philip II of Macedon, the Roman and Byzantine Empires, and, most recently, the Ottoman Empire. In 1834 Athens superseded Nafplio as the capital of independent Greece.

Sights

Acropolis ANCIENT SITE

(Map p620; ☎210 321 0219; adult/child €12/free; ⏲8.30am-8pm Apr-Oct, 8am-5pm Nov-Mar; MAkropoli) Arguably the most important ancient monument in the Western world, the Acropolis attracts multitudes of tourists, so visit in the early morning or late afternoon.

The site was inhabited in Neolithic times and the first temples were built during the Mycenaean era in homage to the goddess Athena. People lived on the Acropolis until the late 6th century BC, but in 510 BC the Delphic oracle declared that the Acropolis should be the province of the gods. When all of the buildings were reduced to ashes by the Persians on the eve of the Battle of Salamis (480 BC), Pericles set about rebuilding a city purely of temples.

Enter near the **Beule Gate**, a Roman arch added in the 3rd century AD. Beyond this lies the **Propylaea**, the enormous columned gate that was the city's entrance in ancient times. Damaged in the 17th century when lightning set off a Turkish gunpowder store, it's since been restored. South of the Propylaea, the small, graceful **Temple of Athena Nike** was been fully restored.

It's the **Parthenon**, however, that epitomises the glory of ancient Greece. Completed in 438 BC, it's unsurpassed in grace and harmony. To achieve the appearance of perfect form, columns become narrower towards the top and the bases curve upward slightly towards the ends – effects that make them look straight. Above the columns are the remains of a Doric frieze, partly destroyed by Venetian shelling in 1687.

The Parthenon was built to house the great statue of Athena commissioned by Pericles, and to serve as the new treasury. In AD 426 the gold-plated 12m-high statue was taken to Constantinople, where it disappeared.

To the north, lies the **Erechtheion** and its much-photographed Caryatids, the six maidens who support its southern portico. These are plaster casts – the originals are in the Acropolis Museum.

On the southern slope of the Acropolis, the importance of theatre in the everyday lives of ancient Athenians is made manifest in the enormous **Theatre of Dionysos** (Map p620). Built between 340 and 330 BC on the site of an earlier theatre dating to the 6th century BC, it held 17,000 people. The **Stoa**

CHEAPER BY THE HALF-DOZEN

The €12 ticket at the Acropolis (valid for four days) includes entry to the other significant ancient sites: Ancient Agora, Roman Agora, Keramikos, Temple of Olympian Zeus and the Theatre of Dionysos.

Anyone aged under 19 years or with an EU student card gets in free. Also free: Sundays from November to March, the first Sunday of April, May, June and October, and national holidays.

of Eumenes (Map p616), built as a shelter and promenade for theatre audiences, runs west to the **Theatre of Herodes Atticus** (Map p620), built in Roman times (open only for performances).

TOP CHOICE **Acropolis Museum** MUSEUM
(Map p616; ☎210 900 0901; www.theacropolismuseum.gr; Dionysiou Areopagitou 15; admission €5; ⏰8am-8pm Tue-Sun; 📶; Ⓜ Akropoli) Don't miss this superb museum on the southern base of the hill, and magnificently reflecting the Parthenon on its glass facade; it houses the surviving treasures of the Acropolis.

Bathed in natural light, the 1st-floor **Archaic Gallery** is a forest of statues, including stunning examples of 6th-century *kore* (maidens). Finds from temples pre-dating the Parthenon include sculptures such as Heracles slaying the Lernaian Hydra, and a lioness devouring a bull.

The museum's crowning glory is the top-floor **Parthenon Gallery**, a glass hall built in alignment with the Parthenon, visible through the windows. It showcases the temple's metopes and 160m frieze shown in sequence for the first time in over 200 years. Interspersed between the golden-hued originals, white plaster replicates the controversial Parthenon Marbles removed by Lord Elgin in 1801 and later sold to the British Museum.

Other highlights include five **Caryatids**, the maiden columns that held up the Erechtheion (the sixth is in the British Museum), a giant floral acroterion and a **movie** illustrating the history of the Acropolis.

The surprisingly good-value **restaurant** has superb views; there's a fine museum **shop**.

Ancient Agora ANCIENT SITE
(Map p620; ☎210 321 0185; Adrianou 24; adult/child €4/free; ⏰8.30am-8pm Apr-Oct, 8am-5.30pm Nov-Mar; Ⓜ Monastiraki) The Ancient Agora was the marketplace of early Athens and the focal point of civic and social life; Socrates spent time here expounding his philosophy. The main monuments of the Agora are the well-preserved **Temple of Hephaestus**, the 11th-century **Church of the Holy Apostles** and the reconstructed **Stoa of Attalos**, which houses the site's excellent museum.

Roman Agora ANCIENT SITE
(Map p620; ☎210 324 5220; cnr Pelopida & Eolou; adult/child €2/free; ⏰8.30am-8pm Apr-Oct, 8am-5.30pm Nov-Mar; Ⓜ Monastiraki) The Romans built their agora just east of the ancient Athenian Agora. The wonderful **Tower of the Winds** was built in the 1st century BC by Syrian astronomer Andronicus. Each side represents a point of the compass and has a relief carving depicting the associated wind.

FREE THRILLS

A simple wander through the streets brings eye candy galore, or take in:

- National Gardens
- Changing of the Guard
- Monastiraki Flea Market
- Sunday Market
- Lykavittos Hill

Temple of Olympian Zeus & Panathenaic Stadium ANCIENT SITES
(Map p616; ☎210 922 6330; adult/child €2/free; ⏰8.30am-8pm Apr-Oct, 8am-5.30pm Nov-Mar; Ⓜ Akropoli) Begun in the 6th century BC, Greece's largest temple is impressive for the sheer size of its Corinthian columns: 17m high with a base diameter of 1.7m. It took more than 700 years to build, with Emperor Hadrian overseeing its completion in AD 131, and sits behind **Hadrian's Arch**. East of the temple, the Panathenaic Stadium, built in the 4th century BC as a venue for the Panathenaic athletic contests, hosted the first modern Olympic Games in 1896.

National Archaeological Museum MUSEUM
(☎210 821 7717; www.namuseum.gr; 28 Oktovriou-Patision 44; adult/child €7/free; ⏰1.30-8pm Mon, 8am-8pm Tue-Sun Apr-Oct, 8.30am-3pm Nov-Mar; Ⓜ Viktoria) One of the world's great museums, the National Archaeological Museum contains significant finds from major archaeological sites throughout Greece. The vast collections include exquisite gold artefacts from Mycenae, spectacular Minoan frescos from Santorini and aquiline Cycladic figurines.

Benaki Museum MUSEUM
(Map p616; ☎210 367 1000; www.benaki.gr; cnr Leoforos Vasilissis Sofias & Koumbari 1; adult/child €6/free, free Thu; ⏰9am-5pm Mon, Wed, Fri & Sat, 9am-midnight Thu, to 3pm Sun; Ⓜ Syntagma) This superb museum houses the extravagant collection of Antoine Benaki, the son of an Alexandrian cotton magnate. Splendid displays include ancient sculpture, Persian,

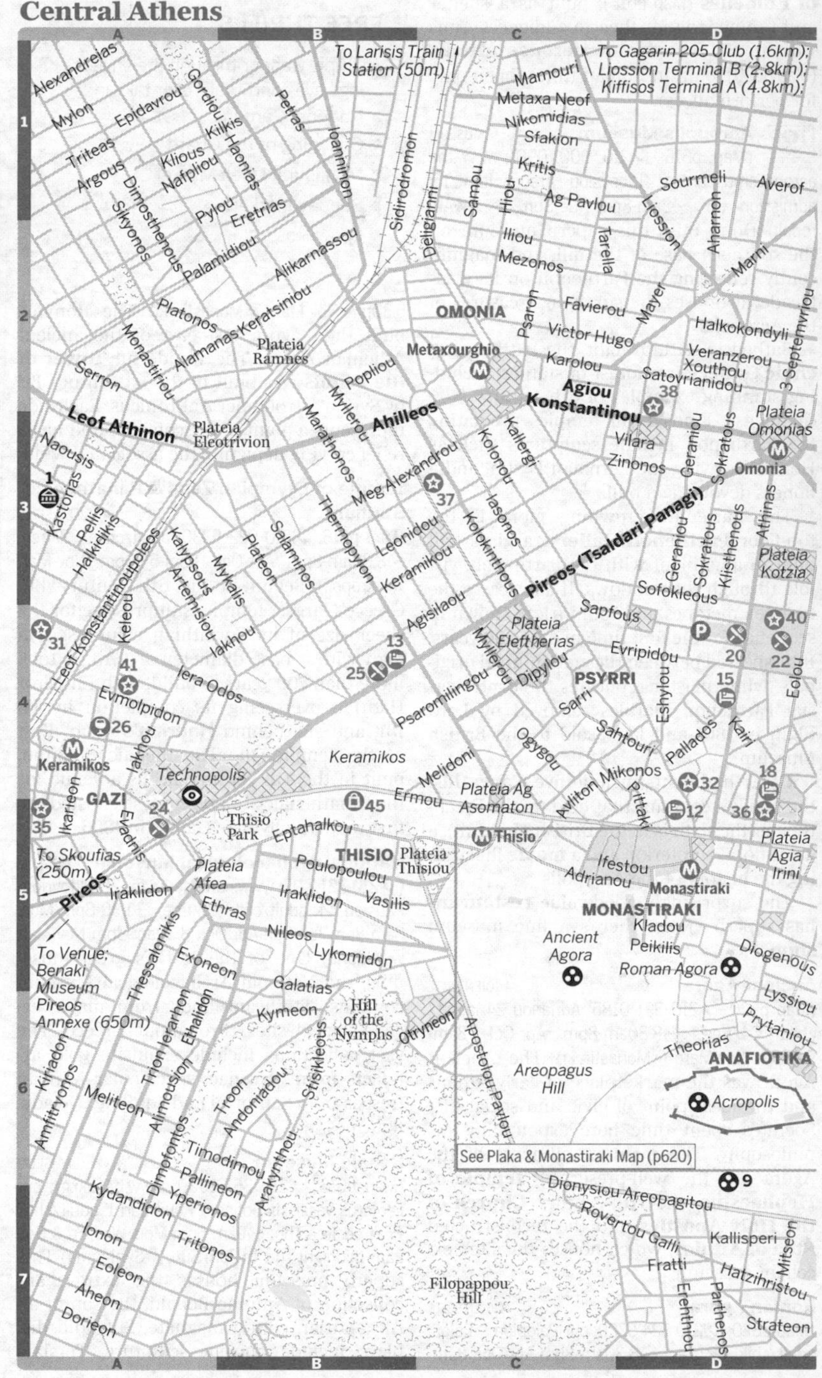
To Larisis Train Station (50m)
To Gagarin 205 Club (1.6km); Liossion Terminal B (2.8km); Kiffisos Terminal A (4.8km)
OMONIA
Metaxourghio
Plateia Ramnes
Leof Athinon
Plateia Eleotrivion
Ahilleos
Agiou Konstantinou
Plateia Omonias
Omonia
Pireos (Tsaldari Panagi)
Plateia Kotzia
Plateia Eleftherias
PSYRRI
Keramikos
GAZI
Technopolis
Thisio Park
Plateia Ag Asomaton
Thisio
THISIO
Plateia Thisiou
Plateia Afea
Plateia Agia Irini
Monastiraki
MONASTIRAKI
Ancient Agora
Roman Agora
Hill of the Nymphs
Areopagus Hill
ANAFIOTIKA
Acropolis
See Plaka & Monastiraki Map (p620)
Filopappou Hill
To Skoufias (250m)
To Venue; Benaki Museum Pireos Annexe (650m)
Dionysiou Areopagitou
Apostolou Pavlou
Ermou
Lekf Konstantinoupoleos
Iera Odos

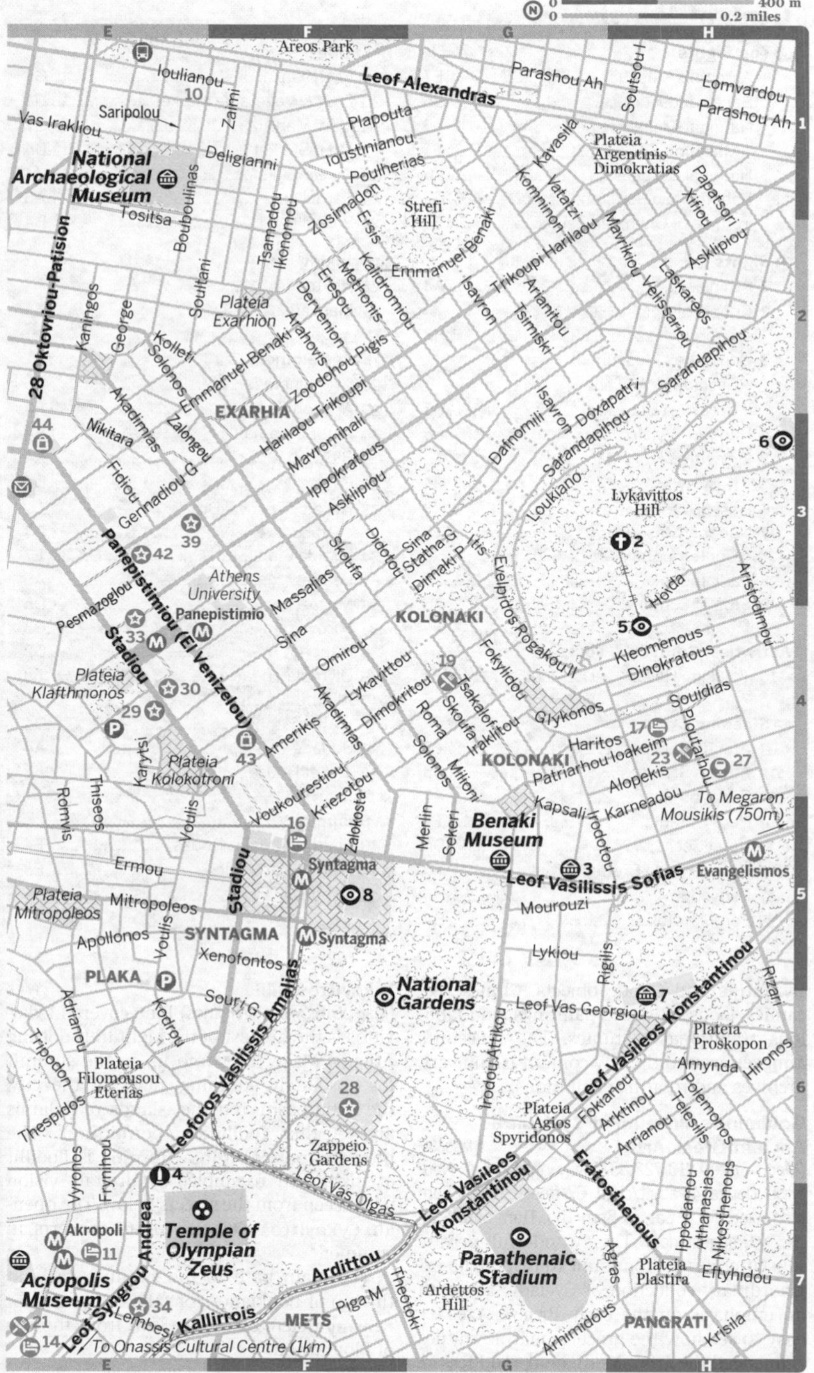

Areos Park
Leof Alexandras
National Archaeological Museum
Plateia Exarhion
EXARHIA
Lykavittos Hill
KOLONAKI
Athens University
Panepistimio
Syntagma
SYNTAGMA
PLAKA
Benaki Museum
Leof Vasilissis Sofias
Evangelismos
National Gardens
Zappeio Gardens
Temple of Olympian Zeus
Akropoli
Acropolis Museum
Panathenaic Stadium
Ardettos Hill
METS
PANGRATI
To Megaron Mousikis (750m)
To Onassis Cultural Centre (1km)

Central Athens

Top Sights

- Acropolis Museum ... E7
- Benaki Museum ... G5
- National Archaeological Museum ... E1
- National Gardens ... F6
- Panathenaic Stadium ... G7
- Temple of Olympian Zeus ... E7

Sights

1 Athinais ... A3
2 Chapel of Agios Georgios ... H3
3 Goulandris Museum of Cycladic & Ancient Greek Art ... G5
4 Hadrian's Arch ... E6
5 Lykavittos Funicular Railway ... H4
6 Lykavittos Theatre ... H3
7 National Museum of Contemporary Art ... H6
8 Parliament ... F5
9 Stoa of Eumenes ... D6

Activities, Courses & Tours

10 Trekking Hellas ... E1

Sleeping

11 Athens Backpackers ... E7
12 Athens Style ... D5
13 Eridanus ... B4
14 Hera Hotel ... E7
15 Hotel Cecil ... D4
16 Hotel Grande Bretagne ... F5
17 Periscope ... H4
18 Tempi Hotel ... D4

Eating

19 Entryfish ... G4
20 Fruit & Vegetable Market ... D4
21 Mani Mani ... E7
22 Meat Market ... D4
23 Oikeio ... H4
24 Sardelles ... A5
25 Varoulko ... B4

Drinking

26 Hoxton ... A4
27 Mai Tai ... H4

Entertainment

28 Aigli Cinema ... F6
29 Apollon Cinema ... E4
30 Astor Cinema ... E4
31 BIG ... A4
32 Envy ... D4
33 Hellenic Festival Box Office ... E4
34 Lamda Club ... E7
35 Letom ... A5
36 Magaze ... D5
37 Mirovolos ... C3
38 National Theatre ... D2
39 Olympia Theatre ... E3
40 Rembetika Stoa Athanaton ... D4
41 Sodade ... A4
42 Ticket House ... E3

Shopping

43 Eleftheroudakis Books ... F4
44 Metropolis Music ... E3
45 Sunday Market ... B5

Byzantine and Coptic objects, Chinese ceramics, icons, El Greco paintings, and fabulous traditional costumes. The museum's annexes around the city contain Islamic art, archives and rotating exhibitions.

Goulandris Museum of Cycladic & Ancient Greek Art MUSEUM
(Map p616; ☎210 722 8321; www.cycladic.gr; Neofytou Douka 4; adult/child €7/free; ⏲10am-5pm Mon, Wed, Fri & Sat, to 8pm Thu, 11am-5pm Sun; wi-fi; Ⓜ Evangelismos) This wonderful private museum was custom-built to display its extraordinary collection of Cycladic art, with an emphasis on the early Bronze Age. It's easy to see how the graceful marble statues influenced the art of Modigliani and Picasso.

Lykavittos Hill PARK
(Map p616; Ⓜ Evangelismos) Pine-covered Lykavittos is the highest of the eight hills dotting Athens. Make the climb up to the summit for absolutely stunning views of the city, the Attic basin and the islands of Salamis and Aegina (pollution permitting). The little **Chapel of Agios Giorgios** is floodlit at night and resembles a fairy-tale vision when seen from the streets below. The open-air **Lykavittos Theatre** hosts concerts in summer.

The main path to the summit starts at the top of Loukianou, or take the **funicular railway** (return €6; ⏲9am-3am) from the top of Ploutarhou.

Parliament & Changing of the Guard CULTURAL RITUAL
(Map p616) In front of the parliament building on Plateia Syntagmatos (Syntagma Sq), the traditionally costumed *evzones* (guards) of the **Tomb of the Unknown Soldier** change every hour on the hour. On Sunday at 11am, a whole platoon marches down Vasilissis Sofias to the tomb, accompanied by a band.

National Gardens PARK
(Map p616; entrances on Leoforos Vasilissis Sofias & Leoforos Vasilissis Amalias; ⌚7am-dusk; MSyntagma) A delightful, shady refuge during summer, these gardens contain a large playground, a duck pond and a tranquil cafe.

Tours

Athens Sightseeing Public Bus Line BUS
(Bus Route 400; tickets €5) Stops at 20 key sites. Buy tickets (valid for 24 hours on all public transport, excluding airport services) on board.

CitySightseeing Athens BUS
(☎210 922 0604; www.city-sightseeing.com; adult/concession €18/8; ⌚every 30min 9am-6pm) Open-top double-decker buses on a 90-minute circuit.

Athens Happy Train TROLLEY
(☎210 725 5400; adult/concession €6/4; ⌚9am-midnight) Hour-long minitrain tours leaving from the top of Ermou.

Trekking Hellas OUTDOOR ACTIVITIES
(☎210 331 0323; www.outdoorsgreece.com; Saripolou 10, Plaka; MSyntagma) Activities from Athens walking tours (€22) to bungee jumping in the Corinth Canal (€60).

Festivals & Events

Hellenic Festival PERFORMING ARTS
(Map p616; ☎210 327 2000; www.greekfestival.gr; box office Panepistimiou 39, Syntagma; ⌚8.30am-4pm Mon-Fri, 9am-2pm Sat; MPanepistimio) The city's most important cultural event runs from mid-June to August. International music, dance and theatre fill venues across Athens and Epidavros' ancient theatre.

Sleeping

Discounts apply in low season, for longer stays and on the internet. Book well ahead for July and August.

CONTEMPORARY ART

Athens is not all ancient art. For a taste of the contemporary, visit:

» **Taf** (The Art Foundation; Map p620; ☎210 323 8757; www.theartfoundation.gr; Normanou 5, Monastiraki) Eclectic art and music gallery.

» **Onassis Cultural Centre** (off Map p616; ☎210 924 9090; www.sgt.gr; Leoforos Syngrou 109, Tavros) This multimillion-euro visual and performing arts centre features theatre, music and dance performances, as well as art exhibits and talks.

» **National Museum of Contemporary Art** (Map p616; ☎210 924 2111; www.emst.gr; Leoforos Vas Georgiou B 17-19, enter from Rigilis; admission €3; ⌚11am-7pm) In 2011, the museum will be moving to the old Fix brewery on Leoforos Syngrou.

Or hit the Gazi neighbourhood for:

» **Technopolis** (☎210 346 7322; Gazi) Former gasworks turned cultural centre.

» **Benaki Museum Pireos Annexe** (☎210 345 3111; www.benaki.gr; Pireos 138, cnr Andronikou, Rouf; ⌚10am-6pm Wed-Sun) Arts and cultural exhibitions.

» **Athinais** (☎210 348 0000; www.athinais.com.gr; Kastorias 36, Gazi; ⌚9am-9pm) Local and international artists. Call ahead for schedule.

Festivals include:

» **Art-Athina** (www.art-athina.gr) International contemporary art fair in May.

» **Athens Biennial** (www.athensbiennial.org) Every two years from June to October.

» **ReMap** (www.remap.org) Parallel event to the Biennial, exhibiting in abandoned buildings.

Plaka & Monastiraki

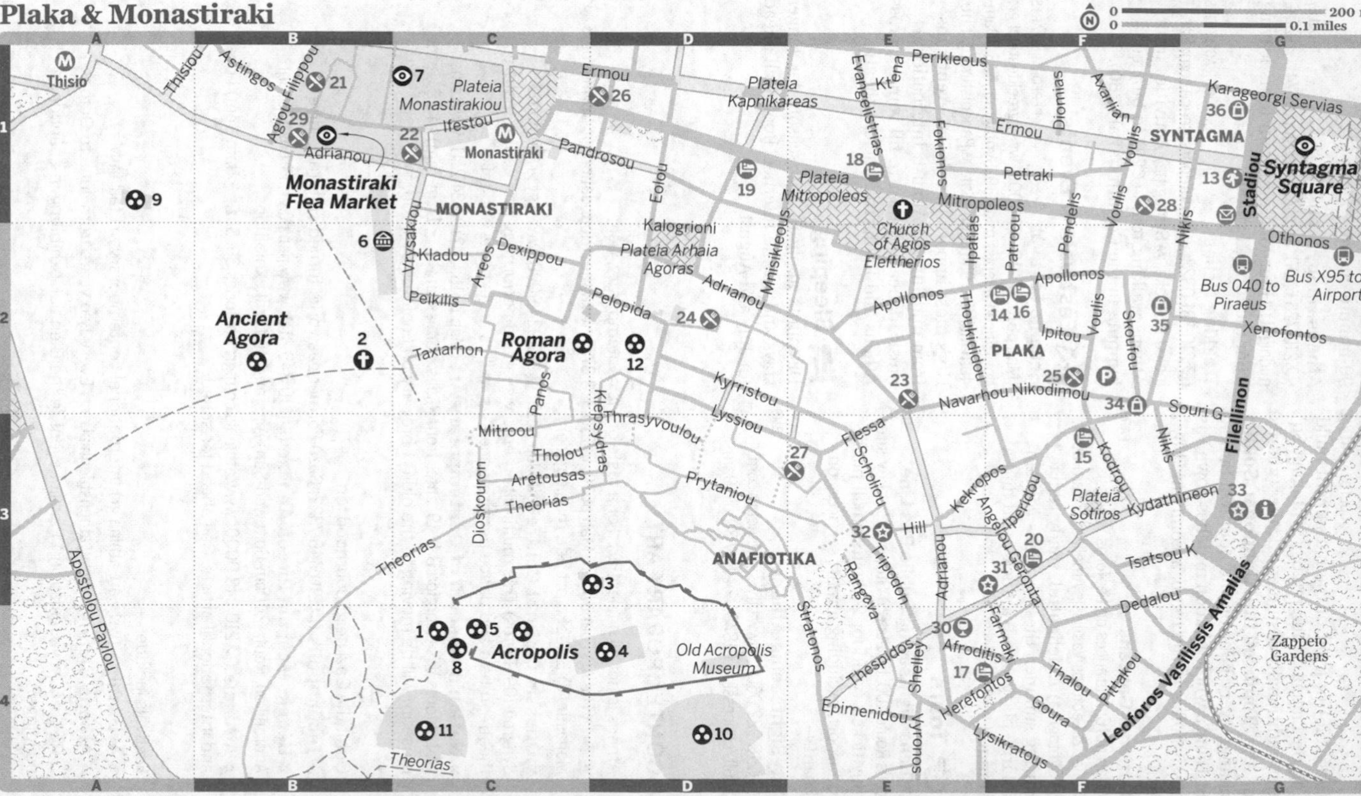

Plaka & Monastiraki

SYNTAGMA & MONASTIRAKI

TOP CHOICE Hotel Grande Bretagne LUXURY HOTEL €€€
(Map p616; ☎210 333 0000; www.grandebretagne.gr; Vasileos Georgiou 1, Syntagma; r/ste from €275/420; P❄@📶🏊; MSyntagma) Dripping with elegance and old-world charm, *the* place to stay in Athens has always has been these deluxe digs. Built in 1862 to accommodate visiting heads of state, it ranks among the great hotels of the world. From the decadent, chandeliered lobby, to the exquisite guestrooms, divine spa and rooftop restaurant, this place is built for pampering.

Magna Grecia BOUTIQUE HOTEL €€
(Map p620; ☎210 324 0314; www.magnagreciahotel.com; Mitropoleos 54, Monastiraki; s/d incl breakfast from €110/130; ❄@📶; MSyntagma) Enjoy Acropolis views from the front rooms and rooftop terrace in a historic building opposite the cathedral. Rooms sport comfortable mattresses and minibars.

Plaka Hotel HOTEL €€
(Map p620; ☎210 322 2096; www.plakahotel.gr; Kapnikareas 7 & Mitropoleos, Monastiraki; s/d/tr incl breakfast €109/135/145; ❄@; MMonastiraki) Folks come here not for the tidy, bland rooms but for the excellent Acropolis views from the rooftop garden and top-floor digs.

Hotel Cecil HOTEL €€
(Map p616; ☎210 321 7079; www.cecil.gr; Athinas 39, Monastiraki; s/d €75/105; ❄; MMonastiraki) Aromatic spices waft into the lobby from nearby Asian markets, but double-pane windows keep the high-ceilinged rooms in this old classical building quiet. Close to Psyrri nightlife.

Tempi Hotel HOTEL €€
(Map p616; ☎210 321 3175; www.tempihotel.gr; Eolou 29, Monastiraki; d/tr €64/78, s/d without bathroom €43/57; 📶; MMonastiraki) No-frills rooms may be tiny, but some have balconies overlooking Plateia Agia Irini. A communal kitchen and nearby markets make it ideal for self-caterers.

PLAKA, MAKRYGIANNI & KOUKAKI

TOP CHOICE Central Hotel BOUTIQUE HOTEL €€
(Map p620; ☎210 323 4357; www.centralhotel.gr; Apollonos 21, Plaka; r incl breakfast

€93-155; ⊖❄@; MSyntagma) Pass through the sleek lobby and by the attentive staff to spacious white rooms hung with original art and decked out with all the mod cons. Some balconies have Acropolis views, as does the rooftop, where you can sunbake and relax in the Jacuzzi.

TOP CHOICE **Hera Hotel** BOUTIQUE HOTEL €€
(Map p616; ☎210 923 6682; www.herahotel.gr; Falirou 9, Makrygianni; r from €115; ❄@; MAkropoli) The interior of this exquisite boutique hotel matches its lovely neoclassical facade. The rooftop garden, restaurant and bar boast spectacular views and it is a short walk to the Acropolis and Plaka.

Athens Backpackers HOSTEL €
(Map p620; ☎210 922 4044; www.backpackers.gr; Makri 12, Makrygianni; dm €24-29, studio from €90; ❄@; MAkropoli) This excellent, popular hostel boasts a rooftop party bar with Acropolis views, kitchen, daily movies, and the friendly Aussie management hosts (free!) barbecues. Breakfast and nonalcoholic drinks are included; long-term storage, laundry and airport pick-up available.

Hotel Acropolis House HOTEL €€
(Map p620; ☎210 322 2344; www.acropolishouse.gr; Kodrou 6-8, Plaka; s incl breakfast €53-73, d €68-91, tr €119; ❄; MSyntagma) This well-situated hotel in a 19th-century house feels more pension than hotel, with a comfy sitting room and hospitable management. Guests chat amicably over breakfast.

Marble House Pension HOTEL €
(off Map p616; ☎210 922 8294; www.marblehouse.gr; Zini 35, Koukaki; s/d/tr €39/49/59, d/tr without bathroom €45/55; ❄@; MSyngrou-Fix) This long-standing Athens favourite is on a quiet cul-de-sac 10 minutes' walk from Plaka. Step through the garden to quiet, spotless rooms. For air-con add €9.

Hotel Hermes BOUTIQUE HOTEL €€
(Map p620; ☎210 323 5514; www.hermeshotel.gr; Apollonos 19, Plaka; s/d/tr incl breakfast €109/135/145; ⊖❄@; MSyntagma) Next to the Central, with similar amenities, but not quite as swish.

Hotel Phaedra HOTEL €€
(Map p620; ☎210 323 8461; www.hotelphaedra.com; Herefontos 16, Plaka; r €65-80; ❄@; MAkropoli) Many of the tasteful, small rooms at this family-run hotel have balconies with Acropolis or church views. Great rooftop terrace.

Student & Travellers' Inn HOSTEL €
(Map p620; ☎210 324 4808; www.studenttravellersinn.com; Kydathineon 16, Plaka; dm €20-25, d €63, without bathroom €58; ❄@; MAkropoli) The mixed-sex dorms may be spartan and housekeeping a bit lean, but extras (laundry, left luggage) make up for it.

PSYRRI & GAZI

Athens Style HOSTEL €
(Map p616; ☎210 322 5010; www.athenstyle.com; Agias Theklas 10, Psyrri; dm incl breakfast €21-25, s/d €51/84, studios €90-124; ❄@; MMonastiraki) This bright, arty hostel, the newest in town, has dorm beds and well-equipped studios. The cool basement lounge holds art exhibitions, a pool table and home cinema; the rooftop bar has Acropolis views.

Eridanus BOUTIQUE HOTEL €€€
(Map p616; ☎210 520 5360; www.eridanus.gr; Pireos 78, Gazi; d incl breakfast from €195; P❄@; MKeramikos) After a late night partying in Gazi or nearby Psyrri, soak in your marble bathtub and lounge around in a fluffy white robe. Helpful staff cater to your every whim; the rooftop garden has Acropolis views.

KOLONAKI

Periscope BOUTIQUE HOTEL €€€
(Map p616; ☎210 729 7200; www.periscope.gr; Haritos 22, Kolonaki; r from €135; ⊖❄@; MEvangelismos) A hip hotel with a cool, edgy look (Mini Cooper seats for chairs in the cafe-bar), this place has comfortable minimalist rooms with all the mod cons and a quiet location.

Eating

In addition to mainstay tavernas, Athens has bistros and swank eateries. Wear your most stylish togs at night: Athenians dress up to eat out. Eat streets include Mitropoleos, Adrianou and Navarchou Apostoli in Monastiraki, the area around Plateia Psyrri and Gazi, near Keramikos metro.

Listings without opening hours specified are open for lunch and dinner daily during high season. For standard business hours, see p692.

The **fruit and vegetable market** (Map p616) on Athinas is opposite the **meat market** (Map p616).

SYNTAGMA & MONASTIRAKI

TOP CHOICE **Tzitzikas & Mermingas** MEZEDHES €€
(Map p620; Mitropoleos 12-14, Syntagma; mezedhes €6-8; MSyntagma) Greek merchan-

dise lines the walls of this cheery, modern *mezedhopoleio*. The great range of delicious and creative *mezedhes* draws a bustling local crowd. Don't miss the decadent honey-coated fried cheese with ham…it's the kind of special dish that will haunt your future dreams.

Café Avyssinia MEZEDHES €€
(Map p620; ☎210 321 7407; Kynetou 7, Monastiraki; mains €8.50-14.50; Ⓜ Monastiraki) Hidden away on the edge of grungy Plateia Avyssinias in the middle of the flea market, this *mezedhopoleio* gets top marks for atmosphere, and the food is not far behind. Often has live music on weekends.

Savas SOUVLAKI €
(Map p620; Mitropoleos 86-88, Monastiraki; gyros €2; Ⓜ Monastiraki) This joint serves enormous grilled-meat plates (€8.50) and the tastiest gyros (pork, beef or chicken) in Athens. Take away or sit down in what becomes one of the city's busiest eat streets late at night.

Also recommended:

Viasos MODERN GREEK €
(Map p620; Adrianou 19) Young local crowds chat over juicy gyros (€2) and generous *mezedhes* (€7 to €12) on one of Athens' most atmospheric pedestrian streets.

Dioskouri MODERN GREEK €
(Map p620; Adrianou 37) Another Adrianou option.

PLAKA & MAKRYGIANNI

Taverna tou Psarra TAVERNA €€
(Map p620; ☎210 321 8734; Eretheos 16, Plaka; mains €8-23; Ⓜ Monastiraki) On a path leading up towards the Acropolis, this gem of a taverna is one of Plaka's best, serving scrumptious *mezedhes* and excellent fish and meat classics on a tree-lined terrace.

Paradosiako TAVERNA €
(Map p620; ☎210 321 4121; Voulis 44a, Plaka; mains €7-14; Ⓜ Syntagma) For great traditional fare, you can't beat this inconspicuous, no-frills taverna on the periphery of Plaka. Choose from daily specials such as delicious shrimp *saganaki*.

Mani Mani REGIONAL CUISINE €
(Map p616; ☎210 921 8180; Falirou 10, Makrygianni; mains €9.50-17; ⏲closed Jul & Aug; Ⓜ Akropoli) Sample cuisine from Mani in the Peloponnese, such as tangy sausage with orange. Most dishes can be ordered as half-serves (at half-price), allowing you to try a wide range.

O Platanos TAVERNA €
(Map p620; ☎210 322 0666; Diogenous 4, Monastiraki, Plaka; mains €7-9; Ⓜ Monastiraki) Laid-back O Platanos (Plane Tree) serves tasty, home-cooked-style Greek cuisine. The lamb dishes are delicious and we love the leafy courtyard.

Eat MODERN GREEK €€
(Map p620; ☎210 324 9129; Adrianou 91, Plaka; mains €8-17; Ⓜ Syntagma) A sleek alternative to the endless traditional tavernas, Eat serves interesting salads and pastas and modern interpretations of Greek classics such as shrimp dolmas with sun-dried tomatoes (€9).

PSYRRI, THISSIO & GAZI

Skoufias REGIONAL CUISINE €
(☎210 341 2252; Vasiliou tou Megalou 50, Rouf; mains €5-9; ⏲9pm-late; Ⓜ Keramikos) This gem of a taverna near the railway line is a little off the beaten track but worth seeking out. The Cretan-influenced menu features eclectic dishes rarely found in the tourist joints: from superb rooster with ouzo to lamb *tsigariasto* (braised) with *horta* (wild greens).

Varoulko SEAFOOD €€€
(Map p616; ☎210 522 8400; www.varoulko.gr; Pireos 80, Gazi; mains €22-30; ⏲closed Sun; Ⓜ Keramikos) For a magical Greek dining experience, you can't beat the winning combination of Acropolis views and delicious seafood by celebrated chef Lefteris Lazarou. This Michelin-starred seafood restaurant remains popular with Athenian celebrities and foodies, who sup on sublime crayfish dolmas wrapped in sorrel leaves in an airy, glass-fronted dining room.

Sardelles SEAFOOD €
(☎210 347 8050; Persefonis 15, Gazi; mains €9.50-15; Ⓜ Keramikos) As the name (sardines) suggests and the novel fishmonger paper tablecloths confirm, this modern fish taverna specialises in seafood *mezedhes*. Outside tables face the illuminated gasworks.

KOLONAKI & PANGRATI

TOP CHOICE **Oikeio** BISTRO €
(Map p616; ☎210 725 9216; Ploutarhou 15, Kolonaki; mains €8-11; Ⓜ Evangelismos) With excellent home-style cooking, this modern taverna lives up to its name ('Homey'). The intimate bistro atmosphere spills out to tables on the pavement for glitterati-watching without the normal high Kolonaki bill. Reservations recommended.

Spondi GOURMET GREEK €€€
(☎210 756 4021; www.spondi.gr; Pyrronos 5, Pangrati; mains €36-50; ⏰8pm-midnight) Dining in this superb restaurant's gorgeous vaulted cellar or in its bougainvillea-draped courtyard in summer is quite an understatedly elegant affair. Chef Arnaud Bignon has won two Michelin stars, creating extravagant seasonal menus using local ingredients and adhering to French technique but embodying vibrant Greek flavours.

Entryfish GOURMET MEZEDHES €€
(Map p616; ☎210 361 7666; Skoufa 52, Kolonaki; mezedhes €11-20; Ⓜ Syntagma) Brush shoulders with CEOs at this packed, swank seafood salon. Funky newsprint and art glass line the walls, and the *mezedhes* all have exquisitely delicate flavours. Reservations recommended.

Drinking

Athenians know how to party. Everyone has their favourite *steki* (hang-out), but expect people to show up after midnight. Head to Psyrri (around Agatharchou), Gazi (around Voutadon and the Keramikos metro station) and Kolonaki (around Ploutarhou and Haritos or Skoufa and Omirou) and explore!

Omonia is best avoided late at night, and although Exarhia has a bohemian bar scene, the neighbourhood has been affected recently by street demonstrations.

Kolonaki has a mind-boggling array of cafes off Plateia Kolonakiou on Skoufa and Tsakalof. Another cafe-thick area is Adrianou, along the Ancient Agora.

TOP CHOICE **Hoxton** BAR
(off Map p616; Voutadon 42, Gazi; Ⓜ Keramikos) Kick back on overstuffed leather couches under modern art in this industrial space that fills up late with bohemians, ruggers and the occasional pop star.

Brettos BAR
(Map p620; ☎210 323 2110; Kydathineon 41, Plaka; Ⓜ Syntagma) This distillery and bar is back-lit by an eye-catching collection of coloured bottles.

Mai-Tai BAR
(Map p616; Ploutarhou 18, Kolonaki; Ⓜ Evangelismos) Jam-packed with well-heeled young Athenians, this is just one in a group of happening spots in Kolonaki.

Entertainment

The *Kathimerini* supplement inside the *International Herald Tribune* contains event listings and a cinema guide, or check www.breathtakingathens.gr, www.ticketservices.gr and www.tickethour.com. **Ticket House** (Map p616; ☎210 360 8366; Panepistimiou 42) sells concert tickets.

Nightclubs

Athenians go clubbing after midnight and dress up. In summer try beachfront venues.

Venue DANCE CLUB
(off Map p616; ☎210 341 1410; www.venue-club.com; Pireos 130, Rouf; ⏰Fri & Sat) Arguably the city's biggest dance club: three-stage dance floor and an energetic crowd.

Envy DANCE CLUB
(Map p616; ☎210 331 7801; Agias Eleousis 3 & Kakourgodikiou, Psyrri; ⏰Wed-Sat) The name changes at this popular club, which plays the latest dance music in Psyrri during winter and takes place at ever-changing beachside spots in summer.

Letom DANCE CLUB
(☎6992240000; Dekeleon 26, Gazi) Late-night clubbers flock to the dance parties with top international and local DJs, and a gay-friendly, hip young crowd.

Akrotiri DANCE CLUB
(☎210 985 9147; Vasileos Georgiou B 5, Agios Kosmas; ⏰10pm-5am) Beach-side with a capacity for 3000, bars and lounges cover multiple levels.

Lava Bore DANCE CLUB
(Map p620; ☎210 324 5335; Filellinon 25, Plaka) A popular place for tourists; open year-round.

Gay & Lesbian Venues

Gay bars cluster in Makrygianni, Psyrri, Gazi, Metaxourghio and Exarhia. Check out www.athensinfoguide.com, www.gay.gr or a copy of the *Greek Gay Guide* booklet at *periptera* (newspaper kiosks).

Lamda Club DANCE CLUB
(Map p616; ☎210 942 4202; Lembesi 15, cnr Leoforos Syngrou, Makrygianni) Athens' best gay dance club gets crowded late.

Sodade DANCE CLUB
(www.sodade.gr; Triptolemou 10, Gazi) Attracts a younger crowd.

BIG BAR
(www.bigbar.gr; Iera Odos 67, Gazi) Hub of Athens' lively bear scene.

Mirovolos RESTAURANT, BAR
(Map p616; ☎210 522 8806; Giatrakou 12, Metaxourghio) Popular lesbian cafe-bar-restaurant.

Magaze CAFE, BAR
(Map p616; Eolou 33, Monastiraki) All-day hangout with Acropolis views from pavement tables; becomes a lively bar after sunset.

Live Music

In summer, concerts rock plazas and parks; some clubs shut down.

JAZZ, ROCK & WORLD MUSIC

TOP CHOICE **Half Note Jazz Club** JAZZ CLUB
(☎210 921 3310; www.halfnote.gr; Trivonianou 17, Mets) Dark, smoky venue for serious jazz.

Gagarin 205 Club MUSIC CLUB
(☎210 854 7601; www.gagarin205.gr; Liossion 205) The city's coolest space attracts interesting international and local acts.

Alavastro Café MUSIC CLUB
(☎210 756 0102; Damareos 78, Pangrati) Eclectic mix of modern jazz, ethnic and Greek music in a casual, intimate venue.

REMBETIKA

Most authentic *rembetika* venues close during summer, but you can see a popularised version at some tavernas in Psyrri.

Rembetika Stoa Athanaton TRADITIONAL MUSIC
(Map p616; ☎210 321 4362; Sofokleous 19; ⊙3.30-6pm & midnight-late Mon-Sat Oct-May) Located above the meat market, this is still *the* place to listen to *rembetika*.

Classical Music, Theatre & Dance

In summer, the excellent Hellenic Festival (p619) swings into action.

Megaron Mousikis CONCERT HALL
(off Map p616; ☎210 728 2333; www.megaron.gr; cnr Leoforos Vasilissis Sofias & Kokkali) Superb concert venue hosting winter performances by local and international artists.

National Theatre DRAMA
(Map p616; ☎210 522 3243; www.n-t.gr; Agiou Konstantinou 22-24, Omonia) Contemporary plays and ancient theatre on the main stage and other venues.

Olympia Theatre OPERA, BALLET
(Map p616; ☎210 361 2461; www.nationalopera.gr; Akadimias 59, Exarhia) November to June: ballet, symphony and the Greek National Opera (www.nationalopera.gr).

Dora Stratou Dance Company DANCE
(Map p620; ☎210 921 4650; www.grdance.org; Filopappou Hill, ticket office Scholiou 8; tickets €15; ⊙9.30pm Tue-Sat, 8.15pm Sun May-Sep) Traditional folk-dancing shows feature more than 75 musicians and dancers in an open-air amphitheatre.

Cinemas

Most cinemas show recent releases in English; tickets cost around €8. In summer, take your movie-going outdoors at Aigli and Cine Paris.

Apollon CINEMA
(Map p616; ☎210 323 6811; Stadiou 19)

Astor CINEMA
(Map p616; ☎210 323 1297; Stadiou 28)

Aigli CINEMA
(Map p616; ☎210 336 9369) Historic open-air cinema in the verdant Zappeio Gardens.

Cine Paris CINEMA
(Map p620; ☎210 322 0721; Kydathineon 22, Plaka) Nab a seat with Acropolis views.

Shopping

Athens is the place to shop for cool jewellery, clothes and shoes, and souvenirs such as backgammon sets, hand-woven textiles, olive oil beauty products, worry beads and ceramics. Find boutiques around Syntagma, from the Attica department store past Voukourestiou and on Ermou; designer brands and cool shops in Kolonaki; and souvenirs, folk art and leather in Plaka and Monastiraki.

Monastiraki Flea Market MARKET
(Map p620) Enthralling; spreads daily from Plateia Monastirakiou (Monastiraki Sq).

Sunday Market MARKET
(Map p616; ⊙7am-2pm Sun) At the end of Ermou, towards Gazi.

Metropolis Music MUSIC
(Map p616; ☎210 383 0804; Panepistimiou 64, Omonia) Well stocked with Greek and international CDs.

Compendium Books BOOKS
(Map p620; ☎210 322 1248; Nikis 28, Plaka; Ⓜ Syntagma) English-language books; excellent selection of Greek history and literature.

Public ELECTRONICS, BOOKS
(Map p620; ☎210 324 6210; Plateia Syntagma; Ⓜ Syntagma) English-language books on 3rd floor.

Eleftheroudakis Books BOOKS
Plaka (Map p620; ☎210 322 9388; Nikis 20; Ⓜ Syntagma); Syntagma (Map p616; ☎210 325 8440; Panepistimiou 17; Ⓜ Syntagma)

Information

Dangers & Annoyances

Like any big city, Athens has its hot spots. Plateia Omonias (Omonia Sq) is home to pickpockets, prostitutes and drug dealers; women should avoid walking alone here at night. Also watch for pickpockets on the metro and at the markets. When there are strikes, picketers tend to march in Plateia Syntagmatos.

When taking taxis, ask the driver to use the meter or negotiate a price in advance. Ignore stories that the hotel you've chosen is closed or full: they're angling for a commission from another hotel.

Bar scams are commonplace, particularly in Plaka and Syntagma. They go something like this: friendly Greek approaches solo male traveller, discovers traveller is new to Athens, and reveals that he, too, is from out of town. However, friendly Greek knows a great bar where they order drinks and equally friendly owner offers another drink. Women appear and more drinks are served; at the end of the night the traveller is hit with an exorbitant bill.

With the recent financial reforms in Greece have come frequent strikes in Athens. If there is a strike while you are here, confirm that the sights you wish to see will be open and the transport you are planning to use will be running.

Emergency

Athens Police Station Central (☎210 770 5711/17; Leoforos Alexandras 173, Ambelokipi; MAmbelokipi); Plateia Syntagmatos (☎210 725 7000)

Police Emergency (☎100)

Tourist Police (☎24hr 171, 210 920 0724; Veïkou 43-45, Koukaki; 8am-10pm)

Visitor Emergency Assistance (☎112) Toll-free, 24 hours; in English.

Internet Access

There are free wireless hot spots at Plateia Syntagmatos, Thisio, Gazi, the port of Piraeus, Starbucks cafes and on the 3rd floor of Public (p625).

Internet Resources

Official visitor site www.breathtakingathens.gr

Media

Kathimerini (www.ekathimerini.com) and *Athens News* (www.athensnews.gr) have English-language coverage.

Medical Services

Ambulance/First-Aid Advice (☎166)

Duty Pharmacies & Hospitals (☎1434, in Greek) Published in *Kathimerini*. Check pharmacy windows for nearest duty pharmacy.

SOS Doctors (☎1016, 210 821 1888; 24hr) Pay service with English-speaking doctors.

Money

Most banks have branches around Plateia Syntagmatos.

Eurochange Syntagma (☎210 331 2462; Karageorgi Servias 2; 8am-9pm; MSyntagma); Monastiraki (☎210 322 2657; Areos 1)

Telephone

Public phones take phonecards, available from kiosks, as are prepaid SIM cards for mobiles.

Tourist Information

EOT (Greek National Tourist Organisation; ☎210 870 7000; www.gnto.gr) Syntagma (Map p620; ☎210 331 0392; Leoforos Vasilissis Amalias 26; 9am-7pm Mon-Fri, 10am-4pm Sat & Sun; MSyntagma); airport (☎210 353 0445; Arrivals Hall; 9am-7pm Mon-Fri, 10am-4pm Sat & Sun); head office (Tsoha 24; 9am-2pm Mon-Fri; MAmbelokipi)

Getting There & Away

Air

Modern **Eleftherios Venizelos International Airport** (ATH; ☎210 353 0000; www.aia.gr), 27km east of Athens, has a 24-hour information desk. For domestic flights:

Aegean Airlines (☎210 626 1000; www.aegeanair.com; Othonos 10, Syntagma)

Athens Airways (☎210 669 6600; www.athensairways.com)

Olympic Air (☎210 926 4444; www.olympicair.com; Filellinon 15, Syntagma)

Boat

Most ferries, hydrofoils and high-speed catamarans leave from the massive port at Piraeus. Some services depart from smaller ports at Rafina and Lavrio.

Bus

Athens has two main intercity **KTEL** (www.ktel.org) bus stations, one 5km and one 7km to the north of Omonia. Get timetables at tourist offices.

Kifissos Terminal A (☎210 512 4910; Kifissou 100) Buses to the Peloponnese, Igoumenitsa, Ionian Islands, Florina, Ioannina, Kastoria, Edessa and Thessaloniki, among other destinations. Bus 051 goes to central Athens (junction of Zinonos and Menandrou, near Omonia) every 15 minutes from 5am to midnight. Taxis to Syntagma cost about €8.

Liossion Terminal B (☎210 831 7153; Liossion 260) Buses to Trikala (for Meteora), Delphi, Larissa, Thiva, Volos and other destinations. To get here, take bus 024 from outside the main gate of the National Gardens on Amalias and ask to get off at Praktoria KTEL. Get off the bus at Liossion 260, turn right onto Gousiou and you'll see the terminal.

Buses for destinations in southern Attica leave from the **Mavromateon Terminal** (☎210 880 8000; Alexandras & 28 Oktovriou-Patision, Pedion Areos), about 250m north of the National Archaeological Museum.

Car & Motorcycle

Syngrou Rd, just south of the Temple of Olympian Zeus, is lined with car-hire firms.

Avis (☎210 322 4951; Leoforos Vasilissis Amalias 48, Makrygianni)

Budget (☎210 921 4771; Leoforos Syngrou 8, Makrygianni)

Europcar (☎210 924 8810; Leoforos Syngrou 43, Makrygianni)

Train

Intercity trains to central and northern Greece depart from the central **Larisis train station**, about 1km northwest of Plateia Omonias.

For the Peloponnese, take the suburban rail to Kiato and change for other OSE services, or check for available lines at the Larisis station.

OSE Offices (☎1110; www.ose.gr) Syntagma (☎210 362 4402; Sina 6; ⏲8am-3pm Mon-Sat); Omonia (☎210 524 0647; Karolou 1; ⏲8am-3pm Mon-Fri)

Getting Around

To/From the Airport

The 24-hour airport information desks are loaded with transport information.

BUS Tickets cost €3.20. Services:

Plateia Syntagmatos Bus X95, 60 to 90 minutes, every 30 minutes, 24 hours (The Syntagma stop is on Othonos St; see Map p620)

Terminal A (Kifissos) Bus Station Bus X93, 35 minutes, every 30 minutes

Metro Line 3 at Ethniki Amyna Bus X94, 25 minutes, every 10 minutes, 7.30am to 11.30pm

Piraeus (Plateia Karaïskaki) Bus X96, 90 minutes, every 20 minutes, 24 hours

METRO Line 3 links the airport to the city centre in around 40 minutes; it operates from Monastiraki from 5.50am to midnight, and from the airport from 5.30am to 11.30pm. Tickets (€6) are valid for all public transport for 90 minutes. Fare for two or more passengers is €5 each.

TAXI Fares vary according to the time of day and level of traffic; expect at least €30 from the airport to the centre, and €40 to Piraeus. Both trips can take up to an hour.

Public Transport

The metro, tram and bus system makes getting around central Athens and to Piraeus easy. Athens' road traffic can be horrendous. Tickets (€1), good for 90 minutes, and a 24-hour travel pass (€3) work on all forms of public transport except for airport services; or get a travel pass. Children aged under six years travel free. People under 18 and over 65 pay half-fare.

Get maps and timetables at EOT tourist offices, **Athens Urban Transport Organisation** (OASA; ☎185; www.oasa.gr; Metsovou 15, Exarhia/Mouseio) or from their website.

BUS & TROLLEYBUS Buses and electric trolleybuses operate every 15 minutes from 5am to midnight. Purchase tickets before boarding (from the metro, a bus-ticket booth or a kiosk). Validate as you board.

Piraeus Buses operate 24 hours: every 20 minutes from 6am to midnight, and then hourly. From Syntagma and Filellinon (see Map p620) to Akti Xaveriou catch Bus 040; from Omonia end of Athinas to Plateia Themistokleous, catch Bus 049.

METRO Trains operate from 5am to midnight: every three minutes during peak periods and every 10 minutes off-peak. Get timetables at www.ametro.gr. Validate tickets as you enter the platforms.

Taxi

Athenian taxis are yellow and hard to hail. The flag fall is €1.05 with an additional surcharge of €1 from ports and train and bus stations, and €3.40 from the airport; then the day rate (tariff 1 on the meter) is €0.60 per kilometre. The night rate (tariff 2 on the meter) is €1.05 per kilometre between midnight and 5am. Baggage costs €0.35 per item over 10kg. The minimum fare is €2.80. Booking a radio taxi costs €1.70 extra.

Athina 1 (☎210 921 2800)

Enotita (☎801 115 1000)

Ikaros (☎210 515 2800)

Train

Fast **suburban rail** (☎1110; www.trainose.com) links Athens with the airport, Piraeus, the outer regions and the northern Peloponnese. It connects to the metro at Larisis, Doukissis Plakentias and Nerantziotissa stations, and goes from the airport to Kiato.

TRAVEL PASS

For short-stay visits, consider the €15 tourist ticket, valid for three days of unlimited travel on all of Athens' public transport, including the metro airport service, and the Athens Sightseeing bus.

Piraeus Πειραιάς

POP 175,700

The highlights of Greece's main port and ferry hub are the otherworldly rows of ferries, ships and hydrofoils filling its seemingly endless quays. It takes around 30 minutes to get here (10km) from Athens' centre by metro, so there's no reason to stay in shabby Piraeus. The Mikrolimano (Small Harbour), with its cafes and fish restaurants, reveals the city's gentler side.

Sleeping

Pireaus Theoxenia LUXURY HOTEL €€€
(☎210 411 2550; www.theoxeniapalace.com; Karaoli Dimitriou 23; d €110-265; ❄@📶) Pireaus' swank, central hotel with plump bathrobes and satellite TV; get the best deals online.

Hotel Triton HOTEL €€
(☎210 417 3457; www.htriton.gr; Tsamadou 8; d €60-68; ❄@) This refurbished hotel with sleek executive-style rooms is a treat compared with Pireaus' usual run-down joints.

Eating

If you're killing time, take trolleybus 20 to Mikrolimano for harbourfront seafood.

Rakadiko TAVERNA €
(☎210 417 8470; Stoa Kouvelou, Karaoli Dimitriou 5; mains €12-20; ⏰Tue-Sat) Dine, quietly, under grapevines, on *mezedhes* from all over Greece. Live *rembetika* on weekends.

Mandragoras MARKET €
(Gounari 14; ⏰7.30am-4pm Mon, Wed, Sat, to 8pm Tue, Thu & Fri) Fantastic array of fresh Greek products.

General Market MARKET €
(⏰6am-4pm Mon-Fri) On Dimosthenous.

Piraeus

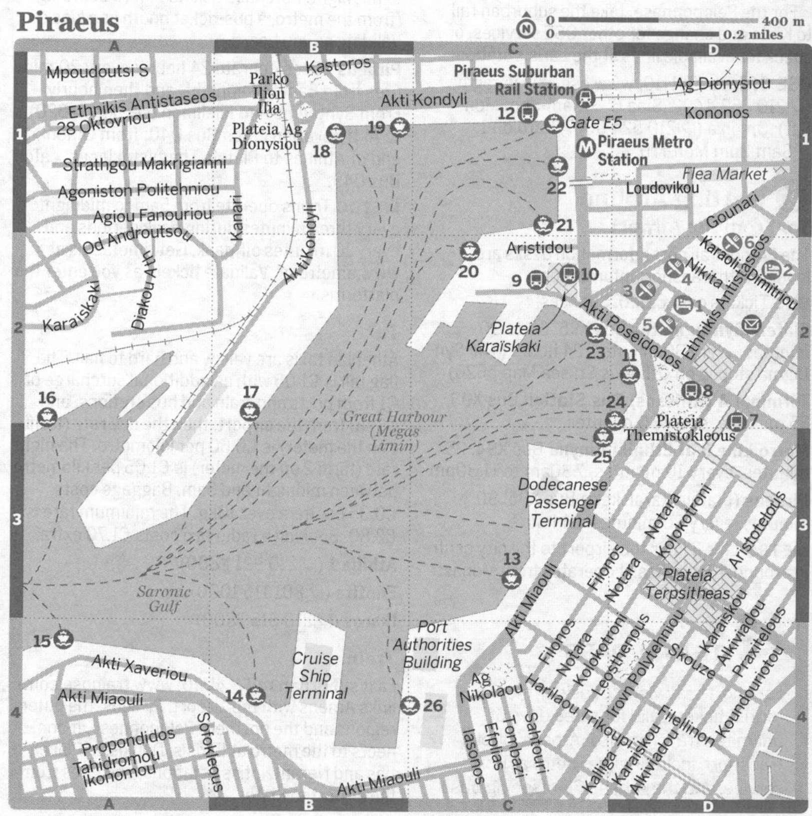

Piraikon SUPERMARKET €
(Ippokratous 1; ⏲8am-8pm Mon-Fri, 8am-4pm Sat)

Information

INTERNET ACCESS Free wi-fi around the port.

LEFT LUGGAGE At the metro station (€3 for 24 hours).

Getting There & Away

Boat

All ferry companies have online timetables and booths on the quays. The main branch of EOT in Athens has a weekly schedule. Schedules are reduced in April, May and October, and are radically cut in winter, especially to smaller islands. When buying tickets, confirm the departure point. See the Getting There & Away sections for each island for more details or contact the **Piraeus Port Authority** (☎1441; www.olp.gr).

Hellenic Seaways (☎210 419 9000; www.hellenicseaways.gr; cnr Akti Kondyli & Elotikou) operates high-speed hydrofoils and catamarans to the Cyclades from early April to the end of October, and year-round services to the Saronic Gulf Islands. Other high-speed services include **Aegean Speedlines** (☎210 969 0950; www.aegeanspeedlines.gr).

Bus

See p698 for Athens buses. The X96 Piraeus–Athens Airport Express (€3.20) leaves from the southwestern corner of Plateia Karaïskaki.

Metro

The fastest and most convenient link to Athens is the metro (€1, 30 minutes, every 10 minutes, 5am to midnight), near the ferries.

Train

Piraeus has a station for Athens' suburban rail.

Getting Around

Local bus 904 runs between the metro station and Zea Marina.

THE PELOPONNESE

ΠΕΛΟΠΟΝΝΗΣΟΣ

The Peloponnese encompasses a breathtaking array of landscapes, villages and ruins, where much of Greek history has played out. It's home to Olympia, birthplace of the Olympic Games; the ancient archaeological sites of magical Epidavros, Mycenae and Corinth; the fairy-tale Byzantine city of Mystras; and ancient Sparta.

Two of Greece's most gorgeous towns grace its shores: Venetian-style Nafplio and romantic Monemvasia. The isolated Mani Peninsula, best known for its wild landscape and people, bristles with fortified tower settlements and is blanketed with a colourful collection of spectacular wildflowers in spring.

Piraeus

Sleeping
1 Hotel Triton D2
2 Piraeus Theoxenia D2

Eating
3 General Market D2
4 Mandragoras D2
5 Piraikon Supermarket D2
6 Rakadiko D2

Transport
7 Bus 040 to Syntagma D2
8 Bus 049 to Omonia D2
9 Bus Station C2
10 Bus X96 to Airport C2
11 Catamarans & Hydrofoils to the Peloponnese & Saronic Gulf D2
12 Free Shuttle Bus to Gates E1 to E3 .... C1
13 Gate E10 .... C3
14 Gate E11 .... B4
15 Gate E12 .... A4
16 Gate E1–Ferries to the Dodecanese A2
17 Gate E2–Ferries to Crete & Northeastern Aegean Islands B2
18 Gate E3 .... B1
19 Gate E4–Ferries to Crete B1
20 Gate E7 .... C2
21 Gate E7–Catamarans to the Cyclades C1
22 Gate E7–Ferries to the Western & Central Cyclades C1
23 Gate E8–Ferries to the Saronic Gulf Islands C2
24 Gate E9–Ferries to the Cyclades D2
25 Gate E9–Ferries to the Cyclades, Samos, Ikaria C3
26 International Ferries C4

Patra ΠΑΤΡΑ

POP 185,700

Greece's third-largest city, Patra is the principal ferry port for the Ionian Islands and Italy. Despite its 3000-year history, ancient sites and vibrant social life, few travellers linger here longer than necessary to transfer to their ferries.

Sights

Kastro CASTLE

(admission free; 8.30am-3pm Tue-Sun) The Byzantine castle, built by the Emperor Justinian, has excellent views to the Ionian Islands.

Archaeological Museum of Patras MUSEUM

(cnr Amerikis & Patras-Athens National Rd; admission free; 8.30am-3pm Tue-Sun) The contemporary buildings here make up the country's second-largest museum and feature objects from prehistoric to Roman times.

Roman Odeon RUINS

(cnr Germanou & Sotiriadou; 8am-3pm Tue-Sun) This impressive place is a magical spot to see a performance.

Festivals

Patras Carnival MARDI GRAS

(www.carnivalpatras.gr) Wild weekend of costume parades and floats in spring.

Sleeping

Primarolia Art Hotel BOUTIQUE HOTEL €€

(2610 624 900; www.arthotel.gr; Othonos Amalias 33; s/d incl breakfast €99/140;) This stylish place oozes individuality, with sleeping spaces ranging from the bold, contemporary and minimalist to the florid, romantic and baroque.

Pension Nikos HOTEL €

(2610 623 757; cnr Patreos 3 & Agiou Andreou 121; s/d/tr €28/38/45, s/d without bathroom €23/33) Marble stairs lead to spotlessly clean rooms smack in the city centre.

Eating & Drinking

There are scores of stylish cafes and fast-food eateries lying between Kolokotroni and Ermou; drinking hot spots cluster on Agios Nikolaos and Radinou (off Riga Fereou). Pedestrianised Trion Navarhon is lined with tavernas.

Kitchen of Kornelia BISTRO €

(2610 272 987; Plateia Kapodistrio 4; mains €8-14; 1.30pm-midnight Tue-Sat, to 5pm Sun) Dig in to Turkish braised beef with aubergine puree (€14) and other delicate specialities in this cool bistro tucked in the corner of a quiet square.

Mythos TAVERNA €

(2610 329 984; cnr Trion Navarhon 181 & Riga Fereou; mains €8-14; 7pm-late) Friendly waiters serve excellent home-cooked Greek classics in a chandelier-strewn town house.

Dia Discount Supermarket SUPERMARKET €

(Agiou Andreou 29; Mon-Sat) Handy for grabbing some food before your ferry departs.

Information

Tourist office (2610 461 741; www.infocenterpatras.gr; Othonos Amalias 6; 8am-10pm) Friendly multilingual staff run Greece's best tourist office, with information on transport, free bicycles and internet access. A kiosk in central Plateia Trion Symahon is open 9am to 4pm.

Tourist Police (2610 455 833; Gounari 52; 7am-9pm)

Getting There & Away

Boat

Schedules vary; the tourist office provides timetables. Ticket agencies line the waterfront.

Strintzis (2610 240 000; www.strintzisferries.gr) routes:

Kefallonia €17.80, 2¾ hours, two daily

Ithaki €17.80, four hours, one daily

Minoan Lines (2610 426 000; www.minoan.gr) and **ANEK Lines** (2610 226 053; www.anek.gr) sail to Corfu (€30.50, seven hours, one daily).

For details of services to Italy, see p696.

Bus

Services from **KTEL Achaia bus station** (2610 623 886; cnr Zaimi 2 & Othonos Amalias):

Athens €17, three hours, half-hourly, via Corinth

Ioannina €20.90, 4½ hours, two daily

Kalamata €20, four hours, two daily

Kalavryta €7.50, two hours, two daily

Pyrgos (for Olympia) €8.80, two hours, 10 daily

Thessaloniki €40, seven hours, four daily

Buses to the Ionian Islands, via the port of Kyllini, leave from the **KTEL Lefkada & Zakynthos bus station** (☎2610 220 993; Othonos Amalias 48) or nearby **KTEL Kefallonia bus station** (☎2610 274 938; Othonos Amalias 58).

Train

Services from **Patra train station** (☎2610 639 108; Othonos Amalias 27):

Athens' Kiato station (connects to suburban rail) regular/intercity express (IC) €3.70/6.90, 2½ hours

Diakofto regular/IC €2.30/4.90, 45 minutes/one hour

Kalamata normal/IC €6.60/11.30, five hours

Pyrgos (for Olympia) normal/IC €3.70/6.30, three/1½ hours

Diakofto–Kalavryta Railway ΔΙΑΚΟΦΤΟ ΚΑΛΑΒΡΥΤΑ

This spectacular rack-and-pinion **train** (☎26910 43228), built in the 1890s, crawls up the deep gorge of the Vouraïkos River from the small coastal town of Diakofto to the mountain resort of Kalavryta, 22km away. It's a thrilling one-hour journey, with dramatic scenery best viewed from any forward-facing seat. There are five trains a day (€9.50) in each direction. They book up, so buy tickets in advance at any train station in Greece. Diakofto is one hour east of Patra on the main train line to Athens (€7). See www.odontotos.com for more information.

Corinth ΚΟΡΙΝΘΟΣ

POP 29,800

Drab, modern Corinth (*ko*-rin-thoss), 6km west of the Corinth Canal, is an uninspiring town; it's better to stay in the village near Ancient Corinth if visiting the ruins.

Sleeping

Hotel Apollon HOTEL €
(☎27410 22587; www.hotelapollongr.com; Damaskinou 2; s/d €35/45; ❄) Basic, handily situated near the bus station and offering good discounts; the best option in town.

Blue Dolphin Camping CAMPING GROUND €
(☎27410 25766; www.camping-blue-dolphin.gr; campsites per tent/adult €5/6.50; ⏲Apr-Sep; 🏊) Has a beach and decent facilities and offers tours. It's at Lecheon, about 4km west of Corinth, just after the ancient Corinth turn-off. Staff will pick you up from train or bus stations.

Getting There & Away

BUSES Buses to Athens (€7.50, 1½ hours, half-hourly) and Ancient Corinth (€1.40, 20 minutes, hourly) leave from the **KTEL Korinthos bus station** (☎27410 75425; Dimocratias 4). Buses to the rest of the Peloponnese leave from the **Corinth Isthmus (Peloponnese) KTEL bus station** (☎27410 83000) on the Peloponnese side of the Corinth Canal. To get there from Corinth, catch one of the frequent local buses to Loutraki.

TRAIN Trains go to Patra (regular/IC €5.70/8.90) and Athens (14 daily, four of which are IC services). The handy *proastiako* suburban train runs goes to Athens airport (€10, one hour, eight daily). At the time of research the inland line to Tripoli was under repair.

Ancient Corinth & Acrocorinth ΑΡΧΑΙΑ ΚΟΡΙΝΘΟΣ & ΑΚΡΟΚΟΡΙΝΘΟΣ

Seven kilometres southwest of Corinth's modern city, the ruins of **Ancient Corinth** (☎27410 31207; site & museum €6; ⏲8am-8pm Apr-Oct, to 3pm Nov-Mar) and its lovely museum

WORTH A TRIP

THE WINE ROAD

The Nemea region, in the rolling hills southwest of Corinth, is one of Greece's premier wine-producing areas, famous for its full-bodied reds from the local *agiorgitiko* grape and a white from *roditis* grapes. Some wineries offer tastings:

» **Skouras** (☎27510 23688; www.skouraswines.com) Northwest of Argos.

» **Ktima Palivou** (☎27460 24190; www.palivos.gr; Ancient Nemea)

» **Lafkioti** (☎27460 31244; www.lafkiotis.gr; Ancient Kleonai) Located 3km east of Ancient Nemea.

» **Gaia Wines** (☎27460 22057; www.gaia-wines.gr; Koutsi) North of Nemea.

lie at the edge of a small village in the midst of fields sweeping to the sea. It was one of ancient Greece's wealthiest cities, but earthquakes and invasions have left only one Greek monument remaining: the imposing **Temple of Apollo**; the rest of the ruins are Roman. **Acrocorinth** (admission free; ⌚8am-3pm), the remains of a citadel built on a massive outcrop of limestone, looms majestically over the site.

The great-value digs at **Tasos Taverna & Rooms** (☎27410 31225; s/d/tr €30/45/55; ❄), 200m from the museum, are spotlessly clean and above an excellent eatery serving Greek classics.

Nafplio ΝΑΥΠΛΙΟ

POP 14,500

Elegant Venetian houses and neoclassical mansions dripping with crimson bougainvillea cascade down Nafplio's hillside to the azure sea. Vibrant cafes, shops and restaurants fill winding pedestrian streets. Crenulated Palamidi Fortress perches above it all. What's not to love?

Sights

Palamidi Fortress FORTRESS

(☎27520 28036; admission €4; ⌚8am-6.45pm Jun-Aug, to 2.45pm Sep-May) Enjoy spectacular views of the town and surrounding coast from the magnificent hilltop fortress built by the Venetians between 1711 and 1714.

Archaeological Museum MUSEUM

(Plateia Syntagmatos; ⌚8.30am-3pm Tue-Sun; adult/concession €2/1) Fine exhibits include fire middens from 32,000 BC and bronze armour from near Mycenae (12th to 13th centuries BC).

Peloponnese Folklore Foundation Museum MUSEUM

(☎27520 28379; 1 Vas Alexandrou St; admission €4; ⌚9am-2.30pm & 5.30-10.30pm) One of Greece's best small museums, with displays of vibrant regional costumes and rotating exhibitions.

Sleeping

Exquisite hotels abound in Nafplio. The Old Town is *the* place to stay, but it has a limited number of budget options. Friday to Sunday town fills up and prices rise; book ahead. Cheaper spots dot the road to Argos and Tolo.

TOP CHOICE **Amfitriti Pension** PENSION €€

(☎27520 96250; www.amfitriti-pension.gr; Kapodistriou 24; d incl breakfast €85-110) Quaint antiques fill these intimate rooms in a house in the Old Town. You can also enjoy stellar views at its nearby sister hotel, **Amfitriti Belvedere**, which is chock full of brightly coloured tapestries and emits a feeling of cheery serenity.

Pension Marianna PENSION €€

(☎27520 24256; www.pensionmarianna.gr; Potamianou 9; s/d/tr incl breakfast €70/85/100; P❄📶) Welcoming owners epitomise Greek *filoxenia* (hospitality) and serve delicious organic breakfasts. Up a steep set of stairs, and tucked under the fortress walls, a dizzying array of rooms intermix with sea-view terraces.

Pension Dimitris Bekas PENSION €

(☎27520 24594; Efthimiopoulou 26; s/d/tr €23/29/40) The only good, central budget option. Clean, homey rooms have a top-value location on the slopes of the Akronafplia, and the owner has a killer baseball-cap collection.

Hotel Grande Bretagne LUXURY HOTEL €€€

(☎27520 96200; www.grandebretagne.com.gr; Filellinon Sq; s/d incl breakfast €130/180) In the heart of Nafplio's cafe action and overlooking the sea, this splendidly restored hotel with high ceilings, antiques and chandeliers radiates plush opulence.

Kapodistrias PENSION €€

(☎27520 29366; www.hotelkapodistrias.gr; Kokinou 20; s/d incl breakfast €50/75; ❄📶) Beautiful rooms, many with elegant canopy beds, come with sea or old-town views.

Adiandi BOUTIQUE HOTEL €€

(☎27520 22073; www.hotel-adiandi.com; Othonos 31; r incl breakfast €110-120; ❄📶) Rooms in this fun and upmarket place are quirkily decorated with artistic door bedheads and contemporary decor. Fantastic farm-fresh breakfasts.

Hotel Byron PENSION €€

(☎27520 22351; www.byronhotel.gr; Platonos 2; d €60-80; ❄) Tucked into two fine Venetian buildings, iron bedsteads, rich carpets and period furniture fill immaculate rooms.

Eating

Nafplio's Old Town streets are loaded with standard tavernas; those on Staïkopoulou and those overlooking the port on Bouboulinas get jam-packed on weekends.

Taverna Aeolos TRADITIONAL GREEK €
(☎27520 26828; V Olgas 30; mains €5-13) This boisterous taverna lined with copper pans gets packed with locals sharing generous mixed-grill plates (€8.50). Live music during summer.

Omorfi Poli GREEK, ITALIAN €
(☎27520 29452; Bouboulinas 75; mains €6-16; ⏲dinner) Greek favourites and *mezedhes* (€5) with a slight Italian twist (there's mushroom risotto), plus friendly service and good wine list.

Antica Gelateria di Roma ICE CREAM €
(☎27520 23520; cnr Farmakopoulou 6 & Komninou) The best (yes, best) traditional gelati outside Italy.

To Kenitrikon CAFE €
(☎27520 29933; Plateia Syntagmatos; mains €4-10) Relax under the shady trees on this pretty square during extensive breakfasts.

Shopping

Nafplio shopping is a delight, with jewellery workshops, boutiques and wonderful regional products, such as honey, wine and handicrafts.

Metallagi JEWELLERY
(☎27520 21267; Sofroni 3) Young jeweller Maria Koitsoidaki handcrafts elegant nature-inspired jewellery from silver, fine metals, gems and stones.

Art Shop CREATIVE ART
(☎27520 29546; Ypsilantou 14) This airy boutique carries a range of carefully selected original art, ceramics, clothes, and kids' painting supplies and games.

Odyssey BOOKS
(☎27520 23430; Plateia Syntagmatos) International papers, magazines and novels.

Information

EMERGENCY **Tourist Police** (☎27520 28131; Kountouridou 16)

TOURIST INFORMATION **Kasteli Travel & Tourist Agency** (☎27520 29395; 38 Vas Konstantinou; ⏲9am-2pm year-round & 6-8pm Jun-Sep) At Syngrou; friendly English-speaking.

Municipal Tourist Office (☎27520 24444; 25 Martiou; ⏲9am-1pm & 4-8pm) Generally unhelpful. A kiosk in Fillenon Sq offers free headsets for walking tours (10am to 1pm and 6pm to 8pm).

Getting There & Away

Services from **KTEL Argolis Bus Station** (☎27520 27323; Syngrou 8):

Argos (for Peloponnese connections) €1.40, 30 minutes, half-hourly

Athens €12, 2½ hours, hourly (via Corinth)

Epidavros €2.60, 45 minutes, four daily

Mycenae €2.60, one hour, two daily

Epidavros ΕΠΙΔΑΥΡΟΣ

Spectacular World Heritage–listed **Epidavros** (☎27530 22006; admission €6; ⏲8am-7pm Apr-Sep, to 5pm Oct-Mar) was the sanctuary of Asclepius, god of medicine. Amid pine-covered hills, the magnificent **theatre** is still a venue during the Hellenic Festival, but don't miss the peaceful **Sanctuary of Asclepius**, an ancient spa and healing centre.

For an early-morning visit to the site, stay at the **Hotel Avaton** (☎27530 22178; s/d €45/69; P❄), just 1km away, at the junction of the road to Kranidi, or go as a day trip from Nafplio (€2.60, 45 minutes, four buses daily).

Mycenae ΜΥΚΗΝΕΣ

Although settled as early as the 6th millennium BC, **Ancient Mycenae** (☎27510 76585; admission €8; ⏲8am-8pm Jun-Sep, to 6pm Oct, to 3pm Nov-May) was at its most powerful from 1600 to 1200 BC. Mycenae's entrance, the **Lion Gate**, is Europe's oldest monumental sculpture. Homer accurately described Mycenae as being 'rich in gold': excavations of **Grave Circle A** by Heinrich Schliemann in the 1870s uncovered magnificent gold treasures, such as the Mask of Agamemnon, now on display at Athens' National Archaeological Museum.

Most people visit on day trips from Nafplio, but the bare **Belle Helene Hotel** (☎27510 76225; Christou Tsounta; d incl breakfast €40) is where Schliemann lived during the excavations.

Two buses go daily to Mycenae from Argos (€1.60, 30 minutes) and Nafplio (€2.60, one hour).

Sparta ΣΠΑΡΤΗ

POP 14,356

Cheerful, unpretentious modern Sparta (*spar*-tee) is at odds with its ancient Spartan image of discipline and deprivation. Although there's little to see, the town makes a convenient base from which to visit Mystras.

WORTH A TRIP

GORGE YOURSELF

The picturesque prefecture of **Arkadia** occupies much of the central Peloponnese and is synonymous with grassy meadows, forested mountains and gurgling streams. West of Tripoli, a tangle of medieval villages and narrow winding roads weave into valleys of dense vegetation beneath the Menalon Mountains. These areas are best accessed by car.

Wonderful walks along the **Lousios Gorge** leave from **Dimitsana** (population 230), a delightful medieval village built amphitheatrically on two hills at the beginning of the gorge. It sits 11km north of **Stemnitsa** (population 412), another gorge gateway and a striking village of stone houses and Byzantine churches.

Trekking Hellas of Arcadia (☎27910 25978, 6974459753; www.trekkinghellas.gr) offers rafting (€50 to €80) on the nearby Lousios and Alfios Rivers, and gorge hikes (€20 to €50).

Leonidio (population 3224), 90km east of Sparta, is dramatically set at the mouth of the **Badron Gorge**. Some older residents still speak Tsakonika, a distinctive dialect from the time of ancient Sparta.

Modern **Hotel Lakonia** (☎27310 28951; www.lakoniahotel.gr; Palaeologou 89; s/d incl breakfast €45/70; ❄📶) maintains comfy, welcoming rooms with spotless bathrooms.

In a cheery yellow building, **Hotel Cecil** (☎27310 24980; Palaeologou 125; s/d €40/55; ❄) has austere rooms with balconies overlooking the quiet end of the strip.

The sweet smell of spices inundates **Restaurant Elysse** (Palaeologou 113; mains €5.50-12), which is run by a friendly Greek-Canadian family. Locals chill out next door at **Café Ouzeri** (mains €2-6).

The **Tourist Police** (☎27310 20492; Theodoritou 20) can provide information.

Sparta's **KTEL Lakonias bus station** (☎27310 26441; cnr Lykourgou & Thivronos), on the east edge of town, services Athens via Corinth (€17.60, 3½ hours, eight daily), Gythio (€4, one hour, five daily), Monemvasia (€9, two hours, three daily) and Mystras (€1.40, 30 minutes, 10 daily).

Mystras ΜΥΣΤΡΑΣ

Magical **Mystras** (☎27310 83377; adult/child €6/3; ⏲8am-7.30pm Apr-Oct, 8.30am-3pm Nov-Mar) was once the effective capital of the Byzantine Empire. Ruins of palaces, monasteries and churches, most of them dating from between 1271 and 1460, nestle at the base of the Taÿgetos Mountains, and are surrounded by verdant olive and orange groves.

Allow half a day to explore the site. While only 7km from Sparta, staying in the village nearby allows you to get there early before it heats up. Enjoy exquisite views and a beautiful swimming pool at **Hotel Byzantion** (☎27310 83309; www.byzantionhotel.gr; s/d €45/65; ❄@🏊), near the main square. Have a decadent escape at **Hotel Pyrgos Mystra** (☎27310 20870; www.pyrgosmystra.com; Manousaki 3; s/d incl breakfast €170/220; ❄), with its lovingly appointed rooms in a restored mansion.

Camp at **Castle View** (☎27310 83303; www.castleview.gr; campsites per adult/tent/car €6/4/4, 2-person bungalow €30, ⏲Apr-Oct; 🏊) about 1km before Mystras village and set in olive trees, or **Camping Paleologio Mystras** (☎27310 22724; campsites per adult/tent/car €7/4/4; 🏊), 2km west of Sparta and approximately 4km from Mystras. Buses will stop outside either if you ask.

Several tavernas serve traditional Greek meals.

Gefyra & Monemvasia ΓΕΦΥΡΑ & ΜΟΝΕΜΒΑΣΙΑ

POP 1320

Slip out along a narrow causeway, up around the edge of a towering rock rising dramatically from the sea and arrive at the exquisite walled village of Monemvasia. Enter the *kastro* (castle), which was separated from mainland Gefyra by an earthquake in AD 375, through a narrow tunnel on foot, and emerge into a stunning (carless) warren of cobblestone streets and stone houses. Beat the throngs of day trippers by staying over.

Signposted steps lead up to the ruins of a **fortress** built by the Venetians in the 16th century, and the Byzantine **Church of Agia Sophia**, perched precariously on the edge of the cliff. Views are spectacular, and wildflowers shoulder-high in spring.

Sleeping & Eating

Staying in a hotel in the *kastro* could be one of the most romantic things you ever do (ask for discounts in low season), but if you're on a tight budget stay in Gefyra.

TOP CHOICE **Hotel Malvasia** HISTORIC HOTEL €€
(☎27320 61113; d/apt from €80/160; ❄👪) A variety of cosy, traditionally decorated rooms and apartments (most with sea views) are scattered around the Old Town.

Hotel Aktaion HOTEL €
(☎27320 61234; s/d €30/40) This clean, sunny hotel, on the Gefyra end of the causeway, has balconies and views of the sea and 'the rock'.

Three traditional Greek tavernas sit cheek to cheek in Monemvasia's old town: **Matoula** (☎27320 61660), **Marianthi** (☎2732 61371) and **To Kanoni** (☎27320 61387). You can't really go wrong (mains €8 to €13).

Taverna O Botsalo TAVERNA
(☎27320 61491; mains €4-9) Just down the wharf on the mainland; serves savoury meals.

Getting There & Away

Buses stop in Gefyra at the friendly **Malvasia Travel** (☎27320 61752), where you can buy tickets. Four daily buses travel to Athens (€27, six hours) via Corinth and Sparta (€9, 2½ hours).

Gythio ΓΥΘΕΙΟ

POP 4490

Gythio (*yee*-thih-o) was once the port of ancient Sparta. Now it's an earthy fishing town on the Lakonian Gulf and gateway to the rugged, much more beautiful Mani Peninsula.

Peaceful **Marathonisi islet**, linked to the mainland by a causeway, is said to be ancient Cranae, where Paris (prince of Troy) and Helen (the wife of Menelaus of Sparta) consummated the love affair that sparked the Trojan War. You'll find the tiny **Museum of Mani History** (☎27330 24484; admission €2; ⏲8am-2.30pm) here in an 18th-century tower.

Sleeping

Camping Meltemi CAMPING GROUND €
(☎27330 23260; www.campingmeltemi.gr; campsites per tent/adult €5/6; ⏲Apr-Oct; 📶🏊) Birds chirp in these idyllic silver olive groves, 3km south of Gythio; private beach, swimming pool and summer beauty contests! The Areopoli bus stops here.

Hotel La Boheme BOUTIQUE HOTEL €
(☎27330 21992; www.labohemehotel.gr; Tzani Tzanitaki; s/d €50/60; P❄@) Sea views, upmarket rooms and a zippy downstairs bar-restaurant draw the crowds.

Xenia Karlaftis Rooms to Rent PENSION €
(☎27330 22719; opposite Marathonisi islet; s/d €25/40) Friendly owner Voula keeps clean rooms and offers kitchen access. Several nearby places are of similar quality if you can't get in here.

Eating

The waterfront is packed with fish tavernas and cafes.

I Gonia TAVERNA €
(Vassilis Pavlou; mains €6-15) Watch all the action while supping on delectable Greek standards. On the corner, opposite the port.

Nissus TAVERNA €
(☎6973384176; mains €10-15; ⏲dinner) Take in fantastic views from this tiny bar-restaurant on Marthonisi islet.

Getting There & Away

BOAT **ANEN Lines** (www.anen.gr) has a weekly summertime ferry to Kissamos, Crete (€22, seven hours) via Kythira (€10, 2½ hours) and Antikythira. Schedules change; check with **Rozakis Travel** (☎27330 22207; rosakigy@otenet.gr; Pavlou 5).

BUS **KTEL Lakonia bus station** (☎27330 22228; cnr Vasileos Georgios & Evrikleos) is on the square near Hotel Aktion. Services:

Areopoli €2.40, 30 minutes, four daily
Athens €21.50, 4½ hours, six daily
Diros Caves €3.30, one hour, one daily
Sparta €3.90, one hour, four daily

The Mani Η ΜΑΝΗ

The exquisite Mani completely lives up to its reputation for rugged beauty, abundant wildflowers in spring and dramatic juxtapositions of sea and the Taÿgetos Mountains (threaded with wonderful walking trails). The Mani occupies the central peninsula of the southern Peloponnese and is divided into two regions: the arid Lakonian (inner) Mani in the south and the verdant Messinian (outer) Mani in the northwest near Kalamata. Explore the winding roads by car.

LAKONIAN MANI

For centuries the Maniots were a law unto themselves, renowned for their fierce independence and their spectacularly murderous internal feuds. To this day, bizarre tower settlements built as refuges during clan wars dot the rocky slopes of Lakonian Mani.

Areopoli (population 774), 30km southwest of Gythio and named after Ares, the god of war, is a warren of cobblestone and ancient towers. Enter a dreamlike courtyard to reach the excellent **Pyrgos Kapetanakas** (☎27330 51233; access off Kapetan Matepan; s/d/tr €50/60/80; ❄), in a splendid tower house built by the powerful Kapetanakas family in 1865. **Tsimova Rooms** (☎27330 51301; Kapetan Matepan; s/d €55/60) is in a renovated tower tucked behind the Church of Taxiarhes.

Step behind the counter to choose from the scrumptious specials at **Nicola's Corner Taverna** (☎27330 51366; Plateia Athanaton; mains €8-10), on the central square.

The **bus station** (☎27330 51229; Plateia Athanaton) services Gythio (€2.80, 30 minutes, four daily), Itilo (for the Messinian Mani, €2, 20 minutes, three daily Monday to Saturday), Gerolimenas (€3.30, 45 minutes, three daily) and the Diros Caves (€1.40, 15 minutes, one daily).

Eleven kilometres south, the extensive, though touristy **Diros Caves** (☎27330 52222; adult/child €12/7; ⏲8.30am-5.30pm Jun-Sep, to 3pm Oct-May) contain a subterranean river. In neighbouring **Pyrgos Dirou**, stay over at chic **Vlyhada** (☎27330 52469; www.vlyhada.gr; d incl breakfast €70; P❄).

Gerolimenas, a tranquil fishing village on a sheltered bay 20km further south, is home to the exceedingly popular boutique **Kyrimai Hotel** (☎27330 54288; www.kyrimai.gr; d from €100; P❄≋). Groovy music and mood lighting fill this exquisitely renovated castle with a seaside swimming pool and top-notch restaurant.

MESSINIAN MANI

Stone hamlets dot aquamarine swimming coves. Silver olive groves climb the foothills to the snow-capped Taÿgetos Mountains. Explore the splendid meandering roads and hiking trails from Itilo to Kalamata.

The people of the enchanting seaside village of **Kardamyli**, 37km south of Kalamata, know how good they've got it. Sir Patrick Leigh Fermor famously wrote about his rambles here in *Mani: Travels in the Southern Peloponnese.* Trekkers come for the magnificent **Vyros Gorge**. Walks are well organised and colour-coded.

Kardamyli has a good choice of small hotels and private rooms for all budgets; book ahead for summer.

Notos Hotel (☎27210 73730; www.notoshotel.gr; studios €95-110; ❄) is really a boutique hamlet of individual stone houses, perched on a hill overlooking the village, the mountains, and the sea! Each elegantly decorated wee house has a fully equipped kitchen, a verandah and a view.

Run by the former housekeeper to Patrick Leigh Fermor, **Lela's Rooms** (☎27210 73541; r €55; ❄) has basic charming rooms on the sea, while the adjoining Lela's Taverna serves up tasty home-style Greek cuisine (mains €10) under pergolas on the water's edge.

Olympia Koumounakou Rooms (☎27210 73623; s/d €30/35) is basic but clean and popular with backpackers, who like the communal kitchen and courtyard.

Beautiful **Elies** (☎27210 73140; mains €6.50-10; ⏲lunch), right by the beach 1km north of town, is worth a lunchtime stop.

Kardamyli is on the main bus route from Itilo to Kalamata (€3.10, one hour) and two to three buses stop daily at the central square.

Olympia ΟΛΥΜΠΙΑ

POP 1000

Tucked alongside the Kladeos River, in fertile delta country, the modern town of Olympia supports the extensive ruins of the same name. The first Olympics were staged here in 776 BC, and every four years thereafter until AD 394 when Emperor Theodosius I banned them. During the competition the city states were bound by a sacred truce to stop fighting and take part in athletic events and cultural exhibitions.

Ancient Olympia (☎26240 22517; adult/child €6/3, site & museum €9/5; ⏲8am-8pm Apr-Oct, 8.30am-3pm Nov-Mar) is dominated by the immense ruined **Temple of Zeus**, to whom the games were dedicated. Don't miss the statue of **Hermes of Praxiteles**, a classical sculpture masterpiece, at the exceptional **Archaeological Museum** (adult/child €6/3; ⏲1.30-8pm Mon, 8am-8pm Tue-Sun Apr-Oct, to 3pm Nov-Mar).

Sparkling-clean **Pension Posidon** (☎26240 22567; www.pensionposidon.gr; Stefanopoulou 9; s/d/tr €35/45/60; ❄) and quiet, spacious **Hotel Pelops** (☎/fax 26240 22543;

www.hotelpelops.gr; Varela 2; s/d/tr incl breakfast €48/60/84;) offer the best value in the centre. Family-run **Best Western Europa** (☎26240 22650; www.hoteleuropa.gr; Drouva 1; s/d €90/130;) perches on a hill above town and has gorgeous sweeping vistas from room balconies and the wonderful swimming pool.

Pitch your tent in the leafy grove at **Camping Diana** (☎26240 22314; campsites per tent/adult €6/8;), 250m west of town.

Tucked beneath the trees, **Taverna Gefsis Melathron** (☎26240 22916; George Douma 3; mains €5-8;) is the best of the ho-hum tavernas for traditional cuisine, including scrumptious vegetarian options and organic wines.

Olympia Municipal Tourist Office (☎26240 23100; Praxitelous Kondyli; 9am-3pm Mon-Fri May-Sep) has transport schedules.

Catch buses at the stop on the north end of town. Northbound buses go via Pyrgos (€1.90, 30 minutes), where you connect to buses for Athens, Corinth and Patra. Two buses go east from Olympia to Tripoli (€11.10, 2½ hours). Trains run daily to Pyrgos (€1, 30 minutes), where you can switch for Athens, Corinth and Patra.

CENTRAL GREECE
ΚΕΝΤΡΙΚΗ ΕΛΛΑΔΑ

This dramatic landscape of deep gorges, rugged mountains and fertile valleys is home to the magical stone pinnacle-topping monasteries of Meteora and the iconic ruins of ancient Delphi, where Alexander the Great sought advice from the Delphic oracle. Established in 1938, **Parnassos National Park** (www.routes.gr), to the north of Delphi, attracts naturalists, hikers and skiers.

Delphi ΔΕΛΦΟΙ

POP 2800

Modern Delphi and its adjoining ruins hang stunningly on the slopes of Mt Parnassos overlooking the shimmering Gulf of Corinth.

The ancient Greeks regarded Delphi as the centre of the world. According to mythology, Zeus released two eagles at opposite ends of the world and they met here. By the 6th century BC, **Ancient Delphi** (☎22650 82312; site or museum €6, combined adult/child €9/5, free Sun Nov-Mar; 1.30-7.45pm Mon, 8am-7.45pm Tue-Sun Apr-Oct, 8.30am-2.45pm Nov-Mar) had become the Sanctuary of Apollo. Thousands of pilgrims flocked here to consult the middle-aged female oracle who sat at the mouth of a fume-emitting chasm. After sacrificing a sheep or goat, pilgrims would ask a question, and a priest would translate the oracle's response into verse. Wars, voyages and business transactions were undertaken on the strength of these prophecies. From the entrance, take the **Sacred Way** up to the **Temple of Apollo**, where the oracle sat. From here the path continues to the **theatre** and **stadium**.

Opposite the main site and down the hill some 100m, don't miss the **Sanctuary of Athena** and the much-photographed **Tholos**, a 4th-century-BC columned rotunda of Pentelic marble.

In the town centre, the welcoming **Hotel Hermes** (☎22650 82318; Vasileon Pavlou-Friderikis 27; s/d incl breakfast €45/60;) has spacious rooms sporting balconies with stunning valley views.

Apollon Camping (☎22650 82762; www.apolloncamping.gr; campsites per person/tent €7.50/4;), 2km west of town, has great facilities, including a restaurant and minimarket.

Specialities at **Taverna Vakhos** (☎22650 83186; Apollonos 31; mains €4.50-11) include stuffed zucchini flowers and rabbit stew. Locals pack **Taverna Gargadouas** (☎22650 82488; Vasileon Pavlou & Friderikis; mains €4-9) for grilled meats and slow-roasted lamb (€7.50).

The **bus station** (☎22660 82317), post office, banks and **tourist office** (☎22650 82900; 7.30am-2.30pm Mon-Fri, 8am-2pm Sat) are all on modern Delphi's main street, Vasileon Pavlou. Six buses a day go to Athens (€13.60, three hours). Take a bus to Lamia (€8.20, two hours, two daily) or Trikala (€13.80, 4½ hours, two daily) to transfer for Meteora.

WORTH A TRIP

PELION PENINSULA

The **Pelion Peninsula**, a dramatic mountain range whose highest peak is Pourianos Stavros (1624m), was inhabited, according to mythology, by half-man and half-horse *kentavri* (centaurs). Today it is a verdant mecca for trekkers. The largely inaccessible eastern flank consists of high cliffs that plunge into the sea. The gentler western flank coils round the Pagasitikos Gulf.

Meteora ΜΕΤΕΩΡΑ

Meteora (meh-*teh*-o-rah) should be a certified Wonder of the World with its magnificent late-14th-century monasteries perched dramatically atop enormous rocky pinnacles. Try not to miss it. The tranquil village of **Kastraki**, 2km from Kalambaka, is the best base for visiting.

While there were once monasteries on all 24 pinnacles, only six are still occupied: **Megalou Meteorou** (Grand Meteoron; ⏲9am-5pm Wed-Mon Apr-Oct, to 4pm Thu-Mon Nov-Mar), **Varlaam** (⏲9am-4pm Wed-Mon Apr-Oct, Thu-Mon Nov-Mar), **Agiou Stefanou** (⏲9am-1.30pm & 3.30-5.30pm Tue-Sun Apr-Oct, 9.30am-1pm & 3-5pm Nov-Mar), **Agias Triados** (Holy Trinity; ⏲9am-5pm Fri-Wed Apr-Oct, 10am-3pm Nov-Mar), **Agiou Nikolaou Anapafsa** (⏲9am-3.30pm Sat-Thu) and **Agias Varvaras Rousanou** (⏲9am-6pm Thu-Tue Apr-Oct, to 4pm Nov-Mar). Admission is €2 for each monastery and strict dress codes apply (no bare shoulders or knees and women must wear skirts; borrow a long skirt at the door if you don't have one). Walk the footpaths between monasteries or drive the back road.

Meteora's stunning rocks are also a climbing mecca. Licensed mountain guide **Lazaros Botelis** (☎24320 79165, 6948043655; meteora@nolimits.com.gr; Kastraki) and mountaineering instructor **Kostas Liolos** (☎6972567582; kliolios@kalampaka.com; Kalambaka) show the way.

Sleeping & Eating

TOP CHOICE **Doupiani House** HOTEL €
(☎24320 75326; www.doupianihouse.com; s/d/tr incl breakfast €40/50/60; P❄@🛜) Gregarious hosts Thanassis and Toula Nakis offer this comfy home from which to explore or simply enjoy the panoramic views. Request a balcony room.

Vrachos Camping CAMPING GROUND €
(☎24320 22293; www.campingmeteora.gr; campsites per tent/adult €7/free; 🏊) Great views, excellent facilities and a good taverna; a short stroll from Kastraki.

Taverna Paradisos TRADITIONAL GREEK €
(☎24320 22723; mains €4-7.50) Look for outstanding traditional meals with spectacular views.

Taverna Gardenia TRADITIONAL GREEK €
(☎24320 22504; Kastrakiou St; mains €4-8) Freshest Greek food served with aplomb and more splendid views. The owners also have good-value, spacious rooms (single/double/triple €35/45/55).

Getting There & Around

Local buses shuttle between Kalambaka and Kastraki (€1.90); a bus goes up to the monasteries in the morning. Hourly buses from Kalambaka go to the transport hub of Trikala (€2, 30 minutes), from where buses go to Ioannina (€13.10, three hours, two daily) and Athens (€27, 4½ hours, seven daily). From Kalambaka, express trains run to Athens (regular/IC €14.60/24.30, 5½hr/4½, two/two daily) and Thessaloniki (€12.10, four hours, three daily).

NORTHERN GREECE ΒΟΡΕΙΑ ΕΛΛΑΔΑ

Northern Greece is stunning, graced as it is with magnificent mountains, thick forests, tranquil lakes and archaeological sites. Most of all, it's easy to get off the beaten track and experience aspects of Greece noticeably different to other mainland areas and the islands.

Thessaloniki ΘΕΣΣΑΛΟΝΙΚΗ

POP 800,800

Dodge cherry sellers in the street, smell spices in the air and enjoy waterfront breezes in Thessaloniki (thess-ah-lo-*nee*-kih), also known as Salonica. The second city of Byzantium and of modern Greece boasts countless Byzantine churches, a smattering of Roman ruins, engaging museums, shopping to rival Athens, fine restaurants and a lively cafe scene and nightlife.

Sights

Historical Sights MONUMENT, CHURCH
Check out the seafront **White Tower** (Lefkos Pyrgos; www.lpth.org; admission free; ⏲8am-3pm Tue-Sun) and wander *hanmams* (Turkish baths) and churches such as the enormous, 5th-century **Church of Agios Dimitrios** (Agiou Dimitriou 97; admission free; ⏲8am-10pm).

Art & Culture
MUSEUMS, GALLERY
The award-winning **Museum of Byzantine Culture** (☎2313 306 400; www.mbp.gr; Leoforos Stratou 2; admission €4; ⏲8am-8pm Tue-Sun, 1.30-8pm Mon) beautifully displays splendid sculptures, mosaics, icons and other intriguing artefacts. The **Archaeological Museum**

(☎2310 830 538; Manoli Andronikou 6; admission €6; ⏲8.30am-8pm) showcases prehistoric, ancient Macedonian and Hellenistic finds.

The compelling **Thessaloniki Centre of Contemporary Art** (www.cact.gr; admission free; ⏲11am-7pm Tue-Sun) and hip **Museum of Photography** (www.thmphoto.gr; admission free; ⏲11am-7pm Tue-Sun), beside the port, are worth an hour.

Sleeping

Steep discounts abound during summer; prices rise during conventions.

Electra Palace Hotel LUXURY HOTEL €€
(☎2310 294 000; www.electrahotels.gr; Plateia Aristotelous 9; d €130-210; ❄@🛜🏊) Dive into five-star seafront pampering: impeccable service, plush rooms, a rooftop bar, indoor and outdoor swimming pools and a *hammam*.

Hotel Pella HOTEL €
(☎2310 524 221; www.pella-hotel.gr; Ionos Dragoumi 63; s/d €40/50; ❄) Quiet and family-run, with spotless rooms.

Hotel Tourist BUSINESS HOTEL €€
(☎2310 270 501; www.touristhotel.gr; Mitropoleos 21; s/d incl breakfast €55/70; ❄@) Spacious rooms in a charming, central, neoclassical building are maintained by friendly staff.

City Hotel BUSINESS HOTEL €€
(☎2310 269 421; www.cityhotel.gr; Komninon 11; s/d incl breakfast €120/135; ❄@🛜) Ask for a light-filled front room in this excellently located sleek, stylish hotel.

Backpacker's Refuge HOSTEL €
(☎6983433591; backpackers_refuge@hotmail.com; Botsari 84; dm per person €15; 🛜) Snug, hostel-like flat with a two-bed and a four-bed dorm. Call, email or SMS ahead, as it's frequently booked.

Hotel Orestias Kastorias HOTEL €
(☎2310 276 517; www.okhotel.gr; Agnostou Stratiotou 14; s/d/tr €38/49/59; ❄@) A friendly favourite with cosy, clean rooms.

Eating

Tavernas dot Plateia Athonos and cafes pack Leoforos Nikis. Head to **Modiano Market** for fresh fruit and vegetables.

Zythos TRADITIONAL GREEK €
(Katouni 5; mains €6-12) Popular with locals, this excellent taverna with friendly staff serves up delicious standards, interesting regional specialities, good wines by the glass and beers on tap. Its second outlet is **Dore Zythos** (☎2310 279 010; Tsirogianni 7), near the White Tower.

Kitchen Bar ECLECTIC INTERNATIONAL €
(☎2310 502 241; Warehouse B, Thessaloniki Port; mains €7-13) This perennial favourite offers both drinks and artfully prepared food, in a sumptuously decorated, renovated warehouse with waterfront tables. Chefs, like style-conscious clientele, are always on display.

O Arhontis FOOD STAND €
(Ermou 26; mains €5; ⏲11am-5pm) Eat delicious grilled sausages and potatoes off butcher's paper at this popular working-class eatery in Modiano Market.

Myrsini CRETAN €
(☎2310 228 300; Tsopela 2; mains €7-10; ⏲Sep-Jun) Hearty portions of delicious Cretan dishes such as roast rabbit and *myzithropitakia* (flaky filo triangles with sweet sheep's milk cheese).

Paparouna CREATIVE GREEK €
(☎2310 510 852; www.paparouna.com; Syngrou 7; mains €8-16; ⏲1pm-1am; 🛜) Built a century ago as a bank, this lively restaurant whips up inventive cuisine like chicken with peppermint and honey.

Turkenlis BAKERY €
(Aristotelous 4) Renowned for *tzoureki* (sweet bread) and a mind-boggling array of sweet-scented confections.

Drinking & Entertainment

Funky bars line Plateia Aristotelous and Leoforos Nikis, while Syngrou and Valaoritou Sts have newer drinking holes.

Spiti Mou BAR
(cnr Egnatia & Leontos Sofou 26; ⏲1pm-late; 🛜) Unmarked entrance and relaxed vibe, with big couches and eclectic tunes.

Lido DISCO
(Frixou 5, Sfageia; ⏲9pm-late) Pumps out R&B, house and more. Like most nightclubs, in summer it operates out on the airport road.

Information

EMERGENCY First-Aid Centre (☎2310 530 530; Navarhou Koundourioti 10)

Tourist Police (☎2310 554 871; 5th fl, Dodekanisou 4; ⏲7.30am-11pm)

TOURIST INFORMATION Office of Tourism Directorate (☎2310 221 100; tour-the@otenet.gr; Tsimiski 136; ⏲8am-8pm Mon-Fri, to 2pm Sat)

Thessaloniki

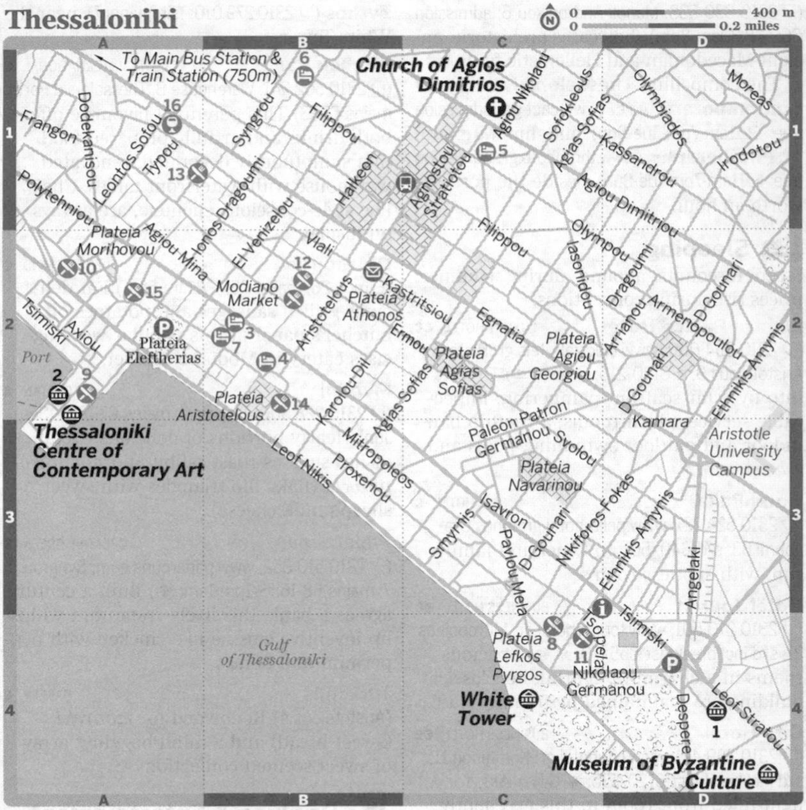

Getting There & Away

Air

Makedonia Airport (SKG; ☎2310 473 212) is 16km southeast of the centre and served by local bus 78 (€0.60, one hour, from 5am to 10pm). Taxis cost €15 (20 minutes).

Olympic Air (☎2310 368 666; Navarhou Koundourioti 1-3) and **Aegean Airlines** (☎2310 280 050; El Venizelou 2) fly throughout Greece. **Astra Airlines** (☎2310 489 392; www.astra-airlines.gr) flies to Chios.

Boat

Weekly ferries go to, among others, Limnos (€25, eight hours), Lesvos (€36, 14 hours) and Chios (€37, 19 hours). **Karaharisis Travel & Shipping Agency** (☎2310 524 544; Navarhou Koundourioti 8) handles tickets.

Bus

The **main bus station** (☎23105 95408; Monastiriou 319) services Athens (€35, 6¼ hours, 10 daily), Ioannina (€28.50, 4¾ hours, six daily) and other destinations. Buses to the Halkidiki Peninsula leave from the **Halkidiki bus terminal** (☎23103 16555; Karakasi 68).

OSE (☎2310 599 100; Aristotelous 26) runs buses to Sofia (€22, seven hours, two to four times daily) and Tirana (€31, twice daily). You can buy tickets from the office on the eastern side of the train station. Buses from the small **KTEL-Asprovalta station** (☎2310 536 260, Irinis 17) serve İstanbul (€45, 9½ hours, two daily).

Train

The **train station** (☎2310 599 421; Monastiriou) serves Athens (regular/IC €28/36, 6¾/5½ hours, seven/10 daily), Alexandroupolis (€13.60, six hours, three daily) and destinations beyond. International trains from Athens (heading to Belgrade, Sofia, İstanbul etc) stop at Thessaloniki. You can get schedules from the **train ticket office** (OSE; ☎2310 598 120; Aristotelous 18) or the station.

Thessaloniki

Top Sights

Church of Agios Dimitrios C1
Museum of Byzantine Culture D4
Thessaloniki Centre of Contemporary Art A2
White Tower C4

Sights

1 Archaeological Museum D4
2 Museum of Photography A2

Sleeping

3 City Hotel B2
4 Electra Palace Hotel B2
5 Hotel Orestias Kastoria C1
6 Hotel Pella B1
7 Hotel Tourist B2

Eating

8 Dore Zythos C4
9 Kitchen Bar A2
10 Krikela's A2
11 Myrsini C4
12 O Arhontis B2
13 Paparouna A1
14 Turkenlis B2
15 Zythos A2

Drinking

16 Spiti Mou A1

Halkidiki ΧΑΛΚΙΔΙΚΗ

Beautiful pine-covered Halkidiki is a three-pronged peninsula that extends into the Aegean Sea, southeast of Thessaloniki. Splendid, if built-up, sandy beaches rim its 500km of coastline. The middle **Sithonian Peninsula** is most spectacular. With camping and rooms to rent, it is more suited to independent travellers than overdeveloped **Kassandra Peninsula**, although Kassandra has the summertime **Sani Jazz Festival** (www.sanifestival.gr). You'll need your own wheels to explore Halkidiki properly.

Halkidiki's third prong is occupied by the all-male Monastic Republic of **Mt Athos** (known in Greek as the Holy Mountain), where 20 monasteries full of priceless treasures stand amid an impressive landscape of gorges, mountains and sea. Only men may visit, a permit is required and the summer waiting list is long. Start months in advance by contacting the Thessaloniki-based **Mt Athos Pilgrims' Bureau** (2310 252 578; fax 2310 222 424; pilgrimsbureau@c-lab.gr; Egnatia 109; 9am-2pm Mon-Fri, 10am-noon Sat).

Alexandroupolis ΑΛΕΞΑΝΔΡΟΥΠΟΛΗ

POP 49,200

Alexandroupolis (ah-lex-an-*dhroo*-po-lih) and nearby Komotini (ko-mo-tih-*nee*) enjoy lively student atmospheres that make for a satisfying stopover on the way to Turkey or Samothraki.

Lavish, waterfront **Hotel Bao Bab** (25510 34823; Alexandroupoli-Komotini Hwy; s/d/tr €40/60/70; P ❄ @), 1km west of town, has large, comfortable rooms and an excellent restaurant. Downtown, **Hotel Marianna** (25510 81456; Malgaron 11; s/d €45/60) has small, clean rooms.

Tuck into today's fresh catch at **Psarotaverna tis Kyra Dimitras** (cnr Kountourioti & Dikastirion; fish €6-11).

Alexandroupoli's cool nightspots change with the whims of its students. Leoforos Dimokratias has trendy bars; cafes line the waterfront.

The **Municipal tourist office** (25510 64184; Leoforos Dimokratias 306; 7.30am-3pm) is helpful.

Getting There & Away

AIR & BOAT Dimokritos Airport is 7km east of town and served by Olympic Air and Aegean Airlines. **Sever Travel** (25510 22555; sever1@otenet.gr; Megalou Alexandrou 24) handles ferry (to Samothraki and Limnos) and airline tickets.

BUS Bus station (25510 26479; Eleftheriou Venizelou 36). Services:

Athens €61, 10 hours, one daily
Thessaloniki €26.50, 3¾ hours, nine daily
İstanbul (Turkey) OSE bus €15, six hours, one daily Tuesday to Sunday

TRAIN Train station (25510 26395). Services:

Athens €49, 14 hours, one daily
Thessaloniki €9, seven hours, six daily
İstanbul €38, seven hours, three daily
Svilengrad (Bulgaria) €7, four hours, one daily

Mt Olympus ΟΛΥΜΠΟΣ ΟΡΟΣ

Just as it did for the ancients, Greece's highest mountain, the cloud-covered lair of the Greek pantheon, fires the visitor's imagination today. The highest of Olympus' eight peaks is **Mytikas** (2917m), popular with trekkers, who use **Litohoro** (elevation 305m), 5km inland from the Athens–Thessaloniki highway, as their base. The main route up takes two days, with a stay overnight at one of the **refuges** (May-Oct). Good protective clothing is essential, even in summer. **EOS** (Greek Alpine Club; 23520 84544; Plateia Kentriki; 9.30am-12.30pm & 6-8pm Mon-Sat Jun-Sep) has information on treks.

The romantic guest house **Xenonas Papanikolaou** (23520 81236; xenpap@otenet.gr; Nikolaou Episkopou Kitrous 1; s/d €45/50;) sits in a flowery garden up in the backstreets, a world away from the tourist crowds.

Olympos Beach Camping (23520 22111; www.olympos-beach.gr; Plaka Litohorou; campsites per adult/tent €7/6, bungalows €45; Apr-Oct) has a funky waterfront lounge and a pleasant beach.

TOP CHOICE **Gastrodromio En Olympio** (23520 21300; Plateia Eleftherias; mains €7-13), one of Greece's best country restaurants, serves up specialities such as *soutzoukakia* (minced meat with cumin and mint) and delicious wild mushrooms with an impressive regional wine list and gorgeous Olympus views.

From the **bus station** (23520 81271) 13 buses daily go to Thessaloniki (€8, 1¼ hours) and three to Athens (€28, 5½ hours). Litohoro's **train station**, 9km away, gets 10 daily trains on the Athens–Volos–Thessaloniki line.

Ioannina ΙΩΑΝΝΙΝΑ

POP 61,700

Charming Ioannina (ih-o-*ah*-nih-nah) on the western shore of Lake Pamvotis at the foot of the Pindos Mountains, was a major intellectual centre during Ottoman rule. Today it's a thriving university town with a lively waterfront cafe scene.

Sights

Kastro OLD QUARTER

The narrow stone streets of the evocative old quarter sit on a small peninsula jutting into the lake. Within its impressive fortifications, **Its Kale**, an inner citadel with lovely grounds and lake views, is home to the splendid **Fetiye Cami** (Victory Mosque), built in 1611, and the gemlike **Byzantine Museum** (26510 25989; admission €3; 8am-5pm Tue-Sun).

Lake Pamvotida LAKE

The lake's serene *nisi* (island) shelters four **monasteries** among its trees. Frequent ferries (€2) leave from near Plateia Mavili.

Sleeping

TOP CHOICE **Filyra** BOUTIQUE HOTEL €€

(26510 83560; http://hotelfilyra.gr; alley off Andronikou Paleologou 18; r €65;) Five Old Town self-catering suites that fill up fast. The affiliated **Traditional Hotel Dafni** (Ioustinianou 12; s/d/q €45/65/90;) is built into the Kastro's outer walls.

Hotel Kastro PENSION €€

(26510 22866; Andronikou Paleologou 57; s/d €75/90;) Ask for a high-ceilinged upstairs room at this quaint hotel, across from Its Kale.

Limnopoula Camping CAMPING GROUND €

(26510 25265; Kanari 10; campsites per tent/adult €4/8; Apr-Oct) Tree-lined and splendidly set on the edge of the lake 2km northwest of town.

Eating & Drinking

Scores of cafes and restaurants line the waterfront. Enjoy a cold beer on a sunny day in Its Kale, at its exquisitely situated cafe (mains €4 to €8).

Taberna To Manteio TRADITIONAL GREEK €

(Plateia Georgiou 15; mains €7-8) Join local families along the flower-filled Its Kale wall for deliciously simple *mezedhes,* salads and grills.

Es Aei GREEK €

(26510 34571; Koundouriotou 50; mains €8-12) This favourite haunt of local and foreign gastronomes combines an Ottoman flair with a unique, glass-roofed dining room.

Ananta BAR

(cnr Anexartisias & Stoa Labei; 9pm-3am) Rock out in the shadows of the long bar.

Information

EOT (tourist office; 26510 41142; Dodonis 39; 7.30am-2.30pm Mon-Fri)

EOS (Greek Alpine Club; 26510 22138; Despotatou Ipirou 2; 7-9pm Mon-Fri)

Getting There & Away

AIR Aegean Airlines (26510 64444) and **Olympic Air** (26510 26518) fly to Athens. Slow buses ply the 2km road into town.

BUS The **station** (26510 26286; Georgiou Papandreou) is 300m north of Plateia Dimokratias. Services:

Athens €35.20, 6½ hours, nine daily

Igoumenitsa €8.80, 1¼ hours, eight daily

Thessaloniki €28.50, 4¾ hours, six daily

Trikala €13.10, 2¼ hours, two daily

Zagorohoria & Vikos Gorge ΤΑ ΖΑΓΟΡΟΧΩΡΙΑ & ΧΑΡΑΔΡΑ ΤΟΥ ΒΙΚΟΥ

Do not miss the spectacular Zagori region, with its deep gorges, abundant wildlife, dense forests and snowcapped mountains. Some 46 charming villages, famous for their grey-slate architecture, and known collectively as the Zagorohoria, are sprinkled across a large expanse of the Pindos Mountains north of Ioannina. These beautifully restored gems were once only connected by stone paths and arching footbridges, but paved roads now wind between them. Get information on walks from Ioannina's EOT and EOS offices. Book ahead during high season (Christmas, Greek Easter and August); prices plummet in low season.

Tiny, carless **Dilofo** makes for a peaceful sojourn, especially if you lodge at excellent **Gaia** (☎26530 22570; www.gaia-dilofo.gr; s/d from €60/100) or **Arhontiko Dilofo** (☎26530 22455; www.dilofo.com; d incl breakfast from €65) and tuck into a delicious meal at **Taverna Lidthos** (mains €6-8), overlooking the village.

Delightful **Monodendri**, known for its special pitta bread, is a popular departure point for treks through dramatic 12km-long, 900m-deep **Vikos Gorge**, with its sheer limestone walls. Get cosy at quaint **Archontiko Zarkada** (☎26530 71305; www.monodendri.com; s/d incl breakfast €40/60), one of Greece's best-value small hotels.

Exquisite inns with attached tavernas abound in remote (but popular) twin villages **Megalo Papingo** and **Mikro Papingo**. Visit the **WWF Information Centre** (Mikro Papingo; 🕙10.30am-6pm Fri-Wed) to learn about the area.

In Megalo Papingo, simple **Lakis** (☎26530 41087; d incl breakfast €65) is a *domatia* (B&B), taverna and store. Stylish **Tsoumani** (☎26530 41893; www.tsoumanisnikos.gr; d from €85) also serves some of the best food around. Two friendly brothers run charming **Xenonas tou Kouli** (☎26530 41115; d €90).

Hide away in Mikro Papingo's sweetly rustic **Xenonas Dias** (☎26530 41257; s/d €60/80) or fabulous, sumptuously minimalist **1700** (☎26530 41179; www.mikropapigo.gr; d from €100) and elegantly appointed **Antalki** (☎26530 41441; www.antalki.gr; d €80-120).

Infrequent buses run to Ioannina from Dilofo (€3.50, three weekly), Monodendri (€3.10, one hour, twice weekly) and the Papingos (€5, two hours, three weekly).

Igoumenitsa ΗΓΟΥΜΕΝΙΤΣΑ

POP 9110

Though tucked beneath verdant hills and lying on the sea, this characterless west-coast port is little more than a ferry hub: keep moving.

If you must stay over, look for *domatia* signs or have a '70s flashback at **Hotel Oscar** (☎26650 23338; Ag Apostolon 149; s/d €30/40; ❄), across from the Corfu ticket booths.

Taverna Emily Akti (Podou 13; mains €6-8) ekes out some character under a pergola near the Corfu ferry quay.

The **bus station** (☎26650 22309; Kyprou 29) services Ioannina (€8.20, 2½ hours, nine daily) and Athens (€33, eight hours, five daily).

Several companies operate **ferries to Corfu** (☎26650 99460) between 5am and 10pm (person/car €7/33, 1½hr, hourly), and hydrofoils in summer. International ferries go to the Italian ports of Ancona, Bari, Brindisi and Venice. Ticket agencies line the port.

SARONIC GULF ISLANDS ΝΗΣΙΑ ΤΟΥ ΣΑΡΩΝΙΚΟΥ

Scattered about the Saronic Gulf, these islands are within easy reach of Athens. The Saronics are named after the mythical King Saron of Argos, a keen hunter who drowned while chasing a deer that had swum into the gulf to escape.

You can either island-hop through the group then return to Piraeus, or carry on to the Peloponnese from any of the islands mentioned.

Aegina ΑΙΓΙΝΑ

POP 13,500

Once a major player in the Hellenic world, thanks to its strategic position at the mouth of the gulf, Aegina (*eh*-yee-nah) now enjoys its position as Greece's premier producer of pistachios. Pick up a bag before you leave!

Bustling **Aegina Town**, on the west coast, is the island's capital and main port. There is no official tourist office, but information can be gleaned at www.aeginagreece.com.

The impressive **Temple of Aphaia** (adult/under 18yr €4/free; 🕙8am-6.30pm) is a well-preserved Doric temple 12km east of Aegina Town. It's said to have served as a model for the construction of the Parthenon. Standing on a pine-clad hill with imposing views out over the gulf, it is well worth a visit. Buses from Aegina Town to the small resort of Agia Marina can drop you at the site.

In Aegina Town, **Hotel Rastoni** (☎22970 27039; www.rastoni.gr; d/tr €90/120; P❄@☎), a boutique hotel with excellent service, gets a big thumbs up for its quiet location, spacious rooms and lovely garden. **Electra Pension** (☎22970 26715; s/d €45/50; ❄) is in a quiet corner of town with rooms that are impeccable and comfy.

A flotilla of ferries (€9.50, 70 minutes) and hydrofoils (€14, 40 minutes) ply the waters between Aegina and Piraeus with great regularity. You can head back to Piraeus, carry on through the Saronic Gulf Islands or take a boat to Methana (€5.70, 40 minutes) on the Peloponnese. There is a good public bus service on the island.

Poros ΠΟΡΟΣ

POP 4500

Only a few hundred metres from the village of Galatas on the shores of the mountainous Peloponnese, Poros is an attractive island with a friendly feel that is worth the effort. **Poros Town**, on the island's southern coast, is a haven for yachties, and with boats from all over tied up along the waterfront, there is a happy mood in the air.

HELLENIC WILDLIFE HOSPITAL

While some Greeks may not appear too environmentally minded, others are making a sterling effort to face the country's ecological problems head on. The **Hellenic Wildlife Hospital** (☎22970 28367; www.ekpaz.gr; ⏲10am-7pm) on the Saronic Gulf island of Aegina is one such place. The centre tackles the damage caused to wild birds and animals due to hunting and pollution, and runs projects such as the release of raptors into the wilds of Crete and Northern Greece. You can visit the centre for free, though donations are appreciated. Better yet, the centre welcomes volunteers and accommodation is supplied.

Seven Brothers Hotel (☎22980 23412; www.7brothers.gr; s/d/tr €55/65/75; ❄@) is conveniently close to the hydrofoil dock. This modern hotel has bright, comfy rooms with balconies and tea- and coffee-making facilities.

There is no tourist office, but also no shortage of businesses hoping to sell you your onward ticket. Hit www.poros.com.gr for extensive information.

There are four ferry (€13.30, 2½ hours) and four hydrofoil (€25.20, one hour) services daily between Poros and Piraeus. The ferries go via Aegina (€8.60, 1¼ hours), while the hydrofoils go direct. Many of the outbound boats head on to Hydra and Spetses. Small boats shuttle back and forth between Poros and Galatas (€1, five minutes) on the Peloponnese.

Hydra ΥΔΡΑ

POP 2900

The catwalk queen of the Saronics, Hydra (*ee*-drah) is a delight. **Hydra Town** has a picturesque horseshoe-shaped harbour with gracious white and pastel stone mansions stacked up the rocky hillsides that surround it. The island is known as a retreat for artists, writers and celebrities, and wears its celebrity with panache.

A major attraction is Hydra's tranquillity. Forget noisy motorbikes keeping you awake half the night! There are no motorised vehicles – apart from two sanitation trucks – and the main forms of transport are foot and donkey.

TOP CHOICE **Pension Erofili** (☎22980 54049; www.pensionerofili.gr; Tombazi; s/d/tr €45/55/65; ❄), tucked away in the inner town, has clean, comfortable rooms and an attractive courtyard. The young family owners add a friendly sparkle. **Hotel Miranda** (☎22980 52230; www.mirandahotel.gr; Miaouli; s/d incl breakfast €120/140; ❄) is worth a splurge. Originally built in 1810 as the mansion of a wealthy Hydriot sea captain, this stylish place retains much of its historical character and is a National Heritage building.

Hydra Town is on the island's north coast. There is no tourist office, but check out www.hydradirect.com for detailed information.

High-speed boat services (€28.40, 1½ hours) connect Hydra with Piraeus seven times daily. There are also services to Ermioni and Porto Heli on the Peloponnese mainland and outbound boats to Spetses.

Spetses ΣΠΕΤΣΕΣ

POP 4000

Spetses is an appealing island that is packed with visitors in summer. Its attractiveness is largely thanks to Spetses-born philanthropist Sotirios Anargyrios, who made a fortune in the US after emigrating in 1848. Anargyrios returned in 1914, bought two-thirds of the then-barren island, planted Aleppo pines, financed the island's road system, and commissioned many of the town's grandest buildings.

Spetses Town, the main port, sprawls along half the northeast coast of the island.

Opposite the small town beach to the east of the ferry quay, **Villa Marina** (☎22980 72646; www.villamarinaspetses.com; s/d €60/75; ❄) is a welcoming place with tidy rooms containing a fridge. Ask for a sea view.

There is no tourist office. See the website www.spetsesdirect.com for more information.

At least six high-speed boats head daily to Piraeus (€39, 2¼ hours). Another option is to carry on to the Peloponnese mainland on boats to Ermioni (€10, one hour) or Porto Heli (€7, 10 minutes).

> **CYCLADIC CONNECTIONS**
>
> For planning purposes, it's worth noting that once the season kicks in, **Hellenic Seaways** (www.hsw.gr) runs daily catamarans up and down the Cyclades, starting from both Piraeus (for Athens) and Iraklio on Crete.
>
> One boat heads south daily from Piraeus to Paros, Naxos, Ios and Santorini, returning along the same route. There's also a daily run from Piraeus to Syros, Tinos and Mykonos.
>
> Heading north from Iraklio, another catamaran runs to Santorini, Ios, Paros, Mykonos and return.
>
> Island-hopping through the Cyclades from Piraeus to Crete (or vice-versa) is getting easier and easier – though ease of travel means there are more people out there doing it!

CYCLADES ΚΥΚΛΑΔΕΣ

The Cyclades (kih-*klah*-dez) are Greek islands to dream about. Named after the rough *kyklos* (circle) they form around the island of Delos, they are rugged outcrops of rock in the azure Aegean, speckled with white cubist buildings and blue-domed Byzantine churches. Throw in sun-blasted golden beaches, more than a dash of hedonism and a fascinating culture, and it's easy to see why many find the Cyclades irresistible.

Some of the islands, such as Mykonos, Ios and Santorini, have seized tourism with great enthusiasm. Prepare to battle the crowds if you turn up at the height of summer. Others are little more than clumps of rock, with a village, secluded coves and a few curious tourists. Ferry services rarely run in winter, while from July to September the Cyclades are vulnerable to the *meltemi*, a fierce northeasterly wind that can cull ferry schedules.

History

Said to have been inhabited since at least 7000 BC, the Cyclades enjoyed a flourishing Bronze Age civilisation (3000–1100 BC), more or less concurrent with the Minoan civilisation. From the 4th century AD, the islands, like the rest of Greece, suffered a series of invasions and occupations. The Turks turned up in 1537 but neglected the Cyclades to the extent that they became backwaters prone to raids by pirates – hence the labyrinthine character of their towns, which was meant to confuse attackers. On some islands the whole population moved into the mountainous interior to escape the pirates, while on others they braved it out on the coast. Consequently, the *hora* (main town) is on the coast on some islands, while on others it is inland.

The Cyclades became part of independent Greece in 1827. During WWII they were occupied by the Italians. Before the revival of the islands' fortunes by the tourist boom that began in the 1970s, many islanders lived in poverty and many more headed for the mainland or emigrated to America or Australia in search of work.

Mykonos ΜΥΚΟΝΟΣ

POP 9700

Sophisticated Mykonos glitters happily under the Aegean sun, shamelessly surviving on tourism. The island has something for everyone, with marvellous beaches, romantic sunsets, chic boutiques, excellent restaurants and bars, and its long-held reputation as a mecca for gay travellers. The maze of white-walled streets in Mykonos Town was designed to confuse pirates, and it certainly manages to captivate and confuse the crowds that consume the island's capital in summer.

Sights & Activities

Mykonos Town NEIGHBOURHOOD

A stroll around Mykonos Town, shuffling through snaking streets with blinding white walls and balconies of flowers is a must for any visitor. **Little Venice**, where the sea laps up to the edge of the restaurants and bars, and Mykonos' famous hilltop row of **windmills** should be included in the spots-to-see list. You're bound to run into one of Mykonos' famous resident pelicans on your walk.

Beaches

The island's most popular beaches are on the southern coast. **Platys Gialos** has wall-to-wall sun lounges, while nudity is not uncommon at **Paradise Beach**, **Super Paradise**, **Agrari** and gay-friendly **Elia**.

Sleeping

Mykonos has two camping areas, both on the south coast. Minibuses from both meet the ferries and buses go regularly into town. Rooms in town fill up quickly in high season.

Hotel Philippi HOTEL €€

(☎22890 22294; chriko@otenet.gr; 25 Kalogera, Mykonos Town; s €60-90, d €75-120; ❄📶) In the heart of the *hora,* Philippi has spacious, bright, clean rooms that open onto a railed verandah overlooking a lush garden. Free wi-fi. An extremely pleasant place to stay.

Paradise Beach Camping CAMPING €

(☎22890 22852; www.paradisemykonos.com; campsites per tent/person €5/10; @🏊) There are lots of options here, including camping, beach cabins and apartments, as well as bars, a swimming pool, games etc. It is skin-to-skin mayhem in summer with a real party atmosphere. The website has it all.

Hotel Lefteris HOTEL €€

(☎22890 27117; www.lefterishotel.gr; 9 Apollonas, Mykonos Town; s/d €95/120, studios €220-260; ❄) Tucked away just up from Taxi Sq, Lefteris has bright, comfy rooms, and a relaxing sun terrace with superb views over town. A good international meeting place.

Poseidon Hotel HOTEL €€

(☎22890 22437; www.poseidonhotelmykonos.gr; Agiou Ioannou, Mykonos Town; s/d/ste €110/130/300; P❄@🏊) In a great location a few hundred metres up from the southern bus station, Poseidon presents more-than-adequate rooms, plush suites and a superb pool area.

Eating

There is no shortage of places to eat and drink in Mykonos Town. Cheap eateries are found around Taxi Sq and the southern bus station. Restaurants offering abundant (but pricey) seafood abound in Little Venice and towards the Delos excursion boats. Mykonos' top touts are its two resident pelicans, who wander the restaurants looking for handouts, often with visitors following them.

TOP CHOICE **Fato a Mano** MEDITERRANEAN €

(☎22890 26256; Meletopoulou Sq; mains €8-15) In the middle of the maze, this place is worth taking the effort to find. It serves up tasty Mediterranean and traditional Greek dishes with pride.

Drinking & Entertainment

The waterfront is perfect for sitting with a drink and watching an interesting array of passers-by, while Little Venice has bars with dreamy views and water lapping below your feet.

Cavo Paradiso CLUB

(☎22890 27205; www.cavoparadiso.gr) For those who want to go the whole hog, this place 300m above Paradise Beach picks up around 2am and boasts a pool the shape of Mykonos. A bus transports clubbers from town in about 15 minutes in summer.

Long feted as a gay travel destination, there are many gay-centric clubs and hang-outs:

Kastro BAR

(Agion Anargyron) In Little Venice, this the spot to start the night with cocktails as the sun sets.

Pierro's CLUB

(Agias Kiriakis) Near Taxi Sq; a popular dance club for rounding off the night.

Information

Tourist information office (☎22890 25250; www.mykonos.gr; ⊙9am-9pm Jul & Aug, 10am-5pm Easter-Jun, Sep & Oct) At the western end of the waterfront, just up from the Delos boat ticket office.

Island Mykonos Travel (☎22890 22232; www.discovergreece.org) On Taxi Sq, where the port

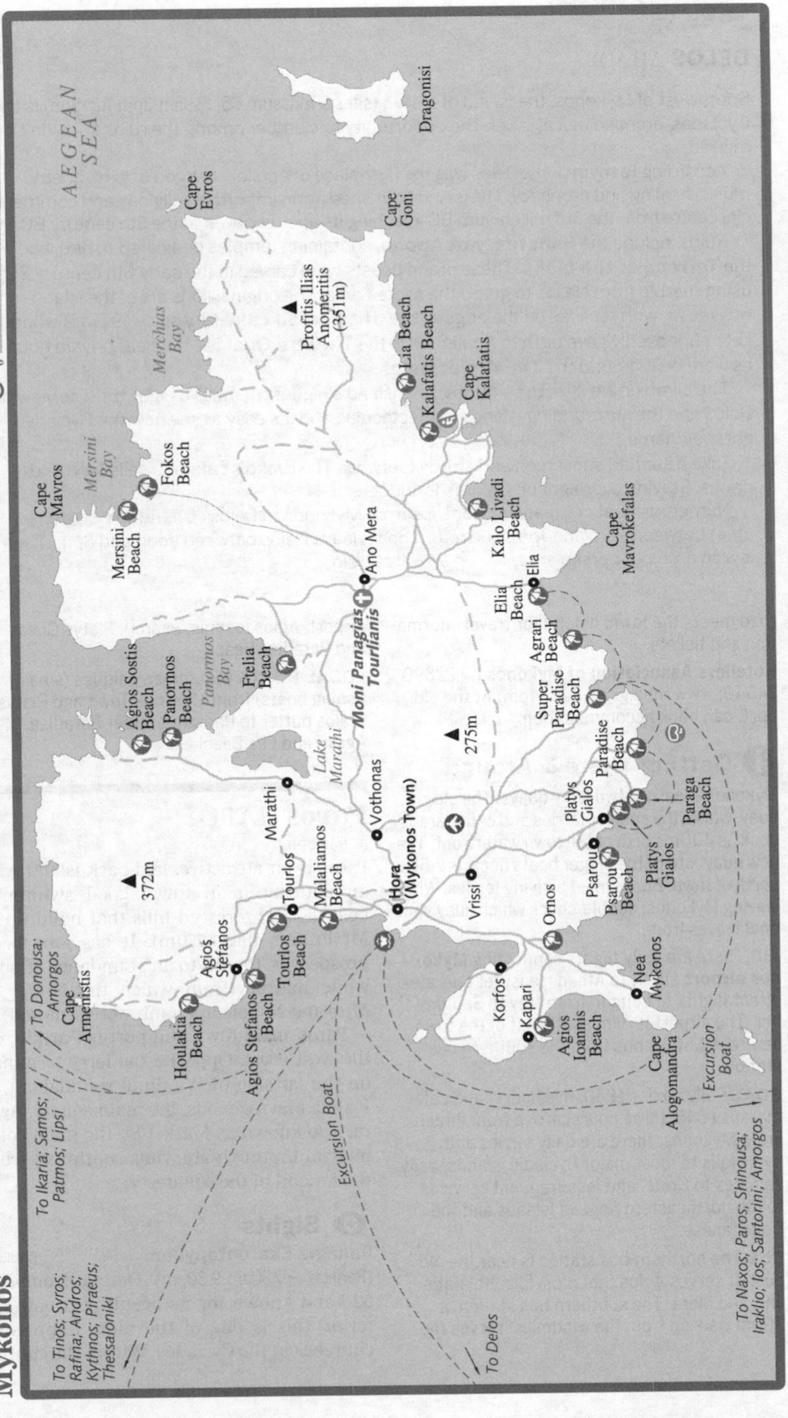

Mykonos

0 5 km
0 3 miles

AEGEAN SEA

To Tinos; Syros; Rafina; Andros; Kythnos; Piraeus; Thessaloniki
To Ikaria; Samos; Patmos; Lipsi
To Donousa; Amorgos
Cape Armenistis
372m
Houlakia Beach
Agios Stefanos
Agios Stefanos Beach
Tourlos Beach
Tourlos
Malaliamos Beach
Excursion Boat
Marathi
Lake Marathi
Agios Sostis Beach
Panormos Beach
Panormos Bay
Ftelia Beach
Cape Mavros
Mersini Bay
Mersini Beach
Fokos Beach
Merchias Bay
Cape Evros
Profitis Ilias Anomeritis (351m)
Moni Panagias Tourlianis
Ano Mera
Vothonas
Hora (Mykonos Town)
275m
Vrissi
To Delos
Korfos
Kapari
Agios Ioannis Beach
Ornos
Psarou
Psarou Beach
Platys Gialos
Platys Gialos
Paraga Beach
Paradise Beach
Super Paradise Beach
Agrari Beach
Elia Beach
Elia
Kalo Livadi Beach
Cape Mavrokefalas
Lia Beach
Kalafatis Beach
Cape Kalafatis
Cape Goni
Dragonisi
Nea Mykonos
Cape Alogomandra
Excursion Boat
To Naxos; Paros; Shinousa; Iraklio; Ios; Santorini; Amorgos

WORTH A TRIP

DELOS ΔΗΛΟΣ

Southwest of Mykonos, the island of **Delos** (sites & museum €5; ⏲9am-3pm Tue-Sun) is the Cyclades' archaeological jewel. The opportunity to clamber among the ruins shouldn't be missed.

According to mythology, Delos was the birthplace of Apollo – the god of light, poetry, music, healing and prophecy. The island flourished as an important religious and commercial centre from the 3rd millennium BC, reaching its apex of power in the 5th century BC.

Ruins include the **Sanctuary of Apollo**, containing temples dedicated to him, and the **Terrace of the Lions**. These proud beasts were carved in the early 6th century BC using marble from Naxos to guard the sacred area. The original lions are in the island's **museum**, with replicas on the original site. The **Sacred Lake** (dry since 1926) is where Leto supposedly gave birth to Apollo, while the **Theatre Quarter** is where private houses were built around the **Theatre of Delos**.

The climb up **Mt Kynthos** (113m), the island's highest point, is a highlight. The view of Delos and the surrounding islands is spectacular, and it's easy to see how the Cyclades got their name.

Take a sunhat, sunscreen and sturdy footwear. The island's cafeteria sells food and drinks. Staying overnight on Delos is forbidden.

Numerous boat companies offer trips from Mykonos to Delos (€15 return, 30 minutes) between 9am and 1pm. The return boats leave Delos between noon and 3pm. There is also a €5 per person entry fee on arrival at Delos.

road meets the town; helpful for travel information and tickets.

Hoteliers Association of Mykonos (☎22890 24540; www.mha.gr; ⏲8am-4pm) At the old port; can book accommodation.

Getting There & Around

Mykonos Town has two ferry quays. The old quay, where the smaller ferries and catamarans dock, is 400m north of the town waterfront. The new quay, where the bigger boats dock, is 2.5km north of town. Buses meet arriving ferries. When leaving Mykonos, double-check which quay your boat leaves from.

AIR There are daily flights connecting **Mykonos airport** (JMK) to Athens. easyJet operates direct flights to London from May to September. The airport is 3km southeast of the town centre; €1.50 by bus from the southern bus station.

BOAT Daily ferries (€30, five hours) and catamarans (€45, three hours) arrive from Piraeus. From Mykonos, there are daily ferries and hydrofoils to most major Cycladic islands, daily services to Crete, and less-frequent services to the northeastern Aegean Islands and the Dodecanese.

BUS The northern bus station is near the old port. It serves Agios Stefanos, Elia, Kalafatis and Ano Mera. The southern bus station, a 300m walk up from the windmills, serves the airport, Agios Ioannis, Psarou, Platys Gialos and Paradise Beach.

LOCAL BOATS In summer, caiques (small fishing boats) from Mykonos Town and Platys Gialos putter to Paradise, Super Paradise, Agrari and Elia Beaches.

Paros ΠΑΡΟΣ

POP 13,000

Paros is an attractive, laid-back island with an enticing main town, good swimming beaches and terraced hills that build up to Mt Profitis Ilias (770m). It has long been prosperous, thanks to an abundance of pure white marble (from which the *Venus de Milo* and Napoleon's tomb were sculpted).

Paros' main town and port is **Parikia**, on the west coast. Opposite the ferry terminal, on the far side of Windmill roundabout, is Plateia Mavrogenous, the main square. Agora, also known as Market St, the main commercial thoroughfare, runs southwest from the far end of the square.

Sights

Panagia Ekatontapyliani CHURCH
(Parikia; ⏲7.30am-9.30pm) Dating from AD 326 and known for its beautiful ornate interior, this is one of the most impressive churches in the Cyclades. Within the church

Paros & Antiparos

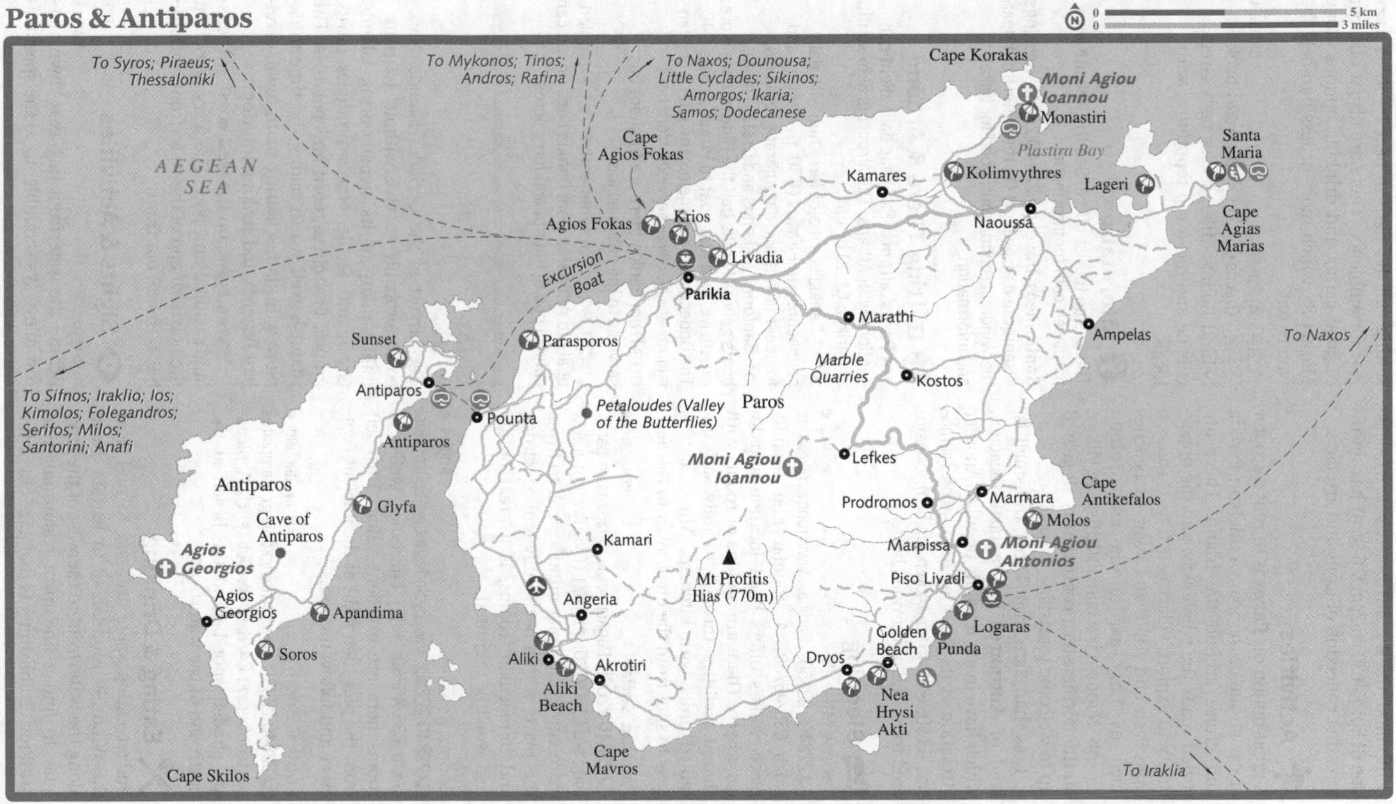

0 5 km
0 3 miles

To Syros; Piraeus; Thessaloniki
To Mykonos; Tinos; Andros; Rafina
To Naxos; Dounousa; Little Cyclades; Sikinos; Amorgos; Ikaria; Samos; Dodecanese
Cape Korakas
Moni Agiou Ioannou
Monastiri
Plastira Bay
Santa Maria
AEGEAN SEA
Cape Agios Fokas
Kamares
Kolimvythres
Lageri
Cape Agias Marias
Agios Fokas
Krios
Naoussa
Livadia
Excursion Boat
Parikia
Marathi
Ampelas
To Naxos
Sunset
Parasporos
Marble Quarries
Kostos
Antiparos
Pounta
Petaloudes (Valley of the Butterflies)
Paros
To Sifnos; Iraklio; Ios; Kimolos; Folegandros; Serifos; Milos; Santorini; Anafi
Antiparos
Lefkes
Moni Agiou Ioannou
Antiparos
Cape Antikefalos
Prodromos
Marmara
Glyfa
Cave of Antiparos
Molos
Kamari
Marpissa
Moni Agiou Antonios
Agios Georgios
Mt Profitis Ilias (770m)
Piso Livadi
Agios Georgios
Angeria
Apandima
Logaras
Golden Beach
Punda
Soros
Aliki
Akrotiri
Dryos
Aliki Beach
Nea Hrysi Akti
Cape Mavros
Cape Skilos
To Iraklia

compound, the **Byzantine Museum** (admission €1.50; ⊙9.30am-2pm & 6-9pm) has an interesting collection of icons and artefacts.

Activities

A great option on **Paros** is to rent a scooter or car at one of the many outlets in Parikia and cruise around the island. There are sealed roads the whole way, and the opportunity to explore villages such as **Naoussa**, **Marpissa** and **Aliki**, and swim at beaches such as **Logaras**, **Punda** and **Golden Beach**. Naoussa is a cute little fishing village on the northeastern coast that is all geared up to welcome tourists.

Less than 2km from Paros, the small island of **Antiparos** has fantastic beaches, which have made it wildly popular. Another attraction is its **Cave of Antiparos** (admission €3.50; ⊙10.45am-3.45pm Jun-Sep), considered to be one of Europe's best.

Sleeping

Rooms Mike ROOMS €
(☎22840 22856; Parikia; www.roomsmike.com; s/d/tr €35/45/60) A popular and friendly place, Mike's offers good location and local advice. There are options of rooms with shared facilities through to fully self-contained units with kitchens. Mike's sign is easy to spot from the quay, away to the left.

Pension Sofia PENSION €€
(☎22840 22085; Parikia; www.sofiapension-paros.com; s/d €100/120; P❄@) If you've got a few extra euros and don't mind a stroll to town, this place, with a beautifully tended garden and immaculate rooms, is a great option that won't be regretted.

Rooms Rena ROOMS €
(☎22840 22220; www.cycladesnet.gr; Epitropakis; s/d/tr €35/45/60; ❄wifi) The quiet, well-kept rooms here are excellent value. Turn left from the pier then right at the ancient cemetery and follow the signs.

Koula Camping CAMPING GROUND €
(☎22840 22801; www.campingkoula.gr; campsites per tent/person €4/8; ⊙Apr-Oct; P wifi) A pleasant shaded spot behind the beach at the north end of the waterfront.

Eating & Drinking

Budget eating spots are easy to find near the Windmill roundabout in Parikia. Head along the waterfront to the west of the ferry quay to find a line-up of restaurants and drinking establishments that gaze out at the setting sun. It's hard to beat **Pebbles Jazz Bar** for ambience. There are also a number of good eating and drinking options along Market St, which more or less parallels the waterfront.

TOP CHOICE **Ephessus** GREEK €
(mains €6-12) On the road back behind Rooms Mike; serves tasty Greek cuisine and has a top reputation with locals.

Information

There is no tourist office. See the website www.parosweb.com for information.

Santorineos Travel (☎22840 24245; bookings@santorineos-travel.gr) On the waterfront near the Windmill roundabout; good for ticketing and information.

Getting There & Around

AIR **Paros' airport** (PAS) has daily flight connections with Athens. The airport is 8km south of Parikia; €1.50 by bus.

BOAT Parikia is a major ferry hub with daily connections to Piraeus (€30, five hours) and frequent ferries and catamarans to Naxos, Ios, Santorini, Mykonos and Crete. The fast boats generally take half the time but are more expensive, eg a fast boat to Piraeus costs €40. The Dodecanese and the northeastern Aegean Islands are also well serviced from here.

BUS From Parikia there are frequent bus services to the entire island.

LOCAL BOATS In summer there are excursion boats to Antiparos from Parikia port, or you can catch a bus to Pounta and ferry across.

Naxos ΝΑΞΟΣ

POP 18,200

The largest of the Cyclades islands, Naxos could probably survive without tourism – unlike many of its neighbouring islands. Green and fertile, Naxos produces olives, grapes, figs, citrus, corn and potatoes. The island is well worth taking the time to explore with its fascinating main town, excellent beaches and striking interior.

Naxos Town, on the west coast, is the island's capital and port. The ferry quay is at the northern end of the waterfront, with the bus terminal out front.

Sights & Activities

Kastro CASTLE
Behind the waterfront in Naxos Town, narrow alleyways scramble up to the spectacu-

Naxos

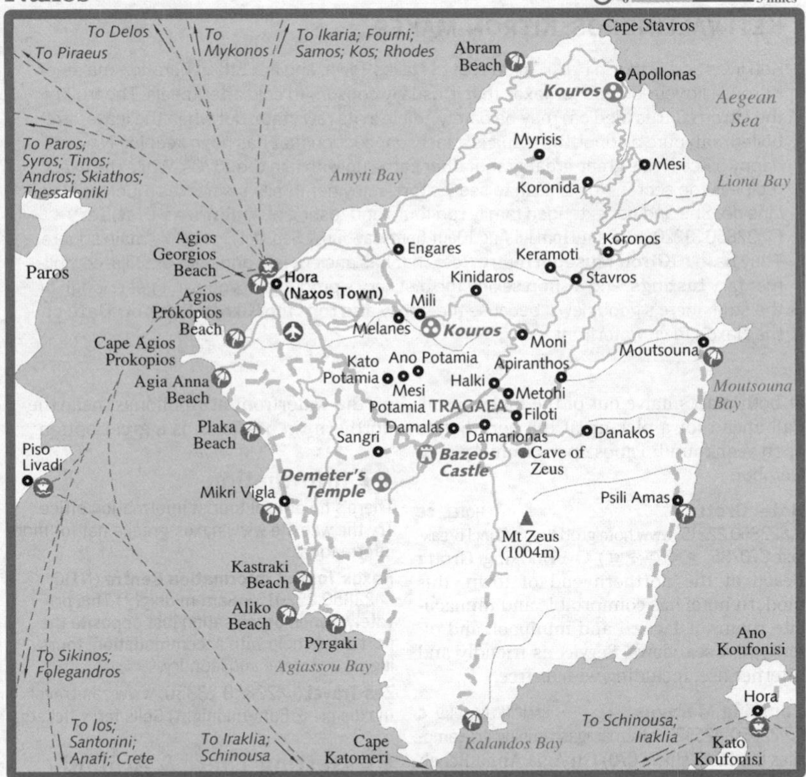

lar hilltop 13th-century *kastro*, where the Venetian Catholics lived. The *kastro* looks out over the town, and has a well-stocked **archaeological museum** (admission €3; ⏲8.30am-3pm Tue-Sun).

Beaches

The beach of **Agios Georgios** is a 10-minute walk south from the main waterfront. Beyond it, wonderful sandy beaches stretch as far south as **Pyrgaki Beach**. **Agia Anna Beach**, 6km from town, and **Plaka Beach** are lined with accommodation and packed in summer.

Villages

A hire car or scooter will help reveal Naxos' dramatic landscape. The **Tragaea** region has tranquil villages, churches atop rocky crags and huge olive groves. **Filoti**, the largest inland settlement, perches on the slopes of **Mt Zeus** (1004m), the highest peak in the Cyclades. The historic village of **Halki**, one-time centre of Naxian commerce, is well worth a visit.

Apollonas is a lovely spot near Naxos' northern tip. There's a **beach**, excellent **taverna**, and the mysterious 10.5m **kouros** (naked male statue), constructed in the 7th century BC, lying abandoned and unfinished in an ancient marble quarry.

Sleeping

TOP CHOICE **Pension Sofi** PENSION €€

(☎22850 23077; www.pensionsofi.gr; r €30-75; ❄) Run by members of the friendly Koufopoulos family, Pension Sofi is in Naxos Town, while their **Studios Panos** (☎22850 26078; www.studiospanos.com; Agios Georgios Beach; r €30-60; ❄) is a 10-minute walk away near Agios Georgios Beach. Prepare yourself to be showered with affection. Guests are met with a glass of family-made wine, and rooms are immaculate with bathroom and kitchen. Highly recommended; rates

LOCAL KNOWLEDGE

KETI VALLINDROS: KITRON-MAKER

Keti lives and works in Halki, 16km east of Naxos Town, and is a 5th-generation maker of Kitron, a liqueur unique to Naxos that is usually consumed cold after meals. The fruit of the citron (Citrus Medica) may be barely edible in its raw state, but when the leaves are boiled with pure alcohol, the result is a tasty concoction that has been keeping Naxians happy since Keti's great-great grandfather came up with it in the 1870s. While the exact recipe is top secret, Keti is keen to see visitors enjoy her family's Kitron as much as Naxians do. She and her extended family run tours and tasting at **Vallindras Distillery** (22850 31220; 10am-11pm Jul-Aug 10am-6pm May-Jun & Sep-Oct) in Halki's main square. They have a **Kitron Museum** (entry free) that has ancient jars and copper stills, complimentary **tastings**, and a **shop** selling the distillery's products. If you can't get enough of the stuff, there's good news, because the family also runs the **Kitron Bar and Café** on the Naxos Town waterfront.

at both places halve out of the high season. Call ahead for a pick-up at the port. Sofi is open year-round; Panos opens from April to October.

Hotel Grotta HOTEL €€
(22850 22215; www.hotelgrotta.gr; s/d incl breakfast €70/85; P❄@☜≋) Overlooking Grotta Beach at the northern end of town, this modern hotel has comfortable and immaculate rooms, a Jacuzzi and minipool, and offers great sea views. Service is friendly and internet use, including wi-fi, is free.

Camping Maragas CAMPING GROUND €
(22850 42552; www.maragascamping.gr; campsites €9, d €45, studio €70) On Agia Anna Beach to the south of town, this place has all sorts of options, including camping, rooms and studios, and there is a restaurant and minimarket on site.

Eating & Drinking

Naxos Town's waterfront is lined with eating and drinking establishments. Head into Market St in the Old Town, just down from the ferry quay, to find quality tavernas. South of the waterfront, but only a few minutes' walk away, Main Sq is home to plenty of excellent eateries.

Metaximas TAVERNA €
(Market St) Serving seafood at its best.

Picasso Mexican Bistro TEX-MEX €
(Agiou Arseniou) Dine on superlative Tex-Mex; near Main Sq.

East West Asian Restaurant ASIAN €
(Odos Komiakis) All your Thai, Chinese and Indian favourites; near Main Sq.

Venetico TAVERNA €
(Apollonas) If you're exploring, every village on the island has a taverna. This one, on the waterfront at Apollonas, near the northern tip of Naxos, is a great option.

Information

There's no official tourist information office. Try the website www.naxos-greece.net for more information.

Naxos Tourist Information Centre (NTIC; 22850 25201; 8am-midnight) This privately owned organisation just opposite the port offers help with accommodation, tours, luggage storage and laundry.

Zas Travel (22850 23330; www.zas-travel-naxos.gr; 8am-midnight) Sells ferry tickets.

Getting There & Around

AIR **Naxos airport** (JNX) has daily flight connections with Athens. The airport is 3km south of town; no buses – a taxi costs €15.

BOAT There are daily ferries (€30, five hours) and catamarans (€45, 3¾ hours) from Naxos to Piraeus, and good ferry and hydrofoil connections to most Cycladic islands and Crete. There are also ferries to Rhodes (€32, 14 hours, twice weekly).

BUS Buses travel to most villages regularly from the bus terminal in front of the port.

CAR & MOTORCYCLE Car and motorcycle rentals are readily available.

Ios ΙΟΣ

POP 1900

Ios has long held a reputation as 'Party Island'. There are wall-to-wall bars and nightclubs in 'the village' (Hora) that thump all night, and fantastic fun facilities at Milopotas Beach that entertain all day. You won't leave disappointed if you're there to party.

But there's more to Ios than just hedonistic activities. British poet and novelist Lawrence Durrell thought highly of Ios as a place of poetry and beauty, and there is an enduring claim that Homer was buried here, with his alleged tomb in the north of the island.

Ios' three population centres are close together on the west coast. Ormos is the port, where ferries arrive. Two kilometres inland and up overlooking the port is 'the village', Hora, while 2km down from Hora to the southeast is Milopotas Beach.

Sights & Activities

The village has an intrinsic charm with its labyrinth of white-walled streets, and it's very easy to get lost, even if you haven't had one too many. Milopotas has everything a resort beach could ask for and parties hard. More and more roads are being upgraded on the island, and a rental car or scooter is becoming a good option for exploring Ios.

Skarkos ARCHAEOLOGICAL SITE
('The Snail'; admission free; 8.30am-3pm Tue-Sun) This new attraction is also an award-winning archaeological triumph for Ios. This Bronze Age settlement crowns a low hill in the plain just to the north of Hora, and its excavations have been opened to the public.

Manganari Beach BEACH
This isolated beach on the south coast is reached by rental vehicle, or by excursion boat or bus in summer. It's a beautiful spot and the drive on Ios' newest sealed road is an experience in itself.

Homer's Tomb TOMB
You'll need your own wheels to get here, 12km north of Hora.

Meltemi Water Sports WATER SPORTS
(22860 91680; www.meltemiwatersports.com) This outfit at Milopotas Beach's far end has rental windsurfers, sailboats and canoes.

Ios

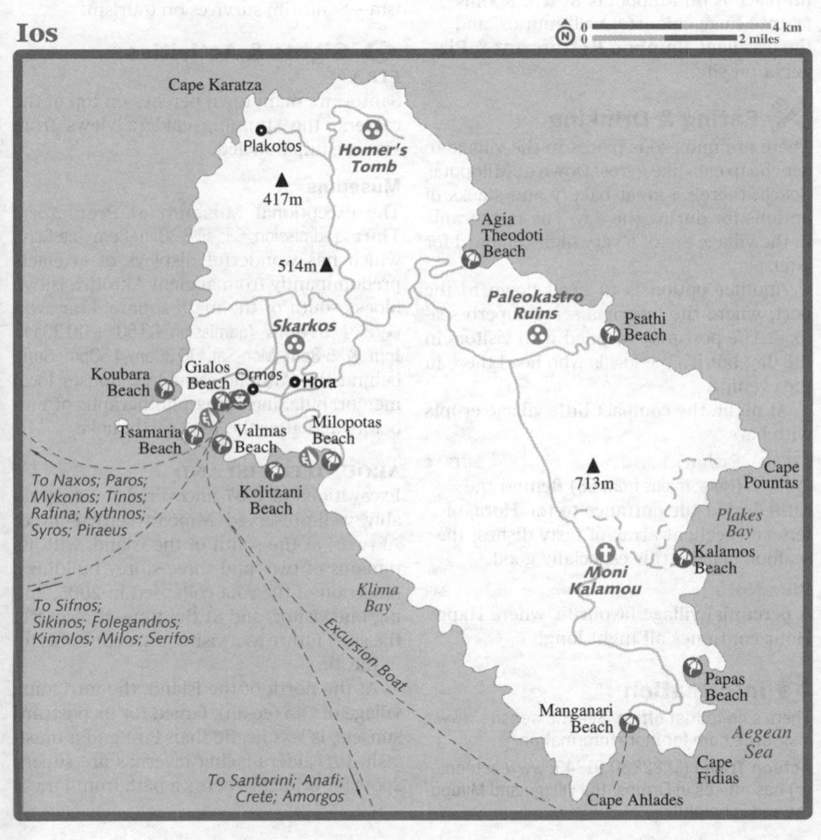

Sleeping

TOP CHOICE Francesco's ROOMS €
(☎22860 91223; www.francescos.net; Hora; dm/s/d €15/40/50; ❄@) A lively meeting place in the village with superlative views from its terrace bar, legendary Francesco's is convenient for party-going, and rates halve out of high season. The party spirit rules here, especially in the new 'giant Jacuzzi'.

Far Out Camping & Beach Club CAMPING GROUND €
(☎22860 91468; www.faroutclub.com; Milopotas; campsites per person €12, bungalows €10-20, studios €90; @≋) Right on Milopotas Beach, this place has tons of options. Facilities include camping, bungalows and hotel rooms, and its pools are open to the public. Details are on the website. It also has rental cars, quad bikes and scooters.

Hotel Nissos Ios HOTEL €€
(☎22860 91610; www.nissosios-hotel.com; Milopotas; s/d/tr €50/70/85; ❄@) This cheerful place is on Milopotas Beach. Rooms feature huge colourful wall murals, and the excellent **Bamboo Restaurant & Pizzeria** on site.

Eating & Drinking

There are numerous places in the village to get cheap eats like gyros. Down at Milopotas Beach, there's a great bakery and stacks of options for during the day. The restaurants in the village are of a very high standard for later.

Another option is to head down to the port, where the tavernas serve superb seafood. The port may be filled with visitors in the day, but it's the locals who head there in the evening.

At night, the compact little village erupts with bars.

TOP CHOICE Pithari GREEK €
(Hora; mains from €8) Behind the cathedral at the entrance to the Hora, offers an excellent array of tasty dishes; the seafood spaghetti is especially good.

Blue Note BAR
A perennial village favourite, where Happy Hour continues all night long!

Information

There's no tourist office. See the website www.iosgreece.com for more information.

Acteon Travel (☎22860 91343; www.acteon.gr) has offices in Ormos, the village and Milopotas and is helpful.

Getting There & Around

BOAT Ios has daily ferry connections with Piraeus (€31.50, seven hours), and being strategically placed between Mykonos and Santorini, there are frequent catamarans and ferries to the major Cycladic islands and Crete.

BUS There are buses every 15 minutes between the port, the village and Milopotas Beach until early morning. Buses head to Manganari Beach in summer (€3 each way).

Santorini (Thira)
ΣΑΝΤΟΡΙΝΗ (ΘΗΡΑ)

POP 13,500

Stunning Santorini is unique and should not be missed. The startling sight of the submerged caldera almost encircled by sheer lava-layered cliffs – topped off by clifftop towns that look like a dusting of icing sugar – will grab your attention and not let it go. If you turn up in high season, though, be prepared for relentless crowds and commercialism – Santorini survives on tourism.

Sights & Activities

FIRA

Santorini's main town perches on top of the caldera; the stunning caldera views from Fira are unparalleled.

Museums

The exceptional **Museum of Prehistoric Thira** (admission €3; ⏲8.30am-8pm Tue-Sun), which has wonderful displays of artefacts predominantly from ancient Akrotiri, is two blocks south of the main square. **Megaron Gyzi Museum** (admission €3.50; ⏲10.30am-1pm & 5-8pm Mon-Sat, 10.30am-4.30pm Sun), behind the Catholic cathedral, houses local memorabilia, including photographs of Fira before and after the 1956 earthquake.

AROUND THE ISLAND

Excavations in 1967 uncovered the remarkably well-preserved Minoan settlement of **Akrotiri** at the south of the island, with its remains of two- and three-storey buildings. A section of the roof collapsed in 2005, killing one visitor, and at the time of research, the site's future as a visitor attraction was up in the air.

At the north of the island, the intriguing village of **Oia** (ee-ah), famed for its postcard sunsets, is less hectic than Fira and a must-visit. Its caldera-facing tavernas are superb spots for brunch. There's a path from Fira to

Oia along the top of the caldera that takes three to four hours to walk.

Santorini's black-sand **beaches** of **Perissa** and **Kamari** sizzle – beach mats are essential.

Of the surrounding islets, only **Thirasia** is inhabited. Visitors can clamber around on volcanic lava on **Nea Kameni** then swim into warm springs in the sea at **Palia Kameni**; there are various excursions available to get you there.

TOP CHOICE **Santo Wines** (☎22860 22596; www.santowines.gr; Pyrgos) is a great spot to try the delectable Assyrtico crisp dry white wine while savouring unbelievable views. Santorini is home to an increasing number of excellent wineries.

Sleeping

Hotel Keti TRADITIONAL HOTEL €€
(☎22860 22324; www.hotelketi.gr; Agiou Mina, Fira; d/tr €95/120; ❄@) Overlooking the caldera, with views to die for, Hotel Keti has traditional rooms carved into the cliffs. Some rooms have Jacuzzis. Head down just before Hotel Atlantis and follow the signs.

Hotel Atlantis HOTEL €€€
(☎22860 22232; www.atlantishotel.gr; Fira; s/d incl breakfast €200/300; P❄@≋) Perfectly

Santorini (Thira)

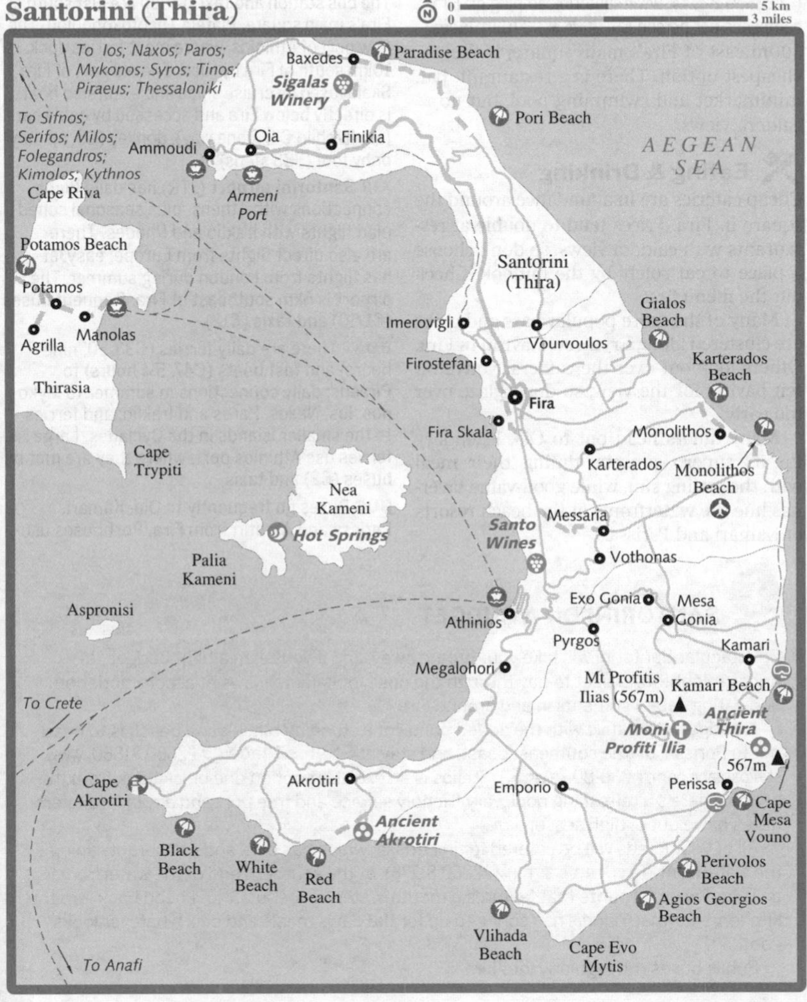

positioned and epitomising Santorini style, Atlantis is the oldest and most impressive place in Fira. With bright, airy rooms, swimming pool, relaxing terraces and lounges, it is a superb place to stay.

Pension Petros PENSION €
(☎22860 22573; www.hotelpetros-santorini.gr; Fira; s/d/tr €60/70/85; ❄) Three hundred metres east of the square, Petros offers decent rooms at good rates, free airport and port transfers, but no caldera views. It's a good budget option, with rates halving outside high season. The friendly family also has other hotels.

Santorini Camping CAMPING GROUND €
(☎22860 22944; www.santorinicamping.gr; Fira; campsites per person €9; P@≋) This place, 500m east of Fira's main square, is the cheapest option. There is a restaurant, bar, minimarket and swimming pool, but no caldera views.

Eating & Drinking

Cheap eateries are in abundance around the square in Fira. Prices tend to double at restaurants with caldera views, so don't choose a place to eat solely by the outlook. Check out the menu first.

Many of the more popular bars and clubs are clustered along Erythrou Stavrou in Fira. Others look out over the caldera; you're often paying for the view, so don't glaze over too early.

Many diners head out to Oia, legendary for its superb sunsets, timing their meal with the setting sun, while good-value tavernas line the waterfronts at the beach resorts of Kamari and Perissa.

Fanari GREEK €
(☎22860 25107; www.fanari-restaurant.gr) On the street leading down to the old port, serves up both tasty traditional dishes and superlative views.

Information

There is no tourist office. Try the website www.santorini.net for more information.

Dakoutros Travel (☎22860 22958; www.dakoutrostravel.gr; ⊙8.30am-10pm) Opposite the taxi station in Fira; extremely helpful and good for ticketing.

Getting There & Around

The bus station and taxi station are just south of Fira's main square, Plateia Theotokopoulou. The new port of Athinios, where most ferries dock, is 10km south of Fira by road. The old port of Fira Skala, used by cruise ships and excursion boats, is directly below Fira and accessed by cable car (adult/child €4/2 one way), donkey (€5, up only) or by foot (588 steps)

AIR **Santorini airport** (JTR) has daily flight connections with Athens, plus seasonal scheduled flights with Iraklio and Rhodes. There are also direct flights from Europe; easyJet has flights from London during summer. The airport is 5km southeast of Fira; frequent buses (€1.50) and taxis (€12).

BOAT There are daily ferries (€33.50, nine hours) and fast boats (€47, 5¼ hours) to Piraeus; daily connections in summer to Mykonos, Ios, Naxos, Paros and Iraklio; and ferries to the smaller islands in the Cyclades. Large ferries use Athinios port, where they are met by buses (€2) and taxis.

BUS Buses go frequently to Oia, Kamari, Perissa and Akrotiri from Fira. Port buses usu-

SANTORINI ON A BUDGET

Spectacular Santorini will take your breath away, and if you're on a tight budget, its prices might too. Expect to pay through the nose for caldera views at accommodation and eating establishments in and around Fira.

A budget alternative with the added bonus of a stunning black-sand beach is to head out to Perissa, on the southeast coast, and stay at **Stelios Place** (☎22860 81860; www.steliosplace.com; r €30-80; P❄≋). Stelios is an excellent option one block back from the beach. There's a refreshing pool, very friendly service and free port and airport transfers. Rates halve out of high season.

All of your needs will be catered for in Perissa, which has bars and restaurants lining the waterfront. **Taverna Lava** (☎22860 81776), at the southern end of the waterfront, is an island-wide favourite that features a mouth-watering menu. Or just head back into the kitchen, see what Yiannis has conjured up for the day's meals and pick whatever looks good.

Public buses run regularly into Fira.

ally leave Fira, Kamari and Perissa one to 1½ hours before ferry departures.

CAR & MOTORCYCLE A rental car or scooter is a great option on Santorini.

CRETE ΚΡΗΤΗ

POP 540,000

Crete is Greece's largest and most southerly island and its size and distance from the rest of Greece give it the feel of a different country. With its dramatic landscape and unique cultural identity, Crete is a delight to explore.

The island is split by a spectacular chain of mountains running east to west. Major towns are on the more hospitable northern coast, while most of the southern coast is too precipitous to support large settlements. The rugged mountainous interior, dotted with caves and sliced by dramatic gorges, offers rigorous hiking and climbing.

While Crete's proud, friendly and hospitable people have enthusiastically embraced tourism, they continue to fiercely protect their traditions and culture – and it is the people that remain a major part of the island's appeal.

For more detailed information, snap up a copy of Lonely Planet's *Crete*. Good websites on Crete include www.interkriti.org, www.infocrete.com and www.explorecrete.com.

History

Crete was the birthplace of Minoan culture, Europe's first advanced civilisation, which flourished between 2800 and 1450 BC. Very little is known of Minoan civilisation, which came to an abrupt end, possibly destroyed by Santorini's volcanic eruption in around 1650 BC. Later, Crete passed from the warlike Dorians to the Romans, and then to the Genoese, who in turn sold it to the Venetians. Under the Venetians, Crete became a refuge for artists, writers and philosophers, who fled after it fell to the Turks. Their influence inspired the young Cretan painter Domenikos Theotokopoulos, who moved to Spain and there won immortality as the great El Greco.

The Turks conquered Crete in 1670. In 1898 Crete became a British protectorate after a series of insurrections and was united with independent Greece in 1913. There was fierce fighting during WWII when a German airborne invasion defeated Allied forces in the 10-day Battle of Crete. A fierce resistance movement drew heavy German reprisals, including the slaughter of whole villages.

Iraklio ΗΡΑΚΛΕΙΟ

POP 131,000

Iraklio (ee-*rah*-klee-oh; often spelt Heraklion), Crete's capital, is a bustling modern city and the fifth-largest in Greece. It has a lively city centre, an excellent archaeological museum and is close to Knossos, Crete's major visitor attraction.

Iraklio's harbours face north into the Sea of Crete. The old harbour is instantly recognisable as it is protected by the old Venetian fortress. The new harbour is 400m east. Plateia Venizelou, known for its Lion Fountain, is the heart of the city, 400m south of the old harbour up 25 Avgoustou.

Sights

Archaeological Museum MUSEUM
(Map p660; Xanthoudidou 2; adult/student €6/3; ⏲8am-1pm Mon, 8am-8pm Tue-Sun) The outstanding Minoan collection here is second only to that of the national museum in Athens. The museum was under long-term reconstruction at the time of research.

Koules Venetian Fortress FORTRESS
(Map p660; admission €2; ⏲9am-6pm Tue-Sun) Protecting the old harbour, this impressive fortress is also known as Rocca al Mare, which, like the city walls, was built by the Venetians in the 16th century.

Battle of Crete Museum MUSEUM
(Map p660; cnr Doukos Beaufort & Hatzidaki; admission free; ⏲8am-3pm) Chronicles the historic WWII battle with photographs, letters, uniforms and weapons.

Sleeping

TOP CHOICE **Lato Boutique Hotel** BOUTIQUE HOTEL €€
(Map p660; ☎28102 28103; www.lato.gr; Epimenidou 15; s/d €100/127; ❄@) This stylish boutique hotel overlooking the waterfront is a top place to stay. Ask for a room with harbour views. The contemporary interior design extends to the bar, breakfast restaurant and **Brilliant** (☎28103 34959), the superb fine-dining restaurant on the ground floor.

Hotel Mirabello HOTEL €
(Map p660; ☎28102 85052; www.mirabello-hotel.gr; Theotokopoulou 20; s/d €35/45; ❄@) A pleasant, relaxed budget hotel on a quiet street in the centre of town, this place is run by an

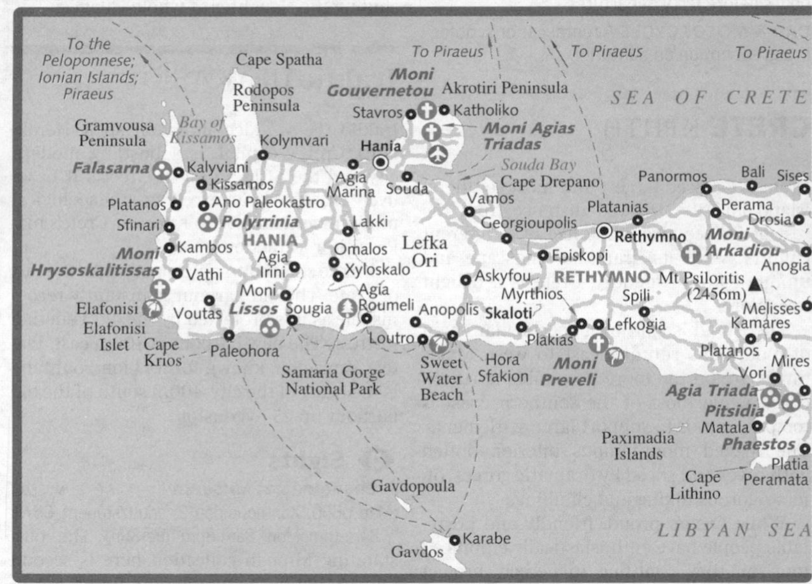

ex-sea captain who has travelled the world. A good-value option. Check out the excellent website.

Rent Rooms Hellas ROOMS €

(Map p660; ☎28102 88851; Handakos 24; dm/d/tr without bathroom €12/30/42) A popular budget choice, this place has a lively atmosphere, packed dorms, a rooftop bar and a bargain breakfast (from €3).

Eating & Drinking

There's a congregation of cheap eateries, bars and cafes in the Plateia Venizelou (Morosini Fountain) and El Greco Park area. The places around the park are packed at night. A bustling, colourful market runs all the way along 1866, with a number of reasonably priced tavernas. Head down towards the old harbour for plenty of seafood options.

Giakoumis Taverna TAVERNA €

(Map p660) One of the best, offering up Cretan specialities hot off the grill.

Ippokambos Ouzerie SEAFOOD €

(Map p660) A local favourite that attracts crowds of seafood lovers.

Café Plus BAR

(Map p660) At the nexus of the pedestrianised zones, this place overflows with locals, especially in the early evening.

Information

TOURIST INFORMATION Tourist office (Map p660; ☎28102 46299; Xanthoudidou 1; ⏲8.30am-8.30pm Apr-Oct, to 3pm Nov-Mar) Opposite the Archaeological Museum.

TRAVEL AGENCIES Skoutelis Travel (☎28102 80808; www.skoutelis.gr; 25 Avgoustou 20) Between Plateia Venizelou and the old harbour; handles airline and ferry bookings, and rents cars.

WEBSITES www.heraklion-city.gr

Getting There & Around

AIR There are many flights departing daily from Iraklio's **Nikos Kazantzakis airport** (HER) for Athens and, in summer, regular flights to Thessaloniki and Rhodes. easyJet has scheduled flights to seven destinations across Europe. Summer sees even more charter flights arrive from all over. The airport is 5km east of town. Bus 1 travels between the airport and city centre (Map p660; €1.20) every 15 minutes from 6am to 1am. It stops at Plateia Eleftherias, across the road from the Archaeological Museum.

BOAT Daily ferries service Piraeus (€37, seven hours), and catamarans head daily to Santorini and continue on to other Cycladic islands. Twice weekly, ferries sail east to Rhodes (€28, 12 hours) via Agios Nikolaos, Sitia, Kassos, Karpathos and Halki.

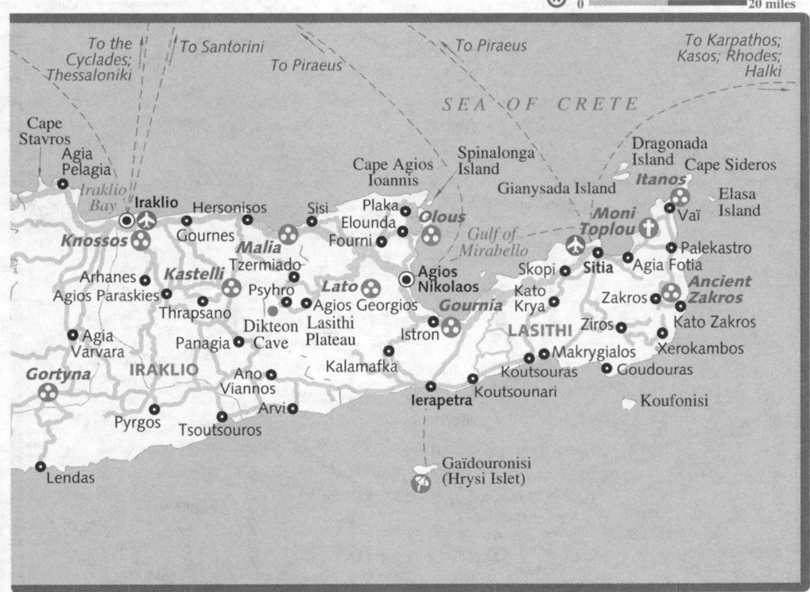

BUS KTEL (www.ktel.org) Runs the buses on Crete; has useful tourist information inside Bus Station A.

Iraklio has two bus stations. The main **Bus Station A** (Map p660) is just inland from the new harbour and serves eastern Crete (Agios Nikolaos, Ierapetra, Sitia, Malia and the Lasithi Plateau), as well as Hania and Rethymno.

Bus Station B (off Map p660), 50m beyond the Hania Gate, serves the southern route (Phaestos, Matala and Anogia).

Check out www.ktel.org for long-distance bus information.

Knossos ΚΝΩΣΣΟΣ

Five kilometres south of Iraklio, **Knossos** (☎28102 31940; admission €6; ⏲8am-7pm Jun-Oct, to 3pm Nov-May) was the capital of Minoan Crete, and is now the island's major tourist attraction.

Knossos (k-nos-*os*) is the most famous of Crete's Minoan sites and is the inspiration for the myth of the Minotaur. According to legend, King Minos of Knossos was given a magnificent white bull to sacrifice to the god Poseidon, but decided to keep it. This enraged Poseidon, who punished the king by causing his wife Pasiphae to fall in love with the animal. The result of this odd union was the Minotaur – half-man and half-bull – who lived in a labyrinth beneath the king's palace, munching on youths and maidens.

In 1900 Arthur Evans uncovered the ruins of Knossos. Although archaeologists tend to disparage Evans' reconstruction, the buildings – incorporating an immense palace, courtyards, private apartments, baths, lively frescos and more – give a fine idea of what a Minoan palace might have looked like.

Buses to Knossos (€1.30, three per hour; 20min) leave from Bus Station A.

Phaestos & Other Minoan Sites ΦΑΙΣΤΟΣ

Phaestos (☎29820 42315; admission €6; ⏲8am-7pm May-Oct, to 5pm Nov-Apr), 63km southwest of Iraklio, is Crete's second-most important Minoan site. While not as impressive as Knossos, Phaestos (fes-*tos*) is still worth a visit for its stunning views of the surrounding Mesara plain and Mt Psiloritis (2456m; also known as Mt Ida). The layout is similar to Knossos, with rooms arranged around a central courtyard. Eight buses a day head to Phaestos from Iraklio's Bus Station B (€5.90, 1½ hours).

Other important Minoan sites can be found at **Malia**, 34km east of Iraklio, where

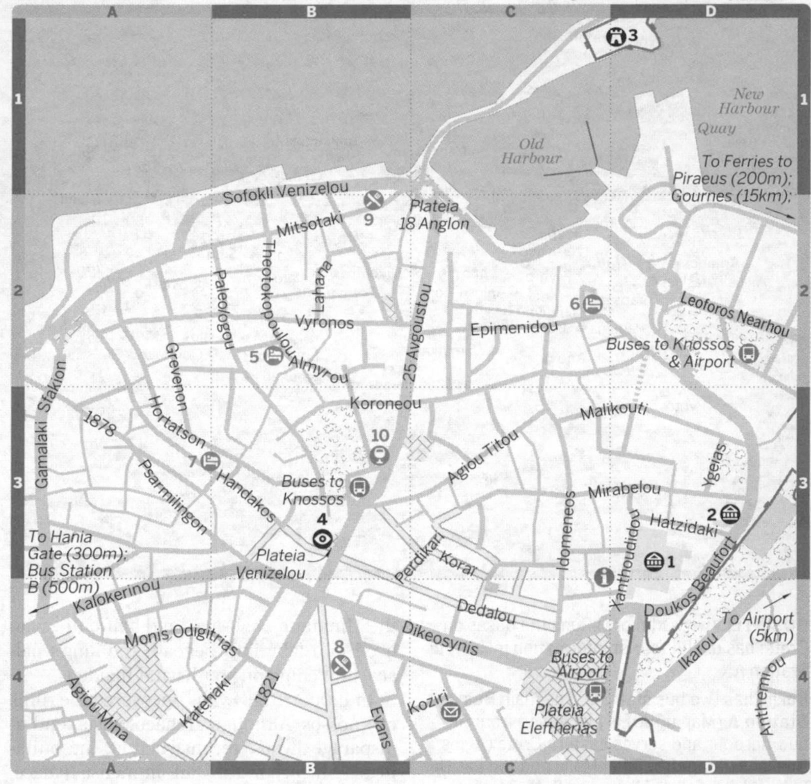

there's a palace complex and adjoining town, and **Zakros**, 40km southeast of Sitia, the last Minoan palace to have been discovered, in 1962.

Rethymno ΡΕΘΥΜΝΟ

POP 28,000

Rethymno (*reth*-im-no) is Crete's third-largest town. It's also one of the island's architectural treasures, due to its stunning fortress and mix of Venetian and Turkish houses in the old quarter. A compact town, most spots of interest are within a small area around the old Venetian harbour.

The old quarter is on a peninsula that juts out into the Sea of Crete; the fortress sits at its head, while the Venetian harbour, ferry quay and beach are on its eastern side. El Venizelou is the main strip along the waterfront and beach. Running parallel behind it is Arkadiou, the main commercial street.

Rethymno's 16th-century **Venetian fortezza** (fortress; Paleokastro Hill; admission €3; ⌚8am-8pm May-Oct) is the site of the city's ancient acropolis and affords great views across the town and mountains. The main gate is on the eastern side of the fortress, opposite the interesting **archaeological museum** (☎28310 54668; admission €3; ⌚8.30am-3pm Tue-Sun), which was once a prison.

Happy Walker (☎28310 52920; www.happywalker.com; Tombazi 56) runs an excellent program of daily walks in the countryside and also longer walking tours.

Sea Front (☎28310 51981; www.rethymnoatcrete.com; Arkadiou 159; d €35-50; ❄) has all sorts of sleeping options and is ideally positioned with beach views and spacious rooms. **Hotel Fortezza** (☎28310 55551; www.fortezza.gr; Melissinou 16; s/d incl breakfast €70/85; P❄≋) is more upmarket; with a refreshing pool, it's in a refurbished old building in the heart of the Old Town. **Rethymno**

Iraklio

Sights

1 Archaeological Museum D3
2 Battle of Crete Museum D3
3 Koules Venetian Fortress D1
4 Lion Fountain B3

Sleeping

5 Hotel Mirabello B2
6 Lato Boutique Hotel C2
7 Rent Rooms Hellas A3

Eating

Brilliant .... (see 6)
8 Giakoumis Taverna B4
9 Ippokambos Ouzeri B2

Drinking

10 Café Plus B3

Youth Hostel (☎28310 22848; www.yhrethymno.com; Tombazi 41; dm €10) is a well-run place with crowded dorms, free hot showers and no curfew.

The **municipal tourist office** (☎28310 29148; www.rethymno.gr; Eleftheriou Venizelou; ⏱9am-8.30pm), on the beach side of El Venizelou, is convenient and helpful. **Ellotia Tours** (☎28310 24533; www.rethymnoatcrete.com; Arkadiou 155) will answer all transport, accommodation and tour inquiries.

There are regular ferries between Piraeus and Rethymno (€30, nine hours), and a high-speed service in summer. Buses depart regularly to Iraklio (€6.5, 1½ hours) and Hania (€6, one hour).

Hania XANIA

POP 53,500

Crete's most romantic, evocative and alluring town, Hania (hahn-*yah*; often spelt Chania) is the former capital and the island's second-largest city. There is a rich mosaic of Venetian and Ottoman architecture, particularly in the area of the old harbour, which lures tourists in droves. Modern Hania retains the exoticism of a city caught between East and West, and is an excellent base for exploring nearby idyllic beaches and a spectacular mountainous interior.

Sights & Activities

Old Harbour HISTORIC DISTRICT

From Plateia 1866, the old harbour is a short walk down Halidon. A stroll around here is a must for any visitor to Hania. It is worth the 1.5km walk around the sea wall to get to the Venetian **lighthouse** (Map p662) at the entrance to the harbour.

Archaeological Museum MUSEUM

(Map p662; Halidon 30; admission €2; ⏱8.30am-3pm Tue-Sun) The museum is housed in a 16th-century Venetian church that the Turks made into a mosque. The building became a movie theatre in 1913 and then was a munitions depot for the Germans during WWII.

Food Market MARKET

(Map p662) Hania's covered food market, in a massive cross-shaped building, is definitely worth an inspection.

Sleeping

TOP CHOICE **Pension Lena** PENSION €

(Map p662; ☎28210 86860; www.lenachania.gr; Ritsou 5; s/d €35/55; ❄) For some real character in where you stay, Lena's pension in an old Turkish building near the mouth of the old harbour is the place to go. Help yourself to one of the appealing rooms if proprietor Lena isn't there – pick from the available ones on the list on the blackboard.

Amphora Hotel HOTEL €€

(Map p662; ☎28210 93224; www.amphora.gr; Parodos Theotokopoulou 20; s/d €95/110; ❄) Most easily found from the waterfront, this is Hania's most historically evocative hotel. Amphora is in an impressively restored Venetian mansion with elegantly decorated rooms around a courtyard. The hotel also runs the **waterfront restaurant**, which ranks as the best along that golden mile.

Camping Hania CAMPING GROUND €

(off Map p662; ☎28210 31138; campsites per tent/person €4/5; P ≋) Take the Kalamaki Beach bus from the east corner of Plateia 1866 (every 15 minutes) to get to this camping ground, which is 3km west of town on the beach. There is a restaurant, bar and minimarket.

Eating & Drinking

The entire waterfront of the old harbour is lined with restaurants and tavernas, many of which qualify as tourist traps. Watch out for touts trying to reel you in. There are a number of good options one street back.

Taverna Tamam TAVERNA €€

(Map p662; ☎28210 58639; Zambeliou 49; 🖉) A taverna in an old converted Turkish bathhouse, with tables that spill out onto the

Hania

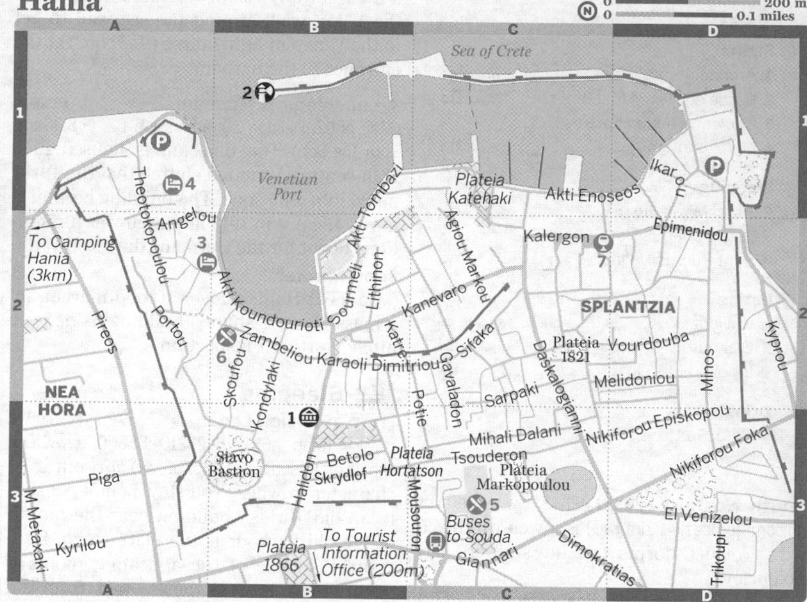

Hania

Sights

1 Archaeological Museum B3
Food Market .... (see 5)
2 Lighthouse B1

Sleeping

3 Amphora Hotel A2
4 Pension Lena A1

Eating

Amphora .... (see 3)
5 Food Market C3
Michelas .... (see 5)
6 Taverna Tamam B2

Drinking

7 Café Kriti C2

street. This place has tasty soups and a superb selection of vegetarian specialities.

TOP CHOICE Michelas CRETAN €
(Map p662; ☎28210 90026; ⏲10am-4pm Mon-Sat) Has authentic Cretan specialities at reasonable prices. This family-run place uses only Cretan ingredients and cooks up a great selection each day that you can peruse, then choose from.

Café Kriti BAR
(Map p662; Kalergon 22; ⏲8pm-late) Near the eastern end of the Venetian harbour, this place is known for its down-to-earth atmosphere and live traditional Cretan music.

Information

TOURIST INFORMATION Tourist information office (off Map p662; ☎28210 36155; Kydonias 29; ⏲8am-2.30pm) Under the Town Hall; is helpful and provides practical information and maps.

TRAVEL AGENCIES Tellus Travel (☎28210 91500; www.tellustravel.gr; Halidon 108; ⏲8am-11pm) Schedules and ticketing; rents out cars.

WEBSITES www.chania.gr

Getting There & Away

AIR There are several flights a day between **Hania airport** (CHQ) and Athens and five flights a week to Thessaloniki. An increasing number of budget airlines are flying directly into Hania; easyJet has flights from London. The airport is 14km east of town on the Akrotiri Peninsula. Taxis to town cost €15; there are few buses.

BOAT Daily ferries sail between Piraeus (€30, nine hours) and the port of Souda, 9km southeast of Hania. There are also increasing numbers of faster boats. Frequent buses (Map p662; €1.30) and taxis (€10) connect town and Souda.

BUS Frequent buses run along Crete's northern coast to Iraklio (€11, 2¾ hours, half-hourly), Rethymno (€6, one hour, half hourly) and Kastelli-Kissamos (€4, one hour, 14 daily); buses run less frequently to Paleohora (€6.50, one hour 50 minutes, four daily), Omalos (€5.90, one hour, three daily) and Hora Sfakion (€6.50, 1½ hours, three daily) from the main bus station on Kydonias.

Hania's bus station is on Kydonias, two blocks southwest of Plateia 1866, one of the city's main squares. Buses for the beaches west of Hania leave from the eastern side of Plateia 1866.

Samaria Gorge ΦΑΡΑΓΓΙ ΤΗΣ ΣΑΜΑΡΙΑΣ

The **Samaria Gorge** (☎28250 67179; admission €5; ⏲6am-3pm May–mid-Oct) is one of Europe's most spectacular gorges and a superb hike. Walkers should take rugged footwear, food, drinks and sun protection for this strenuous five- to six-hour trek.

You can do the walk as part of an excursion tour, or independently by taking the Omalos bus from the main bus station in Hania (€5.90, one hour) to the head of the gorge at Xyloskalo (1230m) at 7.30am, 8.30am and 2pm. It's a 16.7km walk out (all downhill) to Agia Roumeli on the coast, from where you take a boat to Hora Sfakion (€8, 1¼ hours, three daily) and then a bus back to Hania (€6.50, 1½ hours, three daily). You are not allowed to spend the night in the gorge, so you need to complete the walk in a day.

Paleohora & the Southwest Coast ΠΑΛΑΙΟΧΩΡΑ

POP 2200

Paleohora (pal-ee-o-*hor*-a) has a sleepy end-of-the-line feel about it. Isolated and a bit hard to get to, the village is on a peninsula with a sandy beach to the west and a pebbly beach to the east. On summer evenings the main street is closed to traffic and the tavernas move onto the road. If you're after a relaxing few days, Paleohora is a great spot to chill out.

Heading south from the bus stop, you'll find the main street, which is called Eleftheriou Venizelou.

The ruins of the 13th-century **Venetian castle** are worth clambering over, although there's not much left after the fortress was destroyed by the Turks, the pirate Barbarossa in the 16th-century and then the Germans during WWII.

Homestay Anonymous (☎28230 41509; www.cityofpaleochora.gr/cp; s/d/tr €23/28/32; ❄) is a great option with its warm service and communal kitchen. Across the road from the sandy beach, the refurbished **Poseidon Hotel** (☎28230 41374; www.interkriti.net/hotel/paleohora/poseidon; s/d/apt €35/40/50; ❄@) has a mix of tidy double rooms, studios and apartments. **Camping Paleohora** (☎28230 41120; campsites per tent/person €3/5) is 1.5km

BEAT THE CROWDS AT SAMARIA

The Samaria Gorge walk is extremely popular and can get quite crowded, especially in summer. Most walkers have given the gorge a day and are on a rushed trip from Hania and other northern-coast cities.

If you've got a bit of time on your hands, and decide to do things on your own, there are a couple of excellent options.

One is to take the 2pm bus from Hania and spend the night in the Cretan mountains at 1200m above sea level in **Omalos** (population 30) at the very pleasant **Neos Omalos Hotel** (☎28210 67269; www.neos-omalos.gr; s/d €20/30). The hotel's restaurant serves excellent Cretan cuisine and local wine by the litre (€6); there's a shuttle to the start of the gorge track the next morning. Keen hikers may want to stay here a couple of nights and tackle Mt Gingilos (2080m; five hours return from Xyloskalo) before hiking the gorge.

Another option is to leave from Hania in the morning, but let the sprinters go and take your time hiking through this stupendous gorge. When you hit the coast at **Agia Roumeli** (population 125), down a cool beer, take a dip in the refreshing Libyan Sea, savour the tasty Cretan specials at **Faragi Restaurant & Rooms** (☎28250 91225; s/d/tr €20/30/35; ❄) and stay the night in the tidy rooms above the restaurant. The next day you can take a ferry either west to Sougia or Paleohora, or east to Loutro or Hora Sfakion.

northeast of town, near the pebble beach. There's a taverna but no minimarket here.

There are plenty of eating options on the main street. Vegetarians rave about **Third Eye** (mains from €5; ✎), just inland from the sandy beach. Specialities include a tempting range of Greek-Asian fusion dishes.

There's a welcoming **tourist office** (☎28230 41507; ⌚10am-1pm & 6-9pm Wed-Mon May-Oct) on the pebble beach road near the harbour and ferry quay. The opening hours listed here are indicative only! Back on the main street, **Notos Rentals/Tsiskakis Travel** (☎28230 42110; www.notoscar.com; ⌚8am-10pm) handles almost everything, including tickets, rental cars/scooters and internet access.

There are six buses daily between Hania and Paleohora (€6.50, two hours). A bus for Samaria Gorge hikers leaves for Omalos (€5.50, two hours) each morning at 6.15am.

Further east along Crete's southwest coast are **Sougia**, **Agia Roumeli** (at the mouth of the Samaria Gorge), **Loutro** and **Hora Sfakion**. No road links the coastal resorts, but a daily boat from Paleohora to Sougia (€7.50, one hour), Agia Roumeli (€11, 1½ hours), Loutro (€13, 2½ hours) and Hora Sfakion (€14, three hours) connects the villages in summer. The ferry leaves Paleohora at 9.45am and returns from Hora Sfakion at 1pm. It's also possible to walk right along this southern coast.

WORTH A TRIP

LOUTRO

The tiny village of **Loutro** (population 90) is a particularly picturesque spot, curled around the only natural harbour on the southern coast of Crete. It's a great place for a break. With no vehicle access, the only way in is by boat or on foot. Ferries drop in daily from Hora Sfakion to the east, and from Paleohora, Sougia and Agia Roumeli to the west.

Hotel Porto Loutro (☎28250 91433; www.hotelportoloutro.com; s/d/tr incl breakfast €45/55/65; ❄) has tasteful rooms with balconies overlooking the harbour. The village beach, excellent walks, rental kayaks, and boat transfers to Sweetwater Beach will help to fill in a peaceful few days. Take a book and chill out.

Lasithi Plateau ΟΡΟΠΕΔΙΟ ΛΑΣΙΘΙΟΥ

The impressive mountain-fringed Lasithi Plateau in eastern Crete is laid out like an immense patchwork quilt. At 900m above sea level, it is a vast flat expanse of orchards and fields, once dotted with thousands of stone windmills with white canvas sails. There are still plenty of windmills, but most are now of the rusted metal variety and don't work.

There are 20 villages around the periphery of the plain, the largest being **Tzermiado** (population 750), **Agios Georgios** (population 550) and **Psyhro** (population 210).

The **Dikteon Cave** (☎28440 31316; admission €4; ⌚8am-6pm) is where, according to mythology, Rhea hid the newborn Zeus from Cronos, his offspring-gobbling father. The cave, which covers 2200 sq metres and features numerous stalactites and stalagmites, is 1km from the village of Psyhro.

There are daily buses to the area from Iraklio (€5, two hours), though having your own wheels would make life a lot easier.

Agios Nikolaos ΑΓΙΟΣ ΝΙΚΟΛΑΟΣ

POP 11,000

Agios Nikolaos (*ah*-yee-os nih-*ko*-laos) is an attractive former fishing village on Crete's northeast coast. The de facto town centre is around the picturesque **Voulismeni Lake**, which is ringed with cafes and tavernas, and is linked to the sea by a short canal. The ferry port is 150m past the canal.

The two nice little beaches in town, **Kytroplatia** and **Ammos**, get a bit crowded in summer. **Almyros Beach**, about 1km south, gets less so. Agios Nikolaos acts as a base for excursion tours to **Spinalonga Island**. The island's massive fortress was built by the Venetians in 1579 but taken by the Turks in 1715. It later became a leper colony. Nowadays it's a fascinating place to explore. Tours cost around €25.

Pergola Hotel (☎28410 28152; Sarolidi 20; s/d €35-40; ❄) is a friendly family-run place out near the ferry port, with clean rooms, balconies and sea views. **Du Lac Hotel** (☎28410 22711; www.dulachotel.gr; Oktovriou 17; s/d €40/60) is a refurbished hotel in a great location with views out over the lake.

Finding a place to eat will not be a problem. **Taverna Itanos** (☎28410 25340; Kyprou 1;

mains €4-10), tucked away on a backstreet off the main square, is superb, has reasonable prices and offers the opportunity to wander into the kitchen and see what looks good.

The very helpful **municipal tourist office** (☎28410 22357; www.agiosnikolaos.gr; ⌚8am-9pm Apr-Nov) is on the north side of the bridge over the canal and does a good job of finding sleeping options.

Ferries depart for Rhodes (€30, 11 hours) via Sitia, Kasos, Karpathos and Halki twice a week. There are also two weekly ferries to Piraeus (€34, 12 hours). Buses to Iraklio run every 30 minutes (€6.50, 1½ hours).

Sitia ΣΗΤΕΙΑ

POP 8750

Sitia (si-*tee*-a) is a laid-back little town in the northeastern corner of Crete that has escaped much of the tourism frenzy along the north coast. It is on an attractive bay flanked by mountains, and is an easy place to unwind.

The main square, Plateia Iroon Plytehniou, is in the corner of the bay, and recognisable by its palm trees and statue of a dying soldier. The ferry port is about 500m to the northeast.

Porto Belis Travel (☎28430 22370; www.portobelis-crete.gr; Karamanli Aven 34), on the waterfront just before the start of the town beach, is a one-stop shop, handling ticketing, rental cars and scooters, and accommodation bookings in town. It also runs **Porto Belis House** (☎28430 22370; d/q €34/57; ❄) above the travel agency. These rooms are immaculate, have kitchens and look straight out onto the beach.

Hotel Arhontiko (☎28430 28172; Kondylaki 16; d/studio €30/35), two blocks uphill from the port, has spotless rooms with shared bathrooms in a beautifully maintained neoclassical building. **Itanos Hotel** (☎28430 22900; www.itanoshotel.com; Karamanli 4; s/d incl breakfast €42/56; ❄@) is an upmarket establishment next to the square with its own excellent **Itanos Taverna** on the waterfront outside the front door.

The waterfront is lined with tavernas. **Balcony** (☎28430 25084; Foundalidou 19; mains €10-18), a couple of streets back from the waterfront, is the finest dining in Sitia. It's in a charmingly decorated neoclassical building.

The helpful **tourist office** (☎28430 28300; Karamanli; ⌚9.30am-2.30pm & 5-8.30pm Mon-Fri, 9.30am-2pm Sat), on the waterfront, has town maps.

Sitia airport (JSH) has flights to Athens. There are two ferries per week via Kasos, Karpathos and Halki to Rhodes (€27, 14 hours), and two to Piraeus (€32, 14½ hours). There are five buses daily to Iraklio (€13.10, 3½ hours) via Agios Nikolaos (€6.90, 1½ hours).

DODECANESE ΔΩΔΕΚΑΝΗΣΑ

Strung out along the coast of western Turkey, the 12 main islands of the Dodecanese (*dodeca* means 12) have suffered a turbulent past of invasions and occupations that has endowed them with a fascinating diversity.

Conquered successively by the Romans, the Arabs, the Knights of St John, the Turks, the Italians, then liberated from the Germans by British and Greek commandos in 1944, the Dodecanese became part of Greece in 1947. These days, tourists rule.

The islands themselves range from the verdant and mountainous to the rocky and dry. While Rhodes and Kos host highly developed tourism, the more remote islands await those in search of traditional island life.

Rhodes ΡΟΔΟΣ

POP 98,000

Rhodes (Rodos in Greek) is the largest island in the Dodecanese. According to mythology, the sun god Helios chose Rhodes as his bride

TALKING TURKEY

Turkey is so close that it looks like you could swim there from many of the Dodecanese and Northeastern Aegean islands. Here are the boat options:

» Rhodes to Marmaris (see p666)

» Symi to Datça (see p670)

» Kos to Bodrum (see p672)

» Samos to Kuşadasi (near Ephesus; see p673)

» Chios to Çeşme (near İzmir; see p676)

» Lesvos to Dikili (near Ayvalık; see p676)

and bestowed light, warmth and vegetation upon her. The blessing seems to have paid off, for Rhodes produces more flowers and sunny days than most Greek islands. Throw in an east coast of virtually uninterrupted sandy beaches and it's easy to understand why sun-starved northern Europeans flock here.

Getting There & Away

AIR There are plenty of flights daily between Rhodes' **Diagoras airport** (RHO) and Athens, plus less regular flights to Karpathos, Kasos, Kastellorizo, Thessaloniki, Iraklio and Samos. Options are growing. International charter flights swarm in summer, plus budget airlines such as easyJet arrive with scheduled flights. The airport is on the west coast, 16km southwest of Rhodes Town; 25 minutes and €2.20 by bus.

BOAT Rhodes is the main port of the Dodecanese and there is a complex array of departures. There are daily ferries from Rhodes to Piraeus (€53, 13 hours). Most sail via the Dodecanese north of Rhodes, but at least twice a week there is a service via Karpathos, Crete and the Cyclades.

In summer, catamaran services run up and down the Dodecanese daily from Rhodes to Symi, Kos, Kalymnos, Nisyros, Tilos, Patmos and Leros.

TO TURKEY There are boats between Rhodes and Marmaris in Turkey (one-way/return includ-

Rhodes

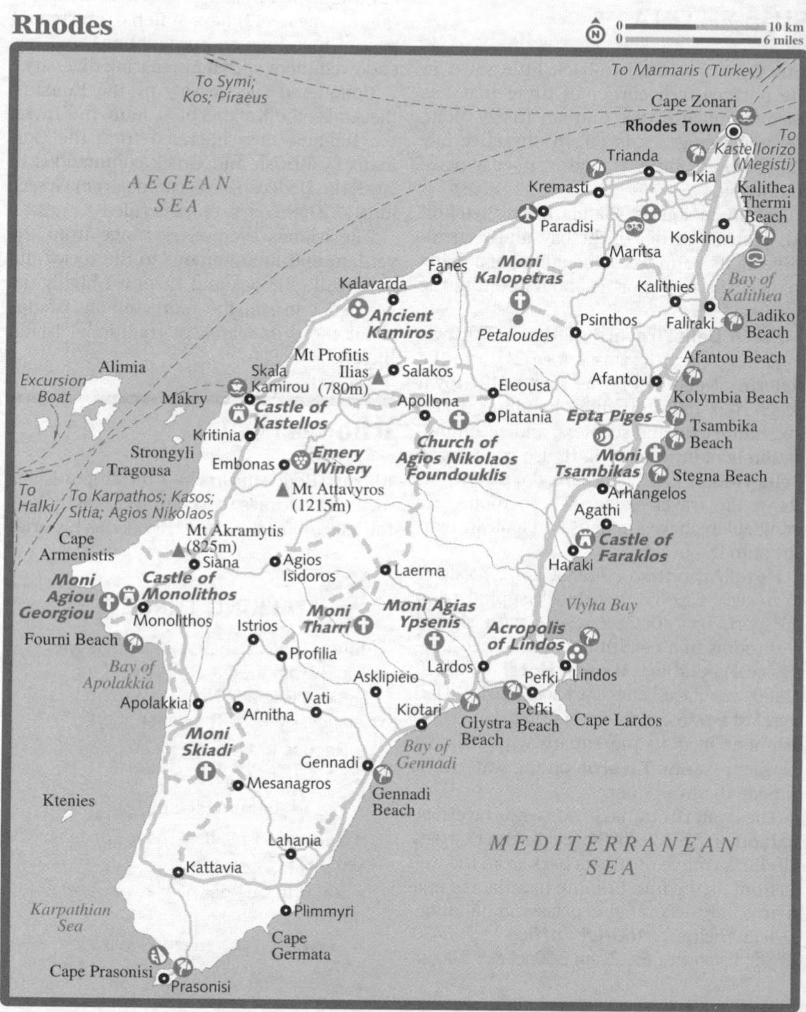

DON'T MISS

OLD TOWN

A wander around Rhodes' World Heritage–listed Old Town is a 'must'. It is reputedly the world's finest surviving example of medieval fortification, with 12m-thick walls. Throngs of visitors pack its busier streets and eating, sleeping and shopping options abound.

The Knights of St John (see p671) lived in the Knights' Quarter in the northern end of the Old Town.

The cobbled **Odos Ippoton** (Ave of the Knights; Map p668) is lined with magnificent medieval buildings, the most imposing of which is the **Palace of the Grand Masters** (Map p668; ☎22410 23359; admission €6; ⏲8.30am-3pm Tue-Sun), which was restored, but never used, as a holiday home for Mussolini.

The 15th-century Knight's Hospital now houses the **Archaeological Museum** (Map p668; ☎22410 27657; Plateia Mousiou; admission €3; ⏲8am-4pm Tue-Sun). The splendid building was restored by the Italians and has an impressive collection that includes the ethereal marble statue *Aphrodite of Rhodes*.

The pink-domed **Mosque of Süleyman** (Map p668), at the top of Sokratous, was built in 1522 to commemorate the Ottoman victory against the knights, then rebuilt in 1808.

You can take a pleasant walk around the imposing walls of the Old Town via the wide and pedestrianised moat walk.

ing port taxes €51/75, 50 minutes). Check www.marmarisinfo.com for up-to-date details.

RHODES TOWN

POP 56,000

Rhodes' capital is Rhodes Town, on the northern tip of the island. Its **Old Town**, the largest inhabited medieval town in Europe, is enclosed within massive walls and is a joy to explore. To the north is **New Town**, the commercial centre. The **town beach**, which looks out at Turkey and can get very crowded in summer, runs around the peninsula at the northern end of New Town.

The main port, **Commercial Harbour**, is east of the Old Town, and is where the big interisland ferries dock. Northwest of here is **Mandraki Harbour**, lined with excursion boats and smaller ferries, hydrofoils and catamarans. It was the supposed site of the Colossus of Rhodes, a 32m-high bronze statue of Apollo built over 12 years (294–282 BC). The statue stood for a mere 65 years before being toppled by an earthquake.

Sleeping

TOP CHOICE **Marco Polo Mansion** BOUTIQUE HOTEL €€
(Map p668; ☎22410 25562; www.marcopolomansion.gr; Agiou Fanouriou 40, Old Town; d €90-150) In a 15th-century building in the Turkish quarter of the Old Town, this place is rich in Ottoman-era colours and features in glossy European magazines. Take a look at the rooms online. Attached is the highly recommended Marco Polo Café, (see boxed text, p669).

Mango Rooms ROOMS €
(Map p668; ☎22410 24877; www.mango.gr; Plateia Dorieos 3, Old Town; s/d/tr €40/50/60; ❄@) A good-value, friendly one-stop shop near the back of the Old Town, Mango has a restaurant, bar and internet cafe down below, six well-kept rooms above, and a sun terrace on top.

Hotel Andreas PENSION €€
(Map p668; ☎22410 34156; www.hotelandreas.com; Omirou 28d, Old Town; s/d €55/70; ❄📶) Tasteful Hotel Andreas has individually decorated rooms and terrific views from its terrace. Rates differ by room; check it all out online, and choose your room before you go. There's a minimum two-night stay, but most stay longer.

Hotel International HOTEL €
(Map p668; ☎22410 24595; diethnes@otenet.gr; 12 Kazouli St, New Town; s/d/tr €45/60/75) In New Town, the International is a friendly family-run operation with immaculately clean and good-value rooms only a few minutes from Rhodes' main town beach. It's a 10-minute stroll to Old Town, and prices drop by a third out of high season.

Eating & Drinking

There's food and drink everywhere you look in Rhodes. Outside the city walls are many cheap places in the New Market, at the southern end of Mandraki Harbour. Head further north into New Town for countless restaurants and bars.

Rhodes Town

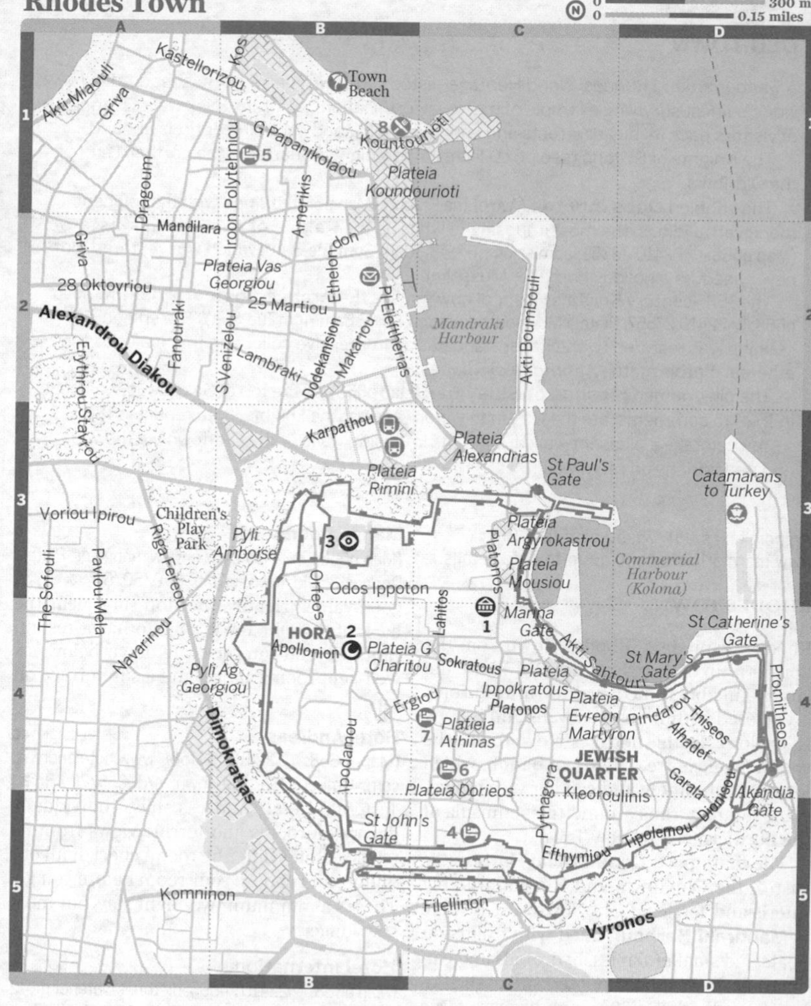

Inside the walls, Old Town has it all in terms of touts and over-priced tavernas trying to separate less savvy tourists from their euro. The back alleys tend to throw up better quality eateries and prices. Delve into the maze and see what you can come up with.

TOP CHOICE **To Meltemi** TAVERNA, SEAFOOD € (Map p666; Kountourioti 8; mains €5-12) At the northern end of Mandraki Harbour is one place worth heading to. Gaze out on Turkey from this beachside taverna where the seafood is superb. Try the grilled calamari stuffed with tomato and feta, and inspect the old photos of Rhodes.

Information

TOURIST INFORMATION Tourist information office (EOT; Map p668; ☎22410 35226; cnr Makariou & Papagou; ⊙8am-2.45pm Mon-Fri) Has brochures, maps and *Rodos News*, a free English-language newspaper.

TRAVEL AGENCIES Triton Holidays (☎22410 21690; www.tritondmc.gr; Plastira 9, Mandraki) In the New Town, this place is exceptionally helpful, handling accommodation bookings, ticketing and rental cars. The island-hopping experts, Triton can provide up-to-date advice in these times of constantly changing flight and boat schedules. E-mail ahead for advice.

WEBSITES www.rodos.gr

Rhodes Town

Sights
1 Archaeological Museum C4
2 Mosque of Süleyman B4
3 Palace of the Grand Masters B3

Sleeping
4 Hotel Andreas C5
5 Hotel International B1
6 Mango Rooms C4
7 Marco Polo Mansion C4

Eating
8 To Meltemi B1

Drinking
Mango Cafe Bar .... (see 6)

Getting Around

BUS Rhodes Town has two bus stations a block apart next to the New Market. The **west-side bus station** serves the airport, Kamiros (€4.60, 55 minutes) and the west coast. The **east-side bus station** serves the east coast, Lindos (€4.70, 1½ hours) and the inland southern villages.

AROUND THE ISLAND

The **Acropolis of Lindos** (admission €6; 8.30am-6pm Tue-Sun), 47km south from Rhodes Town, is an ancient city spectacularly perched atop a 116m-high rocky outcrop. Below is the town of **Lindos**, a tangle of streets with elaborately decorated 17th-century houses.

The extensive ruins of **Kamiros** (admission €4; 8am-5pm Tue-Sun), an ancient Doric city on the west coast, are well preserved, with the remains of houses, baths, a cemetery and a temple, but the site should be visited as much for its lovely setting on a gentle hillside overlooking the sea.

Between Rhodes Town and Lindos, the **beaches** are packed. Venture further south to find good stretches of deserted sandy beach.

Karpathos ΚΑΡΠΑΘΟΣ

POP 6000

The elongated, mountainous island of Karpathos (*kar*-pah-thos), midway between Crete and Rhodes, is a scenic, hype-free place with a cosy port, numerous beaches and unspoilt villages. It is a wealthy island, reputedly receiving more money from emigrants living abroad (mostly in the USA) than any other Greek island.

The main port and capital is **Pigadia**, on the southeast coast. Karpathos has spectacular beaches with some of the clearest turquoise waters to be seen anywhere, particularly **Apella** and **Ahata**, both north of Pigadia, and **Ammoöpi**, 8km south of the capital. The northern village of **Olymbos** is like a living museum. Locals wear traditional outfits and the facades of houses are decorated with bright plaster reliefs. A great option on Karpathos is to hire a car and tour the island in a day on its excellent roads. The 19km stretch from Spoa to Olymbos is expected to finally be sealed by summer 2011.

TOP CHOICE **Elias Rooms** (22450 22446; www.eliasrooms.com; s/d €30/35 s/d apt €35/40) is an excellent accommodation option. Owner Elias is a mine of information and his rooms have great views while being in a quiet part of town. There's a choice of smaller rooms or bigger apartments that are clean and simple. Elias' website can tell you all you need to know about Karpathos and he is happy to provide information by email.

In Pigadia, a booth on the harbour serves as **municipal tourist office** (22450 23835; Jul & Aug). For more information on the island, check out www.inkarpathos.com. **Possi Travel** (22450 22148; possitvl@hotmail.com) on pedestrianised Apodimon Karpathion can suggest local tours and handles air and ferry tickets.

In summer, **Karpathos airport** (AOK), 13km southwest of Pigadia, has daily flights to Rhodes and Athens. With a huge new terminal, international charter flights also wing their way in. There are two ferries a week to Rhodes (€22, four hours) and two to Piraeus (€58, 19 hours) via Crete and the Cyclades. In summer there are daily excursion boats from Pigadia to Ahata and Apella beaches.

DON'T MISS

MARCO POLO CAFÉ

A top spot to eat in Rhodes, and one of our top restaurants for Greece, **Marco Polo Café** (Map p668; 22410 25562; www.marcopolomansion.gr; Agiou Fanouriou 40, Old Town) is worth finding in the backstreets of the Old Town. Owner Efi is as tastefully colourful as her mansion and garden restaurant. This place serves its guests with a rare passion – and the desserts are exquisite!

WORTH A TRIP

TAVERNA UNDER THE TREES *CRAIG MCLACHLAN*

Driving back down the west coast of Karpathos after a swim at Apella, the beach my wife describes as her favourite in Greece, we dropped into Taverna Under the Trees, a standalone place on the remote coastal road which had been highly recommended. I'd been looking for a place under some big trees (as the name suggests!), but as Kosta Ikonomidas explained later, this was his second version of Taverna Under the Trees and as this one had only been open a little over a year, the trees at his new place hadn't grown yet.

My wife and I chose a table with a marvellous view west out over the sea. The only other customers were seated looking east at Karpathos' rugged central mountains. I pointed this out to Kosta.

'Yes, they are Germans and they come every day. One day they look out at the sea, the next they have their backs to it. They have come every day for two weeks!' There's no better recommendation than this, I thought to myself.

Kosta is a Karpathanian character. Along with his family, he immigrated to the US at the age of 17, spent 27 years as a butcher in New York city, then came back to his home village of Piles 14 years ago.

'Karpathos is the second richest Greek island after Chios,' he explained. 'Chios made its money from shipping, but Karpathos became rich by the hard work of its emigrants. People immigrated to the US, Canada and Australia, worked hard, built up businesses, bought property, and Karpathos reaped the benefits. Many sent money to their relatives and family here, while others came back to Karpathos but still earn huge incomes from businesses and properties abroad.'

Taverna Under the Trees is a top spot. Kosta grows his own vegetables and is proud of the quality of the food he serves.

'People come from all over the island for my lamb dishes,' he said proudly. 'I only use the best quality here. Come look in my kitchen!' We had been chatting for a while, and Kosta knew I am a Kiwi. 'Yes, only the best quality,' he said, winking while pulling a vacuum-pack of New Zealand lamb out of the refrigerator!

Look for Kosta and **Taverna Under the Trees** (☎69779 84791) on the coastal road south of Lefkos, but north of the junction to Piles. His calamari is superb, and his smile infectious.

There are also excursions from Pigadia to Diafani, at the north of the island, that include a bus trip to Olymbos.

Local buses can drop you at Ammoöpi beach, but a rental vehicle is a good option.

Symi ΣΥΜΗ

POP 2600

Simply superb, Symi is an inviting island to the north of Rhodes that should be on all island-hopper itineraries. The port town of Gialos is a Greek treasure, with pastel-coloured mansions heaped up the hills surrounding the protective little harbour. Symi is swamped by day trippers from Rhodes, and it's worth staying over to enjoy the island in cruise control. The town is divided into Gialos, the port, and the tranquil *horio* (village) above it, accessible by taxi, bus or 360 steps from the harbour.

There is no tourist office. The best source of information is the free, widely available monthly English-language *Symi Visitor* (www.symivisitor.com), which includes maps of the town.

The **Monastery of Panormitis** (admission free; ⏲dawn-sunset) is a hugely popular complex at the southern end of the island. Its **museum** (admission €1.50) is impressive, but try to avoid the hordes of day trippers who arrive at around 10.30am on excursion boats from Rhodes.

Budget accommodation is scarce. **Rooms Katerina** (☎22460 71813, 69451 30112; d €30; ❄) is excellent, but get in quick as there are only three rooms. There is a communal kitchen with breathtaking views down over the port, and helpful Katerina is happy to answer all your questions.

Pension Catherinettes (☎22460 71671; Julie-symi@otenet.gr; s/d €40/58; ❄@) has airy rooms on the north side of the harbour. It's where the treaty surrendering the Dodecanese to the Allies was signed in 1945. On the waterfront next to the clock tower, **Hotel Nireus** (☎22460 72400; www.nireus-hotel.gr; s/d incl breakfast €80/115; ❄@) is bright, friendly, has free wi-fi and the bonus of being able to swim right out front.

The narrow streets back up the valley from the harbour provide some excellent eating and drinking options. Try to avoid the waterfront spots that cater to flag-following day trippers.

Kalodoukas Holidays (☎22460 71077; www.kalodoukas.gr) handles accommodation bookings, ticketing and has a book of walking trails on the island.

There are frequent boats between Rhodes and Kos that stop at Symi, as well as daily excursion boats from Rhodes. **Symi Tours** (www.symitours.com) runs excursions on Saturdays to Datça in Turkey for €40.

Small taxi boats visit inaccessible east-coast beaches daily in summer, including spectacular Agios Georgious, backed by a 150m sheer cliff.

Kos ΚΩΣ

POP 17,900

Captivating Kos, only 5km from the Turkish peninsula of Bodrum, is popular with history buffs as the birthplace of Hippocrates (460–377 BC), the father of medicine. The island also attracts an entirely different crowd – sun-worshipping beach lovers from northern Europe who flock in on charter flights during summer. Tourism rules the roost, and whether you are there to explore the Castle of the Knights or to party till you drop, Kos should keep you happy for at least a few days.

Kos Town is based around a circular harbour, protected by the imposing Castle of the Knights, at the eastern end of the island. The ferry quay is north of the castle. Akti Koundourioti is the main drag around the harbourfront.

Sights & Activities

Castle of the Knights CASTLE

(☎22420 27927; admission €4; ⏲8am-2.30pm Tue-Sun) Built in the 14th century, this castle protected the knights from the encroaching Ottomans, and was originally separated from town by a moat. That moat is now Finikon, a major street. Entrance to the castle is over the stone bridge behind the Hippocrates Tree.

Asklipieion RUINS

(☎22420 28763; adult/student €4/3; ⏲8am-7:30pm Tue-Sun) On a pine-clad hill 4km southwest of Kos Town stand the extensive ruins of the renowned healing centre where Hippocrates practised medicine. Groups of doctors come from all over the world to visit.

Ancient Agora RUINS

The ancient agora, with the ruins of the **Shrine of Aphrodite** and **Temple of Hercules**, is just off Plateia Eleftherias. North of the agora is the **Hippocrates Plane Tree**, under which the man himself is said to have taught his pupils.

Archaeological Museum MUSEUM

(☎22420 28326; Plateia Eleftherias; admission €3; ⏲8am-2.30pm Tue-Sun) The focus of the collection here is sculpture from excavations around the island.

If the history is all too much, wander around and relax with the Scandinavians at the town **beach** past the northern end of the harbour.

Kos Town has recently developed a number of **bicycle paths** and renting a bike from one of the many places along the waterfront is a great option for getting around town and seeing the sights.

THE KNIGHTS OF ST JOHN

Do some island-hopping in the Dodecanese and you'll quickly realise that the Knights of St John left behind a whole lot of castles.

Originally formed as the Knights Hospitaller in Jerusalem in 1080 to provide care for poor and sick pilgrims, the knights relocated to Rhodes (via Cyprus) after the loss of Jerusalem in the First Crusade. In Rhodes, they ousted the ruling Genoese in 1309, built a stack of castles to protect their new home, then set about irking the neighbours by committing acts of piracy against Ottoman shipping. Sultan Süleyman the Magnificent, not a man you'd want to irk, took offence and set about dislodging the knights from their strongholds. Rhodes capitulated in 1523 and the remaining knights relocated to Malta. They set up there as the Sovereign Military Hospitaller of Jerusalem, of Rhodes, and of Malta.

Sleeping

TOP CHOICE **Hotel Afendoulis** HOTEL €

(☎22420 25321; www.afendoulishotel.com; Evripilou 1; s/d €35/50; ❄@) In a pleasant, quiet area about 500m south of the ferry quay, this well-kept hotel won't disappoint. Run by the charismatic English-speaking Alexis, this is a great place to relax and enjoy Kos. Port and bus station transfers are complimentary, and you can get your laundry done here.

Pension Alexis PENSION €

(☎22420 28798; www.pensionalexis.com; Irodotou 9; s/d €25/35; ❄) This highly recommended place has long been a budget favourite with travellers. It has large rooms, some with shared facilities, and a relaxing veranda and garden. They'll pick you up at the port or bus station for free and there are laundry facilities on site. It's back behind the Dolphin roundabout.

Eating & Drinking

Restaurants line the central waterfront of the old harbour, but you might want to hit the backstreets for value. There are plenty of cheap places to eat on the beach to the north of the harbour, and a dozen discos and clubs around the streets of Diakon and Nafklirou, just north of the agora.

TOP CHOICE **Stadium Restaurant** SEAFOOD €

(☎22420 27880; mains €9-16) On the long waterfront 500m southeast of the castle, Stadium serves succulent seafood at good prices, along with excellent views of Turkey.

Information

TOURIST INFORMATION Municipal tourist office (☎22420 24460; www.kosinfo.gr; Vasileos Georgiou 1; ⊙8am-2.30pm & 3-10pm Mon-Fri, 9am-2pm Sat) On the waterfront directly south of the port; provides maps and accommodation information.

TRAVEL AGENCIES Exas Travel (☎22420 28545; www.exas.gr) Near the Archaeological Museum, in the heart of town, to the southwest of the harbour; handles schedules, ticketing and excursions.

WEBSITES www.kosinfo.gr

Getting There & Around

AIR There are daily flights to Athens from Kos' **Ippokratis airport** (KGS), which is 28km southwest of Kos Town. International charters wing in throughout the summer and easyJet operates scheduled flights from London. Get to/from the airport by bus (€4) or taxi (€25).

BOAT There are frequent ferries from Rhodes to Kos that continue on to Piraeus (€46, 10 hours), as well as ferries heading the opposite way. Daily fast-boat connections head north to Patmos and Samos, and south to Symi and Rhodes.

TO TURKEY In summer boats depart daily for Bodrum in Turkey (€34 return, one hour).

BUS There is a good public bus system on Kos, with the bus station on Kleopatras, near the ruins at the back of town.

MINI-TRAIN Next to the tourist office is a blue mini-train for Asklipion (€5 return, hourly) and a green mini-train that does city tours (€4, 20 minutes).

Patmos ΠΑΤΜΟΣ

POP 3050

Patmos has a sense of 'spirit of place', and with its great beaches and relaxed atmosphere, is a superb place to unwind. For the religiously motivated it is not to be missed. Orthodox and Western Christians have long made pilgrimages to Patmos, for it was here that John the Divine ensconced himself in a cave and wrote the Book of Revelation.

The main town and port of Skala is about halfway down the east coast of Patmos, with a protected harbour. Towering above Skala to the south is the *hora*, crowned by the immense Monastery of St John the Theologian.

Sights & Activities

St John Sites RELIGIOUS SITES

The **Cave of the Apocalypse** (admission free, treasury €6; ⊙8am-1.30pm daily & 4-6pm Tue, Thu & Sun), where St John wrote his divinely inspired Book of Revelation, is halfway between the port and *hora*. Take a bus from the port or hike up the **Byzantine path**, which starts from a signposted spot on the Skala–*hora* road.

The **Monastery of St John the Theologian** (admission free; ⊙8am-1.30pm daily & 4-6pm Tue, Thu & Sun) looks more like a castle than a monastery and tops Patmos like a crown. It exhibits all kinds of monastic treasures.

Beaches BEACHES

Patmos' coastline provides secluded coves, mostly with pebble beaches. The best is **Psili Ammos**, in the south, reached by excursion boat from Skala port. **Lambi Beach**, on the north coast, is a pebble-beach lover's dream come true.

Sleeping

Yvonni Studios ROOMS €
(☎22470 33066; www.12net.gr/yvonni; s/d €35/50) On the western side of Skala, these exceptionally clean and pleasant studios are fully self-contained and big on privacy. Call ahead for a booking or drop into Yvonni's gift shop in Skala and ask for Theo.

Katina's Rooms ROOMS €
(☎22470 31327, 69734 17241; s/d €35/50) The smiling Katina meets most boats and is happy to provide a ride to her four immaculately clean rooms at the northern end of the harbour. Enthusiastic and helpful, she has contacts with other tidy rooms in her neighbourhood if hers are full.

Blue Bay Hotel BOUTIQUE HOTEL €€
(☎22470 31165; www.bluebaypatmos.gr; s/d/tr €78/116/144; ❄@) At the quieter southern end of Skala, this waterfront hotel has superb rooms, internet access, and breakfast included in its rates (which tumble outside of high season).

Information

TOURIST INFORMATION **Tourist office** (☎22470 31666; ⊙8am-6pm Mon-Fri Jun-Sep) In the white building opposite the port in Skala, along with the post office and police station.

TRAVEL AGENCIES **Apollon Travel** (☎22470 31324; apollontravel@stratas.gr) On the waterfront; handles schedules and ticketing.

WEBSITES www.patmosweb.gr; www.patmos-island.com

Getting There & Away

BOAT Patmos is well connected, with ferries to Piraeus (€35, eight hours, two weekly) and south to Rhodes (€32, 7½ hours, two weekly). In summer daily catamarans head south to Kos and Rhodes, and north to Samos.

NORTHEASTERN AEGEAN ISLANDS
ΤΑ ΝΗΣΙΑ ΤΟΥ ΒΟΡΕΙΟ ΑΝΑΤΟΛΙΚΟ ΑΙΓΑΙΟΥ

One of Greece's best-kept secrets, these farflung islands are strewn across the northeastern corner of the Aegean, closer to Turkey than mainland Greece. They harbour unspoilt scenery, welcoming locals, fascinating independent cultures, and remain relatively calm even when other Greek islands are sagging with tourists at the height of summer.

Samos ΣΑΜΟΣ

POP 32,800

A lush mountainous island only 3km from Turkey, Samos has a glorious history as the legendary birthplace of Hera, wife and sister of god-of-all-gods Zeus. Samos was an important centre of Hellenic culture, and the mathematician Pythagoras and storyteller Aesop are among its sons. The island has beaches that bake in summer, and a hinterland that is superb for hiking. Spring brings with it pink flamingos, wildflowers, and orchids that the island grows for export, while summer brings throngs of package tourists.

Getting There & Around

AIR There are daily flights to Athens from **Samos airport** (SMI), 4km west of Pythagorio, plus less regular flights to Iraklio and Thessaloniki. Charter flights wing in from Europe in summer.

BOAT Samos has two main ports: Vathy (Samos Town) in the northeast and Pythagorio on the southeast coast. Those coming from the south by boat generally arrive in Pythagorio. Big ferries use Vathy. Once you're on Samos and have onward tickets, double-check where your boat is leaving from. Buses between the two take 25 minutes.

A maritime hub, Samos offers daily ferries to Piraeus (€35, 13 hours), plus ferries heading north to Chios, west to the Cyclades and south to the Dodecanese. Catamarans head south to Patmos (€20, one hour), carrying on to Leros, Kalymnos and Kos (€34, 3½ hours).

BUS You can get to most of the island's villages and beaches by bus.

CAR & MOTORCYCLE Rental cars and scooters are readily available around the island.

TO TURKEY There are daily ferries to Kuşadasi (for Ephesus) in Turkey (€35/45 one-way/return plus €10 port taxes). Day excursions are also available from April to October. Check with **ITSA Travel** (☎22730 23605; www.itsatravel-samos.gr) in Vathy for up-to-date details.

VATHY (SAMOS TOWN) ΒΑΘΥ ΣΑΜΟΣ

POP 2030

Busy Vathy is an attractive working port town. Most of the action is along Themistokleous Sofouli, the main street that runs along the waterfront. The main square, Plateia Pythagorou, in the middle of the waterfront, is recognisable by its four palm trees and statue of a lion.

The rarely open and hard-to-find **tourist office** (☎22730 28582; ⊙Jun-Sep) is in a side street one block north of the main square.

Samos

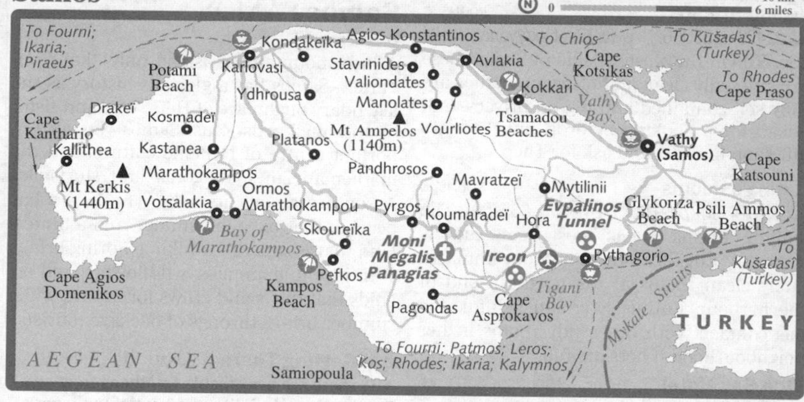

ITSA Travel (☎22730 23605; www.itsatravel.com), opposite the quay, is helpful with travel inquiries, excursions, accommodation and luggage storage. To get to Vathy's bus station, follow the waterfront south and turn left onto Lekati, 250m south of Plateia Pythagorou (just before the police station).

The **Archaeological Museum** (adult/student €3/2; ⏲8.30am-3pm Tue-Sun), by the municipal gardens, is first rate. The highlight is a 5.5m *kouros* statue.

TOP CHOICE **Pythagoras Hotel** (☎22730 28601; www.pythagoras-hotel.com; Kallistratou 12; s/d/tr €20/35/45; P@) is a friendly, great-value place with a convivial atmosphere, run by English-speaking Stelio. There is a restaurant serving tasty home-cooked meals; a bar; satellite TV; and internet access on site. Facing inland, the hotel is 400m to the left of the quay. Call ahead for free pick-up on arrival.

Ino Village Hotel (☎22730 23241; www.inovillagehotel.com; Kalami; s/d/tr incl breakfast €65/80/100; P@) is an impressive, elegant place in the hills north of the ferry quay. Its **Elea Restaurant** on the terrace serves up both invigorated Greek cuisine and views over town and the harbour.

Garden Taverna (☎22730 24033; Manolis Kalomiris; mains €4-9) serves good Greek food in a lovely garden setting; it's up to the left behind the main square.

PYTHAGORIO ΠΥΘΑΓΟΡΕΙΟ

POP 1300

Pretty Pythagorio, 25 minutes south of Vathy by bus, is where you'll disembark if you've come by boat from Patmos. It is a small, enticing town with a yacht-lined harbour and a holiday atmosphere.

The excellent **statue of Pythagoras** and his triangle, on the waterfront opposite the ferry quay, should have you recalling his theorem from your high school maths days. If not, buy a T-shirt emblazoned with it to remind you.

The 1034m-long **Evpalinos Tunnel** (adult/student €4/2; ⏲8.45am-2.45pm Tue-Sun), built in the 6th century BC, was dug by political prisoners and used as an aqueduct to bring water from Mt Ampelos (1140m). In the Middle Ages, locals hid out in it during pirate raids. Part of it can still be explored. It's a 20-minute walk north of town.

Hotel Alexandra (☎22730 61429; Metamorfosis Sotiros 22; d €35), not far from the castle, is a friendly place with cosy rooms and an attractive garden. **Pension Despina** (☎22730 61677; A Nikolaou; s/d €35/50), a block back from the waterfront, offers simple studios and rooms, some with balconies and kitchenettes.

Tavernas and bars line the waterfront. **Poseidon Restaurant** (☎22730 62530; mains from €5), on the small town beach, past the jetty with the Pythagoras statue on it, offers superb seafood. **Iliad Bar** (☎22730 62207; cocktails from €5), on the waterfront, serves wicked cocktails till the wee hours and is run by an expat Kiwi.

The cordial **municipal tourist office** (☎22730 61389; deap5@otenet.gr; ⏲8am-9.30pm) is two blocks from the waterfront on the main street, Lykourgou Logotheti. The bus stop is two blocks further inland on the same street, next to the post office.

Ireon (adult/student €4/3; ⌚8.30am-3pm Tue-Sun), the legendary birthplace of the goddess Hera, is 8km west of Pythagorio. The temple at this World Heritage site was enormous – four times the Parthenon – though only one column remains.

The captivating villages of **Vourliotes** and **Manolates**, on the slopes of imposing Mt Ampelos, northwest of Vathy, are excellent walking territory and have many marked pathways.

Choice beaches include **Tsamadou** on the north coast, **Votsalakia** in the southwest and **Psili Ammos** to the east of Pythagorio. The latter is sandy and stares straight out at Turkey, barely a couple of kilometres away.

Chios ΧΙΟΣ

POP 54,000

Due to its thriving shipping and mastic industries (mastic produces the resin used in chewing gum), Chios (*hee*-os) has never really bothered much with tourism. If you are an off-the-beaten-track type of Greek Islands traveller, you'll find Chios all the more appealing.

Chios Town, on the island's eastern coast, is a working port and home to half the island's inhabitants. A main street runs in a semicircle around the port, with most ferries docking at its northern end. The *kastro* (old Turkish quarter) is to the north of the ferry quay, and Plateia Vounakiou, the main square, is just south and inland from the quay.

Sights & Activities

In Chios Town, **Philip Argenti Museum** (Korais; admission €1.50; ⌚8am-2pm Mon-Thu, 8am-2pm & 5-7.30pm Fri, 8am-12.30pm Sat) contains the treasures of the wealthy Argenti family.

World Heritage-listed **Nea Moni** (New Monastery; admission free; ⌚8am-1pm & 4-8pm) is 14km west of Chios Town and reveals some of the finest Byzantine art in the country, with mosaics dating from the 11th century. The mosaics survived, but the resident monks were massacred by the Turks in 1822. You can see their dented skulls in the chapel at the monastery's entrance.

Those in the ghost village of **Anavatos**, 10km from Nea Moni and built on a precipitous cliff, preferred a different fate, hurling themselves off the cliff rather than being taken captive by the Turks.

Pyrgi, 24km southwest of Chios Town, is one of Greece's most unusual villages. The facades of the town's dwellings are decorated with intricate grey-and-white geometric patterns and motifs. The tiny medieval town of **Mesta**, 10km from Pyrgi and nestled within fortified walls, features cobbled streets, overhead arches and a labyrinth of streets designed to confuse pirates.

Sleeping

TOP CHOICE **Chios Rooms** ROOMS €
(☎22710 20198; www.chiosrooms.gr; Leoforos Egeou 110; s/d/tr €25/35/45) A top location to stay, this place is upstairs in a restored neoclassical house on the waterfront at the southern end of the harbour. It has bright, airy rooms, some with en suite bathrooms, and is being restored lovingly by its Kiwi owner, Don, who is a mine of information on Chios.

Hotel Kyma HOTEL €€
(☎22710 44500; kyma@chi.forthnet.gr; Evgenias Handris 1; s/d/tr incl breakfast €71/90/111; ❄) Around the corner from Chios Rooms, this place occupies a charismatic century-old mansion and is run by the enthusiastic multilingual Theodoris. Ask for a room overlooking the sea.

GUM-CHEWERS FROM WAY BACK

Chios is home to the world's only gum-producing mastic trees and the southern *mastihohoria* (mastic villages) were wealthy for centuries. Not only were they wealthy, but the mastic trees are also said to have saved them when the Turks came and slaughtered the rest of the island's residents. The sultan's reputed fondness for mastic chewing gum – and the rumour that his harem girls used it for keeping their teeth clean and their breath fresh – meant that the *mastihohoria* were spared.

These days, **Masticulture Ecotourism Activities** (☎22710 76084; www.masticulture.com) in the southern village of Mesta, introduces visitors to the local history and culture, including mastic cultivation tours. In Chios Town, on the waterfront, **Mastihashop** sells products such as mastic chewing gum, toothpaste and soaps, and **Mastic Spa** sells mastic-based cosmetics.

Eating

The waterfront has ample options in the way of way of eateries and bars, though for cheap eats, head one street back onto El Venizelou, which is lined with shops. The Plateia Vounakiou area, inland from where the ferries dock, also throws up some good options.

Hotzas Taverna TAVERNA €
(☎22710 42787; Kondyli 3; mains from €5) Up the back of town, Hotzas is known by locals to provide the best Greek fare on the island. Get a local to mark it on a map, and enjoy the walk. It's worth the effort of finding.

Information

TOURIST INFORMATION Municipal tourist office (☎22710 44389; infochio@otenet.gr; Kanari 18; ⏲7am-10pm Apr-Oct, to 4pm Nov-Mar) On the street that runs inland to the main square; provides information on accommodation, schedules and rentals.

TRAVEL AGENCIES Agean Travel (☎22710 41277; aegeantr@otenet.gr; Leoforos Egeou 114) At the southern end of the harbour; handles ticketing.

WEBSITES www.chios.gr

Getting There & Around

AIR There are daily flights from **Chios airport** (JKH) to Athens and five per week to Thessaloniki. The airport is 4km south of Chios Town; there's no bus; a taxi costs €6.

BOAT Ferries sail daily to Piraeus (€32.50, six hours) and Lesvos (€19.50, two hours 15 minutes), and weekly to Thessaloniki (€40, 18 hours). There are two ferries a week south to Samos (€15, three hours).

BUS Chios Town has two bus stations. Blue buses go regularly to local villages and Karfas Beach, and leave from the local bus station at the main square. Buses to Pyrgi (€2.50) and Mesta (€3.50) and other distant points leave from the long-distance bus station on the waterfront near the ferry quay.

TO TURKEY Boats to Turkey run all year from Chios, with daily sailings from July to September to Çeşme (one-way/return €20/30), near İzmir. For details, check out **Miniotis Lines** (☎22710 24670; www.miniotis.gr; Neorion 24).

Lesvos (Mytilini) ΛΕΣΒΟΣ (ΜΥΤΙΛΗΝΗ)

POP 93,500

Lesvos, or Mytilini as it is often called, tends to do things in a big way. The third-largest of the Greek Islands after Crete and Evia, Lesvos produces half the world's ouzo and is home to over 11 million olive trees. Mountainous yet fertile, the island presents excellent hiking and birdwatching opportunities, but remains relatively untouched in terms of tourism development.

Lesvos has always been a centre of philosophy and artistic achievement, and to this day is a spawning ground for innovative ideas in the arts and politics. An excellent source of information on the island is www.greeknet.com.

The two main towns on the island are the capital, Mytilini, on the southeast coast, and attractive Mithymna on the north coast.

Getting There & Away

AIR Written up on flight schedules as Mytilene, Lesvos' **Odysseas airport** (MJT) has daily connections with Athens, plus flights to Thessaloniki and Iraklio. The airport is 8km south of Mytilini town; a taxi costs €8.

BOAT In summer there are daily boats to Piraeus (€30, 12 hours) via Chios, and three boats a week to Thessaloniki (€35, 13 hours).

TO TURKEY There are four ferries a week to Dikeli port, which serves Ayvalik in Turkey (one-way/return €30/45), plus other options. Stop by Zoumboulis Tours (p677) for ticketing and schedules.

MYTILINI ΜΥΤΙΛΗΝΗ

POP 27,300

The capital and main port, Mytilini, is built between two harbours (north and south) with an imposing fortress on the promontory to the east. All ferries dock at the southern harbour, and most of the town's action is around this waterfront. With a large university campus, Mytilini is a lively place year-round.

Sights & Activities

Museums MUSEUMS
Mytilini's excellent neoclassical **Archaeological Museum** (8 Noemvriou; adult/child €3/2; ⏲8.30am-3pm) has a fascinating collection from Neolithic to Roman times.

Theophilos Museum (admission €2; ⏲9am-1pm & 4.30-8pm Tue-Sun), 4km south of Mytilini in Varia village, is a shrine to the prolific folk painter Theophilos. Next door is the **Teriade Museum** (☎22510 23372; admission €2; ⏲8.30am-2pm &5-8pm Tue-Sun), with an astonishing collection of paintings by world-renowned artists.

Fortress FORTRESS
(adult/student €2/1; ⏲8am-2.30pm Tue-Sun) Mytilini's impressive fortress was built in early Byzantine times and enlarged by the

SAPPHO, LESBIANS & LESVOS

Sappho, one of Greece's great ancient poets, was born on Lesvos during the 7th century BC. Most of her work was devoted to love and desire, and the objects of her affection were often female. Because of this, Sappho's name and birthplace have come to be associated with female homosexuality.

These days, Lesvos is visited by many lesbians paying homage to Sappho. The whole island is very gay-friendly, in particular the southwestern beach resort of Skala Eresou, which is built over ancient Eresos, where Sappho was born. The village is well set up to cater to lesbian needs and has a 'Women Together' festival held annually in September. Check out www.sapphotravel.com for details.

There is an excellent statue of Sappho in the main square on the waterfront in Mytilini.

Turks. The pine forest surrounding it is a superb place for a stroll or to have a picnic.

Sleeping

Pension Thalia ROOMS €
(☎22510 24640; Kinikiou 1; s/d €25/30) This pension has clean, bright rooms in a large house. It is about a five-minute walk north of the main square, up Ermou, the road that links the south and north harbours. Follow the signs from the corner of Ermou and Adramytiou.

Hotel Sappho HOTEL €€
(☎22510 22888; Kountourioti 31; s/d/tr €45/60/70) On the waterfront, rooms here are simple but clean. It's easy to find, and has the attraction of a 24-hour reception as ferries into Mytilini tend to arrive at nasty hours.

Porto Lesvos 1 Hotel HOTEL €€
(☎22510 41771; www.portolesvos.gr; Komninaki 21; s/d €60/90; ❄@) This hotel has good rooms and service – right down to robes and slippers – in a restored building one block back from the waterfront.

Eating & Drinking

Mytilini's top spots are a road or two back at the northern end of the harbour.

O Diavlos GREEK €
(☎22510 22020; Ladadika 30) Come here for the best in both local cuisine and art; paintings by local artists line the walls and can be purchased should you get the urge.

Ocean Eleven Bar BAR
(☎22510 27030; Kountourioti 17) Enjoy a cocktail here while watching the mayhem on the waterfront.

Information

TOURIST INFORMATION Tourist office (☎22510 42512; 6 Aristarhou; ⊙9am-1pm Mon-Fri) Located 50m up Aristarhou inland from the quay; offers brochures and maps, but its opening hours are limited.

TRAVEL AGENCIES Tourist Police (☎22510 22776) At the entrance to the quay; helpful if you're outside tourist-office hours.

Zoumboulis Tours (☎22510 37755; Kountourioti 69) On the waterfront, handles flights, boat schedules, ticketing and excursions to Turkey.

WEBSITES www.lesvos.net

Getting Around

BUS Mytilini has two bus stations. For local buses, head along the waterfront to the main square. For long-distance buses, walk 600m from the ferry along the waterfront to El Venizelou and turn right until you reach Agia Irinis park, which is next to the station. There are regular services in summer to Mithymna, Petra, Agiasos, Skala Eresou, Mantamados and Agia Paraskevi.

MITHYMNA ΜΗΘΥΜΝΑ

POP 1500

The gracious, preserved town of Mithymna (known by locals as Molyvos) is 62km north of Mytilini. Cobbled streets canopied by flowering vines wind up the hill below the impressive castle. The town is full of cosy tavernas and genteel stone cottages.

The noble **Genoese castle** (admission €2; ⊙8.30am-7pm Tue-Sun) perches above the town like a crown and affords tremendous views out to Turkey. Pebbly **Mithymna Beach** sits below the town and is good for swimming. Don't forget to stroll down to the harbour.

Eftalou hot springs (public/private bath per person €3.50/5; ⊙public bath 6-8am & 6-10pm, private bath 9am-6pm), 4km from town on the beach, is a superb bathhouse complex with a whitewashed dome and steaming, pebbled pool. There are also private baths where you don't need a bathing suit.

TOP CHOICE **Nassos Guest House** (☎22530 71432; www.nassosguesthouse.com; Arionis; d & tr €20-35; 📶) is an airy, friendly place with shared facilities and a communal kitchen, in an old Turkish house oozing with character. With rapturous views, it's highly recommended. It's easy to spot as it's the only blue house below the castle.

Betty's Restaurant (☎22530 71421; Agora) has superb home-style Greek food, views and atmosphere in a building that was once a notorious bordello. Betty also has a couple of **cottages** (☎22530 71022; www.bettyscottages.molivos.net) with kitchens in her garden that sleep up to four for €50.

From the bus stop, walk straight ahead towards the town for 100m to the helpful **municipal tourist office** (www.mithymna.gr; ⏰8am-9pm Mon-Fri, 9am-7pm Sat & Sun), which has good maps. Some 50m further on, the cobbled main thoroughfare of 17 Noemvriou heads up to the right. Go straight to get to the colourful fishing port.

Buses to Mithymna (€5) take 1¾ hours from Mytilini, though a rental car is a good option.

AROUND THE ISLAND

Southern Lesvos is dominated by **Mt Olympus** (968m) and the very pretty village of **Agiasos**, which has good artisan workshops making everything from handcrafted furniture to pottery.

Western Lesvos is known for its petrified forest, with petrified wood at least 500,000 years old, and for the gay-friendly town of Skala Eresou, the birthplace of Sappho.

SPORADES ΣΠΟΡΑΔΕΣ

Scattered to the southeast of the Pelion Peninsula, to which they were joined in prehistoric times, the 11 islands that make up the Sporades group have mountainous terrain, dense vegetation and are surrounded by scintillatingly clear seas.

The main ports for the Sporades are Volos and Agios Konstantinos on the mainland.

Skiathos ΣΚΙΑΘΟΣ

POP 6150

Lush and green, Skiathos has a beach-resort feel about it. Charter flights bring loads of package tourists, but the island still oozes enjoyment. Skiathos Town and some excellent beaches are on the hospitable south coast, while the north coast is precipitous and less accessible. Skiathos Town was used as a shooting location in the filming of *Mamma Mia*.

Skiathos Town's main thoroughfare is Papadiamanti, named after the 19th-century novelist and short-story writer Alexandros Papadiamanti, who was born here. It runs inland opposite the quay.

Sights & Activities

Beaches

Skiathos has superb beaches, particularly on the south coast. **Koukounaries** is popular with families. A stroll over the headland, **Big Banana Beach** is stunning, but if you want an all-over tan, head a tad further to **Little Banana Beach**, where bathing suits are a rarity.

Boat Trips

At the Old Port in Skiathos Town, there are all sorts of offerings in terms of **boat excursions** – trips to nearby beaches (€10), trips around Skiathos Island (€25) and full-day trips that take in Skopelos, Alonnisos and the Marine Park (€35).

Sleeping

Pension Pandora ROOMS €
(☎24270 24357, 6944137377; www.skiathosinfo.com/accomm/pension-pandora; r €30-70; P ❄) Run by the effervescent Georgina, this family-run place is 10 minutes' walk north of the quay. The spotless rooms have TV, kitchens and balconies. Georgina also has two exceptional apartments just off Papadiamanti.

Camping Koukounaries CAMPING €
(☎24270 49250; campsites per tent/person €4/10) This place, 30 minutes from town by bus at the southwestern end of the island, is at beautiful Koukounaries Beach. There are good facilities, a minimarket and a taverna.

Villa Orsa BOUTIQUE ROOMS €€
(☎24270 22430; s/d incl breakfast €70/80; ❄) Perched above the old harbour, this mansion features traditionally styled rooms and a garden terrace overlooking the sea.

Eating & Drinking

Skiathos Town is brimming with eateries. There are seafood options around the old harbour, and some excellent places up the stairs from there behind the small church.

Skiathos is popular with English visitors who don't want to miss their football; there

MOVIES UNDER THE STARS

Greece has such great weather in summer that not only does it have a history of open-air theatre, there is also an open-air cinema culture. **Cinema Attikon** (☎24720 22352; €7), on Skiathos Town's main street of Papadiamanti, is a great example. You can catch current English-language movies under the stars, sip a beer and practise speed-reading Greek subtitles at the same time! Films are usually shown in their original language in Greece, not dubbed.

A number of other islands have similar outdoor cinemas.

are ample opportunities to consume fish and chips and watch the premier league along Papadiamanti!

Piccolo PIZZA €
(☎24270 22780; mains from €7) Does exquisite pizzas and pastas in a lovely setting.

1901 GREEK €
(☎69485 26701; mains from €7) A superb fine-dining restaurant with a glowing reputation.

Kentavros BAR
(☎24270 22980) A popular drinking spot just off Plateia Papadiamanti. Expect a mellow ambience and mixture of rock, jazz and blues.

Information

TOURIST INFORMATION Tourist information booth (☎24270 23172) At the port, but it opens irregularly.

TRAVEL AGENCIES Heliotropio Travel (☎24270 22430; www.heliotropio.gr) Opposite the ferry quay; handles ticketing and rents cars and scooters.

WEBSITES skiathosinfo.com

Getting There & Around

AIR Along with numerous charter flights from northern Europe, in summer there is a daily flight from Athens to Skiathos. **Skiathos airport** (JSI) is 2km northeast of Skiathos Town.

BOAT There are frequent daily hydrofoils to/from the mainland ports of Volos (€30, 1¼ hours) and Agios Konstantinos (€33, two hours), as well as cheaper ferries. The hydrofoils head to and from Skopelos (€16, 35 minutes) and Alonnisos (€18, one hour). In summer there is a daily hydrofoil to Thessaloniki (€55, 3½ hours).

BUS Crowded buses ply the south-coast road between Skiathos Town and Koukounaries every 30 minutes between 7.30am and 11pm year-round, stopping at all the beaches along the way. The bus stop is at the eastern end of the harbour.

Skopelos ΣΚΟΠΕΛΟΣ

POP 4700

A mountainous island, Skopelos is covered in pine forests, vineyards, olive groves and fruit orchards. While the northwest coast is exposed with high cliffs, the southeast is sheltered and harbours pleasant pebbled beaches. The island's main port and capital of Skopelos Town, on the east coast, skirts a semicircular bay and clambers in tiers up a hillside, culminating in a ruined fortress.

Recent claims to fame for Skopelos are the legendary Skopelos pie, which can be bought all over Greece, and its use as a location for the filming of *Mamma Mia*. The crew took over Skopelos Town's accommodation for a month and filmed at Agnontas and Kastani beaches on the western coast.

TOP CHOICE **Pension Sotos** (☎24240 22549; www.skopelos.net/sotos; s & d €35-55; ❄@📶), in the middle of the waterfront, has big rooms in an enchanting old Skopelete building. There's also a communal kitchen, terrace and courtyard. Check out individual rooms and its different prices online before you go. **Hotel Regina** (☎24240 22138; www.skopelosweb.gr/regina; s/d incl breakfast €40/55; ❄) has bright and cheery rooms with balconies. The hotel's rooftop signage is easily spotted from the waterfront.

Head to Souvlaki Sq, 100m up from the dock, for cheap eats such as gyros and souvlaki. The top spot in town to chill out is under the huge plane tree at **Platanos Jazz Bar** (☎24240 23661) on the waterfront. It's open all day, plays wicked jazz and blues until the late hours, and is the ideal place to recover from, or prepare for, a hangover. Next door is **Taverna Ta Kimata O Angelos** (☎24240 22381), a traditional taverna that is the oldest one on the island.

In Skopelos Town, there is no tourist office, but **Thalpos Holidays** (☎24240 29036; www.holidayislands.com), on the waterfront between the ferry quay and the excursion-boat quay, is handy for accommodation and tours. The bus station is next to the port.

ECOTOURISM ON THE RISE

In a country not noted for its ecological long-sightedness, locals (especially the fishermen) initially struggled with the idea of the **National Marine Park of Alonnisos** when it was established in 1992 to protect the highly endangered Mediterranean monk seal and to promote the recovery of fish stocks.

These days, though, the people of the Sporades have caught on to the advantages of having such a park on their doorstep. Ecotourism is on the rise, with daily excursions on licensed boats into the park from Skiathos, Skopelos and Alonnisos. Though your odds of seeing the shy monk seal aren't great – it's on the list of the 20 most endangered species worldwide – the chances of cruising among pods of dolphins (striped, bottlenose and common) are high.

Excursion boats along the waterfront offer trips into the Marine Park.

Flying Dolphin hydrofoils dash several times a day to Skiathos (€15.50, 45 minutes), Alonnisos (€8.50, 20 minutes), Volos (€26.30, 2¼ hours) and Agios Konstantinos (€44, 2½ hours). Most hydrofoils also call in at Loutraki, the port below Glossa on the northwest coast of the island. There is also a daily ferry along the same route that costs less but takes longer. There are frequent buses from Skopelos Town to Glossa (€4.30, one hour) stopping at all beaches along the way.

Alonnisos ΑΛΟΝΝΗΣΟΣ

POP 2700

Green, serene, attractive Alonnisos is at the end of the line and is thereby the least visited of the Sporades' main islands. The west coast is mostly precipitous cliffs, but the east coast is speckled with pebble-and-sand beaches. The island is well known as a walking destination.

The port village of Patitiri was slapped together in 1965 after an earthquake destroyed the hilltop capital of Alonnisos Town. There are two main thoroughfares; facing inland from the ferry quay, Pelasgon is to the left and Ikion Dolopon is to the far right.

The tiny *hora*, **Old Alonnisos**, is a few kilometres inland. Its streets sprout a profusion of plant life, alluring villas of eclectic design and dramatic vistas.

Pension Pleiades (☎24240 65235; www.pleiadeshotel.gr; s/d €45/50; ❄@) looks out over the harbour and is visible from the quay. The rooms are immaculate, balconied, bright and cheerful. There's also a good restaurant. **Liadromia Hotel** (☎24240 65521; www.liadromia.gr; d/tr/ste €50/70/95; P❄@) is an excellent-value place with tons of character, overlooking Patitiri's harbour. Follow the stairway opposite the National Bank. **Camping Rocks** (☎24240 65410; campsites per person €6) is a shady, basic camping ground. It is a steep hike about 1.5km from the port; go up Pelasgon and take the first road on your left.

There is no tourist office, but on the waterfront, **Alonnisos Travel** (☎24240 66000; www.alonnisostravel.gr) handles boat scheduling and ticketing. **Ikos Travel** (☎24240 65320; www.ikostravel.com) runs a popular round-the-island excursion. The bus stop is on the corner of Ikion Dolopon and the waterfront.

There are ferries with varying regularity connecting Alonnisos to Volos and Agios Konstantinos via Skopelos and Skiathos. Flying Dolphin hydrofoils provide the most regular schedules between the islands. They travel several times a day to Skopelos Town (€9, 20 minutes), Skiathos (€16, 1½ hours), Volos (€38.50, three hours) and Agios Konstantinos (€44, three hours).

The local bus (€1.20) runs to the *hora* every hour.

IONIAN ISLANDS ΤΑ ΕΠΤΑΝΗΣΑ

The idyllic cypress- and fir-covered Ionian Islands stretch down the western coast of Greece from Corfu in the north to Kythira, off the southern tip of the Peloponnese. Mountainous, with dramatic cliff-backed beaches, soft light and turquoise water, they're more Italian in feel, offering a contrasting experience to other Greek islands. Invest in a hire car to get to small villages tucked along quiet back roads. Prices drop in low season.

Corfu ΚΕΡΚΥΡΑ

POP 122,670

Many consider Corfu, or Kerkyra (*ker*-kih-rah) in Greek, to be Greece's most beautiful island – the unfortunate consequence of which is that it's often overrun with crowds.

Getting There & Away

AIR Ioannis Kapodistrias Airport (CFU; ☎26610 30180) is 3km from Corfu Town. **Olympic Air** (☎26610 22962) and **Aegean Airlines** (☎26610 27100) fly daily to Athens and a few times a week to Thessaloniki.

BOAT Ferries go to Igoumenitsa (€7, 1½ hours, hourly). In summer daily ferries and hydrofoils go to Paxi, and international ferries (see p695) stop in Patra (€38, six hours).

BUS Daily buses to Athens (€49, 8½ hours) and Thessaloniki (€45, eight hours) leave from **Avrami long-distance bus station** (☎26610 28927; I Theotoki).

CORFU TOWN

POP 28,692

Built on a promontory and wedged between two fortresses, Corfu's Old Town is a tangle of narrow walking streets through gorgeous Venetian buildings. Explore the winding alleys and surprising plazas in the early morning or late afternoon to avoid the hordes of day trippers seeking souvenirs.

Corfu

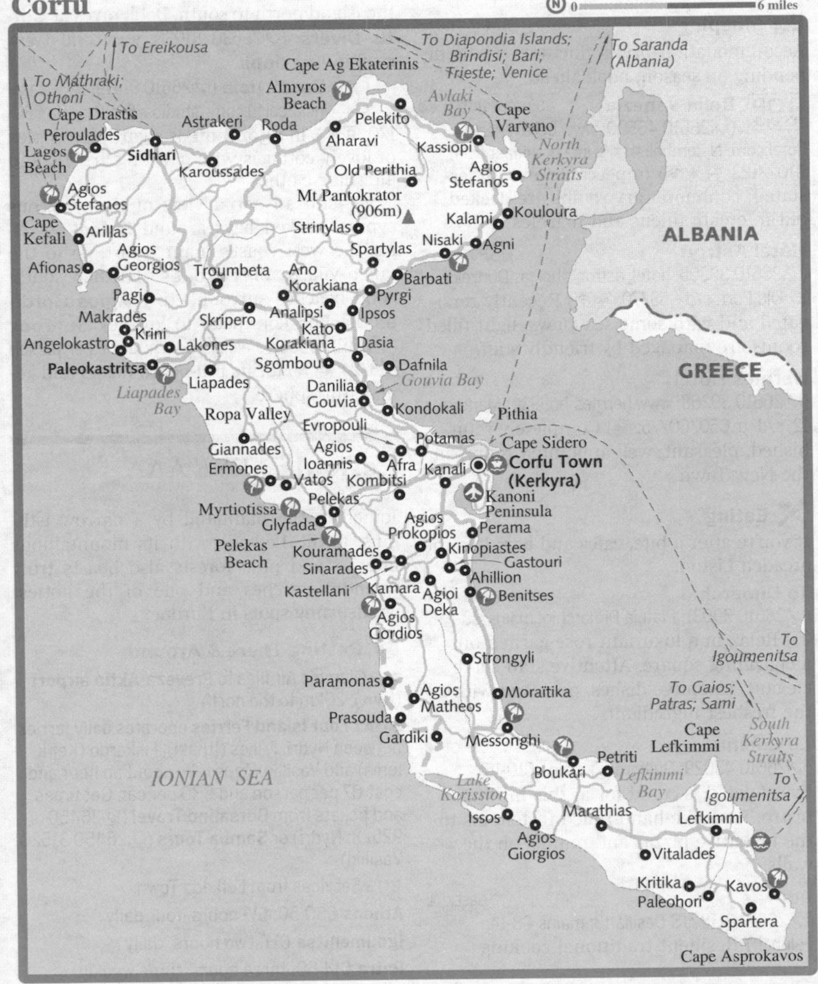

Sights

Palaio Frourio FORTRESS
(Old Fortress; adult/concession €4/2; ⏲8.30am-7pm May-Oct, to 3pm Nov-Mar) The Palaio Frourio stands on an eastern promontory; the **Neo Frourio** (New Fortress) lies to the northwest.

Archaeological Museum MUSEUM
(Vraïla 5; admission €4; ⏲8.30am-3pm Tue-Sun) Houses a collection of finds from Mycenaean to classical times.

Church of Agios Spiridon CHURCH
(Agios Spiridonos) This richly decorated church displays the remains of St Spiridon, paraded through town four times a year.

Sleeping

Accommodation prices fluctuate wildly depending on season; book ahead.

TOP CHOICE **Bella Venezia** BOUTIQUE HOTEL €€
(☎26610 46500; www.bellaveneziahotel.com; N Zambeli 4; s/d incl breakfast from €102/123;) Impeccable and understated; contemporary rooms are decked out in cream linens and marbles.

Hotel Astron HOTEL €€
(☎26610 39505; hotel_astron@hol.gr; Donzelot 15, Old Port; s/d €65/70;) Recently renovated and with some sea views, light-filled rooms are managed by friendly staff.

Hermes Hotel HOTEL €
(☎26610 39268; www.hermes-hotel.gr; Markora 12; s/d/tr €50/60/75;) Completely refurbished, pleasant, well-appointed rooms in the New Town.

Eating

If you're after a bite, cafes and bars line the arcaded Liston.

To Dimarchio ITALIAN, GREEK €€
(☎26610 39031; Plateia Dimarchio; mains €8-25) Relax in a luxuriant rose garden on a charming square. Attentive staff serve elegant, inventive dishes, prepared with the freshest ingredients.

La Cucina ITALIAN, CORFIOT €
(☎26610 45029; Guilford 17; mains €10-15) Every detail is cared for at this intimate bistro, from the hand-rolled tortellonis to the inventive pizzas and murals on the walls.

Rouvás GREEK €
(☎26610 31182; S Desilla 13; mains €8-14; ⏲lunch) Resilient traditional cooking makes this a favourite lunch stop for locals. It even caught the eye of UK celebrity chef Rick Stein for a TV cooking program.

Information

Tourist Police (☎26610 30265; 3rd fl, Samartzi 4)

Getting Around

Blue buses (€0.90 to €1.30) for villages near Corfu Town leave from Plateia San Rocco. Services to other destinations leave from Avrami terminal. A taxi from the airport to the centre costs around €15.

AROUND THE ISLAND

The **Corfu Trail** (www.corfutrail.org) traverses the island north to south. Book dives at **Corfu Divers** (☎26630 81038; www.corfu-divers.com) in **Kassiopi**.

Casa Lucia (☎26610 91419; www.casa-lucia-corfu.com; studios & cottages €60-120; P), in **Sgombou**, is a garden complex of lovely cottages with a strong artistic and alternative ethos.

To gain an aerial view of the gorgeous cypress-backed bays around **Paleokastritsa**, the west coast's main resort, go to the quiet village of **Lakones**. Further south, good beaches surround tiny **Agios Gordios**. Backpackers head to low-key **Sunrock** (☎26610 94637; Pelekas Beach; dm/r per person €18/24; @) for its full-board hostel and genial atmosphere.

Lefkada ΛΕΥΚΑΔΑ

POP 22,500

Joined to the mainland by a narrow isthmus, fertile Lefkada with its mountainous interior and pine forests also boasts truly splendid beaches and one of the hottest windsurfing spots in Europe.

Getting There & Around

AIR Olympic Air flies to **Preveza-Aktio airport** (PVK), 20km to the north.

BOAT **Four Island Ferries** operates daily ferries between Nydri, Frikes (Ithaki), Fiskardo (Keffalonia) and Vasiliki. Trips take about an hour and cost €7 per person and €30 per car. Get times and tickets from **Borsalino Travel** (☎26450 92528; Nydri) or **Samba Tours** (☎26450 31520; Vasiliki).

BUS Services from Lefkada Town:

Athens €30.50, 5½ hours, four daily

Igoumenitsa €11, two hours, daily

Patra €14.50, three hours, three weekly

Preveza €2.70, 30 minutes, six daily
Thessaloniki €39.10, eight hours, two weekly
CAR Rent cars in Lefkada Town, Nydri or Vasiliki.

LEFKADA TOWN

Most travellers' first port of call, Lefkada Town remains laid-back except for August high season. The town's unique earthquake-resistant corrugated-steel architecture somehow blends with its attractive marina, waterfront cafes and vibrant pedestrian thoroughfares.

Sleeping & Eating

Restaurants and cafes line the main street, Dorpfeld, central Lefkas Sq and the waterfront.

Hotel Santa Maura HOTEL €€
(26450 21308; Dorpfeld; s/d/tr incl breakfast €55/75/85;) Think tropical Bahamas with sky-blue and shell-pink interiors and breezy balconies; best rooms on the top floor.

Pension Pirofani HOTEL €€
(26450 25844; Dorpfeld; d €95;) Renovated, sleek rooms have balconies for prime people-watching.

Faei Kairos TRADITIONAL GREEK €
(26450 24045; Golemi; mains €4.50-11) Unashamed nostalgia for the good old days of cinema defines this excellent eatery on Lefkada Town's waterfront.

AROUND THE ISLAND

With its lovely bay, **Nydri** is somewhat blighted by tacky souvenir shops and touristy tavernas. Escape instead to exquisite **Nhion** (26450 41624; Kiafa village; www.neion.gr; d/tr incl breakfast €95/125;), a pristine mountain retreat with stellar views and restored stone buildings.

Lefkada's true gifts are its west-coast beaches. Cliffs drop to broad sweeps of white sand and turquoise waters. Explore! Tiny, bohemian **Agios Nikitas** village draws travellers, but gets very crowded in summer.

Southernmost eucalyptus-scented **Vasiliki** is popular with windsurfers. Organise lessons through **Club Vass** (26450 31588; www.clubvass.com), or guided treks, kayaking and other activities through **Trekking Hellas** (26450 31130; www.trekking.gr). Overlooking the port, **Pension Holidays** (26450 31426; s/d €60/65;) has great-value rooms with kitchens.

Ithaki ΙΘΑΚΗ

POP 3700

Odysseus' long-lost home in Homer's *Odyssey*, Ithaki (ancient Ithaca) remains a verdant, pristine island blessed with cypress-covered hills and beautiful turquoise coves.

Getting There & Away

Ferries run between Frikes, Fiskardo (Keffalonia), Nydri and Vasiliki (Lefkada). Buy tickets at the Frikes dock just before departure. Trips take about 90 minutes and cost €7 per person and €33 per car. Other ferries run to Sami (Keffalonia) and Patras. Check ever-changing routes and schedules at **Delas Tours** (26740 32104; www.ithaca.com.gr; Vathy).

KIONI

Tucked in a tiny, tranquil bay, Kioni is a wonderful place to chill for a few days.

Individuals rent **rooms** (26740 31014; r €40, without bathroom €30), some with kitchens and sea views. **Captain's Apartments** (26740 31481; www.captains-apartments.gr; studio/apt €65/90;) is owned by an affable former merchant navy captain. His shipshape, spacious apartments come with kitchens, satellite TV and balconies overlooking the valley and village.

Several tavernas dot the harbour. Try **Mythos** (mains €6-8) for excellent *pastitsio* and Greek staples. Comfy **Cafe Spavento** also has internet (per hour €4).

AROUND THE ISLAND

The dusty, relaxed port of **Frikes**, where the ferries dock, is a funkier alternative to Kioni and has rooms to rent.

Vathy, Ithaki's small, bustling capital, is the spot for hiring cars and getting cash (no banks in Kioni). Elegant mansions rise from around its bay and **Hotel Perantzada** (26740 33496; www.arthotel.gr/perantzada; Odyssea Androutsou; s/d incl breakfast from €130/150;) occupies two with sensational individually decorated rooms. Charming **Hotel Familia** (26740 33366; www.hotel-familia.com; Odysseos 60; d incl breakfast €140-160;), in a renovated olive press, offers bikes and a bodacious breakfast.

Kefallonia ΚΕΦΑΛΛΟΝΙΑ

POP 39,500

Tranquil cypress- and fir-covered Kefallonia has not succumbed to package tourism to the extent that some of the other Ionian

KEFALLONIA HIGH-SEASON FERRIES

FROM	TO	FARE (€)	DURATION (HR)
Argostoli	Kyllini (Peloponnese)	14	3
Pesada	Agios Nikolaos (Zakynthos)	7	1½
Poros	Kyllini	10	1½
Sami	Bari (Italy)	45	12
Sami	Patra (Peloponnese)	17	2¾
Sami	Piso Aetos & Vathy (Ithaki)	6	45min

Islands have. This largest Ionian island is breathtakingly beautiful with rugged mountain ranges, rich vineyards, soaring coastal cliffs and golden beaches; it remains low-key outside resort areas. Due to the widespread destruction of an earthquake in 1953, much of the island's historic architecture was levelled; Fiskardo is the exception.

Getting There & Around

AIR **Olympic Air** (☎26710 41511) flights go to Athens from **Keffalonia Airport** (EFL; ☎26710 41511), 9km south of Argostoli.

BOAT **Four Island Ferries** operates seasonal routes between Fiskardo, Frikes (Ithaki), Nydri and Vasiliki (Lefkada). In Fiskardo, get tickets from **Nautilus Travel** (☎26740 41440) or the dock before departure. Trips average 90 minutes and cost €7 per person and €30 per car.

BUS Four daily buses connect Argostoli with Athens (€37.10, seven hours), via Patra (€21, four hours)

CAR A car is best for exploring Kefallonia. **Pama Travel** (☎26740 41033; www.pamatravel.com; Fiskardo) rents cars and boats, books accommodation and has internet access.

FISKARDO

Pretty Fiskardo, with its pastel-coloured Venetian buildings set around a picturesque bay, was the only Kefallonian village not to be destroyed by the 1953 earthquake. Despite its popularity with European yachties and upmarket package tourists, it's still peaceful enough to appeal to independent travellers, and is a sublime spot to hang for a few days. Take lovely walks to sheltered coves for swimming.

Sleeping

Archontiko HISTORIC PENSION €€
(☎26740 41342; r from €80; ❄) Overlooking the harbour, people-watch from the balconies of these luxurious rooms in a restored stone mansion.

Faros Suites BOUTIQUE HOTEL €€
(☎26740 41355; www.myrtoscorp.com; ste incl breakfast from €115; ❄@≋) Apartments with fully equipped kitchens, some with sea views, in the next bay over from the village.

Regina's Rooms PENSION €€
(☎26740 41125; d €50-70) On the car park overlooking the village, this budget bargain is ideal for self-caterers. Some of its colourful, breezy rooms have gorgeous bay views or kitchenettes.

Eating

Fiskardo has no shortage of excellent waterside restaurants.

TOP CHOICE **Tassia** SEAFOOD, GREEK €€
(☎26740 41205; mains €10-25) This unassuming but famous Fiskardo institution run by Tassia Dendrinou, celebrated chef and writer, serves up excellent seafood and Greek dishes.

Café Tselenti ITALIAN €€
(☎26740 41344; mains €8-23) Enjoy outstanding Italian classics served by friendly waiters at this place tucked back a bit in a romantic plaza.

Vasso's SEAFOOD €€
(☎26740 41276; mains €10-40) Whether it's fresh grilled fish or pasta with crayfish, Vasso's is *the* place to head for exceptional seafood.

AROUND THE ISLAND

In **Argostoli**, the capital, stay over at **Vivian Villa** (☎26710 23396; www.kefalonia-vivianvilla.gr; Deladetsima 9; s/d/tr €55/70/85, apt €120; ❄) with its big, bright rooms and friendly owners. Sample top Kefallonian cuisine at **Arhontiko** (☎26710 27213; 5 Risospaston; mains €6.50-8.80).

Straddling a slender isthmus on the northwest coast, the petite pastel-coloured village of **Assos** watches over the ruins of a Venetian fortress perched upon a pine-covered peninsula. Splendid **Myrtos Beach**, 13km south of Assos, is spellbinding from above, with postcard views from the precarious roadway.

Zakynthos ΖΑΚΥΝΘΟΣ

POP 38,600

The beautiful island of Zakynthos, or Zante, has stunning coves, dramatic cliffs and extensive beaches, but unfortunately is swamped by package-tour groups, so only a few special spots warrant your time.

Getting There & Around

AIR The **airport** (ZTH; ☎26950 28322) is 6km from Zakynthos Town. **Olympic Air** (☎26950 28322) has daily flights to Athens. easyJet offers occasional flights to Gatwick.

BOAT Get tickets at **Zakynthos Shipping Co-operative** (☎26950 22083/49500; Lombardou 40) in Zakynthos Town. Occasional ferries go to Brindisi, Italy (€69, 15½ hours).

BUS KTEL bus station (☎26950 22255) is west of Zakynthos town. Services:

Athens €23.20, six hours, three daily.

Kefallonia In high season two daily buses go from Pesada to Argostoli, and just two per week go from Agios Nikolaos. Alternatively, cross to Kyllini and catch another ferry to Kefallonia.

Patra €6.80, 3½ hours, four daily.

CAR As bus services are poor, explore the island by car.

Europcar (☎26950 41541; Plateia Agiou Louka, Zakynthos Town).

ZAKYNTHOS TOWN

The island's attractive Venetian capital and port was painstakingly reconstructed after the 1953 earthquake. Its elegant arcades and lively cafe scene make it the best base from which to explore the island.

The peaceful, pine-tree-filled **Kastro** (☎26950 48099; admission €3; ⊙8.30am-2.30pm Tue-Sun), a ruined Venetian fortress high above town, makes for a pleasant outing. The **Byzantine Museum** (☎26950 42714; Plateia Solomou; admission €3; ⊙8.30am-3pm Tue-Sun) houses fabulous ecclesiastical art rescued from churches razed in the earthquake.

Sleeping & Eating

Avoid eating on the touristy Plateia Agiou Markou and do what the locals do: hit Alexandrou Roma for cheap eats. Sweet stores sell *mandolato,* the local soft nougat.

Hotel Strada Marina HOTEL €€
(☎26950 42761; www.stradamarina.gr; Lombardou 14; s/d €60/90; ❄) Well-situated, portside rooms have balconies with sea views.

Camping Zante CAMPING GROUND €
(☎26950 61710; www.zantecamping.gr; Ampula Beach; campsites per person/tent €6/5; @) Decent beachside camping 5km north of Zakynthos Town.

Green Boat Taverna SEAFOOD, GREEK €
(☎26950 22957; Krionerou 50; mains €4-15) Fish and excellent Greek dishes, about 1km north along the waterfront.

Arekia GREEK €
(☎26950 26346; Krioneriou 92; mains €3-10) Munch Greek specialities to the melodies of live *kantades* (serenades), north on the waterfront.

2D SOUVLAKI €
(Alexandrou Roma 32; gyros from €2.50) Delicious gyros and juicy roast chickens.

AROUND THE ISLAND

The **Vasilikos Peninsula** is the pretty green region southeast of Zakynthos Town and fringing **Laganas Bay** with its long, lovely **Gerakas Beach**. The area has been declared a national marine park in order to protect the endangered loggerhead turtles that come ashore to lay their eggs in August, the peak of the tourist invasion. Inform yourself before exploring so as not to accidentally disrupt buried eggs.

TOP CHOICE **Logothetis Organic Farm** (☎26950 35106; http://logothetisfarm.gr; Vasilikos; 1-/2-bedroom cottage €70/150;

ZAKYNTHOS HIGH-SEASON FERRIES

FROM	TO	FARE (€)	DURATION (HR)
Zakynthos Town	Kyllini (Peloponnese)	8.50	1½
Agios Nikolaos	Pesada (Kefallonia)	7	1½
Poros	Kyllini	10	1½

(📶👶) offers tasteful cottages and bicycles, sells organic produce, and arranges horse-riding and sailing.

Cape Keri, near the island's southernmost point, has spectacular views of sheer cliffs and splendid beaches. Keri Beach is overrated. **Tartaruga Camping** (☎26950 51967; www.tartaruga-camping.com; campsites per adult/car/tent €5/3/3.60, r per person €20-50; P❄@), well signed on the road from Laganas to Keri, sprawls through terraced olive groves, pines and plane trees next to the sea.

Continue north and try to arrive early at gorgeous **Limnionas** for swimming in crystal-clear turquoise coves, as there's barely any space to sunbathe on the rocks. The only eatery at the cove, **Taverna Porto Limnionas** (mains €3-15) serves up delicious Greek classics in a sublime setting overlooking the sea.

Many people head to overhyped **Shipwreck Beach** in the northwest. For a sea-level look take a boat from Cape Skinari near Agios Nikolaos, Porto Vromi or Alykes.

UNDERSTAND GREECE

History

With its strategic position at the crossroads of Europe and Asia, Greece has endured a long and turbulent history. During the Bronze Age (3000–1200 BC in Greece), the advanced Cycladic, Minoan and Mycenaean civilisations flourished. The Mycenaeans were swept aside in the 12th century BC by the warrior-like Dorians, who introduced Greece to the Iron Age. The next 400 years are often referred to as the dark ages, a period about which little is known.

By 800 BC, when Homer's *Odyssey* and *Iliad* were first written down, Greece was undergoing a cultural and military revival with the evolution of the city states, the most powerful of which were Athens and Sparta. Greater Greece, Magna Graecia, was created, with southern Italy as an important component. The unified Greeks repelled the Persians twice, at Marathon (490 BC) and Salamis (480 BC). Victory over Persia was followed by unparalleled growth and prosperity known as the classical (or golden) age.

The Golden Age

During this period, Pericles commissioned the Parthenon, Sophocles wrote *Oedipus the King* and Socrates taught young Athenians to think. The golden age ended with the Peloponnesian War (431–404 BC), when the militaristic Spartans defeated the Athenians. They failed to notice the expansion of Macedonia under King Philip II, who easily conquered the war-weary city states.

Philip's ambitions were surpassed by those of his son, Alexander the Great, who marched triumphantly into Asia Minor, Egypt, Persia and what are now parts of Afghanistan and India. In 323 BC he met an untimely death at the age of 33, and his generals divided his empire between themselves.

Roman Rule & the Byzantine Empire

Roman incursions into Greece began in 205 BC. By 146 BC Greece and Macedonia had become Roman provinces. After the subdivision of the Roman Empire into eastern and western empires in AD 395, Greece became part of the Eastern (Byzantine) Empire, based at Constantinople.

In the centuries that followed, Venetians, Franks, Normans, Slavs, Persians, Arabs and, finally, Turks, took turns chipping away at the Byzantine Empire.

ORIGINAL OLYMPICS

The Olympic tradition emerged around the 11th century BC as a paean to the Greek gods, in the form of contests of athletic feats that were attended initially by notable men – and women – who assembled before the sanctuary priests and swore to uphold solemn oaths. By the 8th century BC, the attendance had grown to include a wide confederacy of city states, and the festival morphed into a male-only major event lasting five days at the site of Olympia. A ceremonial truce was enforced for the duration of the games. Crowds of spectators lined the tracks, where competitors vied for victory in athletics, chariot races, wrestling and boxing. Three millennia later, while the scale and scope of the games may have expanded considerably, the basic format has remained essentially unchanged.

The Ottoman Empire & Independence

After the end of the Byzantine Empire in 1453, when Constantinople fell to the Turks, most of Greece became part of the Ottoman Empire. Crete was not captured until 1670, leaving Corfu as the only island not occupied by the Turks. By the 19th century the Ottoman Empire was in decline. The Greeks, seeing nationalism sweep through Europe, fought the War of Independence (1821–22). Greek independence was proclaimed on 13 January 1822, only for arguments among the leaders who had been united against the Turks to escalate into civil war. The Turks, with the help of the Egyptians, tried to retake Greece, but the great powers – Britain, France and Russia – intervened in 1827, and Ioannis Kapodistrias was elected the first Greek president.

Kapodistrias was assassinated in 1831 and the European powers stepped in once again, declaring that Greece should become a monarchy. In January 1833 Otho of Bavaria was installed as king. His ambition, called the Great Idea, was to unite all the lands of the Greek people to the Greek motherland. In 1862 he was peacefully ousted and the Greeks chose George I, a Danish prince, as king.

During WWI Prime Minister Venizelos allied Greece with France and Britain. King Constantine (George's son), who was married to the kaiser's sister Sophia, disputed this and left the country.

Smyrna & WWII

After the war Venizelos resurrected the Great Idea. Underestimating the new-found power of Turkey under the leadership of Atatürk (Mustafa Kemal), he sent forces to occupy Smyrna (the present-day Turkish port of İzmir), with its large Greek population. The army was heavily defeated and this led to a brutal population exchange between the two countries in 1923.

In 1930 George II, Constantine's son, was reinstated as king; he appointed the dictator General Metaxas as prime minister. Metaxas' grandiose ambition was to combine aspects of Greece's ancient and Byzantine past to create a Third Greek Civilisation. However, his chief claim to fame is his celebrated *ohi* (no) to Mussolini's request to allow Italian troops into Greece in 1940.

Greece fell to Germany in 1941 and resistance movements, polarised into royalist and communist factions, staged a bloody civil war lasting until 1949. The civil war was the trigger for a mass exodus that saw almost one million Greeks head off to countries such as Australia, Canada and the USA. Entire villages were abandoned as people gambled on a new start in cities such as Melbourne, Toronto, Chicago and New York.

The Colonels' Coup

Continuing political instability led to the colonels' coup d'état in 1967. The colonels' junta distinguished itself with its appalling brutality, repression and political incompetence. In 1974 it attempted to assassinate Cyprus' leader, Archbishop Makarios, and when he escaped the junta replaced him with the extremist Nikos Samson, prompting Turkey to occupy North Cyprus. The continued Turkish occupation of Cyprus remains one of the most contentious issues in Greek politics. The junta had little choice but to hand back power to the people. In November 1974 a plebiscite voted against restoration of the monarchy. Greece became a republic with the right-wing New Democracy (ND) party taking power.

The 1980s & 1990s

In 1981 Greece entered the European Community (now the EU) as its 10th, smallest and poorest member. Andreas Papandreou's Panhellenic Socialist Movement (Pasok) won the next election, giving Greece its first socialist government. Pasok, which ruled for most of the next two decades, promised the removal of US air bases and withdrawal from NATO, but delivered only rising unemployment and spiralling debt.

Elections in 1990 brought the ND party back to power, but tough economic reforms made the government unpopular and in 1993, Greeks again turned to Pasok and the ailing Papandreou. He had little option but to continue with the austerity program and became equally unpopular until he stood down in 1996 due to ill health. Pasok then abandoned its leftist policies, elected economist and lawyer Costas Simitis as leader, and romped to victory later that year.

The New Millennium

Simitis' government focused strongly on further integration with Europe and in January 2001 admission to the euro club was approved; Greece duly adopted the currency in 2002 and prices have been on the rise ever since.

Greece tilted to the right and in March 2004 elected the ND party led by Costas Karamanlis. This new broom was fortuitous, as the Olympic preparations were running late and suffering budget problems. While the Olympics were successful, Greece is still counting the cost.

During the long hot summer of 2007, forest fires threatened Athens and caused untold damage in the western Peloponnese, Epiros and Evia. Later that year, Karamanlis' government was returned to power for a second term, but amid growing discontent that included massive general strikes and riots, was turfed out in elections in October 2009 in favour of Pasok and George Papandreou, son and grandson of former prime ministers.

Textbooks are being written on Greece's 2010 financial crisis. Simply put, Greece almost fell over from years of over-borrowing, overspending and breaking eurozone rules on deficit management. Financially crippled and looking likely to drag other failing eurozone economies down with it, in May 2010 Greece was on the receiving end of a €110-billion bail-out package to help right the ship. Time will tell if it stays afloat. Needless to say, austerity measures to help balance the budget were not popular, with citizens angry about cuts in spending, pensions and salaries, along with higher taxes.

Greece's foreign policy is dominated by a perceptibly warming, yet still sensitive relationship with Turkey – with Greece continuing to support Turkey's bid to join the EU, despite concerns over Turkish plans to explore for oil and gas in the eastern Aegean.

People

Greece's population has exceeded 11.1 million, with around one-third of the people living in the Greater Athens area and more than two-thirds living in cities – confirming that Greece is now a primarily urban society. Less than 15% live on the islands, the most populous being Crete, Evia and Corfu. Greece has an ageing population and declining birth rate, with big families a thing of the past. Population growth over the last couple of decades is due to a flood of migrants, both legal and illegal.

About 95% of the Greek population belongs to the Greek Orthodox Church. The remainder is split between the Roman Catholic, Protestant, Evangelist, Jewish and Muslim faiths. While older Greeks and those in rural areas tend to be deeply religious, most young people are decidedly more secular.

The Greek year is centred on the saints' days and festivals of the church calendar. Name days (celebrating your namesake saint) are celebrated more than birthdays. Most people are named after a saint, as are boats, suburbs and train stations.

Orthodox Easter is usually at a different time than Easter celebrated by Western churches, though generally in April/May.

RECOGNISE THAT TWANG?

Don't be surprised if your hotel receptionist or waiter speaks perfect English with an Australian twang. A growing stream of young second- and third-generation Greeks are repatriating from the USA, Australia, Canada and other reaches of the Greek diaspora. A huge number of Greeks emigrated during their country's tumultuous history and it is said that over five million people of Greek descent live in 140 countries around the world. Strong sentimental attractions endure and many expat Greeks are involved in the political and cultural life of their ancestral islands, and many retire in Greece.

Arts

The arts have been integral to Greek life since ancient times, with architecture having had the most profound influence. Greek temples, seen throughout history as symbolic of democracy, were the inspiration for architectural movements such as the Italian Renaissance. Today masses of cheap concrete apartment blocks built in the 20th century in Greece's major cities belie this architectural legacy.

Thankfully, the great works of Greek literature are not as easily besmirched. The first and greatest Ancient Greek writer was Homer, author of *Iliad* and *Odyssey,* telling the story of the Trojan War and the subsequent wanderings of Odysseus.

Pindar (c 518–438 BC) is regarded as the pre-eminent lyric poet of ancient Greece and was commissioned to recite his odes at the Olympic Games. The great writers of love poetry were Sappho (6th century BC) and

Alcaeus (5th century BC), both of whom lived on Lesvos. Sappho's poetic descriptions of her affections for women gave rise to the term 'lesbian'.

The Alexandrian Constantine Cavafy (1863–1933) revolutionised Greek poetry by introducing a personal, conversational style. Later, poet George Seferis (1900–71) won the Nobel Prize for literature in 1963, as did Odysseus Elytis (1911–96) in 1979. Nikos Kazantzakis, author of *Zorba the Greek* and numerous novels, plays and poems, is the most famous of 20th-century Greek novelists.

Greece's most famous painter was a young Cretan called Domenikos Theotokopoulos, who moved to Spain in 1577 and became known as the great El Greco. Famous painters of the 20th century include Konstantinos, Partenis and, later, George Bouzianis, whose work can be viewed at the National Art Gallery in Athens.

Music has been a facet of Greek life since ancient times. When visiting Greece today, your trip will inevitably be accompanied by the plucked-string sound of the ubiquitous bouzouki. The bouzouki is one of the main instruments of *rembetika* music – which is in many ways the Greek equivalent of the American blues and has its roots in the sufferings of refugees from Asia Minor in the 1920s.

Dance is also an integral part of Greek life. Whether at a wedding, nightclub or village celebration, traditional dance is widely practised.

Drama continues to feature in domestic arts, particularly in Athens and Thessaloniki. In summer Greek dramas are staged in the ancient theatres where they were originally performed.

Greek film has for many years been associated with the work of film-maker Theo Angelopoulos, who won Cannes' Palme d'Or in 1998 with *An Eternity and One Day*.

Greek TV is dominated by chat shows, sport and foreign movies, only to be interrupted by localised versions of the latest American 'reality TV' hit.

Environment

The Land

Greece sits at the southern tip of the Balkan Peninsula. Of its 1400 islands, only 169 are inhabited. The land mass is 131,944 sq km and Greek territorial waters cover a further 400,000 sq km. Nowhere in Greece is much more than 100km from the sea.

Around 80% of the land is mountainous, with less than a quarter of the country suitable for agriculture.

Greece sits in one of the most seismically active regions in the world – the eastern Mediterranean lies at the meeting point of three continental plates: the Eurasian, African and Arabian. Consequently, Greece has had more than 20,000 earthquakes in the last 40 years, most of them very minor.

Wildlife

The variety of flora in Greece is unrivalled in Europe, with a dazzling array of spectacular wildflowers best seen in the mountains of Crete and the southern Peloponnese.

You won't encounter many animals in the wild, mainly due to hunting. Wild boar, still found in the north, is a favourite target. Squirrels, rabbits, hares, foxes and weasels are all fairly common on the mainland. Reptiles are well represented by snakes, including several poisonous viper species.

Lake Mikri Prespa in Macedonia has the richest colony of fish-eating birds in Europe, while the Dadia Forest Reserve in Thrace counts such majestic birds as the golden eagle and the giant black vulture among its residents.

The brown bear, Europe's largest land mammal, still survives in very small numbers in the mountains of northern Greece, as does the grey wolf.

Europe's rarest mammal, the monk seal, once very common in the Mediterranean Sea, is now on the brink of extinction in Europe. There are about 400 left in Europe, half of which live in Greece. About 40 frequent the Ionian Sea and the rest are found in the Aegean.

The waters around Zakynthos are home to Europe's last large sea turtle colony, that of the loggerhead turtle *(Careta careta)*. The **Sea Turtle Protection Society of Greece** (☎/fax 21052 31342; www.archelon.gr) runs monitoring programs and is always on the look-out for volunteers.

National Parks

While facilities in Greek national parks aren't on par with many other countries, all have refuges and some have marked hiking trails. The most visited parks are Mt Parnitha, north of Athens, and the Samaria

Gorge on Crete. The others are Vikos-Aoös and Prespa National Parks in Epiros; Mt Olympus on the border of Thessaly and Macedonia; and Parnassos and Iti National Parks in central Greece. There is also a national marine park off the coast of Alonnisos, and another around the Bay of Laganas area off Zakynthos.

Environmental Issues

Greece is belatedly becoming environmentally conscious but, regrettably, it's too late for some regions. Deforestation and soil erosion are problems that go back thousands of years, with olive cultivation and goats being the main culprits. Forest fires are also a major problem, with an estimated 250 sq km destroyed every year.

General environmental awareness remains at a depressingly low level, especially where litter is concerned. The problem is particularly bad in rural areas, where roadsides are strewn with aluminium cans and plastic packaging hurled from passing cars. It is somewhat surprising that the waters of the Aegean are as clear as they are considering how many cigarette butts are tossed off ferries.

Food & Drink

Snacks

Greece has a great range of fast-food options. Foremost among them are gyros and souvlaki. The gyros is a giant skewer laden with seasoned meat that grills slowly as it rotates, the meat being steadily trimmed from the outside. Souvlaki are small cubes of meat cooked on a skewer. Both are served wrapped in pitta bread with salad and lashings of tzatziki (a yogurt, cucumber and garlic dip). Other snacks are pretzel rings, spanakopita (spinach and cheese pie) and *tyropitta* (cheese pie).

Starters

Greece is famous for its appetisers, known as *mezedhes* (literally, 'tastes'; meze for short). Standards include tzatziki, *melitzanosalata* (aubergine dip), taramasalata (fish-roe dip), dolmadhes (stuffed vine leaves; dolmas for short), *fasolia* (beans) and *oktapodi* (octopus). A selection of three or four starters represents a good meal and makes an excellent vegetarian option.

Main Dishes

You'll find moussaka (layers of aubergine and mince, topped with béchamel sauce and baked) on every menu, alongside a number of other taverna staples. They include *moschari* (oven-baked veal and potatoes), *keftedes* (meatballs), *stifado* (meat stew), *pastitsio* (baked dish of macaroni with minced meat and béchamel sauce) and *yemista* (either tomatoes or green peppers stuffed with minced meat and rice).

Kalamaria (fried squid) is the most popular (and cheapest) seafood, while *barbouni* (red mullet) and *sifias* (swordfish) tend to be more expensive than meat dishes.

Fortunately for vegetarians, salad is a mainstay of the Greek diet. The most popular is *horiatiki salata,* normally listed on English-language menus as Greek salad. It's a delicious mixed salad comprising cucumbers, peppers, onions, olives, tomatoes and feta cheese. For the full scoop on Greece's legendary feta cheese, check out www.feta.gr.

Desserts

Most Greek desserts are Turkish in origin and are variations on pastry soaked in honey, such as baklava (thin layers of pastry filled with honey and nuts). Delicious Greek yogurt also makes a great dessert, especially with honey.

THE ART OF OUZO

Ouzo is Greece's most famous but misunderstood tipple. While it can be drunk as an aperitif, for most Greeks ouzo has come to embody a way of socialising – best enjoyed during a lazy, extended summer afternoon of seafood *mezedhes* (appetisers) by the beach. Ouzo is sipped slowly and ritually to clean the palate between tastes. It is served in small bottles or *karafakia* (carafes) with water and a bowl of ice cubes – and is commonly drunk on the rocks, diluted with water (it turns a cloudy white). Mixing it with cola is a foreign abomination!

Made from distilled grapes, ouzo is also distilled with residuals from fruit, grains and potatoes, and flavoured with spices, primarily aniseed, giving it that liquorice flavour. The best ouzo is produced on Lesvos and there are more than 360 brands!

NO MORE SMOKE

Legislation that brought in anti-smoking laws similar to those throughout Europe in 2009 was not exactly popular with Greeks, the EU's biggest smokers. Smoking is now officially banned inside public places with the penalty fines placed on the business owners.

Drinks

Bottled mineral water is cheap and available everywhere, as are soft drinks and packaged juices.

Mythos, in its distinctive green bottle, and Alfa, are popular Greek beers.

Greece is traditionally a wine-drinking society. An increasingly good range of wines made from traditional grape varieties is available. Wine enthusiasts should take a look at www.allaboutgreekwine.com. Retsina, wine flavoured with pine-tree resin, is a tasty alternative – though an acquired taste for some. Most tavernas will offer locally made house wines by the carafe.

Metaxa, Greece's dominant brandy, is sweet, while if you are offered some raki, make sure to take a small sip first!

'Greek' coffee should be tried at least once. Don't drink the mudlike grounds at the bottom!

Where to Eat & Drink

The most common variety of restaurant in Greece is the taverna, traditionally an extension of the Greek home table. *Estiatorio* is Greek for restaurant and often has the same dishes as a taverna but with higher prices. A *psistaria* specialises in charcoal-grilled dishes, while a *psarotaverna* specialises in fish. *Ouzeria* (ouzo bars) often have such a range of *mezedhes* that they can be regarded as eateries. For opening hours of restaurants and cafes, see p692. Restaurant listings in this chapter without specified business hours are open for lunch and dinner daily during high season.

Kafeneia are the smoke-filled cafes where men gather to drink 'Greek' coffee, play backgammon and cards, and engage in heated political discussion. Every Greek town you'll visit now has at least one cafe-bar where Greece's youth while away hours over a frappé (frothy ice coffee).

Buying and preparing your own food is easy in Greece – every town of consequence has a supermarket, as well as fruit and vegetable shops.

To have a go at producing your own Greek culinary masterpieces, check out www.gourmed.gr. You'll also find information on the healthy Greek diet at www.mediterranean-diet.gr, while www.oliveoil.gr can tell you all about one of Greece's best-known products.

SURVIVAL GUIDE

Directory A–Z

Accommodation

Hotels Classified as deluxe, or A, B, C, D or E class; ratings seldom seem to have much bearing on the price, which is determined more by season and location.

Domatia Greek equivalent of a B&B, minus the breakfast; don't worry about finding them – owners will find you as they greet ferries and buses shouting 'room!'.

Youth hostels In most major towns and on some islands; **Greek Youth Hostel Organisation** (☎21075 19530; www.athens-yhostel.com).

Camping grounds Generally open from April to October; standard facilities include hot showers, kitchens, restaurants and minimarkets – and often a swimming pool; **Panhellenic Camping Association** (www.panhellenic-camping-union.gr).

Mountain refuges Listed in *Greece Mountain Refuges & Ski Centres*, available free of charge at EOT and EOS (Ellinikos Orivatikos Syndesmos, the Greek Alpine Club) offices.

HAPHAZARD OPENING HOURS

It's worth noting that with businesses associated with tourists, opening hours can be rather haphazard. In high season when there are plenty of visitors around, restaurants, cafes, nightclubs and souvenir shops are pretty much open whenever they think they can do good business. If there are few people around, some businesses will simply close early or won't bother opening at all. And in low season, some places, including some sleeping options, may close up for months at a time.

PRICE RANGES

In this chapter we have used the following price ranges for sleeping options. Prices quoted in listings are for high season (usually July and August) and include a private bathroom.

€€€ more than €150

€€ €60 to €150

€ less than €60

Business Hours

Banks 8am-2.30pm Mon-Thu, 8am-2pm Fri (in cities, also: 3.30-6.30pm Mon-Fri, 8am-1.30pm Sat)

Cafes 10am-midnight

Post offices 7.30am-2pm Mon-Fri (in cities 7.30am-8pm Mon-Fri, 7.30am-2pm Sat)

Restaurants 11am-3pm & 7pm-1am (varies greatly)

Supermarkets 8am-8pm Mon-Fri, 8am-3pm Sat

Street kiosks (*periptera*) early-late Mon-Sun

Children

» It's safe and easy to travel with children in Greece.
» Greeks are very family-orientated.
» Be very careful crossing roads with kids!
» Travel on ferries, buses and trains is free to age four years; half-fare to age 10 (ferries) or 12 (buses and trains).
» You'll find plenty of kids' menus.
» See www.greece4kids.com.

Customs

You may bring the following into Greece duty-free:

» 200 cigarettes or 50 cigars
» 1L of spirits or 2L of wine
» 50ml of perfume
» 250ml of eau de cologne.

It is strictly forbidden to export antiquities (anything over 100 years old) without an export permit.

Embassies & Consulates

Australia (☎210 870 4000; www.greece.embassy.gov.au; 6th fl, Thon Building, cnr Leoforos Alexandras & Leoforos Kifisias, Ambelokipi, Athens)

Canada (☎210 727 3400; www.greece.gc.ca; Genadiou 4, Athens)

Japan (☎210 670 9900; www.gr.emb-japan.go.jp; Ethnikís Antistáseos 46, Halandri, Athens)

New Zealand (☎210 692 4136; www.nzembassy.com; costacot@yahoo.com; Kifisias 76, Ambelokipi, Athens)

UK (☎210 727 2600; http://ukingreece.fco.gov.uk; Ploutarhou 1, Athens)

USA (☎210 721 2951; http://athens.usembassy.gov; Leoforos Vasilissis Sofias 91, Athens)

Food

In this chapter we have used the following price ranges for Eating options:

€€€ more than €40

€€ €15 to €40

€ less than €15

Gay & Lesbian Travellers

» The church plays a significant role in shaping society's views on issues such as sexuality, and homosexuality is generally frowned upon.
» It is wise to be discreet and to avoid open displays of togetherness. That said, Greece is a popular destination for gay travellers.
» Athens has a busy gay scene that packs up and heads to the islands for summer.
» Mykonos has long been famous for its bars, beaches and hedonism.
» A visit to Eresos on Lesvos has become something of a pilgrimage for lesbians.

SEASONAL PRICES

The prices quoted in this chapter for sleeping options are for 'high season' (usually July and August). If you turn up in the 'middle' or 'shoulder seasons' (May and June; September and October) expect to pay significantly less. During 'low season' (late October to late April) prices can be up to 50% cheaper, but a lot of places, especially on the islands, virtually close their shutters for winter. Websites will usually display these differences in price.

Greek accommodation is subject to strict price controls, and by law a notice must be displayed in every room stating the category of the room and the seasonal price. If you think there's something amiss, contact the Tourist Police.

KALIMERA!

Greece is one of those countries where a big smile and some local language can go a long way. If you make an effort, so will the locals. For some more phrases, see the Language chapter (p1227) but also try these basics on for size – they're likely to be all you'll need, and are best if they come with a smile:

» ka·li·me·ra — Good morning
» yia su — Hello
» ef·kha·ri·*sto* — Thank you
» pa·ra·ka·*lo* — Please/You're welcome
» stin i·*yia* mas — Cheers!

Greece is also one of those countries where it pays not to get upset if things don't go your way. There's no point in getting angry with anyone if the ferry is late (or if it doesn't come at all!). You'll likely be met with a stone face and unhelpful service. Relax! You're in Greece!

Internet Access

» Greece has embraced the internet bigtime.
» Charges differ wildly (as does the speed of access).
» Some midrange and most top-end hotels will offer their guests some form of internet connection.
» Laptop-wielding visitors will often be able to connect to wi-fi at hotels and most internet cafes.

Language Courses

For intensive language courses check out the **Athens Centre** (www.athenscentre.gr).

Money

ATMs Everywhere except the smallest villages.

Bargaining While souvenir shops will generally bargain, prices in other shops are normally clearly marked and non-negotiable; accommodation is nearly always negotiable outside peak season, especially for longer stays.

Cash Currency is king at street kiosks and small shops, and especially in the countryside.

Changing currency Banks, post offices and currency exchange offices are all over the places; exchange all major currencies.

Credit cards Generally accepted, but may not be on smaller islands or in small villages.

Tipping The service charge is included on the bill in restaurants, but it is the custom to 'round up the bill'; same for taxis.

Post

» *Tahydromia* (post offices) are easily identified by the yellow sign outside.
» Regular postboxes are yellow; red postboxes are for express mail.
» The postal rate for postcards and airmail letters within the EU is €0.60, to other destinations it's €0.80.

Public Holidays

New Year's Day 1 January

Epiphany 6 January

First Sunday in Lent February

Greek Independence Day 25 March

Good Friday/Easter Sunday March/April

May Day (Protomagia) 1 May

Feast of the Assumption 15 August

Ohi Day 28 October

Christmas Day 25 December

St Stephen's Day 26 December

Safe Travel

» Crime is traditionally low in Greece, but on the rise.
» Watch out for bar scams and *bombes* (spiked drinks).
» Be careful of pickpockets on the Athens metro, around Omonia and at the flea market.
» Thefts from tourists are often committed by other tourists.

Telephone

» Maintained by Organismos Tilepikoinonion Ellados, known as OTE (o-*teh*).

» Public phones are easy to use; pressing the 'i' button brings up the operating instructions in English.
» Public phones are everywhere and all use phonecards.
» For directory inquiries within Greece, call ☎131 or ☎132; for international directory inquiries, it's ☎161 or ☎162.

MOBILE PHONES

» Mobile phones have become the must-have accessory in Greece.
» If you have a compatible GSM phone from a country with a global roaming agreement with Greece, you will be able to use your phone there.
» Make sure you have global roaming activated before you leave your country of residence.
» There are several mobile service providers in Greece; **CosmOTE** (www.cosmote.gr) has the best coverage.
» You can purchase a Greek SIM card for around €20.

PHONE CODES

» Telephone codes are part of the 10-digit number within Greece.
» The landline prefix is 2 and for mobiles it's 6.

PHONECARDS

» All public phones use OTE phonecards; sold at OTE offices and street kiosks.
» Phonecards come in €3, €5 and €10 versions; local calls cost €0.30 for three minutes.
» Discount-card schemes are available, offering much better value for money.

Time

» One time zone throughout Greece.
» Two hours ahead of GMT/UTC.
» Three hours ahead on daylight-savings time: from the last Sunday in March to the last Sunday in October.

MOVING ON?

For tips, recommendations and reviews beyond Greece, head to shop.lonelyplanet.com, where you can purchase downloadable PDFs of the Albania and Turkey chapters from Lonely Planet's *Mediterranean Europe* guide, or the Macedonia and Bulgaria chapters from *Eastern Europe*.

Toilets

» Public toilets are rare, except at airports and bus and train stations.
» Most places have Western-style toilets.
» Some public toilets may be Asian-style squat toilets.
» Greek plumbing can't handle toilet paper! Anything larger than a postage stamp will cause a blockage. Put your used toilet paper, sanitary napkins and tampons in the small bin provided next to every toilet.

Tourist Information

Greek National Tourist Organisation (GNTO; www.gnto.gr) Known as EOT within Greece.

EOT office or **local tourist office** In almost every town of consequence and on many of the islands.

Tourist Police In popular destinations, and can also provide information; head here if you think you've been ripped off.

Travellers with Disabilities

» Most hotels, museums and ancient sites are not wheelchair accessible; the uneven terrain is an issue even for able-bodied people.
» Few facilities for the visually or hearing impaired.
» Check out www.greecetravel.com/handicapped.

Visas

» Visitors from most countries don't need a visa for Greece.
» Countries whose nationals can stay in Greece for up to three months include Australia, Canada, all EU countries, Iceland, Israel, Japan, New Zealand and the USA.

Getting There & Away

Air

» Most visitors arrive by air, mostly into Athens.
» Seventeen international airports in Greece; most handle only summer charter flights to the islands.
» Growing number of scheduled services by budget airlines, eg easyJet flies into Athens, Corfu, Hania, Iraklio, Kos, Mykonos, Rhodes, Santorini, Thessaloniki and Zakynthos

INTERNATIONAL AIRPORTS

CITY	AIRPORT	DESIGNATION
Aktion (for Lefkada)	Aktion National Airport	PVK
Athens	Eleftherios Venizelos Airport	ATH
Corfu	Corfu Intl Airport	CFU
Hania (Crete)	Hania Intl Airport	CHQ
Iraklio	Nikos Kazantzakis Airport	HER
Kalamata	Kalamata Intl Airport	KLX
Karpathos	Karpathos National Airport	AOK
Kavala	Alexander the Great Airport	KVA
Kefallonia	Kefallonia Intl Airport	EFL
Kos	Hippocrates Intl Airport	KGS
Mykonos	Mykonos National Airport	JMK
Rhodes	Diagoras Airport	RHO
Samos	Samos Intl Airport	SMI
Santorini (Thira)	Santorini National Airport	JTR
Skiathos	Skiathos National Airport	JSI
Thessaloniki	Macedonia Airport	SKG
Zakynthos	Zakynthos Intl Airport	ZTH

Greek Airlines flying international routes:

Olympic Air (OA; www.olympicair.com) Privatised version of former Olympic Airlines.

Aegean Airlines (A3; www.aegeanair.com)

Land

BORDER CROSSINGS

You can drive or ride through the following border crossings (the main one is Kakavia):

From Albania:

» Kakavia (60km northwest of Ioannina)
» Sagiada (28km north of Igoumenitsa)
» Mertziani (17km west of Konitsa)
» Krystallopigi (14km west of Kotas)

From Bulgaria:

» Promahonas (109km northeast of Thessaloniki)
» Ormenio (in northeastern Thrace)
» Exohi (50km north of Drama)

From Macedonia:

» Evzoni (68km north of Thessaloniki)
» Niki (16km north of Florina)
» Doïrani (31km north of Kilkis)

From Turkey:

» Kipi (43km east of Alexandroupolis)
» Kastanies (139km northeast of Alexandroupolis)

BUS

The **Hellenic Railways Organisation** (OSE; www.ose.gr) operates:

To Albania Overnight bus between Athens and Tirana (16 hours, daily) via Ioannina and Gjirokastra.

To Bulgaria Athens–Sofia bus (15 hours, six weekly); Thessaloniki-Sofia (7½ hours, four daily).

To Turkey Athens to İstanbul (22 hours, six weekly); stops at Thessaloniki (seven hours) and Alexandroupolis (13 hours).

TRAIN

To Bulgaria Daily train between Sofia and Athens (18 hours) via Thessaloniki.

To Macedonia Two trains daily from Thessaloniki to Skopje (five hours).

To Turkey Daily trains operate between İstanbul and Thessaloniki (12 hours).

To Russia Summer-only direct weekly service from Thessaloniki to Moscow (70 hours).

Sea

Check out ferry routes, schedules and services online at www.greekferries.gr.

ALBANIA

Saranda Petrakis Lines (☎26610 38690; www.ionian-cruises.com) has daily hydrofoils to Corfu (25 minutes).

ITALY

Ancona In summer, there are three daily sailings to Patra (20 hours).

Bari Daily sailings to Patra (14½ hours) via Corfu (eight hours) and Keffalonia (14 hours); also daily to Igoumenitsa (11½ hours).

Brindisi Operates only between April and early October; services to Patra (15 hours), calling in at Igoumenitsa.

Venice In summer, up to 12 weekly sailings to Patra (30 hours) via Corfu (25 hours).

TURKEY

Boat services operate between Turkey's Aegean coast and the Greek Islands:

Rhodes to Marmaris Daily in summer, twice weekly in winter; 50 minutes.

Symi to Datça Saturdays in summer; one hour.

Kos to Bodrum Daily in summer; one hour.

Samos to Kuşadasi Daily in summer, weekly in winter; one hour.

Chios to Çeşme Daily in summer; one hour.

Lesvos to Ayvalik Four times weekly in summer; one hour.

Getting Around

Greece has a comprehensive transport system and is easy to get around.

> **LONDON TO ATHENS OVERLAND**
>
> For overland enthusiasts, a trip from London to Athens can be accomplished in two days, taking in some gorgeous scenery along the way. A sample itinerary from London would see you catching the Eurostar to Paris and then an overnight sleeper train to Bologna in Italy. From there, a coastal train takes you to Bari, where there's an overnight boat to Patra on the Peloponnese. From Patra, it's a 4½-hour train journey to Athens.

Air

Domestic air travel has been very price competitive of late, and it's sometimes cheaper to fly than take the ferry, especially if you book ahead online. A plan to merge Olympic Air and Aegean Airlines was prohibited by the European Commission in January 2011 due to its potential effect on competition and prices.

Domestic Air Carriers

Aegean Airlines (A3; www.aegeanair.com) The big competition offers newer aircraft and similar prices on popular routes.

Astra Airlines (A2; www.astra-airlines.gr) Based in Thessaloniki; a newcomer flying limited routes.

Athens Airways (ZF; www.athensairways.com) New kid on the block.

Olympic Air (OA; www.olympicair.com) Recently privatised; has the most extensive network.

Sky Express (SHE; www.skyexpress.gr) Based in Iraklio, Crete; mainly flies routes that the big two don't.

Bicycle

» Greece has very hilly terrain.
» Summer heat can be stifling.
» Many drivers totally disregard the road rules.

Bicycle tours See www.cyclegreece.gr; bicycles are carried for free on ferries.

Rental bicycles Available at most tourist centres, but these are generally for pedalling around town rather than for serious riding. Prices generally range from €10 to €20 per day.

Boat

FERRY

» Ferries come in all shapes and sizes, from state-of-the-art 'superferries' that run on the major routes, to ageing open ferries that operate local services to outlying islands.
» Newer high-speed ferries are slashing travel times, but cost much more.
» 'Classes' on ferries are largely a thing of the past; you have the option of 'deck class', which is the cheapest ticket, or 'cabin class' with air-con cabins and a decent lounge and restaurant.
» When buying tickets you will automatically be given deck class.

Main Ferry Routes

» Tickets can be bought at the last minute at the dock, but in high season, some boats may be full – plan ahead.

CATAMARAN

» High-speed catamarans have become an important part of the island travel scene.

» Much less prone to cancellation in rough weather.

» Catamaran fares are generally more expensive than ferries and about the same as hydrofoils.

HYDROFOIL

» A faster alternative to ferries on some routes; take half the time, but cost twice as much.

» Most routes will operate only during the high season.

» Tickets for hydrofoils must be bought in advance and they are often sold with seat allocation.

Bus

» Long-distance buses are operated by **KTEL** (Koino Tamio Eispraxeon Leoforion; www.ktel.org).

» Fares are fixed by the government; service routes can be found on the company's website.

» Comfortable, generally run on time, and frequent services on all major routes.

» Reasonably priced – eg Athens–Volos (€25, five hours) and Athens–Patra (€17, three hours).

» Tickets should be bought at least an hour in advance to ensure a seat.

» Buses don't have toilets and refreshments, but stop for a break every couple of hours.

Car & Motorcycle

» A great way to explore areas in Greece that are off the beaten track.

ISLAND-HOPPING

For many, the idea of meandering from island to island by boat in the Greek Islands is the ultimate dream. It's still a lot of fun, but to some extent not what it used to be. Many of those slow, romantic old ferries you may have seen in the movies have disappeared, replaced by big modern people-movers. If you turn up in high season you might find it just as stressful as rush hour back home.

It's still possible to get away from it all, but it will require some thought – head to smaller islands off the beaten path before high season kicks in. Every island has a boat service of some sort!

Boat operations are highly seasonal and based on the tourist trade, so there's not a lot happening in winter. Services pick up from April, and during July and August Greece's seas are a mass of wake and wash.

Summer also brings the *meltemi*, a strong dry northerly wind that can blow for days and cause havoc to ferry schedules.

In any season, changes to schedules can take place at the last minute. Be prepared to be flexible. Boats seldom arrive early, but often arrive late! And some don't come at all. Think of it as part of the fun.

Check out www.greekferries.gr for schedules, costs and links to individual boat company websites.

» Be careful – Greece has the highest road-fatality rate in Europe.
» The road network has improved dramatically in recent years.
» Freeway tolls are fairly hefty.
» Almost all islands are served by car ferries, but they are expensive; costs vary by the size of the vehicle.
» The Greek automobile club, **ELPA** (www.elpa.gr), generally offers reciprocal services to members of other national motoring associations. If your vehicle breaks down, dial ☎104.
» EU-registered vehicles are allowed free entry into Greece for six months without road taxes being due; a green card (international third party insurance) is all that's required.

HIRE

Rental cars

» Available just about anywhere in Greece.
» Better rates with local companies than with the big multinational outfits.
» Check the insurance waivers closely; check how they can assist in case of a breakdown.
» High-season weekly rates start at about €280 for the smallest models, dropping to €200 in winter – add tax and extras.
» Major companies will request a credit-card deposit.
» Minimum driving age in Greece is 18, but most car-hire firms require a driver of 21 or over.

Mopeds & Motorcycles

» Available for hire everywhere.
» Regulations stipulate that you need a valid motorcycle licence stating proficiency for the size of motorcycle you wish to rent – from 50cc upwards.
» Mopeds and 50cc motorcycles range from €10 to €25 per day or from €25 per day for a 250cc motorcycle.
» Outside high season, rates drop considerably.
» Ensure that the bike is in good working order and the brakes work well.
» Check that your travel insurance covers you for injury resulting from motorcycle accidents.

ROAD RULES

» Drive on the right.
» Overtake on the left (not all Greeks do this!).
» Compulsory to wear seatbelts in the front seats, and in the back if they are fitted.
» Drink-driving laws are strict; a blood alcohol content of 0.05% incurs a fine of around €150 and over 0.08% is a criminal offence.

Public Transport

Bus All major towns have local bus systems.

Metro Athens is the only city with a metro system.

Taxi

» Widely available and reasonably priced.

» Yellow city cabs are metered; rates double between midnight and 5am. Grey rural taxis do not have meters; settle on a price before you get in.

» Athens taxi drivers are gifted in their ability to somehow make a little bit extra with every fare. If you have a complaint, note the cab number and contact the Tourist Police.

» Rural taxi drivers are generally honest, friendly and helpful.

Train

» Greece has only two main lines: Athens north to Thessaloniki and Alexandroupolis, and Athens to the Peloponnese

» There are a number of branch lines, eg Pyrgos–Olympia line and the spectacular Diakofto–Kalavryta mountain railway.

» **Greek Railways Organisation** (OSE; www.ose.gr)

» Inter-Rail and Eurail passes are valid; you still need to make a reservation.

» In summer make reservations at least two days in advance.

Ireland

Includes »

Best Places to Eat

» Farmgate Café (p722)
» Winding Stair (p711)
» Fishy Fishy Café (p726)
» Ard Bia at Nimmo's (p737)
» Ginger (p751)

Best Places to Stay

» Isaacs Hostel (p710)
» Number 31 (p711)
» Garnish House (p721)
» Kinlay House (p736)
» Old Rectory (p750)

Why Go?

Few countries have an image so plagued by cliché. From shamrocks and shillelaghs to leprechauns and lovable rogues, there's a plethora of platitudes to wade through before you scramble ashore on the real Ireland.

But it's well worth looking beyond the tourist tat, for the Emerald Isle is one of Europe's gems, a scenic extravaganza of lakes, mountains, sea and sky. From wind-lashed Donegal to picture-postcard County Cork, there are countless opportunities to get outdoors and explore, whether surfing the beach breaks of Bundoran, cycling the coast of Antrim, or hiking the hills of Kerry and Connemara.

There are cultural pleasures too in the land of Joyce and Yeats, U2 and the Undertones. Dublin, Cork and Belfast all have party-on pubs and foot-stomping live-music scenes, while you can enjoy traditional music in the bars of Galway, Doolin and Killarney. So push aside the shamrocks and experience the real Ireland.

When to Go

Dublin

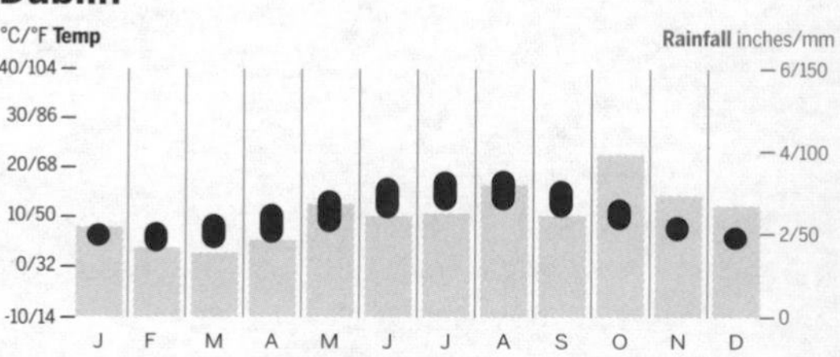

Late March Spring has sprung, landscape is greening, St Patrick's Day festivities beckon.

June Best chance of dry weather, long summer evenings; opera in Wexford, Bloomsday in Dublin.

September–October Summer crowds thin, autumn colours reign, surf's up on the west coast.

Connections

Ireland is just about as far west as you can go in Europe – next stop, North America. But the Emerald Isle can serve as a stepping stone between mainland Europe and the UK. Ferry services run from Roscoff and Cherbourg in northern France to Rosslare (near Wexford) in southeast Ireland. After exploring Ireland you can continue your travels via one of the many ferries linking Ireland with Great Britain: from Rosslare to Fishguard and Pembroke (both in Wales); from Cork to Swansea (Wales); from Dublin or Dun Laoghaire to Holyhead (Wales); from Dublin or Belfast to the Isle of Man and Liverpool (England); from Belfast to Stranraer (Scotland); and from Larne to Troon (April to October only) or Cairnryan (both Scotland).

You can travel direct by coach (via a ferry crossing) from Dublin or Belfast to London and several other UK cities. Budget airlines fly direct from Dublin and Belfast to London, Cardiff, Edinburgh and other UK destinations. For more info, see p765.

ITINERARIES

One Week

Spend a couple of days in Dublin ambling through the excellent national museums, and gorging yourself on Guinness and good company in Temple Bar. Get medieval in Kilkenny before heading on to Cork and discovering why they call it 'The Real Capital'. Meander through lush, idyllic West Cork and take in the friendly spirit and melodious accents of its denizens.

Two Weeks

Follow the one-week itinerary, then make your way from West Cork up to touristy Killarney and the Ring of Kerry on your way to bohemian Galway. Using Galway as your base, explore the alluring Aran Islands and the hills of Connemara. Finally, head north to experience the newly optimistic vibe in fast-changing Belfast.

Essential Food & Drink

» **Champ** Northern Irish dish of ashed potatoes with spring onions (scallions)

» **Colcannon** Mashed potato, milk, cabbage and fried onion

» **Farl** Triangular flatbread in Northern Ireland and Donegal

» **Irish stew** Lamb stew with potatoes, onions and thyme

» **Soda bread** Wonderful bread – white or brown, sweet or savoury – made from very soft Irish flour and buttermilk

» **Stout** Besides Guinness are two other major producers: Murphy's and Beamish & Crawford, both based in Cork city.

» **Irish whiskey** Almost 100 different types are brewed by only three distilleries: Jameson, Bushmills and Cooley.

AT A GLANCE

» **Currency** euro (€) in Republic of Ireland, pound sterling (£) in Northern Ireland

» **Languages** English, Irish Gaelic

» **Money** ATMs widespread; credit cards widely accepted

» **Visas** Schengen rules do not apply; see p765 for information.

Fast Facts

» **Area** 84,421 sq km

» **Population** 6 million

» **Capitals** Dublin (Republic of Ireland), Belfast (Northern Ireland)

» **Emergency** ☎112

» **Telephone** country code Republic of Ireland ☎353, Northern Ireland ☎44; international access code ☎00

Exchange Rates

Australia	A$1	€0.74/ UK£0.65
Canada	C$1	€0.74/ UK£0.63
Euro Zone	€1	UK£0.87
Japan	¥100	€0.87/ UK£0.77
New Zealand	NZ$1	€0.56/ UK£0.45
UK	UK£1	€1.16
USA	US$1	€0.67/ UK£0.60

Set Your Budget

» **Budget hotel room** €60

» **Two-course dinner** €25

» **Pint of beer** €4–5

» **Dublin tram ticket** €2–4

Ireland Highlights

1. Meander through the museums, pubs and literary haunts of **Dublin** (p703), and ask a local, 'Where's the craic?'
2. Hang out in bohemian **Galway** (p736), with its hip cafes and live-music venues
3. Hike along the Causeway Coast and clamber across the **Giant's Causeway** (p754)
4. Take a boat trip to the 6th-century monastery perched atop the wild rocky islet of **Skellig Michael** (p732)
5. Sup a pint of Guinness while tapping your toes to a live music session in one of Dublin's **traditional Irish pubs** (p712).
6. Cycle through the spectacular lake and mountain scenery of the **Gap of Dunloe** (p729)
7. Discover the industrial history of the city that built the world's most famous ocean liner in **Belfast**'s Titanic Quarter (p746)
8. Wander the wild, limestone shores of the remote and craggy **Aran Islands** (p740)

DUBLIN

☎01 / POP 1.1 MILLION

Sitting in a tapas bar on Great George's St, nursing a Guinness or a hangover (or both), you think about what your favourite experience has been in Dublin so far. Was it drinking in Temple Bar with people from dozens of other countries or was it buying fresh vegies at the Asian food market? Was it admiring the Georgian houses along St Stephen's Green or was it wandering the grounds of Trinity College? You never come to an answer, but you do realise that, just as the waters on the banks of the Liffey River seem to rise every day, so does your affection for this city.

The roar of prosperity and the advent of the EU have made it so that all roads lead to Dublin. Visitors swarm in droves like moths to a light bulb – for the historic museums, top-class attractions and Georgian architecture – while immigrants from Eastern Europe, Asia and Africa set up new lives for their families, adding even more depth and complexity to an already rich cultural tapestry. Add a hard-partying nightlife to this mixture and what you get is a city that's constantly changing, and having a rare old time as it does so.

Sights

Dublin is neatly divided by the Liffey River into the more affluent 'south side' and the less prosperous 'north side'. North of the river are O'Connell St, with its needle-shaped Monument of Light, and Gardiner St, with its B&Bs and guest houses. Busáras, the main bus station, and Connolly station, one of the main train stations, are here too.

Immediately south of the river is the bustling Temple Bar district, Trinity College and, just below it, the lovely St Stephen's Green. Pedestrianised Grafton St and its surrounding streets and lanes are crammed with shops and restaurants. About 2km west is Heuston station, the city's other main train station.

Dublin's finest Georgian architecture, including its famed doorways, is found around **St Stephen's Green** (Map p704) and **Merrion Square** (Map p704) just south of Trinity College; both are prime picnic spots when the sun shines.

Trinity College & Book of Kells MUSEUM

(Map p708; www.bookofkells.ie; College Green; admission to college grounds free, Old Library adult/child €9/free; ⏰9.30am-5pm Mon-Sat year-round, 9.30am-4.30pm Sun May-Sep, noon-4.30pm Sun Oct-Apr) Ireland's premier university was founded by Queen Elizabeth I in 1592. Its full name is technically the University of Dublin, but **Trinity College** is the institution's sole college. Until 1793 the students were all Protestants, but today most of them are Catholic. Women were first allowed to matriculate in 1903.

Student-guided **walking tours** (per person €10; ⏰twice per hour 10.45am-3.40pm Mon-Sat & 10.45am-3.15pm Sun mid-May–Sep) depart from inside the main gate on College St. The tour is an especially good deal since it includes admission to the **Old Library** to see the **Book of Kells**, an elaborately illuminated gospel created by monks on the Scottish isle of Iona around AD 800, and the spectacular **Long Room**, an early-18th-century library lined with marble busts of writers and philosophers.

FREE **National Museum of Archaeology** MUSEUM

(Map p708; www.museum.ie; Kildare St; ⏰10am-5pm Tue-Sat, 2-5pm Sun) Among the highlights of the National Museum's archaeology and history branch are its superb collection of **prehistoric gold objects**; the exquisite 12th-century **Ardagh Chalice**, the world's finest

DUBLIN IN...

Two Days

Start by heading to **Trinity College**, where the tour allows you entrance to see the **Book of Kells**. Afterwards, window-shop your way down **Grafton St** while en route to **Fallon & Byrne** for lunch. Walk off the food and wine while marvelling at the Georgian architecture surrounding **St Stephen's Green** before you party your arse off in **Temple Bar**. Then go sleep it off at the gorgeous **Grafton Guesthouse**. Begin your next day with a hearty Irish breakfast before venturing off to view the prehistoric gold at the **National Museum of Archaeology**. Top off your visit by enjoying the best pint of your life at the **Guinness Storehouse**.

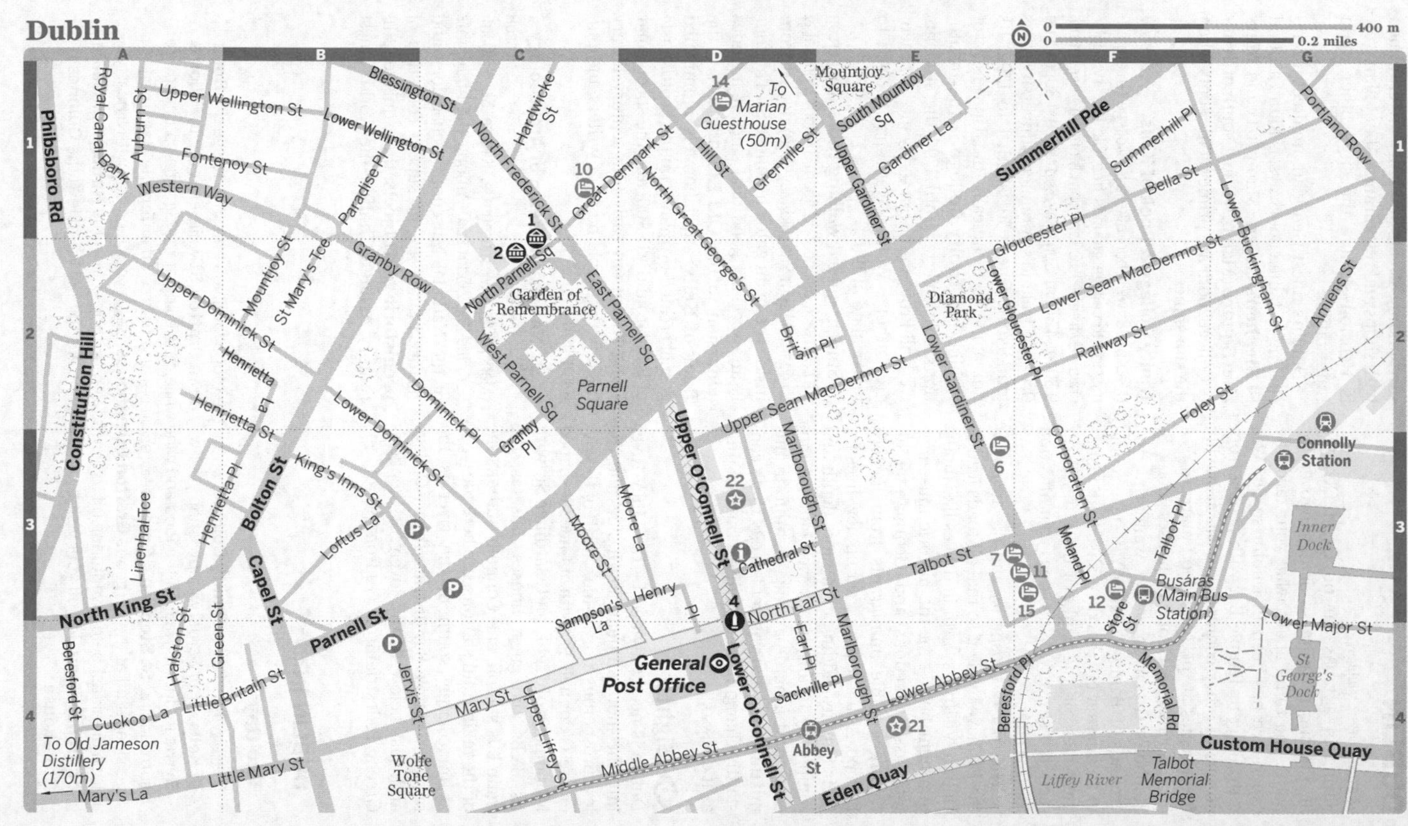

Dublin
0.2 miles
400 m
Phibsboro Rd
Royal Canal Bank
Auburn St
Upper Wellington St
Blessington St
Lower Wellington St
Hardwicke St
North Frederick St
Fontenoy St
Western Way
Paradise Pl
Granby Row
Great Denmark St
North Great George's St
Hill St
Grenville St
To Marian Guesthouse (50m)
Mountjoy Square
South Mountjoy Sq
Upper Gardiner St
Gardiner La
Summerhill Pde
Summerhill Pl
Bella St
Lower Buckingham St
Portland Row
Amiens St
Mountjoy St
St Mary's Tce
Upper Dominick St
North Parnell Sq
Garden of Remembrance
East Parnell Sq
West Parnell Sq
Parnell Square
Granby Pl
Dominick Pl
Lower Dominick St
Henrietta La
Henrietta St
Henrietta Pl
Constitution Hill
Linenhal Tce
Bolton St
King's Inns St
Loftus La
Capel St
North King St
Halston St
Green St
Beresford St
Cuckoo La
Little Britain St
To Old Jameson Distillery (170m)
Mary's La
Little Mary St
Parnell St
Jervis St
Mary St
Upper Liffey St
Wolfe Tone Square
Middle Abbey St
Moore St
Moore La
Sampson's La
Henry Pl
General Post Office
Upper O'Connell St
Lower O'Connell St
Cathedral St
North Earl St
Earl Pl
Sackville Pl
Abbey St
Eden Quay
Marlborough St
Upper Sean MacDermot St
Britain Pl
Lower Gardiner St
Diamond Park
Gloucester Pl
Lower Gloucester Pl
Lower Sean MacDermot St
Railway St
Foley St
Corporation St
Moland Pl
Talbot St
Talbot Pl
Lower Abbey St
Beresford Pl
Memorial Rd
Store St
Busáras (Main Bus Station)
Lower Major St
Connolly Station
Inner Dock
St George's Dock
Custom House Quay
Liffey River
Talbot Memorial Bridge

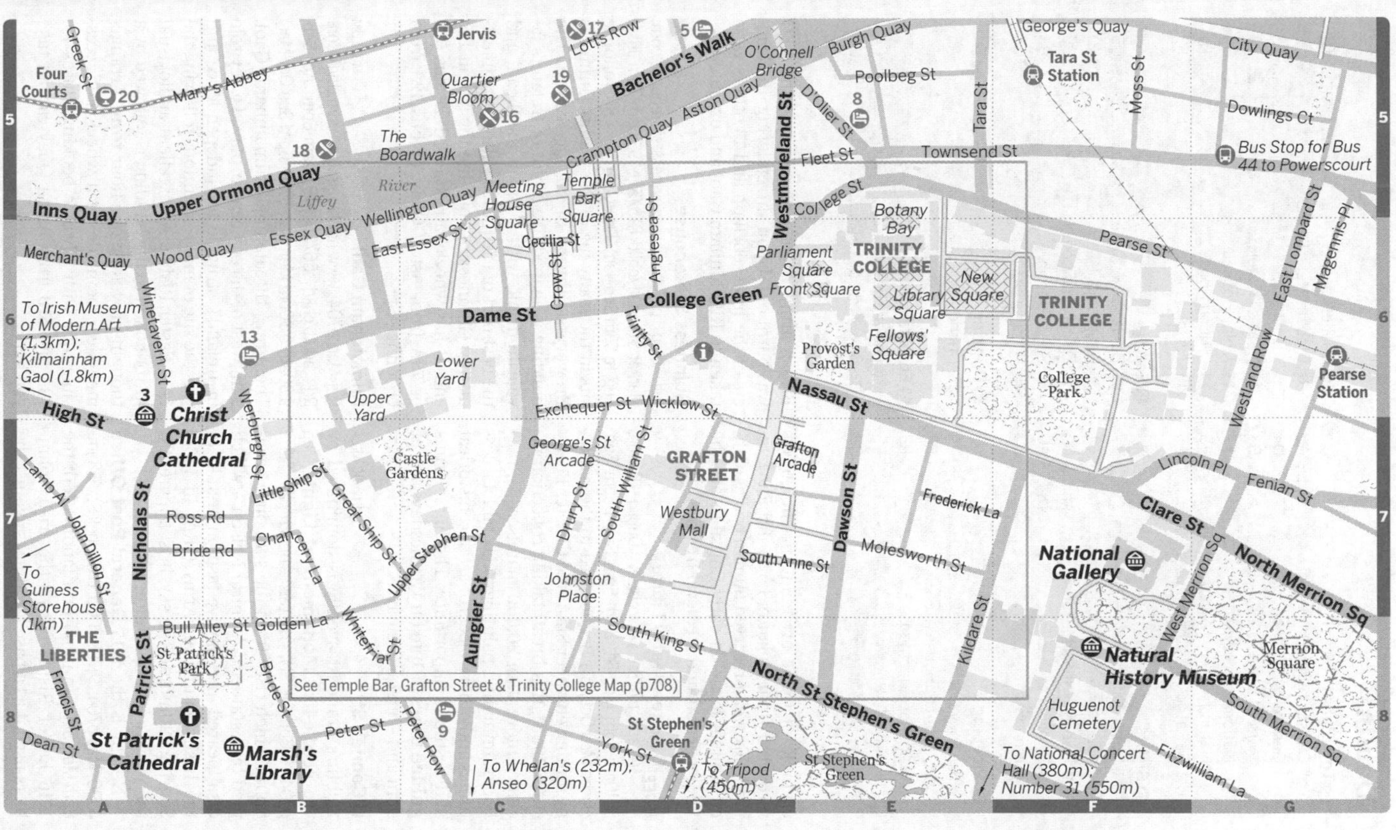
Four Courts
Greek St
20
Mary's Abbey
Jervis
17
Lotts Row
5
Bachelor's Walk
O'Connell Bridge
Burgh Quay
George's Quay
Tara St Station
City Quay
Moss St
Dowlings Ct
Quartier Bloom
19
16
Poolbeg St
D'Olier St
8
Tara St
Bus Stop for Bus 44 to Powerscourt
18
The Boardwalk
Crampton Quay
Aston Quay
Westmoreland St
Fleet St
Townsend St
Inns Quay
Upper Ormond Quay
River Liffey
Meeting House Square
Temple Bar Square
College St
Botany Bay
East Lombard St
Magennis Pl
Merchant's Quay
Wood Quay
Essex Quay
Wellington Quay
East Essex St
Cecilia St
Crow St
Anglesea St
Parliament Square
Front Square
TRINITY COLLEGE
New Square
Library Square
Pearse St
To Irish Museum of Modern Art (1.3km); Kilmainham Gaol (1.8km)
Winetavern St
13
Dame St
College Green
Trinity St
Fellows' Square
Provost's Garden
College Park
Westland Row
Pearse Station
3
Christ Church Cathedral
High St
Werburgh St
Lower Yard
Upper Yard
Nassau St
Exchequer St
Wicklow St
George's St Arcade
Castle Gardens
GRAFTON STREET
Grafton Arcade
Lincoln Pl
Fenian St
Lamb Al
John Dillon St
Nicholas St
Ross Rd
Bride Rd
Little Ship St
Great Ship St
Chancery La
Upper Stephen St
Drury St
South William St
Westbury Mall
Dawson St
Frederick La
Clare St
North Merrion Sq
To Guiness Storehouse (1km)
Aungier St
Johnston Place
South Anne St
Molesworth St
National Gallery
West Merrion Sq
Bull Alley St
Golden La
Whitefriar St
South King St
Kildare St
THE LIBERTIES
Patrick St
St Patrick's Park
Bride St
Natural History Museum
Merrion Square
See Temple Bar, Grafton Street & Trinity College Map (p708)
North St Stephen's Green
Huguenot Cemetery
South Merrion Sq
Francis St
Dean St
St Patrick's Cathedral
Marsh's Library
Peter St
Peter Row
9
St Stephen's Green
York St
To Whelan's (232m); Anseo (320m)
To Tripod (450m)
St Stephen's Green
To National Concert Hall (380m); Number 31 (550m)
Fitzwilliam La
A
B
C
D
E
F
G
5
6
7
8

Dublin

Top Sights

- Christ Church Cathedral A6
- General Post Office D4
- Marsh's Library B8
- National Gallery F7
- Natural History Museum F8
- St Patrick's Cathedral A8

Sights

1 Dublin City Gallery – The Hugh Lane C1
2 Dublin Writers Museum C2
3 Dublinia A6
4 Monument of Light D3

Sleeping

5 Abbey Court Hostel D5
6 Abraham House E3
7 Anchor Guesthouse E3
8 Ashfield House E5
9 Avalon House C8
10 Castle Hotel C1
11 Globetrotters Tourist Hostel F3
12 Isaac's Hostel F3
13 Kinlay House B6
14 Lyndon House D1
15 Townhouse F3

Eating

16 Bar Italia C5
Chapter One .... (see 2)
17 Epicurean Food Hall C5
18 Soup Dragon B5
19 Winding Stair C5

Drinking

20 Hughes' Bar A5

Entertainment

21 Abbey Theatre E4
22 Savoy D3

example of Celtic art; and ancient objects recovered from Ireland's bogs, including remarkably well-preserved human bodies. Other exhibits focus on early Christian art, the Viking period, and medieval Ireland.

FREE **Chester Beatty Library** MUSEUM
(Map p708; www.cbl.ie; Dublin Castle; ⏲10am-5pm Mon-Fri, 11am-5pm Sat, 1-5pm Sun, closed Mon Oct-Apr) Bequeathed to the nation by mining engineer Sir Alfred Chester Beatty (1875–1968), this breathtaking collection includes more than 20,000 manuscripts, rare books, miniature paintings, clay tablets, costumes and other objects of artistic, historical and aesthetic importance. The library runs **guided tours** at 1pm on Wednesdays and at 3pm and 4pm on Sundays.

O'Connell St HISTORIC AREA
Dublin's grandest avenue is dominated by the needle-like **Monument of Light** (Map p704; O'Connell St), better known as 'The Spire', which rises from the spot once occupied by a statue of Admiral Nelson – which disappeared in explosive fashion, thanks to the Irish Republican Army (IRA) in 1966. Soaring 120m into the sky, it is, apparently, the world's tallest sculpture.

Nearby is the 1815 **General Post Office** (GPO; Map p704; ☎705 7000; O'Connell St; ⏲8am-8pm Mon-Sat), an important landmark of the 1916 Easter Rising, when the Irish Volunteers used it as a base for attacks against the British army. After a fierce battle the GPO was burnt out. Upon surrendering, the leaders of the Irish rebellion and 13 others were taken to Kilmainham Gaol and executed.

Guinness Storehouse BREWERY
(off Map p704; www.guinness-storehouse.com; Market St; adult/child €15/5; ⏲9.30am-7pm Jul & Aug, to 5pm Sep-Jun) The Guinness Storehouse sits in the malty fug of the mighty Guinness Brewery southwest of the city centre. The building is shaped like a pint of Ireland's favourite drink, with a bar in the 'head', and the best part of the tour is getting the finest-tasting Guinness of your life for free at the end. It has wheelchair access. Take bus 51B or 78A from Aston Quay, or bus 123 from O'Connell St.

Kilmainham Gaol MUSEUM
(off Map p704; www.heritageireland.com; Inchicore Rd; adult/child €6/2; ⏲9.30am-6pm Apr-Sep, 9.30am-5.30pm Mon-Sat, 10am-6pm Sun Oct-Mar) The grey, threatening Kilmainham Gaol, 2km west of the city centre, played a key role in Ireland's struggle for independence and was the site of mass executions following the 1916 Easter Rising. An excellent audiovisual introduction to the building is followed by a thought-provoking one-hour **tour**. Arrangements can be made for a wheelchair-accessible tour with advance booking. Buses 79, 78A and 51B from Aston Quay can all take you here.

FREE **National Gallery** ART MUSEUM
(Map p704; www.nationalgallery.ie; West Merrion Sq; ⌚9.30am-5.30pm Mon-Wed, Fri & Sat, 9.30am-8.30pm Thu, noon-5.30pm Sun) A magnificent Caravaggio and a breathtaking collection of works by Jack B Yeats – William Butler's younger brother – are the main reasons to visit here. The Millennium wing has a small collection of contemporary Irish works. Free **guided tours** are held at 3pm on Saturday, and 2pm, 3pm and 4pm on Sunday.

Christ Church Cathedral CHURCH
(Map p704; www.cccdub.ie; Christ Church Pl; adult/concession €6/4; ⌚9am-6pm Jun-Aug, 9.45am-5pm Sep-May) Christ Church is the mother of all of Dublin's cathedrals, a simple wood structure until 1169 when the present church was built. In the southern aisle is a monument to Strongbow, a 12th-century Norman warrior. Note the precariously leaning northern wall (it's been that way since 1562).

Next door, connected to the cathedral by an arched walkway, **Dublinia** (Map p704; www.dublinia.ie; adult/child €6.95/4.95; ⌚10am-5pm Apr-Sep, 11am-4pm Mon-Fri, 10am-4pm Sat & Sun Oct-Mar) is a lively attempt to bring medieval Dublin to life, with models of 10 episodes in Dublin's history. It has wheelchair access.

St Patrick's Cathedral CHURCH
(Map p704; www.stpatrickscathedral.ie; St Patrick's Close; adult/family €5.50/15; ⌚9am-6pm Mon-Sat, 9-11am, 12.45-3pm & 4.15-6pm Sun Mar-Oct, 9am-5pm Sat, 10-11am & 12.45-3pm Sun Nov-Feb, closed during times of worship) There was a church on the site of St Patrick's Cathedral as early as the 5th century, but the present building dates from 1191. St Patrick's choir was part of the first group to perform Handel's *Messiah* in 1742, and you can hear their successors sing **Evensong** (⌚5.45pm) most weeknights.

Just around the corner is the antique **Marsh's Library** (Map p704; www.marshlibrary.ie; St Patrick's Close; adult/child €2.50/free; ⌚10am-1pm & 2-5pm Mon & Wed-Fri, 10.30am-1pm Sat), the oldest public library in the country, with an atmosphere that has hardly changed since it opened its doors in 1707.

FREE **Natural History Museum** MUSEUM
(Map p704; www.museum.ie; Merrion St; ⌚10am-5pm Tue-Sat, 2-5pm Sun) Excellent and atmospheric Victorian museum scarcely changed since 1857, when Scottish explorer Dr David Livingstone delivered the opening lecture. Recently reopened after a facelift and reinstatement of grand stone staircase.

Dublin Writers Museum MUSEUM
(Map p704; www.writersmuseum.com; 18-19 Parnell Sq; adult/child €7.50/4.70; ⌚10am-5pm Mon-Sat, 11am-5pm Sun year-round, to 6pm Mon-Fri Jun-Aug) Celebrates the city's role as a literary centre, with displays on Joyce, Swift, Yeats, Wilde, Beckett and others.

Dublin Castle CASTLE
(Map p708; www.dublincastle.ie; adult/concession €4.50/2; ⌚10am-4.45pm Mon-Fri, 2-4.45pm Sat & Sun) The centre of British power in Ireland, dating back to the 13th century; more higgledy-piggledy palace than castle.

FREE **Irish Museum of Modern Art** ART MUSEUM
(off Map p704; www.imma.ie; Military Rd; ⌚10am-5.30pm Tue & Thu-Sat, 10.30am-5.30pm Wed, noon-5.30pm Sun) Renowned for its conceptual installations and temporary exhibitions. Bus 51 or 79 from Aston Quay will get you there.

FREE **Dublin City Gallery – The Hugh Lane** ART MUSEUM
(Map p704; www.hughlane.ie; North Parnell Sq; ⌚10am-6pm Tue-Thu, 10am-5pm Fri & Sat, 11am-5pm Sun) Works by French Impressionists and 20th-century Irish artists; wheelchair accessible.

Old Jameson Distillery WHISKEY DISTILLERY
(off Map p704; www.jamesonwhiskey.com; Bow St; adult/child €13.50/8; ⌚tours 9.30am-6pm) Guided tours cover the entire whiskey-distilling process; tastings follow.

Tours

Bus

Hop-on, hop-off **city tours** costing €16 (tickets valid for 24 hours) are a good way of visiting several major sights in one day. You can start at any stop along the route.

City Sightseeing (www.city-sightseeing.com)

Dublin Bus (www.dublinbus.ie)

Temple Bar, Grafton Street & Trinity College

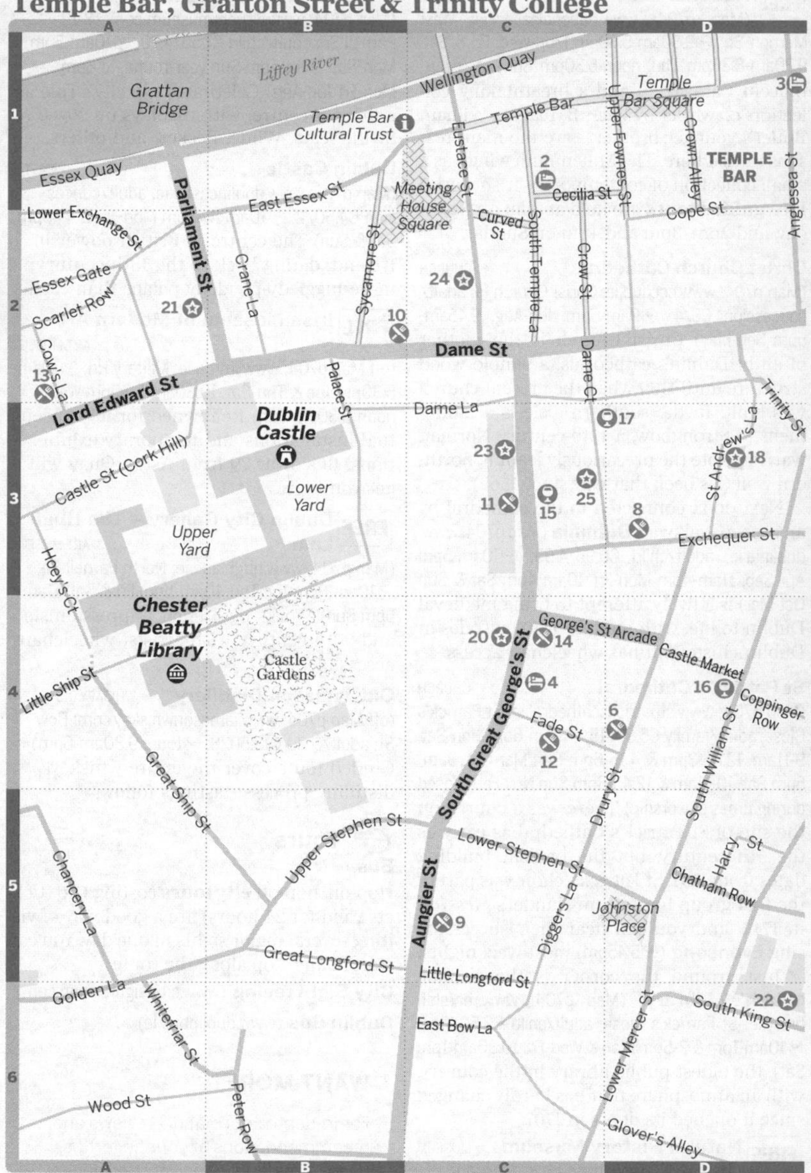

Walking

Each tour lasts two to three hours and costs around €12. Book through Dublin Tourism, hostels or by calling direct.

Dublin Literary Pub Crawl LITERATURE

(☎670 5602; www.dublinpubcrawl.com; ⏲7.30pm daily Apr-Oct, Thu-Sun Nov-Mar) Led by actors performing pieces from Irish literature.

1916 Rebellion Walking Tour HISTORY

(☎086 858 3847; www.1916rising.com; ⏲11.30am Mon-Sat, 1pm Sun Mar-Oct) Visits key sites of the rebellion.

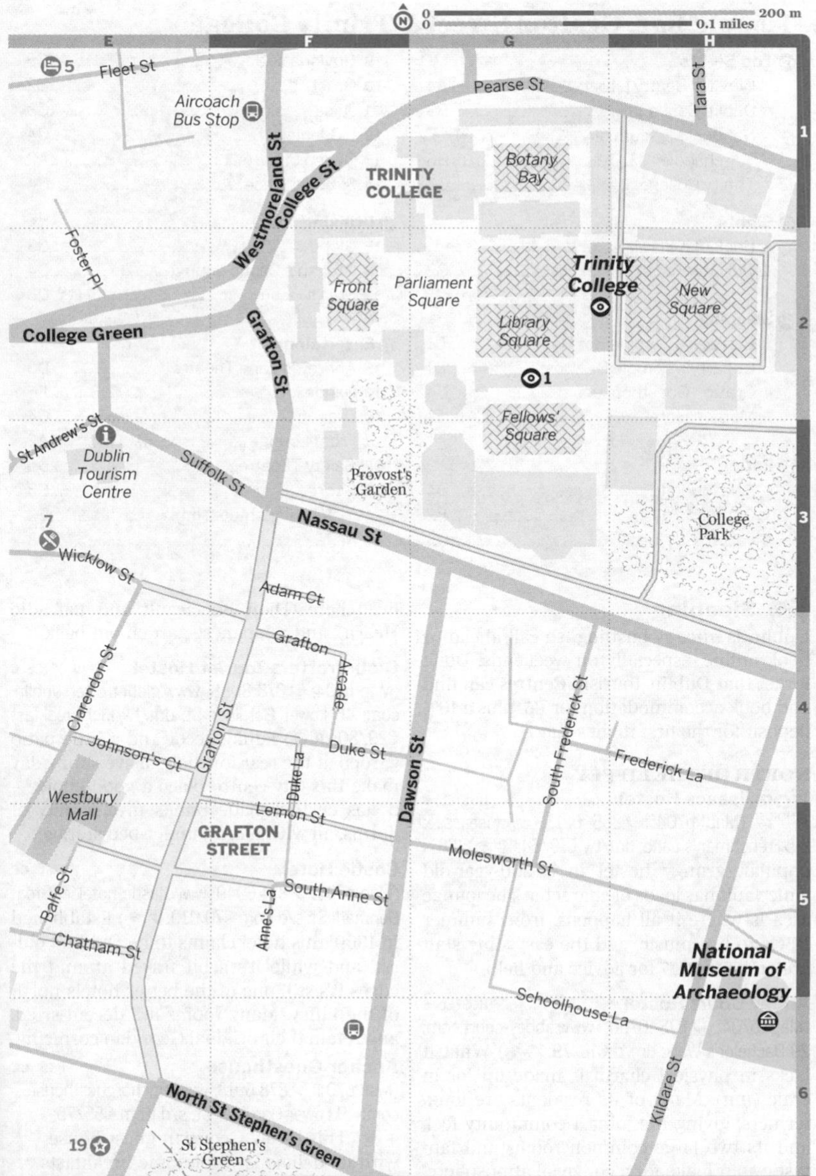

Musical Pub Crawl MUSIC
(☎475 3313; www.discoverdublin.ie; ⏲7.30pm daily Apr-Oct, Thu-Sat Nov-Mar) Irish traditional music explained and demonstrated by two expert musicians in various Temple Bar pubs.

Historical Walking Tours of Dublin HISTORY
(☎087 688 9412; www.historicalinsights.ie; ⏲daily Apr-Oct, Fri-Sun Nov-Mar) 'Seminars on the street' conducted by history graduates of Trinity College Dublin.

Temple Bar, Grafton Street & Trinity College

Sleeping

Dublin is *always* bustling, so call ahead or book online, especially on weekends. Don't forget that Dublin Tourism Centres can find and book accommodation for €5, plus a 10% deposit for the first night's stay.

NORTH OF THE LIFFEY

TOP CHOICE Isaacs Hostel HOSTEL €
(Map p704; ☎855 6215; www.isaacs.ie; 2-5 Frenchman's Lane; dm/tw €19/54; @ 🛜) This popular, grungy hostel in a 200-year-old wine vault has loads of character. The lounge area is where it all happens, from summer BBQs to live music, and the easygoing staff are on hand 24/7 for advice and help.

Abbey Court Hostel HOSTEL €
(Map p704; ☎878 0700; www.abbey-court.com; 29 Bachelor's Walk; dm/d €18/79; @ 🛜) What it lacks in physical charm is made up for in craic (fun). Many of its residents are long-termers, giving the joint a community feel, and its two large common rooms and fantastic staff make for a convivial atmosphere.

Townhouse B&B €€
(Map p704; ☎878 8808; www.townhouseofdublin.com; 47-48 Lower Gardiner St; per person from €40) Elegant but unpretentious, the Georgian Townhouse has beautiful, individually designed bedrooms named after plays by the famous 19th-century playwrights who once lived here (Dion Boucicault and Lafcadio Hearn), and a Japanese garden out back.

Globetrotters Tourist Hostel HOSTEL €
(Map p704; ☎878 8088; www.globetrottersdublin.com; 46 Lower Gardiner St; dm/tw incl breakfast €20/80; P @) Funky decor and a little patio garden at the rear for that elusive sunny day make this city-centre place a good choice – it has custom-made bunks in a variety of dorms, all with handy, under-bed storage.

Castle Hotel HOTEL €€
(Map p704; ☎874 6949; www.castle-hotel.ie; Great Denmark St; s/d from €70/110; P 🛜) Established in 1809, this hotel claims to be Dublin's oldest, and while it's a bit frayed around the edges it's still one of the better hotels north of the Liffey. Many rooms are decent-sized, and retain their original Georgian cornicing.

Anchor Guesthouse B&B €€
(Map p704; ☎878 6913; www.anchorguesthouse.com; 49 Lower Gardiner St; s/d from €55/75; P 🛜) This lovely Georgian guest house, with its delicious wholesome breakfasts and an elegance you won't find in many of the other B&Bs along this stretch, comes highly recommended.

Abraham House HOSTEL €
(Map p704; ☎855 0600; www.abraham-house.ie; 83 Lower Gardiner St; dm incl breakfast €9-20, d incl breakfast €48-60; @ 🛜) Friendly is an understatement at this large and lively

hostel; good rates if you book ahead online. It's close to Connolly Station.

Marian Guesthouse B&B €€
(off Map p704; ☎874 4129; www.marianguesthouse.ie; 21 Upper Gardiner St; per person €30-45; P) Modest but reasonably priced option in the Upper Gardiner St area (north of the city centre).

Lyndon House B&B €€
(Map p704; ☎878 6950; www.lyndonhouse.net; 26 Gardiner Pl; s/d €55/90; P) Another modest but reasonably priced option in the Upper Gardiner St area.

SOUTH OF THE LIFFEY

TOP CHOICE **Number 31** BOUTIQUE HOTEL €€€
(off Map p704; ☎676 5011; www.number31.ie; 31 Leeson Close; s/d/tr from €115/150/225; P) The former dwelling of modernist architect Sam Stephenson (1933–2006) still feels like a 1960s designer pad with sunken sitting room, leather sofas, mirrored bar and floor-to-ceiling windows. A hidden oasis of calm, five minutes' walk from St Stephen's Green. Children under 10 years of age are not allowed here.

Ashfield House HOSTEL €
(Map p704; ☎679 7734; www.ashfieldhouse.ie; 19-20 D'Olier St; dm incl breakfast €9-20, d incl breakfast €48-60; @) Housed in a converted church a stone's throw from Temple Bar and O'Connell Bridge, this hostel feels more like a small hotel, with a good range of private en suite rooms as well as four-, six- and eight-bed dorms.

Barnacles Temple Bar House HOSTEL €
(Map p708; ☎671 6277; www.barnacles.ie; 19 Temple Lane; dm/d from €15/64; @) Plenty bright and immaculately clean, Barnacles' location in the heart of the Temple Bar district makes it a great place to stay if you don't mind the sound of drunken revellers outside your window; rooms at the back are quieter.

Avalon House HOSTEL €
(Map p704; ☎475 0001; www.avalon-house.ie; 55 Aungier St; dm/d €18/60; @) This grand old Victorian building near St Stephen's Green houses a megahostel with four-, 12- and 20-bed mixed dorms on two levels, offering some privacy. There's a large kitchen, several lounges, and a pool room.

Morgan Hotel BOUTIQUE HOTEL €€€
(Map p708; ☎643 7000; www.themorgan.com; 10 Fleet St; r from €110; @) Falling somewhere between *Alice in Wonderland* and a cocaine-and-hooker-fuelled rock-n-roll fantasy, the ubercool Morgan sports a sexy colour scheme of white floors and walls with dark-blue and pink lighting that extends into the bar, the rooms and even the cigar patio.

TOP CHOICE **Grafton Guesthouse** B&B €€
(Map p708; ☎679 2041; www.graftonguesthouse.com; 26-27 South Great George's St; s/d from €70/100;) This Gothic-style building has 17 bright and funky en suite rooms with contemporary fittings, stylish walnut furniture, retro wallpaper and terrific vegie breakfasts.

Kinlay House HOSTEL €
(Map p708; ☎679 6644; www.kinlayhouse.ie; 2-12 Lord Edward St; dm/d from €15/50; @) Big, bustling and always busy, this is not a place for shrinking violets.

Gogarty's Temple Bar Hostel HOSTEL €
(Map p708; ☎671 1822; www.gogartys.ie/hostel; 58-59 Fleet St; dm/d from €15/44;) Lively, party-atmosphere hostel right in the middle of Temple Bar action.

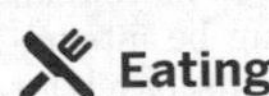

Eating

Dubliners' increased spending power has encouraged many excellent restaurants to take root, while the city's influx of immigrants has stimulated the market for ethnically diverse eateries. The number of good restaurants and cafes north of the Liffey is growing, and many midrange options are concentrated on the southern side of the city centre, especially in the area between Grafton St and South Great George's St.

NORTH OF THE LIFFEY

TOP CHOICE **Winding Stair** IRISH €€
(Map p704; ☎872 7320; www.winding-stair.com; 40 Ormond Quay; mains €22-27; ⊙noon-3.30pm & 5.30-10.30pm daily) This rustic dining room squeezed above a bookshop serves superb Irish grub, from smoked salmon and wheaten bread, to lamb chops with white bean and red onion stew, to sticky pear and ginger steam pud. Hugely popular, so book ahead.

Chapter One FRENCH €€€
(Map p704; ☎873 2266; www.chapteronerestaurant.com; 18-19 North Parnell Sq; mains €32-36; ⊙12.30-2.30pm Tue-Fri, 6-11pm Tue-Sat) Savour fresh Irish produce cooked in classic French style – such as rabbit loin wrapped in pancetta with carrot and black cumin purée, or turbot with fennel and citrus fruit sauce – to the tinkle of a grand piano in the vaulted

basement of the Dublin Writers Museum. Get there between 6pm and 7pm for the three-course Pre-Theatre Special (€37.50).

Soup Dragon CAFE €

(Map p704; 168 Capel St; mains €5-13; ⏲8am-5.30pm Mon-Fri, 11am-5pm Sat) Eat in or take away one of 12 tasty varieties of homemade soups, including shepherd's pie or spicy vegetable gumbo. Bowls come in three different sizes, and prices include fresh bread and a piece of fruit.

Bar Italia ITALIAN €€

(Map p704; 28 Lower Ormond Quay; mains €9-18; ⏲10.30am-11pm Mon-Sat, 1-9pm Sun) One of a new generation of eateries that's showing the more established Italian restaurants how the Old Country really eats. Specialities include ever-changing pasta dishes, homemade risottos and excellent Palombini coffee.

Epicurean Food Hall FOOD HALL €

(Map p704; Lower Liffey St; mains €4-12; ⏲9.30am-5.30pm Mon-Sat) You'll be spoilt for choice in this bustling arcade that houses more than 20 food stalls. The quality can be hit-and-miss, but good choices include Itsabagel (for bagels), El Corte (for coffee) and Istanbul House (for kebabs).

SOUTH OF THE LIFFEY

TOP CHOICE **L'Gueuleton** FRENCH €€

(Map p708; www.lgueuleton.com; 1 Fade St; mains €19-27; ⏲12.30-3pm & 6-10pm Mon-Sat, 1-3pm & 6-9pm Sun) Dubliners just can't get enough of this restaurant's take on French rustic cuisine, which ranges from regulars such as slow-roast pork belly with dauphinoise potatoes, to specials such as warm crayfish salad with paprika and flaked almonds. No reservations – queue for a table, or leave your mobile number and they'll text when a table's ready.

Gruel COMFORT FOOD €

(Map p708; www.gruel.ie; 68a Dame St; mains €5-15; ⏲7am-9.30pm Mon-Fri, 10.30am-10.30pm Sat & Sun) The best budget eatery in town, whether it's for the superfilling lunchtime roast-in-a-roll – a rotating list of slow-roasted organic meats stuffed into a bap and flavoured with homemade relishes – or the evening menu that includes bangers and mash, shepherd's pie, and vegetable tagine.

Fallon & Byrne DELI €€

(Map p708; ☎472 1000; www.fallonandbyrne.com; Exchequer St; mains €6-9; ⏲9am-8pm Mon-Sat, 11am-6pm Sun) Queue for delicious sandwiches at the deli counter in this trendy New York–style food hall, or head upstairs to the chic, buzzy **brasserie** (mains €17-27; ⏲noon-3pm & 6-10pm Mon-Thu, to 11pm Fri & Sat, noon-4pm Sun) with its long red banquettes and diverse menu of beef burgers, steak Béarnaise and sweet potato and nut Wellington (three-course dinner €30 Monday to Friday, and 6pm to 6.30pm Saturday).

Simon's Place SANDWICHES €

(Map p708; cnr George's St Arcade & South Great George's St; sandwiches €4-5; ⏲9am-5.30pm Mon-Sat; 🌿) Simon hasn't had to change his menu of doorstep sandwiches and wholesome vegetarian soups since he first opened shop two decades ago – the grub here is as heartening and legendary as he is.

Cornucopia WHOLEFOODS €€

(Map p708; www.cornucopia.ie; 19 Wicklow St; mains €8-13; ⏲8.30am-9pm Mon-Fri, 8.30am-8pm Sat, noon-7pm Sun; 🌿) For those seeking escape from the Irish cholesterol habit, Cornucopia is a popular, mostly vegan cafe turning out scrumptious healthy goodies. There's even a hot vegetarian breakfast as an alternative to muesli.

Queen of Tarts CAFE €

(Map p708; www.queenoftarts.ie; 3-4 Cow's Lane; mains €5-12; ⏲8am-7pm Mon-Fri, 9am-7pm Sat, 10am-7pm Sun) Pocket-sized Queen of Tarts offers a mouth-watering array of savoury tarts and filled focaccias, fruit crumbles, healthy breakfasts and weekend brunch specials.

Juice VEGETARIAN €€

(Map p708; www.juicerestaurant.ie; 73 South Great George's St; mains €7-16; ⏲11am-11pm; 🌿) A creative vegetarian restaurant, Juice puts an imaginative, California-type spin on all kinds of dishes. The real treat is the selection of delicious fruit smoothies.

Govinda's VEGETARIAN €

(Map p708; www.govindas.ie; 4 Aungier St; mains €7-10; ⏲noon-9pm Mon-Sat; 🌿) This place is totally vegetarian, with a wholesome mix of salads and Indian-influenced hot daily specials.

Asia Market MARKET €

(Map p708; 18 Drury St; ⏲10am-7pm) Heaps of fresh produce and stir-fry sauces, in addition to the usual Asian grocery stand-bys.

Drinking

Temple Bar, Dublin's 'party district', is almost always packed with raucous stag (bachelor) and hen (bachelorette) parties, scantily clad girls, and loud guys from Ohio wearing Guinness T-shirts. If you're just looking to get smashed and hook up with someone from another country, there's no better place in Ireland. If that's not your style, there's plenty to enjoy beyond Temple Bar. In fact, most of the best old-fashioned pubs are outside the district.

TOP CHOICE **Stag's Head** PUB
(Map p708; 1 Dame Ct) Built in 1770, and remodelled in 1895, the Stag's Head is possibly the best traditional pub in Dublin (and therefore the world). You may find yourself philosophising in the ecclesiastical atmosphere, as James Joyce once did. Some of the fitters that worked on this pub probably also worked on churches in the area, so the stained-wood-and-polished-brass similarities are no accident.

Grogan's Castle Lounge PUB
(Map p708; www.groganspub.ie; 15 South William St) A city-centre institution, Grogan's has long been a favourite haunt of Dublin's writers and painters, as well as others from the bohemian, alternative set. Drinks are marginally cheaper in the stone-floored public bar than in the lounge.

Hughes' Bar BAR, LIVE MUSIC
(Map p704; 19 Chancery St) Directly behind Four Courts, this bar has nightly, if impromptu, traditional-music sessions that often result in a closed door – that is, they go on long past official closing time. The pub is also a popular lunchtime spot with barristers working nearby.

Some hipster spots:

Dice Bar BAR
(www.thatsitdublin.com; 79 Queen St;) Co-owned by singer Huey from the band Fun Lovin' Criminals, the Dice Bar looks like something you'd find on New York's Lower East Side.

Anseo BAR
(off Map p704; 28 Lower Camden St) Unpretentious, unaffected and incredibly popular.

Globe BAR
(Map p708; www.globe.ie; 11 South Great George's St;) The granddaddy of Dublin's hipster bars.

☆ Entertainment

For events, reviews and club listings, pick up a copy of the bimonthly freebie *Event Guide* (www.eventguide.ie) or the weekly *In Dublin* (www.indublin.ie) available at cafes and hostels. Thursday's *Irish Times* has a pull-out section called 'The Ticket' that has reviews and listings of all things arty.

Cinemas

Irish Film Institute ART HOUSE
(IFI; Map p708; www.irishfilm.ie; 6 Eustace St) The fantastic IFI has two screens showing classic and art-house films. Wheelchair access available.

Savoy MAINSTREAM
(Map p704; www.omniplex.ie; Upper O'Connell St) A traditional four-screen, first-run cinema.

Gay & Lesbian Venues

Dublin's not a bad place to be gay. Most people in the city centre wouldn't bat an eyelid at cross-dressing or public displays of affection between same-sex couples, but discretion is advised in the suburbs. Check out www.gcn.ie for the latest on Dublin's gay scene.

George BAR
(Map p708; www.thegeorge.ie; 89 South Great George's St) The patriarch of Dublin's gay bars, and an excellent cruising venue, the venerable George has club nights from Wednesday to Saturday, and stand-up comedy on Sunday. It also has a reputation for becoming ever more wild and wacky as the night progresses.

Front Lounge BAR
(Map p708; 33 Parliament St) A lavish, laid-back lounge attracting a mixed upmarket clientele. Drag queen Panti runs the cabaret and karaoke night, Casting Couch, on Tuesday; club nights Friday and Saturday.

Dragon BAR
(Map p708; 64-65 South Great George's St) Dublin's hottest gay disco-bar has colourful Asian decor, comfy booths and a small dance floor that attracts young pre-George revellers.

The following nightspots have regular gay club nights:

Dandelion CLUB
(Map p704; www.welovedandelion.com; St Stephen's Green Shopping Centre, St Stephen's Green West) Glitz (www.queerid.com/glitz), from 11pm Tuesdays.

Andrews Lane Theatre CLUB
(Map p708; www.andrewslane.com; 9-17 St Andrews Lane) Boom! (www.queerid.com/boom) club night from 10pm Saturdays.

Nightclubs

Tripod CLUB, LIVE MUSIC

(off Map p704; www.pod.ie; 35 Harcourt St; ⌚Mon-Sat) Housed in the atmospheric old Harcourt Street station, Tripod integrates three venues (geddit?): a state-of-the-art live rock and pop venue, a smaller dance club and the intimate live venue Crawdaddy.

Rí Rá CLUB

(Map p708; www.rira.ie; Dame Ct; ⌚Mon-Sat) One of the friendlier clubs in the city centre, Rí Rá is full nearly every night with a diverse crowd who come for the mostly funk music downstairs, or more laidback lounge tunes and movies upstairs.

Whelan's LIVE MUSIC

(off Map p704; www.whelanslive.com; 25 Wexford St) A Dublin institution, providing a showcase for Irish singer-songwriters and other lo-fi performers.

Theatre & Classical Music

Abbey Theatre THEATRE

(Map p704; www.abbeytheatre.ie; 26 Lower Abbey St) The famous Abbey is Ireland's national theatre, putting on new Irish works as well as revivals of Irish classics. It's scheduled to move to a new location in docklands before 2016.

National Concert Hall CLASSICAL MUSIC

(off Map p704; www.nch.ie; Earlsfort Tce) Just south of the city centre, Ireland's premier orchestral hall hosts a variety of concerts year-round, including a series of lunchtime concerts from 1.05pm to 2pm on Tuesday from June to August.

Gaiety Theatre MUSICALS

(Map p708; www.gaietytheatre.com; South King St) This popular theatre – which famously staged the 1971 Eurovision Song Contest – hosts, among other things, a program of classical concerts, operas and musicals.

ℹ Information

Medical Services

Doctor on Duty (☎453 9333; www.mediserve.ie; ⌚24hr) Request a doctor to come to your accommodation.

Hickey's Pharmacy (☎873 0427; 55 Lower O'Connell St) Open till 10pm every night.

St James Hospital (☎410 3000; www.stjames.ie; James's St) Dublin's main 24-hour accident and emergency department.

Well Woman Clinic (☎872 8051; www.wellwomancentre.ie; 35 Lower Liffey St; ⌚9.30am-7.30pm Mon, Thu & Fri, 8am-7.30pm Tue & Wed, 10am-4pm Sat) Handles women's health issues and can supply contraception.

Tourist Information

All Dublin tourist offices provide walk-in services only – no phone inquiries. For tourist information by phone, call ☎1850 230 330 from within the Republic.

City Centre Tourist Office (Map p708; 14 O'Connell St; ⌚9am-5pm Mon-Sat)

Dun Laoghaire Tourist Office (Dun Laoghaire ferry port; ⌚10am-1pm & 2-6pm)

Dublin Tourism Centre (Map p708; www.visitdublin.com; St Andrew's Church, 2 Suffolk St; ⌚9am-5.30pm Mon-Sat, 10.30am-3pm Sun year-round, to 7pm Mon-Sat Jul & Aug) Offers tourist information for all of Ireland, as well as accommodation bookings, car hire, maps, and tickets for tours, concerts and more. Ask about the **Dublin Pass** (www.dublinpass.ie), which allows you entrance into more than 30 of Dublin's attractions, as well as some tours and other special offers.

Northern Ireland Tourist Board (NITB; Map p708; ☎605 7732; www.discovernorthernireland.com) Has a desk in the Dublin Tourism Centre; same hours.

Temple Bar Cultural Trust (Map p708; ☎677 2255; www.templebar.ie; 12 East Essex St; ⌚9am-5.30pm Mon-Fri, 10am-5.30pm Sat, noon-3pm Sun) Provides free maps, guides and information on sights within the Temple Bar district.

ℹ Getting There & Away

Air

Dublin airport (DUB; www.dublinairport.com), about 13km north of the city centre, is Ireland's major international gateway, with direct flights from Europe, North America and Asia. Budget airlines including Ryanair and Flybe land here. See p765 for more details.

Boat

There are direct ferries from Holyhead in Wales to **Dublin Port**, 3km northeast of the city centre, and to **Dun Laoghaire**, 13km southeast. Boats also sail direct to Dublin Port from Liverpool and from Douglas, on the Isle of Man. See p766 for more details.

Bus

Busáras (Map p704; www.buseireann.ie; Store St), Dublin's main bus station, is just north of the Liffey. Standard one-way fares from Dublin:

Belfast €15, 2½ hours, hourly

Cork €13, 4½ hours, six daily

Galway €14, 3¾ hours, hourly

Killarney €26, three hours, five daily

The private company **Citylink** (www.citylink.ie) has nonstop services from Dublin airport (picking up at Bachelor's Walk, near O'Connell Bridge, in the city centre) to Galway (€15, three hours, 14 daily).

Train

Iarnród Éireann Travel Centre (☎836 6222, bookings 703 4070; www.irishrail.ie; 35 Lower Abbey St) For travel information and tickets.

Connolly station (Map p704) North of the Liffey; trains to Belfast, Derry, Sligo, other points north and Wexford.

Heuston station South of the Liffey and west of the city centre; trains for Cork, Galway, Killarney, Limerick, and most other points to the south and west.

Regular one-way fares from Dublin:

Belfast from €18, 2¼ hours, up to eight daily

Cork €20, 2¾ hours, hourly

Galway €35, three hours, five daily

Getting Around

To/From the Airport

Aircoach (Map p708; www.aircoach.ie; one-way/return €7/12) Serves various destinations in the city; departs every 10 to 20 minutes from 5am to midnight, hourly through the night.

Airlink Express Coach (www.dublinbus.ie; one-way/return €6/10) Bus 747 runs every 10 to 20 minutes from 6am to midnight to Upper O'Connell St (35 minutes) and the central bus station (Busáras; 45 minutes). Bus 748 runs every 15 to 30 minutes from 6.50am to 10pm to Busáras (30 minutes) and Heuston train station (45 minutes).

Dublin Bus (www.dublinbus.ie; adult/child one-way €2.20/1) A number of buses serve the airport from various points in Dublin, including buses 16A (Rathfarnham), 746 (Dun Laoghaire) and 230 (Portmarnock); all cross the city centre on their way to the airport. Limited luggage capacity.

Taxi A taxi to the city centre should cost around €20 to €25. Some Dublin airport taxi drivers can be unscrupulous, so make sure the meter is on and mention up front that you'll need a meter receipt.

To/From the Ferry Terminals

Buses are timed to coincide with ferries from Dublin Port, leaving Busáras around 1¼ hours before the ferry departure time (one-way €2.50). Dun Laoghaire ferry terminal can be reached by DART, or bus 7, 7A or 8 from Burgh Quay, or bus 46A from Trinity College

Bicycle

Rates begin at around €13/70 a day/week; you'll need a €50 to €200 cash deposit and photo ID.

Neill's Wheels (www.rentabikedublin.com) Various outlets, including Kinlay House and Isaacs Hostel (see Sleeping).

Cycleways (www.cycleways.com; 185-186 Parnell St)

Car

Traffic in Dublin is a nightmare and parking is an expensive headache. There are no free spots to park anywhere in the city centre during business hours (7am to 7pm Monday to Saturday). Better to leave your vehicle at the **Red Cow Park & Ride** just off Exit 9 on the M50 ring road, and take the **Luas tram** into the city centre (€4 return, 30 minutes).

Public Transport

Various public transport passes are available; one day's unlimited bus travel costs €6 (including Airlink); bus and tram costs €7.50; and bus and DART costs €11.

BUS **Dublin Bus** (www.dublinbus.ie) Local buses cost from €1.15 to €2.20 for a single journey. You must pay the exact fare when boarding; drivers don't give change. The Rambler 1 Day (€6) ticket allows one day's unlimited travel on buses including Airlink.

TRAIN **Dublin Area Rapid Transport** (DART; www.irishrail.ie) Provides quick rail access as far north as Howth and south to Bray; Pearse station is handy for central Dublin.

TRAM **Luas** (www.luas.ie) Runs on two (unconnected) lines; the green line runs from the eastern side of St Stephen's Green southeast to Sandyford, and the red line runs from Tallaght to Connolly station, with stops at Heuston station, the National Museum and Busáras. Single fares range from €1.50 to €2.80 depending on how many zones you travel through.

TAXI Taxis in Dublin are expensive; flag fall costs €4.10, plus €1.50 per kilometre. For taxi service, call **National Radio Cabs** (☎677 2222).

AROUND DUBLIN

Dun Laoghaire

☎01 / POP 114,166

Dun Laoghaire (dun-*leary*), 13km south of central Dublin, is a seaside resort and busy harbour with ferry connections to Britain. The B&Bs are slightly cheaper here than in central Dublin, and the fast and frequent train connections make it a convenient stay.

At Sandycove, south of the harbour, is the Martello Tower where James Joyce's epic novel *Ulysses* opens. It now houses the **James Joyce Museum** (The Fortyfoot, Sandycove; adult/child €7.25/4.55; ⏲10am-1pm & 2-5pm

Mon-Sat, 2-6pm Sun Apr-Aug, by arrangement only Sep-Mar). If you fancy a cold saltwater dip, the nearby **Forty Foot Pool** (also mentioned in *Ulysses*) is the place.

Take the Dublin Area Rapid Transport (DART) rail service (€3.80 return, 25 minutes, every 10 to 20 minutes) from Dublin to Dun Laoghaire, then bus 59 to Sandycove Rd, or walk (1km).

Malahide Castle

☎01

Despite the vicissitudes of Irish history, the Talbot family managed to keep **Malahide Castle** (www.malahidecastle.com; adult/child €7.50/4.70; ⏲10am-5pm Mon-Sat year-round, 10am-5pm Sun Apr-Sep, 11am-5pm Sun Oct-Mar) from 1185 through to 1973. The castle is packed with furniture and paintings, and Puck, the family ghost, is still in residence. The extensive **Fry Model Railway** (☎846 2184; adult/child €6/4; ⏲10am-1pm & 2-5pm Tue-Sat, 1-5pm Sun Apr-Sep, closed Oct-Mar) in the castle grounds covers 240 sq metres and recreates Ireland's rail and public transport system (it's actually better than it sounds). Combined tickets (adult/child €11.50/7.50) give admission to the model railway and castle.

Malahide is 13km northeast of Dublin; take the DART rail service from Dublin Connolly to Malahide station (€4, return, 22 minutes, every 10 to 20 minutes).

Brú na Bóinne

☎041

A thousand years older than Stonehenge, the extensive Neolithic necropolis known as Brú na Bóinne (Boyne Palace) is one of the most extraordinary prehistoric sites in Europe. Its tombs date from about 3200 BC, predating the great pyramids of Egypt by six centuries. The complex, including the Newgrange and Knowth passage tombs, can only be visited on a guided walk from the **Brú na Bóinne visitor centre** (www.heritageireland.ie; Donore; adult/child €3/2; ⏲9am-7pm Jun–mid-Sep, 9am-6.30pm May & late Sep, 9.30am-5.30pm Feb, Mar, Apr & Oct, 9.30am-5pm Nov-Jan). At 8.20am during the winter solstice, the rising sun's rays shine directly down Newgrange's long passage and illuminate the chamber for a magical 17 minutes. Arrive early in the summer months as tours tend to fill up.

The site is 50km north of Dublin, signposted off the M1. Take Bus Éireann's 100X or 101 service to Drogheda, then the 163 to Donore (total journey €15 return, 1½ to two hours, five daily), which stops at the gates of the visitor centre. Or use the **Newgrange Shuttlebus** (☎1-800 424 252; www.overthetoptours.com; return €17; ⏲daily).

Guided day tours from Dublin by **Mary Gibbons** (☎086 355 1355; www.newgrangetours.com; tour incl admission €35; ⏲daily) are excellent.

THE SOUTHEAST

The southeast of Ireland is a hell of a lot sunnier and dryer than the rest of the country – it's probably why the Vikings settled here, and certainly a reason why people love to visit. But the weather isn't the only draw – the area is littered with early-Christian ruins such as Glendalough and impressive castles such as Powerscourt. There's also the Wicklow Way, one of many rugged hiking trails that allow you to explore the region's plentiful waterfalls, beaches and mountains. Combine this with artsy towns such as medieval Kilkenny and waterfront Wexford, and you have a region not only diverse, but also bathed in sunlight and warmth – well, by Irish standards at least.

County Wicklow

County Wicklow, situated immediately south of Dublin, has three contenders for the 'best in Ireland' label: best garden (at Powerscourt), best monastic site (at Glendalough) and best walk (the Wicklow Way). Pleasant seaside resorts and beaches – notably at Brittas Bay – straggle along the coast between Bray and Arklow. West towards Sally Gap and due south from here lie the sparsely populated Wicklow Mountains.

POWERSCOURT

In 1974, after major renovations, the 18th-century mansion at **Powerscourt Estate** (www.powerscourt.ie; admission to house free, gardens adult/child €8/5; ⏲9.30am-5.30pm Mar-Oct, to dusk Nov-Feb) burned to the ground when a bird's nest in a chimney caught fire. One wing of the Palladian building remains, with an exhibition room, luxury shops and a delightful terrace cafe, but people come mainly for the gorgeous, 19th-century formal gardens with views east to Great Sugar Loaf (501m).

From the house, a scenic 6km trail leads to **Powerscourt Waterfall** (adult/child €5/3.50; ⌚9.30am-7pm May-Aug, 10.30am-5.30pm Mar, Apr, Sep & Oct, 10.30am-dusk Nov-Feb), at 121m the highest in Ireland. You can also reach the waterfall by road (5km), following signs from the estate entrance.

Powerscourt is 500m south of Enniskerry's main square and about 22km south of Dublin, and is wheelchair accessible. Dublin Bus 44 runs regularly from Townsend St in Dublin to Enniskerry (€4.50, 1¼ hours, every 40 to 50 minutes).

GLENDALOUGH

☎0404 / POP 280

Nestled between two lakes, haunting Glendalough (Gleann dá Loch, meaning 'Valley of the Two Lakes') is one of the most significant monastic sites in Ireland and one of the loveliest spots in the country, with a **round tower**, a **ruined cathedral** and the tiny **Church of St Kevin**.

It was founded in the late 6th century by St Kevin, a bishop who established a monastery on the Upper Lake's southern shore and about whom there is much folklore. During the Middle Ages, when Ireland was known as 'the island of saints and scholars', Glendalough became a monastic city catering to thousands of students and teachers. The site is entered through the only surviving **monastic gateway** in Ireland.

The **Glendalough Visitor Centre** (adult/child €3/1; ⌚9.30am-6pm mid-Mar–mid-Oct, to 5pm mid-Oct–mid-Mar), opposite the Lower Lake car park, has historical displays and a good 20-minute **audiovisual show**. From the Upper Lake (1.5km west of the visitor centre), several good **hiking trails** head into the hills.

Visitors swarm to Glendalough in summer, so it's best to arrive early and/or stay late, preferably on a weekday, as the site is free and open 24 hours. The lower car park gates are locked when the visitor centre closes.

Sleeping

As well as the places listed here, the Glendalough area also has plenty of moderately priced B&Bs.

Glendalough International Hostel HOSTEL €
(☎45342; www.glendaloughinternationalhostel.com; dm €20-24, tw €56; P @) Lying just 600m west of the visitor centre, close to the round tower, this modern hostel attracts outdoorsy types from all over the world, especially during summer. It has great wheelchair accessibility.

Glendalough Hermitage SELF-CATERING €€
(☎45777; www.hermitage.dublindiocese.ie; St Kevin's Parish Church; s/tw €50/75; P) Designed for contemplation, these modest, self-catering bungalows consist of a bedroom, a bathroom, a small kitchen area and an open fire. Visitors of all faiths are welcome, so long as their intentions are meditative; backpackers looking for a cheap bed are not. There is a minimum two-night stay.

Getting There & Away

St Kevin's Bus (www.glendaloughbus.com) runs twice daily to Glendalough (one-way/return €13/20, 1½ hours) from outside the Mansion House on Dawson St in Dublin.

THE WICKLOW WAY

Running for 127km from Marlay Park, Rathfarnham, in southern County Dublin through to Clonegal, County Carlow, the **Wicklow Way** (www.wicklowway.com) is the oldest and most popular of Ireland's long-distance walks. The route is clearly signposted and documented in leaflets and guidebooks; one of the better ones is *The Complete Wicklow Way* by JB Malone. Much of the trail traverses countryside above 500m, so pack proper hiking boots and waterproofs.

The most attractive section of the walk is from Enniskerry to Glendalough (two days). Camping is possible along the route, with permission from local farmers. **Knockree Hostel** (☎01-276 7892; www.knockreeyouthhostel.com; dm/d €19/59; ⌚closed 10am-5pm; P @) is a luxury farm conversion with lovely views, right on the trail 7km west of Enniskerry. The village of **Roundwood**, a good stopover, has a camping ground and some B&Bs.

Wexford

☎053 / POP 9400

Wexford's claustrophobic maze of medieval streets is lined with a mixture of old-time pubs, posh boutiques and modern steel-and-glass buildings. The town's rich and bloody history includes being founded by the Vikings, and being nearly obliterated by Oliver Cromwell.

Wexford is a convenient stopover for those travelling to France or Wales via the Rosslare

Harbour ferry port, 21km southeast of town. It's main attraction, though, is the world-famous **Wexford Opera Festival** (www.wexfordopera.com), an 18-day extravaganza (held in October) that presents rarely performed works to packed audiences in the town's shiny modern **opera house** (www.wexfordoperahouse.ie; 27 High St).

About 4km northwest of Wexford, on the N11 Dublin–Rosslare road at Ferrycarrig, the **Irish National Heritage Park** (www.inhp.com; adult/child €8/4.50; ⌚9.30am-6.30pm) is a theme park that recreates dwellings and everyday life from the Stone Age to the early Norman period; last admission is 1½ hours before closing. A taxi from town will cost about €7.

Sleeping & Eating

Kirwan House HOSTEL €
(☎912 1208; www.wexfordhostel.com; 3 Mary St; dm/d €23/60; @📶) This basic hostel is clean, comfortable and friendly, with a huge kitchen and helpful staff. It's two and a half blocks inland from the tourist office.

Blue Door B&B €€
(☎912 1047; http://indigo.ie/~bluedoor; 18 Lower George St; s/d from €45/80) The breakfasts are a plus at this Georgian townhouse, with smoked salmon and vegetarian alternatives. It's central but quiet, and floor-to-ceiling windows make the bedrooms bright and airy.

Stable Diet CAFE €
(100 South Main St; mains €8-10; ⌚9am-5.30pm Mon-Sat) This bright and busy cafe is famous for its home-baked breads, scones and cakes; the lunch menu consists of freshly made soups and sandwiches, while breakfast choices include French toast with bacon and maple syrup.

Yard BISTRO €€
(☎914 4083; 3 Lower George St; mains lunch €8-12, dinner €18-26; ⌚cafe 9am-6pm, restaurant noon-3pm & 6-10pm) Wexford's top dining spot is a cool, intimate cafe and restaurant that opens to an elegant courtyard beneath a canopy of fairy lights, with a menu of adventurous contemporary cuisine.

SkyView Cafe CAFE €
(Wexford Opera House, 27 High St; mains €5-10; ⌚10am-5pm Mon-Sat) The cafe on the top floor of Wexford's snazzy opera house offers breakfast and lunch accompanied by panoramic views.

Information

Tourist office (☎912 3111; www.discoverireland.ie/wexford; The Quay; ⌚9.15am-1pm & 2-5pm Mon-Fri Nov-Mar, 9am-1pm & 2-6pm Mon-Sat Apr-Oct)

Getting There & Away

BUS Buses depart from the train station.

Dublin €17, 2¾ hours, at least hourly

Rosslare Harbour €5, 30 minutes, at least hourly

TRAIN Wexford's **O'Hanrahan train station** is at the north end of the town centre.

Dublin Connolly €23, 2½ hours, three daily

Rosslare Harbour €5, 25 minutes, three daily

Kilkenny

☎056 / POP 26,500

Built from black limestone flecked with fossil seashells, Kilkenny is known as 'the marble city'. Its picturesque huddle of medieval lanes, strung between castle and cathedral along the bank of the Nore River, is one of the southeast's biggest tourist draws – the narrow streets are often clogged with tour coaches. But it's worth braving the crowds to soak up the atmosphere of one of Ireland's creative crucibles – Kilkenny is a centre for arts and crafts, and home to a host of fine restaurants, cafes, pubs and shops.

Sights

Kilkenny Castle CASTLE
(www.kilkennycastle.ie; adult/child incl tour €6/2.50; ⌚9am-5.30pm Jun-Aug, 9.30am-5.30pm Apr-May & Sep, 9.30am-4.30pm Oct-Mar) Stronghold of the powerful Butler family, Kilkenny Castle has a history dating back to 1172, when the legendary Strongbow erected a wooden tower on the site, though much of its present look dates from the 19th century. Highlights of the guided tour include the painted roof beams of the **Long Gallery**, and the collection of Victorian antiques. There's an excellent **tearoom** in the former castle kitchens, all white marble and gleaming copper.

Craft Centres CRAFTS
The former stables opposite the castle house the **National Craft Gallery** (www.ccoi.ie; Castle Yard; admission free; ⌚10am-5.30pm Tue-Sat year-round, 11am-5.30pm Sun Apr-Dec) and the **Kilkenny Design Centre** (www.kilkennydesign.com; ⌚10am-7pm Mon-Sat, 11am-7pm Sun), showcases for contemporary Irish crafts.

St Canice's Cathedral CHURCH
(www.stcanicescathedral.ie; adult/concession €4/3; ⏲9am-6pm Mon-Sat, 2-6pm Sun Jun-Aug, 10am-1pm & 2-5pm Mon-Sat, 2-6pm Sun Apr-May & Sep, shorter hr Oct-Mar) At the opposite end of town from the castle is Ireland's second-largest cathedral, crammed with medieval monuments and tombs. Outside stands a 30m-tall **round tower** (admission €3; ⏲Apr-Oct), which you can climb – if you're over 12 years of age – for a grand view of the town.

Rothe House MUSEUM
(www.rothehouse.com; Parliament St; adult/child €5/4; ⏲10.30am-5pm Mon-Sat & 3-5pm Sun Apr-Oct, 10.30am-4.30pm Mon-Sat Nov-Mar) Dating from 1594 and now home to a fascinating museum, Rothe House is Ireland's finest example of a Tudor merchant's house, complete with restored medieval garden.

Festivals & Events

Kilkenny is rightly known as the festival capital of Ireland, with several world-class events throughout the year.

Kilkenny Arts Festival ARTS
(www.kilkennyarts.ie) In mid-August the city comes alive with theatre, cinema, music, literature, visual arts, children's events and street spectacles for 10 action-packed days.

Kilkenny Celtic Festival CELTIC
(www.celticfestival.ie) Late September to early October. A celebration of all things 'trad' (traditional) Irish, especially the language.

Sleeping

TOP CHOICE **Celtic House** B&B €€
(☎776 2249; www.celtic-house-bandb.com; 18 Michael St; r €80-90; P@) Artist Angela Byrne extends one of Ireland's warmest welcomes at her spick-and-span B&B. Some of the bright rooms have views of the castle, and Angela's landscapes adorn many of the walls. Guests return time and again – definitely book ahead.

Kilkenny Tourist Hostel HOSTEL €
(☎776 3541; www.kilkennyhostel.ie; 35 Parliament St; dm/tw €17/42; @) Centrally located, within a few steps of half a dozen pubs and restaurants, this hostel has a large kitchen and an atmospheric sitting room with sofas and a turf fire.

Butler B&B €€
(☎776 1178; www.butlercourt.com; Patrick St; r €80-130; @) Where the locals stash their guests, this friendly guest house has 10 nicely appointed rooms opening onto a restful courtyard. Breakfasts are continental and there's a fridge in every room.

Rafter Dempsey's B&B €€
(☎772 2970; www.rafterdempseys.ie; 4 Friary St; r €45-130) This place offers basic B&B accommodation in 16 rooms above a simple pub of the same name, just off High St.

Tree Grove Caravan & Camping Park CAMPING GROUND €
(☎777 0302; www.treegrovecamping.com; campsites per tent & 2 adults €15-20; ⏲Mar–mid-Nov) Located 1.5km south, off the New Ross (R700) road; you can walk into town along a riverside footpath.

Eating

TOP CHOICE **Café Sol** FUSION €€
(☎776 4987; www.cafesolkilkenny.com; William St; mains lunch €9-13, dinner €16-23; ⏲11.30am-9.30pm Mon-Sat, noon-9pm Sun;) The seasonally changing menu at this funky little place lists local sources for most of the produce. The Irish-Mediterranean fusion cuisine, like the bold and edgy artwork on the walls, displays some unexpected combinations, but it works – the place is packed by 1pm, so get in early for lunch. Three-course early-bird menus (€27; 6pm to 7.15pm Sunday to Friday, 5.30pm to 6.15pm Saturday) are great value.

Chez Pierre FRENCH €€
(☎776 4655; 17 Parliament St; mains €5-14, 3-course dinners €26; ⏲10am-4pm Mon-Sat, 10.30am-4pm Sun, 7-9pm Fri & Sat) This neat little bistro does great *tartines* (open sandwiches), soups and sweets during the day, plus classic French dishes for dinner.

Marble City Bar PUB €€
(66 High St; mains €8-15; ⏲noon-9pm) Usual pub-grub standards such as sausage with mash, and fish and chips are raised above the norm here through the use of top-notch ingredients.

Gourmet Store SANDWICHES €
(56 High St; sandwiches €3-4; ⏲9am-6pm Mon-Sat) This classy deli is a good option for picnickers and hostellers.

Drinking & Entertainment

John Cleere's PUB, LIVE MUSIC
(22 Parliament St) Cleere's often has good alternative bands – and the occasional poetry reading – in its theatre out back.

Kyteler's Inn PUB
(27 St Kieran's St) The old house of Dame Kyteler (aka the Witch of Kilkenny) is a

WORTH A TRIP

ROCK OF CASHEL

The **Rock of Cashel** (www.heritageireland.com; adult/child €6/2; ⌚9am-5.30pm mid-Mar–mid-Oct, to 4.30pm mid-Oct–mid-Mar, last admission 45min before closing) is one of Ireland's most spectacular archaeological sites. A prominent green hill, banded with limestone outcrops, it rises from a grassy plain on the outskirts of Cashel town and bristles with ancient fortifications. For more than 1000 years it was a symbol of power, and the seat of kings and churchmen who ruled over the region. Sturdy walls circle an enclosure that contains a complete **round tower**, a roofless **abbey** and the finest 12th-century **Romanesque chapel** in Ireland.

Cashel Lodge and Camping Park (☎062-61003; www.cashel-lodge.com; Dundrum Rd; campsites per person €8, dm/d €20/65; P) is a good place to stay, with terrific views of the Rock.

Bus Éireann (www.buseireann.ie) runs eight buses daily between Cashel and Cork (€12, 1½ hours).

tourist magnet, but an atmospheric pub all the same.

Watergate Theatre THEATRE
(www.watergatetheatre.com; Parliament St) Hosts musical and theatrical productions throughout the year.

Information

Tourist office (☎775 1500; www.kilkennytourism.ie; Rose Inn St; ⌚9am-7pm Mon-Sat & 11am-5pm Sun Jul & Aug, 9.15am-1pm & 2-5pm Mon-Sat Sep-Jun)

Getting There & Away

BUS Buses depart from the train station.

Cork €16, three hours, two daily

Dublin €11, 2¼ hours, five daily

TRAIN **Kilkenny train station** (Dublin Rd) is east of the town centre along John St, next to the MacDonagh Junction shopping mall.

Dublin Heuston from €10, 1¾ hours, eight daily

Galway €59, four hours, one daily (change at Kildare)

THE SOUTHWEST

The southwest comes closest to the misty-eyed vision of Ireland many visitors hold in their imagination – blue lakes and green mountains, blustery beaches, bird-haunted sea cliffs, picturesque hamlets, and welcoming towns where live music sparks up every night. Cork city buzzes with an energy that rivals Dublin's, while Killarney offers a gateway to some of the country's finest scenery.

Cork

☎021 / POP 120,000

There's a reason the locals call Cork (Corcaigh) 'The Real Capital' or 'The People's Republic of Cork'; something special is going on here. The city has long been dismissive of Dublin, and with a burgeoning arts, music and restaurant scene, it has a cultural reputation to rival the capital's. The flurry of urban renewal that began with the city's stint in 2005 as European Capital of Culture has seen new buildings, bars and arts centres spring up all over town. The best of the city is still happily traditional though – snug pubs with live-music sessions most of the week, excellent local produce in an ever-expanding list of restaurants, and a genuinely proud welcome from the locals. North and south of St Patrick's St lie the city's most entertaining quarters: webs of narrow streets crammed with pubs, cafes, restaurants and shops.

Sights

English Market MARKET
(www.corkenglishmarket.ie; Princes St & Grand Pde; ⌚8am-6pm Mon-Sat) It could just as easily be called the Victorian Market for its ornate vaulted ceilings and columns, but the English Market is a true gem, no matter what you name it. Scores of vendors sell some of the very best meat, fish, cheese and takeaway food in the region. On decent days, take your lunch to nearby Bishop Lucey Park, a popular alfresco eating spot.

Cork City Gaol MUSEUM
(www.corkcitygaol.com; Convent Ave; adult/child €7/3.50; ⌚9.30am-6pm Mar-Oct, 10am-5pm Nov-Feb) Closed down in 1923, this vast 19th-cen-

tury prison is now a terrific museum about a terrifying subject. Restored cells, mannequins representing prisoners and guards, and a detailed **audioguide** bring home the horrors of Victorian prison life.

FCrawford Art Gallery ART MUSEUM
(www.crawfordartgallery.ie; Emmet Pl; ⏲10am-5pm Mon-Sat, to 8pm Thu) The 18th-century Cork Customs House is blended with 21st-century Dutch design in this intriguing gallery, a must-see for anyone who enjoys art and architecture. Pieces by Irish artists such as Jack Yeats and Cork's own James Barry sit among a fine permanent collection that includes artists from Continental Europe. The gallery has wheelchair access.

St Finbarre's Cathedral CHURCH
(www.cathedral.cork.anglican.org; Bishop St; adult/child €4/2; ⏲9.30am-5.30pm Mon-Sat, 12.30-5pm Sun Apr-Nov, 10am-12.45pm & 2-5pm Mon-Sat Dec-Mar) Just south of the city centre sits Cork's Protestant cathedral. Built in 1879, this beautiful Gothic Revival structure has a multitude of notable features, including a Golden Angel who sits on the eastern side of the cathedral, and whose job it is to blow her horn at the onset of the Apocalypse.

FREE **Cork Public Museum** MUSEUM
(www.corkcity.ie; Fitzgerald Park; ⏲11am-1pm & 2.15-5pm Mon-Fri, 11am-1pm & 2.15-4pm Sat year-round, 3-5pm Sun Apr-Sep) The city museum has a fine collection of artefacts that trace Cork's past from prehistory to the present, including the city's role in the fight for independence. Bus 8 goes to the University College Cork (UCC) main gates nearby.

Festivals & Events

Guinness Jazz Festival MUSIC
(www.guinnessjazzfestival.com) All-star line-up in venues across town, held in October.

Cork Film Festival FILM
(www.corkfilmfest.org) Eclectic week-long program of international films held in October/November.

Sleeping

TOP CHOICE **Garnish House** B&B €€
(☎427 5111; www.garnish.ie; Western Rd; s/d from €75/86; P 📶) With charming rooms (think flowers and fresh fruit), gourmet breakfasts and hosts who are eager to please, Garnish House is possibly the perfect B&B. From the moment you arrive and are greeted with tea and goodies, until the moment you leave, you will experience nothing short of absolute hospitality.

Brú Bar & Hostel HOSTEL €
(☎455 9667; www.bruhostel.com; 57 MacCurtain St; dm €17-23, d €50-60; P @) Cork's funkiest hostel also has a popular bar and an internet cafe on the premises. This clean and friendly triple treat can be a rocking good time, especially on the weekends.

Kinlay House Shandon HOSTEL €
(☎450 8966; www.kinlayhouse.ie; Bob & Joan's Walk; dm €14-19, s/d from €30/48; @ 📶) This labyrinthine hostel is in a quiet spot near St Anne's Church in Shandon. It has a fun, laid-back atmosphere; services include bureau de change, laundry and luggage storage. Guests can use the next-door gym at a discount.

Cork International Hostel HOSTEL €
(☎454 3289; www.corkinternationalhostel.com; 1-2 Redclyffe, Western Rd; dm €13-18, tw €58; P @) The cheerful staff at this bright and busy An Óige hostel do a great job coping with the constant flow of young travellers. It's 2km from the centre; bus 8 stops outside.

Crawford House B&B €€
(☎427 9000; www.crawfordguesthouse.com; Western Rd; s/d €80/120; P) A top-notch B&B, Crawford House has spacious rooms with king-size beds, gracious furnishings and some bodacious jacuzzis to splash around in. The standard is that of a contemporary hotel, the atmosphere that of a family home.

Sheila's Hostel HOSTEL €
(☎450 5562; www.sheilashostel.ie; 4 Belgrave Pl; dm €14-19, tw €46-54; @ 📶) The sauna, cinema room, coffee shop and super-friendly staff make up for the occasionally cramped atmosphere in this always-heaving hostel.

Oaklands B&B €€
(☎450 0578; 51 Glanmire Rd Lower; s/d €45/70) Close to the train station at the northeastern end of town.

Emerson House B&B €€
(☎450 3647; www.emersonhousecork.com; 2 Clarence Tce, North Summer Hill; r per person from €40; P) Upmarket, gay and lesbian guest house.

Blue Dolphin B&B €€
(☎427 4908; www.bluedolphin.ie; 3 College View, Western Rd; s/d from €50/80; P @) Bright and welcoming, one of several high-quality B&Bs on this strip.

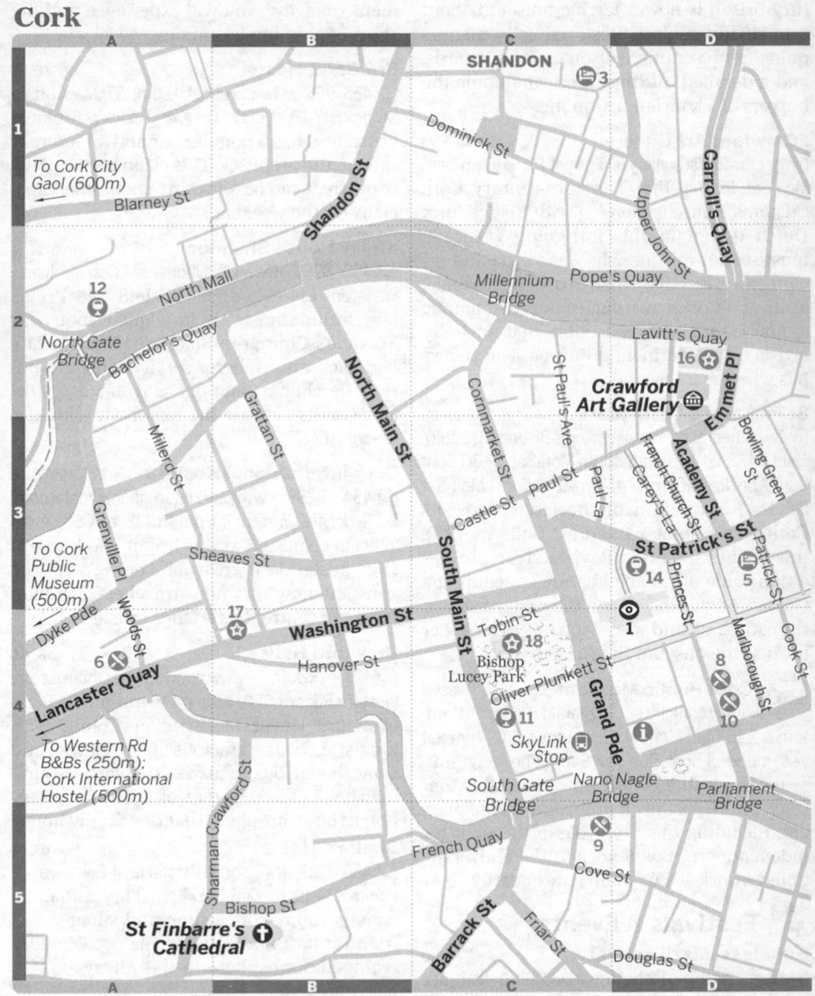

Eating

TOP CHOICE **Farmgate Café** CAFE, BISTRO €€

(www.farmgate.ie; English Market; mains €9-14; ⏲8.30am-10pm Mon-Sat) An unmissable experience at the heart of the English Market, the Farmgate is perched on a balcony overlooking the market below, the source of all that fresh local produce on your plate. Up the stairs and turn left for table service, right for counter service.

Idaho Café CAFE €€

(19 Caroline St; dishes €7-12; ⏲8.30am-5pm) It looks like a trad old caff from the outside, but take a gander at the menu and you'll find all sorts of creative takes on Irish standards. The tea selection includes loads of herbal numbers and there's a good per-glass wine menu.

Wildways ORGANIC €

(www.wildways.net; 21 Princes St; mains €3-7; ⏲8am-5pm Mon-Fri, 8.30am-4pm Sat) Cork's first organic soup and sandwich bar serves such a variety of delicious and healthy food that even the pickiest of eaters can find something scrumptious. If you're around for breakfast, make sure to try the excellent chocolate-chip pancakes.

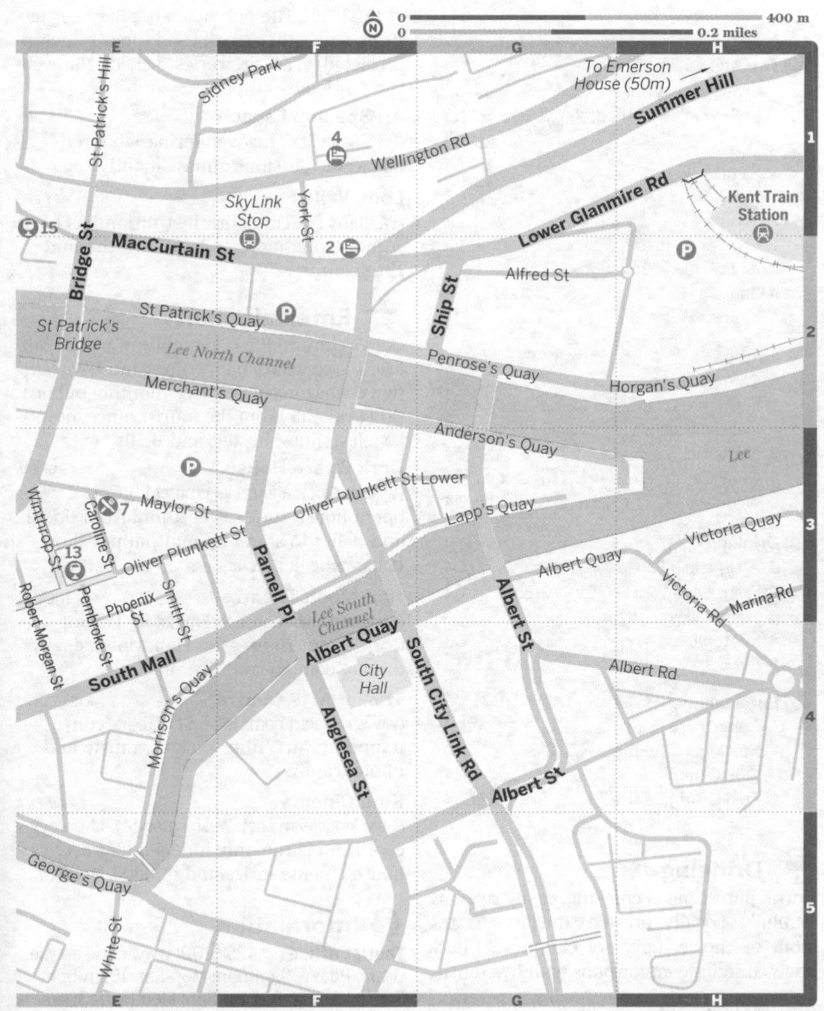

Nash 19 BISTRO €€
(www.nash19.com; Princes St; mains €8-20; ⏲7.30am-5pm Mon-Fri) A sensational bistro with its own food market; local produce is honoured from breakfast to lunch and on to tea. Fresh scones draw in the crowds early; daily specials (soups, salads, desserts etc) and an incredible burger keep them coming throughout the rest of the day.

Quay Co-op VEGETARIAN €
(www.quaycoop.com; 24 Sullivan's Quay; mains €7-11; ⏲9am-9pm Mon-Sat, noon-9pm Sun;) Flying the flag for alternative Cork, this place offers a range of self-service vegie options, all organic, including big breakfasts and rib-sticking soups and casseroles. It also caters for gluten-, dairy- and wheat-free needs, and is amazingly child-friendly.

Café Paradiso VEGETARIAN €€€
(☎427 7939; www.cafeparadiso.ie; 16 Lancaster Quay; mains lunch €14-15, dinner €23-25; ⏲dinner 5.30-10pm Tue-Sat, lunch noon-3pm Fri & Sat) Arguably the best vegetarian restaurant in Ireland, the inventive dishes on offer here will seduce even the most committed carnivore. The pre-theatre menu (till 7pm Tuesday to Friday) offers two/three courses for €24/30.

Cork

Top Sights
- Crawford Art Gallery D2
- St Finbarre's Cathedral B5

Sights
- 1 English Market D4

Sleeping
- 2 Brú Bar & Hostel F2
- 3 Kinlay House Shandon C1
- 4 Sheila's Hostel F1
- 5 Victoria Hotel D3

Eating
- 6 Café Paradiso A4
- Farmgate Café .... (see 1)
- 7 Idaho Cafe E3
- 8 Nash 19 .... D4
- 9 Quay Co-op C5
- 10 Wildways D4

Drinking
- 11 An Spailpín Fánac C4
- 12 Franciscan Well Brewery A2
- 13 Long Valley E3
- 14 Mutton Lane Inn D3
- 15 Sin É E1

Entertainment
- 16 Cork Opera House D2
- Half Moon Theatre .... (see 16)
- 17 Kino Cinema B4
- 18 Triskel Arts Centre C4

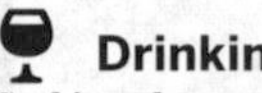

Drinking

Cork's pub scene is cracking, easily rivalling Dublin's. Locally brewed Murphy's is the stout of choice here, not Guinness. Check www.corkgigs.com for pubs with live music.

Mutton Lane Inn PUB
(3 Mutton Lane) With Victorian wallpaper, rock-and-roll posters, and a covered outdoor area for drinking and smoking, Cork's oldest pub is the type of place that you'll wish you had in your home town.

Sin É PUB
(Coburg St) There are no frills or fuss here –just a comfy, sociable pub long on atmosphere and short on pretension. There's music most nights, much of it traditional but with the odd surprise.

Franciscan Well Brewery MICROBREWERY
(www.franciscanwellbrewery.com; 14 North Mall) The best place to enjoy the beer at this microbrewery is in the enormous beer garden at the back. The pub holds regular beer festivals with other small (and often underappreciated) Irish breweries – check the website for details.

An Spailpín Fánach PUB
(28 S Main St) The 'wandering labourer' hosts trad sessions almost nightly.

Long Valley PUB
(Winthrop St) This Cork institution has been going strong more or less since the mid-19th century.

Entertainment

Cork's cultural life is generally of a high calibre. To see what's happening grab *WhazOn?* (www.whazon.com), a free monthly publication available from the tourist office, newsagencies, shops, hostels and B&Bs.

Cork Opera House OPERA
(www.corkoperahouse.ie; Emmet Pl) Cork's opera house stages everything from opera and ballet to stand-up and puppet shows. It has wheelchair access.

Half Moon Theatre THEATRE
(www.corkoperahouse.ie; Emmet Pl) Part of Cork Opera House, the Half Moon stages drama, comedy and live music.

Triskel Arts Centre ARTS CENTRE
(www.triskelart.com; Tobin St) Hosts contemporary art, film, theatre, music and photography.

Kino Cinema CINEMA
(www.kinocinema.net; Washington St) The very cool Kino is the only independent art-house cinema in Ireland outside Dublin.

Information

Tourist office (425 5100; www.corkkerry.ie; Grand Pde; 9am-6pm Mon-Sat, 10am-5pm Sun Jul & Aug, 9.15am-5pm Mon-Fri, 9.30am-4.30pm Sat Sep-Jun)

Getting There & Away

AIR **Cork airport** (www.corkairport.com) is 8km south of the city on the N27. Direct flights to Belfast, Edinburgh, London, Manchester, Amsterdam, Barcelona, Munich, Paris, Warsaw and Rome.

BOAT **Brittany Ferries** (www.brittany-ferries.com) has regular sailings from Cork to Roscoff (France). The ferry terminal is at Ringaskiddy, about 15 minutes by car southeast of the city centre along the N28. See p766 for more details.

BUS **Aircoach** (www.aircoach.ie) provides a direct service to Dublin city and airport from St Patrick Quay (€14, four hours, eight daily). **Cork**

bus station (cnr Merchants Quay & Parnell Pl) is east of the city centre.

Dublin €13, 4½ hours, six daily

Kilkenny €19, three hours, three daily

Killarney €17, 1¾ hours, hourly

TRAIN Cork's **Kent train station** (Glanmire Rd Lower) is across the river.

Dublin €20, 2¾ hours, hourly

Galway €45, five to six hours, seven daily (two or three changes needed)

Killarney €26, 1½ to two hours, nine daily

Getting Around

TO/FROM THE AIRPORT **SkyLink** (www.skylinkcork.com) buses pick up and set down at stops in central Cork (adult/child €5/2.50, 30 minutes, hourly). Otherwise, a taxi costs around €15 to €20.

TO/FROM THE FERRY Taxis cost €28 to €35. Bus Éireann runs a service from the bus station to link up with ferries (bus 223; adult/child €5.50/3.50, 50 minutes). Confirm times at the bus station. There's also a service to Rosslare Harbour (bus 40; adult/child €23.50/16; four to five hours).

BIKE **Cycle Scene** (www.cyclescene.ie; 396 Blarney St) Has bikes for hire from €15/80 per day/week.

Around Cork

BLARNEY

021 / POP 2150

Lying just northwest of Cork, the village of Blarney (An Bhlarna) receives a *gazillion* visitors a year, for one sole reason: **Blarney Castle** (www.blarneycastle.ie; adult/child €10/3.50; 9am-6.30pm Mon-Sat, 9am-5.30pm Sun May-Sep, to dusk daily Oct-Apr). They come to kiss the castle's legendary **Blarney Stone** and get the 'gift of the gab' (Queen Elizabeth I, exasperated with Lord Blarney's ability to talk endlessly without agreeing to her demands, invented the term 'to talk Blarney' back in the 16th century). The stone is up on the battlements, and bending over backwards to kiss it requires a head for heights, although there's someone there to hold you in position. It also helps if you're not germophobic – there's a greasy mark where millions of lips have been before. (The Blarney stain? Sorry.)

Buses run regularly from Cork bus station (€6.20 return, 30 minutes).

COBH

021 / POP 6800

In the wake of the Famine, 2.5 million people emigrated from the port of Cobh (pronounced cove) – go on a grey day and the sense of loss is still almost palpable. When the sun shines, though, you'll see another side to this pretty little town with its **brightly coloured houses** and **seaside promenade**. Be sure to visit the excellent **Cobh, The Queenstown Story** (www.cobhheritage.com; adult/child €7.10/4; 9.30am-5pm Mon-Fri, 9.30am-6pm Sat, 11am-6pm Sun May-Oct, shorter hr Nov-Apr) heritage centre in the old train station. It tells the story of the migrants who sailed from here, and of the town's links with the *Titanic* and the *Lusitania*. Last admission is 30 minutes before closing, and the centre has wheelchair access.

Cobh is 24km southeast of Cork via the N25. Hourly trains (€7 return, 30 minutes) run here from Cork.

KINSALE

021 / POP 2260

The picturesque yachting harbour of Kinsale (Cionn tSáile) is one of the many gems that dot the coastline of County Cork. Kinsale has been labelled the gourmet centre of Ireland and, for such a small place, it certainly contains more than its fair share of international-standard restaurants. It also has lots of craft galleries and shops.

Sights & Activities

Charles Fort RUINS

(www.heritageireland.ie; adult/student €4/2; 10am-6pm mid-Mar–Oct, to 5pm Nov–mid-Mar) Southeast of Kinsale, a scenic 2.5km walk from the town centre, stand the stout ruins of Charles Fort. Built in the 1670s, it is one of the best-preserved star forts in Europe and commands grand coastal views.

You can sail to Charles Fort and up the Bandon River aboard the **Spirit of Kinsale** (086-250 5456; www.kinsaleharbourcruises.com; adult/child €12.50/6). Departure times vary and are weather dependent – check the website or the tourist office for details.

Sleeping

Olde Bakery B&B €€

(477 3012; www.theoldebakerykinsale.com; 56 Lower O'Connell St; r €80) A short walk southwest of the centre is this very friendly place that once was the British garrison bakery. Rooms are a reasonable size, and terrific breakfasts around the kitchen table get everyone chatting.

Dempsey's HOSTEL €

(477 2124; www.hostelkinsale.com; Eastern Rd; dm/tw €15/40;) This basic hostel is the town's

cheapest option, with separate male and female dorms, family rooms, a kitchen, and picnic tables in the front garden. It's the bright-blue house by the petrol station on the road from Cork.

White House B&B €€
(477 2125; www.whitehouse-kinsale.ie; Pearse St; s €65-100, d €100-180; P@) A solid guest house in the town centre, the White House has 10 rooms in warm shades of cream and brown and large, firm beds. The attached **Restaurant d'Antibes** is also excellent.

Eating

TOP CHOICE **Fishy Fishy Café** SEAFOOD €€
(470 0415; www.fishyfishy.ie; Crowley Quay, off Pier Rd; mains €15-24; noon-9pm daily) This seafood restaurant is beautifully understated, with stark white walls splashed with bright artwork and a decked terrace out front. All the fish is caught locally, from the fried haddock in Kinsale beer to the scallops with braised fennel and citrus cream.

Fishy Fishy Chippy SEAFOOD €
(Guardwell; mains €6-10; noon-4.30pm Tue-Sat) If the main restaurant is full (or too expensive), you can get a superb seafood lunch to take away at this chippy a few blocks away near Market Sq. The menu includes beer-battered haddock with chips and salad, and seafood chowder with tarragon and coriander.

Cucina CAFE, BISTRO €€
(www.cucina.ie; 9 Market St; mains €8-14; 9am-5pm Mon-Sat, 9am-3pm Sun, 6-9.30pm Thu-Sat) Laid-back jazz sets the mood at this modern little cafe. Healthy bruschetta, salads and soups, and excellent coffee are served in a simple setting; the evening menu offers dishes such as roast beetroot salad with chorizo and green beans.

Patsy's Corner CAFE €
(Market Sq; mains €3-7; 9am-5.30pm Mon-Sat) Serving homemade soups and pastries alongside fresh sandwiches and salads, Patsy's holds its own as a great corner cafe in a town full of gourmet restaurants.

Information

Tourist office (477 2234; www.kinsale.ie; 1 Pier Rd; 9.30am-1pm & 2.15-5.30pm Mon-Sat Mar-Jun, Sep & Oct, daily Jul & Aug) In the centre of town; opening hours vary, especially in the quieter months.

Getting There & Away

Kinsale is 25km south of Cork; to continue west by bus you have to return to Cork. Buses from Cork (€13 return, 50 minutes, 14 daily Monday to Friday, 11 Saturday, five Sunday) stop near the tourist office.

West Cork

Travelling around west Cork by public transport can be tough. There are at least two daily bus services in summer connecting the main towns, but some routes are not serviced at all during the rest of the year. The trick is to plan ahead at Cork and be prepared to change buses and backtrack – use the online journey planner at www.buseireann.ie. If you're so inclined, hitchhiking is another way to get around West Cork (take the usual safety precautions).

BALTIMORE

028 / POP 400

Just 13km down the Ilen River from Skibbereen, sleepy Baltimore has a population of around 400 that swells enormously during summer. Its main attraction is the ferry to Sherkin and Clear Islands.

Baltimore has plenty of B&Bs, plus the excellent **Top of the Hill Hostel** (20094; www.topofthehillhostel.ie; dm/d €15/44).

The Skibbereen **tourist office** (21766; www.skibbereen.ie; 9am-7pm Jul & Aug, 9am-6pm Mon-Sat Jun & Sep, 9.15am-1pm & 2-5pm Mon-Fri Oct-May) can handle questions about the area.

CLEAR ISLAND

028 / POP 120

Clear Island, or Cape Clear as the locals call it, is the most southerly point of Ireland (apart from Fastnet Rock, 6km to the southwest). It's a Gaeltacht (Irish-speaking) area, with about 120 Irish-speaking inhabitants, one shop, three pubs and its own website, **Oileán Chléire** (Cape Clear Island; www.oilean-chleire.ie). It's a place for quiet walks, birdwatching and hunting down standing stones. There's also a wonderful **storytelling festival** (www.capeclearstorytelling.com) held in early September.

An Óige's **Cape Clear Island Hostel** (41968; www.capeclearhostel.com; Old Coastguard Station, South Harbour; dm €17; @) is in a large white building at the south harbour, or you can camp at **Chléire Haven** (086-197 1956; www.yurt-holidays-ireland.com; per person €10).

Cluain Mara (39153; www.capeclearisland.com; North Harbour; r per person €28-35) and **Ard Na Goithe** (39160; The Glen; per person €35) are both amazingly friendly places in typical island houses. They can be reached by taking the 'bus' (which is actually a silver minivan) from the pier.

The ferries **Cailín Óir** and **Dun Aengus** (☎41923; www.cailinoir.com) sail between Baltimore and Clear Island (weather permitting) three to four times daily in summer and twice daily in winter. The trip takes 45 minutes and costs €16 return (bicycles go for free). In summer ferries to Clear Island also leave from Schull (on the Mizen Head peninsula).

From June to September, the **Karycraft** (☎28278; www.capeclearferries.com; one-way/return €8/14; one to three a day) ferry connects Schull with Clear Island, allowing you to use the island as a stepping stone to travel west.

MIZEN HEAD PENINSULA

☎028

The contorted sea cliffs of Mizen Head provide an alternative scenic objective to the better known and more touristy Ring of Kerry to the north. The road west from the pretty village of **Schull** ends at the **Mizen Head Visitor Centre** (www.mizenhead.net; adult/child €6/3.50; ⏲10am-6pm Jun-Aug, 11am-4pm mid-Mar–May & Sep, 11am-4pm Sat & Sun Oct–mid-Mar), from which a short but spectacular walk leads to **Mizen Head Signal Station**, on a small island connected to the mainland by a 45m-high bridge (you have to pay the visitor-centre admission fee to get to the island). From here you can look down on the pounding sea, striking rock formations and maybe the odd seal.

Stanley House (☎28425; www.stanley-house.net; off Colla Rd; s/d €50/76; ⏲Apr-Sep), just outside of town, has sweeping views of the water from its front lawn, while **Glencairn** (☎28007; susanglencairn@yahoo.ie; Ardmanagh Dr; s/d €45/70), on a cul-de-sac just 100m off Main St, serves up a mighty Irish breakfast.

There are two buses a day from Cork to Schull (€18, 2½ hours).

BEARA PENINSULA

☎027

The Beara Peninsula is a wild, handsome, rocky landscape that's ideal for exploring by foot or bike. Beginning at the attractive Victorian resort of **Glengarriff**, it's possible to drive the 137km **Ring of Beara** in one day, although that would be missing the point. It's also possible to hitchhike around the Ring, which would definitely take more than a day. If you're driving or cycling (leg-power permitting), don't miss the beautiful **Healy Pass**.

Walkers might like to tackle the ruggedly beautiful **Hungry Hill**, made famous by Daphne du Maurier's book of the same name, just outside the pleasant fishing town of **Castletownbere**. Castletownbere is also home to **McCarthy's Bar**, which appears on the cover of the popular book (of the same name) by Pete McCarthy.

The village of **Allihies**, whose colourfully painted houses grace many a postcard and guidebook cover, lies at the centre of an old copper mining area. Its fascinating history is chronicled in the **Allihies Copper Mine Museum** (www.acmm.ie; adult/child €5/2; ⏲10am-5pm daily Apr-Oct). Pick up a copy of the museum leaflet and follow the **Copper Mine Trail**, a waymarked hike among the remains of the old workings.

Sleeping

Murphy's Village Hostel HOSTEL €
(☎63555; www.murphyshostel.com; Main St, Glengarriff; dm/d €15/40; ⏲Jun-Sep) Pleasantly informal hostel in the heart of Glengarriff.

Garranes Farmhouse Hostel HOSTEL €
(☎73147; www.dzogchenbeara.org; Garranes; dm/f €15/40) Between Castletownbere and Allihies, with a breathtaking location high above Bantry Bay. Owned by a Buddhist retreat centre.

Allihies Village Hostel HOSTEL €
(☎71307; www.allihieshostel.net; Allihies; dm/d €18/50; P@) Smart and gleaming hostel among the old copper mines.

Sea View Guesthouse GUEST HOUSE €€
(☎73004; www.seaviewallihies.com; Allihies; s/d €45/75; P) Ten cosy rooms in a tidy yellow building.

Getting There & Away

Bus Éireann's bus 236 runs from Cork to Castletownbere (€20, 3½ hours) via Bantry, Glengarriff and Adrigole, at least three times a week. Bus 282 runs from Kenmare to Ardgroom at least weekly, continuing to Castletownbere (€12, two hours) from mid-June to August only.

Killarney

☎064 / POP 13,500

Killarney is a well-oiled tourism machine in the middle of sublime scenery. Its manufactured tweeness is renowned – the stream of buses arriving to consume soft-toy sham-

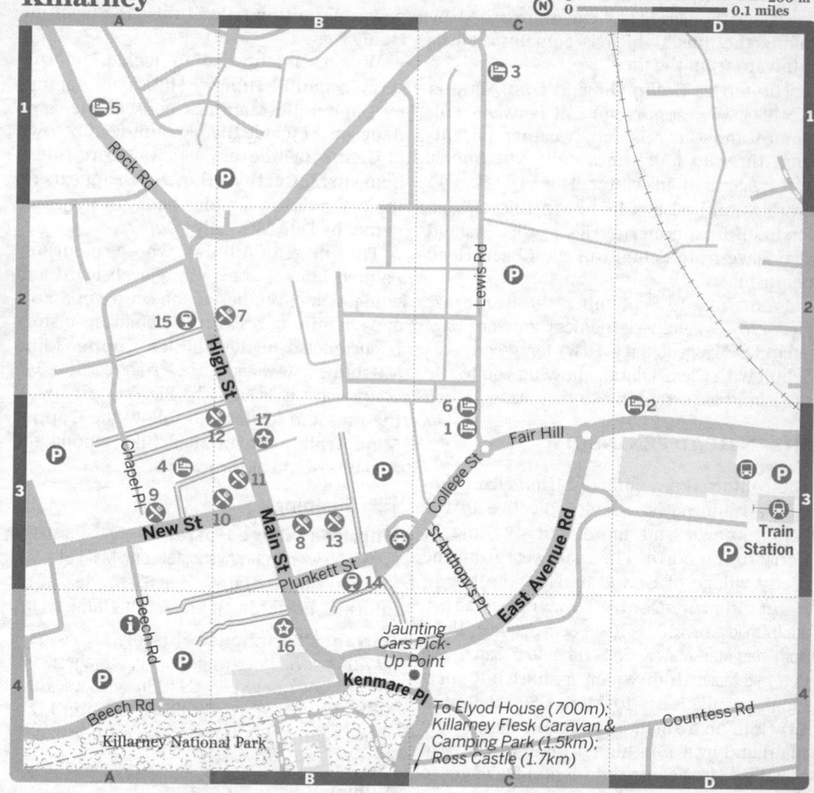

rocks, the placards on street corners pointing to trad-music sessions. However, it has many charms beyond its obvious proximity to lakes, waterfalls, woodland and moors dwarfed by 1000m-plus peaks. In a town that's been practising the tourism game for more than 250 years, competition keeps standards high, and visitors on all budgets can expect to find superb restaurants, great pubs and good accommodation.

Sights & Activities

Most of Killarney's attractions are just outside the town, not actually in it. If you're not on two wheels, the traditional transport is the horse-drawn **jaunting car** (www.killarneyjauntingcars.com), which comes with a driver known as a jarvey. The pick-up point, nicknamed 'the Ha Ha' or 'the Block', is on Kenmare Pl. Tours cost €40 to €70, depending on distance; cars can officially carry up to four people.

Killarney National Park

NATIONAL PARK

Any cynicism engendered by Killarney's shamrock-filled souvenir stores evaporates when you begin to explore the sublime Killarney National Park. Buses rumble up to Ross Castle and Muckross House, but it's possible to flee the rest of tourist-kind while taking in Ireland's largest area of ancient oak woods, panoramic views of its highest mountains, and the country's only wild herd of native red deer.

Lough Leane (the Lower Lake or 'Lake of Learning'), Muckross Lake and the Upper Lake make up about a quarter of the park. Their peaty waters are as rich in wildlife as the surrounding land: cormorants skim across the surface, deer swim out to graze on the islands, and salmon, trout and perch prosper in a pike-free environment.

Designated a Unesco Biosphere Reserve in 1982, the park extends to the southwest of town. There are pedestrian entrances op-

Killarney

Activities, Courses & Tours

O'Connor's Tours (see 17)

Sleeping

1	Fairview	C3
2	Killarney Railway Hostel	D3
3	Kingfisher Lodge	C1
4	Neptune's Killarney Town Hostel	A3
5	Rathmore House	A1
6	Súgán Hostel	C3

Eating

7	Brícín	B2
8	Jam	B3
9	Kathleen's Country Kitchen	A3
10	Revive Café & Wine Bar	B3
11	Sceale Eile	B3
12	Treyvaud's	B3
13	Vanilla Pod	B3

Drinking

14	Courtney's	B3
15	Hussy's	A2

Entertainment

16	Killarney Grand	B4
17	O'Connor's	B3

posite St Mary's Cathedral, with other entrances (for drivers) off the N71.

The restored 14th-century **Ross Castle** (www.heritageireland.ie; adult/child €6/2; ⌚9am-6.30pm Jun-Aug, 9.30am-5.30pm mid-Mar–May & Sep–mid-Oct, 9.30am-4.30pm mid-Oct–mid-Nov) is a 2.5km walk from St Mary's Cathedral. Hour-long **cruises on Lough Leane** (adult/child €10/5) leave the castle daily in summer; you can make bookings at the tourist office. From late September to May boats depart only on demand.

Inisfallen, Lough Leane's largest island, is where the 13th-century *Annals of Inisfallen* were written. The annals, now in the Bodleian Library at Oxford, remain a vital source of information about early Irish history. From Ross Castle you can hire a boat and row to the island to inspect the ruins of a 12th-century **oratory**. Alternatively, boatmen charge around €10 per person for the trip.

The core of Killarney National Park is **Muckross House** (www.muckross-house.ie; adult/child €7/3; ⌚9am-7pm Jul & Aug, to 5.30pm Sep-Jun) and its surrounding estate, donated to the government in 1932. You can pay to tour the house, or walk or cycle around the grounds for free. The house is 5km from central Killarney, set in beautiful gardens; in summer a tourist bus (€10 return) leaves for the house at 1.45pm from O'Connor's pub (High St), returning at 5.15pm.

Gap of Dunloe SCENIC ROUTE

In summer the Gap of Dunloe, a scenic valley squeezed between Purple Mountain and Carrantuohil (at 1040m, Ireland's highest peak), is a tourist bottleneck crammed with coaches depositing crowds of day trippers for one-hour pony-and-trap rides through the pass. Rather than joining the hordes, think about hiring a bike and cycling the route.

Go anticlockwise (going clockwise means a very steep uphill climb), north around Lough Leane to **Kate Kearney's Cottage** (restaurant), then up and through the Gap. An exhilarating downhill ride and a couple of left turns lead to **Lord Brandon's Cottage** (cafe), where you can catch a boat (departs 2pm) to Reen Pier near Ross Castle and a short ride back to town. This should cost about €30, including bike hire; **O'Connors Tours** (☎663 0200; www.gapofdunloetours.com; 7 High St, Killarney) can arrange bus transport to Kate Kearney's, bike hire and boat trip (boat is best booked in advance – if you miss it, it's a long way back to Killarney by road!).

It's also possible to walk through the Gap from Kate Kearney's to Lord Brandon's (12km; allow 2½ hours).

Sleeping

Wherever you stay, book ahead from June to August. Hostels often rent out bikes and offer discounted tours. Finding a room can be tricky during high season, so it may be worth the €5 fee to have the tourist office do the hunting.

Súgán Hostel HOSTEL €

(☎663 3104; www.suganhostelkillarney.com; Lewis Rd; dm/d €17/40) Resembling a hobbit hole, this homely, alcohol-free hostel has a warm fire and equally warm hosts. The atmosphere is nothing short of familial, which makes leaving a hard task. Bicycle hire is €15 a day.

Killarney Railway Hostell HOSTEL €

(☎663 5299; www.killarneyhostel.com; Fair Hill; dm incl breakfast €16-19, s/d 45/54; P@令) This modern hostel near the train station is about as inviting as hostels get, with en suite bathrooms, bunks nestling in nooks, and maps and cycling itineraries adorning the walls. Prices include a basic breakfast.

CLIMBING IRELAND'S HIGHEST HILL

Carrantuohil (1040m), the highest peak in Ireland, lies just 16km west of Killarney. Its summit, marked with a huge steel cross, makes a popular objective for visiting hikers.

The best approach is from **Cronin's Yard** (www.croninsyard.com; Gortboy), a farmhouse with a car park, a tearoom (packed lunches available on request), showers, toilets, and a public telephone. It's at the road's end (OS ref 836873), reached from the N72 via Beaufort, west of Killarney. You may be asked to pay a small fee for using the car park. A broad, easily followed path leads from the car park alongside the Gaddagh River for just over 3km to **Hag's Glen**, a spectacular valley with two small lakes (a worthwhile sight in itself).

From here the popular but hair-raising way to the summit of Carrantuohil lies directly ahead – the **Devil's Ladder**, a gruelling trudge up a badly eroded gully. The ground is loose in places (take great care not to dislodge stones), and in wet conditions the way becomes muddy. From its top, a steep but straightforward hike leads to the summit. The climb takes about six hours return from Cronin's Yard.

Climbing Carrantuohil should never be attempted without a map and compass (and the skills to use them), proper hillwalking boots, waterproofs and spare food and water.

Mountain guide **Con Moriarty** (☎064-662 2681, 087-2214 0002; www.hiddenirelandtours.com) leads guided ascents of Carrantuohil on Wednesday and Saturday for €75 per person (booking essential).

Kingfisher Lodge B&B €€
(☎663 7131; www.kingfisherlodgekillarney.com; Lewis Rd; s/d €65/100; P wi-fi) Lovely back gardens are a highlight at this immaculate B&B, located on a strip with others close to the centre. Walkers will be especially happy here as the owner is a certified guide with years of experience walking and hiking around the region.

Fairview B&B €€
(☎663 4164; www.fairviewkillarney.com; Lewis Rd; s/d €90/130; P @ wi-fi) The Fairview tends towards the boutique end of the guest-house spectrum, with a stylish interior enhanced by luxurious little touches such as plasma TVs and jacuzzis in most of the rooms; your host, James, is possibly the most attentive in Killarney. Rates are substantially discounted in low season, and wheelchair access is available.

Neptune's Killarney Town Hostel HOSTEL €
(☎663 5255; www.neptuneshostel.com; Bishop's Lane, New St; dm €16-20, s/d €40/50; @ wi-fi) Neptune's mixed dorms can sleep over 150, but this central hostel feels much smaller thanks to the roaring fire in reception, free internet access, and the staff's unfailing helpfulness.

Rathmore House B&B €€
(☎663 2829; www.rathmorehousekly.com; Rock Rd; s/d €55/85; ⊙Mar-Nov; P wi-fi) There's a real Irish welcome at this long-established, family-run B&B at the entrance to town.

Elyod House B&B €€
(☎663 6544; www.elyodhouse.ie; Ross Rd; s/d €60/80; P wi-fi) This quietly located modern house is on the road to Ross Castle, a few minutes' walk from town. Rooms are fresh and clean, and the welcome is friendly.

Killarney Flesk Caravan & Camping Park CAMPING GROUND €
(☎663 1704; www.killarneyfleskcamping.com; Muckross Rd; campsites per car, tent & 2 adults €26, hikers per person €10; ⊙mid-Apr-Sep) About 1.5km south of the town centre on the N71 to Kenmare, this camping ground has great views of the mountains.

Eating

Reservations are recommended for evening meals in high season.

TOP CHOICE **Vanilla Pod** MODERN IRISH €€
(☎662 6559; Old Market Lane; mains €8-13, 4-course dinners €35; ⊙9am-6pm Mon-Sat, 6.30-9.30pm Fri & Sat) This little gem of a place serves a range of locally sourced fresh and organic foods, from eggs Benedict for breakfast to slow-roast pork belly for dinner. Bakery items can be enjoyed as a treat all day, especially at the tables out front.

Treyvaud's IRISH €€
(☎663 3062; www.treyvaudsrestaurant.com; 62 High St; mains €17-26; ⊙noon-10pm Tue-Sun, plus 5-10pm Mon May-Sep) A modish restaurant with a strong reputation for subtle dishes

that merge trad Irish with seductive European influences, from fresh seafood chowder to rack of Kerry lamb with rosemary jus.

Brícín IRISH €
(☎663 4902; www.bricin.com; 26 High St; mains €19-26; ⏰6-9pm Tue-Sat) This Celtic deco restaurant doubles as the town museum, with Jonathan Fisher's 18th-century views of the national park taking pride of place. Dishes include Kerry lamb, gourmet nut roast and house speciality *boxty* (potato pancake); the pre-7pm menu offers two courses for €18.

Scéal Eile CAFE €€
(73 High St; mains €9-14; ⏰9.30am-10pm May-Oct, to 6pm Nov-Apr) There's a coffee shop crammed with delectable home baking on the ground floor, while upstairs there's a smart à la carte restaurant, with Irish literary memorabilia decorating the walls, serving traditional Irish cuisine.

Revive Café & Wine Bar CAFE €
(New St; mains €7-9; ⏰9.30am-6pm) This comfortable modern cafe – think chocolate-brown leather armchairs – serves Illy-brand Italian espresso, freshly made sandwiches and delicious, home-baked rhubarb pie.

Jam CAFE €
(77 High St; mains €4-10; ⏰8am-6pm Mon-Sat) This funky little cafe is a healthy pit stop for hot meals, soups, salads, sandwiches, and coffee and cake.

Kathleen's Country Kitchen CAFE €
(New St; breakfasts & lunches €5-11; ⏰9am-5.30pm) The place for a breakfast roll, boiled bacon for lunch and no-nonsense service.

Drinking & Entertainment

Most pubs put on live music, and most nights are lively – even Mondays, when many of the town's hospitality staff are released to the fun side of the bar. Plunkett and College Sts are lined with pubs.

Killarney Grand PUB
(Main St) A great place for authentic music (if you can hear it over the boisterous crowd), the Grand has interesting takes on the traditional thing from 9pm. At 11pm modern bands take over (€6 cover).

O'Connor's PUB
(7 High St) O'Connor's is a tiny but hugely popular pub that stages a mix of trad music, stand-up comedy, readings and pub theatre.

Courtney's PUB
(Plunkett St) With a few nice fireplaces, barrels used as tables and nearly everything made from wood, Courtney's offers the ultimate Irish pub atmosphere.

Hussy's PUB
(High St) Escape the tourist mobs and muse over a pint in this small pub sporting a snug at the entrance and genial drinkers within.

Information

Guide Killarney (€5) is a good monthly 'what's on' guide, available at B&Bs, hostels and the tourist office.

Tourist office (☎663 1633; www.killarney.ie; Beech Rd; ⏰9am-6pm Mon-Sat, 9.15am-1pm & 2-5pm Sun) Busy but efficient; has free map of national park and details of bus services.

Getting There & Around

BIKE O'Sullivan's (www.killarneyrentabike.com; Beech Rd & New St) Bike hire €15/80 per day/week.

BUS Operating from the train station, Bus Éireann has regular services:

Cork €17, 1¾ hours, hourly

Dingle (via Tralee) €14, 2½ hours, five daily

Dublin €26, three hours, five daily

Galway (via Limerick) €24, seven hours, six daily

Rosslare Harbour €28, seven hours, three daily

TAXI Taxis cost roughly €2.65 per kilometre and can be found at the taxi rank on College St.

TRAIN Travelling by train to Cork (€23, 2¼ hours, three daily) or Dublin (€62, six hours, three daily) usually involves changing at Mallow.

Ring of Kerry

☎066

This 179km circuit of the Iveragh Peninsula pops up on every self-respecting tourist itinerary, and for good reason. The road winds past pristine beaches, the island-dotted Atlantic, medieval ruins, mountains and loughs (lakes). Even locals stop their cars to gawk at the rugged coastline – particularly between Waterville and Caherdaniel in the southwest of the peninsula, where the beauty dial is turned up to 11.

Although it can be 'done' in a day by car or bus, or three days by bicycle, the more time you take, the more you'll enjoy it. Tour buses travel the Ring in an anticlockwise direction.

Getting stuck behind one is tedious, so driving in the opposite direction is preferred. Alternatively, you can detour from the main road – the **Ballaghbeama Pass** cuts across the peninsula's central highlands, and has spectacular views and little traffic.

The shorter **Ring of Skellig**, at the end of the peninsula, has fine views of the Skellig Rocks and is free of tourist coaches. You can forgo roads completely by walking the **Kerry Way**, which winds through the Macgillycuddy's Reeks mountains past **Carrantuohil** (p730), Ireland's highest mountain.

Sights

Cahirciveen TOWN

Daniel O'Connell (see p759) was born near Cahirciveen, one of the Ring's larger towns. The excellent, wheelchair-accessible **Barracks Heritage Centre** (www.theoldbarracks.com; adult/student €4/2; ⏲10am-4.30pm Mon-Fri, 11.30am-4.30pm Sat, 1-5pm Sun Jun-Sep, shorter hours in winter) off Bridge St occupies what was once an intimidating Royal Irish Constabulary (RIC) barracks. Exhibits focus on O'Connell and on the Famine's local impact.

Valentia Island ISLAND

South of Cahirciveen the R565 branches west to Valentia Island, the 11km-long jumping-off point for an unforgettable experience: the **Skellig Rocks**, two tiny islands 12km off the coast.

Sleeping

There are plenty of hostels and B&Bs along the Ring. It's wise to book ahead, though, as some places are closed out of season and others fill up quickly.

CAHERCIVEEN

TOP CHOICE **Mannix Point Camping & Caravan Park** CAMPING GROUND €

(☎066-947 2806; www.campinginkerry.com; Mannix Point; campsites per person €10; ⏲Mar-Oct) This place regularly wins awards as the best camping ground in Ireland. With a coastal location, sunset views, and a campers' lounge with peat fire, musical instruments and resident cats, it's easy to see why.

Sive Hostel HOSTEL €

(☎066-947 2717; www.sivehostel.ie; East End, Caherciveen; dm/d €15/40) Simple and sweet, this Independent Holiday Hostels (IHH) affiliate is a good walking base. There's bike storage, a camping area, and it's close to several good pubs.

O'Shea's B&B B&B €€

(☎947 2402; www.osheasbnb.com; Church St, Cahirciveen; s/d €45/70; P) Right in the centre of town, across from the bus stop, O'Shea's is a friendly B&B with a nice view from the back of the house.

BALLINSKELLIGS

Ballinskelligs Inn B&B €€

(☎947 9106; www.ballinskelligsinn.com; Ballinskelligs; s/d €50/90; P) A classic rural inn, this seaside spot is a comfortable place to spend the night after a long day of cycling, hiking or driving. The attached pub-restaurant is rip-roaring fun during summer.

Skellig Hostel HOSTEL €

(☎947 9942; www.skellighostel.com; Ballinskelligs; dm/d €15/52; P) This modern building is a little characterless, but the rooms, lounge and dining room are comfortable, and it's elevated, with sea views.

DON'T MISS

SKELLIG MICHAEL

The vertiginous climb up uninhabited **Skellig Michael** inspires an awe that monks could have clung to life in the meagre beehive-shaped stone huts that stand on the tiny strip of level land on top.

Calm seas permitting, boats run from spring to late summer from Portmagee, just before the bridge to Valentia Island, to Skellig Michael. The standard fare is around €45 return. Advance booking is essential; there are half a dozen boat operators, including **Casey's** (☎947 2437; www.skelligislands.com) and **Sea Quest** (☎947 6214; www.skelligsrock.com).

The **Skellig Experience** (☎947 6306; www.skelligexperience.com; adult/child €5/3; ⏲10am-7pm Jul & Aug, to 6pm May, Jun & Sep, to 5pm Mon-Fri Mar, Apr, Oct & Nov), on Valentia Island beside the bridge from Portmagee, has exhibits on the life and times of the monks who lived on Skellig Michael from the 7th to the 12th centuries. From April to September, a two-hour **cruise** around the Skelligs (without landing) departs from the centre daily at 2.45pm (adult/child €28/15).

Getting Around

Bus Éireann runs a daily **Ring of Kerry bus service** from June to mid-September. Buses leave Killarney at 1.15pm and stop at Killorglin, Glenbeigh, Caherciveen, Waterville, Caherdaniel and Molls Gap, returning to Killarney at 5.40pm (€18).

Travel agencies and hostels in Killarney offer daily tours of the Ring for about €20.

Dingle Peninsula

066

Remote and beautiful, the Dingle Peninsula ends in the Irish mainland's most westerly point. This is a Gaeltacht area – if you're driving, don't bother looking for road signs that say 'Dingle Town'; they all say 'An Daingean', the Irish equivalent.

Centred on pretty Dingle town, the peninsula has a high concentration of ring forts and other ancient ruins; activities on offer range from diving to playing the bodhrán (frame drum). There's an alternative way of life here in the craft shops and cultural centres, trad sessions and folkloric festivals.

DINGLE TOWN

The peninsula's capital (population 1800) is a special place whose charms have long drawn runaways from across the world, making the port town a surprisingly cosmopolitan and creative place. There are loads of cafes, bookshops and art and craft galleries, and a friendly dolphin called Fungie who has lived in the bay for 25 years.

Sights & Activities

Fungie the Dolphin WILDLIFE-WATCHING

The **Dingle Boatmen's Association** (915 2626; www.dingledolphin.com) operates one-hour boat trips to visit Fungie the dolphin. The cost is €16/8 per adult/child (free if Fungie doesn't show, but he usually does). There are also two-hour trips where you can swim with him (€25 per person, wetsuit hire €25 extra). Booking advisable.

Outdoor Activities OUTDOOR ACTIVITIES

Ride the peninsula with **Dingle Horse Riding** (915 2199; www.dinglehorseriding.com; per 30min €15), or learn to surf or windsurf at Brandon Bay by contacting **Jamie Knox Watersports** (713 9411; www.jamieknox.com); a two-hour taster session costs from €45/35 per adult/child, including equipment.

Dingle Oceanworld AQUARIUM

(915 2111; www.dingle-oceanworld.ie; adult/child €12/7; 10am-8.30pm Jul & Aug, to 6pm Sep-Jun) This state-of-the-art aquarium has a walk-through tunnel and touch pool, and is wheelchair accessible; look out for the spectacularly ugly wreck fish.

Dingle Bay Charters CRUISES

(915 1344; www.dinglebaycharters.com) Offers three-hour cruises from the marina to the Blasket Islands (adult/child €40/15).

Sleeping

An Capall Dubh B&B €€

(915 1105; www.ancapalldubh.com; Green St; s/d €65/90; P) Sitting on a cobbled courtyard and entered through a 19th-century stone-built coach entrance, this delightful B&B is a great place to relax after a long day in the outdoors – or a long night in the pub.

Grapevine Hostel HOSTEL €

(915 1434; www.grapevinedingle.com; Dykegate St; dm €16-18, tw €42) Tucked away near the centre of town, the Grapevine is a well-run hostel whose lack of TV encourages guitar singalongs around the fireplace.

Alpine Guesthouse B&B €€

(915 1250; www.alpineguesthouse.com; Mail Rd; s/d €60/110; P) This 45-year-old favourite has bright rooms and a good selection of breakfasts including scrambled eggs and smoked salmon. Friendly owner Paul O'Shea is a mine of Fungie the Dolphin trivia.

Eating

TOP CHOICE **Garden Café** CAFE €€

(www.thegardencafedingle.eu; Green St; mains €8-11; 10am-5pm Mon & Wed-Sat, noon-4pm Sun) A cool little cafe with junk-shop furniture and outdoor tables at the back, the Garden focuses on fresh local produce with lunch dishes such as homemade lasagne, and pear, brie and walnut bruschetta. Best coffee in town too.

Global Village Restaurant INTERNATIONAL €€

(915 2325; Main St; mains €25-30; 6-9.30pm Mar-Oct) With the sophisticated feel of a continental bistro, this restaurant offers a fusion of global recipes gathered by the well-travelled owner-chef. The early bird menu (till 6.45pm) offers three courses for €28.

Goat Street Café CAFE €

(www.thegoatstreetcafe.com; Goat St; mains €5-13; 10am-4pm Mon-Sat, 5.30-8.30pm Tue-Sat) This cheerful little cafe is a popular pit stop for breakfasts of scrambled egg with smoked salmon or pancakes with apple and cinnamon, a lunch of soup, sandwiches or salad, or an evening meal based on the day's catch.

Drinking

Dick Mack's PUB

(Green St) Vestiges of its previous incarnation as a cobbler's workshop line the walls, while drunken revellers sing songs and slap each other's backs. Expect impromptu music sessions.

An Droichead Beag PUB

(www.thesmallbridge.com; Main St) Now this is a pub! Filled with snugs, odd woodwork and a couple of bars, this cavernous place has trad music sessions nightly.

Foxy John's PUB

(Main St) Half hardware store, half old-school pub, Foxy John's is a great place to drop into for a pint, a bag of nails and some good craic. You can also hire a bike here for €10 a day.

Information

Tourist office (915 1188; www.dingle-peninsula.ie; 9am-7pm Jun-Sep, 9am-1pm & 2.15-5pm Mon-Sat Oct-May) At Dingle Town pier.

Getting There & Around

Buses stop outside the car park at the back of the Super Valu store in Dingle Town. Killarney–Tralee–Dingle buses run four times daily Monday to Saturday (€14, 2½ hours).

Dingle has several bike-hire places. **Paddy Walsh** (Dykegate St), next to the Grapevine Hostel, rents bikes for €10 per day.

NORTH & WEST OF DINGLE TOWN

From Dingle follow signs for the **Slea Head Drive**, a scenic coastal road with views of the Blasket Islands that leads to **Dunmore Head**, mainland Ireland's most westerly point. Alternatively, you can head north across the **Connor Pass** (456m), the highest motor road in Ireland, with a spectacular descent on the north side.

Exhibits at Dunquin's excellent **Blasket Centre** (adult/child €4/2; 10am-7pm Jul & Aug, to 6pm Easter-Jun & Sep) celebrate the lives of the former islanders, many of them celebrated musicians, storytellers and writers.

Blasket Islands Tours (915 4864; www.blasketislands.ie) runs ferries from Dunquin to the bleak, uninhabited (since 1953) **Blasket Islands** (€25 return, 20 minutes, seven a day), and also offers 2½-hour **wildlife- and whale-watching cruises** around the islands (adult/child €30/20). Booking is essential.

Dún Chaion Hostel (915 6121; www.anoige.ie; dm €16-19, tw €42; Feb-Nov; P) has a terrific location with stunning views, near the Blasket Centre and not too far from Dunquin Pier, 15km west of Dingle Town. It's closed between 10am and 5pm.

Limerick

061 / POP 54,000

'There once was a city called Limerick...' Umm, no, can't think of anything that rhymes with Limerick. And no one is quite sure why those humorous five-line verses are named after this Irish city, though the name has been in use since the late 19th century.

Limerick (Luimneach) is still trying to shake off a reputation for violence and squalor that was vividly portrayed in Frank McCourt's novel *Angela's Ashes*. Redevelopment was stalled by the 2008 financial crisis, but a couple of interesting sights are worth a brief stop on the way to greener pastures.

Top of the list is the fascinating and unusual **Hunt Museum** (www.huntmuseum.com; Rutland St; adult/child €8/4.25; 10am-5pm Mon-Sat, 2-5pm Sun), which houses a superb collection of Bronze Age, Celtic and medieval artefacts, based on the private collection of antique dealers John and Gertrude Hunt. Half the fun is opening the drawers, where much of the collection is kept, to discover the random treasures hidden within. Look out for the tiny bronze horse by Leonardo da Vinci.

The lofty, echoing rooms of the restored **Georgian House** (www.limerickcivictrust.ie/georgian; 2 Perry Sq; adult/child €8/4; 10am-4pm Mon-Fri) show how Limerick's upper classes once lived. The back garden leads to a coach house that contains a photographic memoir of Limerick and a small but evocative **Ashes Exhibition**, including a reconstruction of Frank McCourt's childhood home.

If you have time for lunch, **DuCarts** (Hunt Museum, Rutland St; mains €5-12; 10am-5pm Mon-Sat, 2-5pm Sun) in the Hunt Museum offers a selection of freshly made salads, soups, sandwiches and hot dishes, all served with a smile.

The **tourist office** (317 522; www.discoverireland.ie/shannon; Arthur's Quay; 9.30am-1pm & 2-5.30pm Mon-Fri, 9.30am-1pm Sat) is near the Shannon River; ask here about *Angela's Ashes* tours.

Getting There & Away

AIR Shannon airport (SNN; www.shannonairport.com) is 24 kilometres west of Limerick. Half-hourly buses connect with Limerick bus and train station (€7).

BUS Bus Éireann services operate from the train station.

Dublin €10, 3¾ hours, hourly

Cork €15, two hours, hourly

Galway €15, 1½ hours, hourly

TRAIN There are regular trains from **Limerick Railway Station** (Parnell St).

Dublin Heuston €26, 2½ hours, six daily

Cork €20, two hours, seven daily (change at Limerick Junction)

THE WEST COAST

The west coast is Ireland at its wildest and most remote, a storm-battered seaboard of soaring sea cliffs and broad surf beaches. Along its length you can explore the eerie lunar landscape of The Burren's limestone plateau, party on in the music pubs of bohemian Galway, and hike the heather-clad hills and bogs of Connemara. The weather is often just as wild as the landscape, but a bit of wind-torn mist and cloud just adds to the atmosphere.

The Burren

The Burren of northern County Clare is a harsh and haunting landscape of bare rock, softened with a sprinkling of rare wildflowers; *Boireann* is Irish for 'Rocky Country', and the name is no exaggeration. The rugged limestone plateau is littered with ancient dolmens, ring forts, round towers, high crosses and a surprisingly diverse range of flora, while rocky foreshores and splendid cliffs line its coast.

Tim Robinson's excellent *Burren Map & Guide* is available at bookshops or tourist offices. If you're stuck for transport, a number of bus tours leave the Galway tourist office every morning for The Burren and the Cliffs of Moher, including **O'Neachtain Tours** (☎091-553 188; www.galway.net/pages/oneachtain-tours). They all cost around €25.

A much better way to explore the Burren, however, is on foot: **Burren Hill Walks** (☎065-707 7168; http://homepage.eircom.net/~burrenhillwalks), based in Ballyvaughan, and **Burren Wild** (☎087-877 9565; www.burrenwalks.com), near Bellharbour, both offer half-day guided walks for €15 to €25 per person.

DOOLIN

☎065 / POP 200

Tiny Doolin – more a scatter of houses than a village proper – is famed for its **music pubs**, and makes a convenient base for exploring The Burren. It's also a gateway for boats to the Aran Islands. In summer it can be difficult to get a bed in Doolin, so book ahead. Some of the hostels rent out bikes for around €10 a day, plus deposit.

Doolin's reputation for top-notch traditional Irish music has spread like wildfire; summer nights find the local pubs packed with an appreciative cosmopolitan crowd.

Sleeping & Eating

Aille River Hostel HOSTEL €
(☎707 4260; www.ailleriverhosteldoolin.ie; dm/d €20/50; mid-Mar–Dec; P@) In a picturesque river spot near the village crossroads, this converted 17th-century farmhouse is the best budget choice. Has turf fires, hot showers, free laundry and good company.

Daly's House B&B €€
(☎707 4242; www.dalys-doolin.com; r per person €32-38; P) What makes B&Bs special is that feeling of someone welcoming you into their home, and here Susan Daly makes you feel truly welcome. Situated 100m off Fisher St, Daly's House has panoramic views of the Cliffs of Moher, a comfy lounge area and even babysitting options.

O'Connor's PUB €€
(Fisherstreet; mains €9-18) The town's most popular pub makes a fine job of Irish standards – the seafood chowder, bacon and cabbage, and fish and chips are all excellent. Beware, however, of bus crowds.

Nagles Doolin Camping CAMPING GROUND €
(☎707 4458; www.doolincamping.com; campsites €20; Apr- Sep;) Sofas in the laundry, smooth grassy pitches, full-on views of the Cliffs of Moher, and Doolin pubs a short distance away – hard to beat!

Doolin Cafe CAFE €€
(Roadford; mains lunch €7, dinner €16-24; noon-3pm & 6-10pm) There's a great atmosphere at this homely but elegant cafe, and great food too, from the full Irish breakfast to a dinner of sirloin steak or grilled sea bass.

Getting There & Away

There are direct buses to Doolin from Limerick, Ennis, Galway and even Dublin; the main Bus

Éireann stop is across from Paddy Moloney's Doolin Hostel. For information on ferries to and from the islands, see p753.

CLIFFS OF MOHER

About 8km south of Doolin are the towering 200m-high Cliffs of Moher, one of Ireland's most famous natural features. In summer the cliffs are overrun with day trippers, so consider staying in Doolin and hiking or biking along The Burren's quiet country lanes, where the views are superb and crowds are never a problem. Either way, be careful along these sheer cliffs, especially in wet or windy weather.

The landscaped **Cliffs of Moher Visitor Centre** (www.cliffsofmoher.ie; adult/child €6/free; ⌚8.30am-7.30pm Jun-Aug, 9am-6pm Mar-May, Sep & Oct, 9am-5pm Nov-Feb) has exhibitions about the cliffs and the environment called the 'Atlantic Edge'. Nearby is **O'Brien's Tower**, which you can climb for €2/1 adult/child. Apparently, local landlord Cornelius O'Brien (1801–57) raised it to impress 'lady visitors'. From the tower walk south or north and the crowds soon disappear. You can also avoid the crowds by visiting after the tourist centre closes.

Galway

☎091 / POP 72,400

Arty and bohemian, Galway (Gaillimh) is legendary around the world for its entertainment scene. Students make up a quarter of the city's population, and brightly painted pubs heave with live music on any given night. Cafes spill out onto cobblestone streets filled with a frenzy of fiddles, banjos, guitars and bodhráns, and jugglers, painters, puppeteers and magicians in outlandish masks enchant passers-by.

Sights & Activities

Galway's city centre is tightly packed between the east bank of the Corrib River and Eyre Sq.

Galway City Museum — FREE — MUSEUM

(www.galwaycitymuseum.ie; Spanish Pde; ⌚10am-5pm daily Jun-Sep, to 5pm Tue-Sat Oct-May) Little remains of Galway's old city walls apart from the **Spanish Arch**, which is right beside the river. The nearby museum has exhibits on the city's history from 1800 to 1950, including an iconic Galway Hooker fishing boat, a collection of currachs (boats made from animal hides) and a controversial statue of Galway-born writer and hell-raiser Pádraic O'Conaire (1883–1928), which was previously in Eyre Sq.

Eyre Square — SQUARE

The focal point of the city centre, Eyre Square is a pleasant green space dotted with statues. In the centre of the square is **Kennedy Park**, honouring a visit by John F Kennedy in 1963.

Shop Street — HISTORIC AREA

Southwest of Eyre Square, the **Collegiate Church of St Nicholas of Myra** dates from 1320 and has several tombs. Also on Shop St, parts of **Lynch Castle**, now a bank, date back to the 14th century. Lynch, so the story goes, was a mayor of Galway in the 15th century who, when his son was condemned for murder, personally acted as hangman. The stone facade that is the **Lynch Memorial Window** (Market St) marks the spot of the deed.

Across the road, in the Bowling Green area, is the **Nora Barnacle House Museum** (8 Bowling Green; admission €3; ⌚10am-5pm mid-May–mid-Sep or by appointment), the former home of the wife and lifelong muse of James Joyce, which displays the couple's letters and photographs.

Salthill Promenade — PROMENADE

A favourite pastime for Galwegians and visitors alike is walking along the seaside promenade running from the edge of the city to Salthill. Stop at **Atlantaquaria** (www.nationalaquarium.ie; Salthill Promenade; adult/child €10.25/6.25; ⌚9am-5pm Mon-Fri, to 6pm Sat & Sun), Ireland's National Aquarium, where kids can pat sea creatures in the touch pools. It's roughly 2km from the city centre.

Festivals & Events

Galway Arts Festival — ARTS

(www.galwayartsfestival.com) Held in July, this is the main event on Galway's calendar.

Galway Oyster Festival — OYSTERS

(www.galwayoysterfest.com) Going strong for more than 50 years now, this festival draws thousands of visitors in late September.

Sleeping

Kinlay House — TOP CHOICE — HOSTEL €

(☎565 244; www.kinlayhouse.ie; Merchant's Rd; dm €16-29, d €54-70; @ wi-fi) The modern, large, wheelchair-accessible Kinlay House is a convenient base, half a block off Eyre Sq. It has clean, spacious rooms and a huge dining-lounge area, which can see all-night revelry. You can book discounted bus tours and Aran Islands ferries at reception.

Skeffington Arms Hotel HOTEL €€
(☎563 173; www.skeffington.ie; Eyre Sq; r €75-190; @ wi-fi) Rooms at the Skeff, overlooking Eyre Sq, are decorated in boutique style but the main reason to stay here is the renowned pub downstairs (with six bars), which also has a lunchtime carvery, an evening restaurant and a classy nightclub.

Barnacle's Quay Street House HOSTEL €
(☎568 644; www.barnacles.ie; 10 Quay St; dm €10-33, d €60-87; @ wi-fi) Set in a medieval townhouse with a modern extension, Barnacle's is at the heart of the action, surrounded by all the pubs, cafes and restaurants you came to Galway for.

St Martin's B&B B&B €
(☎568 286; stmartins@gmail.com; 2 Nun's Island Rd; s/d €45/60) St Martin's is in a great location, with back-window views overlooking the William O'Brien Bridge and a simple garden on the banks of the Corrib. It's in a well-kept townhouse, and the home cooking, comfortable rooms, friendliness and central location make it an ideal choice.

Spanish Arch Hotel HOTEL €€
(☎569 600; www.spanisharchhotel.ie; Quay St; r €69-130; @ wi-fi) In a sensational spot on the main drag, this 20-room boutique hotel is housed in a 16th-century former Carmelite convent. The hotel's solid-timber bar has a great line-up of live music, so rooms at the back, while smaller, are best for a quiet night's sleep.

Griffin Lodge B&B €€
(☎589 440; griffinlodge@eircom.net; 3 Father Griffin Pl; s €45-60, d €55-80; P) You'll be welcomed like a long-lost friend at this family-run B&B, which has eight immaculate rooms in soothing shades of spearmint and moss green.

Sleepzone HOSTEL €
(☎566 999; www.sleepzone.ie; Bóthar na mBan, Wood Quay; dm €15-29, d €50-78, f €60-96; @ wi-fi) Big, busy backpacker base with bureau de change, pool table and BBQ terrace. Party-goers beware: no alcohol is allowed on the premises.

Galway City Hostel HOSTEL €
(☎566 959; www.galwaycityhostel.com; Frenchville Lane; dm €15-21, d €54-80; @ wi-fi) A no-frills but friendly place to stay, right across from the bus station.

Salthill Caravan Park CAMPING GROUND €
(☎523 972; www.salthillcaravanpark.com; campsites per person €10; ⏰Easter-Sep; P) Just west of Salthill, off Salthill Rd, is this scenic spot right on the water. A bus runs the 4km into the city centre every half-hour.

Eating

TOP CHOICE **Ard Bia at Nimmo's** IRISH €€€
(☎561 114; www.ardbia.com; Spanish Arch; mains €17-23; ⏰cafe noon-3pm Wed-Fri, 10am-3.30am Sat, noon-7pm Sun, restaurant 6-10pm Tue-Sat) Tucked behind the Spanish Arch, this informal, cottage-style restaurant with whitewashed interior and mismatched furniture serves some of the finest food in the west of Ireland, from scallops and sea bass to roast Irish lamb. Open as a cafe during the day.

Abalone Restaurant SEAFOOD €€€
(☎534 895; 53 Lower Dominick St; mains €20-30; ⏰6-10pm) There's very fine dining in this tiny yet elegant restaurant. As you'd expect from the name, seafood is the star here, but you'll also find vegetarian treats, steaks and various international dishes.

Food 4 Thought VEGETARIAN €
(Lower Abbeygate St; mains €6-7; ⏰7.30am-6pm Mon-Fri, 8am-6pm Sat, 11.30am-4pm Sun; vegetarian) Head to this new-age cafe for organic and vegetarian sandwiches, savoury scones, and wholesome dishes such as cashew-nut roast and moussaka made with textured vegetable protein.

Griffins Bakery CAFE €
(www.griffinsbakery.com; 21 Shop St; mains €5-13; ⏰8am-7pm Mon-Wed, 8am-8pm Thu-Sat, 9am-8pm Sun) A local institution, Griffins serves up delicious soups, sandwiches, sourdough baps and pizzas in a medieval-style tearoom.

Goya's CAFE €
(2 Kirwan's Lane; mains €5-10; ⏰9.30am-6pm Mon-Sat) Goya's is a Galway treasure hidden down a narrow back alley, with cool pale-blue decor, Segafredo coffee, superb cakes, and hot lunchtime specials.

Also recommended:

Da Tang Noodle House ASIAN €€
(Middle St; mains €11-13; ⏰noon-3pm & 5.30-10pm Mon-Sat, 5.30-10.30pm Sun) This place serves up some tasty Chinese stir-fries

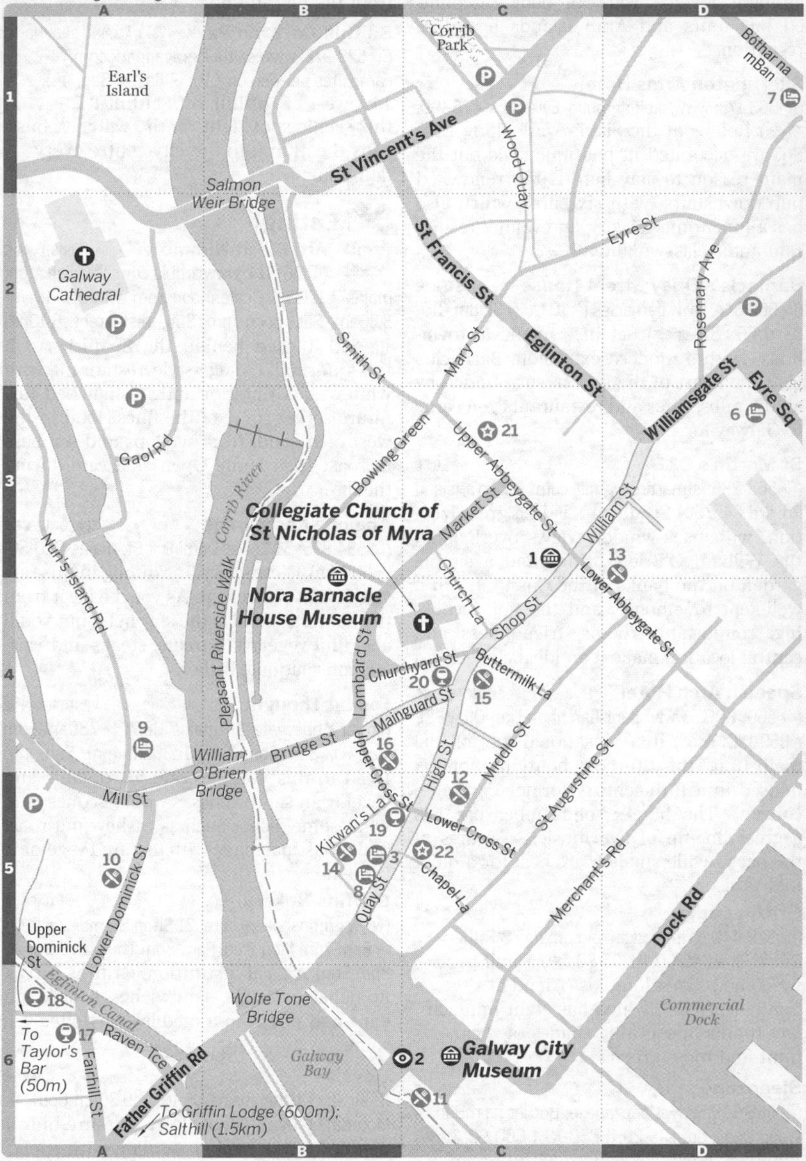

Galway City

A B C D
1 2 3 4 5 6
Corrib Park
Bóthar na mBan
Earl's Island
St Vincent's Ave
Wood Quay
Salmon Weir Bridge
St Francis St
Eyre St
Galway Cathedral
Rosemary Ave
Smith St
Mary St
Eglinton St
Williamsgate St
Eyre Sq
Upper Abbeygate St
Gaol Rd
Bowling Green
Corrib River
William St
Market St
Collegiate Church of St Nicholas of Myra
Nun's Island Rd
Church La
Lower Abbeygate St
Nora Barnacle House Museum
Pleasant Riverside Walk
Shop St
Lombard St
Churchyard St
Buttermilk La
Mainguard St
Bridge St
Middle St
William O'Brien Bridge
High St
Upper Cross St
St Augustine St
Mill St
Kirwan's La
Lower Cross St
Merchant's Rd
Lower Dominick St
Quay St
Chapel La
Dock Rd
Upper Dominick St
Eglinton Canal
Wolfe Tone Bridge
Commercial Dock
To Taylor's Bar (50m)
Raven Tce
Galway Bay
Galway City Museum
Fairhill St
Father Griffin Rd
To Griffin Lodge (600m); Salthill (1.5km)
1 2 3 6 7 8 9 10 11 12 13 14 15 16 17 18 19 20 21 22

and satays in a stylish paper-lantern-lit interior.

Kettle of Fish FISH & CHIPS €
(4 Upper Cross St; mains €8-9; ⌚11am-late) A new-age chipper that boasts of its line-caught fish, including salmon.

Drinking & Entertainment

Most of Galway's pubs see musicians performing a few nights a week, whether playing informally or as headline acts, and many even have live music every night of the week. The free *Galway Advertiser* includes list-

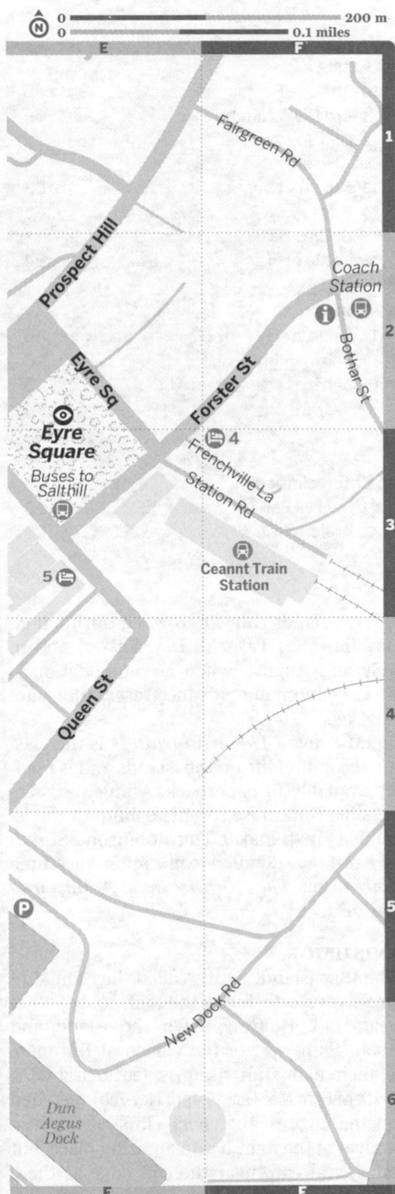

ings of what's on around the city; it's available on Thursday at the tourist office and newsstands around town. The website **Galway City Pub Guide** (www.galwaycitypubguide.com) is another good resource.

Good spots to hear traditional-music sessions include **Monroe's Tavern** (Upper Dominick St), which has set dancing on Tuesday, **Taaffe's Bar** (19 Shop St), **Taylor's Bar** (Upper Dominick St) and **Crane Bar** (2 Sea Rd).

Tig Cóilí PUB

(Mainguard St) Two ceilidh (live-music sessions) a day draw the crowds to this authentic fire-engine-red pub, just off High St. It's where musicians go to get drunk or drunks go to become musicians...or something like that.

Róisín Dubh PUB

(www.roisindubh.net; Upper Dominick St) A superpub complete with vast roof terrace, Róisín Dubh is *the* place to see emerging local indie bands before they hit the big time.

Séhán Ua Neáchtain PUB

(17 Upper Cross St) Known simply as Neáchtains (*nock*-tans), this dusty old pub has a fabulous atmosphere and attracts an eccentric, mixed crowd.

Central Park CLUB

(www.centralparkclub.com; 36 Upper Abbeygate St; ⏲11pm-2am) With seven bars and a capacity of 1000 people, Central Park is a Galway institution, especially among the young-professional crowd.

Druid Theatre THEATRE

(www.druidtheatre.com; Chapel Lane) The long-established Druid Theatre is famed for its experimental works by young Irish playwrights.

ℹ Information

Tourist office (☎537 700; www.irelandwest.ie; Forster St; ⏲9am-5.45pm Jun-Oct, 9am-5.45pm Mon-Sat, 9am-12.45pm Sun Jan-May, Nov & Dec) In summer there can be a long wait to make accommodation bookings.

ℹ Getting There & Around

The bus and train stations are within a stone's throw of Eyre Sq.

BIKE On Yer Bike (www.onyourbikecycles.com; 40 Prospect Hill) Bike hire from €12/60 per day/week.

BUS Bus Éireann buses depart from outside the train station. **Citylink** (www.citylink.ie) and **GoBus** (www.gobus.ie) use the **coach station** (cnr Forster St & Fairgreen Rd) a block northeast.

Clifden €12, 1½ hours, four daily

Doolin €14, 1½ hours, seven daily Monday to Saturday in summer, twice on Sunday

Galway City

Top Sights

Collegiate Church of St Nicholas of Myra ... C4
Eyre Square ... E2
Galway City Museum ... C6
Nora Barnacle House Museum ... B3

Sights

1 Lynch Castle ... C3
Lynch Memorial Window ... (see 1)
2 Spanish Arch ... C6

Sleeping

3 Barnacle's Quay Street House ... B5
4 Galway City Hostel ... F3
5 Kinlay House ... E3
6 Skeffington Arms Hotel ... D3
7 Sleepzone ... D1
8 Spanish Arch Hotel ... B5
9 St Martin's B&B ... A4

Eating

10 Abalone Restaurant ... A5
11 Ard Bia & Nimmo's ... C6
12 Da Tang Noodle House ... C5
13 Food 4 Thought ... D3
14 Goya's ... B5
15 Griffins Bakery ... C4
16 Kettle of Fish ... B4

Drinking

17 Monroe's Tavern ... A6
18 Róisín Dubh ... A6
19 Séhán Ua Neáchtain ... B5
Taaffe's Bar ... (see 15)
20 Tig Coílí ... C4

Entertainment

21 Central Park ... C3
22 Druid Theatre ... C5

Dublin €14, 3¾ hours, hourly

Killarney €22, 4¾ hours, three daily

TRAIN Trains run to and from Dublin (€35, three hours, five daily). You can connect with other trains at Athlone.

Aran Islands

In the last decade the windswept Aran Islands have become one of western Ireland's major attractions. As well as their rugged beauty – they are an extension of The Burren's limestone plateau – the Irish-speaking islands have some of the country's oldest Christian and pre-Christian ruins.

There are three main islands in the group, all inhabited year-round. Most visitors head for long and narrow (14.5km by a maximum 4km) **Inishmór** (or Inishmore). The land slopes up from the relatively sheltered northern shores of the island and plummets on the southern side into the raging Atlantic. **Inishmaan** and **Inisheer** are much smaller and receive far fewer visitors.

On tiny Inisheer, the dense web of drystone walls is almost absurd, with countless kilometres of them separating every patch of rocky land. Though seemingly inhospitable, the islands were actually settled much earlier than the mainland, since agriculture was easier to pursue here than in the densely forested Ireland of the pre-Christian era.

The islands can get crowded during holiday times (St Patrick's Day, Easter) and in July and August, when accommodation is at a premium and advance reservations are advised.

JM Synge's *The Aran Islands* is the classic account of life on the islands and is readily available in paperback. A much less accessible (but more recent) tribute to the islands is map-maker Tim Robinson's *Stones of Aran*. For detailed exploration, pick up a copy of his *The Aran Islands: A Map and Guide*.

INISHMÓR

The 'Big Island', as it's called, has four impressive **stone forts** thought to be 2000 years old. Halfway down the island and about 8km west of the village of Kilronan, semicircular **Dún Aengus** (adult/child €3/1; 10am-6pm Mar-Oct, to 4pm Nov-Feb), perched on the edge of the sheer cliffs, is the best known of the four. It's an amazing place, but take great care near the cliff edge as there are no guard rails.

About 1.5km north is **Dún Eoghanachta**, while halfway back to Kilronan is **Dún Eochla**; both are smaller, perfectly circular ring forts. Directly south of Kilronan and dramatically perched on a promontory is **Dún Dúchathair**, surrounded on three sides by cliffs.

Aran Heritage Centre (Ionad Árann; www.visitaranislands.com; adult/child €3.50/2, incl film €5.50/4; ⏰10am-7pm Jun-Aug, 11am-5pm Apr, May, Sep & Oct), just off the main road leading out of Kilronan, introduces the geology, wildlife, history and culture of the islands. Robert Flaherty's 1934 film *Man of Aran* is screened five times daily.

Kilronan Hostel (☎099-61255; www.kilronanhostel.com; Kilronan; dm €18-27; @📶), perched above Tí Joe Mac's pub, is a friendly hostel just a two-minute walk away from the ferry; staff lend out fishing rods for free and can teach you to play hurling on the beach. **Mainistir House** (☎099-61169; www.mainistirhousearan.com; dm/d €17/50; @📶) is a quirky and colourful 60-bed hostel on the main road north of Kilronan. It caters for both backpackers and families. Book ahead for the great-value organic, largely vegetarian buffet dinners (€16; served 8pm to closing in summer, from 7pm in winter).

Built for the 1930s film of the same name, **Man of Aran Cottage** (☎099-61301; www.manofarancottage.com; s/d €60/90; ⏰Mar-Oct) has authentic stone-and-wood interiors with a genuinely homely feel. It also has a **restaurant** (lunches/dinners from €6/35; ⏰lunch & dinner Jun-Sep, dinner Mar-May & Oct) that serves fresh local fish and organic vegies and herbs from the owners' garden (dinner bookings are essential).

INISHEER

The smallest of the Aran Islands, lying just 8km off the coast from Doolin, is Inisheer (Inis Oírr, or 'Eastern Island'; www.inisoirr-island.com). The 15th-century **O'Brien Castle** (Caislea'n Uí Bhriain) overlooks the beach and harbour.

Brú Radharc Na Mara (☎099-75024; radharcnamara@hotmail.com; dm/d €18/50; ⏰Mar-Oct) is an IHH hostel near the pier. **Radharc an Chláir** (☎099-75019; bridpoil@eircom.net; r €45-75) is a pleasant, modern B&B near O'Brien Castle with views of the Cliffs of Moher and Galway Bay.

INISHMAAN

The least visited of the three islands is peaceful Inishmaan (Inis Meáin, or 'Middle Island'), with a jagged coastline of startling cliffs and empty beaches. The main prehistoric site is **Dún Chonchúir**, a massive oval-shaped stone fort built on a high point and offering views of the island.

There are no hostels on Inishmaan; B&Bs cost about €25 to €50 per person sharing a

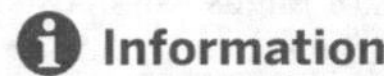

double room; most do evening meals for €25 per person, or you can eat at the island pub.

Information

The **tourist office** (☎099-61263; www.aranislands.ie; ⏰11am-7pm Jun-Sep, 11am-1pm & 2-5pm Mon-Fri, 10am-1pm & 2-5pm Sat & Sun Oct-May) operates year-round at Kilronan, the arrival point and major village of Inishmór. You can leave your luggage and change money here. Around the corner is a Spar **supermarket** with an **ATM**. The Aran Heritage Centre has **internet access**.

Getting There & Away

AIR **Aer Arann** (☎091-593 034; www.aerarannislands.ie) flights from Connemara regional airport at Minna, near Inverin, 38km west of Galway, cost €45 return. Flights serve Inishmór at least five times daily (two or three times daily to the other islands) and take less than 10 minutes. A connecting bus from outside Kinlay House in Galway costs €3 one-way.

BOAT All three islands are served year-round by **Aran Island Ferries** (www.aranislandferries.com; 4 Forster St, Galway); the trip takes around 40 minutes (adult/child €25/13 return). The boat leaves from Rossaveal, 37km west of Galway – it's an extra €7/4 return to catch an Island Ferries bus from near Kinlay House in Galway. Buses leave 1½ hours before ferry departure times and are scheduled to meet arriving ferries. If you have a car, you can go straight to Rossaveal and leave it in the car park for free.

Doolin Ferries (www.doolinferries.com) runs boats to Inishmór (55 minutes) and Inisheer (40 minutes) from Doolin in County Clare for €40 return (April to September only).

Getting Around

Inter-island ferries run from April to September only.

Inisheer and Inishmaan are small enough to explore on foot, but on larger Inishmór bikes are definitely the way to go. **Aran Cycle Hire** (☎099-61132), just up from Kilronan's pier, is one of many bike shops that hire out bikes for €10 per day. The islands are tough on bikes, so check your cruiser carefully before hiring.

Plenty of small operators offer 2½-hour island bus tours for around €10.

Connemara

☎095

With its shimmering black lakes, pale mountains, lonely valleys and more than the occasional rainbow, Connemara in the north-western corner of County Galway is one of the most gorgeous corners of Ireland. This is one of the most important Gaeltacht areas in the country; the lack of English signposting can be confusing at times.

The most scenic routes through Connemara are Oughterard–Recess (via the N59), Recess–Kylemore Abbey (via the R344) and the Leenane–Louisburgh route (via the R335). From Galway, **Lally Tours** (www.lallytours.com) and **O'Neachtain Tours** (www.galway.net/pages/oneachtain-tours) run day-long bus trips through Connemara for around €25 per person.

Sights & Activities

Connemara National Park NATIONAL PARK
(www.connemaranationalpark.ie) Connemara is prime hillwalking country with plenty of wild terrain, none more so than the **Twelve Bens**, a ridge of rugged mountains that form part of Connemara National Park. The park's **visitor centre** (Letterfrack; admission free; 9.30am-6.30pm Jun-Aug, 10am-5.30pm Mar-May & Sep–early Oct) has some interesting displays on bog ecology and history, and is the starting point for short, waymarked hikes.

Connemara Heritage & History Centre HISTORIC BUILDING
(www.connemaraheritage.com; Lettershea; adult/child €8/4; 10am-6pm Apr-Oct) The region's past comes to life at the Connemara Heritage & History Centre. Farmer Dan O'Hara lived here until his eviction from the farm and subsequent emigration to New York, where he ended up selling matches on the street. Its present owners have restored the property, turning it into a window onto lost traditional ways, with demonstrations of bog cutting, thatching, sheep shearing and so on. It's possible to stay at the farmhouse (B&B €36 to €45 per person) in more comfort than Dan ever enjoyed. The homestead is 7km east of Clifden on the N59.

Lough Corrib LAKE
Much of eastern Connemara is occupied by the Republic's largest lake, famous for its trout and salmon fishing. On its western shore is **Aughnanure Castle** (adult/child €3/1; 9.30am-6pm Apr-Oct), a 16th-century tower house overlooking the lough 3km east of the pretty village of Oughterard.

Kylemore Abbey ABBEY
(095-41146; www.kylemoreabbey.com; adult/child €12/free; 9am-5pm) Located on the national park's northern edge is a 19th-century neo-Gothic mansion set beside a lake; the abbey's scenic grounds offer much easier walking.

Sleeping

Ben Lettery Hostel HOSTEL €
(095-51136; www.anoige.ie; Ballinafad; dm €15-20; Mar-Nov; P @) Sitting in the heart of Connemara's wilderness on the N59 halfway between Recess and Clifden, this hostel makes an excellent base for hiking on the Twelve Bens.

Canrawer House Hostel HOSTEL €
(091-552 388; www.oughterardhostel.com; Oughterard; dm/d €17/46; Feb-Oct; P) This attractive modern house at the Clifden end of town is just over 1km down a signposted turning. It offers trout fishing trips for guests on Lough Corrib.

Clifden

POP 1900

Connemara's 'capital', Clifden (An Clochán), is an appealing Victorian-era country town with an oval of streets offering evocative strolls. It presides over the head of the narrow bay where the Owenglin River tumbles down a series of waterfalls into the sea – you can see **salmon leaping the falls** here in season. The surrounding countryside beckons you to walk through woods and above the shoreline. There are craft shops and art galleries tucked among its pubs and restaurants, and the town hosts a popular **arts festival** (www.clifdenartsweek.ie) in September.

Right in the centre of town, **Clifden Town Hostel** (095-21076; www.clifdentownhostel.com; Market St; dm €17-21, d €44) is a cheery IHH hostel set in a cream-coloured house framed by big picture windows.

Also in the centre, **Ben View House** (095-21256; www.benviewhouse.com; Bridge St, Clifden; s €45-60, d €70-90) has an olde-worlde charm provided by timber beams, polished floorboards and old-fashioned hospitality.

There are plenty of eateries to choose from. **Fogerty's** (095-21427; Market St; lunch mains €8-10, 3-course dinners €23; lunch & dinner) is a cosy cottage restaurant serving seafood chowder, steak sandwiches and fish and chips for lunch, with fillet steaks, lamb shank and sea bass for dinner.

There are four express buses daily between Clifden and Galway (two on Sunday). Galway–Westport buses stop in Clifden, as well as at Oughterard, Maam Cross and Recess.

Westport

POP 5400

The lively resort town of Westport (Cathair na Mairt) is a popular stop on the way to/from Sligo or Donegal. It has a tree-lined mall running along the Carrowbeg River, handsome Georgian buildings, an attractive harbour and some good pubs.

Westport's major attraction, **Croagh Patrick**, 7km west of the town, is the hill from which St Patrick performed his snake expulsion (Ireland has been serpent-free ever since). Climbing the 765m peak is a ritual for thousands of pilgrims on the last Sunday of July.

Sleeping & Eating

Old Mill Holiday Hostel HOSTEL €
(☎098-27045; www.oldmillhostel.com; dm/d €19/50; P) In a courtyard off James St sits an 18th-century former brewery that now houses the Old Mill Hostel. The relaxed atmosphere and comfortable beds make it a lovely, family-friendly place to stay.

St Anthony's B&B €€
(☎098-28887; www.st-anthonys.com; Distillery Rd; s/d €45/80; P) Simplicity is the theme at this cosy B&B, where breakfast is delicious and the hosts are gracious. All six rooms are simple and elegant, and two of them have jacuzzis.

Sol Rio INTERNATIONAL €€
(Bridge St; mains €13-25; closed Tue) Excellent Italian, French and Asian dishes at the upstairs restaurant, while the downstairs **cafe** (mains €5-11) serves coffee, cake and tempting lunch dishes such as scrambled egg with asparagus and smoked salmon.

Mill Times Hotel HOTEL €€
(☎098-29200; www.milltimeshotel.ie; Mill St; s/d from €79/98; P wi-fi) Right in the middle of town and close to all the action; some rooms have four-poster beds and jacuzzi tubs.

Information

Tourist office (☎098-25711; www.westporttourism.com; James St; 9am-5.45pm Mon-Fri, 9am-4.45pm Sat) On the main drag.

Getting There & Away

BUS Buses depart from Mill St. Bus Éireann has a counter at the tourist office.

Dublin €19, five hours, three daily

Galway €15, two hours, eight daily

Sligo €17, two hours, two daily

TRAIN The **train station** (Altamount St) is southeast of the town centre. Rail connections to Dublin (€32, €44 on Friday and Sunday, 3½ hours) go via Athlone.

THE NORTHWEST

Ireland's northwest is a paradise for anyone seeking to get off the beaten path. WB Yeats' poetry still echoes through the sleepy towns and prehistoric sites of rustic County Sligo, while the wild and remote beaches of County Donegal offer some of the best surf spots in Europe.

Sligo

POP 17,900

William Butler Yeats (1865–1939) was born in Dublin and educated in London, but his poetry is infused with the landscapes, history and folklore of his mother's native Sligo (Sligeach). He returned many times, and there are plentiful reminders of his presence in this sweet, sleepy town.

The island of **Innisfree**, immortalised in Yeats' poem *The Lake Isle of Innisfree,* is in Lough Gill, southeast of Sligo town.

Sights

FREE **WB Yeats Exhibition** MUSEUM
(www.yeats-sligo.com; 10am-5pm Mon-Fri) Prettily set near Hyde Bridge, the Yeats Building houses the WB Yeats Exhibition, featuring a video presentation and valuable draft manuscripts; the €2 exhibition catalogue makes a good souvenir of Sligo. The charming **tearoom** (10am-5pm Mon-Sat) has outdoor tables overlooking the river.

Grave of WB Yeats CEMETERY
In the churchyard at Drumcliff, 8km north of Sligo, is Yeats' grave. In the 6th century, St Colmcille chose the same location for a monastery – you can still see the stumpy remains of the round tower on the main road nearby. Also in the churchyard is an extraordinary 11th-century **high cross**, carved with intricate biblical scenes. In summer the church shows a 15-minute audiovisual on Yeats and St Colmcille.

Carrowmore megalithic cemetery PREHISTORIC SITE
(www.heritageireland.ie; adult/child €3/1; 10am-6pm Apr-Oct) Located 5km to the southwest

of Sligo is one of the largest Stone Age necropolises in Europe, with more than 60 **stone rings**, **passage tombs** and other Stone Age remains.

A few kilometres northwest from here is the hilltop cairn of **Knocknarea**. About 1000 years younger than Carrowmore, it's said to be the grave of the legendary Maeve, 1st-century-AD Queen of Connaught. Several trails lead to the 328m summit, which commands unrivalled views over the surrounding countryside and coast.

Sleeping & Eating

White House Hostel HOSTEL €
(☎071-914 5160; Markievicz Rd; dm €15; P) This basic but conveniently located hostel is just north of the town centre.

Harbour House HOSTEL €
(☎071-917 1547; www.harbourhousehostel.com; Finisklin Rd; dm/d €20/50; P) For more comfort head to this excellent hostel, which offers a little budget luxury in the form of colourful en suite rooms with TV and firm beds.

Osta CAFE, WINE BAR €
(Garavogue Weir View, Stephen St; mains €7-10; ⊙8am-7pm Mon-Wed, to 8pm Thu-Sat) is a superb cafe and wine bar with a prime location overlooking the river, and outdoor tables in summer.

Fiddler's Creek PUB €€
(Rockwood Pde; mains €10-25; ⊙food noon-3pm & 5.30-10pm) On the opposite side of the river to Osta, this place serves excellent pub grub.

Information

North West Regional Tourism office (☎071-916 1201; www.sligotourism.ie; Temple St; ⊙9am-5pm Mon-Sat Jun-Aug, 9am-5pm Mon-Fri Sep-May) Just south of the town centre.

Getting There & Away

AIR There are daily flights to Dublin from **Sligo airport** (www.sligoairport.com) from €30 one-way.

BUS Bus Éireann has services to Dublin (€17, four hours, four daily) and Westport (€17, two hours, two daily). The Galway–Sligo–Donegal–Derry service runs three times daily (twice on Sundays); it's €16 and 2½ hours to Galway, and €18 and 2½ hours to Derry.

TRAIN The train station is just west of the town centre along Lord Edward St. There are four or five trains daily to Dublin (€32, 3½ hours).

Donegal

You could spend weeks losing yourself in wild and woolly Donegal. Ireland's second-largest county (only Cork is larger), severed from its traditional province when most of Ulster became Northern Ireland, is a land unto itself, a favourite with hikers, surfers and lovers of windswept mountain and coastal scenery.

BUNDORAN

POP 1700

Surfers from all over the world come to Bundoran (Bun Dobhráin) to seek out some of Europe's best beach breaks. Pass by the tacky arcades, fast-food stalls and souvenir shops in the town centre and head for **Tullan Strand**, on the northern edge of town, the focal point of Bundoran's beach scene.

Bundoran Surf Co (www.bundoransurfco.com; Main St; ⊙9.30am-7pm) offers surfing lessons for beginners for €30 (three hours, including equipment). Surf and accommodation packages can also be arranged. If you prefer riding a horse to riding a wave, **Donegal Equestrian Holidays** (www.donegalequestrianholidays.com; Bayview Ave) can provide anything from a one-hour hack (€30) to a full day's trail ride (€110).

Once the holiday home of Viscount Enniskillen, the 300-year-old building housing the **Homefield Hostel** (☎071-984 1288; www.homefieldbackpackers.com; Bayview Ave; dm/d from €20/50; P@) now hosts world travellers year-round. A good B&B option is **Bay View** (☎071-984 1237; cnr Main St & Bayview Ave; s/d €50/70; P), a stately Edwardian townhouse with a view of the ocean.

Main St has no shortage of greasy diners and pubs, but for a better bite venture into **La Sabbia Restaurant** (Homefield Hostel, Bayview Ave; mains €17-25) for impeccable Italian food, or the **Central Bar** (Grand Central Hotel, Main St; mains €8-16) for sensational pub grub.

Bus Éireann buses stop on Main St. There are direct daily services to Sligo (€9, 45 minutes), Galway (€19, 2¼ hours), Donegal (€7, 40 minutes) and more. **Ulsterbus** (www.translink.co.uk) has one daily service Monday to Friday to Belfast via Enniskillen. Feda O'Donnell buses stop two to three times daily, en route to Galway, at the Holyrood Hotel.

The seasonal **tourist office** (☎071-984 1350; Main St; ⊙Jun-Sep, hours vary) is opposite the Holyrood Hotel.

DONEGAL TOWN

POP 2500

Donegal Town (Dún-na-nGall) is more of a gateway to the county than a destination, but it's pleasant enough and worth a visit.

Donegal Castle (adult/child €4/2; ⏰10am-6pm mid-Mar–Oct, 9.30am-4.30pm Fri-Sun Nov & Dec), on a rocky outcrop overlooking the Eske River, stands in ruins but is impressive all the same. About 1.5km south of town is **Donegal Craft Village** (Ballyshannon Rd; ⏰9am-6pm Mon-Sat, 11am-6pm Sun), where you can purchase quality pottery, metalwork, hand-blown glass and other crafts, all made on the premises.

The comfortable IHH **Donegal Town Independent Hostel** (☎074-972 2805; www.donegaltownhostel.com; dm/d €18/46; P 📶) is 1km northwest of town on the Killybegs road (N56). Overlooking the castle and the river, **Bridges B&B** (☎074-972 1082; thebridgesguesthouse@gmail.com; Waterloo Pl; s without bathroom €40, d €70; 📶) offers a friendly welcome and tasty homemade potato bread at breakfast.

Busy **Blueberry Tearoom** (The Diamond; mains €9-11; ⏰9am-7pm Mon-Sat; @) has substantial sandwiches, hot lunches, excellent baked goods, and homemade jams and marmalades; there's a cybercafe upstairs. **Donegal's Famous Chipper** (Upper Main St; fish & chips €7-8; ⏰12.30-11pm Mon & Tue, to 11.30pm Thu-Sun, closed Wed) isn't kidding: it's well known throughout the area for its fabulous fish and chips.

The Diamond (main square) is the centre of town; just south along the Eske River is the **tourist office** (☎074-972 1148; www.discoverireland.ie/northwest; Quay St; ⏰9am-6pm Mon-Sat, noon-4pm Sun Jul & Aug, 9.30am-5.30pm Mon-Sat Sep-Jun).

There are buses to Sligo (€13, 1¼ hours, six daily), Galway (€19, 3½ hours, two to three daily), Derry (€14, 1½ hours), Belfast (€20, 3½ hours) and Dublin (€18, four hours, six daily). The bus stop is on the Diamond, outside the Abbey Hotel.

DON'T MISS

DONEGAL BEER FESTIVAL

If you're in Ireland in autumn, make tracks to Donegal town to indulge in its annual **Beer Festival** (www.donegalfestivals.com), a three-day extravaganza of international ales, open-air rock gigs and resoundingly good craic (fun). It's held in mid- to late September.

SLIEVE LEAGUE

The awe-inspiring cliffs at **Slieve League**, rising 300m above the Atlantic Ocean, are one of Donegal's top sights. To drive to the cliff-edge car park, take the Killybegs–Glencolumbcille road (R263) and, at Carrick, turn left (signposted 'Bunglas'), and then right (signposted 'The Cliffs'). From the parking area at the end of the steep, narrow road (continue through the farm gate), experienced hikers can spend a day walking along the top of the cliffs via the slightly terrifying One Man's Path to Malinbeg, near Glencolumbcille.

IHH's **Derrylahan Hostel** (☎074-973 8079; derrylahan@eircom.net; campsites per person €8, dm/d from €16/40; P @ 📶), on a farm 2km southeast of Carrick, is a convenient base for walkers; call for free pick-up from Kilcar or Carrick. Booking essential November to February.

Tí Linn (Teelin; mains €7-9; ⏰10.30am-5.30pm Easter-Sep, Fri-Tue Feb-Easter & Oct-Nov), at the start of 'The Cliffs' road, is a great lunch stop, serving dishes such as potato farl with smoked salmon and lemon butter.

Once-daily buses (twice daily in July and August) stop at Kilcar and Carrick on the Donegal–Glencolumbcille route.

GLENCOLUMBCILLE

'There's nothing feckin' here!', endearingly blunt locals forewarn visitors to Glencolumbcille (Gleann Cholm Cille). But, with some stunning walks fanning out from the three-pub village, scalloped beaches, an excellent Irish language and culture centre, and a fine little folk museum, chances are you'll disagree.

Approaching Glencolumbcille via the scenic **Glen Gesh Pass** does, however, reinforce just how cut off this starkly beautiful coastal haven is from the rest of the world. You drive past miles and miles of hills and bogs before the ocean appears, followed by a narrow, green valley and the small Gaeltacht village within it.

This spot has been inhabited since 3000 BC and you'll find plenty of **Stone Age remains** throughout the collection of tiny settlements. It's believed that the 6th-century St Colmcille (Columba) founded a monastery here (hence the name, meaning 'Glen of Columba's Church'), and incorporated Stone Age standing stones called turas (after the Irish word for a pilgrimage, or journey) into Christian usage by inscribing them with a cross. At midnight on Colmcille's Feast Day (9 June) penitents walk around the turas and the remains of Colmcille's church before attending Mass at 3am in the local church.

Dooey Hostel (☎074-973 0130; www.dooeyhostel.com; Glencolumbcille; campsites/dm/d €7.50/15/30; P) has character in spades. For one thing, it's owned by an elderly, wild-haired chain-smoker who calls herself 'Mad' Mary O'Donnell. For another, it's literally built into the hillside, with a corridor carved out of the plant-strewn rock face, and jaw-dropping views of the ocean and hills below. No credit cards. If you're driving, turn at the Glenhead Tavern for 1.5km; walkers can take a short cut beside the Folk Village.

Bus 492 runs from Donegal Town to Killybegs (€7.60, 30 minutes) four times daily Monday to Saturday. From there, bus 490 heads west to Glencolumbcille (€7.60, 45 minutes) once daily Monday to Friday and Sunday (twice daily Saturday). In July and August an extra bus runs Monday to Saturday.

NORTHERN IRELAND

POP 1.7 MILLION

When you cross from the Republic into Northern Ireland you notice a couple of changes: the accent is different, the road signs are in miles, and the prices are in pounds sterling. But there's no border checkpoint, no guards, not even a sign to mark the crossing point – the two countries are in a customs union, so there's no passport control, no customs declarations. All of a sudden, you're in the UK.

Dragged down for decades by the violence and uncertainty of the Troubles, Northern Ireland today is a nation rejuvenated. The 1998 Good Friday Agreement laid the groundwork for peace and raised hopes for the future, and since then this UK province has seen a huge influx of investment and redevelopment. Belfast has become a happening place with a famously wild nightlife, while Derry is coming into its own as a cool, artistic city, and the stunning Causeway Coast gets more and more visitors each year.

There are still plenty of reminders of the Troubles – notably the 'peace lines' that still divide Belfast – and the passions that have torn Northern Ireland apart over the decades still run deep. But despite occasional setbacks there is an atmosphere of determined optimism.

Belfast

☎028 / POP 277,000

Once lumped with Beirut, Baghdad and Bosnia as one of the four 'B's for travellers to avoid, Belfast has pulled off a remarkable transformation from bombs-and-bullets pariah to hip-hotels-and-hedonism party town. The city's skyline is in a constant state of flux as redevelopment continues apace. The old shipyards are giving way to the luxury waterfront apartments of the Titanic Quarter; and Victoria Sq, Europe's biggest urban regeneration project, has added a massive city-centre shopping mall to a list of tourist attractions that includes Victorian architecture, a glittering waterfront lined with modern art, foot-stomping music in packed-out pubs and the UK's second-biggest arts festival.

The city centre is compact, with the imposing City Hall in Donegall Sq as the central landmark. The principal shopping district is north of the square. North again, around Donegall St and St Anne's Cathedral, is the bohemian Cathedral Quarter.

South of the square, the so-called Golden Mile stretches for 1km along Great Victoria St, Shaftesbury Sq and Botanic Ave to Queen's University and the leafy suburbs of South Belfast; this area has dozens of restaurants and bars and most of the city's budget and midrange accommodation.

Sights

FREE **Ulster Museum** MUSEUM
(www.ulstermuseum.org.uk; Stranmillis Rd; ⊙10am-5pm Tue-Sun) Recently reopened after a major revamp, the Ulster Museum is now one of Northern Ireland's don't-miss attractions. You could spend several hours browsing the beautifully designed displays, but if you're pressed for time don't miss the following: the **Armada Room**, with artefacts retrieved from the wreck of the Spanish galleon *Girona;* **Takabuti**, a 2500-year-old Egyptian mummy; the **Bann Disc**, a superb example of Celtic design dating from the Iron Age; the **Malone Hoard** of stone axe heads; and the **Snapshot of an Ancient Sea Floor**, a fossilised portion of a 200-million-year-old seabed.

Titanic Quarter HISTORIC AREA
Belfast's **Harland & Wolff shipyards** – whose famous yellow cranes Samson and

Goliath dominate the city's eastern skyline – were the birthplace in 1911 of the *Titanic,* the 'unsinkable' ocean liner that struck an iceberg and sank in 1912. At the time of research construction work had just begun on an 'iconic tourist attraction' rising near the slipway where *Titanic* was built; due to open by 2012 (the centenary of *Titanic's* launch), it will focus both on the ship and also the wider subject of Belfast's maritime heritage.

You can hire a hand-held multimedia device from the Belfast Welcome Centre, which leads you on a self-guided walking tour of the **Titanic Trail** (per device for up to 3hr £8). Highlights include the **SS *Nomadic*** (www.nomadicbelfast.com; Hamilton Graving Dock), the only surviving vessel of the White Star Line (should be open to the public in 2011), and the **Thompson Graving Dock** where the *Titanic* was fitted out. The neighbouring **Pump House** (www.titanictrail.com; guided tour £6; ⏲tours 2pm Mon, Wed, Sat & Sun) contains exhibits and original film of the building of the great ship.

To get a real feel for the area take the Lagan Boat Company's excellent **Titanic Tour** (www.laganboatcompany.com; adult/child £10/8; ⏲12.30pm & 2pm Fri-Mon Mar-Oct, Sat & Sun only Nov & Dec, 3pm Fri-Mon May-Sep).

West Belfast HISTORIC AREA

The Catholic **Falls Rd** and the Protestant **Shankill Rd** have been battlefronts in Belfast's sectarian conflict since the 1970s. Even so, these areas are now quite safe and well worth visiting, if only to see the famous **murals** expressing local political and religious passions, and the infamous **Peace Line** – a 4km-long barrier that divides Catholic and Protestant districts, and which has now been standing longer than the Berlin Wall.

If you don't fancy an organised taxi tour (see p747), pick up a map of the murals from the Belfast Welcome Centre and explore on foot.

> **WANT MORE?**
>
> For in-depth information, reviews and recommendations at your fingertips, head to the Apple App Store to purchase Lonely Planet's *Belfast City Guide* iPhone app.
>
> Alternatively, head to **Lonely Planet** (www.lonelyplanet.com/ireland/northern-ireland/belfast) for planning advice, author recommendations, traveller reviews and insider tips.

FREE **Crown Liquor Saloon** HISTORIC BUILDING

(46 Great Victoria St; ⏲11.30am-11pm Mon-Sat, 12.30-10pm Sun) There are not too many historical monuments that you can enjoy while savouring a pint of beer, but Belfast's most famous pub is one. It was built by Patrick Flanagan in 1885 and displays Victorian architecture at its most extravagant; the snugs are equipped with bells that once connected to a board behind the bar, enabling customers to order drinks without leaving their seats.

Ulster Folk & Transport Museums MUSEUMS

(www.uftm.org.uk; adult/child per museum £6.50/4, both museums £8/4.50; ⏲10am-5pm Tue-Sun Mar-Sep, 10am-4pm Tue-Fri, 11am-4pm Sat & Sun Oct-Feb) Farmhouses, forges, churches and mills, and a complete village have been reconstructed at the **Folk Museum**, with human and animal extras combining to give a strong impression of Irish life over the past few hundred years. A bridge crosses the A2 highway to the **Transport Museum**, which contains various Ulster-related vehicles, including a prototype of the **DeLorean DMC sports car** (of *Back To The Future* fame), and a display on the *Titanic*. It's 11km northeast of the city centre on the A2 Bangor road near Holywood. From Belfast take Ulsterbus 1 or any Bangor-bound train that stops at Cultra station.

FREE **City Hall** HISTORIC BUILDING

(Donegall Sq; ⏲guided tours 11am, 2pm & 3pm Mon-Fri, 2pm & 3pm Sat) Reopened after a massive refurbishment, the Renaissance-style City Hall, completed in 1906, is a testament to the city's industrial prosperity. The highlights of the free guided tour include the sumptuous Italian marble and colourful **stained glass** of the entrance hall and rotunda; an opportunity to sit on the mayor's throne in the **council chamber**; and the idiosyncratic portraits of past lord mayors.

The building is fronted by an especially dour statue of Queen Victoria; her consort, Prince Albert, is commemorated nearby in the **Albert Memorial Clock Tower** (1867), which leans slightly to one side – Belfast's equivalent of Pisa's leaning tower.

Tours

Both **Official Black Taxi Tours** (☎9064 2264; www.belfasttours.com) and **Original Belfast Black Taxi Tours** (☎07751 565359; www.belfasttaxitours.net) offer organised taxi tours of West Belfast, with an even-handed account of the Troubles. They run daily for £8

Belfast

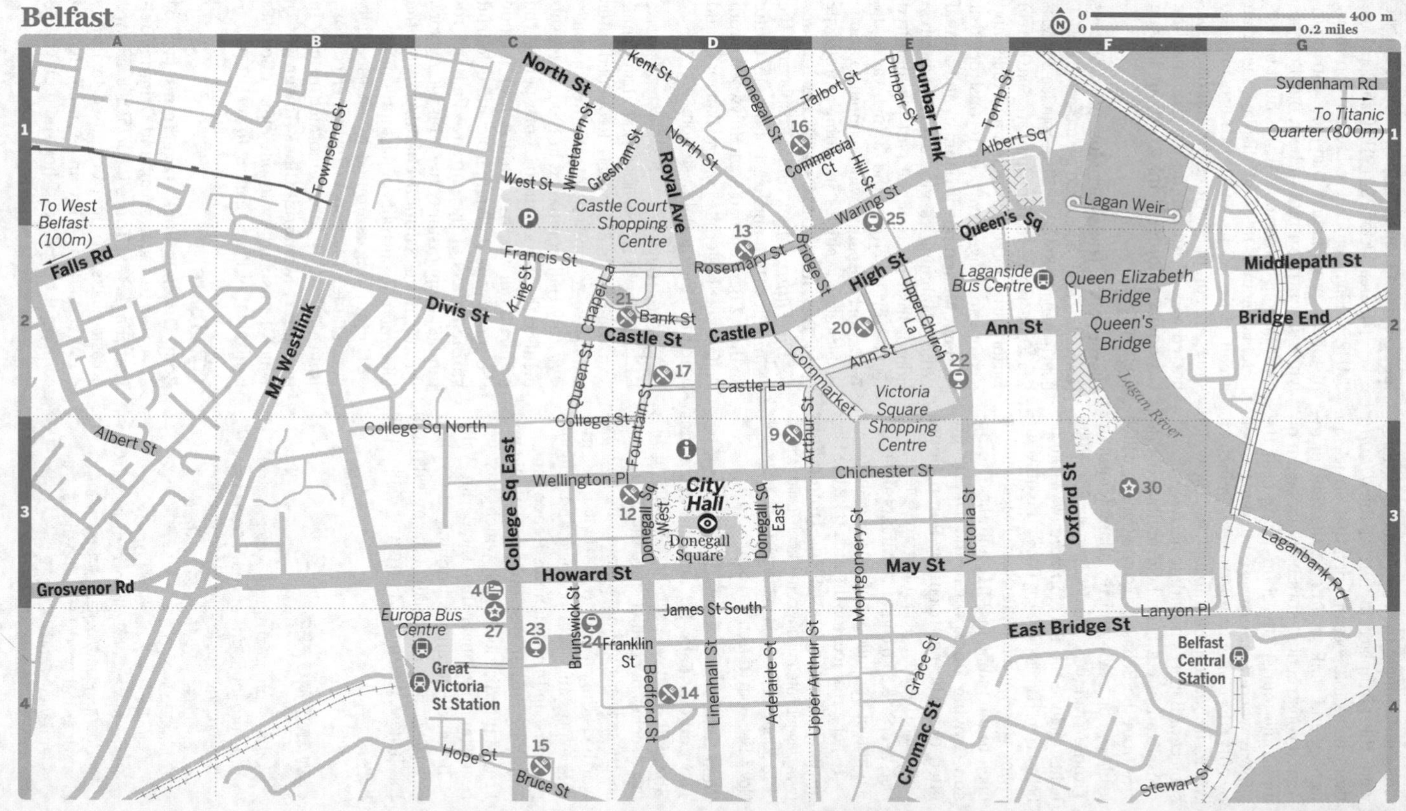
400 m
0.2 miles
A
B
C
D
E
F
G
1
2
3
4
North St
Kent St
Donegall St
Talbot St
Dunbar St
Dunbar Link
Tomb St
Sydenham Rd
To Titanic Quarter (800m)
Townsend St
Winetavern St
Gresham St
Royal Ave
North St
16
Commercial Ct
Hill St
Albert Sq
West St
To West Belfast (100m)
Castle Court Shopping Centre
13
Bridge St
Waring St
25
Queen's Sq
Lagan Weir
Falls Rd
Francis St
Rosemary St
High St
Middlepath St
Laganside Bus Centre
Queen Elizabeth Bridge
King St
Chapel La
21
Bank St
Divis St
Castle St
Castle Pl
20
Upper Church La
Ann St
Bridge End
Queen's Bridge
M1 Westlink
Queen St
17
Ann St
Cornmarket
22
Castle La
Victoria Square Shopping Centre
Lagan River
College Sq North
College St
Fountain St
9
Arthur St
Albert St
Chichester St
Wellington Pl
City Hall
Oxford St
30
College Sq East
12
Donegall Sq West
Donegall Square
Donegall Sq East
Montgomery St
Victoria St
Laganbank Rd
Grosvenor Rd
Howard St
May St
4
Brunswick St
James St South
Lanyon Pl
Europa Bus Centre
27
23
24
Franklin St
East Bridge St
Belfast Central Station
Great Victoria St Station
Bedford St
14
Linenhall St
Adelaide St
Upper Arthur St
Grace St
Cromac St
Hope St
15
Bruce St
Stewart St

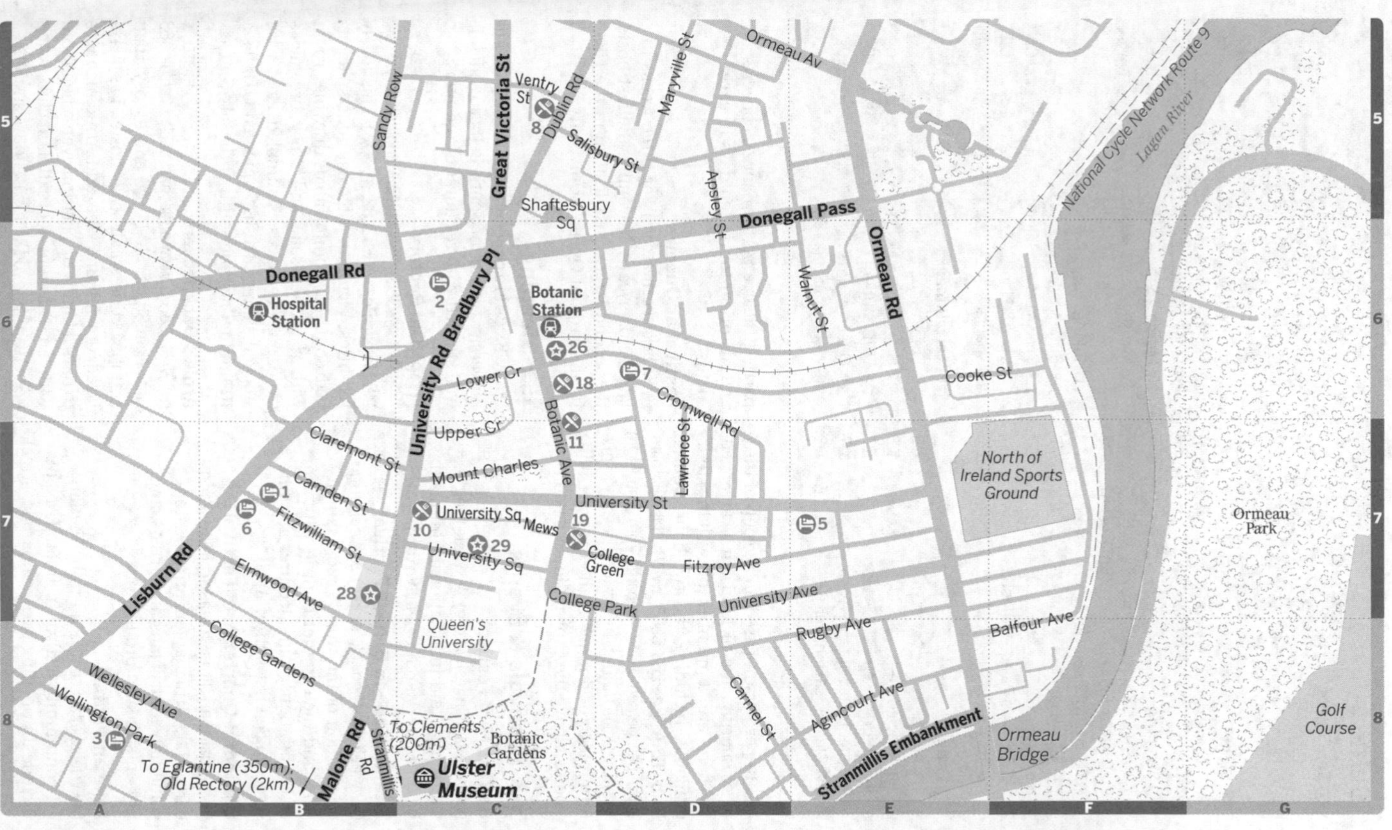

5
6
7
8
A
B
C
D
E
F
G
Sandy Row
Great Victoria St
Ventry St
8
Dublin Rd
Salisbury St
Maryville St
Ormeau Av
Apsley St
Shaftesbury Sq
Donegall Pass
National Cycle Network Route 9
Lagan River
Donegall Rd
Hospital Station
2
University Rd Bradbury Pl
Botanic Station
26
Walnut St
Ormeau Rd
Lower Cr
7
18
Cromwell Rd
Cooke St
Upper Cr
11
Botanic Ave
Lawrence St
Claremont St
Mount Charles
North of Ireland Sports Ground
1
Camden St
University St
6
Fitzwilliam St
University Sq
10
Mews
19
5
Ormeau Park
29
University Sq
College Green
Fitzroy Ave
Lisburn Rd
Elmwood Ave
28
College Park
University Ave
Queen's University
Rugby Ave
Balfour Ave
College Gardens
Wellesley Ave
Carmel St
Agincourt Ave
Wellington Park
3
To Clements (200m)
Botanic Gardens
Stranmillis Embankment
Ormeau Bridge
Golf Course
To Eglantine (350m); Old Rectory (2km)
Malone Rd
Stranmillis Rd
Ulster Museum

Belfast

Top Sights

City Hall ... D3
Ulster Museum ... C8

Sights

Crown Liquor Saloon ... (see 23)

Sleeping

1 Arnie's Backpackers ... B7
2 Belfast International Youth Hostel ... C6
3 Camera Guest House ... A8
4 Fitzwilliam Hotel ... C3
5 Kate's B&B ... E7
6 Paddy's Palace Belfast ... B7
7 Tara Lodge ... D6

Eating

8 Archana ... C5
9 Avoca Cafe ... D3
10 Beatrice Kennedy ... C7
11 Clements (Botanic Ave) ... C7
12 Clements (Donegall Sq) ... D3
13 Clements (Rosemary St) ... D2
14 Deane's Deli Bistro ... D4
15 Ginger ... C4
16 John Hewitt ... D1
17 La Boca ... D2
18 Maggie May's ... C6
19 Molly's Yard ... C7
20 Morning Star ... E2
21 Mourne Seafood Bar ... D2

Drinking

22 Bittle's Bar ... E2
23 Crown Liquor Saloon ... C4
24 Irene & Nan's ... C4
25 Spaniard ... E1

Entertainment

26 Empire Music Hall ... C6
27 Grand Opera House ... C4
28 QUB Student Union ... B7
29 Queen's Film Theatre ... C7
30 Waterfront Hall ... F3

to £10 per person based on a group of three to six sharing, and pick-up can be arranged.

There are a number of walking tours available, including the two-hour **Belfast Pub Tour** (9268 3665; www.belfastpubtours.com; per person £6; departs 7pm Thu, 4pm Sat May-Oct), taking in six of the city's historic pubs, beginning at the Crown Dining Rooms, above the Crown Liquor Saloon.

Festivals & Events

Belfast Film Festival FILM
(www.belfastfilmfestival.org) A week-long festival of Irish and international film-making held in late March or early April.

Titanic Made In Belfast Festival HISTORIC
(www.belfastcity.gov.uk/titanic) A week-long celebration of the world's most famous ship, and the city that built it, with special exhibitions, tours, lectures and film screenings. First half of April.

Cathedral Quarter Arts Festival ARTS
(www.cqaf.com) This fantastic festival, in early May, attracts pioneering writers, comedians, musicians and artists, and presents theatre productions.

Féile an Phobail ARTS
(www.feilebelfast.com) Said to be the largest community festival in Ireland; events include an opening carnival parade, street parties, theatre performances, concerts and historical tours. Ten days in early August.

Festival at Queen's ARTS
(www.belfastfestival.com) For three weeks in late October/early November, Belfast hosts the second-largest arts festival in the UK, in and around Queen's University.

Sleeping

Many B&Bs are concentrated in the pleasant university district of South Belfast, which is well stocked with restaurants and pubs.

TOP CHOICE **Old Rectory** B&B ££
(9066 7882; www.anoldrectory.co.uk; 148 Malone Rd; s/d £52/82; P @) This lovely red-brick Victorian villa has four spacious bedrooms, a comfortable drawing room with a leather sofa, and fancy breakfasts (wild boar sausages, scrambled eggs with smoked salmon, freshly squeezed OJ). It's a 10-minute bus ride south of the city centre.

Arnie's Backpackers HOSTEL £
(9024 2867; www.arniesbackpackers.co.uk; 63 Fitzwilliam St; dm £10-14; @) More cosy than cramped, this small-scale hostel has a relaxed, down-home vibe, and Arnie manages to have a kindly disposition even when faced with an Estonian football fan club who's been drinking vodka for 12 hours straight.

Paddy's Palace Belfast HOSTEL £
(☎9033 3367; www.paddyspalace.com; 68 Lisburn Rd; dm £10-15, d £45; P@) Paddy's offers clean and comfortable dorms, a big, well-equipped kitchen, a bright and homely common room (though the dorms are a bit gloomy) and friendly staff who are happy to point you to the best local pubs. There's no sign outside, so it's easy to miss – bang on the door on Fitzwilliam St, at the corner of Lisburn Rd.

Camera Guest House B&B ££
(☎9066 0026; www.cameraguesthouse.com; 44 Wellington Park; s/d £48/62;) A cosy, welcoming Victorian B&B with an open fire in the drawing room, the Camera is set on a peaceful, tree-lined terrace. The tasty breakfasts are prepared using organic produce, and the friendly couple who own the place are a fount of knowledge on what to see and do in town.

Tara Lodge B&B ££
(☎9059 0900; www.taralodge.com; 36 Cromwell Rd; s/d £70/85; P@) This B&B is a cut above your average South Belfast guest house, with its stylish, minimalist decor; friendly, efficient staff; delicious breakfasts; and 18 bright and cheerful rooms. Great location too, on a quiet side street just a few paces from the buzz of Botanic Ave.

Kate's B&B B&B ££
(☎9028 2091; katesbb127@hotmail.com; 127 University St; per person £30) Kate's is a homely kind of place, from the window boxes bursting with colourful flowers to the cute dining room crammed with bric-a-brac and a couple of resident cats. The bedrooms are basic but comfortable, and only a few minutes' walk from Botanic Ave.

Fitzwilliam Hotel HOTEL £££
(☎9044 2080; www.fitzwilliamhotelbelfast.com; 1-3 Great Victoria St; r from £95; @) A new hotel in a truly central location, the Fitzwilliam pushes all the right style buttons with its use of designer fabrics, cool colours and mood lighting. Bedrooms have crisp linen sheets, fluffy bathrobes and powerful showers, and the staff are unstintingly helpful.

Belfast International Youth Hostel HOSTEL £
(☎9031 5435; www.hini.org.uk; 22-32 Donegall Rd; dm £10-15, s £21-31, tw £29-41; P@) Conveniently sited on the Golden Mile, which means it can be a bit noisy at night when the pubs and clubs empty.

Dundonald Touring Caravan Park CAMPING GROUND £
(☎9080 9100; www.theicebowl.com; 111 Old Dundonald Rd; campsites tent & up to 4 persons £14; ⊙Mar-Oct) Next to the Dundonald Icebowl, 7km east of the city centre (take bus 19 from Donegall Sq West); check in at the Icebowl reception desk.

Eating

There are lots of inexpensive eating places along Botanic Ave in South Belfast, and many pubs offer good-value meals.

TOP CHOICE **Ginger** MODERN IRISH £££
(☎9024 4421; www.gingerbistro.com; 7-8 Hope St; mains £17-22; ⊙noon-3pm Tue-Sat & 5-9pm Mon-Sat) Ginger is a cosy and informal little bistro with an unassuming exterior, serving food that is anything but ordinary – top-quality Irish produce is turned into exquisite dishes such as Indian-seasoned monkfish with mint and lime couscous. The lunch and pre-theatre (5pm to 6.45pm Monday to Friday) menu offers main courses for £8 to £12.

Molly's Yard BISTRO, RESTAURANT ££
(☎9032 2600; www.mollysyard.co.uk; 1 College Green Mews; mains £7-10; ⊙noon-9pm Mon-Thu, noon-6pm Fri & Sat) A restored Victorian stables courtyard is the setting for this cosy bar-bistro with outdoor tables in the yard, a more formal **restaurant** (mains £13-20; ⊙6-9pm Mon-Sat) upstairs, and a seasonal menu focused on fresh local produce. Best to book for dinner.

Mourne Seafood Bar SEAFOOD £
(☎9024 8544; www.mourneseafood.com; 34-36 Bank St; mains £8-18; ⊙noon-5pm Mon, to 9.30pm Tue & Wed, to 10.30pm Thu-Sat, 1-6pm Sun) This informal, publike space, all red brick and dark wood with old oil lamps dangling from the ceiling, is tucked behind a fishmonger's shop, so the locally caught seafood is as fresh as it gets. Hugely popular, so book ahead.

Deane's Deli Bistro BISTRO, DELI ££
(www.michaeldeane.co.uk; 44 Bedford St; mains £11-19; ⊙noon-3pm & 5-9pm Mon & Tue, noon-3pm & 5-10pm Wed-Fri, noon-10pm Sat) Enjoy top-notch nosh by celebrity chef Michael Deane without breaking the bank at this relaxed and informal bistro, with gourmet burgers and posh fish and chips on the menu. Or just grab a sandwich at the next-door deli.

Avoca Café CAFE ££
(41 Arthur St; mains £5-12; ⊙9.30am-5pm Mon-Fri, 9am-5pm Sat, 12.30-5pm Sun) Upstairs in the

Avoca store, this cafe focuses on healthy rolls, wraps, salads and sandwiches to sit in or take away, as well as offering hot lunch specials such as grilled chicken with Mediterranean vegetables.

La Boca ARGENTINIAN ££
(www.labocabelfast.com; 6 Fountain St; tapas £3-5, mains £12-20; ⏲10.30am-7pm Mon-Wed, to 9pm Thu, to 10pm Fri & Sat; 📶) This lively bistro is decked out with Latin American flags and local art, and has an Argentine-themed menu that includes tapas, grilled steak with chimichurri (a sauce of oil, garlic, herbs and spices), and grilled swordfish with chorizo, red pepper and olive dressing.

Maggie May's CAFE £
(www.maggiemaysbelfast.co.uk; 50 Botanic Ave; mains £3-7; ⏲8am-10.30pm Mon-Sat, 10am-10.30pm Sun) This is a classic little cafe with cosy wooden booths, murals of old Belfast, and a host of hungover students wolfing down huge Ulster fries at lunchtime. The all-day breakfast menu runs from tea and toast to eggy bread and maple syrup, while lunch can be soup and a sandwich or steak-and-Guinness pie.

Beatrice Kennedy FUSION, VEGETARIAN £££
(☎9020 2290; www.beatricekennedy.co.uk; 44 University Rd; mains £17-19; ⏲5-10.15pm Tue-Sat, 12.30-2.30pm & 5-8.15pm Sun; 🅥) This is where Queen's students take their parents for a smart dinner. The candlelit Edwardian drawing-room decor sets off a simple menu of superb fusion cuisine, including homemade bread and ice cream; there's also a separate vegetarian menu. From 5pm to 7pm you can get a two-course dinner for just £15.

John Hewitt PUB ££
(www.thejohnhewitt.com; 51 Donegall St; mains £6-9; ⏲food noon-3pm Mon-Sat) Named for the Belfast poet and socialist, this is a modern pub with a traditional atmosphere and a well-earned reputation for excellent food. The menu changes weekly.

Archana INDIAN ££
(www.archana.co.uk; 53 Dublin Rd; mains £7-10; ⏲noon-2pm & 5pm-midnight Mon-Sat, 5-11pm Sun; 🅥) Cosy and unpretentious, with a good range of vegetarian dishes. The thali, a platter of three curries, is good value at £17/11 for the meat/vegie version.

Morning Star PUB £
(www.themorningstarbar.com; 17 Pottinger's Entry; mains £5-15; ⏲noon-9pm Mon-Sat) Famed for its all-you-can-eat lunch buffet (£5; served noon to 4pm).

Clements CAFE £
(62 Botanic Ave; snacks £2-5; ⏲7.30am-10.30pm) Belfast's home-grown answer to Starbucks. Other branches are located on Donegall Sq West, Rosemary St and Stranmillis Rd.

Drinking

Bittle's Bar PUB
(103 Victoria St) A cramped and staunchly traditional bar, Bittle's is a 19th-century triangular red-brick building decorated with paintings of Ireland's literary heroes. Pride of place on the back wall is taken by a large canvas depicting Yeats, Joyce, Behan and Beckett at the bar with glasses of Guinness, and Wilde pulling the pints on the other side.

Spaniard BAR
(www.thespaniardbar.com; 3 Skipper St) Forget 'style': this narrow, crowded bar, which looks as if it's been squeezed into someone's flat, has more atmosphere in one battered sofa than most 'style bars' have in their shiny entirety. Friendly staff, good beer, an eclectic crowd and cool tunes played at a volume that still allows you to talk: bliss.

Irene & Nan's BAR
(www.ireneandnansbelfast.co.uk; 12 Brunswick St) Named after two pensioners from a nearby pub who fancied themselves as glamour queens, Irene & Nan's is a laid-back designer bar with a 1950s retro theme (check out the cool clocks behind the bar), good tunes and good cocktails.

Crown Liquor Saloon PUB
(46 Great Victoria St) Despite being a tourist attraction the Crown still fills up with crowds of locals at lunchtime and in the early evening.

Eglantine PUB
(www.egbar.co.uk; 32 Malone Rd) The 'Eg' is a local institution, and widely reckoned to be the best of Belfast's student pubs.

Entertainment

The Belfast Welcome Centre issues *Whatabout?,* a free monthly guide to Belfast events. Another useful guide is *The Big List* (www.thebiglist.co.uk).

QUB Student Union NIGHTCLUB
(www.qubsu-ents.com; Mandela Hall, Queen's Student Union, University Rd) The student union has various bars and music venues hosting

club nights, live bands and stand-up comedy. The twice-monthly Shine (www.shine.net; Saturday; admission £22) is one of the city's best club nights.

Empire Music Hall LIVE MUSIC
(www.thebelfastempire.com; 42 Botanic Ave) Housed in a converted Victorian church, the Empire is a legendary live-music venue with three floors of entertainment, including a weekly stand-up comedy session on Tuesday nights.

Queen's Film Theatre CINEMA
(QFT; www.queensfilmtheatre.com; 20 University Sq) The QFT is a two-screen art-house cinema, close to the university, and a major venue for the Belfast Film Festival in March.

Rain NIGHTCLUB
(www.rainnightclub.co.uk; 10-14 Tomb St; ⊙9pm-3am) Set in a converted red-brick warehouse, Rain is an opulent and glamorous mainstream nightclub with DJs pumping out commercial music for a mixed, over-21s crowd.

Waterfront Hall CONCERT VENUE
(www.waterfront.co.uk; Lanyon Pl) The impressive 2235-seat Waterfront is Belfast's flagship concert venue, hosting local, national and international performers from pop stars to symphony orchestras.

Lyric Theatre THEATRE
(www.lyrictheatre.co.uk; 55 Ridgeway St) The Lyric, south of the city, stages serious drama; Hollywood star Liam Neeson first trod the boards here. A new theatre building opened in May 2011.

Grand Opera House OPERA
(www.goh.co.uk; 2-4 Great Victoria St) This grand old venue plays host to a mixture of opera, popular musicals and comedy shows.

ℹ Information

Belfast Welcome Centre (☎9024 6609; www.gotobelfast.com; 47 Donegall Pl; ⊙9am-7pm Mon-Sat, 11am-4pm Sun Jun-Sep, 9am-5.30pm Mon-Sat, 11am-4pm Sun Oct-May;) Tourist information for all of Ireland, accommodation bookings, left luggage, and internet access for £1 per 20 minutes.

ℹ Getting There & Away

Air

George Best Belfast City airport (BHD; www.belfastcityairport.com; Airport Rd) Located 6km northeast of the city centre; flights from the UK, Cork and Paris.

Belfast International airport (BFS; www.belfastairport.com) Located 30km northwest of the city; flights from Galway, UK, Europe and New York.

Boat

Ferries to Belfast from Stranraer and Liverpool dock at **Victoria Terminal** (West Bank Rd), 5km north of the city centre; exit the M2 motorway at junction 1. Ferries from the Isle of Man arrive at **Albert Quay** (Serkeley Rd), 2km north of the centre.

Other car ferries to and from Scotland dock at Larne, 30km north of Belfast. For details of ferry services see p766.

Bus

Europa Bus Centre (Great Victoria St) Reached via the Great Northern Mall beside the Europa Hotel. Main terminus for buses to Derry (£10, 1¾ hours, twice hourly), Dublin (£13, three hours, hourly) and destinations in the west and south of Northern Ireland.

Laganside Bus Centre (Oxford St) Near the river. Mainly for buses to County Antrim and eastern County Down.

Aircoach (www.aircoach.ie) Leaves from outside Jury's Hotel on College Sq East, Belfast, for Dublin airport (£12, 2½ hours, hourly).

Train

Belfast has two main train stations: **Great Victoria St** (Great Northern Mall, Great Victoria St), next to the Europa Bus Centre, and **Belfast Central** (East Bridge St), east of the city centre. If you arrive by train at Central Station, your rail ticket entitles you to a free bus ride into the city centre. A local train also connects with Great Victoria St.

Derry £11, 2¼ hours, seven or eight daily

Dublin £28, two hours, eight daily Monday to Saturday, five on Sunday

Larne Harbour £6.20, one hour, hourly

ℹ Getting Around

TO/FROM THE AIRPORTS Airport Express 300 buses link Belfast International airport with the Europa Bus Centre every half-hour (£7, 30 minutes). Alternatively, a taxi costs about £25.

Airport Express 600 buses link George Best Belfast City airport with the Europa Bus Centre (£2, 15 minutes) every 15 or 20 minutes between 6am and 10pm. The taxi fare to the city centre is about £7.

BIKE McConvey Cycles (www.mcconveycycles.com; 182 Ormeau Rd) hires out bikes for £15/60 per day/week. Credit card deposit and photo ID required.

BUS A short trip on a city bus costs £1.40 to £2; a one-day ticket costs £3.50. Most local bus services depart from Donegall Sq, near the City Hall, where there's a ticket kiosk; otherwise, buy a ticket from the driver.

The Belfast–Derry Coastal Road

Ireland isn't short of scenic coastlines, but the Causeway Coast between Portstewart and Ballycastle – climaxing in the spectacular rock formations of the Giant's Causeway – and the Antrim Coast between Ballycastle and Belfast, are as magnificent as they come.

The **Ulsterbus** (☎028-9066 6630; www.translink.co.uk) Antrim Coaster (bus 252) links Belfast with Coleraine (£10, four hours, two daily Monday to Saturday) via Larne, the Glens of Antrim, Ballycastle, the Giant's Causeway, Bushmills, Portrush and Portstewart; a Sunday service operates from July to September only.

From June to September the Causeway Rambler (bus 402) links Coleraine and Carrick-a-Rede (£5.50, 40 minutes, four daily) via Bushmills Distillery, the Giant's Causeway, White Park Bay and Ballintoy. The ticket allows unlimited travel in both directions for one day. Bus 172 runs year-round between Ballycastle and Portrush.

GLENS OF ANTRIM

Between Larne and Ballycastle, the Antrim Coast is characterised by a series of nine beautiful valleys knows as the Glens of Antrim, with lush green fields slung between black basalt crags, and picturesque harbour villages such as **Cushendall** and **Cushendun**. **Glenariff**, with its forest park and waterfalls, has been dubbed 'Queen of the Glens'.

Travelling between Cushendun and Ballycastle (with your own transport), leave the main A2 road for the narrower and more picturesque **Torr Head Scenic Road** (B92), with superb views across to the Scottish coast.

BALLYCASTLE

POP 4000

Ballycastle, where the Atlantic Ocean meets the Irish Sea, is a pleasant harbour town and a natural base for exploring the Antrim and Causeway Coasts.

The IHO **Ballycastle Backpackers** (☎028-2076 3612; www.ballycastlebackpackers.net; 4 North St; dm/tw £15/40; P) is near the waterfront and the main bus stop.

CARRICK-A-REDE ROPE BRIDGE

The 20m-long **rope bridge** (☎028-2076 9839; adult/child £5.40/2.90; ⏲10am-7pm Jun-Aug, to 6pm Mar-May, Sep & Oct, 10.30am-3.30pm Nov & Dec) that connects Carrick-a-Rede Island to the mainland, swaying some 30m above the pounding waves, is a classic test of nerve. The island is the site of a salmon fishery and is a scenic 1.25km walk from the car park. Note that the bridge is closed in high winds.

Sheep Island View Hostel (☎028-2076 9391; www.sheepislandview.com; 42a Main St, Ballintoy; campsites/dm £6/14; P@) offers dorm beds, basic shared accommodation in the camping barn, or a place to pitch a tent. It's on the B15 coast road 1km west of Carrick-a-Rede, and makes an ideal overnight stop if you're hiking between Bushmills and Ballycastle.

GIANT'S CAUSEWAY

This spectacular rock formation – Northern Ireland's only Unesco World Heritage site – is one of Ireland's most impressive and atmospheric landscape features. When you first see it you'll understand why the ancients thought it wasn't a natural feature – the vast expanse of regular, closely packed, hexagonal stone columns looks for all the world like the handiwork of giants.

The more prosaic explanation is that the columns are simply contraction cracks caused by a cooling lava flow some 60 million years ago. The phenomenon is explained in an audiovisual (£1) at the **Causeway Visitors Centre** (☎028-2073 1855; www.giantscausewaycentre.com; ⏲10am-6pm Jul & Aug, 10am-5pm Mar-Jun & Sep & Oct, 10am-4.30pm Nov-Feb).

It costs nothing to visit the site, but car parking is an exorbitant £6. It's an easy 10- to 15-minute walk downhill to the Causeway itself, but a more interesting approach is to follow the clifftop path northeast for 2km to the **Chimney Tops** headland, then descend the **Shepherd's Steps** to the Causeway. For the less mobile, a minibus shuttles from the visitors centre to the Causeway (£2 return).

Bus 172 runs about four times daily (more often in summer and fewer on Sunday) between Portrush and Ballycastle, stopping at the Giant's Causeway. If you can, try to visit the Causeway out of season to avoid the crowds, and experience it at its most evocative.

BUSHMILLS

Bushmills, 4km southwest of the Giant's Causeway, makes a good base for visits to the Causeway Coast, but its real attraction is the **Bushmills Distillery** (☎028-2073 3218; www.bushmills.com; adult/child £6/3; ⊙9.15am-5pm Mon-Sat year-round, 11am-5pm Sun Jul-Sep, noon-5.30pm Sun Mar-Jun & Oct), the world's oldest legal distillery (King James I granted its licence in 1608). A tour of the industrial process is followed by a whiskey-tasting session; tours begin every half-hour or so.

The excellent Hostelling International Northern Ireland (HINI) **Mill Rest Hostel** (☎028-2073 1222; 49 Main St; dm/tw £16.50/39; ⊙daily Mar-Oct, Fri-Sun only Nov-Feb; @) has small dorms and one wheelchair-friendly twin room (reserve in advance).

Derry

☎028 / POP 83,700

Derry or Londonderry? The name you use for Northern Ireland's second-largest city can be a political statement, but today most people just call it Derry, whatever their politics. The 'London' prefix was added in 1613 in recognition of the Corporation of London's role in the 'plantation' of Ulster with Protestant settlers.

In 1968 resentment at the long-running Protestant domination of the city council boiled over into a series of (Catholic-dominated) civil-rights marches. In August 1969 fighting between police and local youths in the poor Catholic Bogside district prompted the UK government to send British troops into Derry. In January 1972 'Bloody Sunday' resulted in the deaths of 13 unarmed Catholic civil-rights marchers in Derry at the hands of the British army, an event that marked the beginning of the Troubles in earnest.

Today Derry is as safe to visit as anywhere else in Northern Ireland, while the Bogside and the inner city have been redeveloped. The city's long, dramatic history is still palpable – in the 17th-century city walls, in the captivating Bogside murals – but it's also a laid-back place with a well-founded reputation for musical excellence, from traditional to cutting-edge contemporary, and a lively arts scene that thrives in the city's many innovative venues.

The centre of old Derry is the walled city on the western bank of the Foyle River. The bus station is just outside the walls at its north end; the modern city centre stretches north from here along Strand Rd. The train station is on the east bank of the Foyle, across Craigavon Bridge, in a district known as the Waterside. The Bogside lies to the west of the walled city.

Sights

FREE City Walls LANDMARK
(www.derryswalls.com) Built between 1613 and 1618, Derry's city wall were the last to be constructed in Europe, and are Ireland's only city walls to survive almost intact. They're about 8m high, 9m thick and encircle the old city for 1.5km. The walls make for a fantastic walk, and provide a grandstand view of the Bogside (itself worth a closer look on foot) and the **People's Gallery**, a series of murals that decorate the gable ends of houses along Rossville St. Painted between 1997 and 2001 by the Bogside Artists, they commemorate key events in the Troubles, including the Battle of the Bogside, Bloody Sunday, and the 1981 hunger strike. The artists now have their own **gallery** (www.bogsideartists.com; cnr Rossville & William Sts; admission free; ⊙9am-6pm daily).

Tower Museum MUSEUM
(www.derrycity.gov.uk/museums; adult/child £4/2.50; ⊙10am-5pm Tue-Sat) O'Doherty's Tower, inside the northern corner of the city walls, is home to the Tower Museum, which traces the story of Derry from the days of St Columbcille to the present, and has an excellent exhibition telling the story of *La Trinidad Valenciera* – a ship of the Spanish Armada which was wrecked at Kinnagoe Bay in Donegal in 1588.

FREE Guildhall HISTORIC BUILDING
(⊙9am-5pm Mon-Fri) Just outside the city walls opposite the Tower Museum, the fine neo-Gothic Guildhall was originally built in 1890 and is noted for its **stained-glass windows**. Guided tours are available in July and August.

Museum of Free Derry MUSEUM
(www.museumoffreederry.org; 55-61 Glenfada Park; adult/concession £3/2; ⊙9am-4.30pm Mon-Fri year-round, 1-4pm Sat Apr-Sep, 1-4pm Sun Jul-Sep) Just off Rossville St, this museum chronicles the history of the Bogside, the civil-rights movement and the events of Bloody Sunday.

St Columb's Cathedral CHURCH
(admission £2; ⊙9am-5pm Mon-Sat Apr-Oct, 9am-1pm & 2-4pm Nov-Mar) Standing at the southern end of the walled city, off Bishop

St Within, this austere cathedral dates from 1628.

Tours

Bogside Artists Tours MURALS
(☎7137 3842; www.bogsideartists.com; per person £4; ⏰tours 10am, noon, 2pm & 4pm daily) Guided walking tours of the famous People's Gallery murals, led by the artists themselves.

City Tours CITY WALLS
(☎7127 1996; www.irishtourguides.com; per person £4) Walking tours of the city walls.

Free Derry Tours HISTORY, POLITICS
(☎0779 328 5972; www.freederry.net; per person £5) Informative walking tours of the Bogside and the walled city.

Sleeping

TOP CHOICE **Saddler's House** B&B ££
(☎7126 9691; www.thesaddlershouse.com; 36 Great James St; s/d £50/60; 📶) Everything in this centrally located Victorian townhouse, from the sharp-witted hosts to their bulldog Bertie, is a joy; it's almost worth visiting Derry just to stay here or at its sister B&B, Merchant's House.

Merchant's House B&B ££
(☎7126 9691; www.thesaddlershouse.com; 16 Queen St; s/d £45/60; 📶) This historic, Georgian-style townhouse has an elegant lounge and dining room with marble fireplaces and antique furniture, TV and coffee-making facilities in all rooms, and homemade marmalade at breakfast; there are even bathrobes in the rooms. Call at Saddler's House first to pick up a key.

Derry City Independent Hostel HOSTEL £
(☎7128 0542; www.derryhostel.com; 44 Great James St; dm/d from £13/36; @📶) Run by experienced backpackers and decorated with souvenirs of their travels around the world, this small, friendly hostel is set in a Georgian townhouse, just a short walk northwest of the bus station.

Derry Palace Hostel HOSTEL £
(☎7130 9051; www.paddyspalace.com; 1 Woodleigh Tce, Asylum Rd; dm/tw from £13/36; P@📶) Part of the Ireland-wide Paddy's Palace chain, this hostel is central, comfortable and as friendly as they come. There's a sunny garden, a good party atmosphere and the staff regularly organise nights out at local pubs with traditional music.

Eating

Encore Brasserie INTERNATIONAL ££
(☎7137 2492; Millennium Forum, Newmarket St; mains £11-14; ⏰noon-4pm & 5-9pm) Set in the lobby of the city's main cultural venue, the Encore is a stylish little place with friendly, efficient service and a crowd-pleasing menu of perennial favourites from homemade lasagne to slow-braised lamb shank. All main courses are £8 from 8pm to 10pm Friday and Saturday.

Café del Mondo CAFE £
(4 Shipquay St; mains £5; ⏰8.30am-5pm Mon-Sat; 📶) A bohemian cafe that serves excellent Fairtrade coffee and a range of healthy lunch dishes, including soups, stews and salads, served with homemade bread.

Café Artisan CAFE £
(18-20 Bishop St Within; mains £3-5; ⏰9.30am-5.30pm Mon-Sat; 📶) This cool little cafe serves delicious homemade soups, deli sandwiches, panini and excellent cappuccinos; and it hosts live jazz on Wednesday evenings.

Drinking & Entertainment

Sandino's CAFE, BAR
(www.sandinos.com; 1 Water St) From the posters of Che to the Free Palestine flag, this relaxed cafe-bar exudes a liberal, left-wing vibe. There are live bands on Friday nights, DJ sessions on Saturdays, and occasional jazz, folk or comedy gigs; check the website for what's on.

Mason's Bar BAR, LIVE MUSIC
(10 Magazine St; cover charge free-£12) Mason's Wednesday- and Friday-night sessions are the place to catch the latest offerings from local bands. There are three or four acts each week, as well as open-mic nights on Mondays, occasional live bands on Saturdays and trad-music sessions on Sundays at 6pm.

Playhouse ARTS CENTRE
(www.derryplayhouse.co.uk; 5-7 Artillery St) Housed in beautifully restored former school buildings with an award-winning modern extension at the rear, this community arts centre stages music, dance and theatre performances by local and international performers.

Millennium Forum THEATRE
(www.millenniumforum.co.uk; New Market St) Ireland's biggest theatre auditorium is a

major venue for dance, drama, concerts, opera and musicals.

Nerve Centre ARTS CENTRE
(www.nerve-centre.org.uk; 7-8 Magazine St) A multimedia arts centre for young, local talent in the fields of music and film. It has a performance area, a theatre, an art-house cinema, a bar and a cafe.

Peadar O'Donnell's PUB, LIVE MUSIC
(63 Waterloo St) Peadar's goes for traditional music sessions nightly and often in the afternoon on weekends, too.

Information

Derry Tourist Information Centre (☎7137 7577; www.derryvisitor.com; 44 Foyle St; ⊙9am-7pm Mon-Fri, 10am-6pm Sat, 10am-5pm Sun Jul-Sep, 9am-5pm Mon-Fri, 10am-5pm Sat Mar-Jun & Oct, 9am-5pm Mon-Fri Nov-Feb) Tourist info for all of Northern Ireland and the Republic, as well as Derry. Also internet access (£1 per 20 minutes), currency exchange and accommodation-booking service.

Getting There & Away

AIR About 13km east of Derry along the A2, the **City of Derry airport** (LDY; www.cityofderryairport.com) has direct flights daily to London Stansted, Dublin, Glasgow Prestwick and Liverpool.

BUS The bus station is just northeast of the city walls, on Foyle St.

Ulsterbus (www.translink.co.uk) service 212, the Maiden City Flyer, is the fastest service between Belfast and Derry (£10, 1¾ hours, every half-hour, fewer on Sunday). Bus 234 goes to Coleraine (£6, one hour, five daily Monday to Friday, two Sunday), where you can connect with the 252 Antrim Coaster service (p757). Bus 274 goes from Derry to Dublin (£16, four hours, every two hours).

Bus Éireann (www.buseireann.ie) service 64 runs from Derry to Galway (£18, 5¼ hours, three daily, two on Sundays) via Donegal and Sligo; another four per day terminate at Sligo.

Lough Swilly Bus Company (www.loughswillybusco.com), with an office upstairs at the Ulsterbus station, serves County Donegal across the border.

Airporter (www.airporter.co.uk) buses run direct from Derry's Quayside Shopping Centre to Belfast International airport (one-way/return £18/28, 1½ hours) and George Best Belfast City airport (one-way/return £18/28, two hours) every 90 minutes Monday to Friday, every two hours at weekends.

TRAIN Derry's **Waterside train station** (always referred to as Londonderry in Northern Ireland timetables) lies across the Foyle River from the city centre, but is connected to it by a free Rail Link bus. Trains to Belfast (£10, 2¼ hours, seven or eight daily Monday to Saturday, four on Sunday) run via Coleraine, where you can change for Portrush (£9, 1¼ hours).

Enniskillen & Lough Erne

☎028

Enniskillen, the main town of County Fermanagh, perches amid the web of waterways that links Upper and Lower Lough Erne, one of Ireland's main centres for boating, canoeing and angling. The town centre is on an island in the Erne River.

Sights

Major sights around Enniskillen include the stately homes of **Castle Coole** (☎6632 2690; Dublin Rd, Enniskillen; adult/child £5.50/2.50; ⊙11am-5pm daily Jul & Aug, Fri-Wed Jun, Sat, Sun & public holidays Apr, May & Sep) and **Florence Court** (☎6634 8249; Swanlinbar Rd, Florencecourt; adult/child £5/2; ⊙11am-5pm daily Jul & Aug, Wed-Mon May, Jun & Sep, Sat, Sun & public holidays Apr & Oct), and the **Marble Arch Caves** (☎6634 8855; www.marblearchcaves.net; Marlbank Scenic Loop, Florencecourt; adult/child £8/5; ⊙10am-5pm Jul & Aug, to 4.30pm Easter-Jun & Sep).

Lower Lough Erne has many interesting early-Christian sites, including the remains of an **Augustinian monastery** and 12th-century **round tower** on **Devenish Island** (☎6862 1588; adult/child return £3/2; ⊙tours 10am, 1pm, 3pm & 5pm daily Apr-Sep), and a small 12th-century church on **White Island** (☎6862 1892; adult/child £3/2; ⊙11am-6pm daily Jul & Aug, 11am-5pm Sat & Sun Apr-Jun & Sep) with six extraordinary Celtic stone figures, thought to date from the 9th century, lined up along the wall like miniature Easter Island statues. Ferries to Devenish depart from Trory Point, 5km north of Enniskillen; boats for White Island leave from Castle Archdale Country Park, 16km northwest of Enniskillen.

Sleeping

Westville Hotel HOTEL ££
(☎6632 0333; www.westvillehotel.co.uk; 14-20 Tempo Rd, Enniskillen; s/d from £80/95; P@≈) The Westville brings a dash of style to Enniskillen's rather staid accommodation scene with its designer fabrics, cool colour combinations, good food and welcoming staff.

WORTH A TRIP

MOURNE MOUNTAINS

The humpbacked hills of the Mourne Mountains form one of the most beautiful corners of Northern Ireland, a distinctive landscape of yellow gorse, grey granite and white-washed cottages, the lower slopes of the hills latticed with a neat patchwork of dry-stone walls cobbled together from huge, rounded granite boulders. The hills were made famous in a popular song penned by Irish songwriter William Percy French in 1896, whose chorus, 'Where the Mountains of Mourne sweep down to the sea', captures perfectly their scenic blend of ocean, sky and hillside.

The Mournes offer some of the best hillwalking in Northern Ireland, detailed in the guidebook *The Mournes: Walks* by Paddy Dillon. You'll also need an Ordnance Survey map, either the 1:50,000 Discoverer Series (Sheet No 29: *The Mournes*) or the 1:25,000 Activity Series *(The Mournes)*.

The main base for exploring the Mournes is the holiday resort of Newcastle, where you'll find plenty of shops, pubs and restaurants. **Newcastle Youth Hostel** (☎028-4372 2133; www.hini.org.uk; 30 Downs Rd; dm £14; ⏲daily Mar-Oct, Fri & Sat nights only Nov & Dec, closed Jan & Feb), housed in an attractive 19th-century villa with sea views, is only a few minutes' walk from the bus station.

Ulsterbus service 20 runs to Newcastle from Belfast's Europa Bus Centre (£7, 1¼ hours, hourly Monday to Saturday, eight Sunday).

Dromard House B&B B&B ££
(☎6638 7250; www.dromardhouse.com; Tamlaght; s/d from £40/58) Roughly 3km along the A4 towards Florence Court sits this lovely traditional Ulster farmhouse on a working organic farm.

Bridges Hostel HOSTEL £
(☎6634 0110; www.hini.org.uk; Belmore St, Enniskillen; dm/tw £17/39; P@🛜) A modern hostel with a great location overlooking a river in the centre of town.

Information

Tourist office (☎6632 3110; www.fermanagh.gov.uk; Wellington Rd; ⏲9am-7pm Mon-Fri Jul & Aug, 9am-5.30pm Mon-Fri Sep-Jun, plus 10am-6pm Sat, 11am-5pm Sun Easter-Sep, 10am-2pm Sat & Sun Oct) About 100m south of the town centre; has internet access (£1 per 20 minutes).

Getting There & Away

Enniskillen's **bus station** (Shore Rd) is across from the tourist office.

Belfast £10, 2¼ hours, hourly Monday to Saturday, two on Sunday

Bundoran £8, 1¼ hours, four daily Monday to Saturday, two on Sunday

Derry £12, 2½ hours, once daily Monday to Friday (via Omagh)

Dublin £18, 3¼ hours, eight daily

UNDERSTAND IRELAND

History

Very Early Irish, Celts & Vikings

The tale of Irish history begins around 10,000 years ago, as the last ice caps melted and the rising sea level cut Ireland off from Britain. Hunter-gatherers may first have traversed the narrowing land bridge, but many more crossed the Irish Sea in small boats. Farming did not reach Ireland until around 4000 BC.

The Celtic warrior tribes who influenced Irish culture came from central Europe around 300 BC and were well ensconced by 100 BC. They had conquered large sections of southern Europe and plundered Rome in the 4th century BC. Known as 'Galli' (Gauls) by the Romans and 'Keltoi' by the Greeks, they were feared by both.

Christian monks, including St Patrick, arrived in Ireland around the 5th century AD, and as the Dark Ages enveloped Europe, Ireland became an outpost of European civilisation. In a land of saints, scholars and missionaries, thriving monasteries produced beautiful illuminated manuscripts, some of which, such as *The Book of Kells* (see p703), survive to this day.

From the end of the 8th century, the rich monasteries were targets of raids by Vikings.

At the height of their power the Vikings ruled Dublin, Waterford and Limerick, but were eventually defeated by legendary Celtic hero Brian Ború, the king of Munster, at the Battle of Clontarf in 1014.

The British Arrive

The Norman conquest of England spread to Ireland in 1169, when Henry II, fearful of the Irish kingdoms' power, dispatched forces to the island.

Oppression of the Catholic Irish got seriously under way in the 1500s when Henry VIII and then Elizabeth I attempted to impose a new Protestant church. Land confiscated from Catholic nobles was given to Protestant settlers from Scotland and England, a policy known as 'the Plantation', sowing the seeds of today's divided Ireland.

In 1685 James II ascended the British throne, but was forced to flee the country because of his outspoken Catholicism. He sought unsuccessfully to regain his crown, which had been handed to the Protestant William of Orange (a Dutchman). William's victory over James at the Battle of the Boyne on 12 July 1690 is commemorated to this day by northern Protestant Orange Parades.

By the 18th century, Ireland's Catholics held less than 15% of the land, and suffered brutal restrictions in employment, education and religion. The United Irishmen began agitating for Irish civil rights under the leadership of young Dublin Protestant and Republican Theobald Wolfe Tone (1763–98). The group was dissolved in 1798 with Wolfe Tone's capture by the British and subsequent suicide.

Ireland's Protestant gentry, alarmed by unrest, sought the security of closer ties with Britain. In 1800 the *Act of Union* was passed, joining Ireland politically with Britain. The Irish parliament voted itself out of existence, and around 100 Irish MPs moved to London's House of Commons.

In the first half of the 19th century, Daniel O'Connell (1775–1847) led Ireland towards greater independence by peaceful means, and won a seat in the British parliament in 1828. Rather than risk a rebellion, the British parliament passed the 1829 *Act of Catholic Emancipation,* allowing Catholics limited voting rights and the right to be elected as MPs.

O'Connell died as Ireland was suffering its greatest tragedy. Successive failures of the potato crop between 1845 and 1851 resulted in the mass starvation and emigration known as Ireland's Great Famine, or the Potato Famine.

Shamefully, during these years there were excellent harvests of crops, such as wheat and dairy produce. But while millions starved, Ireland was forced to export its food to Britain and overseas. About one million died from disease or starvation – some were buried in mass graves, others left where they had dropped. Another million emigrated, and migration continued to reduce the population during the next 100 years.

At the turn of the century, the British parliament began to contemplate Irish home rule, but WWI interrupted the process. Ireland might still have moved, peacefully, towards some sort of home rule but for a bungled uprising in 1916. Though it is now celebrated as a glorious bid for freedom, the Easter Rising was heavy on rhetoric and light on planning on both sides. After the insurrection was put down, a series of trials and executions (15 in all) transformed the ringleaders into martyrs and roused international support for Irish independence.

The Road to Independence

In the 1918 election Irish republicans stood under the banner of Sinn Féin (Ourselves Alone) and won a majority of Irish seats. Ignoring London's parliament, where they were meant to sit, newly elected Sinn Féin deputies declared Ireland independent and formed the Dáil Éireann (Irish assembly), led by Eamon de Valera. The British had not conceded and confrontation was inevitable.

The Anglo-Irish War (1919–21) pitted Sinn Féin and its military wing, the Irish Republican Army (IRA), against the British. The brutal responses of Britain's Black and Tans infantry further roused anti-British sentiment. This was the period when Michael Collins, a charismatic and ruthless leader, masterminded the IRA's campaign of violence (while serving as finance minister in the new Dáil).

After months of negotiations in London, Collins and Arthur Griffith led the delegation that signed the Anglo-Irish Treaty on 6 December 1921. The treaty gave 26 of Ireland's 32 counties their independence, and allowed six largely Protestant counties in Ulster to remain a province of the UK.

The treaty was ratified by the Dáil in January 1922, but passions were so inflamed that within weeks civil war broke out. At issue was the fact that the British monarch remained the nominal head of the new Irish Free State and Irish MPs were required to swear allegiance. To many Irish Catholics, this was a betrayal of republican principles. In the ensuing violence Collins was assassinated in Cork by anti-Treaty forces, while the Free State government briefly imprisoned de Valera.

By 1923 the civil war had ground to a halt, and for nearly 50 years Ireland was relatively peaceful. After boycotting the Dáil for a number of years, de Valera founded Fianna Fáil (Warriors of Ireland), which won a majority in the 1932 election. De Valera introduced a new constitution in 1937 that abolished the oath of British allegiance and claimed sovereignty over the six counties of Ulster. In 1948 the Irish government declared the country a republic and, in 1949, left the British Commonwealth.

The Troubles

According to the Anglo-Irish Treaty, the six counties of Northern Ireland were to be governed by a Northern Irish parliament, which sat at Stormont, near Belfast, from 1920 until 1972.

The Protestant majority made its rule absolute by systematically excluding Catholics from power. This led to the formation of a nonsectarian civil-rights movement in 1967 to campaign for fairer representation for Northern Irish Catholics. In January 1969 civil-rights marchers walked from Belfast to Derry to demand a fairer division of jobs and housing. Just outside Derry, a Protestant mob attacked the mostly Catholic marchers. Further marches, protests and violence followed. Far from keeping the two sides apart, Northern Ireland's mainly Protestant police force, the Royal Ulster Constabulary (RUC), became part of the problem.

Finally, in August 1969, British troops were sent into Derry and Belfast to maintain law and order. Though Catholics initially welcomed the army, it was soon seen as a tool of the Protestant majority. The peaceful civil-rights movement lost ground and the IRA, which had been hibernating, found new, willing recruits for an armed independence struggle.

Thus the so-called Troubles rolled back and forth throughout the 1970s and into the 1980s. Passions reached fever pitch in 1972 when 13 unarmed Catholics were shot dead by British troops in Derry on 'Bloody Sunday' (30 January). Then in 1981, IRA prisoners in Northern Ireland went on a hunger strike to demand the right to be recognised as political prisoners (rather than as terrorists). Ten of them fasted to death, the best known being an elected MP, Bobby Sands.

The waters were further muddied by the IRA splitting into 'official' and 'provisional' wings, from which sprang even more violent republican organisations. Protestant paramilitary organisations, such as the Ulster Volunteer Force (UVF), sprang up in opposition to the IRA and its splinter groups, and violence was met with violence.

Giving Peace a Chance

The 1985 Anglo-Irish Agreement gave the Dublin government an official consultative role in Northern Irish affairs for the first time. The Downing St Declaration of December 1993, signed by Britain and the Republic, moved matters forward, with Britain declaring it had no 'selfish, economic or military interest' in preserving the division of Ireland.

In August 1994 a 'permanent cessation of violence' by the IRA, announced by Sinn Féin's leader Gerry Adams, offered the prospect of peace in Ulster. When Protestant paramilitary forces responded with their own ceasefire in October 1994, most British troops were withdrawn to barracks and roadblocks were removed.

In 1995 the British and Irish governments published two 'framework documents' to lay the groundwork for all-party peace talks. The subsequent negotiations stalled when Britain's Conservative prime minister, John Major, refused to allow all-party talks to start until the IRA decommissioned its weapons. An IRA bomb in the Docklands area of London shattered the negotiations in February 1996. In June, with the IRA's refusal to restore its ceasefire, 'all-party' talks on Ulster's future convened without Sinn Féin.

The peace process regained momentum with the landslide victory in May 1997 of Tony Blair's Labour Party, its massive majority enabling it to act with a freer hand than the previous Conservative government. In June 1997 Britain's new Northern Ireland secretary, Dr Mo Mowlam, promised to admit Sinn Féin to all-party talks following any new ceasefire, which the IRA declared on 20 July 1997.

These talks produced the Good Friday Agreement on 10 April 1998. This agreement allowed the people of Northern Ireland to decide their political future by majority vote, and committed its signatories to 'democratic and peaceful means of resolving differences on political issues'. It established a new Northern Ireland Assembly and high-level political links between the Republic and Northern Ireland. In simultaneous referendums in May 1998 the agreement was approved by 71% of voters in the North and 94% in the South. However, despite these moves towards peace, later that year a bomb planted by the 'Real IRA' killed 28 people in Omagh.

The new assembly was beset by divisions from the outset, which resulted in no less than four suspensions, the latest from 2002 until 2007. After five years of direct rule from London, a deal hammered out between the Democratic Unionist Party and Sinn Féin saw the assembly members finally take their seats in Stormont on 8 May 2007.

Today a cautious optimism prevails and, despite economic recession, occasional flare-ups of sectarian violence, and a renewed bombing campaign by republican splinter groups in Northern Ireland in 2010, the vast majority of people north and south of the border are committed to a peaceful future.

People

The total population of Ireland is around six million: 4.3 million in the Republic and 1.7 million in Northern Ireland. Prior to the 1845–51 Great Famine, the population was around eight million; death and emigration reduced it to around six million, and emigration continued at high levels for the next 100 years. It wasn't until the 1960s that the population began to recover.

Thanks to the EU, Ireland has seen a modest influx of immigrants, mostly from Eastern Europe, within the past five years.

Arts

Literature

The Irish have made an enormous impact on world literature. Important writers include Jonathan Swift, Oscar Wilde, WB Yeats, George Bernard Shaw, James Joyce, Sean O'Casey, Samuel Beckett and Roddy Doyle, whose *Paddy Clarke Ha Ha Ha* won the Booker Prize in 1993. The Ulster-born poet Seamus Heaney was awarded the Nobel Prize for Literature in 1995. Earlier Irish Nobel laureates include Shaw (1925), Yeats (1938) and Beckett (1969). Frank McCourt became a world favourite with his autobiographical *Angela's Ashes* (1996), which won the Pulitzer Prize, and *'Tis* (1999).

Music

Traditional Irish music – played on instruments such as the bodhrán (a flat, goatskin drum), uillean (or 'elbow') pipes, flute and fiddle – is an aspect of Irish culture impossible to miss. Of Irish groups, perhaps the best known are the Chieftains, the Dubliners and the Pogues. Popular Irish singers/musicians who have made it on the international stage include Van Morrison, Thin Lizzy, Sinéad O'Connor, U2, the Cranberries, The Corrs and Damien Rice.

Theatre

Ireland has a rich theatrical history. Dublin's first theatre was founded in Werburgh St in 1637. The literary revival of the late 19th century resulted in the establishment of Dublin's Abbey Theatre, now Ireland's national theatre, which presents works by former greats – WB Yeats, George Bernard Shaw and Sean O'Casey – and promotes modern Irish dramatists. One of the most outstanding playwrights of the last two decades is Frank McGuinness (born 1956),

RELIGION IN IRELAND

Religion has played a pivotal role in Irish history. About 90% of residents in the Republic are Roman Catholic, followed by 3% Protestant, 0.5% Muslim and the rest with no professed religious belief. In Northern Ireland, 53% are Protestant and 44% Catholic.

The Catholic Church has traditionally opposed attempts to liberalise laws governing contraception, divorce and abortion. Today condom machines can be found all over Ireland and divorce is legal, but abortion remains illegal in the Republic. Though still wielding considerable influence in the south, the Church has been weakened recently by drastically declining attendance at church services, by falling numbers of people entering religious life and by paedophile sex scandals. It's now treated with a curious mixture of respect and derision by various sections of the community.

ARCHAEOLOGY

Ireland is packed with archaeological sites that are reminders of its long and dramatic history. You may encounter the following terms:

Cashel A stone ring fort or *rath*.

Dolmen A portal tomb or Stone Age grave consisting of stone 'pillars' supporting a stone roof or capstone.

Passage tomb A megalithic mound-tomb with a narrow stone passage that leads to a burial chamber.

Ring fort or **rath** A circular fort, originally constructed of earth and timber, but later made of stone.

Round tower A tall tower or belfry built as a lookout and place of refuge from the Vikings.

whose plays explore the consequences of 1972's Bloody Sunday on the people of Derry. Other playwrights to watch out for are Martin McDonagh, Brian Friel (of *Dancing at Lughnasa* fame), Conor McPherson, Donal O'Kelly and Enda Walsh.

Environment

Ireland is divided into 32 counties: 26 in the Republic and six in Northern Ireland. The island measures 84,421 sq km (about 83% is the Republic) and stretches 486km north to south and 275km east to west. The jagged coastline extends for 5631km. The midlands of Ireland are flat, rich farmland with huge swaths of peat (which is rapidly being depleted for fuel).

Carrauntuohil (1040m) on the Iveragh Peninsula, County Kerry, is the highest mountain on the island. The Shannon River, the longest in Ireland, flows for 259km before emptying into the Atlantic west of Limerick.

Ireland's rivers and lakes are well stocked with fish, and the island is home to some three-dozen mammal species. The Office of Public Works (OPW) maintains six national parks and 76 nature reserves in the Republic; the Department of the Environment owns or leases more than 40 nature reserves in Northern Ireland.

Food & Drink

In Irish B&B accommodation, breakfasts almost inevitably include 'a fry', a plate consisting of fried eggs, bacon, sausages, black pudding (blood sausage) and tomatoes. Traditional meals (such as Irish stew, often found in pubs) can be cheap and hearty. Potatoes are everywhere, colcannon and champ being two of the tastiest mashes. Seafood is often excellent, especially in the west, and there are some good vegetarian restaurants in cities and larger towns. The panini, an Italian type of sandwich, is so popular here you would think it was traditional.

In Ireland a drink means a beer, either lager or stout. Stout is usually Guinness, although in Cork it can mean a Murphy's or a Beamish. If you haven't developed a taste for stout, a wide variety of lagers are available, including Harp and Smithwicks (don't pronounce the 'w'!). Asking for a Guinness will get you a pint (568mL); if you want a half-pint, ask for a 'glass' or a 'half'.

If someone suggests visiting a pub for its good craic, it means a good time with convivial company. However, if you count cigarettes as an essential part of a good time, you're out of luck – smoking is banned in all public places throughout Ireland.

For standard business hours for restaurants and pubs, see the Survival Guide.

SURVIVAL GUIDE

Directory A–Z

Accommodation

Booking ahead is recommended in peak season (roughly April to October). See the following for booking services:

Fáilte Ireland (Irish Tourist Board; www.discovereireland.ie) Will book accommodation for a 10% room deposit and a fee of €5.

Northern Ireland Tourist Board (NITB; www.discovernorthernireland.com) Books accommodation at no cost but with a 10% deposit upfront.

Gulliver (www.gulliver.ie) Online booking service for both the Republic and Northern Ireland; deposit of 10% and a €5 fee is payable.

PRICE RANGES

In this chapter, prices are listed at high-season rates (low-season rates can be 15% to 20% less), based on two people sharing a double, and include a private bathroom unless otherwise stated.

In the Republic of Ireland section:

€€€ more than €65

€€ €30 to €65

€ less than €30

In the Northern Ireland section:

£££ more than £60

££ £25 to £60

£ less than £25

B&BS

Bed and breakfasts are as Irish as accommodation gets, with seemingly every other house a B&B, sometimes in the strangest locations. Typical costs are around €20 to €40 per person a night (sharing a double room), though more-luxurious B&Bs can cost upwards of €55 per person. Most B&Bs are small, so in summer they quickly fill up.

CAMPING & HOSTELS

Commercial camping grounds typically charge €10 to €20 for a tent and two people. Unless otherwise indicated, prices given in this chapter for 'campsites' are for a tent, car and two people.

Hostels in Ireland can be booked solid in summer. An Óige (meaning 'youth') and Hostelling International Northern Ireland (HINI) are branches of Hostelling International (HI); An Óige has 26 hostels in the Republic, while HINI has six in the North. Other hostel associations include Independent Holiday Hostels (IHH), a cooperative group with about 120 hostels throughout the island, and the Independent Hostels Owners (IHO) association, which has over 100 members around Ireland.

From June to September a dorm bed at most hostels costs €15 to €20, except for the more expensive hostels in Dublin, Belfast and a few other places.

An Óige (www.anoige.ie)

Hostelling International Northern Ireland (HINI; www.hini.org.uk)

Independent Holiday Hostels (IHH; www.hostels-ireland.com)

Independent Hostel Owners in Ireland (IHO; www.independenthostelsireland.com)

Activities

Ireland is great for outdoor activities, and tourist offices have a wide selection of information covering birdwatching (County Donegal and County Wexford), surfing (great along the west coast), scuba diving (West Cork), cycling, fishing, horse riding, sailing, canoeing and many other activities.

Walking is particularly popular, although you must come prepared for wet weather. There are now well over 20 waymarked trails throughout Ireland, one of the most popular being the 132km Wicklow Way (see p717).

Business Hours

Standard business hours are generally the same in both the Republic and Northern Ireland, as below:

Banks 10am-4pm Mon-Fri, to 5pm Thu

Offices 9am-5pm Mon-Fri

Post offices 9am-5.30pm Mon-Fri & 9am-12.30pm Sat in Northern Ireland; 9am-6pm Mon-Fri & 9am-1pm Sat in the Republic. Smaller post offices may close at lunchtime and one day per week.

Pubs 11.30am-11pm Mon-Sat & 12.30-10pm Sun in Northern Ireland, pubs with late licences open until 1am Mon-Sat, and midnight Sun; 10.30am-11.30pm Mon-Thu, 10.30am-12.30am Fri & Sat, noon-11pm Sun in the Republic. All pubs close Christmas Day and Good Friday.

Restaurants noon-10.30pm, many close one day of the week.

Shops 9am-5.30pm or 6pm Mon-Sat (to 8pm Thu and sometimes Fri), noon-6pm Sun (in bigger towns); rural shops may close at lunchtime and one day per week.

Embassies & Consulates

Australia (☎01-664 5300; www.ireland.embassy.gov.au; 7th fl, Fitzwilton House, Wilton Tce, Dublin)

Canada (☎01-234 4000; www.ireland.gc.ca; 7-8 Wilton Tce, Dublin)

New Zealand (☎01-660 4233; www.nzembassy.com; nzconsul@indigo.ie)

UK (☎01-205 3700; www.britishembassy.ie; 29 Merrion Rd, Ballsbridge, Dublin)

USA Republic of Ireland (☎01-668 8777; www.usembassy.ie; 42 Elgin Rd, Ballsbridge, Dublin) Northern Ireland (☎9038 6100; Danesfort House, 223 Stranmillis Rd, Belfast)

Gay & Lesbian Travellers

Despite the decriminalisation of homosexuality a couple of decades ago, gay life is generally neither acknowledged nor understood. Only Dublin and, to a lesser extent, Belfast, Cork, Galway and Limerick have open gay and lesbian communities.

Gay Community News (www.gcn.ie) Free monthly mag available at bars and cafes

National Lesbian & Gay Federation (☎01-671 9076; www.nlgf.ie)

Outhouse Community Centre (☎01-873 4932; www.outhouse.ie; 105 Capel St, Dublin) For gay, lesbian and transgendered people.

Food

The following price indicators are used in this chapter to indicate the cost of a main course at dinner.

In the Republic of Ireland section:

€€€ more than €16

€€ €8 to €16

€ less than €8

In the Northern Ireland section:

£££ more than £15

££ £7 to £15

£ less than £7

Language

While Irish Gaelic is the official language of the Republic of Ireland, it is spoken only in a few rural areas (known as Gaeltacht) mainly in Cork, Donegal, Galway and Kerry. English is the everyday language in the Republic and in Northern Ireland.

Maps

Good-quality maps of Ireland include Michelin's *Ireland Motoring Map* No 923 (1:400,000) and Collins *Touring Map of Ireland*. The more detailed Ordnance Survey *Discovery* series (1:50,000) covers both Northern Ireland and the Republic in 89 sheets (around €8.60 each).

Money

The Irish Republic uses the euro (€), while Northern Ireland uses the British pound sterling (£). Banks offer the best exchange rates; exchange bureaux, open longer, have worse rates and higher commissions. Post offices generally have exchange facilities and are open on Saturday morning.

In Northern Ireland several banks issue their own Northern Irish pound notes, which are equivalent to sterling but not readily accepted in mainland Britain. Many hotels, restaurants and shops in Northern Ireland accept euros.

Ireland is expensive, marginally more so than Britain, but prices vary around the island. Prices for sites and museums are usually 20% to 50% lower for children, students and senior citizens (OAPs); many state-run museums and galleries are free.

For budget travellers, €65 to €70 per day should cover hostel accommodation, getting around, a restaurant meal and a pint.

Fancy hotels and restaurants usually add a 10% or 15% service charge onto bills. Simpler places usually don't add a service charge; if you decide to tip, just round up the bill (or add 10% at most). Taxi drivers do not have to be tipped, but if you do, 10% is more than generous.

Public Holidays

Following is a list of the main public holidays in the Republic, Northern Ireland and both:

New Year's Day 1 January

St Patrick's Day 17 March

Easter (Good Friday to Easter Monday inclusive) March/April

May Holiday First Monday in May

Christmas Day 25 December

St Stephen's Day (Boxing Day) 26 December

NORTHERN IRELAND

Spring Bank Holiday Last Monday in May

Orangemen's Day 12 July (following Monday if 12th is at weekend)

August Bank Holiday Last Monday in August

REPUBLIC OF IRELAND

June Holiday First Monday in June

August Holiday First Monday in August

October Holiday Last Monday in October

Telephone

Local telephone calls from a public phone in the Republic cost a minimum of €0.50 for three minutes; in Northern Ireland a local call costs a minimum of £0.30. Some payphones in Northern Ireland accept euro coins. Prepaid phonecards by Eircom or private operators, available in newsagencies and post offices, work from all payphones and dispense with the need for coins.

To call Northern Ireland from the Republic, do not use ☎0044 as for the rest of the UK. Instead, dial ☎048 and then the local number. To dial the Republic from Northern Ireland, however, use the full international code ☎00-353, then the local number.

You can dial direct to your home-country operator and then reverse charges (collect) or charge the call to a local phone-credit card. From the Republic dial the following codes, then the area code and the number you want. Your home-country operator will come on the line before the call goes through.

Australia ☎1800 550061

France ☎1800 551033

New Zealand ☎1800 550064

UK (BT) ☎1800 550044

USA (AT&T) ☎1800 550000

USA (MCI) ☎1800 551001

USA (Sprint) ☎1800 552001

Reverse-charge calls can also be made from Northern Ireland using the same numbers as you would in mainland Britain.

The mobile (cell-) phone network in Ireland runs on the GSM 900/1800 system compatible with the rest of Europe and Australia, but not the USA. Mobile numbers in the Republic begin with 085, 086 or 087. A local pay-as-you-go SIM for your mobile will cost from around €10, but may work out free after the standard phone-credit refund.

Tourist Information

The Irish tourist board, **Fáilte Ireland** (www.discoverireland.ie), and the **Northern Ireland Tourist Board** (NITB; www.discovernorthernireland.com) operate separately. Both are well organised and helpful, though Fáilte Ireland will not provide any information on places (such as B&Bs and camping grounds) that it has not approved. Every town big enough to have half-a-dozen pubs will have a tourist office, although smaller ones may close in winter. Most will find you a place to stay for a fee of €5.

Tourism Ireland (www.tourismireland.com) handles tourist information for both tourist boards overseas.

Travellers with Disabilities

Guest houses, hotels and sights throughout Ireland are increasingly being adapted for people with disabilities, though facilities are still quite poor by European standards. Fáilte Ireland's various accommodation guides indicate which places are wheelchair accessible, and the NITB publishes *Accessible Accommodation in Northern Ireland.*

Citizens Information Board (☎01-605 90 00; www.citizensinformationboard.ie; George's Quay House, 43 Townsend St, Dublin 4)

Disability Action (☎028-9029 7880; www.disabilityaction.org; Portside Business Park, 189 Airport Rd West, Belfast BT3 9ED).

Visas

Citizens of the EU, Australia, Canada, New Zealand and the US don't need a visa to visit either the Republic or Northern Ireland. EU nationals are allowed to stay indefinitely, while other visitors can usually remain for three to six months. UK nationals born in Britain or Northern Ireland don't need a passport to visit the Republic, but should carry one anyway as identification.

Getting There & Away

Air

There are nonstop flights from Britain, Continental Europe and North America to Dublin, Shannon and Belfast International, and nonstop connections from Britain and Europe to Cork. International departure tax is normally included in the price of your ticket.

International airports in Ireland:

Belfast City (BHD; www.belfastcityairport.com)

Belfast International (BFS; www.belfastairport.com)

Cork (ORK; www.corkairport.com)

Derry (LDY; www.cityofderryairport.com)

Dublin (DUB; www.dublinairport.com)

Kerry (KIR; www.kerryairport.ie)

Knock (NOC; www.irelandwestairport.com)

Shannon (SNN; www.shannonairport.com)

Waterford (WAT; www.flywaterford.com)

Land

National Express and Bus Éireann's Eurolines operate services direct from London and other UK centres to Dublin, Belfast and other cities via various ferry crossings. From London to Dublin or Belfast by bus takes about 12½ hours and costs £45/66 one-way/return standard fare.

National Express (www.nationalexpress.com)

Bus Éireann (www.buseireann.ie)

Sea

There's a wide range of ferry services from Britain and France to Ireland. Prices vary depending on season, time of day, day of the week and length of stay. One-way fares for an adult foot passenger can be as little as £25, but can exceed £75 in summer. For a car plus driver and up to four adult passengers, prices can cost £150 to £300.

Keep an eye out for special deals, discounted return fares and other money savers. And plan ahead – some services are booked up months in advance. **DirectFerries** (www.directferries.co.uk) lists all the available ferry routes and operators.

Ferry operators:

Brittany Ferries (☎021-427 7801, in France 0825 828 828; www.brittanyferries.com) Once weekly April to October.

Celtic Link Ferries (☎040-238084, in France 02 33 43 23 87; www.celticlinkferries.com) Twice-weekly passenger-only service.

Fastnet Line (☎021-437 8892, in the UK 0844 576 8831; www.fastnetline.com) Three or four sailings a week March to November.

Irish Ferries (☎0818-300 400, in the UK 0870 517 1717, in France 01 56 93 43 40; www.irishferries.com) Holyhead ferries up to four a day year-round, from France to Rosslare three times a week, mid-February to December.

Norfolkline (☎01-819 2999, in the UK 0844 499 0007; www.norfolkline.com) Daily sailings year-round.

P&O Irish Sea (☎01-407 3434, in the UK 0871 66 44 999; www.poirishsea.com) Daily sailings year-round.

Steam Packet (☎1800 805055, in the UK 0870 222 1333; www.steam-packet.com) Ferries operate daily Easter to September only.

Stena Line (☎01-204 7777, in the UK 08705 707070; www.stenaline.co.uk) Daily sailings year-round.

DISCOUNTS & PASSES

Eurail Pass Holders get a 50% discount on Irish Ferries crossings to France.

InterRail Pass Holders get a 50% discount on Irish Ferries and Stena Line services.

Britrail Pass Has an option to add on Ireland for an extra fee, including ferry transit.

Getting Around

Travelling around Ireland looks simple, as the distances are short and there's a dense network of roads and railways. But in Ireland, getting from A to B seldom uses a straight line, and public transport can be expensive (particularly trains), infrequent or both. For these reasons having your own transport – either car or bicycle – can be a major advantage.

Air

There are flights within Ireland between Dublin and Belfast, Cork, Derry, Donegal, Galway, Kerry, Shannon and Sligo, as well as a Belfast–Cork service. Most domestic flights take 30 to 50 minutes.

FERRY ROUTES: FRANCE TO IRELAND

ROUTE	OPERATOR	DURATION (HR)	ONE-WAY PASSENGER FARE (€)
Roscoff-Rosslare	Irish Ferries	17	150
Cherbourg-Rosslare	Irish Ferries, Celtic Link	20	60
Roscoff-Cork	Brittany Ferries	14	77

FERRY ROUTES: BRITAIN TO IRELAND

ROUTE	OPERATOR	DURATION (HR)	ONE-WAY PASSENGER FARE (£)
Swansea-Cork	Fastnet Line	12	45
Fishguard-Rosslare	Stena Line	3½	25
Pembroke-Rosslare	Irish Ferries	2	30
Holyhead-Dublin	Stena Line, Irish Ferries	3	26
Holyhead-Dublin (fast boat)	Irish Ferries	1¾	30
Holyhead-Dun Laoghaire	Stena Line	1½	40
Liverpool-Dublin	Norfolkline, P&O Irish Sea	8½	25
Liverpool-Belfast	Norfolkline	8½	40
Douglas (Isle of Man)-Dublin	Steam Packet	2¾	40
Douglas (Isle of Man)-Belfast	Steam Packet	2¾	40
Stranraer-Belfast	Stena Line	3	25
Stranraer-Belfast (fast boat)	Stena Line	2	25
Cairnryan-Larne (fast boat)	P&O Irish Sea	1	24
Troon-Larne (fast boat)	P&O Irish Sea	2	24

Domestic carriers:

Aer Árann (www.aerarann.com)

Aer Lingus (www.aerlingus.com)

Ryanair (www.ryanair.com)

Bicycle

A bike is useful for exploring in rural areas, but beware of traffic on what are often narrow, potholed roads with no space to get out of the way. Note that there is no 'right to roam' as in the UK, and most off-road cycling is technically illegal without the landowner's permission.

Typical bike hire costs are €20 to €25 per day or around €60 to €100 a week. Bags and other equipment can also be hired.

Bicycles can be transported by bus if there is enough room on board; the charge varies. On trains, the cost is €4 to €8 for a one-way journey, but bikes are not allowed on certain routes, including the Dublin Area Rapid Transit (DART).

Raleigh Rent-a-Bike (www.raleigh.ie) Network of agencies all over Ireland; like many local bike shops, they offer one-way hire for an extra charge.

Bus

The Republic of Ireland's national bus line, **Bus Éireann** (☎01-836 6111; www.buseireann.ie), operates services all over the Republic and into Northern Ireland. Fares are much cheaper than train fares. Return trips are usually only slightly more expensive than one-way fares, and special deals (eg same-day returns) are often available. Most intercity buses in Northern Ireland are operated by **Ulsterbus** (☎028-9066 6630; www.translink.co.uk).

DISCOUNTS & PASSES

Bus Éireann offers discounts to ISIC (International Student Identity Cards) holders.

Travel passes for buses in Ireland include:

Open Road Pass (www.buseireann.ie) For bus travel in the Republic. €54 for three days' travel out of six consecutive days; €69 (four out of eight days), €129 (eight out of 16 days); €2234 (15 out of 30 days).

INTERCITY BUS SERVICES

ROUTE	COST	DURATION (HR)	SERVICES PER DAY (MON-SAT)
Belfast-Dublin	£13	3	7
Derry-Belfast	£10	1¾	10+
Derry-Galway	£26	5¼	4
Dublin-Cork	€12	4½	6
Dublin-Donegal	€18	4	5
Dublin-Rosslare	€17	3	12
Dublin-Killarney	€25	6	5
Killarney-Dingle	€14	2	3 or 4
Killarney-Galway	€24	4	6

Irish Rover (www.buseireann.ie) Bus travel on Bus Éireann (Republic) and Ulsterbus (Northern Ireland). €83.50 (for three days' travel out of eight consecutive days); €190 (eight out of 15 days); €280 (15 out of 30 days).

Irish Explorer (www.buseireann.ie) Rail and bus travel in the Republic including DART. €245 for eight days' travel out of 15 consecutive days.

Zone 3 iLink Card (www.translink.co.uk/ilink) Replacement for the Freedom of Northern Ireland pass. Smartcard offering unlimited travel on bus and train in Northern Ireland; one day/one week costs £15/55 plus £1.50 on first purchase (can be topped up).

Car & Motorcycle

HIRE

Car hire in Ireland is expensive, so you're better off booking a package deal from home. In the high season it's wise to book ahead. Extra fees may apply if you cross the North–South border. Automatic cars are more expensive.

People aged under 21 years cannot hire a car; for most hire companies you must be at least 23 and have had a valid driving licence for one year. Some companies will not hire to those aged over 70 or 75. Your own local licence is usually sufficient to hire a car for up to three months.

In the Republic typical weekly high-season hire rates – with insurance, Value-Added Tax (VAT), unlimited distance and collision-damage waiver – cost from €160 for a small car. **Nova Car Hire** (www.rentacar-ireland.com) acts as an agent for Alamo, Budget, European and National, and offers greatly discounted rates.

The international hire companies and major local operators have offices all over Ireland. Recommended firms in Dublin:

Argus Rent-A-Car (☎01-499 9611; www.argusrentals.com)

Dan Dooley Car Hire (☎01-677 2723; www.dan-dooley.ie)

Thrifty Car Rental (☎1800 515800; www.thrifty.ie)

ROAD RULES

Driving is on the left-hand side and you should only overtake (pass) to the right of the vehicle ahead of you. The driver and passengers must wear safety belts, and children under 12 years of age cannot sit in the front. Motorcyclists and passengers must wear helmets; headlights should be dipped.

Minor roads can be potholed and narrow, but the traffic is rarely heavy, except through tourist or commercial towns. Speed limits are posted in mph in Northern Ireland and km/h in the Republic: 110km/h (70mph) on motorways, 100km/h (60mph) on main roads and 50km/h (30mph) or as signposted in towns. Beware of slow-moving tractors and livestock on narrow, winding rural roads. Ireland's blood-alcohol limit is 0.08% and strictly enforced.

Car parks and other specified areas in Ireland are regulated by 'pay and display' tickets or disc parking. Available from most newsagencies, discs are good for one hour. Double yellow lines by the roadside mean no parking at any time, while single yellow lines indicate restrictions (which will be signposted).

Train

The Republic of Ireland's railway system, **Iarnród Éireann** (www.irishrail.ie), has routes radiating out from Dublin, but there is no direct north–south route along the west coast. Tickets can be twice as expensive as the bus, but travel times may be dramatically reduced. Special fares are often available, and a midweek return ticket sometimes costs just a bit more than the single fare; the flip side is that fares may be significantly higher on Friday and Sunday. **Rail Users Ireland** (www.railusers.ie) is more informative than the official website.

Northern Ireland Railways (www.translink.co.uk) has four lines from Belfast, one of which links up with the Republic's rail system.

DISCOUNTS & PASSES

Iarnród Éireann offers discounts to ISIC holders.

Travel passes for trains in Ireland include:

Eurail Pass Valid for train travel in the Republic of Ireland but not in Northern Ireland, 50% discount on Irish Ferries crossings to France.

InterRail Pass 50% discount on train travel within Ireland and on Irish Ferries and Stena Line services.

Britrail Pass Has an option to add on Ireland for an extra fee. The pass also covers ferry transit.

Irish Explorer (www.buseireann.ie) Rail and bus travel in the Republic including DART. €245 for eight days' travel out of 15 consecutive days.

Irish Explorer Rail For train-only travel (five days' travel out of 15). €145 within the Republic only, €180 including Northern Ireland. Not publicised on the www.irishrail.ie website at time of research.

Zone 3 iLink Card (www.translink.co.uk/ilink) Replacement for the Freedom of Northern Ireland pass. Smartcard offering unlimited travel on bus and train in Northern Ireland; one day/one week costs £15/55 plus £1.50 on first purchase (can be topped up).

Italy

Includes »

Best Places to Eat

» Pizzeria da Baffetto (p797)
» Osteria de' Poeti (p834)
» L'Osteria di Giovanni (p845)
» Civico 25 (p856)
» Piccolo Napoli (p876)

Best Places to Stay

» Hotel in Pietra (p870)
» Daphne Inn (p795)
» Ca' Angeli (p824)
» Hostel of the Sun (p862)
» Albergo Miramare (p868)

Why Go?

The land that has turned its lifestyle into a designer accessory, Italy is one of Europe's great seducers. Ever since the days of the 18th-century Grand Tour, travellers have been falling under its spell and still today it stirs strong emotions. The rush of seeing the Colosseum for the first time or cruising down Venice's surreal canals are feelings you'll remember for life.

Of course, Italy is not all about Michelangelo masterpieces and frescoed churches. There's also the food, imitated the world over, and a landscape that boasts beautiful Alpine peaks, stunning coastlines and remote, silent valleys. So if the cities don't do it for you, if their noise, heat and chaos start getting to you – as they get to many locals – change gear and head out to the country for a taste of the sun-kissed slow life.

When to Go

Rome

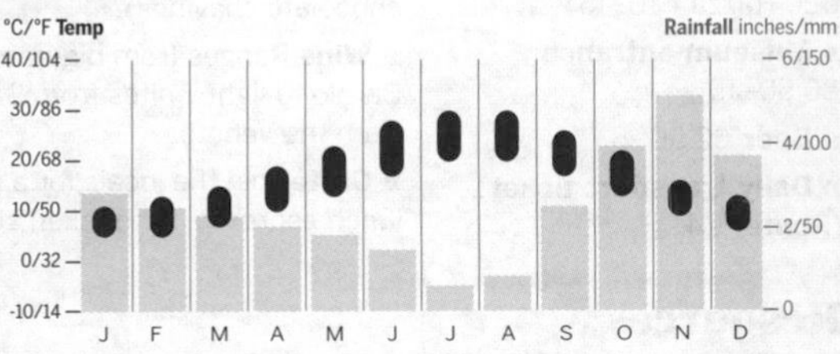

Apr & May Perfect spring temps and a week of free museums and cultural events.

Jul Summer means beach weather and a packed festival calendar.

Oct Enjoy the coast without crowds and some fabulous autumn food.

AT A GLANCE

» **Currency** euro (€)

» **Language** Italian

» **Money** ATMs widespread; credit cards widely accepted

» **Visas** Schengen rules apply

Fast Facts

» **Area** 301,230 sq km

» **Population** 60.34 million

» **Capital** Rome

» **Telephone** country code ☎39; international access code ☎00

» **Emergency** ☎112

Exchange Rates

Australia	A$1	€0.74
Canada	C$1	€0.74
Japan	¥100	€0.87
New Zealand	NZ$1	€0.56
UK	UK£1	€1.16
USA	US$1	€0.67

Set Your Budget

» **Budget hotel room** €55–110 (double)

» **Two-course dinner** from €20 (pizza €10–15)

» **Museum entrance** €6.50–15

» **Beer** €2.50–5

» **Daily transport ticket (Rome)** €4

Resources

» **Delicious Italy** (www.deliciousitaly.com) For foodies

» **Italia** (www.italia.it) Official tourism site

» **Lonely Planet** (www.lonelyplanet.com/italy)

Connections

Milan and Venice are northern Italy's two main transport hubs. From Milan, trains run to cities across Western Europe, including Barcelona, Paris, Zürich and Vienna. Venice is better placed for Eastern Europe, with rail connections to Ljubljana, Zagreb, Belgrade and Budapest. You can also pick up ferries in Venice for Corfu, Igoumenitsa and Patra. Down the east coast, there are ferries from Bari to various Greek ports, as well as to Bar and Dubrovnik. At the other end of the country, Genoa has ferries to Barcelona and Tunis.

ITINERARIES

One week

A one-week whistle-stop tour of Italy is enough to take in some of the country's main cities. After a couple of days exploring Venice's unique canal-scape, head south to Florence, Italy's great Renaissance city. Two days is not long there but it'll whet your appetite for the artistic and architectural treasures that await in Rome.

Two weeks

After the first week, continue south for some sea and southern passion. Spend a day dodging traffic in Naples, a day investigating the ruins at Pompeii and a day or two admiring the Amalfi Coast. Then backtrack to Naples for a ferry to Palermo and the gastronomic delights of Sicily – or perhaps Cagliari and Sardinia's magical beaches, depending on your preference.

Essential Food & Drink

» **Pizza** Two varieties: Roman, with a thin crispy base; and Neapolitan, with a higher, more doughy base. The best are always prepared in a *forno a legna* (wood-fired oven).

» **Gelato** Popular ice-cream flavours include *fragola* (strawberry), *nocciola* (hazelnut) and *stracciatella* (milk with chocolate shavings).

» **Wine** Ranges from big-name reds such as Piedmont's Barolo to light whites from Sardinia and sparkling *prosecco* from the Veneto.

» **Caffè** Join the locals for a morning cappuccino or post-lunch espresso, both taken standing at a bar.

Italy Highlights

1. Lap up the dolce vita in mesmerising **Rome** (774)
2. Take a vaporetto ride past grand but crumbling canalside palaces in **Venice** (p818)
3. Marvel at the Medicis' art collection in the **Uffizi Gallery** (p839) in Florence
4. Dive dreamy waters off **Cala Gonone** (p887) on Sardinia's east coast
5. Hike up an active volcano in the **Aeolian Islands** (p878)
6. Work up an appetite for pizza exploring the baroque backstreets of **Naples** (p858)
7. Blow your mind on baroque architecture in elegant **Lecce** (p872)
8. Explore imperious **Turin** (p809), so much more than Fiat and factories!
9. Delve into frescoed Etruscan tombs in **Tarquinia** (p805)
10. Enjoy a bike ride and picnic atop the medieval city walls in **Lucca** (p852)

ROME

POP 2.72 MILLION

An epic, monumental metropolis, Rome has been in the spotlight for close to 3000 years. As the showcase seat of the Roman Empire, it was the all-powerful *Caput Mundi* (Capital of the World). Later, as the Renaissance capital of the Catholic world, its name sent shivers of holy terror through believers and infidels alike. Some 500 years on, its name still exerts a powerful hold. Fortunately, its reality is every bit as enticing as its reputation. With its architectural and artistic treasures, its romantic corners and noisy, colourful markets, Rome is a city that knows how to impress.

They say a lifetime's not enough for Rome *(Roma, non basta una vita)*. And while it's true that few cities can match its cultural legacy, you don't need to be an expert to enjoy it. In fact, all you have to do is walk its animated streets. Even without trying you'll be swept up in the emotion of a city that has been inspiring artists and lovers since time immemorial.

History

According to legend Rome was founded by Romulus and Remus in 753 BC. Historians debate this, but they do acknowledge that Romulus was the first king of Rome and that the city was an amalgamation of Etruscan, Latin and Sabine settlements on the Palatino, Esquilino and Quirinale Hills. Archaeological discoveries have confirmed the existence of a settlement on the Palatino in that period.

In 509 BC the Roman Republic was founded. Civil war put an end to the republic following the murder of Julius Caesar in 44 BC and a bitter civil war between Octavian and Mark Antony. Octavian emerged victorious and was made the first Roman emperor with the title Augustus.

By AD 100 Rome had a population of 1.5 million and was the *Caput Mundi* (Capital of the World). But by the 5th century decline had set in and in 476 Romulus Augustulus, the last emperor of the Western Roman Empire, was deposed.

By this time Rome's Christian roots had taken firm hold. Christianity had been spreading since the 1st century AD, and under Constantine it received official recognition. Pope Gregory I (590–604) did much to strengthen the Church's grip over the city, laying the foundations for its later role as capital of the Catholic Church.

Under the Renaissance popes of the 15th and 16th centuries, Rome was given an extensive facelift. But trouble was never far away and in 1527 the city was sacked by Spanish forces under Charles V.

Once again Rome needed rebuilding and it was to the 17th-century baroque masters Bernini and Borromini that the city turned. With their exuberant churches, fountains and *palazzi*, these two bitter rivals changed the face of the city. The building boom following the unification of Italy and the declaration of Rome as its capital also profoundly influenced the look of the city, as did Mussolini and hasty post-WWII expansion.

Sights

With more world-class sights than many small nations, Rome can be a daunting prospect. The trick is to relax and not worry about seeing everything – half the fun of the city is just hanging out, enjoying the at-

COLOSSEUM TIPS

Follow these tips to beat the Colosseum queues:

» Buy your ticket from the Palatino entrance (about 250m away at Via di San Gregorio 30) or the Roman Forum entrance (Largo della Salara Vecchia).

» Get the Roma Pass, which is valid for three days and a whole host of sites.

» Book your ticket online at www.pierreci.it (plus booking fee of €1.50).

» Join an official English-language tour – €4 on top of the regular Colosseum ticket price.

Outside the Colosseum, you'll almost certainly be hailed by centurions offering to pose for a photo. They are not doing this for love and will expect payment. There's no set rate but €5 is a perfectly acceptable sum – and that's €5 period, not €5 per person. To avoid ugly scenes always agree on a price beforehand.

ROME IN...

Two Days

Get to grips with ancient Rome at the **Colosseum**, the **Roman Forum** and **Palatino (Palatine Hill)**. Spend the afternoon exploring the **Musei Capitolini** before an evening in **Trastevere**. On day two, hit the Vatican. Marvel at **St Peter's Basilica** and the **Sistine Chapel** in the vast **Vatican Museums**. Afterwards, ditch your guidebook and get happily lost in the animated streets around **Piazza Navona** and the **Pantheon**.

Four Days

With another couple of days you should definitely book a visit to the **Museo e Galleria Borghese** and venture out to **Via Appia Antica** and the catacombs. If you can handle more art, the **Galleria Doria Pamphilj** and the **Museo Nazionale Romano: Palazzo Massimo alle Terme** both merit a visit. In the evenings, join the student drinkers and fashionable diners in San Lorenzo, or let your hair down with a concert at the **Auditorium Parco della Musica**.

mosphere. Most sights are concentrated in the area between Stazione Termini and the Vatican. Halfway between the two, the Pantheon and Piazza Navona lie at the heart of the *centro storico* (historic centre). To the southeast, the Colosseum is an obvious landmark.

ANCIENT ROME

Colosseum RUINS
(Map p780; ☎06 3996 7700; Piazza del Colosseo; adult/EU child incl Roman Forum & Palatino €12/free, audioguide €4; ⊙8.30am-1hr before sunset; MColosseo) Rome's iconic monument is a thrilling sight. The 50,000-seat Colosseum was ancient Rome's most feared arena and is today one of Italy's top draws, attracting between 16,000 and 19,000 people on an average day.

Originally known as the Flavian Amphitheatre, the Colosseum was started by Emperor Vespasian in AD 72 and finished by his son Titus in AD 80. It was clad in travertine and covered by a huge canvas awning that was held aloft by 240 masts. Inside, tiered seating encircled the sand-covered arena, itself built over underground chambers where animals were caged. Games involved gladiators fighting wild animals or each other. But contrary to Hollywood folklore, bouts between gladiators rarely ended in death, as the games' sponsor was required to pay the owner of a killed gladiator 100 times the gladiator's value.

The top tier and underground corridors, known as the hypogeum, have recently been opened to the public. Visits, which cost €8 on top of the normal Colosseum ticket and are by guided tour only, require advance booking.

To the west of the Colosseum, the **Arco di Costantino** was built to celebrate Constantine's victory over rival Maxentius at the battle of Milvian Bridge in 312.

Roman Forum RUINS
(Map p780; Largo della Salara Vecchia; adult/EU child incl Colosseum & Palatino €12/free, audioguide €4; ⊙8.30am-1hr before sunset; MColosseo) Now a collection of fascinating, if rather confusing, ruins, the Roman Forum (Foro Romano) was once the showpiece centre of the Roman Republic. Originally an Etruscan burial ground, it was first developed in the 7th century BC, expanding to become the social, political and commercial core of the Roman world. Its importance declined after the fall of the Roman Empire, until eventually the site was used as pastureland and plundered for marble. The area was system-

ROMA PASS

The **Roma Pass** (www.romapass.it; 3 days €25) provides free admission to two museums or sites (choose from a list of 38), as well as reduced entry to extra sites, unlimited city transport and discounted entry to other exhibitions and events. If you use this for the more expensive sights such as the Colosseum or Musei Capitolini you will save money.

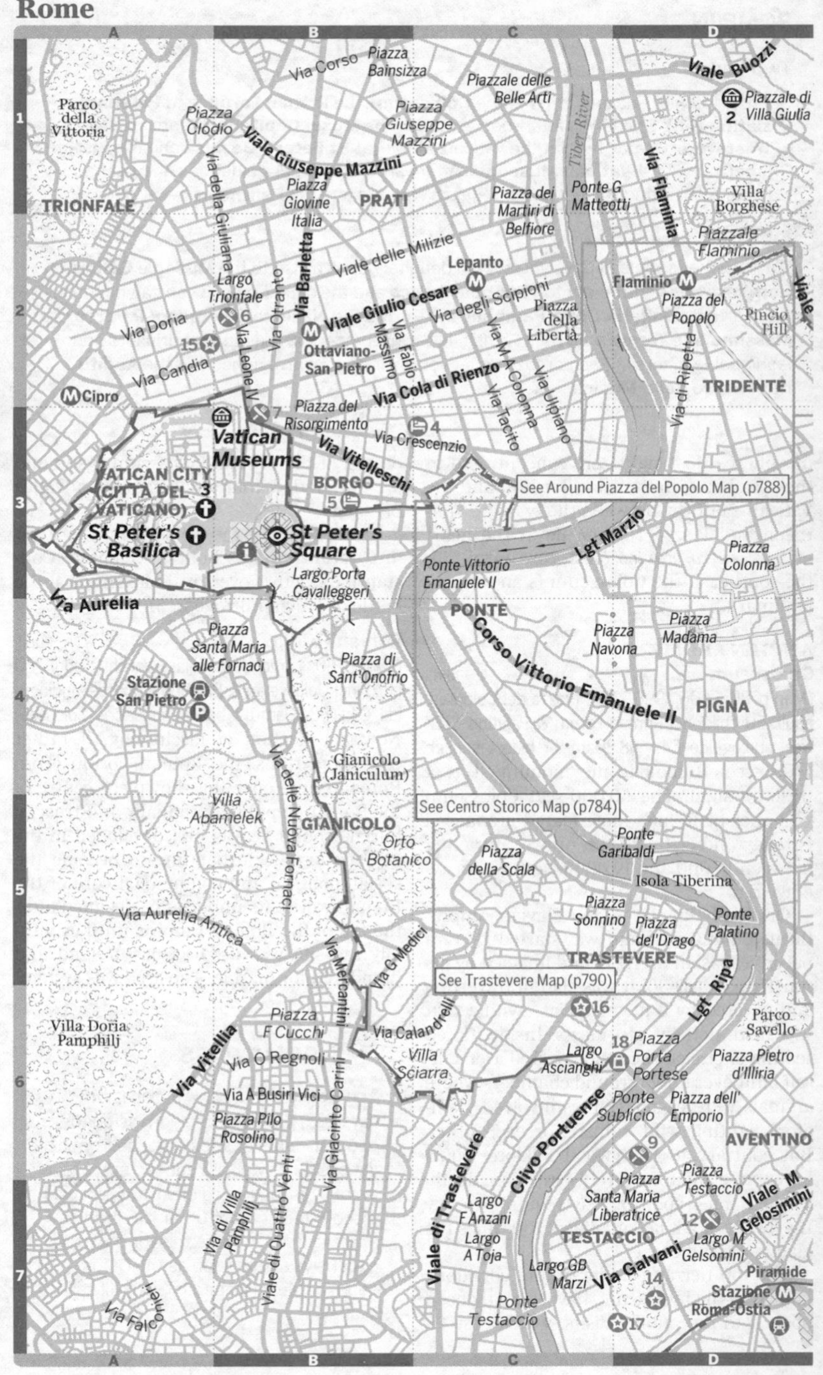
Parco della Vittoria
Piazza Clodio
Via Corso
Piazza Bainsizza
Piazzale delle Belle Arti
Viale Buozzi
Piazzale di Villa Giulia
Piazza Giuseppe Mazzini
Viale Giuseppe Mazzini
Tiber River
Via Flaminia
TRIONFALE
Via della Giuliana
Piazza Giovine Italia
PRATI
Piazza dei Martiri di Belfiore
Ponte G Matteotti
Villa Borghese
Piazzale Flaminio
Viale delle Milizie
Lepanto
Flaminio
Largo Trionfale
Via Barletta
Via Otranto
Viale Giulio Cesare
Via degli Scipioni
Piazza della Libertà
Piazza del Popolo
Pincio Hill
Via Doria
Via Leone IV
Ottaviano-San Pietro
Via Fabio Massimo
Via M A Colonna
Via Candia
Via Cola di Rienzo
Via Ulpiano
Via di Ripetta
TRIDENTE
Cipro
Via Tacito
Piazza del Risorgimento
Via Crescenzio
Vatican Museums
Via Vitelleschi
VATICAN CITY (CITTÀ DEL VATICANO)
BORGO
See Around Piazza del Popolo Map (p788)
St Peter's Basilica
St Peter's Square
Lgt Marzio
Piazza Colonna
Largo Porta Cavalleggeri
Ponte Vittorio Emanuele II
Via Aurelia
PONTE
Piazza Navona
Piazza Madama
Piazza Santa Maria alle Fornaci
Corso Vittorio Emanuele II
Piazza di Sant'Onofrio
Stazione San Pietro
PIGNA
Via delle Nuova Fornaci
Gianicolo (Janiculum)
Villa Abamelek
See Centro Storico Map (p784)
GIANICOLO
Orto Botanico
Ponte Garibaldi
Piazza della Scala
Isola Tiberina
Via Aurelia Antica
Piazza Sonnino
Piazza del'Drago
Ponte Palatino
Via G Medici
Via Mercantini
TRASTEVERE
See Trastevere Map (p790)
Lgt Ripa
Villa Doria Pamphilj
Piazza F Cucchi
Via Calandrelli
Parco Savello
Via Vitellia
Via O Regnoli
Villa Sciarra
Largo Ascianghi
Piazza Porta Portese
Piazza Pietro d'Illiria
Via A Busiri Vici
Ponte Sublicio
Piazza dell' Emporio
Piazza Pilo Rosolino
Clivo Portuense
AVENTINO
Via Giacinto Carini
Viale di Trastevere
Piazza Santa Maria Liberatrice
Piazza Testaccio
Viale di Quattro Venti
Via di Villa Pamphilj
Largo F Anzani
Viale M Gelsomini
Largo A Toja
TESTACCIO
Largo M Gelsomini
Largo GB Marzi
Via Galvani
Piramide
Stazione Roma-Ostia
Via Falconieri
Ponte Testaccio

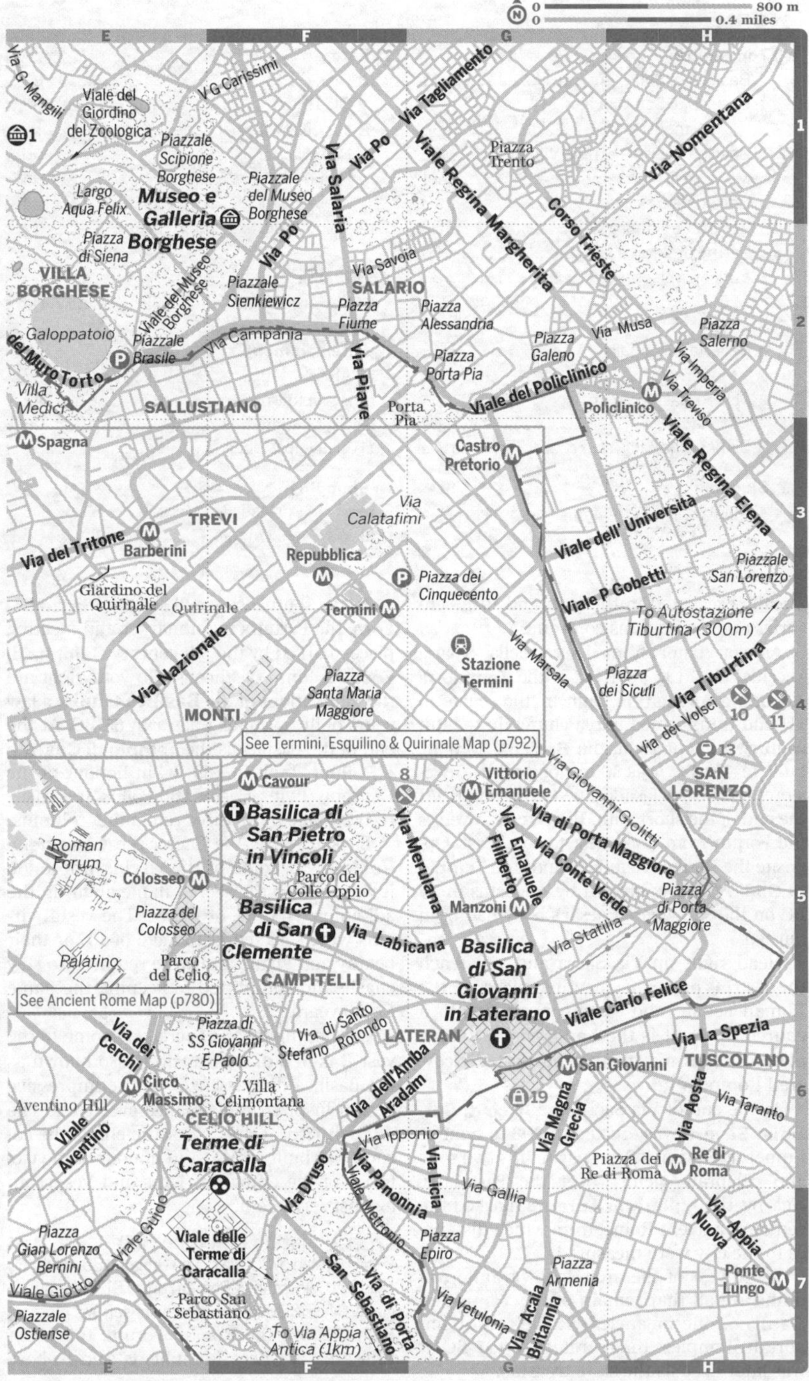
0 800 m
0 0.4 miles
Via G Mangili
Viale del Giordino del Zoologica
V G Carissimi
Via Tagliamento
Via Nomentana
Piazzale Scipione Borghese
Via Po
Viale Regina Margherita
Piazza Trento
Via Salaria
Largo Aqua Felix
Museo e Galleria Borghese
Piazzale del Museo Borghese
Corso Trieste
Piazza di Siena
VILLA BORGHESE
Viale del Museo Borghese
Piazzale Sienkiewicz
Via Savoia
SALARIO
Piazza Fiume
Piazza Alessandria
Galoppatoio
Piazzale Brasile
Via Campania
Via Musa
Piazza Salerno
Piazza Galeno
Piazza Porta Pia
Via Imperia
Via Treviso
del Muro Torto
Villa Medici
Via Piave
Viale del Policlinico
Policlinico
SALLUSTIANO
Porta Pia
Spagna
Castro Pretorio
Viale Regina Elena
Via Calatafimi
TREVI
Viale dell' Università
Via del Tritone
Barberini
Repubblica
Piazzale San Lorenzo
Piazza dei Cinquecento
Viale P Gobetti
Giardino del Quirinale
Quirinale
Termini
To Autostazione Tiburtina (300m)
Via Nazionale
Stazione Termini
Via Marsala
Piazza dei Siculi
Via Tiburtina
Piazza Santa Maria Maggiore
MONTI
10
11
Via dei Volsci
See Termini, Esquilino & Quirinale Map (p792)
13
Cavour
8
Vittorio Emanuele
Via Giovanni Giolitti
SAN LORENZO
Basilica di San Pietro in Vincoli
Via Merulana
Via Emanuele Filiberto
Via di Porta Maggiore
Roman Forum
Colosseo
Parco del Colle Oppio
Via Conte Verde
Piazza di Porta Maggiore
Piazza del Colosseo
Basilica di San Clemente
Manzoni
Via Labicana
Basilica di San Giovanni in Laterano
Via Statilia
Palatino
Parco del Celio
CAMPITELLI
See Ancient Rome Map (p780)
Viale Carlo Felice
Piazza di SS Giovanni E Paolo
Via di Santo Stefano Rotondo
LATERAN
Via dei Cerchi
Via La Spezia
San Giovanni
TUSCOLANO
Circo Massimo
Villa Celimontana
Via dell'Amba Aradam
19
Aventino Hill
CELIO HILL
Via Aosta
Via Taranto
Viale Aventino
Via Ipponio
Via Magna Grecia
Terme di Caracalla
Piazza dei Re di Roma
Re di Roma
Via Druso
Via Pannonia
Via Licia
Via Gallia
Viale Metronio
Via Appia Nuova
Viale Guido
Piazza Gian Lorenzo Bernini
Viale delle Terme di Caracalla
Piazza Epiro
Piazza Armenia
Via di Porta San Sebastiano
Ponte Lungo
Viale Giotto
Parco San Sebastiano
Via Vetulonia
Via Acaia
Britannia
Piazzale Ostiense
To Via Appia Antica (1km)
E
F
G
H
1
2
3
4
5
6
7

Rome

atically excavated in the 18th and 19th centuries and excavations continue.

As you enter from Largo della Salaria Vecchia, ahead to your left is the **Tempio di Antonino e Faustina**, built by the senate in 141 and transformed into a church in the 8th century. To your right, the **Basilica Aemilia**, built in 179 BC, was 100m long with a two-storey porticoed facade lined with shops. At the end of the short path, **Via Sacra** traverses the Forum from northwest to southeast. Opposite the Basilica Aemilia stands the **Tempio di Giulio Cesare**, erected by Augustus in 29 BC on the site where Caesar's body had been burned.

Head right up Via Sacra and you reach the **Curia**, once the meeting place of the Roman senate and later converted into a church. In front is the **Lapis Niger**, a large piece of black marble that purportedly covered Romulus' grave.

At the end of Via Sacra, the **Arco di Settimio Severo** was erected in 203 to honour Emperor Septimus Severus and his two sons and celebrate victory over the Parthians. Nearby, the **Millarium Aureum** marked the centre of ancient Rome, from which distances to the city were measured.

Southwest of the arch, eight granite columns are all that remain of the **Tempio di Saturno**, one of ancient Rome's most important temples. Inaugurated in 497 BC, it was later used as the state treasury.

To the southeast, you'll see the **Piazza del Foro**, the Forum's main market and meeting place, marked by the 7th-century **Colonna di Foca** (Column of Phocus). To your right are the foundations of the **Basilica Giulia**, a law court built by Julius Caesar in 55 BC. At the end of the basilica is the **Tempio di Castore e Polluce**, built in 489 BC in honour of the Heavenly Twins, Castor and Pollux. It is easily recognisable by its three remaining columns.

Back towards Via Sacra, the **Casa delle Vestali** was home of the virgins whose job it was to keep the sacred flame alight in the adjoining **Tempio di Vesta**. The vestal virgins were selected at the age of 10 for their beauty and virtue and were required to stay chaste and committed to keeping the flame for 30 years.

Continuing up Via Sacra, you come to the vast **Basilica di Costantino**, also known as the Basilica di Massenzio, whose impressive design inspired Renaissance architects. The **Arco di Tito**, at the Colosseum end of the Forum, was built in AD 81 in honour of the victories of the emperors Titus and Vespasian against Jerusalem.

TOP CHOICE **Palatino (Palatine Hill)** RUINS
(Map p780; Via di San Gregorio 30; adult/EU child incl Colosseum & Roman Forum €12/free, audioguide €4; 8.30am-1hr before sunset; M Colosseo)
Rising above the Roman Forum, this beautiful area is where Romulus is said to have

founded the city in 753 BC. Archaeological evidence shows that the earliest settlements in the area were in fact on the Palatino and date back to the 8th century BC. This was ancient Rome's poshest neighbourhood and the emperor Augustus lived here all his life. After Rome's fall, it fell into disrepair and in the Middle Ages churches and castles were built over the ruins. During the Renaissance, members of wealthy families established gardens on the hill. Most of the Palatino is covered by the ruins of Emperor Domitian's vast complex, which served as the main imperial palace for 300 years. Divided into the **Domus Flavia** (imperial palace), **Domus Augustana** (the emperor's private residence) and a **stadio** (stadium), it was built by the architect Rabirius in the 1st century AD.

Among the best-preserved buildings on the Palatino is the **Casa di Livia**, home of Augustus' wife Livia, and, in front, Augustus' separate residence, the **Casa di Augusto** (11am-3.30pm Mon, Wed, Sat & Sun), which boasts exceptional frescos.

Museo dei Fori Imperiali MUSEUM

(Map p792; www.mercatiditraiano.it; Via IV Novembre 94; adult/child €9/free; 9am-7pm Tue-Sun; Via IV Novembre) This striking museum brings to life the **Mercati di Traiano**, emperor Trajan's great 2nd-century market complex. From the main hallway, a lift whisks you up to the **Torre delle Milizie** (Militia Tower), a 13th-century red-brick tower, and the upper levels of the vast three-storey semicircular construction that once housed hundreds of traders. From the top there are sweeping views over the Imperial Forums.

Piazza del Campidoglio SQUARE

(Map p780; Piazza Venezia) This striking piazza sits atop the Capitoline Hill (Campidoglio), the lowest of Rome's seven hills. In ancient times, it was home to the city's two most important temples: one dedicated to Juno Moneta and another to Jupiter Capitolinus, where Brutus is said to have hidden after assassinating Caesar. The Michelangelo-designed piazza, accessible by the graceful **Cordonata** staircase, is bordered by **Palazzo Nuovo** on the left, **Palazzo dei Conservatori** on the right, and **Palazzo Senatorio**, the seat of city government since 1143. In the centre, the bronze **statue of Marcus Aurelius** is a copy; the original is in Palazzo Nuovo.

Musei Capitolini MUSEUM

(Capitoline Museums; Map p780; www.museicapitolini.org; Piazza del Campidoglio; adult/child €7.50/free, audioguide €5; 9am-8pm Tue-Sun, last entry 7pm; Piazza Venezia) Housed in Palazzo Nuovo and Palazzo dei Conservatori, the Capitoline Museums are the oldest public museums in the world, dating to 1471. Their collection of classical art is one of Italy's finest, including masterpieces such as the *Lupa capitolina* (She-wolf), a sculpture of Romulus and Remus under a wolf, and the *Galata morente* (Dying Gaul), a moving depiction of a dying Gaul. The **pinacoteca** (art gallery) on the 2nd floor contains paintings by Titian, Tintoretto, Van Dyck, Rubens and Caravaggio.

Chiesa di Santa Maria d'Aracoeli CHURCH

(Map p780; Piazza del Campidoglio 4; 9am-12.30pm & 3-6.30pm; Piazza Venezia) Marking the high point of the Campidoglio, this 6th-century church sits on the site of the Roman temple to Juno Moneta. According to legend it was here that the Tiburtine Sybil told Augustus of the coming birth of Christ, and still today the church has a strong association with the nativity.

Carcere Mamertino CHURCH

(Mamertine Prison; Map p780; closed for restoration; Piazza Venezia) From Piazza del Campidoglio, stairs to the left of Palazzo Senatorio lead down to this ancient prison, now church, where St Peter is said to have miraculously baptised his jailers whilst imprisoned here.

Piazza Venezia SQUARE

Piazza Venezia is dominated by the mountain of white marble that is **Il Vittoriano** (Map p780; Piazza Venezia), aka the Altare della Patria. Begun in 1885 to commemorate Italian unification and honour Victor Emmanuel II, it incorporates the **tomb of the Unknown Soldier**, as well as the **Museo Centrale del Risorgimento** (admission free; 9.30am-6.30pm), documenting Italian unification. For Rome's best 360-degree views, take the **panoramic lift** (adult/concession €7/3.50; 9.30am-6.30pm Mon-Thu, to 7.30pm Fri-Sun) to the top.

Over the square, the 15th-century **Palazzo Venezia** (Via del Plebiscito 118; adult/concession €4/2; 8.30am-7.30pm Tue-Sun) was the first of Rome's great Renaissance *palazzi*. Mussolini had his office here and there's now a museum of medieval and Renaissance art.

Bocca della Verità OFFBEAT SIGHT

(Map p780; Piazza Bocca della Verità 18; 10am-5pm; Via dei Cerchi) A round piece of marble once used as an ancient manhole cover, the Bocca della Verità (Mouth of Truth) is one of Rome's great curiosities. According to

Ancient Rome

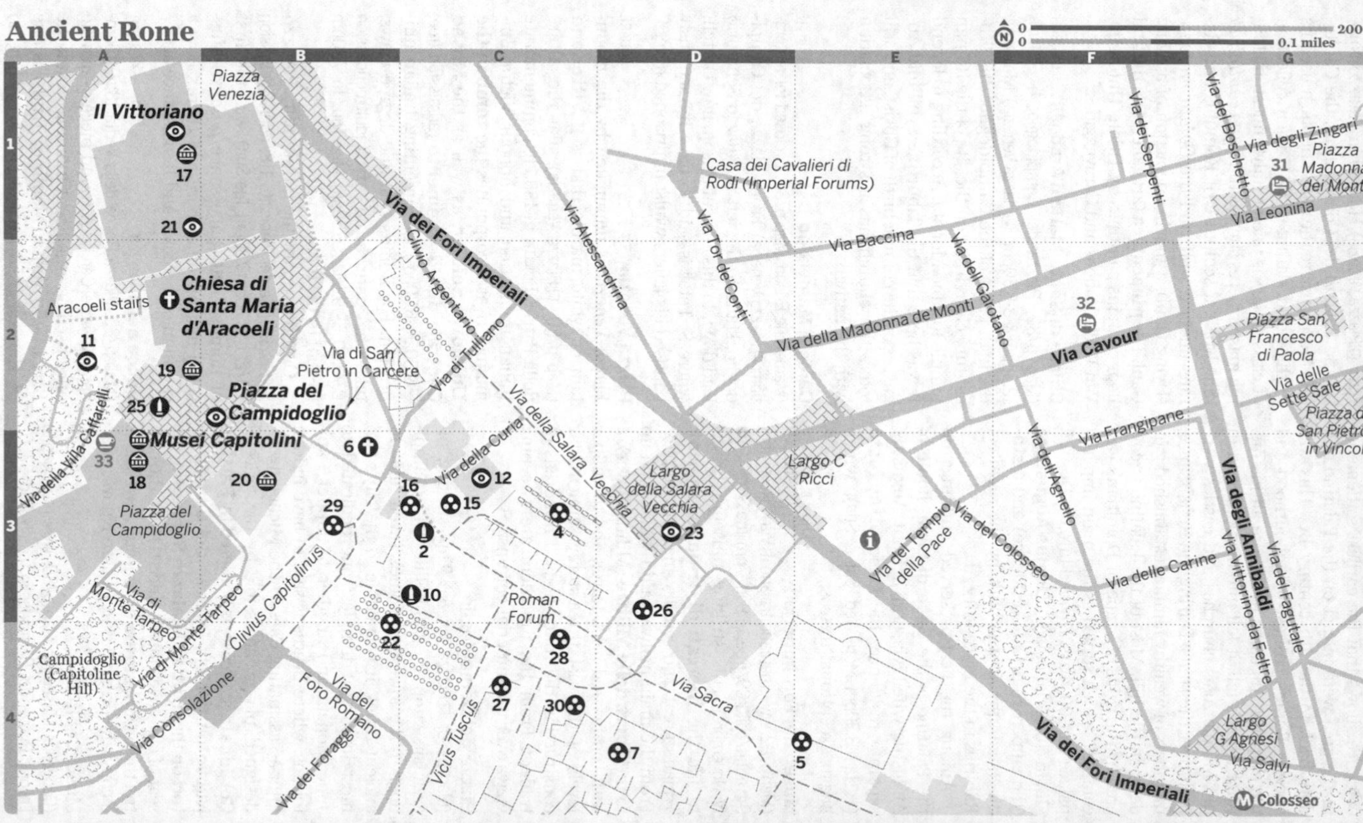

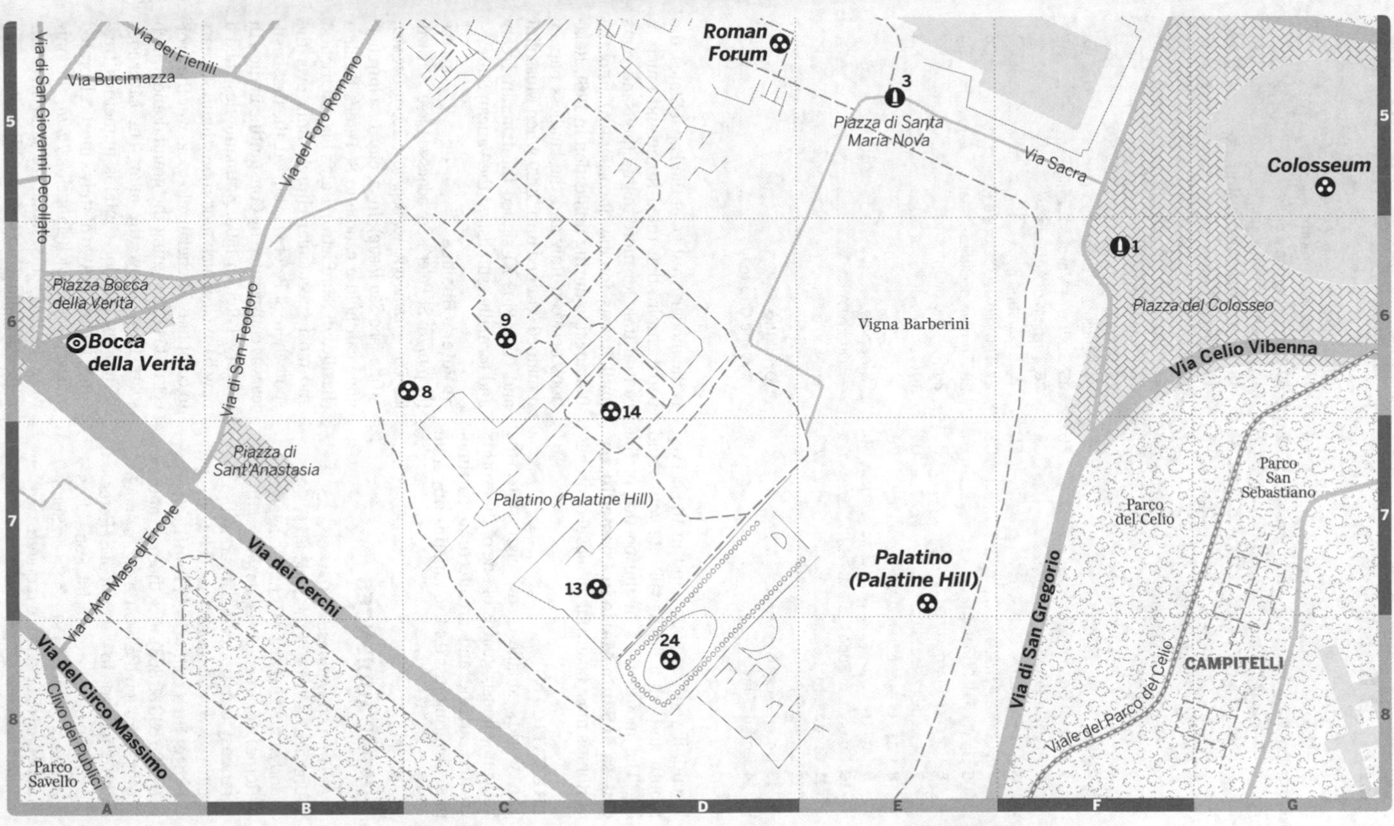
Roman Forum
3
Piazza di Santa Maria Nova
Via Sacra
Colosseum
1
Piazza del Colosseo
Via di San Giovanni Decollato
Via Bucimazza
Via dei Fienili
Via del Foro Romano
Piazza Bocca della Verità
Bocca della Verità
Via di San Teodoro
9
8
14
Vigna Barberini
Via Celio Vibenna
Piazza di Sant'Anastasia
Palatino (Palatine Hill)
Parco San Sebastiano
Parco del Celio
Via d Ara Mass di Ercole
Via dei Cerchi
13
Palatino (Palatine Hill)
Via di San Gregorio
24
CAMPITELLI
Viale del Parco del Celio
Via del Circo Massimo
Clivo dei Publici
Parco Savello
5
6
7
8
A
B
C
D
E
F
G

Ancient Rome

Top Sights

Bocca della Verità A6
Chiesa di Santa Maria d'Aracoeli A2
Colosseum G5
Il Vittoriano A1
Musei Capitolini A3
Palatino (Palatine Hill) E7
Piazza del Campidoglio B2
Roman Forum D5

Sights

1 Arco di Costantino F6
2 Arco di Settimio Severo C3
3 Arco di Tito E5
4 Basilica Aemilia C3
5 Basilica di Constantino E4
6 Carcere Mamertino B3
7 Casa delle Vestali D4
8 Casa di Augusto C6
9 Casa di Livia C6
10 Colonna di Foca C3
11 Cordonata A2
12 Curia C3
13 Domus Augustana C7
14 Domus Flavia D6
15 Lapis Niger C3
16 Millarium Aureum C3
17 Museo Centrale del Risorgimento A1
18 Palazzo dei Conservatori A3
19 Palazzo Nuovo A2
20 Palazzo Senatorio B3
21 Panoramic Lift A1
22 Piazza del Foro B4
23 Roman Forum Entrance D3
24 Stadio D8
25 Statue of Marcus Aurelius A2
26 Tempio di Antonino e Faustina D3
27 Tempio di Castore e Polluce C4
28 Tempio di Giulio Cesare C4
29 Tempio di Saturno B3
30 Tempio di Vesta C4

Sleeping

31 Duca d'Alba G1
32 Nicolas Inn F2

Drinking

33 Caffè Capitolino A3

legend, if you put your hand in the carved mouth and tell a lie, it will bite your hand off. The mouth lives in the portico of the **Chiesa di Santa Maria in Cosmedin**, one of Rome's most beautiful medieval churches.

THE VATICAN

The world's smallest sovereign state, the Vatican jealously guards of one of the world's greatest artistic and architectural patrimonies. Covering just 0.44 sq km, this tiny state is the modern vestige of the Papal States, the papal empire that ruled Rome and much of central Italy for more than a thousand years until it was forcibly incorporated into the Italian state during unification in 1861. Relations between Italy and the landless papacy remained strained until 1929 when Mussolini and Pope Pius XI signed the Lateran Treaty and formally established the Vatican State.

PAPAL AUDIENCES

At 11am on Wednesday, the Pope addresses his flock at the Vatican (in July and August in Castel Gandolfo near Rome). For free tickets, download the request form from the Vatican website (www.vatican.va) and fax it to the **Prefettura della Casa Pontificia** (fax 06 698 85 863). Pick them up at the office through the bronze doors under the colonnade to the right of St Peter's.

When he is in Rome, the Pope blesses the crowd in St Peter's Sq on Sunday at noon. No tickets are required.

St Peter's Basilica CHURCH

(Map p776; St Peter's Sq; admission free, audioguide €5; 7am-7pm Apr-Sep, to 6.30pm Oct-Mar; M Ottaviano-San Pietro) In a city of churches, none can hold a candle to St Peter's Basilica (Basilica di San Pietro), Italy's biggest, richest and most spectacular church. Built over the spot where St Peter was buried, the first basilica was consecrated by Constantine in the 4th century. Later, in 1503, Bramante designed a new basilica, which took more than 150 years to complete. Michelangelo took over the project in 1547, designing the grand dome, which soars 120m above the altar. The cavernous 187m-long interior contains numerous treasures, including two of Italy's most celebrated masterpieces: Michelangelo's *Pietà,* the only work to carry his signature; and Bernini's 29m-high baldachin over the high altar.

Entrance to the **dome** (⌚8am-6pm Apr-Sep, 8am-5pm Oct-Mar) is to the right as you climb the stairs to the basilica's atrium. Make the climb on foot (€5) or by lift (€7).

Note that the basilica is one of Rome's busiest attractions, so expect queues in peak periods. Dress rules and security are stringently enforced, so no shorts, miniskirts or sleeveless tops, and be prepared to have your bags searched.

St Peter's Square SQUARE
(Map p776; Ⓜ Ottaviano-San Pietro) The Vatican's central piazza, St Peter's Sq (Piazza San Pietro) was designed by baroque artist Gian Lorenzo Bernini and laid out between 1656 and 1667. Seen from above it resembles a giant keyhole: two semicircular colonnades, each consisting of four rows of Doric columns, bound by a giant ellipse that straightens out to funnel believers into the basilica. The effect was deliberate – Bernini described the colonnade as representing 'the motherly arms of the church'.

In the centre, the 25m obelisk was brought to Rome by Caligula from Heliopolis in Egypt and later used by Nero as a turning post for the chariot races in his circus.

Vatican Museums ART MUSEUM
(Map p776; ☎06 6988 4676; Viale Vaticano; adult/child €15/free, admission free last Sun of month, audioguide €7; ⌚9am-6pm, last entry 4pm Mon-Sat, to 2pm, last entry 12.30pm last Sun of month; Ⓜ Ottaviano-San Pietro) Boasting one of the world's great art collections, the Vatican Museums are housed in the Palazzo Apostolico Vaticano, a vast 5.5-hectare complex comprising two palaces and three internal courtyards. You'll never manage to explore it all in one day – you'd need several hours just for the highlights – so it pays to be selective. There are several suggested itineraries from the Quattro Cancelli area near the entrance.

Home to some spectacular classical statuary, the **Museo Pio-Clementino** is a must-see. Highlights include the *Apollo belvedere* and the 1st-century *Laocoön,* both in the Cortile Ottagono. Further on, the 175m-long **Galleria delle Carte Geografiche** (Map Gallery) is hung with 40 huge topographical maps. Beyond that are the magnificent **Stanze di Raffaello** (Raphael Rooms), which were once Pope Julius II's private apartments and are decorated with frescos by Raphael. Of the paintings, *La scuola d'Atene* (The School of Athens) in the **Stanza della Segnatura** is considered one of Raphael's great masterpieces.

QUEUE JUMPING AT THE VATICAN MUSEUMS

Here's how to jump the ticket queue – although we can't help with lines for the security checks.

» Book tickets at http://biglietteriamusei.vatican.va/musei/tickets (plus booking fee of €4). You can also book authorised guided tours (adult/concession €31/25).

» Time your visit: Wednesday mornings are a good bet, as everyone is at the Pope's weekly audience at St Peter's; lunchtime is better than the morning; avoid Mondays, when many other museums are shut.

Sistine Chapel
This is the one place in the Vatican Museums that not one of the 4.5 million annual visitors wants to miss. Home to two of the world's most famous works of art, the 15th-century **Sistine Chapel** (Cappella Sistina) is where the papal conclave is locked to elect the Pope. It was originally built in 1484 for Pope Sixtus IV, after whom it is named, but it was Pope Julius II who commissioned Michelangelo to decorate it in 1508. Over the next four years, the artist painted the remarkable *Genesis* (Creation; 1508–12) on the barrel-vaulted ceiling. Twenty-two years later he returned at the behest of Pope Clement VII to paint the *Giudizio universale* (Last Judgment; 1534-41) on the end wall.

The other walls of the chapel were painted by artists including Botticelli, Ghirlandaio, Pinturicchio and Signorelli.

Castel Sant'Angelo CASTLE
(Map p784; Lungotevere Castello 50; adult/EU child €8.50/free; ⌚9am-8pm Tue-Sun; 🚌Piazza Pia) An instantly recognisable landmark, the chunky, round-keeped Castel Sant'Angelo was commissioned by Emperor Hadrian in 123 BC as a mausoleum for himself and his family. In the 6th century, it was converted into a papal fortress, and it's now a museum with an assorted collection of sculptures, paintings, weapons and furniture. The terrace offers fine views.

HISTORIC CENTRE

FREE **Pantheon** MONUMENT
(Map p784; Piazza della Rotonda; audioguide €5; ⌚8.30am-7.30pm Mon-Sat, 9am-6pm Sun, 9am-1pm holidays; 🚌Largo di Torre Argentina) A

Centro Storico (Rome)

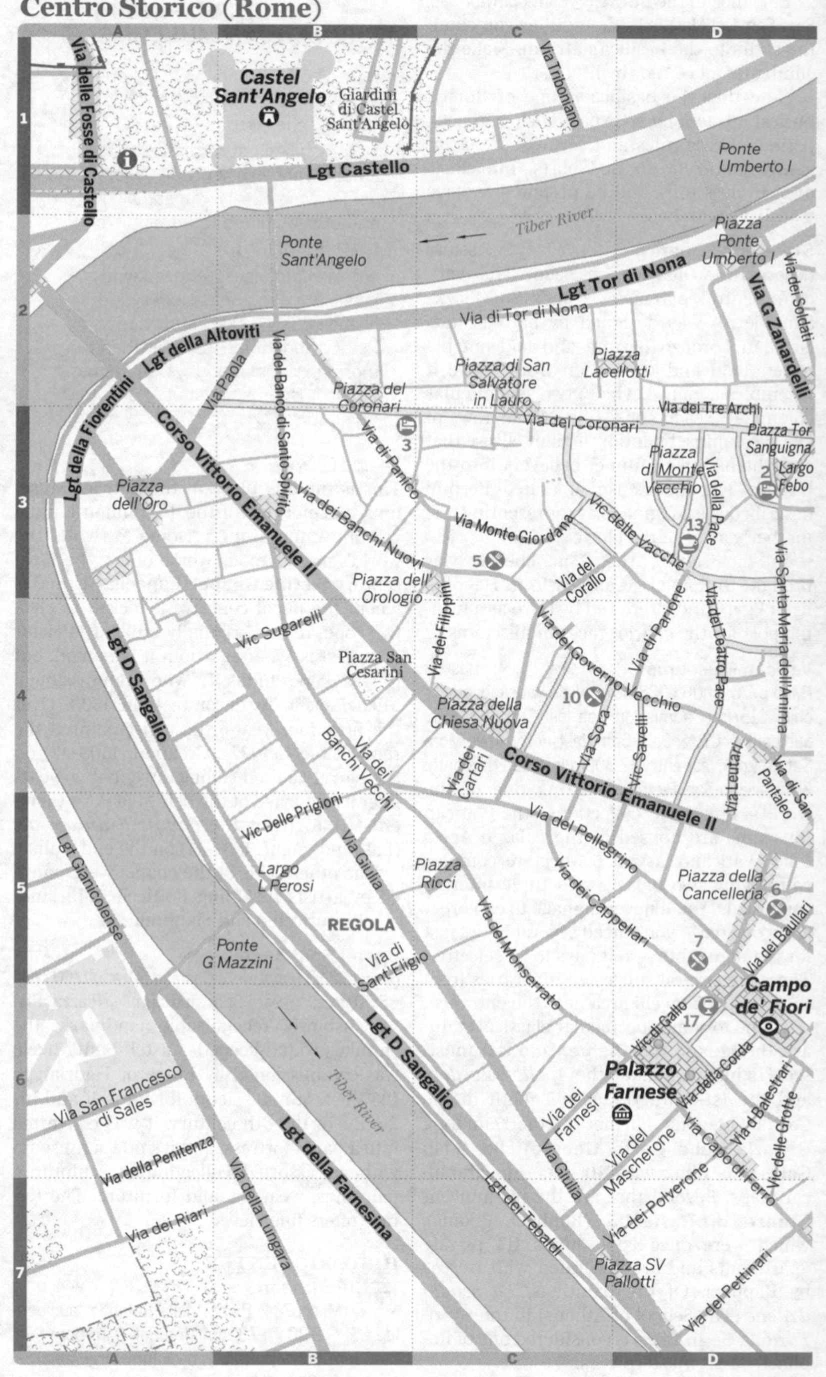

ITALY ROME

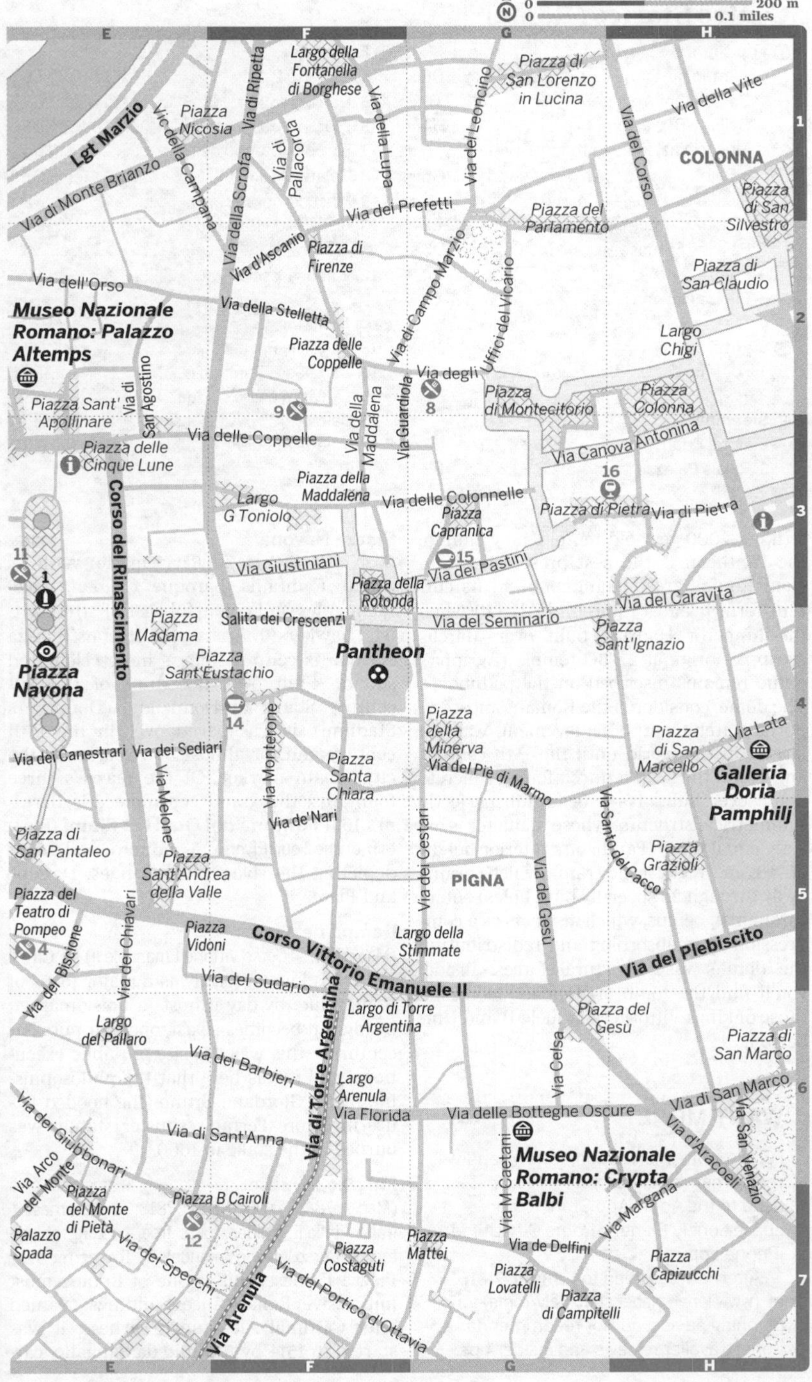

0 200 m
0 0.1 miles
E
F
G
H
1
2
3
4
5
6
7
COLONNA
PIGNA
Lgt Marzio
Via di Monte Brianzo
Piazza Nicosia
Vic della Campana
Via di Ripetta
Largo della Fontanella di Borghese
Via di Pallacorda
Via della Lupa
Via del Leoncino
Piazza di San Lorenzo in Lucina
Via del Corso
Via della Vite
Piazza di San Silvestro
Via dei Prefetti
Piazza del Parlamento
Via della Scrofa
Via d'Ascanio
Piazza di Firenze
Via di Campo Marzio
Uffici del Vicario
Piazza di San Claudio
Via dell'Orso
Via della Stelletta
Museo Nazionale Romano: Palazzo Altemps
Largo Chigi
Piazza delle Coppelle
Via di San Agostino
Via degli
Piazza di Montecitorio
Piazza Colonna
Piazza Sant' Apollinare
9
8
Via della Maddalena
Via Guardiola
Via delle Coppelle
Via Canova Antonina
Piazza delle Cinque Lune
Piazza della Maddalena
16
Largo G Toniolo
Via delle Colonnelle
Piazza Capranica
Piazza di Pietra
Via di Pietra
Corso del Rinascimento
11
1
Via Giustiniani
15
Via dei Pastini
Piazza della Rotonda
Via del Caravita
Piazza Madama
Salita dei Crescenzi
Via del Seminario
Piazza Sant'Ignazio
Pantheon
Piazza Sant'Eustachio
Piazza Navona
14
Piazza della Minerva
Piazza di San Marcello
Via Lata
Via dei Canestrari
Via dei Sediari
Via Monterone
Piazza Santa Chiara
Via del Piè di Marmo
Galleria Doria Pamphilj
Via Melone
Via de'Nari
Via Santo del Cacco
Piazza di San Pantaleo
Piazza Sant'Andrea della Valle
Via dei Cestari
Via del Gesù
Piazza Grazioli
Piazza del Teatro di Pompeo
4
Via dei Chiavari
Piazza Vidoni
Corso Vittorio Emanuele II
Largo della Stimmate
Via del Plebiscito
Via del Biscione
Via del Sudario
Largo di Torre Argentina
Piazza del Gesù
Largo del Pallaro
Piazza di San Marco
Via dei Barbieri
Largo Arenula
Via Celsa
Via Florida
Via delle Botteghe Oscure
Via di San Marco
Via dei Giubbonari
Via di Sant'Anna
Via di Torre Argentina
Via d'Aracoeli
Via San Venazio
Museo Nazionale Romano: Crypta Balbi
Via Arco del Monte
Piazza del Monte di Pietà
Piazza B Cairoli
Via M Caetani
Via Margana
12
Palazzo Spada
Via dei Specchi
Piazza Costaguti
Piazza Mattei
Via de Delfini
Piazza Capizucchi
Piazza Lovatelli
Via del Portico d'Ottavia
Piazza di Campitelli
Via Arenula
ITALY ROME

Centro Storico (Rome)

striking 2000-year-old temple, now church, the Pantheon is the best preserved of ancient Rome's great monuments. In its current form it dates to around AD 120 when the Emperor Hadrian built over Marcus Agrippa's original 27 BC temple (Agrippa's name remains inscribed on the pediment). The dome, considered the Romans' most important architectural achievement, was the largest in the world until the 15th century and is still the largest unreinforced concrete dome ever built. It's a beautiful, perfectly symmetrical structure whose diameter is exactly equal to the Pantheon's interior height of 43.3m. Light (and rain, which drains away through 22 specially built holes) enters through an oculus, which also acts as a compression ring, absorbing and redistributing the dome's vast structural forces. Inside, you'll find the tomb of Raphael, alongside those of kings Vittorio Emanuele II and Umberto I.

WANT MORE?

For in-depth information, reviews and recommendations at your fingertips, head to the Apple App Store to purchase Lonely Planet's *Rome City Guide* iPhone app.

Alternatively, head to **Lonely Planet** (www.lonelyplanet.com/italy/rome) for planning advice, author recommendations, traveller reviews and insider tips.

Piazza Navona SQUARE

(Map p784; Corso del Rinascimento) With its ornate fountains, baroque *palazzi*, pavement cafes and colourful cast of street artists, hawkers, tourists and pigeons, Piazza Navona is central Rome's most celebrated square. Built over the ruins of the 1st-century Stadio di Domiziano (Domitian's Stadium), it was paved over in the 15th century and for almost 300 years was the city's main market. Of the piazza's three fountains, the grand centrepiece is Bernini's 1651 **Fontana dei Quattro Fiumi** (Fountain of the Four Rivers), a monumental affair depicting the rivers Nile, Ganges, Danube and Plate.

Campo de' Fiori SQUARE

(Map p784; Corso Vittorio Emanuele II) 'Il Campo', as it's known locally, is a major focus of Roman life: by day it hosts a noisy market, by night it becomes a vast, open-air pub. For centuries, this was the site of public executions, and it was here that the philosophising monk Giordano Bruno (the hooded figure in Ettore Ferrari's sinister statue) was burned at the stake in 1600.

Palazzo Farnese HISTORIC BUILDING

(Map p784; 06 6889 2818; visitefarnese@france-italia.it; guided tours free, booking obligatory; Corso Vittorio Emanuele II) Towering over Piazza Farnese, this is one of Rome's most impressive Renaissance buildings. Named after Cardinal Alessandro Farnese, it was started in 1514 by Antonio da Sangallo, carried on by Michelangelo and completed by Giacomo della Porta. Inside, frescos by Annibale Carracci are considered to be on a par with Michelangelo's in the Sistine Chapel. Visits are by guided tour only as the *palazzo* is home to the French Embassy. The twin fountains in the piazza are enormous granite baths taken from the Terme di Caracalla.

Galleria Doria Pamphilj ART MUSEUM
(Map p784; www.doriapamphilj.it; Via del Corso 305; adult/concession €9.50/7; 10am-5pm; Piazza Venezia) Behind the grey walls of Palazzo Doria Pamphilj is one of Rome's finest private art collections, with works by Raphael, Tintoretto, Brueghel and Titian. The undisputed masterpiece is the Velázquez portrait of Pope Innocent X, who grumbled that the depiction was 'too real'.

Trevi Fountain FOUNTAIN
(Map p792; M Barberini) Immortalised by Anita Ekberg's sensual dip in Fellini's *La dolce vita,* the Fontana di Trevi is Rome's largest and most famous fountain. The flamboyant baroque ensemble was designed by Nicola Salvi in 1732 and depicts Neptune's chariot being led by Tritons, with sea horses representing the moods of the sea. The water comes from the *aqua virgo,* a 1st-century-BC underground aqueduct, and the name 'Trevi' refers to the *tre vie* (three roads) that converge at the fountain. The custom is to throw a coin into the fountain, thus ensuring your return to Rome. On average about €3000 is chucked away every day.

Galleria Nazionale d'Arte Antica ART MUSEUM
(Map p792; www.galleriaborghese.it; Via delle Quattro Fontane 13; adult/EU child €5/free; 9am-7.30pm Tue-Sun; M Barberini) A must for anyone into Renaissance and baroque art, this sumptuous gallery is housed in Palazzo Barberini, one of Rome's most spectacular *palazzi*. Inside, you'll find works by Raphael, Caravaggio, Guido Reni, Bernini, Filippo Lippi and Holbein, as well as Pietro da Cortona's breathtaking *Trionfo della Divina Provvidenza* (Triumph of Divine Providence) in the main salon.

Spanish Steps MONUMENT
(Map p792; Piazza di Spagna; M Spagna) Rising above **Piazza di Spagna**, the Spanish Steps, aka the Scalinata della Trinità dei Monti, have been a magnet for foreigners since the 18th century. The piazza was named after the Spanish embassy to the Holy See, although the staircase, which was built with French money in 1725, leads to the French church, **Chiesa della Trinità dei Monti**. At the foot of the steps, the fountain of a sinking boat, the *Barcaccia* (1627), is believed to be by Pietro Bernini, father of the more famous Gian Lorenzo. Opposite, **Via dei Condotti** is Rome's top shopping strip.

Piazza del Popolo SQUARE
(Map p788; M Flaminio) This elegant landmark square was laid out in 1538 at the point of convergence of three roads – Via di Ripetta, Via del Corso and Via del Babuino – at what was then Rome's northern entrance. Guarding its southern approach are the twin 17th-century churches of **Santa Maria dei Miracoli** and **Santa Maria in Montesanto**, while on the northern flank is the **Porta del Popolo**, created by Bernini in 1655. In the centre, the 36m-high **obelisk** was brought by Augustus from Heliopolis in ancient Egypt. Rising above the piazza, **Pincio Hill** affords great views.

On the piazza's northern flank, the **Chiesa di Santa Maria del Popolo** (Map p788; 7am-noon & 4-7pm Mon-Sat, 8am-1.30pm & 4.30-7.30pm Sun) is one of Rome's earliest and richest Renaissance churches. The first chapel was built in 1099 to exorcise the ghost of Nero, who was buried on this spot and whose ghost was said to haunt the area, but in its current form it dates to 1472. Inside, the star attractions are the two magnificent Caravaggio paintings: the *Conversione di San Paolo* (Conversion of St Paul) and the *Crocifissione di San Pietro* (Crucifixion of St Peter).

Museo dell'Ara Pacis Augustae MUSEUM
(Map p788; www.arapacis.it; Lungotevere in Augusta; adult/child €6.50/free; 9am-7pm Tue-Sun;

FREE THRILLS

Surprisingly, some of Rome's most famous sights are free:

» Trevi Fountain

» Spanish Steps

» Pantheon

» Bocca della Verità

» All churches, including St Peter's Basilica

» Vatican Museums on the last Sunday of the month.

Around Piazza del Popolo (Rome)

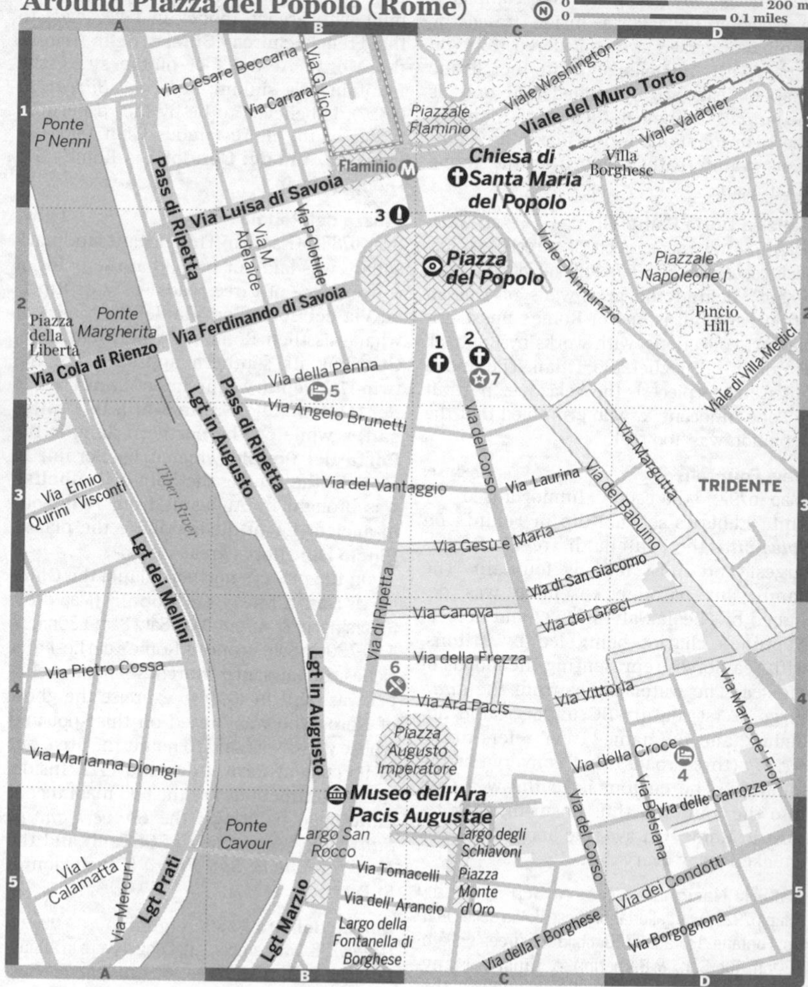

(MFlaminio) The first modern construction in Rome's historic centre, Richard Meier's controversial white pavilion houses the **Ara Pacis Augustae (Altar of Peace)**, one of the most important works of ancient Roman sculpture. The vast marble altar (it measures 11.6m by 10.6m by 3.6m) was completed in 13 BC as a monument to the peace that Augustus established both at home and abroad.

VILLA BORGHESE

Just north of the historic centre, Villa Borghese is Rome's best-known park, a good spot for a picnic and a breath of fresh air. The grounds, which were created in the 17th century by Cardinal Scipione Borghese, are accessible from Piazzale Flaminio, Pincio Hill, and the top of Via Vittorio Veneto. Bike hire is available at various points, typically costing about €5 per hour.

TOP CHOICE Museo e Galleria Borghese

MUSEUM, ART MUSEUM

(Map p776; 06 3 28 10; www.galleriaborghese.it; Piazzale del Museo Borghese; adult/EU child €8.50/2; 8.30am-7.30pm Tue-Sun; Via Pinciana) If you only have time, or inclination, for one art gallery in Rome, make it this one.

Around Piazza del Popolo (Rome)

Housing the 'queen of all private art collections', it boasts paintings by Caravaggio, Botticelli and Raphael, as well as some spectacular sculptures by Gian Lorenzo Bernini. There are too many highlights to list here, but try not to miss Bernini's *Ratto di Proserpina* (Rape of Persephone) and *Apollo e Dafne,* Antonio Canova's *Venere Vincitrice* (Victorious Venus) and the six Caravaggios in room VII. Note that you must book your ticket in advance.

Museo Nazionale Etrusco di Villa Giulia MUSEUM

(Map p776; Piazzale di Villa Giulia; adult/EU child €4/free; 8.30am-7.30pm Tue-Sun; Viale delle Belle Arti) Italy's finest collection of Etruscan treasures is beautifully housed in the 16th-century Villa Giulia. Many of the exhibits come from Etruscan burial tombs in northern Lazio, with standouts including a polychrome terracotta statue of *Apollo* and the 6th-century-BC *Sarcofago degli Sposi* (Sarcophagus of the Betrothed).

Galleria Nazionale d'Arte Moderna ART MUSEUM

(Map p776; www.gnam.beniculturali.it; Viale delle Belle Arti 131; adult/EU child €8/free; 8.30am-7.30pm Tue-Sun; Viale delle Belle Arti) In this vast belle époque palace, you'll find works by some of the most important exponents of modern art, including Canova, Modigliani, De Chirico, Klimt, Pollock and Henry Moore.

TRASTEVERE

Trastevere is one of central Rome's most vivacious neighbourhoods, a tightly packed warren of ochre *palazzi,* ivy-clad facades and photogenic lanes, ideal for aimless wandering. Taking its name from the Latin *trans Tiberium,* meaning over the Tiber, it was originally a working-class district but it has since been gentrified and it is today a trendy hang-out full of bars, trattorias and restaurants.

Basilica di Santa Maria in Trastevere CHURCH

(Map p790; Piazza Santa Maria in Trastevere; 7.30am-8pm; Viale di Trastevere) Nestled in a quiet corner of Piazza Santa Maria in Trastevere, Trastevere's picturesque focal square, this exquisite basilica is believed to be the oldest Roman church dedicated to the Virgin Mary. The original church dates to the 4th century, but a 12th-century makeover saw the addition of a Romanesque bell tower and frescoed facade. Inside it's the glittering 12th-century mosaics that are the main drawcard.

Basilica di Santa Cecilia in Trastevere CHURCH

(Map p790; Piazza di Santa Cecilia; basilica/fresco free/€2.50; basilica 9.30am-1pm & 4-7.15pm, fresco visits 10.15am & 12.30pm Mon-Fri; Viale di Trastevere) The last resting place of St Cecilia, the patron saint of music, this church merits a visit for its spectacular 13th-century fresco – Pietro Cavallini's *The Last Judgement.* Under the main basilica, you can visit excavations of several Roman houses.

TERMINI & ESQUILINO

The largest of Rome's seven hills, Esquilino (Esquiline) extends from the Colosseum up to Stazione Termini, Rome's main transport hub.

Basilica di San Pietro in Vincoli CHURCH

(Map p776; Piazza di San Pietro in Vincoli; 8am-12.30pm & 3-7pm; M Cavour) Pilgrims and art lovers flock to this church, just off Via Cavour, for two reasons: to see the chains worn by St Peter before his crucifixion (hence the church's name – St Peter in Chains) and to marvel at Michelangelo's magnificent *Moses,* the centrepiece of his unfinished tomb of Pope Julius II.

Trastevere (Rome)

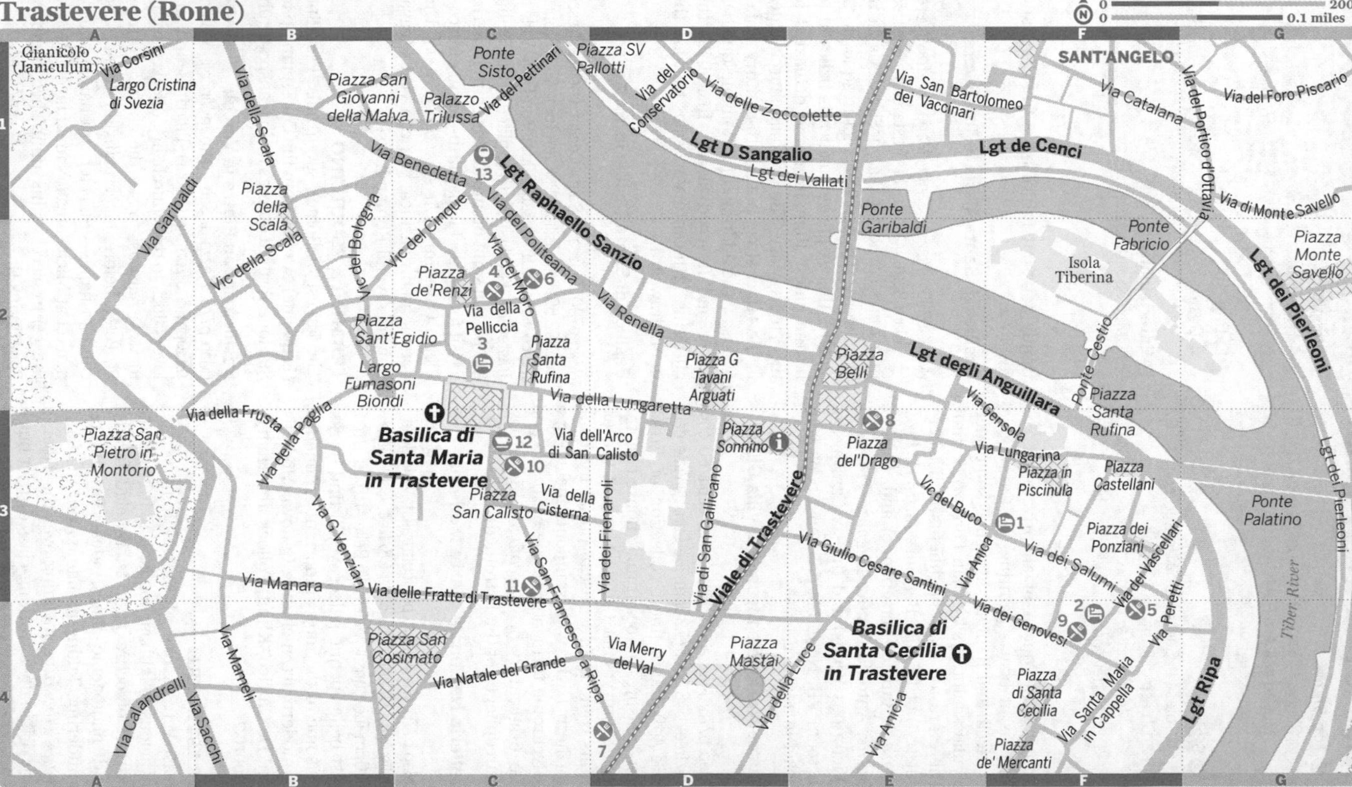

Trastevere (Rome)

Top Sights

Sleeping

Eating

Drinking

Basilica di Santa Maria Maggiore CHURCH
(Map p792; Piazza Santa Maria Maggiore; 7am-7pm; Piazza Santa Maria Maggiore) One of Rome's four patriarchal basilicas, this hulking church was built in 352 on the site of a miraculous snowfall. An architectural hybrid, it has a 14th-century Romanesque belfry, an 18th-century baroque facade, a largely baroque interior and some stunning 5th-century mosaics on the triumphal arch and nave.

Chiesa di Santa Maria degli Angeli CHURCH
(Map p792; Piazza della Repubblica; 7am-6.30pm Mon-Sat, to 7.30pm Sun; M Repubblica) Facing onto Piazza della Repubblica, this cavernous church occupies what was once the central hall of Diocletian's enormous baths complex. Its most interesting feature is the double meridian in the transept.

SAN GIOVANNI & CELIO

Basilica di San Giovanni in Laterano CHURCH
(Map p776; Piazza di San Giovanni in Laterano 4; 7am-6.30pm; M San Giovanni) For a thousand years, this huge white basilica was the most important church in Christendom. Consecrated in 324, it was the first Christian basilica to be built in Rome and until the late 14th century was the Pope's principal residence. Nowadays it's Rome's official cathedral and the Pope's seat as Bishop of Rome. It has been rebuilt various times over the centuries, most notably in the late 18th century, when the monumental facade was added.

Basilica di San Clemente CHURCH
(Map p776; Via di San Giovanni in Laterano; admission basilica/excavations free/€5; 9am-12.30pm & 3-6pm Mon-Sat, noon-6pm Sun; M Colosseo) Nowhere better illustrates the various stages of Rome's ancient history than this fascinating, multi-layered church. Near the Colosseum (head up the hill towards San Giovanni), the 12th-century church at street level was built

MUSEO NAZIONALE ROMANO

Spread over four sites, the **Museo Nazionale Romano** (National Roman Museum) houses one of the world's most important collections of classical art and statuary. A combined ticket including each of the sites costs adult/EU child €7/free and is valid for three days.

» **Palazzo Massimo alle Terme** ART MUSEUM
(Map p792; Largo di Villa Peretti 1; 9am-7.45pm Tue-Sun; M Termini) A fabulous museum with amazing frescos and wall paintings.

» **Terme di Diocleziano** MUSEUM
(Map p792; Via Enrico de Nicola 79; 9am-7.45pm Tue-Sun; M Termini) Housed in the Terme di Diocleziano (Diocletian's Baths), ancient Rome's largest baths complex.

» **Palazzo Altemps** MUSEUM
(Map p784; Piazza Sant'Apollinare 44; 9am-7.45pm Tue-Sun; Corso del Rinascimento) Boasts the best of the museum's classical sculpture, including the famous Ludovisi collection.

» **Crypta Balbi** MUSEUM
(Map p784; Via delle Botteghe Oscure 31; 9am-7.45pm Tue-Sun; Largo di Torre Argentina) Set atop an ancient Roman theatre, the Teatro di Balbus (13 BC).

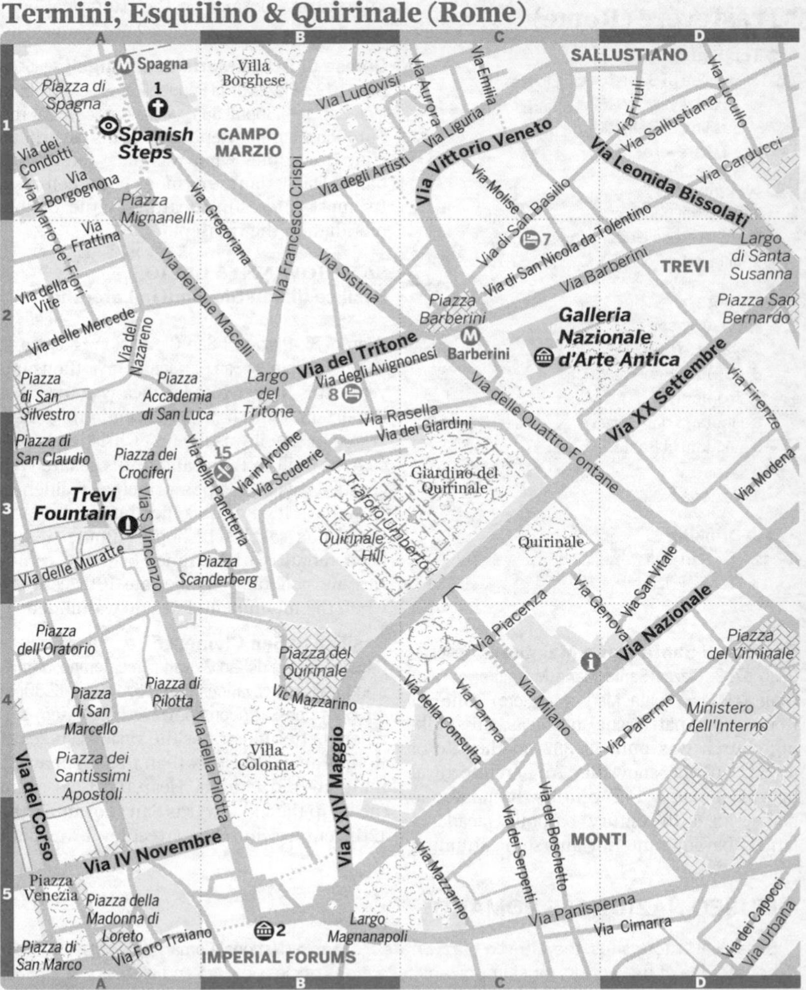

over a 4th-century church that was, in turn, built over a 1st-century Roman house with a temple dedicated to the pagan god Mithras.

Terme di Caracalla RUINS

(Map p776; Via delle Terme di Caracalla 52; adult/EU child €6/free; 9am-1hr before sunset Tue-Sun, to 2pm Mon; Circo Massimo) The vast ruins of the Terme di Caracalla are an awe-inspiring sight. Begun by Caracalla and inaugurated in 217, the 10-hectare leisure complex could hold up to 1600 people and included richly decorated pools, gymnasiums, libraries, shops and gardens. The ruins are now used to stage summer opera.

VIA APPIA ANTICA

The *regina viarum* (queen of roads), Via Appia Antica (Appian Way) is one of the world's oldest roads. Named after Appius Claudius Caecus, who laid the first 90km section in 312 BC, it was extended in 190 BC to reach Brindisi some 540km away on the Adriatic coast. The road, flanked by exclusive residential villas, is rich in ruins and history – this is where Spartacus and 6000 of his slave rebels were crucified in 71 BC, and it's here that you'll find Rome's most celebrated catacombs. These were built as communal burial grounds by the

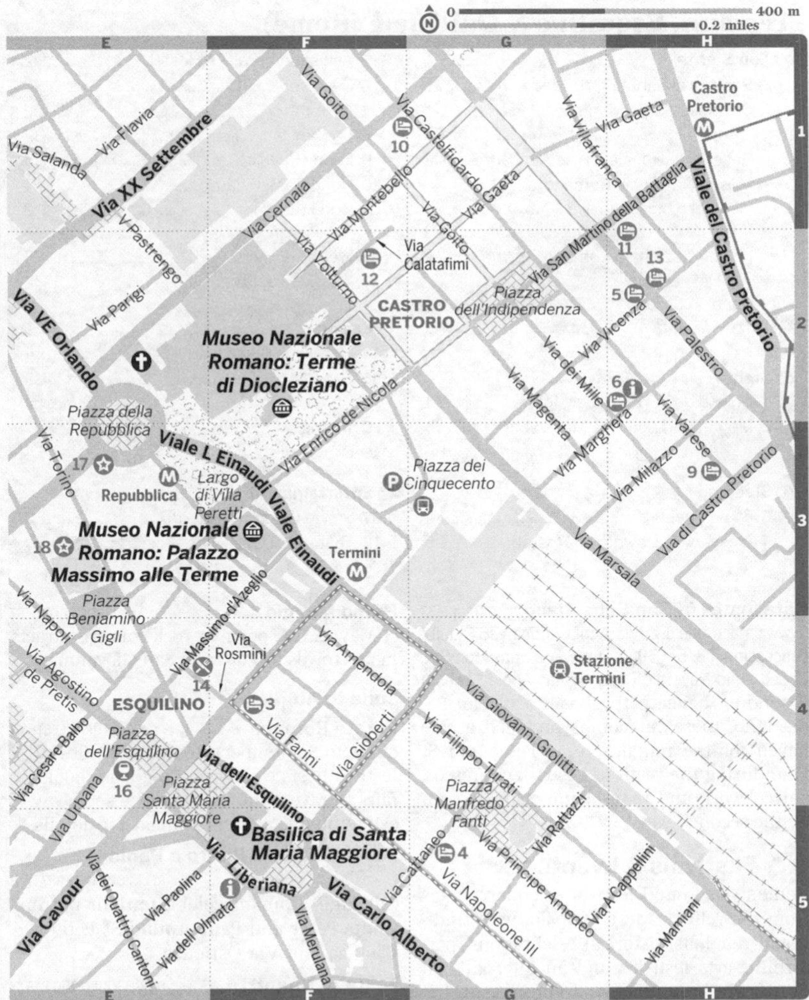

early Christians. Their belief in the Resurrection meant that they couldn't cremate their dead, as was the custom at the time, while persecution meant that they needed somewhere hidden to bury their dead. Roman law also forbade burial within the city walls.

To get to Via Appia Antica, take Metro Line A to Colli Albani, then bus 660, or bus 118 from the Piramide metro station. It's traffic-free on Sunday if you want to walk or cycle it. For information, bike hire or to join a guided tour, head to the **Appia Antica Regional Park Information Point** (☎06 513 53 16; www.parcoappiaantica.org; Via Appia Antica 58-60; ⌚9.30am-1.30pm & 2-5.30pm; 🚌Via Appia Antica).

Catacombs of San Callisto CATACOMBS
(www.catacombe.roma.it; Via Appia Antica 110; adult/child €8/free; ⌚9am-noon & 2-5pm Thu-Tue, closed Feb; 🚌Via Appia Antica) These are Rome's largest, most famous and busiest catacombs. Dating to the end of the 2nd century, they once formed part of a tunnel complex extending for some 20km. Excavations have so far unearthed the tombs of 16 popes and thousands of early Christians.

Termini, Esquilino & Quirinale (Rome)

Top Sights

Basilica di Santa Maria Maggiore F5
Chiesa di Santa Maria degli Angeli E2
Galleria Nazionale d'Arte Antica C2
Museo Nazionale Romano: Palazzo Massimo alle Terme F3
Museo Nazionale Romano: Terme di Diocleziano F2
Spanish Steps A1
Trevi Fountain A3

Sights

1 Chiesa della Trinità dei Monti A1
2 Mercati di Traiano & Museo dei Fori Imperiali B5

Sleeping

3 58 Le Real B&B F4
4 Alessandro Downtown Hostel G5
5 Alessandro Palace Hostel H2
6 Beehive H2
7 Daphne Inn C2
8 Daphne Inn B2
9 Funny Palace H3
10 Hotel Castelfidardo F1
11 Hotel Dolomiti H2
Relais Conte di Cavour .... (see 3)
12 Welrome F2
13 Yellow H2

Eating

14 La Gallina Bianca E4
15 San Crispino B3

Drinking

16 Orbis E4

Entertainment

17 Space Cinema Moderno E3
18 Teatro dell'Opera E3

Catacombs of San Sebastiano CATACOMBS
(www.catacombe.org; Via Appia Antica 136; adult/concession €8/5; 9am-noon & 2-5pm Mon-Sat, closed mid-Nov–mid-Dec; Via Appia Antica) Extending beneath the Basilica di San Sebastiano, these catacombs provided a safe haven for the remains of St Peter and St Paul during the reign of Vespasian. Frescos, stucco work and mausoleums can be seen on the second level.

Festivals & Events

Rome's year-round festival calendar ranges from the religious to the ribald, with traditional religious/historical celebrations, performing-arts festivals and an international film festival. Summer and autumn are the best times to catch an event.

March to May

Easter RELIGIOUS CELEBRATION
On Good Friday the Pope leads a candlelit procession around the Colosseum. At noon on Easter Sunday he blesses the crowds in St Peter's Sq.

Settimana della Cultura CULTURE WEEK
(April & May) Public museums and galleries open free of charge during culture week.

Natale di Roma HISTORIC FESTIVITIES
(21 April) Rome celebrates its birthday with music, historical recreations, fireworks and free entry to many museums.

Primo Maggio ROCK CONCERT
(1 May) A free open-air rock concert attracts huge crowds to Piazza di San Giovanni.

June to August

Estate Romana CULTURAL FESTIVAL
(June to September) Rome's big cultural festival hosts events ranging from book fairs to raves and gay parties – see www.estateromana.comune.roma.it for details.

Festa dei Santi Pietro e Paolo RELIGIOUS CELEBRATION
(29 June) Romans celebrate their patron saints Peter and Paul around St Peter's Basilica and Via Ostiense.

Festa di Noantri NEIGHBOURHOOD PARTY
(last two weeks in July) Trastevere's annual party involves plenty of food, wine, prayer and dancing.

Festa della Madonna della Neve RELIGIOUS CELEBRATION
(5 August) A miraculous 4th-century snowfall is celebrated at the Basilica di Santa Maria Maggiore.

September to November

Romaeuropa MUSIC & DANCE FESTIVAL
(late September to November) International performers take to the stage for Rome's premier music and dance festival – listings on http://romaeuropa.net.

Festival Internazionale del Film di Roma FILM FESTIVAL
(late October) Held at the Auditorium Parco della Musica, Rome's film festival rolls out the red carpet for big-screen big shots – see www.romacinemafest.it.

Sleeping

While there's plenty of choice, accommodation in Rome tends to be expensive. If you can afford it, the best place to stay is in the *centro storico,* but if you're on a tight budget you'll probably end up in the Termini area, where most of the hostels and cheap *pensioni* (guest houses) are located. You'll find a full list of accommodation options (with prices) at www.060608.it.

Always try to book ahead, even if it's just for the first night. But if you arrive without a booking, there's a hotel **reservation service** (☎06 699 10 00; booking fee €3; ⏲7am-10pm) next to the tourist office at Stazione Termini.

ANCIENT ROME

Nicolas Inn B&B €€
(Map p780; ☎06 976 18 483; www.nicolasinn.com; Via Cavour 295; d €100-180; ❄📶) Visitors love this bright B&B at the bottom of Via Cavour, a stone's throw from the Imperial Forums. Run by a welcoming couple, it has four big guestrooms, each with homely furnishings, colourful pictures and en suite bathrooms.

Duca d'Alba HOTEL €€€
(Map p780; ☎06 48 44 71; www.hotelducadalba.it; Via Leonina 14; s €70-210, d €80-260; ❄📶) A refined four-star hotel on an atmospheric cobbled street near Cavour metro station. It's a tight squeeze but the individually decorated guestrooms are sleek and stylish and facilities include a basement fitness room.

THE VATICAN

Hotel Bramante HOTEL €€€
(Map p776; ☎06 688 06 426; www.hotelbramante.com; Via delle Palline 24; s €100-160, d €140-230; ❄📶) Housed in a Renaissance *palazzo* in the shadow of the Vatican walls, this charming hotel is a model of classical elegance. Antique furniture, wood-beamed ceilings, marble bathrooms and fresh flowers combine to create an inviting small-inn feel.

Colors Hotel & Hostel HOSTEL, HOTEL €
(Map p776; ☎06 687 40 30; www.colorshotel.com; Via Boezio 31; dm €25-27, s €50-100, d €55-135; ❄@📶) Fresh from a recent makeover, this laid-back hostel-cum-hotel near the Vatican has cheery, multicoloured dorms (for 18- to 35-year-olds only), attractive private rooms and welcoming staff. Rooms with shared bathrooms are available at cheaper rates. Cash only.

> **DON'T MISS**
>
> **THROUGH THE KEYHOLE**
>
> Up in the **Aventino** district you'll find one of Rome's best views. At the southern end of Via Santa Sabina stands the **Priorato dei Cavalieri di Malta**, the headquarters of the Cavalieri di Malta (Knights of Malta). The building is closed to the public but look through its keyhole and you'll see the dome of St Peter's perfectly aligned at the end of a hedge-lined avenue.

HISTORIC CENTRE

TOP CHOICE **Daphne Inn** BOUTIQUE HOTEL €€
(Map p792; ☎06 874 50 086; www.daphne-rome.com; Via di San Basilio 55 & Via degli Avignonesi 20; s €110-160, d €90-200, ste €320-550; ❄@📶) Daphne is a gem. Spread over two sites near Piazza Barberini, it offers value for money, exceptional service and chic rooms. These come in various shapes and sizes but the overall look is minimalist modern with cooling earth tones and linear, unfussy furniture. Extras include irons and boards, bathrobes and tea- and coffee-making sets.

Hotel Panda HOTEL €
(Map p788; ☎06 678 01 79; www.hotelpanda.it; Via della Croce 35; s €65-80, d €85-110, tr €120-140, ❄📶) A superb position near the Spanish Steps, attractive high-ceilinged rooms and honest rates ensure a year-round stream of travellers to this budget classic. Air-con costs €6 and you can get breakfast at a nearby bar for €5. Cheaper rooms with shared bathrooms are available.

Okapi Rooms HOTEL €€
(Map p788; ☎06 3260 9815; www.okapirooms.it; Via della Penna 57; s €65-80, d €85-120; ❄📶) Occupying a 19th-century town house near Piazza del Popolo, the Okapi is an excellent low-midrange choice. Rooms, which are small and simple, come with cream walls, terracotta-tiled floors and double-glazed windows. Some also have ancient-style carvings and several have tiny terraces.

Relais Palazzo Taverna BOUTIQUE HOTEL €€
(Map p784; ☎06 203 98 064; www.relaispalazzotaverna.com; Via dei Gabrielli 92; s €70-140,

d €100-180; ❄📶) This cracking boutique hotel is superbly located in the heart of the historic centre. Its 11 individually decorated rooms sport a contemporary look with grey parquet floors, hand-printed wallpaper and funky, floral motifs.

Hotel Raphaël LUXURY HOTEL €€€
(Map p784; ☎06 68 28 31; www.raphaelhotel.com; Largo Febo 2; s €160-300, d €220-350; ❄@) An ivy-clad landmark just off Piazza Navona, the Raphaël is a Roman institution. With its gallery lobby – look out for the Picasso ceramics and Miro lithographs – sleek Richard Meier–designed rooms and panoramic rooftop restaurant, it knows how to lay out the red carpet. Breakfast costs extra.

TRASTEVERE

TOP CHOICE **Maria-Rosa Guesthouse** B&B €
(Map p790; ☎338 770 00 67; www.maria-rosa.it; Via dei Vascellari; s €60-70, d €75-85, q €120-130;❄@📶) A home away from home, this is a delightful little B&B on the 3rd floor of a Trastevere town house. It's a simple affair with two guestrooms sharing a single bathroom and a small common area, but the sunlight, pot plants and books create a lovely, warm atmosphere. The owner, Sylvie, is a fount of local knowledge and goes out of her way to help.

Arco del Lauro B&B €€
(Map p790; ☎06 978 40 350; www.arcodellauro.it; Via Arco de' Tolomei 27-29; d €85-145, q €130-180;❄@📶) This friendly B&B is in a medieval *palazzo* in Trastevere's quieter eastern half. The five decent-sized double rooms, all on the ground floor, sport an understated modern look with white walls, parquet and modern furnishings, while the one quad retains a high, wood-beamed ceiling. Reception is open until 3pm, after which you'll need to phone.

Villa della Fonte HOTEL €€
(Map p790; ☎06 580 37 97; www.villafonte.com; Via della Fonte dell'Olio 8; s €90-130, d €130-190; ❄📶) Near Piazza Santa Maria in Trastevere, this charming little hotel is housed in an ivy-clad 17th-century *palazzo*. Its five rooms are small but tastefully decorated with white walls, earth-coloured floors and modern en suite bathrooms.

TERMINI & ESQUILINO

Beehive HOSTEL €
(Map p792; ☎06 447 04 553; www.the-beehive.com; Via Marghera 8; dm €20-25, d €70-80; @📶) A brilliant boutique hostel run by an environmentally conscious American couple, the Beehive boasts stylish decor, a vegetarian cafe (open only for breakfast and Sunday brunch) and a small yoga studio. Beds are in a spotless, eight-person mixed dorm or in one of six double rooms.

58 Le Real B&B B&B €€
(Map p792; ☎06 482 35 66; www.lerealdeluxe.com; Via Cavour 58; r €70-155; ❄📶) This swish nine-room B&B is on the 4th floor of a town house on busy Via Cavour. Rooms are small but stylish with leather armchairs, plasma TVs, Murano chandeliers, polished-wood bedsteads and parquet floors. The same people also run the nearby **Relais Conte di Cavour** (Map p792; ☎06 482 16 38; www.relaiscontedicavour.com; Via Farini 16; r €100-250).

Welrome PENSION €
(Map p792; ☎06 478 24 343; www.welrome.it; Via Calatafimi 15-19; s €50-100, d €60-110; 📶) This is a lovely, low-key hotel not far from Termini. Owner Mary takes great pride in looking after her guests, and her seven rooms provide welcome respite from Rome's relentless streets. Breakfast costs extra, but there are kettles and fridges for guest use.

Hotel Dolomiti HOTEL €€
(Map p792; ☎06 495 72 56; www.hotel-dolomiti.it; Via San Martino della Battaglia 11; s €60-100, d €80-150; ❄@📶) A warm, family-run hotel, the Dolomiti is a reliable choice. Rooms, which are colour coordinated in shades of cream, red and cherry-wood, are spread over three floors of a big *palazzo* not far from Termini.

Funny Palace HOSTEL €
(Map p792; ☎06 447 03 523; www.funnyhostel.com; Via Varese 33; dm €15-25, s €30-70, d €55-100; @) To find this great little backpacker hostel head for the Splashnet laundry, which doubles as the reception and internet point. Upstairs, the mixed dorms are big and well maintained, while the private rooms reveal a simple, homey look. No credit cards.

Alessandro Palace Hostel HOSTEL €
(Map p792; ☎06 44 61 958; www.hostelsalessandro.com; Via Vicenza 42; dm €18-25, d €66-120, tr €58-120; ❄@📶) A long-standing favourite in the Termini area, this slick hostel offers spick-and-span hotel-style rooms, as well as dorms sleeping from four to eight. It's run by a friendly international crew, has 24-hour reception and there's a bar with satellite TV. On the other side of Termini, **Alessandro**

Downtown Hostel (Map p792; ☎06 443 40 147; Via Cattaneo 23) offers more of the same.

Yellow HOSTEL €
(Map p792; ☎06 493 82 682; www.the-yellow.com; Via Palestro 44; dm €18-35; ❄@🛜) In the Termini district, this popular hostel caters to a young, party-loving crowd (there's an age limit – 18 to 40). Dorms, which sleep from four to 12 people in bunk beds, are mixed, and while clean and reasonably sized, they can be noisy. There's no common room but most people hang out in the bar next door.

Hotel Castelfidardo PENSION €
(Map p792; ☎06 446 46 38; www.hotelcastelfidardo.com; Via Castelfidardo 31; s €40-70, d €60-100; ❄🛜) A simple, old-school outfit not far from Stazione Termini.

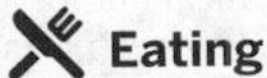

Eating

Eating out is one of the great joys of visiting Rome and everywhere you go you'll find trattorias, pizzerias and restaurants. The focus is very much on traditional Italian cooking, and the vast majority of places, particularly the smaller family-run trattorias, keep to tried-and-tested Roman dishes.

The best places to eat are in the historic centre and Trastevere, but there are also excellent choices in San Lorenzo (the area east of Stazione Termini) and Testaccio. You'll need to choose carefully in the Termini neighbourhood and around the Vatican, as both areas are full of overpriced tourist traps.

Roman specialities include *trippa alla romana* (tripe with potatoes, tomato and pecorino cheese), *fiori di zucca* (fried courgette flowers) and *carciofi alla romana* (artichokes with garlic, mint and parsley). Of the pastas, *cacio e pepe* (with pecorino cheese, black pepper and olive oil) and *all'amatriciana* (with tomato, pancetta and chilli) are Roman favourites.

THE VATICAN

Dino e Tony TRATTORIA €€
(Map p776; ☎06 3973 3284; Via Leone IV 60; mains €12; ⏰Mon-Sat) Something of a rarity, Dino e Tony is an authentic trattoria in the Vatican area. Kick off with the monumental antipasto, a minor meal in its own right, before plunging into its signature dish, *rigatoni all'amatriciana*. Finish up with a *granita di caffé,* a crushed iced coffee served with a full inch of whipped cream.

GELATO GALORE

To get the best out of Rome's *gelaterie* (ice-cream shops) look for the words '*produzione proprio*', meaning 'own production'. As a rough guide, expect to pay between €1.50 and €3.50 for a *cono* (cone) or *coppa* (tub). Here is a choice of the city's finest:

» **San Crispino** (Map p792; Via della Panetteria 42) Near the Trevi Fountain, it serves natural, seasonal flavours – think crema with honey – in tubs only.

» **Old Bridge** (Map p776; Via Bastioni di Michelangelo 5) Just right for a pick-me-up after the Vatican Museums.

» **Tre Scalini** (Map p784; Piazza Navona 30) A Piazza Navona spot famous for *tartufo nero*, a €10 ball of chocolate ice cream filled with chunks of choc and served with cream.

» **Gelateria Giolitti** (Map p784; Via degli Uffici del Vicario 40) Rome's most famous gelateria, near the Pantheon.

HISTORIC CENTRE

TOP CHOICE **Pizzeria da Baffetto** PIZZA €
(Map p784; Via del Governo Vecchio 114; pizzas €6-9; ⏰6.30pm-midnight) For the full-on Roman pizza experience get down to this local institution. Meals here are raucous, chaotic and fast, but the thin-crust pizzas are good and the vibe is fun. To partake, join the queue and wait to be squeezed in wherever there's room. There's also a **Baffetto 2** (Map p784; Piazza del Teatro di Pompeo 18; ⏰6.30pm-12.30am Mon-Fri, 12.30-3.30pm & 6.30pm-12.30am Sat & Sun) near Campo de' Fiori.

Maccheroni TRATTORIA €€
(Map p784; ☎06 6830 7895; Piazza delle Coppelle 44; mains €13; ⏰Mon-Sat) With its classic vintage interior, attractive setting near the Pantheon, and traditional menu, this is the archetypal *centro storico* trattoria. Locals and tourists alike flock here to dine on Roman stalwarts such as *tonnarelli al cacio e pepe* (pasta with cheese and pepper) and *carciofo alla romana* (Roman style artichoke).

Forno di Campo de' Fiori BAKERY €
(Map p784; Campo de' Fiori 22; pizza slices from €2) This is one of Rome's best bakeries, serving bread, panini and delicious straight-from-the-oven pizza *al taglio* (by the slice).

Aficionados claim you should order pizza *bianca* (white pizza), although the panini and pizza *rossa* (with tomato) are just as good.

Ditirambo TRATTORIA €€
(Map p784; ☎06 687 16 26; Piazza della Cancelleria 72; mains €16; ⏰closed Mon lunch; ✓) This hugely popular new-wave trattoria near Campo de' Fiori offers a laid-back, unpretentious atmosphere and innovative, organic cooking. Vegetarians are well catered for, as are seafood fans, with dishes such as turbot roulade with aubergine and mint. Book ahead.

Vineria Roscioli DELICATESSEN, RESTAURANT €€€
(Map p784; ☎06 687 52 87; Via dei Giubbonari 21; mains €20; ⏰Mon-Sat) This deli/restaurant is a foodie paradise. Under the brick arches, you'll find a mouth-watering array of olive oils, conserves, cheeses and hams, while out back the chic restaurant serves sophisticated Italian dishes. Wine buffs can peruse the 1100-strong wine list. Reservations recommended.

Gusto PIZZA, RESTAURANT €€
(Map p788; ☎06 322 62 73; Piazza Augusto Imperatore 9; pizzas/buffet menus €9/10) All exposed brickwork and industrial chic, this big, '90s-style warehouse operation is a lunchtime favourite with office workers, serving everything from thick-crust pizza to cheese platters, salads and overpriced fusion food. At lunch the set menus are a bargain.

Da Tonino TRATTORIA €
(Map p784; Via del Governo Vecchio 18; mains €7; ⏰Mon-Sat) Defiantly old-school, this traditional neighbourhood trattoria sits among the bohemian boutiques and trendy bars on Via del Governo Vecchio. Don't expect frills (or even menus), just tasty Roman cooking served fast and served cheap.

TRASTEVERE

Hostaria dar Buttero TRATTORIA €€
(Map p790; ☎06 580 05 17; Via della Lungaretta; mains €11; ⏰Mon-Sat) On Trastevere's touristy main strip – on the quieter eastern side, though – this is a friendly old-school trattoria. The menu lists all the usual pastas, grilled meats and pizzas (evenings only), but the food is well cooked, the atmosphere is convivial and the prices are inviting. In summer, go for a table in the small back garden.

Osteria da Lucia TRATTORIA €€
(☎06 580 36 01; Vicolo del Mattinato 2; mains €12.50; ⏰Tue-Sun) Hidden away on an atmospheric cobbled backstreet, da Lucia is a terrific neighbourhood trattoria. It's a wonderful place to get your teeth into some authentic Roman soul food, such as *spaghetti alla gricia* (with pancetta and cheese) and tiramisu.

Paris RESTAURANT €€€
(Map p790; ☎06 581 53 78; Piazza San Calisto 7; mains €18; ⏰lunch & dinner Tue-Sat, lunch Sun) Outside of the Jewish Ghetto, this elegant, old-fashioned restaurant is the best place for traditional Roman-Jewish cooking. Specialities include *carciofi alle giudia* (deep-fried artichoke) and *fritto misto con baccalà* (fried vegetables with salted cod).

Da Enzo TRATTORIA €
(Map p790; ☎06 581 83 55; Via dei Vascellari 29; mains €9; ⏰Mon-Sat) Lunching locals queue for a bowl of hearty pasta at this cheery trattoria in Trastevere's eastern streets. It's not the place for a long, lingering meal but for a no-nonsense *rigatoni alla carbonara* (pasta carbonara) it'll do just fine.

Da Augusto TRATTORIA €
(Map p790; Piazza de' Renzi 15; mains €8; ⏰lunch & dinner Mon-Fri, lunch Sat) With a few rickety tables outside and a crowded interior, this earthy Trastevere trattoria is the real McCoy. The menu is rigorously Roman, so expect stalwarts such as *rigatoni all'amatriciana* and *ossobuco con piselli* (ossobuco with peas). Cash only.

Le Mani in Pasta RESTAURANT €€€
(Map p790; ☎06 581 60 17; Via dei Genovesi 37; mains €18; ⏰Tue-Sun) This rustic Trastevere restaurant has an open kitchen that serves up delicious fresh pasta dishes, grilled meats and fresh seafood. It's a well-known spot, so try to book ahead for dinner.

Pizzeria Ivo PIZZERIA €
(Map p790; Via di San Francesco a Ripa 158; pizzas €6; ⏰5.30pm-midnight Wed-Mon) A perennially popular pizzeria, Ivo fits the stereotype. With the TV on in the corner and waiters skilfully manoeuvring plates over the noisy hordes, diners chow down on classic thin-crust pizzas.

Also recommended:

Frontoni DELICATESSEN €
(Map p790; Viale di Trastevere 52-56; pastas €6) Grab a panino at the downstairs deli or head upstairs for a bowl of pasta.

Forno la Renella BAKERY €
(Map p790; Via del Moro 15-16; pizza slices from €2) Choose from the daily batch of wood-fired pizza, bread, and biscuits.

TESTACCIO

Pizzeria Remo PIZZA €

(Map p776; Piazza Santa Maria Liberatice 44; pizzas €6; ⌚7.30pm-1am Mon-Sat) This rowdy Testaccio spot is one of the city's most popular pizzerias. Queues are the norm but the large, thin-crust pizzas and delicious bruschetta (toasted bread drizzled with olive oil and selected toppings) make the wait bearable.

Volpetti Più TAVOLA CALDA €

(Map p776; Via Volta 8; mains €6; ⌚Mon-Sat) Next to the ravishing deli of the same name, this upmarket canteen is one of the few places in town where you can sit down and eat well for less than €15. Grab a tray and choose from the sumptuous spread of pizza, pasta, soup, meat, vegetables and fried nibbles.

TERMINI & ESQUILINO

Pommidoro TRATTORIA €€

(Map p776; ☎06 445 26 92; Piazza dei Sanniti 44; mains €12; ⌚Mon-Sat) A long-standing favourite in the San Lorenzo area east of Termini, Pommidoro continues to win diners over with its no-fuss traditional food. Celebs sometimes drop by – Nicole Kidman and Fabio Capello have both dined here – but it remains an unpretentious spot with a laid-back vibe and excellent food.

Tram Tram TRATTORIA €€

(Map p776; ☎06 49 04 16; Via dei Reti 44; mains €16; ⌚Tue-Sun) Dressed up to look like an old-fashioned trattoria, and named after the trams that rattle past outside, this is a trendy San Lorenzo eatery. It offers traditional dishes with a focus on seafood and rustic southern Italian cuisine. There's also an excellent wine list highlighting Italian producers.

TOP CHOICE **Panella L'Arte del Pane** BAKERY €

(Map p776; Via Merulana 54; pizza slices from €2.50; ⌚8am-midnight Mon-Wed, Fri & Sat, to 2pm Thu, 8.30am-2pm Sun) Not far from the Basilica di Santa Maria Maggiore, this fabulous bakery is a great place for a quick lunch. Once you've chosen from the opulent array of sliced pizza, focaccia, crêpes, and *arancini* (fried rice balls), adjourn to an outdoor table or perch on a stool inside.

La Gallina Bianca RESTAURANT €€

(Map p792; ☎06 474 37 77; Via Rosmini 9; pizzas from €8, mains €15) On a small street off Via Cavour, this choice restaurant offers a welcome respite from the tourist rip-off joints near Termini. It specialises in grilled vegetables and meats, although its supersized salads (€9.50) make for a lovely lunch. Pizza is also available.

Drinking

Drinking in Rome is all about looking the part and enjoying the atmosphere. There are hundreds of bars and cafes across the city, ranging from neighbourhood hang-outs to elegant streetside cafes, dressy lounge bars and Irish-theme pubs. During the day, bars are generally for a quick coffee, often taken standing, while early evening sees the city's hip young drinkers descend on the fashionable watering holes for an *aperitivo* (aperitif).

Much of the action is in the *centro storico*. Campo de' Fiori is popular with young drinkers and can get very rowdy. For a more upmarket scene check out the bars in the lanes around Piazza Navona. Over the river, Trastevere is another popular spot with dozens of bars and pubs. To the east of Termini, San Lorenzo is a favourite of students and bohemian uptowners.

Salotto 42 BAR

(Map p784; www.salotto42.it; Piazza di Pietra; ⌚10am-2am Tue-Sat, to midnight Sun) Run by a Swedish model and her Italian partner, this hip, glamorous lounge bar sports soft sofas, coffee-table books and an excellent *aperitivo* spread. Brunch is also served at weekends.

Caffè Sant'Eustachio CAFE

(Map p784; Piazza Sant'Eustachio 82; ⌚8.30am-1am) This small unassuming place, generally three-deep at the bar, boasts Rome's best coffee. Served sugared and with a layer of froth, the espresso is a smooth, creamy blend with a reassuringly strong caffeine kick.

Freni e Frizioni BAR

(Map p790; Via del Politeama 4-6; www.freniefrizioni.com; ⌚10am-2am) A favourite Trastevere hang-out, housed in a former garage (hence the name – 'brakes and clutches') and spilling out onto a small piazza. The crowd is young and fashionable, the mojitos are great and the *aperitivo* spread well worth investigating.

La Tazza d'Oro CAFE

(Map p784; Via degli Orfani 84-86; ⌚Mon-Sat) A busy, stand-up bar that serves a superb espresso and a range of delicious coffee concoctions, such as *granita di caffè*, a crushed-ice coffee with a big dollop of cream, and *parfait di caffè*, a €3 coffee mousse.

Vineria Reggio WINE BAR
(Map p784; Campo de' Fiori 15; ⏲8.30am-2am Mon-Sat) The coolest of the Campo de' Fiori bars, this place is a good spot to watch the nightly *campo* circus. It has a small, bottle-lined interior and several outside tables.

Caffè Capitolino CAFE
(Map p780; Piazzale Caffarelli) Hidden behind the Capitoline Museums, this stylish rooftop cafe commands memorable views. It's a good place for a museum time out, although you don't need a ticket to drink here – it's accessible via an entrance behind Piazza dei Conservatori.

Bar San Calisto BAR
(Map p790; Piazza San Calisto; ⏲6am-2.30am Mon-Sat) Intellectuals, bohemians, local alcoholics, foreign students – they all flock to this down-at-heel Trastevere landmark for the cheap prices and laid-back atmosphere. It's famous for its chocolate, drunk hot or eaten as ice cream.

Bar della Pace CAFE
(Map p784; Via della Pace 3-7; ⏲8.30am-3am Tue-Sun, 5pm-3am Mon) The archetypal dolce vita bar. With its art nouveau interior, ivy-clad facade and well-dressed customers, it's the very epitome of Italian style.

Bar Arco degli Aurunci BAR
(Map p776; Via degli Aurunci 42; ⏲8am-2am) On a car-free piazza in San Lorenzo, this attractive modern bar is a cool spot for a drink or light meal. Aperitifs are served between 7pm and 9pm.

☆ Entertainment

Rome has a thriving cultural scene, with a year-round calendar of concerts, performances and festivals. In summer, the Estate Romana festival sponsors hundreds of cultural events, many of which are staged in atmospheric parks, piazzas and churches. Autumn is another good time, with festivals dedicated to dance, drama and jazz.

Listings guides include *Roma C'è* (www.romace.it, in Italian; €1) and *Trova Roma*, a free insert with *La Repubblica* newspaper every Thursday. Both are available at newsstands. Up-coming events are also listed on www.turismoroma.it and wwwinromenow.com.

Two good ticket agencies are **Orbis** (Map p792; ☎06 482 74 03; Piazza dell'Esquilino 37; ⏲9.30am-1pm & 4-7.30pm Mon-Fri, 9.30am-1pm Sat), which accepts cash payment only, and the online agency **Hello** (☎800 90 70 80; www.helloticket.it, in Italian).

Classical Music & Opera

Rome's cultural hub and premier concert complex is the **Auditorium Parco della Musica** (☎06 8024 1281; www.auditorium.com; Viale Pietro de Coubertin 34). With its three concert halls and 3000-seat open-air arena, it stages everything from classical-music concerts to tango exhibitions, book readings and film screenings. The auditorium is also home to Rome's top orchestra, the world-class **Orchestra dell'Accademia Nazionale di Santa Cecilia** (☎box office 06 808 20 58; www.santacecilia.it).

The **Accademia Filarmonica Romana** (☎06 320 17 52; www.filarmonicaromana.org) organises classical- and chamber-music concerts, as well as opera, ballet and multimedia events at the **Teatro Olimpico** (☎06 326 59 91; www.teatroolimpico.it; Piazza Gentile da Fabriano 17).

Rome's opera season runs from December to June. The main venue is the **Teatro dell'Opera** (Map p792; ☎box office 06 481 60 255; www.operaroma.it; Piazza Beniamino Gigli 7), which also houses the city's ballet company. Ticket prices tend to be steep. In summer, opera is performed outdoors at the spectacular Terme di Caracalla.

Nightclubs & Live Music

Rome is not one of Europe's great clubbing capitals, but there is action out there. The scene is centred on Testaccio and the Ostiense area, although you'll also find places in Trastevere and the *centro storico*. You'll need to dress the part for the big clubs, which can be tricky to get into, especially for groups of men. Gigs are often listed for 10pm but don't kick off until 11pm, while clubs rarely hot up much before midnight or 1am. Admission is often free but drinks are expensive, typically €10 to €15. Note also that many clubs shut between mid-June and mid-September.

Circolo degli Artisti CLUB, LIVE MUSIC
(www.circolodegliartisti.it; Via Casilina Vecchia 42; ⏲Tue-Sun) Out in the up-coming Pigneto district – to the southeast of Stazione Termini – this fantastic club is a centre of the city's underground music scene, staging big names and emerging talents. It also hosts multimedia performances, film projections and cultural events.

Alexanderplatz JAZZ CLUB
(Map p776; ☎06 397 42 171; www.alexanderplatz.it; Via Ostia 9) Rome's top jazz joint attracts top international performers and a passionate, knowledgeable crowd. In July and August the club ups sticks and transfers to the grounds of Villa Celimontana.

Goa CLUB
(Via Libetta 13; ⊙Tue-Sun) Top international DJs whip the crowd into a frenzy at Rome's top megaclub. Big nights include the Thursday Ultrabeat session, Saturday funky house and the 'Venus Rising' lesbian night every last Sunday of the month.

Villaggio Globale SOCIAL CENTRE
(Map p776; www.vglobale.biz; Lungotevere Testaccio) For a warehouse-party vibe, head to Rome's best-known *centro sociale* (social centre), housed in an ex-slaughterhouse. Live music and DJ sets focus on dancehall, reggae, dubstep and drum'n'bass.

Big Mama BLUES CLUB
(Map p776; ☎06 581 24 51; www.bigmama.it; Vicolo di San Francesco a Ripa 18; ⊙Tue-Sun) This Trastevere basement is Rome's self-styled home of blues. It plays host to the world's top blues musicians and stages soul, jazz and funk.

AKAB CLUB
(Map p776; www.akabcave.com; Via Monte Testaccio 68-69; ⊙Tue-Sat) This is one of the most popular clubs on the Testaccio clubbing strip, with an underground cellar, a chilled garden and a steady supply of house, R&B and techno.

Cinema

Several cinemas show films in English, including the **Space Cinema Moderno** (Map p792; ☎892 11 11; Piazza della Repubblica 45/46), which screens Hollywood blockbusters and big Italian films, and the **Metropolitan** (Map p788; ☎06 320 09 33; Via del Corso 7), a four-screen multiplex near Piazza del Popolo. Expect to pay €7 to €7.50, with discounts on Wednesday.

Shopping

With everything from designer flagship stores to antique emporiums, flea markets and bohemian boutiques, shopping is fun in Rome. For the big-gun designer names head to Via dei Condotti and the area between Piazza di Spagna and Via del Corso. Moving down a euro or two, Via Nazionale, Via del Corso, Via dei Giubbonari and Via Cola di Rienzo are good for midrange clothing stores. For something more left field, try the small fashion boutiques and vintage clothes shops on Via del Governo Vecchio and around Campo de' Fiori. If you're looking for high-quality (read expensive) antiques or gifts, head to Via dei Coronari and Via Margutta. Rome's markets are a great place for bargain hunting. The most famous, **Porta Portese** (Map p776; Piazza Porta Portese; ⊙6am-2pm Sun) is held every Sunday morning near Trastevere, and sells everything from antiques to clothes, bikes, bags and furniture. Near Porta San Giovanni, the **Via Sannio market** (Map p776; Via Sannio; ⊙9am-1.30pm Mon-Sat) sells new and secondhand clothes.

For the best bargains, time your visit to coincide with the *saldi* (sales). Winter sales run from early January to mid-February and summer sales from July to early September.

Information

Emergency

Police station (Questura; ☎06 4 68 61; Via San Vitale 15)

Internet Access

Free wi-fi is now widely available in hostels, B&Bs and hotels across the city. Some also provide laptops/computers for guests' use. You'll find internet cafes across town, although with the recent spread of wi-fi many have shut.

Medical Services

For emergency treatment, go straight to the *pronto soccorso* (casualty) section of an *ospedale* (hospital). Pharmacists will serve prescriptions and can provide basic medical advice.

Ospedale Santo Spirito (☎06 6 83 51; Lungotevere in Sassia 1) Near the Vatican; multilingual staff.

Pharmacy Piazza dei Cinquecento (Piazza dei Cinquecento 49-51; ⊙24hr); Stazione Termini (next to platform 1; ⊙7.30-10.30pm)

Policlinico Umberto I (☎06 499 71; Viale del Policlinico 155) Rome's largest hospital.

Money

ATMs are liberally scattered around the city.

American Express (☎06 6 76 41; Piazza di Spagna 38; ⊙9am-5.30pm Mon-Fri, 9am-12.30pm Sat) Has an ATM and offers exchange facilities and travel services.

Tourist Information

Centro Servizi Pellegrini e Turisti (Map p776; ☎06 698 81 662; St Peter's Sq; ⊙8.30am-6.15pm Mon-Sat) The Vatican's official tourist office.

Enjoy Rome (Map p792; ☎06 445 18 43; www.enjoyrome.com; Via Marghera 8a; ⌚8.30am-7pm Mon-Fri, to 2pm Sat) A private tourist office that arranges tours, airport transfers and hotel reservations.

I Fori di Roma Centro Espositivo Informativo (Map p780; Via dei Fori Imperiali; ⌚9.30am-6.30pm) An information centre dedicated to the Forums.

The Comune di Roma runs a multilingual **tourist information line** (☎06 06 08; ⌚9am-9pm) and information points across the city:

Ciampino airport (International Arrivals; ⌚9am-6.30pm)

Castel Sant'Angelo (Map p784; Piazza Pia; ⌚9.30am-7pm)

Fiumicino airport (International Arrivals; ⌚9am-6.30pm)

Piazza Cinque Lune (Map p784; ⌚9.30am-7pm) Near Piazza Navona.

Piazza Sonnino (Map p790; ⌚9.30am-7pm) In Trastevere.

Santa Maria Maggiore (Map p792; Via dell'Olmata; ⌚9.30am-7pm) Near the Basilica di Santa Maria Maggiore.

Stazione Termini (⌚8am-8.30pm) In the hall parallel to platform 24.

Via Marco Minghetti (Map p784; ⌚9.30am-7pm) Near the Trevi Fountain.

Via Nazionale (⌚9.30am-7pm) In front of the Palazzo delle Esposizioni.

Websites

060608 (www.060608.it) A comprehensive and up-to-date site listing accommodation, attractions, events, and much more.

Pierreci (www.pierreci.it) Has the latest on museums, monuments and exhibitions. Book tickets online here.

Turismo Roma (www.turismoroma.it) Rome Tourist Board's extensive website has plenty of practical information, links and suggestions.

Vatican (www.vatican.va) The Holy See's official website, with practical information on Vatican sites.

Getting There & Away

Air

Rome's main international airport **Leonardo da Vinci** (FCO; ☎06 6 59 51; www.adr.it), better known as Fiumicino, is on the coast 30km west of the city. The much smaller **Ciampino airport** (CIA; ☎06 6 59 51; www.adr.it), 15km southeast of the city centre, is the hub for low-cost carriers including **Ryanair** (www.ryanair.com) and **easyJet** (www.easyjet.com).

Left-luggage (International Arrivals, Terminal 3; per 24hr €6; ⌚6.30am-11.30pm) is available at Fiumicino.

Boat

Rome's port is at Civitavecchia, about 80km north of Rome. The main ferry companies:

Grimaldi Lines (☎081 464 444; www.grimaldi-lines.com) To/from Catania (Sicily), Trapani (Sicily), Porto Torres (Sardinia), Barcelona (Spain), Malta, and Tunis (Tunisia).

Sardinia Ferries (☎199 400 500; www.corsica-ferries.it) To/from Golfo Aranci (Sardinia).

SNAV (☎076 636 63 66; www.snav.it) To/from Palermo (Sicily) and Olbia (Sardinia).

Tirrenia (☎89 21 23; www.tirrenia.it) To/from Arbatax, Cagliari and Olbia (all Sardinia).

Bookings can be made at the Termini-based **Agenzia 365** (⌚7am-9pm), at travel agents or online at www.traghettionline.net. You can also buy directly at the port.

Half-hourly trains depart from Roma Termini to Civitavecchia (€4.50 to €12.50, one hour). On arrival, it's about 700 to the port (to your right) as you exit the station.

Bus

Long-distance national and international buses use the **Autostazione Tiburtina** (Piazzale Tiburtina) in front of Stazione Tiburtina. Take metro line B from Termini to Tiburtina.

You can get tickets from the offices next to the bus terminus or at travel agencies. Bus operators:

Interbus (☎091 34 25 25; www.interbus.it, in Italian) To/from Sicily.

Marozzi (☎080 579 01 11; www.marozzivt.it, in Italian) To/from Sorrento, Bari, Matera and Lecce.

SENA (☎0861 199 19 00; www.senabus.it) To/from Siena and Tuscany.

Sulga (☎800 099 661; www.sulga.it, in Italian) To/from Perugia, Assisi and Ravenna.

Car & Motorcycle

Driving into central Rome is a challenge, involving traffic restrictions, one-way systems, a shortage of street parking, and aggressive drivers.

Rome is circled by the Grande Raccordo Anulare (GRA), to which all autostradas (motorways) connect, including the main A1 north–south artery (the Autostrada del Sole), and the A12, which connects Rome to Civitavecchia and Fiumicino airport.

CAR HIRE Rental cars are available at the airport and Stazione Termini:

Avis (☎06 481 43 73; www.avis.com)

Europcar (☎06 488 28 54; www.europcar.com)

Hertz (☎06 474 03 89; www.hertz.com)

Maggiore National (☎06 488 00 49; www.maggiore.com).

Near Termini, **Bici & Baci** (☎06 482 84 43; www.bicibaci.com; Via del Viminale 5; ⏰8am-7pm) is one of many agencies renting out scooters. Bank on from €19 per day.

Train

Almost all trains arrive at and depart from **Stazione Termini** (Map p792). There are regular connections to other European countries, all major Italian cities, and many smaller towns. Train information is available from the **Sala Viaggiatori** (⏰6am-midnight) next to platform 1, online at www.ferroviedellostato.it, or, if you speak Italian, by calling ☎89 20 21. **Left luggage** (1st 5hr €4, 6-12hr per hr €0.60, 13hr & over per hr €0.20; ⏰6am-11.50pm) is on the lower-ground floor under platform 24.

Rome's second train station is **Stazione Tiburtina**, a short ride away on metro line B.

Getting Around

To/From the Airport

FIUMICINO The easiest way to get to/from the airport is by train but there are also bus services.

Cotral bus (www.cotralspa.it; one-way €4.50 or €7 if bought on bus) Runs to/from Stazione Tiburtina via Stazione Termini. Eight daily departures including night services from Tiburtina at 12.30am, 1.15am, 2.30am and 3.45am and from the airport at 1.15am, 2.15am, 3.30am and 5am. Journey time is 45 minutes to an hour.

FR1 train (one-way €8) Connects the airport to Trastevere, Ostiense and Tiburtina stations. Departures from the airport every 15 minutes (hourly on Sunday and public holidays) between 5.57am and 11.27pm, from Tiburtina between 5.05am and 10.33pm.

Leonardo Express train (adult/child €14/free) Runs to/from platforms 27 and 28 at Stazione Termini. Departures from Termini every 30 minutes between 5.52am and 10.52pm, from the airport between 6.36am and 11.36pm. Journey time is 30 minutes.

SIT bus (☎06 591 68 26; www.sitbusshuttle.it; one-way €8) Regular departures from Via Marsala outside Stazione Termini between 5am and 8.30pm, from the airport between 8.30am and 12.30pm. Tickets available on the bus. Journey time is one hour.

Taxi The set fare to/from the city centre is €40, which is valid for up to four passengers with luggage.

CIAMPINO The best option is to take one of the regular bus services into the city centre. You can also take a bus to Ciampino train station and then pick up a train to Stazione Termini.

Cotral bus (www.cotralspa.it; one-way/return €3.90/6.90) Runs frequent services to/from Ciampino train station (€1.20), where you can connect with trains to Stazione Termini (€1.30) or Anagnina metro station (€1.20).

SIT bus (www.sitbusshuttle.com; one-way/return €6/8) Regular departures from Via Marsala outside Stazione Termini between 4.30am and 9.30pm, from the airport between 7.45am and 11.15pm. Tickets available on the bus. Journey time is 45 minutes.

Taxi The set rate to/from the airport is €30.

Terravision bus (www.terravision.eu; one-way/return €4/8) Twice-hourly departures to/from Via Marsala outside Stazione Termini. From the airport, services are between 8.15am and 12.15pm, from Via Marsala between 4.30am and 9.20pm. Buy tickets at Terracafè in front of the Via Marsala bus stop. Journey time is 40 minutes.

Car & Motorcycle

Most of the historic centre is closed to normal traffic from 6.30am to 6pm Monday to Friday, from 2pm to 6pm Saturday, and from 11pm to 3am Friday to Sunday – see http://atacmobile.it for further details.

PARKING Blue lines denote pay-and-display parking spaces with tickets available from meters (coins only) and *tabacchi* (tobacconists). Expect to pay up to €1.20 per hour between 8am and 8pm (11pm in some places). After 8pm (or 11pm) parking is free until 8am the next morning. If your car gets towed away, check with the **traffic police** (☎06 6 76 91).

Car parks:

Piazzale Partigiani (per hr/day €0.77/5; ⏰6am-11pm)

Stazione Termini (Via Marsala 30; per hr/day €3/26; ⏰6am-1am)

Stazione Tiburtina (Via Pietro l'Eremita; per hr €2; ⏰6am-10pm)

Villa Borghese (Viale del Galoppatoio; per hr/day €1.70/20; ⏰24hr).

Public Transport

Rome's public transport system includes buses, trams, metro and a suburban train network.

TICKETS Valid for all forms of transport and come in various forms:

Single (BIT; €1) Valid for 75 minutes, during which time you can use as many buses or trams as you like but only go once on the metro.

Daily (BIG; €4) Unlimited travel until midnight of the day of purchase.

Three-day (BTI; €11) Unlimited travel for three days.

Weekly (CIS; €16) Unlimited travel for seven days.

Buy tickets at *tabacchi*, newsstands and from vending machines at main bus stops and metro stations. They must be purchased before you start your journey and validated in the yellow machines on buses, at the entrance gates to the metro or at train stations. Ticketless riders risk an on-the-spot €50 fine.

BUSES Buses and trams are run by **ATAC** (☎06 57 003; www.atac.roma.it). The **main bus station** (Map p792; Piazza dei Cinquecento) is in front of Stazione Termini, where there's an **information booth** (⏲7.30am-8pm). Largo di Torre Argentina, Piazza Venezia and Piazza San Silvestro are also important hubs. Buses generally run from about 5.30am until midnight, with limited services throughout the night.

METRO There are two metro lines, A and B, which both pass through Termini. Take line A for the Trevi Fountain (Barberini), Spanish Steps (Spagna), and Vatican (Ottaviano-San Pietro); and line B for the Colosseum (Colosseo) and Circus Maximus (Circo Massimo). Trains run between 5.30am and 11.30pm (to 1.30am on Friday and Saturday).

Taxi

Official licensed taxis are white with the symbol of Rome on the doors. Always go with the metered fare, never an arranged price (the set fares to and from the airports are exceptions). Official rates are posted in taxis.

You can hail a taxi, but it's often easier to wait at a rank or phone for one. There are major taxi ranks at the airports, Stazione Termini and Largo di Torre Argentina. You can book a taxi by phoning the Comune di Roma's automated **taxi line** (☎06 06 09) or calling a taxi company direct:

La Capitale (☎06 49 94)

Pronto Taxi (☎06 66 45)

Radio Taxi (☎06 35 70)

Samarcanda (☎06 55 51)

Tevere (☎06 41 57)

AROUND ROME

Ostia Antica

An easy day trip from Rome, Ostia Antica is well worth a visit. Ostia was ancient Rome's port, and the clearly discernible ruins of restaurants, laundries, shops, houses and public meeting places give a good impression of what life must once have been like in the 100,000-strong town. Founded in the 4th century BC, the port thrived until the 5th century AD, when barbarian invasions and an outbreak of malaria led to its abandonment and slow burial in river silt, thanks to which it has survived so well.

The **ruins** (adult/concession €6.50/3.25; ⏲8.30am-7pm Tue-Sun Apr-Oct, to 6pm Mar, to 5pm Nov, Dec, Jan & Feb) are spread out and you'll need a few hours to do them justice. Highlights include the **Terme di Nettuno** (Baths of Neptune) and adjacent **amphitheatre**, built by Agrippa and later enlarged to hold 3000 people. Behind it, the **Piazzale delle Corporazioni** (Forum of the Corporations) housed Ostia's merchant guilds and is decorated with well-preserved mosaics.

To get to Ostia Antica from Rome take the Ostia Lido train (25 minutes, half-hourly) from Stazione Porta San Paolo next to the Piramide metro station. The journey is covered by standard public-transport tickets. By car, take Via del Mare or Via Ostiense.

Tivoli

POP 55,700

An ancient resort town and playground for the Renaissance rich, hilltop Tivoli is home to two Unesco-listed sites: Villa Adriana, Emperor Hadrian's sprawling summer residence, and Villa d'Este, a Renaissance villa famous for its garden fountains. You can cover both in a day trip from Rome, but it'll be a long day.

Sights

Villa Adriana RUINS

(Hadrian's Villa; adult/EU child €6.50/free, plus possible €3.50 for exhibition; ⏲9am-1hr before sunset) Five kilometres from Tivoli proper, Hadrian's vast 2nd-century complex was one of the largest and most sumptuous villas in the Roman Empire. It was subsequently plundered for building materials, but enough remains to convey its magnificence. Allow several hours to explore it.

Villa d'Este HISTORIC BUILDING, GARDEN

(www.villadestetivoli.info; Piazza Trento; adult/EU child €6.50/free, plus possible €3.50 for exhibition; ⏲8.30am-1hr before sunset Tue-Sun) Up in Tivoli's historic centre, the Renaissance Villa d'Este was built in the 16th century for Cardinal Ippolito d'Este. More than the villa itself, it's the elaborate gardens and their spectacular fountains, including one that plays an organ, that are the main attraction.

Parco Villa Gregoriana PARK
(adult/child €4/2.50; ⏲10am-6.30pm Tue-Sun Apr–mid-Oct, to 2.30pm mid-Oct–Nov & Mar, by appointment rest of year) A short walk from Villa d'Este, this historic park descends down a steep gorge, over which water crashes to the bottom 100m below.

Information

Information is available at the **tourist information kiosk** (☎0774 31 35 36; www.tibursuperbum.it; Piazzale delle Nazioni Unite; ⏲9.30am-5.30pm Tue-Sun) near the bus stop in the historic centre.

Getting There & Away

Tivoli is 30km east of Rome and accessible by Cotral bus (€2, one hour, every 20 minutes) from outside Ponte Mammolo metro station. The fastest route by car is on the Rome–L'Aquila autostrada (A24).

To get to Villa Adriana from Tivoli town centre, take CAT bus 4X (€1, 10 minutes, half-hourly) from Largo Garibaldi.

Tarquinia

POP 16,500

Some 90km northwest of Rome, Tarquinia is an absolute gem, the pick of Lazio's Etruscan towns. The highlight is the magnificent Unesco-listed necropolis, but there's also a fascinating Etruscan museum (the best outside of Rome) and an atmospheric medieval town centre.

Founded in the 12th century BC, Tarquinia grew to rival Athens, and its kings were among the first rulers of the nascent city of Rome. It reached its prime in the 4th century BC, before a century of struggle ended with surrender to Rome in 204 BC.

Sights

TOP CHOICE **Necropolis** ETRUSCAN TOMBS
(Via Ripagretta; admission €6, incl Museo Nazionale Tarquiniense €8; ⏲8.30am-30min before sunset Tue-Sun) This remarkable 7th-century-BC necropolis is one of Italy's most important Etruscan sites. There are reckoned only to be 200 painted Etruscan tombs in the entire country and some 140 of those are in Tarquinia. Of the 6000 tombs that have been excavated since 1489, 19 are currently open to the public, including the **Tomba della Caccia e della Pesca**, the richly decorated **Tomba dei Leopardi** and the **Tomba della Fustigazione** with its erotic depiction of a little friendly S&M.

To get to the necropolis, about 1.5km outside of the town centre, you can either take bus D (€0.60, nine daily) from outside the tourist office or walk – head up Corso Vittorio Emanuele, turn right into Via Porta Tarquinia and follow straight into Via Ripagretta; it'll take about 15 minutes.

Museo Nazionale Tarquiniense MUSEUM
(Piazza Cavour; admission €6, incl necropolis €8; ⏲8.30am-30min before sunset Tue-Sun) Beautifully housed in the 15th-century Palazzo Vitelleschi, this lovely museum is a treasure trove of Etruscan artefacts. Highlights include a stunning terracotta frieze of winged horses (the Cavalli Alati); a room full of painted friezes; displays of sarcophagi, jewellery and amphorae; and some plates embellished with illustrations of acrobatic sex.

Sleeping & Eating

Tarquinia is a long day trip from Rome. If you want to stay overnight, the tourist office can provide accommodation lists. For a bite to eat, **Ristorante Arcadia** (☎0766 85 55 01; Via Mazzini 6; mains €12, tourist menus €14; ⏲Tue-Sun), just behind the museum, is a friendly place serving excellent pasta, seafood and juicy grilled meats.

Information

The helpful **tourist information office** (☎0766 84 92 82; www.tarquiniaturismo.it; Barriera San Giusto; ⏲9am-1pm & 5-10pm Jul & Aug, shorter afternoon hr rest of year) is inside the town's medieval gate.

Getting There & Away

The easiest way to get to Tarquinia from Rome is to take the Pisa train from Termini (€6.20, 1¼ hours, eight daily). At Tarquinia station take bus BC (€0.80, every 30 to 50 minutes) to the town centre.

By car, take the autostrada for Civitavecchia and then Via Aurelia (SS1).

Cerveteri

POP 35,400

With its hilltop *centro storico* and haunting Etruscan tombs, Cerveteri makes a rewarding day trip from Rome. Cerveteri was one of the most important commercial centres in the Mediterranean from the 7th to the 5th century BC. But as Roman power grew, so

Cerveteri's fortunes faded, and in 358 BC the city was annexed by Rome.

Cerveteri's Etruscan tombs are concentrated in the Unesco-listed **Necropoli di Banditaccia** (Piazzale Moretti; admission €6, incl museum €8; ⊙9am-1hr before sunset Tue-Sun), just outside the town centre. The tombs are built into *tumoli* (mounds of earth with carved stone bases), laid out in the form of a town. The best preserved is the 6th-century-BC **Tomba dei Rilievi**, adorned with painted reliefs depicting household items and cooking implements. To get to the necropolis take the white shuttle bus G (€0.77) from next to the tourist information point.

In town, you can dine on tasty regional food at the **Antica Locanda Le Ginestre** (☎06 994 06 72; Piazza Santa Maria 5; mains €20; ⊙Tue-Sun), one of the Lazio region's top restaurants. For a cheaper alternative try **Cavallino Bianco** (☎06 994 06 72; Piazza Risorgimento; mains €8; ⊙closed Tue).

The superhelpful **tourist information point** (☎06 9955 2637; www.etruriaguide.it; Piazza Aldo Moro; ⊙9.30am-12.30pm daily & 5.30-7.30pm Fri & Sat Jun-Sep, 9.30am-12.30pm Mon-Sat Oct-May), by the entrance to the historic centre, has information on local sites, accommodation and transport.

Cerveteri is accessible from Rome by Cotral bus (€3.10, 1¼ hours, every 45 minutes) from outside Cornelia station on metro line A.

NORTHERN ITALY

Italy's well-heeled north is a fascinating area of historical wealth and natural diversity. Bordered by the northern Alps and boasting some of the country's most spectacular coastline, it also encompasses Italy's largest lowland area, the decidedly nonpicturesque Po valley plain. Of the cities it's Venice that hogs the limelight, but in their own way Turin, Genoa and Bologna offer plenty to the open-minded traveller. Verona is justifiably considered one of Italy's most beautiful cities, while the medieval centres of Padua, Ferrara and Ravenna all reward the visitor.

Genoa

POP 611,200

One of the Mediterranean's great ports, Genoa (Genova) is an absorbing city of aristocratic *palazzi*, dark, malodorous alleyways, Gothic architecture and industrial sprawl. Birthplace of Christopher Columbus (1451-1506) and home to Europe's second-largest aquarium (the largest is in Valencia), it was once a powerful maritime republic known as La Superba; nowadays it's a fascinating port that's well worth a stopover, particularly as it's the gateway to the magnificent Cinque Terre National Park.

Sights

Central Genoa is concentrated between the city's two main train stations: Stazione Brignole and Stazione Principe, with most sights in the *centro storico* and Porto Antico (Old Port).

Piazza de Ferrari SQUARE

Genoa's central square is a good place to start exploring the city. Grandiose and impressive, it's centred on an exuberant fountain and flanked by imposing *palazzi* – **Palazzo della Borsa**, Italy's former stock exchange, **Teatro Carlo Felice**, the city's historic opera house, and the huge **Palazzo Ducale** (www.palazzoducale.genova.it; entrance Piazza Giacomo Matteotti), once the seat of the city's rulers but now used to host major art exhibitions. Admission prices and hours depend on the exhibition.

Cattedrale di San Lorenzo CHURCH

(Piazza San Lorenzo; ⊙9am-noon & 3-6pm) A short walk west of Piazza de Ferrari, Genoa's dramatic cathedral is most notable for its black-and-white-triped Italian Gothic facade. It was consecrated in 1118 but the two bell towers and cupola were added in the 16th century.

Acquario di Genova AQUARIUM

(☎010 234 56 78; www.acquariodigenova.it; Ponte Spinola; adult/child €18/12; ⊙8.30am-10pm daily Jul & Aug, 9am-7.30pm Mon-Fri, 8.45am-8.30pm Sat & Sun Mar-Jun, Sep & Oct, 9.30am-7.30pm Mon-Fri, 9.30am-8.30pm Sat & Sun Jan, Feb, Nov & Dec) The main attraction in Genoa's Porto Antico is Europe's second-largest aquarium. Designed by Italian architect Renzo Piano, it houses 5000 animals in six million litres of water.

Renzo Piano was also responsible for two of the port's other landmarks: the **Biosfere** (adult/child €5/3.50; ⊙10am-7pm Apr-Oct, to 5pm Nov-Mar), a giant glass ball housing a tropical ecosystem; and the **Bigo** (adult/child €4/3; ⊙10am-11pm Tue-Sun, 4-11pm Mon Jun-Aug, 10am-6pm Tue-Sun, 2-6pm Mon rest of year), an eye-catching panoramic lift.

Musei di Strada Nuovo MUSEUMS
(Via Garibaldi; adult/concession €8/6; ⌚9am-7pm Tue-Fri, from 10am Sat & Sun) Genoa's main museums are in a series of *palazzi* on Via Garibaldi. The three most important, known collectively as the **Musei di Strada Nuova**, are housed in **Palazzo Bianco** (www.museopalazzobianco.it; Via Garibaldi 11), **Palazzo Rosso** (www.museopalazzorosso.it; Via Garibaldi 18) and **Palazzo Doria-Tursi** (www.museopalazzotursi.it; Via Garibaldi 9). The first two feature works by Flemish, Dutch, Spanish and Italian old masters, while the third displays the personal effects of Niccolò Paganini, Genoa's legendary violinist. Tickets, valid for all three museums, are available from the bookshop in Palazzo Doria-Tursi.

Sleeping

TOP CHOICE **Locanda di Palazzo Cicala** BOUTIQUE HOTEL €€€
(☎010 251 88 24; www.palazzocicala.it; Piazza San Lorenzo 16; s €114-391, d €144-391; ❄@📶) Located in a 16th-century *palazzo* opposite the cathedral, this welcoming boutique hotel has huge high-ceilinged rooms replete with parquet and slick designer furniture. There are also eight apartments available in nearby buildings.

Hotel Bel Soggiorno HOTEL €€
(☎010 54 28 80; www.belsoggiornohotel.com; 2nd fl, Via XX Settembre 19; s €65-110, d €75-135; P❄@📶) Located on Genoa's main shopping strip, this old favourite is an endearing mix of the modern and the antique, with airy, comfortable rooms and modern amenities such as satellite TV and wi-fi.

Albergo Carola PENSION €
(☎010 839 13 40; www.pensionecarola.com; 3rd fl, Via Gropallo 4; s without bathroom €28-35, d €56-70; 📶) Conveniently close to Stazione Brignole, this is a classic old-school *pensione* with simple, well-kept rooms on the 3rd floor of a towering old building. Rates don't include breakfast.

Ostello di Genova HOSTEL €
(☎010 242 24 57; www.ostellogenova.it; Via Costanzi 120; per person dm/s/d €17/27/25) Genoa's HI hostel is a functional, modern affair, some 2km up from the city centre – take bus 40 from Stazione Principe to the end of the line. Check-in is from 2.30pm to midnight and there's a lockout between 11.30am and 2.30pm.

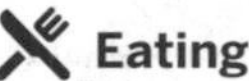

Eating

Ligurian specialities include pesto (a sauce of basil, garlic, pine nuts and Parmesan) served with *trofie* (pasta curls), and focaccia (flat bread made with olive oil). There are numerous restaurants and trattorias in the *centro storico*, while the Porto Antico area is good for cheap takeaways.

Regina Margherita RESTAURANT, PIZZA €€
(☎010 595 57 53; Piazza della Vittoria 89-103; mains €14, pizzas from €5.50) A bright, modern set-up with a two-floor interior and a small outdoor terrace. It's not in a particularly enticing location – on Piazza della Vittoria – but the food is excellent and the service is friendly and efficient. Speciality of the house is the wood-fired Neapolitan pizza.

Osteria San Matteo RESTAURANT €€
(☎010 247 32 82; Piazza San Matteo 4r; mains €12) With its wood beams and exposed-brick walls, this is an inviting *osteria* in the heart of the historic centre. It serves a full menu but it's the reasonably priced seafood that stands out. Particularly tasty are the *acciughe* (anchovies) with potatoes, pine nuts and basil, and the *crema catalana* (crème brûlée).

Antica Cantina i Tre Merli RESTAURANT €€€
(☎010 247 40 95; Vico dietro il Coro Maddalena 26r; mains €19; ⌚closed Sat lunch & Sun) An atmospheric option just off Via Garibaldi, 'The Three Crows' serves Ligurian cuisine with an emphasis on fish. There are a number of regional specialities on offer, including the classic *trofie con pesto* (pasta curls with pesto).

Ristorante Da Rina SEAFOOD €€€
(☎010 246 64 75; www.ristorantedarina.it; Mura delle Grazie 3r; mains €18; ⌚closed Mon & Aug) If you're keen to sample local seafood, this famous place overlooking the port fits the bill. It opened in 1946 and has been a favourite with locals ever since. Reservations recommended.

Drinking & Entertainment

Action centres on the *centro storico*, with a number of good bars clustered around Piazza delle Erbe.

Mcafé CAFE
(Piazza Giacomo Matteotti 9; ⌚8am-10pm Mon-Thu, to 1am Fri, 10am-1am Sat & Sun) This swish cafe by the entrance to the Palazzo Ducale is a good place to sip on something cool as you eye

up fellow drinkers. Upstairs is a restaurant serving set lunch menus (€12) on weekdays and brunch (€16) at the weekend.

Storico Lounge Café CAFE
(Piazza de Ferrari 34/36r; ⏲6am-3am) The *aperitivo* buffet here (5pm to 10pm) is a favourite with the city's fashionable young things, who love congregating at the pavement tables overlooking the Teatro Carlo Felice. There's also a DJ set on Friday and Saturday nights.

Teatro Carlo Felice THEATRE
(☎010 538 12 24; www.carlofelice.it; Passo Eugenio Montale 4) Genoa's historic theatre stages a year-round program of opera, ballet and classical music. Tickets start at about €25.

Information

Tourist offices Airport (☎010 601 52 47; ⏲9am-1pm & 1.30-5.30pm); City centre (☎010 860 61 22; www.turismo.comune.genova.it; Largo Pertini 13; ⏲9.30am-1pm & 2.30-6.30pm); Via Garibaldi (☎010 557 29 03; Via Garibaldi 12r; ⏲9.30am-1pm & 2.30-6.30pm); Antico Porto (⏲10am-7pm)

Getting There & Around

Air

Genoa's **Cristoforo Colombo airport** (GOA; ☎010 6 01 51; www.airport.genova.it; Sestri Ponente) is 6km west of the city. To get there take the **Volabus** (€6, 30min, hourly 5.20am-11.20pm) from Stazione Brignole or Stazione Principe. Buy tickets on board or at tourist offices. A taxi costs €7 per person from Stazione Principe and €8 from Brignole.

Boat

Ferries sail to/from Spain, Sicily, Sardinia, Corsica and Tunisia from the **terminal traghetti** (ferry terminal; www.porto.genova.it; Calata Chiappella), west of the city centre. Ferry companies:

Grandi Navi Veloci (☎010 209 45 91; www.gnv.it) To/from Sardinia (Porto Torres from €25, 11 hours; Olbia from €22, nine to 10 hours), Sicily (Palermo from €83, 20 hours), Barcelona (from €81, 18 hours) and Tunis (from €127, 24 hours).

Moby Lines (☎199 30 30 40; www.mobylines.it) To/from Sardinia (Porto Torres from €24, 10 hours).

Tirrenia (☎800 82 40 79; www.tirrenia.it) To/from Sardinia (Porto Torres from €30, 10 hour; Olbia from €30, 9¾ hours; Arbatax from €27, 14½ hours).

Bus

The main bus terminal is on Piazza della Vittoria, south of Stazione Brignole. Book tickets at **Geotravels** (Piazza della Vittoria 57).

Local buses are run by **AMT** (☎800 08 53 11; www.amt.genova.it). Tickets cost €1.20 and are valid for 90 minutes. Bus 33 runs between Stazione Principe and Stazione Brignole, stopping at Piazza de Ferrari en route.

Train

There are direct trains to Milan (€16.50, 1½ hours, up to 25 daily), Pisa (€16, two hours, up to 15 daily), Rome (€38.50, 5½ hours, nine daily) and Turin (€16, two hours, up to 15 daily). Regional trains to La Spezia service Cinque Terre (€5.30, two hours, up to 21 daily).

It generally makes little difference whether you leave from Brignole or Principe.

Cinque Terre

Liguria's eastern Riviera boasts some of Italy's most dramatic coastline, the highlight of which is the Unesco-listed **Parco Nazionale delle Cinque Terre** (Cinque Terre National Park) just north of La Spezia. Stretching for 18km, this awesome stretch of plunging cliffs and vine-covered hills is named after its five tiny villages: Riomaggiore, Manarola, Corniglia, Vernazza and Monterosso.

It gets very crowded in summer, so try to visit in spring or autumn. You can either visit on a day trip from Genoa or La Spezia, or stay overnight in one of the five villages.

Sights & Activities

The Cinque Terre villages are linked by the 9km **Blue Trail** (Sentiero Azzurro; admission with Cinque Terre Card), a magnificent, mildly challenging five-hour trail. The walk is in four stages, the easiest of which is the first stage from Riomaggiore to Manarola (Via d'Amore, 20 minutes) and the second from Manarola to Corniglia (one hour). For the final two stages, you'll need to be fit and wearing proper walking shoes. The stretch from Corniglia to Vernazza takes approximately 1½ hours and from Vernazza to Monterosso it's two hours. Make sure you bring a hat, sunscreen and plenty of water if walking in hot weather.

The Blue Trail is just one of a network of footpaths and cycle trails that criss-cross the park; details are available from the park offices. If water sports are more your thing, you can hire snorkelling gear (€10 per day) and kayaks (single/double €5/10 per hour) at the **Diving Center 5 Terre** (www.5terrediving.

com; Via San Giacomo) in Riomaggiore. It also offers a snorkelling boat tour for €18.

Sleeping & Eating

L'Eremo Sul Mare B&B €
(☎346 019 58 80; www.eremosulmare.com; Sentiero Azzurro, Vernazza; r €80-110; ❄) This romantic cliffside B&B (its name means Hermitage by the Sea) is beautifully situated on the Blue Trail about 500m uphill from Vernazza train station. It has three rooms, a panoramic sun terrace and a kitchen for guests' use. Cash only.

Ostello 5 Terre HOSTEL €
(☎0187 92 02 15; www.cinqueterre.net/ostello; Via B Riccobaldi 21, Manarola; dm €20-23, d €55-65; ⊙closed Nov-Feb; @) A popular private hostel in Manarola. Beds are in bright six-person single-sex dorms or private rooms with en suite bathrooms. Extras include breakfast (€6) and dinner (€18), laundry facilities and sports kit rental. Book at least a week ahead.

Hotel Ca' d'Andrean HOTEL €
(☎0187 92 00 40; www.cadandrean.it; Via Doscovolo 101, Manarola; s €55-72, d €70-100; ❄) An excellent family-run hotel in the upper part of Manarola. Rooms are big and cool with tiled floors and unobtrusive furniture; some have private terraces. Breakfast (€6) is served in the garden. No credit cards.

Marina Piccola SEAFOOD €€
(☎0187 92 01 03; www.hotelmarinapiccola.com; Via Birolli 120, Manarola; mains €12) Dine on fresh-off-the-boat seafood overlooking the small bay at Manarola. The harbourside setting is ideal for *zuppa di pesce* (fish soup) or seafood risotto. The adjoining hotel has small but comfortable air-conditioned rooms (single/double €87/115).

Trattoria La Lanterna SEAFOOD €€
(☎0187 92 05 89; Via San Giacomo 46, Riomaggiore; mains €16) This busy restaurant is perched above the snug harbour in Riomaggiore. Tables are on a small terrace or in a bright, breezy dining room and the menu features seafood pastas and simple fish dishes.

Information

The park's main **information office** (☎0187 92 06 33; ⊙8am-9.30pm) is to the right as you exit the train station at Riomaggiore. There are other offices in the train stations at Manarola, Corniglia, Vernazza, Monterosso and La Spezia (most open from 8am to 8pm).

Online information is available at www.parconazionale5terre.it and www.cinqueterre.com.

CINQUE TERRE CARD

To walk the Blue Trail (Sentiero Azzurro) coastal path you'll need a Cinque Terre Card. This comes in three forms:

» **Cinque Terre Card** (adult/child 1 day €5/2.50, 2 days €8/4) Available at all park offices.

» **Cinque Terre Treno Card** (adult/child 1 day €8.50/4.30, 2 days €14.70/7.40) Covers the Blue Trail plus unlimited train travel between Levanto and La Spezia, including all five villages.

» **Cinque Terre Card Batello** (adult/child 1 day €19.50/9.80) The Blue Trail and unlimited boat travel within the Area Marina Protetta 5 Terre.

Getting There & Away

Boat

Between July and September, **Golfo Paradiso** (☎0185 77 20 91; www.golfoparadiso.it) operates boat excursions from Genoa's Porto Antico to Vernazza, Monterosso and Riomaggiore. These cost €18 one-way, €33 return.

From late March to October, **Consorzio Marittimo Turistico 5 Terre** (☎0187 73 29 87; www.navigazionegolfodeipoeti.it) runs daily ferries between La Spezia and four of the villages (not Corniglia), costing €16 one-way including all the stops. Return trips are covered by a daily ticket (€23/25 weekdays/weekends).

Train

Regional trains run from Genoa Brignole to Riomaggiore (€4.80, 1½ to two hours, 20 daily), stopping at each of the Cinque Terre villages. The last train back from Riomaggiore to Genoa is at 11.19pm.

Between 4.30am and 11.10pm, one to three trains an hour crawl up the coast from La Spezia to Levanto (€3.30, 30 minutes), stopping at all of the villages en route. If you're doing this journey and you want to walk the Blue Trail, you'll save money buying the Cinque Terre Treno Card.

Turin

POP 908,900

First-time visitors are often surprised by Turin (Torino). Expecting a bleak, industrial sprawl dominated by Fiat factories, they are instead confronted with a dynamic and attractive city full of royal *palazzi*, historic cafes, baroque piazzas and world-class museums. Surprise almost inevitably turns to fascination when they learn of the city's occult aspect. Situated on the 45th parallel, it is said to be one of the three apexes of the white-magic triangle with Lyon and Prague, and also the black-magic counterpart of London and San Francisco.

Sights

Serious sightseers should consider the **Torino & Piedmont Card** (48hr card adult/child €20/10), available at tourist offices, which gives free public transport (not the metro) and discounts or entry to 170 museums, monuments and castles.

Piazza Castello SQUARE

Turin's grandest square is bordered by porticoed promenades and regal palaces. Dominating the piazza, **Palazzo Madama** (www.palazzomadamatorino.it) was the original seat of the Italian parliament. It is now home to the **Museo Civico d'Arte Antica** (Piazza Castello; adult/child €7.50/free; ⏲10am-6pm Tue-Sat, to 8pm Sun), whose impressive collection includes Gothic and early Renaissance paintings and some interesting majolica work. To the north, statues of Castor and Pollux guard the entrance to the enormous and lavishly decorated **Palazzo Reale** (Royal Palace; Piazza Castello; adult/child €6.50/free; ⏲8.30am-7.30pm Tue-Sun), built for Carlo Emanuele II in the mid-17th century. The palace's **Giardino Reale** (Royal Garden; admission free; ⏲9am-1hr before sunset) was designed in 1697 by Louis le Nôtre, noted for his work at Versailles.

A short walk away, **Piazza San Carlo**, known as Turin's drawing room, is famous for its cafes and twin baroque churches **San Carlo** and **Santa Cristina**.

Cattedrale di San Giovanni Battista CHURCH

(Piazza San Giovanni; ⏲8am-noon & 3-7pm Mon-Sat, from 7am Sun) Turin's 15th-century cathedral houses the famous Shroud of Turin *(Sindone)*, supposedly the cloth used to wrap the crucified Christ. A copy is on permanent display in front of the altar, while the real thing is kept in a vacuum-sealed box and rarely revealed.

Mole Antonelliana MUSEUM

(Via Montebello 20) Turin's famous landmark towers 167m over the city skyline. Originally intended as a synagogue, the Mole now houses the enormously enjoyable **Museo Nazionale del Cinema** (www.museocinema.it; adult/child €7/2; ⏲9am-8pm Tue-Fri & Sun, to 11pm Sat) and its comprehensive collection of cinematic memorabilia. Don't miss the glass **panoramic lift** (adult/child €5/3.50; ⏲10am-8pm Tue-Fri & Sun, to 11pm Sat), which whisks you up 85m in 59 seconds. Joint tickets for the museum and lift cost €9/4.50.

Museo Egizio ART MUSEUM

(www.museoegizio.it; Via Accademia delle Scienze 6; adult/child €7.50/free; ⏲8.30am-7.30pm Tue-Sun) This fabulous museum houses an engrossing collection of ancient Egyptian art that is considered the world's most important outside of Cairo and London.

Also recommended:

Pinacoteca Giovanni e Marella Agnelli ART MUSEUM

(www.pinacoteca-agnelli.it; Via Nizza 262; permanent exhibitions adult/child €4/2.50; ⏲10am-7pm Tue-Sun) A Renzo Piano–designed art gallery in the Lingotto, Fiat's former car factory.

Castello di Rivoli Museo d'Arte Contemporanea ART MUSEUM

(www.castellodirivoli.org; Piazza Mafalda di Savoia; adult/child €6.50/free; ⏲10am-5pm Tue-Thu, to 9pm Fri-Sun) A modern art gallery in a castle a few kilometres outside of Turin.

DON'T MISS

HISTORIC CAFES

Turin is home to an impressive array of historic cafes. Don't leave town without propping up the bar and downing an excellent espresso in the following:

Baratti & Milano (Piazza Castello 29; ⏲closed Wed) Serving coffee and confectionary since 1873.

Caffè San Carlo (Piazza San Carlo 156) Dates from 1828.

Caffè Torino (Piazza San Carlo 204) A relative newcomer, this art nouveau gem opened in 1903.

Neuv Caval'd Brônz (Piazza San Carlo 155)

San Tommaso 10 (Via San Tommaso 10; ⏲Mon-Sat) This is where Lavazza started. It now serves an unorthodox array of flavoured coffees as well as all the classics.

Sleeping

TOP CHOICE **Art Hotel Boston** BOUTIQUE HOTEL €€€

(☎011 50 03 59; www.hotelbostontorino.it; Via Massena 70; s €80-150, d €110-190, ste €250-

500; ❄@📶) The Boston's austere facade gives no clues as to its chic modern interior. The public spaces are littered with impressive works of contemporary art, while many of the 86 individually decorated rooms are themed on subjects such as Lavazza coffee, Ayrton Senna and Pablo Picasso.

Hotel Montevecchio HOTEL €€
(☎011 562 00 23; www.hotelmontevecchio.com; Via Montevecchio 13; s €45-90, d €60-120; @📶) Conveniently located about 300m from Porta Nuova train station, this is a friendly, well-run two-star place. Rooms come in sunny shades of yellow, the breakfast buffet is ample and there's a long list of extras, including a laundry service and wi-fi (€10 per day).

L'Orso Poeta B&B €€
(☎011 517 89 96; www.orsopoeta-bed-and-beakfast.it; Corso Vittorio Emanuele II 10; s/d from €70/110; ❄) A welcoming B&B in a historic apartment building by the Po River. Its two small, pastel-shaded rooms have bathrooms and lots of character. Note that it's closed in August, December and January.

Alpi Resort Hotel BUSINESS HOTEL €
(☎011 812 96 77; www.hotelalpiresort.it; Via A Bonafous 5; s €54-65, d €69-85; P❄) A business-like three-star place in an excellent location just off Piazza Vittorio Veneto. Its impeccably clean carpeted rooms are quiet and comfortable, if rather characterless.

Eating & Drinking

Turin has a reputation for magnificent gelato, which you can sample at outlets of **Grom** (⏲11am-midnight Sun-Thu, to 1am Fri & Sat) at Piazza Paleocapa 1d, Via Accademia delle Scienze 4, and Via Garibaldi 11.

Early evening is the time to make for one of the city's cafes and enjoy an *aperitivo* accompanied by a sumptuous buffet (included in the price). The most happening *aperitivo* precinct is Piazza Emanuele Filiberto and environs: try **Pastis** (Piazza Emanuele Filiberto 9) or **I Tre Galli** (Via Sant'Agostino 25; ⏲Mon-Sat). The *aperitivo* drinks cost around €8.

Da Ciro PIZZA €
(☎011 53 19 25; Corso Vinzaglio 17; pizzas from €5.50; ⏲closed Sat lunch & Sun) A favourite of Juventus footballers – ex-Juve legend Ciro Ferrara is a part-owner – this is a little bit of Naples in the north. Diners pile into the cheery, unpretentious interior to tear into delicious wood-fired pizzas. Booking recommended.

Otto Etre Quarti PIZZA, RESTAURANT €€
(☎011 517 63 67; Piazza Solferino 8c; pizzas from €5, mains €12) Claim a table in one of 8¾'s high-ceilinged dining rooms or on the square-side terrace and feast on fab pizzas or tasty pastas such as *paccheri con tonno* (big pasta tubes with tuna).

Information

The city's efficient **tourist office** (☎010 53 51 81; www.turismotorino.org; ⏲9am-7pm daily) has branches at Porta Nuova station, Piazza Castello and Via Giuseppe Verdi near the Mole Antonelliana.

Getting There & Around

In Caselle, 16km northwest of the city centre, **Turin airport** (TRN; ☎011 567 63 61; www.turin-airport.com) serves flights to/from European and national destinations. **Sadem** (☎800 801 600; www.sadem.it, in Italian) runs an airport shuttle (€5.50 or €6 on board, 40 minutes, half-hourly) between the airport and Porta Nuova train station. It operates between 5.15am and 11pm. A taxi costs approximately €35 to €40.

Direct trains connect Turin with Milan (€14.50, two hours, up to 30 daily), Florence (€67, three hours, five daily), Genoa (€15, two hours, up to 20 daily), and Rome (€93, 4¼hr, seven daily).

Milan

POP 1.29 MILLION

Few Italian cities polarise opinion like Milan, Italy's financial and fashion capital. Some people love the cosmopolitan, can-do atmosphere, the vibrant cultural scene and sophisticated shopping; others grumble that it's dirty, ugly and expensive. Certainly, it lacks the picture-postcard beauty of many Italian towns, but in among the urban hustle are some truly great sights – Leonardo da Vinci's *Last Supper,* the immense Duomo, the world-famous La Scala opera house.

Originally founded by Celtic tribes in the 7th century BC, Milan was conquered by the Romans in 222 BC and developed into a major trading and transport centre. From the 13th century it flourished under the rule of two powerful families, the Visconti and the Sforza.

Sights

Milan's main attractions are concentrated in the area between Piazza del Duomo and Castello Sforzesco. To get to the piazza from Stazione Centrale, take the yellow MM3 underground line.

Central Milan

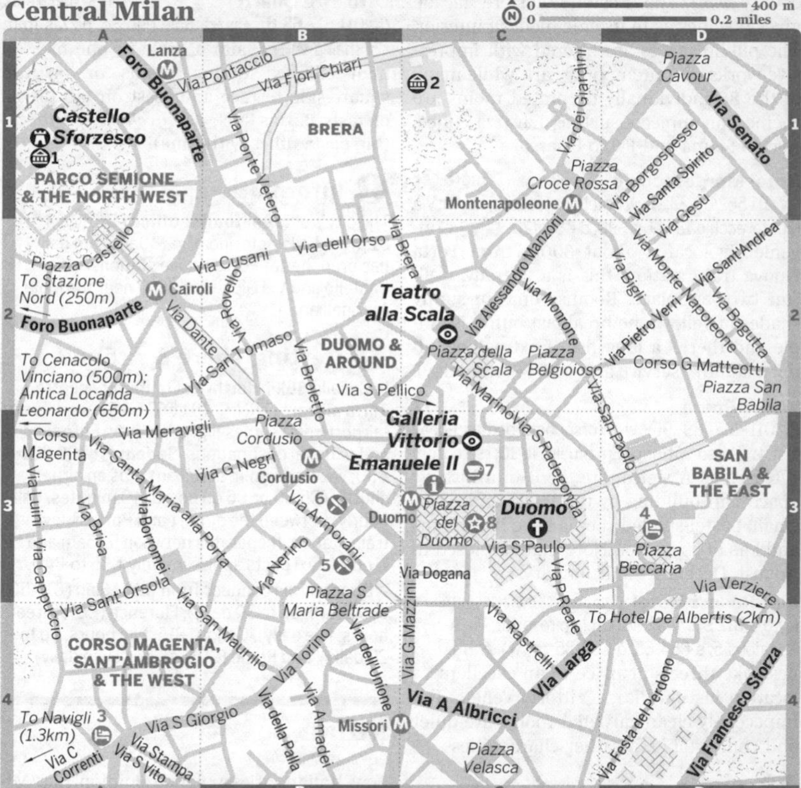

Duomo CHURCH
(Piazza del Duomo; admission free; ⊙7am-7pm) With a capacity of 40,000 people, this is the world's largest Gothic cathedral and the third-largest church in Europe. Commissioned in 1386 to a florid French-Gothic design and finished nearly 600 years later, it's a fairy-tale ensemble of 3400 statues, 135 spires and 155 gargoyles. Climb up to the **roof** (stairs/elevator €5/8; ⊙stairs 9am-5.20pm, lift 9am-9.15pm) for memorable city views.

Galleria Vittorio Emanuele II SHOPPING ARCADE
(Piazza del Duomo) This elegant iron-and-glass shopping arcade opens off the northern flank of Piazza del Duomo. Local tradition claims you can ward off bad luck by grinding your heel into the balls of the mosaic bull on the floor near the central cross.

Teatro alla Scala OPERA HOUSE
(www.teatroallascala.org; Piazza della Scala; admission €5; ⊙9am-12.30pm & 1.30-5.30pm) Milan's legendary opera house hides its sumptuous six-tiered interior behind a surprisingly severe facade. You can peek inside as part of a visit to the theatre's museum providing there are no performances or rehearsals in progress.

The Last Supper (Cenacolo Vinciano) PAINTING
(☎02 9280 0360; www.vivaticket.it; Piazza Santa Maria delle Grazie 2; adult/EU child €6.50/free plus booking fee of €1.50; ⊙8.15am-6.45pm Tue-Sun) Milan's most famous tourist attraction – Leonardo da Vinci's mural of *The Last Supper* – is in the Cenacolo Vinciano, the refectory of the Chiesa di Santa Maria delle Grazie, west of the city centre. To see it you need to book ahead or take a city tour.

FREE **Castello Sforzesco** CASTLE
(www.milanocastello.it; Piazza Castello 3; ⊙7am-7pm) This dramatic 15th-century castle was the Renaissance residence of the Sforza dynasty. It now houses the **Musei del**

Central Milan

Castello (adult/child €3/free; 9am-5.30pm Tue-Sun), a group of museums dedicated to art, sculpture, furniture, archaeology and music. Entry is free on Friday between 2pm and 5.30pm and from Tuesday to Sunday between 4.30pm and 5.30pm.

Pinacoteca di Brera ART MUSEUM
(www.brera.beniculturali.it; Via Brera 28; adult/EU child €11/free; 8.30am-7.15pm Tue-Sun) Art amassed by Napoleon forms the basis for the Pinacoteca's heavyweight collection, which includes Andrea Mantegna's masterpiece, the *Dead Christ* and Raphael's *Betrothal of the Virgin*.

Tours

Autostradale (www.autostradale.it) runs three-hour multilingual bus tours that take in the major sights and include entry to *The Last Supper*. Departures are at 9.30am from Piazza del Duomo every day except Monday. There are also two daily walking tours (€20) between Monday and Saturday, departing from the tourist office on Piazza del Duomo at 10am and 11.30am. Tickets for both tours are available from the tourist office at Piazza del Duomo.

Sleeping

Milan is a business city, which means hotels are expensive and it can be hard to find a room, particularly when trade fairs are on (which is often). Booking is essential at all times.

Antica Locanda Leonardo HOTEL €€
(02 4801 4197; anticalocandaleonardo.com; Corso Magenta 78; s €69-105, d €99-230;) A charming little hotel with characterful rooms and a gregarious, hospitable owner. Housed in a 19th-century *palazzo* near the Cenacolo Vinciano, it's decorated in classic style with polished wood furniture, parquet floors, rugs, and pot plants.

Hotel De Albertis HOTEL €€
(02 738 34 09; www.hoteldealbertis.it; Via De Albertis 7; s €50-100, d €50-160; @) A little way out from the centre in a leafy residential street, this small hotel is a welcoming, family-run affair. There are few frills but rooms are clean, comfortable and quiet. Take bus 92 from Stazione Centrale or tram 27 from the Duomo.

Hotel Nuovo HOTEL €€
(02 8646 4444; www.hotelnuovomilano.com; Piazza Beccaria 6; r €50-150;) In a city where 'cheap' is an ugly word, the Nuovo is a bastion of budget accommodation. Rooms are basic but clean, and the location, just off Corso Vittorio Emanuele II, is a winner. Aircon is only in rooms on the 2nd floor and rates don't include breakfast.

Ariston Hotel HOTEL €€€
(02 7200 0556; www.aristonhotel.com; Largo Carrobbio 2; s €65-380, d €80-380; P@) Claiming to be Milan's first 'ecological hotel', the centrally located Ariston offers smart modern rooms and environmentally friendly touches such as organic breakfasts, all-natural soaps, and free bike hire. Check the website for excellent low-season deals.

Eating & Drinking

Local specialities include *risotto alla milanese* (saffron-infused risotto cooked in bone-marrow stock) and *cotoletta alla milanese* (breaded veal cutlet). There are hundreds of bars and restaurants in Milan but as a general rule, the area around the Duomo is full of smart business-oriented restaurants, Brera is a fashionable bar haunt and the lively Navigli canal district caters to all tastes. Corso Como and environs is another good area for a stylish drink.

Pizzeria Piccola Ischia PIZZA €
(02 204 76 13; Via Morgani 7; pizzas €6.50; closed Wed & lunch Sat & Sun) You might be in the heart of Milan, but this bustling,

boisterous pizzeria is pure Naples. Everything from the wonderful wood-fired pizza to the fried antipasti and exuberant decor screams of the sunny south. It's hugely popular, so expect queues. Also does takeaway.

El Brellin RESTAURANT €€€
(☎02 5810 1351; Via Alzaia Naviglio Grande 14; mains €20, set menus €35-40; ⊙lunch daily, Mon-Sat dinner) Atmosphere-laden El Brellin is set in an 18th-century Navigli laundry. Its candlelit garden is a great place to linger over classic Milanese food whilst watching the evening canalside parade. *Aperitivi* (€8) are served in the bar between 7pm and 9pm.

Rinomata GELATERIA €
(Ripa di Porta Ticinese; ice creams €2.50) If dining in Navigli, skip dessert and grab an ice cream from this historic hole-in-the-wall gelateria. Its fabulous interior features old-fashioned fridges and glass-fronted cabinets filled with cones – and the gelato is good, too.

Peck Italian Bar DESIGNER BAR €€€
(Via Cesare Cantù 3; mains €18; ⊙Mon-Sat) Just around the corner from the legendary **Peck Delicatessen** (www.peck.it; Via Spadari 9; ⊙closed Sun & Mon morning), this bar oozes Milanese style. Black-jacketed bar staff serve coffees, wine and a daily menu of pastas and main courses to a moneyed, well-dressed clientele.

Zucca in Galleria CAFE €
(Galleria Vittorio Emanuele II 21) Grab a coffee (but skip the overpriced food) at the cafe where Giuseppe Verdi used to drink after performances at the Teatro all Scala.

FOOTBALL IN MILAN

Milan is home to Italy's two most successful *calcio* (football) teams: the Berlusconi-owned AC Milan and Internazionale, aka Inter. In recent years, Inter has dominated, winning the Italian championship five times between 2006 and 2010 and romping to victory in the 2010 European Champions League. During the season (September to May), the two clubs play on alternate Sundays at the **Stadio Giuseppe Meazza** (Via Piccolomini 5; Ⓜ Lotto), better known as the San Siro. Match tickets (from €23) are available from branches of Banca Intesa (AC Milan) and Banca Popolare di Milano (Inter). To get to the stadium on match days, take the free shuttle bus from the Lotto (MM1) metro station.

☆ Entertainment

Milan offers a rich and vibrant cultural scene, ranging from opera at La Scala to world-class football and cutting-edge club nights. September is a good time for classical-music fans, as the city co-hosts the **Torino Milano Festival Internazionale della Musica** (www.mitosettembremusica.it).

The opera season at **Teatro alla Scala** (☎02 7200 3744; www.teatroallascala.org; Piazza della Scala) runs from November to July, but you can see theatre, ballet and concerts here year-round, with the exception of August. Tickets are available online or from the **box office** (Galleria del Sagrato, Piazza del Duomo; ⊙noon-6pm) beneath Piazza del Duomo. Bank on €26 to €224 for opera and €19 to €138 for ballet performances.

For jazz, **Blue Note** (☎02 6901 6888; www.bluenotemilano.com; Via Borsieri 37; tickets €20-40) stages top international and Italian performers.

Shopping

For designer clobber head to the so-called Golden Quad, the area around Via della Spiga, Via Sant'Andrea, Via Monte Napoleone and Via Alessandro Manzoni. Street markets are held around the canals, notably on Viale Papiniano on Tuesday mornings and Saturdays.

ℹ Information

Pharmacy (☎02 669 07 35; Stazione Centrale; ⊙24hr)

Police station (Questura; ☎02 6 22 61; Via Fatebenefratelli 11)

Tourist offices Piazza del Duomo (☎02 7740 4343; www.visitamilano.it; Piazza Duomo 19a; ⊙8.45am-1pm & 2-6pm Mon-Sat, 9am-1pm & 2-5pm Sun); Stazione Centrale (☎02 7740 4318; opposite platform 13; ⊙9am-6pm Mon-Sat, to 1pm & 2-5pm Sun) Pick up the free guides *Hello Milano* and *Milanomese*.

ℹ Getting There & Away

Air

Most international flights fly into **Malpensa airport** (MXP; ☎02 23 23 23; www.sea-aeroportimilano.it), about 50km northwest of Milan. Domestic and some European flights use **Linate airport** (LIN; ☎02 23 23 23; www.sea-aeroportimilano.it), about 7km east of the city. Low-cost airlines often use **Orio al Serio airport** (BGY; ☎035 32 63 23; www.sacbo.it), near Bergamo.

Train

Regular daily trains depart **Stazione Centrale** for Venice (€30.15, 2½ hours), Bologna (€41, one hour), Florence (€52, 1¾ hours), Rome (€89, 3½ hours) and other Italian and European cities. Most regional trains stop at Stazione Nord in Piazzale Cadorna. Note that these prices are for the fast Eurostar Alta Velocità services.

Getting Around

To/From the Airport

MALPENSA **Malpensa Shuttle** (www.malpensashuttle.it; adult/concession €7.50/3.75) Buses run to/from Piazza Luigi di Savoia next to Stazione Centrale every 20 minutes between 4.15am and 12.30pm. Buy tickets at Stazione Centrale or the airport. Journey time is 50 minutes.

Malpensa Bus Express (www.autostradale.it; adult/concession €7.50/3.75) To/from Piazza Luigi di Savoia half-hourly between 4.30am and 11pm.The trip takes 50 minutes.

Malpensa Express (www.malpensaexpress.it; adult/concession €11/5.50) Trains from Cadorna underground station half-hourly between 5.57am and 11pm, and then a bus at 11.27pm. Journey time is approximately 35 minutes.

LINATE **Starfly** (www.starfly.net; tickets €4) Buses to/from Piazza Luigi di Savoia half-hourly between 5.40am and 9.30pm. Journey time is 30 minutes. Buy tickets at newsstands or on board.

ATM (www.atm-mi.it; tickets €1) Local bus 73 runs every 10 minutes between 5.35am and 12.35pm from Piazza San Babila.

ORIO AL SERIO **Autostradale** (www.autostradale.it; adult/concession €8.90/4.45) Half-hourly buses to/from Piazza Luigi di Savoia between 4am and 11.30pm. Journey time is one hour.

Bus & Metro

Milan's excellent public transport system is run by **ATM** (www.atm-mi.it). Tickets (€1) are valid for one underground ride or up to 75 minutes' travel on city buses and trams. You can buy them at metro stations, *tabacchi* and newsstands.

Verona

POP 265,400

Wander Verona's atmospheric streets and you'll understand why Shakespeare set *Romeo and Juliet* here – this is one of Italy's most beautiful and romantic cities. Known as *piccola Roma* (little Rome) for its importance in imperial days, its heyday came in the 13th and 14th centuries under the rule of the Della Scala (aka Scaligeri) family, who built *palazzi* and bridges, were patrons to Giotto, Dante and Petrarch, oppressed their subjects and feuded with everyone else. They were eventually deposed in 1387.

Sights

The **Verona Card** (www.veronacard.it; 1/3 days €10/15) covers city transport and the main monuments. It's available from tourist offices and most sights.

Arena di Verona ROMAN AMPHITHEATRE

(www.arena.it; Piazza Brà; adult/concession €6/4.50; ⏲1.30am-7.30pm Mon & 8.30am-7.30pm Tue-Sun Oct-May, 8.30am-3.30pm Jun-Aug) In the corner of Piazza Brà, the 1st-century pink marble Arena di Verona is the third-largest Roman amphitheatre in existence, with a capacity of 20,000. These days it's most famous as Verona's summer opera house (see p816).

Casa di Giulietta LANDMARK

(Via Cappello 23; courtyard free, museum adult/concession €6/4.50; ⏲1.30-7.30pm Mon & 8.30am-7.30pm Tue-Sun) From the Arena, walk along Via Mazzini, the town's premier shopping strip, to Via Cappello and the Casa di Giulietta. This clever tourist attraction was created by local authorities a few decades ago and marketed as Juliet's house. Romantic superstition suggests that rubbing the right breast of Juliet's statue (in the courtyard below the balcony) will bring you a new lover. Further along the street is **Porta Leoni**, one of the city's Roman gates; the other, **Porta Borsari**, is north of the Arena.

Piazzas SQUARES

Set over the city's Roman forum, **Piazza delle Erbe** is lined with sumptuous *palazzi* and filled with touristy market stalls. Through the **Arco della Costa**, the quieter **Piazza dei Signori** is flanked by the **Loggia del Consiglio**, the medieval town hall regarded as Verona's finest Renaissance structure, and **Palazzo degli Scaligeri**, the former residence of the Della Scala family.

Basilica di San Zeno Maggiore CHURCH

(Piazza San Zeno; adult/family €2.50/5; ⏲8.30am-6pm Tue-Sat, 12.30pm-6pm Sun Mar-Oct, 10am-1pm & 1.30-5pm Tue-Sat, 12.30-5pm Sun Nov-Feb) This Romanesque church honours the city's patron saint. Look out for the rose window and Mantegna's triptych of the *Maestà della Vergine* (Majesty of the Virgin), above the high altar.

Sleeping

High-season prices apply during the opera season and it is absolutely essential to book ahead during this period.

Hotel Aurora HOTEL €€
(☎045 59 47 17; www.hotelaurora.biz; Piazza delle Erbe; s €90-135, d €100-160; ❄📶) This top-of-the-range two-star place has friendly staff and clean and comfortable rooms with an understated decor. The lavish breakfast can be enjoyed on a lovely terrace overlooking Piazza delle Erbe.

Appartamenti L'Ospite APARTMENT €€
(☎045 803 69 94; www.lospite.com; Via XX Settembre 3; apt for 1 or 2 persons €55-200, apt for 3 or 4 persons €65-200; ❄📶) Over the river from the *centro storico*, L'Ospite has six self-contained apartments for up to four people. Simple and bright with fully equipped kitchens, they come with wi-fi and are ideal for families.

Ostello Villa Francescatti HOSTEL €
(☎045 59 03 60, fax 045 80 09 127; Salita Fontana del Ferro 15; dm incl breakfast €18.50-20, d €37-40; P) This HI hostel is housed in a 16th-century villa set in extensive grounds. To save yourself a steep uphill walk, take bus 73 from the train station (90 on Sunday). There's a strict 11.30pm curfew.

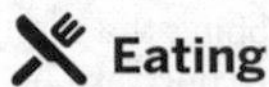

Eating

Boiled meats are a Veronese speciality, as is crisp Soave white wine.

Antica Bottega del Vino WINE BAR €€€
(☎045 800 45 35; www.bottegavini.it; Via Scudo di Francia 3; mains €15-35; ⊙closed Tue) Established in 1890, this wine bar–restaurant is one of the essential stops while you're in town. You can enjoy a glass of wine from a mind-boggling array of choices while standing at the bar, or book a table for a meal. The food is rustic and delicious – freshly made *bigoli all'anatra* (pasta with a duck *ragù*), soupy *risotto all'Amarone* (rice cooked with Amarone wine) and a variety of perfectly cooked meat dishes.

Salumeria G Albertini DELICATESSEN €
(☎045 803 10 74; www.salumeriaalbertini.it; Corso Sant'Anastasia 41; ⊙closed Sun) Albertinis has been the place to source picnic provisions ever since 1939. Its range of local artisan meats, cheese and wine will make an alfresco meal by the river or inside the amphitheatre the stuff of which lasting memories are made.

Al Pompiere TRATTORIA €€
(☎045 803 05 37; www.alpompiere.com; Vicolo Regina d'Ungheria 5; mains €12-24; ⊙Tue-Sat, dinner Mon) There's no secret to the success of this much-loved trattoria – top-notch seasonally inspired food and welcoming surroundings. It's particularly noted for its platters of cheese and *salumi* (home-cured meats).

Entertainment

The opera season at the Roman **Arena** (☎045 800 51 51; www.arena.it; tickets €23-198)

WORTH A TRIP

MANTUA

The beautiful Unesco-listed town of Mantua (Mantova) is an easy day trip from Verona. Best known as the place where Shakespeare exiled Romeo, it was for centuries (1328 to 1707) the stronghold of the Gonzaga family, one of Italy's most powerful Renaissance dynasties.

The **tourist office** (☎0376 43 24 32; www.turismo.mantova.it; Piazza Andrea Mantegna 6; ⊙9am-6pm) is close to the city's major attraction, the enormous **Palazzo Ducale** (www.ducalemantova.org; Piazza Sordello; adult/EU child €6.50/free; ⊙8.30am-7pm Tue-Sun). The highlight of this former seat of the Gonzaga family is the **Camera degli Sposi** (Bridal Chamber), home to extraordinary 15th-century frescos by Andrea Mantegna. To visit the *Camera* you need to book ahead (☎041 241 18 97).

For lunch, sit beneath 15th-century frescos in the vaulted dining room of **Ristorante Masseria** (Piazza Broletto 7; pizza €5-7.50, mains €13; ⊙closed Thu) to enjoy local specialities such as *penne in giallo con zafferano, salsiccia e rosmarino* (pasta tubes with saffron, sausage and rosemary).

The best way to get to Mantua is by regional train from Verona (€2.55, 45 minutes, 16 daily).

runs from late June to the end of August. If you attend a performance make sure you take your own food and drinks (stuff sold in the Arena is outrageously overpriced) and perhaps something to sit on, as the stone seating can be very uncomfortable.

Information

Information is available at the three **tourist offices** (www.tourism.verona.it; airport ☎045 861 91 63; ⌚10am-4pm Mon & Tue, to 5pm Wed-Sat; city centre ☎045 806 86 80; Piazza Brà; ⌚9am-7pm Mon-Sat, 10am-4pm Sun; train station ☎045 800 08 61; ⌚9am-7pm Mon-Sat, to 3pm Sun).

Getting There & Around

Aeroporto di Verona (Valerio Catullo airport; ☎045 809 56 66; www.aeroportidelgarda.it) is 12km outside the city and accessible by bus from the train station (€4.50, 20 minutes, every 20 minutes between 5.40am and 11.10pm). Ryanair flies to **Brescia airport** (VBS; ☎030 965 65 99), from where **CGA** (www.cgabrescia.it) shuttle buses (€11, 45 minutes, one daily) connect to Verona's main train station.

From the main bus terminal in front of the train station, AMT bus 72 leaves Stand F going to Piazza Erbe. Buses 11, 12 and 13 leave Stand A going to the Arena. Tickets cost €1.10 when purchased from the station's *tabacchi* and validated on board and €1.20 if purchased on the bus. A taxi from the train station to the centre costs around €10.

Verona is directly linked by rail to Milan (€17.50, two hours, every 45 minutes), Venice (€18.50, 1¼ hours, half-hourly), Bologna (€13.50, two hours, six daily) and Rome (€64-80.50, 4¼ hours, hourly).

Padua

POP 213,000

The lively university city of Padua (Padova) is a fun place to hang out, but what really makes it special are the stunning frescos in the Cappella degli Scrovegni. From the train station, follow Corso del Popolo and its continuation Corso Garibaldi until you see a park on your left – walk alongside the park, turn left into Via Erimitani and you'll soon come to the *cappella,* which is next to the Chiesa degli Eremitani.

Sights

The **PadovaCard** (www.padovacard.it; 2/3 days for 1 adult & 1 child €15/20), available from tourist offices and participating sights, provides free parking, public transport and entry to many sights, including the Cappella degli Scrovegni (plus €1 booking fee).

Cappella degli Scrovegni CHURCH
(☎049 201 00 20; www.cappelladegliscrovegni.it; Piazza Eremitani 8; tickets incl entry into the adjoining multimedia room & Musei Civici agli Eremitani adult/concession €13/6; ⌚9am-7pm) Don't miss Giotto's extraordinary frescos here; the 38 colourful panels (c 1304–1306) depicting Christ's life cover the chapel from floor to ceiling. It's best to book tickets at least 24 hours in advance, though it's sometimes possible to buy tickets on the spot. Visits are limited to 25 people at one time and last only 15 minutes (20 minutes at night).

From March to November (and also over the Christmas week), the Cappella (but not the Musei Civici agli Eremitani) is open until 10pm every day except Monday. Tickets for these evening openings cost adult/student and child €8/6 – it's also possible to buy a 'double turn' ticket (€12) at these times, which gives you 40 minutes rather than 20.

The picture galleries in the Musei Civici agli Eremitani are home to an impressive collection of paintings and sculptures, including two Giottos.

Basilica di Sant'Antonio CHURCH
(Piazza del Santo; admission free; ⌚6.20am-7.45pm Apr-Oct, to 6.45pm Nov-Feb) On the other side of the *centro storico* to the Capella, this church is home to the surprisingly gaudy **tomb** of St Anthony, Padua's patron saint. It's one of Italy's major pilgrimage sights. To get here, it's a 1km walk from the Cappella degli Scrovegni or a short tram ride on tram No 3, 12 or 18 from the train station (tickets €1.10, available from *tabacchi* or kiosk outside the station).

Sleeping

Belludi 37 BOUTIQUE HOTEL €€
(☎049 66 56 33; www.belludi37.it; Via Luca Belludi 37; s without bathroom €57-80, d €120-150; P❄@) Overlooking the Basilica di Sant'Antonio, this sleek boutique hotel offers good-sized rooms and is known for its personal service. It offers tours of the city's markets and *enoteche* (wine bars), as well as bike hire.

Ostello Città di Padova HOSTEL €
(☎049 875 22 19; www.ostellopadova.it; Via Aleardo Aleardi 30; dm incl breakfast from €19; 📶) Padua's HI hostel has an off-putting institutional feel and rigid opening hours (7.15am to 9.30am and 4.30pm to 11.30pm). Two-, four-, six- and eight-bed rooms are on offer; some have

their own bathroom. Take the tram from the train station to Via Cavaletto, turn right into Via Marin, left at the Torresino church and then right into Via Aleardo.

Albergo Verdi HOTEL €€
(☎049 836 41 63; www.albergoverdipadova.it; Via Dondi dall'Orologio 7; s €40-100, d €40-150; ❄) This modern and centrally located option offers quiet and clean rooms with bright colour schemes and mod cons such as wi-fi (€5 per three hours) and satellite TV.

Eating & Drinking

L'Anfora OSTERIA €€
(☎049 65 66 29; www.osterianfora.it, in Italian; Via dei Sconcin 13; mains €10-15; ⏱closed Sun) The menu at this laid-back *osteria* (tavern) with bare wooden tables and racked wine bottles changes daily and is full of products and dishes typical of Venice. There's sometimes live jazz to accompany your meal – check the website for details.

Antica Osteria dal Capo OSTERIA €€
(☎049 66 31 05; Via degli Obizzi, 2; mains €10-16; ⏱closed Sun all day & lunch Mon) Not far from L'Anfora, this *osteria* offers an atmospheric setting and regional menu.

There are a number of stylish contemporary *enoteche* in Padua that are as popular for *aperitivo* as they are for dinner. Recommended:

Godenda WINE BAR
(☎049 877 41 92; www.godenda.it; Via Squarcione, 4; mains €15; ⏱closed Sun year-round & Mon Apr-Sep) Near Piazza dei Signori.

Enoteca Cortes WINE BAR
(☎049 871 97 97; Riviera Paleocapa 7; mains €16-22; ⏱from 6pm Tue-Sun) Located on a pretty canal to the southwest of the centre.

Information

For tourist information and a copy of the useful, free *Padova Today* magazine, go to one of Padua's three **tourist offices** (www.turismo padova.it; Galleria Pedrocchi ☎049 876 79 27; ⏱9am-1.30pm & 3-7pm Mon-Sat; Piazza del Santo ☎049 875 30 87; ⏱9am-1.30pm & 3-6pm Mon-Sat, 10am-1pm & 3-6pm Sun Apr-Oct only; train station ☎049 875 20 77; ⏱9am-7pm Mon-Sat, to 12.30pm Sun).

Getting There & Away

SITA (☎049 820 68 44; www.sitabus.it, in Italian) buses leave from the new bus station immediately east of the train station going to Venice (€3.55, 45 minutes, hourly) and Marco Polo airport (€3.55, 30 minutes, hourly).

There are regional trains to/from Venice (€2.90, 45 minutes, every 20 minutes), Verona (€4.95, 1½ hours, hourly) and Bologna (€7.45, 1½ hours, hourly). Note that the train information office can be hard to find – it's near Platform 1.

Venice

POP 270,100

Venice (Venezia) is a hauntingly beautiful city. At every turn you're assailed by unforgettable images – tiny bridges crossing limpid canals, delivery barges jostling chintzy gondolas, excited tourists posing for photographs under flocks of pigeons. But to reduce Venice to a set of pictures is as impossible as describing it in sound bites. To gain an understanding of its rich and melancholic culture you really need to walk its hidden back lanes. Parts of the Cannaregio, Dorsoduro and Castello *sestieri* (districts) rarely see many tourists, and you can lose yourself for hours in the streets between the Accademia and the train station. Stroll late at night to feel an eerie atmosphere, redolent of dark passions and dangerous secrets.

Despite its romantic reputation, the reality of modern Venice is a city besieged by rising tides and up to 20 million visitors a year. This and the sky-high property prices mean that most locals live over the lagoon in Mestre.

History

Venice's origins date to the 5th and 6th centuries when barbarian invasions forced the Veneto's inhabitants to seek refuge on the lagoon's islands. First ruled by the Byzantines from Ravenna, it wasn't until 726 that the Venetians elected their first *doge* (duke).

Over successive centuries, the Venetian Republic grew into a great merchant power, dominating half the Mediterranean, the Adriatic and the trade routes to the Levant – it was from Venice that Marco Polo set out for China in 1271. Decline began in the 16th century and in 1797 the city authorities opened the gates to Napoleon, who, in turn, handed the city over to the Austrians. In 1866, Venice was incorporated into the Kingdom of Italy.

Orientation

Everybody gets lost in Venice. With 117 islands, 150-odd canals and 400 bridges (only four of which – the Rialto, the Accademia and, at the train station, the Scalzi and the Calatrava – cross the Grand Canal) it's impossible not to.

It gets worse: Venetian addresses are almost meaningless to all but local posties. Instead of a street and civic number, local addresses often consist of no more than the *sestiere* (Venice is divided into six districts: Cannaregio, Castello, San Marco, Dorsoduro, San Polo and Santa Croce) followed by a long number. Some, however, do have street names and where possible we've provided them. You'll still need to know that a street can be a *calle, ruga* or *salizada;* beside a canal it's a *fondamenta.* A canal is a *rio,* a filled canal-turned-street a *rio terrà,* and a square a *campo* (Piazza San Marco is Venice's only piazza).

The most helpful points of reference are Santa Lucia train station and Piazzale Roma in the northwest and Piazza San Marco (St Mark's Square) in the south. The signposted path from the train station *(ferrovia)* to Piazza San Marco (the nearest Venice has to a main drag) is a good 40- to 50-minute walk.

 Sights

A good way to whet your sightseeing appetite is to take vaporetto (small passenger ferry) No 1 along the **Grand Canal**, which is lined with rococo, Gothic, Moorish and Renaissance palaces. Alight at Piazza San Marco, Venice's most famous sight.

Piazza San Marco SQUARE

(Map p826) Piazza San Marco beautifully encapsulates the splendour of Venice's past and its tourist-fuelled present. Flanked by the arcaded **Procuratie Vecchie** and **Procuratie Nuove**, it's filled for much of the day with tourists, pigeons and policemen. While you're taking it all in, you might see the bronze *mori* (Moors) strike the bell of the 15th-century **Torre dell'Orologio** (clock tower).

But it's to the remarkable **Basilica di San Marco** (Map p826; www.basilicasanmarco.it; Piazza San Marco; admission free; ⌚9.45am-5pm Mon-Sat & 2-5pm Sun Easter-Oct, 9.45am-5pm Mon-Sat & 2-4pm Sun Nov-Easter) that all eyes are drawn. Sporting spangled spires, Byzantine domes, luminous mosaics and lavish marble work, it was originally built to house the remains of St Mark. The original chapel was destroyed by fire in 932 and a new basilica was consecrated in its place in 1094. For the next 500 years it was a work in progress as successive *doges* added mosaics and embellishments looted from the East. Behind the main altar is the **Pala d'Oro** (admission €2.50; ⌚9.45am-5pm Mon-Sat & 2-5pm Sun Easter-Oct, 9.45am-4pm Mon-Sat & 2-4pm Sun Nov-Easter), a stunning gold altarpiece decorated with priceless jewels.

ADMISSION DISCOUNTS

The **Rolling Venice Card** (www.hellovenezia.com; €4) is for visitors aged 14 to 29 years; it offers discounts on food, accommodation, shopping, transport and museums. You can get it at tourist offices, and at HelloVenezia booths throughout the city. You'll need ID.

The **Venice Card Orange** (www.hellovenezia.com; under 30yr 3/7 days €66/87, 30yr & over €73/96) entitles holders to free entry to 12 city museums (including Palazzo Ducale), free entry to the 16 Chorus churches, unlimited use of ACTV public transport, limited use of public toilets, and reduced admissions to various museums and events. It doesn't always represent a saving, so check before buying. It's sold at tourist and HelloVenezia offices.

To visit the museums on Piazza San Marco you'll need to buy either a **Museum Pass** (www.museicivicivenezian.it; adult/EU senior & EU student under 25yr/child under 6yr €18/12/free), which gives entry to the museums on Piazza San Marco and eight other civic museums; or a **San Marco Museum Plus Ticket** (adult/EU senior & EU student under 25yr/child under 6yr €13/7.50/free), which gives entry to the San Marco museums and your choice of one other civic museum. Both are available at participating museums. Discount passes – including an afternoon pass to the museums on Piazza San Marco (adult/EU senior & EU student under 25 years/child under six years €10/4.50/free) – can be purchased in advance at www.veniceconnected.com.

The **Chorus Pass** (www.chorusvenezia.org; adult/student under 29yr/child under 11yr/family €10/7/20/free) covers admission to 16 of Venice's major churches and is available online or at the churches. Otherwise entry to each church costs €3.

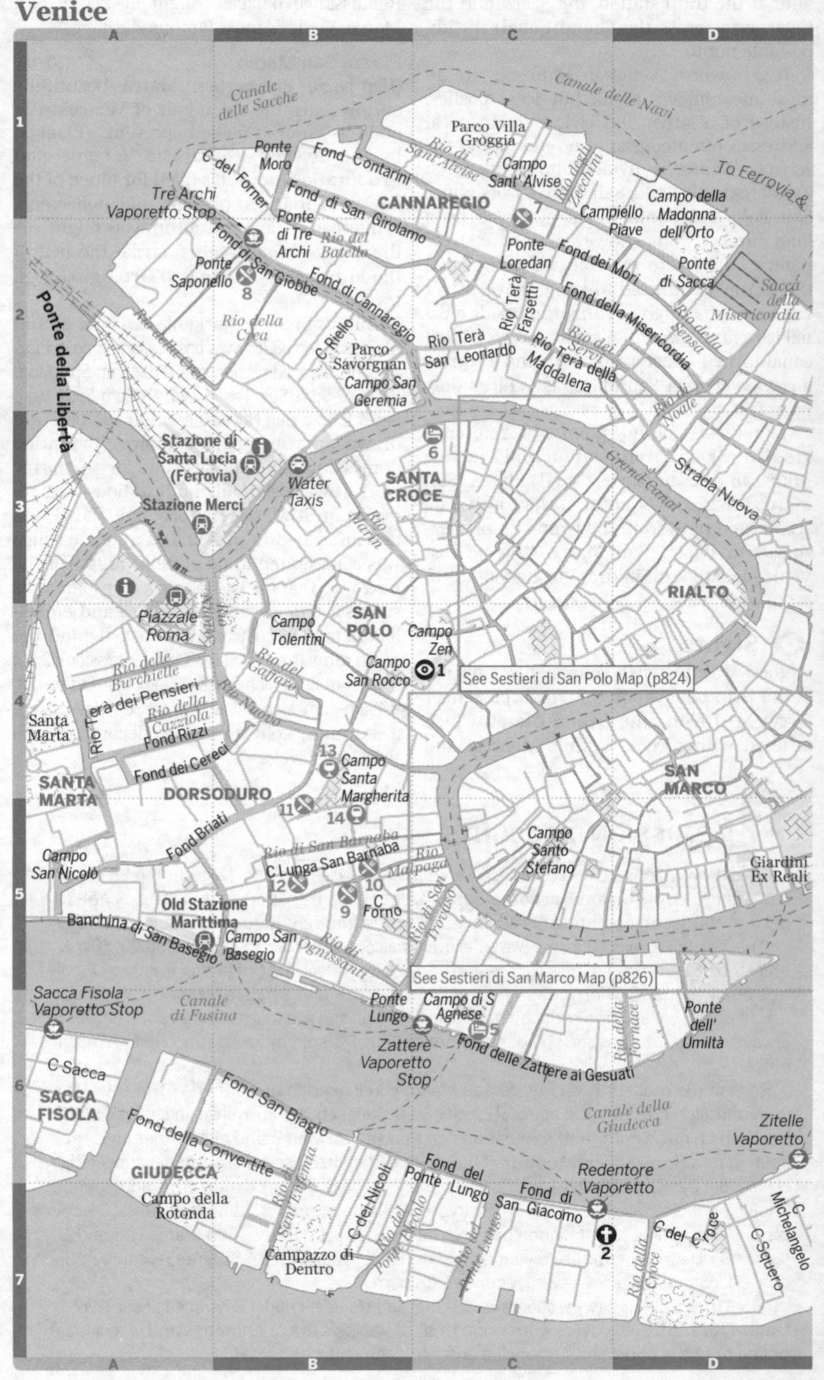
Canale delle Sacche
Canale delle Navi
To Ferrovia &
Parco Villa Groggia
Rio di Sant'Alvise
Campo Sant'Alvise
Rio degli Zecchini
Ponte Moro
Fond Contarini
C del Forner
CANNAREGIO
Tre Archi Vaporetto Stop
Fond di San Girolamo
Ponte di Tre Archi
Rio del Batello
Campiello Piave
Campo della Madonna dell'Orto
Ponte Loredan
Fond dei Mori
Ponte di Sacca
Sacca della Misericordia
Fond di San Giobbe
Ponte Saponello
Fond di Cannaregio
Rio Terà Farsetti
Fond della Misericordia
Rio della Sensa
Ponte della Libertà
Rio della Crea
C Riello
Parco Savorgnan
Rio Terà San Leonardo
Rio dei Servi
Rio Terà della Maddalena
Campo San Geremia
Rio di Noale
Stazione di Santa Lucia (Ferrovia)
Water Taxis
SANTA CROCE
Grand Canal
Strada Nuova
Stazione Merci
Rio Marin
RIALTO
Piazzale Roma
Rio Nuovo
SAN POLO
Campo Tolentini
Campo Zen
Campo San Rocco
See Sestieri di San Polo Map (p824)
Rio delle Burchielle
Rio del Gaffaro
Rio Terà dei Pensieri
Rio della Cazziola
Fond Rizzi
Santa Marta
SANTA MARTA
Fond dei Cereci
DORSODURO
Campo Santa Margherita
SAN MARCO
Fond Briati
Campo Santo Stefano
Rio di San Barnaba
C Lunga San Barnaba
Rio Malpaga
Campo San Nicolò
Giardini Ex Reali
C Forno
Rio di San Trovaso
Old Stazione Marittima
Banchina di San Basegio
Campo San Basegio
Rio di Ognissanti
See Sestieri di San Marco Map (p826)
Sacca Fisola Vaporetto Stop
Canale di Fusina
Ponte Lungo
Campo di S Agnese
Zattere Vaporetto Stop
Rio della Fornace
Ponte dell' Umiltà
Fond delle Zattere ai Gesuati
C Sacca
SACCA FISOLA
Fond San Biagio
Canale della Giudecca
Zitelle Vaporetto
Fond della Convertite
GIUDECCA
Rio di Sant'Eufemia
C dei Nicoli
Fond del Ponte Lungo
Fond di San Giacomo
Redentore Vaporetto
Campo della Rotonda
Rio del Ponte Piccolo
Rio del Ponte Lungo
C del Croce
C Michelangelo
C Squero
Rio della Croce
Campazzo di Dentro
1
2
5
6
7
8
9
10
11
12
13
14

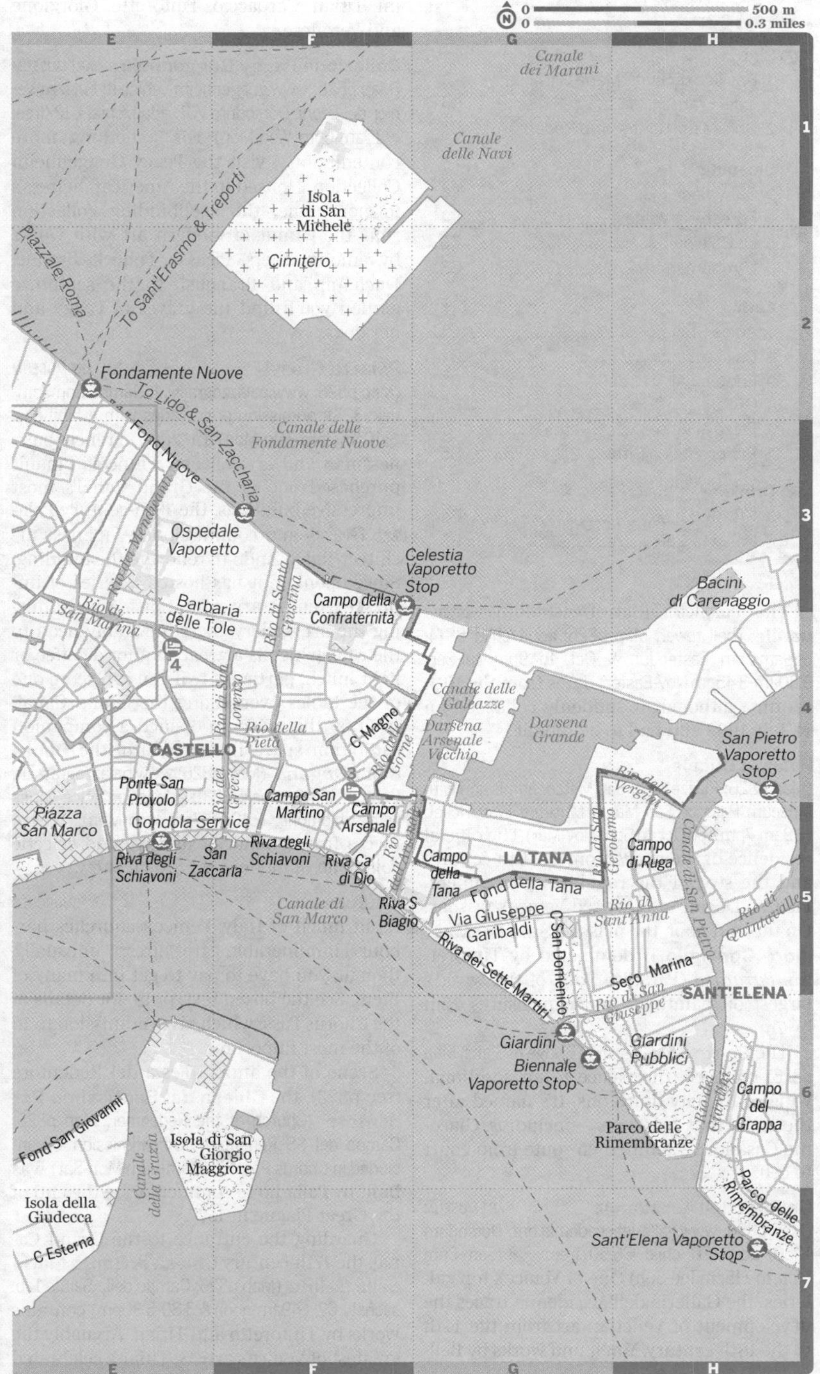

ITALY VENICE

Venice

Sights

Sleeping

Eating

Drinking

The basilica's 99m freestanding **campanile** (bell tower; Map p826; adult/child €8/4; ⏲9am-7pm Easter-Jun & Oct, to 9pm Jul-Sep, 9.30am-3.45pm Nov-Easter) dates from the 10th century, although it suddenly collapsed on 14 July 1902 and had to be rebuilt.

Palazzo Ducale PALACE
(Map p826; Piazzetta di San Marco; admission with Museum Pass or San Marco Museum Plus Ticket; ⏲9am-7pm Apr-Oct, to 6pm Nov-Mar) The official residence of the *doges* from the 9th century and the seat of the republic's government, Palazzo Ducale also housed Venice's prisons. On the 2nd floor, the massive **Sala del Maggiore Consiglio** is dominated by Tintoretto's *Paradiso* (Paradise), one of the world's largest oil paintings, which measures 22m by 7m.

The **Ponte dei Sospiri** (Bridge of Sighs; Map p826) connects the palace to an additional wing of the city dungeons. It's named after the sighs that prisoners – including Giacomo Casanova – emitted en route from court to cell.

Gallerie dell'Accademia ART MUSEUM
(Map p826; www.gallerieaccademia.org; Dorsoduro 1050; adult/EU child €6.50/free; ⏲8.15am-2pm Mon, to 7.15pm Tue-Sun) One of Venice's top galleries, the Galleria dell'Accademia traces the development of Venetian art from the 14th to the 18th century. You'll find works by Bellini, Titian, Carpaccio, Tintoretto, Giorgione and Veronese.

Collezione Peggy Guggenheim ART MUSEUM
(Map p826; www.guggenheim-venice.it; Palazzo Venier dei Leoni, Dorsoduro 701; adult/child €12/free; ⏲10am-6pm Wed-Mon) For something more contemporary, visit the Peggy Guggenheim Collection. Housed in the American heiress's former home, the spellbinding collection runs the gamut of modern art with works by, among others, Picasso, Pollock, Braque, Duchamp and Brancusi. In the sculpture garden you'll find the graves of Peggy and her dogs.

Palazzo Grassi ART MUSEUM
(Map p826; www.palazzograssi.it; Campo San Samuele 3231; admission price varies with exhibitions; ⏲10am-7pm Wed-Mon) In 2005, French businessman and art collector François Pinault purchased one of the Grand Canal's most impressive buildings, the 18th-century Palazzo Grassi, and commissioned Japanese architect Tadeo Ando to renovate the building. Since opening, it has hosted a series of impressive temporary exhibitions. After admiring the art, gallery-goers inevitably head to the cafe, which is a great spot for a coffee or light lunch, particularly if you can score one of the tables overlooking the Grand Canal. In 2009 the museum opened a companion exhibition space in Dorsoduro, the **Punta della Dogana** (Map p826; www.palazzograssi.it; Campo San Samuele 3231; admission price varies with exhibitions; ⏲10am-7pm Wed-Mon), where pieces from Pinault's extensive and eclectic collection of modern art are on show.

Churches CHURCHES
As in much of Italy, Venice's churches harbour innumerable treasures; unusually, though, you have to pay to get into many of them. See the boxed text, p819, for details of the Chorus Pass, which gives admission to 16 of the most important.

Scene of the annual Festa del Redentore (see p823), the **Chiesa del Santissimo Redentore** (Church of the Redeemer; Map p820; Campo del SS Redentore 194; admission €3, included in Chorus Pass; ⏲10am-5pm Mon-Sat) was built by Palladio to commemorate the end of the Great Plague in 1577.

Guarding the entrance to the Grand Canal, the 17th-century **Chiesa di Santa Maria della Salute** (Map p826; Campo della Salute 1/b; sacristy €2; ⏲9am-noon & 3.30-5.30pm) contains works by Tintoretto and Titian. Arguably the greatest of Venice's artists, Titian's celebrated masterpiece the *Assunta* (Assumption; 1518) hangs above the high altar in the **Basilica di Santa Maria Gloriosa dei Frari** (Map p820; Campo dei Frari, San Polo 3004; admission €3, included in Chorus Pass; ⏲10am-6pm Mon-Sat, 1-6pm Sun), the same church in which he's buried.

The Lido BEACH

Unless you're on the Lido for the Venice Film Festival, the main reason to visit is for the beach. Be warned, though, that it's almost impossible to find space on the sand in summer. It's accessible by vaporetti 1, 2, 8, LN, 51, 52, 61 and 62.

Islands ISLANDS

Murano is the home of Venetian glass. Tour a factory for a behind-the-scenes look at production or visit the **Glass Museum** (Fondamenta Giustinian 8; adult/EU concession €6.50/3; ⏲10am-5pm Thu-Tue Nov-Mar, to 6pm Apr-Oct); you'll find it near the Museo vaporetto stop. **Burano**, with its cheery pastel-coloured houses, is renowned for its lace. **Torcello**, the republic's original island settlement, was largely abandoned due to malaria and now counts no more than 80 residents. Its not-to-be-missed Byzantine cathedral, **Santa Maria Assunta** (Piazza Torcello; adult/child €5/free; ⏲10.30am-6pm Mar-Oct, 10am-5pm Nov-Feb), is Venice's oldest.

Vaporetti 41 and 42 service Murano from the San Zaccaria vaporetto stop. Vaporetto LN services Murano and Burano from the vaporetto stop at Fondamente Nove in the northeast of the city. Vaporetto T connects Burano and Torcello.

Activities

Be prepared to pay through the nose for that most quintessential of Venetian experiences, a **gondola ride**. Official rates per gondola (maximum six people) start at €80 (€100 at night) for a short trip including the Rialto but not the Grand Canal, and €120 (€150 at night) for a 50-minute trip including the Grand Canal. Haggling is unlikely to get you a reduction.

If you're a solo traveller in Venice, the cheapest way for you to enjoy a gondola ride is to book in for the two-hour 'Ice-cream & Gondola' tour (€40) offered by **Turismo Ricettivo Veneziano** (www.turive.it). This includes a guided walking tour (conducted in English), a gelato and a 40-minute gondola ride. It leaves from the San Marco tourist office every day at 3pm. The same company offers a 2½hr 'Walking Venice' tour (€35), leaving from the tourist office every day at 9.10am. Both tours run between 1 April and 31 October only.

Festivals & Events

Carnevale RELIGIOUS CELEBRATION

The major event of the year, when some Venetians and loads of tourists don Venetian-made masks and costumes for a week-long party in the lead-up to Ash Wednesday. It's been going since 1268.

Palio delle Quattro Repubbliche Marinare BOAT RACE

Usually held in early June. Venice, Amalfi, Genoa and Pisa take turns to host this historic regatta. It's in Venice in 2015.

Festa del Redentore RELIGIOUS CELEBRATION

Held on the third weekend in July; celebrations climax with a spectacular fireworks display.

Regata Storica GONDALA RACES

Costumed parades precede gondola races on the Grand Canal; held on the first Sunday in September.

Venice Architecture Biennale ARCHITECTURE EXHIBITION

This major architecture shindig is held every even-numbered year from late August to November.

Venice Biennale ART EXHIBITION

This major exhibition of international visual arts is held every odd-numbered year from June to November.

Venice International Film Festival FILM FESTIVAL

(Mostra del Cinema di Venezia) Italy's top film fest is held in late August and September at the Lido's Palazzo del Cinema.

Sleeping

Venice is Italy's most expensive city. It's always advisable to book ahead, especially at weekends, in May and September, and during Carnevale and other holidays.

SAN MARCO

TOP CHOICE **Palazzina Grassi** BOUTIQUE HOTEL €€€

(Map p826; ☎041 528 46 44; www.palazzinagrassi.com; San Marco 3247; rooms from €260; ❄📶) Phillipe Stark has endowed this formidably fashionable hotel with his signature style, and we're pleased to report that his design lives up to the magnificent Grand Canal location. Common areas are lavishly decorated with designer furniture and artworks (as befits a hotel owned by the Pinault

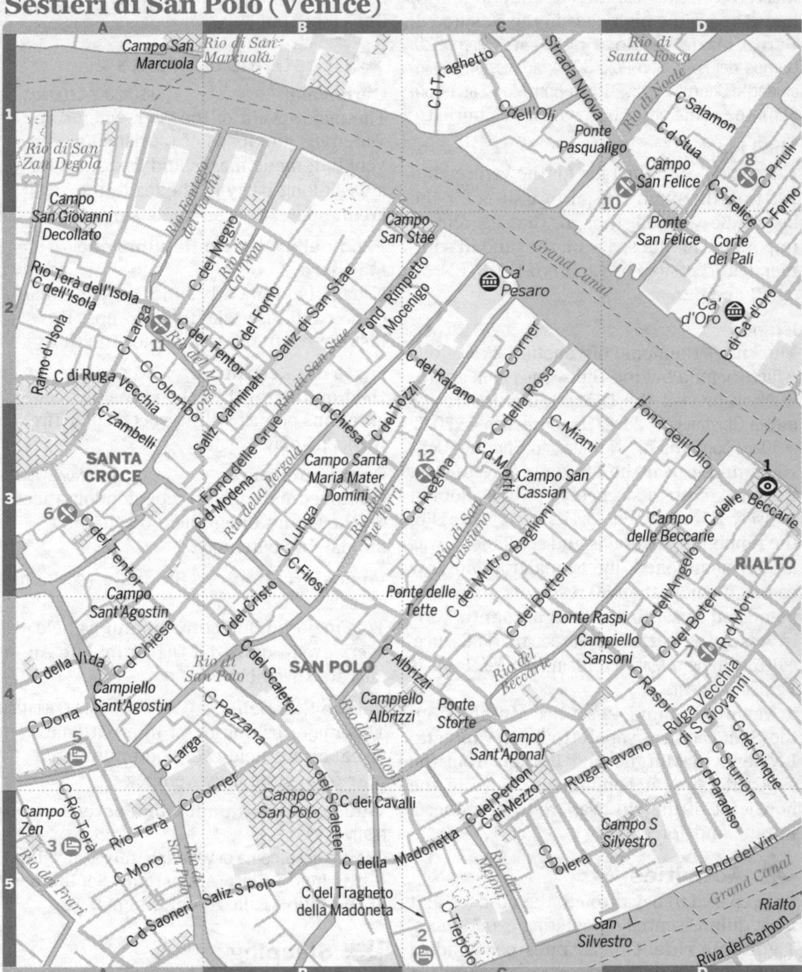

operation) and the light-drenched rooms cleverly use mirrors and white furnishings to maximise space. The hotel's Krug champagne bar is the ultimate in exclusiveness.

Novecento BOUTIQUE HOTEL €€€

(Map p826; ☎041 241 37 65; www.novecento.biz; Celle del Dose, Campo San Maurizio 2683; r €150-300; ❄@📶) The decor here is redolent of the exotic East, and the garden is a gorgeous spot for a leisurely breakfast. The hotel sometimes hosts art exhibitions, meaning that you may well bump into artists and local connoisseurs in the enticing communal lounge.

DORSODURO

La Calcina HOTEL €€

(Map p820; ☎041 520 64 66; www.lacalcina.com; Fondamenta Zattere ai Gesuati 780; s €90-140, d €110-310; ❄) Charming La Calcina offers 29 immaculate and elegant rooms with parquet floors and timber furnishings, and a small garden. In summer, breakfast is served on a terrace overlooking the Guidecca Canal.

SAN POLO & SANTA CROCE

TOP CHOICE **Ca' Angeli** BOUTIQUE HOTEL €€

(Map p824; ☎041 523 24 80; www.caangeli.it; Calle del Tragheto della Madoneta, San Polo 1434;

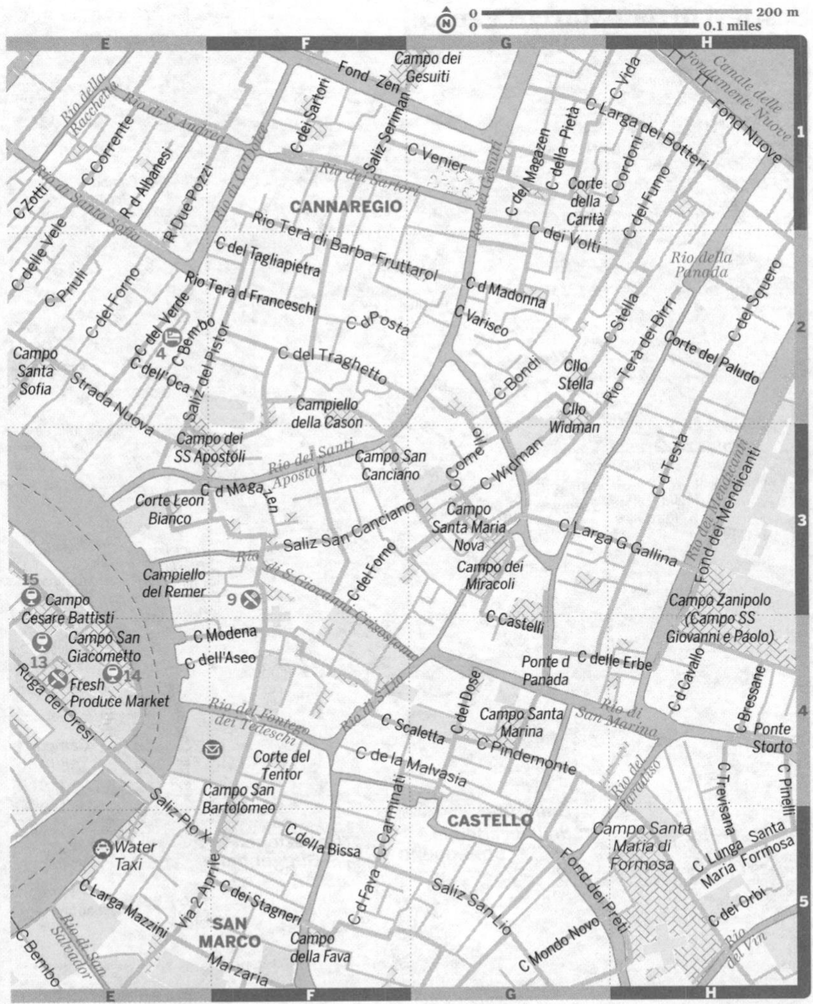

Sestieri di San Polo (Venice)

Sights

1 Rialto Market D3

Sleeping

2 Ca' Angeli C5
3 Hotel Alex A5
4 Hotel Bernardi E2
5 Oltre il Giardino A4

Eating

6 Ae Oche A3
7 All'Arco D4
8 Antica Adelaide D1
9 Fiaschetteria Toscana F3
10 La Cantina D1
11 Osteria La Zucca A2
12 Vecio Fritolin C3

Drinking

13 Al Mercà E4
14 Ancorà E4
15 Muro Venezia E3

Sestieri di San Marco (Venice)

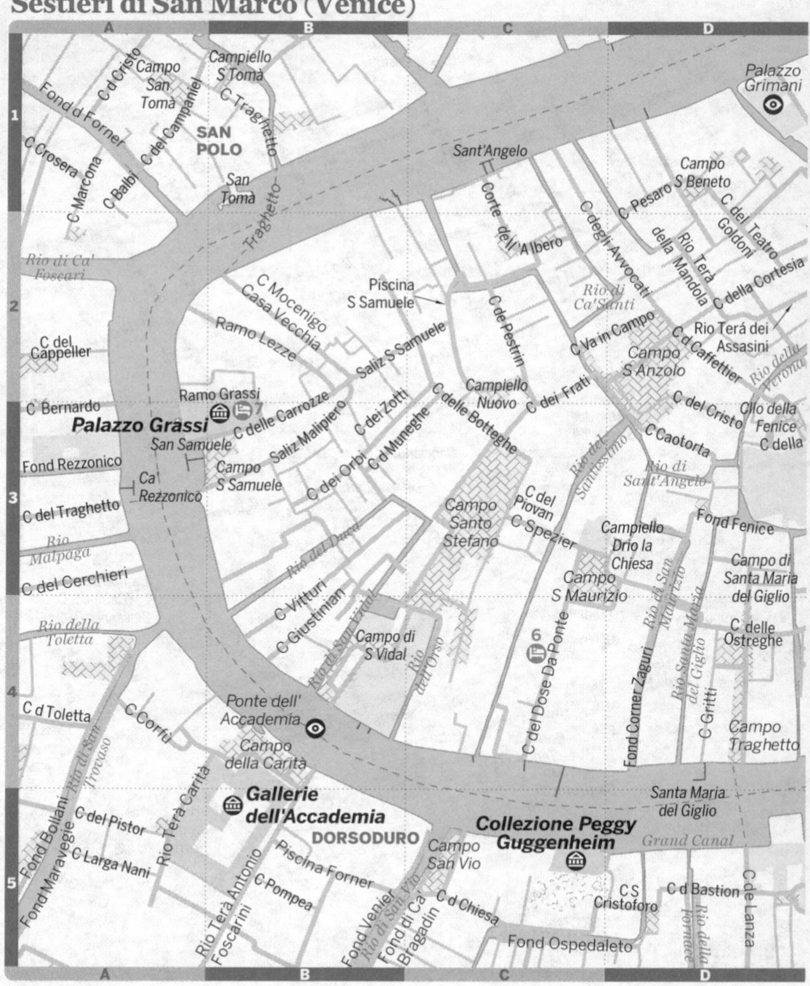

s €85-150, d €105-215, ste €195-315; ❄) A fabulous choice overlooking the Grand Canal, Ca' Angeli is notable for its extremely comfortable rooms, helpful staff and truly magnificent breakfast spread. If you can afford it, opt for a suite overlooking the Grand Canal.

Oltre il Giardino BOUTIQUE HOTEL **€€€**
(Map p824; ☎041 275 00 15; www.oltreilgiardino-venezia.com; Fondamenta Contarini, San Polo 2542; d €150-250, ste €200-500; ❄@) Once home to Alma Mahler, the composer's widow, this gorgeous property boasts a garden with pomegranate, olive and magnolia trees – an idyllic spot for a summer breakfast. The six rooms are charmingly decorated and extremely comfortable.

Hotel Alex PENSION **€**
(Map p824; ☎041 523 13 41; www.hotelalexinvenice.com; Rio Terá, San Polo 2606; s without bathroom €35-56, d without bathroom €40-90, d €60-120) The welcoming Alex is in a quiet spot near Campo dei Frari. Spread over three floors (no lift), most of the rooms are a decent size and all are decorated with simple efficiency.

L'Imbarcadero HOSTEL **€**
(Map p824; ☎392 584 06 00; www.hostelvenice.net; cnr Imbarcadero Riva de Biasio & Calle Zen, Santa Croce; dm/s from €25/65) An easy

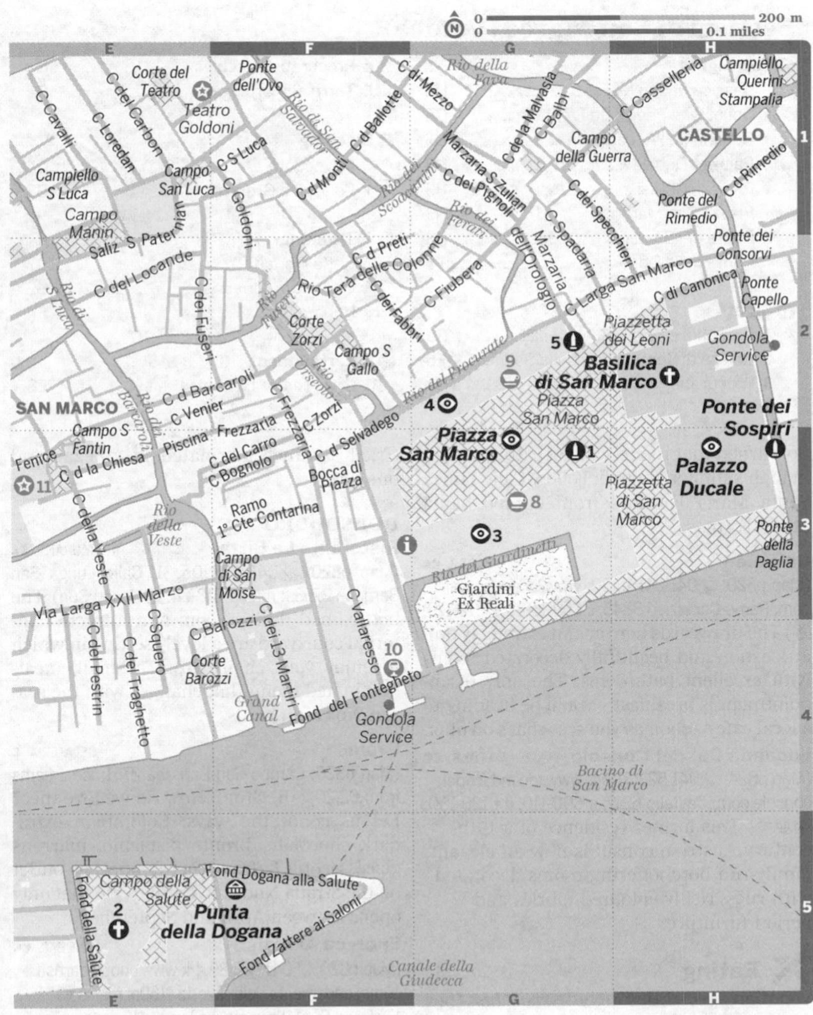

walk from the train station, this friendly hostel in Santa Croce offers clean mixed and female-only dorm rooms and private rooms with shared bathroom.

CANNAREGIO

Hotel Bernardi HOTEL €

(Map p824; ☎041 522 72 57; www.hotelbernardi.com; SS Apostoli Calle dell'Oca 4366; s without bathroom €25-32, d without bathroom €45-62, s €48-72, d €52-85; ❄@) Comfortable rooms (opt for No 25 or 26), hospitable owners and keen prices mean that this top choice is always heavily booked. A recently opened annexe just around the corner (doubles €57 to €90, family rooms €75 to €130) offers large rooms with modern bathrooms, free wi-fi and disabled access.

CASTELLO

Foresteria Valdese HOSTEL €

(Map p820; ☎041 528 67 97; www.foresteriavenezia.it; Centro Culturale P Cavagnis 5170; dm/d from €30/92; @) Run by the Waldensian and Methodist Church and housed in a rambling old mansion close to Piazza San Marco, this hostel is one of the cheapest sleeping options in Venice and so is extremely popular.

Sestieri di San Marco (Venice)

Top Sights

Basilica di San Marco H2
Collezione Peggy Guggenheim C5
Gallerie dell'Accademia B5
Palazzo Ducale H3
Palazzo Grassi B3
Piazza San Marco G3
Ponte dei Sospiri H3
Punta della Dogana F5

Sights

1 Campanile G3
2 Chiesa di Santa Maria della Salute E5
3 Procuratie Nuove G3
4 Procuratie Vecchie G2
5 Torre dell'Orologio G2

Sleeping

6 Novecento C4
7 Palazzina Grassi B3

Drinking

8 Caffè Florian G3
9 Gran Caffè Quadri G2
10 Harry's Bar F4

Entertainment

11 Gran Teatro La Fenice E3

Be warned that rooms can get extremely hot in high summer, though. Follow Calle Lunga Santa Maria Formosa from Campo Santa Maria Formosa.

Ca' Valeri B&B €€

(Map p820; ☎041 241 15 30; www.locandacavaleri.com; Ramo Corazzieri 3845; r €69-169, ste €79-179; ❄) The drawcards here are an extremely quiet location and beautifully decorated rooms with excellent bathrooms. The only disappointment is breakfast – you'll be heading to a local cafe as soon as you see what's on offer.

Locanda Ca' del Console B&B €€

(Map p824; ☎041 523 31 64; www.locandacadelconsole.com; Castello 6217; s €90-110, d €120-180; ❄@☎) This former residence of a 19th-century Austrian consul is now an elegant, family-run hotel offering rooms decorated with rugs, richly coloured fabrics and period furniture.

Eating

Venetian specialities include *risi e bisi* (pea soup thickened with rice) and *sarde di saor* (fried sardines marinated in vinegar and onions).

WANT MORE?

For in-depth information, reviews and recommendations at your fingertips, head to the Apple App Store to purchase Lonely Planet's *Venice & the Veneto City Guide* iPhone app.

Alternatively, head to **Lonely Planet** (www.lonelyplanet.com/italy/venice) for planning advice, author recommendations, traveller reviews and insider tips.

DORSODURO

Ristorante La Bitta RESTAURANT €€

(Map p820; ☎041 523 05 31; Calle Lunga San Barnaba 2753a; mains €18-24; ⊙closed Sun) The bottle-lined dining room and attractive internal courtyard are a lovely setting in which to enjoy your choice from a small, meat-dominated menu that changes with the season. No credit cards.

Grom GELATERIA €

(Map p820; Campo San Barnaba 2761; ice creams from €2.20) Ah, Grom. How do we love thee? Let us count the ways: Colombian extra-dark chocolate, Bronte pistachio, marrons glacé, ricotta & fig... There's another outlet on the Strada Nuova in Cannaregio that only opens between April and September.

Enoteca Ai Artisti WINE BAR €€

(Map p820; ☎041 523 89 44; www.enotecaartisti.com; Fondamenta della Toletta 1169a; mains €15; ⊙closed Sun) This tiny place takes its wine seriously (there's a great choice by the glass) and serves delicious cheeses, bruschetta (toast with toppings) and bowls of pasta.

Pizza al Volo PIZZERIA €

(Map p820; Campo Santa Margherita 2944; pizza slices €2-4) In need of a pizza pit stop? Here's your opportunity. You'll be in the company of a steady stream of interns from the Guggenheim.

SAN POLO & SANTA CROCE

Vecio Fritolin RESTAURANT €€€

(Map p824; ☎041 522 28 81; www.veciofritolin.it; Calle della Regina, Santa Croce 2262; mains €25; ⊙dinner Tue, lunch & dinner Wed-Mon) Traditionally, a *fritolin* was an eatery where diners sat at a common table and tucked into fried seafood and polenta. This is the modern equivalent, only the food is sophisticated, the menu is varied and the decor is stylish rather than rustic. The owners also run a cafe in the Palazzo Grassi.

Osteria La Zucca WINE BAR, RESTAURANT €€
(Map p824; www.lazucca.it; Calle del Tentor, Santa Croce 1762; mains €10; closed Sun;) An unpretentious little restaurant in an out-of-the-way spot, 'The Pumpkin' serves a range of innovative Mediterranean dishes prepared with fresh, seasonal ingredients. Most are small and perfect to share; many are vegetarian.

All'Arco WINE BAR €
(Map p824; Calle dell'Arco, San Polo 436; chiceti €1.50-4; 7.30am-8pm Mon-Sat) Popular with locals, this tiny *osteria* serves delicious bruschetta and a range of good-quality wine by the glass.

Ae Oche PIZZA €
(Map p824; www.aeoche.com; Calle del Tentor, Santa Croce 1552a/b; pizzas €4-9.50) Students adore the Tex-Mex decor and huge pizza list at this bustling place. It's on the main path between the *ferrovia* and San Marco.

CANNAREGIO

Da Marisa TRATTORIA €€
(Map p820; 041 72 02 11; Fondamenta di San Giobbe 652b; lunch incl wine & coffee €15, dinner incl wine & coffee €35-40; lunch daily, dinner Tue & Thu-Sat) You can watch the sun setting over the lagoon from the canalside tables here. Local devotees overlook the fact that service can be brusque, meal times are set (noon and 8pm), credit cards aren't accepted and there's no opportunity to vary the excellent daily menu, which is mostly meat but sometimes seafood.

Fiaschetteria Toscana RESTAURANT €€€
(Map p824; 041 528 52 81; www.fiaschetteriatoscana.it; Salizada S Giovanni Grisostomo 5719; mains €14-32; closed all day Tue & lunch Wed) Don't worry about the name – this old-fashioned favourite near the Rialto specialises in Venetian dishes but varies the formula with a few Tuscan triumphs such as chianina beef fillet in red-wine sauce. Seafood dominates the menu – the house speciality is fried fish 'Serenissima' style – and the desserts are delectable.

Antica Adelaide BAR/TRATTORIA €€
(Map p824; Calle Priuli 3728; mains €10-15) Adelaide has been in the food business since as far back as the 18th century. You can pop in for a drink and *cicheti* (bar snacks) or tuck into a hearty bowl of pasta or full meal.

Anice Stellato TRATTORIA €€€
(Map p820; 041 72 07 44; Fondamenta della Sensa 3272; mains €17.50-23; closed Mon & Tue) In the little-visited historic Jewish Ghetto, this friendly place serves up huge plates of seafood antipasti, delicious pasta dishes and a super-sized house speciality of fried mixed fish with polenta.

La Cantina WINE BAR €
(Map p824; Campo San Felice 3689; chicheti €4-10; closed Mon, 2 weeks Jul & Aug, 2 weeks Jan) Sit at one of the outdoor tables at this *enoteca* (wine bar) and watch the passing traffic promenade up and down the Strada Nuova. A good choice of wines by the glass and classy *chicheti* make it deservedly popular.

Drinking

Al Mercá BAR
(Map p824; Campo Cesare Battisti, San Polo 212-213; closed Sun) One of the city's best bars, this tiny place serves excellent and keenly priced wines by the glass accompanied by a lavish array of *chiceti* – arrive around 6.30pm for the best choice. No seating, just loads of atmosphere.

Muro Venezia BAR
(Map p824; www.murovinoecucina.it; Campo Cesare Battisti, San Polo 222; closed Sun) The centre of a happening nightlife scene in the market squares of the Rialto, Muro is the watering hole of choice for young locals, who spill out into the square with their drinks.

Caffè Florian CAFE
(Map p826; www.caffeflorian.com; Piazza San Marco 56/59) If you think it's worth paying up to four times the usual price for a coffee, emulate Byron, Goethe and Rousseau and pull up a seat at Piazza San Marco's most famous cafe.

Il Caffè BAR
(Map p820; Campo Santa Margherita, Dorsoduro 2963; closed Sun) Popular with foreign and Italian students, this is one of Venice's historic drinking spots. Known to locals as Caffè Rosso because of its red frontage, it's got outdoor seating and serves a great *spritz* (Venetian cocktail made with *prosecco* – Venetian sparkling white, soda water and aperol or campari).

Harry's Bar BAR
(Map p826; www.harrysbarvenezia.com; Calle Vallaresso, San Marco 1323) To drink a Bellini (white-peach pulp and *prosecco*) at the bar

that invented them is an expensive experience to tick off the list rather than a holiday highlight. Nevertheless, this bar to the stars is always full.

Ancorà BAR
(Map p824; Fabbriche Vecchie, San Polo; closed Sun) Enjoy your *aperitivo* with a Grand Canal view while sitting at one of the three outdoor tables on the waterside terrace here.

Gran Caffè Quadri CAFE
(Map p826; www.quadrivenice.com; Piazza San Marco 121) Opposite Florian, Caffè Quadri offers more of the same.

Imagina Café CAFE, BAR
(Map p820; www.imaginacafe.it; Campo San Margherita, Dorsoduro 3126; closed Sun) A constantly changing exhibition program means that patrons can enjoy art with their *aperitivo* at this hip modern bar.

Entertainment

Tickets for the majority of events in Venice are available from **HelloVenezia ticket outlets** (www.hellovenezia.it; 7am-10.45pm), run by the ACTV transport network. You'll find them in front of the train station and at Piazzale Roma.

Gran Teatro La Fenice OPERA HOUSE
(Map p826; for guided tours 041 24 24; www.teatrolafenice.it; Campo San Fantin, San Marco 1977; opera tickets from €20) One of Italy's most important opera houses, the fully restored Fenice is back to its sumptuous best after being destroyed by fire in 1996. The opera season runs from May to November.

Information

Emergency

Police station (Questura; 041 271 55 11; Fondamenta di San Lorenzo, Castello 5053) There's also a small branch at Piazza San Marco 67.

Medical Services

Twenty-four-hour pharmacies are listed in *Un Ospite a Venezia* (A Guest in Venice), a free guide available in many hotels.

Ospedale Civile (Hospital; 041 529 41 04; Campo SS Giovanni e Paolo 6777)

Tourist Information

Pick up the free *Shows & Events* guide at tourist offices. It contains comprehensive city listings and a useful public transport map on the inside back cover. The tourist offices also sell a handy map of the city (€2.50).

Azienda di Promozione Turistica (Venice Tourist Board; central information line 041 529 87 11; www.turismovenezia.it) Lido (Gran Viale Santa Maria Elisabetta 6a; 9am-noon & 3-6pm Jun-Sep); Marco Polo airport (Arrivals Hall; 9am-9pm); Piazza San Marco (Map p826; Piazza San Marco 71f; 9am-3.30pm); Piazzale Roma (Map p820; 9.30am-4.30pm Jun-Sep); train station (Map p820; 8am-6.30pm).

Getting There & Away

Air

Most European and domestic flights land at **Marco Polo airport** (VCE; 041 260 92 60; www.veniceairport.it), 12km outside Venice. Ryanair flies to **Treviso airport** (TSF; 0422 31 51 11; www.trevisoairport.it), about 30km from Venice.

Boat

Minoan Lines (210 414 57 00; www.minoan.gr) runs ferries to Corfu (23½ hours), Igoumenitsa (22 hours) and Patra (36 hours) daily in summer and four times per week in winter. Tickets are priced between €54 and €289.

Bus

ACTV (041 24 24; www.actv.it) buses service surrounding areas, including Mestre, Padua and Treviso. Tickets and information are available at the bus station in Piazzale Roma.

Train

Venice's Stazione di Santa Lucia is directly linked by regional trains to Padua (€2.90, 45 minutes, every 20 minutes), Verona (€18.50, 1¼ hours, half-hourly) and Ferrara (€6.15, 1½ hours, every two hours). It is easily accessible from Bologna, Milan, Rome and Florence. You can also reach points in France, Germany, Austria, Switzerland, Slovenia and Croatia from here.

Getting Around

To/From the Airport

To travel between Venice and Marco Polo airport there are various options. **Alilaguna** (www.alilaguna.com) operates four fast-ferry lines between the airport ferry dock and different parts of the city (€13, 70 minutes, approximately every hour); the Rossa (Red) line goes to Piazza San Marco and the Oro (Gold) line goes to both Rialto and San Marco. Follow the signs from the arrivals hall to the ferry dock, where there is a dedicated ticket office. **ATVO** (041 520 55 30; www.atvo.it, in Italian) runs 'Venezia Express' buses (€3/5.50 one-way/return, 20 minutes, every half-hour) between the airport and Piazzale Roma, and **ACTV** operates bus 5d (€2.50, 25 minutes, every half-hour). Water taxis from the airport cost €100 for up to five passengers; it's an extra €50 to travel via the Grand Canal.

For Treviso airport, take the ATVO Ryanair bus (€5, 70 minutes, 16 daily) from Piazzale Roma two hours and 10 minutes before your flight departure. The last service is at 7.40pm.

Boat

The city's main mode of public transport is the vaporetto. The most useful routes:

1 From Piazzale Roma to the train station and down the Grand Canal to San Marco and the Lido.

2 From S Zaccaria (near San Marco) to the Lido via Giudecca, Piazzale Roma, the train station and the Rialto.

DM From Piazzale Roma to Murano.

LN From Fondamenta Nuove to S Zaccaria via Murano and Burano.

T Runs between Burano and Torcello.

Tickets, available from ACTV booths at the major vaporetti stops, are expensive: €6.50 for a single trip; €16 for 12 hours; €18 for 24 hours; €23 for 36 hours; €28 for two days; €33 for three days; and €50 for seven days. There are significant discounts for holders of the Rolling Venice Card (eg €18 instead of €33 for the three-day ticket) and all tickets are 15% cheaper if you purchase them online (www.veniceconnected.com) in advance of your trip.

The poor man's gondola, *traghetti* (€0.50 per crossing) are used by Venetians to cross the Grand Canal where there's no nearby bridge.

Car & Motorcycle

Vehicles must be parked on Tronchetto or at Piazzale Roma (cars are allowed on the Lido – take car ferry 17 from Tronchetto). The car parks are not cheap – €27 to €30 every 24 hours – so you're better off leaving your car in Mestre and getting a train over to Venice.

Ferrara

POP 134,500

Ferrara retains much of the austere splendour of its Renaissance heyday, when it was the seat of the powerful Este family (1260–1598). Overshadowed by the menacing Castello Estense, the compact medieval centre is atmospheric and lively.

Sights

If you're planning to visit the major monuments, buy a **Museum Card** (adult/concession €17/10), which gives free entry to all municipal museums. It's available from both the Cathedral Museum and Palazzo Schifanoia.

Castello Estense CASTLE
(www.castelloestense.it; Viale Cavour; adult/child €8/free, Lion's Tower extra €2; ⏲9.30am-5.30pm Tue-Sun) Guarding the northern edge of Ferrara's attractive *centro storico*, the stirring Castello Estense is quite a sight with its square towers, moat and drawbridge. It was begun by Nicolò II d'Este in 1385 and became the Este family's residence. Highlights include the **Sala dei Giganti** (Giant's Room) and **Salone dei Giochi** (Games Salon) with frescos by Camillo and Sebastiano Filippi.

Duomo CHURCH
(Piazza Cattedrale; ⏲7.30am-noon & 3-6.30pm Mon-Sat, 7.30am-12.30pm & 3.30-7.30pm Sun) The pink-and-white 12th-century cathedral is most notable for its superb three-tiered marble facade, which combines Romanesque and Gothic architectural styles. The upper tier features a graphic Gothic depiction of the Last Judgement and heaven and hell.

Palazzo Schifanoia HISTORIC BUILDING
(Via Scandiana 23; adult/child €6/free; ⏲9am-6pm Tue-Sun) Famous for its frescos, this is one of Ferrara's earliest Renaissance buildings and another Este palace. In the **Sala dei Mesi** (Room of the Months), the 15th-century frescos are considered among the best examples of their type in Italy.

Sleeping & Eating

You won't need to stay overnight to see Ferrara's sights, but it's a cheap alternative to Bologna, and a viable base for Venice.

Hotel de Prati HOTEL €€
(☎0532 24 19 05; www.hoteldeprati.com; Via Padiglioni 5; s/d €80/120; ❄📶) A charming three-star place on the edge of the *centro storico*. Guestrooms are quietly elegant with wrought-iron bedsteads, high ceilings and classic furniture, while downstairs, the yellow and orange walls stage contemporary art exhibitions.

Pensione Artisti PENSION €
(☎0532 76 10 38; Via Vittoria 66; s/d without bathroom €28/50, d €60) Ferrara's best budget option features scrubbed old-fashioned rooms, kitchen facilities, free bikes and an excellent location in the *centro storico*. The superfriendly owners also ensure a warm welcome. No breakfast.

Ristorante Osteria Balebùste BAR, RESTAURANT €€
(☎0532 76 35 57; Via Vittoria 44; mains €13; ⏲closed Thu) The exposed-brick walls and

high medieval wood ceiling set the atmospheric backdrop for a relaxed meal of well-presented regional food. Particularly good are the meaty main courses. The adjacent bar also serves evening *aperitvi*.

Al Brindisi Wine Bar OSTERIA €€

(Via Adelardi 11; meals €25-30, set lunch menus from €13; ⏲11am-1am) Apparently the oldest *osteria* in the world, this atmospheric wine bar dates to 1435 – Titian and Copernicus both drank here. Alongside the substantial wine list there's an extensive menu of traditional pastas, mains and snacks.

Information

The **tourist office** (☎0532 29 93 03; www.ferrarainfo.com; ⏲9am-1pm & 2-6pm Mon-Sat, 9.30am-1pm & 2-5.30pm Sun) is inside Castello Estense.

Getting There & Around

Ferrara is easy to reach by train. There are regional trains to Bologna (€4, 45 minutes, every 30 to 60 minutes), Venice (€6.15, 1½ hours, every two hours) and nearby Ravenna (€5.70, 1¼ hours, 14 daily).

From the station take bus 1 or 9 for the historic centre.

Bologna

POP 375,000

Boasting a boisterous bonhomie rare in Italy's reserved north, Bologna is worth a few days of anyone's itinerary, not so much for its specific attractions, but for the sheer fun of strolling its animated, arcaded streets. A university town since 1088 (Europe's oldest), it is also one of Italy's foremost foodie destinations. Besides the eponymous *ragù* (bolognese sauce), classic pasta dishes such as tortellini and lasagne were invented here, as was mortadella (aka baloney or Bologna sausage). Treats such as these are enjoyed in welcoming trattorias throughout the city, washed down with fizzy Lambrusco red wine. After dinner, locals love to wander through the city's arcades to their favourite bar or nightclub and party the night away – this is not a town that goes to sleep early.

Sights

Piazza Maggiore SQUARE

Pedestrianised Piazza Maggiore is Bologna's focal showpiece square. On the southern flank, the Gothic **Basilica di San Petronio** (Piazza Maggiore; ⏲7.45am-12.30pm & 3-6pm), currently covered in scaffolding, is dedicated to the city's patron saint, Petronius. Its partially complete facade doesn't diminish its status as the world's fifth-largest basilica. Inside, don't miss Giovanni da Modena's bizarre *I'Inferno* fresco in the fourth chapel on the left.

To the west is the **Palazzo Comunale** (Town Hall), home to the city's art collection, the **Collezioni Comunali d'Arte** (admission free; ⏲9am-3pm Tue-Fri, 10am-6.30pm Sat & Sun) and the **Museo Morandi** (admission free; ⏲9am-3pm Tue-Fri, 10am-6.30pm Sat & Sun) dedicated to the work of Giorgio Morandi.

Adjacent to the square, **Piazza del Nettuno** is named after the **Fontana del Nettuno** (Neptune's Fountain), sculpted by Giambologna in 1566 and featuring an impressively muscled Neptune.

Le Due Torri MEDIEVAL TOWERS

Rising above **Piazza di Porta Ravegnana** are Bologna's two leaning towers, Le Due Torri. The taller of the two, the 97m-high

Bologna

Top Sights

	Basilica di San Domenico	B5
	Basilica di San Petronio	B4
	Le Due Torri	C3
	Piazza Maggiore	B3

Sights

	Collezioni Comunali d'Arte	(see 3)
1	Fontana del Nettuno	B3
2	Museo Civico Archeologico	B4
	Museo Morandi	(see 3)
3	Palazzo Comunale	B3

Sleeping

4	Albergo delle Drapperie	B3
5	Albergo Panorama	A3
6	Hotel Novecento	A4
7	Il Convento dei Fiori di Seta	D6

Eating

8	Il Saraceno	A3
9	La Sorbetteria Castiglione	C6
10	Osteria de' Poeti	C5
11	Pizzeria Belle Arti	D2
12	Trattoria Mariposa	B1

Drinking

13	Café de Paris	C4
14	Caffè degli Orefici	B3
15	La Scuderia	D2

Entertainment

16	Cantina Bentivoglio	D1

Torre degli Asinelli (admission €3; ⌚9am-6pm, to 5pm Nov-Mar), was built between 1109 and 1119 and is now open to the public. Climb the 498 steps for some superb city views. The neighbouring **Torre Garisenda** stands at 48m.

Basilica di San Domenico CHURCH
(Piazza San Domenico 13; ⌚9.30am-12.30pm & 3.30-6.30pm Mon-Sat, 3.30-5.30pm Sun) This 13th-century church is noteworthy for the elaborate sarcophagus of San Domenico, founder of the Dominican order. The tomb stands in the **Capella di San Domenico**,

Bologna

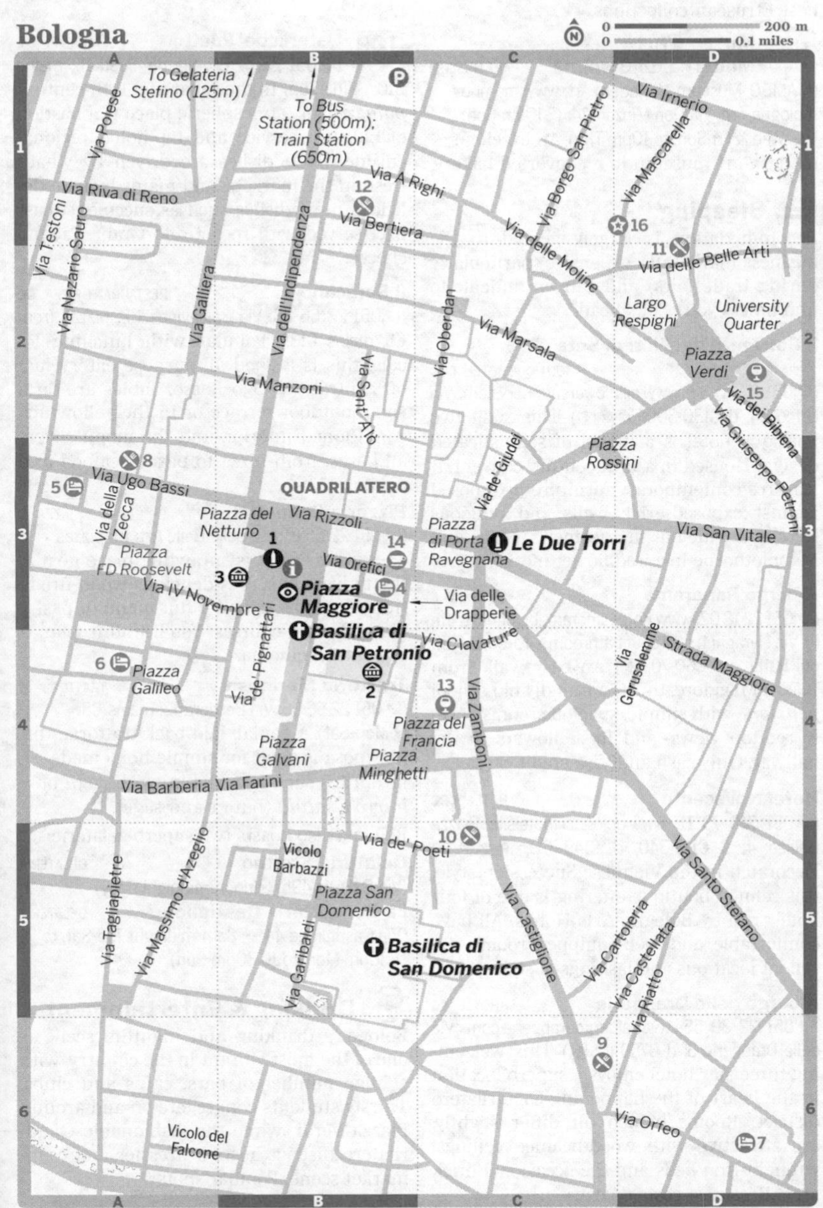

which was designed by Nicolò Pisano and later added to by, among others, Michelangelo.

Also recommended:

FREE **Museo Civico Archeologico** MUSEUM (Via dell'Archiginnasio 2; ⏲9am-3pm Tue-Fri, 10am-6.30pm Sat & Sun) Exhibits Egyptian and Roman artefacts and one of Italy's best Etruscan collections.

FREE **Museo d'Arte Moderna do Bologna** ART MUSEUM (MAMBO, Museum of Modern Art; www.mambo-bologna-org; Via Don Minzoni 14; ⏲10am-6pm Tue, Wed & Fri-Sun, to 10pm Thu) An excellent modern-art museum in a converted bakery.

Sleeping

Accommodation is largely geared to the business market. It's expensive (particularly during trade fairs) and can be difficult to find unless you book ahead.

Il Convento dei Fiori di Seta BOUTIQUE HOTEL €€€
(☎051 27 20 39; www.silkflowersnunnery.com; Via Orfeo 34; d €130-300; ❄@🛜) This seductive boutique hotel is a model of sophisticated design. Housed in a 15th-century convent, it features contemporary furniture juxtaposed against exposed-brick walls and religious frescos, a wine bar in a former sacristy, and Mapplethorpe-inspired flower motifs.

Albergo Panorama PENSION €
(☎051 22 18 02; www.hotelpanoramabologna.it; 4th flr, Via Livraghi 1; s without bathroom €40-50, d without bathroom €60-70; ❄) An easy walk from Piazza Maggiore, this is a friendly old-school *pensione* with simple, spacious rooms, lovely rooftop views, and fresh flowers in the hallway. Only cash and Visa credit cards.

Hotel Novecento HOTEL €€€
(☎051 745 73 11; www.bolognarthotels.it; Piazza Galileo 4; s €113-340, d €149-370; P❄@🛜) Decorated in the Viennese Succession style, this refined boutique offering is one of four hotels run by Bologna Arts Hotels. All have comfortable and well-equipped rooms, excellent locations and lashings of style.

Albergo delle Drapperie HOTEL €€
(☎051 22 39 55; www.albergodrapperie.com; Via delle Drapperie 5; d €75-140; ❄) This welcoming three-star hotel enjoys a superb location in the heart of the happening Quadrilatero district. Rooms, which all differ slightly, are attractive with wood-beamed ceilings, wrought-iron beds and the occasional brick arch. Breakfast costs €5 extra.

Eating

The university district northeast of Via Rizzoli harbours hundreds of restaurants, trattorias, takeaways and cafes catering to hard-up students and gourmet diners alike. For foodie gifts head to the sumptuous delis in the Quadrilatero district east of Piazza Maggiore.

TOP CHOICE **Osteria de' Poeti** RESTAURANT €€
(☎051 23 61 66; Via de' Poeti 1b; mains €10; ⏲Tue-Sun) In the cellar of a 14th-century *palazzo,* this atmospheric place is a bastion of old-style service and top-notch regional cuisine. Pasta dishes are driven by what's fresh in the markets, and mains include delicious meat dishes such as succulent roast beef served with rocket and Grana Padano cheese.

Il Saraceno RESTAURANT, PIZZA €€
(☎051 23 66 28; Via Calcavinazzi 2; pizzas from €5, mains €13,) Popular with lunching locals, this is a good all-purpose eatery just off central Via Ugo Basso. Tables are on a small outdoor terrace or in the yellow air-conditioned interior, and the menu covers all bases, from pizza to pasta, seafood and meats.

Pizzeria Belle Arti PIZZA €
(☎051 22 55 81; Via delle Belle Arti 14; pizzas €5-9, mains €8) This sprawling place near the university serves delicious wood-fired thin-crust pizzas and a full menu of pastas and main courses. You'll find it near the Odeon cinema.

Trattoria Mariposa TRATTORIA €
(☎051 22 56 56; Via Bertiera 12; mains €8; ⏲Mon-Sat) A genial, laid-back trattoria, the Mariposa is good for simple homemade favourites such as tortellini with *ragù* or *burro e salvia* (butter and sage).

Bologna also boasts two superb gelaterie:

Gelateria Stefino GELATERIA
(Via Galleria 49b; ⏲noon-midnight daily)

La Sorbetteria Castiglione GELATERIA
(Via Castiglione 44; ⏲8am-midnight Tue-Sat, to 11.30pm Mon, to 10.30pm Sun).

Drinking & Entertainment

Bologna's drinking and nightlife scene is one of the most vibrant in the country, with a huge number of bars, cafe's and clubs. Thirsty students congregate on and around Piazza Verdi, while the fashionable Quadrilatero district hosts a dressier, more upmarket scene. Popular spots:

Café de Paris BAR

(Piazza del Francia 1c; ⌚8am-1am Mon-Thu, to late Fri & Sat) Modish bar with daily aperitif between 6pm and 10pm.

La Scuderia BAR

(Piazza Verdi 2; ⌚8am-3am Mon-Fri, 5pm-3am Sat) A popular student bar housed in medieval stables.

Caffè degli Orefici CAFE

(Via Orefici 6; ⌚Mon-Sat) A modern cafe next to a historic coffee shop.

Cantina Bentivoglio JAZZ CLUB

(☎051 26 54 16; www.cantinabentivoglio.it; Via Mascarella 4b; ⌚8pm-2am) Music lovers won't want to miss Bologna's top jazz club; it's also a wine bar and restaurant.

Cassero CLUB

(www.cassero.it; Via Don Minzoni 18) Legendary gay and lesbian (but not exclusively) club. Home of Italy's Arcigay movement.

ℹ Information

Ospedale Maggiore (Hospital; ☎051 647 81 11; Largo Nigrisoli 2)

Police station (Questura; ☎051 640 11 11; Piazza Galileo 7)

Tourist information (☎051 23 96 60; www.bolognaturismo.info) Airport (⌚9am-7pm); Piazza Maggiore 1 (⌚9am-7pm)

ℹ Getting There & Around

Air

European and domestic flights arrive at **Guglielmo Marconi airport** (BLQ; ☎051 647 96 15; www.bologna-airport.it), 6km northwest of the city. An Aerobus shuttle (€5, 30 minutes, every 10 minutes) departs from the main train station; buy your ticket at the ATC office behind the taxi rank or on board.

Bus

National and international coaches depart from the **bus station** (Piazza XX Settembre), southeast of the train station. However, for most Italy destinations the train is a better bet.

To get to the centre from the train station take bus A, 25 or 30 (€1).

Train

Bologna is a major rail hub. From the **central train station** (Piazza delle Medaglie d'Oro), fast Eurostar Alta Velocità (ES AV) trains run to: Venice (€28, 1½ hours, hourly), Florence (€24, 40 minutes, half-hourly), Rome (€58, 2¾ hours, half-hourly) and Milan (€41, one hour, hourly).

Ravenna

POP 156,000

Most people visit Ravenna to see its remarkable Unesco-protected mosaics. Relics of the city's golden age as capital of the Western Roman and Byzantine Empires, they are described by Dante in his *Divine Comedy,* much of which was written here. Easily accessible from Bologna, this refined and polished town is worth a day trip at the very least. Its national profile is raised each year during June and July when music concerts are staged as part of the **Ravenna Festival** (www.ravennafestival.org). The involvement of Italy's top conductor, Riccardo Muti, means the classical component is always strong.

👁 Sights

Dante's Tomb TOMB

(Via Dante Alighieri 9; admission free; ⌚9.30am-6.30pm) Dante spent the last 19 years of his life in Ravenna after Florence expelled him in 1302. As a perpetual act of penance, Florence supplies the oil for the lamp that burns in his tomb.

Early Christian Mosaics MOSAICS

Ravenna's mosaics are spread over five sites in the centre: the Basilica di San Vitale, the Mausoleo di Galla Placida, the Basilica di Sant'Appollinare Nuovo, the Museo Arcivescovile and the Battistero Neoniano. These are covered by a single **ticket** (adult/child €8.50/free), which is available at any of the five sites. Outside of town you'll find further mosaics at the Basilica di Sant'Apollinare in Classe. Note that the hours reported here are for April to September; outside of these months they are slightly shorter, typically 9.30am or 10am until 5pm or 5.30pm. Information on Ravenna's main sites is available online at www.ravennamosaici.it.

On the northern edge of the *centro storico,* the sombre exterior of 6th-century **Basilica di San Vitalel** (Via Fiandrini; ⌚9am-7pm) hides a dazzling interior with mosaics depicting Old Testament scenes. In the same complex, the small **Mausoleo di Galla Placidia** (Via Fiandrini; ⌚9am-7pm) contains the city's oldest mosaics. Between March and mid-September there's an extra €2 booking fee for the Mausoleo.

Adjoining Ravenna's unremarkable cathedral, **Museo Arcivescovile** (Piazza Arcivescovado; ⌚9am-7pm) boasts an exquisite 6th-century ivory throne, while next door in the

Battistero Neoniano (Via Battistero; ⏲9am-7pm), the baptism of Christ and the apostles is represented in the domed roof mosaics. To the east, the **Basilica di Sant'Apollinare Nuovo** (Via di Roma; ⏲9am-7pm) boasts, among other things, a superb mosaic depicting a procession of martyrs headed towards Christ and his apostles.

Five kilometres southeast of the city, the apse mosaic of **Basilica di Sant'Apollinare in Classe** (Via Romea Sud, Classe; adult/EU child €3/free; ⏲8.30am-7.30pm Mon-Sat, 1-7.30pm Sun) is a must-see. Take bus 4 (€1) from Piazza Caduti per la Libertà.

Sleeping & Eating

Cá de Vén WINE BAR, RESTAURANT **€€**
(www.cadeven.it; Via Corrado Ricci 24; mains €15; ⏲Tue-Sun) OK, we'll admit it's touristy, but Ravenna's most famous eatery is still an atmospheric spot for a meal and glass of wine. Housed in a cavernous 15th-century *palazzo,* it serves a full menu of regional dishes, including snacks such as *piadine* (flat-bread sandwiches).

Also recommended:

Hotel Sant'Andrea HOTEL **€€**
(☎0544 21 55 64; wwwsantandreahotel.com; Via Cattaneo 33; s €80-100, d €110-140; ❄@) A real find, this charming three-star hotel offers elegant accommodation in a converted convent. A grand wooden staircase leads up to smart, carpeted rooms overlooking a lawned garden.

Ostello Galletti Abbiosi HOSTEL **€**
(☎0544 313 13; www.galletti.ra.it; Via Roma 140; s €46, d €70-92; ❄📶) In an 18th-century town house, this is more hotel than hostel. With high-ceilinged, spacious rooms, polite service and an enviable location, it's an excellent deal.

Ostello Dante HOSTEL **€**
(☎0544 42 11 64; www.hostelravenna.com; Via Nicolodi 12; dm/s/d €16/22/44; @📶) Ravenna's modern HI youth hostel. Take bus 80 or the red 'Metrobus' A from the train station.

Locanda del Melarancio RESTAURANT **€€€**
(www.locandadelmelarancio.it; Via Mentana 33; mains18; ⏲closed Wed) Sophisticated food at popular eatery.

Information

Tourist offices Main office (☎0544 354 04; www.turismo.ravenna.it; Via Salara 8/12; ⏲8.30am-7pm Mon-Sat, 10am-6pm Sun); Teodorico (☎0544 45 15 39; Via delle Industrie 14; ⏲9.30am-12.30pm & 3.30-6.30pm); Classe (☎0544 47 36 61; Via Romea Sud 266, Classe; ⏲9.30am-12.30pm & 3.30-6.30pm) Between October and May hours are slightly shorter, typically closing time is an hour or so earlier.

Getting There & Around

Regional trains connect the city with Bologna (€6.20, 1½ hours, 14 daily) and Ferrara (€5.70, 1¼ hours, 14 daily).

In town, cycling is popular. The tourist office runs a free bike-hire service to visitors aged 18 years or over (take ID).

THE DOLOMITES

A Unesco natural heritage site since 2009, the Dolomites stretch across the northern regions of Trentino-Alto Adige and the Veneto. Their stabbing sawtooth peaks provide some of Italy's most thrilling scenery, as well as superb skiing and hiking.

Ski resorts abound, offering downhill and cross-country skiing as well as snowboarding and other winter sports. Facilities are generally excellent and accommodation is widely available. Ski passes cover either single resorts or a combination of slopes; the most comprehensive is the **Superski Dolomiti pass** (www.dolomitisuperski.com; high season 3/6 days €132/233), which accesses 1220km of runs in 12 valleys.

Hiking opportunities run the gamut from kid-friendly strolls to hard-core mountain treks. Trails are well marked with numbers on red-and-white bands on trees and rocks, or by numbers inside coloured triangles for the four *Alte Vie* (High Routes). Recommended areas include the Alpe di Siusi, a vast plateau above the Val Gardena; the area around Cortina; and Pale di San Martino, accessible from San Martino di Castrozza.

Information

Area-wide information can be obtained from tourist offices in **Trento** (☎0461 21 60 00; www.apt.trento.it; Via Manci 2; ⏲9am-7pm) and **Bolzano** (☎0471 30 70 00; www.bolzano-bozen.it; Piazza Walther 8; ⏲9am-1pm & 2-7pm Mon-Fri, 9am-2pm Sat). The best online resource is www.dolomiti.org.

Getting There & Around

Bolzano airport (BZO; ☎0471 25 52 55; www.abd-airport.it) is only served by a couple of European flights. Otherwise the nearest airports are Verona, Bergamo or Innsbruck in Austria, from where trains run south to Bolzano.

The area's excellent bus network is run by **Trentino Trasporti** (☎0461 82 10 00; www.ttesercizio.it) in Trento; **SAD** (☎800 000 471; www.sii.bz.it) in Alto Adige; and **Dolomiti Bus** (www.dolomitibus.it, in Italian) in the Veneto. During winter, most resorts offer 'ski bus' services.

The main towns and the many ski resorts can be reached directly from cities such as Rome, Florence, Venice, Bologna, Milan and Genoa. Information is available from tourist offices and regional bus stations.

Cortina d'Ampezzo

POP 6110 / ELEV 1224M

Surrounded by some of the Dolomites' most dramatic scenery, Cortina is one of Italy's most famous, fashionable and expensive ski resorts. Predictably it boasts first-class facilities (skiing, skating, sledding, climbing) and superb hiking; less obviously, it has some reasonably priced accommodation. Ask at the **tourist office** (☎0436 32 31; www.infodolomiti.it; Piazzetta San Francesco 8; ⊙9am-12.30pm & 3.30-6.30pm) for listings.

SAD (☎800 000 471; www.sii.bz.it) buses connect Cortina with Dobbiaco, where you can change for Bolzano. **Cortina Express** (☎0436 86 73 50; www.cortinaexpress.it) runs seasonal buses to/from Bologna and Venice, and **ATVO** (www.atvo.it) operates buses to/from Venice, daily between June and August and at weekends the rest of the year. Journey time is about two and a quarter hours for Venice and three hours for Bologna.

Canazei

POP 1870 / ELEV 1460M

One of the best-known resorts in the **Val di Fassa**, Canazei is a great spot for serious skiers. It has 120km of downhill and cross-country runs and is linked to the challenging Sella Ronda ski network. There's even summer skiing on the Marmolada glacier, whose stunning 3342m summit marks the highest point in the Dolomites. Further information is available at the **tourist office** (☎0462 60 96 00; www.fassa.com; Piazza Marconi 5; ⊙8.30am-12.30pm & 3-7pm).

For somewhere to stay overnight, try the **Garni Stella Alpina** (☎0462 60 11 27; www.stella-alpina.net; Via Antermont 6; d €68-128; P@), a traditional guest house with seven warm rooms decked out in local Ladin style.

Canazei is served by year-round **Trentino Trasporti** (☎0461 82 10 00; www.ttesercizio.it) buses from Trento (€5.55, 2½ hours) and seasonal services from Bolzano and the Val Gardena.

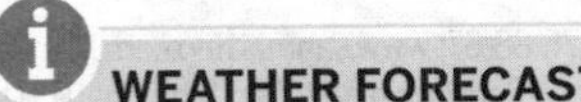

WEATHER FORECAST

Even in summer the weather is extremely changeable in the Alps. Even if it's sweltering when you set off, be prepared for cold, wet weather on even the shortest walks. Essentials include good-quality, worn-in walking boots, a waterproof jacket, warm hat and gloves, light food, plenty of water and a decent map. The best maps are the Tabacco 1:25,000 series, widely available throughout the area.

Val Gardena

Branching northeast off the Val di Fassa, the Val Gardena is a popular skiing area with great facilities and accessible prices. In summer hikers head to the Sella Group and the Alpe di Siusi for rugged, high-altitude walks and to the Vallunga for more accessible family strolls.

The valley's main towns are Ortisei, Santa Cristina and Selva Gardena, all offering plenty of accommodation and easy access to runs. Further information is available online at www.valgardena.it, or from the towns' tourist offices:

Ortisei (☎0471 77 76 00; Via Rezia 1; ⊙8.30am-12.30pm & 2.30-6.30pm Mon-Sat, 10am-noon & 5-6.30pm Sun)

Santa Cristina (☎0471 77 78 00; Via Chemun 9; ⊙8am-noon & 2.30-6.30pm Mon-Sat, 9.30am-noon Sun)

Selva Gardena (☎0471 77 79 00; Via Mëisules 213; ⊙8am-noon & 3-6.30pm Mon-Sat, 9am-noon & 4.30-6.30pm Sun)

The Val Gardena is accessible from Bolzano by year-round **SAD** (☎800 000 471; www.sii.bz.it) buses and from the neighbouring valleys in summer.

San Martino di Castrozza

ELEV 1450M

At the foot of the imposing **Pale di San Martino**, the popular town of San Martino di Castrozza acts as a gateway to the **Parco Naturale Paneveggio – Pale di San Martino** (www.parcopan.org). Its **tourist office**

(☎0439 76 88 67; www.sanmartino.com; Via Passo Rolle 165; ⊙9am-noon & 3-7pm Mon-Sat, 9.30am-12.30pm Sun) is a mine of useful information.

Trentino Trasporti (☎0461 82 10 00; www.ttesercizio.it) buses run to/from Trento.

TUSCANY

Tuscany is one of those places that well and truly lives up to its press. Its fabled rolling landscape has long been considered the embodiment of rural chic, while its cities are home to a significant portfolio of the world's medieval and Renaissance art. Some people never venture beyond Florence, but with some of Italy's most charming towns an easy trip away, to do so would be a waste, particularly as there are so many chances to sample the region's famous food and wine along the way.

Florence

POP 365,700

Poets of the 18th and 19th centuries swooned at the beauty of Florence (Firenze), and once here you'll appreciate why. An essential stop on everyone's Italian itinerary, this Renaissance treasure trove is busy year-round. Fortunately, the huge crowds fail to diminish the city's lustre. A list of its famous sons reads like a Renaissance who's who – under 'M' alone you'll find Medici, Machiavelli and Michelangelo – and its celebrated cityscape lingers in the memory long after you've said your farewells.

History

Many hold that Florentia was founded by Julius Caesar around 59 BC, but archaeological evidence suggests an earlier village, possibly founded by the Etruscans around 200 BC. A rich merchant city by the 12th century, its golden age arrived in the 15th century. Under the Medici prince Lorenzo il Magnifico (1469–92), the city's cultural, artistic and political fecundity culminated in the Renaissance.

The Medici were succeeded in the 18th century by the French House of Lorraine, which ruled until 1860, when the city was incorporated into the kingdom of Italy. From 1865 to 1870, Florence was, in fact, capital of the fledgling kingdom.

During WWII, parts of the city were destroyed by bombing, including all of its bridges except for Ponte Vecchio. In 1966 a devastating flood destroyed or severely damaged many important works of art. More recently, in 1993, the Mafia exploded a massive car bomb, killing five people and destroying part of the Uffizi Gallery. The gallery is currently undergoing a long-overdue €60 million renovation that will result in its exhibition space being doubled. It remains open while these works are occurring, and the estimated date for their completion is 2013.

Sights & Activities

From the main train station, Santa Maria Novella, it's a 550m walk along Via de' Panzani and Via de' Cerretani to the Duomo. From Piazza di San Giovanni, next to the Duomo, Via Roma leads down to Piazza della Repubblica and continues as Via Calimala and Via Por Santa Maria to the Ponte Vecchio.

There are seven major neighbourhoods in the historic centre: Duomo and Piazza della Signoria, Santa Maria Novella, San Lorenzo, San Marco, Santa Croce, Oltrarno and Boboli/San Miniato al Monte. Most of these owe their names to the significant basilicas located within their borders, which make excellent navigational landmarks.

Piazza del Duomo & Around CHURCHES

Pictures don't do justice to the exterior of Florence's Gothic **Duomo** (cathedral; www.duomofirenze.it; ⊙10am-5pm Mon-Wed & Fri, to 3.30pm Thu, to 4.45pm Sat, to 3.30pm 1st Sat of every month, 1.30-4.45pm Sun). While they reproduce the startling colours of the tiered red, green and white marble facade and the beautiful symmetry of the dome, they fail to give any sense of its monumental size. Officially known as the Cattedrale di Santa Maria del Fiore, its construction begun in 1294 by Sienese architect Arnolfo di Cambio, but it wasn't consecrated until 1436. Its most famous feature, the enormous octagonal **Cupola** (dome; admission €8; ⊙8.30am-6.20pm Mon-Fri, to 5pm Sat) was built by Brunelleschi after his design won a public competition in 1420. The interior is decorated with frescos by Vasari and Zuccari, and the stained-glass windows are by Donatello, Paolo Uccello and Lorenzo Ghiberti. The facade is a 19th-century replacement of the unfinished original, pulled down in the 16th century.

Beside the cathedral, the 82m **Campanile** (admission €6; ⊙8.30am-6.50pm) was begun by Giotto in 1334 and completed after his death by Andrea Pisano and Francesco Talenti. The views from the top make the 414-step climb worthwhile.

To the west, the Romanesque **Battistero** (Baptistry; Piazza di San Giovanni; admission €4; ⌚12.15-6.30pm Mon-Sat, 8.30am-1.30pm 1st Sat of every month, 8.30am-1.30pm Sun) is one of the oldest buildings in Florence. Built on the site of a Roman temple between the 5th and 11th centuries, it's famous for its gilded-bronze doors, particularly Lorenzo Ghiberti's *Gate of Paradise*.

Surprisingly overlooked by the crowds, the **Museo dell'Opera del Duomo** (Cathedral Museum; www.operaduomo.firenze.it; admission €6; ⌚9am-6.50pm Mon-Sat & 9am-1pm Sun) on the northern (street) side of the cathedral safeguards treasures that once adorned the Duomo, baptistry and campanile and is one of the city's most impressive museums. Ghiberti's *Gate of Paradise* panels (those on the Baptistry doors are copies) and a Pietà by Michelangelo are in the collection here.

Galleria degli Uffizi (Uffizi Gallery) ART MUSEUM

(www.uffizi.firenze.it; Piazza degli Uffizi 6; adult/EU concession €10/5; ⌚8.15am-6.05pm Tue-Sun) Home to the world's greatest collection of Italian Renaissance art, the Galleria degli Uffizi attracts some 1.5 million visitors annually. They won't all be there when you visit, but unless you've booked a ticket, expect to queue.

The gallery houses the Medici family collection, bequeathed to the city in 1743 on the condition that it never leave the city. Highlights include *La nascita di Venere* (Birth of Venus) and *Allegoria della primavera* (Allegory of Spring) in the Botticelli Rooms (10 to 14); Leonardo da Vinci's *Annunciazione* (Annunciation; room 15); Michelangelo's *Tondo doni* (Holy Family; Room 25); and Titian's *Venere d'Urbino* (Venus of Urbino; Room 28). Elsewhere you'll find works by Giotto, Cimabue, Filippo Lippi, Fra' Angelico, Uccello, Raphael, Andrea del Sarto, Tintoretto and Caravaggio. Tickets are cheaper if there are no temporary exhibitions.

CUTTING THE QUEUES

Sightseeing in Florence inevitably means time spent in queues. You'll never avoid them altogether, but by pre-booking museum tickets you'll save time. For €4 extra per museum you can book tickets for the Uffizi and Galleria dell'Accademia (the two most popular museums) through **Firenze Musei** (☎055 29 48 83; www.firenzemusei.it; ⌚booking line 8.30am-6.30pm Mon-Fri, to 12.30pm Sat, ticket offices 8.15am-6pm daily). Buy ahead of your visit by booking by telephone or online, or purchase in person from the Firenze Musei desks at the Uffizi, Accademia, Palazzo Pitti or Museo di San Marco. There's also a ticket window at the rear of the Chiesa di Orsanmichele.

TOURIST OFFICE CHANGES

As this book was going to press, the APT (Azienda di Promozione Turistica) network across Tuscany had just been disbanded, with individual provinces left to run their own tourist information offices. By the time you read this it's possible that some of the tourist offices in this section might have closed or changed location. We recommend enquiring ahead to avoid disappointment.

Piazza della Signoria SQUARE

Traditional hub of Florence's political life, Piazza della Signoria is dominated by the **Palazzo Vecchio** (Old Palace; www.palazzovecchio-museoragazzi.it; adult/child €6/2; ⌚9am-7pm Fri-Wed, to 2pm Thu), the historical seat of the Florentine government. Characterised by the 94m **Torre d'Arnolfo**, it was designed by Arnolfo di Cambio and built between 1298 and 1340. The **guided tours** (☎055 276 82 24; info.museoragazzi@comune.fi.it) here are great – particularly those for children. Make sure you book in advance.

The statue of *David* outside the *palazzo* is a copy of Michelangelo's original, which stood here until 1873 but is now in the Galleria dell'Accademia. The nearby **Loggia dei Lanzi** is an open-air showcase of sculpture from the 14th and 16th centuries – look out for Giambologna's *Rape of the Sabine Women* (c1583) and Agnolo Gaddi's *Seven Virtues* (1384–89). The loggia is named after the *Lanzichenecchi* (Swiss Guards) who were stationed here in Cosimo I's time.

Ponte Vecchio BRIDGE

The 14th-century Ponte Vecchio was originally flanked by butchers' shops, but when the Medici built a corridor through the bridge to link Palazzo Pitti with Palazzo Vecchio, they

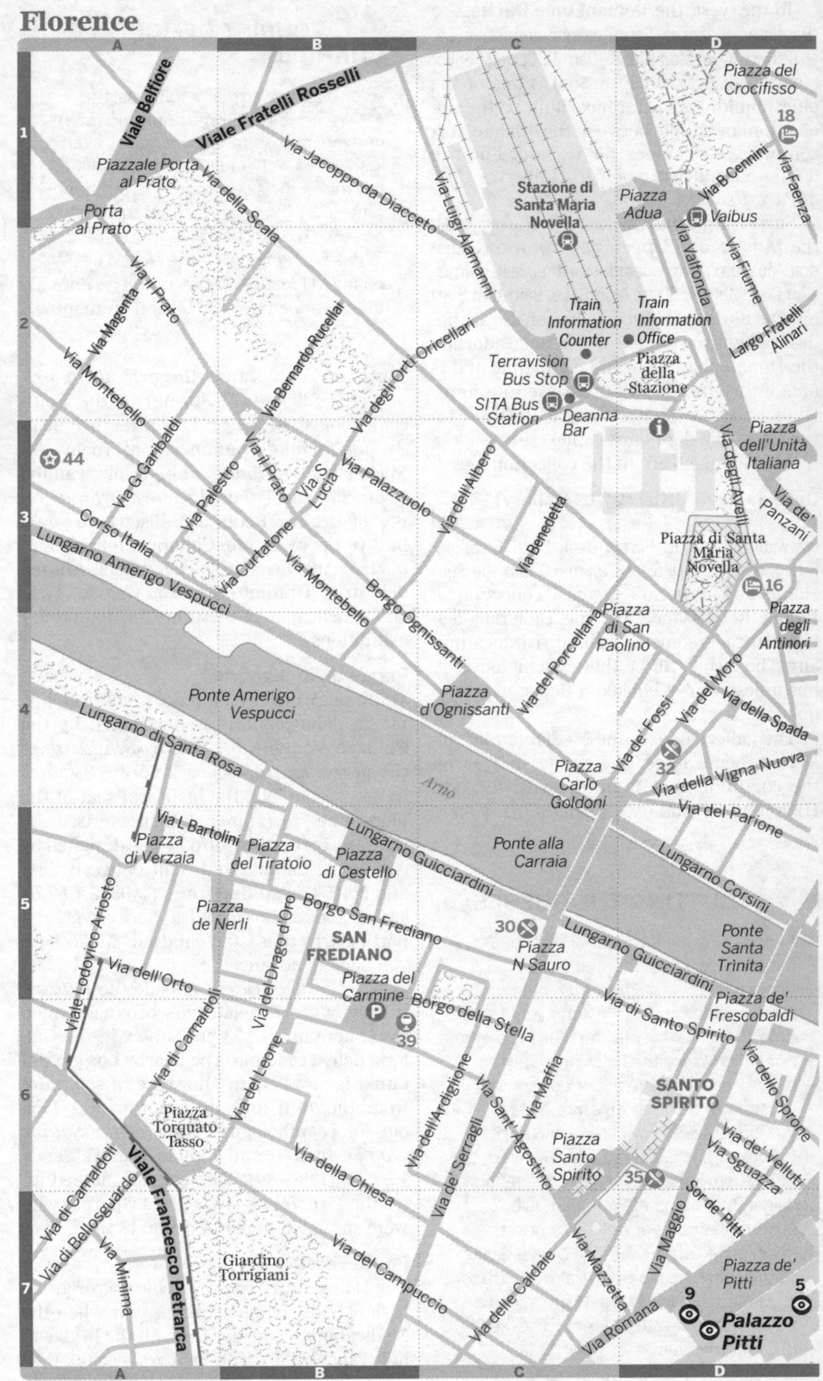
Viale Belfiore
Viale Fratelli Rosselli
Piazzale Porta al Prato
Porta al Prato
Via della Scala
Via Jacopo da Diacceto
Via Luigi Alamanni
Stazione di Santa Maria Novella
Piazza Adua
Via B Cennini
Vaibus
Piazza del Crocifisso
18
Via Faenza
Via Valfonda
Via Fiume
Largo Fratelli Alinari
Train Information Counter
Train Information Office
Terravision Bus Stop
SITA Bus Station
Deanna Bar
Piazza della Stazione
Piazza dell'Unità Italiana
Via de' Panzani
Via degli Avelli
Piazza di Santa Maria Novella
16
Piazza degli Antinori
Via il Prato
Via Magenta
Via Montebello
Via Bernardo Rucellai
Via degli Orti Oricellari
Via G Garibaldi
44
Via Palestro
Via il Prato
Via S Lucia
Via Palazzuolo
Via dell'Albero
Via Benedetta
Corso Italia
Lungarno Amerigo Vespucci
Via Curtatone
Via Montebello
Borgo Ognissanti
Piazza di San Paolino
Via del Porcellana
Piazza d'Ognissanti
Ponte Amerigo Vespucci
Lungarno di Santa Rosa
Via de' Fossi
Via del Moro
Via della Spada
32
Via della Vigna Nuova
Piazza Carlo Goldoni
Arno
Via del Parione
Via L Bartolini
Piazza di Verzaia
Piazza del Tiratoio
Piazza di Cestello
Lungarno Guicciardini
Ponte alla Carraia
Lungarno Corsini
Piazza de Nerli
Borgo San Frediano
Via del Drago d'Oro
SAN FREDIANO
30
Piazza N Sauro
Lungarno Guicciardini
Ponte Santa Trìnita
Viale Lodovico Ariosto
Via dell'Orto
Via di Camaldoli
Piazza del Carmine
39
Borgo della Stella
Via di Santo Spirito
Piazza de' Frescobaldi
Via dello Sprone
Via del Leone
Via dell'Ardiglione
Via Sant' Agostino
Via Maffia
SANTO SPIRITO
Piazza Torquato Tasso
Via della Chiesa
Via de' Serragli
Piazza Santo Spirito
35
Via de' Velluti
Via Sguazza
Sor de' Pitti
Via di Camaldoli
Via di Bellosguardo
Viale Francesco Petrarca
Via Minima
Giardino Torrigiani
Via del Campuccio
Via delle Caldaie
Via Mazzetta
Via Maggio
Piazza de' Pitti
Via Romana
9
5
Palazzo Pitti
A
B
C
D
1
2
3
4
5
6
7

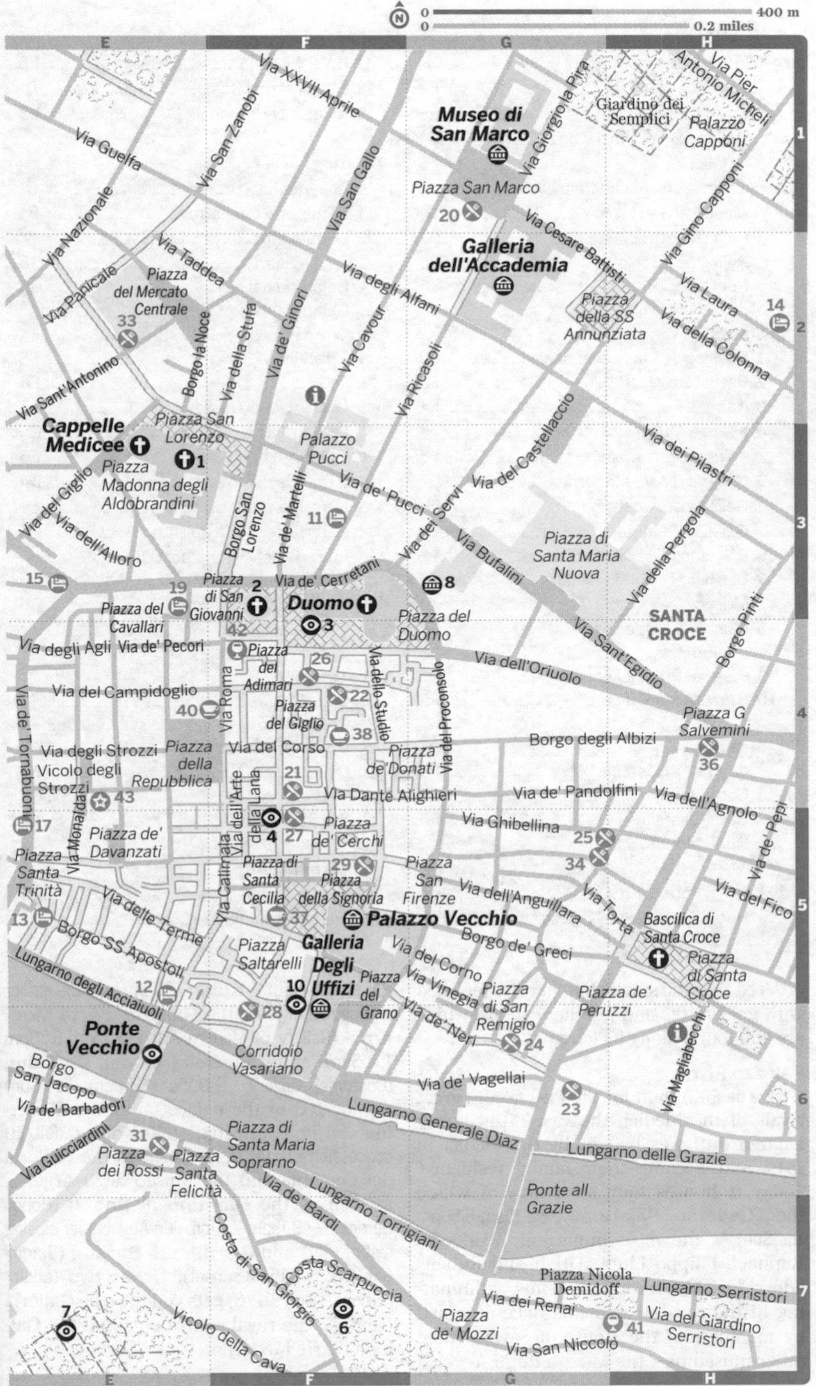

400 m
0.2 miles
Museo di San Marco
Galleria dell'Accademia
Cappelle Medicee
Duomo
Palazzo Vecchio
Galleria Degli Uffizi
Ponte Vecchio
SANTA CROCE
Via XXVII Aprile
Via Guelfa
Via San Zanobi
Via San Gallo
Via Nazionale
Via Panicale
Via Taddea
Piazza del Mercato Centrale
Via della Stufa
Via de' Ginori
Via Cavour
Via degli Alfani
Via Ricasoli
Via Cesare Battisti
Piazza San Marco
Via Giorgio la Pira
Giardino dei Semplici
Via Pier Antonio Micheli
Palazzo Capponi
Via Gino Capponi
Via Laura
Via della Colonna
Piazza della SS Annunziata
Via Sant'Antonino
Borgo la Noce
Piazza San Lorenzo
Piazza Madonna degli Aldobrandini
Palazzo Pucci
Via del Castellaccio
Via dei Pilastri
Via de' Pucci
Via dei Servi
Via Bufalini
Via de' Martelli
Borgo San Lorenzo
Via del Giglio
Via dell'Alloro
Piazza di Santa Maria Nuova
Via della Pergola
Borgo Pinti
Via de' Cerretani
Piazza di San Giovanni
Piazza del Duomo
Piazza del Cavallari
Via degli Agli
Via de' Pecori
Piazza dei Adimari
Via dello Studio
Via dell'Oriuolo
Via Sant'Egidio
Via del Campidoglio
Piazza del Giglio
Via del Proconsolo
Via Roma
Via de' Tornabuoni
Via degli Strozzi
Vicolo degli Strozzi
Piazza della Repubblica
Via del Corso
Piazza de'Donati
Borgo degli Albizi
Piazza G Salvemini
Via Dante Alighieri
Via de' Pandolfini
Via dell'Agnolo
Via Monalda
Via Calimala
Via dell'Arte della Lana
Piazza de' Cerchi
Via Ghibellina
Via de' Pepi
Piazza de' Davanzati
Piazza Santa Trinità
Piazza di Santa Cecilia
Piazza della Signoria
Piazza San Firenze
Via dell'Anguillara
Via Torta
Via del Fico
Via delle Terme
Borgo SS Apostoli
Borgo de' Greci
Bascilica di Santa Croce
Piazza di Santa Croce
Lungarno degli Acciaiuoli
Piazza Saltarelli
Via del Corno
Via Vinegia
Piazza del Grano
Via de' Neri
Piazza di San Remigio
Piazza de' Peruzzi
Via Magliabecchi
Corridoio Vasariano
Via de' Vagellai
Borgo San Jacopo
Via de' Barbadori
Lungarno Generale Diaz
Lungarno delle Grazie
Via Guicciardini
Piazza dei Rossi
Piazza Santa Felicità
Piazza di Santa Maria Soprarno
Via de' Bardi
Lungarno Torrigiani
Ponte all Grazie
Costa di San Giorgio
Costa Scarpuccia
Vicolo della Cava
Piazza Nicola Demidoff
Lungarno Serristori
Via dei Renai
Piazza de' Mozzi
Via San Niccolò
Via del Giardino Serristori

Florence

Top Sights

Cappelle Medicee ... E3
Duomo ... F3
Galleria Degli Uffizi (Uffizi Gallery) ... F6
Galleria dell'Accademia ... G2
Museo di San Marco ... G1
Palazzo Pitti ... D7
Palazzo Vecchio ... F5
Ponte Vecchio ... E6

Sights

1 Basilica di San Lorenzo ... E3
2 Battistero ... F3
3 Campanile ... F4
4 Firenze Musei Ticket Window ... F5
5 Galleria d'Arte Moderna ... D7
Galleria del Costume ... (see 5)
Galleria Palatina ... (see 5)
6 Giardino di Bardini ... F7
7 Giardino di Boboli ... E7
Museo degli Argenti ... (see 5)
8 Museo dell'Opera del Duomo ... G3
9 Palazzo Pitti Ticket Office ... D7
10 Uffizi Ticket Office ... F5

Sleeping

11 Academy Hostel ... F3
12 Continentale ... E5
13 Hotel Cestelli ... E5
14 Hotel Morandi alla Crocetta ... H2
15 Hotel Paris ... E3
16 Hotel Santa Maria Novella ... D3
17 Hotel Scoti ... E5
18 Ostello Archi Rossi ... D1
19 Relais del Duomo ... E3

Eating

20 Accademia Ristorante ... G1
21 Cantinetta dei Verrazzano ... F4
22 Coquinarius ... F4
23 Del Fagioli ... G6
24 Gelateria dei Neri ... G6
25 Gelateria Vivoli ... G5
26 Grom ... F4
27 I Fratellini ... F5
28 'Ino ... F6
29 La Canova di Gustavino ... F5
30 La Carraia ... C5
31 Le Volpi e l'Uva ... E6
32 L'Osteria di Giovanni ... D4
33 Nerbone ... E2
34 Osteria del Caffè Italiano ... G5
Pizzeria del Osteria del Caffè Italiano ... (see 34)
35 Trattoria La Casalinga ... D6
36 Vestri ... H4

Drinking

37 Caffè Rivoire ... F5
38 Chiaroscuro ... F4
39 Dolce Vita ... B6
40 Gilli ... F4
41 Negroni ... H7
42 Old Stove Duomo ... F4

Entertainment

43 Odeon Cinehall ... E4
44 Teatro Comunale ... A3

ordered that the smelly butchers be replaced with goldsmiths and jewellery shops, which are still found along its length.

Palazzo Pitti PALACE
(Piazza de' Pitti) Built for the Pitti family, great rivals of the Medici, the vast 15th-century Palazzo Pitti was bought by the Medici in 1549 and became their family residence. Today it houses four museums, of which the **Galleria Palatina** (8.15am-6.50pm Tue-Sun) is the most important. Works by Raphael, Filippo Lippi, Titian and Rubens adorn lavishly decorated rooms, culminating in the royal apartments once occupied by members of the House of Savoy. Three other museums – the **Museo degli Argenti** (Silver Museum; 8.15am-7.30pm Jun-Aug, earlier closing rest of year), the **Galleria d'Arte Moderna** (Gallery of Modern Art; 8.15am-6.50pm Tue-Sun) and the **Galleria del Costume** (Costume Gallery; 8.15am-6.50pm Tue-Sun) are located in the palace buildings. Ticketing can be confusing: **ticket one** (adult/EU concession €10/5) gets you in to the Galleria del Costume and the Museo degli Argenti, as well as the **Giardino di Boboli** (Boboli Gardens; 8.15am-7.30pm Jun-Aug, earlier closing rest of year) and **Giardino di Bardini** (Bardini Gardens; 8.15am-sunset); **ticket two** (adult/EU concession €12/6) gets you into the Galleria Palatina, the royal apartments and the Galleria d'Arte Moderna.

Galleria dell'Accademia ART MUSEUM
(Via Ricasoli 60; adult/concession €10/5; 8.15am-6.20pm Tue-Sun) The people queuing outside Galleria dell'Accademia are waiting to see *David*, arguably the Western world's most famous sculpture. Michelangelo carved the giant figure from a single block of marble, finishing it in 1504 when he was just 29. The gallery also displays paintings by Florentine artists spanning the 13th to 16th centuries and regularly hosts temporary exhibitions. Tickets are cheaper if there are no temporary exhibitions.

Basilica di San Lorenzo CHURCH
(www.basilicasanlorenzofirenze.com, in Italian; Piazza San Lorenzo; admission €3.50; 10am-5pm Mon-Sat year-round, 1.30-5pm Sun Mar-Oct) One of the city's finest examples of Renaissance architecture, this basilica was built by Brunelleschi in the 15th century and includes his **Sagrestia Vecchia** (Old Sacristy), with sculptural decoration by Donatello.

Around the corner, at the rear of the basilica, is the sumptuous **Cappelle Medicee** (Medici Chapels; Piazza Madonna degli Aldobrandini; adult/concession €6/3; 8.15am-4pm Tue-Sat, 2nd & 4th Mon & 1st, 3rd & 5th Sun of month), the principal burial place of the Medici grand dukes. Its jewel is the incomplete **Sagrestia Nuova**, Michelangelo's first architectural effort, which contains some exquisite sculptures.

Museo di San Marco ART MUSEUM
(Piazza San Marco 1; adult/concession €4/2; 8.15am-1.50pm Tue-Fri, to 4.50pm Sat & 2nd & 4th Sun & 1st, 3rd & 5th Mon of month) Housed in a Dominican monastery, this spiritually uplifting museum is a showcase of the work of Fra' Angelico, who decorated the cells between 1440 and 1441 with deeply devotional frescos to guide the meditation of his fellow friars. Major paintings, including the *Deposition of Christ* (1432) and Fra' Angelico's most famous work, *Annunciation* (c 1440).

Tours

Cycling

The following offer tours of Chianti from Florence, sometimes leaving by minibus and getting on bikes in Chianti and at other times doing the full tour by bike. One-day rides cost between €60 and €90 and are usually available only from March until October.

Florence by Bike BICYCLE
(055 48 89 92; www.florencebybike.it) Guided rides through Chianti plus bike hire (city bike/mountain bike €14.50/21 per day).

I Bike Italy BICYCLE
(055 012 39 94; www.ibikeitaly.com) One- and two-day guided tours in Chianti and a two-hour guided ride around Florence.

I Bike Tuscany BICYCLE
(335 812 07 69; www.ibiketuscany.com) Guided tours around Florence, Chianti and Siena.

Walking Tours

Freya's Florence WALKING
(349 074 89 07; freyasflorence@yahoo.com; €60 per hr for private tours) English-language walking tours with an enthusiastic and expert guide.

Walking Tours of Florence WALKING
(055 264 50 33; www.italy.artviva.com; Via de' Sassetti 1; tours per person from €25) The Artviva outfit offers a range of city tours, all led by English-speaking guides.

Festivals & Events

Scoppio del Carro RELIGIOUS CELEBRATION
(Explosion of the Cart) A cart full of fireworks is exploded in front of the Duomo on Easter Sunday.

Maggio Musicale Fiorentino MUSIC FESTIVAL
(www.maggiofiorentino.com, in Italian) Italy's longest-running music festival, held from April to June.

Festa di San Giovanni RELIGIOUS CELEBRATION
(Feast of St John) Florence's patron saint is celebrated on 24 June with costumed soccer matches on Piazza di Santa Croce and fireworks over Piazzale Michelangelo.

Sleeping

Although there are hundreds of hotels in Florence, it's still prudent to book ahead. Look out for low-season website deals – prices often drop by up to 50%.

WANT MORE?

For in-depth information, reviews and recommendations at your fingertips, head to the Apple App Store to purchase Lonely Planet's *Florence City Guide* iPhone app.

Alternatively, head to **Lonely Planet** (www.lonelyplanet.com/italy/florence) for planning advice, author recommendations, traveller reviews and insider tips.

DUOMO & PIAZZA DELLA SIGNORIA

Relais del Duomo B&B €€
(☉055 21 01 47; www.relaisdelduomo.it, in Italian; Piazza dell'Olio 2; s €48-85, d €70-130; ❄@📶) Florentine B&Bs don't come much better than this one. Located in the shadow of the Duomo, it has four light and airy rooms with attractive furnishings and lovely little bathrooms. Privacy levels are high and management is extremely helpful.

Hotel Cestelli B&B €
(☎055 21 42 13; www.hotelcestelli.com; Borgo SS Apostoli 25; s without bathroom €40-60, d without bathroom €50-80, d €70-100; ☉closed 2 weeks Jan, 3 weeks Aug) Run by Florentine photographer Alessio and his Japanese partner Asumi, this eight-room hotel on the first floor of a 12th-century *palazzo* is wonderfully located. Though dark, the rooms are attractively furnished, quiet and cool.

SANTA MARIA NOVELLA

TOP CHOICE **Hotel Santa Maria Novella** HOTEL €€
(☎055 27 18 40; www.hotelsantamarianovella.it; Piazza di Santa Maria Novella 1; d €135-195, ste €178-235; ❄@📶) The bland exterior of this excellent four-star choice gives no hint of the spacious and elegant rooms within. All are beautifully appointed, featuring marble bathrooms and comfortable beds. The breakfast spread is lavish.

Ostello Archi Rossi HOSTEL €
(☎055 29 08 04; www.hostelarchirossi.com; Via Faenza 94r; dm €21-27, s €40-60, d €60-90; ☉closed 2 weeks Dec; @📶) This ever-busy hostel near Stazione di Santa Maria Novella offers bright dorms with three to nine beds; some are single-sex and all have private bathrooms and keyed lockers. Air-conditioning s in private rooms only. The hostel also offers free walking tours.

Hotel Scoti PENSION €€
(☎055 29 21 28; www.hotelscoti.com; Via de' Tornabuoni 7; s €35-75, d €65-125) On Florence's smartest shopping street, the Scoti is a splendid mix of old-fashioned charm and great value for money. Run with smiling aplomb by Australian Doreen and Italian Carmello, it offers 11 clean and comfortable rooms and an amazing frescoed living room for communal use. Breakfast costs an extra €5.

Continentale BOUTIQUE HOTEL €€€
(☎055 2 72 62; www.lungarnohotels.com; Viccolo dell'Oro 6r; s €240-300, d €290-530; ❄@) Owned by the Ferragamo fashion house and designed by fashionable Florentine architect Michele Bönan, this glamorous hotel references 1950s Italy in its vibrant decor, and is about as hip as Florence gets.

Hotel Paris HOTEL €€
(☎055 28 02 81; www.parishotel.it; Via dei Banchi 2; s €80-125, d €90-180; ❄@📶) This pair of 15th-century palaces is linked on the second floor by a glass walkway. Its comfortable three-star rooms sport high ceilings and Renaissance-style furbelows.

SAN LORENZO

Academy Hostel HOSTEL €
(☎055 23 98 665; www.academyhostel.eu; Via Ricasoli 9; dm €25-38, tw €70-84, s without bathroom €35-45; ❄@📶) The philosophy of this small hostel close to the Duomo is that cheap accommodation shouldn't compromise on comfort. Its dorms (sleeping between three and six) are bright and well set up, with lockers and single beds (no bunks).

Johlea & Johanna B&B €€
(☎055 463 32 92; www.johanna.it; Via San Gallo 80; s €70-120, d €80-170; ❄) This highly regarded B&B has more than a dozen tasteful, individually decorated rooms housed in five historic residences. There are also two charming suite apartments (€92 to €280).

SAN MARCO

Hotel Morandi alla Crocetta BOUTIQUE HOTEL €€
(☎055 234 47 47; www.hotelmorandi.it; Via Laura 50; s €70-109, d €100-169; P❄@📶) This medieval convent-turned-hotel is a stunner. Rooms are charmingly decorated (try for the frescoed No 29) and extremely well equipped. The location is wonderfully quiet.

SAN MINIATO AL MONTE

Campeggio Michelangelo CAMPING GROUND €
(☎055 681 19 77; Viale Michelangelo 80; www.ecvacanze.it; sites per person with tent €10.80, in on-site elevated tent €15.50; P@) Just off Piazzale Michelangelo, this large and well-equipped camping ground is the nearest to the city centre. Take bus 12 from the train station to Piazzale Michelangelo.

Eating

Classic Tuscan dishes include *ribollita,* a heavy vegetable soup, and *bistecca alla fiorentina* (Florentine steak served rare). Chianti is the local tipple.

DUOMO & PIAZZA DELLA SIGNORIA

TOP CHOICE 'Ino SANDWICHES €

(Via dei Georgofili 3r-7r; panini €5-8; ⌚11am-5pm) Short for 'panino', this stylish *paninoteca* (sandwich bar) shop near the Uffizi sources its artisan gourmet ingredients locally and uses them in inventive and delicious ways. A glass of wine is included in the price of every sandwich.

La Canova do Gustavino WINE BAR €€

(Via della Condotta 29r; mains €8-12) The rear dining room of this atmospheric *enoteca* is lined with shelves full of Tuscan wine – the perfect accompaniment to a simple bowl of soup, a bruschetta, a pasta dish or a hearty main.

Cantinetta dei Verrazzano WINE BAR €€

(Via dei Tavolini 18-20; platters €4.50-12, focaccias €3-3.50, panini €1.70-3.90; ⌚noon-9pm Mon-Sat) Come here for focaccia fresh from the oven, perhaps topped with caramelised radicchio or porcini mushrooms. And be sure to wash it down with a glass of wine from the Verrazzano estate in Chianti.

I Fratellini SANDWICHES €

(www.iduefratellini.com; Via dei Cimatori 38r; panini €2.50; ⌚9am-8pm Mon-Sat, closed Fri & Sun 2nd half of Jun & all Aug) I Fratellini is a city institution. Locals flock to its tiny counter for fresh-filled panini ready in the twinkle of an eye, eaten standing in the street.

SANTA MARIA NOVELLA

TOP CHOICE L'Osteria di Giovanni TRATTORIA €€€

(☎055 28 48 97; www.osteriadigiovanni.com, in Italian; Via del Moro 22; mains €18-26; ⌚lunch & dinner Fri-Mon, dinner only Tue-Thu) The house antipasto is a great way to sample Tuscan specialities such as *crostini* and *lardo*, and the *bistecca alla fiorentina* is sensational. Everything a perfect neighbourhood eatery should be, and then some.

Coquinarius WINE BAR €€

(☎055 230 21 53; Via della Oche 15r; mains €15; ☑) Close to Piazza Signoria, this modern *enoteca* is a perfect spot for lunch or a light dinner. The pasta dishes are uniformly good, and there's almost always a few unusual and delicious salads on the menu. Vegetarians will be very happy after a visit here.

SAN LORENZO

Nerbone TAVOLA CALDA €

(☎055 21 99 49; inside Mercato Centrale, Piazza del Mercato Centrale; panini €3-4, mains €5-6.50; ⌚7am-2pm Mon-Sat) This unpretentious market stall has been serving its rustic dishes to queues of shoppers and stallholders since 1872. It's a great place to try local staples such as *trippa alla fiorentina* (€6.50) and *panini con bollito* (a boiled beef bun, €3).

SAN MARCO

Accademia Ristorante TRATTORIA €€

(www.ristoranteaccademia.it, in italian; Piazza San Marco 7r; mains €12-18) There aren't too many decent eateries in this area, which is one of the reasons why this family-run restaurant is perennially packed. Factors such as friendly staff, cheerful decor and consistently good food help, too.

TOP FIVE GELATERIE

There are plenty of places offering *gelato artiginale* (traditional, usually homemade, ice cream and sorbet). Flavours change according to what fruit is in season, and a small cone can cost anywhere from €1.50 to €2.20.

» **La Carraia** (Piazza Nazario Sauro 25; ⌚11am-11pm) Look for the ever-present queue next to the Ponte Carraia, and you will find this fantastic gelateria.

» **Gelateria dei Neri** (22r Via de' Neri; ⌚9am-midnight) Semifreddo-style gelato that is cheaper than its competitors; known for its Giotto (almond, hazelnut and coconut) flavour.

» **Gelateria Vivoli** (Via Isola delle Stinche 7; ⌚7.30am-midnight Tue-Sat, 9am-midnight Sun, closed mid-Aug) Choose a flavour from the huge choice on offer (the chocolate with orange is a perennial favourite) and scoff it in the pretty piazza opposite; tubs only.

» **Grom** (www.grom.it; Via del Campanile at Via delle Oche; ⌚10.30am-11pm, to midnight Apr-Sep) This relative newcomer has taken the city by storm; the flavours are all delectable and many ingredients are organic.

» **Vestri** (www.vestri.it; Borgo degli Albizi 11r; ⌚10.30am-8pm Mon-Sat) Specialises in chocolate; go for the decadent white chocolate with wild strawberries or the chocolate with pepper.

SANTA CROCE

Trattoria Cibrèo (Cibréino) TRATTORIA €€
(www.edizioniteatrodelsalecibreofirenze.it, in Italian; Viadei Macci 122r; mains €13-16; ⏲Tue-Sat, closed Aug) The small dining room here is run with charm and efficiency by a maître d' who will happily explain the menu and suggest a matching wine. *Secondi* comprise a small main dish matched with a side of seasonal vegetables; everything is delicious and exceptionally well priced considering its quality. No reservations and no credit cards.

Del Fagioli TRATTORIA €
(☎055 24 42 85; Corso Tintori 47r; mains €9-10; ⏲Mon-Fri, closed Aug) This Slow Food favourite near the Basilica di Santa Croce is the archetypical Tuscan trattoria. It opened in 1966 and has been serving well-priced bean dishes, soups and roasted meats to throngs of appreciative local workers and residents ever since. No credit cards.

Osteria del Caffè Italiano TRATTORIA €€
(☎055 28 90 20; www.caffeitaliano.it; Via dell'Isola delle Stinche 11-13r; mains €16-25; ⏲Tue-Sun) This old-fashioned *osteria* occupies the ground floor of the 14th-century Palazzo Salviati. It's an excellent spot to try the city's famous *bistecca fiorentina*. The adjoining **Pizzeria del Osteria del Caffè Italiano** (pizzas €8; ⏲dinner only) has a simple dining space and offers a limited menu of three types of pizzas: margherita, napoli and marinara.

OLTRANO

TOP CHOICE **Le Volpi e L'uva** WINE BAR €
(www.levolpieluva.com; Piazza dei Rossi 1; ⏲11am-9pm Mon-Sat) Near the Ponte Vecchio, this intimate *enoteca* has an impressive list of wines by the glass and serves a delectable array of accompanying antipasti, including juicy *prosciutto di Parma, lardo*-topped *crostini* and boutique Tuscan cheeses. There's a tiny outdoor terrace and a small number of bar stools.

Trattoria La Casalinga TRATTORIA €
(Via de' Michelozzi 9r; mains €6-9; ⏲closed Sun) Family run and much loved by locals, this unpretentious and always busy place is one of the city's cheapest trattorias. You'll be relegated behind locals in the queue – it's a fact of life and not worth protesting about – with the eventual reward being hearty and dirt-cheap peasant dishes.

Drinking

Gilli CAFE, BAR
(www.gilli.it; Piazza della Repubblica 39r; ⏲Wed-Mon) The city's grandest cafe, Gilli has been serving excellent coffee and delicious cakes since 1733. Claiming a table on the piazza is *molto* expensive – we prefer standing at the spacious Liberty-style bar.

Old Stove Duomo PUB
(Piazza di San Giovanni 4r) This Irish pub is a magnet for foreign students on holiday, who come here to swill beer and admire the views of the Duomo. Try to snaffle the upstairs balcony table.

James Joyce PUB
(Lungarno Benvenuto Cellini 1r; ⏲6pm-2am, until 3pm Fri & Sat) Guinness on tap and a great beer garden make this somewhat out-of-the-way student favourite worth the walk along the Arno. If you make the trek, consider having dinner at the stylish **Gattabuia Pizzeria** (Lungarno Cellini 13-18r; pizzas €4-12; ⏲dinner daily) next door.

Caffè Rivoire CAFE, BAR
(www.rivoire.it, in Italian; Piazza della Signoria; ⏲closed Mon & 2nd half Jan) Rivoire's terrace has the best view in the city. Settle in for a long *aperitivo* or coffee break – it's worth the high prices.

Chiaroscuro CAFE, BAR
(Via del Corso 36r; ⏲Mon-Sat) Known for its home-roasted coffee, this casual cafe is strategically located between the Duomo and Piazza Signoria. Its *aperitivo* buffet, served between 6pm and 8pm, is excellent.

Dolce Vita BAR
(www.dolcevitaflorence.com; Piazza del Carmine 6r; ⏲5pm-2am Tue-Sun, closed 2 wks Aug) A long-standing Oltrano favourite, 'Sweet Life' serves an *aperitivo* buffet between 7.30pm and 9.30pm, sometimes accompanied by live music.

Negroni BAR
(www.negronibar.com, in Italian; Via dei Renai 17r; ⏲8am-2am Mon-Sat, from 7pm Sun) The famous Florentine cocktail gives its name to this popular bar in the San Nicolò district. Come here after admiring the sun set over the city from Piazzale Michelangelo.

Entertainment

Florence's definitive monthly listings guide, *Firenze Spettacolo* (€1.80), is sold at newsstands.

Concerts, opera and dance are performed year-round at the **Teatro Comunale** (☎800 11 22 11; Corso Italia 16), also the venue for events organised by the Maggio Musicale Fiorentino (see Festivals & Events, p843).

English-language films are screened at the **Odeon Cinehall** (www.cinehall.it, in Italian; Piazza Strozzi 2).

Information

Emergency

Police station (Questura; ☎055 497 71; Via Zara 2)

Medical Services

Dr Stephen Kerr (☎055 28 80 55; www.dr-kerr.com; Piazza Mercato Nuovo 1; 3-5pm Mon-Fri)

Emergency Doctor (Guardia Medica; ☎north of the Arno 055 233 94 56, south of the Arno 055 21 56 16) For a doctor at night, weekends or on public holidays.

Tourist Information

Tourist offices (www.firenzeturismo.it) main office (☎055 29 08 32; Via Cavour 1r; 8.30am-6.30pm Mon-Sat, to 1.30pm Sun); airport (☎055 31 58 74; 8.30am-8.30pm); Santa Croce (☎055 234 04 44; Borgo Santa Croce 29r; 9am-7pm Mon-Sat, to 2pm Sun Mar-Oct, to 5pm Mon-Sat, to 2pm Sun Nov-Feb); Piazza della Stazione (☎055 21 22 45; www.commune.fi.it; Piazza della Stazione 4; 8.30am-7pm Mon-Sat, to 2pm Sun)

Getting There & Away

Air

The main airports serving Florence are **Pisa international airport** (Aeroporto Galileo Galilei; PSA; ☎050 84 93 00; www.pisa-airport.com) and **Bologna airport** (Aeroporto G. Marconi; BLQ; ☎051 647 96 15; www.bologna-airport.it). There's also a small city airport 5km north of Florence, **Florence airport** (Aeroporto Vespucci; FLR; ☎055 306 13 00; www.aeroporto.firenze.it).

Bus

The **SITA bus station** (☎800 37 37 60; www.sitabus.it, in Italian; Via Santa Caterina da Siena 17) is just south of the train station. Buses leave for Siena (€7.10, 1½ hours, every 30 to 60 minutes) and San Gimignano via Poggibonsi (€6.25, 1¼ hours, 14 daily).

Car & Motorcycle

Florence is connected by the A1 *autostrada* to Bologna and Milan in the north and Rome and Naples to the south. The A11 links Florence with Pisa and the coast, and a *superstrada* (expressway) joins the city to Siena.

Train

Florence is well connected by train. There are regular services to/from Pisa (Regional €5.80, 1¼ hours, every 30 minutes), Rome (Eurostar AV, €44, 90 minutes, hourly), Venice (Eurostar AV €52, 1¾ hours, 12 daily) and Milan (Eurostar AV, €16.20, one hour, hourly).

Getting Around

To/From the Airport

Terravision (☎06 321 20 011; www.terravision.it) runs a bus service between the paved bus park in front of the train station and Pisa (Galileo Galilei) airport (adult/child aged five to 12 years €10/4, 70 minutes, 12 daily). Buy your tickets at the Terravision desk inside Deanna Café, opposite. Otherwise there are regular trains (€5.10, 1½ hours, hourly between 6.37am and 8.37pm).

ATAF (☎800 42 45 00; www.ataf.net) runs a shuttle bus (€5, 25 minutes, half-hourly from 5.30am to 11pm) connecting Florence airport with the SITA bus station.

Eurostar's Frecciarossa service travels between Florence and Bologna Centrale train station (€24, 40 minutes, every 30 minutes). Aerobus services travel between Bologna airport and Bologna Centrale (see p835).

Bus

ATAF (☎800 42 45 00; www.ataf.net) buses service the city centre and Fiesole, a small town in the hills 8km northeast of Florence. The most useful terminal is just outside the train station's eastern exit. Take bus 7 for Fiesole, and 12 or 13 for Piazzale Michelangelo. Tickets (90 minutes €1.20) are sold at *tabacchi* and newsstands – you can also buy a 90-minute ticket on board the bus (€2).

Car & Motorcycle

Much of the city centre is restricted to traffic, so the best advice is to leave your car in a car park and use public transport. Details of car parks are available from **Firenze Parcheggi** (☎055 500 19 94; www.firenzeparcheggi.it, in Italian). Note that there is a strict Limited Traffic Zone (ZTL) in the historic centre from 7.30am to 7.30pm Monday to Wednesday and from 7.30am to 6pm and 11.30pm to 4am on Thursday, Friday and Saturday. Fines are hefty if you enter the centre during these times without a special permit having been organised by your hotel in advance. For a map of the ZTL go to www.comune.fi.it/opencms/export/sites/retecivica/materiali/turismo/ztlnov.JPG.

Pisa

POP 87,400

Most people know Pisa as the home of an architectural project gone terribly wrong, but the Leaning Tower is just one of a number of noteworthy sights in this compact and compelling university city.

Pisa's golden age came in the 12th and 13th centuries when it was a maritime power rivalling Genoa and Venice. It was eventually defeated by the Genoese in 1284 and in 1406 it fell to Florence. Under the Medici, the arts and sciences flourished and Galileo Galilei (1564–1642) taught at the university.

Sights & Activities

From Piazza Sant' Antonio, just west of the train station where the bus stands are, the Leaning Tower is a straightforward 1.5km walk – follow Viale F Crispi north, cross the Ponte Solferino over the Arno and continue straight up Via Roma to Campo dei Miracoli.

Pisatour (⌚328 144 68 55; www.pisatour.it; adult/child under 15yr €12/free; ⌚tours Mon & Thu 3pm, Sat 10.30am) offers excellent two-to-three hour English-language guided walking tours around the historic centre and can also organise guides for the Campo dei Miracoli.

Campo dei Miracoli CATHEDRALS

(Field of Miracles) Pisans claim that Campo dei Miracoli is among the most beautiful urban spaces in the world. Certainly, the immaculate walled lawns provide a gorgeous setting for the Cathedral, Baptistry and Tower; on the other hand, few places boast so many tat-waving hawkers.

Forming the centrepiece of the Campo's Romanesque trio, the candy-striped **Cathedral** (Duomo; ⌚10am-12.45pm & 2-5pm Nov-Feb, to 6pm Mar, 1to 8pm Apr-Sep, to 7pm Oct), begun in 1063, has a graceful tiered facade and cavernous interior. The transept's bronze doors are by Bonanno Pisano, and the 16th-century entrance doors are by Giambologna.

To the west, the cupcake-like **Baptistry** (Battistero; ⌚10am-5pm Nov-Feb, 9am-6pm Mar, 8am-8pm Apr-Sep, 9am-7pm Oct) was started in 1153 and completed by Nicola and Giovanni Pisano in 1260. Inside, note Nicola Pisano's beautiful pulpit.

But it's to the campanile, better known as the **Leaning Tower** (Torre Pendente; ⌚10am-4.30pm Dec & Jan, 9.30am-5.30pm Feb, 9am-5.30pm Mar, 8.30am-8pm Apr-Sep, 9am-7pm Oct, 9.30am-5.30pm Nov), that all eyes are drawn. Bonanno Pisano began building in 1173, but almost immediately his plans came a cropper in a layer of shifting soil. Only three of the tower's seven tiers were completed before it started tilting – continuing at a rate of about 1mm per year. By 1990 the lean had reached 5.5 degrees – a tenth of a degree beyond the critical point established by computer models. Stability was finally ensured in 1998 when a combination of biased weighting and soil drilling forced the tower into a safer position. Today it's almost 4.1m off the perpendicular.

Visits are limited to groups of 40 and children under eight years are not allowed entrance; entry times are staggered and queuing is predictably inevitable. It is wise to book ahead.

Flanking the Campo, beautiful **Camposanto cemetery** (⌚10am-5pm Nov-Feb, 9am-6pm Mar, 8am-8pm Apr-Sep, 9am-7pm Oct) is said to contain soil shipped from Calvary during the Crusades. Look out for the 14th-century fresco *The Triumph of Death* on the southern cloister wall.

CAMPO DEI MIRACOLI TICKETING

Ticket pricing for Campo dei Miracoli sights is complicated. Tickets to the **Tower** (€15 at ticket office, €17 when booked online) and **Cathedral** (€2 Mar-Oct, free Nov-Feb) are sold individually, but for the remaining sights combined tickets are available. These cost €5/6/10 for one/two/five sights and cover the Cathedral, Baptistry, Camposanto, Museo dell'Opera del Duomo and Museo delle Sinópie. Entry for children aged under 10 years is free for all sights except the tower. Any ticket will also give access to the multimedia and information areas located in the Museo Dell'Opera del Duomo and Museo delle Sinópie.

Tickets are sold at two **ticket offices** (www.opapisa.it) on the piazza: the central ticket office is located behind the tower and a second office is located in the entrance foyer of the Museo delle Sinópie. To ensure your visit to the tower, book tickets via the website at least 15 days in advance.

Sleeping

Many people visit Pisa on a day trip from Florence, but if you're keen to sample the student bar scene at night there are a few decent overnight options.

Hotel Francesco HOTEL €€
(050 55 54 53; www.hotelfrancesco.com; Via Santa Maria 129; r €60-150;) The best of the hotels lining busy Via Santa Maria (just off Campo dei Miracoli), the small family-run Francesco offers a warm welcome and bright rooms with mod cons. Breakfast isn't included in the price of the room.

Relais Sotto la Torre B&B/HOSTEL €
(050 55 35 59; www.relaisunderthetower.it; cnr Via Santa Maria & Piazza del Duomo; dm €24-25, d without bathroom €52, d €56;) Literally in the shadow of the Leaning Tower, this cross between a B&B and hostel is spread over two buildings and gets mixed reviews from readers. Rooms are all clean, but a few have no windows and reception hours are irregular. You're unlikely to find anything better at this price, though.

Eating & Drinking

The best restaurants are bars are located in the streets around Piazza Dante Alighieri, Piazza Vettovaglie and along the riverbank.

Bar Pasticceria Salza CAFE €
(050 58 02 44; Borgo Stretto 44; 8am-8.30pm Apr-Oct, hr vary Tue-Sun Nov-Mar) Salza has been tempting patrons off Borgo Stretto and into sugar-induced wickedness ever since the 1920s. Claim one of the tables in the arcade, or save some money by standing at the bar – the excellent coffee and dangerously delicious cakes and chocolates will satisfy regardless of where they are sampled.

Il Montino PIZZA €
(Vicolo del Monte 1; cecina €2.40, spuma €1, focaccias €2.50; 10.30am-3pm & 5-10pm Mon-Sat) Students and sophisticates alike adore the *cecina* (chickpea pizza) and *spuma* (sweet, non-alcoholic drink) that are the specialities of this famous pizzeria. Order to go or claim one of the outdoor tables. You'll find it in the laneway behind Caffetiera Ginostra.

Ristoro al Vecchio Teatro TRATTORIA €€
(050 20 21 0; Piazza Dante; set menus €25 & €35, mains €8-12; lunch Mon-Sat, dinner Tue-Sat) The Vecchio Teatro's genial host is proud of his set menu, and for good reason. The four courses are dominated by local seafood specialities and the dessert finale includes a *castagnaccio* (sweet chestnut cake) that has been known to prompt diners to spontaneous applause.

Osteria 050 TRATTORIA €€
(050 54 31 06; www.zerocinquanta.com, in Italian; Via San Francesco 36; closed Sun lunch & Tue) Named after Pisa's phone code, this stylish eatery serves regional specialities made with organic products sourced from the local area and used in season.

Information

For city information, check www.pisaturismo.it or ask at one of the three **tourist offices** (airport 050 50 25 18; 9.30am-11.30pm; city centre 050 4 22 91; Piazza Vittorio Emanuele II 16; 9am-7pm Mon-Sat, to 4pm Sun; Piazza dei Miracoli 334 641 94 08; 9.30am-7.30pm).

Getting There & Away

The city's **Pisa international airport** (Galileo Galilei airport; PSA; 050 84 93 00; www.pisa-airport.com) is linked to the centre by train (€1.10, five minutes, 15 daily), or by the CPT Linea Rossa bus (www.cpt.pisa.it, in Italian; €1, 10 minutes, every 10 minutes). Buy bus tickets at the newsstand at the train station.

Terravision buses depart from the airport to Florence (adult/child five to 12 years €10/4, 70 minutes, 12 daily). **Train Spa** (www.trainspa.it) shuttle buses go to Siena via Empoli (€14, two daily).

Regular trains run to Lucca (Regional €2.40, 30 minutes, every 30 to 60 minutes), Florence (Regional €5.80, 1¼ hours, every 30 minutes), Rome (Eurostar €39.50, three hours, nine daily) and Genoa (InterCity €16, 2½ hours, eight daily).

Siena

POP 54,200

Siena is one of Italy's most enchanting medieval towns. Its walled centre, a beautifully preserved warren of dark lanes punctuated with Gothic *palazzi*, pretty piazzas and eye-catching churches, has at its centre Piazza del Campo (known as Il Campo), the sloping square that is the venue for the city's famous annual horse race, Il Palio.

According to legend, Siena was founded by the sons of Remus. In the Middle Ages its dramatic rise caused political and cultural friction with nearby Florence and the two cities strove to outdo each other with their artistic and architectural achievements. Painters of the Sienese School (most notably in the 13th to 15th centuries) produced significant works of art, many of which are on

Siena

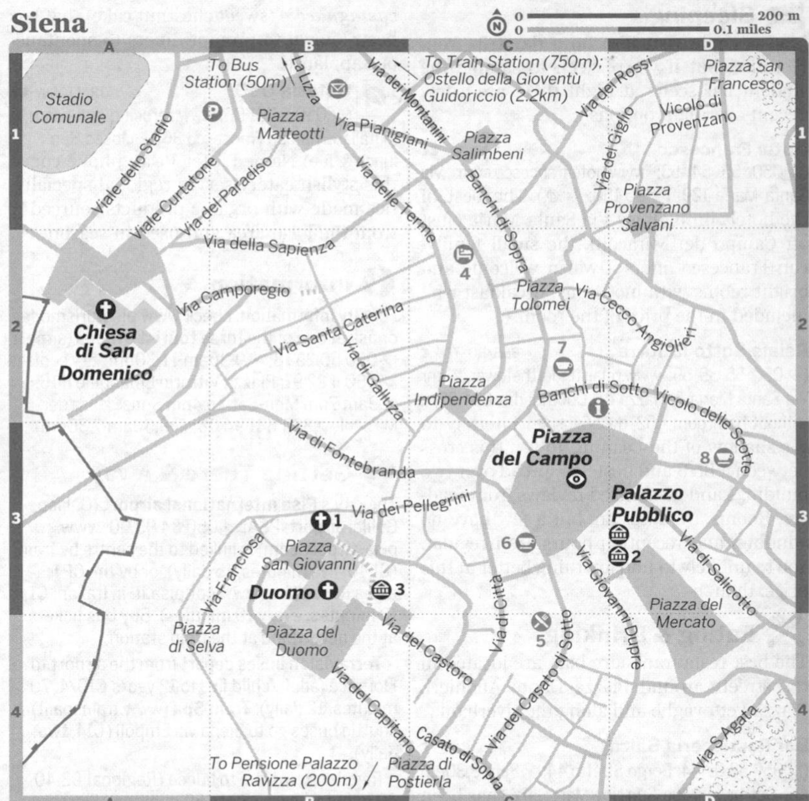

show in the city's impressive museums and churches.

Sights

From the train station take bus 10 (€1) to Piazza Gramsci, from where Piazza del Campo is a short, signposted walk away. From the bus station it's a 10-minute walk up Via La Lizza and Via delle Terme. The centre's main streets – the Banchi di Sopra, Via di Città and Banchi di Sotto – curve around Il Campo. Note that visitors' cars aren't permitted in the centre.

A joint ticket for the Duomo, Battistero, Museo dell'Opera, Diocesan Museum, Crypt and Santa Maria della Scala – all clustered around the Duomo – costs adult/child under 6 years/student/over 65 years €12/free/5/8. See www.operaduomo.siena.it for details.

Piazza del Campo SQUARE

Ever since the 14th century, the slanting, shell-shaped Piazza del Campo has been the city's civic centre. Forming the base of the piazza, the **Palazzo Pubblico** (Palazzo Comunale) is a good example of Sienese Gothic architecture. Inside, the **Museo Civico** (adult/concession €8/4.50; ⏲10am-6.15pm mid-Mar–Oct, to 4.45pm Nov–mid-Mar) houses some extraordinary frescos, including Simone Martini's famous *Maestà* (Virgin Mary in Majesty) and Ambroglio Lorenzetti's *Allegories of Good and Bad Government*. Soaring above the *palazzo* is the 102m (400-step) **Torre del Mangia** (admission €8; ⏲10am-6.15pm mid-Mar–end Oct, to 3.15pm Nov–mid-Mar), which dates from 1297. A combined ticket to the two costs adult/child under 6 years €13/free and is only available at the Torre del Mangia ticket office.

Duomo CHURCH

(Cathedral; Piazza del Duomo; admission €3; ⏲10.30am-7.30pm Mon-Sat & 1.30-5.30pm Sun Mar-May & Sep-Oct, 10.30am-8pm Mon-Sat & 1.30-6pm Sun Jun-Aug, 10.30am-6.30pm Mon-Sat & 1.30-5.30pm Sun Nov-Feb) The spectacular

Siena

Top Sights

Sights

Sleeping

Eating

Drinking

Duomo is one of Italy's Gothic masterpieces. Begun in 1196, it was completed in 1215, although work continued well into the 13th century. Subsequent expansion plans were stymied by the plague of 1348. The striking facade of green, red and white marble was designed by Giovanni Pisano, who also helped his dad, Nicola, craft the cathedral's intricate pulpit. Other noteworthy features include Donatello's bronze of St John the Baptist and statues of St Jerome and Mary Magdalene by Bernini.

Behind the cathedral and down a flight of stairs, the **Battistero** (Baptistry; admission €3; Piazza San Giovanni; 9.30am-7pm Mar-May & Sep-Oct, to 8pm Jun-Aug, 10am-5pm Nov-Feb) has a Gothic facade and a rich interior of 15th-century frescos.

Museo dell'Opera MUSEUM
(Piazza del Duomo; admission €6; 9.30am-7pm Mar-May & Sep-Oct, to 8pm Jun-Aug, to 5pm Nov-Feb) This museum is home to a large collection of Sienese painting and sculpture, including an entire room dedicated to the work of Duccio di Buoninsegna, the most significant painter of the Sienese School.

Chiesa di San Domenico CHURCH
(Piazza San Domenico 1; admission free; 7.30am-1pm & 3-6.30pm) On the western edge of the walled city, this is the last resting place of the head and thumb of St Catherine, Siena's patron saint.

Festivals & Events

Siena's great annual event is the **Palio** (2 Jul & 16 Aug), a pageant culminating in a bareback horse race round Il Campo. The city is divided into 17 *contrade* (districts), of which 10 are chosen annually to compete for the *palio* (silk banner). The only rule in the three-lap race is that jockeys can't tug the reins of other horses.

Sleeping

It's always advisable to book in advance, but for August and the Palio, it's essential.

Pensione Palazzo Ravizza BOUTIQUE HOTEL €€
(0577 28 04 62; www.palazzoravizza.com; Pian dei Mantellini 34; s €95-150, d €115-200; P ❄) *Pensione* is a far too modest title for this intimate, sumptuous place. Occupying a delightful Renaissance *palazzo*, frescoed ceilings and antique furniture co-exist with flat-screen TVs and comprehensive wi-fi coverage. Service is courteous and efficient, and there's a small, leafy garden.

Antica Residenza Cicogna B&B €
(347 007 28 88; www.anticaresidenzacicogna.it; Via dei Termini 67; s €75-90, d €85-100; P ❄) Springless beds, soundproof windows, ornate frescos, antique furniture and a lavish buffet breakfast make this central option justifiably popular. Reception has limited core hours (8am to 1pm), so arrange your arrival in advance.

Ostello della Gioventù Guidoriccio HOSTEL €
(0577 522 12; siena@ostellionline.org; Via Fiorentina 89; per person €20; P @) An inconvenient 20-minute bus ride from the town centre, Siena's HI hostel has 46 neat but dark two-bed rooms. Take bus 10 or 15 from Piazza Gramsci, or 77 from the train station and tell the driver you're after the *ostello*.

Eating & Drinking

Among many traditional Sienese dishes are *panzanella* (summer salad of soaked bread, basil, onion and tomatoes), *pappardelle con la lepre* (ribbon pasta with hare) and panforte (a rich cake of almonds, honey and candied fruit).

Osteria Le Logge RESTAURANT €€€
(0577 4 80 13; www.osterialelogge.it; Via dei Porrione 33; mains €19-24; Mon-Sat) This place changes its menu of creative and delicious Tuscan cuisine almost daily. The downstairs dining room, once a pharmacy, is an

atmospheric space in which to dine and there are also streetside tables.

Hosteria Il Carroccio TRATTORIA €€
(☎0577 4 11 65; Via del Casato di Sotto 32; mains €13-25; ⊙Thu-Tue) Recommended by the prestigious Slow Food movement, Il Carroccio specialises in traditional Sienese cooking. Staples include *pici* (thick spaghetti) and succulent *bistecca di chianina alla brace* (grilled steak).

Caffè Fiorella CAFE €
(Via di Città 13; ⊙Mon-Sat 7am-8pm) Squeeze into this tiny space behind Il Campo to enjoy Siena's best coffee. In summer, the coffee granita with a dollop of cream is a wonderful indulgence.

Pasticceria Nannini CAFE €
(24 Via Banchi di Sopra; ⊙7.30am-11pm) Come here for the finest *cenci* (fried sweet pastry), panforte and *ricciarelli* (almond biscuits) in town, enjoyed with a cup of excellent coffee.

Information

Tourist office (☎0577 28 05 51; www.terresiena.it; Piazza del Campo 56; ⊙9am-7pm).

Getting There & Away

Siena is not on a main train line, so it's easier to arrive by bus. From the bus station on Piazza Gramsci, **Train SPA** (www.trainspa.it) and SITA buses run to/from Florence (€7.10, 1½ hours, every 30 to 60 minutes), Pisa airport (€14, two daily) and San Gimignano (€5.50, 1¼ hours, hourly), either direct or via Poggibonsi.

Sena (☎0577 28 32 03; www.sena.it) operates services to/from Rome (€21, three hours, 10 daily).

Both Train SPA and Sena have ticket offices underneath the piazza.

Lucca

POP 84,200

Lucca is a love-at-first-sight type of place. Hidden behind monumental Renaissance walls, its historic centre is chock-full of handsome churches, excellent restaurants and tempting *pasticcerie*. Founded by the Etruscans, it became a city state in the 12th century and stayed that way for 600 years. Most of its streets and monuments date from this period.

Sights & Activities

From the train station walk across Piazza Ricasoli, cross Viale Regina Margherita and then follow the path across the grass and through the wall to reach the historic centre.

Opera buffs should visit in July and August, when the **Puccini Festival** (☎0584 35 93 22; www.puccinifestival.it; Lucca ticket office Piazza Anfiteatro, tickets €33-160) is held in a purpose-built outdoor theatre in the nearby settlement of Torre del Lago.

City walls CITY WALLS
Lucca's 12m-high city walls were built around the old city in the 16th and 17th centuries and were once defended by 126 cannons. In the 19th century they were crowned with a wide, tree-lined footpath that is now the centre of local Lucchese life. To join the locals in walking, jogging, rollerblading or cycling the 4km-long footpath, access it via Piazzale Verdi or Piazza Santa Maria; bike hire is available at the tourist office at Piazzale Verdi (per hour €2.50) or at one of two bike-rental shops (bikes per hour €2.50, tandems €5.50) at Piazza Santa Maria.

Cattedrale di San Martino CHURCH
(www.museocattedralelucca.it, in Italian; Piazza San Martino; ⊙9.30am-5.45pm Mon-Fri, to 6.45pm Sat, 9am-10.45am & noon-6pm Sun Mar-Oct, 9.30am-4.45pm Mon-Fri, to 6.45pm Sat, 11.20am-11.50am & 1-4.45pm Sun Nov-Feb) The predominantly Romanesque cathedral dates to the 11th century. Its exquisite facade was designed to accommodate the pre-existing campanile, and the reliefs over the left doorway of the portico are believed to be by Nicola Pisano. Inside, there's a magnificent *Last Supper* by Tintoretto.

Chiesa e Battistero dei SS Giovanni e Reparata CHURCH
The 12th-century interior of this deconsecrated church is a hauntingly atmospheric setting for early-evening opera recitals staged by **Puccini e la sua Lucca** (☎340 810 60 42; www.puccinielasualucca.com; adult/concession €17/12), which are held at 7pm every evening from mid-March to October, and on every evening except Thursday from November to mid-March. Professional singers present a one-hour program of arias and duets dominated by the music of Puccini. Tickets are available from the church between 10am and 6pm.

Sleeping

B&B Ai Cipressi B&B €
(☎0583 49 65 71; www.aicipressi.it; Via di Tiglio 126; s €55-79, d €69-99; P❄@☎) Outside Porta Elisa opposite the Sanctuary of Santa Gem-

WORTH A TRIP

SAN GIMIGNANO

Dubbed the medieval Manhattan, San Gimignano is a tiny hilltop town deep in the Tuscan countryside. A mecca for day trippers from Florence and Siena, it owes its nickname to the 11th-century towers that soar above its pristine *centro storico* (historic centre). Originally 72 were built as monuments to the town's wealth but only 14 remain. To avoid the worst of the crowds try to visit midweek, preferably in deep winter.

The **tourist office** (0577 94 00 08; www.sangimignano.com; Piazza del Duomo 1; 9am-1pm & 3-7pm Mar-Oct, to 1pm & 2-6pm Nov-Feb) is a short walk from Piazza dei Martiri di Montemaggio, the nearest San Gimignano has to a bus terminal. On the southern edge of Piazza del Duomo, the **Palazzo Comunale** (Piazza del Duomo; adult/concession €5/4; 9.30am-7pm Mar-Oct, 10am-5.30pm Nov-Feb) houses San Gimignano's art gallery (the **Pinacoteca**) and tallest tower, the **Torre Grossa**. Climb to the top for some unforgettable views.

Nearby, the Romanesque **basilica** (Piazza del Duomo; adult/child €3.50/1.50; 10am-7pm Mon-Fri, to 5.30pm Sat & 12.30-5.30pm Sun Apr-Oct, 10am-5pm Mon-Sat & 12.30-5pm Sun Nov-Mar), known also as the Collegiata, boasts frescos by Ghirlandaio.

While here, be sure to sample the local wine, vernaccia, while marvelling at the spectacular view from the terrace of the **Museo del Vino** (glasses €3-5; 11.30am-6.30pm), located next to the Rocca (fortress).

Regular buses link San Gimignano with Florence (€6.50, 1¼ hours, 14 daily), travelling via Poggibonsi, and Siena (€5.50, 1¼ hours, hourly).

ma Galgani, this motel-style B&B is perfect for travellers with their own car, as it offers free on-site parking. The modern rooms are clean, comfortable and well set up, with good beds and satellite TV.

Affittacamere Stella PENSION €
(0583 31 10 22; www.affittacamerestella.com; Via Pisana Traversa 2; s €45-55, d €60-70;) Just outside the Porta Sant'Anna, this well-regarded guest house in an early-20th-century apartment building offers comfortable and attractive rooms with wooden ceilings, a kitchen for guests' use and private parking. No breakfast.

Ostello San Frediano HOSTEL €
(0583 46 99 57; www.ostellolucca.it; Via della Cavallerizza12; dm €19-21, d €58;) Comfort and service levels are high at this HI-affiliated hostel. There are 141 rooms, a bar and a restaurant. Breakfast costs €3.

Eating

La Pecora Nera TRATTORIA €€
(0583 46 97 38; Piazza San Francesco 4; mains €9-12; closed Mon, Tue dinner, Sun lunch) The only Lucchese restaurant recommended by the Slow Food movement, La Pecora Nera also scores brownie points for social responsibility, as its profits go to fund workshops for young people with Down syndrome.

Taddeucci CAFE €
(www.taddeucci.com; Piazza San Michele 34; 8.30am-7.45pm, closed Thu Nov-Mar) This *pasticceria* is where the traditional Lucchesi treat of *buccellato* was created in 1881. A ring-shaped loaf made with flour, sultanas, aniseed seeds and sugar, it's the perfect accompaniment to a mid-morning or -afternoon espresso.

Forno Giusti BAKERY €
(Via Santa Lucia 20; pizzas & filled focaccias per kg €7-16; 7am-1pm & 4-7.30pm, closed Wed afternoon & all day Sun) The best way to enjoy a Lucchese lunch is to picnic on the walls, particularly if you buy delectable provisions from this excellent bakery.

Information

For tourist information, go to one of Lucca's three **tourist offices** (0583 355 51 00; www.luccatourist.it; Piazza Napoleone (10am-1pm & 2-6pm Mon-Sat); Piazza Santa Maria (9am-7.30pm Apr-Oct, 9am-12.30pm & 3-6.30pm Nov-Mar); Piazza Verdi (9am-7pm).

Getting There & Away

The bus station is near Piazzale Giuseppe Verdi, near Porta Vittorio Emanuele Santa Anna. From the bus station VaiBus buses run to/from Pisa airport (€3, one hour, hourly Monday to Saturday and every two hours Sunday).

Lucca is on the Florence–Pisa–Viareggio train line. Regional trains run to/from Florence (Regional €5.20, 1½ hours, every 30 to 90 minutes) and Pisa (€2.40, 30 minutes, every 30 to 60 minutes).

UMBRIA & LE MARCHE

Dubbed the 'green heart of Italy', the predominantly rural region of Umbria harbours some of Italy's best-preserved historic *borghi* (villages) and many important artistic, religious and architectural treasures. The regional capital, Perugia, provides a convenient base, with Assisi an easy day trip away.

To the east, mountainous Le Marche offers more of the same, its appeal encapsulated in the medieval, fairy-tale centre of Urbino.

Perugia

POP 165,300

With its hilltop medieval centre and international student population, Perugia is Umbria's largest and most cosmopolitan city. There's not a lot to see here, but the presence of the University for Foreigners ensures a buzz that's not always apparent in the region's sleepy hinterland. In July, music fans inundate the city for the prestigious **Umbria Jazz festival** (www.umbriajazz.com).

Perugia has a bloody and lively past. In the Middle Ages, the Baglioni and Oddi families fought for control of the city, while later, as a papal satellite, the city fought with its neighbours. All the while art and culture thrived: painter Perugino and Raphael, his student, both worked here.

The historic centre is on top of the hill, the train station is at the bottom and the regional bus station, Piazza dei Partigiani, is halfway between the two. From Piazza Partigiani there are *scale mobili* (elevators) going up to Piazza Italia, where local buses terminate. From Piazza Italia, pedestrianised Corso Vannucci runs up to Piazza IV Novembre, the city's focal point.

Sights

The **Perugia Città Museo Card** (adult/EU concession €10/6) gives one adult and one child aged under 18 years access to five city museums and is valid for 48 hours.

Piazza IV Novembre SQUARE

Flanking Piazza IV Novembre, the austere 14th-century **Duomo** (Cathedral; Piazza IV Novembre; ⌚7.30am-12.30pm & 4-7pm) has an unfinished two-tone facade and, inside, an altarpiece by Signorelli and sculptures by Duccio.

In the centre of the piazza, the stolid **Fontana Maggiore** was designed by Fra Bevignate and carved by Nicola and Giovanni Pisano between 1275 and 1278.

Palazzo dei Priori PALACE

The Palazzo dei Priori houses Perugia's best museums, including the **Galleria Nazionale dell'Umbria** (www.gallerianazionaleumbria.it, in Italian; Corso Vannucci 19; adult/EU concession €6.50/3.25; ⌚9.30am-7.30pm Mon, 8.30am-7.30pm Tue-Sun), whose collection contains works by local heroes Perugino and Pinturicchio among many others. Close to the *palazzo,* the impressive **Nobile Collegio del Cambio** (Exchange Hall; Corso Vannucci 25; adult/concession €4.50/2.60; ⌚9am-12.30pm & 2.30-5.30pm Mon-Sat, 9am-1pm Sun, closed Mon pm Nov–mid-Mar) is home to impressive frescos by Perugino.

Courses

The **Università per Stranieri** (University for Foreigners; ☎075 574 61; www.unistrapg.it; Piazza Fortebraccio 4) runs hundreds of courses in language, art, history, music and architecture.

Perugia

Top Sights

	Duomo	C2
	Galleria Nazionale dell'Umbria	B3
	Nobile Collegio del Cambio	C3
	Piazza IV Novembre	C2
Sights		
1	Fontana Maggiore	C2
2	Palazzo dei Priori	C3
Activities, Courses & Tours		
3	Università per Stranieri	C1
Sleeping		
4	Centro Internazionale per la Gioventù	D2
5	Primavera Mini Hotel	A2
Eating		
6	Civico 25	D2
7	Pizzeria Mediterranea	C2
Drinking		
8	Punto di Vista	B5
9	Sandri	C3

Sleeping

Primavera Mini Hotel PENSION €

(☎075 572 16 57; www.primaveraminihotel.com; Via Vincioli 8; s €42-65, d €65-75; ❄@☎) On the top floor of a 16th-century *palazzo*, this well-run two-star *pensione* has eight modern rooms that are as clean as they are comfortable (ask for the top-floor room with terrace). Not all rooms have air-con, and breakfast costs an extra €3 to €6. It's deservedly popular, so book well ahead.

Perugia

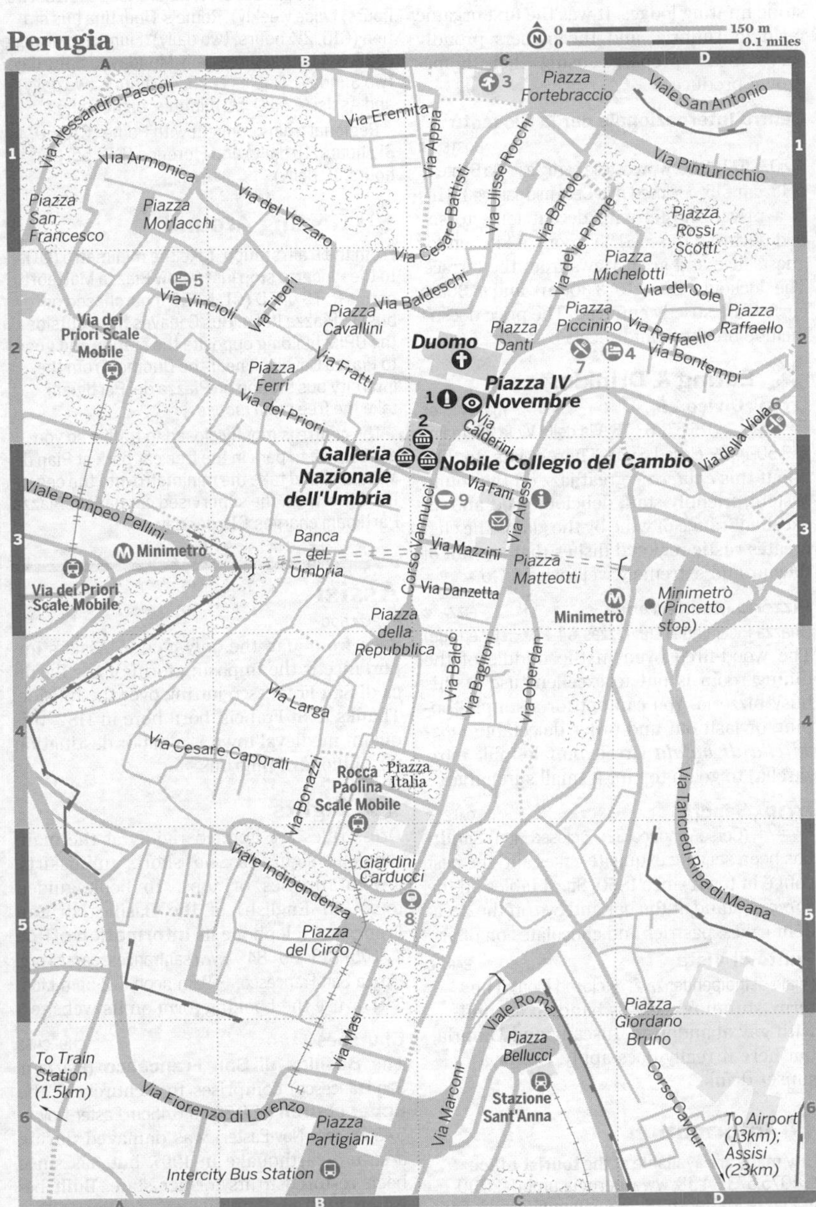

ITALY PERUGIA

Torre Colombaia AGRITURISMO €
(☎075 878 73 41; www.torrecolombaia.it; San Biagio delle Valle; per person incl breakfast/half-board €40/60, self-catering apt €90-125) A 15-minute drive southwest from downtown Perugia, this working farm dates back to the 16th century, and guests stay in restored stone hunting lodges. It was the first organic farm in Umbria, and the owners proudly serve meals prepared using their home-grown produce.

Centro Internazionale per la Gioventù HOSTEL €
(☎075 572 28 80; www.ostello.perugia.it; Via Bontempi 13; dm €15; ⊙closed mid-Dec–mid-Jan; @) This is a private hostel with decent four- to six-bed dorms, a frescoed TV room, a kitchen for guests' use and great views from the terrace. The lockout (11am to 3.30pm) and 3.30am curfew are strictly enforced. The price doesn't include breakfast and sheets cost €2.

Eating & Drinking

TOP CHOICE **Civico 25** WINE BAR €€
(☎075 571 63 76; Via della Viola 25; mains €13.50-14; ⊙closed Sun) There's lots to like about this *enoteca* – great jazz on the sound system, friendly staff, delicious food and an excellent range of wine by the glass. The chef creates rustic regional dishes that are full of flavour and extremely well priced. Go.

Pizzeria Mediterranea PIZZA €
(Piazza Piccinino 11/12; pizzas €4-14; ⊙closed Tue) The wood-fired oven in the middle of the dining room is put to excellent use at this busy pizzeria. You can opt for a simple topping or lash out and order delectable *mozzarella di bufala* (fresh buffalo-milk mozzarella) to go on top for a small surcharge.

TOP CHOICE **Sandri** CAFE €
(Corso Vannucci 32; ⊙closed Mon) Sandri has been serving exquisite cakes and the best coffee in town since 1860. Sit at tables on the *corso* or stand at the bar and eye off the decadent cakes, pastries and chocolates on offer.

Punto di Vista BAR €
(Viale di Indipendenza 2; ⊙closed Mon) The term 'stunning view' is bandied around with gay abandon in Tuscany and Umbria, but here it really does apply. Go for a sunset drink.

Information

City maps are available at the **tourist office** (☎075 573 64 58; www.perugia.umbria2000.it; Piazza Matteotti 18; ⊙8.30am-6.30pm). For information about what's on in town, buy a copy of *Viva Perugia* (€0.80) from a local newsstand.

Getting There & Away

From the intercity bus station on Piazza dei Partigiani, **Sulga** (☎800 09 96 61; www.sulga.it, in Italian) buses depart for Florence (€10.10, two hours, twice weekly), Rome's Tiburtina bus station (€16, 2½ hours, two daily), Fiumicino airport (€23, 3¾ hours, three daily Monday to Saturday, two Sunday), Naples (€25, 4½ hours, two daily) and Assisi (€3.20, 50 minutes, eight daily).

Regional trains connect with Rome (€10.60, 3½ hours, 16 daily) and Florence (€10.55, 2¾ hours, 10 daily).

Getting Around

From the train station, take the minimetrò (€1) to the Pincetto stop just below Piazza Matteotti, or bus R, TS or TD (€1, €1.50 if purchased on bus) to Piazza Italia. Bus C leaves from outside the UPIM building opposite the station and goes to Piazza Cavallini, near the Duomo. From the intercity bus station on Piazza dei Partigiani, take the free *scala mobila*.

The centre is mostly closed to traffic, so you are best off to park in the free car park at Pian di Massiano and take the minimetrò into the centre. Otherwise, the supervised car park at Piazza Partigiani charges €15 per day.

Assisi

POP 27,600

Seen from afar, the only clue to Assisi's importance is the imposing form of the Basilica di San Francesco jutting over the hillside. Thanks to St Francis, born here in 1182, this quaint medieval town is a major destination for millions of pilgrims.

Sights

Dress rules are applied rigidly at the main religious sights, so no shorts, miniskirts, low-cut dresses or tops. To book guided tours (in English) of the Basilica di San Francesco, telephone its **information office** (☎075 819 00 84; www.sanfrancescoassisi.org; Piazza San Francesco; ⊙9am-noon & 2-5pm Mon-Sat) or use the booking form on its website.

Churches CHURCHES
The **Basilica di San Francesco** (Piazza di San Francesco) comprises two churches. The **upper church** (⊙8.30am-6.45pm Easter-Nov, to 5.45pm daily Nov-Easter) was damaged during a severe earthquake in 1997, but has since been restored to its former state. Built between 1230 and 1253 in the Italian Gothic

style, it features superb frescos by Giotto and works by Cimabue and Pietro Cavallini.

Downstairs in the dimly lit **lower church** (6am-6.45pm Easter-Nov, to 5.45pm Nov-Easter), constructed between 1228 and 1230, you'll find a series of colourful frescos by Simone Martini, Cimabue and Pietro Lorenzetti. The crypt where St Francis is buried is below the church.

The 13th-century **Basilica di Santa Chiara** (075 81 22 82; Piazza Santa Chiara; 6.30am-noon & 2-7pm Apr-Oct, to 6pm Nov-Mar) contains the remains of St Clare, friend of St Francis and founder of the Order of Poor Clares.

Sleeping & Eating

You'll need to book ahead during peak times: Easter, August and September, and the Feast of St Francis (3 and 4 October).

Hotel Alexander HOTEL €€
(075 81 61 90; www.hotelalexanderassisi.it; Piazza Chiesa Nuova 6; s €60-80, d €90-120;) Smack-bang in the centre of town, this recently renovated place is a safe choice. There are only nine rooms, but all are clean and well equipped. The roof terrace has great views.

Ostello della Pace HOSTEL €
(075 81 67 67; www.assisihostel.com; Via Valecchie 177; dm €17-19, private room per person €20; @) In a pretty and quiet location between the train station and the Old Town, this family-run HI hostel offers a bar, restaurant, laundry room and bikes for hire.

Trattoria da Erminio TRATTORIA €
(075 81 25 06; www.trattoriadaerminio.it; Via Montecavallo 19; mains €7-11, set menus €16; closed Thu, Feb & first half of Jul) Da Ermino is known for its grilled meats, prepared on a huge fireplace in the main dining area. In summer, tables on the pretty cobbled street are hot property, and no wonder – this is old-fashioned Umbrian dining at its rustic best. You'll find it in the upper town near Piazza Matteotti.

Trattoria Pallotta TRATTORIA €€
(075 81 26 49; Vicolo della Volta Pinta 2; mains €8-16, set menus €16-25; closed Tue) Duck under the frescoed Volta Pinta (Painted Vault) off Piazza del Comune to this brick-vaulted, wood-beamed trattoria. The menu is unapologetically local, featuring homemade *strangozzi* (like tagliatelle), roast pigeon and rabbit stew. There's also an excellent wine list.

Information

Tourist office (075 81 25 34; www.assisi.regioneumbria.eu; Piazza del Comune 22; 8am-2pm & 3-6pm Mon-Sat, 10am-1pm Sun) Supplies maps, brochures and practical information.

Getting There & Away

It is better to travel to Assisi by bus rather than train, as the train station is 4km from Assisi proper, in Santa Maria degli Angeli. Buses arrive at and depart from Piazza Matteotti in the *centro storico*, stopping at Piazza Unita d'Italia below the basilica en route.

Sulga buses connect Assisi with Perugia (€3.20, 50 minutes, eight daily), Rome (€18, three hours, one daily) and Florence (€12.50, 2½ hours, twice weekly).

If you arrive by train, a bus (Linea C, €1, half-hourly) runs between Piazza Matteotti and the station. Regional trains run to Perugia (€2.40, 20 minutes, hourly).

Urbino

POP 15,600

If you visit only one town in Le Marche, make it Urbino. It's difficult to get to, but as you wander its steep, Unesco-protected streets you'll appreciate the effort. Birthplace of Raphael and Bramante and a university town since 1564, it continues to be a bustling centre of culture and learning. In July, it hosts the internationally famous ancient music festival, **Urbino Musica Antica** (www.fima-online.org).

Sights

Interest is centred on Urbino's immaculate hilltop *centro storico*. To get there from the bus terminal on Borgo Mercatale, head up Via Mazzini or take the *ascensore* (lift) up to Via Garibaldi (€0.50).

Palazzo Ducale PALACE
(Piazza Duca Federico; adult/child €4/free; 8.30am-7.15pm Tue-Sun, to 2pm Mon) The town's grand centrepiece is the Renaissance Palazzo Ducale, completed in 1482. Inside, the **Galleria Nazionale delle Marche** features works by Raphael, Paolo Uccello, della Francesca and Verrocchio.

A short walk away is the **Casa Natale di Raffaello** (Via Raffaello 57; admission €3; 9am-1pm & 3-7pm Mon-Sat, 10am-1pm Sun), the house where Raphael spent his first 16 years.

Sleeping & Eating

Albergo Italia HOTEL €€
(☎0722 27 01; www.albergo-italia-urbino.it; Corso Garibaldi 32; s €48-70, d €75-120; ❄@) Right in the heart of the walled town, this place has a bland modern interior offset by helpful staff, a pleasant garden terrace and comfortable rooms.

La Trattoria del Leone TRATTORIA €
(Via Cesare Battisti; mains €10; ⊙dinner daily, lunch Sat & Sun) To dine on classic regional food, head to this unassuming trattoria just off the main square. Expect plenty of salamis and cheese, earthy roast meats and full-blooded red wines.

Information

Tourist offices (☎0722 26 13; www.urbinoculturaturismo.it) Centre (Via Puccinoti 35; ⊙9am-7pm); Bus Terminus (⊙9am-6pm Mon-Sat) Also useful is www.turismo.pesarourbino.it.

Getting There & Around

The only way to get to Urbino by public transport is by bus. **Adriabus** (☎800 66 43 32; www.adriabus.eu) runs up to 20 daily buses to Pesaro (€2.75 to €3), from where you can catch a train to Bologna, and two daily services to Rome (€27, 4¼ hours).

Autolinee Ruocco (☎800 90 15 91; www.viaggiruocco.eu) runs a daily bus to Perugia (€15, 1¾ hours), for which it is essential to book in advance.

SOUTHERN ITALY

A sun-bleached land of spectacular coastlines, windswept hills and proud towns, southern Italy is a robust contrast to the genteel north. Its stunning scenery, graphic ruins and fabulous beaches often go hand in hand with urban sprawl and scruffy coastal development, sometimes in the space of a few kilometres.

Yet for all its troubles, *il mezzogiorno* (the midday sun, as southern Italy is known) has much to offer, specifically the fruitful fusion of architectural, artistic and culinary styles that is the legacy of centuries of foreign dominion.

Naples

POP 963,700

A raucous hell-broth of a city, Naples (Napoli) is loud, anarchic, dirty and edgy. Its manic streets and in-your-face energy leave you disoriented, bewildered and hungry for more. Founded by Greek colonists, it became a thriving Roman city and was later the Bourbon capital of the Kingdom of the Two Sicilies. In the 18th century it was one of Europe's great cities, something you'll readily believe as you marvel at its imperious palaces. Many of Naples' finest *palazzi* now house museums and art galleries, the best of which is the Museo Archeologico Nazionale, one of Italy's premier museums and reason enough for a city stopover.

Naples lazes along the waterfront and is divided into *quartieri* (districts). A convenient point of reference is Stazione Centrale, which forms the eastern flank of Piazza Garibaldi, Naples' ugly transport hub. From Piazza Garibaldi, Corso Umberto I skirts the *centro storico,* which is centred on two parallel roads: Via San Biagio dei Librai and its continuation Via Benedetto Croce (together known as Spaccanapoli); and Via dei Tribunali. West of the *centro storico,* Via Toledo, Naples' main shopping strip, leads down to Piazza del Plebiscito. South of here lies the seafront Santa Lucia district; to the west is Chiaia, an upmarket and extremely fashionable area. Above it all, Vomero is a natural balcony with grand views.

Sights

Centro Storico & Around NEIGHBOURHOOD
If you visit only one museum in southern Italy, make it the **Museo Archeologico Nazionale** (http://museoarcheologiconazionale.campaniabeniculturali.it, in Italian; Piazza Museo Nazionale 19; adult/EU concession €10/5; ⊙9am-7.30pm Wed-Mon), home to one of the world's most important collections of Graeco-Roman antiquities. Many of the exhibits once belonged to the Farnese family, including the colossal *Toro Farnese* (Farnese Bull) and gigantic *Ercole* (Hercules). On the mezzanine floor, *La battaglia di Alessandro contro Dario* (The Battle of Alexander against Darius) is one of many awe-inspiring mosaics from Pompeii.

A short walk south of the museum, Piazza del Gesù Nuovo is flanked by the 16th-century ashlar facade of the **Chiesa del Gesù Nuovo** (⊙7am-1pm & 4-7.30pm) and the **Basilica di Santa Chiara** (www.monasterodisantachiara.eu; Via Santa Chiara 49; ⊙7.30am-1pm & 4-8pm Mon-Sat). This hulking Gothic complex was restored to its original 14th-century look after being severely damaged by WWII bombing. The main attraction in the basilica complex is the tiled **Chiostro delle Clarisse**

(Nuns' Cloisters; admission €5/3.50; ⏲9.30am-5.30pm Mon-Sat, 10am-2.30pm Sun), adjacent to the main basilica.

Just off Via Benedetto Croce, the **Museo Cappella Sansevero** (www.museosansevero.it; Via de Sanctis 19; adult/concession €7/5; ⏲10am-5.40pm Mon & Wed-Sat, to 1.10pm Sun) reveals a sumptuous baroque interior and the *Cristo velato* (Veiled Christ), Giuseppe Sanmartino's incredibly lifelike depiction of Jesus covered by a veil.

Naples' spiritual heart is the **Duomo** (www.duomodinapoli.com; Via Duomo; ⏲8am-12.30pm & 4.30-7pm Mon-Sat, 8.30am-1pm & 5-7.30pm Sun). Built by the Angevins at the end of the 13th century, it has a 19th-century neo-Gothic facade and a largely baroque interior. Inside, the holy of holies is the 17th-century **Cappella di San Gennaro**, containing the head of St Januarius (the city's patron saint) and two vials of his congealed blood. The saint is said to have saved the city from disasters on various occasions.

At the western end of Via dei Tribunali, **Port' Alba** was one of the city's 17th-century gates.

Chiaia & Santa Lucia NEIGHBOURHOOD

At the bottom of Via Toledo, beyond the glass atrium of the **Galleria Umberto I** shopping arcade, Piazza Trieste e Trento leads onto **Piazza del Plebiscito**, Naples' most ostentatious piazza. Forming one side of the square, the rusty-red **Palazzo Reale** (www.palazzorealenapoli.it; Piazza del Plebiscito I; adult/EU concession €4/2; ⏲9am-7pm Thu-Tue) was the official residence of the Bourbon and Savoy kings and now houses a rich collection of baroque and neoclassical furnishings, statues and paintings.

Overlooking the seafront, **Castel Nuovo** is one of Naples' landmark sites, a hulking 13th-century castle known to locals as the Maschio Angioino (Angevin Keep). Inside, the **Museo Civico** (adult/concession €5/4; ⏲9am-7pm Mon-Sat) displays some interesting 14th- and 15th-century frescos and sculptures.

A second castle, the improbably named **Castel dell'Ovo** (Castle of the Egg; Borgo Marinaro; admission free; ⏲8am-6pm Mon-Sat, to 1pm Sun), originally a Norman castle and then an Angevin fortress, marks the eastern end of the *lungomare* (seaside promenade). The strip of seafront here is known as Borgo Marinaro and is now given over to restaurants and bars.

Vomero NEIGHBOURHOOD

The high point (quite literally) of Neapolitan baroque, the stunning **Certosa di San Martino** is one of Naples' must-see sights. Originally a 14th-century Carthusian monastery, it was given a 17th-century facelift by baroque maestro Cosimo Fanzago, and now houses the **Museo Nazionale di San Martino** (Largo San Martino 5; adult/EU concession €8/4; ⏲8.30am-7.30pm Thu-Tue). Highlights include the main church, the Chiostro Grande (Great Cloister), the 'Images and Memories of Naples' exhibit in the Quarto del Priore (Priors' Quarters), and the Sezione Presepiale, dedicated to rare 18th- and 19th-centrury *presepi* (nativity scenes).

It's not worth paying the entrance fee to enter the next-door **Castel Sant' Elmo** – its views are the same as those from the Certosa.

The easiest way up to Vomero is to take the Funicolare Centrale (€1.10) from Stazione Cumana di Montesanto, near Via Toledo.

Capodimonte ART MUSEUM

A 30-minute bus ride from the city centre, Capodimonte is worth a day of anyone's time. The colossal 18th-century Palazzo Reale di Capodimonte houses one of southern Italy's top fine-art museums, and the 130-hectare park is a top picnic spot.

The **Museo di Capodimonte** (Parco di Capodimonte; adult/child €10/5; ⏲8.30am-7.30pm Thu-Tue) is spread over three floors and 160 rooms. You'll never see everything, but a morning should be enough for an abridged tour. With works by Bellini, Botticelli, Titian and Andy Warhol, there's no shortage of talking points, but the piece that many come to see is Caravaggio's striking *Flagellazione* (Flagellation).

Take bus 110, M4 or M5 from Stazione Centrale to get here.

Festivals & Events

The **Festa di San Gennaro** honours the city's patron saint and is held three times a year (first Sunday in May, 19 September and 16 December). Thousands pack into the Duomo to witness the saint's blood liquefy, a miracle said to save the city from potential disasters.

Sleeping

You'll have no problem finding somewhere to stay, though be warned that many places suffer from street noise, and double-glazing isn't common. Most of the budget

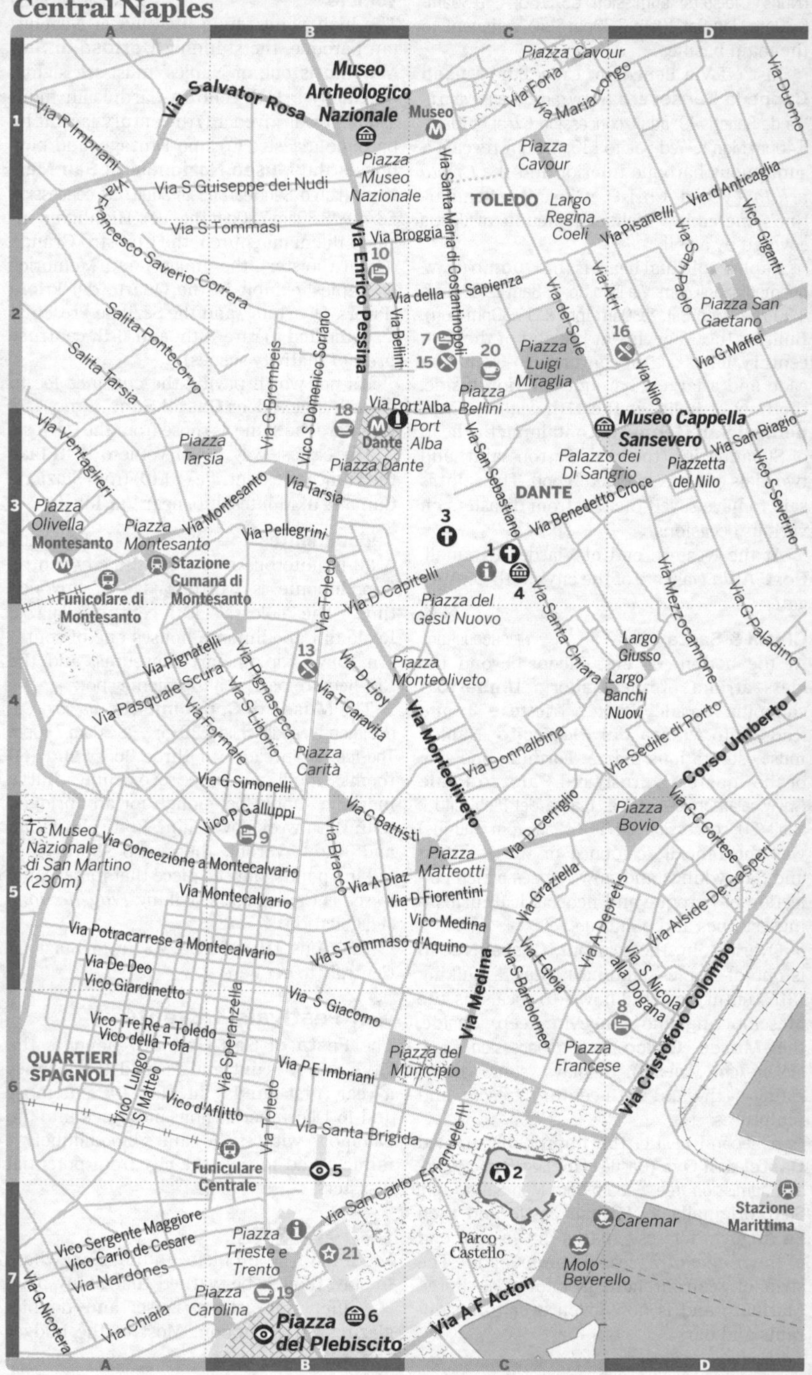

Museo Archeologico Nazionale
Museo
Via Salvator Rosa
Via R Imbriani
Piazza Cavour
Via Foria
Via Maria Longo
Via Duomo
Piazza Cavour
Piazza Museo Nazionale
Via S Guiseppe dei Nudi
Via Francesco Saverio Correra
Via S Tommasi
Via Santa Maria di Costantinopoli
TOLEDO
Largo Regina Coeli
Via d Anticaglia
Via Pisanelli
Via Broggia
Via Enrico Pessina
Via della Sapienza
Via Bellini
Via Atri
Via del Sole
Via San Paolo
Vico Giganti
Piazza San Gaetano
Salita Pontecorvo
Salita Tarsia
Via G Brombeis
Vico S Domenico Soriano
Piazza Luigi Miraglia
Via G Maffei
Via Nilo
Piazza Bellini
Via Port'Alba
Port Alba
Dante
Piazza Dante
Via Ventaglieri
Piazza Tarsia
Museo Cappella Sansevero
Palazzo dei Di Sangrio
Piazzetta del Nilo
Via San Biagio
Vico S Severino
Via Tarsia
Via San Sebastiano
DANTE
Via Benedetto Croce
Piazza Olivella
Montesanto
Piazza Montesanto
Via Montesanto
Via Pellegrini
Stazione Cumana di Montesanto
Funicolare di Montesanto
Via Toledo
Via D Capitelli
Piazza del Gesù Nuovo
Via Santa Chiara
Via Mezzocannone
Via G Paladino
Via Pignatelli
Via Pasquale Scura
Via Pignasecca
Via S Liborio
Via Formale
Via D Lioy
Via T Caravita
Piazza Monteoliveto
Via Monteoliveto
Largo Giusso
Largo Banchi Nuovi
Via Sedile di Porto
Corso Umberto I
Piazza Carità
Via Donnalbina
Via G Simonelli
Vico P Galluppi
Via C Battisti
Via D Cerriglio
Piazza Bovio
Via G C Cortese
To Museo Nazionale di San Martino (230m)
Via Concezione a Montecalvario
Via Bracco
Piazza Matteotti
Via A Diaz
Via Graziella
Via Alside De Gasperi
Via Montecalvario
Via D Fiorentini
Vico Medina
Via Potracarrese a Montecalvario
Via S Tommaso d'Aquino
Via A Depretis
Via De Deo
Vico Giardinetto
Via F Gioia
Via S Bartolomeo
Via S Nicola alla Dogana
Via S Giacomo
Via Medina
Vico Tre Re a Toledo
Vico della Tofa
Via Speranzella
QUARTIERI SPAGNOLI
Piazza del Municipio
Piazza Francese
Via Cristoforo Colombo
Via P E Imbriani
Vico Lungo S Matteo
Vico d'Aflitto
Via Santa Brigida
Funiculare Centrale
Via Emanuele III
Via San Carlo
Stazione Marittima
Caremar
Vico Sergente Maggiore
Vico Cario de Cesare
Via Nardones
Piazza Trieste e Trento
Parco Castello
Molo Beverello
Via G Nicotera
Piazza Carolina
Via Chiaia
Piazza del Plebiscito
Via A F Acton

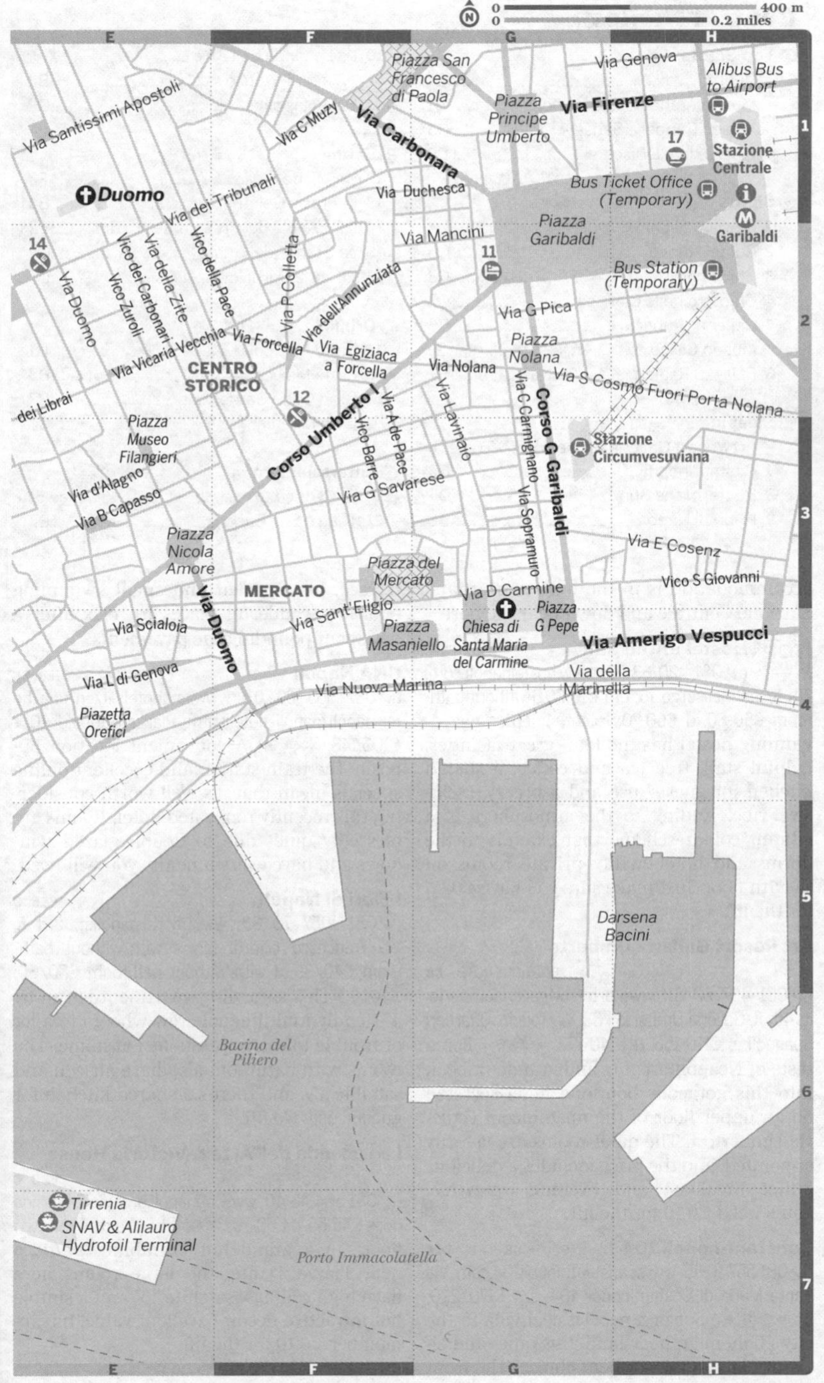
0 400 m
0 0.2 miles
E
F
G
H
1
2
3
4
5
6
7
Piazza San Francesco di Paola
Via Genova
Alibus Bus to Airport
Piazza Principe Umberto
Via Firenze
Via Santissimi Apostoli
Via C Muzy
Via Carbonara
17
Stazione Centrale
Duomo
Via dei Tribunali
Via Duchesca
Bus Ticket Office (Temporary)
Piazza Garibaldi
Garibaldi
Via Mancini
11
14
Vico della Pace
Via P Colletta
Via della Zite
Vico dei Carbonari
Vico Zuroli
Via Duomo
Via dell'Annunziata
Bus Station (Temporary)
Via G Pica
Piazza Nolana
Via Vicaria Vecchia
Via Forcella
Via Egiziaca a Forcella
Via Nolana
CENTRO STORICO
Via S Cosmo Fuori Porta Nolana
dei Librai
12
Corso Umberto I
Via A de Pace
Vico Barre
Via Lavinaio
Via C Carmignano
Corso G Garibaldi
Piazza Museo Filangieri
Stazione Circumvesuviana
Via d'Alagno
Via B Capasso
Via G Savarese
Via Sopramuro
Piazza Nicola Amore
Via E Cosenz
Piazza del Mercato
Vico S Giovanni
MERCATO
Via Duomo
Via D Carmine
Via Sant'Eligio
Piazza G Pepe
Via Scialoia
Piazza Masaniello
Chiesa di Santa Maria del Carmine
Via Amerigo Vespucci
Via L di Genova
Via della Marinella
Via Nuova Marina
Piazetta Orefici
Darsena Bacini
Bacino del Piliero
Tirrenia
SNAV & Alilauro Hydrofoil Terminal
Porto Immacolatella

Central Naples

accommodation is in the ugly area around Stazione Centrale and down near the port.

TOP CHOICE **Hostel of the Sun** HOSTEL €
(☎081 420 63 93; www.hostelnapoli.com; 7th fl, Via Melisurgo 15; dm €16-20,d without bathroom €50-60, d €60-70; ❄@☎) This award-winning hostel has the lot – great facilities, helpful staff, free tea and coffee, a shared kitchen for guests' use and a breezy, inclusive vibe. Adding to the atmosphere is a vibrant colour scheme that extends to the dorms and hotel-quality private rooms on the 5th floor. Just make sure you have €0.05 for the lift.

Art Resort Galleria Umberto BOUTIQUE HOTEL €€
(☎081 497 62 81; www.artresortgalleriaumberto.it; 4th fl, Galleria Umberto I 83, Via Toledo, Quartieri Spagnoli; s €110-156, d €140-193; ❄@☎) For a taste of Neapolitan glitz and grandeur, book into this gorgeous boutique hotel secreted on an upper floor of the magnificent Galleria Umberto I. The quiet rooms are lavishly appointed, and the price includes a delicious buffet breakfast and evening *aperitivo*. You'll need €0.10 for the lift.

Constantinopoli 104 BOUTIQUE HOTEL €€€
(☎081 557 10 35; www.constantinopoli104.com; Via Santa Maria di Costantinopoli 104; s/d €170/220; P❄@☎≋) Set in a neoclassical villa in the city's bohemian heartland, this quiet and elegant place is an excellent choice. The front terrace, lush garden and small swimming pool are wonderful places to relax after a day spent pounding the pavements.

UNA Napoli BUSINESS HOTEL €€
(☎081 563 69 01; www.unahotels.it/en/una_hotel_napoli/napoli_hotels.htm; Piazza Garibaldi 10; r €105-148; ❄@☎) A convenient location opposite the train station and excellent online specials mean that it's well worth considering this recently renovated hotel. Rooms are blessedly quiet due to double-glazed windows and have every amenity you will need.

I Fiori di Napoli B&B €
(☎081 1957 70 83; www.ifioridinapoli.it; 3rd fl, Via Francesco Girardi 92; s with/without bathroom €40/35, d with/without bathroom €80/60; ❄@☎) This sprawling apartment is run by a friendly multilingual crew who go to a lot of trouble to make guests feel at home. The rooms with bathroom also have air-con and satellite TV, and there's a shared kitchen for guests' use. No lift.

La Locanda dell'Arte & Victoria House B&B €
(☎081 564 46 40; www.bbnapoli.org; Via E Pessina 66; s €45-55, d €60-70; ❄@☎) Spread over two floors in a grand but crumbling *palazzo* near Piazza Dante, the large rooms here have high ceilings, satellite TV and a simple but attractive decor. Excellent value, but remember €0.10 for the lift.

Eating

Neapolitans are justifiably proud of their food. The pizza was created here – there are any number of toppings but locals favour margherita (tomato, mozzarella and basil) or marinara (tomato, garlic, oregano and olive oil), cooked in a wood-fired oven. Pizzerias serving the 'real thing' have a sign on their door – *la vera pizza napoletana* (the real Neapolitan pizza).

For something sweet try a *sfogliatella* (a flaky pastry filled with sweet orange-flavoured ricotta, and ideally served warm).

Pizza

Pizzeria Sorbillo PIZZA €
(Via dei Tribunali 32; pizzas from €4; Mon-Sat) The smartest of the Via dei Tribunali pizzerias, the Sorbillo is hugely popular. So much so that eating here is much like sitting down to a meal in rush hour. The hardworking *pizzaioli* (pizza makers) really know their craft – the pizzas are delicious.

Da Michele PIZZA €
(www.damichele.net; Via Cesare Sersale 1/3; pizzas €4-5; 10am-11pm Mon-Sat) The godfather of Neapolitan pizzerias (it opened in 1870), this place near Piazza Garibaldi takes the no-frills ethos to its extremes. It's dingy, old-fashioned and serves only two types of pizza – margherita and marinara.

Il Pizzaiolo del Presidente PIZZA €
(Via dei Tribunali 120/121; pizzas from €4; closed Sun) This is where British uberchef Heston Blumenthal came when he was researching pizza for his TV series *In Search of Perfection*, and for good reason. Be prepared for crowds and service with attitude.

Not Pizza

La Stanza del Gusto WINE BAR €€
(081 40 15 78; www.lastanzadelgusto.com, in Italian; Via Santa Maria di Costantinopoli 100; set menus €35-65, pastas/antipasto platters €14/22; 10.30am-midnight, closed Sun & Mon dinner) Gourmet set menus are served in the upstairs dining room, but the downstairs *enoteca* is more relaxed. We highly recommend the antipasto platters and a thorough investigation of the impressive wine list.

Da Dora SEAFOOD €€€
(081 68 05 19; Via Ferdinando Palasciano 30, Chiaia; mains €12-22; dinner Mon-Sat, lunch Tue-Sat) This Neopolitan institution is known throughout the city for its fresh seafood. The old-fashioned interior is charming, as are the somewhat elderly waiters and the singing chef. Don't miss the seafood antipasto or Dora's famous linguine, made with lobster, squid, clams and prawns.

Fantasia Gelati GELATERIA €
(Via Toledo 381; cones from €2; 7.30am-midnight) It claims to be the '*maesti gelatieri in Napoli*' ('master gelato makers in Naples'), and we thoroughly concur. Make your way to this location or the second store in **Vomero** (Piazza Vanvitelli 22; 7.30am-midnight).

Drinking

TOP CHOICE **Caffè Mexico** CAFE
(Piazza Dante 86; 7am-8.30pm Mon-Sat) This retro gem makes the best coffee in the city. The espresso is served *zuccherato* (sweetened), so request it *amaro* if you drink it unadorned. In summer, the *caffè freddo con panna* (iced coffee with cream) is a treat. There's another branch just near Stazione Centrale at Piazza Garibaldi 70.

Gran Caffè Gambrinus CAFE
(www.caffegambrinus.com; Via Chiaia 1-2; 7am-2am) Naples' most venerable cafe features a showy art nouveau interior and a cast of self-conscious drinkers served by smart, waistcoated waiters. It's great value when you stand at the bar.

Enoteca Belledonne BAR
(www.enotecabelledonne.com; Vico Belledonne a Chiaia 18; 10am-2pm & 7pm-2am Mon, to 2pm & 4.30pm-2am Tue-Sat, 7pm-2am Sun;) Exposed-brick walls, ambient lighting and bottle-lined shelves set the scene at this much-loved Chiaia wine bar. There's also a tempting grazing menu.

Intra Moenia CAFE
(www.intramoenia.it, in Italian; Piazza Bellini 70; 10am-2am) Attracting a bohemian crowd, this arty cafe-cum-bookshop is beautifully located on Piazza Bellini. It's a great place to while away a long summer evening with friends and something cool.

Entertainment

You can buy tickets for most sporting and cultural events at **Box Office** (081 551 91 88; www.boxofficenapoli.it; Galleria Umberto I 17).

Opera fans will enjoy an evening at **Teatro San Carlo** (box office 081 797 23 31; www.teatrosancarlo.it; Via San Carlo 98; box office 10am-7pm Mon-Sat, to 3.30pm Sun; tickets from €25), the oldest opera house in Italy. The opera season runs from December to May and performances of music and ballet are held at other times of the year.

DISCOUNT CARDS

Campania ArteCard (800 600 601; www.campaniaartecard.it; €12-30) gives free or discounted admission to museums in Naples and the whole region. Choose the version that suits you best; some include free public transport. The Napoli e Campi Flegrei card is valid for three days, includes free public transport and will give you free entrance to three museums and 50% disount on the entrance charge for 11 others. Available at participating museums, online or through the call centre.

Information

Dangers & Annoyances

Despite Naples' notoriety as a Mafia hot spot, the city is pretty safe. That said, travellers should be careful about walking alone late at night near Stazione Centrale and Piazza Dante. Petty crime is also widespread – be vigilant for pickpockets and moped bandits, and never leave anything visible in a parked car.

Emergency

Police station (Questura; 081 794 11 11; Via Medina 75)

Medical Services

Ospedale Loreto-Mare (Hospital; 081 254 27 93; Via Amerigo Vespucci 26) On the waterfront, near the train station.

Tourist Information

There are several **tourist information points** (www.inaples.it) around town: Piazza del Gesù Nuovo (081 551 27 01; 9.30am-1.30pm & 2.30-6pm Mon-Sat, 9am-1.30pm Sun); Via Santa Lucia (081 240 09 14; 9am-7pm daily); Via San Carlo (081 40 23 94; 9.30am-1.30pm & 2.30-6pm Mon-Sat, 9am-1.30pm Sun). All stock *Qui Napoli*, a useful bilingual monthly publication with details of sights, transport, accommodation, and major events.

Getting There & Away

Air

Capodichino airport (NAP; 848 88 87 77; www.gesac.it), 7km northeast of the city centre, is southern Italy's main airport. Flights operate to most Italian cities and up to 30 European destinations, as well as New York. Some 27 airlines serve the airport, including Alitalia, Air One, easyJet, Meridiana, Lufthansa, BMI and Air France.

Boat

A fleet of *traghetti* (ferries), *aliscafi* (hydrofoils) and *navi veloci* (fast ships) connect Naples with Sorrento, the bay islands, the Amalfi Coast, Salerno, Sicily and Sardinia. Hydrofoils leave from Molo Beverello and Mergellina; ferries depart from the Porta di Massa ferry terminal.

Tickets for shorter journeys can be bought at Molo Beverello or Mergellina. For longer journeys try ferry company offices at Porto di Massa or a travel agent. You can also buy online.

Qui Napoli lists timetables for Bay of Naples services. Note, however, that ferry services are pared back in winter and adverse sea conditions may affect sailing schedules.

The major companies servicing Naples:

Alì Lauro (081 497 22 38; www.alilauro.it) To/from Sorrento (€10, 35 minutes)

Caremar (081 551 38 82; www.caremar.it, in Italian) To/from Capri (€14.50, 1¼ hours)

Metro del Mare (199 600 700; www.metrodelmare.com) To/from Amalfi (€15, 1½ hours), Positano (€14, 55 minutes), Sorrento (€6.50, 45 minutes) and Salerno (€16, minutes)

NLG (081 552 07 63; www.navlib.it, in Italian) To/from Capri (€16, 30 minutes)

Siremar (89 21 23; www.siremar.it, in Italian) To/from Lipari (€50, 10½ hours)

SNAV (081 428 55 55; www.snav.it, in Italian) To/from Capri (€16, 45 minutes), Palermo (€50, 10 hours)

Tirrenia (081 89 21 23; www.tirrenia.com) To/from Palermo (€50, 10 hours) Cagliari (€55, 16¼ hours)

TTT Lines (081 580 27 44; www.tttlines.it) To/from Catania (€60, 10½ hours)

Bus

Most buses leave from Piazza Garibaldi. **SITA** (199 73 07 49; www.sitabus.it, in Italian) runs buses to Pompeii (€2.40, 40 minutes, hourly), Sorrento (€3.40, one hour 20 minutes, three daily), Positano (€3.40, two hours, three daily), Amalfi (€3.40, two hours, eight daily) and Bari (€20, three hours, one daily). Buy tickets and catch buses from the terminus near Porto di Massa or from the front of Stazione Centrale.

Miccolis (081 200 380; www.miccolis-spa.it, in Italian) serves Lecce (€29, 5½ hours) and Brindisi (€26.60, five hours).

Car & Motorcycle

If you value your sanity, skip driving in Naples. If you want to tempt fate, the city is easily accessible from Rome on the A1 *autostrada*. The Naples–Pompeii–Salerno motorway (A3) connects with the coastal road to Sorrento and the Amalfi Coast.

Train

Naples is southern Italy's main rail hub. Most trains stop at Stazione Centrale, which incorporates Stazione Garibaldi. There are up to 30 trains daily to Rome (InterCity €20.50, 2¼ hours) and some 15 to Salerno (InterCity €7, 35 minutes).

The **Circumvesuviana** (☎800 05 39 39; www.vesuviana.it), accessible through Stazione Centrale, operates trains to Sorrento (€3.40, 65 minutes) via Pompeii (€2.40, 35 minutes) and other towns along the coast. There are about 40 trains daily running between 5am and 10.40pm, with reduced services on Sunday.

Getting Around

To/From the Airport

By public transport you can either take the regular **ANM** (☎800 639 525; www.anm.it) bus 3S (€1.10, 30 minutes, half-hourly) from Piazza Garibaldi, or the Alibus airport shuttle (€3, 20 minutes, every 20 minutes) from Piazza del Municipio or Stazione Centrale.

Taxi fares are set at €19 to/from the historic centre.

Car & Motorcycle

The public car park outside Castel Nuovo charges €1.50 per hour (€2 for successive hours).

Public Transport

You can travel around Naples by bus, metro and funicular. Journeys are covered by the **Unico Napoli ticket** (www.unicocampania.it), which comes in various forms: the standard ticket, valid for 90 minutes, costs €1.10; a daily pass is €3.10; and a weekend daily ticket is €2.60. Note that these tickets are not valid on the Circumvesuviana line.

Taxi

Taxi fares are set at €10.50 between the historic centre and Piazza Garibaldi and €10 from the centre to the port. There's a €3 surcharge after 10pm (€5.50 on Sunday).

Pompeii

An ancient town frozen in its 2000-year-old death throes, Pompeii was a thriving commercial settlement until Mt Vesuvius erupted on 24 August AD 79, burying it under a layer of *lapilli* (burning fragments of pumice stone) and killing some 2000 people. The Unesco-listed **ruins** (☎081 857 53 47; www.pompeiisites.org; adult/EU concession €11/5.50, audioguide €6.50; ⏰8.30am-7.30pm Apr-Oct, to 5pm Nov-Mar, last entry 1½ hr before closing) provide a remarkable model of a working Roman city, complete with temples, a forum, an amphitheatre, apartments, a shopping district and a brothel. Dotted around the 44-hectare site are a number of creepy body casts, made in the late 19th century by pouring plaster into the hollows left by disintegrated bodies. They are so lifelike you can still see clothing folds, hair – even the expressions of terror on their faces.

There is a **tourist office** (☎081 536 32 93; www.pompeiturismo.it; Piazza Porta Marina Inferiore 12; ⏰8am-6pm Mon-Sat, 8.30am-2pm Sun Aug & Sep, 8.30am-3.30pm Mon-Fri, 8.30am-2pm Sat Oct-Jul) just outside the excavations at Porta Marina.

The easiest way to get to Pompeii is by the Ferrovia Circumvesuviana from Naples (€2.40, 35 minutes, half-hourly) or Sorrento (€1.90, 30 minutes, half-hourly). Get off at Pompeii Scavi-Villa dei Misteri; the Porta Marina entrance is nearby.

Capri

POP 7330

The most visited of Naples' Bay islands, Capri is far more interesting than a quick day trip would suggest. Get beyond the glamorous veneer of chichi piazzas and designer boutiques and you'll discover an island of rugged seascapes, desolate Roman ruins and a surprisingly unspoiled rural inland.

Capri's fame dates to Roman times, when Emperor Augustus made it his private playground and Tiberius retired there in AD 27. Its modern incarnation as a tourist destination dates to the early 20th century when it was invaded by an army of European artists, writers and Russian revolutionaries, drawn as much by the beauty of the local boys as the thrilling landscape.

The island is easily reached from Naples and Sorrento. Hydrofoils and ferries dock at Marina Grande, from where it's a short funicular ride up to Capri, the main town. A further bus ride takes you up to Anacapri.

For the best views on the island, take the **seggiovia** (chairlift; one-way/return €7/9; ⏰9.30am-5pm Mar-Oct, 10.30am-3pm Nov-Feb) up from Piazza Vittoria to the summit of **Mt Solaro** (589m), Capri's highest point.

Sights & Activities

Grotta Azzurra CAVE

(Blue Grotto; admission €4; ⏰9am-3pm) Capri's single most famous attraction is the Blue Grotto, a stunning sea cave illuminated by an other-worldly blue light. The best time to visit is in the morning. Boats leave from Marina Grande and the return trip costs €19.50 (€12 for the trip and €7.50 for the row boat into the grotto) plus the entrance fee to the grotto; allow a good hour. You can also take a bus from Viale Tommaso de Tommaso in Anacapri (15 minutes) or walk along Viale Tommaso de Tommaso, Via Pagliaro and Via Grotta Azzurra (50 minutes). Note that the grotto isn't visitable when seas are rough or tides are high.

Giardini di Augusto GARDEN
(Gardens of Augustus; admission free; 9am-1hr before sunset) Once you've explored Capri Town's dinky whitewashed streets, head over to the Giardini di Augusto for some breathtaking views. From here the magnificent **Via Krupp** zigzags vertiginously down to Marina Piccola.

Villa Jovis ANCIENT SITE
(admission €2; 9am-1hr before sunset) East of Capri Town, an hour-long walk along Via Tiberio, are the ruins of the largest and most sumptuous of the island's 12 Roman villas, once Tiberius' main Capri residence. A short walk away, down Via Tiberio and Via Matermània, is **Arco Naturale**, a huge rock arch formed by the pounding sea.

Villa San Michele GARDEN
(081 837 14 01; Via Axel Munthe; admission €6; 9am-6pm May-Sep, to 5pm Oct & Apr, to 3.30pm Nov-Feb, to 4.30pm Mar) Up in Anacapri, Villa San Michele boasts some Roman antiquities and beautiful, panoramic gardens.

Sleeping

Capri has plenty of top-end hotels but few genuinely budget options. Always book ahead, as hotel space is at a premium during summer and many places close in winter.

Hotel La Tosca PENSION €€
(081 837 09 89; www.latoscahotel.com; Via Dalmazio Birago 5; s €48-95, d €75-150; Apr-Oct;) La Tosca is one of the island's top budget hotels. With 10 sparkling white rooms, a central location and a roof terrace with panoramic views, it presses all the right buttons.

Capri Palace HOTEL €€€
(081 978 01 11; www.capripalace.com; Via Capodimonte 2b; s €270-360, d €350-1450; Apr-Nov; @) This fashionable retreat has a stylish Mediterranean-style decor and is full of contemporary art. Guests rarely leave the hotel grounds, taking full advantage of the huge pool, on-site health spa and top-notch **L'Olivo** restaurant.

Hotel Bussola di Hermes HOTEL €€
(081 838 20 10; www.bussolahermes.com; Trav La Vigna 14; s €50-110, d €60-150; @) A hospitable outpost on a quiet Anacapri lane, the year-round Bussola offers recently revamped rooms, some with private terraces and sea views.

Eating & Drinking

Be warned that restaurants on Capri are overpriced and underwhelming. The major exception to this rule (second part only) is L'Olivo restaurant at the Capri Palace Hotel, which is the proud possessor of two Michelin stars.

Da Tonino RESTAURANT €€€
(081 837 67 18; Via Dentecale 12; mains €22-26; closed Wed & Jan-Mar) A tranquil setting and traditional Campanian dishes await at this popular place near Piazetta della Noci. The menu is dominated by seafood – try the grilled calamari or the salt-and-pepper prawns – and there are delicious lemon profiteroles on offer for dessert.

Le Grottelle TRATTORIA €€
(081 837 57 19; Via Arco Naturale 13; mains €15-22; closed mid-Nov–Mar & Wed Sep-Jul) The simple food plays second fiddle to the atmospheric dining areas at Le Grottelle – one in a cave and the other on a terrace with amazing panoramic views. Chat with the waiter about what's fresh from the sea and don't miss the *torta caprese* for dessert.

Pulalli Wine Bar WINE BAR €€
(Piazza Umberto I, 4; closed Tue & Nov-Mar) A ritzy spot for a glass of local *limoncello* (lemon liqueur), Pulalli is perched in the clock tower overlooking 'la Piazzetta', Capri Town's main square. For a grandstand view of the action, snaffle a table on the small terrace. For a good cup of coffee, head to next-door **Piccolo Bar** (Piazza Umberto I, 5; 5am-1.30am).

R Buonocore GELATERIA €
(35 Via Vittorio Emanuele; medium cone €3) Come here for the best gelato in town. You'll find it near the corner of Via Carlo Serena.

Information

Information is available online at www.capri.it, www.capritourism.com or from one of the three **tourist offices** (Anacapri 081 837 15 24; Via

G Orlandi 59; ⏲9am-3pm Mon-Sat; Capri Town ✆081 837 06 86; Piazza Umberto I; ⏲8.30am-8.30pm Mon-Sat, 9am-3pm Sun Apr-Sep, 9am-1pm & 3.30-6.45pm Mon-Sat Nov-Mar; Marina Grande ✆081 837 06 34; ⏲9am-1pm & 3.30-6.45pm Mon-Sat). The offices open occasionally on Sundays in summer between 9am and 3pm.

Getting There & Around

There are year-round hydrofoils and ferries to Capri from Naples and Sorrento. Timetables and fare details are available online at www.capritourism.com; look under 'Shipping timetable'. In Naples, sailing times are published in *Qui Napoli*; in Sorrento you can get timetables from the tourist office (see p868).

From Naples, ferries depart from Porto di Massa and hydrofoils from Molo Beverello and Mergellina. Tickets cost €16 (hydrofoil), €14.50 (fast ferry) and €9.60 (ferry) – see p864 for further details.

From Sorrento, there are more than 25 sailings a day (less in winter). You'll pay €14 for the 20-minute hydrofoil crossing, €9.80 for the 25-minute fast ferry trip.

In summer, hydrofoils and ferries connect Capri with Positano (€15.50 to €16.50) and Amalfi (€15 to €17).

On the island, buses run from Capri Town to/from Marina Grande, Anacapri and Marina Piccola. There are also buses from Marina Grande to Anacapri. Single tickets cost €1.40 on all routes, as does the funicular that links Marina Grande with Capri Town in a four-minute trip.

Taxis between Marina Grande and Capri Town cost €16 and can carry up to six people.

A tour around the island by motorboat (stopping for a swim and at the Grotta Azzurra on the way) costs €160 per group. A reputable operator is **Capri Relax** (www.caprirelaxboats.com), which has a small office near the chemist shop at Marina Grande.

Sorrento

POP 16,600

Overlooking the Bay of Naples and Mt Vesuvius, Sorrento is southern Italy's main package holiday resort. Despite this, and despite the lack of a decent beach, it's an appealing place whose laid-back charm defies all attempts to swamp it in souvenir tat. There are few must-see sights but the *centro storico* is lively and the town makes a good jumping-off point for the Amalfi Coast, Pompeii and Capri.

The centre of town is Piazza Tasso, 300m northwest of the Circumvesuviana train and bus station along Corso Italia. From Marina Piccola, where ferries and hydrofoils dock, walk south along Via Marina Piccola then climb the steps to reach the piazza.

Sights & Activities

You'll probably spend most of your time in the *centro storico*, a tight-knit area of narrow streets lined with loud souvenir stores, cafes, churches and restaurants. To the north, the **Villa Comunale park** (admission free; ⏲8am-midnight Apr-Sep, to 8pm Nov-Mar) commands grand views over the sea to Mt Vesuvius.

The two main swimming spots are **Marina Piccola** and **Marina Grande**, although neither is especially appealing. Nicer by far is **Bagni Regina Giovanna**, a rocky beach set among the ruins of a Roman villa, 2km west of town. To get there take the SITA bus for Massalubrense.

Sleeping

Ulisse Deluxe Hostel HOSTEL €
(✆081 877 47 53; www.ulissedeluxe.com; Via del Mare 22; dm €18-28, d €28-48; P❄@📶) Masquerading as a three-star hotel, this impeccably run hostel offers smart modern rooms and dorms (all with bathroom), access for travellers with disabilities, an internet point (€5 per hour) and a wellness centre. Breakfast costs an extra €6.

Casa Astarita B&B €
(✆081 877 49 06; www.casastarita.com; Corso Italia 67; d €70-110; ❄@) The six rooms in this handsome 18th-century building near Piazza Tasso are individually decorated and have all the mod cons you will need.

Eating & Drinking

Il Buco RESTAURANT €€€
(✆081 878 23 54; www.ilbucoristorante.it; Il Rampa Marina Piccola 5; mains €35-40; ⏲Thu-Tue) Traditional regional specialities are given a modern makeover at Sorrento's best restaurant. Housed in a monks' former wine cellar – hence the name, which means 'the hole' – it well deserves its Michelin star. In summer, seating is outside near one of the city's ancient gates.

L'Antica Trattoria TRATTORIA €€€
(✆081 807 10 82; www.anticatrattoria.it; Via P Reginaldo 33; set 4-course menu €40-46) Another excellent fine-dining option, this place has been pleasing local palettes since 1930. Choose between the tempting four-course set menus on offer (one from the sea and

another from the land), or opt for a gluten-free or vegetarian version.

Il Fauno CAFE €

(Piazza Tasso 13; 7.30am-9pm) Head to Sorrento's main piazza for the best coffee in town.

Information

Tourist information office (081 807 40 33; www.sorrentotourism.com; Via Luigi de Maio 35; 8.45am-6.15pm Mon-Sat, to 12.45 Sun Aug only) In the Circolo dei Forestieri (Foreigners' Club) in front of Marina Piccola.

Getting There & Away

Circumvesuviana trains run half-hourly between Sorrento and Naples (€3.40, 65 minutes) via Pompeii (€1.90). Regular SITA buses leave from the train station for the Amalfi Coast, stopping in Positano (50 minutes) and then Amalfi (1½ hours). Both trips are covered by a 90-minute or greater Unico Costiera travel card.

Sorrento is the main jumping-off point for Capri and ferries/hydrofoils run year-round from Marina Piccola. Get timetables from the tourist office. Tickets cost €14 (hydrofoil) or €9.80 (fast ferry).

Jolly Service and Rent (081 877 34 50; www.sorrentorent.com; Via degli Aranci) rents out cars/scooters from €53/32 per day.

Amalfi Coast

Stretching 50km along the southern side of the Sorrentine Peninsula, the Amalfi Coast (Costiera Amalfitana) is a postcard vision of Mediterranean beauty. Against a shimmering blue backdrop, whitewashed villages and terraced lemon groves cling to vertiginous cliffs backed by the craggy Lattari mountains. This Unesco-protected area is one of Italy's top tourist destinations, attracting hundreds of thousands of visitors each year, 70% of them between June and September.

Getting There & Away

There are two main entry points to the Amalfi Coast: Sorrento and Salerno. Regular SITA buses run from Sorrento to Positano (50 minutes) and Amalfi (1½ hours) and from Salerno to Amalfi (1¼ hours). All trips are covered by a 90-minute or greater Unico Costiera travel card.

Between April and September, **Metrò del Mare** runs boats from Naples to Sorrento (€6.50, 45 minutes), Positano (€14, 55 minutes) and Amalfi (€15, 1½ hours). A trip from Amalfi to Positano costs €9; to Sorrento it's €11. **TravelMar** (089 81 19 86; www.travelmar.it) runs ferries from Amalfi to Salerno (€6) and Positano (€6) and from Salerno to Positano (€10).

By car, take the SS163 coastal road at Vietri sul Mare.

POSITANO

POP 3970

Approaching Positano by boat, you will be greeted by an unforgettable view of colourful, steeply stacked houses packed onto near-vertical green slopes. In town, the main activities are hanging out on the small beach and browsing the expensive boutiques that are scattered around town.

The **tourist office** (089 87 50 67; Via del Saracino 4; 8am-2pm & 3.30-8pm Mon-Sat Apr-Oct, 9am-3pm Mon-Fri Nov-Mar) can provide information on walking in the surrounding hills.

Sleeping & Eating

TOP CHOICE **Albergo Miramare** HOTEL €€€

(089 87 50 02; www.starnet.it/miramare; Via Trara Genoino 29; s €135-150, d €185-250; Mar-Oct;) Every room at this gorgeous hotel has a terrace with sea view, just one of the features that make it a dream holiday destination. Rooms are extremely comfortable, sporting all mod cons, and the common areas include a comfortable lounge and breakfast room with spectacular views.

Villa Flavio Gioia APARTMENT €€

(089 87 52 22; www.villaflaviogioia.it; Piazza Flavio Gioia 2; studio apt €139-199, 1-bedroom apt €169-199, 2-bedroom apt €229-310) Eating out is expensive in Positano, so it makes good financial sense to self-cater for some of your stay. Studio-, one- and two-bedroom apartments are available here year-round and come with equipped kitchenette and sea-facing terrace or balcony.

Hostel Brikette HOSTEL €

(089 87 58 57; www.brikette.com; Via Marconi 358; dm €22-27, d without bathroom €65-70, d €90-110; Easter-Nov; @) Near the bus stop on the coastal road, this is one of the very few hostels on the Amalfi Coast. It's decidedly no-frills, with beds in six- to 20-person dorms and modest private rooms, but there's a terrace for drinks and the views are stunning.

Il San Pietro RESTAURANT €€€

(089 87 54 55; www.ilsanpietro.it; Via Laurito 2; mains €45-55; Apr-Oct) Positano's only claim to haute cuisine has fans throughout Europe. Located in the luxe hotel of the same name, it is a perfect spot for a romantic can-

dlelit dinner. The Michelin-starred chef is Belgian, but has well and truly mastered the Italian culinary repertoire.

Da Vincenzo TRATTORIA €€€
(☎089 87 51 28; www.davincenzo.it; Via Pasitea 172-178; mains €18-30; ⊙dinner daily, lunch Wed-Mon Apr-Nov) The best of the town's trattorias, Da Vincenzo has been serving *cucina di territorio* (cuisine of the territory) since 1958. It does simple dishes well: the fish is always good and the starter of grilled octopus skewers with fried artichokes is a triumph.

AMALFI

POP 5400

An attractive tangle of souvenir shops, dark alleyways and busy piazzas, Amalfi is the coast's main hub. Large-scale tourism has enriched the town, but it maintains a laid-back, small-town vibe, especially outside of the busy summer months.

Looming over the central piazza is the town's landmark **Duomo** (Piazza del Duomo; admission 10am-5pm €2.50, 7.30am-10am & 5pm-7.30pm free; ⊙7.30am-7.30pm), one of the few relics of Amalfi's past as an 11th-century maritime superpower. Between 10am and 5pm, entry is through the adjacent **Chiostro del Paradiso** (Cloisters of Paradise; ⊙9am-7.45pm; adult/child €3/1).

Four kilometres west of town, the **Grotta dello Smeraldo** (Emerald Grotto; admission €5; ⊙9am-4pm) is the local version of Capri's famous sea cave. One-hour boat trips from Amalfi cost €10 return and operate between 9.20am and 3pm daily.

Get details of these and other activities from the **tourist office** (☎089 87 11 07; www.amalfitouristoffice.it; Corso delle Repubbliche Marinare; ⊙9am-1pm & 4-7pm Mon-Fri, to noon Sat).

Sleeping & Eating

A'Scalinatella Hostel HOSTEL €
(☎089 87 14 92; www.hostelscalinatella.com; Piazza Umberto I 5, Atrani; dm without bathroom €25-30, d €70-90; @) A 10-minute walk from Amalfi, this popular budget operation has four-bed dorms, private rooms and apartments scattered across the village. Extras don't run to frills (this place is really basic) but there's a shared kitchen for guest use.

Hotel Lidomare HOTEL €€
(☎089 87 13 32; www.lidomare.it; Largo Duchi Piccolomini 9; s €55-65, d €103-145; ❄📶) Housed in a 14th-century building on a petite piazza, the Lidomare is a lovely, family-run hotel. The spacious rooms are full of character, with majolica tiles and fine old antiques. Some also have Jacuzzis and sea views.

UNICO COSTIERA

If you are travelling in Sorrento and along the Amalfi Coast on a SITA bus, it will save money and time to invest in a Unico Costiera travel card, available for durations of 45 minutes (€2.40) 90 minutes (€3.60), 24 hours (€7.20) and 72 hours (€18). The 24-hour and 72-hour tickets also cover one trip on the city sightseeing bus that travels between Amalfi and Ravello and Amalfi and Maiori. Buy the cards from bars, *tabacchi* and SITA or Circumvesuviana ticket offices.

La Caravella RESTAURANT €€€
(☎089 87 10 29; www.ristorantelacaravella.it; Via Matteo Camera 12; mains €45-55; ⊙Fri-Wed) The location leaves a lot to be desired, but if you're serious about food this is where you should eat when in Amalfi. Michelin starred, it specialises in seafood and has an amazing wine list.

À Sciulia GELATERIA €
(Via Fra Gerardo Sasso 2; ⊙10am-2am Mar–mid-Nov; granitas €3.50) For the best lemon granita on the Amalfi Coast (and that's really saying something), head to this hole in the wall. It's on a set of stairs off Via Lorenzo d'Amalfi – look for benches with lemon-coloured cushions.

Pizzeria Donna Stella PIZZA €
(Salita Rascica 2; pizzas from €6, mains €10; ⊙Tue-Sun) It's well worth searching out this back-alley pizzeria as it boasts one of Amalfi's loveliest settings – a delightful summer garden enclosed by jasmine-clad walls. The food is adequate, but nothing to get excited about – pizzas are your best bet.

Matera

POP 60,400

Set atop two rocky gorges, Matera is one of Italy's most remarkable towns. Dotting the ravines are the famous *sassi* (cave dwellings), where up to half the town's population lived until the late 1950s. Ironically, the *sassi* are now Matera's fortune, attracting visitors from all over the world and inspiring Mel Gibson to film *The Passion of the Christ* here.

WORTH A TRIP

RAVELLO

The refined, polished town of Ravello commands some of the finest views on the Amalfi Coast. A hair-raising 7km road trip from Amalfi, it has been home to an impressive array of bohemians including Wagner, DH Lawrence, Virginia Woolf and Gore Vidal. The main attractions are the beautiful gardens at **Villa Cimbrone** and **Villa Ruffolo**. The **tourist office** (☎089 85 70 96; www.ravellotime.it; Via Roma 18bis; ⏰9am-8pm) can provide details on these and Ravello's famous summer festival.

Regular SITA buses run from Amalfi to Ravello (€3.60; 70 minutes).

Sights & Activities

Sassi CAVE DWELLINGS

Within Matera there are two *sassi* areas, **Barisano** and **Caveoso**. With a map you can explore them on your own, although you might find an audioguide (€8) from Viaggi Lionetti (Via XX Settembre 9) helpful. There are also plenty of agencies offering tours.

Inhabited since the Paleolithic age, the *sassi* were brought to public attention with the publication of Carlo Levi's book *Cristo si é fermato a Eboli* (Christ Stopped at Eboli, 1954). His description of children begging for quinine to stave off endemic malaria shamed the authorities into action and about 15,000 people were forcibly relocated in the late 1950s. In 1993 the *sassi* were declared a Unesco World Heritage site.

Accessible from Via Ridola, **Sasso Caveoso** is the older and more evocative of the two *sassi*. Highlights include the **chiese rupestre** (rock churches) of **Santa Maria de Idris** and **Santa Lucia alle Malve** (both admission free; ⏰9.30am-1.30pm & 4-10pm) with their well-preserved 13th-century Byzantine frescos.

To see how people lived in the *sassi*, the **Casa-Grotta di Vico Solitario** (off Via Bruno Buozzi; admission €1.50; ⏰9am-9pm Apr-Sep, 9.30am-5.30pm Nov-Mar) has been set up to show a typical cave house of 40 years ago.

The countryside outside of Matera, the **Murgia Plateau**, is littered with dozens of Palaeolithic caves and monastic developments. It's best explored with a guide.

Tours

Viaggi Lionetti (☎0835 33 40 33; www.viaggilionetti.com; Via XX Settembre 9) and **Ferula Viaggi** (☎0835 33 65 72; www.ferulaviaggi.it; Via Cappelluti 34) offer guided tours of the *sassi* – about €13 per person for a three-hour tour – as well as excursions into Basilicata.

Sleeping

TOP CHOICE **Hotel in Pietra** BOUTIQUE HOTEL €€

(☎0835 34 40 40; www.hotelinpietra.it; Via San Giovanni Vecchio 22; s €70, d €110-150; ❄) Housed in a 13th-century church in the Sasso Barisano, this is a fabulously seductive boutique hotel. Everything about the place charms, from the glowing butter-yellow stone walls and soaring arches to the chic minimalist decor and rocky bathrooms. Unforgettable.

Sassi Hotel HOTEL €

(☎0835 33 10 09; www.hotelsassi.it; Via San Giovanni Vecchio 89; s/d €70/90, ste €105-125; ❄) In the Barisano, this friendly *sasso* hotel has a range of rooms in a rambling 18th-century *palazzo*. No two are identical, but the best are bright and spacious with tasteful, modern furniture, terraces and panoramic views.

Le Monacelle HOSTEL, HOTEL €

(☎0835 34 40 97; www.lemonacelle.it; Via Riscatto 9/10; dm/s/d/tr/q €17.60/65/86/105/135; @📶) A former monastery near the Duomo, Le Monacelle is a value-for-money hostel-cum-hotel. Rooms are housed in the former cells and retain an air of elegant austerity, while the terrace offers unforgettable *sassi* views.

Eating & Drinking

Il Cantuccio TRATTORIA €€

(☎0835 33 20 90; Via delle Beccherie 33; mains €13; ⏰Tue-Sun) Family-run Il Cantuccio is a Slow Food–recommended trattoria serving creative regional fare. Speciality of the house is a lavish, seven-dish antipasto, which includes a deliciously creamy ricotta with fig syrup and a tasty *caponata* (a sweet-and-sour aubergine ratatouille).

19a Buca Winery? WINE BAR, RESTAURANT €€

(Via Lombardi 3; mains €15; ⏰6pm-midnight Tue-Sat, 11am-3pm & 6pm-midnight Sun) A modish lounge bar–restaurant in an ancient water cistern 13m below Piazza Vittorio Veneto. It's a showy place with contemporary glass and metal decor and a creative, modern menu.

Il Terrazzino TRATTORIA €
(Vico San Giuseppe 7; tourist menus €18, evening pizza menus €6; closed Tue) Just off Piazza Vittorio Veneto, this teeming trattoria does a roaring trade in filling, no-nonsense pastas and simple meat dishes. Get into the swing of things with a rustic antipasto of olives, salami and cheese.

Idris Dolceria GELATERIA
(Via Bruno Buozzi 62; cones €1.80) For ice cream, this tiny place in the Sasso Caveoso serves superb homemade gelato.

Information

Get *sassi* maps from the **tourist information kiosk** (Via Ridola; 9am-12.30pm & 3-6pm) near the entrance to Sasso Caveoso. Online information is available at www.aptbasilicata.it and www.sassiweb.it.

Getting There & Away

The best way to reach Matera is by bus. From Rome's Stazione Tiburtina, **Marozzi** (www.marozzivt.it, in Italian) runs three daily buses (€34.50, 4½ to 6½ hours). Matera's bus terminus is north of Piazza Matteotti near the train station.

By train, the **Ferrovie Appulo Lucano** (080 572 52 29; www.fal-srl.it) runs hourly services to/from Bari (€4, 1¼ hours).

Bari

POP 320,700

Most people visit Bari, Puglia's capital and southern Italy's second city, to pick up a ferry for Greece. And while no one is pretending that this chaotic port is a major must-see destination, it does have a certain, rough-round-the edges charm. There's a buzzing social scene – thanks to the large student population – and a number of architectural gems in the labyrinthine historic centre.

Sights

Bari Vecchia, the Old Town about 1km north of the train station, is where all the major sights are located.

Basilica di San Nicola CHURCH
(Piazza San Nicola; 7am-8.30pm Mon-Sat, to 10pm Sun) Bari's single most important sight, the Basilica di San Nicola is the the first great Norman church in the south and a wonderful example of Puglia's distinct Romanesque style. It was originally built to house the bones of St Nicholas (aka Father Christmas) that were stolen from Myra (in modern-day Turkey) by Baresi fishermen in 1087. His remains still lie in the crypt, ensuring a regular flow of Catholic and Greek Orthodox pilgrims.

Cattedrale San Sabino CHURCH
(Piazza dell'Odegitria; 8am-12.30pm & 4-7.30pm Mon-Sat, 8am-12.30pm & 5-8.30pm Sun) From the basilica it's a short walk to the other impressive Romanesque church. Built in the 11th century, but destroyed and rebuilt a century later, this, not the Basilica di San Nicola, is Bari's main seat of worship.

Castello Svevo CASTLE
(Swabian Castle; Piazza Frederico II di Svevia; admission €2; 8.30am-7.30pm Thu-Tue) On the edge of Bari Vecchia, the brooding, boxlike Castello Svevo dates to Norman times, although much of the present structure was built by Federico II in the 13th century. It now hosts regular art exhibitions.

Sleeping & Eating

Hotel Pensione Giulia PENSION €
(080 521 66 30; www.hotelpensionegiulia.it; Via Crisanzio 12; s/d €60/75, without bathroom €50/65;) Situated near the train station, this old-fashioned, family-run *pensione* has basic, plainly furnished rooms and a homey feel. Air con is available in the rooms with bathroom for €10 extra.

Hotel Costa HOTEL €
(080 521 00 06; www.hotelcostabari.com; Via Crisanzio 12; s/d €63/90;) A modest three-star place with dated decor, decent-sized rooms and a friendly owner. Optional breakfast is €7.50 extra.

TOP CHOICE **Osteria Al Gambero** SEAFOOD €€
(080 521 60 18; Corso Antonio de Tullio; mains €13; Mon-Sat) The seafood in Bari is superb and this characteristic portside restaurant is a cracking place to try it. Join the tourists, devoted locals and occasional celeb for *cavatelli di frutti di mare* (pasta with seafood) followed by oven-baked *spigola* (sea bass).

Information

There's a useful **tourist information point** (080 990 93 41; www.infopointbari.com; Piazza Aldo Moro; 9am-7pm Mon-Sat, 9am-1pm Sun) in front of the train station, and another at the port which opens at 9am and closes according to ferry arrival times.

BRINDISI, GATEWAY TO GREECE

About 115km south of Bari, **Brindisi** has been a gateway to Greece since Roman times. These days various companies operate out of the port, sailing to Corfu, Igoumenitsa, Patra, Kefallonia and Paxos. You can check routes and book tickets at www.traghettigrecia.com.

Brindisi is easily accessible by bus and train from Bari, Lecce, Naples and Rome.

Getting There & Away

Air

Bari is served by **Karol Wojtyla airport** (BRI; ☎080 580 03 58; www.seap-puglia.it), 8km northwest of town in Palese. **Tempesta** (www.autoservizitempesta.it) runs an hourly shuttle bus (€4.15, 30 minutes) between the airport and the train station. Alternatively, take local bus 16 (€0.80, 40 minutes).

Boat

Ferries run from Bari to Greece (Corfu, Igoumenitsa, Patra, Keffallonia), Croatia (Split, Dubrovnik) and Montenegro (Bar). Ferry companies have offices at the port, accessible by bus 20 (€0.80) from the train station. You can also get tickets at **Morfimare Travel Agency** (☎080 578 98 11; Corso Antonio de Tullio 36-40) opposite the port.

Train

Bari is on the main east-coast rail line and there are trains to/from Rome (from €33.50, four to 6½ hours), Brindisi (from €6.80, one hour 20 minutes) and Lecce (from €8.60, 1½ to two hours), as well as many smaller towns in Puglia.

Lecce

POP 94, 800

Lecce's bombastic displays of jaw-dropping baroque architecture are one of southern Italy's highlights. Opulent to the point of excess, the local *barocco leccese* (Lecce baroque) style has earned this urbane city a reputation as the 'Florence of the South'. A lively university town with a vibrant bar scene and a graceful historic centre, Lecce is well worth a stopover.

Sights

Basilica di Santa Croce CHURCH

(☎0832 24 19 57; Via Umberto I; ⏲8am-1pm & 4-9pm) The most celebrated example of Lecce's baroque architecture is the eye-popping Basilica di Santa Croce. It took a team of 16th- and 17th-century craftsmen more than 100 years to create the swirling facade that you see today. If you look carefully you can actually see a profile of Giuseppe Zimbalo, the chief architect, carved into the facade to the left of the rose window.

Piazza del Duomo SQUARE

A short walk from the Basilica, Lecce's showpiece square is yet another orgy of architectural extravagance, much of it down to Giuseppe Zimbalo. He restored the 12th-century **cathedral** (⏲8am-12.30pm & 4-8pm), considered by many to be his masterpiece, and fashioned the 68m-high **bell tower**. Facing the cathedral is the 15th-century **Palazzo Vescovile** (Bishop's Palace) and the 17th-century **Seminario**.

Piazza Sant'Oronzo SQUARE

Lecce's social and commercial hub, Piazza Sant'Oronzo is built round the remains of a 2nd-century **Roman amphitheatre**. Originally this was the largest in Puglia, with a capacity for 15,000 people, but only the lower half of the grandstand survives.

Sleeping

Suite 68 BOUTIQUE B&B €€

(☎0832 30 35 06; www.kalekora.it; Via Prato 7-9; s €60-80, d €80-120; ❄) Decorated with works by local artists, the seven stylish rooms at this city-centre B&B have been designed with immaculate taste. Thoughtful, inventive furniture has been set against sandstone walls and white vaulted ceilings to produce a cool North African feel.

B&B Centro Storico Prestige B&B €

(☎0832 24 33 53; www.bbprestige-lecce.it; Via S Maria del Paradiso 4; s €50-60, d €70-90, apt €65-90; @📶) A cheerful home away from home, this is a cracking little B&B. The irrepressible Renata ushers guests into her lovingly tended 2nd-floor flat, where sunlight floods into understated white guestrooms. There's also a ground-floor apartment for four people and a pretty rooftop terrace.

Centro Storico B&B €

(☎0832 24 27 27; www.bedandbreakfast.lecce.it; Via Vignes 2/b; d €70-80, ste €90-100; P❄📶) A characterful hideaway on the 2nd floor of a 16th-century *palazzo*. The high-ceilinged rooms are bright and colourful, decked out with parquet, wrought-iron beds and thoughtful extras such as kettles and ironing boards. Upstairs, there's a sun terrace where evening wine tastings are held.

Also recommended:

Azzurretta B&B B&B
(☎0832 24 22 11; www.bblecce.it; Via Vignes 2/b; s €31-38, d €56-70; ❄) A smart budget B&B run by the same family as the Centro Storico.

Eating & Drinking

Alle due Corti RESTAURANT €
(☎0832 24 22 23; www.alleduecorti.com; Corte dei Giugni 1; mains €9; ⏲Mon-Sat) This traditional restaurant is a fine place to get to grips with Salento's gastronomic heritage. The menu, written in dialect, features classics such as *la taieddha* (rice, potatoes and mussels) and *pupette alla sucu* (meatballs in tomato sauce).

Vico Patarnello PIZZA, RESTAURANT €
(Vico Mondo Nuovo 2; pizzas €8; ⏲8pm-1.30am Tue-Sun) Follow signs to the Chiesa Greca to find this popular pizzeria-cum-restaurant in the backstreets of the historic centre. With outside seating and a modern interior, it's a lovely spot to munch on pizza or pasta dishes such as *linguine all'astice* (thin pasta ribbons with lobster).

Trattoria Le Zie TRATTORIA €€
(☎0832 24 51 78; Via Colonello Costadura 19; mains €10; ⏲closed Mon & dinner Sun) Also known as 'Cucina Casareccia', this family-run trattoria serves exactly what you hope it will – classic, *nonna*-style cooking. Booking essential.

Of the city's many bars, the **Caffè Letterario** (Via Paladini 48) is a happening spot, and **Caffè Alvino** (Piazza Sant'Oronzo 30; ⏲closed Tue) is the best place for the traditional Leccese pastry, *pasticciotto*.

Information

Tourist office (☎0832 24 80 92; Corso Vittorio Emanuele 24; ⏲9am-1pm & 4-8pm Mon-Sat Apr-Sep, to 7pm Nov-Mar)

Ufficio Informazioni Duomo (☎0832 52 18 77; www.infolecce.it; Piazza del Duomo 2; ⏲9.30am-8pm Mon-Fri, 10am-8pm Sat & Sun) Rents out bikes (per hour/day €3/15) and runs guided tours (per person €7).

Getting There & Away

Lecce is the end of the main southeastern rail line and there are frequent direct trains to/from Brindisi (€2.30, 30 minutes, hourly), Bari (€8.60, 1½ to two hours) and Rome (€62, six hours, seven daily), as well as to points throughout Puglia.

By car, take the SS16 to Bari via Monopoli and Brindisi. For Taranto take the SS7.

SICILY

Everything about the Mediterranean's largest island is extreme – the beauty of the rugged landscape, the robust flavours of the regional cuisine, the relentless summer sun and the all-powerful influence of its criminal underbelly.

Over the centuries, Sicily has seen off a catalogue of foreign invaders, ranging from the Phoenicians and ancient Greeks to the Spanish Bourbons and WWII Allies. All have contributed to the island's cultural landscape, leaving in turn Greek temples, Arab domes, Byzantine mosaics, Norman castles, Angevin churches and baroque facades.

This cultural complexity is complemented by Sicily's volcanic geography. Dominating the east coast, Mt Etna (3329m) is Sicily's most famous volcano, although not its most active; Stromboli usually claims that accolade. All round the island aquamarine seas lap at the craggy coastline, while inland, hilltop towns pepper the timeless countryside.

Getting There & Away

AIR Flights from Italy's mainland cities and a number of European destinations land at Sicily's two main air hubs: Palermo's **Falcone-Borsellino airport** (PMO; www.gesap.it; ☎091 702 01 11) and Catania's **Fontanarossa airport** (CTA; ☎095 723 91 11; www.aeroporo.catania.it). Some carriers to Sicily:

Alitalia (☎06 22 22; www.alitalia.it)

Air One (AP; ☎199 207 080; www.flyairone.it)

easyJet (U2; ☎899 234 589; www.easyjet.com)

Meridiana (IG; ☎89 29 28; www.meridiana.it)

Ryanair (FR; ☎899 678 910; www.ryanair.com)

BOAT Regular car and passenger ferries cross to Sicily (Messina) from Villa San Giovanni in Calabria. The island is also accessible by ferry from Genoa, Livorno, Naples and Cagliari, as well as Malta and Tunisia. The main companies:

Grandi Navi Veloci ☎010 209 45 91; www.gnv.it) To Palermo from Genoa, Civitavecchia, Livorno, Tunis and Malta.

Grimaldi Lines (☎081 49 64 44; www.grimaldi-ferries.com) To Palermo from Tunis and Salerno; to Catania from Genoa, Civitavecchia and Malta; to Trapani from Civitavecchia and Tunis.

SNAV (☎091 601 42 11; www.snav.it) To Palermo from Civitavecchia and Naples.

Tirrenia (☎892 123; www.tirrenia.it) To Palermo from Naples and Cagliari; to Trapani from Cagliari.

Timetables are seasonal, so check with a travel agent or online at www.traghettionline.net. Book well in advance during summer, particularly if you have a car.

For information on ferries going directly to the Aeolian Islands, see p879.

BUS Bus services between Rome and Sicily are operated by **SAIS** (☎800 21 10 20; www.saisautolinee.it, in Italian), **Interbus** (☎0935 224 60; www.interbus.it, in Italian) & **Segesta** (☎091 616 79 19; www.segesta.it in Italian), departing from Rome's Piazza Tiburtina. There are daily buses to Messina (€41, nine hours), Catania (€46, 11 hours), Palermo (€33, 12 hours) and Syracuse (€47, 12 hours).

TRAIN Direct trains run from Milan, Florence, Rome, Naples and Reggio di Calabria to Palermo and Catania. For further information contact **Trenitalia** (☎89 20 21; www.trenitalia.com).

Getting Around

Generally the best way to get around Sicily is by bus. Services are pretty good and most towns are covered. Trains tend to be cheaper on the major routes, but once you're off the coast, they can be painfully slow.

Roads are generally good and autostradas connect major cities.

Palermo

POP 659,500

Exploring this chaotic yet compelling city can be exhausting, but once you've acclimatised to the congested and noisy streets you'll be rewarded with some of southern Italy's most imposing architecture, impressive art galleries, vibrant street markets and an array of tempting restaurants and cafes.

Palermo's centre is large but it's quite manageable to get around on foot. The main street is Via Maqueda, which runs parallel to Via Roma, the busy road running north from the train station. Corso Vittorio Emanuele crosses Via Maqueda at a junction known as the Quattro Canti (Four Corners). You'll find

Central Palermo

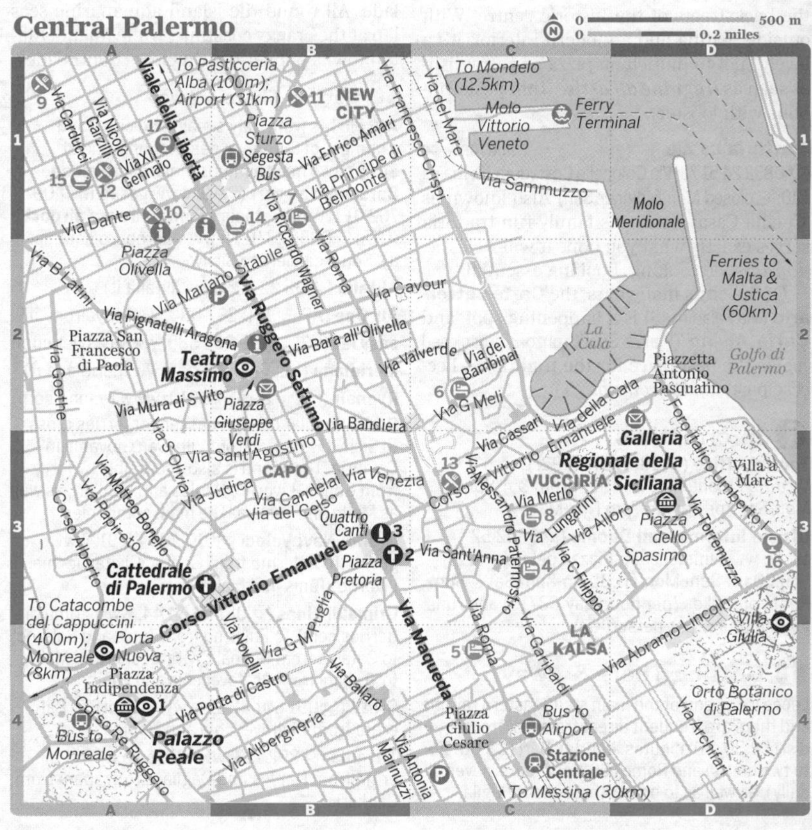

that most sights and hotels are within easy walking distance of this intersection.

Sights

Quattro Canti LANDMARK

The road junction where Palermo's four central districts converge is a good starting point. Locals call the intersection *Il teatro del sole* (Theatre of the Sun), as each of the baroque facades that surround it is lit up during the course of the day. Nearby, Piazza Pretoria is dominated by the ostentatious **Fontana Pretoria**, whose nude nymphs caused outrage when it was bought from Florence in 1573.

Churches CHURCHES

Around the corner from Piazza Pretoria, Piazza Bellini is home to three churches: the **Chiesa di Santa Caterina** (admission €2; 9.30am-1pm & 3-7pm Mon-Sat, to 1.30pm Sun Apr-Nov, to 1.30pm daily Dec-Mar), one of the city's most impressive baroque churches; **La Martorana** (Chiesa di Santa Maria dell'Ammiraglio; 091 616 1692; donation requested; 8.30am-1pm & 3.30-5.30pm Mon-Sat Nov-Feb, to 1pm & 3.30-7pm Mon-Sat Mar-Oct, to 1pm Sun year-round), Palermo's most famous medieval church; and the red-domed **Chiesa Capitolare di San Cataldo** (admission €1.50; 9am-3.30pm Mon-Fri, to 12.30pm Sat & to 1pm Sun), of interest more for its Arab-Norman exterior than its surprisingly bare interior.

A short walk north up Corso Vittorio Emanuele II brings you to the **Cattedrale di Palermo** (www.cattedrale.palermo.it in Italian; Corso Vittorio Emanuele; admission free; 9.30am-1.30pm & 2.30-5.30pm Mon-Sat Nov-Feb, to 5.30pm Mon-Sat Mar-Oct, 8am-1.30pm & 4.30-6pm Sun year-round), a visual riot of arches, cupolas, and crenellations. Modified many times over the centuries, it's a stunning example of Sicily's unique Arab-Norman architectural style.

Palazzo Reale PALACE

(Palazzo dei Normanni; Piazza Indipendenza 1; admission incl Cappella Palatina adult/concession €8.50/6.50; 8.30am-noon & 2-5pm Thu-Sat, Mon & Tue, to 12.30pm Sun) Barely less dramatic than the cathedral is the theatrical seat of the Sicilian parliament. Guided tours lead you to the **Sala di Ruggero II**, the mosaic-decorated bedroom of King Roger II. Downstairs is Palermo's premier tourist attraction, the 12th-century **Cappella Palatina** (Palatine Chapel; 8.15am-5pm Mon-Sat, to 9.45am & 11.15am-12.15pm Sun), a jaw-dropping jewel of Arab-Norman architecture lavishly decorated with exquisite mosaics. Note that if you visit the chapel on a day when the rest of the *palazzo* is closed, the entry price is reduced to adult/concession €7/5.

Galleria Regionale della Siciliana ART MUSEUM

(Sicilian Regional Gallery; www.regione.sicilia.it/beniculturali/palazzoabatellis; Palazzo Abatellis, Via Alloro 4; adult/concession/child & over 65yr €8/4/free; 9am-12.30pm Tue-Sat) The accolade of 'Palermo's best art gallery' has long been bestowed on the Sicilian Regional Gallery, and it is well deserved. Housed in a gorgeous Catalan-Gothic *palazzo*, it is full of treasures and paintings dating from the Middle Ages to the 18th century.

Central Palermo

Top Sights

Cattedrale di Palermo A3
Galleria Regionale della Siciliana D3
Palazzo Reale A4
Teatro Massimo B2

Sights

1 Cappella Palatina A4
Chiesa Capitolare di San Cataldo .. (see 2)
2 Chiesa di Santa Caterina B3
3 Fontana Pretoria B3
La Martorana .... (see 2)

Sleeping

4 Al Giardino Dell'Alloro C3
5 B&B Panormus C4
6 BB22 .... C2
7 Grand Hotel et des Palmes B1
8 San Francesco C3

Eating

9 Cucina A1
10 Fratelli la Bufala A1
11 Piccolo Napoli B1
12 Pizzeria Biondo A1
13 Trattoria Il Maestro del Brodo C3

Drinking

14 Antico Caffè Spinnato B1
15 Cappello Pasticceria A1
16 Kursaal Kalhesa D3
17 Pizzo & Pizzo A1

Teatro Massimo THEATRE

(☎091 609 08 31; Piazza Giuseppe Verdi; www.teatromassimo.it, in Italian; tickets €25-125, 25min guided tours adult/concession €5/3; ⊙tours 10am-2.30pm Tue-Sun) Supposedly the third-largest 19th-century opera house in Europe after Paris and Vienna, the neoclassical Teatro Massimo took over 20 years to build and, in 1897, opened to celebrate the unification of Italy. The theatre has since become a symbol of the triumph and tragedy of Palermo itself. Appropriately enough, the closing scene of *The Godfather III* was filmed here.

Catacombe dei Cappuccini CATACOMBS

(Capuchin Catacombs; Piazza Cappuccini 1; admission €3; ⊙9am-noon & 3-5.30pm, closed Sun pm Nov-Mar) Southwest of the city centre, these macabre catacombs hold the mummified bodies of some 8000 Palermitans who died between the 17th and 19th centuries. To get here, walk west up Corso Vittorio Emmanuele and Via Cappuccini from Piazza Indipendenza and then north into Via Ippolito Pindemonte.

Sleeping

If you're on a budget, B&Bs are a better option than the city's motley array of hostels.

Grand Hotel et Des Palmes HOTEL €€

(☎091 602 81 11; www.grandhoteletdespalmes.it; Via Roma 398; r €115-185; ❄@) This hotel has been the scene of Palermitan intrigues, double-dealings and liaisons ever since it was built in the late 19th century. The grand Liberty-style salons still impress and the recently renovated rooms offer a high level of comfort and amenity. Check the website for specials.

Al Giardino dell'Allaro B&B €

(☎091 617 69 04; www.giardinodellalloro.it; Vicolo San Carlo 8, ang Via Alloro 78; s €35-50, d €75-85; ❄@) Overlooking a tranquil garden in the heart of the Kalsa district, this arty B&B is clean and well maintained. There's a comfortable family suite sleeping four, and five simple doubles, most of which overlook the courtyard.

B&B Panormus B&B €

(☎091 617 58 26; www.bbpanormus.com; Via Roma 72; s €25-65, d €40-100; ❄) Keen prices, a charming host and attractive rooms decorated in the Liberty style make this one of the city's most popular B&Bs. Each of the five impeccably clean rooms has its own private bathroom down the passageway.

San Francesco B&B €

(☎091 888 83 91; www.sanfrancescopalermo.it; Via Merlo 30; s €60 d €80-90; ❄) Run by a friendly young couple, the San Francesco has only three rooms but each is atmospheric. The quiet but central location is hard to beat and the breakfast gets rave reviews from guests.

BB22 BOUTIQUE HOTEL €€

(☎335 790 87 33; www.bb22.it; Largo Cavalieri di Malta 22; s €80-100, d €110-160; ❄📶) Owner Patty hails from Milan, and has endowed this wonderfully located B&B with a generous allocation of that city's sleek designer style.

Eating

Like its architecture, Palermo's food is a unique mix of influences. Traditional yet spicy, it marries the island's superb produce – praised by Homer in *The Odyssey* – with recipes imported by the Arab Saracens in the 9th century. The street food is also superb. Two specialities to try are *arancini* (deep-fried rice balls) and cannoli (pastry tubes filled with sweetened ricotta and candied fruit).

TOP CHOICE **Piccolo Napoli** SEAFOOD €€€

(☎091 32 04 31; Piazetta Mulino al Vento 4; mains €20; ⊙lunch Mon-Sat, dinner Fri & Sat) Known throughout the city for its spectacularly fresh seafood, delectable olives and excellent house wine, Piccolo Napoli is one destination that serious foodies shouldn't miss. The atmosphere is bustling and the genial owner greets most customers by name – a clear sign that once sampled, the food here exerts a true siren's call. Booking is advised.

Cucina TRATTORIA €€

(☎091 626 84 16; Via Principe di Villafranca 54; mains €10; ⊙closed Sun & 2 weeks Aug) This chic eatery offers a welcome alternative to the battalions of Palermitan restaurants offering identical menus (*involtino,* anyone?). Well-executed modern Italian cuisine is on offer and dishes are light, fresh and flavoursome. The loyal clientele queues for lunch but books for dinner.

Pizzeria Biondo PIZZA €

(☎091 58 36 62; Via Nicolò Garzilli 27; pizzas €5-12; ⊙dinner Thu-Tue, closed Aug–mid-Sep) This long-standing favourite has managed to hold its own against the considerable competition posed by the nearby branch of the excellent Fratelli la Bufala chain. Sit in the simple dining room or claim a table on the street to enjoy your choice of pizza from a huge menu.

Trattoria Il Maestro del Brodo TRATTORIA €€

(Via Pannieri 7; mains €14; ⌚lunch Tue-Sun, dinner Fri & Sat) A Slow Food–recommended eatery, this no-frills place in the Vucciria offers a sensational antipasto buffet (€5), delicious soups and an array of ultra-fresh seafood.

For an adrenalin-charged food experience, dive into one of Palermo's legendary markets: **Capo** on Via Sant'Agostino, or **Il Ballaró** in the Albergheria quarter, off Via Maqueda. Both are open from 7am to 8pm Monday to Saturday (to 1pm on Wednesday).

Drinking

Pizzo & Pizzo WINE BAR €€

(Via XII Gennaio 1-5; ⌚Mon-Sat) Patrons are enticed by an extensive and excellent list of wines by the glass, a buzzing atmosphere and a top-notch array of cheeses, cured meats, foie gras and smoked fish.

Cappello Pasticceria CAFE

(Via Niccolò Garzilli 10; ⌚7am-9.30pm Thu-Tue) The chocolates and cakes here are true works of art, as beautiful to look at as they are delicious to eat. There's a boudoir-style salon at the back of the shop.

Antico Caffé Spinnato CAFE

(Via Principe di Belmonte 107-15; ⌚7am-1am) Join Palermo's snappily dressed shoppers for an early-evening drink at this historic cafe. You can sit outside with the pianist or retire to the polished interior to enjoy every imaginable Sicilian drink, ice cream and cake.

Kursaal Kalhesa CAFE, BAR

(www.kursaalkalhesa.it in Italian; Foro Italico Umberto I 21; ⌚noon-3pm & 6pm-1.30am Tue-Fri, noon-1.30am Sat & Sun) The meeting place of choice for the city's avant-garde, Kursaal Kalhesa occupies a remnant of a handsome early-19th-century palace built into the city walls next to the monumental 16th-century Porta dei Greci e dei Bastioni (Door of the Greeks and Bastions).

Information

Emergency

Police station (Questura; ☎091 21 01 11; Piazza della Vittoria)

Medical Services

Ospedale Civico (Hospital; ☎091 666 11 11; Via Carmelo Lazzaro)

Tourist information

The **central tourist office** (☎091 605 83 51; www.palermotourism.com; Piazza Castelnuovo 34; ⌚8.30am-2pm & 2.30-6.30pm Mon-Fri) offers a few brochures on Palermo as well as the *Agenda Turismo*, published annually and containing listings for museums, cultural centres, tour guides and transport companies. There are also tourist information points at **Falcone-Borsellino airport** (☎091 59 16 98; in downstairs hall; ⌚8.30am-7.30pm Mon-Sat) and at **Piazza Bellini**, **Piazza Castelnuovo**, **Piazza della Vittoria** and **Via Cavour** (⌚all 9am-1pm & 3-7pm).

Getting There & Away

National and international flights arrive at **Falcone-Borsellino airport**, 35km west of Palermo. See p898 for details.

The ferry terminal is northeast of the historic centre, off Via Francesco Crispi. Ferries for Cagliari (€51, 14½ hours) and Naples (€50, 10 hours) leave from Molo Vittorio Veneto; for Genoa (€120, 20 hours) from Molo S Lucia. See p898 for further information.

The main intercity bus station is near Via Paolo Balsamo, east of the train station. Sicily's buses are privatised and different routes are serviced by various companies, all of whom have their own ticket offices. Main companies:

Cuffaro (☎091 616 15 10; www.cuffaro.info) To/from Agrigento (€8.10, two hours, nine daily).

Interbus (☎0935 56 51 11; www.interbus.it, in Italian) To/from Syracuse (€13, 3¼ hours, five daily).

SAIS Autolinee (☎091 616 60 28; www.saisautolinee.it, in Italian) To/from Catania (€14.20, 2½ hours, 13 daily).

Regular trains leave from the Stazione Centrale for Messina (€11.55, 3 to 3¾ hours, hourly) via Milazzo (€10.10, 2½ to 3¼ hours), the jumping-off point for the Aeolian Islands. There are also slow services to Catania, Syracuse and Agrigento, as well as to nearby towns such as Cefalù. Long-distance trains go to Reggio di Calabria (€22.40, 5¾ hours, two daily), Naples (€50, 9¼ hours, four daily) and Rome (€61, 11½ hours, seven daily).

Getting Around

To/From the Airport

A half-hourly bus service run by **Prestia e Comandé** (☎091 58 63 51; www.prestiaecomande.it in Italian) connects the airport with the train station via Piazza Politeama. Tickets for the 50-minute journey cost €5.80 and are available on the bus. There's also the hourly Trinacria Express train service (€5.50, 45 minutes) from Stazione Centrale. A taxi to the airport costs €45 (set fare).

WORTH A TRIP

CATTEDRALE DI MONREALE

Just 8km southwest of Palermo, the 12th-century **Cattedrale di Monreale** (Piazza Duomo; admission to cathedral free, north transept & terraces €1.50; ⌚cathedral 8am-6pm, north transept 9am-12.30pm & 3.30-5.30pm) is the finest example of Norman architecture in Sicily. The entire 6400-sq-metre ceiling is covered in mosaics depicting 42 Old Testament stories, including the Creation, Adam and Eve, and Noah and his Ark. It's also worth checking out the tranquil **cloisters** (adult/EU concession 18-25yr/EU child & over 65yr €6/3/free; ⌚9am-6.30pm Tue-Sun).

To get there, take bus 389 from Piazza Indipendenza in Palermo.

Bus

Walking is the best way to get around Palermo's centre but if you want to take a bus, most stop outside or near the train station. Tickets cost €1.20 (€1.60 on bus) and are valid for 90 minutes. There are two small lines – Gialla and Rossa – that operate in the historic centre.

Aeolian Islands

Rising out of the cobalt-blue seas off Sicily's northeastern coast, the Unesco-protected Aeolian Islands (Isole Eolie) have been seducing visitors since Odysseus' time. With their wild, windswept mountains, hissing volcanoes and rich waters, they form a beautiful outdoor playground, ideal for divers, sun seekers and adrenalin junkies.

Part of a huge volcanic ridge, the seven islands (Lipari, Salina, Vulcano, Stromboli, Alicudi, Filicudi and Panarea) represent the very pinnacle of a 3000m-high outcrop that was formed one million years ago. Lipari is the biggest and busiest of the seven, and the main transport hub. From there you can pick up connections to all the other islands, including Vulcano, famous for its therapeutic mud, and Stromboli, whose permanently active volcano supplies spectacular fire shows.

Sights & Activities

Lipari — ISLAND

On Lipari you can explore the volcanic history of the islands at the **Museo Archeologico Eoliano** (adult/child €6/free; ⌚9am-1pm & 3-7pm Mon-Sat, 9am-1.30pm Sun) in the Spanish Aragon-built **citadel**. For sunbathing, head to Canneto and the Spiaggia Bianca or to Porticello for Spiaggia Papesca. Snorkelling and diving are popular – contact **Diving Center La Gorgonia** (☎090 981 26 16; www.lagorgoniadiving.it; Salita San Giuseppe; dives from €32) for equipment and guided dives. For tours of the islands, **Da Massimo Dolce Vita Group** (⌚090 981 30 86, 333 2986624; www.damassimo.it; Via Maurolico 2) offers various packages, ranging from a €15 tour of Lipari and Vulcano to a €80 summit climb of Stromboli.

Vulcano — ISLAND

From Lipari, it's a short boat ride to Vulcano, a malodorous and largely unspoilt island. Most people come here to make the hour-long trek up the **Fossa di Vulcano**, the island's active volcano (€3 for crater entrance), or to wallow in the **Laghetto di Fanghi** mud baths (€2.50 plus €1 for shower).

Stromboli — ISLAND

Famous for its spectacular fireworks, Stromboli's **volcano** is the most active in the region, last exploding in February 2007. To make the tough six- to seven-hour ascent to the 920m summit you are legally required to hire a guide. At the top you're rewarded with incredible views of the Sciara del Fuoco (Trail of Fire) and constantly exploding crater. **Magmatrek** (☎090 986 57 68; www.magmatrek.it) organises afternoon climbs for €28 per person (minimum 10 people).

Sleeping & Eating

Most accommodation is on Lipari. Always try to book ahead, as summer is busy and many places close over winter. Prices fall considerably outside of high season.

LIPARI

Don't immediately dismiss offers by touts at the port – they're often genuine.

Hotel Giardino sul Mare — HOTEL €€€
(☎090 981 10 04; www.giardinosulmare.it; Via Maddalena 65; d €80-230; ⌚Mar-Nov; ❄≋) This friendly family-run hotel sports chichi decor and a superb clifftop location. The pool terrace, situated on the cliff edge, is fabulous, although if you prefer to swim in the sea there's direct access to a rocky platform below.

Diana Brown — PENSION €
(☎090 981 25 84; www.dianabrown.it; Vico Himera 3; s €30-90, d €40-100; ⌚year-round; ❄) Down a tiny back lane, Diana has comfortable rooms

decorated in cheerful summery style. Kettles and fridges are provided and the darker downstairs rooms have a small kitchenette. Breakfast (€5) is served on the solarium.

Osteria Mediterranea TRATTORIA €€
(Corso Vittorio Emanuele; mains €15) Offering excellent value for money, prompt, friendly service and delicious food, this is an excellent choice. Large, juicy olives arrive with the wine, whetting your appetite for the wonderful seafood dishes to follow.

Pescecane PIZZA €
(Via Vittorio Emanuele 223; pizzas from €4.50) One of a number of pizzerias and trattorias on the main strip, this laid-back place serves excellent wood-fired pizzas and typical island food. There's also a great antipasto buffet.

STROMBOLI

La Locanda del Barbablù RESTAURANT, B&B €€€
(☎090 98 61 18; www.barbablu.it; Via Vittorio Emanuele 17-19; set menus €38 & €50; ⊙mid-Apr–mid-Oct) One of Stromboli's top restaurants, this place also has six delightfully eccentric rooms (doubles €140 to €240) decorated with period furniture, silk coverlets and antique tiles.

VULCANO

Hotel Les Sables Noirs HOTEL €€€
(☎090 98 50; www.framonhotels.com; Porto di Ponente; s €95-170, d €150-250; ⊙Apr-Oct; ❄≋) Vulcano's premier hotel sits beachside on the Spiaggia Sabbia Nera. Its large pool is surrounded by gardens and palms, while rooms, many of which have flower-bedecked balconies, are decorated in typical Mediterranean style. The restaurant's panoramic terrace offers sublime sunset views.

Pensione Giara PENSION €€
(☎090 985 22 29; www.pensionelagiara.it; Via Provinciale 18; d €46-144; ⊙Apr-Oct; ❄) Fronted by lemon trees, this is a cheerful, old-school *pensione* on the road from the port to the volcano. It's a modest affair, with sunny white rooms and a rooftop terrace offering impressive volcano views.

Ritrovo Remigio BAR €
(Porto di Levante; cannolo €2) Forget the volcanoes, the beaches, the spectacular views. The single most compelling reason to visit Vulcano is to eat a delectable *cannolo* from this otherwise undistinguished bar-gelateria near the port.

SALINA

Hotel Signum HOTEL €€€
(☎090 984 42 22; www.hotelsignum.it; Via Scalo 15; d €130-280; ⊙end Mar–Oct; ❄≋) Hidden in the tiny hillside lanes of Malfa, this is Salina's best hotel. Everything about the place is perfect, from the antique-clad rooms to the terrace restaurant, from the fabulous wellness centre – complete with natural spa baths – to the stunning infinity pool looking straight out to smoking Stromboli. Check the website for offers.

Information

The islands' only **tourist office** (☎090 988 00 95; www.aasteolie.191.it, in Italian; Corso Vittorio Emanuele 202; ⊙8.30am-1.30pm & 4.30-7.30pm Mon-Fri, 8.30am-1.30pm Sat & Sun Jul & Aug) is on Lipari.

Getting There & Away

The main departure point for the islands is Milazzo. If arriving in Milazzo by train, you'll need to catch a bus (€0.90) or taxi (€13) to the port, 4km from the station. At the port you'll find ticket offices lined up on Corso dei Mille.

Ustica Lines (☎0923 87 38 13; www.ustica lines.it) and **Siremar** (☎892 123; www.siremar .it) run hydrofoils to Vulcano (€14.90, 45 minutes, 17 daily) and on to Lipari (€15.80, one hour). Between June and September departures are almost hourly from 7am to 8pm. There are also direct hydrofoils to Stromboli (€21.45, three hours, eight daily). Siremar also runs ferries to the same destinations. These take up to twice the time and cost about €4 less.

Siremar runs twice-weekly ferries from Naples to Lipari (€50, 10½ hours) and the other islands.

Getting Around

Lipari is the main transport hub, with regular services to Vulcano (ferry/hydrofoil €4.40/5.80, 10/25 minutes), Stromboli (ferry/hydrofoil €12.40/17.80, 1¾/four hours) and the other islands. You can get full timetable information and buy tickets at Lipari's port.

Taormina

POP 11,100

Spectacularly perched on a clifftop terrace, this sophisticated town has a pristine medieval core and grandstand coastal views. Now known as a glitzy resort, it was made famous by Goethe and DH Lawrence, both of whom were former residents. In the 9th century it was Sicily's Byzantine capital.

Sights & Activities

The principal pastime in Taormina is wandering the pretty hilltop streets, browsing the shops and eyeing up fellow holidaymakers.

For a swim you'll need to take the **funivia** (cable car; one-way/return €2/3; ⏲9am-8.15pm, to 1am Apr-Sep) down to Taormina's beach, **Lido Mazzarò**, and the tiny **Isola Bella** set in its own picturesque cove.

SAT (☎0942 2 46 53; www.satgroup.it; Corso Umberto I 73) is one of a number of agencies that organises day trips to Mt Etna, as well as tow Syracuse (€45), Palermo and Cefalù (55), and Agrigento (€50).

Teatro Greco THEATRE
(Via Teatro Greco; adult/concession €6/3; ⏲9am-7pm Mar-Aug, to 6.30pm Apr & Sep, to 5pm Oct & Mar, to 4pm Nov-Feb) Take time to visit the stunning Greek theatre. Built in the 3rd century BC and remodelled 400 years later by the Romans, this perfect horseshoe theatre now hosts summer concerts.

Duomo CHURCH
(⏲9am-noon & 4.30-8pm) On Corso Umberto I, the pedestrianised main drag, people congregate around the ornate baroque fountain and Piazza del Duomo. The Norman-Gothic Duomo is on the eastern side of the piazza.

Villa Comunale GARDEN
(Via Bagnoli Croce; ⏲9am-midnight Apr-Sep, to 10pm Nov-Mar) For some great views, head to this immaculate, colourful garden bursting with Mediterranean flora.

Sleeping & Eating

Hotel Villa Belvedere HOTEL €€
(☎0942 2 37 91; www.villabelvedere.it; Via Bagnoli Croci 79; s €98-130, d €98-200; ⏲end Mar–Nov; P❄≋) The quiet rooms at this historic hotel are simple yet refined, with cream linens and terracotta floors. Guests adore the luxuriant garden, which has a swimming pool and commands majestic sea views.

Le 4 Fontane B&B €
(☎347 075 06 24; www.le4fontane.it; Corso Umberto 231; s €40-50, d €60-90; ❄) Run by a friendly couple, this excellent B&B has three spacious, colourful rooms on the top floor of an old *palazzo* (no lift, though). There's a convenient kitchen and it's perfectly located on Taormina's main drag.

Taormina's Odyssey HOSTEL €
(☎0942 2 45 33; www.taorminaodyssey.com; Via Paternò di Biscari 13; dm/tw from €20/45) Taormina's sole hostel is in a newly constructed building just off Corso Umberto I and features two dorms, four private rooms, a communal kitchen and a large terrace. It's open year-round.

La Piazzetta TRATTORIA €€
(☎094 262 63 17; Via Paladini 5; mains €15-20; ⏲closed Mon Nov-Mar) Ask locals for a recommendation and many will reply '*si mangia bene a* Piazzetta' – 'you eat well at La Piazzetta'. A welcoming family-run outfit with tables on a picturesque square, it serves authentic Sicilian food at honest prices.

Tiramisù PIZZA, TRATTORIA €€
(Via Cappuccini 1, mains €18-24, pizzas from €7; ⏲Wed-Mon) Head to this stylish but unpretentious place near Porta Messina for a simple pizza and beer or for something more elaborate. Just make sure you round things off with one of its trademark tiramisus.

Al Duomo RESTAURANT €€€
(☎094 262 56 56; Vico Ebrei 11; tasting menu €60; ⏲Tue-Sun) Right in the heart of the action, Taormina's best restaurant specialises in traditional regional cuisine. Its terrace is a perfect spot for a romantic dinner.

Information

Tourist office (☎0942 2 32 43; www.gate2taormina.com; Palazzo Corvaja, Corso Umberto I; ⏲8.30am-2pm Mon-Fri & 4-7pm Mon-Thu) Has helpful multilingual staff and plenty of practical information.

Getting There & Away

Taormina is best reached by bus. From the bus terminus on Via Pirandello, Interbus serves Messina (€3.90, 1½ hours, hourly Monday to Saturday, two on Sunday) and **Etna Trasporti** (☎095 53 27 16; www.etna trasporti.it) connects with Catania airport (€5.60, 1½ hours, six daily Monday to Saturday, four on Sunday).

Taormina's train station is some 2km downhill from the main town, making the train a last resort. If you do arrive this way, catch the Interbus service (€1.50) up to town. They run roughly every 30 to 90 minutes, less often on Sunday.

Mt Etna

The dark silhouette of Mt Etna (3329m) broods ominously over the east coast, more or less halfway between Taormina and Catania. One of Europe's highest and most volatile volcanoes, it erupts frequently, most recently in May 2008, spewing out lava and ash from four summit craters and fissures on the mountain's slopes.

By public transport the best way to get to the mountain is to take the daily AST bus from Catania. This departs from in front of the main train station at 8.30am (returning at 4.30pm; €5.15 return) and drops you at the Rifugio Sapienza (1923m), where you can pick up the **Funivia dell'Etna** (cable car €28.50, cable car, bus & guide €53; ⏲9am-4.30pm) to 2500m. From here buses courier you up to the official crater zone (2920m). If you want to walk, allow up to four hours for the round trip.

Gruppo Guide Alpine Etna Sud (☎095 791 47 55; www.etnaguide.com) is one of hundreds of outfits offering guided tours, typically involving 4WD transport and a guided trek. These cost from €45 per person for a half-day tour (usually morning or sunset) and about €60 for a full-day tour.

Armchair excursionists can enjoy Etna views by hopping on a **Ferrovia Circumetnea** train. From Catania it takes two hours to reach Randazzo (www.circumetnea.it; single/return €4.85/7.80) in the mountain's northern reaches. Further Etna information is available from the **municipal tourist office** (☎095 742 55 73; www.comune.catania.it; Via Vittorio Emanuele II 172; ⏲8.15am-7.15pm Mon-Fri, to 12.15pm Sat) in Catania.

If you want to overnight in Catania, **City Lounge B&B** (☎0925 286 17 03; www.city-lounge-bed-and-breakfast.com; Via Gagliani 13; s €35, d €45-65; P@) is an excellent choice. Just five minutes' walk from Piazza del Duomo, it has four thoughtfully decorated guestrooms, a bright communal area and private parking (€5 per night).

Syracuse

POP 124,100

With its gorgeous *centro storico* and gritty ruins, Syracuse (Siracusa) is a baroque beauty with an ancient past. One of Sicily's most visited cities, it was founded in 734 BC by Corinthian settlers and became the dominant Greek city state on the Mediterranean, battling the Carthaginians and Etruscans before falling to the Romans in 212 BC.

If coming by bus, you'll be dropped off at the bus terminal in front of the train station. From here it's about a kilometre walk to Ortygia, the historic centre, where you'll find the best restaurants and hotels – head straight down Corso Umberto. Alternatively, a free shuttle bus connects the station with Piazza Archimede in Ortygia.

Sights

Ortygia HISTORIC AREA

Connected to the town by bridge, the island of Ortygia is an atmospheric warren of elaborate baroque *palazzi*, lively piazzas and busy trattorias. Just off Via Roma, the 7th-century **cathedral** (Piazza del Duomo; ⏲8am-6pm) was built over a pre-existing 5th-century-BC Greek temple, incorporating most of the original columns in its three-aisled structure. Its sumptuous baroque facade was added in the 18th century.

Parco Archeologico della Neapolis ANCIENT SITE

(Viale Paradiso; adult/concession €8/4, incl Museo Archeologico Paolo Orsi €9; ⏲9am-6pm Apr-Sep, to 3pm Mon-Sat, to 1pm Sun Nov-Mar) Syracuse's main attraction is the extensive Parco Archeologico della Neapolis, home to the city's ancient ruins. Hewn out of solid rock, the 5th-century-BC **Greek theatre** is where Aeschylus premiered many of his tragedies. Nearby, the **Orecchio di Dionisio** is an ear-shaped grotto whose perfect acoustics allowed Syracuse's tyrant Dionysius to eavesdrop on his prisoners. On the other side of Via Paradiso, the impressive 2nd-century **Roman amphitheatre** was used for gladiatorial games. The park is a 20-minute walk from the train station.

About 500m east of the archaeological zone, the impressive **Museo Archeologico Paolo Orsi** (Viale Teocrito 66/a; adult/concession €8/4, incl Parco Archeologico della Neapolis €9; ⏲9am-6pm daily Apr-Sep, to 3pm Mon-Sat, to 1pm Sun Nov-Mar) houses Sicily's most extensive archaeological collection.

Sleeping

Alla Giudecca HOTEL €

(☎0931 2 22 55; www.allagiudecca.it; Via Alagona 52; s €60-75, d €80-120; ❄) Located in Ortygia's old Jewish quarter, this gorgeous hotel boasts 23 suites of various sizes. They all differ slightly but the overall look is rustic chic with brick-tiled floors, exposed wood beams and period antiques, and they all have cooking facilities.

Viaggiatori, Viandanti e Sognatori B&B €

(☎0931 2 47 81; www.bedandbreakfastsicily.it; Via Roma 156; s €35-50, d €55-65; ❄) Decorated with verve and boasting a prime location in Ortygia, this is Syracuse's best B&B. There's a lovely bohemian feel, with books and old pieces of antique furniture juxtaposed against silver and purple walls. The same family also runs the more modest **B&B L'Acanto** (☎0931 46 11 29; www.bebsicilia.it; Via Roma 15; s €35-50, d €55-65).

Lol Hostel HOSTEL €
(☎0931 46 50 88; www.lolhostel.com; Via Francesco Crispi 92-96; dm €20-26, d €60-75; ❄@🛜) A terrific modern hostel near the train station, with mixed and female-only dorms and sunny, cheerfully furnished private rooms. All have private bathrooms. There's a charge for internet use, but wi-fi is free.

Eating

Solaria Vini & Liquori WINE BAR €
(www.enotecasolaria.com; Via Roma 86; snacks from €5) This wonderful old-school *enoteca* has rows of dark bottles lined up on floor-to-ceiling shelves. Stop by for a glass of wine and a bite to eat – it serves platters of cheese, olives, prosciutto, anchovies and sardines.

La Gazza Ladra TRATTORIA €
(☎340 060 24 28; Via Cavour 8; mains €12; ⊙Tue-Sun) Hearty, honest fare served in welcoming surroundings at honest prizes. The recipe for success sounds simple but few manage it as well as this friendly, pocket-sized place. Run by a husband-and-wife team, it's recommended by the Slow Food crew.

Jonico-a Rutta 'e Ciauli SEAFOOD €€
(☎0931 6 55 40; Riviera Dioisio il Grande 194; mains €20, pizzas from €5; ⊙closed Tue) It's a long and not particularly enticing hike to this seafront restaurant, but once you're there you'll appreciate the effort, as the sunny terrace offers cooling sea breezes and dreamy views. Fish features heavily on the menu.

Information

There are two tourist offices: the municipal tourist office (☎800 555 000; Via Roma 31; ⊙9am-1pm & 2-5.30pm Mon-Fri, to noon Sat) and the Ortygia tourist office (☎0931 46 42 55; Via Maestranza 33; ⊙8am-2pm & 2.30-5.30pm Mon-Fri, to 2pm Sat).

Getting There & Away

In general, buses are quicker and more convenient than trains. Buses use the terminus in front of the train station. Both Interbus and **AST** (☎0931 46 48 20; www.aziendasicilianatrasporti.it) run to/from Catania (€5.70, 1¼ hours, hourly Monday to Saturday, six Sunday) and Palermo (€13, 3¼ hours, two daily Monday to Saturday, three Sunday).

Trains service Taormina (€7.95, two hours, 10 daily), Catania (€6.10, 1¼ hours, 10 daily) and Messina (€9.45, 2¾ hours, eight daily).

Agrigento

POP 59,200

Agrigento enjoys fame and notoriety in equal measure. Fame for its awe-inspiring Greek temples; notoriety for the rampant *abusivismo* (illegal building) that has overrun the medieval hilltop town with high-rise tower blocks. Agrigento was founded around 581 BC by Greek settlers and became an important trading centre under the Romans and Byzantines.

Intercity buses arrive on Piazzale Rosselli, where you can catch local bus 1, 2 or 3 to the Valley of the Temples. Up in the main town, the **tourist office** (☎800 23 68 37; www.comune.agrigento.it; Piazzale Aldo Moro 1; ⊙8am-2pm Mon-Fri, to 1pm Sat) can provide limited information about the archaeological park.

Sights

Valley of the Temples ARCHAEOLOGICAL SITE
One of the most compelling archaeological sites in southern Europe, this Unesco-listed complex of temples and walls from the ancient city of Akragas was founded here in 581 BC. You'll need a full day to do justice to the **archaeological park** (adult/EU concession €10/free; ⊙8.30am-7pm), divided into eastern and western zones. The most spectacular temples are in the eastern zone. First up is the oldest, the **Tempio di Ercole**, built at the end of the 6th century BC and equivalent in size to the Parthenon. Continuing east, the intact **Tempio della Concordia** was transformed into a Christian church in the 6th century and the **Tempio di Giunone** boasts an impressive sacrificial altar.

Over the road in the western zone, the remains of the 5th-century-BC **Tempio di Giove** suggest just how big the original must have been. In fact, it covered an area of 112m by 56m with 20m-high columns interspersed with *telamoni* (giant male statues), one of which now stands in the Museo Archeologico. Further on, the **Tempio di Castore e Polluce** was partly reconstructed in the 19th century.

North of the temples, on the road up to Agrigento, the **Museo Archeologico** (adult/EU concession €8/free; ⊙9.30am-7pm Tue-Sat, to 1pm Sun & Mon) has a huge collection of well-labelled artefacts.

Sleeping & Eating

Campeggio Internazionale San Leone CAMPING GROUND €
(☎0922 41 11 15; www.campingvalledeitempli.com; Viale Emporium 192, San Leone; sites per person/tent/car €7.50/6/3.50; P@≋) This well-equipped camping ground is on the sea in the small town of San Leone. With a swimming pool, pizzeria and bus shuttle to the temples and nearby beaches, it's got pretty much all you need. Take bus 2 from Agrigento train station.

B&B Atenea 191 B&B €
(☎0922 59 55 94; www.atenea191.com; Via Atenea 191; s €455-60, d €65-85; ❄) A labour of love for the artist owner, the seven rooms at this welcoming B&B are decorated with original paintings and exuberant floral stencils. Two rooms are topped by 18th-century frescos and five have views down to the sea. Breakfast is served on the rooftop patio.

Foresteria Baglio della Luna HOTEL €€€
(☎0922 51 10 61; www.bagliodellaluna.com; Contrada Maddalusa; s €140-210, d €170-250; P❄) The 13th-century watchtower that guards over this romantic four-star hotel houses its showpiece rooms – all cosy wood-panelling, parquet and antique furniture. Over in the main structure, rooms are less showy and diners flock to the excellent hotel restaurant, **Il Déhors**.

Trattoria Pizzeria Manhattan TRATTORIA, PIZZA €
(Salita M Angeli 9; set menus €15-18; ⊙Mon-Sat) Good for straightforward Sicilian cooking, this modest trattoria is halfway up a staircase off Via Ateneo, Agrigento's main street. Help yourself at the antipasto buffet and fill up on spaghetti *alla siciliana* (with tomato, aubergine, basil and salty ricotta). There are two set menus – one with meat, the other with fish.

Café Girasole CAFE €
(Via Atenea 68-70; ⊙Mon-Sat) You can prop up the bar or sit on the small terrace at this great little wine bar, which is popular with lunching locals and the local *aperitivi* set.

Getting There & Away

For most destinations, the bus is the easiest way to get to and from Agrigento. Cuffaro runs buses to Palermo (€8.10, two hours, nine daily Monday to Saturday, three Sunday) and SAIS services go to Catania and Catania airport (€12.20, three hours, at least 10 daily).

SARDINIA

The Mediterranean's second-largest island, Sardinia is a rugged, beautiful place. Tourist interest is largely focused on the coast, which is one of Italy's most impressive, with stunning sandy beaches, crystalline waters and idyllic coves, but venture inland and you'll discover an altogether different island, an island of untamed nature and proud tradition, of dark granite peaks, dizzying valleys and silent cork forests. Adding a sense of mystery are the 7000 *nuraghi* (circular stone towers), that pepper the landscape, all that's left of Sardinia's mysterious prehistoric past.

Sardinia's top coastal resorts, including the celeb-studded Costa Smeralda (Emerald Coast), are among the most expensive holiday destinations on the Med and get extremely busy in peak season. Visit out of high summer, though, and you'll find that space is not a problem and prices compare very favourably with mainland Italy.

You can get round Sardinia on public transport but you'll discover much more with your own wheels.

Getting There & Away

AIR Flights from Italian and European cities serve Sardinia's three main airports: **Elmas** (CAG; ☎070 211 211; www.sogaer.it) in Cagliari; Alghero's **Fertilia** (AHO; ☎079 93 52 82; www.aeroportodialghero.it); and **Olbia Costa Smeralda** (OLB; ☎0789 56 34 44; www.geasar.it).

BOAT Car and passenger ferries sail year-round from various Italian ports, including Civitavecchia, Genoa, Livorno, Naples and Palermo. Several companies ply these routes and services are at their most frequent between June and September. There are also several summer-only routes from Fiumicino. The major routes and the companies that operate them:

Civitavecchia To/from Olbia (Moby Lines, SNAV, Tirrenia); Cagliari (Tirrenia); Golfo Aranci (Sardinia Ferries).

Genoa To/from Porto Torres (Grandi Navi Veloci, Tirrenia); Olbia (Grandi Navi Veloci, Moby Lines, Tirrenia); Arbatax (Tirrenia).

Livorno To/from Olbia (Moby Lines); Golfo Aranci (Sardinia Ferries).

Naples To/from Cagliari (Tirrenia).

Palermo To/from Cagliari (Tirrenia).

For further details, see listings in individual town entries. Online, you can get up-to-date information and book tickets at www.traghettionline.net.

Getting Around

Getting round Sardinia by public transport is time-consuming, but not impossible. In most cases buses are preferable to trains. The main transport provider, **ARST** (☎800 865 042; www.arst.sardegna.it), operates bus and train services across the island, including the **Trenino Verde** (☎800 460 220; www.treninoverde.com), a tiny tourist train that trundles through Sardinia's most inaccessible countryside.

Cagliari

POP 157,300

Sardinia's capital and most cosmopolitan city, Cagliari rises from the sea in a helter-skelter of golden-hued *palazzi,* domes and facades. Yet for all its splendour, it remains what it always has been – a busy working port with a gritty, down-to-earth atmosphere and a vibrant buzz. With its landmark citadel, great restaurants and popular, sandy beach, Cagliari is very much its own city.

Sights & Activities

Cagliari's sights are concentrated in four central districts: Castello, the medieval citadel that towers over the city; Marina, the bustling seafront area; Stampace, which extends westwards of Largo Carlo Felice, modern Cagliari's showpiece street; and Villanova, east of Castello.

Castello HISTORIC NEIGHBOURHOOD

Housed in what was once Cagliari's arsenal, the **Citadella dei Musei** is the city's main museum complex. Of its four museums, the most impressive is the **Museo Archeologico Nazionale** (Piazza dell'Arsenale; adult/child €4/2; ⌚9am-8pm Tue-Sun), whose fabulous *nuraghi* bronzes provide one of the few clues into the island's mysterious native culture.

Guarding the entrance to the Citadella is the 36m-high **Torre di San Pancrazio** (Piazza Indipendenza; adult/concession €4/2.50; ⌚9am-1pm & 3.30-7pm Tue-Sun Apr-Oct, to 4.30pm Tue-Sun Nov-Mar), one of only two existing 14th-century towers.

In the heart of the district stands Cagliari's striking 13th-century cathedral, the **Cattedrale di Santa Maria** (Piazza Palazzo 4; ⌚6.30am-noon & 4-8pm Mon-Sat, 8am-1pm & 4.30-8.30pm Sun). Apart from the bell tower, little remains of the original Gothic structure but it's still an impressive sight with its imitation Pisan-Romanesque facade and baroque interior. Inside, note the imposing Romanesque pulpits.

For the best views in the neighbourhood head to the **Bastione San Remy** (Piazza Costituzione), a monumental terrace, formerly a strong point in the defensive walls, which affords huge panoramas over the city and distant lagoons.

Anfiteatro Romano ROMAN AMPHITHEATRE

(Viale Sant'Ignazio; adult/child €4.30/free; ⌚9.30am-1.30pm Tue-Sat, to 1.30pm & 3.30-5.30pm Sun) To the west of the centre, this 2nd-century amphitheatre is the most important Roman monument in Sardinia. During summer, concerts are staged here.

Spiaggia di Poetto BEACH

A short bus ride from the centre, Cagliari's vibrant beach boasts inviting blue waters and a happening summer bar scene.

Festivals & Events

Cagliari's annual bonanza, the **Festa di Sant'Efisio**, involves four days of costumed processions from 1 May.

Sleeping

Hotel Miramare BOUTIQUE HOTEL **€€€**

(☎070 66 40 21; www.hotelmiramarecagliari.it; Via Roma 59; r €112-280; ❄📶) This boutique four-star place brings a touch of contemporary design to the Sardinian capital. Hidden away in a typical seafront *palazzo,* rooms re-

Cagliari

Top Sights

	Bastione San Remy	D4
	Cattedrale di Santa Maria	D3
	Citadella dei Musei	D1
	Torre di San Pancrazio	D2

Sights

1	Anfiteatro Romano	C1
2	Museo Archeologico Nazionale	D1

Sleeping

3	Albergo Aurora	C4
4	B&B La Marina	C6
5	Hostel Marina	C5
6	Hotel A&R Bundes Jack	B6
7	Hotel Miramare	C6

Eating

8	Da Lillicu	C6
9	Monica e Ahmed	B4
10	Sa Schironada	B5

Drinking

11	Antico Caffè	D5

veal an offbeat look that sets crimson walls and dripping chandeliers against fake zebra-skin chairs and walnut furniture.

Hostel Marina HOSTEL **€**
(☎070 450 97 09; www.aighostels.com; Piazza San Sepolcro 3; dm/s/d €22/30/60; ❄) This cracking HI hostel is in the thick of the Marina district, not a stone's throw from the seafront. It's housed in a converted 15th-century convent and has spacious, sun-filled single-sex dorms, private rooms, and an internal courtyard.

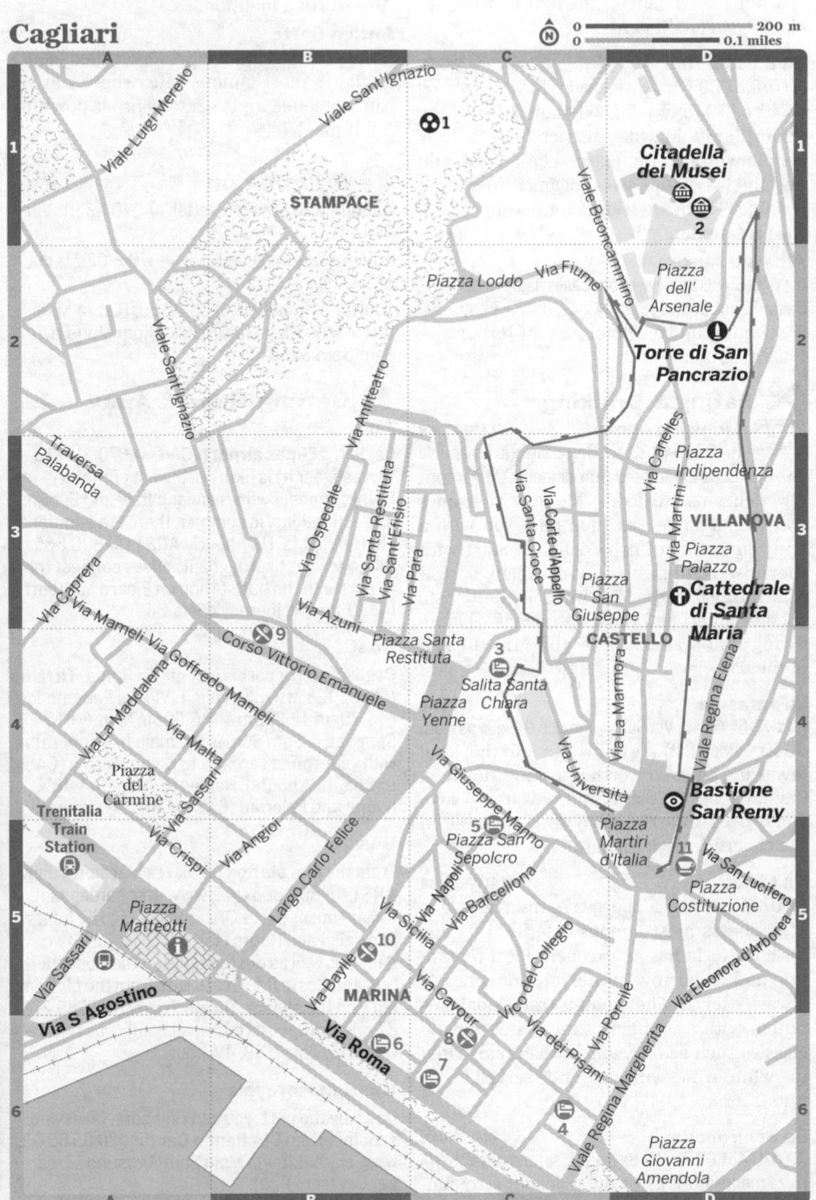

Hotel A&R Bundes Jack PENSION €
(☎070 66 79 70; www.hotelbjvittoria.it; Via Roma 75; s €56-58, d €84-88; ❄) The best budget hotel on the seafront, this is an old-fashioned family-run *pensione*. Run by a garrulous old boy, it has spacious, high-ceilinged rooms decorated with robust family furniture and sparkling chandeliers. Breakfast is not included. No credit cards.

B&B La Marina B&B €
(☎070 67 00 65; www.la-marina.it; Via Porcile 23; s €40, d €70-75; ❄) A good-value B&B in the atmospheric Marina district. The elderly couple who run the place keep a tight ship and the two white, wood-beamed rooms are pristine. There are fridges for guest use.

Also recommended:

Albergo Aurora HOTEL
(☎070 65 86 25; www.hotelcagliariaurora.it; Salita Santa Chiara 19; s €43-49, d €70-75; ❄) A welcoming budget hotel just off buzzing Piazza Yenne.

Eating & Drinking

TOP CHOICE **Monica e Ahmed** SEAFOOD €€
(☎070 640 20 45; Corso Vittorio Emanuele 119; mains €14; ⊙closed Sun dinner) A top spot for delicious seafood. Monica welcomes you with a smile and then plies you with a tempting array of fishy delights. Start with the mixed antipasto – a decadent spread of swordfish carpaccio, mussels, cuttlefish, fried calamari and tuna with beans – before diving into seafood pasta and grilled catch of the day.

Il Fantasma PIZZA €
(☎070 65 67 49; Via San Domenico 94; pizzas from €6.50; ⊙Mon-Sat) It's quite a trek to this local favourite, but well worth it to chow down on Cagliari's best pizza. If you haven't booked, you'll need to arrive early to get a table in the cheerful, brick-lined interior.

Da Lillicu TRATTORIA €€
(☎070 65 29 70; Via Sardegna 78; mains €11) One of Cagliari's most famous eateries, this historic trattoria has an excellent local reputation and its narrow tunnel interior is nearly always packed. The menu is traditional Sardinian with a number of meat and seafood classics such as *burrida* (catfish marinated in white-wine vinegar and served with nuts).

Sa Schironada TRATTORIA €
(☎070 451 07 71; Via Baylle 39; set menus €16-30, pizza menus €5-12) Not the place for a romantic dinner, this big, barn-like trattoria is good for a cheap fill-up. There are various menu options but bear in mind that the antipasto spread is a minor meal in itself, with seafood salads, olives, cheese, salamis and stewed snails.

Also worth a mention:

Antico Caffè CAFE €
(Piazza Costituzione; meals €30; ⊙closed Tue) Cagliari's most famous cafe, where you can sip coffee and cocktails or sit down to a full meal.

Information

Ospedale Brotzu (Hospital; ☎070 53 91; Via Peretti)

Police station (Questura; ☎070 6 02 71; Via Amat Luigi 9)

Tourist office (☎070 66 92 55; Piazza Matteotti; ⊙8.30am-1.30pm & 2-8pm Mon-Fri, 8am-8pm Sat & Sun)

Getting There & Away

Air

Cagliari's **Elmas airport** (CAG; ☎070 211 211; www.sogaer.it) is 6km northwest of the city. Flights connect with mainland Italy and European destinations. In summer, there are additional charter flights. Half-hourly **ARST** (☎800 865 042; www.arst.sardegna.it) buses connect the airport with the bus station on Piazza Matteotti; the 10-minute journey costs €4.

Boat

Cagliari's ferry port is just off Via Roma. **Tirrenia** (☎892 123; www.tirrenia.it; Via dei Ponente 1; ⊙8.30am-12.20pm & 4-6.50pm Mon-Fri, to 6pm Sat, 4-6pm Sun) is the main ferry operator, with year-round services to Civitavecchia (€48 to €58, 16½ hours), Naples (€38 to €44, 16¼ hours) and Palermo (€37 to €44, 14½ hours).

Bus

From the **bus station** on Piazza Matteotti, daily **ARST** (☎800 865 042; www.arst.sardegna.it, in Italian) buses serve Oristano (€6.50, 1½ hours, two daily) and Nuoro (€14.50, 3½ hours, two daily), as well as destinations on the Costa del Sud and Costa Rei. Get tickets from the McDonald's on the square. **Turmo Travel** (☎0789 214 87; www.gruppoturmotravel.com) runs two daily buses to Olbia (€19, 4¼ hours).

Car & Motorcycle

Down by the port, you can rent cars, bikes and scooters from **CIA Rent a Car** (☎070 65 65 03; www.ciarent.it; Via Molo Sant'Agostino 13; car per day from €29).

Train

Trenitalia trains run from the station on Piazza Matteotti to Oristano (€5.95, up to two hours, hourly) and Sassari (€15.75, 4¼ hours, three daily).

Cala Gonone

A popular resort with a small beach and decent accommodation, Cala Gonone makes an excellent base for exploring the spectacular Gulf of Orosei. The coastline, one of Italy's most imperious, is peppered with beaches and sea caves, many of which are only accessible by boat or on foot. Inland, the rugged, difficult terrain is ideal for hikers and climbers.

Sights & Activities

The main activity in Cala Gonone is exploring the coast's coves and caves. You can reach some of these on foot, or by wheeled transport, but the best are only accessible by boat. To hire a boat or join a coastal tour head to the port.

Southern Coast Beaches BEACHES, CAVES

In town, the small beach **Spiaggia Centrale** is good for a quick dip but the best swimming spots are round the coast. **Cala Fuili**, about 3.5km to the south, is a small, rocky inlet backed by a deep green valley. From here you can hike over the clifftops to the stunning **Cala Luna**, about two hours (4km) away on foot. In between the two is the dazzling **Grotta del Bue Marino** (adult/concession €8/4), a complex of stalactite- and stalagmite-filled caves where monk seals used to pup.

Outdoor Activities ACTIVITIES

Outdoor activities are big here and there's excellent diving, snorkelling, rock climbing, mountain biking and hiking. There are various agencies that organise activities, including **Prima Sardegna** (☎0784 93 367; www.primasardegna.com; Lungomare Palmasera 32), which also rents out cars (from €78 per day), scooters (€48 per day), mountain bikes (€24 per day) and kayaks (€30 per day). To hire your own boat reckon on €80 to €120 per day for two people plus €25 or so for petrol extra.

Tours

Operating out of the port, the **Nuovo Consorzio Trasporti Marittimi Calagonone** (☎0784 9 33 05; www.calagononecrociere.it) sails to Cala Luna (€12 to €20) and the Grotta del Bue Marino (€16.50 to €19, including Cala Luna €23 to €32) and runs mini-cruises (€26 to €37) along the coast.

Coop Ghivine (☎349 442 55 52; www.ghivine.com; Via Montebello 5) in nearby Dorgali is one of several cooperatives that organise excursions and guided treks, starting at €35 per person.

Sleeping & Eating

TOP CHOICE **Agriturismo Nuraghe Mannu** AGRITURISMO €

(☎0784 9 32 64; www.agriturismonuraghemannu.com; off the SP 26 Dorgali-Cala Gonone Rd; per person B&B €26-32, half-board €42-46) Immersed in greenery and with blissful sea views, this is the real McCoy, an authentic working farm with four simple double rooms and five tent pitches (€10 to €12 per person). The superb farmhouse restaurant (meals €25 to €35) features plenty of home-produced cheese, salami, pork and wine. Bookings are essential.

Hotel Su Gologone HOTEL €€€

(☎0784 28 75 12; www.sugologone.it; s €115-180, r €120-280; P ❄ ≋) About 20km inland from Cala Gonone, this is a fabulous hacienda-style retreat with rustic rooms in a series of whitewashed cottages. Facilities are top notch and the highly rated restaurant specialises in traditional Sardinian cooking, including a delicious *porceddu* (spit-roasted suckling pig).

Hotel Costa Dorada HOTEL €€

(☎0784 9 33 32; www.hotelcostadorada.it; Lungomare Palmasera 45; per person €54-95; ⊙end Mar–Oct; ❄) The best-looking hotel in town, the flower-clad Costa Dorada offers luxurious sea views and tasteful rooms decorated with local handicrafts. It also has a seafront terrace restaurant (menus €15 to €35) serving fresh seafood and local meat dishes. It's at the southern end of the *lungomare*, just over the road from the beach.

Pop Hotel HOTEL €€

(☎0784 9 31 85; www.hotelpop.it; d €54-128; ❄) This cheerful year-round hotel is yards from the port. Rooms are spacious and sunny and its roadside restaurant, the **Spaghetteria al Porto**, has a huge menu that includes a number of interesting fusion dishes. There are several set menus, otherwise you're looking at around €25 to €35 for a meal.

Camping Cala Gonone CAMPING GROUND €
(☎0784 9 31 65; www.campingcalagonone.it; sites per person incl car & tent €13-19.50, 2-bed bungalow €48-105; ⊙Apr-Oct;) In a pine grove by the entrance to town, this shady camping ground has excellent facilities including a tennis court, bar, barbecue area, pizzeria and swimming pool. Book ahead for August.

Information

Head to the helpful **tourist office** (☎0784 936 96; www.dorgagli.it; Viale Bue Marino 1/a; ⊙9am-9pm Jul & Aug, to 1pm & 3-7pm Easter-Jun & Sep-Oct, to noon rest of year) for maps, accommodation lists and contact details for local guides.

Getting There & Away

There are up to six ARST buses a day from Nuoro to Cala Gonone (€3.50, 70 minutes). If travelling by car, you'll need a good road map, such as *Sardegna* published by the Touring Club Italiano.

Alghero

POP 40,900

A picturesque medieval town, Alghero is the main resort on Sardinia's northwest coast. Surprisingly, though, it's not entirely given over to tourism and it is still an important fishing port. Interest is centred on the *centro storico* with its robust stone ramparts and tight-knit lanes.

Alghero was founded in the 11th century by the Genovese and later became an important outpost of the Aragonese Catalans. Still today the local dialect is a form of Catalan, and the town retains something of a Spanish atmosphere.

Sights & Activities

Centro Storico HISTORIC CENTRE
Alghero's medieval core is a charming mesh of narrow cobbled alleys hemmed in by Spanish Gothic *palazzi*. Of the various churches, the most interesting is the **Chiesa di San Francesco** (Via Carlo Alberto; ⊙7.30am-noon & 5-8.30pm), with its mix of Romanesque and Gothic styles. A short walk away, the **campanile** (bell tower; admission €2; ⊙7pm-9.30pm Tue, Thu & Sat Jul & Aug, 5-8pm Sep, by appointment rest of year) of the Cattedrale di Santa Maria is a fine example of Gothic-Catalan architecture.

Grotte di Nettuno SEA CAVES
(adult/child €12/6; ⊙9am-7pm Apr-Sep, to 6pm Oct, to 1pm Nov-Mar, Nov & Dec) From the port you can take a boat trip along the impressive northern coast to **Capo Caccia** and the grandiose **Grotte di Nettuno** cave complex. The cheapest boat is the **Navisarda ferry** (adult/child return €14/7), which departs hourly between 9am and 5pm from June to September, and three times daily between March and May and in October. Allow 2½ hours for the round trip. Cheaper still, you can get a bus to the caves from Via Catalogna (€3.50 return, 50 minutes, three times daily summer, once winter).

Nuraghe di Palmavera PREHISTORIC RUINS
(admission €3; ⊙9am-7pm May-Sep, to 6pm Apr-Oct, 10am-2pm Nov-Mar) Ten kilometres west of Alghero on the road to Porto Conte, this 3500-year-old *nuraghe* village is well worth a visit.

Sleeping

There's plenty of accommodation in Alghero but you'll need to book between June and September.

Angedras Hotel HOTEL €€
(☎079 973 50 34; www.angedras.it; Via Frank 2; s €53-60, d €75-150;) A model of whitewashed Mediterranean style, the Angedras has cool, airy rooms with big French doors opening on to sunny patios. It's in a quiet residential street within easy walking distance of the historic centre.

Camping La Mariposa CAMPING GROUND €
(☎079 95 03 60; www.lamariposa.it; Via Lido 22; sites per person/tent/car €13/14/6, 4-person bungalows €50-80; ⊙Apr-Oct; @) About 2km north of the centre, this popular camping ground is on the beach amid pine and eucalyptus trees. Alongside the usual facilities (shop,

WORTH A TRIP

BOSA

As much for the getting there as the town itself, a trip to **Bosa** is well worth your time. The 46km road from Alghero is one of Sardinia's great coastal rides, with unforgettable vistas at every turn. Bosa doesn't disappoint either, with its picturesque Old Town rising up from the Temo River.

For the journey, you can rent cars/motorcycles/bikes from **Cicloexpress** (☎079 98 69 50; www.cicloexpress.com; Via Garibaldi, Alghero) for about €75/35/15 per day.

laundry, internet bar, bike hire), there's also an on-site windsurfing centre (www.oceantribe.it).

Hotel San Francesco HOTEL €
(☎079 98 03 30; www.sanfrancescohotel.com; Via Ambrogio Machin 2; s €52-63, d €82-101; ❄@) This year-round hotel is the only one in Alghero's *centro storico*. Housed in an ex-convent, it has plain, modestly decorated rooms set around a 14th-century cloister. Book ahead.

Eating & Drinking

Angedras RESTAURANT €€
(☎079 973 50 78; Bastioni Marco Polo 41; mains €14) Dine in style on Alghero's honey-coloured ramparts. This elegant restaurant, run by the same people as the hotel of the same name, provides a romantic setting for sophisticated and beautifully presented seafood and crisp local wines.

Trattoria Maristella TRATTORIA €€
(☎079 97 81 72; Via Fratelli Kennedy 9; mains €11; ⏲closed Sun dinner) Hospitable and unpretentious, this bustling little trattoria has made a name for itself serving fresh seafood and classic Sardinian staples such as *culurgiones* (ravioli stuffed with potato, pecorino cheese and mint). It gets very busy in peak periods but service is quick and efficient.

Gelateria I Bastioni GELATERIA €
(Bastioni Marco Polo 5; cones €1-3, milkshakes €3.50; ⏲Apr-Oct) It's only a hole in the wall but this gem of a gelateria dishes up superb ice cream. Particularly fab are the fresh fruit flavours, ideally topped by a generous squirt of whipped cream.

Cafe Latino CAFE €
(Bastioni Magellllano 10) On the ramparts overlooking the marina, this cool bar is the ideal place to kick back with a cool drink and while away the long summer evening.

Also recommended:

Il Ghiotto TAVOLA CALDA €
(Piazza Civica 23; mains €5; ⏲Tue-Sun) A fantastic canteen, serving a daily spread of panini, pastas, salads and mains.

Caffè Costantino CAFE €
(Piazza Civica 30; ⏲Thu-Tue) Alghero's ritziest cafe. Come here for coffee and cakes, not main meals.

Information

On the eastern fringe of the *centro storico*, the superhelpful **tourist office** (☎079 97 90 54; www.comune.alghero.ss.it, in Italian; Piazza Porta Terra 9; ⏲8am-8pm Mon-Sat, 10am-1pm Sun) can answer every imaginable question.

Getting There & Away

Alghero's **Fertilia airport** (AHO; ☎079 93 52 82; www.algheroairport.it) is served by a number of low-cost carriers, with connections to mainland Italy and destinations across Europe.

ARST (☎800 865 042; www.arst.sardegna.it, in Italian) Operates hourly buses (€0.70, 20 minutes) between the airport and the bus terminus on Via Cagliari.

Logudoro Tours (☎079 28 17 28; www.logudorotours.it) Runs two daily buses from the airport to Cagliari (€20, 3½ hours) and vice versa.

UNDERSTAND ITALY

History

Despite a history that dates to classical mythology, Italy is actually a very young country. It only came into being with Italian unification in 1861; until then the Italian peninsula had been a complex patchwork of often warring empires, city states and maritime republics.

The Etruscans & Greeks

Of the many Italic tribes that emerged from the Stone Age, the Etruscans left the most enduring mark. By the 7th century BC their city states – places such as Caere (modern-day Cerveteri) and Tarquinii (Tarquinia) – were the dominant forces in central Italy, important Mediterranean powers rivalled only by the Greeks on the south coast. Greek traders had been settling in Italy since the 8th century BC and over the centuries had founded a number of independent city states, collectively known as Magna Graecia. Despite Etruscan attempts to conquer the Greeks, both groups thrived until the 3rd century BC, when legionnaires from the emerging city of Rome came crashing in.

Rise & Fall of Rome

Rome's origins are mired in myth. Romantics hold that the city was founded by Romulus in 753 BC on the site where he and his twin brother Remus had been suckled by a she-wolf. Few historians accept this as fact, although they acknowledge the existence of a settlement on Palatino Hill dating to the 8th century BC and it's generally accepted that Romulus was the first of Rome's seven kings. The last, the Etruscan Tarquinius Superbus, was ousted in 509 BC, paving the way for the creation of the Roman Republic.

The fledgling republic got off to a shaky start but it soon found its feet and by the 2nd century BC it had seen off all its main rivals – the Etruscans, Greeks and Carthaginians – to become the undisputed master of the Western world. The republic's most famous leader was Julius Caesar, a gifted general and ambitious politician whose lust for power eventually proved his, and the republic's, undoing. His assassination on the Ides of March (15 March) in 44 BC sparked off a power struggle between his chosen successor and great-nephew Octavian and Mark Antony, lover of the Egyptian queen Cleopatra. Octavian prevailed and in 27 BC became Augustus, Rome's first emperor.

Augustus, unlike his crazy successors Caligula and Nero, ruled well and Rome flourished, reaching its zenith in the 2nd century AD. But by the 3rd century economic decline and the spread of Christianity were fuelling discontent. Diocletian tried to stop the rot by splitting the empire into eastern and western halves, but when his successor, Constantine (the first Christian emperor), moved his court to Constantinople, Rome's days were numbered. Sacked by the Goths in 410 and plundered by the Vandals in 455, the Western Empire finally fell in 476.

From the Renaissance to the Risorgimento

Medieval Italy was a period of almost constant warfare. While the Papal States fought the Holy Roman Empire for control over Europe's Catholics, the French and Spanish battled over southern Italy, and Italy's prosperous northern city states struggled for territorial gain. Eventually Milan, Venice and Florence, under the powerful Medici family, emerged as regional powers. Against this fractious background, art and culture thrived, and, in the latter half of the 15th century, the Renaissance broke out in Florence. A sweeping intellectual and artistic movement, the Rinascimento soon spread south to Rome before snowballing into a Europe-wide phenomenon.

By the end of the 16th century most of Italy was in foreign hands – the Spanish in the south and the Austrians in the north. Three centuries later, Napoleon's brief Italian interlude gave rise to the Risorgimento (unification movement). With Count Cavour providing the political vision and Garibaldi the military muscle, the movement culminated in the 1861 unification of Italy under King Vittorio Emanuele. In 1870 Rome was wrested from the papacy and became Italy's capital.

Fascism, WWII & the Italian Republic

Following a meteoric rise to power, Benito Mussolini became Italy's leader in 1925, six years after he'd founded his Fascist Party. Invoking Rome's imperial past, he embarked on a disastrous invasion of Abyssinia (modern-day Ethiopia) and, in 1940, entered WWII on Germany's side. Three years later the Allies invaded Sicily and his nation rebelled: King Vittorio Emanuele III had Mussolini arrested and Italy surrendered soon after. Mussolini was killed by Italian partisans in April 1945.

In the aftermath of the war Italy voted to abolish the monarchy, and in 1946 declared itself a constitutional republic.

A founding member of the European Economic Community, Italy enjoyed a largely successful postwar period. Consistent economic growth survived a period of domestic terrorism in the 1970s and continued well into the 1980s.

The Berlusconi Era

The 1990s heralded a period of crisis. In 1992 a minor bribery investigation ballooned into a nationwide corruption scandal known as Tangentopoli ('kickback city'). Top business figures were imprisoned and the main political parties were reduced to tatters, creating a power vacuum into which billionaire media mogul Silvio Berlusconi deftly stepped. A controversial and deeply divisive figure, Berlusconi has dominated Italian public life since his first foray into government in 1994. After a short period as prime minister in 1994, he won the elections in 2001 and went on to become Italy's longest-serving postwar PM. But his tenure was rarely free of controversy as opponents railed against his hold over Italian TV and support for American intervention in the Iraq conflict. The party came to an end in 2006, when, after an acrimonious election campaign, Romano Prodi's centre-left coalition claimed the narrowest of electoral victories.

The Prodi interlude was short-lived, though, and in April 2008, Il Cavaliere (The Knight, as Berlusconi is known) once again returned to the top job, this time beating Walter Veltroni, the former mayor of Rome. In his third period as PM, Berlusconi is currently playing to type, with controversy and scandal never far from the surface. So far, he has survived newspaper stories alleging relationships that he hosted 'bunga-bunga' orgies at his palatial villa near Milan, he has seen a lifelong ally (Marcello Dell'Utri) sentenced to seven years in prison for Mafia links, and he has watched as Italy struggles to cope with the realities of the post-credit-crunch economy. How long he can hang on for will largely depend on the outcome of four trials that he is currently facing on charges ranging from tax fraud and corruption to paying for sex with an underage prostitute and abuse of power.

People

With a population of 60.34 million, Italy is Europe's fourth most populous country after Germany, France and the UK. Almost half of all Italians live in the industrialised north and almost one in five are aged over 65 years. At the other end of the age scale, Italy is dragging its heels. The country has one of the world's lowest birth rates and the average Italian mamma has only 1.3 children, well short of the two per woman that is considered necessary for a population to maintain itself. In fact, were it not for immigration the Italian population would be in decline. Foreign residents now constitute 6.5% of Italy's population.

Traditionally, Italians are very conscious of their regional identity and very family oriented. Times are changing but it's still common for Italian children to remain at home until they marry.

Religion

Up to 80% of Italians consider themselves Catholic, although only about one in three regularly attends church. Similarly, the Vatican remains a powerful voice in national debate, but can't find enough priests for its parish churches. Still, first Communions, church weddings and regular feast days remain an integral part of Italian life.

There are no official figures but it's estimated that there are about 1.3 million Muslims in Italy, making Islam Italy's second religion. Italy also has small but well-established Orthodox, Protestant and Jewish communities.

Arts

Literature

Italian literature runs the gamut from Virgil's *Aeneid,* to the chilling war stories of Primo Levi and the fantastical tales of Italo Calvino.

Dante, whose *Divina commedia* (Divine Comedy) dates to the early 1300s, was one of three 14th-century greats alongside Petrarch and Giovanni Boccaccio, considered the first Italian novelist.

In ensuing centuries, Machiavelli taught how to manipulate power in *Il principe* (The Prince) and Alessandro Manzoni wrote of star-crossed lovers in *I promessi sposi* (The Betrothed).

Italy's southern regions provide rich literary pickings. Giuseppe Tomasi di Lampedusa depicts Sicily's melancholic resignation in *Il gattopardo* (The Leopard), a theme that Leonardo Sciascia later returns to in *Il giorno della civetta* (The Day of the Owl). Carlo Levi denounces southern poverty in *Cristo si é fermato a Eboli* (Christ Stopped at Eboli), an account of his internal exile under the Fascists. More recently, Andrea Camilleri's Sicilian-based Montalbano detective stories have enjoyed great success.

Cinema

The influence of Italian cinema goes well beyond its success at the box office. In creating the spaghetti western Sergio Leone inspired generations of film-makers, as did horror master Dario Argento and art-house genius Michelangelo Antonioni.

The heyday of Italian cinema was the post-WWII period, when the neo-realists Roberto Rossellini, Vittorio de Sica and Luchino Visconti turned their cameras onto the war-weary Italians. Classics of the genre include *Ladri di biciclette* (Bicycle Thieves; 1948) and *Roma città aperta* (Rome Open City; 1945).

Taking a decidedly different turn, Federico Fellini created his own highly visual style and won an international audience with films such as *La dolce vita* (The Sweet Life; 1959).

GET IN THE MOOD

Whet your appetite for an Italian vacation with these films and books:

» *The Terracotta Dog* (Andrea Camilleri) – food-loving Sicilian detective Salvo Montalbano cracks another murder in this enjoyable read.

» *Gomorrah* (Roberto Saviano) – a disturbing exposé of the Neapolitan Camorra.

» *The Leopard* (Giuseppe Tomasi di Lampedusa) – 50 years after it was first published, this is still the best book about Sicily.

» *The Italians* (Luigi Barzini) – no other book better captures the Italian character.

» *The Dark Heart of Italy* (Tobias Jones) – a no-holds barred study of contemporary Italy.

» *Il Postino* (1994) – spectacular Mediterranean scenery sets the stage for this heartbreaking tale of thwarted dreams.

» *Room with a View* (1985) – all repressed emotions and dreamy shots of early-20th-century Florence.

» *The Talented Mr Ripley* (1999) – intrigue and dark doings set against a series of lush Italian backgrounds.

» *Roman Holiday* (1953) – Gregory Peck and Audrey Hepburn scoot around Rome and never get a hair out of place.

» *Pane e Tulipani* (2000) – an eccentric, feel-good romance set in Venice.

Of Italy's contemporary directors, Roberto Benigni won an Oscar for *La vita è bella* (Life is Beautiful; 1997) and Nanni Moretti won Cannes' Palme D'Or for *La stanza del figlio* (The Son's Room; 2001). In 2008 Paolo Sorrentino's *Il divo* (2008) won the Cannes Jury Prize, and *Gomorra* (Gomorrah; 2008), Matteo Garrone's film of Roberto Saviano's best-selling book, took the Festival Grand Prix. More recently, Sabina Guzzanti's *Draquila – L'Italia che trema* (Draquila – Italy Trembles; 2010) provoked heated reaction for its satirical take on Berlusconi's response to the L'Aquila earthquake.

Music

Emotional and highly theatrical, opera has always appealed to Italians. Performances of Verdi and Puccini are regularly staged at legendary theatres such as Milan's Teatro alla La Scala and Naples' Teatro San Carlo.

On the classical front, Antonio Vivaldi (1675–1741) created the concerto in its present form and wrote *Le quattro stagione* (The Four Seasons). In more recent times, the Roman singer Eros Ramazzotti has enjoyed considerable international success with his distinct voice and light pop style.

Architecture & Visual Arts

Everywhere you go in Italy you're faced with reminders of the country's convoluted history. Etruscan tombs at Tarquinia and Greek temples at Agrigento tell of glories long past, while Pompeii's skeletal ruins offer insights into the day-to-day life of ancient Romans. Byzantine mosaics in Ravenna, Venice and Palermo reveal influences sweeping in from the East.

Snowballing through 15th- and 16th-century Europe, the Renaissance left an indelible mark, particularly in Florence and Rome. Filippo Brunelleschi defied the architectural laws of the day to create the dome on Florence's Duomo, and Michelangelo Buonarrotti swept aside all convention to decorate the Sistine Chapel. Contemporaries Leonardo da Vinci and Raphael further brightened the scene.

Controversial and highly influential, Michelangelo Merisi da Caravaggio dominated the late 16th century with his revolutionary use of light and penchant for warts-and-all portraits. There was little warts and all about the 17th-century baroque style, visible in many of Italy's great churches. Witness the Roman works of Gian Lorenzo Bernini and Francesco Borromini, and Lecce's flamboyant *centro storico*.

Signalling a return to sober classical lines, neoclassicism majored in the late 18th and early 19th centuries. Its most famous Italian exponent was Canova, who carved a name for himself with his smooth sensual style.

Rome's Spanish Steps and Trevi Fountain both date to this period.

In sharp contrast to backward-looking neoclassicism, Italian futurism provided a rallying cry for Modernisme, with Giacomo Balla proving hugely influential. Caught up in the Modernista spirit, the 1920s *razionalisti* (rationalists) provided the architectural vision behind the EUR district in Rome.

Continuing in this modernist tradition are Italy's two superstar architects: Renzo Piano, the visionary behind Rome's Auditorium, and Rome-born Massimiliano Fuksas.

Environment

Bound on three sides by four seas (the Adriatic, Ligurian, Tyrrhenian and Ionian), Italy has more than 8000km of coastline. Inland, about 75% of the peninsula is mountainous – the Alps curve around the northern border and the Apennines extend down the boot.

The peninsula and its surrounding seas harbour a rich fauna. You're unlikely to spot them but there are bears, wolves and wildcats in the national parks of central Italy, as well as over 150 types of bird. Swordfish, tuna and dolphins are common along the coastline and although white sharks are known to exist, attacks are rare.

Italy has 24 national parks, covering about 5% of the country, and more than 400 nature reserves, natural parks and wetlands. It also boasts 45 Unesco World Heritage sites, more than any other country in the world.

Environmental Issues

The three most insidious environmental issues affecting Italy are air pollution, waste disposal and coastal development. Heavy industry and high levels of car ownership have combined to produce dense smog and poor air quality. This affects many Italian cities but is especially widespread in the industrialised north.

Inadequate waste disposal is another major cause of pollution, particularly in Naples, where the sight of rubbish rotting on the streets has become sadly familiar. At the heart of the problem lies a chronic lack of facilities – there are insufficient incinerators to burn the refuse and the landfill sights that do exist are generally full, often with waste dumped illegally by organised crime outfits.

Italy's coast has been subject to almost continuous development since the boom in beach tourism in the 1960s and while this has undoubtedly brought short-term advantages, it has also put a great strain on natural resources.

Food & Drink

Despite the ubiquity of pasta and pizza, Italian cuisine is highly regional. Local specialities abound and regional traditions are proudly maintained, so expect pesto in Genoa, pizza in Naples and *ragù* (bolognese sauce) in Bologna. It's the same with wine – Piedmont produces Italy's great reds, Barolo, Barbaresco and Dolcetto, while Tuscany's famous for its Chianti, Brunello and white Vernaccia.

Vegetarians will find delicious fruit and veg in the hundreds of daily markets, and although few restaurants cater specifically to vegetarians, most serve vegetable-based antipasti (starters), pastas, *contorni* (side dishes) and salads.

EARTHQUAKES & VOLCANOES

Italy is one of the world's most earthquake-prone countries. A fault line runs through the entire peninsula – from eastern Sicily, up the Apennines and into the northeastern Alps. The country is usually hit by minor quakes several times a year and devastating earthquakes are not uncommon in central and southern Italy. The most recent, measuring 6.3 on the Richter scale, struck the central region of Abruzzo on 6 April 2009, killing 295 people and leaving up to 55,000 homeless.

Italy's worst 20th-century earthquake hit southern Italy in 1908, when Messina and Reggio di Calabria were destroyed by a seaquake registering seven on the Richter scale. Some 86,000 people were killed by the quake and subsequent tidal wave.

Italy also has six active volcanoes: Stromboli and Vulcano on the Aeolian Islands; Vesuvius, the Campi Flegrei and the island of Ischia near Naples; and Etna on Sicily. Stromboli and Etna are among the world's most active volcanoes, while Vesuvius has not erupted since 1944.

Where to Eat & Drink

The most basic sit-down eatery is a *tavola calda* (literally 'hot table'), which offers canteen-style food. Pizzerias, the best of which have a *forno a legna* (wood-fired oven), serve the obvious but often a full menu as well. For takeaway, a *rosticceria* sells cooked meats and *pizza al taglio* pizza by the slice.

For wine, make for an *enoteca* (wine bar), many of which also serve light snacks and a few hot dishes. Alternatively, most bars and cafes serve *tramezzini* (sandwiches) and panini (bread rolls). A cheaper option is to go to an *alimentari* (delicatessen) and ask them to make a panino with the filling of your choice. At a *pasticceria* you can buy pastries, cakes and biscuits. *Forni* (bakeries) are another good choice for a cheap snack.

For a full meal you'll want a trattoria or a *ristorante*. Traditionally, trattorias were family-run places that served a basic menu of local dishes at affordable prices and thankfully, a few still are. *Ristoranti* offer more choice and smarter service.

Restaurants, all of which are nonsmoking, usually open for lunch from noon to 3pm and for dinner from 7.30pm, earlier in tourist areas.

On the bill expect to be charged for *pane e coperto* (bread and a cover charge). This is standard and is added even if you don't ask for or eat the bread. Typically it ranges from €1 to €4. *Servizio* (service charge) of 10% to 15% might or might not be included; if it's not, tourists are expected to round up the bill or leave 10%.

Habits & Customs

A full Italian meal consists of an antipasto, a *primo* (first course; pasta or rice dish), *secondo* (second/main course; usually meat or fish) with an *insalata* (salad) or *contorno* (vegetable side dish), *dolci* (dessert) and coffee. When eating out it's perfectly acceptable to mix and match any combination and order, say, a *primo* followed by an *insalata* or *contorno*.

Italians don't tend to eat a sit-down *colazione* (breakfast), preferring instead a cappuccino and *cornetto* (pastry filled with custard, chocolate or jam) at a bar. *Pranzo* (lunch) was traditionally the main meal of the day, although many people now have a light lunch and bigger *cena* (dinner). Italians are late diners, often not eating until after 9pm.

SURVIVAL GUIDE

Directory A–Z

Accommodation

The bulk of Italy's accommodation is made up of *alberghi* (hotels) and *pensioni* – often housed in converted apartments. Other options are youth hostels, camping grounds, B&Bs, *agriturismi* (farm-stays), mountain *rifugi* (Alpine refuges), monasteries and villa/apartment rentals.

Prices fluctuate enormously between high and low season. High-season rates apply at Easter, in summer (mid-June to August), and over the Christmas to New Year period. Peak season in the ski resorts runs from December to March.

The north of Italy is generally more expensive than the south.

Many city-centre hotels offer discounts in August to lure clients from the crowded coast. Check hotel websites for last-minute offers.

Many hotels in coastal resorts shut for winter, typically from November to March.

As a rough guide, reckon on at least €55 for a double room in a budget hotel.

PRICE RANGES

In this chapter prices quoted are the minimum-maximum for rooms with a private bathroom, and unless otherwise stated include breakfast. The following price indicators apply (for a high-season double room):

€€€	more than €200
€€	€110 to €200
€	less than €110

B&BS

» There's a huge number of bed and breakfasts (B&Bs) across the country. Quality varies, but the best offer comfort greater than you'd get in a similarly priced hotel room.

» Prices are typically €70 to €180 for a double room.

» Online booking services include **Bed & Breakfast Italia** (☎06 687 86 18; www.bbitalia.it), which has properties all over the country, and **Cross-pollinate** (www.cross-pollinate.com), which has apartments, B&Bs and guest houses in Rome, Florence and Venice.

CAMPING

» Campers are well catered for in Italy.

» Lists of camping grounds are available from local tourist offices or online at www.

campeggi.com, www.camping.it and www.italcamping.it.

» In high season expect to pay up to €20 per person and a further €25 for a tent pitch.

» Independent camping is not permitted in many places.

CONVENTS & MONASTERIES

» Basic accommodation is often available in convents and monasteries.

» The Rome-based **Chiesa di Santa Susanna** (www.santasusanna.org) has a list of convents and monasteries throughout the country.

» You can also try www.monasterystays.com, a specialist online booking service.

FARM-STAYS

» An *agriturismo* (farm-stay) is a good option for a country stay, although you will usually need your own transport.

» Accommodation varies from spartan billets on working farms to palatial suites at luxurious rural retreats.

» For information and lists check out www.agriturist.it or www.agriturismo.com.

HOSTELS

» Official HI-affiliated *ostelli per la gioventù* (youth hostels) are run by the **Italian Youth Hostel Association** (Associazione Italiana Alberghi per la Gioventù; ☎06 487 11 52; www.aighostels.com; Via Cavour 44, Rome). A valid HI card is required for these; you can get one in your home country or directly at hostels.

» There are many privately run hostels offering dorms and private rooms.

» Dorm rates are typically between €15 and €30, with breakfast usually included. Many places also offer dinner for around €10.

REFUGES

» Italy boasts an extensive network of mountain *rifugi*.

» Open from July to September, refuges offer basic dorm-style accommodation, although some larger ones have double rooms.

» Reckon on €20 to €30 per person per night with breakfast included.

» Further information is available from the **Club Alpino Italiano** (CAI; www.cai.it), which owns and runs many of the refuges.

RENTAL ACCOMMODATION

The easiest way to rent an apartment or a holiday villa is through one of the hundreds of specialist agencies. Some options:

Cottages & Castles (www.cottagesandcastles.com.au) Oz-based specialist in villa-style accommodation.

Cottages to Castles (www.cottagestocastles.com) UK operator with properties across the country.

Cuendet (www.cuendet.com) Specialises in villa rentals in Tuscany.

Guest in Italy (www.guestinitaly.com) Has apartments and B&Bs in Rome, Florence and Venice.

Long Travel (www.long-travel.co.uk) Has properties in the south of Italy, Sardinia and Sicily.

Activities

Cycling Tourist offices can provide details on trails and guided rides. The best time is spring. Lonely Planet's *Cycling in Italy* offers practical tips and several detailed itineraries.

Diving There are hundreds of schools offering courses and guided dives for all levels.

Hiking & Walking Thousands of kilometres of *sentieri* (marked trails) criss-cross the country. The hiking season is from June to September. Useful websites include www.cai.it and www.parks.it. Lonely Planet's *Walking in Italy* has descriptions of more than 50 walks.

Skiing Italy's ski season runs from December through to March. Prices are generally high, particularly in the top Alpine resorts – the Apennines are cheaper. The best way to save money is to buy a *settimana bianca* (literally 'white week') package deal, covering seven days' accommodation, food and ski passes.

Business Hours

In this chapter, opening hours have only been provided in Information, Eating, Drinking, Entertainment and Shopping sections when they differ from the following standard hours:

Banks 8.30am-1.30pm & 3-4.30pm Mon-Fri

Bars & Cafes 7.30am-8pm; many open earlier and some stay open until the small hours; pubs often open noon-2am

Discos & Clubs 10pm-4am

Pharmacies 9am-1pm & 4-7.30pm Mon-Fri, to 1pm Sat; outside of these hours, pharmacies open on a rotation basis – all are required to post a list of places open in the vicinity

Post offices major offices 8am-7pm Mon-Fri, to 1.15pm Sat; branch offices 8.30am-2pm Mon-Fri, to 1pm Sat

Restaurants noon-3pm & 7.30-11pm or midnight; most restaurants close one day a week

Shops 9am-1pm & 3.30-7.30pm, or 4-8pm Mon-Sat; in larger cities many chain stores and supermarkets open from 9am to 7.30pm Mon-Sat; some also open Sun morning, typically 9am -1pm; food shops are generally closed Thu afternoon; some other shops are closed Mon morning

Many museums, galleries and archaeological sites operate summer and winter opening hours. Typically, winter hours will apply between November and late March or early April.

Embassies

The following embassies are based in Rome.

Australia (☎06 85 27 21, emergencies ☎800 87 77 90; www.italy.embassy.gov.au; Via Antonio Bosio 5; ⏲9am-5pm Mon-Fri)

New Zealand (☎06 853 75 01; www.nzembassy.com/Italy; Via Clitunno 44; ⏲8.30am-12.30pm & 1.30-5pm Mon-Fri)

UK (☎06 422 00 001; http://ukinitaly.fco.gov.uk; Via XX Settembre 80a; ⏲9.15am-1.30pm Mon-Fri)

USA (☎06 467 41; http://italy.usembassy.gov; Via Vittorio Veneto 119a; ⏲8.30am-noon Mon-Fri)

Food

Throughout this chapter, the following price indicators have been used (prices refer to the cost of a main course):

€€€	more than €18
€€	€10 to €18
€	less than €10

Gay & Lesbian Travellers

» Homosexuality is legal in Italy.
» Homosexuality is well tolerated in major cities but overt displays of affection could attract a negative response, particularly in small towns and in the more conservative south.
» Italy's main gay and lesbian organisation is **Arcigay** (www.arcigay.it, in Italian), based in Bologna.

Internet Access

» Wi-fi is increasingly available and many hotels, hostels, B&Bs and *pensioni* now offer it, either free or for a small charge.
» The [wi-fi] icon in accommodation reviews means wi-fi is available. An @ icon denotes availability of a computer for guest use.
» Access is also available in internet cafes throughout the country, although many have closed in recent years. Charges are typically around €5 per hour.
» To use internet points in Italy you must present photo ID.

Money

» Italy's currency is the euro.
» ATMs, known in Italy as *bancomat*, are widespread and will accept cards displaying the appropriate sign. Visa and MasterCard are widely recognised, as are Cirrus and Maestro; American Express is less common. If you don't have a PIN, some, but not all, banks will advance cash over the counter.
» Credit cards are widely accepted, although they are not as prevalent as in the USA or UK. Many small trattorias, pizzerias and *pensioni* only take cash. Don't assume museums, galleries and the like accept credit cards.
» If your credit/debit card is lost, stolen or swallowed by an ATM, telephone toll-free to block it: **Amex** (☎06 7290 0347); **MasterCard** (☎800 870 866); **Visa** (☎800 81 90 14).
» You're not expected to tip on top of restaurant service charges, but if you think the service warrants it feel free to round up the bill or leave a little extra – 10% is fine. In bars, Italians often leave small change (€0.10 or €0.20).

Post

» Italy's postal system, **Poste Italiane** (☎803 160; www.poste.it), is reasonably reliable.
» The standard service is *posta prioritaria*. Registered mail is known as *posta raccomandata*, insured mail as *posta assicurato*.
» *Francobolli* (stamps) are available at post offices and *tabacchi* (tobacconists) – look for a big white 'T' against a blue/black background. Tobacconists keep regular shop hours.

Public Holidays

Most Italians take their annual holiday in August. This means that many businesses and shops close down for at least a part of the month, usually around Ferragosto (15 August). Easter is another busy holiday.

Public holidays:

New Year's Day (Capodanno) 1 January

Epiphany (Epifania) 6 January

Easter Monday (Pasquetta) March/April

Liberation Day (Giorno delle Liberazione) 25 April

Labour Day (Festa del Lavoro) 1 May

Republic Day (Festa della Repubblica) 2 June

Feast of the Assumption (Ferragosto) 15 August

All Saints' Day (Ognisanti) 1 November

Feast of the Immaculate Conception (Immacolata Concezione) 8 December

Christmas Day (Natale) 25 December

Boxing Day (Festa di Santo Stefano) 26 December

Individual towns also have holidays to celebrate their patron saints:

St Mark (Venice) 25 April

St John the Baptist (Florence, Genoa and Turin) 24 June

Saints Peter and Paul (Rome) 29 June

St Rosalia (Palermo) 15 July

St Janarius (Naples) First Sunday in May, 19 September and 16 December

St Ambrose (Milan) 7 December

Safe Travel

» Petty theft is prevalent in Italy. Be on your guard against pickpockets and moped thieves in popular tourist centres such as Rome, Florence and Venice.
» Watch out for short-changing.
» Road rules are obeyed with discretion, so don't take it for granted that cars will stop at red lights. To cross the road, step confidently into the traffic and walk calmly across.

Telephone

» Area codes are an integral part of all Italian phone numbers and must be dialled even when calling locally. The area codes have been listed in telephone numbers throughout this chapter.
» To call Italy from abroad, dial ☎0039 and then the area code, including the first zero.

ADMISSION PRICES

EU citizens aged between 18 and 25 years, and students from countries with reciprocal arrangements, generally qualify for a discount (usually half-price) at galleries and museums. Under-18s and over-65s often get in free. In all cases you'll need proof of your age, ideally a passport or ID card.

» To call abroad from Italy, dial ☎00, then the relevant country code followed by the telephone number.
» To make a reverse-charge (collect) international call, dial ☎170. All operators speak English.
» You'll find cut-price call centres in all of the main cities. For international calls, their rates are often cheaper than payphones'.
» Skype is available in many internet cafes.

MOBILE PHONES

» Italy uses the GSM 900/1800 network, which is compatible with the rest of Europe and Australia, but not with the North American GSM 1900 or the Japanese system (although some GSM 1900/900 phones do work here).
» If you have a GSM dual- or tri-band cellular phone that you can unlock (check with your service provider), you can buy a *prepagato* (prepaid) SIM card in Italy.
» Companies offering SIM cards include **TIM** (Telecom Italia Mobile; www.tim.it), **Wind** (www.wind.it) and **Vodafone** (www.vodafone.it). You'll need ID to open an account.

PHONE CODES

» Italy's country code is ☎39.
» Mobile phone numbers begin with a three-digit prefix starting with a 3.
» Toll-free (free-phone) numbers are known as *numeri verdi* and start with 800. These are not always available if calling from a mobile phone.

PHONECARDS

To phone from a public payphone you'll need a *scheda telefonica* (telephone card; (€2.50, €5). Buy these at post offices, *tabacchi* and newsstands.

Tourist Information

For pre-trip information, check out the website of the **Ministro del Turismo** (www.italia.

it). The ministry also runs a multilingual telephone information service, **Easy Italy** (☎039 039 039; ⏲9am-10pm).

Tourist offices in Italy are listed throughout this chapter.

Travellers with Disabilities

Italy is not an easy country for travellers with disabilities. Cobbled streets, blocked pavements and tiny lifts all make life difficult. Rome-based **Consorzio Cooperative Integrate** (COIN; ☎06 2326 9231; www.coinsociale.it) is the best point of reference for travellers with disabilities.

Other useful websites:

Handyturismo (www.handyturismo.it) Information on Rome.

Milanopertutti (www.milanopertutti.it) Focuses on Milan.

Terre di Mare (www.terredimare.it) Covers Liguria, including Genoa and the Cinque Terre.

If you're travelling by train, **Trenitalia** (www.ferroviedellostato.it) runs a telephone info line (☎199 30 30 60) with details of assistance available at stations.

Visas

» Schengen visa rules apply for entry to Italy.

» Unless staying in a hotel/B&B/hostel etc, all foreign visitors are supposed to register with the local police within eight days of arrival.

» Non-EU citizens who want to study in Italy must obtain a study visa from their nearest Italian embassy or consulate.

» A *permesso di soggiorno* (permit to stay) is required by all non-EU nationals who stay in Italy longer than three months. You must apply within eight days of arriving in Italy. Check the exact documentary requirements on www.poliziadistato.it.

» EU citizens do not require a *permesso di soggiorno.*

Getting There & Away

Getting to Italy is pretty straightforward. It is well served by Europe's low-cost carriers and there are plenty of bus, train and ferry routes into the country. Flights, tours and rail tickets can be booked online at lonelyplanet.com/bookings.

Air

There are direct intercontinental flights to/from Rome and Milan. European flights also serve regional airports.

Italy's main international airports:

Leonardo da Vinci (www.adr.it) Rome; Italy's main airport, also known as Fiumicino.

Malpensa (www.sea-aeroportimilano.it) Milan's principal airport.

Ciampino (www.adr.it) Rome's second airport. For low-cost European carriers.

Pisa International Galileo Galilei (www.pisa-airport.com) Main gateway for Florence and Tuscany.

Venice Marco Polo (www.veniceairport.it)

Bologna Guglielmo Marconi (www.bologna-airport.it)

Cagliari Elmas (www.sogaer.it)

Naples Capodichino (www.gesac.it)

Palermo Falcone-Borsellino (www.gesap.it)

Italy's national carrier is **Alitalia** (www.alitalia.com).

Land

BORDER CROSSINGS

Italy borders France, Switzerland, Austria and Slovenia. The main points of entry:

From France The coast road from Nice; the Mont Blanc tunnel from Chamonix.

From Switzerland The Grand St Bernard tunnel; the Simplon tunnel; Lötschberg Base tunnel.

From Austria The Brenner Pass.

BUS

Eurolines (www.eurolines.com) operates buses from European destinations to Bologna, Florence, Milan, Naples, Rome, Siena, Turin, Verona, Venice and other Italian cities.

CAR & MOTORCYCLE

If traversing the Alps, note that all the border crossings listed above are open year-round. Other mountain passes are often closed in

MOVING ON?

For further information, head to shop.lonelyplanet.com to purchase a downloadable PDF of the Tunis chapter from Lonely Planet's *Tunisia* guide.

MAIN INTERNATIONAL FERRY ROUTES

FROM	TO	COMPANY	MIN-MAX FARE (€)	DURATION (HR)
Ancona	Igoumenitsa	Minoan, Superfast	73-108	16
Ancona	Patra	Minoan, Superfast	73-108	15½-22
Ancona	Split	Jadrolinija, SNAV	46-90	4½-11
Bari	Igoumenitsa	Agoudimos, Superfast	64-89	8-12
Bari	Patra	Agoudimos, Superfast	64-89	16
Bari	Corfu	Agoudimos	64-85	11
Bari	Kefallonia	Agoudimos	64-85	15½
Bari	Split	Jadrolinija	51-70.50	22
Bari	Dubrovnik	Jadrolinija	46-63.50	10-12
Bari	Bar	Montenegro	50-55	9
Brindisi	Igoumenitsa	Endeavor	36-67	8
Brindisi	Patra	Endeavor	36-75	14
Brindisi	Corfu	Endeavor, Agoudimos	53-73	6½-11½
Brindisi	Kefallonia	Endeavor	61-83	12½
Genoa	Barcelona	GNV	81	18
Genoa	Tunis	GNV	127	24
Venice	Igoumenitsa	Minoan	77-107	23½
Venice	Patra	Minoan	77-107	29½
Venice	Corfu	Minoan	77-107	22

winter and sometimes even in spring and autumn. Make sure you have snow chains in your car.

When driving into Italy always carry proof of ownership of a private vehicle. You'll also need third-party motor insurance. For road rules and other driving information see p900.

TRAIN

International trains connect with various cities:

Milan To/from Barcelona, Paris, Basel, Geneva, Zürich and Vienna.

Rome To/from Paris, Munich and Vienna.

Venice To/from Paris, Basel, Geneva, Lucerne, Vienna, Ljubljana, Zagreb, Belgrade and Budapest.

There are also international trains from Genoa, Turin, Verona, Bologna, Florence and Naples. Details are available online at www.ferroviedellostato.it.

In the UK, the **Rail Europe Travel Centre** (www.raileurope.co.uk) can provide fare information on journeys to/from Italy, most of which require a change at Paris. Another excellent online resource is **The Man in Seat Sixty-One** (www.seat61.com), with an Italy page that details how to travel from London to Italy.

Eurail and Inter-Rail passes are both valid in Italy.

Sea

Dozens of ferry companies connect Italy with other Mediterranean countries. Timetables are seasonal, so always check ahead – you'll find details of routes, companies and online booking on **Traghettiweb** (www.traghettiweb.it).

Prices quoted here are for a one-way *poltrona* (reclinable seat). Holders of Eurail and Inter-Rail passes should check with the ferry company if they are entitled to a discount or free passage.

Major ferry companies:

Agoudimos (www.agoudimos-lines.com)

Endeavor Lines (www.endeavor-lines.com)

Grandi Navi Veloci (www.gnv.it)

Jadrolinija (www.jadrolinija.hr)

Minoan Lines (www.minoanlines.it)

Montenegro (www.montenegrolines.com)

SNAV (www.snav.it)

Superfast Ferries (www.superfast.com)

Tirrenia (www.tirrenia.it)

Getting Around

Air

Domestic flights serve most major Italian cities and the main islands (Sardinia and Sicily), but are relatively expensive. Airlines serving national routes:

Alitalia (☎06 22 22; www.alitalia.it)

Meridiana (☎89 29 28; www.meridiana.it)

easyJet (☎899 23 45 89; www.easyjet.com)

Ryanair (☎899 01 88 80; www.ryanair.com)

Windjet (☎89 20 20; www.volawindjet.it)

The main airports are in Rome, Pisa, Milan, Bologna, Genoa, Turin, Naples, Venice, Catania, Palermo and Cagliari.

Bicycle

» Cycling is a popular pastime in Italy but as a means of everyday transport it's limited to a few cities in the north.

» Tourist offices can generally provide details of designated bike trails and bike hire (bank on at least €10 per day).

» There are no particular road rules for cyclists, although you'd do well to bring a helmet, lights and a small tool kit.

» Bikes can be taken on regional and international trains carrying the bike logo, but you'll need to pay a bike supplement (€3.50 on regional trains, €12 on international trains). Bikes can be carried free if dismantled and stored in a bike bag.

» Bikes generally incur a small supplement on ferries, typically €5 to €10.

Boat

Navi (large ferries) service Sicily and Sardinia; *traghetti* (smaller ferries) and *aliscafi* (hydrofoils) cover the smaller islands.

The main embarkation points for Sardinia are Genoa, Livorno, Civitavecchia and Naples; for Sicily, it's Naples and Villa San Giovanni in Calabria.

Most long-distance ferries travel overnight.

The major domestic ferry companies:

Grandi Navi Veloci (☎010 209 45 91; www.gnv.it) To/from Sardinia and Sicily.

Moby (☎199 30 30 40; www.mobylines.it) To/from Sardinia and Sicily.

Sardinia Ferries (☎199 400 500; www.corsica-ferries.it) To/from Sardinia.

SNAV (☎081 428 55 55; www.snav.it) To/from Sardinia, Sicily, Aeolian Islands, Capri.

Tirrenia (☎892 123; www.tirrenia.it) To/from Sardinia and Sicily.

For details of routes, refer to individual town entries.

Bus

» Italy boasts an extensive and largely reliable bus network.

» Buses are not necessarily cheaper than trains, but in mountainous areas such as Umbria, Sicily and Sardinia they are often the only choice.

» In larger cities, companies have ticket offices or operate through agencies but in most villages and small towns tickets are sold in bars or on the bus.

» Reservations are usually only necessary for high-season long-haul trips.

Car & Motorcycle

» Roads are generally good throughout the country and there's an excellent system of autostradas (motorways).

» There's a toll to use most autostradas, payable in cash or by credit card at exit barriers.

» Autostradas are indicated by an A with a number (eg A1) on a green background; *strade statali* (main roads) are shown by an S or SS and number (eg SS7) against a blue background.

» Italy's motoring organisation **Automobile Club d'Italia** (ACI; www.aci.it) provides 24-hour roadside assistance (☎803 116).

» Cars use unleaded petrol *(benzina senza piombo)* and diesel *(gasolio)*; both are expensive but diesel is slightly cheaper.

DRIVING LICENCES

All EU driving licences are recognised in Italy. Holders of non-EU licences must get an International Driving Permit (IDP) to accompany their national licence.

HIRE

To hire a car:

» You must have a valid driving licence (plus IDP if required).

» You must have had your licence for at least a year.

» You must be aged 21 years or over. Under-25s will often have to pay a young-driver's supplement on top of the usual rates.

» You must have a credit card.

Make sure you understand what is included in the price (unlimited kilometres, tax, insurance, collision damage waiver etc) and what your liabilities are. For the best rental rates, book your car before leaving home. Note also that most cars have manual gear transmission.

The most competitive multinational car-rental agencies:

Avis (☎06 452 10 83 91; www.avisautonoleggio.it)

Budget (☎199 30 73 73; www.budgetautonoleggio.it)

Europcar (☎199 30 70 30; www.europcar.it)

Hertz (☎199 11 22 11; www.hertz.it)

Italy by Car (☎091 380 96 76; www.italybycar.it)

Maggiore (☎199 151 120; www.maggiore.it)

You'll have no trouble hiring a scooter or motorcycle (provided you're over 18); there are rental agencies in all Italian cities. Rates start at about €30 a day for a 50cc scooter.

INSURANCE

If you're driving your own car, you'll need an international insurance certificate, known as a Carta Verde (Green Card), available from your insurance company.

ROAD RULES

» Drive on the right, overtake on the left and give way to cars coming from the right.

» It's obligatory to wear seatbelts, to drive with your headlights on outside built-up areas, and to carry a warning triangle and fluorescent waistcoat in case of breakdown.

» Wearing a helmet is compulsory on all two-wheeled vehicles.

» The blood alcohol limit is 0.05%.

» Unless otherwise indicated, speed limits are as follows:

- *130km/h (in rain 110km/h) on autostradas*
- *110km/h (in rain 90km/h) on all main, non-urban roads*
- *90km/h on secondary, non-urban roads*
- *50km/h in built-up areas*

» Most major Italian cities, including Rome, Bologna, Florence, Milan and Turin, operate restricted traffic zones. You can enter these zones on a *motorino* (moped/scooter) or in a car with foreign registration but not in private or rental cars.

Train

Italy has an extensive rail network. Trains are relatively cheap, and many are fast and comfortable. Most services are run by **Trenitalia** (☎89 20 21; www.ferroviedellostato.it). There are several types of train:

Regionale or interregionale (R) Slow local services.

InterCity (IC) Fast trains between major cities.

Eurostar (ES) Similar to InterCity but faster.

Eurostar Alta Velocità (ES AV) High-speed trains operating on the Turin–Milan–Bologna–Florence–Rome–Naples–Salerno line.

TICKETS

Ticket prices depend on the type of train and class (1st class costs almost double 2nd class). Train prices quoted in this chapter are for the most common trains on any given route – on some routes that might be a slow Regionale train, on others it could be the fast Eurostar Alta Velocità.

» Regional trains are the cheapest.

» InterCity trains require a supplement, which is incorporated in the ticket price. If you have a standard ticket and board an InterCity you will have to pay the difference on board.

» Eurostar and Alta Velocità trains require prior reservation.

» Generally, it's cheaper to buy all local train tickets in Italy – check for yourself on the Trenitalia website.

» Tickets must be validated – in the yellow machines at the entrance to platforms – before boarding trains.

» Children under four years of age travel free, while kids between four and 12 years are entitled to discounts of between 30% and 50%.

Liechtenstein

Includes »

Best Places to Eat

» Torkel (p905)

» Bergrestaurant Sareiserjoch (p907)

Best Places to Stay

» Gasthof Löwen (p905)

» Kulm (p907)

Why Go?

Liechtenstein makes a fabulous trivia subject – *Did you know it is the sixth smallest country in the world?... It's still governed by an iron-willed monarch who lives in a gothic castle on a hill... Yes, it really is the world's largest producer of false teeth.* It's worth visiting this pocket-sized principality solely for the cocktail-party bragging rights, but keep the operation covert. This theme-park micronation takes its independence seriously and would shudder at the thought of being visited for novelty value alone.

Liechtenstein wows with its stunning natural beauty. Measuring just 25km by 6km, it's barely larger than Manhattan, doesn't have an international airport and is reached by public bus from Switzerland and Austria. Vaduz is not the most soulful place on earth, but if you've come this far – coachloads of day trippers do simply for the souvenir passport stamp – venture away from the capital. A riot of hiking and cycling trails offering spectacular views of craggy cliffs, quaint villages and lush green forests awaits you.

When to Go

Vaduz

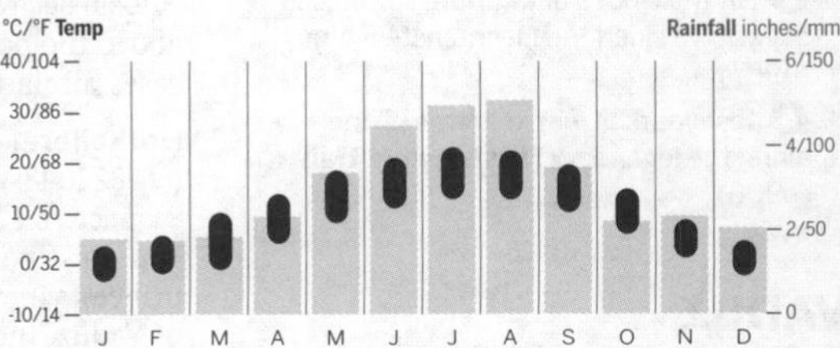

May–Sep Hike to your heart's content, up and away from the busloads of passport-stamp tourists.

Aug Come on the 15th and celebrate the country's national holiday.

Dec–Mar Pummel down snow-covered pistes at its single ski resort.

Liechtenstein Highlights

1. Snap a picture of the **Schloss Vaduz** with its stunning mountain backdrop (p904)
2. Get a souvenir **passport stamp** and send a postcard home (p906)
3. Taste royal wine at the **Hofkellerei des Fürstens**, the prince's own winery (p904)
4. Hit the slopes at **Malbun**, so you can say you've skied the Liechtenstein Alps (p907)
5. Test yourself with extreme hiking along the legendary **Fürstensteig trail** (p906)

VADUZ

POP 5160

Vaduz is the kind of capital city where the butcher knows the baker. With its tidy, quiet streets, lively patio cafes and big Gothic-looking castle on a hill, it feels more like a village than anything else. It's also all that most visitors to Liechtenstein will see, and at times it can feel like its soul has been sold to cater to the whims of the tourist hordes. Souvenir shops, tax-free luxury goods stores and cube-shaped concrete buildings dominate the small, somewhat bland town centre enclosed by Äulestrasse and the pedestrian-only Städtle.

Sights & Activities

Schloss Vaduz CASTLE

(Fürst-Franz-Josef Strasse 150) Although Vaduz Castle is not open to the public, its exterior graces many a photograph and it is worth climbing up the hill for. At the top, there's a magnificent vista of Vaduz with a spectacular mountain backdrop. There's also a network of walking trails along the ridge. For a peek inside the castle grounds, arrive on 15 August (Liechtenstein's national day), when there are magnificent fireworks and the prince invites the entire country over to his place for a glass.

Liechtensteinisches Landesmuseum MUSEUM

(National Museum; ☎239 68 20; www.landesmuseum.li; Städtle 43; adult/concession Sfr8/5, incl Kunstmuseum Sfr15/5; ⊙10am-5pm Tue-Sun, to 8pm Wed) This well-designed museum provides an interesting romp through the principality's history.

Kunstmuseum Liechtenstein MUSEUM

(☎235 03 00; www.kunstmuseum.li; Städtle 32; adult/concession Sfr12/8, incl Landesmuseum Sfr15/5; ⊙10am-5pm Tue-Sun, to 8pm Thu) The mainstay of this museum is contemporary art, not the prince's collection of old masters, which has been relocated to the Palais Liechtenstein museum (p59) in Vienna.

Postmuseum MUSEUM

(☎236 61 05; 1st fl, Städtle 37; admission free; ⊙10am-noon & 1-5pm) On the first floor, above the post office, this museum showcases all national stamps issued since 1912.

Hofkellerei des Fürstens VINEYARD

(☎232 10 18; www.hofkellerei.li; ⊙shop open 8am-noon & 1.30-6.30pm Mon-Fri, 9am-1pm Sat) You must be in a group for a tour at the prince's vineyard, 1km north of the centre of Vaduz. Independent travellers can visit and indulge in a taste at the shop.

Mitteldorf HISTORIC AREA

To see how Vaduz once looked, head northeast from the pedestrian zone to this charming quarter of traditional houses and verdant gardens.

Sleeping

Gasthof Löwen HOTEL $$
(☎238 11 41; www.hotel-loewen.li; Herrengasse 35; s/d Sfr199/299; P wi-fi) Historic and creakily elegant, this six-centuries-old inn has eight spacious rooms with antique furniture and modern bathrooms. There's a cosy bar, fine-dining restaurant and a rear outdoor terrace overlooking grapevines.

Landgasthof Au HOTEL $$
(☎232 11 17; Austrasse 2; s/d Sfr90/140, with shared bathroom Sfr68/110; P) A couple of bus stops south of Vaduz town centre (about a 10-minute walk), this simple, family-run place is a reasonable budget option. A couple of the bigger doubles have terraces.

Camping Mittagspitze CAMPING GROUND $
(☎392 36 77, 392 23 11; www.campingtriesen.li; per adult/child/car Sfr9/4/5, per tent Sfr6-8; ⏲year-round; pool) A well-equipped camping ground in a leafy spot with a restaurant, TV lounge, playground and kiosk, and a swimming pool in summer. Find it 3.5km outside Vaduz, south of Triesen.

SYHA Hostel HOSTEL $
(☎232 50 22; www.youthhostel.ch/schaan; Untere Rütigasse 6; dm/s/d Sfr33/57/84; ⏲Mar-Oct) This hostel caters particularly to cyclists and families. Halfway between Schaan and Vaduz, it's within easy walking distance of both towns. Reception is open from 10am to 5pm.

Landhaus am Giessen HOTEL $$
(☎235 00 35; www.giessen.li; Zollstrasse 16; s/d Sfr100/150; P pool wi-fi) A fairly modern affair with comfortable and good-sized, if comparatively charmless, rooms. It has a sauna and offers massages.

Hotel Falknis HOTEL $
(☎232 63 77; Landstrasse 92; s/d with shared bathroom Sfr55/110; P) Basic rooms located north of the centre – 15 minutes on foot or take the bus.

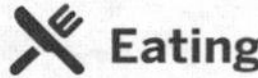

Eating

Pedestrian-only Städtle has a clutch of footpath restaurants and cafes.

TOP CHOICE **Torkel** SWISS $$$
(☎232 44 10; Hintergasse 9; mains Sfr42-60; ⏲lunch & dinner Mon-Fri, dinner Sat) Just above the prince's vineyards sits His Majesty's ivy-clad restaurant. The garden terrace enjoys a wonderful perspective of the castle above, while the ancient, wood-lined interior is cosy in winter. Food mixes classic with modern.

Adler Vaduz INTERNATIONAL $$
(☎232 21 31; www.adler.li; Herrengasse 2; mains Sfr18-50; ⏲lunch & dinner Mon-Fri) A pleasant restaurant in the Hotel Adler, offering a broad selection of cuisine, from pasta to *rindsfilet vom grill auf steinpilzrisotto mit trüffel-rotweinsauce nappiert* (beef steak

NUTS & BOLTS

- **Capital** Vaduz
- **Currency** Swiss franc (Sfr)
- **Area** 155 sq km
- **Telephone codes** country code ☎423; international access code ☎00
- **Emergency** ☎112; ambulance ☎144; fire ☎118; police ☎117
- **Official language** German, although – as in Switzerland – the Swiss-German dialect is the de facto spoken language
- **Visas** Schengen rules apply
- **Exchange rates** A$1 = Sfr0.95; C$1 = 0.93Sfr; €1 = Sfr1.29; ¥100 = Sfr1.12; NZ$1 = Sfr0.68; UK£1 = Sfr1.46; US$1 = Sfr0.87
- **Famous for** dentures, postcards stamped by the country's postal service
- **Phrases** *gruezi* (hello; good day); *merci vielmal* (thank you very much); *adieu* (goodbye); *sprechen sie Englisch?* (do you speak English?)
- **Hostel bed** Sfr40 to Sfr60
- **One-day/week ski pass** Sfr45/205
- **Connections** Austria and Switzerland are the two obvious places to move on to from this tiny nation: to cross the border, hop on a local bus at the Swiss border towns of Buchs or Sargans, or at Austrian next-door-neighbour Feldkirch.

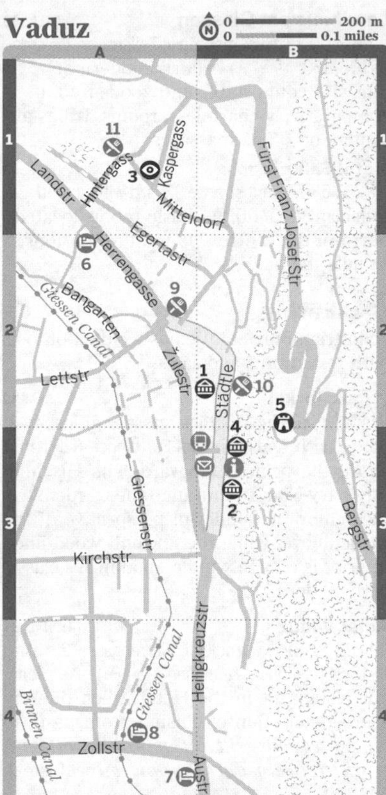

Vaduz

Sights

1 Kunstmuseum Liechtenstein B2
2 Liechtensteinisches Landesmuseum B3
3 Mitteldorf A1
4 Postmuseum B3
5 Schloss Vaduz B2

Sleeping

6 Gasthof Löwen A2
7 Landgasthof Au A4
8 Landhaus am Giessen A4

Eating

9 Adler Vaduz A2
10 Café Wolf B2
Landgasthof Au ....(see 7)
11 Torkel A1

fillet with mushroom risotto and a truffle and red-wine sauce).

Café Wolf INTERNATIONAL **$$**

(232 23 21; Städtle 29; mains Sfr18-50; lunch & dinner) This relaxed cafe and restaurant has pavement tables in summer and a menu that mixes Swiss and international cuisine – anything from pizza to pseudo-Asian dishes.

Landgasthof Au INTERNATIONAL **$$**

(232 11 17; Austrasse 2; mains Sfr18-36; lunch & dinner Wed-Sun) The Landgasthof Au garden restaurant has a good name for its local grub, which ranges from ham omelettes to a couple of vegetarian dishes and a kids' menu.

Information

Liechtenstein Center (239 63 00; www.tourismus.li; Städtle 37; 9am-5pm) This snazzy, modern timber structure is chock-full of information, can recommend excellent day hikes nearby and sells souvenir passport stamps for Sfr3.

Post office (Äulestrasse 38; 7.45am-6pm Mon-Fri, 8-11am Sat)

AROUND VADUZ

Outside Vaduz the air is crisp and clear with a pungent, sweet aroma of cow dung and flowers. The countryside, dotted with tranquil villages and enticing churches set to a craggy alps backdrop, is about as idyllic and relaxing as it gets.

Triesenberg, on a terrace above Vaduz, commands excellent views over the Rhine valley. It has a pretty, onion-domed church and the **Walsermuseum** (262 19 26; www.triesenberg.li; Jonaboda 2; adult/concession Sfr2/1; 7.45-11.45am & 1.30-5.45pm Mon-Fri, 7.45-11am & 1.30-5pm Sat), devoted to the Walser community, whose members came from Switzerland's Valais to settle in the 13th century. Take bus 21 from Vaduz.

There are loads of well-marked **cycling routes** through Liechtenstein (look for signs with a cycle symbol; distances and directions will also be included), as well as 400km of **hiking trails** (see www.wanderwege-llv.li). The most famous is the **Fürstensteig trail**, a rite of passage for nearly every Liechtensteiner. You must be fit and not suffer from vertigo, as the path is narrow in places, reinforced with rope handholds and/or falls away to a sheer drop. The hike, which takes up to four hours, begins at the **Berggasthaus Gaflei** (take bus 22 from Triesenberg). Travel light and wear good shoes.

Malbun

POP 32

Welcome to Liechtenstein's one and only ski resort: found at the end of the road from Vaduz, the 1600m-high resort of Malbun feels like – in the nicest possible sense – the edge of the earth.

The road from Vaduz terminates at Malbun. There is an ATM by the lower bus stop. The **tourist office** (☎263 65 77; www.malbun.li; ⊙9am-noon & 1.30-5pm Mon-Sat, closed mid-Apr–May & Nov–mid-Dec) is on the main street.

Although rather limited in scope – the runs are mostly novice with a few intermediate and cross-country ones thrown in – the skiing is inexpensive for this part of the world and it does offer some bragging rights. Indeed, older British royals such as Prince Charles learned to ski here.

A general ski pass (including the Sareis chair lift) costs Sfr45/205 per day/week for adults and Sfr29/127 for children. One day's equipment rental from **Malbun Sport** (☎263 37 55; www.malbunsport.li; ⊙8am-6pm Mon-Fri, plus Sat & Sun Dec-Mar) costs Sfr60 including skis, shoes and poles.

Hotel Walserhof (☎264 43 23; Sfr140) is a simple mountain house with four doubles and cheerful outdoor dining. **Kulm** (☎237 27 79; www.hotelkulm.com; Sfr180) is a solid chalet with modern double rooms inside the timber house. For gob-smacking mountain views over dinner, it's hard to beat **Bergrestaurant Sareiserjoch** (☎268 21 01; www.sareis.li; mains Sfr20-35; ⊙Jun–mid-Oct & mid-Dec–Apr), at the end of the Sareis chair lift. Go for *käsknöpfli* (cheese-filled dumplings).

UNDERSTAND LIECHTENSTEIN

History

Liechtenstein was created by the merger of the domain of Schellenberg and the county of Vaduz in 1712 by the powerful Liechtenstein family. A principality under the Holy Roman Empire from 1719 to 1806, Liechtenstein finally achieved its full sovereign independence in 1866. A modern constitution was drawn up in 1921, but even today the prince retains the power to dissolve parliament and must approve every act before it becomes law. Prince Franz Josef II was the first ruler to live in the castle above the capital city of Vaduz. He died in 1989 and was succeeded by his son, Prince Hans-Adam II.

Liechtenstein has no military service and its minuscule army was disbanded in 1868. It is known for wine production, postage stamps, dentures and its status as a tax haven. In 2000 Liechtenstein's financial and political institutions were rocked by allegations that money laundering was rife in the country. In response to international outrage, banks agreed to stop allowing customers to bank money anonymously. But the principality remains under pressure to introduce more reforms.

In 2003 Hans-Adam won sweeping powers to dismiss the elected government, appoint judges and reject proposed laws. The following year he handed the day-to-day running of the country to his son Alois.

Scandal rocked the principality again in 2008 when it was discovered that more than 1000 high-flying Germans had evaded tax by depositing large sums of money in trusts run by a Liechtenstein bank partly owned

LIECHTENSTEIN TRIVIA

» Liechtenstein is the only country in the world named after the people who purchased it.

» In its last military engagement in 1866, none of its 80 soldiers was killed. In fact, 81 returned, including a new Italian 'friend'. The army was disbanded soon afterwards.

» Low business taxes means around 75,000 firms, many of them so-called 'letter box companies' with nominal head offices, are registered here – about twice the number of the principality's inhabitants.

» Liechtenstein is Europe's fourth-smallest nation (only the Vatican, Monaco and San Marino are smaller).

» If you ever meet the prince in the pub, make sure he buys a round. The royal family is estimated to be worth UK£3.3 billion.

by the royal family. Liechtenstein didn't dispute that such money could have wound up in its banks (tax evasion is not considered a crime). It was, at that time, considered an uncooperative country by the OECD (that is, a tax haven), but it accused Germany of spying. The country bowed to pressure in 2009 and began exchanging information with the British government. It was removed from the list of uncooperative countries that same year.

Food & Drink

Liechtenstein's cuisine borrows from its larger neighbours, and it is generally good quality but expensive. Basic restaurants provide simple but well-cooked food. Soups are popular and filling, and cheeses form an important part of the diet, as do rösti and wurst.

As in neighbouring Switzerland, restaurants are generally open five or six days a week for lunch and dinner (usually closed between 3pm and 6pm or 7pm). Cafes usually stay open all day, and bars tend to open from lunchtime until around midnight.

SURVIVAL GUIDE

Directory A–Z

Liechtenstein and Switzerland share almost everything, so for more information about Liechtenstein basics, see p1200.

Unlike much of the rest of Europe, smoking in public places has yet to be banned in Liechtenstein, meaning you can freely smoke in hotels, restaurants and so on.

Business Hours

Offices 8am to 5pm, Monday to Friday

Restaurants 11:30am to 2:30pm for lunch, 5pm to 10pm for dinner

Shops 10am to 6 or 7pm Monday to Friday, to 4 or 5pm Saturday, closed on Sunday. Food stores open at 7 or 8am. Smaller shops close for an hour at lunch and tend to shut down around 5pm Monday through Friday.

WANT MORE?

Head to **Lonely Planet** (www.lonelyplanet.com/liechtenstein) for planning advice, author recommendations, traveller reviews and insider tips.

PRICE RANGES

Accommodation prices listed in this chapter are for double rooms with bathrooms during high season. We have used the following symbols to indicate price:

$$$	more than Sfr380
$$	Sfr125 to Sfr380
$	less than Sfr125

The following price indicators for the cost of a main course are used in the listings:

$$$	more than Sfr40
$$	Sfr20 to Sfr40
$	less than Sfr20

Getting There & Away

The nearest airports are Friedrichshafen (Germany) and Zürich (Switzerland), with train connections to the Swiss border towns of Buchs and Sargans. From there, there are usually buses to Vaduz (from Buchs Sfr2.50, Sargans Sfr3.75). Buses also run every 30 minutes from the Austrian border town of Feldkirch; you sometimes have to change at Schaan to reach Vaduz. The Vaduz bus station is on Städtle 38, next to the post office.

A few trains from Buchs to Feldkirch stop at Schaan (bus tickets are valid).

If you're travelling by road, the N16 from Switzerland passes through Liechtenstein via Schaan and ends at Feldkirch. The A13 follows the Rhine along the border. Minor roads cross into Liechtenstein at each motorway exit.

Getting Around

Bus travel is cheap and reliable; all fares cost Sfr2.40, or Sfr3.60 for journeys exceeding 13km (such as Vaduz to Malbun). Grab a timetable from the Vaduz tourist office.

Luxembourg

Includes »

Best Places to Eat

» Caves Gourmandes (p916)
» Mosconi (p916)
» Am Tiirmschen (p916)
» Chiggeri (p916)
» La Table du Pain (p916)
» Am Musée (p916)

Best Places to Stay

» Hôtel Parc Beaux-Arts (p915)
» Melia Luxembourg (p915)
» Hôtel Simoncini (p915)
» HI hostel, Remerschen (boxed text, p915)

Why Go?

Which European nation, just 84km long, consistently rates among the world's three richest countries? Remarkably, the answer is Luxembourg (Luxemburg, Lëtzebuerg). That's quite an achievement for this mostly rural grand duchy that suffered wholesale destruction during WWII. The nation's economic miracle started with steel, but developed with banking – so much so that neighbouring Belgians joke that visitors only come to get their money out. That's unfair. Luxembourg's castle villages and attractively forested hills are popular weekend getaways with lovely forest-shaded hiking trails and well-paved country lanes to keep everything easily accessible. Luxembourg City has a fairy-tale quality to its Unesco-listed historic core. And the vineyards of the Moselle Valley keep the population suitably supplied with fine yet affordable sparkling wine. Welcome to the good life.

When to Go

Luxembourg City

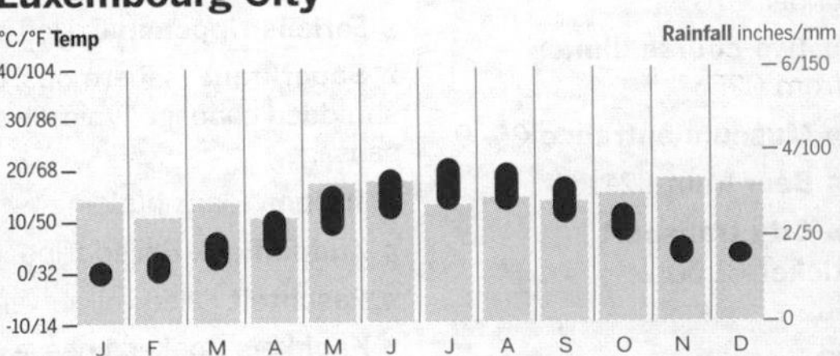

Feb–Mar Bonfires mark the symbolic burning of winter on the first weekend after Carnival.

May–Jun Sprinprozession dancing fills the streets of Echternach on the Tuesday after Whitsun.

Summer & weekends Luxembourg City's business hotels offer bargains; Wiltz arts festival in July.

AT A GLANCE

» **Currency** euro (€)

» **Languages** Lëtzebuergesch, French, German

» **Money** ATMs common in towns (but not villages)

» **Visas** Schengen rules apply

Fast Facts

» **Area** 2586 sq km

» **Population** 492,000

» **Capital** Luxembourg City

» **Telephone** country code ☎352; international access code ☎00

» **Emergency** ☎112

Exchange Rates

Australia	A$1	€0.74
Canada	C$1	€0.74
Japan	¥100	€0.87
New Zealand	NZ$1	€0.56
UK	UK£1	€1.16
USA	US$1	€0.67

Set Your Budget

» **Budget hotel room** under €70

» **Two-course dinner** from €25

» **Museum entrance** €5–9

» **Beer** from €2

» **City transport ticket** €1.50

Resources

» **FAQs** (www.luxembourg.co.uk/faq.html)

» **Official tourism site** (www.ont.lu)

Connections

Luxembourg City has high-speed trains to Paris (around two hours; prebooking compulsory). Express trains run roughly hourly to Brussels (Belgium) via Arlon (Belgium), to Lille (France) via Namur (Belgium), to Koblenz (Germany) via Trier (Germany) and to Basel (Switzerland) via Strasbourg (France). Air links are limited but frequent air-link buses connect the capital to Frankfurt-Hahn airport in Germany and Charleroi airport in Belgium for budget airline flights. Buses also link Luxembourg's Ettelbrück via Wiltz to Bastogne (Belgium).

ITINERARIES

One Day

Wander through Luxembourg City and contrast the craggy ancient heart with its gleaming art galleries and modern museums.

Five Days

Visit Luxembourg City during the weekend while hotel rates are low, then do some wine tasting in the Moselle Valley and go hiking around Echternach. Buses via Beaufort get you to Diekirch to learn more about the country's unlucky WWII history, before finishing up in fairy-tale Vianden. Add a stop at Château de Bourscheid en route if you're driving.

Essential Food & Drink

If the popular local dishes below appeal, Sylvie Bisdorff's *Culinary Luxembourg* has over 100 recipes. If they don't, fear not – Luxembourg City also dishes out varied, international gourmet food.

» **Judd mat gaardebounen** Luxembourg's national dish; smoked pork-neck in a cream-based sauce with chunks of potato and broad beans

» **Ferkels-rippchen** Grilled spare ribs

» **Sauerkraut** (sauermous, choucroute) Pickled, fermented shredded cabbage typically served with cured pork or sausage

» **Traipen** Black pudding

» **Kuddelfleck** Boiled tripe

» **Paschtéit** Filled vol-au-vent

» **Kachkeis** Cooked cheese

» **Kniddelen** 'Dumplings'; often gnocchi-style balls served in various sauces, but the term can also refer to meatballs

» **Fruity white wines** Luxembourg's Moselle Valley produces affordable, high-quality bubbly

» **Lager-style beers** Local lagers include Bofferding, Diekirch, Mousel and Simon Pils

Luxembourg Highlights

1. Wander the capital's famous **Chemin de la Corniche** (p912)
2. Hike into the Tolkeinesque woodlands of **Müllerthal** (p921)
3. Let your imagination reign from the towers of quintessential fortress **Château de Bourscheid** (p920)
4. Step back in time and explore **Vianden** (p918), the most evocative of rural Luxembourg's many appealing castle villages.
5. Pop the fizz with the sparkling wines of Luxembourg's **Moselle Valley** (p921)

LUXEMBOURG CITY

POP 136,000

World Heritage–listed Luxembourg City sits high on a promontory overlooking the deep-cut valleys of the Pétrusse and Alzette Rivers. For a thousand years these gorges were the key to the city's defence. Now they provide visitors with spectacular vistas and enclose the interesting old quarters of Clausen, Pfaffenthal and the Grund.

Sights

OLD TOWN

Within the compact, mostly pedestrianised Old Town all sights are walking distance from each other. Access to the Grund area is easiest using an elevator on Plateau du St-Esprit.

Chemin de la Corniche PROMENADE

This pedestrian promenade has been hailed as 'Europe's most beautiful balcony'. It winds along the course of the 17th-century city ramparts with views across the river canyon towards the hefty fortifications of the **Wenzelsmauer** (Wenceslas Wall). Across Rue Sigefroi, the rampart-top walk continues along Blvd Victor Thorn to the **Dräi Tier** (Triple Gate) tower. En route you'll pass some great viewpoints from which to survey the Pfaffenthal Gorge, spanned to the north by the distinctive **Red Bridge**, officially called Pont Grand-Duchesse Charlotte.

Palais Grand-Ducal PALACE

(17 Rue du Marché-aux-Herbes) A-twitter with photogenic little pointy turrets, this much-extended 1573 royal palace houses the Grand Duke's office, with Luxembourg's parliament occupying the 1859 annex. For a few weeks in midsummer you can get inside the medieval Gothic dining room and sumptuously gilded romanticist upstairs rooms by joining a gently humorous 45-minute **guided tour** (€7; Mon-Sat mid-Jul & Aug). Times vary and prebooking is essential; book at the Luxembourg City Tourist Office. Only one daily tour is in English (typically 4pm) and it sells out fast.

Behind the palace lies the Old Town's most charming knot of **crooked lanes**, while directly west is the contrastingly stately **Place Guillaume II**, lined with 19th-century buildings, including the neoclassical **Hôtel de Ville** (City Hall).

Bock Casemates SUBTERRANEAN FORTIFICATIONS

(Montée de Clausen; adult/child €3/2.50; 10am-5pm Mar-Oct) The Bock is the cliff-top site of Count Sigefroi's once-mighty fort that was Luxembourg's raison d'être. Much of the fortifications were ripped out between 1867 and 1883 following the Treaty of London, but there's a great panorama and beneath the ruins lie the mildly intriguing Casemates, a honeycomb of damp rock galleries and passages carved between 1737 and 1746. Over the years they've housed everything from bakeries to slaughterhouses and garrisons of soldiers. During WWI and WWII they were used as bomb shelters for up to 35,000 people.

Musée d'Histoire de la Ville de Luxembourg MUSEUM

(www.mhvl.lu; 14 Rue du St-Esprit; adult/concession/Luxembourg Card €5/3/free; 10am-6pm Tue-Sun, to 8pm Thu) This engrossing interactive museum of city history hides within a series of 17th-century houses. On Thursday evenings entry is free after 6pm.

MNHA MUSEUM

(Musée National d'Histoire et d'Art; www.mnha.lu; Marché-aux-Poissons; adult/family/LC €5/10/free; 10am-6pm Tue-Sun, to 8pm Thu) Startlingly modern for its Old Town setting, this unusual museum offers a fascinating coverage of art and history. It starts deep in an excavated rocky basement with exhibits of neolithic flints, then sweeps you (somewhat unevenly) through Gallic tomb chambers, Roman mosaics and Napoleonic medals to an excellent, if relatively small, art gallery. Cézanne and Picasso get a look in while Luxembourg's expressionist artist Joseph Kutter (1894–1941) gets a whole floor.

Cathédrale Notre Dame CATHEDRAL

(Blvd Roosevelt; 10am-noon & 2-5.30pm) Most memorable for its unusually elongated black spires, the cathedral contains a tiny yet highly revered Madonna-and-child idol (above the altar) and the graves of the royal family (in the crypt).

LUXEMBOURG CARD

The brilliant value **Luxembourg Card** (www.ont.lu/card-en.html; 1-/2-/3-day adult €10/17/24, family €20/34/48), marked LC in reviews, allows free admission to most of the grand duchy's main attractions and unlimited use of public transport nationwide. You can buy it from tourist offices, museums or certain hotels.

Luxembourg City

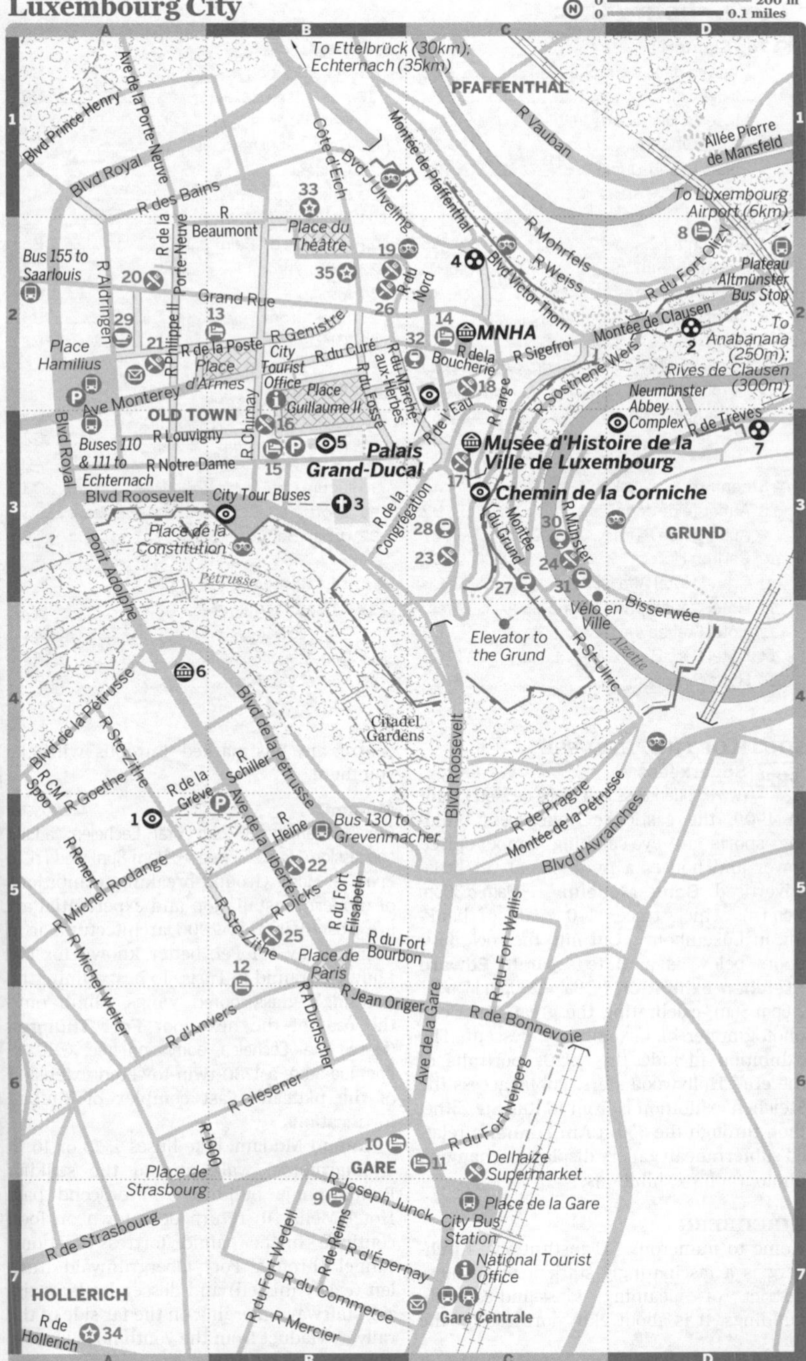

Luxembourg City

Top Sights
Chemin de la Corniche ... C3
MNHA ... C2
Musée d'Histoire de la Ville de Luxembourg ... C3
Palais Grand-Ducal ... C2

Sights
1 Am Tunnel ... A5
Bank Museum ... (see 1)
2 Bock Casemates ... D2
3 Cathédrale Notre Dame ... B3
4 Dräi Tier ... C2
Edward Steichen Exhibition ... (see 1)
5 Hôtel de Ville ... B3
6 Spuerkeess ... A4
7 Wenzelsmauer ... D3

Sleeping
8 Auberge de Jeunesse ... D2
9 Auberge de Reims ... B7
10 Carlton Hôtel ... B6
11 Grand Hotel Alfa ... C6
12 Hôtel Christophe Colomb ... B5
13 Hôtel Français ... B2
14 Hôtel Parc Beaux-Arts ... C2
15 Hôtel Simoncini ... B3

Eating
16 Á La Soupe ... B3
17 Am Musée ... C3
Am Tiirmschen ... (see 18)
18 Caves Gourmandes ... C2
19 Chiggeri ... B2
20 Exki ... A2
21 La Table du Pain ... A2
22 La Table du Pain ... B5
23 Mesa Verde ... C3
24 Mosconi ... C3
25 Restaurant Tibet ... B5
26 Thai Céladon ... B2

Drinking
27 Café des Artistes ... C3
28 d:qliq ... C3
29 L'Interview ... A2
30 Liquid Café ... C3
31 Scott's ... C3
32 Urban Bar ... C2

Entertainment
33 Cinémathèque Municipal ... B1
34 Den Atelier ... A7
35 Secret Garden ... B2

SOUTH OF THE PÉTRUSSE

FREE **Spuerkeess** MUSEUMS
(www.spuerkeess.lu; 1 Place de Metz) Built in 1909, the castlelike Spuerkeess building sports an eye-catching copper-spired tower and houses a professional yet little-advertised **Bank Museum** (9am-5.30pm Mon-Fri), which traces 140 years of banking in Luxembourg. Cut into the rock, four floors below is a quite separate **Edward Steichen exhibition** (9am-5.30pm Mon-Fri, 2-6pm Sun), celebrating the great American photographer of Luxembourg descent. The exhibition includes his 1920s portraits of the era's Hollywood stars. Public access the Steichen exhibition is from 16 Rue Ste-Zithe, then through the 350m **Am Tunnel**, a related subterranean gallery displaying changing photographic exhibitions.

KIRCHBERG

Home to numerous EU institutions, Kirchberg is a fascinatingly stark new business district of gleaming glass-and-concrete buildings. It is about 2km northeast of the centre; any bus marked 'Eurobus' will take you there.

Mudam ART MUSEUM
(www.mudam.lu; 3 Parc Dräi Eechelen; adult/concession/LC €5/3/free; 11am-8pm Wed-Fri, to 6pm Sat-Mon) Ground-breaking exhibitions of modern, installation and experiential art are hosted in this 2006 architectural icon designed by IM Pei, better known for the Louvre pyramid in Paris. To best admire the building's glass-roofed wings, climb onto the roof of the next-door **Fort Thüngen** (Musée Dräi Eechelen; admission free; 10am-4pm Tue-Sun), a 1730 twin-towered extension of the plateau's vast complex of Vauban fortifications.

To find Mudam, take buses 1, 13 or 16 to 'Philharmonie', walk around the striking Philharmonie building and descend past Hotel Melia. To return downtown on foot, continue further amid fortress bastions, tunnel through Fort Obergrünwald, turn left (easily missed) and descend a long zigzag stairway, emerging on the far side of the railway viaduct from the youth hostel.

HAMM

US Military Cemetery CEMETERY

(⏲9am-5pm) In a beautifully maintained graveyard near Hamm lie over 5000 US WWII soldiers, including George S Patton Jr, the audacious general of the US Third Army who played a large part in Luxembourg's 1944 liberation. The site is 4km east of the capital: take bus 15 from Grand Hotel Alfa to Käschtewee (15 minutes, every 20 minutes weekdays, every 40 minutes Sunday), from which it's 10 minutes' walk.

Sleeping

Luxembourg City's accommodation scene is heavy with business options but at weekends and during July and August many places slash their rates, so look for online bargains at these times.

CITY CENTRE

TOP CHOICE **Hôtel Parc Beaux-Arts** BOUTIQUE HOTEL €€€

(☎26 86 76-1; www.parcbeauxarts.lu; 1 Rue Sigefroi; ste Fri-Sun from €149, Mon-Thu €200-465; @) Within a trio of 18th-century houses are 10 gorgeous suites exuding understated luxury. Each features original artworks by contemporary artists, oak floors, Murano crystal lamps and a fresh rose daily.

Hôtel Simoncini HOTEL €€

(☎22 28 44; www.hotelsimoncini.lu; 6 Rue Notre Dame; s/d/tr/ste Mon-Fri €135/160/185/200, Sat & Sun €110/120/145/160; @) With a lobby that doubles as a modern art gallery, this brilliantly central hotel has pristine white rooms with occasional touches of colourful retro-cool.

Hôtel Français HOTEL €€

(☎47 45 34; www.hotelfrancais.lu; 14 Place d'Armes; s/d Mon-Fri €120/140, Sat & Sun €99/125; @) Handily central with 24 presentable, if somewhat small, rooms above a popular, super-central brasserie.

CLAUSEN

Auberge de Jeunesse HOSTEL €

(☎22 68 89; www.youthhostels.lu; 2 Rue du Fort Olizy; HI members dm/s/d €19.90/34.90/51.80 nonmembers €22.90/37.90/57.80; P@) Overshadowed by the railway viaduct, this large modern hostel has no-fuss four- and six-bed rooms, plenty of sitting space and an inexpensive restaurant (four-course meal €9, with vegetarian options). To get here, walk five minutes steeply down from the 'Plateau Altmünster' stop, accessible on bus routes 9 and 14 from the airport or Gare Centrale.

KIRCHBERG

Melia Luxembourg BUSINESS HOTEL €€

(☎27 33 31; www.melia-luxembourg.com; Parc Dräi Eechelen; d weekend/midweek from €90/165;) With Mudam next door and incomparable city views from rooms x01 to x08 on the upper floors, the Melia is a stylish choice indulgently mixing 21st-century and '70s retro motifs. Wi-fi available at per hour/12 hours €4/12. At weekends deals are very good, but Kirchberg can feel oddly abandoned.

STATION AREA

Towards the unexotic Gare Centrale area hotels are generally less expensive, though the cheapest are, not coincidentally, clustered around the tiny red-light district.

Carlton Hôtel HERITAGE HOTEL €€

(☎29 96 60; www.carlton.lu; 9 Rue de Strasbourg; s/d Mon-Fri €110/125, Sat & Sun €70/85; @) Fair value, well modernised rooms in a 1920s building with stained-glass windows in the foyer.

Grand Hotel Alfa CHAIN HOTEL €€€

(☎49 00 11-1; www.mercure.com; 16 Place de la Gare; d €160-220; @) Behind an imposing 1936 facade, the rooms are a bland '90s style and severely over-priced at rack-rates (check the internet for discounts). However, they're an incredible bargain if you score a weekend summer package – from €86 per night, including a Luxembourg Card and a substantial breakfast buffet (normally €18; taken in the hotel's art deco brasserie).

Hôtel Christophe Colomb HOTEL €€

(☎40 84 14-1; www.christophe-colomb.lu; 10 Rue d'Anvers; s/tw/tr Mon-Thu €109/124/134, Fri-Sun €75/85/95;) The neatest of several bland options on Rue d'Anvers with lift, safe, minibar, wi-fi and breakfast included. Parking costs €10.

OUTER HOSTELS

If you don't mind the bus ride there are HI hostels in the pretty castle villages of **Bourglinster** (17km) and **Larochette** (28km), both on Luxembourg City–Diekirch bus route 100. There's also an excellent HI hostel in **Remerschen** (3km north of Schengen on bus route 185), that's handily across the road from an inexpensive wine-tasting bar.

Auberge de Reims CRASH PAD €
(17 Rue Joseph Junck; s/d/tr without bathroom €40/45/50) If saving money is all that counts, these aging but presentably repainted rooms above a downmarket cafe constitute one of several very basic options amid rather seedy bars and peep shows. No reservations. Doors are locked at 2am.

Eating

In summer, pedestrianised streets turn into large open-air dining areas, most notably around tree-shaded Place d'Armes in the Old Town where you'll find everything from €13 Chinese buffets to typical burger chains. Nearby, there are upmarket brasseries stretching down Rue Chimay to the snazzy modern pizzerias on Rue Louvigny. Further south, cheaper terraced places can be found on Place de Paris, including several bar-pizzerias, a sandwich shop and a kebab stand, while nearby Thai and Chinese eateries have meal deals from €7.

For intimate and more original dining options hunt out the alleys and passages collectively nicknamed Ilôt Gourmand, directly behind the palace. The website www.gastronomie.lu is a good restaurant finder.

TOP CHOICE **Caves Gourmandes** FRENCH €€
(46 11 24; www.caves-gourmandes.lu; 32 Rue de l'Eau; mains €15-32, lunch/dinner menus from €15/35) Gently upmarket French and Basque food served in caves dug out of the living rock centuries ago. Directly above is the very refined gourmet restaurant **Bouquet Garni** (www.lebouquetgarni.lu).

Mosconi ITALIAN €€€
(54 69 94; www.mosconi.lu; 13 Rue Münster, Grund; mains €27-34; lunch Tue-Fri, dinner Tue-Sat) Has two Michelin stars and a location as delectable as the upscale Italian food. Reservations and formal dress essential.

Am Tiirmschen LOCAL SPECIALITIES €€
(26 27 07 33; www.amtiirmschen.lu; 32 Rue de l'Eau, Ilôt Gourmand; mains €15-25; noon-2pm Mon-Fri & 7-10.30pm Tue-Sat) This is a great place to sample typical Luxembourg dishes, but they also serve good fish and French options in case your companions don't fancy *kniddelen* (dumplings) or smoked pork. It has a semi-successful mix of old and pseudo-old decor with heavy, bowed beams.

Mesa Verde SEAFOOD, VEGETARIAN €€
(46 41 26; www.mesa.lu; 11 Rue du St-Esprit; mains €20-26; lunch Wed-Fri Sep-Jul, dinner Tue-Sat year-round;) Exotic and imaginative, both in the colours of its psychedelic-carnival decor and the eclectic influences in its imaginative cuisine. Lunch menus start at just €11 but dinners can get pricey. Book ahead.

Am Musée CAFE €
(14 Rue du St-Esprit; sandwiches €3.25, light meals €9.50-13.30; 11am-6pm Tue-Sun) With great views and a peaceful garden terrace, this calm cafe is ideal for nibbling delicious slices of seasonal fruit tart (€3.50) washed down with an inexpensive glass of Moselle wine (from €2.60). Beware, however: the limited meal choices here are preprepared and microwaved.

Chiggeri BRASSERIE, RESTAURANT €€
(22 82 36; www.chiggeri.lu; 15 Rue du Nord; mains €14-35; restaurant noon-2pm & 7.30-10pm Tue-Sun, brasserie 10am-1am Sun-Thu & to 3am Fri & Sat) A historic turreted building with a super summer terrace that offers varied dining and drinking experiences, from the boisterous brasserie-cafe to the classy yet relaxed restaurant with Afro-Aboriginal decor. In 2008, Guinness World Records certified the extraordinary wine list as the world's longest.

Thai Céladon THAI €€
(47 49 34; www.thailand.lu; 1 Rue du Nord; mains €18.50-24; noon-2.30pm Mon-Fri, 7.30-11pm Mon-Sat) Excellent if pricey Thai food served in a chic, minimal Old Town mansion with subtle little neocolonial flourishes.

Restaurant Tibet INDIAN, HIMALAYAN €€
(26 48 59; www.tibetrestaurant.com; 39 Rue St-Zithe; meals €11-16; 11.45am-2pm & 6-11pm) A colourful, incense-scented spot that offers great value weekday lunch buffets (€11; prebook). Meal prices include rice.

Anabanana VEGAN €
(www.anabanana.lu; 117 Rue de la Tour Jacob; sandwich/lunch/dinner €5/12/18; noon-2pm Tue-Fri & 7-9.45pm Tue-Sat;) Quaint, colourful little vegan-fusion restaurant with a fixed dinner choice that changes daily. No alcohol, but juice is €4.50.

Á la Soupe SOUP €
(www.alasoupe.net; Rue Chimay; breakfast €3.50-7, soup €4.50-9; 7am-8.45pm Mon-Sat) Centrally located soup specialist.

La Table du Pain BAKERY, CAFE €
(www.tabledupain.lu; Ville 19 Ave Monterey; baguettes & salads €2.40-12; 7am-6pm Mon-Fri) Convivial rustic bakery-cafe with heavy wooden furniture and a good range of

breakfast options, baguette sandwiches (€2.40 to take away) and big salads. There's a second location at Gare 37 Ave de la Liberté.

Exki ORGANIC, FAST FOOD €

(www.exki.lu; 72 Grand Rue; snacks & light meals €4-7; ⌚7am-7pm Mon-Fri, 8am-6.30pm Sat; wi-fi) Modern self-service cafe offering wholesome organic food and free wi-fi. Before 11am coffee costs €1.

Drinking

Watering holes compete for wealthy youth clientele and ratchet up the music's volume as the evening progresses.

Rives de Clausen NIGHTLIFE AREA

(www.rivesdeclausen.com) Nine themed bar-restaurant clubs together form the city's liveliest youth scene in the recently repurposed former Mousel brewery complex. Options include **Verso** (www.verso.lu), **Life Bar** (www.lifebarclausen.com), **Rock Box** (www.rockbox.lu), very contemporary **Ikki** (www.ikki.lu) and curious, safari-themed **King Wilma** (www.kingwilma.lu), with its skeletal wooden centrepiece. All are side by side so just pick the atmosphere that appeals. On Friday and Saturday nights, shuttle buses running until 3.30am bring revellers back to the Glacis car park (800m northwest of Place d'Armes) and to Rue des Bains.

Urban Bar BAR

(www.urban.lu/urbancity.html; 2 Rue de la Boucherie; ⌚noon-1am Sun-Thu, noon-3am Fri & Sat) It's often standing room only at this hip spot, where waves of '70s retro foam panelling look like ceilings in a Star Trek space pod.

Liquid Café PUB, CAFE

(www.liquid.lu; 17 Rue Münster; ⌚5pm-1am Mon-Fri, 8pm-1am Sat & Sun) Partly candle-lit but utterly unpretentious, this convivial Grund pub-cafe has live jazz Tuesdays and blues gigs Thursdays.

d:qliq BAR, CLUB

(www.dqliq.com; 17 Rue du St-Esprit; ⌚5pm-1am Tue-Thu, 6pm-3am Fri & Sat) Small, graffiti-chic Old Town bar with a varying program of DJs and live, lesser-known bands most weekends, typically electro or house.

Café des Artistes BAR

(22 Montée du Grund; ⌚evenings Tue-Sun) In this atmospheric spot every inch of wall and ceiling is covered with posters old and new and the piano bursts into life Wednesday to Saturday evenings.

L'Interview CAFE

(Rue Aldringen; ⌚7.30am-1am) Full of mirrors and wood panelling, this unpretentious cafe serves great cappuccinos and is popular with a pre-party student-aged crowd by night.

Scott's PUB

(Bisserwée; ⌚11am-1am) Attractive for its outdoor seating perched right above the river.

Entertainment

For entertainment listings see www.agendalux.lu, www.luxembourgticket.lu, www.nightlife-mag.lu or www.rave.lu. Note that the country's two biggest rock/pop music venues, **Rockhal** (www.rockhal.lu) and **Kulturfabrik** (www.kulturfabrik.lu), are both a 20-minute train ride away in Esch-sur-Alzette.

Philharmonie CONCERT HALL

(☎26 32 26 32; www.philharmonie.lu; 1 Place de l'Europe) Out in the Kirchberg, the unique tear-shaped Philharmonie building feels like it might be the check-in area for an interstellar spaceport. It hosts everything from jazz to classical to opera.

Cinémathèque Municipal CINEMA

(☎29 12 59; www.vdl.lu/Cinémathèque-p-1475628.html; 17 Place du Théâtre; adult/concession €3.70/2.40) Art-house offerings with some summer open-air screenings in the courtyard of nearby Théâtre des Capucins.

Secret Garden CLUB

(www.secretgarden.lu; 7 Côte d'Eich; ⌚10pm-1am Tue, to 3am Wed, to 6am Thu-Sat) Lively club carved out of Old Town houses with a garden courtyard to chill out in during fair weather. The €10 admission includes one drink. Bling-tastic cocktail lounge upstairs.

Den Atelier LIVE MUSIC

(☎49 54 66; www.atelier.lu; 56 Rue de Hollerich) Venue for local and visiting groups in what looks from the outside like a glum 1970s factory.

Shopping

For chic boutiques look along Rue Philippe II and Grand Rue in the Old Town. For more affordable chain stores stroll down Ave de la Gare.

Information

Internet Access

Bibliothèque Municipale (3 Rue Génistre; ⌚10am-7pm Tue-Fri, 10am-6pm Sat) Sign up (with ID) for one hour's free internet. No printing.

Cyber Multimedia (8 Rue de Bonnevoie; ⌚9am-8pm Mon-Fri, 10am-8pm Sat, 2-8pm Sun)

Phone House (47 Rue de Strasbourg; per hr €2.50; ⌚2-9pm Mon-Thu, 3-9pm Fri-Sun) Internet, fax and phone service.

Left Luggage

There are **lockers** (Gare Centrale; per day €2-4; ⌚6am-9.30pm) at the far north end of platform 3; inaccessible at night.

Medical

Zitha Klinik (☎49 77 61; www.zitha.lu; 36 Rue Ste-Zithe; ⌚7am-7pm Mon-Fri) is a central clinic where you can see a doctor without appointment. When it's closed go around the corner to **Maison Médicale** (Rue Michel Welter).

Money

ATMs are very widespread but most banks only change money for their customers and there are no exchange booths.

Tourist Information

Luxembourg City Tourist Office (☎22 28 09; www.lcto.lu; Place Guillaume II; ⌚9am-6pm Mon-Sat, 10am-6pm Sun) Free city maps, accommodation help and copious pamphlets. Walking tours depart 2pm summer, 1pm winter.

Luxembourg National Tourist Office (☎42 82 82 20; www.ont.lu; Gare Centrale concourse; ⌚9.30am-12.30pm & 1-5.30pm) City and national information.

Getting There & Away

See p924.

Getting Around

To/From Luxembourg Airport

Luxembourg Airport (www.lux-airport.lu) is 6km east of Place d'Armes. Bus 16 takes 20 minutes from Gare Centrale via Place Hamilius and Philharmonie. Bus 9 takes 30 minutes via Plateau Altmünster (handy for the youth hostel) and Clausen. Both cost €1.50 and run every 15 minutes Monday to Saturday, every half-hour on Sunday until 9pm. A taxi costs around €30.

To/From Other Airports

Flibco (www.flibco.com) shuttlebuses from Gare Centrale run almost around the clock to budget airports Frankfurt-Hahn (€17, two hours) in Germany and Charleroi (€22, 2¼ hours) in Belgium.

Bicycle

SHORT-TERM HIRE Velóh (☎800 611 00; www.en.veloh.lu; membership per week/year €1/15; ⌚24hr) Offers over 50 automated rental pick-up/drop-off stations all over town, 25 of which are equipped with credit-card facilities for paying your initial membership subscription. The idea is to ride the bike from A to B, drop it off at an empty stand, then take a new one (at least five minutes later). The first half-hour is free. Thereafter your credit card is automatically debited €1 per hour, maximum five hours. Return the bike within 24 hours or your credit card will be charged €150. That's reduced to €35 if the bike is stolen, provided you report it to the police and Velóh within 24 hours.

LONG-TERM HIRE Vélo en Ville (☎47 96 23 83; 8 Bisserwée; half-/full day €12.50/20; ⌚8am-8pm Mon-Fri, 10am-8pm Sat & Sun Apr-Sep, 7am-3pm Mon-Fri Oct-Mar) Mountain bikes and free cycle-route pamphlets are available here. If under 26 you get a 20% discount.

Bus

The main bus stand is at Place Hamilius (close to Place d'Armes) for buses going to the Old Town and Gare Centrale, which is the train station. Tickets are sold within Gare Centrale at **Mobiliteitszentral** (☎24 65 24 65; www.mobiliteit.lu; ⌚6am-9pm Mon-Fri, 8am-6pm Sat & Sun), which also has detailed route maps and timetables. Buses usually operate from 5.30am to 10pm. On Friday and Saturday nights there's a limited late-night bus service to 3.30am.

Car & Motorcycle

Much of the Old Town is pedestrianised. The cheapest open-air car park is Glacis, 800m northwest of Place d'Armes. Street parking is free after 6pm and on Sundays. **Autolux** (☎22 11 81; www.autolux.lu; 33 Blvd Prince Henri; ⌚8am-6pm Mon-Fri) rents cars.

AROUND LUXEMBOURG

Hop, skip or jump into the grand duchy: everywhere is easily accessible from the capital. Or, indeed, vice versa.

Vianden

POP 1600

Palace, citadel or fortified cathedral? At first glance it's hard to tell just what it is that towers so grandly above magical little Vianden. In fact it's a vast slate-roofed castle complex whose impregnable stone walls glow golden in the evening's floodlights to create one of Luxembourg's most photogenic scenes. Vianden's appealing Old Town is essentially one road, the cobbled Grand Rue, which rises 700m from the riverside **tourist office** (☎83 42 57 1; www.vianden-info.lu; 1a Rue du Vieux Marché; ⌚8am-noon & 1-5pm Mon-Fri, 10am-2pm some weekends) to the castle gates. Vianden can get over-crowded on summer weekends, but get up early and you'll have the delightful place largely to yourself.

Sights

Château CASTLE

(www.castle-vianden.lu; adult/concession/LC €6/4.50/free; ⏰10am-4pm Nov-Feb, to 5pm Mar & Oct, to 6pm Apr-Sep) The famed castle is entered through a modern exhibition hall, a portcullis gate then takes you upstairs into a vaulted hall full of pikes and armour. The crypt displays plans and models of the castle's various incarnations while some later rooms are furnished in medieval style, including the kitchen and hall 13 with its great fireplace. The 'little palace' shows photos of celebrity visitors, from Mikhail Gorbachev to John Malkovich.

Télésiège CHAIRLIFT

(39 Rue du Sanatorium; one-way/return/LC €2.75/4.50/free; ⏰10am-6pm Easter-Oct, closed some Mon) The chairlift whisks you up a forested hill from the lower bank of the river at the end of Rue Victor Hugo. You arrive at an open-air cafe from which it's a 20-minute woodland stroll down to the castle entrance, or 15 minutes to **Indian Forest Adventure Park** (☎0691 901223; www.vianden-info.lu; admission €15; ⏰Apr-Oct, reservations required) with rope courses, zip lines (€5 extra), forest hikes and climbable trees.

Maison de Victor Hugo HISTORIC HOUSE

(www.victor-hugo.lu; 37 Rue de la Gare; adult/LC €4/free; ⏰11am-5pm Easter & Jul-Aug, weekends only May-Jun & Sep-Oct) Home to French author Victor Hugo for three months in 1871, this little house offers some of the very best castle views, even if you're not excited by the writer's manuscripts and sketches.

Sleeping & Eating

There's ample choice along both Grand Rue and the river banks.

Auberge Aal Veinen HOTEL €

(☎83 43 68; www.hotel-aal-veinen.lu; 114 Grand Rue; s/d €60/80; ⏰closed mid-Dec–mid-Jan; 📶) The eight newly refitted guest rooms are remarkably stylish and well appointed considering they've been inserted into an ultra-quaint barrage of ancient beamwork. The ground-floor restaurant (meals €8 to €27, closed Tuesdays) has a cosy medieval feel and is partly built into the living rock.

Hôtel Heintz HISTORIC INN €€

(☎83 41 55; www.hotel-heintz.lu; 55 Grand Rue; s €52-77, d €62-92; ⏰closed Oct-Easter) Grandfather clocks and historical knick-knacks decorate landings between fine old staircases, while the rear balconies are draped with creeper. Updated guest rooms mix modern art with older furniture. The restaurant is open from 6pm to 7.30pm.

Auberge de Jeunesse HOSTEL €

(☎83 41 77; www.youthhostels.lu; 3 Montée du Château; members dm/s/d €16.20/28.20/42.40, nonmembers €19.20/31.30/48.40; 🚭📶) Located within an archetypal shutter-fronted Vianden mansion close to the château, this standard, well-kept hostel is up near the castle gates. Before lugging your bags up the hill be aware that reception is closed between 10am and 5pm.

Camping de l'Our CAMPING GROUND €

(☎83 45 05; www.camping-our-vianden.lu; 3 Route de Bettel; per adult/child/campsite €5/2.50/5; ⏰Easter-Oct) A quality, 'Category 1' camping ground on the river bank, 1.4km southeast of central Vianden.

Lajolla Lounge CAFE, RESTAURANT €€

(www.lajollalounge.com; 35 Rue de la Gare; snacks €7-12, mains €12-24; ⏰10am-10pm) Behind the Maison de Victor Hugo, the open-air riverside terrace has great castle views, while inside it is unusually fashion-conscious for rural Luxembourg.

Getting There & Away

If arriving by bus hop out at the convenient Vianden–Bréck stop, which is right outside the tourist office. Stay on the bus, if you're heading to Camping de l'Our.

Diekirch Bus 570 (18 minutes) runs twice hourly weekdays; less frequent at weekends.

Clervaux Bus 663 (32 minutes) picks up at 9.16am, 10.46am, 2.46pm and 6.16pm daily.

Echternach

POP 5100

Useful as a hiking base, the ancient town of Echternach has some modest Roman remains, a pretty central square and a gigantic **basilica** (⏰9.30am-6.30pm) that was rebuilt in sombre neo-Romanesque style after suffering merciless WWII bombing. This is Luxembourg's most important religious building, its crypt housing the sacred relics of its founder, the Northumbrian missionary St-Willibrord (AD 658–739). Between

WORTH A TRIP

CASTLES & CASTLE VILLAGES

Vianden is by no means the only town in rural Luxembourg to sport an impressive castle. Some other classics:

Bourscheid

Superbly situated on a lonely rocky bluff amid forested hills, a dreamy array of turrets and towers makes the **Château de Bourscheid** (www.bourscheid.lu; adult/senior/LC €5/4/free; ⏲9.30am-5.30pm Apr–mid-Oct, 11am-4pm mid-Oct–Mar) Luxembourg's most evocative castle. Inside, the site is more ruined than the walls suggest, but from its squat 12th-century keep, classic turret-framed views survey the river bend below. Admission includes a remarkably extensive 90-minute audio tour. The nearest bus stop (on route 545 from Ettelbrück, 8km) is in Bourscheid village. From there the castle is a steep 1.8km descent to the southwest. You'll pass Camping Bourscheid where it's worth following signs between the caravans to find a public-access viewpoint for fabulous views down on the castle. After visiting the castle you could descend another 2km to the N27 road and return to Ettelbrück on bus 550.

Larochette

Two modest rivers cut a dramatic gash in a woodland plateau and little **Larochette** (www.larochette.eu) fell in. Not so its dramatic medieval **castle ruins** (☎83 74 97; Route de Mersch; adult/child €2.50/1; ⏲10am-6pm Easter-Oct), which perch high above on a cliff top accessed by steep stairway paths or by a much gentler 2km double-back road (start off towards Mersch). The village has several hotels and an HI hostel. Hourly bus 100 stops in Larochette between Diekirch (20 minutes) and Luxembourg City (one hour).

Beaufort

Across a pretty, part-wooded valley behind **Beaufort Village** (www.beaufort.lu) are the imposing five-storey ruins of a medieval stone **fortress** (adult/concession/LC €3/2/free, audioguide €3; ⏲9am-6pm Apr-Oct). It lacks Bourscheid's romantic turrets and was bombed during WWII, but there's plenty left to climb. From the Beaufort–Härewiss bus stop it's a 10-minute stroll away. Bus 107 runs to Luxembourg City (1¼ hours), 502 to Diekirch (25 minutes) and 414 to Echternach (18 minutes) or Larochette (25 minutes).

Clervaux

At the centre of this pleasant rural **town** (www.tourisme-clervaux.lu), Clervaux's distinctive, whitewashed castle is a total reconstruction of a 12th-century original that was razed in WWII. It contains the town hall, two minor museums and the world famous **Family of Man exhibition** (www.family-of-man.public.lu), which is due to re-open in 2012. It's a collection of 273 black-and-white mid-20th-century photos from 68 countries, interspersed with wise sayings and quotations. The station, 1km north, has hourly trains to Luxembourg City (52 minutes) via Ettelbrück (26 minutes) and every two hours to Liège (Belgium, 1½ hours). For Vianden (45 minutes) bus 663 departs at 8.30am, 10am, 2pm and 5pm.

Esch-sur-Sûre

Its AD 927 castle tower is very modest, but tiny **Esch-sur-Sûre** (www.petitbourg.lu) is one of Luxembourg's prettiest villages, harmoniously curled upon a knoll in an emerald green loop of the Sûre River. **Hôtel-Restaurant de la Sûre** (☎83 91 10; www.hotel-de-la-sure.lu; 1 Rue du Pont; s/d from €46/66) occupies some of the village's historic houses. Bus 535 from Ettelbrück (40 minutes) runs hourly on weekdays and five times on Sundays.

Wiltz

By Luxembourg standards, Wiltz is a relatively large and slightly banal town, but the grounds of its stately **château** come to life throughout July during the impressive **Wiltz Festival** (www.festivalwiltz.online.lu). Trains take an hour from Luxembourg City.

MÜLLERTHAL TRAILS

West of Echternach, well-signposted **forest trails** (www.mullerthal-trail.lu) take hikers through shoulder-wide microgorges, across trickling streams with mossy banks and past distinctively eroded sandstone formations. This is hardly Bryce Canyon but quaintness trumps grandeur and one almost expects to meet Asterix and his band around the next rocky pinnacle. If you're driving, there are handily accessible tasters right beside the main road either side of Berdorf village (itself utterly uninteresting). Alternatively, try hiking the **E1** (11.7km, four hours), a well-marked circular path that starts up Rue Charly from Echternach bus station and winds through the intriguing **Gorge du Loup**. If this whets your appetite, other Müllerthal trails offer longer alternatives exploring Luxembourg's misleadingly named 'Little Switzerland' – a patchwork of forests and grassy fields (don't imagine even the vaguest hint of an Alpine peak).

the basilica's main door and the **tourist office** (☎72 02 30; wwww.echternach-tourist.lu; Parvis de la Basilique; ⏲9.30am-5.30pm Mon-Fri Sep-Jun, daily Jul & Aug), cross a courtyard flanked by reconstructed 18th-century abbey buildings to find the poorly marked entrance to **Musée de l'Abbaye** (adult/LC €3/free; ⏲10am-noon & 2-6pm). Here, amid ancient codex copies in vaulted subterranean cellars that once housed Europe's foremost medieval scriptorium, you can watch a video about Echternach's unique annual dancing procession, **Sprinprozession**, which is under consideration for Unesco World Heritage status. It is held on the Tuesday after Whitsun, which is the seventh Sunday after Easter.

Hotels and fair-priced street cafes line Rue de la Gare, the pedestrianised street that links the bus station to the main square, Place du Marché, where there's further choice. **Hostellerie de la Basilique** (☎72 94 83; www.hotel-basilique.lu; 7 Place du Marché; s/d/tr €94/121.50/166; ⏲Easter–mid-Nov; ❄@📶) is Echternach's best address, offering 14 tidy rooms with stone-tiled floors and monogrammed linens.

Echternach's modern **HI hostel** (Auberge de Jeunesse; ☎72 01 58; echternach@youthhostels.lu; dm/s €18.20/29, nonmembers €21.20/32; ⏲reception 8am-10am & 5-10pm; P🚭📶) is set in a lakeside country park, offers dinner for €9, and features a popular **climbing wall** (guest/nonguest €3.50/6; ⏲7-10pm Tue, Wed, Fri & Sat). From Echternach's main square head 800m southwest to the fire station (facing the Q8 petrol station), or get off Luxembourg City–Echternach route 110 at bus stop Centre de Secours, then head 1.2km southeast in the direction of Rodenhof (Roudenhaff).

ℹ Getting There & Around

To get around you can hire a mountain bike for a half-/full day for €8/15 from the youth hostel. Bus services to/from Echternach:

Echternach–Luxembourg City Bus 110 (50 minutes, hourly) direct. Bus 111 (55 minutes, hourly) via Berdorf.

Echternach–Diekirch Bus 500 (35 minutes, hourly) direct, or take bus 414 and change in Beaufort.

Diekirch & Ettelbrück

Of many museums commemorating 1944's Battle of the Ardennes, Diekirch's **Musée National d'Histoire Militaire** (www.mnhm.lu; 110 Rue Bamertal; adult/LC €5/free, WWII veterans free; ⏲10am-6pm Apr–mid-Nov, 2-6pm mid-Nov–Mar) is Luxembourg's most comprehensive and visual. Packed full of WWII weaponry, vehicles and memorabilia, numerous well-executed mannequin scenes illustrate the suffering and hardships of that far-from-festive snowy Christmas. It's 10 minutes' walk north of Diekirch's train station. Twice-hourly trains take 40 minutes to Luxembourg City via Ettelbrück (10 minutes), a useful transport hub with bus connections to Bastogne (Belgium) for other major WWII sites.

Moselle Valley

Welcome to wine country. Smothering the Moselle River's steeply rising banks are the neatly clipped vineyards that produce Luxembourg's balanced rieslings, fruity rivaners and excellent crémants (sparkling *méthode traditionelle* wines). The region's various wine towns aren't architecturally memorable but **Ahn** and hillside **Wellenstein** are gently picturesque villages, while bigger **Remich** offers one-hour summer **river cruises** (www.navitours.lu; adult/child/dog €7/4/1). About 1.5km north of Remich's bus terminal, **St-Martin** (☎23 69 97 74; www.cavesstmartin.lu; 53 Route de Stadtbredimus) has wine caves – cool, damp tunnels hewn deep into the rock face. To join their hour-long **tours** (€3.50; ⏰typically 11am, 1pm & 3pm Tue-Sun Apr-Oct) you'll generally need to reserve a spot. In contrast, bookings are unnecessary if you continue to the grand **Caves Bernard-Massard** (☎75 05 45-1; www.bernard-massard.lu; 8 Rue du Pont; ⏰9.30am-6pm Apr-Oct) in central **Grevenmacher** where frequent 20-minute **winery tours** (adult/child from €4/2.50) are multilingual, spiced with humour and culminate in a genteel sampling cafe. Use the Enner der Bréck stop on bus routes 130 or 450.

ℹ Getting There & Away

Luxembourg City–Remich Bus 175 (45 minutes, half-hourly, hourly on Sundays).

Remich–Grevenmacher Bus 450 (30 minutes, hourly except Sundays) Follows the 'wine route'.

Grevenmacher–Luxembourg City (Rue Heine) Bus 130 (55 minutes, up to twice hourly).

Grevenmacher–Echternach Bus 485 (40 minutes hourly, six times on Sundays). Passes Wasserbillig train station (six minutes from Grevenmacher) on the Luxembourg City–Trier–Cologne line.

UNDERSTAND LUXEMBOURG

History

In 963 Count Sigefroi (or Siegfried) of Ardennes built a castle on a promontory in the forested heart of Western Europe – the foundations of what would one day become Luxembourg City. Besieged and rebuilt time and time again, it eventually grew to become one of Europe's strongest fortresses, earning the nickname 'Gibraltar of the North'.

From 1354 the region was an independent duchy but it was conquered by Burgundy in 1443 then later incorporated (like proto-Belgium) into the Hapsburg Empire. Luxembourg City's fortifications proved particularly impressive during the French revolutionary wars, although not quite good enough to survive a seven-month French siege in 1792–93. After Waterloo (1815) Luxembourg was declared a grand duchy under the Dutch king. Its status caused considerable haggling when Belgium declared independence from the Netherlands in 1830, trying to take Luxembourg with it. As a compromise the grand duchy was eventually split (1839) with strategically important Luxembourg City remaining as capital of the Dutch part, albeit garrisoned by Prussian troops. During the 1860s this Prussian presence became a serious bone of contention between France and Germany. In 1867, to defuse a possible war, Luxembourg was declared neutral and had the bulk of its historic fortifications dismantled.

When the Dutch King William III died in 1890 his daughter Wilhelmina became queen of the Netherlands. However, Luxembourg's rules of succession demanded a male ruler. This odd quirk resulted in Luxembourg's previously nominal independence becoming an actual reality.

Germany occupied Luxembourg during both world wars. Liberated in September 1944, it was used at the end of WWII as one of the Allied command centres for the Battle of the Ardennes (see p921). After the war, the government diversified the economy, enabling the little country to ride out a depression in the iron and steel industries during the 1970s and to become a noted financial centre and tax haven. Luxembourg also became home to several key EU institutions. The country enjoys affluence and stability and, despite the global economic downturn, it has one of Europe's healthiest economies.

The grand duchy's royal family is experiencing a similar high. Grand Duke Henri and Grand Duchess Maria Teresa, a Cuban-born commoner who Henri met at university, have further invigorated the role of the ducal family since coming to the throne in 2000.

People

Luxembourgers' national motto, *Mir wëlle bleiwe wat mir sin* (We want to remain what we are), sums up their independent spirit. Some 87% of the population is Roman Catholic, with the church influencing many facets of life, including politics, the media and education. Useful phrases in Lëtzebuergesch (Luxembourg's Germanic language) include *moien* (hello), *äddi* (goodbye), *merci* (thanks). However, with more than a third of Luxembourg's population immigrants (predominantly Portuguese,

Italians and francophones), French is more commonly used as a first language between strangers, while German is also an official language. English is widely understood.

Arts

Luxembourg-born Edward Steichen (1879–1973) was a pioneer of American photography, famed for his 1920s *Vanity Fair* celebrity portraits and later for assembling the Family of Man exhibition, which toured the world before ending up in Clervaux (p920).

When it comes to film, see WWII history through the eyes of Luxembourg's former Grand Duchess in the documentary film, *Charlotte: A Royal at War* (*Lèif Lëtzebuerger*), available on DVD.

In the early 1960s, before pirate radio, Radio Luxembourg was at the forefront of bringing rock music to Europe's youth. Luxembourg has won the Eurovision Song Contest a remarkable five times, though always thanks to foreign performers.

Food & Drink

See p910 for local specialities. Germanic style foods tend to dominate local meals but Luxembourg City offers considerable culinary diversity and ample solace for vegetarians. On weekdays, the lunchtime *plat du jour* (dish of the day) or *menu du jour* (multicourse set menu) are generally great value. Smoking is banned in restaurants (except on terraces) and at lunchtime in cafes.

Environment

Luxembourg is diminutive, 57km by 84km long, divided between the forested Ardennes highlands to the north, and agro-industrial country to the south. About a third of Luxembourg is covered by forests that are home to wild boar, fox and deer.

SURVIVAL GUIDE

Directory A–Z

Accommodation

Tourist offices provide free accommodation brochures and can make bookings for you. The following accommodation types are available:

B&Bs Rare, but farmstays and holiday house rentals are plentiful for those staying awhile (for rentals see, www.gites.lu).

Camping grounds Abundant in the central and northern regions. Officially graded in three categories, but most are Category 1, the best and most expensive.

Hostels Dorm beds in the 10 HI-affiliated hostels (www.youthhostels.lu) cost from around €16 to €20, including breakfast and sheets. HI nonmembers pay €3 per night extra.

Hotels Budget hotels are rare but Luxembourg City's business hotels offer weekend and summer discounts, especially online.

PRICE RANGES

Price ranges are for a midweek double room with ensuite bathroom (or dormitory in hostels) unless otherwise mentioned.

€€€ more than €200

€€ €70 to €200

€ less than €70

Business Hours

Typical opening times:

Banks 8.30am to 4.30pm Monday to Friday, 8.30am to noon Saturday

Post offices 9am to 5pm Monday to Friday, 9am to noon Saturday

Shops 9am to 6pm Monday to Saturday, some close for lunch

Restaurants noon to 2pm and 7pm to 10.30pm

Pubs & bars 11am to 1am

Nightclubs 10pm to 3am

Embassies & Consulates

The nearest Australian, Canadian and New Zealand embassies are located in Belgium.

Australia (www.eu.mission.gov.au)

Canada (www.belgium.gc.ca)

New Zealand (www.nzembassy.com)

UK (☎22 98 64; http://ukinluxembourg.fco.gov.uk; 5 Blvd Joseph II, Luxembourg City)

USA (☎46 01 23; http://luxembourg.usembassy.gov; 22 Blvd Emmanuel Servais, Luxembourg City)

Food

Prices for typical mains are given in our reviews, which use the following price-indicator symbols:

€€€ more than €20

€€ €10 to €20

€ less than €10

Money

ATMs Common in towns but not in villages. Despite all the banks, relatively few offer exchange.

Tipping Not obligatory. Service and taxes are included in all hotel and restaurant prices.

Public Holidays

School holidays are from mid-July to September, the first week of November, two weeks at Christmas, a week at Carnival, two weeks at Easter and a week at Ascension.

New Year's Day 1 January

Easter Monday March/April

May Day 1 May

Ascension Day Fortieth day after Easter

Whit Monday Seventh Monday after Easter

National Day 23 June

Assumption 15 August

All Saints' Day 1 November

Christmas Day 25 December

Telephone

» No area codes are used.

» Call ☎12410 for an international operator.

» Collect calls ☎80 02 00.

Visas

For visa and embassy information see www.mae.lu.

Getting There & Away

Air

From **Luxembourg airport** (LUX; www.luxairport.lu), 6km east of the capital, national carrier **Luxair** (www.luxair.lu) flies to various European destinations including London, Paris and Frankfurt. **Air France** (www.airfrance.lu), **British Airways** (www.ba.com), **KLM** (www.klm.lu), **Lufthansa** (www.lufthansa.lu), **SAS** (www.flysas.com) and **TAP Portugal** (www.flytap.be) also have services.

For budget airline flights take **Flibco** (www.flibco.com) buses from Luxembourg City's Gare Centrale to Germany's Frankfurt-Hahn airport (advance/last-minute purchase €5/17, two hours via Trier, hourly) or Belgium's Charleroi airport (advance/last-minute purchase €5/22, 2½ hours via Arlon).

Car

» Fuel prices are the lowest in Western Europe, so fill her up.

» International driving licences are usually unnecessary; your home licence will suffice.

» Drive on right-hand side.

» Blood-alcohol limit is 0.05%.

» Motorway speed limit is 130km/h.

Bus

Eurolines (☎in the Netherlands 20-560 87 88; www.eurolines.nl) operates buses between Luxembourg City and Amsterdam (nine hours, promo/flexible €20/39) on Mondays, Wednesdays and Fridays but you'll need to make the mandatory prebooking online or by calling the Netherlands.

Local cross-border buses link Bastogne (Belgium) with Ettelbrück and Luxembourg City with Trier and Saarlouis (both in Germany).

Train

International train services from Luxembourg City include the following:

Brussels (€34.60, three hours, eighteen daily)

Koblenz (€37.40 direct, €34.40 changing in Trier, 2¼ hours, hourly)

Paris (€49 to €94.40, 2¼ hours, five daily) TGV (France's high speed train service) with compulsory reservation.

Trier (fast/slow €18.40/15.40, 41/49 minutes, approximately hourly)

Getting Around

Bicycle & Walking

Cycle lanes wind along the Sûre River between Echternach and Diekirch, and along much of the Moselle River. Bikes can be taken aboard trains for free.

Of Luxembourg's 5000km of marked **walking paths** (www.walking.lu), those around Echternach are the most interesting. Tracks marked by white triangles connect the HI hostels. Tourist offices stock regional walking maps.

Train & Bus

From the time you date-stamp it, a €1.50 *kuurzzäitbilljee* (short-time ticket; *billet courte durée*) ticket is valid for two hours for any combination of bus or train within Luxembourg, except to/from border-crossing points. For €4 a *dagesbilljee* (day ticket; *billet longue durée*) is valid all day and until 8am the next morning. If you pay once aboard a train there might be a €1.50 supplement. Upgrading a *kuurzzäitbilljee*/*dagesbilljee* to first class costs just €0.80/2 extra.

The great-value Luxembourg Card (p912) includes unlimited travel plus numerous sights.

Websites www.autobus.lu and www.cfl.lu have timetable information.

The Netherlands

Includes »

Why Go?

Great Dutch artists Rembrandt, Vermeer and Van Gogh have spanned the centuries, and touring Holland you'll see why. Discover clichés such as tulips and windmills, or stroll canals in the midst of 17th-century splendour in beautiful small towns such as Leiden and Delft. Of course, enticing Amsterdam's phenomenal and diverse nightlife is world-famous, from throbbing clubs to quaint brown cafes.

The locals live on bicycles and you can too. Almost every train station has a shop to rent a bike – you'll soon be off on the ubiquitous bike paths, wherever your mood takes you (for more, see p971).

Finally there's the Dutch themselves. Warm, friendly and funny, you'll have a hard time being alone in a cafe as someone will soon strike up a conversation, and usually in English. Revel in Amsterdam, don't miss exquisite Maastricht or pulsing Rotterdam and pick a passel of small towns to add contrast. It's a very big small country.

Best Places to Eat

» Blauw (p958)
» De Ballentent (p955)
» De Haerlemsche Vlaamse (p943)
» Mangerie De Jonge Koekop (p945)
» Muller (p961)

Best Places to Stay

» Hotel Holla (p965)
» Hotel New York (p954)
» Miauw Suites (p935)

When to Go

Amsterdam

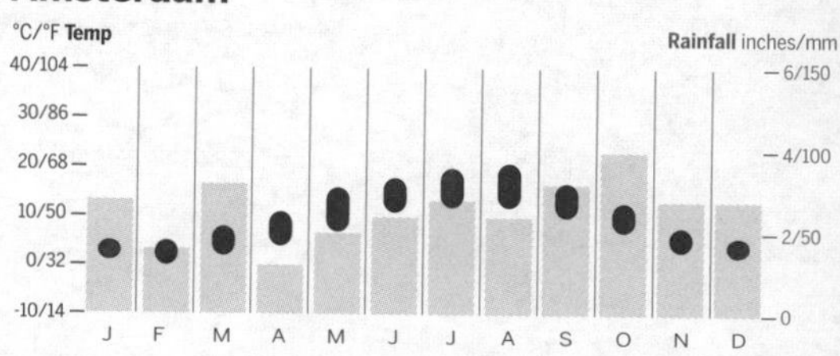

March–May Holland explodes in colour as billions of bulbs bloom.

July Mild summer temps and lots of daylight keep you outside cycling and drinking.

December–February The Dutch passion for ice skating is on display on frozen canals nationwide.

Connections

Train connections to neighbouring countries are good. Amsterdam is linked to Cologne (2½ hours) and Brussels (1¾ hours on the new Thalys/Fyra high-speed line), where you can connect with Eurostar to London. Maastricht is right on the Belgian and German borders; connections to Cologne and Brussels take 1½ hours. It would be easy to put together a circle itinerary that includes the wines of the Moselle Valley in Germany and the beers of Belgium.

ITINERARIES

One Week

Spend three days canal exploring, museum hopping and cafe swooping in Amsterdam. Work your way through the ancient towns of the Randstad and the modern vibe of Rotterdam and save a day for the grandeur of Maastricht.

Two Weeks

Allow four days for Amsterdam's many delights, plus a day trip to the old towns of the north, such as Edam, and a day or two even further north on Texel. Then add a day each at beautiful Delft, regal Hague, cute Utrecht, Rotterdam, and the monumental Delta Project. Finish off with two days in Maastricht.

Essential Food & Drink

» **Vlaamse frites** The iconic French fries smothered in mayonnaise or myriad other gooey sauces.

» **Beer** While the big names like Heineken are ubiquitous, small brewers like Gulpen, Haarlem's Jopen, Bavaria, Drie Ringen, Leeuw and Utrecht are the best.

» **Gouda** The tastiest varieties have strong, complex flavours and are best enjoyed with a bottle of wine or two. Try some *oud* (old) Gouda, hard and rich in flavour and a popular bar snack with mustard. *Oud Amsterdammer* is a real delight, deep orange and crumbly with white crystals of ripeness.

» **Indonesian** The most famous dish is *rijsttafel* (rice table): an array of spicy savoury dishes such as braised beef, pork satay and ribs served with white rice.

» **Erwtensoep** Pea soup rich with onions, carrots, smoked sausage and bacon. Ideally a spoon stuck upright in the pot should remain standing (not served in summer).

» **Kroketten** Croquettes are dough balls with various fillings that are crumbed and deep-fried; the variety called *bitterballen* are a popular brown cafe snack served with mustard.

AT A GLANCE

» **Currency** euro (€)

» **Language** Dutch, English widespread

» **Money** ATMs common, cash preferred for small purchases

» **Visas** Schengen rules apply

Fast Facts

» **Area** 41,526 sq km

» **Population** 16.5 million

» **Capital** Amsterdam

» **Telephone** country code ☎31; international access code ☎00

» **Emergency** ☎112

Exchange Rates

Australia	A$1	€0.74
Canada	C$1	€0.74
Japan	¥100	€0.87
New Zealand	NZ$1	€0.56
UK	UK£1	€1.16
USA	US$1	€0.67

Set Your Budget

» **Midrange hotel double room** €80–150

» **Two-course dinner** €12

» **Heineken** €2.50

» **Coffee-shop joint** €3

» **Bicycle hire** €10 per day

Resources

» **Lonely Planet** (www.lonelyplanet.com/the-netherlands/amsterdam)

» **Netherlands Board of Tourism** (www.holland.com)

» **Windmill Database** (www.molendatabase.nl)

Netherlands Highlights

❶ Stroll canals and soak up one of Europe's most beautiful, vibrant and offbeat old cities, **Amsterdam** (p929)

❷ Immerse yourself in the urban vibe and architecture of **Rotterdam** (p951)

❸ Lose yourself amid the ancient walls and cosmopolitan shops of **Maastricht** (p963)

❹ Take a day trip to evocative **Delft** (p948), where Vermeer found his inspiration

❺ Wander the beautiful tree-lined boulevards and classy museums of **Den Haag** (p945)

❻ Find inspiration at **Leiden** (p943), home of Rembrandt, and the explosion of tulips at nearby Keukenhof Gardens

❼ Go **bike crazy** (p971) across the Netherlands, following dikes along shimmering canals on the world's best network of bike lanes and long-distance routes

❽ Lose a few hours drinking beer in the atmopheric confines of a convivial, uniquely Dutch **brown cafe** (p969)

AMSTERDAM

☎020 / POP 747,000

If Amsterdam were a staid place it would still be one of Europe's most beautiful and historic cities, right up there with Venice and Paris. But add in the qualities that make it Amsterdam – the funky and mellow bars, brown cafes full of characters, pervasive irreverence, whiffs of pot and an open-air marketplace for sleaze and sex – and you have a literally intoxicating mix.

Amsterdam's been a liberal place ever since the Netherlands' Golden Age, when it led European art and trade. Centuries later, in the 1960s, it again led the pack – this time in the principles of tolerance, with broad-minded views on drugs and same-sex relationships taking centre stage.

Wander the 17th-century streets, tour the iconic canals, stop off to enjoy a masterpiece, discover a funky shop and choose from food around the world. Walk or ride a bike around the concentric rings of the centre then explore the historic lanes of the Jordaan district or the Plantage and bask in the many worlds-within-worlds, where nothing ever seems the same twice.

Sights & Activities

Amsterdam is compact, and you can roam the city on foot. Hop on the occasional tram to rest your feet – or stop off in a cafe.

CITY CENTRE

The not-overly-impressive Royal Palace and the square that puts the 'Dam' in Amsterdam anchor Amsterdam's oldest quarter. This is the busiest part of town for tourists: many leave the train station and head straight for the coffee shops and the Red Light District.

Nieuwe Kerk CHURCH

(New Church; Map p930; www.nieuwekerk.nl; Dam; adult/child €5/free; ⌚10am-5pm) Just north of the Royal Palace, the late-Gothic basilica Nieuwe Kerk is the coronation church of Dutch royalty, with a carved oak chancel, a bronze choir screen, a massive, gilded organ and stained-glass windows. It's now used for exhibitions and organ concerts.

Oude Kerk CHURCH

(Old Church; Map p930; www.oudekerk.nl; Oudekerksplein 23; adult/child €7/1; ⌚11am-5pm Mon-Sat, 1-5pm Sun) Amsterdam's oldest building, the 14th-century Oude Kerk was built to honour the city's patron saint, St Nicholas. Inside there's a dramatic Müller organ, gilded oak vaults and impressive stained-glass windows. Watch for the **World Press Photo show** (www.worldpressphoto.org) in late April.

Red Light District DISTRICT

The Red Light District (Map p930) retains the power to make your jaw go limp, even if near-naked prostitutes propositioning passers-by from black-lit windows is the oldest Amsterdam cliché. Note that even in the dark heart of the district there are charming shops and cafes where the only thing that vibrates is your mobile phone. Despite the neon-lit sleaze, the district is tightly regulated and reasonably safe for strolling. The city government has been steadfastly reducing the number of licensed windows.

If you're ready to role play, **Funny Photoshoot** (Map p930; ☎772 4167; www.funnyphotoshoot.nl; Sint Jansstraat; from €25; ⌚by appointment) allows you to dress up (or down) and pose in a re-created prostitute's window.

Amsterdam Museum MUSEUM

(Map p930; www.ahm.nl; Kalverstraat 92; adult/child €10/5; ⌚10am-5pm Mon-Fri, 11am-5pm Sat & Sun) Housed in the old civic orphanage, the Amsterdam Museum takes you through all the fascinating twists and turns of Amsterdam's convoluted history. Look for a recreation of the original Café het Mandje, a touchstone in the gay-rights movement.

Begijnhof HISTORIC COMPLEX

(Map p930; www.begijnhofamsterdam.nl; admission free; ⌚8am-5pm) For a polar opposite, duck into the Begijnhof, an enclosed former convent from the early 14th century. It's a surreal oasis of peace, with tiny houses and postage-stamp gardens around a well-kept courtyard. The Beguines were a Catholic order of unmarried or widowed women who cared for the elderly and lived a religious life

FREE THRILLS

Much of the allure of Amsterdam can be experienced on foot and for free.

» The **Red Light District** can cost you an arm and a leg (or more) but voyeurism is free.

» Regain your inner virtue walking through the **Begijnhof**.

» Find natural peace in the green expanses of **Vondelpark** (p934).

» **Walk the canals** and decide which old gabled house leans the most.

Central Amsterdam

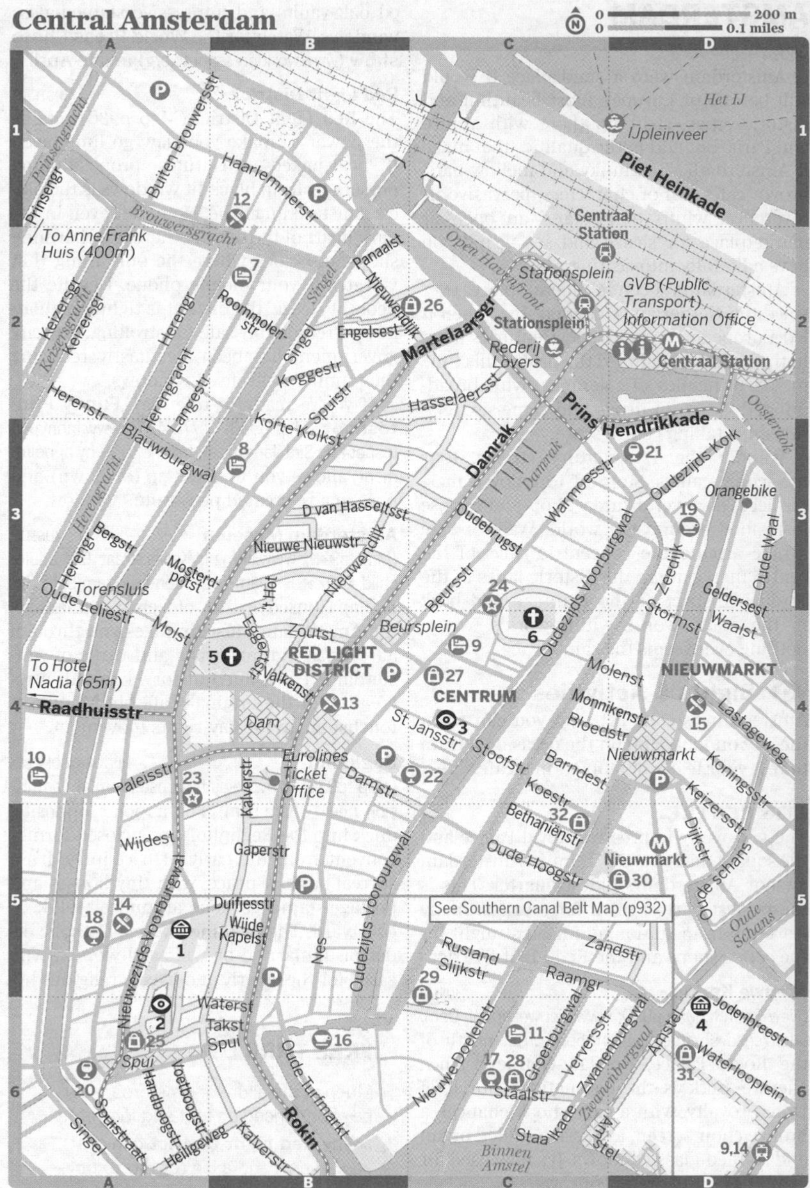

without taking monastic vows. The last died in the 1970s.

CANAL BELT

Created in the 17th century as an upscale neighbourhood, the Canal Belt, especially in the west and south, remains Amsterdam's top district. Wandering here amid architectural treasures and their reflections on the narrow waters of the Prinsengracht, Keizersgracht and Herengracht can cause days to vanish quicker than some of Amsterdam's

Central Amsterdam

Sights

1	Amsterdam Museum	A5
2	Begijnhof	A6
3	Funny Photoshoot	C4
4	Museum Het Rembrandthuis	D6
5	Nieuwe Kerk	B4
6	Oude Kerk	C4

Sleeping

7	Chic & Basic Amsterdam	B2
8	Hotel Brouwer	B3
9	Hotel/Hostel Winston	C4
10	Miauw Suites	A4
11	Stadsdoelen Youth Hostel	C6

Eating

12	De Belhamel	B1
13	De Bijenkorf	B4
14	Lucius	A5
15	Nam Kee	D4

Drinking

16	Crea	B6
17	Doelen	C6
18	Gollem	A5
19	Hofje van Wijs	D3
20	Hoppe	A6
21	In 't Aepjen	D3
22	Proeflokaal Fockink	C4

Entertainment

23	Abraxas	A4
24	Argos	C3

Shopping

25	American Book Center	A6
26	Chills & Thrills	C2
27	Condomerie	C4
28	Juggle	C6
29	Oudemanhuis Book Market	C5
30	t Klompenhuisje	D5
31	Waterlooplein Flea Market	D6
32	Webers	C5

more lurid pursuits. No two buildings are alike, yet they combine in ever-changing, ever-pleasing harmony.

TOP CHOICE **Anne Frank Huis** HISTORIC BUILDING
(off Map p932; Anne Frank House; 556 71 00; www.annefrank.org; Prinsengracht 267; adult/child €8.50/free; 9am-9pm mid-Mar–mid-Sep, to 7pm other times) The Anne Frank Huis, where Anne wrote her famous diary, lures almost a million visitors annually with its secret annexe, reconstruction of Anne's melancholy bedroom, and her actual diary, with its sunnily optimistic writing tempered by quiet despair. Look for the photo of Peter Schiff, her 'one true love'. Try going in the early morning or evening when crowds are lightest; book online to avoid long queues.

FOAM ART MUSEUM
(Map p932; Fotografie Museum Amsterdam; www.foam.nl; Keizersgracht 609; adult/child €8/free; 10am-6pm Sat-Wed, to 9pm Thu & Fri) FOAM is an airy gallery devoted to painting with light. Two storeys of changing exhibitions feature world-renowned photographers such as Sir Cecil Beaton, Annie Leibovitz and Henri Cartier-Bresson.

MUSEUMPLEIN

The genteel streets are a bit bland but what you'll find inside Amsterdam's big three museums will knock your wooden shoes off (if they can ever get them all open again, that is).

TOP CHOICE **Van Gogh Museum** ART MUSEUM
(Map p932; www.vangoghmuseum.nl; Paulus Potterstraat 7; adult/child €14/free; 10am-6pm Sat-Thu, to 10pm Fri) This outstanding museum houses the world's largest Van Gogh collection. Trace the artist's life from his tentative start though to his Japanese phase, and on to the black cloud that descended over him and his work. There's also works by contemporaries Gauguin, Toulouse-Lautrec, Monet and Bernard.

Rijksmuseum MUSEUM
(Map p932; www.rijksmuseum.nl; Stadhouderskade 42; adult/child €12.50/free; 9am-6pm) The nation's most revered museum boasts a collection valued in the billions, but until renovations finish in 2013 (or later) there are only a few masterpieces displayed, including a couple of Vermeers and the crowning glory, Rembrandt's *Nightwatch* (1650). On most days crowds make the entire experience unpleasant. The rooms are tight and you'll find the Louvre's *Mona Lisa* mobs snapping pics with abandon. Save one queue by buying your ticket online.

Stedelijk Museum ART MUSEUM
(Map p932; www.stedelijkindestad.nl; Museumplein) When open, the Stedelijk Museum features around 100,000 pieces, including Impressionist works from Monet, Picasso and Chagall; sculptures from Rodin and Moore; De Stijl landmarks by Mondrian; and pop art from Warhol and Lichtenstein. Renovations and a new other-worldly looking addition

Southern Canal Belt (Amsterdam)

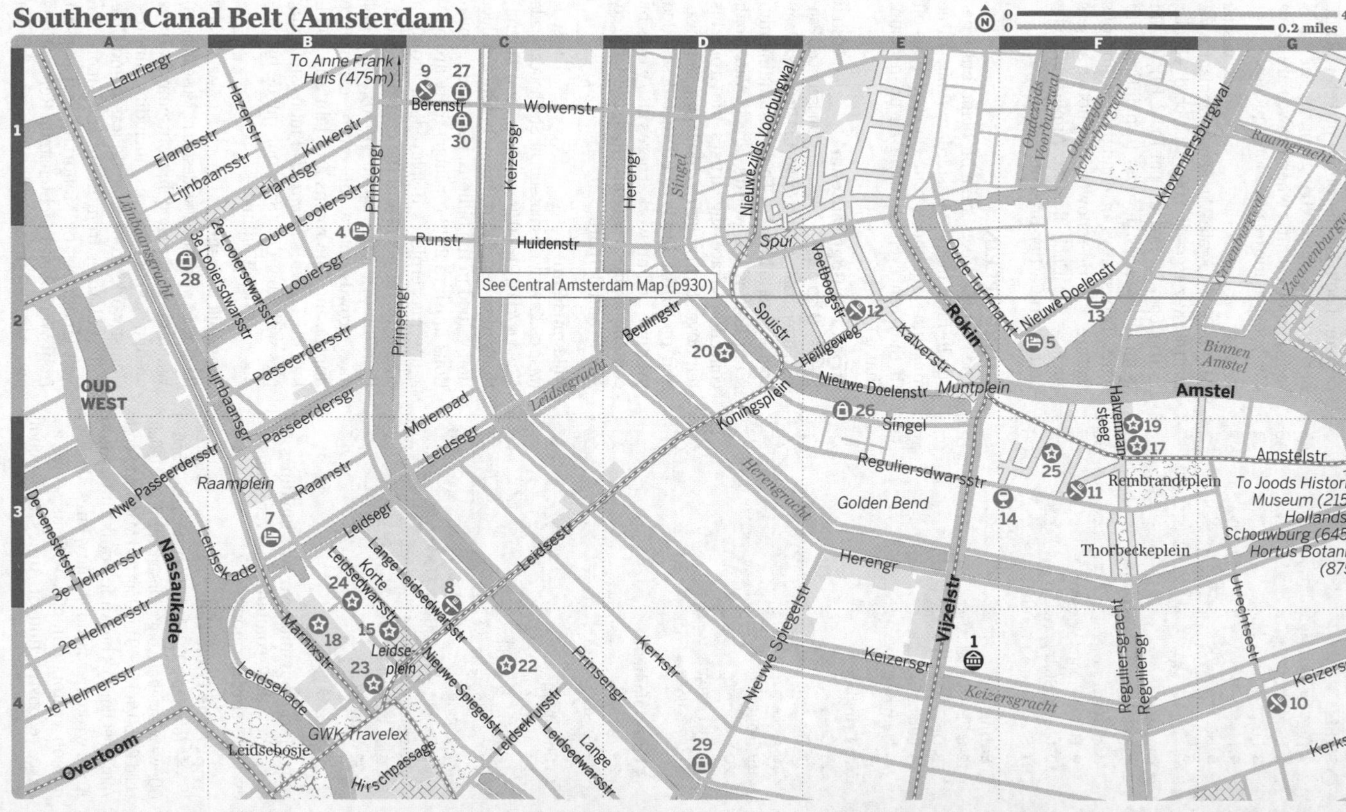

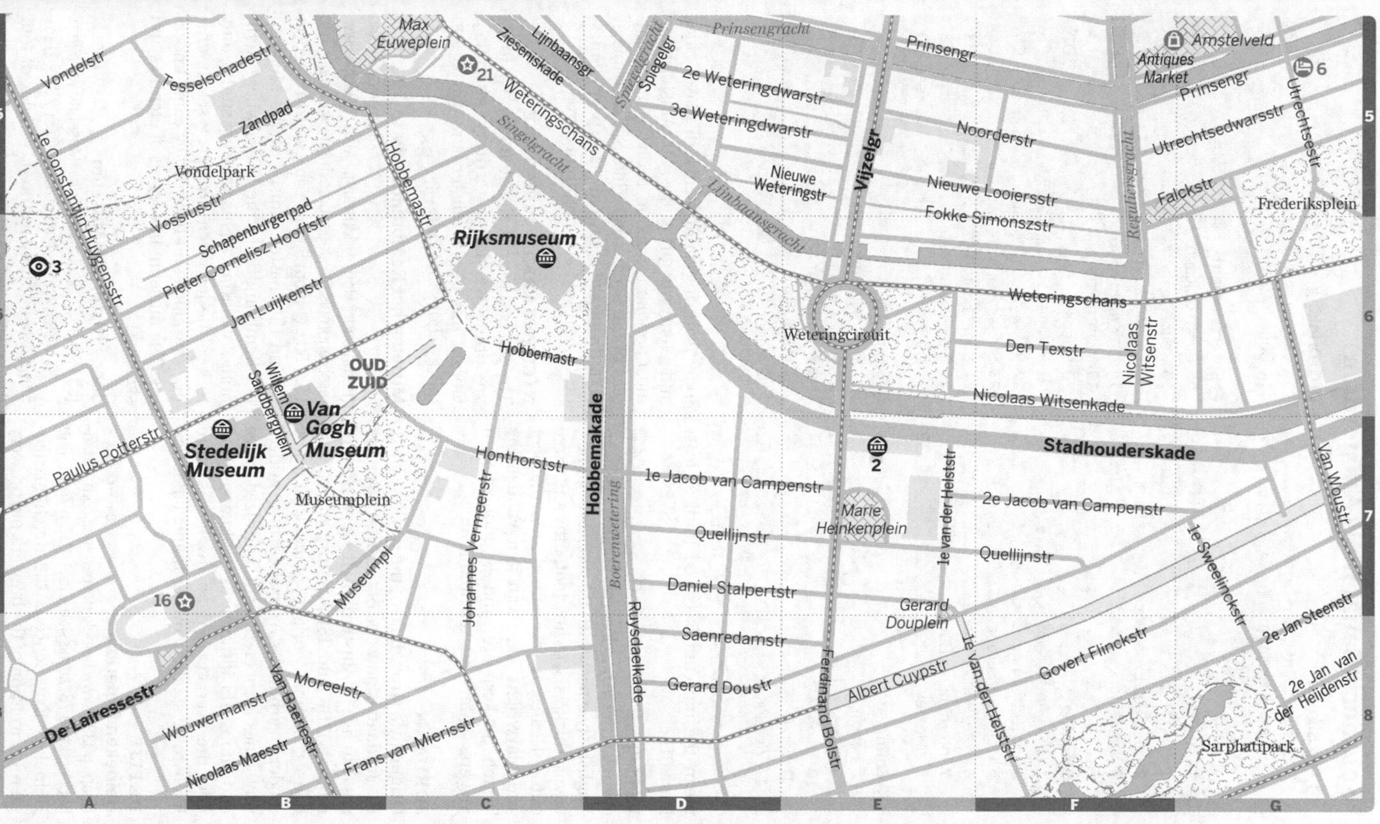

Max Euweplein
21
Lijnbaansgr
Zieseniskade
Weteringschans
Singelgracht
Spiegelgracht
Spiegelgr
Prinsengracht
Prinsengr
2e Weteringdwarstr
3e Weteringdwarstr
Nieuwe Weteringstr
Lijnbaansgracht
Vijzelgr
Noorderstr
Nieuwe Looiersstr
Fokke Simonszstr
Reguliersgracht
Amstelveld
Antiques Market
Prinsengr
6
Utrechtsedwarsstr
Utrechtsestr
Falckstr
Frederiksplein
Vondelstr
Tesselschadestr
Zandpad
Vondelpark
Vossiusstr
Schapenburgerpad
Pieter Cornelisz Hooftstr
1e Constantijn Huygensstr
3
Jan Luijkenstr
Hobbemastr
Rijksmuseum
Hobbemastr
OUD ZUID
Willem Sandbergplein
Van Gogh Museum
Stedelijk Museum
Paulus Potterstr
Museumplein
Museumpl
Honthorststr
Johannes Vermeerstr
Hobbemakade
Boerenwetering
Ruysdaelkade
Weteringschans
Weteringcircuit
Den Texstr
Nicolaas Witsenstr
Nicolaas Witsenkade
Stadhouderskade
2
1e Jacob van Campenstr
2e Jacob van Campenstr
Marie Heinkenplein
1e van der Helststr
Quellijnstr
Quellijnstr
Van Woustr
Daniel Stalpertstr
Saenredamstr
Gerard Doustr
Gerard Douplein
Ferdinand Bolstr
Albert Cuypstr
1e van der Helststr
Govert Flinckstr
1e Sweelinckstr
2e Jan Steenstr
2e Jan van der Heijdenstr
Sarphatipark
16
De Lairessestr
Wouwermanstr
Nicolaas Maesstr
Van Baerlestr
Moreelstr
Frans van Mierisstr
A
B
C
D
E
F
G
5
6
7
8

Southern Canal Belt (Amsterdam)

mean the museum is closed until at least late 2011.

Vondelpark PARK

(Map p932; www.vondelpark.nl) Vondelpark is an English-style park with free concerts, ponds, lawns, thickets, winding footpaths and three outdoor cafes. It was named after the poet and playwright Joost van den Vondel, the 'Dutch Shakespeare', and is popular with joggers, skaters, buskers and lovers.

JORDAAN

Originally a stronghold of the working class, the Jordaan is now one of the most desirable areas to live in Amsterdam. It's a pastiche of modest 17th- and 18th-century merchants' houses, humble workers' homes and a few modern carbuncles, squashed in a grid of tiny lanes peppered with bite-sized cafes and shops. Its intimacy is contagious, and now the average Jordaan dweller is more likely to be a gallery owner than a labourer.

DE PIJP

Heineken Experience BREWERY TOUR

(Map p932; www.heinekenexperience.com; Stadhouderskade 78; admission €15; 11am-7pm) The Heineken Experience is the much-gussied-up reincarnation of the brewer's old brewery tour, featuring multimedia displays, rides and plenty of gift shops. At Amsterdam's most popular attraction, acolytes enjoy samples of the beer, which (like Stella Artois et al) is dismissed as an 'old man's beer' domestically and sold at a premium abroad.

NIEUWMARKT & PLANTAGE

The streets around the Rembrandt House are prime wandering territory, offering a vibrant mix of old Amsterdam, canals and quirky shops and cafes.

Museum het Rembrandthuis HISTORIC BUILDING

(Rembrandt House Museum; Map p930; www.rembrandthuis.nl; Jodenbreestraat 4; adult/child €8/1.50; 10am-5pm) You almost expect to find the master himself at the Museum het Rembrandthuis, the house where Rembrandt van Rijn ran his painting studio, only to lose the lot when profligacy set in, enemies swooped and bankruptcy came knocking. The museum has scores of etchings and sketches.

Joods Historisch Museum MUSEUM

(off Map p932; Jewish Historical Museum; www.jhm.nl; JD Meijerplein 2-4; adult/child €7.50/3; 11am-5pm) A beautifully restored complex of four Ashkenazic synagogues from the 17th and

18th centuries shows the history of Jews in the Netherlands. It vividly captures the vibrant Jewish community snuffed out by WWII.

FREE **Hollandsche Schouwburg** MEMORIAL (off Map p932; Holland Theatre; www.hollandscheschouwburg.nl; Plantage Middenlaan 24; ⌚11am-4pm) After 1942 this theatre became a detention centre for Jews awaiting deportation. Up to 80,000 people passed through here on their way to the death camps. Among the displays, the tale of Bram and Eva Beem is particularly heartbreaking (the Nazis paid a 750 guilder reward – about €15,000 today – for people who betrayed Jews in hiding).

Tours

See p972000 for bike tours as well as canal boat tours of Amsterdam that let you hop on and hop off.

TOP CHOICE **St Nicolaas Boat Club** BOAT TOUR (www.amsterdamboatclub.com; suggested donation €10) The alternative to the big staid boats bumping around the canals, these small boats are piloted by characters as interesting as the passing sights. Have a beer and a smoke and learn about alternative Amsterdam. Departure times vary; sign up at Boom Chicago (p939).

Sleeping

Book ahead for weekends and in summer. Many cheaper places cater specifically to party animals with booze flowing, pot smoking and general mayhem around the clock. Others exude refined old-world charm. Wi-fi is near universal but elevators are not.

DON'T MISS

HORTUS BOTANICUS

Established in 1638, the **Hortus Botanicus** (off Map p932; Botanical Garden; www.dehortus.nl; Plantage Middenlaan 2A; adult/child €7.50/3.50; ⌚9am-5pm Mon-Fri, 10am-5pm Sat & Sun, to 7pm daily Jul & Aug) became a repository for tropical seeds and plants brought by Dutch ships from the East and West Indies. The 4000-plus species are kept in wonderful structures and in compact grounds. Look for Amsterdam's oldest tree plus the alien-like Victoria water lily.

TOP CHOICE **Miauw Suites** HOTEL €€€ (Map p930; ☎717 34 29; www.miauw.com; Hartenstraat 36; r from €150, 2-night minimum; 📶) Located above the same-named fashion shop in the hip Western Canal Belt, Miauw's spacious quarters are just what the doctor ordered for a weekend's shopping blitz. Mixing stylish and vintage decor, suites here are more like one-bedroom flats.

Hotel Amsterdam Wiechmann HOTEL €€ (Map p932; ☎626 33 21; www.hotelwiechmann.nl; Prinsengracht 328; r €65-200; @📶) This family-run hotel occupies three houses on the edge of the Jordaan. It has a marvellous canalside location, cosy but lovingly cared-for rooms furnished with country quilts and chintz. Small singles are good value; breakfast is included and served in a fine corner dining room.

Hotel de l'Europe GRAND HOTEL €€€ (Map p932; ☎531 17 77; www.leurope.nl; Nieuwe Doelenstraat 2-8; r from €250; ❄@🏊) Oozing Victorian elegance, L'Europe welcomes you with a marble lobby, 100 gloriously large rooms (some with terraces, most with canal views) and a sense of serene calm that makes it a blissful oasis amid the hurly-burly. Service is gracious. You can designate your stay carbon-neutral.

Chic & Basic Amsterdam HOTEL €€ (Map p930; ☎522 23 45; www.chicandbasic.com; Herengracht 13-19; s/d from €120/140; @📶) Spread across three canal houses, the modern rooms here merge minimalism with cosiness and flair. The ad-sized photos of skinny models might make you wish you hadn't wolfed down those *frites*, but if you score a Herengracht-facing room all diet thoughts will disappear out the window and into the canal.

Hotel Nadia HOTEL €€ (off Map p930; ☎620 15 50; www.nadia.nl; Raadhuisstraat 51; r €60-150; @📶) This handsome building has a precipitous set of stairs but the energetic staff will tote your luggage up them. Rooms are immaculate and breakfast is included. Rooms to the front have great views of the Westerkerk and the Jordaan.

Hotel Prinsenhof HOTEL € (Map p932; ☎623 17 72; www.hotelprinsenhof.com; Prinsengracht 810; s/d without bathroom €49/69, s/d with bathroom €84/89; 📶) Honest value, this 18th-century house features canal views, rooms with mismatched furniture and 'Captain Hook', the electric luggage hoist. The attic quarters provide top views and are most sought-after.

Hotel/Hostel Winston HOTEL €

(Map p930; ☎623 13 80; www.winston.nl; Warmoesstraat 123; dm €22-42, s €77-100, d €90-120;) With rock 'n' roll rooms, an attached busy club, beer garden and smoking deck, this place hops 24/7. Group dorm rooms sleep up to eight. Most private rooms are 'art' rooms: local artists were given free rein, with results from sci-fi (robots peering at you) to playful and raunchy.

Hotel Brouwer HOTEL €

(Map p930; ☎624 63 58; www.hotelbrouwer.nl; Singel 83; r €60-95;) The eight rooms in this house dating back to 1652 are named for Dutch painters and are simply furnished and boast canal views. There's a mix of Delft-blue tiles and early-20th-century furniture, and a tulip-sized elevator. Breakfast is included; no credit cards.

Stadsdoelen Youth Hostel HOSTEL €

(Map p930; ☎624 68 32; www.stayokay.com; Kloveniersburgwal 97; dm €20-28, s €45-60, d €50-80; @) Efficient and well-run Stadsdoelen is always bustling with backpackers. A mix of 11 ultra-clean, single-sex and mixed rooms (each with up to 17 beds and free lockers) offer a modicum of privacy. There's a big TV room, a hopping bar, a pool table and laundry facilities.

International Budget Hostel HOSTEL €

(Map p932; ☎624 27 84; www.internationalbudgethostel.com; Leidsegracht 76; dm €28-32, tw from €70; @) The canalside location in a former warehouse is close to nightlife. There's a four-person limit in rooms and a cool mix of backpackers from around the world lounging in the common areas. It's clean and the staff have charm that's greater than the prices.

Eating

Amsterdam abounds in food choices. Happy streets for hunting include Utrechtsesraat, Spuistraat and any of the little streets lining and connecting the west canals, such as Berenstraat.

Restaurants

TOP CHOICE **De Belhamel** FRENCH-ITALIAN €€€

(Map p930; Brouwersgracht 60; mains €20-25) In warm weather the canalside tables at the head of the Herengracht are an aphrodisiac, and the sumptuous art nouveau interior provides the perfect backdrop for excellent, French- and Italian-inspired dishes such as silky roast beef.

De Bijenkorf SELF-SERVICE €

(Map p930; Dam 1; 11am-7pm) The city's most fashionable department store has a huge, snazzy restaurant on the 5th floor with a terrace offering rooftop and steeple views. A dozen food stations offer fresh and modern fare.

Pancakes! DUTCH €

(Map p932; Berenstraat 38; mains from €4) A great place to sample Dutch pancakes amid cool shops along the Western Canals, in an atmosphere free of clogs and other kitsch – and there are just as many locals here as tourists. Kids love it.

Lucius SEAFOOD €€€

(Map p930; Spuistraat 247; mains €20-30; dinner) Simple, delicious and consistently full, this seafood place is known for fresh ingredients and for not overdoing the sauce and spice. The interior is all fish tanks and tiles, and service is thorough and efficient.

Tujuh Maret INDONESIAN €€

(Map p932; Utrechtsestraat 73; mains €14-20) Grab a wicker chair and tuck into spicy Sulawesi-style dishes like dried, fried beef or chicken in red-pepper sauce. *Rijsttafel* is laid out according to spice intensity; *makanan kecil* is a mini-*rijsttafel*.

Nam Kee CHINESE €€

(Map p930; Zeedijk 113-116; mains €9-20) It won't win any design awards, but Nam Kee is always the most popular Chinese spot in town. The typically long bilingual menu has all the favourites.

Cafes

Cafes run the spectrum between classic places to update your blog over coffee to full-on pubs. Most have food.

Café de Jaren GRAND CAFE €€

(Map p932; Nieuwe Doelenstraat 20) Watch the Amstel float by from the balcony and waterside terraces of this soaring, bright grand cafe. The great reading table has loads of foreign publications for whiling away hours over beers.

Hofje Van Wijs CAFE €

(Map p930; Zeedijk 43; mains €4-8) The 200-year-old coffee and tea vendor Wijs & Zonen maintains this oasis of a courtyard cafe. Many of the teas are from Indonesia and you can get excellent coffees, cakes and meals.

The place runs a weekly walking tour (3pm Sunday), which covers this once-blighted area.

Crea CAFE €
(Map p930; Turfdraagsterpad 17; mains €4-10) Walking along Grimburgwal, you can't help but notice the prime cafe chairs across the canal. They're part of the University of Amsterdam's cultural centre, a laid-back spot that's a superb urban escape.

Quick Eats

TOP CHOICE **Van Dobben** DUTCH €
(Map p932; Korte Reguliersdwarsstraat 5; mains from €4) Open since the 1940s, the venerable Van Dobben has white tile walls and white-coated counter men who specialise in snappy banter. Trad Dutch fare is the speciality: try the *pekelvlees* (something close to corned beef). The best *kroketten* (croquettes) and pea soup in town.

Vleminckx FRITES €
(Map p932; Voetboogstraat 31; frites from €2; 11am-6pm) This hole-in-the-wall takeaway has drawn hordes for its monumental *frites* since 1887. The standard is smothered in mayonnaise, though you can ask for tomato sauce, peanut sauce or a variety of spicy toppings.

Wil Graanstra Friteshuis FRITES €
(Westermarkt 11; frites from €2; 11am-6pm) This little stall near the Anne Frank Huis has been serving up delectably light and crispy fries with mayo since 1956. Nearby stalls offer local staples such as herring on a stick.

Febo FAST FOOD €
(Map p932; Leidsestraat 94; snacks from €1.50) Insert a few coins in the machine and live the legend. The *bami* rolls are hot as napalm, the *frikadel* frightening and the *kaassoufflé* utterly unsoufflélike. But plucking a treat from the automat windows is a drunken Dutch tradition.

Drinking

A particular Amsterdam joy is discovering your own brown cafe. They are found everywhere, often tucked into the most atmospheric of locations. Many serve food.

TOP CHOICE **Hoppe** BROWN CAFE
(Map p930; Spuistraat 18) This gritty *bruin cafe* has been luring drinkers for more than 300 years. Journalists, bums, socialites and raconteurs toss back brews amid the ancient wood panelling. Most months the energetic crowd spews out from the dark interior and onto the Spui.

> **WANT MORE?**
>
> For in-depth information, reviews and recommendations at your fingertips, head to the Apple App Store to purchase Lonely Planet's *Amsterdam City Guide* iPhone app.

Doelen BROWN CAFE
(Map p930; Kloveniersburgwal 125) On a busy crossroads between the Amstel and De Wallen (the Red Light District), this cafe dates back to 1895 and looks it: carved wooden goat's head, stained-glass lamps, sand on the floor. During fine weather the tables spill across the street for picture-perfect canal views.

Proeflokaal Fockink BAR
(Map p930; Pijlsteeg 31; 3-9pm) This wee tasting house (dating from 1679) serves scores of *jenevers* and liqueurs in an arcade behind Grand Hotel Krasnapolsky. Although there are no seats, it's an intimate place to knock back a taste or two with a friend.

In 't Aepjen BROWN CAFE
(Map p930; Zeedijk 1) Candles burn even during the day at this bar based in a 15th-century house, which is one of the city's two remaining wooden buildings. The name allegedly comes from the bar's role in the 16th and 17th centuries as a crash pad for sailors from the Far East, who often toted *aapjes* (monkeys) with them.

Door 74 BAR
(Map p932; Reguliersdwarsstraat 74) Far and away Amsterdam's best cocktails, served in an elegant but unpretentious atmosphere, behind an unmarked door. It's tiny so getting a seat is a matter of luck but the *gezelligheid* (cosy and cheery) meshes with the hip style in a purely Amsterdam way.

Gollem BAR
(Map p930; Raamsteeg 4) All the brew-related paraphernalia in this miniscule space barely leaves room for the 150 beers and the connoisseurs who come to try them. The bartenders are happy to advise.

Entertainment

Find out what's on in Thursday's papers or the monthly *Time Out Amsterdam*.

GAY & LESBIAN AMSTERDAM

Information

» **Gay News Amsterdam** (www.gayamsterdam.nl) Website and free paper.

» **Pink Point** (www.pinkpoint.org; ⏲noon-6pm Mar-Aug, limited hrs Sep-Feb) On the Keizersgracht, behind the Westerkerk. Part information kiosk, part souvenir shop, with details on myriad gay and lesbian hangouts and social groups, and copies of the candid *Bent Guide*.

Accommodation

Most hotels in town are lesbian and gay friendly, but some cater specifically to queer clientele:

Golden Bear HOTEL €€

(☎624 47 85; www.goldenbear.nl; Kerkstraat 37; r €60-130; 📶) The oldest gay hotel in Amsterdam has been operating since 1948. Straddling two 18th-century buildings, rooms are done up in bright colours, mod-furnishings and minifridges.

Entertainment

Amsterdam's gay scene is among the world's largest. Among the party hubs, Warmoesstraat in the Red Light District hosts the infamous, kink-filled leather and fetish bars, while Rembrandtplein is for traditional pubs and brown cafes, some with a campy bent.

Some possibilities:

Argos BAR

(Map p930; www.argosbar.com; Warmoesstraat 95) Amsterdam's oldest leather bar. Dress code for the regular 'SOS' (Sex On Sunday) party: nude or seminude.

Montmartre BAR

(Map p932; www.cafemontmartre.nl; Halvemaansteeg 17) Beneath outrageous ceiling decorations, patrons sing loudly to Dutch ballads and top-40 songs. It's like a gay Eurovision. Regarded by many as the Benelux's best gay bar.

Coffee Shops

Cafes have coffee, 'coffee shops' are where one buys pot. Smoking regulations mean you can puff pot but not tobacco.

Abraxas COFFEE SHOP

(Map p930; Jonge Roelensteeg 12) The Abraxas management knows what stoners want: mellow music, comfy sofas, rooms with different energy levels, and thick milkshakes. The considerate staff and mellow clientele make this a great place for coffee-shop newbies. Get stoned and send strange emails from the computers.

Rokerij COFFEE SHOP

(Map p932; Lange Leidsedwarsstraat 41) Behind the black hole of an entrance you'll find Asian decor and candlelight for those tired of the Rastafarian vibe. One of many friendly locations.

Nightclubs

Sugar Factory CLUB

(Map p932; www.sugarfactory.nl; Lijnbaansgracht 238) One night it's Balkan beats; another, it's 'wicked jazz sounds' – the Sugar Factory has all kinds of live entertainment. Equally important, the vibe is always welcoming and creative. It's an excellent midsize space, with a smoking lounge upstairs.

Escape CLUB

(Map p932; www.escape.nl; Rembrandtplein 11) Amsterdam's biggest, glitziest club has managed to keep the bass pumping since the '80s. Long lines get longer when a big-name DJ mixes; bouncers are choosey.

Odeon CLUB

(Map p932; www.odeontheater.nl; Singel 460) Set in a skinny canal house, the Odeon has been a creative party spot for decades. Glam but accessible, its club nights are heavy on house and electro.

Live Music

TOP CHOICE **Paradiso** LIVE MUSIC

(Map p932; www.paradiso.nl; Weteringschans 6) This converted church has been a premier rock venue since the '60s. Expect interesting dance music; live shows are followed by DJs or club nights.

Concertgebouw LIVE MUSIC
(Map p932; ☎for tickets 10am-5pm 671 83 45; www.concertgebouw.nl; Concertgebouwplein 2-6) Each year, this neo-Renaissance centre presents around 650 concerts attracting 840,000 visitors, making it the world's busiest concert hall (with reputedly the best acoustics). Holds free 'lunch concerts' at 12.30pm Wednesday, between September and June.

Melkweg LIVE MUSIC
(Map p932; www.melkweg.nl; Lijnbaansgracht 234A) The Milky Way – it's housed in a former dairy – must be Amsterdam's coolest club-gallery-cinema-cafe-concert hall. Its vibrant program of events is so full and varied that it's impossible not to find something you want to go to, from international DJ club nights to live Brazilian jazz.

Theatre

Boom Chicago COMEDY
(Map p932; www.boomchicago.nl; Leidseplein 12) Performs English-language stand-up and improv comedy year-round. See it over dinner and a few drinks. Inspiration is culled from Chicago's legendary Second City.

Stadsschouwburg THEATRE
(Map p932; www.stadsschouwburgamsterdam.nl; Leidseplein 26) Amsterdam's most beautiful theatre was built in 1894. It features large-scale productions, operettas, dance and summer English-language productions and performances.

Sport

Four-time European champion Ajax is the Netherlands' most famous football team. Ajax plays in the **Amsterdam Arena** (www.amsterdamarena.nl; Arena Blvd 11, Bijlmermeer), usually on Saturday evenings and Sunday afternoons August to May. Enjoy a 'World of Ajax' tour.

Cinemas

Amsterdam is a great place to see films from around the world, often in beautiful surrounds.

Movies CINEMA
(www.themovies.nl; Haarlemmerdijk 161) Art-house and indie films are presented in art deco surrounds in Jordaan.

Tuschinskitheater CINEMA
(Map p932; www.pathe.nl/tuschinski; Reguliersbreestraat 26) The place to view blockbusters with a sumptuous art deco interior.

GET UIT & ABOUT

Not sure how to spend your evening? Head to the last-minute ticket desk at the **Uitburo** (Map p932; ☎621 13 11; www.aub.nl; ⏲10am-7.30pm Mon-Sat, noon-7.30pm Sun), in the corner of the Stadsschouwburg on the Leidseplein. Tickets for comedy, dance, concerts, even club nights are often available at a significant discount – and handily marked 'LNP' (language no problem) if understanding Dutch isn't vital.

Shopping

The real pleasure of shopping in Amsterdam is finding some tiny shop selling something you'd find nowhere else. The big department stores cluster around the Dam; chains line the pedestrian (in more ways than one) Kalverstraat. The Red Light District buzzes with vibrating latex creations. Several streets along the Western Canals are dotted with surprising little shops: try Reesstraat and Hartenstraat and the blocks south to Runstraat and Huidenstraat. Several good streets in Nieumarkt have typically eccentric local stores.

CENTRAAL STATION AREA

Chills & Thrills HEADSHOP
(Map p930; Nieuwendijk 17) Herbal trips, truffles, psychoactive cacti, novelty bongs and life-sized alien sculptures.

RED LIGHT DISTRICT

Condomerie CONDOMS
(Map p930; Warmoesstraat 141) Puts the 'pro' back in prophylactic: rarely can you shop for a condom in such a tasteful setting and grapple with so many choices.

Webers FETISH CLOTHING
(Map p930; www.webersholland.nl; Kloveniersburgwal 26) Indulge in top-end versions of every kind of fetish wear imaginable and unimaginable.

WESTERN CANALS

Mendo DESIGNER GOODS
(Map p932; Berenstraat 11) A striking combination of visually stunning books, art, candy and even umbrellas.

DON'T MISS

MARKETS

Markets of just about every description are scattered across the city.

Amsterdam's largest and busiest market, **Albert Cuypmarkt** (www.decuyp.nl; Albert Cuypstraat; ⌚10am-5pm Mon-Sat) is 100 years old. Food of every description, flowers, souvenirs, clothing, hardware and household goods can be found here.

Bloemenmarkt (Map p932; Singel; ⌚9am-5pm, closed Sun Dec-Feb) is a touristy 'floating' flower market that's actually on pilings. Still, at the stalls that actually stock flowers (as opposed to plastic clogs), the vibrant colours burst forth.

You can pick up jewellery, furniture, art and collectables at **De Looier Antiques Market** (Map p932; www.looier.nl; Elandsgracht 109; ⌚11am-5pm Sat-Thu).

A favourite with academics, **Oudemanhuis Book Market** (Map p930; Oudemanhuispoort; ⌚11am-4pm Mon-Fri) is a moody, old, covered alleyway connecting two streets and it's lined with secondhand booksellers.

Waterlooplein Flea Market (Map p930; Waterlooplein; ⌚9am-5pm Mon-Fri, 8.30am-5.30pm Sat) is Amsterdam's most famous flea market: curios, secondhand clothing, music, used footwear, ageing electronic gear, New Age gifts, cheap bicycle parts.

Boekie Woekie BOOKS
(Map p932; Berenstraat 16) Sells books by artists, whether that means a self-published monograph or an illustrated story that's handcrafted right down to the paper.

SOUTHERN CANAL BELT

Eduard Kramer ANTIQUES
(Map p932; Nieuwe Spiegelstraat 64) One of many cute little oddball shops on this street. This one specialises in antique Dutch tiles and lots of other interesting old knick-knacks.

American Book Center BOOKS
(Map p930; Spui 12) Amsterdam's biggest selection of English-language books, travel guides, newspapers and magazines.

NIEUMARKT

Juggle JUGGLING EQUIPMENT
(Map p930; Staalstraat 3) Keeps many balls in the air selling juggling goods.

't Klompenhuisje CLOGS
(Map p930; Nieuwe Hoogstraat 9a) A couple of canals north of Juggle, with surprisingly comfortable, traditional Dutch *klompen* (clogs).

Information

Centrale Doktersdienst (Central Doctors Service; ☎592 34 34; ⌚24hr) Doctor, dentist or pharmacy referrals.

GWK Travelex (Map p930; Centraal Station; ⌚8am-10pm Mon-Sat, 9am-10pm Sun) Exchanges travellers cheques and makes hotel reservations; also at Schiphol.

I Amsterdam Card (www.iamsterdam.com; per 24/48/72hr €38/48/58) Available at VVV tourist offices and some hotels. Includes museum admissions, canal boat trips, discounts at shops, sights and restaurants and a transit pass.

Tourist office (VVV; Map p930; www.iamsterdam.nl; Stationsplein 10; ⌚9am-7pm) Maps, guides and transit passes.

Getting There & Away

Air

Most major airlines serve **Schiphol** (AMS; www.schiphol.nl), 18km southwest of the city centre.

Bus

For details of regional transport in the Netherlands, call the **transport information service** (☎0900-9292; www.9292ov.nl); it costs €0.70 per minute. Fares and travel durations are covered under individual towns in this chapter.

Amsterdam has good long-distance bus links with the rest of Europe.

Eurolines (Map p930; www.eurolines.nl; Rokin 10) tickets can be bought at its office near the Dam, and at most travel agencies and the NS Reisburo (Netherlands Railways Travel Bureau) in Centraal Station. Departures are from the bus station next to Amstelstation.

Train

Amsterdam's main train station is fabled **Centraal Station** (CS; Map p930), with service to the rest of the country and major European cities.

Getting Around

To/From the Airport

A **taxi** into Amsterdam from Schiphol airport takes 25 to 45 minutes and costs about €45.

Trains to Centraal Station leave every few minutes, take 15 to 20 minutes, and cost €4/7 per single/return.

Bicycle

Amsterdam is cycling nirvana: flat, beautiful, with dedicated bike paths. About 150,000 bicycles are stolen each year in Amsterdam, so always lock up. Rental agencies include the following:

Bike City (www.bikecity.nl; Bloemgracht 68-70; per day/week €14/57) In the Jordaan, with no advertising on the bikes – you might pass for a local.

Orangebike (Map p930; www.orangebike.nl; Geldersekade 37; per day/week €10/43) Also offers a range of city tours (from €20).

Boat

Amsterdam's **canal boats** are a popular way to tour the town but most are actually a bit claustrophobic, with steamed-up glass windows surrounding passengers. Look for a boat with an open seating area.

Rederij Lovers (Map p930; www.lovers.nl; Prins Hendrikkade 25-27; adult/child €10/5) Runs several routes that stop at major sights, allowing you to hop on and off; circuits last about an hour.

There are also free **ferries** from behind Centraal Station to destinations around the IJ, notably Amsterdam Noord.

Car & Motorcycle

Amsterdam is horrendous for parking, with charges averaging €5 per hour. Your best bet is to ditch the car at an outlying train station and ride in.

Public Transport

Services – including Amsterdam's iconic **trams** – are run by the local transit authority, the GVB; national railway (NS) tickets are not valid on local transport. The GVB has a highly useful **information office** (Map p930; www.gvb.nl; Stationsplein 10; ⌚7am-9pm Mon-Fri, 8am-9pm Sat & Sun) located across the tram tracks from the Centraal Station main entrance. Keep in mind that you can avoid the often-long lines by buying day passes at the adjoining VVV office instead.

Public transport in Amsterdam uses the *OV-chipkaart* (p973). Cards for one/two hours cost €2.50/3.50 on trams and buses. Better deals are the **unlimited ride tickets** sold by the GVB (from machines and the office), which are good for 24/48/72/96 hours and cost €7/11.50/15.50/19.50.

Night buses take over shortly after midnight, which is when the trams and regular buses stop running.

Taxi

Amsterdam taxis are expensive, even over short journeys. Try **Taxicentrale Amsterdam** (☎677 77 77).

AROUND AMSTERDAM

Aalsmeer

☎0297 / POP 20,000

Here, at the world's biggest **flower auction** (www.floraholland.com; Legmeerdijk 313; adult/child €5/3; ⌚7-10am Mon-Fri), 21 million flowers and plants worth around €6 million change hands daily; the rose is the biggest seller, outselling the tulip three to one. Bidding usually takes place between 7am and 9.30am; Monday, Tuesday and Friday are the best days.

Take Connexxion bus 172 from Amsterdam Centraal Station to the Aalsmeer VBA stop (50 minutes, four times hourly).

Alkmaar

☎072 / POP 93,500

This picturesque town stages its famous **cheese market** (Waagplein; ⌚10am-noon Fri, Apr-early Sep) in the historic main square. The market dates from the 17th century. Dealers in officious white smocks insert a hollow rod to extract cheese samples, sniffing and crumbling for fat and moisture content. Then the porters, wearing colourful hats to signify their cheese guild, heft the cheeses on wooden sledges to a large scale. An average 30 tonnes of cheese is on display at the Alkmaar market at any one time.

Arrive early for more than fleeting glimpses. There are four trains per hour from Amsterdam Centraal (€6.70, 40 minutes).

THE RANDSTAD

When people think of Holland outside of Amsterdam, they are often really thinking about the Randstad. One of the most densely populated places on the planet, it stretches from Amsterdam to Rotterdam and features the classically Dutch towns and cities of Den Haag, Utrecht, Haarlem, Leiden, Delft and Gouda. Most people focus their visit to Holland here, enjoying the peerless cycling network that links the towns amid tulip fields.

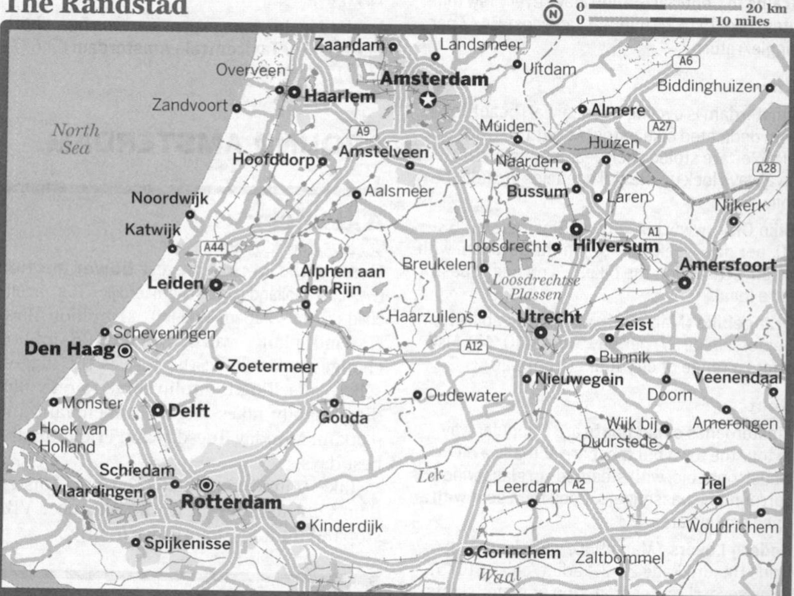

Haarlem

023 / POP 149,000

Haarlem is the Netherlands in microcosm, with canals, gabled buildings and cobblestone streets. Its historic buildings, grand churches, museums, cosy bars, good restaurants and antique shops draw scores of day trippers – it's only 15 minutes by train from Amsterdam.

Sights

A couple of hour's stroll – with stops for refreshments – will cover Haarlem's tidy centre, which radiates out from the **Grote Markt**, where there are markets on many days.

Grote Kerk van St Bavo CHURCH

(www.bavo.nl; Oude Groenmarkt 23; adult/child €2.50/free; 10am-5pm Mon-Sat) This 15th-century Gothic cathedral has a 50m-high steeple that can be seen from almost anywhere in Haarlem. It has a striking Müller organ, 30m high with around 5000 pipes.

Frans Hals Museum ART MUSEUM

(www.franshalsmuseum.nl; Groot Heiligland 62; adult/child €7.50/free; 11am-5pm Tue-Sat, noon-5pm Sun) Kept in an almshouse where Frans Hals spent his final, impoverished years, the superb collection in this museum features Hals' two paintings known collectively as the *Regents & the Regentesses of the Old Men's Alms House* (1664). Among other treasures are ceiling-high illustrations of the human anatomy with biblical and mythological allusions.

FREE **Corrie Ten Boom House** HISTORIC BUILDING

(www.corrietenboom.com; Barteljorisstraat; admission free; 10am-4pm Tue-Sat Apr-Oct, 11am-3pm Nov-Mar) Also known as 'the hiding place', the Corrie Ten Boom House is named for the matriarch of a family that lived here during WWII. In a secret compartment in her bedroom, she hid hundreds of Jews and Dutch resistors until they could escape to safety. In 1944 the family was betrayed and sent to concentration camps, where three died. Later, Corrie Ten Boom toured the world preaching peace. Tours in English held daily.

Sleeping

Looking for a mellow alternative to Amsterdam that doesn't include lighting up? Haarlem is peace personified at night.

Hotel Carillon HOTEL €€

(531 05 91; www.hotelcarillon.com; Grote Markt 27; s/d from €60/80;) Small but tidy white rooms in the shadow of the Grote Kerk are

the hallmark here. A few share bathrooms and cost from €40. Breakfast can be taken in wicker chairs on the sidewalk cafe.

Stempels HOTEL €€
(☎512 39 10; www.stempelsinhaarlem.nl; Klokhuisplein 9; r €90-155; @📶) Haarlem's most interesting lodging has 17 spacious rooms in a gorgeous old printing house on the east side of the Grote Kerk. Small luxuries abound, including a computer in every room, collections of short stories at the bedside and a fine breakfast buffet.

Eating & Drinking

Lange Veerstraat has a bounty of cafes, while Schagchelstraat is lined with restaurants. The Saturday morning market on Grote Markt is one of Holland's best; try the fresh *Stroopwafels* (small caramel-filled waffles).

TOP CHOICE **De Haerlemsche Vlaamse** FAST FOOD €
(Spekstraat 3; frites €2) Practically on the doorstep of the Grote Kerk, this *frites* joint not much bigger than a telephone box is a local institution. Line up for its crispy, golden fries made from fresh potatoes. Choose from one of a dozen sauces, including three kinds of mayonnaise.

Lambermon's Grand Café BISTRO €€
(Korte Veerstraat 1; dishes €8-25) The 'grand' in the name is almost an understatement at this oh-so-chic corner hot spot in a beautiful former fashion store. Bottles of champagne are on ice for sips by the glass; the waitstaff even manages a bit of attitude coupled with elan.

Proeflokaal In den Uiver CAFE €
(Riviervismarkt 13) This nautical-themed old place has shipping knick-knacks and a schooner sailing right over the bar. There's jazz on Thursday and Sunday evenings. It's one of many atmospheric cafes overlooking the Grote Markt.

Information

The **tourist office** (www.vvvhaarlem.nl; Verwulft 11; ⏲9.30am-5.30pm Mon-Fri, 10am-5pm Sat, 11am-3pm Sun Apr-Sep, 9.30am-5.30pm Mon-Fri, 10am-5pm Sat Oct-Mar) is located in a freestanding glass house in the middle of the main shopping district.

Getting There & Away

Trains serve Haarlem's stunning art deco station, a 10-minute walk from the centre.

DESTINATION	PRICE (€)	DURATION (MIN)	FREQUENCY (PER HR)
Amsterdam	3.80	15	5-8
Den Haag	7.30	35-40	4-6
Rotterdam	10.50	50	4

Keukenhof Gardens

One of the Netherlands' top attractions is near Lisse, between Haarlem and Leiden: **Keukenhof** (www.keukenhof.nl; adult/child €14.50/7; ⏲8am-7.30pm mid-Mar–mid-May, last entry 6pm) is the world's largest bulb-flower garden, attracting nearly 800,000 visitors during a season almost as short-lived as the blooms on the millions of multicoloured tulips, daffodils and hyacinths.

Connexxion bus 54 travels from Leiden Centraal Station to Keukenhof (30 minutes, four times per hour).

Leiden

☎071 / POP 116,800

Leiden is a busy, vibrant town that is another popular day trip from Amsterdam. Claims to fame: it's Rembrandt's birthplace, it's home to the Netherlands' oldest university (and 20,000 students) and it's where America's pilgrims raised money to lease the leaky *Mayflower* that took them to the New World in 1620. Large, dignified 17th-century buildings with tall, almost regal windows line the canals.

Sights & Activities

The best way to experience Leiden is by strolling the historic centre, especially along the Rapenburg canal.

Follow the huge steeple to **Pieterskerk** (Pieterskerkhof; ⏲1-4pm), which shines after a grand restoration (a good thing as it's been prone to collapse since it was built in the 14th century). The precinct here is as old-Leiden as you'll get and includes the gabled old **Latin School** (Schoolstraat), which – before it became a commercial building – was graced by a pupil named Rembrandt from 1616 to 1620. Across the plaza, look for the **Gravensteen**, which dates to the 13th century and once was a prison. The gallery facing the plaza was where judges watched executions.

Head east to the 15th-century **St Pancraskerk** (Nieuwstraat), which is surrounded

Leiden

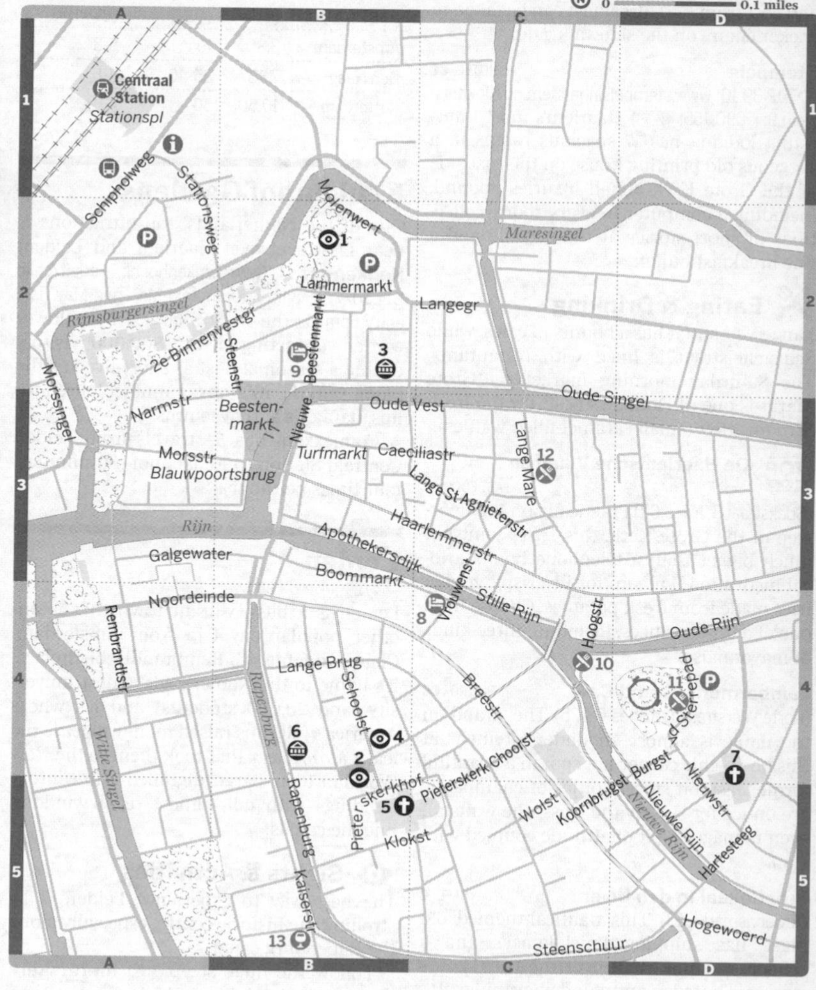

by tiny buildings unchanged since the pilgrims were here in 1620.

Lakenhal MUSEUM

(Cloth Hall; www.lakenhal.nl; Oude Singel 28-32; adult/under 18yr €7.50/free; ⏲10am-5pm Tue-Fri, noon-5pm Sat & Sun) This 17th-century museum has an assortment of paintings by old masters (including a few Rembrandts) as well as some period rooms and temporary exhibits.

De Valk HISTORIC BUILDING

(Falcon; www.molenmuseumdevalk.nl; 2e Binnenvestgracht 1; adult/child €3/2; ⏲10am-5pm Tue-Sat, 1-5pm Sun) Leiden's carefully restored windmill sadly notes that local boy Rembrandt, though a miller's son, didn't paint many windmills.

Rijksmuseum van Oudheden MUSEUM

(National Museum of Antiquities; www.rmo.nl; Rapenburg 28; adult/child €9/free; ⏲10am-5pm Tue-Sun) Hieroglyphs and almost 100 human and animal mummies are the supporting cast to the Temple of Taffeh, a gift from Egypt for Dutch help in rescuing ancient monuments when the Aswan High Dam was built in the 1960s.

Leiden

Sights

1	De Valk	B2
2	Gravensteen	B4
3	Lakenhal	B2
4	Latin School	B4
5	Pieterskerk	B5
6	Rijksmuseum van Oudheden	B4
7	St Pancraskerk	D4

Sleeping

8	Hotel Nieuw Minerva	C4
9	Rembrandt Hotel	B2

Eating

10	Annie's	C4
11	Brasserie Het Koetshuis	D4
12	Mangerie De Jonge Koekop	C3

Drinking

13	Café L'Esperance	B5

Sleeping

Hotel Nieuw Minerva HOTEL €€
(☎512 63 58; www.nieuwminerva.nl; Boommarkt 23; r €80-150; @) The Nieuw Minerva has a traditional look and a quiet canalside location. Some of the 40 rooms even have themed decor – the Rembrandt Room features an old-style walled bed with thick privacy curtains. Stash yourself inside and paint something.

Rembrandt Hotel HOTEL €€
(☎514 42 33; www.rembrandthotel.nl; Nieuwe Beestenmarkt 10; r €85-125; @) Light pouring in the windows makes the white decor of the 20 rooms even brighter at this historic but well-cared-for inn. Rooms have high-speed internet and work desks.

Eating & Drinking

The city-centre canals and narrow old streets abound with choices, although there's little of interest on the walking route in from the station. The sprawling Saturday **market** along Nieuwe Rijn abounds with fresh fare and flowers.

Mangerie De Jonge Koekop BISTRO €€€
(Lange Mare 60; meals from €30; dinner Mon-Sat) Always a popular choice, this bistro has fresh and inventive fare. Dine under the stars at tables outside in summer. Look for the sculpted cow's head on the front, which is as narrow as the first stalk of spring asparagus.

Brasserie Het Koetshuis BISTRO €
(Burgsteeg 13; mains from €8) Right in the shadow of De Burcht (an 11th-century citadel), you can sit on the large terrace and ponder the ramparts or huddle inside at a long table in what was once stables. Cafe classics dominate the long and varied menu.

Café l'Esperance BROWN CAFE €
(Kaiserstraat 1) Long, dark and handsome, all decked out in nostalgic wood panelling *and* overlooking an evocative bend in the canal. Outside tables buzz with frivolity in summer.

Annie's CAFE €
(Hoogstraat 1a; mains from €8; 11am-1am) At the confluence of canals and pedestrian zones, Annie's has a prime water-level location with dozens of tables on a floating pontoon. This classy cafe is good for a drink or a casual meal.

Information

The **tourist office** (www.vvvleiden.nl; Stationsweg 41; 8am-6pm Mon-Fri, 10am-4pm Sat, 11am-3pm Sun), across from the train station, has good maps and historic info.

Getting There & Away

Buses leave from directly in front of Centraal Station. Sample train fares and schedules:

DESTINATION	PRICE (€)	DURATION (MIN)	FREQUENCY (PER HR)
Amsterdam	8	34	6
Den Haag	3.20	10	6
Schiphol Airport	5.30	15	6

Den Haag

☎070 / POP 486,000

Den Haag (The Hague), officially known as 's-Gravenhage (Count's Hedge), is the Dutch seat of government (although Amsterdam is the capital). Wide, tree-lined boulevards like **Lange Voorhout** give Den Hague a suitably regal air: it's the kind of place where the musky aftershave of suave men wearing pink cravats mingles with the frilly scents of sachets sold in pricey boutiques. The many embassies here plus various international courts of justice – which keep Den Haag in the news – give the city a worldly air. Nightlife thrives with fun seekers on international assignment and its museums include one exquisite star.

Sights & Activities

TOP CHOICE **Mauritshuis** ART MUSEUM
(www.mauritshuis.nl; Korte Vijverberg 8; adult/child €11/free; ⌚10am-5pm Tue-Sat, 11am-5pm Sun) For a painless introduction to Dutch and Flemish art, visit this small museum in a jewel-box of an old palace. Highlights include the Dutch *Mona Lisa:* Vermeer's *Girl with a Pearl Earring*. Rembrandts include a wistful self-portrait from the year of his death, 1669. Even if you're just passing Den Haag on the train, it's well worth hopping off to visit.

Binnenhof PALACE
(⌚10am-4pm Mon-Sat) The royal palace adjoins the Mauritshuis and is surrounded by parliamentary buildings that have long been at the heart of Dutch politics. The sterile central courtyard was once used for executions. A highlight of the complex is the 13th-century Gothic **Ridderzaal** (Knights' Hall).

Grote Kerk CHURCH
(Rond de Grote Kerk 12) Dating from 1450, this modest church has a fine pulpit that was constructed 100 years later. The neighbouring 1565 **old town hall** is a splendid example of Dutch Renaissance architecture.

Gemeentemuseum ART MUSEUM
(Municipal Museum; www.gemeentemuseum.nl; Stadhouderslaan 41; adult/child €10/free; ⌚11am-5pm Tue-Sun) Admirers of De Stijl and Piet Mondrian mustn't miss this Berlage-designed museum. Mondrian's unfinished *Victory Boogie Woogie* takes pride of place (as it should: the museum paid €30 million for it) and there are also a few Picassos and other works by some of the better-known names of the 20th century. Take tram 17 from Centraal Station and Holland Spoor station.

Den Haag Centre

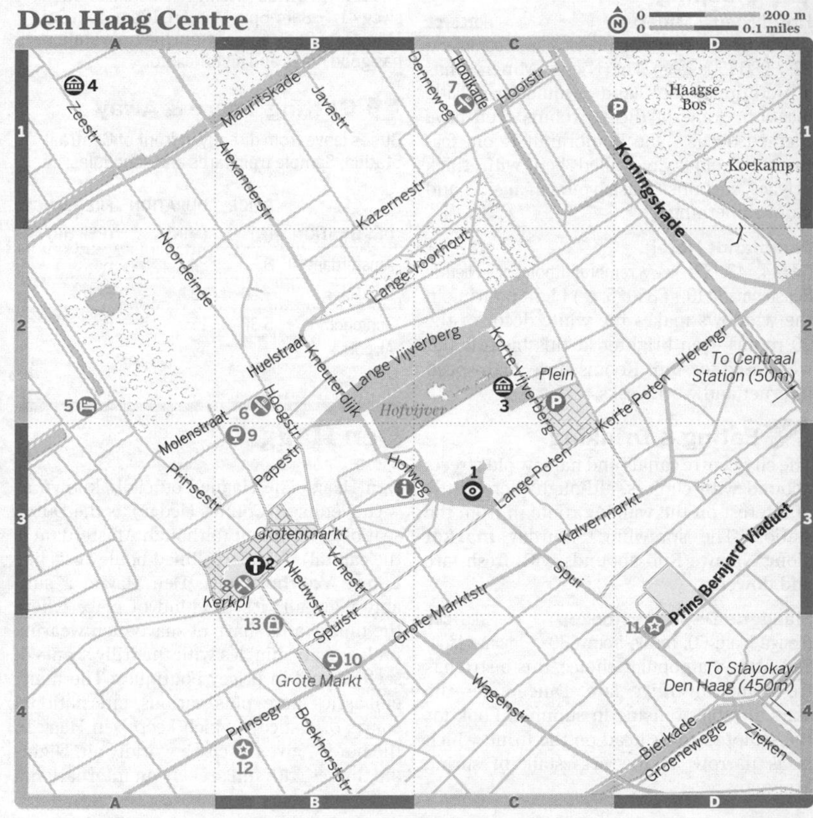

Madurodam TOURIST ATTRACTION

(www.madurodam.nl; George Maduroplein 1; adult/child €15/11; ⌚9am-6pm) In a hurry? This miniaturised Netherlands – complete with 1:25-scale versions of Schiphol, Amsterdam, windmills and tulips, Rotterdam harbour and the Delta dikes – is yet another example of the Dutch passion for recreating their reality artificially.

Panorama Mesdag PAINTING

(www.panorama-mesdag.nl; Zeestraat 65; adult/child €6.50/3; ⌚10am-5pm Mon-Sat, noon-5pm Sun & holidays) The *Panorama* (1881) is a gigantic 360-degree painting of Scheveningen, painted by Hendrik Willem Mesdag. It's viewed from a fake dune, with real sand, birdsong and wave sounds. Masterful achievement aside, you could just head 4km west to the real thing.

Scheveningen BEACH

(www.scheveningen.nl) On warm days the sands get oversubscribed by mobs of sun seekers but there's commercial relief in a slew of diversions that would warm the cockles of a Blackpool or Atlantic City huckster. Escape the madness on paved bike paths that run for miles through desolate dunes. Trams 1, 9 and 11 heading west serve Scheveningen but it's more pleasantly approached at the end of a 15- to 20-minute (4km) bike ride that will take you past the lush homes of some of Den Haag's most well-heeled residents.

Den Haag Centre

Sights

1 Binnenhof ... C3
2 Grote Kerk ... B3
3 Mauritshuis ... C2
4 Panorama Mesdag ... A1

Sleeping

5 Hotel La Ville ... A2

Eating

6 Brasserie 't Ogenblik ... B2
7 Les Ombrelles ... C1
8 Zebedeüs ... B3

Drinking

9 Café De Oude Mol ... B3
10 De Zwarte Ruiter ... B4

Entertainment

11 Nederlands Dans Theater ... D4
12 Paard van Troje ... B4

Shopping

13 Stanley & Livingstone ... B4

Sleeping

Discreet and subtly elegant hotels are scattered throughout the centre.

Hotel Sebel BOUTIQUE HOTEL €€

(☎385 92 00; www.hotelsebel.nl; Prins Hendrikplein 20; r €80-150; 📶) This 33-room boutique hotel is in a proud art nouveau corner building. Everything has been tastefully updated and the lobby is downright minimalist. The cheapest rooms let you touch the walls...all at once; better are the garden rooms with terraces. It's on tram line 17 from Centraal Station and Holland Spoor station.

Hotel La Ville HOTEL €€

(☎346 36 57; www.hotellaville.nl; Veenkade 5-6; r €45-125; 📶) The 21 rooms here are the best deal close to the centre. Things are basic white but spotless and comfortable; some rooms share bathrooms. Apartments have basic cooking facilities and there's a small cafe.

Stayokay Den Haag HOSTEL €

(☎315 78 88; www.stayokay.com/denhaag; Scheepmakerstraat 27; dm from €23; @) This 220-bed branch of the Stayokay hostel chain has all the usual facilities, including a bar, restaurant, internet and games. It's around 15-minutes' walk from Den Haag HS station.

Eating & Drinking

All those expats on expense accounts support a diverse and thriving cafe culture. The cobbled streets and canals off Denneweg are an excellent place to stroll hungry.

TOP CHOICE **Les Ombrelles** SEAFOOD €€€

(☎365 87 89; www.lesombrelles.nl; Hooistraat 4; mains €15-30; ⌚lunch Mon-Fri, dinner Mon-Sat) At a confluence of canals in one of the city's most charming districts, this long-running favourite sets up tables across the shady plaza. The tank with live crabs tells you that this is seafood country, and the very long menu abounds with choice.

De Zwarte Ruiter CAFE €

(The Black Rider; Grote Markt 27; snacks from €4) The Rider faces off with the competing Boterwaag across the Markt like rival kings of cool. We call this one the winner, with its terrace and art deco mezzanine – light-filled, split-level and cavernous – and boisterous crowds of commoners, diplomats and, no doubt, the odd international jewel thief.

Mero BISTRO €€€
(☎352 36 00; Vissershavenweg 61, Scheveningen; mains €20-30; ⏰lunch Tue-Fri, dinner Tue-Sat) Industrial chic is the style at this harbourside brasserie serving the best fish in the area. The bold crustacean art on the walls is matched by the bold flavours on the plate. Near tram 11.

Brasserie 't Ogenblik BISTRO €€
(Molenstraat 4c; mains €6-15) Servers zip about at this ever-popular cafe at the confluence of several pedestrianised shopping streets (in summer, tables are set up along voyeur-friendly Hoogstraat). Coffees and teas offer refreshment, and a creative line-up of salads, sandwiches, soups and more offer sustenance.

Café De Oude Mol CAFE €
(Oude Molstraat 61; snacks from €3) Some of the *oude* (old) *National Geographics* piled in the window actually predate the crusty yet genial characters arrayed around the bar. Pass through the ivy-covered door and you'll find Den Haag without the pretence.

Zebedeüs CAFE €
(Rond de Grote Kerk 8; meals from €7) Built right into the walls of the Grote Kerk, this bright cafe is a day-tripper's dream, with huge, fresh sandwiches served all day. Grab one of many tree-shaded tables outside or relax with a coffee and a newspaper at the big tables within.

☆ Entertainment

Nederlands Dans Theater DANCE
(www.ndt.nl; Schedeldoekshaven 60) This world-famous dance company has two main components: NDT1, the main troupe of 30 dancers; and NDT2, a small group of 16 dancers under 23.

Paard van Troje CLUB
(www.paard.nl; Prinsegracht 12) This eclectic venue has club nights and live music, as well as a cafe. The program's also eclectic: everything from booty-shaking DJs to cutting-edge house to flamenco.

Shopping

Grote Markstraat is fittingly the street for large stores. Interesting shops and oddball boutiques line Hoogstraat, Noordeinde and Heulstraat; the real treats are along Prinsestraat. Grab the latest Lonely Planet guide at **Stanley & Livingstone** (☎365 73 06; Schoolstraat 21), an excellent travel bookshop.

Information

The **tourist office** (www.denhaag.com; Hofweg 1; ⏰9.30am-6pm Mon-Fri, to 5pm Sat, 11am-5pm Sun) sells tickets for local events and has internet access.

Getting There & Around

Most **trains** start/stop their journeys from **Den Haag Centraal Station** (CS). But some through trains only stop at **Den Haag HS** (Holland Spoor) station just south of the centre. Sample train fares:

DESTINATION	PRICE (€)	DURATION (MIN)	FREQUENCY (PER HR)
Amsterdam	10	50	4
Rotterdam	4.30	25	4
Schiphol	7.30	30	4

A useful **day pass** for local trams costs €6.70 but you have to wait in often-long ticket queues at CS and HS.

Delft

☎015 / POP 96,600

Compact, charming and relaxed, Delft may be the perfect Dutch day trip. Founded around 1100, it maintains tangible links to its romantic past despite the pressures of modernisation and tourist hordes. Many of the canalside vistas could be scenes from the *Girl with a Pearl Earring,* the novel about Golden Age painter Johannes Vermeer, which was made into a movie (and partially shot here) in 2003. His *View of Delft* is an enigmatic vision of the town (it hangs in the Mauritshuis in Den Haag). Delft is also famous for its 'delftware', the distinctive blue-and-white pottery originally duplicated from Chinese porcelain by 17th-century artisans.

Sights

The 14th-century **Nieuwe Kerk** (www.nieuwekerk-delft.nl; Markt; adult/child €3.50/1.50; ⏰9am-6pm Apr-Oct, 11am-4pm Nov-Mar, closed Sun) houses the crypt of the Dutch royal family and the mausoleum of Willem the Silent. The fee includes entrance to the **Oude Kerk** (www.oudekerk-delft.nl; Heilige Geestkerkhof; ⏰9am-6pm Apr-Oct, 11am-4pm Nov-Mar, closed Sun). The latter, 800 years old, is a surreal sight: its tower leans 2m from the vertical. Among the tombs inside is Vermeer's. The

DON'T MISS

GOUDA

Its association with cheesy comestibles has made Gouda famous – the town's namesake fermented curd is among the Netherlands' best-known exports. But Gouda, the town, has a bit more to it than that. It enjoyed economic success and decline in the same manner as the rest of Holland from the 16th century onwards.

The **central Markt** is one of the largest such squares in the Netherlands. Right in the middle is the mid-15th-century **town hall**. Constructed from shimmering sandstone, this regal Gothic structure bespeaks the wealth Gouda enjoyed from the cloth trade when it was built.

On the north side of the Markt, you can't miss the **Waag**, a former cheese-weighing house built in 1668. If you have any doubt about its use, check out the reliefs carved into the side showing the cheese being weighed. It houses the **Kaaswaag** (adult/child €3.50/3; ⏲1-5pm Tue-Sun Apr-Oct), a museum that follows the history of the cheese trade in the Netherlands.

Just south of the Markt is **Sint Janskerk** (Achter de Kerk; adult/child €2.50/1.75; ⏲10am-5pm). The church itself had chequered beginnings: it burned down with ungodly regularity every 100 years or so from 1361 until the mid-16th century, when what you see today was completed. The stained-glass windows are renowned.

Gouda is on the busy train line between Utrecht (€5.70, 20 minutes) and Rotterdam (€4.50, 20 minutes).

town hall and the **Waag** on the Markt are right out of the 17th century.

Vermeer Centre Delft TOURIST ATTRACTION
(Voldersgracht 21; adult/child €7/3; ⏲10am-5pm) The nonprolific painter (only 35 works are firmly attributed to him) stars at this touristy attraction, which looks at his artistry and life in detail but actually has none of his paintings.

Municipal Museum het Prinsenhof MUSEUM
(www.prinsenhof-delft.nl; St Agathaplein 1; adult/child €7.50/free; ⏲10am-5pm Tue-Sat, 1-5pm Sun) This museum, in a former convent where Willem the Silent was assassinated in 1584, displays various objects telling the story of the 80-year war with Spain, as well as 17th-century paintings.

de Candelaer STUDIO
(www.candelaer.nl; Kerkstraat 13; ⏲9am-5.30pm Mon-Fri, 9am-5pm Sat year-round, 9am-5pm Sun Mar-May) Just five artists produce iconic Delftware here. When it's quiet they'll give you a detailed tour of the manufacturing process.

Royal Delft FACTORY
(www.royaldelft.com; Rotterdamseweg 196; ⏲9am-5pm daily Apr-Oct, closed Sun Nov-Mar) The only original Delftware factory, operating since the 1650s. Bus 129 from the train station stops nearby at Jaffalaan, or it's a 15-minute walk.

Sleeping

Compact in size and oh-so-charming, Delft makes a good base for exploring much of Holland, with frequent and fast train services putting towns from Leiden to Rotterdam less than 20 minutes away.

Hotel Coen HOTEL €€
(☎214 59 14; www.hotelcoendelft.nl; Coenderstraat 47; r from €80; @📶) Just behind the train station but removed from the construction, this family-run hotel has 55 beds in a variety of rooms, from budget singles as thin as your wallet to grander doubles.

Hotel de Ark HOTEL €€
(☎215 79 99; www.deark.nl; Koornmarkt 65; r €115-160; @📶) Four 17th-century canalside houses have been turned into this gracious and luxurious small hotel. Rooms are reached by elevator and have vintage beauty that isn't stuffy. Out back there's a small garden; nearby are apartments for longer stays.

Eating & Drinking

De Visbanken SEAFOOD STAND €
(Camaretten 2; snacks from €3; ⏲10am-6pm) Someone has been selling fish on this spot since 1342. The present vendors line the display cases in the old open-air pavilion with all manner of things fishy. Enjoy marinated and smoked treats or go for something fried.

Delft

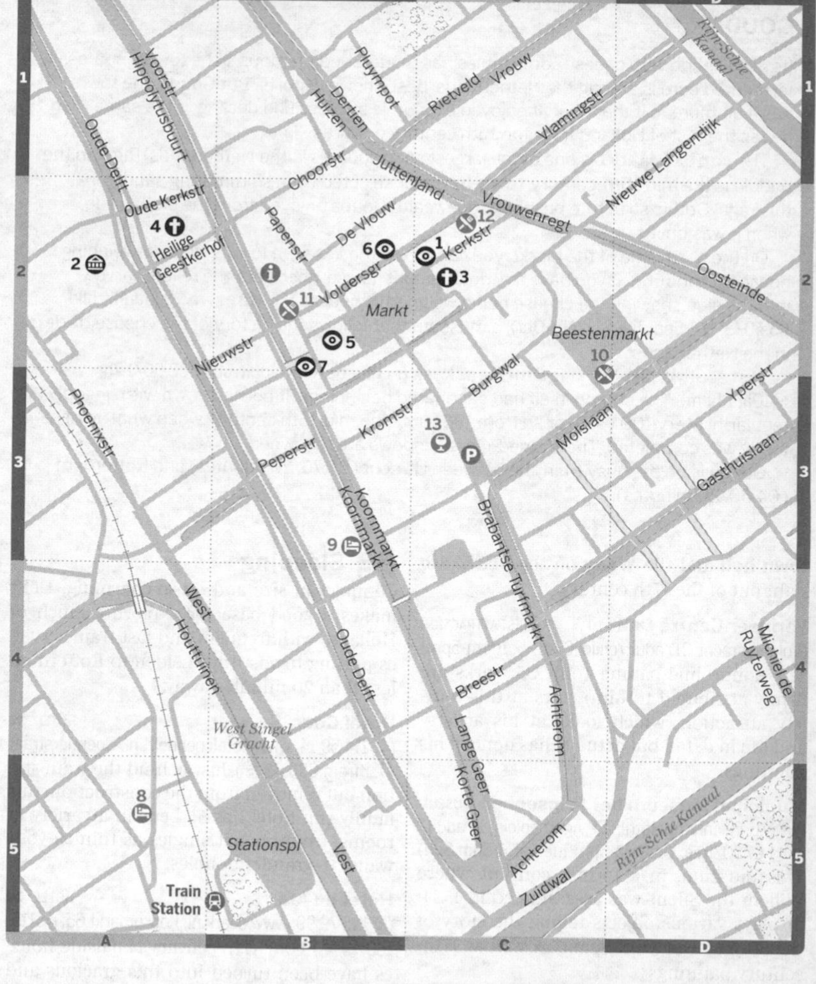

Delft

Sights

1 De Candelaer ... C2
2 Municipal Museum Het Prinsenhof ... A2
3 Nieuwe Kerk ... C2
4 Oude Kerk ... A2
5 Town Hall ... B2
6 Vermeer Centre Delft ... B2
7 Waag ... B2

Sleeping

8 Hotel Coen ... A5
9 Hotel de Ark ... B3

Eating

10 Barrique ... C3
11 De Visbanken ... B2
12 Eetcafé De Ruif ... C2

Drinking

13 Locus Publicus ... C3

Eetcafé De Ruif BISTRO €€

(Kerkstraat 22; mains €12-18; lunch & dinner) Wonderfully rustic, with a low ceiling and canal views from a rear terrace. Try the much-loved local Stellendam shrimps. At night it's a popular place for a glass of this or that, with or without shrimp.

Barrique CAFE €

(Beestenmarkt 33; meals from €8) Just east of the Markt, cafes sprawl across the shady Beestenmarkt. Where pigs were once sold (1449–1972), it's now home to fun-filled consumption. This slick cafe specialises in wine for the beer-weary, tapas and smooth jazz.

Locus Publicus PUB

(Brabantse Turfmarkt 67) Glowing from within, this beer cafe has more than 200 beers. It's charming and filled with cheery locals who quaff their way through the list.

Information

The **tourist office** (0900-515 15 55; www.delft.nl; Hippolytusbuurt 4; 10am-4pm Mon, 9am-6pm Tue-Fri, to 5pm Sat, to 4pm Sun) has free internet; the thematic walking guides are excellent.

Getting There & Away

The area around the **train station** will be a vast construction site for years to come as the lines are moved underground. Sample train fares:

DESTINATION	PRICE (€)	DURATION (MIN)	FREQUENCY (PER HR)
Amsterdam	11.60	60	2
Den Haag	2.50	12	4
Rotterdam	3.20	12	4

Rotterdam

010 / POP 606,000

Rotterdam bursts with energy. Vibrant nightlife, a diverse, multi-ethnic community, an intensely interesting maritime tradition and a wealth of top-class museums all make it a must-see part of any visit to Holland, especially if you are passing by on the new high-speed trains.

The Netherlands' 'second city', Rotterdam was bombed flat during WWII and spent the following decades rebuilding. You won't find the classic Dutch medieval centre here – it was swept away along with the other rubble and detritus of war. In its place is an architectural aesthetic that's unique in Europe, a progressive, perpetual-motion approach to architecture that's clearly a result of the city's postwar, postmodern, anything-goes philosophy (a fine example of this is the Paul McCarthy statue titled *Santa with Butt Plug* that the city placed in the main shopping district).

Sights & Activities

Rotterdam is split by the vast Nieuwe Maas shipping channel, which is crossed by a series of tunnels and bridges, notably the fabulously postmodern Erasmusbrug. The centre is on the north side of the water and is easily strolled. The historic neighbourhood of Delfshaven is 3km west.

TOP CHOICE **Museum Boijmans van Beuningen** MUSEUM

(www.boijmans.nl; Museumpark 18-20; adult/child €9/free, Wed free; 11am-5pm Tue-Sun) Museum Boijmans van Beuningen is among Europe's very finest museums and has a permanent collection taking in Dutch and European art (Bosch, Van Eyck, Rembrandt, Tintoretto, Titian and Bruegel's *Tower of Babel*). The surrealist wing features ephemera, paraphernalia and famous works from Dalí, Duchamp, Magritte, Man Ray and more.

Architecture NOTABLE BUILDINGS

Like those mod visions of the future that never seem to come to pass, Rotterdam's architecture is both fanciful and arresting.

The **Overblaak Development** (1978–84), designed by Piet Blom, is marked by its pencil-shaped tower and arresting up-ended, cube-shaped apartments. One unit, the **Kijk-Kubus Museum-House** (www.kubuswoning.nl; adult/child €2.50/1.50; 11am-5pm), lets you see what its like to live at odd angles.

Designed by Ben van Berkel, the 1996 800m-long **Erasmusbrug** bridge is a city icon. Nearby, on the south bank, look for **KPN Telecom headquarters**, built in 2000 and designed by Renzo Piano, who also designed Paris' Pompidou Centre. The building leans at a sharp angle, seemingly resting on a long pole. There's also the very tall new **MaasToren** and **De Rotterdam**, which broke ground in 2009 and will be the largest building in the country.

Historisch Museum het Schielandhuis MUSEUM

(www.hmr.rotterdam.nl; Korte Hoogstraat 31; adult/child €5/free; 11am-5pm Tue-Sun) Located in one of the city's few surviving 17th-century buildings, exhibits focus on everyday life

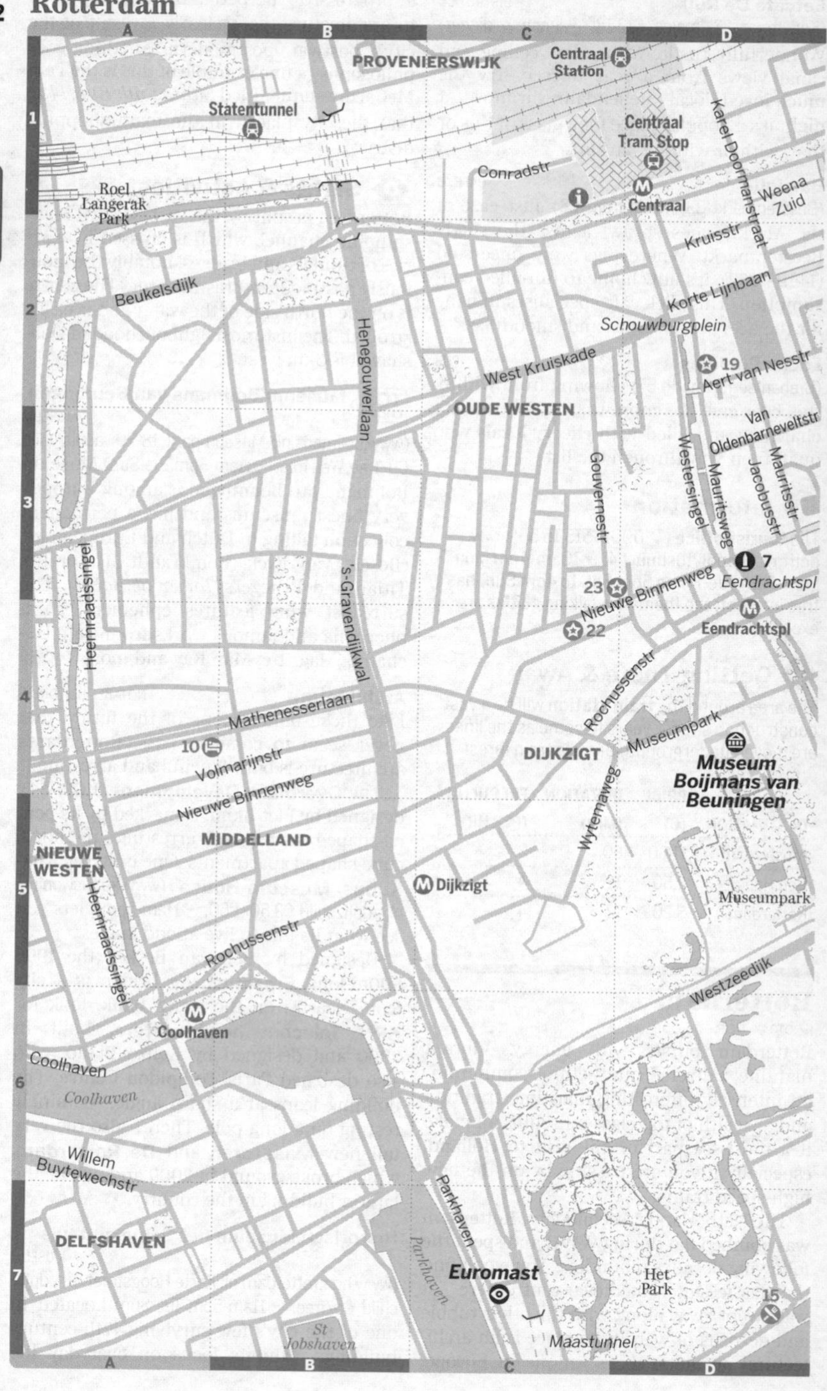
A
B
C
D
1
2
3
4
5
6
7
PROVENIERSWIJK
Centraal Station
Statentunnel
Centraal Tram Stop
Conradstr
Centraal
Roel Langerak Park
Karel Doormanstraat
Weena Zuid
Kruisstr
Beukelsdijk
Korte Lijnbaan
Schouwburgplein
Henegouwerlaan
West Kruiskade
19
Aert van Nesstr
OUDE WESTEN
Van Oldenbarneveltstr
Westersingel
Mauritsweg
Jacobusstr
Mauritsstr
Gouvernestr
7
Eendrachtspl
23
Nieuwe Binnenweg
22
Eendrachtspl
Heemraadssingel
's-Gravendijkwal
Rochussenstr
Mathenesserlaan
Museumpark
10
DIJKZIGT
Volmarijnstr
Museum Boijmans van Beuningen
Nieuwe Binnenweg
Wytemaweg
MIDDELLAND
NIEUWE WESTEN
Dijkzigt
Museumpark
Heemraadssingel
Rochussenstr
Westzeedijk
Coolhaven
Coolhaven
Coolhaven
Willem Buytewechstr
Parkhaven
DELFSHAVEN
Parkhaven
Euromast
Het Park
15
St Jobshaven
Maastunnel

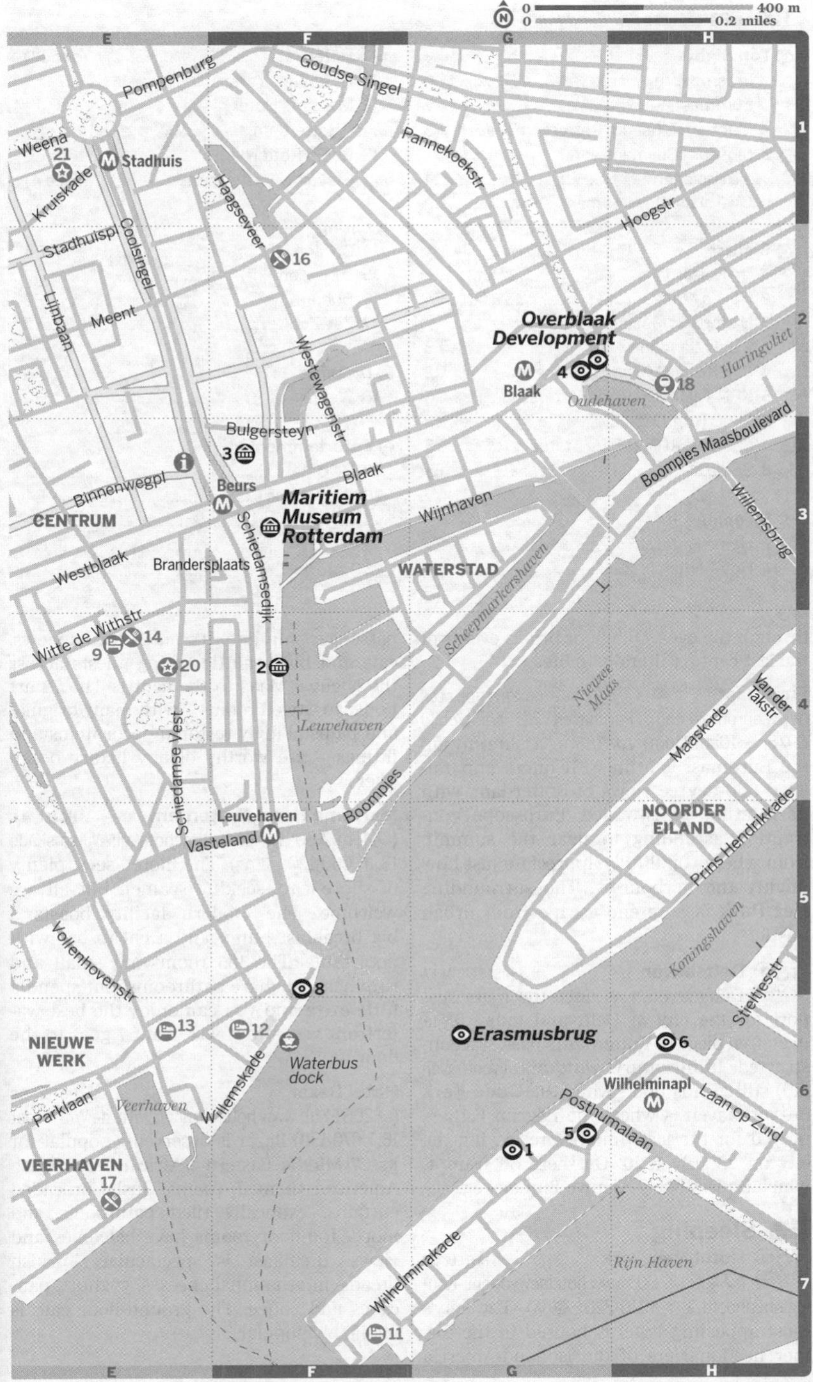
0 400 m
0 0.2 miles
E
F
G
H
1
2
3
4
5
6
7
Pompenburg
Goudse Singel
Pannekoekstr
Weena
21
Stadhuis
Kruiskade
Haagseveer
Hoogstr
Stadhuispl
Coolsingel
16
Lijnbaan
Meent
Westewagenstr
Overblaak Development
Blaak
4
18
Haringvliet
Oudehaven
Bulgersteyn
3
Boompjes Maasboulevard
Blaak
Binnenwegpl
Beurs
Maritiem Museum Rotterdam
Wijnhaven
CENTRUM
Schiedamsedijk
Willemsbrug
Westblaak
Brandersplaats
WATERSTAD
Scheepmakershaven
Witte de Withstr
14
9
20
2
Nieuwe Maas
Van der Takstr
Leuvehaven
Maaskade
Schiedamse Vest
Boompjes
Leuvehaven
NOORDER EILAND
Vasteland
Prins Hendrikkade
Vollenhovenstr
Koningshaven
8
Stieltjesstr
13
12
Erasmusbrug
6
NIEUWE WERK
Waterbus dock
Willemskade
Wilhelminapl
Laan op Zuid
Parklaan
Veerhaven
Posthumalaan
5
1
VEERHAVEN
17
Wilhelminakade
Rijn Haven
11

Rotterdam

Top Sights

	Erasmusbrug	G6
	Euromast	C7
	Maritiem Museum Rotterdam	F3
	Museum Boijmans van Beuningen	D4
	Overblaak Development	G2

Sights

1	De Rotterdam	G6
2	Haven Museum	F4
3	Historisch Museum Het Schielandhuis	F3
4	Kijk-Kubus Museum-House	G2
5	KPN Telecom Headquarters	G6
6	MaasToren	H6
7	Santa With Butt Plug Statue	D3
8	Spido	F5

Sleeping

9	Home Hotel	E4
10	Hotel Amar	A4
	Hotel Bazar	(see 14)
11	Hotel New York	F7
12	Maritime Hotel Rotterdam	F6
13	Room Rotterdam	E6
	Stayokay Rotterdam	(see 4)

Eating

14	Bazar	E4
15	De Ballentent	D7
16	Dudok	F2
17	Zee Zout	E7

Drinking

18	Weimar	H2

Entertainment

19	De Unie	D2
20	Gay Palace	E4
21	off_corso	E1
22	Pluto	C4
23	Rotown	C3

through the ages. One floor brings events of the last century literally to life.

Euromast OBSERVATION DECK
(www.euromast.com; Parkhaven 20; adult/child €9/6; ⏲10am-11pm) At 185m, a shimmy up the Euromast is a must. It offers unparalleled 360-degree views of Rotterdam, with its rotating, glass-walled 'Euroscope' contraption ascending to near the summit, from where you'll fully appreciate just how mighty the harbour is. The surrounding **Het Park** is a serene escape from urban bustle.

TOP CHOICE **Delfshaven** HISTORIC AREA
Delfshaven was once the main seaport for the city of Delft and today it's a twee-free piece of Rotterdam's past. A reconstructed 18th-century **windmill** (Voorhaven 210) still grinds flour, while the **Oude Kerk** on Voorhaven is where the Pilgrim Fathers prayed for the last time before leaving the city on 22 July 1620. Get here on tram 4, which cruises lively Nieuwe Binnenweg.

Sleeping

TOP CHOICE **Hotel New York** HOTEL €€
(☎439 05 00; www.hotelnewyork.nl; Koninginnenhoofd 1; r €110-220; @📶) The city's most appealing hotel is housed in the former headquarters of the Holland-America passenger-ship line. It's noted for its views, cafe and boat shuttle taking guests across the Nieuwe Maas to the centre. The 72 art nouveau–styled rooms – with many original and painstakingly restored decor items and fittings – are worthy of any luxury ocean liner.

Maritime Hotel Rotterdam HOTEL €€
(☎411 92 60; www.maritimehotel.nl; Willemskade 13; r €60-120; @📶) The hotel sees plenty of shore-leave-seeking seamen but all are welcome. The modern facility boasts a big breakfast buffet and a cheap bar with pool table. The 135 rooms are small and the cheapest share bathrooms, but spend a little extra and you can enjoy the best waterfront views in town. Tram 7 goes to the door.

Hotel Bazar HOTEL €€
(☎206 51 51; www.hotelbazar.nl; Witte de Withstraat 16; r €70-130) Bazar is deservedly popular for its 27 Middle Eastern–, African- and South American–themed rooms: lush, brocaded curtains, exotically tiled bathrooms and more. Top-floor rooms have balconies and views. Breakfast is spectacular: Turkish breads, international cheeses, yoghurt, pancakes and coffee. The ground-floor cafe is justifiably popular.

Home Hotel STUDIOS €€
(☎411 21 21, 414 21 50; www.homehotel.nl; Witte de Withstraat 38; r from €80) More than 85 studio apartments are available for rent in various buildings in one of Rotterdam's most appealing neighbourhoods. Some have wi-fi but all have cooking facilities. Rates fall for multiple nights and many people stay by the week or month.

Stayokay Rotterdam HOSTEL €
(☎436 57 63; www.stayokay.com/rotterdam; Overblaak 85-87; dm €17-25, r from €65; @☎) Those odd angles you see at this hostel may not be to do with what you just smoked; this posh hostel is within the landmark Overblaak development. There are 245 beds in oddly shaped rooms that sleep two to eight. Some have air con and those on the top floor have cool views.

Hotel Amar HOTEL €
(☎425 57 95; www.amarhotel.nl; Mathenesserlaan 316; r €50-90; @☎) Small place is in a leafy neighbourhood close to Delfshaven, the Museumplein and good nightlife. Rooms are simple, comfy and share bathrooms.

Room Rotterdam HOSTEL €
(☎282 72 77; www.roomrotterdam.nl; Van Vollenhovensraat 62; dm from €17; @☎) A popular hostel with 16 dorm rooms, each with two to 10 beds. Each has its own decor, ranging from 'Dutch Delight' to 'Love'.

Eating

CENTRAL ROTTERDAM

Look for myriad eating choices in Veerhaven, Witte de Single, Nieuwe Binnenweg and Oude Haven.

TOP CHOICE **De Ballentent** DUTCH €
(www.deballentent.nl; Parkkade 1; meals from €5; ⌚9am-11pm) Rotterdam's best waterfront pub-cafe is also a great spot for a meal. Dine on one of two terraces or inside. Mussels, schnitzels and more line the menu but the real speciality here are *bals,* huge homemade meatloafy meatballs.

Bazar MIDDLE EASTERN €€
(Witte de Withstraat 16; mains €7-15) On the ground floor of the inventive Hotel Bazar, this eatery comes up with creative Middle Eastern fusion fare that complements the stylised decor. Dolmades haven't tasted this good any place west of Istanbul.

Zee Zout SEAFOOD €€€
(www.restaurantzeezout.nl; Westerkade 11b; meals from €45; ⌚lunch Tue-Fri, dinner Tue-Sat) The name means sea salt, and that's all you need to know. Well, actually, details such as the superbly prepared fresh fish, wrap-around windows, outside seating with waterfront views and polished service are also key.

Dudok GRAND CAFE €€
(Meent 88; dishes €6-20) There are always crowds at this sprawling brasserie near the

MARITIME ROTTERDAM

Rotterdam has embraced the sea, shipping and trade since the 16th century. Harbour tours of Europe's busiest port are fascinating, while museums and exhibits on the water bring this heritage to life.

Maritiem Museum Rotterdam MUSEUM
(www.maritiemmuseum.nl; Leuvehaven 1; adult/child €7.50/4; ⌚10am-5pm Tue-Sat, 11am-5pm Sun year-round, plus 10am-5pm Mon Jul & Aug) This engaging museum looks at the Netherlands' rich maritime traditions. There's an array of models that any youngster would love to take into the tub, plus more interesting and explanatory displays.

Haven Museum OPEN-AIR MUSEUM
(Leuvehaven 50; admission free; ⌚visitors centre 10am-5pm Tue-Sun) All manner of old and historic ships moored in the basin just south of the Maritiem Museum. You can wander the quays around the clock.

Oude Haven HISTORIC AREA
Near the Overblaak Development and the Blaak train, metro and tram station, the oldest part of the harbour dates from the 14th century. Historic boats are moored here and you can often see restorations in progress.

Spido HARBOUR CRUISE
(www.spido.nl; Willemsplein 85; adult/child €9.50/6; ⌚9.30am-5pm Jun-Sep, shorter hr Oct-May) Offers daily harbour tours.

centre. Inside it's all high ceilings and walls of glass; outside you have your pick of an array of tables lining the street. Meals range from breakfast to snacks to cafe fare such as soups and pasta.

DELFSHAVEN

Historic and appealing, Delfshaven is a vibrant, multi-ethnic neighbourhood with many cafes and bars, especially along the canal near the Oude Kerk.

Het Eethuisje DUTCH €

(Mathenesserdijk 436; mains €8-10) Trad Dutch food is served from this little storefront near the canal. Utterly tourist-free. Tuck into meaty fare served with rib-sticking starchy sides.

Stadsbrouwerij De Pelgrim DUTCH €€

(Aelbrechtkolk 12; mains €7-20) It's named for the religious folk who passed through on their way to America and you can make your own voyage through the various beers brewed in the vintage surrounds. Meals range from casual lunches to more ambitious multicourse dinners.

Drinking

De Oude Sluis BROWN CAFE

(Havenstraat 7, Delfshaven) The view up the canal from the tables outside goes right out to Delfshaven's windmill at this ideal brown cafe. Inside you'll find good beers on tap, including the hoppy Brigand IPA.

Weimar CAFE

(Haringvliet 637) Named for the Hotel Weimer that stood here and was blasted to rubble in 1940, this is one of scores of waterside cafes in Oude Haven. Have a wander and pick one or several, depending on your mood. The Weimar is one of the more gracious.

Entertainment

Rotterdam draws clubgoers from across Europe.

Rotown BAR

(www.rotown.nl; Nieuwe Binnenweg 17-19) A smooth bar, a dependable live-rock venue, an agreeable outdoor cafe and the anchor of Rotterdam's most interesting street. The musical program features new local talent, established international acts and crossover experiments.

Gay Palace CLUB

(www.gay-palace.nl; Schiedamsesingel 139) And here we have Rotterdam's only gay nightclub, with four floors of throbbing dance action – with different scenes on each floor – to work you into a sweat.

off_corso CLUB

(www.off-corso.nl; Kruiskade 22) This is where it's at: bleeding-edge local and international DJs mashing up a high-fibre electronic diet of bleeps 'n' beats. Art displays provide diversions at this prototypical Rotterdam club.

De Unie VENUE

(www.deunie.nu; Mauritsweg 35) Truly cultural, this landmark venue is a vision in white, which provides a blank slate for events from cabaret to forums about taxation and the middle class to acoustic folk.

Pluto COFFEE SHOP

(www.pluto.nl; Nieuwe Binnenweg 54) Space, not the Disney dog, is the inspiration at this head shop, which sells every kind of pot accessory and goods to fill them.

Information

The Rotterdam Welcome Card (from €9) offers discounts for sights, hotels and restaurants and

DON'T MISS

BLOWING IN THE WIND

In 1740 a series of windmills were built to drain a polder about 12km southeast of Rotterdam. Today 19 of the Dutch icons survive at **Kinderdijk** (www.kinderdijk.nl), which is a Unesco monument. You can wander the dikes for over 3km amid the spinning sails and visit inside one of the **windmills** (adult/child €3.50/2; 9.30am-5.30pm). It's a good bicycle ride; you can rent bikes once there or travel from Rotterdam (16km); get a map from the tourist office.

A fantastic day trip is by the **Waterbus** (www.waterbus.nl; Willemskade; day pass adult/child €11.50/7). The fast ferries leave from Rotterdam every 30 minutes and a connection puts you at Kinderdijk, 1km from the first mill. After the visit, continue by ferry to utterly charming **Dordrecht** and then return to Rotterdam by train.

free public transport. Buy it from the tourist office.

Tourist office (www.rotterdam.info) City (Coolsingel 197; ⌚9am-6pm Mon-Sat, 10am-5pm Sun); Groothandelsgebouw (Weena; ⌚9am-5.30pm Mon-Sat, 10am-5pm Sun) Free internet; pick up the essential *R Zine*. The main (city) branch is located in the City Information Centre, with a good display on architecture since the war and a huge town model. A second location is near the train station in the landmark Groothandelsgebouw.

Use-It (www.use-it.nl; Schaatsbaan 41-45; ⌚9am-6pm Tue-Sun mid-May–mid-Sep, to 5pm Tue-Sat mid-Sep–mid-May) Offbeat independent tourist organisation all but lost amid the station construction. Books cheap accommodation and publishes the excellent *Simply the Best* budget guide.

Getting There & Away

The area around **Rotterdam Centraal Station** will be one big construction site until the stunning new station – set above and below ground – is completed in 2013.

DESTINATION	PRICE (€)	DURATION (MIN)	FREQUENCY (PER HR)
Amsterdam via Leiden	13.30	65	5
Amsterdam (high speed)	21	40	2
Brussels	27-43	75-107	1
Schiphol	10.70	47	3
Utrecht	9.10	40	4

Getting Around

Rotterdam's trams, buses and metro are provided by **RET** (www.ret.nl). Most converge in front of CS, where there is an **information booth** (⌚6am-11pm Mon-Fri, 8am-11pm Sat & Sun) that also sells tickets. There are other information windows in the major metro stations. Day passes are €6.

Rent bikes from Use-it (p957) for €6 per day.

Utrecht

☎030 / POP 302,000

Utrecht is one of the Netherlands' oldest cities and boasts a beautiful, vibrant, old-world city centre, ringed by striking 13th-century canal wharves. The wharves, well below street level, are unique to Utrecht. Canalside streets alongside brim with shops, restaurants and cafes.

Initial impressions may be less auspicious. When you step off the train you'll find yourself lost in the maze that is the Hoog Catharijne shopping centre. The Hoog is huge...and it's attached to the station...and it seemingly goes on forever...and ever. It's really a nightmare but a vast construction project (www.cu2030.nl) is transforming the entire area.

The city's student community of 40,000 is the largest in the country. Saturdays are mad with shoppers and day trippers in from every polder in the region. In contrast, Sunday mornings are a fab time to immerse yourself in the moody charms or empty streets echoing with church bells.

Sights

Focus your wanderings on the **Domplein** and south along the tree-lined **Oudegracht**. The tourist office has a good booklet that covers Utrecht's myriad small museums, which feature everything from waste water to old trains.

Domtoren HISTORIC BUILDING

(www.domtoren.nl; Domplein; adult/child €8/4.50; ⌚11am-4pm) The Domtoren is 112m high, with 465 steps. It's a tough haul to the top but well worth the exertion: the tower gives unbeatable city views. The guided tour in Dutch and English is detailed and gives privileged insight into this beautiful structure. Buy tickets nearby at the tourist office.

Centraal Museum MUSEUM

(www.centraalmuseum.nl; Nicolaaskerkhof 10; adult/child €9/4; ⌚11am-5pm Tue-Sun) This museum has a wide-ranging collection: applied arts dating back to the 17th century as well as paintings by some of the Utrecht School artists. There's even a 12th-century boat that was dug out of the local mud and a 400-year-old dollhouse. Admission also includes the following:

Dick Bruna Huis

(www.dickbrunahuis.nl; Nicolaaskerkhof 10) One of Utrecht's favourite sons, author and illustrator Dick Bruna is the creator of beloved cartoon rabbit Miffy and she naturally takes pride of place at his **studio** across from the museum. Kids get a huge kick out of it, but so do adults who appreciate superlative graphic design.

Rietveld-Schröderhuis

This Unesco-recognised **landmark house** is just outside the centre. Built in 1924 by

Utrecht architect Gerrit Rietveld, it is a stark example of 'form follows function'. There's a €3 surcharge for the mandatory tour; the museum will give you a map for the pleasant 25-minute stroll to the house or loan you a free bike.

Museum Catharijneconvent MUSEUM
(www.catharijneconvent.nl; Nieuwegracht 63; adult/child €11.50/7.25; ⏲10am-5pm Tue-Fri, 11am-5pm Sat & Sun) This museum has the finest collection of medieval religious art in the Netherlands, housed in a Gothic former convent and an 18th-century canalside house. Look for the Rembrandt and, if you're lucky, you'll find a temporary exhibition to match the stir caused by the recent one on phallic art.

Sleeping

B&B Utrecht B&B €
(☎065 043 48 84; www.hostelutrecht.nl; Lucas Bolwerk 4; dm from €21, r from €60; @) Straddling the border between hostel and hotel, this spotless inn in an elegant old building has an internal Ikea vibe. Breakfast is free, as is use of a huge range of musical instruments. Bikes are rented.

Grand Hotel Karel V HOTEL €€€
(☎233 75 55; www.karelv.nl; Geertebolwerk 1, off Walsteeg; r €140-300; ❄@📶) The lushest accommodation in Utrecht can be found in this former knights' gathering hall from the 14th century. The service and decor are understated. The 117 rooms are split between the old manor and a new wing. Taking tea in the walled garden is sublime.

Strowis Budget Hostel HOSTEL €
(☎238 02 80; www.strowis.nl; Boothstraat 8; dm from €16, r €63; @📶) This 17th-century building is near the town centre and has been lovingly restored and converted into a hostel (four- to 14-bed rooms). It has a cosy bar and rents bikes.

Eating

When Utrecht groans with visiting mobs, you can escape down to the waterside canal piers with a picnic.

TOP CHOICE **Blauw** INDONESIAN €€€
(www.restaurantblauw.nl; Springweg 64; set menu from €20; ⏲dinner) Blauw is *the* place for stylish Indonesian food in Utrecht. Young and old alike enjoy spicy, fresh fare amid the stunning red decor that mixes vintage art with hip minimalism.

Deeg MEDITERRANEAN €€€
(www.restaurantdeeg.nl; Lange Nieuwstraat 71; menus from €34; ⏲dinner) A charming corner location in the museum quarter is but the first draw at this casual bistro, which has nightly set menus that change regularly. Fresh local produce gets a Mediterranean accent and many items – such as the cheeses – are organic.

Oudaen CAFE €€
(www.oudaen.nl; Oudegracht 99; mains €8-22) The best choice on this busy stretch of the canal. Set in a restored 14th-century banquet hall, it has a varied menu of salads, steaks and seafood. Best of all, it brews its own beer, which you can enjoy under the high ceilings or outside on the canal.

Drinking

TOP CHOICE **ACU** BAR
(www.acu.nl; Voorstraat 71; ✎) Billing itself as a 'political cultural centre', ACU is a classic student dive. It combines bar, disco,

DON'T MISS

HOGE VELUWE NATIONAL PARK

The **Hoge Veluwe** (www.hogeveluwe.nl; adult/child/car €8/4/6; ⏲8am-10pm summer, 9am-6pm winter) is the Netherlands' largest national park, featuring a mix of forests and woods, shifting sands and heathery moors, along with red deer, wild boar and mouflon (wild sheep).

It features the world-class **Kröller-Müller Museum** (☎0318-59 12 41; www.kmm.nl; Houtkampweg 6; park admission plus adult/child €8/4; ⏲10am-5pm Tue-Sun), which has a superb collection of works by Van Gogh, as well as other pieces by Picasso, Renoir and Manet.

From Arnhem train station (Utrecht to Arnhem by train: €9.40, 37 minutes, four per hour), take bus 2 (15 minutes, every 30 minutes) to the Schaarsbergen park entrance (stop: Koningsweg). Various buses run inside the park to the museum.

WORTH A TRIP

THE DUTCH VS THE SEA

The disastrous 1953 flood was the impetus for the country's enormous Delta Project, which began shortly after and was finished decades later. The southwest river deltas were blocked using a network of dams, dikes and a remarkable 3.2km storm-surge barrier, which is lowered in rough conditions.

The **Waterland Neeltje Jans** (www.neeltjejans.nl; admission Nov-Mar €14, Apr-Oct €19; ⏲10am-5.30pm) is located near the main surge barrier. You can still explore the absorbing exhibits about floods, dams and plucky Dutch courage in battling the sea, but now the complex also includes other amusements, such as seals, a water park, fake beach and the worrisomely named thrill ride: the Moby Dick. For a big blow, try the hurricane simulator.

The entire sandy, wind-blown, wave-tossed region has coastal sections that are part of the **National Park Oosterschelde** (www.npoosterschelde.nl; visitor centre admission free; ⏲10am-5pm); there's a small information booth in the building across the N57 from Waterland. Bus 133 stops at the Waterland Neeltje Jans on its run from Middelburg station (30 minutes, every 30 minutes).

lecture hall and more. Argue about whether Trotsky was too conservative while downing organic vegan food.

Café Ledig Erf PUB
(Tolsteegbrug 3) This classy pub overlooks a confluence of canals (and other cafes) at the southern tip of town. The terrace vies with the beer list in offering the most joy. The autumn bock beer fest is a winner.

't Oude Pothuys BROWN CAFE
(Oudegracht 279) Small and dark, this basement pub has nightly music – jam sessions with locals trying their hand at rock and jazz. Totally refurbished, enjoy drinks on the canalside pier.

Information

The **tourist office** (www.utrechtyourway.nl; Domplein 9; ⏲10am-6pm Mon-Fri, 10am-5pm Sat, noon-5pm Sun) sells maps and tours of the nearby Domtoren.

Getting There & Away

Utrecht is easily walked (once you escape the shopping mall). The **train station** is a major connection point and is Holland's busiest. It is on the line linking Amsterdam to Cologne. Sample train fares:

DESTINATION	PRICE (€)	DURATION (MIN)	FREQUENCY (PER HR)
Amsterdam	6.70	30	4
Maastricht	23.50	120	2
Rotterdam	9.10	40	4

THE DELTA REGION

The province of Zeeland (Sea Land) is three slivers of land nestling in the middle of a vast delta through which many of Europe's rivers drain; it dominates this peaceful corner of the Netherlands. As you survey the calm, flat landscape, consider that the region was home to two massive waterborne tragedies. In 1421 the St Elizabeth's Day flood killed more than 100,000 people; and in 1953, yet another flood laid waste to 2000 lives and 800km of dikes, leaving 500,000 homeless and leading to the Delta Project, among the world's greatest engineering feats.

Middelburg

☎0118 / POP 48,000

Middelburg, Zeeland's sleepy medieval capital, is a friendly, low-key settlement: not exactly flush with nightlife, but perfect for exploring a region that is quintessentially Dutch.

Sights

This pretty, airy little town is eminently suitable for walking, with cobblestones and snaking alleyways leading in and away from the town square, which hosts a famous **market** on Thursday.

The sizable **Abdij** complex dates from the 12th century and houses the regional government as well as three churches and two museums. Climb **Lange Jan** (admission €4), a 91m-high tower dating from the 14th century. The revamped **Zeeuws**

Museum (www.zeeuwsmuseum.nl; adult/child €8/free; ⌚10am-5pm Tue-Sun), in the former monks' dormitories, features traditional garb, which must have been an expensive burden for people barely eking out a living farming.

The **Stadhuis** (city hall; adult/child €4.25/3.75; ⌚tours 11.30am & 3.15pm) grabs the eye: it's staggeringly beautiful. The Gothic side facing the Markt is from the 1400s, while the classical Noordstraat segment dates from the 1600s.

Sleeping & Eating

Hotel Aan De Dam HOTEL €€
(☎64 37 73; www.hotelaandedam.nl; Dam 31; r €80-140; 📶) An opulent 1652 mansion has been converted into Middelburg's most appealing hotel. The seven rooms are mostly very large and have period decor that's been tricked out with modern conveniences – such as luxurious bathrooms as opposed to chamber pots. It overlooks a canal and small park.

Het Princenjagt HOTEL €
(☎61 34 16; www.hotelhetprincenjagt.nl; Nederstraat 2; r €40-80; 📶) This eight-room B&B has a kitchen for guests and a jaunty location by the marina. Touches include a little toaster on each table at breakfast and nice chairs for slouching in the rooms.

Peper & Zout SEAFOOD €€
(www.peperenzout.com; Lange Noordstraat 8; mains €12-25; ⌚closed Wed) The cute fishy tiles outside tell you what's on the menu inside. Excellent seafood that changes by the season is the draw here, as is the cheery owner.

De Mug PUB €€
(www.demug.nl; Vlasmarkt 54-56; mains €16-21; ⌚dinner Tue-Sat) Don't be fooled by the Heineken signs; the beer list is long and boasts many rare Trappist varieties. Also try the Mug Bitter, which is heavy on the hops. The menu goes well with the brews: hearty seafood and meat plus more simple fare for snacking.

Getting There & Away

Middelburg is near the end of a long train line from Rotterdam (€19, 1½ hours) via Roosendaal.

THE NORTH & EAST

This region includes Friesland, which, once upon a time, incorporated regions of the Netherlands, northern Germany and Denmark, until it became part of the united Netherlands. The land is spongy and green, dotted with cows, lakes and centuries-old churches. Though the Frisian language is similar to Dutch, pronunciation is entirely different. Apparently Frisian is the closest language to English, although English speakers will not understand it. As the Frisians themselves say: 'As milk is to cheese, are English and Frise'.

Groningen

☎050 / POP 185,000

It may be a long way from Amsterdam, but Groningen's a vibrant, youthful city, boasting all you'd expect of a progressive Dutch metropolis – its 20,000-strong student population (which has been around since 1614 when the university first opened) sees to that. There are also the requisite art museums, theatre, and classical concerts, as well as sublime scenes of gabled houses reflected in silent canals.

Sights & Activities

The **Grote Markt** is nothing special but the nearby **Vismarkt** has more intimate charms. Just west, **Aa-kerk** (A-Kerkhof) has parts dating to the 15th century and was a seamen's church, as this was the old harbour area. **Oude Boteringestraat** has a number of appealing buildings dating from the 17th and 18th centuries.

Groninger Museum MUSEUM
(www.groningermuseum.nl; Museumeiland 1; adult/child €10/3; ⌚10am-5pm Tue-Sun, to 10pm Fri) The striking, polymorphous and recently rehabbed local museum occupies three islands in the middle of the canal in front of the station, and hosts contemporary design and photography exhibitions alongside classic Golden Age Dutch paintings.

Martinikerk CATHEDRAL
(Grote Markt; admission €1; ⌚11am-5pm Mon-Sat mid-Apr–mid-Nov) The 16th-century Martinikerk, at the northern corner of the Grote Markt, is eye-catching. Its 96m-high tower, the Martinitoren, is considered to have one of the most finely balanced profiles in the country. A climb (admission €3; purchase ticket at tourist office) to the top yields sweeping views.

Noordelijk Scheepvaartmuseum MUSEUM
(Northern Shipping Museum; www.noordelijkscheepvaartmuseum.nl; Brugstraat 24-26; adult/

child €4/2.50; ⌚10am-5pm Tue-Sat, 1-5pm Sun) The Noordelijk Scheepvaartmuseum is laid out over several floors of buildings that once comprised a 16th-century distillery. Highlights include an intricately carved replica of the church at Paramaribo – the capital of former Dutch colony Suriname – in a bottle (room 3).

Sleeping

Hotel Schimmelpenninck Huys HOTEL €€
(☎318 95 02; www.schimmelpenninckhuys.nl; Oosterstraat 53; r €80-120; 📶) The Schimmelpenninck is Groningen's grande dame, and like a dowager of a certain age, it sprawls in several directions; in this case to three sides of its block. Antique-filled common areas lead to a serene courtyard and bistro. Rooms range from simple, standard doubles to suites with antique pieces and chandeliers.

Hotel Garni Friesland HOTEL €
(☎312 13 07; www.hotelfriesland.nl; Kleine Pelsterstraat 4; r €40-100; 📶) The Friesland is bare bones, but it's central and the prices are unbeatable. Service is friendly and amenable, and the 17 rooms are adequate. Some bathrooms are down the hall.

Eating & Drinking

Groningen has no fixed opening hours for cafes and bars, so party on! The **organic food market** (Vismarkt; ⌚Tue) is a regional favourite.

TOP CHOICE **Muller** FUSION €€€
(☎318 32 08; www.restaurantmuller.nl; Grote Kromme Elleboog 13; menus from €60; ⌚dinner Tue-Sat) You can enjoy the show here for free by watching the artistry in the kitchen from the windows on the street. But, really, why settle for half? Menus change regularly and include delights such as lobster, scallops, lamb and much more. One of the region's best.

't Feithhuis GRAND CAFE €€
(www.restaurant-feithhuis.nl; Martinikerkhof 10; mains €8-16) In a leafy pedestrian quarter just off the Grote Markt, this stylish grand cafe has a wide terrace outside and a stark, woodsy interior. Food ranges from bagels to complex sandwiches and Mediterranean-flavoured mains.

Roezemoes BROWN CAFE
(Gedempte Zuiderdiep 15) You can tell this gem of a brown cafe has been around a while; the bullet holes from the 1672 invasion attempt are a dead giveaway. Come evening, expect to find late-night drinking and the occasional blues band.

De Pintelier BAR
(Kleine Kromme Elleboog 9) Step back to the 1920s at this cosy bar where the selection

WORTH A TRIP

DEVENTER

Deventer was already a bustling mercantile port as far back as AD 800, and it maintained its prosperous trading ties for centuries, evidence of which you'll see everywhere in its sumptuously detailed old buildings.

The **Brink** is the main square and Deventer's commercial heart. The town's famous **Waag**, the 1528 weigh house in the middle of the square, was restored in 2003. Look for the cauldron on the north side – a gruesome and well-supported legend tells of a 16th-century clerk boiled alive in it, after he was discovered substituting cheap metals for precious ones in the local money supply.

The **Grote of Lebuïnuskerk** (admission €3; ⌚11am-5pm Mon-Sat) is the city's main church. It stands on a site where other churches were razed by flames and other catastrophes time and again, before the present Gothic structure was built between 1450 and 1530 during the Hanseatic League era.

Deventer is so well preserved that most streets will have something to see. On **Assenstraat** and **Polstraat** there are wall carvings and window decorations created over several centuries.

The **tourist office** (☎69 14 10; www.vvvdeventer.nl; Brink 56; ⌚10am-5pm Tue-Sat, 1-5pm Sun & Mon) sells excellent walking guides and shares space with a small museum inside the Waag.

Deventer is at the junction of several minor train lines, including one to Utrecht (€12.60, one hour).

of beer and *jenevers* (ginlike liqueur) reads like an encyclopedia. Its long wooden bar and thicket of tables are timeless.

Entertainment

Vera CLUB
(www.vera-groningen.nl; Oosterstraat 44; ⊙Thu-Sat) Legendary club at which to see the next big rock act: U2 played to 30-odd people in the early 1980s; Nirvana later gave a performance to a crowd of 60. Motto: 'club for the international pop underground'.

Information

The **tourist office** (www.vvvgroningen.nl; Grote Markt 25; ⊙9am-6pm Mon-Sat year-round, 11am-3pm Sun Jun-Aug) sells excellent walking-tour maps in English (€1.50).

Getting There & Away

Sample train schedules:

DESTINATION	PRICE (€)	DURATION (MIN)	FREQUENCY (PER HR)
Utrecht	24.80	120	1
Zwolle	15.90	69	3

Texel

☎0222 / POP 13,700

Texel (*tes*-sel) is a natural playground of broad white beaches, lush nature reserves, forests and picture-book villages. Some 25km long and 9km wide, it's just 3km off the coast of Noord Holland and makes a superb getaway from the mainland rush. Beauty and isolation are in abundance. The beaches seem to go on forever while inland there's **De Dennen**, a dark and leafy forest. Most villages exude charm, although tourist hub **De Koog** is more redolent with fudge.

Sights & Activities

Duinen van Texel National Park is a patchwork of varied dunescape running along the entire west coast of the island. Salt fens and heath alternate with velvety, grass-covered dunes. Much of the area is bird sanctuary and accessible only on foot. Pause at the excellent **Ecomare** (www.ecomare.nl; Ruyslaan 92, De Koog; adult/child €9/6; ⊙9am-5pm), a nature centre devoted to the preservation and understanding of Texel's wildlife.

Sleeping & Eating

Although Texel has an astounding 46,000 beds, book ahead, especially in July and August. Eating opportunities abound in season.

Bij Jef HOTEL €€
(☎31 96 23; www.bijjef.nl; Herenstraat 34, Den Hoorn; r from €100; wi-fi) The nine simple, yet stylish, rooms here come with a bathtub, views of the countryside and a sun-drenched balcony. However, the real star is the sumptuous **restaurant** (menus from €65), which has an ever-changing menu created from local produce, meats and seafood. Try for a garden table.

't Anker HOTEL €€
(☎31 62 74; www.t-anker.texel.com; Kikkertstraat 24, De Cocksdorp; s/d from €46/90; wi-fi) This small, family-run hotel is full of charm and cheer, and has basic yet comfy rooms. Its lush garden is just an appetiser for the Roggesloot nature reserve close by, and Texel's iconic lighthouse, which is just a healthy stroll away.

Information

The **tourist office** (www.texel.net; Emmalaan 66, Den Burg; ⊙9am-5.30pm Mon-Fri, to 5pm Sat) books rooms and has loads of advice for hikers, bikers and nude sunbathers.

Getting There & Away

Trains from Amsterdam to Den Helder (€13, 1¼ hours) are met by a bus that connects with the **car ferry** (www.teso.nl; adult/child/car return €4/2/38; ⊙6.30am-9pm), which then makes the crossing in 20 minutes. Local **buses** criss-cross Texel.

THE SOUTHEAST

The Dutch Southeast includes Noord Brabant, the country's largest province, primarily a land of agriculture and industry peppered with a few historic towns, including Den Bosch. The long and narrow Limburg province is home to Maastricht, contender for the title of finest Dutch city, as well as the presence of – wait for it – hills.

Den Bosch

☎073 / POP 138,000

This sweet old town has a top-notch church, outstanding cafes, cave-like canals and atmospheric streets. The official name is 's-

Hertogenbosch (Duke's Forest), but everyone calls it Den Bosch (den *boss*). It's also the birthplace of 15th-century painter Hieronymous Bosch, who took his name from the town. It's ideal for a day trip.

Sights

St Janskathedraal (www.sint-jan.nl; Choorstraat 1; admission free; ⏲8am-5pm), one of the finest Gothic churches in the Netherlands, took from 1380 to 1530 to complete. Look for the menagerie of oddball characters carved in stone above the flying buttresses.

You can find traces of Bosch in his city today. There's a **statue** of him in front of the Stadhuis. More interestingly, the **Jheronimus Bosch Art Center** (www.jheronimusbosch-artcenter.nl; Jeroen Boschplein 2; adult/child €6/3; ⏲10am-5pm Tue-Sun) re-creates all of his works and uses interactive exhibits to explore his work and life.

Canals in Den Bosch are different from the others you've been seeing: many have long stretches where they pass under buildings, plazas and roads. These tunnels add spice to the usual canal tours and have inspired more than one tunnel-of-love moment. **Binnendieze** (www.binnendieze.nl; Molenstraat 15a; adult/child €6/3; ⏲tickets 9.30am-5pm Apr-Oct) runs various fascinating, 50-minute tours of the centre's canals. Walking tours are also on offer.

Eating & Drinking

Jan de Groot BAKERY €

(Stationsweg 24; treats from €2) The crowds know this is *the* place to get a *Bossche bol* (Den Bosch ball). It's a chocolate-coated cake the size of a softball, filled with sweetened fresh cream. It may be the best thing on your tongue all day.

Artisan BISTRO €€€

(Verwerstraat 24; menus from €34; ⏲noon-10pm Tue-Sun) Fresh fare sourced locally. Lunches feature imaginative sandwiches, salads and specials (about €8). Dinner brings out the kitchen skills with seasonal menus that can range from mussels to roasts. Between meals, enjoy a glass of wine in the courtyard.

Information

The **tourist office** (www.vvvdenbosch.nl; Markt 77; ⏲1-6pm Mon, 9.30am-6pm Tue-Fri, 9am-5pm Sat) has good walking and cycling maps.

Getting There & Away

Sample train fares:

DESTINATION	PRICE (€)	DURATION (MIN)	FREQUENCY (PER HR)
Amsterdam	13.40	60	2
Maastricht	18.80	85	2
Utrecht	8	30	4

Maastricht

☎043 / POP 120,000

The Netherlands' other great old city couldn't be further from Amsterdam and the pearls of the Randstad and still be in the country. Granted, Maastricht sits on a little geographic appendage dangling down like an appendix but it is well worth the time to journey here from the northwest (and you can easily continue on to Belgium and Germany).

Among the 1650 listed historic buildings, look for Spanish and Roman ruins, French and Belgian twists in the architecture, splendid food and the small-town cosmopolitan flair that made Maastricht a natural location for the signing of the namesake treaty, which created the modern EU in 1992.

Sights & Activities

Maastricht's delights are scattered along both banks of the Maas. The best approach is to just start strolling. The city's ruins, old fortifications, museums and cafes (and the odd surprise) reward walkers. **Onze Lieve Vrouweplein** is an intimate cafe-filled square named after its church, which still attracts pilgrims. The busy pedestrian **Sint Servaasbrug** dates from the 13th-century and links Maastricht's centre with the Wyck district.

Bonnefantenmuseum ART MUSEUM

(www.bonnefantenmuseum.nl; Ave Cèramique 250; adult/child €8/free; ⏲11am-5pm Tue-Sun) This postmodern fantasy features a striking 28m tower that houses various provocative exhibits. The collection combines Flemish masterpieces from the 16th and 17th centuries with modern works.

Vrijthof HISTORIC SQUARE

The large square of Vrijthof is surrounded by lively cafes and cultural institutions. It's dominated by **Sint Servaasbasiliek** (admission €2; ⏲10am-5pm Mon-Sat, 12.30-5pm Sun), a pastiche of architecture dating from 1000. Duck around the back to the serene cloister garden and the **Treasury** (schatkamer; adult/child €4/free; ⏲10am-5pm Mon-Sat, 12.30-5pm Sun), where much of the gold artwork dates from the 12th century.

Maastricht

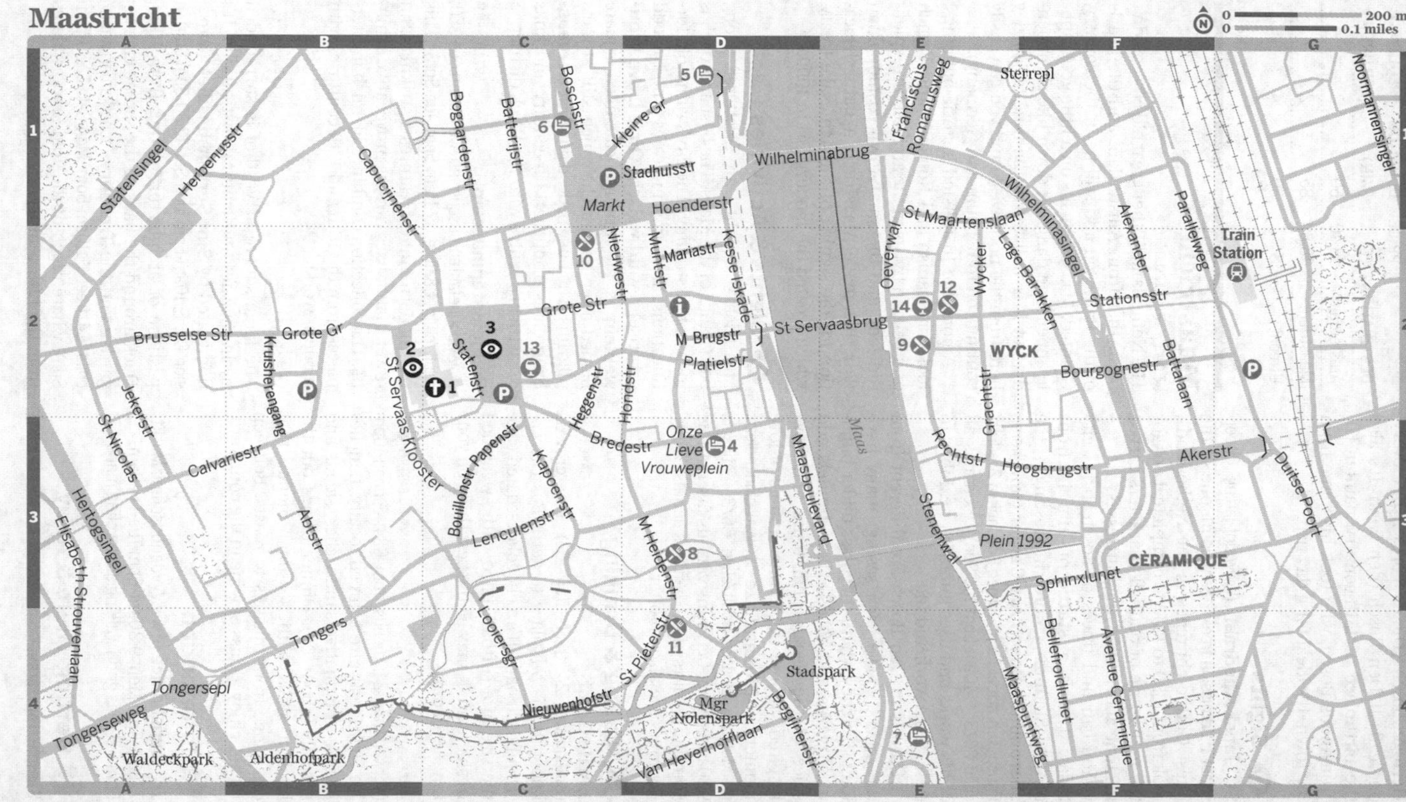
0 200 m
0 0.1 miles
Statensingel
Herbenusstr
Capucijnenstr
Bogaardenstr
Batterijstr
Boschstr
Kleine Gr
Stadhuisstr
Markt
Hoenderstr
Nieuwestr
Muntstr
Mariastr
Kesse Iskade
Wilhelminabrug
Francíscus Romanusweg
Sterrepl
Noormannensingel
St Maartenslaan
Wilhelminasingel
Alexander
Parallelweg
Train Station
Oeverwal
Wycker
Lage Barakken
Stationsstr
St Servaasbrug
M Brugstr
Grote Str
Brusselse Str
Grote Gr
Kruisherengang
St Servaas Klooster
Statenstr
Platielstr
WYCK
Bourgognestr
Battalaan
Jekerstr
St Nicolas
Calvariestr
Bouillonstr
Papenstr
Kapoenstr
Heggenstr
Hondstr
Bredestr
Onze Lieve Vrouweplein
Maasboulevard
Maas
Rechtstr
Grachtstr
Hoogbrugstr
Akerstr
Duitse Poort
Hertogsingel
Elisabeth Strouvenlaan
Abtstr
Lenculenstr
M Heidenstr
Stenenwal
Plein 1992
CÈRAMIQUE
Sphinxlunet
Tongers
Looiersgr
St Pieterstr
Stadspark
Tongersepl
Tongerseweg
Nieuwenhofstr
Mgr Nolenspark
Begijnenstr
Waldeckpark
Aldenhofpark
Van Heyerhofflaan
Maaspuntweg
Bellefroidlunet
Avenue Céramique

Maastricht

Sights
1 Sint Servaasbasiliek C2
2 Treasury B2
3 Vrijthof C2

Sleeping
4 Hotel Derlon D3
5 Hotel d'Orangerie D1
6 Hotel Holla C1
7 Stayokay Maastricht E4

Eating
8 Bisschopsmolen D3
9 Gadjah Mas E2
10 Reitz C2
11 Sjieke D4
12 Zondag E2

Drinking
13 In Den Ouden Vogelstruys C2
14 Take One E2

Sint Pietersberg FORT & TUNNELS
(www.maastrichtunderground.nl; adult/child €5/4; tour times vary by season) Much of Maastricht is riddled with defensive tunnels dug into the soft sandstone during the many sieges over the centuries; some date to Roman times. The best place to see the tunnels is on a tour of Sint Pietersberg, a Roman fort 2km south of Helpoort. This is a beautiful area, pastoral and peaceful, and the fort is an arresting sight peeking over the hillside.

Festivals & Events

Carnaval is celebrated with greater vigour in Maastricht than anywhere else in Europe, save Venice (Italy) and Sitges (Spain). The orgy of partying and carousing begins the Friday before Shrove Tuesday and lasts until the last person collapses some time on the following Wednesday.

Sleeping

TOP CHOICE **Hotel Holla** HOTEL €
(321 35 23; www.hotelholla.nl; Boschstraat 104-106; r €50-90; @) In an elegant 1855 building, the 24 stylish rooms here are well-appointed for the price. Adding to the excellent value is the ground-floor cafe, which serves excellent coffee in smart surrounds.

Hotel d'Orangerie HOTEL €€
(326 11 11; www.hotel-orangerie.nl; Kleine Gracht 4; r €90-160) There's a gracious elegance about this hotel in a stately building dating back to 1752. The welcome is genuine. The 22 rooms come in various levels of ornate decor. Take breakfast in the airy courtyard.

Hotel Derlon HOTEL €€€
(321 67 70; www.derlon.com; Onze Lieve Vrouweplein 6; r from €200; @) The sleekly luxurious and smartly suave Derlon boasts 48 rooms with designer fittings. The breakfast room is in the basement, built around Roman ruins. A pampering and indulgent experience.

Stayokay Maastricht HOSTEL €
(750 17 90; www.stayokay.com/maastricht; Maasboulevard 101; dm from €20, r from €55; @) A stunner of a hostel with a large terrace right on the Maas. Choose from one of the 199 beds in dorms and private rooms. It's just south of the centre in a park.

Eating

Excellent restaurants are even more common than old fortifications in Maastricht.

Bisschopsmolen CAFE €
(Stenebrug 1-3; meals €5-12; lunch) How cool is this? A working water wheel powers a vintage flour mill that supplies an adjoining bakery. The loaves come in many forms and are joined by other tasty treats (direct from the ovens that are on view out back). The cafe has sandwiches and other in-house creations. You can self-tour the mill and see how flour's been made for eons.

Sjieke DUTCH €€
(St Pieterstraat 13; meals €12-25; dinner) This cosy corner spot turns out traditional Dutch fare, including hearty stews, roasts, fresh fish and more. In summer there's a thicket of tables in the park across the street. Have a red beer and pick out the stars through the trees.

Gadjah Mas INDONESIAN €€
(Rechtstraat 42; mains €17-25; dinner) The Rechtstraat, east of the river, is one of the best streets for dining in Maastricht. This small and lovely Indonesian bistro has *rijsttafels* that break with the cliched norm. Flavours are bright and spices are not skimped.

Zondag CAFE €
(www.cafezondag.nl; mains €6-12; Wycker Brugstraat 42) Funky mellow tunes through the day segue to jazzier, harder sounds at night. It's light, airy, beautifully tiled and the food couldn't be fresher. Choose from a huge range of sandwiches and baked goods by day.

Reitz FRITES €

(Markt 75; frites €2) Join the queues at this iconic French-fries stall, which has been serving perfectly scrumptious *frites* under the classic neon sign for decades.

Drinking

TOP CHOICE **Take One** BROWN CAFE

(www.takeonebiercafe.nl, in Dutch; Rechtstraat 28) Cramped and narrow from the outside, this 1930s tavern has well over 100 beers from the most obscure parts of Benelux. It's run by husband-and-wife team Peet Seerden and Méry Willemsen, who help you select the beer most appropriate to your tastes.

In Den Ouden Vogelstruys PUB

(www.vogelstruys.nl; Vrijthof 15) Overlooking the cathedral across the square is this antique bar, the top choice among many. The entrance has big, old, heavy red curtains, while inside the bar there are big, old, heavy light fittings, and big, old, heavy Trappist beer. (But the local cheese is light and creamy...)

Information

ANWB (Wycker Brugstraat 24; ⏲9.30am-6pm Mon-Fri, to 5pm Sat) Has a tourist office info desk; convenient to the train station.

Tourist office (www.vvvmaastricht.nl; Kleine Straat 1; ⏲9am-6pm Mon-Sat year-round, 11am-3pm Sun May-Oct) In the 15th-century Dinghuis; offers excellent walking-tour brochures.

Getting There & Away

Regular **trains** link Maastricht to Brussels (€30, 1½ hours) via Liege; with connections, Cologne (€25) is two hours away. Sample Dutch train fares:

DESTINATION	PRICE (€)	DURATION (MIN)	FREQUENCY (PER HR)
Amsterdam	26.60	150	2
Den Bosch	18.80	85	2
Utrecht	23.50	120	2

UNDERSTAND THE NETHERLANDS

History

Although the Netherlands is geographically tiny, it has been a major player in world affairs throughout the ages – often unwittingly. While the nation's borders have been repeatedly sliced and diced, the Dutch themselves have blitzed distant lands. Away from conflict, the Netherlands has made a stellar contribution to the visual arts and has initiated many world firsts in 'social engineering'.

The Early Years

The Netherlands' early history is bound with that of Belgium and Luxembourg – the three were known as the Low Countries until the 16th century. In 1579 provinces in the northern Low Countries formed the United Provinces, which was the basis for the Netherlands today. They were opposed to the Spanish rule that was in place, while the southern regions, which eventually became Belgium, were open to compromise. The United Provinces fought the Spanish in the 80-year-long Revolt of the Netherlands, which ended in 1648 with a treaty that recognised them as an independent republic.

The Golden Age & the United Kingdom

The Netherlands' Golden Age lasted from about 1580 to 1740. The era's wealth was generated by the Dutch East India Company, which sent ships to the Far East for spices and other exotic goods, while colonising the Cape of Good Hope and Indonesia and establishing trading posts throughout Asia. Later the West Indies Company sailed to West Africa and the Americas. A number of Caribbean islands were also captured in a bid to thwart the Spanish. One unfortunate by-product of Dutch colonisation was the extinction of the dodo in Mauritius, largely due to introduced species.

The wealthy merchant class supported scores of artists, including Vermeer, Steen, Hals and Rembrandt. The sciences thrived: Christiaan Huygens, for example, discovered Saturn's rings and invented the pendulum clock.

In 1795 the French invaded. When occupation ended in 1815, the United Kingdom of the Netherlands – incorporating Belgium and Luxembourg – was born. Earlier that year prostitution was legalised in the Netherlands by Napoleon (who wanted to control STDs), though it took until 1988 for the Dutch to define it as a legal profession and to allow prostitutes to join trade unions.

In 1830 the Belgians rebelled and became independent, and Luxembourg was split be-

DUTCH JEWS

Before WWII the Netherlands was home to 140,000 Jews, of whom about two-thirds lived in Amsterdam. During the war, the occupying Nazis brought about the almost complete annihilation of the Dutch Jewish community. Less than 30,000 survived the war (25,000 in hiding and 5000 in the camps), and Amsterdam's Jewish quarter was left a ghost town.

Estimates put the current Jewish population of the Netherlands at between 41,000 and 45,000, almost half living in Amsterdam.

Jewish history is recounted at several museums in Amsterdam, including the **Anne Frank Huis** (p931), a must-see for visitors; the **Joods Historisch Museum** (p934), which covers the sweep of the Dutch Jewish experience; and **Hollandsche Schouwburg** (p935), where Jews were held before being deported.

tween Belgium and the Netherlands. Nine years later the Dutch part gained independence and officially became Luxembourg.

World Wars & Beyond

The Netherlands stayed neutral in WWI and tried to repeat the feat in WWII, only to be invaded by the Germans. Rotterdam was levelled, Dutch industry was commandeered for war purposes, and thousands of Dutch men were sent to work in Nazi factories in Germany.

Indonesia won independence from the Netherlands in 1949, despite Dutch military opposition. Suriname followed, peacefully, in 1975. The Antilles has close ties with the Netherlands but is self-ruled.

In 1953 a high spring tide and severe storm breached Zeeland's dikes, drowning 2000 people. Under the Delta Project (see the boxed text, p959) a massive engineering project was created to prevent the tragedy from repeating.

In the 1960s Amsterdam became Europe's radical heart, giving rise to the riotous squatters' movement and the promiscuity that lingers today.

Although cannabis was decriminalised in the Netherlands in 1976, it took 27 years for this ruling to be taken to its logical conclusion. In 2003 the Netherlands became the first country to legalise prescriptions of medicinal cannabis, intended as a pain reliever for cancer and multiple sclerosis sufferers, among others.

Maastricht Treaty to Present Day

Perhaps because of the devastating Nazi occupation, the Dutch have largely embraced European integration. In 1992 European Community members met in Maastricht to sign the treaty that created the EU.

In 1993 the Netherlands became the first country to regulate doctor-assisted euthanasia, and in 2000 the practice was legalised under stringent guidelines. That year the Netherlands also became the first nation in the world to legalise same-sex marriages.

As the Netherlands has become ever more crowded, immigration has become a political hot potato. In 2002 right-wing politician Pim Fortuyn, an advocate of zero immigration, was shot dead a few days before the Dutch general election.

In 2004 there was another high-profile assassination. Theo van Gogh, an inflammatory right-wing film-maker and columnist was killed in Amsterdam. A note was impaled to his body with the knife, threatening the government, Dutch politician Ayaan Hirsi Ali and Jewish groups. The murderer was an Islamic Moroccan; when Van Gogh died, he was finishing off a film about Fortuyn. Van Gogh was known for his controversial statements about Muslims, and he had received death threats after he made a short film, *Submission* (written by outspoken ex-Muslim Hirsi Ali), detailing the abuse of four Muslim women.

The famously tolerant Dutch have moved to the right somewhat in recent years. The notorious coffee shops and legal red light districts are under fire as the populace tires of antisocial behaviour associated with both – and often perpetrated by foreigners.

In 2010 elections, no party came close to a majority and months were spent forming a rather tenuous centre-right coalition with Mark Rutte as prime minister.

Meanwhile Den Haag stays in the news as war-crimes trials move forward for people such as Radovan Karadzic in the city's various international courts.

Although disappointed by the loss, the country was very proud to see the Orange team reach the 2010 World Cup finals.

Arts

Visual Arts

The Netherlands claims a superb artistic heritage: many non-Dutch would be able to name at least one famous Dutch painter.

From the 15th century, Hieronymus Bosch's nightmarish works can be seen as an antecedent of surrealism. During the Golden Age, Rembrandt emerged with the brightest glow of all, creating shimmering religious scenes, in-demand portraits and contemplative landscapes. Frans Hals (1582–1666) captured his subjects in unguarded moments, and Jan Vermeer (1632–75) concentrated on everyday occurrences in middle-class homes, giving a proto-cinematographic quality to his compositions.

Vincent van Gogh's (1853–90) revolutionary use of colour, coarse brushwork and layered contours established him on a higher plane than his contemporaries, yet he only sold one work while alive. A bit later, Piet Mondrian (1872–1944), along with Theo van Doesburg, founded the De Stijl movement; his style of abstract rectangular compositions came to be known as neoplasticism.

MC Escher's (1902–72) graphic art still has uncanny power: a waterfall simultaneously flows up and down; a building folds in on itself. It's popular with mathematicians and stoners alike.

Architecture

Few countries have exerted more influence on architecture than the Netherlands. Thick walls, small windows and round arches are some of the major characteristics of the Romanesque style (900–1250), while pointed arches, ribbed vaulting and dizzying heights were trademarks of the Gothic era (c 1250–1600). The Netherlands excelled in Mannerism (1520–1600), a sort of toned-down baroque.

From the mid-17th century onwards Dutch architecture began to influence France and England, but during the 1700s Dutch architects deferred to all things French, except during the Napoleonic Wars in the late 18th century when designers, influenced by Greek and Roman blueprints, came up with neoclassicism, known for its order, symmetry and simplicity.

Many big projects from the 1850s onward were neo-Gothic, harking back to the grand Gothic cathedrals. One of the leading architects of this period was Pierre Cuypers, who built Amsterdam Centraal Station and the Rijksmuseum.

As the 20th century approached, Hendrik Petrus Berlage, the father of modern Dutch architecture, unleashed on the nation spartan, utilitarian designs that did away with frivolous ornamentation, such as the Gemeentemuseum in Den Haag.

Functionalism (1927–70) drew influence from Germany's Bauhaus School, the American Frank Lloyd Wright and France's Le Corbusier. Since the 1980s numerous 'isms', such as structuralism, neorationalism, postmodernism and supermodernism, have taken root, especially in Rotterdam, where city planners have encouraged bold designs that range from Piet Blom's startling cube-shaped apartments to Ben van Berkel's graceful Erasmusbrug bridge. Rotterdam is also home to Rem Koolhaas, perhaps the best-known contemporary Dutch architect, as well as MVRDV, a firm known for its space-saving schemes such as 40-storey pig farms.

Music

In the early '90s gabber, an extreme mutation of techno originating in Rotterdam, was unleashed. Gabber raised beats per minute to heart-attack levels, giving the finger to purists with its sheer fetishisation of sensation.

The Dutch also have a major presence in the populist world-DJ rankings with the likes of Tiësto, while the North Sea Jazz Festival, the world's largest jazz fest, is held each summer in Rotterdam.

Pop festivals come out of the woodwork in the warmer months: the gargantuan Parkpop draws around 350,000 ravers to Den Haag. Dance Valley in Spaarnwoude near Amsterdam pulls up to 100 live acts and DJs.

Environment

The Netherlands' land mass now encompasses 41,526 sq km, roughly half the size of Scotland, and half of it lies at or below sea level in the form of polders (stretches of land reclaimed from the sea). If the Netherlands lost its 2400km of dikes and dunes the large cities would be inundated, so pumping stations run around the clock to drain off excess water. Rising water levels due to climate change is a huge concern.

The Netherlands' highest point, the Vaalserberg, is in the province of Limburg, at a grand elevation of 321m.

Food & Drink

Dutch Dishes

Dutch food is hearty and designed to line the stomach; dishes include *stamppot* (mashed pot) – potatoes mashed with kale, endive or sauerkraut and served with smoked sausage or pork strips. *Hutspot* (hotchpotch) is similar, but with potatoes, carrots, onions and braised meat.

The Dutch consume almost 17kg of cheese per person per year (nearly two-thirds of it is Gouda). Look for aged varieties, often sold in brown cafes as snacks and at street markets.

Seafood is found at street stalls, including raw, slightly salted herring cut into bite-sized pieces and served with onion and pickles. Smoked eel and *kibbeling* (deep-fried cod parings) are also popular.

For the greatest hits of Dutch cuisine, see p927.

Drinks

Lager beer is the staple drink, served cool and topped by a big head of froth. Some places serve half-litre mugs to please tourists. More bars are serving interesting beers from a growing number of small Dutch and Belgian brewers. Look for hoppy Jopen from Haarlem.

Dutch *jenever,* or gin, is made from juniper berries and drunk chilled from a shot glass filled to the brim. Most people prefer *jonge* (young) *jenever,* which is smoother; the strong juniper flavour of *oude* (old) *jenever* can be an acquired taste.

EAT EARLY

The Dutch eat dinner early – popular places fill up by 7pm and most kitchens close by 10pm (9pm outside of Amsterdam and Rotterdam). Lunch tends to be more of a snack, and just a half-hour break is common. Coffee breaks are frequent.

Where to Eat & Drink

As well as restaurants, there are *eetcafes,* which are affordable, small and popular pub-like eateries. Eating venues are smokefree.

'Cafe' means a pub, also known as a *kroeg.* They generally serve food, and many have outdoor terraces. The most famous type is the cosy *bruin cafe* (brown cafe) – the name comes from smoke stains on the walls, although pretenders make do with brown paint. The best ooze the uniquely Dutch concept of *gezelligheld,* which is one of those words that defies easy translation but which combines cosy, fun and quaint with an overlay of familiarity and good cheer.

Grand cafes are more spacious, have comfortable furniture and are very popular.

Broodjeszaken (sandwich shops) and snack bars are everywhere. Munchies are squelched around the clock at fast-food joints such as Febo, where deep-fried snacks sing their siren song from behind coin-operated doors.

For more on opening hours, see p970.

SURVIVAL GUIDE

Directory A–Z

Accommodation

Always book accommodation ahead, especially during high season; note that many visitors choose to stay in Amsterdam even if travelling elsewhere. The tourist offices operate booking services; when booking for two, make it clear whether you want two single (twin) beds or a double bed.

Many Dutch hotels have steep, perilous stairs but no lifts, although most top-end and some midrange hotels are exceptions.

Lists of camping grounds are available from the tourist offices. Expect to pay roughly €10 to €20 for two people and a tent overnight, plus €3 to €6 for a car. The camping grounds have plenty of caravan hook-ups.

Stayokay (☎020-501 31 33; www.stayokay.com) is the Dutch hostelling association. A youth-hostel card costs €15 at the hostels; nonmembers pay an extra €2.50 per night and after six nights you become a member. The usual HI discounts apply.

PRICE RANGES

In this chapter, prices include private bathrooms unless otherwise stated and are quoted at high-season rates. Breakfast is not included unless specified. Most room are nonsmoking.

€€€ more than €150

€€ €80 to €150

€ less than €80

Business Hours

Banks & government offices 9.30am-4pm Mon-Fri

Bars & cafes 11am-1am

Clubs Mostly 10pm-4am

Museums Most closed Monday

Post offices 9am-6pm Mon-Fri

Restaurants 10am-10pm or 11am-10pm, with a 3-6pm break

Shops Noon-6pm Mon, 9am-6pm Tue-Sat (also Sun in large cities), to 9pm Thu; supermarkets to 8pm

Discount Cards

Available from the museums themselves, a *Museumkaart* gives access to 400 museums across the country for €40 (€20 for under 25s).

Embassies & Consulates

Australia (070-310 82 00; www.netherlands.embassy.gov.au; Carnegielaan 4, Den Haag)

Canada (070-311 16 00; www.netherlands.gc.ca; Sophialaan 7, Den Haag)

New Zealand (070-346 93 24; www.nzembassy.com; Eisenhowerlaan 77, Den Haag)

UK (www.ukinspain.fco.gov.uk) Amsterdam (676 43 43; Koningslaan 44) The Hague (070-427 04 27; Lange Voorhout 10)

USA Amsterdam (575 53 30; http://amsterdam.usconsulate.gov; Museumplein 19) The Hague (070-310 22 09; http://thehague.usembassy.gov; Lange Voorhout 102)

Food

The following price categories for the cost of a main course are used in the listings in this chapter.

€€€ more than €20

€€ €10 to €20

€ less than €10

Legal Matters

Drugs are actually illegal in the Netherlands. Possession of soft drugs up to 5g is tolerated but larger amounts can get you jailed. Hard drugs are treated as a serious crime.

Smoking is banned in all public places, including most bars (except for tiny family-run pubs). In a uniquely Dutch solution, you can still smoke pot in coffee shops as long as there's no tobacco mixed in.

TIPPING

Tipping is not essential as restaurants, hotels, bars etc include a service charge on their bills. A little extra is always welcomed though, and it's an excellent way to compliment the service (if you feel it needs complimenting). The tip can be anything from rounding up to the nearest euro, to 10% of the bill.

Money

ATMS

Automatic teller machines can be found outside banks and at train stations.

CREDIT CARDS

All major international cards are recognised, and you will find that most hotels, restaurants and major stores accept them (although *not* the Dutch railway). But always check first to avoid, as they say, disappointment. Shops may levy a 5% surcharge (or more) on credit cards to offset the commissions charged by card providers.

Public Holidays

Public holidays in the Netherlands:

Nieuwjaarsdag New Year's Day

Goede Vrijdag Good Friday

Eerste Paasdag Easter Sunday

Tweede Paasdag Easter Monday

Koninginnedag (Queen's Day) 30 April

Bevrijdingsdag (Liberation Day) 5 May

Hemelvaartsdag Ascension Day

Eerste Pinksterdag Whit Sunday (Pentecost)

Tweede Pinksterdag Whit Monday

Eerste Kerstdag (Christmas Day) 25 December

Tweede Kerstdag (Boxing Day) 26 December

Safe Travel

The Netherlands is a safe country, but be sensible all the same: don't leave valuables in cars and *always* lock your bike. Never buy drugs on the street: you'll get ripped off or mugged and it's illegal. And don't light up joints just anywhere – stick to coffee shops.

Telephone

Most public phones will accept credit cards as well as various phonecards.

Country code ☎31

Collect call (gesprek) domestic ☎0800 01 01; international ☎0800 04 10

International access code ☎00

International directory inquiries ☎0900 84 18

National directory inquiries ☎1888

Operator assistance ☎0800 04 10

Getting There & Away

Air

Huge **Schiphol Airport** (AMS; www.schiphol.nl) is the Netherlands' main international airport. **Rotterdam Airport** (RTM; www.rotterdamthehagueairport.nl) and **Eindhoven Airport** (EIN; www.eindhovenairport.nl) are small.

Land

BUS

The most extensive European bus network is maintained by **Eurolines** (www.eurolines.com). It offers a variety of passes with prices that vary by time of year.

Busabout (www.busabout.com) is a UK-based budget alternative. It runs coaches on circuits in Continental Europe, including one through Amsterdam; passes are available in a variety of flavours.

THE NETHERLANDS BY BIKE

The Netherlands has more than 20,000km of dedicated **bike paths** *(fietspaden)*, which makes it the most bike-friendly place on the planet. You can criss-cross the country on the motorways of cycling: the **LF routes**. Standing for *landelijke fietsroutes* (long-distance routes), but virtually always simply called LF, there are more than 25 routes comprising close to 7000km. All are well marked by distinctive green-and-white signs.

The best overall maps are the widely available Falk/VVV *Fietskaart met Knooppuntennetwerk* (cycling network) maps, a series of 20 that blanket the country in 1:50,000 scale, and cost €8. The keys are in English and they are highly detailed and very easy to use. Every bike lane, path and other route is shown, along with distances.

Web Resources

» **Cycling in the Netherlands** (http://holland.cyclingaroundtheworld.nl) Superb English-language site with a vast amount of useful and inspiring information.

» **Landelijke Fietsroutes** (www.landelijkefietsroutes.nl, in Dutch) Dutch site that lists all the LF routes and gives basic details and an outline of each.

» **Startpagina** (http://fiets.startpagina.nl, in Dutch) Dutch site that lists every conceivable website associated with cycling in the Netherlands.

Bike Rentals

Independent rental shops are available in abundance. Many day trippers avail themselves of the train-station bicycle shops, called **Rijwiel shops** (www.ov-fiets.nl), which are found in more than 100 stations. Operating long hours (6am to midnight is common), the shops hire out bikes from €6 to €8 per day, with discounts by the week. You'll have to show an ID and leave a deposit (usually €25 to €100). The shops also usually offer repairs, sell new bikes and have secured bike parking (from per day/week €1.10/4.40).

On Trains

You may bring your bicycle onto any train as long as there is room; a day pass for bikes (*dagkaart fiets;* €6) is valid.

TRAINS & TRIBULATIONS

Buying a train ticket is the hardest part of riding Dutch trains. Among the challenges:

» Only some ticket machines accept cash, and those are coins-only, meaning that buying a ticket to go any distance will require a pocketful of change.

» Ticket machines that accept plastic will not work with most non-Dutch credit and ATM cards.

» Ticket windows (excepting one each at Schiphol and Amsterdam) do not accept credit or ATM cards, although they will accept paper euros. Lines are often long and there is a surcharge for the often-unavoidable need to use a ticket window.

» Deeply discounted tickets for Hispeed and Fyra trains sold on the web require a Dutch credit card, a policy unheard of in other countries. And the cheap fares can't be bought at ticket windows.

» The once-popular *Voordeelurenabonnement*, good for a 40% discount on train travel, is now sold only to people with Dutch bank accounts.

CAR & MOTORCYCLE

You'll need the vehicle's registration papers, third-party insurance and an international driver's permit in addition to your domestic licence. The national auto club, **ANWB** (www.anwb.nl), has offices across the country and will provide info if you can show an auto-club card from your home country (eg AAA in the US or AA in the UK).

TRAIN

The Netherlands has good train links to Germany, Belgium and France. All Eurail, InterRail, Europass and Flexipass tickets are valid on the Dutch national train service, **Nederlandse Spoorwegen** (Netherlands Railway, NS; www.ns.nl). Many international services, including those on the high-speed line to Belgium, are operated under the **Hispeed** (www.nshispeed.nl) and **Fyra** (www.fyra.com) brands. In addition, **Thalys** (www.thalys.com) fast trains serve Brussels (where you can connect to Eurostar) and Paris. Major Dutch train stations have international ticket offices and, in peak periods, it's wise to reserve seats in advance.

Finally open (years late and far over budget), the high-speed line from Amsterdam (via Schipol and Rotterdam) speeds travel times to Antwerp (70 minutes), Brussels (1¾ hours) and Paris (three hours).

German ICE high-speed trains run six times a day between Amsterdam and Cologne (2½ hours) via Utrecht. Many continue on to Frankfurt (four hours) via Frankfurt Airport.

Sea

There are several companies operating car/passenger ferries between the Netherlands and the UK:

DFDS Seaways (www.dfds.co.uk) Sails between Newcastle and IJmuiden, which is close to Amsterdam.

P&O Ferries (www.poferries.com) Operates an overnight ferry every evening between Hull and Europoort (near Rotterdam).

Stena Line (www.stenaline.co.uk) Sails between Harwich and Hoek van Holland.

Getting Around

Boat

Ferries connect the mainland with the five Frisian Islands, including Texel. Other ferries span the Westerschelde in the south of Zeeland, providing road links to the bit of the Netherlands south of here as well as to Belgium. These are popular with people using the Zeebrugge ferry terminal and run frequently year-round.

Car & Motorcycle

HIRE

Outside Amsterdam, car-hire companies can be in inconvenient locations if you're arriving by train. You must be at least 23 years of age to hire a car in the Netherlands. Some car-hire firms levy a small surcharge for drivers under 25. You'll need to show a valid driving licence when renting a car in the Netherlands.

ROAD RULES

Traffic travels on the right and the minimum driving age is 18 for vehicles and 16 for motorcycles. Seat belts are required and children under 12 must ride in the back if there's room. Trams always have the right of way and, if turning right, bikes have priority.

Speed limits are 50km/h in built-up areas, 80km/h in the country, 100km/h on major through-roads, and 120km/h on freeways (sometimes 100km/h, clearly indicated). The blood-alcohol limit when driving is 0.05%.

Public Transport

National public transport info is available by phone (☎0900 9292) and on the web (www.9292ov.nl).

The new universal form of transport payment in the Netherlands, the **OV-chipkaart** (www.ov-chipkaart.nl) is a smartcard that you use in place of cash. Visitors can buy one from vending machines in stations or at ticket windows. Each card stores the value of your payment and deducts the cost of trips as you use it. Refill from machines or ticket windows (although the latter are often thronged).

When you enter and exit a bus, tram or train, you hold the card against a reader at the doors or station gates. The system then calculates your fare and deducts it from the card. Fares for the chip cards are much lower than a ticket bought from the driver or conductor on buses and trams. You can also buy OV-chipkaarts good for unlimited use for one or more days and this is often the most convenient option.

Train

The train network is run by **NS** (Nederlandse Spoorwegen; www.ns.nl). First-class sections are barely different from 2nd-class areas, but they are less crowded. Trains are fast and frequent and serve most places of interest. Distances are short. Most train stations have lockers operated by credit cards (average cost €4).

TICKETS

Enkele reis One way; you can break your journey along the direct route.

Dagretour Day return; 10% to 15% cheaper than two one-way tickets.

Weekendretour Weekend return; costs the same as a normal return and is valid from 7pm Friday to 4am Monday.

Dagkaart Day pass; allows unlimited train travel throughout the country. Only good value if you're planning to spend the day on the train.

Portugal

Includes »

Best Places to Eat

» 100 Maneiras (p988)

» Fortaleza do Guincho (p996)

» Café Ingles (p1000)

» A Grade (p1013)

» Taberna do Valentim (p1016)

Best Places to Stay

» Solar dos Mouros (p983)

» Pensão Residencial Sintra (p995)

» Palace Hotel do Buçaco (p1009)

» Guest House Douro (p1012)

» Hotel de Peneda (p1017)

Why Go?

Medieval castles, frozen-in-time villages, captivating cities and golden-sand beaches: the Portugal experience can mean many things. History, great food and wine, idyllic scenery and blazing nightlife are just the beginning...

Portugal's capital, Lisbon, and its northern rival, Porto, are gems among the urban streetscapes of Europe. Both are magical places for the wanderer, with picturesque views over the river, rattling trams and atmospheric lanes that hide boutiques and old-school record shops, stylish lounges and a vibrant mix of restaurants, fado clubs and open-air cafes.

Outside the cities, Portugal's landscape unfolds in all its variegated beauty. Here you can stay overnight in converted hilltop fortresses fronting age-old vineyards, hike amid granite peaks or explore historic villages of the little-visited hinterland. More than 800km of coast offers more outdoor enticements. You can gaze out over dramatic end-of-the-world cliffs, surf stellar breaks off dune-covered beaches or laze peacefully on sandy islands fronting calm blue seas.

When to Go

Lisbon

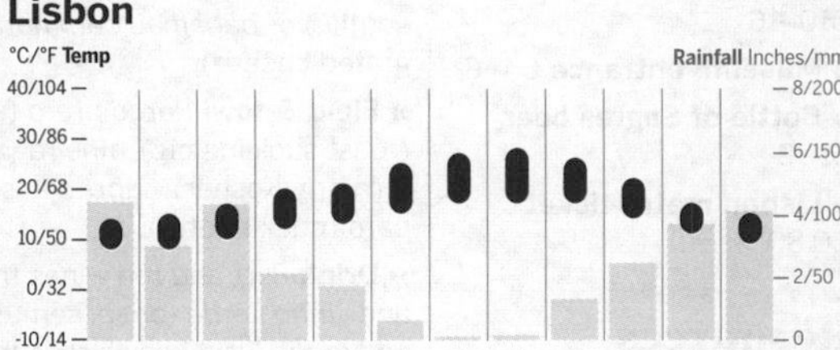

Apr & May Sunny days and wildflowers set the stage for hiking and outdoor activities.

Jun–Aug Lovely and lively, with a packed festival calendar and steamy beach days.

Late Sep & Oct Crisp mornings and sunny days; prices dip, crowds disperse.

AT A GLANCE

» **Currency** euro (€)

» **Language** Portuguese

» **Money** ATMs widespread; banks open Mon-Fri

» **Visas** Schengen rules apply

Fast Facts

» **Area** 91,470 sq km

» **Population** 10.8 million

» **Capital** Lisbon

» **Telephone** country code ☎351; international access code ☎00

» **Emergency** ☎112

Exchange Rates

Australia	A$1	€0.74
Canada	C$1	€0.74
Japan	¥100	€0.87
New Zealand	NZ$1	€0.56
UK	UK£1	€1.16
USA	US$1	€0.67

Set Your Budget

» **Budget hotel room** €40

» **Two-course dinner** €10–16

» **Museum entrance** €4–6

» **Bottle of Sagres beer** €2–3

» **Lisbon metro ticket** €0.80

Resources

» **Lonely Planet** (www.lonelyplanet.com/portugal/lisbon)

» **Portugal Tourism** (www.visitportugal.com) Official tourism site

Connections

Travelling overland from Portugal entails a trip through Spain. Good places to cross the (invisible) border include ferry crossing from Vila Real de Santo António in The Algarve, with onward connections to Seville. There are also links from Elvas (going across to Badajoz) and rail links from Valença do Minho in the north (heading up to Santiago de Compostela in Galicia). See p1021 for more details.

ITINERARIES

One Week

Devote three days to Lisbon, including a night of fado in the Alfama, bar-hopping in Bairro Alto and Unesco-gazing and pastry-eating in Belém. Spend a day taking in the wooded wonderland of Sintra, before continuing to Porto, gateway to the magical wine-growing region of the Douro valley. Wind up your week in the picturesque lanes of Coimbra, Portugal's own Cambridge.

Two Weeks

On week two, stroll the historic lanes of Évora and visit the nearby megaliths. Take in magical hilltop castle towns like Monsaraz and scenic Castelo de Vide before hitting The Algarve. Travel along the coast, visiting the pretty beach-surrounded towns of Tavira, Faro, Lagos and Sagres. End the grand tour with a bang in Lisbon.

Essential Food & Drink

» **Seafood** Char-grilled *lulas* (squid), *polvo* (octopus) or *sardinhas* (sardines). Other treats: *cataplana* (seafood and sausage cooked in a copper pot), *caldeirada* (hearty fish stew) and *açorda de mariscos* (bread stew with shrimp).

» **Cod for all seasons** Portuguese have dozens of ways to prepare *bacalhau* (salted cod). Try *bacalhau a brás* (grated cod fried with potatoes and eggs), *bacalhau espiritual* (cod soufflé) or *bacalhau com natas* (baked cod with cream and grated cheese).

» **Field & fowl** *Porco preto* (sweet 'black' pork), *leitão* (roast suckling pig), *alheira* (bread and meat sausage – formerly Kosher), *cabrito assado* (roast kid) and *arroz de pato* (duck risotto).

» **Drink** Port and red wines from the Douro valley, *alvarinho* and *vinho verde* (crisp, semi-sparkling wine) from the Minho and great, little-known reds from the Alentejo and the Beiras (particularly the Dão region).

» **Pastries** The *pastel de nata* (custard tart) is legendary, especially in Belém. Other delicacies: *travesseiros* (almond and egg pastries) and *queijadas* (mini-cheese pastries).

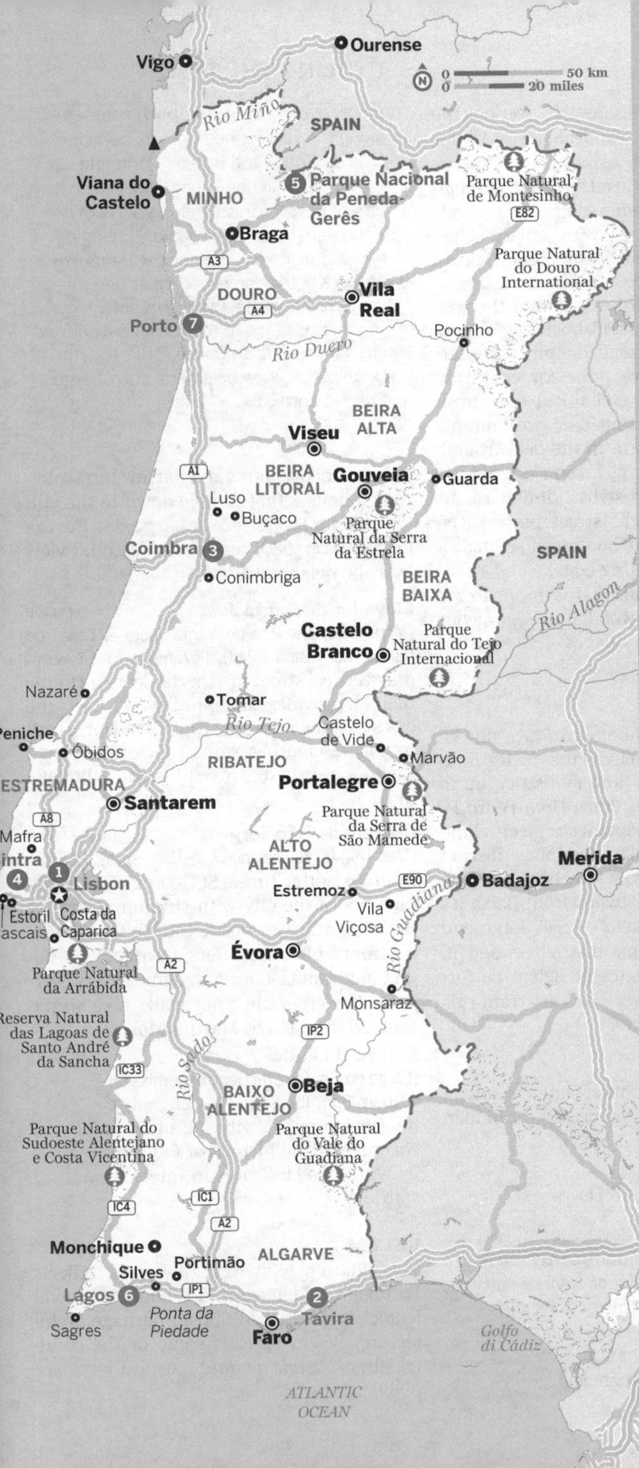

Portugal Highlights

1. Follow the sound of fado spilling from the lamplit lanes of the **Alfama** (p978), an enchanting old-world neighbourhood in the heart of Lisbon
2. Take in the laid-back charms of **Tavira** (p998), before hitting some of The Algarve's prettiest beaches
3. Catch live music in a backstreet bar in **Coimbra** (p1007), a festive university town with a stunning medieval centre
4. Explore the wooded hills of **Sintra** (p994), studded with fairy-tale-like palaces, villas and gardens
5. Conquer the trails of the ruggedly scenic **Parque Nacional da Peneda-Gerês** (p1017)
6. Enjoy heady beach days in **Lagos** (p999), a surf-loving town with a vibrant drinking and dining scene
7. Explore the Unesco World Heritage–listed centre of **Porto** (p1009), sampling velvety ports at riverside wine lodges

LISBON

POP 580,000

Spread across steep hillsides that overlook the Rio Tejo, Lisbon has captivated visitors for centuries. Windswept vistas at breathtaking heights reveal the city in all its beauty: Roman and Moorish ruins, white-domed cathedrals and grand plazas lined with sun-drenched cafes. The real delight of discovery, though, is delving into the narrow cobblestone lanes.

As bright-yellow trams clatter through curvy tree-lined streets, Lisboetas (residents of Lisbon) stroll through lamplit old quarters, much as they've done for centuries. Village-life gossip is exchanged over fresh bread and wine at tiny patio restaurants as fado singers perform in the background. In other parts of town, Lisbon reveals her youthful alter ego at stylish dining rooms and lounges, late-night street parties, riverside nightspots and boutiques selling all things classic and cutting-edge.

Just outside Lisbon, there's more to explore: enchanting woodlands, gorgeous beaches and seaside villages – all ripe for discovery.

Sights

At the riverfront is the grand Praça do Comércio. Behind it march the pedestrian-filled streets of Baixa (lower) district, up to Praça da Figueira and Praça Dom Pedro IV (aka Rossio). From Baixa it's a steep climb west, through swanky shopping district Chiado, into the narrow streets of nightlife haven Bairro Alto. Eastward from Baixa it's another climb to Castelo de São Jorge and the labyrinthine Alfama district around it. The World Heritage sites of Belém lie further west along the river – an easy tram-ride from Praça do Comércio.

BAIXA & ALFAMA

Alfama is Lisbon's Moorish time capsule: a medina-like district of tangled alleys, hidden palm-shaded squares and narrow terracotta-roofed houses that tumble down to the glittering Tejo. The terrace at **Largo das Portas do Sol** (Map p980) provides a splendid view over the neighbourhood.

Elevador de Santa Justa ELEVATOR
(Map p984; cnr Rua de Santa Justa & Largo do Carmo; admission €2.80; 7am-11pm) Lisbon's only vertical street lift, this lanky neo-Gothic marvel provides sweeping views over the city's skyline. From the top, it's a short stroll to the fascinating ruins of **Convento do Carmo**, mostly destroyed in an earthquake in 1755.

Castelo de São Jorge CASTLE RUINS
(Map p984; admission €7; 9am-9pm) Dating from Visigothic times, St George's Castle sits high above the city with stunning views of the city and river. Inside the Ulysses Tower, a **camera obscura** offers a unique 360-degree angle on Lisbon, with demos every half-hour. If you'd rather not walk, take scenic tram 28 from Largo Martim Moniz.

Museu do Fado MUSEUM
(Largo do Chafariz de Dentro; admission €3; 10am-6pm Tue-Sun) This engaging museum provides vibrant audiovisual coverage of the history of fado from its working-class roots to international stardom.

BELÉM

This quarter, 6km west of Rossio, reflects Portugal's golden age and is home to several iconic sights. In addition to heritage architecture, Belém spreads some of the country's best *pastéis de nata* (custard tarts; see p989).

CYCLING THE TEJO

A new **cycling/jogging path** courses along the Tejo for nearly 7km, between Cais do Sodré and Belém. Complete with artful touches – including the poetry of Pessoa printed along parts of it – the path traverses a rapidly changing landscape, taking in ageing warehouses that are being converted into open-air cafes, restaurants and nightspots.

A handy place to rent bikes is a short stroll from Cais do Sodré: **Bike Iberia** (Map p984; www.bikeiberia.com; Largo Corpo Santo 5).

LISBOA CARD

If you're planning on doing a lot of sightseeing, this **discount card** represents excellent value. It offers free entry to key museums and attractions, plus unlimited use of public transport. The 24-/48-/72hr versions cost €17/27/34; it's available at tourist offices.

To reach Belém, hop aboard tram 15 from Praça da Figueira or Praça do Comércio.

Mosteiro dos Jerónimos MONASTERY

(Map p980; Praça do Império; admission €6; ⏲10am-6pm Tue-Sun) Dating from 1496, this Unesco World Heritage site is one of Lisbon's icons, and is a soaring extravaganza of Manueline architecture with stunning carvings and ceramic tiles.

Museu Colecção Berardo ART MUSEUM

(Map p980; www.museuberardo.pt; Praça do Império; admission free; ⏲10am-7pm Sat-Thu, to 10pm Fri) Houses an impressive collection of abstract, surrealist and pop art, along with some of the city's best temporary exhibits. There's also a great indoor-outdoor cafe.

Torre de Belém TOWER

(off Map p980; admission €4; ⏲10am-5pm Tue-Sun) Another of Belém's Unesco World Heritage–listed wonders, the Tower of Belém symbolises the voyages that made Portugal powerful. Brave the cramped winding staircase to the turret for fantastic river views.

SALDANHA

Museu Calouste Gulbenkian MUSEUM

(Map p980; Avenida de Berna 45; admission €4; ⏲10am-6pm Tue-Sun) This celebrated museum showcases an epic collection of Eastern and Western art: Egyptian mummy masks, Mesopotamian urns, Qing porcelain and paintings by Rembrandt, Renoir and Monet.

Centro de Arte Moderna ART MUSEUM

(Modern Art Centre; Map p980; Rua Dr Nicaulau de Bettencourt; admission €4; ⏲10am-6pm Tue-Sun) In a sculpture-dotted garden alongside Museu Calouste Gulbenkian, the modern art museum contains a stellar collection of 20th-century Portuguese art.

SANTA APOLÓNIA & LAPA

The museums listed here are west and east of the city centre, but well worth visiting.

Museu Nacional do Azulejo MUSEUM

(Map p980; Rua Madre de Deus 4; admission €5; ⏲10am-6pm Wed-Sun, 2-6pm Tue) Languishing in a sumptuous 17th-century convent, this museum showcases Portugal's artful *azulejos* (ceramic tiles), with a fascinating 36m-long panel depicting pre-earthquake Lisbon.

Museu Nacional de Arte Antiga ART MUSEUM

(Ancient Art Museum; Map p980; Rua das Janelas Verdes; admission €5; ⏲10am-6pm Wed-Sun, 2-6pm Tue) Set in a lemon-fronted, 17th-century palace, this museum presents a star-studded collection of European and Asian paintings and decorative arts.

PARQUE DAS NAÇÕES

The former Expo '98 site, a revitalised 2km-long waterfront area in the northeast,

LISBON IN...

Two Days

Take a roller-coaster ride on tram 28, hopping off to scale the ramparts of **Castelo de São Jorge**. Sample Portugal's finest at **Wine Bar do Castelo**, then stroll the picturesque lanes of **Alfama**, pausing for a pick-me-up in arty **Pois Café**. Glimpse the fortress-like **Sé** cathedral en route to shopping in pedestrianised **Baixa**. By night, return to lantern-lit Alfama for first-rate fado at Mesa de Frades.

On day two, breakfast on cinnamon-dusted pastries in **Belém**, then explore the fantastical Manueline cloisters of **Mosteiro dos Jerónimos**. River-gaze from the **Torre de Belém** and see cutting-edge art at the **Museu Colecção Berardo**. Head back for sundowners and magical views at **Noobai Café**, dinner at **100 Maneiras** and bar crawling in **Bairro Alto**.

Four Days

Go window-shopping and cafe-hopping in well-heeled **Chiado**, then head to futuristic **Parque das Nações** for riverfront gardens and the head-spinning **Oceanário**. That night, dine at **Bocca** or **Olivier**, then go dancing in clubbing temple **Lux**.

On day four, catch the train to **Sintra**, for walks through boulder-speckled woodlands to fairy-tale palaces. Back in **Rossio**, toast your trip with cherry liqueur at **A Ginjinha** and alfresco dining at **Chapitô**.

Greater Lisbon

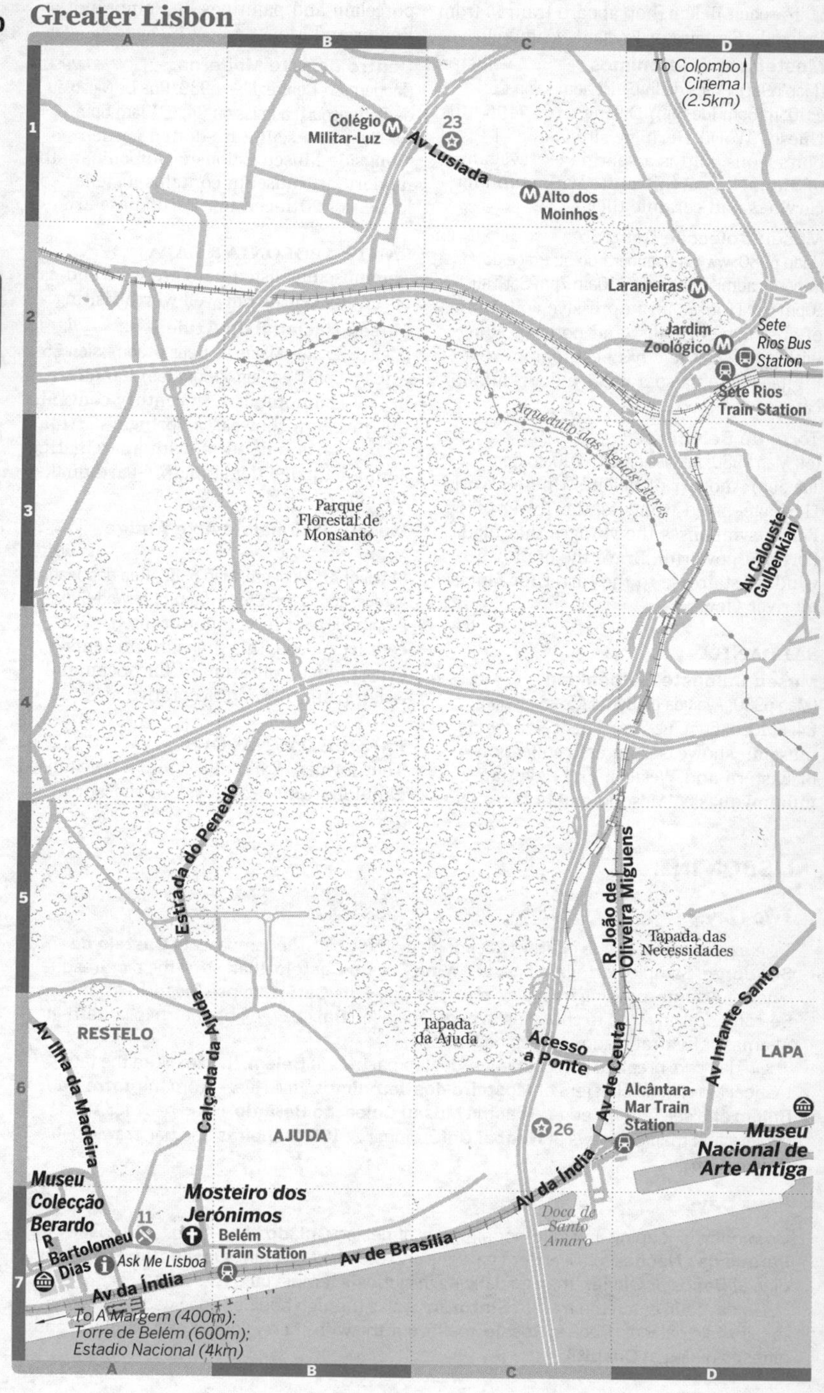

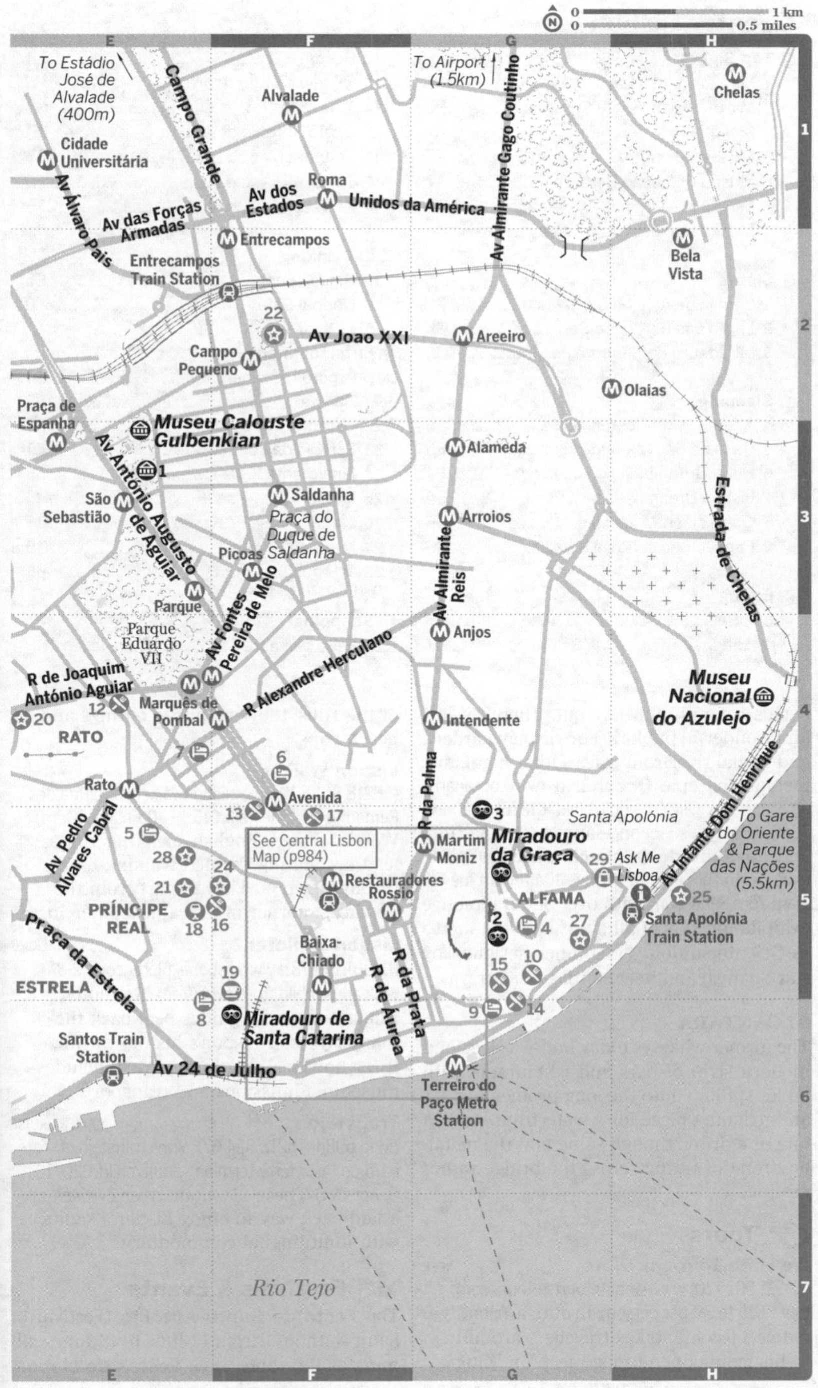
0 1 km
0 0.5 miles
To Estádio José de Alvalade (400m)
To Airport (1.5km)
Campo Grande
Alvalade
Av Almirante Gago Coutinho
Chelas
Cidade Universitária
Av Álvaro Pais
Roma
Av dos Estados
Unidos da América
Av das Forças Armadas
Entrecampos
Bela Vista
Entrecampos Train Station
22
Av Joao XXI
Areeiro
Campo Pequeno
Olaias
Praça de Espanha
Museu Calouste Gulbenkian
Av António Augusto de Aguiar
Alameda
1
Saldanha
São Sebastião
Praça do Duque de Saldanha
Arroios
Estrada de Chelas
Picoas
Av Fontes Pereira de Melo
Av Almirante Reis
Parque
Parque Eduardo VII
Anjos
R Alexandre Herculano
R de Joaquim António Aguiar
Museu Nacional do Azulejo
12
20
Marquês de Pombal
Intendente
RATO
7
6
Rato
R da Palma
Av Infante Dom Henrique
13
Avenida
17
3
Santa Apolónia
To Gare do Oriente & Parque das Nações (5.5km)
Av Pedro Álvares Cabral
5
See Central Lisbon Map (p984)
Martim Moniz
Miradouro da Graça
28
24
29
Ask Me Lisboa
Restauradores
21
Rossio
ALFAMA
25
PRÍNCIPE REAL
18
16
2
4
27
Santa Apolónia Train Station
Praça da Estrela
Baixa-Chiado
R da Prata
R de Áurea
15
10
ESTRELA
19
8
Miradouro de Santa Catarina
9
14
Santos Train Station
Av 24 de Julho
Terreiro do Paço Metro Station
Rio Tejo
E
F
G
H
1
2
3
4
5
6
7
PORTUGAL LISBON

Greater Lisbon

Top Sights
Miradouro da Graça ... G5
Miradouro de Santa Catarina ... F6
Mosteiro dos Jerónimos ... A7
Museu Calouste Gulbenkian ... E3
Museu Colecção Berardo ... A7
Museu Nacional de Arte Antiga ... D6
Museu Nacional do Azulejo ... H4

Sights
1 Centro de Arte Moderna ... E3
2 Largo das Portas do Sol ... G5
3 Miradouro da Senhora do Monte ... G5

Sleeping
4 Alfama Patio Hostel ... G5
5 Casa de São Mamede ... E5
6 Hotel Britania ... F4
7 Lisbon Dreams ... E4
8 Oasis Lisboa ... E6
9 Pensão São João da Praça ... G6

Eating
10 A Baîuca ... G5
11 Antiga Confeitaria de Belém ... A7
12 Bocca ... E4
13 Cervejaria Ribadouro ... F5
14 Pois Café ... G6
Santo Antonio de Alfama ... (see 15)
15 Senhora Mãe ... G5
16 Terra ... F5
17 Zé Varunca ... F5

Drinking
18 Cinco Lounge ... E5
19 Noobai Café ... F5

Entertainment
20 Amoreiras Cinema ... E4
21 Bar 106 ... E5
22 Campo Pequeno ... F2
23 Estádio da Luz ... C1
24 Finalmente ... F5
25 Lux ... H5
26 LX Factory ... C6
27 Mesa de Frades ... G5
28 Trumps ... E5

Shopping
29 Feira da Ladra ... G5

equals a family fun day out. There's weird and wonderful public art on display, gardens and casual riverfront cafes. Other highlights include the epic **Oceanário** (www.oceanario.pt; Doca dos Olivais; adult/child €12/6; 10am-7pm), Europe's second-largest oceanarium, and **Pavilhão do Conhecimento** (Living Science Centre; adult/child €7/4; 10am-6pm Tue-Fri, 11am-7pm Sat & Sun) with over 300 interactive exhibits for kids of all ages. Take the metro to Oriente station – a stunner designed by star Spanish architect Santiago Calatrava.

ALCÂNTARA

The former wharves today house a sleek and modern strip of bars and restaurants with tables spilling onto the long promenade. It's an intriguing place for a waterfront stroll, a bite or a drink, though some find the metallic drone of traffic across the bridge rather grating.

Tours

We Hate Tourism Tours JEEP
(911 501 720; www.wehatetourismtours.com; tours €15 to 30 per person) Bruno, a friendly native Lisboeta, takes travellers around in his iconic open-topped jeep on 'King of the Hills' tours, nightlife outings and beach trips.

Lisbon Walker WALKING
(218 861 840; www.lisbonwalker.com; Rua dos Remédios 84; 3hr walk €15; 10am & 2.30pm) Well-informed, English-speaking guides lead fascinating themed walking tours through Lisbon. They depart from the northeast corner of Praça do Comércio.

Lisbon Explorer WALKING
(961 198 781; www.lisbonexplorer.com; 2-3hr walk adult/child from €34/free) Top-notch English-speaking guides peel back the many layers of Lisbon's history during three-hour walking tours. Price includes museum admissions and transport.

Transtejo RIVER CRUISE
(Map p984; 218 824 671; www.transtejo.pt; Terreiro do Paço ferry terminal; adult/child €20/10; Apr-Oct) These 2½-hour river cruises are a laid-back way to enjoy Lisbon's sights with multilingual commentary.

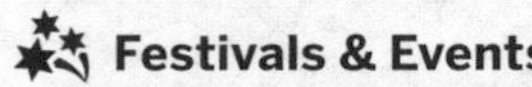

Festivals & Events

The **Festa de Santo António** (Festival of Saint Anthony), from 12 June to 13 June, culminates the three-week **Festas de Lisboa**, with processions and dozens of street parties; it's liveliest in the Alfama.

Sleeping

Lisbon has seriously raised the slumber stakes recently with a new crop of design-conscious boutique hotels and upmarket backpacker digs. Book ahead during high season (July to mid-September).

BAIXA & ROSSIO

Lavra Guest House GUEST HOUSE €€
(Map p984; ☎218 820 000; www.lavra.pt; Calçada de Santana 182, Rossio; s/d from €40/50;) Set in a former convent, the Lavra Guest house has a range of rooms, from basic quarters facing onto an inner courtyard, to brighter rooms with wood floors and tiny balconies.

Lisbon Story Guesthouse GUEST HOUSE €€
(Map p984; ☎211 529 313; www.lisbonstoryguesthouse.com; Largo de São Domingos 18, Rossio; d without bathroom incl breakfast €45-80; @) Overlooking the Praça São Domingos is a small, welcoming guest house with small, well-maintained rooms and a shoe-free lounge, with throw pillows and low tables.

Goodnight Hostel HOSTEL €
(Map p984; ☎213 430 139; www.goodnighthostel.com; Rua dos Correiros 113, Baixa; dm/d €20/50; @) Set in a converted 18th-century town house, this glam hostel rocks with its fab location and retro design. The high-ceilinged dorms offer vertigo-inducing views over Baixa.

Lounge Hostel HOSTEL €
(Map p984; ☎213 462 061; www.lisbonloungehostel.com; Rua de São Nicolau 41, Baixa; dm/d incl breakfast €20/60; @) These ultrahip Baixa digs have a party vibe. Bed down in immaculate dorms and meet like-minded travellers in the funky lounge watched over by a wacky moose head.

Travellers House HOSTEL €
(Map p984; ☎210 115 922; www.travellershouse.com; Rua Augusta 89, Baixa; dm from €22; @) This superfriendly hostel is set in a converted 250-year-old house and offers cosy dorms, a retro lounge with beanbags, an internet corner and a communal kitchen.

Residencial Florescente GUEST HOUSE €€
(Map p984; ☎213 426 609; www.residencialflorescente.com; Rua das Portas de Santo Antão 99, Rossio; s/d from €45/65; @) On a vibrant street lined with alfresco restaurants, lemon-fronted Florescente has comfy rooms in muted tones with shiny new bathrooms. It's a two-minute walk from Rossio.

Pensão Imperial GUEST HOUSE €
(Map p984; ☎213 420 166; Praça dos Restauradores 78, Rossio; s/d €25/40) Cheery Imperial has a terrific location over the main square. The high-ceilinged rooms with simple wooden furniture are nothing flash, but some have flower-draped balconies overlooking the *praça*.

ALFAMA

Alfama Patio Hostel HOSTEL €
(Map p980; ☎218 883 127; www.flashhostel.com; Escola Gerais 3; dm/d from €17/60; @) Located in the heart of the Alfama, this place attracts a cool, laid-back crowd. There are loads of activities (pub crawls, day trips to the beach), plus barbecues on the garden-like patio.

Solar dos Mouros BOUTIQUE HOTEL €€€
(Map p984; ☎218 854 940; www.solardosmouros.pt; Rua do Milagre de Santo António 4; d from €120-240;) Affording river or castle views, the 12 rooms at this boutique charmer bear the imprint of artist Luís Lemos and offer high-end trappings, plus a tiny water garden.

FREE LISBOA

Aside from the Castelo de São Jorge, all the sights in the Lisbon section have free entrance on Sundays from 10am to 2pm. For a free cultural fix on other days, make for Belém's **Museu Colecção Berardo** for great art exhibits, **Museu do Teatro Romano** (Roman Theatre Museum; Map p984; Pátio do Aljube 5; 10am-1pm & 2-6pm Tue-Sun) for Roman theatre ruins, and the fortresslike **Sé** (cathedral; Map p984), built in 1150 on the site of a mosque. For more Roman ruins, take a free tour of the **Núcleo Arqueológico** (Map p984; Rua dos Correeiros 9; 10am-5pm Mon-Sat), which contains a web of tunnels hidden under the Baixa. The new **Museu de Design e da Moda** (Map p984; Rua Augusta 24; 10am-8pm Tue-Sun) exhibits eye-catching furniture, industrial design and couture dating to the 1930s.

Central Lisbon

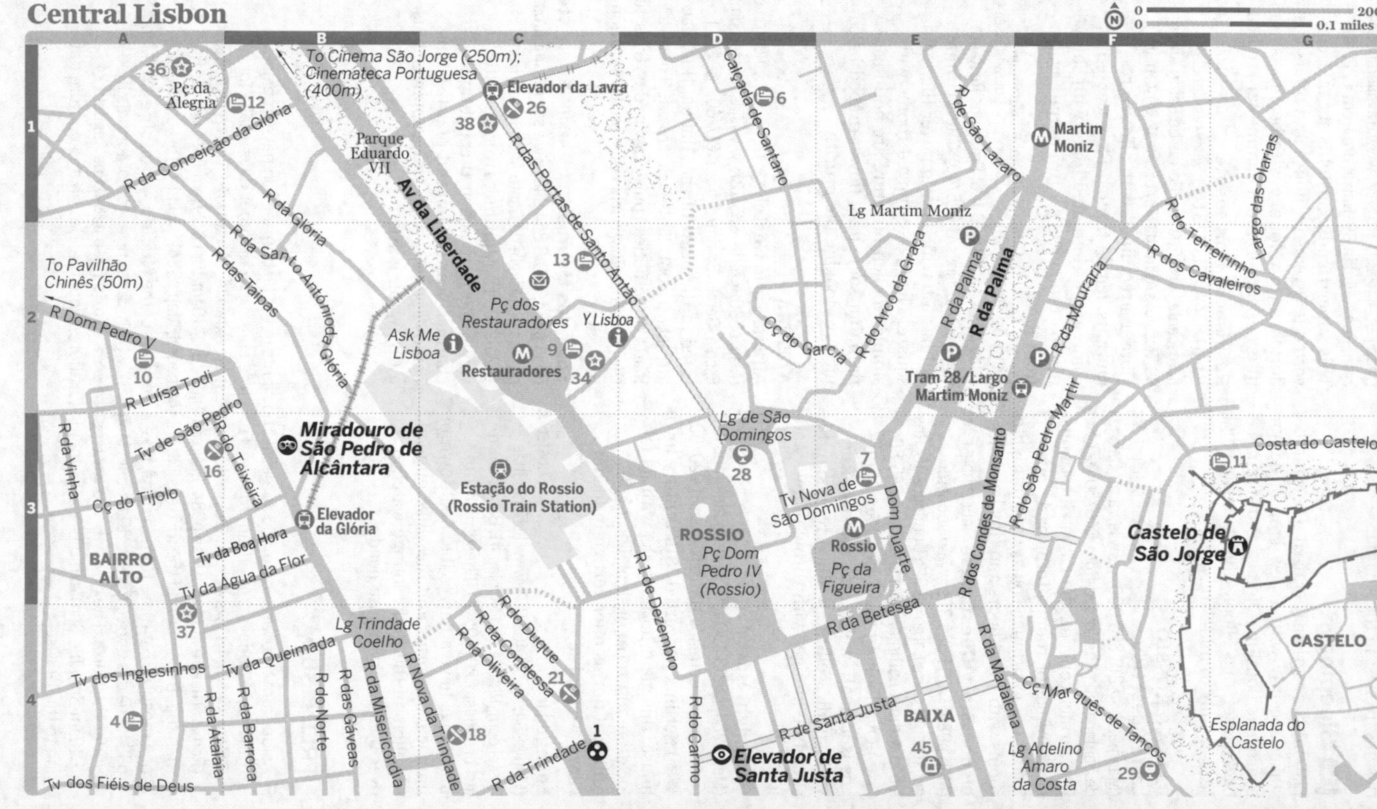

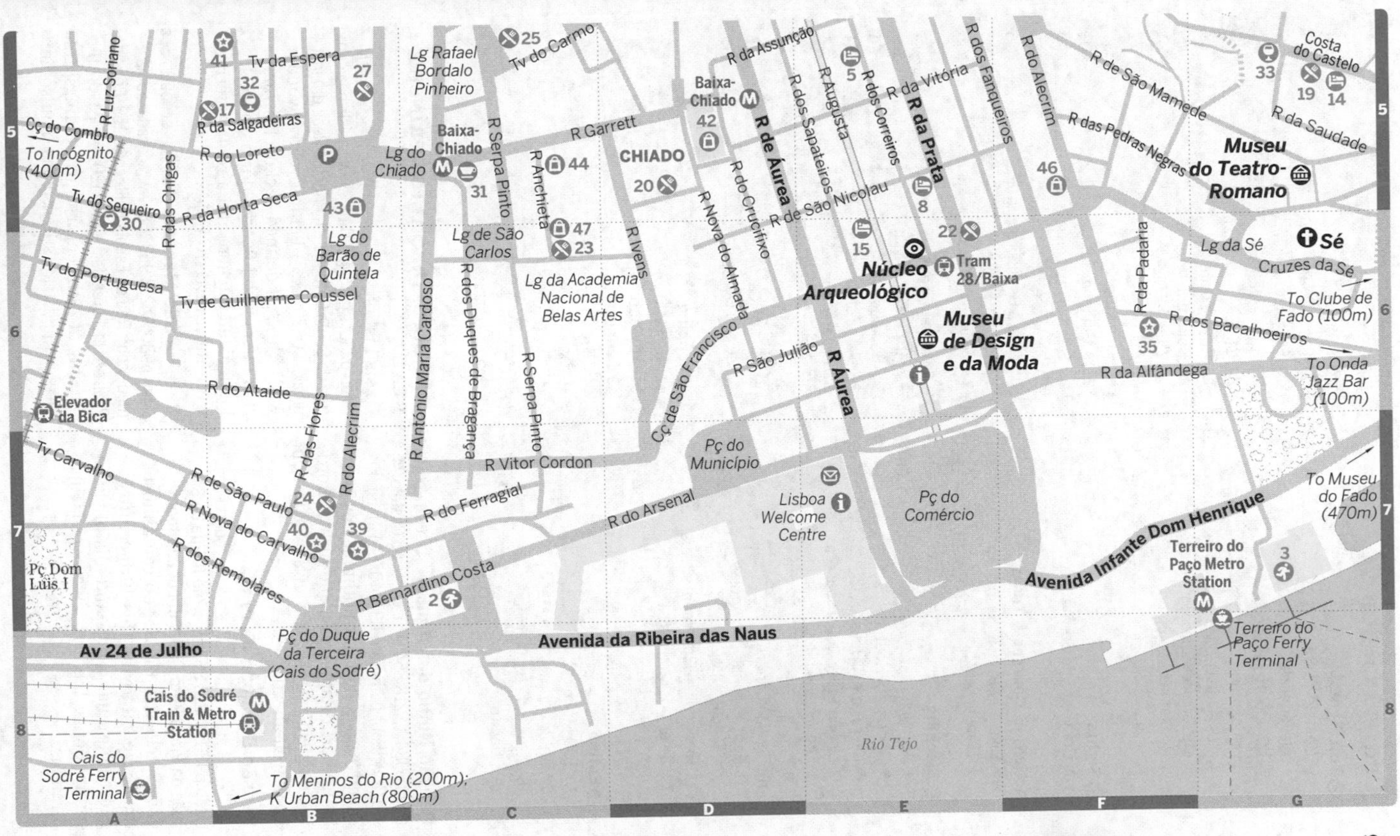
41
Tv da Espera
32
27
17
R da Salgadeiras
R Luz Soriano
25
Tv do Carmo
Lg Rafael Bordalo Pinheiro
Cç do Combro
To Incógnito (400m)
R do Loreto
R das Chigas
Baixa-Chiado
Lg do Chiado
31
R Serpa Pinto
R Garrett
R Anchieta
44
CHIADO
20
Baixa-Chiado
42
R da Assunção
R de Áurea
R dos Sapateiros
R Augusta
5
R dos Correiros
R da Vitória
R da Prata
R dos Fanqueiros
R do Alecrim
R de São Mamede
R das Pedras Negras
Costa do Castelo
33
19
14
R da Saudade
Museu do Teatro-Romano
46
Tv do Sequeiro
30
R da Horta Seca
43
Lg do Barão de Quintela
Lg de São Carlos
47
23
R Ivens
R Nova do Almada
R do Crucifixo
R de São Nicolau
8
15
22
Núcleo Arqueológico
Tram 28/Baixa
R da Padaria
Lg da Sé
Sé
Cruzes da Sé
To Clube de Fado (100m)
Tv do Portuguesa
Tv de Guilherme Coussel
Lg da Academia Nacional de Belas Artes
Museu de Design e da Moda
R dos Bacalhoeiros
35
To Onda Jazz Bar (100m)
R da Alfândega
R São Julião
R Áurea
Cç de São Francisco
R António Maria Cardoso
R dos Duques de Bragança
R Serpa Pinto
R do Ataide
Elevador da Bica
R das Flores
R do Alecrim
R Vitor Cordon
Pç do Município
Tv Carvalho
R de São Paulo
24
R Nova do Carvalho
40
39
R do Ferragial
R do Arsenal
Lisboa Welcome Centre
Pç do Comércio
To Museu do Fado (470m)
Avenida Infante Dom Henrique
Terreiro do Paço Metro Station
3
Pç Dom Luís I
R dos Remolares
R Bernardino Costa
2
Av 24 de Julho
Pç do Duque da Terceira (Cais do Sodré)
Avenida da Ribeira das Naus
Terreiro do Paço Ferry Terminal
Cais do Sodré Train & Metro Station
Cais do Sodré Ferry Terminal
To Meninos do Rio (200m); K Urban Beach (800m)
Rio Tejo

Central Lisbon

Top Sights

Castelo de São Jorge G3
Elevador de Santa Justa D4
Miradouro de São Pedro de Alcântara B3
Museu de Design e da Moda E6
Museu do Teatro Romano G5
Núcleo Arqueológico E6
Sé G6

Sights

1 Convento do Carmo C4

Activities, Courses & Tours

2 Bike Iberia C7
3 Transtejo G7

Sleeping

4 Anjo Azul A4
5 Goodnight Hostel E5
6 Lavra Guest House D1
7 Lisbon Story Guesthouse E3
8 Lounge Hostel E5
9 Pensão Imperial C2
10 Pensão Londres A2
11 Pensão Ninho das Águias G3
12 Residencial Alegria B1
13 Residencial Florescente C2
14 Solar dos Mouros G5
15 Travellers House E6

Eating

16 100 Maneiras A3
17 Antigo Primeiro de Maio B5
18 Cervejaria da Trindade C4
19 Chapitô G5
20 Fábulas D5
21 Faca & Garfo C4
22 Fragoleto E6
23 Kaffee Haus C6
24 Olivier B7
25 Royale Café C5
26 Solar dos Presuntos C1
27 Tavares Rico B5

Drinking

28 A Ginjinha D3
29 Bar das Imagens F4
30 Bicaense A5
31 Café a Brasileira C5
32 Maria Caxuxa B5
33 Wine Bar do Castelo G5

Entertainment

34 ABEP Ticket Kiosk C2
35 Bacalhoeiro F6
36 Cabaret Maxime A1
37 Catacumbas A4
38 Crew Hassan C1
39 Discoteca Jamaica B7
40 Music Box B7
41 Zé dos Bois B5

Shopping

42 Armazéns do Chiado D5
43 Fábrica Sant'Anna B5
44 Livraria Bertrand C5
45 Outra Face da Lua E4
46 Santos Ofícios F5
47 Vida Portuguesa C6

Pensão Ninho das Águias GUEST HOUSE €
(Map p984; ☎218 854 070; Costa do Castelo 74; s/d/tr without bathroom €30/40/60) It isn't called 'eagle's nest' for nothing: this guest house has a Rapunzel-esque turret affording magical 360-degree views over Lisbon. Book well ahead.

Pensão São João da Praça GUEST HOUSE €
(Map p980; ☎218 862 591; 2nd fl, Rua de São João da Praça 97; d €50, without bathroom €35) So close to the *Sé* you can almost touch the gargoyles, this 19th-century guest house has a pick-and-mix of clean, sunny rooms; the best have river-facing verandas.

CHIADO, BAIRRO ALTO & PRÍNCIPE REAL

Oasis Lisboa HOSTEL €
(Map p980; ☎213 478 044; www.oasislisboa.com; Rua de Santa Catarina 24, Principe Real; dm incl breakfast €20; @📶) Behind yellow wonder walls, this self-defined backpacker mansion offers wood-floored dorms, a sleek lounge and kitchen, and a rooftop terrace with impressive river views.

Casa de São Mamede GUEST HOUSE €€€
(Map p980; ☎213 963 166; www.casadesaomamede.com; Rua da Escola Politécnica 159, Principe Real; s/d incl breakfast €100/120; ❄) A soothing stay in 18th-century surroundings; this former magistrate's house has handsome

original tiles and elegant antique-clad rooms.

Pensão Londres GUEST HOUSE €€
(Map p984; ☎213 462 203; www.pensaolondres.com.pt; Rua Dom Pedro V 53, Bairro Alto; s/d €50/75) This friendly and popular place has old-fashioned appeal with large, high-ceilinged, carpeted rooms. Those on the 4th floor have fine views.

Anjo Azul GUEST HOUSE €€
(Map p984; ☎213 478 069; www.anjoazul.com; Rua Luz Soriano 75, Bairro Alto; d €50-80; @) This gay-friendly hotel has rooms from scarlet-and-black love nests with heart pillows to chocolate-caramel numbers.

AVENIDA DE LIBERDADE, RATO & MARQUÊS DE POMBAL

Lisbon Dreams GUEST HOUSE €€
(Map p980; ☎213 872 393; www.lisbondreamsguesthouse.com; Rua Rodrigo da Fonseca 29, Rato; s/d/tr without bathroom incl breakfast €40/60/75; @ 📶) On a quiet street lined with jacaranda trees, Lisbon Dreams offers excellent value for its bright modern rooms with high ceilings and high-end mattresses. Bathrooms are shared, but spotlessly clean.

Hotel Britania HOTEL €€€
(Map p980; ☎213 155 016; www.heritage.pt; Rua Rodrigues Sampaio 17; d from €160; ❄ @ 📶) Art deco rules the waves at the affable, top-rated Britania, a boutique gem near Avenida da Liberdade. Cassiano Branco put his modernist stamp on the rooms with chrome lamps, plaid fabrics and shiny marble bathrooms.

Residencial Alegria GUEST HOUSE €€
(Map p984; ☎213 220 670; www.alegrianet.com; Praça da Alegria 12; d €58-78; ❄) Overlooking a palm-dotted plaza, this lemon-fronted belle époque gem has airy and peaceful rooms, with antique-filled corridors.

Eating

New-generation chefs, first-rate ingredients and a generous pinch of old-world spice have put the Portuguese capital on the gastronomic map. You'll find everything from ubercool sushi lounges to designer Michelin-starred restaurants.

BAIXA & ROSSIO

Solar dos Presuntos PORTUGUESE €€€
(Map p984; ☎213 424 253; Rua das Portas de Santo Antão 150, Rossio; mains €15-24; ⏲lunch & dinner Mon-Sat) Renowned for its excellent seafood as well as its smoked and grilled meats, this buzzing restaurant serves up memorable prawn and lobster curry, salt-baked sea bass and delectable seafood paella, among other great picks.

WORTH A TRIP

COSTA DA CAPARICA

Located 10km southwest of Lisbon, Costa da Caparica's seemingly never-ending beach attracts sun-worshipping Lisboetas craving all-over tans, surfer dudes keen to ride Atlantic waves, and day-tripping families seeking clean sea and soft sand. It hasn't escaped development, but head south and the high-rises soon give way to pine forests and mellow beach-shack cafes.

During the summer a **narrow-gauge railway** runs the length of the beach for 20 stops. The nearer beaches, including **Praia do Norte** and **Praia do São Sebastião**, are great for families, while the further ones are younger and trendier, including **Praia da Sereia** (stop 15), with its cool beachfront bar, Bar Waikiki. **Praia do Castelo** (stop 11) and **Praia da Bela Vista** (stop 17) are more-secluded gay and nudist havens.

The **main beach** (called Praia do CDS, or Centro Desportivo de Surf) is lined with cafes, bars and surfing clubs along its promenade.

If you decide to stay overnight, there are a handful of decent lodgings in town, including simple but comfy **Residencial Mar e Sol** (☎212 900 017; www.residencialmaresol.com; Rua dos Pescadores 42; s/d €45/65; ❄ @ 📶).

The best way to get here is by **ferry to Cacilhas** from Lisbon's Cais do Sodré, where bus 135 runs to Costa da Caparica town (€3, 30 to 45 minutes, every 30 to 60 minutes).

Sport-minded folk can also get there by bike and ferry, by riding along the **Tejo bike path** 7km from Cais do Sodré to Belém, taking the ferry from there to Trafaria, then continuing on another **new bike path** (also separate from traffic) that runs for another 6km down to Costa da Caparica.

HEAVENLY VIEWS

Lisbon's *miradouros* (view points) provide memorable settings to take in the panorama. Some have outdoor cafes attached.

» **Largo das Portas do Sol** (Map p980) With a stylish bar and cafe.

» **Miradouro da Graça** (Map p980) A pine-fringed square that's perfect for sundowners.

» **Miradouro da Senhora do Monte** (Map p980) The highest lookout, with memorable castle views.

» **Miradouro de São Pedro de Alcântara** (Map p984) Drinks and sweeping views on the edge of Bairro Alto.

» **Miradouro de Santa Catarina** (Map p980) Youthful spot with guitar-playing rebels, artful graffiti and first-rate eating/drinking spot (Noobai Café) attached.

Fragoleto ICE CREAM €
(Map p984; Rua da Prata 74, Baixa; scoop €1.90; ⏲9am-8pm Mon-Sat) For tasty gelato, head for pint-sized Fragoleto. Manuela makes authentic ice cream using fresh, seasonal fruit.

ALFAMA

Santo António de Alfama PORTUGUESE €€
(Map p980; ☎218 881 328; Beco de Saõ Miguel 7; mains €13-16; ⏲lunch & dinner) With a lovely front courtyard and atmospheric interior, this bistro is one of the Alfama's stars, with tasty appetisers (gorgonzola-stuffed mushrooms, roasted aubergines with yoghurt), as well as more filling traditional Portuguese dishes.

Chapitô CONTEMPORARY €€
(Map p984; ☎218 867 334; Costa do Castelo 7; tapas €4-5, mains €10-17; ⏲7.30pm-2am Mon-Fri, noon-2am Sat & Sun) Chapitô's tree-filled courtyard hums with arty types tucking into tapas or barbecued steaks. Zebra and giraffe prints glam up the top-floor restaurant, affording mesmerising views over Lisbon.

Pois Café CAFE €
(Map p980; Rua de São João da Praça 93; mains €5-12; ⏲11am-8pm Tue-Sun) Boasting a laid-back boho vibe, Pois Café has creative salads, sandwiches and tangy juices. Its sofas invite lazy afternoons spent reading novels and sipping coffee.

Senhora Mãe CONTEMPORARY €€
(Map p980; Largo de São Martinho 6-7; mains €10-18; ⏲lunch & dinner) A pleasant front patio and a stylish interior set the scene for seasonally inspired dishes, such as ravioli in cuttlefish ink or duck breast with lemongrass.

AVENIDA DE LIBERDADE, RATO & MARQUÊS DE POMBAL

Zé Varunca PORTUGUESE €€
(Map p980; Rua de São José 54; mains €10-13; ⏲lunch & dinner Mon-Sat) This charming, rustically decorated restaurant specialises in Alentejo cooking, with a changing menu of regional favourites such as roast pork with clam sauce and *migas de bacalhau* (a bread-based dish cooked with cod).

Bocca FUSION €€€
(Map p980; ☎213 808 383; Rua Rodrigo da Fonseca 87, Marques de Pombal; mains €15-30; ⏲lunch & dinner Tue-Sat) This elegant, award-winning restaurant serves beautifully turned-out meat and seafood dishes. The gastrobar serves inventive plates meant for sharing, as well as tasty cocktails. Superb wine list.

Cervejaria Ribadouro SEAFOOD €€
(Map p980; ☎213 549 411; Rua do Salitre 2; mains €8-20; ⏲lunch & dinner) This bustling beer hall is popular with local seafood fans. The shellfish are plucked fresh from the tank, weighed and cooked to lip-smacking perfection.

CHIADO, BAIRRO ALTO & PRÍNCIPE REAL

TOP CHOICE **100 Maneiras** FUSION €€€
(Map p984; ☎210 990 475; Rua do Teixeira 35, Bairro Alta; tasting menus €35; ⏲dinner Mon-Sat) One of Lisbon's best-rated restaurants, 100 Maneiras has no menu, just a 10-course tasting menu that changes daily and features creative, delicately prepared dishes. There's a lively buzz to the elegant and small space. Reservations essential.

Olivier FRENCH €€€
(Map p984; ☎213 422 916; Rua do Alecrim 23, Chiado; mains €19-27, tasting menus €38; ⏲dinner Mon-Sat) Lisbon masterchef Olivier da Costa continues to wow diners at this intimate Chiado restaurant, with its beautifully prepared French-inspired dishes served

amid gilded banquettes, low-hanging chandeliers and vintage wallpaper. Reservations recommended.

Fábulas CAFE €

(Map p984; Calçada Nova de São Francisco 14, Chiado; mains €6-10; ⏲10am-midnight Mon-Sat, 10am-8pm Sun; @) Exposed stone walls, low lighting and twisting corridors that open onto cosy nooks and crannies do indeed conjure a storybook fable *(fábula)*. Sink into a comfy couch with coffee or wine, or have a meal – salads, pasta, burritos, crêpes and daily specials.

Faca & Garfo PORTUGUESE €

(Map p984; Rua da Condessa 2, Chiado; mains €6-8; ⏲lunch & dinner Mon-Sat) The sweet *azulejo*-filled Faca & Garfo (which means 'knife and fork') serves carefully prepared Portuguese recipes at reasonable prices. Try the authentic *alheira de Mirandela* (chicken sausage) or the *bife à casa* (steak with cream and port wine sauce).

Terra VEGETARIAN €€

(Map p980; Rua da Palmeira 15, Principe Real; buffets €15; ⏲lunch Sat & Sun, dinner Tue-Sun;) Terra is famed for its superb vegetarian buffet (including vegan options) of salads, kebabs and curries, plus organic wines and juices. A fountain gurgles in the tree-shaded courtyard, lit by twinkling lights after dark.

Antigo Primeiro de Maio PORTUGUESE €€

(Map p984; Rua da Atalaia 8, Bairro Alta; mains €10-12; ⏲dinner Mon-Sat, lunch Mon-Fri) Always packed with regulars, this small festive *tasca* (tavern) serves excellent traditional Portuguese dishes, amid tiled walls, a garrulous crowd and harried-but-friendly waiters.

Tavares Rico PORTUGUESE €€€

(Map p984; ☎213 421 112; Rua da Misericórdia 37, Chiado; mains €32-38, tasting menus €90; ⏲lunch & dinner Tue-Sat) Tavares is the fairest of them all, with its all-gold 18th-century interior lit by chandeliers. Signature dishes such as scallops with Alentejo bacon marry well with Portuguese wines.

Kaffee Haus CAFE €

(Map p984; Rua Anchieta 3, Chiado; mains €6-10; ⏲11am-midnight Tue-Thu, 11am-2am Fri & Sat, 11am-8pm Sun) Overlooking a peaceful corner of Chiado, this cool but unpretentious cafe has daily chalkboard specials – big salads, tasty schnitzels, strudels, cakes and more.

Royale Café CAFE €

(Map p984; ☎213 469 125; Largo Rafael Bordalo Pinheiro 29, Chiado; snacks €4-6; ⏲10am-midnight Mon-Sat, to 8pm Sun) This chichi cafe has a pleasant vine-clad courtyard that's ideal for drinks and create-your-own sandwiches.

Cervejaria da Trindade PORTUGUESE €€

(Map p984; ☎213 423 506; Rua Nova da Trindade 20c, Chiado; mains €8-20) This 13th-century monastery turned clattering beer hall oozes atmosphere with its vaults and *azulejos*. Feast on humungous steaks or lobster stew, washed down with foaming beer.

BELÉM

A Margem FUSION €€

(off Map p980; ☎918 225 584; Doca do Bom Sucesso; salads €10-12; ⏲10am-1am) Well sited near the river's edge, this small, sun-drenched cube of glass and white stone boasts an open patio and large windows facing the Tejo. Locals come for fresh salads, cheese plates, bruschetta and other light bites, as well as wine and cocktails.

Antiga Confeitaria de Belém PATISSERIE €

(Map p980; ☎213 637 423; Rua de Belém 86-88) A classically tiled and elegant cafe with probably the best *pastéis de nata* on earth. Delicious! Since 1837, this patisserie has been transporting locals to sugar-coated nirvana with heavenly *pastéis de belém*: crisp pastry nests filled with custard cream, baked at 400 degrees for that perfect golden crust, then lightly dusted with cinnamon. Admire *azulejos* in the vaulted rooms or devour a still-warm tart at the counter to try to guess the secret ingredient.

Drinking

All-night street parties in Bairro Alto, sunset drinks from high Alfama terraces, and sumptuous art deco cafes scattered about Chiado – Lisbon has many enticing options for imbibers.

Pavilhão Chinês LOUNGE BAR
(off Map p984; Rua Dom Pedro V 89-91, Principe Real) An old curiosity shop of a bar with oil paintings and model spitfires dangling from the ceiling, and cabinets brimming with glittering Venetian masks and Action Men. Play pool or bag a comfy armchair with port or beer in hand.

Bicaense BAR
(Map p984; Rua da Bica de Duarte Belo 42a, Bica) Indie kids have a soft spot for this chilled Santa Catarina haunt, kitted out with retro radios, projectors and squishy beanbags. DJs spin house to the preclubbing crowd and the back room stages occasional gigs.

Wine Bar do Castelo WINE BAR
(Map p984; Rua Bartolomeu de Gusmão 13, Castelo; ⌚noon-11pm) Near the entrance to the Castelo de São Jorge, this welcoming place serves more than 150 Portuguese wines by the glass, along with gourmet smoked meats, cheeses, olives and other tasty accompaniments.

Cinco Lounge LOUNGE BAR
(Map p980; Rua Ruben António Leitão 17, Principe Real; ⌚9pm-2am Tue-Sat) Take an award-winning London-born mixologist, add a candlelit, gold-kissed setting and give it a funky twist and you have Cinco Lounge. Come for the laid-back scene and legendary cocktails.

Meninos do Rio OUTDOOR BAR
(off Map p984; Rua da Cintura do Porto de Lisboa, Armação 255, Santos; ⌚12.30pm-1am Sun-Thu, to 4am Fri & Sat) Perched on the river's edge, Meninos do Rio has palm trees, wooden decks, reggae-playing DJs and tropical cocktails, giving it a vibe that's more Caribbean than Iberian.

Maria Caxuxa BAR
(Map p984; Rua Barroca 6, Bairro Alto; ⌚8am-2am) Maria Caxuxa has effortless style, its several rooms decked with giant mixers, *azulejo*-lined walls and 1950s armchairs and sofas, as funk-laden jazz plays overhead.

Café a Brasileira CAFE, BAR
(Map p984; ☎213 469 547; Rua Garrett 120, Chiado; ⌚8am-2am) An historic watering hole for Lisbon's 19th-century greats, with warm wooden innards and a busy counter serving daytime coffees and pints at night.

Bar das Imagens BAR
(Map p984; Calçada Marquês de Tancos 1, Castelo; ⌚11am-2am Tue-Sat, 3-11pm Sun) With a terrace affording vertigo-inducing views over the city, this cheery bar serves potent Cuba libres and other well-prepared cocktails.

Noobai Café CAFE, BAR
(Map p980; Miradouro de Santa Catarina, Santa Catarina; ⌚noon-midnight) Lisbon's best-kept secret is next to Miradouro de Santa Catarina, with a laid-back vibe, jazzy beats and magnificent views from the terrace.

A Ginjinha BAR
(Map p984; Largo de Saõ Domingos 8, Rossio; ⌚9am-10pm) Join a wide swath of society for a refreshingly potent quaff of *ginjinha* (cherry brandy) at this tiny bar-stand-up counter near Rossio.

☆ Entertainment

For the latest goings-on, pick up the weekly *Time Out Lisboa* (www.timeout.pt) from bookstores, or the free monthly *Follow me Lisboa* or the *Agenda Cultural Lisboa* from the tourist office.

Live Music

Zé dos Bois ALTERNATIVE
(Map p984; ☎213 430 205; www.zedosbois.org; Rua da Barroca 59, Bairro Alta) Focusing on tomorrow's performing arts and music trends, Zé dos Bois is an experimental venue with a laid-back courtyard. This boho haunt has hosted bands such as Black Dice and Animal Collective.

Onda Jazz Bar JAZZ
(off Map p984; www.ondajazz.com; Arco de Jesus 7, Alfama) This vaulted cellar features a menu of mainstream jazz, plus more-eclectic beats of bands hailing from Brazil and Africa.

Catacumbas JAZZ
(Map p984; Travessa da Água da Flor 43, Bairro Alta) Moodily lit and festooned with portraits of legends such as Miles Davis, this den is jam-packed when it hosts live jazz on Thursday night.

Nightclubs

Cover charges for nightclubs vary from €5 to €20.

Lux NIGHTCLUB
(Map p980; www.luxfragil.com; Avenida Infante Dom Henrique, Santo Apolónia) Lisbon's ice-cool, must-see club, Lux is run by ex-Frágil maestro Marcel Reis and is part-owned by John Malkovich. Lux hosts big-name DJs and a fine roof terrace overlooking the Tejo.

PORTUGUESE SOUL

Infused by Moorish song and the ditties of homesick sailors, bluesy, bittersweet **fado** encapsulates the Lisbon psyche like nothing else. The uniquely Portuguese style was born in the Alfama, still the best place in Lisbon to hear it live. Minimum consumption charges range from €15 to €25 per person.

» **A Baîuca** (Map p980; Rua de São Miguel 20; ⏲dinner Thu-Mon) On a good night, walking into A Baîuca is like gatecrashing a family party. It's a special place with *fado vadio,* where locals take a turn and spectators hiss if anyone dares to chat during the singing.

» **Clube de Fado** (off Map p984; ☎218 852 704; www.clube-de-fado.com; Rua de São João da Praça; ⏲9pm-2.30am Mon-Sat) Hosts the cream of the fado crop in vaulted, dimly lit surrounds. Big-name *fadistas* perform here alongside celebrated guitarists.

» **Mesa de Frades** (Map p980; ☎917 029 436; www.mesadefrades.com; Rua dos Remédios 139a; admission from €15; ⏲dinner Wed-Mon) A magical place to hear fado, tiny Mesa de Frades used to be a chapel. It's tiled with exquisite *azulejos* and has just a handful of tables. Reserve ahead.

Music Box
NIGHTCLUB

(Map p984; Rua Nova do Carvalho 24, Cais do Sodré; www.musicboxlisboa.com) Under the brick arches on Rua Nova do Carvalho lies one of Lisbon's hottest clubs. Music Box hosts loud and bouncy club nights with music shifting from electro to rock, plus ear-splitting gigs by rising bands.

Incógnito
NIGHTCLUB

(off Map p984; Rua Poiais de São Bento 37, Santa Catarina) No-sign, pint-sized Incógnito offers an alternative vibe and DJs thrashing out indie rock and electro-pop. Sweat it out with a fun crowd on the tiny basement dance floor, or breathe more easily in the loft bar upstairs.

Discoteca Jamaica
NIGHTCLUB

(Map p984; Rua Nova do Carvalho, Cais do Sodré; ⏲11pm-4am) Gay and straight, black and white, young and old – everyone has a soft spot for this offbeat club. It gets going around 2am at weekends with DJs pumping out reggae, hip hop and retro.

Cabaret Maxime
NIGHTCLUB

(Map p984; www.cabaret-maxime.com; Praça da Alegria 58) Young Lisboetas flock to this former strip club for DJ nights of old-school tunes, or loud, sweaty gigs of established and upcoming local bands.

K Urban Beach
NIGHTCLUB

(off Map p984; www.grupo-k.pt; Cais da Viscondessa, Santos) Jutting out over the Tejo, this stylish and airy club has a lively dance floor, a restaurant and outdoor seating that makes fine use of its scenic riverside setting.

Alternative Culture

Lisbon may flirt with high culture and embrace fado, but she also has an ongoing relationship with the underdog. Individuality trumps conformity and alternative culture rules in these offbeat cultural centres.

LX Factory
ART SPACE

(Map p980; www.lxfactory.com; Rua Rodrigues de Faria 103, Alcântara) Lisbon's new hub of creativity hosts a dynamic menu of events from live concerts and film screenings to fashion shows and art exhibitions. There's a rustically cool cafe as well as a restaurant, bookshop and design-minded shops. Weekend nights see parties with a dance- and art-loving crowd.

Crew Hassan
ECLECTIC

(Map p984; Rua das Portas de Santo Antão 159, Rossio; @🖉) Alternative types dig Crew Hassan's graffiti, threadbare sofas, cheap veggie fare and free internet. Its line-up spans films, gigs, exhibitions and DJs playing music from reggae to minimalist techno.

Bacalhoeiro
BAR

(Map p984; ☎218 864 891; Rua dos Bacalhoeiros 125, Baixa; 📶) Nonconformist, laid-back Bacalhoeiro shelters a cosy bar and hosts everything from alternative gigs to film screenings, salsa nights and themed parties. Free wi-fi.

Gay & Lesbian Venues

Lisbon has a relaxed yet flourishing gay scene with an annual Gay Pride Festival in

June. Visit www.gaylisbon4u.com for more listings.

Bar 106 BAR
(Map p980; www.bar106.com; Rua de São Marçal 106) Young and fun with an upbeat, pre-clubbing vibe and crazy events such as Sunday's message party.

Finalmente NIGHTCLUB
(Map p980; Rua da Palmeira 38) This popular club has a tiny dance floor, nightly drag shows and wall-to-wall crowds.

Trumps NIGHTCLUB
(Map p980; www.trumps.pt; Rua da Imprensa Nacional 104b) Lisbon's hottest gay club, with cruisy corners, a sizeable dance floor and events from live music to drag.

Cinemas

Lisbon's cinematic standouts are the grand **São Jorge** (off Map p984; Avenida da Liberdade 175) and, just around the corner, **Cinemateca Portuguesa** (off Map p984; www.cinemateca.pt; Rua Barata Salgueiro 39); both screen offbeat, art-house, world and old films. For Hollywood fare, visit multiscreen **Amoreiras Cinema** (Map p980; Amoreiras Shopping Centre, Avenida Eng Duarte Pacheco) or **Colombo Cinema** (off Map p980; Centro Colombo, Avenida Lusíada).

Sport

Lisbon's football teams are Benfica, Belenenses and Sporting. Euro 2004 led to the upgrading of the 65,000-seat **Estádio da Luz** (Map p980) and the construction of the 54,000-seat **Estádio Nacional** (Map p980). Bullfights are staged on Thursday from May to October at **Campo Pequeno** (Map p980; Avenida da República; tickets €10-75). Tickets are available at **ABEP ticket kiosk** (Map p984; Praça dos Restauradores). State-of-the-art stadium **Estádio José de Alvalade** (off Map p984; Rua Prof Fernando da Fonseca) seats 54,000 and is just north of the university. Take the metro to Campo Grande.

Shopping

Shops in Lisbon are a mix of the classic and the wild, with antiques, stuck-in-time button and tinned-fish shops, and edgy boutiques all sprinkled across the hilly landscape. Rua Garrett and nearby Largo do Chiado, across Rua da Misericórdia, are home to some of Lisbon's oldest and most upmarket boutiques. Meanwhile, Bairro Alto attracts vinyl lovers and vintage fans to its cluster of late-opening boutiques.

Feira da Ladra MARKET
(Map p980; Campo de Santa Clara, Alfama; 7am-5pm Sat) You'll find old records, coins, jewellery, vintage postcards, dog-eared poetry books and other attic treasure/trash at this lively Saturday market.

Vida Portuguesa PORTUGUESE PRODUCTS
(Map p984; Rua Anchieta 11, Chiado) With high ceilings and polished cabinets, this store lures nostalgics with all-Portuguese products, from retro-wrapped Tricona sardines to lime-oil soap and Bordallo Pinheiro porcelain swallows.

Santos Oficios HANDICRAFTS
(Map p984; Rua da Madalena 87, Baixa) Touristy but fine selection of Portuguese folk art.

Armazéns do Chiado MALL
(Map p984; Rua do Carmo 2, Chiado) A convenient, well-concealed shopping complex. The Fnac here is good for books, music and booking concert tickets.

Outra Face da Lua VINTAGE
(Map p984; Rua da Assunção 22, Baixa) A fun-to-explore vintage shop in Baixa, with a cafe inside.

Fábrica Sant'Ana HANDICRAFTS
(Map p984; Rua do Alecrim 95, Chiado) Great spot for purchasing fabulous new and old *azulejos*.

Livraria Bertrand BOOKS
(Map p984; 213 421 941; Rua Garrett 73, Chiado) Bertrand has Portuguese and foreign-language books amid 18th-century charm.

Information

Emergency

Police, Fire & Ambulance 119

Police station (217 654 242; Rua Capelo 13)

Tourist police (213 421 634; Palácio Foz, Praça dos Restauradores; 24hr)

Internet Access

If you're packing a laptop, these cafes offer free wireless surfing:

Mar Adentro (Rua do Alecrim 35)

Brown's Coffee Shop (Rua da Vitória 86)

Fábulas (Calçada Nova de São Francisco 14)

Sans laptop, head to the following places, which charge around €2 to €3 per hour:

Cyber Bica (Rua dos Duques de Bragança; 11am-midnight Mon-Fri)

Portugal Telecom (Praça Rossio 68; 8am-11pm)

WORTH A TRIP

PARQUE NATURAL DA ARRÁBIDA

Thickly green, hilly and edged by gleamingly clean, golden beaches and chiselled cliffs, the Arrábida Natural Park stretches along the southeastern coast of the Setúbal Peninsula, some 40km south of Lisbon. Highlights here are the long, golden beaches of windsurfer hot-spot **Figueirinha** and the sheltered bay of **Galapo**. Most stunning of all is **Portinho da Arrábida** with fine sand, azure waters and a small 17th-century fort built to protect the monks from Barbary pirates.

Further west lies the former fishing village turned resort town of **Sesimbra**, with a fine beach, a hilltop castle and good seafood restaurants. Keep heading west to reach the haunting **Cabo Espichel**, home to a desolate church and striking ocean views over the cliffs.

Your best option for getting here and exploring the area is to rent a car. Be warned: parking is tricky near the beaches.

Web Café (Rua do Diário de Notícias 126; ⌚7pm-2am)

Internet Resources

www.timeout.pt Details on upcoming gigs, cultural events and interesting commentary, in Portuguese.

www.askmelisboa.com Multilingual site with info on discount cards.

www.golisbon.com Up-to-date info on sightseeing, eating, nightlife and events.

www.visitlisboa.com Lisbon's comprehensive tourism website, with the low-down on sightseeing, transport and accommodation.

Medical Services

Farmácia Estácio (Rossio 62) A central pharmacy.

British Hospital (☎217 213 400; Rua Tomás da Fonseca) English-speaking staff and doctors.

Money

Cota Câmbios (Rossio 41) One of the best exchange rates in town.

Post

Main post office (Map p984; Praça do Comércio)

Post office (Map p984; Praça dos Restauradores)

Telephone

Portugal Telecom (Rossio 68; ⌚8am-11pm)

Tourist Information

Ask Me Lisboa (Map p984; www.askmelisboa.com; Praça dos Restauradores; ⌚9am-8pm) The largest and most helpful tourist office. Can book accommodation or reserve rental cars.

Y Lisboa (Map p984; www.askmelisboa.com; Praça dos Restauradores; ⌚9am-8pm)

Lisboa Welcome Centre (Map p984; www.visitlisboa.com; Praça do Comércio; ⌚9am-6pm)

Information kiosks (Map p984; near Rua Conceição; ⌚10am-1pm & 2-6pm); Santa Apolónia (door 47, inside train station; ⌚8am-1pm Tue-Sat); Belém (Map p984; Largo dos Jernónimos; ⌚10am-1pm & 2-6pm Tue-Sat); Airport (⌚7am-midnight)

Getting There & Away

Air

Around 6km north of the centre, **Aeroporto de Lisboa** (Lisbon Airport; Map p980; www.ana.pt) operates direct flights to many European cities.

Bus

Lisbon's long-distance bus terminal is **Sete Rios** (Map p980; Rua das Laranjeiras), conveniently linked to both Jardim Zoológico metro station and Sete Rios train station. The big carriers, **Rede Expressos** (☎213 581 460; www.rede-expressos.pt) and **Eva** (☎213 581 466; www.eva-bus.com), run frequent services to almost every major town.

The other major terminal is **Gare do Oriente** (at Oriente metro and train station), concentrating on services to the north and to Spain. The biggest companies operating from here are **Renex** (☎218 956 836; www.renex.pt) and the Spanish operator **Avanza** (☎218 940 250; www.avanzabus.com).

Train

Santa Apolónia station (Map p980) is the terminus for northern and central Portugal. You can catch trains from Santa Apolónia to Gare do Oriente train station, which has departures to The Algarve and international destinations. **Cais do Sodré station** (Map p984) is for Belém, Cascais and Estoril. **Rossio station**

(Map p984) is the terminal for trains to Sintra via Queluz.

For fares and schedules visit www.cp.pt.

Getting Around

To/From the Airport

The **AeroBus** (91) runs every 20 minutes from 7.45am to 8.15pm, taking 30 to 45 minutes between the airport and Cais do Sodré; buy your ticket (€3.50) on the bus. A **taxi** into town is about €10 to €14.

Car & Motorcycle

On the outskirts of the city there are cheap (or free) **car parks** near Parque das Nações and Belém. The most central underground car park is at Praça dos Restauradores, costing around €10 to €12 per day. On Saturday afternoons and Sunday, parking is normally free in the pay-and-display areas in the centre.

Public Transport

A 24-hour **Bilhete Carris/Metro** (€3.75) gives unlimited travel on all buses, trams, metros and funiculars. Pick it up from Carris kiosks and metro stations.

BUS, TRAM & FUNICULAR Buses and trams run from 6am to 1am, with a few all-night services. Pick up a transport map from tourist offices or Carris kiosks. A single ticket costs €1.40 on board or €0.81 if you buy a refillable *Viva Viagem* card (€0.50), available at Carris offices and in metro stations.

There are three funiculars:

Elevador da Bica (Map p984)

Elevador da Glória (Map p984)

Elevador do Lavra (Map p984)

Don't leave the city without riding **tram 28** from Largo Martim Moniz through the narrow streets of the Alfama; tram 12 goes from Praça da Figueira out to Belém.

FERRY Car, bicycle and passenger ferries leave frequently from the **Cais do Sodré ferry terminal** (Map p984) to Cacilhas (€0.81, 10 minutes), a transfer point for some buses to Setúbal. From **Terreiro do Paço terminal** catamarans zip across to Montijo (€2.10, every 30 minutes) and Seixal (€1.75, every 30 minutes).

METRO The **metro** (www.metrolisboa.pt; 1-/2-zone single €0.85/1.15; ⏲6.30am-1am) is useful for hops across town and to the Parque das Nações. Buy tickets from metro ticket machines, which have English-language menus.

Taxi

Lisbon's taxis are metered and best hired from taxi ranks. Beware of rip-offs from the airport. From Rossio to Belém is around €8 and to the castle about €6. To call one, try **Rádio Táxis** (☎218 119 000) or **Autocoope** (☎217 932 756).

AROUND LISBON

Sintra

POP 26,400

Lord Byron called this hilltop town a 'glorious Eden' and, although best appreciated at dusk when the coach tours have left, it *is* a magnificent place. Less than an hour west of Lisbon, Sintra was the traditional summer retreat of Portugal's kings. Today it's a fairytale setting of stunning palaces and manors surrounded by rolling green countryside.

Sights & Activities

Although the whole town resembles a historical theme park, there are several compulsory eye-catching sights. Most are free or discounted with the Lisboa Card (see p978).

TOP CHOICE **Quinta da Regaleira** VILLA, GARDENS
(www.regaleira.pt; Rua Barbosa du Bocage; adult/child €6/3; ⏲10am-8pm) Exploring this neo-Manueline manor and gardens is like delving into another world. The villa has ferociously carved fireplaces, frescos and Venetian glass mosaics with wild mythological and Knights Templar symbols. The playful gardens hide fountains, grottoes, lakes and underground caverns. All routes seem to lead to the 30m-deep initiation well, **Poço Iniciáto**, with mysterious hollowed-out underground galleries lit by fairy lights.

Palácio Nacional de Sintra PALACE
(Largo Rainha Dona Amélia; admission €7; ⏲10am-5.30pm Thu-Tue) The whimsical interior of Sintra's iconic twin-chimney palace is a mix of Moorish and Manueline styles, with arabesque courtyards, barley-twist columns and stunning 15th- and 16th-century geometric *azulejos*.

Castelo dos Mouros CASTLE
(adult/child €6/5; ⏲10am-8pm) An energetic, 3km greenery-flanked hike from the

SINTRA BY BIKE

One new way to see the sights is via electric bicycle, offered by **MVP** (www.mvp.pt; ⏲10am-6pm) in the Torre do Relógio near the tourist office in Sintra. Half-day rental costs €19, which is great value considering it includes free admission to four sites, including Castelo dos Mouros, Palácio Nacional da Pena and Monserrate Park.

centre, the 8th-century ruined ramparts of this castle provide fine views.

Palácio Nacional da Pena PALACE
(adult/child €8/6; ⏲10am-7pm) This exuberantly kitsch palace is a further 800m from the Castelo dos Mouros, and is a an architectural extravaganza crammed with curious treasures.

Museu de Arte Moderna MUSEUM
(www.berardocollection.com; Avenida Heliodoro Salgado; admission free; ⏲10am-6pm Tue-Sun) This first-rate museum hosts rotating exhibitions covering the entire modern-art spectrum, from kinetic and pop art to surrealism and expressionism.

Monserrate Park GARDENS, PALACE
(www.parquesdesintra.pt; adult/child €6/5; ⏲9.30am-8pm) This wild, rambling 30-hectare wooded garden 3.5km west of Sintra bristles with exotic foliage. A manicured lawn sweeps up to the whimsical, 19th-century Moorish-inspired **palácio** (⏲10am-1pm & 2-6.30pm).

Sleeping

Pensão Residencial Sintra GUEST HOUSE €€
(☎219 230 738; www.residencialsintra.blogspot.com; Travessa dos Avelares 12; d incl breakfast from €80; @☎≋) This stately 1850s manor overlooks rambling gardens and an inviting pool, and offers captivating views to the castle. The bright, high-ceilinged rooms are decorated in crisp hues with shiny wood floors.

Lawrence's Hotel GUEST HOUSE €€
(☎219 105 500; www.lawrenceshotel.com; Rua Consiglieri Pedroso 38-40; d/ste from €90/180; ❄@) Lord Byron once stayed at this 18th-century mansion turned boutique hotel. It oozes charm in its lantern-lit, vaulted corridors, snug bar and individually designed rooms, decorated with *azulejos* and antique trunks. Lawrence's has an excellent restaurant.

Casa de Hóspedes Dona Maria da Parreirinha GUEST HOUSE €
(☎219 232 490; Rua João de Deus 12-14; d €45-55) A short walk from the train station, this small, homely guest house has old-fashioned but spotless rooms, with big windows, dark-wood furnishings and floral fabrics.

Eating & Drinking

Sintra is famous for its luscious pastries, including *queijadas* (crisp pastry shells filled with marzipan-like cheese, sugar, flour and cinnamon) and *travesseiros* (light rolled and folded puff pastries filled with almond-and-egg yolk cream). Sample the goods at **Fábrica das Verdadeiras Queijadas da Sapa** (Alameda Volta do Duche 12; ⏲closed Mon) and **Casa Piriquita** (Rua das Padarias 1-5; ⏲closed Wed).

Tulhas PORTUGUESE €€
(Rua Gil Vicente 4; mains €9-14; ⏲closed Wed) This converted grain warehouse is dark, tiled and quaint, with twisted chandeliers and a relaxed, cosy atmosphere. It's renowned for its *bacalhau com natas* (shredded cod with cream and potato).

Tasca do Xico TAPAS €€
(Rua Arco do Teixeira 6; tapas €4-6; ⏲noon-10pm Tue-Sun) On a quiet lane in the old quarter, the petite Tasca do Xico prepares tasty tapas plates (prawns with garlic, mussels in vinaigrette) as well as a few heartier changing specials such as grilled fresh fish of the day.

Saudade CAFE €
(Avenida Dr Miguel Bombardo 8; snacks €2-4; ⏲8am-10pm Tue-Sun) This former bakery has cherub-covered ceilings and a rambling interior, making it a fine spot for pastries or lighter fare (with a different soup, salad, fish and meat dish of the day). A gallery features changing art exhibitions.

Information

Tourist office (www.cm-sintra.pt; Praça da República 23; ⏲9am-7pm) Has useful maps and can help with accommodation.

Getting There & Away

The **Lisbon–Sintra railway** terminates in Sintra, a 1km scenic walk northeast of the town's historic centre. Sintra's **bus station**, and another train station, are a further 1km east in the new town Portela de Sintra. Frequent **shuttle buses** link the historic centre with the bus station.

Train services (€2, 40 minutes, every 15 minutes) run between Sintra and Lisbon's Rossio station. Buses run regularly from Sintra to Cascais (€3.50, 60 minutes), Estoril (€3.50, 40 minutes) and Mafra (45 minutes).

On Fridays to Sundays in summer, Sintra's restored electric tram, the **Elétrico de Sintra** (one-way €2) offers convenient access to the coast, departing about hourly from Rua Alves Roçadas near Portela de Sintra train station, arriving at Praia das Maçãs 45 minutes later.

Getting Around

A handy bus for accessing the castle is the hop-on, hop-off **Scotturb bus** 434 (€4.60), which runs from the train station via Sintra-Vila to Castelo dos Mouros (10 minutes), Palácio da Pena (15 minutes) and back.

A **taxi** to Pena or Monserrate costs around €16 return.

Cascais

POP 33,400

Cascais is a handsome seaside resort with elegant buildings, an atmospheric Old Town and a happy abundance of restaurants and bars.

Sights & Activities

Coast & Beaches COAST, BEACHES

Cascais' three sandy bays – **Praia da Conceição**, **Praia da Rainha** and **Praia da Ribeira** – are great for a sunbake or a tingly Atlantic dip, but attract crowds in summer.

Estoril is a somewhat faded resort 2km east of Cascais with a popular sandy beach and Europe's largest **casino** (www.casino-estoril.pt).

The sea roars into the coast at **Boca do Inferno** (Hell's Mouth), 2km west of Cascais. Spectacular **Cabo da Roca**, Europe's westernmost point, is 16km from Cascais and Sintra and is served by buses from both towns.

Casa das Histórias Paula Rego GALLERY

(www.casadashistoriaspaularego.com; Avenida da República 300; admission free; ⏲10am-8pm) Sintra's stellar new attraction showcases the evocative, twisted fairy-tale-like paintings of Paula Rego, one of Portugal's finest living artists.

Museu Condes de Castro Guimarães MUSEUM

(admission €2; ⏲10am-5pm Tue-Sun) The picturesque gardens of **Parque Marechal Carmona** (Avenida Rei Humberto II) house this museum in a whimsical early-19th-century mansion, complete with castle turrets and Arabic cloister.

Sleeping & Eating

Fortaleza do Guincho LUXURY HOTEL €€€

(☎214 870 491; www.guinchotel.pt; Estrada do Guincho; d incl breakfast from €205; ❄@📶) Set in a 17th-century fortress perched over the sea, this dramatic five-star guest house has small but beautifully set rooms with solid antique furnishings. The superb **restaurant** (mains around €32) has a Michelin star.

Residencial Solar Dom Carlos GUEST HOUSE €€

(☎214 828 115; www.solardomcarlos.pt; Rua Latino Coelho 104; s/d €55/70; P@) Hidden down a sleepy alley, this 16th-century former royal residence turned guest house retains lots of original features, from chandeliers to wood beams, *azulejos* and a frescoed breakfast room.

Cascais Beach Hostel HOSTEL €

(☎309 906 421; www.cascaisbeachhostel.com; Rua da Vista Alegre 10; dm/d €20/50; @📶🏊) Central for Cascais' beaches and nightlife, this hostel has wood-floored rooms, a lounge, communal kitchen and pool.

Confraria Sushi JAPANESE €€

(Rua Luís Xavier Palmeirim 16; mains €8-13; ⏲noon-midnight Tue-Sun) This art-slung cafe, jazzed up with technicolour glass chandeliers, is a fun spot for sushi and tasty salads. Patio seating.

Apeadeiro SEAFOOD €€

(Avenida Vasco da Gama 252; mains €7-12) With walls hung with fishing nets, this sunny restaurant is known for its superb chargrilled fish – shrimp piri-piri is delicious.

Information

Tourist office (www.visiteestoril.com; Rua Visconde de Luz 14) Can provide accommodation lists and bus timetables.

Getting There & Around

Trains run frequently to Cascais via Estoril (€1.70, 40 minutes) from Cais do Sodré station in Lisbon.

> **BIKE TO THE BEACH**
>
> **Free bikes** are available from 8am to 7pm from a kiosk on Largo da Estação near the train station (bring ID). There's a bicycle path that runs the entire 9km stretch from Cascais to wild **Guincho beach**, a popular surf spot.

THE ALGARVE

Love it or loathe it, it's easy to see the allure of The Algarve: breathtaking cliffs, golden sands, scalloped bays and long sandy islands. Although overdevelopment has blighted parts of the coast, head inland and you'll land solidly in lovely Portuguese countryside once again. Algarve highlights include the forested slopes of Monchique, pretty riverside town of Tavira and windswept, historic Sagres. Underrated Faro is the regional capital.

The Algarve

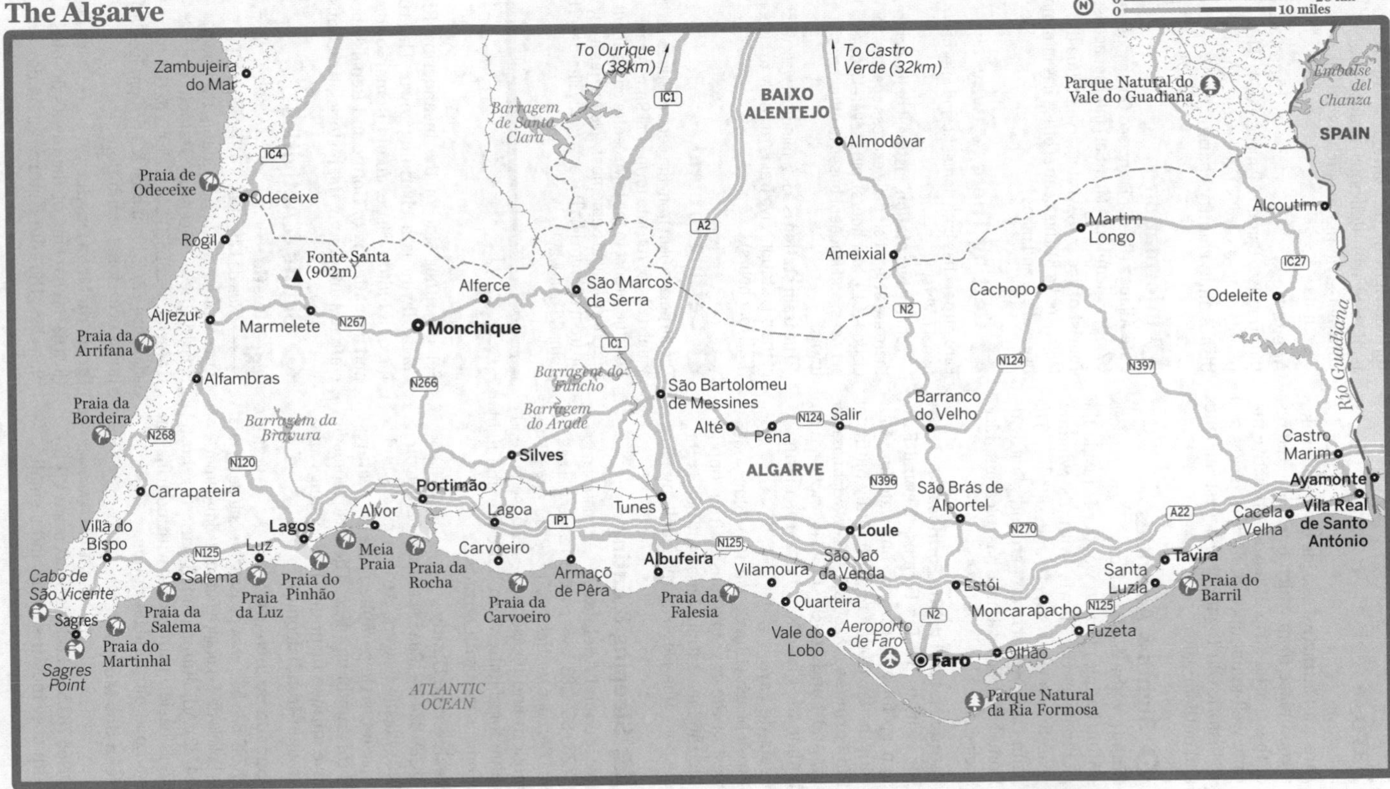
0 20 km
0 10 miles
Zambujeira do Mar
Praia de Odeceixe
Odeceixe
Rogil
Fonte Santa (902m)
Aljezur
Marmelete
Praia da Arrifana
Alfambras
Praia da Bordeira
Carrapateira
Villa do Bispo
Cabo de São Vicente
Sagres
Sagres Point
Praia do Martinhal
Praia da Salema
Salema
Luz
Praia da Luz
Lagos
Praia do Pinhão
Meia Praia
Alvor
Portimão
Praia da Rocha
Carvoeiro
Praia da Carvoeiro
Lagoa
Silves
Armaçõ de Pêra
Monchique
Alferce
São Marcos da Serra
Barragem de Santa Clara
Barragem do Funcho
Barragem do Arade
Barragem da Bravura
To Ourique (38km)
To Castro Verde (32km)
BAIXO ALENTEJO
Almodôvar
Ameixial
São Bartolomeu de Messines
Alté
Pena
Salir
Barranco do Velho
ALGARVE
Tunes
Albufeira
Praia da Falesia
Vilamoura
São Jaõ da Venda
Quarteira
Vale do Lobo
Aeroporto de Faro
Loule
São Brás de Alportel
Estói
Faro
Olhão
Moncarapacho
Fuzeta
Parque Natural da Ria Formosa
Santa Luzia
Tavira
Praia do Barril
Cacela Velha
Vila Real de Santo António
Ayamonte
Castro Marim
Cachopo
Martim Longo
Odeleite
Alcoutim
Parque Natural do Vale do Guadiana
Embalse del Chanza
SPAIN
Rio Guadiana
ATLANTIC OCEAN
IC4
N267
N266
N268
N120
N125
IC1
A2
N2
N124
N396
N270
IP1
A22
N397
IC27

Faro

POP 58,000

Faro is an attractive seaside town and makes a good place from which to explore the rest of this coastal strip. It has an attractive marina, well-maintained parks and plazas and an historic Old Town full of pedestrian lanes and outdoor cafes.

Sights & Activities

Cidade Velha & Waterfront OLD TOWN

An intriguing place to wander is inside the picturesque Old Town, with its winding, peaceful cobbled streets and squares. The palm-clad **waterfront** around Praça de Dom Francisco Gomes has pleasant kick-back cafes.

Parque Natural da Ria Formosa PARK

For visits to the Ria Formosa Natural Park, sign up for a boating or birdwatching tour with the environmentally friendly outfits of **Ria Formosa** (☎289 817 466; www.formosamar.pt) and **Lands** (☎967 073 846; www.lands.pt), both in the Clube Naval in Faro's marina.

Praia de Faro BEACH

Faro's beach (Ilha de Faro), is 6km southwest of the city; take bus 16 from opposite the bus station. Less crowded is the unspoilt Ilha Deserta, reachable by ferry.

Sleeping & Eating

Residencial Adelaide GUEST HOUSE €€

(☎289 802 383; www.adelaideresidencial.net; Rua Cruz dos Mestres 9; s/d €40/50; ❄ 📶) This modern and pleasant guest house is good value for slightly worn but clean and light rooms, some with terraces.

Residencial Dandy GUEST HOUSE €€

(☎289 824 791; Rua Filipe Alistão 62; d from €40) Plastic flowers, African masks and museum-style paraphernalia are features of this rambling place. The best rooms have antique furniture, high ceilings and wrought-iron balconies.

Pousada da Juventude HOSTEL €

(☎289 826 521; www.pousadasjuventude.pt; Rua da Polícia de Segurança Pública 1; dm/d from €14/32) Adjoining a small park, this hostel offers basic, clean rooms with no frills but is a good ultrabudget option.

Mesa dos Mouros PORTUGUESE, INTERNATIONAL €€€

(☎966 784 536; Largo da Sé 10; mains €11-18) With cosy indoor seating and a small terrace right by the cathedral, this place is blessed with delicious seafood and gourmet-style mains such as rabbit with chestnuts.

Adega Nova PORTUGUESE €€

(Rua Francisco Barreto 24; mains €6-14) This popular place serves tasty meat and fish dishes amid country charm.

Information

Café Aliança (Rua Dr Francisco Gomes; per hr €2.50; ⏲8am-10pm Mon-Sat) Internet access.

Tourist office (www.visitalgarve.pt; Rua da Misericórdia 8) This central office has informative leaflets and maps.

Getting There & Away

Faro airport has both domestic and international flights.

From the **bus station**, just west of the centre, there are at least six daily express coaches to Lisbon (€19, four hours), plus several slower services, and frequent buses to other coastal towns.

The **train station** is a few minutes' walk west of the bus station. Five trains run daily to Lisbon (€21, four hours).

Getting Around

The **airport** is 6km from the centre. **Buses** 14 and 16 (€1.65) run into town until 9pm. A **taxi** from the airport to the town centre costs about €12. From May to September, five **ferries** a day run from to/from Ilha Deserta (www.ilha-deserta.com; €5 one-way).

Tavira

POP 12,600

Set on either side of the meandering Rio Gilão, Tavira is a charming town. The ruins of a hilltop castle, an old Roman bridge and a smattering of Gothic and Renaissance churches are among the historic attractions.

Sights & Activities

FREE **Castle** CASTLE

(Rua da Liberdade; ⏲10am-5pm) Tavira's ruined castle dominates the town. Nearby, the 16th-century **Palácio da Galeria** (☎281 320 540; Calçada da Galeria; admission €2; ⏲10am-noon & 3-6.30pm Tue-Sat) holds occasional exhibitions.

Igreja da Misericórdia CHURCH

(Rua da Galeria) One of the town's 30-plus churches, the 16th-century Igreja da

Misericórdia is among the most striking in The Algarve.

Ilha da Tavira ISLAND, BEACH
An island beach connected to the mainland by a ferry at Quatro Águas. Walk the 2km or take the (summer-only) bus from the bus station.

Casa Abilio BIKE HIRE
(Rua João Vaz Corte Real 23; per day around €7) Enjoy pedal power with a rented bike.

Sport Nautica KAYAKING
(Rua Jacques Pessoa 26; per half-/full day €15/25) Rent kayaks for a paddle along the river.

Sleeping & Eating

Pensão Residencial Lagôas GUEST HOUSE €
(281 322 252; Rua Almirante Cândido dos Reis 24; s/d from €20/30) A long-standing favourite, friendly Lagôas has small (some cramped), spotless rooms. There's a plant-filled courtyard and good terrace views.

Residencial Princesa do Gilão GUEST HOUSE €€
(281 325 171; Rua Borda d'Água de Aguiar 10; s/d €50/60;) This '80s-style place on the river has tight but neat rooms with identical decor. Go for a room with a river view.

Pensão Residencial Castelo GUEST HOUSE €€
(281 320 790; Rua da Liberdade 22; s/d €40/60;) Castelo offers nicely furnished rooms with spotless tile floors. Some also have balconies and castle views.

Restaurante Bica SEAFOOD €€
(Rua Almirante Cândido dos Reis 24; mains €7-16) Deservedly popular, Bica serves splendid food, such as fresh grilled fish, which diners enjoy with inexpensive but decent Borba wine.

Bistro 'oPorto' INTERNATIONAL €€
(Rua Dr José Pires Padinha 180; mains €10-14; lunch & dinner Tue-Sat) An intimate bar and a relaxed riverside setting make for a pleasant time at this French-owned spot. Dishes combine Portuguese and French flavours and vegetarians are usually catered for.

Information

Câmara municipal (town hall; Praça da Republica; 9am-8pm Mon-Fri, 10am-1pm Sat) Free internet access.

Tourist office (Rua da Galeria 9) Can help with accommodation

Getting There & Away

Some 15 **trains** and six express **buses** run daily between Faro and Tavira (€3.20, one hour).

Lagos

POP 17,500

In summer the pretty fishing port of Lagos has a party vibe; its picturesque cobbled streets and pretty nearby beaches pack with revellers and sun-seekers.

Sights & Activities

Museu Municipal MUSEUM
(Rua General Alberto da Silveira; admission €3; 9.30am-12.30pm & 2-5pm Tue-Sun) The municipal museum houses an eclectic mix of archaeological and ecclesiastical treasures (and oddities). Admission includes the adjacent **Igreja de Santo António**, one of the best baroque churches in Portugal.

Beaches BEACHES
The beach scene includes **Meia Praia**, a vast strip to the east; **Praia da Luz** to the west; and the smaller **Praia do Pinhão**.

Blue Ocean OUTDOOR ACTIVITIES
(964 665 667; www.blue-ocean-divers.de) Organises diving, kayaking and snorkelling safaris. Along the promenade, fishermen can offer motorboat jaunts to nearby grottoes.

Kayak Adventures KAYAKING
(www.kayakadventures-lagos.com) Offers kayaking trips from Batata Beach.

Sleeping

Pensão Marazul GUEST HOUSE €€
(282 770 230; www.pensaomarazul.com; Rua 25 de Abril 13; s/d from €40/50;) Draws a good mix of foreign travellers to its small but cheerfully painted rooms – the best of which offer sea views.

Sol a Sol HOTEL €€
(282 761 290; www.residencialsolasol.com; Rua Lançarote de Freitas 22; s/d/tr from €60/65/80) This central, small hotel has neat rooms with tiny balconies and views over the town.

Pousada da Juventude HOSTEL €
(282 761 970; www.pousadasjuventude.pt; Rua Lançarote de Freitas 50; dm €16, d €43, without bathroom €35;) One of Portugal's best, this well-run hostel is a great place to meet other travellers.

Eating

A Forja TOP CHOICE PORTUGUESE €€
(Rua dos Ferreiros 17; mains €7-15; lunch & dinner Sun-Fri) This buzzing place pulls in the crowds for its hearty, top-quality traditional food. Plates of the day are always reliable, as are the fish dishes.

Casinha do Petisco PORTUGUESE, SEAFOOD €€
(Rua da Oliveira 51; mains €7-12; Mon-Sat) This tiny traditional gem comes highly recommended by locals for its seafood grills and shellfish dishes.

Information

Café Gélibar (Rua Lançarote de Freitas 43; per hr €3; 9am-10pm) Sip coffee while emailing.

Tourist office (www.visitalgarve.pt; Praça Gil Eanes) In the centre of town.

Getting There & Away

Bus and **train** services depart frequently for other Algarve towns, and around eight times daily to Lisbon (€20, 4¼ hours).

Getting Around

A **bus service** (tickets €1-2; 7am-8pm Mon-Sat) provides useful connections to the beaches of Meia Praia and Luz. Rent bicycles and motorbikes from **Motorent** (289 769 716; www.motorent.pt; Rua Victor Costa e Silva; bike/motorcycle per day from €10/50).

Monchique

POP 2800

High above the coast, in cooler mountainous woodlands, the picturesque hamlet of Monchique makes a lovely base for exploring, with some excellent options for walking, cycling and canoeing.

Sights & Activities

Caldas de Monchique, 6km south, is a peaceful hamlet with a **spa resort** (www.monchiquetermas.com). Some 8km west is The Algarve's 'rooftop', the 902m **Fóia** peak atop the Serra de Monchique, with heady views through a forest of radio masts.

Igreja Matriz CHURCH
(Rua da Igreja) This church features a stunning Manueline portal, with its stone seemingly tied in knots. Keep climbing to reach the ruins of the 17th-century Franciscan monastery, **Nossa Senhora do Desterro**, which overlooks the town from its wooded hilltop.

Outdoor Tours OUTDOOR ACTIVITIES
(282 969 520, 916 736 226; www.outdoor-tours.com; Mexilhoeira Grande; trips from €20) Offers cycling, kayaking and walking trips.

Sleeping & Eating

Residencial Miradouro GUEST HOUSE €
(282 912 163; Rua dos Combatentes do Ultramar; s/d/tr €35/40/50) This 1970s hilltop place offers sweeping, breezy views and neat rooms, some with balcony.

A Charrete PORTUGUESE €€
(Rua Dr Samora Gil 30-34; mains €9-16; lunch & dinner Thu-Tue) Touted as the town's best eatery for its regional specialities, this place serves reliably good cuisine amid country rustic charm.

Information

Tourist office (Largo de São Sebastião; 9.30am-1pm & 2-5.30pm Mon-Fri) Uphill from the bus stop.

Getting There & Away

There are five to nine **buses** daily from Portimão (€2.80, 45 minutes) to Monchique.

Silves

POP 10,800

The one-time capital of Moorish Algarve, Silves is a pretty town of jumbling orange rooftops scattered above the banks of the Rio Arade. Clamber around the ramparts of its fairy-tale **castle** for superb views.

Sleeping & Eating

Residencial Ponte Romana GUEST HOUSE €
(282 443 275; Horta da Cruz; s/d €20/35) Floral-themed rooms beside the Roman bridge, with castle views and a cavernous bar-restaurant full of old-timers and Portuguese families.

Quinta da Figueirinha RURAL INN €€
(282 440 700; www.qdf.pt; 2-/4-/6-person apt €64/92/125;) Four kilometres outside of Silves, this 36-hectare organic farm offers simple apartments in idyllic, farmlike surroundings.

Café Ingles CAFE, BAR €€
(mains €7-14;) Situated at the castle entrance, this funky English-owned place has vegetarian dishes, homemade soups, pasta and wood-fired pizza. In summer there's live music at weekends.

Information

No Name Internet (Rua Pintor Bernardo Marques; per hr €2) Internet access.

Getting There & Away

Silves **train station** is 2km from town; trains from Lagos (€2.15, 35 minutes) stop eight times daily (from Faro, change at Tunes), to be met by local buses. Four to seven **buses** run daily connecting Silves and Albufeira (€3.75, 40 minutes).

Sagres

POP 1940

The small, elongated village of Sagres has an end-of-the-world feel with its sea-carved cliffs and empty, wind-whipped fortress high above the ocean.

Sights & Activities

Coast & Beaches COAST, BEACHES

Visit Europe's southwestern-most point, the **Cabo de São Vicente** (Cape St Vincent), 6km to the west. A solitary lighthouse stands on this barren cape.

This coast is ideal for surfing; hire windsurfing gear at sand-dune fringed **Praia do Martinhal**. You can sign up for surfing lessons, hire bikes and arrange canoe trips with **Sagres Natura** (www.sagresnatura.com; Rua São Vicente). **DiversCape** (965 559 073; www.diverscape.com; Porto da Balereira) organises diving trips.

Fortaleza de Sagres FORT

(adult/child €3/1.50; 10am-8.30pm) Sagres' fort offers breathtaking views over the seaside cliffs. According to legend, this is where Henry the Navigator established his navigation school and primed the early Portuguese explorers.

Sleeping & Eating

Casa do Cabo de Santa Maria GUEST HOUSE €€

(282 624 722; casacabosantamaria@sapo.pt; Rua Patrão António Faústino; r/apt from €50/80) These squeaky-clean rooms and apartments might not have sweeping views, but they are handsome and nicely furnished.

TOP CHOICE **A Tasca** SEAFOOD €€€

(Porto da Baleeira; mains €12-25; lunch & dinner Thu-Tue) Overlooking the marina, this cosy place whips up tasty *cataplana* (seafood and sausage cooked in a copper pot) and other seafood dishes, best enjoyed on the sunny terrace.

Information

Tourist office (Rua Comandante Matoso; Tue-Sat) Central to town.

Getting There & Away

Frequent **buses** run daily to Sagres from Lagos (€3.50, one hour), with fewer on Sunday. Two continue out to Cabo de São Vicente on weekdays.

CENTRAL PORTUGAL

The vast centre of Portugal is a rugged swath of rolling hillsides, whitewashed villages and olive groves and cork trees. Richly historic, it is scattered with prehistoric remains and medieval castles. It's also home to one of Portugal's most architecturally rich towns, Évora, as well as several spectacular walled villages. There are fine local wines and, for the more energetic, plenty of outdoor exploring in the dramatic Beiras region.

Évora

POP 56,500

Évora is an enchanting place to delve into the past. Inside the 14th-century walls, Évora's narrow, winding lanes lead to a striking medieval cathedral, a Roman temple and a picturesque town square. These old-fashioned good-looks are the backdrop to a lively student town surrounded by wineries and dramatic countryside.

Sights & Activities

Sé CHURCH

(Largo do Marquês de Marialva; admission €2-5; 9am-noon & 2-5pm) Évora's cathedral has fabulous cloisters and a museum jam-packed with ecclesiastical treasures.

Templo Romano RUINS

(Temple of Diana; Largo do Conde de Vila Flor) Once part of the Roman Forum; it's a heady slice of drama right in town.

Capela dos Ossos OSSUARY

(Praça 1 de Maio; admission €2; 9am-1pm & 2.30-6pm) Built from the skeletons of several thousand people, the ghoulish Chapel of Bones in the Igreja de São Francisco provides a real *Addams Family* day out.

Sleeping

TOP CHOICE **Albergaria Calvario** BOUTIQUE HOTEL €€€

(266 745 930; Travessa dos Lagares 3; d/studio incl breakfast €108/125) Elegant, friendly and

Évora

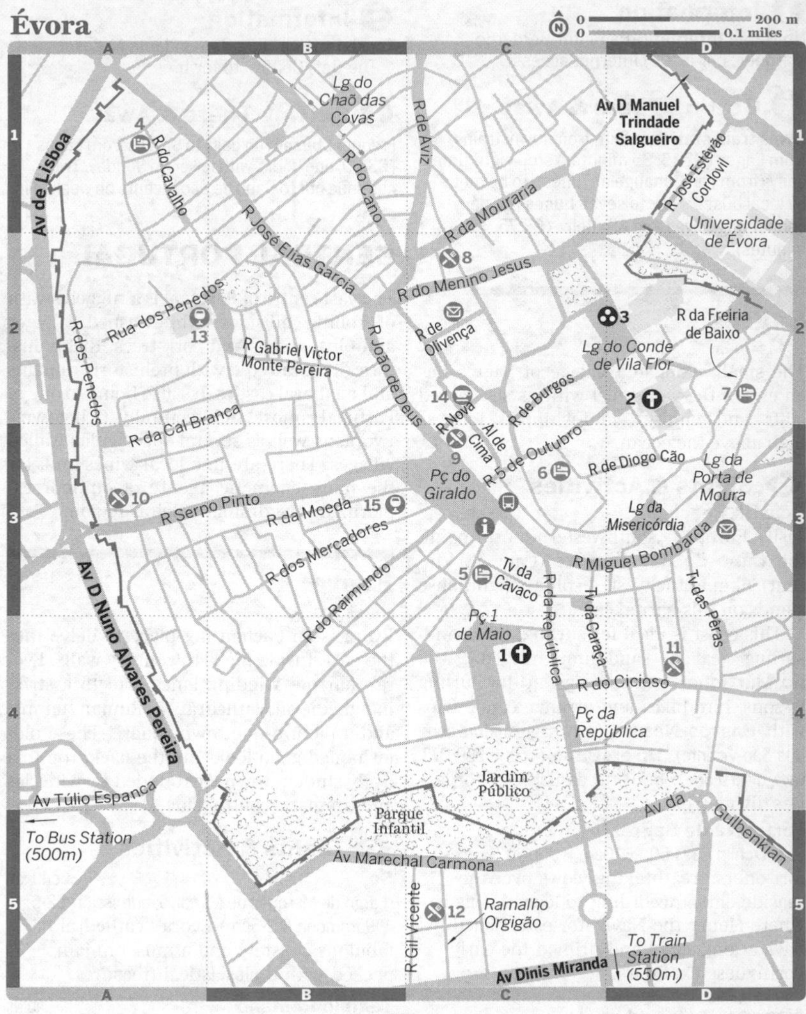

comfortable, this place has an ambience that travellers adore. Pleasant lounge areas, books and classical music, plus comfortable beds and flat-screen TVs, ensure a homely stay. Breakfasts are excellent.

Residencial Policarpo GUEST HOUSE €€
(☎266 702 424; www.pensaopolicarpo.com; Rua da Freiria de Baixo 16; d €57, without bathroom €35; P @) This former 16th-century home is charming and atmospheric, if somewhat faded. The guest rooms are decorated with a mix of carved wooden – as well as traditionally hand-painted – Alentejan furniture.

Casa dos Teles GUEST HOUSE €
(☎266 702 453; Rua Romão Ramalho 27; d €30-40; ❄) These nine rooms – mostly light and airy – are good value; quieter rooms at the back overlook a pretty courtyard.

Residencial Diana GUEST HOUSE €€
(☎266 702 008; Rua de Diogo Cão 2; d €55, without bathroom €47; ❄ 📶) The Diana is slightly long in the tooth now, with saggy mattresses and grannylike decor. Nevertheless, it's still somewhat charming in a high-ceilinged-and-wood-floored kind of way.

Évora

Sights

Capela dos Ossos .... (see 1)
1 Igreja de São Francisco C4
2 Sé D2
3 Templo Romano D2

Sleeping

4 Albergaria Calvario A1
5 Casa dos Teles C3
6 Residencial Diana C3
7 Residencial Policarpo D2

Eating

8 Botequim da Mouraria C2
9 Café Arcada C3
10 Dom Joaquim A3
11 Pastelaria Couventual Pão de Rala D4
12 Vinho e Noz C5

Drinking

13 Bar do Teatro A2
14 Cup of Joe C2
15 Oficin@Bar B3

Eating

Botequim da Mouraria PORTUGUESE €€
(266 746 775; Rua da Mouraria 16a; mains €12.50-14; lunch & dinner Mon-Fri, lunch Sat) Poke around the old Moorish quarter to find this cosy spot serving some of Évora's finest food and wine. There are no reservations, just 12 stools at a counter. Rumour is that it's moving to larger premises.

Dom Joaquim PORTUGUESE €€
(266 731 105; Rua dos Penedos 6; mains €11-13; lunch & dinner Thu-Tue) Amid stone walls and modern artwork, Dom Joaquim serves excellent traditional cuisine including meats (game and succulent, fall-off-the bone oven lamb) and seafood dishes.

Vinho e Noz PORTUGUESE €€
(Ramalho Orgigão 12; mains €9-11; lunch & dinner Mon-Sat) This delightful family-run place has professional service, a large wine list and good-quality cuisine.

Café Arcada CAFE, RESTAURANT €
(Praça do Giraldo 10; meals €7-10; breakfast, lunch & dinner) An Évora institution, serving up coffee, crêpes and cakes, with outdoor tables on the plaza.

Pastelaria Conventual Pão de Rala PASTISSERIE €
(Rua do Cicioso 47; 7.30am-8pm) Specialises in heavenly pastries, all made on the premises.

Drinking

Cup of Joe CAFE, BAR €
(Praça de Sertório 3; noon-2am) Part of a coffee chain, this attractive cafe has peaceful outdoor seating overlooking a plaza. Electronic music and a friendly cocktail-sipping crowd arrive by night.

Bar do Teatro BAR
(Praça Joaquim António de Aguiar; 8pm-2am) This small, inviting bar has high ceilings and old-world decor that sees a friendly mixed crowd.

Oficin@Bar BAR
(Rua da Moeda 27; 8pm-2am Mon-Sat) Attracting all ages, this is a small, relaxed bar with jazz and blues playing in the background.

Information

Câmara municipal (town hall; 9am-12.30pm & 2-5pm Mon-Fri) Free internet.

Tourist office (www.cm-evora.pt; Praça do Giraldo 73) Has an excellent city map.

Getting There & Away

Évora has six to 12 **buses** daily to Lisbon (€12, two hours) and three to Faro (€16, five hours), departing from the station off Avenida São Sebastião (700m southwest of the centre). At the time of research the **train station** (600m south of the Jardim Público) was closed. When operating, trains head to Lisbon, Beja, Lagos and Faro.

Monsaraz

POP 20

In a dizzy setting high above the plain, this walled village has a moody medieval feel and magnificent views.

The **Museu de Arte Sacra** (Plaça Dom Nuno Álvares; admission €1.80; 10am-6pm) has a good display of religious artefacts; the 15th-century fresco here is quite superb. Situated 3km north of town is **Menhir of Outeiro**, one of the tallest megalithic monuments ever discovered.

There are several places to stay in town, including the friendly **Casa Paroquial** (266 557 181; Rua Direita 4; s/d/tr €35/40/70),

WORTH A TRIP

MEGALITHS

Ancient Greek for 'big stones', **megaliths** are found all over the ancient landscape that surrounds Évora. Such prehistoric structures, built around 5000 to 6000 years ago, dot the European Atlantic coast, but here in Alentejo there is an astounding number of Neolithic remains. Dolmens (Neolithic stone tombs, or *antas* in Portuguese) were probably temples and/or tombs, covered with a large flat stone and usually built on hilltops or near water. Menhirs (individual standing stones) point to fertility rites, while *cromeleques* (cromlechs, stone circles) were also places of worship.

Évora's tourist office sells a *Historical Itineraries* leaflet (€1.05) that details many sites. Dolmen devotees can buy the book *Paisagens Arqueologicas A Oeste de Évora*, which has English summaries.

The star attraction is the **Cromeleque dos Almendres**, the Iberian peninsula's most important megalithic group. The site consists of a huge oval of some 95 rounded granite monoliths – some of which are engraved with symbolic markings – spread down a rough slope. They were erected over different periods, it seems with geometric and astral consideration, probably for social gatherings or sacred rituals. Some 15km west of Évora, it's an extraordinary site to visit.

Two and a half kilometres before Cromeleque dos Almendres stands **Menhir dos Almendres**, a single stone about 4m high, with some very faint carvings near the top. Look for the sign; to reach the menhir you must walk for a few hundred metres from the road.

To get to this area, your only option is to rent a car or bike (note that about 5km of the route is rough and remote). Stop by the tourist office for exact driving directions.

with wooden trimmings, whitewashed walls and heavy wooden furniture.

Eat before 8pm as the town tucks up early to bed. **Cafe-Restaurante Lumumba** (Rua Direita 12; mains €7-9; ⏰lunch & dinner) is a small local favourite for its pleasant atmosphere, decent mains and terrace with views.

The **tourist office** (☎266 557 136; Praça Dom Nuno Álvares) can offer advice on accommodation.

Up to four daily **buses** connect Monsaraz with Reguengos de Monsaraz (€3, 35 minutes, Monday to Friday), with connections to Évora.

Estremoz

POP 9000

One of three marble towns in these parts, Estremoz has an attractive centre set with peaceful plazas, orange-tree-lined lanes and a hilltop castle and convent. In its prime, the town was one of the most strongly fortified in Portugal, with its very own palace (now a luxurious *pousada;* upmarket inn).

Sights

Museu Municipal MUSEUM
(Largo D Dinis; adult/child €1.50/free; ⏰9am-12.30pm & 2-5.30pm Tue-Sun) In a beautiful 17th-century almshouse, the municipal museum specialises in fascinating pottery figurines, including an entire Easter parade.

Palácio Ducal PALACE
(Terreiro do Paça, Vila Viçosa; admission €6; ⏰2.30-5.30pm Tue, 10am-1pm & 2.30-5.30pm Wed-Sun) Located in another marble town 17km from Estremoz, this magnificent ancestral home of the dukes of Bragança is rich with *azulejos*, frescoed ceilings and elaborate tapestries.

Sleeping & Eating

Residencial O Gadanha GUEST HOUSE €
(☎268 339 110; www.residencialogadanha.com; Largo General Graça 56; s/d/tr €20/32.50/42.50; ❄) This whitewashed house offers excellent value for its bright, fresh and clean rooms overlooking the square.

Adega do Isaías PORTUGUESE €€
(Rua do Almeida 21; mains €8-12; ⏰lunch & dinner Mon-Sat) This award-winning, rustic *tasca* serves tender fish, meat and Alentejan specialities inside a wine cellar crammed with tables and huge wine jars.

Information

Tourist office (www.cm-estremoz.pt; Rossio Marquês de Pombal) Just south of Rossio.

Getting There & Away

Estremoz is linked to Évora by three local **buses** (€4, 1¼ hours), Monday to Friday.

Peniche

POP 16,000

Popular for its nearby surfing beaches and also as a jumping-off point for the beautiful Ilhas Berlengas nature reserve, the coastal city of Peniche remains a working port, giving it a slightly grittier and more 'lived-in' feel than its beach-resort neighbours. It has a walled historic centre and lovely beaches east of town.

From the bus station, it's a 10-minute walk west to the historic centre.

Sights

Fortress FORTRESS

(admission free) Peniche's imposing 16th-century fortress served as one of dictator Salazar's infamous jails for political prisoners and was later a temporary home for African refugees. The on-site **museum** (admission €1.50) houses the chilling interrogation chambers and cells on the top floor.

Islands ISLANDS

About 5km to the northeast of Peniche is the scenic island-village of **Baleal**, connected to the mainland village of Casais do Baleal by a causeway. The fantastic sweep of sandy beach here offers some fine surfing. Surf schools dot the sands, as do several bar-restaurants.

Sitting about 10km offshore from Peniche, **Berlenga Grande** is a spectacular, rocky and remote island, with twisting, shocked-rock formations and gaping caverns. It's the only island of the Berlenga archipelago you can visit; the group consists of three tiny islands surrounded by clear, calm, dark-blue waters full of shipwrecks – great for snorkelling and diving. Several outfits make the 40-minute trip to the island, including **Viamar** (☎262 785 646; www.viamar-berlenga.com; return adult/child €18/10).

Activities

Surfing

Surf camps offer week-long instruction (from €250 to 450 per week including lodging) as well as individual two-hour classes (€50), plus board and wetsuit hire. Well-established names include **Baleal Surfcamp** (www.balealsurfcamp.com), **Maximum Surfcamp** (www.maximumsurfcamp.com) and **Peniche Surfcamp** (www.penichesurfcamp.com).

Diving

There are good diving opportunities around Peniche, and especially around Berlenga. Expect to pay about €60 to €70 for two dives (less around Peniche) with **Acuasuboeste** (www.acuasuboeste.com; Porto de Pesca) or **Haliotis** (www.haliotis.pt; Avenida Monsenhor Bastos).

Kitesurfing

Kitesurfing is big in Peniche. **Peniche Kite & Surf Center** (www.penichekitecenter.com) offers lessons with equipment for €70.

Sleeping

TOP CHOICE **Casa das Marés** B&B €€

(☎262 769 255/200/371; www.casadasmares2.com, www.casadasmares1.com; Praia do Baleal; d €80; wi-fi) At the picturesque, windswept tip of Baleal, this imposing house features three unique adjoining B&Bs run by three sisters. The breezy, inviting rooms all have great sea views, and the entire place is loaded with character. Worth reserving ahead.

WORTH A TRIP

CASTELO DE VIDE

A worthy detour north of Estremoz is the hilltop, story-book town **Castelo de Vide**, noted for its picturesque houses with Gothic doorways. Highlights are the **Judiaria** (Old Jewish Quarter), the **medieval backstreets** and (yet another) castle-top **view**. Try to spend a night here heading skywards to **Marvão** (population 190), a fabulous mountain-top walled village 12km from Castelo de Vide. There are charming guest houses in the area, including the good-value **Casa de Hóspedes Melanie** (☎245 901 632; Largo do Paça Novo 3; s/d/tr €25/35/45; air-con) in Castelo de Vide, and the very elegant **Quinta do Barrieiro** (☎245 964 308; www.quintadobarrieiro.com; d from €85; air-con wi-fi pool) in Marvão.

On weekdays, three **buses** run from Portalegre to Castelo de Vide (€2.50 to €5, 20 minutes) and two to Marvão (€2.50, 45 minutes). There are three buses connecting Estremoz and Portalegre (€5 to €9, 50 to 80 minutes).

Peniche Hostel HOSTEL €
(☎969 008 689; www.penichehostel.com; Rua Arquitecto Paulino Montês 6; dm/d €20/45; @☎) This cosy welcoming hostel, only five minutes' walk from the bus station, has colourfully decorated rooms overlooking the town wall. Surfboards and bikes are available for hire, and there's an attached surf school.

Mar e Sol HOTEL €€
(☎919 543 105; www.restaurantemaresol.com; d/q €80/130; ⊙mid-Apr–Oct) One of two places to stay on the island of Berlenga Grande, with simple rooms just a few steps above Berlenga's boat dock. Book well ahead.

Eating

Restaurante A Sardinha SEAFOOD €€
(Rua Vasco da Gama 81; mains €6.50-12.50; ⊙lunch & dinner) This simple place on a narrow street parallel to Largo da Ribeira does a roaring trade with locals and tourists alike.

Hó Amaral PORTUGUESE €€
(Rua Dr Francisco Seia 7; mains €8-14; ⊙lunch & dinner Fri-Wed) Still going strong after 35 years, this snug wood-panelled eatery reliably does some of the best seafood in Peniche.

Getting There & Away

Peniche's **bus station** (☎968 903 861) is located 400m northeast of the tourist office (cross the Ponte Velha connecting the town to the isthmus). Buses go to Lisbon (€8.20, 1½ hours, every one to two hours), Coimbra (€13, 2¾ hours, three daily) and Óbidos (€2.75, 40 minutes, five to 13 daily).

Óbidos

POP 3100

This exquisite walled village was a wedding gift from Dom Dinis to his wife Dona Isabel (beats a fondue set), and its historic centre is a delightful place to wander. Highlights include the **Igreja de Santa Maria** (Rua Direita), with fine *azulejos*, and views from the town walls.

Sleeping & Eating

Bar Lagar da Mouraria BAR, RESTAURANT €
(Rua da Mouraria; mains €8-10; ⊙11am-2am) Housed in a former winery, with beamed ceiling, a flagstone floor and seats around a massive old winepress, this charmer has a menu of tapas, cheese, sausage, sandwiches, fish soup or daily specials.

Casa de São Thiago B&B €€
(☎262 959 587; www.casas-sthiago.com; Largo de São Thiago; s/d €65/80) This charming labyrinth of trim 18th-century rooms and flower-filled courtyards sits in the shadow of the castle.

Óbido Sol GUEST HOUSE €
(☎262 959 188; Rua Direita 40; d €40-50) This neatly kept Old Town guest house has cosy and comfortable rooms surrounding a snug living room.

Information

Espaço Internet (Rua Direita 107) Free internet access.

Tourist office (Rua Direita) This helpful tourist office is just outside Porta da Vila, the town's main entrance gate.

Getting There & Away

There are direct **buses** Monday to Friday from Lisbon (€7, 70 minutes).

Nazaré

POP 16,000

With a warren of narrow cobbled lanes running down to a wide, cliff-backed beach, Nazaré is Estremadura's most picturesque coastal resort. The town centre is jammed with seafood restaurants, bars and local women in traditional dress hawking rooms for rent.

Sights & Activities

The **beaches** here are superb, although swimmers should be aware of dangerous currents. Climb or take the funicular to the clifftop **Sítio**, with its cluster of fishermen's cottages and great view.

Historic Monasteries ARCHITECTURE
Two of Portugal's big-time architectural masterpieces are close by. Follow the signs to Alcobaça where, right in the centre of town, is the immense **Mosteiro de Santa Maria de Alcobaça** (admission €6; ⊙9am-7pm) dating from 1178; don't miss the colossal former kitchen.

Batalha's massive **Mosteiro de Santa Maria de Vitória** (admission €6; ⊙9am-6pm), dating from 1388, is among the supreme achievements of Manueline architecture.

Sleeping & Eating

Many townspeople rent out rooms; doubles start at €35.

Vila Conde Fidalgo GUEST HOUSE €
(☎262 552 361; http://condefidalgo.planetaclix.pt; Avenida da Independência Nacional 21a; d/apt from €45/50) This pretty little complex uphill a few blocks from the beach is built around a series of flower-filled courtyards. Rooms all have kitchenettes.

Adega Oceano HOTEL €€
(☎262 561 161; www.adegaoceano.com, in Portuguese; Avenida da República 51; d €50-60; ❄📶) This little oceanfront place offers pleasantly set rooms – renovated modern rooms in back, beach-view quarters in front.

TOP CHOICE **A Tasquinha** SEAFOOD €€
(Rua Adrião Batalha 54; mains €6.50-11; ⏱lunch & dinner Tue-Sun) This enormously popular family-run tavern serves high-quality seafood at reasonable prices. Expect queues on summer nights.

ℹ Information

Tourist office (www.cm-nazare.pt) At the end of Avenida da República.

ℹ Getting There & Away

Nazaré has numerous **bus** connections to Lisbon (€9.50, two hours).

Tomar

POP 16,000

A charming town straddling a river, Tomar has the notoriety of being home to the Knights Templar; check out their headquarters, the outstanding monastery **Convento de Cristo** (admission €6; ⏱9am-6pm). Other rarities include a magnificent 17th-century **Aqueduto de Pegões** (aqueduct) and a medieval **synagogue** (Rua Dr Joaquim Jacinto 73; admission free; ⏱10am-7pm Tue-Sun). The town is backed by the dense greenery of the **Mata Nacional dos Sete Montes** (Seven Hills National Forest).

Sleeping & Eating

Residencial União GUEST HOUSE €
(☎249 323 161; www.hotel-ami.com/hotel/uniao; Rua Serpa Pinto 94; s/d/q €25/38/45; 📶) Tomar's most atmospheric budget choice, this once-grand town house features large and sprucely maintained rooms with antique furniture and fixtures.

Estalagem de Santa Iria INN €€
(☎249 313 326; www.estalagemsantairia.com; Mouchão Parque; s/d/ste €65/85/125; 📶) Centrally located on an island in Tomar's lovely riverside park, this '40s-style inn has large comfortable rooms, most with balconies overlooking the leafy grounds or the river.

Calça Perra INTERNATIONAL €€
(Rua Pedro Dias 59; mains €8-13; ⏱lunch & dinner Tue-Sun) A charming backstreet eatery with a diverse and innovative menu and occasional fado nights.

Restaurante Bela Vista PORTUGUESE €€
(Rua Marquês de Pombal 68; mains €6-11; ⏱lunch & dinner Wed-Sun, lunch Mon) With a lovely riverside terrace and standard Portuguese fare.

ℹ Information

Tourist office (Avenida Dr Cândido Madureira) Can provide town and forest maps.

ℹ Getting There & Away

Frequent **trains** run to Lisbon (€8.35, two hours).

Coimbra

POP 101,000

Coimbra is a dynamic, fashionable, yet comfortably lived-in city, with a student life centred on the magnificent 13th-century university. Aesthetically eclectic, there are elegant shopping streets, ancient stone walls and backstreet alleys with hidden *tascas* and fado bars. Coimbra was the birth and burial place of Portugal's first king, and was the country's most important city when the Moors captured Lisbon.

Sights & Activities

Igreja de Santa Cruz MONASTERY
(Praça 8 de Maio; admission €2.50; ⏱9am-noon & 2-5pm Mon-Sat) Located at the bottom of the hill in the Old Town, the monastery has a fabulous ornate pulpit and medieval royal tombs. It can be reached via the **elevator** (one-way €1.60) by the market.

Velha Universidade UNIVERSITY
(Old University; admission €7; ⏱10am-noon & 2-5pm) The old university is unmissable in its grandeur. You can visit the library with its gorgeous book-lined hallways and the Manueline chapel dating back to 1517.

O Pioneiro do Mondego KAYAKING
(www.opioneirodomondego.com) Rents out kayaks for paddling the Rio Mondego between Penacova and Torres de Mondego, an 18km trip costing €20 per person.

WORTH A TRIP

ROMAN RUINS

Conimbriga, 16km south of Coimbra, is the site of the well-preserved ruins of a **Roman town** (9am-8pm), including mosaic floors, elaborate baths and trickling fountains. It's a fascinating place to explore, with a good **museum** (admission €4; 10am-6pm Tue-Sun) that describes the once-flourishing and later abandoned town. There's a sunny cafe on site. Frequent buses run to Condeixa, 2km from the site; there are also two direct buses (€2.15) from Coimbra.

Festivals & Events

Coimbra's annual highlight is **Queima das Fitas**, a boozy week of fado and revelry that begins on the first Thursday in May when students celebrate the end of the academic year.

Sleeping

TOP CHOICE **Casa Pombal Guest House** BOUTIQUE GUEST HOUSE €€
(239 835 175; www.casapombal.com; Rua das Flores 18; d €68, without bathroom €52; @) This winning, Dutch-run guest house squeezes tons of charm into a small space. Ample morning buffet.

Pensão-Restaurante Flôr de Coimbra GUEST HOUSE €
(239 823 865; flordecoimbrahr.com.sapo.pt; Rua do Poço 5; s/d/tr €50/60/70, without bathroom €20/35/45;) This once-grand 19th-century home with its own restaurant offers loads of character in a great location.

Grande Hostel de Coimbra HOSTEL €
(239 108 212; www.grandehostelcoimbra.com; Rua Antero Quental 196; dm/d €18/40; @) You won't find a hostel more laid-back than this and it's hard to beat the location in a grand, century-old town house near the nightlife of Coimbra's university campus.

Eating & Drinking

Self-caterers should stop by the modern **Mercado Municipal Dom Pedro V** (Rua Olímpio Nicolau Rui Fernandes; Mon-Sat) for fruit, vegetables and more.

Restaurante Zé Manel PORTUGUESE €€
(Beco do Forno 12; mains €7-9; lunch & dinner Mon-Fri, lunch Sat) Great food, huge servings and a zany atmosphere, with walls papered with diners' comments, cartoons and poems.

Restaurante Zé Neto PORTUGUESE €€
(Rua das Azeiteiras 8; mains €6-10; lunch & dinner Mon-Sat) This marvellous family-run place specialises in homemade Portuguese standards, including *cabrito* (kid).

Italia ITALIAN €€
(Parque Dr Manuel de Braga; mains €8-15; noon-midnight) Expand your midriff at this excellent Italian restaurant on the riverfront with laden dishes of excellent pizza and pasta.

Café Santa Cruz CAFE €€
(Praça 8 de Maio; Mon-Sat) Former chapel that has been resurrected into one of Portugal's most atmospheric cafes.

Entertainment

Coimbra-style fado is more cerebral than the Lisbon variety, and its adherents are staunchly protective.

TOP CHOICE **Á Capella** FADO HOUSE
(www.acapella.com.pt; Rua Corpo de Deus; admission incl 1 drink €10; 10pm-2am) Housed in a fabulous 14th-century former chapel, Á Capella regularly hosts the city's most renowned fado musicians.

Via Latina DANCE CLUB
(Rua Almeida Garrett 1; Tue-Sat) Fires up to a steamy dance pit late at night.

Information

Espaço Internet (Praça 8 de Maio 37; 10am-2pm & 3-8pm) Free internet access.

Tourist office (Praça da Porta Férrea)

Getting There & Away

At least a dozen **buses** and as many **trains** run daily from Lisbon (€12, 2½ hours) and Porto (€11, 1½ hours), plus frequent buses from Faro and Évora, via Lisbon. The main train stations are **Coimbra B**, 2km northwest of the centre, and central **Coimbra A**. Most long-distance trains call at Coimbra B. The **bus station** (Avenida Fernão Magalhães) is about 400m northeast of the centre.

Luso & the Buçaco Forest

POP 2000

This sylvan region harbours a lush forest of century-old trees surrounded by countryside that's dappled with heather, wildflowers and leafy ferns. There's even a fairy-tale palace here, a 1907 neo-Manueline extravagance, where visitors can dine or stay overnight. Buçaco was chosen as a retreat by 16th-century monks, and it surrounds the lovely spa town of Luso.

The **Maloclinic Spa** (www.maloclinicspa.com; Rua Álvaro Castelões) offers a range of treatments.

Sleeping & Eating

Palace Hotel do Buçaco HOTEL €€€

(☎231 937 970; www.palacehoteldobussaco.com; Mata Nacional do Buçaco; standard/superior d midweek €150/170, weekend €175/200; P ❄) Live a real-life fairy tale and stay at this ostentatious palace complete with gargoyles, ornamental garden and turrets. The elegant restaurant offers seven-course menus for around €40.

Hotelaria Alegre BOUTIQUE HOTEL €€

(☎231 930 256; www.alegrehotels.com; Rua Emídio Navarro 2; s €40-45, d €55-65; P 📶 🏊) This grand, peach-coloured 19th-century town house has polished period furniture and other appealing touches. There's a formal parlour and vine-draped garden with pool.

Information

Tourist office (Avenida Emídio Navarro 136; ⊙Mon-Sat) Has maps and leaflets about the forest and trails.

Getting There & Away

Buses to/from Coimbra (€3.20, 45 minutes) run four times daily each weekday and twice daily on Saturdays.

Serra da Estrela

The forested Serra da Estrela has a raw natural beauty and offers some of the country's best hiking. This is Portugal's highest mainland mountain range (1993m), and the source of its two great rivers: Rio Mondego and Rio Zêzere. The town of **Manteigas** makes a great base for hiking and exploring the area (plus skiing in winter). The **main park office** (☎275 980 060; pnse@icn.pt; Rua 1 de Maio 2; Manteigas; ⊙Mon-Fri) provides details of popular walks in the Parque Natural da Serra da Estrela; additional offices are at Seia, Gouveia and Guarda.

Sleeping

Casa das Obras B&B €€

(☎275 981 155; www.casadasobras.pt; Rua Teles de Vasconcelos, Manteigas; r summer/winter €64/80; P 📶 🏊) This lovely 18th-century town house has antique-filled rooms, and a pool in a grassy courtyard across the street.

Albergaria Berne HOTEL €€

(☎275 981 351; www.albergariaberne.com; Quinta de Santo António, Manteigas; s/d from €35/55; P ❄ @ 📶 🏊) Going for a Swiss feel, this lovely hotel has wood-accented rooms, some with balconies and views of Manteigas and the mountains above.

Getting There & Around

Two regular weekday **buses** connect Manteigas with Guarda, from where there are onward services to Coimbra and Lisbon.No buses cross the park, although you can go around it. At least two buses link Seia, Gouveia and Guarda daily.

THE NORTH

Beneath the edge of Spanish Galicia, northern Portugal is a land of lush river valleys, sparkling coastline, granite peaks and virgin forests. This region is also gluttony for wine lovers: it's the home of the sprightly *vinho verde* wine and ancient vineyards along the dramatic Rio Douro. Gateway to the north is Porto, a beguiling riverside city blending both medieval and modern attractions. Smaller towns and villages also offer cultural allure, from majestic Braga, the country's religious heart, to the seaside beauty Viana do Castelo.

Porto

POP 263,000

At the mouth of the Rio Douro, the hilly city of Porto presents a jumble of styles, eras and attitudes: narrow medieval alleyways, extravagant baroque churches, prim little squares, and wide boulevards lined with beaux-arts edifices. A lively walkable city with chatter in the air and a tangible sense of history, Porto's old-world riverfront district is a Unesco World Heritage site. Across the water twinkle the neon signs of Vila Nova de Gaia, the headquarters of the major port manufacturers.

Sights

Head for the riverfront Ribeira district for an atmospheric stroll around, checking out the gritty local bars, sunny restaurants and river cruises.

Porto

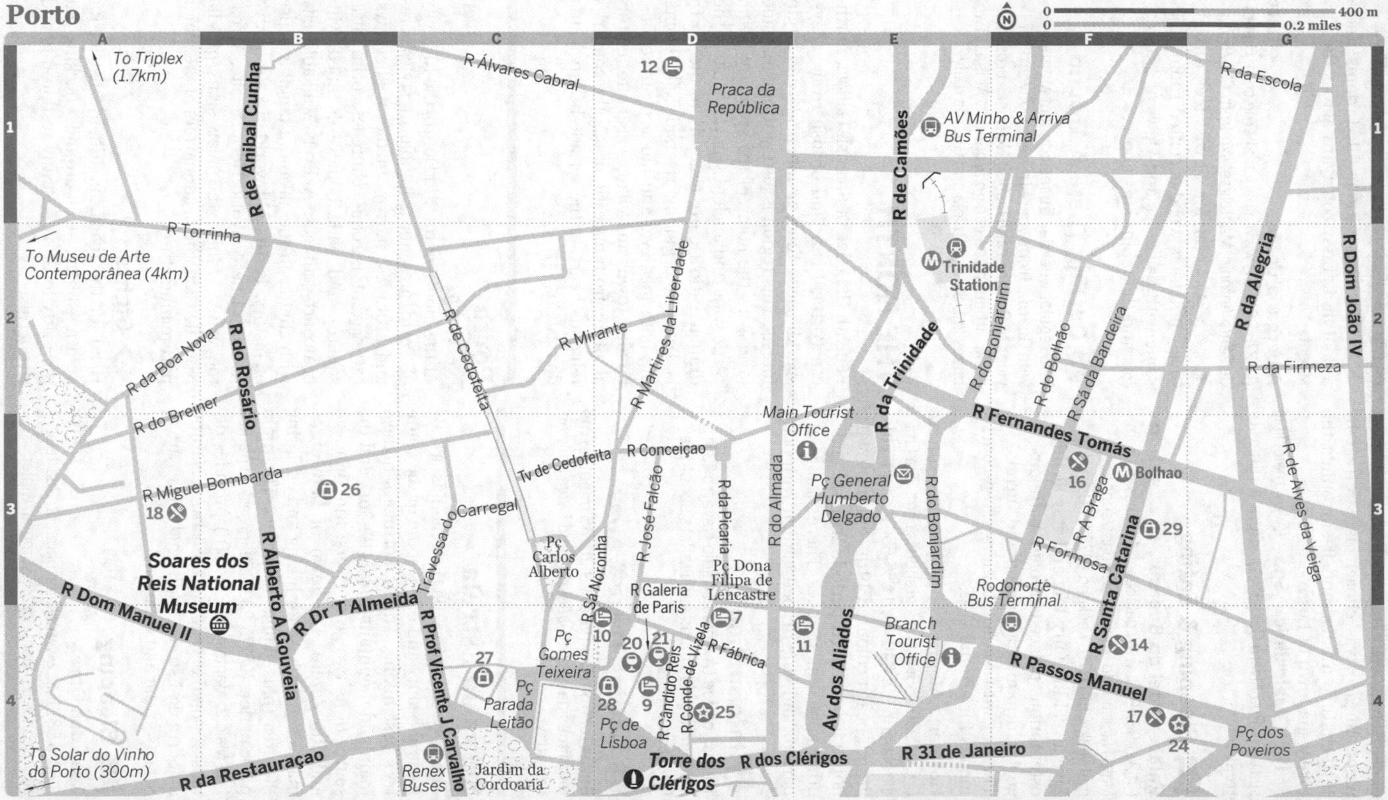

400 m
0.2 miles

To Triplex (1.7km)
To Museu de Arte Contemporânea (4km)
To Solar do Vinho do Porto (300m)
R Álvares Cabral
Praca da República
12
AV Minho & Arriva Bus Terminal
R da Escola
R de Camões
R Torrinha
R de Anibal Cunha
Trinidade Station
R da Alegria
R Dom João IV
R da Boa Nova
R do Rosário
R de Cedofeita
R Mirante
R Martires da Liberdade
R do Bonjardim
R do Bolhão
R Sá da Bandeira
R da Firmeza
R do Breiner
R da Trinidade
Main Tourist Office
R Fernandes Tomás
R de Alves da Veiga
R Conceiçao
Tv de Cedofeita
R Miguel Bombarda
26
18
16
Bolhao
Pç General Humberto Delgado
R José Falcão
R da Picaria
R do Almada
R A Braga
29
Travessa do Carregal
Pç Carlos Alberto
R Formosa
R Santa Catarina
Soares dos Reis National Museum
R Dom Manuel II
R Alberto A Gouveia
R Dr T Almeida
R Sá Noronha
R Galeria de Paris
Pç Dona Filipa de Lencastre
7
11
Av dos Aliados
Rodonorte Bus Terminal
Branch Tourist Office
14
R Prof Vicente J Carvalho
27
10
20
21
R Fábrica
R Passos Manuel
Pç Gomes Teixeira
28
9
R Cândido Reis
R Conde de Vizela
25
17
24
Pç dos Poveiros
Pç Parada Leitão
Pç de Lisboa
R da Restauraçao
Renex Buses
Jardim da Cordoaria
Torre dos Clérigos
R dos Clérigos
R 31 de Janeiro

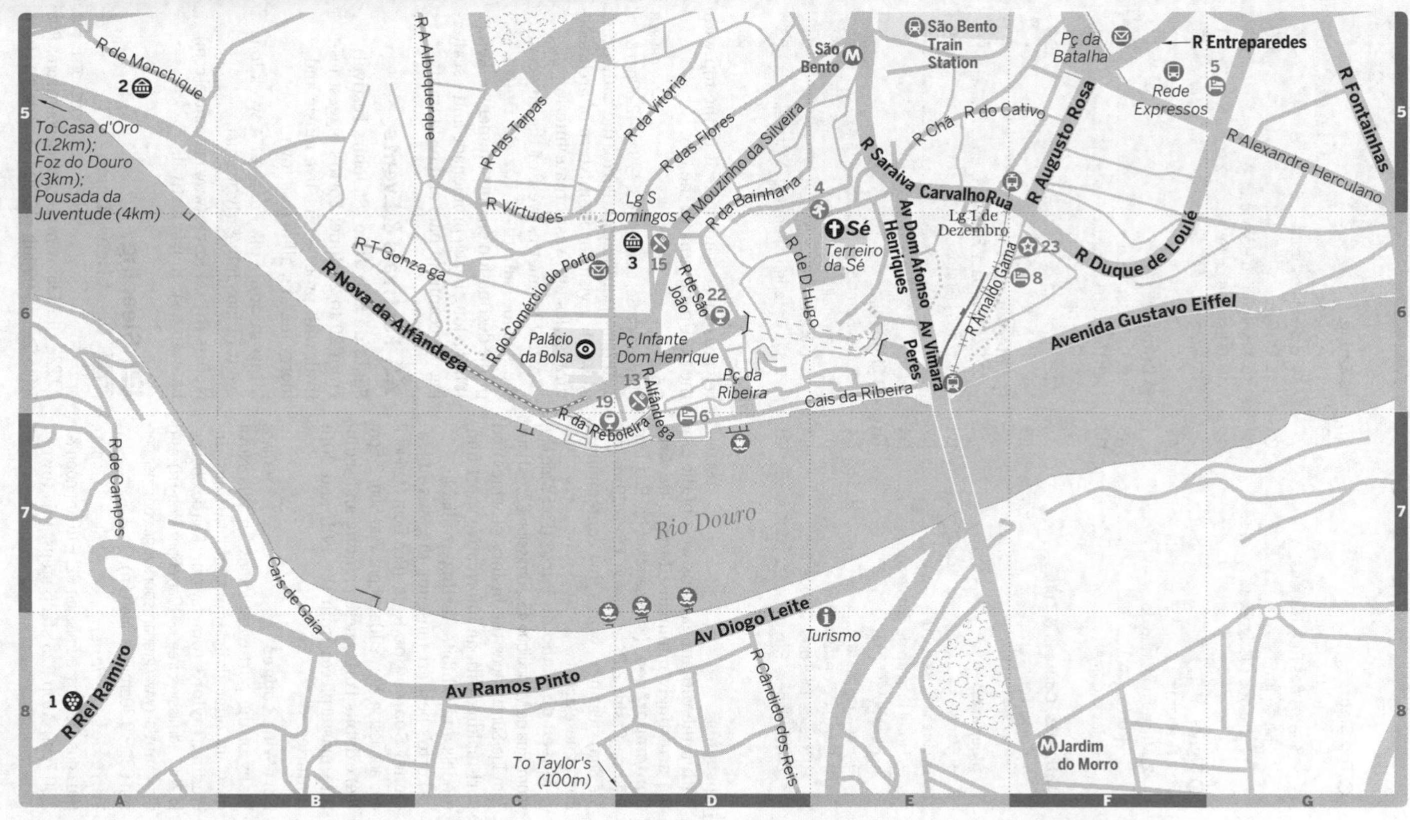

R de Monchique
To Casa d'Oro (1.2km); Foz do Douro (3km); Pousada da Juventude (4km)
R A Albuquerque
R das Taipas
R da Vitória
R das Flores
R Mouzinho da Silveira
R da Bainharia
R Virtudes
Lg S Domingos
R T Gonzaga
R do Comércio do Porto
R Nova da Alfândega
Palácio da Bolsa
Pç Infante Dom Henrique
R de São João
R Alfândega
R da Reboleira
Pç da Ribeira
Cais da Ribeira
São Bento
São Bento Train Station
Sé
Terreiro da Sé
R de D Hugo
Av Dom Afonso Henriques
Av Vimara Peres
R Saraiva Carvalho
Rua
R Chã
R do Cativo
Lg 1 de Dezembro
R Arnaldo Gama
R Augusto Rosa
R Duque de Loulé
Avenida Gustavo Eiffel
Pç da Batalha
R Entreparedes
Rede Expressos
R Alexandre Herculano
R Fontainhas
Rio Douro
R de Campos
Cais de Gaia
R Rei Ramiro
Av Ramos Pinto
Av Diogo Leite
Turismo
R Cândido dos Reis
To Taylor's (100m)
Jardim do Morro

Porto

Top Sights
Sé ... E6
Soares dos Reis National Museum ... B4
Torre dos Clérigos ... D4

Sights
1 Graham's ... A8
2 Museu do Vinho do Porto ... A5
3 Palacio das Artes ... D6

Activities, Courses & Tours
4 Porto Tours ... E5

Sleeping
5 6Only ... G5
6 Guesthouse Douro ... D7
7 Hotel Infante de Sagres ... D4
8 Pensão Astória ... F6
9 Pensão Cristal ... D4
10 Porto Downtown Hostel ... D4
11 Residencial dos Aliados ... E4
12 Residencial Rex ... D1

Eating
13 A Grade ... D6
14 Café Majestic ... F4
15 DOP ... D6
16 Mercado do Bolhão ... F3
17 O Escondidinho ... F4
18 Rota do Chá ... A3

Drinking
19 Café Bar O Cais ... C7
20 Casa do Livro ... D4
21 Galeria de Paris ... D4
22 Vinologia ... D6

Entertainment
23 Hot Five Jazz & Blues Club ... F6
24 Maus Hábitos ... F4
25 Plano B ... D4

Shopping
26 CC Bombarda ... B3
27 Garrafeira do Carmo ... C4
28 Livraria Lello ... D4
29 Via Caterina Shopping Centre ... F3

Museums MUSEUMS
Within the verdant gardens west of the city, the arrestingly minimalist **Museu de Arte Contemporânea** (www.serralves.pt; Rua Dom João de Castro 210; admission €5; ⏲10am-7pm Tue-Sun) features works by contemporary Portuguese artists.

Museu do Vinho do Porto (Port Wine Museum; Rua de Monchique 45; admission €2; ⏲11am-7pm Tue-Sun) traces the history of wine- and port-making with an informative short film, models and exhibits. Tastings available.

Porto's best art museum, the **Museu Nacional Soares dos Reis** (Rua Dom Manuel II 44; admission €6; ⏲10am-6pm Wed-Sun, 2-6pm Tue) exhibits Portuguese painting and sculpture masterpieces from the 19th and 20th centuries.

Port-Wine Lodges TASTINGS
Many of the port-wine lodges in Vila Nova de Gaia offer daily tours and tastings, including **Taylor's** (www.taylor.pt; Rua do Choupelo 250; admission free; ⏲10am-6pm Mon-Fri) and **Graham's** (www.grahamsportlodge.com; per person €3; ⏲9.30am-6pm Mon-Fri).

Torre dos Clérigos TOWER
(Rua dos Clérigos; admission €2; ⏲10am-noon & 2.30-7pm) Atop 225 steep steps, this tower rewards those who make it to the top with the best panorama of the city.

Sé CHURCH
(Terreiro da Sé; cloisters €3; ⏲9am-12.30pm & 2.30-7pm) Dominating Porto, the cathedral is worth a visit for its mixture of architectural styles and vast ornate interior.

A few kilometres west of the city centre, the seaside suburb of **Foz do Douro** is a prime destination on hot summer weekends. It has a long beach promenade and a scattering of oceanfront bars and restaurants.

Festivals & Events

Festa de São João (St John's Festival) From 20 to 24 June; Porto's biggest festival, with processions, live music and merry-making all across town.

International Folk Festival A week-long event in late July/early August.

Noites Ritual Rock (www.noitesritual.com) Late August; music festival.

Sleeping

TOP CHOICE **Guest House Douro** BOUTIQUE HOTEL €€€
(☎222 015 135; www.guesthousedouro.com; Rua Fonte Taurina 99-101; r €130-170; ❄@📶) In a

restored relic overlooking the Douro, these eight rooms have been blessed with gorgeous wood floors, plush queen beds and marble baths; the best have river views. There's a 1am curfew.

TOP CHOICE **6 Only** GUEST HOUSE €€
(☎222 013 971; www.6only.pt; Rua Duque de Loulé 97; d €70-80; @☎) This beautifully restored guest house has just six rooms, all with simple but stylish details that effortlessly blend old (such as wrought-iron decorative balconies) with new (free in-room wi-fi). There's a lounge, a Zen-like courtyard and friendly staff.

Pensão Cristal GUEST HOUSE €
(☎222 002 100; www.pensaocristal.com; Rua Galeria de Paris 48; r €35-60; P❄☎) Pensão Cristal has narrow, artwork-lined corridors and cosy rooms with wood furnishings. It sits on a romantic street that can get rowdy on weekends when the nearby galleries and bars get rolling.

Residencial Rex GUEST HOUSE €
(☎222 074 590; www.residencialrex.com; Praça da República 117; r €48-60; P❄) Residencial Rex is set in a 150 year-old belle-époque manor with a wide range of rooms. Floors two and three are best, with handsome old details, high ceilings and plenty of space.

Pousada da Juventude HOSTEL €
(☎226 177 257; www.microsites.juventude.gov.pt; Rua Paulo da Gama 551; ⊙24hr; dm/r €14/30; P@☎) In a bright, modern building on bluffs above the Rio Douro, the crown jewel of Portugal's hostels offers basic but handsome doubles with sweeping views of the river, as well as clean, well-maintained dorms. It's 4km from central Porto.

Hotel Infante de Sagres BOUTIQUE HOTEL €€€
(☎223 398 500; www.hotelinfantesagres.pt; Praça Dona Filipa de Lencastre 62; s/d from €175/195; ❄☎) An exquisite time warp, with well-coiffed doormen, crystal chandeliers and ornately decorated common areas, this place feels like a royal getaway in the heart of the city.

Pensão Astória GUEST HOUSE €
(☎222 008 175; Rua Arnaldo Gama 56; r €25-35) In an austere but elegant town house above the Rio Douro, this spotless place has old-world charm; several rooms have superb views. Reservations recommended.

Residencial dos Aliados GUEST HOUSE €
(☎222 004 853; www.residencialaliados.com; Rua Elísio de Melo 27; r €40-70; ❄☎) Set in one of Porto's marvellous beaux-arts buildings, offering spiffy rooms with polished wooden floors, decent beds and dark wood furnishings.

Porto Downtown Hostel HOSTEL €
(☎222 018 094; www.portodowntownhostel.com; Praça Guilherme Gomes Fernandes 66; r €16-19; P❄☎) This popular hostel has large sunlit dorms with new beds, and common areas with shag rugs and beanbag chairs strewn about.

Eating

TOP CHOICE **A Grade** PORTUGUESE €€
(☎223 321 130; Rua da Saoicolau 9; mains €10-20; ⊙lunch & dinner Mon-Sat) Both a humble mum-and-dad operation and a masterwork of traditional fare, with standouts such as baked octopus in butter and wine, roast veal and grilled seafood casseroles. Reservations recommended.

DOP PORTUGUESE €€
(☎222 014 313; www.ruipaula.com; Largo S Domingos 18; mains €25-50; ⊙lunch & dinner) Sit at the 'long table' and watch the chef prepare tapas tableside, or find a romantic corner and linger over duck risotto and a bottle of Douro red. Porto's upper crust digs it.

Casa d'Oro ITALIAN €€
(Alameda Bastio Teles 797; pizzas €8-12; ⊙lunch & dinner) A concrete and glass clay-oven pizzeria leaning over the Rio Douro just upriver from the mouth. It does terrific pizzas including *diavola* (spicy salami and oregano), *Vesuvio* (sausage and broccoli) and *fichi e prosciutto* (prosciutto and fig).

O Escondidinho PORTUGUESE €€
(www.escondidinho.com.pt; Rua Passos Manuel 144; mains €13-20; ⊙lunch & dinner) Amid *azulejos,* dark wood furnishings and starched white place settings, O Escondidinho serves excellent traditional cuisine.

Mercado do Bolhão MARKET €
(Rua Formosa; ⊙8am-5pm Mon-Fri, to 1pm Sat) Fruit, vegies, cheese and deli goodies in a 19th-century wrought-iron building.

Café Majestic CAFE €
(Rua Santa Catarina 112; ⊙9.30am-midnight Mon-Sat) An art-nouveau extravagance where old souls linger over afternoon tea.

Rota do Chá CAFE €
(Rua Miguel Bombarda 457; ⊙noon-8pm Mon-Thu, noon-midnight Fri & Sat, 1-8pm Sun; ✎) This proudly bohemian cafe has a verdant

PORT WINE PRIMER

With its intense flavours, silky textures and appealing sweetness, port wine is easy to love, especially when taken with its proper accompaniments: cheese, nuts and dried fruit.

It was probably Roman soldiers who first planted grapes in the Douro valley some 2000 years ago, but tradition credits the discovery of port itself to 17th-century British merchants. With their country at war with France, they turned to their old ally Portugal to meet their wine habit. According to legend, the British threw in some brandy with grape juice, both to take off the wine's bite and preserve it for shipment back to England – and port wine was the result.

but rustic back garden and a magnificent tea selection.

Drinking

There are dozens of bars on Praça da Ribeira and along the adjacent quay. On warm nights the outdoor tables get packed.

Casa do Livro LOUNGE BAR

(Rua Galeria de Paris 85; ⌚11.30am-2am Mon-Sat) Vintage wallpaper, gilded mirrors and walls of books give a discreet charm to this perfectly lit bar. On weekends DJs spin funk, soul and retro sounds in the back room for pretty people.

Vinologia WINE BAR

(Rua de São João 46) This oaky, subterranean wine bar is an excellent place to sample Porto's fine quaffs.

Café Bar O Cais BAR

(Rua Fonte Taurina 2a) A loyal following crowds the funky, classic-rock-drenched basement bar with old stone walls and vinyl booths.

Solar do Vinho do Porto WINE BAR, RESTAURANT

(Rua Entre Quintas 220) In a 19th-century house near the Palácio de Cristal, this upmarket spot has a manicured garden with picturesque views of the Douro and hundreds of ports by the glass.

Galeria de Paris BAR, CAFE

(Rua Galeria de Paris 56) A whimsically decorated bar (and daytime lunch buffet), with toys, old phones and other memorabilia lining the walls, which shake to a hip-hop soundtrack.

☆ Entertainment

Plano B GALLERY, CAFE, BAR

(Rua Cândido dos Reis 30; ⌚closed Aug) This creative space has an art gallery and cafe, with a cosy downstairs space where DJs and live bands hold court.

Maus Hábitos NIGHTCLUB

(www.maushabitos.com; 4th fl, Rua Passos Manuel 178) This bohemian, multiroom space hosts art exhibits, while live bands and DJs work the back stage.

Triplex NIGHTCLUB

(www.triplex.com.pt; Avenida Boavista 911) In a pink, three-storey mansion, Triplex has a regular line-up of '80s, electronica and '60s sounds (plus karaoke on Thursday).

Hot Five Jazz & Blues Club JAZZ

(www.hotfive.eu; Largo Actor Dias 51; ⌚10pm-3am Wed-Sun) Hosts live jazz and blues as well as acoustic, folk and all-out jam sessions.

Shopping

Major shopping areas are eastward around the Bolhão market and Rua Santa Catarina.

Via Catarina Shopping Centre MALL

(Rua Santa Catarina) The best central shopping mall, in a tasteful building.

CC Bombarda GALLERIA

(Rua Miguel Bombarda) For something a little edgier, visit this gallery of stores selling urban wear, stylish home knick-knacks, Portuguese indie rock and other hipster-pleasing delights.

Garrafeira do Carmo PORT

(Rua do Carmo 17) Port is, naturally, a popular purchase in this town. This knowledgeable shop has a good selection.

Livraria Lello BOOKS

(Rua das Carmelitas 144) Even if you're not after books, don't miss this 1906 neo-Gothic confection

Information

Santo António Hospital (☎222 077 500; Largo Prof Abel Salazar) Has English-speaking staff.

On Web (Praça General Humberto Delgado 291; per hr €1.80; ⌚10am-2am Mon-Sat, 3pm-2am Sun) Internet access.

Main post office (Praça General Humberto Delgado) Across from the main tourist office.

Branch tourist office (Rua Infante Dom Henrique 63) Small but helpful office.

Main tourist office (www.portoturismo.pt; Rua Clube dos Fenianos 25) Opposite the *câmara municipal*.

 Getting There & Away

Air

Porto is connected by daily flights from Lisbon and London, and direct links from other European cities, particularly with easyJet and Ryanair.

Bus

Porto has many private bus companies leaving from different terminals; the main tourist office can help. In general, for Lisbon (€18) and The Algarve the choice is **Renex** (www.renex.pt; Campo Mártires de Pátria 37) or **Rede Expressos** (www.rede-expressos.pt; Rua Alexandre Herculano 370).

Three companies operate from or near Praceto Régulo Magauanha, off Rua Dr Alfredo Magalhães: **Transdev-Norte** goes to Braga (€5); **AV Minho** to Viana do Castelo (€7).

Train

Porto is a northern Portugal rail hub with three stations. Most international trains, and all intercity links, start at **Campanhã**, 2km east of the centre. Inter-regional and regional services depart from Campanhã or the central **São Bento station** (Praça Almeida Garrett). Frequent local trains connect these two.

At **São Bento station** you can book tickets to any other destination.

Getting Around

To/From the Airport

The **metro's 'violet' line** provides handy service to the airport. A one-way ride to the centre costs €1.50 and takes about 45 minutes. A daytime **taxi** costs €20 to €25 to/from the centre.

Public Transport

Save money on transport by purchasing a refillable **Andante Card** (€0.50), valid for transport on buses, metro, funicular and tram.

BUS Central hubs of Porto's extensive bus system include Jardim da Cordoaria, Praça da Liberdade and São Bento station. Tickets are cheapest from STCP kiosks or newsagents (€1.80 return within Porto). Tickets bought on the bus are one-way €1.50. There's also a €5 day pass available.

FUNICULAR A panoramic funicular shuttles up and down a steep incline from Avenida Gustavo Eiffel to Rua Augusto Rosa (€0.90, from 8am to 8pm).

METRO Porto's **metro** (www.metrodoporto.pt) currently comprises four metropolitan lines that all converge at the Trinidade stop. Tickets cost €1.50 for a single ride, and €1 with an Andante Card.

TRAM Porto has three antique trams that trundle around town. The most useful line, 1E, travels along the Douro towards the Foz district.

Taxi

To cross town, expect to pay between €5 and €7. There's a 20% surcharge at night, and an additional charge to leave city limits, which includes Vila Nova de Gaia. There are taxi ranks throughout the centre or you can call a **radio taxi** (☎225 076 400).

Along the Douro

Portugal's best-known river flows through the country's rural heartland. In the upper reaches, port-wine grapes are grown on steep terraced hills, punctuated by remote stone villages and, in spring, splashes of dazzling white almond blossom.

The Rio Douro is navigable right across Portugal. Highly recommended is the train journey from Porto to Pinhão (€9, 2½ hours, five trains daily), the last 70km clinging to the river's edge; trains continue to Pocinho (from Porto €10.65, 3½ hours). **Porto Tours** (☎222 000 073; www.portotours.com; Torre Medieval, Calçada Pedro Pitões 15), situated next to Porto's cathedral, can arrange tours, including idyllic Douro cruises. Cyclists and drivers can choose river-hugging roads along either bank, and visit wineries along the way (check out www.rvp.pt for an extensive list of wineries open to visitors). You can also stay overnight in scenic wine lodges among the vineyards.

Viana do Castelo

POP 37,500

The jewel of the Costa Verde (Green Coast), Viana do Castelo has both an appealing medieval centre and lovely beaches just outside the city. In addition to its natural beauty, Viana do Castelo whips up some excellent seafood and hosts some magnificent traditional festivals, including the spectacular **Festa de Nossa Senhora da Agonia** in August.

Sights

The stately heart of town is **Praça da República**, with its delicate fountain and grandiose buildings, including the 16th-century **Misericórdia**, a former almshouse.

Templo do Sagrado Coração de Jesus CHURCH
(Temple of the Sacred Heart of Jesus; admission free; ⌚8am-7pm Apr-Sep) Atop Santa Luzia Hill, the Temple of the Sacred Heart of Jesus offers a grand panorama across the river. It's a steep 2km climb; you can also catch a ride on the newly restored funicular railway (one-way/return €2/3).

Praia do Cabedelo BEACH
Viana's enormous arcing beach is one of the Minho's best, with little development to spoil its charm. It's across the river from town, best reached by **ferry** (adult/child €1.20/0.60; ⌚hourly 9am to 6pm) from the pier south of Largo 5 de Outubro.

Sleeping

Margarida da Praça BOUTIQUE HOTEL €€
(☎258 809 630; www.margaridadapraca.com; Largo 5 Outubre; r €65-75; ❄📶) Fantastically whimsical, this friendly boutique inn offers colourful rooms accented by candelabra lanterns and lush duvets.

Residencial Jardim GUEST HOUSE €€
(☎258 828 915; www.residencialjardim.com.sapo.pt; Largo 5 de Outubro 68; d €65; ❄📶) This stately 19th-century town house has spacious rooms with wood floors and French windows overlooking the historic centre or the river.

Pousada da Juventude Gil Eannes HOSTEL €
(☎258 821 582; www.pousadasjuventude.pt; Gil Eannes; dm/s/d €10/16/24; 📶) Sleep in the bowels of a huge, creaky hospital ship where men were stitched up and underwent emergency dentistry. This floating hostel scores well for novelty, but has few amenities.

Eating

TOP CHOICE **Taberna do Valentim** SEAFOOD €€
(Rua Monsignor Daniel Machado 180; mains €12-15; ⌚lunch & dinner Mon-Sat) In the old fishermen's neighbourhood, this fantastic seafood restaurant serves grilled fish by the kilogram, and rich seafood stews – *arroz de tamboril* (monkfish rice) and *caldeirada* (fish stew).

Restaurante Zefa Carqueja GRILL €€
(Campo do Castelo; mains €8-25; ⌚lunch & dinner) Barbecue aficionados should seek this casual grill house for some of the best barbecue chicken and ribs in northern Portugal.

Information

Tourist office (Rua Hospital Velho) Handily located in the old centre.

Getting There & Away

Five to 10 **trains** go daily to Porto (€5 to €8, two hours), as well as express **buses** (€7, 2¼ hours).

Braga

POP 133,000

Portugal's third-largest city boasts a fine array of churches, their splendid baroque facades looming above the old plazas and narrow lanes of the historic centre. Lively cafes, trim little boutiques, and some good restaurants add to the appeal.

Sights

It's an easy day trip to **Guimarães** with its medieval town centre and a palace of the dukes of Bragança. It's also a short jaunt to **Barcelos**, a town famed for its sprawling Thursday market.

Sé CHURCH
(Rua Dom Paio Mendes; admission free; ⌚8.30am-6.30pm) In the centre of Braga, this is one of Portugal's most extraordinary cathedrals, with roots dating back a thousand years. Within the cathedral you can also visit the **treasury** (€2) and **choir** (€2).

Escadaria do Bom Jesus RELIGIOUS SITE
At Bom Jesus do Monte, a hilltop pilgrimage site 5km from Braga, is an extraordinary stairway, with allegorical fountains, chapels and a superb view. City bus 2 (€1.50) runs frequently from Braga to the site, where you can climb the steps (pilgrims sometimes do this on their knees) or ascend by funicular railway (€1.20).

Sleeping

TOP CHOICE **Casa Santa Zita** GUEST HOUSE €
(☎253 618 331; Rua São João 20; s/d €30/40) This impeccably kept pilgrims' lodge (look for the small tile reading 'Sta Zita') has bright, spotless rooms and an air of palpable serenity. Midnight curfew.

Albergaria da Sé GUEST HOUSE €€
(☎253 214 502; www.albergaria-da-se.com.pt; Rua Gonçalo Pereira 39; s/d from €45/55; P❄) Around the corner from the cathedral, this friendly three-storey guest house has darkwood floors and airy rooms.

Eating & Drinking

Livraria Café CAFE €

(Avenida Central 118; mains €4-6; 9am-7.30pm Mon-Sat) Tucked inside the bookshop Centésima Página, this charming cafe serves tasty quiches, salads and desserts. Outdoor tables are in the pleasantly rustic garden.

Cozinha da Sé PORTUGUESE €€

(Rua Dom Frei Caetano Brandão 95; mains €7-10; Tue-Sun) Sé serves traditional, high-quality dishes (including one vegetarian selection).

Taperia Palatu SPANISH, PORTUGUESE €€

(Rua Dom Afonso Henrique 35; mains €8-12; Mon-Sat) A Spanish/Portuguese couple serves up delectable Spanish tapas and classic Portuguese dishes in an airy courtyard.

Information

Tourist office (www.cm-braga.pt; Praça da República 1) Can help with accommodation and maps.

Getting There & Away

Trains arrive regularly from Lisbon (€31, 3¼ hours), Coimbra (€19, 2¼ hours) and Porto (€2.20, 1¼ hours), and there are daily connections north to Viana do Castelo. Daily **bus** services link Braga to Porto (€4.50, 1¼ hours) and Lisbon (€19, five hours). **Car hire** is available at **AVIC** (253 203 910; Rua Gabriel Pereira de Castro 28; Mon-Fri), with prices starting at €35 per day.

Parque Nacional da Peneda-Gerês

Spread across four impressive granite massifs, this vast park encompasses boulder-strewn peaks, precipitous valleys, gorse-clad moorlands and forests of oak and pine. It also shelters more than 100 granite villages that, in many ways, have changed little since Portugal's founding in the 12th century. For nature lovers the stunning scenery here is unmatched in Portugal for camping, hiking and other outdoor adventures. The park's main centre is at Vila do Gerês, a sleepy, hot-spring village.

Activities

Hiking

There are trails and footpaths through the park, some between villages with accommodation. Leaflets detailing these are available from the park offices.

Day hikes around Vila do Gerês are popular. An adventurous option is the **old Roman road** from Mata do Albergaria (10km up-valley from Vila do Gerês), past the **Vilarinho das Furnas** reservoir to Campo do Gerês. More distant destinations include **Ermida** and **Cabril**, both with simple accommodation.

Cycling & Horse Riding

Mountain bikes can be hired in Campo do Gerês (15km northeast of Vila do Gerês) from **Equi Campo** (253 357 022, www.equicampo.com; per hr/day €5/18; 10am-7pm). Guides here also lead horse-riding trips, hikes and combination hiking/climbing/abseiling excursions.

Water Sports

Rio Caldo, 8km south of Vila do Gerês, is the base for water sports on the Caniçada reservoir. English-run **AML** (Água Montanha e Lazer; 965 000 917; www.aguamontanha.com; Lugar de Paredes) rents kayaks, pedal boats, rowing boats and small motorboats. It also organises kayaking trips along the Albufeira de Salamonde.

Sleeping & Eating

Vila do Gerês has plenty of *pensões* (guest houses), but you may find vacancies are limited; many are block-booked by spa patients in summer.

TOP CHOICE **Hotel de Peneda** BOUTIQUE HOTEL €€

(251 460 040; www.hotelpeneda.com; Lugar da Peneda; r €40-75; P) Set in the Serra da Peneda in the northern reaches of the park, this mountain lodge has a waterfall backdrop, a gushing creek beneath and ultra-cosy rooms with blonde-wood floors and views of quaint Peneda village across the ravine. The restaurant is decent.

Pousada da Juventude de Vilarinho das Furnas HOSTEL €

(253 351 339; www.pousadasjuventude.pt; dm/bungalow €13/50; P@) Campo's woodland hostel began life as a temporary dam-workers' camp and now offers a spotless selection of spartan dormitories, simply furnished doubles (with bathrooms) and roomier bungalows with kitchen units.

Quinta Souto-Linho RURAL INN €€

(253 392 000; www.oocities.com/souto_linho; d €50-60; P) This delightful Victorian manor house in Vila do Gerês has four

simply but tastefully remodelled rooms with hardwood floors; some have views. There's also a swimming pool with fine vistas.

Parque Campismo de Cerdeira CAMPING GROUND €
(☎253 351 005; www.parquecerdeira.com; camping per person/tent/car €5/4/4.50, bungalows €50-65; ⏰year-round; P) In Campo de Gerês, this place has oak-shaded sites, laundry, pool, minimarket and a particularly good restaurant. The ecofriendly bungalows have French doors opening onto unrivalled mountain views.

Information

The head park office is **Adere-PG** (www.adere-pg.pt; ⏰Mon-Fri) in Ponte de Barca. Obtain park information and reserve cottages and other park accommodation through here. Other Adere-PG stations are at Mezio and Lamas de Mouro.

Getting There & Away

Because of the lack of transport within the park, it's good to have your own wheels. You can rent cars in Braga.

UNDERSTAND PORTUGAL

History

Portugal has an early history of occupation, stretching back to 700 BC when the Celts arrived on the Iberian peninsula, followed by the Phoenicians, Greeks, Romans, Visigoths, Moors and Christians.

Life Under the Moors

The Moors ruled southern Portugal for more than 400 years, and some scholars describe that time as a golden age. The Arabs introduced irrigation, previously unknown in Europe. Two Egyptian agronomists came to Iberia in the 10th century and wrote manuals on land management, animal husbandry, plant and crop cultivation and irrigation designs. They also introduced bananas, rice, coconuts, maize and sugar cane. They also encouraged small-scale, cooperatively run communities, specialising in olive oil and wine production and food markets – still embraced in many parts of Portugal.

The Moors opened schools and set about campaigns to achieve mass literacy (in Arabic of course), as well as the teaching of maths, geography and history. Medicine reached new levels of sophistication. There was also a degree of religious tolerance that evaporated when the Christian crusaders came to power. Much to the chagrin of Christian slave owners, slavery was not permitted in the Islamic kingdom – making it a refuge for runaway slaves. Muslims, Christians and Jews all peacefully coexisted, at times even collaborating together, creating the most scientifically and artistically advanced society the world had ever known up until that time.

Age of Discovery

The 15th century marked a golden era in Portuguese history, when Portuguese explorers helped transform the small kingdom into a great imperial power.

The third son of King João I, Henrique 'O Navegador' (Henry the Navigator, 1394–1460) played a pivotal role in establishing Portugal's maritime dominance. As governor of The Algarve he assembled the very best sailors, map-makers, shipbuilders, instrument-makers and astronomers.

By 1431, Portuguese explorers discovered the islands of Madeira and the Azores, followed by Gil Eanes' 1534 voyage beyond Cape Bojador in West Africa, breaking a maritime superstition that this was the end of the world. More achievements followed over the next century. In 1488, Portuguese sailors, under navigator Bartolomeu Dias, were the first Europeans to sail around Africa's southern tip and into the Indian Ocean. This was followed by the epic voyage in 1497–98 when Vasco da Gama reached southern India, and in 1500 when Cabral discovered Brazil. With gold and slaves from Africa and spices from the East, Portugal was soon rolling in riches. As its explorers reached Timor, China and eventually Japan, Portugal cemented its power with garrison ports and trading posts. The monarchy, taking its 'royal fifth' of profits, became the wealthiest in Europe, and the lavish Manueline architectural style symbolised the exuberance of the age.

The Salazar Years

In 1908 King Carlos and his eldest son were assassinated in Lisbon. Two years later Portugal became a republic, which set the stage for an enormous power struggle. Over the next 16 years, chaos ruled, with an astounding 45 different governments coming to power, often the result of military intervention. Another coup in 1926 brought forth new names and faces, most significantly António de Oliveira Salazar, a finance minister who would rise up through the ranks to become prime minister – a post he would hold for 36 years.

Salazar hastily enforced his 'New State' – a republic that was nationalistic, Catholic, authoritarian and essentially repressive. All political parties were banned except for the loyalist National Union, which ran the show, and the National Assembly. Strikes were banned and propaganda, censorship and brute force kept society in order. The new secret police, Polícia Internacional e de Defesa do Estado (PIDE), inspired terror and suppressed opposition by imprisonment and torture. Various attempted coups during Salazar's rule came to nothing. The only good news was a dramatic economic turnaround, with surging industrial growth through the 1950s and 1960s.

Decolonisation finally brought the Salazarist era to a close. Independence movements in Portugal's African colonies led to costly and unpopular military interventions. In 1974, military officers reluctant to continue fighting bloody colonial wars staged a nearly bloodless coup – later nicknamed the Revolution of the Carnations (after victorious soldiers stuck carnations in their rifle barrels). Carnations are still a national symbol of freedom.

Arts

Music

The best-known form of Portuguese music is the melancholy, nostalgic songs called fado (literally 'fate') said to have originated from troubadour and African slave songs. The late Amália Rodrigues was the Edith Piaf of Portuguese fado. Today it is Mariza who has captured the public's imagination with her extraordinary voice and fresh contemporary image. Lisbon's Alfama district has plenty of fado houses (see the boxed text, p991), ranging from the grandiose and tourist-conscious to small family affairs.

Architecture

Unique to Portugal is Manueline architecture, named after its patron King Manuel I (1495–1521). It symbolises the zest for discovery of that era and is hugely flamboyant, characterised by fantastic spiralling columns and elaborate carving and ornamentation.

Visual Arts

Portugal's stunning painted *azulejo* tiles coat contemporary life, covering everything from houses to churches. The art form dates from Moorish times and reached a peak in the late 19th century when the art nouveau and art deco movements provided fantastic facades and interiors. Lisbon has its very own *azulejo* museum (p979).

Environment

Portugal has made astounding gains in transforming itself from a nation powered largely by fossil fuels to one powered by solar, wind and hydropower. In 2005, only 17% of electricity in Portugal's grid came from green energy. By 2010, the figure had risen to 45% – a gain unprecedented elsewhere in Europe. In 2008 the world's largest solar farm opened in the Alentejo, powering 30,000 homes. Portugal also has numerous wind farms and has even launched the world's first 'wave farm' to harness the ocean's power, just north of Porto. By the time you read this, Portugal may have realised its goal of becoming the first country with a nationwide grid of charging stations for electric cars.

SURVIVAL GUIDE

Directory A–Z

Accommodation

There's an excellent range of good-value, inviting accommodation in Portugal. Budget places provide some of Western Europe's cheapest rooms, while you'll find atmospheric, accommodation in farms, palaces, castles, mansions and rustic town houses – usually giving good mileage for your euro.

PRICE RANGES

We list high-season rates for a double room; breakfast is generally not included.

€€€	more than €100
€€	€50 to €100
€	less than €50

ECOTOURISM & FARMSTAYS

Turismo de Habitação (www.turihab.pt) is a private network of historic, heritage or rustic properties, ranging from 17th-century manors to quaint farmhouses or self-catering cottages. Doubles run from about €60 to €120.

SEASONS

Rates in this chapter are for high season.

» **High season:** mid-June to mid-September.

» **Mid-season:** May to mid-June and mid-September to October.

» **Low season:** November to April.

POUSADAS

These are government-run former castles, monasteries or palaces, often in spectacular locations. For details contact tourist offices or **Pousadas de Portugal** (www.pousadas.pt).

GUEST HOUSES

The most common types are the *residencial* and the *pensão:* usually simple, family-owned operations. Some have cheaper rooms with shared bathrooms.

HOSTELS

Portugal has a growing number of hostels, particularly in Lisbon. Nationwide, Portugal has over 30 *pousadas da juventude* (youth hostels; www.pousadasjuventude.pt) within the Hostelling International (HI) system.

CAMPING

For detailed listings of campsites nationwide, pick up the **Roteiro Campista** (www.roteiro-campista.pt; €7), updated annually and sold at bookshops. The swishest places are run by **Orbitur** (www.orbitur.pt) and **Inatel** (www.inatel.pt).

Activities

Cycling and **mountain-biking** trips are becoming popular in Portugal; good starting points are Tavira in The Algarve, Sintra and Setúbal in central Portugal and Parque Nacional da Peneda-Gerês in the north.

Fine country **walks** are found in Parque Nacional da Peneda-Gerês, Serra da Estrela. The ambitious can follow the 240km walking trail **Via Algarviana** (www.viaalgarviana.org) across southern Portugal.

Popular **water sports** include surfing, windsurfing, canoeing, rafting and water skiing. For local specialists, see Lagos, Sagres, Tavira, Coimbra and Parque Nacional da Peneda-Gerês.

Modest alpine **skiing** is possible at Torre in the Serra da Estrela, usually from January through to March.

Business Hours

Reviews in this chapter don't list hours unless they differ from these standard hours:

Banks 8.30am to 3pm Monday to Friday

Bars 7pm to 2am

Cafes 9am to 7pm

Malls 10am to 10pm

Nightclubs 11pm to 4am Thursday to Saturday

Post offices 8.30am to 4pm Monday to Friday

Restaurants noon to 3pm & 7pm to 10pm

Shops 9.30am to noon & 2pm to 7pm Monday to Friday, 10am to 1pm Saturday

Sights 10am to 12.30pm & 2-5pm Tuesday to Sunday

Discount Cards

If you plan to do a lot of sightseeing in Portugal's main cities, the **Lisboa Card** (p978) and **Porto Card** are sensible investments. Sold at tourist offices, these cards offer discounts or free admission to many attractions, and free travel on public transport.

Embassies & Consulates

Australia (☎213 101 500; www.portugal.embassy.gov.au; 2nd fl, Av da Liberdade 200, Lisbon)

Canada Lisbon (☎213 164 600; www.canadainternational.gc.ca; 3rd fl, Av da Liberdade 198, Lisbon); Faro (☎289 803 757; Rua Frei Lourenço de Santa Maria 1, Faro)

Ireland (☎213 929 440; www.embassyofireland.pt; Rua da Imprensa a Estrela 1, Lisbon)

New Zealand Madrid (☎34 915 230 226; www.nzembassy.com) The nearest New Zealand embassy is in Madrid.

UK (☎213 924 000; www.ukinportugal.fco.gov.uk; Rua de Saõ Bernardo 33, Lisbon) Also in Portimaõ.

USA (☎217 273 300; http://portugal.usembassy.gov; Av das Forças Armadas, 1600-081 Lisbon)

Food

There is a great range of offerings for diners of all budgets in Portugal. For a small cost, you'll be able to eat daily specials (pork, chicken, fried fish) at casual, family-style restaurants. Midrange offerings can be found at popular Portuguese eateries serving traditional fare such as *bacalhau* dishes, as well as vegetarian and international fare.

With a budget of €15 per main and up, diners can sample some of the country's best restaurants.

The following price indicators (per main course) are used in this chapter:

€€€ more than €14

€€ €9 to €14

€ less than €9

Money

There are numerous banks with ATMs located throughout Portugal. Credit cards are accepted in midrange and top-end hotels, restaurants and shops.

Public Holidays

New Year's Day 1 January

Carnaval Tuesday February/March – the day before Ash Wednesday

Good Friday March/April

Liberty Day 25 April – celebrating the 1974 revolution

Labour Day 1 May

Corpus Christi May/June – 9th Thursday after Easter

Portugal Day 10 June – also known as Camões and Communities Day

Feast of the Assumption 15 August

Republic Day 5 October – commemorating the 1910 declaration of the Portuguese Republic

All Saints' Day 1 November

Independence Day 1 December – commemorating the 1640 restoration of independence from Spain

Feast of the Immaculate Conception 8 December

Christmas Day 25 December

Telephone

Portugal's country code is ☎351. There are no regional area codes. Mobile phone numbers within Portugal have nine digits and begin with ☎9.

All Portuguese phone numbers consist of nine digits. These include area codes, which always need to be dialled. For general information dial ☎118, and for reverse-charge (collect) calls dial ☎120.

Phonecards are the most reliable and cheapest way of making a phone call from a telephone booth. They are sold at post offices, newsagents and tobacconists in denominations of €5 and €10.

Visas

EU nationals need only a valid passport or identity card for entry to Portugal, and can stay indefinitely. Citizens of Australia, Canada, New Zealand and the US can stay for up to 90 days in any half-year without a visa. Others, including nationals of South Africa, need a visa unless they're the spouse or child of an EU citizen.

Getting There & Away

Air

TAP (www.tap.pt) is Portugal's international flag carrier as well as its main domestic airline. Portugal's main airports:

Lisbon (LIS; ☎218 413 500; www.ana-aeroportos.pt)

Porto (OPO; ☎229 432 400; www.ana-aeroportos.pt)

Faro (FAO; ☎289 800 800; www.ana-aeroportos.pt)

Land

BUS

UK–Portugal and France–Portugal Eurolines services cross to Portugal via northwest Spain; see the boxed text in this section for routes and fares. Some operators:

Alsa (www.alsa.es)

Avanza (www.avanzabus.com)

Damas (www.damas-sa.es)

Eurolines (www.eurolines.com)

Eva (www.eva-bus.com)

CAR & MOTORCYCLE

There is no border control in Portugal. For more information about driving in Portugal, see p1022.

TRAIN

The most popular train link from Spain is on the Sud Express, operated by **Renfe** (www.renfe.com; one-way tickets from €59), which has a nightly sleeper service between Madrid and Lisbon. Badajoz (Spain)–Elvas–Lisbon is slow and there is only one regional service daily, but the scenery is stunning. Coming from Galicia, in the northwest of Spain, travellers can go from Vigo to Valença do Minho (Portugal) and continue on to Porto.

SPAIN TO PORTUGAL BUS SERVICES

FROM	TO	VIA	COST (€)	DURATION (HRS)	COMPANY
Madrid	Porto	Guarda	50	8½	Eurolines
Madrid	Lisbon	Évora	50	8	Eurolines, Avanza, Alsa
Barcelona	Lisbon	Évora	100	18	Eurolines
Madrid	Lisbon	Évora	45	8	Eurolines
Sevilla	Lisbon	Évora	48	7	Eurolines, Alsa, Eva, Damas
Sevilla	Faro	Huelva	20	4½	Eva, Damas

From France, there's Lisbon service via Irún (Spain) that takes around 20 hours (one-way tickets from €136). For trains from Paris, contact **SNCF** (www.sncf.com).

Getting Around

Air

TAP Portugal (TAP; www.flytap.com) has daily Lisbon–Faro flights (under an hour) year-round. Overall, however, flights within Portugal are poor value; it is a lot cheaper and not terribly time-consuming to travel by bus or train.

Bicycle

Mountain biking is a fine way to explore the country, although given the Portuguese penchant for overtaking on blind corners, it can be dangerous on lesser roads. Bicycle lanes are rare: veteran cyclists recommend the Parque Nacional da Peneda-Gerês (p1017). A handful of towns have bike-hire outfits (from €10 to €20 a day). If you're bringing your own, pack plenty of spare inner tubes. Bicycles can be taken free on all regional and inter-regional trains as accompanied baggage. They can also go on a few suburban services on weekends. Most domestic bus lines won't accept bikes.

Boat

Portugal is not big on water-borne transport as a rule; however, there are river cruises along the Rio Douro from Porto (p1015), Lisbon's river trips (p982) and commuter ferries.

Bus

A host of small private bus operators, most amalgamated into regional companies, run a dense network of services across the country. Among the largest companies are **Rede Expressos** (www.rede-expressos.pt), **Rodonorte** (www.rodonorte.pt) and The Algarve line **Eva** (www.eva-bus.com).

Most bus-station ticket desks will give you a computer printout of fares, and services and schedules are usually posted at major stations.

CLASSES

Expressos Comfortable, fast buses between major cities

Rápidas Quick regional buses

Carreiras Marked CR, slow, stopping at every crossroad

COSTS

Travelling by bus in Portugal is fairly inexpensive. A Lisbon–Faro express bus costs around €20; Lisbon–Porto costs about €18. Both take four hours. An under-26 card should get you a small discount on long-distance services.

Car & Motorcycle

AUTOMOBILE ASSOCIATIONS

Automóvel Clube de Portugal (ACP; ☎213 180 100; www.acp.pt) has a reciprocal arrangement with better-known foreign automobile clubs, including AA and RAC. It provides medical, legal and breakdown assistance. The 24-hour emergency help number is ☎707 509 510.

HIRE

To hire a car in Portugal you must be at least 25 years old and have held your home licence for over a year (some companies allow younger drivers at higher rates). To hire a scooter of up to 50cc you must be over 18 years old and have a valid driving licence. For more powerful scooters and motorbikes you must have a valid driving licence covering these vehicles from your home country.

INSURANCE

Although most car-insurance companies within the EU will cover taking your car to Portugal, it is prudent to consider extra cover for assistance in case your car breaks down. The minimum insurance required is third party.

ROAD RULES

The various speed limits for cars and motorcycles are 50km/h within cities and public centres, 90km/h on normal roads and 120km/h on motorways (but 50km/h, 70km/h and 100km/h for motorcycles with sidecars).

Driving is on the right side of the road. Drivers and front passengers in cars must wear seatbelts. Motorcyclists and passengers must wear helmets, and motorcycles must have headlights on day and night. Using a mobile phone while driving could result in a fine.

Drink-driving laws are strict in Portugal, with a maximum legal blood-alcohol level of 0.05%.

Train

Caminhos de Ferro Portugueses (www.cp.pt) is the statewide train network and is generally efficient.

There are four main types of long-distance service. Note that international services are marked IN on timetables.

Regional (marked R on timetables) Slow trains that stop everywhere

Interregional (IR) Reasonably fast trains

Intercidade (IC) or **rápido** Express trains

Alfa Pendular Deluxe, marginally faster and much pricier service.

Spain

Includes »

Best Places to Eat

» Arzak (p1087)

» La Cuchara de San Telmo (p1087)

» Mercado de San Miguel (p1040)

» Le Pepica (p1099)

Best Places to Stay

» Casa Morisca Hotel (p1121)

» Pensión Bellas Artes (p1086)

» Hospedería La Gran Casa Mudéjar (p1055)

» Hotel Constanza (p1074)

Why Go?

Passionate, sophisticated and devoted to living the good life, Spain is at once a stereotype come to life and a country more diverse than you ever imagined.

Spanish landscapes stir the soul, from the jagged Pyrenees and wildly beautiful cliffs of the Atlantic northwest to charming Mediterranean coves, while astonishing architecture spans the ages at seemingly every turn. Spain's cities march to a beguiling beat, rushing headlong into the 21st century even as timeless villages serve as beautiful signposts to Old Spain. And then there's one of Europe's most celebrated (and varied) gastronomic scenes.

But above all, Spain lives very much in the present. Perhaps you'll sense it along a crowded after-midnight street when all the world has come out to play. Or maybe that moment will come when a flamenco performer touches something deep in your soul. Whenever it happens, you'll find yourself nodding in recognition: *this* is Spain.

When to Go

Madrid

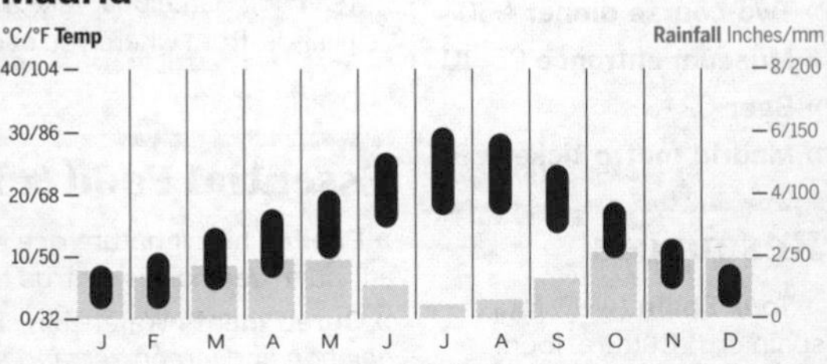

Mar–Apr Spring wildflowers, Semana Santa processions and mild southern temps

May & Sep Mild and often balmy weather but without the crowds of high summer

Jun–Sep Spaniards hit the coast in warm weather, but quiet corners still abound

AT A GLANCE

» **Currency** euro

» **Language** Spanish (Castellano), Catalan, Basque, Galician (Gallego)

» **Money** ATMs everywhere

» **Visas** Schengen rules apply

Fast Facts

» **Area** 504,782 sq km

» **Population** 46 million

» **Capital** Madrid

» **Telephone** country code ☎34; international access code ☎00

» **Emergency** ☎112

Exchange Rates

Australia	A$1	€0.74
Canada	C$1	€0.74
Japan	¥100	€0.87
New Zealand	NZ$1	€0.56
UK	UK£1	€1.16
USA	US$1	€0.67

Set Your Budget

» **Budget hotel room** €60

» **Two-course dinner** €30

» **Museum entrance** €6–10

» **Beer** €2–3

» **Madrid metro ticket** €9

Resources

» **Tour Spain** (www.tourspain.org) Culture, food, hotels and transport links

» **Turespaña** (www.spain.info) Official tourism site

» **Lonely Planet** (www.lonelyplanet.com/spain)

Connections

Spanish airports are among Europe's best connected, while the typical overland route leads many travellers from France over the Pyrenees into Spain. Rather than taking the main road/rail route along the Mediterranean coast (or between Biarritz and San Sebastián), you could follow lesser known, pretty routes over the mountains. There's nothing to stop you carrying on to Portugal: numerous roads and the Madrid–Lisbon rail line connect the two countries.

The most obvious sea journeys lead across the Strait of Gibraltar to Morocco. The most common routes connect Algeciras or Tarifa with Tangier, from where there's plenty of transport deeper into Morocco. Car ferries also connect Barcelona with Italian (and occasionally Moroccan) ports. For transport details, turn to p1145.

There are two main rail lines to Spain from Paris, one to Madrid (to be upgraded to a high-speed service by 2012) via the Basque Country, and another to Barcelona. The latter connects with services to the French Riviera and Switzerland. New rail links are also cutting travel time between southern France and Barcelona.

ITINERARIES

One Week

Marvel at Barcelona's art nouveau–influenced Modernista architecture and seaside style before taking the train to San Sebastián, with a stop in Zaragoza on the way. Head on to Bilbao for the Guggenheim Museum and end the trip living it up in Madrid's legendary night scene.

One Month

Fly into Seville and embark on a route exploring the town and picture-perfect Ronda, Granada and Córdoba. Take the train to Madrid, from where you can check out Toledo, Salamanca and Segovia. Make east for the coast and Valencia, detour northwest into the postcard-perfect villages of Aragón and the Pyrenees, then travel east into Catalonia, spending time in Tarragona before reaching Barcelona. Take a plane or boat for the Balearic Islands, from where you can get a flight home.

Essential Food & Drink

» **Paella** This signature rice dish comes in infinite varieties, although Valencia is its true home.

» **Cured meats** Wafer-thin slices of *chorizo, lomo, salchichón* and *jamón serrano* appear on most Spanish tables.

» **Tapas** These bite-sized morsels range from uncomplicated Spanish staples to pure gastronomic innovation.

» **Olive oil** Spain is the world's largest producer of olive oil.

» **Wine** Spain has the largest area of wine cultivation in the world. La Rioja and Ribera del Duero are the best-known wine-growing regions.

MADRID

POP 3.6 MILLION

No city on earth is more alive than Madrid, a beguiling place whose sheer energy carries a simple message: this city knows how to live. Explore the old streets of the centre, relax in the plazas, soak up the culture in its excellent art museums, and spend at least one night in the city's legendary nightlife scene.

History

Established as a Moorish garrison in 854, Madrid was little more than a muddy, mediocre village when King Felipe II declared it Spain's capital in 1561. That began to change when it became the permanent home of the previously roaming Spanish court.

Despite being home to generations of nobles, the city was a squalid grid of unpaved alleys and dirty buildings until the 18th century, when King Carlos III turned his attention to public works. With 175,000 inhabitants under Carlos' rule, Madrid had become Europe's fifth largest capital.

The postcivil war 1940s and '50s were trying times for the capital, with rampant poverty. When Spain's dictator, General Franco, died in 1975, the city exploded with creativity and life, giving Madrileños the party-hard reputation they still cherish.

Terrorist bombs rocked Madrid in March 2004, just before national elections, and killed 191 commuters on four trains. In 2007 two people died in a Basque terrorist bomb attack at the city's airport. With remarkable aplomb, the city quickly returned to business as usual on both occasions.

Orientation

In Spain, all roads lead to Madrid's Plaza de la Puerta del Sol, kilometre zero. South of the plaza is the oldest part of the city, with Plaza Mayor and Los Austrias to the southwest and the busy streets of the Huertas *barrio* (district or quarter of a town or city) to the southeast. Also to the south lie La Latina and Lavapiés.

North of the plaza is the east–west thoroughfare Gran Vía, the gay *barrio* (neighbourhood) Chueca and gritty Malasaña. East are the city's big three art museums on Paseo del Prado, El Retiro park and upmarket Salamanca.

Sights & Activities

Get under the city's skin by walking its streets, sipping coffee and beer in its plazas and relaxing in its parks. Madrid de los Austrias, the maze of mostly 15th- and 16th-century streets that surround Plaza Mayor, is the city's oldest district. Tapas-crazy La Latina, alternative Chueca, bar-riddled Huertas and Malasaña, and chic Salamanca are other districts that reward pedestrian exploration.

Build in time for three of Europe's top art collections at the Prado, Reina Sofía and Thyssen-Bornemisza museums, as well as a visit to the Palacio Real.

Museo del Prado — ART MUSEUM

(Map p1034; www.museodelprado.es; Paseo del Prado; adult/student/child under 18yr & EU senior over 65yr €8/4/free, free to all 6-8pm Tue-Sat & 5-8pm Sun; ⌚9am-8pm Tue-Sun; Ⓜ Banco de España)
Spain's premier art museum, the Prado is a seemingly endless parade of priceless works from Spain and beyond. The 1785 neoclassical Palacio de Villanueva opened as a museum in 1819.

The collection is roughly divided into eight major collections: Spanish paintings (1100–1850), Flemish paintings (1430–1700), Italian paintings (1300–1800), French paintings (1600–1800), German paintings (1450–1800), sculptures, decorative arts, and drawings and prints. There is generous coverage of Spanish greats including Goya, Velázquez and El Greco. Prized works include Velázquez' masterpiece *Las Meninas* (depicting maids of honour attending the daughter of King Felipe IV, and Velázquez himself painting portraits of the queen and king) and *El Jardín de las Delicias* (The Garden of Earthly Delights), a three-panelled painting by Hieronymus Bosch of the creation of man, the pleasures of the world, and hell.

Goya's *El Dos de Mayo* and *El Tres de Mayo* rank among Madrid's most emblematic paintings; they bring to life the 1808 anti-French revolt and subsequent execution of insurgents in Madrid. Also worth tracking down is his dark and disturbing *Las Pinturas Negras* (Black Paintings), so-called because of the dark browns and black that dominate and for the distorted animalesque appearance of their characters.

Other masters on show include Peter Paul Rubens, Pieter Bruegel, Rembrandt, Anton van Dyck, Dürer, Rafael, Titian, Tintoretto, Sorolla, Gainsborough, Fra Angelico and Tiepolo.

From the 1st floor of the Palacio de Villanueva, passageways lead to the Edificio Jerónimos, the Prado's modern extension. The main hall contains information counters, a bookshop and a cafe. Rooms A and B

Spain Highlights

1. Explore the **Alhambra** (p1121), an exquisite Islamic palace complex in Granada
2. Visit Gaudí's singular work in progress, Barcelona's **La Sagrada Família** (p1069), a cathedral that truly defies imagination
3. Wander amid the horseshoe arches of Córdoba's **Mezquita** (p1118), close to perfection wrought in stone
4. Eat your way through **San Sebastián** (p1086), a gourmand's paradise with an idyllic setting
5. Join the pilgrims making their way to magnificent **Santiago de Compostela** (p1094)
6. Soak up the scent of orange blossom, admire the architecture and surrender to the party atmosphere in sunny **Seville** (p1112)
7. Discover the impossibly beautiful Mediterranean beaches and coves of **Menorca** (p1110)
8. Spend your days in some of Europe's best art galleries and nights amid its best nightlife in **Madrid** (p1027)
9. Be carried away by the soulful strains of live **flamenco** (p1139)

Bordeaux
FRANCE
Avignon
Nîmes
Montpellier
Toulouse
BASQUE COUNTRY
San Sebastián
Irún
NAVARRA
Golfe de Beauduc
Vitoria
Pamplona
Perpignan
Miranda de Ebro
Andorra la Vella
ANDORRA
Jaca
Figueres
Logroño
Calahorra
Huesca
CATALONIA
Girona
Fornells
Costa Brava
Manresa
Tossa de Mar
Soria
Lleida
Zaragoza
Barcelona
CASTILLA Y LEÓN
Sitges
Tarragona
ARAGÓN
Guadalajara
Alcalá de Henares
Teruel
Madrid
Aranjuez
Cuenca
Ciutadella de Menorca
Menorca
Maó
Mallorca
Inca
Artà
Manacor
Sagunto
Alcázar de San Juan
VALENCIA
Valencia
Palma de Mallorca
Alginet
Balearic Islands
Manzanares
Albacete
Ibiza
Denia
Valdepeñas
Benidorm
Alicante
Elche
Cieza
Murcia
MURCIA
Costa Blanca
MEDITERRANEAN SEA
Cartagena
Guadix
Granada
Mojácar
Costa Cálida
Almería
Adra
Cabo de Gata
Costa De Almería
ALGERIA
AP1
AP68
A9
AP2
A23
AP7
A3
A7
A91
0 300 km
0 200 miles

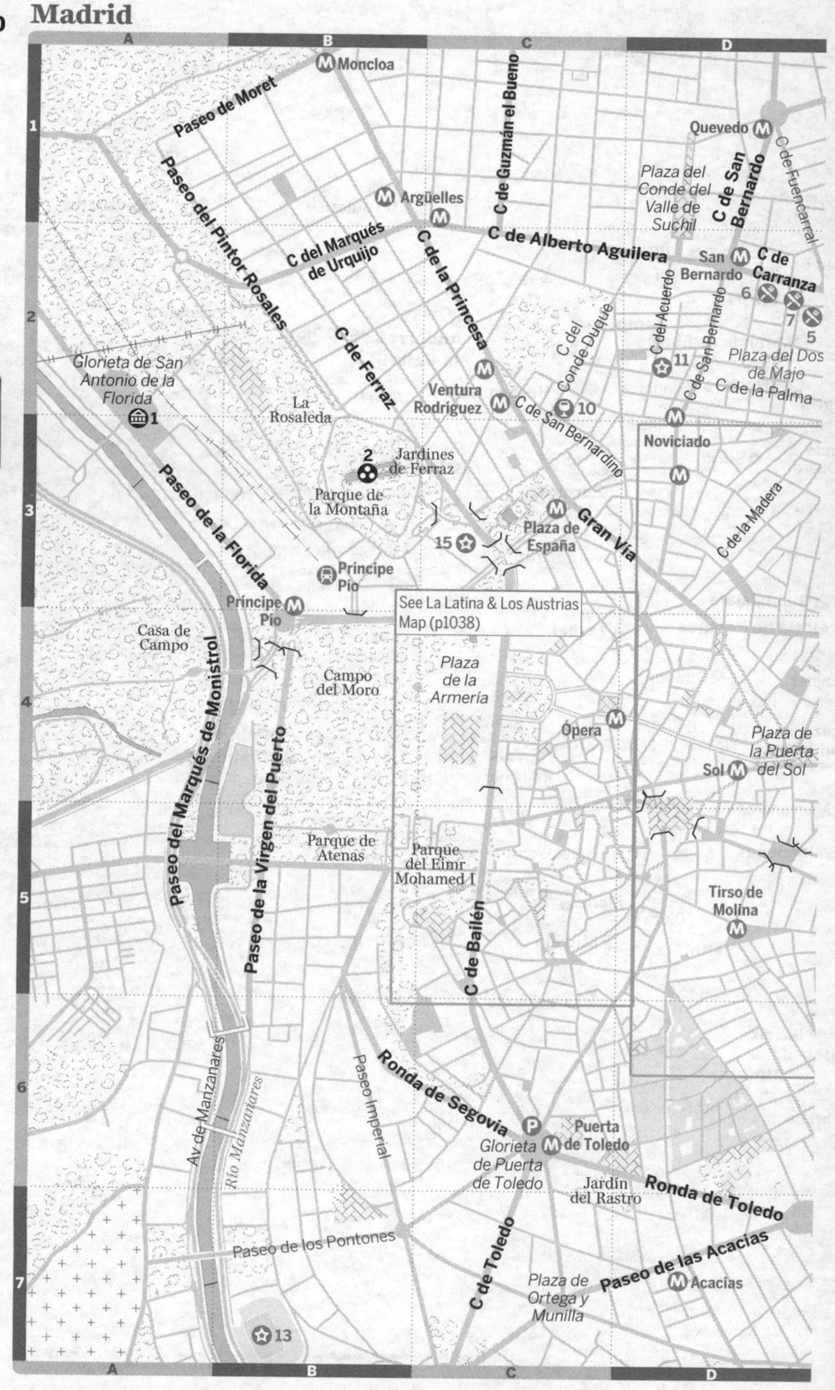
Moncloa
Paseo de Moret
C de Guzmán el Bueno
Quevedo
C de Fuencarral
Paseo del Pintor Rosales
Argüelles
Plaza del Conde del Valle de Suchil
C de San Bernardo
C del Marqués de Urquijo
C de la Princesa
C de Alberto Aguilera
San Bernardo
C de Carranza
C del Acuerdo
C del Conde Duque
C de San Bernardo
C de Ferraz
Plaza del Dos de Majo
C de la Palma
Glorieta de San Antonio de la Florida
La Rosaleda
Ventura Rodríguez
C de San Bernardino
Noviciado
Jardines de Ferraz
Parque de la Montaña
Paseo de la Florida
Plaza de España
Gran Vía
C de la Madera
Príncipe Pío
See La Latina & Los Austrias Map (p1038)
Casa de Campo
Campo del Moro
Plaza de la Armería
Paseo del Marqués de Monistrol
Ópera
Plaza de la Puerta del Sol
Sol
Paseo de la Virgen del Puerto
Parque de Atenas
Parque del Emir Mohamed I
Tirso de Molina
C de Bailén
Av de Manzanares
Río Manzanares
Paseo Imperial
Ronda de Segovia
Puerta de Toledo
Glorieta de Puerta de Toledo
Jardín del Rastro
Ronda de Toledo
Paseo de los Pontones
C de Toledo
Paseo de las Acacias
Acacias
Plaza de Ortega y Munilla

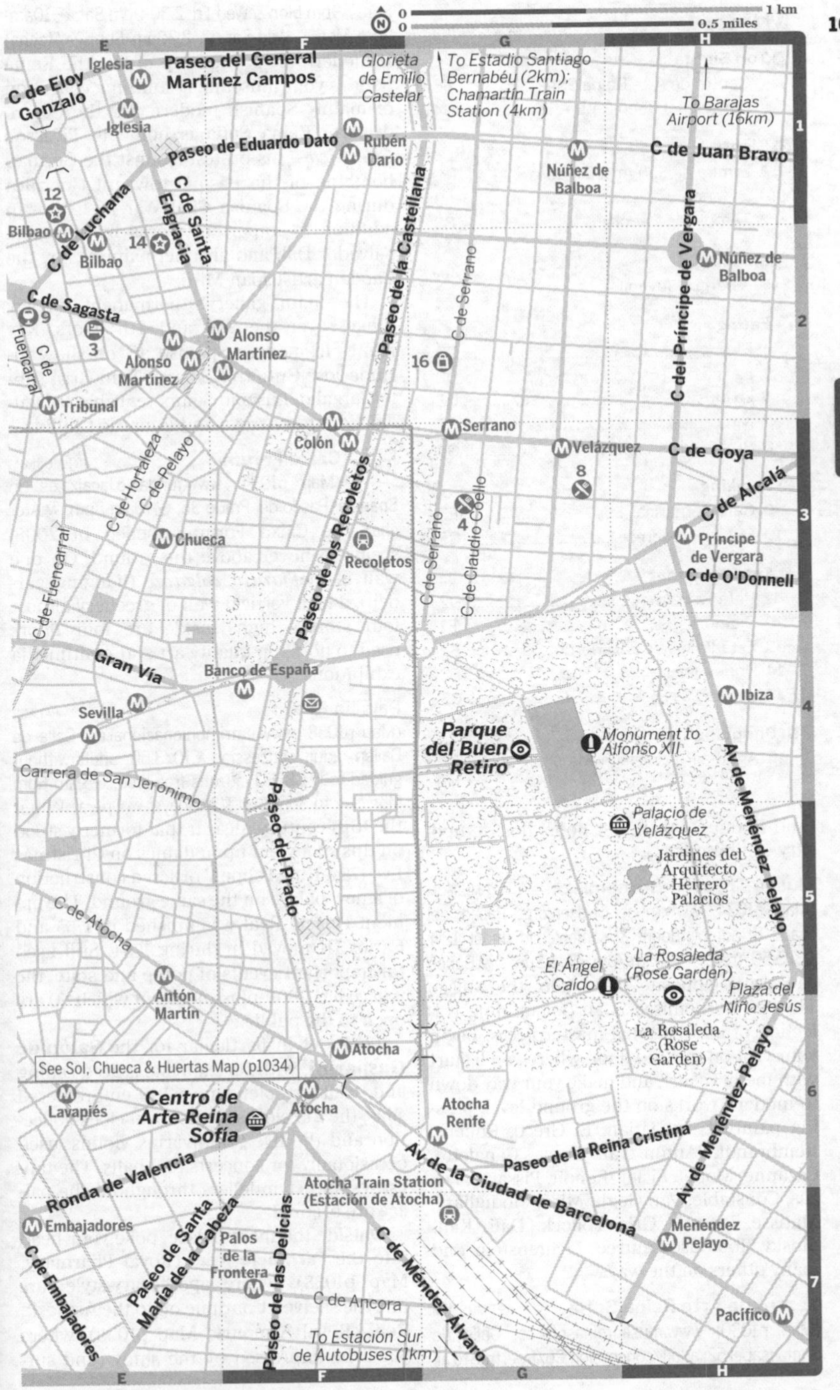

0 1 km
0 0.5 miles
Paseo del General Martínez Campos
Glorieta de Emilio Castelar
To Estadio Santiago Bernabéu (2km); Chamartín Train Station (4km)
To Barajas Airport (16km)
C de Eloy Gonzalo
Iglesia
Paseo de Eduardo Dato
Rubén Darío
Núñez de Balboa
C de Juan Bravo
C de Santa Engracia
C de Luchana
Bilbao
Paseo de la Castellana
C de Serrano
C del Príncipe de Vergara
C de Sagasta
C de Fuencarral
Alonso Martínez
Tribunal
Colón
Serrano
Velázquez
C de Goya
C de Hortaleza
C de Pelayo
Paseo de los Recoletos
C de Claudio Coello
C de Alcalá
Chueca
Recoletos
Príncipe de Vergara
C de O'Donnell
Gran Vía
Banco de España
Sevilla
Ibiza
Parque del Buen Retiro
Monument to Alfonso XII
Carrera de San Jerónimo
Paseo del Prado
Palacio de Velázquez
Av de Menéndez Pelayo
Jardines del Arquitecto Herrero Palacios
C de Atocha
El Ángel Caído
La Rosaleda (Rose Garden)
Plaza del Niño Jesús
Antón Martín
Atocha
See Sol, Chueca & Huertas Map (p1034)
Lavapiés
Centro de Arte Reina Sofía
Atocha Renfe
Paseo de la Reina Cristina
Ronda de Valencia
Av de la Ciudad de Barcelona
Atocha Train Station (Estación de Atocha)
Embajadores
Paseo de Santa María de la Cabeza
Palos de la Frontera
Paseo de las Delicias
C de Méndez Álvaro
Menéndez Pelayo
C de Embajadores
C de Ancora
Pacífico
To Estación Sur de Autobuses (1km)

Madrid

Top Sights

Sights

Sleeping

Eating

Drinking

Entertainment

Shopping

(and Room C on the 1st floor) host temporary exhibitions.

Museo Thyssen-Bornemisza ART MUSEUM
(Map p1034; www.museothyssen.org; Paseo del Prado 8; adult/student & senior/child under 12yr €8/5.50/free; 10am-7pm Tue-Sun; M Banco de España) Opposite the Prado, the Museo Thyssen-Bornemisza is an outstanding collection of international masterpieces. Begin your visit on the 2nd floor, where you'll start with medieval art, and make your way down to modern works on the ground level, passing paintings by Titian, El Greco, Rubens, Rembrandt, Anton van Dyck, Canaletto, Cézanne, Monet, Sisley, Renoir, Pissarro, Degas, Constable, Van Gogh, Miró, Modigliani, Matisse, Picasso, Gris, Pollock, Dalí, Kandinsky, Toulouse-Lautrec, Lichtenstein and many others on the way.

Centro de Arte Reina Sofía ART MUSEUM
(Map p1030; www.museoreinasofia.es; Calle de Santa Isabel 52; adult/concession €6/free, free to all Sun, 7-9pm Mon & Wed-Fri, 2.30-9pm Sat; 10am-9pm Mon & Wed-Sat, to 2.30pm Sun; M Atocha) If modern art is your cup of tea, the Reina Sofía is your museum. A stunning collection of mainly Spanish modern art, the Centro de Arte Reina Sofía is home to Picasso's *Guernica* – his protest against the German bombing of the Basque town of Guernica during the Spanish Civil War in 1937 – in addition to important works by surrealist Salvador Dalí and abstract paintings by the Catalan artist Joan Miró.

The main gallery's permanent display ranges over the 2nd and 4th floors. Key names in modern Spanish art on show include José Gutiérrez Solana, Juan Gris, Pablo Gargallo, Eusebio Sempere, Pablo Palazuelo, Eduardo Arroyo and Eduardo Chillida.

FREE **Caixa Forum** ART MUSEUM
(Map p1034; www.fundacio.lacaixa.es, in Spanish; Paseo del Prado 36; 10am-8pm; M Atocha) The Caixa Forum, opened in 2008, seems to hover above the ground. On one wall is the *jardín colgante* (hanging garden), a lush vertical wall of greenery almost four storeys high. Inside are four floors used to hold top-quality art and multimedia exhibitions.

Palacio Real PALACE
(Map p1038; www.patrimonionacional.es; Calle de Bailén; adult/concession €10/3.50, adult without guided tour €8, EU citizens free Wed; 9am-6pm Mon-Sat, to 3pm Sun & holidays; M Ópera) When the 16th-century Alcázar that formerly stood on this spot went up in flames on Christmas Eve 1734, King Felipe V ordered construction of a new palace on the same ground. The opulent Palacio Real was finished in 1755 and Carlos III moved in during 1764. Still used for important events of pomp and state, the palace has 2800-plus rooms, of which 50 are open to the public.

Look out in particular for the **Salón de Gasparini**, with its exquisite stucco ceiling and walls resplendent with embroidered silks, the 215 clocks of the royal clock collection and the five Stradivarius violins, used occasionally for concerts and balls. The tapestries and chandeliers throughout the palace are original.

Outside the main palace, poke your head into the **Farmacia Real** (Royal Pharmacy; Map p1038), where apothecary-style jars line the shelves. Continue on to the **Armería Real** (Royal Armoury; Map p1038), where you'll be impressed by the shiny (and surprisingly tiny!) royal suits of armour, most of them from the 16th and 17th centuries.

Plaza Mayor SQUARE

Ringed with cafes and restaurants, and packed with people day and night, the 17th-century arcaded Plaza Mayor (Map p1034) is an elegant and bustling square.

Designed in 1619 by Juan Gómez de Mora, the plaza's first public ceremony was the beatification of San Isidro Labrador, Madrid's patron saint. Thereafter, bullfights watched by 50,000 spectators were a recurring spectacle until 1878, while the autos-da-fé (the ritual condemnation of heretics) of the Spanish Inquisition also took place here. Fire largely destroyed the square in 1790, but it was rebuilt and became an important market and hub of city life. Today, the uniformly ochre-tinted apartments with wrought-iron balconies are offset by the exquisite frescos of the 17th-century **Real Casa de la Panadería** (Royal Bakery); the frescos were added in 1992.

Churches CHURCHES

The **Catedral de Nuestra Señora de la Almudena** (Map p1038; Calle de Bailén; admission free; ⌚9am-8.30pm; Ⓜ Ópera) is just across the plaza from the Palacio Real. Finished in 1992 after a century, the cathedral is cavernous and laden with more adornment than charm. It's possible to climb to the cathedral's summit with fine views. En route you climb up through the cathedral's museum; follow the signs to the **Museo de la Catedral y Cúpola** (Map p1038; adult/child €6/4; ⌚10am-2.30pm Mon-Sat) on the northern facade that faces the Palacio Real.

The cathedral is less captivating than the imposing 18th-century **Basílica de San Francisco El Grande** (Map p1038; Plaza de San Francisco 1; adult/concession €3/2; ⌚mass 8am-12.30pm & 4-6pm Mon-Sat; Ⓜ La Latina or Puerta de Toledo).

Convento de las Descalzas Reales CONVENT

(Convent of the Barefoot Royals; Map p1034; www.patrimonionacional.es; Plaza de las Descalzas 3; adult/child €5/2.50, EU citizens free Wed; ⌚10.30am-12.45pm & 4-5.45pm Tue-Thu & Sat, 10.30am-12.45pm Fri, 11am-1.45pm Sun; Ⓜ Ópera or Sol) Opulent inside though with a rather plain plateresque exterior, the Convento de las Descalzas Reales was founded in 1559 by Juana of Austria. Daughter of Spain's King Carlos I and Isabel of Portugal, Juana transformed one of her mother's palaces into the noblewomen's convent of choice. On the obligatory guided tour you'll see a gaudily frescoed Renaissance stairway, a number of extraordinary tapestries based on works by Rubens, and a wonderful painting entitled *The Voyage of the 11,000 Virgins*. Some 33 nuns still live here and there are 33 chapels dotted around the convent.

Parque del Buen Retiro GARDENS

(Map p1030; ⌚6am-midnight May-Sep, to 11pm Oct-Apr; Ⓜ Retiro, Príncipe de Vergara, Ibiza or Atocha) The splendid gardens of El Retiro are littered with marble monuments, landscaped lawns, the occasional elegant building and abundant greenery. It's quiet and contemplative during the week, but comes to life on weekends.

The focal point for so much of El Retiro's life is the artificial lake (*estanque*), which is watched over by the massive ornamental structure of the **Monument to Alfonso XII** on the east side of the lake, complete with marble lions.

Hidden among the trees south of the lake, the late-19th-century **Palacio de Cristal**, a magnificent metal and glass structure that is arguably El Retiro's most beautiful architectural monument, is now used for temporary exhibitions. Just north of here, the 1883 **Palacio de Velázquez** is also used for temporary exhibitions.

At the southern end of the park, near **La Rosaleda** (Rose Garden) with its more than 4000 roses, is a statue of **El Ángel Caído** (the Fallen Angel, aka Lucifer), one of the few statues to the devil anywhere in the world. It sits 666m above sea level...

In the northeastern corner of the park is the **Ermita de San Isidro**, a small country chapel noteworthy as one of the few, albeit modest, examples of Romanesque architecture in Madrid.

Just outside the park is the **Real Jardín Botánico** (Royal Botanical Garden; Map p1034; Plaza de Bravo Murillo 2; adult/concession/child €2.50/1.25/free; ⌚10am-9pm May-Aug; Ⓜ Atocha).

Other Sights

The frescoed ceilings of the **Ermita de San Antonio de la Florida** (Map p1030; Glorieta de San Antonio de la Florida 5; admission free; ⌚9.30am-8pm Tue-Fri, 10am-2pm Sat & Sun, hr vary Jul & Aug; Ⓜ Príncipe Pío) are one of Madrid's most surprising secrets. In the southern of the two small chapels you can see Goya's work in its original setting, rendered in 1798. The painter is buried in front of the altar.

Sol, Chueca & Huertas (Madrid)

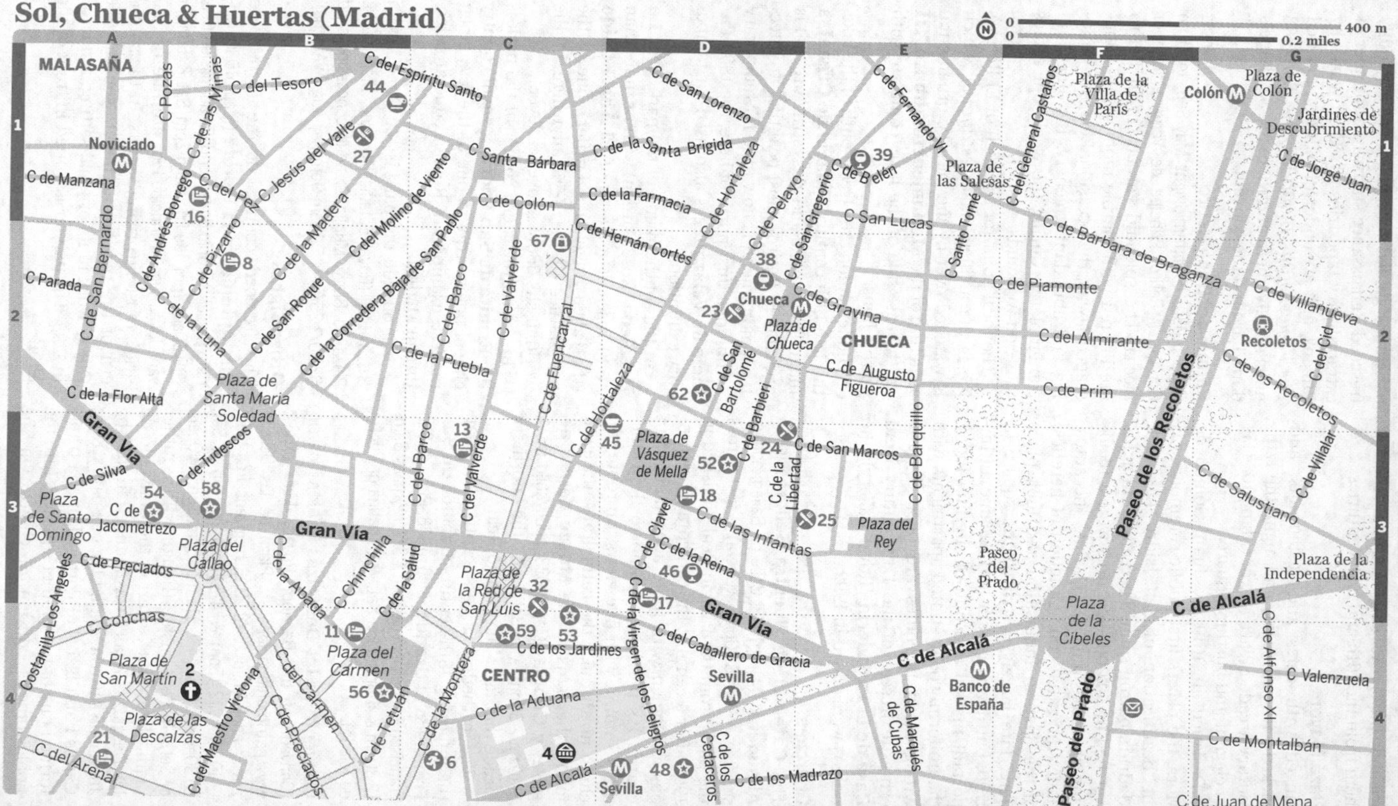

0 400 m
0 0.2 miles
A B C D E F G
1 2 3 4
MALASAÑA
Noviciado
C de Manzana
C Pozas
C de las Minas
C del Tesoro
C del Espíritu Santo
44
27
C Jesús del Valle
C del Pez
16
C de Andrés Borrego
C de San Bernardo
C Parada
C de Pizarro
8
C de la Madera
C del Molino de Viento
C de la Corredera Baja de San Pablo
C de San Roque
C de la Luna
C de la Flor Alta
Plaza de Santa Maria Soledad
Gran Vía
C de Tudescos
C de Silva
Plaza de Santo Domingo
54
C de Jacometrezo
58
Plaza del Callao
C de Preciados
Costanilla Los Angeles
C Conchas
Plaza de San Martín
2
Plaza de las Descalzas
21
C del Arenal
C del Maestro Victoria
C del Carmen
C de Preciados
C de la Abada
C Chinchilla
C de la Salud
11
Plaza del Carmen
56
C de Tetuán
C de la Montera
6
C Santa Bárbara
C de Colón
C del Barco
C de Valverde
67
C de la Puebla
13
C del Barco
C del Valverde
C de Fuencarral
Plaza de la Red de San Luis
32
59
53
C de los Jardines
CENTRO
C de la Aduana
4
C de Alcalá
Sevilla
C de San Lorenzo
C de la Santa Brigida
C de la Farmacia
C de Hernán Cortés
C de Hortaleza
45
Plaza de Vásquez de Mella
18
C de Clavel
C de la Reina
46
17
C de la Virgen de los Peligros
48
C de los Cedaceros
C de los Madrazo
C del Caballero de Gracia
Sevilla
C de Hortaleza
C de Pelayo
C de San Gregorio
38
Chueca
23
Plaza de Chueca
C de Gravina
C de San Bartolomé
62
C de Barbieri
52
24
C de la Libertad
25
C de las Infantas
C de San Marcos
CHUECA
C de Augusto Figueroa
C de Belén
39
C San Lucas
C de Fernando VI
C Santo Tomé
Plaza de las Salesas
C del General Castaños
C de Piamonte
C del Almirante
C de Prim
C de Barquillo
Plaza del Rey
C de Marqués de Cubas
Banco de España
Paseo del Prado
C de Bárbara de Braganza
Plaza de la Villa de París
Colón
Plaza de Colón
Jardines de Descubrimiento
C de Jorge Juan
C de Villanueva
Recoletos
C del Cid
C de los Recoletos
Paseo de los Recoletos
C de Villalar
C de Salustiano
Plaza de la Independencia
Plaza de la Cibeles
C de Alcalá
C de Alfonso XI
C Valenzuela
Paseo del Prado
C de Montalbán
C de Juan de Mena

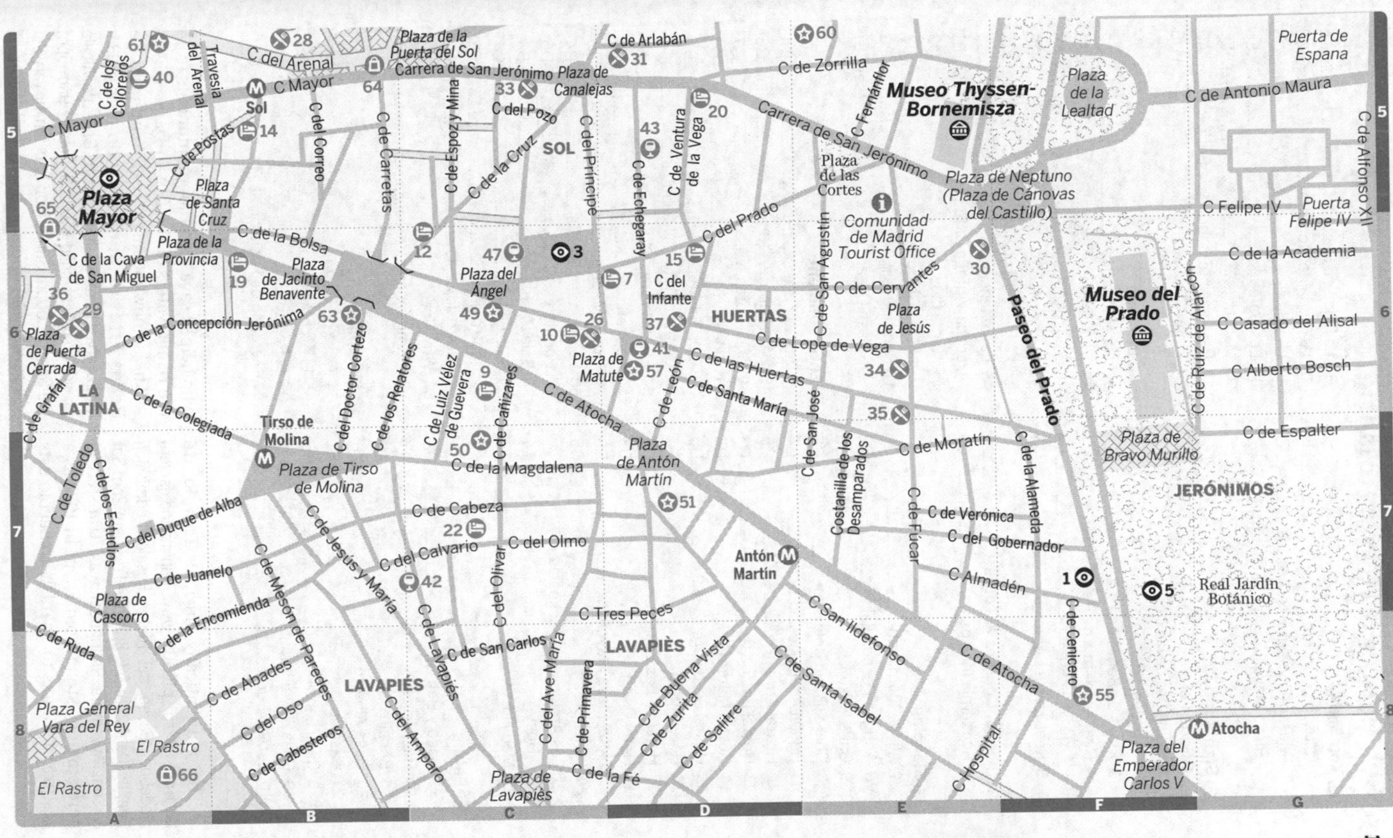
Plaza Mayor
C Mayor
C de los Coloreros
Travesia del Arenal
C del Arenal
Sol
C de Postas
Plaza de Santa Cruz
Plaza de la Provincia
C de la Cava de San Miguel
Plaza de Puerta Cerrada
LA LATINA
C de Grafal
C de Toledo
C de los Estudios
C de la Concepción Jerónima
C de la Colegiada
C del Duque de Alba
C de Juanelo
Plaza de Cascorro
C de la Encomienda
C de Ruda
Plaza General Vara del Rey
El Rastro
El Rastro
C de Abades
C del Oso
C de Cabesteros
C de Mesón de Paredes
LAVAPIÉS
C del Amparo
Plaza de la Puerta del Sol
Carrera de San Jerónimo
Plaza de Canalejas
C del Correo
C de Carretas
C de Espoz y Mina
C del Pozo
C de la Cruz
SOL
C de la Bolsa
Plaza de Jacinto Benavente
Plaza del Ángel
C del Doctor Cortezo
C de los Relatores
C de Luiz Vélez de Guevera
C de Cañizares
Tirso de Molina
Plaza de Tirso de Molina
C de la Magdalena
C de Cabeza
C del Calvario
C de Jesús y María
C del Olmo
C del Olivar
C de Lavapiés
C de San Carlos
C Tres Peces
LAVAPIÈS
C del Ave María
C de Primavera
C de Buena Vista
C de Zurita
C de Salitre
Plaza de Lavapiès
C de la Fé
C de Arlabán
C del Príncipe
C de Echegaray
C de Ventura de la Vega
C del Prado
C del Infante
HUERTAS
Plaza de Matute
C de León
C de Atocha
C de las Huertas
C de Santa María
Plaza de Antón Martín
Antón Martín
C de Zorrilla
C Fernanflor
Carrera de San Jerónimo
Plaza de las Cortes
C de San Agustín
Comunidad de Madrid Tourist Office
C de Cervantes
Plaza de Jesús
C de Lope de Vega
C de San José
Costanilla de los Desamparados
C de Fúcar
C de Moratín
C de la Alameda
C de Verónica
C del Gobernador
C Almadén
C San Ildefonso
C de Santa Isabel
C Hospital
C de Atocha
C de Cenicero
Museo Thyssen-Bornemisza
Plaza de la Lealtad
Plaza de Neptuno (Plaza de Cánovas del Castillo)
Paseo del Prado
Museo del Prado
C de Ruiz de Alarcón
Plaza de Bravo Murillo
JERÓNIMOS
Real Jardín Botánico
Atocha
Plaza del Emperador Carlos V
Puerta de Espana
C de Antonio Maura
C de Alfonso XII
C Felipe IV
Puerta Felipe IV
C de la Academia
C Casado del Alisal
C Alberto Bosch
C de Espalter
A
B
C
D
E
F
G
5
6
7
8

Sol, Chueca & Huertas (Madrid)

Top Sights

Museo del Prado ... F6
Museo Thyssen-Bornemisza ... E5
Plaza Mayor ... A5

Sights

1 Caixa Forum ... F7
2 Convento de las Descalzas Reales ... A4
3 Plaza de Santa Ana ... C6
4 Real Academia de Bellas Artes de San Fernando ... C4
5 Real Jardín Botánico ... F7

Activities, Courses & Tours

6 Academia Inhispania ... C4

Sleeping

7 Alicia Room Mate ... D6
8 Antigua Posada del Pez ... B2
9 Cat's Hostel ... C6
10 Chic & Basic Colors ... C6
11 Hostal Acapulco ... B4
12 Hostal Adriano ... C6
13 Hostal La Zona ... C3
14 Hostal Madrid ... B5
15 Hostal Sardinero ... D6
16 Hotel Abalú ... A1
17 Hotel de Las Letras ... D3
18 Hotel Óscar ... D3
19 Hotel Plaza Mayor ... B6
20 Hotel Urban ... D5
21 Los Amigos Sol Backpackers' Hostel ... A4
22 Mad Hostel ... C7

Eating

23 Baco y Beto ... D2
24 Bazaar ... D3
25 Bocaito ... E3
26 Casa Alberto ... C6
27 Casa Julio ... B1
28 Casa Labra ... B5
29 Casa Revuelta ... A6
30 Estado Puro ... E6
31 La Finca de Susana ... D5
32 La Gloria de Montera ... C3
33 Lhardy ... C5
34 Los Gatos ... E6
35 Maceiras ... E6
36 Restaurante Sobrino de Botín ... A6
37 Vinos González ... D6

Drinking

38 Café Acuarela ... D2
39 Café Belén ... E1
40 Chocolatería de San Ginés ... A5
41 El Imperfecto ... D6
42 La Escalera de Jacob ... C7
43 La Venencia ... D5
44 Lolina Vintage Café ... B1
45 Mamá Inés ... D3
46 Museo Chicote ... D3
47 Penthouse ... C6
Splash Óscar ... (see 18)

Entertainment

48 Adraba ... D4
49 Café Central ... C6
50 Casa Patas ... C7
51 Cine Doré ... D7
52 Club 54 Studio ... D3
53 Costello Café & Niteclub ... C4
54 El Berlín Jazz Club ... A3
55 Kapital ... F8
Liquid Madrid ... (see 52)
56 Localidades Galicia ... B4
57 Popular ... D6
58 Sala Bash/Ohm ... B3
59 Sala El Sol ... C4
60 Teatro de la Zarzuela ... E5
61 Teatro Joy Eslava ... A5
62 Why Not? ... D2
63 Yelmo Cineplex Ideal ... B6

Shopping

64 Casa de Diego ... B5
65 El Arco Artesanía ... A5
66 El Rastro ... A8
67 Mercado de Fuencarral ... C2

SPAIN MADRID

The authentically ancient **Templo de Debod** (Map p1030; www.munimadrid.es/templodebod; Paseo del Pintor Rosales; admission free; ⏲10am-2pm & 6-8pm Tue-Fri, 10am-2pm Sat & Sun; Ⓜ Ventura Rodríguez) was transferred here stone by stone from Egypt in 1972 as a gesture of thanks to Spanish archaeologists who helped save Egyptian monuments from the rising waters of the Aswan Dam.

The somewhat fusty **Real Academia de Bellas Artes de San Fernando** (Map p1034; http://rabasf.insde.es, in Spanish; Calle de Alcalá 13; adult/student/child €3/1.50/free; ⏲9am-5pm Tue-Sat, to 2.30pm Sun & Mon Sep-Jun, hr vary Jul & Aug; Ⓜ Sevilla) offers a broad collection of

WANT MORE?

For in-depth information, reviews and recommendations at your fingertips, head to the Apple App Store to purchase Lonely Planet's *Madrid City Guide* iPhone app.

Alternatively, head to **Lonely Planet** (www.lonelyplanet.com/spain/madrid) for planning advice, author recommendations, traveller reviews and insider tips.

old and modern masters, including works by Zurbarán, El Greco, Rubens, Tintoretto, Goya, Sorolla and Juan Gris.

Madrid also some lovely public squares, among them **Plaza de Oriente** (Map p1038; MÓpera), **Plaza de la Villa** (Map p1038; MÓpera or Sol), **Plaza de la Paja** (Map p1038; MLa Latina) and **Plaza de Santa Ana** (Map p1034; MSol, Sevilla or Antón Martín).

Courses

There's no shortage of places to learn Spanish in Madrid.

Academia Inhispania LANGUAGE SCHOOL
(Map p1034; www.inhispania.com; Calle de la Montera 10-12; MSol)

Academia Madrid Plus LANGUAGE SCHOOL
(Map p1038; www.madridplus.es; 6th fl, Calle del Arenal 21; MÓpera)

Tours

The Centro de Turismo de Madrid offers **Descubre Madrid** (Discover Madrid; ☎91 588 29 06; www.esmadrid.com/descubremadrid; walking tours adult/concession €3.90/3.12, bus tours €6.45/5.05, bicycle tours €3.90/3.12 plus €6 bike rental), with dozens of guided walking, cycling and bus itineraries.

Festivals & Events

Madrid's social calendar is packed with festivals and special events. Major holidays and festivals:

Fiesta de San Isidro CITY FESTIVAL
Street parties, parades, bullfights and other fun events honour Madrid's patron saint on and around 15 May.

Veranos de la Villa SUMMER FESTIVAL
Madrid's town hall stages a series of cultural events, shows and exhibitions known as Summers in the City, in July and August.

Suma Flamenca FLAMENCO
A soul-filled flamenco festival that draws some of the biggest names in the genre to the Teatros del Canal in May or June.

Sleeping

Madrid has high-quality accommodation across all price ranges. Where you decide to stay will play an important role in your experience of Madrid. Los Austrias, Sol and Centro put you in the heart of the busy downtown area, while La Latina (the best *barrio* for tapas), Lavapiés and Huertas (good for nightlife) are ideal for those who love Madrid nights and don't want to stagger too far to get back to their hotel. You don't have to be gay to stay in Chueca, but you'll love it if you are, while Malasaña is another inner-city *barrio* with great restaurants and bars.

LOS AUSTRIAS, SOL & CENTRO

TOP CHOICE **Hotel Meninas** BOUTIQUE HOTEL €€
(Map p1038; ☎91 541 28 05; www.hotelmeninas.com; Calle de Campomanes 7; s/d from €109/129; MÓpera; ❄📶) Inside a refurbished 19th-century mansion, the Meninas combines old-world comfort with modern, minimalist style. The colour scheme is blacks, whites and greys, with dark-wood floors and splashes of fuchsia and lime-green.

TOP CHOICE **Cat's Hostel** HOSTEL €
(Map p1034; ☎91 369 28 07; www.catshostel.com; Calle de Cañizares 6; dm/d from €15/42; MAntón Martín; ❄@) Forming part of a 17th-century palace, the internal courtyard here is Madrid's finest – lavish Andalucian tilework, a fountain, a spectacular glass ceiling and stunning Islamic decoration, surrounded on four sides by an open balcony. There's a super-cool basement bar with free internet connections and fiestas, often with live music.

Hostal Madrid BUDGET HOTEL, APARTMENTS €
(Map p1034; ☎91 522 00 60; www.hostal-madrid.info; 2nd fl, Calle de Esparteros 6; s €40-60, d €50-78, apt €60-150; MSol) Nineteen excellent apartments here range in size from 33 sq metres to 200 sq metres, each with a fully equipped kitchen, sitting area, bathroom and, in some, an expansive terrace with good rooftop views. The double *hostal* (budget hotel) rooms are comfortable and well-sized, and the service is extremely friendly.

Mad Hostel HOSTEL €
(Map p1034; ☎91 506 48 40; www.madhostel.com; Calle de Cabeza 24; dm from €15; MAntón

La Latina & Los Austrias (Madrid)

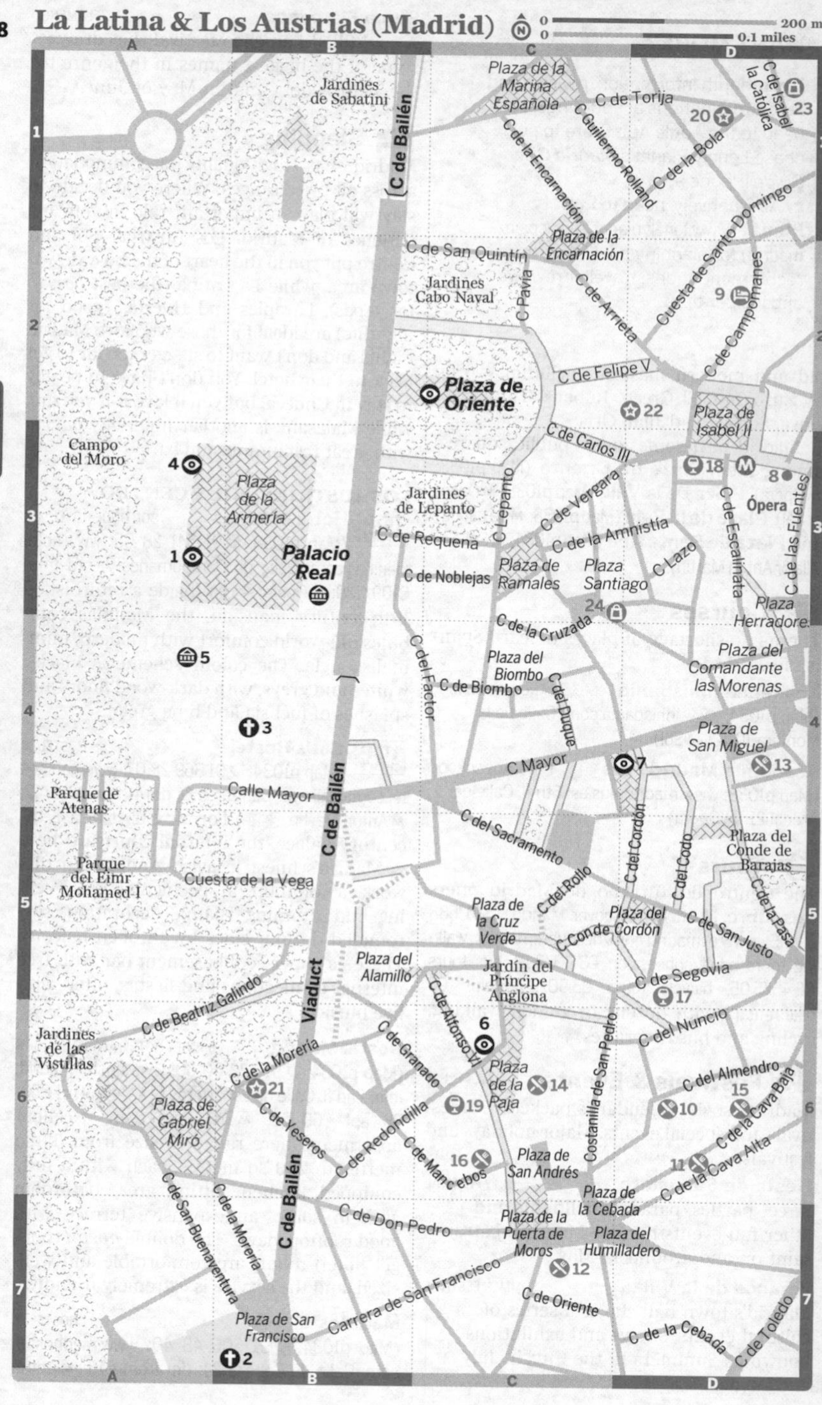

La Latina & Los Austrias (Madrid)

Martín; ❄@) From the same people who brought you Cat's Hostel, Mad Hostel is less distinguished architecturally but a similar deal. The 1st-floor courtyard – with retractable roof – is a wonderful place to chill, while the four- to eight-bed rooms are smallish but new and clean. There's a small rooftop gym equipped with state-of-the-art equipment.

Hotel Plaza Mayor HOTEL €€
(Map p1034; ☎91 360 06 06; www.h-plazamayor.com; Calle de Atocha 2; s/d from €50/60; MSol or Tirso de Molina; ❄) Stylish decor, charming original elements of a 150-year-old building and helpful staff are selling points here. The rooms are attractive, some with a light colour scheme and wrought-iron furniture. The attic rooms have great views.

Los Amigos Sol Backpackers' Hostel HOSTEL €
(Map p1034; ☎91 559 24 72; www.losamigoshostel.com; 4th fl, Calle de Arenal 26; dm €17-20; MÓpera or Sol; @) If you arrive in Madrid keen for company, this could be the place for you – lots of students stay here, the staff are savvy (and speak English) and there are bright dorm-style rooms (with free lockers). Prices include breakfast and there's a kitchen for use by guests.

Hostal Acapulco BUDGET HOTEL €
(Map p1034; ☎91 531 19 45; www.hostalacapulco.com; Calle de la Salud 13; s/d/tr €52/62/79; MGran Vía; ❄☁) This immaculate little *hostal* has marble floors, renovated bathrooms, double-glazed windows and comfortable beds. Street-facing rooms have balconies overlooking sunny Plaza del Carmen.

Hotel de Las Letras HOTEL €€
(Map p1034; ☎91 523 79 80; www.hoteldelasletras.com; Gran Vía 11; d from €100; MGran Via) Hotel de las Letras started the rooftop hotel-bar trend in Madrid. The bar's wonderful, but the whole hotel is excellent with individually styled rooms, each with literary quotes scribbled on the walls.

HUERTAS & ATOCHA

TOP CHOICE **Alicia Room Mate** BOUTIQUE HOTEL €€
(Map p1034; ☎91 389 60 95; www.room-matehoteles.com; Calle del Prado 2; d €105-165; MSol, Sevilla or Antón Martín; ❄☁) With beautiful, spacious rooms, Alicia overlooks Plaza de Santa Ana. It has an ultra-modern look and the downstairs bar is oh-so-cool.

Hotel Urban LUXURY HOTEL €€€
(Map p1034; ☎91 787 77 70; www.derbyhotels.com; Carrera de San Jerónimo 34; d from €190; MSevilla; ❄☁☐) The towering glass edifice of Hotel Urban is the epitome of art-inspired designer

cool. Dark-wood floors and dark walls are offset by plenty of light, while the bathrooms have wonderful designer fittings. The rooftop swimming pool is Madrid's best.

Hostal Sardinero BUDGET HOTEL €
(Map p1034; ☎91 429 57 56; www.hostalsardinero.com; Calle del Prado 16; s/d from €42/50; Ⓜ Sol or Antón Martín; ❄) A change of owners here has brought more than just a fresh lick of paint, new mattresses and new TVs. The cheerful rooms, which have high ceilings, air-conditioning, a safe, hairdryer and renovated bathroom, are complemented nicely by the equally cheerful Nieves and Jimmy who are attentive without being in your face.

Chic & Basic Colors BUDGET HOTEL €€
(Map p1034; ☎91 429 69 35; www.chicandbasic.com; 2nd fl, Calle de las Huertas 14; s/d/apt from €62/78/96; Ⓜ Antón Martín; ❄ 📶 ✉) It's all about colours here at this fine little *hostal*. The rooms are white in a minimalist style with free internet, flat-screen TVs, dark hardwood floors with a bright colour scheme superimposed on top, with every room a different shade. It's all very comfortable, contemporary and casual.

Hostal Adriano BUDGET HOTEL €
(Map p1034; ☎91 521 13 39; www.hostaladriano.com; 4th fl, Calle de la Cruz 26; s/d/tr €53/65/85; Ⓜ Sol) They don't come any better than this bright and cheerful *hostal* wedged in the streets that mark the boundary between Sol and Huertas. Most rooms are well sized and each has its own colour scheme.

MALASAÑA & CHUECA

TOP CHOICE **Hotel Óscar** BOUTIQUE HOTEL €€
(Map p1034; ☎91 701 11 73; www.room-matehoteles.com; Plaza de Vázquez de Mella 12; d €90-200; Ⓜ Gran Vía; ❄ 📶 ✉) Simply outstanding, Hotel Óscar's designer rooms ooze style and sophistication. Some have floor-to-ceiling murals, the lighting is always funky and the colour scheme is awash with pinks, lime-greens, oranges or a more minimalist black-and-white. The facade – with thousands of hanging Coca-Cola bottles – is a striking local landmark; there's a fine street-level tapas bar and a rooftop terrace.

TOP CHOICE **Antigua Posada del Pez** HOSTEL €€
(Map p1034; ☎91 531 42 96; www.antiguaposadadelpez.com; Calle de Pizarro 16; s €40-120, d €50-150; Ⓜ Noviciado) This place inhabits the shell of a historic Malasaña building, but the rooms are slick and contemporary with designer bathrooms. You're also just a few steps up the hill from Calle del Pez, one of Malasaña's most happening streets. It's an exceptionally good deal, even when prices head upwards.

Hotel Abalú BOUTIQUE HOTEL €€
(Map p1034; ☎91 531 47 44; www.hotelabalu.com; Calle del Pez 19; s/d/ste from €74/90/140; Ⓜ Noviciado; ❄ 📶) Hotel Abalú is an oasis of style amid Malasaña's time-worn feel. Each room has its own design drawn from the imagination of Luis Delgado, from retro chintz to Zen, baroque to pure white, and most aesthetics in between. Some of the suites have jacuzzis and large-screen home cinemas.

Hostal La Zona HOSTEL €
(Map p1034; ☎91 521 99 04; www.hostallazona.com; 1st fl, Calle de Valverde 7; s/d/tr €50/60/85; Ⓜ Gran Vía; ❄ 📶) Catering primarily to a gay clientele, the stylish Hostal La Zona has exposed brickwork, wooden pillars and a subtle colour scheme. Other highlights include free internet, helpful staff and air-conditioning/heating in every room.

Albergue Juvenil HOSTEL €
(Map p1030; ☎91 593 96 88; www.ajmadrid.es; Calle de Mejía Lequerica 21; dm €19-25; Ⓜ Bilbao or Alonso Martínez; ❄ 📶) The Albergue's dorms are spotless, no dorm houses more than six beds (and each has its own bathroom), and facilities include a pool table, a gym, wheelchair access, free internet, laundry and a TV/DVD room.

Eating

It's possible to find just about any kind of cuisine and eatery in Madrid, from ageless traditional to trendy fusion. Madrid is a focal point of cooking from around the country and is particularly attached to seafood; despite not having a sea, Madrid has the world's second-largest fish market (after Tokyo).

From the chaotic tapas bars of La Latina to countless neighbourhood favourites, you'll have no trouble tracking down specialities like *cochinillo asado* (roast suckling pig) or *cocido madrileño* (a hearty stew made of beans and various animals' innards).

LOS AUSTRIAS, SOL & CENTRO

TOP CHOICE **Mercado de San Miguel** FOOD MARKET €€
(Map p1038; www.casinodemadrid.es; Plaza de San Miguel; meals €15-35; ⏲10am-midnight Sun-Wed, to 2am Thu-Sat; Ⓜ Sol) One of Madrid's oldest and most beautiful markets, the Mercado de

San Miguel has undergone a stunning major renovation and bills itself as a 'culinary cultural centre'. Within the early-20th-century glass walls, the market has become an inviting space strewn with tables (difficult to nab) where you can enjoy the freshest food or a drink. Apart from the fresh fish corner, you can order tapas at most of the counter bars.

Restaurante Sobrino de Botín TRADITIONAL SPANISH €€
(Map p1034; ☎91 366 42 17; www.botin.es; Calle de los Cuchilleros 17; meals €40-45; Ⓜ La Latina or Sol) It's not every day that you can eat in the oldest restaurant in the world (1725), which also appears in many novels about Madrid, most notably Hemingway's *The Sun Also Rises*. The secret of its staying power is fine *cochinillo* (suckling pig; €22.90) and *cordero asado* (roast lamb; €22.90) cooked in wood-fired ovens. Eating in the vaulted cellar is a treat.

La Gloria de Montera SPANISH €€
(Map p1034; Calle del Caballero de Gracia 10; meals €25-30; Ⓜ Gran Vía) Minimalist style, tasty Mediterranean dishes and great prices mean that you'll probably have to wait in line (no reservations taken) to eat here.

LA LATINA & LAVAPIÉS

This area is best known for its tapas bars; see the boxed text, p1042.

TOP CHOICE **Naïa Restaurante** FUSION €€
(Map p1038; ☎91 366 27 83; www.naiarestaurante.com, in Spanish; Plaza de la Paja 3; meals €30-35; ⌚lunch & dinner Tue-Sun; Ⓜ La Latina) On the lovely Plaza de la Paja, Naïa has a real buzz about it, with a cooking laboratory overseen by Carlos López Reyes, delightful modern Spanish food and a chill-out lounge downstairs. The emphasis throughout is on natural ingredients, healthy cooking and exciting tastes.

TOP CHOICE **Viva La Vida** VEGETARIAN €
(Map p1038; www.vivalavida.vg; Costanilla de San Andrés 16; veg buffet €2.10 per 100g; ⌚noon-midnight; Ⓜ La Latina; ✍) This organic food shop has as its centrepiece an enticing vegetarian buffet with hot and cold food that's always filled with flavour. On the cusp of Plaza de la Paja, it's a great place at any time of the day, especially outside normal Spanish eating hours.

Casa Lucio TRADITIONAL SPANISH €€
(Map p1038; ☎91 365 32 52; www.casalucio.es, in Spanish; Calle de la Cava Baja 35; meals €45-50; ⌚lunch & dinner Sun-Fri, dinner Sat, closed Aug; Ⓜ La Latina) Lucio has been wowing *madrileños* with his light touch, quality ingredients and home-style local cooking for ages – think seafood, roasted meats and eggs (a Lucio speciality) in abundance.

HUERTAS & ATOCHA

TOP CHOICE **Vinos González** TAPAS, DELICATESSEN €€
(Map p1034; Calle de León 12; meals €20-25; ⌚9am-midnight Tue-Thu, to 1am Fri & Sat; Ⓜ Antón Martín) Ever dreamed of a deli where you could choose a tasty morsel and sit down and eat it right there? Well, here you can. On offer are a tempting array of cheeses, cured meats and other typically Spanish delicacies.

TOP CHOICE **Casa Alberto** TRADITIONAL SPANISH €€
(Map p1034; ☎91 429 93 56; www.casaalberto.es, in Spanish; Calle de las Huertas 18; meals €25-30; ⌚noon-1.30am Tue-Sat, to 4pm Sun; Ⓜ Antón Martín) One of the most atmospheric old *tabernas* of Madrid, Casa Alberto has been around since 1827. The secret to its staying power is vermouth on tap, excellent tapas and fine sit-down meals; *rabo de toro* (bull's tail) is a good order.

Maceiras GALICIAN €€
(Map p1034; Calle de las Huertas 66; meals €20-30; Ⓜ Antón Martín) Galician tapas (think octopus, green peppers etc) never tasted so good as in this agreeably rustic bar down the bottom of the Huertas hill, especially when washed down with a crisp white Ribeiro.

Lhardy TRADITIONAL SPANISH €€€
(Map p1034; ☎91 521 33 85; www.lhardy.com; Carrera de San Jerónimo 8; meals €60-70; ⌚lunch & dinner Mon-Sat, lunch Sun, closed Aug; Ⓜ Sol or Sevilla) This Madrid landmark (since 1839) is an elegant treasure trove of takeaway gourmet tapas. Upstairs is the upscale preserve of house specialities such as pheasant in grape juice and lemon soufflé. It's expensive, but the quality and service are unimpeachable.

La Finca de Susana MEDITERRANEAN €€
(Map p1034; www.lafinca-restaurant.com; Calle de Arlabán 4; meals €20-25; Ⓜ Sevilla) It's difficult to find a better combination of price, quality cooking and classy atmosphere anywhere in Huertas. The softly lit dining area is bathed in greenery and the sometimes innovative, sometimes traditional food draws a hip young crowd. It doesn't take reservations.

MALASAÑA & CHUECA

TOP CHOICE **La Musa** SPANISH FUSION €€
(Map p1030; www.lamusa.com.es; Calle de Manuela Malasaña 18; meals €25-30; ⌚9am-1.30am

A TAPAS TOUR OF MADRID

Madrid's home of tapas is La Latina, especially along Calle de la Cava Baja and the surrounding streets. **Almendro 13** (Map p1038; Calle del Almendro 13; meals €15-20; MLa Latina) is famous for quality rather than frilly elaborations, with cured meats, cheeses, tortillas and *huevos rotos* (literally, 'broken eggs') the house specialities. Down on Calle de la Cava Baja, **Txacolina** (Map p1038; Calle de la Cava Baja 26; meals €15-20; lunch & dinner Sat, dinner Mon & Wed-Fri; MLa Latina) does some of the biggest *pintxos* (Basque tapas) you'll find. Not far away, **Juanalaloca** (Map p1038; Plaza de la Puerta de Moros 4; meals €25-35; lunch & dinner Tue-Sun, dinner Mon; MLa Latina) does a magnificent *tortilla de patatas* (potato and onion omelette).

In the centre, for *bacalao* (cod) the historic **Casa Labra** (Map p1034; Calle de Tetuán 11; meals €15-20; 11am-3.30pm & 6-11pm; MSol) and **Casa Revuelta** (Map p1034; Calle de Latoneros 3; meals €15-20; 10.30am-4pm & 7-11pm Mon & Wed-Sat, 10.30am-4pm Sun, closed Aug; MLa Latina or Sol) have no peers.

Down the bottom of the Huertas hill, **Los Gatos** (Map p1034; Calle de Jesús 2; meals €25-30; noon-1am Sun-Thu, to 2am Fri & Sat; MAntón Martín) has eclectic decor and terrific canapés. Nearby, along the Paseo del Prado, there's super-cool **Estado Puro** (Map p1034; www.tapasenestadopuro.com, in Spanish; Plaza de Cánovas del Castillo 4; tapas €1.95-9.50; 11am-1am Tue-Sat, to 4pm Sun; MBanco de España or Atocha) with gourmet tapas inspired by Catalonia's world-famous El Bulli restaurant. In Salamanca, **Biotza** (Map p1030; Calle de Claudio Coello 27; 9am-midnight Mon-Thu, to 1am Fri & Sat; MSerrano) offers creative Basque *pintxos* in stylish surrounds.

Chueca is another stellar tapas *barrio*. Don't miss **Bocaito** (Map p1034; Calle de la Libertad 4-6; meals €20-25; lunch & dinner Mon-Fri, dinner Sat; MChueca), another purveyor of Andalucian *jamón* (ham) and seafood. **Casa Julio** (Map p1034; Calle de la Madera 37; meals €10-15; lunch & dinner Mon-Sat; MTribunal) is widely touted as the home of Madrid's best *croquetas* (croquettes). Another brilliant choice is **Baco y Beto** (Map p1034; www.bacoybeto.com, in Spanish; Calle de Pelayo 24; meals €20-25; lunch & dinner Fri & Sat, dinner Mon-Thu; MChueca).

Sun-Thu, to 2.30am Fri & Sat; MSan Bernardo) Snug yet loud, a favourite of Madrid's hip young crowd yet utterly unpretentious, La Musa is all about designer decor, lounge music on the sound system and food (breakfast, lunch or dinner) that is always fun and filled with flavour. The menu is divided into three types of tapas – hot, cold and BBQ.

TOP CHOICE Bazaar MODERN SPANISH €€
(Map p1034; www.restaurantbazaar.com; Calle de la Libertad 21; meals €20-25; MChueca) Bazaar's popularity among the well-heeled and often-famous shows no sign of abating. Its pristine white interior design with theatre lighting may draw a crowd that looks like it stepped out of the pages of *Hola!* magazine, but the food is extremely well priced and innovative. No reservations.

Nina MODERN SPANISH €€
(Map p1030; 91 591 00 46; Calle de Manuela Malasaña 10; meals €30-40; MBilbao) Sophisticated, intimate and wildly popular, Nina has an extensive menu (available in English) of nouvelle Mediterranean cuisine that doesn't miss a trick. We like the decor, all exposed brick and subtle lighting, we love just about everything on the menu, but we adore the honey-and-*sobrasada*-sausage-glazed grilled ostrich steak with a salmon and raspberry crust.

La Isla del Tesoro VEGETARIAN €€
(Map p1030; 91 593 14 40; www.isladeltesoro.net; Calle de Manuela Malasaña 3; meals €30-40; MBilbao;) La Isla del Tesoro is loaded with quirky charm – the dining area is like someone's fantasy of a secret garden come to life. The cooking here is assured and wide-ranging in its influences; the jungle burger is typical in a menu that's full of surprises.

SALAMANCA

Sula Madrid SPANISH FUSION €€€
(Map p1030; 91 781 61 97; www.sula.es; Calle de Jorge Juan 33; meals €60-70; lunch & dinner Mon-Sat; MVelázquez) A gastronomic temple that combines stellar cooking with clean-lined sophistication, Sula Madrid – a gourmet food store, super-stylish tapas bar and top-notch restaurant all rolled into one – is

one of our favourite top-end restaurants in Madrid. It serves a range of Mediterranean dishes – some traditional, some with the most creative of twists – that you won't find anywhere else.

 Drinking

Madrid lives life on its streets and plazas, and bar-hopping is a pastime enjoyed by young and old alike. If you're after the more traditional, with tiled walls and flamenco tunes, head to Huertas. For gay-friendly drinking holes, Chueca is the place. Malasaña caters to a grungy, funky crowd, while La Latina has friendly bars that guarantee atmosphere most nights of the week. In summer, the terrace bars that pop up all over the city are unbeatable.

The bulk of Madrid bars open to 2am Sunday to Thursday, and to 3am or 3.30am Friday and Saturday.

LOS AUSTRIAS & CENTRO

TOP CHOICE **Museo Chicote** COCKTAIL BAR
(Map p1034; www.museo-chicote.com; Gran Vía 12; ⏲6pm-3am Mon-Thu, to 3.30am Fri & Sat; MGran Vía) The founder of this Madrid landmark is said to have invented more than a hundred cocktails, which the likes of Hemingway, Ava Gardner, Grace Kelly, Sophia Loren and Frank Sinatra all enjoyed at one time or another. It's at its best after midnight when a lounge atmosphere takes over, couples cuddle on the curved benches and some of the city's best DJs do their stuff.

Café del Real BAR-CAFE
(Map p1038; Plaza de Isabel II 2; ⏲9am-1am Mon-Thu, to 3am Fri & Sat; MÓpera) One of the nicest bar-cafes in central Madrid, this place serves a rich variety of creative coffees and a few cocktails to a soundtrack of chill-out music. The best seats are upstairs, where the low ceilings, wooden beams and leather chairs make a great place to pass an afternoon.

MADRID'S FAVOURITE POSTCLUBBING MUNCHIES

Chocolatería de San Ginés (Map p1034; Pasadizo de San Ginés 5; ⏲9.30am-7am Mon-Fri, 9am-7am Fri & Sat; MSol) Join the sugar-searching throngs who end the night at this legendary bar, famous for its freshly fried *churros* (fried sticks of dough) and syrupy hot chocolate.

LA LATINA & LAVAPIÉS

Delic BAR-CAFE
(Map p1038; Costanilla de San Andrés 14; ⏲11am-2am Sun & Tue-Thu, 7pm-2am Mon, 11am-2.30am Fri & Sat; MLa Latina) We could go on for hours about this long-standing cafe-bar, but we'll reduce it to its most basic elements: nursing an exceptionally good mojito (€8) or three on a warm summer's evening at Delic's outdoor tables on one of Madrid's prettiest plazas is one of life's great pleasures.

La Escalera de Jacob COCKTAIL BAR
(Map p1034; Calle de Lavapiés 11; ⏲6pm-2am; MAntón Martín or Tirso de Molina) With magicians, storytellers, children's theatre (on Saturdays and Sundays at noon) and live jazz and other musical genres, 'Jacob's Ladder' is one of Madrid's most original bars. And regardless of what's on, it's worth stopping by here for creative cocktails that you won't find anywhere else.

Café del Nuncio BAR-CAFE
(Map p1030; Calle de Segovia 9; ⏲noon-2am Sun-Thu, to 3am Fri & Sat; MLa Latina) Café del Nuncio straggles down a stairway passage to Calle de Segovia. You can drink on one of several cosy levels inside or, better still in summer, enjoy the outdoor seating that one local reviewer likened to a slice of Rome.

HUERTAS & ATOCHA

TOP CHOICE **Penthouse** COCKTAIL BAR
(Map p1034; 7th fl, Plaza de Santa Ana 14; ⏲9pm-1.30am Mon-Wed, to 2am Thu, to 2.30am Fri & Sat, 5pm-1.30am Sun; MAntón Martín or Sol) High above the Plaza de Santa Ana, this sybaritic rooftop cocktail bar has terrific views over Madrid's rooftops. It's a place for sophisticates, with chill-out areas strewn with cushions, funky DJs and a dress policy designed to sort out the classy from the wannabes.

TOP CHOICE **La Venencia** WINE BAR
(Map p1034; Calle de Echegaray 7; ⏲1-3.30pm & 7.30pm-1.30am; MSol) This is how sherry bars should be – old-world, drinks poured straight from the dusty wooden barrels and none of the frenetic activity for which Huertas is famous. La Venencia is a *barrio* classic, with fine sherry from Sanlúcar and *manzanilla* from Jeréz.

El Imperfecto BAR
(Map p1034; Plaza de Matute 2; ⏲3pm-2am Sun-Thu, to 3am Fri & Sat; MAntón Martín) Its name notwithstanding, the 'Imperfect One' is our ideal Huertas bar, with live jazz most

Tuesdays at 9pm and a drinks menu as long as a saxophone, ranging from cocktails (€6.50) and spirits to milkshakes, teas and creative coffees.

MALASAÑA & CHUECA

TOP CHOICE **Café Comercial** CAFE
(Map p1030; Glorieta de Bilbao 7; 7.30am-midnight Mon, to 1am Tue-Thu, to 2am Fri, 8.30am-2am Sat, 9am-midnight Sun; M Bilbao) This glorious old Madrid cafe proudly fights a rearguard action against progress with heavy leather seats, abundant marble and old-style waiters. As close as Madrid came to the intellectual cafes of Paris' Left Bank, Café Comercial now has a clientele that has broadened to include just about anyone.

Splash Óscar BAR
(Map p1034; Plaza de Vázquez de Mella 12; 4.30pm-12.30am; M Gran Vía) Another of Madrid's stunning rooftop terraces (although this one with a small swimming pool), atop Hotel Óscar, this chilled space with gorgeous skyline views has become a cause célèbre among A-list celebrities.

Kabokla BAR
(www.kabokla.es, in Spanish; Calle de San Vicente Ferrer 55; 10pm-1am Tue-Thu, 6pm-3am Fri, 2.30-6.30pm & 10.30pm-3.30am Sat, 2.30pm-10pm Sun; M Noviciado) Run by Brazilians and dedicated to all things Brazilian, Kabokla is terrific. When there's no live music, the DJ gets the crowd dancing. It also serves Madrid's smoothest caipirinhas.

El Jardín Secreto BAR
(Map p1030; Calle del Conde Duque 2; 5.30pm-12.30am Sun-Thu & Sun, 6.30pm-2.30am Fri & Sat; M Plaza de España) 'The Secret Garden' is all about intimacy and romance in a *barrio* that's one of Madrid's best-kept secrets. Lit by Spanish designer candles, draped in organza from India and serving up chocolates from the Caribbean, it never misses a beat.

Café Belén BAR
(Map p1034; Calle de Belén 5; 3.30pm-3am; M Chueca) Café Belén is cool in all the right places – lounge and chill-out music, dim lighting, a great range of drinks (the mojitos are especially good) and a low-key crowd that's the height of casual sophistication.

Lolina Vintage Café CAFE
(Map p1034; Calle del Espíritu Santo 9; 10am-1am Sun-Tue, to 2am Wed, to 2.30am Thu-Sat; M Tribunal) Lolina Vintage Café seems to have captured the essence of Malasaña in one small space. With a studied retro look (comfy old-style chairs and sofas, gilded mirrors and 1970s-era wallpaper), it confirms that the new Malasaña is not unlike the old but a whole lot more sophisticated.

☆ Entertainment

The **Guía del Ocio** (www.guiadelocio.com, in Spanish; €1) is the city's classic weekly listings magazine. Also good are **Metropoli** (www.abc.es/metropolis, in Spanish) and **On Madrid** (www.elpais.com, in Spanish), respectively *ABC's* and *El País'* Friday listings supplements.

Nightclubs

No *barrio* is without a decent club or disco, but the most popular dance spots are in the centre. Don't expect dance clubs or *discotecas* (nightclubs) to get going until after 1am at the earliest. Standard entry fee is €10, which usually includes the first drink, although megaclubs and swankier places charge a few euros more.

Teatro Joy Eslava CLUB
(Map p1034; www.joy-eslava.com; Calle del Arenal 11; admission €12-15; 11.30pm-6am; M Sol) The only things guaranteed at this grand old Madrid dance club (housed in a 19th-century theatre) are a crowd and the fact that it will be open. (The club claims to have opened every single day for the past 29 years.) The music and the crowd are a mixed bag, but queues are long and invariably include locals and tourists, and even the occasional *famoso*.

Charada CLUB
(Map p1038; www.charadaclubdebaile.com, in Spanish; Calle de la Bola 13; admission €10-15; midnight-6am Thu-Sat; M Santo Domingo) Charada took the Madrid nightlife scene by storm in 2009 and has never looked back. Its decor is New York chic (with no hint of its former existence as a brothel), the cocktails are highly original, the clientele is well-heeled and often famous, and it's the home turntable for some of the best house DJs in town.

Adraba CLUB
(Map p1034; www.fsmgroup.es, in Spanish; Calle de Alcalá 20; admission €15-18; midnight-6am Wed-Sun; M Sevilla) This historic nightclub finally reopened to much fanfare in 2010 and rapidly re-established itself as one of the city's best. The designer decor is stunning and there are five nights of dancing with a sophisticated crowd. Whatever the night, the resident DJs are among the best in Madrid.

Kapital CLUB
(Map p1034; www.grupo-kapital.com, in Spanish; Calle de Atocha 125; admission €20; ⌚6-10pm & midnight-6am Thu-Sun; Ⓜ Atocha) One of the most famous megaclubs in Madrid, this massive seven-storey nightclub has something for everyone: from cocktail bars and dance music to karaoke, salsa, hip hop and more chilled spaces for R&B and soul, as well as a section devoted to 'Made in Spain' music.

Cinemas

Cine Doré CINEMA
(Map p1034; Calle de Santa Isabel 3; ⌚Tue-Sun; Ⓜ Antón Martín) The National Film Library offers fantastic classic and vanguard films for just €2.50.

Yelmo Cineplex Ideal SPANISH CINEMA
(Map p1034; www.yelmocines.es, in Spanish; Calle del Doctor Cortezo 6; Ⓜ Sol or Tirso de Molina) Close to Plaza Mayor; offers a wide selection of films.

Theatre

Madrid has a lively cultural scene, with concerts and shows taking place throughout the city.

Teatro de la Zarzuela THEATRE
(Map p1034; ☎91 524 54 00; teatrodelazarzuela.mcu.es; Calle de Jovellanos 4; Ⓜ Banco de España) This theatre, built in 1856, is the premier place to see *zarzuela,* a very Spanish mixture of dance, music and theatre. It also hosts a smattering of classical music and opera, as well as the cutting-edge Compañía Nacional de Danza.

Teatro Real OPERA
(Map p1038; ☎902 244 848; www.teatro-real.com, in Spanish; Plaza de Oriente; Ⓜ Ópera) The Teatro Real is the city's grandest stage for elaborate operas and ballets. You'll pay as little as €15 for a spot so far away you will need a telescope, although the sound quality is consistent throughout.

Live Music

FLAMENCO

Many of flamenco's top names perform in Madrid, making it an excellent place to see interpretations of the art.

Corral de la Morería FLAMENCO
(Map p1038; ☎91 365 84 46; www.corraldelamoreria.com; Calle de la Morería 17; admission €27-37; ⌚8.30pm-2.30am, shows 10pm & midnight Sun-Fri, 7pm, 10pm & midnight Sat; Ⓜ Ópera) One of the most prestigious flamenco stages in Madrid, with 50 years as a leading flamenco venue and top performers most nights. The stage area has a rustic feel, and tables are pushed up close. We'd steer clear of the overpriced restaurant, but the performances have a far higher price to quality ratio.

Las Tablas FLAMENCO
(Map p1030; ☎91 542 05 20; www.lastablasmadrid.com; Plaza de España 9; admission €24; ⌚shows 10.30pm Sun-Thu, 8pm & 10pm Fri & Sat; Ⓜ Plaza de España) Las Tablas has quickly earned a reputation for quality flamenco. Most nights you'll see a classic flamenco show, with plenty of throaty singing and soul-baring dancing. Antonia Moya and Marisol Navarro, leading lights in the flamenco world, are regular performers.

Casa Patas FLAMENCO
(Map p1034; ☎91 369 04 96; www.casapatas.com, in Spanish; Calle de Cañizares 10; admission €30-35; ⌚shows 10.30pm Mon-Thu, 9pm & midnight Fri & Sat; Ⓜ Antón Martín or Tirso de Molina) One of the

GAY & LESBIAN MADRID

The heartbeat of gay Madrid is the inner-city *barrio* of Chueca, where Madrid didn't just come out of the closet, but ripped the doors off in the process.

A good place to get the low-down is the laid-back **Mamá Inés** (Map p1034; www.mamaines.com, in Spanish; Calle de Hortaleza 22; ⌚10am-2pm Sun-Thu, to 3am Fri & Sat; Ⓜ Gran Vía or Chueca). **Café Acuarela** (Map p1034; Calle de Gravina 10; ⌚11am-2am Sun-Thu, to 3am Fri & Sat; Ⓜ Chueca) is another dimly lit centrepiece of gay Madrid.

Two of the most popular Chueca nightspots are **Club 54 Studio** (Map p1034; www.studio54madrid.com, in Spanish; Calle de Barbieri 7; ⌚11.30pm-3.30am Thu-Sat; Ⓜ Chueca), modelled on the famous New York club Studio 54, and **Liquid Madrid** (Map p1034; www.liquid.es; Calle de Barbieri 7; ⌚9am-3am Mon-Thu, to 3.30am Fri & Sat; Ⓜ Chueca). **Why Not?** (Map p1034; Calle de San Bartolomé 7; admission €10; ⌚10.30pm-6am; Ⓜ Chueca) is the sort of place where nothing's left to the imagination. Another club popular with a predominantly gay crowd is **Sala Bash/Ohm** (Map p1034; Plaza del Callao 4; ⌚midnight-6am Fri & Sat; Ⓜ Callao).

top flamenco stages in Madrid, this *tablao* always offers unimpeachable quality.

JAZZ

Café Central JAZZ CLUB
(Map p1034; ☎91 369 41 43; www.cafecentralmadrid.com, in Spanish; Plaza del Angel 10; admission €10-15; ⊙1pm-2.30am Sun-Thu, 1.30pm-3.30am Fri & Sat; Ⓜ Antón Martín or Sol) This art deco bar has consistently been voted one of the best jazz venues in the world by leading jazz magazines, and with almost 9000 gigs under its belt, it rarely misses a beat. Shows start at 10pm and tickets go on sale an hour before the set starts.

FREE **Populart** JAZZ CLUB
(Map p1034; www.populart.es, in Spanish; Calle de las Huertas 22; ⊙6pm-2.30am Sun-Fri, to 3.30am Fri & Sat; Ⓜ Antón Martín or Sol) One of Madrid's classic jazz clubs, this place offers a low-key atmosphere and top-quality music – mostly jazz, but with occasional blues, swing and even flamenco thrown into the mix. Shows start at 10.15pm, but if you want a seat get here early.

El Berlín Jazz Club JAZZ CLUB
(Map p1034; ☎91 521 57 52; www.cafeberlin.es, in Spanish; Calle de Jacometrezo 4; admission €6-10; ⊙7pm-2.30am Tue-Sun; Ⓜ Callao or Santo Domingo) El Berlín has been something of a Madrid jazz stalwart since the 1950s and it's all about classic jazz with none of the fusion performances that you find elsewhere. The headline acts take to the stage at 11.30pm on Fridays and Saturdays, with other performances sprinkled throughout the week.

OTHER LIVE MUSIC

Costello Café & Niteclub LIVE MUSIC
(Map p1034; www.costelloclub.com; Calle del Caballero de Gracia 10; admission €5-10; ⊙6pm-1am Sun-Wed, to 2.30am Thu-Sat; Ⓜ Gran Vía) Very cool. Costello Café & Niteclub is smooth-as-silk ambience wedded with an innovative mix of pop, rock and fusion in Warholesque surrounds. There's live music every night of the week (except Sundays) at 9.30pm, with resident and visiting DJs until closing time from Thursday to Saturday.

Sala El Sol LIVE MUSIC
(Map p1034; www.elsolmad.com, in Spanish; Calle de los Jardines 3; admission €8-25; ⊙11pm-5.30am Tue-Sat Jul-Sep; Ⓜ Gran Vía) Madrid institutions don't come any more beloved than Sala El Sol. It opened in 1979, and quickly established itself as a leading stage for all the icons of the era. The music rocks and rolls and usually resurrects the '70s and '80s while soul and funk also get a run.

Café La Palma LIVE MUSIC
(Map p1030; www.cafelapalma.com, in Spanish; Calle de la Palma 62; admission under €12; ⊙4.30pm-3am Sun-Thu, to 3.30am Fri & Sat; Ⓜ Noviciado) It's amazing how much variety Café La Palma has packed into its labyrinth of rooms. Live shows featuring hot local bands are held at the back, while DJs mix up the front. You might find live music other nights, but there are always two shows at 10pm and midnight from Thursday to Saturday.

Clamores LIVE MUSIC
(Map p1030; www.clamores.es, in Spanish; Calle de Alburquerque 14; admission €5-15; ⊙6pm-3am; Ⓜ Bilbao) This one-time classic jazz cafe has morphed into one of the most diverse live music stages in Madrid. Jazz is still a staple, but world music, flamenco, soul fusion, singer-songwriter, pop and rock all make regular appearances. Live shows can begin as early as 9pm.

FREE **Honky Tonk** LIVE MUSIC
(Map p1030; www.clubhonky.com, in Spanish; Calle de Covarrubias 24; ⊙9pm-5am; Ⓜ Alonso Martínez) Despite the name, this is a great place to see local rock 'n' roll, though many acts have a little country or blues thrown into the mix too. It's a fun vibe in a smallish club that's been around since the heady 1980s. Arrive early as it fills up fast.

Sport

Get tickets to football matches and bullfights from box offices or through agents such as **Localidades Galicia** (Map p1034; ☎91 531 91 31; www.bullfightticketsmadrid.com; Plaza del Carmen 1; ⊙9.30am-1pm & 4.30-7pm Mon-Sat, 9.30am-1pm Sun; Ⓜ Sol).

FOOTBALL

Estadio Santiago Bernabéu FOOTBALL STADIUM
(off Map p1030; www.realmadrid.com; Avenida de Concha Espina 1; tour adult/under 14yr €15/10; ⊙10am-7pm Mon-Sat, 10.30am-6.30pm Sun; Ⓜ Santiago Bernabéu) The legendary Real Madrid plays at this stadium. Fans can visit the stadium and take an interesting tour through the presidential box, dressing room and field. The all-important telephone number for booking game tickets (which you later pick up at Gate 42) is ☎902 32 43 24, which only works if you're calling from within Spain.

Estadio Vicente Calderón FOOTBALL STADIUM
(Map p1030; www.clubatleticodemadrid.com; Paseo de la Virgin del Puerto; Ⓜ Pirámides) This is home

to Atlético de Madrid, whose fans are famed as being some of the country's most devoted.

BULLFIGHTING

Plaza de Toros Las Ventas BULLFIGHTING
(☎91 356 22 00; www.las-ventas.com, in Spanish; Calle de Alcalá 237; tours €7; ⏲tours 10am-2pm; Ⓜ Ventas) Some of Spain's top *toreros* swing their capes in Plaza de Toros Las Ventas, east of Parque del Buen Retiro. Fights are held every Sunday afternoon from mid-May through October. Get tickets (from €5 unshaded standing-room only) at the plaza box office, Localidades Galicia, or from official ticket agents on Calle Victoria close to the Plaza de la Puerta del Sol. For excellent tours of the bullring in English and Spanish, contact **Tauro Tour** (☎91 556 92 37; gregorio@trazopublicidad.es; 4th fl, Paseo de la Castellana 115).

Shopping

The key to shopping Madrid-style is knowing where to look. Salamanca is the home of upmarket fashions, with chic boutiques lining up to showcase the best that Spanish and international designers have to offer. Some of it spills over into Chueca, but Malasaña is Salamanca's true alter ego, home to fashion that's as funky as it is offbeat and ideal for that studied underground look that will fit right in with Madrid's hedonistic after-dark crowd. Central Madrid – Sol, Huertas or La Latina – offers plenty of individual surprises.

During *las rebajas,* the annual winter and summer sales, prices are slashed on just about everything. The winter sales begin around 7 January and last well into February. Summer sales begin in early July and last into August.

Shops may (and many do) open on the first Sunday of every month and throughout December.

Antigua Casa Talavera TRADITIONAL CERAMICS
(Map p1038; Calle de Isabel la Católica 2; ⏲10am-1.30pm & 5-8pm Mon-Fri, to 1.30pm Sat; Ⓜ Santo Domingo) The extraordinary tiled facade of this wonderful old shop conceals an Aladdin's Cave of ceramics from all over Spain. This is not the mass-produced stuff aimed at the tourist market, but comes from the small family potters of Andalucía and Toledo.

El Arco Artesanía SOUVENIRS
(Map p1034; Plaza Mayor 9; ⏲11am-9pm; Ⓜ Sol or La Latina) This original shop in the southwestern corner of Plaza Mayor sells an outstanding array of homemade designer souvenirs, from stone and glasswork to jewellery and home fittings.

El Flamenco Vive FLAMENCO
(Map p1038; www.elflamencovive.es; Calle Conde de Lemos 7; ⏲10am-2pm & 5-9pm Mon-Sat; Ⓜ Ópera) This temple to flamenco has it all: guitars, songbooks, well-priced CDs, polka-dotted dancing costumes, shoes, colourful plastic jewellery and even literature about flamenco.

Casa de Diego HANDICRAFTS, ACCESSORIES
(Map p1034; www.casadediego.com; Plaza de la Puerta del Sol 12; ⏲9.30am-8pm Mon-Sat; Ⓜ Sol) This classic shop has been around since 1858, selling and repairing Spanish fans, shawls, umbrellas and canes. Service is old-style and the staff occasionally grumpy, but the fans are works of antique art.

El Rastro MARKET
(Map p1034; Calle de la Ribera de Curtidores; ⏲8am-3pm Sun; Ⓜ La Latina, Puerta de Toledo or Tirso de Molina) A Sunday morning at El Rastro, Europe's largest flea market, is a Madrid institution. You could easily spend an entire morning inching your way down the Calle de la Ribera de Curtidores and through the maze of streets that hosts El Rastro flea market every Sunday morning. For every 10 pieces of junk, there's a real gem (we spotted a lost masterpiece: an Underwood typewriter) waiting to be found. A word of warning: pickpockets love El Rastro as much as everyone else.

Agatha Ruiz de la Prada CLOTHING
(Map p1030; www.agatharuizdelaprada.com; Calle de Serrano 27; ⏲10am-8.30pm Mon-Sat; Ⓜ Serrano) This boutique has to be seen to be believed, with pinks, yellows and oranges at every turn. It's fun and exuberant, but it's not just for kids: it's also serious and highly original fashion. Agatha Ruiz de la Prada is one of the enduring icons of 1980s Madrid.

Mercado de Fuencarral CLOTHING
(Map p1034; www.mdf.es, in Spanish; Calle de Fuencarral 45; ⏲11am-9pm Mon-Sat; Ⓜ Tribunal) Madrid's home of alternative club cool is still going strong, revelling in its reverse snobbery. With shops like Fuck, Ugly Shop and Black Kiss, it's funky, grungy and filled to the rafters with torn T-shirts and more black leather and silver studs than you'll ever need.

Information

Dangers & Annoyances

Madrid is a generally safe city although, as in most European cities, you should be wary of pickpockets in the city centre, on the Metro and around major tourist sights.

Prostitution along Calle de la Montera and in the Casa del Campo park means that you need to exercise extra caution in these areas.

For details about common scams, see the Spain Directory A–Z (p1144).

Discount Cards

The **Madrid Card** (☎91 360 47 72; www.madrid card.com; 1/2/3 days €47/60/74) includes free entry to more than 40 museums in and around Madrid and discounts on public transport. The cheaper version (1/2/3 days for €31/35/39) covers just cultural sights.

Emergency

Emergency (☎112)

Policía Nacional (☎091)

Servicio de Atención al Turista Extranjero (Foreign Tourist Assistance Service; ☎91 548 85 37, 91 548 80 08; www.esmadrid.com/satemadrid; Calle de Leganitos 19; ⏲9am-10pm; Ⓜ Plaza de España or Santo Domingo)

Internet Access

Café Comercial (Glorieta de Bilbao 7; per 50min €1; ⏲7.30am-midnight Mon, to 1am Tue-Thu, to 2am Fri, 8.30am-2am Sat, 9am-midnight Sun; Ⓜ Bilbao) One of Madrid's grandest old cafes with internet upstairs.

Centro de Turismo de Madrid (www.esmadrid.com) Free internet for up to 15 minutes at the branch on Plaza Mayor, or free and unlimited access at the Plaza de Colón branch.

Left Luggage

At Madrid's Barajas airport, there are three **consignas** (left-luggage offices; ⏲24hr). In either, you pay €3.85 for the first 24-hour period (or fraction thereof). Thereafter, it costs €3.83/4.93 per day per small/large bag. Similar services operate for similar prices at Atocha and Chamartín train stations (open 7am to 11pm).

Medical Services

Anglo-American Medical Unit (Unidad Medica; ☎91 435 18 23; www.unidadmedica.com; Calle del Conde de Aranda 1; ⏲9am-8pm Mon-Fri, 10am-1pm Sat for emergencies; Ⓜ Retiro) Private clinic with Spanish- and English-speaking staff. Consultations cost around €125.

Farmacia Mayor (☎91 366; Calle Mayor 13; ⏲24hr; Ⓜ Sol)

Money

Like all Spanish cities, Madrid is fairly crawling with bank branches equipped with ATMs. As a rule, exchange bureaux have longer hours but worse rates and steeper commissions.

Post

Main post office (www.correos.es; Plaza de la Cibeles; ⏲8.30am-9.30pm Mon-Fri, to 2pm Sat; Ⓜ Banco de España)

Tourist Information

Centro de Turismo de Madrid (www.esmadrid.com; Plaza Mayor 27; ⏲9.30am-8.30pm; Ⓜ Sol) Excellent city tourist office with a smaller office underneath Plaza de Colón and information points at Plaza de la Cibeles, Plaza de Callao, outside the Centro de Arte Reina Sofía and at the T4 terminal at Barajas airport.

Regional tourist office (www.turismomadrid.es; Calle del Duque de Medinaceli 2; ⏲8am-8pm Mon-Sat, 9am-2pm Sun; Ⓜ Banco de España) Further offices at Barajas airport (T1 and T4), and Chamartín and Atocha train stations.

Getting There & Away

Air

Madrid's international Barajas airport (MAD), 15km northeast of the city, is a busy place, with flights coming in from all over Europe and beyond.

Bus

Estación Sur de Autobuses (☎91 468 42 00; www.estaciondeautobuses.com, in Spanish; Calle de Méndez Álvaro 83; Ⓜ Méndez Álvaro), just south of the M-30 ring road, is the city's principal bus station. It serves most destinations to the south and many in other parts of the country. Major bus companies:

ALSA (☎902 422 242; www.alsa.es)

Avanzabus (☎902 020 052; www.avanza bus.com)

Car & Motorcycle

The city is surrounded by two main ring roads, the outermost M-40 and the inner M-30; there are also two additional partial ring roads, the M-45 and the more-distant M-50.

Train

Madrid is served by two main train stations. The bigger of the two is **Puerta de Atocha** (Ⓜ Atocha Renfe), at the southern end of the city centre. **Chamartín train station** (Ⓜ Chamartín) lies in the north of the city. The bulk of trains for Spanish destinations depart from Atocha, especially those going south. International services arrive at and leave from Chamartín. For bookings, contact **Renfe** (☎902 24 02 02; www.renfe.es) at either station.

High-speed Tren de Alta Velocidad Española (AVE) services connect Madrid with Seville (via Córdoba), Valladolid (via Segovia), Toledo, Valencia, Málaga and Barcelona (via Zaragoza and Tarragona).

Getting Around

To/From the Airport

METRO Line 8 of the metro (entrances in T2 and T4) runs to the Nuevos Ministerios transport interchange, which connects with lines 10 and 6. It operates from 6.05am to 2am. A single ticket costs €1 (10-ride Metrobús ticket €9); there's an additional €1 supplement if you're travelling to/from the airport. The journey to Nuevos Ministerios takes around 15 minutes, around 25 minutes from T4.

BUS At time of publication, a new 24-hour bus service between Plaza de la Cibeles and the airport was due to start.

AeroCITY (☎91 747 75 70; www.aerocity.com; €5-19 per person) is a private minibus service that takes you door-to-door between central Madrid and the airport.

TAXI A taxi to the city centre will cost you around €25 in total (up to €35 from T4), depending on traffic and where you're going; in addition to what the meter reads, you pay a €5.50 airport supplement.

Public Transport

Madrid's **metro** (www.metromadrid.es) is extensive and well maintained. A single ride costs €1 and a 10-ride ticket is €9. The metro is quick, clean, relatively safe and runs from 6am until 2am.

The bus system is also good; contact **EMT** (www.emtmadrid.es) for more information. Twenty-six night-bus *búhos* (owls) routes operate from midnight to 6am, with all routes originating in Plaza de la Cibeles.

Taxi

You can pick up a taxi at ranks throughout town or simply flag one down. Flag fall is €2.05 from 6am to 10pm daily, €2.20 from 10pm to 6am Sunday to Friday and €3.10 from 10pm Saturday to 6am Sunday. Several supplementary charges, usually posted inside the taxi, apply; these include €5.50 to/from the airport and €2.95 from taxi ranks at train and bus stations.

Radio-Teléfono Taxi (☎91 547 82 00, 91 547 82 00; www.radiotelefono-taxi.com)

Tele-Taxi (☎91 371 21 31, 902 501 130)

AROUND MADRID

The Comunidad de Madrid, the province surrounding the capital, has some of Spain's finest royal palaces and gardens that make for easy day trips from the capital.

Places worth exploring include the royal palace complex at **San Lorenzo de El Escorial** (www.patrimonionacional.es; admission €8, EU citizens free Wed; ⏲10am-6pm Apr-Sep, 10am-5pm Oct-Mar, closed Mon). Check also at www.sanlorenzoturismo.org.

Other worthwhile excursions include **Aranjuez** (www.aranjuez.es, in Spanish), with its **royal palace** (www.patrimonionacional.es; adult/child €5/2.50, EU citizens free Wed, gardens free; ⏲palace 10am-6.15pm Tue-Sun, gardens 8am-8.30pm); the traditional village of **Chinchón** (www.ciudad-chinchon.com); and the university town (and birthplace of Miguel de Cervantes), **Alcalá de Henares** (www.turismoalcala.com, in Spanish).

CASTILLA Y LEÓN

Spain's Castilian heartland, Castilla y León is littered with hilltop towns sporting magnificent Gothic cathedrals, monumental city walls and mouth-watering restaurants.

Ávila

POP 56,9000

Ávila's old city, surrounded by imposing city walls comprising eight monumental gates, 88 watchtowers and more than 2500 turrets, is one of the best-preserved medieval bastions in all of Spain. It's a perfect place to spend a day strolling narrow laneways and soaking up history. The city is known as the birthplace of Santa Teresa, a mystical writer and reformer of the Carmelite order.

Sights

Murallas CITY WALLS

(adult/child €4/2.50; ⏲10am-8pm Tue-Sun) Don't even *think* of leaving town without enjoying the walk along the top of Ávila's 12th-century *murallas*. The two access points are at **Puerta del Alcázar** and **Puerta de los Leales**, which allow walks of 300m and 1200m respectively. The same ticket allows you to climb both sections; the last ones are sold at 7.30pm.

Cathedral CHURCH

(Plaza de la Catedral; admission €4; ⏲10am-7pm Mon-Fri, to 8pm Sat, noon-6pm Sun) Embedded into the eastern city walls, the splendid 12th-century cathedral was the first Gothic-style church built in Spain. It boasts rich walnut choir stalls and a long, narrow central nave that makes the soaring ceilings seem all the more majestic.

FREE **Convento de Santa Teresa** MUSEUM

(⏲8.45am-1.30pm & 3.30-9pm Tue-Sun) The convent was built in 1636 at the birthplace of 16th-century mystic and ascetic, Santa Teresa. It's home to relics, including a piece of the saint's ring finger, as well as a small museum about her life.

Sleeping

TOP CHOICE Hotel Las Leyendas HISTORIC HOTEL €€
(920 35 20 42; www.lasleyendas.es; Calle de Francisco Gallego 3; s/d €69/89;) Occupying the house of 16th-century Ávila nobility, this intimate hotel overflows with period touches (original wooden beams, exposed brick and stonework) wedded to modern amenities.

Hotel El Rastro HISTORIC HOTEL €€
(920 35 22 25; www.elrastroavila.com; Calle Cepedas; s/d from €55/65;) Not to be confused with the *hostal* (budget hotel) of the same name, this superb choice is located in a former 16th-century palace. Natural stone, exposed brickwork and a warm colour scheme of earth colours exude a calming understated elegance. The rooms are spacious and stylish.

Hostal Arco San Vicente BUDGET HOTEL €€
(920 22 24 98; www.arcosanvicente.com; Calle de López Núñez 6; s/d €55/65;) This gleaming *hostal* has small blue carpeted rooms with pale paintwork and wrought-iron bed heads. The location, just inside Puerta de San Vicente, and the parking (€10), are additional perks.

Eating & Drinking

Ávila is famous for its *chuleton de Ávila* (T-bone steak) and *judías del barco de Ávila* (white beans, often with chorizo, in a thick sauce).

Hostería Las Cancelas REGIONAL €€
(920 21 22 49; www.lascancelas.com; Calle de la Cruz Vieja 6; meals €30-40; lunch & dinner Feb-Dec) Part of the hotel of the same name, this courtyard restaurant occupies a delightful interior patio dating back to the 15th century. It's renowned for being a mainstay of Ávila cuisine, and traditional meals are prepared with a salutary attention to detail. Reservations recommended.

Restaurante Reyes Católicos REGIONAL €€
(www.restaurante-reyescatolicos.com, in Spanish; Calle de los Reyes Católicos 6; menú del día €15, meals €25-35) Fronted by a popular tapas bar, this place has bright decor and an accomplished kitchen that churns out traditional dishes that benefit from a creative tweak.

TOP CHOICE La Bodeguita de San Segundo WINE BAR
(www.vinoavila.com, in Spanish; Calle de San Segundo 19; 11am-midnight Thu-Tue) Situated in the 16th-century Casa de la Misericordia, this superb wine bar is standing-room only most nights and more tranquil in the quieter afternoon hours.

Information

Centro de Recepción de Visitantes (tourist office; www.avilaturismo.com; Avenida de Madrid 39; 8am-8pm)

Regional tourist office (www.turismocastillayleon.com; Calle San Segundo 17; 9am-8pm Sun-Thu, 9am-9pm Fri & Sat).

Getting There & Away

BUS From Ávila's bus station, there are frequent services to Segovia (€5.45, 55 minutes) and Salamanca (€6.76, 1½ hours).

TRAIN More than 30 trains run daily to Madrid (from €8.25, 1¼ to two hours) and to Salamanca (€9.65, one to 1½ hours, nine daily).

Salamanca

POP 155,600

Whether floodlit by night or bathed in midday sun, Salamanca is a dream destination. This is a city of rare architectural splendour, awash with golden sandstone overlaid with Latin inscriptions in ochre, and with an extraordinary virtuosity of plateresque and Renaissance styles. The monumental highlights are many, with the exceptional Plaza Mayor (illuminated to stunning effect at night) an unforgettable highlight. But this is also Castilla's liveliest city, home to a massive Spanish and international student population who throng the streets at night and provide the city with so much youth and vitality.

Sights & Activities

TOP CHOICE Plaza Mayor SQUARE
The harmonious Plaza Mayor was completed in 1755 to a design by Alberto Churriguera, one of the clan behind an at times overblown variant of the baroque style that bears their name.

FREE Catedral Nueva & Catedral Vieja CHURCHES
Curiously, Salamanca is home to two cathedrals: the newer and larger cathedral was built beside the old Romanesque one instead of on top of it, as was the norm. The

Catedral Nueva (New Cathedral; Plaza de Anaya; admission free; ⏲9am-8pm), completed in 1733, is a late-Gothic masterpiece that took 220 years to build. Its magnificent Renaissance doorways stand out. For fine views over Salamanca, head to the southwestern corner of the cathedral facade and the **Puerta de la Torre** (Ieronimus; Plaza de Juan XXIII; admission €3.25; ⏲10am-7.15pm), from where stairs lead up through the tower.

The largely Romanesque **Catedral Vieja** (Old Cathedral; admission €4.75; ⏲10am-7.30pm) is a 12th-century temple with a stunning 15th-century altarpiece whose 53 panels depict scenes from the life of Christ and Mary, topped by a representation of the Final Judgement. The entrance is inside the Catedral Nueva.

Universidad Civil UNIVERSITY
(Calle de los Libreros; adult/student €4/2, Mon morning free; ⏲9.30am-1pm & 4-7pm Mon-Fri, 9.30am-1pm & 4-6.30pm Sat, 10am-1pm Sun) The Universidad Civil is a tapestry in sandstone, bursting with images of mythical heroes, religious scenes and coats of arms. It's dominated in the centre by busts of Fernando and Isabel. You can visit the old classrooms and one of the oldest university libraries in Europe.

Other Sights OTHER SIGHTS
Salamanca's other stand-out buildings include the glorious **Casa de las Conchas** (Calle de la Compañia 2; admission free; ⏲9am-9pm Mon-Fri, 9am-2pm & 4-7pm Sat, 10am-2pm & 4-7pm Sun), a city symbol since it was built in the 15th century. The church at the **Convento de San Esteban** (adult/child €3/2; ⏲10am-1.15pm & 4-7.15pm) has an extraordinary altar-like facade with the stoning of San Esteban (St Stephen) as its central motif.

Quiet streets lead away to the northeast to the **Convento de Santa Clara** (admission €3; ⏲9.30am-2pm & 4.15-7pm Mon-Fri, 9.30am-3pm Sat & Sun). This much-modified convent started life as a Romanesque structure and you can climb up some stairs to inspect at close quarters the 14th- and 15th-century *artesonado* (Mudéjar ceiling).

Sleeping

TOP CHOICE **Microtel Placentinos** BOUTIQUE HOTEL €€
(☎923 28 15 31; www.microtelplacentinos.com; Calle de Placentinos 9; s/d incl breakfast €80/95; ❄📶) One of Salamanca's most charming boutique hotels, Microtel Placentinos is tucked away on a quiet street and has rooms with exposed stone walls and wooden beams. The service is faultless, and the overall atmosphere one of intimacy and discretion.

Aparthotel El Toboso APARTMENT HOTEL €
(☎923 27 14 62; www.hoteltoboso.com; Calle del Clavel 7; s/d/tr from €30/52/82, 3-/4-/5-person self-contained apt €76/84/93; ❄📶) These rooms have a homey spare-room feel and are super value, especially the enormous apartments which come with kitchens (including washing machines) and renovated bathrooms.

Hostal Concejo HOTEL €€
(☎923 21 47 37; www.hconcejo.com, in Spanish; Plaza de la Libertad 1; s/d/tr €45/62/80; P❄@📶) A cut above the average *hostal*, the stylish Concejo has polished-wood floors, tasteful furnishings and a superb central location. Try and snag one of the corner rooms (like number 104) with its traditional glassed-in balcony, complete with table, chairs and people-watching views.

Hostal Catedral BUDGET HOTEL €
(☎923 27 06 14; Rúa Mayor 46; s/d €30/48; ❄) Just across from the cathedrals, this pleasing *hostal* has just six extremely pretty, clean-as-a-whistle, bright rooms with showers. All look out onto the street or cathedral, which is a real bonus, as is the motherly owner, who treats her visitors as honoured guests.

Eating & Drinking

Mesón Las Conchas GRILLED MEATS €€
(Rúa Mayor 16; meals €25-30) Enjoy a choice of outdoor tables (in summer), an atmospheric bar or the upstairs, wood-beamed dining area. The bar caters mainly to locals who know their *embutidos* (cured meats). For sit-down meals, there's a good mix of roasts and *raciones* (large tapas servings).

FIND THE FROG

The university's facade is an ornate mass of sculptures and carvings, and hidden among this 16th-century plateresque creation is a tiny stone frog. Legend says that those who find the frog will have good luck in studies, life and love. If you don't want any help, look away now... It's sitting on a skull on the pillar that runs up the right-hand side of the facade.

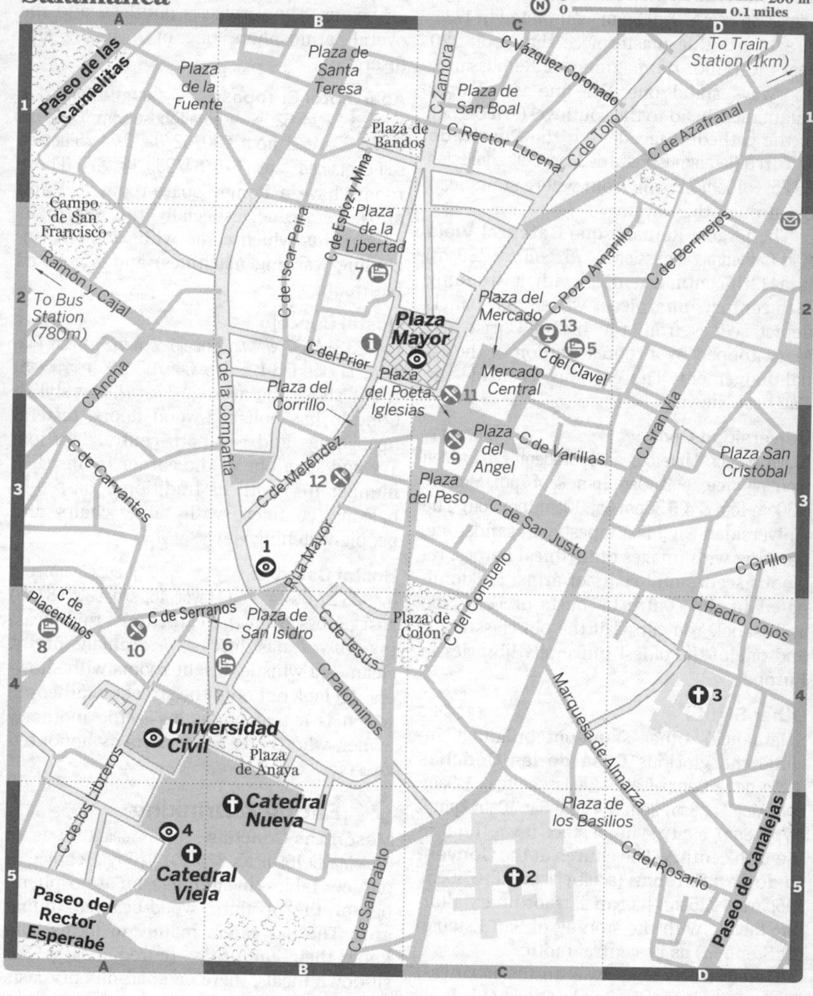

SPAIN CASTILLA Y LEÓN

Mesón Cervantes CASTILIAN €€
(Plaza Mayor 15; meals €15-20; ⏲10am-midnight) Another great place where you can eat at the outdoor tables on the plaza, but the dark wooden beams and atmospheric buzz of the Spanish crowd on the 1st floor should be experienced at least once. The food's a mix of salads and *raciones*.

El Pecado MODERN CREATIVE €€
(☎923 26 65 58; Plaza del Poeta Iglesias 12; meals €40, menú de degustación €45; ⊜) A trendy place that regularly attracts Spanish celebrities (eg Pedro Almodóvar and Ferran Adrià), El Pecado ('The Sin') has an intimate dining room and quirky, creative menu. The hallmarks are fresh tastes, intriguing combinations and dishes that regularly change according to what is fresh in the market that day. Reservations recommended.

Mandala Café MODERN MEDITERRANEAN €
(Calle de Serranos 9-11; menú €10;) Cool and casual Mandala specialises in a superb daily menu with choices like black rice with prawns and *calamares* (squid), and vegetarian moussaka. There are also more salads than you can shake a carrot stick at, as well as cakes and fancy ice creams.

Salamanca

Top Sights

Catedral Nueva B5
Catedral Vieja A5
Plaza Mayor C2
Universidad Civil A4

Sights

1 Casa de las Conchas B3
2 Convento de San Esteban C5
3 Convento de Santa Clara D4
4 Puerta de la Torre A5

Sleeping

5 Aparthotel El Toboso C2
6 Hostal Catedral B4
7 Hostal Concejo B2
8 Microtel Placentinos A4

Eating

9 El Pecado C3
10 Mandala Café A4
11 Mesón Cervantes C2
12 Mesón Las Conchas B3

Drinking

13 Tío Vivo C2

TOP CHOICE **Tío Vivo** MUSIC BAR
(Calle del Clavel 3; ⏲4pm-late) Sip drinks by flickering candlelight to a background of '80s music, enjoying the whimsical decor of carousel horses and oddball antiquities. There's live music Tuesdays to Thursdays from midnight.

Information

Municipal tourist office (www.salamanca.es; Plaza Mayor 14; ⏲9am-2pm & 4.30-8pm Mon-Fri, 10am-8pm Sat, 10am-2pm Sun)

Regional tourist office (www.turismocastillayleon.com; Casa de las Conchas, Rúa Mayor; ⏲9am-8pm Sun-Thu, 9am-9pm Fri & Sat)

Getting There & Away

BUS Buses run from the **bus station** (Avenida de Filiberto Villalobos 71-85) to Madrid (regular/express €14.80/21.90, three/2½ hours, hourly), Ávila (€6.76, 1½ hours, one to four daily) and Segovia (€10.96, 2¾ hours, two daily).

TRAIN Up to eight trains depart daily for Madrid's Chamartín station (€19.10, 2½ hours) via Ávila (€9.65, one hour). The train station is about 1km beyond Plaza de España.

Segovia

POP 56,100

Unesco World Heritage–listed Segovia has a stunning monument to Roman grandeur and a castle said to have inspired Walt Disney, and is otherwise a city of warm terracotta and sandstone hues set amid the rolling hills of Castilla.

Sights

TOP CHOICE **Acueducto** ROMAN AQUEDUCT
El Acueducto, an 894m-long engineering wonder that looks like an enormous comb of stone blocks plunged into the lower end of old Segovia, is the obvious starting point of a tour of town. This Roman aqueduct is 28m high and was built without a drop of mortar – just good old Roman know-how.

TOP CHOICE **Alcázar** CASTLE
(www.alcazardesegovia.com; Plaza de la Reina Victoria Eugenia; adult/child €4/3, tower €2, EU citizens free 3rd Tue of month; ⏲10am-7pm Apr-Sep) The fortified and fairytale Alcázar is perched dramatically on the edge of Segovia. Roman foundations are buried somewhere underneath the splendour, but what we see today is a 13th-century structure that burned down in 1862 and was subsequently rebuilt. Inside is a collection of armour and military gear, but even better are the ornate interiors of the reception rooms and the 360-degree views from the **Torre de Juan II**.

Catedral CHURCH
(Plaza Mayor; adult/child €3/2, free 9.30am-1.15pm Sun; ⏲9.30am-6.30pm) In the heart of town, the resplendent late-Gothic Catedral was started in 1525 and completed a mere 200 years later. The Cristo del Consuelo **chapel** houses a magnificent Romanesque doorway preserved from the original church that burned down.

Iglesia de Vera Cruz CHURCH
(Carretera de Zamarramala; admission €1.75; ⏲10.30am-1.30pm & 4-7pm Tue-Sun, closed Nov) The most interesting of Segovia's numerous churches, and one of the best preserved of its kind in Europe, is the 12-sided Iglesia de la Vera Cruz. Built in the 13th century by the Knights Templar and based on the Church of the Holy Sepulchre in Jerusalem, it long

Segovia

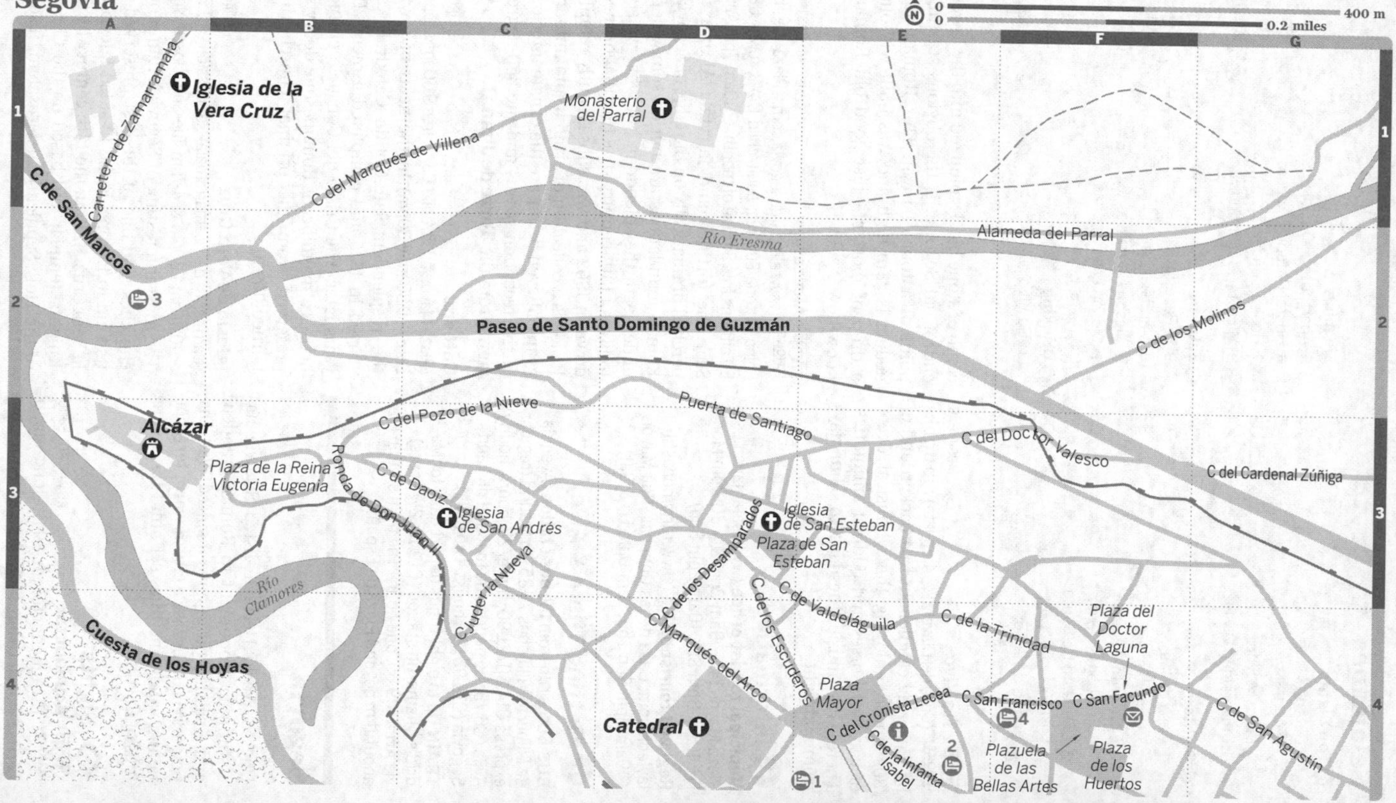

Iglesia de la Vera Cruz
Carretera de Zamarramala
Monasterio del Parral
C del Marqués de Villena
C de San Marcos
Río Eresma
Alameda del Parral
3
Paseo de Santo Domingo de Guzmán
C de los Molinos
Alcázar
C del Pozo de la Nieve
Puerta de Santiago
C del Doctor Valesco
C del Cardenal Zúñiga
Plaza de la Reina Victoria Eugenia
Ronda de Don Juan II
C de Daoiz
Iglesia de San Andrés
Iglesia de San Esteban
Plaza de San Esteban
C de los Desamparados
C Judería Nueva
Río Clamores
C de Valdeláguila
C de la Trinidad
C de los Escuderos
C Marqués del Arco
Cuesta de los Hoyas
Plaza Mayor
Catedral
C del Cronista Lecea
C San Francisco
C San Facundo
Plaza del Doctor Laguna
C de San Agustín
C de la Infanta Isabel
Plazuela de las Bellas Artes
Plaza de los Huertos
1
2
4
0 400 m
0 0.2 miles

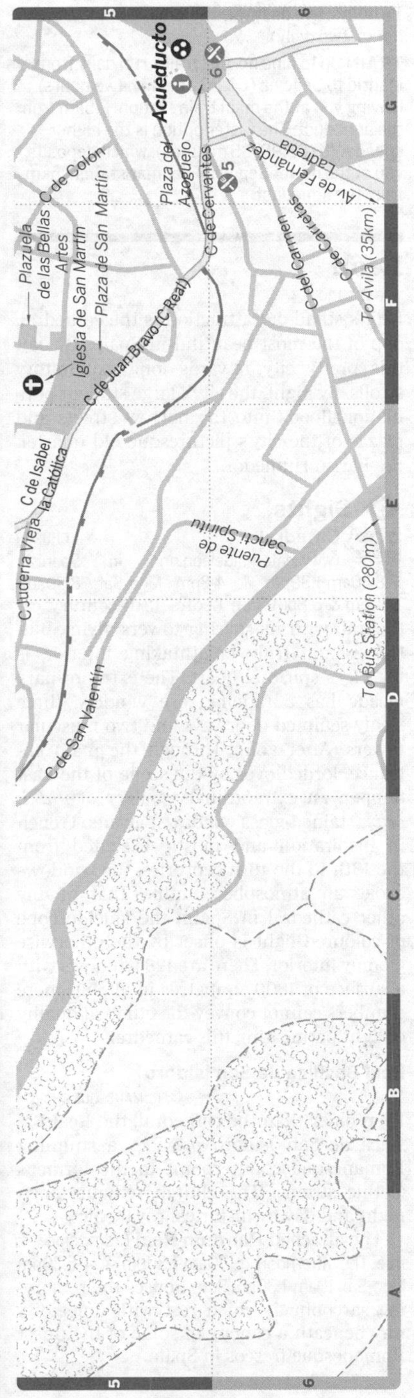

housed what was said to be a piece of the Vera Cruz (True Cross).

Sleeping

TOP CHOICE **Hospedería La Gran Casa Mudéjar** HISTORIC HOTEL €€
(921 46 62 50; www.lacasamudejar.com; Calle de Isabel la Católica 8; r €90;) Spread over two buildings, this place has been magnificently renovated, blending genuine 15th-century Mudéjar carved wooden ceilings in some rooms with modern amenities. In the newer wing, where the building dates from the 19th century, the rooms on the top floors have fine mountain views.

Hotel Alcázar BOUTIQUE HOTEL €€€
(921 43 85 68; www.alcazar-hotel.com; Calle de San Marcos 5; s/d incl breakfast €135/163;) Sitting by the riverbank in the valley beneath the Alcázar, this charming, tranquil little hotel has lavish rooms beautifully styled to suit those who love old-world luxury. Breakfast on the back terrace is a lovely way to pass the morning, and there's an intimacy and graciousness about the whole experience.

Hostal Fornos BUDGET HOTEL €
(921 46 01 98; www.hostalfornos.com, in Spanish; Calle de la Infanta Isabel 13; s/d €41/55;) This tidy little *hostal* is a cut above most places in this price category. It has a cheerful air and rooms with a fresh white-linen-and-wicker-chair look. Some are larger than others, but the value is unbeatable.

Natura – La Hostería BUDGET HOTEL €
(921 46 67 10; www.naturadesegovia.com, in Spanish; Calle de Colón 5-7; r €60;) An eclectic choice a few streets back from Plaza Mayor. The owner obviously has a penchant

Segovia

Top Sights

Acueducto G5
Alcázar A3
Catedral D4
Iglesia de la Vera Cruz A1

Sleeping

1 Hospedería La Gran Casa Mudéjar E4
2 Hostal Fornos E4
3 Hotel Alcázar A2
4 Natura–La Hostería F4

Eating

5 Casa Duque G6
6 Mesón de Cándido G6
Restaurante El Fogón Sefardí ...... (see 1)

for Dalí prints and the rooms have plenty of character, with chunky wooden furnishings and bright paintwork.

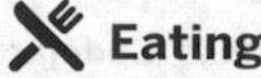

Eating

Segovianos love their pigs to the point of obsession. Just about every restaurant proudly boasts its *horno de asar* (roasts). The main speciality is *cochinillo asado* (roast suckling pig), but *judiones de la granja* (butter beans with pork chunks) also looms large on menus. Reservations are always recommended.

TOP CHOICE **Restaurante El Fogón Sefardí** SEPHARDIC €€

(☎921 46 62 50; www.lacasamudejar.com; Calle de Isabel la Católica 8; meals €30-40;) This is one of the most original places in town, serving Sephardic cuisine in a restaurant with an intimate patio or in a splendid dining hall with original 15th-century Mudéjar flourishes. The theme in the bar is equally diverse, with dishes from all the continents.

TOP CHOICE **Casa Duque** GRILLED MEATS €€

(☎921 46 24 87; www.restauranteduque.es; Calle de Cervantes 12; menús del día €21-40, meals €25-35) They've been serving *cochinillo asado* here since the 1890s. For the uninitiated, try the *menú segoviano* (€31), which includes *cochinillo,* or the *menú gastronómico* (€40). Downstairs is the informal *cueva* (cave), where you can get tapas and full-bodied *cazuelas* (stews).

Mesón de Cándido GRILLED MEATS €€

(☎921 42 81 03; www.mesondecandido.es; Plaza del Azoguejo 5; meals €30-40;) Set in a delightful 18th-century building in the shadow of the aqueduct, Mesón de Cándido is famous throughout Spain for its suckling pig and the more unusual roast boar with apple.

Information

Centro de Recepción de Visitantes (tourist office; www.turismodesegovia.com; Plaza del Azoguejo 1; ⏲10am-7pm Sun-Fri, 10am-8pm Sat). Guided city tours (two hours 15 minutes, €12 per person) depart daily at 11.15am (minimum of four persons).

Regional tourist office (www.segoviaturismo.es; Plaza Mayor 10; ⏲9am-8pm Sun-Thu, 9am-9pm Fri & Sat)

Getting There & Away

BUS Buses run half-hourly to Segovia from Madrid's Paseo de la Florida bus stop (€6.70, 1½ hours). Buses also run to/from Ávila (€5.45, 1¼ hours, five daily) and Salamanca (€10.96, 2¾ hours, two daily).

TRAIN Up to nine normal trains run daily from Madrid to Segovia (€6.50 one way, two hours), leaving you at the main train station, 2.5km from the aqueduct. The faster option is the high-speed AVE (€9.90, 35 minutes), which deposits you at the newer Segovia-Guiomar station, 5km from the aqueduct.

León

POP 135,100

León's stand-out attraction is the cathedral, one of the most beautiful in Spain. By day, this pretty city rewards long exploratory strolls. By night, the city's large student population floods into the narrow streets and plazas of the city's picturesque old quarter, the Barrio Húmedo.

Sights

TOP CHOICE **Catedral** CHURCH

(www.catedraldeleon.org, in Spanish; ⏲8.30am-1.30pm & 4-8pm Mon-Sat, 8.30am-2.30pm & 5-8pm Sun) León's 13th-century cathedral, with its soaring towers, flying buttresses and truly breathtaking interior, is the city's spiritual heart. The extraordinary facade has a radiant rose window, three richly sculpted doorways and two muscular towers. After going through the main entrance, lorded over by the scene of the Last Supper, an extraordinary gallery of *vidrieras* (stained-glass windows) awaits. French in inspiration and mostly executed from the 13th to the 16th centuries, the windows evoke an atmosphere unlike that of any other cathedral in Spain; the kaleidoscope of coloured light is offset by the otherwise gloomy interior. There are 128 windows with a surface of 1800 sq metres in all, but mere numbers cannot convey the ethereal quality of light permeating this cathedral.

Real Basílica de San Isidoro ROMANESQUE CHURCH

Even older than the cathedral, the Real Basílica de San Isidoro provides a stunning Romanesque counterpoint to the former's Gothic strains. The church remains open night and day by historical royal edict.

The attached **Panteón Real** (admission €4, free Thu afternoon; ⏲10am-1.30pm & 4-6.30pm Mon-Sat, 10am-1.30pm Sun) houses the remaining sarcophagi, which rest with quiet dignity beneath a canopy of some of the finest Romanesque frescos in Spain.

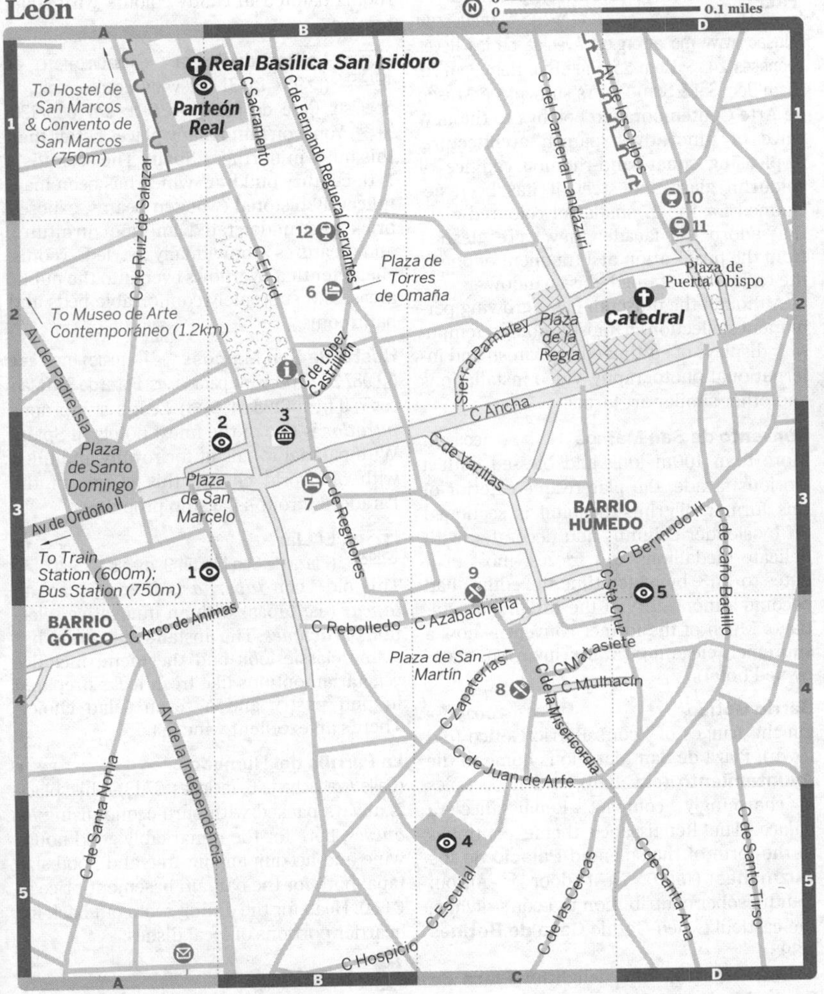

León

Top Sights

Catedral D2
Panteón Real A1
Real Basílica San Isidoro A1

Sights

1 Ayuntamiento A3
2 Casa de Botines B3
3 Palacio de los Guzmanes B3
4 Plaza de Santa María del Camino C5
5 Plaza Mayor D3

Sleeping

6 Hostal San Martín B2
7 La Posada Regia B3

Eating

8 El Llar C4
9 La Parrilla del Humedo C3

Drinking

10 Big John's D1
11 Ébanno D2
12 Ékole Café B2

FREE **Museo de Arte Contemporáneo** ART MUSEUM

(Musac; www.musac.org.es; Avenida de los Reyes Leóneses 24; ⌚11am-8pm Tue-Thu, 11am-9pm Fri, 10am-9pm Sat & Sun) León's showpiece Museo de Arte Contemporáneo belongs to the new wave of innovative Spanish architecture. A pleasing square-and-rhombus edifice of colourful glass and steel, it has been acclaimed for the 37 shades of coloured glass that adorn the facade; they were gleaned from the pixelisation of a fragment of one of the cathedral's stained-glass windows.

Although the museum has a growing permanent collection, it mostly houses temporary displays of cutting-edge Spanish and international photography, video installations and other similar art forms.

Convento de San Marcos CONVENT

More than 100m long and blessed with a glorious facade, the plateresque exterior of this former pilgrims' hospital is sectioned off by slender columns and decorated with delicate medallions and friezes; most of it dates to 1513, by which time the edifice had become a monastery of the Knights of Santiago. Much of the former convent is now a supremely elegant *parador* (luxurious state-owned hotel).

Barrio Gótico HISTORIC QUARTER

On the fringes of León's Barrio Gótico (old town), Plaza de San Marcelo is home to the **Ayuntamiento** (city hall), which occupies a charmingly compact Renaissance-era palace. The Renaissance theme continues in the form of the splendid **Palacio de los Guzmanes** (1560). Next door is Antoni Gaudí's sober contribution to León's skyline, the castlelike, neo-Gothic **Casa de Botines** (1893).

Down the hill, the delightful **Plaza de Santa María del Camino** (also known as Plaza del Grano) feels like a cobblestone Castilian village square. At the northeastern end of the old town in Barrio Húmedo is the beautiful and time-worn 17th-century **Plaza Mayor**.

Sleeping & Eating

TOP CHOICE **Hostal San Martín** HOTEL €

(☎987 87 51 87; www.sanmartinhostales.com; 2nd fl, Plaza de Torres de Omaña 1; s/d/tr €31/43/55, s without bathroom €20) In a splendid central position, this recently overhauled 18th-century building has light, airy rooms painted in candy colours with small terraces.

TOP CHOICE **La Posada Regia** HISTORIC HOTEL €€

(☎987 21 31 73; www.regialeon.com, in Spanish; Calle de Regidores 9-11; s/d €65/120; ❄📶) You won't find many places better than this hotel in northern Spain. The secret is a 14th-century building, which has been magnificently restored (wooden beams, exposed brick and understated antique furniture), and features individually styled rooms, character that overflows even into the public areas, and supremely comfortable beds and bathrooms.

Hostal de San Marcos HISTORIC HOTEL €€€

(☎987 23 73 00; www.parador.es; Plaza de San Marcos 7; d from €198; ❄@📶) León's sumptuous *parador* is one of the finest hotels in Spain. With palatial rooms fit for royalty and filled with old-world charm, this is one of the Paradores group's flagship properties.

TOP CHOICE **El Llar** TAPAS €€

(Plaza de San Martín 9; meals €25-30; 🖉) This old León *taberna* is a great place to *tapear* (eat tapas) with an innovative selection of *raciones*. The upstairs restaurant has a fine classic look and the menu includes vegetarian options like fresh leeks prepared in puff pastry and a seven salad choice. There's an excellent wine list.

La Parrilla del Humedo TAPAS €

(Calle Azabacheria 6; raciones €7-13) This place is always packed with euro-economising *leonéses,* here for the remarkably good house wine and accompanying free and good-size tapa; both for the bargain basement price of €1.50. Head for the dining room out back for heartier portions of local dishes.

Drinking

The Barrio Húmedo's night-time epicentre is Plaza de San Martín – prise open the door of any bar here or in the surrounding streets (especially Calle de Juan de Arfe and Calle de la Misericordia), inch your way to the bar and you're unlikely to want to leave until closing time.

Tucked away behind the cathedral to the east, **Big John's** (Avenida de los Cubos 4; ⌚7pm-2am) is a jazz hang-out with a vigorous sound mix including bebop, Latin and Dixieland, while adjacent **Ébanno** (Avenida de los Cubos 2; ⌚4pm-late) is classy and as good for laptop-toting wi-fi hunters as for late-night sophisticates. Elsewhere, **Ékole Café** (Plaza de Torres de Omaña; ⌚4.30pm-1.30am Sun-Thu, 4.30pm-3.30am Fri & Sat) is another favourite León drinking hole with an old Parisian feel.

Information

Tourist office (www.turismocastillayleon.com; Calle el Cid 2; ⌚9am-8pm)

Getting There & Away

BUS From the **bus station** (Paseo del Ingeniero Sáez de Miera), there are numerous daily buses to Madrid (€22, 3½ hours) and Burgos (€14.10, 3¾ hours).

TRAIN Regular daily trains travel to Burgos (from €20.10, two hours), Oviedo (from €18.80, two hours), Madrid (from €28.30, 4¼ hours) and Barcelona (from €68.40, nine hours).

Burgos

POP 174,100

The legendary warrior El Cid was born just outside Burgos and is buried in its magnificent cathedral. The grey-stone architecture, fortifying cuisine and extreme climate can make Burgos edgy, but below the surface lies vibrant nightlife, good restaurants and, when the sun's shining, pretty streetscapes.

Sights

TOP CHOICE **Catedral** CHURCH

(Plaza del Rey Fernando; adult/child €5/2.50; ⌚9.30am-6.30pm) The Unesco World Heritage–listed cathedral is a masterpiece. It had humble origins as a modest Romanesque church, but work began on a grander scale in 1221. Remarkably, within 40 years most of the French Gothic structure that you see today had been completed. Probably the most impressive of the portals is the **Puerta del Sarmental**, the main entrance for visitors, although the honour could also go to the **Puerta de la Coronería**, on the northwestern side.

Inside the main sanctuary a host of other chapels showcase the diversity of the interior, from the light and airy **Capilla de la Presentación** to the **Capilla de la Concepción** with its impossibly gilded 15th-century altar. The main altar is a typically overwhelming piece of gold-encrusted extravagance, while directly beneath the star-vaulted central dome lies the **tomb of El Cid**. The **Capilla del Condestable**, behind the main altar, is a remarkable late-15th-century production.

Monasterio de las Huelgas MONASTERY

(guided tours adult/child €5/2.50, free Wed; ⌚10am-1pm & 3.45-5.30pm Tue-Sat, 10.30am-2pm Sun) A 30-minute walk west of the city centre on the southern bank of Río Arlanzón, this monastery was once among the most prominent monasteries in Spain. Founded in 1187 by Eleanor of Aquitaine, daughter of Henry II of England and wife of Alfonso VIII of Castilla, it's still home to 35 Cistercian nuns. This veritable royal pantheon contains the tombs of numerous kings and queens, as well as a spectacular gilded Renaissance altar.

Sleeping & Eating

TOP CHOICE **Hotel Norte y Londres** HISTORIC HOTEL €€

(☎947 26 41 25; www.hotelnorteylondres.com; Plaza de Alonso Martínez 10; s/d €66/100; P@) Set in a former 16th-century palace and with understated period charm, this fine hotel promises spacious rooms with antique furnishings, polished wooden floors and pretty balconies; those on the 4th floor are more modern.

Hotel Jacobeo HOTEL €

(☎947 26 01 02; www.hoteljacobeo.com; Calle de San Juan 24; s/d incl breakfast €47/58;) This stylish small hotel has gleaming rooms of burgundy-and-white washed walls, terracotta tiles and parquet floors. Bathrooms are well equipped, if on the small side.

Hotel Meson del Cid HISTORIC HOTEL €€

(☎947 20 87 15; www.mesondelcid.es; Plaza de Santa María 8; s/d €70/100; P) Housed in the oldest nonmunicipal building in the city (dating from 1483), the rooms have burgundy-and-cream fabrics, aptly combined with dark wood furnishings and terracotta tiles. Most have stunning front-row views of the cathedral. The dated bathrooms are due for a slick makeover in 2011.

TOP CHOICE **Cervecería Morito** TAPAS €

(Calle de la Sombrerería 27; tapas €3, raciones €5-7) Cervecería Morito is the undisputed king of Burgos tapas bars and it's always crowded. A typical order is *alpargata* (lashings of cured ham with bread, tomato and olive oil) or *calamares fritos* (fried calamari).

La Fabula MODERN CASTILIAN €€

(☎947 26 30 92; Calle de la Puebla 18; menú del día €15, meals €25-30) With local celebrity chef Isabel Alvarez at the helm, fabulous La Fabula offers innovative slimmed-down dishes in a bright, modern dining room filled with classical music.

Information

Municipal tourist office (www.aytoburgos.es, in Spanish; Plaza del Rey Fernando 2; ⊙10am-2pm & 4.30-7.30pm Mon-Fri, 10am-1.30pm & 4-7.30pm Sat & Sun)

Regional tourist office (www.turismocastillayleon.com; Plaza de Alonso Martínez 7; ⊙9am-8pm Sun-Thu, 9am-9pm Fri & Sat)

Getting There & Away

BUS From Burgos' **bus station** (Calle de Miranda 4) regular buses run to Madrid (€16.25, 2¾ hours), Bilbao (€11.86, two hours) and León (€14.10, 3¾ hours).

TRAIN Burgos is connected to Madrid (from €25.60, four hours, up to seven daily), Bilbao (from €18.70, three hours, five daily), León (from €20.10, two hours, four daily) and Salamanca (from €20.90, 2½ hours, three daily).

CASTILLA-LA MANCHA

Known as the stomping ground of Don Quijote and Sancho Panza, Castilla-La Mancha conjures up images of lonely windmills, medieval castles and bleak, treeless plains. The characters of Miguel de Cevantes provide the literary context, but the richly historic cities of Toledo and Cuenca are the most compelling reasons to visit.

Toledo

POP 82,300

Toledo is Spain's equivalent of a downsized Rome. Commanding a hill rising above the Tajo River, it's crammed with monuments that attest to the waves of conquerors and communities – Roman, Visigoth, Jewish, Muslim and Christian – who have called the city home during its turbulent history. It's one of the country's major tourist attractions.

Sights

TOP CHOICE **Catedral de Toledo** CHURCH

(Plaza del Ayuntamiento; adult/child €7/free; ⊙10.30am-6.30pm Mon-Sat, 2-6.30pm Sun) Toledo's cathedral dominates the skyline, reflecting the city's historical significance as the heart of Catholic Spain. Within its hefty stone walls there are stained-glass windows, tombs of kings, and art in the sacristy by the likes of El Greco, Zurbarán, Crespi, Titian, Rubens and Velázquez. Behind the main altar lies a mesmerising piece of 18th-century Churrigueresque baroque, the **Transparente**. Look out for the **Custodia de Arfe**, by the celebrated 16th-century goldsmith Enrique de Arfe. With 18kg of pure gold and 183kg of silver, this 16th-century conceit bristles with some 260 statuettes.

Sinagoga del Tránsito SYNAGOGUE

(www.museosefardi.net, in Spanish; Calle Samuel Leví; adult/child €2.40/1.20, audioguide €3; ⊙10am-9pm Tue-Sat, 10am-2pm Sun) Toledo's former *judería* (Jewish quarter) was once home to 11 synagogues. Tragically, the bulk of Toledo's Jews were expelled in 1492. This magnificent synagogue was built in 1355 by special permission of Pedro I (construction of synagogues was prohibited in Christian Spain). The synagogue now houses the **Museo Sefardi** (⊙10am-9pm Tue-Sat, 10am-2pm Sun).

San Juan de los Reyes MONASTERY

(Calle San Juan de los Reyes 2; admission €2.30; ⊙10am-6pm) North of the synagogues lies the early-17th-century Franciscan monastery and church of San Juan de los Reyes, notable for its delightful cloisters. Provocatively built in the heart of the Jewish quarter, the monastery was founded by Isabel and Fernando to demonstrate the supremacy of the Catholic faith. The rulers had planned to be buried here but, when they took the greater prize of Granada in 1492 they opted for the purpose-built Capilla Real. Throughout the church and cloister the coat of arms of Isabel and Fernando dominates, and the chains of Christian prisoners liberated in Granada dangle from the outside walls. The prevalent late-Flemish Gothic style is enhanced with lavish Isabelline ornament, counterbalanced by Mudéjar decoration.

Sinagoga de Santa María La Blanca SYNAGOGUE

(Calle de los Reyes Católicos 4; admission €2.30; ⊙10am-6pm) This more modest synagogue is characterised by the horseshoe arches that delineate the five naves – classic Almohad architecture.

FREE **Museo de Santa Cruz** MUSEUM

(Calle de Cervantes 3; ⊙10am-6.30pm Mon-Sat, 10am-2pm Sun) Just off the Plaza de Zocodover, the 16th-century Museo de Santa Cruz is a beguiling combination of Gothic and Spanish Renaissance styles. The cloisters and carved wooden ceilings are superb, as are the upstairs displays of Spanish ceramics. The ground-level gallery contains a number of El Grecos, a painting attributed to Goya *(Cristo Crucificado)* and the wonderful 15th-century *Tapestry of the Astrolabes.*

Iglesia de Santo Tomé CHURCH
(www.santotome.org; Plaza del Conde; admission €2.30; 10am-6pm) This otherwise modest church contains El Greco's masterpiece, *El Entierro del Conde de Orgaz* (The Burial of the Count of Orgaz). When the count was buried in 1322, Saints Augustine and Stephen supposedly descended from heaven to attend the funeral. El Greco's work depicts the event, complete with miracle guests including himself, his son and Cervantes.

Mezquita del Cristo de la Luz MOSQUE
(Cuesta de Carmelitas Descalzos 10; admission €1.90; 2-8pm Fri, 10am-2pm & 3-8pm Sat & Sun) On the northern slopes of town you'll find a modest, yet beautiful, mosque. Built in the 10th century, it suffered the usual fate of being converted to a church (hence the religious frescos), but the original vaulting and arches survived.

Sleeping

Accommodation is often full, especially from Easter to September.

TOP CHOICE **Casa de Cisneros** BOUTIQUE HOTEL €€
(925 22 88 28; www.hostal-casa-de-cisneros.com; Calle del Cardenal Cisneros; s/d €50/80;) Across from the cathedral, this seductive hotel is built on the site of an 11th-century Islamic palace, parts of which can be spied via a glass porthole in the lobby floor. In comparison, this building is a 16th-century youngster with pretty stone-and-wood-beamed rooms and voguish en suite bathrooms.

Hostal Santo Tomé BUDGET HOTEL €
(925 22 17 12; www.hostalsantotome.com; Calle de Santo Tomé 13; s/d €42/55;) This good-value *hostal*, above a souvenir shop, has larger-than-most rooms with pale-wood floors and furniture, plus bathrooms with five-star attitude offering extras like shoe polish and hairdryers.

Hostal del Cardenal HISTORIC HOTEL €€
(925 22 49 00; www.hostaldelcardenal.com; Paseo de Recaredo 24; s/d €77/113;) A wonderful 18th-century mansion with soft ochre-coloured walls, arches and columns. The rooms are grand, yet welcoming, with dark furniture, plush fabrics and parquet floors. Several overlook the glorious terraced gardens.

La Posada de Manolo BOUTIQUE HOTEL €€
(925 28 22 50; www.laposadademanolo.com; Calle de Sixto Ramón Parro 8; s/d incl breakfast €42/66;) This memorable hotel has themed each floor with furnishings and decor reflecting one of the three cultures of Toledo: Christian, Islamic and Jewish. There are stunning views of the old town and cathedral from the terrace.

Parador Nacional Conde de Orgaz HISTORIC HOTEL €€€
(925 22 18 50; www.parador.es; Cerro del Emperador; s/d €171/159;) High above the southern bank of Río Tajo, Toledo's low-rise *parador* boasts a classy interior and breathtaking city views. To get here, cross the Puente de Alcántara bridge and follow the signs.

Eating

TOP CHOICE **Aurelio** TRADITIONAL SPANISH €€€
(925 22 13 92; Plaza del Ayuntamiento 4; meals €35-45; lunch & dinner Tue-Sat, lunch Mon) The three restaurants under this name are among the best of Toledo's top-end eateries (the other locations are Calle de la Sinagoga 1 and 6). Game, fresh produce and traditional dishes are prepared with panache. Reservations recommended.

Alfileritos 24 MODERN INTERNATIONAL €€
(www.alfileritos24.com; Calle de los Alfileritos 24; meals €25-35;) The 14th-century surroundings of columns, beams and barrel-vault ceilings are snazzily coupled with modern artwork and bright dining rooms spread over four floors. The menu demonstrates an innovative flourish in the kitchen.

La Abadía LIGHT DISHES €€
(www.abadiatoledo.com; Plaza de San Nicolás 3; meals €25-30;) In a former 16th-century palace, this atmospheric bar and restaurant has arches, niches and subtle lighting spread over a warren of brick-and-stone-clad rooms. The menu includes various lightweight dishes like *verduras a la parrilla* (grilled fresh vegetables) – perfect for small appetites.

Palacios TRADITIONAL SPANISH €
(Calle Alfonso X el Sabio 3; menú €13.90, meals €14-18) An unpretentious place where stained glass, beams and efficient old-fashioned service combine with traditional no-nonsense cuisine. Hungry? Try a gut-busting bowl of homestyle *judías con perdiz* (white beans with partridge) for starters.

Toledo

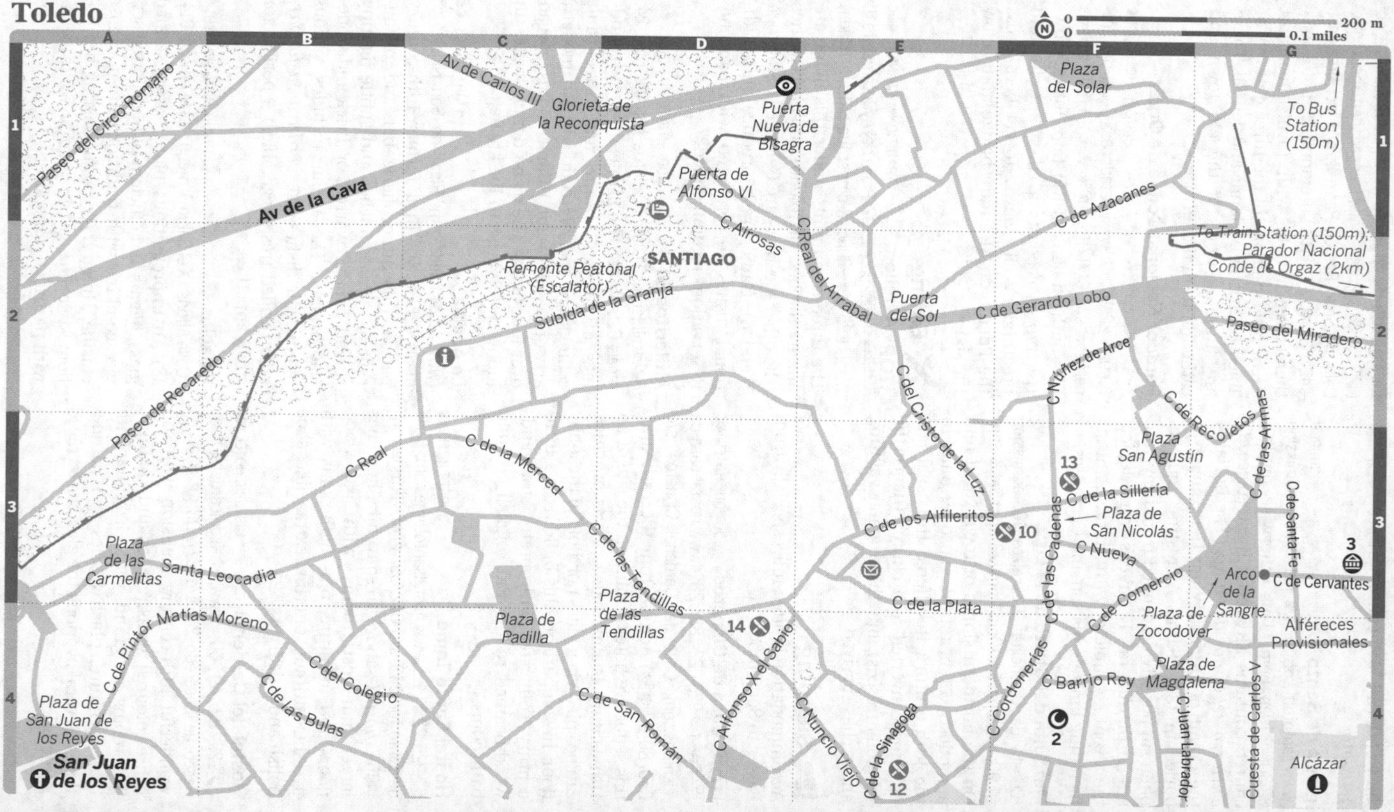

0 200 m
0 0.1 miles
A B C D E F G
1 2 3 4
Paseo del Circo Romano
Av de Carlos III
Glorieta de la Reconquista
Puerta Nueva de Bisagra
Plaza del Solar
To Bus Station (150m)
Puerta de Alfonso VI
Av de la Cava
7
C Airosas
C de Azacanes
To Train Station (150m); Parador Nacional Conde de Orgaz (2km)
SANTIAGO
Remonte Peatonal (Escalator)
C Real del Arrabal
Subida de la Granja
Puerta del Sol
C de Gerardo Lobo
Paseo del Miradero
Paseo de Recaredo
C Núñez de Arce
C del Cristo de la Luz
C de Recoletos
C de las Armas
Plaza San Agustín
13
C de la Sillería
C Real
C de la Merced
C de los Alfileritos
10
Plaza de San Nicolás
C de Santa Fe
C Nueva
3
Plaza de las Carmelitas
Santa Leocadia
C de las Tendillas
C de las Cadenas
C de Comercio
Arco de la Sangre
C de Cervantes
C de la Plata
Plaza de las Tendillas
Plaza de Padilla
14
Plaza de Zocodover
Alféreces Provisionales
C de Pintor Matías Moreno
C del Colegio
C Alfonso X el Sabio
C Cordonerías
C Barrio Rey
Plaza de Magdalena
C de las Bulas
C de San Román
C Nuncio Viejo
C de la Sinagoga
2
C Juan Labrador
Cuesta de Carlos V
Plaza de San Juan de los Reyes
San Juan de los Reyes
12
Alcázar

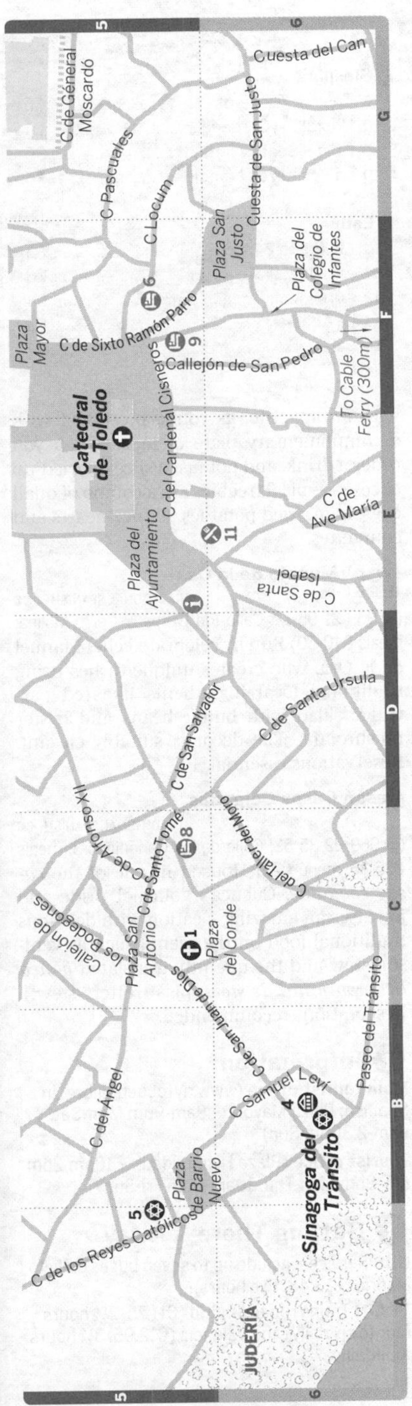

Information

Main tourist office (www.toledoturismo.com; Plaza del Ayuntamiento; ⌚10.30am-2.30pm Mon, 10.30am-2.30pm & 4.30-7pm Tue-Sun)

Provincial tourist office (www.diputoledo.es; Subida de la Granja; ⌚10am-5pm Mon-Sat, 10am-3pm Sun)

Getting There & Away

For most major destinations, you'll need to backtrack to Madrid.

BUS From Toledo's **bus station** (Avenida de Castilla La Mancha), buses depart for Madrid (from €5.25,one to 1½ hours) every half-hour from 6am to 10pm daily (less often on Sunday). There are also services on weekdays and Sunday to Cuenca (€11.40, 2¼ hours).

TRAIN The high-speed AVE service runs every hour or so to Madrid (€9.90, 30 minutes).

Cuenca

POP 53,000

A World Heritage site, Cuenca is one of Spain's most memorable small cities, its old centre a stage set of evocative medieval buildings. Most emblematic are the *casas colgadas,* the hanging houses.

Sights & Activities

TOP CHOICE Casas Colgadas — HISTORIC BUILDINGS

Cuenca's *casas colgadas* jut out precariously over the steep defile of Río Huécar. Dating from the 16th century, the houses with their layers of wooden balconies seem to emerge from the rock as if an extension of the cliffs. One of the finest restored examples now houses the **Museo de Arte Abstracto Español** (Museum of Abstract Art; www.march.es; adult/child €3/free; ⌚11am-2pm & 4-6pm Tue-Fri, 11am-2pm & 4-8pm Sat, 11am-2.30pm Sun), an impressive contemporary art museum, whose constantly evolving displays include works by Chillida, Tápies, Millares and the extraordinary landscapes by Eusebio Sempere (1924–85), which really capture the colourful patterned plains of La Mancha. For the best views of the *casas colgadas,* cross the **Puente de San Pablo** footbridge, or walk to the **mirador** at the northernmost tip of the old town.

Museo de la Semana Santa — MUSEUM

(Calle Andrés de Cabrera; adult/child €3/free; ⌚11am-2pm & 4.30-7.30pm Wed-Sat; 👪) The next best thing to experiencing Semana Santa (Easter) first-hand, spread over two floors are audiovisual displays showing the

Toledo

Top Sights

Catedral de Toledo........E5
San Juan de los Reyes........A4
Sinagoga del Tránsito........B6

Sights

1 Iglesia de Santo Tomé........C5
2 Mezquita del Cristo de la Luz........F4
3 Museo de Santa Cruz........G3
4 Museo Sefardi........B6
5 Sinagoga de Santa María La Blanca........A5

Sleeping

6 Casa de Cisneros........F5
7 Hostal del Cardenal........D1
8 Hostal Santo Tomé........C5
9 La Posada de Manolo........F5

Eating

10 Alfileritos 24........F3
11 Aurelio........E6
12 Aurelio........E4
13 La Abadía........F3
14 Palacios........D4

processions by local brotherhoods, against a background of sombre music.

Sleeping

TOP CHOICE Posada de San José HISTORIC HOTEL €

(☎969 21 13 00; www.posadasanjose.com; Ronda de Julián Romero 4; s/d without bathroom €30/43, d from €82) Owned by Antonio and his Canadian wife, Jennifer, this 17th-century former choir school retains an extraordinary monastic charm with its labyrinth of rooms, crumbling portal, uneven floors and original tiles. The cheaper rooms are in the former priests' cells, while the more costly doubles combine homey comfort with sumptuous old-word charm. Several have balconies with dramatic views of the gorge.

Hostal San Pedro BUDGET HOTEL €

(☎969 23 45 43, 628 407601; www.hostalsanpedro.es; Calle San Pedro 34; s/d €35/60) At this well-priced and well-positioned *hostal,* rooms have butter-coloured paintwork, wrought-iron bed heads and rustic wood furniture; the bathrooms are shiny and modern. The owners live elsewhere, so be sure to call before you show up.

Parador HISTORIC HOTEL €€

(☎969 23 23 20; www.parador.es; Calle de Hoz de Huécar; d €143; P❄) This majestic former convent commands stunning views of the *casas colgadas.* The aesthetically revamped rooms have a luxury corporate feel, while the public areas are headily historic with giant tapestries and antiques.

Eating

TOP CHOICE La Bodeguilla de Basilio TAPAS €

(Calle Fray Luis de León 3; raciones €10-13; ⊙lunch & dinner Mon-Sat, lunch Sun) Arrive here with an appetite, as you're presented with a complimentary plate of tapas when you order a drink, and not just a slice of dried-up cheese – typical freebies are a combo of quail eggs, ham, fried potatoes, lettuce hearts and courgettes.

TOP CHOICE Manolo de la Osa TRADITIONAL SPANISH €€€

(☎969 21 95 12; Calle Río Gritos 5, Cerro Molina; meals €40-50) Run by celebrated chef Manuel de la Osa, who creates unique dishes using traditional local ingredients like red partridge salad with butter beans and oyster mushrooms. The decor is suitably elegant. Reservations essential.

Mesón Casas Colgadas TRADITIONAL SPANISH €€

(☎969 22 35 52; Calle de los Canónigos 3; meals €25-35, menú €27) Housed in one of the *casas colgadas,* Cuenca's gourmet pride and joy fuses an amazing location with delicious traditional food on the menu, such as venison stew and the quaintly translated *boned little pork hands stew* (pigs trotters stew!). Reservations recommended.

Information

Main tourist office (www.aytocuenca.org, in Spanish; Plaza Mayor; ⊙9am-9pm Mon-Sat, 9am-2.30pm Sun)

Tourist office (Plaza Hispanidad; ⊙10am-2pm & 5-8pm Mon-Thu, 10am-8pm Fri-Sun)

Getting There & Away

BUS Services include up to seven buses daily to Madrid (€13.48, two hours).

TRAIN Trains run to Madrid (€11.75, 2½ hours, four to six daily) and Valencia (€12.95, 3¼ hours, four daily).

CATALONIA

Home to stylish Barcelona, ancient Tarragona, romantic Girona, and countless alluring destinations along the coast, in the Pyrenees and in the rural interior, Catalonia (Catalunya in Catalan, Cataluña in Castilian) is a treasure box waiting to be opened.

Barcelona

POP 1.62 MILLION

Barcelona is one of Europe's coolest cities. Despite two millennia of history it's a forward-thinking place, always on the cutting edge of art, design and cuisine. Whether you explore its medieval palaces and plazas, gawk at the Modernista masterpieces, shop for designer duds along its bustling boulevards, sample its exciting nightlife or just soak up the sun on the beaches, you'll find it hard not to fall in love with this vibrant city.

As much as Barcelona is a visual feast, it will also lead you into culinary temptation. Anything from traditional Catalan cooking through the latest in avant-garde new Spanish cuisine will have your appetite in overdrive.

Central Plaça de Catalunya marks the divide between historic and modern Barcelona. From here, the pedestrian boulevard La Rambla shoots southeast to the sea, with the busy Barri Gòtic (Gothic Quarter) and El Raval districts hugging it on either side. To the northwest spreads L'Eixample, laced with Modernista marvels and endless shopping and dining options.

Sights & Activities

La Rambla HISTORIC AREA

Spain's most famous boulevard, the part-pedestrianised La Rambla, explodes with life. Stretching from **Plaça de Catalunya** (Map p1070) to the waterfront, it's lined with street artists, newsstands and vendors selling everything from mice to magnolias.

The colourful **Mercat de la Boqueria** (Map p1070; La Rambla; 8am-8pm Mon-Sat; M Liceu), a fresh food market with a Modernista entrance, is one of La Rambla's highlights. Nearby, stop for a tour of the **Gran Teatre del Liceu** (Map p1070; 93 485 99 14; www.liceubarcelona.com; La Rambla dels Caputxins 51-59; admission with/without guide €8.70/4; guided tour 10am, unguided visits 11.30am, noon, 12.30pm & 1pm; M Liceu), the city's fabulous opera house.

Also stop at the **Plaça Reial** (Map p1070; M Liceu), a grand 19th-century square surrounded by arcades lined with restaurants and bars. At the waterfront end of La Rambla stands the **Mirador de Colom** (Map p1070; M Drassanes), a statue of Columbus atop a tall pedestal.

Barri Gòtic HISTORIC AREA

Barcelona's Gothic **Catedral** (Map p1070; Plaça de la Seu; admission free, special visit €5; 8am-12.45pm & 5.15-8pm, special visit 1-5pm Mon-Sat, 2-5pm Sun & holidays; M Jaume I) was built atop the ruins of an 11th-century Romanesque church. Highlights include the cool cloister, the crypt tomb of martyr Santa Eulàlia (one of Barcelona's two patron saints), the choir stalls (€2.20), the lift to the rooftop (€2.20) and the modest art collection in the **Sala Capitular** (chapterhouse; admission €2). You only pay the individual prices if you visit outside the special visiting hours.

Not far from the cathedral is pretty **Plaça del Rei** and the fascinating **Museu d'Història de Barcelona** (Map p1070; www.museuhistoria.bcn.cat; Carrer del Veguer; adult/senior & student/child under 7yr €7/5/free, free for all from 4pm 1st Sat of month & from 3pm Sun; 10am-8pm Tue-Sun, to 3pm holidays; M Jaume I), where you can visit a 4000-sq-metre excavated site of Roman Barcelona under the plaza. The museum encompasses historic buildings including the **Palau Reial Major** (Main Royal Palace), once a residence of the kings of Catalonia and Aragón, and its **Saló del Tinell** (Great Hall).

The area between Carrer dels Banys Nous, to the east of the church, and Plaça de Sant Jaume is known as the Call, and was Barcelona's **Jewish quarter** from at least the 11th century until anti-Semitism saw the Jews expelled from it in 1424. Here the sparse remains of what is purported to be the medieval **Sinagoga Major** (Main Synagogue; Map p1070; www.calldebarcelona.org; Carrer de Marlet 5; admission by €2 donation; 10.30am-6pm Mon-Fri, to 3pm Sat & Sun; M Liceu) have been revealed.

El Raval NEIGHBOURHOOD

To the west of La Rambla is El Raval district, a once-seedy, now-funky area overflowing with cool bars and shops. Visit the **Museu d'Art Contemporani de Barcelona** (Macba; Map p1070; 93 412 08 10 www.macba.cat; Plaça dels Àngels 1; adult/concession €7.50/6; 11am-8pm Mon & Wed, to midnight Thu-Fri, 10am-8pm Sat, 10am-3pm Sun & holidays; M Universitat), which has an impressive collection of international contemporary art.

Barcelona

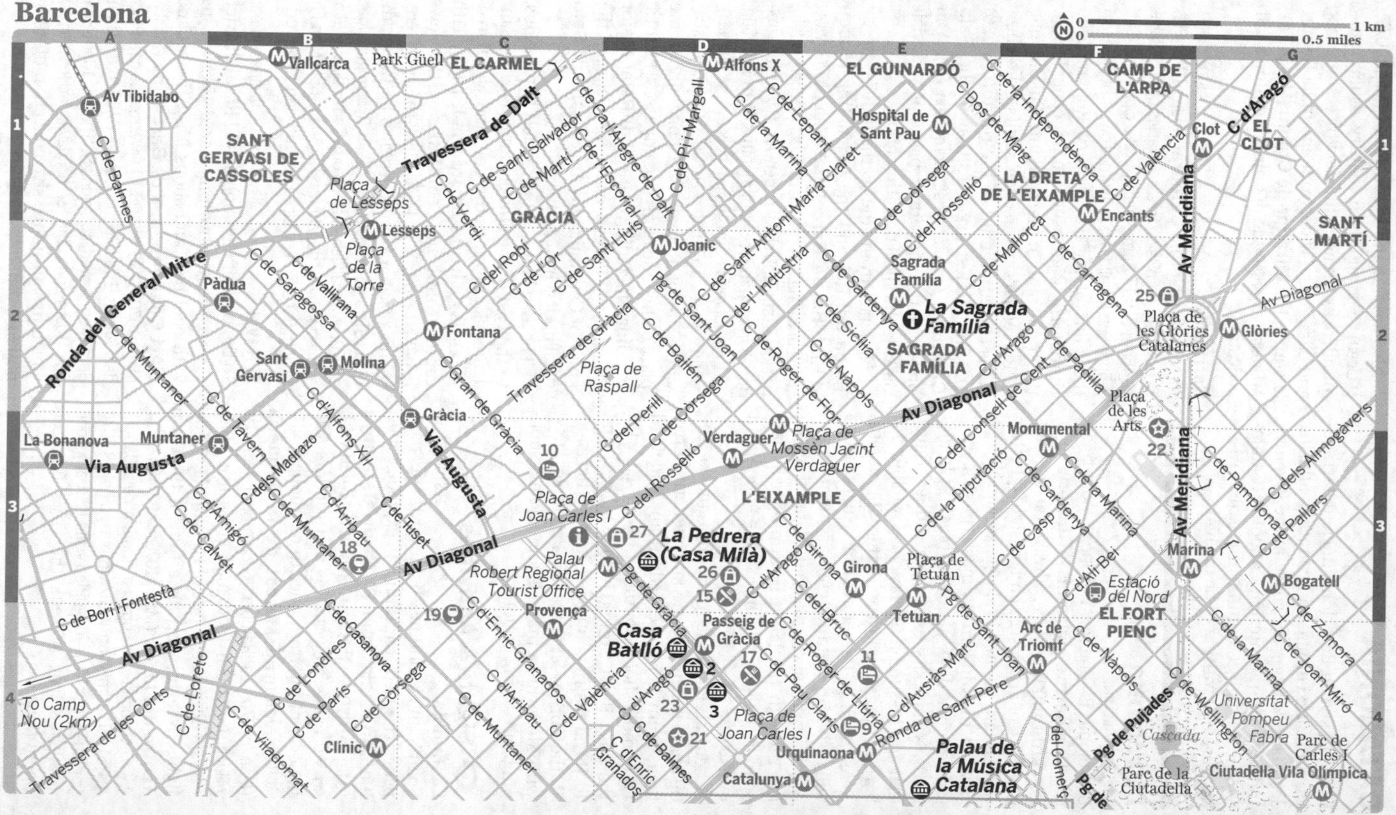

0 — 1 km
0 — 0.5 miles

A B C D E F G
1 2 3 4

Vallcarca
Park Güell
EL CARMEL
Alfons X
EL GUINARDÓ
CAMP DE L'ARPA
Av Tibidabo
C de Balmes
SANT GERVASI DE CASSOLES
Travessera de Dalt
Plaça de Lesseps
Lesseps
Plaça de la Torre
C de Verdi
C de Sant Salvador
C de Martí
C de Ca l'Alegre de Dalt
C de l'Escorial
C de Pi i Margall
C de Lepant
C de la Marina
Hospital de Sant Pau
C Dos de Maig
C de la Independència
Clot
C d'Aragó
EL CLOT
C de València
LA DRETA DE L'EIXAMPLE
Encants
Av Meridiana
SANT MARTÍ
GRÀCIA
C del Robí
C de l'Or
C de Sant Lluís
Joanic
C de Sant Antoni Maria Claret
C de Còrsega
C del Rosselló
C de Mallorca
C de Cartagena
Ronda del General Mitre
Pàdua
C de Saragossa
C de Vallirana
Fontana
C de l'Indústria
Pg de Sant Joan
C de Sardenya
Sagrada Família
La Sagrada Família
SAGRADA FAMÍLIA
C de Sicília
25
Plaça de les Glòries Catalanes
Glòries
Av Diagonal
C de Muntaner
Sant Gervasi
Molina
Travessera de Gràcia
Plaça de Raspall
C de Bailèn
C de Roger de Flor
C de Nàpols
C d'Aragó
C de Padilla
Gràcia
C Gran de Gràcia
C d'Alfons XII
Via Augusta
C de Tavern
La Bonanova
Muntaner
C dels Madrazo
C del Perill
C de Còrsega
Verdaguer
Plaça de Mossèn Jacint Verdaguer
Av Diagonal
C del Consell de Cent
Monumental
Plaça de les Arts
22
C dels Almogàvers
10
C d'Amigó
C de Calvet
C de Muntaner
C d'Aribau
C de Tuset
C del Rosselló
L'EIXAMPLE
C de la Diputació
C de Sardenya
C de la Marina
C de Pamplona
C de Pallars
Plaça de Joan Carles I
27
La Pedrera (Casa Milà)
C de Girona
Girona
Plaça de Tetuan
C de Casp
Marina
18
Palau Robert Regional Tourist Office
26
15
C d'Aragó
C del Bruc
Tetuan
C d'Alí Bei
Estació del Nord
Bogatell
EL FORT PIENC
C de Bori i Fontestà
19
C d'Enric Granados
Provença
Pg de Gràcia
Passeig de Gràcia
Casa Batlló
2
17
C de Roger de Llúria
11
Pg de Sant Joan
Arc de Triomf
C de Nàpols
C de la Marina
C de Zamora
C de Joan Miró
Av Diagonal
C de Loreto
C de Londres
C de Casanova
C de València
23
3
C de Pau Claris
C d'Ausiàs Marc
Ronda de Sant Pere
C de Wellington
Pg de Pujades
Universitat Pompeu Fabra
Cascada
Parc de Carles I
To Camp Nou (2km)
Travessera de les Corts
C de Viladomat
C de París
C de Còrsega
Clínic
C de Muntaner
C d'Aribau
C de Balmes
C d'Enric Granados
21
Plaça de Joan Carles I
9
Urquinaona
Catalunya
Palau de la Música Catalana
C del Comerç
Pg de
Parc de la Ciutadella
Ciutadella Vila Olímpica

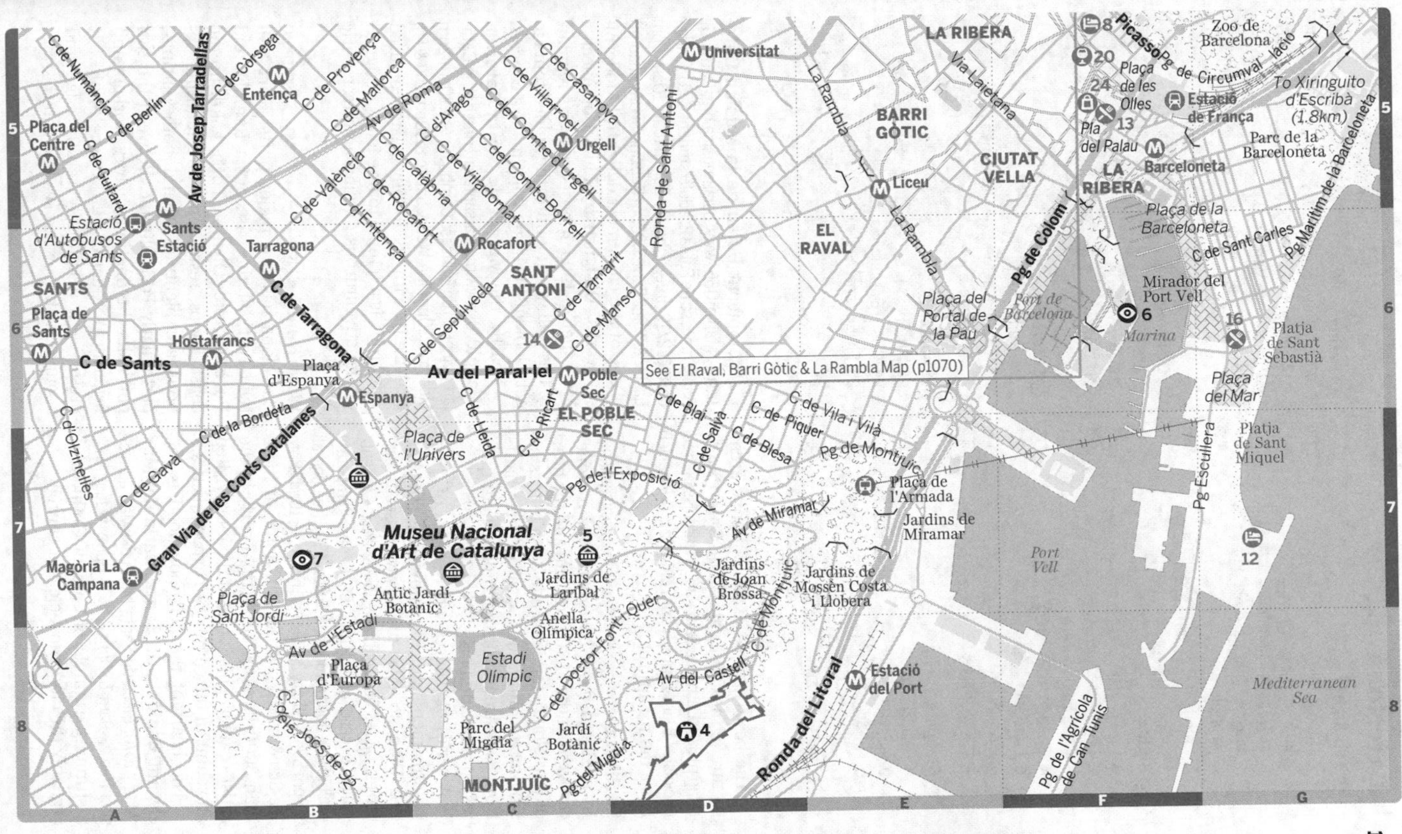

See El Raval, Barri Gòtic & La Rambla Map (p1070)
To Xiringuito d'Escribà (1.8km)
Mediterranean Sea
Port Vell
Port de Barcelona
Marina
LA RIBERA
BARRI GÒTIC
CIUTAT VELLA
EL RAVAL
SANT ANTONI
EL POBLE SEC
SANTS
MONTJUÏC
Pg de Colom
La Rambla
Via Laietana
Ronda de Sant Antoni
Ronda del Litoral
Av del Paral·lel
Gran Via de les Corts Catalanes
C de Tarragona
C de Sants
Av de Josep Tarradellas
Pg Marítim de la Barceloneta
Pg de Circumval·lació
Pg Escullera
Pg de l'Agrícola
Pg de Can Tunis
Pg de Montjuïc
Av de Miramar
C de Montjuïc
Av del Castell
C del Doctor Font i Quer
Pg del Migdia
Av de l'Estadi
C dels Jocs de 92
Pg de l'Exposició
C de Vila i Vilà
C de Piquer
C de Blesa
C de Blai
C de Salvà
C de Ricart
C de Lleida
C de Sepúlveda
C de Mansó
C de Tamarit
C de Casanova
C de Villarroel
C del Comte d'Urgell
C del Comte Borrell
C de Viladomat
C d'Aragó
C de Calàbria
C de Rocafort
C d'Entença
C de Mallorca
C de València
C de Provença
C de Còrsega
Av de Roma
C de Berlín
C de Numància
C de Guitard
C de la Bordeta
C de Gavà
C d'Olzinelles
C de Sant Carles
Universitat
Liceu
Urgell
Rocafort
Poble Sec
Espanya
Tarragona
Entença
Hostafrancs
Sants Estació
Plaça de Sants
Plaça del Centre
Estació d'Autobusos de Sants
Magòria La Campana
Estació del Port
Barceloneta
Estació de França
Zoo de Barcelona
Parc de la Barceloneta
Plaça de la Barceloneta
Mirador del Port Vell
Platja de Sant Sebastià
Platja de Sant Miquel
Plaça del Mar
Plaça del Portal de la Pau
Plaça de l'Armada
Jardins de Miramar
Jardins de Mossèn Costa i Llobera
Jardins de Joan Brossa
Jardins de Laribal
Anella Olímpica
Estadi Olímpic
Jardí Botànic
Antic Jardí Botànic
Parc del Migdia
Museu Nacional d'Art de Catalunya
Plaça de l'Univers
Plaça d'Espanya
Plaça d'Europa
Plaça de Sant Jordi
Plaça de les Olles
Pla del Palau
Picasso

Barcelona

Top Sights
Casa Batlló D4
La Pedrera (Casa Milà) D3
La Sagrada Família E2
Museu Nacional d'Art de Catalunya C7
Palau de la Música Catalana E4

Sights
1 CaixaForum B7
2 Casa Amatller D4
3 Casa Lleó Morera D4
4 Castell de Montjuïc D8
5 Fundació Joan Miró C7
6 L'Aquàrium F6
7 Poble Espanyol B7

Sleeping
8 Chic & Basic F5
9 Hostal Goya E4
10 Hotel Casa Fuster C3
11 Hotel Constanza E4
12 W Barcelona G7

Eating
13 Cal Pep F5
14 Inopia C6
15 Relais de Venise D3
16 Suquet de l'Almirall G6
17 Tapaç 24 .... D4

Drinking
18 Berlin B3
19 Dry Martini C4
20 Gimlet F5

Entertainment
21 Arena Madre D4
22 Teatre Nacional de Catalunya F3
Terrazza .... (see 7)

Shopping
23 Antonio Miró D4
24 Custo Barcelona F5
25 Els Encants Vells F2
26 Joan Murrià D3
27 Vinçon D3

The best example of Romanesque architecture in the city, **Església de Sant Pau** (Map p1070; Carrer de Sant Pau 101; admission free; ⏲cloister 10am-1pm & 4-7pm Mon-Sat; Ⓜ Paral.lel) has a dainty little cloister.

La Ribera NEIGHBOURHOOD

In medieval days, La Ribera was a stone's throw from the Mediterranean and the heart of Barcelona's foreign trade, with homes belonging to numerous wealthy merchants. Now it's a trendy district full of boutiques, restaurants and bars.

A series of palaces where some of those wealthy merchants lived now house the **Museu Picasso** (Map p1070; www.museupicasso.bcn.es; Carrer de Montcada 15-23; adult/student/senior & child under 16yr €9/6/free, temporary exhibitions adult/student €5.80/2.90, free for all 3-8pm Sun & all day 1st Sun of month; ⏲10am-8pm Tue-Sun & holidays; Ⓜ Jaume I), home to more than 3000 Picassos, most from early in the artist's career. This is one of the most visited museums in the country, so expect queues.

The heart of the neighbourhood is the elegant **Església de Santa Maria del Mar** (Map p1070; Plaça de Santa Maria del Mar; admission free; ⏲9am-1.30pm & 4.30-8pm; Ⓜ Jaume I), a stunning example of Catalan Gothic and arguably the city's most elegant church.

The opulent **Palau de la Música Catalana** (Map p1066; www.palaumusica.org; Carrer de Sant Francesc de Paula 2; adult/student & EU senior/child €12/10/free; ⏲hourly 50min tours 10am-6pm Easter & Aug, 10am-3.30pm Sep-Jul; Ⓜ Urquinaona) is one of the city's most delightful Modernista works. Designed by Lluís Domènech i Montaner in 1905, it hosts concerts regularly. It is well worth joining the guided tours to get a look inside if you don't make a concert.

Nearby, the **Mercat de Santa Caterina** (Map p1070; www.mercatsantacaterina.net, in Catalan; Avinguda de Francesc Cambó 16; ⏲7.30am-2pm Mon, to 3.30pm Tue, Wed & Sat, to 8.30pm Thu & Fri; Ⓜ Jaume I), with its loopily pastel-coloured wavy roof, is a temple to fine foods designed by the adventurous Catalan architect Enric Miralles.

Waterfront SEAFRONT

Barcelona has two major ports: **Port Vell** (Old Port), at the base of La Rambla, and **Port Olímpic** (Olympic Port), 1.5km up the coast. Shops, restaurants and nightlife options are plentiful around both marinas, particularly Port Olímpic. Between the two ports sits the onetime factory workers and fishermen's quarter, **La Barceloneta**. It preserves a delightfully scruffy edge and abounds with crowded seafood eateries.

At the end of Moll d'Espanya in Port Vell is **L'Aquàrium** (Map p1066; www.aquarium bcn.com; Moll d'Espanya; adult/senior over 60yr/child 4-12yr/under 4yr €17.50/14.50/12.50/free; ⌚9.30am-11pm Jul & Aug; Ⓜ Drassanes), with its 80m-long shark tunnel. Short of diving among them (which can be arranged), this is as close as you can get to a set of shark teeth without being bitten.

Barcelona boasts 4km of city *platjas* (beaches), beginning with the gritty **Platja de la Barceloneta** and continuing north-east, beyond Port Olímpic, with a series of cleaner, more attractive strands. All get packed in summer.

L'Eixample NEIGHBOURHOOD

Modernisme, the Catalan version of art nouveau, transformed Barcelona's cityscape in the early 20th century. Most Modernista works were built in L'Eixample, the grid-plan district that was developed from the 1870s on.

Modernisme's star architect was the eccentric Antoni Gaudí (1852–1926), a devout Catholic whose work is full of references to nature and Christianity. His masterpiece, **La Sagrada Família** (Expiatory Temple of the Holy Family; Map p1066; ☎93 207 30 31; www.sagrada familia.org; Carrer de Mallorca 401; adult/senior & student/child to 10yr €12/10/free, combined with Casa-Museu Gaudí in Park Güell €14/12/free; ⌚9am-8pm Apr-Sep, to 6pm Oct-Mar; Ⓜ Sagrada Família), is a work in progress and Barcelona's most famous building. Construction began in 1882 and could be completed in 2020. Gaudí spent 40 years working on the church, though he only saw the crypt, the apse and the nativity facade completed. Eventually there'll be 18 towers, all more than 100m high, representing the 12 apostles, four evangelists and Mary, Mother of God, plus the tallest tower (170m) standing for Jesus Christ. Climb high inside some of the towers (or take the elevator, €2) for a new perspective.

Gaudí's **La Pedrera** (Casa Milà; Map p1066; www.fundaciocaixacatalunya.es; Carrer de Provença 261-265; adult/student & EU senior/child under 13yr €10/6/free; ⌚9am-8pm; Ⓜ Diagonal) is his best-known secular creation, named (it translates as The Quarry) because of its uneven grey-stone facade, which ripples around the corner of Carrer de Provença. The wave effect is emphasised by elaborate wrought-iron balconies. Inside, you can visit a museum about Gaudí and his work, a Modernista apartment and the surreal rooftop with its bizarre chimneys.

Just down the street is the unique facade of the **Casa Batlló** (Map p1066; www.casabatllo.es; Passeig de Gràcia 43; adult/student, child 7-18yr & senior/child under 7yr €17.80/14.25/free; ⌚9am-8pm; Ⓜ Passeig de Gràcia), an allegory for the legend of St George (Sant Jordi in Catalan) the dragon-slayer. On the same block are two other Modernista gems, **Casa Amatller** (Passeig de Gràcia 41) by Josep Puig i Cadafalch and the **Casa Lleó Morera** (Passeig de Gràcia 35) by Lluís Domènech i Montaner.

High up in the Gràcia district sits Gaudí's enchanting **Park Güell** (Carrer d'Olot 7; admission free; ⌚10am-9pm; Ⓜ Lesseps or Vallcarca, 🚌24), originally designed to be a self-contained community with houses, schools and shops. The project flopped, but we're left with a Dr Seuss–style playground filled with colourful mosaics and Gaudí-designed paths and plazas.

The website www.rutadelmodernisme.com is a great resource on Modernisme in Barcelona.

Montjuïc NEIGHBOURHOOD

Southwest of the city centre and with views out to sea and over the city, Montjuïc serves as a Central Park of sorts and is a great place for a jog or stroll. It's dominated by the **Castell de Montjuïc** (Map p1066), a one-time fortress with great views. Buses 50, 55 and 61 all head up here. A local bus, the PM (Parc de Montjuïc) line, does a circle trip from Plaça d'Espanya to the *castell*. Cable cars and a funicular line also access the area.

Museu Nacional d'Art de Catalunya (Map p1066; www.mnac.cat; Mirador del Palau Nacional; adult/student/senior & child under 15yr €8.50/6/free, 1st Sun of month free; ⌚10am-7pm Tue-Sat, to 2.30pm Sun & holidays; Ⓜ Espanya) is a broad panoply of Catalan and European art. The Romanesque frescos are truly stunning.

El Raval, Barri Gòtic & La Rambla (Barcelona)

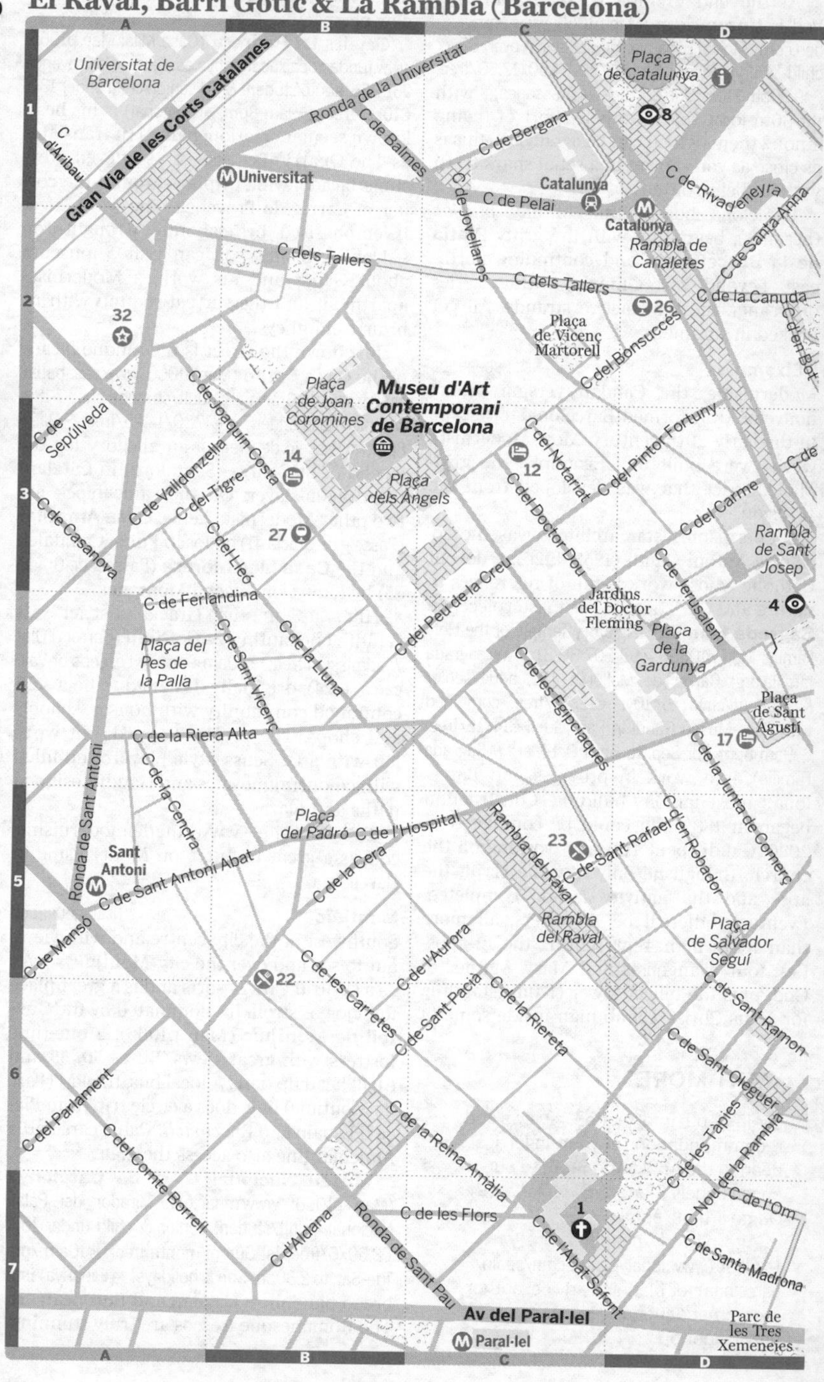

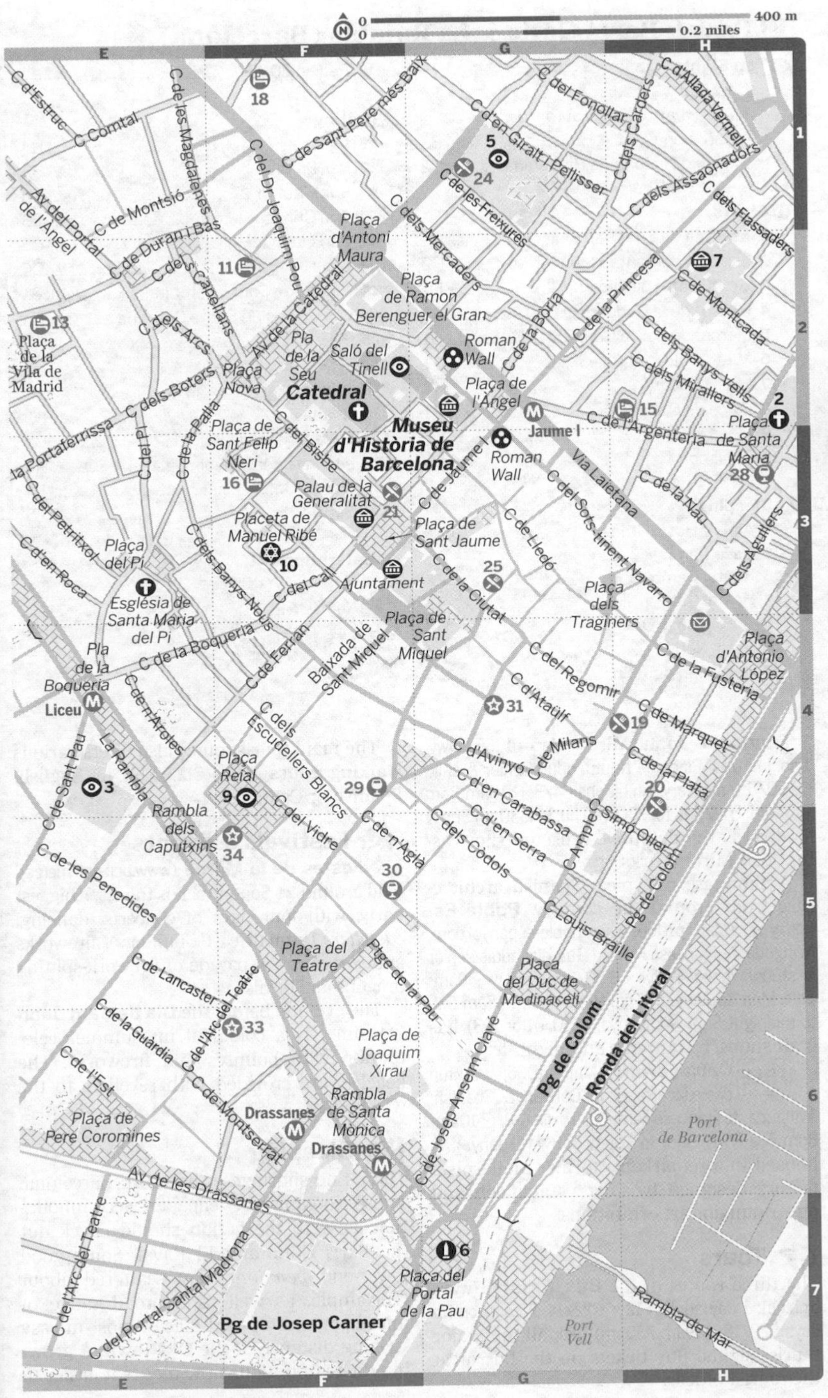
0 400 m
0 0.2 miles
C d'Estruc
C Comtal
C de les Magdalenes
C de Sant Pere més Baix
C del Fonollar
C dels Carders
C d'Allada Vermell
C d'en Giralt i Pellisser
C dels Assaonadors
C de les Freixures
C dels Flassaders
C del Dr Joaquim Pou
Av del Portal de l'Àngel
C de Montsió
C de Duran i Bas
C dels Capellans
Plaça d'Antoni Maura
C dels Mercaders
Plaça de Ramon Berenguer el Gran
C de la Princesa
C de Montcada
Av de la Catedral
C dels Arcs
Plaça de la Vila de Madrid
Pla de la Seu
Saló del Tinell
Roman Wall
C de la Bòria
C dels Banys Vells
C dels Miralers
Plaça Nova
C dels Boters
Catedral
Plaça de l'Àngel
Jaume I
C de l'Argenteria
Plaça de Santa Maria
Museu d'Història de Barcelona
la Portaferrissa
C de la Palla
Plaça de Sant Felip Neri
C del Bisbe
C de Jaume I
Roman Wall
Via Laietana
C del Sots-tinent Navarro
C de la Nau
C del Pi
C del Petritxol
Palau de la Generalitat
Placeta de Manuel Ribé
Plaça de Sant Jaume
C de Lledó
C dels Agullers
C d'en Roca
Plaça del Pi
C dels Banys Nous
C del Call
Ajuntament
C de la Ciutat
Plaça dels Traginers
Església de Santa Maria del Pi
C de la Boqueria
Baixada de Sant Miquel
Plaça de Sant Miquel
Plaça d'Antonio López
C de Ferran
C del Regomir
C de la Fusteria
Pla de la Boqueria
Liceu
C de n'Aroles
C dels Escudellers Blancs
C d'Ataülf
C de Marquet
C de Sant Pau
La Rambla
Plaça Reial
C de Milans
C d'Avinyó
C de la Plata
Rambla dels Caputxins
C del Vidre
C de n'Aglà
C d'en Carabassa
C d'en Serra
C dels Còdols
C Ample
C Simó Oller
Pg de Colom
C de les Penedides
C Louis Braille
Plaça del Teatre
Ptge de la Pau
Plaça del Duc de Medinaceli
C de Lancaster
C de l'Arc del Teatre
C de la Guàrdia
Plaça de Joaquim Xirau
C de Josep Anselm Clavé
Pg de Colom
Ronda del Litoral
C de l'Est
C de Montserrat
Rambla de Santa Mònica
Drassanes
Drassanes
Port de Barcelona
Plaça de Pere Coromines
Av de les Drassanes
C de l'Arc del Teatre
C del Portal Santa Madrona
Plaça del Portal de la Pau
Pg de Josep Carner
Port Vell
Rambla de Mar

El Raval, Barri Gòtic & La Rambla (Barcelona)

Top Sights
Catedral ... F2
Museu d'Art Contemporani de Barcelona ... B3
Museu d'Història de Barcelona ... G2

Sights
1 Església de Sant Pau ... C7
2 Església de Santa Maria del Mar ... H2
3 Gran Teatre del Liceu ... E4
4 Mercat de la Boqueria ... D4
5 Mercat de Santa Caterina ... G1
6 Mirador de Colom ... G7
7 Museu Picasso ... H2
8 Plaça de Catalunya ... D1
9 Plaça Reial ... F4
10 Sinagoga Major ... F3

Sleeping
11 Alberg Hostal Itaca ... F2
12 Casa Camper ... C3
13 Hostal Campi ... E2
14 Hostal Gat Raval ... B3
15 Hotel Banys Oriental ... H2
16 Hotel Neri ... F3
17 Hotel San Agustín ... D4
18 Pensió 2000 ... F1

Eating
19 Agut ... H4
20 Bar Celta ... H4
Bar Pinotxo ... (see 4)
21 Can Conesa ... F3
22 Can Lluís ... B5
23 Casa Leopoldo ... C5
24 Cuines de Santa Caterina ... G1
Les Cuines de Santa Caterina ... (see 5)
25 Pla ... G3

Drinking
26 Boadas ... D2
27 Casa Almirall ... B3
28 La Vinya del Senyor ... H3
29 Marula Café ... F4
30 Soul Club ... F5

Entertainment
31 Harlem Jazz Club ... G4
32 Metro ... A2
33 Moog ... F6
34 Sala Tarantos ... F5

Fundació Joan Miró (Map p1066; www.bcn.fjmiro.es; Plaça de Neptu; adult/senior & child €8.50/6, temporary exhibitions €4/3; ⏲10am-8pm Tue-Wed, Fri & Sat, to 9.30pm Thu, to 2.30pm Sun & holidays) is the definitive museum showcasing Joan Miró's works.

A showcase of typical Spanish architecture from around the country, **Poble Espanyol** (Map p1066; www.poble-espanyol.com; Avinguda de Francesc Ferrer i Guàrdia; adult/senior & student/child 4-12yr €8.50/6.50/5.50; ⏲9am-8pm Mon, to 2am Tue-Thu, to 4am Fri, to 5am Sat, to midnight Sun; Ⓜ Espanya, 🚌 50, 61 or 193) has craft shops, restaurants and nightlife.

FREE **CaixaForum** (Map p1066; www.fundacio.lacaixa.es, in Catalan & Spanish; Avinguda de Francesc Ferrer i Guàrdia 6-8; ⏲10am-8pm Tue-Fri & Sun, to 10pm Sat; Ⓜ Espanya) is housed in a remarkable former Modernista factory designed by Puig i Cadafalch and puts on major art exhibitions.

Tours

The three routes of the **Bus Turístic** (www.tmb.net; 1 day adult/4-12yr €22/14, 2 consecutive days €29/18; ⏲9am-7.30pm) link all the major tourist sights. Buy tickets on the bus or at the tourist office.

The main tourist office also offers various **walking tours** (tours €12.50-19) in English, Spanish or Catalan.

Festivals & Events

The **Festes de la Mercè** (www.bcn.cat/merce), held around 24 September, is the city's biggest party, with four days of concerts, dancing, *castellers* (human castle-builders), fireworks and *correfocs* – a parade of firework-spitting dragons and devils.

The evening before the **Dia de Sant Joan** (24 June) is a colourful midsummer celebration with bonfires and fireworks. The beaches are crowded with revellers to the wee hours.

Sleeping

There's no shortage of hotels in Barcelona. Those looking for cheaper accommodation close to the action should check out the Barri Gòtic and El Raval. Some good lower-end *pensiones* are scattered about L'Eixample, as well as a broad range of midrange and top-end places, most in easy striking distance of the Old Town. A growing range of options now makes it easier to stay in La Ribera and near the beaches at La Barceloneta.

Numerous private apartment-rental companies operate in Barcelona. These can often be a better deal than staying in a hotel. Start your search at **Aparteasy** (93 451 67 66; www.aparteasy.com), **Barcelona On Line** (902 887 017, 93 343 79 93; www.barcelona-on-line.es) and **Rent a Flat in Barcelona** (93 342 73 00; www.rentaflatinbarcelona.com).

LA RAMBLA & BARRI GÒTIC

Hotel Neri HOTEL €€€
(Map p1070; 93 304 06 55; www.hotelneri.com; Carrer de Sant Sever 5; d from €235; MLiceu;) Occupying a beautifully adapted, centuries-old building, this stunningly renovated medieval mansion combines historic stone walls with sexy plasma TVs. Downstairs is a fine restaurant, and you can take a drink and catch some rays on the roof deck.

Alberg Hostel Itaca HOSTEL €
(Map p1070; 93 301 97 51; www.itacahostel.com; Carrer de Ripoll 21; dm €14-20, d €55; MJaume I;) A bright, quiet hostel near La Catedral, Itaca has spacious dorms (sleeping six, eight or 12 people), with parquet floors, spring colours and a couple of doubles with private bathroom.

Hostal Campi BUDGET HOTEL €
(Map p1070; 93 301 35 45; www.hostalcampi.com; Carrer de la Canuda 4; d €67, s/d without bathroom €34/57; MCatalunya) An excellent bottom-end deal. The best rooms are the doubles with their own loo and shower. Although basic, they are extremely roomy and bright.

EL RAVAL

Hotel San Agustín HOTEL €€
(Map p1070; 93 318 16 58; www.hotelsa.com; Plaça de Sant Agustí 3; s €123-144, d €171; MLiceu;) Once an 18th-century monastery, this hotel opened in 1840, making it the city's oldest. The location is perfect: a quick stroll off La Rambla on a curious square. Rooms sparkle, are mostly spacious and light, and have parquet floors.

Hostal Gat Raval BUDGET HOTEL €€
(Map p1070; 93 481 66 70; www.gataccommodation.com; Carrer de Joaquín Costa 44; d €82, s/d without bathroom €58/74; MUniversitat;) There's a pea-green and lemon-lime colour scheme in this hip, young, 2nd-floor hostel-style lodgings deep in El Raval. Rooms are pleasant, secure and each is behind a green door, but only some have private bathroom.

Casa Camper HOTEL €€€
(Map p1070; 93 342 62 80; www.casacamper.com; Carrer d'Elisabets 11; s/d €228/255; MLiceu;) Run by the Mallorcan shoe people in the better end of El Raval, these designer digs offer rooms with a few surprises, like the Vinçon furniture. Across the corridor from each room is a separate, private sitting room, with balcony, TV and hammock.

LA RIBERA & LA BARCELONETA

TOP CHOICE **Hotel Banys Orientals** BOUTIQUE HOTEL €€
(Map p1070; 93 268 84 60; www.hotelbanysorientals.com; Carrer de l'Argenteria 37; s/d €93/107; MJaume I;) Cool blues and aquamarines combine with dark-hued parquet floors to lend this boutique beauty an understated charm. All rooms – admittedly on the small side but impeccably presented – look onto the street or back lanes.

Chic & Basic HOTEL €€
(Map p1066; 93 295 46 52; www.chicandbasic.com; Carrer de la Princesa 50; s €96, d €132-171; MJaume I;) In a completely renovated building are 31 spotlessly white rooms. They have high ceilings, enormous beds (room types are classed as M, L and XL!) and lots of detailed touches (LED lighting, TFT TV screens and the retention of many beautiful old features of the original building, such as the marble staircase).

Pensió 2000 BUDGET HOTEL €
(Map p1070; 93 310 74 66; www.pensio2000.com; Carrer de Sant Pere més Alt 6; s/d €52/65, without bathroom €35/45; MUrquinaona;) Sitting in front of the Modernista chocolate box that is the Palau de la Música Catalana, this cheerful *pensión,* with its seven canary-yellow rooms, is a conveniently placed option. Two rooms (the pick) have their own bathroom. You can also take time out on the little terrace.

W Barcelona HOTEL €€€
(Map p1066; 93 295 28 00; www.w-barcelona.com; Plaça de la Rosa del Vents 1; r 283-385; MBarceloneta, 17, 39, 57 or 64;) In an admirable location at the end of a beach, this spinnaker-shaped glass tower offers all sorts of rooms. Guests flit between the gym, infinity pool (with bar) and Bliss@spa. There's avant-garde dining on the 2nd floor in the Bravo restaurant and hip cocktail sipping with stunning views in the Eclipse bar.

L'EIXAMPLE

TOP CHOICE Hotel Constanza BOUTIQUE HOTEL €€
(Map p1066; ☎93 270 19 10; www.hotelconstanza.com; Carrer del Bruc 33; s/d €110/130; MGirona or Urquinaona; ❄@) Constanza is a boutique belle that has stolen the heart of many a visitor to Barcelona. Even smaller singles are made to feel special with broad mirrors and strong colours (reds and yellows, with black furniture). Suites and studios are further options. The terrace is a nice spot to relax for a while, looking over the rooftops of L'Eixample.

Hostal Goya BUDGET HOTEL €€
(Map p1066; ☎93 302 25 65; www.hostalgoya.com; Carrer de Pau Claris 74; s €70, d €96-113; MPasseig de Gràcia; ❄) The Goya is a gem of a spot on the chichi side of l'Eixample and a short stroll from Plaça de Catalunya. Rooms have parquet floors and a light colour scheme that varies from room to room. In the bathrooms, the original mosaic floors have largely been retained, combined with contemporary design features.

Hotel Casa Fuster HOTEL €€€
(Map p1066; ☎93 255 30 00, 902 202345; www.hotelcasafuster.com; Passeig de Gràcia 132; s/d from €294/321; MDiagonal; P❄@) It is hard to believe the wrecking ball once threatened this Modernista mansion turned luxury hotel. Standard rooms are plush if smallish. Period features have been lovingly restored and complemented with hydromassage tubs and king-sized beds.

Eating

Barcelona is foodie heaven. The city has firmly established itself as one of Europe's gourmet capitals, and innovative, cutting-edge restaurants abound. Some of the most creative chefs are one-time students of world-renowned chef Ferran Adrià, whose influence on the city's cuisine is strong.

Although Barcelona has a reputation as a hot spot of 'new Spanish cuisine', you'll still find local eateries serving up time-honoured local grub, from squid-ink *fideuà* (a satisfying paella-like noodle dish) through pigs' trotters, rabbit with snails, and *butifarra* (a tasty local sausage).

LA RAMBLA & BARRI GÒTIC

Skip the overpriced traps along La Rambla and get into the winding lanes of the Barri Gòtic.

Bar Celta TAPAS €€
(Map p1070; ☎93 315 00 06; Carrer de la Mercè 16; meals €20-25; ⏲noon-midnight Tue-Sun; MDrassanes) Specialists in *pulpo* (octopus) and other seaside delights from Galicia in the country's northwest; the waiters waste no time in serving up bottles of crisp white Ribeiro wine to wash down the *raciones*.

Agut CATALAN €€
(Map p1070; ☎93 315 17 09; Carrer d'En Gignàs 16; meals €35; ⏲lunch & dinner Tue-Sat, lunch Sun; ❄) Contemporary paintings set a contrast with the fine traditional Catalan dishes offered in this timeless restaurant. You might start with something like the *bouillabaisse con cigalitas de playa* (little seawater crayfish) for €11 and follow with an oak-grilled meat dish.

Pla MODERN SPANISH €€
(Map p1070; ☎93 412 65 52; www.pla-repla.com; Carrer de Bellafila 5; meals €45-50; ⏲dinner; ❄) In this modern den of inventive cooking with music worthy of a club, the chefs present deliciously strange combinations such as *bacallà amb salsa de pomes verdes* (cod in a green apple sauce). Exotic meats like kangaroo turn up on the menu too.

Can Conesa SNACKS €
(Map p1070; ☎93 310 57 95; Carrer de la Llibreteria 1; rolls & toasted sandwiches €3-5; ⏲Mon-Sat; MJaume I) This place has been doling out delicious *entrepans* (bread rolls with filling), frankfurters and toasted sandwiches here for more than 50 years – *barcelonins* swear by it and queue for them.

EL RAVAL

Bar Pinotxo TAPAS €€
(Map p1070; Mercat de la Boqueria; meals €20; ⏲6am-5pm Mon-Sat Sep-Jul; MLiceu) Of the half-dozen or so tapas bars and informal eateries within the market, this one near the Rambla entrance is about the most popular. Roll up to the bar and enjoy some people-watching as you munch on tapas assembled from the products on sale at the stalls around you.

Can Lluís CATALAN €€
(Map p1070; ☎93 441 11 87: Carrer de la Cera 49; meals €30-35; ⏲Mon-Sat Sep-Jul; MSant Antoni) Three generations have kept this spick-and-span old-time classic in business since 1929. Beneath the olive green beams in the back dining room you can see the spot where an anarchist's bomb went off in 1946, killing the then owner. Expect fresh fish and seafood.

Casa Leopoldo CATALAN €€
(Map p1070; ☎93 441 30 14; www.casaleopoldo.com; Carrer de Sant Rafael 24; meals €50; ⊙lunch & dinner Tue-Sat, lunch Sun Sep-Jul; ⊜) Several rambling dining areas with magnificent tiled walls and exposed timber-beam ceilings make this a fine option. The seafood menu is extensive and the local wine list strong. This is an old-town classic beloved of writers and artists down the decades.

LA RIBERA & WATERFRONT

La Barceloneta is the place to go for seafood; Passeig Joan de Borbó is lined with eateries but locals head for the back lanes.

TOP CHOICE **Xiringuito d'Escribà** SEAFOOD €€
(off Map p1066; ☎93 221 07 29; www.escriba.es; Ronda Litoral 42, Platja de Bogatell; meals €40-50; ⊙lunch; MLlacuna) The Barcelona pastry family serves up top-quality seafood at this popular waterfront eatery. This is one of the few places where one person can order from the selection of paella and *fideuá* (normally a minimum of two people).

Cal Pep TAPAS €€
(Map p1066; ☎93 310 79 61; www.calpep.com; Plaça de les Olles 8; meals €45-50; ⊙lunch Tue-Sat, dinner Mon-Fri Sep-Jul; MBarceloneta; ⊜) It's getting a foot in the door here that's the problem. And if you want one of the five tables out the back, you'll need to call ahead. Most people are happy elbowing their way to the bar for some of the tastiest gourmet seafood tapas in town.

Les Cuines de Santa Caterina INTERNATIONAL €€
(Map p1070; ☎93 268 99 18; www.cuinessantacaterina.com; Mercat de Santa Caterina; meals €25-30; MJaume I; ⊜✎) Peck at the sushi bar, tuck into classic rice dishes or go vegetarian in this busy market restaurant in the Mercat de Santa Caterina. A drawback is the speed with which they whisk barely finished plates away from you, but the range of dishes and bustling atmosphere are fun. It doesn't take reservations, so it's first come first served.

Suquet de l'Almirall SEAFOOD €€
(Map p1066; ☎93 221 62 33; Passeig de Joan de Borbó 65; meals €45-50; ⊙lunch & dinner Tue-Sat, lunch Sun; MBarceloneta, 🚌17, 39, 57 or 64; ⊜) A family business run by one of the acolytes of Ferran Adrià's El Bulli restaurant, the order of the day is top-class seafood. A good option is the pica pica marinera (a seafood mix; €38) or you could opt for the tasting menu (€44).

L'EIXAMPLE & GRÀCIA

TOP CHOICE **Tapaç 24** TAPAS €€
(Map p1066; www.carlesabellan.com; Carrer de la Diputació 269; meals €30-35; ⊙9am-midnight Mon-Sat; MPasseig de Gràcia) Specials in this basement tapas temple include the *bikini* (toasted ham and cheese sandwich – here the ham is cured and the truffle makes all the difference!), a thick black *arròs negre de sípia* (squid ink black rice) and, for dessert, *xocolata amb pa, sal i oli* (delicious balls of chocolate in olive oil with a touch of salt and wafer).

Inopia TAPAS €€
(Map p1066; ☎93 424 52 31; www.barinopia.com; Carrer de Tamarit 104; meals €25-30; ⊙dinner Tue-Sat, lunch Sat; MRocafort) Albert Adrià, brother of star chef Ferran, has his hands full with this constantly busy gourmet tapas temple. Select a *pintxo de cuixa de pollastre a l'ast* (chunk of rotisserie chicken thigh) or the lightly fried, tempura-style vegetables. Wash down with house red or Moritz beer.

Relais de Venise MEAT €€
(Map p1066; ☎93 467 21 62; Carrer de Pau Claris 142; meals €35; ⊙Sep-Jul; MPasseig de Gràcia; ⊜) There's just one dish, a succulent beef entrecôte with a secret 'sauce Porte-Maillot' (named after the location of the original restaurant in Paris), chips and salad. It is served in slices and in two waves so that it doesn't go cold.

Drinking

Barcelona abounds with day-time cafes, laid-back lounges and lively night-time bars. Closing time is generally 2am from Sunday to Thursday and 3am Friday and Saturday.

BARRI GÒTIC

TOP CHOICE **Soul Club** MUSIC BAR
(Map p1070; Carrer Nou de Sant Francesc 7; ⊙10pm-2.30am Mon-Thu, to 3am Fri & Sat, 8pm-2.30am Sun; MDrassanes) Each night the DJs change the musical theme, which ranges from deep funk to Latin grooves. The tiny front bar is for drinking and chatting (get in early for a stool or the sole lounge). Out back is where the dancing is done.

Marula Café BAR
(Map p1070; www.marulacafe.com; Carrer dels Escudellers 49; ⊙11pm-5am Sun-Thu, to 5.30am Fri & Sat; MLiceu) A fantastic new funk find in the heart of the Barri Gòtic, Marula will transport you to the 1970s and the best in black music, mostly funk and soul. James

Brown fans will think they've died and gone to heaven.

EL RAVAL

Boadas COCKTAIL BAR
(Map p1070; Carrer dels Tallers 1; noon-2am Mon-Thu, to 3am Fri & Sat; M Catalunya) Inside the unprepossessing entrance is one of the city's oldest cocktail bars (famed for its daiquiris). The bow-tied waiters have been serving up their poison since 1933; Joan Miró and Hemingway tippled here.

Casa Almirall BAR
(Map p1070; Carrer de Joaquín Costa 33; 5.30pm-2.30am Sun-Thu, 7pm-3am Fri & Sat; M Universitat) In business since the 1860s, this unchanged corner bar is dark and intriguing, with Modernista decor and a mixed clientele. There are some great original pieces in here, like the marble counter.

LA RIBERA

Gimlet COCKTAIL BAR
(Map p1066; Carrer del Rec 24; 10pm-3am; M Jaume I) White-jacketed bar staff with all the appropriate aplomb will whip you up a gimlet or any other classic cocktail (around €10) your heart desires. Barcelona cocktail guru Javier Muelas is behind this and several other cocktail bars around the city, so you can be sure of excellent drinks, some with a creative twist.

La Vinya del Senyor WINE BAR
(Map p1070; Plaça de Santa Maria del Mar 5; noon-1am Tue-Sun; M Jaume I) The wine list is as long as *War and Peace,* and the terrace lies in the shadow of Santa Maria del Mar. You can crowd inside the tiny wine bar itself or take a bottle upstairs.

L'EIXAMPLE & GRÀCIA

Berlin BAR
(Map p1066; Carrer de Muntaner 240; 10am-2am Mon-Wed, to 2.30am Thu, to 3am Fri & Sat; M Diagonal or Hospital Clínic) This elegant corner bar attracts waves of night animals starting up for a long night. In warmer weather you can sit outside on the footpath, or head downstairs into the basement if the bar's too crowded.

Dry Martini COCKTAIL BAR
(Map p1066; www.drymartinibcn.com; Carrer del Consell de Cent 247; 5pm-3am; FGC Provença) Well-dressed waiters serve up the best dry martini in town, or whatever else your heart desires, in this classic cocktail lounge. Sink into a leather lounge and nurse a huge G&T.

☆ Entertainment

To keep up with what's on, pick up a copy of the weekly listings magazine, *Guía del Ocio* (€1) from newsstands.

Nightclubs

Barcelona clubs are spread a little more thinly than bars across the city. They tend to open from around midnight until 6am. Entry can cost from nothing to €20 (one drink usually included).

TOP CHOICE **Elephant** CLUB
(www.elephantbcn.com, in Spanish; Passeig dels Til.lers 1; Wed, Thu & Sun free, Fri & Sat €15; 11.30pm-3am Wed, to 5am Thu-Sun; M Palau Reial; P) Getting in here is like being invited to some private Beverly Hills party. Models and wannabes mix freely, as do the drinks. A big tentlike dance space is the focus but mingle around the various garden bars too.

TOP CHOICE **Terrrazza** CLUB
(Map p1066; www.laterrrazza.com; Avinguda de Francesc Ferrer i Guàrdia; admission €10-20; midnight-5am Thu, to 6am Fri & Sat; M Espanya) One of the city's top summertime dance locations, Terrrazza attracts squadrons of the beautiful people, locals and foreigners alike, for a full-on night of music and cocktails partly under the stars inside the Poble Espanyol complex.

Moog CLUB
(Map p1070; www.masimas.com/moog; Carrer de l'Arc del Teatre 3; admission €10; midnight-5am; M Drassanes) This fun, minuscule club is a downtown hit. In the main downstairs dance area, DJs dish out house, techno and electro, while upstairs you can groove to indie and occasional classic pop.

Gay & Lesbian Venues

Barcelona's gay and lesbian scene is concentrated in the blocks around Carrers de Muntaner and Consell de Cent (dubbed Gayxample). Here you'll find ambience every night of the week in the bars, discos and drag clubs.

Party hard at classic gay discos such as **Arena Madre** (Map p1066; www.arenadisco.com, in Spanish; Carrer de Balmes 32; M Universitat) and **Metro** (Map p1070; www.metrodiscobcn.com; Carrer de Sepúlveda 185; 1am-5am Mon, midnight-5am Sun & Tue-Thu, midnight-6am Fri & Sat; M Universitat).

Theatre

Most theatre in the city is in Catalan.

There are quite a few venues that stage vanguard drama and dance, including the

Teatre Nacional de Catalunya (Map p1066; ☎93 306 57 00; www.tnc.cat; Plaça de les Arts 1; admission €12-32; ⊙box office 3-7pm Wed-Fri, to 8.30pm Sat, to 5pm Sun & 1hr before show; MGlòries or Monumental).

Live Music

TOP CHOICE **Harlem Jazz Club** JAZZ
(Map p1070; www.harlemjazzclub.es; Carrer de la Comtessa de Sobradiel 8; admission up to €10; ⊙8pm-4am Tue-Thu & Sun, to 5am Fri & Sat; MDrassanes) This narrow, smoky, old-town dive is one of the best spots in town for jazz. Every now and then it mixes it up with a little rock, Latin or blues. There are usually two sessions in an evening.

Sala Tarantos FLAMENCO
(Map p1070; ☎93 319 17 89; www.masimas.net; Plaça Reial 17; admission from €7; ⊙performances 8.30pm, 9.30pm & 10.30pm; MLiceu) This basement locale is the stage for some of the best flamenco to pass through Barcelona.

Sport

FC Barcelona (Barça for aficionados) has one of the best stadiums in Europe – the 99,000-capacity **Camp Nou** (off Map p1066; ☎902 189 900; Carrer d'Aristides Maillol; ⊙box office 9am-1.30pm & 3.30-6pm Mon-Fri; MPalau Reial or Collblanc) in the west of the city. Tickets for national-league games are available at the stadium, by phone or online. For the latter two options, nonmembers must book 15 days before the match.

Shopping

Most mainstream fashion stores are along a shopping 'axis' that runs from Plaça de Catalunya along Passeig de Gràcia, then left (west) along Avinguda Diagonal.

The El Born area in La Ribera is awash with tiny boutiques, especially those purveying young, fun fashion. There are plenty of shops scattered throughout the Barri Gòtic (stroll Carrer d'Avinyò and Carrer de Portaferrissa). For secondhand stuff, head for El Raval, especially Carrer de la Riera Baixa.

Joan Murrià FOOD & DRINK
(Map p1066; www.murria.cat; Carrer de Roger de Llúria 85; MPasseig de Gràcia) Ramon Casas designed the Modernista shop-front ads for this delicious delicatessen, where the shelves groan under the weight of speciality food from around Catalonia and beyond.

Els Encants Vells MARKET
('The Old Charms'; Map p1066; www.encantsbcn.com, in Catalan; Plaça de les Glòries Catalanes; ⊙7am-6pm Mon, Wed, Fri & Sat; MGlòries) Bargain hunters love this free-for-all flea market.

Vinçon HOMEWARES
(Map p1066; www.vincon.com; Passeig de Gràcia 96; ⊙10am-8.30pm Mon-Sat; MDiagonal) Vinçon has the slickest designs in furniture and household goods, local and imported. The building once belonged to the Modernista artist Ramon Casas.

Antonio Miró CLOTHING
(Map p1066; www.antoniomiro.es, in Spanish; Carrer del Consell de Cent 349; ⊙10am-8pm Mon-Sat; MPasseig de Gràcia) Mr Miró is one of Barcelona's haute-couture kings. He concentrates on light, natural fibres to produce smart, unpretentious men's and women's fashion. High-end evening dresses and shimmering, smart suits lead the way.

Custo Barcelona CLOTHING
(Map p1066; www.custo-barcelona.com; Plaça de les Olles 7; MJaume I) Custo bewitches people the world over with a youthful, psychedelic panoply of women's and men's fashion. It has several branches around town.

Information

Dangers & Annoyances

Purse snatching and pickpocketing are major problems, especially around Plaça de Catalunya, La Rambla and Plaça Reial. See p1144 for more information on general safety.

Emergency

Tourists who want to report thefts need to go to the Catalan police, known as the **Mossos d'Esquadra** (☎088; Carrer Nou de la Rambla 80), or the **Guàrdia Urbana** (Local Police; ☎092; La Rambla 43).

In an emergency, call ☎112.

Internet Access

Bornet (Carrer de Barra Ferro 3; per hr/10hr €2.80/20; ⊙10am-11pm Mon-Fri, 2pm-11pm Sat & Sun & holidays; MJaume I) A cool little internet centre-cum-art gallery.

Medical Services

Call ☎010 to find the nearest late-opening duty pharmacy.

Farmàcia Clapés (La Rambla 98; MLiceu)

Hospital Clínic i Provincial (☎93 227 54 00; Carrer de Villarroel 170; MHospital Clínic)

Money

Banks (with ATMs) and foreign-exchange offices abound in Barcelona. **Interchange** (Rambla dels Caputxins 74; ⊙9am-11pm; MLiceu) represents American Express.

Post

Main post office (Plaça d'Antoni López; 8.30am-9.30pm Mon-Fri, to 2pm Sat; Jaume I)

Tourist Information

Oficina d'Informació de Turisme de Barcelona Main branch (www.barcelonaturisme.com; Plaça de Catalunya 17-S underground; 9am-9pm); Aeroport del Prat (Terminals 1, 2B and 2A arrivals halls; 9am-9pm); Estació Sants (8am-8pm late Jun–late Sep, 8am-8pm Mon-Fri, 8am-2pm Sat, Sun & holidays Oct-May; Sants Estació); Town hall (Carrer de la Ciutat 2; 9am-8pm Mon-Fri, 10am-8pm Sat, 10am-2pm Sun & holidays; Jaume I)

Regional tourist office (www.gencat.net/probert; Passeig de Gràcia 107; 10am-7pm Mon-Sat, to 2.30pm Sun; Diagonal)

Getting There & Away

Air

Barcelona's airport, **El Prat de Llobregat** (902 404 704; www.aena.es), is 12km southwest of the city centre. Barcelona is a big international and domestic destination, with direct flights from North America as well as many European cities.

Boat

Regular passenger and vehicular ferries to/from the Balearic Islands, operated by **Acciona Trasmediterránea** (902 454 645; www.trasmediterranea.es), dock along both sides of the Moll de Barcelona wharf in Port Vell; see p1147 for further information.

The Grimaldi group's **Grandi Navi Veloci** (in Italy 010 209 4591; www1.gnv.it; Drassanes) runs high-speed, thrice-weekly luxury ferries between Barcelona and Genoa, while **Grimaldi Ferries** (902 531 333, in Italy 081 496444; www.grimaldi-lines.com) operates similar services to Civitavecchia (near Rome), Livorno (Tuscany) and Porto Torres (northwest Sardinia).

Bus

The main terminal for most domestic and international buses is the **Estació del Nord** (902 303 222; www.barcelonanord.com; Carrer d'Ali Bei 80; Arc de Triomf). ALSA goes to Madrid (€28.18, eight hours, up to 16 daily), Valencia (€25.34, 4½ to 6½ hours, up to 14 daily) and many other destinations.

Eurolines (www.eurolines.com) also offers international services from Estació del Nord and **Estació d'Autobusos de Sants** (Carrer de Viriat), which is next to Estació Sants Barcelona.

Car & Motorcycle

Autopistas (tollways) head out of Barcelona in most directions, including the C31/C32 to the southern Costa Brava; the C32 to Sitges; the C16 to Manresa (with a turn-off for Montserrat); and the AP7 north to Girona, Figueres and France, and south to Tarragona and Valencia (turn off along the AP2 for Lleida, Zaragoza and Madrid).

Train

Virtually all trains travelling to and from destinations within Spain stop at **Estació Sants** (Sants-Estació). High-speed trains to Madrid via Lleida and Zaragoza take as little as two hours and 40 minutes; prices vary wildly. Other trains run to Valencia (€38.50 to €43.10, three to 4½ hours, 15 daily) and Burgos (from €49, six to seven hours, four daily).

There are also international connections with French cities from the same station.

Getting Around

To/From the Airport

The **A1 Aerobús** (93 415 60 20; one way €5) runs from Terminal 1 to Plaça de Catalunya from 6.05am to 1.05am, taking 30 to 40 minutes. A2 Aerobús does the same run from Terminal 2, from 6am to 12.30am. Buy tickets on the bus.

Renfe's R2 Nord train line runs between the airport and Passeig de Gràcia (via Estació Sants) in central Barcelona (about 35 minutes). Tickets cost €3, unless you have a T-10 multitrip public-transport ticket.

A taxi to/from the centre, about a half-hour ride depending on traffic, costs around €20 to €25.

Public Transport

Barcelona's metro system spreads its tentacles around the city in such a way that most places of interest are within a 10-minute walk of a station. Buses and suburban trains are needed only for a few destinations. A single metro, bus or suburban train ride costs €1.40, but a T-1 ticket, valid for 10 rides, costs €7.85.

Taxi

Barcelona's black-and-yellow taxis are plentiful and reasonably priced. The flag fall is €2. If you can't find a street taxi, call 93 303 30 33.

Monestir de Montserrat

The monks who built the Monestir de Montserrat (Monastery of the Serrated Mountain), 50km northwest of Barcelona, chose a spectacular spot. The Benedictine **monastery** (www.abadiamontserrat.net; 9am-6pm) sits on the side of a 1236m-high mountain of weird, bulbous peaks. The monastery was founded in 1025 and pilgrims still come from all over Christendom to kiss the Black

Virgin (La Moreneta), the 12th-century wooden sculpture of the Virgin Mary.

The **Museu de Montserrat** (Plaça de Santa Maria; adult/student €6.50/5.50; ⊙10am-6pm) has an excellent collection, ranging from an Egyptian mummy to art by El Greco, Monet, Degas and Picasso.

If you're around the basilica at the right time, you'll catch a brief performance by the **Montserrat Boys' Choir** (Escolania; www.escolania.net; admission free; ⊙performances 1pm & 6.45pm Mon-Fri, 11am & 6.45pm Sun Sep-Jun).

You can explore the mountain above the monastery on a web of paths leading to some of the peaks and to 13 empty and rather dilapidated hermitages. Running every 20 minutes, the **Funicular de Sant Joan** (one way/return €4.50/7.20; ⊙10am-5.40pm Apr-Oct, to 7pm mid-Jul–Aug, to 4.30pm Mar & Nov, 11am-4.30pm Dec, closed Jan-Feb) will carry you up the first 250m from the monastery.

Getting There & Away

Montserrat is an easy day trip from Barcelona. The R5 line trains operated by FGC run from Plaça d'Espanya station in Barcelona to Monistrol de Montserrat up to 18 times daily starting at 5.16am. They connect with the rack-and-pinion train, or **cremallera** (www.cremallerademontserrat.com), which takes 17 minutes to make the upwards journey and costs €5.15/8.20 one way/return.

Girona

POP 92,200

A tight huddle of ancient arcaded houses, grand churches, climbing cobbled streets and medieval baths, all enclosed by defensive walls and a lazy river, constitute a powerful reason for visiting north Catalonia's largest city, Girona (Castilian: Gerona).

Sights & Activities

Catedral CHURCH

The billowing baroque facade of the cathedral stands at the head of a majestic flight of steps rising from Plaça de la Catedral. Repeatedly rebuilt and altered down the centuries, it has Europe's widest Gothic nave (23m). The cathedral's **museum** (www.catedraldegirona.org; adult/under 7yr €5/free, admission free Sun; ⊙10am-8pm Apr-Oct, to 7pm Nov-Mar, 10am-2pm Sun & holidays), through the door marked 'Claustre Tresor', contains the masterly Romanesque *Tapís de la Creació* (Tapestry of the Creation) and a Mozarabic illuminated *Beatus* manuscript, dating from 975. The fee for the museum also admits you to the beautiful 12th-century Romanesque **cloister**.

TOP CHOICE **Passeig Arqueològic** GARDENS

Across the street from the Banys Àrabs, steps lead up into some heavenly gardens where town and plants merge into one organic masterpiece. The gardens follow the city walls up to the 18th-century Portal de Sant Cristòfol gate, from where you can walk back down to the cathedral.

The Call HISTORIC DISTRICT

Until 1492 Girona was home to Catalonia's second-most important medieval Jewish community (after Barcelona), and its Jewish quarter, the Call, was centred on Carrer de la Força. For an idea of medieval Jewish life and culture, visit the **Museu d'Història dels Jueus de Girona** (Jewish History Museum, aka the Centre Bonastruc Ça Porta; Carrer de la Força 8; adult/child €2/free; ⊙10am-8pm Mon-Sat Jun-Oct, 10am-6pm Mon-Sat Nov-May, 10am-3pm Sun & holidays).

Sleeping & Eating

TOP CHOICE **Hotel Llegendes de Girona** HOTEL €€€

(☎972 22 09 05; www.llegendeshotel.com; Portal de la Barca 4; d €123, 'Fountain of Lovers' room

NO MORE BULLS?

On 28 July 2010 Catalonia became the first region in mainland Spain to ban bullfighting; the Canary Islands voted to make bullfighting illegal in 1991. The vote, which came as a result of a 180,000-strong petition, follows moves by 23 municipalities (including Barcelona) who have declared themselves to be antibullfighting cities in recent years. With Catalonia never the strongest bastion of bullfighting tradition and with Spain's major national political parties opposing Catalonia's ban, the chances of other Spanish regions following suit seem remote. However, other factors do pose a significant (albeit longer-term) threat to bullfighting. Recent surveys have found that around 50% of Spaniards oppose bullfighting, with the figures much higher among younger Spaniards. The recent global economic crisis has also taken its toll – there was a 50% drop in the number of bullfights in 2009, with many small towns forced to cancel their annual fiestas.

€288;) This new hotel has so many hi-tech gadgets it's like sleeping in the Space Shuttle. The rooms are supremely comfortable and the all-glass bathrooms with huge rain showers are minimalist. In each room is a little book detailing different tantric sex positions and in three of the rooms is an 'Eros' sofa…

Bed & Breakfast Bells Oficis B&B €€
(972 22 81 70; www.bellsoficis.com; Carrer dels Germans Busquets 2; r incl breakfast €35-85;) Up the wobbly winding staircase of an old building you'll discover six very desirable rooms. Some have unusual pebble art in the bathroom whilst others share bathrooms and some have views over the street.

Gro Hostel Girona HOSTEL €
(972 31 20 45; www.equity-point.com; Plaça Catalunya 23; dm incl breakfast from €20, without bathroom from €18;) Part of a small chain of hostels (the others are in Barcelona and Madrid), it offers not just the cheapest night's kip in Girona but is also a great-value, colourful and friendly hostel in its own right.

TOP CHOICE **Restaurant Txalaka** BASQUE €€
(972 22 59 75; Carrer Bonastruc de Porta 4; menú €33, mains €15-20, pintxos €2.50-4; closed Sun) For sensational Basque cooking and *pintxos* (Basque tapas) washed down with txakoli (the fizzy, white wine from the Basque coast), poured from a great height the way it's supposed to be, don't miss this popular place on the edge of the new town.

L'Alqueria RICE DISHES €€
(972 22 18 82; www.restaurantalqueria.com; Carrer Ginesta 8; mains €15-20; lunch & dinner Wed-Sat, lunch Tue & Sun, closed Mon) This smart new restaurant serves the finest *arrós negre* (rice cooked in cuttlefish ink) and *arrós a la Catalan* in the city. It's wise to book ahead.

Information

Tourist office (www.girona.cat; Jōan Maragall 2; 8am-8pm Mon-Fri, 8am-2pm & 4-8pm Sat, 9am-2pm Sun)

Getting There & Away

AIR Girona-Costa Brava airport, 11km south of the centre and just off the AP7 and A2, is Ryanair's Spanish hub.

TRAIN There are more than 20 trains per day to Figueres (€10.50 to €13.70, 30 to 40 minutes) and Barcelona (from €14.90, 1½ hours).

The Costa Brava

The Costa Brava (Rugged Coast) was Catalonia's first tourist centre, and after you visit its rocky coastline, romantic coves, turquoise waters and former fishing villages, you'll see why. Overdevelopment has ruined some stretches but much of the coast retains its spectacular beauty.

Sights & Activities

The Costa Brava is all about picturesque inlets and coves – and there are many. Although buses run along much of the coast, the best way to uncover some of these gems is with your own wheels.

The first truly pretty stop on the Costa Brava when heading northeast from Barcelona is **Tossa de Mar**, with its golden beach, ochre medieval village core and nearby coves. The coast road on to **Sant Feliu de Guíxols** is spectacular.

Further north are three gorgeous beach towns near Palafrugell: **Tamariu** (the small-

DALÍ'S CATALONIA

A short train ride north of Girona, Figueres is home to the zany **Teatre-Museu Dalí** (www.salvador-dali.org; Plaça de Gala i Salvador Dalí 5; adult/under 9yr €11/free; 9am-8pm Jul-Sep, 9.30am-6pm Mar-Jun & Oct, 10.30am-6pm Nov-Feb, closed Mon Oct-Jun), housed in a 19th-century theatre converted by Salvador Dalí (who was born here). 'Theatre-museum' is an apt label for this multidimensional trip through one of the most fertile (or disturbed) imaginations of the 20th century. It's full of surprises, tricks and illusions, and contains a substantial portion of Dalí's life's work.

Dalí fans will want to travel south to visit the equally kooky **Castell de Púbol** (972 48 86 55; www.salvador-dali.org; La Pera; adult/under 9yr €7/free; 10am-8pm, closed Jan–mid-Mar & Mon outside high season) at La Pera, 22km northwest of Palafrugell, and the **Casa Museu Dalí** (972 25 10 15; www.salvador-dali.org; Port Lligat; adult/child €10/free) at his summer getaway in Port Lligat (1.25km from Cadaqués), where entry is by advance reservation only.

est, least crowded and most exclusive), **Llafranc** (the biggest and busiest) and **Calella de Palafrugell**. There are further fine beaches and coves on the coast near Begur, a little further north.

North of the Costa Brava's main dive centre, **L'Estartit**, are the ruins of the Greek and Roman town of **Empúries** (www.mac.cat; adult/child €3/free; ⌚10am-8pm Jun-Sep, to 6pm Oct-May), 2km outside **L'Escala**.

Cadaqués, at the end of an agonising series of hairpin bends one hour from Figueres, is postcard perfect. Beaches are of the pebbly variety, so people spend a lot of time sitting at waterfront cafes or strolling. It's a pleasant 2km walk from central Cadaqués to Port Lligat, where you'll find Dalí's summer residence. Some 10km northeast of Cadaqués is **Cap de Creus**, an impressive cape that is Spain's easternmost point.

Of the many historic towns inland from the Costa Brava, the pretty walled town of **Pals**, 6km inland from Begur, and the nearby impeccably preserved medieval hamlet of **Peratallada** are the most charming.

Sleeping & Eating

TOSSA DE MAR

TOP CHOICE **Hostal Cap d'Or** HOTEL €€
(☎972 34 00 81; www.hotelcapdor.com; Passeig de la Vila Vella 1; s/d incl breakfast €53/96; P❄📶) Rub up against the town's history in this spot right in front of the walls. Rooms are lovingly decorated in sea blues and whites, and the best look straight onto the beach.

Hotel Canaima HOTEL €€
(☎972 34 09 95; www.hotelcanaima.com; Avendia de la Palma 24; s/d incl breakfast €37.50/75; ❄📶) Surrounded by super-sized package holiday hotels, this little family-run hotel offers something refreshingly different. Rooms are big and bright with little balconies and there's a laid-back cafe downstairs.

CADAQUÉS

TOP CHOICE **Hostal Vehí** BUDGET HOTEL €€
(☎972 25 84 70; www.hostalvehi.com; Carrer de l'Església 5; s/d €77, without bathroom €30/55; ❄) Near the church in the heart of the old town, this simple but engaging *pensión* with clean as a whistle rooms tends to be booked up for July and August. Easily the cheapest deal in town, it's also about the best. In fact the only drawback we can come up with is that it's a pain to get to if you have a lot of luggage. Breakfast is €6 extra.

Information

There are tourist offices in **Palafrugell** (☎972 61 44 75; Carrer de les Voltes 6; ⌚10am-8pm Jul-Aug, shorter hours rest of year) and other towns on the coast and inland.

Getting There & Away

Sarfa (☎902 30 20 25; www.sarfa.com) runs buses from Barcelona, Girona and Figueres to most towns along the Costa Brava.

Tarragona

POP 134,160

Barcelona's senior in Roman times and a lesser medieval city, Tarragona is a provincial sort of place with some outstanding attractions: Catalonia's finest Roman ruins, a magnificent medieval cathedral in a pretty Old Town, and some decent beaches.

Sights & Activities

Museu d'Història de Tarragona ROMAN RUINS
(MHT; www.museutgn.com; adult/child per site €3/free, incl all MHT sites €10; ⌚9am-9pm Mon-Sat, to 3pm Sun Easter-Oct, shorter hours rest of year) To call the four sites that make up the Museu d'História de Tarragona a museum is somewhat misleading as there are, in fact, four separate Roman sites (which since 2000 together have constituted a Unesco World Heritage site).

Start with the **Pretori i Circ Romans** (Plaça del Rei), which includes part of the vaults of the Roman circus, where chariot races were held. Near the beach is the crown jewel of Tarragona's Roman sites, the well-preserved **Amfiteatre Romà** (Plaça d'Arce Ochotorena), where gladiators battled each other, wild animals or Russell Crowe to the death. Southeast of Carrer de Lleida are remains of the **Fòrum Romà** (Carrer del Cardenal Cervantes), dominated by several imposing columns. The **Passeig Arqueològic** is a peaceful walk around part of the perimeter of the old town between two lines of city walls; the inner ones are mainly Roman.

Museu Nacional Arqueològic de Tarragona MUSEUM
(www.mnat.es; Plaça del Rei 5; adult/child €2.40/free; ⌚10am-8pm Tue-Sat, 10am-2pm Sun & holidays Jun-Sep, shorter hours rest of year) This carefully presented museum gives further insight into Roman Tarraco. Exhibits include part of the Roman city walls, mosaics, frescos, sculpture and pottery.

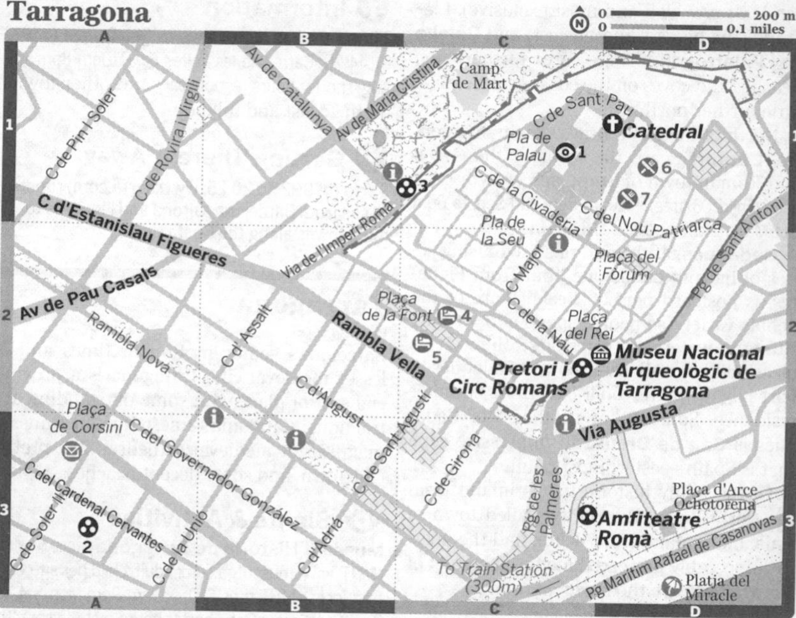

Tarragona

Top Sights

- Amfiteatre Romà ... C3
- Catedral ... D1
- Museu Nacional Arqueològic de Tarragona ... D2
- Pretori i Circ Romans ... C2

Sights

1. Entrance to Catedral, Cloister ... C1
2. Fòrum Romà ... A3
3. Passeig Arqueològic ... C1

Sleeping

4. Hotel Plaça de la Font ... C2
5. Pensió Forum ... C2

Eating

6. Aq ... D1
7. Quim Quima ... D1

Catedral CHURCH

(Pla de la Seu; adult/child €3.80/1.20; ⊙10am-7pm Mon-Sat, shorter hours Jul–mid-Oct) Sitting grandly at the top of the old town, Tarragona's cathedral demands a solid chunk of your time. Built between 1171 and 1331 on the site of a Roman temple, it combines Romanesque and Gothic features, as typified by the main facade on Pla de la Seu. The entrance is by the cloister on the northwest flank of the building. The cloister and its perfectly presented gardens have Gothic vaulting and Romanesque carved capitals.

Sleeping & Eating

Look for tapas bars and inexpensive cafes on the Plaça de la Font. The Moll de Pescadors (Fishermen's Wharf) is the place to go for seafood restaurants.

Pensió Forum PENSION €

(☎977 23 1718; Plaça de la Font 37; s/d €26/38) The small but oh so colourful rooms at this helpful pension perch above a restaurant and overlook the main square – views of which can be enjoyed from one of the rooms with a balcony.

Hotel Plaça de la Font HOTEL €€

(☎977 24 61 34; www.hotelpdelafont.com; Plaça de la Font 26; s/d €55/70; ❄) Although a trifle cramped, the rooms here have a pleasing modern look, with soft colours, sturdy beds and, in the case of half of the rooms, little balconies overlooking the square.

Aq MODERN CATALONIAN €€

(☎977 21 59 54; Carrer de les Coques 7; mains €15, menú del día from €18; ⊙Tue-Sat) A bubbly designer haunt with stark colour contrasts (black, lemon and cream linen), slick lines and intriguing international plays on traditional cooking.

Quim Quima INTERNATIONAL €€
(☎977 25 21 21; Carrer de les Coques 1bis; meals €35, menú del día from €19.90; ⏱lunch Tue-Thu, lunch & dinner Fri & Sat) This renovated medieval mansion makes a marvellous setting for a meal. The playful menu is wide-ranging, including sausage-and-cheese crêpes and lasagne.

Information

Regional tourist office (Carrer de Fortuny 4; ⏱9am-2pm & 4-6.30pm Mon-Fri, 9am-2pm Sat)

Tourist office (www.tarragonaturisme.cat; Carrer Major 39; ⏱10am-8pm Mon-Sat, 10am-2pm Sun Jul-Oct, 10am-2pm & 4-7pm Mon-Sat)

Getting There & Away

BUS Bus services run to Barcelona, Valencia, Zaragoza, Madrid, Alicante, Pamplona, the main Andalucian cities, Andorra and the north coast. The bus station is around 1.5km northwest of the old town.

TRAIN At least 16 regional trains per day run to/from Barcelona's Passeig de Gràcia via Sants. The cheapest fares cost €13.80 to an average of €20 and the journey takes one to 1½ hours.

ARAGÓN, BASQUE COUNTRY & NAVARRA

This northeast area of Spain is brimming with fascinating destinations: the arid hills and proud history of Aragón; the lush coastline and gourmet delights of the Basque Country (País Vasco); and the wine country and famous festivals of Navarra.

Aragón

Zaragoza is the capital of the expansive Aragón region, though by no means is the city its only attraction. The national parks and pretty towns of the Pyrenees are well worth exploring too.

ZARAGOZA

POP 624,700 / ELEV 200M

Sitting on the banks of the mighty Ebro River, Zaragoza (a contraction of Caesaraugusta, the name the Romans gave to this city when they founded it in 14 BC) is a busy regional capital with a seemingly voracious appetite for eating out and late-night revelry. The historic old centre, crowned by the majestic Basílica del Pilar, throws up echoes of its Roman and Muslim past. The Old Town is also home to El Tubo (The Tube), a maze of streets with countless tapas bars and cafes.

Sights

FREE **Basílica de Nuestra Señora del Pilar** CHURCH
(Plaza del Pilar s/n; ⏱7am-8.30pm) Brace yourself for the saintly and the solemn in this great baroque cavern of Catholicism. It was here on 2 January 40 that Santiago (St James the Apostle) is believed to have seen the Virgin Mary descend atop a marble *pilar* (pillar). A chapel was built around the remaining pillar, followed by a series of ever-more-grandiose churches, culminating in the enormous basilica that you see today. Originally designed in 1681, it was greatly modified in the 18th century and the towers were not finished until the early 20th century. The exterior, with its splendid main dome lording over a flurry of 10 mini domes, each encased in chunky blue, green, yellow and white tiles, creates a kind of rugged Byzantine effect.

A **lift** (admission €2; ⏱10am-1.30pm & 4-6.30pm Tue-Sun) whisks you most of the way up the north tower (Torre Pilar) for fine views.

TOP CHOICE **Aljafería** PALACE
(Calle de los Diputados; adult/under 12yr €3/free, free Sun; ⏱10am-2pm Sat-Wed, 4.30-8pm Mon-Wed, Fri & Sat Jul & Aug, shorter hours rest of year) La Aljafería is Spain's finest Islamic-era edifice outside Andalucía. It's not in the league of Granada's Alhambra or Córdoba's Mezquita, but it's nonetheless a glorious monument. The Aljafería was built as a pleasure palace for Zaragoza's Islamic rulers, chiefly in the 11th century. After the city passed into Christian hands in 1118, Zaragoza's Christian rulers made alterations.

Inside the main gate, cross the rather dull introductory courtyard into a second, the **Patio de Santa Isabel**, once the central courtyard of the Islamic palace. Here you're confronted by the delicate interwoven arches typical of the geometric mastery of Islamic architecture.

La Seo CHURCH
(Catedral de San Salvador; Plaza de la Seo; admission €4; ⏱10am-6pm Tue-Fri, 10am-2pm & 3-6pm Sat, 10-11.30am & 2.30-6pm Sun Jun-Sep) La Seo may lack the fame of the Basílica de Nuestra Señora del Pilar, but its interior is easily

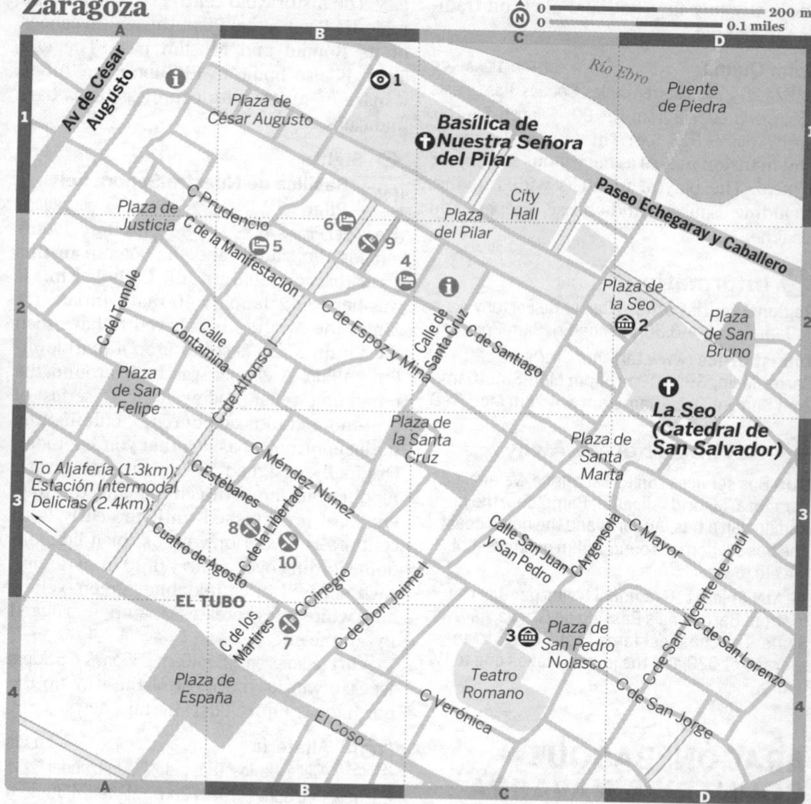

its architectural superior. Built between the 12th and 17th centuries, it displays a fabulous spread of architectural styles from Romanesque to baroque.

Museo del Foro de Caesaraugusta MUSEUM

(Plaza de la Seo 2; admission €2.50; 9am-8.30pm Tue-Sat, 10am-2pm Sun Jun-Sep, shorter hours rest of year) The trapezoid building on Plaza de la Seo is the entrance to an excellent reconstruction of part of Roman Caesaraugusta's forum, now well below ground level.

Museo del Teatro de Caesaraugusta ROMAN THEATRE, MUSEUM

(Calle de San Jorge 12; admission €3.50; 9am-8.30pm Tue-Sat, to 1.30pm Sun) Discovered during the excavation of a building site in 1972, the ruins of Zaragoza's Roman theatre are the focus of this interesting museum; the theatre once seated 6000 spectators.

Sleeping

TOP CHOICE **Hotel Las Torres** HOTEL €€

(Hotel Nastasi Basic ZGZ; 976 39 42 50; www.nastasibasiczgzhotel.com; Plaza del Pilar 11; s/d incl breakfast from €65/75;) This is easily Zaragoza's best place to stay. The rooms are designer cool with dazzling white furnishings and daring wallpaper. The bathroom have hydromassage showers, and the views of the square and basilica from the balconies in most rooms are simply stunning.

Hotel San Valero HOTEL €

(976 29 86 21; www.hotelsanvalero.com; Calle de la Manifestación 27; d €40-48;) It's difficult to believe the prices here. Centrally located, the rooms have a designer feel and while some could be larger, the value is unimpeachable. In short, it's a boutique hotel feel for *hostal* prices.

Zaragoza

Top Sights

Sights

Sleeping

Eating

Sabinas APARTMENTS €€
(☎976 20 47 10; www.sabina.es; Calle de Alfonso I 43; d/apt from €58/68; P❄📶) Apartments with a kitchen and sitting room styled with a contemporary look and a location a few steps off Plaza del Pilar make this a terrific option. The bathrooms are lovely and the price is extraordinarily good considering the location and size of the rooms. Standard doubles with a microwave are also available.

Eating & Drinking

Zaragoza has some terrific tapas bars, with dozens of places on or close to Plaza de Santa Marta. Otherwise the narrow streets of El Tubo, north of Plaza de España, are tapas central.

Calle del Temple, southwest of Plaza del Pilar, is the spiritual home of Zaragoza's roaring nightlife. This is where the city's students head out to drink. There are more bars lined up along this street than anywhere else in Aragón.

TOP CHOICE **Casa Pascualillo** TAPAS €
(Calle de la Libertad 5; meals €15-25; ⏲lunch & dinner Tue-Sat, lunch Sun) The bar here groans under the weight of every tapa variety imaginable, with seafood and meat in abundance; the house speciality is El Pascualillo, a 'small' *bocadillo* (filled roll) of *jamón,* mushrooms and onion.

Taberna Doña Casta TAPAS €€
(Calle Estébanes 6; ⏲Tue-Sun) If you like your tapas without too many frills, this enduringly popular and informal *taberna* could become your culinary home in Zaragoza. The bottle of wine and six tapas for €23 is a terrific way to meet all your gastronomic needs at a reasonable price. The specialities are *croquetas* (croquettes) and egg-based dishes.

Casa Lac REGIONAL, TAPAS €€
(☎976 29 90 25; Calle de los Mártires 12; meals €30-35; ⏲Wed-Mon) The grand old lady of the Zaragoza dining scene, Casa Lac pays homage to the 19th century (it opened in 1825) with its seigniorial decor and impeccable service. The food revolves around Aragonese staples, although the lamb carpaccio with foie gras shows Casa Lac isn't averse to a little experimentation. Dine upstairs with the Who's Who of Zaragoza society, or downstairs in the more informal tapas bar.

El Rincón de Aragón REGIONAL €€
(☎976 20 11 63; Calle de Santiago 3-5; meals €20-35) There's no time for unnecessary elaborations here – the decor is basic and the food stripped down to its essence – but the eating is top-notch and ideal for finding out why people get excited about Aragonese cooking. One house speciality among many is the *ternasco asado con patatas a la pobre* (roasted suckling lamb ribs with 'poor man's potatoes').

Information

Municipal tourist office (www.zaragozaturismo.es; ⏲9am-9pm mid-Jun–mid-Oct, 10am-8pm mid-Oct–mid-Jun)

Oficina de Turismo de Aragón (www.turismodearagon.com; Avenida de César Augusto 25; ⏲9am-2pm & 5-8pm Mon-Fri, from 10am Sat & Sun)

Getting There & Away

AIR **Zaragoza-Sanjurjo airport** (☎976 71 23 00) has domestic and international flights.

BUS Services from the bus station attached to the Estación Intermodal Delicias train station include Madrid (from €14.47, 3¾ hours) and Barcelona (€13.71, 3¾ hours).

TRAIN Zaragoza's **Estación Intermodal Delicias** (Calle Rioja 33) is connected by almost hourly high-speed AVE services to Madrid (€58.20, 1½ hours, 10 daily) and Barcelona (€63.70, from 1½ hours). There are also trains to Valencia (€28.60, 4½ hours, three daily) and Teruel (€15.90, 2¼ hours, four daily).

Around Aragón

In Aragón's south, little visited **Teruel** is home to some stunning Mudéjar architecture. Nearby, **Albarracín** is one of Spain's most beautiful villages.

In the north, the Pyrenees dominate and the **Parque Nacional de Ordesa y Monte Perdido** is excellent for hiking; the pretty village of **Torla** is the gateway. South of the hamlet of **La Besurta** is the great Maladeta massif, a superb challenge for experienced climbers. This forbidding line of icy peaks, with glaciers suspended from the higher crests, culminates in **Aneto** (3404m), the highest peak in the Pyrenees. There are plenty of hiking and climbing options for all levels in these mountain parks bordering France. Another enchanting base for exploration in the region is **Aínsa**, a hilltop village of stone houses.

In Aragón's northwest, **Sos del Rey Católico** is another gorgeous stone village draped along a ridge.

Basque Country

The Basques, whose language is believed to be among the world's oldest, claim two of Spain's most interesting cities – San Sebastián and Bilbao – as their own. Stately San Sebastián offers a slick seaside position and some of the best food Spain has to offer. The extraordinary Guggenheim Bilbao museum is that city's centrepiece.

SAN SEBASTIÁN

POP 183,300

Stylish San Sebastián (Donostia in Basque) has the air of an upscale resort, complete with an idyllic location on the shell-shaped Bahía de la Concha. The natural setting – crystalline waters, a flawless beach, green hills on all sides – is captivating. But this is one of Spain's true culinary capitals, with more Michelin stars per capita here than anywhere else on earth.

Sights & Activities

Beaches & Isla de Santa Clara BEACHES

Fulfilling almost every idea of how a perfect city beach should be formed, **Playa de la Concha** and its westerly extension **Playa de Ondarreta** are easily among the best city beaches in Europe. The **Isla de Santa Clara**, about 700m from the beach, is accessible by boats that run every half-hour from June to September. Less popular, but just as showy, **Playa de Gros**, east of Río Urumea, is the city's main surf beach.

Museo Chillida Leku MUSEUM, PARK

(www.museochillidaleku.com; adult/child €8.50/free; ⌚10.30am-8pm Mon-Sat, to 3pm Sun Jul & Aug, shorter hours rest of year) This open-air museum, south of San Sebastián, is the most engaging museum in rural Basque Country. Amid the beech, oak and magnolia trees, you'll find 40 sculptures of granite and iron created by the renowned Basque sculptor Eduardo Chillida. Many more of Chillida's works appear inside the renovated 16th-century farmhouse.

To get here, take the G2 bus (€1.35) for Hernani from Calle de Okendo in San Sebastián and get off at Zabalaga.

Aquarium AQUARIUM

(www.aquariumss.com; Paseo del Muelle 34; adult/4-12yr €12/6; ⌚10am-8pm Mon-Fri, to 9pm Sat & Sun Apr-Jun & Sep, shorter hours rest of year) In the city's excellent aquarium you'll fear for your life as huge sharks bear down on you, and be tripped out by fancy fluoro jellyfish. The highlights of a visit are the cinema screen–sized deep ocean and coral reef exhibits, and the long tunnel, around which swim monsters of the deep.

Monte Igueldo LOOKOUT

The views from the summit of Monte Igueldo, just west of town, will make you feel like a circling hawk staring over the vast panorama of the Bahía de la Concha and the surrounding coastline and mountains. The best way to get there is via the old-world **funicular railway** (return adult/under 7yr €2.60/1.90; ⌚10am-10pm mid-Jul & Aug, shorter hours rest of year).

Monte Urgull CASTLE, MUSEUM

You can walk to the top of Monte Urgull, topped by low castle walls and a grand statue of Christ, by taking a path from Plaza de Zuloaga or from behind the aquarium. The views are breathtaking. The castle houses the well-presented **Mirando a San Sebastián** (admission free; ⌚11am-8pm May–mid-Sep, shorter hours rest of year), a small museum focusing on the city's history.

Sleeping

TOP CHOICE **Pensión Bellas Artes** BOUTIQUE HOTEL €€

(☎943 47 49 05; www.pension-bellasartes.com; Calle de Urbieta 64; s/d from €75/95; 📶) To call this magnificent place a mere *pensión* is to do it something of a disservice. Its spacious rooms (some with glassed-in balconies) with exposed stone walls and excellent bathrooms should be the envy of many a more expensive hotel. It also has to be the friendliest hotel in town – the staff seem to genuinely love their job and city, and want to help you get the most out of your visit.

Pensión Aida BOUTIQUE HOTEL €€
(943 32 78 00; www.pensionesconencanto.com; Calle de Iztueta 9; s/d €59/82, studio €145;) The owners of this excellent *pensión* read the rule book on what makes a good hotel and have complied exactly. The rooms are bright and bold, full of exposed stone, and everything smells fresh and clean. The communal area, stuffed with soft sofas and mountains of information, is a big plus.

Pensión Amaiur Ostatua BOUTIQUE HOTEL €
(943 42 96 54; www.pensionamaiur.com; Calle de 31 de Agosto 44; s without bathroom €40-45, d without bathroom €50-65;) Sprawling over three-floors of an old townhouse this excellent *pensión* continues to improve. The rooms, all of which share bathrooms, are fairly small but have had a great deal of thought put into them, and every room and every floor is different – maybe you'll get one with chintzy wallpaper or maybe you'll go for one with brazen primary colours.

Pensión Altair PENSIÓN €€
(943 29 31 33; www.pension-altair.com; Calle Padre Larroca 3; s/d €60/84;) This brand-new *pensión* might well be the future of the San Sebastián accommodation scene. A beautifully restored townhouse with unusual arched windows that look like they've come from a church, and spacious minimalist rooms that are a world away from the fusty decor of the old town *pensións*. Reception is closed between 1.30pm and 5pm.

Eating

San Sebastián is paradise for food lovers. Considered the birthplace of *nueva cocina española* (Spanish nouvelle cuisine), this area is home to some of the country's top chefs. Yet not all the good food is pricey. Head to the Parte Vieja for San Sebastián's *pintxos*, Basque-style tapas.

Do what the locals do – crawls of the city centre's bars. *Pintxo* etiquette is simple. Ask for a plate and point out what *pintxos* (bar snacks – more like tasty mounds of food on little slices of baguette) you want. Keep the toothpicks and go back for as many as you'd like. Accompany with *txakoli*, a cloudy white wine poured like cider to create a little fizz. When you're ready to pay, hand over the plate with all the toothpicks and tell bar staff how many drinks you've had. It's an honour system that has stood the test of time. Expect to pay €2.50 to €3.50 for a *pintxo* and *txakoli*.

TOP CHOICE **La Cuchara de San Telmo** TAPAS €
(Calle de 31 de Agosto 28) This unfussy, hidden-away (and hard to find) bar offers miniature *nueva cocina vasca* (Basque nouvelle cuisine) from a supremely creative kitchen, where chefs Alex Montiel and Iñaki Gulin conjure up such delights as *carrílera de ternera al vino tinto* (calf cheeks in red wine), with meat so tender it starts to dissolve almost before it's past your lips.

TOP CHOICE **Arzak** BASQUE FINE DINING €€€
(943 27 84 65; www.arzak.info; Avenida Alcalde Jose Elosegui 273; meals around €150; closed last 2 weeks Jun & all Nov) With three shining Michelin stars, acclaimed chef Juan Mari Arzak takes some beating when it comes to *nueva cocina vasca* and his restaurant is, not surprisingly, considered one of the best places to eat in Spain. Arzak is now assisted by his daughter Elena and they never cease to innovate. Reservations, well in advance, are obligatory. The restaurant is about 1.5km east of San Sebastián.

Astelana TAPAS €
(Calle de Iñigo 1) The *pintxos* draped across the counter in this bar, tucked into the corner of Plaza de la Constitución, stand out as some of the best in the city. Many of them are a fusion of Basque and Asian inspirations, but the best of all are perhaps the foie gras–based treats.

Restaurante Alberto SEAFOOD €
(943 42 88 84; Calle de 31 de Agosto 19; menú €14; closed Tue) A charming old seafood restaurant with a fishmonger-style window display of the day's catch. It's small, dark and friendly, but much of the fish is sold by the kilo so bring a friend.

La Mejíllonera TAPAS €
(Calle del Puerto 15) If you thought mussels came only with garlic sauce, come here and discover mussels (from €3) by the thousand in all their glorious forms. Mussels not for you? Opt for the calamari and spicy *patatas bravas*. We promise you won't regret it.

Information

Street signs are in Basque and Spanish.

Oficina de Turismo (943 48 11 66; www.sansebastianturismo.com; Alameda de Blvd 8;

San Sebastián

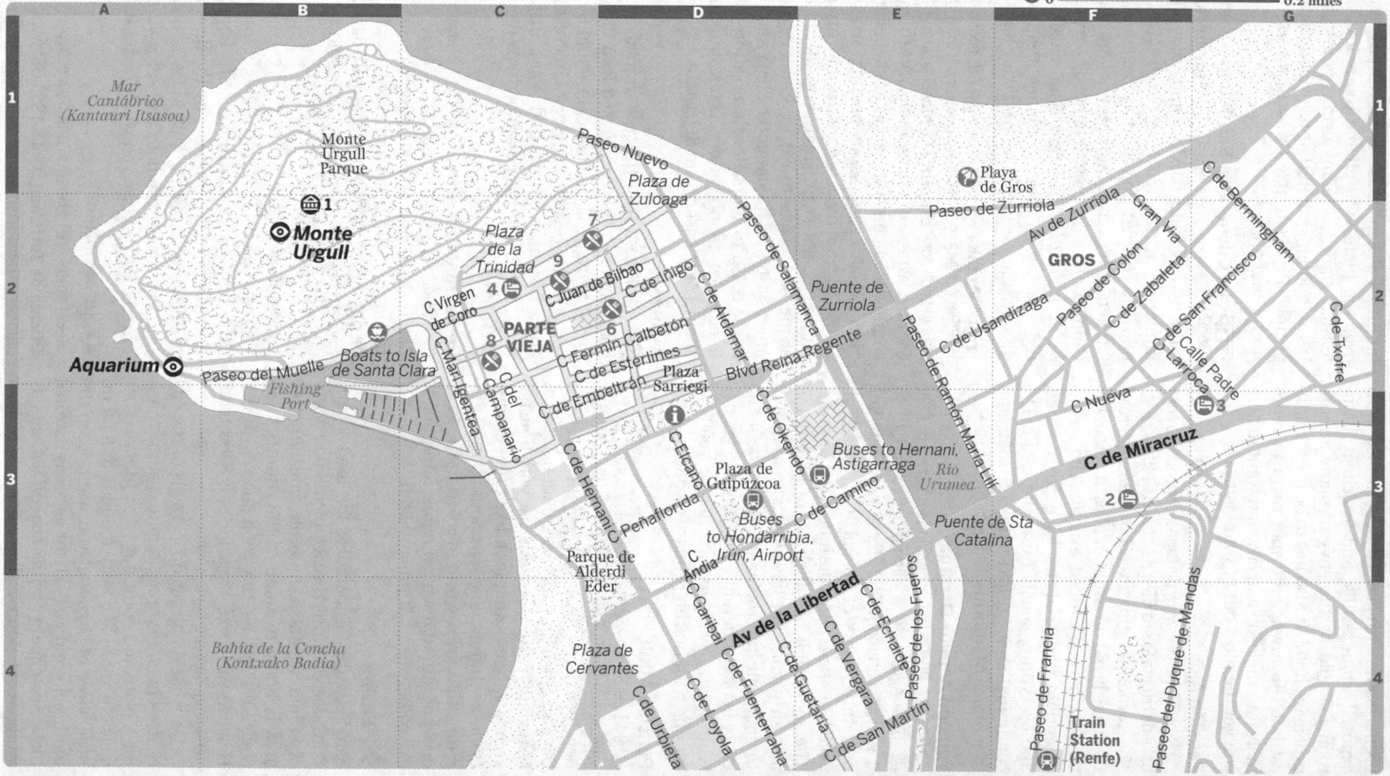

0 – 400 m
0 – 0.2 miles

A B C D E F G
1 2 3 4

Mar Cantábrico (Kantauri Itsasoa)
Monte Urgull Parque
1
Monte Urgull
Aquarium
Paseo del Muelle
Fishing Port
Boats to Isla de Santa Clara
C Virgen de Coro
C Mari Igentea
C del Campanario
Plaza de la Trinidad
4
9
7
8
6
PARTE VIEJA
C Juan de Bilbao
C de Iñigo
C Fermín Calbetón
C de Esterlines
C de Embeltrán
Plaza Sarriegi
Paseo Nuevo
Plaza de Zuloaga
C de Aldamar
Paseo de Salamanca
Puente de Zurriola
Blvd Reina Regente
C de Hernani
C Elcano
C de Okendo
C Peñaflorida
Plaza de Guipúzcoa
Buses to Hondarribia, Irún, Airport
Buses to Hernani, Astigarraga
C de Camino
Río Urumea
Parque de Alderdi Eder
C Andia
C Garibai
Av de la Libertad
C de Echaide
Paseo de los Fueros
Plaza de Cervantes
C de Urbieta
C de Loyola
C de Fuenterrabia
C de Guetaria
C de Vergara
C de San Martín
Bahía de la Concha (Kontxako Badia)
Puente de Sta Catalina
Paseo de Ramón María Lili
C de Usandizaga
Playa de Gros
Paseo de Zurriola
Av de Zurriola
GROS
Paseo de Colón
C de Zabaleta
Gran Via
C de Bermingham
C de San Francisco
Calle Padre C Larroca
3
C de Txofre
C Nueva
C de Miracruz
2
Paseo de Francia
Train Station (Renfe)
Paseo del Duque de Mandas

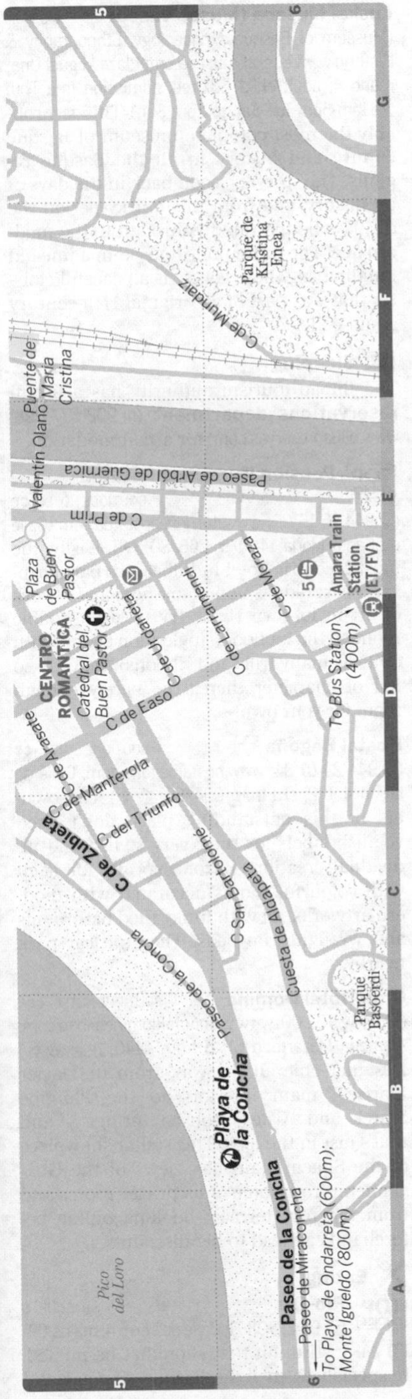

⌚9am-8pm Mon-Sat, 10am-7pm Sun Jun-Sep, 9am-1.30pm & 3.30-7pm Mon-Thu, 9.30am-7pm Fri & Sat, 10am-2pm Sun Oct-May)

ℹ Getting There & Away

AIR The city's **airport** (☎902 40 47 04; www.aena.es) is 22km out of town, near Hondarribia. There are regular flights to Madrid and occasional charters to European cities.

BUS Daily bus services leave for Bilbao (€7.06 to €14, one hour), Bilbao Airport (€15.40, 1¼ hours), Biarritz (France; €8.50, 1¼ hours), Madrid (from €31.99, five hours) and Pamplona (€6.88, one hour).

TRAIN The main **Renfe train station** (Paseo de Francia) is just across Río Urumea. There are regular services to Madrid (from €52.60, five hours) and Barcelona (from €36.90, eight hours). There's only one direct train to Paris, but there are plenty more from the Spanish/French border town of Irun (or sometimes Hendaye) (€1.80, 25 minutes), which is also served by **Eusko Tren/Ferrocarril Vasco** (www.euskotren.es, in Spanish & Basque). Trains depart every half-hour from Amara train station, about 1km south of the city centre.

BILBAO

POP 354,200

The commercial hub of the Basque Country, Bilbao (Bilbo in Basque) is best known for the magnificent Guggenheim Museum. An architectural masterpiece by Frank Gehry, the museum was the catalyst of a turn-around that saw Bilbao transformed from an industrial port city into a vibrant cultural centre. After visiting this must-see temple to modern art, spend time exploring Bilbao's

San Sebastián

Top Sights

Aquarium ... A2
Monte Urgull ... B2
Playa de la Concha ... B6

Sights

1 Mirando a San Sebastián ... B2

Sleeping

2 Pensión Aida ... F3
3 Pension Altair ... G3
4 Pensión Amaiur Ostatua ... C2
5 Pensión Bellas Artes ... E6

Eating

6 Astelana ... D2
7 La Cuchara de San Telmo ... C2
8 La Mejillonera ... C2
9 Restaurante Alberto ... C2

Casco Viejo (Old Quarter), a grid of elegant streets dotted with shops, cafes, *pintxos* bars and several small but worthy museums.

Sights

TOP CHOICE **Museo Guggenheim** ART MUSEUM
(www.guggenheim-bilbao.es; Avenida Abandoibarra 2; adult/child €13/free; ⊙10am-8pm Jul & Aug, closed Mon Sep-Jun) Opened in September 1997, Bilbao's Museo Guggenheim lifted modern architecture and Bilbao into the 21st century – with sensation. Some might say, probably quite rightly, that structure overwhelms function here and that the Guggenheim is more famous for its architecture than its content. But Canadian architect Frank Gehry's inspired use of flowing canopies, cliffs, promontories, ship shapes, towers and flying fins is irresistible. The interior of the Guggenheim is purposefully vast. The cathedral-like atrium is more than 45m high. Light pours in through the glass cliffs. Permanent exhibits fill the ground floor and include such wonders as mazes of metal and phrases of light reaching for the skies.

For most people, though, it is the temporary exhibitions that are the main attraction (check the Guggenheim's website for a full program of upcoming exhibitions).

Museo de Bellas Artes ART MUSEUM
(Fine Arts Museum; www.museobilbao.com; Plaza del Museo 2; adult/child €6/free, admission free Wed; ⊙10am-8pm Tue-Sun) A mere five minutes from Museo Guggenheim is Bilbao's Museo de Bellas Artes. There are three main subcollections: Classical art, with works by Murillo, Zurbarán, El Greco, Goya and van Dyck; Contemporary art, featuring works by Gauguin, Francis Bacon and Anthony Caro; and Basque art, with the works of the great sculptors Jorge de Oteiza and Eduardo Chillida, and also strong paintings by the likes of Ignacio Zuloago and Juan de Echevarria.

Casco Viejo OLD TOWN
The compact Casco Viejo, Bilbao's atmospheric old quarter, is full of charming streets, boisterous bars, and plenty of quirky and independent shops. At the heart of the Casco are Bilbao's original 'seven streets', Las Siete Calles, which date from the 1400s.

The 14th-century Gothic **Catedral de Santiago** (⊙10am-1pm & 4-7pm Tue-Sat, 10.30am-1.30pm Sun) has a splendid Renaissance portico and pretty little cloister. Further north, the 19th-century arcaded **Plaza Nueva** is a rewarding *pintxo* haunt.

Euskal Museoa (Museo Vasco) MUSEUM
(Museum of Basque Archaeology, Ethnography & History; www.euskal-museoa.org; Plaza Miguel Unamuno 4; adult/child €3/free, admission free Thu; ⊙11am-5pm Tue-Sat, to 2pm Sun) This is probably the most complete museum of Basque culture and history in all the Basque regions. The story kicks off back in the days of prehistory, and from this murky period the displays bound rapidly through to the modern age. The museum is housed in a fine old building, at whose centre is a peaceful cloister that was part of an original 17th-century Jesuit college.

Sleeping

The Bilbao tourism authority has a useful **reservations department** (☎902 877 298; www.bilbaoreservas.com) for accommodation.

TOP CHOICE **Pensión Iturrienea Ostatua** BOUTIQUE HOTEL €€
(☎944 16 15 00; www.iturrieneaostatua.com; Calle de Santa María 14; d/tr €66/80;) Easily the most eccentric hotel in Bilbao, it's part farmyard, part old-fashioned toyshop, and a work of art in its own right. Try to get a double room on the 1st floor (singles don't come with quite as many frills and ribbons); they are so full of character there'll be barely enough room for your own!

Hostal Begoña BOUTIQUE HOTEL €€
(☎944 23 01 34; www.hostalbegona.com; Calle de la Amistad 2; s/d from €54/63; @) The owners of this outstanding place don't need voguish labels for their very stylish and individual creation. Begoña speaks for itself with colourful rooms decorated with modern artworks, all with funky tiled bathrooms and wrought-iron beds. There's a car park nearby.

Gran Hotel Domine BOUTIQUE HOTEL €€€
(☎944 25 33 00; www.granhoteldominebilbao.com; Alameda Mazarredo 61; d from €140; P@) Designer chic all the way, from the Javier Mariscal main interiors to the Philippe Starck and Arne Jacobsen fittings – and that's just in the loos. This stellar showpiece of the Silken chain has views of the Guggenheim from some of its pricier rooms and from the roof terrace. Booking online beforehand can lead to big discounts.

Eating

TOP CHOICE **Rio-Oja** BASQUE €
(☎944 15 08 71; Calle de Perro 4; mains €9-12) An institution that shouldn't be missed. It specialises in light Basque seafood and

heavy inland fare, but to most foreigners the sheep brains and squid floating in pools of its own ink are the makings of a culinary adventure story they'll be recounting for years. Don't worry, though: it really does taste much better than it sounds.

TOP CHOICE **Restaurante Guggenheim** BASQUE FINE DINING €€€
(☎944 23 93 33; www.restauranteguggenheim.com; bistro menu €20, restaurant menu €75, mains €30-35 ⊙closed Mon & Christmas period) El Goog's modernist, chic restaurant and cafe are under the direction of super chef Josean Martínez Alija. Needless to say, the *nueva cocina vasca* is breathtaking, and the ever-changing menu includes such mouth-waterers as Iberian pork meatballs with carrot juice and curry. Even the olives are vintage classics: all come from thousand-year-old olive trees! Reservations are essential in the evening, but at lunch it's a first-come, first-served basis from 1.30pm.

Café Iruña BASQUE €
(cnr Calles de Colón de Larreátegui & Berástegui; menú del día €13.50) Moorish style and a century of gossip are the defining characteristics of this grand old dame. It's the perfect place to indulge in a bit of people-watching and while you're at it you might as well also indulge in a meal or, in the evening, some *pinchos morunos* (spicy kebabs with bread; €2.20).

Information

Tourist office (www.bilbao.net/bilbaoturismo; Plaza del Ensanche 11; ⊙9am-2pm & 4-7.30pm Mon-Fri) Other branches at the Teatro Arriaga, Museo Guggenheim and airport.

Getting There & Away

AIR Bilbao's airport (BIO), with domestic and a handful of international flights, is near Sondika, 12km northeast of the city. The airport bus Bizkaibus A3247 (€1.20, 30 minutes) runs to/from Termibus (bus station), where there is a tram stop and a metro station.

TRAIN Two Renfe trains runs daily to Madrid (from €48.60, six hours) and Barcelona (€62.30, six hours) from the Abando train station. Slow **FEVE** (www.feve.es) trains run from Concordia station next door, heading west into Cantabria and Asturias.

BUS Regular bus services operate to/from Madrid (€27.17, 4¾ hours), Barcelona (€41.90, seven hours), Pamplona (€13.40, two hours) and Santander (from €6.71, 1¼ hours).

Navarra

Navarra, historically and culturally linked to the Basque Country, is known for its fine wines and for the Sanfermines festival in Pamplona.

PAMPLONA

POP 195,800

Immortalised by Ernest Hemingway in *The Sun Also Rises*, the pre-Pyrenean city of Pamplona (Iruña in Basque) is home of the wild Sanfermines (aka Encierro or Running of the Bulls) festival, but is also an extremely walkable city that's managed to mix the charm of old plazas and buildings with modern shops and a lively nightlife.

Sights

Cathedral CHURCH
(Calle Dormitalería; guided tours adult/child €4.40/2.60; ⊙10am-7pm Mon-Fri, to 2pm Sat mid-Jul–mid-Sep, closed for lunch mid-Sep–mid-Jul) Pamplona's main cathedral stands on a rise just inside the city ramparts amid a dark thicket of narrow streets. It's a late-medieval Gothic gem spoiled only by its rather dull neoclassical facade, an 18th-century appendage. The real joys are the vast interior and the Gothic cloister, where there is marvellous delicacy in the stonework.

Ciudadela & Parks PARK
(Avenida del Ejército) The walls and bulwarks of the grand fortified citadel, the star-shaped Ciudadela, lurk amid the verdant grass and trees in what is now a charming park, the portal to three more parks that unfold to the north and lend the city a beautiful green escape.

Museo Oteiza MUSEUM
(www.museooteiza.org; Calle de la Cuesta 7; adult/student/child €4/2/free, all admission free Fri;

SURVIVING SANFERMINES

The Sanfermines festival is held from 6 to 14 July, when Pamplona is overrun with thrill-seekers, curious onlookers and, yes, bulls. The Encierro (Running of the Bulls) begins at 8am daily, when bulls are let loose from the Coralillos Santo Domingo. The 825m race lasts just three minutes, so don't be late. The safest place to watch the Encierro is on TV. If that's too tame for you, try to sweet-talk your way onto a balcony or book a room in a hotel with views.

⏲11am-7pm Tue-Sat, to 3pm Sun Jun-Sep) Around 9km northeast of Pamplona in the town of Alzuza, this impressive museum contains almost 3000 pieces by the renowned Navarran sculptor Jorge Oteiza. As well as his workshop, this beautifully designed gallery incorporates the artist's former home in a lovely rural setting. Three buses a day run to Alzuza from Pamplona's bus station.

Sleeping

Accommodation is hard to come by during Sanfermines – book months in advance. Prices below don't reflect the huge (up to fivefold) mark-up you'll find in mid-July.

TOP CHOICE Palacio Guendulain HISTORIC HOTEL €€€
(☎948 22 55 22; www.palacioguendulain.com; Calle Zapatería 53; d from €128; P❄📶) To call this stunning new hotel sumptuous is an understatement. Inside the converted former home of the Viceroy of New Granada, the rooms contain 'Princess and the Pea' soft beds, enormous showers and regal armchairs.

Hotel Puerta del Camino BOUTIQUE HOTEL €€
(☎948 22 66 88; www.hotelpuertadelcamino.com; Calle dos de Mayo 4; s/d €70/82; P❄@) A very stylish new hotel inside a converted convent (clearly the nuns appreciated the finer things in life!) beside the northern gates to the old city. The functional rooms have clean, modern lines and it's positioned in one of the prettier, and quieter, parts of town.

Habitaciones Mendi PENSION €
(☎948 22 52 97; Calle de las Navas de Tolosa 9; s/d €30/45) Full of the spirits of Pamplona past, this charming little guesthouse is a real find. Creaky, wobbly wooden staircases and equally creaky chintzy rooms make it just like being at your gran's, and the woman running it will cluck over you as if she were your gran.

Eating & Drinking

Central streets such as Calle de San Nicolás and Calle de la Estafeta are lined with tapas bars, many of which morph into nightspots on weekends.

Baserri BASQUE €
(Calle de San Nicolás 32; menú del día €14) This place has won enough pintxo awards that we could fill this entire book listing them. As you'd expect from such a certificate-studded bar, the pintxos are superb but sadly the full meals play something of a second fiddle in comparison.

Casa Otaño BASQUE €
(☎948 22 50 95; Calle de San Nicolás 5; mains €15-18) A little pricier than many on this street but worth the extra. Its formal atmosphere is eased by the dazzling array of pink and red flowers spilling off the balcony. Great dishes range from the locally caught trout to heavenly duck dishes.

Mesón Pirineo BASQUE €
(Calle de la Estafeta 41; mains €12-16) There's nothing fancy and modern about this place; it's just old Navarran style and superb *pintxos* all the way.

Café Iruña HISTORIC CAFE
(Plaza del Castillo 44) Opened on the eve of Sanfermines in 1888, Café Iruña's dominant position, powerful sense of history and frilly belle époque decor make this by far the most famous and popular watering hole in the city.

Information

Tourist office (www.turismo.navarra.es; Calle de Esclava 1; ⏲9am-8pm Mon-Sat, to 2pm Sun)

Getting There & Away

AIR Pamplona's **airport** (☎948 16 87 00), about 7km south of the city, has regular flights to Madrid and Barcelona. Bus 21 (€1.10) travels between the city (from the bus station) and the airport.

BUS From the **main bus station** (Calle Conde Oliveto 8), buses leave for Bilbao (€13.40, two hours) and San Sebastián (€6.88, one hour).

TRAIN Pamplona's train station is linked to the city centre by bus 9 from Paseo de Sarasate every 15 minutes. Trains run to/from Madrid (€56, three hours, four daily) and San Sebastián (from €20.40, two hours, two daily).

CANTABRIA, ASTURIAS & GALICIA

With a landscape reminiscent of parts of the British Isles, 'Green Spain' offers great walks in national parks, seafood feasts in sophisticated towns and oodles of opportunities to plunge into the ice-cold waters of the Bay of Biscay.

Cantabria

Some 34km west of the regional capital, Santander, **Santillana del Mar** (www.santillanadelmar.com) is a bijou medieval village and the obvious overnight base for visiting the nearby Cueva de Altamira.

The country's finest prehistoric art, in the Cueva de Altamira, 2km southwest of Santillana del Mar, is off-limits to all but the scientific community. Since 2001, however, the **Museo Altamira** (http://museodealtamira.mcu.es; adult/child, EU senior or student €3/free, Sun & from 2.30pm Sat free; ⌚9.30am-8pm Tue-Sat, to 3pm Sun & holidays) has allowed all comers to view the inspired, 14,500-year-old depictions of bison, horses and other beasts (or rather, their replicas) in this full-size, dazzling re-creation of the cave's most interesting chamber, the Sala de Polícromos (Polychrome Hall).

Buses run three to four times a day from Santander to Santilla del Mar.

Oviedo

POP 190,000

The elegant parks and modern shopping streets of Asturias' capital are agreeably offset by what remains of the *casco antiguo* (old town).

Just outside the city (within 3km) is a scattering of 9th-century, pre-Romanesque buildings, including the **Iglesia de San Julián de los Prados**, **Palacio de Santa María del Naranco** and the **Iglesia de San Miguel de Lillo**. Get information from the tourist offices in town.

Sights

Catedral de San Salvador CHURCH

FREE The mainly Gothic cathedral is home to the **Cámara Santa** (museum & cloister €3.50, free Thu afternoon); ⌚10am-1pm & 4-6pm Mon-Sat), a chapel built by Alfonso II to house holy relics. It contains some key symbols of medieval Spanish Christianity: Alfonso II presented the Cruz de los Ángeles (Cross of the Angels) to Oviedo in 808, and it's still the city's emblem; a century later, Alfonso III donated the Cruz de la Victoria (Cross of Victory), which in turn became the sign of Asturias.

Old Town HISTORIC AREA

The Old Town's nooks and crannies include **Plaza de la Constitución**, capped at one end by the Iglesia de San Isidoro and fronted by an eclectic collection of old shops, cafes and the 17th-century *ayuntamiento*. To the south, past the **Mercado El Fontán** food market, arcaded **Plaza Fontán** is equipped with a couple of *sidrerías* (cider houses). Other little squares include Plaza de Trascorrales, Plaza de Riego and Plaza del Paraguas.

WORTH A TRIP

PICOS DE EUROPA

These jagged mountains straddling Asturias, Cantabria and northeast Castilla y León amount to some of the finest walking country in Spain.

They comprise three limestone massifs (whose highest peak rises 2648m). The 647-sq-km **Parque Nacional de los Picos de Europa** (www.picosdeeuropa.com, in Spanish) covers all three massifs and is Spain's second-biggest national park.

There are numerous places to stay and eat all over the mountains. Getting here and around by bus can be slow going but the Picos are accessible from Santander and Oviedo (the latter is easier) by bus.

Sleeping & Eating

Oviedo's *sidrería* rules include getting good food at reasonable prices. Calle de la Gascona is a particularly happy hunting ground.

Hotel de la Reconquista HOTEL €€€

(☎985 24 11 00; www.hoteldelareconquista.com; Calle de Gil de Jaz 16; s/d from €131/157; P ⊜ ❄ @ ᯤ) The city's top lodgings, two blocks northwest of Campo de San Francisco, started life as an 18th-century hospice. Rooms come in different shapes and sizes, with timber furniture, floor-to-ceiling windows, and gentle ochre and white colour schemes.

Hotel Santa Cruz HOTEL €€

(☎985 22 37 11; www.santacruzoviedo.com; Calle de Marqués de Santa Cruz 6; s/d €50/65; P ⊜ ᯤ) Only a couple of rooms overlook the lovely big green park across the street, and there's nothing inspired about the decor. But with well-sized, spotless rooms, friendly reception and a central location, this amounts to decent value.

La Puerta Nueva MEDITERRANEAN €€

TOP CHOICE (☎985 22 52 27; Calle de Leopoldo Alas 2; meals €40-60; ⌚lunch daily, dinner Thu-Sat; ⊜) A gourmet experience, mixing northern with Mediterranean cooking in a homey, welcoming atmosphere. The best option is to tackle one of the tasting menus.

Tierra Astur SIDRERÍA €€

(☎985 20 25 02; Calle de la Gascona 1; meals €20-30) An especially atmospheric *sidrería* restaurant, Tierra Astur is famed for its grilled meats and prize-winning cider. Folks queue for tables, or give up and settle for tapas at the bar. Platters of Asturian sausage, cheese or ham are a good starter option.

Information

Oficina Municipal de Turismo (Plaza de la Constitución 4; ⏲9.30am-7.30pm)

Regional tourist office (www.infoasturias.com; Calle de Cimadevilla 4; ⏲10am-8pm Mon-Fri, to 7pm Sat & Sun, closed Sun mid-Sep–Jun)

Getting There & Away

AIR The **Aeropuerto de Asturias** (☎902 404704) is at Santiago del Monte, 47km northwest of Oviedo and 40km west of Gijón. There are flights to European cities and around Spain. Buses run hourly to/from Oviedo's ALSA bus station (€6.35, 45 minutes).

BUS From the **ALSA bus station** (☎902 422242; Calle de Pepe Cosmen), 300m northeast of the train station, direct services head to Gijón (€2.15, 30 minutes) every 10 or 15 minutes. Other daily buses head to Asturian towns, Galicia, Cantabria and elsewhere.

TRAIN One **station** (Avenida de Santander) serves both train companies, Renfe and FEVE (for buses to Santander and Bilbao), the latter located on the upper level. **Renfe** (www.renfe.com) runs trains to León, Madrid and Barcelona at least once daily. For Gijón, Renfe *cercanías* (€2.75, 35 minutes) go once or twice an hour.

Santiago de Compostela

POP 79,000

The supposed burial place of St James (Santiago), Santiago de Compostela is a bewitching city. Christian pilgrims journeying along the Camino de Santiago often end up mute with wonder on entering its medieval centre. Fortunately, they usually regain their verbal capacities over a celebratory late-night foray into the city's lively bar scene.

Sights

Catedral de Santiago de Compostela CHURCH

(Praza do Obradoiro; www.catedraldesantiago.es; ⏲7am-9pm) The grand heart of Santiago, the cathedral soars above the city centre in a splendid jumble of moss-covered spires and statues. Though Galicia's grandest monument was built piecemeal through the centuries, its beauty is only enhanced by the mix of Romanesque, baroque and Gothic flourishes. What you see today is actually the fourth church to stand on this spot. The bulk of it was built between 1075 and 1211, in Romanesque style with a traditional Latin-cross layout and three naves.

The main entrance is via the lavish staircase and facade on the Praza do Obradoiro, or through the south door on Praza de Praterías. The baroque Obradoiro facade was erected in the 18th century partly to protect the cathedral's original entrance, which is now just inside it – the artistically unparalleled **Pórtico de la Gloria** (Galician: Porta da Gloria), with its 200 Romanesque sculptures by Maestro Mateo.

Towards the far (west) end of the cathedral's main nave, to the right of the Churrigueresque **Altar Mayor** (Main Altar), a small staircase leads up above the altar to a 13th-century **statue of Santiago**, which the faithful queue up to embrace.

A special pilgrims' Mass is celebrated at noon daily. Other high-altar Masses take place at 10am, 6pm and (except Sunday) 7.30pm.

For an unforgettable bird's-eye view of the city, take the **cathedral rooftop tour** (☎981 55 29 85; www.santiagoturismo.com; per person €10; ⏲10am-2pm & 4-8pm).

Museo da Catedral MUSEUM

(Cathedral Museum; www.catedraldesantiago.es; Praza do Obradoiro; adult/student & pilgrim/child €5/3/free; ⏲10am-2pm & 4-8pm, closed Sun afternoon) The many-roomed Museo da Catedral, entered to the right of the Obradoiro facade, spreads over four floors and includes the cathedral's large 16th-century Gothic/plateresque cloister. You'll see Maestro Mateo's original stone choir (destroyed in 1603 but recently pieced back together), rooms of tapestries including a set from designs by Goya, the lavishly decorated 18th-century *sala capitular* (chapter house), and the richly decorated crypt beneath the Pórtico de la Gloria.

Around the Cathedral PLAZAS

The cathedral is surrounded by handsome plazas that invite you to wander through them. The grand **Praza do Obradoiro** (Workshop Plaza), to which most arriving Camino pilgrims instinctively find their way, earned its name from the stonemasons' workshops set up here while the cathedral was being built. At its northern end, the Renaissance **Hostal dos Reis Católicos** was built in the early 16th century. Today it shelters well-off travellers instead, as a luxurious *parador*. Along the western side of the square is the elegant 18th-century **Pazo de Raxoi**, now the city hall.

Around the corner, **Praza das Praterías** (Silversmiths' Square) is marked with the **Fuente de los Caballos** (1829) fountain, with the cathedral's south facade at the top of the steps. Curiously, the **Casa do Cabildo**, facing it on the lower side of the square, is no more than a 3m-deep facade, erected in 1758 to embellish the plaza.

FREE **Museo das Peregrinacións** MUSEUM
(www.mdperegrinacions.com; Rúa de San Miguel 4; 10am-8pm Tue-Fri, 10.30am-1.30pm & 5-8pm Sat, 10.30am-1.30pm Sun) This fine museum explores the pilgrim culture that has so shaped Santiago. Look out for the fascinating illuminated map showing pilgrimage destinations across the world.

Sleeping

Casa-Hotel As Artes HOTEL €€
(981 55 52 54; www.asartes.com; Travesía de Dos Puertas 2; r €102-130;) On a quiet street close to the cathedral, As Artes' lovely stone-walled rooms exude a romantic rustic air. Breakfast (€10.80) is served in a homey dining room overlooking the street.

Parador Hostal dos Reis Católicos HOTEL €€€
(981 58 22 00; www.parador.es; Praza do Obradoiro 1; r incl breakfast from €190;) Opened in 1509 and rubbing shoulders with the cathedral, the palatial *parador* is Santiago's top hotel. Even if you don't book one of its regal rooms, stop in for tea at the elegant cafe.

Hotel Airas Nunes HOTEL €€
(981 56 93 50; www.pousadasdecompostela.com; Rúa do Vilar 17; d €97;) For laid-back elegance, this is a great choice, though it can be hard to get a room. The spiralling granite staircase leads to 10 appealing rooms with garnet-and-green colour schemes, buttery yellow walls, warm wooden furniture and wood-beam ceilings.

Meiga Backpackers HOSTEL €
(981 57 08 46; www.meiga-backpackers.es; Rúa dos Basquiños 67; dm incl breakfast €17-18;) Clean, colourful, friendly and handily placed between the bus station and city centre, Meiga has spacious bunk dorms, a kitchen, a garden and no curfew. It's the only place you need consider if you're on the budget backpacking trail – unless you want a private room, in which case **Meiga Backpackers Pension** (981 59 64 01; www.meiga-backpackers.es; Rúa da República del Salvador 32; d €36-42;), in the new town, could fit the bill nicely.

Eating

A Curtidoría GALICIAN €€
(981 55 43 42; Rúa da Conga 2-3; meals €25-50; closed Sun dinner;) Understatedly stylish and a favourite lunch spot with locals, A Curtidoría overlooks four streets from its two dining rooms and specialises in inventive but uncomplicated fish, meat and rice dishes like crab-stuffed peppers, grilled turbot with glazed vegies or entrecôte with wild mushroom sauce.

Mesón Ó 42 TAPAS €
(Rúa do Franco 42; raciones €5-18) With a solid list of favourite local *raciones* like *empanadas* (pies), shellfish, octopus and tortillas, as well as fish, meat and rice dishes, this popular place stands out from the crowd with its well-prepared food and good service.

Casa Rosalía TAPAS €
(Rúa do Franco 10; raciones €4-16) With a more contemporary style than other nearby bars, Rosalía draws crowds for tapas and *raciones* like scallop-and-monkfish brochette or Galician cheese salad. A selection of tempting snacks (€1.10 to €1.60) is ranged along the bar.

Drinking

If you're after tapas and wine, graze along Rúa do Franco and Rúa da Raíña. For people-watching, hit the cafes along Praza da Quintana and Rúa do Vilar. The liveliest area lies east of Praza da Quintana, especially along Rúa de San Paio de Antealtares, known as a hot spot for live music.

Information

City tourist office (www.santiagoturismo.com; Rúa do Vilar 63; 9am-9pm)

Pilgrims' Reception Office (Oficina de Acogida de Peregrinos; 981 56 88 46; www.peregrinossantiago.es; Rúa do Vilar 1; 9am-8pm)

Regional tourist office (www.turgalicia.es; Rúa do Vilar 30-32; 10am-8pm Mon-Fri, 11am-2pm & 5-7pm Sat, 11am-2pm Sun)

Getting There & Around

AIR Flights from various Spanish and European destinations land at **Lavacolla airport** (981 54 75 00). Up to 36 Empresa Freire buses (€1.80) run daily between Lavacolla airport and Rúa do Doutor Teixeiro, in the new town southwest of Praza de Galicia.

Santiago de Compostela

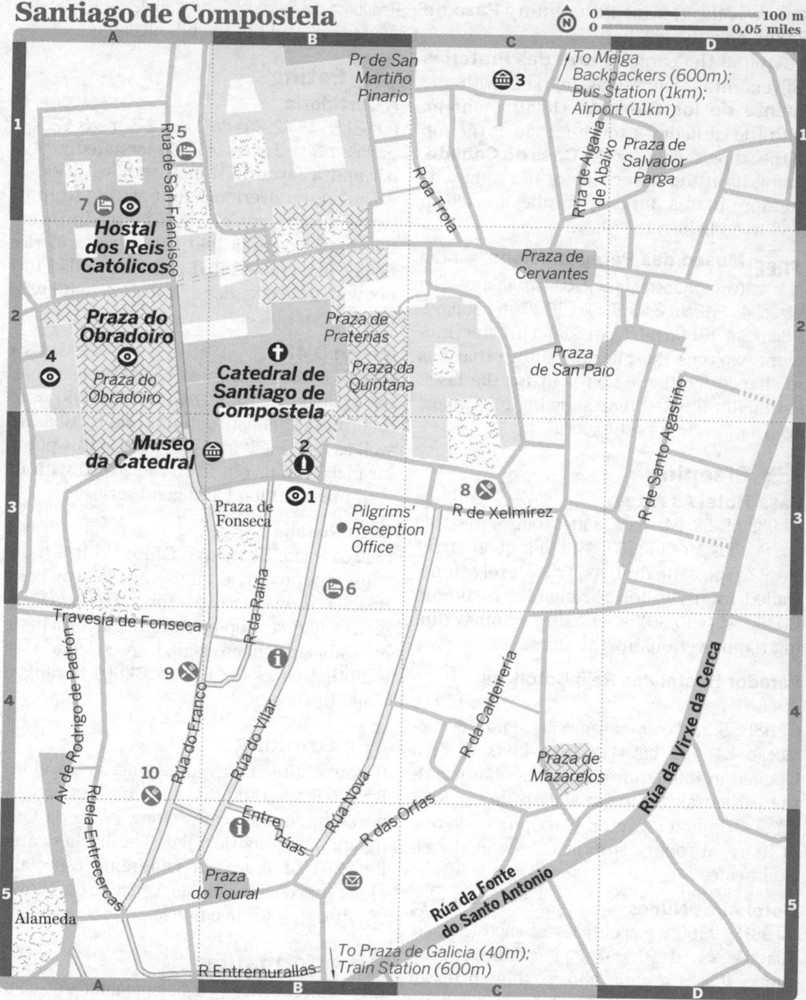

BUS The **bus station** (☎981 54 24 16; www.tussa.org, in Spanish; Praza de Camilo Díaz Baliño) is about a 20-minute walk northeast of the centre. Castromil-Monbus runs to destinations throughout Galicia. ALSA has services to Oviedo (€26 to €43, 4¾ to 5½ hours), San Sebastián (€58, 12½ to 13½ hours), León (€23 to €27, six hours) and Madrid (€42 to €60, eight to 9¾ hours). ALSA also has direct daily services to Porto (€29, three hours) and Lisbon (€50, seven to nine hours).

TRAIN From the **train station** (Avenida de Lugo), regional trains run up and down the coast, while a daytime Talgo and an overnight Trenhotel head to Madrid (€49.50, nine hours).

Around Galicia

Galicia's dramatic Atlantic coastline is one of Spain's best-kept secrets, with wild and precipitous cliffs and isolated fishing villages. The lively port city of **A Coruña** has a lovely city beach and fabulous seafood (a recurring Galician theme). It's also the gateway to the stirring landscapes of the **Costa da Morte** and **Rías Altas**; the latter's highlight among many is probably **Cabo Ortegal**. Inland Galicia is also worth exploring, especially the old town of **Lugo**, surrounded by what many consider to be the world's best preserved Roman walls.

Santiago de Compostela

VALENCIA & MURCIA

A warm climate, an abundance of seaside resorts, and interesting cities make this area of Spain a popular destination. The beaches of the Costa Blanca (White Coast) draw most of the visitors, but venture beyond the shore to get a real feel for the region.

Valencia

POP 814,200

Valencia, where paella first simmered over a wood fire, is a vibrant, friendly, slightly chaotic place. It has two outstanding fine-arts museums, an accessible old quarter, Europe's newest cultural and scientific complex, and one of Spain's most exciting nightlife scenes.

Head to the Barrio del Carmen, Valencia's oldest quarter, for quirky shops and the best nightlife. Other key areas are the nearby Plaza del Ayuntamiento, the Plaza de la Reina and the Plaza de la Virgen.

Sights & Activities

TOP CHOICE Ciudad de las Artes y las Ciencias SCIENCE CENTRE

(City of Arts & Sciences; reservations 902 10 00 31; www.cac.es; combined ticket adult/child €31.50/24) The aesthetically stunning City of Arts & Sciences occupies a massive 350,000-sq-metre swath of the old Turia riverbed. It's mostly the work of stellar local architect, the world-renowned Santiago Calatrava. The complex includes the **Oceanogràfic** (adult/child €24/18; 10am-6pm), a stunning aquarium; **Hemisfèric** (adult/child €7.50/5.80), a planetarium and IMAX cinema; **Museo de las Ciencias Príncipe Felipe** (adult/child €7.50/6; 10am-7pm), an interactive science museum; and the extraordinary **Palau de les Arts Reina Sofía** (www.lesarts.com; Autovía a El Saler) concert hall. It's 3km southeast of the Plaza de la Virgen; take bus 35 from Plaza del Ayuntamiento or bus 95 from Torres de Serranos or Plaza de América.

Barrio del Carmen HISTORIC AREA

You'll see Valencia's best face by simply wandering around the Barrio del Carmen. Valencia's Romanesque-Gothic-baroque-Renaissance **catedral** (adult/child incl audioguide €4/2.70; 10am-5.30pm Mon-Sat, 2-5.30pm Sun) is a compendium of centuries of architectural history and home to the **Capilla del Santo Cáliz**, a chapel said to contain the Holy Grail (the chalice Christ supposedly used in the last supper). Climb the 207 stairs of the **Micalet bell tower** (Miguelete bell tower; adult/child €2/1; 10am-7pm) for sweeping city views.

Plaza del Mercado HISTORIC PLAZA

Over on Plaza del Mercado, two emblematic buildings, each a masterpiece of its era, face each other. Valencia's Modernista covered market, the **Mercado Central** (7.30am-2.30pm Mon-Sat) recently scrubbed and glowing as new, was constructed in 1928. With over 900 stalls, it's a swirl of smells, movement and colour. **La Lonja** (10am-2pm & 4.30-8.30pm Mon-Sat, 10am-3pm Sun) is a splendid late-15th-century building, a Unesco World Heritage site and was originally Valencia's silk and commodity exchange.

Instituto Valenciano de Arte Moderno (IVAM) CONTEMPORARY ART MUSEUM

(www.ivam.es; Calle de Guillem de Castro 118; adult/child €2/1; 10am-8pm Tue-Sun) IVAM (*ee-bam*) hosts excellent temporary exhibitions and houses an impressive permanent collection of 20th-century Spanish art.

FREE Museo de Bellas Artes FINE ARTS MUSEUM

(Calle San Pío V 9; 10am-8pm Tue-Sun) Bright and spacious, the Museo de Bellas Artes ranks among Spain's best. Highlights include the

Valencia City

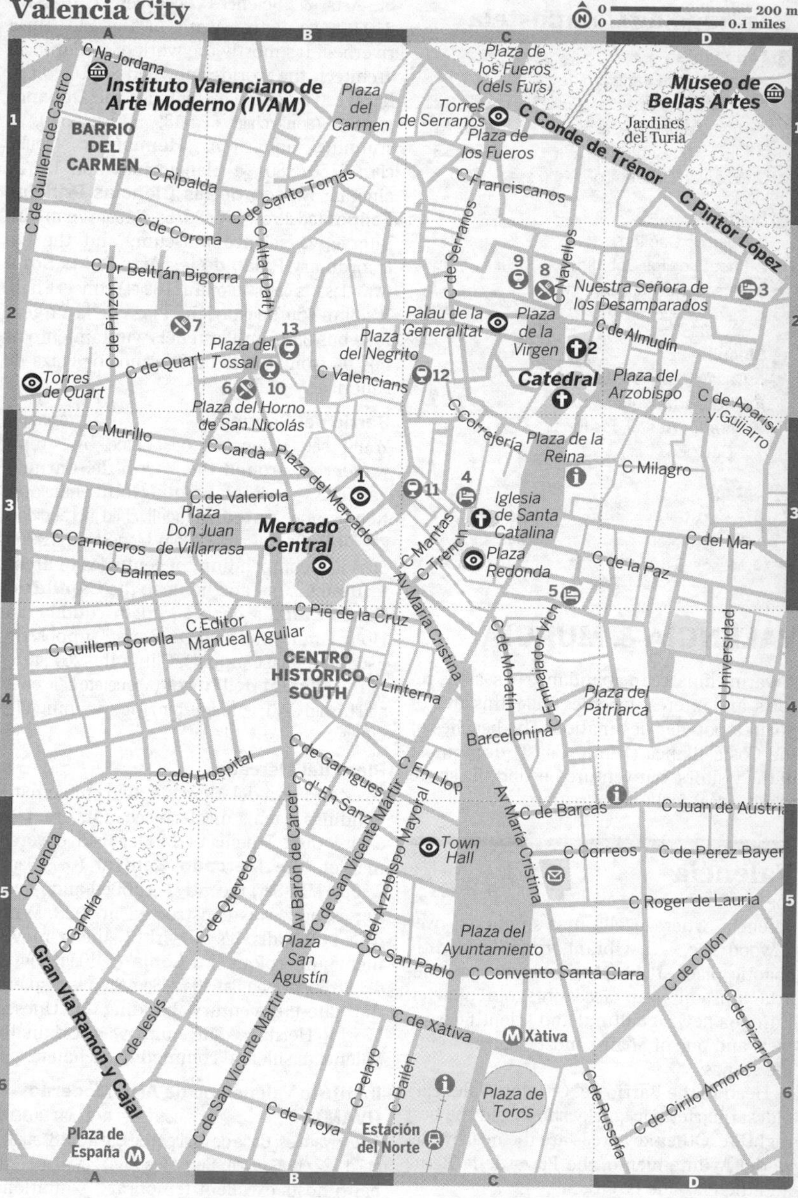

grandiose Roman *Mosaic of the Nine Muses,* a collection of magnificent late-medieval altarpieces and works by El Greco, Goya, Velázquez, Murillo, Ribalta and artists such as Sorolla and Pinazo of the Valencian Impressionist school.

Beaches

Playa de la Malvarrosa runs into **Playa de las Arenas**. Each is bordered by the **Paseo Marítimo** promenade and a string of restaurants. **Playa El Salér**, 10km south, is backed by shady pine woods. **Autocares**

Valenca City

Top Sights
- Catedral ... C2
- Instituto Valenciano de Arte Moderno (IVAM) ... A1
- Mercado Central ... B3
- Museo de Bellas Artes ... D1

Sights
1. La Lonja ... B3
2. Nuestra Señora de los Desamparados ... C2

Sleeping
3. Ad Hoc ... D2
4. Hostal Antigua Morellana ... C3
5. Petit Palace Bristol ... C3

Eating
6. Bar Pilar ... B2
7. L'Hamadríada ... A2
8. Seu-Xerea ... C2

Drinking
9. Café de las Horas ... C2
10. Café Infanta ... B2
11. Café Lisboa ... C3
12. Café-Bar Negrito ... C2
13. Sant Jaume ... B2

Herca (☎96 349 12 50; www.autocaresherca.com, in Spanish) buses run between Valencia and Perelló hourly (half-hourly in summer), calling by El Salér village. The beaches lie east and southeast of the city centre.

Sleeping

TOP CHOICE **Ad Hoc** HOTEL €€
(☎96 391 91 40; www.adhochoteles.com; Calle Boix 4; s €65-101, d €76-125; ❄📶) Friendly, welcoming Ad Hoc offers comfort and charm deep within the old quarter. The late-19th-century building has been restored to its former splendour with great sensitivity.

TOP CHOICE **Petit Palace Bristol** BOUTIQUE HOTEL €€
(☎96 394 51 00; www.hthoteles.com; Calle Abadía San Martín 3; r €60-130; ❄@📶) Hip and minimalist, this lovely boutique hotel, a comprehensively made-over 19th-century mansion, retains the best of its past and does a particularly scrumptious buffet breakfast. Free bikes for guests.

Chill Art Jardín Botánico BOUTIQUE HOTEL €€
(☎96 315 40 12; www.hoteljardinbotanico.com; Calle Doctor Peset Cervera 6; s €94-133, d €94-149; ❄📶) Welcoming and megacool, this intimate, 16-room hotel is furnished with great flair. Candles flicker in the lounge and each bedroom has original artwork. The Instituto Valenciano de Arte Moderno (IVAM) is nearby.

Hostal Antigua Morellana BUDGET HOTEL €
(☎96 391 57 73; www.hostalam.com; Calle En Bou 2; s €45-55, d €55-65; ❄) The friendly, family-run 18-room Hostal Antigua Morellana is tucked away near the central market. Occupying a renovated 18th-century *posada* (where wealthier merchants could spend the night), it has cosy, good-sized rooms, most with balconies.

Neptuno HOTEL €€€
(☎96 356 77 77; www.hotelneptunovalencia.com; Paseo de Neptuno 2; s €115-135, d €128-148; ❄📶) Neptuno, ultramodern and ultracool, overlooks the beach and leisure port. It's ideal for mixing cultural tourism with a little beach frolicking.

Eating

At weekends, locals in their hundreds head for Las Arenas, just north of the port, where a long line of restaurants overlooking the beach all serve up authentic paella in a three-course meal costing around €15.

TOP CHOICE **La Pepica** SEAFOOD €€
(☎96 371 03 66; Paseo Neptuno 6; meals around €25; ⊙lunch & dinner Mon-Sat, lunch Sun) More expensive than its competitors, La Pepica is renowned for its rice dishes and seafood. Here, Ernest Hemingway, among many other luminaries, once strutted. Between courses, browse through the photos and tributes that plaster the walls.

TOP CHOICE **Tridente** SPANISH FUSION €€€
(☎96 371 03 66; Paseo Neptuno; menú €45-65, mains €22-30; ⊙Tue-Sat & lunch Sun) Begin with an aperitif on the broad beachfront terrace, then move inside, where there's an ample à la carte selection but you won't find details of the day's *menús* in front of you – they're delivered orally by the maître d', who speaks good English. Dishes with their combinations of colours and blending of sweet and savoury are creative and delightfully presented, and portions are generous.

BURN BABY BURN

In mid-March, Valencia hosts one of Europe's wildest street parties: **Las Fallas de San José** (www.fallas.es, in Spanish). For one week (12 to 19 March), the city is engulfed by an anarchic swirl of fireworks, music, festive bonfires and all-night partying. On the final night, giant *ninots* (effigies), many of political and social personages, are torched in the main plaza.

If you're not in Valencia then, see the *ninots* saved from the flames by popular vote at the **Museo Fallero** (Plaza Monteolivete 4; adult/child €2/1; ⏲10am-2pm & 4.30-8pm Tue-Sat, 10am-3pm Sun).

Bar Pilar TAPAS €
(C del Moro Zeit 13; ⏲noon-midnight) Cramped, earthy Bar Pilar is great for hearty tapas and *clóchinas,* small, juicy local mussels, available between May and August. For the rest of the year, *mejillones* are served, altogether fatter if less tasty. Ask for an *entero,* a platterful in a spicy broth that you scoop up with a spare shell.

Seu-Xerea MEDITERRANEAN €€
(☎96 392 40 00; www.seuxerea.com; Calle Conde Almodóvar 4; menú €22-50, mains €16-19; ⏲lunch & dinner Mon-Fri, dinner Sat) This welcoming restaurant has a creative, regularly changing à la carte menu that features dishes both international and rooted in Spain. Wines are uniformly excellent.

L'Hamadríada MEDITERRANEAN €€
(☎96 326 08 91; www.hamadriada.com, in Spanish; Plaza Vicente Iborra; lunch menú €13, menús €18-22, mains €12.50-16; ⏲lunch Sun-Tue, lunch & dinner Wed-Sat) Staff are well informed and attentive at the Wood Nymph, a local favourite. This slim white rectangle of a place does an innovative midday *menú,* perfectly simmered rice dishes, and grills where the meat, like the vegetables, is of prime quality.

Drinking

The Barrio del Carmen, the university area (around Avenidas de Aragón and Blasco Ibáñez), the area around the Mercado de Abastos and, in summer, the new port area and Malvarrosa are all jumping with bars and clubs.

TOP CHOICE **Sant Jaume** CAFE BAR
(Plaza del Tossal) A converted pharmacy, its 1st floor is all quiet crannies and poky passageways

Café-Bar Negrito CAFE BAR
(Plaza del Negrito) Recently redesigned, it traditionally attracts a more left-wing, intellectual clientele.

Café Lisboa CAFE BAR
(Plaza del Doctor Collado 9) Another lively, student-oriented bar with a large, street-side terrace.

Café Infanta CAFE BAR
(Plaza del Tossal) The interior is a clutter of cinema memorabilia while its external terrace is great for people-watching.

Café de las Horas COCKTAIL BAR
(Calle Conde de Almodóvar 1) Offers a high baroque interior, tapestries, candelabras, music of all genres and a long list of exotic cocktails.

☆ Entertainment

Terraza Umbracle LOUNGE, CLUB
(⏲midnight-6.30am Thu-Sat mid-May–mid-Oct) At the southern end of the Umbracle walkway within the City of Arts and Sciences, this is a cool, sophisticated spot to spend a hot summer night. Catch the evening breeze under the stars on the terrace, then drop below to **MYA**, a top-of-the-line club with an awesome sound system. Admission (€20 including first drink) covers both venues.

Dub Club CLUB
(Calle Jesús 91; ⏲Thu-Sun) 'We play music not noise' is the slogan of this funky dive with its long, narrow bar giving onto a packed dance floor. And it indeed offers great music and great variety including live jazz jamming, reggae, dub, drum'n'bass, funk, breakbeat and more. It's around 1km southwest of the Plaza de la Virgen, just off Avenida Giorgeta.

Black Note LIVE MUSIC
(Calle Polo y Peyrolón 15) Valencia city's most active jazz venue, Black Note has live music Monday to Thursday and good canned jazz, blues and soul on Friday and Saturday. Admission, including first drink, costs from €6 to €15 depending on who's grooving. It's 1.5km east of the Plaza de la Virgen, just off Avenida de Aragón.

Information

Regional tourist office (www.comunitatvalenciana.com; Calle Paz 48; ⏲9am-8pm Mon-Sat, 10am-2pm Sun)

Turismo Valencia (VLC) (www.turisvalencia.es; Plaza de la Reina 19; ⏲9am-7pm Mon-Sat, 10am-2pm Sun)

Getting There & Away

AIR Valencia's **Aeropuerto de Manises** (☎96 159 85 00) is 10km west of the city centre. It's served by metro lines 3 and 5. Budget flights serve major European destinations.

BOAT Acciona Trasmediterránea (www.acciona-trasmediterranea.es) operates car and passenger ferries to Ibiza, Mallorca and Menorca; see p1147.

BUS Valencia's **bus station** (☎96 346 62 66) is beside the riverbed on Avenida Menéndez Pidal. **Avanza** (www.avanzabus.com) operates hourly bus services to/from Madrid (€18 to €27, four hours). **ALSA** (www.alsa.es) has numerous buses to/from Barcelona (€26 to €30, 4½ hours) and Alicante (€21, 2½ hours), most passing by Benidorm (€14.50, 1¾ hours).

TRAIN From Valencia's Estación del Norte, major destinations include Alicante (€29, 1¾ hours, eight daily) and Barcelona (€39 to €43, three to 3½ hours, at least 12 daily). The AVE, the high-speed train, now links Madrid and Valencia, with up to 15 high-speed services daily and a journey time of around 1¾ hours.

Getting Around

Metro line 5 connects the airport, city centre and port. The high-speed tram leaves from the FGV tram station, 500m north of the cathedral, at the Pont de Fusta. This is a pleasant way to get to the beach, the paella restaurants of Las Arenas and the port.

Alicante

POP 334,800

With its elegant, palm-lined boulevards, lively nightlife scene and easy-to-access beaches, Alicante (Alacant in Valenciano) is an all-in-one Spanish city. The city is at its most charming at night, when tapas bars and taverns in El Barrio (the Old Quarter) come alive.

Sights & Activities

TOP CHOICE Castillo de Santa Bárbara CASTLE
(10am-10pm) There are sweeping views over the city from this 16th-century castle, which will soon house the **Museo de la Ciudad de Alicante (MUSA)**, a new museum recounting the history of the city. A lift/elevator, reached by a footbridge opposite Playa del Postiguet, rises through the bowels of the mountain.

TOP CHOICE Museo de Arte Contemporáneo de Alicante (MACA) ART MUSEUM
(Plaza Sta María 3; admission free; 10am-8pm Tue-Sat, to 2pm Sun) Closed for many years while its premises, the splendid 17th-century Casa de la Asegurada, were renovated and enlarged, this splendid museum has an excellent collection of 20th-century Spanish art, including works by Dalí, Miró, Chillida, Sempere, Tàpies and Picasso.

Beaches BEACHES
Immediately north of the port is the sandy beach of **Playa del Postiguet**. Easily reached by tram, **Playa de San Juan** is larger and usually less crowded.

Sleeping

TOP CHOICE Hostal Les Monges Palace BUDGET HOTEL €
(☎96 521 50 46; www.lesmonges.net; Calle San Agustín 4; s €30-44, d €45-59;) This agreeably quirky place is a treasure with its winding corridors, tiles, mosaics and antique furniture. Each room is individually decorated and reception couldn't be more welcoming. Look out for the small Dalí original beside the reception desk.

Guest House Antonio BOUTIQUE BUDGET HOTEL €
(☎650 718353; www.guesthousealicante.com; Calle Segura 20; s €35-40, d €45-50;) A magnificent budget choice: eight large, tastefully decorated rooms, each with a safe, full-size fridge and free beverage-making facilities. The five apartments (€70 to €80), two with their own patio, have a mini-kitchen and washing machine, and are exceptional value.

Eating & Drinking

The old quarter around Catedral de San Nicolás is wall-to-wall bars. Down by the harbour, the Paseo del Puerto, tranquil by day, is a double-decker line of bars, cafes and night-time discos.

TOP CHOICE Piripi VALENCIAN €€
(☎96 522 79 40; Avenida Oscar Esplá 30; mains €12-26) This highly regarded restaurant is strong on rice, seafood and fish, which arrives fresh and daily from the wholesale markets of Denia and Santa Pola. There's a huge variety of tapas and a *valenciano* speciality that changes daily. It's around 500m west of Plaza de Calvo Sotelo.

El Trellat MODERN SPANISH €
(Calle de Capitán Segarra 19; lunch menú €10, dinner menús €10-25; lunch Mon-Sat, dinner Fri & Sat) Beside the covered market, this small, friendly place has exceptionally creative, flexible *menús:* a serve-yourself first-course buffet, then an ample choice of inventive mains.

Alicante

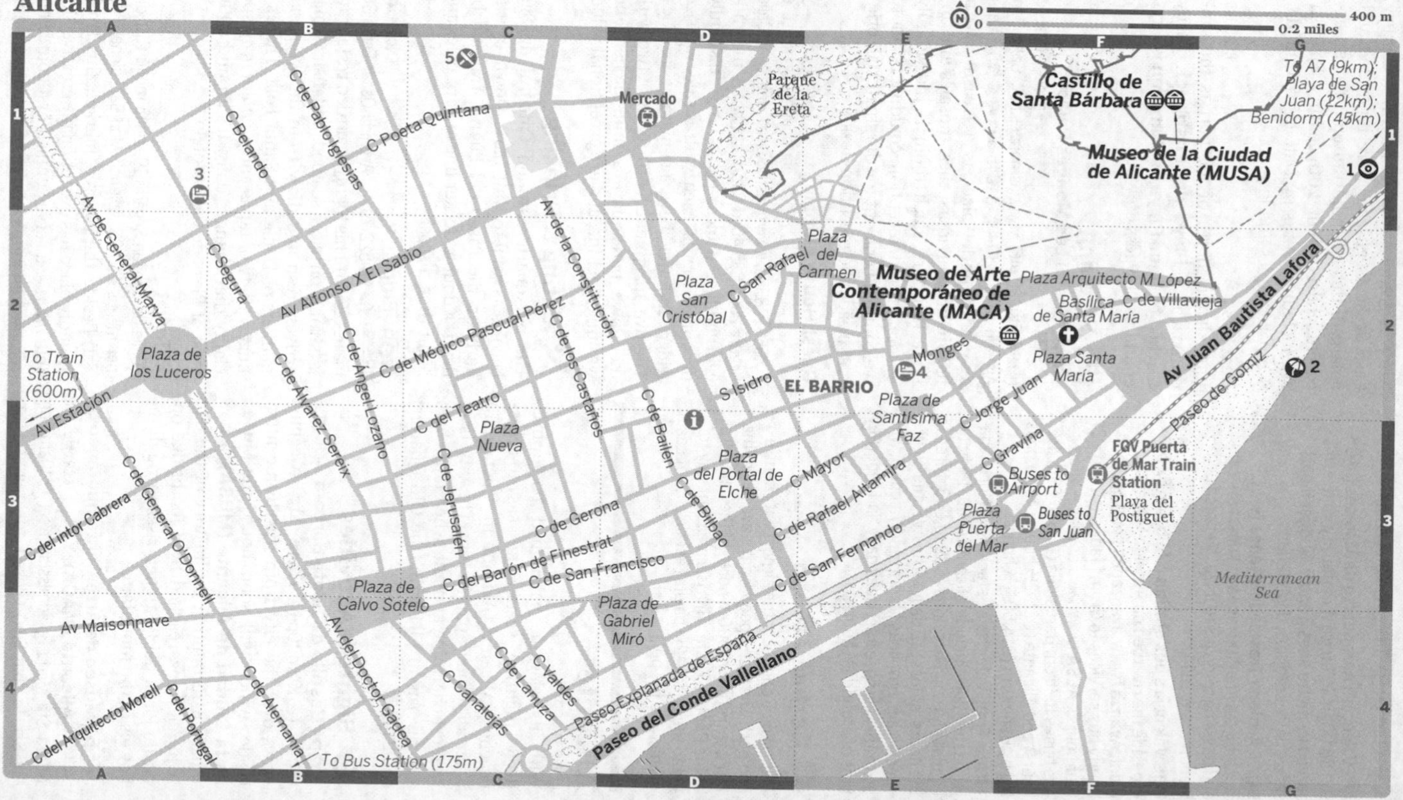

0 400 m
0 0.2 miles
Castillo de Santa Bárbara
Museo de la Ciudad de Alicante (MUSA)
To A7 (9km); Playa de San Juan (22km); Benidorm (45km)
Parque de la Ereta
Mercado
C Poeta Quintana
C de Pablo Iglesias
C Belando
C Segura
Av de General Marva
Av Alfonso X El Sabio
Av de la Constitución
C de los Castaños
C de Médico Pascual Pérez
C de Ángel Lozano
C de Álvarez Sereix
Plaza de los Luceros
To Train Station (600m)
Av Estación
Plaza del Carmen
C San Rafael
Plaza San Cristóbal
Museo de Arte Contemporáneo de Alicante (MACA)
Plaza Arquitecto M López
Basílica de Santa María
C de Villavieja
Plaza Santa María
Av Juan Bautista Lafora
Paseo de Gomiz
Monges
EL BARRIO
S Isidro
Plaza de Santísima Faz
C Jorge Juan
C Gravina
C del Teatro
Plaza Nueva
C de Bailén
Plaza del Portal de Elche
C Mayor
C de Bilbao
C de Rafael Altamira
C de Jerusalén
C de Gerona
C del Barón de Finestrat
C de San Francisco
C de San Fernando
Buses to Airport
Buses to San Juan
Plaza Puerta del Mar
FGV Puerta de Mar Train Station
Playa del Postiguet
Mediterranean Sea
C del intor Cabrera
C de General O'Donnell
Plaza de Calvo Sotelo
Plaza de Gabriel Miró
Av Maisonnave
Av del Doctor Gadea
C Canalejas
C de Lanuza
C Valdés
Paseo Explanada de España
Paseo del Conde Vallellano
C del Arquitecto Morell
C del Portugal
C de Alemania
To Bus Station (175m)

Alicante

Information

Municipal tourist office (www.alicanteturismo.com) Branches at the bus station and train station.

Regional tourist office (Rambla de Méndez Núñez 23; 9am-8pm Mon-Sat, 10am-2pm Sun)

Getting There & Away

AIR Alicante's **El Altet airport**, gateway to the Costa Blanca, is around 12km southwest of the centre. It's served by budget airlines, charters and scheduled flights from all over Europe.

BUS Destinations include Madrid (€27.50, 5¼ hours, at least 10 daily), Murcia (€5.50, one hour, at least seven daily) and Valencia (€21, 2½ hours, 10 daily).

TRAIN Destinations from the main **Renfe Estación de Madrid** (Avenida de Salamanca) include Barcelona (€55, five hours, eight daily), Madrid (€45, 3¾ hours, seven daily), Murcia (€4.50, 1¼ hours, hourly) and Valencia (€29, 1¾ hours, eight daily).

TRAM (www.fgvalicante.com) Tram line 1 goes to Benidorm (€4.40, one hour, every 30 minutes). Catch it from the Mercado stop beside the covered market, changing at La Isleta or Lucentum.

Costa Blanca

Clean white beaches, bright sunshine and a rockin' nightlife have made the **Costa Blanca** (www.costablanca.org) one of Europe's favourite summer playgrounds. Many resorts are shamefully overbuilt, but it is still possible to discover charming towns and unspoilt coastline. Some of the best towns to explore include **Benidorm**, a highrise nightlife hot spot in summer (but filled to the brim with pensioners the rest of the year); **Altea**, whose church with its pretty blue-tiled dome is its crowning glory; and **Calpe**, known for the Gibraltar-like **Peñon de Ifach** (332m). All are accessible by train from Alicante.

Murcia

With its rural interior, small coastal resorts and lively capital city, **Murcia** (www.murciaturistica.es) is as authentically Spanish as it gets. A conservative province, Murcia is known for its fabulous local produce, rich tapas and unusually warm coast.

MURCIA

POP 433,850

Murcia is a laid-back provincial capital that comes alive during the weekend *paseo* (stroll). Bypassed by most tourists and treated as a country cousin by too many Spaniards, the city nevertheless merits a visit. Head for the river, the cathedral and the surrounding pedestrian streets.

Sights & Activities

TOP CHOICE **Real Casino de Murcia** HISTORIC BUILDING
(www.casinodemurcia.com; Calle Trapería 18; admission €5; 11.30am-9pm) Murcia's resplendent casino first opened as a gentlemen's club in 1847. The building is a fabulous combination of historical design and opulence, providing an evocative glimpse of bygone aristocratic grandeur.

FREE **Catedral de Santa María** CHURCH
(Plaza del Cardinal Belluga; 7am-1pm & 5-8pm) Murcia's cathedral was built in 1394 on the site of a mosque. The initial Gothic architecture was given a playful baroque facelift in 1748. The 15th-century **Capilla de los Vélez** is a highlight; the chapel's flutes and curls resemble piped icing.

Sleeping & Eating

TOP CHOICE **Hotel Casa Emilio** HOTEL €
(968 22 06 31; www.hotelcasaemilio.com; Alameda de Colón 9; s/d €45/50; P ❄ ☎) Across from the Floridablanca gardens, near the river, this is an attractively designed and well-maintained hotel with spacious, brightly lit rooms, large bathrooms and good firm mattresses.

Arco de San Juan HISTORIC HOTEL €€
(968 21 04 55; www.arcosanjuan.com; Plaza de Ceballos 10; s/d €75/130; P) This four-star hotel in a former 18th-century palace hints at its palatial past with a massive 5m-high original door and some hefty repro columns. The rooms are classic and comfortable, with hardwood details and classy fabrics.

Figón de Alfaro TAPAS €
(Calle Alfaro 7; meals €12-15; lunch & dinner Mon-Sat, lunch Sun) Popular with all ages and budgets, Figón de Alfaro offers a chaotic bar area or a more sedate interconnecting dining room. Choose from full meals, a range of juicy *montaditos* (minirolls) or innovative one-offs such as *pastel de berejena con salsa de calabacín* (aubergine pie with a courgette sauce).

Los Zagales SPANISH €
(Calle Polo Medina 4; meals €10-15) Lying within confessional distance of the cathedral (since 1926), Los Zagales dishes up superb, inexpensive tapas, *raciones, platos combinados,* homemade desserts (and homemade chips). This is where the locals eat, so you may have to wait for a table. It's worth it.

Los Arroces del Romea RICE DISHES €€
(Plaza Romea; meals €20-25;) Watch the speciality paella-style rice dishes being prepared in cartwheel-sized pans over the flames while you munch on circular *murciano* bread drizzled with olive oil.

Information

Tourist office (www.murciaciudad.com; Plaza del Cardenal Belluga; 10am-2pm & 5-9pm Mon-Sat, 10am-2pm Sun)

Getting There & Away

AIR Murcia's San Javier airport is closer to Cartagena than Murcia city. There are numerous flights to/from the UK.

TRAIN Up to five trains travel daily to/from Madrid (€44.60, 4¼ hours).

BALEARIC ISLANDS

POP 1.07 MILLION

The Balearic Islands (Illes Balears in Catalan) adorn the glittering Mediterranean waters off Spain's eastern coastline. Beach tourism destinations *par excellence,* each of the four islands has a quite distinct identity and they have managed to retain much of their individual character and beauty. All boast beaches second to none in the Med but each offers reasons for exploring inland too.

Check out websites like www.illesbalears.es, www.platgesdebalears.com and www.balearsculturaltour.com.

Getting There & Away

Air

In summer, charter and regular flights converge on Palma de Mallorca and Ibiza from all over Europe. Major operators from the Spanish mainland include **Iberia** (www.iberia.es), **Air Europa** (www.aireuropa.com), **Spanair** (www.spanair.com), **Air Berlin** (www.airberlin.com) and **Vueling** (www.vueling.com).

Boat

Compare prices and look for deals at **Direct Ferries** (www.directferries.es). Ferries serving the Balearic Islands:

Acciona Trasmediterránea (902 454 645; www.trasmediterranea.es)

Baleària (902 160 180; www.balearia.com)

Cala Ratjada Tours (902 100 444; www.calaratjadatours.es, in Spanish)

Iscomar (902 119 128; www.iscomar.com)

The main ferry routes to the mainland:

Ibiza (Ibiza City) To/from Barcelona (Acciona Trasmediterránea, Baleària), Valencia (Acciona Trasmediterránea)

Ibiza (Sant Antoni) To/from Denia and Barcelona (Baleària), Valencia (Acciona Trasmediterránea, Baleària)

Mallorca (Palma de Mallorca) To/from Barcelona and Valencia (Acciona Trasmediterránea, Baleària), Denia (Baleària)

Menorca (Maó) To/from Barcelona and Valencia (Acciona Trasmediterránea, Baleària)

The main interisland ferry routes:

Ibiza (Ibiza City) To/from Palma de Mallorca (Acciona Trasmediterránea and Baleària)

Mallorca (Cala Ratjada) To/from Ciutadella (Cala Ratjada Tours)

Mallorca (Palma de Mallorca) To/from Ibiza City (Acciona Trasmediterránea and Baleària) and Maó (Acciona Trasmediterránea and Baleària)

Mallorca (Port d'Alcúdia) To/from Ciutadella (Iscomar)

Menorca (Ciutadella) To/from Cala Ratjada (Cala Ratjada Tours) and Port d'Alcúdia (Iscomar)

Menorca (Maó) To/from Palma de Mallorca (Acciona Trasmediterránea and Baleària)

Mallorca

The sunny, warm hues of the medieval heart of Palma de Mallorca (pop 401,300), the archipelago's capital, make a great introduction to the islands. The northwest coast, dominated by the Serra de Tramuntana mountain range, is a beautiful region of olive groves, pine forests and ochre villages, with a spectacularly rugged coastline. Most of Mallorca's best beaches are on the north and east coasts, and although many have been swallowed up by tourist developments, you can still find the occasional exception. There is also a scattering of fine beaches along the south coast.

Getting Around

BUS Most of the island is accessible by bus from Palma. All buses depart from or near the **bus station** (Carrer d'Eusebi Estada).

TRAIN Two train lines run from Plaça d'Espanya in Palma de Mallorca. The popular, old train runs to Sóller, a pretty ride. A standard train line runs inland to Inca (€1.80, 40 minutes, every half-hour), where the line splits with a branch to Sa Pobla (€2.40, one hour, hourly) and another to Manacor (€2.40, 1¼ hours, hourly).

PALMA DE MALLORCA

Sights & Activities

TOP CHOICE Cathedral CHURCH

(La Seu; Carrer del Palau Reial 9; adult/child €4/3; ⌚10am-5.15pm Mon-Fri, 10am-2.15pm Sat) This awesome structure, completed in 1601, is predominantly Gothic, apart from the main facade (replaced after an earthquake in 1851) and parts of the interior. The cathedral's interior is stunning, with ranks of slender columns supporting the soaring ceiling and framing three levels of elaborate stained-glass windows. The front altar's centrepiece, a light, twisting wrought-iron sculpture suspended from the ceiling, is one of Gaudí's more eccentric creations. For once, Gaudí is upstaged by the island's top contemporary artist, Miquel Barceló, who reworked the **Capella del Santíssim i Sant Pere**, at the head of the south aisle, in a dream-fantasy, swirling ceramic rendition of the miracle of the loaves and fishes.

Palau de l'Almudaina PALACE

(Carrer del Palau Reial s/n; adult/child €3.20/2.30, audioguide €2.50; ⌚10am-5.45pm Mon-Fri, to 1.15pm Sat) Originally an Islamic fort, this mighty construction was converted into a residence for the Mallorcan monarchs at the end of the 13th century. It is still occasionally used for official functions when King Juan Carlos is in town. At other times, you can wander through a series of cavernous and austere stone-walled rooms, a chapel with a rare Romanesque entrance, and upstairs royal apartments adorned with Flemish tapestries and period furniture.

Es Baluard ART MUSEUM

(Museu d'Art Modern i Contemporani; www.esbaluard.org, in Spanish; Porta de Santa Catalina 10; adult/child €6/4.50, temporary exhibitions €4/3; ⌚10am-8pm Tue-Sun) This 21st-century concrete complex nests within Palma's grand Renaissance-era seaward fortifications. A playful game of light, surfaces and perspective, it makes the perfect framework for the works within.

Palau March ART MUSEUM

(www.fundbmarch.es; Carrer de Palau Reial 18; adult/child €3.60/free; ⌚10am-6pm Mon-Fri, to 2pm Sat) This house, palatial by any definition, contains sculptures by 20th-century greats such as Henry Moore, Auguste Rodin, Barbara Hepworth and Eduardo Chillida which grace the outdoor terrace. Within is a set of Salvador Dalí prints.

FREE Museu d'Art Espanyol Contemporani ART MUSEUM

(Museu Fundació Juan March; www.march.es/arte/palma; Carrer de Sant Miquel 11; ⌚10am-6.30pm Mon-Fri, 10.30am-2pm Sat) On permanent display within this 18th-century mansion are some 70 pieces that together constitute a veritable who's who of mostly 20th-century artists, including Picasso, Miró, Juan Gris (of cubism fame), Dalí and the sculptor Julio González.

Sleeping

TOP CHOICE Hotel Santa Clara BOUTIQUE HOTEL €€€

(☎971 72 92 31; www.santaclarahotel.es; Carrer de Sant Alonso 16; s/d from €155/210; ❄@📶) Boutique meets antique in this historic mansion, respectfully converted, where subdued greys, steely silvers and cream blend harmoniously with the warm stone walls, ample spaces and high ceilings of the original structure.

Hotel Born HISTORIC HOTEL €€

(☎971 71 29 42; www.hotelborn.com; Carrer de Sant Jaume 3; s incl breakfast €52, d €76-97; ❄@📶) A superb place in the heart of the city, this hotel is in an 18th-century palace. Rooms combine elegance and history with all mod cons. The best have an engaging view onto the palm-shaded patio.

Palma de Mallorca

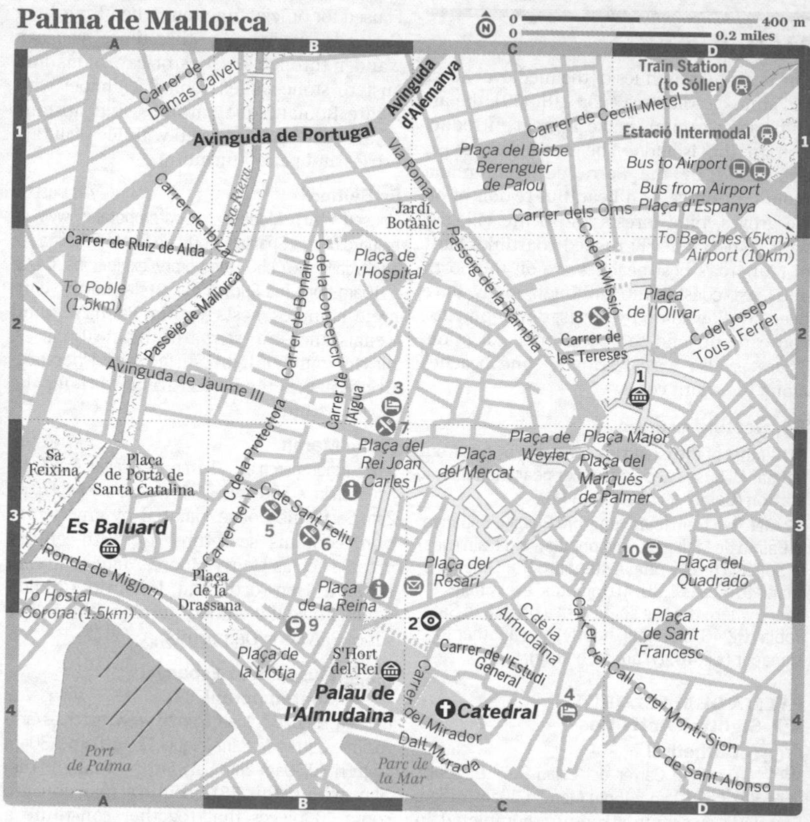

Hostal Corona HOTEL €
(☎971 73 19 35; www.hostal-corona.com; Carrer de Josep Villalonga 22; s €30, d €45-60) With its palm trees and cornucopia of plants, the generous courtyard garden of this little hotel (the house was once a private villa) has a faraway feel. Rooms are simple, with timber furnishings and old tiled floors.

Eating

TOP CHOICE **Simply Fosh** INTERNATIONAL €€
(☎971 72 01 14; www.simplyfosh.com; Carrer de la Missió 7a; mains €14-26, dinner menús €52; Mon-Sat) It's great gourmet cuisine at the restaurant of Michelin-starred British chef Marc Fosh. Quality is sustained right down to the cheese board, with its selection of the very best that Spain offers.

La Bodeguilla SPANISH €€
(☎971 71 82 74; www.la-bodeguilla.com; Carrer de Sant Jaume 3; mains €17.50-19.50; Mon-Sat) This gourmet restaurant does creative interpretations of dishes from across Spain (such as *cochinillo,* suckling pig, from Segovia, and *lechazo,* young lamb, baked Córdoba-style in rosemary).

Bon Lloc VEGETARIAN €
(☎971 71 86 17; www.bonllocrestaurant.com, in Spanish; Carrer de Sant Feliu 7; menús €13.50; lunch Mon-Sat;) This 100% vegetarian place, where all produce is organic, is light, open and airy. There are no agonising decisions – just a satisfying, take-it-or-leave-it four-course menú. It's hugely popular so do ring to reserve.

13% TAPAS €
(www.13porciento.com; Carrer Sant Feliu 13a; meals around €15;) At the quieter end of the old town, this L-shaped barn of a place is both wine and tapas bar. Most items are organic and there's plenty of choice for vegetarians. Wines are displayed on racks and all can be purchased (both bar and takeaway prices are quoted so you know exactly the mark-up).

Palma de Mallorca

Drinking & Entertainment

The old quarter is the city's most vibrant nightlife zone. Particularly along the narrow streets between Plaça de la Reina and Plaça de la Drassana, you'll find an enormous selection of bars, pubs and bodegas. According to a much flouted law, bars should shut by 1am Sunday to Thursday (3am Friday and Saturday).

Vamos 365 (www.vamosmallorca365.com), a monthly freebie, has its finger on Palma's night-time pulse.

TOP CHOICE **Puro Beach** BAR
(www.purobeach.com; 11am-2am Apr-Oct) This uber-laid-back, sunset chill lounge has a tapering outdoor promontory with an all-white bar that's perfect for sunset cocktails, DJ sessions and fusion food escapes. It is just a two-minute walk east of Cala Estancia (itself just east of Ca'n Pastilla). It's southeast of Palma de Mallorca along the coast.

Ca'n Joan de S'Aigo CAFE
(Carrer de Can Sanç 10; 8am-9pm Wed-Mon) Dating from 1700, this is *the* place for a hot chocolate (€1.40) in what can only be described as an antique-filled milk bar. The house speciality is *quart,* a feather-soft sponge cake that children love with almond-flavoured ice cream.

Abaco BAR
(www.bar-abaco.com, in Spanish; Carrer de Sant Joan 1; from 9pm) Behind a set of ancient timber doors is the bar of your wildest dreams. Inside, a typical Mallorcan patio and candlelit courtyard are crammed with elaborate floral arrangements, cascading towers of fresh fruit and bizarre artworks.

Information

Consell de Mallorca tourist office (971 71 22 16; www.infomallorca.net; Plaça de la Reina 2; 8am-8pm Mon-Fri, 9am-2pm Sat)

Municipal tourist office (902 102365; 9am-8pm Mon-Sat) Main office (Casal Solleric, Passeig d'es Born 27); branch office (train station)

AROUND MALLORCA

Mallorca's northwestern coast is a world away from the high-rise tourism on the other side of the island. Dominated by the Serra de Tramuntana, it's a beautiful region of olive groves, pine forests and small villages with shuttered stone buildings. There are a couple of highlights for drivers: the hair-raising road down to the small port of **Sa Calobra**, and the amazing trip along the peninsula leading to the island's northern tip, **Cap Formentor**.

Sóller is a good place to base yourself for hiking and the nearby village of **Fornalutx** is one of the prettiest on Mallorca.

From Sóller, it's a 10km walk to the beautiful hilltop village of **Deià** (www.deia.info), where Robert Graves, poet and author of *I Claudius*, lived for most of his life. From the village, you can scramble down to the small shingle beach of **Cala de Deià**. Boasting a fine monastery and pretty streets, **Valldemossa** (www.valldemossa.com) is further southwest down the coast.

Further east, **Pollença** and **Artà** are attractive inland towns. Nice beaches include those at **Cala Sant Vicenç**, **Cala Mondragó** and around **Cala Llombards**.

Sleeping & Eating

The **Consell de Mallorca tourist office** (971 71 22 16; www.infomallorca.net; Plaça de la Reina 2; 8am-8pm Mon-Fri, 9am-2pm Sat) in Palma can supply information on rural and other types of accommodation around the island.

DEIÀ

Hostal Miramar HOTEL €€

(☎971 63 90 84; www.pensionmiramar.com; Carrer de Ca'n Oliver; r incl breakfast €84, without bathroom €75; ⊙Mar–mid-Nov) Hidden within the lush vegetation above the main road and with views across to Deià's hillside church and sea beyond, this 19th-century stone house with gardens is a shady retreat with nine rooms.

El Barrigón de Xelini TAPAS €

(Avinguda del Arxiduc Lluís Salvador 19; meals €20; ⊙Tue-Sun) You never quite know what to expect here, but tapas, more than 50 kinds drawn from all over Spain, are at the core. It has a penchant for mains of lamb too. On summer weekends, there's live jazz.

SÓLLER

The Sóller area has plenty of boutique hotels in historic buildings or country houses; many are listed on www.sollernet.com.

Hotel El Guía HOTEL €€

(☎971 63 02 27; www.sollernet.com/elguia; Carrer del Castanyer 2; s/d €53/84) Right beside the train station and family run, this is a good place to meet fellow walkers. Its bright, simple rooms feature timber trims and modern bathrooms, and it runs a creditable restaurant.

Ca's Carreter MALLORCAN €€

(☎971 63 51 33; Carrer del Cetre 9; menús €12, mains €16; ⊙lunch & dinner Tue-Sat, lunch Sun) Set in a leafy cart workshop (founded in 1914), this is a cool and welcoming spot for modest local cooking, with fresh fish and meat options.

EAST COAST

Hostal Playa Mondragó BUDGET HOTEL €€

(☎971 65 77 52; www.playamondrago.com; Cala Mondragó; s/d incl breakfast €63/96; ⊙Easter-Oct; ❄ 📶 🏊) Barely 50m back from one of the beaches, it's a tranquil option and the better rooms have balconies and fine sea views.

Ibiza

Ibiza (Eivissa in Catalan) is an island of extremes. Its formidable party reputation is completely justified, with some of the world's greatest clubs attracting hedonists from the world over. The interior and northeast of the island, however, are another world. Peaceful country drives, hilly green territory, a sprinkling of mostly laid-back beaches and coves, and some wonderful inland accommodation and eateries, are light years from the ecstasy-fuelled madness of the clubs that dominate the west.

Getting Around

AIR Ibiza's airport (Aeroport d'Eivissa), just 7km southwest of Ibiza City, receives direct flights from all over Europe.

BOAT Hourly ferries (one way/return €3.50/6) run to/from Playa d'en Bossa and Figueretes from May to October. Boats to Cala Llonga, Santa Eulària d'es Riu and Es Canar (all €13 return) run up to six times daily from May to mid-October.

BUS Buses to other parts of the island depart from the new bus station (nearing completion when we last visited) on Avenide de la Pau.

IBIZA CITY

Sights & Activities

Ibiza City's port area of **Sa Penya** is crammed with funky and trashy clothing boutiques and arty-crafty market stalls. From here, you can wander up into **D'Alt Vila**, the atmospheric old walled town.

Ramparts HISTORIC AREA

A ramp leads from Plaça de Sa Font in Sa Penya up to the 1585 **Portal de ses Taules** gateway, the main entrance. The walls consist of seven artillery bastions joined by thick protective walls up to 22m in height. You can **walk** the entire perimeter of these impressive Renaissance-era walls, designed to withstand heavy artillery, and enjoy great views along the way.

Catedral CHURCH

Ibiza's cathedral elegantly combines several styles: the original 14th-century structure is Catalan Gothic but the sacristy was added in 1592, and a major baroque renovation took place in the 18th century.

Centre d'Interpretació Madina Yasiba MUSEUM

(Carrer Major 2; adult/child €2/1.50; ⊙10am-2pm & 6-8pm Tue-Sat, 10am-2pm Sun) A small display that replicates the medieval Muslim city of Madina Yasiba (Ibiza City), prior to the island's fall to Christian forces in 1235. Artefacts, audiovisuals and maps help transport us to those times.

Sleeping

Many of Ibiza City's hotels and *hostales* are closed in the low season and heavily booked between April and October. Make sure you book ahead.

Hotel La Ventana HISTORIC HOTEL €€€
(☎971 30 35 37; www.laventanaibiza.com; Carrer de Sa Carossa 13; d from €165;) This charming 15th-century mansion is set on a little tree-shaded square in the old town. Some rooms come with stylish four-poster beds and mosquito nets. The rooftop terrace, trim gardens and restaurant are welcome extras.

Hostal La Marina BUDGET HOTEL €€
(☎971 31 01 72; www.hostal-lamarina.com; Carrer de Barcelona 7; r €68-125;) Looking onto both the waterfront and bar-lined Carrer de Barcelona, this mid-19th-century building has all sorts of brightly coloured rooms. A handful of singles and some doubles look onto the street (with the predictable noise problem), with pricier doubles and attics with terraces and panoramic port and/or town views.

Casa de Huéspedes Navarro BUDGET HOTEL €
(☎971 31 07 71; Carrer de sa Creu 20; s/d without bathroom €28/55; May-Oct) Right in the thick of things, this simple option has eight rooms at the top of a long flight of stairs. The front rooms have harbour views, interior ones are quite dark (but cool in summer) and there's a sunny rooftop terrace. Bathrooms are shared but spotless.

Eating

TOP CHOICE Comidas Bar San Juan MEDITERRANEAN €
(Carrer de Guillem de Montgrí 8; meals €15-20; Mon-Sat) A family-run operation with two small dining rooms, this simple eatery offers outstanding value, with fish dishes for around €10 and many small mains for €6 or less. It doesn't take reservations so do arrive early.

Restaurant of Hotel Mirador de Dalt Vila GOURMET €€
(☎971 30 30 45; Plaça d'Espanya 4; menú €45, mains €26-30; Easter-Dec) At this intimate – do reserve – restaurant with its painted barrel ceiling and original canvases around the walls, you'll dine magnificently. Service is discreet yet friendly, dishes are creative, colourful and delightfully presented.

Drinking

Sa Penya is the nightlife centre. Dozens of bars keep the port area jumping. Alternatively, various bars at Platja d'en Bossa combine sounds, sand, sea and sangria.

Discobus (www.discobus.es; per person €3; midnight-6am Jun-Sep) runs around the major discos, bars and hotels in Ibiza City, Platja d'en Bossa, Sant Rafel, Es Canar, Santa Eulària and Sant Antoni.

Teatro Pereira MUSIC BAR
(www.teatropereyra.com; Carrer del Comte de Rosselló 3; 8am-4am) Away from the waterfront hubbub, this hugely atmospheric place, all stained wood and iron girders, was once the foyer of the long-abandoned 1893 theatre at its rear. Packed most nights with a more eclectic crowd than the standard preclubbing bunch, it offers nightly live music sessions. By day, it's a stylish place for a drink or snack.

Bora Bora Beach Club BEACH BAR
(noon-4am May-Sep) At Platja d'en Bossa, about 2km from the old town, this is *the* place – a long beachside bar where sun- and fun-worshippers work off hangovers and prepare new ones. Entry's free and the ambience is chilled, with low-key club sounds wafting over the sand.

Information

Tourist office Main office (www.ibiza.travel; Passeig de Vara de Rei 1; 9am-8pm Mon-Fri, to 7pm Sat); D'Alt Vila office (Carrer Major 2; 9am-8pm Mon-Sat, to 3pm Sun)

AROUND IBIZA

Ibiza has numerous unspoiled and relatively undeveloped beaches. **Cala de Boix**, on the northeastern coast, is the only black-sand beach on the island, while further north are the lovely beaches of **S'Aigua Blanca**.

On the north coast near Portinatx, **Cala Xarraca** is in a picturesque, secluded bay, and near Port de Sant Miquel is the attractive **Cala Benirrás**.

In the southwest, **Cala d'Hort** has a spectacular setting overlooking two rugged rock islets, Es Verda and Es Verdranell.

The best thing about rowdy **Sant Antoni**, the island's second biggest town and north of Ibiza City, is heading to the small rock-and-sand strip on the north shore to join hundreds of others for sunset drinks at a string of chilled bars. The best known remains **Café del Mar** (www.cafedelmar.es; 4pm-1am), our favourite, but it's further north along the pedestrian walkway.

Local **buses** (www.ibizabus.com) run to most destinations between May and October.

Sleeping & Eating

Check out rural accommodation at www.ibizaruralvillas.com and www.casasruralesibiza.com (in Spanish). For more standard

Ibiza City (Eivissa)

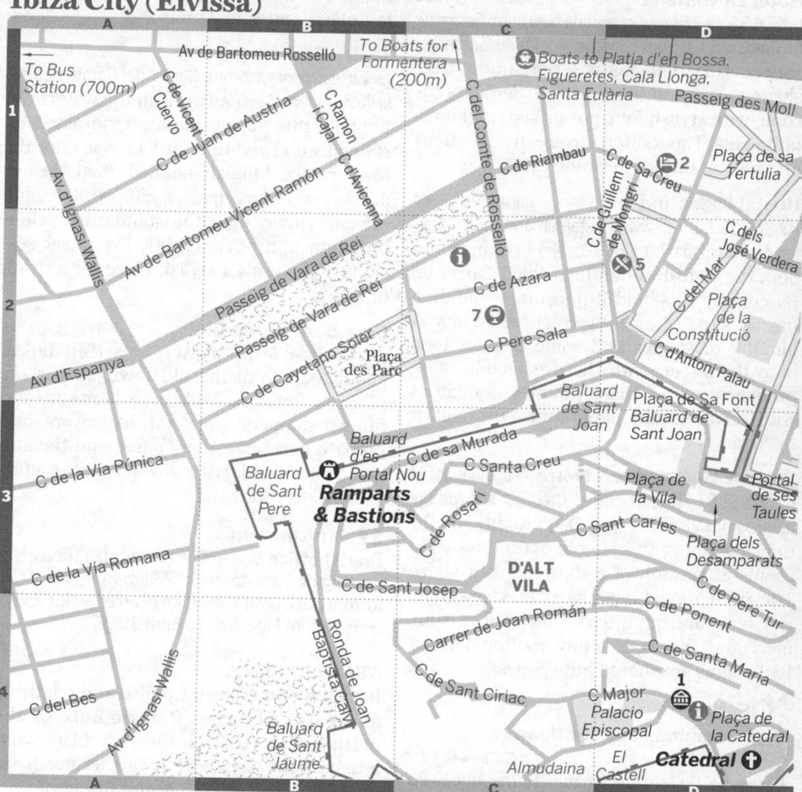

accommodation, start at www.ibizahotels guide.com.

TOP CHOICE Hostal Cala Boix BUDGET HOTEL €€
(☎971 33 52 24; www.hostalcalaboix.com; d incl breakfast €80; ⊙May-Oct; ❄) Set uphill and back from the beach, this solitary place has big, cheap rooms and a hearty restaurant. On the beach you'll find a daytime bar in summer.

Hostal Es Alocs BUDGET HOTEL €
(☎971 33 50 79; www.hostalalocs.com; s/d €35/65; ⊙May-Oct) Right on the beach at Platja Es Figueral. Rooms are simple, over a couple of floors. Downstairs it has a bar-restaurant with shady terrace.

Bar Anita BAR-RESTAURANT €
(mains €8-16) A timeless tavern opposite the village church in inland Sant Carles, this place offers anything from pizza to slabs of *entrecote con salsa de pimiento* (entrecôte in a pepper sauce; €15).

Menorca

Renowned for its pristine beaches and archaeological sites, tranquil Menorca was declared a Biosphere Reserve by Unesco in 1993. The capital, Maó, is known as Mahón in Castilian.

Getting Around

TO/FROM THE AIRPORT Bus 10 (€1.60) runs between Menorca's airport, 7km southwest of Maó, and the city's bus station every half-hour. A taxi costs around €15.

BUS You can get to most destinations from Maó, but, with a few exceptions, services are infrequent and sluggish.

Sights & Activities

Maó absorbs most of the tourist traffic. North of Maó, a drive across a lunar landscape leads to the lighthouse at **Cap de Favàritx**. South of the cape stretch some

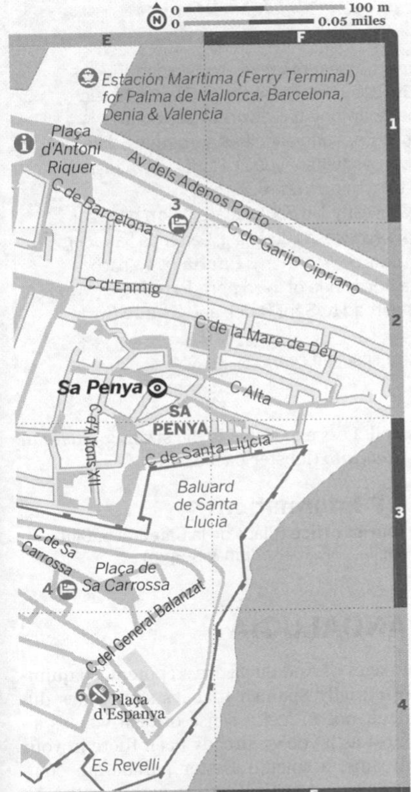

fine sandy bays and beaches, including **Cala Presili** and **Platja d'en Tortuga**, reachable on foot.

Ciutadella, with its smaller harbour and historic buildings, has a more distinctly Spanish feel to it and is the more attractive of the two. A narrow country road leads south of Ciutadella (follow the 'Platges' sign from the *ronda*, or ring road) and then forks twice to reach some of the island's loveliest beaches: (from west to east) **Arenal de Son Saura**, **Cala en Turqueta**, **Es Talaier**, **Cala Macarelleta** and **Cala Macarella**. As with most beaches, you'll need your own transport.

In the centre of the island, the 357m-high **Monte Toro** has great views; on a clear day you can see Mallorca.

On the northern coast, the picturesque town of **Fornells** is on a large bay popular with windsurfers.

Ibiza City (Eivissa)

Top Sights
Catedral D4
Ramparts & Bastions B3
Sa Penya E2

Sights
1 Centre d'Interpretació Madina Yabisa D4

Sleeping
2 Casa de Huéspedes Navarro D1
3 Hostal La Marina E1
4 Hotel La Ventana E3

Eating
5 Comidas Bar San Juan D2
6 Restaurant of Hotel Mirador de Dalt Vila E4

Drinking
7 Teatro Pereira C2

Sleeping

Many accommodation options on the island are closed between November and April.

MAÓ

TOP CHOICE **Casa Alberti** HISTORIC HOTEL **€€**
(☎971 35 42 10; Carrer d'Isabel II 9; www.casalberti.com; s/d incl breakfast from €80/100; ⏰Easter-Oct) Climb the central stairs with their striking wrought-iron banisters to your vast room with its white walls and whitest of white sheets. Each of the six bedrooms within this 18th-century mansion is furnished with traditional items, while bathrooms are designer-cool and contemporary.

CIUTADELLA

Hotel Gèminis HOTEL **€€**
(☎971 38 46 44; www.hotelgeminismenorca.com; Carrer de Josepa Rossinyol 4; s/d €65/96;) A friendly, stylish two-star place on a backstreet, this graceful, three-storey, rose-and-white lodging offers comfortable if somewhat neutral rooms just a short walk away from the city centre.

Hostal-Residencia Oasis BUDGET HOTEL **€**
(☎971 38 21 97; Carrer de Sant Isidre 33; s/d €35/45) Run by a delightful elderly couple, this quiet place is close to the heart of the old quarter. Rooms, mostly with bathroom, are set beside a spacious garden courtyard. Their furnishings, though still trim, are from deep into the last century.

CLUBBING IN IBIZA

In summer (late May to the end of September), the west of the island is a continuous party from sunset to sunrise and back again. In 2009 the International Dance Music Awards ranked two Ibiza clubs, Pacha and Space, among their worldwide top five.

The clubs operate nightly from around 1am to 6am and each has something different. Theme nights, fancy-dress parties and foam parties (where you are half-drowned in the stuff) are regular features. Admission can cost anything from €25 to €60.

The best include **Amnesia** (www.amnesia.es; ⏲early Jun-Sep), located 4km north of Ibiza City on the road to Sant Rafel; **Es Paradis** (www.esparadis.com; Carrer de Salvador Espriu 2, Sant Antoni; ⏲mid-May–Sep) in Sant Antoni de Portmany; **Pacha** (www.pacha.com; ⏲nightly Jun-Sep, Fri & Sat Oct-May), on the north side of Ibiza port; **Privilege** (www.privilegeibiza.com), 5km north of Ibiza City on the road to Sant Rafel; and **Space** (www.space-ibiza.es; ⏲Jun–mid-Oct).

A good website is **Ibiza Spotlight** (www.ibiza-spotlight.com).

Eating & Drinking

The ports in both Maó and Ciutadella are lined with bars and restaurants.

MAÓ

El Varadero SPANISH €€
(☎971 35 20 74; Moll de Llevant 4; mains €11.50-17; ⏲Easter-Nov) With such a splendid vista from the harbourside terrace, it must be tempting to simply sit on your laurels. But El Varadero doesn't. There's a range of tempting rice dishes and a short, select choice of fish and meat mains. If a full meal is too much, drop by for a tapa or two with a glass of wine and savour the view.

CIUTADELLA

TOP CHOICE **Cas Ferrer de Sa Font** MENORCAN €€
(☎971 48 07 84; www.casferrer.com; Carrer del Portal de Sa Font 16; meals €35; ⏲Tue-Sun) Nowhere on the island will you find more authentic Menorcan cuisine based upon meats and vegetables from the owner's organic farm. Dine on the delightful interior patio of this charming 18th-century building or inside, below beams and soft curves, in what was once a blacksmith's forge.

Café des Museu COCKTAIL BAR
(Carreró d'es Palau 4; ⏲10pm-3.30am) In the old town, this charming cocktail bar tucked away down a tight lane occasionally hosts live gigs – anything from acid jazz to bossanova.

FORNELLS

Es Port SEAFOOD €€
(☎971 37 64 03; Passeig Marítim 5; meals €30-35; ⏲Sat-Thu Easter-Oct) Some fine fresh fish and seafood are done here. Of course, it does *caldereta de llagosta* (lobster stew; €64) as well. Less expensive is the sizzling *paella de llomanto* (lobster paella; €35).

Information

Tourist office (Plaça de la Catedral 5, Ciutadella; ⏲8.30am-3pm & 5-9pm)

ANDALUCÍA

Images of Andalucía are so potent, so quintessentially Spanish that it's sometimes difficult not to feel a sense of déjà vu. It's almost as if you've already been there in your dreams: a solemn Easter parade, an ebullient spring festival, exotic nights in the Alhambra. In the stark light of day the picture is no less compelling.

Seville

POP 703,000

A sexy, gutsy and gorgeous city, Seville is home to two of Spain's most colourful festivals, fascinating and distinctive *barrios* (neighbourhoods) and a local population that lives life to the fullest. A fiery place (as you'll soon see in its packed and noisy tapas bars), it is also hot climatewise – avoid July and August!

Sights & Activities

Cathedral & Giralda CHURCH
(adult/concession/under 16yr €8/2/free; ⏲11am-5.30pm Mon-Sat, 2.30-6.30pm Sun Sep-Jun, 9.30am-4.30pm Mon-Sat, 2.30-6.30pm Sun Jul & Aug) After Seville fell to the Christians in 1248, its main mosque was used as a church until 1401, when it was knocked down to make way for what would become one of

the world's largest cathedrals and an icon of Gothic architecture. The building wasn't completed until 1507. Over 90m high, the perfectly proportioned and exquisitely decorated **La Giralda** was the minaret of the mosque that stood on the site before the cathedral. The views from the summit are exceptional.

Inside, the **Capilla de San Antonio** contains Murillo's large 1666 canvas depicting the vision of St Anthony of Padua. Inside the southern door stands the elaborate **tomb of Christopher Columbus**, which Spain transferred here from Cuba in 1902. Towards the east end of the main nave is the **Capilla Mayor**, whose Gothic altarpiece is the jewel of the cathedral and reckoned to be the biggest altarpiece in the world with more than 1000 carved biblical figures. The **Sacristía de los Cálices** (Sacristy of the Chalices) contains Goya's 1817 painting of the Seville martyrs *Santas Justa y Rufina*. The room's centrepiece is the **Custodia de Juan de Arfe**, a huge 475kg silver monstrance made in the 1580s by Renaissance metalsmith Juan de Arfe. Displayed in a glass case are the city keys handed to the conquering Fernando III in 1248.

Alcázar CASTLE

(adult/child & concession €7.50/free; ⌚9.30am-7pm Apr-Sep, to 6pm Oct-Mar) Seville's Alcázar, a royal residence for many centuries, was founded in 913 as a Muslim fortress. The Alcázar has been expanded and rebuilt many times in its 11 centuries of existence. The Catholic Monarchs, Fernando and Isabel, set up court here in the 1480s as they prepared for the conquest of Granada. Later rulers created the Alcázar's lovely gardens. The Alcázar's highlights include exquisitely adorned patios and the showpiece **Palacio de Don Pedro**.

FREE **Archivo de Indias** MUSEUM

(Calle Santo Tomás, ⌚10am-4pm Mon-Sat, to 2pm Sun & holidays) On the western side of Plaza del Triunfo, the Archivo de Indias is the main archive on Spain's American empire, with 80 million pages of documents dating from 1492 through to the end of the empire in the 19th century: a most effective statement of Spain's power and influence during its Golden Age.

Barrio de Santa Cruz HISTORIC DISTRICT

Seville's medieval *judería*, east of the cathedral and Alcázar, is today a tangle of atmospheric, winding streets and lovely plant-decked plazas perfumed with orange blossom. Among its most characteristic plazas is **Plaza de Santa Cruz**, which gives the *barrio* its name. **Plaza de Doña Elvira** is another romantic perch, especially in the evening.

Museo del Baile Flamenco MUSEUM

(www.museoflamenco.com; Calle Manuel Rojas Marcos 3; adult/child €10/6; ⌚9.30am-7pm) The brainchild of Sevillana flamenco dancer Cristina Hoyos, Seville's newest museum is spread over three floors of an 18th-century palace, although at €10 a pop it's more than a little overpriced. Exhibits include sketches, paintings, photos of erstwhile (and contemporary) flamenco greats, plus a collection of dresses and shawls.

Parque de María Luisa & Plaza de España PARK

(⌚8am-10pm) A large area south of the tobacco factory was transformed for Seville's 1929 international fair, the Exposición Iberoamericana, when architects adorned it with fantastical buildings, many of them harking back to Seville's past glory or imitating the native styles of Spain's former colonies. In its midst is the large Parque de María Luisa, a living expression of Seville's Moorish and Christian past.

Festivals & Events

The first of Seville's two great festivals is **Semana Santa**, the week leading up to Easter Sunday. Throughout the week, thousands of members of religious brotherhoods parade in penitents' garb with tall, pointed *capirotes* (hoods) accompanying sacred images through the city, while huge crowds look on.

The **Feria de Abril**, a week in late April, is a welcome release after this solemnity: the festivities involve six days of music, dancing, horse riding and traditional dress, plus daily bullfights.

The city also stages Spain's largest flamenco festival, the month-long **Bienal de Flamenco**. It's held in September in even-numbered years.

WANT MORE?

For in-depth information, reviews and recommendations at your fingertips, head to the Apple App Store to purchase Lonely Planet's *Seville City Guide* iPhone app.

Seville

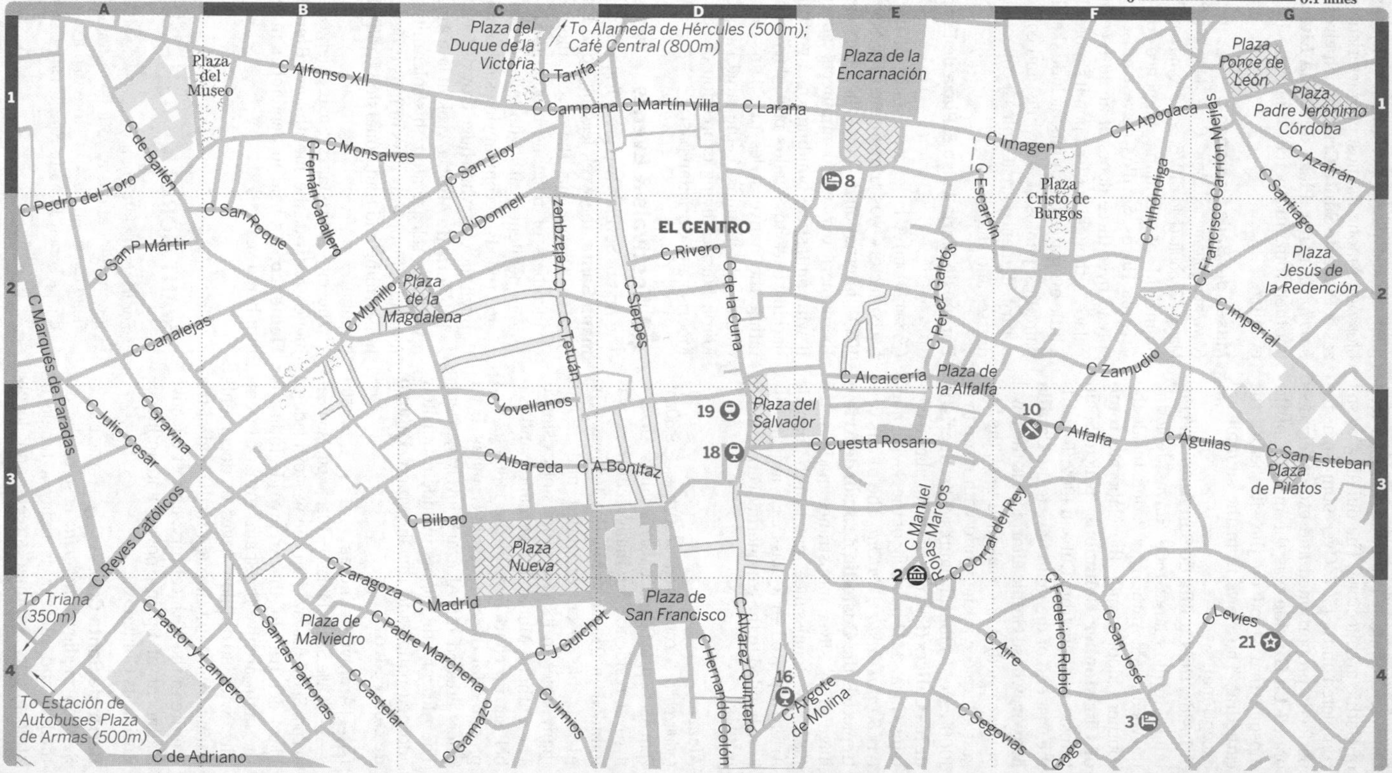

0 200 m
0 0.1 miles
A B C D E F G
1 2 3 4
Plaza del Duque de la Victoria
To Alameda de Hércules (500m); Café Central (800m)
Plaza de la Encarnación
Plaza Ponce de León
Plaza Padre Jerónimo Córdoba
Plaza del Museo
C Alfonso XII
C Tarifa
C Campana
C Martín Villa
C Laraña
C A Apodaca
C Imagen
C Azafrán
C Santiago
C Francisco Carrión Mejías
C Alhóndiga
Plaza Cristo de Burgos
C Escarpín
8
C de Bailén
C Monsalves
C Fernán Caballero
C San Eloy
C O'Donnell
C Velázquez
C Pedro del Toro
C San Roque
EL CENTRO
C Rivero
C San P Mártir
Plaza Jesús de la Redención
C Pérez Galdós
C Murillo
Plaza de la Magdalena
C Sierpes
C de la Cuna
C Imperial
C Marqués de Paradas
C Canalejas
C Tetuán
C Alcaicería
Plaza de la Alfalfa
C Zamudio
C Julio César
C Gravina
C Jovellanos
19
Plaza del Salvador
10
C Alfalfa
C Águilas
C San Esteban
Plaza de Pilatos
18
C Cuesta Rosario
C Albareda
C A Bonifaz
C Reyes Católicos
C Bilbao
C Manuel Rojas Marcos
C Corral del Rey
Plaza Nueva
2
C Zaragoza
C Madrid
Plaza de San Francisco
C Federico Rubio
C San José
C Levíes
To Triana (350m)
C Pastor y Landero
C Santas Patronas
Plaza de Malviedro
C Padre Marchena
C J Guichot
C Álvarez Quintero
C Hernando Colón
C Aire
21
16
C Argote de Molina
C Castelar
C Jimios
C Segovias
To Estación de Autobuses Plaza de Armas (500m)
C Garnazo
C de Adriano
3
Gago

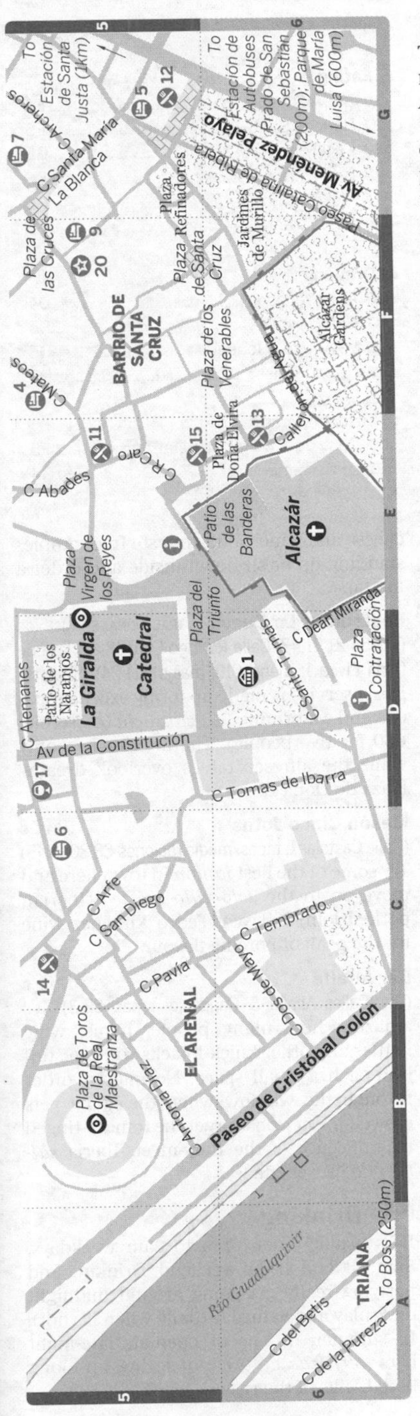

Sleeping

There's plenty of accommodation in the Barrio de Santa Cruz (close to the Alcázar), El Arenal and El Centro.

Prices over Semana Santa and the Feria de Abril can be up to double the high-season prices cited here. Accommodation is often full on weekends and is always booked solid during festivals, so book well ahead.

Hotel Amadeus HOTEL €€
(954 50 14 43; www.hotelamadeussevilla.com; Calle Farnesio 6; s/d €85/95; P ❄ wi-fi) This musician family converted their 18th-century mansion into a stylish hotel with 14 elegant rooms of which Mozart would have been proud. A couple of the newer rooms have been soundproofed for piano or violin practice.

Las Casas de la Judería HOTEL €€€
(954 41 51 50; www.casasypalacios.com; Callejón Dos Hermanas 7; s/d from €140/175; P ❄ wi-fi) At last a five-star that might actually be worth it. Countless patios and corridors link this veritable palace that was once 18 different houses situated on the cusp of the Santa Cruz quarter. The decor is exquisite, from the trickling fountains to the antique furniture and paintings.

Hotel Puerta de Sevilla HOTEL €€
(954 98 72 70; www.hotelpuertadesevilla.com; Calle Puerta de la Carne 2; s/d €66/86; P ❄ @ wi-fi) A small shiny hotel in a great location, the Puerta de Sevilla has tin-glazed painted *azulejos* tiles, flower-pattern textiles and wrought-iron beds, all for one star. An extra bonus is the first-class but friendly service.

Pensión San Pancracio PENSIÓN €
(954 41 31 04; Plaza de las Cruces 9; d €50, s/d without bathroom €25/35) An ideal budget option in Santa Cruz, this old rambling family house has plenty of different room options (all cheap) and a pleasant flower-bedecked patio/lobby. Friendliness makes up for the lack of luxury.

Hotel Simón HOTEL €€
(954 22 66 60; www.hotelsimonsevilla.com; Calle García de Vinuesa 19; s €60-70, d €95-110; ❄) A typically grand 18th-century Sevillan house, with an ornate patio and spotless and comfortable rooms, this place gleams way above its two-star rating. Some of the rooms are embellished with rich *azulejos* tile-work.

Oasis Backpackers' Hostel HOSTEL €
(954 29 37 77; www.oasissevilla.com; Plaza de la Encarnación 29; dm/d incl breakfast €15/50; ❄ @ wi-fi)

Seville

Top Sights

- Alcazár E6
- Catedral D5
- La Giralda D5

Sights

1 Archivo de Indias D6
2 Museo del Baile Flamenco E3

Sleeping

3 Hotel Amadeus F4
4 Hotel Goya F5
5 Hotel Puerta de Sevilla G5
6 Hotel Simón C5
7 Las Casas de la Judería G5
8 Oasis Backpackers' Hostel E1
9 Pensión San Pancracio F5

Eating

10 Bar Alfalfa F3
11 Bodega Santa Cruz E5
12 Catalina G5
13 Extraverde E6
14 Mesón Cinco Jotas C5
15 Restaurante La Cueva E5

Drinking

16 Antigüedades D4
17 Casa Morales D5
18 La Antigua Bodeguita D3
19 La Sapotales D3

Entertainment

20 Casa de la Memoria de Al-Andalus F5
21 La Carbonería G4

Seville's offbeat, buzzing backpacker central offers 24-hour free internet access. The new location is in Plaza Encarnación, a narrow street behind the Church of the Anunciación. Each dorm bed has a personal safe, and there is a small rooftop pool. There's no curfew. This is Spain!

Hotel Goya HOTEL €
(☎954 21 11 70 www.hotelgoyasevilla.com; Calle Mateos Gago 31; s/d €40/60;) The gleaming Goya is more popular than ever. Book ahead.

Eating

TOP CHOICE Catalina TAPAS €
(Paseo Catalina de Ribera 4; raciones €10) If your view of tapas is 'glorified bar snacks'; then your ideas could be blown out of the water here with a creative mix of just about every ingredient known to Iberian cooking. Start with the goat's cheese, aubergine and paprika special.

Bodega Santa Cruz TAPAS €
(Calle Mateos Gago; tapas €1.50-2) Forever crowded and with a mountain of paper on the floor, this place is usually standing room only with tapas and drinks enjoyed alfresco as you dodge the marching army of tourists squeezing through Santa Cruz's narrow streets.

Extraverde TAPAS €
(Plaza de Doña Elvira 8; tapas €2.50-4; ⏲10.30am-11.30pm) New on the scene, Extraverde is a unique bar/shop specialising in Andalucian products such as olive oil, cheese and wine. You can taste free samples standing up or sit down inside and order a full tapa.

Restaurant La Cueva TRADITIONAL SPANISH €€
(☎954 21 31 43; Calle Rodrigo Caro 18 & Plaza de Doña Elvira 1; menú €16, mains €11-24) Slightly frosty service is made up for by excellent paella and a storming fish *zarzuela* (casserole; €30 for two people). The interior is roomy while the alfresco tables overlook dreamy Plaza de Doña Elvira.

Mesón Cinco Jotas TAPAS €
(Calle Castelar 1; tapas/media raciones €3.80/9.45) Try some of the best *jamón* in town here and move on to the *solomillo ibérico* (Iberian pork sirloin) in sweet Pedro Ximénez wine for the peak of porcine flavour.

Bar Alfalfa TAPAS €
(Cnr Calles Alfalfa & Candilejo; tapas €2-3) It's amazing how many people, hams, wine bottles and other knick-knacks you can stuff into such a small space. No matter; order through the window when the going gets crowded. You won't forget the tomato-tinged magnificence of the Italy-meets-Iberia *salmorejo* bruschetta.

Drinking

Bars usually open 6pm to 2am weekdays, 8pm till 3am at the weekend. Drinking and partying really get going around midnight on Friday and Saturday (daily when it's hot). In summer, dozens of open-air late-night bars *(terrazas de verano)* spring up along both banks of the river.

Plaza del Salvador is brimful of drinkers from mid-evening to 1am. Grab a drink from **La Antigua Bodeguita** or **La Sapotales** next door and sit on the steps of the Parroquia del Salvador.

Antigüedades BAR
(Calle Argote de Molina 40) Blending mellow beats with offbeat decor, the tiled window seats with a view of the busy street are the best place to nurse your drink.

Casa Morales BAR
(Garcia de Vinuesa 11) Founded in 1850, not much has changed in this defiantly old-world bar, with charming anachronisms wherever you look. Towering clay *tinajas* (wine storage jars) carry the chalked-up tapas choices of the day. Locals sweat it out on summer nights like true *sevillanos*.

Café Central BAR
(Alameda de Hércules 64) One of the oldest and most popular along the street, Central has yellow bar lights, wooden flea-market chairs and a massive crowd that gathers at weekends.

☆ Entertainment

Seville is arguably Spain's flamenco capital and you're most likely to catch a spontaneous atmosphere (of unpredictable quality) in one of the bars staging regular nights of flamenco with no admission fee. *Soleares,* Flamenco's truest *cante jondo* (deep song), was first concocted in Triana; head here to find some of the more authentic clubs.

TOP CHOICE **La Carbonería** FLAMENCO BAR
(Calle Levíes 18; admission free; ⏲8pm-4am) During the day there is no indication that this happening place is anything but a large garage. But come 8pm and this converted coal yard in the Barrio de Santa Cruz reveals two large bars, and nightly live flamenco (11pm and midnight) for no extra charge.

Casa de la Memoria de Al-Andalus FLAMENCO SHOW
(☎954 56 06 70; Calle Ximénez de Enciso 28; tickets €15; ⏲9pm) This place in Santa Cruz is probably the most intimate and authentic nightly *tablao* (flamenco show), offering a wide variety of flamenco styles in a room of shifting shadows. Space is limited to 100, so reserve tickets in advance.

Casa Anselma FLAMENCO BAR
(Pagés de Corro 49, Triana; ⏲midnight to late Mon-Sat) If you can squeeze in past the foreboding form of Anselma (a celebrated Triana flamenco dancer) at the door, you'll quickly realise that anything can happen in here. Casa Anslema (beware: there's no sign, just a doorway embellished with *azulejos* tiles) is the antithesis of a tourist flamenco *tablao,* with cheek-to-jowl crowds, thick cigarette smoke, zero amplification and spontaneous outbreaks of dexterous dancing. Pure magic.

 Information

Discover Sevilla (www.discoversevilla.com)
Explore Seville (www.exploreseville.com)
Regional tourist office Avenida de la Constitución (Avenida de la Constitución 21; ⏲9am-7pm Mon-Fri, 10am-2pm & 3-7pm Sat, 10am-2pm Sun, closed holidays); Estación de Santa Justa (⏲9am-8pm Mon-Fri, 10am-2pm Sat & Sun, closed holidays)
Seville Tourism (www.turismo.sevilla.org)
Turismo Sevilla (www.turismosevilla.org; Plaza del Triunfo 1; ⏲10.30am-7pm Mon-Fri)

 Getting There & Away

Air

A range of domestic and international flights land in Seville's **Aeropuerto San Pablo**, 7km from the city centre.

Bus

From the **Estación de Autobuses Prado de San Sebastián** (Plaza San Sebastián), there are 12 or more buses daily to/from Cádiz (€11.50, 1¾ hours), Córdoba (€10, two hours), Granada (€19, 3½ hours), Ronda (€11, 2½ hours, five or more daily) and Málaga (€15.75, 2¾ hours).

From the **Estación de Autobuses Plaza de Armas** (Avenida del Cristo de la Expiración), destinations include Madrid (€18.65, six hours, 14 daily), Mérida (€13, three hours, 12 daily), Cáceres (€15, four hours, six daily) and Portugal.

Train

The modern, efficient **Estación de Santa Justa** (Avenida Kansas City) is 1.5km northeast of the city centre. There's also a city-centre **Renfe ticket office** (Calle Zaragoza 29).

Twenty or more superfast AVE trains, reaching speeds of 280km/h, whiz daily to/from Madrid (€80.70, 2½ hours) and to Barcelona (€130, 6½ hours, one daily). Other services include Barcelona (€61 to €88, 10½ to 13 hours, three daily), Cádiz (€12.75, 1¾ hours, 13 daily), Córdoba (€16 to €32, 40 minutes to 1½ hours, 21 or more daily), Granada (€24, three hours, four daily), Málaga (€19.10 to €36.40, 2½ hours, five daily) and Mérida (€14, five hours, one daily).

Getting Around

Los Amarillos (www.losamarillos.es) runs buses between the airport and the Avenida del Cid near the San Sebastión bus station (€2.20 to €2.50, at 15 and 45 minutes past the hour). A taxi costs about €20.

Buses run by Seville's urban transport authority **Tussam** (www.tussam.es), C1, C2, C3 and C4, do useful circular routes linking the main transport terminals and the city centre.

Tussam's **Tranvia** (www.tussam.es, in Spanish), the city's sleek tram service, was launched in 2007. Individual rides cost €1.20, or you can buy a *Bono* (travel pass offering five rides for €5) from many newspaper stands and tobacconists.

SeVici (902 01 10 32; www.sevici.es; 7am-9pm) is a cycle-hire network comprising almost 200 fully automated pick-up/drop-off points dotted all over the city (clearly shown on a nifty folding pocket map). A one-week subscription costs €5. Your first 30 minutes cycling is free, the next hour costs €1, second and subsequent hours are €2 per hour.

Córdoba

POP 302,000

Córdoba was once one of the most enlightened Islamic cities on earth, and enough remains to place it in the contemporary top three Andalucian draws. The centrepiece is the gigantic and exquisitely rendered Mezquita. Surrounding it is an intricate web of winding streets, geranium-sprouting flower boxes and cool intimate patios that are at their most beguiling in late spring.

Sights & Activities

TOP CHOICE **Mezquita** CHURCH, MOSQUE

(adult/child €8/4, free 8.30-10am Mon-Sat; 10am-7pm Mon-Sat Apr-Oct, 9-10.45am & 1.30-6.30pm Sun) Founded in 785, Córdoba's gigantic mosque is a wonderful architectural hybrid with delicate horseshoe arches making this unlike anywhere else in Spain. The main entrance is the **Puerta del Perdón**, a 14th-century Mudéjar gateway, with the

Córdoba

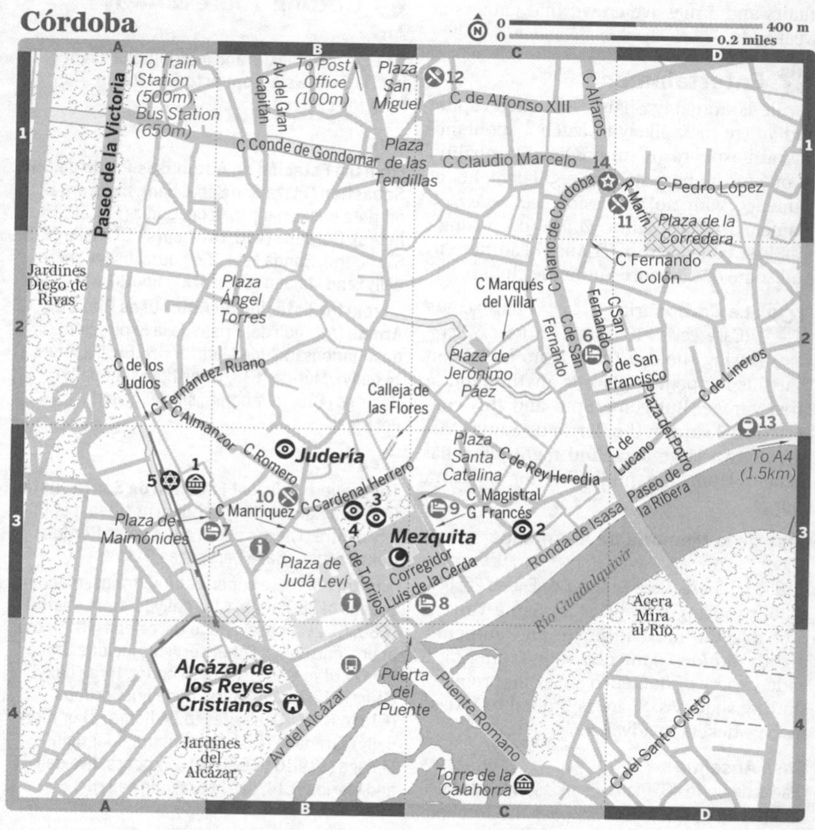

ticket office immediately inside. Also inside the gateway is the aptly named **Patio de los Naranjos** (Courtyard of the Orange Trees). Once inside, you can see straight ahead to the **mihrab**, the prayer niche in the mosque's *qibla* (the wall indicating the direction of Mecca) that was the focus of prayer. The first 12 transverse aisles inside the entrance, a forest of pillars and arches, comprise the original **8th-century mosque**.

Judería HISTORIC DISTRICT

The medieval *judería*, extending northwest from the Mezquita almost to Avenida del Gran Capitán, is today a maze of narrow streets and whitewashed buildings with flowery window boxes. The beautiful little 14th-century **Sinagoga** (Calle de los Judíos 20; adult/EU citizen €0.30/free; ⏲9.30am-2pm & 3.30-5.30pm Tue-Sat, 9.30am-1.30pm Sun & holidays) is one of only three surviving medieval synagogues in Spain and the only one in Andalucía.

In the heart of the *judería*, and once connected by an underground tunnel to the Sinagoga, is the 14th-century **Casa de Sefarad** (www.casadesefarad.es; admission €4; ⏲10am-6pm Mon-Sat, 11am-2pm Sun) This small, beautiful museum is devoted to reviving interest in the Spanish Sephardic-Judaic tradition.

Alcázar de los Reyes Cristianos CASTLE

(Castle of the Christian Monarchs; Campo Santo de Los Mártires s/n; adult/concession €4/2, free Fri; ⏲10am-2pm & 5.30-7.30pm Tue-Sat, 9.30am-2.30pm Sun & holidays) Just southwest of the Mezquita, the Alcázar began as a palace and fort for Alfonso X in the 13th century. From 1490 to 1821 the Inquisition operated from here. Today its gardens are among the most beautiful in Andalucía.

Hammam Baños Árabes BATHHOUSE

(☎957 48 47 46; www.hammamspain.com/cordoba; Calle del Corregidor Luis de la Cerda 51; bath/bath & massage €26/33; ⏲2hr sessions 10am, noon, 2pm, 4pm, 6pm, 8pm & 10pm) Follow the lead of the medieval Cordobans and dip your toe in the beautifully renovated Arab baths, where you can enjoy an aromatherapy massage, with tea, hookah and Arabic sweets in the cafe later.

Medina Azahara ISLAMIC RUINS

(Madinat al-Zahra; adult/EU citizen €1.50/free; ⏲10am-6.30pm Tue-Sat, to 8.30pm May–mid-Sep, to 2pm Sun) Even in the cicada-shrill heat and stillness of a summer afternoon, the Medina Azahara whispers of the power and vision of its founder, Abd ar-Rahman III. The self-proclaimed caliph began the construction of a magnificent new capital 8km west of Córdoba around 936, and took up full residence around 945. Medina Azahara was a resounding declaration of his status, a magnificent trapping of power. It was destroyed in the 11th century and just 10% of the site has been excavated. A taxi costs €37 for the return trip, with one hour to view the site, or you can book a three-hour coach tour for €6.50 to €10 through many Córdoba hotels.

Sleeping

TOP CHOICE **Hotel Hacienda Posada de Vallina** HOTEL €€

(☎957 49 87 50; ww.hhposadadevallinacordoba.com; Calle del Corregidor Luís de la Cerda 83; s/d €50/70; P❄@🛜) In an enviable nook on

Córdoba

Top Sights

Alcázar de los Reyes Cristianos B4
Judería B3
Mezquita B3

Sights

1 Casa de Sefarad A3
2 Hammam Baños Árabes C3
3 Patio de los Naranjos B3
4 Puerta del Perdón B3
5 Sinagoga A3

Sleeping

6 Hostal La Fuente C2
7 Hotel Amistad Córdoba B3
8 Hotel Hacienda Posada de Vallina C3
9 Hotel Mezquita C3

Eating

10 Casa Pepe de la Judería B3
11 Taberna Salinas D1
12 Taberna San Miguel El Pisto C1

Drinking

13 Amapola D2

Entertainment

14 Jazz Café C1

the quiet side of the Mezquita (the building actually predates it), this cleverly renovated hotel uses portraits and period furniture to enhance a plush and modern interior. The rooms make you feel comfortable but in-period (ie medieval Córdoba). Columbus allegedly once stayed here.

Hotel Amistad Córdoba HOTEL €€€
(☎957 42 03 35; www.nh-hoteles.com; Plaza de Maimónides 3; s/d €125; P❄@☎) Occupying two 18th-century mansions with original Mudéjar patios, the Amistad is part of the modern NH chain with elegant rooms and all the requisite luxury hotel facilities including babysitting. Closed at the time of research, but renovations will have been completed by the time you read this.

Hostal La Fuente HOTEL €
(☎957 48 78 27; www.hostallafuente.com; Calle San Fernando 51; s/d €35/50; ❄@☎) A journeyman hotel, though in Córdoba this means you get an airy patio, *azulejos* tiles, exposed brick and interesting architectural details. The rooms are clean and comfortable, and the staff quietly helpful.

Hotel Mezquita HOTEL €€
(☎957 47 55 85; hotelmezquita.com; Plaza Santa Catalina 1; s/d €42/74; ❄) One of the best-value places in town, this hotel is right opposite the Mezquita itself. The 16th-century mansion has sparkling bathrooms and elegant rooms, some with views of the great mosque across the street.

Eating & Drinking

Córdoba's liveliest bars are mostly scattered around the newer parts of town and come alive at about 11pm or midnight on weekends. Most bars in the medieval centre close around midnight.

TOP CHOICE **Taberna San Miguel El Pisto** TAPAS €
(Plaza San Miguel 1; tapas €3, media raciones €5-10; ⊙closed Sun & Aug) Stand aside Seville. Fine wine, great atmosphere, professional old-school waiters, zero pretension and a clamorous yet handsome decor make El Pisto (the barrel) a Córdoban and Andalucian tapa classic. You can squeeze in at the bar or grab a jug of wine and grab a table out back.

Taberna Salinas TAPAS €
(Calle Tundidores 3; tapas/raciones €2.50/8; ⊙closed Sun & Aug) Dating back to 1879, this large patio restaurant fills up fast. Try the delicious aubergines with honey or potatoes with garlic. The tavern side is quieter in the early evening, and the friendly bar staff will fill your glass with local Montilla whenever you look thirsty.

Casa Pepe de la Judería ANDALUCIAN €€€
(☎957 20 07 44; Calle Romero 1; tapas/media raciones €2.50-9.50, mains €11-18, menú €27) A great roof terrace with views of the Mezquita and a labyrinth of busy dining rooms. Down a complimentary glass of Montilla before launching into the house specials, including Cordoban oxtails or venison fillets.

Amapola BAR
(Paseo de la Ribera 9; ⊙9am-3pm Mon-Fri, 5pm-4am Sat & Sun) This is where the young and beautiful lounge on green leather sofas consuming elaborate cocktails. DJs spin until the small hours.

Jazz Café LIVE MUSIC
(Calle Espartería; ⊙8am-late) This fabulous, cavernous bar full of black-and-white jazz photos puts on regular free live jazz and jam sessions.It's also a good place for an early-morning hangover cure.

Information

Municipal tourist office (Plaza de Judá Levi; ⊙8.30am-2.30pm Mon-Fri)

Regional tourist office (Calle de Torrijos 10; ⊙9am-7.30pm Mon-Fri, 9.30am-3pm Sat, Sun & holidays)

Getting There & Away

BUS The **bus station** (Glorieta de las Tres Culturas) is 1km northwest of Plaza de las Tendillas. Destinations include Seville (€10.36, 1¾ hours, six daily), Granada (€12.52, 2½ hours, seven daily) and Málaga (€12.75, 2¾ hours, five daily).

TRAIN From Córdoba's **train station** (Avenida de América), destinations include Seville (€10.60 to €32.10, 40 to 90 minutes, 23 or more daily), Madrid (€52 to €66.30, 1¾ to 6¼ hours, 23 or more daily), Málaga (€21 to €39.60, one to 2½ hours, nine daily) and Barcelona (€59.40 to €133, 10½ hours, four daily).

Granada

POP 300,000 / ELEV 685M

Granada's eight centuries as a Muslim capital are symbolised in its keynote emblem, the remarkable Alhambra, one of the most graceful architectural achievements in the Muslim world. Islam was never completely expunged here, and today it seems more present than ever in the shops, restaurants, tearooms and mosque of a growing North African community in and around the maze of the Albayzín. The tapas bars fill to bursting with hungry and thirsty revellers, while flamenco dives resound to the heart-wrenching tones of the south.

Sights & Activities

TOP CHOICE **Alhambra** PALACE

(☎902 44 12 21; www.alhambra-tickets.es, www.servicaixa.com; adult/EU senior/EU student/ under 8yr €12/9/9/free, Generalife only €6; ⏲8.30am-8pm 16 Mar-31 Oct, to 6pm 1 Nov-14 Mar) The mighty Alhambra is breathtaking. Much has been written about its fortress, palace, patios and gardens, but nothing can really prepare you for seeing the real thing.

The **Alcazaba**, the Alhambra's fortress, dates from the 11th to the 13th centuries. There are spectacular views from the tops of its towers. The **Palacio Nazaríes** (Nasrid Palace), built for Granada's Muslim rulers in their 13th- to 15th-century heyday, is the centrepiece of the Alhambra. The beauty of its patios and intricacy of its stuccoes and woodwork, epitomised by the **Patio de los Leones** (Patio of the Lions) and **Sala de las Dos Hermanas** (Hall of the Two Sisters), are stunning. The **Generalife** (Palace Gardens) is a great spot to relax and contemplate the complex from a little distance.

The Palacio Nazaríes is also open for **night visits** (⏲10pm-11.30pm Tue-Sat Mar-Oct, 8pm-9.30pm Fri & Sat Nov-Feb). Book for night visits the same way as for day visits.

Albayzín HISTORIC AREA

Exploring the narrow, hilly streets of the Albayzín, the old Moorish quarter across the river from the Alhambra, is the perfect complement to the Alhambra. The cobblestone streets are lined with gorgeous *cármenes* (large mansions with walled gardens, from the Arabic *karm* for garden). It survived as the Muslim quarter for several decades after the Christian conquest in 1492.

Head uphill to reach the **Mirador de San Nicolás** – a viewpoint with breathtaking vistas and a relaxed scene.

Capilla Real HISTORIC BUILDING

(www.capillareal.granada.com; Calle Oficios; admission €3.50; ⏲10.30am-1.30pm & 4-7.30pm Mon-Sat, 11am-1.30pm & 4-7pm Sun Apr-Oct) It's well worth exploring the streets and lanes surrounding Plaza Bib-Rambla, and visiting the chapel where Fernando and Isabel, the Christian monarchs who conquered Granada in 1492, are buried. The sacristy contains a small but impressive **museum** with royal memorabilia and lovely artworks, including Botticelli's *Prayer in the Garden of Olives*.

Next door to the chapel is Granada's **Catedral** (admission €3.50; ⏲10.45am-1.30pm & 4-8pm Mon-Sat, 4-8pm Sun), which dates from the early 16th century.

Sleeping

TOP CHOICE **Casa Morisca Hotel** HISTORIC HOTEL €€€

(☎958 22 11 00; www.hotelcasamorisca.com; Cuesta de la Victoria 9; d interior/exterior €118/148; ❄@📶) The Morisca could easily compete with the finest of Marrakech's *riads* with its 14 Alhambra-esque rooms occupying a gorgeous late-15th-century Albayzín mansion. Everything is arranged around an atmospheric patio with an ornamental pool and overlooking wooden galleries. The pinnacle: an exquisite Mirador suite, affording views of the great palace it-

ALHAMBRA TICKETS

Up to 6600 tickets to the Alhambra are available for each day. About one-third of these are sold at the ticket office on the day, but they sell out early and you need to start queuing by 7am to be reasonably sure of getting one. It's highly advisable to book in advance (you pay €1 extra per ticket). You can book up to a year ahead in two ways:

» **Alhambra Advance Booking** (☎national calls 902 88 80 01, international calls 0034 934 92 37 50; www.alhambra-tickets.es; ⏲8am-9pm)

» **Servicaixa** (www.servicaixa.com) Online booking in Spanish and English. You can also buy tickets in advance from Servicaixa cash machines (8am to 7pm March to October, 8am to 5pm November to February), but only in the Alhambra grounds

For internet or phone bookings you need a Visa card, MasterCard or Eurocard. You receive a reference number, which you must show, along with your passport, national identity card or credit card, at the Alhambra ticket office when you pick up the ticket on the day of your visit.

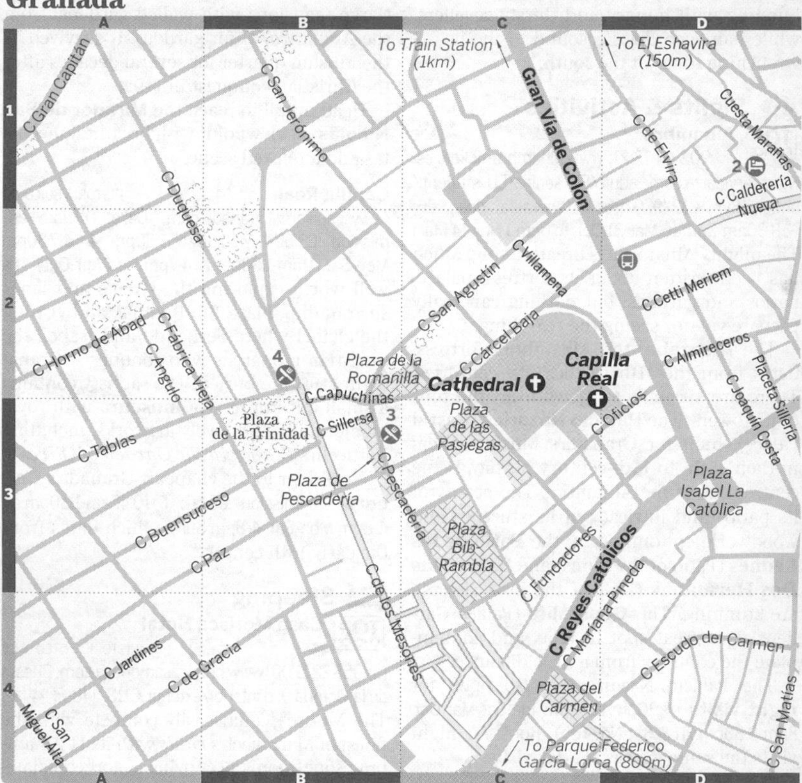

self. It's around 600m northeast of the Iglesia de Santa Ana, just off the Carrera del Darro.

Carmen de la Alcubilla HISTORIC HOTEL €€€
(958 21 55 51; www.alcubilladelcaracol.com; Aire Alta 12; s/d €100/120;) Tranquil Granadian beauty, this time perched on the Realejo hill in a restored Carmen (house with an internal garden) with a terraced garden overflowing with jasmine and lemon trees. The house is (almost refreshingly) light on antiques, but the views of the Sierra Nevada are stunning and the service flawless. It's on one of the southern slopes of the Alhambra, south of the Cuesta de Gomérez.

Parador de Granada HISTORIC HOTEL €€€
(958 22 14 40; www.parador.es; Calle Real de la Alhambra; r €315;) The most expensive *parador* in Spain can't be beaten for its location within the walls of the Alhambra and its historical connections (it was a former convent). Live like a Nasrid king, for one night at least. Book ahead.

Hotel Casa del Capitel Nazarí HISTORIC HOTEL €€
(958 21 52 60; www.hotelcasacapitel.com; Cuesta Aceituneros 6; s/d €88/110;) More Albayzín magic in a 1503 Renaissance palace which is as much architectural history lesson as plush hotel. Rooms have Moroccan inflections and the courtyard hosts art exhibits.

Hostal Molinos HOTEL €
(958 22 73 67; www.hotelmolinos.es; Calle Molinos 12; s/d/tr €29/32/45;) Don't let the 'narrowest hotel in the world' moniker put you off (and yes, it actually is – and has a certificate from the *Guinness Book of Records* to prove it): there's plenty of breathing space in Molino's nine rooms and warm hospitality in its information-stacked lobby. Situated at the

Granada

Top Sights

Albayzín E1
Alhambra F2
Capilla Real C2
Cathedral C2

Sleeping

1 Hotel Casa del Capitel Nazarí F1
2 Oasis Backpackers' Hostel D1

Eating

3 Oliver B3
4 Reca B2
5 Restaurante Arrayanes E1

foot of the Realejo, it makes an economical central option.

Oasis Backpackers' Hostel HOSTEL €
(958 21 58 48; www.oasisgranada.com; Placeta Correo Viejo 3; dm/d €18/40;) Bohemian digs in a bohemian quarter, Oasis is seconds away from the bars on Calle de Elvira. There's free internet access, a rooftop terrace and personal safes. As backpacker's hostels go, it's a gem.

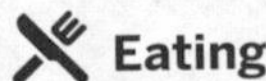

Eating

Granada is one of the last bastions of that fantastic practice of free tapas with every drink, and some have an international flavour. The labyrinthine Albayzín holds a wealth of eateries tucked away in the narrow streets. Calle Caldereria Nueva is a fascinating muddle of *teterías* (tearooms) and Arabic-influenced takeaways.

TOP CHOICE **Restaurante Arrayanes** MOROCCAN €
(958 22 84 01; Cuesta Marañas 4; mains €8.50-19; from 8pm) The best Moroccan food in a city that is well known for its Moorish throwbacks? Recline on lavish patterned seating, try the rich fruity tagine casseroles and make your decision. No alcohol.

Parador de Granada INTERNATIONAL €€
(958 22 14 40; Calle Real de la Alhambra; mains €19-22; 8am-11pm) Even a jaded, jilted, world-weary cynic would come over all romantic in this dreamy setting. The Spanish food has Moroccan and French influences, and it tastes all the better for being taken inside the Alhambra.

El Ají MODERN SPANISH €
(San Miguel Bajo 9; mains €12-20;) A cool, modern (tiny) interior, soft jazz, and a menu of nontraditional meat and vegetarian choices make Ají different in the way that only Granada can be. It's at the western end of the Albayzín, off Calle de Santa Isabel La Real.

Reca TAPAS €
(Plaza de la Trinidad; raciones €8; closed Tue) A tapas classic rightly famous for its *salmorejo* (thicker version of gazpacho) and its all-through-the-afternoon food service.

Oliver SEAFOOD €
(Calle Pescadería 12; mains €12-18; closed Sun) Sandwiched in between Plazas Bib-Rambla and Trinidad, this is a favourite lunchtime office-worker stop, revered for its fried fish.

Entertainment

The excellent monthly *Guía de Granada* (€1), available from kiosks, lists entertainment venues and tapas bars.

Situated above and to the northwest of the city centre, and offering panoramic views over the Alhambra, the Sacromonte is Granada's centuries-old *gitano* (Roma) quarter. The Sacromonte caves harbour touristy flamenco haunts, which you can prebook through hotels and travel agencies; some offer free transport. Try the Friday or Saturday midnight shows at **Los Tarantos** (☎day 958 22 45 25, night 958 22 24 92; Camino del Sacromonte 9; admission €24) for a lively experience.

Peña de la Platería FLAMENCO
(Placeta de Toqueros 7) Buried deep in the Albayzín warren, this is a genuine aficionados' club with a large outdoor patio. Dramatic 9.30pm performances take place on Thursday or Saturday in an adjacent room and cost €12.

El Eshavira LIVE MUSIC
(Postigo de la Cuna 2; ⏲from 10pm) Duck down a spooky alley to this shadowy haunt of flamenco and jazz. It is jam-packed on Thursday and Sunday, the performance nights.

Information

Regional tourist office (www.turismodegranada.org; Plaza de Mariana Pineda 10; ⏲9am-8pm Mon-Fri, 10am-2pm & 4-7pm Sat, 10am-3pm Sun May-Sep)

Municipal tourist office (www.granadatur.com; Calle Almona del Campillo, 2; ⏲9am-7pm Mon-Fri, to 6pm Sat, 10am-2pm Sun)

Getting There & Away

AIR Destinations from Granada's airport include Madrid, Barcelona, Milan and Bologna. **Autocares J González** (www.autocaresjosegonzalez.com) runs buses between the airport and the city centre (€3, five daily) on Gran Vía de Colón.

BUS Granada's **bus station** (Carretera de Jaén) is 3km northwest of the city centre. **Alsina Graells** (☎902 42 22 42; www.alsa.es) runs to Córdoba (€12.50, 2¾ hours direct, nine daily), Seville (€19.30, three hours direct, eight daily), Málaga (€9.75, 1½ hours direct, 16 daily) and Madrid (€16.30, five to six hours, 10 to 13 daily).

TRAIN The **train station** (Avenida de Andaluces) is 1.5km west of the centre. Trains run to/from Seville (€23.85, three hours, four daily), Almería (€15.90, 2¼ hours, four daily), Ronda (€13.50, three hours, three daily), Algeciras (€20.10, 4½ hours, three daily), Madrid (€66.80, four to five hours, one or two daily), Valencia (€50.60, 7½ to eight hours, one daily) and Barcelona (€62.10, 12 hours, one daily).

Costa de Almería

The coast east of Almería in eastern Andalucía is perhaps the last section of Spain's Mediterranean coast where you can have a beach to yourself. This is Spain's sunniest region – even in late March it can be warm enough to strip off and take in the rays.

Sights & Activities

Alcazaba FORTRESS
(Calle Almanzor s/n; adult/EU citizen €1.50/free; ⏲9am-8.30pm Tue-Sun Apr-Oct, to 6.30pm Tue-Sun Nov-Mar) An enormous 10th-century Muslim fortress, the Alcazaba is the highlight of Almería City.

Cabo de Gata BEACHES
The best thing about the region is the wonderful coastline and semidesert scenery of the **Cabo de Gata** promontory. All along the 50km coast from El Cabo de Gata village to Agua Amarga, some of the most beautiful and empty beaches on the Mediterranean alternate with precipitous cliffs and scattered villages. The main village is laid-back **San José**, with excellent beaches nearby, such as **Playa de los Genoveses** and **Playa de Mónsul**.

Sleeping & Eating

ALMERÍA CITY

TOP CHOICE **Hotel Costasol** HOTEL €
(☎950 23 40 11; www.hotelcostasol.com; Paseo de Almería 58; r €54; P❄@☎) It's amazing what some red colour accents and a clean, simple but funky refurb can do. Factor in the sleek reception, enormous bathrooms, spacious communal areas and stylish basement restaurant, and you won't find a better hotel for this price in Andalucía.

Hotel Torreluz HOTEL €€
(☎950 23 43 99; www.torreluz.com; Plaza de las Flores 2 & 3; s/d 2-star €39/64, 3-star €56/74; P❄☎) Burnt-plum-coloured walls, comfortable beds and good prices make this one of Almería's best-value places to stay.

CABO DE GATA

Sanctuario San Jośe HOTEL €€
(☎902 87 73 88; www.elsantuariosanjose.es; Camino de Calahiguera 9, San José; s/d €64/79; P❄) This refurbished 28-room brilliant-white hotel offers minimal yet friendly design with attractive lounging and dining terraces. Its Anicette restaurant (mains €15 to €24) has a strong reputation locally.

Hostal Sol Bahía HOTEL €€
(☎950 38 03 07; Avenida de San José, San José; d €40-70; ❄) The Sol Bahía and its sister establishment, Hostal Bahía Plaza across the street, are in the centre of San José and have functional, clean rooms in bright, modern buildings.

Restaurante Mediterraneo SEAFOOD €€
(Puerto Deportivo de San José, San José; mains €10-22) Last stop in a run of similarly good seafood restaurants near the marina, this one has particularly friendly staff and a less frantic atmosphere than some of its neighbours.

ℹ Information

Regional tourist office (Parque de Nicolás Salmerón, Almería City; ⏲9am-7pm Mon-Fri, 10am-2pm Sat & Sun)

ℹ Getting There & Away

AIR Almería **airport** (☎950 21 37 00), 10km east of the city centre, receives flights from several European countries, as well as Barcelona, Madrid and Melilla.

BOAT There are daily sailings to/from Melilla, Nador (Morocco) and Ghazaouet (Algeria). The tourist office has details.

BUS Destinations served from Almería's **bus station** (☎950 26 20 98) include Granada (€13.45, 2¼ hours, 10 daily), Málaga (€16, 3¼ hours, 10 daily), Murcia (€17.25, 2½ hours, 10 daily), Madrid (€25, seven hours, five daily) and Valencia (€35.65, 8½ hours, five daily).

TRAIN Daily trains run to Granada (€15.90, 2¼ hours), Seville (€38.15, 5½ hours) and Madrid (€44.10, 6¾ hours).

Málaga

POP 720,000

The exuberant port city of Málaga may be uncomfortably close to the overdeveloped Costa del Sol, but it's a wonderful amalgam of old Andalucian town and modern metropolis. The centre presents the visitor with narrow, old streets and wide, leafy boulevards, beautiful gardens and impressive monuments, fashionable shops and a burgeoning cultural life. The city's terrific bars and nightlife, the last word in Málaga *joie de vivre*, stay open very late.

Sights & Activities

TOP CHOICE **Museo Picasso Málaga** ART MUSEUM
(☎902 44 33 77; www.museopicassomalaga.org; Palacio de Buenavista, Calle San Agustín 8; permanent/temporary collection €6/4.50, combinted ticket €8, seniors & under-26 students half-price; ⏲10am-8pm Tue-Thu & Sun, to 9pm Fri & Sat; 👪) The hottest attraction on Málaga's tourist scene is tucked away on a pedestrian street in what was medieval Málaga's *judería*. The Museo Picasso Málaga has 204 Picasso works and also stages high-quality temporary exhibitions on Picasso themes. The Picasso paintings, drawings, engravings, sculptures and ceramics on show (many never previously on public display) span almost every phase and influence of the artist's colourful career. Picasso was born in Málaga in 1881 but moved to northern Spain with his family when he was nine.

Casa Natal de Picasso (Plaza de la Merced 15; admission €1; ⏲9.30am-8pm), Picasso's birthplace, is a centre for exhibitions and academic research on contemporary art, with a few compelling items of personal memorabilia and a well-stocked shop. Entrance is free with the Picasso museum combined ticket.

Cathedral CHURCH
(www.3planalfa.es/catedralmalaga; Calle Molina Lario; admission €3.50; ⏲10am-5.30pm Mon-Fri, to 5pm Fri, closed Sun & holidays) Preserved rather magnificently, like an unfinished Beethoven symphony, Málaga's cathedral was begun in the 16th century on the former site of the main mosque and never properly completed. Consequently the building exhibits a mishmash of architectural styles absorbed over two centuries of construction. The entrance is on Calle Císter.

Alcazaba CASTLE
(Calle Alcazabilla; admission €2.10, incl Castillo de Gibralfaro €3.40; ⏲9.30am-8pm Tue-Sun Apr-Oct) At the lower, western end of the Gibralfaro hill, the wheelchair-accessible Alcazaba was the palace-fortress of Málaga's Muslim governors, dating from 1057. The brick path winds uphill, interspersed with arches and stone walls, and is refreshingly cool in summer. Roman artefacts and fleeting views of the harbour and city enliven the walk, while honeysuckle, roses and jasmine perfume the air.

Castillo de Gibralfaro CASTLE
(admission €2.10; ⏲9am-9pm Apr-Sep, to 6pm Oct-Mar) Above the Alcazaba rises the older Castillo de Gibralfaro, built by Abd ar-Rahman I, the 8th-century Cordoban emir, and rebuilt in the 14th and 15th centuries. Nothing much remains of the castle's interior,

Málaga

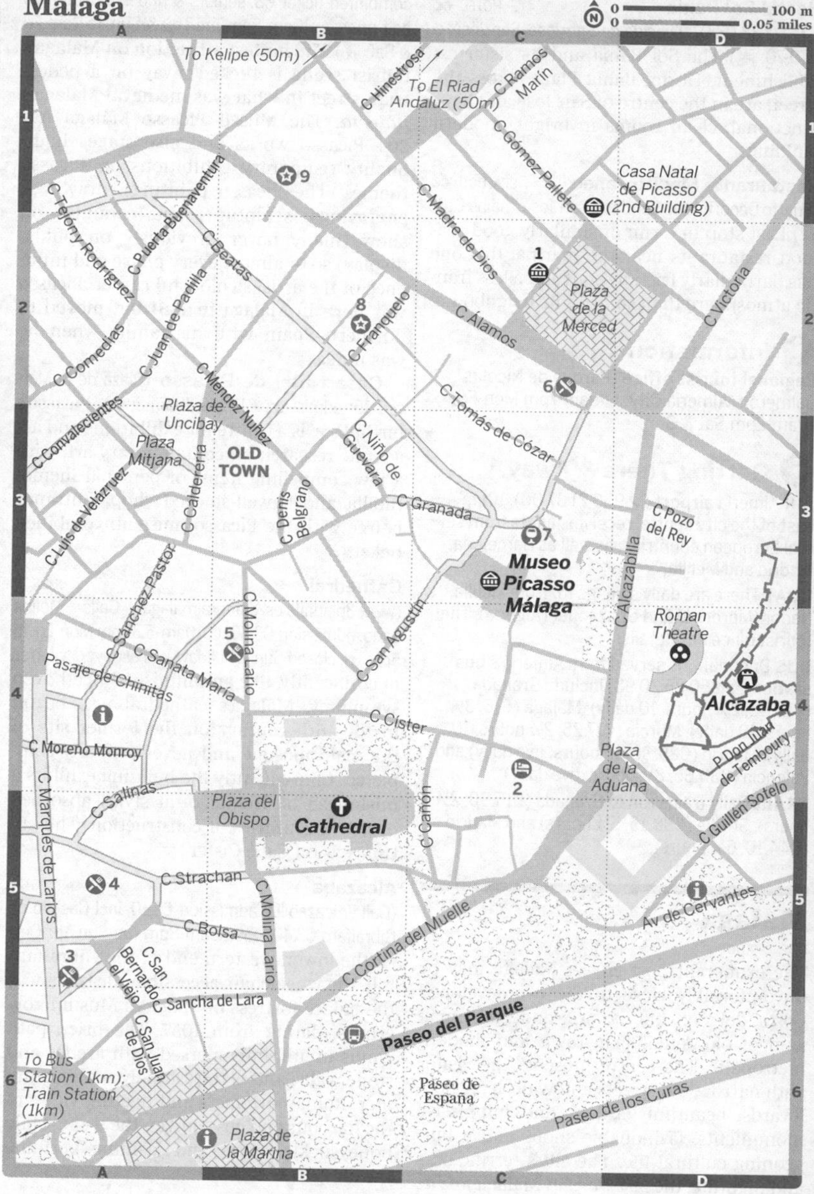

but the walkway around the ramparts affords exhilarating views and there's a tiny museum with a military focus.

Beaches BEACHES

Sandy city beaches stretch several kilometres in each direction from the port. **Playa de la Malagueta**, handy to the city centre, has some excellent bars and restaurants close by. **Playa de Pedregalejo** and **Playa del Palo**, about 4km east of the centre, are popular and reachable by bus 11 from Paseo del Parque.

Málaga

Top Sights

Sights

Sleeping

Eating

Drinking

Entertainment

Sleeping

El Riad Andaluz HOTEL €€

(952 21 36 40; www.elriadandaluz.com; Calle Hinestrosa 24; s/d €70/86;) Colourful and exotic, this gorgeous restored monastery in the Centro Historico offers eight rooms with Moroccan decor set around an atmospheric patio, with tea and coffee on tap all day.

Parador Málaga Gibralfaro HOTEL €€€

(952 22 19 02; www.parador.es; Castillo de Gibralfaro; r €160-171;) With an unbeatable location up on the pine-forested Gibralfaro hill, Málaga's modern but rustic *parador* provides spectacular views of city and harbour from its upper floors, excellent terrace restaurant and rooftop pool.

Hotel Sur HOTEL €€

(952 22 48 03; www.hotel-sur.com; Calle Trinidad Grund 13; s/d/tr €52/76/100, s/d without bathroom €39/49;) A good location a goal kick away from the Plaza de la Marina adds kudos to the plain but pristine Hotel Sur's portfolio. More are added with friendly, polite staff and the availability of wi-fi in all of the rooms. It's around 250m southwest of Plaza de la Marina, off Alameda Principal.

Hotel Carlos V HOTEL €

(952 21 51 20; www.hotel-carlosvmalaga.com; Calle Císter 10; s/d €36/59;) Close to the cathedral and Picasso Museum, the Carlos V is enduringly popular. Renovated in 2008, bathrooms sparkle in their new uniform of cream-and-white tiles. Excellent standard for the price and helpful staff make this hotel a winner.

Eating

Most of the best eating places are sandwiched in the narrow streets between Calle Marqués de Larios and the cathedral.

La Rebaná TAPAS €

(Calle Molina Lario 5; tapas €4.20-8.50, raciones €7-11.50) A great, noisy tapas bar near the Picasso Museum and the cathedral. Dark wood, tall windows and exposed brick walls create a modern, minimal but laid-back space. Try the foie gras with salted nougat for a unique tapa.

Gorki TAPAS €€

(Calle Strachan 6; platos combinados €7.50-16) A popular upmarket tapas bar with pavement tables and a modern interior full of wine-barrel tables and stools. Creative tapas have a more *Sevillano* twist and the clientele is young and trendy.

Café Lepanto CAFE, SNACKS €

(Calle Marqués de Larios 7) An old-world Italianate coffee/ice-cream bar that serves as Málaga's top *confitería,* Lepanto is insanely popular, probably because most of its sweets and pastries are highly addictive. Enjoy them in the art nouveau–embellished interior, served by athletic waiters in waistcoats.

Lechuga TAPAS €

(Plaza de la Merced 1; tapas €2.50-3.50, raciones €8-10;) In this calm retreat, vegetables reign supreme and the chef does wonderful things with them, as with hummus, Indian-style *bhajis* and various inventive salads.

Drinking & Entertainment

On weekend nights, the web of narrow old streets north of Plaza de la Constitución comes alive. Look for bars around Plaza de la Merced, Plaza Mitjana and Plaza de Uncibay.

Málaga's substantial flamenco heritage has its nexus to the northwest of Plaza de la Merced. Venues here include **Kelipe** (692 82 98 85; www.kelipe.net; Calle Pena 11), a flamenco centre which puts on *muy puro* performances Thursday to Saturday at 9.30pm; entry of €15 includes one drink and tapa; reserve ahead. Intensive weekend courses in guitar and dance are also held. **Amargo** (Calle R Franquillo 3) offers Friday and Saturday night gigs, while **Vino Mio** (Calle Alamos) is a small restaurant with an international menu where musicians and dancers fill the wait for the food.

TOP CHOICE **Bodegas El Pimpi** BAR
(Calle Granada 62; ⏲11am-2am) A Málaga institution with a warren of charming rooms and mini patios, El Pimpi attracts a boisterous crowd of all nationalities and generations with its sweet wine and traditional music. Look out for the flamenco (last Monday of the month) and the signed photo of a young-looking Tony Blair.

Information

Municipal tourist office (www.malagaturismo.com, in Spanish) Plaza de la Marina (⏲9am-8pm Mar-Sep, to 6pm Oct-Feb); Casita del Jardinero (Avenida de Cervantes 1; ⏲9am-8pm Mar-Sep, to 6pm Oct-Feb)

Regional tourist office (Pasaje de Chinitas 4; www.andalucia.org; ⏲9am-7.30pm Mon-Fri, 10am-7pm Sat, 10am-2pm Sun)

Getting There & Away

AIR Málaga's busy **airport** (☎952 04 88 38), the main international gateway to Andalucía, receives flights by dozens of airlines from around Europe. The Aeropuerto train station on the Málaga–Fuengirola line is a five-minute walk from the airport. Trains run about every half-hour to Málaga-Renfe station (€2, 11 minutes) and Málaga-Centro station.

BUS Málaga's **bus station** (Paseo de los Tilos) is 1km southwest of the city centre. Frequent buses go to Seville (€16, 2½ hours), Granada (€9.75, 1½ to two hours), Córdoba (€12.50, 2½ hours) and Ronda (€9.50, 2½ hours).

TRAIN **Málaga-Renfe** (Explanada de la Estación), the main station, is around the corner from the bus station. The superfast AVE service runs to Madrid (€76.40 to €85, 2½ hours, six daily). Trains also go to Córdoba (€21 to €44, one hour, 10 daily), Seville (€19.10 to €36.40, 2½ hours, five daily) and Barcelona (€62.70 to €138, 13 or 6½ hours, two daily).

Ronda

POP 37,000 / ELEV 744M

Perched on an inland plateau riven by the 100m fissure of El Tajo gorge and surrounded by the beautiful Serranía de Ronda, Ronda is the most dramatically sited of Andalucía's *pueblos blancos* (white villages).

Sights & Activities

The **Plaza de Toros** (built 1785), considered the national home of bullfighting, is a mecca for aficionados; inside is the small but fascinating **Museo Taurino** (Calle Virgen de la Paz; admission €6; ⏲10am-8pm Apr-Sep, to 6pm Oct-Mar).

The amazing 18th-century **Puente Nuevo** (New Bridge) is an incredible engineering feat crossing the gorge to the originally Muslim Old Town (La Ciudad). At the **Casa del Rey Moro** (House of the Moorish King; Calle Santo Domingo 17), a romantically crumbling 18th-century house, supposedly built over the remains of an Islamic palace, you can visit the cliff-top gardens and climb down La Mina, a Muslim-era stairway cut inside the rock, right to the bottom of the gorge.

Also well worth a visit are the beautiful 13th-century **Baños Arabes** (Arab Baths; Hoyo San Miguel; admission €3, free on Sun; ⏲10am-7pm Mon-Fri, to 3pm Sat & Sun). Nearby, the amusing **Museo del Bandolero** (Calle de Armiñán 65; admission €3; ⏲10.30am-8pm Apr-Sep, to 6pm Oct-Mar) is dedicated to the banditry for which central Andalucía was renowned in the 19th century.

Sleeping & Eating

Hotel San Francisco HOTEL €
(☎952 87 32 99; www.hotelsanfranciscoronda.com; Calle María Cabrera 18; s/d incl breakfast €38/60; ❄) This is the best budget option in Ronda, offering a warm welcome. It was recently refurbished and upgraded from *hostal* to hotel, with facilities to match including wheelchair access.

Hotel Alavera de los Baños HOTEL €€
(☎952 87 91 43; www.alaveradelosbanos.com; Hoyo San Miguel s/n; s/d incl breakfast €70/95; ❄≋) A magical hotel with style echoes of the Arab baths next door, this one-time tannery looks like it was decorated by a departing Moor, with a flower-filled patio and pool. The sultan-sized baths are carved from a type of stucco, and their pink tinge is due to natural pigments.

Parador de Ronda HOTEL €€€
(☎952 87 75 00; www.parador.es; Plaza de España s/n; r €160-171; P❄@≋) Acres of shining marble and deep-cushioned furniture give this modern *parador* a certain appeal. The terrace is a wonderful place to drink in views of the gorge with your coffee or wine, especially at night.

TOP CHOICE **Bodega San Francisco** TAPAS €
(Calle Ruedo Alameda; raciones €6-10) Taking price, food quality, ambience and local-to-tourist ratio into account, this is the best eating joint in town – hands down.

It's situated in the Barrio San Francisco just outside the old Carlos V gate and gets regular rave reviews from travellers who have sought it out.

Information

Municipal tourist office (www.turismoderonda.es; Paseo de Blas Infante; ⌚10am-7.30pm Mon-Fri May-Sep, to 6pm Oct-Apr, 10.15am-2pm & 3.30-6.30pm Sat, Sun & holidays)

Regional tourist office (www.andalucia.org; Plaza de España 1; ⌚9am-7.30pm Mon-Fri May-Sep, to 6pm Oct-Apr, 10am-2pm Sat)

Getting There & Away

BUS From the **bus station** (Plaza Concepción García Redondo 2), there are frequent services to/from Málaga (€9.20, two hours), Seville (€10.85, 2½ hours), Cádiz (€13.85, 2½ hours) and Málaga (€10.21, 1½ hours, at least three daily).

TRAIN From the **train station** (Avenida de Andalucía), trains run to/from Algeciras (€7.40 to €18.70, 1¾ hours, six daily), Granada (€13.50, 2½ hours, three daily), Córdoba (€31.50, 2½ hours, two daily) and Málaga (€9.75, two hours, one daily except Sunday).

Algeciras

POP 111,300

An unattractive industrial and fishing town between Tarifa and Gibraltar, Algeciras is the major port linking Spain with Morocco. Keep your wits about you, and ignore the legions of moneychangers, drug-pushers and ticket-hawkers who hang out here. The **tourist office** (Calle Juan de la Cierva s/n; ⌚9am-7.30pm Mon-Fri, 9.30am-3pm Sat & Sun) is near the port.

Getting There & Away

BOAT FRS (☎956 68 18 30; www.frs.es) runs the fastest ferry services from Algeciras to Tangier (passenger/car/motorcycle €37/93/31, 70 minutes, eight daily).

BUS The bus station is on Calle San Bernardo. **Comes** (☎956 65 34 56) has buses for La Línea (for Gibraltar; €2, 30 minutes) every half-hour, Tarifa (€2, 30 minutes, 13 daily), Cádiz (€11, 2½ hours, 13 daily) and Seville (€17, 2½ hours, six daily).

TRAIN The **train station** (☎956 63 10 05) runs services to/from Madrid (€68.70, six or 11 hours, two daily) and Granada (€20.20, four hours, three daily).

Cádiz

POP 128,600

Cádiz, widely considered the oldest continuously inhabited settlement in Europe, is crammed onto the head of a promontory like an overcrowded ocean liner. Columbus sailed from here on his second and fourth voyages, and after his success in the Americas, the town grew into Spain's richest and most cosmopolitan city in the 18th century. The best time to visit is during the February *carnaval* (carnival), which rivals Rio in terms of outrageous exuberance.

Sights & Activities

Catedral — CHURCH

(Plaza de la Catedral; adult/student €5/3, free 7-8pm Tue-Fri, 11am-1pm Sun; ⌚10am-6.30pm Mon-Sat, 1.30-6.30pm Sun) The yellow-domed 18th-century cathedral is the city's most striking landmark. From a separate entrance on Plaza de la Catedral, climb to the top of the **Torre de Poniente** (Western Tower; adult/child/senior €4/3/3; ⌚10am-6pm, to 8pm mid-Jun–mid-Sep) for marvellous vistas.

You can also get your bearings by climbing up the baroque **Torre Tavira** (Calle Marqués del Real Tesoro 10; adult/student €4/3.30; ⌚10am-6pm, to 8pm mid-Jun–mid-Sep), the highest of Cádiz' old watchtowers, which features sweeping views of the city.

Museo de Cádiz — MUSEUM

(Plaza de Mina; adult/EU citizen €1.50/free; ⌚2.30-8.30pm Tue, 9am-8.30pm Wed-Sat, 9.30am-2.30pm Sun) The Museo de Cádiz has a magnificent collection of archaeological remains, as well as an excellent fine-art collection.

For more history, the city's lively **central market** (Plaza de las Flores) is on the site of a former Phoenician temple.

Playa de la Victoria — BEACH

The broad, sandy Playa de la Victoria, a lovely Atlantic beach, stretches about 4km along the peninsula from its beginning 1.5km beyond the Puertas de Tierra. Bus 1 'Plaza España–Cortadura' from Plaza de España will get you there.

Sleeping & Eating

TOP CHOICE Hotel Argantonio — HOTEL €€

(☎956 21 16 40; www.hotelargantonio.com; Calle Argantonio 3; s/d incl breakfast €90/107; ❄@📶) A very attractive small new hotel in the old city with an appealing Mudéjar accent to its decor. Staff are welcoming, and

SPAIN ALGECIRAS

the rooms are comfortable with wi-fi access and flat-screen TVs.

Hospedería Las Cortes de Cádiz HOTEL €€€ (☎956 21 26 68; www.hotellascortes.com; Calle San Francisco 9; s/d incl breakfast €107/148; P❄@📶) This excellent hotel occupies a remodelled 1850s mansion. The 36 rooms, each themed around a figure, place or event associated with the Cortes de Cádiz, sport classical furnishings and modern comforts. The hotel also has a roof terrace, Jacuzzi and small gym.

Casa Caracol HOSTEL € (☎956 26 11 66; www.caracolcasa.com; Calle Suárez de Salazar 4; dm/hammock incl breakfast €16/10; @📶) Casa Caracol is the only backpacker hostel in the old town. Friendly, as only Cádiz can be, it has bunk dorms for four and eight, a communal kitchen and a roof terrace with hammocks. Green initiatives include recycling, water efficiency and plans for solar panels.

Arrocería La Pepa RICE DISHES €€ (☎956 26 38 21; Paseo Maritimo 14; paella per person €12-17) To get a decent paella you have to leave the old town behind and head a few kilometres southeast along Playa de la Victoria – an appetite-rousing predinner walk or a quick ride on the number 1 bus. Either method is worth it. The fish in La Pepa's seafood paella tastes as if it's just jumped the 100 or so metres from the Atlantic onto your plate.

El Aljibe TAPAS €€ (www.pablogrosso.com; Calle Plocia 25; tapas €2-3.50, mains €10-15) Cadiz-native chef Pablo Grosso concocts delicious combinations of the traditional and the adventurous. Try the pheasant breast stuffed with dates and the *solomillo ibérico* (Iberian pork sirloin) with Emmental cheese, ham and piquant peppers. You can enjoy his creations as tapas in the stone-walled downstairs bar.

Information

Municipal tourist office (Paseo de Canalejas s/n; ⌚8.30am-6pm Mon-Fri, 9am-5pm Sat & Sun)

Regional tourist office (Avenida Ramón de Carranza s/n; ⌚9am-7.30pm Mon-Fri, 10am-2pm Sat, Sun & holidays)

Getting There & Away

BUS Destinations include Seville (€11, 1¾ hours, 10 daily), Tarifa (€8.46, two hours, five daily), Ronda (€13, three hours, two daily), Málaga (€20, four hours, six daily) and Granada (€28, five hours, four daily).

TRAIN From the **train station** (☎902 24 02 02) trains run daily to Seville (€12.75, two hours), three per day to Córdoba (€23.85 to €38.20, three hours) and two to Madrid (€70, five hours). High-speed AVE services to Madrid are slated for commencement by 2012.

Tarifa

POP 17,700

Windy, laid-back Tarifa is so close to Africa that you can almost hear the call to prayer issuing from Morocco's minarets. The town is a bohemian haven of cafes and crumbling Moorish ruins. There's also a lively windsurfing and kitesurfing scene.

Stretching west are the long, sandy (and largely deserted) beaches of the Costa de la Luz (Coast of Light), backed by cool pine forests and green hills.

Sights

A wander round the old town's narrow streets, of mainly Islamic origin, is an appetiser for Morocco. The Mudéjar **Puerta de Jerez** was built after the Reconquista. Wind your way to the mainly 15th-century **Iglesia de San Mateo** (Calle Sancho IV El Bravo; ⌚9am-1pm & 5.30-8.30pm). South of the church, the **Mirador El Estrecho**, atop part of the castle walls, has spectacular views across to Africa, only 14km away. The 10th-century **Castillo de Guzmán** (Calle Guzmán El Bueno; admission €2; ⌚11am-4pm) is also worth a wander; tickets for the latter must be bought at the tourist office.

Activities

Beaches

On the isthmus leading out to Isla de las Palomas, tiny **Playa Chica** lives up to its name. Spectacular **Playa de los Lances** is a different matter stretching northwest for 10km to the huge sand dune at **Ensenada de Valdevaqueros**.

Kitesurfing & Windsurfing

Tarifa now has around 30 kitesurf and windsurf schools, many of them with offices or shops along Calle Batalla del Salado or on Calle Mar Adriático. Most rent equipment and run classes. Most of the action occurs along the coast between Tarifa and Punta Paloma, 11km northwest.

Horse Riding

Located on Playa de los Lances, **Aventura Ecuestre** (956 23 66 32; www.aventuraecuestre.com; Hotel Dos Mares, N340 Km79.5) and **Hurricane Hípica** (646 964279; Hurricane Hotel, N340 Km78) both rent well-kept horses with excellent guides. An hour's beach ride costs €30. Three- or four-hour inland rides cost €70.

Whale-watching

The Strait of Gibraltar is a top site for viewing whales and dolphins. Killer whales visit in July and August, huge sperm and fin whales lurk here from spring to autumn, and pilot whales and three types of dolphin stay all year. Several organisations in Tarifa run daily two- to 2½-hour boat trips to observe these marine mammals, and most offer a free second trip if you don't at least see dolphins. **Firmm** (956 62 70 08; www.firmm.org; Calle Pedro Cortés 4; Mar-Oct) is the best and uses every trip to record data.

Sleeping & Eating

TOP CHOICE Posada La Sacristía HISTORIC HOTEL €€
(956 68 17 59; www.lasacristia.net; Calle San Donato 8; r incl breakfast €115-135) Tarifa's most elegant accommodation is in a beautifully renovated 17th-century townhouse with both Moorish and Thai Buddhist influences. The 10 white rooms have some lovely details.

Hostal Africa HOTEL €
(956 68 02 20; Calle María Antonia Toledo 12; s/d €50/65, without bathroom €35/50; closed 24 Dec-31 Jan) The well-travelled owners of this revamped house know just what travellers need. Rooms are attractive and there's an expansive terrace with wonderful views. Short-term storage for boards, bicycles and baggage is available.

Arte Vida Hotel HOTEL €€€
(956 68 52 46; www.hotelartevidatarifa.com; N340 Km79.3; s/d incl breakfast €120/140; P) The stylish Arte Vida, just over 5km from the town centre, combines attractive, medium-sized rooms with an excellent restaurant that has stunning views. Its grassy garden opens right onto the beach.

Chilimoso ARABIC €
(Calle Peso 6; dishes €4-6;) This tiny place serves tasty vegan and vegetarian food with oriental leanings. Try the falafel with hummus, tzatziki and salad.

Mandrágora MOROCCAN, ARABIC €€
(956 68 12 91; Calle Independencia 3; Mains €12-18; from 8pm Mon-Sat) Follow the 'listed in Lonely Planet' sign to this intimate place with its Moroccan-Arabic-inspired menu. Try the fruity lamb tagine or monkfish in a wild mushroom sauce.

Information

Tourist office (www.aytotarifa.com, in Spanish; Paseo de la Alameda; 10am-2pm daily, 4-6pm Mon-Fri Oct-May, 6-8pm Mon-Fri Jun-Sep)

Getting There & Away

BUS Comes (956 68 40 38; Calle Batalla del Salado 13) runs daily buses to Cádiz (€8.45, 1¾ hours), Algeciras (€2, 30 minutes), La Línea de la Concepción (for Gibraltar; €3.83, 45 minutes), Seville (€17.05, three hours) and Málaga (€12.75, two hours).

BOAT FRS (956 68 18 30; www.frs.es; Estación Marítima) runs fast ferries between Tarifa and Tangier (passenger/car/motorcycle €37/93/31, 35 minutes, eight daily).

GIBRALTAR

POP 28,000

The British colony of Gibraltar is like 1960s Britain on a sunny day, with Bobbies, double-decker buses and fried-egg-and-chip-style eateries. In British hands since 1713, the island was the starting point for the Muslim conquest of Iberia a thousand years earlier. Spain has never fully accepted UK control of the island but, for the moment at least, talk of joint sovereignty seems to have gone cold. Inhabitants speak English and Spanish, and signs are in English.

Sights & Activities

In town, the **Gibraltar Museum** (Bomb House Lane; adult/under 12yr £2/1; 10am-6pm Mon-Fri, to 2pm Sat), with its interesting historical collection and Muslim-era bathhouse, is worth a peek.

The large **Upper Rock Nature Reserve** (adult/child incl attractions £10/5, vehicle £2, pedestrian excl attractions £0.50; 9.30am-7.15pm, last entry 6.45pm), covering most of the upper rock, has spectacular views. The rock's most famous inhabitants are its colony of Barbary macaques, the only wild primates in Europe. Some of these hang around the **Apes' Den** near the middle cable-car station; others can often be seen at the top station or Great Siege Tunnels. Other attractions include **St**

Michael's Cave, a large natural grotto renowned for its stalagmites and stalactites, and the **Great Siege Tunnels**, a series of galleries hewn from the rock by the British during the Great Siege by the Spaniards (1779–83) to provide new gun emplacements.

Dolphin-watching is an option from April to September. Most boats go from Watergardens Quay or adjacent Marina Bay. The trips last about 1½ hours and cost around £20 per adult. Tourist offices have full details.

Sleeping & Eating

Compared with Spain, expect to pay through the nose for accommodation and food.

Bristol Hotel HOTEL €€
(☎76800; www.bristolhotel.gi; 10 Cathedral Sq; s/d/tr £63/81/93; P❄📶🏊) Veterans of bucket-and-spade British seaside holidays can wax nostalgic at the stuck-in-the-'70s Bristol with its creaking floorboards, red patterned carpets and Hi-de-Hi reception staff. Arrivals from other climes will enjoy the attractive walled garden, small swimming pool and prime location just off the main street.

Cannon Hotel HOTEL €€
(☎51711; www.cannonhotel.gi; 9 Cannon Lane; d incl breakfast £47, s/d without bathroom £26.50/38.50) This is a small, budget-priced hotel right in the main shopping area that recalls a kind of Britain of yesteryear with its flowery decor.

Clipper BRITISH €€
(78B Irish Town; mains £3.50-9; 🍴) Full of that ubiquitous naval decor, the Clipper offers real pub grub, genuine atmosphere and Premier League football on big-screen TV. Picture a little piece of Portsmouth floated round the Bay of Biscay to keep the Brits happy. Full English breakfast is served from 9.30am to 11am.

House of Sacarello INTERNATIONAL €€
(57 Irish Town; daily specials £7-11.50; ⏰9am-7.30pm Mon-Fri, to 3pm Sat, closed Sun) A restaurant with many hats (and nooks) in a converted coffee warehouse that serves light lunches, pastas, salads, quiche and soup. Or you can linger over afternoon tea between 3pm and 7.30pm.

Information

Money

The currency is the Gibraltar pound. You can also use euros or pounds sterling.

Telephone

To dial Gibraltar from Spain, you precede the five-digit local number with the code ☎00350; from other countries, dial the international access code, then the Gibraltar country code (☎350) and local number. To phone Spain from Gibraltar, just dial the nine-digit Spanish number.

Tourist Information

Gibraltar Tourist Board (www.gibraltar.gov.uk; Duke of Kent House, Cathedral Sq; ⏰9am-5.30pm Mon-Thu, to 5.15pm Fri)

Tourist office (Grand Casemates Sq; ⏰9am-5.30pm Mon-Fri, 10am-3pm Sat, to 1pm Sun & holidays)

Visas

To enter Gibraltar, you need a passport or EU national identity card. EU, USA, Canadian, Australian, New Zealand and South African passport-holders are among those who do not need visas for Gibraltar.

Getting There & Away

AIR easyJet (www.easyjet.com) flies approximately 15 times weekly from London Gatwick, **British Airways** (www.ba.com) operate seven weekly flights from London Heathrow and **Monarch Airlines** (www.flymonarch.com) flies daily to/from London Luton and thrice weekly to/from Manchester.

BUS There are no regular buses to Gibraltar, but La Línea de la Concepción bus station is only a five-minute walk from the border.

CAR & MOTORCYCLE Snaking vehicle queues at the 24-hour border and congested traffic in Gibraltar often make it easier to park in La Línea and walk across the border. To take a car into Gibraltar (free) you need an insurance certificate, registration document, nationality plate and driving licence.

FERRY Transcoma (☎in Spain 902 10 41 01, in Gibraltar 200 61 720; www.transcomalines.com) operates ferries between Algerciras and Gibraltar (one way/return €8/14, five daily).

EXTREMADURA

A sparsely populated stretch of vast skies and open plains, Extremadura is far enough from most beaten tourist trails to give you a genuine sense of exploration.

Trujillo

POP 9800

With its medieval architecture, leafy courtyards, fruit gardens, churches and convents, Trujillo truly is one of the most captivating small towns in Spain. It can't be much bigger now than it was in 1529, when its most famous son, Francisco Pizarro, set off with his three brothers and a few buddies for an expedition that culminated in the bloody conquest of the Incan empire.

Sights

Plaza Mayor SQUARE

A large equestrian **Pizarro statue** by American Charles Rumsey looks down over the spectacular Plaza Mayor. On the plaza's south side, carved images of Pizarro and his lover Inés Yupanqui (sister of the Inca emperor Atahualpa) decorate the corner of the 16th-century **Palacio de la Conquista**. Through a twisting alley above the Palacio de la Conquista is the **Palacio Juan Pizarro de Orellana** (admission free; 10am-1pm & 4.30-6.30pm Mon-Sat, 10am-12.30pm Sun), converted from miniature fortress to Renaissance mansion by one of the Pizarro cousin conquistadors. Overlooking the Plaza Mayor from the northeast corner is the 16th-century **Iglesia de San Martín** (adult/under 12yr €1.40/free; 10am-2pm & 4-7pm) with delicate Gothic ceiling tracing, stunning stained-glass windows and a grand organ (climb up to the choir loft for the best view).

Upper Town HISTORIC AREA

The 900m of walls circling the upper town date from Muslim times and it was here that the newly settled noble families built their mansions and churches after the Reconquista.

The 13th-century **Iglesia de Santa María la Mayor** (adult/under 12yr €1.40/free; 10am-2pm & 4-7pm) has a mainly Gothic nave and a Romanesque tower that you can ascend (all 106 steps) for fabulous views.

At the top of the hill, Trujillo's impressive **castle** (adult/under 12yr €1.40/free; 10am-2pm & 4-7pm) has 10th-century Muslim origins (evident by the horseshoe-arch gateway just inside the main entrance) and was later strengthened by the Christians. Patrol the battlements for magnificent 360-degree sweeping views.

Sleeping & Eating

TOP CHOICE **Posada Dos Orillas** HISTORIC HOTEL €€

(927 65 90 79; www.dosorillas.com; Calle de Cambrones 6; d €70-90 Sun-Thu, €80-107 Fri & Sat) This tastefully renovated 16th-century mansion in the walled town once served as a silk-weaving centre. The rooms replicate Spanish colonial taste; those in the older wing bear the names of the 'seven Trujillos' of Extremadura and the Americas. It has a pleasant courtyard restaurant.

El Mirador de las Monjas HOTEL €€

(927 65 92 23; www.elmiradordelasmonjas.com, in Spanish; Plaza de Santiago 2; s/d incl breakfast €50/60 Mon-Thu, €60/70 Fri-Sun) High in the old town, this contemporary six-room *hostería* has large, minimalist rooms with clean lines and stylish bathrooms.

TOP CHOICE **Restaurante La Troya** TRADITIONAL SPANISH €

(Plaza Mayor 10; set menú €15) Mention Trujillo to anyone in Spain and chances are they'll have heard of La Troya – the restaurant is an *extremeño* institution. You will be directed to one of several dining areas and there be presented with plates of tortilla, chorizo, cheese and salad, followed by a three-course menu (with truly gargantuan portions), including wine and water.

Restaurante Pizarro TRADITIONAL SPANISH €€

(Plaza Mayor 13; meals €30-40; Wed-Mon) Next door to La Troya, much quieter and with arguably better food (they've been winning gastronomic awards since 1985). The dining room is pleasantly unpretentious, while the menu includes dishes like chicken stuffed with truffles, and *frito de cordero* (lamb stew).

Information

Tourist office (www.trujillo.es, in Spanish; Plaza Mayor s/n; 10am-2pm & 4-7pm Oct-May, 10am-2pm & 5-8pm Jun-Sep)

Getting There & Away

The **bus station** (927 32 12 02; Avenida de Miajadas) is 500m south of Plaza Mayor. There are services to/from Madrid (€19.30 to €31.40, three to 4¼ hours, five daily), Cáceres (€4.20, 40 minutes, eight daily) and Mérida (€8.15, 1½ hours, three daily).

Cáceres

POP 89,100

Cáceres' *ciudad monumental* (old town), built in the 15th and 16th centuries, is perfectly preserved. The town's action centres on Plaza Mayor, at the foot of the Old Town, and busy Avenida de España, a short distance south.

Sights & Activities

Plaza de Santa María
SQUARE

Enter the Old Town from Plaza Mayor through the 18th-century **Arco de la Estrella**, built with a wide span for the passage of carriages. The 15th-century Gothic cathedral, **Concatedral de Santa María** (Plaza de Santa María; admission €1; ⌚9.30am-2pm & 5.30-8.30pm Mon-Sat, 9.30-11.50am & 5.30-7.15pm Sun May-Sep), creates an impressive opening scene. Climb the **bell tower** (€1) for stunning views.

Also on the plaza are the **Palacio Episcopal** (Bishop's Palace), the **Palacio de Mayoralgo** and the **Palacio de Ovando**, all in 16th-century Renaissance style. Heading back through Arco de la Estrella, you can climb the 12th-century **Torre de Bujaco** (Plaza Mayor; adult/under 12yr €2/free; ⌚10am-2pm & 5.30-8.30pm Mon-Sat, 10am-2pm Sun Apr-Sep, 10am-2pm & 4.30-7.30pm Mon-Sat, 10am-2pm Sun Oct-Mar) for good stork's-eye views of the Plaza Mayor.

Plaza de San Mateo & Plaza de las Veletas
SQUARE

From Plaza de San Jorge, Cuesta de la Compañía climbs to Plaza de San Mateo and the **Iglesia de San Mateo**, traditionally the church of the land-owning nobility and built on the site of the town's mosque.

Below the square is the excellent **Museo de Cáceres** (Plaza de las Veletas 1; adult/EU citizens €1.20/free; ⌚9am-2.30pm & 5-8.15pm Tue-Sat, 10.15am-2.30pm Sun) in a 16th-century mansion built over an evocative 12th-century *aljibe* (cistern), the only surviving element of Cáceres' Muslim castle. It has an impressive archaeological section and an excellent fine-arts display (open only in the mornings), with works by Picasso, Miró, Tapiès and other renowned Spanish painters and sculptors.

Sleeping & Eating

Hotel Casa Don Fernando
BOUTIQUE HOTEL €€

(☎927 21 42 79; www.casadonfernando.com; Plaza Mayor 30; d €60-140; ❄📶) Arguably the classiest midrange choice in Cáceres, this boutique hotel sits on Plaza Mayor directly opposite the Arco de la Estrella. Spread over four floors, there are rooms on each floor with plaza views, and the designer rooms and bathrooms are tastefully chic. Parking is €9.

Hotel Iberia
HOTEL €

(☎927 24 76 34; www.iberiahotel.com, in Spanish; Calle de los Pintores 2; s/d €46/60; ❄) Located in an 18th-century former palace just off Plaza Mayor, this friendly and family-run 36-room hotel has public areas that look like an old-world museum piece, decorated with antique furnishings. The rooms are more subdued with parquet floors, cream walls and pale-grey tiled bathrooms.

Mesón El Asador
TRADITIONAL SPANISH €€

(Calle de Moret 34; raciones €6-8, meals €20-30, set menus €15-26; ⌚closed Sun) Enter the dining room and you get the picture right away: one wall is covered with hung hams. It's often packed to the rafters with locals, not least because you won't taste better roast pork (or lamb) in town. Its bar also serves *bocadillos* and a wide range of *raciones,* while the *menú especial* (€26) is terrific value.

Restaurante Torre de Sande
FUSION €€

(☎927 21 11 47; www.torredesande.com, in Spanish; Calle Condes 3; meals €35-45; ⌚lunch & dinner Tue-Sat, lunch Sun) Dine in the pretty courtyard on dishes like *salmorejo de cerezas del jerte con queso de cabra* (cherry-based cold soup with goat's cheese) at this elegant gourmet restaurant. More modestly, stop for a drink and a tapa (€4) at the interconnecting Tapería.

Information

Junta de Extremadura tourist office (www.turismoextremadura.com; Plaza Mayor 3; ⌚8.30am-2.30pm & 4-6pm or 5-7pm Mon-Fri, 10am-2pm Sat & Sun)

Municipal tourist office (Calle de los Olmos 3; ⌚10am-2pm & 4.30-7.30pm or 5.30-8.30pm)

Getting There & Away

BUS The **bus station** (⌚927 23 25 50; Carretera de Sevilla) has services to Trujillo (€4.20, 40 minutes, eight daily) and Mérida (€5.35, 50 minutes, two to four daily).

TRAIN Up to five trains per day run to/from Madrid (€25.80 to €38.50, four hours), Plasencia (€5.55, 1½ hours) and Mérida (from €4.30, one hour).

Mérida

POP 74,900

Once the biggest city in Roman Spain, Mérida is home to more ruins of that age than anywhere else in the country and is a wonderful spot to spend a few archaeologically inclined days.

Sights

Roman Remains
RUINS

The **Teatro Romano** (Calle Alvarez S. de Buruaga; adult/under 12yr €8/free; ⌚9.30am-7.30pm Jun-Sep, 9.30am-1.45pm & 4-6.15pm Oct-May), built around 15 BC to seat 6000 spectators and set in lovely gardens, has a dramatic and well-preserved two-tier backdrop of Corinthian stone columns; the stage's facade (*scaenae frons*) was inaugurated in AD 105. The theatre hosts performances during the Festival del Teatro Clásico in summer. The adjoining **Anfiteatro**, opened in 8 BC for gladiatorial contests, had a capacity of 14,000.

Los Columbarios (Calle del Ensanche s/n; adult/under 12yr €4/free; ⌚9.30am-1.45pm & 5-7.15pm Jun-Sep, 9.30am-1.45pm & 4-6.15pm Oct-May) is a Roman funeral site. A footpath connects it with the **Casa del Mitreo** (Calle Oviedo s/n; adult/under 12yr €4/free; ⌚9.30am-1.45pm & 5-7.15pm Jun-Sep, 9.30am-1.45pm & 4-6.15pm Oct-May), a 2nd-century Roman house with several intricate mosaics and a well-preserved fresco.

Don't miss the extraordinarily powerful spectacle of the **Puente Romano** over the Río Guadiana, which at 792m in length with 60 granite arches is one of the longest bridges built by the Romans.

The **Templo de Diana** (Calle de Sagasta) stood in the municipal forum, where the city government was based. The restored **Pórtico del Foro**, the municipal forum's portico, is just along the road.

Museo Nacional de Arte Romano
MUSEUM

(museoarteromano.es; Calle de José Ramón Mélida; adult/child €3/free, EU seniors & students free; ⌚9.30am-3.30pm & 5.30-8.30pm Tue-Sun Jul-Sep, shorter hours rest of year) On no account miss this fabulous museum which has a superb collection of statues, mosaics, frescos, coins and other Roman artefacts. Designed by the architect Rafael Moneo, the soaring brick structure makes a remarkable home for the collection.

Alcazaba
FORTRESS

(Calle Graciano; adult/child €4/free; ⌚9.30am-1.45pm & 5-7.15pm Jun-Sep, 9.30am-1.45pm & 4-6.15pm Oct-May) This large Muslim fort was built in AD 835 on a site already occupied by the Romans and Visigoths. Down below, its *aljibe* (cistern) incorporates marble and stone slabs with Visigothic decoration that were recycled by the Muslims, while the ramparts look out over the Guadiana and down into the Alcazaba's gardens. The 15th-century monastery in its northeast corner now serves as the Junta de Extremadura's presidential offices.

Sleeping & Eating

TOP CHOICE La Flor de al-Andalus
BUDGET HOTEL €

(☎924 31 33 56; www.laflordeal-andalus.es, in Spanish; Avenida de Extremadura 6; s/d €33/45; ❄📶) If only all *hostales* were this good. Opened in May 2010 and describing itself as a 'boutique *hostal*', La Flor de al-Andalus has beautifully decorated rooms in Andalucían style, friendly service and a good location within walking distance of all the main sites. The buffet breakfast costs just €3.

TOP CHOICE Hotel Adealba
HOTEL €€

(☎924 38 83 08; www.hoteladealba.com; Calle Romero Leal 18; d incl breakfast from €96.30; 🚭📶❄) Opened in 2009, this stunning hotel occupies a 19th-century townhouse close to the Templo de Diana and does so with a classy, contemporary look. The designer rooms have strong, contrasting colours and there's a pillow menu to choose from. Parking is €12.

Tabula Calda
TRADITIONAL SPANISH €€

(www.tabulacalda.com; Calle Romero Leal 11; meals €20-25; ⌚lunch & dinner Mon-Sat, lunch Sun) This inviting space with tilework and abundant greenery serves up well-priced meals (including *menús* from €12 to €24.50) that cover most Spanish staples. The cooking effortlessly combines traditional home cooking, thoughtful presentation and subtle innovations.

Convivium
TAPAS, TRADITIONAL SPANISH €

(Calle de Sagasta 21; tortillinas €1, meals €15-20) Head straight for the pretty patio with tables set under a large lemon tree at this informal place where the speciality is *tortillinas* (mini omelettes with fillings including cod, salami, spinach, aubergines and prawns). The *tortillina*, gazpacho and drink for €2.50 has to be Mérida's best deal.

Information

Municipal tourist office (www.merida.es, in Spanish; Paseo de José Álvarez Sáenz de Buruaga s/n; ⌚9.30am-2pm & 5-7.30pm)

Getting There & Away

BUS From the **bus station** (☎924 37 14 04; Avenida de la Libertad), destinations include Seville (€13.10, 2½ hours, five daily), Cáceres (€5.35,

50 minutes, two to four daily), Trujillo (€8.15, 1¼ hours, three daily) and Madrid (€22.15 to €27, four to five hours, eight daily).

TRAIN Trains to Madrid (€31.80 to €36.30, 4½ to 6½ hours, five daily), Cáceres (from €4.30, one hour, six daily) and Seville (€14.10, four hours, one daily).

UNDERSTAND SPAIN

History

Ancient Civilisations

Spain's story is one of European history's grand epics, and it's a story that begins further back than most – the oldest pieces of human bone in Europe (dating back a mere 780,000 years) have been found in Spain, in the Sierra de Atapuerca near Burgos.

The point at which Spanish history really gets interesting, however, is when the great civilisations of the Ancient Mediterranean began to colonise what we now know as the Iberian Peninsula, from around 1000 BC. The sea-going Phoenicians founded a great seafaring empire which depended on the establishment of ports around the Mediterranean rim. One of these ports, Cádiz (p1129), is widely believed to Europe's oldest continuously inhabited settlement.

The Romans arrived in the 3rd century BC and while they took 200 years to subdue the peninsula, they would hold it for six centuries. Called Hispania, Roman Spain became an integral part of the Roman Empire, with its impact upon language, architecture and religion lasting to this day. Reminders of Roman times include Segovia's aqueduct (p1053), the ancient theatres and other monuments of Mérida (p1134) and Tarragona (p1081), and the ruins of Zaragoza (p1083).

Muslim Spain & the Reconquista

In 711 Muslim armies invaded the peninsula, most of which they would end up occupying. Muslim dominion would last almost 800 years in parts of Spain. In Islamic Spain (known as al-Andalus), arts and sciences prospered, new crops and agricultural techniques were introduced, and palaces, mosques, schools, public baths and gardens were built. The spirit of these times lives on most powerfully in Andalucía.

In 1085 Alfonso VI, king of Castile, took Toledo, the first definitive victory of the Reconquista (the struggle to wrestle Spain into Christian hands). By the mid-13th century, the Christians had taken most of the peninsula, except for the emirate of Granada.

The kingdoms of Castile and Aragón emerged as Christian Spain's two main powers, and in 1469 they were united by the marriage of Isabel, princess of Castile, and Fernando, heir to Aragón's throne. Known as the Catholic Monarchs, they laid the foundations for the Spanish Golden Age, but were also responsible for one of the darkest hours in Spain's history – the Spanish Inquisition, a witch-hunt to expel or execute Jews and other non-Christians. In 1492 the last Muslim ruler of Granada surrendered to them, marking the end of the Reconquista. In the same year, Jews were expelled from Spain, with Muslims sent into exile eight years later.

The Golden Age

In the same year that marked the end of the Reconquista, Christopher Columbus (Colón in Castilian) landed in the Bahamas and later Cuba. He never guessed he'd discovered new continents and changed the course of history. His voyages sparked a period of exploration and exploitation that was to yield Spain enormous wealth, while destroying the ancient American empires. Over the centuries that followed, Spain's growing confidence was reflected in an extravagant cultural outpouring, producing towering figures such as Velázquez and Cervantes. For three centuries, gold and silver from the New World were used to finance the rapid expansion of the Spanish empire but were not enough to prevent its slow decline. By the 18th century, the mighty Spanish empire was on its way out, the life sucked out of it by a series of unwise kings, a self-seeking noble class and ceaseless warfare.

Struggle for the Soul of Spain

By the early 19th century, Spain's royal court had descended into internecine squabbles over succession to the Spanish throne. The consequences for the rest of the country were profound.

In 1807–08 Napoleon's forces occupied a weakened Spain, and King Carlos IV abdicated without a fight. In his place Napoleon installed his own brother, Joseph Bonaparte. The Spaniards retaliated with a five-year war of independence (in which British forces under the Duke of Wellington played a key role). The French were expelled in 1813 after defeat at Vitoria. A Bourbon, Fernando VII, was restored to the Spanish throne – despite periods of interruption to their rule, the Bourbon royal family rule Spain to this day.

Independence may have been restored, but Spain spent much of the next century embroiled in wars at home and abroad. The Spanish-American War of 1898 marked the end of the Spanish empire. The USA crushed Spanish arms and took over its last overseas possessions – Cuba, Puerto Rico, Guam and the Philippines. Spain was in a dire state.

Franco's Spain

Begun in the 19th century, the battle between conservatives and liberals, and between monarchists and republicans came to a head in July 1936 when Nationalist plotters in the army rose against the Republican government, launching a civil war (1936–39) that would create bitter wounds that are still healing today. The Nationalists, led by General Francisco Franco (who stood at the head of an alliance of the army, Church and the Fascist-style Falange Party), received military support from Nazi Germany and Fascist Italy, while the elected Republican government received support from the Soviet Union and other foreign leftists.

The war ended in 1939, with Franco the victor. Some 350,000 Spaniards died in the war, most of them on the battlefield but many others in executions, prison camps or simply from disease and starvation. After the war, thousands of Republicans were executed, jailed or forced into exile, and Franco's 36-year dictatorship began with Spain isolated internationally and crippled by recession. It wasn't until the 1950s and '60s, when the rise in tourism and a treaty with the USA combined to provide much-needed funds, that the country began to recover, although Franco retained an iron grip over the country.

The New Spain

Franco died in 1975, having named Juan Carlos, the grandson of Alfonso XIII, as his successor. Despite Franco's careful grooming, King Juan Carlos opted for the creation of a constitutional monarchy and a democratic government. The first elections were held in 1977 and a new constitution was drafted in 1978. It was a dramatic shift and although deep schisms remain to this day, the country's democratic transition has been an extraordinary success.

Post-Franco Spain bore little resemblance to what went before and the country revelled in its new-found freedoms with all the zeal of an ex-convent schoolgirl. Seemingly everything – from political parties to drugs – was legalised and the 1980s, despite the spectre of killings by the Basque terrorist group ETA, was a period of great cultural innovation and Spain's reputation as Europe's party capital was born. Spain joined the European Community (EC) in 1986 and celebrated its return to the world stage in style in 1992, with Expo '92 in Seville and the Olympic Games in Barcelona.

At a political level, Spain was ruled from 1982 until 1996 by the Partido Socialista Obrero Español (Spanish Socialist Party; PSOE) of Felipe González. By 1996 the PSOE government stood accused of corruption and was swept from power by the centre-right Partido Popular (Popular Party; PP), led by José María Aznar. The PP went on to establish programs of economic decentralisation and liberalisation.

Spain Today

Long accustomed to terrorist attacks by ETA (which has killed more than 800 people in the past four decades), Spain was nonetheless shaken to its core by the largest-ever terrorist attack on Spanish soil (later claimed by al-Qaeda), in Madrid on 11 March 2004. In national elections held three days later, the PP lost the presidential election to the PSOE. Among his first actions as president, José Luís Rodríguez Zapatero withdrew Spanish troops from Iraq.

The Socialists embarked on something of a social revolution, legalising gay marriage, regularising the status of hundreds of thousands of illegal immigrants, removing the Church's role in religious education in schools, making abortions easier to obtain, and pushing through a law aimed at investigating the crimes and executions of the Franco years; the latter broke the 'pact of silence' that had prevailed throughout the transition to democracy in the late 1970s.

Zapatero also opened the way to increased devolution of powers to the regions but, again, not without controversy. The opposition PP took special exception to Catalonia's new Estatut (autonomy statutes). Indeed, the PP maintained a divisive campaign against the government until the 2008 elections, which Zapatero also won.

Within months of his re-election, years of economic boom came shuddering to an end amid the global financial crisis; unemployment jumped from around 7% in 2007 to above 20% in 2010. With the economy deep in recession, the Socialists' popularity plummeted. National elections are due in 2012.

Good news may be hard to come by, but the announcement of a ceasefire by a much-weakened ETA in September 2010 was welcomed by the government and opposition alike. Although ETA has returned to arms after similar ceasefires in the past, the move has nonetheless raised much-needed hopes that at least one source of conflict within Spanish society may soon come to an end.

People

Spain has a population of approximately 46 million, descended from all the many peoples who have settled here over the millennia, among them Iberians, Celts, Romans, Jews, Visigoths, Berbers, Arabs and 20th-century immigrants from across the globe. The biggest cities are Madrid (3.6 million), Barcelona (1.62 million), Valencia (814,200) and Seville (703,000). Each region proudly preserves its own unique culture, and some – Catalonia and the Basque Country in particular – display a fiercely independent spirit.

Religion

Only about 20% of Spaniards are regular churchgoers, but Catholicism is deeply ingrained in the culture and an estimated 94% of Spaniards identify themselves as Catholics. As the writer Unamuno said, 'Here in Spain we are all Catholics, even the atheists'.

However, many Spaniards have a deep-seated scepticism about the Church. During the civil war and the four decades of Franco's rule, the Catholic Church was, for the most part, a strong supporter of his policies and church-going was practically obligatory – those who shunned the Church were often treated as outcasts or targeted as delinquents by Franco's police. The Church retains a powerful public voice in national debates.

Spain's most significant (and growing) religious communities after the Catholics are Protestants and Muslims.

Arts

Literature

Miguel de Cervantes' novel *Don Quijote* is the masterpiece of the literary flowering of the 16th and 17th centuries, not to mention one of the world's great works of fiction.

The next high point of in the early 20th century grew out of the crisis of the Spanish-American War that spawned the intellectual Generation of '98. The towering figure was poet and playwright Federico García Lorca, who won international acclaim before he was murdered in the civil war for his Republican sympathies.

Popular contemporary authors include Arturo Pérez Reverte, whose *Capitán Alatriste* books are international best-sellers. Another writer with a broad following is Javier Marías. He has kept the country in thrall these past years with his 1500-page trilogy, *Tu Rostro Mañana* (Your Face Tomorrow).

Cinema

Modern Spanish cinema's best-known director is Pedro Almodóvar, whose humorous, cutting-edge films are often set amid the great explosion of drugs and creativity that occurred in Madrid in the 1980s. His *Todo Sobre Mi Madre* (All About My Mother; 1999) and *Habla Con Ella* (Talk to Her; 2002) are both Oscar winners, while *Volver* (2006) is his most acclaimed recent work.

Alejandro Amenábar, the young Chilean-born director of *Abre los Ojos* (Open Your Eyes; 1997), *The Others* (2001) and the Oscar-winning *Mar Adentro* (The Sea Inside; 2004), is Almodóvar's main competition for Spain's 'best director' title. That latter film's star, Javier Bardem, won the Oscar for Best Supporting Actor in the Coen brothers' disturbing *No Country for Old Men* in 2008.

Woody Allen set his *Vicky Cristina Barcelona* (2008), a light romantic comedy, largely in Barcelona; the Madrid-born actress Penélope Cruz won an Oscar for Best Supporting Actress for her role in the film.

Architecture

Spain resembles an open-air gallery that spans some of history's most important architectural styles.

The Muslims left behind some of the most splendid buildings in the Islamic world, particularly in Andalucía. Examples include Granada's Alhambra (p1121), Córdoba's Mezquita (p1118) and Seville's Alcázar (p1113) – the latter is an example of Mudéjar architecture, the name given to Islamic artistry built in Christian-held territory. Outside of Andalucía, Zaragoza's Aljafería (p1083) captures the same spirit, albeit on a smaller scale.

The first main Christian architectural movement was Romanesque, best seen in churches and monasteries across the north of the country. Later came the great Gothic cathedrals, such as those in Toledo (p1060), Burgos (p1059), León (p1056), Ávila (p1049), Salamanca (p1050) and Seville (p1112) of the 12th to 16th centuries. Spain then followed the usual path to baroque (17th and 18th centuries) and neoclassicism (19th century).

Around the turn of the 20th century, Catalonia produced its startling Modernista movement, so many of whose buildings adorn Barcelona's streets; Antoni Gaudí's La Sagrada Família (p1074) is the most stunning example.

Of the daring contemporary structures appearing all over Spain, Valencia's Ciudad de las Artes y las Ciencias (p1097) and Bilbao's Guggenheim (p1090) are the most eye-catching.

Painting

Spain's painters rank among some of history's best-known European masters.

The giants of Spain's Golden Age (around 1550 to 1650) were Toledo-based El Greco (originally from Crete) and Diego Velázquez, considered Spain's best painter by greats including Picasso and Dalí. El Greco and Velázquez are well represented in Madrid's Museo del Prado (p1027), as is the genius of the 18th and 19th centuries, Francisco Goya. Goya's versatility ranged from unflattering royal portraits and anguished war scenes to bullfight etchings and tapestry designs.

Catalonia was the powerhouse of early-20th-century Spanish art, claiming the hugely prolific Pablo Picasso (although born in Málaga, Andalucía), the colourful symbolist Joan Miró and surrealist Salvador Dalí. To get inside the latter's world, head for Figueres or the Castell de Púbol (for both, see the boxed text, p1080). The two major museums dedicated to Picasso's work are the Museu Picasso (p1076) in Barcelona and the Museo Picasso Málaga (p1125), while his signature *Guernica* and other works are found in Madrid's Centro de Arte Reina Sofía (p1032). The Reina Sofía also has works by Joan Miró, as does the Fundació Joan Miró (p1069).

Important artists of the late 20th century include the Basque sculptor Eduardo Chillida; his Museo Chillida Leku (p1086) is south of San Sebastián.

Flamenco

Most musical historians speculate that flamenco probably dates back to a fusion of songs brought to Spain by the *gitanos* (Roma people or gypsies) with music and verses from North Africa crossing into medieval Muslim Andalucía. Flamenco as we now know it first took recognisable form in the 18th and early 19th centuries among *gitanos* in western Andalucía. Suitably, for a place considered the cradle of the genre, the Seville–Jerez de la Frontera–Cádiz axis is still considered the flamenco heartland and it's here, purists believe, that you must go for the most authentic flamenco experience.

Environment

The Land

Spain is a geographically diverse country, with landscapes ranging from the near-deserts of Almería to the emerald green countryside of Asturias and deep coastal inlets of Galicia, from the rolling sunbaked plains of Castilla-La Mancha to the rugged Pyrenees. The country covers 84% of the Iberian Peninsula and spreads over 505,370 sq km, about 40% of which is high *meseta* (tableland).

FLAMENCO – THE ESSENTIAL ELEMENTS

A flamenco singer is known as a *cantaor* (male) or *cantaora* (female); a dancer is a *bailaor/a*. Most of the songs and dances are performed to a blood-rush of guitar from the *tocaor/a* (flamenco guitarist). Percussion is provided by tapping feet, clapping hands and sometimes castanets. Flamenco *coplas* (songs) come in many different types, from the anguished *soleá* or the intensely despairing *siguiriya* to the livelier *alegría* or the upbeat *bulería*. The first flamenco was *cante jondo* (deep song), an anguished instrument of expression for a group on the margins of society. *Jondura* (depth) is still the essence of pure flamenco.

The traditional flamenco costume – shawl, fan and long frilly bata de cola (tail gown) for women, flat Cordoban hats and tight black trousers for men – dates from Andalucian fashions in the late 19th century.

Wildlife

The brown bear, wolf, Iberian lynx (the world's most endangered cat species, although it's making a hesitant and much-assisted comeback) and wild boar all survive in Spain, although only the boar exists in abundance. Spain's high mountains harbour the chamois and Spanish ibex, and big birds of prey such as eagles, vultures and lammergeier. The marshy Ebro Delta and Guadalquivir estuary are important for waterbirds, among them the spectacular greater flamingo.

Environmental Issues

Spain faces some of the most pressing environmental issues of our time. Drought, massive overdevelopment of its coastlines, overexploitation of scarce water resources by tourism projects and intensive agriculture, and spiralling emissions of greenhouse gases are all major concerns. It's a slightly more nuanced picture than first appears – Spain is a leading player in the wind-power industry, it has locked away around 40,000 sq km of protected areas, including 14 national parks, and its system of public transport is outstanding – but the apparent absence of any meaningful political will to tackle these issues is storing up problems for future generations.

Food & Drink

Reset your stomach's clock in Spain unless you want to eat alone, with other tourists or, in some cases, not at all.

Most Spaniards start the day with a light *desayuno* (breakfast), perhaps coffee with a *tostada* (piece of toast) or *pastel/bollo* (pastry), although they might stop in a bar later for a mid-morning *bocadillo* (baguette). *La comida* (lunch) is usually the main meal of the day, eaten between about 2pm and 4pm. The *cena* (evening meal) is usually lighter and most locals won't sit down for it before 9pm. The further south you go, the later start times tend to be – anything from 10pm to midnight!

Staples & Specialities

The variety in Spanish cuisines is quite extraordinary, and each region has its own styles and specialities. One of the most characteristic dishes, from the Valencia region, is paella – rice, seafood, the odd vegetable and often chicken or meat, all simmered together and traditionally coloured yellow with saffron. *Jamón serrano* (cured ham) is a delicacy available in many different qualities.

Many would argue that tapas are Spain's greatest culinary gift to the world, not least because the possibilities are endless. Anything can be a tapa, from a handful of olives or a piece of *tortilla de patatas* (potato and onion omelette) to more elaborate and often intensely surprising combinations of tastes. For tapas, the cities of Andalucía are usually (but not always) bastions of tradition, while the undoubted king of tapas destinations is San Sebastián (p1087), in Basque country, where they call tapas '*pintxos*'. It all comes together in Madrid (see the boxed text, p1042).

Drinks

Start the day with a strong coffee, either as a *cafe con leche* (half-coffee, half-milk), *cafe solo* (short black, espresso-like) or *cafe cortado* (short black with a little milk).

The most common way to order a *cerveza* (beer) is to ask for a *caña* (small draught beer). In Basque Country this is a *zurrito*. A larger beer (about 300mL) is often called a *tubo*. All these words apply to *cerveza de barril* (draught beer) – if you just ask for a *cerveza* you're likely to get bottled beer, which is a little more expensive.

Vino (wine) comes *blanco* (white), *tinto* (red) or *rosado* (rosé). Exciting wine regions include Penedès, Priorat, Ribera del Duero and La Rioja. There are also many regional specialities, such as *jerez* (sherry) in Jerez de la Frontera and *cava* (a sparkling wine) in Catalonia. Sangria, a sweet punch made of red wine, fruit and spirits, is a summer drink and especially popular with tourists. *Tinto de verano,* a kind of wine shandy, is a summer alternative.

Agua del grifo (tap water) is usually safe to drink.

Where to Eat & Drink

Bars and cafes are open all day (see p1142 for detailed hours), serving coffees, pastries, *bocadillos* and usually tapas (which generally cost from €1.50 to €4). You can also order *raciones,* a large-sized serving of these snacks.

Spaniards like to eat out, and restaurants (which come in different styles and with different names such as *taberna, mesón, tasca* and *restaurante*) abound even in small towns. At lunchtime, most places

JAMÓN – A PRIMER

Unlike Italian prosciutto, Spanish *jamón* is a bold, deep red and well marbled with buttery fat. Like wines and olive oil, Spanish *jamón* is subject to a strict series of classifications. *Jamón serrano* refers to *jamón* made from white-coated pigs introduced to Spain in the 1950s. Once salted and semidried by the cold, dry winds of the Spanish sierra, most now go through a similar process of curing and drying in a climate-controlled shed for around a year. *Jamón serrano* accounts for approximately 90% of cured ham in Spain.

Jamón ibérico – more expensive and generally regarded as the elite of Spanish hams – comes from a black-coated pig indigenous to the Iberian Peninsula and a descendant of the wild boar. If the pig gains at least 50% of its body weight during the acorn-eating season, it can be classified as *jamón ibérico de bellota*, the most sought-after designation for *jamón*.

offer a *menú del día* – a fixed-price lunch menu and the traveller's best friend. For €8 to €12 you typically get three courses, bread and a drink. The *plato combinado* (combined plate) is a cousin of the *menú* and usually includes a meat dish with some vegetables.

After dinner, head for the bars where you can get coffee and tea. A *bar de copas* will sell beer and an endless array of *combinados* (drinks like vodka and orange or rum and Coke) and sometimes more sophisticated cocktails.

As of 1 January 2011, all bars and restaurants are smoke-free.

Vegetarians & Vegans

Vegetarians may have to be creative in Spain. You'll find dedicated vegetarian restaurants in larger cities and important student centres. Otherwise, most traditional restaurants will offer salads and egg tortillas, but little else for non-carnivores. Even salads may come laden with sausages or tuna. Pasta and pizza are readily available, as is seafood for those who eat it. Vegans will have an especially hard time away from the big cities (and not an easy time in them).

Directory A–Z

Accommodation

In this chapter, budget options include everything from dorm-style youth hostels to family-style *pensiones* and slightly better-heeled *hostales*. At the upper end of this category you'll find rooms with air-conditioning and private bathrooms. Midrange *hostales* and hotels are more comfortable and most offer standard hotel services. Business hotels, trendy boutique hotels and luxury hotels are usually in the top-end category.

Virtually all accommodation prices are subject to IVA *(impuesto sobre el valor añadido)*, the Spanish version of value-added tax, which is 7%. This may or may not be included in the quoted price. To check, ask: *Está incluido el IVA?* (Is IVA included?)

PRICE RANGES

Our reviews refer to double rooms with a private bathroom, except in hostels or where otherwise specified. Quoted rates are for **high season**, which is generally May to September (though this varies greatly from region to region).

€€€ more than €120 (more than €200 for Madrid/Barcelona)

€€ €60 to €120 (€70 to €200 for Madrid/Barcelona)

€ less than €60 (less than €70 for Madrid/Barcelona)

CAMPING

Spain has around 1000 officially graded *campings* (camping grounds) and they vary greatly in service, cleanliness and style. They're officially rated as first class (1ªC), second class (2ªC) or third class (3ªC). Camping grounds usually charge per person, per tent and per vehicle – typically €5 to €9 for each. Many camping grounds close from around October to Easter.

Useful websites:

Campings Online (www.campingsonline.com/espana) Booking service.

Campinguía (www.campinguia.com) Contains comments (mostly in Spanish) and links.

Guía Camping (www.guiacampingfecc.com) Online version of the annual *Guía Camping* (€13.60), which is available in bookshops around the country.

HOTELS, HOSTALES & PENSIONES

Most options fall into the categories of hotels (one to five stars, full amenities), *hostales* (high-end guesthouses with private bathroom; one to three stars) or *pensiones* (guesthouses, usually with shared bathroom; one to three stars).

Among the more tempting hotels for those with a little fiscal room to manoeuvre are the 90 or so **paradores** (☎in Spain 902 547 979; www.parador.es), a state-funded chain of hotels in often stunning locations, among them towering castles and former medieval convents. Boutique hotels are also all the rage.

YOUTH HOSTELS

Albergues juveniles (youth hostels) are cheap places to stay, especially for lone travellers. Expect to pay from €15 to €28 per night, depending on location, age and season. Spain's Hostelling International (HI) organisation, **Red Española de Albergues Juveniles** (REAJ; www.reaj.com), has around 250 youth hostels throughout Spain. Official hostels require HI membership (you can buy a membership card at virtually all hostels) and many have curfews.

Activities

HIKING

Spain is a hiker's paradise. You can read more about some of the best treks in the country in Lonely Planet's *Walking in Spain*. Useful for hiking, especially in the Pyrenees, are maps by Editorial Alpina. The series combines information booklets with detailed maps. Buy them at bookshops, sports shops and sometimes at petrol stations near hiking areas.

Throughout Spain, you'll find GR (*Grandes Recorridos,* or long distance) trails. These are indicated with red-and-white markers. The Camino de Santiago (St James' Way, with several branches) is perhaps Spain's best-known long-distance walk. In addition to this world-famous pilgrimage route across northern Spain, some of Spain's best hiking is in the Pyrenees, Picos de Europa and Andalucía.

SKIING

Skiing is cheaper but less varied than in much of the rest of Europe. The season runs from December to mid-April. The best resorts are in the Pyrenees, especially in northwest Catalonia and in Aragón. The Sierra Nevada in Andalucía offers the most southerly skiing in Western Europe.

SURFING, WINDSURFING & KITESURFING

The Basque Country has good surf spots, including San Sebastián, Zarautz and the legendary left at Mundaka. Tarifa (p1130), with its long beaches and ceaseless wind, is generally considered to be the windsurfing capital of Europe. It's also a top spot for kitesurfing.

Business Hours

Reviews in this guidebook won't list business hours unless they differ from the following standards:

Banks 8.30am to 2pm Monday to Friday; some also open 4pm to 7pm Thursday and 9am and 1pm Saturday

Central post offices 8.30am to 9.30pm Monday to Friday, 8.30am to 2pm Saturday

Nightclubs midnight or 1am to 5am or 6am

Restaurants lunch 1pm to 4pm, dinner 8.30pm to midnight or later

Shops 10am to 2pm and 4.30pm to 7.30pm or 5pm to 8pm; big supermarkets and department stores generally open from 10am to 10pm Monday to Saturday

Embassies & Consulates

Australia (☎91 353 66 00; www.spain.embassy.gov.au; 24th fl, Paseo de la Castellana 259D, Madrid)

Canada (☎91 382 84 00; www.espana.gc.ca; Torre Espacio, Paseo de la Castellana 259D, Madrid)

Japan (☎91 590 76 00; www.es.emb-japan.go.jp; Calle de Serrano 109, Madrid)

New Zealand (☎91 523 02 26; www.nzembassy.com; Calle del Pinar 7, Madrid)

UK (☎91 714 63 00; http://ukinspain.fco.gov.uk; Torre Espacio, Paseo de la Castellana 259D, Madrid)

USA (☎91 587 22 00; http://madrid.usembassy.gov; Calle de Serrano 75, Madrid)

Food

Throughout this chapter, each place to eat is accompanied by one of the following symbols (the price relates to a three-course meal with house wine per person):

€€€	more than €50
€€	€20 to €50
€	less than €20

Gay & Lesbian Travellers

Homosexuality is legal in Spain. In 2005 the Socialist president, José Luis Rodríguez Zapatero, gave the country's conservative Catholic foundations a shake with the legalisation of same-sex marriages in Spain.

Lesbians and gay men generally keep a fairly low profile, but are quite open in the cities. Madrid (see the boxed text, p1045), Barcelona (p1076), Sitges, Torremolinos and Ibiza have particularly lively scenes.

Internet Access

Wi-fi is increasingly available at most hotels and in some cafes, restaurants and airports; generally (but not always) free.

Good cybercafes are increasingly hard to find; ask at the local tourist office. Prices per hour range from €1.50 to €3.

Language Courses

Among the more popular places to learn Spanish are Barcelona, Granada, Madrid, Salamanca and Seville.

The **Escuela Oficial de Idiomas** (EOI; www.eeooiinet.com, in Spanish) is a nationwide institution teaching Spanish and other local languages. On the website's opening page, hit 'Centros' under 'Comunidad' and then 'Centros en la Red' to get to a list of schools.

Legal Matters

Drugs Cannabis is legal but only for personal use and in very small quantities. Public consumption of any drug is illegal.

Legal driving age 18

Legal drinking age 18

Smoking Not permitted in any enclosed public space, including bars, restaurants and nightclubs.

Maps

If you're driving around Spain, consider investing in a road atlas with detailed road maps as well as maps of all the main towns and cities. Most travel shops stock them. Otherwise, some of the best maps for travellers are by Michelin, which produces the 1:1,000,000 *Spain Portugal* map and six 1:400,000 regional maps covering the whole country. Also good are the GeoCenter maps published by Germany's RV Verlag.

Money

ATMs Many credit and debit cards can be used for withdrawing money from *cajeros automáticos* (automatic teller machines) that display the relevant symbols such as Visa, MasterCard, Cirrus etc.

Cash Most banks will exchange major foreign currencies and offer the best rates. Ask about commissions and take your passport.

Credit & Debit Cards Can be used to pay for most purchases. You'll often be asked to show your passport or some other form of identification. The most widely accepted cards are Visa and MasterCard.

Moneychangers Exchange offices, indicated by the word *cambio* (exchange), offer longer opening hours than banks, but worse exchange rates and higher commissions.

Taxes & Refunds In Spain, value-added tax (VAT) is known as IVA (*ee*-ba; *impuesto sobre el valor añadido*). Visitors are entitled to a refund of the 16% IVA on purchases costing more than €90.16 from any shop if they are taking them out of the EU within three months.

Tipping Menu prices include a service charge. Most people leave some small change. Taxi drivers don't have to be tipped but a little rounding up won't go amiss.

Travellers Cheques Can be changed (for a commission) at most banks and exchange offices.

Post

The Spanish postal system, **Correos** (☎902 197 197; www.correos.es), is generally reliable, if a little slow at times. Ordinary mail to other Western European countries can take up to a week (although often as little as three days); to North America up to 10 days; and to Australia or New Zealand (NZ) between 10 days and three weeks.

Sellos (stamps) are sold at most *estancos* (tobacconists' shops with 'Tabacos' in yellow letters on a maroon background), as well as post offices.

A postcard or letter weighing up to 20g costs €1.07 from Spain to other European countries, and €1.38 to the rest of the world.

Public Holidays

The two main periods when Spaniards go on holida&y are Semana Santa (the week leading up to Easter Sunday) and July or August. At these times accommodation can be scarce and transport heavily booked.

There are at least 14 official holidays a year – some observed nationwide, some locally. National holidays:

Año Nuevo (New Year's Day) 1 January

Viernes Santo (Good Friday) March/April

Fiesta del Trabajo (Labour Day) 1 May

La Asunción (Feast of the Assumption) 15 August

Fiesta Nacional de España (National Day) 12 October

La Inmaculada Concepción (Feast of the Immaculate Conception) 8 December

Navidad (Christmas) 25 December

Regional governments set five holidays and local councils two more. Common dates:

Epifanía (Epiphany) or **Día de los Reyes Magos** (Three Kings' Day) 6 January

Día de San José (St Joseph's Day) 19 March

Jueves Santo (Good Thursday) March/April. Not observed in Catalonia and Valencia.

Corpus Christi June. The Thursday after the eighth Sunday after Easter Sunday.

Día de San Juan Bautista (Feast of St John the Baptist) 24 June

Día de Santiago Apóstol (Feast of St James the Apostle) 25 July

Día de Todos los Santos (All Saints Day) 1 November

Día de la Constitución (Constitution Day) 6 December

Safe Travel

Most visitors to Spain never feel remotely threatened, but a sufficient number have unpleasant experiences to warrant an alert. The main thing to be wary of is petty theft (which may of course not seem so petty if your passport, cash, travellers cheques, credit card and camera go missing). Stay alert and you can avoid most thievery techniques. Algeciras, Barcelona, Madrid and Seville are the worst offenders, as are popular beaches in summer (never leave belongings unattended). Common scams include the following:

» Kids crowding around you asking for directions or help.

» A person pointing out bird droppings on your shoulder (some substance their friend has sprinkled on you) – as they help clean it off they are probably emptying your pockets.

» The guys who tell you that you have a flat tyre. While your new friend and you check the tyre, his pal is emptying the car.

» The classic snatch-and-run. Never leave your purse, bag, wallet, mobile phone etc unattended or alone on a table.

» An old classic: the ladies offering flowers for good luck. We don't know how they do it, but your pockets always wind up empty.

Telephone

Blue public payphones are common and fairly easy to use. They accept coins, phonecards and, in some cases, credit cards. Phonecards come in €6 and €12 denominations and, like postage stamps, are sold at post offices and tobacconists.

International reverse-charge (collect) calls are simple to make: dial ☎900 99 followed by the appropriate code. For example: ☎900 99 00 61 for Australia, ☎900 99 00 44 for the UK, ☎900 99 00 11 (AT&T) for the USA etc.

To speak to an English-speaking Spanish international operator, dial ☎1008 (for calls within Europe) or ☎1005 (rest of the world).

MOBILE PHONES

All Spanish mobile phone companies (Telefónica's MoviStar, Orange and Vodafone) offer *prepagado* (prepaid) accounts for mobiles. The SIM card costs from €50, which includes some prepaid phone time.

Mobile phone numbers in Spain start with the number 6.

PHONE CODES

Telephone codes in Spain are an integral part of the phone number. All numbers are nine digits and you just dial that nine-digit number.

Numbers starting with 900 are national toll-free numbers, while those starting 901 to 905 come with varying costs; most can only be dialled from within Spain. In a similar category are numbers starting with 800, 803, 806 and 807.

Tourist Information

All cities and many smaller towns have an *oficina de turismo*. In the country's provincial capitals you'll sometimes find more than one tourist office – one specialising in information on the city alone, the other carrying mostly provincial or regional information. National and natural parks also often have visitor centres offering useful information.

Turespaña (www.spain.info) is the country's national tourism body.

Visas

Spain is one of 25 member countries of the Schengen Convention and Schengen visa rules apply.

Citizens or residents of EU & Schengen countries No visa required.

Citizens or residents of Australia, Canada, Israel, Japan, NZ and the USA No visa required for tourist visits of up to 90 days.

Other countries Check with a Spanish embassy or consulate.

To work or study in Spain A special visa may be required – contact a Spanish embassy or consulate before travel.

Work

Norwegian, Swiss, Icelandic and EU nationals may work in Spain without a visa. Everyone else is supposed to obtain a work permit (from a Spanish consulate in their country of residence) and, if they plan to stay more than 90 days, a residence visa. These procedures can be complex.

Teaching English is an obvious option; a TEFL (Teaching English as a Foreign Language) certificate will be a big help. Other possibilities include summer bar and restaurant work, as well as getting work on yachts in major ports.

Getting There & Away

Entering the Country

Immigration and customs checks usually involve a minimum of fuss, although there are exceptions. Your vehicle could be searched on arrival from Morocco; they're looking for controlled substances. Expect long delays at these borders, especially in summer.

The tiny principality of Andorra is not in the EU, so border controls (and rigorous customs checks for contraband) remain in place.

Air

Flights from all over Europe, including numerous budget airlines, serve main Spanish airports. All of Spain's airports share the user-friendly website and flight information telephone number of **Aena** (☎902 404 704; www.aena.es), the national airports authority. For more information on each airport on Aena's website, choose English and click on the drop-down menu of airports. Each airport's page has details on practical information (such as parking and public transport) and a full list of (and links to) airlines using that airport.

Madrid's Aeropuerto de Barajas is Spain's busiest (and Europe's fourth-busiest) airport. Other major airports include Barcelona's Aeroport del Prat (BCN) and the airports of Palma de Mallorca (PMI), Málaga (AGP), Alicante (ALC), Girona (GRO), Valencia (VLC), Ibiza (IBZ), Seville (SVQ), Bilbao (BIO) and Zaragoza (ZAZ).

You'll find a list of major airlines operating throughout Europe on p1219.

Land

Spain shares land borders with France, Portugal and Andorra.

Apart from shorter cross-border services, **Eurolines** (www.eurolines.com) is the main operator of international bus services to Spain from most of Western Europe and Morocco.

In addition to the rail services connecting Spain with France and Portugal, there are direct trains between Zurich and Barcelona (via Bern, Geneva, Perpignan and Girona), and between Milan and Barcelona (via Turin, Perpignan and Girona). For these and other services, visit the website of **Renfe** (☎for international trips 902 24 34 02; www.renfe.com), the Spanish national railway company.

ANDORRA

Regular buses connect Andorra with Barcelona (including winter ski buses and direct services to the airport) and other destinations in Spain (including Madrid) and France.

FRANCE

Bus

Eurolines (www.eurolines.fr) heads to Spain from Paris and more than 20 other French cities and towns. It connects with Madrid (17¾ hours), Barcelona (14¾ hours) and many other destinations. There's at least one departure per day for main destinations.

Car & Motorcycle

The main road crossing into Spain from France is the highway that links up with Spain's AP7 tollway, which runs down to Barcelona and follows the Spanish coast south (with a branch, the AP2, going to Madrid via Zaragoza). A series of links cut across the Pyrenees from France and Andorra into Spain, as does a coastal route that runs from Biarritz in France into the Spanish Basque Country.

Train

The main rail lines into Spain cross the Franco–Spanish frontier along the Mediterranean coast and via the Basque Country. Another minor route runs inland across the Pyrenees from Latour-de-Carol to Barcelona.

In addition to the options listed below, TGV (high-speed) trains connect Paris Montparnasse with Irún, where you change to a normal train for the Basque Country and on towards Madrid. Up to three TGVs also put you on track to Barcelona (leaving from Paris Gare de Lyon), with a change at Montpellier or Narbonne.

There are plans for a high-speed rail link between Madrid and Paris by 2012. Major cross-border services in the meantime:

Paris Austerlitz to Madrid Chamartín (chair/sleeper class €166.50/194.20, 13½ hours, one daily) *Trenhotel Francisco de Goya* runs via Orléans, Blois, Poitiers, Vitoria, Burgos and Valladolid.

Paris Austerlitz to Barcelona Estacio de Franca (sleeper class €188, 12 hours, one daily) *Trenhotel Joan Miró* runs via Orléans, Limoges, Figueres and Girona.

Montpellier to Lorca (twice daily) Talgo service along the Mediterranean coast via Girona, Barcelona, Tarragona, Valencia, Alicante, Murcia and Cartagena.

PORTUGAL

Bus

Avanza (☎in Spain & Portugal 902 02 09 99; www.avanzabus.com) runs two daily buses between Lisbon and Madrid (€55.25, 7½ to nine hours, two daily).

Other bus services run north via Porto to Tui, Santiago de Compostela and A Coruña in Galicia. Local buses cross the border from towns such as Huelva in Andalucía, Badajoz in Extremadura and Ourense in Galicia.

Car & Motorcycle

The A5 freeway linking Madrid with Badajoz crosses the Portuguese frontier and continues on to Lisbon, and there are many other road connections up and down the length of the Hispano–Portuguese frontier.

Train

From Portugal, the main line runs from Lisbon across Extremadura to Madrid.

Lisbon–Madrid chair/sleeper class €58.60/83.20, 10½ hours, one daily

Lisbon–Irún chair/sleeper class €68.80/96.60, 14½ hours, one daily

Sea

Ferries run to mainland Spain regularly from the Canary Islands, Italy, North Africa (Algeria, Morocco and the Spanish enclaves of Ceuta and Melilla) and the UK. Most services are run by the Spanish national ferry company, **Acciona Trasmediterránea** (☎902 45 46 45; www.trasmediterranea.es). You can take vehicles on the following routes.

ALGERIA

Acciona Trasmediterránea runs the following services from late June to mid-September:

Almería–Ghazaouet eight hours, four weekly

Almería–Oran eight hours, two weekly

ITALY

Barcelona–Genoa 18 hours, three weekly

Barcelona–Civitavecchia (near Rome) 20½ hours, six to seven weekly

Barcelona–Livorno (Tuscany) 19½ hours, three weekly

Barcelona–Porto Torres (Sardinia) 12 hours, one daily

MOROCCO

In addition to the following services, there are also ferries to the Spanish enclaves of Melilla (from Almería and Málaga) and Ceuta (from Algeciras).

Tangier–Algeciras (70 minutes, up to eight daily) Buses from several Moroccan cities converge on Tangier to make the ferry crossing to Algeciras, and then fan out to the main Spanish centres.

Tangier–Barcelona 24 hours, weekly

Tangier–Tarifa 35 minutes, up to eight daily

Nador–Almería five to eight hours, up to three daily

For further information, head to shop.lonelyplanet.com to purchase a downloadable PDF of the Morocco chapter from Lonely Planet's *Mediterranean Europe* guide.

UK

From mid-March to mid-November, **Brittany Ferries** (☎0871 244 0744; www.brittany-ferries.co.uk) runs the following services:

Plymouth–Santander 24 to 35 hours, weekly

Portsmouth–Santander 24 to 35 hours, three weekly

Getting Around

Students and seniors are eligible for discounts of 30% to 50% on most types of transport within Spain.

Air

Domestic Spanish routes are operated by the following airlines:

Air Berlin (www.airberlin.com) German budget airline with flights from Madrid to Valencia, Palma de Mallorca, Seville, Jerez de la Frontera and Asturias.

Air Europa (www.aireuropa.com) Dozens of domestic Spanish routes.

easyJet (www.easyjet.com) To Ibiza from Madrid and Bilbao.

Iberia (www.iberia.es) Spain's national airline and its subsidiary, Iberia Regional-Air Nostrum, covering most of Spain.

Ryanair (www.ryanair.com) More than a dozen domestic Spanish routes.

Spanair (www.spanair.com) Numerous domestic Spanish services.

Vueling (www.vueling.com) Spanish low-cost company with loads of domestic flights within Spain.

Bicycle

Finding bikes to rent in Spain is a hit-and-miss affair, so it's best to bring your own. Getting hold of spare parts in case you need them, however, shouldn't be a problem.

All regional trains have space for carrying bikes, and they're also permitted on most *cercanías* (local area trains around big cities such as Madrid and Barcelona). On long-distance trains there are more restrictions. As a rule, you have to be travelling overnight in a sleeper or couchette to have the (dismantled) bike accepted as normal luggage.

Boat

Regular ferries connect the Spanish mainland with the Balearic Islands. For more details, see p1147.

Bus

Spain's bus network is operated by countless independent companies, and reaches into the most remote towns and villages. Many towns and cities have one main station for arrivals and departures, which usually has an information desk. Tourist offices can also help with information on bus services.

Local services can get you nearly anywhere, but most buses connecting rural towns aren't geared to tourist needs. Frequent weekday services drop off to a trickle (or nothing) on Saturday and Sunday. It's not necessary, and often not possible, to make advance reservations for local bus journeys. It is, however, a good idea to turn up at least 30 minutes before the bus leaves to guarantee a seat.

Generally, bus fares are cheaper than on the faster, long-distance trains. For longer trips, you can and should buy your ticket in advance.

Among the hundreds of bus companies operating in Spain, the following have the largest networks:

ALSA (☎902 422 242; www.alsa.es)

Avanza (☎902 020 999; www.avanzabus.com)

Car & Motorcycle

Spain's roads vary enormously but are generally good. Fastest are the *autopistas;* on some, you have to pay hefty tolls. Minor routes can be slow going but are usually more scenic. Trying to find a parking spot in larger towns and cities can be a nightmare. *Grúas* (tow trucks) can and will tow your car. The cost of bailing out a car can be €200 or more.

Spanish cities do not have parking meters at every spot. Instead, if you park in a blue or green zone (frequently from 8am to 2pm or from 4pm to 8pm), you obtain a ticket from a street-side meter, which may be a block away. Display the ticket on the dashboard.

Petrol stations are easy to find along highways and *autopistas*.

AUTOMOBILE ASSOCIATIONS

The **Real Automóvil Club de España** (RACE; ☎902 404 545; www.race.es) is the national automobile club. They may well come to assist you in case of a breakdown, but in any event you should obtain an emergency telephone number for Spain from your own insurer.

DRIVING LICENCES

All EU member states' driving licences are recognised. Other foreign licences should be accompanied by an International Driving Permit. These are available from automobile clubs in your country and valid for 12 months.

HIRE

To rent a car in Spain you have to have a licence, be aged 21 or over and have a credit or debit card. Rates vary widely: the best deals tend to be in major tourist areas, including airports. Prices are especially competitive in the Balearic Islands. Expect a compact car to cost from €30 and up per day. See p1221 for information on major car-hire companies.

INSURANCE

Third-party motor insurance is a minimum requirement and it is compulsory to have an internationally recognised proof of insurance, which can be obtained from your insurer. Also ask your insurer for a European Accident Statement form, which can simplify matters in the event of an accident.

ROAD RULES

Blood-alcohol limit 0.05%.

Legal driving age for cars 18.

Legal driving age for motorcycles & scooters 16 (80cc and over) or 14 (50cc and under). A licence is required.

Motorcyclists Must use headlights at all times and wear a helmet if riding a bike of 125cc or more.

Side of the road Drive on the right.

Speed limits In built-up areas 50km/h (and in some cases, such as inner-city Barcelona, 30km/h), which increases to 100km/h on major roads and up to 120km/h on *autovías* and *autopistas* (toll-free and tolled dual-lane highways, respectively). Cars towing caravans are restricted to a maximum speed of 80km/h.

Train

Renfe (☎902 240 202; www.renfe.es) is the national railway company. Trains are mostly modern and comfortable, and late arrivals are the exception rather than the rule. The high-speed network is in constant expansion.

You can buy tickets and make reservations online, at stations, at travel agencies displaying the Renfe logo and in Renfe offices in many city centres.

Passes are valid for all long-distance Renfe trains; Inter-Rail users pay supplements on Talgo, InterCity and AVE trains. All passholders making reservations pay a small fee.

Among Spain's numerous types of trains:

Alaris, Altaria, Alvia, Arco and Avant Long-distance intermediate-speed services.

Cercanías For short hops and services to outlying suburbs and satellite towns in Madrid, Barcelona and 11 other cities.

Euromed Similar to the AVE trains, they connect Barcelona with Valencia and Alicante.

Regionales Trains operating within one region, usually stopping at all stations.

Talgo and Intercity Slower long-distance trains.

Tren de Alta Velocidad Española (AVE) High-speed trains that link Madrid with Barcelona, Burgos, Córdoba, Cuenca, Huesca, Lerida, Málaga, Seville, Valencia, Valladolid and Zaragoza. There is also a Barcelona–Seville service. In coming years Madrid–Cádiz and Madrid–Bilbao should come on line.

Trenhotel Overnight trains with sleeper berths.

CLASSES & COSTS

All long-distance trains have 2nd and 1st classes, known as *turista* and *preferente*, respectively. The latter is 20% to 40% more expensive.

Fares vary enormously depending on the service (faster trains cost considerably more) and, in the case of some high-speed services such as the AVE, on the time and day of travel. Tickets for AVE trains are by far the most expensive. A one-way trip in 2nd class from Madrid to Barcelona (on which route only AVE trains run) could cost as must as €115 (it works out slightly cheaper if you book online).

Children aged between four and 12 years are entitled to a 40% discount; those aged under four travel for free (except on high-speed trains, for which they pay the same as those aged four to 12). Buying a return ticket often gives you a 10% to 20% discount on the return trip. Students and people up to 25 years of age with a Euro<26 Card (Carnet Joven in Spain) are entitled to 20% to 25% off most ticket prices.

On overnight trips within Spain on *trenhoteles* it's worth paying extra for a *litera* (couchette; a sleeping berth in a six- or four-bed compartment) or, if available, single or double cabins in *preferente* or *gran clase* class. The cost depends on the class of accommodation, type of train and length of journey.

RESERVATIONS

Reservations are recommended for long-distance trips; you can make them in train stations, Renfe offices, travel agencies and online. A growing number of stations let you pick up prebooked tickets from machines scattered about the station concourse.

Switzerland

Includes »

Best Places to Eat

- » Atrio Vulcanelli (p1187)
- » Lötschberg AOC (p1170)
- » Osteria Chiara (p1191)

Best Places to Stay

- » Pension für Dich (p1183)
- » Hôtel Masson (p1163)
- » Mountain Hostel (p1177)

Why Go?

What giddy romance Zermatt, St Moritz and other glitterati-encrusted names evoke.

This is *Sonderfall Schweiz* ('special case Switzerland'), a privileged neutral country set apart from others, proudly idiosyncratic, insular and unique. Blessed with gargantuan cultural diversity, its four official languages alone say it all.

The Swiss don't do half-measures: Zürich, their most gregarious urban centre, has cutting-edge art, legendary nightlife and one of the world's highest living standards. The national passion for sweat, stamina and clingy Lycra takes 65-year-olds across 2500m-high mountain passes for Sunday strolls, sees giggly three-year-olds skiing rings around grown-ups, prompts locals done with 'ordinary' marathons to sprint backwards up mountains – all in the name of good old-fashioned fun.

So don't depend just on your postcard images of Bern's chocolate-box architecture, the majestic Matterhorn or the thundering Rheinfall – Switzerland is a place that's so outrageously beautiful it simply must be seen to be believed.

When to Go

Geneva

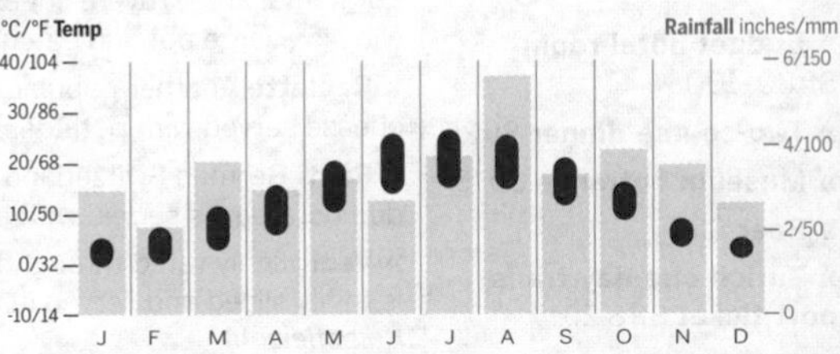

Dec–early Apr Carve through powder and drink glühwein at an alpine resort

May–Sep Hike in the shadow of the Matterhorn and be wowed by its mesmerising stance

Aug Celebrate Swiss National Day on 1 August and witness Swiss national pride in full force

AT A GLANCE

» **Currency** Swiss franc (Sfr)

» **Languages** French, German, Italian, Romansch

» **Money** ATMs readily available

» **Visas** Schengen rules apply

Fast Facts

» **Area** 41,285 sq km

» **Population** 7.8 million

» **Capital** Bern

» **Telephone** country code ☎41; international access code ☎00

» **Emergency** police ☎117; fire ☎118; ambulance ☎144

Exchange Rates

Australia	A$1	Sfr0.95
Canada	C$1	Sfr0.93
Euro Zone	€1	Sfr1.29
Japan	¥100	Sfr1.12
New Zealand	NZ$1	Sfr0.68
UK	UK£1	Sfr1.46
USA	US$1	Sfr0.87

Set Your Budget

» **Budget hotel room** Sfr80–100

» **Two-course dinner** Sfr25

» **Museum entrance** Sfr15

» **Beer** Sfr5

» **Zurich one-day transport ticket** Sfr8.20

Resources

» **swissinfo** (www.swissinfo.ch)

» **MySwitzerland** (www.myswitzerland.com)

Connections

Landlocked between France, Germany, Austria, Liechtenstein and Italy, Switzerland's a doddle to move on from. Geneva city buses run as far as the French border (a couple cross into France, continuing along the southern shore of Lake Geneva) and there are plenty of direct train connections from Geneva and Zurich to Paris, as well as Hamburg, Milan and Barcelona. There are also TGV links from Geneva and Zurich. Cosmopolitan Zürich enjoys as many international rail connections, including daily trains to/from Stuttgart, Munich and Innsbruck. In northern Switzerland, Basel is the major European rail hub, with separate train stations serving France and Germany. Then, of course, there is Italy, a mere hop and a skip from Locarno in Italianate Ticino.

ITINERARIES

One Week

Starting in vibrant Zürich, shop famous Bahnhofstrasse and hit the bars of Züri-West. Next, head to the Jungfrau region to explore some kick-ass alpine scenery (think James Bond racing an avalanche down a sheer snowy rock face). Take a pit stop in beautiful Lucerne before finishing up in country capital Bern.

Two Weeks

As above, then head west for French-immersion lessons in Geneva or lakeside Lausanne. Explore the Neuchâtel and Fribourg cantons, stopping in Gruyères to dip into a cheesy fondue and overdose on meringues drowned in thick double cream. Zip to Zermatt or across to St Moritz to frolic in snow or green meadows, then loop east to taste the Italian side of Switzerland.

Essential Food & Drink

» **Fondue** Switzerland's best-known dish, in which melted Emmental and Gruyère cheese are combined with white wine in a large pot and eaten with bread cubes.

» **Raclette** Another popular artery-hardener of melted cheese served with potatoes.

» **Rösti** German Switzerland's national dish of fried shredded potatoes is served with everything.

» **Veal** Highly rated throughout the country; in Zürich, veal is thinly sliced and served in a cream sauce *(Gschnetzeltes Kalbsfleisch)*.

» **Bündnerfleisch** Dried beef, smoked and thinly sliced.

» **Wurst** Like their northern neighbours, the Swiss also munch on a wide variety of sausages.

GENEVA

POP 185,700

Supersleek, slick and cosmopolitan, Geneva (Genève in French, Genf in German) is a rare breed of city. It's one of Europe's priciest. Its people chatter in every language under the sun (184 nationalities comprise 45% of the city's population) and it's constantly thought of as the Swiss capital – which it isn't. This gem of a city superbly strung around the sparkling shores of Europe's largest alpine lake is, in fact, only Switzerland's second-largest city.

Yet the whole world is here: the UN, International Red Cross, International Labour Organization, World Health Organization – 200-odd governmental and nongovernmental international organisations fill the city's plush hotels with big-name guests, feast on an incredulous choice of cuisine and help prop up the overload of banks, jewellers and chocolate shops for which Geneva is known. Strolling manicured city parks, lake sailing and skiing next door in the Alps are weekend pursuits.

Sights & Activities

The city centre is so compact it's easy to see many of the main sights on foot.

Lake Geneva LAKE

Begin your exploration of Europe's largest alpine lake by having a coffee on **Île Rousseau**, where a statue honours the celebrated freethinker. Cross to the southern side of the lake and walk west to the **Horloge Fleurie** (Flower Clock; Quai du Général-Guisan) in the Jardin Anglais. Geneva's most photographed clock, crafted from 6500 flowers, has ticked since 1955 and sports the world's longest second hand (2.5m).

The 140m-tall **Jet d'Eau** on the lake's southern shore is impossible to miss. At any one time there are 7 tonnes of water in the air, shooting up with incredible force – 200km/h, 1360 horsepower – to create its sky-high plume, kissed by a rainbow on sunny days.

Old Town HISTORIC AREA

The main street, Grand-Rue, shelters the **Espace Rousseau** at No 40, where the 18th-century philosopher was born.

Nearby, the part-Romanesque, part-Gothic **Cathédrale de St-Pierre** is where Protestant John Calvin preached from 1536 to 1564. Beneath the cathedral is the **site archéologique** (☎022 311 75 74; www.site-archeologique.ch; Cour St-Pierre 6; adult/child Sfr8/4; ⏲10am-5pm Tue-Sun), an interactive space safeguarding fine 4th-century mosaics and a 5th-century baptismal font.

You can trace Calvin's life in the neighbouring **Musée Internationale de la Réforme** (International Museum of the Reformation; ☎022 310 24 31; www.musee-reforme.ch; Rue du Clootre 4; adult/student/child Sfr8/3/2; ⏲10am-5pm Tue-Sun).

Palais des Nations LANDMARK

(☎022 907 48 96; www.unog.ch; Ave de la Paix 14; tours Sfr10; ⏲10am-noon & 2-4pm Apr-Oct, to 5pm Jul & Aug, 10am-noon & 2-4pm Mon-Fri Nov-Mar) The art deco Palais des Nations is the European arm of the UN and the home of 3000 international civil servants. You can see where decisions about world affairs are made on the hour-long tour. Afterwards check out the extensive gardens – don't miss the towering grey monument coated with heat-resistant titanium donated by the USSR to commemorate the conquest of space. An ID or passport is obligatory for admission.

FREE **International Red Cross & Red Crescent Museum** MUSEUM

(Musée Internationale de la Croix Rouge et du Croissant-Rouge; ☎022 748 95 25; www.micr.org; Ave de la Paix 17; ⏲10am-5pm Wed-Mon) A compelling multimedia trawl through atrocities perpetuated by humanity in recent history. Against the long litany of war and nastiness, documented in films, photos, sculptures and soundtracks, are set the noble aims of the organisation.

Other Museums MUSEUMS

Konrad Witz's *La pêche miraculeuse* (c 1440–44) portraying Christ walking on water on Lake Geneva is a highlight of the **Musée d'Art et d'Histoire** (☎022 418 26 00; http://mah.ville-ge.ch; Rue Charles Galland 2; permanent collection free, temporary exhibition fees vary; ⏲10am-5pm Tue-Sun). The particularly

GENEVA IN TWO DAYS

Explore the left-bank **parks**, **gardens** and **Jet d'Eau**, then hit the **Old Town** for lunch and a stroll. Tummy full, take in a **museum**, followed by a dip in the water and an aperitif at **Bains des Pâquis**. On day two, plan a tour of **CERN** or **Palais des Nations**, followed by another stroll along the lake.

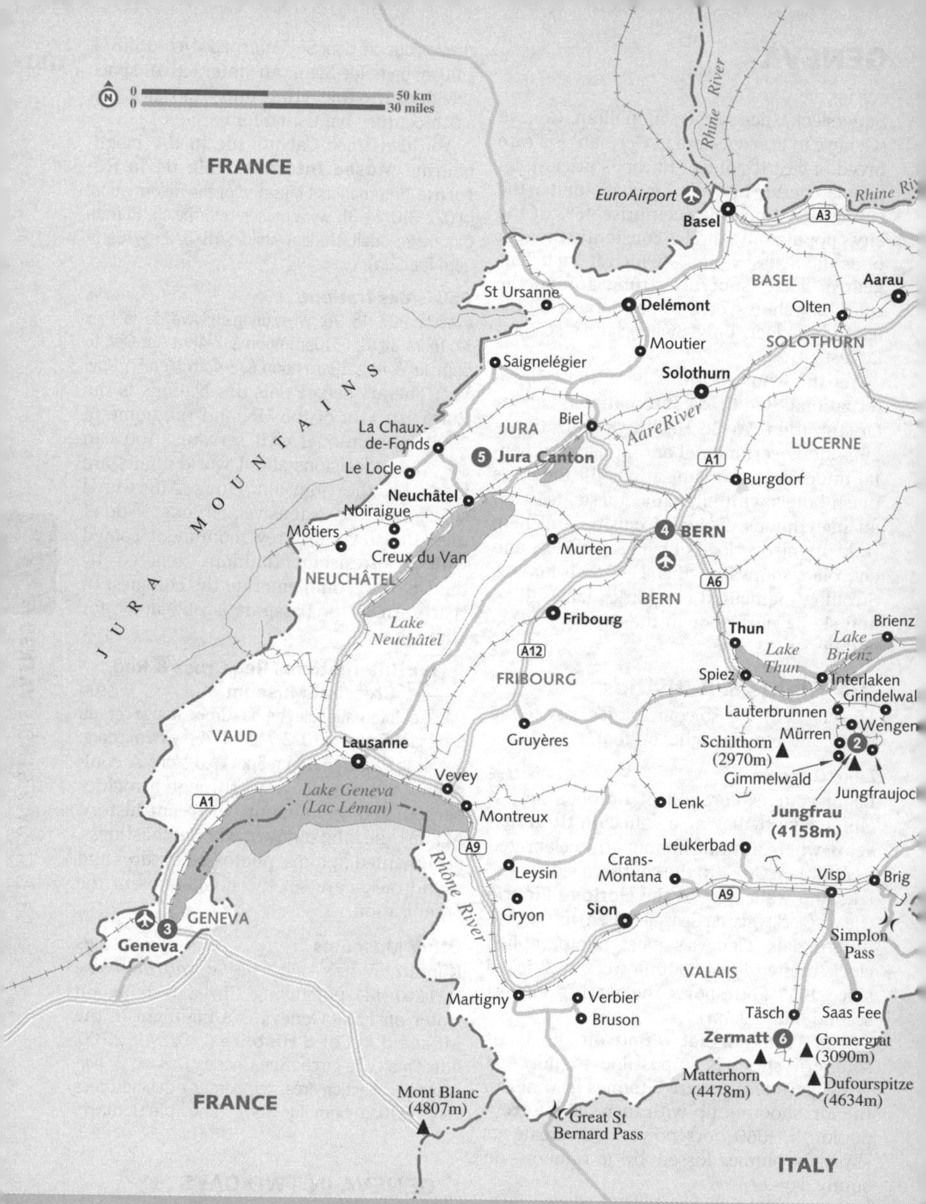

0 50 km
0 30 miles
FRANCE
Rhine River
EuroAirport
Basel
Rhine River
A3
BASEL
Aarau
St Ursanne
Delémont
Olten
Moutier
SOLOTHURN
Saignelégier
Solothurn
J U R A M O U N T A I N S
La Chaux-de-Fonds
JURA
Biel
Aare River
LUCERNE
5 Jura Canton
A1
Le Locle
Burgdorf
Neuchâtel
Noiraigue
Môtiers
4 BERN
Murten
Creux du Van
NEUCHÂTEL
A6
BERN
Fribourg
Thun
Brienz
Lake Neuchâtel
Lake Thun
Lake Brienz
A12
Spiez
Interlaken
FRIBOURG
Grindelwal
Lauterbrunnen
Wengen
VAUD
Mürren
Schilthorn (2970m)
Gruyères
Lausanne
2
Gimmelwald
Vevey
Lake Geneva (Lac Léman)
Jungfraujoc
A1
Montreux
Lenk
Jungfrau (4158m)
A9
Leukerbad
Rhône River
Leysin
Crans-Montana
Visp
Brig
A9
Gryon
Sion
3
GENEVA
Geneva
Simplon Pass
VALAIS
Martigny
Verbier
Täsch
Saas Fee
Bruson
Zermatt 6
Gornergrat (3090m)
Matterhorn (4478m)
Dufourspitze (4634m)
FRANCE
Mont Blanc (4807m)
Great St Bernard Pass
ITALY

Highlights

1 Hit the hip bars of **Zurich** (p1179) and relax the next day with a stroll along the city's sublime lake.

2 Be wowed by the Eiger's monstrous north face on a ride to the 'top of Europe', 3471m **Jungfraujoch** (p1179).

3 Get wet with a fountain dash beneath Geneva's **Jet d'Eau** (p1151) or a soak in a white-chocolate bath.

4 Be surprised by Swiss capital **Bern** (p1167): think medieval charm, folkloric fountains and a pulsating party scene.

5 Sleep in hay in the mysterious green hills and thick, dark forests of the clover-shaped **Jura canton** (p1165).

6 Gape at the iconic Matterhorn and wander around the car-free alpine village of **Zermatt** (p1165).

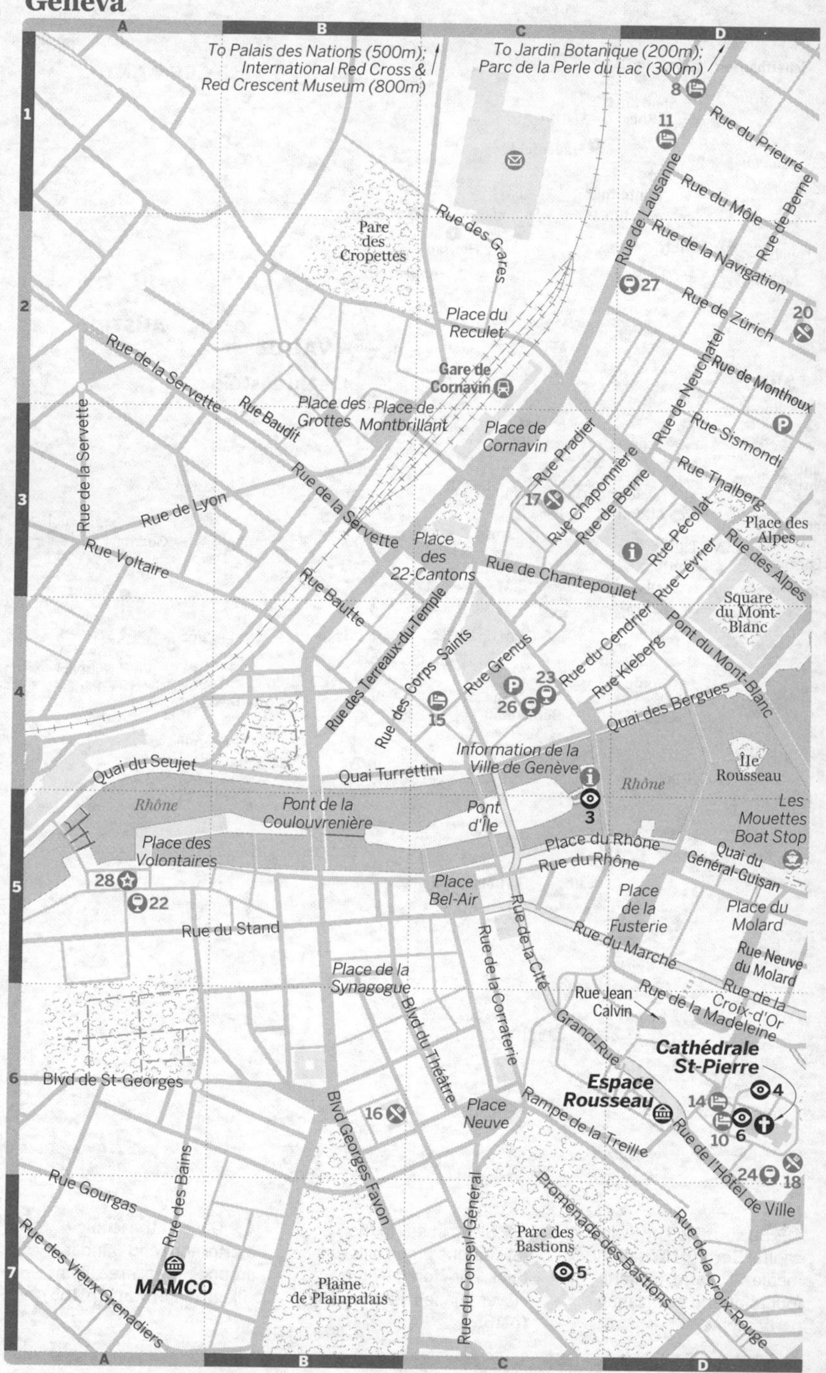

To Palais des Nations (500m); International Red Cross & Red Crescent Museum (800m)
To Jardin Botanique (200m); Parc de la Perle du Lac (300m)
Rue du Prieuré
Rue du Môle
Rue de Berne
Rue de Lausanne
Rue de la Navigation
Rue de Zürich
Rue de Neuchatel
Rue de Monthoux
Rue Sismondi
Rue Thalberg
Place des Alpes
Rue des Alpes
Square du Mont-Blanc
Pont du Mont-Blanc
Parc des Cropettes
Rue des Gares
Place du Reculet
Gare de Cornavin
Rue de la Servette
Rue Baudit
Place des Grottes
Place de Montbrillant
Place de Cornavin
Rue Pradier
Rue Chaponnière
Rue de Berne
Rue Pécolat
Rue Lévrier
Rue de la Servette
Rue de Lyon
Rue Voltaire
Place des 22-Cantons
Rue de Chantepoulet
Rue Bautte
Rue des Terreaux-du-Temple
Rue des Corps Saints
Rue Grenus
Rue du Cendrier
Rue Kleberg
Quai des Bergues
Île Rousseau
Quai du Seujet
Quai Turrettini
Information de la Ville de Genève
Rhône
Pont de la Coulouvrenière
Pont d'Île
Les Mouettes Boat Stop
Place des Volontaires
Place du Rhône
Rue du Rhône
Quai du Général-Guisan
Place Bel-Air
Place de la Fusterie
Place du Molard
Rue du Stand
Rue de la Cité
Rue de la Corraterie
Rue du Marché
Rue Neuve du Molard
Place de la Synagogue
Rue Jean Calvin
Rue de la Croix-d'Or
Rue de la Madeleine
Grand-Rue
Cathédrale St-Pierre
Blvd du Théâtre
Blvd de St-Georges
Espace Rousseau
Place Neuve
Blvd Georges Favon
Rampe de la Treille
Rue de l'Hôtel de Ville
Rue Gourgas
Rue des Bains
Rue du Conseil-Général
Promenade des Bastions
Parc des Bastions
Rue de la Croix-Rouge
Rue des Vieux Grenadiers
MAMCO
Plaine de Plainpalais

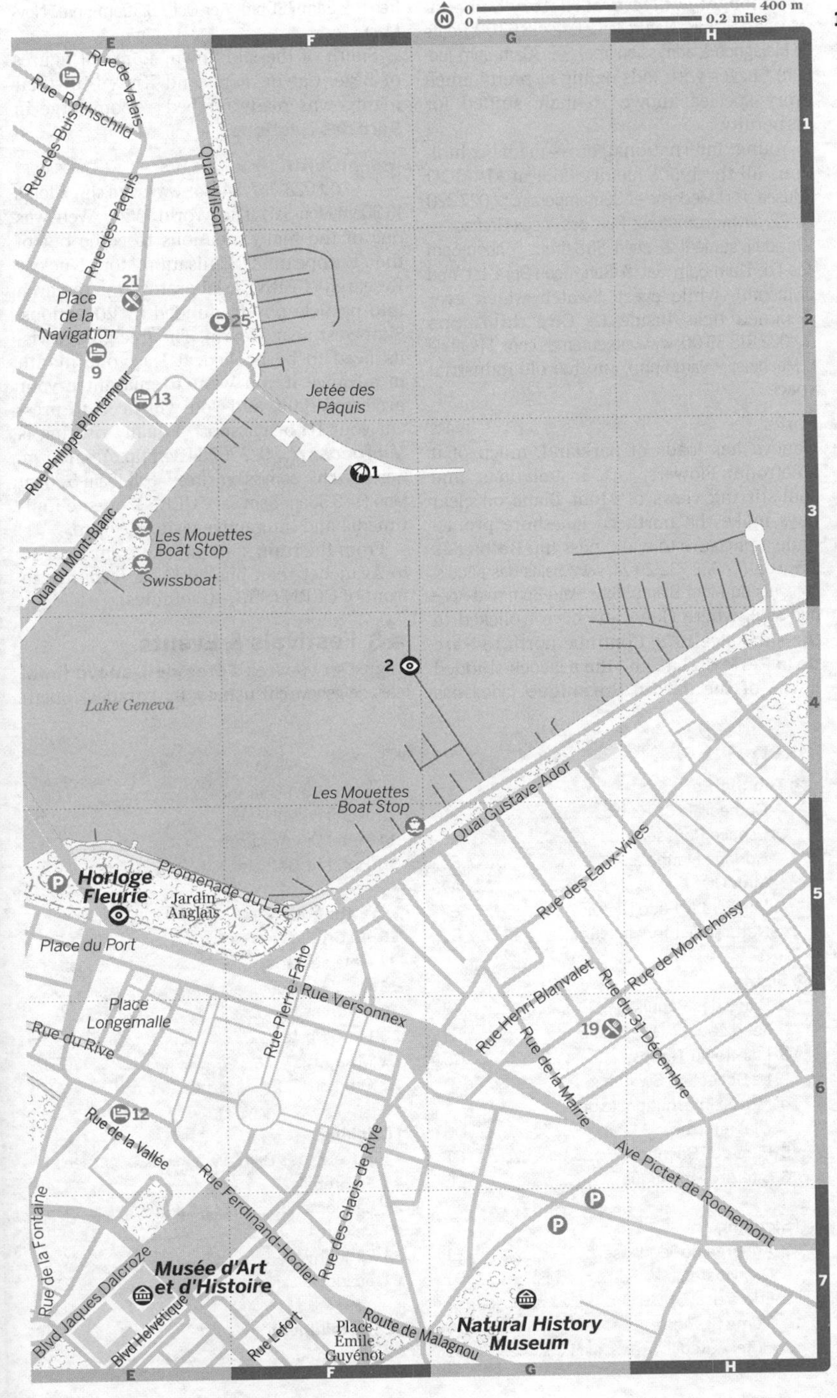

0 400 m
0 0.2 miles
E
F
G
H
1
2
3
4
5
6
7
Rue de Valais
Rue Rothschild
Rue des Buis
Rue des Pâquis
Quai Wilson
Place de la Navigation
Rue Philippe Plantamour
Quai du Mont-Blanc
Jetée des Pâquis
Les Mouettes Boat Stop
Swissboat
Lake Geneva
Les Mouettes Boat Stop
Quai Gustave-Ador
Horloge Fleurie
Jardin Anglais
Promenade du Lac
Place du Port
Rue des Eaux-Vives
Rue de Montchoisy
Rue Pierre-Fatio
Rue Versonnex
Rue Henri Blanvalet
Rue du 31 Décembre
Rue de la Mairie
Place Longemalle
Rue du Rive
Rue de la Vallée
Ave Pictet de Rochemont
Rue Ferdinand-Hodler
Rue des Glacis de Rive
Rue de la Fontaine
Blvd Jacques Dalcroze
Musée d'Art et d'Histoire
Blvd Helvétique
Rue Lefort
Place Émile Guyénot
Route de Malagnou
Natural History Museum
1
2
7
9
12
13
19
21
25

well thought-out **Natural History Museum** (Musée d'Histoire Naturelle; 022 418 63 00; Route de Malagnou 1; admission free; 9.30am-5pm Tue-Sun) buzzes with kids ogling at pretty much every species known to man, stuffed for perpetuity.

Young, international, cross-media exhibitions fill the 1950s factory floor at **MAMCO** (Musée d'Art Moderne et Contemporain; 022 320 61 22; www.mamco.ch; Rue des Vieux-Grenadiers 10; adult/student & child Sfr8/free; noon-6pm Tue-Fri, 11am-6pm Sat & Sun, noon-9pm 1st Wed of month), while every Swatch watch ever designed ticks inside **La Cité du Temps** (022 818 39 00; www.citedutemps.com; 1 Pont de la Machine; 9am-6pm), another old industrial space.

Parks PARKS

Geneva has loads of parkland, much of it lakefront. Flowers, art installations and soul-stirring views of Mont Blanc on clear days make the northern lakeshore promenade a pleasure to walk: pass hip **Bains des Pâquis** (022 732 29 74; www.bains-des-paquis.ch; Quai du Mont-Blanc 30; 9am-8pm mid-Apr–mid-Sep), where Genevans have frolicked in the sun since 1872. Continue north to **Parc de la Perle du Lac** and the peacock-studded lawns of the **Jardin Botanique** (admission free; 8am-7.30pm Apr-Oct, 9.30am-5pm Nov-Mar).

South of the Old Town, 4.5m-tall figures of Bèze, Calvin, Farel and Knox – in their nightgowns ready for bed – loom large in **Parc des Bastions**.

FREE **CERN** LABORATORY

(022 767 84 84; www.cern.ch; tours 10.30am Mon-Sat) The World Wide Web was one of the many creations to come out of the European Organisation for Nuclear Research (CERN), a laboratory for research into particle physics funded by 20 nations, 8km west near Meyrin. The free guided visits need to be booked at least one month in advance if you want to guarantee your preferred date, and you will need to present your ID or passport. Equally riveting is **Microcosm** (022 767 84 84; http://microcosm.web.cern.ch; admission free; 8.15am-5.30pm Mon-Fri, 8.30am-5pm Sat), CERN's on-site multimedia and interactive visitors centre.

From the train station, take tram 14 or 16 to Avanchet then bus 56 to its terminus in front of CERN (Sfr3, 40 minutes).

Festivals & Events

August's two-week **Fêtes de Genève** (www.fetes-de-geneve.ch) ushers in parades, open-

Geneva

Top Sights

- Cathédrale St-Pierre ... D6
- Espace Rousseau ... D6
- Horloge Fleurie ... E5
- MAMCO ... A7
- Musée d'Art et d'Histoire ... E7
- Natural History Museum ... G7

Sights

1 Bains des Pâquis ... F3
2 Jet d'Eau ... F4
3 La Cité du Temps ... C5
La Collection Swatch ... (see 3)
4 Musée Internationale de la Réforme ... D6
5 Parc des Bastions ... C7
6 Site Archéologique ... D6

Sleeping

7 Auberge de Jeunesse ... E1
8 City Hostel ... D1
9 Edelweiss ... E2
10 Hôme St-Pierre ... D6
11 Hôtel Auteuil ... D1
12 Hôtel Bel'Esperance ... E6
13 Hôtel de la Cloche ... E2
14 Hôtel Les Armures ... D6
15 Hotel St-Gervais ... C4

Eating

16 Au Grütli ... B6
17 Café de Paris ... C3
18 Chez Ma Cousine ... D6
19 L'Adresse ... G6
20 Les 5 Portes ... D2
21 Mikado ... E2
22 Omnibus ... A5

Drinking

Buvette des Bains ... (see 1)
23 La Bretelle ... C4
24 La Clémence ... D6
25 Paillote ... F2
26 Piment Vert ... C4
27 Scandale ... D2

Entertainment

28 L'Usine ... A5

FREE THRILLS

Bags of fabulous things to see and do in Geneva don't cost a cent. Our favourite freebies:

» Dashing like mad under the iconic **Jet d'Eau**

» Getting lost in the **Old Town**

» Commiserating over the dark side of humanity at the **International Red Cross & Red Crescent Museum**

» Admiring every species of tiger known to man in the **Natural History Museum**

» Hobnobbing with big-bang scientists at **CERN**

» Going green in the **Jardin Botanique**

» Flopping on the beach on the **Bains de Pâquis** jetty

» **Pedalling** along the lake into France or towards Lausanne

air concerts, lakeside merry-go-rounds and fireworks. On 11 December, the **Escalade** celebrates the foiling of an invasion by the Duke of Savoy in 1602 with a costumed parade, the smashing and eating of chocolate cauldrons, and a day of running races around the Old Town.

Sleeping

When checking-in, ask for your free public transport ticket covering unlimited bus travel for the duration of your hotel stay.

Hôtel de la Cloche HOTEL **$**
(022 732 94 81; www.geneva-hotel.ch/cloche; Rue de la Cloche 6; s/d from Sfr95/110, without bathroom from Sfr65/98;) Elegant fireplaces, bourgeois furnishings, wooden floors and the odd chandelier add a touch of grandeur to this old-fashioned one-star hotel.

Hôme St-Pierre HOSTEL **$**
(022 310 37 07; www.homestpierre.ch; Cour St-Pierre 4; dm Sfr31, s/d without bathroom Sfr48/72; reception 9am-noon & 4-8pm Mon-Sat, 9am-noon Sat; @) This boarding house was founded by the German Lutheran Church in 1874. Women are its primary clientele – just six dorm beds are up for grabs for six lucky guys – and the rooftop terrace that crowns the place is magical.

Hotel St-Gervais HOTEL **$$**
(022 732 45 72; www.stgervais-geneva.ch; Rue des Corps-Saints 20; d from Sfr140, s/d without bathroom from Sfr105/119; reception 7am-11pm) Travellers with jumbo-sized suitcases beware: scaling the seven floors in the pocket-handkerchief lift of this quaint choice near the train station is a squash and a squeeze. Renovated rooms are on the 1st and 7th floors.

Hôtel Bel'Esperance HOTEL **$$**
(022 818 37 37; www.hotel-bel-esperance.ch; Rue de la Vallée 1; s/d from Sfr105/154; reception 7am-10pm; @) This two-star hotel is a two-second flit to the Old Town. Rooms are quiet and cared for, and those on the 1st floor share a kitchen. Ride the lift to the 5th floor to flop on a chair on a flower-filled rooftop terrace. Free wi-fi.

La Cour des Augustins HOTEL **$$$**
(022 322 21 00; www.lacourdesaugustins.com; s/d from Sfr175/250; Rue Jean-Violette 15; P@) South of the centre and disguised by a 19th-century facade, the crisp white interior of this 'boutique gallery hotel' sports the latest technology and screams cutting edge.

Edelweiss HOTEL **$$$**
(022 544 51 51; www.manotel.com; Place de la Navigation 2; d from Sfr290;) Plunge yourself into the heart of the Swiss Alps *en ville* at this Heidi-style hideout, with its big cuddly St Bernard, fireplace and chalet-styled restaurant.

Hôtel Auteuil HOTEL **$$$**
(022 544 22 22; www.manotel.com; Rue de Lausanne 33; d from Sfr350; P@) The star of this design-driven hotel near the station is its collection of B&W photos of 1950s film stars in Geneva. Grab *The Book* from reception to find out precisely who's who where. Free wi-fi.

Hôtel Les Armures HOTEL **$$$**
(022 310 91 72; www.hotel-les-armures.ch; Rue du Puits-St-Pierre 1; s/d from Sfr450/720; P@) This slumbering 17th-century beauty oozes history from every last ceiling beam. Beautifully placed in the heart of Geneva's Old Town, it has an intimate and refined atmosphere.

WANT MORE?

Head to **Lonely Planet** (www.lonely planet.com/switzerland/geneva) for planning advice, author recommendations, traveller reviews and insider tips.

City Hostel HOSTEL $
(☎022 901 15 00; www.cityhostel.ch; Rue de Ferrier 2; dm from Sfr32, s/d from Sfr61; ⊙reception 7.30am-noon & 1pm-midnight; P⊖@) Spanking clean is the trademark of this well-organised hostel, where two-bed dorms give travellers a chance to double up cheaply. Rates include sheets, towels and use of the kitchen, TV room and a free locker.

Auberge de Jeunesse HOSTEL $
(☎022 732 62 60; www.yh-geneva.ch; Rue Rothschild 28-30; dm Sfr29, d from Sfr85; ⊙6.30-10am & 2pm-1am Jun-Sep, 6.30-10am & 4pm-midnight Oct-May; @) Dorms max out at 12 beds.

Eating

Geneva flaunts ethnic food galore. For the culinary curious with no fortune to blow, the Pâquis area cooks up cuisine from most corners of the globe in cheapish eateries. In the Old Town, terrace cafes and restaurants crowd Geneva's oldest square, medieval Place du Bourg-de-Four. Near the station, Scandale is a hot lunchtime spot. For quintessential Swiss fondue (Sfr32) and yodelling, **Edelweiss** (☎022 544 51 51; www.manotel.com; Place de la Navigation 2) is *the* address.

Chez Ma Cousine INTERNATIONAL $
(☎022 310 96 96; www.chezmacousine.ch; Place du Bourg-de-Four 6; mains Sfr14-17; ⊙lunch & dinner) *'On y mange du poulet'* (we eat chicken) is the strap line of this student institution that appeals for one good reason – generously handsome, homely portions of chicken, potatoes and salad at an unbeatable price.

Omnibus INTERNATIONAL $$
(☎022 321 44 45; www.omnibus-cafe.ch; Rue de la Coulouvrenière 23; mains Sfr19-45; ⊙lunch & dinner Mon-Fri, dinner Sat & Sun) Don't be fooled by the graffiti-plastered facade of this Rhône-side space. Inside, a maze of retro rooms seduces on first sight. Its business card is a recycled bus ticket.

L'Adresse INTERNATIONAL $$
(☎022 736 32 32; www.ladresse.ch; Rue du 31 Decembre 32; mains Sfr24-37; ⊙lunch & dinner Tue-Sat) An urban loft with rooftop terrace and hybrid lifestyle boutique–contemporary bistro, this hip address is at home in converted artist workshops. *The* address for lunch, brunch or (in their words) Saturday slunch...

Au Grütli INTERNATIONAL $$
(☎022 328 98 68; www.cafedu grutli.ch; Rue du Général Dufour 16; mains Sfr28-36; ⊙breakfast, lunch & dinner Mon-Fri, dinner Sat & Sun) Indonesian lamb, moussaka, scallops with ginger and citrus fruits or Provençal chicken are among the international flavours at this razor-sharp theatre restaurant.

Café de Paris FRENCH $$
(rue du Mont Blanc 26; mains Sfr40; ⊙lunch & dinner) A memorable dining experience since 1930. Everyone goes for the same thing here: green salad, beef steak with a killer-calorie herb and butter sauce, and as many fries as you can handle.

Les 5 Portes FRENCH $
(☎022 731 84 38; Rue de Zürich 5; mains Sfr16-22; ⊙breakfast, lunch & dinner Mon-Fri, lunch & dinner Sat & Sun) The Five Doors is a fashionable Pâquis port of call that embraces every mood and moment.

Mikado JAPANESE $
(☎022 732 47 74; Rue de l'Ancien Port 9; sushi Sfr2.50, mains Sfr6.50; ⊙lunch & dinner Tue-Sat) If it's authenticity, speed and tasty fast food on a red lacquered tray you want, this Japanese delicatessen hits the spot.

Drinking & Entertainment

Pâquis, the district in between the train station and lake, is particularly well endowed with bars. In summer the **paillote** (Quai du Mont-Blanc 30; ⊙to midnight), with wooden tables inches from the water, gets crammed.

Scandale BAR
(☎022 731 83 73; www.scandale.ch; Rue de Lausanne 24; ⊙11am-2am Tue-Fri, 5pm-2am Sat) Retro 1950s furnishings in a cavernous interior with comfy sofas ensures this lounge bar is never empty. Happenings include art exhibitions, Saturday-night DJs and bands.

Buvette des Bains BAR
(☎022 738 16 16; www.bains-des-paquis.ch; Quai du Mont-Blanc 30; ⊙8am-10pm) Meet Genevans at this earthy beach bar at Bains des Pâquis. Dining is on trays and in summer alfresco.

La Bretelle BAR
(☎022 732 75 96; Rue des Étuves 17; ⊙6pm-2am) Little has changed since the 1970s, when

this legendary bar opened. Live accordion accompanies French chansons most nights.

La Clémence BAR
(☎022 312 24 98; www.laclemence.ch; Place du Bourg-de-Four 20; ⏲7am-1am Mon-Thu & Sun, to 2am Fri & Sat) Indulge in a glass of local wine or an artisanal beer at this venerable cafe-bar located on Geneva's loveliest square.

La Plage BAR
(☎022 342 20 98; Rue Vautier 19; ⏲11am-1am Mon-Thu, 10am-2am Fri & Sat, 5pm-1am Sun) With bare wood tables, checked lino floor, green wooden shutters and tables outside, the Beach in Carouge is a timeless drinking hole.

L'Usine CLUB
(☎022 781 34 90; www.usine.ch; Place des Volontaires 4) This grungy and youthful converted gold-roughing factory entertains with dance nights, art happenings, theatre, cabaret and club nights.

Piment Vert BAR
(☎022 731 93 03; www.pimentvert.ch; Place De-Grenus 4; ⏲11.30am-2.45pm & 5.30-10pm Mon-Fri, noon-4pm Sat) Fast, fresh, and trendy sums up this hybrid Indian-Sri Lankan bar.

Le Chat Noir LIVE MUSIC
(☎022 343 49 98; www.chatnoir.ch, in French; Rue Vautier 13; ⏲Tue-Sat) Nightly jazz, rock, funk and salsa gigs.

Le Déclic CLUB
(☎022 320 59 40; www.ledeclic.ch; Blvd du Pont d'Arve 28; ⏲5pm-2am Mon-Fri, 9pm-2am Sat) Gay nightclub.

Ciné Lac CINEMA
(www.cinelac.ch, in French; adult/under 14yr Sfr17/14; ⏲Jul & Aug) Glorious summertime open-air cinema with a screen set up on the lakeside.

Information

Cantonal Hospital (☎022 372 33 11; emergency 022 372 81 20; www.hug-ge.ch; Rue Micheli du Crest 24)

Police station (☎117; Rue de Berne 6)

Post office (Rue du Mont-Blanc 18; ⏲7.30am-6pm Mon-Fri, 9am-4pm Sat)

SOS Médecins à Domicile (☎022 748 49 50; www.sos-medecins.ch, in French) Home/hotel doctor calls.

Tourist office (☎022 909 70 00; www.geneve-tourisme.ch; Rue du Mont-Blanc 18; ⏲10am-6pm Mon, 9am-6pm Tue-Sat)

Getting There & Away

AIR **Aéroport International de Genève** (GVA; ☎0900 57 15 00; www.gva.ch), 4km from town, has connections to major European cities and many others worldwide. It is also an easyJet hub.

BOAT **CGN** (Compagnie Générale de Navigation; ☎0848 811 848; www.cgn.ch) operates a steamer service from its Jardin Anglais jetty to other villages on Lake Geneva. Many only sail May to September, including those to/from Lausanne (Sfr37.60, 3½ hours). Eurail and Swiss Pass holders are valid on CGN boats or there is a one-day CGN boat pass (Sfr49).

BUS International buses depart from the **bus station** (☎0900 320 320, 022 732 02 30; www.coach-station.com; Place Dorcière).

TRAIN Trains run to most Swiss towns including at least hourly to/from Lausanne (Sfr20.60, 40 minutes), Bern (Sfr46, 1¾ hours) and Zürich (Sfr80, 2¾ hours).

International daily rail connections from Geneva include Paris (TGV from Sfr130, 3½ hours),

WORTH A TRIP

ZEN OUT IN GRYON & LEYSIN

Trek off the beaten track to lap up Swiss alpine charm in untouched **Gryon** (1130m), with great meadow hiking trails and **Chalet Martin** (☎024 498 33 21; Chalet Martin; www.gryon.com; dm/d from Sfr25/70; P@), a Swiss-Australian-run hostel that travellers give rave reviews. The vibe is strictly laid-back and the place organises dozens of activities – paragliding, skiing and chocolate tasting included. Take a train from Lausanne to Bex (Sfr17.40, 40 minutes, hourly), then the cogwheel train to Gryon (Sfr6.20, 30 minutes, hourly). The hostel is a five-minute signposted walk from the train stop.

Equally Zen is **Leysin**, a hub for skiers, boarders and hikers who can't sing the praises highly enough of **Hiking Sheep** (☎024 494 35 35; www.hikingsheep.com; dm/d Sfr30/80; P❄@). The tall, art deco house has a kitchen, great communal facilities, a pine-forested backyard and breathtaking views from its balconies. Find it a two-minute walk from Leysin-Grand Hôtel train station. Ride the cogwheel train from Aigle (Sfr10.80, 30 minutes, hourly), in turn linked by train with Lausanne (Sfr14.80, 30 minutes, hourly).

Hamburg (from Sfr278, 9½ hours), Milan (from Sfr97, 4½ hours) and Barcelona (from Sfr125, 10 hours).

Getting Around

TO/FROM THE AIRPORT Getting from the airport is easy with regular trains into Gare de Cornavin (Sfr3, eight minutes). Slower bus 10 (Sfr3) does the same 5km trip. A metered taxi costs Sfr30 to Sfr50.

Bicycle Pick up a bike at Genève Roule (%022 740 13 43; www.geneveroule.ch; Place de Montbrillant 17; h8am-6pm Mon-Sat) or its seasonal Jetée des Pâquis pick-up point for Sfr12/20 per day/weekend. May to October, borrow a bike (with advertisements on it) for free.

PUBLIC TRANSPORT Buses, trams, trains and boats service the city, and ticket dispensers are found at all stops. Tickets cost Sfr2 (within one zone, 30 minutes) or Sfr3 (two zones, one hour), and a city/canton day pass is Sfr7/12. The same tickets are also valid on the yellow shuttle boats known as Les Mouettes (the seagulls) that criss-cross the lake every 10 minutes between 7.30am and 6pm.

LAKE GENEVA REGION

East of Geneva, Western Europe's biggest lake stretches like a giant liquid mirror between French-speaking Switzerland on its northern shore and France to the south. Known as Lake Geneva by many and Lac Léman to Francophones, the Swiss side of the lake cossets the elegant city of Lausanne, the pretty palm tree–studded Riviera resort of Montreux, and the marvellous emerald spectacle of vines marching up steep hillsides in strict unison.

Lausanne

POP 125,900

In a fabulous location overlooking Lake Geneva, Lausanne is an enchanting beauty with several distinct personalities: the former fishing village of Ouchy, with its summer beach-resort feel; Place St-François, with stylish, cobblestone shopping streets; and Flon, a warehouse district of bars, galleries and boutiques. It's also got a few amazing sights. One of the country's grandest Gothic cathedrals dominates its medieval centre.

The **tourist office** (021 613 73 21; www.lausanne-tourisme.ch; Place de la Navigation 4; 9am-6pm Oct-Mar, to 8pm Apr-Sep) neighbours Ouchy metro station and has a **branch office** (Place de la Gare 9; 9am-7pm) at the train station.

Sights & Activities

Musée de l'Art Brut MUSEUM
(021 315 25 70; www.artbrut.ch; Ave des Bergières 11-13; adult/student/child Sfr10/5/free, 1st Sat of month free; 11am-6pm Tue-Sun Sep-Jun, daily Jul & Aug) This alluring museum showcases a fascinating amalgam of 15,000 works of art created by untrained artists – psychiatric patients, eccentrics and incarcerated criminals. The works offer a striking variety, at times a surprising technical capacity and in some cases an inspirational world view. Biographies and explanations are in English. The museum is about 600m northwest of Place St François; take bus 2 or 3 to the Beaulieu stop.

Musée Olympique MUSEUM
(021 621 65 11; www.museum.olympic.org; Quai d'Ouchy 1; adult/student/child Sfr15/10/free; 9am-6pm Apr-Oct, 9am-6pm Tue-Sun Nov-Mar) Lausanne is home to the International Olympic Committee, and sports aficionados can immerse themselves in archival footage, interactive computers and memorabilia at the information-packed Musée Olympique.

Cathédrale de Notre Dame CHURCH
(7am-7pm Mon-Fri, 8am-7pm Sat & Sun Apr-Aug, 7am-5.30pm Sep-Mar) This glorious Gothic cathedral is arguably the finest in Switzerland. Built in the 12th and 13th centuries, highlights include the stunningly detailed carved portal, vaulted ceilings and archways, and carefully restored stained-glass windows.

Sleeping

Hotel guests get a Lausanne Transport Card covering unlimited use of public transport for the duration of their stay.

Lausanne Guest House GUEST HOUSE $
(021 601 80 00; www.lausanne-guesthouse.ch; Chemin des Épinettes 4; dm Sfr36, s/d Sfr96/125, without bathroom Sfr86/105; P@) An attractive mansion converted into quality backpacking accommodation near the train station. Many rooms have lake views and some of the building's energy is solar.

Hôtel du Port HOTEL $$$
(021 612 04 44; www.hotel-du-port.ch; Place du Port 5; s/d from Sfr165/195;) A perfect location in Ouchy, just back from the lake, makes this a good choice. The best doubles peep at the lake and suites slumber on the 3rd floor.

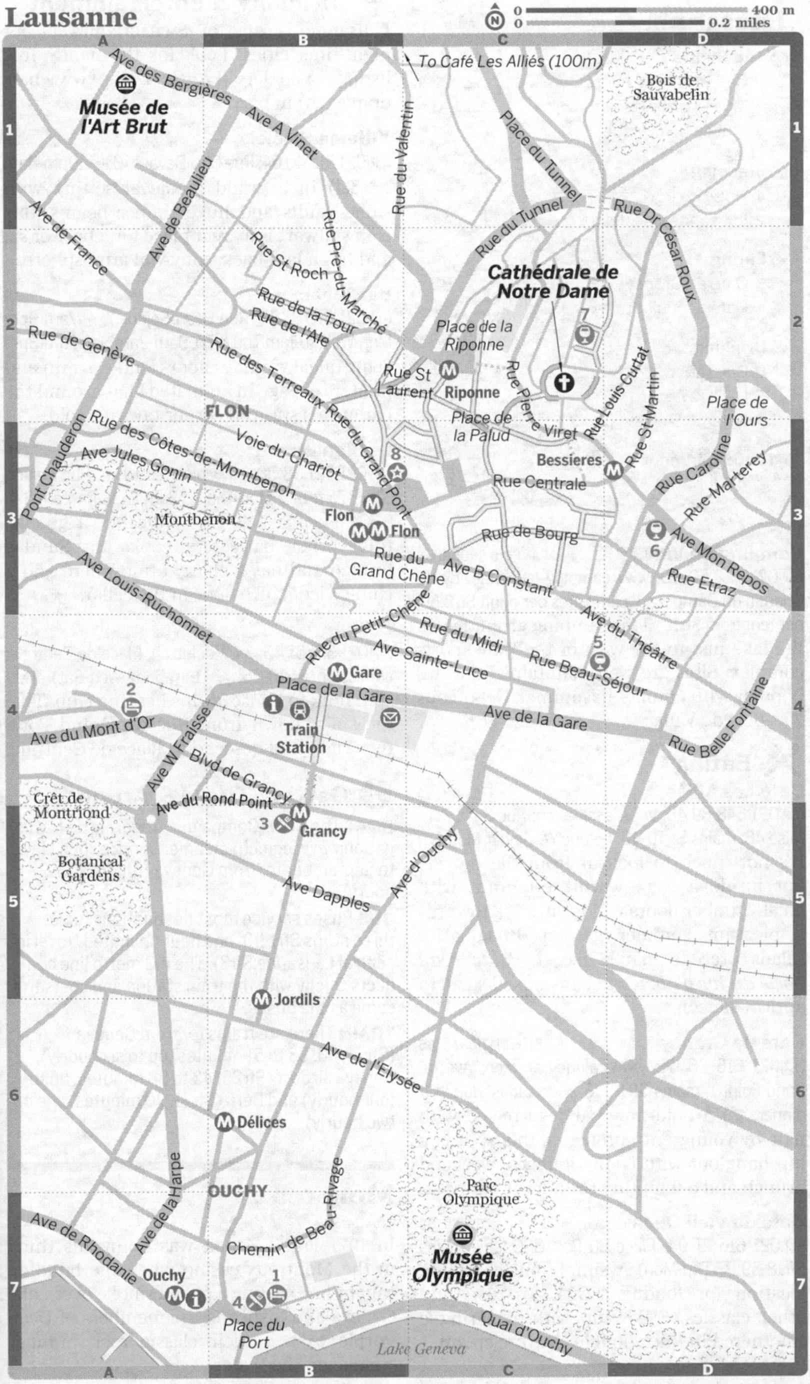

0 400 m
0 0.2 miles

A B C D

To Café Les Alliés (100m)

Musée de l'Art Brut
Ave des Bergières
Ave A Vinet
Rue du Valentin
Place du Tunnel
Bois de Sauvabelin
Ave de Beaulieu
Ave de France
Rue Pré-du-Marché
Rue St Roch
Rue du Tunnel
Rue Dr César Roux
Cathédrale de Notre Dame
Rue de la Tour
Rue de l'Ale
Rue de Genève
Rue des Terreaux
Place de la Riponne
7
Rue St Laurent
Riponne
Rue Pierre Viret
Rue Louis Curtat
Rue St Martin
Place de l'Ours
FLON
Rue des Côtes-de-Montbenon
Rue du Grand Pont
Place de la Palud
Voie du Chariot
Ave Jules Gonin
8
Bessières
Rue Caroline
Rue Marterey
Pont Chauderon
Rue Centrale
Montbenon
Flon
Flon
Rue de Bourg
6
Ave Mon Repos
Rue du Grand Chêne
Ave B Constant
Rue Etraz
Ave Louis-Ruchonnet
Rue du Petit-Chêne
Rue du Midi
Ave du Théatre
5
Ave Sainte-Luce
Rue Beau-Séjour
Gare
Place de la Gare
2
Train Station
Ave de la Gare
Rue Belle Fontaine
Ave du Mont d'Or
Ave W Fraisse
Blvd de Grancy
Crêt de Montriond
Ave du Rond Point
3
Grancy
Botanical Gardens
Ave d'Ouchy
Ave Dapples
Jordils
Ave de l'Elysée
Délices
Ave de la Harpe
OUCHY
Chemin de Beau-Rivage
Parc Olympique
Ave de Rhodanie
Musée Olympique
Ouchy
1
4
Place du Port
Quai d'Ouchy
Lake Geneva

Lausanne

Top Sights

	Cathédrale de Notre Dame	C2
	Musée de l'Art Brut	A1
	Musée Olympique	C7

Sleeping

1	Hôtel du Port	B7
2	Lausanne GuestHouse	A4

Eating

3	Café de Grancy	B5
4	Café du Vieil Ouchy	B7

Drinking

5	Bar Tabac	C4
6	Le Bleu Lézard	D3
7	XIIleme Siècle	C2

Entertainment

8	D-Club	B3

Camping de Vidy CAMPING GROUND **$**
(021 622 50 00; www.camping lausannevidy.ch; Chemin du Camping 3; campsites per adult Sfr8.50, per tent from Sfr12) This camping ground is on the lake just to the west of the Vidy sports complex. Sites are well maintained and it's popular with families in summer. Get off bus 2 at Bois de Vaux.

Eating

Café Les Alliés FRENCH **$$**
(021 648 69 40; www.lesallies.ch; Rue de la Pontaise 48; mains Sfr19-40; lunch & dinner Mon-Fri) It's not much to look at from the outside but inside a cosy, warm restaurant with creaky timber floors winds out back towards a pleasant summer garden. Imaginative salads precede mains like *steak de veau poêlé au jus d'abricots* (pan-cooked steak in apricot sauce).

Café de Grancy INTERNATIONAL **$$**
(021 616 86 66; www.cafédegrancy.ch; Ave du Rond Point 1; mains Sfr18-36; breakfast, lunch & dinner;) An old-time bar resurrected with flair by young entrepreneurs, this spot is a hip hang-out with comfy lounges, weekend brunch and a tempting restaurant out back.

Café du Vieil Ouchy SWISS **$$**
(021 616 21 94; Place du Port 3, Ouchy; mains Sfr18-39; Thu-Mon) A simple but charming location for fondue (Sfr24.50), rösti and other classics. Follow up with a meringue smothered in thick double Gruyère cream.

Drinking & Entertainment

Lausanne is one of Switzerland's busier night-time cities. Look for the handy free listings booklet *What's Up* (www.whats upmag.ch) in bars.

XIIleme Siècle PUB
(021 312 40 64; Rue Cité-Devant 10; 10pm-4am Tue-Sat) In a grand medieval setting with stone vaults and huge timber beams, this cosy stalwart is a great place for a beer or six and has a laid-back, convivial atmosphere.

Bar Tabac BAR
(021 312 33 16; Rue Beau Séjour 7; 7am-9pm Mon-Wed, to 1am Thu & Fri, 9am-2am Sat, 9am-3pm Sun) Squeaky timber floors lend warmth and punters engage in animated chat around the bar at this spruced corner tavern of old.

Le Bleu Lézard BAR
(021 321 38 30; www.bleu-lezard.ch; Rue Enning 10; 7am-1am Mon-Thu, to 2am Fri, 8am-2am Sat, 9.30am-1am Sun;) An oldie but a goodie, this corner bar-eatery cooks up Sunday brunch and has a chatty atmosphere and a club-styled dance floor in the cellar.

D-Club CLUB
(021 351 51 40; www.dclub.ch; Place de Centrale; admission Sfr10-25; 11pm-5am Wed-Sat) DJs spin funk to house at this heaving club. Take the stairs down from Rue du Grand Pont, turn right and descend to Place de Centrale.

Getting There & Around

BOAT The **CGN** (Compagnie Générale de Navigation; www.cgn.ch) steamer service runs May to September to/from Geneva (Sfr37.60, 3½ hours).

BUS Buses service most destinations (up to three stops Sfr1.90, one hour unlimited travel in central Lausanne Sfr3). The m2 metro line connects Ouchy with the train station and costs the same as the buses.

TRAIN There are trains to/from Geneva (Sfr20.60, 33 to 51 minutes, up to six hourly), Geneva airport (Sfr25, 42 to 58 minutes, up to four hourly) and Bern (Sfr31, 70 minutes, one or two hourly).

Montreux

POP 24,600

In 1971 Frank Zappa was doing his thing in the Montreux casino when the building caught fire, casting a pall of smoke over Lake Geneva and inspiring the members of Deep Purple to pen their classic rock number 'Smoke on the Water'.

The showpiece of the Swiss Riviera has been an inspiration to writers, artists and musicians for centuries. Famous one-time residents include Lord Byron, Ernest Hemingway and the Shelleys. It's easy to see why: Montreux boasts stunning Alp views, tidy rows of pastel buildings and Switzerland's most extraordinary castle.

Each year crowds throng to the **Montreux Jazz Festival** (www.montreuxjazz.com) for a fortnight in early July. Free concerts take place every day, but big-name gigs cost (Sfr40 to Sfr100).

Sights

Château de Chillon CASTLE

(☎021 966 89 10; www.chillon.ch; Ave de Chillon 21; adult/student/child Sfr12/10/6; ⏰9am-7pm Apr-Sep, 9.30am-6pm Mar & Oct, 10am-4pm Nov-Feb, last entry 1hr before close) Originally constructed on the shores of Lake Geneva in the 11th century, Château de Chillon was brought to the world's attention by Lord Byron and the world has been filing past ever since. Spend at least a couple of hours exploring its numerous courtyards, towers, dungeons and halls filled with arms, period furniture and artwork.

The castle is a 45-minute lakefront walk from Montreux. Otherwise trolley bus 1 (Sfr2.30) passes every 10 minutes.

Sleeping & Eating

Hôtel Masson HOTEL $$

(☎021 966 00 44; www.hotelmasson.ch; Rue Bonivard 5; d from Sfr120; P📶) In 1829, this vintner's mansion was converted into a hotel. Its old charm has remained intact and the hotel, set in magnificent grounds, is on the Swiss Heritage list of most beautiful hotels in the country. Find it in the hills southeast of Montreux.

Auberge de Jeunesse HOSTEL $

(☎021 963 49 34; Passage de l'Auberge 8, Territet; dm from Sfr33; ⏰mid-Feb–mid-Nov; @) This chirpy hostel is a 30-minute walk along the lake clockwise from the tourist office (or take the local train to Territet or bus 1).

Hôtel La Rouvenaz HOTEL $$

(☎021 963 27 36; Rue du Marché 1; s/d from Sfr130/190; @📶) A simple, family-run spot with 12 rooms and its own Italian restaurant, you cannot get any closer to the lake or the heart of the action.

Montagnard SWISS $$

(☎021 964 83 49; www.montagnard.ch; mains Sfr22-28; ⏰Wed-Sun) For a taste of country fare in a timber farmhouse with gardens, head to this restaurant in the village of Villard-sur-Chamby, a 9.5km taxi ride from central Montreux.

FAIRYLAND ABSINTHE

It was in the deepest darkest depths of the Val de Travers – dubbed the Pays des Fées (Fairyland) – that the magical green drink absinthe was first distilled in 1740; it was first produced commercially in 1797 (although it was a Frenchman called Pernod who made the first known bitter green liqueur just a few kilometres across the French–Swiss border in Pontarlier).

From 1910, following Switzerland's prohibition of the wickedly alcoholic and ruthlessly bitter aniseed drink, distillers of the so-called 'devil in the bottle' in the Val de Travers moved underground. In 1990 the great-grandson of a preprohibition distiller in Môtiers came up with Switzerland's first legal aniseed liqueur since 1910 – albeit one which was only 45% proof alcohol (instead of 50% to 75%) and which scarcely contained thujone (the offensive chemical found in wormwood, said to be the root of absinthe's devilish nature). An *extrait d'absinthe* (absinthe extract) quickly followed and in 2005, following Switzerland's lifting of its absinthe ban, the **Blackmint – Distillerie Kübler & Wyss** (☎032 861 14 69; www.blackmint.ch; Rue du Château 7) in Môtiers distilled its first true and authentic batch of the mythical *fée verte* (green fairy) from valley-grown wormwood. Mix one part crystal-clear liqueur with five parts water to make it green (and wait for light and floaty feelings to hit, as was the case after the first glass we shared with friends back home!).

Swilling the green fairy, aka absinthe, at the bar aboard an old steam train as it puffs the length of the Val de Travers is particularly evocative. Jump aboard in Neuchâtel with **Vapeur Val de Travers** (☎032 863 24 07; www.rvt-historique-ch; Rue de la Gare 19, Travers; day trips with lunch Sfr75).

Café du Grütli SWISS $$
(☎021 963 42 65; Rue du Grand Chêne 8; mains Sfr18-30; ⏲Wed-Mon) This cheerful little eatery is hidden in the old part of town and provides good home cooking. Think rösti with ham, hearty meat dishes, salads and the inevitable fondue.

Getting There & Away

There are trains to Geneva (Sfr28, 70 minutes, hourly) and Lausanne (Sfr10.20, 25 minutes, three hourly). Make the scenic journey to Interlaken via the GoldenPass Panoramic, with changes at Zweisimmen and Spiez (Sfr80, three hours, daily; rail passes valid).

Gruyères

With its riot of 15th- to 17th-century houses, cobbled heart, and menus of cheese and featherweight meringues drowned in thick cream, Gruyères is so dreamy even Sleeping Beauty wouldn't wake up.

Sights & Activities

Maison du Gruyère CHEESERY
(☎026 921 84 00; www.lamaisondugruyere.ch; adult/under 12yr Sfr7/3; ⏲9am-7pm Apr-Sep, to 6pm Oct-Mar) The beans about Gruyères' hard name-protected cheese, made for centuries in its surrounding alpine pastures, are spilled here in Pringy, 1.5km away. The cheese-making takes place several times daily and can be watched through glass windows.

FREE **Fromagerie d'Alpage de Moléson** CHEESERY
(☎026 921 10 44; ⏲9.30am-10pm mid-May–mid-Oct) At this 17th-century mountain chalet, 5km southwest of Gruyères in Moléson-sur-Gruyères (elevation 1100m), cheese is made a couple of times a day in summer using old-fashioned methods.

Musée HR Giger MUSEUM
(☎026 921 22 00; adult/child Sfr10/5; ⏲10am-6pm Apr-Oct, to 5pm Tue-Sun Nov-Mar) Fans of the *Alien* movies will relish this shrine to HR Giger's expansive imagination in a 16th-century mansion. Finish with a drink in the Giger-style bar opposite.

Sentier des Fromageries WALK
For more cheese-making, hike through green Gruyères pastures to a couple of tiny mountain huts where shepherds make cheese in summer along the Sentier des Fromageries (7km to 8km, two hours). The **tourist office** (☎026 921 10 30; www.gruyeres.ch, in French; Rue du Bourg 1; ⏲10.30am-noon & 1.30-4.30pm Mon-Fri, plus 9am-5pm Sat & Sun Jul–mid-Sep) has details.

Château CASTLE
(☎026 921 21 02; www.chateau-gruyeres.ch; adult/child Sfr9.50/3; ⏲9am-6pm Apr-Oct, 10am-

WORTH A TRIP

NEUCHÂTEL

Its Old Town sandstone elegance, the airy Gallic nonchalance of its cafe life and the gay lakeside air that breezes along the shoreline of its glittering lake make Neuchâtel disarmingly charming. The small university town, complete with its own spirited *comune libre* (free commune), is compact enough to discover on foot, while the French spoken here is said to be Switzerland's purest. Not just that: Neuchâtel's town observatory gives the official time-check for all of Switzerland.

The pedestrian zone and Place Pury (the local bus hub) are about 1km from the train station; walk down the hill along Ave de la Gare. The lakeside **tourist office** (☎032 889 68 90; www.neuchateltourism.ch; Hôtel des Postes, Place du Port; ⏲9am-noon & 1.30-5.30pm Mon-Fri, to noon Sat Sep-Jun, 9am-6.30pm Mon-Fri, 9am-4pm Sat, 10am-2pm Sun Jul & Aug) is next to the post office.

The 15th-century **Chateau de Neuchâtel** (☎032 889 60 00; guided tours free; ⏲10am-noon & 2-4pm Mon-Sat, 2-4pm Sun Apr-Sep) and the adjoining **Collegiate Church** are the centrepieces of the Old Town. The striking cenotaph of 15 statues dates from 1372. Scale the nearby **prison tower** (☎032 717 71 02; Rue Jehanne de Hochberg 5; admission Sfr1; ⏲8am-6pm Apr-Sep) for broad views of town and lake.

Visit the **Musée d'Art et d'Histoire** (☎032 717 79 25; www.mahn.ch, in French; Esplanade Léopold Robert 1; adult/under 16yr Sfr8/free, Wed free; ⏲11am-6pm Tue-Sun) to see beloved 18th-century clockwork figures.

Trains serve Geneva (Sfr38, 70 minutes, hourly), Bern (Sfr18.20, 35 minutes, hourly) and other destinations.

WORTH A TRIP

THE JURA

The grandest towns in this clover-shaped canton are little more than enchanting villages. Deep, mysterious forests and impossible green clearings succeed one another across the low mountains of the Jura and some 1200km of marked paths across the canton give hikers plenty of scope. This is the place to escape.

Its capital is **Delémont**, though there is little reason to linger. Head instead 12km northwest to stroll around contemporary art and installations at the open-air sculpture park **La Balade de Séprais** (www.balade-seprais.ch). Or feast on thin crisp *tartes flambées* and apple cake to die for at **Hôtel-Restaurant de la Demi Lune** (☎032 461 35 31; Place Roger Schaffter; s/d from Sfr95/100) in **St Ursanne**, a drop-dead-gorgeous medieval village with a 12th-century Gothic church, 16th-century town gate, clusters of ancient houses and a lovely stone bridge crossing the Doubs River.

The **tourist office** (☎032 420 47 73; Place Roger Schaffter; ⏰10am-noon & 2-5pm Mon-Fri, 10am-4pm Sat & Sun) offers up heaps of information on river kayaking, canoeing and walking.

From Delémont there are trains heading to St Ursanne (Sfr6.80, 20 minutes, hourly), from where you can continue to Porrentuy (Sfr4.80, 12 minutes).

4.30pm Nov-Feb) The ab fab turreted castle is Gruyères' crowning glory.

Eating

Chalet de Gruyères SWISS $$

(☎026 921 21 54; www.chalet-gruyeres.ch, in French; Rue du Château 53; fondues & raclettes Sfr30; ⏰lunch & dinner) Dip into a *moitié-moitié* (mix of Gruyère and soft local vacherin) at this cosy, cowbell-strewn restaurant where fondue is the star of every menu, irrespective of season (locals only eat fondue in winter).

Getting There & Away

Gruyères can be reached by hourly bus or train (Sfr17.20, 40 minutes to one hour) from Fribourg to Bulle, then another hourly bus or train (Sfr3.50, 15 to 20 minutes). The village is a 10-minute walk uphill from the train station.

VALAIS

Matterhorn country: an intoxicating land that seduces the toughest of critics with its endless panoramic vistas and breathtaking views. This is an earthy part of southern Switzerland where farmers were so poor a century ago they didn't have two francs to rub together, yet today it's a jet-set land where celebrities sip Sfr10,000 champagne cocktails from ice-carved goblets.

An area of extraordinary natural beauty, the outdoors here is so great it never goes out of fashion. Switzerland's 10 highest mountains – all over 4000m – rise to the sky here, while snow fiends ski and board in one of Europe's top resorts, Zermatt. When snows melt and valleys turn lush green, hiking opportunities are boundless.

Zermatt

POP 5800

Since the mid-19th century, Zermatt has starred among Switzerland's glitziest resorts. Today it attracts intrepid mountaineers and hikers, skiers who cruise at snail's pace, spellbound by the scenery, and style-conscious darlings flashing designer togs in the lounge bars. But all are smitten with the Matterhorn (4478m), the Alps' most famous peak and an unfathomable monolith synonymous with Switzerland that you simply can't quite stop looking at.

Sights & Activities

Gornergrat MOUNTAIN

Alpine views of Gornergrat (3090m) from the cable cars and gondolas are uniformly breathtaking, especially from the **cogwheel train** (one way Sfr38), which takes 35 to 45 minutes with two to three departures per hour. Sit on the right-hand side to gawp at the Matterhorn. Alternatively, hike from Zermatt to Gornergrat in five hours.

Cemetery CEMETERY

A walk in Zermatt's cemetery is a sobering experience for any would-be mountaineer, as numerous monuments tell of untimely deaths on Monte Rosa and the Matterhorn.

Matterhorn Museum MUSEUM
(☎027 967 41 00; www.matterhornmuseum.ch; Kirchplatz; adult/student/10-16yr/under 10yr Sfr10/8/5/free; ⏲11am-6pm mid-Dec–Sep, 2-6pm Oct, closed Nov–mid-Dec) On 13 July 1865 Edward Whymper led the first successful ascent of the mountain. The climb took 32 hours but the descent was marred by tragedy when four team members crashed to their deaths in a 1200m fall down the North Wall. Visit the museum to see the infamous rope that broke.

Alpin Center SKI SCHOOL
(☎027 966 24 60; www.alpincenter-zermatt.ch; Bahnhofstrasse 58; ⏲8.30am-noon & 3-7pm mid-Nov–Apr & Jul-Sep) Climbs led by mountain guides can be arranged to major 4000ers, including Breithorn (Sfr165), Riffelhorn (Sfr257) and, for experts willing to acclimatise for a week, Matterhorn (Sfr998). The program also covers multiday hikes, glacier hikes to Gorner (Sfr120), snowshoeing (Sfr140) and ice-climbing (Sfr175).

Skiing SKIING
For skiers and snowboarders, Zermatt is cruising heaven, with mostly long, scenic red runs, plus a scattering of blues for ski virgins and knuckle-whitening black runs for experts. The three main skiing areas are **Rothorn**, **Stockhorn** (good for mogul fans) and **Klein Matterhorn** (snowboarding freestyle park and half-pipe) – holding 300km of ski runs in all, with free buses shuttling skiers between areas. February to April is peak time. Snow can be sketchy in early summer but lifts are significantly quieter.

A day pass covering all ski lifts in Zermatt (excluding Cervinia) costs Sfr67/57/34 per adult/student/child and Sfr75/64/38 including Cervinia.

Klein Matterhorn SKIING
Klein Matterhorn is topped by Europe's highest cable-car station (3820m), providing access to Europe's highest skiing, Switzerland's most extensive summer skiing (25km of runs) and deep powder at the Italian resort of **Cervinia**. Broad and exhilarating, the No 7 run down from the border is a must-ski. Don't forget your passport.

If the weather is fine, take the lift up to the summit of Klein Matterhorn (3883m) for top-of-the-beanstalk views over the Swiss Alps (from Mont Blanc to Aletschhorn) and deep into Italy.

Sleeping & Eating

Most places close May to mid-June and again from October to mid-November.

Berggasthaus Trift HOSTEL $
(☎079 408 70 20; dm/d with half-board Sfr66/152; ⏲Jul-Sep) It's a trudge to this 2337m-high mountain hut but the hike is outstanding. The alpine haven is run by Hugo (a whiz on the alphorn) and Fabienne, who serve treats such as home-cured beef and oven-warm apple tart on the terrace. Get the camera ready for when the sun sets over Monte Rosa.

Hotel Bahnhof HOTEL $$
(☎027 967 24 06; www.hotelbahnhof.com; Bahnhofstrasse; dm Sfr40, s/d Sfr70/110; wi-fi) Opposite the station, these spruce budget digs have a lounge, a snazzy open-plan kitchen and proper beds that are a godsend after scaling or schussing down mountains all day. Free wi-fi.

Zermatt SYHA Hostel HOSTEL $
(☎027 967 23 20; Staldenweg 5; dm/d from Sfr48/110; @) Question: how many hostels have the Matterhorn peeking through the window in the morning? Answer: one. And if that doesn't convince you, the modern dorms, sunny terrace and first-rate facilities should.

Whymper Stube SWISS $$
(☎027 967 22 96; Bahnhofstrasse 80; mains Sfr23-42) The mantra at this alpine classic serving the tastiest fondue in Zermatt (including variations with pears and gorgonzola): gorge today, climb tomorrow.

Bayard Metzgerei SWISS $
(☎027 967 22 66; Bahnhofstrasse 9; sausages from Sfr6; ⏲noon-6.30pm Jul-Sep, 4-6.30pm Dec-Mar) Follow your nose to this butcher's grill for to-go bratwurst, chicken and other carnivorous bites.

Drinking

Papperla Pub PUB
(☎027 967 40 40; Steinmattstrasse 34; ⏲11am-11.30pm; wi-fi) Rammed with sloshed skiers, this pub blends pulsating music with lethal Jägermeister bombs and good vibes. Squeeze in, slam shots, then shuffle downstairs to Schneewittchen club (open to 4am) for more of the same.

Hennu Stall BAR
(☎027 966 35 10; Klein Matterhorn; ⏲2-7pm) Last one down to this snow-bound 'chicken run' is a rotten egg. Hennu is the wildest après-ski shack on Klein Matterhorn. A metre-long

'ski' of shots will make you cluck all the way down to Zermatt.

Igloo Bar BAR

(Gornergrat; www.iglu-dorf.ch; ⏲10am-4pm) Sub-zero sippers sunbathe, stare wide-mouthed at the Matterhorn and guzzle glühwein amid the ice sculptures at this igloo bar. It's on the run from Gornergrat to Riffelberg.

Information

The **tourist office** (☎027 966 81 00; www.zermatt.ch; Bahnhofplatz 5; ⏲8.30am-6pm Mon-Sat, 8.30am-noon & 1.30-6pm Sun mid-Jun–Sep, 8.30am-noon & 1.30-6pm Mon-Sat, 9.30am-noon & 4-6pm Sun Oct–mid-Jun) has all the bumph.

Getting There & Around

CAR Zermatt is car-free, and dinky electric vehicles are used to transport goods and serve as taxis around town. Drivers have to leave their vehicles in one of the garages or the open-air car park in Tδsch (Sfr13.50 per day) and take the train (Sfr7.60, 12 minutes) into Zermatt.

TRAIN Trains depart roughly every 20 minutes from Brig (Sfr35, 1½ hours), stopping at Vispen route. Zermatt is also the starting point of the *Glacier Express* to Graubünden, one of the most spectacular train rides in the world.

BERN

POP 123,400

One of the planet's most underrated capitals, Bern is a fabulous find. With the genteel old soul of a Renaissance man and the heart of a high-flying 21st-century gal, the riverside city is both medieval and modern. The 15th-century Old Town is gorgeous enough to sweep you off your feet and make you forget the century (it's definitely worthy of its 1983 Unesco World Heritage site protection order). But the edgy vintage boutiques, artsy-intellectual bars and Renzo Piano's futuristic art museum crammed with Paul Klee pieces slam you firmly back into the present.

Sights

Old Town HISTORIC AREA

Bern's flag-bedecked medieval centre is an attraction in its own right, with 6km of covered arcades and cellar shops/bars descending from the streets. After a devastating fire in 1405, the wooden city was rebuilt in today's sandstone.

Bern's **Zytglogge** (clock tower) is a focal point; crowds congregate around to watch its revolving figures twirl at four minutes before the hour, after which the actual chimes begin. Tours enter the tower to see the clock mechanism from May to October; contact the tourist office for details.

Equally enchanting are the 11 decorative **fountains** (1545) depicting historical and folkloric characters. Most are along Marktgasse as it becomes Kramgasse and Gerechtigkeitsgasse, but the most famous lies in Kornhausplatz: the **Kindlifresserbrunnen** (Ogre Fountain) of a giant snacking...on children.

Inside the 15th-century Gothic **Münster** (cathedral; www.bernermuenster.ch; tower adult/7-16yr Sfr5/2, audioguide Sfr5; ⏲10am-5pm Mon-Sat, 11.30am-5pm Sun summer, noon-4pm Mon-Fri, 10am-5pm Sat, 11.30am-4pm winter, tower closes 30min earlier), a 344-step hike up the lofty spire – Switzerland's tallest – is worth the climb.

Paul Klee Centre MUSEUM

(☎031 359 01 01; www.zpk.org; Monument in Fruchtland 3; adult/6-16yr Sfr18/6, audioguides Sfr5; ⏲10am-5pm Tue-Sun) Bern's Guggenheim, the fabulous Zentrum Paul Klee is an eye-catching 150m-long building designed by Renzo Piano 3km east on the outskirts of town. Inside the three-peak structure, the middle 'hill' showcases 4000 rotating works from Paul Klee's prodigious and often playful career. Interactive computer displays built into the seating mean you can get the low-down on all the Swiss-born artist's major pieces, and music audioguides (Sfr5) take visitors on one-hour DIY musical tours of his work.

In the basement of another 'hill' is **Kindermuseum Creaviva**, an inspired children's museum where kids can experiment with hands-on art exhibits (included in admission price) or sign up for a one-hour art workshop (Sfr15).

In the grounds, a walk through fields takes visitors past a stream of modern and contemporary sculptures, including works by Yoko Ono and Sol Lewitt; the walk also affords views of the museum's wave-like living roof sections.

Take bus 12 from Bubenbergplatz to Zentrum Paul Klee (Sfr3.80; sit on the right for the best views of the city on your way out there). By car the museum is right next to the Bern-Ostring exit of the A6.

Einstein Museum MUSEUM

(☎031 312 00 91; www.einstein-bern.ch; Kramgasse 49; adult/student Sfr6/4.50; ⏲10am-7pm Mon-Fri, to 4pm Sat Feb-Dec) The world's most famous

Bern

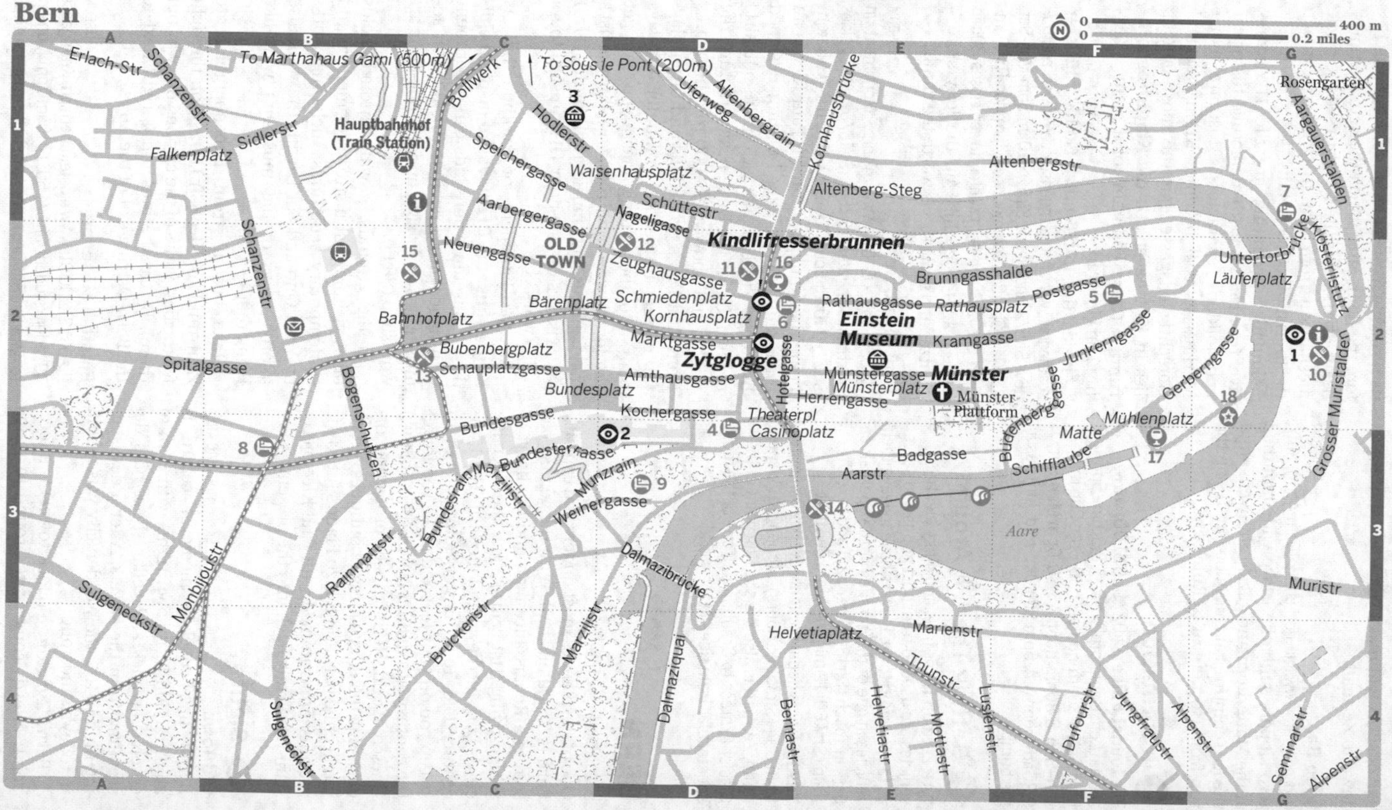
0 400 m
0 0.2 miles
To Marthahaus Garni (500m)
To Sous le Pont (200m)
Erlach-Str
Schanzenstr
Sidlerstr
Falkenplatz
Hauptbahnhof (Train Station)
Bollwerk
Hodlerstr
Speichergasse
Waisenhausplatz
Aarbergergasse
Neuengasse
OLD TOWN
Schüttestr
Nageligasse
Zeughausgasse
Bärenplatz
Bahnhofplatz
Bubenbergplatz
Schauplatzgasse
Spitalgasse
Bogenschutzen
Bundesplatz
Bundesgasse
Amthausgasse
Kochergasse
Marktgasse
Kornhausplatz
Schmiedenplatz
Zytglogge
Kindlifresserbrunnen
Theaterpl
Casinoplatz
Hotelgasse
Uferweg
Altenbergrain
Kornhausbrücke
Altenberg-Steg
Altenbergstr
Rathausgasse
Rathausplatz
Brunngasshalde
Postgasse
Einstein Museum
Kramgasse
Münstergasse
Münsterplatz
Herrengasse
Münster
Münster Plattform
Junkerngasse
Badgasse
Aarstr
Budenberggasse
Matte
Schifflaube
Mühlenplatz
Gerberngasse
Aare
Untertorbrücke
Läuferplatz
Klösterlistutz
Rosengarten
Aargauerstalden
Grosser Muristalden
Muristr
Bundesterrasse
Bundesrain
Marzilistr
Munzrain
Weihergasse
Dalmazibrücke
Dalmaziquai
Rainmattstr
Monbijoustr
Sulgeneckstr
Brückenstr
Helvetiaplatz
Marienstr
Thunstr
Bernastr
Helvetiastr
Mottastr
Lusienstr
Dufourstr
Jungfraustr
Alpenstr
Seminarstr
1
2
3
4
5
6
7
8
9
10
11
12
13
14
15
16
17
18

Bern

Top Sights

	Einstein Museum	E2
	Kindlifresserbrunnen	D2
	Münster	E2
	Zytglogge	D2

Sights

1	Bärengraben	G2
2	Houses of Parliament	D3
3	Kunstmuseum	C1

Sleeping

4	Bellevue Palace	D3
5	Hotel Belle Epoque	F2
6	Hotel Glocke Backpackers Bern	D2
7	Hotel Landhaus	G1
8	Hotel National	B3
9	SYHA Hostel	D3

Eating

10	Altes Tramdepot	G2
11	Kornhauskeller	D2
12	Lőtschberg AOC	D2
13	Markthalle	C2
14	Terrasse & Casa	E3
15	Tibits	C2

Drinking

16	Café des Pyrénées	D2
17	Silo Bar	F3

Entertainment

18	Wasserwerk	G2

scientist developed his theory of relativity in Bern in 1905. Find out more at the Einstein Haus, in the humble apartment where Einstein lived between 1903 and 1905 while working as a low-paid clerk in the Bern patent office. Multimedia displays now flesh out the story of the subsequent general equation – $E=MC^2$, or energy equals mass times the speed of light squared – that fundamentally changed humankind's understanding of space, time and the universe. Upstairs, a 20-minute biographical film tells Einstein's life story.

FREE **Houses of Parliament** HISTORIC SITE
(☎031 332 85 22; www.parliament.ch; Bundesplatz; ⊙hourly tours 9am-4pm Mon-Sat) The 1902 Bundeshäuser, home of the Swiss Federal Assembly, is impressively ornate, with statues of the nation's founding fathers, a stained-glass dome adorned with cantonal emblems and a huge 214-bulb chandelier. Tours are offered when parliament is in recess; otherwise watch from the public gallery. Bring your passport to get in.

Bärengraben BEAR PARK
(www.baerenpark-bern.ch, in German; ⊙9.30am-5pm) Bern was founded in 1191 by Berchtold V and named for the unfortunate bear (*bärn* in local dialect) that was his first hunting victim. The bear remains the city's heraldic mascot, hence the bear pits. Since 2009 the bears live in a new, spacious, riverside park. Beware: don't feed the bears anything random, but do buy a paper cone of fresh fruit (Sfr3).

Kunstmuseum MUSEUM
(☎031 328 09 44; www.kunstmuseumbern.ch, in German; Hodlerstrasse 8-12; adult/student main collection Sfr8/5, temporary exhibitions Sfr8-18; ⊙10am-9pm Tue, to 5pm Wed-Sun) The permanent collection at the Museum of Fine Arts includes works by Italian artists such as Fra Angelico, Swiss artists such as Ferdinand Hodler, and works by Picasso and Dalí.

Sleeping

The tourist office makes hotel reservations (for free) and has information on 'three nights for the price of two' deals.

Marthahaus Garni HOTEL $
(☎031 332 41 35; www.marthahaus.ch; Wyttenbachstrasse 22a; s/d Sfr115/145, without bathroom from Sfr70/105;) Plum in a leafy residential location, this five-storey building feels like a friendly boarding house. Clean, simple rooms are very white with a smattering of modern art, plus there's a kitchen.

Hotel Landhaus HOTEL $$
(☎031 331 41 66; www.landhausbern.ch; Altenbergstrasse 4; dm from Sfr33, d from Sfr160, without bathroom from Sfr120;) Backed by the grassy slope of a city park and fronted by the river and Old Town spires, this historic hotel oozes character. Its soulful ground-floor restaurant, a tad bohemian, draws a staunchly local crowd.

Bellevue Palace HOTEL $$$
(☎031 320 45 45; www.bellevue-palace.ch; Kochergasse 3-5; s/d from Sfr360/390;) Bern's power brokers and international statesmen such as Nelson Mandela gravitate towards Bern's only five-star hotel. Near the parliament, it's *the* address to impress. Cheaper weekend rates.

Hotel National HOTEL $
(☎031 381 19 88; www.nationalbern.ch, in German; Hirschengraben 24; s/d Sfr100/140, without bath-

room from Sfr60/120; @) The quaint, charming National wouldn't be out of place in Paris, with its wrought-iron lift, lavender sprigs and Persian rugs over creaky wooden floors.

Hotel Innere Enge HOTEL $$$
(☎031 309 61 11; www.zghotels.ch; Engestrasse 54; d from Sfr240; P@) It might not be city centre, but this jazz hotel north of the city centre is unique. Run with passion by Bern Jazz Festival organiser Hans Zurbrügg and wife Marianne Gauer, a top Swiss hotel-interior designer, the place oozes panache. Don't miss its cellar jazz bar.

Hotel Belle Epoque HOTEL $$$
(☎031 311 43 36; www.belle-epoque.ch; Gerechtigkeitsgasse 18; s/d from Sfr250/350; @) Standards are so exacting at this romantic hotel with art deco furnishings that modern aberrations are cleverly hidden – dig the TV in the steamer-trunk-style cupboard – so as not to spoil the look.

Hotel Glocke Backpackers Bern HOSTEL $
(☎031 311 37 71; www.bernbackpackers.com; Rathausgasse 75; dm Sfr34-45; reception 8-11am & 3-10pm; @) Its Old Town location makes this many backpackers' first choice, although street noise might irritate light sleepers.

SYHA Hostel HOSTEL $
(☎031 326 11 11; www.youthhostel.ch/bern; Weihergasse 4; dm from Sfr33; reception 7am-noon & 2pm-midnight; @) Prettily set across from the river, this well-organised hostel sports clean dorms and a leafy terrace with red seating and ping-pong table. Free bike rental May to October (Sfr20 deposit).

Eating

Waterside or Old Town, Bern cooks up a delicious choice of dining handy for all budgets.

Lötschberg AOC SWISS $$
(☎031 311 34 55; Zeughausgasse 16; mains Sfr14-28) Take an all-Swiss wine and beer list, add cheese specialities from the Valais (including fondue and raclette, of course), decorate the cheerful yellow walls with circular, wood wine racks, add chequered tablecloths and you have one of the most dynamic Swiss restaurants in the country. This popular, casual spot, favoured by locals and visitors alike, serves exceptional Swiss fare without the kitsch and is as great for a bite and a glass of wine as it is for a full sit-down meal.

Altes Tramdepot SWISS $
(☎031 368 14 15; Am Bärengraben; mains Sfr16-20; lunch & dinner) Even locals recommend this cavernous microbrewery by the bear pits. Swiss specialities snuggle up to wok-cooked stir-fries, pasta and international dishes on its bistro-styled menu.

Du Nord INTERNATIONAL $$
(☎031 332 23 38; www.dunord-bern.ch; Lorrainestrasse 2; mains Sfr20-36; closed Sun) This gay-friendly space with good-value international kitchen and bar buzzes with Bern's hippest and the occasional gig. Find it crowned by a pretty pink, fairy-tale turret.

TOP QUICK EATS

This student-busy city has some super quick-eat options, oozing atmosphere and even a table thrown in for a highly affordable price. You'll pay less than Sfr15 for a full meal.

Munch between meals on a *brezel* (pretzel; around Sfr3) smothered in salt crystals or sunflower, pumpkin or sesame seeds from kiosks at the train station; or a bag of piping-hot chestnuts crunched to the tune of the astronomical clock striking.

Markthalle (Bubenbergplatz 9; 6.30am-11.30pm Mon-Wed, to 12.30am Thu & Fri, 7.30am-12.30am Sat;) Buzzing in atmosphere and quick-snack action, this covered market arcade is jam-packed with eateries from around the world: curries, vegetarian, wok stir-fries, *bruschette*, noodles, pizza, south Indian, Turkish, Middle Eastern...you name it, it's here. Eat standing at bars or around plastic tables.

Sous le Pont (www.souslepont.ch) Grab fries, falafel or a *schnitzelb* from the graffiti-covered hole-in-the-wall next to the eponymous cafe-bar and dine at the graffiti-covered table in the graffiti-covered courtyard. Beer costs Sfr3.80/5.20 per 300/500dL glass.

Tibits (☎031 312 91 11; Bahnhofplatz 10; 6.30am-11.30pm Mon-Wed, 6.30am-midnight Thu-Sat, 8am-11pm Sun;) This vegetarian buffet restaurant inside the train station is just the ticket for a quick healthy meal, any size, any time of day. Serve yourself, get it weighed and pay accordingly.

Terrasse & Casa ITALIAN $$
(☎031 350 50 01; www.schwellenmaetteli.ch; Dammaziquai 11; mains Sfr29-44; ⊙Terrasse open daily, Casa closed Mon) Dubbed 'Bern's Riviera', this twinset of classy hang-outs on the Aare is an experience. Terrasse is a glass shoebox with wooden decking over the water and sun-loungers overlooking a weir, while Casa serves Italian food in a country-styled timber-framed house.

Kornhauskeller SWISS $$$
(☎031 327 72 72; Kornhausplatz 18; mains Sfr32-52; ⊙lunch & dinner Mon-Sat, dinner Sun) Dress well and dine fine beneath vaulted frescoed arches at Bern's former granary, where beautiful people sip cocktails alongside historic stained-glass on the mezzanine above.

Drinking & Entertainment

For an earthy drink with old-generation locals, order one at the marble-topped bar inside the **Markthalle** (Bubenbergplatz 9).

Sous le Pont BAR
(☎031 306 69 55; www.souslepont.ch; Neubrückstrasse 8; ⊙11.30am-2.30pm & 6pm-2.30am Tue-Thu, 11.30am-2.30pm & 7pm-2am Fri, 7pm-2.30am Sat) Delve into the grungy underground scene around the station in the bar of semi-chaotic alternative-arts centre, Reitschule. Find it in an old stone, graffiti-covered building – an old riding school built in 1897 – by the railway bridge.

Silo Bar BAR
(☎031 311 54 12; www.silobar.ch, in German; Mühlenplatz 11; ⊙10pm-3.30am Thu-Sat) By the water in the hip Matte quarter, Bern's monumental 19th-century corn house throbs with mainstream hits and a lively predominantly student set – *the* place to drink, dance and party.

Café des Pyrénées BAR
(☎031 311 30 63; Kornhausplatz 17; ⊙Mon-Sat) With its mix of wine-quaffing trendies and beer-loving students, this Bohemian joint feels like a Parisian cafe-bar.

Wasserwerk CLUB
(☎031 312 12 31; www.wasser werkclub.ch; Wasserwerkgasse 5; ⊙10pm-late Thu-Sat) Bern's main techno venue with bar, club and occasional live music.

Information

BernCard (per 24/48/72hr Sfr20/31/38) Discount card providing admission to permanent collections at 27 museums, free public transport and city-tour discounts.

Bern Tourismus (☎031 328 12 12; www.berninfo.com; Bahnhoftplatz; ⊙9am-8.30pm Jun-Sep, 9am-6.30pm Mon-Sat, 10am-5pm Sun Oct-May) Street-level floor of the train station. City tours, free hotel bookings, internet access (per hour Sfr12).

Post office (Schanzenstrasse 4; ⊙7.30am-9pm Mon-Fri, 8am-4pm Sat, 4-9pm Sun)

Tourist office (☎031 328 12 12; Bärengraben; ⊙9am-6pm Jun-Sep, 10am-4pm Mar-May & Oct, 11am-4pm Nov-Feb) By the bear pits.

Getting There & Around

AIR **Bern-Belp airport** (BRN; ☎031 960 21 21; www.alpar.ch), 9km southeast of the city centre, is a small airport with direct flights to/from Munich (from where there are onward connections pretty much everywhere) with Lufthansa and Southampton in the UK with Fly Be. **Airport shuttles** (☎031 971 28 88, 079 651 70 70) coordinated with flight departures pick up/drop off at the train station (Sfr15, 20 minutes).

BICYCLE Pedal around with a bike, micro-scooter or skateboard from **Bern Rollt** (☎079 277 28 57; www.bernrollt.ch; 1st 4hr free, then per hr Sfr1; ⊙7.30am-9.30pm May-Oct), which has kiosks inside the train station, at the western end of Zeughausgasse and just off Bubenbergplatz on Hirschengrasse.

PUBLIC TRANSPORT Bus and tram tickets are available from ticket machines at stops, and cost Sfr2 (maximum six stops) or Sfr3.80 for a single journey within zones 1 and 2. **Moonliner** (☎031 321 88 12; www.moonliner.ch, in German) night buses transport night owls from Bahnhofplatz two or three times between midnight and 3.30am on Friday and Saturday nights. Fares start at Sfr5.

TRAINS Hourly trains connect to most Swiss towns, including Geneva (Sfr46, 1¾ hours), Basel (Sfr37, 70 minutes) and Zürich (Sfr46, one hour).

CENTRAL SWITZERLAND & BERNESE OBERLAND

The Bernese Oberland should come with a health warning – caution: may cause trembling in the north face of Eiger, uncontrollable bouts of euphoria at the foot of Jungfrau, 007 delusions at Schilthorn and A-list fever in Gstaad. Mark Twain wrote that no opiate compared to walking through this landscape – and he should know – and even when sober, the electric-green spruce forests, mountains so big they'll swallow you up, surreal china-blue skies, swirling glaciers and turquoise lakes seem hallucinatory. Up at Europe's highest station, Jungfraujoch, husky yapping mingles with Bollywood beats. Yet just paces away, the serpentine Aletsch Glacier flicks out its tongue and you're surrounded by 4000m turrets and frosty stillness.

Lucerne

POP 59,500

Recipe for a gorgeous Swiss city: take a cobalt lake ringed by mountains of myth, add a medieval Old Town and sprinkle with covered bridges, sunny plazas, candy-coloured houses and waterfront promenades. Lucerne is bright, beautiful and has been little Miss Popular since the likes of Goethe, Queen Victoria and Wagner savoured her views in the 19th century. Legend has it that an angel with a light showed the first settlers where to build a chapel in Lucerne, and today it still has amazing grace.

Sights

Old Town HISTORIC AREA

Your first port of call should be the medieval Old Town, with its ancient rampart walls and towers, 15th-century buildings with painted facades and the two much-photographed covered bridges. **Kapellbrücke** (Chapel Bridge), dating from 1333, is Lucerne's best-known landmark. It's famous for its distinctive water tower and the spectacular 1993 fire that nearly destroyed it. Though it has been rebuilt, fire damage is still obvious on the 17th-century pictorial panels under the roof. In better condition, but rather dark and dour, are the *Dance of Death* panels under the roofline of **Spreuerbrücke** (Spreuer Bridge).

Sammlung Rosengart MUSEUM

(041 220 16 60; www.rosengart.ch; Pilatusstrasse 10; adult/student Sfr18/16; 10am-6pm Apr-Oct, 11am-5pm Nov-Mar) Lucerne's blockbuster cultural attraction is the Rosengart Col-

Lucerne

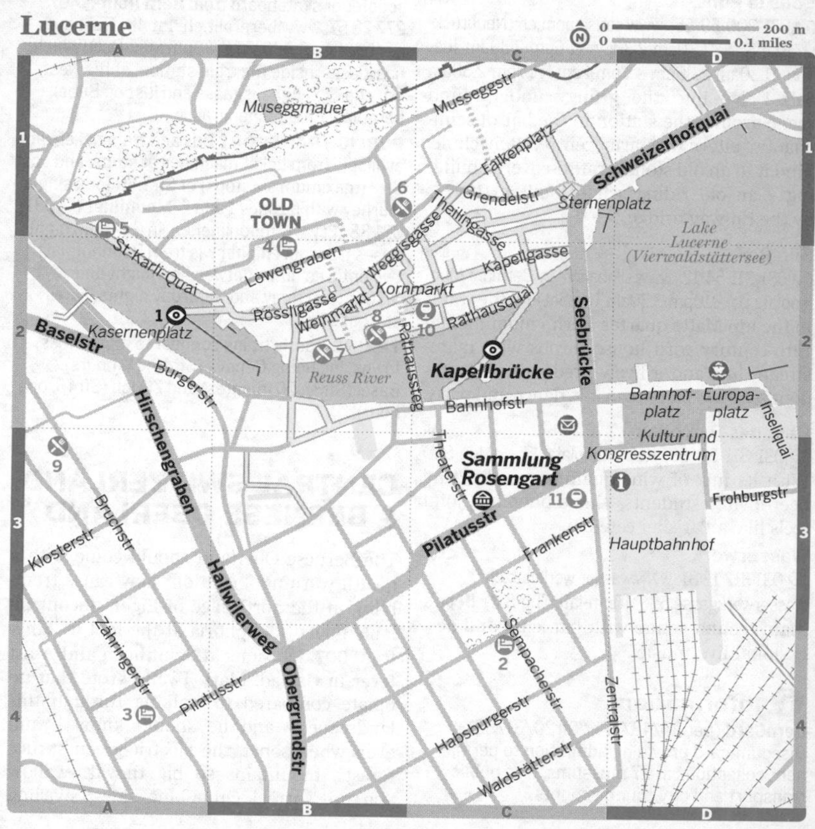

lection, occupying a graceful neoclassical pile. It showcases the outstanding stash of Angela Rosengart, a Swiss art dealer and close friend of Picasso. Alongside works by the great Spanish master are paintings and sketches by Cézanne, Klee, Kandinsky, Miró, Matisse and Monet. Standouts include Joan Miró's electric-blue *Dancer II* (1925) and Paul Klee's childlike *X-chen* (1938).

Complementing this collection are some 200 photographs by David Douglas Duncan of the last 17 years of Picasso's life with his family in their home on the French Riviera. It's a uniquely revealing series and principally a portrait of the artist as an impish craftsman, lover and father.

Verkehrshaus MUSEUM
(☎041 370 44 44; www.verkehrshaus.ch; Lidostrasse 5; adult/child Sfr24/12; ⌚9am-6pm Apr-Oct, 10am-5pm Nov-Mar) Planes, trains and automobiles are the name of the game in the huge, family-oriented Transport Museum, east of the city centre, which is devoted to Switzerland's proud transport history. Space rockets, a communications display, simulators, a planetarium, an **IMAX cinema** (www.imax.ch; adult/child Sfr18/14) and the **Swiss Arena** – a gigantic 1:20,000 walkable map of Switzerland, taken from aerial photos, where you can delight in leaping over the Alps – all help make this Switzerland's most popular museum. Take bus 6, 8 or 24 from Bahnhofplatz.

Lucerne

Top Sights
- Kapellbrücke C2
- Sammlung Rosengart C3

Sights
- 1 Spreuerbrücke A2

Sleeping
- 2 Hotel Alpha A4
- 3 Jailhotel Löwengraben B2
- 4 The Hotel C4
- 5 Tourist Hotel A1

Eating
- 6 Jazzkantine B1
- 7 La Terraza B2
- 8 Restaurant Schiff B2
- 9 Schützengarten A3

Drinking
- 10 Rathaus Bräuerei C2
- 11 Roadhouse C3

Activities

Strandbad Lido SWIMMING
(☎041 370 38 06; www.lido-luzern.ch; Lidostrasse 6a; adult/child Sfr6/3; ⌚9am-8pm mid-May–Sep) Perfect for a splash or sunbathe, this lakefront beach has a playground, volleyball court and heated outdoor pool. Or swim for free on the other bank of the lake by Seepark, off Alpenquai.

Outventure ADVENTURE SPORTS
(☎041 611 14 41; www.outventure.ch; Stans) Outventure tempts adrenalin junkies with pursuits including tandem paragliding (Sfr150), canyoning (from Sfr110), glacier trekking (Sfr150) and canoeing on Lake Lucerne (Sfr115).

Bike Rental CYCLING
(☎041 51 227 32 61; half-/full day Sfr25/33) Bikes can be rented at the train station. Check out the routes circumnavigating the lake; an easygoing and scenic option is the 16km pedal to Winkel via Kastanienbaum.

Festivals & Events

Lucerne's six-day **Fasnacht** celebrations are more boisterous and fun than Basel's carnival. The party kicks off on 'Dirty Thursday' with the emergence of the character 'Fritschi' from a window in the town hall, when bands of musicians and revellers take to the streets. The carnival moves through raucous celebrations climaxing on Mardi Gras (Fat Tuesday), and is over on Ash Wednesday.

June's **Jodler Fest Luzern** (www.jodlerfestluzern.ch) is a classic alpine shindig: think 12,000 Swiss yodellers, alphorn players and flag throwers.

Sleeping

Backpackers Lucerne HOSTEL $
(☎041 360 04 20; www.backpackerslucerne.ch; Alpenquai 42; dm/d from Sfr33/70; ⌚reception 7-10am & 4-11pm; @📶) It's backpacker heaven: right on the lake, this soulful place has artslung walls, bubbly staff, a well-equipped kitchen and immaculate dorms with balconies. It's a 15-minute walk southeast of the station.

Hotel Alpha HOTEL $
(☎041 240 42 80; www.hotelalpha.ch; Zähringerstrasse 24; s/d from Sfr75/110; @📶) Easy on the eye and wallet, this hotel is in a quiet residential area 10 minutes' walk from the centre. Rooms are simple, light and spotlessly clean.

Bed and Breakfast B&B $
(041 310 15 14; www.thebandb.ch; Taubenhausstrasse 34; s/d Sfr80/120; Mar-Oct; P) This friendly B&B feels like a private home, with stylish, contemporary rooms – crisp white bedding, scatter cushions and hot pink and lime accents. Unwind in the flowery garden or with a soak in the old-fashioned tub. Free wi-fi is another bonus. Take bus 1 to Eichof.

Tourist Hotel HOTEL $$
(041 410 24 74; www.touristhotel.ch; St-Karli-Quai 12; dm from Sfr40, s/d Sfr140/220, without bathroom from Sfr80/120; P@) Don't be put off by the uninspired name and pease-pudding green facade of this central, riverfront cheapie. Dorms are basic, but rooms cheery, with bold paint jobs, parquet floors and flatscreen TVs.

Jailhotel Löwengraben HOTEL $$
(041 410 78 30; www.jailhotel.ch; Löwengraben 18; s/d from Sfr120/150;) This former prison has novelty value, but you might get a jailhouse shock when you enter your cell to find barred windows, bare floorboards and a prefab bathroom. It's fun for a laugh and its location is stellar, but it ain't great for quality shut-eye with thumping techno in Alcatraz club downstairs to 3am.

The Hotel HOTEL $$$
(041 226 86 86; www.the-hotel.ch; Sempacherstrasse 14; ste from Sfr420; @) Streamlined and jet black, 10 vampy suites reveal stainless-steel fittings, open-plan bathrooms peeking through to garden foliage, and stills from movie classics gracing the ceilings at this Jean Nouvel creation. Downstairs Bam Bou is one of Lucerne's hippest restaurants.

SYHA hostel HOSTEL $
(041 420 88 00; www.youthhostel.ch/luzern; Sedelstrasse 12; dm/d from Sfr33/82; check-in 2pm-midnight summer, from 4pm winter; P@) These HI digs are modern, well run and clean, and value-for-money meals are available throughout the day. Take bus 18 from the train station to Jugendherberge.

Eating & Drinking

Many places in Lucerne double as bars and restaurants. Places open for breakfast and stay open until late in the evening. Self-caterers should head to Hertensteinstrasse, where cheap eats are plentiful from snack stands (and frankly, you won't find much in the way of cheap sit-down eats in this town).

Restaurant Schiff SWISS $$
(041 418 52 52; Unter der Egg 8; mains Sfr20-45) Under the waterfront arcades and lit by tea lights at night, this restaurant has bags of charm. Try fish from Lake Lucerne and some of the city's most celebrated *Chögalipaschtetli* (vol-au-vents stuffed with meat and mushrooms).

Jazzkantine ITALIAN $
(041 410 73 73; Grabenstrasse 8; mains Sfr15-22; 7am-12.30am Mon-Sat, 4pm-12.30am Sun) Stainless-steel bar, sturdy wooden tables and chalkboard menus – this is an arty haunt. Go for tasty *bruschette* or more ambitious dishes like penne vodka. Saturday-night gigs follow weeknight jazz workshops.

La Terraza ITALIAN $$
(041 410 36 31; Metzgerrainle 9; mains Sfr18-45) Set in a 12th-century building that has housed fish sellers, dukes and scribes over the years, La Terraza oozes atmosphere. Think *bella* Italia with an urban edge. When the sun's out, sit on the riverfront terrace for favourites like clam-and-rocket spaghetti.

Schützengarten INTERNATIONAL $$
(041 240 01 10; Bruchstrasse 20; mains Sfr19-45; Mon-Sat;) As well as a cracking sense of humour, Schützengarten has smiley service, wood-panelled surrounds, appetising vegetarian and vegan dishes, and organic wine. Sit on the vine-strewn terrace in summer.

Rathaus Bräuerei PUB
(041 410 52 57; Unter den Egg 2; 8am-midnight Mon-Sat, to 11pm Sun) Sip home-brewed beer under the vaulted arches of this buzzy tavern, or nab a pavement table and watch the river flow.

Roadhouse BAR
(041 220 27 27; www.roadhouse.ch; Pilatusstrasse 1; 11am-4am) Roadhouse plays solid rock to a young, fun crowd. Check out Wednesday night's jam sessions, where anyone with an instrument or voice (preferably both) can take the stand.

Information

Lucerne Card (24/48/72hr Sfr19/27/33) If you are planning to visit several museums, it's worth buying a Lucerne Card, available at the tourist office. It gets you 50% discount on museum admissions, unlimited use of public transport and other reductions.

Luzern Tourism (041 227 17 17; www.luzern.com; Zentralstrasse 5; 8.30am-7.30pm Mon-Fri, 9am-7.30pm Sat & Sun mid-Jun–mid-Sep,

9am-6.30pm daily May–mid-Jun & mid-Sep–Oct, 8.30am-5.30pm Mon-Fri, 9am-1pm Sat & Sun Nov-Apr) Accessed from platform 3 of the train station.

Surfers Island (☎041 412 00 44; Weinmarkt 15; per hr Sfr10; ⏲10am-7pm Mon-Fri, to 4pm Sat) Internet access.

Getting There & Away

Frequent trains connect Lucerne to Interlaken West (Sfr33.40, two hours, via the scenic Brünig Pass), Bern (Sfr35, 1¾ hours), Lugano (Sfr55, 2¾ hours), Geneva (Sfr72, 3¾ hours, via Olten or Langnau) and Zürich (Sfr23, one hour).

Interlaken

POP 5300

Once Interlaken made the Victorians swoon with its dreamy mountain vistas, viewed from the chandelier-lit confines of its grand hotels. Today it makes daredevils scream with its adrenalin-loaded adventures. Straddling the glittering Lakes Thun and Brienz, and dazzled by the pearly whites of Eiger, Mönch and Jungfrau, the scenery here is mind-blowing. Particularly, some say, if you're abseiling waterfalls, thrashing white water or gliding soundlessly above 4000m peaks.

Though the streets are filled with enough yodelling kitsch to make Heidi cringe, Interlaken still makes a terrific base for exploring the Bernese Oberland. Its adventure capital status has spawned a breed of funky bars, party-mad hostels and restaurants serving flavours more imaginative than fondue.

Activities

Tempted to hurl yourself off a bridge, down a cliff or along a raging river? You're in the right place. Switzerland is the world's second-biggest adventure-sports mecca, nipping at New Zealand's sprightly heels, and Interlaken is its busiest hub.

Almost every heart-stopping pursuit you can think of is offered here (although the activities take place in the greater Jungfrau Region). You can white-water raft on the Lütschine, Simme and Saane Rivers; go canyoning in the Saxetet, Grimsel or Chli Schliere gorges; and canyon-jump at the Gletscherschlucht near Grindelwald. If that doesn't grab you, there's paragliding, glacier bungee jumping, skydiving, ice-climbing, hydro-speeding and zorbing, where you're strapped into a giant plastic ball and sent spinning down a hill.

Prices are from Sfr90 for rock climbing, Sfr95 for zorbing, Sfr110 for rafting or canyoning, Sfr120 for hydro-speeding, Sfr130 for bungee jumping, Sfr160 for paragliding, Sfr195 for hang-gliding and Sfr430 for skydiving. Most excursions are without incident, but there's always a small risk and it's wise to ask about safety records and procedures. Major operators able to arrange most sports:

Alpin Center ADVENTURE SPORTS
(☎033 823 55 23; www.alpincenter.ch; Hauptstrasse 16)

Alpinraft ADVENTURE SPORTS
(☎033 823 41 00; www.alpinraft.ch; Hauptstrasse 7)

Outdoor Interlaken ADVENTURE SPORTS
(☎033 826 77 19; www.outdoor-interlaken.ch; Hauptstrasse 15)

Swissraft ADVENTURE SPORTS
(☎033 821 66 55; www.swissraft-activity.ch; Obere Jungfraustrasse 72)

Sleeping

Hotel Rugenpark B&B $
(☎033 822 36 61; www.rugenpark.ch; Rugenparkstrasse 19; s/d from Sfr85/130, without bathroom from Sfr65/105; ⏲closed Nov–mid-Dec; P⊖@) Chris and Ursula have worked magic to transform this into a sweet B&B. Rooms are humble, but the place is spotless and has been enlivened with colourful butterflies, beads and travel trinkets. Quiz your knowledgeable hosts for help and local tips.

Funny Farm GUESTHOUSE $
(☎033 828 12 81; www.funny-farm.ch; Hauptstrasse 36; P@≋) Funny Farm is halfway between a squat and an island shipwreck. The ramshackle art nouveau house, surrounded by makeshift bars and a swimming pool, is patrolled by Spliff, the lovably dopey St Bernard. Dorms are a bit faded and musty, but guests don't care; they're here for the party and revel in such anarchism. Closed during 2011; check the website for details.

Schlaf im Stroh FARMSTAY $
(☎033 822 04 31; www.uelisi.ch; Lanzenen 30; ⏲May-Sep; P) Our readers have been singing the praises of this friendly farm for years. Bring your sleeping bag to snooze in the straw and wake up to a hearty breakfast. Kids adore the resident cats, goats and rabbits. It's 15 minutes' walk from Interlaken Ost station along the Aare River (upstream). Closed during 2011; check the website for details.

RiverLodge & Camping TCS CAMPING GROUND $
(☎033 822 44 34; Brienzstrasse 24; campsites per adult/tent Sfr10/9; ⏲May–mid-Oct; 📶) Facing the Aare River and handy for Interlaken Ost train station, this camping ground and hostel duo offer first-class facilities, including a communal kitchen and laundry. Rent bikes and kayaks here.

Victoria-Jungfrau Grand Hotel & Spa HOTEL $$$
(☎033 828 28 28; www.victoria-jungfrau.ch; Höheweg 41; s/d from Sfr560/680, d with Jungfrau views from Sfr780; P) The reverent hush and impeccable service evoke an era when only royalty and the seriously wealthy travelled. A perfect melding of well-preserved Victorian features and modern luxury make this Interlaken's answer to Raffles.

Balmer's Herberge HOSTEL $
(☎033 822 19 61; www.balmers.ch; Hauptstrasse 23; dm from Sfr29, s/d Sfr45/78; P@📶) Adrenalin junkies hail Balmer's for its fun frat-house vibe. These party-mad digs offer beer-garden happy hours, wrap lunches, pumping bar with DJs, and chill-out hammocks for nursing a hangover.

Backpackers Villa Sonnenhof HOSTEL $
(☎033 826 71 71; www.villa.ch; Alpenstrasse 16; dm from Sfr35; ⏲reception 7am-11pm; @) While most Interlaken hostels are charged with more energy than a Duracell bunny, this homely place recharges your batteries. The olive-fronted villa exudes Victorian flair with stucco and vintage steamer trunks, immaculate dorms, well-equipped kitchen and leafy garden.

Post Hardmannli HOTEL $$
(☎033 822 89 19; www.post-hardermannli.ch; s/d Sfr100/155; P) An affable Swiss-Kiwi couple, Andreas and Kim, run this rustic chalet. Rooms are simple yet comfy, decorated with pine and chintzy pastels. Cheaper rooms forgo balconies and Jungfrau views. The home-grown farm produce at breakfast is a real treat.

Eating & Drinking

Am Marktplatz is scattered with bakeries and bistros with alfresco seating. The bars at Balmer's and Funny Farm are easily the liveliest drinking holes for revved-up 20-something travellers. You'll find a mixed crowd in the Happy Inn.

Benacus SWISS $$
(☎033 821 20 20; www.benacus.ch; Stadthausplatz; mains Sfr20-33; ⏲closed Sun, lunch Sat) Supercool Benacus is a breath of urban air with its glass walls, slick wine-red sofas, lounge music and street-facing terrace. The TV show 'Funky Kitchen Club' is filmed here. The menu stars creative flavours like potato and star anise soup, and Aargau chicken with caramelised pak choi.

Belvédère Brasserie SWISS $$
(☎033 828 91 00; Höheweg 95; mains Sfr17-36) Yes it's attached to the rather boring-looking Hapimag, but this brasserie has an upbeat modern decor and a terrace with Jungfrau views. It serves up international favourites such as veal in merlot sauce, alongside a handful of Swiss stalwarts such as fondue and rösti.

Goldener Anker INTERNATIONAL $$
(☎033 822 16 72; www.anker.ch, in German; Marktgasse 57; mains Sfr18-41; ⏲dinner) This beamed restaurant, locals will whisper in your ear, is the best in town. Globetrotters include everything from sizzling fajitas to red snapper and ostrich steaks. It also has a roster of live bands.

Sandwich Bar SWISS $
(☎033 821 63 25; Rosenstrasse 5; snacks Sfr4-9; ⏲7.30am-7pm Mon-Fri, 8am-5pm Sat) This snack bar is an untouristy gem. Choose your bread and get creative with fillings (our favourite is *Bündnerfleisch* with sundried tomatoes and parmesan). Otherwise try soups, salads and locally made ice cream.

Information

The **post office** (Postplatz; ⏲8am-noon & 1.45-6pm Mon-Fri, 8.30-11am Sat) and **tourist office** (☎033 826 53 00; www.interlakentourism.ch; Höheweg 37; ⏲8am-7pm Mon-Fri, 8am-5pm Sat, 10am-noon & 5-7pm Sun Jul–mid-Sep, 8am-noon & 1.30-6pm Mon-Fri, 9am-noon Sat rest of year) are near Interlaken West.

Getting There & Away

The only way south for vehicles without a detour around the mountains is the car-carrying train from Kandersteg, south of Spiez.

Trains to Grindelwald (Sfr10.20, 40 minutes, hourly), Lauterbrunnen (Sfr7, 20 minutes, hourly) and Lucerne (Sfr30, two hours, hourly) depart from Interlaken Ost. Trains to Brig (Sfr41, 1½ hours, hourly) and Montreux via Bern or Visp (Sfr57 to Sfr67, 2¾ hours, hourly) leave from either Interlaken West or Ost.

Jungfrau Region

If the Bernese Oberland is Switzerland's Alpine heart, the Jungfrau region is where yours will skip a beat. Presided over by glacier-encrusted monoliths Eiger, Mönch and Jungfrau (Ogre, Monk and Virgin), the scenery stirs the soul and strains the neck muscles. It's a magnet for skiers and snowboarders with its 200km of pistes; a one-day ski pass for Kleine Scheidegg-Männlichen, Grindelwald-First, or Mürren-Schilthorn costs Sfr59. Come summer, hundreds of kilometres of walking trails allow you to capture the landscape from many angles, but it never looks less than astonishing.

The Lauterbrunnen Valley branches out from Interlaken with sheer rock faces and towering mountains on either side, attracting an army of hikers and mountain bikers. Cowbells echo in the valley and every house and hostel has a postcard-worthy view. Many visitors choose to visit this valley on a day trip from Interlaken.

GRINDELWALD

POP 3800

Once a simple farming village nestled in a valley under the north face of the Eiger, Grindelwald's charms were discovered by skiers and hikers in the late 19th century, making it one of Switzerland's oldest and the Jungfrau's largest resorts. It has lost none of its appeal over the decades, with archetypal alpine chalets and verdant pastures set against an Oscar-worthy backdrop.

Grindelwald tourist office (☎033 854 12 12; www.grindelwald.ch; Dorfstrasse; ⊙8am-noon & 1.30-6pm Mon-Fri, 9am-noon & 1.30-5pm Sat & Sun summer & winter, 8am-noon & 1.30-5pm Mon-Fri, 9am-noon Sat rest of year) is at the Sportzentrum, 200m from the train station.

Hourly trains link Grindelwald with Interlaken Ost (Sfr10.20, 40 minutes, hourly).

Sights & Activities

Oberer Gletscher GLACIER

(Upper Glacier; adult/child Sfr6/3; ⊙9am-6pm mid-May–Oct) The shimmering, slowly melting Oberer Gletscher is a 1½-hour hike from the village, or catch a bus (marked Terrasen Weg-Oberer Gletscher) to Hotel-Restaurant Wetterhorn. Walk 10 minutes from the bus stop, then pant up 890 log stairs to reach a terrace offering dramatic vistas. A crowd-puller is the vertiginous hanging bridge spanning the gorge.

Gletscherschlucht GLACIER

(Glacier Gorge; admission Sfr7; ⊙10am-5pm May-Oct, to 6pm Jul & Aug) Turbulent waters carve a path through the craggy Gletscherschlucht, a 30-minute walk south of the centre. A footpath weaves through tunnels hacked into cliffs – a popular spot for canyon- and bungee-jumping expeditions.

Grindelwald-First SKIING

First is the main skiing area, with runs stretching from **Oberjoch** at 2486m to the village at 1050m. In the summer it caters to **hikers** with 90km of trails at about 1200m, 48km of which are open year-round.

Catch the longest **cable car** (☎033 854 80 80; www.maennlichen.ch) in Europe from Grindelwald-Grund to Männlichen (single/return Sfr31/Sfr51), where there are more extraordinary views and hikes.

Sleeping & Eating

Mountain Hostel HOSTEL $

(☎033 854 38 38; www.mountainhostel.ch; dm Sfr37-42, d Sfr92-102; P) Near the Männlichen cable-car station, this is a good base for sports junkies. Cyclists are especially welcome. Rates include free ice-skating and swimming at a nearby facility.

SYHA Hostel HOSTEL $

(☎033 853 10 09; www.youthhostel.ch/grindelwald; Terrassenweg; dm Sfr31.50-38.50, d Sfr108, d without bathroom Sfr80; ⊙reception 7.30-10am & 4-10pm; @) This excellent hostel is in a cosy wooden chalet perched high on a hill, with magnificent views. Avoid the 20-minute slog from the train station by taking the Terrassenweg-bound bus to the Gaggi Säge stop.

SLEEP SUSTAINABLY

Perched above Grindelwald village, eco-friendly chalet **Naturfreundehaus** (☎033 853 13 33; www.naturfreundehaeuser.ch; Terrassenweg; dm/s/d Sfr36/46/72; ⊙closed low season; P), whose name suitably translates as the House of Friends of Nature, is a green gem. Most folk have a cat or dog; Vreni and Heinz have Mono the trout as family pet. Creaking floors lead up to cute pine-panelled rooms, including a shoebox single – Switzerland's smallest, so they say. Try an Eiger coffee with amaretto or a homemade mint cordial in the quirky cafe downstairs. The garden has wonderful views to Eiger and Wetterhorn.

Memory SWISS $$
(☎033 854 31 31; Dorfstrasse; mains Sfr16-28; ⊙11.30am-10.30pm) Always packed, the Eiger Hotel's unpretentious restaurant rolls out tasty Swiss grub such as rösti and fondue. Try to bag a table on the street-facing terrace.

C & M SWISS $$
(☎033 853 07 10; mains Sfr20-35; ⊙Wed-Mon) Just as appetising as the menu are the stupendous views to Unterer Gletscher from this gallery-style cafe's sunny terrace. Enjoy a salad, coffee and cake, or seasonally inspired dishes such as venison stew with dumplings and bilberry-stuffed apple.

GIMMELWALD

POP 118

Decades ago some anonymous backpacker scribbled these words in the guestbook at the Mountain Hostel: 'If heaven isn't what it's cracked up to be, send me back to Gimmelwald.' Enough said. When the sun is out in Gimmelwald, this pipsqueak of a village will simply take your breath away. Once a secret bolthole for hikers and adventurers keen to escape the region's worst tourist excesses, Gimmelwald gets a fair whack of foot traffic these days – though even the presence of crowds can't diminish its scintillating, classic Swiss scenery and outdoorsy charm.

The surrounding hiking trails include one down from Mürren (30 to 40 minutes) and one up from Stechelberg (1¼ hours). Cable cars are also an option (Mürren or Stechelberg Sfr5.60).

After a long summer hike, bed down at **Pension Berggeist** (☎033 855 17 30; www.berggeist.ch; dm/d Sfr15/40), a dead-simple and rustic place with bargain rooms, priceless views and sandwiches sold by the centimetre to please every pocket. Book all kinds of activities here, from skydiving to llama trekking.

Or there's the backpacking legend **Mountain Hostel** (☎033 855 17 04; www.mountainhostel.com; dm Sfr20; ⊙reception 8.30am-noon & 6-11pm Apr-Nov; @) A soak in its outdoor whirlpool with stunning views hits the spot every time. (And don't forget to sign the guestbook!) **Esther's Guest House** (☎033 855 54 88; www.esthersguesthouse.ch; s/d Sfr45/100; @) is a sweet B&B with a tiny shop inside, where you can stock up on local goodies like Gimmelwald salami and Stechelberg honey.

MÜRREN

POP 438

Arrive on a clear evening when the sun hangs low on the horizon, and you'll think you've died and gone to heaven. Car-free Mürren *is* storybook Switzerland.

In summer, the **Allmendhubel funicular** (single/return Sfr12/7.40) takes you above Mürren to a panoramic restaurant. From here, you can set out on many walks, including the famous **Northface Trail** (1½ hours) via Schiltalp to the west, with spellbinding views of the Lauterbrunnen Valley and monstrous Eiger north face – bring binoculars to spy intrepid climbers. There's also a kid-friendly **Adventure Trail** (one hour).

The **tourist office** (☎033 856 86 86; www.wengen-muerren.ch; ⊙8.30am-7pm Mon-Sat, to 8pm Thu, to 6pm Sun high season, to 7pm Mon-Sat, to 5pm Sun shoulder seasons, 8.30am-noon & 1-5pm Mon-Fri low season) is in the sports centre.

Sleeping options include **Eiger Guesthouse** (☎033 856 54 60; www.eigerguesthouse.com; dm Sfr40-70, d Sfr160, without bathroom Sfr120; @), by the train station, with the downstairs pub serving tasty grub; and **Hotel Jungfrau** (☎033 856 64 64; www.hoteljungfrau.ch; s Sfr88-110, d Sfr270-300; @), overlooking the nursery slopes from its perch above Mürren. It dates to 1894 and has a beamed lounge with open fire. Ten out of 10 to much-lauded chalet **Hotel Alpenruh** (☎033 856 88 00; www.alpenruh-muerren.ch; s/d Sfr145/270; @), for service, food and unbeatable views to Jungfrau massif.

Tham's (☎033 856 01 10; mains Sfr15-28; ⊙dinner) serves Asian fare cooked by a former five-star chef who's literally taken to the hills to escape.

SCHILTHORN

There's a tremendous 360-degree panorama available from the 2970m **Schilthorn** (www.schilthorn.ch). On a clear day, you can see from Titlis to Mont Blanc and across to the German Black Forest. Yet you may find that some visitors seem more preoccupied with practising their delivery of the immortal line, 'The name's Bond – James Bond' than they are in taking in the 200 or so peaks before them. Don't be surprised: this is where some scenes from *On Her Majesty's Secret Service* were shot in the 1960s, as the fairly tacky **Touristorama** below the Piz Gloria revolving restaurant reminds you.

Buy a Sfr116 excursion trip (Half-Fare Card and Eurail Pass 50% off, Swiss Pass 65% off) going to Lauterbrunnen, Grütschalp, Mürren, Schilthorn and returning through Stechelberg to Interlaken. A return from Lauterbrunnen (via Grütschalp) and Mürren costs about Sfr100, as does the return journey via the Stechelberg cable car.

JUNGFRAUJOCH

Sure, the world wants to see Jungfraujoch (3471m) and yes, tickets are expensive, but don't let that stop you. It's a once-in-a-lifetime trip and there's a reason why two million people a year visit this Holy Grail, Europe's highest train station. The icy wilderness of swirling glaciers and 4000m turrets that unfolds is truly enchanting.

Clear good weather is essential for the trip; check www.jungfrau.ch or call ☎033 828 79 31 and don't forget warm clothing, sunglasses and sunscreen. Up top, when you tire of the view (is this possible?), dash downhill on a snow disc (free), zip across the frozen plateau on a flying fox (Sfr20), enjoy a bit of tame skiing or boarding (Sfr33), drive a team of Greenland dogs or do your best Tiger-Woods-in-moon-boots impersonation with a round of glacier golf. It isn't cheap at Sfr10 a shot, but get a hole-in-one and you win the Sfr100,000 jackpot (which, mysteriously, nobody has yet won).

From Interlaken Ost, journey time is 2½ hours each way (Sfr177.80 return, Swiss Pass/Eurail Sfr133). The last train back is at 5.50pm in summer, 4.40pm in winter. However, there's a cheaper 'good morning' ticket of Sfr153.80 (Swiss/Eurail Pass discounts available) if you take the first train (6am from Interlaken Ost) and leave the summit by 12.30pm. Between 1 November and 30 April the reduction is valid for both the 6am and 7.05am trains, and the 12.30pm restriction doesn't apply.

ZÜRICH

POP 365,400

Zürich used to be Europe's best-kept secret. Conservative bankers and perfect, medieval landmarks stood at the forefront, with no hint that a city as cool and hip as Berlin or Amsterdam lurked within this financial centre's impeccably clean streets. But somewhere between ranking as the top city in the world for quality life seven years running, hosting Europe's largest street party and erecting a flagship store made entirely of 16 stacked shipping containers, the secret got out and the international press started writing about the real Zürich: a cool, stylish and surprising city.

You can eat a traditional wurst while pondering a swim in the postcard-perfect lake dotted with majestic swans, inspect Le Corbusier's last architectural construction, get lost in cobbled streets lined with half-timbered, sloping landmarks, sip a cocktail atop an ancient tower with a view of the Alps or go clubbing in a former powdered-milk warehouse.

WANT MORE?

Head to **Lonely Planet** (www.lonelyplanet.com/switzerland/zurich) for planning advice, author recommendations, traveller reviews and insider tips.

Sights

Old Town HISTORIC AREA

Explore the cobbled streets of the pedestrian Old Town lining both sides of the river.

The bank vaults beneath **Bahnhofstrasse**, the city's most elegant street, are said to be crammed with gold and silver. Indulge in affluent Züricher-watching and ogle at the luxury shops selling watches, clocks, chocolates, furs, porcelain and fashion labels galore.

On Sundays all of Zürich strolls around the lake – the locals are on to something, and one short meander tells you why (it's simply sublime, relaxing and on a clear day you'll glimpse the Alps in the distance).

Fraumünster CHURCH

(www.fraumuenster.ch; Münsterplatz; ⏲9am-6pm May-Sep, 10am-5pm Oct-Apr) On the west bank of the Limmat River, the 13th-century Fraumünster is Zürich's most noteworthy attraction, with some of the most distinctive and attractive stained-glass windows in the world.

Grossmünster CHURCH

(Grossmünsterplatz; www.grossmuenster.ch; ⏲9am-6pm mid-Mar–Oct, 10am-5pm Nov–mid-Mar, tower closed Sun morning mid-Mar–Oct & Sun Nov–mid-Mar) Across the river, the dual-towered Grossmünster was where, in the 16th century, the Protestant preacher Huldrych Zwingli first spread his message of 'pray and work' during the Reformation – a

Zürich

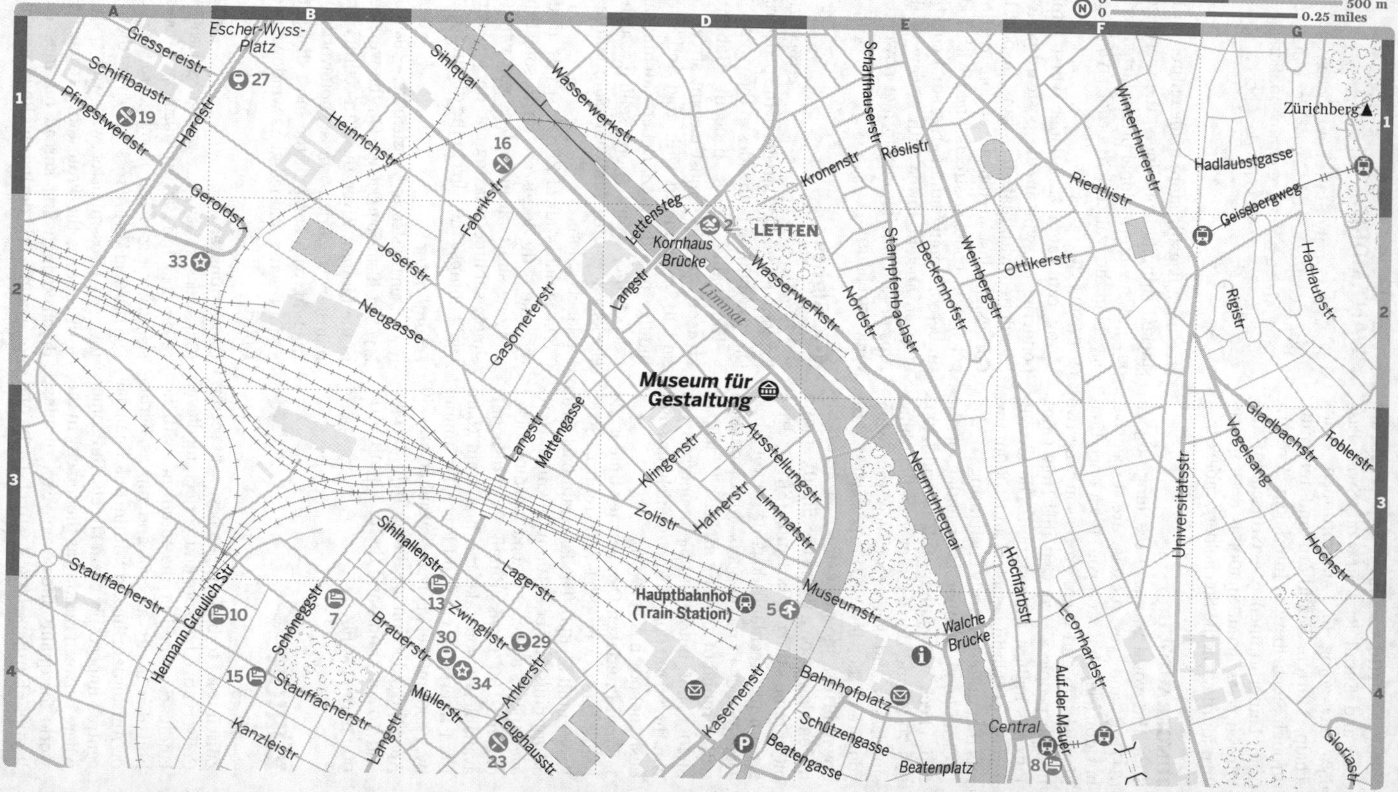

0 500 m
0 0.25 miles

A B C D E F G
1 2 3 4

Escher-Wyss-Platz
Giessereistr
Schiffbaustr
Pfingstweidstr
Hardstr
Heinrichstr
Sihlquai
Wasserwerkstr
Geroldstr
Josefstr
Fabrikstr
Neugasse
Gasometerstr
Langstr
Mattengasse
Lettensteg
Kornhaus Brücke
Limmat
LETTEN
Wasserwerkstr
Kronenstr
Röslistr
Schaffhauserstr
Nordstr
Stampfenbachstr
Beckenhofstr
Weinbergstr
Ottikerstr
Riedtlistr
Winterthurerstr
Hadlaubstgasse
Geissbergweg
Hadlaubstr
Rigistr
Zürichberg
Museum für Gestaltung
Klingenstr
Ausstellungstr
Zolistr
Hafnerstr
Limmatstr
Neumühlequai
Hochfarbstr
Universitätstr
Gladbachstr
Vogelsang
Toblerstr
Hochstr
Leonhardstr
Gloriastr
Stauffacherstr
Hermann Greulich Str
Schöneggstr
Sihlhallenstr
Lagerstr
Zwinglistr
Brauerstr
Müllerstr
Ankerstr
Zeughausstr
Stauffacherstr
Kanzleistr
Langstr
Hauptbahnhof (Train Station)
Museumstr
Walche Brücke
Kasernenstr
Bahnhofplatz
Schützengasse
Beatengasse
Beatenplatz
Central
Auf der Mauer
2 5 7 8 10 13 15 16 19 23 27 29 30 33 34

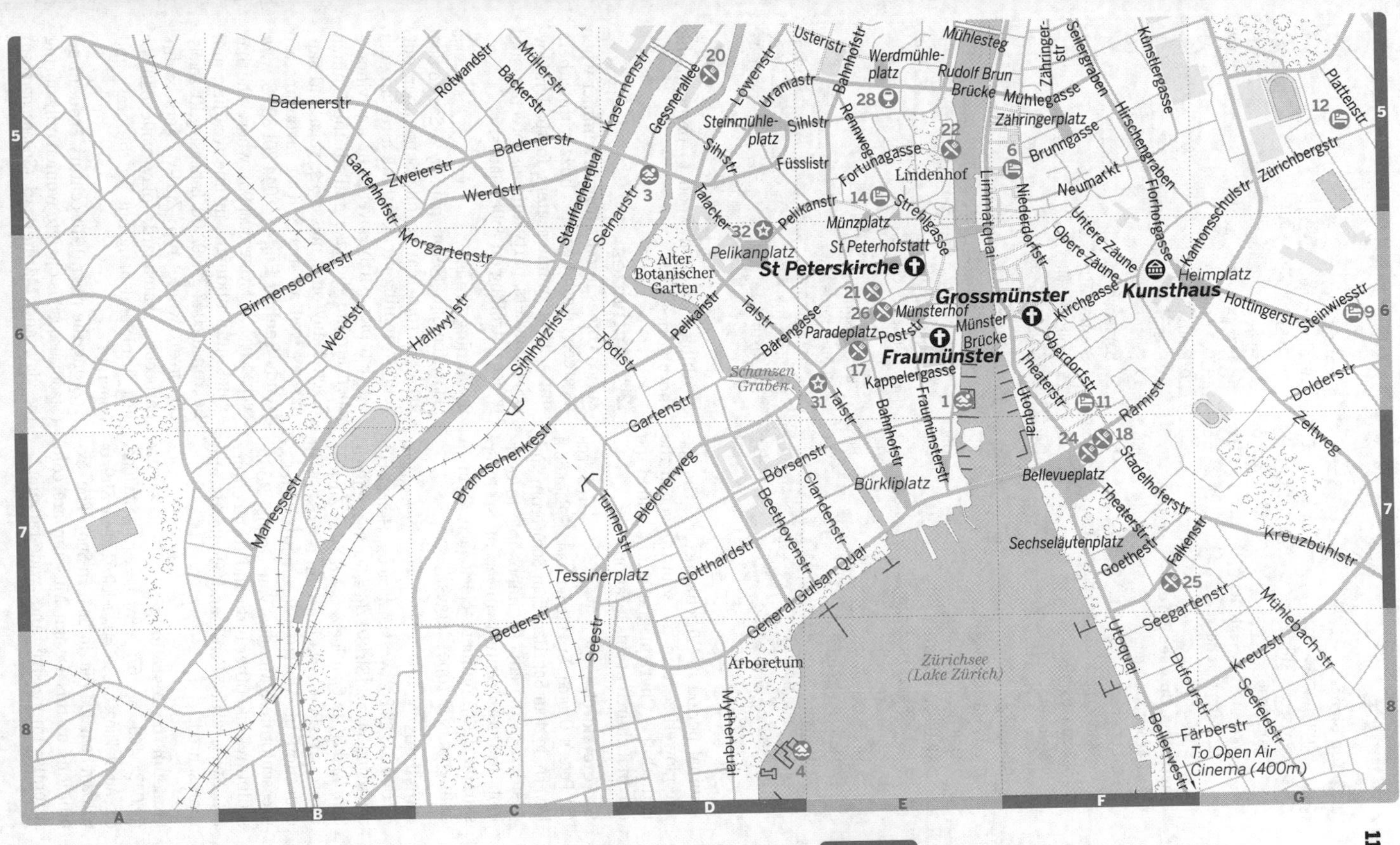

SWITZERLAND ZÜRICH

Zürich

Top Sights

- Fraumünster E6
- Grossmünster F6
- Kunsthaus F6
- Museum für Gestaltung D2
- St Peterskirche E6

Activities, Courses & Tours

1 Frauenbad E6
2 Letten D2
3 Männerbad D5
4 Seebad Enge D8
5 Velogate D4

Sleeping

6 City Backpacker F5
7 Dakini B4
8 Hotel du Théâtre F4
9 Hotel Foyer Hottingen G6
10 Hotel Greulich B4
11 Hotel Otter F6
12 Hotel Plattenhof G5
13 Hotel Rothaus C4
14 Hotel Widder E5
15 Pension für Dich B4

Eating

16 Alpenrose C1
Café für Dich .... (see 15)
17 Café Sprüngli E6
18 Kronenhalle F7
19 Les Halles A1
20 Reithalle D5
21 Restaurant Zum Kropf E6
22 Schipfe 16 .... E5
23 Seidenspinner C4
24 Sternen Grill F7
25 Tibits by Hiltl F7
26 Zeughauskeller E6

Drinking

27 Hard One B1
28 Jules Vernon Panorama Bar E5
29 Liquid C4
30 Longstreet Bar C4

Entertainment

31 Alte Börse E6
32 Kaufleuten D6
33 Supermarket A2
34 Zukunft C4

seminal period in Zürich's history. The figure glowering from the south tower of the cathedral is Charlemagne, who founded the original church at this location.

St Peterskirche CHURCH
(St Peter's Church; St Peterhofstatt; ⏲8am-6pm Mon-Fri, to 4pm Sat, 11am-5pm Sun) From any position in the city, it's impossible to overlook the 13th-century tower of St Peterskirche. Its prominent clock face, 8.7m in diameter, is Europe's largest.

Kunsthaus MUSEUM
(☎044 253 84 84; www.kunsthaus.ch; Heimplatz 1; adult/student/child Sfr18/8/free, Sun free; ⏲10am-8pm Wed-Fri, to 6pm Tue & Sat & Sun) Zürich's impressive Fine Arts Museum boasts a rich collection of Alberto Giacometti stick-figure sculptures, Monets, Van Goghs, Rodin sculptures and other 19th- and 20th-century art. Swiss artist Ferdinand Hodler is also represented.

Museum für Gestaltung MUSEUM
(☎043 446 67 67; www.museum-gestaltung.ch; Ausstellungstrasse 60; adult/student Sfr9/6; ⏲10am-8pm Tue-Thu, to 5pm Fri-Sun) The exhibitions at this Design Museum are consistently impressive and wide-ranging – anything from Bollywood to photographic short stories.

Activities

Zürich comes into its own in summer when its green lakeshore parks buzz with bathers, sun-seekers, in-line skaters, footballers, lovers, picnickers, party animals, preeners and police patrolling on rollerblades!

Swimming Areas SWIMMING
(admission Sfr6; ⏲9am-7pm May & Sep, to 8pm Jun-Aug) From May to mid-September, outdoor swimming areas – think a rectangular wooden pier partly covered by a pavilion – open around the lake and up the Limmat River. Many offer massages, yoga and saunas, as well as snacks. Our favourites are trendy **Seebad Enge** (☎044 201 38 89; www.seebadenge.ch; Mythenquai 95), where the bar opens until midnight in fine weather; and **Letten** (☎044 362 92 00; Lettensteg 10; admission free), where hip Züri-Westers swim, barbecue, skateboard, play volleyball or just drink and hang out on the grass and concrete.

Along the river, 19th-century **Frauenbad** (Stadthausquai) is open to women only during the day, and **Männerbad** (Schanzengraben) is men-only. Both open their trendy bars to both sexes at night – leave shoes at the entrance and drink with feet dipped in the water!

Festivals & Events

Zürich celebrates spring with **Sechseläuten** (www.sechselaeuten.ch), which sees guild members in historical costume parade down the streets on the third Monday in April, climaxing with the burning of a fireworks-filled 'snowman' (Böögg) to mark winter's end.

August's **Street Parade** (www.street-parade.ch) is Europe's largest street party in any given year, attracting well over half a million ravers.

Sleeping

Pension für Dich PENSION $
(044 317 91 60; www.fuerdich.ch; Stauffacherstrasse 141; d without bathroom from Sfr95;) These simple but fabulous apartments have been converted into comfy rooms – think retro furnishings meets Ikea. A number of rooms have balconies, and breakfast can be had for a steal at its cafe downstairs, plus you're smack in the centre of the Kreis 4 nightlife action. There's no reception – just head to the bar in the cafe.

Hotel Widder HOTEL $$$
(044 224 25 26; www.widderhotel.ch; Rennweg 7; s/d from Sfr530/725; P@) A stylish hotel in the equally grand Augustiner district, the Widder is a pleasing fusion of modernity and traditional charm. Rooms and public areas across the eight town houses that make up this place are stuffed with art and designer furniture.

ONCE A TRUCK TARPAULIN, NOW A BAG

Freitag (043-3669520; Geroldstrasse 17; 11am-7.30pm Mon-Fri, 11am-5pm Sat), run by two ambitious Swiss dudes, proves everything can have a second life. Choose an industrial-looking messenger bag, travelling tote or women's purse made from 100% recycled materials (truck tarps, seat belts etc) in this flagship store housed in a 26m-high stack of retired shipping containers in Züri-West. Even if you can't afford the pricey bags, hike up to the alfresco viewing platform in the top container.

Camping Seebucht CAMPING GROUND $
(044 482 16 12; www.camping-zurich.ch; Seestrasse 559; campsites per adult/tent Sfr7.50/11; May-Sep) On the western shore of the lake, 4km from the city centre, this camping ground has good facilities. Take bus 161 or 165 from Bürkliplatz.

Hotel Foyer Hottingen HOTEL $
(044 256 19 19; www.hotel-foyer-hottingen.ch; Hottingerstrasse 31; dm from Sfr45, s from Sfr130, without bathroom from Sfr115;) Rooms are clinical but excellent value; some have a balcony. Each floor has showers and communal kitchen, and on the top floor is a dorm for women only, with a roof terrace.

SYHA hostel HOSTEL $
(043 399 78 00; www.youthhostel.ch; Mütschellenstrasse 114, Wollishofen; dm from Sfr42, s/d from Sfr107/127; @) This bulbous, purple-red hostel features a swish 24-hour reception/dining hall, flat-screen TVs and sparkling modern bathrooms. Dorms are small. Take tram 7 to Morgental, or S-Bahn to Wollishofen.

Dakini B&B $
(044 291 42 20; www.dakini.ch; Brauerstrasse 87; s/d from Sfr80/140; @) This relaxed B&B attracts a bohemian crowd of artists and performers, academics and trendy tourists who don't bat an eyelid at its location near the red-light district. Take tram 8 to Bäckeranlange.

Hotel Rothaus HOTEL $$
(043 322 10 58; www.hotelrothaus.ch; Sihlhallenstrasse 1; s/d from Sfr100/130;) Smack in the middle of the Langstrasse action, you'd never guess this cheerful red brick place was once a brothel. A variety of fresh, airy rooms are complemented by a busy little eatery-bar downstairs.

Hotel Otter HOTEL $$
(044 251 22 07; www.wueste.ch; Oberdorfstrasse 7; s/d/apt from Sfr125/155/200;) A true gem, the Otter has 17 rooms variously decorated with pink satin sheets and plastic beads, raised beds, wall murals and in one instance a hammock. A popular bar, the Wüste, is downstairs.

Hotel du Thèâtre HOTEL $
(044-2672670; www.hotel-du-theatre.ch; Seilergraben 69; s/d from Sfr100/110;) Located in the lively Niederdorf and within walking distance to the train station, this friendly boutique hotel is decorated with designer furniture and old film stills (an ode to the hotel's past – in the 1950s it was a combined

theatre and hotel). Tranquillity prevails here and the staff are more than happy to give guests insider tips on local restaurants and bars.

Hotel Greulich HOTEL **$$$**
(043 243 42 43; www.greulich.ch; Hermann Greulich Strasse 56; s/d from Sfr190/255;) The curving blue-grey walls lend these designer digs in a quieter part of Kreis 4 a retro art deco touch. Minimalist off-white rooms are laid out in facing bungalows along two sides of an austere courtyard.

Hotel Plattenhof HOTEL **$$$**
(044 251 19 10; www.plattenhof.ch; Plattenstrasse 26; s/d from Sfr190/255; P) This place manages to be cool without looking pretentious. It features a youthful, vaguely Japanese style, with low beds and mood lighting in its newest rooms. Even the older rooms are stylishly minimalist. Take tram 6 to Platte.

City Backpacker HOSTEL **$**
(044 251 90 15; www.city-backpacker.ch; Niederdorfstrasse 5; dm Sfr35, s/d from Sfr75/115; reception closed noon-3pm; @) This youthful party hostel is friendly and well equipped, if a trifle cramped. Overcome the claustrophobia in summer by hanging out on the roof terrace – the best spot in Zürich to wind down at sunset with a few cold beers.

Eating

Zürich has a thriving cafe culture and hundreds of restaurants – explore Niederdorfstrasse and its nearby backstreets.

Zeughauskeller SWISS **$$**
(044 211 26 90; www.zeughauskeller.ch; Bahnhofstrasse 28a; mains Sfr18-35; 11.30am-11pm;) The menu at this huge, atmospheric beer hall – set inside a former armoury (look for the shields and various protective antiques hanging from the walls) – offers 20 different kinds of sausages in eight languages, as well as numerous other Swiss specialities of a carnivorous and vegetarian variety. It's a local institution and well loved by the lunch crowd, so expect queues during the week between noon and 2pm.

Cafe für Dich CAFE **$**
(044 317 91 60 Stauffacherstrasse 141; Zähringerplatz 11; snacks Sfr5-9; 6pm-midnight Mon, 9am-midnight Tue-Sun) This laid-back cafe in Kreis 4 could easily be in San Francisco or Brooklyn, with its no-nonsense come-and-hang-out vibe. Occasional one-man-band live music and poetry readings keep the atmosphere serious but fun, and it's a fab spot to grab a tea, single malt, local beer or a small snack (olives, quiches) throughout the day and eve.

Restaurant Zum Kropf SWISS **$$**
(044 221 18 05; www.zumkropf.ch; In Gassen 16; mains Sfr23-48; closed Sun) Notable for its historic interior, with marble columns, stained glass and ceiling murals, Kropf has been favoured by locals since 1888 for its hearty Swiss staples and fine beers.

Les Halles INTERNATIONAL **$$**
(044 273 11 25; www.les-halles.ch; Pfingstweidstrasse 6; mains Sfr22-31; 11am-midnight Mon-Wed, to 1am Thu-Sat) One of several chirpy bar-restaurants in revamped factory buildings, this is the best place in town to tuck into *moules mit frites* (mussels and fries). Hang at the bustling bar and shop at the market.

Reithalle INTERNATIONAL **$$**
(044 212 07 66; www.restaurant-reithalle.ch; Gessnerallee 8; mains Sfr22-35; lunch & dinner Mon-Fri, dinner Sat & Sun) Fancy dining in stables in a former barracks complex? The walls at this boisterous, convivial spot are still lined with the cavalry horses' feeding and drinking troughs. Cuisine is copious Swiss and international, and tables are cleared at 11.30pm when the place morphs into a dance club.

Alpenrose SWISS **$$**
(044 271 39 19; Fabrikstrasse 12; mains Sfr24-42; Mon-Sat) With its timber-clad walls, 'no polka dancing' warning and fine cuisine from regions all over Switzerland, this place makes for an inspired meal out. Try risotto from Ticino, *pizokel* (a kind of long and especially savoury *spätzli*, or dumpling) from Graubünden or freshly fished local perch filets. Reservations essential.

Seidenspinner MODERN EUROPEAN **$$$**
(044 241 07 00; www.seidenspinner.ch; Ankerstrasse 120; mains Sfr29-55; lunch & dinner Tue-Fri, dinner Sat) A favourite with the media and fashion crowd, Silk-spinner boasts an extravagant interior with huge flower arrangements and shards of mirrored glass. European cooking dominates.

Kronenhalle SWISS **$$$**
(044 251 66 69; Rämistrasse 4; mains Sfr32-87; lunch & dinner) Haunt of city movers and shakers in suits, with an old-world feel, the Crown Hall is a brasserie where impeccably mannered waiters move discreetly beneath Chagall, Miro, Matisse and Picasso originals.

Café Sprüngli SWISS $

(☎044 224 47 31; www.spruengli.ch; Bahnhofstrasse 21; mains Sfr9-15; ⏲7am-6.30pm Mon-Fri, 8am-6pm Sat, 9.30am-5.30pm Sun) Indulge in cakes, chocolate and coffee at this epicentre of sweet Switzerland, in business since 1836. You can have a light lunch too but whatever you do, don't fail to check out the chocolate shop heaven around the corner on Paradeplatz.

Tibits by Hiltl INTERNATIONAL $

(☎044 260 32 22; www.tibits.ch; Seefeldstrasse 2; meals per 100g Sfr3.80, mains from Sfr10; ⏲6.30am-midnight Mon-Fri, 8am-midnight Sat, 9am-midnight Sun; 🥬) Tibits is where with-it, health-conscious Zürichers eat light. Think tasty vegetarian buffet, fresh fruit juices, coffees and cake – take your pick and pay at the counter.

Sternen Grill SWISS $

(Theatrestrasse 22; snacks from Sfr6; ⏲11.30am-midnight) This is the city's most famous – and busiest – sausage stand; just follow the crowds streaming into Bellevueplatz for a tasty greasefest.

Schipfe 16 INTERNATIONAL $

(☎044 211 21 22; Schipfe 16; menus Sfr17-20; ⏲lunch Mon-Fri) Overlooking the Limmat River from the historic Schipfe area, Schipfe 16 is a good-natured canteen-style spot for a humble speed lunch.

Drinking & Entertainment

Buzzing drinking options congregate in the happening Kreis 4 district (the former red light district known as the Langstrasse area – it's safe to wander though you may be offered drugs or sex – with loads of popular bars quietly humming off its side streets) and Kreis 5 district, together known as Züri-West. Mid-May to mid-September, Wednesday to Sunday, the trendy water bars at the **lake baths** are hot places to hang bare-footed. Clubbers should dress well and be prepared to cough up Sfr15 to Sfr30 admission.

For a month from mid-July, there's an extremely popular waterside **open-air cinema** (☎0800 078078; www.orangecinema.ch; Zürichhorn).

Jules Verne Panorama Bar BAR

(☎044-8886666; Uraniastrasse 9; ⏲11am-midnight Mon-Fri, 11.30am-midnight Sat, 4-11pm Sun) Served on the top floor of a round observatory tower, the jumbo cocktails are almost as impressive as the 360-degree view. Best for an early drink around sunset – later in the evening elbow-room is non-existent.

Longstreet Bar BAR

(☎044 241 21 72; www.longstreetbar.ch; Langstrasse 92; ⏲8pm-3am Tue-Thu, to 4am Fri & Sat, to 2am Sun) Run by the guy seemingly behind half Zürich's nightlife, this purple-felt lined one-time cabaret is now a throbbing music bar with DJs. Count the thousands of light bulbs.

Liquid CLUB

(☎079 446 73 66; www.liquid-bar.ch; Zwinglistrasse 12; ⏲5pm-1am Mon-Thu, to 3am Fri, 7pm-3am Sat) With its striped wallpaper and plastic chairs moulded in the shape of boiled eggs broken in half, this is kitsch at its best – a hip backdrop for lounge-oriented music nights.

Hard One BAR

(☎044 444 10 00; www.hardone.ch; Hardstrasse 260; admission free-Sfr15; ⏲6pm-2am Tue-Thu, to 4am Fri & Sat) The punters flock to this glass cube of a lounge bar for great views and weekend gigs.

Zukunft CLUB

(www.zukunft.ch; Dienerstrasse 33; ⏲11pm-late Thu-Sat) Look for a modest queue (there's no name) and head downstairs to this literally underground dance bar, where a broad range of electro and other dance music keep a mixed crowd happy.

Supermarket CLUB

(☎044 440 20 05; www.supermarket.li; Geroldstrasse 17; ⏲11pm-late Thu-Sat) Looking like an innocent little house, Supermarket boasts three cosy lounge bars around the dance floor, a covered back courtyard and an interesting roster of DJs playing house. The crowd is mid-20s.

Kaufleuten CLUB

(☎044-2253322; Pelikanplatz 18; ⏲from 11pm Thu-Sat) Two floors, four bars and a dance floor adjacent to the art deco stage of this former theatre keep this a perennial favourite among all age groups year after year. Dress to impress.

Alte Börse CLUB

(www.alteboerse.com; Bleicherweg 5; ⏲10pm-late Thu-Sat) Hundreds of dance fanatics cram into this club in a respectable town-centre building for intense electronic sessions with DJs from all over the world. It also gets in occasional live acts.

Information

Police station (☎044 216 71 11; Bahnhofquai 3)

Post office (train station; ⏲7am-9pm)

University Hospital (☎044 255 11 11, 044 255 21 11; www.usz.ch; Rämistrasse 100) Casualty medical service.

Zürich Tourism (☎044 215 40 00, hotel reservations 044 215 40 40; www.zuerich.com; train station; ⏲8am-8.30pm Mon-Sat, 8.30am-6.30pm Sun May-Oct, 8.30am-7pm Mon-Sat, 9am-6.30pm Sun Nov-Apr)

ZürichCard (per 24/72hr Sfr17/24) Discount card available from the tourist office and airport train station; provides free public transport, free museum admission and more.

Getting There & Away

AIR Zürich airport (ZRH; ☎043 816 22 11; www.zurich-airport.com), 10km north of the centre, is a small international hub with two terminals.

CAR The A3 approaches Zürich from the south along the shore of Lake Zürich. The A1 is the fastest route from Bern and Basel.

TRAIN Direct daily trains run to Stuttgart (Sfr76, three hours), Munich (Sfr104, 4½ hours) and Innsbruck (Sfr79, four hours) plus many other international destinations. There are regular direct departures to most major Swiss towns, such as Lucerne (Sfr23, 46 to 50 minutes), Bern (Sfr46, 57 minutes) and Basel (Sfr31, 55 minutes).

Getting Around

TO/FROM THE AIRPORT Up to nine trains an hour yo-yo between the airport and main train station between 6am and midnight (Sfr6, nine to 14 minutes).

BICYCLE City bikes (www.zuerirollt.ch) can be picked up at **Velogate** (train station; ⏲8am-9.30pm) for free if you bring the bike back after six hours or pay Sfr5 per day.

BOAT April to October **lake steamers** (☎044 487 13 33; www.zsg.ch) depart from Bürkliplatz.

PUBLIC TRANSPORT There is a comprehensive, unified bus, tram and S-Bahn service in the city, which includes boats plying the Limmat River. Short trips under five stops are Sfr2.40. A 24-hour pass for the centre is Sfr7.80. For unlimited travel within the canton, including extended tours of the lake, a day pass costs Sfr30.40.

NORTHERN SWITZERLAND

This region is left off most people's Switzerland itineraries – precisely why you should visit! Sure, it is known for industry and commerce, but it also has some great attractions. Breathe in the sweet (OK slightly stinky) odours of black-and-white cows as you roll through the bucolic countryside. Take time to explore the tiny rural towns set among green rolling hills, and on Lake Constance (Bodensee) and the Rhine (Rhein) River on the German border.

Basel

POP 165,100

Strangely, given its northerly location, Basel has some of the hottest weather in the country, so you should visit in the summer. When the mercury starts rising the city sheds its notorious reserve and just cuts loose. As locals bob along in the fast-moving Rhine River, cool off in the city's numerous fountains, whiz by on motor scooters, and dine and drink on overcrowded pavements, you could almost be in Italy, rather than on the dual border with France and Germany.

Basel's (Bâle in French) idyllic Old Town and many enticing galleries and museums are top draws any time of year. The famous Renaissance humanist Erasmus of Rotterdam was associated with the city and his tomb rests in the cathedral.

Sights & Activities

Old Town HISTORIC AREA

With its cobbled streets, colourful fountains, medieval churches and stately buildings, the Old Town is a wonderful place to wander. In Marktplatz check out the impressive rust-coloured **Rathaus** (Town Hall), with frescoed courtyard. The 12th-century **Münster** (cathedral; ⏲10am-5pm), southeast from Marktplatz, is another highlight, with Gothic spires and Romanesque St Gallus doorway.

Theaterplatz is a crowd-pleaser, with a curious **fountain**, designed by Swiss sculptor Jean Tinguely. His madcap scrap-metal machines perform a peculiar water dance, delighting children and weary travellers alike. Also check out the 700-year-old **Spalentor** gate tower, a remnant of the town's old city walls, with a massive portal and grotesque gargoyles.

Kunstmuseum ART MUSEUM

(Museum of Fine Arts; ☎061 206 62 62; www.kunstmuseumbasel.ch; St Alban-Graben 16; adult/student/child Sfr12.50/5/free, 1st Sun of month free; ⏲10am-5pm Tue-Sun) Art lovers can ogle at Switzerland's largest art collection, including works by Klee and Picasso.

Fondation Beyeler ART MUSEUM

(☎061 645 97 00; www.beyeler.com; Baselstrasse 101, Riehen; adult/student/child Sfr25/12/6;

⏲10am-6pm, to 8pm Wed) The art space to really knock your socks off is the Fondation Beyeler, in an open-plan building by Italian architect Renzo Piano. The quality of its 19th- and 20th-century paintings is matched only by the way Miró and Max Ernst sculptures are juxtaposed with similar tribal figures. Take tram 6 to Riehen.

Festivals & Events

Basel's huge **Fasnacht** spring carnival kicks off at 4am on the Monday after Ash Wednesday with the **Morgestraich**: streetlights are extinguished and a procession of masked, costumed revellers wends its way through town. Restaurants and bars stay open all night and the streets positively throb with festivities.

Sleeping

Hotels are often full during Basel's trade fairs and conventions; book ahead. Guests receive a free Mobility Pass upon checking in, meaning free travel on public transport.

Hotel Stadthof HOTEL **$**
(☎061 261 87 11; www.stadthof.ch; Gerbergasse 84; s/d from Sfr75/125) Book ahead to snag a room at this spartan but decent central hotel, located above a pizzeria on an Old Town square. The cheaper rooms share toilet and shower.

Au Violon HOTEL **$**
(☎061 269 87 11; www.au-violon.com; Im Lohnhof 4; s/d from Sfr120/140; ⊖ ᯤ) Quaint, atmospheric Au Violon was a prison from 1835 to 1995. Most of the rooms are two cells rolled into one and overlook a cobblestone courtyard or the cathedral. Sitting atop a leafy hilltop, its restaurant is equally appealing.

Hotel Krafft HOTEL **$**
(☎061 690 91 30; www.hotelkrafft.ch; Rheingasse 12; s/d from Sfr75/125; ᯤ) Design-savvy urbanites adore this place. Sculptural chandeliers dangle in the creaky-floored dining room (for fine food) overlooking the Rhine, and stainless-steel water bars adorn each landing of the spiral stairs.

Basel Backpack HOSTEL **$**
(☎061 333 00 37; www.baselbackpack.ch; Dornacherstrasse 192; dm Sfr32, s/d from Sfr80/100; ⊖@) Converted from a factory, this independent hostel south of the main train station has cheerful, colour-coded eight-bed dorms and more sedate doubles and family rooms.

SYHA Basel City Youth Hostel HOSTEL **$**
(☎061 365 99 60; www.youthhostel.ch/basel.city; Pfeffingerstasse 8; dm Sfr35.50, s/d Sfr79/95; ⏲reception 7am-noon & 3-11pm; @) A convenient hostel in former post office buildings, it's across from the train station. Rooms have up to four beds and there's space aplenty – including a summertime interior courtyard.

Eating

Atrio Vulcanelli INTERNATIONAL **$$**
(☎061 683 06 80; www.vulcanelli.ch; Erlenmattstrasse 5; mains Sfr16-36; ⏲dinner Wed-Sat) Nautical and cabaret meets bohemian in this vast, high-ceilinged space-cum-bistro north of the Old Town. Its hodgepodge of creaky wood tables and decadent candelabras keeps things cosy and the seasonal cuisine is spot on. In summer after dinner, head over to the open-air **beach bar** (⏲10pm-5am Fri & Sat) down the street, which morphs into a club in the wee hours.

Acqua ITALIAN **$$**
(☎061 564 66 66; www.acquabasilea.ch; Binningerstrasse 14; mains Sfr17-42; ⏲lunch & dinner Tue-Fri, dinner Sat) For a glam postindustrial experience, head to these converted waterworks. Cuisine is Tuscan and Basel's beautiful people drink in the attached lounge bar or on the summer terrace.

Druck Punkt BISTRO **$$**
(☎061 261 50 22; St Johanns Vorstadt 19; mains Sfr17-25; ⏲Mon-Fri) This converted print shop makes an unpretentious bistro, with chalky walls and heavy wooden tables.

Parterre INTERNATIONAL **$$**
(☎061 695 89 98; www.parterre.net; Klybeckstrasse 1b; mains Sfr16-38; ⏲dinner Mon-Sat) Unusual dishes such as lake salmon in saffron sauce with potato gratin and cabbage stud the menu in this slightly alternative place overlooking a park. Snacks and light meals are served throughout the day.

Oliv MEDITERRANEAN **$$**
(☎061 283 03 03; www.restaurantoliv.ch; Bachlettenstrasse 1; mains Sfr25-39; ⏲lunch & dinner Tue-Fri, dinner Sat) A trendy hang-out not far from the zoo, Oliv leans towards fresh and varied Mediterranean cooking. Unusually, dainty appetites can order half portions.

St Alban Stübli SWISS **$$$**
(☎061 272 54 15; www.st-alban-stuebli.ch; St Alban Vorstadt 74; mains Sfr40-59; ⏲Mon-Fri) Set in a lovely quiet street, this is your quintessential cosy local tavern with dim yellow lighting,

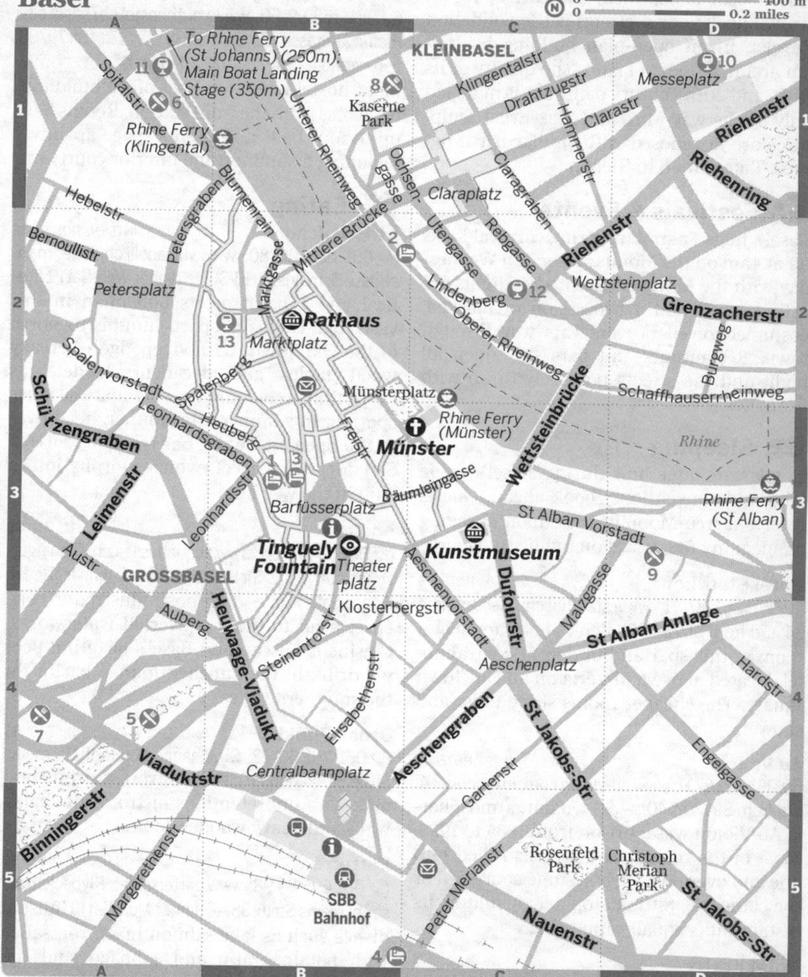

plenty of timber and fine linen. Food fuses local with French.

Drinking & Entertainment

Steinenvorstadt and Barfüsserplatz teem with teens and 20-somethings on the weekends. A faint whiff of grunge floats around Kleinbasel, the area around Rheingasse and Utengasse, with a few watering holes and something of a red-light zone to lend it edge.

Bar Rouge BAR

(☎061 361 30 21; www.barrouge.ch; Level 31, Messeplatz 10; ⌚5pm-1am Mon-Wed, to 2am Thu, to 4am Fri & Sat) This plush red bar with panoramic views from the 31st floor of the ugly glass Messeturm (trade fair tower) is the city's most memorable. Hipsters, and a few suits early on weekday evenings, come to appreciate the regular DJs and films.

Hirscheneck BAR

(☎061 692 73 33; Lindenberg 23; ⌚9am-midnight Sun-Thu, 10am-2am Fri & Sat) A relaxed, grungy, almost knockabout place with an urban vibe (try to spot someone *without* piercings), this corner bar has tables on the footpath and regular gigs and DJs.

Basel

Top Sights

Sleeping

Eating

Drinking

Zum Roten Engel CAFE-BAR
(☎061 261 20 08; Andreasplatz 15; ⏲9am-midnight Mon-Sat, 10am-10pm Sun) Spilling onto an irresistible, tiny cobblestone square, this student haunt is perfect for a latte by day or glass of wine come dusk.

Cargo-Bar CLUB
(☎061 321 00 72; www.cargobar.ch; St Johanns Rheinweg 46; ⏲4pm-1am Sun-Thu, to 2.30am Fri & Sat) A nice halfway house between cool and alternative, located in a tucked-away spot on the river. There are lots of art installations, live gigs, video shows and DJs.

Information

Post office (Rüdengasse 1; ⏲7.30am-6.30pm Mon-Wed, to 7pm Thu-Fri, 8am-5pm Sat)

Tourist office (☎061 268 68 68; www.basel.com; Stadt-Casino, Barfüsserplatz, Steinenberg 14; ⏲8.30am-6.30pm Mon-Fri, 9am-5pm Sat, 9am-4pm Sun)

Getting There & Away

AIR The **EuroAirport** (BSL or MLH; ☎061 325 31 11; www.euroairport.com), 5km northwest of town in France, is the main airport for Basel.

TRAIN Basel is a major European rail hub, with two main train stations: the Swiss-French SBB (south bank) and the BBF (north bank) for trains to/from Germany.

Destinations include Paris (from Sfr70, 3½ to five hours). Local trains to the Black Forest stop only at BBF, though fast EC services stop at SBB too. Main destinations along this route are Amsterdam (from Sfr180, eight hours, daily), Frankfurt (from Sfr137, three hours, daily) and Hamburg (from Sfr220, 6½ to 7½ hours, daily).

Services within Switzerland from SBB include Geneva (Sfr69, 2¾ hours, twice hourly) and Zürich (Sfr31, 55 minutes to 1¾ hours, twice hourly).

Getting Around

Bus 50 links the airport and SBB train station (Sfr6.60, 20 minutes). The trip by **taxi** (☎061 691 77 88) costs around Sfr40.

Appenzellerland

The Appenzellers are the butt of many a cruel joke by their fellow Swiss, a little like Tasmanians in Australia or Newfoundlanders in Canada. As Swiss Germans say, Appenzellers *hätte ä langi Laitig* (have a very long cable). It takes a while after you tug for them to get the message. And indeed, there's no denying that the Appenzellcanton is still firmly rooted in tradition: Innerrhoden continues to hold a yearly open-air parliament and didn't permit women to vote until 1991.

Such devotion to rural tradition has an upside: locals go to great lengths to preserve their heritage. This area of impossibly green valleys, thick forests and mighty mountains is dotted with timeless villages and criss-crossed by endless hiking and cycling paths.

The pastel-hued village of **Appenzell** is a feast for the eyes and the stomach. Behind the gaily decorative coloured facades of its traditional buildings lie cafes, cake shops, cheese shops, delicatessens, butchers and restaurants all offering local specialities. Don your lazy hat and enjoy a long slow lunch and wander!

The train station is 400m from the town centre, home to the **tourist office** (☎071 788 96 41; www.appenzell.ch; Hauptgasse 4; ⏲9am-noon & 1.30-6pm Mon-Fri, 10am-noon & 2-5pm Sat & Sun Apr-Oct, 9am-noon & 2-5pm Mon-Fri, 2-5pm Sat & Sun Nov-Mar).

Hotel Appenzell (☎071 788 15 15; www.hotel-appenzell.ch; Landsgemeindeplatz; s/d Sfr130/220; ⊜) sits in a brightly decorated, typical Appenzeller building and is a solid choice to both sleep and sample seasonal cuisine, including vegetarian dishes and the local strong-smelling Appenzell cheese.

There is a train to St Gallen (Sfr10.80, 50 minutes, twice hourly).

WORTH A TRIP

SHAFFHAUSEN & THE RHINE

Schaffhausen is the kind of quaint medieval town one more readily associates with Germany (perhaps no coincidence given how close the border is). Ornate frescos and oriel windows adorn pastel-coloured houses in the pedestrian-only Altstadt (Old Town), home to the **tourist office** (☎052 632 40 20; www.schaffhausen-tourismus.ch, www.shtotal.info; Herrenacker 15; ⏰9.30am-6pm Mon-Fri, to 4pm Sat Jun-Sep, to 2pm Sun Jun-Aug, to 5pm Mon-Fri, to 1pm Sat Oct-May).

Prime views preen their feathers atop the 16th-century **Munot fortress** (admission free; ⏰8am-8pm May-Sep, 9am-5pm Oct-Apr), a 15-minute uphill walk through vineyards from town.

Westward along the river on foot (40 minutes) or aboard bus 1 to Neuhausen is **Rheinfall** (Rhine Falls), waterfalls that, though only 23m tall, are deemed Europe's largest. The amount of water thundering down is extraordinary.

The 45km **boat trip** (☎052 634 08 88; www.urh.ch or www.riverticket.ch; Freier Platz; single/return Sfr21/30; ⏰Mar-Oct) from Schaffhausen to Konstanz sails past one of the Rhine's more beautiful stretches. It passes meadows, castles and ancient villages, including **Stein am Rhein**, 20km to the east, where you could easily wear out your camera snapping pictures of the buildings in the picture-perfect Rathausplatz.

Direct hourly trains run to/from Schaffhausen and Zürich (Sfr18.20, 40 minutes).

TICINO

This is the Switzerland that Heidi never mentioned: the summer air is rich, hot (and smokefree thanks to a cantonwide ban on smoking in public places since 2007) and the peacock-proud posers propel their scooters in and out of traffic. Italian weather, Italian style. And that's not to mention the Italian ice cream, Italian pizza, Italian architecture and Italian language.

South of the Alps, Ticino (Tessin in German and French) has a distinct look. The canton manages to perfectly fuse Swiss cool with Italian passion, as evidenced by a lusty love for Italian comfort food and full-bodied wines that's balanced by a healthy respect for rules and regulations.

Locarno

POP 15,600

The rambling red enclave of Italianate town houses, piazzas and arcades ending at the northern end of Lake Maggiore, coupled with more hours of sunshine than anywhere else in Switzerland, give this laid-back town a summer resort atmosphere. The lowest town in Switzerland, it seemed like a soothing spot to host the 1925 peace conference that was intended to bring stability to Europe after WWI.

Five minutes' walk west of the train station is the town's heart, Piazza Grande, and the **tourist office** (☎091 791 00 91; www.maggiore.ch; Largo Zorzi 1; ⏰9am-6pm Mon-Fri, 10am-6pm Sat, 10am-1.30pm & 2.30-5pm Sun mid-Mar–Oct, 9.30am-noon & 1.30-5pm Mon-Fri, 10am-noon & 1.30-5pm Sat Nov–mid-Mar) nearby.

Sights & Activities

Madonna del Sasso SANCTUARY

Don't miss the formidable Madonna del Sasso, located up on the hill, with panoramic views of the lake and town. The sanctuary was built after the Virgin Mary allegedly appeared in a vision in 1480. It features a church with 15th-century paintings, a small museum and several distinctive statues.

There is a funicular from the town centre, but the 20-minute climb is not demanding (take Via al Sasso off Via Cappuccini) and you pass some shrines on the way.

Festivals & Events

In August more than 150,000 film buffs hit town for the two-week **International Film Festival** (www.pardo.ch). Cinemas are used during the day but at night films are shown in the open-air on a giant screen in the Piazza Grande.

Sleeping

Camping Delta CAMPING GROUND $

(☎091 751 60 81; www.campingdelta.com; Via Respini 7; campsites Sfr47-57, plus per adult/senior & student/child Sfr20/17/6; ⏰Mar-Oct) Although pricey, this camping ground has great facilities and is brilliantly located between the shores of Lago Maggiore and the Maggia River.

Vecchia Locarno HOTEL $
(☎091 751 65 02; www.hotel-vecchia-locarno.ch; Via della Motta 10; s/d without bathroom from Sfr55/100) Rooms are gathered around a sunny internal courtyard, evoking a Mediterranean mood, and some have Old Town views. Digs are simple but comfortable.

Eating & Drinking

Lake Maggiore has a great variety of fresh and tasty fish, including *persico* (perch) and *corigone* (whitefish).

Osteria Chiara ITALIAN $$
(☎091 743 32 96; Vicolo della Chiara 1; mains Sfr16-30; ⏲Tue-Sat) Tucked away on a cobbled lane, this has all the cosy feel of a grotto. Sit at granite tables beneath the pergola or at timber tables by the fireplace for chunky pasta and mostly meat dishes. From the lake follow the signs up Vicolo dei Nessi.

Bar Sport BAR
(Via della Posta 4; ⏲8am-1am Mon-Fri, 10am-1am Sat, 2pm-1am Sun) A run-of-the-mill place by day, this rough-and-tumble bar with red-walled dance space out the back and beer garden is a huge hit with night owls. A few other bars loiter nearby.

Getting There & Away

The St Gotthard Pass provides the road link (A2) to central Switzerland. There are trains from Brig (Sfr51, 2½ hours, hourly) that pass through Italy en route; change trains at Domodossola across the border and bring your passport.

THESE BOOTS ARE MADE FOR WALKING...NOT

Hiking trails abound around Appenzell. One more unusual one is the **Barefoot Path** from Gonten, 5km west of Appenzell, to Gontenbad (one hour), for which you really don't need shoes – think lush green moors and meadows. In Gontenbad, dip in mud-laden water from the moors at **Natur-Moorbad** (☎071 795 31 23; www.naturmoorbad.ch; admission Sfr20; Gontenbad), a moor bath dating to 1740, whose wholly natural products relieve stress or skin conditions (adding in nettles, ferns and other plants) or simply serve to luxuriate loved ones with sweet rose baths (Sfr86 for two).

Lugano

POP 51,900

There is a distinct vibrant snappiness in the air in Lugano, Switzerland's southernmost tourist town, where visitors unravel the spaghetti maze of cobblestone streets while locals toil in stuffy banks – this is the country's third-most important banking centre.

A sophisticated slice of Italian life with colourful markets, upmarket shops, interlocking *piazze* and lakeside parks, lucky Lugano lounges on the northern shore of Lake Lugano, at the feet of Mounts San Salvatore and Bré. Read: a superb base for lake trips, water sports and hillside hikes.

The Centro Storico (Old Town) is a 10-minute walk downhill from the train station; take the stairs or the funicular (Sfr1.10). The **tourist office** (☎091 913 32 32; www.lugano-tourism.ch; Riva Giocondo Albertolli; ⏲9am-7pm Mon-Fri, to 5pm Sat, 10am-5pm Sun Apr-Oct, 9am-noon & 2-5.30pm Mon-Fri, 10am-12.30pm & 1.30-5pm Sat Nov-Mar) runs a **booth** (⏲2-7pm Mon-Sat) at the station.

Sights & Activities

Wander through the mostly porticoed lanes woven around the busy main square, Piazza della Riforma (which is even more lively when the Tuesday- and Friday-morning markets are held). Via Nassa is the main shopping street and indicates there is no shortage of cash in this town.

Chiesa di Santa Maria degli Angioli CHURCH
(St Mary of the Angels; Piazza Luini; ⏲8am-5pm) The simple Romanesque Chiesa di Santa Maria degli Angioli, against which a now-crumbling former hotel was built, contains two frescos by Bernardino Luini dating from 1529. Covering the entire wall that divides the church in two is a grand didactic illustration of the Crucifixion. The closer you look, the more scenes of Christ's Passion are revealed, along with others of Christ being taken down from the Cross and the Resurrection. The power and vivacity of the colours are astounding.

Museo del Cioccolato Alprose MUSEUM
(☎091 611 88 88; www.alprose.ch; Via Rompada 36, Caslano; adult/child Sfr3/1; ⏲9am-5.30pm Mon-Fri, to 4.30pm Sat & Sun) Chomp on a chocolate-coated history lesson: watch the sweet substance being made and taste it for free. Get there by the Ferrovia Ponte Tresa train (Sfr7).

WORTH A TRIP

BELLINZONA'S UNESCO CASTLES

Ticino's capital is a quiet stunner. Strategically placed at the conversion point of several valleys leading down from the Alps, Bellinzona is visually unique. Inhabited since Neolithic times, it is dominated by three grey-stone, fairy-tale medieval castles that have attracted everyone from Swiss invaders to painters such as JMW Turner. Turner may have liked the place, but Bellinzona has a surprisingly low tourist profile, in spite of its castles together forming a Unesco World Heritage site.

The **tourist office** (☎091 825 21 31; www.bellinzonaturismo.ch; Piazza Nosetto; ⏰9am-6pm Mon-Fri, to noon Sat, reduced hours in winter), in the restored Renaissance town hall, can provide information on Bellinzona and the whole canton.

You can roam the ramparts of the two larger castles, **Castelgrande** or **Castello di Montebello**, both of which are still in great condition and offer panoramic views of the town and countryside.

Alternatively, seize the rare opportunity to dine in a Unesco World Heritage site at medieval **Castelgrande** (☎091 826 23 53; www.castelgrande.ch; Castelgrande; mains Sfr35-60; ⏰Tue-Sun).

Bellinzona is on the train route connecting Locarno (Sfr8.20, 20 to 25 minutes) and Lugano (Sfr11.80, 26 to 30 minutes).

Boat Trips BOAT TRIPS

Take a boat trip to one of the photogenic villages hugging the shoreline – car-free **Gandria** is popular – and feast on traditional Ticinese dishes in your pick of quintessential Ticinese grottos.

Sleeping

Many hotels close for part of the winter.

Hotel Pestalozzi HOTEL $$

(☎091 921 46 46; www.pestalozzi-lugano.ch; Piazza Indipendenza 9; s/d Sfr108/190, without bathroom Sfr68/112; ❄📶) This renovated art nouveau building is home to rooms with reds, blues and creams dominating the decor. Cheaper ones have a shared bathroom in the corridor.

Hotel Montarina HOTEL $$

(☎091 966 72 72; www.montarina.ch; Via Montarina 1; s/d from Sfr85/125; P📶🏊) Behind the train station, this charming hotel has airy rooms, timber floors and antiques. Some rooms have kitchens and the garden is pool-clad.

Hostel Montarina HOSTEL $

(☎091 966 72 72; www.montarina.ch; Via Montarina 1; dm from Sfr34) Hostel Montarina has simple rooms with four to 16 bunk beds. A buffet breakfast is available for Sfr12.

SYHA hostel HOSTEL $

(☎091 966 27 28; www.luganoyouth hostel.ch; Via Cantonale 13, Savosa; dm/s/d Sfr29/70/98; ⏰mid-Mar–Oct; 🏊) Housed in Villa Savosa, this is one of Switzerland's more enticing youth hostels. Take bus 5 to Crocifisso.

Eating

For pizza or overpriced pasta, any of the places around Piazza della Riforma are pleasant and lively enough.

Bottegone del Vino ITALIAN $$

(☎091 922 76 89; Via Magatti 3; mains Sfr27-42; ⏰Mon-Sat) Favoured by the local banking brigade at lunchtime, this is a great place to taste fine local wines over a well-prepared meal. The menu changes daily and knowledgeable waiters fuss around the tables, only too happy to suggest the perfect Ticino tipple.

Grand Café Al Porto INTERNATIONAL $$$

(☎091 910 51 30; Via Pessina 3; mains Sfr31-48; ⏰8am-6.30pm Mon-Sat) This cafe, which began life way back in 1803, has several fine rooms for dining inside. Be sure to head upstairs to take a peek into the frescoed Cenacolo Fiorentino, once a monastery dining hall.

Al Lido INTERNATIONAL $$

(☎091 971 55 00; Viale Castagnola; snacks Sfr9-15, mains Sfr19-32; ⏰brunch & dinner Wed-Sat) Lugano's lakeside beach restaurant is hot for Sunday buffet brunch (Sfr37) and its Wednesday-evening version (same price), with DJ thrown in.

L'Antica Osteria del Porto REGIONAL $$

(☎091 971 42 00; Via Foce 9; mains Sfr22-41; ⏰Wed-Mon) Set back from the sailing club, this is the place to savour local fish and Ticinese dishes.

Drinking & Entertainment

Soho Café COCKTAIL BAR
(☎091 922 60 80; Corso Pestalozzi 3; ⏲7am-1am Mon-Fri, 4pm-1am Sat) Good-looking Lugano townies crowd into this long, orange-lit bar for cocktails. Chilled DJ music creates a pleasant buzz. The problem might be squeezing through to the bar!

New Orleans Club CLUB
(☎091 921 44 77; www.neworleansclublugano.com; Piazza Indipendenza 1; ⏲5pm-1am Mon-Sat) A lively spot Thursday to Saturday night with Latin, hip-hop and disco nights.

Getting There & Around

AIR From **Agno airport** (☎091 612 11 11; www.lugano-airport.ch), **Darwin Airline** (www.darwinairline.com) flies to Rome (Fiumicino), Geneva and Olbia (in Sardinia). **Flybaboo** (www.flybaboo.com) flies regularly to Geneva and **Swiss** (www.swiss.com) to Zürich.

BUS To St Moritz, one postal bus runs direct via Italy at least Friday to Sunday (Sfr69, four hours, daily late June to mid-October and late December to early January). Reserve at the bus station, the train station information office or on ☎091 807 85 20. All postal buses leave from the main bus depot at Via Serafino Balestra, but you can pick up the St Moritz and some other buses outside the train station 15 minutes later.

TRAIN Lugano is on the same road and rail route as Bellinzona.

GRAUBÜNDEN

Don't be fooled by Graubünden's diminutive size on a map. This is topographic origami at its finest. Unfold the rippled landscape to find an outdoor adventurer's paradise riddled with more than 11,000km of walking trails, 600-plus lakes and 1500km of downhill ski slopes – including super swanky St Moritz and backpacker mecca Flims-Laax. Linguistically wired to flick from Italian to German to Romansch, locals keep you guessing too.

Flims-Laax

They say if the snow ain't falling anywhere else, you'll surely find some around Flims-Laax. These towns, along with tiny Falera, 20km west of Chur, form a single ski area known as the **Weisses Arena** (White Arena), with 220km of slopes catering for all levels. Laax in particular is a mecca for snowboarders, who spice up the local nightlife too. The resort is barely two hours by train and bus (less by car) from Zürich airport.

The main **tourist office** (☎081 920 92 00; www.flims.com in summer, www.laax.com in winter; Via Nova; ⏲8am-6pm Mon-Fri, to noon Sat mid-Jun–mid-Aug, to 5pm Mon-Sat mid-Dec–mid-Apr) is in Flims-Dorf.

Activities

Skiing SKIING
The ski slopes range as high as 3000m and are mostly intermediate or easy, although there are some 45km of more challenging runs. A one-day ski pass includes ski buses and costs Sfr62 (plus Sfr5 for the KeyCard that you use to access the lifts).

Laax SNOWBOARDING
Laax was the first Swiss resort to allow snowboarders to use the lifts back in 1985, and remains a mecca for snowsurfers, with two huge half-pipes (one said to be the biggest in the world) and a freestyle park huddled around the unfortunately named Crap Sogn Gion peak. The season starts in late October

KIRSCH & KISSES

It is just melted cheese and bread, right? Wrong. You'll find two variations of fondue dominating most menus: *moitié-moitié,* a mix of vacherin and Gruyère cheeses (a slightly nutty concoction) or pure vacherin (smooth and creamy). In both versions, the finely grated cheese is added to a *caquelon* (a special ceramic pot) with a clove of garlic rubbed along its sides. White wine and a touch of kirsch (cherry schnapps) are carefully added until the cheese reaches an ideal consistency – not too thin, not too thick. Then you begin dipping bread into the mixture.

A common error is frequently made by foreigners who drink beer with the dish – this is a bad idea. Beer simply sits on top of the cheese in your stomach, resulting in an unpleasant (and often sleepless) night holding your belly. Do as the locals do and drink hot tea or wine, or better yet, dip the cubes of bread into kirsch before hitting the cheese. But make sure you stir carefully, unless you have a crush on one of your dinner companions that is: per Swiss tradition, if you lose your bread in the pot, you must kiss the person seated on your left.

on the glacier and, depending on snowfalls, in mid-December elsewhere.

Vorderrhein RIVER RAFTING
In summer try river rafting on a turbulent 17km stretch of the Vorderrhein between Ilanz and Reichenau. It will take you through the **Rheinschlucht** (Rhine Gorge), somewhat optimistically dubbed Switzerland's Grand Canyon, but impressive enough for all that. **Swissraft** (081 911 52 50; www.swissraft.ch) offers half-/full-day rafting for Sfr109/160.

Sleeping & Eating

Sleep? Dream on.

Riders Palace HOTEL $$
(081 927 97 00; www.riderspalace.ch; Laax Murschetg; dm Sfr30-60, d Sfr180-280) It may resemble an oversized Rubik's cube, but Riders Palace is a curious slice of designer cool with bare concrete walls and fluorescent lighting. Choose between basic five-bed dorms, slick rooms with Philippe Starck tubs or hi-tech suites complete with PlayStation and Dolby surround. Find it 200m from the Laax lifts.

La Vacca SWISS $$$
(081 927 99 62; Plaun Station, Laax-Murschetg lifts; mains Sfr40-70; late Dec–mid-Apr) Experience the raw funk of La Vacca, a tipi where cowhide-draped chairs surround a roaring open fire. Forget stringy fondue; the menu is as exciting as the design – think melt-in-your-mouth bison steaks paired with full-bodied Argentine wines.

Drinking

In the drinking stakes, there's the too-cool lobby bar with DJs at **Riders Palace** (4pm-4am) or the **Crap Bar** (081 927 99 45; Laax-Murschetg lifts; 4pm-2am), the place to slam shots, check your email and shimmy in your snow-boots after a day pounding powder.

Getting There & Away

Postal buses run to Flims and the other villages in the White Arena area hourly from Chur (Sfr12.80 to Flims Dorf, 30 minutes). A free local shuttle bus connects the three villages.

St Moritz

POP 5100

Switzerland's original winter wonderland and the cradle of Alpine tourism, St Moritz (San Murezzan in Romansch) has been luring royals, the filthy rich and moneyed wannabes since 1864. With its smugly perfect lake and aloof mountains, the town looks a million dollars. Still waiting to make your first billion? Stay in St Moritz Bad.

Yet despite the Gucci set propping up the bars and celebs bashing the pistes (A-listers such as Kate Moss and George Clooney included), this resort isn't all show. The real riches lie outdoors with superb carving on Corviglia, hairy black runs on Diavolezza and miles of hiking trails when the powder melts.

Activities

Skiers and snowboarders will revel in the 350km of runs in three key areas. Avid cross-country skiers can glide through snow-dusted woodlands and plains on 160km of groomed trails. See www.skiengadin.ch for the complete skiing low-down.

You can also hike or try your hand at golf (including on the frozen lake in winter), tennis, in-line skating, fishing, horse riding, sailing, windsurfing and river rafting, to mention just a few activities. The tourist office has a list of prices and contacts.

Corviglia & Signal SKIING
For groomed slopes with big mountain vistas, head to Corviglia (2486m), accessible by funicular from Dorf. From Bad a cable car goes to Signal (shorter queues), giving access to the slopes of Piz Nair. A ski pass for both areas costs Sfr67 (child/youth Sfr23/45) for one day.

Diavolezza SKIING
Silhouetted by glaciated 4000ers, Diavolezza (2978m) is a must-ski for free-riders and fans of jaw-dropping descents.

Sleeping & Eating

Chesa Chantarella HOTEL $$
(081 833 33 55; www.chesachantarella.ch; Via Salastrains; s/d from Sfr120/210; Jun-Sep & Dec-Apr; P) Sitting above the town, this is a lively choice with bright, modern rooms. Sip hot chocolate on the terrace, venture down to the wine cellar or dine on hearty local fare in the restaurant.

Hotel Waldhaus am See HOTEL $$$
(081 836 60 00; www.waldhaus-am-see.ch; s/d from Sfr180/330; P@) Overlooking the lake, this friendly pad has light-flooded rooms with pine furnishings and floral fabrics, many with enticing lake and mountain views. There's a sauna and a restaurant serving appetising grill specialities.

Jugendherberge St Moritz HOSTEL $
(☎081 836 61 11; www.youthhostel.ch/st.moritz; Stille Via Surpunt 60; dm/d from Sfr55/140; @) Budget beds are gold-dust rare in St Moritz, but you'll find one at this hostel edging the forest. The four-bed dorms and doubles are quiet and clean. There's a kiosk, games room and laundrette.

Hatecke SWISS $$
(☎081 864 11 75; www.hatecke.ch; snacks & mains Sfr16-28; ⏲9am-6.30pm Mon-Fri, to 6pm Sat) Edible art is the only way to describe the organic, locally sourced delicacies at Hatecke. *Bündnerfleisch* and venison ham are carved into wafer-thin slices on a century-old slicing machine in this speciality shop. Sit on a sheepskin stool in the funky cafe next door to lunch on delicious Engadine beef carpaccio or *Bündnerfleisch* with truffle oil.

Engiadina SWISS $$
(☎081 833 32 65; Plazza da Scuola 2; fondue Sfr29-46; ⏲Mon-Sat) A proper locals' place, Engiadina is famous for fondue, and that's the best thing to eat here. Champagne gives the melted cheese a kick. It's open year-round.

Drinking

Around 20 bars and clubs pulsate in winter. While you shuffle to the beat, your wallet might also waltz itself wafer-thin: nights out in St Moritz can be nasty on the banknotes.

Roo Bar BAR
(☎081 837 50 50; Via Traunter Plazzas 7; ⏲2-8pm Dec-Apr) After a hard day's skiing or boarding, snow bums fill the terrace of this après-ski joint at Hauser's Hotel. Hip hop, techno and copious quantities of schnapps fuel the party.

Bobby's Pub PUB
(☎081 834 42 83; Via dal Bagn 50a; ⏲9.30am-1.30am) This laid-back and friendly English-style watering hole serves 30 different brews and attracts young snowboarders in season. It's among the few places open year-round.

Information

The **tourist office** (☎081 837 33 33; www.stmoritz.ch; Via Maistra 12; ⏲9am-6.30pm Mon-Fri, 9am-noon & 1.30-6pm Sat, 4-6pm Sun Dec-Easter & mid-Jun–mid-Sep, 9am-noon & 2-6pm Mon-Fri, 9am-noon Sat rest of year) has all the usual traveller info.

Getting There & Away

BUS The *Palm Express* postal bus runs to Lugano (Sfr69 or Sfr20 with Swiss Travel pass, four hours, daily summer; Friday, Saturday and Sunday winter); advance reservations are obligatory(☎058 386 31 66).

TRAIN The **Glacier Express** (www.glacierexpress.ch) plies one of Switzerland's most famous scenic train routes, connecting St Moritz to Zermatt (Sfr138 plus Sfr15 or Sfr30 reservation fee in summer, 7½ hours, daily) via the 2033m Oberalp Pass. It covers 290km and crosses 291 bridges. Novelty drink glasses in the dining car have sloping bases to compensate for the hills – remember to keep turning them around!

Swiss National Park

The road west from Müstair stretches 34km over the Ofenpass (Pass dal Fuorn, 2149m), through the thick woods of Switzerland's only **national park** (www.nationalpark.ch; ⏲Jun-Oct) and on to **Zernez** and the hands-on **Swiss National Park Centre** (☎081 851 41 41; www.nationalpark.ch; adult/child Sfr7/3; ⏲8.30am-6pm Jun-Oct, 9am-noon & 2-5pm Nov-May), where you can explore a marmot hole, eyeball adders in the vivarium and learn about conservation and environmental change.

The national park was established in 1914 – the first such park in Europe – and spans 172 sq km. 'Nature gone wild' pretty much sums it up: think dolomite peaks, shimmering glaciers, larch woodlands, gentian-flecked pastures, clear waterfalls, and high moors strung with topaz lakes. Zernez **tourist office** (☎081 856 13 00; Chasa Fuchina) has hike details, including the three-hour hike from S-chanf to Trupchun (popular in autumn when you might spy rutting deer) and the Naturlehrpfad circuit near **Il Fuorn**, where bearded vultures can be sighted.

Entry to the park and its car parks is free. Walkers can enter by trails from Zernez, S-chanf and Scuol. Conservation is paramount here, so stick to footpaths and respect regulations prohibiting camping, littering, lighting fires, cycling, picking flowers and disturbing the animals.

Sleeping & Eating

There are several hotels and restaurants in Zernez and a couple in the park itself.

Hotel Bär & Post HOTEL $
(☎081 851 55 00; www.baer-post.ch; dm/s/d from Sfr19/88/70) Welcoming all-comers since 1905, these central digs have inviting rooms with lots of stone, pine and downy duvets,

plus basic bunk rooms. There's also a sauna and a rustic restaurant, dishing up good steaks and pasta.

Chamanna Cluozza HOSTEL $
(☎081 856 12 35; dm/d with half-board Sfr60/138; ⊙late Jun–mid-Oct) For peace and a cracking location, you can't beat this forest hideaway. Dorms are great for walkers eager to hit the trail first thing. It's a three-hour-odd hike from Zernez.

Il Fuorn HOTEL $$
(☎081 856 12 26; www.ilfuorn.ch; s/d Sfr120/199, without bathroom Sfr95/150; half-board extra Sfr30; ⊙May-Oct) In the heart of the national park, this guesthouse has light, comfy rooms with loads of pine. Trout and game are big on the *stübli* (cosy Swiss bistro) menu.

ℹ Getting There & Away

Trains run regularly from Zernez to St Moritz (Sfr17.40, 50 minutes), stopping at S-chanf, Zuoz and Celerina. For the latter and St Moritz, change at Samedan.

UNDERSTAND SWITZERLAND

History

The region's first inhabitants were a Celtic tribe, the Helvetii. The Romans arrived in 107 BC via the Great St Bernard Pass, but were gradually driven back by the Germanic Alemanni tribe, which settled in the region in the 5th century AD. Burgundians and Franks also came to the area, and Christianity was gradually introduced.

The territory was united under the Holy Roman Empire in 1032, but central control was never tight, and neighbouring nobles fought each other for local influence. Rudolph I spearheaded the Germanic Habsburg expansion and gradually brought the squabbling nobles to heel.

The Swiss Confederation

Upon Rudolph's death in 1291, local leaders saw a chance to gain independence. The forest communities of Uri, Schwyz and Nidwalden formed an alliance on 1 August 1291, which is seen as the origin of the Swiss Confederation (their struggles against the Habsburgs are idealised in the legend of William Tell). This union's success prompted other communities to join: Lucerne (1332), followed by Zürich (1351), Glarus and Zug (1352), and Bern (1353).

Encouraged by successes against the Habsburgs, the Swiss acquired a taste for territorial expansion and more land was seized. Fribourg, Solothurn, Basel, Schaffhausen and Appenzell joined the confederation, and the Swiss gained independence from the Holy Roman Emperor Maximilian I after their victory at Dornach in 1499.

Eventually, the Swiss over-extended themselves when they took on a superior force of French and Venetians at Marignano in 1515 and lost. Realising they could no longer compete against better-equipped larger powers, they declared their neutrality. Even so, Swiss mercenaries continued to serve in other armies for centuries, and earned an unrivalled reputation for skill and courage.

The Reformation during the 16th century caused upheaval throughout Europe. The Protestant teachings of Luther, Zwingli and Calvin spread quickly, although the inaugural cantons remained Catholic. This caused internal unrest that dragged on for centuries.

The French Republic invaded Switzerland in 1798 and established the Helvetic Republic. The Swiss vehemently resisted such centralised control, causing Napoleon to restore the former confederation of cantons in 1803. Yet France still retained overall jurisdiction. Following Napoleon's defeat by the British and Prussians at Waterloo, Switzerland finally gained independence.

The Modern State

Throughout the gradual move towards one nation, each canton remained fiercely independent, to the extent of controlling coinage and postal services. The cantons lost these powers in 1848, when a new federal constitution was agreed upon, with Bern as the capital. The Federal Assembly was set up to take care of national issues, but the cantons retained legislative (Grand Council) and executive (States Council) powers to deal with local matters.

Having achieved political stability, Switzerland could concentrate on economic and social matters. Poor in mineral resources, it developed industries dependent on highly skilled labour. A network of railways and roads was built, opening up previously inaccessible regions of the Alps and helping the development of tourism.

The Swiss carefully guarded their neutrality in the 20th century. Their only involvement in WWI was organising units of the Red Cross (founded in Geneva in 1863 by Henri Dunant). Switzerland did join the League of Nations after peace was won, but only on the condition that its involvement was financial and economic rather than military. Apart from some accidental bombing, WWII left Switzerland largely unscathed.

While the rest of Europe was still recovering from the war, Switzerland was able to forge ahead from an already powerful commercial, financial and industrial base. Zürich developed as an international banking and insurance centre, while the World Health Organization (WHO) and many other international bodies set up headquarters in Geneva. Switzerland's much-vaunted neutrality led it to decline joining either the UN or EU, but the country became one of the world's richest and most respected.

Then, in the late 1990s, a series of scandals forced Switzerland to begin reforming its famously secretive banking industry. In 1995, after pressure from Jewish groups, Swiss banks announced that they had discovered millions of dollars lying in dormant pre-1945 accounts, belonging to Holocaust victims and survivors. Three years later, amid allegations they'd been sitting on the money without seriously trying to trace its owners, the two largest banks, UBS and Credit Suisse, agreed to pay US$1.25 billion in compensation to Holocaust survivors and their families.

New Millennium

The year 2001 was truly Switzerland's *annus horribilis*. The financial collapse of the national airline Swissair, a canyoning accident in the Bernese Oberland killing 21 tourists, an unprecedented gun massacre in the Zug parliament and a fatal fire in the Gotthard Tunnel within 12 months all prompted intense soul-searching. Four years on, devastating floods prompted a more pragmatic debate on what should be done.

Since the new millennium, historically isolated Switzerland has recognised the universal challenges it faces and has slowly but surely started reaching out to the world. In 2002 it became the 190th member of the UN and in 2005 it finally joined Europe's 'Schengen' passport-free travel zone, a move that did not actually come into effect until December 2008 for overland arrivals and March 2009 for airport arrivals. Yet few expect the country to even consider joining either the EU – something French-speaking cantons would welcome – or the euro single currency any time soon (if ever).

Banking confidentiality, dating to the Middle Ages here, was enshrined in law in 1934 when numbered (rather than named) bank accounts were introduced. However, in 2004, the country made another concession to that veil of secrecy when it agreed to tax accounts held in Switzerland by EU citizens.

In late 2008, the country's privileged banking sector even gave itself a scare. As

IT ALL HAPPENED IN SWITZERLAND

» Albert Einstein came up with his theories of relativity and the famous formula $E=MC^2$ in Bern in 1905.

» Switzerland gave birth to the World Wide Web at the acclaimed CERN (European Centre for Nuclear Research) institute outside Geneva.

» The first acid trip took place in Switzerland. In 1943 chemist Albert Hofmann was conducting tests for a migraine cure in Basel when he accidentally absorbed the lysergic acid diethylamide, or LSD, compound through his fingertips.

» Of the 800 or so films produced by India's huge movie-making industry each year, more are shot in Switzerland than in any other foreign country. 'For the Indian public, Switzerland is the land of their dreams,' film star Raj Mukherjee has said. Favourite destination shoots include the Bernese Oberland, Central Switzerland and Geneva.

» Switzerland's central Alpine region possesses one of Europe's richest traditions of myth and legend. Pontius Pilate is said to rise out of the lake on Mt Pilatus, near Lucerne, every Good Friday (the day he condemned Jesus Christ) to wash blood from his hands – and anybody who witnesses this event will allegedly die within the year. Tiny 'wild folk' with supernatural powers, called Chlyni Lüüt, were once reputed to inhabit Mt Rigi, also near Lucerne. Their children's spleens were removed at birth, giving them the ability to leap around mountain slopes.

the subprime mortgage scandal fired shock waves through the world's financial markets, Switzerland's two largest banks – UBS and Credit Suisse – were forced to admit heavy losses too. The government waded in with a US$60 billion package to bail out UBS, to the horror of most Swiss, who howled in protest at the huge bonuses paid in preceding years to those very bank managers who'd risked all – and cocked up.

Switzerland Today

In keeping with Western European trends, the Swiss banned smoking on public transport in 2005 and in 2007 Ticino became the first canton to outlaw smoking in all public places. In 2009 smoking was banned in all restaurants and bars across the country. In November of the same year, Switzerland again made headlines when 57% of the country voted to ban the construction of all new minarets in Switzerland. The move – backed by the Swiss Peoples Party (SVP) but opposed by the government – was ultimately accepted in the end by the Swiss government and implemented into law. In 2010, voters also approved a referendum initiative to deport all foreigners who had committed a serious crime.

People

Switzerland's name may stand for everything from knives to watches, but don't expect this nation to take a stand for anyone other than itself. Militarily neutral for centuries, and armed to the teeth to make sure it stays that way, in Switzerland it's the Swiss Way or the highway.

With a population of almost 7.8 million, Switzerland averages 176 people per sq km. Zürich is the largest city, followed by Geneva, Basel and Bern. Most people are of Germanic origin, as reflected in the breakdown of the four national languages (see p1202). Around 20% of residents in Switzerland are not Swiss citizens.

The Swiss are polite, law-abiding people who usually see no good reason to break the rules. Living quietly with your neighbours is a national obsession. Good manners infuse the national psyche, and politeness is the cornerstone of all social intercourse. Always shake hands when being introduced to a Swiss, and kiss on both cheeks to greet and say goodbye to friends. Don't forget to greet shopkeepers when entering shops. When drinking with the Swiss, always wait until everyone has their drink and toast each of your companions, looking them in the eye and clinking glasses. Drinking before the toast is unforgivable, and will lead to seven years of bad sex…or so the superstition goes. Don't say you weren't warned.

In a few mountain regions such as Valais, people still wear traditional rural costumes, but dressing up is usually reserved for festivals. Yodelling, playing the alphorn and Swiss wrestling are also part of the alpine tradition.

Religion

The split between Roman Catholicism (42%) and Protestantism (35%) roughly follows cantonal lines. Strong Protestant areas include Zürich, Geneva, Vaud, Bern and Neuchâtel; Valais, Ticino, Fribourg, Lucerne and the Jura are predominantly Catholic.

Just over 4% of the population is Muslim.

Arts

Many foreign writers and artists, including Voltaire, Byron, Shelley and Turner, have visited and settled in Switzerland. Local and international artists pouring into Zürich during WWI spawned its Dadaist movement.

Paul Klee (1879–1940) is the best-known native painter. He created bold, hard-lined abstract works. The writings of Genevan philosopher Jean-Jacques Rousseau (1712–78) played an important part in the development of democracy. Critically acclaimed postwar dramatists and novelists Max Frisch (1911–91) and Friedrich Dürrenmatt (1921–90) entertained readers with their dark satire, tragi-comedies and morality plays. On the musical front, Arthur Honegger (1892–1955) is Switzerland's most recognised composer.

The Swiss have made important contributions to graphic design and commercial art. Anyone who's ever used a computer will have interacted with their fonts, from Helvetica to Frutiger to Univers.

The father of modern architecture, Le Corbusier (1887–1965), who designed Notre Dame du Haut chapel at Ronchamps in France, Chandigarh in India and the UN headquarters in New York, was Swiss. One of the most-acclaimed contemporary architectural teams on earth, Jacques Herzog and Pierre de Meuron, live and work in Basel. Winners of the prestigious Pritzker Prize in

2001, this pair created London's acclaimed Tate Modern museum building.

Gothic and Renaissance architecture are prevalent in urban areas, especially Bern. Rural Swiss houses vary according to region, but are generally characterised by ridged roofs with wide, overhanging eaves, and balconies and verandahs enlivened by colourful floral displays, especially geraniums.

To the chagrin of many, Switzerland also sports some pretty artistic graffiti. Giant intricately spray-painted patterns (along with less savoury pieces) grace buildings scattered along railway tracks near train stations.

Environment

Mountains make up 70% of Switzerland's 41,285 sq km. Farming is intensive and cows graze on the upper slopes as soon as the retreating snow line permits.

Europe's highest elevations smugly sit here. The Dufourspitze (4634m) of Monte Rosa in the Alps is Switzerland's highest point, but the Matterhorn (4478m), with its Toblerone-shaped cap is better known. Then of course there's Mont Blanc (4807m), a hulk of a mountain – Europe's highest – shared with France and Italy.

Switzerland's 1800 glaciers cover a 2000-sq-km area, but global warming means they're melting rapidly. The country's most famous mass of ice, rock and snow – the 23km-long Aletsch Glacier – shrunk 114.6m in 2006 alone and could shrink 80% by 2100 if things don't change, say experts: 600 people posed nude on the glacier in 2007 for a photo by New Yorker Spencer Tunick as part of a Greenpeace campaign calling for governments worldwide to act quickly.

The St Gotthard Mountains in central Switzerland are the source of many lakes and rivers, including the Rhine and the Rhône. The Jura Mountains straddle the border with France, and peak at around 1700m. Between the two is the Mittelland, a region of hills also known as the Swiss Plateau, criss-crossed by rivers, ravines and winding valleys.

The ibex, with its huge curved ridged horns is the most distinctive alpine animal. In all some 12,000 of this type of mountain goat roam Switzerland and prime ibex-spotting terrain is the country's only national park (169 sq km), unimaginatively called the Swiss National Park.

Switzerland is extremely environmentally friendly: its citizens produce less than 400kg of waste each per year (half the figure for the USA), are diligent recyclers and are actively encouraged to use public transport. Moreover, pioneering green travel networks integrate the country's nonmotorised traffic routes: **SwitzerlandMobility** (www.switzerlandmobility.ch) maps out 169 routes for walkers (6300km), cyclists (8500km), mountain bikers (3300km), roller-bladers or -skaters (1000km) and canoeists (250km) countrywide – all perfectly signposted and easy to follow.

GOIN' GREEN WITH THE ECO-ANGELS

Many Swiss resorts have been polishing their eco-halos recently in a bid to offset the impact of skiing. To further plan your environmentally friendly ski trip and reduce your carbon snowprint, see **Save Our Snow** (www.saveoursnow.com) and the **Association of Car-Free Swiss Resorts** (www.gast.org, in German).

Whiter-than-white ski resorts in Graubünden include **Arosa** (www.arosa.ch), a one-hour train journey from Chur, which runs on nearly 100% renewable energy, operates free shuttle buses and boasts Switzerland's first carbon offsetting policy; **Flims-Laax** (p1193), which makes snow using hydroelectricity and recycled water; and **St Moritz** (p1194), with its clean-energy policy, pedestrian zones and efficient public transport network.

Gstaad (www.gstaad.ch) has a pedestrianised centre, excellent public transport and makes huge efforts to preserve its natural surroundings in the Bernese Oberland. Valais skiers can carve with a clear conscience in **Verbier** (www.verbier.ch), where energy-efficient snow-grooming machines use biodiesel fuel. In the Jungfrau region, **Zermatt** (p1165) is a whiter-than-white green classic with its car-free and eco-sound building policies, free shuttle buses and 60% hydroelectricity. Other notable wholly car-free resorts include **Saas Fee** (www.saas-fee.ch) near Zermatt, **Wengen** and **Mürren** (p1178) near Lauterbrunnen, and Valais' **Bettmeralp** (www.bettmeralp.ch).

Reinventing the Alps is the hot topic at higher altitudes. Most pressing is not so much how to be green, how to be ecological, how to burn clean energy – Swiss eco-angels have that sorted. Rather, it is what must be done to keep ski resorts sustainable as the globe warms: experts say you can forget sure-thing snow below 1500m by 2050.

Food & Drink

Staples & Specialities

Lactose intolerants will struggle in this dairy-obsessed country, which makes some of the world's most delectable chocolate and where cheese is a way of life. The best-known Swiss dish is fondue, in which melted Emmental and Gruyère are combined with white wine in a large pot and eaten with bread cubes. Another popular artery-hardener is raclette, melted cheese served with potatoes. Rösti (fried shredded potatoes) is German Switzerland's national dish, and is served with everything.

Many dishes are meaty, and veal is highly rated throughout the country. In Zürich it is thinly sliced and served in a cream sauce *(Gschnetzeltes Kalbsfleisch). Bündnerfleisch* is dried beef, smoked and thinly sliced. Like their northern neighbours, the Swiss also munch on a wide variety of *wurst* (sausage).

Wine is considered an essential accompaniment to lunch and dinner. Local vintages are generally good quality, but you might not have heard of them, as they are rarely exported. The main growing regions are Italian- and French-speaking areas, particularly in Valais and by Lakes Neuchâtel and Geneva.

Where to Eat & Drink

Buffet-style restaurant chains, such as Manora, have a huge selection of freshly cooked food at low prices. Migros and Coop are the main supermarket chains. Street stalls are a good place to pick up cheap eats – you'll find kebabs and sandwiches everywhere. Bratwurst and pretzel stands (sometimes the pretzels are even stuffed with meats and cheeses) also abound in German cantons.

Restaurants sometimes close between meals (generally from 3pm to 5pm), although this is becoming rare in large cities, and tend to have a closing day, often Monday. Cafes usually stay open all day. Bars are open from lunchtime until at least midnight. Clubs get going after 10pm and close around 4am.

In cities and larger towns there are dedicated vegetarian restaurants. Most eateries offer a small selection of meatless options too, including large salad plates.

SURVIVAL GUIDE

Directory A–Z

Accommodation

From palatial palaces and castles to mountain refuges, nuclear bunkers, icy igloos or simple haylofts, Switzerland sports traditional and creative accommodation in every price range. Moreover, an increasing number of places are green when it comes to eco-friendly heating, lighting, waste disposal and so on. Online, www.myswitzerland.com is a great resource for tracking down accommodation.

The prices may seem steep – even the most inexpensive places are pricey compared with other parts of Europe. The upside is that hostels, hotels and B&Bs almost always include a generous breakfast in their price and the standard of accommodation is high, divine fluffy feather duvet included.

In both Switzerland and Lichtenstein, many budget hotels have cheaper rooms with shared toilet and shower facilities, and more expensive rooms with private bathroom. For a budget double with bathroom expect to pay up to Sfr150; midrange places will set you back anywhere from Sfr150 to Sfr250, while top-end places priced from Sfr250 offer pure, unadulterated, time-honoured Swiss luxury, with gasp-worthy price tag to match.

Rates in cities and towns stay constant most of the year. In mountain resorts prices are seasonal:

Low season mid-September to mid-December, mid-April to mid-June

Mid-season January to mid-February, mid-June to early July, September

High season July to August, Christmas, mid-February to Easter

PRICE RANGES

Our reviews refer to double rooms with a private bathroom, except in hostels or where otherwise specified. Quoted rates are for high season.

$$$ more than Sfr250

$$ Sfr150 to Sfr250

$ less than Sfr150

HAY BARNS

If you're looking for a way to experience life on a Swiss farm, **Aventure sur la Paille/Schlaf im Stroh** (☎041 678 12 86; www.abenteuer-stroh.ch) offers the ultimate adventure. When their cows are out to pasture in summer, or indeed even after they've been brought in for the winter come early October, farmers charge travellers Sfr20 to Sfr30 per adult and Sfr10 to Sfr20 per child to sleep on straw in their hay barns or lofts (listen to the jangle of cow or goat bells beneath your head!). Farmers provide cotton undersheets (to avoid straw pricks) and woolly blankets for extra warmth, but guests need their own sleeping bags and pocket torch. Nightly rates include a farmhouse breakfast; shower and evening meals are extras.

HOSTELS

Switzerland has two types of hostels: **Swiss Youth Hostels** (SYHA; www.youthhostel.ch), affiliated with Hostelling International (HI), where nonmembers pay an additional 'guest fee' of Sfr6, and independent hostels which can be more charismatic. Prices listed in this book for SYHA hostels do not include the guest fee. On average a dorm bed in either type costs Sfr30 to Sfr40, including sheets.

There are another 80 hostels in the shape of alpine chalet or rural farmhouse that offer hostel-style accommodation under the green umbrella group **Naturfreundehaus** (Friends of Nature; www.nfhouse.org).

Activities

There are dozens of ski resorts throughout the Alps, pre-Alps and Jura, and 200-odd different ski schools. Equipment hire is available at resorts, and ski passes allow unlimited use of mountain transport.

There is simply no better way to enjoy Switzerland's spectacular scenery than to walk through it. There are 50,000km of designated paths, often with a convenient inn or cafe located en route. Yellow signs marking the trail make it difficult to get lost, and each provides an average walking time to the next destination. Slightly more strenuous mountain paths have white-red-white markers. The **Schweizer Alpen-Club** (SAC; ☎031 370 1818; www.sac-cas.ch, in German; Monbijoustrasse 61, Bern) maintains huts for overnight stays at altitude and can also help with extra information.

You can water-ski, sail and windsurf on most lakes, and rafting on many Alpine rivers, including the Rhine and the Rhône. And there are more than 350 lake beaches.

Bungee jumping, paragliding, canyoning and other high-adrenalin sports are widely available throughout Switzerland, especially in the Interlaken area.

Business Hours

Reviews in this guidebook won't list business hours unless they differ from the following standards:

Banks 8.30am to 5pm Monday to Fri; 8am to noon Saturday

Clubs from roughly 9pm to late

Pubs & cafes 5pm to midnight; to 2am on weekends

Restaurants 11am to 2.30pm, 5pm to 11pm

Shops 8am to noon & 2pm to 6.30pm Monday to Friday , to 9pm Thursday or Friday in towns, 8am to 5pm Saturday

Electricity

Swiss sockets are recessed, hexagonally shaped and incompatible with most plugs from abroad (including 'universal' adapters).

Embassies & Consulates

Embassies are in Bern while cities such as Zürich and Geneva have several consulates. Neither Australia nor New Zealand has an embassy in Switzerland, but each has a consulate in Geneva. For a comprehensive list, see www.eda.admin.ch.

Australia (☎022 799 91 00; www.australia.ch; Chemin des Fins 2, Geneva)

Canada Bern (☎031 357 32 00; www.canada-ambassade.ch; Kirchenfeldstrasse 88); Geneva (☎022 919 92 00; 5 Ave de l'Ariana)

New Zealand (☎022 929 03 50; Chemin des Fins 2, Grand-Saconnex, Geneva)

UK Bern (☎031 359 77 00; http://ukinswitzerland.fco.gov.uk/en; Thunstrasse 50); Geneva (☎022 918 24 00; Ave Louis Casai 50); Zürich (☎01 383 65 60; Hegibachstrasse 47)

USA Bern (☎031 357 70 11; http://bern.usembassy.gov; Sulgeneckstrasse 19); Geneva (☎022 840 51 60; Rue François Versonnex 7); Zürich (☎043 499 29 60; Dufourstrasse 101)

Festivals & Events

There are more events than we could possibly list; check www.switzerland.com for a complete listing.

February

Fasnacht A lively spring carnival of wild parties and parades is celebrated countrywide, but with particular enthusiasm in Basel and Lucerne.

March

Combats de Reines March to October, the lower Valais stages traditional cow fights known as the Combats de Reines.

April

Landsgemeinde On the last Sunday in April, the people of Appenzell gather in the main square to take part in a unique open-air parliament.

July

Montreux Jazz Festival (www.montreuxjazz.com) Big-name rock/jazz acts hit town for this famous festival, held during the first two weeks of July.

August

National Day On 1 August celebrations and fireworks mark the country's National Day.

Street Parade (www.streetparade.ch) Zürich lets its hair down in the second week of August with an enormous techno parade with 30 lovemobiles and more than half a million excited ravers.

October

Vintage Festivals Down a couple in wine-growing regions such as Neuchâtel and Lugano in early October.

November

Onion Market Bern takes on a carnival atmosphere for a unique market day held on the fourth Monday of November.

December

L'Escalade (www.escalade.ch) This historical festival in Geneva (11 December) celebrates deliverance from would-be conquerors.

Gay & Lesbian Travellers

Attitudes toward homosexuality are reasonably tolerant in Switzerland. Zürich and Geneva have particularly lively gay scenes.

Online listing guides:

Cruiser magazine (www.cruiser.ch)

Pink Cross (www.pinkcross.ch)

Food

The following price indicators for the cost of a main course are used in the listings:

$$$	more than Sfr40
$$	Sfr20 to Sfr40
$	less than Sfr20

Internet Resources

Switzerland has a strong presence on the internet, with most tourist-related businesses having their own website; a good place to start is **Switzerland Tourism** (www.myswitzerland.com), with many useful links. Tune into the latest beat on **Glocals** (www.glocals.com), Switzerland's savviest urbanites tell you where the party is!

Language

Located in the corner of Europe where Germany, France and Italy meet, Switzerland is a linguistic melting pot with three official federal languages: German (spoken by 64% of the population), French (19%) and Italian (8%). Swiss 'German' speakers write standard or 'high' German, but speak their own language: Schwyzertütsch has no official written form and is mostly unintelligible to outsiders.

A fourth language, Romansch, is spoken by less than 1% of the population, mainly in the canton of Graubünden. Derived from Latin, it's a linguistic relic that has survived in the isolation of mountain valleys. Romansch was recognised as a national language by referendum in 1938 and given federal protection in 1996.

English-speakers will have few problems being understood in the German-speaking parts. However, it is simple courtesy to greet people with the Swiss-German *grüezi* and to enquire *Sprechen Sie Englisch?* (Do you speak English?) before launching into English.

In French Switzerland you shouldn't have too many problems either, unlike in Italian-speaking Switzerland, where few speak anything other than Italian and some French and/or German.

Money

Swiss francs are divided into 100 centimes (*Rappen* in German-speaking Switzerland).

Language Areas

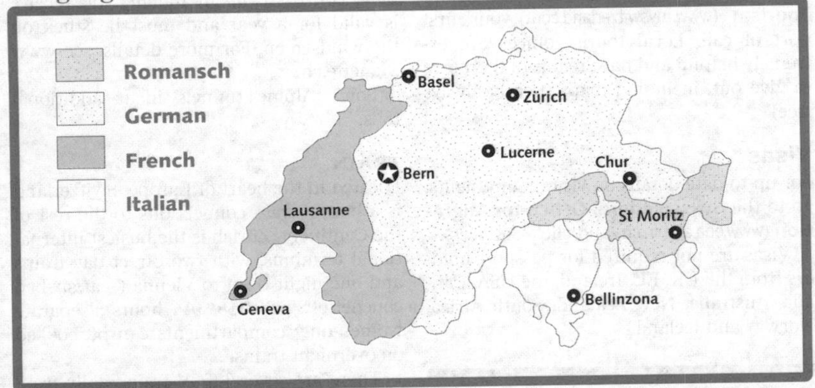

There are notes for 10, 20, 50, 100, 200 and 1000 francs, and coins for five, 10, 20 and 50 centimes, as well as for one, two and five francs.

All major travellers cheques and credit cards are accepted. Nearly all train stations have currency-exchange facilities open daily and ATMs are everywhere.

There's no need to tip in Switzerland, unless you feel the service was superlative. Tips are included in meal prices.

Post

Postcards and letters sent to Europe cost Sfr1.30/1.20 priority/economy; to elsewhere they cost Sfr1.80/1.40.

Post office opening times vary. Typically they open 7.30am to noon and 2pm to 6.30pm Monday to Friday and until 11am Saturday.

Public Holidays

New Year's Day 1 January

Easter March/April (Good Friday, Easter Sunday and Monday)

Ascension Day 40th day after Easter

Whit Sunday & Monday Seventh week after Easter

National Day 1 August

Christmas Day 25 December

St Stephen's Day 26 December

Telephone

Area codes do not exist in Switzerland or Liechtenstein. Although the numbers for a particular city or town share the same three-digit prefix (for example Bern 031, Geneva 022), numbers always must be dialled in full, even when calling from next door – literally.

Mobile phone numbers start with the code 079. To find a phone number in Switzerland, check the phone book (http://tel.local.ch/en); dial ☎1812 (connection charge 80c plus 10c a minute) to speak to a machine; or ☎1811 (connection charge Sfr1.50, Sfr0.70 for the first minute and Sfr0.22 per minute thereafter) for a real person; the latter also finds international telephone numbers.

National telephone provider **Swisscom** (http://fr.swisscom.ch) operates the world's densest network of public phone booths. Minimum charge for a call is Sfr0.50 and phones take Swiss franc or euro coins, and phonecards, sold at post offices, newsagencies etc. Many booths also accept major credit cards.

The normal/cheap tariff for international dialling to fixed-line phones is Sfr0.12/0.10 per minute for several countries, including Australia, Britain, Canada, New Zealand and the USA; and Sfr0.25/0.20 to countries including Ireland, Japan and the Netherlands.

Save money by buying a prepaid Swisscom card worth Sfr10, Sfr20, Sfr50 and Sfr100. Or look for prepaid cards from rival operators such as **Mobile Zone** (www.mobilezone.ch, in German, French & Italian).

Prepaid local SIM cards (Sfr30 to Sfr100) are available from the three network operators (you'll need your passport when you buy):

Orange (www.orange.ch)

Sunrise (www.sunrise.ch)

Swisscom Mobile (www.swisscom-mobile.ch)

Tourist Information

Make the Swiss tourist board **Switzerland Tourism** (www.myswitzerland.com) your first port of call. Local tourist offices are extremely helpful and have reams of literature to give out, including maps (nearly always free).

Visas

For up-to-date details on visa requirements, go to the **Swiss Federal Office for Migration** (www.eda.admin.ch) and click 'Services'.

Visas are not required for passport holders from the UK, EU, Ireland, the USA, Canada, Australia, New Zealand, South Africa, Norway and Iceland.

Getting There & Away

Air

The main international airports:

EuroAirport (MLH or BSL; +33 3 89 90 31 11; www.euroairport.com) France-based, serving Basel as well as Mulhouse in France and Freiburg, Germany.

Geneva International airport (GVA; 0900 57 15 00; www.gva.ch)

Zürich airport (ZRH; 043 816 22 11, SMS 9292 message ZRH plus flight number for flight information; www.zurich-airport.com)

Lake

Switzerland can be reached by steamer from several lakes.

Lake Constance (Switzerland (071 466 78 88; www.sbsag.ch); Austria (05574 42868; www.bodenseeschifffahrt.at); Germany (07531 3640 389; www.bsb-online.com) From Germany.

Lake Geneva (0848 811 848; www.cgn.ch) From France.

Lago Maggiore (091 751 61 40; www.navigazionelaghi.it) From Italy.

Land

CAR & MOTORCYCLE

Roads into Switzerland are good despite the difficulty of the terrain, but special care is needed to negotiate mountain passes.

Upon entering Switzerland you will need to decide whether you wish to use the motorways: there is a one-off charge of Sfr40 payable in cash, including euros, at the border or, better still, in advance through Switzerland Tourism or a motoring organisation. The sticker (*vignette* in French and German, *contrassegno* in Italian) you receive is valid for a year and must be stuck on the windscreen. For more details, see www.vignette.ch.

Some Alpine tunnels incur additional tolls.

TRAIN

Located in the heart of Europe, Switzerland is a hub of train connections to the rest of the Continent. Zürich is the busiest international terminus, with two direct day trains and one night train to Vienna (seat/six-bed couchette Sfr123/148, 9½ hours); separate women-only compartments can be booked on overnight trains.

There are several TGV trains daily from Paris to several cities including Geneva (€77, 3½ hours), Lausanne (€92 to €120, 3½ to four hours), Bern (€106 to €132, 4½ hours), Basel (€91, 3¾ hours) and Zurich (from €140; 4½ hours). Most connections from Germany, including from Frankfurt and Berlin, pass though Zürich or Basel.

Trains between Switzerland and Italy are operated by both Swiss and Italian national railways. Eurail and Interail passes are valid, and Swiss Pass holders get 20% discount. Nearly all connections to/from Italy pass through Milan before branching off to Zürich (Sfr97, 3¾ hour), Lucerne (Sfr97, 3½ hour), Bern (Sfr87.80, 3½ hour) or Lausanne (Sfr84, 3¾ hour).

Getting Around

Air

Swiss International Air Lines (www.swiss.com) serves the major hubs of EuroAirport (Basel), Geneva and Zürich airports, with return fares fluctuating wildly in price – anything from Sfr70 to Sfr300; and Swiss no-frills carrier **Fly Baboo** (www.flybaboo.com) flies Geneva-Lugano.

Bicycle

You can hire bikes from most train stations with **Rent-a-Bike** (041 925 11 70; www.rent-a-bike.ch, in French & German; per day Sfr33) and return to any station with a rental office. Bikes can be transported on most trains; station-rented bikes travel free (maximum five bikes per train), otherwise you need a bike pass (one day Sfr15, with Swiss travel pass Sfr10). Bern, Geneva and Zürich offer free bike loans from their train stations.

Local tourist offices often have good cycling information.

Bus

Yellow postal buses are a supplement to the rail network, following postal routes and linking towns to the more inaccessible regions in the mountains. In all, routes cover some 8000km of terrain. Services are regular, and departures tie in with train arrivals. Postbus stations are next to train stations and offer destination and timetable information.

Car

The **Swiss Touring Club** (Touring Club der Schweiz; ☎022 417 24 24; www.tcs.ch), Switzerland's largest motoring organisation, is affiliated with the AA in Britain and has reciprocal agreements with motoring organisations worldwide.

You do not need an International Driving Permit to operate a vehicle in Switzerland. A licence from your home country is sufficient. There are numerous petrol stations and garages throughout Switzerland if you break down.

For the best deals on car hire, prebook; particularly competitive rates are often found on **Auto Europe** (www.autoeurope.com).

When driving in Switzerland, be prepared for winding roads, high passes and long tunnels. Normal speed limits are 50km/h in towns, 120km/h on motorways, 100km/h on semimotorways (designated by roadside rectangular pictograms showing a white car on a green background) and 80km/h on other roads. Mountain roads are well maintained but you should stay in low gear whenever possible and remember that ascending traffic has the right of way over descending traffic, and postbuses always have right of way. Snow chains are recommended during winter. Use dipped lights in *all* road tunnels. Some minor Alpine passes are closed from November to May – check with the local tourist offices before setting off.

Switzerland is tough on drink-driving; if your blood alcohol level is over 0.05% you face a large fine or imprisonment.

Train

The Swiss rail network consists of a combination of state-run and private lines, and

PASSES & DISCOUNTS

Swiss public transport is an efficient, fully integrated and comprehensive system, which incorporates trains, buses, boats and funiculars. Convenient discount passes make the system even more appealing – on extensive travel within Switzerland the following national travel passes generally offer betters savings than Eurail or Inter Rail passes. Find comprehensive information on all of them at http://traintickets.myswitzerland.com.

The **Swiss Pass** (www.swisstravelsystem.ch) is the best deal for big travellers, allowing unlimited travel on almost every train, boat and bus service in the country, and on trams and buses in 38 towns. Reductions of 50% apply on funiculars, cable cars and private railways, such as Jungfrau Railways. These passes are available for four days (Sfr260), eight days (Sfr376), 15 days (Sfr455), 22 days (Sfr525) and one month (Sfr578); prices are for 2nd-class tickets. If you are under 26, buy the **Swiss Youth Pass** equivalent, 25% cheaper in each instance. The **Swiss Flexi Pass** allows free, unlimited trips for three to six days within a month and costs Sfr249 to Sfr397 (2nd class). With either pass, two people travelling together get 15% off. Passes also allow you free admission to all Swiss museums, making them an even better bargain.

The **Swiss Card** allows a free return journey from your arrival point to any destination in Switzerland, 50% off rail, boat and bus excursions, and reductions on mountain railways. It costs Sfr182 (2nd class) or Sfr255 (1st class) and it is valid for a month. The **Half-Fare Card** is a similar deal, minus the free return trip. It costs Sfr99 for one month.

The **Family Card** gives free travel for children aged under 16 if they're accompanied by a parent and is available free to pass purchasers.

All these passes are best purchased online before arrival in Switzerland at www.swisstravelsystem.com or in the UK from the **Swiss Travel Centre** (☎0207 420 49 00; 30 Bedford St, London WC2E 9ED). In Switzerland larger train-station offices sell travel passes.

covers 5000km. Trains are clean, reliable and frequent, and are as fast as the terrain will allow. Prices are high, and if you plan on taking more than one or two train trips it's best to purchase a travel pass. All fares quoted in this chapter are for 2nd class; 1st-class fares are about 65% higher. All major stations are connected by hourly departures, but services stop from around midnight to 6am.

Most train stations offer luggage storage at a counter (around Sfr5 per piece) or in 24hr lockers (Sfr3 to Sfr10), and have excellent information counters. Train schedules are revised yearly; double-check details before travelling either online with **Swiss Federal Railways** (www.rail.ch, www.sbb.ch/en), abbreviated to SBB/CFF/FFS in German/French/Italian. Or call its **Rail Service** (☎0900 300 300, per min Sfr1.19).

Survival Guide

Directory A–Z

Readers should note there are two types of directories in this book: the Regional Directory and individual country directories. The bookwide Directory A–Z serves as a comprehensive resource for the whole of Western Europe. The country directories appear at the end of each country chapter and are a round-up of specific details pertaining to that country. Some subjects will be covered in both directories (eg general accommodation options are outlined here, but prices are covered in the country directories).

Accommodation

Where you stay in Western Europe may be one of the highlights of your trip. Quirky family-run inns, manic city hostels, and low-key beach resorts are just some of the places where you'll make both new memories and, more than likely, new friends.

The cheapest places to stay in Western Europe are camping grounds, followed by hostels and accommodation in student dormitories. Cheap chain hotels are popping up across the region, but pensions, private rooms and B&Bs have much more character and are often good value. Self-catering apartments and cottages are worth considering when travelling with a group, especially if you plan to stay somewhere for a while. During peak holiday periods, accommodation can be hard to find, and it's advisable to book ahead. Even camping grounds can fill up, especially in or around big cities.

Accommodation listings in this guide have been listed in order of preference. See the country directories for more details about local accommodation.

B&Bs & Guest Houses

There's a huge range of accommodation above the hostel level. In the UK and Ireland, B&Bs – where you get bed and breakfast in a private home – are real bargains. In some areas every second house will have a B&B sign out the front.

In other countries, similar private accommodation – though often without breakfast – may go under the name of pension, guest house, *Gasthaus*, *Zimmerfrei*, *chambre d'hôte* and so on. Although the majority of guest houses are simple affairs and not the potpourri-scented luxuries North Americans may be used to, there are more expensive ones around.

With this type of accommodation especially, make certain that the place is centrally located and not in some dull and distant suburb.

Camping

Camping is immensely popular in Western Europe and provides the cheapest form of accommodation. There's usually a charge per tent or site, per person and per vehicle. National tourist offices often provide booklets or brochures listing camping grounds throughout their countries.

In large cities, most camping grounds will be some distance from the centre. For this reason camping is most popular with people who have their own transport. If you're on foot, the money you save by camping can quickly be eaten up by the cost of commuting to and from a town centre. Many camping grounds rent bungalows or cottages accommodating from two to eight people.

Camping other than at designated camping grounds

BOOK YOUR STAY ONLINE

For more accommodation reviews by Lonely Planet authors, check out hotels.lonelyplanet.com/europe. You'll find independent reviews, as well as recommendations on the best places to stay. Best of all, you can book online.

is difficult; there are few places in Western Europe where you can pitch a tent away from prying eyes, and you usually need permission from the local authorities (the police or local council office) or from the owner of the land.

In some countries, such as Austria, the UK, France and Germany, free camping is illegal on all but private land; in Greece it's illegal altogether.

Hostels

Hostels offer the cheapest (secure) roof over your head in Western Europe, and you don't have to be a youngster to use them.

HOSTELLING INTERNATIONAL

Most hostels are part of the national Youth Hostel Association (YHA), which is affiliated with **Hostelling International** (HI; www.hihostels.com) – once called the International Youth Hostel Federation (IYHF). The name change was made, in part, to de-emphasise the youth aspect. The HI website has links to all the national organisations and you can use it to book beds or rooms in advance. You can join YHA or HI in advance or at the hostels. Members usually pay about 10% less on rates.

At a hostel, you get a bed in a dorm or a private room plus the use of communal facilities, which often include a kitchen where you can prepare your own meals. You are often required to have a sleeping sheet; simply using your sleeping bag is not permitted. If you don't have your own approved sleeping sheet, you can usually hire or buy one. Many hostels now ban use of sleeping bags because of problems with bed bugs.

Hostels vary widely in character, but increased competition from other forms of accommodation, particularly the emergence of privately owned hostels, have prompted many places to improve their facilities and cut back on rules and regulations.

The trend is moving toward smaller dormitories with just four to six beds. Single and double rooms with private bathrooms are common and it's not unusual to find entire families at hostels.

PRIVATE HOSTELS

There are many private hostelling organisations in Western Europe and hundreds of unaffiliated backpacker hostels. Private hostels have fewer rules (eg no curfew, no daytime lockout), more self-catering kitchens and a much lower number of large, noisy school groups. They often also have a much more party-friendly vibe.

However, whereas HI hostels must meet minimum safety and cleanliness standards, private hostels do not, which means that facilities vary greatly (although some, such as Germany's Menninger chain, are slickly run and have luxe trappings). Dorms in some private hostels, especially in Germanic countries, can be mixed gender. Most private hostels now have small dorm rooms of three to eight beds, and private singles and doubles.

The following websites are recommended as resources for hostellers; all of them have booking engines, helpful advice from fellow travellers and excellent tips for novices.

Europe's Famous Hostels (www.famoushostels.com)

Hostel Planet (www.hostelplanet.com)

Hostel World (www.hostelworld.com)

Hostelling International (www.hihostels.com)

Hostels.com (www.hostels.com)

Hostelz (www.hostelz.com)

EMERGENCY NUMBERS

The EU-wide general emergency number is ☎112 (but ☎999 in the UK); see the Fast Facts or Nuts & Bolts box at the start of each country chapter for more details.

Hotels

From fabulous five-star icons to workaday cheapies, the range of hotels in Western Europe is immense. You'll often find inexpensive hotels clustered around bus and train station areas, which are always good places to start hunting; but these can be charmless and scruffy. Look for moderately priced places closer to the interesting parts of town.

Check your hotel room and bathroom before you agree to stay, and make sure you know what it's going to cost – discounts are often available for groups or for longer stays. Ask about breakfast; sometimes it's included, sometimes it's not.

If you think a room is too expensive, ask if there's anything cheaper; hotel owners often try to steer you towards more expensive options, and you can sometimes find affordable rooms in some of Western Europe's famous old hotels simply by asking. They may be in the attic or have a weird shape but can be great value. In southern Europe in particular, hotel owners may be open to a little bargaining if times are slack.

Besides big booking sites such as **Hotels.com** (www.hotels.com), we've had good luck with the following discount booking sites:

DHR (www.dhr.com)

Direct Rooms (www.directrooms.com)

Hotel Club (www.hotelclub.net)

Hotel Info (www.hotel.info)
HRS (www.hrs.com)
LateRooms (www.laterooms.com)

Rental Accommodation

Rentals can be both advantageous and fun for families travelling together or for those staying in one place for a few nights. You can have your own chic Left Bank apartment in Paris or a villa in Tuscany with a pool – and often at cheaper rates than for hotels.

You'll have the freedom of coming and going whenever you like without worrying about curfews and strict checkout times, plus a feeling of coming 'home' after a hard day of sightseeing. All rentals should be equipped with kitchens (or at least a kitchenette), which can save on the food bill and allow you to peruse the neighbourhood markets and shops, eating like the locals do. Some are a little more upmarket with laundry facilities, parking and even daily maid services.

For leads, try the following websites:

Holiday Havens (www.holidayhavens.co.uk)
Holiday-Rentals (www.holiday-rentals.uk)
Homelidays (www.homelidays.com)
Vacations-Abroad (www.vacations-abroad.com)
Vacation Rentals By Owner (www.vrbo.com)

Resorts

From foreboding Irish mansions to grand Swiss hotels, Western Europe has many fabled resorts, where travellers try to avoid ever checking out. Ask about deals and rooms that are cheaper than the average.

Activities

Europe offers countless opportunities to indulge in more active pursuits than simply snapping photos and posting them to your blog. The varied geography and climate supports the full range of outdoor activities: boating, windsurfing, skiing, fishing, hiking, cycling and mountaineering. For local information, see the individual country chapters.

Boating

Europe's many lakes, rivers and diverse coastlines offer a variety of boating options unmatched anywhere in the world. You can houseboat in France, kayak in Switzerland, charter a yacht in Greece, row on a peaceful Alpine lake, join a Danube River cruise from Amsterdam to Vienna, rent a sailing boat on the Côte d'Azur or dream away on a canal boat along the extraordinary canal network of Britain (or Ireland, or France) – the possibilities are endless. See individual country chapters for more details.

Cycling

Along with hiking, cycling is the best way to really get close to the scenery and the people, keeping yourself fit in the process. It's also a good way to get around many cities and towns.

Much of Western Europe is ideally suited to cycling. In the northwest, the flat terrain ensures that bicycles are a popular form of everyday transport, though rampant headwinds often spoil the fun. In the rest of the region, hills and mountains can make for heavy going, but this is offset by the dense concentration of things to see. Cycling is a great way to explore many of the Mediterranean islands, though the heat can get to you after a while.

Popular cycling areas include the Belgian Ardennes, the west of Ireland, much of The Netherlands (the world's most bike-friendly nation), the coasts of Sardinia and Puglia, anywhere in the Alps (for those fit enough), and the south of France.

Usually your bike can fly with you, albeit in the cargo hold. Check with your airline. Alternatively, places to hire/rent are myriad.

See p1219 for more information on bicycle touring, and the Activities and Getting Around sections in individual country chapters for rental tips and ideas on places to peddle.

Hiking

Keen hikers can spend a lifetime exploring Western Europe's many exciting trails. Popular routes feature places to stay, often far up on some breathtakingly gorgeous peak.

Highlights include:

The Alps Spanning Switzerland, Austria, Germany and Italy, with echoes of Heidi, bell-ringing dairy cows and trails organised with Swiss precision.

Italian Dolomites Like the Alps but less crowded and with better food.

Pyrenees Follow the trails of partisans through hills with Gallic-Iberian flavours.

Corsica & Sardinia Sun-drenched rugged beauty, with a Mediterranean view around every corner.

Northern Portugal A glass of port awaits after a day on the trail.

Scotland's West Highland Way Brambles, moors and locations from *Monty Python and the Holy Grail*.

Ramblers (www.ramblers.org.uk) is a non-profit organisation that promotes long-distance walking in the UK and can help you with maps and information. The British-based **Ramblers Holidays** (www.ramblersholidays.co.uk) offers hiking-oriented trips in Europe and elsewhere. For shorter day hikes, local tourist offices are usually excellent resources. Just ask.

Every country in Western Europe has national parks and other interesting areas or attractions that may qualify as a hiker's paradise, depending on your preferences. Guided hikes are often available for those who prefer expert leadership.

Skiing

In winter Europeans take to the pistes, flocking to hundreds of resorts located in the Alps and Pyrenees for downhill skiing and snowboarding. Cross-country skiing is also very popular in some areas.

Equipment hire (or even purchase) can be relatively cheap if you follow the tips in this guide, and the hassle of bringing your own skis may not be worth it. As a rule, a skiing holiday in Europe will work out to be about twice as expensive as a summer holiday of the same length.

The skiing season generally lasts from early December to late March, though at higher altitudes it may extend an extra month either side. Snow conditions can vary greatly from one year to the next and from region to region, but January and February tend to be the best (and busiest) months.

Ski resorts in the French and Swiss Alps offer legendary skiing and facilities but are also the most expensive. Expect high prices in the German Alps too. Austria is generally slightly cheaper than France and Switzerland (especially in Carinthia). Prices in the Italian Alps are similar to Austria (with some upmarket exceptions such as Cortina d'Ampezzo) and can be relatively cheap given the right package.

For comprehensive reports on ski conditions, try www.onthesnow.com.

Windsurfing

Windsurfing is a European passion, practised most places there's water and sand (which is also a commentary on the breezy nature of Western European beaches). It's easy to rent sailboards in many tourist centres, and courses are usually available for beginners.

Business Hours

Standard business hours vary hugely in Western Europe, where dinner means midnight in Madrid and 7pm in Holland. Some countries have embraced Sunday shopping and others haven't. See the country chapter directories for details.

Children

Europe is the home of *Little Red Riding Hood, Cinderella, King Arthur, Tintin* et al, and is a great place to travel with kids. Successful travel with young children requires some careful planning and effort. Don't try to overdo things; even for adults, packing too much sightseeing into the time available can cause problems. Make sure your activities include the kids as well – balance that day at the Louvre with a day at Disneyland Paris. Include children in the trip planning; if they've helped to work out where you will be going they will be much more interested when they get there.

Most car-hire firms in Western Europe have children's safety seats for hire at a nominal cost, but it's essential that you book them in advance. The same goes for high chairs and cots (cribs); they're standard in most restaurants and hotels but numbers are limited. The choice of baby food, formulas, soy and cow's milk, disposable nappies (diapers) and the like is good in all Western European supermarkets.

Customs Regulations

Duty-free goods are not sold to those travelling from one EU country to another. For goods purchased at airports or on ferries *outside* the EU, the usual allowances apply for tobacco (200 cigarettes, 50 cigars or 250g of loose tobacco) – although some countries have reduced this to curb smoking – and alcohol (1L of spirits or 2L of liquor with less than 22% alcohol by volume; 4L of wine). The total value of these goods cannot exceed €300.

Do not confuse these with duty-paid items (including alcohol and tobacco) bought at normal shops and supermarkets in another EU country, where certain goods might be more expensive. (Alcoholic beverages in France, for example, are cheaper than in the UK.)

Discount Cards

Camping Card International

The **Camping Card International** (CCI; www.anwbonline.com) is a camping ground ID that can be used instead of a passport when checking into a camping ground and includes third-party insurance. As a result, many camping grounds offer a small discount (usually 5% to 10%) if you sign in with one.

CCIs are issued by automobile associations, camping federations or sometimes on the spot at camping grounds.

Senior Cards

Museums and various other sights and attractions (including public swimming pools and spas), as well as transport companies, frequently offer discounts to retired people, old-age pensioners and/or those over 60.

Make sure you bring proof of age; that suave signor in Italy or that polite Parisian mademoiselle is not going to believe you're not a day over 39.

Student & Youth Cards

The **International Student Travel Confederation** (ISTC; www.istc.org) issues three cards for students, teachers and under-26s, offering thousands of worldwide discounts on transport, museum entry, youth hostels and even some restaurants. These cards are: the ISIC (International Student Identity Card), the ITIC (International Teacher Identity Card) and the IYTC (International Youth Travel Card). You can check the full list of discounts and where to apply for the cards on the ISTC website. Issuing offices include **STA Travel** (www.statravel.com). Most places, however, will also accept regular student identity cards.

For people under 30, there's also the **European Youth Card** (www.euro26.org) which has scores of discounts.

Electricity

Voltages & Cycles

Most of Europe runs on 220V/50Hz AC (as opposed to, say, North America, where the electricity is 120V/60 Hz AC). Chargers for phones, iPods and laptops *usually* can handle any type of electricity. If in doubt, read the tiny print. .

Plugs & Sockets

For most of the countries in this book you'll need a plug converter that looks like one of these shown here. If you don't get one before travelling, try the shops in airports and train stations when you arrive.

The main exception is Switzerland, which uses electrical sockets that are recessed, hexagonally shaped and generally incompatible with most plugs from abroad (including 'universal' adapters).

CONTINENTAL EUROPE

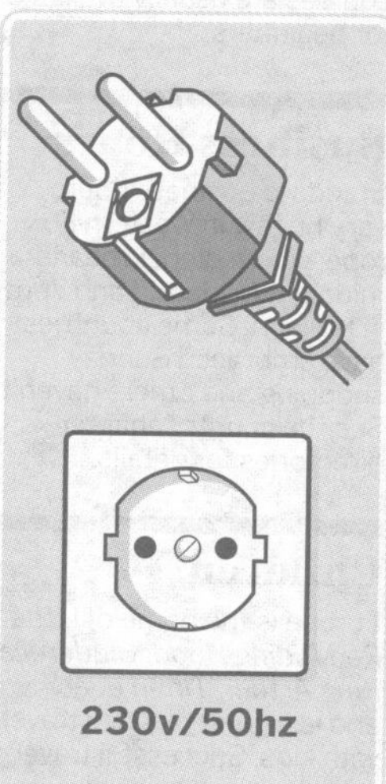

BRITAIN & IRELAND

Embassies & Consulates

As a tourist, it is vitally important that you understand what your own embassy (the embassy of the country of which you are a citizen) can and cannot do. Generally speaking, embassies won't be much help in emergencies if the trouble you're in is even remotely your fault.

Remember that you are bound by the laws of the country that you are in. Your embassy will show little sympathy if you end up in jail after committing a crime locally, even if such actions are legal in your own country.

In genuine emergencies you might get some assistance, but only if other channels have been exhausted. For example, if you need to get home urgently, a free ticket is exceedingly unlikely as the embassy would expect you to have insurance. If you have all your money and documents stolen, the embassy might assist with getting a new passport, but a loan for onward travel is almost always out of the question.

Locations

Nations such as Australia, Canada, New Zealand and the US have embassies and consulates across Western Europe in capitals and major cities.

You can find locations using these websites:

Australia (www.dfat.gov.au)
Canada (www.international.gc.ca)
New Zealand (www.mfat.govt.nz)
United Kingdom (www.fco.gov.uk)
United States (www.travel.state.gov)

Gay & Lesbian Travellers

In cosmopolitan centres in Western Europe you'll find very liberal attitudes toward homosexuality. Belgium, The Netherlands and Spain have legalised full same-sex marriages. Many other countries allow civil partnerships that grant all or most of the rights of marriage.

London, Paris, Berlin, Madrid, Lisbon and Amsterdam have thriving gay communities and pride events. The Greek islands of Mykonos and Lesvos are popular gay beach destinations.

The following websites are useful:

Damron (www.damron.com) The USA's leading gay publisher offers guides to world cities.

Gay Journey (www.gayjourney.com) A mishmash of travel-related information including lists of gay-friendly hotels in Europe.

International Lesbian and Gay Association (www.ilga.org) Campaigning group with some country-specific information on homosexual issues (not always up to date) and a conference calendar.

Spartacus International Gay Guide (www.spartacusworld.com) A male-only directory of gay entertainment venues in Europe and the rest of the world.

Health

It is unlikely that you will encounter unusual health problems in Western Europe, and if you do, standards of care are world-class. It's also important to have health insurance for your trip; for more information, see Insurance.

A few travelling tips:

» Bring medications in their original, clearly labelled containers.

» Bring a list of your prescriptions (photocopies of the containers are good) including generic names, so you can get replacements if your bags go on holiday – carry this info separately.

» If you have health problems that may need treatment, bring a signed and dated letter from your physician describing your medical conditions and medications.

» If carrying syringes or needles, have a physician's letter documenting their medical necessity.

» If you need vision correction, carry a spare pair of contact lenses or glasses, and/or take your optical prescription with you.

Recommended Vaccinations

No jabs are necessary for Western Europe. However, the World Health Organization (WHO) recommends that all travellers should be covered for diphtheria, tetanus, measles, mumps, rubella and polio, regardless of their destination.

Insurance

It's foolhardy to travel without insurance to cover theft, loss and medical problems. Start by seeing what your own insurance covers, be it medical, home owner's or renter's. You may find that many aspects of travel in Western Europe are covered. You may also find gaping holes. If you need to purchase coverage, there's a wide variety of policies, so check the small print. Some policies specifically exclude 'dangerous activities', which can include scuba diving, motorcycling, winter sports, adventure sports or even hiking. Some pay doctors or hospitals directly, but most require you to pay upfront, save the documentation and then claim later. Some policies also ask you to call back (reverse charges) to a centre in your home country, where an immediate assessment of your problem is made. Check that the policy covers ambulances or an emergency flight home.

If you're an EU citizen, the European Health Insurance Card (EHIC) covers you for most medical care. EHIC will not cover you for non-emergencies or emergency repatriation. Citizens of other countries should find out if there is a reciprocal arrangement for free medical care between their country and the country visited. If you do need health insurance, strongly consider a policy that covers you for the worst possible scenario. Find out in advance if your insurance plan will make payments directly to providers or reimburse you later for overseas health expenditures. The former option is generally preferable, as it doesn't require you to pay out-of-pocket costs in a foreign country.

The policies handled by **STA Travel** (www.statravel.com) and other student travel agencies are usually good value. In the UK, the website **Money Supermarket** (www.moneysupermarket.com) does an automated comparison of 450 partner policies and comes up with the best for your needs.

Worldwide travel insurance is available at lonelyplanet.com/travel_services. You can buy, extend and claim online anytime – even if you're already on the road.

Internet Access

The number of internet cafes is plummeting. You'll still find them in tourist areas and around big train stations. Otherwise you may end up at online gaming parlours where you can compose an email asking for money from home or bragging about the cute local you met in a pub while boys blast aliens all around you. When in doubt, ask at a tourist office.

» Hostels, hotels and other accommodation usually have wi-fi (WLAN in Germany).

» Wi-fi access is best the further north in Western Europe you go (Greece and Portugal are laggards).

» Wi-fi is often free in hostels and midrange places, while

costing €20 or more at top end hotels.

» Internet access places may add a surcharge of €1 to €5 per hour for using Skype.

Legal Matters

Most Western European police are friendly and helpful, especially if you have been a victim of a crime. You are required by law to prove your identity if asked by police, so always carry your passport, or an identity card if you're an EU citizen.

Illegal Drugs

Narcotics are sometimes openly available in Europe, but that doesn't mean they're legal. The Netherlands is famed for its liberal attitudes, with 'coffee shops' openly selling cannabis. However, even there it's a case of the police turning a blind eye. Possession of cannabis is decriminalised but not legalised (except for medicinal use). Don't take this relaxed attitude as an invitation to buy harder drugs; if you get caught, you'll be punished. In Belgium, the possession of up to 5g of cannabis is legal but selling the drug isn't, so if you get caught at the point of sale you could be in trouble. In Portugal, the possession of *all* drugs has been decriminalised. Once again, however, selling is illegal.

Smoking

Cigarette-smoking bans have been progressively introduced across Europe. Although outdoor seating has long been a tradition at European cafes, it's gained new popularity given that most Western European countries have banned smoking in public places, including restaurants and bars. Some hotels still allow smoking in rooms in a few countries, so if you're a non-smoker it's worth asking if you can get a no-smoking room when reserving. If you're a smoker, the easiest strategy is to assume you can't and then light up with relish if you see locals puffing away.

Media

Newspapers & Magazines

Keeping up with the news in English is obviously no problem in the UK or Ireland. In larger towns in the rest of Western Europe you can buy the excellent *International Herald Tribune*, as well as the colourful but superficial *USA Today*. Among other English-language newspapers widely available are the *Guardian*, the *Financial Times* and the *Times*. Also readily available are *Time Magazine* and the *Economist*.

Radio & TV

If you're close to the northwest coast of France, you can pick up British radio stations including BBC's Radio 4. There are also numerous English-language broadcasts, and even BBC World Service and Voice of America (VOA) rebroadcasts on local AM and FM radio stations. Otherwise, you can pick up a mixture of the BBC World Service and BBC for Europe on medium wave at 648kHz AM in Benelux (Belgium, The Netherlands and Luxembourg) and parts of France and Germany.

Money

For security and flexibility, diversify your source of funds. Carry an ATM card, credit card and cash. See p1216 for info on carrying money safely.

ATMs

Every country in this book has international ATMs allowing you to withdraw cash directly from your home account, and this is the most common way European travellers access their money. You should always have a back-up option, however, as some travellers have reported glitches with ATMs in various countries, even when their card worked elsewhere across Western Europe. In some remote villages, ATMs might be scarce too.

When you withdraw money from an ATM the amounts are converted and dispensed in local currency but there

MINIMISING ATM CHARGES

When you withdraw cash from an ATM overseas there are several ways you can get hit. Firstly, most banks add a hidden 2.75% loading to what's called the 'Visa/Mastercard wholesale' or 'interbank' exchange rate. In short, they're giving you a worse exchange rate than strictly necessary. Additionally, some banks charge their customers a cash withdrawal fee (usually 2% with a minimum €2 or more). If you're really unlucky, the bank at the foreign end might charge you as well. Triple whammy. If you use a credit card in ATMs you'll also pay interest – usually quite high – on the cash withdrawn.

Most experts agree that having the right bankcard is still cheaper than exchanging cash directly. If your bank levies fees, then making larger, less frequent withdrawals is better. It's also worth seeing if your bank has reciprocal agreements with banks where you are going that minimise ATM fees.

will be fees. If you're uncertain, ask your bank.

Finally, don't forget your normal security procedures: cover the keypad when entering your PIN and make sure there are no unusual devices (which might copy your card's information) attached to the machine. If your card disappears and the screen goes blank before you've even entered your PIN, don't enter it – especially if a 'helpful' bystander tells you to do so. If you can't retrieve your card, call your bank's emergency number as soon as possible.

THE EURO

The euro is the official currency used in 16 of the 27 EU states: Austria, Belgium, Cyprus, Finland, France, Germany, Greece, Ireland, Italy, Luxembourg, Malta, The Netherlands, Portugal, Slovakia, Slovenia and Spain. Denmark, Britain, Switzerland and Sweden have held out against adopting the euro for political reasons.

The euro is divided into 100 cents and has the same value in all EU member countries. There are seven euro notes (5, 10, 20, 50, 100, 200 and 500 euros) and eight euro coins (1 and 2 euros, then 1, 2, 5, 10, 20 and 50 cents). One side is standard for all euro coins and the other side bears a national emblem of participating countries.

Cash

Nothing beats cash for convenience...or risk. If you lose it, it's gone forever and very few travel insurers will come to your rescue. Those that do will limit the amount to somewhere around €300 or £200.

If flying into Western Europe from elsewhere, you'll find ATMs and currency exchanges in the arrivals area of the airport. There is no reason to get local currency before arriving in Western Europe, especially as exchange rates in your home country are likely to be abysmal.

Credit Cards

Credit cards are handy for major purchases such as air or rail tickets, and offer a lifeline in certain emergencies.

Visa and MasterCard/Eurocard are more widely accepted in Europe than Amex and Diners Club. There are, however, regional differences in the general acceptability of credit cards. In the UK, for example, you can usually flash your plastic in the most humble of budget restaurants; in Germany some restaurants don't take credit cards. Cards are not widely accepted off the beaten track.

As with ATM cards, banks have loaded up credit cards with hidden charges for foreign purchases. Cash withdrawals on a credit card are almost always a much worse idea than using an ATM card due to the fees and high interest rates. Plus, purchases in different currencies are likely to draw various conversion surcharges that are simply there to add to the bank's profit. These can run up to 5% or more. Your best bet is to check these things before leaving.

International Transfers

International bank transfers are good for secure one-off movements of large amounts of money, but they might take three to five days and there will be a fee (about £25 in the UK, for example).

In an emergency, it's quicker and easier to have money wired via **Western Union** (www.westernunion.com) or **MoneyGram** (www.moneygram.com). All are quite costly.

Money Exchange

In general, US dollars and UK pounds are the easiest currencies to exchange in Western Europe. Get rid of Scottish and Welsh pounds before leaving the UK; nobody outside Britain will touch them.

Most airports, central train stations, big hotels and many border posts have banking facilities outside regular business hours, at times on a 24-hour basis. Post offices in Western Europe often perform banking tasks, tend to be open longer hours and outnumber banks in remote places.

The best exchange rates are usually at banks. *Bureaux de changes* usually – but not always – offer worse rates or charge higher commissions. Hotels are almost always the worst places to change money.

Taxes & Refunds

Sales tax applies to many goods and services in Western Europe (although the amount – 10% to 20% – is already built into the price of the item). Luckily, when non-EU residents spend more than a certain amount (around €75) they can usually reclaim that tax when leaving the country.

Making a tax-back claim is straightforward. First, make sure the shop offers duty-free sales (often a sign will be displayed reading 'Tax-Free Shopping'). When making your purchase ask the shop attendant for a tax-refund voucher, filled in with the correct amount and the date. This can be used to claim a refund directly at international airports (beware, however, of very long lines), or be stamped at ferry ports or border crossings and mailed back for a refund.

None of this applies to EU residents. Even an American citizen living in London is not entitled to a rebate on items bought in Paris. Conversely, an EU-passport holder living in New York is.

Tipping

Adding another 5% to 10% to a bill at a restaurant or cafe for good service is common across Western Europe. See individual country directories for additional details.

Travellers Cheques

Travellers cheques have been largely replaced by international ATMs and it's often difficult to find places that cash them.

Safe Travel

On the whole, you should experience few problems travelling in Western Europe – even alone – as the region is well developed and relatively safe. But do exercise common sense. Whatever you do, don't leave friends and relatives back home worrying about how to get in touch with you in case of an emergency. Work out a list of places where they can contact you or, best of all, phone home now and then or email.

Also, leave a record (ie a photocopy) of your passport, credit and ATM cards and other important documents in a safe place. You can scan your documents and credit cards and post the file somewhere safe online, perhaps by emailing it to yourself. This gives you access from anywhere and saves you from having both the originals and copies lost. If things are stolen or lost, replacement is much easier when you have the vital details available.

Drugs

Always treat drugs with caution. There are a lot of drugs available in Western Europe, sometimes quite openly (particularly in the Netherlands), but that doesn't mean they're legal. Even a little hashish can cause a great deal of trouble in some places. See each chapter's regional directory for more details on local laws.

Theft

Theft happens in Western Europe; be wary of theft by other travellers, too. The most important things to secure are your passport, papers, tickets and money, in that order.

You can lessen the risks further by being careful of 'snatch thieves', who go for cameras and shoulder bags. They sometimes operate from motorcycles or scooters and expertly slash the strap before you have a chance to react. A small day pack is better, but watch your rear. Be very careful at cafes and bars; loop the strap of your bag around your leg while seated.

Pickpockets are most active in dense crowds, especially in busy train stations and on public transport during peak hours. A common ploy is for one person to distract you while another zips through your pockets. Beware of gangs of kids – who can look either dishevelled or well dressed – madly waving newspapers and demanding attention. In the blink of an eye, a wallet or camera can go missing. And a jacket or purse left on the back of a chair is an invitation for theft.

Scams

See the individual chapters for scams by country. Generally, be aware of shopkeepers in touristy places who may short-change you.

Telephone

Treat your hotel phone and its often hidden and outrageous rates the same way you'd treat a thief. Using wi-fi in the room for Skype is the most common way to connect.

Mobile Phones

Travellers can easily purchase prepaid mobile phones (from £20/€30) or SIM cards (from £5/€10). GSM phones can be used throughout all countries in Western Europe. Mobile shops are everywhere. Shops in large train stations are especially adept at getting visitors set up.

You can bring your mobile phone from home and buy a local SIM card to enjoy cheap local calling rates if it is a) unlocked and b) compatible with European GSM networks. Check first.

If you bring your mobile phone from home:

» Check international roaming rates in advance; often they are very expensive.

» Check roaming fees for data usage for email and web connections; users of smart phones (eg iPhones) can get socked with huge fees.

Phone Codes

For individual country codes see the Fast Facts or Nuts & Bolts box at the start of each country chapter.

Time

Greenwich Mean Time/ UTC Britain, Ireland

Central European Time (GMT/UTC +1hr) Andorra, Austria, Belgium, France, Germany, Greece, Italy, Liechtenstein, Luxembourg, The Netherlands, Portugal, Spain, Switzerland

East European Time (GMT/ UTC +2hrs) Greece

Daylight Saving Time/ Summer Time Last Sunday in March to the last Sunday in October

Tourist Information

Tourist offices in Western Europe are common and almost universally helpful. They can find accommodation, issue maps, advise on sights and activities and help with more obscure queries such as, 'Where can I wash my clothes?'. You'll find details for the relevant local office in almost every city and town listing in this book.

Visas

Most readers of this book will have very little to do with visas. While border procedures between EU and non-EU countries can still be thorough, citizens of Australia, Canada, New Zealand and the USA don't need visas for tourist visits to the UK or any Schengen country. With a valid passport you should be able to visit Western European countries for up to three months, provided you have some sort of onward or return ticket and/or 'sufficient means of support' (money).

For those who do require visas, it's important to remember that these will have a 'use-by' date, and you'll be refused entry after that period has elapsed. It may not be checked when entering these countries overland, but major problems can arise if it is requested during your stay or on departure and you can't produce it.

Schengen Visa Rules

As per the Schengen Agreement, there are no passport controls at borders between the following countries:

- Austria
- Belgium
- Czech Republic
- Denmark
- Estonia
- Finland
- France
- Germany
- Greece
- Hungary
- Iceland
- Italy
- Latvia
- Lithuania
- Liechtenstein
- Luxembourg
- Malta
- The Netherlands
- Norway
- Portugal
- Slovakia
- Slovenia
- Spain
- Sweden
- Switzerland

(At the time of writing, Bulgaria and Romania were scheduled to become member nations in October 2011). Think of this zone as one country in terms of your three-month stay. It won't work to try to stay in each of the countries for three months.

Visa details are given in each country chapter. Schengen countries use the phrase 'Schengen rules apply'.

If you are planning to stay in Western Europe for longer than three months, make sure you leave the Schengen zone before your 90 days are up (say by a jaunt to the UK or Ireland) and then return, getting a new entrance stamp in your passport.

Weights & Measures

The metric system is used throughout Western Europe. In Britain, however, non-metric equivalents are common (distances continue to be given in miles and beer is sold in pints, not litres).

Transport

GETTING THERE & AWAY

Part of the adventure is figuring out how to get to Western Europe, and in these days of cut-throat competition among airlines there are plenty of opportunities to find cheap tickets to a variety of gateway cities.

Options for reaching Western Europe by land or sea are few. International strife has lead to the closure of most land routes from Asia, while watery options are limited to the odd cruise ship from the USA.

Flights, tours and rail tickets can be booked online at www.lonelyplanet.com/bookings.

Air

Western Europe is well-served by just about every major airline in the world; the main gateways include airports in London, Paris, Amsterdam, Frankfurt and Rome. However, with connections you can reach scores of airports across the continent. Once in Europe you can take advantage of cheap fares for getting around at a good price, although trains will be better for two environments: yours and the planet's.

For details on specific airports, see the Transport sections of the individual country chapters.

Land

You can easily get to Western Europe from the rest of Europe by road, bus or train. Things become more complicated, however, the further away you're coming from.

Train

It *is* possible to get to Western Europe by train from central and eastern Asia, but count on spending at least eight days doing it. Four different train lines wind their way to Moscow: the Trans-Siberian (9297km from Vladivostok), the Trans-Mongolian (7860km from Beijing) and the Trans-Manchurian (9001km from Beijing) all use the same tracks across Siberia but have different routes east of Lake Baikal, while the Trans-Kazakhstan (another Trans-Siberian line) runs between Moscow and Urumqi in northwestern China. Prices vary enormously depending on where you buy the ticket and what's included – advertised 2nd-class fares cost around £600 from Beijing to Moscow.

There are many travel options between Western Europe and Moscow as well as other Eastern European countries and the Baltics. Poland, the Czech Republic and Hungary all have myriad rail links.

Sea

Ferries

There are many ferries crossing the Mediterranean between Africa and Western Europe. The ferry you take will depend on your travels in Africa, but the options include Spain–Morocco, France–Morocco, France–Tunisia and Italy–Tunisia. There are also ferries between Greece and Israel via Cyprus. Ferries also serve Germany from all the Scandinavian countries.

Passenger Ships

Cunard's **Queen Mary 2** (www.cunard.com) sails between New York and Southampton (England) several times a year; the trip takes six nights each way and costs under US$3000 for two people in a standard double cabin. Deals abound. Other cruise lines have occasional crossings as well.

GETTING AROUND

Travel within most of the EU, whether by air, rail or car, is made easier owing to the Schengen Agreement, which abolished border controls between most EU countries. All travellers must still carry a passport; there are two passport-control lines – EU and non-EU nationals.

Britain and Ireland are among the few EU countries currently outside the agreement (even non-EU Switzerland has joined).

Discount airlines are revolutionising the way people

cover long distances within Europe. However, hopping on a plane deprives you the fun of travelling by train and the cultural experiences of navigating train stations, and there are important concerns about carbon emissions.

Air

Getting around Western Europe by air is very popular thanks to the proliferation of discount airlines and cheap fares. It's possible to go from London to Berlin at times for less than €30; fares around Europe for less than €100 are common. More interestingly, dozens of tiny airports across Europe now boast airline services, so a trip to Italy doesn't mean choosing between Milan and Rome, but rather scores of airports up and down the 'boot'.

It's possible to put together a practical itinerary that might bounce from London to the south of Spain to Italy to Amsterdam in a two-week period, all at an affordable price and avoiding endless train rides.

Airlines in Western Europe

Although many people first think of budget airlines when they consider a cheap ticket in Western Europe, you should compare all carriers, including established ones like British Airways and Lufthansa, which serve major airports close to main destinations. Deals crop up in the dangdest places.

Major budget airlines in Western Europe are listed following. See the Transport sections of individual country chapters for scores of smaller airlines with more limited service.

Air Berlin (www.airberlin.com) Hubs in Germany; service across Europe.

easyJet (www.easyjet.com) Flies to major airports across Europe.

Germanwings (www.germanwings.com) Hubs in Germany; service across Europe.

Ryanair (www.ryanair.com) Flies to scores of destinations across Europe, but confirm your destination airport is not a deserted airfield out in the sticks.

Vueling (www.vueling.com) Serves a broad swath of Europe from its Spanish hubs.

The best place to buy cheap airline tickets is on the internet. In fact, many airlines only sell their cheapest tickets online. Various websites compare fares across a range of airlines within Europe, including the following:

- » www.cheapoair.com
- » www.kayak.com
- » www.skyscanner.net
- » www.sidestep.com

Air Passes

The three major airline alliances each offer various schemes where you can purchase flights within Europe if you fly to Europe with one of the member carriers. Typically these cost about US$65 to US$100 per flight.

oneworld (www.oneworld.com)

SkyTeam (www.skyteam.com)

Star Alliance (www.staralliance.com)

Bicycle

A tour of Western Europe by bike may seem like a daunting prospect but help is at hand. The **Cyclists' Touring Club** (CTC; www.ctc.org.uk) is based in the UK and offers members an information service on all matters associated with cycling, including cycling conditions, detailed routes, itineraries and maps.

The key to a successful cycling trip is to travel light. What you carry should be determined by your destination and the type of trip you're taking. Even for the most basic trip, it's worth carrying the tools necessary for repairing a puncture. Bicycle shops are found everywhere, but you still might want to pack the following if you don't want to rely on others:

- » Allen keys
- » spanners
- » spare brake and gear cables
- » spare spokes
- » strong adhesive tape

Wearing a helmet is not always compulsory but is

DISCOUNT AIRLINES

With cheap fares come many caveats. Some of the barebones airlines are just that – expect nonreclining seats, nonexistent legroom and nonexistent window shades. At some far-flung airports, customer service may also be nonexistent – same goes for convenience. If you really want to go to Carcassonne in the south of France, then getting a €20 ticket from London will be a dream come true. But if you want to go to Frankfurt in Germany and end up buying a ticket to 'Frankfurt-Hahn', you will find yourself at a small airport 70km west of Frankfurt and two hours away by bus. Also beware of discount airline websites such as those of Air Berlin and Germanwings, which show nonstop flights that are actually connections.

In this book you will find dozens of airports with budget carrier service. Check their websites to confirm the latest details as budget-flight routes can change often.

CLIMATE CHANGE & TRAVEL

Every form of transport that relies on carbon-based fuel generates CO_2, the main cause of human-induced climate change. Modern travel is dependent on aeroplanes, which might use less fuel per kilometre per person than most cars but travel much greater distances. The altitude at which aircraft emit gases (including CO_2) and particles also contributes to their climate change impact. Many websites offer 'carbon calculators' that allow people to estimate the carbon emissions generated by their journey and, for those who wish to do so, to offset the impact of the greenhouse gases emitted with contributions to portfolios of climate-friendly initiatives throughout the world. Lonely Planet offsets the carbon footprint of all staff and author travel.

advised. A seasoned cyclist can average about 80km a day, but this depends on the terrain and how much you are carrying.

For more information on cycling, see the bicycle coverage in the Transport sections of individual country chapters.

Hire

It's easy to hire bicycles in Western Europe and you can often negotiate good deals. Rental periods vary. Local tourist offices, hostels and hotels will have information on rental outlets. Occasionally you can drop off the bicycle at a different location so you don't have to double back on your route.

Urban bike-hire schemes, where you check out a bike from one stand and return it to another after brief use, have taken off in cities as huge as London and Paris.

Purchase

For major cycling tours it's best to have a bike you're familiar with, so consider bringing your own rather than buying one on arrival. If you can't be bothered with the hassle of transporting your own, there are plenty of places to buy bikes in Western Europe (shops sell them new and secondhand).

Transporting a Bicycle

If you want to use your own bicycle in Western Europe, you should be able to take it with you on the plane. Check with the airline for details before you buy your ticket as each one has a different policy.

Within Western Europe, bikes can sometimes be taken onto a train with you, subject to a small supplementary fee. See the Transport sections in the individual country chapters for more detail.

Fast trains can rarely accommodate bicycles; you might need to send it as registered luggage, and it may end up on a different train from the one you take (as is often the case in France and Spain). Eurostar charges £22 to send a bike as registered luggage on its routes. Reserve in advance. You can transport your bicycle with you on Eurotunnel through the Channel Tunnel.

The UK-based **Bike Express** (www.bike-express.co.uk) is a coach service on which cyclists can travel with their bicycles. It runs in the summer in the UK, France and Spain, with 49 pick-up and drop-off points.

Boat

Multiple ferry companies compete on the main ferry routes, and the resulting service is comprehensive but complicated. The same ferry company can have a host of different prices for the same route, depending on the time of day or year, the validity of the ticket or the length of your vehicle. It's worth planning (and booking) ahead where possible as there may be special reductions on off-peak crossings and advance-purchase tickets. Most ferry companies adjust prices according to the level of demand (so-called 'fluid' or 'dynamic' pricing), so it may pay to offer alternative travel dates. Vehicle tickets usually include the driver and a full complement of passengers.

The main areas of ferry service for users of this book are between Ireland and the UK; Ireland and France; the UK and the Continent (especially France but also Belgium, the Netherlands and Spain); and Italy and Greece.

Compare fares and routes using **ferrysavers.com** (www.ferrysavers.com).

Rail-pass holders are entitled to discounts or free travel on some lines. If you take your vehicle on board, you are usually denied access to it during the voyage.

Bus

Buses sometimes have the edge in terms of costs, but are generally slower and much less comfortable than trains and not as quick or sometimes as cheap as airlines.

Eurolines

Europe's largest network of international buses is provided by a consortium of bus companies that operates under the name **Eurolines** (www.eurolines.com). There are many services and it's possible to travel very far for less than €100. Eurolines' various affiliates offer many national and regional bus passes.

For more information about long-distance buses, see the Transport sections in the individual country chapters.

Busabout

Busabout (www.busabout.com) operates buses that complete set circuits around Europe, stopping at major cities. You get unlimited travel per sector and can 'hop-on/hop-off' at any scheduled stop, then resume with a later bus. Buses are often oversubscribed, so prebook each sector to avoid being stranded.

Departures are about every two days from April to October. The circuits cover all countries in continental Western Europe, and you can pay to add on Greece, Scandinavia and/or a London–Paris link.

Passes allowing you to cover a lot of territory start at less than US$600.

Campervan

A popular way to tour Europe is for three or four people to band together to buy or rent a campervan. London is the usual embarkation point. Some good British publications and websites to check out for campervan purchases and rentals include the following:

Loot (www.loot.com)

Auto Trader (www.autotrader.co.uk)

Worldwide Motorhome Hire (www.worldwide-motorhome-hire.com)

Campervans usually feature a fixed high-top or elevating roof and two to five bunk beds. Apart from the essential gas cooker, professional conversions may include a sink, a fridge and built-in cupboards. Prices and facilities vary considerably and it's certainly worth getting advice from a mechanic to see if you are being offered a fair price. Getting a mechanical check (costing from £40) is also a good idea. Once on the road, you should be able to keep your budget lower than a backpacker using trains, but don't forget to set some money aside for emergency repairs.

The main advantage of travelling by campervan is flexibility. Transport, accommodation and storage are all taken care of. Unfortunately, the self-contained factor can also prove to be one of the downsides. Conditions can get very cramped, tempers can become frayed and your romantic, hippy-style trail may dissolve into the campervan trip from hell.

Car

Travelling with your own vehicle allows increased flexibility and the option to get off the beaten track. Unfortunately, cars can be the proverbial ball-and-chain in city centres when you have to negotiate one-way streets or find somewhere to park amid a confusing concrete jungle and a welter of insanely expensive parking options.

Automobile Associations

Perish the thought of ever breaking down in some remote rural village in the Pyrenees or the isolated Irish countryside. But it happens. Should you find yourself in a predicament, you can contact the local automobile association for emergency assistance if it has an agreement with the auto club in your home country (and if you're a member!). These associations can provide a variety of roadside services such as petrol refills, flat-tyre repair and towing, plus predeparture information such as maps and itineraries and even an accommodation reservation service. Check with the main automobile association in your home country for coverage options.

Driving Licences

Proof of ownership of a private vehicle should always be carried (a Vehicle Registration Document for British-registered cars) when touring Europe. An EU driving licence is acceptable for driving throughout Europe.

Many non-European driving licences are valid in Europe. Some travel websites and auto clubs advise carrying an International Driving Permit (IDP), but this costly multilingual document sold by national auto clubs is not necessary in Western Europe – especially not to rent a car.

Fuel

Fuel prices can vary enormously from country to country (though it's always more expensive than in North America or Australia) and may bear little relation to the general cost of living. For fuel prices across the EU, surf over to the **AA Ireland** (www.aaroadwatch.ie/eupetrolprices) website.

Unleaded petrol and diesel are available across Western Europe.

Hire

The big international rental companies will give you reliable service and a good standard of vehicle. Usually you will have the option of returning the car to a different outlet at the end of the rental period. Rates vary widely but expect to pay somewhere between €25 and €70 per day. Prebook for the lowest rates – if you walk into an office and ask for a car on the spot, you will pay much more. For really good deals, prepay for your rental. Fly/drive combinations and other programs are worth looking into. Major companies in

Western Europe include the following:

Avis (www.avis.com)

Budget (www.budget.com)

Europcar (www.europcar.com)

Hertz (www.hertz.com)

» Rental brokers can be a lot cheaper than the major rental firms. Good companies to try include the following:

Auto Europe (www.autoeurope.com)

AutosAbroad (www.autosabroad.com)

holiday autos car hire (www.holidayautos.com)

Kemwel (www.kemwel.com)

» No matter where you rent from, it is imperative to understand exactly what is included in your rental agreement (collision waiver, unlimited mileage etc). Make sure you are covered with an adequate insurance policy. And take note: less than 4% of European cars have automatic transmissions, so if you're afraid of a stick, you'll pay more than double for your car.

The minimum age to rent a vehicle is usually 21 or even 23, and you'll need a credit card.

Insurance

Third-party motor insurance is compulsory in Europe if you are driving your own car (rental cars usually come with insurance). Most UK motor-insurance policies automatically provide this for EU countries. Get your insurer to issue a Green Card (which may cost extra), which is an internationally recognised proof of insurance, and check that it lists all the countries you intend to visit.

Also ask your insurer for a European Accident Statement form, which can simplify things if the worst happens. Never sign statements you can't understand – insist on a translation and sign only if it's acceptable.

It's a good investment to take out a European motoring-assistance policy, such as the AA Five Star Service or the RAC European Motoring Assistance. Expect to pay about £50 for 14 days' cover, with a 10% discount for association members. Non-Europeans might find it cheaper to arrange international coverage with their national motoring organisation before leaving home. Ask your motoring organisation for details about free services offered by affiliated organisations around Western Europe.

Every vehicle travelling across an international border should display a sticker showing its country of registration. Car rental/hire agencies usually ensure cars are properly equipped; when in doubt, ask. UK drivers should contact the following for more information:

AA (www.theaa.com)

RAC (www.rac.co.uk)

Purchase

Britain is probably the best place to buy a vehicle as secondhand prices are good and, whether buying privately or from a dealer, if you're an English-speaker the absence of language difficulties will help you establish what you are getting and what guarantees you can expect in the event of a breakdown.

Some good British papers to check out for vehicle purchases are **Loot** (www.loot.com) and **AutoTrader** (www.autotrader.co.uk).

Bear in mind that you will be getting a car with the steering wheel on the right-hand side in Britain. If you want left-hand drive and can afford to buy new, prices are usually reasonable in Greece, France, Germany, Belgium, Luxembourg and the Netherlands.

For a real adventure consider buying a new car at the source. European car companies such as BMW, Mercedes and Volvo will sell the same model of car you'd buy in your home country but let you pick it up at the factory in Europe and drive it on a holiday. The company then has it shipped to your hometown.

Road Conditions

Conditions and types of roads vary across Western Europe, but it is possible to make some generalisations. The fastest routes are four- or six-lane dual carriageways/highways, ie two or three lanes either side (motorway, autobahn, autoroute, autostrada etc). These roads are great for speed and comfort but driving can be dull, with little or no interesting scenery. Some of these roads incur expensive tolls (eg in Italy, France and Spain) or have a general tax for usage (Switzerland and Austria), but there will usually be an alternative route you can take. Motorways and other primary routes are almost always in good condition.

Road surfaces on minor routes are not perfect in some countries (eg Greece), although normally they will be more than adequate. These roads are narrower and progress is generally much slower. To compensate, you can expect much better scenery and plenty of interesting villages along the way.

Road Rules

Automobile associations can supply members with country-by-country information about motoring regulations, or they may produce motoring guidebooks for general sale.

With the exception of Britain and Ireland, driving is on the right-hand side of the road.

Take care with speed limits, as they vary from country to country. You may be surprised at the apparent disregard of traffic regulations in some places (particularly in Italy and Greece), but as a visitor it is always best to be cautious. In many countries, driving infringements are subject to an on-the-spot fine; always ask for a receipt.

European drink-driving laws are particularly strict. The blood-alcohol concentration (BAC) limit when driving is between 0.05% and 0.08%, but in certain areas it can be 0%. See the individual country chapters for more detail on traffic laws.

Hitching

Hitching is never entirely safe in any country and we don't recommend it. Travellers who decide to hitch should understand they are taking a small but potentially serious risk. Key points to remember:

» Hitch in pairs; it will be safer.

» Solo women should never hitch.

» Don't hitch from city centres; take public transport to suburban exit routes.

» Hitching is usually illegal on motorways – stand on the slip roads or approach drivers at petrol stations and truck stops.

» Look presentable and cheerful, and make a cardboard sign indicating your intended destination in the local language.

» Never hitch where drivers can't stop in good time or without causing an obstruction. At dusk, give up and think about finding somewhere to stay.

It is sometimes possible to arrange a lift in advance: scan student noticeboards in colleges or contact car-sharing agencies. Such agencies are particularly popular in Germany where they're called *Mitfahrzentrale*.

Motorcycle

With its good-quality winding roads, stunning scenery and an active motorcycling scene, Western Europe is made for motorcycle touring. The weather is not always reliable, though, so make sure your wet-weather gear is up to scratch. The wearing of helmets for rider and passenger is compulsory everywhere in Western Europe. See the Transport sections of individual country chapters for additional rules.

On ferries, motorcyclists can sometimes be squeezed on board without a reservation, although booking ahead is certainly advisable during peak travelling periods.

Take note of local customs about parking motorcycles on footpaths. Although this is illegal in some countries, the police usually turn a blind eye as long as the vehicle doesn't obstruct pedestrians. Don't try this in Britain – your feeble excuses to traffic wardens will fall on deaf ears.

If you are thinking of touring Europe on a motorcycle, contact the **British Motorcyclists Federation** (☎0116-284 5380; www.bmf.co.uk) for help and advice. An excellent source of information for travellers interested in more adventurous biking activities can be found at **Horizons Unlimited** (www.horizonsunlimited.com).

Motorcycle and moped rental is easy in countries such as Italy, Spain, Greece and in the south of France. In tourist areas just ask around for nearby rental agencies.

Public Transport

Most Western European cities have excellent public transport systems, which comprise some combination of metros (subways), trains, trams and buses. Service is usually comprehensive. Major airports generally have fast-train or metro links to the city centre. See the individual country chapters for more information.

Taxi

Taxis in Western Europe are metered and rates are generally high. There might also be supplements (depending on the country) for things such as luggage, the time of day, the location at which you boarded and for extra passengers. Good public transport networks make the use of taxis almost unnecessary, but if you need one in a hurry they can usually be found idling near train stations or outside big hotels. Spain, Greece and Portugal have lower fares, which makes taking a taxi more viable.

Don't underestimate the local knowledge that can be gleaned from taxi drivers. They can often tell you about the liveliest places in town and know all about events happening during your stay.

Tours

Package tours, whether tailor-made or bog-standard, cater for all tastes, interests and ages. The internet is an excellent resource for finding unusual tours that might not receive media or trade attention. Many people have had memorable trips on tours organised by cultural institutions like the **US Smithsonian Institution** (www.smithsonian.com) which run tours lead by experts in fields such as art. Try searching for your own interest (eg walking) with 'Europe tour' and see what you get.

Train

Trains are a popular way of getting around: they are comfortable, frequent and generally on time. The Channel Tunnel makes it possible to get from Britain to continental Europe using **Eurostar** (www.eurostar.com). See individual country chapters for more detail.

For many people, travel in Europe would not be travel in Europe without trains. But note that the traditional image of compartments with little wine-bottle holders and various colourful characters roaming the corridor has been completely replaced by fast, modern trains that are more like much-more-comfortable versions of airliners. Diners have mostly been replaced by snack bars or trolleys, although most people buy their food before boarding.

Information

Every national railway has a website with a vast amount of schedule and fare information. Other recommended websites include the following:

DB Bahn (www.bahn.de) Excellent schedule and fare information in English for trains not just in Germany but across Europe.

Man In Seat Sixty-one (www.seat61.com) Invaluable train descriptions and details of journeys to the far reaches of the continent.

If you plan to travel extensively by train, you might enjoy the Thomas Cook *European Rail Timetable*, which gives a cleverly condensed listing of train schedules that indicate where extra fees apply or where reservations are necessary. The timetable is updated monthly and is available from **Thomas Cook** (www.thomascookpublishing.com) outlets and bookshops in the UK (order online elsewhere in the world).

Note that European trains sometimes split en route in order to service two destinations, so even if you know you're on the right train, make sure you're in the correct carriage too.

Tickets

Normal international tickets are valid for two months and you can make as many stops as you like en route. Used this way, a ticket from Paris to Vienna can serve as a mini–rail pass, as long as you stay on the route shown on the ticket.

Check out the Transport sections of the country chapters for various discount schemes within countries.

DISCOUNT TRAIN TICKETS ONLINE

Many railways offer cheap ticket deals through their websites. It's always worth checking online for the same kinds of sales we now expect from budget airlines, including advance-purchase reductions, one-off promotions and special circular-route tickets.

How you actually receive the discount train tickets you've purchased online varies. Common methods include the following:

» Reservation number issued with the reservation which you use at a station ticket-vending machine (some UK lines).

» Credit card you used to purchase the tickets at a station ticket-vending machine (France, but non-French credit-card holders must retrieve their tickets at a ticket window).

» Ticket is emailed to buyer who then prints it out (Germany).

» Nonlocal credit cards aren't accepted online and you can't buy the discounted fares at the station (the Netherlands).

High-speed Trains

Western European trains (outside of Greece and Portugal) are often fast, frequent and usually comfortable. High-speed networks (300km/h or more) continue to expand and have given the airlines major competition on many routes.

Some sample travel times include the following:

ROUTE	DURATION
Amsterdam–Paris	3hr
Barcelona–Madrid	3hr
Brussels–Cologne	2¼hr
London–Paris	2¼hr
Milan–Rome	4hr
Nuremberg–Munich	1hr
Paris–Frankfurt	3¾hr
Paris–Marseille	3hr
Zürich–Milan	3¾hr

Major high-speed trains that cross borders include the following:

Eurostar (www.eurostar.com) Links beautiful St Pancras station in London to Brussels and Paris in about two hours.

ICE (www.bahn.de) The fast trains of the German railways span the country and extend to Paris, Brussels, Amsterdam, Vienna and Switzerland.

TGV (www.sncf.com) The legendary fast trains of France reach Belgium, Luxembourg, Germany, Switzerland and Italy.

Thalys (www.thalys.com) Links Paris with Brussels, Amsterdam and Cologne.

Other Trains

See the Transport sections of the individual country chapters for full details on national train services but it does bear reiterating: you'll have a splendid holiday in Western Europe if you rely entirely on the convenient, comfortable trains.

NIGHT TRAINS

The romantic image of the European night train is becoming a lot less common with the popularity of budget airlines; however, you can still find a good network of routes from the north to Italy. Besides the national railways:

Artesia (www.artesia.eu) Runs services between Paris and Rome and points in between.

Caledonian Sleeper (www.scotrail.co.uk) Links London overnight with Scotland (as far north as Inverness and Aberdeen).

City Night Line (www.citynightline.de) Operates night trains from Germany and the Netherlands south through Switzerland and Austria into Italy as well as France.

On the trains, look for these types of accommodation:

Couchette Bunks that are comfortable enough, if lacking a bit in privacy. There are four per compartment in 1st class or six in 2nd class. A bunk costs around €15 for most international trains, irrespective of the length of the journey.

Sleepers (wagon-lits) The most comfortable option, offering beds for one or two passengers in 1st class, and two or three passengers in 2nd class. Charges vary depending on the journey, but they are significantly more expensive than couchettes. Expect to pay at least €100 per person.

EXPRESS TRAINS

Slower but still reasonably fast trains that cross borders are often called **EuroCity** (EC) or **InterCity** (IC). Reaching speeds of up to 200km/h or more, they are comfortable and frequent. A good example is Austria's **Railjet** service, which reaches Munich and Zurich.

EURAIL PASSES

GLOBAL PASS	15 DAYS	1 MONTH
Adult (1st or 2nd class)	US$795	US$1265
Under-26 (2nd class only)	US$519	US$819

FLEXI PASS	10 DAYS IN 2 MONTHS	15 DAYS IN 2 MONTHS
Adult (1st or 2nd class)	US$939	US$1229
Under-26 (2nd class only)	US$609	US$799

Reservations

At weekends and during holidays and the summer, it's a good idea to reserve seats on trains (which costs about €3 to €5). Standing at the end of the car for five hours is not what holiday dreams are made of. Some heavily discounted tickets bought online may include an assigned seat on a train, but most regular tickets are good for any train on the route.

You can usually reserve ahead of time using a ticket machine in stations or at a ticket window. On many high-speed trains – such as France's TGVs – reservations are mandatory.

Pass-holders should note that reservations are a good idea for the same reasons. Just because your pricey pass lets you hop-on/hop-off at will, there's no guarantee that you'll have a seat.

Train Passes

Think carefully about purchasing a rail pass. In particular, prices for the multitude of Eurail passes have become quite expensive. Spend a little time online checking the national railways' websites and determine what it would cost to do your trip by buying the tickets separately. More often than not, you'll find that you'll spend less than if you buy a Eurail pass.

Shop around as pass prices can vary between different outlets. Once purchased, take care of your pass as it cannot be replaced or refunded if lost or stolen. Passes get reductions on Eurostar through the Channel Tunnel and on certain ferry routes (eg between France and Ireland). In the USA, **Rail Europe** (www.raileurope.com) sells a variety of rail passes; note that its individual train tickets tend to be more expensive than what you'll pay buying from railways online or in stations.

EURAIL

There are so many different **Eurail** (www.eurail.com) passes to choose from and such a wide variety of areas and time periods covered that you need to have a good idea of your itinerary before purchasing one. These passes can only be bought by residents of non-European countries and are supposed to be purchased before arriving in Europe. There are two flavours: one for adults, one for people under 26 (see the boxed text for prices).

Eurail passes are valid for unlimited travel on national railways and some private lines in the Western European countries of Austria, Belgium, France, Germany, Greece, Ireland, Italy, Luxembourg, the Netherlands, Portugal, Spain and Switzerland (including Liechtenstein), plus several

INTERRAIL PASSES

PASS TYPE	ADULT 1ST CLASS	ADULT 2ND CLASS	UNDER-26 2ND CLASS
5 days of travel within 10 days	€389	€259	€169
10 days of travel within 22 days	€559	€369	€249
Unlimited travel for 1 month	€719	€479	€319

more neighbouring ones. They are also valid on some ferries between Italy and Greece. Reductions are given on some other ferry routes and on river/lake steamer services in various countries and on the Eurostar to/from the UK. The UK is *not* covered by Eurail – it has its own Britrail pass (p312).

Pass types include the following:

Eurail Global All the European countries (despite the much grander-sounding name) for a set number of consecutive days.

Eurail Flexi Offers travel for a set number of days within a period of time.

Eurail Saver Two to five people travelling together as a group for the entire trip can save about 15% on the various pass types above.

Eurail Selectpass Buyers choose which neighbouring countries it covers and for how long. Options are myriad and can offer significant savings over the other passes if, for example, you are only going to three or four countries. Use the Eurail website to calculate these.

Extra Fees

Eurail likes to promote the hop-on/hop-off any train aspect of their passes. But when it comes to the most desirable high-speed trains this is not always the case. While German ICE trains may be used at will, French TGVs require a seat reservation and the catch is that these are not always available to pass holders on all trains. In addition, some of the high-speed services like Thalys trains require a fairly hefty surcharge from pass users (1st class/2nd class €41/€26).

INTERRAIL

The **InterRail** (www.interrailnet.com) pass is available to European residents of more than six months' standing (passport identification is required). Terms and conditions vary slightly from country to country, but in the country of origin there is a discount of around 50% on the normal fares. The pass covers up to 30 countries.

InterRail passes are generally cheaper than Eurail, but most high-speed trains require that you also buy a seat reservation and pay a supplement of €3 to €40 depending on the route. InterRail passes are also available for individual countries. Compare these to passes offered by the national railways.

NATIONAL RAIL PASSES

If you're intending to travel extensively within one country, check what national rail passes are available as these can sometimes save you a lot of money; details can be found in the individual country chapters. In a large country such as Germany where you might be covering long distances, a pass can make sense, whereas in a small country such as the Netherlands it won't.

Language

WANT MORE?

For in-depth language information and handy phrases, check out Lonely Planet's *Western Europe Phrasebook*. You'll find it at **shop.lonelyplanet.com**, or you can buy Lonely Planet's iPhone phrasebooks at the Apple App Store.

This chapter offers basic vocabulary to help you get around Western Europe. If you read our coloured pronunciation guides as if they were English, you'll be understood.

Note that, in our pronunciation guides, the stressed syllables are indicated with italics. Also, kh and gh represent a throaty sound (as in the Scottish *loch*) wherever they appear in our guides.

DUTCH

Dutch is spoken in The Netherlands and the northern part of Belgium (Flanders).

Hello.	*Dag.*	dakh
Goodbye.	*Dag.*	dakh
Please.	*Alstublieft.*	al·stew·*bleeft*
Thank you.	*Dank u.*	dangk ew
Yes./No.	*Ja./Nee.*	yaa/ney
Help!	*Help!*	help
Cheers!	*Proost!*	prohst

I don't understand.
Ik begrijp het niet. — ik buh·*khreyp* huht neet

How much is it?
Hoeveel kost het? — hoo·*veyl* kost huht

Where's ...?
Waar is ...? — waar is ...

Where are the toilets?
Waar zijn de toiletten? — waar zeyn duh twa·*le*·tuhn

FRENCH

French is spoken in France, Switzerland, Luxembourg and the southern part of Belgium (Wallonia).

The r sound is a throaty one and there are nasal vowels (pronounced as if you're trying to force the sound through your nose) which are indicated in our guides with o or u followed by an almost inaudible nasal consonant sound m, n or ng. Syllables in French words are, for the most part, equally stressed.

Hello.	*Bonjour.*	bon·zhoor
Goodbye.	*Au revoir.*	o·rer·vwa
Please.	*S'il vous plaît.*	seel voo play
Thank you.	*Merci.*	mair·see
Yes./No.	*Oui./Non.*	wee/non
Help!	*Au secours!*	o skoor
Cheers!	*Santé!*	son·tay

I don't understand.
Je ne comprends pas. — zher ner kom·pron pa

How much is it?
C'est combien? — say kom·byun

Where's ...?
Où est ...? — oo ay ...

Where are the toilets?
Où sont les toilettes? — oo son ley twa·let

GERMAN

German has official status in Germany, Austria, Liechtenstein, Switzerland, Luxembourg and Belgium.

Hello.

(in general)	*Guten Tag.*	*goo*·ten taak
(in Austria)	*Servus.*	*zer*·vus
(in Switzerland)	*Grüezi.*	*grew*·e·tsi

Goodbye.	*Auf Wiedersehen.*	owf *vee*·der·zey·en
Please.	*Bitte.*	*bi*·te
Thank you.	*Danke.*	*dang*·ke
Yes./No.	*Ja./Nein.*	yaa/nain
Help!	*Hilfe!*	*hil*·fe
Cheers!	*Prost!*	prawst

I don't understand.
Ich verstehe nicht. ikh fer·*shtey*·e nikht

How much is it?
Wie viel kostet das? vee feel *kos*·tet das

Where's ...?
Wo ist ...? vaw ist ...

Where are the toilets?
Wo ist die Toilette? vo ist dee to·a·*le*·te

GREEK

Greek is the language of mainland Greece and its islands (as well as a co-official language of Cyprus).

Hello.	Γεια σου.	yia su
Goodbye.	Αντίο.	a·*di*·o
Please.	Παρακαλώ.	pa·ra·ka·*lo*
Thank you.	Ευχαριστώ.	ef·kha·ri·*sto*
Yes./No.	Ναι./Οχι.	ne/*o*·hi
Help!	Βοήθεια!	vo·*i*·thia
Cheers!	Στην υγειά μας!	stin i·*yia* mas

I don't understand.
Δεν καταλαβαίνω. dhen ka·ta·la·*ve*·no

How much is it?
Πόσο κάνει; *po*·so *ka*·ni

Where's ...?
Που είναι . . . ? pu *i*·ne ...

Where are the toilets?
Που είναι η τουαλέτα; pu *i*·ne i tu·a·*le*·ta

ITALIAN

The language of Italy also has official status – and is spoken – in Switzerland.

Hello.	*Buongiorno.*	bwon·*jor*·no
Goodbye.	*Arrivederci.*	a·ree·ve·*der*·chee
Please.	*Per favore.*	per fa·*vo*·re
Thank you.	*Grazie.*	*gra*·tsye
Yes./No.	*Sì./No.*	see/no
Help!	*Aiuto!*	ai·*yoo*·to
Cheers!	*Salute!*	sa·*loo*·te

I don't understand.
Non capisco. non ka·*pee*·sko

How much is it?
Quant'è? kwan·*te*

Where's ... ?
Dov'è ... ? do·*ve* ...

Where are the toilets?
Dove sono i gabinetti? *do*·ve *so*·no ee ga·bee·*ne*·tee

PORTUGUESE

Most vowel sounds in Portugal's language have a nasal version (ie pronounced as if you're trying to force the sound through your nose), which is indicated in our pronunciation guides with ng after the vowel.

Hello.	*Olá.*	o·*laa*
Goodbye.	*Adeus.*	a·de·*oosh*
Please.	*Por favor.*	poor fa·*vor*
Thank you.	*Obrigado.* (m) *Obrigada.* (f)	o·bree·*gaa*·doo o·bree·*gaa*·da
Yes./No.	*Sim./Não.*	seeng/nowng
Help!	*Socorro!*	soo·*ko*·rroo
Cheers!	*Saúde!*	sa·*oo*·de

I don't understand.
Não entendo. nowng eng·*teng*·doo

How much is it?
Quanto custa? *kwang*·too *koosh*·ta

Where's ...?
Onde é ...? *ong*·de e ...

Where are the toilets?
Onde é a casa de banho? *ong*·de e a *kaa*·za de *ba*·nyoo

SPANISH

Spanish is the main language of Spain. Note that the th sound is pronounced 'with a lisp'.

Hello.	*Hola.*	*o*·la
Goodbye.	*Adiós.*	a·*dyos*
Yes./No.	*Sí./No.*	see/no
Please.	*Por favor.*	por fa·*vor*
Thank you.	*Gracias.*	*gra*·thyas
Cheers!	*¡Salud!*	sa·*loo*
Help!	*¡Socorro!*	so·*ko*·ro

I don't understand.
Yo no entiendo. yo no en·*tyen*·do

How much is it?
¿Cuánto cuesta? *kwan*·to *kwes*·ta

Where's ...?
¿Dónde está ...? *don*·de es·*ta* ...

Where are the toilets?
¿Dónde están los servicios? *don*·de es·*tan* los ser·*vee*·thyos

behind the scenes

SEND US YOUR FEEDBACK

We love to hear from travellers – your comments keep us on our toes and help make our books better. Our well-travelled team reads every word on what you loved or loathed about this book. Although we cannot reply individually to postal submissions, we always guarantee that your feedback goes straight to the appropriate authors, in time for the next edition. Each person who sends us information is thanked in the next edition – and the most useful submissions are rewarded with a free book.

Visit **lonelyplanet.com/contact** to submit your updates and suggestions or to ask for help. Our award-winning website also features inspirational travel stories, news and discussions.

Note: We may edit, reproduce and incorporate your comments in Lonely Planet products such as guidebooks, websites and digital products, so let us know if you don't want your comments reproduced or your name acknowledged. For a copy of our privacy policy visit lonelyplanet.com/privacy.

OUR READERS

Many thanks to the travellers who used the last edition and wrote to us with helpful hints, useful advice and interesting anecdotes:

Paul Beach, Nathan Billington, Colette Coumont, Blaž Cugmas, Gaetan, Brian Gettings, Arnon Golan, Julian Gonzalez, Hamish Gray, Florian Hinz, Lisa Johann, Russell Kim, Michelle Kirby, Christian Louis, Marshall Mckinney, Kevin Paxter, Aileen Traves, Roald van Stijn, Rachel Waldman, Jeff White, Aprilianto Wiria

AUTHOR THANKS

Ryan Ver Berkmoes

Thanks to all the authors who worked so hard on this new-look Lonely Planet guidebook. Great job all! Meanwhile, in Germany Angela Cullen was a dear as always and I'm happy to see she still prefers Harry over a chihuahua. It was good to get back on track with Alan Wissenburg. Thanks to Birgit Borowski and Dr Eva Missler in Stuttgart. And thanks to Claudia Stehle as always for taking me to the dark depths of the BF. Samuel L Bronkowitz gets a nod as does Erin, the Kona-Denny's girl.

Alexis Averbuck

Once again, extensive, grateful thanks are due to Alexandra Stamopoulou for all of her insightful tips. Marijke Verstrepen and Margarita Kontzia provided helpful advice on festivals and hot happenings around the country. Dimitris Foussekis always shows me something new. And thank you Anthy and Costas for making Athens feel like home. Special thanks are also due to Craig McLachlan for seamlessly pulling our chapter together.

Kerry Christiani

Special thanks go to my husband, Andy, for being with me every step of the way on this book. I'd also like to thank all the tourism professionals who made the road to research silky-smooth, especially Sabine Günterseder (Upper Austria Tourism), Monika Reichel (Salzburg Information) and Nicholas Boekdrukker (Innsbruck Tourism). At Lonely Planet, thanks go to Jo Potts, Herman So and my co-authors for being so great to work with.

Mark Elliott

A million mercis to my beloved wife, Danielle Systermans, and to all our Benelux friends who have taught me so much over the years. Many thanks to Jan van Akker, David de Graef, Valerie De Kerpel, Lesley Devos, Guy Jacobs, Ludovic Desmet, Rémi Durand, Wieland de Hoon, Hans Rossel, Matthieu Segard and Brandon Noble. Endless thanks to my unbeatable family back in England, whose love and inspiration gave me the joy and freedom to live and learn.

David Else

As always, massive appreciation goes to my wife, Corinne, for joining me on many of my research trips around Britain, and for not minding when I locked myself away for 12 hours at a time to write this book – and for bringing coffee when it got nearer to 18 hours. Thanks also to Ryan and the other authors who worked with me on this book, to the helpful team of commissioning editors at Lonely Planet's London office, and of course to the production editors and cartographers in Melbourne who brought this book to final fruition.

Duncan Garwood

Grazie to all the friends and family who helped me out on this job: Lorenzo and Viviana, Pino and Andrea, Luigi, Sonia and Giacomo, Antonello and Dora. Thanks also to tourist office staff: Daniela Pinna (Cagliari), Tiziana (Cala Gonone), Patrizia (Alghero), Ilaria Lucentini (Cerveteri), Caterina Gucciardo (Mantua), Chiara De Angelis (Urbino), Laura Longa (Bari), the ladies at Genoa, and Mikaela Bandini (Matera). A big thank you to fellow author Virginia Maxwell and coordinating maestro Ryan Ver Berkmoes. Finally, a huge hug to Lidia, Ben and Nick.

Anthony Ham

In eight years of living in Madrid, I have been welcomed and assisted by too many people to name and whose lives and stories have become a treasured part of the fabric of my own. It was my great fortune a week after arriving in Madrid to meet my wife and soulmate, Marina, who has made this city a true place of the heart. And to my daughters, Carlota and Valentina: truly you are Madrid's greatest gift of all.

Virginia Maxwell

Duncan Garwood and Ryan Ver Berkmoes gave me encouragement, expert advice and extended deadlines, for which I was extremely grateful. *Grazie mille!* Thanks also to my favourite travelling companion, Max Handsaker; to Peter, for looking after the home front; and to Shelley, Roger, Moss, Dennis, Sophia, Theo, Freya, Filippo, Fabrizio and Elisabetta.

Craig McLachlan

A hearty thanks to all those who helped me out on the road, but most of all to my exceptionally beautiful wife, Yuriko, who let me know when I'd had enough Mythos each day! (And who also limited my daily intake of gyros pitta.)

Miles Roddis

Lots of thanks to Ingrid, who skied the slopes, rode the moguls and chipped in with valuable après-ski advice as I scurried my way around the tiny land of Andorra. Major thank-yous as well to particularly helpful tourist office staff Carolina (Andorra la Vella), Eva (Ordino) and Aret, Sonia and Ingrid (Canillo).

Caroline Sieg

Thanks to my parents for instilling in me a lifelong zest for travel. Thanks mucho to Lucy Monie for giving me this gig and *merci viel mal* to all my friends – old and new – for wining and dining with me across the country. And last but not least, thanks to Jules and Thresher, for all those memories that never go out of style.

Regis St Louis

Big thanks to coordinating maestro Ryan Ver Berkmoes and *Portugal* 8 co-authors Kate, Gregor and Adam, who proved a stellar team to work with. In Portugal, I'd like to thank João for deep insight into Lisboa, Paolo for the enlightening Castelo walk and the memorable meals, Bruno for the radical UMM experience, and the many locals who shared tips along the way. As always, *beijos* to Cassandra and daughters Magdalena and Genevieve for their support.

Nicola Williams

Kudos to the exceptional commitment, creativity and cooperation of the *France* 9 team of authors, whose prose I cut and manicured to create the France chapter of this guide. *Un grand merci* to Parisians Laure Chouillou and Sophie Maisonnier, and at-home *bisous* to Matthias and our three wonderfully travel-happy children: Niko (nine), Mischa (six) and Kaya (10 months).

Neil Wilson

Thanks to the friendly and helpful tourist office staff all over Ireland, and to all those folk in pubs and on the road who offered advice and recommendations.

ACKNOWLEDGMENTS

Climate map data adapted from Peel MC, Finlayson BL & McMahon TA (2007) 'Updated World Map of the Köppen-Geiger Climate Classification', *Hydrology and Earth System Sciences*, 11, 163344.

Cover photograph: Vase of sunflowers and an antique chair, Roussillon, France, Europe/ Barbara Van Zanten

Many of the images in this guide are available for licensing from Lonely Planet Images: www.lonelyplanetimages.com.

THIS BOOK

Many people have helped to create this 10th edition of Lonely Planet's Western Europe guidebook, which is part of Lonely Planet's Europe series. Other titles in this series include *Eastern Europe*, *Mediterranean Europe*, *Central Europe*, *Scandinavia* and *Europe on a Shoestring*. Lonely Planet also publishes phrasebooks for these regions. This guidebook was commissioned in Lonely Planet's London office, and produced by the following:

Commissioning Editors Lucy Monie, Paula Hardy, Joe Bindloss

Coordinating Editors Ali Lemer, Anna Metcalfe

Coordinating Cartographer Valentina Kremenchutskaya

Coordinating Layout Designer Carlos Solarte

Managing Editors Bruce Evans, Kirsten Rawlings

Managing Cartographers Amanda Sierp, Herman So

Managing Layout Designer Celia Wood

Assisting Editors Janet Austin, Andrew Bain, Alice Barker, Kate Daly, Victoria Harrison, Kim Hutchins, Gabby Innes, Bella Li, Robyn Loughnane, Charles Rawlings-Way, Simon Sellars, Matty Soccio, Fionnuala Twomey, Jeanette Wall

Assisting Cartographers Anita Banh, Ildiko Bogdanovits, Csanad Csutoros, Di Duggan, Jennifer Johnston, Eve Kelly, Anthony Phelan

Assisting Layout Designers Yvonne Bischofberger, Wibowo Rusli

Cover Research Naomi Parker

Internal Image Research Aude Vauconsant

Indexers Susie Ashworth, Sonya Mithen

Language Content Branislava Vladisavljevic

Thanks to Mark Adams, Imogen Bannister, David Connolly, Melanie Dankel, Stefanie Di Trocchio, Janine Eberle, Ryan Evans, Joshua Geoghegan, Mark Germanchis, Michelle Glynn, Lauren Hunt, Laura Jane, David Kemp, Yvonne Kirk, Nic Lehman, John Mazzocchi, Wayne Murphy, Adrian Persoglia, Lachlan Ross, Michael Ruff, Julie Sheridan, Laura Stansfeld, John Taufa, Sam Trafford, Juan Winata, Emily K Wolman, Nick Wood

index

A

000 Map pages
000 Photo pages

B

000 Map pages
000 Photo pages

C

D

000 Map pages
000 Photo pages

000 Map pages
000 Photo pages

N

O

P

000 Map pages
000 Photo pages

T

U

000 Map pages
000 Photo pages

how to use this book

These symbols will help you find the listings you want:

- Sights
- Activities
- Courses
- Tours
- Festivals & Events
- Sleeping
- Eating
- Drinking
- Entertainment
- Shopping
- Information/ Transport

These symbols give you the vital information for each listing:

- Telephone Numbers
- Opening Hours
- Parking
- Nonsmoking
- Air-Conditioning
- Internet Access
- Wi-Fi Access
- Swimming Pool
- Vegetarian Selection
- English-Language Menu
- Family-Friendly
- Pet-Friendly
- Bus
- Ferry
- Metro
- Subway
- London Tube
- Tram
- Train

Reviews are organised by author preference.

Look out for these icons:

TOP CHOICE Our author's recommendation

FREE No payment required

A green or sustainable option

Our authors have nominated these places as demonstrating a strong commitment to sustainability – for example by supporting local communities and producers, operating in an environmentally friendly way, or supporting conservation projects.

Map Legend

Sights
- Beach
- Buddhist
- Castle
- Christian
- Hindu
- Islamic
- Jewish
- Monument
- Museum/Gallery
- Ruin
- Winery/Vineyard
- Zoo
- Other Sight

Activities, Courses & Tours
- Diving/Snorkelling
- Canoeing/Kayaking
- Skiing
- Surfing
- Swimming/Pool
- Walking
- Windsurfing
- Other Activity/ Course/Tour

Sleeping
- Sleeping
- Camping

Eating
- Eating

Drinking
- Drinking
- Cafe

Entertainment
- Entertainment

Shopping
- Shopping

Information
- Post Office
- Tourist Information

Transport
- Airport
- Border Crossing
- Bus
- Cable Car/ Funicular
- Cycling
- Ferry
- Metro
- Monorail
- Parking
- S-Bahn
- Taxi
- Train/Railway
- Tram
- Tube Station
- U-Bahn
- Other Transport

Routes
- Tollway
- Freeway
- Primary
- Secondary
- Tertiary
- Lane
- Unsealed Road
- Plaza/Mall
- Steps
- Tunnel
- Pedestrian Overpass
- Walking Tour
- Walking Tour Detour
- Path

Boundaries
- International
- State/Province
- Disputed
- Regional/Suburb
- Marine Park
- Cliff
- Wall

Population
- Capital (National)
- Capital (State/Province)
- City/Large Town
- Town/Village

Geographic
- Hut/Shelter
- Lighthouse
- Lookout
- Mountain/Volcano
- Oasis
- Park
- Pass
- Picnic Area
- Waterfall

Hydrography
- River/Creek
- Intermittent River
- Swamp/Mangrove
- Reef
- Canal
- Water
- Dry/Salt/ Intermittent Lake
- Glacier

Areas
- Beach/Desert
- Cemetery (Christian)
- Cemetery (Other)
- Park/Forest
- Sportsground
- Sight (Building)
- Top Sight (Building)

Regis St Louis

Portugal Regis' long-time admiration for wine, rugged coastlines and melancholic music made him easy prey for Portugal. He has travelled extensively across the country, most recently fêting Lisbon's favourite saint at the Festa de Santo Antonio, exploring gorgeous beaches in the Parque Natural da Arrábida and eating too many *pasteis de nata* (including six in one day – oops). Regis is the coordinating author of Lonely Planet's *Portugal*, and his travel essays have appeared in newspapers, in-flight magazines and online. He lives in Brooklyn, New York.

Read more about Regis at:
lonelyplanet.com/members/regisstlouis

Nicola Williams

France Nicola Williams has lived in France and written about it for more than a decade. From her hillside home on the southern shore of Lake Geneva, it's a quick flit to the Alps (call her a ski fiend...), Paris (...art buff), Provence (...food and wine lover). Paris this time meant stylish apartment living in St-Germain des Prés with husband extraordinaire Matthias and three trilingual kids with ants in their pants. Nicola blogs at tripalong.wordpress.com and tweets at @Tripalong.

Read more about Nicola at:
lonelyplanet.com/members/nicolawilliams

Neil Wilson

Ireland Neil's first experiences of Ireland were a sailing trip to Kinsale in 1990 and a tour of Northern Ireland's Antrim coast in 1994. Since then he has returned regularly for holidays, hiking trips and guidebook research – this time round he finally climbed Carrantuohil, Ireland's highest peak. Neil is a full-time travel writer based in Edinburgh, Scotland, and has written around 50 guidebooks, including working on the last four editions of Lonely Planet's *Ireland* guide.

Read more about Neil at:
lonelyplanet.com/members/neilwilson

David Else

Britain David is a professional travel writer and the author of more than 40 guidebooks, including numerous editions of Lonely Planet's *Great Britain* and *England* guides, and *Walking in Britain*. His knowledge comes from a lifetime of travel around the country, often on foot – a passion dating from university years, when heading for the hills was always more attractive than visiting the library. Originally from London, David has lived in Yorkshire, Wales and Derbyshire, and is currently based on the southern edge of the Cotswolds.

Read more about David at:
lonelyplanet.com/members/davidelse

Duncan Garwood

Italy Since moving to Italy in 1997, Duncan has travelled the length and breadth of the country numerous times, contributing to a raft of Lonely Planet's *Italy* guides as well as newspapers and magazines. Each trip throws up special memories; this time it was a perfect beach moment in Sardinia – driving down a rough dirt track to find a deserted strip of sand lapped by limpid aquamarine waters. He currently lives in the Alban hills just outside of Rome.

Read more about Duncan at:
lonelyplanet.com/members/duncangarwood

Anthony Ham

Spain In 2002, Anthony arrived in Madrid on a one-way ticket and has called the city home ever since. He now lives with his *madrileña* wife and two daughters overlooking their favourite plaza in the city. He has written more than 50 guidebooks for Lonely Planet, including *Spain* and *Madrid*. Researching this guide allowed him to rediscover his home city afresh (Malasaña is his new favourite *barrio*) and he particularly enjoyed losing himself in the villages of Aragón.

Read more about Anthony at:
lonelyplanet.com/members/anthony_ham

Virginia Maxwell

Italy Virginia has been travelling regularly in Italy for over 20 years, inspired by a love of Renaissance arts and architecture and an all-abiding passion for the country's food and wine. She is the coordinating author of Lonely Planet's *Tuscany & Umbria* book and has covered Rome, Lazio and Tuscany for the *Italy* guidebook.

Read more about Virginia at:
lonelyplanet.com/members/virginiamaxwell

Craig McLachlan

Greece Craig has researched the Greek Islands for four of the most recent Lonely Planet guidebooks on Greece. He is also a regular visitor to Greece as a tour leader, mainly guiding hiking groups in the mountains and gorges of Crete and around the Cyclades. A Kiwi, Craig spends the southern-hemisphere summer running an outdoor adventure company in Queenstown before heading north for the winter as a 'freelance anything'. He is also a karate instructor and Japanese interpreter. Check out www.craigmclachlan.com.

Read more about Craig at:
lonelyplanet.com/members/craigmclachlan

Miles Roddis

Andorra Living in Valencia, on Spain's Mediterranean coast, Miles loses count of the times he's nipped up to Andorra for a skiing weekend or a summertime camping and walking break – though never, ever to shop. He has written or contributed to more than 50 Lonely Planet titles, including both general and walking guides, covering Andorra's immediate neighbours, Spain and France.

Read more about Miles at:
lonelyplanet.com/members/serranoham

Caroline Sieg

Germany, Liechtenstein, Switzerland Half-Swiss, half-American, Caroline's relationship with Switzerland began when she and her family first moved to Lucerne at age five. Several moves back and forth across the Atlantic ended when she relocated to Zurich for high school and several years beyond that, including working a season in a ski resort in the Valais. These days, Caroline heads to Switzerland as often as possible – to ski, indulge in cheese and chocolate or to simply meander along Lake Zürich.

Read more about Caroline at:
lonelyplanet.com/members/carolinesieg

OUR STORY

A beat-up old car, a few dollars in the pocket and a sense of adventure. In 1972 that's all Tony and Maureen Wheeler needed for the trip of a lifetime – across Europe and Asia overland to Australia. It took several months, and at the end – broke but inspired – they sat at their kitchen table writing and stapling together their first travel guide, *Across Asia on the Cheap*. Within a week they'd sold 1500 copies. Lonely Planet was born.

Today, Lonely Planet has offices in Melbourne, London and Oakland, with more than 600 staff and writers. We share Tony's belief that 'a great guidebook should do three things: inform, educate and amuse'.

OUR WRITERS

Ryan Ver Berkmoes

Coordinating Author; Germany, Netherlands Ryan Ver Berkmoes once lived in Germany, spending three years in Frankfurt editing a magazine until he got a chance for a new career: as a Lonely Planet author. One of his first jobs was working on the Germany chapter of the fourth edition of this very book. Later he worked on the first edition of Lonely Planet's *The Netherlands*, a country where they pronounce his name better than he can. He continues to write about both. These days he lives in Portland, Oregon. Follow him at ryanverberkmoes.com. He tweets at @ryanvb.

Read more about Ryan at:
lonelyplanet.com/members/ryanverberkmoes

Alexis Averbuck

Greece Alexis Averbuck lives in Hydra, Greece and makes any excuse she can to travel the isolated back roads of her adopted land. She is committed to dispelling the stereotype that Greece is simply a string of sandy beaches. A travel writer for two decades, Alexis has lived in Antarctica for a year, crossed the Pacific by sailboat and written books on her journeys through Asia and the Americas. She's also a painter – see her work at www.alexisaverbuck.com.

Read more about Alexis at:
lonelyplanet.com/members/alexisaverbuck

Kerry Christiani

Austria Born in Essex, Kerry now lives in the Black Forest, Germany. On her second visit to Austria for Lonely Planet she discovered the truth about the von Trapps in Salzburg, sweated out a rare heatwave in the Alps and climbed (almost) every mountain – and in doing so fell for the country and its great outdoors all over again. Kerry's wanderlust has taken her to six continents, inspiring numerous articles and some 20 guidebooks, including Lonely Planet's *Germany*, *Switzerland* and *France*.

Read more about Kerry at:
lonelyplanet.com/members/kerrychristiani

Mark Elliott

Belgium, Luxembourg In 1995, a chance encounter at a Turkmenistan camel market saw British-born author Mark Elliott tumble into the arms of his Belgian bride-to-be. He followed her home and is now well into a second decade living in the Benelux, still revelling in the crazy carnivals, fabulous festivals, classic castles and brilliant beer cafes that make this area one of the world's most underestimated destinations.

Read more about Mark at:
lonelyplanet.com/members/markelliottauthor

OVER PAGE MORE WRITERS

Published by Lonely Planet Publications Pty Ltd
ABN 36 005 607 983
10th edition – Oct 2011
ISBN 978 1 74179 679 7

10 9 8 7 6 5 4 3 2 1
Printed in Singapore